THE EUROPA DIRECTORY OF

INTERNATIONAL ORGANIZATIONS

2002

THE EUROPA DIRECTORY OF
INTERNATIONAL ORGANIZATIONS
2002

4TH EDITION

Routledge
Taylor & Francis Group
LONDON AND NEW YORK

First published 2002 by Europa Publications
Fourth edition 2002

Published 2014
by Routledge
2 Park Square, Milton Park, Abingdon, Oxon OX14 4RN

and by Routledge
711 Third Avenue, New York, NY, 10017, USA

Routledge is an imprint of the Taylor & Francis Group, an informa business

ISBN 13: 978-1-85743-110-0 (hbk)

ISSN 1465-4628

Editors: Catriona Appeatu Holman, Helen Canton
Contributors: Yzanne MacKay, Juliet Summerscale
Editorial Support: Simon Chapman, Phil McIntyre

Imageset by MPG Dataworld

FOREWORD

The fourth edition of the EUROPA DIRECTORY OF INTERNATIONAL ORGANIZATIONS offers readers a comprehensive guide to international organizations and an essential understanding of the framework of international affairs. It provides, in a single volume, detailed coverage of the most important intergovernmental groupings, as well as more concise details of some 1,500 other entities. Extensive general background information gives a historical and legal perspective to the international system.

The steadfast process of globalization evident in recent years has given rise to a renewed determination by governments to co-operate in order to ensure their own economic and political stability, and consequently to a structure of international security, cultural, economic, political and trading arrangements of unprecedented complexity. A new introductory essay by Clive Archer offers a concise history of these developments, and a clear overview of the structure and functioning of the international system. The 11 September 2001 terrorist attacks on the USA highlighted the significant challenges facing international organizations in the areas of international security and law—a theme explored in William Hopkinson's essay—as well as their irreversible role in determining the global political and economic agenda. The development of modern international organizations is recorded in a chronology in Part One. Part One also contains a listing of days, weeks, years and decades sponsored by international organizations, which focus world-wide attention on specific themes.

The United Nations is covered in depth, in Part Two, reflecting its status as the world's largest intergovernmental body. Detailed information on the structure, membership and activities of all major offices, programmes and agencies is given. Similar information is provided, in Part Three, for other major international organizations. These bodies, of course, do not operate in isolation and there is an increasing level of collaboration and even integration of functions between organizations. However, the structured approach of these principal sections is intended to provide the reader with an accessible overview of each organization as accurately and clearly as possible. Briefer details of other international organizations appear in Part Four where, for ease of reference, they are listed according to subject. An index to all organizations appearing in Parts Two, Three and Four is to be found at the back of the volume.

Several articles incorporate the text of an organization's founding treaty or other significant document that shaped its future structure and objectives. Other important international treaties are positioned so as to be of most interest or use to the reader; usually this is where an organization has been actively involved in its formulation, even if not bearing any legal responsibility for its implementation or supervision. Separately documented are lists of key resolutions adopted by the UN General Assembly and Security Council, to be found after the entry for each organ, which aim to place the activities and development of these bodies, in particular the UN's peace-keeping role, within a broader context.

The book concludes, in Part Five, with a Who's Who section, providing biographical information on the principal officers and other key personalities in international organizations at the start of the 21st century.

All the information in this publication has been extensively researched and verified. Despite the many advances in electronic research, direct contact with and assistance from the organizations themselves is often the only way to ensure detailed and reliable information, for which the editors remain entirely grateful.

May 2002

ACKNOWLEDGEMENTS

The reproduction of texts, and summaries of texts, of international treaties, founding documents and intergovernmental declarations is gratefully acknowledged.

The editors also wish to thank the many individuals and organizations whose interest and co-operation helped in the preparation of this publication, and all those who have replied to Europa's questionnaires, which, for many organizations, remain the primary source of information. Their generous assistance is recognized as being invaluable in presenting consistently accurate and up-to-date material.

CONTENTS

PART FOUR

Other International Organizations

Listed by subject

PART FIVE

Who's Who in International Organizations

ABBREVIATIONS

Abog.	Abogado (Lawyer)
Acad.	Academician; Academy
ACP	African, Caribbean and Pacific (countries)
ADB	African Development Bank; Asian Development Bank
Adm.	Admiral
admin.	administration
AFESD	Arab Fund for Economic and Social Development
AH	anno Hegirae
a.i.	ad interim
AIA	ASEAN Investment Area
AIDS	acquired immunodeficiency syndrome
Al.	Aleja (Alley, Avenue)
ALADI	Asociación Latinoamericana de Integración
Alt.	Alternate
amalg.	amalgamated
Apdo	Apartado (Post Box)
APEC	Asia-Pacific Economic Co-operation
approx.	approximately
Apt	Apartment
ASEAN	Association of South East Asian Nations
ASEM	Asia-Europe Meeting
asscn	association
assoc.	associate
asst	assistant
Aug.	August
auth.	authorized
Ave	Avenue
Avda	Avenida (Avenue)
Avv.	Avvocato (Lawyer)
BA	Bachelor of Arts
Bd	Board
Bd, Bld, Blv., Blvd	Boulevard
b/d	barrels per day
BIS	Bank for International Settlements
Bldg	Building
BP	Boîte postale (Post Box)
br.(s)	branch(es)
Brig.	Brigadier
BSE	bovine spongiform encephalopathy
bte	boîte (box)
BSEC	(Organization of the) Black Sea Economic Co-operation
bul.	bulvar (boulevard)
c.	circa; cuadra(s) (block(s)); child, children
CACM	Central American Common Market
Cad.	Caddesi (Street)
CAN	Comunidad Andina de Naciones
CAP	Common Agricultural Policy; Consolidated Inter-agency Appeal Process
cap.	capital
Capt.	Captain
CARICOM	Caribbean Community and Common Market
CBSS	Council of Baltic Sea States
Cdre	Commodore
Cen.	Central
CEO	Chief Executive Officer
CET	common external tariff
CFA	Communauté Financière Africaine; Co-opération Financière en Afrique centrale
CFP	Common Fisheries Policy; Communauté française du Pacifique; Comptoirs français du Pacifique
CFSP	Common Foreign and Security Policy
CGAP	Consultative Group to Assist the Poorest
CGIAR	Consultative Group on International Agricultural Research
Chair.	Chairman/person/woman
Cia	Companhia
Cía	Compañía
CICP	Centre for International Crime Prevention
Cie	Compagnie
c.i.f.	cost, insurance and freight
C-in-C	Commander-in-Chief
circ.	circulation
CIS	Commonwealth of Independent States
CJTF	Combined Joint Task Force
cm	centimetre(s)
CMAG	Commonwealth Ministerial Action Goup on the Harare Declaration
Cnr	Corner
c/o	care of
Co	Company; County
Col	Colonel
Col.	Colonia
Coll.	College
COMESA	Common Market for Eastern and Southern Africa
Comm.	Commission; Commendatore
Commdr	Commander
Commdt	Commandant
Commr	Commissioner
Confed.	Confederation
Cont.	Contador (Accountant)
COP	Conference of the Parties
Corpn	Corporation
CP	Case Postale; Caixa Postal; Casella Postale (Post Box)
Cres.	Crescent
CSCE	Conference on Security and Co-operation in Europe
CTBT	Comprehensive (Nuclear) Test Ban Treaty
Cttee	Committee
cu	cubic
cwt	hundredweight
d.	daughter(s)
DC	District of Columbia; Distrito Central
Dec.	December
Del.	Delegación
Dem.	Democratic; Democrat
Dep.	Deputy
dep.	deposits
Dept	Department
devt	development
DF	Distrito Federal
Diag.	Diagonal
Dir	Director
Div.	Division(al)
DN	Distrito Nacional
Doc.	Docent
DOMREP	Mission of the Representative of the Secretary-General in the Dominican Republic
DOTS	direct observation treatment; short-course
Dott.	Dottore
DPRK	Democratic People's Republic of Korea
Dr	Doctor
Dr.	Drive
Dra	Doctora
Drs	Doctorandus
dwt	dead weight tons
E	East; Eastern
EBRD	European Bank for Reconstruction and Development
EC	European Community
ECA	(United Nations) Economic Commission for Africa
ECE	(United Nations) Economic Commission for Europe
ECLAC	(United Nations) Economic Commission for Latin America and the Caribbean
ECO	Economic Co-operation Organization
Econ.	Economic; Economics; Economist
ECOSOC	(United Nations) Economic and Social Council
ECOWAS	Economic Community of West African States
ECU	European Currency Unit
ed.	educated
EDI	Economic Development Institute
Edif.	Edificio (Building)
edn	edition
EEA	European Economic Area
EEC	European Economic Community
EFTA	European Free Trade Association
e.g.	exempli gratia (for example)
EIB	European Investment Bank
EMS	European Monetary System
EMU	economic and monetary union
Eng.	Engineer; Engineering

ABBREVIATIONS

ERM	exchange rate mechanism
ESA	European Space Agency
Esc.	Escuela; Escudos; Escritorio
ESCAP	(United Nations) Economic and Social Commission for Asia and the Pacific
ESCWA	(United Nations) Economic and Social Commission for Western Asia
ESDI	European Security and Defence Identity
ESDP	European Security and Defence Policy
esq.	esquina (corner)
est.	established; estimate; estimated
etc.	et cetera
EU	European Union
excl.	excluding
exec.	executive
Ext.	Extension
f.	founded
fax	facsimile
FAO	Food and Agriculture Organization
FATF	Financial Action Task Force on Money Laundering
Feb.	February
Fed.	Federation; Federal
FM	frequency modulation
fmrly	formerly
f.o.b.	free on board
Fr	Father
Fr.	Franc
FRY	Federal Republic of Yugoslavia
ft	foot (feet)
FTAA	Free Trade Area of the Americas
FYRM	former Yugoslav republic of Macedonia
g	gram(s)
GATT	General Agreement on Tariffs and Trade
GCC	Gulf Co-operation Council
GDP	gross domestic product
Gdns	Gardens
GEF	Global Environment Facility
Gen.	General
GIEWS	Global Information and Early Warning System
GM	genetically modified
GMT	Greenwich Mean Time
GNP	gross national product
Gov.	Governor
Govt	Government
GPML	UN Global Programme Against Money Laundering
grt	gross registered tons
GWh	gigawatt hours
ha	hectares
HE	His/Her Eminence; His/Her Excellency
HEWS	Humanitarian Early Warning System
HIPC	heavily indebted poor country
HIV	human immunodeficiency virus
hl	hectolitre(s)
HM	His/Her Majesty
Hon.	Honorary; Honourable
HQ	Headquarters
HRH	His/Her Royal Highness
IAEA	International Atomic Energy Agency
IASC	Inter-Agency Standing Committee
IBRD	International Bank for Reconstruction and Development (World Bank)
ICAO	International Civil Aviation Organization
ICC	International Chamber of Commerce; International Criminal Court
ICFTU	International Confederation of Free Trade Unions
ICJ	International Court of Justice
ICRC	International Committee of the Red Cross
ICSID	International Centre for Settlement of Investment Disputes
ICTR	International Criminal Tribunal for Rwanda
ICTY	International Criminal Tribunal for the former Yugoslavia
IDA	International Development Association
IDB	Inter-American Development Bank
IDP	internally displaced person
i.e.	id est (that is to say)
IFAD	International Fund for Agricultural Development
IFC	International Finance Corporation
IGAD	Intergovernmental Authority on Development
ILO	International Labour Organization/Office
IMF	International Monetary Fund
IMO	International Maritime Organization
in (ins)	inch (inches)
Inc, Incorp., Incd	Incorporated
incl.	including
Ind.	Independent
Ing.	Engineer
INSAG	International Nuclear Safety Advisory Group
Insp.	Inspector
Inst.	Institute
Int.	International
IOC	International Olympic Committee
IOM	International Organization for Migration
IPM	Integrated Pest Management
IPU	Inter-Parliamentary Union
irreg.	irregular
Is	Islands
ISIC	International Standard Industrial Classification
IT	information technology
ITU	International Telecommunication Union
Jan.	January
Jnr	Junior
Jr	Jonkheer (Netherlands); Junior
Jt	Joint
kg	kilogram(s)
kHz	kilohertz
km	kilometre(s)
kv.	kvartal (apartment block); kvartira (apartment)
kW	kilowatt(s)
kWh	kilowatt hours
LAIA	Latin American Integration Association
lb	pound(s)
LDCs	Least Developed Countries
Lic.	Licenciado
Licda	Licenciada
Lt, Lieut	Lieutenant
Ltd	Limited
m	metre(s)
m.	married; million
Maj.	Major
Man.	Manager; managing
mem.	member
MEP	Member of the European Parliament
Mercosul	Mercado Comun do Sul (Southern Common Market)
Mercosur	Mercado Común del Sur (Southern Common Market)
MFN	most favoured nation
mfrs	manufacturers
Mgr	Monseigneur; Monsignor
MHz	megahertz
MIGA	Multilateral Investment Guarantee Agency
Mil.	Military
Min.	Minister; Ministry
MINUGUA	United Nations Verification Mission in Guatemala
MINURCA	United Nations Mission in the Central African Republic
MINURSO	United Nations Mission for the Referendum in Western Sahara
MIPONUH	United Nations Civilian Police Mission in Haiti
Mlle	Mademoiselle
mm	millimetre(s)
Mme	Madame
MONUA	United Nations Observer Mission in Angola
MONUC	United Nations Mission in the Democratic Republic of the Congo
MOU	Memorandum of Understanding
MP	Member of Parliament
MSS	Manuscripts
MW	megawatt(s); medium wave
MWh	megawatt hour(s)
N	North; Northern
n.a.	not available
nab.	naberezhnaya (embankment, quai)
NAFTA	North American Free Trade Agreement
nám.	náměstí (square)
Nat.	National
NATO	North Atlantic Treaty Organization
NCO	Non-Commissioned Officer
NEPAD	New Partnership for Africa's Development
NGO	non-governmental organization
no	número (number)
no.	number
Nov.	November
NPT	(Nuclear) Non-Proliferation Treaty
NPV	net present value

nr	near
nrt	net registered tons
NSW	New South Wales
NY	New York
NZ	New Zealand
OAPEC	Organization of Arab Petroleum Exporting Countries
OAS	Organization of American States
OAU	Organization of African Unity
OCHA	Office for the Co-ordination of Humanitarian Affairs
Oct.	October
OECD	Organisation for Economic Co-operation and Development
OECS	Organisation of East Caribbean States
Of.	Oficina (Office)
OHCHR	Office of the United Nations High Commissioner for Human Rights
OIC	Organization of the Islamic Conference
ONUC	United Nations Operation in the Congo
ONUCA	United Nations Observer Group in Central America
ONUMOZ	United Nations Operation in Mozambique
ONUSAL	United Nations Observer Mission in El Salvador
OPEC	Organization of the Petroleum Exporting Countries
opp.	opposite
Org.	Organization
OSCE	Organization for Security and Co-operation in Europe
p.	page
p.a.	per annum
Parl.	Parliament(ary)
pas.	passazh (passage)
per.	pereulok (lane, alley)
Perm. Rep.	Permanent Representative
PIC	Prior Informed Consent
PF	Postfach (Post Box)
PK	Post Box (Turkish)
PKO	peace-keeping operation
pl.	platz; place; ploshchad (square)
PLC	Public Limited Company
PLO	Palestine Liberation Organization
PMB	Private Mail Bag
PNA	Palestinian National Authority
POB	Post Office Box
pr.	prospekt (avenue)
Pres.	President
PRSP	Poverty Reduction Strategy Paper(s)
Prin.	Principal
Prof.	Professor
Propr	Proprietor
Prov.	Province; Provincial; Provinciale (Dutch)
Pte	Private
Pty	Proprietary
p.u.	paid up
publ.	publication; published
Publr	Publisher
Pvt.	Private
q.v.	quod vide (to which refer)
Rd	Road
reg., regd	register; registered
reorg.	reorganized
Rep.	Republic; Republican; Representative
Repub.	Republic
res	reserve(s)
retd	retired
Rev.	Reverend
Rm	Room
Rt	Right
S	South; Southern; San
s.	son(s)
SA	Société Anonyme, Sociedad Anónima (Limited Company); South Australia
SAARC	South Asian Association for Regional Co-operation
SADC	Southern African Development Community
SAR	Special Administrative Region
SDR(s)	Special Drawing Right(s)
Sec.	Secretary
Secr.	Secretariat
Sen.	Senior; Senator
Sept.	September
SICA	Sistema de la Integración Centroamericana
SITC	Standard International Trade Classification
SJ	Society of Jesus
SMEs	small and medium-sized enterprises
Soc.	Society
Sok.	Sokak (Street)
Sq.	Square
sq	square (in measurements)
Sr	Senior; Señor
Sra	Señora
St	Saint; Street
Sta	Santa
Ste	Sainte
subs.	subscriptions; subscribed
Supt	Superintendent
TD	Teachta Dála (Member of Parliament)
tech., techn.	technical
tel.	telephone
Treas.	Treasurer
TV	television
u.	utca (street)
u/a	unit of account
UAE	United Arab Emirates
UDEAC	Union Douanière et Economique de l'Afrique Centrale
UEE	Unidade Económica Estatal
UEMOA	Union économique et monétaire ouest-africaine
UK	United Kingdom
ul.	ulitsa (street)
UN	United Nations
UNAMIC	United Nations Advance Mission in Cambodia
UNAMIR	United Nations Assistance Mission for Rwanda
UNAMSIL	United Nations Mission in Sierra Leone
UNASOG	United Nations Aouzou Strip Observer Group
UNAVEM	United Nations Angola Verification Mission
UNCED	United Nations Conference on Environment and Development
UNCRO	United Nations Confidence Restoration Operation in Croatia
UNCTAD	United Nations Conference on Trade and Development
UNDCP	United Nations International Drug Control Programme
UNDOF	United Nations Disengagement Observer Force
UNDP	United Nations Development Programme
UNEF	United Nations Emergency Force
UNEP	United Nations Environment Programme
UNESCO	United Nations Educational, Scientific and Cultural Organization
UNFICYP	United Nations Peace-keeping Force in Cyprus
UNGOMAP	United Nations Good Offices Mission in Afghanistan and Pakistan
UNHCHR	United Nations High Commissioner for Human Rights
UNHCR	United Nations High Commissioner for Refugees
UNICEF	United Nations Children's Fund
UNIDO	United Nations Industrial Development Organization
UNIFEM	UN Development Fund for Woment
UNIFIL	United Nations Interim Force in Lebanon
UNIIMOG	United Nations Iran-Iraq Military Observer Group
UNIKOM	United Nations Iraq-Kuwait Observation Mission
UNIPOM	United Nations India-Pakistan Observation Mission
Univ.	University
UNMEE	UN Mission in Ethiopia and Eritrea
UNMIBH	United Nations Mission in Bosnia and Herzegovina
UNMIH	United Nations Mission in Haiti
UNMIK	United Nations Interim Administration Mission in Kosovo
UNMOGIP	United Nations Military Observer Group in India and Pakistan
UNMOP	United Nations Mission of Observers in Prevlaka
UNMOT	United Nations Mission of Observers in Tajikistan
UNMOVIC	United Nations Monitoring, Verification and Inspection Commission
UNOGIL	United Nations Observation Group in Lebanon
UNOMIG	United Nations Observer Mission in Georgia
UNOMIL	United Nations Observer Mission in Liberia
UNOMSIL	United Nations Observer Mission in Sierra Leone
UNOMUR	United Nations Observer Mission Uganda-Rwanda
UNOPS	UN Office for Project Services
UNOSOM	United Nations Operation in Somalia
UNPA	United Nations Protected Area
UNPREDEP	United Nations Preventive Deployment Force
UNPROFOR	United Nations Protection Force

UNRWA	United Nations Relief and Works Agency for Palestine Refugees in the Near East
UNSCOM	United Nations Special Commission
UNSF	United Nations Security Force in West New Guinea (New Irian)
UNSMIH	United Nations Support Mission in Haiti
UNTAC	United Nations Transitional Authority in Cambodia
UNTAES	United Nations Transitional Administration for Eastern Slavonia, Baranja and Western Sirmium
UNTAET	United Nations Transitional Administration in East Timor
UNTAG	United Nations Transition Group
UNTMIH	United Nations Transition Mission in Haiti
UNTSO	United Nations Truce Supervision Organization
UNYOM	United Nations Yemen Observation Mission
UPU	Universal Postal Union
USA	United States of America
USAID	United States Agency for International Development
USSR	Union of Soviet Socialist Republics
UNITA	Uniâo Nacional para a Independência Total de Angola
VAT	Value-added Tax
Ven.	Venerable
VI	(US) Virgin Islands
viz.	videlicet (namely)
Vn	Veien (Street)
vol.(s)	volume(s)
vul.	vulitsa (street)
W	West; Western
WA	Western Australia; Washington (State)
WCL	World Confederation of Labour
WEU	Western European Union
WFP	World Food Programme
WFTU	World Federation of Trade Unions
WHO	World Health Organization
WIPO	World Intellectual Property Organization
WMO	World Meteorological Organization
WTO	World Trade Organization
yr	year

INTERNATIONAL TELEPHONE CODES

To make international calls to telephone and fax numbers listed in *The Europa Directory of International Organizations*, dial the international code of the country from which you are calling, followed by the appropriate country code for the organization you wish to call (listed below), followed by the area code (if applicable) and telephone or fax number listed in the entry.

	Country code	Time difference hours + or − Greenwich Mean Time (GMT)*
Afghanistan	93	+4½
Albania	355	+1
Algeria	213	+1
Andorra	376	+1
Angola	244	+1
Antigua and Barbuda	1 268	−4
Argentina	54	−3
Armenia	374	+4
Australia	61	+7 to +10
Australian External Territories:		
Christmas Island	61	+10
Cocos (Keeling) Islands	61	+10
Norfolk Island	672	+11½
Austria	43	+1
Azerbaijan	994	+5
The Bahamas	1 242	−5
Bahrain	973	+3
Bangladesh	880	+6
Barbados	1 246	−4
Belarus	375	+2
Belgium	32	+1
Belize	501	−6
Benin	229	+1
Bhutan	975	+6
Bolivia	591	−4
Bosnia and Herzegovina	387	+1
Botswana	267	+2
Brazil	55	−3 to −4
Brunei	673	+8
Bulgaria	359	+2
Burkina Faso	226	0
Burundi	257	+2
Cambodia	855	+7
Cameroon	237	+1
Canada	1	−3½ to −8
Cape Verde	238	−1
Central African Republic	236	+1
Chad	235	+1
Chile	56	−4
China, People's Republic	86	+8
Special Administrative Regions:		
Hong Kong	852	+8
Macau	853	+8
China (Taiwan)	886	+8
Colombia	57	−5
Comoros	269	+3
Congo, Democratic Republic	243	+1
Congo, Republic	242	+1
Costa Rica	506	−6
Côte d'Ivoire	225	0
Croatia	385	+1
Cuba	53	−5
Cyprus	357	+2
'Turkish Republic of Northern Cyprus'	90 392	+2
Czech Republic	420	+1
Denmark	45	+1
Danish External Territories:		
Faroe Islands	298	0
Greenland	299	−1 to −4
Djibouti	253	+3
Dominica	1 767	−4
Dominican Republic	1 809	−4
East Timor	670	+8
Ecuador	593	−5
Egypt	20	+2
El Salvador	503	−6
Equatorial Guinea	240	+1
Eritrea	291	+3
Estonia	372	+2
Ethiopia	251	+3
Fiji	679	+12
Finland	358	+2
Finnish External Territory:		
Åland Islands	358	+2
France	33	+1
French Overseas Departments:		
French Guiana	594	−3
Guadeloupe	590	−4
Martinique	596	−4
Réunion	262	+4
French Overseas Collectivités Territoriales:		
Mayotte	269	+3
Saint Pierre and Miquelon	508	−3
French Overseas Territories:		
French Polynesia	689	−10
New Caledonia	687	+11
Wallis and Futuna Islands	681	+12
Gabon	241	+1
The Gambia	220	0
Georgia	995	+4
Germany	49	+1
Ghana	233	0
Greece	30	+2
Grenada	1 473	−4
Guatemala	502	−6
Guinea	224	0
Guinea-Bissau	245	0
Guyana	592	−4
Haiti	509	−5
Honduras	504	−6
Hungary	36	+1
Iceland	354	0
India	91	+5½
Indonesia	62	+7 to +8
Iran	98	+3½
Iraq	964	+3
Ireland	353	0
Israel	972	+2
Italy	39	+1
Jamaica	1 876	−5
Japan	81	+9
Jordan	962	+2
Kazakhstan	7	+6
Kenya	254	+3
Kiribati	686	+12
Korea, Democratic People's Republic (North Korea)	850	+9

	Country code	Time difference hours + or − Greenwich Mean Time (GMT)*
Korea, Republic (South Korea)	82	+9
Kuwait	965	+3
Kyrgyzstan	996	+5
Laos	856	+7
Latvia	371	+2
Lebanon	961	+2
Lesotho	266	+2
Liberia	231	0
Libya	218	+1
Liechtenstein	423	+1
Lithuania	370	+2
Luxembourg	352	+1
Macedonia, former Yugoslav republic	389	+1
Madagascar	261	+3
Malawi	265	+2
Malaysia	60	+8
Maldives	960	+5
Mali	223	0
Malta	356	+1
Marshall Islands	692	+12
Mauritania	222	0
Mauritius	230	+4
Mexico	52	−6 to −7
Micronesia, Federated States	691	+10 to +11
Moldova	373	+2
Monaco	377	+1
Mongolia	976	+8
Morocco	212	0
Mozambique	258	+2
Myanmar	95	+6½
Namibia	264	+2
Nauru	674	+12
Nepal	977	+5½
The Netherlands	31	+1
Netherlands Dependencies:		
Aruba	297	−4
Netherlands Antilles	599	−4
New Zealand	64	+12
New Zealand's Dependent and Associated Territories:		
Cook Islands	682	−10½
Niue	683	−11
Nicaragua	505	−6
Niger	227	+1
Nigeria	234	+1
Norway	47	+1
Norwegian External Territory:		
Svalbard	47	+1
Oman	968	+4
Pakistan	92	+5
Palau	680	+9
Panama	507	−5
Papua New Guinea	675	+10
Paraguay	595	−4
Peru	51	−5
The Philippines	63	+8
Poland	48	+1
Portugal	351	1
Qatar	974	+3
Romania	40	+2
Russia	7	+2 to +12
Rwanda	250	+2
Saint Christopher and Nevis	1 869	−4
Saint Lucia	1 758	−4
Saint Vincent and the Grenadines	1 784	−4
Samoa	685	−11
San Marino	378	+1
São Tomé and Príncipe	239	0
Saudi Arabia	966	+3

	Country code	Time difference hours + or − Greenwich Mean Time (GMT)*
Senegal	221	0
Seychelles	248	+4
Sierra Leone	232	0
Singapore	65	+8
Slovakia	421	+1
Slovenia	386	+1
Solomon Islands	677	+11
Somalia	252	+3
South Africa	27	+2
Spain	34	+1
Sri Lanka	94	+5½
Sudan	249	+2
Suriname	597	−3
Swaziland	268	+2
Sweden	46	+1
Switzerland	41	+1
Syria	963	+2
Tajikistan	992	+5
Tanzania	255	+3
Thailand	66	+7
Togo	228	0
Tonga	676	+13
Trinidad and Tobago	1 868	−4
Tunisia	216	+1
Turkey	90	+2
Turkmenistan	993	+5
Tuvalu	688	+12
Uganda	256	+3
Ukraine	380	+2
United Arab Emirates	971	+4
United Kingdom	44	0
United Kingdom Crown Dependencies	44	0
United Kingdom Overseas Territories:		
Anguilla	1 264	−4
Ascension Island	247	0
Bermuda	1 441	−4
British Virgin Islands	1 284	−4
Cayman Islands	1 345	−5
Diego Garcia (British Indian Ocean Territory)	246	+5
Falkland Islands	500	−4
Gibraltar	350	+1
Montserrat	1 664	−4
Saint Helena	290	0
Turks and Caicos Islands	1 649	−5
United States of America	1	−5 to −10
United States Commonwealth Territories:		
Northern Mariana Islands	1 670	+10
Puerto Rico	1 787	−4
United States External Territories:		
American Samoa	684	−11
Guam	1 671	+10
United States Virgin Islands	1 340	−4
Uruguay	598	−3
Uzbekistan	998	+5
Vanuatu	678	+11
Vatican City	39	+1
Venezuela	58	−4
Viet Nam	84	+7
Yemen	967	+3
Yugoslavia	381	+1
Zambia	260	+2
Zimbabwe	263	+2

* The times listed compare the standard (winter) times in the various countries. Some countries adopt Summer (Daylight Saving) Time—i.e. +1 hour—for part of the year.

PART ONE

Background Information

AN INTRODUCTION TO INTERNATIONAL ORGANIZATIONS

CLIVE ARCHER*

The international organizations most often seen in the media, such as the United Nations, NATO, European Union and the International Olympic Committee, have a wide range of activities and are also quite different in their history, size and nature. Yet they have in common the name 'international organization'. An international organization can be defined as *a formal, continuous structure established by agreement between members (governmental and/or non-governmental) from two or more sovereign states with the aim of pursuing the common interest of the membership.* This definition places an emphasis on membership, which does not have to be that of governments, the structure, i.e. it should be more permanent than a conference, and the pursuit of the members' interests, meaning that the organization should not just exist for the convenience of one member. The wide range of international organizations have become an integral part of the international system since they first appeared on the scene over 180 years ago.

HISTORY

The Beginnings

The first international organizations were established in the 19th century. The earliest was probably the commission established by the Convention of Octroi in 1804 to administer the navigation of the River Rhine, but this became a victim of the Napoleonic wars. It was re-established in 1831, 10 years after a similar international commission for the Elbe was set up. The European Danube Commission was established in 1856, the International Telegraph Union (which became the International Telecommunication Union—ITU) in 1865, with a formal secretariat established in 1868, and the General Postal Union (later the Universal Postal Union—UPU) in 1874. Before such organizations could exist, four preconditions needed to be fulfilled: a number of states functioning as independent political units had to exist; they had to have a substantial measure of contact between themselves; there had to be an awareness of problems that could arise from their co-existence and of the possibilities from co-operation; and there had to be a recognition that relations could be regulated by such institutions as international organizations. Greater ease of travel in the 19th century brought more frequent contact between states. The growth of internationalized commerce prompted the rise of international agencies to help manage it, such as the river commissions. Public organizations were joined by private ones, for example the International Institute of Agriculture, the World Anti-Slavery Convention and the Universal Peace Congress. According to the Union of International Associations, the number of intergovernmental organizations increased from seven in the 1870s to 37 by 1909, but the number of international non-governmental organizations was already 176 by that date.

The Paris Conference of 1856, at the end of the Crimean War, included a number of declarations covering free trade, naval warfare, the abolition of privateering, blockades and flags of neutrality in wartime. These were agreed not just by the European Great Powers but also by a number of smaller states and non-European countries such as China, Turkey, Japan and Mexico. Many of these states also attended a conference in 1889 in The Hague called to discuss disarmament; 44 states were present at the second Hague Conference, held in 1907. These gatherings established a panel of arbitrators to help settle disputes between states. However, these meetings and organizations did little to ameliorate tension between the main powers in Europe which led to the slide towards war in August 1914.

The First World War and the League of Nations

The First World War of 1914–1918 saw immense slaughter and destruction in Europe and the collapse of four empires—the German, Austro-Hungarian, Turkish and Russian. However, the conduct of the war from the French and British, and later American, side involved close co-operation between these states Several institutions were established, such as the Supreme War Council, served by a secretariat, as well as a range of inter-Allied councils covering economic, military and political aspects of the war. After the USA entered the war, President Woodrow Wilson issued his 'Fourteen Points', one of which was a commitment to 'a general association of nations' to be set up after the war. The British and French administrations had their own schemes for such an organization that would try to prevent a major war from occurring. These ideas were discussed at the Versailles Peace Conference in 1919.

The League of Nations, the main international organization that emerged from Versailles, drew on these plans as well as the wartime and 19th century experience. The Assembly of the League was similar to the Hague gatherings, with each state having one vote. Its Council was more like the Supreme War Council, including the major powers, though it also had some representation from other states, while the secretariat was also similar to that which served the Supreme War Council.

The League has often been seen as an institutionalization of the pre-war diplomacy. However, its founding document, the Covenant, attempted something more advanced. Under Article 11 any threat of war was declared a matter of concern for the whole League, with the League taking 'any action that may be deemed wise and effectual to safeguard the peace of nations'. Furthermore, Articles 12–16 outlined how states might conduct their relations by taking any disputes to the newly-established Permanent Court of International Justice, arbitration, conciliation or mediation, and by allowing a breathing space before resorting to war, unlike in August 1914. States resorting to war in contravention of these articles would be deemed to have committed an act of war against all other League members and would be subject to sanctions. Other parts of the Covenant dealt with matters such as open diplomacy, disarmament, former German colonies, and economic and social issues.

Though President Wilson was one of the founding fathers of the League, he was unable to get US membership accepted by the Senate, and the USA never joined the League, compromising its effectiveness from the start.

The Inter-war period

At first, it seemed that the League of Nations was a useful, though modest, addition to international diplomacy. It helped solve disputes between Finland and Sweden in 1920, Greece and Bulgaria in 1925 and between Turkey and Iraq. It also brought the questions of refugees and the treatment of minorities to international attention. By the end of the 1920s it was turning its attention to the issue of disarmament.

Nevertheless, the League had two major structural deficiencies. The first was that of membership. As well as the absence of the USA, the Soviet Union only joined in 1935, by which time Germany, Italy and Japan had left. The second was that the Covenant was part of the Versailles Peace Conference and was seen as a victors' charter. It was thus a source of discontent for Germany, especially after Hitler came to power in 1933 with a determination to unravel both the Peace Treaty and the works of the League. Two other powers that had been on the winning side in 1919 felt that the settlement had not given them enough: both Italy and Japan had not received the overseas possessions they expected. In 1931 Japan occupied the northern part of China, Manchuria, and in 1935 Italy invaded Abyssinia (Ethiopia), then

*Clive Archer is Research Professor in the Department of Politics and Philosophy at Manchester Metropolitan University and is Chair of the University Association for Contemporary European Studies. He is author of *International Organizations* (London: Routledge, 2001, 3rd ed.).

one of the few independent states in Africa. In the first case, the League did little, and in the second it imposed sanctions against Italy, but these were ineffective. As Hitler expanded Germany's power over its neighbours, the League proved unable to act. Only in September 1939 were the British and the French ready to challenge Germany over its invasion of Poland, and this led to the start of the Second World War and the demise of the League of Nations.

The Second World War and the United Nations

The Second World War saw the effective end of the League of Nations and many other international organizations (although the International Committee of the Red Cross undertook important work between the belligerents in Europe overseeing the rules regarding prisoners of war and aiding the treatment and repatriation of injured combatants). The war was also the crucible for the formation of the post-war political structure, when, in a series of meetings, the Allies (the Soviet Union, United Kingdom and the USA, later joined by China and France) decided on the creation of a United Nations Organization (UNO).

The UNO (later shortened to UN) was established in June 1945, at an international conference held in San Francisco, USA, with 50 founding members. After the experience of the League of Nations, the new organization was negotiated during the war and was not tied to any specific peace treaty. Superficially the structure of the UN resembled that of the League. There was a Security Council, of which the Allied Powers had permanent membership; a General Assembly, with all states being allowed membership; a secretariat; and the International Court of Justice, which took over from the Permanent Court of International Justice. There was also an Economic and Social Council and a Trusteeship Council, which oversaw the administration of the colonies of the defeated states. A key difference from the League system was that the Security Council had the prime responsibility for matters of peace and security, something that was not clear about the League Council. Furthermore, the UN Secretary-General had the right to bring security matters to the notice of the Security Council and had wider political powers than his League predecessor.

The UN Security Council was empowered to act when it was agreed that there had been an act of aggression, a breach of the peace or a threat to the peace, a question that was to be settled by a majority of the Council members, but with no Permanent Member voting against (exercising a veto). The Security Council could then resolve, under Chapter Seven of the UN Charter, what sanctions, diplomatic action or armed action should be taken, and all member states were obliged to follow such resolutions. Unlike the fairly legalistic process of the League, the UN peace and security system rested more on political decisions, wherein lay both its strength and weakness.

The Cold War period

In the post-Second World War period, the UN survived and expanded, especially after the increase in sovereign states resulting from decolonization in the 1960s and 1970s and the fragmentation of the Soviet Union after 1991. By 1955 there were 76 members, 100 by the end of the 1960s, 157 by 1982 and 189 by 2002.
During the period 1945–89 the UN reflected the major political and economic conditions in the wider world. First, the division between the market-oriented West, led by the USA, and the state-controlled economies of the Soviet Union-led Eastern bloc affected the workings of the UN. By 1947 efforts by the Western states to pass resolutions through the Security Council were vetoed by the Soviet Union, a trend that continued until well into the 1980s. The main exception was in June 1950 after the invasion of the Republic of Korea (South Korea) by communist forces from North Korea. The USA, as the protector of South Korea, brought the matter before the Security Council while the Soviet Union was absent, owing to a dispute regarding the new communist government in Beijing which had not been seated as the representative of China. The Security Council declared the North Korean action to be aggression and instituted military action against the aggressors. However, many of the disputes between East and West, such as those over Berlin in the 1950s and 1960s, Viet Nam in the 1960s and 1970s, or Cuba in 1952, have been directly negotiated between the USA and its allies and the Soviet Union, and only incidentally involved the Security Council.

The other main development during this period was the growth of the southern hemisphere as a political presence. Decolonization in Asia in the late 1940s and 1950s, was followed by a similar process in Africa and the Caribbean in the 1960s and 1970s. These new countries formed a so-called Third World bloc between the East and West, and used their numbers in the UN General Assembly to place issues reflecting their own interests on the agenda. These questions mainly reflected the economic and social disparities between the richer Western nations and the Third World. During the late 1960s and 1970s the developing countries of the Third World used organizations such as the UN Conference on Trade and Development (UNCTAD) to advance their concerns in the face of the domination of world economic co-operation by the Bretton Woods institutions. These institutions — the International Bank for Reconstruction and Development (IBRD, or the World Bank), the International Monetary Fund (IMF) and the General Agreement on Tariffs and Trade, and their associated agencies—were established immediately after the Second World War and were dominated by Western states, especially the USA. The Third World states felt excluded from institutions in which they had little say, and turned to the UN and UNCTAD to press for greater control of their own natural resources, better trade conditions and a reduction in Third World debts. They had some success during the 1970s when their proposals were backed by the Organization of Petroleum Exporting Countries (OPEC), the membership of which was sympathetic to the general political aims of the Third World and which had some economic clout because of the rising oil prices.

By the 1980s much of this momentum had been lost and the Third World ('the South') had to wait until the end of the millennium for debt relief to be placed on the agendas of organizations dominated by 'the North', such as the Bretton Woods institutions, European Union (EU) and the Group of Seven (G7) meetings of seven of the most wealthy industrialized states (the USA, United Kingdom, Canada, France, Germany, Italy and Japan). Many non-governmental organizations such as Caritas, Oxfam and Save the Children played a key role in campaigning for these countries and organizations to consider debt cancellations.

After the Cold War

By the mid-1980s the Soviet Union, under the leadership of Mikhail Gorbachev, had decided that 'the arms race' with the West that was central to the Cold War could no longer be afforded, let alone won. This led to a number of co-operative agreements between East and West and, eventually, the emergence of new political structures, for example the transformation of the Conference on Security and Co-operation in Europe into a permanent organization, the OSCE. From 1989 to 1991, the Soviet bloc in Eastern Europe and then the Soviet Union itself collapsed, ending the Cold War. The deadlock in the Security Council of the UN had already been ended with Gorbachev's new approach and the UN took on a new lease of life, establishing peace-keeping operations in places such as Central America (with the UN acronym ONUCA, 1989-92), Cambodia (UNAMIC, 1991-92) and between Iran and Iraq (UNIIMOG, 1988-91). When Iraq invaded Kuwait in August 1990, the Security Council united in opposition to his action, imposed sanctions on Iraq and supported the establishment of a coalition of forces, led by the USA, to expel Iraqi troops from Kuwait and establish an observation mission (UNIKOM) between the two states from April 1991. After Yugoslavia collapsed into conflict in 1991, the UN joined with the European Communities (later the European Union) to broker peace between the new states and various factions within these states, but with little success. US-led intervention in the mid-1990s led to a settlement and the establishment of UN peace missions in Bosnia and Herzegovina (UNMIBH, from 1995), Croatia (UNCRO, 1995–96, UNTAES, 1996–98), the Federal Republic of Yugoslavia (UNPROFOR, 1992–95) and the former Yugoslav republic of Macedonia (UNPREDEP, 1995–99). After the US-led action in Kosovo and Metohija in 1999, a UN administration was established for that province (UNMIK). UN missions were also used in Africa (Sierra Leone, UNAMSIL; the Democratic Republic of the Congo, MONUC, both from 1999), East Timor (UNTAET, from October 1999) and Tajikistan (UNMOT, 1994–2000).

While the end of the Cold War provided many opportunities for the UN to be involved in peace operations, and the Security Council showed some willingness in providing the mandate for such activities, the UN has not become as dominant in peace and security matters as some have wished. Many of the conflicts (such as those in former Yugoslavia) have been within, rather than between, states, and the permanent members of the Security Council have sometimes been reluctant to sanction UN action in civil wars. Furthermore, the UN has lacked resources, especially as a number of key countries, notably Russia and the USA, did not pay their full dues during the 1990s. Finally, the most powerful state, the USA, has refused to place its military forces under UN control, and action in a number of areas has therefore depended on the willingness of US administrations to be involved. Action against terrorist networks and against the Taliban government of Afghanistan at the end of 2001, was another demonstration of a US-led operation that acted with the consent of the Security Council.

A further phenomenon in the 1990s was the rise of regional international organizations. Some new ones, such as the Council for Baltic Sea States and the Arctic Council, covered geographically defined areas. Existing regional agencies, such as ECOWAS in West Africa, and ASEAN in South-East Asia became more active. A whole range of organizations, such as the Committee of the Regions, the European Community Humanitarian Office and the European Bank for Reconstruction and Development, were in one form or another associated with the European Union, which in itself forms a system of governance that includes a number of international organizations.

More generally, the 1990s saw a fluctuation in the number of international organizations. While the number of intergovernmental organizations rose from 289 in 1970 to some 380 by 1990, the total fell to about 250 by 2000, reflecting a closer questioning of costs and benefits of international organizations by governments during the 1990s. However the growth in the number of international non-governmental organizations continued apace. It had already risen from 1,470 in 1964 to 4,676 in 1985, and by 1999 the total was 5,825, according to the *Yearbook of International Organizations* (Union of International Associations).

TYPES OF INTERNATIONAL ORGANIZATIONS

International organizations can be classified in a number of ways. The three main methods of dividing them are by types of membership, aims and activities, and by structure.

Membership

Though the rise of international organizations had to wait until the establishment of a system of sovereign states that had frequent contact with each other, the membership of international organizations is not limited to states represented by their governments. An important distinction is between the kinds of international organizations that are interstate, or intergovernmental, and those whose membership is non-governmental. A further category has mixed membership.

Intergovernmental organizations (IGOs). According to the UN Economic and Social Council (ECOSOC), there is a distinction between intergovernmental organizations (IGOs) and international non-governmental organizations (INGOs—sometimes shortened to NGOs). IGOs are created by intergovernmental agreement and their members are governments or their agents. The terms 'intergovernmental organization' and 'interstate organization' are interchangeable.

International non-governmental organizations (INGOs). What are often called 'international organizations' sometimes contain members that are not states or governmental representatives but are drawn from groups, associations, organizations or individuals from within the state. These non-governmental actors are performing on the international stage and their activities give rise to transnational interaction.

Transnational organizations (TNOs). These are established when such relationships between more than two participants become institutionalized by agreement into a formal, continuous structure in order to pursue the common interests of the participants, one of which is not an agent of government or an international organization. In contrast to an intergovernmental organization, a TNO must have a non-state actor for at least one of its members.

Three sorts of TNOs can be identified. The genuine INGO is an organization with only non-governmental members. These bring together the representatives of like-minded groups from more than two countries, examples of which are the International Olympic Committee, the World Council of Churches, the Soroptimist International, the Salvation Army and the Universal Esperanto Association. A hybrid INGO has some governmental and some non-governmental representation. If established by a treaty between governments, it is an IGO, for example the International Labour Organization (ILO) which has trade union and management (i.e. non-governmental) membership as well as governmental representatives. However, some INGOs have a mixed membership and are not the result of a purely intergovernmental agreement, for example the International Council of Scientific Unions. The transgovernmental organization is set up by governmental actors not controlled by the central foreign policy organs of their governments. Examples include the International Union of Local Authorities (IULA), the International Council for the Exploration of the Sea (ICES), the International Criminal Police Organization (Interpol), and the Inter-Parliamentary Union.

A fourth category of TNOs is sometimes mentioned: that of the business international non-governmental organizations (BINGOs), alternatively called multinational enterprises or corporations. However these are normally excluded from the term 'international organization' on the following grounds: that ECOSOC does so; that they reflect the workings, albeit across frontiers, of one corporation domiciled in one state; and that they are profit-making organizations.

Aims and Activities

A common way of classifying international organizations is by examining what they do. The aims of most international organizations can be seen in the basic document that establishes them, such as a treaty or agreement. The record of the international organization can also be examined to see whether the organization has lived up to its aims. International organizations are quite often divided into those that have general aims—the UN being the most obvious example—and specialized organizations, including many members of the UN family such as the World Health Organization (WHO), the Food and Agriculture Organization (FAO) and the UN Children's Fund (UNICEF). Also, international organizations may have aims and activities that encourage co-operative behaviour, such as the Nordic Council, and/or they may aim at reducing conflict between members, as in the case of the UN, the Organization of African Unity and the League of Arab States.

Structure

An easy way to distinguish between the variety of international organizations is to look at the structure of their institutions. The early international organizations in the 19th century had simple structures. The Universal Postal Union and the International Telegraph Union (see above) both had permanent administrative offices and policy-making meetings of the representatives of member states every few years. The League of Nations, with its secretariat, council, assembly and court was more complicated and this institutional edifice was built on by the UN which added a Trusteeship Council and an Economic and Social Council as well as a host of committees and agencies. A number of organizations have judicial bodies attached to them—such as the European Court of Human Rights of the Council of Europe—and a few have parliamentary organs, such as the Consultative Assembly of the Council of Europe and the directly-elected European Parliament of the European Union.

Power within the various organs of an international organizations may be divided unequally. In IGOs, the member states often try to retain the greatest power for the organ within which they are represented. However, not all members carry the same clout. In the UN there are the five permanent members of the Security Council—the USA, Russia, the People's Republic of China, the United Kingdom and France, in effect the main powers at the end of the Second World War—who have the privileged position of being able to veto any Security Council resolution by casting a negative vote. Those providing large capital subscriptions to the IMF and the IBRD have the most votes on their governing bodies, which are thus controlled by the industrialized states. Power may also fluctuate between the institutions of an international organization that represent the interests of the member states (especially the more powerful ones) and those that represent the wider interests of the organization. There has thus been a tension within the UN between the Security Council, in which Great Power interests dominate, and the Secretary-General's office. When the Security Council was paralysed by power divisions during the Cold War, the Secretaries-General tried to develop their powers and influence. Dag Hammarskjöld, who served as Secretary-General from 1953 to 1961, played an important role in developing the office, though both the Soviet Union and the USA attempted to prevent successive Secretaries-General from taking too much power.

ROLES OF INTERNATIONAL ORGANIZATIONS

Instrument of the membership

The most common role played by international organizations in the global system is that of being used by the membership for their own ends. In the case of IGOs, the member states not only may try to limit the power of independent action by the institutions of international organizations but will also vie with other members to get the most out of any particular international organization. However, multilateral co-operation offers possibilities that individual states would not have if they acted separately. This means that there is often an ambiguity in states' policies towards international organizations. While membership offers new opportunities, it also brings responsibilities and restraints. Furthermore, the ability of a state to use an organization for its own ends may change over time. For example, the USA was able to use the UN for its own diplomatic needs during the first eight years of its existence as it had a Secretary-General sympathetic to its aims and a General Assembly on which it could normally rely. Only in the Security Council could the Soviet Union veto US resolutions. Later in the 1960s and 1970s, the majority of the General Assembly, consisting of developing states, were critical of US policies, and the Secretaries-General—U Thant and Kurt Waldheim—were more even-handed in their dealings with the power blocs. Consequently US administrations became less able and willing to use the UN as a diplomatic instrument.

Forums for activity

A second role for international organizations is that of an arena within which the members meet, debate and act. Especially during the Cold War the UN was often used as an 'arena for combat' between East and West and also between North and South in the late 1960s and 1970s. This was aided by the arrangement of states into blocs—the West consisting of the NATO states and countries such as Australia and New Zealand, the East consisting of the Soviet bloc, and the South covering most of the states of Asia, Africa and Latin America. Other organizations were established to act as platforms for particular interests: OPEC being the forum for petroleum exporting states.

International actors

International organizations are sometimes seen as independent actors on the world scene. Thus the organization as a whole is seen as separate from its membership. The media often talk about the 'UN taking action' or 'OPEC increasing prices' thus confirming the image of international organizations acting apart from their membership. Though all international organizations are dependent on their membership, not least for finance and other resources, they have institutional frameworks that allow them to achieve more than if their members acted separately or, indeed, just co-operated on an *ad hoc* basis. Depending on the strength of the institutions of the organization, such as a secretariat or a court, international organizations can sometimes act contrary to the wishes of at least some of their members, though they would be risking their very existence by doing this for any length of time. Even some INGOs are seen as effective independent actors on the world scene. The International Committee of the Red Cross and Red Crescent is a good example, and it has now been joined by a number of humanitarian organizations such as Médecins sans Frontières, Oxfam and Caritas.

FUNCTIONS OF INTERNATIONAL ORGANIZATIONS

Recruitment

On the whole, the functions that international organizations perform help to maintain the international system within which they exist. One task that they aid is that of recruitment of participants in the international political system. By consisting of the representatives of sovereign states, the very existence of IGOs has encouraged non-self-governing territories to achieve independence. This has allowed them to gain access to organizations where they can promote their state's interests. Thus many small territories have pressed for independence and membership of the UN. Furthermore, INGOs have recruited groups and individuals so that they may act more effectively at the international level, and their effectiveness is recognized by a number of leading IGOs such as ECOSCO, the ILO, UNESCO and UNCTAD, in which they are provided with consultative status.

Aggregation of views

Organizations such as trade unions, charities, interest groups and political parties within national political systems help to aggregate viewpoints on a wide range of subjects from the national minimum wage and aid for the developing world to the moral aspects of genetic research and the benefits of privatization or nationalization. Most often this aggregation of interests is aimed at national (or regional) governments. Such interests aggregated at the international level by international organizations are faced with the lack of a central body that allocates values and resources, a government. However, values and resources are allocated internationally but by a diffuse system consisting of more than 180 states, international organizations themselves and the international markets. International organizations in all three roles mentioned above—instruments for members, forums and actors—can aggregate opinion and articulate it more or less effectively. Shipowners put forward their views to governments and agencies through the International Chamber of Shipping, religious groups have the forum of the World Council of Churches to express their opinions, and the labour movement attempts to advance workers' rights through the ILO.

Norms and Socialization

International organizations have played an important role in spreading certain norms and values throughout the world. The UN Charter in its Preamble expresses particular values such as 'faith in fundamental human rights' and in 'the equal rights of men and women and of nations large and small'. The Universal Declaration of Human Rights adopted by the UN General Assembly in 1948 'as a common standard of achievement for all peoples and all nations' has references to personal, social and economic rights. Furthermore, the UN helped to de-legitimize European colonialism and to outlaw white-ruled South Africa for its policy of apartheid or separate treatment of whites and blacks. The role of socialization by which societies decide what is acceptable and inculcate beliefs and behaviour into their members is often undertaken within states by families, voluntary groups and even governments. Internationally, it is quite often religions or multinational companies that can act as agents of socialization. International organizations can contribute to the process, but are often in competition with more powerful state and commercial forces. The International Olympic Committee tries to further the values of competitive sport world-wide, and the various Nordic associations, as well as the Nordic Council, have helped to produce a common feeling among the citizens of the five Nordic states. Also international organizations have helped to socialize governments. Organizations such as the League of Nations and United Nations have tried, with mixed success, to persuade some governments—often those with revolutionary credentials such as the Soviet Union, the People's Republic of China, or Iran after 1979—to behave in a way more acceptable to the rest of the international community. The Federal Republic of Yugoslavia under President Milošović was not allowed UN membership until the downfall of its turbulent leader in 2000. Some commentators view the World Trade Organization as an effective socializing instrument by which the former-Soviet bloc states and Third World countries are persuaded to accept the rigours of freer trade and the market economy.

Rules

At the national level, rule-making is the task of governments and parliaments. Though the UN is far from being either a world government or parliament, this does not mean that rules are not made, implemented and adjudicated internationally. This may be seen within the UN system when the General Assembly adopts a convention relating to the rules of diplomatic practice or the Third UN Conference on the Law of the Sea concludes a comprehensive agreement affecting the world's oceans. Organizations such as the International Bureau of Weights and Measures, the UPU and the Metric Union have had over a hundred years of experience of making international rules in their functional areas. Many of their rules, concerning the implementation of common standards, have been accepted because of their usefulness in international trade, for example. However, there are other international organizations that have wider rule-application capabilities. The International Committee of the Red Cross and Red Crescent has helped to supervise the rules of war and conflict across the globe. Amnesty International and a host of other INGOs have tried to make sure that human rights are respected. The International Atomic Energy Agency has wide powers to monitor the spread of fissionable material. International organizations also have rule-adjudication functions. The International Court of Justice makes judgments about claims between states. The European Court of Human Rights (of the Council of Europe) and the European Court of Justice (of the European Union) can make rulings that directly affect individuals in the member states.

Operations

International organizations undertake a number of functional activities. These includes banking (the Bank for International Settlements, the European Bank for Reconstruction and Development), providing aid (the humanitarian INGOs and several UN specialized agencies), helping refugees (the UN High Commissioner for Refugees) and running technical services (INTELSAT, the World Weather Watch of the World Meteorological Organization). A number of INGOs also run operations, especially in developing countries where they help clear land mines, feed refugees or encourage rural development.

CONCLUSIONS

International organizations have grown considerably since their inception in the early 19th century. The most rapid and continuous growth has been in international non-governmental organizations, with the number of inter-governmental organizations seeming to have peaked in the early 1990s. These organizations, ranging from the UN network down to the humblest of INGOs, can be instruments for their members, meeting-places and actors. They cover a wide role of functions in the international system including making and applying rules and carrying out a number of activities often associated with governments. International organizations have attempted, with mixed success, to tackle the wide range of global problems such as conflict, poverty, illness, environmental degradation and ignorance. Their effectiveness is constrained not just by the enormity of their tasks but also because of their own organizational shortcomings and the reluctance of member states to give them resources. Nevertheless, they are a part of the way that the world is run and are likely to continue to develop into the 21st century.

CHALLENGES FACING THE INTERNATIONAL SYSTEM IN THE 21st CENTURY

WILLIAM HOPKINSON*

Reflection on the great changes that have taken place in international affairs and in the role and activities of international organizations would in any case be appropriate at the start of a new millennium, and is particularly apt given the major terrorist attacks perpetrated against the USA on 11 September 2001 and all consequent military and diplomatic action. It has been variously suggested that the nature of the world has been irrevocably changed by the attacks; that they will in time be seen as the first blows in a great struggle of the poor South against the rich North; or that they have induced a new concord in international affairs in which all the major players are united on one side and will co-operate in an unprecedented fashion. All of those hypotheses seem exaggerations. Domestic perceptions of security in the USA have changed, and, given the weight of the USA in international relations, that will have some impact. Moreover, Russia seems finally to have opted for the West as its preferred partner. Beyond this, however, the world post-11 September seems very similar to the one which existed before. The persistent problems of the Middle East, of Africa, of the Indian subcontinent, and of global warming and other environmental degradation remain, as do the economic and political issues arising from globalization.

The nature of international relations altered almost beyond recognition in the course of the 20th century, and to a very significant degree after 1950. The issues, the players, and the manner of play are now very different. Some of these developments have followed from technological or economic changes, as in the processes of globalization: it is now often more appropriate to speak of *global* rather than international politics. Others stem from political or geopolitical changes of a more traditional sort, though often of an unprecedented magnitude. The two greatest of these were the process of decolonization, which redrew the world map and changed the numbers and kinds of state actors, and then, after a longish interval, the collapse of the Soviet Empire, which heralded the end of the Cold War and the consequent revolution in European security issues.

Security nevertheless remains at the heart of international relations: it is the necessary prior condition of all other objectives. However, the meaning of international security has changed, expanding to encompass more actors and more kinds of actor, and very different threats. Not least among these is the threat to stability and order posed by not the strong state but the weak. The risk of state collapse is now of much greater concern than previously, both to immediate neighbours and to the wider international community. Such collapse may provide scope for ethnic conflict or for the rise of warlords. As in Afghanistan, it may also provide a lodgement for major terrorist activities. Trans-border criminal operations are another significant factor with far-reaching impact. Terrorism, trafficking and other criminal activities are now often found to be very closely interlinked. The recrudescence of violence, including both ethnic strife and terrorism, has compelled consideration of its causes, and of potential solutions. The search for these is a pressing issue, as demonstrated by the state of the Middle East peace process, Chechnya, Iraq, the lack of stability in many Muslim states, the major problems in parts of sub-Saharan Africa and now the emergence of large-scale global terrorism. The waging of war against the Taliban in Afghanistan has prompted further consideration of the application of military force in distant locations, regarding both the suitability of this and possible means of achieving it, as well as further consideration of the problems of asymmetric warfare. All this has major implications for the role of, and indeed the very existence of, international organizations.

Early announcements after the Cold War that the shape of the future was unequivocally clear and that it was to be either the end of history, or a coming clash of civilizations, or an overwhelming wave of unifying globalization, or a new Middle Ages, have been followed by more nuanced responses. A recent development has been the reaction against globalization and the market economy manifested in the demonstrations that were held in Seattle and Washington in 1999 and 2000 against the WTO and IMF, respectively, and were repeated during 2001 against other meetings of influential economic organizations. This kind of protest, involving groups from both developing and industrialized countries, shows every sign of continuing. It clearly indicates the increasingly intimate relationship between international relations and economic and societal issues. No longer are the former the sole preserve of chancelleries and ministries of foreign affairs: the organization of international economic meetings must now take into account the likelihood of disruption by external pressures, both physical and political.

THE CHALLENGES AHEAD

As international actions in the Balkans and Afghanistan have demonstrated, the mechanisms for dealing with the new security agenda include not only conciliation and political negotiation, but also outside intervention, whose purposes may include the relief of humanitarian disasters, peace enforcement, or more traditional concerns such as the replacement of regimes that support hostile forces or activities. Indeed, a principal theme of international relations in the early 21st century is likely to remain the question of intervention: who can do what to whom, on what basis, and to what end.

Military intervention requires effective armed forces able to operate at a distance. Few countries have had force projection capabilities of any significance in recent years. Most have been concerned to defend their own territories, and have had at best only a very limited capacity to go beyond that. The USA, however, has long had major capabilities, and is still unparalleled in those. The two years culminating in the Nice Summit of the European Union (EU) at the end of 2000 saw the determination of European nations, led by the United Kingdom and France, to acquire at least modest ability to project power away from the home country, and to sustain their operations for some time. To achieve that they need armed forces that are mobile, flexible, and can be supplied and commanded far from their bases. Therefore they also need improved transport and communication assets. The latest developments point to the possible realization of the long-sought European Security and Defence Identity, or now rather, in an EU rather than a NATO context, the Common European Security and Defence Policy with a link to the Common Foreign and Security Policy. The full development of such a policy, and of the necessary military assets, is still, however, a very long way away. Meanwhile, both in terms of capability and domestic political acceptability, intervention remains much more a US than a European phenomenon. Nevertheless, whether or not the Europeans are ultimately successful in their aim, their efforts are likely to have implications both for the question of intervention and for transatlantic relations.

Despite some multilateralist gestures engendered by the events of 11 September 2001, the new administration in Washington may in fact prove to be both more unilateralist and, in some senses, more isolationist than its predecessor. The Bush administration appears unilateralist in the sense of being likely to pursue what it perceives as US interests outside international frameworks except when the latter clearly conform to its own concerns. It may be isolationist in the sense of showing even more reluctance than its predecessor to commit its military to situations where

*William Hopkinson (formerly Assistant Under Secretary of State at the UK Ministry of Defence and Deputy Director and Director of Studies at the Royal Institute of International Affairs, London, UK) writes and lectures on international relations and security.

the USA does not have a direct and vital national interest, and may look to the Europeans to do more while still expecting them to follow the US lead in most security issues. These factors, and the extent of European capabilities, will have an impact on the nature of future interventions.

Some of the gravest security crises of recent years have arisen in Africa, where timely intervention might have saved many lives. However, the capabilities for constructive intervention of most countries there are far more limited even than those of the Europeans. Nevertheless, during the 1990s several multinational operations were successfully mobilized there, under the banner of sub-regional organizations; these still tended to be dominated by one major power, giving rise to the inherent complications of a government pursuing its own political agenda. A further significant development was the British military intervention in Sierra Leone: far from being condemned as neo-colonialism, as might have been expected only a few years earlier, this was widely welcomed as a major step towards creating order and stability.

The US intervention in Afghanistan represented in some ways a reversion to an earlier pattern of events. In response to an act of aggression a great power was successful in removing an offending regime (in this case one that had sheltered the perpetrators of the attack). More difficult will be achieving the ultimate aim of defeating terrorism. Terrorism is a broad term, covering a wide spectrum of actors and goals, ranging from the deranged individual, through organized groups with definable agendas, to millennial groups who have no achievable objective. Combating terrorism requires successful intelligence work, good policing, effective legal and judicial procedures, and, in some circumstances, limited military engagement. In an interconnected world, effective international co-operation is essential, not least in tracing and curtailing financial flows. In the case of the groups with political agendas, attention must be paid to the motivating factors. Even in other cases it is necessary to have regard to background social, economic and political factors, and to consider whether alleviation of those might reduce the incentives or opportunities for terrorism. Despite the weight currently directed at countering this problem, it is not clear as yet how effective the ongoing efforts will be or what role will be played by intervention in states aiding terrorism. Another form of outside intervention, the need for which has been clearly demonstrated but whose execution has been problematic, concerns the provision of humanitarian assistance to populations affected by natural disasters. In recent years, for example, flooding, storms and earthquakes in Honduras, the Indian subcontinent, Western Asia, Mozambique and Venezuela have wrought widespread devastation, overstretching the capabilities of the countries concerned. International assistance has been forthcoming, but real difficulties have been evident in assembling the necessary skills and equipment. The role of non-governmental organizations (NGOs) in providing immediate relief and in assisting with the subsequent rebuilding of society has often been crucial, although forging their efforts into a coherent whole can be an arduous process. In future, global climate change may increase the incidence of such crises. Undoubtedly the direct and indirect pressures of population growth will magnify the effects: expanding deforestation will increase the risk of floods, while cities will be larger and the numbers afflicted greater, etc.

The changes in thinking on intervention have occurred in a rather irregular and not entirely coherent manner. They have been influenced by the revolution in communications through which far-away disasters, or what may be seen as unacceptable oppressions, are brought more or less instantaneously into the homes of concerned and relatively vocal citizens who firmly believe that something must be done. This feeling may not always be moderated either by an appreciation of the full background, or by an understanding of what could usefully be achieved. It is, nevertheless, a real political fact. In order to address it international law is already, to some extent, developing through specific negotiated treaties, for example by the establishment of the International Criminal Court (ICC), agreed by representatives of some 120 countries in Rome in 1998. However, that kind of progress may not be sufficient; what may be termed customary law may have to develop in parallel, and more quickly than before.

The development of international law seems likely to be a second major theme of the coming years. If this is to deal with current security issues and present widespread political concerns it will have to advance beyond where the UN Charter now rests. In particular, international law will have to address matters which, at the time of the Charter's agreement, were regarded as solely for domestic decision. There is a certain oddity in that, for the Charter was drafted in the context of a struggle against a regime whose treatment of its own population was to give rise to an international tribunal and trials for crimes against humanity. Nevertheless, in the age of great power politics internal matters were reserved for sovereign states. Whilst that perspective still finds strong echoes in Asia, in Russia and in many segments of US opinion (in the latter case often rather oddly co-existing with a belief in the USA's right to intervene), political opinion in many places has now moved on.

The scope for, and the pace of, the development of international law will be strongly affected by the approach of the new Bush administration in Washington. Whilst seeking to draw tighter the networks necessary to defeat major terrorism, or at least to limit its effects, the US seems very reluctant to accept restraints upon its own freedoms of action. As a consequence of US attitudes the pace of the creation of new rules and norms by treaty may slow down significantly; there is even a risk of some regression. The USA's sense of exceptionalism—that, no matter what applies to others, its government, including Congress, can accept no external restraints upon US sovereignty—is deeply ingrained. A society in which lawyers exercise exceptional influence seems, nonetheless, ill at ease with the prospect of an enhanced role for international law.

The third great area to be considered is the growth in the number of non-state actors that are present in one form or another on the international stage. Some are supra-national in the sense of UN agencies, or regional organizations; some are sub-national. The proposal for a special court in Sierra Leone envisaged a new type of international organization, a joint national and international tribunal, with roles for both the UN and the national government. Without prophesying the end of the nation state, we are seeing the creation of new kinds of political organization. The EU is one outstanding example; another (very different) is Bosnia and Herzegovina, where relatively strong entities enjoy something like *de facto* sovereignty within a weak outer envelope. The future of Kosovo may provide a further example of a new kind of political entity. It remains to be seen what stable entity, if any, can be created in post-Taliban Afghanistan.

Over the coming years most conflicts seem likely to involve not nation states fighting each other, but clashes within states, or between groups within different states. Such conflict is now a more usual source of instability and loss of life than inter-state warfare. This gives added importance to the growth in numbers and importance of sub-state groups or entities as international actors. These include organizations which help to alleviate suffering and resolve conflict but also those which engender it. Thus they include NGOs and corporations but also major criminal associations, such as those concerned with the production and transportation of illegal drugs. The wealthiest of these can deploy technology and armaments powerful enough to threaten the very security of some nations, and to pose a challenge even to the resources of the USA. This capacity has also been demonstrated by terrorist groups, notably by bin Laden and al-Qa'ida.

All three of the elements outlined above, intervention, the advance of international law, and the greatly increased importance of non-state actors, come together in the issue of failed states. In some instances, states which had a recognized international existence, membership of the UN, and so on, have ceased to function in any meaningful way, either as guardians of the well-being of their people, or as entities able to engage in wider international relations. There is nothing new in this phenomenon, except that in time past the major powers could either ignore the breakdown and regard the failed state as part of the uncivilized area of the world, or they could intervene to colonize or police the area in question. Improvements in communications and global interaction make it much less easy to ignore breakdowns than before. Public opinion in favour of action and large movements of refugees pressurize governments in the more fortunate parts of the world to respond. Despite very deep disorder in some places it is no longer generally acceptable to regard anywhere as a place where the rules of civilized conduct have no relevance. On the other hand, colonialism has not generally been regarded as an acceptable option as it once would have been, either with domestic audiences, or with world opinion. (In view of events in the Balkans, there are some indications that this attitude is starting to change, although the new protectorates there entail multinational duty rather than imperial glory.) Thus, against the cry that something must be done, failed states raise in an acute form the issues of the responsibilities and powers of the international community, and of the individual actors within it.

THE POLITICS OF INTERVENTION

The key question in armed intervention concerns specifying the circumstances in which it is justified. Subsidiary questions are then how that justification is to be established or demonstrated, what is to be done, and by whom. The UN Security Council may authorize intervention if it believes that there is a threat to international peace or security. Internal strife, or some other symptom of a failing state, may pose problems to neighbouring countries from violence, or tides of refugees, or both, spilling over their borders. There may be fears about weapons of mass destruction becoming freed from effective control, or about adverse environmental impact. In many instances such threats make for a colourable case for the Security Council's authorizing intervention. As well as action by the Security Council the UN Charter also authorizes, under Article 51, self-defence against aggression, at any rate pending the Security Council's taking a decisive lead. That may justify certain interventions, either by a state directly threatened, or by its allies, though the number of instances to which this Article will apply are *prima facie* limited. Nevertheless, the US intervention against the Afghan regime that sheltered terrorists may point the way to a further extension of doctrines of intervening in failed or failing states.

Whether the Security Council in fact authorizes intervention will be influenced, of course, almost as much by politics, and especially by relations between the five permanent members, as by the facts on the ground. The events of 11 September 2001 and subsequent fight against terrorism may have permanently affected those relationships; however, on balance that appears improbable, although Russia has moved to a closer relationship with the West that seems likely to endure. If a permanent member uses its veto, Security Council action will be blocked, whatever the facts; and if, for whatever reason, the Security Council does not give its authorization, then a gap in legal authority or political legitimacy, as these have hitherto been understood, may well occur. Nevertheless, a continuing feeling that something must be done, either because of the degree of human suffering involved, or because the breakdown of order, including the existence of a terrorist haven, may pose a threat either to the international community as a whole, or to the interests of particular states, may lead some nations to conclude that they must intervene, irrespective of the lack of Security Council agreement.

On the other hand, the facts may hardly support the existence of the purported threat to international peace or security from the action or state of affairs to remedy which a Security Council resolution is sought, but if the Security Council can agree upon it, there will, politically and effectively, be a valid basis for intervention. The Security Council is its own judge in that the processes are essentially political not legal. If there is authorization there can be no effective challenge to the merits of an intervention, or questioning of whether it was strictly justified within the terms of the UN Charter. There can, of course, be challenges, as there were over Iraq, as to whether an earlier Security Council resolution still authorizes intervention, but again those are of a political rather than juridical nature. However, even if it is agreed that something should be done, there may be real problems in deciding on a course that really helps to resolve the crisis. For example, the declaration by the UN of Safe Areas in Bosnia and Herzegovina was hardly an assistance to conflict resolution or the rebuilding of civil society, since there were real difficulties in the application of the decision to the situation on the ground.

Even when it is known that a particular course of action would help, and there are no political obstacles put in its way, there may still be real difficulties in implementing it. This has been demonstrated by responses to natural disasters. Many organizations may wish to assist but may inadvertently impede each other's activities. Some organizations may favour a particular group, while governments may be anxious to demonstrate their own credentials. Operations may be hampered by a lack of trained personnel, of supplies, of transport with which to reach an area and function therein, or of the kind of engineering support required to repair roads or restore water supplies. Since in all types of humanitarian or state-building intervention international organizations, such as the agencies of the UN and NGOs, are likely to play a vital role, better preparation in terms of equipment, training and, in so far as is possible, co-ordination, is essential.

Where there is civil strife many of the same problems may be present, and there will be additional complications. There are very real limits to what NGOs can achieve in areas of active conflict. There will often be a pressing need for military or gendarmerie action. However, no nation may be willing to expose its armed forces to risk. Even where there is a willingness to act, there may be a shortage of resources, whether financial or logistical or of necessary skills. The UN has experienced severe financial shortfalls and has problems with command and control of military operations. There are few other established institutions for providing resources from the international community in a regular way for conflict resolution. Even if the resources are available, there may be problems in applying them effectively, either because of a lack of appropriate information, or because of structural inefficiencies in how the UN and its agencies operate. Moreover, at the national level, most ministries of foreign affairs are lacking in financial means, while ministries of defence often regard their resources as confined to national defence. NATO is capable of much of the necessary military planning, but is not appropriate for all circumstances. In cases where it is not, or where major members are unwilling to act, because of lack of resources or for political reasons, there is at present no other multinational military organization capable of undertaking the most complex operations. In due course the EU may develop sufficient capabilities, but that lies at best some years ahead.

The USA as a global force

As the possessors of unrivalled and in some ways unique military capabilities, and as inheritors, at any rate *inter alia*, of a tradition of viewing themselves as different from other powers, as a special nation, many in the US political classes feel on the one hand empowered to act when their judgement is satisfied, and on the other reluctant to accept the restraints which international bodies not subject to their own institutions may seek to impose. The final decade of the 20th century saw intervention by bombing in Iraq because of that regime's failure to meet the UN's requirements on the dismantling of its weapons of mass destruction, and the policing, again by air power, of no-fly zones imposed to restrict that country's ability to oppress its own population. In the Balkans, after the creation by intervention of what is, in effect, a new sort of political entity in Bosnia and Herzegovina, there has been intervention over the treatment by Serbia of the Albanian population in its southern province of Kosovo and, of a rather different sort, in Macedonia. In all except the last of these examples the US was a major player, both politically and militarily. Without its capabilities the interventions could not have been mounted, at least in the form in which they were.

The Kosovo case raised even more difficult questions than that of Iraq. In the latter there had been earlier UN involvement following external aggression by the Iraqi regime. The events in Serbia, however, concerned the treatment by a sovereign state of part of its own population. Even more significantly, there was no specific UN Security Council mandate for action. At the end of 2001, the intervention in Afghanistan was even more unilateral in execution, albeit endorsed by a wide political coalition. The USA put together a network of support which included a small degree of military contribution from its allies but also, more importantly from its point of view, political engagement from China, Russia and many Muslim states. With the application of its own military power, largely air assets and special forces, in support of local elements, it was able to topple the Taliban regime.

The USA will also almost certainly remain extremely reluctant to risk its own servicemen while continuing to emphasize air power and other high-technology means of attacking opponents from a distance. Such methods hardly make for a successful recipe for intervention in complex and messy situations of internal strife or domestic disorder, even when there is general agreement on its justification. The usual requirement is to engage in numbers on the ground, both to police the situation and to gather intelligence. Moreover, the military element of any intervention should be there to serve wider political ends; that means that it should be subsumed in a wider political plan. When general agreement is lacking, the preferred US approach may make for great international friction, and may offer little hope of producing an enduring outcome better than the pre-existing state of affairs.

Problems of single power leadership

US tendencies towards exceptionalism (which may be amplified under the new regime in Washington) manifest themselves not only in questions of military intervention but also in a self-image as an automatic diplomatic and political leader. Indeed, these tendencies go further, manifesting themselves in attempts to impose US legislation on others (as over sanctions in respect of, for example, Cuba, Iran and Libya), while resisting others' jurisdiction over American citizens or activities (for example, the difficulties with the statute of the ICC and with the verification provisions of the Chemical Weapons Convention). It may be that the rest of the international community will, perhaps perforce, tolerate, or even continue to welcome, a degree of US unilateral leadership. After all, despite some grievous mistakes, the USA has been, in many places and on many occasions, a force for good. In the longer term, however, such a reaction must be doubtful, especially given the increasing assertiveness of Asian players such as China and India and the strong reactions against Western approaches to economics and social issues, particularly in the Islamic world. For example, the follow-up to the intervention in Afghanistan will require particularly careful handling if there is not to be adverse reaction in Muslim societies. In any case, all power corrupts, and there is no reason to think that over time, with an unfettered capability to interfere, the USA would remain immune from that.

A separate concern is that US interest, stimulated like that of other nations by media attention, and sometimes ignorant of issues on which the media has not focused, may be too erratic to be tolerable as the sole long-term mainstay of international engagement. There may well be issues of vital importance to particular nations or regions which, quite understandably, do not seize the attention of the USA. It will still be necessary for the international community to have the means to deal with them. Moreover, some of the domestic political pressures which influence its foreign policy are already all too likely to distort that policy away from what is in the USA's own interests, let alone those of the rest of the world. Its role in the Middle East Peace Process is an example. There, one of the major issues is US reluctance to intervene in a way consistent with UN Security Council resolutions, as well as its tendency to use its veto to prevent the Security Council from addressing the problem. More generally, and not confined to the USA, there are real issues about the impact of democratic and popular pressures on international relations which have not been thought through. As a consequence of those, the difficulties in the modern world confronting all nations and groups of nations attempting to pursue consistent long-term policies are great but rarely acknowledged.

THE DEVELOPMENT OF INTERNATIONAL LAW

Great powers have, of course, always intervened in particular cases in the business of their neighbours, and sometimes in the business of those far away. The classic depiction of a system of sovereign states who did not interfere in each other's internal affairs, and which operated in a universe of international actors bound by a few rules of international law, was always an oversimplification. The rules applied, on the whole, only as regards developed nations, and in their fullness only to relatively strong players. In the 19th-century it was not only Metternich, the Austrian Chancellor, but also Gladstone, the British Prime Minister, who could call for interference in other nations' business. The then Great Powers intervened and interfered in the Ottoman Empire, in China, and elsewhere. There came significant changes after the First World War and the foundation of the League of Nations, but again these were not so far-reaching even in principle as they at first appeared. From that period dates the first real outlawing of aggression as an instrument of policy, and some significant recognition of the right of self-determination. However, colonial government was not outlawed, and great pressure could be brought on sovereign states to change not only their policies, but even their borders, as in the case of Czechoslovakia in 1938.

It would be naïve to expect that, whatever the legal framework, great powers would cease to wield influence, sometimes very significant influence, over their neighbours and others, while resisting interference in their own affairs. That was acknowledged at the creation of the UN by the powers given to the permanent members of the Security Council, which represented a step forward from the constitution of the League of Nations. Now, however, what is desirable, indeed necessary, is to extend the limitations on unilateral great power action, and to reinforce the role and rule of law in international affairs. It would be in the interests of the West, including the US, to do that, while Western views on conduct and governance are still in the ascendant. If it has a vision of world order it would do well to get this enshrined in enduring mechanisms during the next few decades. It will not be in the West's long-term interest to foster the notion that unilateral intervention by the strong is the way forward. Nothing lasts forever; empires rise and fall. Half a century hence, the relative power of the USA may be reduced, and that of other nations on the increase. US citizens will not welcome unilateralism when, without international legal sanction, say, Chinese marines land in the Persian Gulf to protect China's energy supplies, or a resurgent Russia presses on or over its southern borders to quell what it sees as destabilizing upheaval. If one accepts that values which might be described as Western, at least in origin (i.e. an emphasis on human rights, the belief in the rule of law not of men), are really valid, then it would be in the interests of all nations and all peoples to fix them in the international system as firmly as possible. That will require further erosion of the 19th-century concept of sovereignty (as generally understood), and the extension of the role of international organizations.

The growth of feeling, since at least the post-Second World War Nuremberg Trials, up to and including the trials in The Hague, Netherlands, in respect of crimes committed in the former Yugoslavia, and the creation of the ICC, that certain behaviour cannot be viewed simply as a domestic matter, suggests that further development of international law is required. However, intervention in cases of civil war or internal strife poses particular difficulties: the struggle may be especially bitter; there may be no solution; and it may be impossible to identify who is doing what in the conflict. Moreover, according to the wording of the UN Charter, not only is the Security Council apparently not authorized to act in such cases, it appears actually forbidden to do so, internal matters being excluded from its competence by Article 2. Yet it is precisely such matters that, in the light of the experience of Kosovo, not to mention the Taliban regime in Afghanistan, are most likely to agitate public opinion and so lead to calls for intervention. If the Security Council fails to act, for whatever reason, then the choice may be some form of unilateral action, or neglect of a situation which may be producing consequences that are felt to be intolerable.

However, legal development is not some kind of universal panacea. At the end of a period of civil conflict, prosecution of criminals may be necessary in order to rebuild society. On the other hand, it may also serve to impede that very reconstruction. In the case of Spain, officials of the Franco era have generally been consigned to oblivion and *de facto* indemnity. That has apparently suited the evolution of Spanish society to a democratic and liberal present. In the case of South Africa, forgiveness has (in general) followed confession. In Chile, the outgoing head of state, Gen. Augusto Pinochet, struck a bargain which allowed for peaceful transition to a democracy, admittedly fragile but, nevertheless, working. The subsequent attempts to extradite him to Spain raised another aspect of this complex set of issues. It is generally in everyone's interest to bring about a peaceful transfer of power. Nothing seems more likely to induce a dictator to hold on to power than making clear that when he has given up office he is liable to be brought to trial. The issues here are genuinely difficult: there is a need to avoid lessening the disincentives to seizing power unlawfully, so there is a need to make clear that wrongdoing may be punished. However, whether prosecution necessarily serves the greatest good in particular circumstances is a matter, ultimately, for political judgement. That judgement will often be difficult, as will the question of whose political judgement should prevail: that of those directly involved, or that of the wider international community (or some part of it).

The major state actors will need to address these and other issues as they endeavour to formulate policies that will bring Serbia and Iraq back into the fold. Serbia seems to be making good progress and Milošević has been sent for trial in The Hague without significant adverse reaction in the country he once ruled.

Saddam Hussein may be deserving of punishment; attempting to seize and try him, however, quite apart from arguments of feasibility, might provide neither the greatest benefit to the well-being of his people nor expedite a final resolution of the threat that he poses. On the other hand, if his regime is not to be toppled by force, the present set of sanctions and sporadic air action will have to be modified. They are attracting widespread odium (whether logically or not) for the sufferings of the Iraqi people, without significantly hurting the leadership's ability to control the country (indeed, they are probably reinforcing it.)

Intervention against domestic oppression does not exhaust the cases where legal development may be necessary. Even where no crime within the scope of the ICC has been committed, or when there is no knowledge of who may have committed a crime, there may be such loss of life or suffering, whether caused by action or inaction of a government, or by non-state actors, or by natural disaster, that entering into a country to stabilize the situation may be considered to be a political imperative. Regional organizations may act in such cases, or individual states, or groups of them. However, without a much greater sense of what is generally permissible such action is obviously open to grave abuse, and could end up by being destabilizing rather than a benefit. Hence the need is for international law to grow, as well as for the development of appropriate practices for giving international political legitimacy.

THE GROWTH OF NON-STATE ENTITIES

Both of the above needs affect, and are affected by, the third great area of interest, the growth in numbers and importance of non-state actors. Classically, international law was concerned with relations between states. However, new agents and new forms of power now crowd the stage. The global reach of large corporations has squeezed state power steadily for a generation. From the other side, the old state-centric security order is being altered both by newly-empowered non-state actors and also by a range of powerful factors, which are not conscious agents but are the consequence of pressure in a closely interlinked world, as in the case of the demonstrators against the WTO and globalization generally.

This power shift has placed new issues on the security agenda; it has also produced new forms of interaction. There are problems of unintended synergy between factors and actors, and of partial mutual misunderstandings between individuals, groups and societies. The forces of globalization are simultaneously unifying and fragmenting. Under the influence of the information technology revolution and the changes in the world economy, which are in part a consequence of it, individuals, sub-state groups and non-state organizations can become greatly empowered. China needs to embrace the technological revolution to enable its economy to prosper, but is finding already that its power to control the dissemination of ideas or the co-ordination of action is diminishing. Meanwhile, the same revolution can give the state unparalleled capabilities for intervention in the lives of individuals or the activities of groups and organizations. States' legitimate endeavours to control or monitor activities which threaten their security may also pose problems for privacy and freedom. This will present real difficulties in the context of a major international drive against terrorism.

International relations can no longer be regarded, if it ever could, as a Newtonian study of billiard balls rolling around a universe regulated only by a few simple laws. The actors are of various and diverse kinds; the relations between them are subject not only to laws different from those of the past, but also to laws which are changing. The reactions go down to lower levels of organization; the impact of far away events at low levels can have an effect, at great distance, on high policy.

Private corporations have long had significant influence, and not just in the economic sphere. Now they can frequently be direct actors in security. Their engagement ranges from logistic contracting for developed states with first class armed forces, through the provision of armed guards for government and commercial activities in places where law and order have broken down, to the provision of actual armed forces for governments whose states have failed. Africa has seen the most significant sorts of development at that end of the spectrum. Many NGOs and governments have great reservations about the engagement of what they see simply as mercenaries. However, if a government cannot recruit and train effective forces, it may nevertheless still need internal and external armed protection. Governments must still retain responsibility for the actions of such hired organizations, which themselves must be made subject to the normal rules and laws applicable to regular forces. It is not sufficient simply to condemn the practice of using them; the needs of those who hire them must be addressed. That is another aspect of the problem of the failed state, and an area where serious thought is required.

Meanwhile, there has been a great growth in the numbers and influence of NGOs, essentially private-sector organizations, charities, pressure groups and political actors which may be national or international, world-wide or local, in their focus. Some, such as Oxfam, are long established; others have come into being in response to particular recent crises. Relations with governments and international organizations, and with each other, can be strained. NGOs are not easily regulated in their activities. They are not responsible in the sense that democratic governments generally are; sometimes their single issue focus can lead to pressures which emphasize only one aspect of a complex situation. They may thus lead the media to a particular view of events, clash with forces or organizations charged with stabilization or pacification, and press ahead with their own schemes even if that causes major problems for other actors. All that said, NGOs often have good, if not the best, information about a complex situation. Furthermore, they may be able to respond faster than governments or official agencies, or act when governments cannot. The influence that NGOs can bring to bear will often make a significant contribution, and not just to humanitarian problems. Those wishing to address a range of disasters or violations of human rights must work with them and sometimes through them; at the very least, it will generally be impossible to ignore them and their personnel in planning and executing operations in troubled places.

Since governments and international organizations like the UN have to take cognizance of NGOs, it is not unreasonable to look for a degree of reciprocity. That is not to ask them to forgo their independence of governments, but to recognize that governments have a legitimacy of their own, as does the UN. Governments can err and frequently have, but they are still principal actors on the international scene, and many have a degree of democratic legitimacy to which no NGO can aspire. Moreover, the military, who will be involved in many crises, with their discipline, and even with their lethal force, are not necessarily to be accounted as hostile to men of virtue and good will. They may have been asked to undertake a thankless peace-keeping task in which they must be impartial. They may have many lives to protect, and have to order priorities between one set of issues and another. Such ordering of priorities is not itself a ground for criticism, even if it does not accord with an NGO's view of the world.

CONCLUSION

The international system changed out of recognition in the 20th century, and the lines of development in the first quarter of the next are already clear. The coming changes may not be so great as those since 1900, but they will nevertheless be very substantial. Over the last 20 years serious concern has become widespread about the proliferation of weapons of mass destruction and about international terrorism. These issues will continue to demand and to receive great attention. Perspectives are currently affected by the attacks of 11 September 2001; in the medium term it may be that those are seen as, on the whole, symptoms of deeper issues rather than of first-rate importance in themselves. Certainly, the underlying problems that existed before that date are almost all still there and still need resolution. Meanwhile, the need for intervention in sovereign states (whether to protect human rights, or for humanitarian purposes in response to natural disasters, or to deal with crime and terrorism), new actors and changed forms of political organization, and the development of international law, all point to new roles and duties for international organizations and institutions, and an obligation for them to embrace the challenges and to adapt effectively.

The traditional focus of international law on states has changed, and will have to change further. There are now many more sorts of actor, and a much wider set of concerns, not all of which are adequately provided for by present arrangements. There is a need to fit the NGOs, which are present in so many crises, and which have acquired in public estimation so much legitimacy, into a coherent relationship, in the various areas where they are engaged, so that they do not impede or imperil other actors, or each other. The issues are political in the widest sense; and there is much to do to enable the full capabilities of the international community to be brought to bear on particular problems.

The role of the media and of popular opinion will be vital in the new century. Very few countries nowadays can conduct their international relations without public support. However, a background of engaged reporting and potentially volatile public opinion does not facilitate the formation and pursuit of consistent policies directed to strategic ends. Reconciling long- and short-term aims, and national interest with media concerns, will pose severe tests for statesmen.

The development of international organizations and of international law will be profoundly affected by the line adopted by the US Government. The USA is the one remaining superpower and the new administration may reinforce tendencies towards unilateralism and some aspects of isolationism. Meanwhile, there are indications that the Europeans will be more actively engaged across the full spectrum of security activity, though major investment of resources, and great developments in policy harmonization, are still required for that.

THE DEVELOPMENT OF INTERNATIONAL ORGANIZATIONS: A CHRONOLOGY

1863

17 Feb. First meeting of the International Committee of the Red Cross (ICRC), as the International Committee for the Relief of Wounded Soldiers.

26 Oct. First international conference organized by the ICRC.

1864

22 Aug. Geneva Convention for the Amelioration of the Condition of Soldiers Wounded in Armies in the Field signed.

1865

17 May International Telegraph Convention signed in Paris, establishing the International Telegraph Union; present name—International Telecommunication Union—adopted in 1934 (became a specialized agency of the UN on 15 Oct. 1947).

1874

9 Oct. General Postal Union established (name changed to Universal Postal Union in 1878; became a specialized agency of the UN on 1 July 1948).

1889

31 Oct. Inter-Parliamentary Union established (initially as the Inter-Parliamentary Conference for International Arbitration).

1890

14 April International Union of American Republics founded, at first International American Conference, held in Washington, DC, USA.

1894

23 June International Olympic Committee established.

1899

18 May–29 July International Peace Conference held in The Hague (Convention for the Pacific Settlement of International Disputes signed).

1906

6 July Geneva Convention signed, extending the provisions of the first Convention to naval warfare.

1907

18 Oct. Convention respecting laws and customs of war on land (Hague Rules) signed at second Hague Peace Conference.

1914

Aug. Outbreak of World War I.

1918

18 Jan. US President Wilson outlined the objectives of a peace settlement, which included provisions for the establishment of an association of nations to strengthen international relations and help maintain peace.

11 Nov. Armistice declared, ending World War I.

1919

5 May League of Red Cross Societies established (became League of Red Cross and Red Crescent Societies in 1983; current name—International Federation of the Red Cross and Red Crescent Societies—adopted in 1991).

28 June Versailles Peace Treaty signed, incorporating the Covenant establishing a League of Nations.
International Labour Organization established by Part XIII of the Treaty of Versailles, to assume the functions of the International Labour Office (became a specialized agency of the UN on 14 Dec. 1946).

1920

10 Jan. Covenant establishing the League of Nations entered into force.

13 Dec. Statute of the Permanent Court of International Justice adopted (formally operational 15 Dec. 1922–31 Dec. 1945).

1921

19 June International Federation of Christian Trade Unions established (renamed World Confederation of Labour Oct. 1968).

20 Aug. First High Commissioner for Refugees appointed, by League of Nations.

21 Nov.–6 Feb. 1922 Washington Conference, during which treaties were concluded relating to China's territorial integrity, the use of chemical weapons and limitations on naval armaments.

1925

18 Dec. International Bureau of Education established (became an intergovernmental org. on 25 July 1929; incorporated into UNESCO in 1961).

1926

26 Sept. Slavery Convention signed by representatives of 36 nations, in Geneva.

1928

27 Aug. Kellogg-Briand Pact, renouncing war as an instrument of national policy, signed (based on the initiative of the US and French ministers of foreign affairs; entered into effect 24 July 1929).

26 Sept. General Act for the Pacific Settlement of International Disputes adopted by the General Assembly of the League of Nations.

1929

27 July Geneva Convention relating to the Treatment of Prisoners of War signed.

1930

13 March–12 April (Second) Conference on Codification of International Law held in The Hague.

17 May Bank for International Settlements established.

1939

1 Sept. German invasion of Poland, marking the start of World War II.

1941

14 Aug. Atlantic Charter signed by the US President Roosevelt and British Prime Minister Winston Churchill, proposing a set of principles for international collaboration in maintaining peace and security.

1942

1 Jan. Declaration by United Nations signed by representatives of 26 nations (pledged to continue fighting together against the Axis powers).

1943

18 May–3 June United Nations Conference on Food and Agriculture held in Hot Springs, Virginia, USA; proposed a world programme and creation of a Food and Agriculture Organization.

9 Nov. Agreement on establishment of an interim United Nations Relief and Rehabilitation Administration to extend emergency assistance to liberated countries.

1944

1–22 July United Nations Monetary and Financial Conference held in Bretton Woods, New Hampshire, USA: representatives of 45 countries formulated proposals relating to post-war international payment problems, and endorsed establishment of the International Monetary Fund (IMF) and International Bank for Reconstruction and Development (IBRD).

21 Sept.– Dumbarton Oaks Conference Washington, DC,

7 Oct. USA: China, United Kingdom, USA and USSR agreed on aims, structure and functioning of a world organization.

1945

22 March Pact of League of Arab States signed (entered into force 10 May 1945).

8 May Unconditional surrender of Germany, ending war in Europe.

26 June Charter of the United Nations signed by representatives of 50 nations.

6 Aug. First use of atomic bomb during warfare, on Hiroshima, Japan.

2 Sept. Unconditional surrender of Japan.

3 Oct. World Federation of Trade Unions established.

16 Oct. Food and Agriculture Organization established (incorporating the International Institute of Agriculture, an intergovernmental body established 7 June 1905).

24 Oct. UN Charter entered into force, formally establishing the United Nations.

16 Nov. Constitution adopted establishing a UN Educational, Scientific and Cultural Organization (UNESCO) (entered into force 4 Nov. 1946).

20 Nov. International Military Tribunal initiated trial proceedings in Nuremberg, Germany, against principal military officers in the former Nazi regime (continued functioning until 1 Oct. 1946).

27 Dec. Articles of Agreement establishing the IMF and IBRD adopted.

1946

10 Jan. First meeting of the UN General Assembly, held in London, United Kingdom.

13 Jan. UN Economic and Social Council (ECOSOC) formally constituted.

17 Jan. First meeting of the UN Security Council.

24 Jan. UN Atomic Energy Commission established (suspended 22 June 1948 after differences between the USA and USSR).

1 Feb. First Secretary-General of the United Nations, Trygve Lie, took office.

6 Feb. International Court of Justice inaugurated.

25 June IBRD commenced operations.

11 Dec. UN International Children's Emergency Fund (UNICEF) established (mandate extended in 1950; name and mandate amended in 1953 to become UN Children's Fund, retaining the same acronym).

15 Dec. International Refugees Organization (IRO) established (assumed responsibility from the UN Relief and Rehabilitation Administration).

1947

1 March IMF commenced operations.

28 March UN Economic Commission for Europe established by ECOSOC as the first regional commission of the UN (commenced operations in May 1947; became a permanent organ of the UN in 1951).

UN Economic Commission for Asia and the Far East (ECAFE) established (commenced operations in June 1948; name changed to UN Economic Commission for Asia and the Pacific (ESCAP) in Aug. 1974).

4 April International Civil Aviation Organization established, following ratification of the Chicago Convention on International Civil Aviation, signed 7 Dec. 1944.

11 Oct. Convention on establishment of World Meteorological Organization signed, assuming functions of the International Meteorological Organization (f. 1873) (convention entered into force 23 March 1950; became a specialized agency of the UN on 20 Dec. 1951).

30 Oct. General Agreement on Tariffs and Trade signed (entered into force on 1 Jan. 1948, establishing multilateral rules for trade).

1948

25 Feb. UN Economic Commission for Latin America established (redesignated Economic Commission for Latin America and the Caribbean (ECLAC) in July 1984).

6 March Inter-governmental Maritime Consultative Organization established at the conclusion of a UN Maritime Conference.

17 March Treaty of Economic, Social and Cultural Collaboration and Collective Self-Defence (The Brussels Treaty) signed by France, Belgium, Luxembourg, the Netherlands and the United Kingdom.

24 March Charter for an International Trade Organization (ITO) signed at the end of the International Conference on Trade and Employment, held in Havana, Cuba. (The establishment of the ITO was subsequently postponed indefinitely.)

7 April Constitution establishing World Health Organization entered into force (signed July 1946).

16 April Organisation for European Economic Co-operation (OEEC) established, in connection with the post-war Marshall Plan for economic reconstruction.

2 May Organization of American States established, as a successor to the International Union of American Republics.

29 May UN Security Council resolved to deploy first group of UN military observers in order to supervise a halt in the hostilities between Palestinian Arabs and the newly-proclaimed state of Israel. (The United Nations Truce Supervision Organization was deployed in June.)

25 June European and US commands began collaboration to deliver by air humanitarian provisions to Berlin, Germany, which had been isolated by a Soviet blockade (the so-called 'Berlin Airlift'; continued to 30 Sept. 1949).

22 Aug. World Council of Churches established.

1 Dec. United Nations Relief for Palestinian Refugees established.

9 Dec. Convention on the Prevention and Punishment of the Crime of Genocide adopted by the UN General Assembly.

10 Dec. Universal Declaration of Human Rights adopted by the UN General Assembly.

1949

25 Jan. Council for Mutual Economic Assistance (CMEA or Comecon) established to support economic development of the USSR and countries of Eastern Europe.

4 April North Atlantic Treaty signed in Washington, DC, USA, institutionalizing the Atlantic Alliance and providing a legal basis for the establishment of the North Atlantic Treaty Organization (NATO).

5 May Statute establishing Council of Europe signed (entered into force 3 August 1949).

12 Aug. Convention on the Protection of Civilian Populations in Time of War (Fourth Geneva Convention), together with revisions of previous Geneva Conventions, adopted at the conclusion of a Diplomatic Conference (initiated 21 April 1949).

8 Dec. United Nations Relief and Works Agency for Palestine Refugees (UNRWA) established to succeed earlier programme (began operations in May 1950).

1950

7 July UN Security Council authorized the establishment of a unified multinational force to restore peace in Korea, under the command of the USA.

4 Nov. Convention for the Protection of Human Rights and Fundamental Freedoms (European Convention on Human Rights) adopted by the Council of Europe; entered into force on 3 Nov. 1953.

1951

1 Jan. Office of the United Nations High Commissioner for Refugees began operations, assuming the functions of the IRO.

18 April Treaty of Paris signed, establishing a European Coal and Steel Community.

28 July Convention relating to the Status of Refugees adopted.

5 Dec. Provisional Intergovernmental Committee for Movement and Migrants from Europe established (mandate extended and name changed to become Intergovernmental Committee for European Migration in Nov. 1952, later Intergovernmental Committee for Migration; constitution changing name to International Organization for Migration entered into force in Nov. 1989).

1952

March Nordic Council inaugurated.

1954

23 Oct. Treaty of Brussels modified, providing for establishment of a Western European Union.

1955

6 May Western European Union formally established.

14 May Warsaw Treaty of Friendship, Co-operation and Mutual Assistance (the Warsaw Pact) signed by USSR and six Eastern European countries.

1956

24 July International Finance Corporation (IFC) established as an affiliate of the IBRD.

1957

25 March Treaty of Rome establishing a European Economic Community and a European Atomic Energy Community signed (entered into force 1 January 1958).

3 June Council of Arab Economic Unity established (first meeting held in 1964).

29 July Statute establishing International Atomic Energy Agency (IAEA) entered into force (approved 23 Oct. 1956).

1958

17 March Convention establishing Inter-Governmental Maritime Consultative Organization entered into force (became a specialized agency of the UN on 13 Jan. 1959; present name, International Maritime Organization, adopted in May 1982).

1959

8 April Agreement to establish an Inter-American Development Bank adopted (entered into force 30 Dec. 1959).

20 Nov. Declaration on the Rights of the Child adopted by UN General Assembly.

1 Dec. Antarctic Treaty signed by 12 countries, banning weapons testing on the continent and guaranteeing its use solely for peaceful purposes (entered into force 23 June 1961).

1960

18 Feb. Montevideo Treaty signed, constituting Latin American Free Trade Association (LAFTA).

3 May Convention establishing European Free Trade Association entered into force (signed in Jan. 1960).

10–14 Sept. Conference held in Baghdad, Iraq, established Organization of the Petroleum Exporting Countries (OPEC).

24 Sept. International Development Association established.

1 Oct. Inter-American Development Bank commenced operations.

14 Dec. Convention on the establishment of an Organisation for Economic Co-operation and Development, to supersede the OEEC, signed.

15 Dec. General Treaty of Central American Economic Integration signed (ratified Sept. 1963, creating Central American Common Market).

1961

24 Nov. World Food Programme established (commenced operations 1 Jan. 1963).

1962

23 March Treaty of Nordic Co-operation (Helsinki Treaty) signed.

1963

25 May Charter establishing Organization of African Unity (OAU) adopted.

4 Aug. Agreement establishing African Development Bank signed (entered into force 10 Sept. 1964; Bank commenced operations on 1 July 1966).

1964

30 Dec. UN Conference on Trade and Development established as a permanent organ of the General Assembly.

1965

23 June First Secretary-General of the Commonwealth appointed (following decision in 1964 by Commonwealth Heads of Government to establish a permanent secretariat).

22 Nov. UN General Assembly approved the establishment of a United Nations Development Programme, by merger of the UN Special Fund and the Expanded Programme of Technical Assistance (created in 1949), effective from 1 Jan. 1966.

21 Dec. International Convention on the Elimination of All Forms of Racial Discrimination adopted (entered into force 4 Jan. 1969).

1966

14 Oct. International Centre for the Settlement of Investment Disputes established.

24 Nov. Asian Development Bank established (commenced operations 19 Dec. 1966).

16 Dec. International Covenants on Economic, Social and Cultural Rights and on Civil and Political Rights adopted by UN General Assembly.

1967

1 Jan. UN Industrial Development Organization established, on the basis of a resolution of the General Assembly adopted on 17 Nov. 1966 (became a specialized agency of the UN on 1 Jan. 1986).

14 Feb. Treaty for the Prohibition of Nuclear Weapons in Latin America (the Tlatelolco Treaty) signed (entered into force on 22 April 1968, establishing the first nuclear-free zone in a populated region).

14 July Convention establishing the World Intellectual Property Organization (WIPO) adopted; entered into force on 26 April 1970. (WIPO became a specialized agency of the UN in December 1974.)

8 Aug. Declaration establishing the Association of South East Asian Nations (ASEAN) signed in Bangkok, Thailand.

1968

9 Jan. Organization of Arab Petroleum Exporting Countries established.

1 May Caribbean Free Trade Area (CARIFTA) established (on basis of agreement signed between Antigua, Barbados and Guyana on 15 Dec. 1965).

12 June Treaty on the Non-Proliferation of Nuclear Weapons (NPT) adopted by UN General Assembly (entered into force 1970).

1969

26 May Agreement signed by Bolivia, Chile, Colombia, Ecuador and Peru to establish a common market (Andean Pact).

10 Sept. OAU Convention on Refugees signed.

22 Nov. American Convention on Human Rights adopted.

1971

25 May Organization of the Islamic Conference formally inaugurated.

5 Aug. First South Pacific Forum, held in Wellington, New Zealand.

25 Oct. People's Republic of China assumed a permanent seat on the UN Security Council, following recognition by the General Assembly of it being a permanent member of the UN (in place of the Republic of China, which had held the seat in the Security Council since 1949).

1972

10 April Convention on the Prohibition of the Develop-

ment, Production and Stockpiling of Bacteriological (biological) and Toxin Weapons and on their Destruction (Biological Weapons Convention) opened for signature (entered into force 26 March 1975).

15 Dec. United Nations Environment Programme established.

18 Dec. United Nations Fund for Population Activities (UNFPA, established as the Trust Fund for Population Activities in 1967) designated a fund of the UN General Assembly; name changed to United Nations Population Fund in 1987, retaining the same acronym.

1973

17 April South Pacific Trade Bureau established to service South Pacific Forum meetings (changed name to South Pacific Forum Secretariat in 1988, and to Pacific Islands Forum Secretariat in 2000—when the annual South Pacific Forum was renamed Pacific Islands Forum).

4 July Treaty of Chaguaramas signed, establishing a Caribbean Community and Common Market (CARICOM) to supersede CARIFTA.

9 Aug. UN Economic Commission for Western Asia established (commenced operations 1 January 1974; renamed Economic and Social Commission for Western Asia (ESCWA) in 1985).

1974

12 Aug. Agreement establishing Islamic Development Bank signed.

Dec. World Food Council established.

1975

28 Feb. First Lomé Convention signed between EC and 46 African, Caribbean and Pacific (ACP) countries (replacing Yaoundé Conventions 1965/70 and Arusha Convention 1968).

28 May Treaty establishing Economic Community of West African States (ECOWAS) signed in Lagos, Nigeria.

31 May European Space Agency established (succeeding European Launcher Development Organization and the European Space Research Organization, established in 1962).

3 July–2 Aug. Conference on Security and Co-operation in Europe, held in Helsinki, Finland. Concluded the Helsinki Final Act on East–West Relations, signed by representatives of 35 nations.

1976

1 Jan. OPEC Fund for International Development began operations.

1977

2 Feb. Agreement establishing Arab Monetary Fund entered into force.

8 June Additional Protocols to the 1949 Geneva Conventions adopted, relating to the protection of victims of international and non-international conflicts.

30 Nov. Agreement establishing International Fund for Agricultural Development entered into force.

1978

Oct. UN Centre for Human Settlements (Habitat) established (renamed UN Human Settlements Programme in Jan. 2002).

1980

1 April Southern African Development Co-ordination Conference (SADCC) established (succeeded by Southern African Development Community in 1992).

8 May Eradication of smallpox declared by the 33rd World Health Assembly.

13 Aug. Latin American Integration Association established (succeeding LAFTA).

1981

25 May Co-operation Council for Arab States of the Gulf (GCC) inaugurated.

27 June African Charter on Human and People's Rights signed (entered into force 21 Oct. 1986).

22 Dec. Preferential Trade Area for Eastern and Southern African States (PTA) established.

1982

22 May IMCO transformed into International Maritime Organization.

10 Dec. UN Convention on the Law of the Sea signed in Montego Bay, Jamaica.

1984

10 Dec. Convention against Torture and other Cruel, Inhuman or Degrading Treatment or Punishment adopted by UN General Assembly.

1985

6 Aug. South Pacific Nuclear Free Zone Treaty (Rarotonga Treaty) signed in Cook Islands (entered into force 11 Dec. 1986).

1988

12 April Convention establishing Multilateral Investment Guarantee Agency entered into force.

1989

7 Nov. Inaugural meeting of Asia-Pacific Economic Co-operation (APEC), in Canberra, Australia.

20 Nov. Convention on the Rights of the Child adopted by the UN General Assembly.

1990

Aug. First multinational forces of the Economic Community of West African States (ECOMOG) dispatched, to Liberia.

1991

26 March Treaty of Asunción signed establishing the Southern Common Market (Mercosur).

3 April UN Special Commission (UNSCOM) established to monitor and eliminate Iraq's weapons of mass destruction.

15 April European Bank for Reconstruction and Development inaugurated.

3 June Treaty to establish an African Economic Community signed.

1 July Warsaw Pact countries agreed to end political functions of the Pact (its military institutions having already been abandoned).

30 Sept. Council for Mutual Economic Assistance formally dissolved.

8 Dec. Commonwealth of Independent States established by signature of the Minsk Agreement by Russia, Belarus and Ukraine; other republics joined on 21 Dec. giving formal recognition that the USSR had ceased to exist.

24 Dec. Russia assumed USSR's permanent seat in the Security Council and in all other UN organs.

1992

21 Feb. UN Security Council authorized initial mandate for UN peace-keepers in the former Yugoslavia.

3 July UNHCR initiated an emergency airlift to provide humanitarian assistance to Sarajevo, Bosnia and Herzegovina (had become the longest humanitarian airlift in history by the time it ended on 9 Jan. 1996).

17 Aug. Members of SADCC signed a treaty establishing a successor organization, the South African Development Community (treaty entered into effect 5 Oct. 1993).

1993

13 Jan. Convention on the Prohibition of the Development, Production, Stockpiling and Use of Chemical Weapons and on their Destruction signed (entered into force 29 April 1997).

25 May UN Security Council adopted statute of an International Tribunal for the Prosecution of Persons Responsible for Serious Violations of International Humanitarian Law Committed in the Territory of the Former Yugoslavia (the International Criminal Tribunal for the former Yugoslavia—ICTY).

1 Nov. Treaty on European Union (Maastricht Treaty) entered into force.

20 Dec. Position of UN High Commissioner for Human Rights established by the UN General Assembly.

1994

1 Jan. North American Free Trade Agreement (NAFTA) entered into force.

11 Jan. Partnership for Peace initiative launched by NATO.

9 Feb. NATO endorsed the principle of air strikes against artillery positions responsible for attacks on civilian targets in the former Yugoslavia, to be activated at the request of the UN Secretary-General.

1 Nov. Trusteeship Council suspended.

8 Nov. International Criminal Tribunal for Rwanda established.

16 Nov. UN Convention on the Law of the Sea entered into force, providing for the establishment of the International Seabed Authority.

6 Dec. CSCE transformed into Organization for Security and Co-operation in Europe (OSCE); authorized the grouping's first peace-keeping operation, to supervise a cease-fire in Nagorny-Karabakh.

8 Dec. Common Market for Eastern and Southern African (COMESA) established, succeeding the PTA.

1995

1 Jan. World Trade Organization formally established. Mercosur became fully operational.

11 May States party to the 1968 Nuclear Non-Proliferation Treaty agreed to extend its provisions indefinitely.

15 Dec. South-East Asia Nuclear Weapons Free Zone treaty signed (entered into force 27 March 1997).

20 Dec. Responsibility for maintaining peace and stability in Bosnia and Herzegovina transferred from the UN Protection Force (UNPROFOR) to a NATO-led Implementation Force (later Stabilization Force).

1996

1 Jan. Joint UN Programme on HIV/AIDS (UNAIDS) became operational.

10 March Protocol to the Cartagena Agreement signed in Trujillo, Peru, establishing a Community of Andean Nations.

21 March Charter of the Intergovernmental Authority on Development—IGAD adopted; IGAD superseded the Intergovernmental Authority on Drought and Development, established in 1986.

11 April African Nuclear Weapons Free Zone Treaty (Pelindaba Treaty) signed in Cairo, Egypt.

24 Sept. Comprehensive Test Ban Treaty signed.

1997

27 May Founding Act on Mutual Relations, Co-operation and Security signed between Russia and NATO (provided for the establishment of a Permanent Joint Council).

18 Sept. Convention on the Prohibition of the Use, Stockpiling, Production and Transfer of Anti-Personnel Land Mines and on their Destruction (Ottawa Convention) concluded; opened for signature 3 Dec.

1998

17 July Statute for an International Criminal Court adopted, in Rome, Italy. (The Statute received its 60th ratification on 11 April 2002, enabling its entry into force on 1 July.)

2 Sept. First judgment by an international court for the crime of genocide passed by the International Criminal Tribunal for Rwanda.

1999

1 Jan. Single currency ('euro') adopted by 11 (later 12) countries of the EU.

1 March Ottawa Convention entered into force.

12 March Czech Republic, Hungary and Poland admitted as full members of NATO.

24 March NATO initiated its first military offensive against a sovereign state (the Federal Republic of Yugoslavia).

10 June UN Security Council authorized the deployment of an international security presence in Kosovo and Metohija (with NATO participation under unified command) and the establishment of an international civilian presence, the UN Interim Administration Mission in Kosovo (UNMIK). For the first time other organizations (the OSCE and EU) were mandated to co-ordinate aspects of a mission under the UN's overall jurisdiction.

25 Oct. UN Security Council authorized the establishment of the UN Transitional Administration in East Timor (UNTAET), with a mandate to govern East Timor during its transition to independence from Indonesia. (The military component of UNTAET assumed formal command of military operations in the territory in February 2000.)

17 Dec. UN Monitoring, Verification and Inspection Commission (UNMOVIC) established, replacing UNSCOM.

2000

23 June Cotonou Agreement concluded between the EU and 78 African, Caribbean and Pacific (ACP) states, replacing the fourth Lomé Convention.

7 July Treaty re-establishing the East African Community (signed by the heads of state of Kenya, Tanzania and Uganda on 30 November 1999) entered into force.

6–8 Sept. Millennium Summit of UN heads of state or government convened to review challenges confronting the UN in the 21st century.

1 Nov. Federal Republic of Yugoslavia assumed the seat in the UN General Assembly previously occupied by the former Yugoslavia.

2001

26 Feb. Treaty of Nice signed by EU ministers of foreign affairs.

26 May Constitutive Act of the African Union (signed 11 July 2000 in Lomé, Togo, by OAU heads of state and government) entered into force.

12 Sept. Following major terrorist attacks against targets in the USA, NATO's North Atlantic Council invoked for the first time Article 5 of the organization's founding treaty, concerning collective self-defence, which stipulates that an armed attack against one NATO member on European or North American territory is considered as an attack against all the allies.

9–14 Nov. Fourth WTO ministerial conference, convened in Doha, Qatar: Doha Declaration adopted, incorporating new negotiating agenda and work programme; People's Republic of China and Taiwan admitted as WTO members.

10 Dec. Centennial Nobel Peace Prize awarded, in two equal portions, to the United Nations and to its Secretary-General, Kofi Annan.

2002

1 Jan. 'Euro' banknotes and coins entered into circulation in the 12 'Euro Area' countries of the EU (with, following a short dual circulation period, 28 February as the final deadline for the withdrawal of former national currencies).
United Nations System Staff College became operational

10 Jan. International Security Assistance Force (authorized for a six-month period by the UN Security Council on 20 December 2001) formally established to aid the Afghan Interim Authority with the maintanence of security in and around Kabul; initial command was to be exercized by the United Kingdom.

INTERNATIONAL OBSERVANCES

(Mainly sponsored by the UN. Other sponsoring organizations are indicated in parentheses.)

Days and Weeks

January

30	World Leprosy Day

February

2	World Wetlands Day (Ramsar Convention on Wetlands)
21	International Mother Language Day

March

8	International Day for Women's Rights and International Peace
(2nd Mon.)	Commonwealth Day (Commonwealth Secretariat)
15	World Consumer Rights Day (Consumers International)
21	International Day for the Elimination of Racial Discrimination
21	World Poetry Day
21–27	Week of Solidarity with the Peoples Struggling against Racism and Racial Discrimination
22	World Day for Water
23	World Meteorological Day
24	World Tuberculosis Day
27	World Theatre Day (International Theatre Institute and UNESCO)

April

2	International Children's Book Day (International Board on Books for Young People)
7	World Health Day
14	Pan-American Day (OAS)
23	World Book and Copyright Day
23	Africa Malaria Day
26	World Intellectual Property Day

May

3	World Press Freedom Day
8	International Red Cross Day (ICRC)
15	International Day of Families
17	World Telecommunication Day
21	World Day for Cultural Development
25	Africa Day (OAU)
25–31	Week of Solidarity with the Peoples of All Non-Self-Governing Territories
31	World No Tobacco Day

June

4	International Day of Innocent Children Victims of Aggression
5	World Environment Day
8	World Oceans Day
17	World Day to Combat Desertification and Drought
20	Africa Refugee Day (OAU)
	World Refugee Day
26	UN International Day in Support of Victims of Torture
	International Day against Drug Abuse and Illicit Trafficking

July

(1st Sat.)	International Day of Co-operatives
11	World Population Day

August

3	Friendship Day
9	International Day of the World's Indigenous People
12	International Youth Day
17	SADC Day (Southern African Development Community)
23	International Day for the Remembrance of the Slave Trade and its Abolition

September

8	International Literacy Day
16	International Day for the Preservation of the Ozone Layer
(3rd Tues.)	International Day of Peace (opening of new session of the UN General Assembly)
24	World Heart Day (World Heart Federation, UNESCO and WHO)
(Final week)	World Maritime Day

October

1	International Day of Older Persons
4–10	World Space Week
5	International Teachers' Day
(1st Mon.)	World Habitat Day
9	World Post Day
10	World Mental Health Day
	World Standards Day (International Organization for Standardization)
(2nd Wed.)	International Day for Natural Disaster Reduction
15	World Rural Women's Day
(3rd week)	European Week for Safety and Health at Work (European Union)
16	World Food Day
17	International Day for the Eradication of Poverty
24	United Nations Day
	World Development Information Day
24–30	Disarmament Week

November

9–14	International Week of Science and Peace
14	World Diabetes Day (International Diabetes Federation and WHO)
16	International Day for Tolerance
20	Africa Industrialization Day
	Universal Children's Day
21	World Television Day
22	World Humanitarian Day
25	International Day for the Elimination of Violence against Women
28	ECO Day (Economic Co-operation Organization)
29	International Day of Solidarity with the Palestinian People

December

1	World Aids Day
2	International Day for the Abolition of Slavery
3	International Day of Disabled Persons
5	International Volunteer Day for Economic and Social Development
7	International Civil Aviation Day
8	International Migrants Day
	SAARC Day (South Asian Association for Regional Co-operation)
10	Human Rights Day
11	World Asthma Day (Global Initiative for Asthma)
(2nd Sun.)	International Children's Day of Broadcasting
18	International Migrants' Day
29	International Day for Biological Diversity

Years

2001
European Year of Languages (European Union)
International Year of Mobilization against Racism, Racial Discrimination, Xenophobia and Related Intolerance
International Year of Volunteers
UN Year of Dialogue among Civilizations

2002
International Year of Ecotourism
International Year of Mountains

2003
International Year of Freshwater

2005
International Year of Microcredit

Decades

1993–2003
Third Decade to Combat Racism and Racial Discrimination
Asian and Pacific Decade of Disabled Persons
Second Industrial Development Decade for Africa

1994–2004
International Decade of the World's Indigenous People

1995–2004
UN Decade for Human Rights Education

1997–2006
First United Nations Decade for the Eradication of Poverty

2001–2010
International Decade for a Culture of Peace and Non-violence for the Children of the World
Second International Decade for the Eradication of Colonialism

PART TWO

The United Nations

THE UNITED NATIONS

Address: United Nations, New York, NY 10017, USA.

Telephone: (212) 963-1234; **fax:** (212) 963-4879; **internet:** www.un.org.

The United Nations was founded in 1945 to maintain international peace and security and to develop international co-operation in addressing economic, social, cultural and humanitarian problems.

The United Nations was a name devised by President Franklin D. Roosevelt of the USA. It was first used in the Declaration by United Nations of 1 January 1942, when representatives of 26 nations pledged their governments to continue fighting together against the Axis powers.

The United Nations Charter (see p. 62) was drawn up by the representatives of 50 countries at the United Nations Conference on International Organization, which met at San Francisco from 25 April to 26 June 1945. The representatives deliberated on the basis of proposals put forward by representatives of China, the USSR, the United Kingdom and the USA at Dumbarton Oaks in August–October 1944. The Charter was signed on 26 June 1945. Poland, not represented at the Conference, signed it later but nevertheless became one of the original 51 members.

The United Nations officially came into existence on 24 October 1945, when the Charter had been ratified by China, France, the USSR, the United Kingdom and the USA, and by a majority of other signatories. United Nations Day is celebrated annually on 24 October.

The UN's chief administrative officer is the Secretary-General, elected for a five-year term by the General Assembly on the recommendation of the Security Council. He acts in that capacity at all meetings of the General Assembly, the Security Council, the Economic and Social Council, and the Trusteeship Council, and performs such other functions as are entrusted to him by those organs. He is required to submit an annual report to the General Assembly and may bring to the attention of the Security Council any matter which, in his opinion, may threaten international peace.

Secretary-General (1997–2006): Kofi Annan (Ghana).

Membership

MEMBERS OF THE UNITED NATIONS

(with assessments for percentage contributions to the UN budget for 2003, and year of admission)

Afghanistan	0.00900	1946
Albania	0.00300	1955
Algeria	0.07000	1962
Andorra	0.00400	1993
Angola	0.00200	1976
Antigua and Barbuda	0.00200	1981
Argentina	1.45900	1945
Armenia	0.00200	1992
Australia	1.62700	1945
Austria	0.94700	1955
Azerbaijan	0.00400	1992
Bahamas	0.01200	1973
Bahrain	0.01800	1971
Bangladesh	0.01000	1974
Barbados	0.00900	1966
Belarus[1]	0.01900	1945
Belgium	1.12900	1945
Belize	0.00100	1981
Benin	0.00200	1960
Bhutan	0.00100	1971
Bolivia	0.00800	1945
Bosnia and Herzegovina	0.00400	1992
Botswana	0.01000	1966
Brazil	2.39000	1945
Brunei	0.03300	1984
Bulgaria	0.01300	1955
Burkina Faso	0.00200	1960
Burundi	0.00100	1962
Cambodia	0.00200	1955
Cameroon	0.00900	1960
Canada	2.55800	1945
Cape Verde	0.00100	1975
Central African Republic	0.00100	1960
Chad	0.00100	1960
Chile	0.21200	1945
China, People's Republic	1.53200	1945
Colombia	0.20100	1945
Comoros	0.00100	1975
Congo, Democratic Republic	0.00400	1960
Congo, Republic	0.00100	1960
Costa Rica	0.02000	1945
Côte d'Ivoire	0.00900	1960
Croatia	0.03900	1992
Cuba	0.03000	1945
Cyprus	0.03800	1960
Czech Republic[2]	0.20300	1993
Denmark	0.74900	1945
Djibouti	0.00100	1977
Dominica	0.00100	1978
Dominican Republic	0.02300	1945
Ecuador	0.02500	1945
Egypt	0.08100	1945
El Salvador	0.01800	1945
Equatorial Guinea	0.00100	1968
Eritrea	0.00100	1993
Estonia	0.01000	1991
Ethiopia	0.00400	1945
Fiji	0.00400	1970
Finland	0.52200	1955
France	6.46600	1945
Gabon	0.01400	1960
The Gambia	0.00100	1965
Georgia	0.00500	1992
Germany	9.76900	1973
Ghana	0.00500	1957
Greece	0.53900	1945
Grenada	0.00100	1974
Guatemala	0.02700	1945
Guinea	0.00300	1958
Guinea-Bissau	0.00100	1974
Guyana	0.00100	1966
Haiti	0.00200	1945
Honduras	0.00500	1945
Hungary	0.12000	1955
Iceland	0.03300	1946
India	0.34100	1945
Indonesia	0.20000	1950
Iran	0.27200	1945
Iraq	0.13600	1945
Ireland	0.29400	1955
Israel	0.41500	1949
Italy	5.06475	1955
Jamaica	0.00400	1962
Japan	19.51575	1956
Jordan	0.00800	1955
Kazakhstan	0.02800	1992
Kenya	0.00800	1963
Kiribati	0.00100	1999
Korea, Democratic People's Republic	0.00900	1991
Korea, Republic	1.85100	1991
Kuwait	0.14700	1963
Kyrgyzstan	0.00100	1992
Laos	0.00100	1955
Latvia	0.01000	1991
Lebanon	0.01200	1945
Lesotho	0.00100	1966
Liberia	0.00100	1945
Libya	0.06700	1955

Liechtenstein	0.00600	1990
Lithuania	0.01700	1991
Luxembourg	0.08000	1945
Macedonia, former Yugoslav republic	0.00600	1993
Madagascar	0.00300	1960
Malawi	0.00200	1964
Malaysia	0.23500	1957
Maldives	0.00100	1965
Mali	0.00200	1960
Malta	0.01500	1964
Marshall Islands	0.00100	1991
Mauritania	0.00100	1961
Mauritius	0.01100	1968
Mexico	1.08600	1945
Micronesia, Federated States	0.00100	1991
Moldova	0.00200	1992
Monaco	0.00400	1993
Mongolia	0.00100	1961
Morocco	0.04400	1956
Mozambique	0.00100	1975
Myanmar	0.01000	1948
Namibia	0.00700	1990
Nauru	0.00100	1999
Nepal	0.00400	1955
Netherlands	1.73800	1945
New Zealand	0.24100	1945
Nicaragua	0.00100	1945
Niger	0.00100	1960
Nigeria	0.06800	1960
Norway	0.64600	1945
Oman	0.06100	1971
Pakistan	0.06100	1947
Palau	0.00100	1994
Panama	0.01800	1945
Papua New Guinea	0.00600	1975
Paraguay	0.01600	1945
Peru	0.11800	1945
Philippines	0.1000	1945
Poland	0.37800	1945
Portugal	0.46200	1955
Qatar	0.03400	1971
Romania	0.05800	1955
Russia[3]	1.20000	1945
Rwanda	0.00100	1962
Saint Christopher and Nevis	0.00100	1983
Saint Lucia	0.00200	1979
Saint Vincent and the Grenadines	0.00100	1980
Samoa (formerly Western Samoa)	0.00100	1976
San Marino	0.00200	1992
São Tomé and Príncipe	0.00100	1975
Saudi Arabia	0.55400	1945
Senegal	0.00500	1960
Seychelles	0.00200	1976
Sierra Leone	0.00100	1961
Singapore	0.39300	1965
Slovakia[2]	0.04300	1993
Slovenia	0.08100	1992
Solomon Islands	0.00100	1978
Somalia	0.00100	1960
South Africa	0.40800	1945
Spain	2.51875	1955
Sri Lanka	0.01600	1955
Sudan	0.00600	1956
Suriname	0.00200	1975
Swaziland	0.00200	1968
Sweden	1.02675	1946
Syria	0.08000	1945
Tajikistan	0.00100	1992
Tanzania	0.00400	1961
Thailand	0.29400	1946
Togo	0.00100	1960
Tonga	0.00100	1999
Trinidad and Tobago	0.01600	1962
Tunisia	0.03000	1956
Turkey	0.44000	1945
Turkmenistan	0.00300	1992
Tuvalu	0.00100	2000
Uganda	0.00500	1962
Ukraine[1]	0.05300	1945
United Arab Emirates	0.20200	1971
United Kingdom	5.53600	1945
USA	22.00000	1945
Uruguay	0.08000	1945
Uzbekistan	0.01100	1992
Vanuatu	0.00100	1981
Venezuela	0.20800	1945
Viet Nam	0.01600	1977
Yemen[4]	0.00600	1947/67
Yugoslavia[5]	0.02000	1945
Zambia	0.00200	1964
Zimbabwe	0.00800	1980

Total Membership: 189 (March 2002)

[1] Until December 1991 both Belarus and Ukraine were integral parts of the USSR and not independent countries, but had separate UN membership.

[2] Czechoslovakia, which had been a member of the UN since 1945, ceased to exist as a single state on 31 December 1992. In January 1993, as Czechoslovakia's legal successors, the Czech Republic and Slovakia were granted UN membership, and seats on subsidiary bodies that had previously been held by Czechoslovakia were divided between the two successor states.

[3] Russia assumed the USSR's seat in the General Assembly and its permanent seat on the Security Council (see p. 38) in December 1991, following the USSR's dissolution.

[4] The Yemen Arab Republic (admitted to the UN as Yemen in 1947) and the People's Democratic Republic of Yemen (admitted as Southern Yemen in 1967) merged to form the Republic of Yemen in May 1990.

[5] The Socialist Federal Republic of Yugoslavia was an original member of the UN until its dissolution following the establishment and subsequent admission to the UN of Bosnia and Herzegovina, Croatia and Slovenia (and, later, the former Yugoslav republic of Macedonia). In September 1992 the UN General Assembly voted to suspend Yugoslavia, then comprising only the two republics of Serbia and Montenegro and renamed the Federal Republic of Yugoslavia, from participation in its proceedings until the new Yugoslav state had applied and been accepted to fill the seat in the UN occupied by the former Yugoslavia; this was achieved on 1 November 2000.

SOVEREIGN COUNTRIES NOT IN THE UNITED NATIONS

(March 2002)

China (Taiwan)
Switzerland
Vatican City (Holy See)

Diplomatic Representation

MEMBER STATES' PERMANENT MISSIONS TO THE UNITED NATIONS

(with Permanent Representatives—April 2002)

Afghanistan: 360 Lexington Ave, 11th Floor, New York, NY 10017; tel. (212) 972-1212; fax (212) 972-1216; e-mail afgwatan@aol.com; Dr RAVAN A. G. FARHÂDI.

Albania: 320 East 79th St, New York, NY 10021; tel. (212) 249-2059; fax (212) 535-2917; e-mail albania@un.int; AGIM NESHO.

Algeria: 326 East 48th St, New York, NY 10017; tel. (212) 750-1960; fax (212) 759-9538; e-mail algeria@un.int; internet www.algeria-un.org; ABDALLAH BAALI.

Andorra: 2 United Nations Plaza, 25th Floor, New York, NY 10017; tel. (212) 750-8064; fax (212) 750-6630; e-mail andorra@un.int; JULI MINOVES TRIQUELL.

Angola: 125 East 73rd St, New York, NY 10021; tel. (212) 861-5656; fax (212) 861-9295; e-mail angola@un.int; ISMAEL ABRAÃO GASPAR MARTINS.

Antigua and Barbuda: 610 Fifth Ave, Suite 311, New York, NY 10020; tel. (212) 541-4117; fax (212) 757-1607; e-mail antigua@un.int; internet www.un.int/antigua; Dr PATRICK ALBERT LEWIS.

Argentina: 1 United Nations Plaza, 25th Floor, New York, NY 10017; tel. (212) 688-6300; fax (212) 980-8395; e-mail argentina @un.int; internet www.un.int/argentina; ARNOLDO M. LISTRE.

Armenia: 119 East 36th St, New York, NY 10016; tel. (212) 686-9079; fax (212) 686-3934; e-mail armenia@un.int; Dr MOVSES ABELIAN.

Australia: 150 East 42nd St, 33rd Floor, New York, NY 10017; tel. (212) 351-6600; fax (212) 351-6610; e-mail australia@un.int; internet www.un.int/australia; JOHN DAUTH.

Austria: 823 United Nations Plaza, 8th Floor, New York, NY 10017; tel. (212) 949-1840; fax (212) 953-1302; e-mail austria@un.int; internet www.un.int/austria; GERHARD PFLANZELTER.

Azerbaijan: 866 United Nations Plaza, Suite 560, New York, NY 10017; tel. (212) 371-2559; fax (212) 371-2784; e-mail azerbaijan@un.int; internet www.un.int/azerbaijan; YASHAR ALIYEV.

Bahamas: 231 East 46th St, New York, NY 10017; tel. (212) 421-6925; fax (212) 759-2135; e-mail bahamas@un.int; ANTHONY CHARLES ROLLE.

Bahrain: 866 Second Ave, 14th/15th Floor, New York, NY 10017; tel. (212) 223-6300; fax (212) 319-0687; e-mail bahrain @un.int; JASSIM MOHAMMED BUALLAY.

Bangladesh: 821 United Nations Plaza, 8th Floor, New York, NY 10017; tel. (212) 867-3434; fax (212) 972-4038; e-mail bangladesh@un.int; internet www.un.int/bangladesh; IFTEKHAR AHMED CHOWDHURY.

Barbados: 800 Second Ave, 2nd Floor, New York, NY 10017; tel. (212) 867-8431; fax (212) 986-1030; e-mail barbados@un.int; JUNE YVONNE CLARKE.

Belarus: 136 East 67th St, New York, NY 10021; tel. (212) 535-3420; fax (212) 734-4810; e-mail belarus@un.int; internet www.un.int/belarus; SERGEI LING.

Belgium: 823 United Nations Plaza, 4th Floor, New York, NY 10017; tel. (212) 378-6300; fax (212) 681-7618; e-mail belgium @un.int; internet www.un.int/belgium; JEAN DE RUYT.

Belize: 800 Second Ave, Suite 400G, New York, NY 10017; tel. (212) 599-0233; fax (212) 599-3391; e-mail belize@un.int; MICHAEL ANTHONY ASHCROFT.

Benin: 4 East 73rd St, New York, NY 10021; tel. (212) 249-6014; fax (212) 734-4735; e-mail benin@un.int; JOËL WASSI ADECHI.

Bhutan: 2 United Nations Plaza, 27th Floor, New York, NY 10017; tel. (212) 826-1919; fax (212) 826-2998; e-mail bhutan@ un.int; Lyonpo OM PRADHAN.

Bolivia: 211 East 43rd St, 8th Floor (Room 802), New York, NY 10017; tel. (212) 682-8132; fax (212) 682-8133; e-mail bolivia@ un.int; JAVIER MURILLO DE LA ROCHA.

Bosnia and Herzegovina: 866 United Nations Plaza, Suite 580, New York, NY 10017; tel. (212) 751-9015; fax (212) 751-9019; e-mail bosnia@un.int; internet www.un.int/bosnia; MIRZA KUSLJUGIC.

Botswana: 103 East 37th St, New York, NY 10016; tel. (212) 889-2277; fax (212) 725-5061; e-mail botswana@un.int; LEGWAILA JOSEPH LEGWAILA.

Brazil: 747 Third Ave, 9th Floor, New York, NY 10017; tel. (212) 372-2600; fax (212) 371-5716; e-mail braun@lbrasonu.org; internet www.un.int/brazil; GELSON FONSECA, Jr.

Brunei: 771 First Ave, New York, NY 10017; tel. (212) 697-3465; fax (212) 697-9889; e-mail brunei@un.int; SERBINI ALI.

Bulgaria: 11 East 84th St, New York, NY 10028; tel. (212) 737-4790; fax (212) 472-9865; e-mail bulgaria@un.int; internet www.un.int/bulgaria; STEFAN TAFROV.

Burkina Faso: 115 East 73rd St, New York, NY 10021; tel. (212) 288-7515; fax (212) 772-3562; e-mail burkinafaso@un.int; MICHEL KAFANDO.

Burundi: 336 East 45th St, 12th Floor, New York, NY 10017; tel. (212) 499-0001; fax (212) 499-0006; e-mail burundi@un.int; MARC NTETURUYE.

Cambodia: 866 United Nations Plaza, Suite 420, New York, NY 10017; tel. (212) 223-0676; fax (212) 223-0425; e-mail cambodia @un.int; internet www.un.int/cambodia; OUCH BORITH.

Cameroon: 22 East 73rd St, New York, NY 10021; tel. (212) 794-2295; fax (212) 249-0533; e-mail cameroon@un.int; MARTIN BELINGA EBOUTOU.

Canada: 1 Dag Hammarskjöld Plaza, 885 Second Ave, 14th Floor, New York, NY 10017; tel. (212) 848-1100; fax (212) 848-1195; e-mail canada@un.int; internet www.un.int/canada; PAUL HEINBECKER.

Cape Verde: 27 East 69th St, New York, NY 10021; tel. (212) 472-0333; fax (212) 794-1398; e-mail capeverde@un.int; LUIS DE MATOS MONTEIRO DA FONSECA.

Central African Republic: 386 Park Ave South, Room 1114, New York, NY 10016; tel. (212) 679-8089; fax (212) 545-8326; e-mail caf@un.int; ANTONIO DEINDE FERNANDEZ.

Chad: 211 East 43rd St, Suite 1703, New York, NY 10017; tel. (212) 986-0980; fax (212) 986-0152; e-mail chad@un.int; LAOTEGGUELNODJI KOUMTOG.

Chile: 3 Dag Hammarskjöld Plaza, 305 East 47th St, 10th/11th Floor, New York, NY 10017; tel. (212) 832-3323; fax (212) 832-8714; e-mail chile@un.int; JUAN GABRIEL VALDES.

China, People's Republic: 350 East 35th St, New York, NY 10016; tel. (212) 655-6100; fax (212) 634-7626; e-mail china@ un.int; internet www.china-un.org/eng/index.html; WANG YING-FAN.

Colombia: 140 East 57th St, 5th Floor, New York, NY 10022; tel. (212) 355-7776; fax (212) 371-2813; e-mail colombia@un.int; internet www.un.int/colombia; ALFONSO VALDIVIESO.

Comoros: 420 East 50th St, New York, NY 10022; tel. (212) 972-8010; fax (212) 983-4712; e-mail comoros@un.int; internet www.un.int/comoros; Chargé d'affaires a.i. MAHMOUD MOHAMED ABOUD.

Congo, Democratic Republic: 866 United Nations Plaza, Suite 511, New York, NY 10017; tel. (212) 319-8061; fax (212) 319-8232; e-mail drcongo@un.int; internet www.un.int/drcongo; CHRISTIAN ATOKI ILEKA.

Congo, Republic: 14 East 65th St, New York, NY 10021; tel. (212) 744-7840; fax (212) 744-7975; e-mail congo@un.int; BASILE IKOUEBE.

Costa Rica: 211 East 43rd St, Room 903, New York, NY 10017; tel. (212) 986-6373; fax (212) 986-6842; e-mail costarica@un.int; BERND NIEHAUS.

Côte d'Ivoire: 46 East 74th St, New York, NY 10021; tel. (212) 717-5555; fax (212) 717-4492; e-mail ivorycoast@un.int; internet www.un.int/cotedivoire; DJESSAN PHILIPPE DJANGONE-BI.

Croatia: 820 Second Ave, 19th Floor, New York, NY 10017; tel. (212) 986-1585; fax (212) 986-2011; e-mail croatia@un.int; internet www.un.int/croatia; Dr IVAN ŠIMONOVIĆ.

Cuba: 315 Lexington Ave and 38th St, New York, NY 10016; tel. (212) 689-7215; fax (212) 779-1697; e-mail cuba@un.int; internet www.un.int/cuba; RAFAEL DAUSA CESPEDES.

Cyprus: 13 East 40th St, New York, NY 10016; tel. (212) 481-6023; fax (212) 685-7316; e-mail cyprus@un.int; internet www.un.int/cyprus; SOTIRIOS ZACKHEOS.

Czech Republic: 1109–1111 Madison Ave, New York, NY 10028; tel. (212) 535-8814; fax (212) 772-0586; e-mail czechrepublic@un.int; HYNEK KMONICEK.

Denmark: 1 Dag Hammarskjöld Plaza, 885 Second Ave, 18th Floor, New York, NY 10017; tel. (212) 308-7009; fax (212) 308-3384; e-mail denmark@un.int; internet www.un.int/denmark; ELLEN MARGRETHE LØJ.

Djibouti: 866 United Nations Plaza, Suite 4011, New York, NY 10017; tel. (212) 753-3163; fax (212) 223-1276; e-mail djibouti@nyct.net; ROBLE OLHAYE.

Dominica: 800 Second Ave, Suite 400H, New York, NY 10017; tel. (212) 949-0853; fax (212) 808-4975; e-mail dominica@ un.int; SIMON PAUL RICHARDS.

Dominican Republic: 144 East 44th St, 4th Floor, New York, NY 10017; tel. (212) 867-0833; fax (212) 986-4694; e-mail dr@un.int; PEDRO PADILLA TONOS.

Ecuador: 866 United Nations Plaza, Room 516, New York, NY 10017; tel. (212) 935-1680; fax (212) 935-1835; e-mail ecuador @un.int; internet www.un.int/ecuador; LUIS CHIRIBOGA.

Egypt: 304 East 44th St, New York, NY 10017; tel. (212) 503-0300; fax (212) 949-5999; e-mail egypt@un.int; AHMED ABOUL GHEIT.

El Salvador: 46 Park Ave, New York, NY 10016; tel. (212) 679-1616; fax (212) 725-7831; e-mail elsalvador@un.int; JOSÉ ROBERTO ANDINO-SALAZAR.

Equatorial Guinea: 57 Magnolia Ave, Mount Vernon, NY 10553; tel. (914) 667-8999; fax (914) 667-8778; e-mail eqguinea@un.int; TEODORO BIYOGO NSUE.

Eritrea: 800 Second Ave, 18th Floor, New York, NY 10017; tel. (212) 687-3390; fax (212) 687-3138; e-mail eritrea@un.int; AHMED TAHIR BADURI.

Estonia: 600 Third Ave, 26th Floor, New York, NY 10016; tel. (212) 883-0640; fax (212) 883-0648; e-mail estonia@un.int; MERLE PAJULA.

Ethiopia: 866 Second Ave, 3rd Floor, New York, NY 10017; tel. (212) 421-1830; fax (212) 754-0360; e-mail ethiopia@un.int; internet www.un.int/ethiopia; FISSEHA YIMER.

Fiji: 630 Third Ave, 7th Floor, New York, NY 10017; tel. (212) 687-4130; fax (212) 687-3963; e-mail fiji@un.int; AMRAIYA NAIDU.

Finland: 866 United Nations Plaza, Suite 222, New York, NY 10017; tel. (212) 355-2100; fax (212) 759-6156; e-mail finland @un.int; internet www.un.int/finland; MARJATTA RASI.

France: 1 Dag Hammarskjöld Plaza, 245 East 47th St, 44th Floor, New York, NY 10017; tel. (212) 308-5700; fax (212) 421-6889; e-mail france@un.int; internet www.un.int/france; JEAN-DAVID LEVITTE.

Gabon: 18 East 41st St, 9th Floor, New York, NY 10017; tel. (212) 686-9720; fax (212) 689-5769; e-mail gabon@un.int; DENIS DANGUE RÉWAKA.

The Gambia: 800 Second Ave, Suite 400F, New York, NY 10017; tel. (212) 949-6640; fax (212) 808-4975; e-mail gambia @un.int; CRISPIN GREY-JOHNSON.

Georgia: 1 United Nations Plaza, 26th Floor, New York, NY 10021; tel. (212) 759-1949; fax (212) 759-1832; e-mail georgia @un.int; internet www.un.int/georgia/index.html; Dr PETER P. CHKHEIDZE.

Germany: 871 United Nations Plaza, New York, NY 10017; tel. (212) 940-0400; fax (212) 940-0402; e-mail germany@un.int; internet www.germany-info.org/UN; Prof. Dr DIETER KASTRUP.

Ghana: 19 East 47th St, New York, NY 10017; tel. (212) 832-1300; fax (212) 751-6743; e-mail ghanaperm@aol.com; NANA EFFAH-APENTENG.

Greece: 866 Second Ave, 13th Floor, New York, NY 10017; tel. (212) 888-6900; fax (212) 888-4440; e-mail greece@un.int; internet www.un.int/greece; ADAMANTIOS VASSILAKIS.

Grenada: 800 Second Ave, Suite 400K, New York, NY 10017; tel. (212) 599-0301; fax (212) 599-1540; e-mail grenada@un.int; Dr LAMUEL A. STANISLAUS.

Guatemala: 57 Park Ave, New York, NY 10016; tel. (212) 679-4760; fax (212) 685-8741; e-mail guatemala@un.int; internet www.un.int/guatemala; GERT ROSENTHAL.

Guinea: 140 East 39th St, New York, NY 10016; tel. (212) 687-8115; fax (212) 687-8248; e-mail guinea@un.int; FRANÇOIS LONSENY FALL.

Guinea-Bissau: 211 East 43rd St, Room 704, New York, NY 10017; tel. (212) 338-9394; fax (212) 293-0264; e-mail guinea -bissau@un.int; Chargé d'affaires a.i. JOÃO SOARES.

Guyana: 866 United Nations Plaza, Suite 555, New York, NY 10017; tel. (212) 527-3232; fax (212) 935-7548; e-mail guyana@ un.int; GERT ROSENTHAL.

Haiti: 801 Second Ave, Room 600, New York, NY 10017; tel. (212) 370-4840; fax (212) 661-8698; e-mail haiti@un.int; JEAN-CLAUDE ALEXANDRE.

Honduras: 866 United Nations Plaza, Suite 417, New York, NY 10017; tel. (212) 752-3370; fax (212) 223-0498; e-mail honduras @un.int; ANGEL EDMUNDO ORELLANA MERCADO.

Hungary: 227 East 52nd St, New York, NY 10022; tel. (212) 752-0209; fax (212) 755-5395; e-mail hungary@un.int; internet www.un.int/hungary; LASZLO MOLNAR.

Iceland: 800 Third Ave, 36th Floor, New York, NY 10022; tel. (212) 593-2700; fax (212) 593-6269; e-mail icecon.ny@utn.stjr.is; THORSTEINN INGÓLFSSON.

India: 235 East 43rd St, New York, NY 10017; tel. (212) 490-9660; fax (212) 490-9656; e-mail india@un.int; internet www.un.int/india; KAMALESH SHARMA.

Indonesia: 325 East 38th St, New York, NY 10016; tel. (212) 972-8333; fax (212) 972-9780; e-mail indonesia2@un.int; internet www.un.int/indonesia; MAKMUR WIDODO.

Iran: 622 Third Ave, 34th Floor, New York, NY 10017; tel. (212) 687-2020; fax (212) 867-7086; e-mail iran@un.int; internet www.un.int/iran; SEYED MOHAMMAD HADI NEJAD-HOSSEINIAN.

Iraq: 14 East 79th St, New York, NY 10021; tel. (212) 737-4433; fax (212) 772-1794; e-mail iraq@un.int; internet www.iraqi -mission.org; MOHAMMED ALDOURI.

Ireland: 1 Dag Hammarskjöld Plaza, 885 Second Ave, 19th Floor, New York, NY 10017; tel. (212) 421-6934; fax (212) 752-4726; e-mail ireland@un.int; RICHARD RYAN.

Israel: 800 Second Ave, New York, NY 10017; tel. (212) 499-5510; fax (212) 499-5515; e-mail israel@un.int; internet www .israel-un.org; YEHUDA LANCRY.

Italy: 2 United Nations Plaza, 24th Floor, New York, NY 10017; tel. (212) 486-9191; fax (212) 486-1036; e-mail italy@un.int; internet www.italyun.org; SERGIO VENTO.

Jamaica: 767 Third Ave, 9th Floor, New York, NY 10017; tel. (212) 935-7509; fax (212) 935-7607; e-mail jamaica@un.int; internet www.un.int/jamaica; PATRICIA DURRANT.

Japan: 866 United Nations Plaza, 2nd Floor, New York, NY 10017; tel. (212) 223-4300; fax (212) 751-1966; e-mail mis sion@un-japan.org; internet www.un.int/japan; YUKIO SATOH.

Jordan: 866 United Nations Plaza, Suite 552, New York, NY 10017; tel. (212) 832-9553; fax (212) 832-5346; e-mail jordan@ un.int; Prince ZEID RA'AD ZEID AL-HUSSEIN.

Kazakhstan: 866 United Nations Plaza, Suite 586, New York, NY 10017; tel. (212) 230-1900; fax (212) 230-1172; e-mail kazakhstan@un.int; internet www.un.int/kazakhstan; MADINA JARBUSSYNOVA.

Kenya: 866 United Nations Plaza, Room 486, New York, NY 10017; tel. (212) 421-4740; fax (212) 486-1985; e-mail kenyamis siontoun@usa.net; BOB F. JALANGO.

Korea, Democratic People's Republic: 820 Second Ave, 13th Floor, New York, NY 10017; tel. (212) 972-3105; fax (212) 972-3154; dprk@un.int; PAK GIL YON.

Korea, Republic: 335 East 45th St, New York, NY 10017; tel. (212) 439-4000; fax (212) 986-1083; e-mail korea@un.int; internet www.un.int/korea; SUN JOUN YOUNG.

Kuwait: 321 East 44th St, New York, NY 10017; tel. (212) 973-4300; fax (212) 370-1733; e-mail kuwait@kuwaitmission.com; internet www.kuwaitmission.com; MOHAMMAD A. ABULHASAN.

Kyrgyzstan: 866 United Nations Plaza, Suite 477, New York, NY 10017; tel. (212) 486-4214; fax (212) 486-5259; e-mail kyrgyzstan@un.int; KAMIL BAIALINOV.

Laos: 317 East 51st St, New York, NY 10022; tel. (212) 832-2734; fax (212) 750-0039; e-mail laos@un.int; internet www.un.int/lao; ALOUNKÈO KITTIKHOUN.

Latvia: 333 East 50th St, New York, NY 10022; tel. (212) 838-8877; fax (212) 838-8920; e-mail latvia@un.int; GINTS JEGERMANIS.

Lebanon: 866 United Nations Plaza, Room 531–533, New York, NY 10017; tel. (212) 355-5460; fax (212) 838-2819; e-mail lebanon@un.int; Chargé d'affaires a.i. Dr HIGHAM HAMDAN.

Lesotho: 204 East 39th St, New York, NY 10016; tel. (212) 661-1690; fax (212) 682-4388; e-mail lesotho@un.int; internet www.un.int/lesotho; LEBOHANG KENNETH MOLEKO.

Liberia: 820 Second Ave, 13th Floor, New York, NY 10017; tel. (212) 687-1033; fax (212) 687-1035; e-mail liberia@un.int; LAMI KAWAH.

Libya: 309-315 East 48th St, New York, NY 10017; tel. (212) 752-5775; fax (212) 593-4787; e-mail info@libya-un.org; internet www.un.int/libya; ABUZED OMAR DORDA.

Liechtenstein: 633 Third Avenue, 27th Floor, New York, NY 10017; tel. (212) 599-0220; fax (212) 599-0064; e-mail liechtenstein@un.int; internet www.un.int/liechtenstein; CLAUDIA FRITSCHE.

Lithuania: 420 Fifth Ave, 3rd Floor, New York, NY 10018; tel. (212) 354-7820; fax (212) 354-7833; e-mail lithuania@un.int; internet www.un.int/lithuania; GEDIMINAS SERKSNYS.

Luxembourg: 17 Beekman Pl., New York, NY 10022; tel. (212) 935-3589; fax (212) 935-5896; e-mail luxembourg@un.int; internet www.un.int/luxembourg; HUBERT WURTH.

Macedonia, former Yugoslav republic: 866 United Nations Plaza, Suite 517, New York, NY 10017; tel. (212) 308-8504; fax (212) 308-8724; e-mail macedonia@un.int; SRGJAN KERIM.

Madagascar: 820 Second Ave, Suite 800, New York, NY 10017; tel. (212) 986-9491; fax (212) 986-6271; e-mail madagascar@un.int; JEAN DELACROIX BAKONIARIVO.

Malawi: 600 Third Ave, 21st Floor, New York, NY 10016; tel. (212) 949-0180; fax (212) 599-5021; e-mail malawi@un.int; ISAAC CHIKWEKWERE LAMBA.

Malaysia: 313 East 43rd St, New York, NY 10017; tel. (212) 986-6310; fax (212) 490-8576; email malaysia@un.int; internet www.un.int/Malaysia; AGAM HASMY.

Maldives: 800 Second Ave, Suite 400E, New York, NY 10017; tel. (212) 599-6195; fax (212) 661-6405; e-mail maldives@un.int; internet www.un.int/maldives; HUSSAIN SHIHAB.

Mali: 111 East 69th St, New York, NY 10021; tel. (212) 737-4150; fax (212) 472-3778; e-mail mali@un.int; MOCTAR OUANE.

Malta: 249 East 35th St, New York, NY 10016; tel. (212) 725-2345; fax (212) 779-7097; e-mail malta@un.int; WALTER BALZAN.

Marshall Islands: 800 Second Ave, 18th Floor, New York, NY 10017; tel. (212) 983-3040; fax (212) 983-3202; e-mail marshall islands@un.int; ALFRED CAPELLE.

Mauritania: 211 East 43rd St, Suite 2000, New York, NY 10017; tel. (212) 986-7963; fax (212) 986-8419; e-mail mauritania@un.int; MAHFOUDH OULD DEDDACH.

Mauritius: 211 East 43rd St, 15th Floor, New York, NY 10017; tel. (212) 949-0190; fax (212) 697-3829; e-mail mauritius@un.int; JAGDISH KOONJUL.

Mexico: 2 United Nations Plaza, 28th Floor, New York, NY 10017; tel. (212) 752-0220; fax (212) 688-8862; e-mail mexico@un.int; internet www.un.int/mexico; ADOLFO MIGUEL AGUILAR ZINSER.

Micronesia, Federated States: 820 Second Ave, Suite 17A, New York, NY 10017; tel. (212) 697-8370; fax (212) 697-8295; e-mail micronesia@un.int; MASAO NAKAYAMA.

Moldova: 573-577 Third Ave, New York, NY 10016; tel. (212) 682-3523; fax (212) 682-6274; e-mail moldova@un.int; internet www.un.int/modova; Chargé d'affaires Dr ION BOTNARU.

Monaco: 866 United Nations Plaza, Suite 520, New York, NY 10017; tel. (212) 832-0721; fax (212) 832-5358; e-mail monaco@un.int; www.un.int/monaco; JACQUES LOUIS BOISSON.

Mongolia: 6 East 77th St, New York, NY 10021; tel. (212) 861-9460; fax (212) 861-9464; e-mail mongolia@un.int; internet www.un.int/mongolia; JARGALSAIKHANY ENKHSAIKHAN.

Morocco: 866 Second Ave, 6th and 7th Floors, New York, NY 10017; tel. (212) 421-1580; fax (212) 980-1512; e-mail morocco@un.int; MOHAMED BENNOUNA.

Mozambique: 420 East 50th St, New York, NY 10022; tel. (212) 644-5965; fax (212) 644-5972; e-mail mozambique@un.int; internet www.un.int/mozambique; CARLOS DOS SANTOS.

Myanmar: 10 East 77th St, New York, NY 10021; tel. (212) 535-1310; fax (212) 737-2421; e-mail myanmar@un.int; KYAW TINT SWE.

Namibia: 135 East 36th St, New York, NY 10016; tel. (212) 685-2003; fax (212) 685-1561; e-mail namibia@un.int; internet www.un.int/namibia; MARTIN ANDJABA.

Nauru: 800 Second Ave, Suite 400D, New York, NY 10017; tel. (212) 937-0074; fax (212) 937-0079; VINCI NEIL CLODUMAR.

Nepal: 820 Second Ave, Suite 17B, New York, NY 10017; tel. (212) 370-3988; fax (212) 953-2038; e-mail nepal@un.int; internet www.un.int/nepal; MURARI RAJ SHARMA.

Netherlands: 235 East 45th St, 16th Floor, New York, NY 10017; tel. (212) 697-5547; fax (212) 370-1954; e-mail netherlands@un.int; internet www.pvnewyork.org; DIRK JAN VAN DER BERG.

New Zealand: 1 United Nations Plaza, 25th Floor, New York, NY 10017; tel. (212) 826-1960; fax (212) 758-0827; e-mail nz@un.int; internet www.un.int/newzealand; DON MACKAY.

Nicaragua: 820 Second Ave, 8th Floor, New York, NY 10017; tel. (212) 490-7997; fax (212) 286-0815; e-mail nicaragua@un.int; internet www.un.int/nicaragua; EDUARDO J. SEVILLA SOMOZA.

Niger: 417 East 50th St, New York, NY 10022; tel. (212) 421-3260; fax (212) 753-6931; e-mail niger@un.int; OUSMANE MOUTARI.

Nigeria: 828 Second Ave, New York, NY 10017; tel. (212) 953-9130; fax (212) 697-1970; e-mail nigeria@un.int; ARTHUR C. I. MBANEFO.

Norway: 825 Third Ave, 39th Floor, New York, NY 10022; tel. (212) 421-0280; fax (212) 688-0554; e-mail delun.@mfa.no; internet www.un.norway-un.org; OLE PETER KOLBY.

Oman: 866 United Nations Plaza, Suite 540, New York, NY 10017; tel. (212) 355-3505; fax (212) 644-0070; e-mail oman@un.int; FUAD MUBARAK AL-HINAI.

Pakistan: 8 East 65th St, New York, NY 10021; tel. (212) 879-8600; fax (212) 744-7348; e-mail pakistan@un.int; internet www.un.int/pakistan; SHAMSHAD AHMAD.

Palau: New York; e-mail palau@un.int.

Panama: 866 United Nations Plaza, Suite 4030, New York, NY 10017; tel. (212) 421-5420; fax (212) 421-2694; e-mail panama@un.int; RAMÓN A. MORALES.

Papua New Guinea: 201 East 42nd St, Suite 405, New York, NY 10017; tel. (212) 557-5001; fax (212) 557-5009; e-mail png@un.int; PETER DICKSON DONIGI.

Paraguay: 211 East 43rd St, Suite 400, New York, NY 10017; tel. (212) 687-3490; fax (212) 818-1282; e-mail paraguay@un.int; ELADIO LOIZAGA.

Peru: 820 Second Ave, Suite 1600, New York, NY 10017; tel. (212) 687-3336; fax (212) 972-6975; e-mail peru@un.int; OSWALDO DE RIVERO.

Philippines: 556 Fifth Ave, 5th Floor, New York, NY 10036; tel. (212) 764-1300; fax (212) 840-8602; e-mail misunphil@aol.com; ALFONSO TIAOQUI YUCHENGCO.

Poland: 9 East 66th St, New York, NY 10021; tel. (212) 744-2506; fax (212) 517-6771; e-mail poland@un.int; internet www.un.int/poland; JANUSZ STANCZYK.

Portugal: 866 Second Ave, 9th Floor, New York, NY 10017; tel. (212) 759-9444; fax (212) 355-1124; e-mail portugal@un.int; internet www.un.int/portugal; FRANCISCO SEIXAS DA COSTA.

Qatar: 809 United Nations Plaza, 4th Floor, New York, NY 10017; tel. (212) 486-9335; fax (212) 758-4952; e-mail qatar@un.int; Chargé d'affaires a.i. JAMAL NASSIR SULTAN AL-BADER.

Romania: 573–577 Third Ave, New York, NY 10016; tel. (212) 682-3273; fax (212) 682-9746; e-mail romania@un.int; internet www.un.int/romania; ALEXANDRU A. NICULESCU.

Russia: 136 East 67th St, New York, NY 10021; tel. (212) 861-4900; fax (212) 628-0252; e-mail rusun@un.int; internet www.un.int/russia; SERGEI V. LAVROV.

Rwanda: 124 East 39th St, New York, NY 10016; tel. (212) 679-9010; fax (212) 679-9133; e-mail rwanda@un.int; ANASTASE GASANA.

Saint Christopher and Nevis: 414 East 75th St, 5th Floor, New York, NY 10021; tel. (212) 535-1235; fax (212) 535-6858; e-mail sknmission@aol.com; Dr JOSEPH R. CHRISTMAS.

Saint Lucia: 800 Second Ave, 9th Floor, New York, NY 10017; tel. (212) 697-9360; fax (212) 697-4993; e-mail stlucia@un.int; internet www.un.int/stlucia; EARL STEPHEN HUNTLEY.

Saint Vincent and the Grenadines: 801 Second Ave, 21st Floor, New York, NY 10017; tel. (212) 687-4490; fax (212) 949-5946; e-mail stvg@un.int; MARGARET HUGHES FERRARI.

Samoa: 800 Second Ave, Suite 400J, New York, NY 10017; tel. (212) 599-6196; fax (212) 599-0797; e-mail samoa@un.int; TUILOMA NERONI SLADE.

San Marino: 327 East 50th St, New York, NY 10022; tel. (212) 751-1234; fax (212) 751-1436; e-mail sanmarino@un.int; GIAN NICOLA FILIPPI BALESTRA.

São Tomé and Príncipe: 400 Park Ave, 7th Floor, New York, NY 10022; tel. (212) 317-0533; fax (212) 317-0580; e-mail stp@un.int; Chargé d'affaires a.i. DOMINGOS AUGUSTO FERREIRA.

Saudi Arabia: 405 Lexington Ave, 56th Floor, New York, NY 10017; tel. (212) 697-4830; fax (212) 983-4895; e-mail saudiarabia@un.int; internet www.saudi-un-ny.org; FAWZI BIN ABDUL MAJEED SHOBOKSHI.

Senegal: 238 East 68th St, New York, NY 10021; tel. (212) 517-9030; fax (212) 517-7628; e-mail senegal@un.int; PAPA LOUIS FALL.

Seychelles: 800 Second Ave, Room 400C, New York, NY 10017; tel. (212) 972-1785; fax (212) 972-1786; e-mail seychelles@un.int; CLAUDE MOREL.

Sierra Leone: 245 East 49th St, New York, NY 10017; tel. (212) 688-1656; fax (212) 688-4924; e-mail sierraleone@un.int; IBRAHIM M'BABA KAMARA.

Singapore: 231 East 51st St, New York, NY 10022; tel. (212) 826-0840; fax (212) 826-2964; e-mail singapore@un.int; internet www.mfa.gov.sg/newyork; KISHORE MAHBUBANI.

Slovakia: 866 United Nations Plaza, Suite 494, New York, NY 10017; tel. (212) 980-1558; fax (212) 980-3295; e-mail slovakia@un.int; PETER TOMKA.

Slovenia: 600 Third Ave, 24th Floor, New York, NY 10016; tel. (212) 370-3007; fax (212) 370-1824; e-mail slovenia@un.int; internet www.un.int/slovenia; Dr ERNEST PETRIČ.

Solomon Islands: 800 Second Ave, Suite 400L, New York, NY 10017; tel. (212) 599-6193; fax (212) 661-8925; e-mail solomonislands@un.int; Chargé d'affaires a.i. JEREMIAH MANELE.

Somalia: 425 East 61st St, Suite 702, New York, NY 10021; tel. (212) 688-9410; fax (212) 759-0651; e-mail somalia@un.int; AHMED ABDI HASHI.

South Africa: 333 East 38th St, 9th Floor, New York, NY 10016; tel. (212) 213-5583; fax (212) 692-2498; e-mail southafrica@un.int; internet www.southafrica-newyork.net/pmun.index.htm; DUMISANA SHADRACK KUMALO.

Spain: 823 United Nations Plaza, 9th Floor, New York, NY 10017; tel. (212) 661-1050; fax (212) 949-7247; e-mail spain@un.int; internet www.spainun.org; INOCENCIO F. ARIAS.

Sri Lanka: 630 Third Ave, 20th Floor, New York, NY 10017; tel. (212) 986-7040; fax (212) 986-1838; e-mail srilanka@un.int; CHITHAMBARANATHAN MAHENDRAN.

Sudan: 655 Third Ave, Suite 500-510, New York, NY 10017; tel. (212) 573-6033; fax (212) 573-6160; e-mail sudan@un.int; ELFATIH MOHAMED AHMED ERWA.

Suriname: 866 United Nations Plaza, Suite 320, New York, NY 10017; tel. (212) 826-0660; fax (212) 980-7029; e-mail suriname@un.int; internet www.un.int/suriname; IRMA KLEIN-LEOMBAN TOBING.

Swaziland: 408 East 50th St, New York, NY 10022; tel. (212) 371-8910; fax (212) 754-2755; e-mail swaziland@un.int; CLIFFORD SIBUSIO MAMBA.

Sweden: 1 Dag Hammarskjöld Plaza, 885 Second Ave, 46th Floor, New York, NY 10017; tel. (212) 583-2500; fax (212) 832-0389; e-mail sweden@un.int; internet www.un.int/sweden; PIERRE SCHORI.

Syria: 820 Second Ave, 15th Floor, New York, NY 10017; tel. (212) 661-1313; fax (212) 983-4439; e-mail syria@un.int; Dr MIKHAIL WEHBE.

Tajikistan: 136 East 67th St, New York, NY 10021; tel. (212) 744-2196; fax (212) 472-7645; e-mail tajikistan@un.int; RASHID ALIMOV.

Tanzania: 205 East 42nd St, 13th Floor, New York, NY 10017; tel. (212) 972-9160; fax (212) 682-5232; e-mail tanzania@un.int; DAUDI NGELAUTWA MWAKAWAGO.

Thailand: 351 East 52nd St, New York, NY 10022; tel. (212) 754-2230; fax (212) 754-2535; e-mail thailand@un.int; CHUCHAI KASEMSARN.

Togo: 112 East 40th St, New York, NY 10016; tel. (212) 490-3455; fax (212) 983-6684; e-mail togo@un.int; ROLAND YAO KPOTSRA.

Tonga: 800 Second Ave, Suite 400B, New York, NY 10017; tel. (212) 5996190; fax (212) 8084975; S. TU'A TAUMOEPEAU-TUPOU.

Trinidad and Tobago: 820 Second Ave, 5th Floor, New York, NY 10017; tel. (212) 697-7620; fax (212) 682-3580; e-mail tto@un.int; GEORGE W. MCKENZIE.

Tunisia: 31 Beekman Pl., New York, NY 10022; tel. (212) 751-7503; fax (212) 751-0569; e-mail tunisia@un.int; internet www.tunisiaonline.com/tunisia-un/index.html; NOUREDDINE MEJDOUB.

Turkey: 821 United Nations Plaza, 10th Floor, New York, NY 10017; tel. (212) 949-0150; fax (212) 949-0086; e-mail turkey@un.int; internet www.un.int/turkey; MEHMET UMIT PAMIR.

Turkmenistan: 866 United Nations Plaza, Suite 424, New York, NY 10021; tel. (212) 486-8908; fax (212) 486-2521; e-mail turkmenistan@un.int; AKSOLTAN T. ATAEVA.

Tuvalu: ENELE SOSENE SOPOAGA.

Uganda: 336 East 45th St, New York, NY 10017; tel. (212) 949-0110; fax (212) 687-4517; e-mail uganda@un.int; internet www.un.int/uganda; Prof. MATIA MULAMBA SEMAKULA KIWANUKA.

Ukraine: 220 East 51st St, New York, NY 10022; tel. (212) 759-7003; fax (212) 355-9455; e-mail ukraine@un.int; internet www.uamission.og; VALERIY P. KUCHINSKY.

United Arab Emirates: 747 Third Ave, 36th Floor, New York, NY 10017; tel. (212) 371-0480; fax (212) 371-4923; e-mail uae@un.int; ABDULAZIZ NASSER R. AL-SHAMSI.

United Kingdom: 1 Dag Hammarskjöld Plaza, 885 2nd Ave, New York, NY 10017; tel. (212) 745-9200; fax (212) 745-9316; e-mail uk@un.int; internet www.ukun.org; Sir JEREMY GREENSTOCK.

USA: 799 United Nations Plaza, New York, NY 10017; tel. (212) 415-4000; fax (212) 415-4443; e-mail usa@un.int; internet www.un.int/usa; JOHN DIMITRI NEGROPONTE.

Uruguay: 866 United Nations Plaza, Suite 322, New York, NY 10017; tel. (212) 593-0935; fax (212) 593-0935; e-mail uruguay@un.int; internet www.un.int/uruguay; FELIPE H.PAOLILLO.

Uzbekistan: 866 United Nations Plaza, Suite 326, New York, NY 10017; tel. (212) 486-4242; fax (212) 486-7998; e-mail uzbekistan@un.int; ALISHER VOHIDOV.

Vanuatu: 866 United Nations Plaza, 3rd Floor, New York, NY 10017; tel. (212) 425-9600; fax (212) 425-9653; e-mail vanuatu@un.int; Chargé d'affaires a.i. SELWYN ARUTANGAI.

Venezuela: 335 East 46th St, New York, NY 10017; tel. (212) 557-2055; fax (212) 557-3528; e-mail venezuela@un.int; internet www.un.int/venezuela; MILOS ALCALAY.

Viet Nam: 866 United Nations Plaza, Suite 435, New York, NY 10017; tel. (212) 644-0594; fax (212) 644-5732; e-mail vietnam@un.int; internet www.un.int/vietnam; NGUYEN THANH CHAU.

Yemen: 413 East 51st St, New York, NY 10022; tel. (212) 355-1730; fax (212) 750-9613; e-mail yemen@un.int; ABDALLA SALEH AL-ASHTAL.

Yugoslavia: 854 Fifth Ave, New York, NY 10021; tel. (212) 879-8700; fax (212) 879-8705; e-mail yugoslavia@un.int; internet www.un.int/yugoslavia; DEJAN SAHOVIĆ.

Zambia: 237 East 52nd St, New York, NY 10022; tel. (212) 888-5770; fax (212) 888-5213; e-mail zambia@un.int; internet www.un.int/zambia; MWELWA C. MUSAMBACHI.

Zimbabwe: 128 East 56th St, New York, NY 10022; tel. (212) 980-9511; fax (212) 308-6705; e-mail zimbabwe@un.int; T. J. B. JOKONYA.

OBSERVERS

Non-member states, inter-governmental organizations, etc., which have received an invitation to participate in the sessions and the work of the General Assembly as Observers, maintaining permanent offices at the UN.

Non-member states

Holy See: 25 East 39th St, New York, NY 10016; tel. (212) 370-7885; fax (212) 370-9622; e-mail holysee@un.int; Most Rev. RENATO RAFFAELE MARTINO, Titular Archbishop of Segermes.

Switzerland: 633 Third Ave, 29th Floor, New York, NY 10017; tel. (212) 286-1540; fax (212) 286-1555; e-mail switzerland@un.int.; JENO C. A. STAEHELIN.

Inter-governmental organizations*

Asian-African Legal Consultative Committee: 404 East 66th St, Apt 12C, New York, NY 10021; tel. (212) 734-7608; e-mail aalcc@un.int; K. BHAGWAT-SINGH.

Caribbean Community: 97-40 62nd Drive, 15K, Rego Park, NY 11374-1336; tel. and fax (718) 896-1179; e-mail caribcomun@un.int; HAMID MOHAMMED.

Commonwealth Secretariat: 800 Second Ave, 4th Floor, New York, NY 10017; tel. (212) 599-6190; fax (212) 808-4975; e-mail comsec@thecommonwealth.org.

European Community: Delegation of the European Commission, 3 Dag Hammarskjöld Plaza, 12th Floor, 305 East 47th St, New York, NY 10017; tel. (212) 371-3804; fax (212) 758-2718; e-mail ec@un.int; Liaison Office of the General Secretariat of the Council of Ministers of the European Union, 345 East 46th St, 6th Floor, New York, NY 10017; tel. (212) 292-8600; fax (212) 681-6266; the Observer is the Permanent Representative to the UN of the country currently exercising the Presidency of the Council of Ministers of the European Union.

La Francophonie: 801 Second Ave, Suite 605, New York, NY 10017; tel. (212) 867-6771; fax (212) 867-3840; e-mail francophonie@un.int; RIDHA BOUABID.

International Organization for Migration: 122 East 42nd St, Suite 1610, New York, NY 10168; tel. (212) 681-7000; fax (212) 867-5887; e-mail unobserver@iom.int; ROBERT G. PAIVA.

International Seabed Authority: 1 United Nations Plaza, Room 1140, New York, NY 10017; tel. (212) 963-6470; fax (212) 963-0908.

International Tribunal for the Law of the Sea: 1 United Nations Plaza, Room 1140, New York, NY 10017, tel. (212) 963-6480; fax (212) 963-0908.

League of Arab States: 747 Third Ave, 35th Floor, New York, NY 10017; tel. (212) 838-8700; fax (212) 355-3909; e-mail las@un.int; Dr HUSSEIN A. HASSOUNA.

Organization of African Unity: 346 East 50th St, New York, NY 10022; tel. (212) 319-5490; fax (212) 319-7135; e-mail oau@un.int; AMADOU KÉBÉ.

Organization of the Islamic Conference: 130 East 40th St, 5th Floor, New York, NY 10016; tel. (212) 883-0140; fax (212) 883-0143; e-mail oic@un.int; internet www.un.int/oic; MOKHTAR LAMANI.

World Conservation Union—IUCN: 406 West 66th St, New York, NY 10021; tel. and fax (212) 734-7608.

* The following inter-governmental organizations have a standing invitation to participate as Observers, but do not maintain permanent offices at the United Nations:

- African, Caribbean and Pacific Group of States
- African Development Bank
- Agency for the Prohibition of Nuclear Weapons in Latin America and the Caribbean
- Andean Community
- Association of Caribbean States
- Central American Integration System
- Commonwealth of Independent States
- Council of Europe
- Economic Co-operation Organization
- International Criminal Police Organization (Interpol)
- Latin American Economic System
- Latin American Parliament
- Organisation for Economic Co-operation and Development
- Organization for Security and Co-operation in Europe
- Organization of American States
- Organization of the Black Sea Economic Co-operation
- Permanent Court of Arbitration
- Pacific Islands Forum

Other observers

International Committee of the Red Cross: 801 Second Ave, 18th Floor, New York, NY 10017; tel. (212) 599-6021; fax (212) 599-6009; e-mail redcrosscommittee@un.int; SYLVIE JUNOD.

International Federation of Red Cross and Red Crescent Societies: 800 Second Ave, 3rd Floor, Suite 355, New York, NY 10017; tel. (212) 338-0161; fax (212) 338-9832; e-mail redcross@un.int; ENTCHO GOSPODINOV.

Palestine: 115 East 65th St, New York, NY 10021; tel. (212) 288-8500; fax (212) 517-2377; e-mail mission@palestine-un.org; internet www.palestine-un.org; Dr NASSER AL-KIDWA.

Sovereign Military Order of Malta: 416 East 47th St, 8th Floor, New York, NY 10017; tel. (212) 355-6213; fax (212) 355-4014; e-mail sm-malta@un.int; JOSÉ ANTONIO LINATI-BOSCH.

United Nations Information Centres/Services

Afghanistan: (temporarily inactive).

Algeria: 9A rue Emile Payen, Hydra, Algiers; tel. (2) 691212; fax (2) 692315; e-mail unic.dz@undp.org; internet www.unic.org.dz.

Argentina: Junín 1940, 1°, 1113 Buenos Aires; tel. (1) 803-7671; fax (1) 804-7545; e-mail buenosaires@unic.org.ar; internet www.unic.org.ar (also covers Uruguay).

Australia: POB 4045, 46-48 York St, 5th Floor, Sydney, NSW 2001; tel. (2) 9262-5111; fax (2) 9262-5886; e-mail unsyd@ozemail.com.au (also covers Fiji, Kiribati, Nauru, New Zealand, Samoa, Tonga, Tuvalu and Vanuatu).

Austria: POB 500, Vienna International Centre, 1400 Vienna; tel. (1) 26060-4666; fax (1) 26060-5899; e-mail unis@unis.unvienna.org; internet www.unis.unvienna.org (also covers Hungary, Slovakia and Slovenia).

Bahrain: POB 26004, Bldg 69, Rd 1901, Manama 319; tel. (973) 311-676; fax (973) 311-692; e-mail unic@batelco.com.bh (also covers Qatar and the United Arab Emirates).

Bangladesh: POB 3658, House 60, Rd 11A, Dhanmondi, Dhaka 1209; tel. (2) 8118600; fax (2) 8112343; e-mail unicdha@citechco.net; internet www.unicdhaka.org.

Belgium: Montoyerstraat 14, 1000 Brussels; tel. (2) 289-28-90; fax (2) 502-40-61; e-mail unic@unbenelux.org; internet www.unbenelux.org (also covers Luxembourg, the Netherlands and the European Union institutions).

Bolivia: Apdo 9072, Calle 14 esq. S. Bustamante, Ed. Metrobol II, Calacoto, La Paz; tel. (2) 2795544; fax (2) 2795963; e-mail unicbol@nu.org.bo; internet www.no.org.bo/cinu.

Brazil: Palacio Itamaraty, Avda Marechal Floriano 196, 20080-002 Rio de Janeiro; tel. (21) 253-2211; fax (21) 233-5753; e-mail infounic@unicrio.org.br; internet www.unicrio.org.br.

Burkina Faso: BP 135, ave Georges Konseiga, Secteur no 4, Ouagadougou; tel. 30-60-76; fax 31-13-22; e-mail cinu.oui@fasonet.bf; internet www.cinu-burkina.org (also covers Chad, Mali and Niger).

Burundi: BP 2160, ave de la Révolution 117, Bujumbura; tel. (2) 225018; fax (2) 241798; e-mail unicbuj@cbinf.com.

Cameroon: PB 836, Immeuble Kamdem, rue Joseph Clère, Yaoundé; tel. 22-50-43; fax 23-51-73; e-mail unic@un.cm (also covers the Central African Republic and Gabon).

Chile: Edif. Naciones Unidas, Avda Dag Hammarskjöld, Casilla 179-D, Santiago; tel. (2) 210-2000; fax (2) 208-1946; e-mail dpisantiago@eclac.cl.

Colombia: Apdo Aéreo 058964; Calle 100, No. 8A-55, 10°, Santafé de Bogotá 2; tel. (1) 257-6044; fax (1) 257-6244; e-mail uniccol@mbox.unicc.org; internet www.onucolombia.org (also covers Ecuador and Venezuela).

Congo, Democratic Republic: PB 7248, Batîment Deuxième République, blvd du 30 juin, Kinshasa; tel. (12) 33431; fax (871) 761-274432; e-mail amisi.ramazani@undp.org.

Congo, Republic: POB 13210, ave Foch, Case ORTF 15, Brazzaville; tel. 814447; fax 812744; e-mail prosper.mihindou@undp.org.

Czech Republic: nam. Kinských 6, 150 00 Prague 5; tel. (2) 57199831; fax (2) 47316761; e-mail unicprg@terminal.cz; internet www.unicprague.cz.

Denmark: Midtermolen 3, 2100 Copenhagen Ø; tel. 35-46-73-00; fax 35-46-73-01; e-mail unic@un.dk; internet www.un.dk (also covers Finland, Iceland, Norway and Sweden).

Egypt: POB 982, World Trade Centre, 1191 Corniche El Nil, Boulak, Cairo; tel. (2) 5315593; fax (2) 3553705; e-mail info@unic-eg.org; internet www.unic-eg.org (also covers Saudi Arabia).

El Salvador: (temporarily inactive).

Ethiopia: POB 3001, Africa Hall, Addis Ababa; tel. (1) 515826; fax (1) 510365; e-mail ecainfo@un.org.

France: 1 rue Miollis, 75732 Paris Cédex 15; tel. 1-45-68-10-00; fax 1-43-06-46-78; e-mail unic.paris@unesco.org; internet www.onu.fr.

Germany: 53175 Bonn, Haus Cartanjen, Martin-Luther-King-Str. 8; 53153 Bonn; tel. (228) 815-2770; fax (228) 815-2777; e-mail unic@uno.de; internet www.uno.de.

Ghana: POB 2339, Gamel Abdul Nassar/Liberia Roads, Accra; tel. (21) 666851; fax (21) 665578; e-mail info@unicar.org.gh (also covers Sierra Leone).

Greece: 36 Amalia Ave, 105 58; Athens; tel. (1) 5230640; fax (1) 5233639; e-mail unicgre@mbox.unicc.org; internet www.unic.gr (also covers Cyprus and Israel).

India: 55 Lodi Estate, New Delhi 110 003; tel. (11) 462-8877; fax (11) 462-0293; internet www.unic.org.in (also covers Bhutan).

Indonesia: Gedung Dewan Pers, 5th Floor, 32–34 Jalan Kebon Sirih, Jakarta; tel. (21) 3900292; fax (21) 3900274; e-mail unicjak@cbn.net.id.

Iran: POB 15875-4557; 185 Ghaem Magham Farahani Ave, Tehran 15868; tel. (21) 873-1534; fax (21) 204-4523; e-mail unic@unic.un.or.ir.

Italy: Palazzetto Venezia, Piazza San Marco 50, 00186 Rome; tel. (06) 6789907; fax (06) 6793337; e-mail onuitalia@onuitalia.it; internet www.onuitalia.it (also covers the Holy See, Malta and San Marino).

Japan: UNU Bldg, 8th Floor, 53-70 Jingumae S-chome, Shibuya-ku, Tokyo 150 0001; tel. (3) 5467-4451; fax (3) 5467-4455; e-mail unic@untokyo.jp; internet www.unic.or.jp (also covers Palau).

Kenya: POB 30552, United Nations Office, Gigiri, Nairobi; tel. (2) 623292; fax (2) 624349; e-mail unic@unep.org (also covers Seychelles and Uganda).

Lebanon: Riad es-Solh Sq., POB 4656, Chouran, Beirut; tel. (1) 981301; fax (1) 981516; e-mail friji@escwa.org.lb (also covers Jordan, Kuwait and Syria).

Lesotho: POB 301, Maseru 100; tel. 312496; fax 310042; e-mail unicmaseru@undp.org.

Liberia: Dubar Bldg, Virginia, Monrovia; tel. 226194.

Libya: POB 286, Shara Muzzafar al-Aftas, Hay al-Andalous, Tripoli; tel. (21) 4777885; fax (21) 4777343; e-mail fo.lby@undp.org.

Madagascar: PB 1348, 22 rue Rainitovo, Antasahavola, Antananarivo; tel. (20) 2224115; fax (20) 33315; internet www.onu.dts.mg.

Mexico: Presidente Masaryk 29, 6°, México 11 570, DF; tel. (5) 250-1364; fax (5) 203-8638; e-mail infounic@un.org.mx; internet www.cinu.org.mx (also covers Cuba and the Dominican Republic).

Morocco: BP 601, zankat Tarik Ibnou Zind (Angle rue Roudana) 6, Rabat; tel. (7) 7686-33; fax (7) 7683-77; e-mail cinu@fusion.net.ma; internet www.cinu.org.ma.

Myanmar: POB 230, 6 Natmauk Rd, Yangon; tel. (1) 292619; fax (1) 292911; e-mail unic.myanmar@undp.org.

Namibia: Private Bag 13351, Paratus Bldg, 372 Independence Ave, Windhoek; tel. (61) 233034; fax (61) 233036; e-mail unic@un.na.

Nepal: POB 107, UN House, Kathmandu; tel. (1) 524366; fax (1) 523991; e-mail registry.np@undp.org.

Nicaragua: Apdo 3260, Palacio de la Cultura, Managua; tel. (2) 664253; fax (2) 222362; e-mail cedoc@sdnnic.org.ni.

Nigeria: POB 1068, 17 Kingsway Rd, Ikoyi, Lagos; tel. 269-4886; fax (1) 269-1934; e-mail uniclag@unicnig.org.

Pakistan: POB 1107, House No. 26, 88th St, G-6/3, Islamabad; tel. (51) 270610; fax (51) 271856; e-mail unic@isb.paknet; com.pk; internet www.un.org.pk/unic.

Panama: POB 6-9083, El Dorado; Banco Central Hispano Edif., 1°, Calle Gerardo Ortega y Av. Samuel Lewis, Panama City; tel. (7) 233-0557; fax (7) 223-2198; e-mail cinup@cciglobal.net.pa; internet www.onu.org.pa/cinup.

Paraguay: Casilla de Correo 1107, Edif. City, 3°, Asunción; tel. (21) 614443; fax (21) 449611; e-mail unic@undp.org.py.

Peru: POB 14-0199, Lord Cochrane 130, San Isidro, Lima 27; tel. (1) 441-8745; fax (1) 441-8735; e-mail informes@uniclima.org.pe.

Philippines: NEDA Bldg, Ground Floor, 106 Amorsolo St, Legaspi Village, Makati City, Manila; tel. (2) 8920611; fax (2) 8163011; e-mail infocentre@unicmanila.org (also covers Papua New Guinea and Solomon Islands).

Poland: 00-608 Warsaw, Al. Niepodległości 186; 02-514 Warsaw, POB 1; tel. (22) 8259245; fax (22) 8255785; e-mail unic.pl@undp.org; internet www.unic.un.org.pl.

Portugal: Rua Latino Coelho No. 1, Edif. Aviz, Bloco A1, 10°, 1000 Lisbon; tel. (1) 319-0790; fax (1) 352-0559; e-mail uniclisbon@onuportugal.pt; internet www.onuportugal.pt.

Romania: POB 1-701, 16 Aurel Vlaicu St, Bucharest; tel. (1) 2113242; fax (1) 2113506; e-mail unic@undp.ro.

Russia: 4/16 Glazovsky Per., Moscow; tel. (095) 241-2894; fax (095) 230-2138; e-mail dpi-moscow@unic.ru; internet www.unic.ru.

Senegal: BP 154, Immeuble UNESCO, 12 ave Roume, Dakar; tel. 823-30-70; fax 822-26-79; e-mail cinu.dakar@sentoo.sn (also covers Cape Verde, Côte d'Ivoire, The Gambia, Guinea, Guinea-Bissau and Mauritania).

South Africa: Metro Park Bldg, 351 Schoeman St, POB 12677, Pretoria 0126; tel. (12) 338-5077; fax (12) 320-1122; e-mail unic@un.org.za.

Spain: Avda General Perón 32-1°, 28020 Madrid; tel. (91) 5558087; fax (91) 5971231; e-mail unicspa@mbox.unicc.org.

Sri Lanka: POB 1505, 202–204 Bauddhaloka Mawatha, Colombo 7; tel. (1) 580691; fax (1) 581116; e-mail anusha.atukorale@undp.org.

Sudan: POB 1992, UN Compound, Gamma'a Ave, Khartoum; tel. (11) 773121; fax (11) 773128; e-mail fo.sdn@un.org (also covers Somalia).

Switzerland: Palais des Nations, 1211 Geneva 10; tel. (22) 917-2300, fax (22) 917-0030; e-mail dpi_geneva@unog.ch; internet www.unog.ch/unis/unis1.htm (also covers Bulgaria).

Tanzania: POB 9224, Old Boma Bldg, Morogoro Rd/Sokoine Drive, Dar es Salaam; tel. (22) 2119510; fax (22) 2112923; e-mail unic.urt@raha.com.

Thailand: ESCAP, United Nations Bldg, Rajdamnern Ave, Bangkok 10200; tel. (2) 288-1234; fax (2) 288-1000; e-mail unisbkk.unescap@un.org; internet www.unescap.org/unic (also covers Cambodia, Hong Kong, Laos, Malaysia, Singapore and Viet Nam).

Togo: BP 911, 107 blvd du 13 janvier, Lomé; tel. and fax 212306; e-mail cinutogo@laposte.tg (also covers Benin).

Trinidad and Tobago: POB 130, Bretton Hall, 16 Victoria Ave, Port of Spain; tel. 623-4813; fax 623-4332; e-mail unicpos@unicpos.org.tt (also covers Antigua and Barbuda, the Bahamas, Barbados, Belize, Dominica, Grenada, Guyana, Jamaica, the Netherlands Antilles, Saint Christopher and Nevis, Saint Lucia, Saint Vincent and the Grenadines and Suriname).

Tunisia: BP 863, 61 blvd Bab-Benat, Tunis; tel. (1) 560-203; fax (1) 568-811; e-mail unic.tunis@planet.tn; internet www.unic-tunis.intl.tn.

Turkey: PK 407, 197 Atatürk Bulvarı, Ankara; tel. (312) 4268113; fax (312) 4689719; e-mail unic@un.org.tr; internet www.un.org.tr/unic.html.

United Kingdom: Millbank Tower, 21st Floor, 21-24 Millbank, London, SW1P 4QH; tel. (20) 7630-1981; fax (20) 7976-6478; e-mail info@uniclondon.org; internet www.unitednations.org.uk (also covers Ireland).

USA: 1775 K St, NW, Suite 400, Washington, DC 20006; tel. (202) 331-8670; fax (202) 331-9191; e-mail unicwash@unicwash.org; internet www.unicwash.org.

Yemen: POB 237, Handhal St, 4 Al-Boniya Arca, San'a; tel. (1) 274000; fax (1) 274043; e-mail unicyem@ynet.ye.

Zambia: POB 32905, Lusaka 10101; tel. (1) 228487; fax (1) 222958; unic@zamnet.zam (also covers Botswana, Malawi and Swaziland).

Zimbabwe: POB 4408, Sanders House, 2nd Floor, First St/Jason Moyo Ave, Harare; tel. (4) 777060; fax (4) 750476; e-mail unic@samara.co.uk; internet www.samara.co.zw/unic.

OTHER UNITED NATIONS OFFICES

Armenia: 375001 Yerevan, 14 Karl Libknekht St, 1st Floor; tel. and fax (2) 15-16-47; e-mail dpi@undp.am; internet www.undpi.am.

Azerbaijan: 370001 Baku, 3 Isteglialiyat St; tel. (12) 98-98-88; fax (12) 98-32-35; e-mail dpi@un.azeri.com; internet www.un-az.org/dpi.

Belarus: 220050 Minsk, 17 Kirov St, 6th Floor; tel. 2278149; fax 22260340; e-mail dpi_by@un.dp.org; internet www.un.minsk.by.

Eritrea: POB 5366, Andinet St, Zone 4 Admin. 07, Airport Rd, Asmara; tel. (1) 182166; fax (1) 1801081; e-mail fo.eri@undp.org.

Georgia: 380079 Tbilisi, Eristavi St 9; tel. (32) 998558; fax (32) 250271; e-mail registry.ge@undp.org.ge.

Kazakhstan: 480100 Almaty, Tole bi 67; tel. (3272) 69-53-27; fax (3272) 58-26-54; e-mail registry.kz@un.indp.org.

Ukraine: 252020 Kiev, 6 Klovsky Uzviz, 1; tel. (44) 253-55-59; fax (44) 253-26-07; e-mail registry@unkiev.ua; internet www.un.kiev.ua.

Uzbekistan: 700029 Tashkent, 4 Taras Shevchenko St; tel. (371) 139-48-35; fax (371) 133-09-77; e-mail fouzb@fouzb.undp.org; internet www.undp.uz.

Conferences

Global conferences are convened regularly by the United Nations. Special sessions of the General Assembly (see p. 33) assess progress achieved in the implementation of conference action plans. The following conferences and special sessions were scheduled for 2001–02:

Third UN Conference on the Least Developed Countries (May 2001: Brussels, Belgium).

Special Session of the General Assembly on the Implementation of the Outcome of the UN Conference on Human Settlements—Habitat 11 (June 2001).

Special Session of the General Assembly on the Problem of HIV/AIDS in All its Aspects (June 2001).

UN Conference on the Illicit Trade in Small Arms and Light Weapons in All its Aspects (July 2001: United Nations, New York).

World Conference Against Racism, Racial Discrimination, Xenophobia and Related Intolerence (Aug./Sept. 2001: Durban, South Africa).

Conference on Facilitating the Entry into Force of the Comprehensive Nuclear Test Ban Treaty (Nov. 2001: United Nations, New York).

International Conference on Financing for Development (March 2002: Monterrey, Mexico).

Second World Assembly on Ageing (April 2002: Madrid, Spain).

Special Session of the General Assembly on Children (May 2002).

World Summit on Sustainable Development (Sept. 2002: Johannesburg, South Africa).

Co-ordinating Bodies

The 27-member United Nations System Chief Executives Board for Co-ordination—CEB, founded in 1946 as the Administrative Committee on Co-ordination and renamed in 2001, convenes at least twice a year under the chairmanship of the Secretary General to co-ordinate UN system-wide policies, activities and management issues. In 1997 the United Nations Development Group (UNDG) was established, under the chairmanship of the Administrator of UNDP (q.v.), uniting the heads of some 20 UN funds, programmes and departments concerned with sustainable development, in order to promote coherent policy at country level. Project management services are provided throughout the UN system of entities and organizations, as well as to certain bilateral donors, international financial institutions and governments, by the United Nations Office for Project Services—UNOPS. UNOPS, founded in 1995 and a member of the UNDG, is self-financing and in 2000 delivered services valued at US $471m. in respect of more that 2,600 projects. The Inter-Agency Standing Committee—IASC, founded in 1992, comprises the executive heads of 17 leading UN and other agencies and NGO consortia, who convene at least twice a year under the leadership of the Emergency Relief Co-ordinator (see OCHA, p. 84). It co-ordinates and administers the international response to complex and major humanitarian disasters, and the development of relevant policies.

Finance

The majority of the UN's peace-keeping operations (q.v.) are financed separately from the UN's regular budget by assessed contributions from member states.

In recent years the UN has suffered financial difficulties, owing to an expansion of the organization's political and humanitarian activities and delay on the part of member states in paying their contributions. In 1993 the UN Secretary-General formulated a series of economy measures to be applied throughout the organization, in order to avert a financial crisis. However, the fragility of the UN's financial situation persisted, partly owing to delays in the process between approval of a peace-keeping operation and receipt of contributions for that budget. At 31 December 2001 members owed the UN some US $2,110m., compared with $2,260m. at the end of the previous year, of which $1,823m. was for peace-keeping operations and $44m. for international tribunals. Of the total amount of unpaid assessments the USA owed $1,456m. During 2001, however, 135 members paid their regular budget assessments in full and total receipts from member states amounted to the highest level of contributions in the organization's history.

In 1997 a US business executive announced a donation of US $1,000m., to be paid in regular instalments over a 10-year period, to finance humanitarian and environmental programmes. A UN International Partnership Trust Fund was established to administer the donation. In the same year the UN Secretary-General pledged to implement administrative reforms of the UN and proposed a reduction in the organization's budget. A Development Account was established in December under the Secretary-General's reform programme; administrative savings were to be channelled through this to finance development projects. In late 1999 the Secretary-General stated that a further reduction in the UN budget would compromise the organization's capacity to implement mandated activities. In December 2000 the General Assembly approved a restructuring of scale of assessment calculations, the methodology and accuracy of which had been contested in recent years, particularly by the USA, which owed about two-thirds of the unpaid contributions. For the period 2001–03 the level of US contributions to the regular annual budget was to be reduced from 25% to 22%, while annual contributions were to be raised for several nations with rapidly developing economies. The budget for 2002–03 totalled $2,625.2m., compared with $2,535.7m. in the previous biennium.

TWO-YEAR BUDGET OF THE UNITED NATIONS (US $'000)

	2002–03
Overall policy-making, direction and co-ordination	499,141.1
Political affairs	248,094.1
International justice and law	59,103.1
International co-operation for development	273,137.6
Regional co-operation for development	335,182.7
Human rights and humanitarian affairs	123,457.5
Public information	144,719.2
Common support services	428,530.5
Internal oversight	20,296.9
Jointly-financed activities and special expenses	77,777.1
Capital expenditures	45,423.6
Staff assessment	348,250.3
Development Account	13,065.0
Total	2,625,178.7

United Nations Publications

Africa Recovery (quarterly).

Annual Report of the Secretary-General on the Work of the Organization.

Basic Facts About the United Nations.

Demographic Yearbook.

Development Update (2 a month).

Index to Proceedings (of the General Assembly; the Security Council; the Economic and Social Council; the Trusteeship Council).

International Law Catalogue.

Monthly Bulletin of Statistics.

Population and Vital Statistics Report (quarterly).

Statistical Yearbook (also on CD-Rom).

The UN Chronicle (quarterly).

United Nations Disarmament Yearbook.

United Nations Juridical Yearbook.

World Economic and Social Survey.

World Situation and Prospects.

World Statistics Pocketbook.

Yearbook of the United Nations.

Other UN publications are listed in the chapters dealing with the agencies concerned.

Secretariat

According to the UN Charter the Secretary-General is the chief administrative officer of the organization, and he may appoint further Secretariat staff as required. The principal departments and officers of the Secretariat are listed below. The chief administrative staff of the UN Regional Commissions and of all the subsidiary organs of the UN are also members of the Secretariat staff and are listed in the appropriate chapters. The Secretariat staff also includes a number of special missions and special appointments, including some of senior rank.

In November 2000 the total number of staff of the Secretariat holding appointments continuing for a year or more was approximately 13,891, including those serving away from the headquarters, but excluding staff working for the UN specialized agencies and subsidiary organs.

In July 1997 the Secretary-General initiated a comprehensive reform of the administration of the UN and abolished some 1,000 Secretariat posts. A Senior Management Group was established as part of a new Secretariat leadership and management structure, to enhance day-to-day efficiency and accountability. The reforms aimed to restructure the Secretariat's substantive work programme around the UN's five core missions, i.e. peace and security, economic and social affairs, development co-operation, humanitarian affairs and human rights. During 1997 the Centre for Human Rights and the Office of the High Commissioner for Human Rights were consolidated into a single office under the reform process, while a new Office for Drug Control and Crime Prevention was established, within the framework of the UN Office in Vienna, to integrate efforts to combat crime, drug abuse and terrorism. A new Office of the Iraq Programme was established in October to undertake and co-ordinate activities relating to the oil-for-food programme (see Security Council, p. 39). In December the General Assembly endorsed a recommendation of the Secretary-General to create the position of Deputy Secretary-General, who was to assist in the management of Secretariat operations, in particular the ongoing reform process, and represent the Secretary-General as required.

SECRETARY-GENERAL

KOFI ANNAN (Ghana).

DEPUTY SECRETARY-GENERAL

LOUISE FRÉCHETTE (Canada).

EXECUTIVE OFFICE OF THE SECRETARY-GENERAL

Under-Secretary-General, Chief of Staff: S. IQBAL RIZA (Pakistan).

Assistant Secretary-General, Special Adviser: JOHN G. RUGGIE.

Assistant Secretary-General, External Relations: GILLIAN SORENSEN (USA).

DEPARTMENT FOR DISARMAMENT AFFAIRS

Under-Secretary-General: JAYANTHA DHANAPALA (Sri Lanka).

DEPARTMENT OF ECONOMIC AND SOCIAL AFFAIRS

Under-Secretary-General: NITIN DESAI (India).

Assistant Secretary-General, Special Adviser on Gender Issues and the Advancement of Women: ANGELA KING (Jamaica).

Assistant Secretary-General, Policy Co-ordination and Inter-Agency Affairs: PATRIZIO CIVILI (Italy).

DEPARTMENT OF GENERAL ASSEMBLY AFFAIRS AND CONFERENCE SERVICES

Under-Secretary-General: JIN YONGJIAN (China).

Assistant Secretary-General: FEDERICO RIESCO (Chile).

DEPARTMENT OF MANAGEMENT

Under-Secretary-General: JOSEPH E. CONNOR (USA).

Assistant Secretary-General, Controller: JEAN-PIERRE HALBWACHS (Mauritius).

Assistant Secretary-General, Human Resources: RAFIAH SALIM (Malaysia).

Assistant Secretary-General, Central Support: TOSHIYUKI NIWA (Japan).

DEPARTMENT OF PEACE-KEEPING OPERATIONS

Under-Secretary-General: JEAN-MARIE GUEHENNO (France).

Assistant Secretary-General: HÉDI ANNABI (Tunisia).

Assistant Secretary-General: HOCINE MEDILI (acting) (Algeria).

DEPARTMENT OF POLITICAL AFFAIRS

Under-Secretary-General: Sir KIERAN PRENDERGAST (United Kingdom).

Assistant Secretary-General: DANILO TÜRK (Slovenia).

Assistant Secretary-General: TULIAMENI KALOMEH (Namibia).

DEPARTMENT OF PUBLIC INFORMATION

Interim Head: SHASHI THAROOR (India).

OFFICE FOR THE CO-ORDINATION OF HUMANITARIAN AFFAIRS

Under-Secretary-General for Humanitarian Affairs and Emergency Relief Co-ordinator: KENZO OSHIMA (Japan).

OFFICE FOR DRUG CONTROL AND CRIME PREVENTION

Under-Secretary-General: ANTONIO MARIA COSTA (Italy).

OFFICE OF INTERNAL OVERSIGHT SERVICES

Under-Secretary-General: DILEEP NAIR (Singapore).

OFFICE OF THE IRAQ PROGRAMME

Assistant Secretary-General: BENON V. SEVAN (Cyprus).

OFFICE OF LEGAL AFFAIRS

Under-Secretary-General, The Legal Counsel: HANS CORELL (Sweden).

Assistant Secretary-General: RALPH ZACKLIN (United Kingdom).

OFFICE OF SECURITY CO-ORDINATION

Assistant Secretary-General: BENON V. SEVAN (Cyprus).

OFFICE OF THE SPECIAL REPRESENTATIVE OF THE SECRETARY-GENERAL FOR CHILDREN AND ARMED CONFLICT

Under-Secretary-General: OLARA OTUNNU (Uganda).

OFFICE OF THE UNITED NATIONS HIGH COMMISSIONER FOR HUMAN RIGHTS

Address: Palais des Nations, 1211 Geneva 10, Switzerland.

Telephone: (22) 9179353; **fax:** (22) 9179012; **internet:** www.unhchr.ch.

High Commissioner: MARY ROBINSON (Ireland).

GENEVA OFFICE

Address: Palais des Nations, 1211 Geneva 10, Switzerland.

Telephone: (22) 9171234; 412962; **fax:** (22) 9170123; **internet:** www.unog.ch.

Director-General: SERGEI ORDZONIKIDZE (Russia).

NAIROBI OFFICE

Address: POB 30552, Nairobi, Kenya.

Telephone: (2) 623292; **fax:** (2) 624349.

Director-General: Dr KLAUS TÖPFER (Germany).

VIENNA OFFICE

Address: Vienna International Centre, POB 500, 1400 Vienna, Austria.

Telephone: (1) 26060-0; **fax:** (1) 26333-89; **internet:** www.un.or.at.

Director-General: ANTONIO MARIA COSTA (Italy) (from June 2002).

General Assembly

The General Assembly was established as a principal organ of the United Nations under the UN Charter (see p. 62). It first met on 10 January 1946. It is the main deliberative organ of the United Nations, and the only one composed of representatives of all the UN member states. Each delegation consists of not more than five representatives and five alternates, with as many advisers as may be required. The Assembly meets regularly for three months each year, and special sessions may also be held. It has specific responsibility for electing the Secretary-General and members of other UN councils and organs, and for approving the UN budget and the assessments for financial contributions by member states. It is also empowered to make recommendations (but not binding decisions) on questions of international security and co-operation.

The regular session of the General Assembly commences in mid-September. After the election of its President and other officers, the Assembly opens its general debate, a two-week period during which the head of each delegation makes a formal statement of his or her government's views on major world issues. Since 1997 the Secretary-General has presented his report on the work of the UN at the start of the general debate. The Assembly then begins examination of the principal items on its agenda: it acts directly on a few agenda items, but most business is handled by the six Main Committees (listed below), which study and debate each item and present draft resolutions to the Assembly. After a review of the report of each Main Committee, the Assembly formally approves or rejects the Committee's recommendations. On designated 'important questions', such as recommendations on international peace and security, the admission of new members to the United Nations, or budgetary questions, a two-thirds majority is needed for adoption of a resolution. Other questions may be decided by a simple majority. In the Assembly, each member has one vote. Voting in the Assembly is sometimes replaced by an effort to find consensus among member states, in order to strengthen support for the Assembly's decisions: the President consults delegations in private to find out whether they are willing to agree to adoption of a resolution without a vote; if they are, the President can declare that a resolution has been so adopted.

Special sessions of the Assembly may be held to discuss issues which require particular attention (e.g. illicit drugs) and 'emergency special sessions' may also be convened to discuss situations on which the UN Security Council has been unable to reach a decision (for example, in 2000 on Israel's construction of new settlements in east Jerusalem). A special session of the Assembly entitled Gender Equality, Development and Peace for the 21st Century, reviewing the UN Fourth World Conference on Women, held at Beijing, People's Republic of China, in 1995, was held in June 2000. During that month a special session reviewing the World Summit for Social Development, held at Copenhagen in 1995, was also convened. Two special sessions took place in June 2001: the first assessed the outcome of the UN Conference on Human Settlements (Habitat II, held in Istanbul, Turkey, in 1996), and the second considered issues related to the global epidemic of HIV/AIDS. A special session on children, with the aim of reviewing progress made since the World Summit for Children, held in 1990, and the adoption in 1989 of the Convention on the Rights of the Child, was scheduled to have taken place in September 2001. This was postponed, however, following terrorist attacks against targets in the USA, until May 2002.

The Assembly's 55th session was designated as the Millennium Assembly. In early September 2000 a Millennium Summit of UN heads of state or government was convened to debate 'The Role of the United Nations in the 21st Century'. The Millennium Summit issued a declaration identifying the values, principles and goals that should guide the organization in key areas including peace, development, environment, human rights, protection of the vulnerable, and the special needs of the African continent; and specified six fundamental values underlying international relations: freedom; equality; solidarity; tolerance; respect for nature; and a sense of shared responsibility for the global economy and social development. Reform of the Security Council and the need for increased UN co-operation with the private sector, non-governmental organizations and civil society in pursuing its goals were addressed in the Declaration. It also requested regular reviews of the summit.

In September 1992 the Federal Republic of Yugoslavia (which in April had formally replaced the Socialist Federal Republic of Yugoslavia, although comprising only two of the six former Yugoslav republics) was suspended from the proceedings of the General Assembly. The Assembly required the new Yugoslav state to apply to occupy the former Yugoslavia's seat in the UN. This was achieved in November 2000.

President of 56th Session (from September 2001): Dr HAN SEUNG SOO (Republic of Korea).

MAIN COMMITTEES

There are six Main Committees, on which all members have a right to be represented. Each Committee includes an elected Chairperson and two Vice-Chairs.

First Committee: Disarmament and International Security.

Second Committee: Economic and Financial.

Third Committee: Social, Humanitarian and Cultural.

Fourth Committee: Special Political and Decolonization.

Fifth Committee: Administrative and Budgetary.

Sixth Committee: Legal.

OTHER SESSIONAL COMMITTEES

General Committee: f. 1946; composed of 28 members, including the Assembly President, the 21 Vice-Presidents of the Assembly and the Chairs of the six Main Committees.

Credentials Committee: f. 1946; composed of nine members appointed at each Assembly session.

POLITICAL AND SECURITY MATTERS

Special Committee on Peace-keeping Operations: f. 1965; 34 appointed members.

Disarmament Commission: f. 1978 (replacing body f. 1952); 61 members.

UN Scientific Committee on the Effects of Atomic Radiation: f. 1955; 21 members.

Committee on the Peaceful Uses of Outer Space: f. 1959; 61 members; has a Legal Sub-Committee and a Scientific and Technical Sub-Committee.

Ad Hoc Committee on the Indian Ocean: f. 1972; 44 members.

Committee on the Exercise of the Inalienable Rights of the Palestinian People: f. 1975; 25 members.

Special Committee on the Implementation of the Declaration on Decolonization: f. 1961; 24 members.

DEVELOPMENT

Commission on Science and Technology for Development: f. 1992; 33 members.

Committee on Energy and Natural Resources Development: f. 1998; 24 members.

United Nations Environment Programme (UNEP) Governing Council: f. 1972; 58 members (see p. 104).

LEGAL QUESTIONS

International Law Commission: f. 1947; 34 members elected for a five-year term; originally established in 1946 as the Committee on the Progressive Development of International Law and its Codification.

Advisory Committee on the UN Programme of Assistance in Teaching, Study, Dissemination and Wider Appreciation of International Law: f. 1965; 25 members.

UN Commission on International Trade Law: f. 1966; 36 members.

Special Committee on the Charter of the United Nations and on the Strengthening of the Role of the Organization: f. 1975; composed of all UN members.

There is also a UN Administrative Tribunal and a Committee on Applications for Review of Administrative Tribunal Judgments.

ADMINISTRATIVE AND FINANCIAL QUESTIONS

Advisory Committee on Administrative and Budgetary Questions: f. 1946; 16 members appointed for three-year terms.

Committee on Contributions: f. 1946; 18 members appointed for three-year terms.

International Civil Service Commission: f. 1972; 15 members appointed for four-year terms.

Committee on Information: f. 1978, formerly the Committee to review UN Policies and Activities; 95 members.

There is also a Board of Auditors, Investments Committee, UN Joint Staff Pension Board, Joint Inspection Unit, UN Staff Pension Committee, Committee on Conferences, and Committee for Programme and Co-ordination.

GENERAL ASSEMBLY RESOLUTIONS

(Adoption of Agreements, Conventions, Declarations, Protocols and other instruments)

Note: Until 1976 resolutions of the General Assembly were numbered consecutively, with the session of the Assembly indicated in parentheses. Since that date (i.e. from the 31st regular session of the Assembly) a new numbering sequence has been established at the beginning of each session. Thus each resolution is numbered according to the session in which it was adopted, followed by its chronological position within that session. Resolutions adopted in special or emergency session are identified with an 'S' or 'ES', respectively.

Resolution 22 (I): Adopted 13 Feb. 1946. General Convention on Privileges and Immunities of the UN.

Resolution 54 (I): Adopted 19 Nov. 1946. Transfer to the UN of power exercised by the League of Nations under the International Agreements, Conventions and Protocols on Narcotic Drugs, including a Protocol amending the Agreements, Conventions and Protocols on Narcotic Drugs.

Resolution 84 (I): Adopted 11 Dec. 1946. Agreement between the UN and the Carnegie Foundation concerning the use of the premises of the Peace Palace at The Hague by the International Court of Justice.

Resolution 169 (II): Adopted 31 Oct. 1947. Agreement between the UN and the USA regarding the headquarters of the UN.

Resolution 179 (II): Adopted 21 Nov. 1947. Co-ordination of the privileges and immunities of the UN and of the specialized agencies of the UN, including the General Convention on Privileges and Immunities of the UN.

Resolution 211 (III): Adopted 8 Oct. 1948. International provisions for the control of certain drugs including a protocol bringing under international control drugs outside the scope of the Convention of 13 July 1931 for Limiting the Manufacture and Regulating the Distribution of Narcotic Drugs, as amended by the Protocol contained in Resolution 54 (I).

Resolution 217 (III): Adopted 10 Dec. 1948. International Bill of Human Rights, including the Universal Declaration of Human Rights.

Resolution 260 (III): Adopted 9 Dec. 1948. Convention on the Prevention and Punishment of the Crime of Genocide.

Resolution 317 (IV): Adopted 2 Dec. 1949. Convention for the Suppression of the Traffic in Persons and of the Exploitation of the Prostitution of others.

Resolution 428 (V): Adopted 14 Dec. 1950. Statute of the Office of the UN High Commissioner for Refugees.

Resolution 630 (VII): Adopted 16 Dec. 1952. Convention on the International Right of Correction.

Resolution 640 (VII): Adopted 20 Dec. 1952. Convention on the Political Rights of Women.

Resolution 1040 (XI): Adopted 29 Jan. 1957. Convention on the Nationality of Married Women.

Resolution 1386 (XIV): Adopted 20 Nov. 1959. Declaration of the Rights of the Child.

Resolution 1514 (XV): Adopted 14 Dec. 1960. Declaration on the Granting of Independence to Colonial Countries and Peoples.

Resolution 1541 (XV): Adopted 15 Dec. 1960. Principles which should guide members in determining whether or not an obligation exists to transmit the information called for under Article 73e of the Charter, in respect of such territories whose people have not yet attained a full measure of independence.

Resolution 1653 (XVI): Adopted 24 Nov. 1961. Declaration on the Prohibition of the Use of Nuclear and Thermonuclear Weapons.

Resolution 1763 (XVII): Adopted 7 Nov. 1962. Draft Convention and draft Recommendation on Consent to Marriage, Minimum Age for Marriages and Registration of Marriages.

Resolution 1904 (XVIII): Adopted 20 Nov. 1963. UN Declaration on the Elimination of all forms of Racial Discrimination.

Resolution 1962 (XVIII): Adopted 13 Dec. 1963. Declaration of Legal Principles governing the Activities of States in the Exploration and Use of Outer Space.

Resolution 2018 (XX): Adopted 1 Nov. 1965. Recommendation on Consent to Marriage, Minimum Age for Marriage and Registration of Marriages.

Resolution 2037 (XX): Adopted 7 Dec. 1965. Declaration on the Promotion among Youth of the Ideals of Peace, Mutual Respect and Understanding between Peoples.

Resolution 2106 (XX): Adopted 21 Dec. 1965. International Convention on the Elimination of all forms of Racial Discrimination.

Resolution 2131 (XX): Adopted 21 Dec. 1965. Declaration on the Inadmissibility of Intervention in the Domestic Affairs of States and the Protection of their Independence and Sovereignty.

Resolution 2200 (XXI): Adopted 16 Dec. 1966. International Covenant on Economic, Social and Cultural Rights, Civil and Political Rights and Optional Protocol to the International Covenant on Civil and Political Rights.

Resolution 2222 (XXI): Adopted 19 Dec. 1966. Treaty on Principles governing the Activities of States in the Exploration and Use of Outer Space, including the Moon and other Celestial Bodies.

Resolution 2263 (XXII): Adopted 7 Nov. 1967. Declaration on the Elimination of Discrimination against Women.

Resolution 2312 (XXII): Adopted 14 Dec. 1967. Declaration on Territorial Asylum.

Resolution 2345 (XXII): Adopted 19 Dec. 1967. Agreement on the Rescue of Astronauts, the Return of Astronauts and the Return of Objects launched into Outer Space.

Resolution 2373 (XXII): Adopted 12 June 1968. Treaty on the Non-proliferation of Nuclear Weapons.

Resolution 2391 (XXIII): Adopted 26 Nov. 1968. Convention on the Non-applicability of Statutory Limitations to War Crimes and Crimes against Humanity.

Resolution 2530 (XXIV): Adopted 8 Dec. 1969. Convention on Special Missions and Optional Protocol concerning the Compulsory Settlement of Disputes.

Resolution 2542 (XXIV): Adopted 11 Dec. 1969. Declaration on Social Progress and Development.

Resolution 2625 (XXV): Adopted 24 Oct. 1970. Declaration on Principles of International Law concerning Friendly Relations and Co-operation among States in accordance with the Charter of the UN.

Resolution 2626 (XXV): Adopted 24 Oct. 1970. International Development Strategy for the Second UN Development Decade.

Resolution 2627 (XXV): Adopted 24 Oct. 1970. Declaration on the Occasion of the 25th Anniversary of the UN.

Resolution 2660 (XXV): Adopted 7 Dec. 1970. Treaty on the Prohibition of the Emplacement of Nuclear Weapons and other Weapons of Mass Destruction on the Seabed and the Ocean Floor and in the Subsoil thereof.

Resolution 2734 (XXV): Adopted 16 Dec. 1970. Declaration on the Strengthening of International Security.

Resolution 2749 (XXV): Adopted 17 Dec. 1970. Declaration of Principles governing the Seabed and the Ocean Floor, and the Subsoil thereof, beyond the Limits of National Jurisdiction.

Resolution 2777 (XXVI): Adopted 29 Nov. 1971. Convention on International Liability for Damage caused by Space Objects.

Resolution 2826 (XXVI): Adopted 16 Dec. 1971. Convention on the Prohibition of the Development, Production and Stockpiling of Bacteriological (Biological) and Toxin Weapons and on their Destruction.

Resolution 2832 (XXVI): Adopted 16 Dec. 1971. Declaration of the Indian Ocean as a Zone of Peace.

Resolution 2856 (XXVI): Adopted 20 Dec. 1971. Declaration on the Rights of Mentally Retarded Persons.

Resolution 2902 (XXVI): Adopted 22 December 1971. Supplementary Agreement between the UN and the Carnegie Foundation concerning the use of the premises of the Peace Palace at The Hague by the International Court of Justice.

Resolution 3068 (XXVIII): Adopted 30 Nov. 1973. International Convention on the Suppression and Punishment of the Crime of Apartheid.

Resolution 3074 (XXVIII): Adopted 3 Dec. 1973. Principles of international co-operation in the detection, arrest, extradition and punishment of persons guilty of war crimes and crimes against humanity.

Resolution 3166 (XXVIII): Adopted 14 Dec. 1973. Convention on the Prevention and Punishment of Crimes against Internationally Protected Persons, including Diplomatic Agents.

Resolution 3201 (S-VI): Adopted 1 May 1974. Declaration on the Establishment of a New International Economic Order.

Resolution 3235 (XXIX): Adopted 12 Nov. 1974. Convention on the Registration of Objects launched into Outer Space.

Resolution 3281 (XXIX): Adopted 12 Dec. 1974. Charter of Economic Rights and Duties of States.

Resolution 3314 (XXIX): Adopted 14 Dec. 1974. Definition of Aggression.

Resolution 3318 (XXIX): Adopted 14 Dec. 1974. Declaration on the Protection of Women and Children in Emergency and Armed Conflict.

Resolution 3346 (XXIX): Adopted 17 Dec. 1974. Agreement between the UN and the World Intellectual Property Organization (WIPO).

Resolution 3384 (XXX): Adopted 10 Nov. 1975. Declaration on the Use of Scientific and Technological Progress in the Interests of Peace and for the Benefit of Mankind.

Resolution 3447 (XXX): Adopted 9 Dec. 1975. Declaration on the Rights of Disabled Persons.

Resolution 3452 (XXX): Adopted 9 Dec. 1975. Declaration on the Protection of all Persons from being subjected to Torture and other Cruel, Inhuman or Degrading Treatment or Punishment.

Resolution 31/72: Adopted 10 Dec. 1976. Convention on the Prohibition of Military or any other Hostile Use of Environmental Modification Techniques.

Resolution 32/105: Adopted 14 Dec. 1977. International Declaration against Apartheid in Sports.

Resolution 32/107: Adopted 15 Dec. 1977. Agreement between the UN and the International Fund for Agricultural Development (IFAD).

Resolution 32/155: Adopted 19 Dec. 1977. Declaration on the Deepening and Consolidation of International *Détente.*

Resolution 32/156: Adopted 19 Dec. 1977. Agreement on Co-operation and Relationships between the UN and the World Tourism Organization (WTO).

Resolution S-9/2: Adopted 3 May 1978. Declaration on Namibia.

Resolution 33/73: Adopted 15 Dec. 1978. Declaration on the Preparation of Societies for Life in Peace.

Resolution 33/162: Adopted 20 Dec. 1978. Charter of Rights for Migrant Workers in Southern Africa.

Resolution 34/68: Adopted 5 Dec. 1979. Agreement governing the Activities of States on the Moon and other Celestial Bodies.

Resolution 34/88: Adopted 11 Dec. 1979. Declaration on International Co-operation for Disarmament.

Resolution 34/93: Adopted 12 Dec. 1979. Declaration on South Africa.

Resolution 34/146: Adopted 17 Dec. 1979. International Convention against the Taking of Hostages.

Resolution 34/169: Adopted 17 Dec. 1979. Code of Conduct for law-enforcement officials.

Resolution 34/180: Adopted 18 Dec. 1979. Convention on the Elimination of all forms of Discrimination against Women.

Resolution 35/46: Adopted 3 Dec. 1980. Declaration of the 1980s as the Second Disarmament Decade.

Resolution 35/55: Adopted 5 Dec. 1980. International Agreement for the Establishment of the University for Peace and Charter of the University of Peace.

Resolution 35/56: Adopted 5 Dec. 1980. International Development Strategy for the Third UN Development Decade.

Resolution 36/55: Adopted 25 Nov. 1981. Declaration on the Elimination of all forms of Intolerance and of Discrimination based on Religion or Belief.

Resolution 36/100: Adopted 9 Dec. 1981. Declaration on the Prevention of Nuclear Catastrophe.

Resolution 36/103: Adopted 9 Dec. 1981. Declaration on the Inadmissibility of Intervention and Interference in the Internal Affairs of States.

Resolution 37/7: Adopted 28 Oct. 1982. World Charter for Nature.

Resolution 37/10: Adopted 15 Nov. 1982. Manila Declaration on the Peaceful Settlement of International Disputes.

Resolution 37/63: Adopted 3 Dec. 1982. Declaration on the Participation of Women in Promoting International Peace and Co-operation.

Resolution 37/92: Adopted 10 Dec. 1982. Principles governing the use by states of artificial earth satellites for international direct television broadcasting.

Resolution 37/194: Adopted 18 Dec. 1982. Principles of medical ethics relevant to the role of health personnel, particularly physicians, in the protection of prisoners and detainees against torture and other cruel, inhuman or degrading treatment or punishment.

Resolution 39/11: Adopted 12 Nov. 1984. Declaration on the Right of Peoples to Peace.

Resolution 39/29: Adopted 3 Dec. 1984. Declaration on the Critical Economic Situation in Africa.

Resolution 39/46: Adopted 10 Dec. 1984. Convention against Torture and other Cruel, Inhuman or Degrading Treatment or Punishment.

Resolution 39/142: Adopted 14 Dec. 1984. Declaration on the Control of Drugs-trafficking and Drug Abuse.

Resolution 40/33: Adopted 29 Nov. 1985. UN standard minimum rules for the administration of juvenile justice (The Beijing Rules).

Resolution 40/34: Adopted 29 Nov. 1985. Declaration of Basic Principles of Justice for Victims of Crime and Abuse of Power.

Resolution 40/64: Adopted 10 Dec. 1985. International Convention against Apartheid in Sports.

Resolution 40/144: Adopted 13 Dec. 1985. Declaration on the Human Rights of Individuals who are not Nationals of the Country in which they live.

Resolution 40/180: Adopted 17 Dec. 1985. Agreement between the UN and the UN Industrial Development Organization (UNIDO).

Resolution 41/65: Adopted 3 Dec. 1986. Principles relating to remote sensing of the earth from outer space.

Resolution 41/85: Adopted 3 Dec. 1986. Declaration on Social and Legal Principles Relating to the Protection and Welfare of Children, with special reference to Foster Placement and Adoption Nationally and Internationally.

Resolution 41/128: Adopted 4 Dec. 1986. Declaration on the Right to Development.

Resolution 42/22: Adopted 18 Nov. 1987. Declaration on the Enhancement of the Effectiveness of the Principle of Refraining from the Threat or Use of Force in International Relations.

Resolution 42/186: Adopted 11 Dec. 1987. Environmental perspective to 2000 and beyond.

Resolution 43/51: Adopted 5 Dec. 1988. Declaration on the Prevention and Removal of Disputes and Situations which may threaten International Peace and Security and on the Role of the UN in this Field.

Resolution 43/165: Adopted 9 Dec. 1988. UN Convention on International Bills of Exchange and International Promissory Notes.

Resolution 43/173: Adopted 9 Dec. 1988. Body of principles for the protection of all persons under any form of detention or imprisonment.

Resolution 44/25: Adopted 20 Nov. 1989. Convention on the Rights of the Child.

Resolution 44/34: Adopted 4 Dec. 1989. International Convention against the Recruitment, Use, Financing and Training of Mercenaries.

Resolution S-16/1: Adopted 14 Dec. 1989. Declaration on Apartheid and its Destructive Consequences in Southern Africa.

Resolution 44/114: Adopted 15 Dec. 1989. Principles that should govern further actions of states in the field of the 'freezing' and reduction of military budgets.

Resolution 44/128: Adopted 15 Dec. 1989. International Covenant on Civil and Political Rights: Second Optional Protocol aiming at the Abolition of the Death Penalty.

Resolution S-18/3: Adopted 1 May 1990. Declaration on International Economic Co-operation, in particular the Revitalization of Economic Growth and Development of the Developing Countries.

Resolution 45/62: Adopted 4 Dec. 1990. Declaration of the 1990s as the Third Disarmament Decade.

Resolution 45/95: Adopted 14 Dec. 1990. Guide-lines for the regulation of computerized data files.

Resolution 45/110: Adopted 14 Dec. 1990. UN standard minimum rules for non-custodial measures (The Tokyo Rules).

Resolution 45/111: Adopted 14 Dec. 1990. Basic principles for the treatment of prisoners.

Resolution 45/112: Adopted 14 Dec. 1990. UN guide-lines for the prevention of juvenile delinquency.

Resolution 45/113: Adopted 14 Dec. 1990. UN rules for the protection of juveniles deprived of their liberty.

Resolution 45/116: Adopted 14 Dec. 1990. Model Treaty on Extradition.

Resolution 45/117: Adopted 14 Dec. 1990. Model Treaty on Mutual Assistance in Criminal Matters and Optional Protocol concerning the Proceeds of Crime.

Resolution 45/118: Adopted 14 Dec. 1990. Model Treaty on the Transfer of Proceedings in Criminal Matters.

Resolution 45/119: Adopted 14 Dec. 1990. Model Treaty on the Transfer of Supervision of Offenders Conditionally Sentenced or Conditionally Released.

Resolution 45/158: Adopted 18 Dec. 1990. International Convention on the Protection of the Rights of All Migrant Workers and Members of their Families.

Resolution 45/199: Adopted 21 Dec. 1990. International Development Strategy for the Fourth UN Development Decade.

Resolution 46/59: Adopted 9 Dec. 1991. Declaration on Fact-finding by the UN in the Field of the Maintenance of International Peace and Security.

Resolution 46/91: Adopted 16 Dec. 1991. UN principles for older persons.

Resolution 46/119: Adopted 17 Dec. 1991. Principles for the protection of persons with mental illness and for the improvement of mental health care.

Resolution 46/151: Adopted 18 Dec. 1991. UN new agenda for the development of Africa in the 1990s.

Resolution 46/152: Adopted 18 Dec. 1991. Statement of Principles and Programme of Action of the UN Crime Prevention and Criminal Justice Programme.

Resolution 47/5: Adopted 16 Oct. 1992. Proclamation on Ageing.

Resolution 47/68: Adopted 14 Dec. 1992. Principles relevant to the use of nuclear power sources in outer space.

Resolution 47/133: Adopted 18 Dec. 1992. Declaration on the Protection of all Persons from Enforced Disappearance.

Resolution 47/135: Adopted 18 Dec. 1992. Declaration on the Rights of Persons belonging to National or Ethnic, Religious and Linguistic Minorities.

Resolution 48/96: Adopted 20 Dec. 1993. Standard rules on the equalization of opportunities for persons with disabilities.

Resolution 48/104: Adopted 20 Dec. 1993. Declaration on the Elimination of Violence against Women.

Resolution 48/134: Adopted 20 Dec. 1993. Principles relating to the status of national institutions for the promotion and protection of human rights (Paris Principles).

Resolution 48/263: Adopted 28 July 1994. Agreement relating to the implementation of part XI of the UN Convention on the Law of the Sea.

Resolution 49/57: Adopted 9 Dec. 1994. Declaration on the Enhancement of Co-operation between the UN and Regional

Arrangements or Agencies in the Maintenance of International Peace and Security.

Resolution 49/59: Adopted 9 Dec. 1994. Convention on the Safety of UN and associated Personnel.

Resolution 49/60: Adopted 9 Dec. 1994. Declaration on Measures to Eliminate International Terrorism.

Resolution 50/5: Adopted 18 Oct. 1995. Declaration in Commemoration of the 50th Anniversary of the end of the Second World War.

Resolution 50/6: Adopted 24 Oct. 1995. Declaration on the Occasion of the 50th Anniversary of the UN.

Resolution 50/48: Adopted 11 Dec. 1995. UN Convention on Independent Guarantees and Stand-by Letters of Credit.

Resolution 50/50: Adopted 11 Dec. 1995. UN model rules for the conciliation of disputes between states.

Resolution 51/59: Adopted 12 Dec. 1996. International Code of Conduct for public officials.

Resolution 51/60: Adopted 12 Dec. 1996. UN Declaration on Crime and Public Security.

Resolution 51/122: Adopted 13 Dec. 1996. Declaration on International Co-operation in the Exploration and Use of Outer Space for the Benefit and in the Interest of all States, taking into Particular Account the Needs of Developing Countries.

Resolution 51/162: Adopted 16 Dec. 1996. Model law on electronic commerce.

Resolution 51/191: Adopted 16 Dec. 1996. UN Declaration against Corruption and Bribery in International Commercial Transactions.

Resolution 51/210: Adopted 17 Dec. 1996. Declaration to supplement the Declaration on Measures to Eliminate International Terrorism of 1994.

Resolution 51/229: Adopted 21 May 1997. Convention on the Law of the Non-navigational Uses of International Watercourses.

Resolution 51/240: Adopted 20 June 1997. Agenda for Development.

Resolution 52/27: Adopted 26 Nov. 1997. Agreement concerning the Relationship between the UN and the International Seabed Authority.

Resolution 52/86: Adopted 12 Dec. 1997. Model strategies and practical measures on the elimination of violence against women in the field of crime prevention and criminal justice.

Resolution 52/158: Adopted 15 Dec. 1997. Model law on cross-border insolvency.

Resolution 52/164: Adopted 15 Dec. 1997. International Convention for the Suppression of Terrorist Bombings.

Resolution S-20/3: Adopted 10 June 1998. Declaration on the Guiding Principles of Drug Demand Reduction.

Resolution 52/251: Adopted 8 Sept. 1998. Agreement on Co-operation and the Relationship between the UN and the International Tribunal for the Law of the Sea.

Resolution 53/2: Adopted 6 Oct. 1998. Declaration on the Occasion of the 50th Anniversary of UN Peace-keeping.

Resolution 53/101: Adopted 8 Dec. 1998. Principles and guidelines for international negotiations.

Resolution 53/144: Adopted 9 Dec. 1998. Declaration on the Right and Responsibility of Individuals, Groups and Organs of Society to Promote and Protect Universally Recognized Human Rights and Fundamental Freedoms.

Resolution 54/4: Adopted 6 Oct. 1999. Optional Protocol to the Convention on the Elimination of All Forms of Discrimination against Women (Resolution 34/180).

Resolution 54/109: Adopted 9 Dec. 1999. International Convention for the Suppression of the Financing of Terrorism.

Resolution 54/263: Adopted 16 May 2000. Optional Protocol to the Convention on the Rights of the Child concerning the involvement of children in armed conflict, and Optional Protocol on the sale of children, child prostitution and child pornography.

Resolution S-22/2: Adopted 12 June 2000. Declaration on state of progress of and initiatives for the future implementation of the Programme of Action for the Sustainable Development of Small Island Developing States.

Resolution 54/280: Adopted 30 June 2000. Agreement to regulate the relationship between the United Nations and the Preparatory Commission for the Comprehensive Nuclear Test Ban Treaty Organization.

Resolution 55/2: Adopted 8 Sept. 2000. United Nations Millennium Declaration.

Resolution 55/25: Adopted 15 Nov. 2000. United Nations Convention against Transnational Organized Crime; two additional Protocols.

Resolution 55/59: Adopted 4 Dec. 2000. Vienna Declaration on Crime and Justice: Meeting the Challenges of the Twenty-first Century.

Resolution 55/153: Adopted 12 Dec. 2000. Articles on nationality of natural persons in relation to the succession of states.

Resolution 55/255: Adopted 31 May 2001. Protocol against the Illicit Manufacturing of and Trafficking in Firearms, their Parts and Components and Ammunition, supplementing theUN Convention against Transnational Organized Crime.

Resolution S-25/2: Adopted 9 June 2001. Declaration on Cities and other Human Settlements in the New Millennium.

Resolution S-26/2: Adopted 27 June 2001. Declaration of Commitment on HIV/AIDS.

Resolution 55/278: Adopted 12 July 2001. Statute of the UN System Staff College in Turin, Italy.

Resolution 55/283: Adopted 7 Sept. 2001. Agreement concerning the relationship between the UN and the Organization for the Prohibition of Chemical Weapons.

Resolution 56/6: Adopted 9 Nov. 2001. Global Agenda for Dialogue among Civilizations.

Security Council

The Security Council was established as a principal organ under the United Nations Charter (see p. 62); its first meeting was held on 17 January 1946. Its task is to promote international peace and security in all parts of the world.

MEMBERS

Permanent members:

People's Republic of China, France, Russia, United Kingdom, USA.

The remaining 10 members are normally elected (five each year) by the General Assembly for two-year periods (five countries from Africa and Asia, two from Latin America, one from eastern Europe, and two from western Europe and others).

Non-permanent members as at 1 January 2002:

Colombia, Ireland, Mauritius, Norway, Singapore (term expires 31 December 2002).

Bulgaria, Cameroon, Guinea, Mexico, Syria (term expires 31 December 2003).

Rotation of the Presidency in 2002:

Mauritius (January); Mexico (February); Norway (March); Russia (April); Singapore (May); Syria (June); United Kingdom (July); USA (August); Bulgaria (September); Cameroon (October); China (November); Colombia (December).

ORGANIZATION

The Security Council has the right to investigate any dispute or situation which might lead to friction between two or more countries, and such disputes or situations may be brought to the Council's attention either by one of its members, by any member state, by the General Assembly, by the Secretary-General or even, under certain conditions, by a state which is not a member of the United Nations.

The Council has the right to recommend ways and means of peaceful settlement and, in certain circumstances, the actual terms of settlement. In the event of a threat to or breach of international peace or an act of aggression, the Council has powers to take 'enforcement' measures in order to restore international peace and security. These include severance of communications and of economic and diplomatic relations and, if required, action by air, land and sea forces.

All members of the United Nations are pledged by the Charter to make available to the Security Council, on its call and in accordance with special agreements, the armed forces, assistance and facilities necessary to maintain international peace and security. These agreements, however, have not yet been concluded.

The Council is organized to be able to function continuously. The Presidency of the Council is held monthly in turn by the member states in English alphabetical order. Each member of the Council has one vote. On procedural matters decisions are made by the affirmative vote of any nine members. For decisions on other matters the required nine affirmative votes must include the votes of the five permanent members. This is the rule of 'great power unanimity' popularly known as the 'veto' privilege. In practice, an abstention by one of the permanent members is not regarded as a veto. Any member, whether permanent or non-permanent, must abstain from voting in any decision concerning the pacific settlement of a dispute to which it is a party. Any member of the UN that is party to a dispute under consideration by the Council may participate in the Council's discussions without a vote.

ACTIVITIES

In January 1992 the first ever summit meeting of the Security Council was convened, and was attended by the heads of state or government of 13 of its 15 members, and by the ministers of foreign affairs of the remaining two. The subject of the summit meeting, which was presented in a report drafted by the Secretary-General (entitled 'An Agenda for Peace') was the UN's role in preventive diplomacy, peace-keeping and peace-making.

Consideration of reform of the Security Council commenced in 1993 at the 48th Session of the General Assembly, which established a Working Group to assess the issue. In October 1994 a general debate of the General Assembly revealed widespread support for expanding the Security Council to 20 seats and awarding permanent membership to Japan and Germany. In March the President of the General Assembly formally introduced a proposal for reform, which envisaged a Council consisting of 24 members, including five new permanent members and four new non-permanent members. In September 2000 the UN Millennium Summit declared support for continued discussions on reform of the Council. A summit meeting of the Council convened during the Millennium Summit issued a declaration on ensuring an effective role for the Council in maintaining international peace and security, with particular reference to Africa.

As the UN organ primarily responsible for maintaining peace and security, the Security Council is empowered to deploy UN forces in the event that a dispute leads to fighting. It may also authorize the use of military force by a coalition of member states or a regional organization. During 2001 the Security Council continued to monitor closely all existing peace-keeping missions and the situations in countries where missions were being undertaken, and to authorize extensions of their mandates accordingly. In March the Council authorized an increase in the military component of the mission in Sierra Leone (UNAMSIL) to 17,500. The mandate of the mission in the Democratic Republic of the Congo (MONUC) was revised in June to provide for the establishment of a civilian police component and a planning section to co-ordinate the process of disarmament, demobilization, repatriation and reintegration. (For details of UN observer missions and peace-keeping operations, see pp. 124–135.)

The imposition of sanctions by the Security Council as a means of targeting regimes and groupings that are deemed to threaten international peace and security has increased significantly in recent years and has been subjected to widespread scrutiny regarding enforceability and the potential adverse humanitarian consequences for general populations. In the latter respect the Council has, since 1999, incorporated clauses on humanitarian assessment in its resolutions; the sanctions that took effect against the Taliban in Afghanistan in January 2001 (see below) were the first to entail mandatory monitoring of the humanitarian impact. In 2000 a proposal was submitted to the Council regarding the establishment of a permanent body to monitor sanctions violations. The UN Secretary-General established a special committee in April 2000 to evaluate sanctions policy. A draft version of the committee's final report, issued in February 2001, recommended that future Security Council resolutions enforcing sanctions should clearly specify intended goals and targets, include incentives to reward partial compliance, and focus in particular on the finances of leaders. In April 2000 the Council authorized the establishment of a temporary monitoring mechanism to investigate alleged violations of the sanctions imposed against the UNITA rebels in Angola, owing to their failure to implement earlier Council resolutions demanding compliance with the obligations of the peace process in that country. The mandate of the mechanism was extended in 2001. In mid-2000 the Council's sanctions committee organized a public hearing to assess the role played in the conflict by the illicit diamond trade; the participants included representatives of interested states, regional and international organizations, the global diamond industry and of civil society, as well as individual experts. (It had become evident that the ongoing conflicts in Sierra Leone and Angola were fuelled by rebel groups' illegal exploitation of diamond resources and use of the proceeds derived therefrom to purchase armaments.) In July 2000 the Council voted to prohibit the exportation of all rough diamonds from Sierra Leone that had not been officially certified by that country's Government. This measure was extended by the Council in December 2001 for a period of 11 months, from January 2002. In December a panel of experts appointed by the Council issued a report on the connections between the illicit exportation of diamonds from

Sierra Leone and the international trade in armaments. In March 2001 the Council banned the purchase of diamonds exported from Liberia, and demanded that the Liberian authorities refrain from purchasing so-called 'conflict diamonds' from illegal sources and cease providing support to rebel organizations, with particular reference to the main rebel grouping active in Sierra Leone. The Council re-imposed an embargo on the sale or supply of armaments to Liberia (a previous arms embargo, implemented in 1992, was terminated) and imposed diplomatic restrictions on high-level Liberian government officials. These sanctions came into effect in May. In June the Council decided to exempt certain non-lethal equipment from the embargo against Somalia, in order to facilitate the delivery of humanitarian assistance. In September the Council terminated an arms embargo against the Federal Republic of Yugoslavia, which had been imposed in March 1998 to foster peace and stability in the province of Kosovo and Metohija. Later in that month the sanctions that had been imposed against Sudan in 1996 were terminated in recognition of that country's accession to international conventions of the elimination of terrorism and the implementation of other measures to comply with Council demands.

In March 1998 the Security Council held an open meeting to discuss sanctions that had been imposed against Libya in 1992 and 1993 as a consequence of that country's refusal to extradite for trial two people (alleged to be Libyan intelligence agents) suspected of bombing a US passenger airline over the United Kingdom in 1988. In August 1998 the Council endorsed a proposal to convene a trial under Scottish jurisdiction at a court in the Netherlands, and resolved to suspend all punitive measures against Libya once the authorities in that country had surrendered the suspects. In April 1999, following a period of intensive negotiations, facilitated by the South African President, Nelson Mandela, and representatives of the Saudi Arabian Government, Libya released the two suspects, who were escorted to the Netherlands by the UN's Legal Counsel. On their arrival, and transfer to Scottish custody, the suspension of sanctions against Libya came into effect. The trial commenced in May 2000; in January 2001 one of the accused was acquitted and the other found guilty of complicity in the bombing. A condition of the termination of the sanctions was that Libya should 'demonstrate by concrete actions its renunciation of terrorism'; as the Libyan authorities continued to deny any liability for the Lockerbie attack following the January 2001 verdict, the sanctions were not immediately fully withdrawn.

In December 1996 the Security Council approved the implementation of Resolution 986, which was adopted in April 1995, to provide for the limited sale of Iraqi petroleum to enable the purchase of humanitarian supplies and the provision of contributions to the UN Compensation Committee (which had been established to settle claims against Iraq resulting from the Gulf War). Exports of petroleum up to a value of US $1,000m. every 90 days were to be permitted under the agreement; the Council was responsible for renewing the mandate of the agreement and for approving contracts for the sale of petroleum and the purchase of food and medical goods. The situation in Iraq was monitored by the UN Special Commission (UNSCOM), which had been established in 1991 to monitor the disposal of weapons. In February 1998, despite ongoing tensions between the Iraqi Government and UNSCOM, the Council approved a resolution expanding the so-called oil-for-food programme to allow for sales of petroleum up to a value of $5,256m. every 180 days (superseding a resolution to extend the programme at its existing level, which was authorized in December 1997). The new agreement entered into force on 1 June 1998, following the Secretary-General's approval of a new distribution plan. In mid-December UNSCOM's chairman, Richard Butler, reported to the Security Council regarding Iraq's continued failure to co-operate with UN inspectors and ordered the withdrawal of all UNSCOM personnel from Iraq. The US and United Kingdom Governments responded to Butler's report by conducting extensive airstrikes against Iraqi military targets; however, their action was condemned by some governments for having been undertaken without explicit Security Council authorization. In October 1999 the Council agreed to permit Iraq to generate a further $3,040m. in the next 180-day period of the oil-for-food agreement, accounting for the shortfall of authorized revenue that had not yet been generated. In mid-December the Council approved a six-month extension of the programme. A few days later it adopted a resolution establishing a new policy towards Iraq. The resolution provided for an unlimited ceiling on petroleum exports under the agreed humanitarian programme, and for a suspension of sanctions dependent upon Iraq's co-operation with a new arms inspection body, the UN Monitoring, Verification and Inspection Commission (UNMOVIC) that was to replace UNSCOM. At the end of March 2000 the Council doubled the maximum permitted revenue that Iraq might use to purchase petroleum industry spare parts and other equipment under the ongoing programme. In that month, during a Council meeting on Iraq, the Secretary-General stated that the oil-for-food programme represented a moral dilemma for the UN as it appeared insufficiently to meet the humanitarian requirements of the Iraqi population. The UN's economic sanctions, which no longer commanded widespread international support and had prompted the resignations (in October 1998 and March 2000) of two successive Chief UN Relief Co-ordinators for Iraq as well as continuing opposition within the Council from the People's Republic of China, France and Russia, were robustly challenged by the Iraqi regime during 2000 and early 2001. In November 2000 Iraq demanded the right to impose a surcharge on its exports under the oil-for-food programme, and in January 2001 an oil pipeline between Iraq and Syria was reportedly re-opened without recourse to the Council's sanctions committee. In early December 2000 the Iraqi regime, while agreeing the terms of the next (ninth) 180-day phase of the programme, temporarily suspended exports of petroleum once again during a dispute with the sanctions committee over the pricing mechanism for its oil sales. It was reported in mid-December that the Iraqi administration had implemented the illicit surcharge. The Council urged buyers of Iraqi oil not to pay the premium. A new sanctions regime was discussed during 2001. This envisaged facilitating the transfer of civilian and humanitarian goods to Iraq, while tightening border checks for military or other illegal trading. Disagreements among Council members concerned the extra responsibility placed on Iraq's neighbouring countries and the compilation of a list of 'controlled' items requiring special approval to be imported into Iraq. The existing oil-for-food scheme was extended in early July after Russia confirmed that it would veto the new proposals. A further extension was granted in November; however, the Council approved a draft list of goods for review which it intended to enter into effect on 30 May 2002. The new measures remained under consideration in early 2002.

In mid-October 1999 the Council issued a resolution in which it condemned suspected illegal terrorist-related activities undertaken in Taliban-controlled areas of Afghanistan, including the training of terrorists and, in particular, the shielding of those suspected of organizing the bomb attacks against the US embassies in Kenya and Tanzania in August 1998. The Council demanded that the main suspects be extradited for trial and resolved to impose punitive measures against the Taliban authorities if these conditions were not met within one month. Consequently, an embargo on all Taliban-controlled overseas funds and international flights of the national airline entered into effect in November 1999. In December 2000 the Council authorized the imposition of an arms embargo on the area of Afghanistan under Taliban control, and resolved that all member states should 'freeze' the funds and assets of all individuals and entities accused of complicity in the 1998 terrorist bombings. In addition, the Council banned the supply to the Taliban-controlled area of a specific chemical believed to be used there in the production of illegal narcotic drugs. The new sanctions took effect in January 2001. In July the Council established a monitoring mechanism to strengthen the enforcement of the sanctions by Afghanistan's neighbouring countries.

On 12 September 2001 the Security Council expressed its unequivocal condemnation of the terrorist attacks against targets in the USA, which had occurred on the previous day. It expressed its readiness to combat terrorism and reiterated the right to individual or collective self-defence in accordance with the UN Charter. At the end of September the Council determined to establish a Counter-Terrorism Committee to monitor a range of measures to combat international terrorism, including greater international co-operation and suppressing the financing of terrorist groups. A special session of the Council at ministerial level was convened on the issue of terrorism in mid-November. Further debate on Afghanistan, where it was believed the Taliban authorities had sheltered those responsible for the attacks, confirmed Council support for a UN role in assisting the country to establish a transitional administration leading to the formation of a new multi-ethnic government. In December the Council endorsed an agreement on provisional political arrangements concluded by representatives of Afghan groups meeting in Bonn, Germany, and, later in that month, authorized the establishment of an International Security Assistance Force to help to maintain a secure environment in the capital, Kabul, and surrounding areas. In January 2002 the Council terminated all restrictions against Ariana Afghan Airlines.

During 2001 the Council provided a forum for discussion of the situation in the Middle East, and the escalating violence in the West Bank and Gaza and in Israel. However, disagreement among its permanent members prevented an agreement on action. In March and December the USA vetoed a draft resolution in support of the establishment of an international observer force. Other open debates held during the year included consideration of the situation in East Timor and the exploitation of natural resources in the Democratic Republic of the Congo, as well as general discussions concerning civilians in armed conflict, women, peace and security, small arms and light weapons, conflict prevention, and HIV/AIDS. Presidential statements were issued on several of these issues. In January a public meeting was held on co-operation between the UN and peace-keeping troop-contributing countries. A working group was subsequently established to consider the issue and a Council resolution on means to strengthen this co-operation was approved in June. In August the Council adopted as a resolution a comprehensive consideration of the role of the Council in the prevention of armed conflict. In November a resolution was adopted outlining specific commitments and measures to protect children from the effects of armed conflict and to meet their humanitarian needs.

COMMITTEES

In February 2002 there were two **Standing Committees**, each composed of representatives of all Council member states:

Committee of Experts on Rules of Procedure (studies and advises on rules of procedure and other technical matters);

Committee on the Admission of New Members.

***Ad hoc* Committees**, which are established as needed, comprise all Council members and meet in closed session:

Governing Council of the UN Compensation Commission established by Security Council Resolution 692 (1991).

Security Council Committee on Council Meetings away from Headquarters.

Security Council Committee established pursuant to Resolution 1373 (2001) concerning Counter-Terrorism.

Within this category are the Sanctions Committees, which may be established to oversee economic or political enforcement measures, imposed by the Security Council to maintain or restore international peace and security. At February 2002 the following committees were operational:

Security Council Committee established pursuant to Resolution 1243 (2001) concerning Liberia;

Security Council Committee established pursuant to Resolution 1267 (1999) concerning Afghanistan;

Security Council Committee established pursuant to Resolution 1132 (1997) concerning Sierra Leone;

Security Council Committee established pursuant to Resolution 918 (1994) concerning Rwanda;

Security Council Committee established pursuant to Resolution 864 (1993) concerning the situation in Angola;

Security Council Committee established pursuant to Resolution 751 (1992) concerning Somalia;

Security Council Committee established pursuant to Resolution 748 (1992) concerning Libya;

Security Council Committee established pursuant to Resolution 661 (1990) concerning the situation between Iraq and Kuwait.

INTERNATIONAL TRIBUNALS

In May 1993 the Security Council, acting under Article VII of the UN Charter, adopted Resolution 827, which established an *ad hoc* 'war crimes' tribunal. The so-called International Tribunal for the Prosecution of Persons Responsible for Serious Violations of International Humanitarian Law Committed in the Territory of the Former Yugoslavia (also referred to as the International Criminal Tribunal for the former Yugoslavia—ICTY) was inaugurated in The Hague, Netherlands, in November, comprising a prosecutor and 11 judges sitting in two trial chambers and one appeals chamber. In May 1998 the Security Council authorized the establishment of a third trial chamber, and the election of three new judges, in order to expand the capacity of the Tribunal. In November 2000 the Security Council authorized the enlargement of the appeals chamber and agreed to establish a reserve of 27 additional judges to serve as required. Public hearings were initiated in November 1994. The first trial proceedings commenced in May 1996, and the first sentence was imposed by the Tribunal in November. In July and November 1995 the Tribunal formally charged the Bosnian Serb political and military leaders Radovan Karadžić and Gen. Ratko Mladić, on two separate indictments, with genocide and crimes against humanity, and in July 1996 issued international warrants for their arrest. They remained at large in early 2002. In April 2000 Momčilo Krajišnik, a senior associate of Karadžić, was detained by the ICTY, charged with genocide, war crimes and crimes against humanity. Biljana Plavšić, a further former Bosnian Serb political leader, surrendered to the Tribunal in January 2001, also indicted on charges of genocide, war crimes and crimes against humanity. In the following month three Bosnian Serb former soldiers were convicted by the ICTY of utilizing mass rape and the sexual enslavement of women as instruments of terror in wartime. In mid-1998 the ICTY began investigating reported acts of violence against civilians committed by both sides in the conflict in the southern Serbian province of Kosovo and Metohija. In early 1999 there were reports of large-scale organized killings, rape and expulsion of the local Albanian population by Serbian forces. In April ICTY personnel visited refugee camps in neighbouring countries in order to compile evidence of the atrocities, and obtained intelligence information from NATO members regarding those responsible for the incidents. In May the then President of the Federal Republic of Yugoslavia (FRY), Slobodan Milošević, was indicted, along with three senior government ministers and the chief-of-staff of the army, charged with crimes against humanity and violations of the customs of war committed in Kosovo since 1 January 1999; international warrants were issued for their arrests. In June, following the establishment of an international force to secure peace in Kosovo, the ICTY established teams of experts to investigate alleged atrocities at 529 identified grave sites. The new FRY administration, which had assumed power following legislative and presidential elections in late 2000, contested the impartiality of the ICTY, proposing that Milošević and other members of the former regime should be tried before a national court. In April 2001 Milošević was arrested by the local authorities in Belgrade. Under increasing international pressure, the Federal Government approved his extradition in June, and he was immediately transferred to the ICTY, where he was formally charged with crimes against humanity committed in Kosovo in 1999. A further indictment of crimes against humanity committed in Croatia during 1999–92 was confirmed in October, and a third indictment, which included charges of genocide committed in Bosnia and Herzegovina in 1999–95, was confirmed in November. In early February 2002 the Appeals Chamber ordered that the three indictments be considered in a single trial. The trial commenced later in that month. Milošević, however, continued to protest at the illegality of his arrest and refused to recognize the jurisdiction of the Court. In August 2001 the ICTY passed its first sentence of genocide, convicting a former Bosnian Serb military commander, Gen. Radislav Kristić, for his role in the deaths of up to 8,000 Bosnian Muslim men and boys in Srebreniča in July 1995. At February 2002 44 individuals were being detained by the ICTY, six had been provisionally released, while 30 arrest warrants remained outstanding. At that time 67 of the accused had appeared in proceedings before the Tribunal, of whom 15 were awaiting appeal, 11 had received a final sentence and five had been acquitted or found not guilty. Three people had already served their sentence.

President of the ICTY: CLAUDE JORDA (France).

Registrar: HANS HOLTHUIS (Netherlands).

Address: Public Information Unit, POB 13888, 2501 The Hague, Netherlands.

Telephone: (70) 512-5233; **fax:** (70) 512-5355; **internet:** www.un.org/icty.

In November 1994 the Security Council adopted Resolution 955, establishing an International Criminal Tribunal for Rwanda (ICTR) to prosecute persons responsible for genocide and other serious violations of humanitarian law that had been committed in Rwanda and by Rwandans in neighbouring states. The Tribunal was to consist of two three-member trial chambers and one appeals chamber, and was to be served by the same Prosecutor as that of the ICTY. Its temporal jurisdiction was limited to the period 1 January to 31 December 1994. In April 1998 the Security Council authorized the establishment of a third three-member trial chamber. The Security Council authorized the enlargement of the appeals chamber and approved the election of two further judges to the Tribunal in November 2000. A high security Detention Facility has been built within the compound of the prison in Arusha. The first plenary session of the Tribunal was held in The Hague in June 1995; formal proceedings at its permanent headquarters in Arusha, Tanzania, were initiated in November. The first trial of persons charged by the Tribunal commenced in January 1997, and sentences were imposed in July. During that year the proceedings of the ICTR were undermined by reports of mismanagement and the need for administrative reforms. In September 1998 the former Rwandan Prime Minister, Jean Kambanda, and a former mayor of Taba, Jean-Paul Akayesu, both Hutu extremists, were found guilty of genocide and crimes against humanity; Kambanda subsequently became the first person ever to be sentenced under the 1948 Convention on the Prevention and Punishment of the Crime of Genocide. In October 2000 the Tribunal rejected an appeal by Kambanda. In November 1999 the Rwandan Government temporarily suspended co-operation with the Tribunal in protest at a decision of the appeals chamber to release an indicted former government official owing to procedural delays. (The appeals chamber subsequently reversed this decision.) By November 2001 some 74 people had been indicted by the ICTR, of whom 52 had been detained in custody. Eight individuals had been sentenced by the Tribunal at January 2002 and one person had been acquitted. Seven trials, involving 17 individuals, were under way at that time.

President of the ICTR: NAVANETHEM PILLAY (South Africa).

Registrar: Adama Dieng (Senegal).

Address: Arusha International Conference Centre, POB 6016, Arusha, Tanzania.

Telephone: (57) 4207; **fax:** (57) 4000; **e-mail:** public@un.org; **internet:** www. ictr.org.

Both Tribunals are supported by teams of investigators and human rights experts working in the field to collect forensic and other evidence in order to uphold indictments. Evidence of mass graves resulting from large-scale unlawful killings has been uncovered in both regions.

Chief Prosecutor: CARLA DEL PONTE (Switzerland).

SECURITY COUNCIL RESOLUTIONS

Resolution 1: Adopted 25 Jan. 1946. Agreed to convene the Military Staff Committee established by the UN to provide advice and assistance to the Security Council and comprising the Chiefs of Staff of permanent members of the Security Council or their representatives.

Resolution 8: Adopted 29 Aug. 1946. Endorsed the admission of Afghanistan, Iceland and Sweden to the UN.

Resolution 13: Adopted 12 Dec. 1946. Endorsed the admission of Thailand to the UN.

Resolution 16: Adopted 10 Jan. 1947. Constituted a Free Territory of Trieste (in Italy).

Resolution 21: Adopted 2 April 1947. Designated the Pacific Islands, formerly held under a Japanese mandate, as a strategic area and placed them under the International Trusteeship System, with the USA as administering authority.

Resolution 27: Adopted 1 Aug. 1947. Requested that Indonesia and the Netherlands observe an immediate cease-fire and resolve their conflict peacefully.

Resolution 29: Adopted 12 Aug. 1947. Endorsed the admission of Pakistan and Yemen to the UN.

Resolution 30: Adopted 25 Aug. 1947. Recognized measures taken by the Governments of Indonesia and the Netherlands to comply with Resolution 27, a statement by the Netherlands of its intention to request career consuls in Batavia (Jakarta) to report on the situation in Indonesia and to organize a sovereign, democratic United States of Indonesia, and a request by Indonesia for the deployment of a Commission of Observers.

Resolution 35: Adopted 3 Oct. 1947. Requested that the Secretary-General deploy a three-member Committee of Good Offices to facilitate a settlement between Indonesia and the Netherlands.

Resolution 38: Adopted 17 Jan. 1948. Requested the Governments of India and Pakistan to implement measures to improve the situation in the disputed Indian state of Jammu and Kashmir.

Resolution 39: Adopted 20 Jan. 1948. Established a three-member investigatory and mediatory Commission for India and Pakistan, with one member to be selected by the Government of India and one by the Government of Pakistan, for deployment to the disputed state of Jammu and Kashmir.

Resolution 41: Adopted 28 Feb. 1948. Welcomed the Truce Agreement signed by the Governments of Indonesia and the Netherlands.

Resolution 43: Adopted 1 April 1948. Requested the Arab and Jewish communities to halt the violent disorder in Palestine. Requested the Jewish Agency for Palestine and the Arab Higher Committee to make available a representative to facilitate a truce.

Resolution 45: Adopted 10 April 1948. Endorsed the admission of Burma (Myanmar) to the UN.

Resolution 46: Adopted 17 April 1948. Requested all parties involved in the situation in Palestine and the governments of member states to facilitate a truce by means of the cessation of military activity, co-operation with the United Kingdom in its role as the administering authority, and the avoidance of actions likely to obstruct or damage Holy Places in Palestine.

Resolution 47: Adopted 21 April 1948. Increased membership of the Commission for India and Pakistan to five, and requested its immediate deployment. Made recommendations for the restoration of peace to the disputed state of Jammu and Kashmir, and requested that the Indian Government establish a Plebiscite Administration to hold a popular vote on the accession of the state to India or Pakistan. Authorized the Commission to establish a military observer group in Jammu and Kashmir.

Resolution 48: Adopted 23 April 1948. Established a Security Council Truce Commission for Palestine, to monitor the implementation of Resolution 46.

Resolution 49: Adopted 22 May 1948. Demanded that a cease-fire be observed in Palestine. Requested all parties to facilitate the work of a UN Mediator appointed by the General Assembly.

Resolution 50: Adopted 29 May 1948. Requested all those involved in the situation in Palestine to observe a cease-fire for a four-week period. Urged Governments to refrain from sending troops or weapons to the area. Stated that any violation of the cease-fire could lead to action under the provisions of the Charter of the UN. Agreed to dispatch a number of military observers to Palestine to assist the UN Mediator and the Security Council Truce Commission.

Resolution 53: Adopted 7 July 1948. Appealed for the cease-fire in Palestine to be maintained.

Resolution 54: Adopted 15 July 1948. Determined that the situation in Palestine constituted a threat to peace under Article 39 of the UN Charter. Requested all those involved to co-operate with the UN Mediator in Palestine and to observe an immediate cease-fire, which was to remain in force pending a transition to peace. Requested the UN Mediator in Palestine to monitor the truce and investigate alleged breaches of the cease-fire.

Resolution 56: Adopted 19 Aug. 1948. Declared the authorities involved in the situation in Palestine to be responsible for preventing all violations of the truce and obliged them to convict any person acting in breach of it.

Resolution 57: Adopted 18 Sept. 1948. Expressed shock at the assassination of the UN Mediator in Palestine.

Resolution 61: Adopted 4 Nov. 1948. Requested governments involved in the situation in Palestine to withdraw any forces which had advanced beyond demarcation lines fixed by the Acting Mediator in Palestine, and to establish demilitarized, neutral zones to ensure the full observance of the cease-fire. Appointed a five-member Committee to advise the Acting Mediator.

Resolution 62: Adopted 16 Nov. 1948. Imposed an armistice in Palestine, with the establishment of permanent demarcation lines.

Resolution 63: Adopted 24 Dec. 1948. Expressed concern at the resumption of hostilities in Indonesia, and requested the Governments of Indonesia and the Netherlands to observe an immediate cease-fire. Demanded the release of the President of Indonesia and other political detainees.

Resolution 66: Adopted 29 Dec. 1948. Ordered the observation of an immediate cease-fire in Palestine and the implementation of Resolution 61, following an outbreak of hostilities on 22 Dec.

Resolution 67: Adopted 28 Jan. 1949. Demanded the cessation of military operations by the Governments of Indonesia and the Netherlands and the release of all political prisoners. Recommended the establishment of an interim federal government by 15 March, the holding of elections to select representatives to an Indonesian constituent assembly by 1 Oct. and the transfer of sovereignty from the Netherlands to the United States of Indonesia by 1 July 1950. Decided that the Committee of Good Offices was to become the UN Commission for Indonesia, to be assisted by the Consular Committee.

Resolution 69: Adopted 4 March 1949. Endorsed the admission of Israel to the UN.

Resolution 73: Adopted 11 Aug. 1949. Requested all those involved in the conflict in Palestine to support the work of the Conciliation Commission for Palestine. Concluded that the Armistice Agreements reached superseded Resolutions 50 and 54. Reaffirmed a request for an unconditional cease-fire to be observed. Relieved the Acting Mediator in Palestine from further duties and confirmed that the implementation of each agreement was to be monitored by a Mixed Armistice Commission, the chairman of which was to be the Chief of Staff of the UN Truce Supervision Organization (UNTSO) in Palestine, or his representative.

Resolution 80: Adopted 14 March 1950. Commended the Governments of India and Pakistan for effecting a cessation of hostilities, establishing a cease-fire line and agreeing upon the appointment of a Plebiscite Administrator for the disputed state of Jammu and Kashmir, and requested the two Governments to undertake a demilitarization programme and to appoint a UN Representative to assume the duties of the UN Commission for India and Pakistan.

Resolution 82: Adopted 25 June 1950. Condemned the invasion of the Republic of Korea (South Korea) and demanded an immediate cease-fire and the withdrawal of North Korean troops. Requested the UN Commission on Korea to monitor the situation.

Resolution 83: Adopted 27 June 1950. Appealed for assistance to enable the Republic of Korea (South Korea) to repel North Korean forces, and to restore peace and stability to the region.

Resolution 84: Adopted 7 July 1950. Welcomed the prompt military and other assistance provided to the Republic of Korea (South Korea) by member states. Recommended that the military forces provided form a unified command under the USA.

Resolution 85: Adopted 31 July 1950. Requested the unified force (officially entitled the United Nations Command) to determine the humanitarian needs of the population of North Korea.

Resolution 86: Adopted 26 Sept. 1950. Endorsed the admission of Indonesia to the UN.

Resolution 89: Adopted 17 Nov. 1950. Reminded all parties to the situation in Palestine to resolve disputes according to the procedures established by the Armistice Agreements, which envisaged permanent peace for Palestine.

Resolution 91: Adopted 30 March 1951. Instructed the UN Representative for India and Pakistan to effect the demilitarization of the disputed state of Jammu and Kashmir, on the basis of resolutions made by the UN Commission for India and Pakistan in Aug. 1948 and Jan. 1949.

Resolution 92: Adopted 8 May 1951. Expressed concern at the resumption of violence in the demilitarized zone established by the Israel–Syria Armistice Agreement of 20 July 1949, and demanded that an immediate cease-fire be observed.

Resolution 93: Adopted 18 May 1951. Instructed the Governments of Israel and Syria strictly to observe their Armistice Agreement and to inform the Mixed Armistice Commission of any grievances.

Resolution 95: Adopted 1 Sept. 1951. Requested the Egyptian Government to remove restrictions imposed on the movement of commercial ships through the Suez Canal to Israeli and other ports in contravention of the Egypt–Israel Armistice Agreement.

Resolution 96: Adopted 10 Nov. 1951. Welcomed an agreement by the Governments of India and Pakistan to determine the accession of the disputed state of Jammu and Kashmir by means of a plebiscite and urged both parties to resolve the issues remaining.

Resolution 101: Adopted 24 Nov. 1953. Condemned retaliatory action taken by Israel against Jordan as constituting a violation of the cease-fire provisions of Resolution 54 and of the Israeli–Jordan Armistice Agreement.

Resolution 106: Adopted 29 March 1955. Condemned an attack by Israel against Egypt on 6 March as constituting a threat to the Egypt–Israel Armistice Agreement.

Resolution 108: Adopted 8 Sept. 1955. Expressed concern at the cessation of negotiations between Egypt and Israel, and deplored the resumption of violence along the armistice demarcation line established between the two countries in Feb. 1949.

Resolution 109: Adopted 14 Dec. 1955. Endorsed the admission of Albania, Austria, Bulgaria, Cambodia, Ceylon (now Sri Lanka), Finland, Hungary, Ireland, Italy, Jordan, Laos, Libya, Nepal, Portugal, Romania and Spain to the UN.

Resolution 111: Adopted 19 Jan. 1956. Condemned an attack by Israel against Syria in Dec. as constituting a violation of the cease-fire provisions of Resolution 54 and the Israel–Syria Armistice Agreement.

Resolution 112: Adopted 6 Feb. 1956. Endorsed the admission of Sudan to the UN.

Resolution 113: Adopted 4 April 1956. Concluded that the situation in the Middle East constituted a threat to peace in the region and requested the Secretary-General to arrange for the implementation of measures to reduce tension, including the withdrawal of forces from armistice demarcation lines, freedom of movement for UN observers and arrangements for the detection of violation of the Armistice Agreements.

Resolution 115: Adopted 20 July 1956. Endorsed the admission of Morocco to the UN.

Resolution 116: Adopted 26 July 1956. Endorsed the admission of Tunisia to the UN.

Resolution 118: Adopted 13 Oct. 1956. Agreed that a settlement of the dispute concerning the Suez Canal should ensure free movement through the Canal, be unrelated to political issues, and respect the sovereignty of Egypt, with tolls and charges to be decided between Egypt and the users of the Canal.

Resolution 121: Adopted 12 Dec. 1956. Endorsed the admission of Japan to the UN.

Resolution 123: Adopted 21 Feb. 1957. Requested the President of the Security Council to examine with the Governments of India and Pakistan proposals for resolving the dispute over the state of Jammu and Kashmir.

Resolution 124: Adopted 7 March 1957. Endorsed the admission of Ghana to the UN.

Resolution 125: Adopted 5 Sept. 1957. Endorsed the admission of Malaya (now Malaysia) to the UN.

Resolution 127: Adopted 22 Jan. 1958. Instructed the Chief of Staff of the Truce Supervision Organization in Palestine to regulate civilian activity between the demarcation lines of Israel and Jordan and to perform a survey of property ownership in the zone, in order to ensure that one party's property was not used by another without permission.

Resolution 128: Adopted 11 June 1958. Agreed to deploy a UN Observation Group in Lebanon (UNOGIL) to ensure that no illegal penetration of weapons or military personnel from the United Arab Republic (Egypt and Syria) was taking place.

Resolution 131: Adopted 9 Dec. 1958. Endorsed the admission of Guinea to the UN.

Resolution 133: Adopted 26 Jan. 1960. Endorsed the admission of Cameroon to the UN.

Resolution 134: Adopted 1 April 1960. Condemned the violent repression of demonstrators against racial discrimination in South Africa, and requested that South Africa abandon its policy of apartheid and seek to promote racial equality.

Resolution 135: Adopted 27 May 1960. Requested the Governments of France, the United Kingdom, the USA and the USSR to resume negotiations for a peaceful solution to existing problems, including nuclear disarmament and the cessation of nuclear weapons tests.

Resolution 136: Adopted 31 May 1960. Endorsed the admission of Togo to the UN.

Resolution 139: Adopted 28 June 1960. Endorsed the admission of Mali to the UN.

Resolution 140: Adopted 29 June 1960. Endorsed the admission of Malagasy (now Madagascar) to the UN.

Resolution 141: Adopted 5 July 1960. Endorsed the admission of Somalia to the UN.

Resolution 142: Adopted 7 July 1960. Endorsed the admission of the Republic of the Congo (now the Democratic Republic of the Congo (DRC, previously Zaire) to the UN.

Resolution 143: Adopted 14 July 1960. Demanded that the Belgian Government withdraw its troops from the newly independent territory of the (Democratic) Republic of the Congo and authorized the Secretary-General to dispatch UN troops to the region to maintain order.

Resolution 146: Adopted 9 Aug. 1960. Demanded that the Belgian Government withdraw its troops from the province of Katanga in the (Democratic) Republic of the Congo and allow the UN force to gain access to it.

Resolution 147: Adopted 23 Aug. 1960. Endorsed the admission of Dahomey (now Benin) to the UN.

Resolution 148: Adopted 23 Aug. 1960. Endorsed the admission of Niger to the UN.

Resolution 149: Adopted 23 Aug. 1960. Endorsed the admission of Upper Volta (now Burkina Faso) to the UN.

Resolution 150: Adopted 23 Aug. 1960. Endorsed the admission of Côte d'Ivoire to the UN.

Resolution 151: Adopted 23 Aug. 1960. Endorsed the admission of Chad to the UN.

Resolution 152: Adopted 23 Aug. 1960. Endorsed the admission of the Republic of the Congo (Brazzaville) to the UN.

Resolution 153: Adopted 23 Aug. 1960. Endorsed the admission of Gabon to the UN.

Resolution 154: Adopted 23 Aug. 1960. Endorsed the admission of the Central African Republic to the UN.

Resolution 155: Adopted 24 Aug. 1960. Endorsed the admission of Cyprus to the UN.

Resolution 158: Adopted 28 Sept. 1960. Endorsed the admission of Senegal to the UN.

Resolution 159: Adopted 28 Sept. 1960. Endorsed the admission of Mali to the UN.

Resolution 160: Adopted 7 Oct. 1960. Endorsed the admission of Nigeria to the UN.

Resolution 161: Adopted 21 Feb. 1961. Following the killing of the leaders of the (Democratic) Republic of the Congo, urged that measures be implemented to prevent the re-occurrence of civil war, that all troops, other than those under UN command, be withdrawn, and that an investigation into the assassinations be undertaken. Urged that Parliament be convened and that the Congolese forces be brought under control to prevent any further deterioration of the situation in the (Democratic) Republic of the Congo.

Resolution 163: Adopted 9 June 1961. Deplored the violent repression by Portuguese forces of a nationalist rebellion in Angola. Requested a Sub-committee on the Situation in Angola to implement its mandate promptly.

Resolution 165: Adopted 26 Sept. 1961. Endorsed the admission of Sierra Leone to the UN.

Resolution 166: Adopted 25 Oct. 1961. Endorsed the admission of the Mongolian People's Republic (Mongolia) to the UN.

Resolution 167: Adopted 25 Oct. 1961. Endorsed the admission of Mauritania to the UN.

Resolution 168: Adopted 3 Nov. 1961. Endorsed the appointment of U Thant as acting Secretary-General of the UN (following the death, in an aircraft accident, of Dag Hammarskjöld).

Resolution 169: Adopted 24 Nov. 1961. Condemned the Belgian Government's support for the secession of the Katanga region in the (Democratic) Republic of the Congo, and all armed attacks against UN forces, and demanded their immediate cessation.

Resolution 170: Adopted 14 Dec. 1961. Endorsed the admission of Tanganyika (now part of Tanzania) to the UN.

Resolution 171: Adopted 9 April 1962. Condemned an outbreak of hostilities between Israel and Syria in March. Requested that both parties co-operate with the Chief of Staff and abide by the new cease-fire agreement and the provisions of the Israel–Syria Armistice Agreement.

Resolution 172: Adopted 26 July 1962. Endorsed the admission of Rwanda to the UN.

Resolution 173: Adopted 26 July 1962. Endorsed the admission of Burundi to the UN.

Resolution 174: Adopted 12 Sept. 1962. Endorsed the admission of Jamaica to the UN.

Resolution 175: Adopted 12 Sept. 1962. Endorsed the admission of Trinidad and Tobago to the UN.

Resolution 176: Adopted 4 Oct. 1962. Endorsed the admission of Algeria to the UN.

Resolution 177: Adopted 15 Oct. 1962. Endorsed the admission of Uganda to the UN.

Resolution 179: Adopted 11 June 1963. Authorized the establishment of the UN Yemen Observation Mission.

Resolution 180: Adopted 31 July 1963. Confirmed General Assembly Resolution 1514 (XV). Declared Portugal's policy of claiming the territories administered by it to be 'inalienable' overseas possessions to be in contravention of the Charter of the UN. Demanded that Portugal recognize the right of the people under its administration to self-determination and independence, that it cease all acts of repression and evacuate its forces from the territories concerned, that it introduce an unconditional political amnesty, that it commence negotiations with the aim of transferring power to elected political institutions and that it, ultimately, grant independence to its overseas possessions. Requested all member states to refrain from providing the Portuguese Government with assistance that might enable it to continue to repress territories under its administration.

Resolution 181: Adopted 7 Aug. 1963. Declared South Africa's racial policy to be in contravention of the Charter of the UN and requested that it abandon the apartheid regime in compliance with Resolution 134. Established an arms embargo against South Africa.

Resolution 182: Adopted 4 Dec. 1963. Condemned South Africa's refusal to comply with previous resolutions and requested the Government to abolish discriminatory and repressive measures and release all political prisoners.

Resolution 184: Adopted 16 Dec. 1963. Endorsed the admission of Zanzibar (now part of Tanzania) to the UN.

Resolution 185: Adopted 16 Dec. 1963. Endorsed the admission of Kenya to the UN.

Resolution 186: Adopted 4 March 1964. Established a UN Peace-keeping Force in Cyprus (UNFICYP) and appointed a UN Mediator to promote a peaceful settlement to the dispute between the Greek and Turkish Cypriot communities.

Resolution 189: Adopted 4 June 1964. Condemned armed incursions into Cambodia by units of the Vietnamese army. Deployed three observers to Cambodia and Viet Nam to consider measures to prevent further hostilities.

Resolution 191: Adopted 18 June 1964. Reiterated its condemnation of apartheid and appealed to the South African Government to release opponents of the apartheid regime and abolish all charges brought against them.

Resolution 193: Adopted 9 Aug. 1964. Appealed for an immediate cease-fire to be observed in Cyprus, and requested the Government of Turkey to halt its use of military force.

Resolution 195: Adopted 9 Oct. 1964. Endorsed the admission of Malawi to the UN.

Resolution 196: Adopted 30 Oct. 1964. Endorsed the admission of Malta to the UN.

Resolution 197: Adopted 30 Oct. 1964. Endorsed the admission of Zambia to the UN.

Resolution 200: Adopted 15 March 1965. Endorsed the admission of Gambia to the UN.

Resolution 202: Adopted 6 May 1965. Expressed concern at the situation in Southern Rhodesia, following elections at which the white-supremacist party, the Rhodesian Front (RF), which sought full independence from the United Kingdom and the retention of a minority-rule constitution, won all seats.

Resolution 203: Adopted 14 May 1965. Authorized a mission of the representative of the Secretary-General in the Dominican Republic (DOMREP) to report on the conflict in that country.

Resolution 209: Adopted 4 Sept. 1965. Requested the Governments of India and Pakistan to observe a cease-fire and to co-operate with the UN Military Observer Group in India and Pakistan (UNMOGIP), following a deterioration in the situation along the cease-fire line in the disputed state of Jammu and Kashmir.

Resolution 211: Adopted 20 Sept. 1965. Demanded that India and Pakistan observe a cease-fire agreement over the disputed state of Jammu and Kashmir. Requested the Secretary-General to dispatch an Observation Mission to supervise the cease-fire and the withdrawal of military forces.

Resolution 212: Adopted 20 Sept. 1965. Endorsed the admission of the Maldives to the UN.

Resolution 213: Adopted 20 Sept. 1965. Endorsed the admission of Singapore to the UN.

Resolution 215: Adopted 5 Nov. 1965. Reaffirmed Resolution 211 and requested the Governments of India and Pakistan to instruct their armed forces to halt military activity and violations of the cease-fire agreement in Jammu and Kashmir and to meet a representative of the Secretary-General to establish a plan for the withdrawal of troops.

Resolution 216: Adopted 12 Nov. 1965. Condemned the unilateral declaration of independence made by the white minority party, the Rhodesian Front (RF), in Southern Rhodesia, and requested member states to refrain from recognizing the new regime.

Resolution 217: Adopted 20 Nov. 1965. Reiterated its condemnation of the declaration of independence in Rhodesia and declared it to be legally invalid. Requested the United Kingdom to resolve the situation in Rhodesia and to allow the population to determine its own future, in compliance with General Assembly Resolution 1514 (XV). Urged member states to avoid establishing economic links with Rhodesia.

Resolution 223: Adopted 21 June 1966. Endorsed the admission of Guyana to the UN.

Resolution 224: Adopted 14 Oct. 1966. Endorsed the admission of Botswana to the UN.

Resolution 225: Adopted 14 Oct. 1966. Endorsed the admission of Lesotho to the UN.

Resolution 229: Adopted 2 Dec. 1966. Endorsed the appointment of U Thant as Secretary-General of the UN.

Resolution 230: Adopted 7 Dec. 1966. Endorsed the admission of Barbados to the UN.

Resolution 232: Adopted 16 Dec. 1966. Determined that the rebellion in Rhodesia constituted a threat to international peace and security and imposed mandatory economic sanctions against that country.

Resolution 233: Adopted 6 June 1967. Requested a cease-fire to be observed by Israeli forces and Egypt, Iraq, Jordan and Syria (following the initiation by Israel of what came to be known as the 'Six-Day War').

Resolution 237: Adopted 14 June 1967. Demanded the Government of Israel to treat humanely prisoners of war, to ensure the security and welfare of the inhabitants of areas affected by the recent military operations and to facilitate the return of those displaced by the hostilities.

Resolution 239: Adopted 10 July 1967. Condemned all member states permitting or tolerating the recruitment of mercenaries and the provision of facilities to them, with the objective of overthrowing the governments of member states. In particular, requested governments to ensure that their territories were not used for the recruitment, training and transit of mercenaries seeking to overthrow the Government of the DRC.

Resolution 242: Adopted 22 Nov. 1967. Refined principles for peace in the Middle East by means of the withdrawal of Israeli forces from the Occupied Territories and acknowledgement of the sovereignty, territorial integrity and political independence of all countries in the region. Established that the problem of refugees had to be resolved and requested a Special Representative to be deployed to the Middle East to promote a peaceful settlement.

Resolution 243: Adopted 12 Dec. 1967. Endorsed the admission of Southern Yemen to the UN.

Resolution 248: Adopted 24 March 1968. Condemned military action taken against Jordan by Israeli forces, in contravention of UN resolutions and the Charter of the UN, and reaffirmed Resolution 237.

Resolution 249: Adopted 18 April 1968. Endorsed the admission of Mauritius to the UN.

Resolution 252: Adopted 21 May 1968. Condemned Israel's refusal to comply with UN resolutions and declared invalid all legislative and administrative measures taken by Israel in Jerusalem, including the expropriation of land and property. Urgently requested Israel to rescind those measures and to refrain from taking further action of that kind.

Resolution 253: Adopted 29 May 1968. Condemned acts of political oppression undertaken by the Rhodesian regime and demanded the United Kingdom, as administering authority, to end the rebellion. Strengthened economic sanctions against Rhodesia and prohibited member states from permitting those connected with the regime to enter their territories. Established a Committee to monitor the implementation of sanctions.

Resolution 255: Adopted 19 June 1968. Welcomed the intention of a number of member states with nuclear weapons to assist non-nuclear-weapon states party to the Treaty on the Non-proliferation of Nuclear Weapons (adopted by General Assembly Resolution 2373 (XXII)) should they be subjected to a threat of aggression by a nuclear state.

Resolution 257: Adopted 11 Sept. 1968. Endorsed the admission of Swaziland to the UN.

Resolution 260: Adopted 6 Nov. 1968. Endorsed the admission of Equatorial Guinea to the UN.

Resolution 262: Adopted 31 Dec. 1968. Condemned Israel for a raid on Beirut airport in Lebanon, which destroyed 13 Lebanese aircraft.

Resolution 264: Adopted 20 March 1969. Recognized that the General Assembly had terminated South Africa's mandate over Namibia and assumed responsibility for the territory until it gained independence. Declared South Africa's continued presence in Namibia to be illegal and demanded its withdrawal.

Resolution 267: Adopted 3 July 1969. Reaffirmed Resolution 252 and deplored Israel's refusal to comply with UN resolutions. Requested Israel to rescind all measures purporting to alter the status of Jerusalem.

Resolution 269: Adopted 12 Aug. 1969. Reaffirmed Resolution 264 and asserted that the Security Council was to meet to discuss further measures, should South Africa refuse to comply with its provisions by 4 Oct.

Resolution 277: Adopted 18 March 1970. Condemned Rhodesia for declaring itself a republic and demanded member states to withhold recognition of the Rhodesian regime. Reiterated the United Kingdom's responsibility for Rhodesia and demanded that member states sever all relations with Rhodesia and terminate transport services to and from that country.

Resolution 282: Adopted 23 July 1970. Reasserted its opposition to the apartheid regime of South Africa. Strengthened the arms embargo imposed against South Africa and condemned all violations of it.

Resolution 283: Adopted 29 July 1970. Requested member states formally to withdraw recognition of South Africa's authority over Namibia and to end all commercial and industrial investments in Namibia. Requested the General Assembly to establish a UN fund for Namibia.

Resolution 284: Adopted 29 July 1970. Requested the International Court of Justice to provide an advisory opinion on the legal consequences of South Africa's continued presence in Namibia.

Resolution 286: Adopted 9 Sept. 1970. Demanded the immediate release of all hijacked passengers and crews and requested that member states take all possible legal measures to prevent terrorist interference with international civil air travel.

Resolution 287: Adopted 10 Oct. 1970. Endorsed the admission of Fiji to the UN.

Resolution 292: Adopted 10 Feb. 1971. Endorsed the admission of Bhutan to the UN.

Resolution 294: Adopted 15 July 1971. Condemned acts of hostility perpetrated by the army of Portuguese Guinea (now Guinea-Bissau) against Senegal from 1967. Approved the establishment of a special mission to monitor the situation along the border between the two countries.

Resolution 296: Adopted 18 Aug. 1971. Endorsed the admission of Bahrain to the UN.

Resolution 297: Adopted 15 Sept. 1971. Endorsed the admission of Qatar to the UN.

Resolution 298: Adopted 25 Sept. 1971. Reaffirmed Resolutions 252 and 267 and condemned Israel's refusal to comply with UN resolutions. Confirmed all administrative and legislative actions by Israel which altered the status of Jerusalem to be invalid.

Resolution 299: Adopted 30 Sept. 1971. Endorsed the admission of Oman to the UN.

Resolution 301: Adopted 20 Oct. 1971. Condemned actions taken by the Government of South Africa to destroy the unity and territorial integrity of Namibia, including the establishment of 'Bantustans'. Supported the advisory opinion of the International Court of Justice (ICJ), which ruled that South Africa's presence in Namibia was illegal and that it should withdraw immediately. Requested all states to refrain from observing treaties or from entering into diplomatic relations with South Africa.

Resolution 304: Adopted 8 Dec. 1971. Endorsed the admission of the United Arab Emirates to the UN.

Resolution 306: Adopted 21 Dec. 1971. Endorsed the appointment of Kurt Waldheim as Secretary-General of the UN.

Resolution 307: Adopted 21 Dec. 1971. Demanded the strict observation of the cease-fire agreement for the disputed Indian state of Jammu and Kashmir, while troops were withdrawn. Appealed for international humanitarian aid.

Resolution 310: Adopted 4 Feb. 1972. Condemned South Africa's refusal to comply with Security Council resolutions and its repression of labourers in Namibia. Reaffirmed the illegality of South Africa's continued occupation of Namibia. Requested all member states with business interests in Namibia to ensure that they complied with the provisions of the Universal Declaration of Human Rights.

Resolution 312: Adopted 4 Feb. 1972. Requested Portugal to recognize the right of its territories to self-determination and independence, in accordance with General Assembly Resolution 1514 (XV). Demanded that Portugal end its colonial wars and its repression of Angola, Portuguese Guinea (now Guinea-Bissau) and Mozambique.

Resolution 313: Adopted 28 Feb. 1972. Demanded that Israel withdraw from Lebanese territory.

Resolution 320: Adopted 29 Sept. 1972. Expressed concern that a number of member states were ignoring the sanctions imposed against Rhodesia by Resolution 253, and urged the USA in particular to comply with its provisions.

Resolution 321: Adopted 23 Oct. 1972. Condemned a border attack on Senegal by the Portuguese army, and warned that the Security Council would consider taking further action if Portugal refused to comply with its resolutions.

Resolution 323: Adopted 6 Dec. 1972. Noted that the majority of Namibian people consulted voiced their support for national independence through the withdrawal of the South African administration and the abolition of its 'homelands' policy.

Resolution 326: Adopted 2 Feb. 1973. Condemned the acts of hostility perpetrated against Zambia by the regime of Rhodesia, in collaboration with the regime of South Africa, and condemned Rhodesia's acts of internal political repression. Demanded that the United Kingdom, as administrator of Rhodesia, implement measures to prevent further such actions. Agreed to deploy a special mission to assess the situation in the region.

Resolution 328: Adopted 10 March 1973. Endorsed the conclusions of the special mission established by Resolution 326. Affirmed that the Zimbabwean people should be permitted to exercise their right to self-determination in accordance with General Assembly Resolution 1514 (XV) and reiterated demands for the withdrawal of South African troops from Rhodesia.

Resolution 333: Adopted 22 May 1973. Strengthened sanctions imposed against Rhodesia.

Resolution 335: Adopted 22 June 1973. Endorsed the admission of the German Democratic Republic and the Federal Republic of Germany to the UN.

Resolution 336: Adopted 18 July 1973. Endorsed the admission of the Bahamas to the UN.

Resolution 338: Adopted 22 Oct. 1973. Demanded a cease-fire agreement between Israel and the Arab states. Reaffirmed the principles of Resolution 242.

Resolution 340: Adopted 25 Oct. 1973. Approved the establishment of a second UN Emergency Force (UNEF II) in the Middle East to assist in efforts for the establishment of peace.

Resolution 341: Adopted 27 Oct. 1973. Approved UNEF's mandate in the Middle East.

Resolution 347: Adopted 24 April 1974. Condemned the Israeli invasion of Lebanon and asked Israel to refrain from further acts of violence and to release all abducted Lebanese civilians.

Resolution 350: Adopted 31 May 1974. Welcomed the Agreement on Disengagement negotiated between Israeli and Syrian forces in the context of Resolution 338, and established a United Nations Disengagement Observer Force (UNDOF).

Resolution 351: Adopted 10 June 1974. Endorsed the admission of Bangladesh to the UN.

Resolution 352: Adopted 21 June 1974. Endorsed the admission of Grenada to the UN.

Resolution 353: Adopted 20 July 1974. Requested all states to recognize the sovereignty, independence and territorial integrity of Cyprus. Demanded an immediate cease-fire and the cessation of foreign military intervention in that country, and requested that Greece, Turkey and the United Kingdom commence negotiations for the restoration of peace and constitutional government to Cyprus. Requested that all parties co-operate fully with the UN Peace-keeping Force in Cyprus.

Resolution 356: Adopted 12 Aug. 1974. Endorsed the admission of Guinea-Bissau to the UN.

Resolution 360: Adopted 16 Aug. 1974. Expressed regret at the unilateral military action taken against Cyprus by Turkey, urged compliance with the provisions of previous resolutions, and requested the resumption of negotiations, as described in Resolution 353.

Resolution 361: Adopted 30 Aug. 1974. Commended the negotiations between the two community leaders in Cyprus. Expressed concern for persons displaced as a result of the situation and requested the provision of emergency humanitarian assistance to Cyprus.

Resolution 366: Adopted 17 Dec. 1974. Demanded that South Africa comply with the ruling of the International Court of Justice that confirmed its presence in Namibia to be illegal, that it withdraw its administration and transfer power to the Namibian people, and that it release all Namibian political prisoners, abolish the application of all racially and politically discriminatory practices, and allow the return of exiled Namibians to their country.

Resolution 367: Adopted 12 March 1975. Expressed concern that the unilateral declaration of a 'Federated Turkish State' in Cyprus could compromise continued negotiations, and requested that the Secretary-General undertake efforts to resume negotiations.

Resolution 372: Adopted 18 Aug. 1975. Endorsed the admission of Cape Verde to the UN.

Resolution 373: Adopted 18 Aug. 1975. Endorsed the admission of São Tomé and Príncipe to the UN.

Resolution 374: Adopted 18 Aug. 1975. Endorsed the admission of Mozambique to the UN.

Resolution 375: Adopted 18 Aug. 1975. Endorsed the admission of Papua New Guinea to the UN.

Resolution 376: Adopted 17 Oct. 1975. Endorsed the admission of the Comoros to the UN.

Resolution 377: Adopted 22 Oct. 1975. Requested that the Secretary-General enter into consultations with the parties involved with the situation in Spanish (Western) Sahara.

Resolution 379: Adopted 2 Nov. 1975. Advised all parties concerned with the situation in Spanish (Western) Sahara to avoid action that could increase tension in the area and requested the Secretary-General to intensify consultations with the parties involved.

Resolution 380: Adopted 6 Nov. 1975. Expressed disapproval of the Moroccan 'Green March' on Spanish (Western) Sahara, and demanded that Morocco withdraw all participants from the territory. Urged all parties involved to co-operate fully with the Secretary-General.

Resolution 382: Adopted 1 Dec. 1975. Endorsed the admission of Suriname to the UN.

Resolution 384: Adopted 22 Dec. 1975. Demanded that the territorial integrity and right to self-determination of East Timor be respected, and that the Government of Indonesia withdraw its troops from the territory. Requested that the Secretary-General deploy a Special Representative to East Timor.

Resolution 385: Adopted 30 Jan. 1976. Condemned South Africa's failure to comply with Resolutions 264, 269 and 366 and reaffirmed their terms. Condemned the country's illegal use of Namibia as a military base. Demanded that South Africa end its policy of 'Bantustans' and 'homelands'. Condemned South Africa's evasion of UN demands for free elections in Namibia and demanded that it make a formal declaration accepting provisions for elections to be held.

Resolution 386: Adopted 17 March 1976. Praised Mozambique's decision to impose economic sanctions on Rhodesia, condemned the aggression by the illegal regime in Rhodesia against Mozambique, and appealed to member states and UN bodies to assist Mozambique in its economic situation.

Resolution 387: Adopted 31 March 1976. Condemned aggression against Angola by South African forces and the use of Namibia as a military base. Demanded that South Africa respect Angola's independence, sovereignty and territorial integrity, and compensate Angola for losses incurred by its invasion.

Resolution 388: Adopted 6 April 1976. Resolved that member states should make sure not to insure any products in Rhodesia, or exported from or intended for importation to Rhodesia, in contravention of Resolution 253. Compelled member states to ensure that no trade marks or franchise agreements were entered into with Rhodesian enterprises.

Resolution 389: Adopted 22 April 1976. Reiterated Resolution 384 and requested that the Secretary-General's Special Representative continue the mission assigned to him.

Resolution 392: Adopted 19 June 1976. Condemned the South African regime for the violent repression of demonstrators against racial discrimination, including school children, on 16 June, and expressed its sympathy to the victims of this violence. Reaffirmed that the doctrine of apartheid constituted a crime against humanity, and requested the Government to end violence against African people and eliminate racial discrimination.

Resolution 393: Adopted 30 July 1976. Condemned South Africa for an attack on Zambia on 11 July and demanded that it respect Zambia's independence, sovereignty, territorial integrity and air space. Reiterated the demand that South Africa end its use of Namibia as a military base. Commended Zambia for its support of Namibia and declared that the liberation of Namibia and Rhodesia and the elimination of apartheid in South Africa were necessary for peace in the region.

Resolution 394: Adopted 16 Aug. 1976. Endorsed the admission of the Seychelles to the UN.

Resolution 395: Adopted 25 Aug. 1976. Requested that Greece and Turkey seek to reduce tensions and resume direct negotiations concerning the dispute over the extent of each country's jurisdiction of the Aegean Sea.

Resolution 397: Adopted 22 Nov. 1976. Endorsed the admission of Angola to the UN.

Resolution 399: Adopted 1 Dec. 1976. Endorsed the admission of (Western) Samoa to the UN.

Resolution 400: Adopted 7 Dec. 1976. Endorsed the appointment of Kurt Waldheim as Secretary-General of the UN for a second term of office.

Resolution 402: Adopted 22 Dec. 1976. Commended Lesotho for its refusal to recognize South Africa's proclamation of an 'independent' Transkei 'Bantustan'. Demanded the immediate reopening of border posts with Lesotho by the Transkeian authorities and condemned all actions intended to compel Lesotho to recognize the Transkei. Appealed to member states and UN bodies to provide assistance to Lesotho.

Resolution 403: Adopted 14 Jan. 1977. Condemned all provocation, harassment and political repression by the illegal regime in Rhodesia against Botswana, and demanded the immediate cessation of all hostilities. Deplored all acts of collaboration and collusion sustaining the illegal regime in Rhodesia. Agreed to dispatch a Mission to Botswana to establish the assistance required and to arrange for the provision of financial assistance.

Resolution 404: Adopted 8 Feb. 1977. Affirmed that the territorial integrity and political independence of Benin must be respected. Agreed to deploy a three-member Special Mission to Benin to investigate the invasion of the capital on 16 January.

Resolution 405: Adopted 14 April 1977. Acknowledged the work of the Special Mission to Benin. Condemned the act of aggression perpetrated against Benin on 16 January and agreed to gather more information on the mercenaries. Reaffirmed Resolution 239. Requested member states to be alert to the danger posed by mercenaries, and to consider implementing measures to prohibit the domestic recruitment, training and transit of mercenaries.

Resolution 406: Adopted 25 May 1977. Expressed support for the Government of Botswana and endorsed the recommendations of the Mission to Botswana. Welcomed the establishment by the Secretary-General of an account for contributions to Botswana.

Resolution 407: Adopted 25 May 1977. Expressed appreciation to the Secretary-General for his arrangement of a Mission to Lesotho to establish the assistance required, and endorsed the recommendations of that Mission. Welcomed the establishment by the Secretary-General of an account for contributions to Lesotho.

Resolution 409: Adopted 27 May 1977. Agreed that Member States should forbid the use or transfer of funds by the illegal regime in Rhodesia.

Resolution 411: Adopted 30 June 1977. Reiterated Resolution 386 and condemned the continued aggression carried out by Rhodesia against Mozambique. Condemned South Africa for its support of Rhodesia, reaffirmed that its regime constituted a source of instability in the region and requested that member states cease the provision of support to the regime. Reaffirmed the right of the people of Zimbabwe to self-determination and independence. Appealed to member states to provide assistance to Mozambique to allow it to increase its defence capabilities.

Resolution 412: Adopted 7 July 1977. Endorsed the admission of Djibouti to the UN.

Resolution 413: Adopted 20 July 1977. Endorsed the admission of Viet Nam to the UN.

Resolution 414: Adopted 15 Sept. 1977. Expressed concern at developments in the new Famagusta area of Cyprus and requested that the two communities in Cyprus resume negotiations under the auspices of the Secretary-General.

Resolution 415: Adopted 29 Sept. 1977. Requested the appointment of a representative to undertake discussions with the British Resident Commissioner, and other parties, concerning military and other arrangements required to enable a transition to majority rule in Rhodesia.

Resolution 417: Adopted 31 Oct. 1977. Condemned the South African authorities for the violent repression of black people and opponents of racial discrimination. Demanded that the Government release those imprisoned under arbitrary security laws, remove bans on organizations and media opposed to apartheid and abolish the policies of apartheid and 'Bantustans' and the 'Bantu' education system.

Resolution 418: Adopted 4 Nov. 1977. Imposed a mandatory arms embargo against South Africa.

Resolution 419: Adopted 24 Nov. 1977. Reaffirmed Resolution 405 and requested that member states gather information concerning the mercenaries involved in the attack on Benin of 16 Jan. and appealed for the provision of assistance to that country. Acknowledged the Government of Benin's wish to bring the mercenaries to justice.

Resolution 421: Adopted 9 Dec. 1977. Established a Security Council Committee to monitor and strengthen the implementation of the mandatory arms embargo against South Africa.

Resolution 423: Adopted 14 March 1978. Condemned the attempts of the minority regime in Rhodesia to maintain power and declared unacceptable any internal agreement concluded under that regime. Requested that the UK Government take the necessary measures to end the regime. Declared that the replacement of the police and military forces and the holding of free and fair elections under the auspices of the UN were required to restore legality to the country.

Resolution 424: Adopted 17 March 1978. Condemned the invasion of Zambia on 6 March by Rhodesian troops. Reiterated that the freedom of Namibia and Zimbabwe, and the elimination of the apartheid regime in South Africa were required to attain peace in the region. Demanded that the UK Government act promptly to end the illegal regime in Rhodesia.

Resolution 425: Adopted 19 March 1978. Demanded that Israel respect Lebanese territorial integrity, sovereignty and independence and withdraw its troops following an invasion of southern Lebanon. Established a UN Interim Force in Lebanon (UNIFIL) to assist in the restoration of peace.

Resolution 427: Adopted 3 May 1978. Criticized attacks carried out against UN troops in Lebanon.

Resolution 428: Adopted 6 May 1978. Condemned the invasion of Angola on 4 May by South African troops and their use of Namibia as a military base. Demanded that South Africa respect Angola's integrity, sovereignty and independence and withdrawal unconditionally from both Angola and Namibia. Decided to reconvene in the event of any further attacks on Angola.

Resolution 431: Adopted 27 July 1978. Requested the appointment by the Secretary-General of a Special Representative for Namibia, to facilitate its independence.

Resolution 432: Adopted 27 July 1978. Voiced support for the reintegration of Walvis Bay by Namibia, in order to ensure the territory's integrity and unity. Demanded that South Africa refrain from using Walvis Bay in a way likely to threaten Namibia's economy or independence.

Resolution 433: Adopted 17 Aug. 1978. Endorsed the admission of the Solomon Islands to the UN.

Resolution 435: Adopted 28 Sept. 1978. Endorsed proposals for the evacuation of South African forces from Namibia and for the election of a constituent assembly in Namibia under UN supervision. Established a UN Transition Assistance Group (UNTAG).

Resolution 436: Adopted 6 Oct. 1978. Requested all those involved in the conflict in Lebanon to implement an immediate cease-fire and to permit the International Committee of the Red Cross to gain access to the area of conflict.

Resolution 437: Adopted 10 Oct. 1978. Expressed regret at the decision by the US Government to permit members of the Rhodesian regime, including its leader, Ian Smith, to enter the USA in contravention of Resolution 253, and requested that the USA observe the provisions of Security Council resolutions.

Resolution 439: Adopted 13 Nov. 1978. Condemned South Africa for holding unilateral elections in Namibia between 4 and 8 Dec., in contravention of Resolutions 385 and 435, and declared the results to be invalid. Requested South Africa to cancel further elections scheduled to take place in Dec. and to comply with Security Council resolutions.

Resolution 442: Adopted 6 Dec. 1978. Endorsed the admission of Dominica to the UN.

Resolution 445: Adopted 8 March 1979. Condemned Rhodesian regime for invasions of Angola, Mozambique and Zambia and requested that member states provide assistance to those three countries in order to increase their defence capabilities. Requested that the UK Government take action to prevent illegal executions in Rhodesia. Criticized the elections scheduled to be held in the territory in April and declared them invalid.

Resolution 446: Adopted 22 March 1979. Declared invalid the settlements established by Israel in Palestine and other Arab territories from 1967, and deplored Israel's contravention of Security Council resolutions. Established a three-member Commission to examine the situation in the Occupied Territories.

Resolution 447: Adopted 28 March 1979. Condemned the sustained invasions of Angola by South African troops and their continued use of Namibia as a military base. Demanded that South Africa respect Angola's integrity, sovereignty and independence and abandon its armed invasions. Requested that member states provide assistance to Angola to strengthen its defence capabilities.

Resolution 448: Adopted 30 April 1979. Condemned elections held in Rhodesia and declared the results to be invalid.

Resolution 452: Adopted 14 June 1979. Accepted the recommendations of the Commission established by Resolution 446 and requested that Israel halt the establishment of settlements in those territories, including Jerusalem.

Resolution 453: Adopted 12 Sept. 1979. Endorsed the admission of St Lucia to the UN.

Resolution 455: Adopted 23 Nov. 1979. Condemned Rhodesia's continued invasions of Zambia and condemned South Africa for its collaboration. Demanded that the UK Government act promptly to dissolve the Rhodesian regime. Requested compensation for Zambia, and assistance from member states.

Resolution 457: Adopted 4 Dec. 1979. Demanded that the Government of Iran release hostages held in the US embassy in Tehran and requested that the Governments of Iran and the USA peacefully resolve their differences.

Resolution 460: Adopted 21 Dec. 1979. Agreed to remove sanctions implemented against Rhodesia by previous resolutions and to dissolve the Committee established by Resolution 253. Requested all parties to respect the provisions of agreements reached and requested the UK Government to ensure that troops remained in Rhodesia, other than those agreed upon by the Lancaster House Conference.

Resolution 463: Adopted 2 Feb. 1980. Requested that the United Kingdom effect the immediate withdrawal of all South African forces from Rhodesia, and condemned the South African regime for its interference. Demanded that the UK Government ensure full participation in the forthcoming elections by Zimbabweans, through the return of exiles and refugees, the release of political prisoners, compliance with the provisions of the Lancaster House Agreement, equal treatment of all parties and the termination of inappropriate emergency measures.

Resolution 464: Adopted 19 Feb. 1980. Endorsed the admission of St Vincent and the Grenadines to the UN.

Resolution 465: Adopted 1 March 1980. Deplored Israel's refusal to co-operate with the Security Council Commission, its formal rejection of Resolutions 446 and 452 and its refusal to allow the Mayor of Hebron to appear before the Security Council. Declared invalid the settlements established by Israel in Palestine and other Arab territories from 1967, and deplored Israel's continuing settlement policy.

Resolution 466: Adopted 11 April 1980. Condemned South Africa's intensified invasions of Zambia and demanded that it evacuate its troops. Warned South Africa that continued aggression would provoke further action by the Security Council.

Resolution 467: Adopted 24 April 1980. Condemned Israel's contravention of resolutions concerning its invasion of Lebanon (including Resolution 425) and all acts of hostility in Lebanon and towards UNIFIL, including an attack on UNIFIL headquarters. Requested that a meeting of the Israel–Lebanon Mixed Armistice Commission (ILMAC) be convened in the hope of reaffirming the General Armistice Agreement.

Resolution 468: Adopted 8 May 1980. Demanded that Israel allow the return of illegally expelled Palestinian leaders, the Mayors of Hebron and Halhoul and the Judge of Hebron.

Resolution 473: Adopted 13 June 1980. Condemned the South African regime for the continued violent repression of black people and opponents of apartheid. Expressed support for the victims of racial discrimination. Demanded that the Government release those imprisoned for their opposition to apartheid, including Nelson Mandela, remove bans on political parties, organizations and the media opposed to apartheid, halt all political trials, abolish the policy of apartheid and introduce equal opportunities for all South Africans. Reiterated Resolution 418.

Resolution 476: Adopted 30 June 1980. Reaffirmed the need for Israel to end its continued occupation of Arab territories, including Jerusalem, and reiterated that all changes made to Jerusalem were invalid. Deplored Israel's contravention of UN resolutions and requested that, henceforth, it comply with them.

Resolution 477: Adopted 30 July 1980. Endorsed the admission of Zimbabwe to the UN.

Resolution 478: Adopted 20 Aug. 1980. Announced its refusal to recognize a 'basic law' by Israel, which made East Jerusalem part of an undivided Jerusalem, and requested that member states withdraw all diplomatic missions established in Jerusalem.

Resolution 479: Adopted 28 Sept. 1980. Requested that Iran and Iraq halt the use of force and resolve their differences by peaceful means.

Resolution 487: Adopted 19 June 1981. Condemned an air attack by Israel on the Iraqi nuclear research centre on 7 June as representing a serious threat to the International Atomic Energy Agency (IAEA) safeguards regime and requested that Israel adhere to IAEA safeguards.

Resolution 489: Adopted 8 July 1981. Endorsed the admission of Vanuatu to the UN.

Resolution 490: Adopted 21 July 1981. Requested an immediate cease-fire in Lebanon.

Resolution 491: Adopted 23 Sept. 1981. Endorsed the admission of Belize to the UN.

Resolution 492: Adopted 10 Nov. 1981. Endorsed the admission of Antigua and Barbuda to the UN.

Resolution 494: Adopted 11 Dec. 1981. Endorsed the appointment of Javier Pérez de Cuéllar as Secretary-General of the UN.

Resolution 496: Adopted 15 Dec. 1981. Condemned an attempt by mercenaries on 25 Nov. to overthrow the Government of the Seychelles and agreed to send a three-member Commission of Inquiry to investigate the events.

Resolution 497: Adopted 17 Dec. 1981. Declared invalid Israel's formal annexation of the occupied Syrian Golan Heights.

Resolution 502: Adopted 3 April 1982. Demanded an immediate cease-fire in the Falkland (Malvinas) Islands, the withdrawal of all Argentine troops and a diplomatic solution to the dispute between the UK and Argentina concerning the islands.

Resolution 504: Adopted 30 April 1982. Requested that a fund be established to aid the peace-keeping force of the Organization of African Unity (OAU) in Chad.

Resolution 505: Adopted 26 May 1982. Requested the Secretary-General to seek to negotiate a cease-fire agreement for the Falkland (Malvinas) Islands between the Argentine and UK Governments.

Resolution 509: Adopted 6 June 1982. Demanded that Israel immediately evacuate its military troops from Lebanon and requested all parties to observe an immediate cease-fire in Lebanon, following the escalation of hostilities.

Resolution 512: Adopted 19 June 1982. Expressed concern at the suffering of both Lebanese and Palestinian refugees and appealed for the provision of humanitarian assistance and for those involved in the conflict to respect the rights of civilians and to facilitate the distribution of aid.

Resolution 513: Adopted 4 July 1982. Reaffirmed Resolution 512, and requested that access be restored to vital facilities, including water, electricity, food and medicine, in South Lebanon and West Beirut.

Resolution 514: Adopted 12 July 1982. Recalled Resolution 479, requesting a cease-fire in the war between Iran and Iraq. Agreed to deploy a group of observers to the region to monitor the cease-fire and the withdrawal of troops.

Resolution 515: Adopted 29 July 1982. Requested that the Israeli Government remove restrictions preventing the distribution of humanitarian supplies to the civilian population of Beirut, Lebanon.

Resolution 516: Adopted 1 Aug. 1982. Reaffirmed previous resolutions regarding military activity in Lebanon and at the Israel–Lebanon border and demanded a cease-fire. Authorized the deployment of UN observers to monitor the situation in the Beirut area.

Resolution 517: Adopted 4 Aug. 1982. Following the invasion of Beirut by Israeli troops on 3 Aug., reconfirmed demands for an immediate cease-fire and the evacuation of Israeli forces.

Resolution 518: Adopted 12 Aug. 1982. Reiterated demands for the cessation of hostilities in Lebanon and the removal of restrictions preventing the distribution of humanitarian supplies in Beirut.

Resolution 520: Adopted 17 Sept. 1982. Condemned the assassination of the elected President of Lebanon, and demanded the evacuation of Israeli troops from Beirut, following an invasion on 15 Sept.

Resolution 521: Adopted 19 Sept. 1982. Condemned the massacre of Palestinian refugees in Beirut, Lebanon. Authorized an increase in the number of UN observers in the vicinity of Beirut, from 10 to 50. Established a Commission of Investigation to Lebanon.

Resolution 527: Adopted 15 Dec. 1982. Condemned armed hostilities perpetrated by South African troops against Lesotho, and demanded that it provide compensation for damage caused. Affirmed the right of Lesotho to shelter victims of apartheid.

Resolution 532: Adopted 31 May 1983. Mandated the Secretary-General to undertake consultations in Namibia with the aim of implementing Resolution 435.

Resolution 537: Adopted 22 Sept. 1983. Endorsed the admission of St Vincent and the Grenadines to the UN.

Resolution 539: Adopted 28 Oct. 1983. Condemned South Africa's continued occupation of Namibia and its obstruction of Resolution 435 through its support for the policy of 'linkage' (whereby South Africa insisted on the withdrawal of Cuban troops from Angola prior to the implementation of Resolution 435).

Resolution 541: Adopted 18 Nov. 1983. Condemned the unilateral declaration of an independent 'Turkish Republic of Northern Cyprus' ('TRNC') by the Turkish Cypriot authorities and demanded its withdrawal. Requested that member states withhold recognition of the 'TRNC'.

Resolution 548: Adopted 24 Feb. 1984. Endorsed the admission of Brunei to the UN.

Resolution 550: Adopted 11 May 1984. Reaffirmed Resolution 541. Condemned the establishment of diplomatic links between the 'TRNC' and Turkey, and plans for a referendum to approve a new constitution and elections to a constituent assembly.

Resolution 552: Adopted 1 June 1984. Condemned attacks by Iran against Saudi Arabian and Kuwaiti commercial ships in the Gulf and reaffirmed their right to free navigation.

Resolution 554: Adopted 17 Aug. 1984. Declared the new Constitution of South Africa, which provided for the election of people of mixed race and of Asian origin, to be invalid and contrary to the principles of the UN Charter. Reiterated that the elimination of apartheid and the holding of elections under universal adult suffrage were required to resolve the situation in that country. Requested governments not to recognize the results of elections to be held under the apartheid regime.

Resolution 556: Adopted 23 Oct. 1984. Condemned the killing and wounding of those demonstrating against the new Constitution in South Africa.

Resolution 558: Adopted 13 Dec. 1984. Requested member states to refrain from importing arms and military vehicles manufactured in South Africa.

Resolution 560: Adopted 12 March 1985. Condemned the South African apartheid regime for the killing of those protesting against their forced removal from certain areas and the arbitrary arrest of members of opposition organizations and demanded the release of all political prisoners.

Resolution 566: Adopted 19 June 1985. Declared illegal the establishment of a 'Transnational Government of National Unity' by the South African regime in Windhoek, Namibia, and condemned South Africa's continued obstruction of Resolution 435. Mandated the Secretary-General to resume discussions with South Africa, with the aim of implementing the Resolution. Proposed that member states impose voluntary sanctions against South Africa.

Resolution 567: Adopted 20 June 1985. Condemned South Africa for the resumption of violence against Angola. Demanded that it evacuate its troops and refrain from using Namibia as a military base.

Resolution 568: Adopted 21 June 1985. Condemned a military attack on the capital of Botswana by South African forces. Requested the Secretary-General to dispatch an investigatory mission to Botswana to assess the damage caused and to propose measures to increase Botswana's capacity to assist South African refugees.

Resolution 569: Adopted 26 July 1985. Condemned the mass arrest of opponents of apartheid and the declaration of a state of emergency in 36 magisterial districts by the South African Government. Reaffirmed the need to eliminate apartheid and reiterated the proposal that member states adopt sanctions against South Africa.

Resolution 573: Adopted 4 Oct. 1985. Condemned Israel for an attack against the headquarters of the Palestine Liberation Organization (PLO) in Tunisia.

Resolution 574: Adopted 7 Oct. 1985. Condemned South Africa for an armed incursion into Angola, its continued occupation of parts of Angola and its continued use of Namibia as a military base. Demanded that South Africa halt all hostilities and evacuate its troops from Angolan territory. Affirmed Angola's right to defend its sovereignty, territorial integrity and independence. Requested all member states fully to implement Resolution 418.

Resolution 579: Adopted 18 Dec. 1985. Condemned abduction and the taking of hostages. Emphasized the obligation of member states to secure the release of those abducted or taken hostage on their territory. Urged all member states to become party to the relevant conventions.

Resolution 580: Adopted 30 Dec. 1985. Condemned South Africa for the deaths of nine people (including six South African refugees) in Lesotho. Affirmed the right of Lesotho to shelter victims of apartheid and appealed for economic assistance for Lesotho. Demanded that South Africa abolish the apartheid regime.

Resolution 581: Adopted 13 Feb. 1986. Condemned South Africa for threats made to other southern African countries and the escalation of violence in the region. Reiterated demands for the abolishment of apartheid.

Resolution 582: Adopted 24 Feb. 1986. Implicitly blamed Iraq for initiating the conflict with Iran and condemned the continuance and escalation of the conflict. Demanded that both parties observe an immediate cease-fire.

Resolution 587: Adopted 23 Sept. 1986. Condemned attacks made against the UN Interim Force in Lebanon.

Resolution 589: Adopted 10 Oct. 1986. Endorsed the appointment of Javier Pérez de Cuéllar as Secretary-General of the UN for a second term of office.

Resolution 591: Adopted 28 Nov. 1986. Strengthened the arms embargo against South Africa.

Resolution 592: Adopted 8 Dec. 1986. Requested Israel to abide by the Geneva Convention relative to the Protection of Civilian Persons in Time of War, following an attack on university students by the Israeli armed forces.

Resolution 598: Adopted 20 July 1987. In response to the escalating tensions between Iran and Iraq, including the bombing of neutral shipping and the use of chemical weapons, urged an immediate cease-fire, the withdrawal of military forces to international boundaries, and the co-operation of both parties in mediation efforts to achieve a peace settlement.

Resolution 601: Adopted 30 Oct. 1987. Condemned South Africa's continued occupation of Namibia and its refusal to comply with Security Council resolutions, in particular resolutions 385 and 435. Welcomed the professed willingness of the Namibian nationalist organization, the South West Africa People's Organization (SWAPO), to observe a cease-fire with South Africa.

Resolution 602: Adopted 25 Nov. 1987. Reiterated condemnation of South Africa's continued attacks on Angola and its occupation of parts of Angola and Namibia, and the entry into Angola of the South African President. Repeated demands for a cease-fire and mandated the Secretary-General to monitor the evacuation of South African forces from Angola.

Resolution 605: Adopted 22 Dec. 1987. Deplored the killing of Palestinian civilians by the Israeli armed forces.

Resolution 607: Adopted 5 Jan 1988. Appealed to Israel to refrain from deporting Palestinian civilians from the Occupied Territories.

Resolution 608: Adopted 14 Jan. 1988. Demanded that Israel withdraw the order to deport Palestinian civilians and to ensure the safe return to the Occupied Territories of those already deported.

Resolution 611: Adopted 25 April 1988. Condemned the assassination by Israel of the military commander of the Palestine Liberation Organization (PLO) in Tunisia.

Resolution 612: Adopted 9 May 1988. Emphasized the need for Iran and Iraq urgently to observe the Protocol for the Prohibition of the Use in War of Asphyxiating, Poisonous or Other Gases, and of Bacteriological Methods of Warfare.

Resolution 616: Adopted 20 July 1988. Expressed distress and regret at the shooting down of an Iranian civilian aircraft mistakenly identified as an attacking fighter aircraft by US forces.

Resolution 619: Adopted 9 Aug. 1988. Established a UN Iran–Iraq Military Observer Group (UNIIMOG) to monitor the cease-fire between the two countries.

Resolution 620: Adopted 26 Aug. 1988. Condemned the continued use of chemical weapons by Iran and Iraq, in contravention of Resolution 612.

Resolution 621: Adopted 20 Sept. 1988. Authorized the appointment of a special representative for Western Sahara, following the provisional acceptance in Aug. by Morocco and a national liberation movement, the Polisario Front, of a peace plan proposed by the Secretary-General.

Resolution 622: Adopted 31 Oct. 1988. Agreed to deploy military officers from existing UN operations to assist in a UN Good Offices Mission in Afghanistan and Pakistan (UNGOMAP).

Resolution 626: Adopted 20 Dec. 1988. Established a UN Angola Verification Mission (UNAVEM) to monitor the withdrawal of Cuban troops from Angola.

Resolution 628: Adopted 16 Jan. 1989. Welcomed a bilateral agreement between Angola and Cuba for the withdrawal of Cuban troops from Angola, and a tripartite accord between Angola, Cuba and South Africa for the implementation of Resolution 435 from 1 April.

Resolution 635: Adopted 14 June 1989. Condemned all illegal and terrorist acts affecting civil aviation and requested all member states to co-operate to devise and implement measures to prevent terrorist acts, including the use of explosives.

Resolution 644: Adopted 7 Nov. 1989. Established a UN Observer Group in Central America (UNOCA) to monitor compliance with the 'Tela' peace accord in Nicaragua, to prevent cross-border incursions by rebel groups and to assist in supervising the forthcoming Nicaraguan elections.

Resolution 650: Adopted 27 March 1990. Increased the strength of the UN Observer Group in Central America (UNOCA), in order to facilitate the demobilization of the Nicaraguan resistance forces.

Resolution 652: Adopted 17 April 1990. Endorsed the admission of Namibia to the UN.

Resolution 660: Adopted 2 Aug. 1990. Demanded the immediate and unconditional withdrawal of Iraqi forces from Kuwait.

Resolution 661: Adopted 6 Aug. 1990. Imposed mandatory economic sanctions against Iraq and the occupied areas of Kuwait, with exemptions for food and medical supplies, owing to Iraq's refusal to comply with Resolution 660. Established a Security Council Committee to monitor the implementation of sanctions.

Resolution 662: Adopted 9 Aug. 1990. Declared Iraq's annexation of Kuwait to be 'null and void'.

Resolution 663: Adopted 14 Aug. 1990. Endorsed the admission of Liechtenstein to the UN.

Resolution 664: Adopted 18 Aug. 1990. Demanded that Iraq allow the safe evacuation of foreign nationals from Iraq and Kuwait, and permit consular officials to gain access to those nationals.

Resolution 667: Adopted 16 Sept. 1990. Condemned acts of aggression perpetrated by Iraq against diplomatic premises and staff in Kuwait, including the abduction of foreign nationals. Stated Iraq's decision to close diplomatic and consular missions in Kuwait and to withdraw their immunity and privileges to be in contravention of international law.

Resolution 668: Adopted 20 Sept. 1990. Endorsed the framework for a comprehensive settlement in Cambodia.

Resolution 672: Adopted 12 Oct. 1990. Condemned the killing of Palestinians by Israeli police in Jerusalem, following clashes with Jewish worshippers. Voted to dispatch a mission of observers to Israel to investigate the killings.

Resolution 673: Adopted 24 Oct. 1990. Deplored Israel's refusal to co-operate with the mission of observers established by Resolution 672.

Resolution 677: Adopted 28 Nov. 1990. Condemned Iraqi attempts to alter the demographic character of Kuwait and to destroy Kuwait's civil records.

Resolution 678: Adopted 29 Nov. 1990. Authorized member states to use all necessary means to enforce the withdrawal of Iraqi forces from Kuwait after 15 Jan. 1991.

Resolution 681: Adopted 20 Dec. 1990. Deplored the Israeli Government's decision to resume the deportation of Palestinian civilians in the Occupied Territories. Requested the UN Secretary-General, in co-operation with the International Committee of the Red Cross, to consider convening a conference to examine the enforcement of the Geneva Convention in relation to the protection of Palestinian civilians under Israeli occupation.

Resolution 683: Adopted 22 Dec. 1990. Terminated the trusteeship agreements for the Pacific Islands of the Marshall Islands, the Federated States of Micronesia, and the Northern Mariana Islands, as established by Resolution 21.

Resolution 686: Adopted 2 March 1991. Required Iraq to repeal all laws and decrees concerning the annexation of Kuwait. Dictated terms for a permanent cease-fire in Kuwait, including the release of all prisoners of war.

Resolution 687: Adopted 3 April 1991. Extended the terms for a cease-fire in Kuwait. Demanded that both Iraq and Kuwait recognize the inviolability of the Iraq–Kuwait border and established an Iraq–Kuwait Boundary Demarcation Commission. Requested the deployment of UN observers to the area. Linked the removal of sanctions against Iraq to the elimination of its non-conventional weaponry, as certified by a UN Special Commission (UNSCOM). Required Iraq to renounce international terrorism, and to accept proposals for the establishment of a war reparation fund to be derived from Iraqi petroleum revenues.

Resolution 688: Adopted 5 April 1991. Condemned the repression of the Iraqi civilian population in Iraq, particularly in the Kurdish populated areas.

Resolution 689: Adopted 9 April 1991. Established an Observation Mission (UNIKOM) to monitor the demilitarized zone between Iraq and Kuwait.

Resolution 690: Adopted 29 April 1991. Approved the establishment of a UN Mission for the Referendum in Western Sahara (MINURSO) to verify a cease-fire in Western Sahara and to organize a plan for a referendum on self-determination.

Resolution 692: Adopted 20 May 1991. Decided to establish a UN Compensation Commission (UNCC) to administer a fund for victims of Iraqi aggression, which was to be financed by a levy on Iraqi petroleum revenues, as detailed in Resolution 687.

Resolution 693: Adopted 20 May 1991. Approved the establishment of a UN Observer Mission in El Salvador (ONUSAL) to verify accords reached between the Government of El Salvador and the guerrilla organization, the Frente Farabundo Martí para la Liberación Nacional (FMLN).

Resolution 696: Adopted 30 May 1991. Agreed to prolong the presence of the UN Angola Verification Mission (UNAVEM), as UNAVEM II, with a mandate to ensure the implementation of the peace accords concluded in Angola.

Resolution 702: Adopted 8 Aug. 1991. Endorsed the admission of the Democratic People's Republic of Korea and of the Republic of Korea to the UN.

Resolution 703: Adopted 9 Aug. 1991. Endorsed the admission of the Federated States of Micronesia to the UN.

Resolution 704: Adopted 9 Aug. 1991. Endorsed the admission of the Marshall Islands to the UN.

Resolution 705: Adopted 15 Aug. 1991. Agreed that war reparations to be paid by Iraq should not exceed 30% of the annual value of its exports of petroleum and petroleum products.

Resolution 706: Adopted 15 Aug. 1991. Proposed authorizing member states to allow the import of Iraqi petroleum worth up to US $1,600m. over a six-month period, to be paid into an escrow account controlled by the UN and to be used for humanitarian needs and war reparations.

Resolution 707: Adopted 15 Aug. 1991. Condemned Iraq's failure to comply with UN weapons inspectors and its safeguards agreement with the International Atomic Energy Agency (IAEA). Demanded that Iraq disclose details of all non-conventional weaponry, that it allow members of a UN Special Commission (UNSCOM) and the IAEA to gain unrestricted access to all the necessary areas and records, and that it halt all its nuclear activities.

Resolution 709: Adopted 12 Sept. 1991. Endorsed the admission of Estonia to the UN.

Resolution 710: Adopted 12 Sept. 1991. Endorsed the admission of Latvia to the UN.

Resolution 711: Adopted 12 Sept. 1991. Endorsed the admission of Lithuania to the UN.

Resolution 712: Adopted 19 Sept. 1991. Approved Resolution 706.

Resolution 713: Adopted 25 Sept. 1991. Imposed an arms embargo against Yugoslavia and demanded that all hostilities in that country end immediately.

Resolution 714: Adopted 30 Sept. 1991. Commended a framework peace agreement between the Government of El Salvador and the opposition FMLN movement, reached in New York, under the auspices of the UN.

Resolution 715: Adopted 11 Oct. 1991. Established the terms under which the UN Special Commission (UNSCOM) was to inspect Iraqi weapons.

Resolution 717: Adopted 16 Oct. 1991. Agreed to establish a peace-keeping operation, the UN Advance Mission in Cambodia (UNAMIC).

Resolution 718: Adopted 31 Oct. 1991. Welcomed the agreements signed in Paris for a comprehensive settlement of the conflict in Cambodia. Authorized the Secretary-General to dispatch a special representative to Cambodia.

Resolution 720: Adopted 21 Nov. 1991. Endorsed the appointment of Dr Boutros Boutros-Ghali as Secretary-General of the UN.

Resolution 724: Adopted 15 Dec. 1991. Endorsed a proposal by the Secretary-General to dispatch to Yugoslavia an advance contingent of peace-keeping troops, as part of the mission of his Personal Envoy. Established a Committee to supervise implementation of the arms embargo against Yugoslavia.

Resolution 727: Adopted 8 Jan. 1992. Deplored the deaths in Yugoslavia of five members of the European Community Monitoring Mission. Endorsed a proposal by the Secretary-General to dispatch to Yugoslavia up to 50 military liaison officers to help maintain the cease-fire.

Resolution 728: Adopted 8 Jan. 1992. Endorsed a proposal by the Secretary-General for the mandate of the UN Advance Mission in Cambodia to be extended to include mine-clearing operations.

Resolution 729: Adopted 14 Jan. 1992. Agreed to extend the mandate of the UN Observer Mission in El Salvador (ONUSAL) to include the verification and monitoring of the formal cease-fire agreement to be signed between the Government of El Salvador and the FMLN. Requested the Secretary-General to increase the strength of ONUSAL.

Resolution 731: Adopted 21 Jan. 1992. Demanded Libya's compliance with requests for the extradition of two Libyan nationals alleged to be responsible for the bombing of a civilian aircraft over Scotland in 1988, and its co-operation with a French inquiry into an aircraft bombing over Niger in 1989.

Resolution 732: Adopted 23 Jan. 1992. Endorsed the admission of Kazakhstan to the UN.

Resolution 733: Adopted 23 Jan. 1992. Urged all those involved in the conflict in Somalia to observe an immediate cease-fire and imposed an arms embargo against Somalia.

Resolution 735: Adopted 29 Jan. 1992. Endorsed the admission of Armenia to the UN.

Resolution 736: Adopted 29 Jan. 1992. Endorsed the admission of Kyrgyzstan to the UN.

Resolution 737: Adopted 29 Jan. 1992. Endorsed the admission of Uzbekistan to the UN.

Resolution 738: Adopted 29 Jan. 1992. Endorsed the admission of Tajikistan to the UN.

Resolution 739: Adopted 29 Jan. 1992. Endorsed the admission of Moldova to the UN.

Resolution 741: Adopted 7 Feb. 1992. Endorsed the admission of Turkmenistan to the UN.

Resolution 742: Adopted 14 Feb. 1992. Endorsed the admission of Azerbaijan to the UN.

Resolution 743: Adopted 21 Feb. 1992. Approved the establishment of a UN Protection Force (UNPROFOR) in response to the escalating conflict in Yugoslavia.

Resolution 744: Adopted 25 Feb. 1992. Endorsed the admission of San Marino to the UN.

Resolution 745: Adopted 28 Feb. 1992. Authorized the dispatch of a peace-keeping force to Cambodia to establish a UN Transitional Authority in Cambodia (UNTAC), replacing the UN Advance Mission in Cambodia. Requested that an election be held in Cambodia by May 1993.

Resolution 746: Adopted 17 March 1992. Urged all Somali factions to observe the cease-fire agreements signed, including an agreement to permit the presence of an observer mission to monitor the implementation of the cease-fire. Endorsed the decision of the Secretary-General urgently to dispatch a technical mission to Somalia to survey the situation.

Resolution 748: Adopted 31 March 1992. Agreed to impose economic sanctions against Libya, including an international air embargo, the prohibition of trade in arms and a reduction in its diplomatic personnel, if it refused to comply with the provisions of Resolution 731 and commit itself to the renunciation of terrorism by 15 April. Established a Security Council Committee to monitor the implementation of sanctions.

Resolution 750: Adopted 10 April 1992. Endorsed a 'set of ideas' on Cyprus compiled by the Secretary-General, which advocated uninterrupted negotiations until a settlement was reached.

Resolution 751: Adopted 24 April 1992. Established a 50-member UN Operation in Somalia (UNOSOM) to monitor the cease-fire in Somalia. Agreed in principle to establish a UN security force for deployment to Somalia, and welcomed the Secretary-General's intention to appoint a Special Representative to Somalia. Established a Security Council Committee to monitor the implementation of the arms embargo against Somalia.

Resolution 752: Adopted 15 May 1992. Demanded an immediate cease-fire in Bosnia and Herzegovina and the cessation of all forms of external interference. Requested the withdrawal and the disarming of the Yugoslav People's Army and all irregular forces in Bosnia and Herzegovina. Emphasized the need for humanitarian assistance to the country.

Resolution 753: Adopted 18 May 1992. Endorsed the admission of Croatia to the UN.

Resolution 754: Adopted 18 May 1992. Endorsed the admission of Slovenia to the UN.

Resolution 755: Adopted 20 May 1992. Endorsed the admission of Bosnia and Herzegovina to the UN.

Resolution 757: Adopted 30 May 1992. Imposed economic sanctions against the Federal Republic of Yugoslavia for its continuing involvement in the conflict in Bosnia and Herzegovina, in contravention of Resolution 752.

Resolution 761: Adopted 29 June 1992. Authorized the immediate deployment of additional troops of the UN Protection Force (UNPROFOR) in order to protect Sarajevo airport in Bosnia and Herzegovina, following its surrender to UN authority for humanitarian purposes. Requested all parties involved in the conflict to observe an unconditional cease-fire.

Resolution 762: Adopted 30 June 1992. Required Croatian forces to end all hostilities and to withdraw to the positions held prior to 21 June and to refrain from entering Serbian areas, following the launch of a series of offensives in those areas. Authorized an increase in the number of military observers and civilian police-forces affiliated to the UN Protection Force.

Resolution 763: Adopted 6 July 1992. Endorsed the admission of Georgia to the UN.

Resolution 764: Adopted 13 July 1992. Authorized the deployment to Sarajevo, Bosnia and Herzegovina, of additional UN troops.

Resolution 765: Adopted 16 July 1992. Endorsed the appointment of a special representative to facilitate mediation in South Africa, owing to the escalation of violence.

Resolution 766: Adopted 21 July 1992. Deplored violations of the cease-fire agreement in Cambodia and the lack of co-operation experienced by the UN Transitional Authority in Cambodia (UNTAC).

Resolution 767: Adopted 27 July 1992. Requested that an urgent airlift operation be organized to facilitate the provision of humanitarian assistance to the population of Somalia and urged all those involved in the conflict to co-operate with the UN in order to aid the distribution of humanitarian supplies. Reaffirmed the arms embargo against Somalia.

Resolution 769: Adopted 7 Aug. 1992. Authorized an increase in the number of the troops of the UN Protection Force. Condemned the abuses of human rights taking place in the Federal Republic of Yugoslavia.

Resolution 770: Adopted 13 Aug. 1992. Reaffirmed the demand for a cease-fire in Bosnia and Herzegovina. Demanded unimpeded access to detention camps in Bosnia and Herzegovina for the International Committee of the Red Cross and authorized member states to take all necessary measures to ensure the delivery of humanitarian aid. Expressed concern at the conditions of civilians imprisoned in camps, prisons and detention centres in that country.

Resolution 771: Adopted 13 Aug. 1992. Emphasized that those responsible for abusing human rights in the Federal Republic of Yugoslavia (FRY) would be held personally responsible. Strongly condemned all violations of international humanitarian law, including 'ethnic cleansing' (the expulsion of an ethnic group or groups in an attempt to create a homogenous population). Requested member states and appropriate organizations to gather substantiated evidence of human rights violations carried out in the FRY.

Resolution 772: Adopted 17 Aug. 1992. Authorized the deployment of a UN Observer Mission in South Africa.

Resolution 775: Adopted 28 Aug. 1992. Authorized the deployment of an additional 3,500 troops for the UN Operation in Somalia (UNOSOM).

Resolution 777: Adopted 19 Sept. 1992. Prohibited the Federal Republic of Yugoslavia from continuing the membership of the former Socialist Federal Republic of Yugoslavia in the UN, and demanded that it apply for membership and discontinue its participation at the General Assembly.

Resolution 778: Adopted 2 Oct. 1992. Permitted the confiscation of oil-related Iraqi assets in member states.

Resolution 779: Adopted 6 Oct. 1992. Authorized the UN Protection Force to monitor the withdrawal of the Yugoslav army from Croatia, the demilitarization of the Prevlaka peninsula and the removal of weapons from adjacent areas of Croatia and Montenegro.

Resolution 780: Adopted 6 Oct. 1992. Requested the Secretary-General to establish a Committee of Experts to investigate the evidence of human rights abuses in the Federal Republic of Yugoslavia received as a result of Resolution 771.

Resolution 781: Adopted 9 Oct. 1992. Imposed a ban on military flights in Bosnia and Herzegovina's airspace in order to facilitate the provision of humanitarian assistance and the cessation of hostilities.

Resolution 788: Adopted 19 Nov. 1992. Imposed a mandatory embargo on the supply of armaments to Liberia, owing to the civil war, and authorized the Secretary-General to dispatch a special representative to that country.

Resolution 789: Adopted 25 Nov. 1992. Following the suspension of negotiations over Cyprus, requested that the Turkish Cypriots adopt a position consistent with the 'set of ideas' proposed by the Secretary-General.

Resolution 790: Adopted 30 Nov. 1992. Condemned the non-co-operation of the Party of Democratic Kampuchea (PDK) with the UN Transitional Authority in Cambodia. Approved an embargo on petroleum supplies to the PDK and endorsed a ban on the export of timber (the party's principal source of income).

Resolution 794: Adopted 3 Dec. 1992. Reiterated demands for a cease-fire in Somalia and condemned those impeding the distribution of humanitarian assistance. Endorsed a US proposal to lead a Unified Task Force to restore security to Somalia.

Resolution 795: Adopted 11 Dec. 1992. Approved the deployment a UN Protection Force contingent to the former Yugoslav republic of Macedonia to monitor its borders with the Federal Republic of Yugoslavia.

Resolution 797: Adopted 16 Dec. 1992. Established a UN Operation in Mozambique (ONUMOZ) to monitor demobilization and the creation of a new national defence force, and to supervise elections.

Resolution 798: Adopted 18 Dec. 1992. Condemned acts of 'unspeakable brutality' in Bosnia and Herzegovina, following allegations of the large-scale organized rape of Muslim women detained by Serb forces, and demanded access to and the closure of the detention camps.

Resolution 799: Adopted 18 Dec. 1992. Condemned Israel for the large-scale deportation of Palestinian civilians and demanded the return of the deportees to Israel.

Resolution 800: Adopted 8 Jan. 1993. Endorsed the admission of Slovakia to the UN.

Resolution 801: Adopted 8 Jan. 1993. Endorsed the admission of the Czech Republic to the UN.

Resolution 802: Adopted 25 Jan. 1993. Ordered Croatian forces to withdraw from areas protected by the UN Protection Force (UNPROFOR), following an offensive across UN peace-keeping lines, and ordered Serbian forces to return weapons reclaimed from UNPROFOR storage areas for defence purposes.

Resolution 808: Adopted 22 Feb. 1993. Provided for the establishment of an international tribunal to prosecute persons responsible for serious violations of international humanitarian law committed in the former Yugoslavia since 1991.

Resolution 809: Adopted 2 March 1993. Outlined a new plan for a resolution to the dispute with the Moroccan Government over Western Sahara, providing for a referendum on self-determination to take place by the end of the year.

Resolution 811: Adopted 12 March 1993. Condemned the continued violations of peace accords in Angola by the African nationalist group União Nacional para a Independência Total de Angola (UNITA). Demanded that UNITA recognize the results of elections held in Sept. 1992 and demanded that a cease-fire be observed throughout Angola. Condemned attacks on members of the UN Angola Verification Mission (UNAVEM II).

Resolution 813: Adopted 26 March 1993. Condemned attacks upon the forces of the Economic Community of West African States (ECOWAS) in Liberia. Declared its willingness to take action against factions failing to comply with the 'Yamoussoukro' peace accord of Oct. 1991.

Resolution 814: Adopted 26 March 1993. Requested the Secretary-General to arrange the provision of humanitarian assistance to Somalia, to assist in the repatriation of refugees, to promote the re-establishment of national and regional institutions and the police force and to help to develop a mine-clearance programme. Approved the establishment of the UN Operation in Somalia II (UNOSOM II) to replace the Unified Task Force, established by Resolution 794 to enforce peace in Somalia.

Resolution 816: Adopted 31 March 1993. Extended the ban on flights imposed by Resolution 781. Authorized member states to take all necessary measures to enforce the 'no-fly zone' applying to Bosnian airspace.

Resolution 817: Adopted 7 April 1993. Endorsed the admission of Macedonia to the UN, as 'The Former Yugoslav Republic of Macedonia', owing to a dispute with Greece regarding the use of the name 'Macedonia'.

Resolution 818: Adopted 14 April 1993. Expressed concern at the delays in the implementation of the peace process in Mozambique, and urged the Government of Mozambique and the opposition guerrilla group, Resistência Nacional Moçambicana (RENAMO), to finalize a timetable for the implementation of the General Peace Agreement. Requested both sides to guarantee freedom of movement for members of the UN Operation in Mozambique.

Resolution 820: Adopted 17 April 1993. Commended the acceptance of a peace plan for Bosnia and Herzegovina by two parties. Expressed concern at the refusal of the Bosnian Serb Assembly to accept the plan and provided for the strengthening of sanctions.

Resolution 822: Adopted 30 April 1993. Demanded the withdrawal of Armenian forces from Azerbaijan and demanded that a cease-fire between the two parties be observed. Requested that negotiations to resolve the conflict be resumed and requested unrestricted access for humanitarian supplies.

Resolution 824: Adopted 6 May 1993. Established six 'safe areas' in Bosnia and Herzegovina (Sarajevo, Bihać, Tuzla, Goražde, Srebreniča and Žepa) to protect the civilian population from Serb attack, and demanded an immediate cease-fire to be observed in and around those areas.

Resolution 825: Adopted 11 May 1993. Urged the Democratic People's Republic of Korea to reconsider its decision to withdraw from the Treaty on the Non-Proliferation of Nuclear Weapons and requested it to allow an inspection of its nuclear facilities to be carried out by the International Atomic Energy Agency.

Resolution 827: Adopted 25 May 1993. Approved the statute of the International Criminal Tribunal for the former Republic of Yugoslavia (ICTY).

Resolution 828: Adopted 26 May 1993. Endorsed the admission of Eritrea to the UN.

Resolution 829: Adopted 26 May 1993. Endorsed the admission of Monaco to the UN.

Resolution 832: Adopted 27 May 1993. Extended the mandate of the UN Observer Mission in El Salvador (ONUSAL) to include the observation of elections in that country.

Resolution 836: Adopted 4 June 1993. Extended the mandate of the UN Protection Force (UNPROFOR) to allow it to use force in response to attacks on 'safe areas' in Bosnia and Herzegovina. Authorized member states to act nationally or through regional organizations to use air power to assist UNPROFOR to carry out its mandate.

Resolution 837: Adopted 6 June 1993. Condemned an armed attack which killed 24 members of the UN Operation in Somalia (UNOSOM II) and sought to bring to justice those responsible. Reiterated the need for all Somali parties to disarm and to comply with agreements.

Resolution 840: Adopted 15 June 1993. Endorsed the results of elections held in Cambodia and certified that they were free and fair.

Resolution 841: Adopted 16 June 1993. Imposed a mandatory world-wide arms and petroleum embargo against Haiti, in response to the continuing political crisis in that country.

Resolution 846: Adopted 22 June 1993. Approved the establishment of a UN Observer Mission Uganda–Rwanda (UNOMUR) to be deployed on the Ugandan side of the border in order to prevent military supplies reaching Rwandan rebels.

Resolution 848: Adopted 8 July 1993. Endorsed the admission of Andorra to the UN.

Resolution 851: Adopted 15 July 1993. Reiterated demands for the African nationalist group União Nacional para a Independência Total de Angola (UNITA) to cease military activity and to recognize the results of the elections held in Angola in Sept. 1992, and warned that an economic embargo would be imposed against UNITA if a cease-fire were not observed by 15 Sept.

Resolution 858: Adopted 24 Aug. 1993. Approved the establishment of a UN Observer Mission in Georgia (UNOMIG) to monitor and verify compliance with a cease-fire agreement.

Resolution 860: Adopted 27 Aug. 1993. Confirmed that the mandate of the UN Transition Authority in Cambodia (UNTAC) would be terminated upon the creation of a new government in Cambodia in Sept.

Resolution 861: Adopted 27 Aug. 1993. Suspended the arms and petroleum embargo against Haiti, owing to the reinstatement of the elected President.

Resolution 864: Adopted 15 Sept. 1993. Listed economic sanctions to be imposed against the nationalist UNITA movement in Angola, unless a cease-fire was established within 10 days, and established a Security Council Committee to monitor their implementation.

Resolution 866: Adopted 22 Sept. 1993. Approved the establishment of a UN Observer Mission in Liberia (UNOMIL), to co-operate with the military observers of the Economic Community of West African States (ECOWAS) in monitoring the transition to peace.

Resolution 867: Adopted 23 Sept. 1993. Approved the establishment of a UN Mission in Haiti (UNMIH), to advise in the creation of a new police force and the modernization of the army.

Resolution 868: Adopted 29 Sept. 1993. Condemned the increasing number of attacks against UN personnel, and determined that for the purposes of future missions the Security Council would require host countries to ensure the security of all UN personnel.

Resolution 871: Adopted 4 Oct. 1993. Acknowledged the Secretary-General's decision to create three subordinate commands for Bosnia and Herzegovina, Croatia and the 'former Yugoslav republic of Macedonia' within the UN Protection Force (UNPROFOR). Condemned continuing armed hostilities in Bosnia and Herzegovina and Croatia and authorized UNPROFOR to use force if necessary.

Resolution 872: Adopted 5 Oct. 1993. Provided for the establishment of a UN Assistance Mission to Rwanda (UNAMIR), with a mandate to monitor observance of the cease-fire agreement, to contribute to the safety of the capital, to assist with mine-clearance, and to facilitate the repatriation of refugees, into which the UN Observer Mission Uganda–Rwanda was to be integrated.

Resolution 873: Adopted 13 Oct. 1993. Agreed to re-impose an arms and petroleum embargo against Haiti, owing to violations of the 'Governors' Island' peace accord signed in July.

Resolution 875: Adopted 16 Oct. 1993. Condemned the assassination of government officials in Haiti and appealed to member states to ensure full implementation of the embargo imposed against that country, in particular by monitoring the cargoes of incoming ships.

Resolution 876: Adopted 19 Oct. 1993. Affirmed the territorial integrity and sovereignty of Georgia, and condemned the violation of the cease-fire agreement by Abkhazia in July and the murder of the Chairman of the Defence Council and Council of Ministers of the Autonomous Republic of Abkhazia.

Resolution 880: Adopted 4 Nov. 1993. Welcomed the accession of the King of Cambodia and new Royal Government and confirmed that the withdrawal of the UN Transition Authority in Cambodia (UNTAC) would be completed by mid-Nov., with exceptions for the mine-clearance and training units, medical personnel and military police.

Resolution 883: Adopted 11 Nov. 1993. Provided for economic sanctions against Libya to be strengthened in the event of Libya's non-compliance with Resolutions 731 and 748 by 1 Dec., including the closure of Libyan Arab Airlines' offices abroad, a ban on the sale of equipment and services for the civil aviation sector, the sequestration of financial resources held overseas, a ban on the sale to Libya of specified items for use in the petroleum and gas industries, and a reduction in personnel levels at Libyan diplomatic missions.

Resolution 897: Adopted 4 Feb. 1994. Revised the mandate of the UN Operation in Somalia (UNOSOM II) to include assisting the implementation of the 'Addis Ababa' peace accords, protecting ports and airports and assisting the reorganization of the police and judicial services. Reduced the strength of UNOSOM II to a maximum of 22,000 troops.

Resolution 900: Adopted 4 March 1994. Requested the Secretary-General to establish a voluntary trust fund for Bosnia and Herzegovina and to appoint an official to work with the Government of that country to restore essential public services to the capital.

Resolution 912: Adopted 21 April 1994. Expressed regret at the deaths of the Presidents of Burundi and Rwanda on 6 April, following the shooting down of the Rwandan presidential aircraft, and at the subsequent violence and political assassinations. Condemned the continuing violence and attacks against the UN Assistance Mission in Rwanda (UNAMIR) and altered UNAMIR's mandate to enable it to facilitate negotiations towards an immediate cease-fire and to assist in the resumption of humanitarian assistance.

Resolution 913: Adopted 22 April 1994. Condemned the continued shelling of the 'safe area' of Goražde by Serb forces in Bosnia and Herzegovina and demanded the observation of an immediate cease-fire.

Resolution 914: Adopted 27 April 1994. Authorized the strength of the UN Protection Force (UNPROFOR) to be increased by up to 6,500 troops.

Resolution 917: Adopted 6 May 1994. Imposed extended sanctions against Haiti from 21 May, including a ban on international trade (with exemptions for food and medicine), reduced air links, visa restrictions for certain officials, and a provision preventing members of the regime from gaining access to assets held outside Haiti.

Resolution 918: Adopted 17 May 1994. Imposed an arms embargo against Rwanda and established a Security Council Committee to monitor its implementation. Revised the mandate of the UN Assistance Mission for Rwanda (UNAMIR) to include the protection of refugees and displaced persons and the provision of security for the distribution of humanitarian supplies.

Resolution 919: Adopted 25 May 1994. Removed the mandatory arms embargo and other restrictions imposed against South Africa by Resolution 418 and other resolutions, and dissolved the Committee established by Resolution 421.

Resolution 924: Adopted 1 June 1994. Demanded a cease-fire and the resumption of negotiations to end the conflict in the Yemen and ordered a UN commission of inquiry to be dispatched to the region.

Resolution 925: Adopted 8 June 1994. Endorsed proposals for the deployment of additional battalions of the UN Assistance Mission in Rwanda (UNAMIR) and the establishment of a Trust Fund for Rwanda.

Resolution 929: Adopted 22 June 1994. Authorized the establishment of a multinational force in Rwanda for humanitarian purposes, pending the arrival of the necessary forces for UNAMIR.

Resolution 935: Adopted 1 July 1994. Requested the Secretary-General to establish a Commission of Experts to investigate evidence of violations of international humanitarian law in Rwanda and urged member states and humanitarian organizations to make available all relevant substantiated information.

Resolution 937: Adopted 21 July 1994. Authorized the UN Observer Mission in Georgia to be increased in strength, with an extended mandate to include monitoring the cease-fire agreement and the withdrawal of Georgian troops beyond the boundaries of Abkhazia.

Resolution 939: Adopted 29 July 1994. Reiterated that the status quo in Cyprus was unacceptable and advocated a new initiative by the Secretary-General for a solution to the conflict, based on a single nationality, international identity and sovereignty.

Resolution 940: Adopted 31 July 1994. Authorized the establishment in Haiti of a multinational force, under unified command, to restore the legitimately elected President and government authorities by 'all necessary means'. Approved the deployment of a UN Mission in Haiti (UNMIH), once stability had been achieved, to maintain security, facilitate the electoral process and to provide training for the Haitian army and police force.

Resolution 941: Adopted 23 Sept. 1994. Emphasized the policy of 'ethnic cleansing' to be a violation of international humanitarian law (with particular regard to the activities of Bosnian Serb forces).

Resolution 942: Adopted 23 Sept. 1994. Imposed sanctions on those areas of Bosnia and Herzegovina controlled by Serb forces, owing to the refusal of the Bosnian Serb party to accept a proposal for a territorial settlement.

Resolution 943: Adopted 23 Sept. 1994. Partially suspended sanctions imposed against the Federal Republic of Yugoslavia (FRY), with the border between the FRY and Bosnia and Herzegovina to remain closed, with exceptions for food, medical supplies and essential clothing.

Resolution 944: Adopted 29 Sept. 1994. Ordered the deployment of the UN Mission in Haiti established by Resolution 940. Agreed to remove all the sanctions imposed against Haiti upon the return of its exiled President, who was to resume his duties.

Resolution 948: Adopted 15 Oct. 1994. Welcomed the return from exile of the President of Haiti.

Resolution 949: Adopted 15 Oct. 1994. Demanded that the evacuation of Iraqi forces recently transferred to southern Iraq be completed immediately and stipulated that Iraq must not employ its forces in a manner that could constitute a threat to its neighbours or to UN operations in Iraq.

Resolution 955: Adopted 8 Nov. 1994. Approved the establishment of an international tribunal for the prosecution of persons responsible for serious violations of international humanitarian law in Rwanda or in neighbouring states during 1994 (the so-called International Criminal Tribunal for Rwanda—ICTR).

Resolution 956: Adopted 10 Nov. 1994. Terminated the trusteeship agreement for the Pacific Island of Palau, as established by Resolution 21.

Resolution 958: Adopted 19 Nov. 1994. Extended the provisions of Resolution 836 to Croatia.

Resolution 960: Adopted 21 Nov. 1994. Welcomed and endorsed as free and fair elections held in Mozambique in Oct.

Resolution 963: Adopted 29 Nov. 1994. Endorsed the admission of Palau to the UN.

Resolution 965: Adopted 30 Nov. 1994. Expanded the mandate of the UN Assistance Mission for Rwanda to include responsibility for the safety of personnel of the ICTR and human rights officers, including full-time protection for the Prosecutor's Office, and for the establishment and training of a new national police force.

Resolution 968: Adopted 16 Dec. 1994. Approved the establishment of a UN Mission of Observers in Tajikistan (UNMOT) to monitor a cease-fire agreement.

Resolution 975: Adopted 30 Jan. 1995. Approved the deployment of the UN Mission in Haiti (UNMIH) to succeed the incumbent multinational force by 31 March and the creation of a trust fund to support the Haitian national police.

Resolution 976: Adopted 8 Feb. 1995. Approved the establishment of a new Angola Verification Mission (UNAVEM III), with some 7,000 military troops, to assist in the restoration of peace to Angola upon the cessation of hostilities.

Resolution 977: Adopted 22 Feb. 1995. Designated Arusha, Tanzania, as the seat for the ICTR.

Resolution 981: Adopted 31 March 1995. Approved the establishment of a peace-keeping force, in Croatia, the UN Confidence Restoration Operation in Croatia (UNCRO).

Resolution 983: Adopted 31 March 1995. Resolved that the UN operation in the former Yugoslav republic of Macedonia would, henceforth, be known as the UN Preventive Deployment Force (UNPREDEP).

Resolution 985: Adopted 13 April 1995. Decided to establish a Security Council Committee to verify compliance with the arms embargo imposed on Liberia by Resolution 788.

Resolution 986: Adopted 14 April 1995. Approved the partial resumption of Iraqi petroleum exports, to generate funds for necessary humanitarian supplies, under an 'oil-for-food' agreement which provided for the export of petroleum valued at up to US $1,000m. every 90 days.

Resolution 990: Adopted 28 April 1995. Authorized the deployment of the UN Confidence Restoration Operation in Croatia (UNCRO).

Resolution 991: Adopted 28 April 1995. Affirmed that the mandate of the UN Observer Mission in El Salvador (ONUSAL) was to terminate on 30 April.

Resolution 994: Adopted 17 May 1995. Condemned the unacceptable treatment of the UN Confidence Restoration Operation in Croatia (UNCRO) and stressed the need for an early restoration of its authority.

Resolution 997: Adopted 9 June 1995. Reduced the strength of the UN Assistance Mission for Rwanda (UNAMIR) from 5,586 troops to 2,200.

Resolution 1001: Adopted 30 June 1995. Renewed the mandate of the UN Observer Mission in Liberia (UNOMIL) and urged parties to install a Council of State, to re-establish a comprehensive cease-fire and to create a timetable for the implementation of the Akosombo and Accra peace accords.

Resolution 1004: Adopted 12 July 1995. Demanded the immediate withdrawal of Bosnian Serbs from the designated 'safe area' of Srebreniča and the release of members of the UN Protection Force who had been taken hostage.

Resolution 1005: Adopted 17 July 1995. Authorized the supply of restricted amounts of explosives to Rwanda for mine-clearance purposes.

Resolution 1009: Adopted 10 Aug. 1995. Demanded a cease-fire, full compliance with UN resolutions and respect for the Serb population in Croatia and requested that international humanitarian organizations be allowed access to it.

Resolution 1011: Adopted 16 Aug. 1995. Authorized the removal of restrictions imposed by Resolution 918, to allow the sale and supply of arms to the Government of Rwanda through specified points of entry, until Sept. 1996.

Resolution 1012: Adopted 28 Aug. 1995. Authorized the establishment of a commission of inquiry to investigate the assassination of the President of Burundi in Oct. 1993 and subsequent acts of violence, and to recommend measures to bring to justice the perpetrators.

Resolution 1013: Adopted 7 Sept. 1995. Authorized the establishment of an international commission of inquiry to gather information concerning the provision of arms and military training to former Rwandan government forces in the Great Lakes region, in contravention of Security Council resolutions, and to recommend measures to prevent the illegal flow of arms.

Resolution 1020: Adopted 10 Nov. 1995. Adjusted the mandate of the UN Observer Mission in Liberia to comprise support for Economic Community of West African States (ECOWAS) troops, the Liberian National Transitional Government (LNTG) and humanitarian assistance, the investigation of violations of cease-fire agreements and human rights, the monitoring of compliance with peace accords, the provision of assistance for the maintenance of assembly sites and the observation of elections.

Resolution 1021: Adopted 22 Nov. 1995. Authorized the phased removal of the arms embargo imposed against the Federal Republic of Yugoslavia (FRY) by Resolution 713, upon confirmation that the General Framework Agreement for Peace in Bosnia and Herzegovina in Dayton, Ohio, USA, had been signed by Bosnia and Herzegovina, Croatia and the FRY.

Resolution 1022: Adopted 22 Nov. 1995. Suspended indefinitely all measures imposed against the Federal Republic of Yugoslavia, owing to the signature of the General Framework Agreement for Peace in Bosnia and Herzegovina in Dayton, Ohio, USA. Measures imposed against the Bosnian Serb party were to be removed following confirmation by the commander of the international force to be deployed to the region of the withdrawal of Bosnian Serb forces beyond specified zones of separation.

Resolution 1023: Adopted 22 Nov. 1995. Welcomed the signature of the Basic Agreement on the Region of Eastern Slavonia, Baranja and Western Sirmium, by representatives of the Croatian Government and Eastern Slavonian Serbs, whereby Eastern Slavonia was to be administered by a transitional administration appointed by the UN prior to its re-integration into Croatia.

Resolution 1025: Adopted 30 Nov. 1995. Decided to terminate the mandate of the UN Confidence Restoration Operation (UNCRO) on 15 Jan. 1996, or upon the deployment of a transitional peace-keeping force to Eastern Slavonia, as required by the Basic Agreement on the Region of Eastern Slavonia, Baranja and Western Sirmium.

Resolution 1026: Adopted 30 Nov. 1995. Established a deadline of 31 Jan. 1996 for the withdrawal of the UN Protection Force from Bosnia and Herzegovina.

Resolution 1029: Adopted 12 Dec. 1995. Adjusted the mandate of the UN Assistance Mission for Rwanda to include the repatriation of Rwandan refugees and the protection of members of the ICTR pending the implementation of alternative measures and approved a reduction in strength to 1,200 troops.

Resolution 1034: Adopted 21 Dec. 1995. Condemned continued violations of international humanitarian law in the Federal Republic of Yugoslavia, in particular those carried out by Bosnian Serbs and paramilitary forces in Banja Luka, Sanskimost, Srebreniča and Žepa.

Resolution 1035: Adopted 21 Dec. 1995. Approved the establishment of a UN civilian police force, the International Police Task Force (IPTF), to assist with the implementation of the General Framework Agreement for Peace in Bosnia and Herzegovina after the replacement of the UN Protection Force by a multinational 'implementation force' (IFOR).

Resolution 1037: Adopted 15 Jan. 1996. Established a UN Transitional Administration for Eastern Slavonia, Baranja and Western Sirmium (UNTAES) to replace the UN Confidence Restoration Operation in Croatia (UNCRO).

Resolution 1038: Adopted 15 Jan. 1996. Endorsed the continued presence of UN observers in the Prevlaka peninsula.

Resolution 1044: Adopted 31 Jan. 1996. Condemned an attempt to assassinate the President of Egypt in Addis Ababa, Ethiopia, in June 1995, and demanded that the Government of Sudan comply with a request by the Organization of African Unity for the extradition of the three individuals implicated in the attack.

Resolution 1048: Adopted 29 Feb. 1996. Welcomed the democratic election of a new president in Haiti and decided to reduce the strength of the UN Mission in Haiti to 1,200 troops and 300 civil police.

Resolution 1049: Adopted 5 March 1996. Condemned hostilities in Burundi and appealed for negotiations to take place. Requested states to help to identify and close radio stations encouraging violence and suggested that a UN radio station be established. Urged the Organization of African Unity to increase the strength of the Observer Mission in Burundi.

Resolution 1050: Adopted 8 March 1996. Endorsed plans for the withdrawal of the UN Assistance Mission in Rwanda and requested a UN office to be maintained in Rwanda to support the Government with national reconciliation, to assist the strengthening of the judicial system and to facilitate the return of refugees.

Resolution 1051: Adopted 27 March 1996. Approved a monitoring mechanism for Iraqi exports and imports.

Resolution 1052: Adopted 18 April 1996. Condemned the shelling by Israeli forces of a base of the UN Interim Force in Lebanon, which resulted in the deaths of a large number of Lebanese civilians and demanded an immediate cease-fire.

Resolution 1053: Adopted 23 April 1996. Demanded countries in the Great Lakes region to ensure that their territories were not used as military bases by armed groups, and to prevent the sale of arms to former Rwandan government forces or militia groups.

Resolution 1054: Adopted 26 April 1996. Imposed a range of diplomatic sanctions against Sudan, owing to the failure of the Sudanese Government to comply with the provisions of Resolution 1044.

Resolution 1060: Adopted 12 June 1996. Deplored Iraq's refusal to allow weapons inspectors of the UN Special Commission to gain access to specified sites.

Resolution 1063: Adopted 28 June 1996. Established a UN Support Mission in Haiti (UNSMIH) to replace and reduce the strength of the existing UN mission.

Resolution 1065: Adopted 12 July 1996. Expressed concern at the lack of progress towards a political settlement to the conflict in Abkhazia, Georgia, and voiced support for Georgia's territorial integrity.

Resolution 1070: Adopted 16 Aug. 1996. Imposed a further air embargo against Sudan.

Resolution 1072: Adopted 30 Aug. 1996. Condemned the overthrow of the Government of Burundi and appealed for a cessation of hostilities and a return to constitutional order in that country.

Resolution 1073: Adopted 28 Sept. 1996. Demanded the cessation of hostilities between members of the Palestinian security forces, Palestinian civilians and the Israeli army and urged the resumption of negotiations within the Middle East peace process, following the Israeli Government's decision to open a tunnel running under a mosque in East Jerusalem.

Resolution 1074: Adopted 1 Oct. 1996. Definitively removed the sanctions regime imposed against the Federal Republic of Yugoslavia and the Serb Republic by Resolution 1022, following the holding of elections in Bosnia and Herzegovina in Sept.

Resolution 1076: Adopted 22 Oct. 1996. Demanded the cessation of armed hostilities in Afghanistan and appealed to member states to refrain from supplying arms to parties to the conflict. Denounced discrimination against the female population and other violations of human rights in that country.

Resolution 1078: Adopted 9 Nov. 1996. Approved the establishment of a multinational humanitarian task force in eastern Zaire.

Resolution 1090: Adopted 13 Dec. 1996. Endorsed the appointment of Kofi Annan as Secretary-General of the UN.

Resolution 1097: Adopted 18 Feb. 1997. Endorsed a peace plan for eastern Zaire, which advocated an immediate cease-fire, the evacuation of external forces, respect for the sovereignty and territorial integrity of Zaire and other states in the Great Lakes region, security for refugees and displaced people and negotiations towards a peaceful settlement.

Resolution 1101: Adopted 28 March 1997. Condemned escalating hostilities in Albania, between insurgents and government troops, and endorsed a European Union initiative for the establishment of a multinational force to supervise humanitarian aid operations.

Resolution 1106: Adopted 16 April 1997. Welcomed the inauguration of the new Government of National Unity and Reconciliation in Angola on 11 April and urged the prompt completion of the remaining military aspects of the peace process and the full reinstatement of a state administration.

Resolution 1111: Adopted 4 June 1997. Extended the 'oil-for-food' agreement with Iraq approved by Resolution 986.

Resolution 1115: Adopted 21 June 1997. Condemned Iraq's repeated obstruction of the UN Special Commission (UNSCOM) weapons inspectors and demanded that they be allowed unconditional and unrestricted access to all requested areas, equipment, facilities, records and transport.

Resolution 1118: Adopted 30 June 1997. Approved the establishment of a UN Observer Mission in Angola (MONUA), to succeed the UN Angola Verification Mission, to oversee the implementation of the remaining provisions of the peace accord.

Resolution 1121: Adopted 22 July 1997. Established a Dag Hammarskjöld Medal to pay tribute to those killed while in the service of UN peace-keeping operations.

Resolution 1123: Adopted 30 July 1997. Approved the establishment of a UN Transition Mission in Haiti (UNTMIH), including 250 police and 50 soldiers, to replace the UN Support Mission in Haiti.

Resolution 1125: Adopted 6 Aug. 1997. Authorized the activities of the Inter-African Mission to Monitor the Implementation of the Bangui Agreements (MISAB) in the Central African Republic.

Resolution 1127: Adopted 28 Aug. 1997. Adopted new sanctions against the União Nacional para a Independência Total de Angola (UNITA), to come into effect on 30 Sept., owing to its failure to meet the requirements stipulated as part of the peace process.

Resolution 1129: Adopted 12 Sept. 1997. Approved continued Iraqi petroleum exports under the 'oil-for-food' agreement, although under modified terms, owing to an earlier interruption of exports.

Resolution 1130: Adopted 29 Sept. 1997. Postponed the implementation of sanctions against União Nacional para a Independência Total de Angola (UNITA), owing to the partial restoration of the state administration in several districts in Angola.

Resolution 1132: Adopted 8 Oct. 1997. Demanded the restoration of the democratically elected Government in Sierra Leone and the cessation of violence by the military junta. Imposed sanctions against Sierra Leone, including an embargo on the import of armaments and petroleum products, and established a Security Council Committee to monitor those sanctions.

Resolution 1134: Adopted 23 Oct. 1997. Condemned Iraq's refusal to comply with the UN Special Commission (UNSCOM) and warned that non-co-operation with UNSCOM would lead to the imposition of travel restrictions on Iraqi officials.

Resolution 1137: Adopted 12 Nov. 1997. Activated the travel restrictions on Iraqi officials proposed by Resolution 1134. Stipulated that Iraq should retract its decision to expel US weapons inspectors and warned that further intransigence could provoke possible military action.

Resolution 1141: Adopted 28 Nov. 1997. Established a UN Civilian Police Mission in Haiti (MIPONUH) of some 300 police to succeed the UN Transition Mission in Haiti.

Resolution 1145: Adopted 19 Dec. 1997. Established a UN Police Support Group to oversee the work of the Croatian police in the Danube region, in particular with regard to the return of displaced persons, following the withdrawal of the UN Transitional Administration for Eastern Slavonia, Baranja and Western Sirmium (UNTAES).

Resolution 1153: Adopted 20 Feb. 1998. Increased the maximum permitted revenue from Iraqi exports of petroleum under the 'oil-for-food' programme to US $5,256m. over a six-month period.

Resolution 1154: Adopted 2 March 1998. Endorsed the Memorandum of Understanding between the UN Secretary-General and Iraq concerning co-operation with UN Special Commission (UNSCOM) and International Atomic Energy Agency (IAEA) experts and threatened extreme consequences if the agreement were reneged upon by Iraq.

Resolution 1156: Adopted 16 March 1998. Welcomed the return from exile and reinstatement of the President of Sierra Leone and voted to end the embargo on imports of petroleum products to that country.

Resolution 1157: Adopted 20 March 1998. Endorsed a gradual reduction in the strength of the UN Observer Mission in Angola.

Resolution 1158: Adopted 25 March 1998. Authorized additional exports of Iraqi petroleum of up to a total of US $1,400m. over a 90-day period.

Resolution 1159: Adopted 27 March 1998. Approved the establishment of a UN Mission in Central African Republic (MINURCA) to assume responsibility from the Inter-African Mission to Monitor the Implementation of the Bangui Agreements (MISAB).

Resolution 1160: Adopted 31 March 1998. Demanded that the Federal Republic of Yugoslavia (FRY) undertake measures to resolve the conflict between Serbs and the ethnic Albanian majority in the Serbian province of Kosovo and Metohija. Imposed an arms embargo against the FRY and established a Security Council Committee to monitor its implementation.

Resolution 1161: Adopted 9 April 1998. Re-established the international commission of inquiry created by Resolution 1013 to gather information concerning arms sales to former Rwandan government forces in the Great Lakes region and to recommend measures to prevent the illegal flow of arms.

Resolution 1162: Adopted 17 April 1998. Authorized the deployment of military and security personnel to Sierra Leone.

Resolution 1165: Adopted 30 April 1998. Approved the establishment of a third three-member trial chamber for the ICTR.

Resolution 1166: Adopted 13 May 1998. Approved the establishment of a third three-member trial chamber of the ICTY.

Resolution 1171: Adopted 5 June 1998. Removed the arms embargo imposed against the Government of Sierra Leone.

Resolution 1172: Adopted 6 June 1998. Condemned nuclear tests undertaken by India and Pakistan in May. Encouraged states to refrain from exporting equipment, materials and technology that could assist the nuclear weapon and ballistic missile programmes of those two countries.

Resolution 1173: Adopted 12 June 1998. Condemned the União Nacional para a Independência Total de Angola (UNITA) for its failure to comply with the provisions of the Lusaka Protocol and Security Council resolutions. Decided to impose sanctions against UNITA, including 'freezing' its funds in other countries, halting official contacts with its leaders and preventing the export from Angola of all diamonds not controlled by the Government's Certificate of Origin regime.

Resolution 1175: Adopted 19 June 1998. Authorized the export to Iraq of oil-production parts and equipment to enable Iraq to export sufficient quantities of petroleum to fulfil Resolution 1153.

Resolution 1177: Adopted 26 June 1998. Condemned the use of force in the border dispute between Ethiopia and Eritrea.

Resolution 1181: Adopted 13 July 1998. Approved the establishment of a UN Observer Mission in Sierra Leone (UNOMSIL) to monitor the security situation and the disarmament of former combatants.

Resolution 1184: Adopted 16 July 1998. Approved the creation by the UN Mission in Bosnia and Herzegovina of a programme to monitor and assess the court system in that country as part of a legal reform programme.

Resolution 1189: Adopted 13 Aug. 1998. Condemned terrorist attacks carried out against the US embassies in Nairobi, Kenya, and in Dar es Salaam, Tanzania, on 7 Aug.

Resolution 1192: Adopted 27 Aug. 1998. Welcomed an initiative for the trial before a Scottish court convened in the Netherlands of the two Libyan nationals alleged to be responsible for the bombing of civilian aircraft Pan Am flight 103 over Scotland in 1988.

Resolution 1193: Adopted 28 Aug. 1998. Expressed concern at the continued conflict in Afghanistan and demanded the cessation of armed hostilities and the resumption of direct negotiations. Condemnation attacks on UN personnel in the territories occupied by the Taliban.

Resolution 1194: Adopted 9 Sept. 1998. Condemned the decision by Iraq to suspend co-operation with the UN Special Commission and the International Atomic Energy Agency, in contravention of Security Council resolutions and the Memorandum of Understanding signed in Feb. between the Secretary-General and Iraq.

Resolution 1197: Adopted 18 Sept. 1998. Appealed for measures to improve peace-keeping mechanisms within the Organization of African Unity through the establishment of an early warning system in Africa and a UN Preventative Action Liaison Office.

Resolution 1199: Adopted 23 Sept. 1998. Demanded the observation and maintenance of an immediate cease-fire in the province of Kosovo and Metohija, the withdrawal of Serbian security forces, unrestricted access for humanitarian agencies and negotiations to end the conflict in the Federal Republic of Yugoslavia.

Resolution 1201: Adopted 15 Oct. 1998. Endorsed the decision by the authorities of the Central African Republic to conduct legislative elections and agreed to expand the mandate of the UN Mission in the Central African Republic to include support for the conduct of elections.

Resolution 1203: Adopted 24 Oct. 1998. Endorsed two agreements signed with the North Atlantic Treaty Organization (NATO) and the Organization for Security and Co-operation in Europe (OSCE) by the Yugoslav authorities, providing for the establishment of NATO and OSCE verification missions in the province of Kosovo and Metohija.

Resolution 1205: Adopted 5 Nov. 1998. Condemned the decision made by Iraq on 31 Oct. to cease co-operation with the UN Special Commission and demanded that it reverse it immediately.

Resolution 1207: Adopted 17 Nov. 1998. Condemned the Federal Republic of Yugoslavia's failure to execute three arrest warrants issued by the ICTY and demanded their immediate execution.

Resolution 1208: Adopted 19 Nov. 1998. Urged the international community to support host African states to enhance their protection and treatment of refugees in camps.

Resolution 1209: Adopted 19 Nov. 1998. Considered the problem of the illicit flow of armaments in Africa.

Resolution 1214: Adopted 8 Dec. 1998. Condemned violence perpetrated by the Taliban in Afghanistan and reiterated demands for a cease-fire and for the resumption of negotiations. Approved the establishment of a civil affairs unit within the UN Special Mission to Afghanistan to deter human rights violations in Afghanistan.

Resolution 1216: Adopted 21 Dec. 1998. Expressed appreciation for the accords reached in Aug. and Nov. 1998 between the Government of Guinea-Bissau and the self-proclaimed 'military junta for the consolidation of democracy, peace and justice' and demanded that they be implemented fully.

Resolution 1219: Adopted 31 Dec. 1998. Expressed concern at the crash of UN flight 806 in Angola and at the increased number of aircraft disappearing over territory controlled by the União Nacional para a Independência Total de Angola (UNITA). Deplored UNITA's lack of co-operation with crash investigators and demanded that the UN be allowed access to the territory where the crash took place.

Resolution 1221: Adopted 12 Jan. 1999. Condemned the shooting down of a second UN aircraft over territory controlled by UNITA in Angola. Affirmed its determination to carry out an investigation of the circumstances of the two crashes and demanded that UNITA comply with Resolution 1219. Emphasized the member states' obligation to comply with sanctions imposed against UNITA.

Resolution 1226: Adopted 29 Jan. 1999. Expressed concern at the escalating risk of armed conflict in the border dispute between Eritrea and Ethiopia, and support for the mediation efforts of the Organization of African Unity (OAU).

Resolution 1227: Adopted 10 Feb. 1999. Condemned the use of force in the conflict between Eritrea and Ethiopia and demanded a cease-fire and the resumption of negotiations. Urged member states to refrain from providing arms to either of the countries involved in the dispute.

Resolution 1233: Adopted 6 April 1999. Approved establishment of a Post-Conflict Peace Building Support Office in Guinea-Bissau, headed by a Representative of the UN Secretary-General, to help consolidate peace, following the inauguration of a new Government of National Unity in that country.

Resolution 1234: Adopted 9 April 1999. Reiterated concern at the ongoing fighting in the Democratic Republic of the Congo, and demanded the withdrawal of all foreign forces from the country and the initiation of peace negotiations.

Resolution 1239: Adopted 14 May 1999. Urged safe and unrestricted access for all humanitarian personnel throughout the Federal Republic of Yugoslavia in order to guarantee refugees and displaced persons the right to return home.

Resolution 1244: Adopted 10 June 1999. Authorized the deployment of international civilian and security personnel to Kosovo and Metohija, under UN auspices, and outlined the terms of a political settlement for the province based on the general principles agreed by ministers of foreign affairs of the Group of Eight (G-8) industrialized nations on 6 May. The authorized force, comprising mainly NATO personnel, was to be responsible for ensuring the withdrawal of all Serbian military, police and paramilitary forces, and preventing their return and any new hostilities, and for demobilizing Kosovo Albanian groups. The civilian operation (the UN Interim Administration in Kosovo and Metohija—UNMIK), under the control of a Special Representative of the UN Secretary-General, was to provide an interim administration to supervise the development of democratic, self-governing institutions.

Resolution 1246: Adopted 11 June 1999. Established a UN Mission in East Timor (UNAMET) to organize and conduct a popular poll on the political future of the territory, following agreements concluded between Indonesia, Portugal and the UN on 5 May.

Resolution 1248: Adopted 25 June 1999. Endorsed the admission of Kiribati to the UN.

Resolution 1249: Adopted 25 June 1999. Endorsed the admission of Nauru to the UN.

Resolution 1253: Adopted 28 July 1999. Endorsed the admission of Tonga to the UN.

Resolution 1261: Adopted 25 Aug. 1999. Expressed concern at the impact of armed conflict on children and the long-term consequences of this for durable peace and stability. Condemned the targeting of children in situations of armed conflict, including killing, maiming, sexual violence, abduction and forced displacement, the recruitment and use of child soldiers and attacks on places such as hospitals and schools.

Resolution 1265: Adopted 17 Sept. 1999. Condemned the deliberate targeting of civilians in situations of armed conflict as well as attacks on objects protected under international law. Called upon all parties to put an end to such practices. Decided to establish immediately a mechanism to review further the recommendations contained in the report by the UN Secretary-General on the protection of civilians in armed conflict.

Resolution 1266: Adopted 4 Oct. 1999. Permitted Iraq to increase exports under current phase of the 'oil-for-food' programme to compensate for deficits in two previous phases.

Resolution 1267: Adopted 15 Oct. 1999. Demanded that the Taliban in Afghanistan deliver those accused of co-ordinating the 1998 terrorist bombings of the US embassies in Kenya and Tanzania to appropriate authorities in order that they might be brought to justice in one of the countries where they had been indicted. Decided that, if this demand were not met by 14 Nov. 1999, all member states should 'freeze' funds owned or controlled by the Taliban and prohibit the take-off and landing on their territory of Taliban-owned aircraft.

Resolution 1270: Adopted 22 Oct. 1999. Authorized the establishment of the UN Mission in Sierra Leone (UNAMSIL), mandated to co-operate with all parties to the peace agreement signed in July at Lomé, Togo, to assist with the disarmament, demobilization and reintegration of former combatants, and to establish a presence at key locations.

Resolution 1272: Adopted 25 Oct. 1999. Authorized the establishment of the UN Transitional Administration in East Timor (UNTAET), empowered to exercise all legislative and executive authority over the territory, including the administration of justice.

Resolution 1279: Adopted 30 Nov. 1999. Authorized the establishment of the UN Mission in the DRC (MONUC), mandated to establish contacts with the signatories to the Lusaka cease-fire agreement (concluded in Aug. 1999 by the parties to the conflict in the DRC) and to liaise with the Joint Military Commission, established under the agreement to enforce the cessation of hostilities. Also mandated to provide information on security conditions and to facilitate the delivery of humanitarian aid.

Resolution 1284: Adopted 17 Dec. 1999. Authorized the formation of the UN Monitoring, Verification and Inspection Commission (UNMOVIC) to establish and operate a reinforced system for overseeing the elimination of weapons of mass destruction in Iraq. Authorized member states to permit the importation of any volume of petroleum and petroleum products originating in Iraq and to permit financial and other essential transactions relating thereto. Stipulated conditions relating to the eventual suspension of sanctions against Iraq.

Resolution 1286: Adopted 19 Jan. 2000. Condemned continuing violence in Burundi, emphasizing attacks against civilians, in particular the murder of UN personnel and Burundi civilians in Oct. 1999. Urged that the perpetrators be brought to justice swiftly. Urged all parties to end the ongoing armed conflict.

Resolution 1289: Adopted 7 Feb. 2000. Approved the expansion of the military component of UNAMSIL. Revised UNAMSIL's mandate to provide security at key locations in Sierra Leone.

Resolution 1290: Adopted 17 Feb. 2000. Endorsed the admission of Tuvalu to the UN.

Resolution 1293: Adopted 31 March 2000. Doubled the maximum permitted revenue that Iraq might use to purchase oil industry spare parts and equipment under the 'oil-for-food' programme.

Resolution 1295: Adopted 18 April 2000. Reiterated the demand that UNITA comply with its obligations under the Lusaka Protocol and with previous Security Council resolutions. Emphasized concern at violations of sanctions imposed against UNITA and stressed the obligation of all member states to comply fully with these. Authorized the establishment of a temporary mechanism to monitor the sanctions violations.

Resolution 1298: Adopted 17 May 2000. Condemned the continuing conflict between Eritrea and Ethiopia. Demanded the immediate cessation of all military actions and avoidance of further use of force. Demanded the resumption of peace talks under the auspices of the OAU. Imposed an embargo on the sale or supply of arms and related material to Eritrea or Ethiopia.

Resolution 1299: Adopted 19 May 2000. Authorized the rapid reinforcement of the military component of UNAMSIL, providing for a total of 13,000 personnel.

Resolution 1306: Adopted 5 July 2000. Prohibited the exportation from Sierra Leone of rough diamonds not officially certified by that country's Government.

Resolution 1308: Adopted 17 July 2000. Expressed concern at the potentially damaging impact of HIV and AIDS on the health of personnel deployed to UN peace-keeping operations. Requested the Secretary-General to facilitate the provision of education on disease prevention to such personnel. Urged support from member states and encouraged UNAIDS to strengthen co-operation with member states.

Resolution 1310: Adopted 27 July 2000. Welcomed verification by the Secretary-General of Israel's removal of violations of the troop withdrawal line at its border with Lebanon. Welcomed the establishment by the Lebanon Government of checkpoints in the area vacated by the Israeli forces.

Resolution 1312: Adopted 31 July 2000. Authorized the establishment of the UN Mission in Ethiopia and Eritrea (UNMEE) to liaise with the parties to, and facilitate and verify compliance with, the cease-fire agreement signed in Algiers in mid-June relating to those countries' two-year border conflict.

Resolution 1315: Adopted 14 Aug. 2000. Requested the Secretary-General to negotiate an agreement with the Sierra Leone Government on the establishment of an international tribunal to try those accused of perpetrating crimes against humanity, war crimes and other serious violations of international law within the territory of that country.

Resolution 1318: Adopted 7 Sept. 2000. Declaration of the Millennium Summit Meeting of the Security Council on ensuring an effective role for the Council in the maintenance of international peace and security, with particular reference to promoting peace and sustainable development in Africa. Addressed the root causes of conflicts and the contributory effects of the illicit exploitation and sale of commodities and the illegal trade in armaments; welcomed the report issued in Aug. by the Panel on UN Peace Operations.

Resolution 1319: Adopted 8 Sept. 2000. Condemned the murder of three UNHCR personnel by Indonesian militia in West Timor.

Resolution 1320: Adopted 15 Sept. 2000. Authorized the expansion of UNMEE, emphasizing that the mission's mandate would be terminated on completion of the process to delimit and demarcate the Eritrea-Ethiopia border.

Resolution 1322: Adopted 7 Oct. 2000. Deplored the provocation at holy sites in Jerusalem and the subsequent fatal violent incidents. Condemned the escalation of violence and, in particular, the excessive use of force against Palestinians. Called upon Israel to abide by the obligations of the Geneva Conventions and urged a cessation of violence and an immediate resumption of the peace process. Stressed the importance of establishing a mechanism for an objective inquiry into the recent events.

Resolution 1325: Adopted 31 Oct. 2000. Invited the Secretary-General to report to the Security Council on the impact of armed conflict on women and girls, the role of women in peace-building, and on gender dimensions in peace processes and conflict resolution. Urged the improved protection of women and girls in armed conflict situations. Recommended more female appointments at all levels of UN peace-keeping activities, and increased participation by women in decision-making processes at national, regional and international level.

Resolution 1326: Adopted 31 Oct. 2000. Endorsed the admission of the Federal Republic of Yugoslavia to the UN.

Resolution 1327: Adopted 13 Nov. 2000. Agreed, having considered the report of the Panel on UN Peace Operations, to adopt several guide-lines aimed at improving the Council's management of UN peace-keeping activities. Requested the Secretary-General, in consultation with UN member states, to prepare a comprehensive operational doctrine for the military component of peace-keeping operations.

Resolution 1329: Adopted 30 Nov. 2000. Authorized the expansion of the appeals chambers at both the ICTR and ICTY, and approved the appointment of two further judges to the ICTR and the establishment of a pool of 27 *ad litem* judges at the ICTY.

Resolution 1333: Adopted 19 Dec. 2000. Demanded that the Taliban in Afghanistan comply with Resolution 1267. Imposed an embargo on the direct or indirect supply, sale or transfer of arms and related material to that part of the territory of Afghanistan under Taliban control. Decided that all member states should refrain from providing technical advice, assistance or training relating to Taliban military activities, close all Taliban offices and offices of Ariana Afghan Airlines in their territories, and that all states must 'freeze' the funds and assets of Osama bin Laden (believed to be responsible for the 1998 attacks on US embassies in Kenya and Tanzania) and of all associated individuals and entities. Also prohibited the supply to the Taliban-controlled area of a specific chemical believed to be used there in the production of illegal narcotic drugs.

Resolution 1338: Adopted 31 Jan. 2001. Urged the international community to provide financial and technical assistance to East Timor for institution-building and the establishment of a Defence Force.

Resolution 1341: Adopted 22 Feb. 2001. Required the full disengagement of foreign troops from the Democratic Republic of the Congo. Expressed the intention to send a Council mission to that country in order to monitor the situation and the implementation of the peace accord.

Resolution 1343: Adopted 7 March 2001. Demanded that Liberia cease to support the members or activities of the Revolutionary United Front of Sierra Leone, or of other armed rebel groups in the region, and that all neighbouring countries undertake efforts to maintain the security of border areas. Demanded that the Liberian Government comply with Resolution 1306. Terminated the existing arms embargo against Liberia (under the terms of resolution 788), but imposed a further embargo on the sale of armaments and related material to Liberia and on the export of diamonds from that country, and travel restrictions on senior Liberian officials and their spouses, to be effective from 7 May 2001 if the above demands had not been met.

Resolution 1346: Adopted 30 March 2001. Approved an increase in the military component of the UN Mission in Sierra Leone (UNAMSIL) to 17,500, and a revised concept of operations, in order to implement the process of disarmament, demobilization and reintegration. Urged UNAMSIL to maintain its support for returning refugees and displaced persons.

Resolution 1352: Adopted 1 June 2001. Expressed its intention to consider new arrangements for the sale or supply of goods to Iraq, and the facilitation of trade and economic co-operation with Iraq in civilian sectors.

Resolution 1353: Adopted 13 June 2001. Adopted decisions and recommendations of the Statement of principles on co-operation with troop-contributing countries, which aimed to strengthen relations between the UN and those countries and to enhance the effectiveness of peace-keeping operations.

Resolution 1355: Adopted 15 June 2001. Reiterated demands for all sides in the Democratic Republic of the Congo to respect the Lusaka cease-fire agreement, including the withdrawal of foreign troops, the cessation of aid to or co-operation with armed groups, and the end to the training and use of child soldiers. Urged neighbouring countries to co-operate in support of peace in the region. Approved the establishment of a civilian police component of the UN Organization Mission in the DRC (MONUC) and for an increase in the number of human rights personnel.

Resolution 1356: Adopted 19 June 2001. Approved certain exemptions (for non-lethal equipment) to the sanctions imposed against Somalia by Resolution 733.

Resolution 1358: Adopted 27 June 2001. Recommended to the General Assembly the appointment of Kofi Annan for a second term of office as UN Secretary-General, from 1 Jan. 2002 to 31 Dec. 2006.

Resolution 1363: Adopted 30 July 2001. Established a mechanism to monitor implementation of Council-imposed sanctions against the Taliban regime in Afghanistan and to assist neighbouring countries to increase their capacity to implement the measures. The mechanism was to comprise a five-member Monitoring Group, and a Sanctions Enforcement Support Team, of up to 15 members, to be located in bordering countries.

Resolution 1366: Adopted 30 Aug. 2001. Considered current and future aspects of the role of the Security Council in the prevention of armed conflict, on the basis of a report by the Secretary-General. Expressed support for the development of a comprehensive conflict prevention strategy, and the Council's willingness to consider preventive deployment missions.

Resolution 1367: Adopted 10 Sept. 2001. Terminated the prohibitions on the sale or supply of arms to the Federal Republic of Yugoslavia, established by Resolution 1160.

Resolution 1368: Adopted 12 Sept. 2001. Unequivocally condemned the terrorist attacks of 11 Sept. against targets in the USA. Called upon all states to co-operate in bringing the perpetrators, organizers and sponsors of the attacks to justice, and expressed readiness to respond to the events as necessary and to combat all forms of terrorism. Reiterated the inherent right of individual or collective self-defence as recognized by the UN Charter.

Resolution 1369: Adopted 14 Sept. 2001. Outlined the obligations of Ethiopia and Eritrea to support the UN mission there and the implementation of the Algiers peace agreements, including the pursuit of confidence-building measures.

Resolution 1372: Adopted 28 Sept. 2001. Terminated the sanctions imposed against Sudan by Resolutions 1054 and 1070 in 1996, in response to the efforts of the Government of Sudan to comply with the provisions of Security Council resolutions and its accession to international conventions for the elimination of international terrorism.

Resolution 1373: Adopted 28 Sept. 2001. Approved measures and strategies to combat the threat of international terrorism, including obligations on states to freeze the assets of any individual or group involved in terrorist activities, to deny them safe haven, to co-operate in the exchange of information and in criminal investigations, and to impose stricter border controls. Established a Counter-Terrorism Committee to monitor implementation of the resolution.

Resolution 1376: Adopted 9 Nov. 2001. Outlined the progress of the peace process in the Democratic Republic of the Congo. Expressed support for the new phase in deployment of the UN mission in that country in order to oversee the process of disarmament, demobilization, repatriation, resettlement and reintegration, although emphasized that this required the demilitarization of Kisangani as well as freedom of movement throughout the country.

Resolution 1377: Adopted 12 Nov. 2001. Adopted a ministerial declaration on the global effort to combat terrorism. Urged all states to intensify co-operation and all efforts to eliminate international terrorism and to become parties to international conventions relating to terrorism.

Resolution 1378: Adopted 14 Nov. 2001. Determined that the UN should play a central role in supporting the efforts of Afghanistan to establish a transitional administration prior to the formation of a new, multi-ethnic government. Expressed support for the activities of the Secretary-General's Special Representative on Afghanistan, Lakhdar Brahimi, with overall authority for the humanitarian, human rights and political efforts of the UN in that country. Urged all states to provide humanitarian and longer-term assistance to Afghanistan.

Resolution 1379: Adopted 20 Nov. 2001. Considered all means to support children affected by armed conflict, and to extend protection wherever possible.

Resolution 1383: Adopted 6 Dec. 2001. Endorsed the agreement on provisional arrangements in Afghanistan reached between representatives of the Northern Alliance and other Afghan groups meeting in Bonn, Germany. Declared willingness to take any necessary action to support the interim institutions and to support the full implementation of the agreement.

Resolution 1386: Adopted 20 Dec. 2001. Authorized the establishment of an International Security Assistance Force, as envisaged in the Bonn Agreement, to assist the Interim Authority in Afghanistan to maintain a security in the capital, Kabul, and in the surrounding areas. Requested Afghan groupings to implement their commitment to withdraw all military units from Kabul.

Resolution 1388: Adopted 15 Jan. 2002. Decided that the air embargo and the freezing of assets controlled by the Taliban no longer applied to Ariana Afghan Airlines, and terminated measures to close all overseas offices of the airline (imposed by Resolution 1333).

Resolution 1389: Adopted 16 Jan. 2002. Mandated UNAMSIL to assist with the conduct of elections in Sierra Leone, and authorized an expansion of the UN civilian police component to support the national police in undertaking election-related activities.

Resolution 1390: Adopted 16 Jan. 2002. Determined that all states adopt certain measures against the terrorist network led by Osama bin Laden, members of the Taliban and any individual or groups associated with them, including the freezing of all assets, preventing their entry or transit, and preventing the sale or supply of arms-related material. Measures to be overseen by the Monitoring Group established under Resolution 1363.

Resolution 1397: Adopted 12 March 2002. Envisaged separate states of Israel and Palestine, based on secure and internationally recognized borders. Expressed grave concern at the continued, escalating hostilities in the Middle East region and demanded an immediate end to all acts of violence. Urged both sides to co-operate in the implementation of the Tenet work plan and the Mitchell Report recommendations, with the aim of resuming negotiations for a political settlement.

Resolution 1401: Adopted 28 March 2002. Established a UN Assistance Mission in Afghanistan (UNAMA), for an initial 12-month period, on the basis of a report of the Secretary-General. (It was to have a two-pillar mandate relating to political affairs and to relief and assistance.) Reaffirmed support for the Secretary-General's Special Representative to Afghanistan, Lakhdar Brahimi, and endorsed his full authority over planning and conduct of UN activities in that country.

Resolution 1402: Adopted 1 April 2002. Called upon Israel and the Palestine Authority to implement a cease-fire, following further violent attacks by both sides, and to co-operate with the US Special Envoy and other diplomatic efforts to implement the Tenet work plan and, ultimately, to resume peace negotiations. Called for the withdrawal of Israeli troops from Palestinian cities, including Ramallah.

Resolution 1405: Adopted 19 April 2002. Expressed concern at the humanitarian situation in Palestine, and in particular in the Jenin refugee camp. Urged the removal of all restrictions on operations of humanitarian organizations and endorsed the dispatch of a UN fact-finding team to investigate recent events in Jenin.

Trusteeship Council

The Trusteeship Council (comprising the People's Republic of China—a non-active member until May 1989, France, Russia, the United Kingdom and the USA) was established to supervise United Nations Trust Territories through their administering authorities and to promote the political, economic, social and educational advancement of their inhabitants towards self-government or independence (see Charter, p. 62). On 1 October 1994 the last territory remaining under UN trusteeship, the Republic of Palau (part of the archipelago of the Caroline Islands), declared its independence under a compact of free association with the USA, its administering authority. The Security Council terminated the Trusteeship Agreement on 10 November, having determined that the objectives of the agreement had been fully attained. On 1 November the Trusteeship Council formally suspended its operations; thereafter it was to be convened on an extraordinary basis as required.

Economic and Social Council—ECOSOC

ECOSOC promotes world co-operation on economic, social, cultural and humanitarian problems. (See Charter, p. 62.)

MEMBERS

Fifty-four members are elected by the General Assembly for three-year terms: 18 are elected each year. Membership is allotted by regions as follows: Africa 14 members, western Europe and others 13, Asia 11, Latin America 10, eastern Europe 6.

President: IVAN ŠIMONOVIĆ (Croatia).

ORGANIZATION

The Council, which meets annually for four to five weeks between May and July, alternately in New York and Geneva, is mainly a central policy-making and co-ordinating organ. It has a co-ordinating function between the UN and the specialized agencies, and also makes consultative arrangements with approved voluntary or non-governmental organizations which work within the sphere of its activities. The Council has functional and regional commissions to carry out much of its detailed work.

During 1999 ECOSOC pursued discussions with the IMF and World Bank regarding the socio-economic aspects of globalization and increased co-operation for development.

SESSIONAL COMMITTEES

Each sessional committee comprises the 54 members of the Council: there is a First (Economic) Committee, a Second (Social) Committee and a Third (Programme and Co-ordination) Committee.

FUNCTIONAL COMMISSIONS

Commission on Crime Prevention and Criminal Justice: f. 1992; aims to formulate an international convention on crime prevention and criminal justice; 40 members.

Commission on Human Rights: f. 1946; seeks greater respect for the basic rights of man, the prevention of discrimination and the protection of minorities; reviews specific instances of human rights violation and dispatches rapporteurs to investigate allegations of abuses in particular countries; provides policy guidance; works on declarations, conventions and other instruments of international law; meets annually for six weeks; 53 members. There is a Sub-Commission on the Promotion and Protection of Human Rights, comprising working groups on issues such as slavery, indigenous populations, detention and communications.

Commission on Narcotic Drugs: f. 1946; mainly concerned in combating illicit traffic; 53 members. There is a Sub-Commission on Illicit Drug Traffic and Related Matters in the Near and Middle East.

Commission on Population and Development: f. 1946; advises the Council on population matters and their relation to socio-economic conditions; 47 members.

Commission on Science and Technology for Development: f. 1992; works on the restructuring of the UN in the economic, social and related fields; 33 members.

Commission for Social Development: f. 1946 as the Social Commission; advises ECOSOC on issues of social and community development; 46 members.

Commission on the Status of Women: f. 1946; aims at equality of political, economic and social rights for women, and supports the right of women to live free of violence; 45 members.

Commission on Sustainable Development: f. 1993 to oversee integration into the UN's work of the objectives set out in 'Agenda 21', the programme of action agreed by the UN Conference on Environment and Development in June 1992; 53 members.

Statistical Commission: Standardizes terminology and procedure in statistics and promotes the development of national statistics; 24 members.

COMMITTEES AND SUBSIDIARY BODIES

Commission on Human Settlements: f. 1977.

Committee for Development Policy: f. 1965.

Committee on Energy and Natural Resources for Development: f. 1998.

Committee on Negotiations with Intergovernmental Agencies: f. 1946.

Committee on Non-Governmental Organizations: f. 1946.

Committee for Programme and Co-ordination: f. 1962.

REGIONAL COMMISSIONS

(see pp. 73–83)

Economic Commission for Africa—ECA.

Economic Commission for Europe—ECE.

Economic Commission for Latin America and the Caribbean—ECLAC.

Economic and Social Commission for Asia and the Pacific—ESCAP.

Economic and Social Commission for Western Asia—ESCWA.

RELATED BODIES

Board of Trustees of the International Research and Training Institute for Women (INSTRAW): 11 members (see p. 139).

International Narcotics Control Board: f. 1964; 13 members.

UNDP/UNFPA Executive Board: 36 members, elected by ECOSOC (see p. 100).

UNHCR Executive Committee: 53 members, elected by ECOSOC (see p. 108).

UNICEF Executive Board: 36 members, elected by ECOSOC (see p. 89).

WFP Executive Board: one-half of the 36 members are elected by ECOSOC, one-half by the FAO; governing body of the World Food Programme (see p. 141).

International Court of Justice

Address: Peace Palace, Carnegieplein 2, 2517 KJ The Hague, Netherlands.

Telephone: (70) 302-23-23; **fax:** (70) 364-99-28; **e-mail:** information@icj-cij.org; **internet:** www.icj-cij.org.

Established in 1945, the Court is the principal judicial organ of the UN. All members of the UN, and also Switzerland, are parties to the Statute of the Court. (See Charter, p. 62.)

THE JUDGES

(March 2002; in order of precedence)

	Term Ends*
President: GILBERT GUILLAUME (France)	2009
Vice-President: SHI JIUYONG (People's Republic of China)	2003
Judges:	
SHIGERU ODA (Japan)	2003
RAYMOND RANJEVA (Madagascar)	2009
GÉZA HERCZEGH (Hungary)	2003
CARL-AUGUST FLEISCHHAUER (Germany)	2003
ABDUL G. KOROMA (Sierra Leone)	2003
VLADLEN S. VERESHCHETIN (Russia)	2006
ROSALYN HIGGINS (United Kingdom)	2009
GONZALO PARRA-ARANGUREN (Venezuela)	2009
PIETER H. KOOIJMANS (Netherlands)	2006
JOSÉ FRANCISCO REZEK (Brazil)	2006
AWN SHAWKAT AL-KHASAWNEH (Jordan)	2009
THOMAS BUERGENTHAL (USA)	2009
NABIL ELARABY (Egypt)	2006
Registrar: PHILIPPE COUVREUR (Belgium)	

* Each term ends on 5 February of the year indicated.

The Court is composed of 15 judges, each of a different nationality, elected with an absolute majority by both the General Assembly and the Security Council. Representation of the main forms of civilization and the different legal systems of the world are borne in mind in their election. Candidates are nominated by national panels of jurists.

The judges are elected for nine years and may be re-elected; elections for five seats are held every three years. The Court elects its President and Vice-President for each three-year period. Members may not have any political, administrative, or other professional occupation, and may not sit in any case with which they have been otherwise connected than as a judge of the Court. For the purposes of a case, each side—consisting of one or more States—may, unless the Bench already includes a judge with a corresponding nationality, choose a person from outside the Court to sit as a judge on terms of equality with the Members. Judicial decisions are taken by a majority of the judges present, subject to a quorum of nine Members. The President has a casting vote.

FUNCTIONS

The International Court of Justice operates in accordance with a Statute which is an integral part of the UN Charter. Only States may be parties in cases before the Court; those not parties to the Statute may have access in certain circumstances and under conditions laid down by the Security Council.

The Jurisdiction of the Court comprises:

1. All cases which the parties refer to it jointly by special agreement (indicated in the list below by a stroke between the names of the parties).

2. All matters concerning which a treaty or convention in force provides for reference to the Court. About 700 bilateral or multilateral agreements make such provision. Among the more noteworthy: Treaty of Peace with Japan (1951), European Convention for Peaceful Settlement of Disputes (1957), Single Convention on Narcotic Drugs (1961), Protocol relating to the Status of Refugees (1967), Hague Convention on the Suppression of the Unlawful Seizure of Aircraft (1970).

3. Legal disputes between States which have recognized the jurisdiction of the Court as compulsory for specified classes of dispute. Declarations by the following 63 States accepting the compulsory jurisdiction of the Court are in force: Australia, Austria, Barbados, Belgium, Botswana, Bulgaria, Cambodia (Kampuchea), Cameroon, Canada, Colombia, the Democratic Republic of the Congo, Costa Rica, Cyprus, Denmark, the Dominican Republic, Egypt, Estonia, Finland, The Gambia, Georgia, Greece, Guinea, Guinea-Bissau, Haiti, Honduras, Hungary, India, Japan, Kenya, Lesotho, Liberia, Liechtenstein, Luxembourg, Madagascar, Malawi, Malta, Mauritius, Mexico, Nauru, the Netherlands, New Zealand, Nicaragua, Nigeria, Norway, Pakistan, Panama, Paraguay, the Philippines, Poland, Portugal, Senegal, Somalia, Spain, Sudan, Suriname, Swaziland, Sweden, Switzerland, Togo, Uganda, the United Kingdom, Uruguay, and the Federal Republic of Yugoslavia.

Disputes as to whether the Court has jurisdiction are settled by the Court.

Judgments are without appeal, but are binding only for the particular case and between the parties. States appearing before the Court undertake to comply with its Judgment. If a party to a case fails to do so, the other party may apply to the Security Council, which may make recommendations or decide upon measures to give effect to the Judgment.

Advisory opinions on legal questions may be requested by the General Assembly, the Security Council or, if so authorized by the Assembly, other United Nations organs or specialized agencies.

Rules of Court governing procedure are made by the Court under a power conferred by the Statute.

In July 1993 the Court established a seven-member Chamber for Environmental Matters, in view of the world-wide expansion of environmental law and protection.

CONSIDERED CASES

Judgments

Since 1946 more than 80 cases have been referred to the Court by States. Some were removed from the list as a result of settlement or discontinuance, or on the grounds of a lack of basis for jurisdiction. Cases which have been the subject of a Judgment by the Court include: Monetary Gold Removed from Rome in 1943 (Italy *v.* France, United Kingdom and USA); Sovereignty over Certain Frontier Land (Belgium/Netherlands); Arbitral Award made by the King of Spain on 23 December 1906 (Honduras *v.* Nicaragua); Temple of Preah Vihear (Cambodia *v.* Thailand); South West Africa (Ethiopia and Liberia *v.* South Africa); Northern Cameroons (Cameroon *v.* United Kingdom); North Sea Continental Shelf (Federal Republic of Germany/Denmark and Netherlands); Appeal relating to the Jurisdiction of the ICAO Council (India *v.* Pakistan); Fisheries Jurisdiction (United Kingdom *v.* Iceland; Federal Republic of Germany *v.* Iceland); Nuclear Tests (Australia *v.* France; New Zealand *v.* France); Aegean Sea Continental Shelf (Greece *v.* Turkey); United States of America Diplomatic and Consular Staff in Tehran (USA *v.* Iran); Continental Shelf (Tunisia/Libya); Delimitation of the Maritime Boundary in the Gulf of Maine Area (Canada/USA); Continental Shelf (Libya/Malta); Application for revision and interpretation of the Judgment of 24 February 1982 in the case concerning the Continental Shelf (Tunisia *v.* Libya); Military and Paramilitary Activities in and against Nicaragua (Nicaragua *v.* USA); Frontier Dispute (Burkina Faso/Mali); Delimitation of Maritime Boundary (Denmark *v.* Norway); Maritime Boundaries (Guinea-Bissau *v.* Senegal); Elettronica Sicula SpA (USA *v.* Italy); Land, Island and Maritime Frontier Dispute (El Salvador/Honduras) (in one aspect of which Nicaragua was permitted to intervene); Delimitation of Maritime Boundary in the area between Greenland and Jan Mayen island (Denmark *v.* Norway); Maritime Delimitation and Territorial Questions between Qatar and Bahrain (Qatar *v.*

Bahrain); Territorial Dispute (Libya/Chad); East Timor (Portugal *v.* Australia); the Gabčíkovo-Nagymaros Hydroelectric Project (Hungary *v.* Slovakia), aspects of which were still under consideration in early 2002; Fisheries Jurisdiction (Spain *v.* Canada); Delimitation of the Boundary around Kasikili Sedudu Island (Botswana *v.* Namibia); and La Grand case (Germany *v.* USA).

Other cases remaining under consideration, or pending before the Court, in early 2002 were: cases brought by Libya against the United Kingdom and the USA concerning questions of interpretation and application of the 1971 Montreal Convention arising from the aerial incident at Lockerbie, United Kingdom, in 1988; a case brought by Iran against the USA concerning the destruction of oil platforms; cases brought by Bosnia and Herzegovina and Croatia against the Federal Republic of Yugoslavia (FRY) concerning the application of the 1948 Convention on the Prevention and Punishment of the Crime of Genocide and an application, brought by the FRY, for revision of a judgment in 1996; a case brought by Cameroon against Nigeria concerning the land and maritime boundary between those two states, as well as a case concerning the interpretation of the Judgment of the Court on its jurisdiction in that case; a case concerning sovereignty over Pulau Ligatan and Pulau Sipadan brought by Indonesia and Malaysia; a case brought by Guinea against the Democratic Republic of the Congo (DRC) concerning the treatment of a Guinean business executive, Ahmadou Sadio Diallo; cases concerning the legality of the use of force brought by the FRY against Belgium, Canada, France, Germany, Italy, the Netherlands, Portugal and the United Kingdom; a case brought by the DRC against Uganda, regarding armed activities on the territory of the DRC; dispute between Nicaragua and Honduras concerning maritime delimitation in the Caribbean Sea; a case brought by the DRC against Belgium regarding the issuing by a Belgian examining judge of an international arrest warrant against a Congolese government minister; a case brought by Liechtenstein against Germany regarding compensation for property of Liechtenstein nationals seized as a consequence of the Second World War; and a case brought by Nicaragua against Colombia concerning territory and maritime delimitation in the western Caribbean.

Advisory Opinions

Matters on which the Court has delivered an Advisory Opinion at the request of the United Nations General Assembly, or an organ thereof, include the following: Condition of Admission of a State to Membership in the United Nations; Competence of the General Assembly for the Admission of a State to the United Nations; Interpretation of the Peace Treaties with Bulgaria, Hungary and Romania; International Status of South West Africa; Reservations to the Convention on the Prevention and Punishment of the Crime of Genocide; Effect of Awards of Compensation Made by the United Nations Administrative Tribunal (UNAT); Western Sahara; Application for Review of UNAT Judgment No. 333; Applicability of the Obligation to Arbitrate under Section 21 of the United Nations Headquarters Agreement of 26 June 1947 (relating to the closure of the Observer Mission to the United Nations maintained by the Palestine Liberation Organization).

An Advisory Opinion has been given at the request of the Security Council: Legal Consequences for States of the continued presence of South Africa in Namibia (South West Africa) notwithstanding Security Council resolution 276 (1970).

In 1989 (at the request of the UN Economic and Social Council—ECOSOC) the Court gave an Advisory Opinion on the Applicability of Article 6, Section 22, of the Convention on the Privileges and Immunities of the United Nations. The Court has also, at the request of UNESCO, given an Advisory Opinion on Judgments of the Administrative Tribunal of the ILO upon Complaints made against UNESCO, and on the Constitution of the Maritime Safety Committee of the Inter-Governmental Maritime Consultative Organization, at the request of IMCO. In July 1996 the Court delivered Advisory Opinions on the Legality of the Use by a State of Nuclear Weapons in Armed Conflict, requested by WHO, and on the Legality of the Use or Threat of Nuclear Weapons, requested by the UN General Assembly. In April 1999 the Court delivered an Advisory Opinion, requested by ECOSOC, on the Difference Relating to Immunity from Legal Process of a Special Rapporteur of the Commission on Human Rights.

Finance

The UN budget appropriation for the Court for the two year period 2002–03 amounted to US $23,837m.

Publications

Acts and Documents, No. 5 (contains Statute and Rules of the Court, the Resolution concerning its internal judicial practice and other documents).

Bibliography (annually).

Pleadings (Written Pleadings and Statements, Oral Proceedings, Correspondence): series.

Reports (Judgments, Opinions and Orders): series.

Yearbook.

Charter of the United Nations

(Signed 26 June 1945)

We the peoples of the United Nations determined

to save succeeding generations from the scourge of war, which twice in our lifetime has brought untold sorrow to mankind, and

to reaffirm faith in fundamental human rights, in the dignity and worth of the human person, in the equal rights of men and women and of nations large and small, and

to establish conditions under which justice and respect for the obligations arising from treaties and other sources of international law can be maintained, and

to promote social progress and better standards of life in larger freedom,

And for these ends

to practise tolerance and live together in peace with one another as good neighbours, and

to unite our strength to maintain international peace and security, and

to ensure, by the acceptance of principles and the institution of methods, that armed force shall not be used, save in the common interest, and

to employ international machinery for the promotion of the economic and social advancement of all peoples,

Have resolved to combine our efforts to accomplish these aims.

Accordingly, our respective Governments, through representatives assembled in the city of San Francisco, who have exhibited their full powers found to be in good and due form, have agreed to the present Charter of the United Nations and do hereby establish an international organization to be known as the United Nations.

I. PURPOSES AND PRINCIPLES

Article 1

The Purposes of the United Nations are:

1. To maintain international peace and security, and to that end: to take effective collective measures for the prevention and

removal of threats to the peace, and for the suppression of acts of aggression or other breaches of the peace, and to bring about by peaceful means, and in conformity with the principles of justice and international law, adjustment or settlement of international disputes or situations which might lead to a breach of the peace:

2. To develop friendly relations among nations based on respect for the principle of equal rights and self-determination of peoples, and to take other appropriate measures to strengthen universal peace;

3. To achieve international co-operation in solving international problems of an economic, social, cultural, or humanitarian character, and in promoting and encouraging respect for human rights and for fundamental freedoms for all without distinction as to race, sex, language, or religion; and

4. To be a centre for harmonizing the accusations of nations in the attainment of these common ends.

Article 2

The Organization and its Members, in pursuit of the Purposes stated in Article 1, shall act in accordance with the following Principles.

1. The Organization is based on the principle of the sovereign equality of all its Members.

2. All Members, in order to ensure to all of them the rights and benefits resulting from membership, shall fulfil in good faith the obligations assumed by them in accordance with the present Charter.

3. All Members shall settle their international disputes by peaceful means in such a manner that international peace and security, and justice, are not endangered.

4. All Members shall refrain in their international relations from the threat or use of force against the territorial integrity or political independence of any state, or in any manner inconsistent with the Purposes of the United Nations.

5. All Members shall give the United Nations every assistance in any action it takes in accordance with the present Charter, and shall refrain from giving assistance to any state against which the United Nations is taking preventive or enforcement action.

6. The Organization shall ensure that states which are not Members of the United Nations act in accordance with these Principles so far as may be necessary for the maintenance of international peace and security.

7. Nothing contained in the present Charter shall authorize the United Nations to intervene in matters which are essentially within the domestic jurisdiction of any state or shall require the Members to submit such matters to settlement under the present Charter; but this principle shall not prejudice the application of enforcement measures under Chapter VII.

II. MEMBERSHIP

Article 3

The original Members of the United Nations shall be the states which, having participated in the United Nations Conference on International Organization at San Francisco, or having previously signed the Declaration by United Nations of January 1, 1942, sign the present Charter and ratify it in accordance with Article 110.

Article 4

1. Membership in the United Nations is open to all other peace-loving states which accept the obligations contained in the present Charter and, in the judgement of the Organization, are able and willing to carry out these obligations.

2. The admission of any such state to membership in the United Nations will be effected by a decision of the General Assembly upon the recommendation of the Security Council.

Article 5

A member of the United Nations against which preventive or enforcement action has been taken by the Security Council may be suspended from the exercise of the rights and privileges of membership by the General Assembly upon the recommendation of the Security Council. The exercise of these rights and privileges may be restored by the Security Council.

Article 6

A Member of the United Nations which has persistently violated the Principles contained in the present Charter may be expelled from the Organization by the General Assembly upon the recommendation of the Security Council.

III. ORGANS

Article 7

1. There are established as the principal organs of the United Nations: a General Assembly, a Security Council, an Economic and Social Council, a Trusteeship Council, an International Court of Justice, and a Secretariat.

2. Such subsidiary organs as may be found necessary may be established in accordance with the present Charter.

Article 8

The United Nations shall place no restrictions on the eligibility of men and women to participate in any capacity and under conditions of equality in its principal and subsidiary organs.

IV. THE GENERAL ASSEMBLY

Composition

Article 9

1. The General Assembly shall consist of all the Members of the United Nations.

2. Each Member shall have not more than five representatives in the General Assembly.

Functions and Powers

Article 10

The General Assembly may discuss any questions or any matters within the scope of the present Charter or relating to the powers and functions of any organs provided for in the present Charter, and, except as provided in Article 12, may make recommendations to the Members of the United Nations or to the Security Council or to both on any such questions or matters.

Article 11

1. The General Assembly may consider the general principles of co-operation in the maintenance of international peace and security, including the principles governing disarmament and the regulation of armaments, and may make recommendations with regard to such principles to the Members or to the Security Council or to both.

2. The General Assembly may discuss any questions relating to the maintenance of international peace and security brought before it by any Member of the United Nations, or by the Security Council, or by a state which is not a Member of the United Nations in accordance with Article 35, paragraph 2, and, except as provided in Article 12, may make recommendations with regard to any such question to the state or states concerned or to the Security Council or both. Any such question on which action is necessary shall be referred to the Security Council by the General Assembly either before or after discussion.

3. The General Assembly may call the attention of the Security Council to situations which are likely to endanger international peace and security.

4. The powers of the General Assembly set forth in this Article shall not limit the general scope of Article 10.

Article 12

1. While the Security Council is exercising in respect of any dispute or situation the functions assigned to it in the present Charter, the General Assembly shall not make any recommendations with regard to that dispute or situation unless the Security Council so requests.

2. The Secretary-General, with the consent of the Security Council, shall notify the General Assembly at each session of any matters relative to the maintenance of international peace and security which are being dealt with by the Security Council and shall similarly notify the General Assembly, or the Members of the United Nations if the General Assembly is not in session, immediately the Security Council ceases to deal with such matters.

Article 13

1. The General Assembly shall initiate studies and make recommendations for the purpose of:

(a) promoting international co-operation in the political field and encouraging the progressive development of international law and its codification;

(b) promoting international co-operation in the economic, social, cultural, educational, and health fields, and assisting in the realization of human rights and fundamental freedoms for all without distinction as to race, sex, language, or religion.

2. The further responsibilities, functions and powers of the General Assembly with respect to matters mentioned in paragraph 1(b) above are set forth in Chapters IX and X.

Article 14

Subject to the provision of Article 12, the General Assembly may recommend measures for the peaceful adjustment of any situation, regardless of origin, which it deems likely to impair the general welfare or friendly relations among nations, including situations resulting from a violation of the provisions of the present Charter setting forth the Purposes and Principles of the United Nations.

Article 15

1. The General Assembly shall receive and consider annual and special reports from the Security Council; these reports shall include an account of the measures that the Security Council has decided upon or taken to maintain international peace and security.

2. The General Assembly shall receive and consider reports from the other organs of the United Nations.

Article 16

The General Assembly shall perform such functions with respect to the international trusteeship system as are assigned to it under Chapters XII and XIII, including the approval of the trusteeship agreements for areas not designated as strategic.

Article 17

1. The General Assembly shall consider and approve the budget of the Organization.

2. The expenses of the Organization shall be borne by the Members as apportioned by the General Assembly.

3. The General Assembly shall consider and approve any financial and budgetary arrangements with specialized agencies referred to in Article 57 and shall examine the administrative budgets of such specialized agencies with a view to making recommendations to the agencies concerned.

Voting

Article 18

1. Each Member of the General Assembly shall have one vote.

2. Decisions of the General Assembly on important questions shall be made by a two-thirds majority of the members present and voting. These questions shall include: recommendations with respect to the maintenance of international peace and security, the election of the non-permanent Members of the Security Council, the election of the Members of the Economic and Social Council, the election of Members of the Trusteeship Council in accordance with paragraph 1(c) of Article 86, the admission of new Members to the United Nations, the suspension of the rights and privileges of membership, the expulsion of Members, questions relating to the operation of the trusteeship system, and budgetary questions.

3. Decisions on other questions, including the determination of additional categories of questions to be decided by a two-thirds majority, shall be made by a majority of the members present and voting.

Article 19

A Member of the United Nations which is in arrears in the payment of its financial contributions to the Organization shall have no vote in the General Assembly if the amount of its arrears equals or exceeds the amount of the contributions due from it for the preceding two full years. The General Assembly may, nevertheless, permit such a Member to vote if it is satisfied that the failure to pay is due to conditions beyond the control of the Member.

Procedure

Article 20

The General Assembly shall meet in regular annual sessions and in such special sessions as occasion may require. Special sessions shall be convoked by the Secretary-General at the request of the Security Council or of a majority of the members of the United Nations.

Article 21

The General Assembly shall adopt its own rules of procedure. It shall elect its President for each session.

Article 22

The General Assembly may establish such subsidiary organs as it deems necessary for the performance of its functions.

V. THE SECURITY COUNCIL

Composition

Article 23

1. The Security Council shall consist of 11 Members of the United Nations. The Republic of China*, France, the Union of Soviet Socialist Republics†, the United Kingdom of Great Britain and Northern Ireland, and the United States of America shall be permanent members of the Security Council. The General Assembly shall elect six other Members of the United Nations to be non-permanent members of the Security Council, due regard being specially paid, in the first instance to the contribution of Members of the United Nations to the maintenance of international peace and security and to the other purposes of the Organization, and also to equitable geographical distribution.

2. The non-permanent members of the Security Council shall be elected for a term of two years. In the first election of the non-permanent members, however, three shall be chosen for a term of one year. A retiring member shall not be eligible for immediate re-election.

3. Each member of the Security Council shall have one representative.

Functions and Powers

Article 24

1. In order to ensure prompt and effective action by the United Nations, its Members confer on the Security Council primary responsibility for the maintenance of international peace and security, and agree that in carrying out its duties under this responsibility the Security Council acts on their behalf.

2. In discharging these duties the Security Council shall act in accordance with the Purposes and Principles of the United Nations. The specific powers granted to the Security Council for the discharge of these duties are laid down in Chapters VI, VII, VIII and XII.

3. The Security Council shall submit annual and, when necessary, special reports to the General Assembly for its consideration.

Article 25

The Members of the United Nations agree to accept and carry out the decisions of the Security Council in accordance with the present Charter.

Article 26

In order to promote the establishment and maintenance of international peace and security with the least diversion for armaments of the world's human and economic resources, the Security Council shall be responsible for formulating, with the assistance of the Military Staff Committee referred to in Article 47, plans

* From 1971 the Chinese seat in the UN General Assembly and its permanent seat in the Security Council were occupied by the People's Republic of China.

† In December 1991 Russia assumed the former USSR's seat in the UN General Assembly and its permanent seat in the Security Council.

to be submitted to the Members of the United Nations for the establishment of a system for the regulation of armaments.

Voting

Article 27

1. Each member of the Security Council shall have one vote.

2. Decisions of the Security Council on procedural matters shall be made by an affirmative vote of seven members.

3. Decisions of the Security Council on all other matters shall be made by an affirmative vote of seven members including the concurring votes of the permanent members; provided that, in decisions under Chapter VI, and under paragraph 3 of Article 52, a party to a dispute shall abstain from voting.

Procedure

Article 28

1. The Security Council shall be so organized as to be able to function continuously. Each member of the Security Council shall for this purpose be represented at all times at the seat of the Organization.

2. The Security Council shall hold periodic meetings at which each of its members may, if it so desires, be represented by a member of the government or by some other specially designated representative.

3. The Security Council may hold meetings at such places other than the seat of the Organization as in its judgment will best facilitate its work.

Article 29

The Security Council may establish such subsidiary organs as it deems necessary for the performance of its functions.

Article 30

The Security Council shall adopt its own rules of procedure, including the method of selecting its President.

Article 31

Any Member of the United Nations which is not a member of the Security Council may participate, without vote, in the discussion of any question brought before the Security Council whenever the latter considers that the interests of that Member are specially affected.

Article 32

Any Member of the United Nations which is not a member of the Security Council or any state which is not a Member of the United Nations, if it is a party to a dispute under consideration by the Security Council, shall be invited to participate, without vote, in the discussion relating to the dispute. The Security Council shall lay down such conditions as it deems just for the participation of a state which is not a Member of the United Nations.

VI. PACIFIC SETTLEMENT OF DISPUTES

Article 33

1. The parties to any dispute, the continuance of which is likely to endanger the maintenance of international peace and security, shall, first of all, seek a solution by negotiation, enquiry, mediation, conciliation, arbitration, judicial settlement, resort to regional agencies or arrangements, or other peaceful means of their own choice.

2. The Security Council shall, when it deems necessary, call upon the parties to settle their disputes by such means.

Article 34

The Security Council may investigate any dispute, or any situation which might lead to international friction or give rise to a dispute, in order to determine whether the continuance of the dispute or situation is likely to endanger the maintenance of international peace and security.

Article 35

1. Any Member of the United Nations may bring any dispute, or any situation of the nature referred to in Article 34, to the attention of the Security Council or of the General Assembly.

2. A state which is not a Member of the United Nations may bring to the attention of the Security Council or of the General Assembly any dispute to which it is a party if it accepts in advance, for the purposes of the dispute, the obligations of pacific settlement provided in the present Charter.

3. The proceedings of the General Assembly in respect of matters brought to its attention under this Article will be subject to the provisions of Articles 11 and 12.

Article 36

1. The Security Council may, at any stage of a dispute of the nature referred to in Article 33 or of a situation of like nature, recommend appropriate procedures or methods of adjustment.

2. The Security Council should take into consideration any procedures for the settlement of the dispute which have already been adopted by the parties.

3. In making recommendations under this Article the Security Council should also take into consideration that legal disputes should as a general rule be referred by the parties to the International Court of Justice in accordance with the provisions of the statute of the Court.

Article 37

1. Should the parties to a dispute of the nature referred to in Article 33, fail to settle it by the means indicated in that Article, they shall refer it to the Security Council.

2. If the Security Council deems that the continuance of the dispute is in fact likely to endanger the maintenance of international peace and security, it shall decide whether to take action under Article 36 or to recommend such terms of settlement as it may consider appropriate.

Article 38

Without prejudice to the provisions of Articles 33 to 37, the Security Council may, if all the parties to any dispute so request, make recommendations to the parties with a view to a pacific settlement of the dispute.

VII. ACTION WITH RESPECT TO THREATS TO THE PEACE, BREACHES OF THE PEACE, AND ACTS OF AGGRESSION

Article 39

The Security Council shall determine the existence of any threat to the peace, breach of the peace, or act of aggression and shall make recommendations, or decide what measures shall be taken in accordance with Articles 41 and 42, to maintain or restore international peace and security.

Article 40

In order to prevent an aggravation of the situation, the Security Council may, before making the recommendations or deciding upon the measures provided for in Article 39, call upon the parties concerned to comply with such provisional measures as it deems necessary or desirable. Such provisional measures shall be without prejudice to the rights, claims, or position of the parties concerned. The Security Council shall duly take account of failure to comply with such provisional measures.

Article 41

The Security Council may decide what measures not involving the use of armed force are to be employed to give effect to its decisions, and it may call upon the Members of the United Nations to apply such measures. These may include complete or partial interruption of economic relations and of rail, sea, air, postal, telegraphic, radio, and other means of communication, and the severance of diplomatic relations.

Article 42

Should the Security Council consider that measures provided for in Article 41 would be inadequate or have proved to be inadequate, it may take such action by air, sea, or land forces as may be necessary to maintain or restore international peace and security. Such action may include demonstrations, blockade, and other operations by air, sea, or land forces of Members of the United Nations.

Article 43

1. All Members of the United Nations, in order to contribute to the maintenance of international peace and security, undertake to make available to the Security Council, on its call and in accordance with a special agreement or agreements, armed forces, assistance, and facilities, including rights of passage, necessary for the purpose of maintaining international peace and security.

2. Such agreement or agreements shall govern the numbers and types of forces, their degree of readiness and general location, and the nature of the facilities and assistance to be provided.

3. The agreement or agreements shall be negotiated as soon as possible on the initiative of the Security Council. They shall be concluded between the Security Council and Members or between the Security Council and groups of Members and shall be subject to ratification by the signatory states in accordance with their respective constitutional processes.

Article 44

When the Security Council has decided to use force it shall, before calling upon a Member not represented on it to provide armed forces in fulfilment of the obligations assumed under Article 43, invite that Member, if the Member so desires, to participate in the decisions of the Security Council concerning the employment of contingents of that Member's armed forces.

Article 45

In order to enable the United Nations to take urgent military measures, Members shall hold immediately available national air-force contingents for combined international enforcement action. The strength and degree of readiness of these contingents and plans for their combined action shall be determined, within the limits laid down in the special agreement and agreements referred to in Article 43, by the Security Council with the assistance of the Military Staff Committee.

Article 46

Plans for the application of armed force shall be made by the Security Council with the assistance of the Military Staff Committee.

Article 47

1. There shall be established a Military Staff Committee to advise and assist the Security Council on all questions relating to the Security Council's military requirements for the maintenance of international peace and security, the employment and command of forces placed at its disposal, the regulation of armaments, and possible disarmament.

2. The Military Staff Committee shall consist of the Chiefs of Staff of the permanent members of the Security Council or their representatives. Any Member of the United Nations not permanently represented on the Committee shall be invited by the Committee to be associated with it when the efficient discharge of the Committee's responsibilities requires the participation of that Member in its work.

3. The Military Staff Committee shall be responsible under the Security Council for the strategic direction of any armed forces placed at the disposal of the Security Council. Questions relating to the command of such forces shall be worked out subsequently.

4. The Military Staff Committee, with the authorization of the Security Council and after consultation with appropriate regional agencies, may establish regional sub-committees.

Article 48

1. The action required to carry out the decisions of the Security Council for the maintenance of international peace and security shall be taken by all the Members of the United Nations or by some of them, as the Security Council may determine.

2. Such decisions shall be carried out by the Members of the United Nations directly and through their action in the appropriate international agencies of which they are members.

Article 49

The Members of the United Nations shall join in affording mutual assistance in carrying out the measures decided upon by the Security Council.

Article 50

If preventive or enforcement measures against any state are taken by the Security Council, any other state, whether a Member of the United Nations or not, which finds itself confronted with special economic problems arising from the carrying out of those measures shall have the right to consult the Security Council with regard to a solution of those problems.

Article 51

Nothing in the present Charter shall impair the inherent right of individual or collective self-defence if an armed attack occurs against a Member of the United Nations, until the Security Council has taken measures necessary to maintain international peace and security. Measures taken by Members in the exercise of this right of self-defence shall be immediately reported to the Security Council and shall not in any way affect the authority and responsibility of the Security Council under the present Charter to take at any time such action as it deems necessary in order to maintain or restore international peace and security.

VIII. REGIONAL ARRANGEMENTS

Article 52

1. Nothing in the present Charter precludes the existence of regional arrangements or agencies for dealing with such matters relating to the maintenance of international peace and security as are appropriate for regional action, provided that such arrangements or agencies and their activities are consistent with the Purposes and Principles of the United Nations.

2. The Members of the United Nations entering into such arrangements or constituting such agencies shall make every effort to achieve pacific settlement of local disputes through such regional agencies before referring them to the Security Council.

3. The Security Council shall encourage the development of pacific settlement of local disputes through such regional arrangements or by such regional agencies either on the initiative of the states concerned or by reference from the Security Council.

4. This Article in no way impairs the application of Articles 34 and 35.

Article 53

1. The Security Council shall, where appropriate, utilize such regional arrangements or agencies for enforcement action under its authority. But no enforcement action shall be taken under regional arrangements or by regional agencies without the authorization of the Security Council, with the exception of measures against any enemy state, as defined in paragraph 2 of this Article, provided for pursuant to Article 107 or in regional arrangements directed against renewal of aggressive policy on the part of any such state, until such time as the Organization may, on request of the Governments concerned, be charged with the responsibility for preventing further aggression by such a state.

2. The term enemy state as used in paragraph 1 of this Article applies to any state which during the Second World War has been an enemy of any signatory of the present Charter.

Article 54

The Security Council shall at all times be kept fully informed of activities undertaken or in contemplation under regional arrangements or by regional agencies for the maintenance of international peace and security.

IX. INTERNATIONAL ECONOMIC AND SOCIAL CO-OPERATION

Article 55

With a view to the creation of conditions of stability and well-being which are necessary for peaceful and friendly relations among nations based on respect for the principle of equal rights and self-determination of peoples, the United Nations shall promote:

(a) higher standards of living, full employment, and conditions of economic and social progress and development;

(b) solutions of international economic, social, health, and related problems; and international cultural and educational co-operation; and

(c) universal respect for, and observance of, human rights and fundamental freedoms for all without distinction as to race, sex, language, or religion.

Article 56

All Members pledge themselves to take joint and separate action in co-operation with the Organization for the achievement of the purposes set forth in Article 55.

Article 57

1. The various specialized agencies, established by intergovernmental agreement and having wide international responsibilities, as defined in their basic instruments, in economic, social, cultural, educational, health, and related fields, shall be brought into relationship with the United Nations in accordance with the provisions of Article 63.

2. Such agencies thus brought into relationship with the United Nations are hereinafter referred to as specialized agencies.

Article 58

The Organization shall make recommendations for the co-ordination of the policies and activities of the specialized agencies.

Article 59

The Organization shall, where appropriate, initiate negotiations among the states concerned for the creation of any new specialized agencies required for the accomplishment of the purposes set forth in Article 55.

Article 60

Responsibility for the discharge of the functions of the Organization set forth in this Chapter shall be vested in the General Assembly and, under the authority of the General Assembly, in the Economic and Social Council, which shall have for this purpose the powers set forth in Chapter X.

X. THE ECONOMIC AND SOCIAL COUNCIL

Composition

Article 61

1. The Economic and Social Council shall consist of 18 Members of the United Nations elected by the General Assembly.

2. Subject to the provisions of paragraph 3, six members of the Economic and Social Council shall be elected each year for a term of three years. A retiring member shall be eligible for immediate re-election.

3. At the first election, 18 members of the Economic and Social Council shall be chosen. The term of office of six members so chosen shall expire at the end of one year, and of six other members at the end of two years, in accordance with arrangements made by the General Assembly.

4. Each member of the Economic and Social Council shall have one representative.

Functions and Powers

Article 62

1. The Economic and Social Council may make or initiate studies and reports with respect to international economic, social, cultural, educational, health, and related matters and may make recommendations with respect to any such matters to the General Assembly, to the Members of the United Nations, and to the specialized agencies concerned.

2. It may make recommendations for the purpose of promoting respect for, and observance of, human rights and fundamental freedoms for all.

3. It may prepare draft conventions for submission to the General Assembly, with respect to matters falling within its competence.

4. It may call, in accordance with the rules prescribed by the United Nations, international conferences on matters falling within its competence.

Article 63

1. The Economic and Social Council may enter into agreements with any of the agencies referred to in Article 57, defining the terms on which the agency concerned shall be brought into relationship with the United Nations. Such agreements shall be subject to approval by the General Assembly.

2. It may co-ordinate the activities of the specialized agencies through consultation with and recommendations to such agencies and through recommendations to the General Assembly and to the Members of the United Nations.

Article 64

1. The Economic and Social Council may take appropriate steps to obtain regular reports from the specialized agencies. It may make arrangements with the Members of the United Nations and with specialized agencies to obtain reports on the steps taken to give effect to its own recommendations and to recommendations on matters falling within its competence made by the General Assembly.

2. It may communicate its observations on these reports to the General Assembly.

Article 65

The Economic and Social Council may furnish information to the Security Council and shall assist the Security Council upon its request.

Article 66

1. The Economic and Social Council shall perform such functions as fall within its competence in connection with the carrying out of the recommendations of the General Assembly.

2. It may, with the approval of the General Assembly, perform services at the request of Members of the United Nations and at the request of specialized agencies.

3. It shall perform such other functions as are specified elsewhere in the present Charter or as may be assigned to it by the General Assembly.

Voting

Article 67

1. Each member of the Economic and Social Council shall have one vote.

2. Decisions of the Economic and Social Council shall be made by a majority of the members present and voting.

Procedure

Article 68

The Economic and Social Council shall set up commissions in economic and social fields and for the promotion of human rights, and such other commissions as may be required for the performance of its functions.

Article 69

The Economic and Social Council shall invite any Member of the United Nations to participate, without vote, in its deliberations on any matter of particular concern to that Member.

Article 70

The Economic and Social Council may make arrangements for representatives of the specialized agencies to participate, without vote, in its deliberations and in those of the commissions established by it, and for its representatives to participate in the deliberations of the specialized agencies.

Article 71

The Economic and Social Council may make suitable arrangements for consultation with non-governmental organizations which are concerned with matters within its competence. Such arrangements may be made with international organizations and, where appropriate, with national organizations after consultation with the Member of the United Nations concerned.

Article 72

1. The Economic and Social Council shall adopt its own rules of procedure, including the method of selecting its President.

2. The Economic and Social Council shall meet as required in accordance with its rules, which shall include provision for the convening of meetings on the request of a majority of its members.

XI. NON-SELF-GOVERNING TERRITORIES

Article 73

Members of the United Nations which have or assume responsibilities for the administration of territories whose peoples have not yet attained a full measure of self-government recognize the principle that the interests of the inhabitants of these territories are paramount, and accept as a sacred trust the obligation to promote to the utmost, within the system of international peace and security established by the present Charter, the well-being of the inhabitants of these territories, and, to this end:

(a) to ensure, with due respect for the culture of the peoples concerned, their political, economic, social, and educational advancement, their just treatment, and their protection against abuses;

(b) to develop self-government, to take due account of the political aspirations of the peoples, and to assist them in the progressive development of their free political institutions, according to the particular circumstances of each territory and its peoples and their varying stages of advancement;

(c) to further international peace and security;

(d) to promote constructive measures of development, to encourage research, and to co-operate with one another and, when and where appropriate, with specialized international bodies with a view to the practical achievement of the social, economic, and scientific purposes set forth in this Article; and

(e) to transmit regularly to the Secretary-General for information purposes, subject to such limitations as security and constitutional considerations may require, statistical and other information, of a technical nature relating to economic, social, and educational conditions in the territories for which they are respectively responsible other than those territories to which Chapters XII and XIII apply.

Article 74

Members of the United Nations also agree that their policy in respect of the territories to which this Chapter applies, no less than in respect of their metropolitan areas, must be based on the general principles of good-neighbourliness, due account being taken of the interests and well-being of the rest of the world, in social, economic, and commercial matters.

XII. INTERNATIONAL TRUSTEESHIP SYSTEM

Article 75

The United Nations shall establish under its authority an international trusteeship system for the administration and supervision of such territories as may be placed thereunder by subsequent individual agreements. These territories are hereinafter referred to as trust territories.

Article 76

The basic objectives of the trusteeship system, in accordance with the Purposes of the United Nations laid down in Article 1 of the present Charter, shall be:

(a) to further international peace and security;

(b) to promote the political, economic, social, and educational advancement of the inhabitants of the trust territories, and their progressive development towards self-government or independence as may be appropriate to the particular circumstances of each territory and its peoples and the freely expressed wishes of the peoples concerned, and as may be provided by the terms of each trusteeship agreement;

(c) to encourage respect for human rights and for fundamental freedoms for all without distinction as to race, sex, language, or religion, and to encourage recognition of the interdependence of the peoples of the world; and

(d) to ensure equal treatment in social, economic, and commercial matters for all Members of the United Nations and their nationals, and also equal treatment for the latter in the administration of justice, without prejudice to the attainment of the foregoing objectives and subject to the provisions of Article 80.

Article 77

1. The trusteeship system shall apply to such territories in the following categories as may be placed thereunder by means of trusteeship agreements.

(a) territories now held under mandate;

(b) territories which may be detached from enemy states as a result of the Second World War; and

(c) territories voluntarily placed under the system by states responsible for their administration.

2. It will be a matter for subsequent agreement as to which territories in the foregoing categories will be brought under the trusteeship system and upon what terms.

Article 78

The trusteeship system shall not apply to territories which have become Members of the United Nations, relationship among which shall be based on respect for the principle of sovereign equality.

Article 79

The terms of trusteeship for each territory to be placed under the trusteeship system, including any alteration or amendment, shall be agreed upon by the states directly concerned, including the mandatory power in the case of territories held under mandate by a Member of the United Nations, and shall be approved as provided for in Articles 83 and 85.

Article 80

1. Except as may be agreed upon in individual trusteeship agreements, made under Articles 77, 79, and 81, placing each territory under the trusteeship system, and until such agreements have been concluded, nothing in this Chapter shall be construed in or of itself to alter in any manner the rights whatsoever of any states or any peoples or the terms of existing international instruments to which Members of the United Nations may respectively be parties.

2. Paragraph 1 of this Article shall not be interpreted as giving grounds for delay or postponement of the negotiation and conclusion of agreements for placing mandated and other territories under the trusteeship system as provided for in Article 77.

Article 81

The trusteeship agreement shall in each case include the terms under which the trust territory will be administered and designate the authority which will exercise the administration of the trust territory. Such authority, hereinafter called the administering authority, may be one or more states or the Organization itself.

Article 82

There may be designated, in any trusteeship agreement, a strategic area or areas which may include part or all of the trust territory to which the agreement applies, without prejudice to any special agreement or agreements made under Article 43.

Article 83

1. All functions of the United Nations relating to strategic areas, including the approval of the terms of the trusteeship agreements and of their alteration or amendment, shall be exercised by the Security Council.

2. The basic objectives set forth in Article 76 shall be applicable to the people of each strategic area.

3. The Security Council shall, subject to the provisions of the trusteeship agreements and without prejudice to security considerations, avail itself of the assistance of the Trusteeship Council to perform those functions of the United Nations under the trusteeship system relating to political, economic, social, and educational matters in the strategic areas.

Article 84

It shall be the duty of the administering authority to ensure that the trust territory shall play its part in the maintenance of international peace and security. To this end the administering authority may make use of volunteer forces, facilities, and assistance from the trust territory in carrying out the obligations towards the Security Council undertaken in this regard by the administering authority, as well as for local defence and the maintenance of law and order within the trust territory.

Article 85

1. The functions of the United Nations with regard to trusteeship agreements for all areas not designated as strategic, including

the approval of the terms of the trusteeship agreements and of their alteration or amendment, shall be exercised by the General Assembly.

2. The Trusteeship Council, operating under the authority of the General Assembly, shall assist the General Assembly in carrying out these functions.

XIII. THE TRUSTEESHIP COUNCIL*

Composition

Article 86

1. The Trusteeship Council shall consist of the following Members of the United Nations:

(a) those Members administering trust territories:

(b) such of those Members mentioned by name in Article 23 as are not administering trust territories; and

(c) as many other Members elected for three-year terms by the General Assembly as may be necessary to ensure that the total number of members of the Trusteeship Council is equally divided between those Members of the United Nations which administer trust territories and those which do not.

2. Each member of the Trusteeship Council shall designate one specially qualified person to represent it therein.

Functions and Powers

Article 87

The General Assembly and, under its authority, the Trusteeship Council, in carrying out their functions, may:

(a) consider reports submitted by the administering authority;

(b) accept petitions and examine them in consultation with the administering authority;

(c) provide for periodic visits to the respective trust territories at times agreed upon with the administering authority; and

(d) take these and other actions in conformity with the terms of the trusteeship agreements.

Article 88

The Trusteeship Council shall formulate a questionnaire on the political, economic, social, and educational advancement of the inhabitants of each trust territory, and the administering authority for each trust territory within the competence of the General Assembly shall make an annual report to the General Assembly upon the basis of such questionnaire.

Voting

Article 89

1. Each member of the Trusteeship Council shall have one vote.

2. Decisions of the Trusteeship Council shall be made by a majority of the members present and voting.

Procedure

Article 90

1. The Trusteeship Council shall adopt its own rules of procedure, including the method of selecting its President.

2. The Trusteeship Council shall meet as required in accordance with its rules, which shall include provision for the convening of meetings on the request of a majority of its members.

Article 91

The Trusteeship Council shall, when appropriate, avail itself of the assistance of the Economic and Social Council and of the specialized agencies in regard to matters with which they are respectively concerned.

* On 1 October 1994 the Republic of Palau, the last remaining territory under UN trusteeship, became independent. The Trusteeship Council formally suspended operations on 1 November; subsequently it was to be convened, as required, on an extraordinary basis.

XIV. THE INTERNATIONAL COURT OF JUSTICE

Article 92

The International Court of Justice shall be the principal judicial organ of the United Nations. It shall function in accordance with the annexed Statute, which is based upon the Statute of the Permanent Court of International Justice and forms an integral part of the present Charter.

Article 93

1. All Members of the United Nations are *ipso facto* parties to the Statute of the International Court of Justice.

2. A state which is not a Member of the United Nations may become a party to the Statute of the International Court of Justice on condition to be determined in each case by the General Assembly upon the recommendation of the Security Council.

Article 94

1. Each Member of the United Nations undertakes to comply with the decision of the International Court of Justice in any case to which it is a party.

2. If any party to a case fails to perform the obligations incumbent upon it under a judgment rendered by the Court, the other party may have recourse to the Security Council, which may, if it deems necessary, make recommendations or decide upon measures to be taken to give effect to the judgment.

Article 95

Nothing in the present Charter shall prevent Members of the United Nations from entrusting the solution of their differences to other tribunals by virtue of agreements already in existence or which may be concluded in the future.

Article 96

1. The General Assembly or the Security Council may request the International Court of Justice to give an advisory opinion on any legal question.

2. Other organs of the United Nations and specialized agencies, which may at any time be so authorized by the General Assembly, may also request advisory opinions of the Court on legal questions arising within the scope of their activities.

XV. THE SECRETARIAT

Article 97

The Secretariat shall comprise a Secretary-General and such staff as the Organization may require. The Secretary-General shall be appointed by the General Assembly upon the recommendation of the Security Council. He shall be the chief administrative officer of the Organization.

Article 98

The Secretary-General shall act in that capacity in all meetings of the General Assembly, of the Security Council, of the Economic and Social Council, and of the Trusteeship Council, and shall perform such other functions as are entrusted to him by these organs. The Secretary-General shall make an annual report to the General Assembly on the work of the Organization.

Article 99

The Secretary-General may bring to the attention of the Security Council any matter which in his opinion may threaten the maintenance of international peace and security.

Article 100

1. In the performance of their duties the Secretary-General and the staff shall not seek or receive instructions from any government or from any other authority external to the Organization. They shall refrain from any action which might reflect on their position as international officials responsible only to the Organization.

2. Each Member of the United Nations undertakes to respect the exclusively international character of the responsibilities of the Secretary-General and the staff and not to seek to influence them in the discharge of their responsibilities.

Article 101

1. The staff shall be appointed by the Secretary-General under regulations established by the General Assembly.

2. Appropriate staffs shall be permanently assigned to the Economic and Social Council, the Trusteeship Council, and, as required, to other organs of the United Nations. These staffs shall form a part of the Secretariat.

3. The paramount consideration in the employment of the staff and in the determination of the conditions of service shall be the necessity of securing the highest standards of efficiency, competence, and integrity. Due regard shall be paid to the importance of recruiting the staff on as wide a geographical basis as possible.

XVI. MISCELLANEOUS PROVISIONS

Article 102

1. Every treaty and every international agreement entered into by any Member of the United Nations after the present Charter comes into force shall as soon as possible be registered with the Secretariat and published by it.

2. No party to any such treaty or international agreement which has not been registered in accordance with the provisions of paragraph 1 of this Article may invoke that treaty or agreement before any organ of the United Nations.

Article 103

In the event of a conflict between the obligations of the Members of the United Nations under the present Charter and their obligations under any other international agreement, their obligations under the present Charter shall prevail.

Article 104

The Organization shall enjoy in the territory of each of its Members such legal capacity as may be necessary for the exercise of its functions and the fulfilment of its purposes.

Article 105

1. The Organization shall enjoy in the territory of each of its Members such privileges and immunities as are necessary for the fulfilment of its purposes.

2. Representatives of the Members of the United Nations and officials of the Organization shall similarly enjoy such privileges and immunities as are necessary for the independent exercise of their functions in connection with the Organization.

3. The General Assembly may make recommendations with a view to determining the details of the application of paragraphs 1 and 2 of this Article or may propose conventions to the Members of the United Nations for this purpose.

XVII. TRANSITIONAL SECURITY ARRANGEMENTS

Article 106

Pending the coming into force of such special agreements referred to in Article 43 as in the opinion of the Security Council enable it to begin the exercise of its responsibilities under Article 42, the parties to the Four-Nation Declaration signed at Moscow, October 30, 1943, and France, shall, in accordance with the provisions of paragraph 5 of that Declaration, consult with one another and as occasion requires with other Members of the United Nations with a view to such joint action on behalf of the Organization as may be necessary for the purpose of maintaining international peace and security.

Article 107

Nothing in the present Charter shall invalidate or preclude action, in relation to any state which during the Second World War has been an enemy of any signatory to the present Charter, taken or authorized as a result of that war by the Governments having responsibility for such action.

XVIII. AMENDMENTS

Article 108

Amendments to the present Charter shall come into force for all Members of the United Nations when they have been adopted by a vote of two-thirds of the members of the General Assembly and ratified in accordance with their respective constitutional processes by two-thirds of the Members of the United Nations, including all the permanent members of the Security Council.

Article 109

1. A General Conference of the Members of the United Nations for the purpose of reviewing the present Charter may be held at a date and place to be fixed by a two-thirds vote of the members of the General Assembly and by a vote of any seven members of the Security Council. Each Member of the United Nations shall have one vote in the conference.

2. Any alteration of the present Charter recommended by a two-thirds vote of the conference shall take effect when ratified in accordance with their respective constitutional processes by two-thirds of the Members of the United Nations including all the permanent members of the Security Council.

3. If such a conference has not been held before the tenth annual session of the General Assembly following the coming into force of the present Charter, the proposal to call such a conference shall be placed on the agenda of that session of the General Assembly, and the conference shall be held if so decided by a majority vote of the members of the General Assembly and by a vote of any seven members of the Security Council.

XIX. RATIFICATION AND SIGNATURE

Article 110

1. The present Charter shall be ratified by the signatory states in accordance with their respective constitutional processes.

2. The ratifications shall be deposited with the Government of the United States of America, which shall notify all the signatory states of each deposit as well as the Secretary-General of the Organization when he has been appointed.

3. The present Charter shall come into force upon the deposit of ratifications by the Republic of China, France, the Union of Soviet Socialist Republics, the United Kingdom of Great Britain and Northern Ireland, and the United States of America, and by a majority of the other signatory states. A protocol of the ratifications deposited shall thereupon be drawn up by the Government of the United States of America which shall communicate copies thereof to all the signatory states.

4. The states signatory to the present Charter which ratify it after it has come into force will become original Members of the United Nations on the date of the deposit of their respective ratifications.

Article 111

The present Charter, of which the Chinese, French, Russian, English, and Spanish texts are equally authentic, shall remain deposited in the archives of the Government of the United States of America. Duly certified copies thereof shall be transmitted by that Government to the Governments of the other signatory states.

IN FAITH WHEREOF the representatives of the Governments of the United Nations have signed the present Charter.

DONE at the city of San Francisco the twenty-sixth day of June, one thousand nine hundred and forty-five.

Amendments

The following amendments to Articles 23 and 27 of the Charter came into force in August 1965.

Article 23

1. The Security Council shall consist of 15 Members of the United Nations. The Republic of China, France, the Union of Soviet Socialist Republics, the United Kingdom of Great Britain and Northern Ireland, and the United States of America shall be permanent members of the Security Council. The General Assembly shall elect 10 other Members of the United Nations to be non-permanent members of the Security Council, due regard being specially paid, in the first instance to the contribution of Members of the United Nations to the maintenance of international peace and security and to the other purposes of the Organization, and also to equitable geographical distribution.

2. The non-permanent members of the Security Council shall be elected for a term of two years. In the first election of the non-permanent members after the increase of the membership of the Security Council from 11 to 15, two of the four additional members shall be chosen for a term of one year. A retiring member shall not be eligible for immediate re-election.

3. Each member of the Security Council shall have one representative.

Article 27

1. Each member of the Security Council shall have one vote.

2. Decisions of the Security Council on procedural matters shall be made by an affirmative vote of nine members.

3. Decisions of the Security Council on all other matters shall be made by an affirmative vote of nine members including the concurring votes of the permanent members; provided that, in decisions under Chapter VI and under paragraph 3 of Article 52, a party to a dispute shall abstain from voting.

The following amendments to Article 61 of the Charter came into force in September 1973.

Article 61

1. The Economic and Social Council shall consist of 54 Members of the United Nations elected by the General Assembly.

2. Subject to the provisions of paragraph 3, 18 members of the Economic and Social Council shall be elected each year for a term of three years. A retiring member shall be eligible for immediate re-election.

3. At the first election after the increase in the membership of the Economic and Social Council from 27 to 54 members, in addition to the members elected in place of the nine members whose term of office expires at the end of that year, 27 additional members shall be elected. Of these 27 additional members, the term of office of nine members so elected shall expire at the end of one year, and of nine other members at the end of two years, in accordance with arrangements made by the General Assembly.

4. Each member of the Economic and Social Council shall have one representative.

The following amendment to Paragraph 1 of Article 109 of the Charter came into force in June 1968.

Article 109

1. A General Conference of the Members of the United Nations for the purpose of reviewing the present Charter may be held at a date and place to be fixed by a two-thirds vote of the members of the General Assembly and by a vote of any nine members of the Security Council. Each Member of the United Nations shall have one vote in the conference.

Universal Declaration of Human Rights

(Adopted 10 December 1948)

Whereas recognition of the inherent dignity and of the equal and inalienable rights of all members of the human family is the foundation of freedom, justice and peace in the world,

Whereas disregard and contempt for human rights have resulted in barbarous acts which have outraged the conscience of mankind, and the advent of a world in which human beings shall enjoy freedom of speech and belief and freedom from fear and want has been proclaimed as the highest aspiration of the common people,

Whereas it is essential, if man is not to be compelled to have recourse, as a last resort, to rebellion against tyranny and oppression, that human rights should be protected by the rule of law,

Whereas it is essential to promote the development of friendly relations between nations,

Whereas the peoples of the United Nations have in the Charter reaffirmed their faith in fundamental human rights, in the dignity and worth of the human person and in the equal rights of men and women and have determined to promote social progress and better standards of life in larger freedom,

Whereas Member States have pledged themselves to achieve, in co-operation with the United Nations, the promotion of universal respect for and observance of human rights and fundamental freedoms,

Whereas a common understanding of these rights and freedoms is of the greatest importance for the full realization of this pledge,

Now, therefore,

The General Assembly

Proclaims this Universal Declaration of Human Rights as a common standard of achievement for all peoples and all nations, to the end that every individual and every organ of society, keeping this Declaration constantly in mind, shall strive by teaching and education to promote respect for these rights and freedoms and by progressive measures, national and international, to secure their universal and effective recognition and observance, both among the peoples of Member States themselves and among the peoples of territories under their jurisdiction.

Article 1

All human beings are born free and equal in dignity and rights. They are endowed with reason and conscience and should act towards one another in a spirit of brotherhood.

Article 2

Everyone is entitled to all the rights and freedoms set forth in this Declaration, without distinction of any kind, such as race, colour, sex, language, religion, political or other opinion, national or social origin, property, birth or other status.

Furthermore, no distinction shall be made on the basis of the political, jurisdictional or international status of the country or territory to which a person belongs, whether it be independent, trust, non-self-governing or under any other limitation of sovereignty.

Article 3

Everyone has the right to life, liberty and security of person.

Article 4

No one shall be held in slavery or servitude; slavery and the slave trade shall be prohibited in all their forms.

Article 5

No one shall be subjected to torture or to cruel, inhuman or degrading treatment or punishment.

Article 6

Everyone has the right to recognition everywhere as a person before the law.

Article 7

All are equal before the law and are entitled without any discrimination to equal protection of the law. All are entitled to equal protection against any discrimination in violation of this Declaration and against any incitement to such discrimination.

Article 8

Everyone has the right to an effective remedy by the competent national tribunals for acts violating the fundamental rights granted him by the constitution or by law.

Article 9

No one shall be subjected to arbitrary arrest, detention or exile.

Article 10

Everyone is entitled in full equality to a fair and public hearing by an independent and impartial tribunal, in a determination of his rights and obligations and of any criminal charge against him.

Article 11

1. Everyone charged with a penal offence has the right to be presumed innocent until proved guilty according to law in a public trial at which he has had all the guarantees necessary for his defence.

2. No one shall be held guilty of any penal offence on account of any act or omission which did not constitute a penal offence, under national or international law, at the time when it was committed. Nor shall a heavier penalty be imposed than the one that was applicable at the time the penal offence was committed.

Article 12

No one shall be subjected to arbitrary interference with his privacy, family, home or correspondence, nor to attacks upon his honour and reputation. Everyone has the right to the protection of the law against such interference or attacks.

Article 13

1. Everyone has the right to freedom of movement and residence within the borders of each state.
2. Everyone has the right to leave any country, including his own, and to return to his country.

Article 14

1. Everyone has the right to seek and to enjoy in other countries asylum from persecution.
2. This right may not be invoked in the case of prosecutions genuinely arising from non-political crimes or from acts contrary to the purposes and principles of the United Nations.

Article 15

1. Everyone has the right to a nationality.
2. No one shall be arbitrarily deprived of his nationality nor denied the right to change his nationality.

Article 16

1. Men and women of full age, without any limitation due to race, nationality or religion, have the right to marry and to found a family. They are entitled to equal rights as to marriage, during marriage and at its dissolution.
2. Marriage shall be entered into only with the free and full consent of the intending spouses.
3. The family is the natural and fundamental group unit of society and is entitled to protection by society and the State.

Article 17

1. Everyone has the right to own property alone as well as in association with others.
2. No one shall be arbitrarily deprived of his property.

Article 18

Everyone has the right to freedom of thought, conscience and religion; this right includes freedom to change his religion or belief, and freedom, either alone or in community with others and in public or private, to manifest his religion or belief in teaching, practice, worship and observance.

Article 19

Everyone has the right to freedom of opinion and expression; this right includes freedom to hold opinions without interference and to seek, receive and impart information and ideas through any media and regardless of frontiers.

Article 20

1. Everyone has the right to freedom of peaceful assembly and association.
2. No one may be compelled to belong to an association.

Article 21

1. Everyone has the right to take part in the government of his country, directly or through freely chosen repesentatives.
2. Everyone has the right of equal access to public service in his country.
3. The will of the people shall be the basis of the authority of government; this will shall be expressed in periodic and genuine elections which shall be by universal and equal suffrage and shall be held by secret vote or by equivalent free voting procedures.

Article 22

Everyone, as a member of society, has the right to social security and is entitled to realization, through national effort and international co-operation and in accordance with the organization and resources of each State, of the economic, social and cultural rights indispensable for his dignity and the free development of his personality.

Article 23

1. Everyone has the right to work, to free choice of employment, to just and favourable conditions of work and to protection against unemployment.
2. Everyone, without any discrimination, has the right to equal pay for equal work.
3. Everyone who works has the right to just and favourable remuneration ensuring for himself and his family an existence worthy of human dignity, and supplemented, if necessary, by other means of social protection.
4. Everyone has the right to form and to join trade unions for the protection of his interests.

Article 24

Everyone has the right to rest and leisure, including reasonable limitation of working hours and periodic holidays with pay.

Article 25

1. Everyone has the right to a standard of living adequate for the health and well-being of himself and of his family, including food, clothing, housing and medical care and necessary social services, and the right to security in the event of unemployment, sickness, disability, widowhood, old age or other lack of livelihood in circumstances beyond his control.
2. Motherhood and childhood are entitled to special care and assistance. All children, whether born in or out of wedlock, shall enjoy the same social protection.

Article 26

1. Everyone has the right to education. Education shall be free, at least in the elementary and fundamental stages. Elementary education shall be compulsory. Technical and professional education shall be made generally available and higher education shall be equally accessible to all on the basis of merit.
2. Education shall be directed to the full development of the human personality and to the strengthening of respect for human rights and fundamental freedoms. It shall promote understanding, tolerance and friendship among all nations, racial or religious groups, and shall further the activities of the United Nations for the maintenance of peace.
3. Parents have a prior right to choose the kind of education that shall be given to their children.

Article 27

1. Everyone has the right freely to participate in the cultural life of the community, to enjoy the arts and to share in scientific advancement and its benefits.
2. Everyone has the right to the protection of the moral and material interests resulting from any scientific, literary or artistic production of which he is the author.

Article 28

Everyone is entitled to a social and international order in which the rights and freedoms set forth in this Declaration can be fully realized.

Article 29

1. Everyone has duties to the community in which alone the free and full development of his personality is possible.
2. In the exercise of his rights and freedoms, everyone shall be subject only to such limitations as are determined by law solely for the purpose of securing due recognition and respect for the rights and freedoms of others and of meeting the just requirements of morality, public order and the general welfare in a democratic society.
3. These rights and freedoms may in no case be exercised contrary to the purposes and principles of the United Nations.

Article 30

Nothing in this Declaration may be interpreted as implying for any State, group or person any right to engage in any activity or to perform any act aimed at the destruction of any of the rights and freedoms set forth herein.

UNITED NATIONS REGIONAL COMMISSIONS

Economic Commission for Europe—ECE

Address: Palais des Nations, 1211 Geneva 10, Switzerland.

Telephone: (22) 9174444; **fax:** (22) 9170505; **e-mail:** info .ece@unece.org; **internet:** www.unece.org.

The UN Economic Commission for Europe was established in 1947. It provides a regional forum for governments from European countries, the USA, Canada, Israel and central Asian republics to study the economic, environmental and technological problems of the region and to recommend courses of action. ECE is also active in the formulation of international legal instruments and the setting of international norms and standards.

MEMBERS

Albania	Liechtenstein
Andorra	Lithuania
Armenia	Luxembourg
Austria	Macedonia, former Yugoslav republic
Azerbaijan	Malta
Belarus	Moldova
Belgium	Monaco
Bosnia and Herzegovina	Netherlands
Bulgaria	Norway
Canada	Poland
Croatia	Portugal
Cyprus	Romania
Czech Republic	Russia
Denmark	San Marino
Estonia	Slovakia
Finland	Slovenia
France	Spain
Georgia	Sweden
Germany	Switzerland
Greece	Tajikistan
Hungary	Turkey
Iceland	Turkmenistan
Ireland	Ukraine
Israel	United Kingdom
Italy	USA
Kazakhstan	Uzbekistan
Kyrgyzstan	Yugoslavia
Latvia	

Organization

(March 2002)

COMMISSION

ECE, with ECAFE (now ESCAP), was the earliest of the five regional economic commissions set up by the UN Economic and Social Council. The Commission holds an annual plenary session and several informal sessions, and meetings of subsidiary bodies are convened throughout the year.

Chairman (2002): KÁLMÁN PETÖCZ (Slovakia).

SECRETARIAT

The secretariat services the meetings of the Commission and its subsidiary bodies and publishes periodic surveys and reviews, including a number of specialized statistical bulletins on timber, housing, building, and transport (see list of publications below). It maintains close and regular liaison with the United Nations Secretariat in New York, with the secretariats of the other UN regional commissions and of other UN organizations, including the UN Specialized Agencies, and with other intergovernmental organizations. The Executive Secretary also carries out secretarial functions for the Executive Body of the 1979 Convention on Long-range Transboundary Air Pollution and its protocols. The ECE and UN Secretariats also service the ECOSOC Committee of Experts on the Transport of Dangerous Goods.

Executive Secretary: BRIGITA SCHMÖGNEROVÁ (Slovakia).

Activities

The guiding principle of ECE activities is the promotion of sustainable development. Within this framework, ECE's main objectives are to provide assistance to countries of central and eastern Europe in their transition from centrally-planned to market economies and to achieve the integration of all members into the European and global economies. Environmental protection, transport, statistics, trade facilitation and economic analysis are all principal topics in the ECE work programme, which also includes activities in the fields of timber, energy, trade, industry, and human settlements.

The 52nd plenary session of the ECE, held in April 1997, introduced a programme of reform, reducing the number of principal subsidiary bodies from 14 to seven, in order to concentrate resources on the core areas of work listed below, assisted by sub-committees and groups of experts. The Commission also determined to strengthen economic co-operation within Europe and to enhance co-operation and dialogue with other sub-regional organizations.

Committee on Environmental Policy: Provides policy direction for the ECE region and promotes co-operation among member governments in developing and implementing policies for environmental protection, rational use of natural resources, and sustainable development; supports the integration of environmental policy into sectoral policies; seeks solutions to environmental problems, particularly those of a transboundary nature; assists in strengthening environmental management capabilities, particularly in countries in transition; prepares ministerial conferences (normally held every four years—2003: Kiev, Ukraine); develops and promotes the implementation of international agreements on the environment; and assesses national policies and legislation.

Committee on Human Settlements: Reviews trends and policies in the field of human settlements; undertakes studies and organizes seminars; promotes international co-operation in the field of housing and urban and regional research; assists the countries of central and eastern Europe, which are currently in the process of economic transition, in reformulating their policies relating to housing, land management, sustainable human settlements, and planning and development.

Committee on Sustainable Energy: Exchanges information on general energy problems; work programme comprises activities including labelling classification systems and related legal and policy frameworks; liberalization of energy markets, pricing policies and supply security; development of regional sustainable energy strategies for the 21st century; rational use of energy, efficiency and conservation; energy infrastructure including interconnection of electric power and gas networks; coal and thermal power generation in the context of sustainable energy development; Energy Efficiency project; promotion and development of a market-based Gas Industry in Economics in Transition—Gas Centre project; and technical assistance and operational activities in energy for the benefit of countries with economies in transition.

Committee for Trade, Industry and Enterprise Development: A forum for studying means of expanding and diversifying trade among European countries, as well as with countries in other regions, and for drawing up recommendations on how to achieve these ends. Analyses trends, problems and prospects in intra-European trade; explores means of encouraging the flow of international direct investment into the newly opening economies of central and eastern Europe; promotes new or improved methods of trading by means of marketing, industrial co-operation, contractual guides, and the facilitation of international trade procedures (notably through the Electronic Data Interchange for Administration, Commerce and Transport—UN/EDIFACT, a flexible single international standard).

Conference of European Statisticians: Promotes improvement of national statistics and their international comparability in economic, social, demographic and environmental fields; promotes co-ordination of statistical activities of international organizations active in Europe and North America; and responds to the increasing need for international statistical co-operation both within the ECE region and between the region and other regions. Works very closely with the OECD and the EU.

Inland Transport Committee: Promotes a coherent, efficient, safe and sustainable transport system through the development of international agreements, conventions and other instruments covering a wide range of questions relating to road, rail, inland water and combined transport, including infrastructure, border-crossing facilitation, road traffic safety, requirements for the construction of road vehicles and other transport regulations, particularly in the fields of transport of dangerous goods and perishable foodstuffs. Also considers transport trends and economics and compiles transport statistics. Assists central and eastern European countries, as well as ECE member states from central Asia, in developing their transport systems and infrastructures.

Timber Committee: Regularly reviews markets for forest products; analyses long-term trends and prospects for forestry and timber; keeps under review developments in the forest industries, including environmental and energy-related aspects. Subsidiary bodies run jointly with FAO deal with forest technology, management and training and with forest economics and statistics.

SUB-REGIONAL PROGRAMMES

Southeast European Co-operative Initiative—SECI: initiated in December 1996, in order to encourage co-operation among countries of the sub-region and to facilitate their access to the process of European integration. Nine *ad hoc* Project Groups have been established to undertake preparations for the following selected projects: trade facilitation; transport infrastructure, in particular road and rail networks; financial policies to promote small and medium-sized enterprises; co-operation to combat crime and corruption; energy efficiency demonstration zone networks; interconnection of natural gas networks; co-operation among securities markets; and the recovery programme for rivers, lakes and adjacent seas (with particular emphasis on the Danube River Basin). Activities are overseen by a SECI Agenda Committee and a SECI Business Advisory Council. Participating countries: Albania, Bosnia and Herzegovina, Bulgaria, Croatia, Greece, Hungary, the former Yugoslav republic of Macedonia, Moldova, Romania, Slovenia and Turkey.

Special Programme for the Economies of Central Asia—SPECA: initiated in March 1998 as a joint programme of the ECE and ESCAP. Aims to strengthen sub-regional co-operation, in particular in the following areas: the development of transport infrastructure and facilitation of cross-border activities; the rational use of energy and water; regional development and attraction of foreign investment; and development of multiple routes for pipeline transportation of hydrocarbons to global markets. Participating countries: Kazakhstan, Kyrgyzstan, Tajikistan, Turkmenistan and Uzbekistan.

Finance

ECE's budget for the two years 2002–03 was US $40.0m.

Publications

ECE Annual Report.

Annual Bulletin of Housing and Building Statistics for Europe and North America.

Annual Bulletin of Transport Statistics for Europe and North America.

ECE Highlights (quarterly).

The ECE in the Age of Change.

Economic Survey of Europe (2 a year).

Statistical Journal of the UNECE (quarterly).

Statistical Standards and Studies.

Statistics of Road Traffic Accidents in Europe and North America.

Timber Bulletin (6 a year).

Timber Committee Yearbook (annually).

Trends in Europe and North America: Statistical Yearbook of the ECE (annually).

UN Manual of Tests and Criteria of Dangerous Goods.

UN Recommendations on the Transport of Dangerous Goods.

Women and Men in Europe and North America.

World Robotics (annually).

Studies on air pollution, forestry and timber, water, gas, energy; environmental performance reviews; country profiles on the housing sector; transport agreements; customs conventions; maps; trade and investment briefings and guides; fertility and family surveys; statistical bulletins.

Reports, proceedings of meetings, technical documents, codes of conduct, codes of practice, guide-lines to governments, etc.

Economic and Social Commission for Asia and the Pacific—ESCAP

Address: United Nations Bldg, Rajdamnern Ave, Bangkok 10200, Thailand.

Telephone: (2) 288-1234; **fax:** (2) 288-1000; **e-mail:** unisbkk.unescap@un.org; **internet:** www.unescap.org.

The Commission was founded in 1947 to encourage the economic and social development of Asia and the Far East; it was originally known as the Economic Commission for Asia and the Far East (ECAFE). The title ESCAP, which replaced ECAFE, was adopted after a reorganization in 1974.

MEMBERS

Afghanistan	Korea, Democratic People's Republic	Papua New Guinea
Armenia	Korea, Republic	Philippines
Australia	Kyrgyzstan	Russia
Azerbaijan	Laos	Samoa
Bangladesh	Malaysia	Singapore
Bhutan	Maldives	Solomon Islands
Brunei	Marshall Islands	Sri Lanka
Cambodia	Micronesia, Federated States	Tajikistan
China, People's Republic	Mongolia	Thailand
Fiji	Myanmar	Tonga
France	Nauru	Turkey
Georgia	Nepal	Turkmenistan
India	Netherlands	Tuvalu
Indonesia	New Zealand	United Kingdom
Iran	Pakistan	USA
Japan	Palau	Uzbekistan
Kazakhstan		Vanuatu
Kiribati		Viet Nam

ASSOCIATE MEMBERS

American Samoa	Hong Kong	Northern Mariana Islands
Cook Islands	Macao	
French Polynesia	New Caledonia	
Guam	Niue	

Organization

(March 2002)

COMMISSION

The Commission meets annually at ministerial level to examine the region's problems, to review progress, to establish priorities and to decide upon the recommendations of the Executive Secretary or the subsidiary bodies of the Commission.

Ministerial and intergovernmental conferences on specific issues may be held on an *ad hoc* basis with the approval of the Commission, although, from 1998, no more than one ministerial conference and five intergovernmental conferences may be held during one year.

COMMITTEES AND SPECIAL BODIES

The following advise the Commission and help to oversee the work of the Secretariat:

Committee on the Environment and Natural Resources Development: meets annually.

Committee on Regional Economic-Co-operation: meets every two years, with a high-level Steering Group, which meets annually to discuss and develop policy options.

Committee on Socio-economic Measures to Alleviate Poverty in Rural and Urban Areas: meets annually.

Committee on Statistics: meets every two years.

Committee on Transport, Communications, Tourism and Infrastructure Development: meets annually.

Special Body on Least-Developed and Land-locked Developing Countries: meets every two years.

Special Body on Pacific Island Developing Countries: meets every two years.

In addition, an Advisory Committee of permanent representatives and other representatives designated by members of the Commission functions as an advisory body.

SECRETARIAT

The Secretariat operates under the guidance of the Commission and its subsidiary bodies. It consists of two servicing divisions, covering administration and programme management, in addition to the following substantive divisions: Development research and policy analysis; International trade and industry; Environment and natural resources development; Social development; Population and rural and urban development; Transport, communications, tourism and infrastructure development; and Statistics.

The Secretariat also includes the ESCAP/UNCTAD Joint Unit on Transnational Corporations and the UN information services.

Executive Secretary: KIM HAK-SU (Republic of Korea).

SUB-REGIONAL OFFICE

ESCAP Pacific Operations Centre (EPOC): Private Bag 004, Port Vila, Vanuatu; tel. 23458; fax 23921; e-mail escappoc@ascap.org.vu; f. 1984, to provide effective advisory and technical assistance at a sub-regional level and to identify the needs of island countries. Dir NIKENIKE VUROBARAVU.

Activities

ESCAP acts as a UN regional centre, providing the only intergovernmental forum for the whole of Asia and the Pacific, and executing a wide range of development programmes through technical assistance, advisory services to governments, research, training and information.

In 1992 ESCAP began to reorganize its programme activities and conference structures in order to reflect and serve the region's evolving development needs. The approach that was adopted focused on regional economic co-operation, poverty alleviation through economic growth and social development, and environmental and sustainable development.

Regional economic co-operation. Provides technical assistance and advisory services. Aims to enhance institutional capacity-building; gives special emphasis to the needs of least developed, land-locked and island developing countries, and to economies in transition in accelerating their industrial and technological advancement, promoting their exports, and furthering their integration into the region's economy; supports the development of electronic commerce and other information technologies in the region; and promotes the intra-regional and inter-subregional exchange of trade, investment and technology through the strengthening of institutional support services such as regional information networks.

Development research and policy analysis. Aims to increase the understanding of the economic and social development situation in the region, with particular attention given to sustainable economic growth, poverty alleviation, the integration of environmental concerns into macroeconomic decisions and policy-making processes, and enhancing the position of the region's disadvantaged economies. The sub-programme is responsible for the provision of technical assistance, and the production of relevant documents and publications.

Social development. The main objective of the sub-programme is to assess and respond to regional trends and challenges in social policy and human resources development, with particular attention to the planning and delivery of social services and training programmes for disadvantaged groups, including the poor, youths, women, the disabled, and the elderly. Implements global and regional mandates, such as the Programme of Action of the World Summit for Social Development and the Jakarta

Plan of Action on Human Resources Development and Action for the Asian and Pacific Decade of Disabled Persons 1993–2002. In addition, the sub-programme aims to strengthen the capacity of public and non-government institutions to address the problems of marginalized social groups and to foster partnerships between governments, the private sector, community organizations and all other involved bodies. In 1998 ESCAP initiated a programme of assistance in establishing a regional network of Social Development Management Information Systems (SOMIS). Feasibility studies were conducted in three pilot countries in 1998–2000. In 2001 ESCAP undertook regional preparations for a World Summit on Sustainable Development, which was to be held in Johannesburg, South Africa, in September 2002.

Population and rural and urban development. Aims to assess and strengthen the capabilities of local institutions in rural and urban development, as well as increasing the capacity of governmental and non-governmental organizations to develop new approaches to poverty alleviation and to support food security for rural households. Promotes the correct use of agro-chemicals in order to increase food supply and to achieve sustainable agricultural development and administers the Fertilizer Advisory Development and Information Network for Asia and the Pacific (FADINAP). Rural employment opportunities and the access of the poor to land, credit and other productive assets are also considered by the sub-programme. Undertakes technical co-operation and research in the areas of ageing, female economic migration and reproductive health, and prepares specific publications relating to population. Implements global and regional mandates, such as the Programme of Action of the International Conference on Population and Development. The Secretariat co-ordinates the Asia-Pacific Population Information Network (POPIN).

Environment and natural resources development. Concerned with strengthening national capabilities to achieve environmentally-sound and sustainable development by integrating economic concerns, such as the sustainable management of natural resources, into economic planning and policies. The sub-programme was responsible for implementation of the Regional Action Programme for Environmentally Sound and Sustainable Development for the period 1996–2000. Other activities have included the promotion of integrated water resources development and management, including water quality and a reduction in water-related natural disasters; strengthening the formulation of policies in the sustainable development of land and mineral resources; the consideration of energy resource options, such as rural energy supply, energy conservation and the planning of power networks; and promotion of the use of space technology applications for environmental management, natural disaster monitoring and sustainable development.

Transport, communications, tourism and infrastructure development. Aims to develop inter- and intra-regional transport links to enhance trade and tourism, mainly through implementation of an Asian Land Transport Infrastructure Development project. Other activities are aimed at improving the planning process in developing infrastructure facilities and services, in accordance with the regional action programme of the New Delhi Action Plan on Infrastructure Development in Asia and the Pacific, which was adopted at a ministerial conference held in October 1996, and at enhancing private sector involvement in national infrastructure development through financing, management, operations and risk-sharing. A Ministerial Conference on Infrastructure Development was organized by ESCAP in November 2001. The meeting concluded a memorandum of understanding, initially signed by ESCAP, Kazakhstan, the Republic of Korea, Mongolia and Russia, to facilitate the transport of container goods along the Trans-Asian Railway. The sub-programme aims to reduce the adverse environmental impact of the provision of infrastructure facilities and to promote more equitable and easier access to social amenities. Tourism concerns include the development of human resources, improved policy planning for tourism development, greater investment in the industry, and minimizing the environmental impact of tourism.

Statistics. Provides training and advice in priority areas, including national accounts statistics, gender statistics, population censuses and surveys, and the management of statistical systems. Supports co-ordination throughout the region of the development, implementation and revision of selected international statistical standards. Disseminates comparable socio-economic statistics, with increased use of the electronic media, promotes the use of modern information technology in the public sector and trains senior-level officials in the effective management of information technology.

Throughout all the sub-programmes, ESCAP aims to focus particular attention on the needs and concerns of least developed, land-locked and island developing nations, and economies in transition in the region.

CO-OPERATION WITH THE ASIAN DEVELOPMENT BANK

In July 1993 a memorandum of understanding was signed by ESCAP and the Asian Development Bank (ADB—q.v.), outlining priority areas of co-operation between the two organizations. These were: regional and sub-regional co-operation; issues concerning the least-developed, land-locked and island developing member countries; poverty alleviation; women in development; population; human resource development; the environment and natural resource management; statistics and data bases; economic analysis; transport and communications; and industrial restructuring and privatization. The two organizations were to co-operate in organizing workshops, seminars and conferences, in implementing joint projects, and in exchanging information and data on a regular basis.

ASSOCIATED BODIES

Asian and Pacific Centre for Transfer of Technology: Off New Qutab Institutional Area, POB 4575, New Delhi 110 016, India; tel. (11) 6966509; fax (11) 6856274; e-mail infocentre@apctt.org; internet www.apctt.org; f. 1977 to assist countries of the ESCAP region by strengthening their capacity to develop, transfer and adopt technologies relevant to the region, and to identify and to promote regional technology development and transfer. Dir Dr JÜRGEN H. BISCHOFF. Publs *Asia Pacific Tech Monitor, VATIS Updates on Biotechnology, Food Processing, Ozone Layer Protection, Non-Conventional Energy,* and *Waste Technology* (each every 2 months), *International Technology and Business Opportunities Update* (quarterly).

ESCAP/WMO Typhoon Committee: c/o UNDP, POB 7285, ADC, Pasay City, Metro Manila, Philippines; tel. (632) 3733443; fax (2) 3733419; e-mail tcs@philonline.com; f. 1968; an intergovernmental body sponsored by ESCAP and WMO for mitigation of typhoon damage. It aims at establishing efficient typhoon and flood warning systems through improved meteorological and telecommunication facilities. Other activities include promotion of disaster preparedness, training of personnel and co-ordination of research. The committee's programme is supported from national resources and also by UNDP and other international and bilateral assistance. Mems: Cambodia, People's Republic of China, Hong Kong, Japan, Democratic People's Republic of Korea, Republic of Korea, Laos, Macao, Malaysia, Philippines, Singapore, Thailand, USA, Viet Nam. Co-ordinator of Secretariat: Dr ROMAN L. KINTANAR.

Regional Co-ordination Centre for Research and Development of Coarse Grains, Pulses, Roots and Tuber Crops in the Tropics of Asia and the Pacific (CGPRT Centre): Jalan Merdeka 145, Bogor 16111, Indonesia; tel. (251) 343277; fax (251) 336290; e-mail cgprt@indo.net.id; internet www.cgprt.org.sg; f. 1981; initiates and promotes research, training and publications on the production, marketing and use of these crops. Dir Dr NOBUYOSHI MAENO. Publs *Palawija News* (quarterly), working paper series, monograph series and statistical profiles.

Statistical Institute for Asia and the Pacific: 2-2 Wakaba 3-chome, Mihama-ku, Chiba-shi, Chiba 261-8787, Japan; tel. (43) 2999782; fax (43) 2999780; e-mail staff@unsiap.or.jp; internet www.unsiap.or.jp; f. 1970; trains government statisticians; prepares teaching materials, provides facilities for special studies and research of a statistical nature, assists in the development of training on official statistics in national and sub-regional centres. Dir TOMAS P. AFRICA (Philippines).

WMO/ESCAP Panel on Tropical Cyclones: Technical Support Unit, c/o Pakistan Meteorological Dept, POB 1214, H-8, Islamabad, Pakistan; tel. (51) 9257314; fax (51) 432588; e-mail tsupmd@hotmail.com; f. 1973 to mitigate damage caused by tropical cyclones in the Bay of Bengal and the Arabian Sea; mems: Bangladesh, India, Maldives, Myanmar, Pakistan, Sri Lanka, Thailand. Co-ordinator of Secretariat Dr QAMAR-UZ-ZAMAN CHAUDHRY.

Finance

For the two-year period 2000–01 ESCAP's regular budget, an appropriation from the UN budget, was US $57.0m. (compared with $67.5m. in 1998–99). The regular budget is supplemented annually by funds from various sources for technical assistance.

Publications

Annual Report.

Agro-chemicals News in Brief (quarterly).

Asia-Pacific Development Journal (2 a year).

Asia-Pacific in Figures (annually).

Asia-Pacific Population Journal (quarterly).

Asia-Pacific Remote Sensing and GIS Journal (2 a year).

Atlas of Mineral Resources of the ESCAP Region.

Confluence (water resources newsletter, 2 a year).

Economic and Social Survey of Asia and the Pacific (annually).

Environmental News Briefing (every 2 months).

ESCAP Energy News (2 a year).

ESCAP Human Resources Development Newsletter (2 a year).

ESCAP Population Data Sheet (annually).

ESCAP Tourism Newsletter (2 a year).

Fertilizer Trade Information Monthly Bulletin.

Foreign Trade Statistics of Asia and the Pacific (annually).

Government Computerization Newsletter (irregular).

Industry and Technology Development News for Asia and the Pacific (annually).

Poverty Alleviation Initiatives (quarterly).

Regional Network for Agricultural Machinery Newsletter (3 a year).

Small Industry Bulletin for Asia and the Pacific (annually).

Social Development Newsletter (2 a year).

Space Technology Applications Newsletter (quarterly).

Statistical Indicators for Asia and the Pacific (quarterly).

Statistical Newsletter (quarterly).

Statistical Yearbook for Asia and the Pacific.

Trade and Investment Information Bulletin (monthly).

Transport and Communications Bulletin for Asia and the Pacific (annually).

Water Resources Journal (quarterly).

Bibliographies; country and trade profiles; commodity prices; statistics.

Economic Commission for Latin America and the Caribbean—ECLAC

Address: Edif. Naciones Unidas, Avda Dag Hammarskjöld, Casilla 179D, Santiago, Chile.

Telephone: (2) 2102000; **fax:** (2) 2080252; **e-mail:** dpisantiago@eclac.cl; **internet:** www.eclac.org.

The UN Economic Commission for Latin America was founded in 1948 to co-ordinate policies for the promotion of economic development in the Latin American region. The current name of the Commission was adopted in 1984.

MEMBERS

Antigua and Barbuda	Costa Rica	Haiti
Argentina	Cuba	Honduras
Bahamas	Dominica	Italy
Barbados	Dominican Republic	Jamaica
Belize	Ecuador	Mexico
Bolivia	El Salvador	Netherlands
Brazil	France	Nicaragua
Canada	Grenada	Panama
Chile	Guatemala	Paraguay
Colombia	Guyana	Peru
Saint Christopher and Nevis	Spain	Portugal
Saint Lucia	Suriname	United Kingdom
Saint Vincent and the Grenadines	Trinidad and Tobago	USA
		Uruguay
		Venezuela

ASSOCIATE MEMBERS

Anguilla	Montserrat	Puerto Rico
Aruba	Netherlands Antilles	United States Virgin Islands
British Virgin Islands		

Organization

(March 2002)

COMMISSION

The Commission normally meets every two years in one of the Latin American capitals. The 28th session of the Commission was held in Mexico City in April 2000, and the 29th session was to be held in Brasilia in May 2002. The Commission has established the following permanent bodies:

Caribbean Development and Co-operation Committee.

Central American Development and Co-operation Committee.

Committee of High-Level Government Experts.

Committee of the Whole.

Regional Conference on the Integration of Women into the Economic and Social Development of Latin America and the Caribbean.

Regional Council for Planning.

SECRETARIAT

The Secretariat employs more than 500 staff and is headed by the the Offices of the Executive Secretary and of the Secretary of the Commission. ECLAC's work programme is carried out by the following divisions: Economic Development; Social Development; International Trade and Integration; Production, Productivity and Management; Statistics and Economic Projections; Environment and Human Settlements; Natural Resources and Infrastructure; Documents and Publications; and Population. There are also units for information and conference services, women and development and special studies, an electronic information section, and a support division of administration.

Executive Secretary: JOSÉ ANTONIO OCAMPO (Colombia).

Secretary of the Commission: DANIEL BLANCHARD.

SUB-REGIONAL OFFICES

Caribbean: 63 Park St, Chic Bldg, 3rd Floor, POB 1113, Port of Spain, Trinidad and Tobago; tel. 623-5595; fax 623-8486; e-mail registry@eclacpos.org; internet www.eclacpos.org; f. 1956; covers non-Spanish-speaking Caribbean countries; Dir LEN ISHMAEL.

Central America and Spanish-speaking Caribbean: Avda Presidente Masaryk 29, 11570 México, DF; tel. (5) 250-1555; fax (5) 531-1151; e-mail cepal@un.org.mx; internet www.eclac

.org.mx; f. 1951; covers Central America and Spanish-speaking Caribbean countries; Dir REBECA GRYNSPAN.

There are also national offices, in Santafé de Bogotá, Brasília, Buenos Aires and Montevideo and a liaison office in Washington, DC.

Activities

ECLAC collaborates with regional governments in the investigation and analysis of regional and national economic problems, and provides guidance in the formulation of development plans. Its activities include research; analysis; publication of information; provision of technical assistance; participation in seminars and conferences; training courses; and co-operation with national, regional and international organizations.

The 26th session of the Commission, which was held in San José, Costa Rica, in April 1996, considered means of strengthening the economic and social development of the region, within the framework of a document prepared by ECLAC's Secretariat, and adopted a resolution which defined ECLAC as a centre of excellence, charged with undertaking an analysis of specific aspects of the development process, in collaboration with member governments. The meeting also reviewed the impact on ECLAC of the ongoing process of reform throughout the UN system. In May 1998 the 27th session of the Commission, held in Oranjestad, Aruba, approved the ongoing reform programme, and in particular efforts to enhance the effectiveness and transparency of ECLAC's activities. The main topics of debate at the meeting were public finances, fiscal management and social and economic development. The Commission adopted a Fiscal Covenant, incorporating measures to consolidate fiscal adjustment and to strengthen public management, democracy and social equity, which was to be implemented throughout the region and provide the framework for further debate at national and regional level. ECLAC's 28th session, convened in Mexico City in April 2000, debated a document prepared by the Secretariat which proposed that the pursuit of social equity, sustainable development and 'active citizenship' (with emphasis on the roles of education and employment) should form the basis of future policy-making in the region.

ECLAC works closely with other agencies within the UN system and with other regional and multinational organizations. ECLAC is co-operating with the OAS and the Inter-American Development Bank in the servicing of intergovernmental groups undertaking preparatory work for the establishment of a Free Trade Area of the Americas. In May 2001 ECLAC hosted the first meeting of the Americas Statistics Conference. In January 2002 ECLAC hosted an Interregional Conference on Financing for Development, held in Mexico City, which it had organized as part of the negotiating process prior to the World Summit on Financing for Development, scheduled to be held in March.

Latin American and Caribbean Institute for Economic and Social Planning—ILPES: Edif. Naciones Unidas, Avda Dag Hammarskjöld, Casilla 1567, Santiago, Chile; tel. (2) 2102506; fax (2) 2066104; e-mail pdekock@eclac.cl; www.eclac.org/ilpes; f. 1962; supports regional governments through the provision of training, advisory services and research in the field of public planning policy and co-ordination. Dir FERNANDO SÁNCHEZ-ALBAVERA.

Latin American Demographic Centre—CELADE: Edif. Naciones Unidas, Avda Dag Hammarskjöld, Casilla 179D, Santiago, Chile; tel. (2) 2102002; fax (2) 2080252; e-mail djaspers @eclac.cl; internet www.eclac.org/celade; f. 1957, became an integral part of ECLAC in 1975; provides technical assistance to governments, universities and research centres in demographic analysis, population policies, integration of population factors in development planning, and data processing; conducts three-month courses on demographic analysis for development and various national and regional seminars; provides demographic estimates and projections, documentation, data processing, computer packages and training. Dir DANIEL S. BLANCHARD.

Finance

For the two-year period 2000–01 ECLAC's regular budget, an appropriation from the UN, amounted to US $78.9m. In addition, extrabudgetary activities are financed by governments, other organizations, and UN agencies, including UNDP, UNFPA and UNICEF.

Publications

Boletín del Banco de Datos del CELADE (annually).

Boletín demográfico (2 a year).

Boletín de Facilitación del Comercio y el Transporte (every 2 months).

CEPAL Review (Spanish and English, 3 a year).

CEPALINDEX (annually).

Co-operation and Development (Spanish and English, quarterly).

DOCPAL Resúmenes (population studies, 2 a year).

ECLAC Notes/Notas de la CEPAL (every 2 months).

Economic Panorama of Latin America (annually).

Economic Survey of Latin America and the Caribbean (Spanish and English, annually).

Foreign Investment in Latin America and the Caribbean (annually).

Latin American Projections 2001-02.

Notas de Población (2 a year).

PLANINDEX (2 a year).

Preliminary Overview of the Economies of Latin America and the Caribbean (annually).

Social Panorama of Latin America (annually).

Statistical Yearbook for Latin America and the Caribbean (Spanish and English).

Studies, reports, bibliographical bulletins.

Economic Commission for Africa—ECA

Address: Africa Hall, POB 3001, Addis Ababa, Ethiopia.

Telephone: (1) 517200; **fax:** (1) 514416; **e-mail:** ecainfo@uneca.org; **internet:** www.uneca.org.

The UN Economic Commission for Africa was founded in 1958 by a resolution of the UN Economic and Social Council (ECOSOC) to initiate and take part in measures for facilitating Africa's economic development.

MEMBERS

Algeria	Eritrea	Niger
Angola	Ethiopia	Nigeria
Benin	Gabon	Rwanda
Botswana	The Gambia	São Tomé and Príncipe
Burkina Faso	Ghana	Senegal
Burundi	Guinea	Seychelles
Cameroon	Guinea-Bissau	Sierra Leone
Cape Verde	Kenya	Somalia
Central African Republic	Lesotho	South Africa
Chad	Liberia	Sudan
Comoros	Libya	Swaziland
Congo, Democratic Republic	Madagascar	Tanzania
Congo, Republic	Malawi	Togo
Côte d'Ivoire	Mali	Tunisia
Djibouti	Mauritania	Uganda
Egypt	Mauritius	Zambia
Equatorial Guinea	Morocco	Zimbabwe
	Mozambique	
	Namibia	

Organization

(March 2002)

COMMISSION

The Commission may only act with the agreement of the government of the country concerned. It is also empowered to make recommendations on any matter within its competence directly to the government of the member or associate member concerned, to governments admitted in a consultative capacity, and to the UN Specialized Agencies. The Commission is required to submit for prior consideration by ECOSOC any of its proposals for actions that would be likely to have important effects on the international economy.

CONFERENCE OF MINISTERS

The Conference, which meets every two years, is attended by ministers responsible for economic or financial affairs, planning and development of governments of member states, and is the main deliberative body of the Commission.

The Commission's responsibility to promote concerted action for the economic and social development of Africa is vested primarily in the Conference, which considers matters of general policy and the priorities to be assigned to the Commission's programmes, considers inter-African and international economic policy, and makes recommendations to member states in connection with such matters.

OTHER POLICY-MAKING BODIES

A Conference of Ministers of Finance and a Conference of Ministers responsible for economic and social development and planning meet in alternate years to formulate policy recommendations. Each is served by a committee of experts. Five intergovernmental committees of experts attached to the Sub-regional Development Centres (see below) meet annually and report to the Commission through a Technical Preparatory Committee of the Whole, which was established in 1979 to deal with matters submitted for the consideration of the Conference.

Seven other committees meet regularly to consider issues relating to the following policy areas: women and development; development information; sustainable development; human development and civil society; industry and private sector development; natural resources and science and technology; and regional co-operation and integration.

SECRETARIAT

The Secretariat provides the services necessary for the meeting of the Conference of Ministers and the meetings of the Commission's subsidiary bodies, carries out the resolutions and implements the programmes adopted there. It comprises an Office of the Executive Secretary, the African Centre for Women and the following eight divisions: Food Security and Sustainable Development; Development Management; Development Information Services; Regional Co-operation and Integration; Programme Planning, Finance and Evaluation; Economic and Social Policy; Human Resources and System Management; Conference and General Services.

Executive Secretary: KINGSLEY Y. AMOAKO (Ghana).

SUB-REGIONAL DEVELOPMENT CENTRES

Multinational Programming and Operational Centres (MULPOCs) were established, in 1977, to implement regional development programmes. In May 1997 the Commission decided to transform the MULPOCs into Sub-regional Development Centres (SRDCs) in order to enable member states to play a more effective role in the process of African integration and to facilitate the integration efforts of the other UN agencies active in the sub-regions. In addition, the SRDCs were to act as the operational arms of ECA at national and sub-regional levels: to ensure harmony between the objectives of sub-regional and regional programmes and those defined by the Commission; to provide advisory services; to facilitate sub-regional economic co-operation, integration and development; to collect and disseminate information; to stimulate policy dialogue; and to promote gender issues.

Central Africa: POB 836, Yaoundé, Cameroon; tel. 23-14-61; fax 23-31-85; e-mail srdc@camnet.cm; Dir ADDO IRO.

Eastern Africa: POB 4654, Kigali, Rwanda; tel. 86549; fax 86546; e-mail easrdc@rwandatel1.rwanda1.com; Dir MBAYE DIOUF.

Northern Africa: POB 316, Tangier, Morocco; tel. (39) 322346; fax (39) 340357; e-mail srdc-na@uneca.org; Dir ABDELOUAHAB REZIG.

Southern Africa: POB 30647, Lusaka, Zambia; tel. (1) 228503; fax (1) 236949; e-mail uneca@zamnet.zm; Dir Dr ROBERT M. OKELLO.

West Africa: POB 744, Niamey, Niger; tel. 72-29-61; fax 72-28-94; e-mail srdcwest@eca.ne; Dir JEGGAN C. SENGHOR.

Activities

The Commission's activities are designed to encourage sustainable socio-economic development in Africa and to increase economic co-operation among African countries and between Africa and other parts of the world. The Secretariat has been guided in its efforts by major regional strategies including the Abuja Treaty establishing the African Economic Community signed under the aegis of the Organization of African Unity in 1991, the UN System-wide Special Initiative on Africa (launched in 1996, see below), and the UN New Agenda for the Development of Africa covering the period 1991–2000. ECA's main programme areas for the period 1996–2001 were based on an Agenda for Action, which was announced by the OAU Council of Ministers in March 1995 and adopted by African heads of state in June, with the stated aim of 'relaunching Africa's economic and social development'. The five overall objectives were to facilitate economic and social policy analysis and implementation; to ensure food security and sustainable development; to strengthen development management; to harness information for development; and to promote regional co-operation and integration. In all its activities ECA aimed to promote the themes of capacity-building and of fostering leadership and the empowerment of women in Africa. In May 1998 ECA's African Centre for Women inaugurated a new Fund for African Women's Development to support capacity-building activities.

DEVELOPMENT INFORMATION SERVICES

Until 1997 regional development information management was promoted through the Pan-African Development Information System (PADIS, established in 1980 and known until 1989 as the Pan-African Documentation and Information Service). In 1997 the Development Information Services Division (DISD) was created, with responsibility for co-ordinating the implementation of the Harnessing Information Technology for Africa project (in the context of the UN System-wide Special Initiative on Africa) and for the implementation of the African Information Society Initiative (AISI), a framework for creating an information and communications infrastructure; for overseeing quality enhancement and dissemination of statistical databases; for improving access to information by means of enhanced library and documentation services and output; and by strengthening geo-information systems for sustainable development. In addition, ECA encourages member governments to liberalize the telecommunications sector and stimulate imports of computers in order to enable the expansion of information technology throughout Africa. ECA manages the Information Technology Centre for Africa, based in Addis Ababa.

Regional statistical development activities are managed through the Co-ordinating Committee on African Statistical Development (CASD, established in 1992). The CASD facilitates the harmonization of statistical systems and methodologies at regional and national level; establishes mechanisms for the continuous exchange of information between governments, national agencies and regional and sub-regional bodies, and all bilateral and multilateral agencies; identifies and proposes new lines of action; and informs the Conference of African Planners, Statisticians and Population and Information Specialists on the progress of the Addis Ababa Plan of Action for Statistical Development in the 1990s (adopted in 1992). In May 1997 five task forces were established to undertake the CASD's activities; these covered the following areas: improving e-mail connectivity; monitoring the implementation of the Addis Ababa Plan of Action; strengthening statistical training programme for Africa (STPA) centres; assisting with the formation of census and household survey data service centres in two–five pilot countries, and with the establishment of a similar regional ECA service centre; and establishing live databases, comprising core macro and sectoral statistical indicators, initially as a pilot project in two–five countries, with eventual links to a regional database facility.

ECA assists its member states in (i) population data collection and data processing; (ii) analysis of demographic data obtained from censuses or surveys; (iii) training demographers at the Regional Institute for Population Studies (RIPS) in Accra, Ghana, and at the Institut de formation et de recherche démographiques (IFORD) in Yaoundé, Cameroon; (iv) formulation of population policies and integrating population variables in development planning, through advisory missions and through the organization of national seminars on population and development; and (v) dissemination of demographic information. The strengthening of national population policies was an important element of ECA's objective of ensuring food security in African countries.

In August 2000 ECA launched the Africa Knowledge Networks Forum (AKNF). The Forum, to be convened on an annual basis under ECA auspices, was to facilitate co-operation in information-sharing and research between professional research and development networks, and also between these and policy-makers, educators, civil society organizations and the private sector. It was to provide technical support to the ADF process (see below).

DEVELOPMENT MANAGEMENT

ECA aims to assist governments, public corporations, universities and the private sector in improving their financial management; strengthening policy-making and analytical capacities; adopting measures to redress skill shortages; enhancing human resources development and utilization; and promoting social development through programmes focusing on youth, people with disabilities and the elderly. The Secretariat organizes training workshops, seminars and conferences at national, subregional and regional levels for ministers, public administrators and senior policy-makers, as well as for private and non-governmental organizations. ECA aims to increase the participation of women in economic development and incorporates this objective into its administrative activities and work programmes.

Following the failure to implement many of the proposals under the UN Industrial Development Decade for Africa (IDDA, 1980–90) and the UN Programme of Action for African Economic Recovery and Development (1986–90), a second IDDA was adopted by the Conference of African Ministers of Industry in July 1991. The main objectives of IDDA II (1993–2003) included the consolidation and rehabilitation of existing industries, the expansion of new investments, and the promotion of small-scale industries and technological capabilities. In June 1996 a conference, organized by ECA, was held in Accra, Ghana, with the aim of reviving private investment in Africa in order to stimulate the private sector and promote future economic development. In October 1999 the first African Development Forum (ADF) was held in Addis Ababa, Ethiopia. The ADF process was initiated by ECA to formulate an agenda for effective, sustainable development in African countries through dialogue and partnership between governments, academics, the private sector, donor agencies etc. It was intended that the process would focus towards an annual meeting concerned with a specific development issue. The first Forum was convened on the theme 'The Challenge to Africa of Globalization and the Information Age'. It reviewed the AISI (see above) and formulated country action plans and work programmes. The four issues addressed were: strengthening Africa's information infrastructure; Africa and the information economy; information and communication technologies for improved governance; and democratizing access to the information society. The second ADF, convened in October 2000, in Addis Ababa, on the theme 'AIDS: the Greatest Leadership Challenge', addressed the impact on Africa of the HIV/AIDS epidemic and issued a Consensus and Plan of Action. The third ADF, held in March 2002, addressed the theme 'Defining Priorities for Regional Integration'.

In 1997 ECA hosted the first of a series of meetings on good governance, in the context of the UN System-wide Special Initiative on Africa. The second African Governance Forum (AGF II) was held in Accra, Ghana, in June 1998. The Forum focused on accountability and transparency, which participants agreed were essential elements in promoting development in Africa and should involve commitment from both governments and civil organizations. AGF III was convened in June 1999 in Bamako, Mali, to consider issues relating to conflict prevention, management and governance. The fourth AGF, which took place in Kampala, Uganda, in September 2000, focused on parliamentary processes and their role in consolidating good governance on the continent.

The ECA was to be the main body responsible for identifying and preparing programmes on economic and corporate governance under the New Partnership for African Development (NEPAD), established in accordance with a decision of the OAU summit of heads of state and government held in July 2001.

ECONOMIC AND SOCIAL POLICY

The Economic and Social Policy division concentrates on the following areas: economic policy analysis, trade and debt, social policy and poverty analysis, and the co-ordination and monitoring of special issues and programmes. Monitoring economic and social trends in the African region and studying the development problems concerning it are among the fundamental tasks of the Commission, while the special issues programme updates legislative bodies regarding the progress made in the implementation of initiatives affecting the continent. Every year the Commission publishes the *Survey of Economic and Social Conditions in Africa* and the *Economic Report on Africa.*

The Commission gives assistance to governments in general economic analysis, fiscal, financial and monetary management, trade liberalization, regional integration and planning. ECA's work on economic planning has been broadened in recent years, in order to give more emphasis to macro-economic management in a mixed economy approach: a project is being undertaken to develop short-term forecasting and policy models to support economic management. The Commission has also undertaken a major study of the informal sector in African countries. Special assistance is given to least-developed, land-locked and island countries which have a much lower income level than other countries and which are faced with heavier constraints. Studies are also undertaken to assist longer-term planning.

In May 1994 ECA ministers of economic and social development and of planning, meeting in Addis Ababa, adopted a *Framework Agenda for Building and Utilizing Critical Capacities in Africa*. The agenda aimed to identify new priority areas to stimulate development by, for example, strengthening management structures, a more efficient use of a country's physical infrastructure and by expanding processing or manufacturing facilities.

ECA aims to strengthen African participation in international negotiations. To this end, assistance has been provided to member states in the ongoing multilateral trade negotiations under the World Trade Organization; in the annual conferences of the IMF and the World Bank; in negotiations with the EU; and in meetings related to economic co-operation among developing countries. Studies have been prepared on problems and prospects likely to arise for the African region from the implementation of the Common Fund for Commodities and the Generalized System of Trade Preferences (both supervised by UNCTAD); the impacts of exchange-rate fluctuations on the economies of African countries; and on the long-term implications of different debt arrangements for African economies. ECA assists individual member states by undertaking studies on domestic trade, expansion of intra-African trade, trans-national corporations, integration of women in trade and development, and strengthening the capacities of state-trading organizations. ECA encourages the diversification of production, the liberalization of cross-border trade and the expansion of domestic trade structures, within regional economic groupings, in order to promote intra-African trade. ECA also helps to organize regional and 'All-Africa' trade fairs.

In March/April 1997 the Conference of African Ministers of Finance, meeting in Addis Ababa, reviewed a new initiative of the World Bank and IMF to assist the world's 41 most heavily indebted poor countries, of which 33 were identified as being in sub-Saharan Africa. While the Conference recognized the importance of the involvement of multilateral institutions in assisting African economies to achieve a sustainable level of development, it criticized aspects of the structural adjustment programmes imposed by the institutions and advocated more flexible criteria to determine eligibility for the new scheme.

ECA aims to improve the socio-economic prospects of women through the promotion of equal access to resources and opportunities and equal participation in decision-making.

FOOD SECURITY AND SUSTAINABLE DEVELOPMENT

In the early 1990s reports were compiled on the development, implementation and sound management of environmental programmes at national, sub-regional and regional levels. ECA members adopted a common African position for the UN Conference on Environment and Development, held in June 1992. In 1995 ECA published its first comprehensive report and statistical survey of human development issues in African countries. The *Human Development in Africa Report*, which was to be published every two years, aimed to demonstrate levels of development attained, particularly in the education and child health sectors, to identify areas of concern and to encourage further action by policy-makers and development experts. ECA is actively involved in the promotion of food security in African countries through raising awareness of the relationship between population, food security, the environment and sustainable development; encouraging the advancement of science and technology in member states; and providing policy analysis support and technical advisory services.

PROGRAMME PLANNING, FINANCE AND EVALUATION

ECA provides guidance in the formulation of policies towards the achievement of Africa's development objectives to the policy-making organs of the UN and OAU. It contributes to the work of the General Assembly and other specialized agencies by providing an African perspective in the preparation of development strategies. In March 1996 the UN announced its System-wide Special Initiative on Africa to mobilize resources and to implement a series of political and economic development objectives over a 10-year period. ECA's Executive Secretary is the Co-Chair, with the Administrator of the UNDP, of the Steering Committee for the Initiative.

REGIONAL CO-OPERATION AND INTEGRATION

The Regional Co-operation and Integration Division administers the transport and communications and mineral and energy sectors, in addition to its activities concerning the Sub-regional Development Centres (SRDCs—see above), the integrated development of transboundary water resources, and facilitating and enhancing the process of regional economic integration.

ECA was appointed lead agency for the second United Nations Transport and Communications Decade in Africa (UNTACDA II), covering the period 1991–2000. The principal aim of UNTACDA II was the establishment of an efficient, integrated transport and communications system in Africa. The specific objectives of the programme included: (i) the removal of physical and non-physical barriers to intra-African trade and travel, and improvement in the road transport sector; (ii) improvement in the efficiency and financial viability of railways; (iii) development of Africa's shipping capacity and improvement in the performance of Africa's ports; (iv) development of integrated transport systems for each lake and river basin; (v) improvement of integration of all modes of transport in order to carry cargo in one chain of transport smoothly; (vi) integration of African airlines, and restructuring of civil aviation and airport management authorities; (vii) improvement in the quality and availability of transport in urban areas; (viii) development of integrated regional telecommunications networks; (ix) development of broadcasting services, with the aim of supporting socio-economic development; and (x) expansion of Africa's postal network. ECA is the co-ordinator, with the World Bank, of a regional Road Management Initiative, which was launched in 1988. By early 1996 13 African countries were receiving assistance under the initiative, which sought to encourage a partnership between the public and private sectors to manage and maintain road infrastructure more efficiently and thus to improve country-wide communications and transportation activities. The third African road safety congress was held in April 1997, in Pretoria, South Africa. The congress, which was jointly organized by ECA and the OECD, aimed to increase awareness of the need to adopt an integrated approach to road safety problems. During 1998/99 transport activities included consideration of a new African air transport policy, workshops on port restructuring, and regional and country analyses of transport trends and reforms.

The Fourth Regional Conference on the Development and Utilization of Mineral Resources in Africa, held in March 1991, adopted an action plan that included the formulation of national mineral exploitation policies; and the promotion of the gemstone industry, small-scale mining and the iron and steel industry. ECA supports the Southern African Mineral Resources Development Centre in Dar-es-Salaam, Tanzania, and the Central African Mineral Development Centre in Brazzaville, Republic of the Congo, which provide advisory and laboratory services to their respective member states.

ECA's Energy Programme provides assistance to member states in the development of indigenous energy resources and the formulation of energy policies to extricate member states from continued energy crises. In 1997 ECA strengthened co-operation with the World Energy Council and agreed to help implement the Council's African Energy Programme.

ECA assists member states in the assessment and use of water resources and the development of river and lake basins common to more than one country. ECA encourages co-operation between countries with regard to water issues and collaborates with other UN agencies and regional organizations to promote technical and economic co-operation in this area. ECA has been particularly active in efforts to promote the integrated development of the water resources of the Zambezi river basin and of Lake Victoria.

In all of its activities ECA aims to strengthen institutional capacities in order to support the process of regional integration, and aims to assist countries to implement existing co-operative agreements, for example by promoting the harmonization of macroeconomic and taxation policies and the removal of non-tariff barriers to trade.

ASSOCIATED BODY

Information Technology Centre for Africa (ITCA): POB 3001, Addis Ababa, Ethiopia; tel. (1) 314520; fax (1) 515829; e-mail mfaye@uneca.org; internet www.uneca.org/itca; aims to strengthen the continent's communications infrastructure and promote the use of information and communications technologies in planning and policy-making; stages exhibitions and provides training facilities.

Finance

For the two-year period 2000–01 ECA's regular budget, an appropriation from the UN budget, was an estimated US $78.5m.

Publications

Africa in Figures.
African Statistical Yearbook.
African Trade Bulletin (2 a year).
African Women's Report (annually).
Africa's Population and Development Bulletin.
Compendium of Intra-African and Related Foreign Trade Statistics.
Directory of African Statisticians (every 2 years).
ECA Development Policy Review.
ECA Environment Newsletter (3 a year).
ECANews (monthly).
Economic Report on Africa (annually).
Focus on African Industry (2 a year).
GenderNet (annually).
Human Development in Africa Report (every 2 years).
Human Rights Education.
Report of the Executive Secretary (every 2 years).
Survey of Economic and Social Conditions in Africa (annually).
Country reports, policy and discussion papers, reports of conferences and meetings, training series, working paper series.

Economic and Social Commission for Western Asia—ESCWA

Address: Riad es-Solh Sq., POB 11-8575, Beirut, Lebanon.

Telephone: (1) 981301; **fax:** (1) 981510; **e-mail:** unescwa@escwa.org.lb; **internet:** www.escwa.org.lb.

The UN Economic Commission for Western Asia was established in 1974 by a resolution of the UN Economic and Social Council (ECOSOC), to provide facilities of a wider scope for those countries previously served by the UN Economic and Social Office in Beirut (UNESOB). The name 'Economic and Social Commission for Western Asia' (ESCWA) was adopted in 1985.

MEMBERS

Bahrain	Palestine
Egypt	Qatar
Iraq	Saudi Arabia
Jordan	Syria
Kuwait	United Arab Emirates
Lebanon	Yemen
Oman	

Organization

(March 2002)

COMMISSION

The sessions of the Commission (held every two years) are attended by delegates from member states. Representatives of UN bodies and specialized agencies, regional organizations, other UN member states, and non-governmental organizations having consultative status with ECOSOC may attend as observers.

PREPARATORY COMMITTEE

The Committee, formerly the Technical Committee, has the task of reviewing programming issues and presenting recommendations in that regard to the sessions of the Commission. It is the principal subsidiary body of the Commission and functions as its policy-making structure. Six specialized inter-governmental committees have been established to consider specific areas of activity, to report on these to the Preparatory Committee and to assist the Committee in formulating ESCWA's medium-term work programmes.

Statistics Committee: established in 1992; meets every two years.

Committee on Social Development: established in 1994; meets every two years.

Committee on Energy: established in 1995; meets every two years.

Committee on Water Resources: established in 1995; meets every two years.

Committee on Transport: established in 1997; meets annually.

Committee on Liberalization of Foreign Trade and Economic Globalization: established in 1997; meets every two years.

SECRETARIAT

The Secretariat comprises an Executive Secretary, a Deputy Executive Secretary, a Senior Adviser and Secretary of the Commission, an Information Services Unit and divisions for administrative services and programme planning and technical co-operation. ESCWA's technical and substantive activities are undertaken by the following divisions: energy, natural resources and environment; social development issues and policies; economic development issues and policies; sectoral issues and policies; and statistics.

Executive Secretary: MERVAT M. TALLAWY (Egypt).

Activities

ESCWA is responsible for proposing policies and actions to support development and to further economic co-operation and integration in western Asia. ESCWA undertakes or sponsors studies of economic social and development issues of the region, collects and disseminates information, and provides advisory services to member states in various fields of economic and social development. It also organizes conferences and intergovernmental and export group meetings and sponsors training workshops and seminars.

Much of ESCWA's work is carried out in co-operation with other UN bodies, as well as with other international and regional organizations, for example the League of Arab States (q.v.) the Co-operation Council for the Arab States of the Gulf (q.v.) and the Organization of the Islamic Conference (OIC, q.v.). In April 2001 ESCWA convened an inaugural consultative meeting with representatives of more than 100 non-governmental organizations, in order to strengthen co-operation with civil society.

ESCWA works within the framework of medium-term plans, which are divided into two-year programmes of action and priorities. The Commission restructured its work programme in the mid-1990s, which focused ESCWA activities from 15 to five sub-programmes. A further reorganization of the sub-programmes was implemented in 1997 to provide the framework for activities in the medium-term period 1998–2001. In May 2001 the Commission approved a work programme for 2002–03 on the basis of the existing sub-programme structure.

MANAGEMENT OF NATURAL RESOURCES AND ENVIRONMENT

The main objective of the sub-programme is to promote regional co-ordination and co-operation in the management of natural resources, in particular water resources and energy, and the protection of the environment. Work in this area aims to counter the problem of an increasing shortage of freshwater resources and deterioration in water quality resulting from population growth, agricultural land-use and socio-economic development, by supporting measures for more rational use and conservation of water resources, and by promoting public awareness and community participation in water and environmental protection projects. In addition, ESCWA assists governments in the formulation and implementation of capacity-building programmes and the development of surface and groundwater resources. In 2002–03 ESCWA aimed to promote greater co-operation among member and non-member countries in the management and use of shared water resources.

ESCWA supports co-operation in the establishment of electricity distribution and supply networks throughout the region and promotes the use of alternative sources of energy and the development of new and renewable energy technologies. Similarly, ESCWA promotes the application of environmentally sound technologies in order to achieve sustainable development, as well as measures to recycle resources, minimize waste and reduce the environmental impact of transport operations and energy use. Under the sub-programme ESCWA collaborates with national, regional and international organizations in monitoring and reporting on emerging environmental issues and to pursue implementation of Agenda 21, which was adopted at the June 1992 UN Conference on Environment and Development, with particular regard to land and water resource management and conservation.

IMPROVEMENT OF THE QUALITY OF LIFE

ESCWA's key areas of activity in this sub-programme are population, sustainable human development, the advancement of women and gender equality, and human settlements. The sub-programme was designed to pursue the implementation of recommendations relevant to the region of the four UN world conferences held on these themes during the mid-1990s.

ESCWA's objectives with regard to population are to increase awareness and understanding of links between population factors and poverty, human rights and the environment, and to strengthen the capacities of member states to analyse and assess demographic trends and migration. In the area of human development ESCWA aims to further the alleviation of poverty and to generate a sustainable approach to development through, for example, greater involvement of community groups in decision-making and projects to strengthen production and income-generating capabilities. The sub-programme incorporates activities to ensure all gender-related recommendations of the four world conferences could be pursued in the region, including support for the role of the family and assistance to organizations for monitoring and promoting the advancement of women. With regard to human settlements, the objectives of the sub-programme are to monitor and identify problems resulting from rapid urbanization and social change, to promote understanding and awareness of the problems and needs of human settlements, and to strengthen the capacity of governments in the region in formulating appropriate policies and strategies for sustainable human settlement development. In 2002–03 ESCWA's priorities were to develop and promote social policies and strategies with the emphasis on family cohesion, the advancement of women, poverty reduction, disabled and ageing populations, population dynamics, and the security of tenure. It also aimed to promote transparent and accountable governance, based on greater participation of civil society.

ECONOMIC DEVELOPMENT AND GLOBAL CHANGES

During the period 2002–03 ESCWA aimed to assist member states to achieve sustainable economic development in the region and to integrate more fully into the world economy. Under the sub-programme ESCWA aimed to assist member countries to identify the challenges and opportunities created by the World Trade Organization and other regional groupings, in particular with regard to free trade areas, the liberalization and management of financial markets, and the promotion of foreign direct investment. It also intended to improve the analysis of economic developments and the formulation of economic management policies, as well as to provide guidance on alternative development strategies to reduce the dominance of the petroleum sector.

CO-ORDINATION OF POLICIES AND HARMONIZATION OF NORMS AND REGULATIONS FOR SECTORAL DEVELOPMENT

This sub-programme is concerned with the harmonization of standards throughout the region in the areas of transport, industry, agriculture and technology. ESCWA aims to promote co-operation among member states in transport and infrastructure policies and greater uniformity of safety and legal standards, the latter with a view to facilitating border crossings between countries in the region. ESCWA, similarly, aims to assist local industries to meet regional and international standards and regulations, as well as to improve the competitiveness of industries through the development of skills and policies and greater co-operation with other national and regional support institutions. In May 2001 ESCWA member states adopted an Agreement on International Transport System in the Arab Mashreq, which had been formulated by the Secretariat with the aim of establishing a unified transportation network linking all countries in the region. In 2002–03 ESCWA envisaged pursuing activities to promote the harmonization of norms and standards for sustainable development within the region. ESCWA also aimed to provide support for the co-ordination of sectoral policies, in particular with regard to poverty-related issues, and to develop and disseminate related statistics, information and electronic data.

CO-ORDINATION AND HARMONIZATION OF STATISTICS AND INFORMATION DEVELOPMENT

In the medium-term ESCWA intended to develop the statistical systems of member states in order to improve the relevance and accuracy of economic and social data, and to implement measures to make the information more accessible to planners and researchers. Priorities for the biennium 2002–03 included activities to improve human and institutional capacities, in particular in the use of statistical tools for data analysis, to expand the adoption and implementation of international statistical methods, and to promote co-operation to further the regional harmonization of statistics.

Finance

ESCWA's share of the UN budget for the two years 2000–01 was US $50.3m., compared with $49.5m. for the previous biennium.

Publications

All publications are annual, unless otherwise indicated.

Agriculture and Development in Western Asia.

ESCWA Update (monthly).

External Trade Bulletin of the ESCWA Region.

National Accounts Studies of the ESCWA Region.

Population Bulletin of the ESCWA Region.

Prices and Financial Statistics in the ESCWA Region.

Socio-economic Data Sheet (every 2 years).

Statistical Abstract of the ESCWA Region.

Survey of Economic and Social Developments in the ESCWA Region.

Transport Bulletin.

Weekly News.

OTHER UNITED NATIONS BODIES

Office for the Co-ordination of Humanitarian Affairs—OCHA

Address: United Nations Plaza, New York, NY 10017, USA.

Telephone: (212) 963-1234; **fax:** (212) 963-1312; **e-mail:** ochany@un.org; **internet:** www.reliefweb.int/ocha_ol/.

OCHA was established in January 1998 as part of the UN Secretariat, with a mandate to co-ordinate international humanitarian assistance and to provide policy and other advice on humanitarian issues. It replaced the Department of Humanitarian Affairs, established in 1992.

Organization

(March 2002)

OCHA has headquarters in New York, and in Geneva, Switzerland, and it maintains a field presence in 34 locations. In 2002 there were 188 staff at the headquarters (of whom 57 were regular staff and 131 were extrabudgetary), 58 project staff, and 172 international and 486 national field staff.

Under Secretary-General for Humanitarian Affairs and Emergency Relief Co-ordinator: KENZO OSHIMA (Japan).

Activities

OCHA's mandate is to work with UN agencies, governments, intergovernmental humanitarian organizations and non-governmental organizations to ensure that a prompt, co-ordinated and effective response to emergency situations is provided. OCHA reaches agreement with other UN bodies regarding the division of responsibilities, which may include field missions to assess requirements, organizing Consolidated Inter-agency Appeals for financial assistance, and mobilizing other resources. The Emergency Relief Co-ordinator is the principal adviser to the UN Secretary-General on humanitarian issues. He chairs the Inter-Agency Standing Committee (IASC), which co-ordinates and administers the international response to humanitarian disasters and the development of relevant policies. The Co-ordinator also acts as Convener of the Executive Committee for Humanitarian Affairs, which provides a forum for humanitarian agencies, as well as the political and peace-keeping departments of the UN Secretariat, to exchange information on emergency situations and humanitarian issues. In 2001 OCHA began to implement the recommendations of an internal review process aimed at strengthening its three core functions of co-ordination, advocacy and policy development. During that year OCHA also began to develop a new strategic planning process.

OCHA monitors developments throughout the world and undertakes contingency planning to enable it to respond immediately to emergency situations. It maintains internet-based Integrated Regional Information Networks (IRINs). The first IRIN was created in 1995 in Nairobi, Kenya, to disseminate information on the humanitarian situation in central and east Africa. Additional IRINs have since been established in Abidjan, Côte d'Ivoire, and Johannesburg, South Africa, in order to provide accurate information concerning developments in western and southern Africa. An IRIN for central Asia, operating from Islamabad, Pakistan, was inaugurated in August 2000. A complementary service, ReliefWeb, which was launched in 1996, monitors crises and publishes the information obtained on the internet. IRIN and ReliefWeb together form part of OCHA's Policy, Analysis and Information Division, based in New York. In addition, OCHA holds a number of conferences and workshops.

OCHA administers a Disaster Response System, which monitors field situations, liaises with UN Resident Co-ordinators world-wide and undertakes disaster-preparedness activities. UN Disaster Assessment and Co-ordination (UNDAC) teams, established by OCHA with the aid of donor governments, are available for immediate deployment to help to determine requirements and to co-ordinate assistance in those countries affected by disasters, for example by establishing reliable telecommunications and securing other logistical support. OCHA maintains a Central Register of Disaster Management Capacities, which may be available for international assistance. In addition, emergency equipment and supplies are held at a military airport in Brindisi, Italy, ready for emergency dispatch. OCHA also issues Situation Reports to inform the international community of any emergency situation, the type and level of assistance required and action being undertaken.

OCHA facilitates the Consolidated Inter-agency Appeal Process (CAP), which aims to organize a co-ordinated response to resource mobilization following humanitarian crises. Under guide-lines adopted by the IASC in 1994, the CAP was clearly defined as a programming mechanism rather than simply an appeal process. Technical guide-lines adopted in 1999 established a framework for developing a Common Humanitarian Action Plan (CHAP) to address a crisis, co-ordinating the relevant inter-agency appeal (on the basis of the CHAP), and preparing strategic monitoring reports. CAP appeals for 2002, seeking an estimated US $2,500m., were issued in November 2001; they concerned 18 complex humanitarian crises affecting some 33m. people. A Central Emergency Revolving Fund (CERF), under the authority of the Emergency Relief Co-ordinator, enables humanitarian agencies to provide an immediate response to emergencies, before donor contributions become available. Agencies borrowing from the fund are required to reimburse the amount loaned within a certain period of time, which is not to exceed one year.

Finance

OCHA's budgetary requirements for 2002 were an estimated US $70m., of which about $9m. was to be provided from the regular budget of the UN.

Publication

OCHA News (weekly).

Office for Drug Control and Crime Prevention—ODCCP

Address: Vienna International Centre, POB 500, A-1400 Vienna, Austria.

Telephone: (1) 26060-0; **fax:** (1) 26060-5866; **e-mail:** odccp@odccp.org; **internet:** www.odccp.org.

The Office was established in November 1997 to strengthen the UN's integrated approach to issues relating to drug control, crime prevention and international terrorism. It comprises two principal components: the United Nations International Drug Control Programme and the Centre for International Crime Prevention, both headed by the ODCCP Executive Director.

In March 1999 a new UN Global Programme against Money Laundering (GPML) was established within the framework of the ODCCP to assist governments with formulating legislation against money laundering and establishing and maintaining appropriate frameworks to counter the problem. GPML activities include the provision of technical assistance, training, and the collection, research and analysis of crime data. The Programme, in collaboration with other governmental organizations, law enforcement agencies and academic institutions, co-ordinates the International Money Laundering Information Network (IMoLIN), an internet-based information resource. IMoLIN incorporates the Anti-Money Laundering International Database (a comprehensive database on money-laundering legislation throughout the world that constituted a key element in ODCCP activities in support of the elaboration of the International Convention against Transnational Organized Crime—see below). At the first GPML Forum, held in the Cayman Islands in March 2000, the governments of 31 participating 'offshore' financial centres agreed in principle to adopt internationally-accepted standards of financial regulation and measures against money laundering.

The ODCCP's Terrorism Prevention Branch, established in 1999, researches trends in terrorist activity and assists countries with improving their capabilities to investigate and prevent acts of terrorism. The Branch promotes international co-operation in combating the problem, is compiling a database on global terrorism, and has initiated a study into the connections between terrorist activity and other forms of crime.

Executive Director: ANTONIO MARIA COSTA (Italy) (from June 2002).

UNITED NATIONS INTERNATIONAL DRUG CONTROL PROGRAMME—UNDCP

UNDCP was established in 1991 to co-ordinate the activities of all UN specialized agencies and programmes in matters of international drug control. The structures of the former Division of Narcotic Drugs, the UN Fund for Drug Abuse Control and the secretariat of the International Narcotics Control Board (see below) were integrated into the new body. Accordingly, UNDCP became the focal point for promoting the UN Decade Against Drug Abuse (1991–2000) and for assisting member states to implement the Global Programme of Action that was adopted by the General Assembly in 1990 with the objective of achieving an international society free of illicit drugs and drug abuse. At a special summit meeting of the UN General Assembly, held in June 1998, heads of state and representatives of some 150 countries adopted a global strategy, formulated on the basis of UNDCP proposals, to reduce significantly the production of illicit substances by 2008, and to strengthen drug prevention, treatment and rehabilitation programmes by 2003. UNDCP subsequently launched two programmes that aimed to facilitate the realization of these objectives by improving and standardizing the compilation and analysis of data. A four-year Global Monitoring Programme of Illicit Crops, covering the period January 2000–December 2003, was to employ a combination of satellite sensing (with the assistance of the European Space Agency, q.v.), aerial surveillance and ground-level surveys of regions known to have high levels of illicit crop cultivation, in order to provide a reliable collection and analysis mechanism for data on the production of illicit substances. Governments were to be encouraged to use the information obtained in the formulation of comprehensive national monitoring systems. The Global Assessment Programme on Drug Abuse (GAP), also covering the period January 2000–December 2003, was to establish one global and nine regional drug abuse data systems to collect and evaluate data on the extent of and patterns of illegal substance abuse.

UNDCP serves as an international centre of expertise and information on drug abuse control, with the capacity to provide legal and technical assistance in relevant areas of concern. The Programme supports governments in efforts to strengthen their institutional capacities for drug control (for example, drug identification and drug law enforcement training) and to prepare and implement national drug control 'action plans'. Efforts to enhance regional co-operation in the control of narcotics are also supported. Through these national and regional strategies UNDCP aims to reduce the demand for illicit drugs, to suppress trafficking in these substances and to reduce the production of drugs, for example by creating alternative sources of income for farmers economically dependent on the production of illicit narcotic crops. This latter approach has been successfully applied in Laos, reducing the levels of opium cultivation, and in the coca-growing regions of Peru, Bolivia and Colombia.

UNDCP sponsors activities to generate public awareness of the harmful effects of drug abuse, as part of its efforts to reduce the demand for illicit drugs. In 1998 UNDCP established the Global Youth Network project, which aims to involve young people in drug-abuse prevention activities. UNDCP also works with governments, as well as non-governmental and private organizations, in the detection, treatment, rehabilitation and social reintegration of drug addicts. UNDCP undertakes research to monitor the drugs problem: for example, assessing the characteristics of drug-takers and the substances being used in order to help identify people at risk of becoming drug-takers and to enhance the effectiveness of national programmes to address the issue (see also the GAP, above).

UNDCP promotes implementation of the following major treaties which govern the international drug control system: the Single Convention on Narcotic Drugs (1961) and a Protocol amending the Convention (1972); the Convention on Psychotropic Substances (1971); and the UN Convention against Illicit Traffic in Narcotic Drugs and Psychotropic Substances (1988). Among other important provisions, these treaties aim to restrict severely the production of narcotic drugs, while ensuring an adequate supply for medical and scientific purposes, to prevent profits obtained from the illegal sale of drugs being diverted into legal usage and to secure the extradition of drug-traffickers and the transfer of proceedings for criminal prosecution. UNDCP assists countries to adapt their national legislation and drug policies to facilitate their compliance with these conventions and to enhance co-ordinated inter-governmental efforts to control the movement of narcotic drugs. UNDCP services meetings of the International Narcotics Control Board, an independent body responsible for promoting and monitoring government compliance with the provisions of the drug control treaties, and of the Commission on Narcotic Drugs, which, as a functional committee of ECOSOC (q.v.), is the main policy-making organ within the UN system on issues relating to international drug abuse control.

UNDCP co-operates closely with other international, regional and non-governmental organizations and maintains dialogue with agencies advocating drug abuse control. In April 1999 UNDCP became the seventh co-sponsor of the Joint UN Programme on HIV/AIDS (UNAIDS), which was established on 1 January 1996 by UNICEF, UNDP, UNFPA, UNESCO, WHO and the World Bank. UNDCP's participation was in recognition of the importance of international drug control efforts in preventing the spread of HIV/AIDS. (ILO became the eighth co-sponsor in 2001.)

Finance

The UNDCP Fund receives an allocation from the regular budget of the UN, although voluntary contributions from member states and private organizations represent the majority of its resources. The proposed budget for the two-year period 2002–03 amounted to US $168.4m., including programme expenditure of $130.0m. Voluntary contributions provide about 90% of budgetary resources.

Publications

Bulletin on Narcotics (quarterly).

Global Illicit Drug Trends.

ODCCP Update (quarterly).

Technical Series.

World Drug Report.

CENTRE FOR INTERNATIONAL CRIME PREVENTION—CICP

The CICP, established in 1997, is the UN body responsible for crime prevention, criminal justice and criminal law reform. It oversees the application of international standards and norms relating to these areas, for example the Minimum Rules for the Treatment of Prisoners, Conventions against Torture, and Other Cruel, Inhuman or Degrading Treatment or Punishment, and Safeguards Guaranteeing the Protection of the Rights of Those Facing the Death Penalty. The Centre provides member states with technical assistance to strengthen national capacities to establish appropriate legal and criminal justice systems and to combat transnational organized crime (see below). The CICP supports the Commission on Crime Prevention and Criminal Justice, a functional committee of ECOSOC which provides guidance in developing global anti-crime policies. In 1999 the CICP initiated three new programmes: a Global Programme against Corruption, a three-year Global Programme against Trafficking in Human Beings (trafficking in human beings for sexual exploitation or forced labour is regarded as the fastest-growing area of international organized crime), and a Global Programme on Organized Crime, which aimed to analyse emerging transnational criminal organizations and assist countries to formulate strategies to combat the problem. The CICP supported member states in the preparation of the UN Convention against Transnational Organized Crime, which was adopted by the General Assembly in August 2000; the so-called Palermo Convention, with two additional Protocols on trafficking in human beings and the smuggling of migrants, was opened for signature in December at a UN conference on combating organized crime held in Sicily, Italy. By January 2002 the Convention had been signed by 140 states and ratified by seven. In that month the CICP participated in a preparatory meeting on the formulation of a UN Convention against Corruption.

The CICP promotes research and undertakes studies of new forms of crime prevention, in collaboration with the UN Interregional Crime and Justice Research Institute (UNICRI, q.v.). It also maintains a UN Crime and Justice Information Network database (UNCJIN), which provides information on national crime statistics, publications and links to other relevant intergovernmental agencies and research and academic institutes.

Following the major terrorist attacks perpetrated against targets in the USA in September 2001 several UN member states urged that the CICP and the ODCCP's Terrorism Prevention Branch be strengthened to combat potential future global terrorist threats.

Finance

The Centre has an annual administrative budget of US $3m., and approximately $3m. is budgeted annually for projects.

Publications

Forum on Crime and Society.

Global Report on Crime and Justice.

The United Nations and Juvenile Justice: A Guide to International Standards and Best Practices.

Office of the United Nations High Commissioner for Human Rights—OHCHR

Address: Palais Wilson, 52 rue de Paquis, 1201 Geneva, Switzerland.

Telephone: (22) 9179290; **fax:** (22) 9179022; **e-mail:** scrt.hchr@unog.ch; **internet:** www.unhchr.ch.

The Office is a body of the UN Secretariat and is the focal point for UN human rights activities. Since September 1997 it has incorporated the Centre for Human Rights.

Organization

(March 2002)

HIGH COMMISSIONER

In December 1993 the UN General Assembly decided to establish the position of a United Nations High Commissioner for Human Rights (UNHCHR) following a recommendation of the World Conference on Human Rights, held in Vienna, Austria, in June of that year. The High Commissioner, who is the UN official with principal responsibility for UN human rights activities, is appointed by the UN Secretary-General, with the approval of the General Assembly, for a four-year term in office, renewable for one term.

High Commissioner: MARY ROBINSON (Ireland).

Deputy to the High Commissioner: Dr BERTRAND GANGAPERSAND RAMCHARAN (Guyana).

ADMINISTRATION

The work of the Office is conducted by the following branches: Research and Right to Development, responsible for human rights policy development, undertaking research and providing information to the High Commissioner and other human rights experts, working groups, etc.; Support Services, which provides administrative support to UN human rights mechanisms, including the Commission on Human Rights and its working groups, and the Sub-commission on the Promotion and Protection of Human Rights and its working groups; and Activities and Programmes, which conducts field operations, provides advice and technical assistance to governments, and implements special procedures relating to human rights concerns. The Office also comprises a Staff Office, an Administrative Section and a branch office in New York, USA.

FIELD PRESENCES

As the Office's involvement in field work has expanded, a substantial structure of field presences has developed to strengthen this aspect of the Office's work. In early 2002 there were field presences in 20 countries, covering the following areas: Abkhazia (Georgia), Afghanistan, Angola, Bosnia and Herzegovina, Burundi, Cambodia, Central African Republic, Chad, Colombia, Croatia, the Democratic Republic of the Congo, Gaza (Emerging Palestinian Autonomous Areas), Guatemala, Guinea-Bissau, Liberia, Madagascar, Sierra Leone, Somalia, South Africa and the provinces of Kosovo and Serbia (Federal Republic of Yugoslavia).

Activities

The mandate of the OHCHR incorporates the following functions and responsibilities: the promotion and protection of human rights throughout the world; the reinforcement of international co-operation in the field of human rights; the promotion of universal ratification and implementation of international standards; the establishment of a dialogue with governments to ensure respect for human rights; and co-ordination of efforts by other UN programmes and organs to promote respect for human rights. The Office may study and react to cases of serious violations of human rights, and may undertake diplomatic efforts to prevent violations. It also produces educational and other information material to enhance understanding of human rights. The Office was the lead agency in undertaking preparations for the World Conference against Racism, Racial Discrimination, Xenophobia and Related Intolerance, convened in Durban, South Africa, in August/September 2001 and attended by representatives of 168 governments. The following five core themes were addressed at Durban: sources, causes, forms and contemporary manifestations of racism; victims; prevention, education and protection measures; provision of remedies and redress (i.e. compensation); and future strategies to achieve full and effective equality. The Conference adopted the 'Durban Declaration' and a Programme of Action, in accordance with which national plans of action were to be implemented by participating states: universal ratification of the International Convention on the Elimination of all Forms of Racism (ICERD) was to be aimed for by 2005, with the broadest possible ratification of other human rights instruments, and national legislation was to be improved in line with the ICERD. An interim anti-discrimination unit was to be established within the OHCHR on the recommendation of the Conference. The Office was to play a leading role in following up the Programme of Action.

OHCHR field offices and operations ('field presences'—see above) undertake a variety of activities, such as training and other technical assistance, support for Special Rapporteurs (usually appointed by the Commission on Human Rights to investigate human rights emergencies), monitoring and fact-finding. Increasingly they provide support to conflict prevention, peace-making, peace-keeping and peace-building activities. From 2002 OHCHR was to organize the provision of human rights training to military and police personnel attached to peace-keeping missions.

In January 2000 OHCHR established a quick response desk to co-ordinate urgent appeals for assistance in addressing human rights emergencies. The High Commissioner issues reports on human rights emergencies to the Commission on Human Rights. During 2001 the High Commissioner presented reports on her investigations into allegations of violations of human rights in Chechnya, Colombia, East Timor, Sierra Leone, and the West Bank and Gaza.

TECHNICAL CO-OPERATION PROGRAMME

The UN Technical Co-operation Programme in the Field of Human Rights was established in 1955 to assist states, at their request, to strengthen their capacities in the observance of democracy, human rights, and the rule of law. Examples of work undertaken within the framework of the programme include training courses and workshops on good governance and the observance of human rights, expert advisory services on the incorporation of international human rights standards into national legislation and policies and on the formulation of national plans of action for the promotion and protection of human rights, fellowships, the provision of information and documentation, and consideration of promoting a human rights culture. In recent years the Programme, one of the key components of OHCHR's activities, has expanded to undertake UN system-wide human rights support activities, for example in the area of peace-keeping (see above).

Finance

The Office is financed from the regular budget of the UN, as well as by a number of voluntary and trust funds. OHCHR launched its first annual appeal to the international community for voluntary contributions in 2000. For 2002 some US $22.5m. was provisionally allocated under the regular budget, while OHCHR appealed for $55.8m. in voluntary contributions.

Publications

Annual Report.

Fact sheet series.

Human Rights Quarterly.

Human rights study series.

Professional training series.

Other reference material, reports, proceedings of conferences, workshops, etc.

United Nations Human Settlements Programme—UN-Habitat

Address: POB 30030, Nairobi, Kenya.

Telephone: (2) 621234; **fax:** (2) 624266; **e-mail:** infohabitat@unhabitat.org; **internet:** www.unhabitat.org.

UN-Habitat (formerly the United Nations Centre for Human Settlements, UNCHS-Habitat, established in October 1978 to service the intergovernmental Commission on Human Settlements) became a full UN programme in January 2002, in accordance with a decision of the General Assembly in December 2001. UN-Habitat serves as a focus for human settlements activities in the UN system.

Organization

(March 2002)

GOVERNING COUNCIL

The Governing Council (formerly the Commission on Human Settlements) meets once every two years and has 58 members, serving for four years. Sixteen members are from Africa, 13 from Asia, six from eastern European countries, 10 from Latin America and 13 from western Europe and other countries. It is served by an inter-sessional subsidiary body, the Committee of Permanent Representatives to UN-Habitat. The Governing Council reports to the UN General Assembly through ECOSOC (q.v.).

SECRETARIAT

The Secretariat services the Governing Council, implements its resolutions and ensures the integration and co-ordination of technical co-operation, research and policy advice. Its Work Programme incorporates the following priority areas, as defined by the Governing Council: Shelter and social services; Urban management; Environment and infrastructure; and Assessment, information and monitoring. The Secretariat is responsible for monitoring the implementation of the objectives of the Second UN Conference on Human Settlements, Habitat II, which was held in Istanbul, Turkey, in June 1996.

Executive Director: ANNA KAJUMULO TIBAIJUKA (Tanzania).

Activities

UN-Habitat supports and conducts capacity-building and operational research, provides technical co-operation and policy advice, and disseminates information with the aim of strengthening the development and management of human settlements. Nearly one-half of the world's population lives in towns and cities.

In June 1996 representatives of 171 national governments and of more than 500 municipal authorities attending Habitat II adopted a Global Plan of Action (the 'Habitat Agenda'), which incorporated detailed programmes of action to realize economic and social development and environmental sustainability, and endorsed the conference's objectives of ensuring 'adequate shelter for all' and 'sustainable human settlements development in an urbanizing world'. UN-Habitat provides the leadership and serves as a focal point for the implementation of the Agenda. In 1999 UNCHS (Habitat) approved a set of 23 resolutions to reduce poverty, improve shelter and environmental conditions, promote good governance, and improve the status of women. A special session of the UN General Assembly, entitled Istanbul + 5, was held in June 2001 to report on the implementation of the recommendations of the Habitat II conference. The special session adopted a Declaration on Cities and Other Human Settlements in the New Millennium that reaffirmed commitment to the objectives of the Habitat Agenda and urged an intensification of efforts towards eradicating widespread poverty, which was identified as the main impediment to achieving these, and towards promoting good governance. The special session also resolved to increase international co-operation in several other areas, including addressing HIV/AIDS, urban crime and violence, environmental issues, and the problems posed by conflicts and refugees; and recommended the enhancement of the status and role of UNCHS (Habitat). Consequently, in December 2001 the General Assembly authorized the elevation of the body to a full UN programme with a strengthened mandate to address and implement the Habitat Agenda and, in January 2002, UN-Habitat was inaugurated.

UN-Habitat maintains a Global Urban Observatory to monitor implementation of the Habitat Agenda and to report on local and national plans of action, international and regional support programmes and ongoing research and development. The Observatory, which incorporates the Best Practices and Local Leadership Programme and the Urban Indicators Programme, operates through an international network of regional and national institutions, all of which provide local training in appropriate data collection methods and in the development, adoption and maintenance of reliable information systems.

The Programme—then UNCHS (Habitat)—was the co-ordinating agency for the implementation of the Global Strategy for Shelter to the Year 2000 (GSS), adopted by the General Assembly in 1988. The GSS aimed to facilitate the construction and improvement of housing for all, in particular by and for the poorest in society, and promoted the use of legal and other incentives to encourage non-governmental parties to become engaged in housing and urban development.

Through its Women in Human Settlements Development Programme, which was established in 1990, the Programme—then UNCHS (Habitat)—ensured that the issue of human settlements was included in the agenda of the UN Fourth World Conference on Women, which was held in Beijing, People's Republic of China, in September 1995, and successfully incorporated the right of women to ownership of land and property into the Global Platform for Action which resulted from the conference. An advisory board, the Huairou Commission, comprising women from 'grass-roots' groups, non-governmental organizations (NGOs), the UN and research and political institutions, has since been established to ensure a link between the Beijing and Habitat Agendas and the inclusion of gender issues in the follow-up to Habitat II.

UN-Habitat participates in implementing the human settlements component of Agenda 21, which was adopted at the UN Conference on Environment and Development in June 1992, and is also responsible for the chapter of Agenda 21 that refers to solid waste management and sewage-related issues. The Programme implements a programme entitled 'Localizing Agenda 21', to assist local authorities in developing countries to address local environmental and infrastructure-related problems. It also collaborates with national governments, private-sector and non-governmental institutions and UN bodies to achieve the objectives of Agenda 21. The Settlement Infrastructure and Environment Programme was initiated in 1992 to support developing countries in improving the environment of human settlements through policy advice and planning, infrastructure management and enhancing awareness of environmental and health concerns in areas such as water, sanitation, waste management and transport. An Urban Management Programme aims to strengthen the contribution of cities and towns in developing countries towards human development, including economic growth, social advancements, the reduction of poverty and the improvement of the environment. The Programme, which is active in 120 cities, is an international technical co-operation project, of which UN-Habitat is the executing agency, the World Bank is an associated agency, while UNDP provides core funding and monitoring. The Programme is operated through regional offices, in collaboration with bilateral and multilateral support agencies, and brings together national and local authorities, community leaders and representatives of the private sector to consider specific issues and solutions to urban problems. The related Safer Cities Programme was initiated in 1996. A Sustainable Cities Programme, operated jointly with UNEP, is concerned with incorporating environmental issues into urban planning and management, in order to ensure sustainable and equitable development. The Programme is active in some 20 cities world-wide, although a prepared series of policy guide-lines is used in many others. Some 95% of the Programme's resources are spent at city level to strengthen the capacities of municipal authorities and their public-, private- and community-sector partners in the field of environmental planning and management, with the objective that the concepts and approaches of the Programme are replicated throughout the region. UN-Habitat was to provide the secretariat of the inaugural World Urban Forum, scheduled to be held in April/May 2002 with participation by national governments and Habitat Agenda partners. The World Urban Forum, which represents a merger of the former Urban Environment Forum and International Forum on Urban Poverty, aims to promote international co-operation in shelter and urban development issues. In addition, UN-Habitat supports training and other activities designed to strengthen management development (in particular in the provision and maintenance of services and facilities) at local and community level.

Increasingly the Programme is being called upon to contribute to the relief, rehabilitation and development activities undertaken by the UN in areas affected by regional and civil conflict. It has been actively involved in the reconstruction of human settlements and other development activities in Afghanistan, as well as contributing to reconstruction programmes in East Timor, Iraq, Myanmar, Rwanda and Somalia. It administers a Housing and Property Directorate that was established in January 2000 in post-conflict Kosovo and Metohija, within the framework of the UN's interim administration in the province. UN-Habitat also provides assessment and technical support in the aftermath of natural disasters. Reconstruction and recovery activities are co-ordinated by the Risk and Disaster Management Unit.

Finance

UN-Habitat's work programme is financed from the UN regular budget, the Habitat and Human Settlements Foundation and from extra-budgetary resources. The approved budget for the two-year period 2002–03 amounted to US $24m.

Publications

Global Report on Human Settlements (annually).

Habitat Debate (quarterly).

Technical reports and studies, occasional papers, bibliographies, directories.

United Nations Children's Fund—UNICEF

Address: 3 United Nations Plaza, New York, NY 10017, USA.

Telephone: (212) 326-7000; **fax:** (212) 888-7465; **e-mail:** netmaster@unicef.org; **internet:** www.unicef.org.

UNICEF was established in 1946 by the UN General Assembly as the UN International Children's Emergency Fund, to meet the emergency needs of children in post-war Europe and China. In 1950 its mandate was changed to respond to the needs of children in developing countries. In 1953 the General Assembly decided that UNICEF should continue its work, as a permanent arm of the UN system, with an emphasis on programmes giving long-term benefits to children everywhere, particularly those in developing countries. In 1965 UNICEF was awarded the Nobel Peace Prize.

Organization

(March 2002)

EXECUTIVE BOARD

The Executive Board, as the governing body of UNICEF, comprises 36 member governments from all regions, elected in rotation for a three-year term by ECOSOC. The Board establishes policy, reviews programmes and approves expenditure. It reports to the General Assembly through ECOSOC.

SECRETARIAT

The Executive Director of UNICEF is appointed by the UN Secretary-General in consultation with the Executive Board. The administration of UNICEF and the appointment and direction of staff are the responsibility of the Executive Director, under policy directives laid down by the Executive Board, and under a broad authority delegated to the Executive Director by the Secretary-General. In December 2001 there were some 5,600 UNICEF staff positions, of which about 85% were in the field.

Executive Director: CAROL BELLAMY (USA).

UNICEF REGIONAL OFFICES

UNICEF has a network of eight regional and 126 field offices serving 162 countries and territories. Its offices in Tokyo, Japan, and Brussels, Belgium, support fund-raising activities; UNICEF's supply division is administered from the office in Copenhagen, Demark. A research centre concerned with child development is based in Florence, Italy.

The Americas and the Caribbean: Apdo 3667, Balboa Ancon, Panamá, Panama; tel. (507) 317-0257; fax (507) 317-0257; e-mail unicef@sinfo.net; internet www.uniceflac.org.

Central and Eastern Europe, Commonwealth of Independent States and Baltic States: Palais des Nations, 1211 Geneva, Switzerland; tel. (22) 9095600; fax (22) 9095909.

East Asia and the Pacific: POB 2-154, Bangkok 10200, Thailand; tel. (2) 2805931; fax (2) 2803563; e-mail eapro@unicef.org.

Eastern and Southern Africa: POB 44145, Nairobi, Kenya; tel. (2) 621234; fax (2) 622678; e-mail nairobiro@unicef.org.

Europe: Palais des Nations, 1211 Geneva 10, Switzerland; tel. (22) 9095111; fax (22) 9095900.

Middle East and North Africa: POB 1551, UNICEF House, Tla'a al-Ali al Dahak Bin Soufian St, 11821 Amman, Jordan; tel. (6) 5539977; fax (6) 5538880; e-mail menaro@unicef.org.jo.

South Asia: POB 5815, Leknath Marg, Kathmandu, Nepal; tel. 417082; fax 419479; e-mail rosa@unicef.org.

West and Central Africa: BP 443, Abidjan 04, Côte d'Ivoire; tel. 213131; fax 227607; e-mail wcaro@unicef.org.

OTHER UNICEF OFFICES

UNICEF Innocenti Research Centre: Piazza SS. Annunziata 2, 50122 Florence, Italy; tel. (055) 20330; fax (055) 244817; e-mail florence@unicef.org; internet www.unicef-icdc.org.

Belgium: rue Montoyer 14, 1000 Brussels; tel. (2) 5132251; fax (2) 5132290; e-mail brussels@unicef.org.

UNICEF Supply Division: UNICEF Plads, Freeport 2100, Copenhagen; tel. (45) 35273527; fax (45) 35269421; e-mail supply@unicef.dk; internet www.supply.unicef.dk.

Japan: UN Bldg, 8th Floor, 53-70, Jingumae 5-chome, Shibuya-ku, Tokyo 150, Japan; tel. (3) 5467-4431; fax (3) 5467-4437; e-mail unicefjp@sepia.ocn.ne.jp.

NATIONAL COMMITTEES

UNICEF is supported by 37 National Committees, mostly in industrialized countries, whose volunteer members, numbering more than 100,000, raise money through various activities, including the sale of greetings cards. The Committees also undertake advocacy and awareness campaigns on a number of issues and provide an important link with the general public.

Activities

UNICEF is dedicated to the well-being of children and women and works for the realization and protection of their rights within the frameworks of the Convention on the Rights of the Child, which was adopted by the UN General Assembly in 1989 and by 2002 was almost universally ratified, and of the Convention on the Elimination of All Forms of Discrimination Against Women, adopted by the UN General Assembly in 1979. Promoting the full implementation of the Conventions, UNICEF aims to ensure that children world-wide are given the best possible start in life and attain a good level of basic education, and that adolescents are given every opportunity to develop their capabilities and participate successfully in society. The Fund also continues to provide relief and rehabilitation assistance in emergencies. Through its extensive field network in some 162 developing countries and territories, UNICEF undertakes, in co-ordination with governments, local communities and other aid organizations, programmes in health, nutrition, education, water and sanitation, the environment, gender issues and development, and other fields of importance to children. Emphasis is placed on low-cost, community-based programmes. UNICEF programmes are increasingly focused on supporting children and women during critical periods of their life, when intervention can make a lasting difference, i.e. early childhood, the primary school years, adolescence and the reproductive years. Priorities include early years development, immunization strategies, girls' education, combating the spread and impact of HIV/AIDS, and strengthening the protection of children against violence, exploitation and abuse.

UNICEF was instrumental in organizing the World Summit for Children, held in September 1990 and attended by representatives from more than 150 countries, including 71 heads of state or government. The Summit produced a Plan of Action which recognized the rights of the young to 'first call' on their countries' resources and formulated objectives for the year 2000, including: (i) a reduction of the 1990 mortality rates for infants and children under five years by one-third, or to 50–70 per 1,000 live births, whichever is lower; (ii) a reduction of the 1990 maternal mortality rate by one-half; (iii) a reduction by one-half of the 1990 rate for severe malnutrition among children under the age of five; (iv) universal access to safe drinking water and to sanitary means of excreta disposal; and (v) universal access to basic education and completion of primary education by at least 80% of children. UNICEF supported the efforts of governments to achieve progress towards these objectives. UNICEF has played a leading role in helping governments and other partners prepare for the UN General Assembly Special Session on Children, scheduled to take place in May 2002 to assess the outcome of the 1990 summit and to adopt a set of actions and objectives for the next 10 years.

In 2000 UNICEF launched a new initiative, the Global Movement for Children—comprising governments, private- and public-sector bodies, and individuals—which aimed to rally world-wide support to improve the lives of all children and adolescents. In April 2001 a 'Say Yes for Children' campaign was adopted by the Global Movement, identifying 10 critical actions required to further its objectives. These were: eliminating all forms of discrimination and exclusion; putting children first; ensuring a caring environment for every child; fighting HIV/AIDS; eradicating violence against and abuse and exploitation of children; listening to children's views; universal eduation; protecting children from war; safeguarding the earth for children; and combating poverty. UNICEF was to co-ordinate the campaign.

UNICEF, in co-operation with other UN agencies, promotes universal access to and completion of basic and good quality education. The Fund, with UNESCO, UNDP, UNFPA and the World Bank, co-sponsored the World Conference on Education for All, held in Thailand in March 1990, and undertook efforts to achieve the objectives formulated by the conference, which included the elimination of disparities in education between boys and girls. UNICEF participated in and fully supports the objectives and framework for action adopted by the follow-up World Education Forum in Dakar, Senegal, in April 2000. The Fund supports education projects in sub-Saharan Africa, South Asia and countries in the Middle East and North Africa, and implements a Girls' Education Programme in more than 60 developing countries, which aims to increase the enrolment of girls in primary schools. More than 120m. children world-wide, of whom nearly 53% are girls, remain deprived of basic education.

Through UNICEF's efforts the needs and interests of children were incorporated into Agenda 21, which was adopted as a plan of action for sustainable development at the UN Conference on Environment and Development, held in June 1992. In mid-1997, at the UN General Assembly's Special Session on Sustainable Development, UNICEF highlighted the need to improve safe water supply, sanitation and hygiene, and thereby reduce the risk of diarrhoea and other water-borne diseases, as fundamental to fulfilment of child rights. The Fund has supported initiatives to provide the benefits of safe water, sanitation and hygiene education to communities in developing countries. UNICEF also works with UNEP to promote environment issues of common concern and with the World Wide Fund for Nature to support the conservation of local ecosystems.

UNICEF aims to break the cycle of poverty by advocating for the provision of increased development aid to developing countries, and aims to help poor countries obtain debt relief and to ensure access to basic social services. To this end it supports NetAid, an internet-based strategy to promote sustainable development and combat extreme poverty. UNICEF is the leading agency in promoting the 20/20 initiative, which was endorsed at the World Summit for Social Development, held in Copenhagen, Denmark, in March 1995. The initiative encourages the governments of developing and donor countries to allocate at least 20% of their domestic budgets and official development aid respectively, to health care, primary education and low-cost safe water and sanitation.

UNICEF, which vigorously opposes the exploitation of children as a violation of their basic human rights, works with ILO and other partners to promote an end to exploitative and hazardous child labour, and supports special projects to provide education, counselling and care for the estimated 250m. children between the ages of five and 14 years working in developing countries. UNICEF played a major role at the World Congress against Commercial Sexual Exploitation of Children, held in Stockholm, Sweden, in 1996, which adopted a Declaration and Agenda for Action to end the sexual exploitation of children. UNICEF also actively participated in the International Conference on Child Labour held in Oslo, Norway, in November 1997. The Conference adopted an Agenda for Action to eliminate the worst forms of child labour, including slavery-like practices, forced labour, commercial sexual exploitation and the use of children in drugs-trafficking and other hazardous forms of work. UNICEF supports the 1999 ILO Worst Forms of Child Labour Convention, which aims at the prohibition and immediate elimination of the worst forms of child labour. In 1999 UNICEF launched a global initiative, Education as a Preventive Strategy Against Child Labour, with the aim of providing education to children forced to miss school because of work. The Fund helped to draft and promotes full ratification and implementation of an Optional Protocol to the Convention of the Rights of the Child concerning the sale of children, child prostitution and pornography, which was adopted in May 2000 and entered into force in January 2002. UNICEF co-sponsored and actively participated in the Second Congress Against Commercial Sexual Exploitation of Children held in Yokohama, Japan, in December 2001.

Child health is UNICEF's largest programme sector, accounting for some 40% of programme expenditure in 2000. UNICEF estimates that around 10m. children under five years of age die each year, mainly in developing countries, and the majority from largely preventable causes. UNICEF has worked with WHO and other partners to increase global immunization coverage against the following six diseases: measles, poliomyelitis, tuberculosis, diphtheria, whooping cough and tetanus. In 2000 UNICEF, in partnership with WHO, governments and other partners, helped to immunize 550m. children under five years of age in 53 countries against polio. In January of that year UNICEF, WHO, the World Bank and a number of public- and private-sector partners launched the Global Alliance for Vaccines and Immunization (GAVI), which aimed to protect children of all nationalities and socio-economic groups against vaccine-preventable diseases. GAVI's strategy included improving access to sustainable immunization services, expanding the use of existing vaccines, accelerating the development and introduction of new vaccines and technologies and promoting immunization coverage as a focus of international development efforts. UNICEF and WHO also work in conjunction on the Integrated Management of Childhood Illness programme to control diarrhoeal dehydration, a major cause of death among children under five years of age in the developing world. UNICEF-assisted programmes for the control of diarrhoeal diseases promote the low-cost manufacture and distribution of pre-packaged salts or home-made solutions. The use of 'oral rehydration therapy' has risen significantly in recent years, and is believed to prevent more than 1m. child deaths annually. During 1990–2000 diarrhoea-related deaths were reduced by one-half. UNICEF also promotes the need to improve sanitation and access to safe water supplies in developing nations in order to reduce the risk of diarrhoea and other water-borne diseases (see 20/20 initiative, above). To control acute respiratory infections, another leading cause of death in children under five in developing countries, UNICEF works with WHO in training health workers to diagnose and treat the associated diseases. As a result, child deaths from pneumonia and other respiratory infections have been reduced by one-half since 1990. Around 1m. children die from malaria every year, mainly in sub-Saharan Africa. In October 1998 UNICEF, together with WHO, UNDP and the World Bank, inaugurated a new global campaign, Roll Back Malaria, to fight the disease. UNICEF supports control programmes in more than 30 countries.

According to UNICEF estimates, around 27% of children under five years of age are underweight, while each year malnutrition contributes to about one-half of the child deaths in that age group and leaves millions of others with physical and mental disabilities. More than 2,000m. people world-wide (mainly women and children in developing countries) are estimated to be deficient in one or more essential vitamins and minerals, such as vitamin A, iodine and iron. UNICEF supports national efforts to reduce malnutrition, for example, fortifying staple foods with micronutrients, widening women's access to education, improving household food security and basic health services, and promoting sound child-care and feeding practices. Since 1991 more than 15,000 hospitals in at least 136 countries have been designated 'baby-friendly', having implemented a set of UNICEF and WHO recommendations entitled '10 steps to successful breast-feeding'. In 1996 UNICEF expressed its concern at the impact of international economic embargoes on child health, citing as an example the extensive levels of child malnutrition recorded in Iraq. UNICEF remains actively concerned at the levels of child malnutrition and accompanying diseases in Iraq and in the Democratic People's Republic of Korea, which has also suffered severe food shortages centres.

UNICEF estimates that almost 515,000 women die every year during pregnancy or childbirth, largely because of inadequate maternal health care. For every maternal death, approximately 30 further women suffer permanent injuries or chronic disabilities as a result of complications during pregnancy or childbirth. With its partners in the Safe Motherhood Initiative—UNFPA, WHO, the World Bank, the International Planned Parenthood Federation, the Population Council, and Family Care International—

UNICEF promotes measures to reduce maternal mortality and morbidity, including improving access to quality reproductive health services, educating communities about safe motherhood and the rights of women, training midwives, and expanding access to family planning services.

UNICEF is concerned at the danger posed by HIV/AIDS to the realization of children's rights. It is estimated that one-half of all new HIV infections occur in young people. At the end of 2001 11.8m. young people, aged 15 to 24 years, were living with HIV/AIDS. Some 800,000 children under 15 were newly infected during that year, while 580,000 died as a result of AIDS. UNICEF's priorities in this area include prevention of infection among young people, reduction in mother-to-child transmission, care and protection of orphans and other vulnerable children, and care and support for children, young people and parents living with HIV/AIDS. UNICEF works closely in this field with governments and co-operates with other UN agencies in the Joint UN Programme on HIV/AIDS (UNAIDS), which became operational on 1 January 1996.

UNICEF provides emergency relief assistance, supports education, health, mine-awareness and psychosocial activities and helps to demobilize and rehabilitate child soldiers in countries and territories affected by violence and social disintegration. It assists children orphaned or separated from their parents and made homeless through armed conflict. In recent years several such emergency operations have been undertaken, including in Afghanistan, Angola, Burundi, Kosovo, Liberia, Sierra Leone and Sudan. In 1999 UNICEF adopted a Peace and Security Agenda to help guide international efforts in this field. Emergency education assistance includes the provision of 'Edukits' in refugee camps and the reconstruction of school buildings. In the area of health the Fund co-operates with WHO to arrange 'days of tranquility' in order to facilitate the immunization of children in conflict zones. Psychosocial assistance activities include special programmes to assist traumatized children and help unaccompanied children to be reunited with parents or extended families. An estimated 300,000 children are involved in armed conflicts as soldiers, porters and forced labourers. UNICEF encourages ratification of the Optional Protocol to the Convention on the Rights of the Child on the involvement of children in armed conflict, which was adopted by the General Assembly in May 2000 and entered into force in February 2002, and bans the compulsory recruitment of combatants below 18 years. The Fund also urges states to make unequivocal statements endorsing 18 as the minimum age of voluntary recruitment to the armed forces. UNICEF was an active participant in the so-called 'Ottawa' process (supported by the Canadian Government) to negotiate an international ban on anti-personnel land-mines which, it was estimated, killed and maimed between 8,000 and 10,000 children every year. The Convention on the Prohibition of the Use, Stockpiling, Production and Transfer of Anti-Personnel Mines and on their Destruction was adopted in December 1997 and entered into force in March 1999. By October 2001 the Convention had been ratified by 122 countries. UNICEF is committed to campaigning for its universal ratification and full implementation, and also supports mine-awareness campaigns.

Finance

UNICEF is funded by voluntary contributions from governments and non-governmental and private-sector sources. Total income in 2000 amounted to US $1,139m., of which 64% was from governments and intergovernmental organizations. Total expenditure in 2000 amounted to $1,111m.

UNICEF's income is divided into contributions for 'regular resources' (used for country programmes of co-operation approved by the Executive Board, programme support, and management and administration costs) and contributions for 'other resources' (for special purposes, including expanding the outreach of country programmes of co-operation and ensuring capacity to deliver critical assistance to women and children for example during humanitarian crises). In 2000 contributions for 'regular resources' totalled US $563m. and those for 'other resources' amounted to $576m.

Publications

Facts and Figures (in English, French and Spanish).

The State of the World's Children (annually, in Arabic, English, French, Russian and Spanish and about 30 other national languages).

UNICEF Annual Report (in English, French and Spanish).

UNICEF at a Glance (annually, in English, French and Spanish).

Reports; series on children and women; nutrition; education; children's rights; children in wars and disasters; working children; water; sanitation and the environment; analyses of the situation of children and women in individual developing countries.

Convention on the Rights of the Child

(Adopted by the General Assembly on 20 November 1989)

PREAMBLE

The States Parties to the present Convention,

Considering that, in accordance with the principles proclaimed in the Charter of the United Nations, recognition of the inherent dignity and of the equal and inalienable rights of all members of the human family is the foundation of freedom, justice and peace in the world,

Bearing in mind that the peoples of the United Nations have, in the Charter, reaffirmed their faith in fundamental human rights and in the dignity and worth of the human person, and have determined to promote social progress and better standards of life in larger freedom,

Recognizing that the United Nations has, in the Universal Declaration of Human Rights and in the International Covenants on Human Rights, proclaimed and agreed that everyone is entitled to all the rights and freedoms set forth therein, without distinction of any kind, such as race, colour, sex, language, religion, political or other opinion, national or social origin, property, birth or other status,

Recalling that, in the Universal Declaration of Human Rights, the United Nations has proclaimed that childhood is entitled to special care and assistance,

Convinced that the family, as the fundamental group of society and the natural environment for the growth and well-being of all its members and particularly children, should be afforded the necessary protection and assistance so that it can fully assume its responsibilities within the community,

Recognizing that the child, for the full and harmonious development of his or her personality, should grow up in a family environment, in an atmosphere of happiness, love and understanding,

Considering that the child should be fully prepared to live an individual life in society, and brought up in the spirit of the ideals proclaimed in the Charter of the United Nations, and in particular in the spirit of peace, dignity, tolerance, freedom, equality and solidarity,

Bearing in mind that the need to extend particular care to the child has been stated in the Geneva Declaration of the Rights of the Child of 1924 and in the Declaration of the Rights of the Child adopted by the General Assembly on 20 November 1959 and recognized in the Universal Declaration of Human Rights, in the International Covenant on Civil and Political Rights (in particular in articles 23 and 24), in the International Covenant on Economic, Social and Cultural Rights (in particular in article 10) and in the statutes and relevant instruments of specialized agencies and international organizations concerned with the welfare of children,

Bearing in mind that, as indicated in the Declaration of the Rights of the Child, 'the child, by reason of his physical and mental immaturity, needs special safeguards and care, including appropriate legal protection, before as well as after birth',

Recalling the provisions of the Declaration on Social and Legal Principles relating to the Protection and Welfare of Children, with Special Reference to Foster Placement and Adoption Nationally and Internationally; the United Nations Standard Minimum

Rules for the Administration of Juvenile Justice (The Beijing Rules); and the Declaration on the Protection of Women and Children in Emergency and Armed Conflict,

Recognizing that, in all countries in the world, there are children living in exceptionally difficult conditions, and that such children need special consideration,

Taking due account of the importance of the traditions and cultural values of each people for the protection and harmonious development of the child,

Recognizing the importance of international co-operation for improving the living conditions of children in every country, in particular in the developing countries,

Have agreed as follows:

PART I

Article 1

For the purposes of the present Convention, a child means every human being below the age of eighteen years unless, under the law applicable to the child, majority is attained earlier.

Article 2

1. States Parties shall respect and ensure the rights set forth in the present Convention to each child within their jurisdiction without discrimination of any kind, irrespective of the child's or his or her parent's or legal guardian's race, colour, sex, language, religion, political or other opinion, national, ethnic or social origin, property, disability, birth or other status.

2. States Parties shall take all appropriate measures to ensure that the child is protected against all forms of discrimination or punishment on the basis of the status, activities, expressed opinions, or beliefs of the child's parents, legal guardians, or family members.

Article 3

1. In all actions concerning children, whether undertaken by public or private social welfare institutions, courts of law, administrative authorities or legislative bodies, the best interests of the child shall be a primary consideration.

2. States Parties undertake to ensure the child such protection and care as is necessary for his or her well-being, taking into account the rights and duties of his or her parents, legal guardians, or other individuals legally responsible for him or her, and, to this end, shall take all appropriate legislative and administrative measures.

3. States Parties shall ensure that the institutions, services and facilities responsible for the care or protection of children shall conform with the standards established by competent authorities, particularly in the areas of safety, health, in the number and suitability of their staff, as well as competent supervision.

Article 4

States Parties shall undertake all appropriate legislative, administrative, and other measures for the implementation of the rights recognized in the present Convention. With regard to economic, social and cultural rights, States Parties shall undertake such measures to the maximum extent of their available resources and, where needed, within the framework of international co-operation.

Article 5

States Parties shall respect the responsibilities, rights and duties of parents or, where applicable, the members of the extended family or community as provided for by local custom, legal guardians or other persons legally responsible for the child, to provide, in a manner consistent with the evolving capacities of the child, appropriate direction and guidance in the exercise by the child of the rights recognized in the present Convention.

Article 6

1. States Parties recognize that every child has the inherent right to life.

2. States Parties shall ensure to the maximum extent possible the survival and development of the child.

Article 7

1. The child shall be registered immediately after birth and shall have the right from birth to a name, the right to acquire a nationality and, as far as possible, the right to know and be cared for by his or her parents.

2. States Parties shall ensure the implementation of these rights in accordance with their national law and their obligations under the relevant international instruments in this field, in particular where the child would otherwise be stateless.

Article 8

1. States Parties undertake to respect the right of the child to preserve his or her identity, including nationality, name and family relations as recognized by law without unlawful interference.

2. Where a child is legally deprived of some or all of the elements of his or her identity, States Parties shall provide appropriate assistance and protection, with a view to re-establishing speedily his or her identity.

Article 9

1. States Parties shall ensure that a child shall not be separated from his or her parents against their will, except when competent authorities subject to judicial review determine, in accordance with applicable law and procedures, that such separation is necessary for the best interests of the child. Such determination may be necessary in a particular case such as one involving abuse or neglect of the child by the parents, or one where the parents are living separately and a decision must be made as to the child's place of residence.

2. In any proceedings pursuant to paragraph 1 of the present article, all interested parties shall be given an opportunity to participate in the proceedings and make their views known.

3. States Parties shall respect the right of the child who is separated from one or both parents to maintain personal relations and direct contact with both parents on a regular basis, except if it is contrary to the child's best interests.

4. Where such separation results from any action initiated by a State Party, such as the detention, imprisonment, exile, deportation or death (including death arising from any cause while the person is in the custody of the State) of one or both parents or of the child, that State Party shall, upon request, provide the parents, the child or, if appropriate, another member of the family with the essential information concerning the whereabouts of the absent member(s) of the family unless the provision of the information would be detrimental to the well-being of the child. States Parties shall further ensure that the submission of such a request shall of itself entail no adverse consequences for the person(s) concerned.

Article 10

1. In accordance with the obligation of States Parties under article 9, paragraph 1, applications by a child or his or her parents to enter or leave a State Party for the purpose of family reunification shall be dealt with by States Parties in a positive, humane and expeditious manner. States Parties shall further ensure that the submission of such a request shall entail no adverse consequences for the applicants and for the members of their family.

2. A child whose parents reside in different States shall have the right to maintain on a regular basis, save in exceptional circumstances, personal relations and direct contacts with both parents. Towards that end and in accordance with the obligation of States Parties under article 9, paragraph 1, States Parties shall respect the right of the child and his or her parents to leave any country, including their own, and to enter their own country. The right to leave any country shall be subject only to such restrictions as are prescribed by law and which are necessary to protect the national security, public order (ordre public), public health or morals or the rights and freedoms of others and are consistent with the other rights recognized in the present Convention.

Article 11

1. States Parties shall take measures to combat the illicit transfer and non-return of children abroad.

2. To this end, States Parties shall promote the conclusion of bilateral or multilateral agreements or accession to existing agreements.

Article 12

1. States Parties shall assure to the child who is capable of forming his or her own views the right to express those views freely in all matters affecting the child, the views of the child being given due weight in accordance with the age and maturity of the child.

2. For this purpose, the child shall in particular be provided the opportunity to be heard in any judicial and administrative proceedings affecting the child, either directly, or through a representative or an appropriate body, in a manner consistent with the procedural rules of national law.

Article 13

1. The child shall have the right to freedom of expression; this right shall include freedom to seek, receive and impart information and ideas of all kinds, regardless of frontiers, either orally, in writing or in print, in the form of art, or through any other media of the child's choice.

2. The exercise of this right may be subject to certain restrictions, but these shall only be such as are provided by law and are necessary:

(a) For respect of the rights or reputations of others; or

(b) For the protection of national security or of public order (ordre public), or of public health or morals.

Article 14

1. States Parties shall respect the right of the child to freedom of thought, conscience and religion.

2. States Parties shall respect the rights and duties of the parents and, when applicable, legal guardians, to provide direction to the child in the exercise of his or her right in a manner consistent with the evolving capacities of the child.

3. Freedom to manifest one's religion or beliefs may be subject only to such limitations as are prescribed by law and are necessary to protect public safety, order, health or morals, or the fundamental rights and freedoms of others.

Article 15

1. States Parties recognize the rights of the child to freedom of association and to freedom of peaceful assembly.

2. No restrictions may be placed on the exercise of these rights other than those imposed in conformity with the law and which are necessary in a democratic society in the interests of national security or public safety, public order (ordre public), the protection of public health or morals or the protection of the rights and freedoms of others.

Article 16

1. No child shall be subjected to arbitrary or unlawful interference with his or her privacy, family, home or correspondence, nor to unlawful attacks on his or her honour and reputation.

2. The child has the right to the protection of the law against such interference or attacks.

Article 17

States Parties recognize the important function performed by the mass media and shall ensure that the child has access to information and material from a diversity of national and international sources, especially those aimed at the promotion of his or her social, spiritual and moral well-being and physical and mental health. To this end, States Parties shall:

(a) Encourage the mass media to disseminate information and material of social and cultural benefit to the child and in accordance with the spirit of article 29;

(b) Encourage international co-operation in the production, exchange and dissemination of such information and material from a diversity of cultural, national and international sources;

(c) Encourage the production and dissemination of children's books;

(d) Encourage the mass media to have particular regard to the linguistic needs of the child who belongs to a minority group or who is indigenous;

(e) Encourage the development of appropriate guidelines for the protection of the child from information and material injurious to his or her well-being, bearing in mind the provisions of articles 13 and 18.

Article 18

1. States Parties shall use their best efforts to ensure recognition of the principle that both parents have common responsibilities for the upbringing and development of the child. Parents or, as the case may be, legal guardians, have the primary responsibility for the upbringing and development of the child. The best interests of the child will be their basic concern.

2. For the purpose of guaranteeing and promoting the rights set forth in the present Convention, States Parties shall render appropriate assistance to parents and legal guardians in the performance of their child-rearing responsibilities and shall ensure the development of institutions, facilities and services for the care of children.

3. States Parties shall take all appropriate measures to ensure that children of working parents have the right to benefit from child-care services and facilities for which they are eligible.

Article 19

1. States Parties shall take all appropriate legislative, administrative, social and educational measures to protect the child from all forms of physical or mental violence, injury or abuse, neglect or negligent treatment, maltreatment or exploitation, including sexual abuse, while in the care of parent(s), legal guardian(s) or any other person who has the care of the child.

2. Such protective measures should, as appropriate, include effective procedures for the establishment of social programmes to provide necessary support for the child and for those who have the care of the child, as well as for other forms of prevention and for identification, reporting, referral, investigation, treatment and follow-up of instances of child maltreatment described heretofore, and, as appropriate, for judicial involvement.

Article 20

1. A child temporarily or permanently deprived of his or her family environment, or in whose own best interests cannot be allowed to remain in that environment, shall be entitled to special protection and assistance provided by the State.

2. States Parties shall in accordance with their national laws ensure alternative care for such a child.

3. Such care could include, *inter alia*, foster placement, *kafalah* of Islamic law, adoption or if necessary placement in suitable institutions for the care of children. When considering solutions, due regard shall be paid to the desirability of continuity in a child's upbringing and to the child's ethnic, religious, cultural and linguistic background.

Article 21

States Parties that recognize and/or permit the system of adoption shall ensure that the best interests of the child shall be the paramount consideration and they shall:

(a) Ensure that the adoption of a child is authorized only by competent authorities who determine, in accordance with applicable law and procedures and on the basis of all pertinent and reliable information, that the adoption is permissible in view of the child's status concerning parents, relatives and legal guardians and that, if required, the persons concerned have given their informed consent to the adoption on the basis of such counselling as may be necessary;

(b) Recognize that inter-country adoption may be considered as an alternative means of a child's care, if the child cannot be placed in a foster or an adoptive family or cannot in any suitable manner be cared for in the child's country of origin;

(c) Ensure that the child concerned by inter-country adoption enjoys safeguards and standards equivalent to those existing in the case of national adoption;

(d) Take all appropriate measures to ensure that, in inter-country adoption, the placement does not result in improper financial gain for those involved in it;

(e) Promote, where appropriate, the objectives of the present article by concluding bilateral or multilateral arrangements or agreements, and endeavour, within this framework, to ensure that the placement of the child in another country is carried out by competent authorities or organs.

Article 22

1. States Parties shall take appropriate measures to ensure that a child who is seeking refugee status or who is considered a

refugee in accordance with applicable international or domestic law and procedures shall, whether unaccompanied or accompanied by his or her parents or by any other person, receive appropriate protection and humanitarian assistance in the enjoyment of applicable rights set forth in the present Convention and in other international human rights or humanitarian instruments to which the said States are Parties.

2. For the purpose, States Parties shall provide, as they consider appropriate, co-operation in any efforts by the United Nations and other competent intergovernmental organizations or non-governmental organizations co-operating with the United Nations to protect and assist such a child and to trace the parents or other members of the family of any refugee child in order to obtain information necessary for reunification with his or her family. In cases where no parents or other members of the family can be found, the child shall be accorded the same protection as any other child permanently or temporarily deprived of his or her family environment for any reason, as set forth in the present Convention.

Article 23

1. States Parties recognize that a mentally or physically disabled child should enjoy a full and decent life, in conditions which ensure dignity, promote self-reliance and facilitate the child's active participation in the community.

2. States Parties recognize the right of the disabled child to special care and shall encourage and ensure the extension, subject to available resources, to the eligible child and those responsible for his or her care, of assistance for which application is made and which is appropriate to the child's condition and to the circumstances of the parents or others caring for the child.

3. Recognizing the special needs of a disabled child, assistance extended in accordance with paragraph 2 of the present article shall be provided free of charge, whenever possible, taking into account the financial resources of the parents or others caring for the child, and shall be designed to ensure that the disabled child has effective access to and receives education, training, health care services, rehabilitation services, preparation for employment and recreation opportunities in a manner conducive to the child's achieving the fullest possible social integration and individual development, including his or her cultural and spiritual development.

4. States Parties shall promote, in the spirit of international co-operation, the exchange of appropriate information in the field of preventive health care and of medical, psychological and functional treatment of disabled children, including dissemination of and access to information concerning methods of rehabilitation, education and vocational services, with the aim of enabling States Parties to improve their capabilities and skills to widen their experience in these areas. In this regard, particular account shall be taken of the needs of developing countries.

Article 24

1. States Parties recognize the right of the child to the enjoyment of the highest attainable standard of health and to facilities for the treatment of illness and rehabilitation of health. States Parties shall strive to ensure that no child is deprived of his or her right of access to such health care services.

2. States Parties shall pursue full implementation of this right and, in particular, shall take appropriate measures:

(a) To diminish infant and child mortality;

(b) To ensure the provision of necessary medical assistance and health care to all children with emphasis on the development of primary health care;

(c) To combat disease and malnutrition, including within the framework of primary health care, through, *inter alia,* the application of readily available technology and through the provision of adequate nutritious foods and clean drinking-water, taking into consideration the dangers and risks of environmental pollution;

(d) To ensure appropriate pre-natal and post-natal health care for mothers;

(e) To ensure that all segments of society, in particular parents and children, are informed, have access to education and are supported in the use of basic knowledge of child health and nutrition, the advantages of breast-feeding, hygiene and environmental sanitation and the prevention of accidents;

(f) To develop preventive health care, guidance for parents and family planning education and services.

3. States Parties shall take all effective and appropriate measures with a view to abolishing traditional practices prejudicial to the health of children.

4. States Parties undertake to promote and encourage international co-operation with a view to achieving progressively the full realization of the right recognized in the present article. In this regard, particular account shall be taken of the needs of developing countries.

Article 25

States Parties recognize the right of a child who has been placed by the competent authorities for the purposes of care, protection or treatment of his or her physical or mental health, to a periodic review of the treatment provided to the child and all other circumstances relevant to his or her placement.

Article 26

1. States Parties shall recognize for every child the right to benefit from social security, including social insurance, and shall take the necessary measures to achieve the full realization of this right in accordance with their national law.

2. The benefits should, where appropriate, be granted, taking into account the resources and the circumstances of the child and persons having responsibility for the maintenance of the child, as well as any other consideration relevant to an application for benefits made by or on behalf of the child.

Article 27

1. States Parties recognize the right of every child to a standard of living adequate for the child's physical, mental, spiritual, moral and social development.

2. The parent(s) or others responsible for the child have the primary responsibility to secure, within their abilities and financial capacities, the conditions of living necessary for the child's development.

3. States Parties, in accordance with national conditions and within their means, shall take appropriate measures to assist parents and others responsible for the child to implement this right and shall in case of need provide material assistance and support programmes, particularly with regard to nutrition, clothing and housing.

4. States Parties shall take all appropriate measures to secure the recovery of maintenance for the child from the parents or other persons having financial responsibility for the child, both within the State Party and from abroad. In particular, where the person having financial responsibility for the child lives in a State different from that of the child, States Parties shall promote the accession to international agreements or the conclusion of such agreements, as well as the making of other appropriate arrangements.

Article 28

1. States Parties recognize the right of the child to education, and with a view to achieving this right progressively and on the basis of equal opportunity, they shall, in particular:

(a) Make primary education compulsory and available free to all;

(b) Encourage the development of different forms of secondary education, including general and vocational education, make them available and accessible to every child, and take appropriate measures such as the introduction of free education and offering financial assistance in case of need;

(c) Make higher education accessible to all on the basis of capacity by every appropriate means;

(d) Make educational and vocational information and guidance available and accessible to all children;

(e) Take measures to encourage regular attendance at schools and the reduction of drop-out rates.

2. States Parties shall take all appropriate measures to ensure that school discipline is administered in a manner consistent with the child's human dignity and in conformity with the present Convention.

3. States Parties shall promote and encourage international co-operation in matters relating to education, in particular with a view to contributing to the elimination of ignorance and illiteracy throughout the world and facilitating access to scientific and technical knowledge and modern teaching methods. In this regard, particular account shall be taken of the needs of developing countries.

Article 29

1. States Parties agree that the education of the child shall be directed to:

(a) The development of the child's personality, talents and mental and physical abilities to their fullest potential;

(b) The development of respect for human rights and fundamental freedoms, and for the principles enshrined in the Charter of the United Nations;

(c) The development of respect for the child's parents, his or her own cultural identity, language and values, for the national values of the country in which the child is living, the country from which he or she may originate, and for civilizations different from his or her own;

(d) The preparation of the child for responsible life in a free society, in the spirit of understanding, peace, tolerance, equality of sexes, and friendship among all peoples, ethnic, national and religious groups and persons of indigenous origin;

(e) The development of respect for the natural environment.

2. No part of the present article or article 28 shall be construed so as to interfere with the liberty of individuals and bodies to establish and direct educational institutions, subject always to the observance of the principle set forth in paragraph 1 of the present article and to the requirements that the education given in such institutions shall conform to such minimum standards as may be laid down by the State.

Article 30

In those States in which ethnic, religious or linguistic minorities or persons of indigenous origin exist, a child belonging to such a minority or who is indigenous shall not be denied the right, in community with other members of his or her group, to enjoy his or her own culture, to profess and practise his or her own religion, or to use his or her own language.

Article 31

1. States Parties recognize the right of the child to rest and leisure, to engage in play and recreational activities appropriate to the age of the child and to participate freely in cultural life and the arts.

2. States Parties shall respect and promote the right of the child to participate fully in cultural and artistic life and shall encourage the provision of appropriate and equal opportunities for cultural, artistic, recreational and leisure activity.

Article 32

1. States Parties recognize the right of the child to be protected from economic exploitation and from performing any work that is likely to be hazardous or to interfere with the child's education, or to be harmful to the child's health or physical, mental, spiritual, moral or social development.

2. States Parties shall take legislative, administrative, social and educational measures to ensure the implementation of the present article. To this end, and having regard to the relevant provisions of other international instruments, States Parties shall in particular:

(a) Provide for a minimum age or minimum ages for admission to employment;

(b) Provide for appropriate regulation of the hours and conditions of employment;

(c) Provide for appropriate penalties or other sanctions to ensure the effective enforcement of the present article.

Article 33

States Parties shall take all appropriate measures, including legislative, administrative, social and educational measures, to protect children from the illicit use of narcotic drugs and psychotropic substances as defined in the relevant international treaties, and to prevent the use of children in the illicit production and trafficking of such substances.

Article 34

States Parties undertake to protect the child from all forms of sexual exploitation and sexual abuse. For these purposes, States Parties shall in particular take all appropriate national, bilateral and multilateral measures to prevent:

(a) The inducement or coercion of a child to engage in any unlawful sexual activity;

(b) The exploitative use of children in prostitution or other unlawful sexual practices;

(c) The exploitative use of children in pornographic performances and materials.

Article 35

States Parties shall take all appropriate national, bilateral and multilateral measures to prevent the abduction of, the sale of or traffic in children for any purpose or in any form.

Article 36

States Parties shall protect the child against all other forms of exploitation prejudicial to any aspects of the child's welfare.

Article 37

States Parties shall ensure that:

(a) No child shall be subjected to torture or other cruel, inhuman or degrading treatment or punishment. Neither capital punishment nor life imprisonment without possibility of release shall be imposed for offences committed by persons below eighteen years of age;

(b) No child shall be deprived of his or her liberty unlawfully or arbitrarily. The arrest, detention or imprisonment of a child shall be in conformity with the law and shall be used only as a measure of last resort and for the shortest appropriate period of time;

(c) Every child deprived of liberty shall be treated with humanity and respect for the inherent dignity of the human person, and in a manner which takes into account the needs of persons of his or her age. In particular, every child deprived of liberty shall be separated from adults unless it is considered in the child's best interest not to do so and shall have the right to maintain contact with his or her family through correspondence and visits, save in exceptional circumstances;

(d) Every child deprived of his or her liberty shall have the right to prompt access to legal and other appropriate assistance, as well as the right to challenge the legality of the deprivation of his or her liberty before a court or other competent, independent and impartial authority, and to a prompt decision on any such action.

Article 38

1. States Parties undertake to respect and to ensure respect for rules of international humanitarian law applicable to them in armed conflicts which are relevant to the child.

2. States Parties shall take all feasible measures to ensure that persons who have not attained the age of fifteen years do not take a direct part in hostilities.

3. States Parties shall refrain from recruiting any person who has not attained the age of fifteen years into their armed forces. In recruiting among those persons who have attained the age of fifteen years but who have not attained the age of eighteen years, States Parties shall endeavour to give priority to those who are oldest.

4. In accordance with their obligations under international humanitarian law to protect the civilian population in armed conflicts, States Parties shall take all feasible measures to ensure protection and care of children who are affected by an armed conflict.

Article 39

States Parties shall take all appropriate measures to promote physical and psychological recovery and social reintegration of a child victim of: any form of neglect, exploitation, or abuse; torture or any other form of cruel, inhuman or degrading treatment or punishment; or armed conflicts. Such recovery and reintegration shall take place in an environment which fosters the health, self-respect and dignity of the child.

Article 40

1. States Parties recognize the right of every child alleged as, accused of, or recognized as having infringed the penal law to be treated in a manner consistent with the promotion of the child's sense of dignity and worth, which reinforces the child's respect for the human rights and fundamental freedoms of others and which takes into account the child's age and the desirability of promoting the child's reintegration and the child's assuming a constructive role in society.

2. To this end, and having regard to the relevant provisions of international instruments, States Parties shall, in particular, ensure that:

(a) No child shall be alleged as, be accused of, or recognized as having infringed the penal law by reason of acts or omissions that were not prohibited by national or international law at the time they were committed;

(b) Every child alleged as or accused of having infringed the penal law has at least the following guarantees:

(i) To be presumed innocent until proven guilty according to law;

(ii) To be informed promptly and directly of the charges against him or her, and, if appropriate, through his or her parents or legal guardians, and to have legal or other appropriate assistance in the preparation and presentation of his or her defence;

(iii) To have the matter determined without delay by a competent, independent and impartial authority or judicial body in a fair hearing according to law, in the presence of legal or other appropriate assistance and, unless it is considered not to be in the best interest of the child, in particular, taking into account his or her age or situation, his or her parents or legal guardians;

(iv) Not to be compelled to give testimony or to confess guilt; to examine or have examined adverse witnesses and to obtain the participation and examination of witnesses on his or her behalf under conditions of equality;

(v) If considered to have infringed the penal law, to have this decision and any measures imposed in consequence thereof reviewed by a higher competent, independent and impartial authority or judicial body according to law;

(vi) To have the free assistance of an interpreter if the child cannot understand or speak the language used;

(vii) To have his or her privacy fully respected at all stages of the proceedings.

3. States Parties shall seek to promote the establishment of laws, procedures, authorities and institutions specifically applicable to children alleged as, accused of, or recognized as having infringed the penal law, and, in particular:

(a) The establishment of a minimum age below which children shall be presumed not to have the capacity to infringe the penal law;

(b) Whenever appropriate and desirable, measures for dealing with such children without resorting to judicial proceedings, providing that human rights and legal safeguards are fully respected.

4. A variety of dispositions, such as care, guidance and supervision orders; counselling; probation; foster care; education and vocational training programmes and other alternatives to institutional care shall be available to ensure that children are dealt with in a manner appropriate to their well-being and proportionate both to their circumstances and the offence.

Article 41

Nothing in the present Convention shall affect any provisions which are more conducive to the realization of the rights of the child and which may be contained in:

(a) The law of a State party; or

(b) International law in force for that State.

PART II

Article 42

States Parties undertake to make the principles and provisions of the Convention widely known, by appropriate and active means, to adults and children alike.

Article 43

1. For the purpose of examining the progress made by States Parties in achieving the realization of the obligations undertaken in the present Convention, there shall be established a Committee on the Rights of the Child, which shall carry out the functions hereinafter provided.

2. The Committee shall consist of 10 experts of high moral standing and recognized competence in the field covered by this Convention. The members of the Committee shall be elected by States Parties from among their nationals and shall serve in their personal capacity, consideration being given to equitable geographical distribution, as well as to the principal legal systems.

3. The members of the Committee shall be elected by secret ballot from a list of persons nominated by States Parties. Each State Party may nominate one person from among its own nationals.

4. The initial election to the Committee shall be held no later than six months after the date of the entry into force of the present Convention and thereafter every second year. At least four months before the date of each election, the Secretary-General of the United Nations shall address a letter to States Parties inviting them to submit their nominations within two months. The Secretary-General shall subsequently prepare a list in alphabetical order of all persons thus nominated, indicating States Parties which have nominated them, and shall submit it to the States Parties to the present Convention.

5. The elections shall be held at meetings of States Parties convened by the Secretary-General at United Nations Headquarters. At those meetings, for which two-thirds of States Parties shall constitute a quorum, the persons elected to the Committee shall be those who obtain the largest number of votes and an absolute majority of the votes of the representatives of States Parties present and voting.

6. The members of the Committee shall be elected for a term of four years. They shall be eligible for re-election if renominated. The term of five of the members elected at the first election shall expire at the end of two years; immediately after the first election, the names of these five members shall be chosen by lot by the Chairman of the meeting.

7. If a member of the Committee dies or resigns or declares that for any other cause he or she can no longer perform the duties of the Committee, the State Party which nominated the member shall appoint another expert from among its nationals to serve for the remainder of the term, subject to the approval of the Committee.

8. The Committee shall establish its own rules of procedure.

9. The Committee shall elect its officers for a period of two years.

10. The meetings of the Committee shall normally be held at United Nations Headquarters or at any other convenient place as determined by the Committee. The Committee shall normally meet annually. The duration of the meetings of the Committee shall be detemined, and reviewed, if necessary, by a meeting of the States Parties to the present Convention, subject to the approval of the General Assembly.

11. The Secretary-General of the United Nations shall provide the necessary staff and facilities for the effective performance of the functions of the Committee under the present Convention.

12. With the approval of the General Assembly, the members of the Committee established under the present Convention shall receive emoluments from the United Nations resources on such terms and conditions as the Assembly may decide.

Article 44

1. States Parties undertake to submit to the Committee, through the Secretary-General of the United Nations, reports on the measures they have adopted which give effect to the rights recog nized herein and on the progress made on the enjoyment of those rights:

(a) Within two years of the entry into force of the Convention for the State Party concerned,

(b) Thereafter every five years.

2. Reports made under the present article shall indicate factors and difficulties, if any, affecting the degree of fulfilment of the obligations under the present Convention. Reports shall also

contain sufficient information to provide the Committee with a comprehensive understanding of the implementation of the Convention in the country concerned.

3. A State Party which has submitted a comprehensive initial report to the Committee need not in its subsequent reports submitted in accordance with paragraph 1(b) of the present article repeat basic information previously provided.

4. The Committee may request from States Parties further information relevant to the implementation of the Convention.

5. The Committee shall submit to the General Assembly, through the Economic and Social Council, every two years, reports on its activities.

6. States Parties shall make their reports widely available to the public in their own countries.

Article 45

In order to foster the effective implementation of the Convention and to encourage international co-operation in the field covered by the Convention:

(a) The specialized agencies, the United Nations Children's Fund and other United Nations organs shall be entitled to be represented at the consideration of the implementation of such provisions of the present Convention as fall within the scope of their mandate. The Committee may invite the specialized agencies, the United Nations Children's Fund and other competent bodies as it may consider appropriate to provide expert advice on the implementation of the Convention in areas falling within the scope of their respective mandates. The Committee may invite the specialized agencies, the United Nations Children's Fund and other United Nations organs to submit reports on the implementation of the Convention in areas falling within the scope of their activities;

(b) The Committee shall transmit, as it may consider appropriate, to the specialized agencies, the United Nations Children's Fund and other competent bodies, any reports from States Parties that contain a request, or indicate a need, for technical advice or assistance, along with the Committee's observations and suggestions, if any, on these requests or indications;

(c) The Committee may recommend to the General Assembly to request the Secretary-General to undertake on its behalf studies on specific issues relating to the rights of the child;

(d) The Committee may make suggestions and general recommendations based on information received pursuant to articles 44 and 45 of the present Convention. Such suggestions and general recommendations shall be transmitted to any State Party concerned and reported to the General Assembly, together with comments, if any, from States Parties.

PART III

Article 46

The present Convention shall be open for signature by all States.

Article 47

The present Convention is subject to ratification. Instruments of ratification shall be deposited with the Secretary-General of the United Nations.

Article 48

The present Convention shall remain open for accession by any State. The instruments of accession shall be deposited with the Secretary-General of the United Nations.

Article 49

1. The present Convention shall enter into force on the thirtieth day following the date of deposit with the Secretary-General of the United Nations of the twentieth instrument of ratification or accession.

2. For each State ratifying or acceding to the Convention after the deposit of the twentieth instrument of ratification or accession, the Convention shall enter into force on the thirtieth day after the deposit by such State of its instrument of ratification or accession.

Article 50

1. Any State Party may propose an amendment and file it with the Secretary-General of the United Nations. The Secretary-General shall thereupon communicate the proposed amendment to States Parties, with a request that they indicate whether they favour a conference of States Parties for the purpose of considering and voting upon the proposals. In the event that, within four months from the date of such communication, at least one-third of the States Parties favour such a conference, the Secretary-General shall convene the conference under the auspices of the United Nations. Any amendment adopted by a majority of States Parties present and voting at the conference shall be submitted to the General Assembly for approval.

2. An amendment adopted in accordance with paragraph 1 of the present article shall enter into force when it has been approved by the General Assembly of the United Nations and accepted by a two-thirds majority of States Parties.

3. When an amendment enters into force, it shall be binding on those States Parties which have accepted it, other States Parties still being bound by the provisions of the present Convention and any earlier amendments which they have accepted.

Article 51

1. The Secretary-General of the United Nations shall receive and circulate to all States the text of reservations made by States at the time of ratification or accession.

2. A reservation incompatible with the object and purpose of the present Convention shall not be permitted.

3. Reservations may be withdrawn at any time by notification to that effect addressed to the Secretary-General of the United Nations, who shall then inform all States. Such notification shall take effect on the date on which it is received by the Secretary-General.

Article 52

A State Party may denounce the present Convention by written notification to the Secretary-General of the United Nations. Denunciation becomes effective one year after the date of receipt of the notification by the Secretary-General.

Article 53

The Secretary-General of the United Nations is designated as the depositary of the present Convention.

Article 54

The original of the present Convention, of which the Arabic, Chinese, English, French, Russian and Spanish texts are equally authentic, shall be deposited with the Secretary-General of the United Nations.

In witness thereof the undersigned plenipotentiaries, being duly authorized thereto by their respective Governments, have signed the present Convention.

United Nations Conference on Trade and Development—UNCTAD

Address: Palais des Nations, 1211 Geneva 10, Switzerland.

Telephone: (22) 9071234; **fax:** (22) 9070057; **e-mail:** ers@unctad.org; **internet:** www.unctad.org.

UNCTAD was established in December 1964. It is the principal instrument of the UN General Assembly concerned with trade and development, and is the focal point within the UN system for integrated activities relating to trade, finance, technology, investment and sustainable development. It aims to maximize the trade and development opportunities of developing countries, in particular least-developed countries, and to assist them to adapt to the increasing globalization and liberalization of the world economy.

Organization

(March 2002)

CONFERENCE

The Conference is the organization's highest policy-making body and normally meets every four years at ministerial level in order to formulate major policy guide-lines and to decide on UNCTAD's forthcoming programme of work. Tenth session: Bangkok, Thailand, February 2000. All 189 UN member states are members of UNCTAD (as well as Switzerland and the Holy See), while many intergovernmental and non-governmental organizations participate in its work as observers.

TRADE AND DEVELOPMENT BOARD

The Trade and Development Board is the executive body of UNCTAD. It comprises elected representatives from 146 UNCTAD member states and is responsible for ensuring the overall consistency of UNCTAD's activities, as well as those of its subsidiary bodies. The Board meets for a regular annual session lasting about 10 days, at which it examines global economic issues. It also reviews the implementation of the Programme of Action for the Least-Developed Countries and the UN New Agenda for the Development of Africa in the 1990s (UNNADF), with particular attention given to lessons that may be drawn from successful development experiences. The final review of UNNADF was due to take place in 2002. The Board may also meet a further three times a year in order to address management or institutional matters.

COMMISSIONS

The Trade and Development Board has three Commissions: the Commission on Trade in Goods and Services and Commodities; the Commission on Investment, Technology and Related Financial Issues; and the Commission on Enterprise, Business Facilitation and Development. The Commissions meet once a year in regular session and may convene up to 10 Expert Meetings a year on specific issues.

SECRETARIAT

The secretariat comprises the following Divisions: Globalization and Development Strategies; International Trade in Goods and Services and Commodities; Investment, Technology and Enterprise Development; Services Infrastructure for Development and Trade Efficiency. It also incorporates the Office of the Special Co-ordinator for Least Developed, Land-locked, and Small Island Developing States.

The UNCTAD secretariat undertakes policy analysis; monitoring, implementation and follow-up of decisions of intergovernmental bodies; technical co-operation in support of UNCTAD's policy objectives; and information exchanges and consultations of various types.

Secretary-General: RUBENS RICÚPERO (Brazil).

Activities

During the 1980s UNCTAD focused on its role in providing a forum for the negotiation of international agreements on commodities. (Such agreements are designed to ensure the stabilization of conditions in the trade of the commodities concerned.) UNCTAD's facilitation of international commodity agreements has subsequently continued but has been superseded as a priority by other activities (see below). Under UNCTAD's auspices agreements have been negotiated or renegotiated on cocoa (1975, 1980, 1986 and 1993), jute (1982 and 1989), olive oil (1986), rubber (1979, 1987 and 1995), sugar (1977 and 1992), tin (1981) and tropical timber (1994). The establishment of the Common Fund for Commodities was agreed by UNCTAD in 1980, and the Fund came into operation in September 1989 (see p. 527).

By the early 1990s several commodity agreements had lapsed and the conclusion of the GATT Uruguay Round of trade talks in December 1993 and the changes in international trading structures that had already taken place were deemed to necessitate a substantial reorientation of UNCTAD's role. Following restructuring agreed at the eighth session of the Conference in Cartagena, Colombia, in February 1992, further changes to UNCTAD's focus and organization were approved at the ninth Conference. In particular, UNCTAD was to give special attention to assisting developing countries in taking advantage of the increased liberalization of world trade under the GATT and World Trade Organization agreements (q.v.). Concern was expressed that the world's poorest countries would be even further marginalized if they were not given additional support to enable them to begin to compete with more successful economies. During 1996 a Trust Fund for the Least Developed Countries was established, with an initial target figure of US $5m., with the aim of assisting those countries to become integrated into the world economy. UNCTAD has been mandated as the organ within the UN system responsible for negotiating a multilateral framework governing direct foreign investment that would protect the interests of the poorest countries, taking account of the work already undertaken by OECD in this area. In UNCTAD's revised approach, encouragement of foreign direct investment and of domestic private enterprise in developing countries and countries in transition have become central to the agency's work. UNCTAD is increasingly seeking the input and participation of non-governmental groups, such as academics, non-governmental organizations (NGOs) and business representatives, in its intergovernmental machinery, where appropriate. In November 1998 UNCTAD organized a Partners for Development summit meeting, with the aim of identifying development projects of interest to the private sector and facilitating co-operation between private companies, banks and development bodies. Some 2,700 representatives of the private sector, NGOs, academic institutions and governments from 172 countries attended the conference, which was held in Lyon, France. During the meeting the UNCTAD secretariat concluded 18 partnership agreements with private and public organizations, covering the following areas of activity: international transport; investment promotion; electronic commerce; the promotion of small and medium-sized enterprises and of entrepreneurship; conservation of biodiversity and sustainable development; and agricultural commodities. The 10th session of the Conference, held in February 2000 in Bangkok, Thailand, debated developmental strategies relating to globalization. The Conference issued the Bangkok Declaration, which stated the importance of promoting equitable and sustainable development in view of increasing global interdependence, trade liberalization and advances in technology. The Declaration emphasized commitment to a fair, non-discriminatory and fully-integrated multilateral trading system that would not tolerate the marginalization of the world's least developed economies, and urged that the next round of multilateral trade negotiations address development issues. The Declaration noted the need for increased policy coherence at national and international level, and for more effective co-operation and co-ordination among multilateral institutions. It recommended open debate on global development issues by all development partners, including the private sector, NGOs, academics and politicians. The Conference also adopted a plan of action which assessed the consequences of globalization for development, recommended measures to be implemented by the international community, and provided guide-lines for UNCTAD's future work programme.

The Commission on Trade in Goods and Services and Commodities examines ways of maximizing the positive impact of globalization and liberalization on sustainable development by assisting in the effective integration of developing countries into the international trading system. In the field of services, where developing countries suffer from deficiencies in the customs, financial and communications sectors, the Commission recommends ways for countries to overcome problems in these areas. In the field of commodities, the Commission promotes diversification, to reduce dependence on single commodities, transparency in commodity markets and the sustainable management of commodity resources. During the 1990s UNCTAD undertook research into the design and implementation of a multilateral system to trade emissions of so-called greenhouse gases. In June 1997, in co-operation with the Earth Council, UNCTAD established a Greenhouse Gas Emissions Trading Policy Forum to support the development of a plurilateral emissions market. In June 1999 the International Emissions Trading Association (IETA) was established, sponsored by UNCTAD and the Earth Council. The IETA, which was envisaged as a successor to the Forum, comprised commercial companies, business organizations and regional and national trading associations, as well as invited international organizations, research institutes and NGOs. It was to serve as a forum for the exchange of information and ideas relating to international emissions trading and as a means of developing the market in emission permit trading, which was scheduled to be launched in 2008. During the initial phase of the IETA's operations UNCTAD provided temporary secretariat support.

UNCTAD is responsible for the Generalized System of Preferences (GSP), initiated in 1971, whereby a proportion of both agricultural and manufactured goods that are exported by developing countries receive preferential tariff treatment by certain developed countries, Russia and several central European countries. UNCTAD monitors changes in and amendments to national GSP schemes and reviews the use of these schemes by beneficiary developing countries. In addition, the Commission on Trade in Goods and Services and Commodities (see above) is responsible for providing a forum to examine the operation of schemes, the benefits they offer and the future role of the GSP. In March 2001 the European Union introduced a new initiative, the so-called Everything but Arms scheme, to amend the GSP regime in member countries to provide free market access to all products from LDCs (see below), except arms and munitions, and with special provisions for rice, sugar and bananas. UNCTAD's database of trade control measures has been made available through a Trade Analysis and Information System (TRAINS).

The Commission on Investment, Technology and Related Financial Issues provides a forum to help general understanding of trends in the flow of foreign direct investment, which is considered one of the principal instruments for the integration of developing economies into the global system, and assists developing countries in improving their overall investment climate. The Commission examines issues related to competition law and assists developing countries in formulating competition policies. The Commission also undertakes the functions of the former ECOSOC Commission on International Investment and Transnational Corporations, which aimed to provide an understanding of the nature of foreign direct investment and transnational corporations, to secure effective international agreements and to strengthen the capacity of developing countries in their dealings with transnational corporations through an integrated approach, including research, information and technical assistance. A subsidiary body—the Intergovernmental Group of Experts on International Standards of Accounting and Reporting—aimed to improve the availability of information disclosed by transnational corporations. In November 1997 the UN General Assembly endorsed a proposal of the UN Secretary-General that the Group report directly through the UNCTAD Commission on Investment, Technology and Related Financial Issues.

The Commission on Enterprise, Business Facilitation and Development advises countries on policy-related issues and training activities concerning the development of entrepreneurship. It facilitates the exchange of experiences on the formulation and implementation of enterprise development strategies, including privatization, public-sector co-operation and the special problems relating to enterprise development in countries in economic transition. The Commission oversees the Global Trade Point Network (GTPNet), which was launched in 1994 as an electronic source of trade-related information. In 2001 the Network was assisting in the introduction of e-commerce practices in developing countries.

UNCTAD's work in the field of shipping and maritime activity resulted in the adoption of the UN Convention on a Code of Conduct for Liner Conferences (effective from 1983), which provides for the national shipping lines of developing countries to participate on an equal basis with the shipping lines of developed countries. Other UNCTAD initiatives have resulted in the adoption of the UN Convention on the Carriage of Goods by Sea (Hamburg Rules—1978), the UN Convention on International Multimodal Transport (1980), the UN Convention on Conditions for Registration of Ships (1986), and the International Convention on Maritime Liens and Mortgages. This last Convention was adopted in May 1993 in Geneva by a UN International Maritime Organization Conference of Plenipotentiaries, and its objectives were to encourage international uniformity in the field of maritime liens and mortgages and to improve conditions for ship financing. Technical co-operation and training projects, financed by UNDP and additional funds from bilateral donors, constitute an important component of UNCTAD's work in the fields of ports and multimodal transport and have resulted in the development of specialized courses. A software package Advance Cargo Information System (ACIS), enables shipping lines and railway companies to track the movement of cargo. Through the use of ACIS and the Automated System for Customs Data (ASYCUDA), operational in more than 80 countries, UNCTAD aims to enhance the effective exchange of information in order to counter customs fraud.

UNCTAD aims to give particular attention to the needs of the world's 49 least developed countries (LDCs—as defined by the UN). The eighth session of the Conference requested that detailed analyses of the socio-economic situations and domestic policies of the LDCs, their resource needs, and external factors affecting their economies be undertaken as part of UNCTAD's work programme. The ninth session determined that particular attention be given to the problems of the LDCs in all areas of UNCTAD's work. The 10th session focused on the impact of globalization on developing economies and on means of improving trade opportunities for the LDCs. UNCTAD served as the secretariat for the Third UN Conference on the Least Developed Countries, which took place in Brussels, Belgium, in May 2001. The Conference, which was attended by more than 6,500 participants from governments, NGOs and other elements of civil society, considered issues including governance, peace and social stability, enhancing productive capacities, intellectual property and development, infrastructure development, and financing growth and development. A Programme of Action for 2001–10, which had been elaborated by LDCs and their development partners, was adopted by the Conference.

UNCTAD provides assistance to developing countries in the area of debt-management, and in seeking debt relief from their creditors. UNCTAD is responsible for the software component of a joint programme with the World Bank to extend technical co-operation to developing countries in the field of debt management. The assistance is based on the development and distribution of software (the Debt Management and Financial Analysis System—DMFAS) designed to enable debtor countries to analyse data, make projections, and to plan strategies for debt repayment and reorganization. UNCTAD provides training for operators in the use of the software, and for senior officials, to increase their awareness of institutional reforms which might be necessary for effective debt management.

The Secretariat provided technical assistance to developing countries in connection with the Uruguay Round of multilateral trade negotiations (see WTO). The International Trade Centre in Geneva is operated jointly by WTO and UNCTAD. In February 2002 UNCTAD initiated a new capacity-building and technical assistance programme to help developing countries in trade negotiations resulting from the WTO meeting in Doha, Qatar, in November 2001.

Since May 1993 UNCTAD has serviced the ECOSOC Commission on Science and Technology for Development, which provides a forum for discussion of the following issues relating to science and technology for development: technology for small-scale economic activities to address the basic needs of low-income countries; gender implications of science and technology for developing countries; science and technology and the environment; the contribution of technologies to industrialization in developing countries; and the role of information technologies, in particular in relation to developing countries. The Commission meets every two years.

Finance

The operational expenses of UNCTAD are borne by the regular budget of the UN, and amount to approximately US $45m. annually. Technical co-operation activities, financed from extra-budgetary resources, amount to some $24m. annually.

Publications

E-commerce and Development Report (annually).

Handbook of Statistics (annually, also available on CD-ROM).

The Least Developed Countries Report (annually).

Monthly Commodity Price Bulletin.

Review of Maritime Transport (annually).

Trade and Development Report (annually).

Transnational Corporations (3 a year).

UNCTAD Commodity Yearbook.

UNCTAD News (3 a year).

World Commodity Survey.

World Investment Report (annually).

United Nations Development Programme—UNDP

Address: One United Nations Plaza, New York, NY 10017, USA.

Telephone: (212) 906-5295; **fax:** (212) 906-5364; **e-mail:** hq@undp.org; **internet:** www.undp.org.

The Programme was established in 1965 by the UN General Assembly. Its central mission is to help countries to eradicate poverty and achieve a sustainable level of human development, an approach to economic growth that encompasses individual well-being and choice, equitable distribution of the benefits of development, and conservation of the environment. UNDP advocates for a more inclusive global economy.

Organization

(March 2002)

UNDP is responsible to the UN General Assembly, to which it reports through ECOSOC.

EXECUTIVE BOARD

The Executive Board is responsible for providing intergovernmental support to, and supervision of, the activities of UNDP and the UN Population Fund (UNFPA). It comprises 36 members: eight from Africa, seven from Asia, four from eastern Europe, five from Latin America and the Caribbean and 12 from western Europe and other countries.

SECRETARIAT

In recent years UNDP has implemented a process aimed at restructuring and improving the efficiency of its administration. Offices and divisions at the Secretariat include: an Operations Support Group; Offices of the United Nations Development Group, the Human Development Report, Audit and Performance Review, and Communications; and Bureaux for Crisis Prevention and Recovery, Resources and Strategic Partnerships, Development Policy, and Management. Five regional bureaux, all headed by an assistant administrator, cover: Africa; Asia and the Pacific; the Arab states; Latin America and the Caribbean; and Europe and the Commonwealth of Independent States. There is also a Division for Global and Interregional Programmes.

Administrator: MARK MALLOCH BROWN (United Kingdom).

Associate Administrator: Dr ZÉPHIRIN DIABRÉ (Burkina Faso).

COUNTRY OFFICES

In almost every country receiving UNDP assistance there is an office, headed by the UNDP Resident Representative, who usually also serves as UN Resident Co-ordinator, responsible for the co-ordination of all UN technical assistance and operational development activities, advising the Government on formulating the country programme, ensuring that field activities are undertaken, and acting as the leader of the UN team of experts working in the country. The offices function as the primary presence of the UN in most developing countries.

Activities

As the world's largest source of grant technical assistance for developing countries, UNDP provides advisory and support services to governments and UN teams. Assistance is mostly non-monetary, comprising the provision of experts' services, consultancies, equipment and training for local workers, including fellowships for advanced study abroad. UNDP supports programme countries in attracting aid and utilizing it efficiently. The Programme is committed to allocating some 88% of its regular resources to low-income developing countries. Developing countries themselves contribute significantly to the total project costs in terms of personnel, facilities, equipment and supplies.

Since the mid-1990s UNDP has strengthened its focus on results, streamlining its management practices and promoting clearly defined objectives for the advancement of sustainable human development. Under 'UNDP 2001', an extensive internal process of reform initiated during the late 1990s, UNDP placed increased emphasis on its activities in the field and on performance and accountability, focusing on the following priority areas: democratic governance; poverty reduction; crisis prevention and recovery; energy and environment; promotion of information and communications technology; and combating HIV/AIDS. In 2001 UNDP established six Thematic Trust Funds, covering each of these areas, to enable increased support of thematic programme activities. Gender equality and the provision of country-level aid co-ordination services are also important focus areas. In accordance with the more results-oriented approach developed under the 'UNDP 2001' process the Programme has introduced a new Multi-Year Funding Framework (MYFF), the first phase of which covers the period 2000–03. The MYFF outlines the country-driven goals around which funding is to be mobilized, integrating programme objectives, resources, budget and outcomes. It provides the basis for the Administrator's Business Plans for the same duration and enables policy coherence in the implementation of programmes at country, regional and global levels. A Results-Oriented Annual Report (ROAR) was produced for the first time in 2000 from data compiled by country offices and regional programmes. It was hoped that UNDP's greater focus on performance would generate increased voluntary contributions from donors, thereby strengthening the Programme's core resource base. In September 2000 the first ever Ministerial

Meeting of ministers of development co-operation and foreign affairs and other senior officials from donor and programme countries, convened in New York, USA, endorsed UNDP's shift to a results-based orientation.

From the mid-1990s UNDP also determined to assume a more active and integrative role within the UN system-wide development framework. UNDP Resident Representatives—usually also serving as UN Resident Co-ordinators, with responsibility for managing inter-agency co-operation on sustainable human development initatives at country level—were to play a focal role in implementing this approach. In order to promote its co-ordinating function UNDP allocated increased resources to training and skill-sharing programmes. In late 1997 the UNDP Administrator was appointed to chair the UN Development Group (UNDG), which was established as part of a series of structural reform measures initiated by the UN Secretary-General, with the aim of strengthening collaboration between all UN funds, programmes and bodies concerned with development. The UNDG promotes coherent policy at country level through the system of UN Resident Co-ordinators (see above), the Common Country Assessment mechanism (CCA, a country-based process for evaluating national development situations), and the UN Development Assistance Framework (UNDAF, the foundation for planning and co-ordinating development operations at country level, based on the CCA). Within the framework of the Administrator's Business Plans for 2000–03 a new Bureau for Resources and Strategic Partnerships was established to build and strengthen working partnerships with other UN bodies, donor and programme countries, international financial institutions and development banks, civil society organizations and the private sector. The Bureau was also to serve UNDPs Regional Bureaux and country offices through the exchange of information and promotion of partnership strategies.

UNDP has a catalyst and co-ordinating function as the focus of UN system-wide efforts to achieve the so-called Millennium Goals, pledged by governments attending a summit meeting of the UN General Assembly in September 2000. The objectives included a reduction by 50% in the number of people with income of less than US $1 a day and those suffering from hunger and lack of safe drinking water by 2015. Other commitments made concerned equal access to education for girls and boys, the provision of universal primary education, the reduction of maternal mortality by 75%, and the reversal of the spread of HIV/AIDS and other diseases.

UNDP aims to help governments to reassess their development priorities and to design initiatives for sustainable human development. UNDP country officers support the formulation of national human development reports (NHDRs), which aim to facilitate activities such as policy-making, the allocation of resources and monitoring progress towards poverty eradication and sustainable development. In addition, the preparation of Advisory Notes and Country Co-operation Frameworks by UNDP officials help to highlight country-specific aspects of poverty eradiction and national strategic priorities. In January 1998 the Executive Board adopted eight guiding principles relating to sustainable human development that were to be implemented by all country offices, in order to ensure a focus to UNDP activities. A network of Sub-regional Resource Facilities (SURFs) has been established to strengthen and co-ordinate UNDP's technical assistance services. Since 1990 UNDP has published an annual *Human Development Report*, incorporating a Human Development Index, which ranks countries in terms of human development, using three key indicators: life expectancy, adult literacy and basic income required for a decent standard of living. In 1997 a Human Poverty Index and a Gender-related Development Index, which assesses gender equality on the basis of life expectancy, education and income, were introduced into the Report for the first time.

UNDP's activities to facilitate poverty eradication include support for capacity-building programmes and initiatives to generate sustainable livelihoods, for example by improving access to credit, land and technologies, and the promotion of strategies to improve education and health provision for the poorest elements of populations (with a focus on women and girls). In 1996 UNDP launched the Poverty Strategies Initiative (PSI) to strengthen national capacities to assess and monitor the extent of poverty and to combat the problem. All PSI projects were to involve representatives of governments, the private sector, social organizations and research institutions in policy debate and formulation. In early 1997 a UNDP scheme to support private-sector and community-based initiatives to generate employment opportunities, MicroStart, became operational. UNDP supports the Caribbean Project Development Facility and the Africa Project Development Facility, which are administered by the International Finance Corporation (q.v.) and which aim to develop the private sector in these regions in order to generate jobs and sustainable livelihoods. With the World Bank, UNDP helps governments of developing countries applying for international debt relief to draft Poverty Reduction Stategy Papers.

Approximately one-quarter of all UNDP programme resources support national efforts to ensure efficient and accountable governance and to build effective relations between the state, the private sector and civil society, which are essential to achieving sustainable development. UNDP undertakes assessment missions to help ensure free and fair elections and works to promote human rights, a transparent and competent public sector, a competent judicial system and decentralized government and decision-making. Within the context of the UN System-wide Special Initiative on Africa, UNDP supports the Africa Governance Forum which convenes annually to consider aspects of governance and development. In July 1997 UNDP organized an International Conference on Governance for Sustainable Growth and Equity, which was held in New York, USA, and attended by more than 1,000 representatives of national and local authorities and the business and non-governmental sectors. At the Conference UNDP initiated a four-year programme to promote activities and to encourage new approaches in support of good governance. In May/June 1999 a World Conference on Governance was held in Manila, the Philippines, attended by some 1,000 government officials and representatives of the private sector and non-governmental organizations. UNDP sponsored a series of meetings held on the subject of Building Capacities for Governance. In April UNDP and the Office of the High Commissioner for Human Rights launched a joint programme to strengthen capacity-building in order to promote the integration of human rights issues into activities concerned with sustainable human development.

UNDP plays a role in developing the agenda for international co-operation on environmental and energy issues, focusing on the relationship between energy policies, environmental protection, poverty and development. UNDP supports the development of national programmes that emphasize the sustainable management of natural resources, for example through its Sustainable Energy Initiative, which promotes more efficient use of energy resources and the introduction of renewable alternatives to conventional fuels. UNDP is also concerned with forest management, the aquatic environment and sustainable agriculture and food security. Within UNDP's framework of urban development activities the Local Initiative Facility for Urban Environment (LIFE) undertakes small-scale environmental projects in low-income communities, in collaboration with local authorities and community-based groups. Other initiatives include the Urban Management Programme and the Public-Private Partnerships Programme for the Urban Environment, which aimed to generate funds, promote research and support new technologies to enhance sustainable environments in urban areas. In 1996 UNDP initiated a process of collaboration between city authorities world-wide to promote implementation of the commitments made at the 1995 Copenhagen summit for social development (see below) and to help to combat aspects of poverty and other urban problems, such as poor housing, transport, the management of waste disposal, water supply and sanitation. The first Forum of the so-called World Alliance of Cities Against Poverty was convened in October 1998, in Lyon, France. The second Forum took place in April 2000 in Geneva, Switzerland.

UNDP collaborates with other UN agencies in countries in crisis and with special circumstances to promote relief and development efforts, in order to secure the foundations for sustainable human development and thereby increase national capabilities to prevent or pre-empt future crises. In particular, UNDP is concerned to achieve reconciliation, reintegration and reconstruction in affected countries, as well as to support emergency interventions and management and delivery of programme aid. In 1995 the Executive Board decided that 5% of total UNDP regular resources be allocated to countries in 'special development situations', i.e. urgently requiring major, integrated external support. Special development initiatives include the demobilization of former combatants, rehabilitation of communities for the sustainable reintegration of returning populations, the restoration and strengthening of democratic institutions, and clearance of anti-personnel land-mines. UNDP has established a mine action unit within its Bureau for Crisis Prevention and Recovery (formerly the Emergency Response Division), in order to strengthen national de-mining capabilities. In December 1996 UNDP launched the Civilian Reconstruction Teams programme, creating some 5,000 jobs for former combatants in Liberia to work on the rehabilitation of that country's infrastructure. In January 2002 UNDP, the World Bank and the Asian Development Bank announced the results of a jointly-prepared preliminary 'needs assessment' report for reconstruction efforts in Afghanistan: it was estimated that US $15,000m. in donor financing would be required over 10 years, of which $5,000m. would need to be provided in the first 2.5 years. UNDP is the focal point within the UN system for strengthening national capacities for natural disaster reduction (prevention, preparedness and mitigation relating to natural, environmental and technological hazards). UNDP's Disaster Management Programme oversees the system-wide Disaster Management Training Programme.

UNDP is a co-sponsor, jointly with WHO, the World Bank, UNICEF, UNESCO, UNDCP, ILO and UNFPA, of a Joint UN Programme on HIV and AIDS, which became operational on 1 January 1996. UNAIDS co-ordinates UNDP's HIV and Development Programme. Within the UN system UNDP also has responsibility for co-ordinating activities following global UN conferences. In March 1995 government representatives attending the World Summit for Social Development, which was held in Copenhagen, Denmark, approved initiatives to promote the eradication of poverty, to increase and reallocate official development assistance to basic social programmes and to promote equal access to education. The Programme of Action adopted at the meeting advocated that UNDP support the implementation of social development programmes, co-ordinate these efforts through its field offices and organize efforts on the part of the UN system to stimulate capacity-building at local, national and regional levels. The PSI (see above) was introduced following the summit. A special session of the General Assembly to review the implementation of the summit's objectives was convened in June 2000. Following the UN Fourth World Conference on Women, held in Beijing, People's Republic of China, in September 1995, UNDP led inter-agency efforts to ensure the full participation of women in all economic, political and professional activities, and assisted with further situation analysis and training activities. (UNDP also created a Gender in Development Office to ensure that women participate more fully in UNDP-sponsored activities.) In June 2000 a special session of the General Assembly (Beijing + 5) was convened to review the conference. UNDP played an important role, at both national and international levels, in preparing for the second UN Conference on Human Settlements (Habitat II), which was held in Istanbul, Turkey, in June 1996 (see the UN Human Settlements Programme, p. 87). At the conference UNDP announced the establishment of a new facility, which was designed to promote private-sector investment in urban infrastructure. A special session of the UN General Assembly, entitled Istanbul + 5, was held in June 2001 to report on the implementation of the recommendations of the Habitat II conference.

UNDP aims to ensure that, rather than creating an ever-widening 'digital divide', ongoing rapid advancements in information technology are harnessed by poorer countries to accelerate progress in achieving sustainable human development. UNDP advises governments on technology policy, promotes digital entrepreneurship in programme countries and works with private-sector partners to provide reliable and affordable communications networks. The Bureau for Development Policy operates the Information Technology for Development Programme, which aims to promote sustainable human development through increased utilization of information and communications technologies globally. The Programme aims to establish technology access centres in developing countries. A Sustainable Development Networking Programme focuses on expanding internet connectivity in poorer countries through building national capacities and supporting local internet sites. UNDP has used mobile internet units to train people even in isolated rural areas. In 1999 UNDP, in collaboration with an international communications company, Cisco Systems, and other partners, launched NetAid, an internet-based forum (accessible at www.netaid.org) for mobilizing and co-ordinating fundraising and other activities aimed at alleviating poverty and promoting sustainable human development in the developing world. With Cisco Systems and other partners, UNDP has worked to establish academies of information technology to support training and capacity-building in developing countries. By February 2002 70 academies had been established in 34 countries. UNDP and the World Bank jointly host the secretariat of the Digital Opportunity Task Force, a partnership between industrialized and developing countries, business and non-governmental organizations that was established in 2000.

In 1996 UNDP implemented its first corporate communications and advocacy strategy, which aimed to generate public awareness of the activities of the UN system, to promote debate on development issues and to mobilize resources by increasing public and donor appreciation of UNDP. UNDP sponsors the International Day for the Eradication of Poverty, held annually on 17 October.

Finance

UNDP and its various funds and programmes (see below) are financed by the voluntary contributions of members of the United Nations and the Programme's participating agencies, as well as through cost-sharing by recipient governments and third-party donors. In 2000 total voluntary contributions amounted to an estimated US $2,400m, of which $634m. was for regular (core) resources (compared with $681m. in 1999). Donor co-finance, including trust funds and cost-sharing by third parties, amounted to $571m. in 2000, while cost-sharing by programme country governments amounted to more than $900m. It was hoped that the introduction of the new Multi-Year Funding Framework for the four-year period 2000–03 and of Results-Oriented Annual Reports from 2000 (see above) would increase UNDP's resource base by stimulating an increase in voluntary contributions. In 2000 field programme expenditure under UNDP's regular programme totalled $1,458m.

Publications

Annual Report of the Administrator.

Choices (quarterly).

Global Public Goods: International Co-operation in the 21st Century.

Human Development Report (annually, also available on CD-ROM).

Poverty Report (annually).

Associated Funds and Programmes

UNDP is the central funding, planning and co-ordinating body for technical co-operation within the UN system. A number of associated funds and programmes, financed separately by means of voluntary contributions, provide specific services through the UNDP network. UNDP manages a trust fund to promote economic and technical co-operation among developing countries.

CAPACITY 21

UNDP initiated Capacity 21 at the UN Conference on Environment and Development, which was held in June 1992, to support developing countries in preparing and implementing policies for sustainable development. Capacity 21 promotes new approaches to development, through national development strategies, community-based management and training programmes.

GLOBAL ENVIRONMENT FACILITY—GEF

The GEF, which is managed jointly by UNDP, the World Bank and UNEP, began operations in 1991 for an initial pilot phase covering 1991–94. Its aim is to support projects concerning climate change, the conservation of biological diversity, the protection of international waters, and reducing the depletion of the ozone layer in the atmosphere. UNDP is responsible for capacity-building, targeted research, pre-investment activities and technical assistance. UNDP also administers the Small Grants Programme of the GEF, which supports community-based activities by local non-governmental organizations. During the pilot phase of the GEF total funding was US $1,500m. In 1994 representatives of 34 countries agreed to provide $2,000m. to replenish GEF funds. In 1998 36 donor countries pledged $2,750m. for the next replenishment of GEF funds (GEF-2), covering the period 1 July 1998–30 June 2002. Negotiations for the third replenishment commenced in October 2000. At 30 June 2000 the GEF portfolio comprised 165 projects; 94 projects had been completed at that time. During 1991–99 some $939m. in funding was approved for the GEF-UNDP project portfolio.

Internet: www.gefweb.org.

MONTREAL PROTOCOL

UNDP assists countries to eliminate the use of ozone-depleting substances (ODS), in accordance with the Montreal Protocol to the Vienna Convention for the Protection of the Ozone Layer (see p. 106), through the design, monitoring and evaluation of ODS phase-out projects and programmes. In particular, UNDP provides technical assistance and training, national capacity-building and demonstration projects and technology transfer investment projects. By mid-2001, through the Executive Committee of the Montreal Protocol, UNDP had completed 822 projects and activities concerned with eliminating ozone-depleting substances.

UNDP DRYLANDS DEVELOPMENT CENTRE—DDC

The Centre, based in Nairobi, Kenya, was established in February 2002, superseding the former UN Office to Combat Desertification and Drought (UNSO). (UNSO had been established following the conclusion, in October 1994, of the UN Convention to Combat Desertification in Those Countries Experiencing Serious Drought and/or Desertification, Particularly in Africa; in turn, UNSO had replaced the former UN Sudano-Sahelian Office.) The DDC was to focus on the following areas: ensuring that national development planning takes account of the needs of dryland communities, particularly in poverty reduction strategies; helping countries to cope with the effects of climate variability, especially drought, and to prepare for future climate change; and addressing local issues affecting the utilization of resources.

Director: PHILIP DOBIE.

PROGRAMME OF ASSISTANCE TO THE PALESTINIAN PEOPLE—PAPP

PAPP, established in 1978, is committed to strengthening newly-created institutions in the Israeli-occupied Territories and emerging Palestinian autonomous areas, to creating employment opportunities and to stimulating private and public investment in the area to enhance trade and export potential. Examples of PAPP activities include the following: construction of sewage collection networks and systems in the northern Gaza Strip; provision of water to 500,000 people in rural and urban areas of the West Bank and Gaza; construction of schools, youth and health centres; support to vegetable and fish traders through the construction of cold storage and packing facilities; and provision of loans to strengthen industry and commerce.

Internet: www.papp.undp.org.

UNITED NATIONS CAPITAL DEVELOPMENT FUND—UNCDF

The Fund was established in 1966 and became fully operational in 1974. It invests in poor communities in least-developed countries through local governance projects and microfinance operations, with the aim of increasing such communities' access to essential local infrastructure and services and thereby improving their productive capacities and self-reliance. UNDCF encourages participation by local people and local governments in the planning, implementation and monitoring of projects. The Fund aims to promote the interests of women in community projects and to enhance their earning capacities. By 1999 56 countries had received UNCDF assistance. In 1998 the Fund nominated 15 less-developed countries in which to concentrate subsequent programmes. A Special Unit for Microfinance (SUM), established in 1997 as a joint UNDP/UNCDF operation, was fully integrated into UNCDF in 1999. UNDCF/SUM helps to develop financial services for poor communities and supports UNDP's MicroStart initiative. UNCDF's annual programming budget amounts to some US $40m.

Internet: www.undp.org/uncdf.

Executive Secretary: NORMAND LAUZON.

UNITED NATIONS DEVELOPMENT FUND FOR WOMEN—UNIFEM

UNIFEM is the UN's lead agency in addressing the issues relating to women in development and promoting the rights of women world-wide. The Fund provides direct financial and technical support to enable low-income women in developing countries to increase earnings, gain access to labour-saving technologies and otherwise improve the quality of their lives. It also funds activities that include women in decision-making related to mainstream development projects. In 2000 UNIFEM approved 77 new projects and continued to support some 159 ongoing programmes world-wide. UNIFEM has supported the preparation of national reports in 30 countries and used the priorities identified in these reports and in other regional initiatives to formulate a Women's Development Agenda for the 21st century. Through these efforts, UNIFEM played an active role in the preparation for the UN Fourth World Conference on Women, which was held in Beijing, People's Republic of China, in September 1995. UNIFEM participated at a special session of the General Assembly convened in June 2000 to review the conference, entitled Women 2000: Gender Equality, Development and Peace for the 21st Century (Beijing + 5). In March 2001 UNIFEM, in collaboration with International Alert, launched a Millennium Peace Prize for Women. In January 2002 UNIFEM appealed for US $12m. to support women's leadership in the ongoing peace-building and reconstruction process in Afghanistan. Programme expenditure in 2000 totalled $25.4m.

Headquarters: 304 East 45th St, 15th Floor, New York, NY 10017, USA; tel. (212) 906-6400; fax (212) 906-6705; e-mail unifem@undp.org; internet www.unifem.undp.org.

Director: NOELEEN HEYZER (Singapore).

UNITED NATIONS VOLUNTEERS—UNV

The United Nations Volunteers is an important source of middle-level skills for the UN development system supplied at modest cost, particularly in the least-developed countries. Volunteers expand the scope of UNDP project activities by supplementing the work of international and host-country experts and by extending the influence of projects to local community levels. UNV also supports technical co-operation within and among the developing countries by encouraging volunteers from the countries themselves and by forming regional exchange teams comprising such volunteers. UNV is involved in areas such as peace-building, elections, human rights, humanitarian relief and community-based environmental programmes, in addition to development activities. The UN General Assembly designated 2001 as the International Year of Volunteers.

The UN International Short-term Advisory (UNISTAR) Programme, which is the private-sector development arm of UNV, has increasingly focused its attention on countries in the process of economic transition. Since 1994 UNV has administered UNDP's Transfer of Knowledge Through Expatriate Nationals (TOKTEN) programme, which was initiated in 1977 to enable specialists and professionals from developing countries to contribute to development efforts in their countries of origin through short-term technical assignments.

At 31 January 2002 2,946 UNVs were serving in 132 countries. At that time the total number of people who had served under the initiative amounted to more than 30,000 in some 140 countries.

Headquarters: POB 260111, 53153 Bonn, Germany; tel. (228) 8152000; fax (228) 8152001; e-mail information@unvolunteers.org; internet www.unvolunteers.org.

Executive Co-ordinator: SHARON CAPELING-ALAKIJA.

United Nations Environment Programme—UNEP

Address: POB 30552, Nairobi, Kenya.

Telephone: (2) 621234; **fax:** (2) 624489; **e-mail:** cpiinfo@unep.org; **internet:** www.unep.org.

The United Nations Environment Programme was established in 1972 by the UN General Assembly, following recommendations of the 1972 UN Conference on the Human Environment, in Stockholm, Sweden, to encourage international co-operation in matters relating to the human environment.

Organization

(March 2002)

GOVERNING COUNCIL

The main functions of the Governing Council, which meets every two years, are to promote international co-operation in the field of the environment and to provide general policy guidance for the direction and co-ordination of environmental programmes within the UN system. It comprises representatives of 58 states, elected by the UN General Assembly, for four-year terms, on a regional basis. The Council is assisted in its work by a Committee of Permanent Representatives.

HIGH-LEVEL COMMITTEE OF MINISTERS AND OFFICIALS IN CHARGE OF THE ENVIRONMENT

The Committee was established by the Governing Council in 1997, with a mandate to consider the international environmental agenda and to make recommendations to the Council on reform and policy issues. In addition, the Committee, comprising 36 elected members, was to provide guidance and advice to the Executive Director, to enhance UNEP's collaboration and co-operation with other multilateral bodies and to help to mobilize financial resources for UNEP.

SECRETARIAT

Offices and divisions at UNEP headquarters include the the Office of the Executive Director; the Secretariat for Governing Bodies; Offices for Evaluation and Oversight, Programme Co-ordination and Management, and Resource Mobilization; and divisions of communications and public information, early warning and assessment, policy development and law, policy implementation, technology and industry and economics, regional co-operation and representation, environmental conventions, and GEF co-ordination.

Executive Director: Dr KLAUS TÖPFER (Germany).

REGIONAL OFFICES

Africa: POB 30552, Nairobi, Kenya; tel. (2) 624283; fax (2) 623928; internet www.unep.org/roa.

Asia and the Pacific: UN Bldg, 10th Floor, Rajdamnern Ave, Bangkok 10200, Thailand; tel. (2) 288-1870; fax (2) 280-3829; e-mail uneproap@un.org.

Europe: 15 chemin des Anémones, 1219 Châtelaine, Geneva, Switzerland; tel. (22) 9178279; fax (22) 9178024; e-mail roe@unep.ch; internet www.unep.ch.

Latin America and the Caribbean: Blvd de los Virreyes 155, Lomas Virreyes, 11000 México, DF, Mexico; tel. (5) 2024841; fax (5) 2020950; e-mail unepnet@rolac.unep.mx; internet www.rolac.unep.mx.

North America: 1707 H St NW, Washington, DC 20006, USA; tel. (202) 785-0465; fax (202) 785-2096; e-mail uneprona@un.org; internet www.rona.unep.org.

West Asia: POB 10880, Manama, Bahrain; tel. 276072; fax 276075; e-mail myunrowa@batelco.com.bh.

OTHER OFFICES

Convention on International Trade in Endangered Species of Wild Fauna and Flora (CITES): 15 chemin des Anémones, 1219 Châtelaine, Geneva, Switzerland; tel. (22) 9178139; fax (22) 7973417; e-mail cites@unep.ch; internet www.cites.org; Sec.-Gen. WILLEM WOUTER WIJNSTEKERS (Netherlands).

Global Programme of Action for the Protection of the Marine Environment from Land-based Activities: POB 16227, 2500 The Hague, Netherlands; tel. (70) 3114460; fax (70) 3456648; e-mail gpa@unep.nl; internet www.gpa.unep.org; Co-ordinator Dr VEERLE VANDEWEERD.

New York Office: DC-2 Bldg, Room 0803, 2 United Nations Plaza, New York, NY 10017, USA; tel. (212) 963-8210; fax (212) 963-7341; internet www.nyo.unep.org.

Regional Co-ordinating Unit for East Asian Seas: UN Bldg, 10th Floor, Rajdamnern Ave, Bangkok 10200, Thailand; tel. (2) 288-1860; fax (2) 281-2428; e-mail kirkman.unescap@un.org; Co-ordinator HUGH KIRKMAN.

Regional Co-ordinating Unit for the Caribbean Environment Programme: 14-20 Port Royal St, Kingston, Jamaica; tel. 9229267; fax 9229292; e-mail uneprcuja@cwjamaica.com; internet www.cep.unep.org; Co-ordinator NELSON ANDRADE COLMENARES.

Secretariat of the Basel Convention: CP 356, 15 chemin des Anémones, 1219 Châtelaine, Geneva, Switzerland; tel. (22) 9178218; fax (22) 7973454; e-mail sbc@unep.ch; internet www.unep.ch/basel; Exec. Sec. SACHIKO KUWABARA-YAMAMOTO.

Secretariat of the Convention on Biological Diversity: World Trade Centre, 393 St Jacques St West, Suite 300, Montréal, QC, Canada H2Y 1N9; tel. (514) 288-2220; fax (514) 288-6588; e-mail secretariat@biodiv.org; internet www.biodiv.org; Exec. Sec. HAMDALLAH ZEDAN.

Secretariat of the Multilateral Fund for the Implementation of the Montreal Protocol: 1800 McGill College Ave, 27th Floor, Montréal, QC, Canada H3A 3J6; tel. (514) 282-1122; fax (514) 282-0068; e-mail secretariat@unmfs.org; internet unmfs.org; Chief OMAR EL-ARINI.

UNEP Arab League Liaison Office: POB 212, Cairo, Egypt; tel. (2) 3361349; fax (2) 3370658.

UNEP/CMS (Convention on the Conservation of Migratory Species of Wild Animals) **Secretariat:** Martin-Luther-King-Str. 8, 53175 Bonn, Germany; tel. (228) 8152401; fax (228) 8152449; e-mail cms@unep.de; internet www.wcmc.org.uk/cms; Exec. Sec. ARNULF MÜLLER-HELMBRECHT.

UNEP Chemicals: International Environment House, 11–13 chemin des Anémones, 1219 Châtelaine, Geneva, Switzerland; tel. (22) 9171234; fax (22) 7973460; e-mail opereira@unep.ch; internet www.chem.unep.ch; Dir JAMES B. WILLIS.

UNEP Co-ordinating Unit for the Mediterranean Action Plan (MEDU): Leoforos Vassileos Konstantinou 48, POB 18019, 11610 Athens, Greece; tel. (1) 7273100; fax (1) 7253196; e-mail unepmedu@unepmap.gr; internet www.unepmap.org; Co-ordinator LUCIEN CHABASON.

UNEP Division of Technology, Industry and Economics: Tour Mirabeau, 39–43, Quai André Citroën, 75739 Paris Cédex 15, France; tel. 1-44-37-14-41; fax 1-44-37-14-74; e-mail unep.tie@unep.fr; internet www.uneptie.org/; Dir JACQUELINE ALOISI DE LARDEREL.

UNEP International Environmental Technology Centre: 2-110 Ryokuchi koen, Tsurumi-ku, Osaka 538-0036, Japan; tel. (6) 6915-4581; fax (6) 6915-0304; e-mail ietc@unep.or.jp; internet www.unep.or.jp; Dir STEVE HALLS.

UNEP Ozone Secretariat: POB 30552, Nairobi, Kenya; tel. (2) 623850; fax (2) 623913; e-mail ozoneinfo@unep.org; internet www.unep.org/ozone/; Officer-in-Charge MICHAEL GRABER.

UNEP Secretariat for the UN Scientific Committee on the Effects of Atomic Radiation: Vienna International Centre, Wagramerstrasse 5, POB 500, 1400 Vienna, Austria; tel. (1) 26060-4330; fax (1) 26060-5902; e-mail norman.gentner@unvienna.un.or.at; internet www.unscear.org; Sec. Dr NORMAN GENTNER.

Activities

UNEP serves as a focal point for environmental action within the UN system. It aims to maintain a constant watch on the changing state of the environment; to analyse the trends; to assess the problems using a wide range of data and techniques; and to promote projects leading to environmentally sound development. It plays a catalytic and co-ordinating role within and beyond the UN system. Many UNEP projects are implemented in co-operation with other UN agencies, particularly UNDP, the World Bank group, FAO, UNESCO and WHO. About 45 intergovernmental organizations outside the UN system and 60 international non-governmental organizations have official observer status on UNEP's Governing Council, and, through the Environment Liaison Centre in Nairobi, UNEP is linked to more than 6,000 non-governmental bodies concerned with the environment. UNEP also sponsors international conferences, programmes, plans and agreements regarding all aspects of the environment.

In February 1997 the Governing Council, at its 19th session, adopted a ministerial declaration (the Nairobi Declaration) on UNEP's future role and mandate, which recognized the organization as the principal UN body working in the field of the environment and as the leading global environmental authority, setting and overseeing the international environmental agenda. In June a special session of the UN General Assembly, referred to as the 'Rio + 5', was convened to review the state of the environment and progress achieved in implementing the objectives of the UN Conference on Environment and Development (UNCED), held in Rio de Janeiro, Brazil, in June 1992. The meeting adopted a Programme for Further Implementation of Agenda 21 (a programme of activities to promote sustainable development, adopted by UNCED) in order to intensify efforts in areas such as energy, freshwater resources and technology transfer. The meeting confirmed UNEP's essential role in advancing the Programme and as a global authority promoting a coherent legal and political approach to the environmental challenges of sustainable development. An extensive process of restructuring and realignment of functions was subsequently initiated by UNEP, and a new organizational structure reflecting the decisions of the Nairobi Declaration was implemented during 1999. UNEP has played a leading role in preparing for the World Summit on Sustainable Development ('Rio + 10'), scheduled to be held in August/September 2002 in Johannesburg, South Africa, to assess strategies for strengthening the implementation of Agenda 21.

In May 2000 UNEP sponsored the first annual Global Ministerial Environment Forum, held in Malmö, Sweden, and attended by environment ministers and other government delegates from more than 130 countries. Participants reviewed policy issues in the field of the environment and addressed issues such as the impact on the environment of population growth, the depletion of earth's natural resources, climate change and the need for fresh water supplies. The Forum issued the Malmö Declaration, which identified the effective implementation of international agreements on environmental matters at national level as the most pressing challenge for policy-makers. The Declaration emphasized the importance of mobilizing domestic and international resources and urged increased co-operation from civil society and the private sector in achieving sustainable development.

ENVIRONMENTAL ASSESSMENT AND EARLY WARNING

The Nairobi Declaration resolved that the strengthening of UNEP's information, monitoring and assessment capabilities was a crucial element of the organization's restructuring, in order to help establish priorities for international, national and regional action, and to ensure the efficient and accurate dissemination of emerging environmental trends and emergencies.

In 1995 UNEP launched the Global Environment Outlook (GEO) process of environmental assessment. UNEP is assisted in its analysis of the state of the global environment by an extensive network of collaborating centres. Reports on the process are issued every two–three years. (The first Global Environment Outlook, GEO-I, was published in January 1997, and the second, GEO 2000, in September 1999.) UNEP is leading a major Global International Waters Assessment to consider all aspects of the world's water-related issues, in particular problems of shared transboundary waters, and of future sustainable management of water resources. UNEP is also a sponsoring agency of the Joint Group of Experts on the Scientific Aspects of Marine Environmental Pollution and contributes to the preparation of reports on the state of the marine environment and on the impact of land-based activities on that environment. In November 1995 UNEP published a Global Biodiversity Assessment, which was the first comprehensive study of biological resources throughout the world. The UNEP-World Conservation Monitoring Centre (UNEP-WCMC), established in June 2000, provides biodiversity-related assessment.

UNEP's environmental information network includes the Global Resource Information Database (GRID), which converts collected data into information usable by decision-makers. The INFOTERRA programme facilitates the exchange of environmental information through an extensive network of national 'focal points'. By early 2002 177 countries were participating in the network. Through INFOTERRA UNEP promotes public access to environmental information, as well as participation in environmental concerns. UNEP aims to establish in every developing region an Environment and Natural Resource Information Network (ENRIN) in order to make available technical advice and manage environmental information and data for improved decision-making and action-planning in countries most in need of assistance. UNEP aims to integrate its information resources in order to improve access to information and to promote its international exchange. This has been pursued through UNEPnet, an internet-based interactive environmental information- and data-sharing facility, and Mercure, a telecommunications service using satellite technology to link a network of 16 earth stations throughout the world.

UNEP's information, monitoring and assessment structures also serve to enhance early-warning capabilities and to provide accurate information during an environmental emergency.

POLICY DEVELOPMENT AND LAW

UNEP aims to promote the development of policy tools and guidelines in order to achieve the sustainable management of the world environment. At a national level it assists governments to develop and implement appropriate environmental instruments and aims to co-ordinate policy initiatives. Training workshops in various aspects of environmental law and its applications are conducted. UNEP supports the development of new legal, economic and other policy instruments to improve the effectiveness of existing environmental agreements.

UNEP was instrumental in the drafting of a Convention on Biological Diversity (CBD) to preserve the immense variety of plant and animal species, in particular those threatened with extinction. The Convention entered into force at the end of 1993; by March 2002 182 countries and the European Community were parties to the CBD. The CBD's Cartagena Protocol on Biosafety (so-called as it had been addressed at an extraordinary session of parties to the CBD convened in Cartagena, Colombia, in February 1999) was adopted at a meeting of parties to the CBD held in Montreal, Canada, in January 2000. The Protocol regulates the transboundary movement and use of living modified organisms resulting from biotechnology (such as genetically modified—GM—seeds and crops), in order to reduce any potential adverse effects on biodiversity and human health. It establishes an Advanced Informed Agreement procedure to govern the import of such organisms. By March 2002 the Protocol had been ratified by 13 states. In January 2002 UNEP launched a major project aimed at supporting developing countries with assessing the potential health and environmental risks and benefits of GM crops, in preparation for the Protocol's entry into force. In February the parties to the CBD and other partners convened a conference, in Montreal, to address ways in which the traditional knowledge and practices of local communities could be preserved and used to conserve highly-threatened species and ecosystems. UNEP supports co-operation for biodiversity assessment and management in selected developing regions and for the development of strategies for the conservation and sustainable exploitation of individual threatened species (e.g. the Global Tiger Action Plan). It also provides assistance for the preparation of individual country studies and strategies to strengthen national biodiversity management and research. UNEP administers the Convention on International Trade in Endangered Species of Wild Flora and Fauna (CITES), which entered into force in 1975.

In October 1994 87 countries, meeting under UN auspices, signed a Convention to Combat Desertification (see UNDP Drylands Development Centre, p. 103), which aimed to provide a legal framework to counter the degradation of drylands. An estimated 75% of all drylands have suffered some land degradation, affecting approximately 1,000m. people in 110 countries. UNEP continues to support the implementation of the Convention, as part of its efforts to protect land resources. UNEP also aims to improve the assessment of dryland degradation and desertification in co-operation with governments and other international bodies, as well as identifying the causes of degradation and measures to overcome these.

UNEP is the lead UN agency for promoting environmentally sustainable water management. It regards the unsustainable use of water as the most urgent environmental and sustainable development issue, and estimates that two-thirds of the world's population will suffer chronic water shortages by 2025, owing to rising demand for drinking water as a result of growing populations, decreasing quality of water because of pollution, and increasing requirements of industries and agriculture. In 2000 UNEP adopted a new water policy and strategy, comprising assessment, management and co-ordination components. The Global International Waters Assessment (see above) is the primary framework for the assessment component. The management component includes the Global Programme of Action (GPA) for the Protection of the Marine Environment from Land-based Activities (adopted in November 1995), and UNEP's freshwater programme and regional seas programme. The GPA for the Protection of the Marine Environment for Land-based Activities focuses on the effects of activities such as pollution on freshwater resources, marine biodiversity and the coastal ecosystems of small-island developing states. UNEP aims to develop a similar global instrument to ensure the integrated management of freshwater resources. It promotes international co-operation in the management of river basins and coastal areas and for the development of tools and guide-lines to achieve the sustainable management of freshwater and coastal resources. UNEP provides scientific, technical and administrative support to facilitate the implementation and co-ordination of 14 regional seas conventions and 13 regional plans of action, and is developing a strategy to strengthen collaboration in their implementation. The new water policy and strategy emphasizes the need for improved co-ordination of existing activities. UNEP aims to play an enhanced role within relevant co-ordination mechanisms, such as the UN open-ended informal consultation process on oceans and the law of the sea.

In 1996 UNEP, in collaboration with FAO, began to work towards promoting and formulating a legally-binding international convention on prior informed consent (PIC) for hazardous chemicals and pesticides in international trade, extending a voluntary PIC procedure of information exchange undertaken by more than 100 governments since 1991. The Convention was adopted at a conference held in Rotterdam, Netherlands, in September 1998, and was to enter into force on being ratified by 50 signatory states. It aimed to reduce risks to human health and the environment by restricting the production, export and use of hazardous substances and enhancing information exchange procedures.

In conjunction with UN-Habitat, UNDP, the World Bank and other organizations and institutions, UNEP promotes environmental concerns in urban planning and management through the Sustainable Cities Programme, as well as regional workshops concerned with urban pollution and the impact of transportation systems. In 1994 UNEP inaugurated an International Environmental Technology Centre (IETC), with offices in Osaka and Shiga, Japan, in order to strengthen the capabilities of developing countries and countries with economies in transition to promote environmentally-sound management of cities and freshwater reservoirs through technology co-operation and partnerships.

UNEP has played a key role in global efforts to combat risks to the ozone layer, resultant climatic changes and atmospheric pollution. UNEP worked in collaboration with the World Meteorological Organization to formulate the UN Framework Convention on Climate Change (UNFCCC), with the aim of reducing the emission of gases that have a warming effect on the atmosphere, and has remained an active participant in the ongoing process to review and enforce its implementation (see WMO, p. 198, for further details, including on the Kyoto Protocol to the UNFCCC). UNEP was the lead agency in formulating the 1987 Montreal Protocol to the Vienna Convention for the Protection of the Ozone Layer (1985), which provided for a 50% reduction in the production of chlorofluorocarbons (CFCs) by 2000. An amendment to the Protocol was adopted in 1990, which required complete cessation of the production of CFCs by 2000 in industrialized countries and by 2010 in developing countries; these deadlines were advanced to 1996 and 2006, respectively, in November 1992. In 1997 the ninth Conference of the Parties (COP) to the Vienna Convention adopted a further amendment which aimed to introduce a licensing system for all controlled substances. The eleventh COP, meeting in Beijing, People's Republic of China, in November/December 1999, adopted the Beijing Amendment, which imposed tighter controls on the import and export of hydrochlorofluorocarbons, and on the production and consumption of bromochloromethane (Halon-1011, an industrial solvent and fire extinguisher). The Beijing Amendment entered into force in December 2001. A Multilateral Fund for the Implementation of the Montreal Protocol was established in June 1990 to promote the use of suitable technologies and the transfer of technologies to developing countries. UNEP, UNDP, the World Bank and UNIDO are the sponsors of the Fund, which by July 2001 had approved financing for some 3,850 projects in 124 developing countries at a cost of US $1,200m. Commitments of $440m. were made to the fourth replenishment of the Fund, covering the three-year period 2000–02.

POLICY IMPLEMENTATION

UNEP's Division of Environmental Policy Implementation incorporates two main functions: technical co-operation and response to environmental emergencies.

With the UN Office for the Co-ordination of Humanitarian Assistance, UNEP has established a joint Environment Unit to mobilize and co-ordinate international assistance and expertise for countries facing environmental emergencies and natural disasters. In mid-1999 UNEP and UN-Habitat jointly established a Balkan Task Force (subsequently renamed UNEP Balkans Unit) to assess the environmental impact of NATO's aerial offensive against the Federal Republic of Yugoslavia. In November 2000 the Unit led a field assessment to evaluate reports of environmental contamination by debris from NATO ammunition containing depleted uranium. A final report, issued by UNEP in March 2001, concluded that there was no evidence of widespread contaminiation of the ground surface by depleted uranium and that the radiological and toxicological risk to the local population was negligible. It stated, however, that considerable scientific uncertainties remained, for example as to the safety of groundwater and the longer-term behaviour of depleted uranium in the environment, and recommended precautionary action. In December 2001 UNEP established a new Post-conflict Assessment Unit, which replaced, and extended the scope of, the Balkans Unit. In early 2002 the Post-conflict Assessment Unit was undertaking activities in Afghanistan as well as the Balkans.

UNEP, together with UNDP and the World Bank, is an implementing agency of the Global Environment Facility (GEF, see p. 102), which was established in 1991 as a mechanism for international co-operation in projects concerned with biological diversity, climate change, international waters and depletion of the ozone layer. UNEP services the Scientific and Technical Advisory Panel, which provides expert advice on GEF programmes and operational strategies.

TECHNOLOGY, INDUSTRY AND ECONOMICS

The use of inappropriate industrial technologies and the widespread adoption of unsustainable production and consumption patterns have been identified as being inefficient in the use of renewable resources and wasteful, in particular in the use of energy and water. UNEP aims to encourage governments and the private sector to develop and adopt policies and practices that are cleaner and safer, make efficient use of natural resources, incorporate environmental costs, ensure the environmentally sound management of chemicals, and reduce pollution and risks to human health and the environment. In collaboration with other organizations and agencies UNEP works to define and formulate international guidelines and agreements to address these issues. UNEP also promotes the transfer of appropriate technologies and organizes conferences and training workshops to provide sustainable production practices. Relevant information is disseminated through the International Cleaner Production Information Clearing House. UNEP, together with UNIDO, has established eight National Cleaner Production Centres to promote a preventive approach to industrial pollution control. In October 1998 UNEP adopted an International Declaration on Cleaner Production, with a commitment to implement cleaner and more sustainable production methods and to monitor results; the Declaration had 267 signatories at December 2001, including representatives of 45 governments. In 1997 UNEP and the Coalition for Environmentally Responsible Economies launched the Global Reporting Initiative, which, with participation by corporations, business associations and other organizations and stakeholders, develops guide-lines for voluntary reporting by companies on their economic, environmental and social performance.

UNEP provides institutional servicing to the Basel Convention on the Control of Transboundary Movements of Hazardous Wastes and their Disposal, which was adopted in 1989 with the aim of preventing the disposal of wastes from industrialized countries in countries that have no processing facilities. In March 1994 the second meeting of parties to the Convention agreed to ban exportation of hazardous wastes between OECD and non-OECD countries by the end of 1997. The third meeting of parties to the Convention, held in 1995, proposed that the ban should be incorporated into the Convention as an amendment. The resulting so-called Ban Amendment required ratification by three-quarters of the 62 signatory states present at the time of adoption before it could enter into effect; by March 2002 the Ban Amendment had been ratified by 29 parties. The fourth full meeting of parties to the Convention, held in February 1998, attempted to clarify the classification and listing of hazardous wastes. At March 2002 the number of parties to the Convention totalled 149. In December 1999 132 states adopted a Protocol to the Convention to address issues relating to liability and compensation for damages from waste exports. The governments also agreed to establish a multilateral fund to finance immediate clean-up operations following any environmental accident.

The UNEP Chemicals office was established to promote the sound management of hazardous substances, central to which was the International Register of Potentially Toxic Chemicals (IRPTC). UNEP aims to facilitate access to data on chemicals and hazardous wastes, in order to assess and control health and environmental risks, by using the IRPTC as a clearing house facility of relevant information and by publishing information and technical reports on the impact of the use of chemicals.

UNEP's OzonAction Programme works to promote information exchange, training and technological awareness. Its objective is to strengthen the capacity of governments and industry in developing countries to undertake measures towards the cost-effective phasing-out of ozone-depleting substances. UNEP also encourages the development of alternative and renewable sources of energy. To achieve this, UNEP is supporting the establishment of a network of centres to research and exchange information of environmentally-sound energy technology resources.

REGIONAL CO-OPERATION AND REPRESENTATION

UNEP maintains six regional offices. These work to initiate and promote UNEP objectives and to ensure that all programme formulation and delivery meets the specific needs of countries and regions. They also provide a focal point for building national, sub-regional and regional partnership and enhancing local participation in UNEP initiatives. Following UNEP's reorganization a co-ordination office was established at headquarters to promote regional policy integration, to co-ordinate programme planning, and to provide necessary services to the regional offices.

UNEP provides administrative support to several regional conventions, for example the Lusaka Agreement on Co-operative Enforcement Operations Directed at Illegal Trade in Wild Flora and Fauna, which entered into force in December 1996 having been concluded under UNEP auspices in order to strengthen the implementation of the CBD and CITES in Eastern and Central Africa. UNEP also organizes conferences, workshops and seminars at national and regional levels, and may extend advisory services or technical assistance to individual governments.

CONVENTIONS

UNEP aims to develop and promote international environmental legislation in order to pursue an integrated response to global environmental issues, to enhance collaboration among existing convention secetariats, and to co-ordinate support to implement the work programmes of international instruments.

UNEP has been an active participant in the formulation of several major conventions (see above). The Division of Environmental Conventions is mandated to assist the Division of Policy Development and Law in the formulation of new agreements or protocols to existing conventions. Following the successful adoption of the Rotterdam Convention in September 1998, UNEP played a leading role in formulating a multilateral agreement to reduce and ultimately eliminate the manufacture and use of Persistent Organic Pollutants (POPs), which are considered to be a major global environmental hazard. The agreement on POPs, concluded in December 2000 at a conference sponsored by UNEP in Johannesburg, South Africa, was opened for signature in May 2001.

UNEP has been designated to provide secretariat functions to a number of global and regional environmental conventions (see above for list of offices).

COMMUNICATIONS AND PUBLIC INFORMATION

UNEP's public education campaigns and outreach programmes promote community involvement in environmental issues. Further communication of environmental concerns is undertaken through the media, an information centre service and special promotional events, including World Environment Day, photograph competitions, and the awarding of the Sasakawa Prize (to recognize distinguished service to the environment by individuals and groups) and of the Global 500 Award for Environmental Achievement. In 1996 UNEP initiated a Global Environment Citizenship Programme to promote acknowledgment of the environmental responsibilities of all sectors of society.

Finance

UNEP derives its finances from the regular budget of the United Nations and from voluntary contributions to the Environment Fund. A budget of US $119.9m. was authorized for the two-year period 2002–03, of which $100m. was for programme activities (see below), $14.9m. for management and administration, and $5m. for fund programme reserves.

APPROVED BUDGET FOR FUND PROGRAMME ACTIVITIES, 2002–03

	(US $'000)
Environmental Assessment and Early Warning	23,000
Policy Development and Law	13,925
Policy Implementation	8,000
Technology, Industry and Economics	21,350
Regional Co-operation and Representation	21,025
Environment Conventions	6,975
Communications and Public Information	5,725
Total	100,000

Publications

Annual Report.

APELL Newsletter (2 a year).

Cleaner Production Newsletter (2 a year).

Climate Change Bulletin (quarterly).

Connect (UNESCO-UNEP newsletter on environmental degradation, quarterly).

EarthViews (quarterly).

Environment Forum (quarterly).

Environmental Law Bulletin (2 a year).

Financial Services Initiative (2 a year).

GEF News (quarterly).

Global Environment Outlook (every 2–3 years).

Global Water Review.

GPA Newsletter.

IETC Insight (3 a year).

Industry and Environment Review (quarterly).

Leave it to Us (children's magazine, 2 a year).

Managing Hazardous Waste (2 a year).
Our Planet (quarterly).
OzonAction Newsletter (quarterly).
Tierramerica (weekly).
Tourism Focus (2 a year).
UNEP Chemicals Newsletter (2 a year).
UNEP Update (monthly).
World Atlas of Coral Reefs.
World Atlas of Desertification.
Studies, reports, legal texts, technical guide-lines, etc.

United Nations High Commissioner for Refugees—UNHCR

Address: CP 2500, 1211 Geneva 2 dépôt, Switzerland.

Telephone: (22) 7398111; **fax:** (22) 7397312; **e-mail:** unhcr@unhcr.ch; **internet:** www.unhcr.ch.

The Office of the High Commissioner was established in 1951 to provide international protection for refugees and to seek durable solutions to their problems.

Organization

(March 2002)

HIGH COMMISSIONER

The High Commissioner is elected by the United Nations General Assembly on the nomination of the Secretary-General, and is responsible to the General Assembly and to the UN Economic and Social Council (ECOSOC).

High Commissioner: RUUD LUBBERS (Netherlands).

Deputy High Commissioner: MARY ANN WYRSCH (USA).

EXECUTIVE COMMITTEE

The Executive Committee of the High Commissioner's Programme (ExCom), established by ECOSOC, gives the High Commissioner policy directives in respect of material assistance programmes and advice in the field of international protection. In addition, it oversees UNHCR's general policies and use of funds. ExCom, which comprises representatives of 57 states, both members and non-members of the UN, meets once a year.

ADMINISTRATION

Headquarters include the Executive Office, comprising the offices of the High Commissioner, the Deputy High Commissioner and the Assistant High Commissioner. There are separate offices for the Inspector General, the Special Envoy in the former Yugoslavia, and the Director of the UNHCR liaison office in New York. The other principal administrative units are the Division of Communication and Information, the Department of International Protection, the Division of Resource Management, and the Department of Operations, which is responsible for the five regional bureaux covering Africa; Asia and the Pacific; Europe; the Americas and the Caribbean; and Central Asia, South-West Asia, North Africa and the Middle East. At July 2001 there were 289 UNHCR field offices in 123 countries. At that time UNHCR employed 5,192 people, including short-term staff, of whom 4,272 (or 82%) were working in the field.

Activities

The competence of the High Commissioner extends to any person who, owing to well-founded fear of being persecuted for reasons of race, religion, nationality or political opinion, is outside the country of his or her nationality and is unable or, owing to such fear or for reasons other than personal convenience, remains unwilling to accept the protection of that country; or who, not having a nationality and being outside the country of his or her former habitual residence, is unable or, owing to such fear or for reasons other than personal convenience, is unwilling to return to it. This competence may be extended, by resolutions of the UN General Assembly and decisions of ExCom, to cover certain other 'persons of concern', in addition to refugees meeting these criteria. Refugees who are assisted by other UN agencies, or who have the same rights or obligations as nationals of their country of residence, are outside the mandate of UNHCR.

In recent years there has been a significant shift in UNHCR's focus of activities. Increasingly UNHCR is called upon to support people who have been displaced within their own country (i.e. with similar needs to those of refugees but who have not crossed an international border) or those threatened with displacement as a result of armed conflict. In addition, it is providing greater support to refugees who have returned to their country of origin, to assist their reintegration, and is working to enable the local community to support the returnees, frequently through the implementation of Quick Impact Projects (QIPs). At December 2000 the refugee population world-wide provisionally totalled 12.1m. and UNHCR was concerned with an estimated further 897,000 asylum-seekers, 793,000 recently returned refugees and 7.3m. others (of whom an estimated 5.3m. were internally displaced persons—IDPs).

The first annual World Refugee Day, sponsored by UNHCR, was held on 20 June 2001.

INTERNATIONAL PROTECTION

As laid down in the Statute of the Office, UNHCR's primary function is to extend international protection to refugees and its second function is to seek durable solutions to their problems. In the exercise of its mandate UNHCR seeks to ensure that refugees and asylum-seekers are protected against *refoulement* (forcible return), that they receive asylum, and that they are treated according to internationally recognized standards. UNHCR pursues these objectives by a variety of means that include promoting the conclusion and ratification by states of international conventions for the protection of refugees. UNHCR promotes the adoption of liberal practices of asylum by states, so that refugees and asylum-seekers are granted admission, at least on a temporary basis.

The most comprehensive instrument concerning refugees that has been elaborated at the international level is the 1951 United Nations Convention relating to the Status of Refugees. This Convention, the scope of which was extended by a Protocol adopted in 1967, defines the rights and duties of refugees and contains provisions dealing with a variety of matters which affect the day-to-day lives of refugees. The application of the Convention and its Protocol is supervised by UNHCR. Important provisions for the treatment of refugees are also contained in a number of instruments adopted at the regional level. These include the OAU Convention of 1969 Governing the Specific Aspects of Refugee Problems, the European Agreement on the Abolition of Visas for Refugees, and the 1969 American Convention on Human Rights.

UNHCR has actively encouraged states to accede to the 1951 United Nations Refugee Convention and the 1967 Protocol: 141 states had acceded to either or both of these basic refugee instruments by January 2002. An increasing number of states have also adopted domestic legislation and/or administrative measures to implement the international instruments, particularly in the field of procedures for the determination of refugee status. UNHCR has sought to address the specific needs of refugee women and children, and has also attempted to deal with the problem of military attacks on refugee camps, by adopting and encouraging the acceptance of a set of principles to ensure the safety of refugees. In recent years it has formulated a strategy designed to address the fundamental causes of refugee flows. In 2001, in response to widespread concern about perceived high numbers of asylum-seekers and large-scale international economic migration and human trafficking, UNHCR initiated a series of Global Consultations on International Protection with the signatories to the 1951 Convention and 1967 Protocol, and other interested parties, with a view to strengthening both the application and scope of international refugee legislation. In July 2001 the High Commissioner urged the fair treatment of asylum-seekers in industrialized countries pending the outcome of their applications. He condemned the practice of detaining them, supported the introduction of new clearly defined systems for dealing separately with asylum-seekers and economic migrants, and expressed concern at instances of manipulation and misreporting of the issues involved by politicians and the media. Following the major terrorist attacks perpetrated in September against targets in the USA, UNHCR issued a list of concerns relating to possible negative consequences for asylum-seekers and refugees, including the threat of increased xenophobia and discrimination.

ASSISTANCE ACTIVITIES

UNHCR assistance activities, excepting a small number of so-called Supplementary Programmes, are financed from the Unified Annual Programme Budget.

The first phase of an assistance operation uses UNHCR's capacity of emergency preparedness and response. This enables UNHCR to address the immediate needs of refugees at short notice, for example, by employing specially-trained emergency teams and maintaining stockpiles of basic equipment, medical aid and materials. A significant proportion of UNHCR expenditure is allocated to the next phase of an operation, providing 'care and maintenance' in stable refugee circumstances. This assistance can take various forms, including the provision of food, shelter, medical care and essential supplies. Also covered in many instances are basic services, including education and counselling.

POPULATIONS OF CONCERN TO UNHCR BY REGION* ('000 persons, at 31 December 2000, provisional figures)

	Refugees†	Asylum-seekers	Returned refugees‡	Others of concern§	Total
Africa	3,611	90	279	1,356	5,336
Asia	5,378	47	349	2,670	8,445
Europe	2,424	333	164	2,728	5,649
Latin America	38	3	1	534	576
North America	629	417	—	—	1,045
Oceania	68	7	—	0.0	76
Total	12,148	897	793	7,288	21,126

* In accordance with the regional classification of the UN's Department for Economic and Social Affairs, under which Africa includes countries of North Africa, and Asia incorporates Cyprus and Turkey and all countries of the Middle East not located on the African continent. Latin America covers Central and South America and the Caribbean.

† Includes persons recognized as refugees under international law, and also people receiving temporary protection and assistance outside their country but who have not been formally recognized as refugees.

‡ Refugees who returned to their place of origin during 2000.

§ Mainly internally displaced persons (IDPs) and former IDPs who returned to their place of origin during 2000.

POPULATIONS OF CONCERN TO UNHCR BY COUNTRY* ('000 persons, at 31 December 2000, provisional figures)

	Refugees	Asylum-seekers	Returned refugees†	Others of concern†
Africa				
Algeria	169.7	—	—	—
Angola	12.1	0.9	8.8	257.5
Congo, Democratic Republic	332.5	0.1	14.8	3.0
Congo, Republic	123.2	0.9	5.6	—
Côte d'Ivoire	120.7	2.2	—	—
Eritrea	2.0	—	68.0	366.8
Ethiopia	198.0	0.0	2.9	—
Guinea	433.1	—	—	—
Kenya	206.1	8.7	4.9	—
Liberia	69.3	—	42.4	124.0
Sierra Leone	6.5	0.5	40.9	500.0
Sudan	401.0	3.2	0.3	—
Tanzania	680.9	21.4	0.0	—
Uganda	236.6	2.5	0.4	—
Zambia	250.9	0.2	0.2	—
Asia				
Afghanistan	—	0.0	292.5	758.6
Armenia	280.6	—	—	—
Azerbaijan	0.3	3.4	0.0	624.1
China, People's Republic‡	294.1	0.0	0.0	—
Georgia	7.6	—	0.0	272.5
India	170.9	0.1	0.0	—
Indonesia	122.6	0.4	0.8	0.0
Iran	1,868.0	12.2	0.1	—
Iraq	127.8	0.9	3.7	—
Kazakhstan	20.4	1.2	0.0	160.0
Kuwait	2.8	0.1	—	138.0
Nepal	127.2	0.0	—	—
Pakistan	2,001.5	0.6	—	—
Sri Lanka	0.0	0.0	0.0	706.5
Thailand	105.0	0.4	0.0	0.0
Europe				
Belarus	0.5	0.4	—	160.0
Bosnia and Herzegovina	38.2	0.1	18.7	577.6
France	129.7§	—	—	—
Germany	906.0	70.3	—	—
Netherlands	146.0§	84.5	—	—
Russia	26.3	0.7	0.0	1,315
Sweden	157.2§	—	—	—
Switzerland	57.7	27.5	—	—
Ukraine	3.0	0.1	0.0	261.1
United Kingdom	149.8§	66.2	—	—
Yugoslavia	484.4	0.0	124.5	352.5
Latin America				
Colombia	0.2	0.0	0.3	525.0
North America				
Canada	121.5§	30.2	—	—
USA	507.3§	386.3	0.0	—

* The list includes only those countries having 100,000 or more persons of concern to UNHCR.

† See table above for definitions.

‡ Excluding Hong Kong Special Administrative Region.

§ Figure estimated by UNHCR on the basis of previous average annual arrivals and/or recognition of asylum-seekers.

As far as possible, assistance is geared towards the identification and implementation of durable solutions to refugee problems—this being the second statutory responsibility of UNHCR. Such solutions generally take one of three forms: voluntary repatriation, local integration or resettlement in another country. Voluntary repatriation is increasingly the preferred solution, given the easing of political tension in many regions from which refugees have fled. Where voluntary repatriation is feasible, the Office assists refugees to overcome obstacles preventing their return to their country of origin. This may be done through negotiations with governments involved, or by providing funds either for the physical movement of refugees or for the rehabilitation of returnees once back in their own country.

ORIGIN OF MAJOR REFUGEE POPULATIONS AND PERSONS IN REFUGEE-LIKE SITUATIONS*
('000 persons, 31 December 2000, provisional figures)

Origin	Refugees
Afghanistan	3,567.2
Burundi	567.0
Iraq	497.4
Sudan	485.5
Bosnia and Herzegovina	454.7
Somalia	441.6
Angola	421.2
Sierra Leone	401.8

* Information on the origin of refugees is not available for a number of, mainly industrialized, countries. Data exclude some 3.9m. Palestinian refugees who come under the mandate of UNRWA (q.v.). Palestinians who are outside the UNRWA area of operation, for example those in Iraq and Libya, are considered to be of concern to UNHCR.

When voluntary repatriation is not an option, efforts are made to assist refugees to integrate locally and to become self-supporting in their countries of asylum. This may be done either by granting loans to refugees, or by assisting them, through vocational training or in other ways, to learn a skill and to establish themselves in gainful occupations. One major form of assistance to help refugees re-establish themselves outside camps is the provision of housing. In cases where resettlement through emigration is the only viable solution to a refugee problem, UNHCR negotiates with governments in an endeavour to obtain suitable resettlement opportunities, to encourage liberalization of admission criteria and to draw up special immigration schemes. During 2000 an estimated 39,500 refugees were resettled under UNHCR auspices.

In the early 1990s UNHCR aimed to consolidate efforts to integrate certain priorities into its programme planning and implementation, as a standard discipline in all phases of assistance. The considerations include awareness of specific problems confronting refugee women, the needs of refugee children, the environmental impact of refugee programmes and long-term development objectives. In an effort to improve the effectiveness of its programmes, UNHCR has initiated a process of delegating authority, as well as responsibility for operational budgets, to its regional and field representatives, increasing flexibility and accountability. An Evaluation and Policy Analysis Unit, established in 1999, reviews systematically UNHCR's operational effectiveness.

EAST ASIA, SOUTH ASIA AND THE PACIFIC

In June 1989 an international conference was convened by UNHCR in Geneva to discuss the ongoing problem of refugees and displaced persons in and from the Indo-Chinese peninsula. The participants adopted the Comprehensive Plan of Action (CPA) for Indo-Chinese Refugees, which provided for the 'screening' of all Vietnamese arrivals in the region to determine their refugee status, the resettlement of 'genuine' refugees and the repatriation (described as voluntary 'in the first instance') of those deemed to be economic migrants. A steering committee of the international conference met regularly to supervise the plan. In March 1996 UNHCR confirmed that it was to terminate funding for the refugee camps (except those in Hong Kong) at the end of June to coincide with the formal conclusion of the CPA; however, it pledged to support transitional arrangements regarding the completion of the repatriation process and maintenance of the remaining Vietnamese 'non-refugees' during the post-CPA phase-out period, as well as to continue its support for the reintegration and monitoring of returning nationals in Viet Nam and Laos. The prospect of forcible repatriation provoked rioting and violent protests in many camps throughout the region. By mid-1996 more than 88,000 Vietnamese and 22,000 Laotians had returned to their countries of origin under the framework of the CPA, with Malaysia and Singapore having completed the repatriation process. In late July the Philippines Government agreed to permit the remaining camp residents to settle permanently in that country. In September the remaining Vietnamese refugees detained on the island of Galang, in Indonesia, were repatriated, and in February 1997 the last camp for Vietnamese refugees in Thailand was formally closed. In mid-June of that year the main Vietnamese detention camp in Hong Kong was closed. However, the scheduled repatriation of all remaining Vietnamese before the transfer of sovereignty of the territory to the People's Republic of China (PRC) at the end of June was not achieved. In early 1998 the Hong Kong authorities formally terminated the policy of granting a port of first asylum to Vietnamese 'boat people'. In February 2000 UNHCR, which had proposed the integration of the remaining Vietnamese as a final durable solution to the situation, welcomed a decision by the Hong Kong authorities to offer permanent residency status to the occupants of the last remaining Vietnamese detention camp (totalling 973 refugees and 435 'non-refugees'). By the end of May, when the camp was closed, more than 200 Vietnamese had failed to apply for residency. At 31 December 2000 UNHCR was providing assistance to an estimated further 294,060 Vietnamese refugees in mainland PRC. In 1995, in accordance with an agreement concluded with the PRC Government, UNHCR initiated a programme to redirect its local assistance to promote long-term self-sufficiency in the poorest settlements, including support for revolving-fund rural credit schemes. UNHCR favours the local integration of the majority of the Vietnamese refugee population in the PRC as a durable solution to the situation.

The conclusion of a political settlement of the conflict in Cambodia in October 1991 made possible the eventual repatriation of some 370,000 Cambodian refugees and displaced persons. A land-mine survey was undertaken in order to identify the risk to returnees posed by unexploded mines (mine clearance was subsequently undertaken under UN auspices). The actual repatriation operation began in March 1992 and was completed in April 1993. At the same time, however, thousands of ethnic Vietnamese (of whom there were estimated to be 200,000 in Cambodia) were fleeing to Viet Nam, as a result of violence perpetrated against them by Cambodian armed groups. In March 1994, 25,000 supporters of the Khmers Rouges in Cambodia fled across the border into Thailand, following advances by government forces. The refugees were immediately repatriated by the Thai armed forces into Khmer Rouge territory, which was inaccessible to aid agencies. In July 1997 armed conflict between opposing political forces in northern Cambodia resulted in large-scale population movements. A voluntary repatriation programme was initiated in October, and in late March 1999 UNHCR announced that the last Cambodian refugees had left camps in Thailand, the majority having been repatriated to north-western Cambodia. A new UNHCR programme was initiated to monitor the welfare of returnees and assist in their reintegration; this was terminated at the end of 2000.

A temporary cessation of hostilities between the Sri Lankan Government and Tamil separatists in early 1995 greatly facilitated UNHCR's ongoing efforts to repatriate Sri Lankan Tamils who had fled to India. However, later in that year an offensive by Sri Lankan government troops in the northern Jaffna peninsula caused a massive displacement of the local Tamil population and effectively ended the repatriation process. Increasing insecurity during late 1999 and 2000 prompted further population displacements. However, fewer movements were recorded in 2001. In July UNHCR suspended its activities in Mallavi, northern Sri Lanka, owing to security concerns. At 31 December 2000 there were an estimated 706,510 Sri Lankan IDPs of concern to UNHCR, and an estimated 67,000 Sri Lankan refugees remaining in India. India's total refugee population, of some 170,940, provisionally, at December 2000, also included 92,340 refugees from the PRC (mainly Tibetans), and 12,760 Afghans.

In 1991–92 thousands of people of Nepalese ethnic origin living in Bhutan sought refuge from alleged persecution by fleeing to Nepal. By 2000 there were an estimated 98,900 Bhutanese refugees in Nepal, of whom the majority were receiving UNHCR assistance in the form of food, shelter, medical care and water. In December 2000 Bhutan and Nepal reached agreement on a joint verification mechanism for the repatriation of the refugees, which had been hitherto the principal issue precluding a resolution of the situation. Progress towards settling a remaining disagreement concerning categorizing the refugees was achieved during 2001. The first verification of Bhutanese refugees was undertaken in March, and it was envisaged that voluntary repatriations would commence during 2002.

From April 1991 increasing numbers of Rohingya Muslims in Myanmar fled into Bangladesh to escape the brutality and killings perpetrated by the Myanma armed forces. UNHCR launched an international appeal for financial aid for the refugees, at the request of Bangladesh, and collaborated with other UN agencies in providing humanitarian assistance. In May 1993 UNHCR and Bangladesh signed a memorandum of understanding, whereby UNHCR would be able to monitor the repatriation process of the estimated 270,000 Myanmar refugees and ensure that people were returning of their own free will. In November a memorandum of understanding, signed with the Myanma Government, secured UNHCR access to the returnees. The first refugees returned to Myanmar with UNHCR assistance at the end of April 1994. They and all subsequent returnees were provided with a small amount of cash, housing grants and two months' food rations, and were supported by several small-scale reintegration projects. In January 1997 the Bangladesh and Myanma Governments agreed to conclude the mass repatriation programme by the end of March, later extended to August. In July, in advance of the revised deadline, Rohingya activists initiated a hunger-strike in protest at alleged efforts by the Bangladesh authorities to repatriate forcibly the remaining refugees. The repatriation process resumed in November 1998, although by the end of 2000 an estimated 21,520 Myanma refugees still remained in camps in Bangladesh. Attempts by UNHCR to find a local solution for those unwilling to return to Myanmar have been met with resistance by the Bangladeshi Government.

In the early 1990s members of ethnic minorities in Myanmar attempted to flee attacks by government troops into Thailand; however, the Thai Government refused to recognize them as refugees or to offer them humanitarian assistance. The border camps remained vulnerable to attacks by rival Karen (Kayin) factions and by Myanma Government forces. In December 1997 Thailand and Myanmar agreed to commence 'screening' the refugees to determine those who had fled persecution and those who were economic migrants. By the end of 2000 there were an estimated 104,570 people in camps along the Myanma–Thai border, the majority of whom were Karen refugees.

In April 1999, following the announcement by the Indonesian Government, in January, that it would consider a form of autonomy or independence for East Timor, some 26,000 Indonesian settlers left their homes as a result of clashes between opposing groups and uncertainty regarding the future of the territory. The popular referendum on the issue, conducted at the end of August, and the resulting victory for the independence movement, provoked a violent reaction by pro-integration militia. UNHCR staff, along with other international personnel, were forced to evacuate the territory in early September. At that time there were reports of forced mass deportations of East Timorese to West Timor, while a large number of others fled their homes into remote mountainous areas of East Timor. In mid-September UNHCR staff visited West Timor to review the state of refugee camps, allegedly under the control of militia, and to persuade the authorities to permit access for humanitarian personnel. It was estimated that 250,000–260,000 East Timorese had fled to West Timor, of whom some 230,000 were registered in 28 camps at the end of September. At that time there were also reportedly 190,000–300,000 people displaced within East Timor, although the International Committee of the Red Cross estimated that a total of 800,000 people, or some 94% of the population, had been displaced, or deported, during the crisis. The arrival of multinational troops, from 20 September, helped to stabilize the region and enable the safe receipt and distribution of food supplies, prompting several thousands to return from hiding. Most homes, however, along with almost all other buildings in the capital, Dili, had been destroyed. In October UNHCR, together with the International Organization for Migration, initiated a repatriation programme for the refugees in West Timor. However, despite an undertaking by the Indonesian Government in mid-October that it would ensure the safety of all refugees and international humanitarian personnel, persistent intimidation by anti-independence militia impeded the registration and repatriation processes. The operation was also hindered by the Indonesian Government's decision to reduce the provision of food aid to the camps from the beginning of July 2000. UNHCR initially aimed to complete the operation by mid-2001, prior to the staging of elections to a Constituent Assembly by the UN Transitional Administration in East Timor (UNTAET, q.v.). However, in early September 2000 UNHCR suspended its activities in West Timor, following the murder by militiamen of three of its personnel. A UN Security Council resolution, adopted soon afterwards, deplored this incident and strongly urged the Indonesian authorities to disable the militia and to guarantee the future security of all refugees and humanitarian personnel. In mid-September UNTAET and the Indonesian Government signed a Memorandum of Understanding on co-operation in resolving the refugee crisis. However, despite a subsequent operation by the Indonesian security forces to disarm the militia, intimidation of East Timorese refugees reportedly persisted, and UNHCR did not redeploy personnel to West Timor. The Office has, however, liaised with other humanitarian organizations to facilitate continuing voluntary repatriations, which have been encouraged by the Indonesian authorities. By the end of November 2001 nearly 190,000 East Timorese refugees were reported to have returned to East Timor since late 1999, while around 70,000 were believed to remain in West Timorese camps. At the beginning of January 2002 the Indonesian Government terminated the provision of food assistance to the latter. UNHCR's operation in East Timor has aimed to promote the safe voluntary repatriation of refugees, monitor returnees, support their reintegration through the implementation of QIPs, pursue efforts towards sustainable development and the rehabilitation of communities, and to promote reconciliation and respect for human rights. It was envisaged that UNHCR's assistance activities in the territory (which was scheduled to achieve full independence in May) would be phased out by mid-2002; thereafter only the Dili office was to remain open, with a mandate to support East Timor's accession to the international instruments of protection and the development of new national refugee protection legislation.

Hostilities between Muslim separatists and government forces in the autonomous Mindanao region of southern Philippines, which escalated in March 2000, displaced several hundred thousand people during that year, mainly temporarily. UNHCR provided some technical assistance to the Philippines authorities to help ameliorate the situation; by the end of 2000 there remained an estimated displaced population of 140,000.

In late August 2001 UNHCR expressed concern when the Australian authorities refused entry into that country to some 430 Afghan asylum-seekers who had been rescued at sea by a Norwegian vessel near the Australian external territory of Christmas Island. In September the Afghans were removed on an Australian naval ship to Nauru, Papua New Guinea and New Zealand. At the request of the Nauru authorities, UNHCR dispatched a team there to assist with ascertaining the refugee status and resettlement needs of members of the group. Further groups of asylum-seekers at sea were subsquently similarly redirected, mainly to Nauru and Papua New Guinea; in mid-September the Australian Government successfully appealed a ruling by the Federal Court of Australia demanding that it reverse its decision, and stricter legislation aimed at deterring future asylum-seekers was swiftly adopted, including removing the external territories from Australia's migration zone. At 31 December 2000 Australia was sheltering an estimated 4,920 asylum-seekers. In February 2002 the High Commissioner urged the Australian Government to reconsider its policy of holding asylum-seekers in detention centres pending the outcome of their applications, following widely-publicized protests by a number of such detainees against allegedly unsatisfactory conditions and delays in processing their applications. UNHCR aimed to undertake public awareness activities in Australia during that year.

CENTRAL ASIA, SOUTH-WEST ASIA, NORTH AFRICA AND THE MIDDLE EAST

From 1979, as a result of civil strife in Afghanistan, there was a massive movement of refugees from that country into Pakistan and Iran, creating the world's largest refugee population, which reached a peak of almost 6.3m. people in 1992. In 1988 UNHCR agreed to provide assistance for the voluntary repatriation of refugees, both in ensuring the rights of the returning population and in providing material assistance such as transport, immunization, and supplies of food and other essentials. In April 1992, following the establishment of a new Government in Afghanistan, refugees began to repatriate in substantial numbers (hitherto only a small proportion had returned), although, meanwhile, large numbers of people continued to flee into Pakistan as a result of continuing insecurity. From October 1996 an escalation of hostilities in northern and western regions of Afghanistan resulted in further massive population displacement. During 1997 UNHCR operated a pilot scheme to organize group repatriations to specific areas in Afghanistan, under the protection of international observers; despite initial successes, however, the scheme was suspended in late 1998. In early 1998 UNHCR initiated a new monitoring system to evaluate the situation of returnees in Afghanistan. By the end of the year the total number of returnees from Iran and Pakistan since 1988 amounted to more than 4.2m. In recent years UNHCR, with other UN agencies, attempted to meet the immediate needs of IDPs and recent returnees (estimated to total 758,630 and 292,480 respectively at 31 December 2000) through systematic monitoring (see above) and, for example, by initiating small-scale multi-sectoral QIPs to improve shelter, rural water supply and local infrastructure; organizing income-generating and capacity-building activities; and providing food and tools. However, the ongoing civil conflict, as well as successive severe droughts and harsh winter conditions, caused renewed population displacement, precluding a settlement of the Afghan refugee situation and entailing immense difficulties in undertaking comprehensive relief efforts. Activities were disrupted by periodic withdrawals of UN international personnel owing to security concerns. The humanitarian crisis worsened considerably during 2000. At the end of that year an estimated 1.3m. Afghan refugees were sheltering in Iran (unchanged since the end of 1999), 2m. in Pakistan (compared with 1.2m. at end-1999), 15,350 in Tajikistan, and some 12,760 in India. In mid-2001 UNHCR warned that the food insecurity in the country was continuing to deteriorate, and that population movements were ongoing. In September, prompted by the threat of impending military action directed by a US-led global coalition against targets in the Taliban-administered areas of Afghanistan, UNHCR launched a US $252m. appeal to finance an emergency relief operation to cope with a potentially large further movement of Afghan refugees and IDPs. Although all surrounding countries imposed 'closed border' policies (with Pakistan reportedly permitting limited entry to Afghans in possession of correct travel documentation), it was envisaged that, were the security situation to deteriorate significantly, large numbers of Afghans might attempt to cross into the surrounding countries (mainly Iran and Pakistan) at unsecured points of entry. UNHCR urged the adoption of more liberal border policies and began substantially to reinforce its presence in Iran and Pakistan. Activities being undertaken included the supply of basic relief items such as tents and health and hygiene kits, and assistance with the provision of community services such as education for school-age children. The construction and maintenance of new camps near the Pakistan-Afghanistan border was initiated in co-operation with the Pakistan Government and other agencies, and it was also planned to construct new refugee shelters in Iran. Emergency contingency plans were also formulated for a relief initiative to assist a projected further 500,000 IDPs (in addition to the large numbers of people already displaced) inside Afghanistan. Large population movements out of cities were reported from the start of the international political crisis. An estimated 6m. Afghans (about one-quarter of the total population) were believed to be extremely vulnerable, requiring urgent food aid and other relief supplies. In mid-September all foreign UN field staff were withdrawn from Afghanistan for security reasons; meanwhile, in order to address the humanitarian situation, a Crisis Group was established by several UN agencies, including UNHCR, and a crisis management structure came into operation at UNHCR headquarters. In October (when air strikes were initiated against Afghanistan) UNHCR opened a staging camp at a major crossing point on the Afghanistan-Pakistan border, and put in place a system for monitoring new refugee arrivals (implemented by local people rather than by UNHCR personnel). It was estimated that from October 2001–January 2002 about 50,000 Afghan refugees entered Pakistan officially, while about 150,000 crossed into the country at unofficial border points; many reportedly sought refuge with friends and relatives. Much smaller movements into Iran were reported. Spontaneous repatriations also occurred during that period (reportedly partly owing to the poor conditions at many camps in Pakistan), and UNHCR-assisted IDP returns were also undertaken. UNHCR resumed operations within Afghanistan in mid-November 2001, distributing supplies and implementating QIPs, for example aimed at providing warm winter clothing. From that month some 130,000 Afghan refugees in Pakistan were relocated from inadequate accommodation to new camps. In January 2002 the new interim Afghan administration accepted a draft proposal by UNHCR concerning the logistics of planned future phased mass voluntary returns of Afghan refugees from Iran and Pakistan; it was subsequently announced that UNHCR would organize voluntary repatriations from the end of March, while also providing assistance packages to those returning before then. It was envisaged that tripartite accords on repatriation would subsequently be concluded by UNHCR and the Afghan authorities with Iran and Pakistan. A proposed draft declaration of amnesties and guarantees for returnees was also considered. UNHCR aimed to focus its protection activities primarily on refugees and returnees, while also providing some limited assistance to IDPs. It was recognized that continuing insecurity, Afghanistan's devastated infrastructure and the presence of land-mines could impede the progress of mass repatriations; in early 2002 UNHCR was assisting with rehabilitation projects in co-operation with partner agencies. By February four UNHCR offices were operating in Afghanistan. During 2001 Afghans represented the largest national group submitting new applications for asylum in industrialized countries world-wide.

In late 1992 people began to flee civil conflict in Tajikistan and to seek refuge in Afghanistan. During 1993 an emergency UNHCR operation established a reception camp to provide the 60,000 Tajik refugees with basic assistance, and began to move them away from the border area to safety. In December a tripartite agreement was concluded by UNHCR and the Tajik and Afghan Governments regarding the security of refugees returning to Tajikistan. UNHCR monitored the repatriation process and provided materials for the construction of almost 20,000 homes. The operation was concluded by the end of 1997. Nevertheless, at the end of 2000, there were still nearly 60,000 Tajik refugees remaining in other countries of the former USSR, of whom 14,120 were receiving assistance from UNHCR. Security concerns regarding returnees prompted the Tajikistan authorities to suspend repatriation operations temporarily in 2000. In late 2001 emergency relief supplies were dispatched to UNHCR's offices in Tajikistan, Turkmenistan and Uzbekistan as a contingency measure to prepare for a possible influx of refugees from Afghanistan, owing to the ongoing US military airstrikes targeting areas of that country.

In March–May 1991, following the war against Iraq by a multinational force, and the subsequent Iraqi suppression of resistance in Kurdish areas in the north of the country, there was a massive movement of some 1.5m., mainly Kurdish, refugees, into Iran and Turkey. UNHCR was designated the principal UN agency to seek to alleviate the crisis. In May the refugees began to return to Iraq in huge numbers, and UNHCR assisted in their repatriation, establishing relief stations along their routes from Iran and Turkey. By the end of the year, however, negotiations between the Kurds and the Iraqi Government had broken down and refugees were once again entering Iran in large numbers, following the resumption of the violent suppression of Kurdish activists. In April 1994 UNHCR initiated a programme to provide food and relief assistance to Turkish Kurds who had fled into northern Iraq. In September 1996 fighting escalated among the Kurdish factions in northern Iraq. By the time a cease-fire agreement was concluded in November some 65,000 Iraqi Kurds had fled across the border into Iran. UNHCR, together with the Iranian Government, provided these new refugees with basic humanitarian supplies. By the end of the year, however, the majority of refugees had returned to Iraq, owing to poor conditions in the temporary settlements, security concerns at being located in the border region and pressure from the Iranian authorities. UNHCR announced its intention to withdraw from the Atroush camp in northern Iraq, which housed an estimated 15,000 Turkish Kurds, following several breaches of security in the camp, and expressed its concern at the political vacuum in the region resulting from the factional conflict. UNHCR proceeded to transfer

3,500 people to other local settlements, and continued to provide humanitarian assistance to those refugees who had settled closer to Iraqi-controlled territory but who had been refused asylum. During 1997–2000 some 2,200 Turkish Kurds repatriated from Iraq with assistance from UNHCR. At 31 December 2000 the refugee population in Iraq amounted to an estimated 127,787, of whom about 36,000 were assisted by UNHCR. The total refugee population included some 90,000 Palestinians, 23,890 Iranian Kurds and 12,640 Turkish Kurds. In addition, there were an estimated 3,715 recently returned refugees in Iraq of concern to UNHCR. At that time there was still a substantial Iraqi refugee population in the region, totalling an estimated 497,350, of whom 386,000 were in Iran. At the end of 2000 Iran remained the principal country of asylum in the world, hosting some 1.9m. refugees, mainly from Afghanistan and Iraq. In March 2001 the Governments of Iran and Iraq concluded a bilateral accord on repatriating to those countries 5,000 Iranians and 5,000 Iraqis; UNHCR was to assist with the implementation of the agreement.

Following the war to liberate Kuwait UNHCR gave protection and assistance to Iraqis, Bidoon (stateless people) and Palestinians who were forced to leave that country. In May 2000 the Kuwaiti authorities determined that all remaining resident Bidoon should register officially with the national authorities by 27 June; while it was agreed that citizenship requirement restrictions would be eased for some 36,000 Bidoon who had been enumerated at a population census in 1965, the remaining stateless residents (numbering an estimated 75,000) were to be required to apply for short-term residency permits. At 31 December there were, provisionally, 2,776 registered refugees in Kuwait, mainly Iraqis and Palestinians. In that year it was estimated that an additional 138,000 people in Kuwait were of concern to UNHCR.

In late 2001, following the terrorist attacks perpetrated against targets in the USA in September and subequent threat of action by a US-led global coalition against countries suspected of harbouring and promoting terrorist organizations, UNHCR reassessed its emergency preparedness in the Middle East.

UNHCR co-ordinates humanitarian assistance for the estimated 165,000 Sahrawis registered as refugees in four camps in the Tindouf area of Algeria. In September 1997 an agreement was reached on implementing the 1991 Settlement Plan for the Western Sahara. Accordingly, UNHCR was to help organize the registration and safe return of some 120,000 Sahrawi refugees provisionally identified as eligible to vote in the planned referendum on the future of the territory. In addition, UNHCR was to facilitate the reintegration of the returnees and monitor their rehabilitation. By early 2002, however, little progress had been achieved towards the implementation of the Settlement Plan.

In June 1992 people fleeing the civil war and famine in Somalia began arriving in Yemen in large numbers. UNHCR set up camps to accommodate some 50,000 refugees, providing them with shelter, food, water and sanitation. As a result of civil conflict in Yemen in mid-1994 a large camp in the south of the country was demolished and other refugees had to be relocated, while the Yemeni authorities initiated a campaign of forcible repatriation. During 1998–mid-2000 the refugee population in Yemen expanded owing to an influx of Somalis fleeing civil conflict and, to a lesser extent, people displaced by the 1998–2000 Eritrea–Ethiopia border conflict. The relocation of refugees to a newly-constructed camp at al-Kharaz, central Yemen, commenced in late 2000. At December 2000 Yemen was hosting an estimated 61,960 refugees, of whom 556,520 were from Somalia.

From 1974–97 UNHCR acted as co-ordinator of the UN Humanitarian Programme of Assistance for Cyprus, assisting people displaced as a consequence of the division of the island. During the period 1987–97 UNHCR focused on the implementation of bi-communal projects to strengthen local infrastructures. From December 1999 UNHCR ceased to designate IDPs in Cyprus (estimated to number 265,000 in that year) as 'of concern'.

AFRICA

UNHCR has provided assistance to refugee and internally displaced populations in many parts of the continent where civil conflict, drought, extreme poverty, violations of human rights or environmental degradation have forced people to flee their home regions. The majority of African refugees and returnees are located in countries that are themselves suffering major economic problems and are thus unable to provide the basic requirements of the uprooted people. Furthermore, UNHCR has often failed to receive adequate international financial support to implement effective relief programmes.

East Africa

The Horn of Africa, afflicted by famine, separatist violence and ethnic conflict, has experienced large-scale population movements in recent years. Following the overthrow of the regime of former Somali president Siad Barre in January 1991 hundreds of thousands of Somalis fled to neighbouring countries. In 1992 UNHCR initiated a repatriation programme for the massive Somali and Ethiopian refugee populations in Kenya, which included assistance with reconstruction projects and the provision of food to returnees and displaced persons. However, continuing instability in many areas of Somalia impeded the completion of the repatriation process to that country and resulted in further population displacement. Some 25,910 Somali refugees repatriated from Ethiopia to Somalia with UNHCR assistance in 1999, and an estimated 67,000 in 2000. It was hoped that the conclusion of the Somali national reconciliation conference in August 2000 would accelerate repatriations, although southern areas of the country subsequently remained unstable, with their absorption capacities also undermined by a lack of basic services and persistent drought. During 2001 UNHCR, with other partners, was implementing community-based QIPs, which aimed to facilitate long-term self-reliance for returnees by improving local education and health provision, water supply and productive capacity. At 31 December 2000 there remained an estimated total Somali refugee population of 441,605, of whom 137,216 were in Kenya and 121,096 were in Ethiopia. By November 1997 UNHCR estimated that some 600,000 Ethiopians had repatriated from neighbouring countries, either by spontaneous or organized movements. The voluntary repatriation operation of Ethiopian refugees from Sudan (which commenced in 1993) was concluded in mid-1998. With effect from 1 March 2000 UNHCR withdrew the automatic refugee status of Ethiopians who left their country before 1991. From late 1999 until March 2000 transportation and rehabilitation assistance were offered to those concerned who wished to repatriate. At 31 December 2000 there remained an estimated total Ethiopian refugee population of 43,578, of whom some 19,131 remained in Sudan. At that time Ethiopia itself was hosting a total of 197,959 refugees (mainly Somalis, see above), while Kenya was sheltering 206,106 (also mainly Somalis).

From 1992 some 500,000 Eritreans took refuge in Sudan as a result of separatist conflicts; however, by 1995 an estimated 125,000 had returned spontaneously, in particular following Eritrea's accession to independence in May 1993. A UNHCR repatriation programme to assist the remaining refugees, which had been delayed for various political, security and funding considerations, was initiated in November 1994. Its implementation was, however, hindered by a shortfall in donor funding and by disputes between the Eritrean and Sudanese Governments, and Sudan continued to host substantial numbers of Eritrean refugees. Renewed conflict between Ethiopia and Eritrea, which commenced in 1998, had, by mid-1999, resulted in the displacement of some 350,000 Eritreans and 300,000 Ethiopians. Meanwhile, UNHCR continued to negotiate with the Eritrean Government to permit an organized, voluntary repatriation of refugees from Sudan. In mid-2000, following an escalation of the conflict in May, UNHCR reported that some 95,000 Eritreans had sought refuge in Sudan, while smaller numbers had fled to Djibouti and Yemen. Following the conclusion of a cease-fire agreement between Eritrea and Ethiopia in June, UNHCR initiated an operation in December to repatriate the most recent wave of Eritrean refugees from Sudan, and also inaugurated a scheme (which had been scheduled to start in May) to repatriate 147,000 long-term refugees. During the latter part of 2000 25,000 Eritreans repatriated from Sudan with UNHCR assistance, and a further 5,000 returned in spontaneous movements. At 31 December the total number of Eritreans sheltering in Sudan was estimated at 368,969, of whom 174,302 were receiving UNHCR assistance, while there were also an estimated 366,834 Eritrean IDPs of concern to the Office. UNHCR aimed to assist with the repatriation of 62,000 recent and long-term Eritrean refugees from Sudan in 2001, and of a further 90,000 in 2002. By late

2001 most IDPs had returned home. Meanwhile, UNHCR and other agencies were collaborating to rehabilitate areas of Eritrea that were receiving returnees.

At 31 December 2000 an estimated 485,540 Sudanese remained exiled as refugees, mainly in Uganda, the Central African Republic, Kenya, the Democratic Republic of the Congo and Ethiopia, owing to continuing unrest in southern Sudan. The Ugandan Government, hosting an estimated 192,160 of these refugees at that time, has provided new resettlement sites and, jointly with UNHCR and other partners, has developed a Self-Reliance Strategy, which envisages achieving self-sufficiency for the long-term refugee population through integrating services for refugees into existing local structures.

West Africa

In West Africa the refugee population increased by one-third during 1992 and the first half of 1993, with the addition of new refugees fleeing Togo, Liberia and Senegal. In accordance with a Liberian peace agreement, signed in July 1993, UNHCR was responsible for the repatriation of Liberian refugees who had fled to Guinea, Côte d'Ivoire and Sierra Leone during the civil conflict. UNHCR also began to provide emergency relief to displaced persons within the country. Persisting political insecurity prevented any solution to the refugee problem, and in mid-1996 UNHCR suspended its preparatory activities for a repatriation and reintegration operation, owing to an escalation in hostilities. In early 1997 the prospect of a peaceful settlement in Liberia prompted a spontaneous movement of refugees returning home, and in April UNHCR initiated an organized repatriation of Liberian refugees from Ghana. Improved security conditions in Liberia, following the establishment of a democratically-elected government in August and the consolidation of the peace settlement, were expected to accelerate the return of refugees and other displaced persons. In the event the process was hindered slightly by logistical difficulties and the persisting volatility of some border regions. During 1998 and 1999 an estimated 15,000 Liberians fled to Guinea from insecurity in the Lofa area of northern Liberia; meanwhile, UNHCR was forced to suspend its operations in Lofa. By the end of 1999 some 343,000 Liberians were reported to have returned, 128,200 with UNHCR assistance. UNHCR has organized QIPs to facilitate the reintegration of the returnees. Mounting insecurity in southern Guinea from September 2000 (see below) accelerated the return of Liberian refugees from camps there. At 31 December there were still an estimated 273,200 Liberian refugees, of whom 117,750 were in Côte d'Ivoire and 123,990 in Guinea. At that time there were also some 42,360 recently returned Liberian refugees and 110,690 Liberian IDPs of concern to UNHCR.

Further large-scale population displacement in West Africa followed an escalation of violence in Sierra Leone in early 1995. By December 1996 there were nearly 370,000 Sierra Leonean refugees in Liberia and Guinea, while a further 654,600 internally displaced Sierra Leoneans were of concern to UNHCR. The repatriation of Sierra Leonean refugees from Liberia was initiated in February 1997. However, the programme was suspended in May, owing to renewed political violence, which forced UNHCR staff to evacuate the country, and the seizure of power by military forces. Thousands of people fled to other parts of the country, as well as to Guinea and Liberia, to escape the hostilities. Following the intervention of the ECOMOG multinational force (see ECOWAS p. 306) and the conclusion of a peace agreement in October, residents of the Sierra Leone capital, Freetown, who had been displaced by the conflict, began to return. In February 1998 ECOMOG troops took control of Freetown from the rebel military forces, and in the following month the elected President, Ahmed Tejan Kabbah, was reinstated as Head of State. None the less, large numbers of Sierra Leoneans continued to cross the borders into neighbouring countries, owing to ongoing violence in the northern and eastern regions of the country and severe food shortages. In early 1999 anti-government forces again advanced on Freetown, prompting heavy fighting with ECOMOG troops and the displacement of thousands more civilians. In February a reported 200,000 people fled the town of Kenema in southeastern Sierra Leone following attacks by rebel militia. In May a cease-fire agreement was concluded between the Government and opposition forces, and a formal peace accord was signed in early July under which the rebels were to be disarmed, demobilized and reintegrated into society; however, the agreement broke down in May 2000. The resumption of hostilities delayed a planned repatriation programme and displaced an estimated 50,000 thousand people from their homes. Meanwhile, persistent insecurity in northeastern and some border areas of Sierra Leone prompted further movements of Sierra Leonean refugees to Guinea during 2000. From September, however, unrest in southern Guinea (see below) caused some Sierra Leonean refugees who had been sheltering in camps there to repatriate. A new cease-fire agreement, entailing the recommencement of the disarmament, demobilization and reintegration plan, was signed by the Sierra Leone Government and the rebels in early November. At 31 December there were an estimated 309,070 Sierra Leonean refugees in Guinea and 69,230 in Liberia. There were also 200,000 recently returned refugees in Sierra Leone of concern to UNHCR and an estimated displaced population of 300,000. In early 2001 UNHCR organized radio broadcasts to southern Guinea warning Sierra Leoneans against attempting to escape the unrest there by returning over the land border into northeastern and other border areas of Sierra Leone, which remained volatile. During that year the Office assisted returns by sea from the Guinean capital Conakry to Freetown. It was hoped that following legislative and presidential elections scheduled to take place in Sierra Leone in May 2002 UNHCR-assisted voluntary repatriations of refugees would accelerate. UNHCR is involved in short-term programmes aimed at reintegrating returnees into local communities.

In August 2000 the security sitiuation in southern border areas of Guinea deteriorated owing to increasing insurgencies by rebels from Liberia and Sierra Leone, which displaced a large number of Guineans from their homes and also endangered an estimated 460,000 mainly Liberian and Sierra Leonean refugees (see above) accommodated in Guinean camps. In mid-September UNHCR and other aid organizations withdrew their international personnel and suspended food distribution in these areas following the murder by armed rebels of a member of UNHCR staff. Insecurity, hunger and mounting hostility from elements of the local population subsequently led significant numbers of refugees to flee the unprotected camps. Many sought to reach northern Guinea, while some returned spontaneously to their countries of origin. Following an escalation in fighting between Guinean government forces and insurgent rebels in early December refugee movements intensified; however, it was reported that an estimated 180,000 refugees and 70,000 IDPs remained stranded without humanitarian assistance in the southwestern Bec de Perroquet area. Later in December UNHCR dispatched emergency teams to assist with the relocation of refugees who had escaped the conflict zone. In February 2001 the High Commissioner negotiated with the parties to the conflict for the establishment of a humanitarian 'lifeline' to enable the delivery of assistance to and possible evacuation of the refugees and IDPs trapped at Bec de Perroquet: convoys of food aid began to reach the area at the end of that month. Meanwhile, UNHCR opened new refugee settlements in central Guinea and, supported by the Guinean authorities, dispatched search teams into Bec de Perroquet in an attempt to find and evacuate refugees still stranded there; from February–late May some 54,000 refugees were relocated. UNHCR withdrew from Bec de Perroquet at the end of May. From March refugee camps were guarded by Guinean security personnel, with some practical support from UNHCR (including the provision of communications equipment and transport); an agreement formalizing this arrangement was signed by the Office and the Guinean authorities in October.

In June 1998 UNHCR expressed concern at the outbreak of fighting in Guinea-Bissau, which had prompted the majority of the capital's population of some 300,000 to flee into the surrounding countryside and generated concern for the safety of the estimated 15,000 Senegalese refugees who had been based in camps in Guinea-Bissau since 1992. UNHCR staff attempted to monitor the movements of the population, and, despite the border between Guinea and Guinea-Bissau officially being declared closed, estimated that some 12,000 people crossed into the neighbouring country during June 1998. A cease-fire was agreed between the conflicting forces in August; however, there was renewed conflict in October prompting further population displacement. UNHCR staff attempted to distribute mosquito nets and other non-food supplies to the displaced population, but, along with other humanitarian personnel, they were repeatedly obliged to evacuate the country owing to the ongoing violence. A peace accord was concluded in November. During the first half of 1999 UNHCR repatriated all Guinea-Bissau refugees from Guinea. In early 1994 some 40,000 Tuareg nomads, who had fled from northern Mali into Burkina Faso, received protection and material assistance from two newly-established UNHCR field offices. During 1995 large numbers of the Malian refugee population (totalling some 175,000) returned spontaneously from camps in Mauritania, Burkina Faso and Algeria, owing to political developments in Mali. An organized repatriation of the remaining refugees was initiated in 1996. In November UNHCR signed an agreement with the Malian and Nigerien Governments establishing the conditions of repatriation of 25,000 Tuareg refugees living in Niger. By 31 December 2000 almost all Malian refugees in the region had repatriated.

Central Africa

Since 1993 the Great Lakes region of Central Africa has experienced massive population displacement, causing immense operational challenges and demands on the resources of international humanitarian and relief agencies. In October of that year a military coup in Burundi prompted some 580,000 people to flee into Rwanda and Tanzania, although many had returned by early 1994. By May, however, an estimated 860,000 people from Burundi and Rwanda had fled to neighbouring states (following a resurgence of ethnic violence in both countries), including 250,000 mainly Rwandan Tutsi refugees who entered Tanzania over a 24-hour period in late April in the most rapid mass exodus hitherto witnessed by UNHCR. In May UNHCR began an immediate operation to airlift emergency supplies to the refugees. Despite overcrowding in camps and a high incidence of cholera and dysentery (particularly in camps in eastern Zaire, where many thousands of Rwandan Hutus had sought refuge following the establishment of a new Rwandan Government in July) large numbers of refugees refused to accept UNHCR-assisted repatriation, owing to fears of reprisal ethnic killings. In September reports of mass ethnic violence in Rwanda, which were disputed by some UN agencies, continued to disrupt UNHCR's policy of repatriation and to prompt returnees to cross the border back into Zaire. Security in the refugee camps, which was undermined by the presence of military and political elements of the former Rwandan regime, remained an outstanding concern of UNHCR. A resurgence of violence in Burundi, in February 1995, provoked further mass population movements. However, in March the Tanzanian authorities, reportedly frustrated at the lack of international assistance for the refugees and the environmental degradation resulting from the camps, closed Tanzania's border with Burundi, thus preventing the admission into the country of some 100,000 Rwandan Hutu refugees who were fleeing camps in Burundi. While persisting disturbances in Rwanda disrupted UNHCR's repatriation programme, in April Rwandan government troops employed intimidation tactics to force some 90,000 internally displaced Hutus to leave a heavily-populated camp in the south-west of the country; other small camps were closed. In August the Zairean Government initiated a programme of forcible repatriation of the estimated 1m. Rwandan and 70,000 Burundian Hutu refugees remaining in the country, which prompted as many as 100,000 refugees to flee the camps into the surrounding countryside. Following widespread international condemnation of the forcible repatriation and expressions of concern for the welfare of the remaining refugees, the Zairean Government suspended the programme, having first received an assurance that UNHCR would assume responsibility for the repatriation of all the refugees by the end of 1995 (although in December the Government accepted that its deadline could not be achieved). In September Rwanda agreed to strengthen its reception facilities and to provide greater security and protection for returnees, in collaboration with UNHCR, in order to prepare for any large-scale repatriation. UNHCR, meanwhile, expanded its information campaign to promote the return of refugees, and enhanced its facilities at official border entry points. In December UNHCR negotiated an agreement between the Rwandan and Tanzanian authorities concerning the repatriation of the estimated 500,000 Rwandans remaining in camps in Tanzania. UNHCR agreed to establish a separate camp in north-west Tanzania in order to accommodate elements of the refugee population that might disrupt the repatriation programme. The repatriation of Rwandan refugees from all host countries was affected by reports of reprisals against Hutu returnees by the Tutsi-dominated Government in Rwanda. In February 1996 the Zairean Government renewed its efforts to accelerate the repatriation process, owing to concerns that the camps were becoming permanent settlements and that they were being used to train and rearm a Hutu militia. In July the Burundian Government forcibly repatriated 15,000 Rwandan refugees, having announced the closure of all remaining refugee camps. The repatriation programme, which was condemned by UNHCR, was suspended by the country's new military authorities, but only after many more thousands of refugees had been obliged to return to Rwanda and up to 30,000 had fled to Tanzania.

In October 1996 an escalation of hostilities between Zairean government forces, accused by Rwanda of arming the Hutu *Interahamwe* militia, and Zairean (Banyamulenge) Tutsis, who had been the focus of increasingly violent assaults, resulted in an extreme humanitarian crisis. Some 250,000 refugees fled 12 camps in the east of the country, including 90,000 Burundians who returned home. An estimated 500,000 refugees regrouped in Muganga camp, west of Goma, although with insufficient relief assistance, following the temporary evacuation of international aid workers. UNHCR appealed to all Rwandan Hutu refugees to return home, and issued assurances of the presence of human rights observers in Rwanda to enhance their security. In mid-November, with the apparent withdrawal of *Interahamwe* forces, and the advance of the Tutsi-dominated Alliance des forces démocratiques pour la libération du Congo–Zaïre (AFDL), more than 600,000 refugees unexpectedly returned to Rwanda; however, concern remained on the part of the international community for the substantial number of Rwandan Hutu refugees at large in eastern Zaire. Further mass movement of Rwandan refugee populations occurred in December, owing to the threat of forcible repatriation by the Tanzanian Government, which had announced its intention of closing all camps by the end of the year. UNHCR initiated a repatriation programme; however, 200,000 refugees, unwilling to return to Rwanda, fled their camps. The majority of the refugees were later identified by the Tanzanian national army and escorted to the Rwandan border. By the end of December some 483,000 refugees had returned to Rwanda from Tanzania.

In February 1997 violence in Zaire escalated, prompting some 56,000 Zaireans to flee into Tanzania and disrupting the distribution of essential humanitarian supplies to refugees remaining in Zaire. An estimated 170,000 refugees abandoned their temporary encampment at Tingi-Tingi, fearing attacks by the advancing AFDL forces. About 75,000 reassembled at Ubundu, south of Kisangani, while the fate of the other refugees remained uncertain. In March and April reports of attacks on refugee camps, by AFDL forces and local Zaireans, resulted in large numbers of people fleeing into the surrounding countryside, with the consequent deaths of many of the most vulnerable members of the refugee population from disease and starvation. At the end of April the leader of the AFDL, Laurent-Désiré Kabila, ordered the repatriation of all Rwandan Hutu refugees by the UN within 60 days. Emergency air and land operations to evacuate some 185,000 refugees who had regrouped into temporary settlements were initiated a few days later. The repatriation process, however, was hindered by administrative and logistical difficulties and lack of co-operation on the part of the AFDL forces. By June an estimated 215,000 Rwandans were still missing or dispersed throughout the former Zaire (renamed the Democratic Republic of the Congo—DRC—by the AFDL in May). In the following months relations between the Kabila Government and UNHCR deteriorated as a result of several incidences of forcible repatriations of refugees to Rwanda and reports that the authorities were hindering a UN investigation into alleged abuses of the human rights of Rwandan Hutu refugees by AFDL forces. In August an agreement was concluded to provide for the voluntary repatriation of some 75,000 Congolese refugees remaining in Tanzania, under UNHCR supervision. However, the conflict that erupted in the DRC in August 1998 (see below) led to further large population movements. The repatriation of the estimated 260,000 Burundians remaining in Tanzania was also impeded, from early 1998, by an escalation of violence, which destabilized areas of return for both refugees and internally displaced persons. In December 1997 a tripartite agreement was signed to provide for the organized repatriation of the remaining Congolese refugees in Rwanda, with both Governments agreeing to observe strict conditions of security for the refugees on both sides of the border.

During the late 1990s UNHCR resolved to work, in co-operation with UNDP and WFP, to rehabilitate areas previously inhabited by refugees in countries of asylum and undertook to repair roads, bridges and other essential transport infrastructure, improve water and sanitation facilities, and strengthen the education sector. However, the political stability of the region remained extremely uncertain, and, from August 1998, DRC government forces and rebels became involved in a civil war in which the militaries of several regional governments were also implicated. From late 1998 substantial numbers of DRC nationals fled to neighbouring countries (mainly Tanzania and Zambia) or were displaced within the DRC. Meanwhile, the DRC, in turn, was hosting a significant foreign refugee population. Although a cease-fire agreement was signed by all parties to the conflict in July 1999, this was not implemented until early 2001, when Kabila was assassinated and succeeded as President by his son, Maj.-Gen. Joseph Kabila. The implementation of a plan for the phased disengagement of local and foreign forces, finalized in December 2000, was initiated in 2001, as a result of which UNHCR made preparatory plans for eventual mass refugee returns. The major populations of concern to UNHCR in the Great Lakes region at 31 December 2000 were, provisionally, as follows: 332,464 refugees in the DRC; 56,000 IDPs in Burundi; and a refugee population of 680,862 remaining in Tanzania, which was coping with new influxes of refugees, mainly from Burundi, and also from the DRC and Rwanda. The security of international aid personnel in the Great Lakes region has been of conern; UNHCR suspended all non-essential operations in Burundi from October 1999–April 2000, following the murder there of two UN personnel. In 2001 UNHCR was providing education, environmental protection and healthcare programmes at camps in Tanzania. The Office aimed to continue to facilitate some 200,000 repatriations to Burundi and a smaller number of returns to Rwanda in 2002.

In mid-1997 an estimated 40,000 refugees from the Republic of the Congo fled to the DRC, following a short-lived outbreak of civil conflict. In December a memorandum of understanding was signed by representatives of the two Governments and of UNHCR, providing for their immediate repatriation. From late 1998 the resumption of conflict in the Republic of the Congo disrupted UNHCR humanitarian efforts in that country and caused 60,000 Congolese to seek refuge in the DRC, 11,900 to flee to Gabon, and the internal displacement of as many as 400,000 people. Following the agreement of a cease-fire in December the majority of IDPs returned home. A tripartite accord on the repatriation of refugees remaining in Gabon to the Republic of the Congo was adopted by the two Governments and UNHCR in 2001. UNHCR aimed to cease repatriation support by the end of 2002, by which time it was envisaged that most refugees would have returned. During 2000 more than 80,000 refugees from the DRC sought protection in the Republic of the Congo.

Southern Africa

In 1994 continuing civil conflict in Angola caused some 370,000 people to leave their home areas. Prior to the signing of a peace settlement in November, UNHCR provided assistance to 112,000 IDPs and returnees, although military activities, which hindered accessibility, undermined the effectiveness of the assistance programme. In mid-1995, following a consolidation of the peace process in Angola, UNHCR appealed for US $44m. to support the voluntary repatriation of Angolan refugees over a two-and-a-half-year operation. Implementation of the repatriation programme was delayed, however, reportedly owing to poor accommodation and other facilities for returnees, limited progress in confining and disarming opposition troops and the continued hazard of land-mines throughout the country. During 1997 an estimated 53,000 Angolans voluntarily returned from the DRC and Zambia, bringing the total returnees since mid-1995 to some 130,000. In November 1997 UNHCR resolved to implement an operation to provide for the repatriation and reintegration of the remaining Angolan refugees by June 1999. UNHCR allocated $15.7m. to support the repatriation process and other activities in Angola, including strengthening the country's road infrastructure, monitoring areas of return, the implementation of reintegration projects and promoting links with other development programmes. In May 1998, however, the security situation in Angola deteriorated, and at the end of June UNHCR declared a temporary suspension of the repatriation operation. The renewed violence also resulted in further population displacement: by December at least 90,000 people had been displaced within Angola and 40,000 had fled to the DRC. By April 1999 a further 21,500 Angolan refugees had arrived in the DRC, and, from October a new influx of Angolan refugees, numbering more than 40,000, reached that country; at that time some 26,000 Angolans also crossed into Zambia, and 5,000 into Namibia. Refugee movements out of Angola continued during 2000. By December an estimated 421,160 Angolans were sheltering in neighbouring countries, including 198,150 in Zambia and 175,420 in the DRC. In July of that year UNHCR expanded its operations in Angola to support IDPs by providing emergency humanitarian assistance and helping IDP communities and local administrations with the provision of basic services, demining and the rehabilitation of local infrastructures. At the end of 2000 UNHCR was providing assistance to some 257,508 Angolan IDPs. It was estimated that in all some 3m.–4m. Angolans had been displaced from their homes during the 1980s and 1990s. In 2002 the Office aimed to provide limited support to IDPs and returnees, and to provide basic assistance, including food and primary education, for the estimated 12,000 refugees and asylum-seekers (mainly from the DRC) sheltering in the country.

THE AMERICAS AND THE CARIBBEAN

The International Conference on Central American Refugees — (CIREFCA), held in Guatemala in May 1989, adopted a plan of action for the voluntary repatriation of refugees in the region, and established national co-ordinating committees to assist in this process. At that time there were some 150,000 refugees receiving UNHCR assistance, and a further estimated 1.8m. other refugees and displaced persons. The repatriation process initiated by CIREFCA was formally concluded in June 1994. UNHCR's efforts in the region have subsequently emphasized legal issues and refugee protection, while assisting governments to formulate national legislation on asylum and refugees. At the end of 2000 the outstanding population of concern to UNHCR in Central America was an estimated 18,450 mainly Guatemalan refugees remaining in Mexico. At that time Costa Rica was hosting a refugee population of some 5,520, the majority of whom were from Nicaragua. In the first half of 2001 around 2,500 Colombians applied for asylum in Costa Rica.

In 1999 the Colombian Government approved an operational plan proposed by UNHCR to address a massive population displacement that had arisen in that country in recent years (escalating from 1997), as a consequence of ongoing internal conflict and alleged human rights abuses committed by armed groups. At the end of 2000 some 525,000 IDPs were of concern to UNHCR and believed to require urgent assistance; many of these had congregated near Colombia's borders with Ecuador, Panama and Venezuela. Small influxes of Colombian refugees had entered neighbouring countries. During 2000 UNHCR monitored cross-border population movements, assisted with the implementation of an IDP registration plan, supported a pilot early warning project to forecast future population movements, and provided training in emergency response to displacements. In 2001 the Office's main concerns in Colombia included supporting ongoing changes in the country's institutional framework for IDPs; enhancing the implementation at community-level of national policy on IDPs; and improving the co-ordination of concerned international agencies. UNHCR and UNICEF (q.v.) have co-operated to improve the provision of education to displaced children.

Canada and the USA are major countries of resettlement for refugees. UNHCR provides counselling and legal services for asylum-seekers in these countries. At 31 December 2000 the estimated refugee populations totalled 121,460 in Canada and 507,290 in the USA, while asylum-seekers numbered 30,180 and 386,330 respectively.

EUROPE

The political changes in eastern and central Europe during the early 1990s resulted in a dramatic increase in the number of asylum-seekers and displaced people in the region. UNHCR was the agency designated by the UN Secretary-General to lead the UN relief operation to assist those affected by the conflict in the former Yugoslavia. It was responsible for the supply of food and other humanitarian aid to the besieged capital of Bosnia and Herzegovina, Sarajevo, and to Muslim and Croatian enclaves in the country, under the armed escort of the UN Protection Force. Assistance was provided not only to Bosnian refugees in Croatia and displaced people within Bosnia and Herzegovina's borders, but also, in order to forestall further movements of people, to civilians whose survival was threatened. The operation was often seriously hampered by armed attacks (resulting, in some cases, in fatalities), distribution difficulties and underfunding from international donors. The Dayton peace agreement, which was signed in December 1995 bringing an end to the conflict, secured the right for all refugees and displaced persons freely to choose their place of residence within the new territorial arrangements of Bosnia and Herzegovina. Thus, the immediate effect of the peace accord was further population displacement, including a mass exodus of almost the entire Serb population of Sarajevo. Under the peace accord, UNHCR was responsible for planning and implementing the repatriation of all Bosnian refugees and displaced persons, then estimated at 2m.; however, there were still immense obstacles to freedom of movement, in particular for minorities wishing to return to an area dominated by a different politico-ethnic faction. By the end of 2000 there was still an estimated total Bosnian refugee population of some 454,680, of whom some 214,440 were receiving assistance from UNHCR. The majority of the Bosnian refugee population were in the Federal Republic of Yugoslavia (FRY). In addition, there were 18,720 recently returned refugees and 59,350 returned IDPs of concern to UNHCR in Bosnia and Herzegovina, as well as 518,250 IDPs who had yet to return home. Returns by refugees and IDPs (including significant numbers of minorities) accelerated during 2000, owing to an improvement in security conditions.

From March 1998 attacks by Serbian forces against members of a separatist movement in the southern Serbian province of Kosovo and Metohija resulted in large-scale population displacement. Of particular concern were some 50,000 people who had fled to the surrounding mountains, close to the Albanian border, without shelter or adequate provisions. In October the withdrawal of Serbian troops and the involvement of the international community in the provision of aid and monitoring of the situation in Kosovo was thought to have prompted substantial numbers to have returned home. However, in December there were reports of renewed attacks by Serbian forces on the local Albanian population, which persisted into 1999. The failure of peace negotiations prompted further displacement, and in late March an estimated 95,000 people fled their homes following the withdrawal of international observers of the OSCE and the commencement of a NATO operation, which aimed to halt the Serbian attacks and compel the FRY to agree to a peace settlement. By mid-April UNHCR estimated that up to 1.3m. Kosovar Albanians had been displaced since the fighting began in 1998, with reports that thousands had been forcibly expelled by Serbian troops in recent weeks. UNHCR attempted to provide emergency relief to the thousands of refugees who fled to neighbouring countries, and expressed concern for those remaining in the province, of whom up to 400,000 were thought to be living without shelter. In early April 1999 UNHCR condemned the decision of the authorities in the former Yugoslav republic of Macedonia (FYRM) forcibly to evacuate some 30,000 refugees from camps in Blace, near the FRY border, and subsequently to close the border to further refugees. At that time UNHCR helped to co-ordinate an international effort to evacuate substantial numbers of the refugees to third countries, and issued essential identity and travel documents. In Albania UNHCR funded transport to relocate an estimated 250,000 people from the border town of Kukës, where resources and the local infrastructure were strained by the massive population influx, to other sites throughout the country. At the start of June the Kosovar refugee population totalled some 443,300 people in Albania, 247,800 in the FYRM, 69,300 in Montenegro, and 21,700 in Bosnia and Herzegovina, while at least 40,000 had been temporarily resettled in more than 20 other countries. In mid-June, following a cease-fire accord and an agreement by the FRY to withdraw all forces and paramilitary units, UNHCR initiated a large-scale registration operation of Kosovar refugees and began to deliver emergency provisions to assist the displaced population within Kosovo. Despite warnings of anti-personnel devices and lack of shelter, UNHCR estimated that some 477,000 refugees had returned in a spontaneous repatriation movement by the end of June. Meanwhile, local Serbs began to move out of the province; by August an estimated 137,000 Serbs had left Kosovo, fearing reprisal attacks by returning ethnic Albanians. In September UNHCR estimated that one-third of all homes in Kosovo had been destroyed or seriously damaged during the conflict, prompting concerns regarding the welfare of returning refugees and IDPs in the coming winter months. UNHCR began to distribute 'shelter kits' to assist the process of reconstruction of homes, and proceeded to accelerate the distribution of blankets and winter clothing, as well as of fuel and other essential supplies, throughout Serbia and Montenegro. By the end of 1999 the majority of refugees had returned to Kosovo. In mid-2000 UNHCR scaled down its emergency humanitarian activities in Kosovo and provided a UN Humanitarian Co-ordinator to oversee the transition to reconstruction and development, in co-operation with the UN Interim Administration Mission in Kosovo (UNMIK).

In response to the mounting insecurity in the FYRM from early 2001, as conflict escalated between ethnic Albanian rebels and government troops, some 74,000 Macedonian refugees fled to Kosovo (of whom about 15,000 repatriated promptly) and 5,000 to southern Serbia during February–July, while over that period a further 34,500 people were displaced from their homes. In June UNHCR appealed for funds to finance the provision of emergency humanitarian assistance to the Macedonian refugees, and opened a registration centre in Kosovo. There were further repatriations following the conclusion in August of a framework peace agreement between the opposing parties, although continuing insecurity precluded mass returns.

In December 1992 UNHCR dispatched teams to establish offices in both Armenia and Azerbaijan to assist people displaced as a result of the war between the two countries and to provide immediate relief. A cease-fire was signed between the two sides in May 1994, although violations of the accord were subsequently reported and relations between the two countries remained tense. At the end of 2000 the region was still supporting a massive displaced population, including an estimated 280,580 Azerbaijani refugees in Armenia and 572,450 IDPs of concern to UNHCR in Azerbaijan. UNHCR's humanitarian activities have focused on improving shelter, in particular for the most vulnerable among the refugee population, and promoting economic self-sufficiency and stability. In Georgia, where almost 300,000 people left their homes as a result of civil conflict from 1991, UNHCR has attempted to encourage income-generating activities among the displaced population, to increase the Georgian Government's capacity to support those people and to assist the rehabilitation of people returning to their areas of origin. In late 1999 an estimated 7,000 refugees fleeing insecurity in Chechnya (see below) entered Georgia; during 2001 UNHCR periodically delivered supplies to the Chechen refugees. From 1994 UNHCR pursued a process to establish a comprehensive approach to the problems of refugees, returnees, IDPs and migrants in the Commonwealth of Independent States. A regional conference convened in Geneva, Switzerland, in May 1996, endorsed a framework of activities aimed at managing migratory flows and at developing institutional capacities to prevent mass population displacements. At that time it was estimated that more than 9m. former citizens of the USSR had relocated since its disintegration as a result of conflict, economic pressures and ecological disasters.

In March 1995 UNHCR initiated an assistance programme for people displaced as a result of conflict in the separatist republic of Chechnya (Russian Federation), as part of a UN inter-agency relief effort, in collaboration with the International Committee of the Red Cross (ICRC, q.v.). UNHCR continued its activities in 1996, at the request of the Russian Government, at which time the displaced population within Chechnya and in the surrounding republics totalled 490,000. During 1997 UNHCR provided re-integration assistance to 25,000 people who returned to

Chechnya, despite reports of sporadic violence. The security situation in the region deteriorated sharply in mid-1999, following a series of border clashes and incursions by Chechen separatist forces into the neighbouring republic of Dagestan. In September Russian military aircraft began an aerial offensive against suspected rebel targets in Chechnya, and at the end of the month ground troops moved into the republic. By November an estimated 225,000 Chechens had fled to neighbouring Ingushetiya. UNHCR dispatched food supplies to assist these and, from February 2000, periodically sent relief convoys into Chechnya, where there was still a substantial displaced population; the adverse security situation, however, prevented other UNHCR deployment within Chechnya. In late 2000 UNHCR assisted with the construction of the first tented camp to provide adequate winter shelter for Chechens in Ingushetiya; many others were being sheltered in local homes. About 150,000 Chechens remained in Ingushetiya in the second half of 2001.

CO-OPERATION WITH OTHER ORGANIZATIONS

UNHCR works closely with other UN agencies, intergovernmental organizations and non-governmental organizations (NGOs) to increase the scope and effectiveness of its operations. Within the UN system UNHCR co-operates, principally, with the World Food Programme in the distribution of food aid, UNICEF and the World Health Organization in the provision of family welfare and child immunization programmes, OCHA in the delivery of emergency humanitarian relief, UNDP in development-related activities and the preparation of guide-lines for the continuum of emergency assistance to development programmes, and the Office of the UN High Commissioner for Human Rights. UNHCR also has close working relationships with the International Committee of the Red Cross and the International Organization for Migration. In 2001 UNHCR worked with 537 NGOs as 'implementing partners', enabling UNHCR to broaden the use of its resources while maintaining a co-ordinating role in the provision of assistance.

TRAINING

UNHCR organizes training programmes and workshops to enhance the capabilities of field workers and non-UNHCR staff, in the following areas: the identification and registration of refugees; people-orientated planning; resettlement procedures and policies; emergency response and management; security awareness; stress management; and the dissemination of information through the electronic media.

Finance

The United Nations' regular budget finances a proportion of UNHCR's administrative expenditure. The majority of UNHCR's programme expenditure (about 98%) is funded by voluntary contributions, mainly from governments. The Private Sector and Public Affairs Service, established in 2001, aims to increase funding from non-governmental donor sources, for example by developing partnerships with foundations and corporations. Following approval of the Unified Annual Programme Budget any subsequently-identified requirements are managed in the form of Supplementary Programmes, financed by separate appeals. The programme budget for 2002 amounted to US $828.6m.

Publications

Refugees (quarterly, in English, French, German, Italian, Japanese and Spanish).

Refugee Survey Quarterly.

The State of the World's Refugees (every 2 years).

UNHCR Handbook for Emergencies.

Press releases, reports.

Convention relating to the Status of Refugees

(28 July 1951)

PREAMBLE

The High Contracting Parties

Considering that the Charter of the United Nations and the Universal Declaration of Human Rights approved on 10 December 1948 by the General Assembly have affirmed the principle that human beings shall enjoy fundamental rights and freedoms without discrimination,

Considering that the United Nations has, on various occasions, manifested its profound concern for refugees and endeavoured to assure refugees the widest possible exercise of these fundamental rights and freedoms,

Considering that it is desirable to revise and consolidate previous international agreements relating to the status of refugees and to extend the scope of and protection accorded by such instruments by means of a new agreement,

Considering that the grant of asylum may place unduly heavy burdens on certain countries, and that a satisfactory solution of a problem of which the United Nations has recognized the international scope and nature cannot therefore be achieved without international co-operation,

Expressing the wish that all States, recognizing the social and humanitarian nature of the problem of refugees will do everything within their power to prevent this problem from becoming a cause of tension between States,

Noting that the United Nations High Commissioner for Refugees is charged with the task of supervising international conventions providing for the protection of refugees, and recognizing that the effective co-ordination of measures taken to deal with this problem will depend upon the co-operation of States with the High Commissioner,

Have agreed as follows:

I. GENERAL PROVISIONS

Article 1

Definition of the term "Refugee".

A. For the purposes of the present Convention, the term "refugee" shall apply to any person who:

(1) Has been considered a refugee under the Arrangements of 12 May 1926 and 30 June 1928 or under the Conventions of 28 October 1933 and 10 February 1938, the Protocol of 14 September 1939 or the Constitution of the International Refugee Organization; Decisions of non-eligibility taken by the International Refugee Organization during the period of its activities shall not prevent the status of refugee being accorded to persons who fulfil the conditions of paragraph 2 of this section;

(2) As a result of events occurring before 1 January 1951 and owing to well-founded fear of being persecuted for reasons of race, religion, nationality, membership of a particular social group or political opinion, is outside the country of his nationality and is unable or, owing to such fear, is unwilling to avail himself of the protection of that country; or who, not having a nationality and being outside the country of his former habitual residence as a result of such events, is unable or, owing to such fear, is unwilling to return to it.

In the case of a person who has more than one nationality, the term "the country of his nationality" shall mean each of the countries of which he is a national, and a person shall not be deemed to be lacking the protection of the country of his nationality if, without any valid reason based on well-founded fear, he has not availed himself of the protection of one of the countries of which he is a national.

B. (1) For the purposes of this Convention, the words "events occurring before 1 January 1951" in Article 1, Section A, shall be understood to mean either (a) 'events occurring in Europe before 1 January 1951'; or (b) 'events occurring in Europe or elsewhere before 1 January 1951'; and each Contracting State shall make a declaration at the time of signature, ratification or accession, specifying which of these meanings it applies for the purpose of its obligations under this Convention;

(2) Any Contracting State which has adopted alternative (a) may at any time extend its obligations by adopting alternative (b) by means of a notification addressed to the Secretary-General of the United Nations.

C. This Convention shall cease to apply to any person falling under the terms of Section A if:

(1) He has voluntarily re-availed himself of the protection of the country of his nationality; or

(2) Having lost his nationality, he has voluntarily re-acquired it; or

(3) He has acquired a new nationality, and enjoys the protection of the country of his new nationality; or

(4) He has voluntarily re-established himself in the country which he left or outside which he remained owing to fear of persecution; or

(5) He can no longer, because the circumstances in connection with which he has been recognized as a refugee have ceased to exist, continue to refuse to avail himself of the protection of the country of his nationality;

Provided that this paragraph shall not apply to a refugee falling under Section A(1) of this Article who is able to invoke compelling reasons arising out of previous persecution for refusing to avail himself of the protection of the country of nationality;

(6) Being a person who has no nationality he is, because the circumstances in connection with which he has been recognized as a refugee have ceased to exist, able to return to the country of his former habitual residence;

Provided that this paragraph shall not apply to a refugee falling under section A(1) of this Article who is able to invoke compelling reasons arising out of previous persecution for refusing to return to the country of his former habitual residence.

D. This Convention shall not apply to persons who are at present receiving from organs or agencies of the United Nations other than the United Nations High Commissioner for Refugees protection or assistance.

When such protection or assistance has ceased for any reason, without the position of such persons being definitively settled in accordance with the relevant resolutions adopted by the General Assembly of the United Nations, these persons shall ipso facto be entitled to the benefits of this Convention.

E. This Convention shall not apply to a person who is recognized by the competent authorities of the country in which he has taken residence as having the rights and obligations which are attached to the possession of the nationality of that country.

F. The provisions of this Convention shall not apply to any person with respect to whom there are serious reasons for considering that:

(a) He has committed a crime against peace, a war crime, or a crime against humanity, as defined in the international instruments drawn up to make provision in respect of such crimes;
(b) he has committed a serious non-political crime outside the country of refuge prior to his admission to that country as a refugee;
(c) he has been guilty of acts contrary to the purposes and principles of the United Nations.

Article 2

General obligations.

Every refugee has duties to the country in which he finds himself, which require in particular that he conform to its laws and regulations as well as to measures taken for the maintenance of public order.

Article 3

Non-discrimination.

The Contracting States shall apply the provisions of this Convention to refugees without discrimination as to race, religion or country of origin.

Article 4

Religion.

The Contracting States shall accord to refugees within their territories treatment at least as favourable as that accorded to their nationals with respect to freedom to practise their religion and freedom as regards the religious education of their children.

Article 5

Rights granted apart from this Convention.

Nothing in this Convention shall be deemed to impair any rights and benefits granted by a Contracting State to refugees apart from this Convention.

Article 6

The term "in the same circumstances".

For the purposes of this Convention, the term "in the same circumstances" implies that any requirements (including requirements as to length and conditions of sojourn or residence) which the particular individual would have to fulfil for the enjoyment of the right in question, if he were not a refugee, must be fulfilled by him, with the exception of requirements which by their nature a refugee is incapable of fulfilling.

Article 7

Exemption from reciprocity.

1. Except where this Convention contains more favourable provisions, a Contracting State shall accord to refugees the same treatment as is accorded to aliens generally.

2. After a period of three years' residence, all refugees shall enjoy exemption from legislative reciprocity in the territory of the Contracting States.

3. Each Contracting State shall continue to accord to refugees the rights and benefits to which they were already entitled, in the absence of reciprocity, at the date of entry into force of this Convention for that State.

4. The Contracting States shall consider favourably the possibility of according to refugees, in the absence of reciprocity, rights and benefits beyond those to which they are entitled according to paragraphs 2 and 3, and to extending exemption from reciprocity to refugees who do not fulfil the conditions provided for in paragraphs 2 and 3.

5. The provisions of paragraphs 2 and 3 apply both to the rights and benefits referred to in Articles 13, 18, 19, 21 and 22 of this Convention and to rights and benefits for which this Convention does not provide.

Article 8

Exemption from exceptional measures.

With regard to exceptional measures which may be taken against the person, property or interests of nationals of a foreign State, the Contracting States shall not apply such measures to a refugee who is formally a national of the said State solely on account of such nationality. Contracting States which, under their legislation, are prevented from applying the general principle expressed in this Article, shall, in appropriate cases, grant exemptions in favour of such refugees.

Article 9

Provisional measures.

Nothing in this Convention shall prevent a Contracting State, in time of war or other grave and exceptional circumstances, from taking provisionally measures which it considers to be essential to the national security in the case of a particular person, pending a determination by the Contracting State that that person is in fact a refugee and that the continuance of such measures is necessary in his case in the interests of national security.

Article 10

Continuity of residence.

1. Where a refugee has been forcibly displaced during the Second World War and removed to the territory of a Contracting State, and is resident there, the period of such enforced sojourn shall be considered to have been lawful residence within that territory.

2. Where a refugee has been forcibly displaced during the Second World War from the territory of a Contracting State and has, prior to the date of entry into force of this Convention, returned there for the purpose of taking up residence, the period of

residence before and after such enforced displacement shall be regarded as one uninterrupted period for any purposes for which uninterrupted residence is required.

Article 11

Refugee seamen.

In the case of refugees regularly serving as crew members on board a ship flying the flag of a Contracting State, that State shall give sympathetic consideration to their establishment on its territory and the issue of travel documents to them or their temporary admission to its territory particularly with a view to facilitating their establishment in another country.

II. JURIDICAL STATUS

Article 12

Personal status.

1. The personal status of a refugee shall be governed by the law of the country of his domicile or, if he has no domicile, by the law of the country of his residence.

2. Rights previously acquired by a refugee and dependent on personal status, more particularly rights attaching to marriage, shall be respected by a Contracting State, subject to compliance, if this be necessary, with the formalities required by the law of that State, provided that the right in question is one which would have been recognized by the law of that State had he not become a refugee.

Article 13

Movable and immovable property.

The Contracting States shall accord to a refugee treatment as favourable as possible and, in any event, not less favourable than that accorded to aliens generally in the same circumstances, as regards the acquisition of movable and immovable property and other rights pertaining thereto, and to leases and other contracts relating to movable and immovable property.

Article 14

Artistic rights and industrial property.

In respect of the protection of industrial property, such as inventions, designs or models, trade marks, trade names, and of rights in literary, artistic, and scientific works, a refugee shall be accorded in the country in which he has his habitual residence the same protection as is accorded to nationals of that country. In the territory of any other Contracting State, he shall be accorded the same protection as is accorded in that territory to nationals of the country in which he has his habitual residence.

Article 15

Right of association.

As regards non-political and non-profit-making associations and trade unions the Contracting States shall accord to refugees lawfully staying in their territory the most favourable treatment accorded to nationals of a foreign country, in the same circumstances.

Article 16

Access to courts.

1. A refugee shall have free access to the courts of law on the territory of all Contracting States.

2. A refugee shall enjoy in the Contracting State in which he has his habitual residence the same treatment as a national in matters pertaining to access to the Courts, including legal assistance and exemption from *cautio judicatem solvi.*

3. A refugee shall be accorded in the matters referred to in paragraph 2 in countries other than that in which he has his habitual residence the treatment granted to a national of the country of his habitual residence.

III. GAINFUL EMPLOYMENT

Article 17

Wage-earning employment.

1. The Contracting States shall accord to refugees lawfully staying in their territory the most favourable treatment accorded to nationals of a foreign country in the same circumstances, as regards the right to engage in wage-earning employment.

2. In any case, restrictive measures imposed on aliens or the employment of aliens for the protection of the national labour market shall not be applied to a refugee who was already exempt from them at the date of entry into force of this Convention for the Contracting State concerned, or who fulfils one of the following conditions: (a) He has completed three years' residence in the country, (b) He has a spouse possessing the nationality of the country of residence. A refugee may not invoke the benefits of this provision if he has abandoned his spouse, (c) He has one or more children possessing the nationality of the country of residence.

3. The Contracting States shall give sympathetic consideration to assimilating the rights of all refugees with regard to wage-earning employment to those of nationals, and in particular of those refugees who have entered their territory pursuant to programmes of labour recruitment or under immigration schemes.

Article 18

Self-employment.

The Contracting States shall accord to a refugee lawfully in their territory treatment as favourable as possible and, in any event, not less favourable than that accorded to aliens generally in the same circumstances, as regards the right to engage on his own account in agriculture, industry, handicrafts and commerce and to establish commercial and industrial companies.

Article 19

Liberal professions.

1. Each Contracting State shall accord to refugees lawfully staying in their territory who hold diplomas recognized by the competent authorities of that State, and who are desirous of practising a liberal profession, treatment as favourable as possible and, in any event, not less favourable than that accorded to aliens generally in the same circumstances.

2. The Contracting States shall use their best endeavours consistently with their laws and constitutions to secure the settlement of such refugees in the territories, other than the metropolitan territory, for whose international relations they are responsible.

IV. WELFARE

Article 20

Rationing.

Where a rationing system exists, which applies to the population at large and regulates the general distribution of products in short supply, refugees shall be accorded the same treatment as nationals.

Article 21

Housing.

As regards housing, the Contracting States, in so far as the matter is regulated by laws or regulations or is subject to the control of public authorities, shall accord to refugees lawfully staying in their territory treatment as favourable as possible and, in any event, not less favourable than that accorded to aliens generally in the same circumstances.

Article 22

Public education.

(1) The Contracting States shall accord to refugees the same treatment as is accorded to nationals with respect to elementary education.

(2) The Contracting States shall accord to refugees treatment as favourable as possible, and, in any event, not less favourable than that accorded to aliens generally in the same circumstances, with respect to education other than elementary education and, in particular, as regards access to studies, the recognition of foreign school certificates, diplomas and degrees, the remission of fees and charges and the award of scholarships.

Article 23

Public relief.

The Contracting States shall accord to refugees lawfully staying in their territory the same treatment with respect to public relief and assistance as is accorded to their nationals.

Article 24

Labour legislation and social security.

(1) The Contracting States shall accord to refugees lawfully staying in their territory the same treatment as is accorded to nationals in respect of the following matters:

(2) The right to compensation for the death of a refugee resulting from employment injury or from occupational disease shall not be affected by the fact that the residence of the beneficiary is outside the territory of the Contracting State.

(3) The Contracting States shall extend to refugees the benefits of agreements concluded between them, or which may be concluded between them in the future, concerning the maintenance of acquired rights and rights in the process of acquisition in regard to social security, subject only to the conditions which apply to nationals of the States signatory to the agreements in question.

(4) The Contracting States will give sympathetic consideration to extending to refugees so far as possible the benefits of similar agreements which may at any time be in force between such Contracting States and non-contracting States.

V. ADMINISTRATIVE MEASURES

Article 25

Administrative assistance.

(1) When the exercise of a right by a refugee would normally require the assistance of authorities of a foreign country to whom he cannot have recourse, the Contracting States in whose territory he is residing shall arrange that such assistance be afforded to him by their own authorities or by an international authority.

(2) The authority or authorities mentioned in paragraph 1 shall deliver or cause to be delivered under their supervision to refugees such documents or certifications as would normally be delivered to aliens by or through their national authorities.

(3) Documents or certifications so delivered shall stand in the stead of the official instruments delivered to aliens by or through their national authorities, and shall be given credence in the absence of proof to the contrary.

(4) Subject to such exceptional treatment as may be granted to indigent persons, fees may be charged for the services mentioned herein, but such fees shall be moderate and commensurate with those charged to nationals for similar services.

(5) The provisions of this Article shall be without prejudice to Articles 27 and 28.

Article 26

Freedom of movement.

Each Contracting State shall accord to refugees lawfully in its territory the right to choose their place of residence and to move freely within its territory, subject to any regulations applicable to aliens generally in the same circumstances.

Article 27

Identity papers.

The Contracting States shall issue identity papers to any refugee in their territory who does not possess a valid travel document.

Article 28

Travel documents.

(1) The Contracting States shall issue to refugees lawfully staying in their territory travel documents for the purpose of travel outside their territory unless compelling reasons of national security or public order otherwise require, and the provisions of the Schedule to this Convention shall apply with respect to such documents. The Contracting States may issue such a travel document to any other refugee in their territory; they shall in particular give sympathetic consideration to the issue of such a travel document to refugees in their territory who are unable to obtain a travel document from the country of their lawful residence.

(2) Travel documents issued to refugees under previous international agreements by parties thereto shall be recognized and treated by the Contracting States in the same way as if they had been issued pursuant to this article.

Article 29

Fiscal charges.

(1) The Contracting States shall not impose upon refugee duties, charges or taxes, of any description whatsoever, other or higher than those which are or may be levied on their nationals in similar situations.

(2) Nothing in the above paragraph shall prevent the application to refugees of the laws and regulations concerning charges in respect of the issue to aliens of administrative documents including identity papers.

Article 30

Transfer of assets.

(1) A Contracting State shall, in conformity with its laws and regulations, permit refugees to transfer assets which they have brought into its territory, to another country where they have been admitted for the purposes of resettlement.

(2) A Contracting State shall give sympathetic consideration to the application of refugees for permission to transfer assets wherever they may be and which are necessary for their resettlement in another country to which they have been admitted.

Article 31

Refugees unlawfully in the country of refuge.

(1) The Contracting States shall not impose penalties, on account of their illegal entry or presence, on refugees who, coming directly from a territory where their life or freedom was threatened in the sense of Article 1, enter or are present in their territory without authorization, provided they present themselves without delay to the authorities and show good cause for their illegal entry or presence.

(2) The Contracting States shall not apply to the movements of such refugees restrictions other than those which are necessary and such restrictions shall only be applied until their status in the country is regularized or they obtain admission into another country. The Contracting States shall allow such refugees a reasonable period and all the necessary facilities to obtain admission into another country.

Article 32

Expulsion.

(1) The Contracting States shall not expel a refugee lawfully in their territory save on grounds of national security or public order.

(2) The expulsion of such a refugee shall be only in pursuance of a decision reached in accordance with due process of law. Except where compelling reasons of national security otherwise require, the refugee shall be allowed to submit evidence to clear himself, and to appeal to and be represented for the purpose before competent authority or a person or persons specially designated by the competent authority.

(3) The Contracting States shall allow such a refugee a reasonable period within which to seek legal admission into another country. The Contracting States reserve the right to apply during that period such internal measures as they may deem necessary.

Article 33

Prohibition of expulsion or return ('refoulement').

(1) No Contracting State shall expel or return ('refouler') a refugee in any manner whatsoever to the frontiers of territories where his life or freedom would be threatened on account of his race, religion, nationality, membership of a particular social group or political opinion.

(2) The benefit of the present provision may not, however, be claimed by a refugee whom there are reasonable grounds for regarding as a danger to the security of the country in which he is, or who, having been convicted by a final judgment of a particularly serious crime, constitutes a danger to the community of that country.

Article 34

Naturalization.

The Contracting States shall as far as possible facilitate the assimilation and naturalization of refugees. They shall in particular make every effort to expedite naturalization proceedings and to reduce as far as possible the charges and costs of such proceedings.

VI. EXECUTORY AND TRANSITORY PROVISIONS

Article 35

Co-operation of the national authorities with the United Nations.

(1) The Contracting States undertake to co-operate with the Office of the United Nations High Commissioner for Refugees, or any other agency of the United Nations which may succeed

it, in the exercise of its functions, and shall in particular facilitate its duty of supervising the application of the provisions of this Convention.

(2) In order to enable the Office of the High Commissioner, or any other agency of the United Nations which may succeed it, to make reports to the competent organs of the United Nations, the Contracting States undertake to provide them in the appropriate form with information and statistical data requested concerning:

Article 36

Information on national legislation.

The Contracting States shall communicate to the Secretary-General of the United Nations the laws and regulations which they may adopt to ensure the application of this Convention.

Article 37

Relation to previous Conventions.

Without prejudice to Article 28, paragraph 2, of this Convention, this Convention replaces, as between parties to it, the Arrangements of 5 July 1922, 31 May 1924, 12 May 1926, 30 June 1928 and 30 July 1935, the Conventions of 28 October 1933 and 10 February 1938, the Protocol of 14 September 1939 and the Agreement of 15 October 1946.

VII. FINAL CLAUSES

Article 38

Settlement of disputes.

Any dispute between parties to this Convention relating to its interpretation or application, which cannot be settled by other means, shall be referred to the International Court of Justice at the request of any one of the parties to the dispute.

Article 39

Signature, ratification and accession.

(1) This Convention shall be opened for signature at Geneva on 28 July 1951 and shall hereafter be deposited with the Secretary-General of the United Nations. It shall be open for signature at the European Office of the United Nations from 28 July to 31 August 1951 and shall be re-opened for signature at the Headquarters of the United Nations from 17 September 1951 to 31 December 1952.

(2) This Convention shall be open for signature on behalf of all States Members of the United Nations, and also on behalf of any other State invited to attend the Conference of Plenipotentiaries on the Status of Refugees and Stateless Persons or to which an invitation to sign will have been addressed by the General Assembly. It shall be ratified and the instruments of ratification shall be deposited with the Secretary-General of the United Nations.

(3) This Convention shall be open from 28 July 1951 for accession by the States referred to in paragraph 2 of this Article. Accession shall be effected by the deposit of an instrument of accession with the Secretary-General of the United Nations.

Article 40

Territorial application clause.

(1) Any state may, at the time of signature, ratification or accession, declare that this Convention shall extend to all or any of the territories for the international relations of which it is responsible. Such a declaration shall take effect when the Convention enters into force for the State concerned.

(2) At any time thereafter any such extension shall be made by notification addressed to the Secretary-General of the United Nations and shall take effect as from the ninetieth day after the day of receipt by the Secretary-General of the United Nations of this notification, or as from the date of entry into force of the Convention for the State concerned, whichever is the later.

(3) With respect to those territories to which this Convention is not extended at the time of signature, ratification or accession, each State concerned shall consider the possibility of taking the necessary steps in order to extend the application of this Convention to such territories, subject, where necessary for constitutional reasons, to the consent of the governments of such territories.

Article 41

Federal clause.

In the case of a Federal or non-unitary State, the following provisions shall apply:

1. With respect to those Articles of this Convention that come within the legislative jurisdiction of constituent States, provinces or cantons which are not, under the constitutional system of the federation, bound to take legislative action, the Federal Government shall bring such Articles with a favourable recommendation to the notice of the appropriate authorities of States, provinces or cantons at the earliest possible moment.

2. A Federal State Party to this Convention shall, at the request of any other Contracting State transmitted through the Secretary-General of the United Nations, supply a statement of the law and practice of the Federation and its constituent units in regard to any particular provision of the Convention showing the extent to which effect has been given to that provision by legislative or other action.

Article 42

Reservations.

(1) At the time of signature, ratification or accession, any State may make reservations to articles of the Convention other than to Articles 1, 3, 4, 16(1), 33, 36–46 inclusive.

(2) Any State making a reservation in accordance with paragraph 1 of this article may at any time withdraw the reservation by a communication to that effect addressed to the Secretary-General of the United Nations.

Article 43

Entry into force.

(1) This Convention shall come into force on the ninetieth day following the day of deposit of the sixth instrument of ratification or accession.

(2) For each State ratifying or acceding to the Convention after the deposit of the sixth instrument of ratification or accession, the Convention shall enter into force on the ninetieth day following the date of deposit by such State of its instrument of ratification or accession.

Article 44

Denunciation.

(1) Any Contracting State may denounce this Convention at any time by a notification addressed to the Secretary-General of the United Nations.

(2) Such denunciation shall take effect for the Contracting State concerned one year from the date upon which it is received by the Secretary-General of the United Nations.

(3) Any State which has made a declaration or notification under Article 40 may, at any time thereafter, by a notification to the Secretary-General of the United Nations, declare that the Convention shall cease to extend to such territory one year after the date of receipt of the notification by the Secretary-General.

Article 45

Revision.

(1) Any Contracting State may request revision of this Convention at any time by a notification addressed to the Secretary-General of the United Nations.

(2) The General Assembly of the United Nations shall recommend the steps, if any, to be taken in respect of such request.

Article 46

Notifications by the Secretary-General of the United Nations.

The Secretary-General of the United Nations shall inform all Members of the United Nations and non-member States referred to in Article 39:

IN FAITH WHEREOF the undersigned, duly authorized, have signed this Convention on behalf of their respective Governments,

DONE at GENEVA, this twenty-eighth day of July, one thousand nine hundred and fifty-one, in a single copy, of which the English and French texts are equally authentic and which shall remain deposited in the archives of the United Nations, and certified true copies of which shall be delivered to all Members of the United Nations and to the non-member States referred to in Article 39.

Protocol relating to the Status of Refugees

(signed 31 January 1967)

The States Parties to the present Protocol,

Considering that the Convention relating to the Status of Refugees done at Geneva on 28 July 1951 (hereinafter referred to as the Convention) covers only those persons who have become refugees as a result of events occurring before 1 January 1951,

Considering that new refugee situations have arisen since the Convention was adopted and that the refugees concerned may therefore not fall within the scope of the Convention,

Considering that it is desirable that equal status should be enjoyed by all refugees covered by the definition in the Convention irrespective of the dateline 1 January 1951,

Have agreed as follows:

Article 1

General provision.

1. The States Parties to the present Protocol undertake to apply Articles 2 to 34 inclusive of the Convention to refugees as hereinafter defined.

2. For the purpose of the present Protocol, the term 'refugee' shall, except as regards the application of paragraph 3 of this Article, mean any person within the definition of Article 1 of the Convention as if the words 'As a result of events occurring before 1 January 1951 and . . . 'and the words' . . . a result of such events', in Article 1 A (2) were omitted.

3. The present Protocol shall be applied by the States Parties hereto without any geographic limitation, save that existing declarations made by States already Parties to the Convention in accordance with Article 1 B (1)(a) of the Convention, shall, unless extended under Article 1 B (2) thereof, apply also under the present Protocol.

Article 2

Co-operation of the national authorities with the United Nations.

1. The States Parties to the present Protocol undertake to co-operate with the Office of the United Nations High Commissioner for Refugees, or any other agency of the United Nations which may succeed it, in the exercise of its functions, and shall in particular facilitate its duty of supervising the application of the provisions of the present Protocol.

2. In order to enable the Office of the High Commissioner, or any other agency of the United Nations which may succeed it, to make reports to the competent organs of the United Nations, the States Parties to the present Protocol undertake to provide them with the information and statistical data requested, in the appropriate form, concerning: (a) The condition of refugees; (b) The implementation of the present Protocol; (c) Laws, regulations and decrees which are, or may hereafter be, in force relating to refugees.

Article 3

Information on national legislation.

The States Parties to the present Protocol shall communicate to the Secretary-General of the United Nations the laws and regulations which they may adopt to ensure the application of the present Protocol.

Article 4

Settlement of disputes.

Any dispute between States Parties to the present Protocol which relates to its interpretation or application and which cannot be settled by other means shall be referred to the International Court of Justice at the request of any one of the parties to the dispute.

Article 5

Accession.

The present Protocol shall be open for accession on behalf of all States Parties to the Convention and of any other State Member of the United Nations or member of any of the specialized agencies or to which an invitation to accede may have been addressed by the General Assembly of the United Nations. Accession shall be effected by the deposit of an instrument of accession with the Secretary-General of the United Nations.

Article 6

Federal clause.

In the case of a Federal or non-unitary State, the following provisions shall apply:

(a) With respect to those articles of the Convention to be applied in accordance with Article 1, paragraph 1, of the present Protocol that come within the legislative jurisdiction of the federal legislative authority, the obligations of the Federal Government shall to this extent be the same as those of States Parties which are not Federal States;

(b) With respect to those articles of the Convention to be applied in accordance with Article 1, paragraph 1, of the present Protocol that come within the legislative jurisdiction of constituent States, provinces or cantons which are not, under the constitutional system of the federation, bound to take legislative action, the Federal Government shall bring such articles with a favourable recommendation to the notice of the appropriate authorities of States, provinces or cantons at the earliest possible moment;

(c) A Federal State Party to the present Protocol shall, at the request of any other State Party hereto transmitted through the Secretary-General of the United Nations, supply a statement of the law and practice of the Federation and its constituent units in regard to any particular provision of the Convention to be applied in accordance with Article 1, paragraph 1, of the present Protocol, showing the extent to which effect has been given to that provision by legislative or other action.

Article 7

Reservations and declarations.

1. At the time of accession, any State may make reservations in respect of Article 4 of the present Protocol and in respect of the application in accordance with Article 1 of the present Protocol of any provisions of the Convention other than those contained in Articles 1, 3, 4, 16(1) and 33 thereof, provided that in the case of a State Party to the Convention reservations made under this Article shall not extend to refugees in respect of whom the Convention applies.

2. Reservations made by States Parties to the Convention in accordance with Article 42 thereof shall, unless withdrawn, be applicable in relation to their obligations under the present Protocol.

3. Any State making a reservation in accordance with paragraph 1 of this Article may at any time withdraw such reservation by a communication to that effect addressed to the Secretary-General of the United Nations.

4. Declarations made under Article 40, paragraphs 1 and 2, of the Convention by a State Party thereto which accedes to the present Protocol shall be deemed to apply in respect of the present Protocol, unless upon accession a notification to the contrary is addressed by the State Party concerned to the Secretary-General of the United Nations. The provisions of Article 40, paragraphs 2 and 3, and of Article 44, paragraph 3, of the Convention shall be deemed to apply *mutatis mutandis* to the present Protocol.

Articles 8–11

Entry into force, denunciation, notifications etc.

United Nations Peace-keeping Operations

Address: Department of Peace-keeping Operations, Room S-3727-B, United Nations, New York, NY 10017, USA.

Telephone: (212) 963-8077; **fax:** (212) 963-9222; **internet:** www.un.org/Depts/dpko/.

United Nations peace-keeping operations have been conceived as instruments of conflict control. The UN has used these operations in various conflicts, with the consent of the parties involved, to maintain international peace and security, without prejudice to the positions or claims of parties, in order to facilitate the search for political settlements through peaceful means such as mediation and the good offices of the Secretary-General. Each operation is established with a specific mandate, which requires periodic review by the Security Council. United Nations peace-keeping operations fall into two categories: peace-keeping forces and observer missions.

Peace-keeping forces are composed of contingents of military and civilian personnel, made available by member states. These forces assist in preventing the recurrence of fighting, restoring and maintaining peace, and promoting a return to normal conditions. To this end, peace-keeping forces are authorized as necessary to undertake negotiations, persuasion, observation and fact-finding. They conduct patrols and interpose physically between the opposing parties. Peace-keeping forces are permitted to use their weapons only in self-defence.

Military observer missions are composed of officers (usually unarmed), who are made available, on the Secretary-General's request, by member states. A mission's function is to observe and report to the Secretary-General (who, in turn, informs the UN Security Council) on the maintenance of a cease-fire, to investigate violations and to do what it can to improve the situation.

Peace-keeping forces and observer missions must at all times maintain complete impartiality and avoid any action that might affect the claims or positions of the parties. In January 1995 the UN Secretary-General presented a report to the Security Council, reassessing the UN's role in peace-keeping. The document stipulated that UN forces in conflict areas should not be responsible for peace-enforcement duties, and included a proposal for the establishment of a 'rapid reaction' force which would be ready for deployment within a month of being authorized by the Security Council. In September 1997 the UN Secretary-General established a staff to plan and organize the formation of the so-called UN Stand-by Forces High Readiness Brigade (SHIRBRIG), to be based in Denmark. SHIRBRIG was declared available to the UN in January 2000; by that time Argentina, Austria, Canada, Denmark, Italy, the Netherlands, Norway, Poland, Romania and Sweden had formally committed troops to the force. SHIRBRIG became fully operational in late 2000 with the deployment of troops to the newly-authorized UN Mission in Ethiopia and Eritrea (UNMEE, see below). A Stand-by Arrangements System (UNSAS) became operational in 1994; at the end of 2001 some 69 countries were participating in the system by making available specialized civilian and military personnel, as well as other services and equipment. In August 2000 a report on UN peace-keeping activities prepared by a team of experts appointed by the Secretary-General assessed the aims and requirements of peace-keeping operations and recommended several measures to improve the performance of the Department of Peace-Keeping Operations (DPKO), focusing on its planning and management capacity from the inception of an operation through to post-conflict peace-building activities, and on its rapid response capability. Proposed reforms included the establishment of a body to improve co-ordination of information and strategic analysis requirements; the promotion of partnership arrangements between member states (within the context of UNSAS, see above) enabling the formation of several coherent multinational brigades, and improved monitoring of the preparedness of potential troop contributor nations, with a view to facilitating the effective deployment of most operations within 30 days of their authorization in a Security Council resolution; the adoption of 'on-call' reserve lists to ensure the prompt deployment of civilian police and specialists; the preparation of a global logistics support strategy; and a restructuring of the DPKO to improve administrative efficiency. The study also urged an increase in resources for funding peace-keeping operations and the adoption of a more flexible financing mechanism, and emphasized the importance of the UN's conflict prevention activities. In November the Security Council, having welcomed the report, adopted guidelines aimed at improving its management of peace-keeping operations, including providing missions with clear and achievable mandates. In June 2001 the Council adopted a resolution incorporating a Statement of principles on co-operation with troop-contributing countries, which aimed to strengthen the relationship between those countries and the UN and to enhance the effectiveness of peace-keeping operations.

The UN's peace-keeping forces and observer missions are financed in most cases by assessed contributions from member states of the organization. In recent years a significant expansion in the UN's peace-keeping activities has been accompanied by a perpetual financial crisis within the organization, as a result of the increased financial burden and some member states' delaying payment. By 31 December 2001 outstanding assessed contributions to the peace-keeping budget amounted to some US $1,900m.

By February 2002 the UN had undertaken a total of 54 peace-keeping operations, of which 13 were authorized in the period 1948–88 and 41 since 1988, reaching a peak in 1993 with a total deployment of more than 80,000 troops from 77 countries. At early 2002 87 countries were contributing some 47,095 military personnel and civilian police to the 15 ongoing operations.

UNITED NATIONS DISENGAGEMENT OBSERVER FORCE—UNDOF

Headquarters: Camp Faouar, Syria.

Commander: Maj.-Gen. Bo Wranker (Sweden).

UNDOF was established for an initial period of six months by a UN Security Council resolution in May 1974, following the signature in Geneva of a disengagement agreement between Syrian and Israeli forces. The mandate has since been extended by successive resolutions. The initial task of the Force was to take over territory evacuated in stages by the Israeli troops, in accordance with the disengagement agreement, to hand over territory to Syrian troops, and to establish an area of separation on the Golan Heights.

UNDOF continues to monitor the area of separation; it carries out inspections of the areas of limited armaments and forces; uses its best efforts to maintain the cease-fire; and undertakes activities of a humanitarian nature, such as arranging the transfer of prisoners and war-dead between Syria and Israel. The Force operates exclusively on Syrian territory.

At 31 January 2002 the Force comprised 1,032 troops; it is assisted by approximately 80 military observers of UNTSO's Observer Group Golan, and supported by 127 international and local civilian personnel. Further UNTSO military observers help UNDOF in the performance of its tasks, as required. The General Assembly appropriated US $35.7m. to cover the cost of the operation for the period 1 July 2001–30 June 2002.

UNITED NATIONS INTERIM ADMINISTRATION MISSION IN KOSOVO—UNMIK

Headquarters: Priština, Kosovo, Yugoslavia.

Special Representative of the UN Secretary-General and Head of Mission: Michael Steiner (Germany).

Principal Deputy Special Representative of the UN Secretary-General: Charles H. Brayshaw (USA).

Deputy Special Representative for Police and Justice: Jean-Christian Cady (France).

Deputy Special Representative for the Interim Civil Administration: Thomas Koenigs (Germany).

Deputy Special Representative for (OSCE) Institution Building in Kosovo: DAAN EVERTS (Netherlands).

Deputy Special Representative for (EU) Reconstruction in Kosovo: ANDY BEARPARK (United Kingdom).

In June 1999 NATO suspended a 10-week aerial offensive against the Federal Republic of Yugoslavia, following an agreement by the Serbian authorities to withdraw all security and paramilitary forces from the southern province of Kosovo and Metohija, where Serbian repression of a separatist movement had prompted a humanitarian crisis and co-ordinated international action to resolve the conflict. On 10 June the UN Security Council adopted Resolution 1244, which outlined the terms of a political settlement for Kosovo and provided for the deployment of international civilian and security personnel. The security presence, termed the Kosovo Peace Implementation Force (KFOR), was to be led by NATO, while the UN was to oversee all civilian operations. UNMIK was established under the terms of Resolution 1244 as the supreme legal and executive authority in Kosovo, with responsibility for all civil administration and for facilitating the reconstruction and rehabilitation of the province as an autonomous region. For the first time in a UN operation other organizations were mandated to co-ordinate aspects of the mission in Kosovo, under the UN's overall jurisdiction. The four key elements, or Pillars, of UNMIK were humanitarian affairs (led by UNHCR); the interim civil administration; democratization and institution-building (OSCE); and economic reconstruction (EU). At the end of the first year of UNMIK's presence the element of humanitarian assistance was phased out. A new Pillar I, concerned with police and justice, was established in May 2001, under the direct leadership of the UN. On arriving in the province at the end of June 1999 UNMIK and KFOR established a Joint Implementation Commission to co-ordinate and supervise the demilitarization of the Kosovo Liberation Army. UNMIK initiated a mass information campaign (and later administered new radio stations in Kosovo) to urge co-operation with the international personnel in the province and tolerance for all ethnic communities. A Mine Co-ordinating Centre supervised efforts to deactivate anti-personnel devices and to ensure the safety of the returning ethnic Albanian population. In mid-July the UN Secretary-General's permanent Special Representative took office, and chaired the first meeting of the Kosovo Transitional Council (KTC), which had been established by the UN as a multi-ethnic consultative organ, the highest political body under UNMIK, to help to restore law and order in the province and to reintegrate the local administrative infrastructure. In August a Joint Advisory Council on Legislative Matters was constituted, with representatives of UNMIK and the local judiciary, in order to consider measures to eliminate discrimination from the province's legal framework. At the end of July UNMIK personnel began to supervise customs controls at Kosovo's international borders. Other developments in the first few months of UNMIK's deployment included the establishment of joint commissions on energy and public utilities, education, and health, a Technical Advisory Commission on establishing a judiciary and prosecution service, and, in October, the establishment of a Fuel Supervisory Board to administer the import, sale and distribution of petroleum. Central financial institutions for the province were inaugurated in November. In the same month UNMIK established a Housing and Property Directorate and Claims Commission in order to resolve residential property disputes. In September the KTC agreed to establish a Joint Security Committee, in response to concerns at the escalation of violence in the province, in particular attacks on remaining Serbian civilians. In mid-October a UN worker was murdered, reportedly by ethnic Albanians who had identified him as a local Serb. In November the Special Representative appealed for additional funds and police officers to counter further ethnic violence. In mid-December the leaders of the three main political groupings in Kosovo agreed on provisional power-sharing arrangements with UNMIK for the administration of Kosovo until the holding of elections, scheduled for 2000. The agreement on the so-called Kosovo-UNMIK Joint Interim Administrative Structure established an eight-member executive Interim Administrative Council and a framework of administrative departments. The KTC was to maintain its consultative role. In January 2000 UNMIK oversaw the inauguration of the Kosovo Protection Corps, a civilian agency comprising mainly former members of the newly-demilitarized Kosovo Liberation Army, which was to provide an emergency response service and a humanitarian assistance capacity, to assist in de-mining operations and contribute to rebuilding local infrastructure. In August UNMIK, in view of its mandate to assist with the regeneration of the local economy, concluded an agreement with a multinational consortium to rehabilitate the important Trepca non-ferrous mining complex. During mid-2000 UNMIK organized the voter registration process for the forthcoming territory-wide municipal elections. These were held on 28 October with a strong voter turnout, although participation by minority communities was low. In mid-December the Supreme Court of Kosovo was inaugurated, comprising 16 judges appointed by the Special Representative of the UN Secretary-General. During 2000 UNMIK police and KFOR co-operated in conducting joint security operations; the establishment of a special security task force to combat ethnically-motivated political violence, comprising senior UNMIK police and KFOR members, was agreed in June. From January 2001 UNMIK international travel documents were distributed to Kosovars without Yugoslav passports. From early June, in response to ongoing concern at violence between ethnic Albanians and security forces in the former Yugoslav republic of Macedonia (FYRM), UNMIK designated 19 authorized crossing points at Kosovo's international borders with Albania and the FYRM, and its boundaries with Montenegro and Serbia. In mid-May the Special Representative of the Secretary-General signed the Constitutional Framework on Interim Self-Government, providing for the establishment of a Constitutional Assembly; elections to the proposed Assembly were scheduled to take place in mid-November. UNMIK undertook efforts to register voters, in particular those from minority ethnic groups, and to continue to facilitate the return of displaced persons to their home communities. The last session of the KTC was held in October, and a general election was conducted, as scheduled, on 17 November. In December the Special Representative of the Secretary-General inaugurated the new 120-member Assembly. By February 2002, however, there was still no agreement by the Assembly on the positions of President or Prime Minister.

At mid-January 2002 UNMIK comprised 4,519 civilian police officers, 37 military personnel, and an additional 1,178 international civilian personnel and 3,397 local civilian personnel. The General Assembly apportioned US $413.4m. to finance the operation during the period 1 July 2001–30 June 2002.

UNITED NATIONS INTERIM FORCE IN LEBANON—UNIFIL

Headquarters: Naqoura, Lebanon.

Personal Representative of the UN Secretary-General for Southern Lebanon: STAFFAN DE MISTURA (Sweden).

Commander: Maj.-Gen. LALIT MOHAN TEWARI (India).

UNIFIL was established by UN Security Council Resolution 425 in March 1978, following an invasion of Lebanon by Israeli forces. The force was mandated to confirm the withdrawal of Israeli forces, to restore international peace and security, and to assist the Government of Lebanon in ensuring the return of its effective authority in southern Lebanon. UNIFIL also extended humanitarian assistance to the population of the area, particularly following the second Israeli invasion of Lebanon in 1982. UNIFIL has provided civilians with food, water, fuel; medical and dental services; and some veterinary assistance. In April 1992, in accordance with its mandate, UNIFIL completed the transfer of part of its zone of operations to the control of the Lebanese army.

In March 1998 the Israeli Government announced that it recognized Security Council Resolution 425, requiring the unconditional withdrawal of its forces from southern Lebanon. It stipulated, however, that any withdrawal of its troops must be conditional on receiving security guarantees from the Lebanese authorities. A formal decision to this effect, adopted on 1 April, was rejected by the Lebanese and Syrian Governments. In mid-April 2000 the Israeli Government formally notified the UN Secretary-General of its intention to comply forthwith and in full with Resolution 425. Later in that month the UN Secretary-General dispatched a team of experts to study the technical aspects of the impending implementation of Resolution 425, and sent a delegation, led by both his Special Co-ordinator for the Middle East Peace Process, Terje Roed Larsen, and the Commander of UNIFIL, to consult with regional Governments and groupings. The withdrawal of Israeli troops commenced in mid-May, and the final contingent was reported to have left Lebanon on 24 May. Meanwhile, the Security Council endorsed an operational plan to enable UNIFIL to verify the withdrawal. All concerned parties were urged to co-operate with UNIFIL in order to ensure the full implementation of the resolution. In accordance with its mandate, UNIFIL was to be disbanded following the resumption by the Lebanese Government of effective authority and the normal responsibilities of a state throughout the area, including the re-establishment of law and order structures. In mid-June the UN Secretary-General confirmed that Israeli forces had been fully evacuated from southern Lebanon. Soon afterwards UNIFIL reported several Israeli violations of the line of withdrawal, the so-called Blue Line. The Israeli Government agreed to rectify these by the end of July, and on 24 July the UN Secretary-General confirmed that no serious violations remained. UNIFIL, reinforced with additional troops, patrolled the area vacated by the Israeli forces, monitored the line of withdrawal, undertook demining activities, and continued to provide humanitarian assistance. From August the Lebanese Government deployed a Joint Security Force to the area and began re-establishing local administrative structures and reintegrating basic services into the rest of the country. However, the authorities declined to deploy military personnel along the border zone, on the grounds that a comprehensive peace agreement with Israel would first need to be achieved. In November, following two serious violations of the Blue Line in the previous month by both Israeli troops and Hezbollah militia, the Security Council urged the Lebanese Government to take effective control of the whole area vacated by Israel and to assume international responsibilities. In January 2001 the UN Secretary-General reported that UNIFIL no longer exercised control over the area of operation, which remained relatively stable. The Security Council endorsed his proposals to reconfigure the Force in order to focus on its remaining mandate of maintaining and observing the cease-fire along the line of withdrawal. An initial reduction in the Force's strength to 4,550 troops was to be effected by July. During the year several incidents involving Hezbollah attacks on Israeli military positions and frequent air violations of the area of withdrawal by Israeli military aircraft were reported. UNIFIL remained as an observer presence, and by mid-2002 was expected to have a reduced force strength of some 2,000 troops.

At 31 January 2002 the Force comprised 3,494 troops, assisted by some 50 military observers of UNTSO's Observer Group Lebanon, and also by some 459 international and local civilian staff. The General Assembly appropriation for the operation for the period 1 July 2001–30 June 2002 amounted to US $143.3m.

UNITED NATIONS IRAQ-KUWAIT OBSERVATION MISSION—UNIKOM

Headquarters: Umm Qasr, Kuwait.

Commander: Maj.-Gen. MIGUEL ANGEL MORENO (Argentina).

UNIKOM was established by a UN Security Council resolution (initially for a six-month period) in April 1991, to monitor a 200-km demilitarized zone along the border between Iraq and Kuwait. The task of the mission was to deter violations of the border, to monitor the Khor Abdullah waterway between Iraq and Kuwait, and to prevent military activity within the zone. In February 1993 the Security Council adopted a resolution to strengthen UNIKOM, following incursions into Kuwaiti territory by Iraqi personnel. The resolution enabled the use of physical action to prevent or redress violations of the demilitarized zone or the newly-defined boundary between Iraq and Kuwait. UNIKOM assisted with the relocation of Iraqi citizens from Kuwait, which was completed in February 1994; has provided technical support to other UN operations in the area, especially the Iraq–Kuwait Boundary Demarcation Commission (which was terminated in 1993); and facilitates the humanitarian activities of the International Committee of the Red Cross. A maritime operation to monitor the Khor Abdullah waterway commenced in February 2000.

At 31 January 2002 UNIKOM comprised 905 troops and 192 military observers, assisted by some 220 international and local civilian support staff. The UN General Assembly appropriated US $52.8m. for the maintenance of the mission for the period 1 July 2001–30 June 2002; two-thirds of UNIKOM's total costs are funded by voluntary contributions from Kuwait.

UNITED NATIONS MILITARY OBSERVER GROUP IN INDIA AND PAKISTAN—UNMOGIP

Headquarters: Rawalpindi, Pakistan (November–April), Srinagar, India (May–October).

Chief Military Observer: Maj.-Gen. HERMANN K. LOIDOLT (Austria).

The Group was established in 1948 by UN Security Council resolutions aiming to restore peace in the region of Jammu and Kashmir, the status of which had become a matter of dispute between the Governments of India and Pakistan. Following a cease-fire which came into effect in January 1949, the military observers of UNMOGIP were deployed to assist in its observance. There is no periodic review of UNMOGIP's mandate. In 1971, following the signature of a new cease-fire agreement, India claimed that UNMOGIP's mandate had lapsed, since it was originally intended to monitor the agreement reached in 1949. Pakistan, however, regarded UNMOGIP's mission as unchanged, and the Group's activities have continued, although they have been somewhat restricted on the Indian side of the 'line of control', which was agreed by India and Pakistan in 1972.

At 31 January 2002 there were 45 military observers deployed on both sides of the 'line of control', supported by 54 international and local civilian personnel. The operation was allocated US $6.2m. from the regular budget of the UN for 2002.

UNITED NATIONS MISSION FOR THE REFERENDUM IN WESTERN SAHARA—MINURSO

Headquarters: el-Aaiún, Western Sahara.

Special Representative of the UN Secretary-General and Chief of Mission: WILLIAM LACY SWING (USA).

Personal Envoy of the UN Secretary-General: JAMES A. BAKER, III (USA).

Commander: Brig.-Gen. CLAUDE BUZE (Belgium).

In April 1991 the UN Security Council endorsed the establishment of MINURSO to verify a cease-fire in the disputed territory of Western Sahara, which came into effect in September 1991, and to implement a settlement plan, involving the repatriation of Western Saharan refugees (in co-ordination with UNHCR), the release of all Sahrawi political prisoners, and and the organization of a referendum on the future of the territory. Western Sahara is claimed by Morocco, the administering power since 1975, and by the Algerian-supported Frente Popular para la Liberación de Saguia el Hamra y Río de Oro—Frente Polisario. Although originally envisaged for January 1992, the referendum was postponed indefinitely. In 1992 and 1993 the Secretary-General's Special Representative organized negotiations between the Frente Polisario and the Moroccan Government, who were in serious disagreement regarding criteria for eligibility to vote in the plebiscite (in particular, the Moroccan Government insisted that more than 100,000 members of ethnic groups who had been forced to leave the territory under Spanish rule prior to the last official census in 1974, the results of which were to be used as a basis for voter registration, should be allowed to participate in a referendum). Nevertheless, in March 1993 the Security Council advocated that further efforts should be made to compile a satisfactory electoral list and to resolve the outstanding differences on procedural issues. An Identification Commission was consequently established to begin the process of voter registration, although this was obstructed by the failure of the Moroccan Government and the Frente Polisario to pursue political dialogue. The identification and registration operation was formally initiated in August 1994; however, the process was complicated by the dispersed nature of the Western Saharan population. In December 1995 the UN Secretary-General reported that the identification of voters had stalled, owing to persistent obstruction of the process on the part of the Moroccan and Frente Polisario authorities; at the end of May 1996 the Security Council endorsed a recommendation of the Secretary-General to suspend the identification process until all sides demonstrate their willingness to co-operate with the mission. The Security Council decided that MINURSO's operational capacity should be reduced by 20%, with sufficient troops retained to monitor and verify the cease-fire.

In early 1997 the new Secretary-General of the UN, Kofi Annan, attempted to revive the possibility of an imminent resolution of the dispute, amid increasing concerns that the opposing authorities were preparing for a resumption of hostilities in the event of a collapse of the existing cease-fire, and appointed James Baker, a former US Secretary of State, as his Personal Envoy to the region. In June Baker obtained the support of Morocco and the Frente Polisario, as well as Algeria and Mauritania (which border the disputed territory), to conduct further negotiations in order to advance the referendum process. Direct talks between senior representatives of the Moroccan Government and the Frente Polisario authorities were initiated later in that month, in Lisbon, Portugal, under the auspices of the UN, and attended by Algeria and Mauritania in an observer capacity. In September the two sides concluded an agreement which aimed to resolve the outstanding issues of contention and enable the referendum to be conducted in late 1998. The agreement included a commitment by both parties to identify eligible Sahrawi voters on an individual basis, in accordance with the results of the 1974 census, and a code of conduct to ensure the impartiality of the poll. In October 1997 the Security Council endorsed a recommendation of the Secretary-General to increase the strength of the mission, to enable it to supervise nine identification centres. The process of voter identification resumed in December 1997. The agenda for the settlement plan envisaged that the identification process would be followed by a process of appeal, the publication of a final list of voters, and then by a transitional period, under UN authority, during which all Sahrawi refugees would be repatriated. The referendum was scheduled to be conducted in December 1998. In January 1998 the Security Council approved the deployment of an engineering unit to support MINURSO in its demining activities. During that year ongoing disputes regarding the eligibility of members of three Saharan tribal groups caused significant delays in the identification process.

By early September 1998 the initial identification process had been completed, with a total of 147,350 voters identified, including 87,238 since December 1997. However, the issue of the eligibility of 65,000 members of the three disputed tribal groups remained unresolved. In October the Security Council endorsed a series of measures proposed by the Secretary-General to advance the referendum, including a strengthened Identification Commission to consider requests from any applicant from the disputed tribal groups on an individual basis. The proposals also incorporated the need for an agreement by both sides with UNHCR with regard to arrangements for the repatriation of refugees. In November, following a visit to the region by the Secretary-General, the Frente Polisario accepted the proposals, and in March 1999 the Moroccan Government signed an agreement with the UN to secure the legal basis of the MINURSO operation. In May the Moroccan Government and the Frente Polisario agreed in principle to a draft plan of action for cross-border confidence measures. A new timetable envisaged the referendum being held on 31 July 2000. In July 1999 the UN published the first part of a provisional list of 84,251 qualified voters. The appeals process then commenced. In late November almost 200 Moroccan prisoners of war were released by the Frente Polisario authorities, following a series of negotiations led by the Special Representative of the UN Secretary-General. The identification of applicants from the three disputed Saharan tribal groups was completed at the end of December. In January 2000 the second, final part of the provisional list of qualified voters was issued, and a six-week appeals process ensued. In December 1999 the Security Council acknowledged that persisting disagreements obstructing the implementation of the settlement plan (mainly concerning the processing and analysis of appeals, the release of remaining prisoners and the repatriation of refugees) precluded any possibility of conducting the referendum before 2002. In June 2001 the Personal Envoy of the Secretary-General elaborated a draft Framework Agreement on the Status of Western Sahara, which envisaged the disputed area remaining part of Morocco, but with substantial devolution of authority. Any referendum would be postponed. The Security Council, while granting an extension of MINURSO's mandate until November, authorized Baker to discuss the proposals with all concerned parties. In November the Security Council, at the insistence of the Frente Polisario, requested the opinion of the UN Legal Counsel regarding the legality of two short-term reconnaissance licences granted by Morocco to international petroleum companies for operation in the Western Sahara. In that month the Council extended MINURSO's mandate until the end of February 2002. In January the new Special Representative of the UN Secretary-General, William Lacy Swing, visited the region and met with leaders of both sides. He welcomed the release by the Frente Polisario of a further 115 Moroccan prisoners, but urged both sides to release all long-term detainees. In February the Security Council extended MINURSO's mandate until 30 April; however, with no further progress towards a political agreement having been made, the mission's future was under consideration.

The mission has headquarters in the north and south of the disputed territory, and there is a liaison office in Tindouf, Algeria, which was established in order to maintain contact with the Frente Polisario (which is based in Algeria) and the Algerian Government.

At 4 January 2002 MINURSO comprised 203 military observers, 27 troops and 26 civilian police observers, supported by 315 international and local civilian personnel. The General Assembly appropriation to cover the cost of the mission for the period 1 July 2001–30 June 2002 amounted to US $50.5m.

UNITED NATIONS MISSION IN BOSNIA AND HERZEGOVINA—UNMIBH

Headquarters: Sarajevo, Bosnia and Herzegovina.

Special Representative of the Secretary-General and Co-ordinator of UN Operations in Bosnia and Herzegovina: JACQUES PAUL KLEIN (USA).

Deputy Special Representative of the UN Secretary-General: (vacant).

Commissioner of the UN International Police Task Force: Gen. VINCENT COEURDEROY (France).

In February 1992 the UN established a Protection Force (UNPROFOR), in response to the escalating conflict in the former Yugoslavia, which became one of the largest operations ever mounted by the UN. UNPROFOR assumed responsibility for monitoring the withdrawal of anti-aircraft and heavy weapons by both Bosnian Muslims and Serbs to agreed locations within Bosnia and Herzegovina, the delivery of humanitarian assistance and monitoring compliance with the prohibition on military flights in Bosnian airspace. In December 1995 leaders of the warring parties in the former Yugoslavia signed a peace accord, which had been concluded in the previous month in Dayton, USA. UNPROFOR's mandate was terminated a few days later, when a new multinational force under NATO command (the Implementation Force—IFOR) assumed authority for implementation of the peace accord, for a 12-month period, on 20 December.

On 21 December 1995 the Security Council agreed on the establishment of the UN International Police Task Force (IPTF) and a UN civilian office, in accordance with the Dayton peace agreement. The operation subsequently became known as the UN Mission in Bosnia and Herzegovina (UNMIBH), with the broad mandate to contribute to the establishment of the rule of law in Bosnia and Herzegovina The IPTF's tasks included: restructuring and reform of the local police in Bosnia and Herzegovina to establish a professional, multi-ethnic force; the provision of basic and specialized training of police officers and personnel; assessing threats to public order and advising on the capability of law enforcement agencies to deal with such threats; and monitoring and providing support to the Bosnian police forces in the execution of their duties. A Human Rights Office was established to investigate and act upon any violations of human rights by law enforcement personnel and to maintain a registry of local police officers. The UN Co-ordinator was to exercise authority over the IPTF Commissioner and to co-ordinate other UN activities in Bosnia and Herzegovina relating to humanitarian relief and refugees, demining, elections and economic reconstruction. UNMIBH was to co-operate closely with IFOR and, later, with its successor operation, the Stabilization Force (SFOR), which became operational in December 1996. In March 1996 the Security Council authorized the deployment of five military liaison officers, in order to strengthen liaison arrangements with IFOR. Prior to and during legislative elections, which were held throughout Bosnia and Herzegovina in mid-September, the IPTF assisted IFOR in providing protection to refugees and displaced people returning to vote in their towns of origin. At the international conference to review implementation of the Dayton agreement, which was held in mid-November, it was agreed that the IPTF's mandate was to be strengthened, granting it enhanced powers to investigate the Bosnian police in both sectors of the country. In March 1997 the Security Council authorized the strengthening of the IPTF by an additional 186 police officers and 11 civilian monitors in order to monitor, restructure and train the local police force in the contested north-eastern city of Brčko, which was temporarily under international supervision. During September UNMIBH co-operated with SFOR and an election monitoring group to assist safe and democratic voting in municipal elections in the Bosnian Federation, and monitored the movement of voters within the region and across boundary lines. In May 1998 the Security Council authorized the deployment of an additional 30 IPTF monitors to conduct a series of intensive training programmes for the local police in Bosnia and Herzegovina. In July the Security Council endorsed the establishment of a new programme, within UNMIBH's mandate, to assess and monitor the judicial system in Bosnia and Herzegovina and to promote the rule of law. The Council authorized the deployment of 26 legal experts to undertake the programme. UNMIBH has pursued efforts to establish a State Border Service, equipped to help to counter illegal immigration, smuggling and activities linked to international terrorism. By the end of 2001 an estimated 75% of Bosnian borders, including the international airports, were under the control of the Service. In July 2001 UNMIBH initiated a Special Anti-Trafficking Operations project to counter the problem of trade in women for prostitution. The Security Council has successively renewed UNMIBH's mandate, including that of the IPTF. In June 2001 the mission's mandate was extended until 21 June 2002. In December 2001 the Secretary-General observed that UNMIBH was making progress towards completing its core mandate by the end of 2002, and a smaller, non-UN, successor mission was under consideration. In February 2002 the EU confirmed its intention to provide an EU Police Mission (EUPM), from 1 January 2003, to assume responsibility from UNMIBH.

At 31 January 2002 UNMIBH comprised 1,590 civilian police officers and three military liaison officers, as well as 1,922 international and local civilian personnel. The General Assembly appropriation for the period 1 July 2001 to 30 June 2002, which included the budgets of the UN Mission of Observers in Prevlaka and of UN liaison offices in Belgrade and Zagreb, amounted to US $144.7m.

UNITED NATIONS MISSION IN ETHIOPIA AND ERITREA—UNMEE

Headquarters: Asmara, Eritrea; Addis Ababa, Ethiopia.

Special Representative of the Secretary-General and Head of Mission: LEGWAILA JOSEPH LEGWAILA (Botswana).

Commander: Maj.-Gen. PATRICK C. CAMMAERT (Netherlands).

At the end of July 2000 the Security Council authorized the establishment of UNMEE to facilitate compliance with and verify a cease-fire agreement that had been signed by the Governments of Eritrea and Ethiopia in mid-June (having been mediated by the Organization of African Unity—OAU, q.v.), with a view to settling a two-year border conflict between the two countries. In mid-September the Security Council authorized the deployment of up to 4,200 military personnel (including 220 military observers) to the operation, which was given an initial six-month mandate. The Security Council emphasized that UNMEE's mandate would be terminated on completion of the process to delimit and demarcate the Eritrea-Ethiopia border. In December the Eritrean and Ethiopian authorities concluded a full peace accord. In February 2001 the Military Co-ordination Commission (which had been established jointly by the UN and the OAU in accordance with the cease-fire accord to address military and technical aspects of the peace process, and had met for the first time in December 2000) agreed a timetable to enable Eritrean and Ethiopian forces, monitored by UNMEE, to redeploy in order to establish a 25-km temporary security zone in the border area; the security zone was declared operational in mid-April 2001. UNMEE was subsequently to continue to monitor both forces, to co-ordinate and provide technical assistance for demining activities in the vacated and adjacent areas, and to co-ordinate local humanitarian and human rights activities by UN and other agencies. From mid-2001 UNMEE repeatedly protested against alleged restrictions placed on its freedom of movement by the Eritrean authorities in areas adjoining the security zone; these impeded the mission's capability to monitor the redeployment of that country's forces. In January 2002 the Security Council, noting that Eritrea had started to permit UNMEE delegates to visit certain parts of the adjacent areas on submission of 24 hours' notice, urged that the mission be allowed full freedom of movement. The Council also requested that the Eritrean Government disclose details of an alleged continuing military and police presence within the temporary security zone, and that it conclude a status of forces agreement with the Secretary-General. In March UNMEE's mandate was extended for a further six months, until 15 September.

At 31 January 2002 UNMEE comprised 3,790 troops, 214 military observers, 121 staff officers, 10 national support personnel, and 472 international and local civilian personnel. The proposed budget for the mission amounted to US $200.3m. for the period 1 July 2001 to 30 June 2002.

UNITED NATIONS MISSION IN SIERRA LEONE—UNAMSIL

Headquarters: Freetown, Sierra Leone.

Special Representative of the Secretary-General and Chief of Mission: OLUYEMI ADENIJI (Nigeria).

Commander: Lt-Gen. DANIEL ISHMAEL OPANDE (Kenya).

Chief Military Observer: Maj.-Gen. SYED ATHAR ALI (Pakistan).

In July 1998 the Security Council established a UN observer mission in Sierra Leone (UNOMSIL) to monitor the military and security situation in that country following the restoration of a democratically-elected government. UNOMSIL was authorized to oversee the disarmament and demobilization of former combatants, as well as the voluntary disarmament of members of the civilian defence force, and to assist in monitoring respect for international humanitarian law. The Special Representative, with the civilian component of the mission, was authorized to advise the Sierra Leonean authorities on police practice, training and reform, and to help to address the country's human rights needs. UNOMSIL was to work closely with forces of the Economic Community for West African States (ECOWAS) in promoting peace and national reconciliation. In January 1999, following a sudden escalation of hostilities, the UN Security Council extended the mandate of UNOMSIL for a further two months, although it acknowledged that several UNOMSIL military observers, together with civilian support staff, would withdraw to Conakry, Guinea, until the security situation improved. In March the Security Council condemned the ongoing violation of human rights in Sierra Leone and urged all neighbouring countries to prevent the cross-border supply of armaments to anti-government forces. None the less, the Council extended the mission's mandate until mid-June and, subsequently, until mid-December. In August the Security Council authorized a provisional expansion of UNOMSIL of up to 210 military observers, in order to support the implementation of a peace agreement which had been signed by the parties to the Sierra Leone conflict in July, in Lomé, Togo. In October the Council authorized the establishment of the UN Mission in Sierra Leone (UNAMSIL), comprising up to 6,000 military personnel, to help to consolidate peace in that country. UNAMSIL was mandated to co-operate with the Sierra Leonean Government and all other parties to enforce the cease-fire accord and Lomé peace agreement, to implement a plan for the disarmament, demobilization and reintegration of all former combatants, and to facilitate the delivery of humanitarian assistance. The mission was to assume responsibility for all civilian, political and military components of UNOMSIL, the mandate of which was terminated with immediate effect. In February 2000 the Council expanded UNAMSIL's mandate to include the provision of security at key locations and government installations, assistance to the Sierra Leone law enforcement authorities, and the safe keeping and subsequent disposal of military equipment collected from former combatants. The Council also enlarged the mission's authorized strength from 6,000 to 11,100 military personnel.

During early 2000, in contravention of the Lomé accord, Sierra Leone rebels repeatedly obstructed the implementation of the disarmament and demobilization programme. In May, following an attack on a contingent of UNAMSIL troops in the previous month, rebels killed several mission personnel and captured and detained a large number of others (reportedly as many as 500); these were all released later in the month. In response to the breakdown in security the United Kingdom deployed a force in Sierra Leone in early May, with a mandate to evacuate British nationals; the presence of the British troops was also regarded, however, as a deterrent to any escalation in rebel activities pending the arrival of UNAMSIL reinforcements. In mid-May the Security Council approved a further increase in the mission's authorized strength, providing for a total of 13,000 military personnel. The United Kingdom withdrew most of its force in the following month, leaving a small contingent to train Sierra Leone government troops and undertake security duties. In mid-July UNAMSIL mounted a successful operation to release 233 of its personnel, who had been surrounded by rebels in eastern Sierra Leone since the end of May. The Security Council adopted a resolution in July banning the direct and indirect importation of rough diamonds from rebel-controlled areas of Sierra Leone, following mounting concern at the role played by illicit diamond exploitation in motivating and funding anti-government activities. In August the Security Council recommended that UNAMSIL should be strengthened to enable it to secure approach routes to the Lungi and Freetown peninsulas and to counter continuing attacks by armed rebels. The Security Council asked the Secretary-General to assess the number of additional troops that would be required to achieve this. A new cease-fire agreement, entailing the recommencement of the disarmament, demobilization and reintegration plan, was signed by the Sierra Leone Government and the principal rebel group in early November. In March 2001 the Council expanded the mission's authorized maximum strength to 17,500 military personnel and also approved a revised concept of operations that envisaged the deployment of UNAMSIL troops, government representatives, and international humanitarian personnel into rebel-controlled areas, with a view to re-establishing basic services and the authority of the state. In December the Security Council noted that the Sierra Leone Government, assisted by UNAMSIL, had yet to establish full authority over the rebel-dominated diamond-producing areas of the country. In January 2002 the Security Council welcomed the significant progress that had been achieved in the implementation of the disarmament, demobilization and reintegration plan, including the official completion of the disarmament element during that month. In early 2002 a newly-established interim electoral component of UNAMSIL was supporting the Sierra Leone Government and National Electoral Commission in undertaking preparations for legislative and presidential elections that were scheduled to take place in May. UNAMSIL offices were to be established in each of Sierra Leone's five electoral regions. In March the mission's mandate was extended until 30 September 2002.

At 31 January 2002 UNAMSIL comprised 17,099 troops and 245 military observers, assisted by 56 civilian police and 838 international and local civilian personnel. The proposed budget for the mission amounted to US $699.2m. for the period 1 July 2001 to 31 July 2002.

UNITED NATIONS MISSION IN THE DEMOCRATIC REPUBLIC OF THE CONGO—MONUC

Headquarters: Kinshasa, Democratic Republic of the Congo.

Special Representative of the UN Secretary-General and Chief of Mission: AMOS NAMANGA NGONGI (Cameroon).

Commander: Maj.-Gen. MOUNTAGA DIALLO (Senegal).

In August 1999 the UN Security Council authorized the deployment of up to 90 military liaison personnel to support implementation of a cease-fire agreement for the Democratic Republic of the Congo (DRC) which had been signed in Lusaka, Zambia, in July, by the heads of state of the DRC, Angola, Namibia, Rwanda, Uganda and Zimbabwe. The Council approved the establishment of MONUC in late November. With an initial mandate until 1 March 2000, the mission was, in co-operation with a Joint Military Commission comprising representatives of the parties to the conflict, to oversee the implementation of the agreement, including monitoring the cease-fire and the disengagement of forces. The mission was also mandated to facilitate the delivery of humanitarian assistance and to develop a mine action plan and undertake emergency demining activities. The first phase of MONUC's operations entailed the deployment of unarmed liaison and technical assessment officers, as well as other multidisciplinary personnel, previously authorized by the Council, to the capitals of the states party to the Lusaka accord and, where possible, to rebel group headquarters. In February 2000 the Security Council authorized the expansion of the mission to comprise up to 5,537 military personnel, including up to 500 observers, thereby enabling the commencement of the second phase of the operation, under which military observers were to be dispatched to the DRC to monitor and verify the cease-fire and disengagement of forces. In April a sub-plan on military disengagement and redeployment was agreed in Kampala, Uganda, by the parties to the conflict and, in December, a revised sub-plan was adopted in Harare, Zimbabwe. However, by early 2001 the Lusaka cease-fire accord and Kampala and Harare sub-plans remained to be implemented and only a small contingent of MONUC observers had been deployed in the DRC. In mid-February the Security Council adopted a resolution demanding that the parties to the conflict commence the phased disengagement and redeployment of their forces by mid-March and stipulating that plans for the full withdrawal of foreign troops and the disarmament, demobilization and resettlement of militia must be prepared and adopted by mid-May. The resolution raised the maximum number of military observers to 550, to be stationed around four regional headquarters; the deployment of up to 1,900 armed security personnel to protect these bases was also authorized. River boat units were to be deployed to assist with the transportation of observers and supplies and to reinforce the mission's presence; it was hoped that commercial activity along river routes would thus also be supported. In mid-March the initial phase of military disgagement was reported to have commenced. Small contingents of MONUC troops were deployed in the DRC from March, including, in the following month, to the strategic rebel-occupied northeastern town of Kisangani. In June the Security Council approved a revised concept of operations for MONUC, entailing the establishment of a civilian police element, enhancing the mission's presence in Kisangani and strengthening its logistic support capabilities. In February 2002 the UN Secretary-General reported that 55 teams of military observers were stationed in the DRC. Preparations were under way for implementing the mission's third phase of operations, which was to entail the deployment of a full peace-keeping force to oversee the complete withdrawal of foreign troops from DRC territory and the disarmament, demobilization and reintegration of rebel forces. MONUC's mandate has been successively extended, most recently to 15 June 2002.

At 31 January 2002 MONUC comprised 2,933 troops, 438 military observers and 13 civilian police, assisted by 780 international and local civilian personnel. The proposed budget for the mission amounted to US $393.2m. for the period 1 July 2001–31 March 2002, funded from a Special Account comprising assessed contributions from UN member states.

UNITED NATIONS MISSION OF OBSERVERS IN PREVLAKA—UNMOP

Headquarters: Cavtat, Croatia.

Chief Military Observer: Col RODOLFO SERGIO MUJICA (Argentina).

UNMOP was authorized by the Security Council in January 1996, following the termination of the mandate of the UN

Confidence Restoration Operation, to assume responsibility for monitoring the demilitarization of the Prevlaka peninsula in Croatia, which had been occupied by the Serbian-dominated Yugoslav People's Army. UNMOP became operational on 1 February. While political tensions persisted throughout 1996, the UN Secretary-General reported that UNMOP's presence in the region had facilitated the process of bilateral negotiations between Croatia and the Federal Republic of Yugoslavia (FRY). During 1997 the Security Council urged both parties to refrain from provocative actions in Prevlaka, to cease any violations of the demilitarized zone and to co-operate fully with UNMOP. The Council also reiterated the urgency of removing anti-personnel land-mines from areas patrolled by UNMOP in order to improve the safety and security of the region and ensure freedom of movement to enable UNMOP to implement its mandate. By December it was reported that the demining process had been completed in the entire UN-controlled territory. In June 2001 the Presidents of the FRY and Croatia agreed to strengthen the process of normalizing relations between the two countries and to facilitate the free movement of people and goods. Bilateral consultations towards a settlement of the Prevlaka issue were subsequently held. In November the ministers of foreign affairs of the two countries declared their intention to establish an inter-state commission to address the outstanding issues concerning common borders. In January 2002, despite concern at reports of ongoing violations of the demilitarized region, the Security Council extended UNMOP's mandate for a further six month period, until mid-July 2002.

At 31 January 2002 UNMOP comprised 27 military observers and nine civilian support staff. The annual cost of UNMOP is included in the budget of the UN Mission in Bosnia and Herzegovina (see above), from which it also derives its administrative support.

UNITED NATIONS OBSERVER MISSION IN GEORGIA—UNOMIG

Headquarters: Sukhumi, Georgia.

Special Representative of the UN Secretary-General and Head of Mission: DIETER BODEN (Germany).

Chief Military Observer: Maj.-Gen. ANIS AHMED BAJWA (Pakistan).

UNOMIG was established in August 1993 to verify compliance with a cease-fire agreement, signed in July between the Government of Georgia and Abkhazian forces. The mission was the UN's first undertaking in the former USSR. In October the UN Secretary-General stated that a breakdown in the cease-fire agreement had invalidated UNOMIG's mandate. He proposed, however, to maintain, for information purposes, the eight-strong UNOMIG team in the city of Sukhumi, which had been seized by Abkhazian separatist forces in late September. In late December the Security Council authorized the deployment of additional military observers in response to the signing of a memorandum of understanding by the conflicting parties earlier that month. Further peace negotiations, which were conducted in January–March 1994 under the authority of the UN Secretary-General's Special Envoy, achieved no political consensus. While the Security Council approved new resolutions to prolong the existence of UNOMIG, the full deployment of a peace-keeping force remained dependent on progress in the peace process. In July the Security Council endorsed the establishment of a peace-keeping force, consisting of 3,000 troops from the Commonwealth of Independent States (CIS, q.v.), to verify a cease-fire agreement that had been signed in May. At the same time the Security Council increased the authorized strength of the mission from 88 to 136 military observers and expanded UNOMIG's mandate to incorporate the following tasks: to monitor and verify the implementation of the agreement and to investigate reported violations; to observe the CIS forces; to verify that troops and heavy military equipment remain outside the security zone and the restricted weapons zone; to monitor the storage of the military equipment withdrawn from the restricted zones; to monitor the withdrawal of Georgian troops from the Kodori Gorge region to locations beyond the Abkhazian frontiers; and to patrol regularly the Kodori Gorge. Peace negotiations were pursued in 1995, despite periodic outbreaks of violence in Abkhazia. In July 1996 the Security Council urged the Abkhazian side to accelerate significantly the process of voluntary return of Georgian refugees and displaced persons to Abkhazia. In October the Council decided to establish a human rights office as part of UNOMIG. In May 1997 the Security Council issued a Presidential Statement urging greater efforts towards achieving a peaceful solution to the dispute. The Statement endorsed a proposal of the UN Secretary-General to strengthen the political element of UNOMIG to enable the mission to assume a more active role in furthering a negotiated settlement. In July direct discussions between representatives of the Georgian and Abkhazian authorities, the first in more than two years, were held under UN auspices. In early 1998 the security situation in Abkhazia deteriorated. Following an outbreak of violence in May the conflicting parties signed a cease-fire accord, which incorporated an agreement that UNOMIG and CIS forces would continue to work to create a secure environment to allow for the return of displaced persons to the Gali region of Abkhazia. In addition, the UN Security Council urged both parties to establish a protection unit to ensure the safety of UN military observers. In December 2000, following a series of detentions and hostage-takings of Mission personnel in the Kodori Gorge during late 1999 and 2000, UNOMIG suspended patrols of that area. Reviewing the operation in January 2001 the UN Secretary-General expressed concern at the recent recurrent abductions and urged the Abkhazian side to cease imposing restrictions on the mission's freedom of movement. Although contacts between the Georgian and Abkhazian authorities continued in 2001, progress towards the conclusion of a durable political settlement remained stalled by an *impasse* between the two sides regarding the future political status of Abkhazia. A Programme of Action on confidence-building measures was concluded in March; however, the negotiation process was interrupted from April, owing to increasing insecurity in the conflict zone and the ongoing activities of illegal armed groups. In October a UNOMIG helicopter was shot down in the Kodori Gorge, resulting in the deaths of nine people. UNOMIG suspended its patrols of the area. In January 2002 a protocol was signed between the conflicting parties providing for the withdrawal of Georgian troops from the Kodori valley and the resumption of UN patrols, with effect from 1 February. In spite of persisting concerns regarding the security and freedom of movement of UN personnel, at the end of January the Security Council granted UNOMIG's mandate a further six-month extension.

At 31 January 2002 UNOMIG comprised 106 military observers, supported by 262 international and local civilian personnel. The General Assembly budget appropriation for the mission for the period 1 July 2001–30 June 2002 amounted to US $27.9m.

UNITED NATIONS PEACE-KEEPING FORCE IN CYPRUS—UNFICYP

Headquarters: Nicosia, Cyprus.

Special Adviser to the UN Secretary-General: ALVARO DE SOTO (Peru).

Acting Special Representative of the UN Secretary-General and Chief of Mission: ZBIGNIEW WLOSOWICZ (Poland).

Commander: Maj.-Gen. JIN HA HWANG (Republic of Korea).

UNFICYP was established in March 1964 by a UN Security Council resolution (initially for a three-month duration, subsequently periodically extended) to prevent a recurrence of fighting between the Greek and Turkish Cypriot communities, and to contribute to the maintenance of law and order and a return to normal conditions. The Force controls a 180-km buffer zone, established (following the Turkish intervention in 1974) between the cease-fire lines of the Turkish forces and the Cyprus National Guard. It is mandated to investigate and act upon all violations of the cease-fire and buffer zone. The Force also performs humanitarian functions, such as facilitating the supply of electricity and water across the cease-fire lines, and offering emergency medical services. In August 1996 serious hostilities between elements of the two communities in the UN-controlled buffer zone resulted in the deaths of two people and injuries to many others, including 12 UN personnel. Following further intercommunal violence,

UNFICYP advocated the prohibition of all weapons and military posts along the length of the buffer zone. The Force also proposed additional humanitarian measures to improve the conditions of minority groups living in the two parts of the island. In reports to the Security Council, the UN Secretary-General has consistently recognized UNFICYP as being indispensable to maintaining calm on the island and to creating the best conditions for his good offices. In July 1997 a new series of direct negotiations between the leaders of the two communities was initiated, under the auspices of the UN Secretary-General's Special Adviser; however, the talks were suspended at the end of that year. In November 1999 the leaders of the two communities agreed to participate in proximity negotiations, to be mediated by the UN. The first round of these took place in New York, in December. A second and third round were convened in Geneva, Switzerland, in February and July 2000, respectively. A fourth round of proximity talks was held in New York in September and a fifth round in Geneva, in November. In December 2001 the leaders of the two communities met together, in the presence of the Special Adviser, and agreed to begin a series of direct talks in January 2002. An intensive dialogue between the two sides was ongoing in early 2002.

At 31 January 2002 UNFICYP had an operational strength of 1,198 military personnel and 35 civilian police officers, supported by 146 international and local civilian staff. Over the period 1 July 2001–30 June 2002 the proposed cost of maintaining the force amounted to US $42.4m., of which some $22.3m. was to be met by assessed contributions from UN member states, with voluntary contributions from the Governments of Cyprus and of Greece to amount to $13.6m. and $6.5m. respectively.

UNITED NATIONS TRANSITIONAL ADMINISTRATION IN EAST TIMOR—UNTAET

Headquarters: Dili, East Timor.

Special Representative of the UN Secretary-General and Transitional Administrator: SÉRGIO VIEIRA DE MELLO (Brazil).

Commander: Lt-Gen. WINAI PHATTIYAKUL (Thailand).

In May 1999 Indonesia and Portugal signed an accord, under UN auspices, providing for a 'popular consultation' to determine the future status of East Timor, a former Portuguese colony which had been governed by Indonesia since 1976. The poll was to be organized by the UN, offering eligible voters a form of political autonomy or full independence from Indonesia, the outcome of which would then be endorsed by the Indonesian Government and implemented by a UN transitional authority. Under the agreement, Indonesia was to be responsible for maintaining peace and security in the territory and to ensure that voting was conducted without intimidation or violence, while the UN was to provide additional unarmed civilian and police personnel. In June the Security Council formally authorized the establishment of a UN Mission in East Timor (UNAMET), which was to comprise up to 280 police advisers and 50 military liaison officers, with an initial mandate until 31 August (later extended). The poll, which was initially scheduled for early August, was twice postponed, owing to security concerns; however, registration of voters commenced in mid-July. In late August the UN Security Council condemned the violent attacks and intimidatory tactics of militia groups favouring support for Indonesia, and acknowledged reports that Indonesian officers had failed to prevent the decline in law and order, but determined that the vote should proceed. The Council also resolved to expand UNAMET's presence in September to 460 police officers and 300 military liaison officers. The poll was conducted on 30 August. The security situation in the territory declined dramatically following the popular consultation, and on 1 September the Security Council convened an emergency meeting to condemn, and demand the arrest of, those responsible for violent attacks on UN staff, pro-independence supporters and foreign journalists. The civil unrest and indiscriminate killings escalated after the announcement of the results of the poll, which identified some 78.5% of East Timorese voters in favour of independence, and resulted in mass population displacement. A further meeting of Security Council members, held on 5 September, resolved to send a five-member mission to discuss the situation with the Indonesian Government. The failure of a curfew, imposed by the Indonesian authorities a few days later, to restore security prompted the UN to evacuate almost all its remaining staff. In mid-September, following international condemnation of the situation and intense diplomatic pressure, the Indonesian Government reversed its earlier opposition to a proposal by the Australian Government and agreed to permit foreign troops to help restore order in East Timor. The Security Council subsequently authorized the establishment of a multinational force, under unified command, with a mandate to restore peace and security in the territory, until replaced by a UN peace-keeping operation. The so-called International Force for East Timor (INTERFET) was also mandated to protect and support UNAMET and to facilitate humanitarian operations. In late September INTERFET assumed formal control of the territory, while UNAMET re-established its headquarters in Dili. In late October, following ratification of the results of the popular poll by the Indonesian People's Consultative Assembly, the Security Council voted to establish a UN Transitional Administration in East Timor (UNTAET) to oversee the transition to independence and govern the territory on an interim basis. UNTAET was to exercise all judicial and executive authority in East Timor. The Transitional Administration's mandate authorized it to provide security and maintain law and order in the territory; to assume responsibility for the co-ordination and provision of humanitarian assistance; to establish an effective administration; to assist in the development of civil and social services and to promote capacity-building for self-government; and to assist in the creation of conditions for sustainable development. The responsibilities and personnel of UNAMET were incorporated into UNTAET. Military command was transferred from INTERFET to UNTAET in February 2000. In December 1999 a National Consultative Council (NCC), including the UNTAET Transitional Administrator and other UNTAET senior officials, as well as representatives of East Timorese political groupings, was established to advise UNTAET. In July 2000 a Transitional Cabinet was formed, comprising both local and UNTAET representatives. An advisory East Timor National Council, composed entirely of East Timorese, was inaugurated in October, superseding the NCC. In early August UNTAET launched a new governing structure, the East Timor Transitional Administration (ETTA). ETTA was to comprise (under the authority of the Transitional Administrator) the Transitional Cabinet, the East Timor National Council and the judicial system, thereby incorporating both UNTAET and East Timorese representatives. In January 2001 the UN Secretary-General presented a report to the Security Council outlining recommendations to enable elections to a new permanent East Timorese legislative structure to be staged later in 2001; the report envisaged the attainment of full independence for the territory by the end of the year. In late January a Special Panel for Serious Crimes, which had been established by UNTAET to investigate and prosecute crimes relating to the unrest in the territory during January–October 1999, passed its first sentence on an Indonesian militia member. The first trial of those charged with crimes against humanity opened in July. UNTAET's mandate was extended in January until 31 January 2002. In March 2001 a working group on post-UNTAET planning was formed to assess the level of external assistance that would be required by the East Timorese authorities following independence. Elections to an 88-member Constituent Assembly were organized by UNTAET on 30 August; an independent electoral commission subsequently declared these to have been conducted freely and fairly. (Prior to the elections UNTAET had developed a framework to facilitate the territory-wide provision of civic education, initiated a voter education programme and established an election resource centre.) In September UNTAET transferred responsibility for the Constitutional Commission to the newly-formed Assembly. On 20 September the East Timorese Council of Ministers of the Second Transitional Government was inaugurated, replacing the Transitional Cabinet. The new Council of Ministers was to govern the territory during the remainder of the transition to independence and was empowered to formulate policies, oversee the developing public administration structures, and to consult with the Transitional Administrator on the promulgation of new legislation. The Transitional Administrator retained final executive and legislative authority over the territory. In October the Constituent Assembly approved 20 May 2002 as the date for the transfer of sovereignty from UNTAET to fully independent, elected institutions. UNTAET subsequently began a gradual reduction of its peace-keeping component, with the aim of reducing troop levels to 5,000 by independence. The first battalion of an East Timor Defence Force was inaugurated in October. In January 2002 the UN Security Council extended UNTAET's mandate until 20 May. Plans for a successor mission were under consideration.

At 31 January 2002 UNTAET comprised 6,266 troops, 1,259 civilian police officers and 118 military observers, supported by 2,613 international and local civilian personnel. The budget appropriation for the operation in the period 1 July 2001–30 June 2002 amounted to US $476.8m.; this was funded from a Special Account comprising assessed contributions from UN member states.

UNITED NATIONS TRUCE SUPERVISION ORGANIZATION—UNTSO

Headquarters: Government House, Jerusalem.

Chief-of-Staff: Maj.-Gen. CARL A. DODD (Ireland).

UNTSO was established initially to supervise the truce called by the UN Security Council in Palestine in May 1948 and has assisted in the application of the 1949 Armistice Agreements. Its activities have evolved over the years, in response to developments in the Middle East and in accordance with the relevant resolutions of the Security Council. There is no periodic renewal procedure for UNTSO's mandate.

UNTSO observers assist UN peace-keeping forces in the Middle East, at present UNIFIL and UNDOF (see above). The mission maintains offices in Beirut, Lebanon, and Damascus, Syria. In addition, UNTSO operates a number of outposts in the Sinai region of Egypt to maintain a UN presence there. UNTSO observers have been available at short notice to form the nucleus of new peace-keeping operations.

The operational strength of UNTSO at 30 November 2001 was 153 military observers, supported by 209 international and local civilian staff. UNTSO expenditures are covered by the regular budget of the United Nations. The cost of the operation in 2002 was estimated to be US $23.2m.

United Nations Peace-keeping Operations and Observer Missions

(A listing of all current and completed operations, in chronological order)

UNITED NATIONS TRUCE SUPERVISION ORGANIZATION—UNTSO

Mandated to supervise the peace agreements in Palestine. (See above for the operation's ongoing role in the Middle East.)

Duration: June 1948–.

Headquarters: Government House, Jerusalem.

UNITED NATIONS MILITARY OBSERVER GROUP IN INDIA AND PAKISTAN—UNMOGIP

Established to help to restore peace in the disputed region of Jammu and Kashmir. Activities are ongoing (see above).

Duration: January 1949–.

Headquarters: Rawalpindi, Pakistan (November–April), Srinagar, India (May–October).

FIRST UNITED NATIONS EMERGENCY FORCE—UNEF I

Aimed to secure and supervise the withdrawal of foreign troops from Egyptian territory and the cessation of hostilities between Egypt and Israel, and to maintain peaceful conditions in the area.

Duration: November 1956–June 1967.

Headquarters: Gaza.

UNITED NATIONS OBSERVATION GROUP IN LEBANON—UNOGIL

Established to supervise the border between Lebanon and Syria, and, in particular, to ensure that there were no illegal crossings or supply of armaments.

Duration: June 1958–December 1958.

Headquarters: Beirut, Lebanon.

UNITED NATIONS OPERATION IN THE CONGO—ONUC

Established, initially, to oversee the withdrawal of Belgian forces and the maintenance of law and order. Also aimed to maintain the territorial integrity of the Congo and prevent civil conflict or interference by foreign troops. After the withdrawal of the UN military contingent civilian operations continued, under the authority of the UN Technical Assistance Board.

Duration: July 1960–June 1964.

Headquarters: Léopoldville, Republic of the Congo (now Kinshasa, the Democratic Republic of the Congo).

UNITED NATIONS SECURITY FORCE IN WEST NEW GUINEA (NEW IRIAN)—UNSF

Mandated to maintain peace and security during the transitional period pending transfer of the territory (previously under Dutch rule) to Indonesia.

Duration: October 1962–April 1963.

Headquarters: Hollandia, West New Guinea (now Jayapura, Irian Jaya).

UNITED NATIONS YEMEN OBSERVATION MISSION—UNYOM

Established to observe the disengagement agreement and to secure the withdrawal of all foreign troops.

Duration: July 1963–September 1964.

Headquarters: San'a, Yemen.

UNITED NATIONS PEACE-KEEPING FORCE IN CYPRUS—UNFICYP

Established to prevent further fighting between the Greek and Turkish Cypriot communities and to help to maintain law and order. Ongoing activities include supervision of a buffer-zone and other humanitarian tasks (see above).

Duration: March 1964–.

Headquarters: Nicosia, Cyprus.

MISSION OF THE REPRESENTATIVE OF THE SECRETARY-GENERAL IN THE DOMINICAN REPUBLIC—DOMREP

Established to oversee a cease-fire between opposition movements.

Duration: May 1965–October 1966.

Headquarters: Santo Domingo, Dominican Republic.

UNITED NATIONS INDIA-PAKISTAN OBSERVATION MISSION—UNIPOM

Established following the renewal of hostilities between India and Pakistan to supervise the cease-fire lines and the withdrawal of all armed personnel along the international border in areas outside of Kashmir.

Duration: September 1965–March 1966.

Headquarters: Amritsar, India; Lahore, Pakistan.

SECOND UNITED NATIONS EMERGENCY FORCE—UNEF II

Established after the Arab–Israeli war to supervise a full cease-fire. Following peace agreements concluded in January 1994 and September 1995 UNEF supervised the redeployment of Egyptian and Israeli forces and established buffer zones in the region of the Suez Canal and in the Sinai Peninsula.

Duration: October 1973–July 1979.

Headquarters: Ismailia, Egypt.

UNITED NATIONS DISENGAGEMENT OBSERVER FORCE—UNDOF

Established, initially, to supervise the disengagement of Syrian and Israeli forces, to monitor the withdrawal of Israeli troops and to establish an area of separation in the Golan Heights. Activities are ongoing (see above).

Duration: June 1974–.

Headquarters: Damascus, Syria.

UNITED NATIONS INTERIM FORCE IN LEBANON—UNIFIL

Mandated to oversee the withdrawal of Israeli forces from southern Lebanon and to consolidate peace and security in the region. Activities are ongoing (see above).

Duration: March 1978–.

Headquarters: Naqoura, Lebanon.

UNITED NATIONS GOOD OFFICES MISSION IN AFGHANISTAN AND PAKISTAN—UNGOMAP

Established to monitor the withdrawal of Soviet troops from Afghanistan, as well as the non-interference and non-intervention of troops between Afghanistan and Pakistan, in accordance with a peace accord signed in April 1988.

Duration: May 1988–March 1990.

Headquarters: Kabul, Afghanistan; Islamabad, Pakistan.

UNITED NATIONS IRAN-IRAQ MILITARY OBSERVER GROUP—UNIIMOG

Its principal tasks were to monitor compliance with the cease-fire agreement, supervise the withdrawal of troops to internationally-recognized boundaries, and facilitate confidence-building and other measures to reduce tensions between the two sides.

Duration: August 1988–February 1991.

Headquarters: Baghdad, Iraq.

UNITED NATIONS ANGOLA VERIFICATION MISSION I—UNAVEM I

Mandated to verify the redeployment of Cuban troops, and their phased and eventual withdrawal from Angola.

Duration: January 1989–June 1991.

Headquarters: Luanda, Angola.

UNITED NATIONS TRANSITION GROUP—UNTAG

Mandated to supervise democratic elections in Namibia and to ensure a peaceful transition to independence, in accordance with a UN Security Council resolution adopted in September 1978. The resolution was finally implemented in April 1989.

Duration: April 1989–March 1990.

Headquarters: Windhoek, Namibia.

UNITED NATIONS OBSERVER GROUP IN CENTRAL AMERICA—ONUCA

Established to verify undertakings by five Central American Governments (those of Costa Rica, El Salvador, Guatemala, Honduras and Nicaragua) to cease aid to irregular forces, and to refrain from the use of the territory of one state for attacks on another.

Duration: November 1989–January 1992.

Headquarters: Tegucigalpa, Honduras.

UNITED NATIONS IRAQ-KUWAIT OBSERVATION MISSION—UNIKOM

Mandated to monitor the demilitarized zone along the border between Iraq and Kuwait (see above).

Duration: April 1991–.

Headquarters: Umm Qasr, Iraq.

UNITED NATIONS MISSION FOR THE REFERENDUM IN WESTERN SAHARA—MINURSO

Responsible for the monitoring of a cease-fire, and for the organization and supervision of a referendum on the future of the disputed territory. Activities are ongoing (see above).

Duration: April 1991–.

Headquarters: el-Aaiún, Western Sahara.

UNITED NATIONS ANGOLA VERIFICATION MISSION II—UNAVEM II

Established by the enlargement of the original UNAVEM mandate to enable the mission to perform new verification tasks arising from Peace Accords. The mission also observed general elections, held in September 1992, under an enlarged mandate.

Duration: June 1991–February 1995.

Headquarters: Luanda, Angola.

UNITED NATIONS OBSERVER MISSION IN EL SALVADOR—ONUSAL

Mandated to monitor agreements concluded between the Government and opposition FMLN forces in El Salvador, and, in particular, the Agreement on Human Rights.

Duration: July 1991–April 1995.

Headquarters: San Salvador, El Salvador.

UNITED NATIONS ADVANCE MISSION IN CAMBODIA—UNAMIC

Established to monitor the cease-fire, following the conclusion of a peace settlement between Government and opposition factions. Absorbed into UNTAC (see above).

Duration: October 1991–March 1992.

Headquarters: Phnom Penh, Cambodia.

UNITED NATIONS PROTECTION FORCE—UNPROFOR

Established to ensure the withdrawal of Yugoslav forces from Croatia and the demilitarization of three Serbian-held enclaves. Its mandate was subsequently enlarged to ensure the safe delivery of humanitarian assistance within Bosnia and Herzegovina, the withdrawal of Yugoslav troops from the Prevlaka peninsula in Croatia, and the removal of heavy weapons from neighbouring areas in Croatia and Montenegro. UNPROFOR also monitored compliance with the prohibition on military flights in Bosnian airspace.

Duration: March 1992–December 1995.

Headquarters: Zagreb, Croatia.

UNITED NATIONS TRANSITIONAL AUTHORITY IN CAMBODIA—UNTAC

Mandated to organize and oversee democratic elections in Cambodia, and to supervise the administration of the country during the transitional period prior to the establishment of an elected government. Other duties included assisting the disarmament of Cambodian warring factions, the repatriation and resettlement of refugees, and the rehabilitation of the country's infrastructure.

Duration: March 1992–September 1993.

Headquarters: Phnom Penh, Cambodia.

UNITED NATIONS OPERATION IN SOMALIA I—UNOSOM I

Responsible for monitoring a cease-fire between the principal warring factions in Somalia, promoting a political settlement, and the distribution of humanitarian aid. In December 1992 the UN Security Council endorsed the dispatch of a multinational force, under US command, to create a secure environment for the provision of humanitarian relief. UNOSOM remained responsible for humanitarian assistance and the political aspects of efforts to establish peace in Somalia.

Duration: April 1992–March 1993.

Headquarters: Mogadishu, Somalia.

UNITED NATIONS OPERATION IN MOZAMBIQUE—ONUMOZ

Established to facilitate implementation of a peace agreement, signed in October 1992, between the Government and opposition RENAMO movement, including verification of the cessation of hostilities, supervision of the separation, demobilization and disarmament of forces, co-ordination of humanitarian operations, and organization of general elections.

Duration: December 1992–December 1994.

Headquarters: Maputo, Mozambique.

UNITED NATIONS OPERATION IN SOMALIA II—UNOSOM II

Assumed control from the multinational force for the restoration and enforcement of peace, stability and law and order, as well as the rehabilitation of the country's political, economic and social structures and the enforcement of the disarmament of Somalia's principal conflicting factions.

Duration: March 1993–March 1995.

Headquarters: Mogadishu, Somalia.

UNITED NATIONS OBSERVER MISSION UGANDA-RWANDA—UNOMUR

Established to monitor the border between Uganda and Rwanda, in order to prohibit the illegal supply of military assistance to Rwanda.

Duration: June 1993–September 1994.

Headquarters: Kabale, Uganda.

UNITED NATIONS OBSERVER MISSION IN GEORGIA—UNOMIG

Established to monitor a cease-fire between Georgian and separatist Abkhazian forces. Under an enlarged mandate the mission was to monitor and verify implementation of a new agreement, signed in May 1994. It co-operates with troops from the Commonwealth of Independent States to facilitate the return of refugees and other displaced persons. Activities are ongoing (see above).

Duration: August 1993–.

Headquarters: Sukhumi, Georgia.

UNITED NATIONS OBSERVER MISSION IN LIBERIA—UNOMIL

Established to verify implementation of a peace agreement signed by the conflicting parties in Liberia, including a lasting cease-fire and the disengagement of forces.

Duration: September 1993–September 1997.

Headquarters: Monrovia, Liberia.

UNITED NATIONS MISSION IN HAITI—UNMIH

Established to maintain order during the transition of power from the military authorities to Haiti's exiled President Aristide. Under an enlarged mandate the mission provided technical assistance and monitored national elections.

Duration: September 1993–June 1996.

Headquarters: Port-au-Prince, Haiti.

UNITED NATIONS ASSISTANCE MISSION FOR RWANDA—UNAMIR

Mandated to monitor a cease-fire agreement, signed in August 1993 and to help to maintain peace and security during the transitional peace process until the establishment of a new government. Its mandate was enlarged in May 1994, following the eruption of ethnic violence, to establish secure humanitarian areas and provide security for relief operations.

Duration: October 1993–March 1996.

Headquarters: Kigali, Rwanda.

UNITED NATIONS AOUZOU STRIP OBSERVER GROUP—UNASOG

Established to verify the withdrawal of Libyan forces from the Aouzou Strip, in accordance with a decision of the International Court of Justice.

Duration: May 1994–June 1994.

Headquarters: Chad.

UNITED NATIONS MISSION OF OBSERVERS IN TAJIKISTAN—UNMOT

Mandated to monitor a cease-fire agreement signed by the Tajik Government and opposition forces in September 1994, and subsequent peace accords, to facilitate the provision of humanitarian assistance, and to support the preparation of elections and the holding of a referendum.

Duration: December 1994–May 2000.

Headquarters: Dushanbe, Tajikistan.

UNITED NATIONS ANGOLA VERIFICATION MISSION III—UNAVEM III

Mandated to supervise and monitor the terms of a new peace accord (the Lusaka Protocol) and to assist in the process of national reconciliation, reconstruction and mine-clearance.

Duration: February 1995–June 1997.

Headquarters: Luanda, Angola.

UNITED NATIONS CONFIDENCE RESTORATION OPERATION IN CROATIA—UNCRO

Replaced UNPROFOR personnel in the disputed regions of Western Slavonia, Krajina, Eastern Slavonia and the Prevlaka peninsula, with the aim of enforcing a cease-fire, maintaining peace and freedom of movement, and monitoring the deployment of troops and weapons.

Duration: March 1995–January 1996.

Headquarters: Zagreb, Croatia.

UNITED NATIONS PREVENTIVE DEPLOYMENT FORCE—UNPREDEP

Assumed the functions of the UNPROFOR contingent in the former Yugoslav republic of Macedonia, with the objective of upholding the stability of the territory.

Duration: March 1995–February 1999.

Headquarters: Skopje, the former Yugoslav republic of Macedonia.

UNITED NATIONS MISSION IN BOSNIA AND HERZEGOVINA—UNMIBH

Incorporates the United Nations International Police Task Force and a United Nations civilian office. (See above for ongoing activities.)

Duration: December 1995–.

Headquarters: Sarajevo, Bosnia and Herzegovina.

UNITED NATIONS TRANSITIONAL ADMINISTRATION FOR EASTERN SLAVONIA, BARANJA AND WESTERN SIRMIUM—UNTAES

Established to supervise the demilitarization of the region and its reintegration into Croatia, over a two-year period.

Duration: January 1996–January 1998.

Headquarters: Vukovar, Croatia.

UNITED NATIONS MISSION OF OBSERVERS IN PREVLAKA—UNMOP

Assumed responsibility from UNCRO for monitoring the demilitarization of the Prevlaka peninsula. Activities are ongoing (see above).

Duration: January 1996–.

Headquarters: Dubrovnik, Croatia.

UNITED NATIONS SUPPORT MISSION IN HAITI—UNSMIH

Continued the UN's presence in Haiti, after the expiry of UNMIH's mandate, in order to assist the Government to maintain a secure and stable environment and to strengthen the national police force.

Duration: July 1996–July 1997.

Headquarters: Port-au-Prince, Haiti.

UNITED NATIONS VERIFICATION MISSION IN GUATEMALA—MINUGUA

Dispatched as a military attachment to the UN Mission for the Verification of Human Rights in Guatemala (authorized by the UN General Assembly) to verify a cease-fire agreement signed between the Government and opposition forces.

Duration: January 1997–May 1997.

Headquarters: Guatemala City, Guatemala.

UNITED NATIONS OBSERVER MISSION IN ANGOLA—MONUA

Succeeded UNAVEM III with responsibility for overseeing the remaining tasks of the Lusaka peace accord, including the demobilization of the opposition UNITA forces and reinstatement of state administration throughout the country.

Duration: July 1997–February 1999.

Headquarters: Luanda, Angola.

UNITED NATIONS TRANSITION MISSION IN HAITI—UNTMIH

Mandated to undertake specialist police training and to ensure the safety and freedom of movement of UN personnel working in the country.

Duration: August 1997–November 1997.

Headquarters: Port-au-Prince, Haiti.

UNITED NATIONS CIVILIAN POLICE MISSION IN HAITI—MIPONUH

Established to complete UNTMIH's mandate of providing training and other technical assistance for law enforcement bodies and to support the process of national reconciliation.

Duration: December 1997–March 2000.

Headquarters: Port-au-Prince, Haiti.

UNITED NATIONS CIVILIAN POLICE SUPPORT GROUP

Established to monitor the activities of the Croatian police force and the welfare of populations returning to the Danube region following the withdrawal of UNTAES personnel.

Duration: January 1998–October 1998.

Headquarters: Vukovar and Zagreb, Croatia.

UNITED NATIONS MISSION IN THE CENTRAL AFRICAN REPUBLIC—MINURCA

Assumed authority from a multinational force, with the aim of securing a peaceful environment, including the disarmament of rebel soldiers and other combatants, and of supporting preparations for legislative elections. Its mandate was enlarged in October 1998 to include support for the conduct of elections.

Duration: March 1998–February 2000.

Headquarters: Bangui, Central African Republic.

UNITED NATIONS OBSERVER MISSION IN SIERRA LEONE—UNOMSIL

Aimed to promote stability and security in Sierra Leone following the restoration of a democratically-elected government, including monitoring the disarmament and demobilization of opposition forces and respect for human rights.

Duration: July 1998–October 1999.

Headquarters: Freetown, Sierra Leone.

UNITED NATIONS INTERIM ADMINISTRATION MISSION IN KOSOVO—UNMIK

Established as the supreme legal and executive authority in the province of Kosovo and Metohija, following the withdrawal of Serbian security and paramilitary forces from the province and the subsequent suspension by NATO of its aerial offensive against the Federal Republic of Yugoslavia. Activities are ongoing (see above).

Duration: June 1999–.

Headquarters: Priština, Kosovo, Yugoslavia.

UNITED NATIONS MISSION IN SIERRA LEONE—UNAMSIL

Mandated to assist with the implementation of a peace accord signed by the Sierra Leone Government and rebel groups, to enforce a plan for the disarmament and demobilization of all former combatants and to facilitate the delivery of humanitarian assistance. Activities are ongoing (see above).

Duration: October 1999–.

Headquarters: Freetown, Sierra Leone.

UNITED NATIONS TRANSITIONAL ADMINISTRATION IN EAST TIMOR—UNTAET

Established to exercise all judicial and executive authority in East Timor, following the organization by the UN of a popular referendum at which a majority of East Timorese voted in favour of independence for their territory. Activities are ongoing (see above).

Duration: October 1999–.

Headquarters: Dili, East Timor.

UNITED NATIONS MISSION IN THE DEMOCRATIC REPUBLIC OF THE CONGO—MONUC

Mandated to assist with the implementation of a cease-fire agreement in the Democratic Republic of the Congo. Activities are ongoing (see above).

Duration: November 1999–.

Headquarters: Kinshasa, Democratic Republic of the Congo.

UNITED NATIONS MISSION IN ETHIOPIA AND ERITREA—UNMEE

Mandated to assist with the implementation of a cease-fire agreement between Eritrea and Ethiopia. Activities are ongoing (see above).

Duration: July 2000–.

Headquarters: Asmara, Eritrea; Addis Ababa, Ethiopia.

United Nations Population Fund—UNFPA

Address: 220 East 42nd St, New York, NY 10017, USA.

Telephone: (212) 297-5020; **fax:** (212) 297-4911; **internet:** www.unfpa.org.

Created in 1967 as the Trust Fund for Population Activities, the UN Fund for Population Activities (UNFPA) was established as a Fund of the UN General Assembly in 1972 and was made a subsidiary organ of the UN General Assembly in 1979, with the UNDP Governing Council (now the Executive Board) designated as its governing body. In 1987 UNFPA's name was changed to the United Nations Population Fund (retaining the same acronym).

Organization

(March 2002)

EXECUTIVE DIRECTOR

The Executive Director, who has the rank of Under-Secretary-General of the UN, is responsible for the overall direction of the Fund, working closely with governments, other United Nations bodies and agencies, and non-governmental and international organizations to ensure the most effective programming and use of resources in population activities.

Executive Director: THORAYA A. OBAID (Saudi Arabia).

EXECUTING AGENCIES

UNFPA provides financial and technical assistance to developing countries at their request. In many projects assistance is extended through member organizations of the UN system (in particular, FAO, ILO, UNESCO, WHO), although projects are executed increasingly by national governments themselves. The Fund may also call on the services of international, regional and national non-governmental and training organizations, as well as research institutions. In addition, eight UNFPA regional technical support teams, composed of experts from the UN, its specialized agencies and non-governmental organizations, assist countries at all stages of project/programme development and implementation.

FIELD ORGANIZATION

UNFPA operates field offices, each headed by an UNFPA Representative, in 105 countries. In other countries UNFPA uses UNDP's field structure of Resident Representatives as the main mechanism for performing its work. The field offices assist governments in formulating requests for aid and co-ordinate the work of the executing agencies in any given country or area. UNFPA has eight regional technical support teams (see above). At 1 January 2001 there were 839 UNFPA staff members worldwide, of whom 628 were in the field.

Activities

The major functions of UNFPA, according to its mandate, are: to advance the knowledge and capacity to respond to needs in population and family planning; to promote awareness of population problems in developed and developing countries and possible strategies to deal with them; to assist countries, at their request, in dealing with their population problems, in the forms and means best suited to the individual countries' requirements; and to play a leading role in the UN system in promoting population programmes and support and co-ordinate projects.

In co-operation with the UN Population Division, UNFPA played an important role in preparing for and conducting the International Conference on Population and Development (ICPD), held in Cairo, Egypt, in September 1994. UNFPA's then Executive Director, Dr Nafis Sadik, acted as Secretary-General of the Conference, which was attended by representatives of 182 countries. The Fund was appointed as the lead body within the UN system responsible for following up and implementing the Programme of Action adopted by the ICPD. This outlined the objectives to be pursued for the next 20 years (despite reservations recorded by the representatives of some predominantly Roman Catholic and Islamic countries, concerning sections which they regarded as endorsing abortion and sexual promiscuity). The Programme's objectives envisaged universal access to reproductive health and family planning services, a reduction in infant, child and maternal mortality, a life expectancy at birth of 75 years or more, and universal access to primary education for all children by 2015. The Programme emphasized the necessity of empowering and educating women, in order to achieve successful sustainable human development. Annual expenditure required for the implementation of the objectives was estimated to amount to US $17,000m. in 2000, increasing to $21,700m. in 2015: of these amounts, the international community or donor countries would need to contribute about one-third. During 1995 UNFPA undertook to redefine its programme directions, resource allocations and policy guide-lines in order to implement effectively the recommendations of the ICPD Programme of Action. The Executive Board subsequently endorsed the following as core programme areas: Reproductive Health, including Family Planning and Sexual Health; Population and Development Strategies; and Advocacy (for example, human rights, education, basic health services and the empowerment of women). A special session of the UN General Assembly (entitled ICPD + 5 and attended by delegates from 177 countries) was held in June/July 1999 to assess progress in achieving the objectives of the Cairo Conference and to identify priorities for future action. In February UNFPA had organized a forum, held in The Hague, Netherlands, to review implementation of the ICPD Programme of Action in preparation for the special session. ICPD + 5 adopted several key actions for further implementation of the Programme of Action. These included advancing understanding of the connections between poverty, gender inequalities, health, education, the environment, financial and human resources, and development; focusing on the economic and social implications of demographic change; greater incorporation of gender issues into social and development policies and greater involvement of women in decision-making processes; greater support for HIV/AIDS prevention activities; and strengthened political commitment to the reproductive health of adolescents. Several new benchmarks were adopted by the special session, including the achievement of 60% availability of contraceptives and reproductive health care services by 2005, 80% by 2010, with universal availability by 2015.

UNFPA recognizes that improving reproductive health is an essential requirement for improving the general welfare of the population and the basis for empowering women and achieving sustainable social and economic development. The ICPD succeeded in raising the political prominence of reproductive health issues and stimulating consideration by governments of measures to strengthen and restructure their health services and policies. UNFPA encourages the integration of family planning into all maternal, child and other reproductive health care. Its efforts to improve the quality of these services include support for the training of health-care personnel and promoting greater accessibility. Many reproductive health projects focus on the reduction of maternal mortality, which was included as a central objective of the ICPD Programme, and recognized as a legitimate element of international human rights instruments concerning the right to life/survival. The ICPD reported that the leading cause of maternal deaths (i.e. those related to pregnancy, which amount to about 600,000 each year) was unsafe abortions, and urged governments to confront the issue as a major public health concern. UNFPA is also concerned with reducing the use of abortion (i.e. its use as a means of family planning), and with preventing infertility, reproductive tract infections and sexually-transmitted diseases, including HIV/AIDS. Special attention is given to the specific needs of adolescents, for example through education and counselling initiatives, and to women in emergency situations. UNFPA distributes reproductive health supplies (including home delivery kits), with a focus on HIV-prevention, to regions affected by conflict or natural disaster. UNFPA also supports research into contraceptives and training in contraceptive technology. The Fund's Global Initiative on Reproductive Health Commodity Management organizes in-depth studies on national contraceptive requirements and aims to ensure an adequate supply of contraceptives and reproductive health supplies to developing countries. UNFPA encourages partnerships between private-sector interests and the governments of developing nations, with a view to making affordable commercial contraceptive products more easily available to consumers and thereby enabling governments to direct subsidies at the poorest sectors of society.

UNFPA helps countries to formulate and implement comprehensive population policies as a central part of any strategies to achieve sustainable development. The Fund aims to ensure that the needs and concerns of women are incorporated into development and population policies. Under this programme area UNFPA provides assistance and training for national statistical offices in undertaking basic data collection, for example censuses and demographic surveys. UNFPA also provides assistance for analysis of demographic and socio-economic data, for research on population trends and for the formulation of government policies. It supports a programme of fellowships in demographic analysis, data processing and cartography.

UNFPA's advocacy role is incorporated into all its programming activities in support of the objectives of the ICPD. Consequently, the Fund aims to encourage the participation of women at all levels of decision- and policy-making and supports programmes that improve the access of all girls and women to education and grant women equal access to land, credit and employment opportunities. UNFPA's annual *State of World Population Report* has consistently focused on the improved welfare of women as an issue of basic human rights; this includes the eradication of all forms of gender discrimination, entitlement to reproductive choice and a zero-tolerance approach to the protection of women from sexual and domestic violence and coercion. UNFPA helps to promote awareness of these objectives and to incorporate them into national programmes. In 1997 UNFPA appointed a special ambassador to generate international awareness of the dangers of female genital mutilation. UNFPA emphasizes the role of knowledge and prevention in combating the spread of HIV/AIDS. There are special programmes on youth, on ageing and on migration, and the Fund is currently increasing educational and research activities in the area of population and the environment. UNFPA attempts to increase awareness of the issue of population through regional and national seminars, publications (see below) and audio-visual aids, participation in conferences, and through a pro-active relationship with the mass media. In 1999 UNFPA promoted observance of 12 October as the symbolic day on which the world's population was estimated to reach 6,000m.

In 1995 UNFPA actively participated in the World Summit for Social Development, an international conference held in Copenhagen, Denmark, in March, and the UN Fourth World Conference on Women, held in Beijing, People's Republic of China, in September, at which the key concepts of the ICPD Programme were emphasized and reinforced. In 1996 UNFPA contributed to the second UN Conference on Human Settlements (Habitat II), which was held in Istanbul, Turkey, in June, by reporting on current trends in urbanization and population distribution and their link to human settlements. UNFPA is participating in the UN System-wide Special Initiative on Africa that was initiated by the UN Secretary-General in March 1996. UNFPA's principal involvement is to assist countries to implement efforts for reproductive health and to promote the integration of population considerations into development planning. UNFPA collaborates with other UN agencies and international experts to develop a reliable, multidisciplinary set of indicators to measure progress towards achieving the objectives of different global conferences and to help formulate reproductive health programmes and monitor their success. UNFPA co-operates with other UN agencies in the Joint UN Programme on HIV/AIDS (UNAIDS), which became operational on 1 January 1996. The Fund organized a high-level panel discussion on the theme 'Gender and HIV/AIDS' at the UN General Assembly special session on HIV/AIDS held in June 2001.

Finance

UNFPA is supported entirely by voluntary contributions from donor countries. In 2000 UNFPA's income totalled US $366.1m. of which $262.5m. was for regular resources and $103.6m. for multi- and bilateral co-financing activities. Project expenditure in 2000 totalled $255.6m., compared with $316.6m. in 1999. Of total programme expenditure in 2000, about 63% was allocated to reproductive health care, 24% to population and development strategies and 9% to advocacy.

Publications

Annual Report.

AIDS Update (annually).

Dispatches (10 a year, in English, French and Spanish).

Inventory of Population Projects in Developing Countries around the World (annually in English and French).

Populi (quarterly, in English, French and Spanish).

State of World Population Report (annually).

Reports and reference works; videotapes and radio programmes.

United Nations Relief and Works Agency for Palestine Refugees in the Near East—UNRWA

Addresses: Gamal Abd an-Nasser St, Gaza City;
Bayader Wadi Seer, POB 140157, Amman 11814, Jordan.

Telephone (Gaza City): (7) 6777333; **fax:** (7) 6777555.
Telephone (Amman): (6) 5826171; **fax:** (6) 5826177.

E-mail: unrwapio@unrwa.org; **internet:** www.un.org/unrwa/.

UNRWA was established by the UN General Assembly to provide relief, health, education and welfare services for Palestine refugees in the Near East, initially on a short-term basis. UNRWA began operations in May 1950 and, in the absence of a solution to the refugee problem, its mandate has subsequently been extended by the General Assembly, most recently until 30 June 2002.

Organization

(March 2002)

UNRWA employs an international staff of about 120 and more than 22,500 local staff, mainly Palestine refugees. In mid-1996 the agency's headquarters were relocated, from Vienna, Austria, to Gaza and Jordan. The Commissioner-General is the head of all UNRWA operations and reports directly to the UN General Assembly. UNRWA has no governing body, but its activities are reviewed annually by a 10-member Advisory Commission comprising representatives of the governments of:

Belgium	Jordan	Turkey
Egypt	Lebanon	United Kingdom
France	Syria	USA
Japan		

Commissioner-General: PETER HANSEN (Denmark).

FIELD OFFICES

Each field office is headed by a director and has departments responsible for education, health and relief and social services programmes, finance, administration, supply and transport, legal affairs and public information.

Gaza: POB 61; Al Azhar Rd, Rimal Quarter, Gaza City; tel. (7) 2824508; fax (7) 6777444.

Jordan: POB 484; Al Zubeidi Bldg, Mustafa Bin Abdullah St, Tla'a Al-Ali, Amman; tel. (6) 5607194; fax (6) 5685476.

Lebanon: POB 11-0947, Beirut 1107 2060; Bir Hassan, Ghobeiri, Beirut; tel. (1) 822415; fax (1) 840469.

Syria: POB 4313; UN Compound, Mezzah Highway/Beirut Rd, Damascus; tel. (11) 6133035; fax (11) 6133047.

West Bank: POB 19149; Sheik Jarrah Qtr, East Jerusalem; tel. (2) 5890400; fax (2) 5322714.

LIAISON OFFICES

Egypt: 2 Dar-el-Shifa St, Garden City, POB 227, Cairo; tel. (2) 354-8502; fax (2) 354-8504.

Switzerland: Rm 92-93 Annexe Le Bocage, Palais des Nations, 1211 Geneva; tel. (22) 9171166; fax (22) 9170956.

USA: 2 United Nations Plaza, Room DC 2-1755, New York, NY 10017; tel. (212) 963-2255; fax (212) 935-7899.

Activities

ASSISTANCE ACTIVITIES

Since 1950 UNRWA has been the main provider of relief, health, education and social services for Palestine refugees in Lebanon, Syria, Jordan, the West Bank and the Gaza Strip. For UNRWA's purposes, a Palestine refugee is one whose normal residence was in Palestine for a minimum of two years before the 1948 conflict and who, as a result of the Arab–Israeli hostilities, lost his or her home and means of livelihood. To be eligible for assistance, a refugee must reside in one of the five areas in which UNRWA operates and be in need. A refugee's descendants who fulfil certain criteria are also eligible for UNRWA assistance. At 30 June 2001 UNRWA was providing essential services to 3,874,738 registered refugees (see table). Of these, an estimated 1,235,315 (32%) were living in 59 camps serviced by the Agency, while the remaining refugees had settled in the towns and villages already existing.

UNRWA's three principal areas of activity are education; health; and relief and social services. Some 81% of the Agency's 2001 general fund budget was devoted to these three operational programmes.

Education accounted for 54% of UNRWA's 2001 budget. In the 2000/2001 school year there were 477,216 pupils enrolled in 639 UNRWA schools, and 14,877 educational staff. UNRWA also operated eight vocational and teacher-training centres, which provided a total of 4,704 training places. UNRWA awarded 431 scholarships for study at Arab universities in 2000/2001. Technical co-operation for the Agency's education programme is provided by UNESCO.

Health services accounted for 18% of UNRWA's 2001 general fund budget. At mid-2001 there were 122 primary health care units providing outpatient medical care, disease prevention and control, maternal and child health care and family planning services, of which 85 also offered dental care. At that time annual patient visits to UNRWA medical units numbered 7.7m., while the number of health staff totalled 3,438. UNRWA also operates a small hospital in the West Bank and offers assistance towards emergency and other secondary treatment, mainly through contractual agreements with non-governmental and private hospitals. Technical assistance for the health programme is provided by WHO.

Relief and social services accounted for 10% of UNRWA's general fund budget for 2001. These services comprise the distribution of food rations, the provision of emergency shelter and the organization of welfare programmes for the poorest refugees (at 30 June 2001 217,388 refugees, or 5.6% of the total registered refugee population, were eligible to receive special hardship assistance). In 2000 UNRWA provided technical and financial support to 71 women's programme centres, 27 youth activity centres and 36 community-based rehabilitation centres.

In order to encourage Palestinian self-reliance the Agency issues grants to ailing businesses and loans to families who qualify as special hardship cases. Between 1983 and early 1993 608 such grants and loans were made. In 1991 UNRWA launched an income generation programme, which provides capital loans to small businesses and micro-enterprises with the objective of creating sustainable employment and eliminating poverty, particularly in the Occupied Territories. By 30 June 2001 44,068 loans, with a total estimated value of US $58.6m., had been issued to new and existing Palestinian-owned enterprises.

SPECIAL PROGRAMMES

Following the signing of the Declaration of Principles by the Palestine Liberation Organization and the Israeli Government in September 1993, UNRWA initiated a Peace Implementation Programme (PIP) to improve services and infrastructure for Palestinian refugees. In September 1994 the first phase of the programme (PIP I) was concluded after the receipt of US $93.2m. in pledged donations. PIP I projects included the construction of 33 schools and 24 classrooms and specialized education rooms, the rehabilitation of 4,700 shelters, the upgrading of solid waste disposal facilities throughout the Gaza Strip and feasibility studies for two sewerage systems. It was estimated that these projects created more than 5,500 jobs in the Gaza Strip for an average period of four months each. By the end of 2000 the total number of PIP projects, including those under the second phase of the programme (PIP II), amounted to 496, while funds received or pledged to the Programme totalled $255.6m.

Since 1993 UNRWA has been engaged in the construction, equipping and commissioning of a 232-bed hospital in the Gaza Strip, with funds from the European Union and its member states. The outpatient facilities opened in July 2000. The hospital and an affiliated nursing college were to be integrated into the health care system of the Palestinian National Authority, once the process of commissioning had been completed.

AID TO DISPLACED PERSONS

After the renewal of Arab–Israeli hostilities in the Middle East in June 1967, hundreds of thousands of people fled from the fighting and from Israeli-occupied areas to east Jordan, Syria and Egypt. UNRWA provided emergency relief for displaced refugees and was additionally empowered by a UN General Assembly resolution to provide 'humanitarian assistance, as far as practicable, on an emergency basis and as a temporary measure' for those persons other than Palestine refugees who were newly displaced and in urgent need. In practice, UNRWA lacked the funds to aid the other displaced persons and the main burden of supporting them devolved on the Arab governments concerned. The Agency, as requested by the Government of Jordan in 1967 and on that Government's behalf, distributes rations to displaced persons in Jordan who are not registered refugees of 1948.

RECENT EMERGENCIES

In November 2000 UNRWA launched an emergency humanitarian appeal for US $39.1m. in additional funds to assist Palestinian refugees affected by the most recent escalation of violence in the region and the Israeli-imposed blockade on Palestinian Authority-controlled territory. UNRWA became the lead agency with responsibility for the co-ordination and delivery of emergency assistance, as well as for monitoring the immediate needs of the local populations. A second appeal was made by the Agency in April 2001, for some $37.2m., and a third emergency appeal, for $77m., was issued in June to provide basic food and medical supplies until the end of the year. The additional resources were also required to fund a programme of emergency workdays, which aimed to provide employment and income for labourers with dependents, while improving the local infrastructure. In addition, UNRWA intended to provide extra schooling days to make up for those missed because of the fighting, trauma counselling for children, and post-injury rehabilitation. In mid-January 2002 UNRWA reacted immediately to assess the needs of refugees following the demolition of 54 shelters by Israeli forces, and provided emergency supplies, including tents, blankets, mats and food.

STATISTICS

Refugees Registered with UNRWA (30 June 2001)

Country	Number	% of total
Jordan	1,639,718	42.3
Gaza Strip	852,626	22.0
West Bank	607,770	15.7
Syria	391,651	10.1
Lebanon	382,973	9.9
Total	3,874,738	100.0

Finance

UNRWA is financed almost entirely by voluntary contributions from governments and the European Union, the remainder being provided by UN bodies, non-governmental organizations, business corporations and private sources, which also contribute to extrabudgetary activities. UNRWA's general fund budget for 2001 amounted to US $310.4m. The proposed 2002 budget amounted to $330.7m.

Publication

Annual Report of the Commissioner-General of UNRWA.

United Nations Training and Research Institutes

UNITED NATIONS INSTITUTE FOR DISARMAMENT RESEARCH—UNIDIR

Address: Palais des Nations, 1211 Geneva 10, Switzerland.

Telephone: (22) 9173186; **fax:** (22) 9170176; **e-mail:** unidir@unog.ch; **internet:** www.unog.ch/unidir.

UNIDIR is an autonomous institution within the United Nations. It was established by the General Assembly in 1980 for the purpose of undertaking independent research on disarmament and related problems, particularly international security issues. UNIDIR's statute became effective on 1 January 1985.

The work of the Institute is based on the following objectives: to provide the international community with more diversified and complete data on problems relating to international security, the armaments race and disarmament in all fields, so as to facilitate progress towards greater global security and towards economic and social development for all peoples; to promote informed participation by all states in disarmament efforts; to assist ongoing negotiations on disarmament, and continuing efforts to ensure greater international security at a progressively lower level of armaments, in particular nuclear weapons, by means of objective studies and analyses; and to conduct long-term research on disarmament in order to provide a general insight into the problems involved and to stimulate new initiatives for negotiations.

The work programme of UNIDIR is reviewed annually and is subject to approval by its Board of Trustees. During 2001 UNIDIR conducted research and organized seminars on a range of issues, including: peace-building and practical disarmament in West Africa; the costs of disarmament; contemporary issues in arms control and disarmament (the so-called Geneva Forum); development of the *UNIDIR Handbook on Arms Control* and the *Handbook on Verification and Compliance*; tactical nuclear weapons; and fissile materials. Research projects are conducted within the Institute, or commissioned to individual experts or research organizations. For some major studies, multinational groups of experts are established. The Institute offers internships, in connection with its research programme. UNIDIR maintains a database on research institutes (DATARIs) in the field of international security (accessible at dataris.sipri.org).

The Institute is financed mainly by voluntary contributions from governments and public or private organizations. A contribution to the costs of the Director and staff may be provided from the UN regular budget.

The Director of UNIDIR reports annually to the General Assembly on the activities of the Institute. The UN Secretary-General's Advisory Board on Disarmament Studies functions as UNIDIR's Board of Trustees.

Director: PATRICIA LEWIS (United Kingdom).

Publications: *Disarmament Forum* (quarterly), *UNIDIR Newsletter* (quarterly); research reports (6 a year); research papers (irregular).

UNITED NATIONS INSTITUTE FOR TRAINING AND RESEARCH—UNITAR

Address: Palais des Nations, 1211 Geneva 10, Switzerland.

Telephone: (22) 9171234; **fax:** (22) 9178047; **e-mail:** info@unitar.org; **internet:** www.unitar.org.

UNITAR was established in 1963, as an autonomous body within the United Nations, in order to enhance the effectiveness of the latter body in achieving its major objectives. In recent years the main focus of the Institute has shifted to training, with basic research being conducted only if extra-budgetary funds are made available. Training is provided at various levels for personnel on assignments under the United Nations and its specialized agencies or under organizations operating in related fields. In 2001 UNITAR programmes included courses on the management of international affairs; the application of environmental law; debt, financial management and negotiation; foreign economic relations; chemicals and waste management; climate change; information and communication technologies; and the special needs of women and children in and after conflict. Most training programmes are designed and conducted in Geneva. In October 2001 UNITAR, in collaboration with the authorities in Hiroshima, Japan, initiated the Hiroshima Programmes, which aimed to organize training activities in the Asia and Pacific region to promote peace and security and economic and social development.

UNITAR offers a fellowship programme in peace-making and preventive diplomacy to provide advanced training for international and national civil servants in conflict analysis and mediation. It also organizes, jointly with the UN Office for Legal Affairs, an annual fellowship programme in international law.

UNITAR is financed by voluntary contributions from UN member states, by donations from foundations and other non-governmental sources, and by income generated by its Reserve Fund.

Executive Director: MARCEL A. BOISARD (Switzerland).

UNITED NATIONS INTERNATIONAL RESEARCH AND TRAINING INSTITUTE FOR THE ADVANCEMENT OF WOMEN—INSTRAW

Address: Calle César Nicolás Pensón 102-A, POB 21747, Santo Domingo, Dominican Republic.

Telephone: (809) 685-2111; **fax:** (809) 685-2117; **e-mail:** instraw.hq.sd@codetel.net.do; **internet:** www.un-instraw.org.

The Institute was established by ECOSOC, and endorsed by the General Assembly, in 1976, following a recommendation of the World Conference on the International Women's Year (1975). INSTRAW provides training, conducts research and collects and disseminates relevant information in order to stimulate and to assist the advancement of women and their integration in the development process, both as participants and beneficiaries. In 1999 INSTRAW initiated a process of restructuring to implement a strategic mandate to use new information and communication technologies. In June 2000 INSTRAW inaugurated the Gender Awareness Information and Networking System (GAINS), an internet-based database on research and training materials. During the two-year period 2001–02 INSTRAW's work programme focused on: building partnerships for gender equality; women and men in the information society; and the impact of globalization.

INSTRAW is an autonomous body of the UN, funded by voluntary contributions from UN member states, inter- and non-governmental organizations, foundations and other private sources. An 11-member Board of Trustees meets annually to formulate the principles and guide-lines for the activities of INSTRAW and to consider the current work progamme and budget proposals, and reports to ECOSOC. INSTRAW maintains a liaison office at the UN Secretariat in New York.

Officer-in-Charge: TATJANA SIKOSKA.

Publications: *INSTRAW News* (2 a year); training materials, research studies.

UNITED NATIONS INTERREGIONAL CRIME AND JUSTICE RESEARCH INSTITUTE—UNICRI

Address: Viale Maestri del Lavoro 10, 10127 Turin, Italy.

Telephone: (011) 6537111; **fax:** (011) 6313368; **e-mail:** unicri@unicri.it; **internet:** www.unicri.it.

The Institute was established in 1968 as the United Nations Social Defence Research Institute. Its present name was adopted by a resolution of ECOSOC in 1989. The Institute undertakes research, training and information activities in the fields of crime prevention and criminal justice, at international, regional and national levels.

In collaboration with national governments, UNICRI aims to establish a reliable base of knowledge and information on organized crime; to identify strategies for the prevention and control of crime, within the framework of contributing to socio-economic development and protecting human rights; and to design systems to support policy formulation, implementation and evaluation. UNICRI organizes workshops and conferences, and promotes the exchange of information through its international documentation centre on criminology.

UNICRI is funded by the United Nations Crime Prevention and Criminal Justice Fund, which is financed by voluntary contributions from UN member states, non-governmental organizations, academic institutions and other concerned bodies.

Director: ALBERTO BRADANINI (Italy).

UNITED NATIONS RESEARCH INSTITUTE FOR SOCIAL DEVELOPMENT—UNRISD

Address: Palais des Nations, 1211 Geneva 10, Switzerland.

Telephone: (22) 9173020; **fax:** (22) 9170650; **e-mail:** info@unrisd.org; **internet:** www.unrisd.org.

UNRISD was established in 1963 as an autonomous body within the United Nations, to conduct multi-disciplinary research into the social dimensions of contemporary problems affecting development.

The Institute aims to provide governments, development agencies, grass-roots organizations and scholars with a better understanding of how development policies and processes of economic, social and environmental change affect different social groups.

UNRISD research is undertaken in collaboration with a network of national research teams drawn from local universities and research institutions. UNRISD aims to promote and strengthen research capacities in developing countries. During the period 2000–03 its research programme was to include the following projects: gender, poverty and well-being; social policy in a development context; neoliberalism and institutional reform in East Asia; technocratic policy making and democratization; public sector reform and crisis-ridden states; community perspectives on urban governance; grassroots movements and initiatives for land reform; information technologies and social development; and business responsibility for sustainable development.

The Institute is supported by voluntary grants from governments, and also receives financing from other UN organizations, and from various other national and international agencies.

Director: THANDIKA MKANDAWIRE (Sweden).

Publications: *UNRISD Social Development News* (quarterly), discussion papers and monographs.

UNITED NATIONS SYSTEM STAFF COLLEGE

Address: Viale Maestri del Lavoro 10, 10127 Turin, Italy.

Telephone: (011) 3936797; **fax:** (011) 6936349; **e-mail:** unscp@itcilo.it; **internet:** www.unssc.org/unscp.

In July 2001 the UN General Assembly approved a statute for the College, which, it envisaged, would provide knowledge management, training and continuous learning opportunities for all UN personnel. The inaugural meeting of the Board of Governors was held in November, and the College formally began operations on 1 January 2002. It aimed to promote the exchange of knowledge and shared learning, to administer learning and training workshops, as well as distance learning opportunities, to provide support and expert advice, and to act as a clearing house for learning activities. The College's work programme for 2002 included activities in the following areas: capacity-building for development—UN system challenges for the 21st century; commu-nication training; distance learning for population; early warning and preventive measures: building UN capacity; global learning network on partnerships; induction/orientation training; human rights training; and resident co-ordinator system training.

Director: JOHN MACHIN (United Kingdom).

UNITED NATIONS UNIVERSITY—UNU

Address: 53–70, Jingumae 5-chome, Shibuya-ku, Tokyo 150-8925, Japan.

Telephone: (3) 3499-2811; **fax:** (3) 3499-2828; **e-mail:** mbox@hq.unu.edu; **internet:** www.unu.edu.

The University is sponsored jointly by the United Nations and UNESCO. It is an autonomous institution within the United Nations, guaranteed academic freedom by a charter approved by the General Assembly in 1973. It is governed by a 28-member University Council of scholars and scientists, of whom 24 are appointed by the Secretary-General of the UN and the Director-General of UNESCO (who, together with the Executive Director of UNITAR, are *ex-officio* members of the Council; the Rector is also on the Council). The University is not traditional in the sense of having students or awarding degrees, but works through networks of collaborating institutions and individuals. These include Associated Institutions (universities and research institutes linked with the UNU under general agreements of co-operation). The UNU undertakes multi-disciplinary research on problems that are the concern of the United Nations and its agencies, and works to strengthen research and training capabilities in developing countries. It provides post-graduate fellowships for scientists and scholars from developing countries, and conducts various training activities in association with its programme. Its main thematic programme areas are peace; governance; development; science, technology and society; and environment.

The UNU's research and training centres and programmes include the World Institute of Development Economics Research (UNU/WIDER) in Helsinki, Finland, the Institute for New Technologies (UNU/INTECH) in Maastricht, Netherlands, the International Institute for Software Technology (UNU/IIST) in Macau, the UNU Institute for Natural Resources in Africa in Accra, Ghana (UNU/INRA—with a mineral resources unit in Lusaka, Zambia), the UNU Programme for Biotechnology in Latin America and the Caribbean (UNU/BIOLAC), based in Caracas, Venezuela, the UNU International Leadership Academy (UNU/ILA) in Amman, Jordan, the Institute of Advanced Studies (UNU/IAS), based in Tokyo, Japan, and the UNU International Network on Water, Environment and Health (UNU/INWEH) in Ontario, Canada.

The UNU is financed by voluntary contributions from UN member states. The budget for 2000 amounted to US $35.9m.

Rector: Prof. HANS J. A. VAN GINKEL (Netherlands).

Publications: *UNU Nexions* (regular newsletter), *WIDERAngle* (2 a year), *Africa Research* (2 a year), regular journals, abstracts, research papers.

UNIVERSITY FOR PEACE

Address: POB 138, Ciudad Colón, Costa Rica.

Telephone: 249-1072; **fax:** 249-1929; **e-mail:** info@upeace.org; **internet** www.upeace.org.

The University for Peace was established by the United Nations in 1980 to conduct research on, *inter alia*, disarmament, mediation, the resolution of conflicts, the preservation of the environment, international relations, peace education and human rights.

The Council of the University (the governing body, comprising 15 members) was reconstituted in March 1999, meeting for the first time since 1994. In May 1999 the Council initiated a programme of extensive reforms and expansion. A programme of short courses was reintroduced in 2001, and new Masters degrees in International Law and the Settlement of Disputes and in Human Rights Studies were developed, and scheduled to commence in September 2002. A University for Peace Centre and Policy Institute was established in Geneva, Switzerland, in 2000, and an Institute for Media, Peace and Security was established, with temporary headquarters in Paris, France, in 2001.

Rector and Chief Executive Officer: MARTIN LEES (United Kingdom).

Publications: *Dialogue*, *Infopaz*.

World Food Programme—WFP

Address: Via Cesare Giulio Viola 68, Parco dei Medici, 00148 Rome, Italy.

Telephone: (06) 6513-1; **fax:** (06) 6590-632; **e-mail:** wfpinfo@wfp.org; **internet:** www.wfp.org.

WFP, the food aid organization of the United Nations, became operational in 1963. It provides relief assistance to victims of natural and man-made disasters, and supplies food aid to people in developing countries to eradicate chronic undernourishment, to support social development and to promote self-reliant communities.

Organization

(March 2002)

EXECUTIVE BOARD

The governing body of WFP is the Executive Board, comprising 36 members, 18 of whom are elected by the UN Economic and Social Council (ECOSOC) and 18 by the Council of the Food and Agriculture Organization (FAO). The Board meets four times each year at WFP headquarters.

SECRETARIAT

WFP's Executive Director is appointed jointly by the UN Secretary-General and the Director-General of FAO and is responsible for the management and administration of the Programme. In 2000 there were 2,533 permanent staff members, of whom about 75% were working in the field. WFP administers some 87 country offices, in order to provide operational, financial and management support at a more local level, and has established seven regional bureaux, located in Bangkok, Thailand (for Asia), Cairo, Egypt (for the Middle East, Central Asia and the Mediterranean), Rome, Italy (for Eastern Europe), Managua, Nicaragua (for Latin America and the Caribbean), Yaoundé, Cameroon (for Central Africa), Kampala, Uganda (for Eastern and Southern Africa), and Dakar, Senegal (for West Africa).

Executive Director: JAMES T. MORRIS (USA).

Activities

WFP is the only multilateral organization with a mandate to use food aid as a resource. It is the second largest source of assistance in the UN, after the World Bank group, in terms of actual transfers of resources, and the largest source of grant aid in the UN system. WFP handles more than one-third of the world's food aid. WFP is also the largest contributor to South–South trade within the UN system, through the purchase of food and services from developing countries. WFP's mission is to provide food aid to save lives in refugee and other emergency situations, to improve the nutrition and quality of life of vulnerable groups and to help to develop assets and promote the self-reliance of poor families and communities. WFP aims to focus its efforts on the world's poorest countries and to provide at least 90% of its total assistance to those designated as 'low-income food-deficit'. It also endeavours to address the specific nutritional needs of women and to increase their access to food and development resources. At the World Food Summit, held in November 1996, WFP endorsed the commitment to reduce by 50% the number of undernourished people, no later than 2015. In 2000 WFP delivered a total of 3.7m. metric tons of food assistance, reaching an estimated 83m. people in 83 countries.

In the early 1990s there was a substantial shift in the balance between emergency relief and development assistance provided by WFP, owing to the growing needs of victims of drought and other natural disasters, refugees and displaced persons. By 1994 two-thirds of all food aid was for relief assistance and one-third for development, representing a direct reversal of the allocations five years previously. In addition, there was a noticeable increase in aid given to those in need as a result of civil war, compared with commitments for victims of natural disasters. Accordingly, WFP has developed a range of mechanisms to enhance its preparedness for emergency situations and to improve its capacity for responding effectively to situations as they arise. A new programme of emergency response training was inaugurated in 2000, while security concerns for personnel was incorporated as a new element into all general planning and training activities. Through its Vulnerability Analysis and Mapping (VAM) project, WFP aims to identify potentially vulnerable groups by providing information on food security and the capacity of different groups for coping with shortages, and to enhance emergency contingency-planning and long-term assistance objectives. By 2001 VAM field units were operational in more than 50 countries. WFP also co-operates with FAO to conduct Joint Crop and Food Supply Assessment Missions, 25 of which were undertaken in 2000 in Africa and Asia. The key elements of WFP's emergency response capacity are its strategic stores of food and logistics equipment, stand-by arrangements to enable the rapid deployment of personnel, communications and other essential equipment, and the Augmented Logistics Intervention Team for Emergencies (ALITE), which undertakes capacity assessments and contingency-planning. In 2000 a new UN Humanitarian Response Depot was opened in Brindisi, Italy, under the direction of WFP experts, for the storage of essential rapid response equipment. In that year WFP also led efforts, undertaken with other UN humanitarian agencies, for the design and application of local UN Joint Logistics Centre facilities, which aimed to co-ordinate resources in an emergency situation.

In 2000 WFP humanitarian relief benefited some 25m. people affected by war and civil unrest and 36m. victims of earthquakes, drought, floods and other natural disasters. In that year the main focus of WFP relief activities was sub-Saharan Africa, which accounted for 65% of total emergency operational expenditure. In March WFP initiated a six-month emergency operation to provide food to an estimated 1m. people who had lost their homes as a result of flooding in Mozambique. In the same month the UN Secretary-General appointed WFP's Executive Director as his Special Envoy for the drought in the Horn of Africa. Some 1m. metric tons of food aid was subsequently mobilized to meet the food and non-food needs of 16m. affected people in Kenya, Somalia and Tanzania. Other major emergency operations undertaken in 2000 included the provision of aid to some 900,000 people in Cambodia, Laos and Viet Nam affected by flooding of the Mekong River, support for communities in south-west Bangladesh who were also victims of severe floods, the provision of aid to 230,000 displaced people in Colombia, and emergency assistance to some 1.2m. people in Serbia, Kosovo and Metohija, Montenegro, Albania and the former Yugoslav republic of Macedonia. In recent years WFP has been actively concerned with the food situation in the Democratic People's Republic of Korea

(DPRK), which has required substantial levels of emergency food supplies, owing to natural disasters and consistently poor harvests. By mid-1999 an estimated 1.5m.–3.5m. people had died of starvation in the DPRK since 1995. During 2000 an estimated 9.4m. people in the DPRK received WFP assistance. In November 2001 WFP requested support for its seventh emergency operation in the DPRK, which aimed to provide food aid to 6.4m. people during 2002, at a cost of US $214m. An additional long-standing concern of WFP has been Afghanistan, where civil conflict and severe drought have caused massive food insecurity and population displacement. In March 2001 WFP launched an appeal for $76m. to fund a new one-year emergency operation to assist 3.8m. people. In August WFP reported a substantial cereal deficit in the country and identified widespread pre-famine conditions. Accordingly, the operation was expanded to provide assistance to 5.5m. people, with new funding requirements amounting to $151m., in order to meet its objectives, which included delivering food to those threatened with starvation, providing subsidized bread to urban communities, and encouraging farmers to engage in productive activities. In mid-September, however, the delivery of food aid to Afghanistan was suspended and all international personnel were withdrawn owing to a deterioration in the security situation and expectation of imminent military action by a US-led coalition against the Taliban regime. Food shipments to northern areas of the country were resumed later in that month. Meanwhile, in readiness for a predicted mass influx of refugees from Afghanistan were international military action to be initiated, WFP staff were mobilized in neighbouring countries and emergency supplies stockpiled in border regions. The first delivery of humanitarian supplies by air was undertaken in late October. By mid-December, despite the withdrawal of the Taliban authorities, the distribution of aid to an estimated 7.5m. Afghans in need was still seriously hampered by poor rural infrastructure, adverse weather conditions and ongoing security concerns.

Through its development activities, WFP aims to alleviate poverty in developing countries by promoting self-reliant families and communities. Food is supplied, for example, as an incentive in development self-help schemes and as part-wages in labour-intensive projects of many kinds. In all its projects WFP aims to assist the most vulnerable groups and to ensure that beneficiaries have an adequate and balanced diet. Activities supported by the Programme include the settlement and resettlement of groups and communities; land reclamation and improvement; irrigation; the development of forestry and dairy farming; road construction; training of hospital staff; community development; and human resources development such as feeding expectant or nursing mothers and schoolchildren, and support for education, training and health programmes. During 2000 WFP supported 189 development projects in 59 countries, which benefited some 22m. people. School feeding projects benefited 12.3m. children during that year. In 2001 WFP initiated a new Global School Feeding Campaign to strengthen international co-operation to expand educational opportunities for poor children and to improve the quality of the teaching environment.

Following a comprehensive evaluation of its activities, WFP is increasingly focused on linking its relief and development activities to provide a continuum between short-term relief and longer-term rehabilitation and development. In order to achieve this objective, WFP aims to integrate elements that strengthen disaster mitigation into development projects, including soil conservation, reafforestation, irrigation infrastructure and transport construction and rehabilitation and to promote capacity-building elements within relief operations, e.g. training, income-generating activities and environmental protection measures. In 1999 WFP adopted a new Food Aid and Development policy, which aims to use food assistance both to cover immediate requirements and to create conditions conducive to enhancing the long-term food security of vulnerable populations. During that year WFP began implementing Protracted Relief and Recovery Operations (PRROs), where the emphasis is on fostering stability, rehabilitation and long-term development for victims of natural disasters, displaced persons and refugees. PRROs were to be introduced no later than 18 months after the initial emergency operation, and to last no more than three years. When undertaken in collaboration with UNHCR and other international agencies, WFP was to be responsible for mobilizing basic food commodities and for related transport, handling and storage costs. In 2000 93 PRROs, involving the provision of 936,000 metric tons of food, were being undertaken in 39 countries.

OPERATIONAL EXPENDITURE IN 2000, BY REGION AND TYPE* (US $ '000, provisional figures)

Region	Development	Relief	Special operations	Total (incl. others†)
Sub-Saharan Africa	78,480	775,061	19,858	888,120
Asia	82,843	298,324	4,818	391,719
Latin America and the Caribbean	30,596	13,994	—	45,226
North Africa and the Middle East	23,293	13,379	12,574	54,771
Europe and the CIS	—	102,814	-165	102,899
Total	215,212	1,203,573	37,084	1,491,035‡

* Excludes programme support and administrative costs.
† Trust fund expenditures.
‡ Includes operational expenditures that cannot be apportioned by project operation.

Finance

The Programme is funded by voluntary contributions from donor countries and intergovernmental bodies such as the European Union. Contributions are made in the form of commodities, finance and services (particularly shipping). Commitments to the International Emergency Food Reserve (IEFR), from which WFP provides the majority of its food supplies, and to the Immediate Response Account of the IEFR (IRA) are also made on a voluntary basis by donors. WFP's operational expenditure in 2000 amounted to some US $1,491m., while administrative costs totalled $108m.

Publications

Annual Report.
Food and Nutrition Handbook.
School Feeding Handbook.

SPECIALIZED AGENCIES WITHIN THE UN SYSTEM

Food and Agriculture Organization of the United Nations—FAO

Address: Viale delle Terme di Caracalla, 00100 Rome, Italy.

Telephone: (06) 57051; **fax:** (06) 5705-3152; **e-mail:** fao.hq@fao.org; **internet:** www.fao.org.

FAO, the first specialized agency of the UN to be founded after the Second World War, aims to alleviate malnutrition and hunger, and serves as a co-ordinating agency for development programmes in the whole range of food and agriculture, including forestry and fisheries. It helps developing countries to promote educational and training facilities and the creation of appropriate institutions.

MEMBERS

183 members (including the European Union as a member organization): see Table on pp. 211–213.

Organization

(March 2002)

CONFERENCE

The governing body is the FAO Conference of member nations. It meets every two years, formulates policy, determines the Organization's programme and budget on a biennial basis, and elects new members. It also elects the Director-General of the Secretariat and the Independent Chairman of the Council. Every other year, FAO also holds conferences in each of its five regions (see below).

COUNCIL

The FAO Council is composed of representatives of 49 member nations, elected by the Conference for staggered three-year terms. It is the interim governing body of FAO between sessions of the Conference. The most important standing Committees of the Council are: the Finance and Programme Committees, the Committee on Commodity Problems, the Committee on Fisheries, the Committee on Agriculture and the Committee on Forestry.

SECRETARIAT

The total number of budgeted staff posts at FAO headquarters in 2001 was 1,888 (891 professional staff and 997 general staff), while staff posts in field, regional and country offices numbered 1,394. Work is supervised by the following Departments: Administration and Finance; General Affairs and Information; Economic and Social Policy; Agriculture; Forestry; Fisheries; Sustainable Development; and Technical Co-operation.

Director-General: JACQUES DIOUF (Senegal).

REGIONAL OFFICES

Africa: UN Agency Bldg, North Maxwell Rd, POB 1628, Accra, Ghana; tel. (21) 666851; fax (21) 668427; e-mail fao-raf@fao.org; Regional Rep. Bamidele F. DADA.

Asia and the Pacific: Maliwan Mansion, Phra Atit Rd, Bangkok 10200, Thailand; tel. (2) 281-7844; fax (2) 280-0445; e-mail fao-rap@fao.org; internet www.or.th; Regional Rep. R. B. SINGH.

Europe: Viale delle Terme di Caracalla, Room A-304, 00100 Rome, Italy; tel. (06) 570-51; fax (06) 570-53152; Regional Rep. CLAUDE FORTHOMME.

Latin America and the Caribbean: Avda Dag Hammarskjöld 3241, Casilla 10095, Vitacura, Santiago, Chile; tel. (2) 337-2100; fax (2) 337-2101; e-mail fao-rlc@field.fao.org; internet www.rlc.fao.org; Regional Rep. GUSTAVO GORDILLO DE ANDA.

Near East: 11 El-Eslah el-Zerai St, Dokki, POB 2223, Cairo, Egypt; tel. (2) 3372229; fax (2) 7495981; e-mail fao-rne@field .fao.org; Regional Rep. ATIF YEHEYA BUKHARI.

In addition, the following Sub-regional Offices are operational: in Harare, Zimbabwe (for Southern and Eastern Africa); in Bridgetown, Barbados (for the Caribbean); in Tunis, Tunisia (for North Africa); in Budapest, Hungary (for Central and Eastern Europe); and in Apia, Samoa (for the Pacific Islands).

JOINT DIVISIONS AND LIAISON OFFICES

Joint ECA/FAO Agriculture Division: Africa Hall, POB 3001, Addis Ababa, Ethiopia; tel. (1) 510406; fax (1) 514416.

Joint ECE/FAO Timber Section: Palais des Nations, 1211 Geneva 10, Switzerland; tel. (22) 917-2874; fax (22) 917-0041.

Joint ESCWA/FAO Agriculture Division: POB 927115, Amman, Jordan; tel. (6) 606847; fax (6) 674261.

Joint IAEA/FAO Division of Nuclear Techniques in Food and Agriculture: Wagramerstrasse 5, 1400 Vienna, Austria; tel. (1) 20600; fax (1) 20607.

European Union: 21 ave du Boulevard, 1210 Brussels, Belgium; tel. (2) 203-8852; e-mail fao-lobr@field.fao.org; Dir M. R. DE MONTALEMBERT.

Japan: 6F Yokohama International Organizations Centre, Pacifico-Yokohama, 1-1-1, Minato Mirai, Nishi-ku, Yokohama 220-0012; tel. (45) 222-1101; fax (45) 222-1103.

North America: Suite 300, 2175 K St, NW, Washington, DC 20437, USA; tel. (202) 653-2400; fax (202) 653-5760; e-mail fao-lowa@fao.org; Dir C. H. RIEMENSCHNEIDER.

United Nations: Suite DC1-1125, 1 United Nations Plaza, New York, NY 10017, USA; tel. (212) 963-6036; fax (212) 963-5425; Dir HOWARD W. HJORT.

Activities

FAO aims to raise levels of nutrition and standards of living, by improving the production and distribution of food and other commodities derived from farms, fisheries and forests. FAO's ultimate objective is the achievement of world food security, 'Food for All'. The organization provides technical information, advice and assistance by disseminating information; acting as a neutral forum for discussion of food and agricultural issues; advising governments on policy and planning; and developing capacity directly in the field.

In November 1996 FAO hosted the World Food Summit, which was held in Rome and was attended by heads of state and senior government representatives of 186 countries. Participants approved the Rome Declaration on World Food Security and the World Food Summit Plan of Action, with the aim of halving the number of people afflicted by undernutrition, at that time estimated to total 828m. world-wide, by no later than 2015. A review conference to assess progress in achieving the goals of the summit, entitled World Food Summit: Five Years Later, was scheduled to be held in June 2002.

In November 1999 the FAO Conference approved a long-term Strategic Framework for the period 2000–15, which emphasized national and international co-operation in pursuing the goals of the 1996 World Food Summit. The Framework promoted interdisciplinarity and partnership, and defined three main global objectives: constant access by all people to sufficient nutritionally adequate and safe food to ensure that levels of undernourishment were reduced by 50% by 2015 (see above); the continued contribution of sustainable agriculture and rural development to economic and social progress and well-being; and the conservation, improvement and sustainable use of natural resources. It identified five corporate strategies (each supported by several strategic objectives), covering the following areas: reducing food insecurity and rural poverty; ensuring enabling policy and regulatory frameworks for food, agriculture, fisheries and forestry; creating sustainable increases in the supply and availability of agricultural, fisheries and forestry products; conserving and enhancing sustainable use of the natural resource base; and generating knowledge. The November 2001 FAO Conference adopted a medium-term plan covering 2002–07 and a work programme for 2000–03, both on the basis of the Strategic Framework.

FAO organizes an annual series of fund-raising events, 'TeleFood', some of which are broadcast on television and the internet, in order to raise public awareness of the problems of hunger and malnutrition. Since its inception in 1997 public donations to TeleFood have exceeded US $9m., financing more than 1,000 'grass-roots' projects in more than 100 countries. The projects have provided tools, seeds and other essential supplies directly to small-scale farmers, and have been especially aimed at helping women.

In 1999 FAO signed a memorandum of understanding with UNAIDS on strengthening co-operation. In December 2001 FAO, IFAD and WFP determined to strengthen inter-agency collaboration in developing strategies to combat the threat posed by the HIV/AIDS epidemic to food security, nutrition and rural livelihoods. During that month experts from those organizations and UNAIDS held a technical consultation on means of mitigating the impact of HIV/AIDS on agriculture and rural communities in affected areas.

The Technical Cooperation Department has responsibility for FAO's operational activities, including policy development assistance to member countries; investment support; and the management of activities associated with the development and implementation of country, sub-regional and regional programmes. The Department manages the technical co-operation programme (TCP, which funds 13% of FAO's field programme expenditures), and mobilizes resources.

AGRICULTURE

FAO's most important area of activity is crop production, accounting annually for about one-quarter of total field programme expenditure. FAO assists developing countries in increasing agricultural production, by means of a number of methods, including improved seeds and fertilizer use, soil conservation and reforestation, better water resource management techniques, upgrading storage facilities, and improvements in processing and marketing. FAO places special emphasis on the cultivation of under-exploited traditional food crops, such as cassava, sweet potato and plantains.

In 1985 the FAO Conference approved an International Code of Conduct on the Distribution and Use of Pesticides, and in 1989 the Conference adopted an additional clause concerning 'Prior Informed Consent' (PIC), whereby international shipments of newly banned or restricted pesticides should not proceed without the agreement of importing countries. Under the clause, FAO aims to inform governments about the hazards of toxic chemicals and to urge them to take proper measures to curb trade in highly toxic agrochemicals while keeping the pesticides industry informed of control actions. In 1996 FAO, in collaboration with UNEP, publicized a new initiative which aimed to increase awareness of, and to promote international action on, obsolete and hazardous stocks of pesticides remaining throughout the world (estimated in 2001 to total some 500,000 metric tons). In September 1998 a new legally-binding treaty on trade in hazardous chemicals and pesticides was adopted at an international conference held in Rotterdam, Netherlands. The so-called Rotterdam Convention required that hazardous chemicals and pesticides banned or severely restricted in at least two countries should not be exported unless explicitly agreed by the importing country. It also identified certain pesticide formulations as too dangerous to be used by farmers in developing countries, and incorporated an obligation that countries halt national production of those hazardous compounds. The treaty was to enter into force on being ratified by 50 signatory states. FAO was co-operating with UNEP to provide an interim secretariat for the Convention. In July 1999 a conference on the Rotterdam Convention, held in Rome, established an Interim Chemical Review Committee with responsibility for recommending the inclusion of chemicals or pesticide formulations in the PIC procedure. By March 2002 the treaty had been ratified by 20 states. As part of its continued efforts to reduce the environmental risks posed by over-reliance on pesticides, FAO has extended to other regions its Integrated Pest Management (IPM) programme in Asia and the Pacific on the use of safer and more effective methods of pest control, such as biological control methods and natural predators (including spiders and wasps), to avert pests. In February 2001 FAO warned that some 30% of pesticides sold in developing countries did not meet internationally accepted quality standards.

FAO's Joint Division with the International Atomic Energy Agency (IAEA) tests controlled-release formulas of pesticides and herbicides that gradually free their substances and can limit the amount of agrochemicals needed to protect crops. The Joint FAO-IAEA Division is engaged in exploring biotechnologies and in developing non-toxic fertilizers (especially those that are locally available) and improved strains of food crops (especially from indigenous varieties). In the area of animal production and health, the Joint Division has developed progesterone-measuring and disease diagnostic kits, of which thousands have been delivered to developing countries. FAO's plant nutrition activities aim to promote nutrient management, such as the Integrated Plant Nutritions Systems (IPNS), which are based on the recycling of nutrients through crop production and the efficient use of mineral fertilizers.

The conservation and sustainable use of plant and animal genetic resources are promoted by FAO's Global System for Plant Genetic Resources, which includes five databases, and the Global Strategy on the Management of Farm Animal Genetic Resources. An FAO programme supports the establishment of gene banks, designed to maintain the world's biological diversity by preserving animal and plant species threatened with extinction. FAO, jointly with UNEP, has published a document listing the current state of global livestock genetic diversity. In June 1996 representatives of more than 150 governments convened in Leipzig, Germany, at a meeting organized by FAO (and hosted by the German Government) to consider the use and conservation of plant genetic resources as an essential means of enhancing food security. The meeting adopted a Global Plan of Action, which included measures to strengthen the development of plant varieties and to promote the use and availability of local varieties and locally-adapted crops to farmers, in particular following a natural disaster, war or civil conflict. In November 2001 the FAO Conference adopted the International Treaty on Plant Genetic Resources for Food and Agriculture, which was to provide a framework to ensure access to plant genetic resources and to related knowledge, technologies and funding. The Treaty was to enter into force once it had been ratified by 40 signatory states.

An Emergency Prevention System for Transboundary Animal and Plant Pests and Diseases (EMPRES) was established in 1994 to strengthen FAO's activities in the prevention, control and, where possible, eradication of pests and highly contagious livestock diseases (which the system categorizes as epidemic diseases of strategic importance, such as rinderpest or foot-and-mouth; diseases requiring tactical attention at international or regional level, e.g. Rift Valley fever; and emerging diseases, e.g. bovine spongiform encephalopathy—BSE). During 1994 EMPRES published guide-lines on all aspects of desert locust monitoring, commissioned an evaluation of recent control efforts and prepared a concept paper on desert locust management. FAO has assumed responsibility for technical leadership and co-ordination of the Global Rinderpest Eradication Programme (GREP), which has the objective of eliminating the disease by 2010. Following technical consulations in late 1998, an Intensified GREP was launched. In November 1997 FAO initiated a Programme Against African Trypanosomiasis, which aimed to counter the disease affecting cattle in almost one-third of Africa. EMPRES promotes Good Emergency Management Practices (GEMP) in animal health. The system is guided by the annual meeting of the EMPRES Expert Consultation.

FAO's organic agriculture programme provides technical assistance and policy advice on the production, certification and trade of organic produce. In July 2001 the FAO/WHO Codex Alimentarius Commission adopted guide-lines on organic livestock production, covering organic breeding methods, the elimination of growth hormones and certain chemicals in veterinary medicines, and the use of good quality organic feed with no meat or bone meal content.

ENVIRONMENT

At the UN Conference on Environment and Development (UNCED), held in Rio de Janeiro, Brazil, in June 1992, FAO participated in several working parties and supported the adoption of Agenda 21, a programme of activities to promote sustainable development. FAO is responsible for the chapters of Agenda 21 concerning water resources, forests, fragile mountain ecosystems and sustainable agriculture and rural development. FAO was designated by the UN General Assembly as the lead agency for co-ordinating the International Year of Mountains (2002), which aimed to raise awareness of mountain ecosystems and to promote the conservation and sustainable development of mountainous regions.

FISHERIES

FAO's Fisheries Department consists of a multi-disciplinary body of experts who are involved in every aspect of fisheries development from coastal surveys, conservation management and use of aquatic genetic resources, improvement of production, processing and storage, to the compilation and analysis of statistics, development of computer databases, improvement of fishing gear, institution-building and training. In November 1993 the FAO Conference adopted an agreement to improve the monitoring and control of fishing vessels operating on the high seas that are registered under 'flags of convenience', in order to ensure their compliance with internationally accepted marine conservation and management measures. In March 1995 a ministerial meeting of fisheries adopted the Rome Consensus on World Fisheries, which identified a need for immediate action to eliminate overfishing and to rebuild and enhance depleting fish stocks. In November the FAO Conference adopted a Code of Conduct for Responsible Fishing, which incorporated many global fisheries and aquaculture issues (including fisheries resource conservation and development, fish catches, seafood and fish processing, commercialization, trade and research) to promote the sustainable development of the sector. In February 1999 the FAO Committee on Fisheries adopted new international measures, within the framework of the Code of Conduct, in order to reduce over-exploitation of the world's fish resources, as well as plans of action for the conservation and management of sharks and the reduction in the incidental catch of seabirds in longline fisheries. The voluntary measures were endorsed at a ministerial meeting, held in March and attended by representatives of some 126 countries, which issued a declaration to promote the implementation of the Code of Conduct and to achieve sustainable management of fisheries and aquaculture. In March 2001 FAO adopted an international plan of action to address the continuing problem of so-called illegal, unreported and unregulated fishing (IUU). In that year FAO estimated that about one-half of major marine fish stocks were fully exploited, one-quarter under-exploited, at least 15% over-exploited, and 10% depleted or recovering from depletion. IUU was estimated to account for up to 30% of total catches in certain fisheries. In October FAO and the Icelandic Government jointly organized the Reykjavik Conference on Responsible Fisheries in the Marine Ecosystem, which adopted a declaration on pursuing responsible and sustainable fishing activities in the context of ecosystem-based fisheries management (EBFM). EBFM involves determining the boundaries of individual marine ecosystems, and maintaining or rebuilding the habitats and biodiversity of each of these so that all species will be supported at levels of maximum production. FAO promotes aquaculture (which contributed to 31% of global fish landings in 1999) as a valuable source of animal protein and income-generating activity for rural communities. In February 2000 FAO and the Network of Aquaculture Centres in Asia and the Pacific (NACA, q.v.) jointly convened a Conference on Aquaculture in the Third Millennium, which was held in Bangkok, Thailand, and attended by participants representing more than 200 governmental and non-governmental organizations. The Conference debated global trends in aquaculture and future policy measures to ensure the sustainable development of the sector. It adopted the Bangkok Declaration and Strategy for Aquaculture Beyond 2000. In December 2001 FAO issued a report based on the technical proceedings of the conference.

FORESTRY

FAO focuses on the contribution of forestry to food security, on effective and responsible forest management and on maintaining a balance between the economic, ecological and social benefits of forest resources. The Organization has helped to develop national forestry programmes and to promote the sustainable development of all types of forest. FAO administers the global Forests, Trees and People Programme, which promotes the sustainable management of tree and forest resources, based on local knowledge and management practices, in order to improve the livelihoods of rural people in developing countries. FAO's Strategic Plan for Forestry was approved in March 1999; its main objectives were to maintain the environmental diversity of forests, to realise the economic potential of forests and trees within a sustainable framework, and to expand access to information on forestry. In March 2001 FAO and the International Tropical Timber Organization (q.v.) jointly convened a meeting of international experts on forest fire management.

NUTRITION

The International Conference on Nutrition, sponsored by FAO and WHO, took place in Rome in December 1992. It approved a World Declaration on Nutrition and a Plan of Action, aimed at promoting efforts to combat malnutrition as a development priority. Since the conference, more than 100 countries have formulated national plans of action for nutrition, many of which were based on existing development plans such as comprehensive food security initiatives, national poverty alleviation programmes and action plans to attain the targets set by the World Summit for Children in September 1990. In October 1996 FAO, WHO and other partners jointly organized the first World Congress on Calcium and Vitamin D in Human Life, held in Rome. In January 2001 a joint team of FAO and WHO experts issued a report concerning the allergenicity of foods derived from biotechnology (i.e. genetically modified—GM foods). In July the Codex Alimentarius Commission agreed the first global principles for assessing the safety of GM foods, and approved a series of maximum levels of environmental contaminants in food. At that time FAO was considering establishing a food safety and quality facility to assist least-developed countries with updating national food safety systems. FAO and WHO jointly convened a Global Forum of Food Safety Regulators in Marrakech, Morocco, in January 2002.

PROCESSING AND MARKETING

An estimated 20% of all food harvested is lost before it can be consumed, and in some developing countries the proportion is much higher. FAO helps reduce immediate post-harvest losses, with the introduction of improved processing methods and storage systems. It also advises on the distribution and marketing of agricultural produce and on the selection and preparation of foods for optimum nutrition. Many of these activities form part of wider rural development projects. Many developing countries rely on agricultural products as their main source of foreign earnings, but the terms under which they are traded are usually more favourable to the industrialized countries. FAO continues to favour the elimination of export subsidies and related discriminatory practices, such as protectionist measures that hamper international trade in agricultural commodities. FAO has organized regional workshops and national projects in order to help member states to implement World Trade Organization regulations, in particular with regard to agricultural policy, intellectual property rights, sanitary and phytosanitary measures, technical barriers to trade and the international standards of the Codex Alimentarius. FAO evaluates new market trends and helps to develop improved plant and animal quarantine procedures. In November 1997 the FAO Conference adopted new guide-lines on surveillance and on export certification systems in order to harmonize plant quarantine standards. In August 1999 FAO announced the establishment of a new forum, PhAction, to promote post-harvest research and the development of effective post-harvest services and infrastructure.

FOOD SECURITY

FAO's policy on food security aims to encourage the production of adequate food supplies, to maximize stability in the flow of supplies, and to ensure access on the part of those who need them. In 1994 FAO initiated the Special Programme for Food

Security (SPFS), designed to assist low-income countries with a food deficit to increase food production and productivity as rapidly as possible, primarily through the widespread adoption by farmers of improved production technologies, with emphasis on areas of high potential. FAO was actively involved in the formulation of the Plan of Action on food security that was adopted at the World Food Summit in November 1996, and was to be responsible for monitoring and promoting its implementation. In March 1999 FAO signed agreements with the International Fund for Agricultural Development (IFAD) and WFP (see below) that aimed to increase co-operation within the framework of the SPFS. A budget of US $10m. was allocated to the SPFS for the two-year period 1998–99. In early 2002 the SPFS was operational in 67 countries categorized as 'low-income food-deficit', of which 38 were in Africa. The Programme promotes South-South co-operation to improve food security and the exchange of knowledge and experience. By December 2001 25 bilateral co-operation agreements were in force, for example, between Pakistan and Swaziland and Viet Nam and Benin.

FAO's Global Information and Early Warning System (GIEWS), which become operational in 1975, maintains a database on and monitors the crop and food outlook at global, regional, national and sub-national levels in order to detect emerging food supply difficulties and disasters and to ensure rapid intervention in countries experiencing food supply shortages. It publishes regular reports on the weather conditions and crop prospects in sub-Saharan Africa and in the Sahel region, issues special alerts which describe the situation in countries or subregions experiencing food difficulties, and recommends an appropriate international response. In October 1999 FAO published the first annual *State of Food Insecurity in the World*, based on data compiled by a new Food Insecurity and Vulnerability Information and Mapping Systems programme.

An Inter-Agency Task Force on the UN Response to Long-Term Food Security, Agricultural Development and Related Aspects in the Horn of Africa, appointed by the UN Secretary-General in April 2000, is chaired by the Director-General of FAO.

FAO INVESTMENT CENTRE

The Investment Centre was established in 1964 to help countries to prepare viable investment projects that will attract external financing. The Centre focuses its evaluation of projects on two fundamental concerns: the promotion of sustainable activities for land management, forestry development and environmental protection, and the alleviation of rural poverty. In 1998–99 76 projects were approved, representing a total investment of some US $4,670m.

EMERGENCY RELIEF

FAO works to rehabilitate agricultural production following natural and man-made disasters by providing emergency seed, tools, and technical and other assistance. Jointly with the United Nations, FAO is responsible for the World Food Programme (WFP, q.v.), which provides emergency food supplies and food aid in support of development projects. In 2000 FAO's Special Relief Operations Service approved 104 projects in 41 countries.

INFORMATION

FAO collects, analyses, interprets and disseminates information through various media, including an extensive internet site. It issues regular statistical reports, commodity studies, and technical manuals in local languages (see list of publications below). Other materials produced by the FAO include information booklets, reference papers, reports of meetings, training manuals and audiovisuals.

FAO's internet-based interactive World Agricultural Information Centre (WAICENT) offers access to agricultural publications, technical documentation, codes of conduct, data, statistics and multimedia resources. FAO compiles and co-ordinates an extensive range of international databases on agriculture, fisheries, forestry, food and statistics, the most important of these being AGRIS (the International Information System for the Agricultural Sciences and Technology) and CARIS (the Current Agricultural Research Information System). Statistical databases include the GLOBEFISH databank and electronic library, FISHDAB (the Fisheries Statistical Database), FORIS (Forest Resources Information System), and GIS (the Geographic Information System). In addition, FAOSTAT (formerly AGROSTAT) provides access to updated figures in six agriculture-related topics.

FAO Councils and Commissions

(Based at the Rome headquarters unless otherwise indicated.)

African Commission on Agricultural Statistics: c/o FAO Regional Office for Africa, POB 1628, Accra, Ghana: f. 1961 to advise member countries on the development and standardization of food and agricultural statistics; 37 member states.

African Forestry and Wildlife Commission: f. 1959 to advise on the formulation of forest policy and to review and co-ordinate its implementation on a regional level; to exchange information and advise on technical problems; 42 member states.

Asia and Pacific Commission on Agricultural Statistics: c/o FAO Regional Office, Maliwan Mansion, Phra Atit Rd, Bangkok 10200, Thailand; f. 1962 to review the state of food and agricultural statistics in the region and to advise member countries on the development and standardization of agricultural statistics; 25 member states.

Asia and Pacific Plant Protection Commission: c/o FAO Regional Office, Maliwan Mansion, Phra Atit Rd, Bangkok 10200, Thailand; f. 1956 (new title 1983) to strengthen international co-operation in plant protection to prevent the introduction and spread of destructive plant diseases and pests; 25 member states.

Asia-Pacific Fishery Commission: c/o FAO Regional Office, Maliwan Mansion, Phra Atit Rd, Bangkok 10200, Thailand; f. 1948 to develop fisheries, encourage and co-ordinate research, disseminate information, recommend projects to governments, propose standards in technique and management measures; 20 member states.

Asia-Pacific Forestry Commission: f. 1949 to advise on the formulation of forest policy, and review and co-ordinate its implementation throughout the region; to exchange information and advise on technical problems; 29 member states.

Caribbean Plant Protection Commission: f. 1967 to preserve the existing plant resources of the area.

Commission on African Animal Trypanosomiasis: f. 1979 to develop and implement programmes to combat this disease; 39 member states.

Commission for Controlling the Desert Locust in the Eastern Region of its Distribution Area in South West Asia: f. 1964 to carry out all possible measures to control plagues of the desert locust in Afghanistan, India, Iran and Pakistan.

Commission for Controlling the Desert Locust in the Near East: c/o FAO Regional Office for the Near East, POB 2223, Cairo, Egypt; f. 1967 to promote national and international research and action with respect to the control of the desert locust in the Near East.

Commission for Controlling the Desert Locust in North-West Africa: f. 1971 to promote research on control of the desert locust in NW Africa.

Commission on Fertilizers: f. 1973 to provide guidance on the effective distribution and use of fertilizers.

Commission for Inland Fisheries of Latin America: f. 1976 to promote, co-ordinate and assist national and regional fishery and limnological surveys and programmes of research and development leading to the rational utilization of inland fishery resources.

Commission on Plant Genetic Resources: f. 1983 to provide advice on programmes dealing with crop improvement through plant genetic resources.

European Commission on Agriculture: f. 1949 to encourage and facilitate action and co-operation in technological agricultural problems among member states and between international organizations concerned with agricultural technology in Europe.

European Commission for the Control of Foot-and-Mouth Disease: f. 1953 to promote national and international action for the control of the disease in Europe and its final eradication.

European Forestry Commission: f. 1947 to advise on the formulation of forest policy and to review and co-ordinate its implementation on a regional level; to exchange information and to make recommendations; 27 member states.

European Inland Fisheries Advisory Commission: f. 1957 to promote improvements in inland fisheries and to advise member governments and FAO on inland fishery matters.

FAO Regional Commission on Farm Management for Asia and the Far East: c/o FAO Regional Office, Maliwan Mansion, Phra Atit Rd, Bangkok 10200, Thailand; f. 1959 to stimulate and co-ordinate farm management research and extension activities and to serve as a clearing-house for the exchange of information and experience among the member countries in the region.

FAO/WHO Codex Alimentarius Commission: f. 1962 to make proposals for the co-ordination of all international food standards work and to publish a code of international food standards; established Intergovernmental Task Force on Foods Derived from Biotechnology in 1999; 165 member states.

General Fisheries Council for the Mediterranean—GFCM: f. 1952 to develop aquatic resources, to encourage and co-ordinate research in the fishing and allied industries, to assemble and publish information, and to recommend the standardization of equipment, techniques and nomenclature.

Indian Ocean Fishery Commission: f. 1967 to promote national programmes, research and development activities, and to examine management problems; 41 member states.

International Poplar Commission: f. 1947 to study scientific, technical, social and economic aspects of poplar and willow cultivation; to promote the exchange of ideas and material between research workers, producers and users; to arrange joint research programmes, congresses, study tours; to make recommendations to the FAO Conference and to National Poplar Commissions.

International Rice Commission: f. 1948 to promote national and international action on production, conservation, distribution and consumption of rice, except matters relating to international trade; 61 member states.

Joint FAO/WHO/OAU Regional Food and Nutrition Commission for Africa: c/o FAO Regional Office for Africa, POB 1628, Accra, Ghana; f. 1962 to provide liaison in matters concerning food and nutrition, and to review food and nutritional problems in Africa; 43 member states.

Latin American and Caribbean Forestry Commission: f. 1948 to advise on formulation of forest policy and review and co-ordinate its implementation throughout the region; to exchange information and advise on technical problems; 31 member states.

Near East Forestry Commission: f. 1953 to advise on formulation of forest policy and review and co-ordinate its implementation throughout the region; to exchange information and advise on technical problems; 20 member states.

Near East Regional Commission on Agriculture: c/o FAO Regional Office, POB 2223, Cairo, Egypt; f. 1983 to conduct periodic reviews of agricultural problems in the region; to promote the formulation and implementation of regional and national policies and programmes for improving production of crops and livestock; to strengthen the management of crops, livestock and supporting services and research; to promote the transfer of technology and regional technical co-operation; and to provide guidance on training and human resources development.

North American Forestry Commission: f. 1959 to advise on the formulation and co-ordination of national forest policies in Canada, Mexico and the USA; to exchange information and to advise on technical problems; three member states.

Regional Animal Production and Health Commission for Asia and the Pacific: c/o FAO Regional Office, Maliwan Mansion, Phra Atit Rd, Bangkok 10200, Thailand; f. 1973 to promote livestock development in general, and national and international research and action with respect to animal health and husbandry problems in the region; 14 member states.

Regional Commission on Land and Water Use in the Near East: f. 1967 to review the current situation with regard to land and water use in the region; to identify the main problems concerning the development of land and water resources which require research and study and to consider other related matters.

Regional Fisheries Advisory Commission for the South West Atlantic: f. 1961 to advise FAO on fisheries in the South West Atlantic area, to advise member countries (Argentina, Brazil and Uruguay) on the administration and rational exploitation of marine and inland resources; to assist in the collection and dissemination of data, in training, and to promote liaison and co-operation.

Western Central Atlantic Fishery Commission: f. 1973 to assist international co-operation for the conservation, development and utilization of the living resources, especially shrimps, of the Western Central Atlantic.

Finance

FAO's Regular Programme, which is financed by contributions from member governments, covers the cost of FAO's Secretariat, its Technical Co-operation Programme (TCP) and part of the cost of several special action programmes. The proposed budget for the two years 2002–2003 totalled US $652m. Much of FAO's technical assistance programme is funded from extra-budgetary sources. The single largest contributor is the United Nations Development Programme (UNDP), which in 1999 accounted for $26m., or 8.7% of field project expenditures. More important are the trust funds that come mainly from donor countries and international financing institutions. They totalled $228m., or 76.5% of field project expenditures in 1999. FAO's contribution under the TCP (FAO's regular budgetary funds for the Field Programme) was $39m., or 13% of field project expenditures, while the Organization's contribution under the Special Programme for Food Security was $5m., or some 1.7% of the total $298m.

Publications

Animal Health Yearbook.

Commodity Review and Outlook (annually).

Environment and Energy Bulletin.

Ethical Issues in Food and Agriculture.

Fertilizer Yearbook.

Food Crops and Shortages (6 a year).

Food Outlook (5 a year).

Forest Resources Assessment.

Plant Protection Bulletin (quarterly).

Production Yearbook.

Quarterly Bulletin of Statistics.

The State of Food and Agriculture (annually).

The State of Food Insecurity in the World (annually).

The State of World Fisheries and Aquaculture (every two years).

The State of the World's Forests (every 2 years).

Trade Yearbook.

Unasylva (quarterly).

Yearbook of Fishery Statistics.

Yearbook of Forest Products.

World Animal Review (quarterly).

World Watch List for Domestic Animal Diversity.

Commodity reviews; studies; manuals.

International Atomic Energy Agency—IAEA

Address: POB 100, Wagramerstrasse 5, 1400 Vienna, Austria.
Telephone: (1) 26000; **fax:** (1) 26007; **e-mail:** official.mail@iaea.org; **internet:** www.iaea.org/worldatom.

The International Atomic Energy Agency (IAEA) is an intergovernmental organization, established in 1957 in accordance with a decision of the General Assembly of the United Nations. Although it is autonomous, the IAEA is administratively a member of the United Nations, and reports on its activities once a year to the UN General Assembly. Its main objectives are to enlarge the contribution of atomic energy to peace, health and prosperity throughout the world and to ensure, so far as it is able, that assistance provided by it or at its request or under its supervision or control is not used in such a way as to further any military purpose.

MEMBERS

133 members: see Table on pp. 211–213.

Organization

(March 2002)

GENERAL CONFERENCE

The Conference, comprising representatives of all member states, convenes each year for general debate on the Agency's policy, budget and programme. It elects members to the Board of Governors, and approves the appointment of the Director-General; it admits new member states.

BOARD OF GOVERNORS

The Board of Governors consists of 35 member states: 22 elected by the General Conference for two-year periods and 13 designated by the Board from among member states which are advanced in nuclear technology. It is the principal policy-making body of the Agency and is responsible to the General Conference. Under its own authority, the Board approves all safeguards agreements, important projects and safety standards. In 1999 the General Conference adopted a resolution on expanding the Board's membership to 43, to include 18 states designated as the most advanced in nuclear technology. The resolution required ratification by two-thirds of member states to come into effect.

SECRETARIAT

The Secretariat, comprising about 2,200 staff, is headed by the Director-General, who is assisted by six Deputy Directors-General. The Secretariat is divided into six departments: Technical Co-operation; Nuclear Energy; Nuclear Safety; Nuclear Sciences and Applications; Safeguards; Management. A Standing Advisory Group on Safeguards Implementation advises the Director-General on technical aspects of safeguards.

Director-General: Dr MOHAMMAD EL-BARADEI (Egypt).

Activities

The IAEA's functions can be divided into two main categories: technical co-operation (assisting research on and practical application of atomic energy for peaceful uses); and safeguards (ensuring that special fissionable and other materials, services, equipment and information made available by the Agency or at its request or under its supervision are not used for any military purpose).

TECHNICAL CO-OPERATION AND TRAINING

The IAEA provides assistance in the form of experts, training and equipment to technical co-operation projects and applications world-wide, with an emphasis on radiation protection and safety-related activities. Training is provided to scientists, and experts and lecturers are assigned to provide specialized help on specific nuclear applications.

FOOD AND AGRICULTURE

In co-operation with FAO (q.v.), the Agency conducts programmes of applied research on the use of radiation and isotopes in fields including: efficiency in the use of water and fertilizers; improvement of food crops by induced mutations; eradication or control of destructive insects by the introduction of sterilized insects (radiation-based Sterile Insect Technique); improvement of livestock nutrition and health; studies on improving efficacy and reducing residues of pesticides, and increasing utilization of agricultural wastes; and food preservation by irradiation. The programmes are implemented by the Joint FAO/IAEA Division of Nuclear Techniques in Food and Agriculture and by the FAO/IAEA Agriculture and Biotechnology Laboratory, based at IAEA's laboratory complex in Seibersdorf, Austria. A new Training and Reference Centre for Food and Pesticide Control opened at Seibersdorf in mid-1999. The Centre was to support the implementation of national legislation and trade agreements ensuring the quality and safety of food products in international trade.

LIFE SCIENCES

In co-operation with the World Health Organization (WHO, q.v.), IAEA promotes the use of nuclear techniques in medicine, biology and health-related environmental research, provides training, and conducts research on techniques for improving the accuracy of radiation dosimetry.

In 2001 the IAEA/WHO Network of Secondary Standard Dosimetry Laboratories (SSDLs) comprised 80 laboratories in 62 member states. The Agency's Dosimetry Laboratory in Seibersdorf performs dose inter-comparisons for both SSDLs and radiotherapy centres. The IAEA undertakes maintenance plans for nuclear laboratories; national programmes of quality control for nuclear medicine instruments; quality control of radioimmunoassay techniques; radiation sterilization of medical supplies; and improvement of cancer therapy.

PHYSICAL AND CHEMICAL SCIENCES

The Agency's programme in physical sciences includes industrial applications of isotopes and radiation technology; application of nuclear techniques to mineral exploration and exploitation; radiopharmaceuticals; and hydrology, involving the use of isotope techniques for assessment of water resources. Nuclear data services are provided, and training is given for nuclear scientists from developing countries. The Physics, Chemistry and Instrumentation Laboratory at Seibersdorf supports the Agency's research in human health, industry, water resources and environment.

NUCLEAR POWER

At the end of 2000 there were 438 nuclear power plants in operation throughout the world, providing about 16% of total electrical energy generated during the year. There were also 31 reactors under construction. The Agency helps developing member states to introduce nuclear-powered electricity-generating plants through assistance with planning, feasibility studies, surveys of manpower and infrastructure, and safety measures. It publishes books on numerous aspects of nuclear power, and provides training courses on safety in nuclear power plants and other topics. An energy data bank collects and disseminates information on nuclear technology, and a power-reactor information system monitors the technical performance of nuclear power plants. There is increasing interest in the use of nuclear reactors for seawater desalination and radiation hydrology techniques to provide potable water. In July 1992 the EC, Japan, Russia and the USA signed an agreement to co-operate in the engineering design of an International Thermonuclear Experimental Reactor (ITER). The project aimed to demonstrate the scientific and technological feasibility of fusion energy, with the aim of providing a source of clean, abundant energy in the 21st century. An Extension Agreement, signed in 1998, provided for the continuation of the project. In November 2000 the International Project on Innovative Nuclear Reactors and Fuel Cycles (INPRO) was inaugurated. INPRO aimed to promote nuclear energy as a means of meeting future sustainable energy requirements and to facilitate the exchange of information by member states to advance innovations in nuclear technology.

RADIOACTIVE WASTE MANAGEMENT

The Agency provides practical help to member states in the management of radioactive waste. The Waste Management Advisory Programme (WAMAP) was established in 1987, and undertakes advisory missions in member states. A code of practice to prevent the illegal dumping of radioactive waste was drafted in 1989, and another on the international trans-boundary movement of waste was drafted in 1990. A ban on the dumping of radioactive waste at sea came into effect in February 1994, under the Convention on the Prevention of Marine Pollution by Dumping of Wastes and Other Matters (see IMO, p. 169). The IAEA was to determine radioactive levels, for purposes of the Convention, and provide assistance to countries for the safe disposal of radioactive wastes.

In September 1997 IAEA adopted a Joint Convention on the Safety of Spent Fuel Management and on the Safety of Radioactive Waste Management. The first internationally-binding legal device to address such issues, the Convention was to ensure the safe storage and disposal of nuclear and radioactive waste, during both the construction and operation of a nuclear power plant, as well as following its closure. The Convention entered into force in June 2001, and had been ratified by 27 parties at February 2002.

NUCLEAR SAFETY

The IAEA's nuclear safety programme encourages international co-operation in the exchange of information, promoting implementation of its safety standards and providing advisory safety services. It includes the IAEA International Nuclear Event Scale; the Incident Reporting System; an emergency preparedness programme (which maintains an Emergency Response Centre); operational safety review teams; the 15-member International Nuclear Safety Advisory Group (INSAG); the Radiation Protection Advisory Team; and a safety research co-ordination programme. The safety review teams provide member states with advice on achieving and maintaining a high level of safety in the operation of nuclear power plants, while research programmes establish risk criteria for the nuclear fuel cycle and identify cost-effective means to reduce risks in energy systems. At that time 53 member states had agreed to report all nuclear events, incidents and accidents according to the International Nuclear Event Scale. In May the Director-General initiated a review of the Agency's nuclear strategy, proposing the development of national safety profiles, more active promotion of safety services and improved co-operation at governmental and non-governmental levels.

The revised edition of the Basic Safety Standards for Radiation Protection (IAEA Safety Series No. 9) was approved in 1994. The Nuclear Safety Standards programme, initiated in 1974 with five codes of practice and more than 60 safety guides, was revised in 1987 and again in 1995.

During 2000 the IAEA's Technical Co-operation Programme organized more than 100 educational and training courses in the field of nuclear safety and radiation protection.

Following a serious accident at the Chornobyl (Chernobyl) nuclear power plant in Ukraine (then part of the USSR) in April 1986, two conventions were formulated by the IAEA and entered into force in October. The first, the Convention on Early Notification of a Nuclear Accident, commits parties to provide information about nuclear accidents with possible trans-boundary effects at the earliest opportunity (it had 87 parties by February 2002); and the second commits parties to endeavour to provide assistance in the event of a nuclear accident or radiological emergency (this had 83 parties by February 2002). During 1990 the IAEA organized an assessment of the consequences of the Chernobyl accident, undertaken by an international team of experts, who reported to an international conference on the effects of the accident, convened at the IAEA headquarters in Vienna in May 1991. In February 1993 INSAG published an updated report on the Chernobyl incident, which emphasized the role of design factors in the accident, and the need to implement safety measures in the RBMK-type reactor. In March 1994 an IAEA expert mission visited Chernobyl and reported continuing serious deficiencies in safety at the defunct reactor and the units remaining in operation. An international conference reviewing the radiological consequences of the accident, 10 years after the event, was held in April 1996, co-sponsored by the IAEA, WHO and the European Commission. The last of the Chernobyl plant's three operating units was officially closed in December 2000. The IAEA was to offer a wide range of assistance during Chernobyl's decommissioning period, the first stage of which was expected to have a duration of five years.

In September 1999 the IAEA activated its Emergency Response Centre, following a serious incident at a fuel conversion facility in Tokaimura, Japan. The Centre was used to process information from the Japanese authorities and to ensure accurate reporting of the event. In October a three-member IAEA team of experts visited the site to undertake a preliminary investigation into the causes and consequences of the accident.

An International Convention on Nuclear Safety was adopted at an IAEA conference in June 1994. The Convention applies to land-based civil nuclear power plants: adherents commit themselves to fundamental principles of safety, and maintain legislative frameworks governing nuclear safety. The Convention entered into force in October 1996. The first Review Meeting of Contracting Parties to the Convention was held in April 1999. By February 2002 53 states had ratified the Convention.

In September 1997 more than 80 member states adopted a protocol to revise the 1963 Vienna Convention on Civil Liability for Nuclear Damage, fixing the minimum limit of liability for the operator of a nuclear reactor at 300m. Special Drawing Rights (SDRs, the accounting units of the IMF) in the event of an accident. The amended protocol also extended the length of time during which claims may be brought for loss of life or injury. The amended protocol had been signed by 15 countries and ratified by four at February 2002. A Convention on Supplementary Compensation for Nuclear Damage established a further compensatory fund to provide for the payment of damages following an accident; contributions to the Fund were to be calculated on the basis of the nuclear capacity of each member state. The Convention had 13 signatories and three contracting states by February 2002.

In July 1996 the IAEA co-ordinated a study on the radiological situation at the Mururoa and Fangatauta atolls, following the French nuclear test programmes in the South Pacific. Results published in May 1998 concluded there was no radiological health risk and that neither remedial action nor continued environmental monitoring was necessary.

The IAEA is developing a training course on measurement methods and risk analysis relating to the presence of depleted uranium (which can be used in ammunition) in post-conflict areas. In November 2000 IAEA specialists participated in a fact-finding mission organized by UNEP in Kosovo and Metohija, which aimed to assess the environmental and health consequences of the use of depleted uranium in ammunition by NATO during its aerial offensive against the Federal Republic of Yugoslavia in 1999. (A report on the situation was published by UNEP in March 2001.)

In May 2001 IAEA convened an international conference to address the protection of nuclear material and radioactive sources from illegal trafficking. In September, in view of the perpetration of major terrorist attacks against targets in the USA during that month, the IAEA General Conference addressed the potential for nuclear-related terrorism. It adopted a resolution that emphasized the importance of the physical protection of nuclear material in preventing its illicit use or the sabotage of nuclear facilities and nuclear materials. Three main potential threats were identified: the acquisition by a terrorist group of a nuclear weapon; acquisition of nuclear material to construct a nuclear weapon or cause a radiological hazard; and violent acts against nuclear facilities to cause a radiological hazard. The Board of Governors was subsequently considering plans to expand the Agency's programmes for nuclear security, including strengthening border monitoring and increasing the Emergency Response Centre's capacity to react in the event of a nuclear-related terrorist attack. It was estimated that the Agency's upgraded nuclear security activities would require significant additional annual funding. An IAEA special session on nuclear terrorism was held in November.

DISSEMINATION OF INFORMATION

The International Nuclear Information System (INIS), which was established in 1970, provides a computerized indexing and abstracting service. Information on the peaceful uses of atomic energy is collected by member states and international organizations and sent to the IAEA for processing and dissemination (see list of publications below). The IAEA also co-operates with FAO in an information system for agriculture (AGRIS) and with the World Federation of Nuclear Medicine and Biology, and the non-profit Cochrane Collaboration, in maintaining an electronic database of best practice in nuclear medicine. The IAEA Nuclear Data Section provides cost-free data centre services and co-operates with other national and regional nuclear and atomic data centres in the systematic world-wide collection, compilation, dissemination and exchange of nuclear reaction data, nuclear structure and decay data, and atomic and molecular data for fusion.

SAFEGUARDS

The Treaty on the Non-Proliferation of Nuclear Weapons (known also as the Non-Proliferation Treaty or NPT), which entered into force in 1970, requires each 'non-nuclear-weapon state' (one which had not manufactured and exploded a nuclear weapon or other nuclear explosive device prior to 1 January 1967) which is a party to the Treaty to conclude a safeguards agreement with the IAEA. Under such an agreement, the state undertakes to accept IAEA safeguards on all nuclear material in all its peaceful nuclear activities for the purpose of verifying that such material is not diverted to nuclear weapons or other nuclear explosive devices. In May 1995 the Review and Extension Conference of parties to the NPT agreed to extend the NPT indefinitely, and reaffirmed support for the IAEA's role in verification and the transfer of peaceful nuclear technologies. At the next review conference, held in April/May 2000, the five 'nuclear-weapon states'— the People's Republic of China, France, Russia, the United Kingdom and the USA—issued a joint statement pledging their commitment to the ultimate goal of complete nuclear disarmament under effective international controls. By February 2002 182 non-nuclear-weapon states and the five nuclear-weapon states had ratified and acceded to the Treaty, but a number of non-nuclear-weapon states had not complied, within the prescribed time-limit, with their obligations under the Treaty regarding the conclusion of the relevant safeguards agreement with the Agency.

The five nuclear-weapon states have concluded safeguards agreements with the Agency that permit the application of IAEA safeguards to all their nuclear activities, excluding those with 'direct national significance'. A Comprehensive Nuclear Test Ban Treaty (CTBT) was opened for signature in September 1996, having been adopted by the UN General Assembly. The Treaty was to enter into international law upon ratification by all 44 nations with known nuclear capabilities. A separate verification organization was to be established, based in Vienna. A Preparatory Commission for the treaty organization became operational in 1997. By March 2002 165 countries had signed the CTBT and 90 had ratified it, including 31 of the 44 states with nuclear capabilities. However, the US Senate rejected ratification of the CTBT in October 1999.

The IAEA administers full applications of safeguards in relation to a number of regional nuclear weapons treaties. By December 2001 31 of the 32 states party to the Treaty for the prohibition of Nuclear Weapons in Latin America (Tlatelolco Treaty) had concluded safeguards agreements with the Agency, as had all 11 signatories of the South Pacific Nuclear-Free Zone Treaty (Rarotonga Treaty). In late 1998 IAEA safeguards agreements were in force with seven of the nine states party to the Treaty in the South-East Asia Nuclear-Weapon Free Zone (Treaty of Bangkok). In April 1996 an African Nuclear-Weapon Free Zone Treaty (the Pelindaba Treaty) was signed by 43 states at a ceremony in Cairo, Egypt. The IAEA provided technical and legal advice during the negotiations on the Treaty, which committed countries to renouncing the development, acquisition, testing or stationing of nuclear arms on their territories and prohibited all dumping of imported radioactive waste. At the end of 2000 224 IAEA safeguards agreements were in force with 141 states. Of these, 71 states had declared significant nuclear activities and were under inspection. At the end of the same year there were 1,094 nuclear installations and locations containing nuclear material subject to IAEA safeguards. During 2000 the IAEA established an imagery database of nuclear sites; digital image surveillance systems had been installed in 24 countries by the end of the year. A total of 2,467 inspections were conducted in 2000. Expenditure on the Safeguards Regular Budget for that year was US $70.6m; extrabudgetary programme expenditure amounted to $10.3m.

In April 1992 the Democratic People's Republic of Korea (DPRK) ratified a safeguards agreement with the IAEA. In late 1992 and early 1993, however, the IAEA unsuccessfully requested access to two non-declared sites in the DPRK, where it was suspected that material capable of being used for the manufacture of nuclear weapons was stored. In March 1993 the DPRK announced its intention of withdrawing from the NPT: it suspended its withdrawal in June, but continued to refuse full access to its nuclear facilities for IAEA inspectors. In May 1994 the DPRK began to refuel an experimental nuclear power reactor at Yongbyon, but refused to allow the IAEA to analyse the spent fuel rods in order to ascertain whether plutonium had been obtained from the reactor for possible military use. In June the IAEA Board of Governors halted IAEA technical assistance to the DPRK (except medical assistance) because of continuous violation of the NPT safeguards agreements. In the same month the DPRK withdrew from the IAEA (though not from the NPT); however, it allowed IAEA inspectors to remain at the Yongbyon site to conduct safeguards activites. In October the Governments of the DPRK and the USA concluded an agreement whereby the former agreed to halt construction of two new nuclear reactors, on condition that it received international aid for the construction of two 'light water' reactors (which could not produce materials for the manufacture of nuclear weapons). The DPRK also agreed to allow IAEA inspections of all its nuclear sites, but only after the installation of one of the 'light water' reactors had been completed (entailing a significant time lapse). In November IAEA inspectors visited the DPRK to initiate verification of the suspension of the country's nuclear programme, in accordance with the agreement concluded in the previous month. From 1995 the IAEA pursued technical discussions with the DPRK authorities as part of the Agency's efforts to achieve the full compliance of the DPRK with the IAEA safeguards agreement. By the end of 1999 the canning of spent fuel rods from the Yongbyon nuclear power reactor was completed. However, little overall progress had been achieved, owing to the obstruction of inspectors by the authorities in that country, including their refusal to provide samples for analysis. The IAEA was unable to verify the suspension of the nuclear programme and declared that the DPRK continued to be in non-compliance with its NPT safeguards agreement. In January 2002 the DPRK permitted a low-level inspection of the Yongbyon site by an IAEA technical team. It was envisaged at that time that the new 'light water' reactors would become operational by 2008.

In April 1991 the UN Security Council requested the IAEA to conduct investigations into Iraq's capacity to produce nuclear weapons, following the end of the war between Iraq and the UN-authorized, US-led multinational force. The IAEA was to work closely with a UN Special Commission of experts (UNSCOM, q.v.), established by the Security Council, whose task was to inspect and dismantle Iraq's weapons of mass destruction (including chemical and biological weapons). In July the IAEA declared that Iraq had violated its safeguards agreement with the IAEA by not submitting nuclear material and relevant facilities in its uranium-enrichment programme to the Agency's inspection. This was the first time that a state party to the NPT had been condemned for concealing a programme of this nature. In October the sixth inspection team, composed of UNSCOM and representatives of the IAEA, was reported to have obtained conclusive documentary evidence that Iraq had a programme for developing nuclear weapons. By February 1994 all declared stocks of nuclear-weapons-grade material had been removed from Iraq. Subsequently, the IAEA pursued a programme of long-term surveillance of nuclear activity in Iraq, under a mandate issued by the UN Security Council. In September 1996 Iraq submitted to the IAEA a 'full, final and complete' declaration of its nuclear activities. However, in September–October 1997 the IAEA recommended that Iraq disclose further equipment, materials and information relating to its nuclear programme. In April 1998 IAEA technical experts were part of a special group that entered eight presidential sites in Iraq to collect baseline data, in accordance with a Memorandum of Understanding concluded between the UN Secretary-General and the Iraqi authorities in February. The accord aimed to ensure full Iraqi co-operation with UNSCOM and IAEA personnel. In August, however, Iraq suspended co-operation with UN inspectors, which prevented IAEA from implementing its programme of ongoing monitoring and verification (OMV) activities. Iraq's action was condemned by the IAEA General Conference in September. In October IAEA reported that while there was no evidence of Iraq having produced nuclear weapons or having retained or obtained a capability for the production of nuclear weapons, the Agency was unable to guarantee that all items had been found. All IAEA inspectors were temporarily relocated from Iraq to Bahrain in November, in accordance with a decision to withdraw UNSCOM personnel owing to Iraq's failure to agree to resume co-operation. In March 2000 UNSCOM was replaced by a new arms inspection body, the UN Monitoring, Verification and Inspection Commission (UNMOVIC). Although the IAEA carried out inventory verifications of nuclear material in Iraq in January 2000, January 2001 and January 2002, pursuant to Iraq's NTP safeguards agreement, full inspection activities in conjunction with UNMOVIC remained suspended in early 2002. In early March an Iraqi government delegation met the UN Secretary-General and the head of UNMOVIC; no agreement was reached, however, on the resumption of inspection activities.

In late 1997 the IAEA began inspections in the USA to verify the conversion for peaceful uses of nuclear material released from the military sector. In 1998 the United Kingdom announced that substantial quantities of nuclear material previously in its military programme would become available for verification under its voluntary offer safeguards agreement.

In June 1995 the Board of Governors approved measures to strengthen the safeguards system, including allowing inspection teams greater access to suspected nuclear sites and to information on nuclear activities in member states, reducing the notice time for inspections by removing visa requirements for inspectors and using environmental monitoring (i.e. soil, water and air samples) to test for signs of radioactivity. In April 1996 the IAEA initiated a programme to prevent and combat illicit trafficking of nuclear weapons, and in May 1998 the IAEA and the World Customs Organization (q.v.) signed a Memorandum of Understanding to enhance co-operation in the prevention of illicit nuclear trafficking. In May 1997 the Board of Governors adopted a model additional protocol approving measures to strengthen safeguards further, in order to ensure the compliance of non-nuclear-weapon states with IAEA commitments. The new protocol compelled member states to provide inspection teams with improved access to information concerning existing and planned nuclear activities, and to allow access to locations other than known nuclear sites within that country's territory. By March 2001 18 states had ratified additional protocols to their safeguards agreements.

IAEA's Safeguards Analytical Laboratory analyses nuclear fuel-cycle samples collected by IAEA safeguards inspectors. The Agency's Marine Environment Laboratory, in Monaco, studies radionuclides and other ocean pollutants.

NUCLEAR FUEL CYCLE

The Agency promotes the exchange of information between member states on technical, safety, environmental, and economic aspects of nuclear fuel cycle technology, including uranium prospecting and the treatment and disposal of radioactive waste; it provides assistance to member states in the planning, implementation and operation of nuclear fuel cycle facilities and assists in the development of advanced nuclear fuel cycle technology. Every two years, in collaboration with the OECD, the Agency prepares estimates of world uranium resources, demand and production.

Finance

The Agency is financed by regular and voluntary contributions from member states. Expenditure approved under the regular budget for 2002 amounted to some US $245m., and the target for voluntary contributions to finance the IAEA technical assistance and co-operation programme in that year was $73m.

Publications

Annual Report.

IAEA Bulletin (quarterly).

IAEA Newsbriefs (every 2 months).

IAEA Yearbook.

INIS Atomindex (bibliography, 2 a month).

INIS Reference Series.

INSAG Series.

Legal Series.

Meetings on Atomic Energy (quarterly).

The Nuclear Fuel Cycle Information System: A Directory of Nuclear Fuel Cycle Facilities.

Nuclear Fusion (monthly).

Nuclear Safety Review (annually).

Panel Proceedings Series.

Publications Catalogue (annually).

Safety Series.

Technical Directories.

Technical Reports Series.

Treaty on the Non-Proliferation of Nuclear Weapons

(Signed 1 July 1968)

The States concluding this Treaty, hereinafter referred to as the 'Parties to the Treaty',

Considering the devastation that would be visited upon all mankind by a nuclear war and the consequent need to make every effort to avert the danger of such a war and to take measures to safeguard the security of peoples,

Believing that the proliferation of nuclear weapons would seriously enhance the danger of nuclear war,

In conformity with resolutions of the United Nations General Assembly calling for the conclusion of an agreement on the prevention of wider dissemination of nuclear weapons,

Undertaking to co-operate in facilitating the application of International Atomic Energy Agency safeguards on peaceful nuclear activities,

Expressing their support for research, development and other efforts to further the application, within the framework of the International Atomic Energy Agency safeguards system, of the principle of safeguarding effectively the flow of source and special fissionable materials by use of instruments and other techniques at certain strategic points,

Affirming the principle that the benefits of peaceful applications of nuclear technology, including any technological by-products which may be derived by nuclear-weapon States from the development of nuclear explosive devices, should be available for peaceful purposes to all Parties of the Treaty, whether nuclear-weapon or non-nuclear-weapon States,

Convinced that, in furtherance of this principle, all Parties to the Treaty are entitled to participate in the fullest possible exchange of scientific information for, and to contribute alone or in co-operation with other States to, the further development of the applications of atomic energy for peaceful purposes,

Declaring their intention to achieve at the earliest possible date the cessation of the nuclear arms race and to undertake effective measures in the direction of nuclear disarmament,

Urging the co-operation of all States in the attainment of this objective,

Recalling the determination expressed by the Parties to the 1963 Treaty banning nuclear weapon tests in the atmosphere, in outer space and under water in its Preamble to seek to achieve the discontinuance of all test explosions of nuclear weapons for all time and to continue negotiations to this end,

Desiring to further the easing of international tension and the strengthening of trust between States in order to facilitate the cessation of the manufacture of nuclear weapons, the liquidation of all their existing stockpiles, and the elimination from national arsenals of nuclear weapons and the means of their delivery pursuant to a Treaty on general and complete disarmament under strict and effective international control,

Recalling that, in accordance with the Charter of the United Nations, States must refrain in their international relations from the threat or use of force against the territorial integrity or political independence of any State, or in any other manner inconsistent with the Purposes of the United Nations, and that the establishment and maintenance of international peace and security are to be promoted with the least diversion for armaments of the world's human and economic resources,

Have agreed as follows:

Article I

Each nuclear-weapon State Party to the Treaty undertakes not to transfer to any recipient whatsoever nuclear weapons or other nuclear explosive devices or control over such weapons or explosive devices directly, or indirectly; and not in any way to assist, encourage, or induce any non-nuclear-weapon State to manufacture or otherwise acquire nuclear weapons or other nuclear explosive devices, or control over such weapons or explosive devices.

Article II

Each non-nuclear-weapon State Party to the Treaty undertakes not to receive the transfer from any transferor whatsoever of nuclear weapons or other nuclear explosive devices or of control over such weapons or explosive devices directly, or indirectly; not to manufacture or otherwise acquire nuclear weapons or other nuclear explosive devices; and not to seek or receive any assistance in the manufacture of nuclear weapons or other nuclear explosive devices.

Article III

1. Each non-nuclear-weapon State Party to the Treaty undertakes to accept safeguards, as set forth in an agreement to be negotiated and concluded with the International Atomic Energy Agency in accordance with the Statute of the International Atomic Energy Agency and the Agency's safeguards system, for the exclusive purpose of verification of the fulfilment of its obligations assumed under this Treaty with a view to preventing diversion of nuclear energy from peaceful uses to nuclear weapons or other nuclear explosive devices. Procedures for the safeguards required by this article shall be followed with respect to source or special fissionable material whether it is being produced, processed or used in any principal nuclear facility or is outside any such facility. The safeguards required by this article shall be applied to all source or special fissionable material in all peaceful nuclear activities within the territory of such State, under its jurisdiction, or carried out under its control anywhere.

2. Each State Party to the Treaty undertakes not to provide: (a) source or special fissionable material, or (b) equipment or material especially designed or prepared for the processing, use or production of special fissionable material, to any non-nuclear-weapon State for peaceful purposes, unless the source or special fissionable material shall be subject to the safeguards required by this article.

3. The safeguards required by this article shall be implemented in a manner designed to comply with article IV of this Treaty, and to avoid hampering the economic or technological development of the Parties or international co-operation in the field of peaceful nuclear activities, including the international exchange of nuclear material and equipment for the processing, use or production of nuclear material for peaceful purposes in accordance with the provisions of this article and the principle of safeguarding set forth in the Preamble of the Treaty.

4. Non-nuclear-weapon States Party to the Treaty shall conclude agreements with the International Atomic Energy Agency to meet the requirements of this article either individually or together with other States in accordance with the Statute of the International Atomic Energy Agency. Negotiation of such agreements shall commence within 180 days from the original entry into force of this Treaty. For States depositing their instruments of ratification or accession after the 180-day period, negotiation of such agreements shall commence not later than the date of such deposit. Such agreements shall enter into force not later than eighteen months after the date of initiation of negotiations.

Article IV

1. Nothing in this Treaty shall be interpreted as affecting the inalienable right of all the Parties to the Treaty to develop research, production and use of nuclear energy for peaceful purposes without discrimination and in conformity with articles I and II of this Treaty.

2. All the Parties to the Treaty undertake to facilitate, and have the right to participate in, the fullest possible exchange of equipment, materials and scientific and technological information for the peaceful uses of nuclear energy. Parties to the Treaty in a position to do so shall also co-operate in contributing alone or together with other States or international organizations to the further development of the applications of nuclear energy for peaceful purposes, especially in the territories of non-nuclear-weapon States Party to the Treaty, with due consideration for the needs of the developing areas of the world.

Article V

Each party to the Treaty undertakes to take appropriate measures to ensure that, in accordance with this Treaty, under appropriate international observation and through appropriate international procedures, potential benefits from any peaceful applications of nuclear explosions will be made available to non-nuclear-weapon States Party to the Treaty on a nondiscriminatory basis and that the charge to such Parties for the explosive devices used will be as low as possible and exclude any charge for research and development. Non-nuclear-weapon States Party to the Treaty shall be able to obtain such benefits, pursuant to a special international agreement or agreements, through an appropriate international body with adequate representation of non-nuclear-weapon States. Negotiations on this subject shall commence as soon as possible after the Treaty enters into force. Non-nuclear-weapon States Party to the Treaty so desiring may also obtain such benefits pursuant to bilateral agreements.

Article VI

Each of the Parties to the Treaty undertakes to pursue negotiations in good faith on effective measures relating to cessation of the nuclear arms race at an early date and to nuclear disarmament, and on a Treaty on general and complete disarmament under strict and effective international control.

Article VII

Nothing in this Treaty affects the right of any group of States to conclude regional treaties in order to assure the total absence of nuclear weapons in their respective territories.

Article VIII

1. Any Party to the Treaty may propose amendments to this Treaty. The text of any proposed amendment shall be submitted to the Depositary Governments which shall circulate it to all Parties to the Treaty. Thereupon, if requested to do so by one-third or more of the Parties to the Treaty, the Depositary Governments shall convene a conference, to which they shall invite all the Parties to the Treaty, to consider such an amendment.

2. Any amendment to this Treaty must be approved by a majority of the votes of all the Parties to the Treaty, including the votes of all nuclear-weapon States Party to the Treaty and all other Parties which, on the date the amendment is circulated, are members of the Board of Governors of the International Atomic Energy Agency. The amendment shall enter into force for each Party that deposits its instrument of ratification of the amendment upon the deposit of such instruments of ratification by a majority of all the Parties, including the instruments of ratification of all nuclear-weapon States Party to the Treaty and all other Parties which, on the date the amendment is circulated, are members of the Board of Governors of the International Atomic Energy Agency. Thereafter, it shall enter into force for any other Party upon the deposit of its instrument of ratification of the amendment.

3. Five years after the entry into force of this Treaty, a conference of Parties to the Treaty shall be held in Geneva, Switzerland, in order to review the operation of this Treaty with a view to assuring that the purposes of the Preamble and the provisions of the Treaty are being realized. At intervals of five years thereafter, a majority of the Parties to the Treaty may obtain, by submitting a proposal to this effect to the Depositary Governments, the convening of further conferences with the same objective of reviewing the operation of the Treaty.

Article IX

1. This Treaty shall be open to all States for signature. Any State which does not sign the Treaty before its entry into force in accordance with paragraph 3 of this article may accede to it at any time.

2. This Treaty shall be subject to ratification by signatory States. Instruments of ratification and instruments of accession shall be deposited with the Governments of the United States of America, the United Kingdom of Great Britain and Northern Ireland and the Union of Soviet Socialist Republics, which are hereby designated the Depositary Governments.

3. This Treaty shall enter into force after its ratification by the States, the Governments of which are designated Depositaries of the Treaty, and forty other States signatory to this Treaty and the deposit of their instruments of ratification. For the purposes of this Treaty, a nuclear-weapon State is one which has manufactured and exploded a nuclear weapon or other nuclear explosive device prior to January 1 1967.
4. For States whose instruments of ratification or accession are deposited subsequent to the entry into force of this Treaty, it shall enter into force on the date of the deposit of their instruments of ratification or accession.
5. The Depositary Governments shall promptly inform all signatory and acceding States of the date of each signature, the date of deposit of each instrument of ratification or of accession, the date of the entry into force of this Treaty, and the date of receipt of any requests for convening a conference or other notices.
6. This Treaty shall be registered by the Depositary Governments pursuant to article 102 of the Charter of the United Nations.

Article X

1. Each Party shall in exercising its national sovereignty have the right to withdraw from the Treaty if it decides that extraordinary events, related to the subject matter of this Treaty, have jeopardized the supreme interests of its country. It shall give notice of such withdrawal to all other Parties to the Treaty and to the United Nations Security Council three months in advance. Such notice shall include a statement of the extraordinary events it regards as having jeopardized its supreme interests.
2. Twenty-five years after the entry into force of the Treaty, a conference shall be convened to decide whether the Treaty shall continue in force indefinitely, or shall be extended for an additional fixed period or periods. The decision shall be taken by a majority of the Parties to the Treaty.

Article XI

This Treaty, the English, Russian, French, Spanish and Chinese texts of which are equally authentic, shall be deposited in the archives of the Depositary Governments. Duly certified copies of this Treaty shall be transmitted by the Depositary Govenments to the Governments of the signatory and acceding States.

In witness whereof the undersigned, duly authorized, have signed this Treaty.

Done in triplicate, at the cities of Washington, London and Moscow, this first day of July one thousand nine hundred sixty-eight.

International Bank for Reconstruction and Development—IBRD (World Bank)

Address: 1818 H St, NW, Washington, DC 20433, USA.
Telephone: (202) 477-1234; **fax:** (202) 477-6391; **e-mail:** pic@worldbank.org; **internet:** www.worldbank.org.

The IBRD was established in December 1945. Initially it was concerned with post-war reconstruction in Europe; since then its aim has been to assist the economic development of member nations by making loans where private capital is not available on reasonable terms to finance productive investments. Loans are made either directly to governments, or to private enterprises with the guarantee of their governments. The World Bank, as it is commonly known, comprises the IBRD and the International Development Association (IDA, q.v.). The affiliated group of institutions, comprising the IBRD, the IDA, the International Finance Corporation (IFC, q.v.), the Multilateral Investment Guarantee Agency (MIGA, q.v.) and the International Centre for Settlement of Investment Disputes (ICSID, see below), is now referred to as the World Bank Group.

MEMBERS

There are 183 members: see Table on pp. 211–213. Only members of the International Monetary Fund (IMF, q.v.) may be considered for membership in the World Bank. Subscriptions to the capital stock of the Bank are based on each member's quota in the IMF, which is designed to reflect the country's relative economic strength. Voting rights are related to shareholdings.

Organization

(March 2002)

Officers and staff of the IBRD serve concurrently as officers and staff in the IDA. The World Bank has offices in New York, Brussels, Paris (for Europe), Frankfurt, London, Geneva and Tokyo, as well as in more than 100 countries. Country Directors are located in some 28 country offices.

BOARD OF GOVERNORS

The Board of Governors consists of one Governor appointed by each member nation. Typically, a Governor is the country's finance minister, central bank governor, or a minister or an official of comparable rank. The Board normally meets once a year.

EXECUTIVE DIRECTORS

With the exception of certain powers specifically reserved to them by the Articles of Agreement, the Governors of the Bank have delegated their powers for the conduct of the general operations of the World Bank to a Board of Executive Directors which performs its duties on a full-time basis at the Bank's headquarters. There are 24 Executive Directors (see table below); each Director selects an Alternate. Five Directors are appointed by the five members having the largest number of shares of capital stock, and the rest are elected by the Governors representing the other members. The President of the Bank is Chairman of the Board.

The Executive Directors fulfil dual responsibilities. First, they represent the interests of their country or groups of countries. Second, they exercise their authority as delegated by the Governors in overseeing the policies of the Bank and evaluating completed projects. Since the Bank operates on the basis of consensus (formal votes are rare), this dual role involves frequent communication and consultations with governments so as to reflect accurately their views in Board discussions.

The Directors consider and decide on Bank policy and on all loan and credit proposals. They are also responsible for presentation to the Board of Governors at its Annual Meetings of an audit of accounts, an administrative budget, the *Annual Report* on the operations and policies of the World Bank, and any other matter that, in their judgement, requires submission to the Board of Governors. Matters may be submitted to the Governors at the Annual Meetings or at any time between Annual Meetings.

PRINCIPAL OFFICERS

The principal officers of the Bank are the President of the Bank, four Managing Directors, two Senior Vice-Presidents and 23 Vice-Presidents.

President and Chairman of Executive Directors: JAMES D. WOLFENSOHN (USA).

Managing Directors: SHENGMAN ZHANG (People's Republic of China), PETER L. WOICKE (Germany), JEFFREY GOLDSTEIN (USA), Dr MAMPHELA RAMPHELE (South Africa).

Vice-President and Corporate Secretary: CHEIKH IBRAHIMA FALL (Senegal).

Activities

FINANCIAL OPERATIONS

IBRD capital is derived from members' subscriptions to capital shares, the calculation of which is based on their quotas in the International Monetary Fund (q.v.). At 30 June 2001 the total subscribed capital of the IBRD was US $189,505m., of which the paid-in portion was $11,476m. (6.1%); the remainder is subject to call if required. Most of the IBRD's lendable funds come from its borrowing, on commercial terms, in world capital markets, and also from its retained earnings and the flow of repayments on its loans. IBRD loans carry a variable interest rate, rather than a rate fixed at the time of borrowing.

IBRD loans usually have a 'grace period' of five years and are repayable over 15 years or fewer. Loans are made to governments, or must be guaranteed by the government concerned, and are normally made for projects likely to offer a commercially viable rate of return. In 1980 the World Bank introduced structural adjustment lending, which (instead of financing specific projects) supports programmes and changes necessary to modify the structure of an economy so that it can restore or maintain its growth and viability in its balance of payments over the medium term.

The IBRD and IDA together made 225 new lending and investment commitments totalling US $17,250.6m. during the year ending 30 June 2001, compared with 223 (amounting to $15,276.2m.) in the previous year. During 2000/01 the IBRD alone approved commitments totalling $10,487.1m. (compared with $10,918.7m. in the previous year), of which $4,806.7m. (46%) was allocated to Latin America and the Caribbean, $2,154.1m. (21%) to Europe and Central Asia, and $2,035.0m. (19%) to South Asia (see table). An additional $104.8m. was committed through Trust Funds for 17 special financing operations for East Timor, Gaza and the West Bank, Kosovo, and the Federal Republic of Yugoslavia. Disbursements by the IBRD in the year ending 30 June 2001 amounted to $11,784m.(For details of IDA operations, see separate chapter on IDA.)

IBRD operations are supported by medium- and long-term borrowings in international capital markets. During the year ending 30 June 2001 the IBRD's net income amounted to US $1,489m.

The World Bank's primary objectives are the achievement of sustainable economic growth and the reduction of poverty in developing countries. In the context of stimulating economic growth the Bank promotes both private-sector development and human resource development and has attempted to respond to the growing demands by developing countries for assistance in these areas. In March 1997 the Board of Executive Directors endorsed a 'Strategic Compact', providing for a programme of reforms, to be implemented over a period of 30 months, to increase the effectiveness of the Bank in achieving its central objective of poverty reduction. The reforms included greater decentralization of decision-making, and investment in front-line operations, enhancing the administration of loans, and improving access to information and co-ordination of Bank activities through a knowledge management system comprising four thematic networks: the Human Development Network; the Environmentally and Socially Sustainable Development Network; the Finance, Private Sector and Infrastructure Development Network; and the Poverty Reduction and Economic Management Network. In July the World Bank initiated a review to assess the economic and social impact of its work in developing countries. In 2000/01 the Bank adopted a new two-year Strategic Framework which emphasized two essential approaches for Bank support: strengthening the investment climate and prospects for sustainable development in a country, and supporting investment in the poor. In September 2001 the Bank announced that it was to join the UN as a full partner in implementing the so-called Millennium Development Goals, and was to make them central to its development agenda. The objectives, which were approved by governments attending a special session of the UN General Assembly in September 2000, included a reduction by 50% in the number of people with an income of less than US $1 a day and those suffering from hunger and lack of safe drinking water by 2015.

The Bank's efforts to reduce poverty include the compilation of country-specific assessments and the formulation of country assistance strategies (CASs) to review and guide the Bank's country programmes. Since August 1998 the Bank has published CASs, with the approval of the government concerned. In 1998/99 the Bank's Executive Directors endorsed a Comprehensive Development Framework (CDF) to effect a new approach to development assistance based on partnerships and country responsibility, with an emphasis on the interdependence of the social, structural, human, governmental, economic and environmental elements of development. The Framework, which aimed to enhance the overall effectiveness of development assistance, was formulated after a series of consultative meetings organized by the Bank and attended by representatives of governments, donor agencies, financial institutions, non-governmental organizations, the private sector and academics.

In December 1999 the Bank introduced a new approach to implement the principles of the CDF, as part of its strategy to enhance the debt relief scheme for heavily indebted poor countries (see below). Applicant countries were requested to formulate a national strategy to reduce poverty, to be presented in the form of a Poverty Reduction Strategy Papers (PRSP). In cases where there might be some delay in issuing a full PRSP, it was permissible for a country to submit a less detailed 'interim' PRSP (I-PRSP) in order to secure the preliminary qualification for debt relief. During 2000/01 32 countries issued full and interim PRSPs for consideration by the Bank and IMF, compared with 12 in the previous year. During that year the Bank introduced a new Poverty Reduction Support Credit to help low-income countries to implement the policy and institutional reforms outlined in their PRSP. The first credits were approved for Uganda and Viet Nam in May and June respectively. It was envisaged that in 2001/02 each CAS presented for an IDA country would be based on a PRSP. In January 2002 a PRSP public review conference, attended by more than 200 representatives of donor agencies, civil society groups, and developing country organizations was held as part of an ongoing review of the scheme by the Bank and the IMF.

In September 1996 the World Bank/IMF Development Committee endorsed a joint initiative to assist heavily indebted poor countries (HIPCs) to reduce their debt burden to a sustainable level, in order to make more resources available for poverty reduction and economic growth. A new Trust Fund was established by the World Bank in November to finance the initiative. The Fund, consisting of an initial allocation of US $500m. from the IBRD surplus and other contributions from multilateral creditors, was to be administered by IDA. Of the 41 HIPCs identified by the Bank, 33 were in sub-Saharan Africa. In April 1997 the World Bank and the IMF announced that Uganda was to be the first beneficiary of the initiative, enabling the Ugandan Government to reduce its external debt by some 20%, or an estimated $338m. In early 1999 the World Bank and IMF initiated a comprehensive review of the HIPC initiative. By April meetings of the Group of Seven industrialized nations (G-7) and of the governing bodies of the Bank and IMF indicated a consensus that the scheme needed to be amended and strengthened, in order to allow more countries to benefit from the initiative, to accelerate the process by which a country may qualify for assistance, and to enhance the effectiveness of debt relief. In June the G-7 and Russia, meeting in Cologne, Germany, agreed to increase contributions to the HIPC Trust Fund and to cancel substantial amounts of outstanding debt, and proposed more flexible terms for eligibility. In September the Bank and IMF reached an agreement on an enhanced HIPC scheme, with further revenue to be generated through the revaluation of a percentage of IMF gold reserves. Under the enhanced initiative it was agreed that, during the initial phase of the process to ensure suitability for debt relief, each applicant country should formulate a PRSP, and should demonstrate prudent financial management in the implementation of the strategy for at least one year, with support from the IDA and IMF. At the pivotal 'decision point' of the process, having thus developed and successfully applied the poverty reduction strategy, applicant countries still deemed to have an unsustainable level of debt were to qualify for interim debt relief from the IMF and IDA, as well as relief on highly concessional terms from other official bilateral creditors and multilateral institutions. During the ensuing 'interim period' countries were required successfully to implement further economic and social development reforms, as a final demonstration of suitability for securing full debt relief at the 'completion point' of the scheme. Data produced at the decision point was to form the base for calculating the final debt relief (in contrast to the original initiative, which based its calculations on projections of a country's debt stock at the completion point). In the majority of cases a sustainable level of debt was targeted at 150% of the net present value (NPV) of the debt in relation to total annual exports (compared with 200%–250% under the original initiative). Other countries

EXECUTIVE DIRECTORS AND THEIR VOTING POWER (30 June 2001)

		IBRD		IDA	
Executive Director	Casting Votes of	Total votes	% of total	Total votes	% of total
Appointed:					
CAROLE BROOKINS*	USA	265,219	16.45	1,865,737	14.46
YUZO HARADA	Japan	127,250	7.89	1,414,996	10.96
HELMUT SCHAFFER	Germany	72,649	4.51	913,474	7.08
PIERRE DUQUESNE*	France	69,647	4.32	561,248	4.35
TOM SCHOLAR†	United Kingdom	69,647	4.32	641,302	4.97
Elected:					
PHILIPPE M. PEETERS (Belgium)	Austria, Belarus‡, Belgium, Czech Republic, Hungary, Kazakhstan, Luxembourg, Slovakia, Slovenia, Turkey	77,669	4.82	580,627	4.50
MOISES PINEDA (Mexico)	Costa Rica, El Salvador, Guatemala, Honduras, Mexico, Nicaragua, Spain, Venezuela‡	72,786	4.51	285,452	2.21
PIETER STEK (Netherlands)	Armenia, Bosnia and Herzegovina, Bulgaria‡, Croatia, Cyprus, Georgia, Israel, the former Yugoslav republic of Macedonia, Moldova, Netherlands, Romania‡, Ukraine‡	72,208	4.48	471,373	3.65
TERRIE O'LEARY (Canada)	Antigua and Barbuda‡, The Bahamas‡, Barbados‡, Belize, Canada, Dominica, Grenada, Guyana, Ireland, Jamaica‡, Saint Christopher and Nevis, Saint Lucia, Saint Vincent and the Grenadines	62,217	3.86	551,237	4.27
JAIME RUIZ (Colombia)	Brazil, Colombia, Dominican Republic, Ecuador, Haiti, Panama, Philippines, Suriname‡, Trinidad and Tobago	58,124	3.61	374,936	2.91
FRANCO PASSACANTANDO (Italy)	Albania, Greece, Italy, Malta‡, Portugal, San Marino‡	55,938	3.47	507,328	3.93
NEIL F. HYDEN (Australia)	Australia, Cambodia, Kiribati, Republic of Korea, Marshall Islands, Federated States of Micronesia, Mongolia, New Zealand, Palau, Papua New Guinea, Samoa, Solomon Islands,Vanuatu	55,800	3.46	386,903	3.00
BALMIKI PRASAD SINGH (India)	Bangladesh, Bhutan, India, Sri Lanka	54,945	3.41	546,804	4.24
AHMED SADOUDI (Algeria)	Algeria, Ghana, Iran, Iraq, Morocco, Pakistan, Tunisia	54,052	3.35	253,710	1.97
FINN JØNCK (Denmark)	Denmark, Estonia‡, Finland, Iceland, Latvia, Lithuania‡, Norway, Sweden	54,039	3.35	637,035	4.94
GIRMAI ABRAHAM (Eritrea)	Angola, Botswana, Burundi, Eritrea, The Gambia, Kenya, Lesotho, Liberia, Malawi, Mozambique, Namibia‡, Nigeria, Seychelles‡, Sierra Leone, South Africa, Sudan, Swaziland, Tanzania, Uganda, Zambia, Zimbabwe	53,962	3.35	475,933	3.69
MATTHIAS MEYER (Switzerland)	Azerbaijan, Kyrgyzstan, Poland, Switzerland, Tajikistan, Turkmenistan‡, Uzbekistan	46,096	2.86	453,949	3.52
ZU GUANGYAO	People's Republic of China	45,049	2.79	247,345	1.92
YAHYA ABDULLAH M. ALYAHYA	Saudi Arabia	45,045	2.79	458,383	3.55
ANDREI BUGROV	Russia	45,045	2.79	35,887	0.28
KHALID M. AL-SAAD (Kuwait)	Bahrain‡, Egypt, Jordan, Kuwait, Lebanon, Libya, Maldives, Oman, Qatar‡, Syria, United Arab Emirates, Yemen	43,984	2.73	283,971	2.20
ABDUL AZIZ M. YAACOB (Malaysia)	Brunei‡, Fiji, Indonesia, Laos, Malaysia, Myanmar, Nepal, Singapore‡, Thailand, Tonga, Viet Nam	41,096	2.55	345,372	2.68
MARIO SOTO-PLATERO (Uruguay)	Argentina, Bolivia, Chile, Paraguay, Peru, Uruguay‡	37,499	2.33	237,131	1.84
BASSARY TOURÉ (Mali)	Benin, Burkina Faso, Cameroon, Cape Verde, Central African Republic, Chad, Comoros, Democratic Republic of the Congo, Republic of the Congo, Côte d'Ivoire, Djibouti, Equatorial Guinea, Gabon, Guinea, Guinea-Bissau, Madagascar, Mali, Mauritania, Mauritius, Niger, Rwanda, São Tomé and Príncipe, Senegal, Togo	32,252	2.00	374,898	2.91

Note: Afghanistan (550 votes in IBRD and 13,557 in IDA), Ethiopia (1,228 votes in IBRD and 23,053 in IDA) and Somalia (802 votes in IBRD and 10,506 in IDA) did not participate in the 2000 regular election of Executive Directors. The Federal Republic of Yugoslavia (1,847 votes in IBRD and 25,109 in IDA) became a member after that election.

* Took office 20 August 2001.

† Took office January 2002.

‡ Member of IBRD only (not IDA).

with a lower debt-to-export ratio were to be eligible for assistance under the scheme, providing that their export earnings were at least 30% of GDP (lowered from 40% under the original initiative) and government revenue at least 15% of GDP (reduced from 20%). At February 2002 four countries (Bolivia, Mozambique, Tanzania and Uganda) had reached completion point under the enhanced HIPC initiative, while 22 countries had reached their decision point (including Côte d'Ivoire, reached under the original scheme). At that time a total of US $24,347m. in NPV terms had been committed, of which the Bank's share was $6,203m.

During 2000/01 the World Bank strengthened its efforts to counter the problem of HIV and AIDS in developing countries. In September 2000 a new Multi-Country HIV/AIDS Programme for Africa (MAP) was launched, in collaboration with UNAIDS and other major donor agencies and non-governmental organizations. Some US $500m. was allocated to the initiative and was used to support efforts in seven countries. In February 2002 the Bank approved an additional $500m. for a second phase of MAP, which was envisaged to assist HIV/AIDS schemes in a further 12 countries, as well as regional activities. During 2000/01 the Bank also approved two operations under an HIV/AIDS initiative for the Caribbean. In November 2001 the Bank appointed its first Global HIV/AIDS Adviser. In addition to providing financial services, the Bank also undertakes analytical and advisory services, and supports learning and capacity-building, in particular through the World Bank Institute (see below), the Staff Exchange Programme and knowledge-sharing initiatives.

TECHNICAL ASSISTANCE

The provision of technical assistance to member countries has become a major component of World Bank activities. The economic and sector work (ESW) undertaken by the Bank is the vehicle for considerable technical assistance. In addition, project loans and credits may include funds earmarked specifically for feasibility studies, resource surveys, management or planning advice, and training.

The Bank serves as an executing agency for projects financed by the UN Development Programme. It also administers projects financed by various trust funds.

Technical assistance (usually reimbursable) is also extended to countries that do not need Bank financial support, e.g. for training and transfer of technology. The Bank encourages the use of local consultants to assist with projects and stimulate institutional capability.

The Project Preparation Facility (PPF) was established in 1975 to provide cash advances to prepare projects that may be financed by the Bank. In December 1994 the PPF's commitment authority was increased from US $220m. to $250m. In 1992 the Bank established an Institutional Development Fund (IDF), which became operational on 1 July; the purpose of the Fund was to provide rapid, small-scale financial assistance, to a maximum value of $500,000, for capacity-building proposals.

In March 1996 a new programme to co-ordinate development efforts in Africa was announced by the UN Secretary-General. The World Bank was to facilitate the mobilization of the estimated US $25,000m. required to achieve the objectives of the Special Initiative over a 10-year period. In addition, the Bank was to provide technical assistance to enable countries to devise economic plans (in particular following a period of civil conflict), agricultural development programmes and a common strategy for African countries to strengthen the management capacities of the public sector.

ECONOMIC RESEARCH AND STUDIES

In the 1990s the World Bank's research, conducted by its own research staff, was increasingly concerned with providing information to reinforce the Bank's expanding advisory role to developing countries and to improve policy in the Bank's borrowing countries. The principal areas of current research focus on issues such as maintaining sustainable growth while protecting the environment and the poorest sectors of society, encouraging the development of the private sector, and reducing and decentralizing government activities.

Consultative Group on International Agricultural Research—CGIAR: founded in 1971 under the sponsorship of the World Bank, FAO and UNDP. (In 1995 UNEP was invited to become the fourth sponsoring member.)The Bank is chairman of the Group (which includes governments, private foundations and multilateral development agencies) and provides its secretariat. The Group was formed to raise financial support for international agricultural research work for improving crops and animal production in the developing countries; it supports 16 research centres. Its work is focused on the following five research areas: increasing productivity; protecting the environment; saving biodiversity; improving policies; and strengthening national research. Its 2000 budget amounted to US $331m. Dir FRANCISCO REIFSCHNEIDER (Brazil).

CO-OPERATION WITH OTHER ORGANIZATIONS

The World Bank co-operates closely with other UN bodies, at the project level, particularly in the design of social funds and social action programmes. It collaborates with the IMF in implementing economic adjustment programmes in developing countries. The Bank holds regular consultations with the European Union and OECD on development issues, and the Bank-NGO Committee provides an annual forum for discussion with non-governmental organizations (NGOs). In September 1995 the Bank initiated the Information for Development Programme (InfoDev) with the aim of fostering partnerships between governments, multilateral institutions and private-sector experts in order to promote reform and investment in developing countries through improved access to information technology.

In June 1995 the World Bank joined other international donors (including regional development banks, other UN bodies, Canada, France, the Netherlands and the USA) in establishing a Consultative Group to Assist the Poorest (CGAP), which was to channel funds to the most needy through grass-roots agencies. An initial credit of approximately US $200m. was committed by the donors. The Bank manages the CGAP Secretariat, which is responsible for the administration of external funding and for the evaluation and approval of project financing. In addition, the CGAP was to provide training and information services on microfinance for policy-makers and practitioners.

In 1997 a Partnerships Group was established to strengthen the Bank's work with development institutions, representatives of civil society and the private sector. The Group established a new Development Grant Facility, which became operational in October, to support partnership initiatives and to co-ordinate all of the Bank's grant-making activities. Also in 1997 the Bank, in partnership with the IMF, UNCTAD, UNDP, the World Trade Organization (WTO) and International Trade Commission, established an Integrated Framework for Trade-related Assistance to Least Developed Countries, at the request of the WTO, to assist those countries to integrate into the global trading system and improve basic trading capabilities. Strengthening co-operation with external partners was a fundamental element of the Comprehensive Development Framework, which was adopted in 1998/99 (see above).

The Bank is a lead organization in providing reconstruction assistance following natural disasters or conflicts, usually in collaboration with other UN agencies or international organizations, and through special trust funds. In April 1999 the World Bank and the IMF convened an international meeting of governments and agencies to review the immediate response of the international community to meet the humanitarian, economic and financial needs of the six Balkan countries most affected by the conflict in Kosovo and Metohija, a southern province of Serbia (Federal Republic of Yugoslavia—FRY). The meeting also aimed to consider areas for future co-operation and measures to promote economic recovery and growth in those countries. In July the World Bank and European Commission organized an international conference to mobilize funds for post-conflict rehabilitation in Kosovo. A new trust fund for the FRY became operational in 2000/01. In November 2001 the Bank worked with UNDP and the Asian Development Bank to assess the needs of Afghanistan following the removal of the Taliban authorities in that country. At an International Conference on Reconstruction Assistance to Afghanistan, held in Tokyo, Japan, in January 2002, the Bank's President proposed extending US $500m. in assistance over a 30-month period, and providing an immediate amount of $50m.–$70m. in grants.

The Bank conducts co-financing and aid co-ordination projects with official aid agencies, export credit institutions, and commercial banks. During the year ending 30 June 2001 a total of 131 IBRD and IDA projects involved co-financers' contributions amounting to US $5,470m.

EVALUATION

The Operations Evaluation Department is an independent unit within the World Bank, which studies and publishes the results of projects after a loan has been fully disbursed, so as to identify problems and possible improvements in future activities. In 1996 a Quality Assurance Group was established to monitor the effectiveness of the Bank's operations and performance.

In September 1993 the Bank's Board of Executive Directors agreed to establish an independent Inspection Panel, consistent with the Bank's objective of improving project implementation and accountability. The panel, which became operational in

September 1994, was to conduct independent investigations and report on complaints concerning the design, appraisal and implementation of development projects supported by the Bank. By the end of 2001 the panel had received 22 formal requests for inspection, and had undertaken 12 investigations.

IBRD INSTITUTIONS

World Bank Institute—WBI: founded in March 1999 by merger of the Bank's Learning and Leadership Centre, previously responsible for internal staff training, and the Economic Development Institute (EDI), which had been established in 1955 to train government officials concerned with development programmes and policies. The new Institute aimed to emphasize the Bank's priority areas through the provision of training courses and seminars relating to poverty, crisis response, good governance and anti-corruption strategies. The Institute was also to take the lead in co-ordinating a process of consultation and dialogue with researchers and other representatives of civil society to examine poverty for the 2000/01 *World Development Report.* During 1999/2000 the WBI expanded its programmes through distance learning, global knowledge networks, and use of new technologies. Under the EDI a World Links for Development programme was initiated to connect schools in developing countries with partner establishments in industrialized nations via the internet. A new initiative, Global Development Learning Network, aimed to expand access to information and learning opportunities through the internet, videoconferences and organized exchanges. Vice-Pres. FRANNIE LÉAUTIER (Tanzania/France).

International Centre for Settlement of Investment Disputes—ICSID: founded in 1966 under the Convention of the Settlement of Investment Disputes between States and Nationals of Other States. The Convention was designed to encourage the growth of private foreign investment for economic development, by creating the possibility, always subject to the consent of both parties, for a Contracting State and a foreign investor who is a national of another Contracting State to settle any legal dispute that might arise out of such an investment by conciliation and/or arbitration before an impartial, international forum. The governing body of the Centre is its Administrative Council, composed of one representative of each Contracting State, all of whom have equal voting power. The President of the World Bank is (*ex officio*) the non-voting Chairman of the Administrative Council.

At the end of February 2002 134 countries had signed and ratified the Convention to become ICSID Contracting States. At 30 June 2001 87 cases had been registered by the Centre, of which 38 were pending. Sec.-Gen. KO-YUNG TUNG (Japan).

Publications

Abstracts of Current Studies: The World Bank Research Program (annually).

Annual Report on Operations Evaluation.

Annual Report on Portfolio Performance.

Annual Review of Development Effectiveness.

EDI Annual Report.

Global Commodity Markets (quarterly).

Global Development Finance (annually, also on CD-Rom and online).

Global Economic Prospects (annually).

ICSID Annual Report.

ICSID Review—Foreign Investment Law Journal (2 a year).

Joint BIS-IMF-OECD-World Bank Statistics on External Debt (quarterly, also available on the internet at www.worldbank.org/data/jointdebt.html).

New Products and Outreach (EDI, annually).

News from ICSID (2 a year).

Poverty Reduction Strategies Newsletter (quarterly).

Research News (quarterly).

Staff Working Papers.

Transition (every 2 months).

World Bank Annual Report.

World Bank Atlas (annually).

World Bank Economic Review (3 a year).

The World Bank and the Environment (annually).

World Bank Research Observer.

World Development Indicators (annually, also on CD-Rom and online).

World Development Report (annually, also on CD-Rom).

World Bank Statistics

LENDING OPERATIONS, BY PURPOSE
(projects approved, year ending 30 June; US $ million)

	2000	2001
Agriculture	1,336.7	1,456.8
Economic policy	1,286.7	1,323.8
Education	684.0	794.1
Electric power and other energy	994.2	824.4
Environment	514.1	515.9
Finance	1,676.5	2,231.3
Health, nutrition and population	987.0	1,047.8
Mining and other extractive activities	54.5	36.0
Petroleum and gas	167.0	81.6
Private-sector development	163.9	507.3
Public-sector management	2,442.5	2,570.6
Social protection	990.0	1,672.5
Telecommunications	109.3	65.0
Transportation	1,690.0	2,969.9
Urban development	621.7	549.5
Water supply and sanitation	903.6	554.0
Multisector	654.5	50.1
Total	15,276.2	17,250.6

Note: Total does not include special financing of US $104.8m. provided by the Trust Funds for East Timor, Gaza and the West Bank, Kosovo, and the Federal Republic of Yugoslavia.

IBRD INCOME AND EXPENDITURE
(US $ million, year ending 30 June)

Revenue	2000	2001
Income from loans:		
Interest	8,041	8,052
Commitment charges	112	91
Income from investments and securities	1,759	1,701
Other income	133	171
Total income	10,045	10,015

Expenditure	2000	2001
Interest on borrowings	6,978	6,988
Amortization of issuance and prepayment costs	150	164
Interest on securities sold under repurchase agreements and payable-for-cash collateral received	4	6
Administrative expenses	935	859
Contributions to special programmes	126	147
Provision for loan losses	-166	676
Other financial expenses	27	31
Total	8,054	8,871
Operating income	1,991	1,144
Effects of adjustment and accounting charge	—	345
Net income	1,991	1,489

IBRD LOANS AND IDA CREDITS APPROVED, BY SECTOR AND REGION (1 July 2000–30 June 2001; US $ million)

Sector	Africa	East Asia and Pacific	South Asia	Europe and Central Asia	Latin America and the Caribbean	Middle East and North Africa	Total
Agriculture	362.3	193.5	231.8	234.5	359.5	75.2	1,456.8
Economic policy	540.3	250.0	350.0	183.5	—	—	1,323.8
Education	74.9	7.6	192.6	90.3	362.7	66.0	794.1
Electric power and other energy	—	30.0	630.0	164.4	—	—	824.4
Environment	22.0	4.8	5.0	32.2	451.9	—	515.9
Finance	204.4	8.0	181.3	853.5	984.1	—	2,231.3
Health, nutrition and population	384.2	108.2	70.0	30.0	455.4	—	1,047.8
Mining and other extractive activities	18.0	—	—	—	—	18.0	36.0
Petroleum and gas	72.0	—	—	9.6	—	—	81.6
Private-sector development	462.2	—	—	19.8	25.3	—	507.3
Public-sector management	382.2	—	182.6	66.4	1,795.7	143.7	2,570.6
Social protection	453.7	378.4	—	439.0	381.4	20.0	1,672.5
Telecommunications	—	—	—	—	—	65.0	65.0
Transportation	99.0	729.0	1,333.0	303.8	422.5	82.6	2,969.9
Urban development	40.0	389.3	4.7	85.0	13.5	17.0	549.5
Water supply and sanitation	254.4	—	65.5	176.1	38.0	20.0	554.0
Multisector	—	35.0	—	5.0	10.1	—	50.1
Total	3,369.6	2,133.8	3,246.5	2,693.1	5,300.1	507.5	17,250.6
of which: IBRD	—	1,136.1	2,035.0	2,154.1	4,806.7	355.2	10,487.1
IDA	3,369.6	997.7	1,211.5	539.0	493.4	152.3	6,763.5
Number of operations	59	24	24	54	50	14	225

Note: Totals do not include special financing of US $104.8m. provided by the Trust Funds for East Timor, Gaza and the West Bank, Kosovo, and the Federal Republic of Yugoslavia.

IBRD OPERATIONS AND RESOURCES, 1997–2001 (US $ million, years ending 30 June)

	1996/97	1997/98	1998/99	1999/2000	2000/01
Loans approved	14,525	21,086	22,182	10,919	10,487
Gross disbursements	13,998	19,232	18,205	10,918	11,784
New medium- to long-term borrowings	15,139	27,748	21,846	15,206	17,223
Net income	1,285	1,243	1,518	1,991	1,489
Subscribed capital	182,426	186,436	188,220	188,606	189,505
Net loans and callable guarantees outstanding	105,954	106,947	117,694	117,181	115,390

Source: *World Bank Annual Report 2001.*

International Development Association—IDA

Address: 1818 H Street, NW, Washington, DC 20433, USA.

Telephone: (202) 477-1234; **fax:** (202) 477-6391; **internet:** www.worldbank.org/ida.

The International Development Association began operations in November 1960. Affiliated to the IBRD (see above), IDA advances capital to the poorer developing member countries on more flexible terms than those offered by the IBRD.

MEMBERS

162 members: see Table on pp. 211–213.

Organization

(March 2002)

Officers and staff of the IBRD serve concurrently as officers and staff of IDA.

President and Chairman of Executive Directors: JAMES D. WOLFENSOHN (*ex officio*).

Activities

IDA assistance is aimed at the poorer developing countries (i.e. those with an annual GNP per head of less than US $885 in 2000 dollars qualified for assistance in 2001/02). Under IDA lending conditions, credits can be extended to countries whose balance of payments could not sustain the burden of repayment required for IBRD loans. Terms are more favourable than those provided by the IBRD; credits are for a period of 35 or 40 years, with a 'grace period' of 10 years, and carry no interest charges. At 1 January 2002 79 countries were eligible for IDA assistance, including several small-island economies with a GNP per head greater than $885, but which would otherwise have little or no access to Bank funds, and 14 so-called 'blend borrowers' (such as India), which are entitled to borrow from both the IDA and IBRD. IDA administers a Trust Fund, which was established in November 1996 as part of a World Bank/IMF initiative to assist heavily indebted poor countries (HIPCs, see IBRD).

IDA's total development resources, consisting of members' subscriptions and supplementary resources (additional subscriptions and contributions), are replenished periodically by contributions from the more affluent member countries. In November 1998 representatives of 39 donor countries agreed to provide US $11,600m. for the 12th replenishment of IDA funds, enabling total lending to amount to an estimated $20,500m. in the period July 1999–June 2002. The new IDA-12 resources were to be directed towards the following objectives: investing in people; promoting good governance; promoting broad-based growth; and protecting the environment. Discussions regarding the 13th replenishment of IDA funds commenced in February 2001.

During the year ending 30 June 2001 IDA credits totalling US $6,763.5m. were approved. Of total IDA assistance during that year, $3,369.6m. (49.8%) was for Africa, $1,211.5m. (17.9%) for South Asia, and $997.7m. (14.8%) for East Asia and the Pacific (see table on p. 158). The largest borrowers of IDA credits were Ethiopia ($666.8m. for seven projects), Viet Nam ($629.1m. for four projects) and India ($520.3m. for six projects). More than one-half of IDA lending was for investment projects, in particular for the provision of basic social services, while some 25% was in the form of adjustment credits.

Publication

Annual Report.

IDA OPERATIONS AND RESOURCES, 1997–2001 (US $ million, years ending 30 June)

	1996/97	1997/98	1998/99	1999/2000	2000/01
Commitments	4,622	7,508*	6,812*	4,358*	6,764*
Disbursements	5,979	5,630	6,023	5,177	5,492

* Excluding HIPC development grants.

Source: *World Bank Annual Report 2001.*

International Finance Corporation—IFC

Address: 2121 Pennsylvania Ave, NW, Washington, DC 20433, USA.

Telephone: (202) 477-1234; **fax:** (202) 974-4384; **e-mail:** information@ifc.org; **internet:** www.ifc.org.

IFC was founded in 1956 as a member of the World Bank Group to stimulate economic growth in developing countries by financing private-sector investments, mobilizing capital in international financial markets, and providing technical assistance and advice to governments and businesses.

MEMBERS

175 members: see Table on pp. 211–213.

Organization

(March 2002)

IFC is a separate legal entity in the World Bank Group. Executive Directors of the World Bank also serve as Directors of IFC. The President of the World Bank is *ex officio* Chairman of the IFC Board of Directors, which has appointed him President of IFC. Subject to his overall supervision, the day-to-day operations of IFC are conducted by its staff under the direction of the Executive Vice-President.

PRINCIPAL OFFICERS

President: JAMES D. WOLFENSOHN (USA).

Executive Vice-President: PETER L. WOICKE (Germany).

REGIONAL AND INDUSTRY DEPARTMENTS

Seven Regional Departments cover: sub-Saharan Africa; East Asia and the Pacific; South Asia; Central and Eastern Europe; Southern Europe and Central Asia; Latin America and the Caribbean; and the Middle East and North Africa. These aim to develop strategies for member countries, promote businesses, and strengthen relations with governments and the private sector. The Industry Departments include Agribusiness; the Global Financial Markets Group; Global Information and Communications Technologies (jointly managed with the World Bank); the Global Practice Group for Social Sectors; Infrastructure; Mining (jointly managed with the World Bank); Petroleum, Gas and Chemicals (jointly managed with the World Bank); Power; Private Equity and Investment Funds; Small and Medium Enterprises (jointly managed with the World Bank); Syndications and International Securities; and Trust Funds.

REGIONAL AND RESIDENT MISSIONS

There are Regional and Resident Missions in Argentina, Australia, Bangladesh, Brazil (for Latin America and the Caribbean), Cambodia, Cameroon, People's Republic of China, Colombia, Côte d'Ivoire (for West and Central Africa), Egypt (for the Middle East and North Africa), Ghana, Guatemala, India (for South Asia), Kenya (for East Africa), Republic of Korea, Mexico, Nepal, Nigeria, Poland, Russia (for Central and Eastern Europe), South Africa (for Southern Africa), Thailand, Turkey, Viet Nam and Zimbabwe. There are also Special Representatives in France, Germany, Japan and the United Kingdom (for Europe), and other programme co-ordinators, managers and investment officers in more than 30 additional countries.

Activities

IFC aims to promote economic development in developing member countries by assisting the growth of private enterprise and effective capital markets. It finances private sector projects, through loans, the purchase of equity, quasi-equity products, and risk management services, and assists governments to create conditions that stimulate the flow of domestic and foreign private savings and investment. IFC also mobilizes additional resources from other financial institutions, in particular through syndicated loans, thus providing access to international capital markets. IFC provides a range of advisory services to help to improve the investment climate in developing countries and offers technical assistance to private enterprises and governments.

To be eligible for financing, projects must be profitable for investors, as well as financially and economically viable, must benefit the economy of the country concerned, and must comply with IFC's environmental and social guide-lines. IFC aims to promote best corporate governance and management methods and sustainable business practices, and encourages partnerships between governments, non-governmental organizations and community groups. IFC may provide finance for a project that is partly state-owned, provided that there is participation by the private sector and that the project is operated on a commercial basis.

IFC's authorized capital is US $2,450m. At 30 June 2001 paid-in capital was $2,360m. The World Bank was originally the principal source of borrowed funds, but IFC also borrows from private capital markets. IFC's net income amounted to $345m. in 2000/01, compared with $380m. in the previous year.

In the year ending 30 June 2001 project financing approved by IFC amounted to US $5,357m. for 240 projects (compared with $5,846m. for 259 projects in the previous year). Of the total approved, $3,742m. was for IFC's own account, while $1,615m. was in the form of loan syndications and underwriting of securities issues and investment funds by more than 100 participant banks and institutional investors. Generally, the IFC limits its financing to less than 25% of the total cost of a project, but may take up to a 35% stake in a venture (although never as a majority shareholder). Disbursements for IFC's account amounted to $1,535m. in 2000/01 (compared with $2,210m. in the previous year).

Projects approved during 2000/01 were located in 75 countries and regions. The largest proportion of total financing by IFC was allocated to Latin America and the Caribbean (26%); the Middle East and North Africa received 24%, Asia and the Pacific 20%, sub-Saharan Africa 16%, and Europe and Central Asia 13%. The Corporation invests in a wide variety of business and financial institutions in a broad range of sectors. In 2000/01 almost one-third of total financing committed (30%) was for financial services. Other financing was for utilities and transportation (21%), information technologies (18%), petroleum, gas and mining (8%), industrial and consumer products (4%), non-metallic mineral product manufacturing (4%), health care and education (4%), chemicals (3%), and others (9%).

IFC offers risk-management services, assisting institutions in avoiding financial risks that arise from changes in interest rates, in exchange rates or in commodity prices. In 2000/01 IFC approved eight risk-management projects for companies and banks, bringing the total number of projects approved since the introduction of the service in 1990 to 98 in 38 countries.

In 1999/2000 the IFC and World Bank advisory services were integrated into the Private Sector Advisory Services (PSAS). The PSAS advises governments and private enterprises on policy, transaction implementation and foreign direct investment. The Foreign Investment Advisory Service (FIAS), established in 1986, provides advice on promoting foreign investment and strengthening the country's investment framework at the request of governments. During 2000/01 FIAS completed 48 advisory projects, including six regional assignments to assist groups of countries to co-ordinate their foreign direct investment strategies and investment promotion activities. Under the Technical Assistance Trust Funds Program (TATF), established in 1988, IFC manages resources contributed by various governments and agencies to provide finance for feasibility studies, project identification studies and other types of technical assistance relating to project preparation. By 30 June 2001 the TATF had financed more than 1,000 technical assistance projects.

IFC has helped to establish several regional facilities which aim to assist small-scale entrepreneurs to develop business proposals and generate funding for their projects. For each of the facilities listed below IFC is the executing agency, and their activities are co-ordinated by the Small and Medium Enterprise (SME) Department. The Africa Project Development Facility

(APDF) was established in 1986 by IFC, UNDP and the African Development Bank, and has headquarters in Johannesburg, South Africa, with other offices in Cape Town (South Africa), Cameroon, Ghana, Kenya, and Nigeria. The Facility also promotes capacity-building for SMEs, local business associations and financial institutions. It works closely with the African Management Services Company (AMSCo, established in 1989, with headquarters in Amsterdam, the Netherlands) which helps to find qualified senior executives and technical personnel to work with African companies, assist in the training of local managers, and provide management support The South Pacific Project Facility, based in Sydney, Australia, was established in 1991, mainly to assist local businesses in the IFC Pacific Island member countries. A separate office in Port Moresby, Papua New Guinea, was opened in 1997. The Mekong Project Development Facility was inaugurated in 1995, and became operational in 1997, specifically to support the development of SMEs in Cambodia, Laos and Viet Nam.

In September 2000 the Southeast Europe Enterprise Development (SEED) initiative was formally launched at its headquarters in Sarajevo, Bosnia and Herzegovina, as a five-year scheme to support the development of the private-sector in Albania, Bosnia and Herzegovina, Kosovo, the former Yugoslav republic of Macedonia, and the Federal Republic of Yugoslavia. In June of that year the IFC approved the establishment of a China Project Development Facility to support the development of SMEs within the People's Republic of China. The Facility's headquarters in Chengdu, Sichuan Province, was expected to become operational in 2001/2002. Both these initiatives highlighted the following three strategic targets: to provide support services at enterprise level; to assist the development of local private sector support institutions; and to advocate ways to improve the business-enabling environment.

Publications

Annual Report.
Emerging Stock Markets Factbook (annually).
Impact (quarterly).
Lessons of Experience (series).
Results on the Ground (series).
Review of Small Businesses (annually).
Discussion papers and technical documents.

IFC OPERATIONS AND RESOURCES, 1992–2001 (fiscal years ending 30 June)

	1992	1993	1994	1995	1996	1997	1998	1999	2000	2001
Approved investments										
Number of new projects	167	185	231	213	264	276	304	255	259	240
Total financing (US $ million)	3,226	3,936	4,287	5,467	8,118	6,722	5,905	5,280	5,846	5,357
Total project costs* (US $ million)	12,000	17,422	15,839	19,352	19,633	17,945	15,726	15,578	21,136	16,427
Disbursements (IFC's own account, US $ million)	1,114	1,106	1,537	1,808	2,053	2,003	2,054	2,102	2,210	1,535
Resources and income (US $ million)										
Borrowings	5,114	5,565	6,531	7,993	8,956	10,123	11,162	12,429	14,919	15,457
Paid-in capital.	1,251	1,423	1,658	1,875	2,076	2,229	2,337	2,350	2,358	2,360
Retained earnings	1,138	1,280	1,538	1,726	2,071	2,503	2,749	2,998	3,378	3,723
Net income	180	142	258	188	346	432	246	249	380	345

* Including investment mobilized from other sources.
Source: *IFC Annual Report 2001.*

Multilateral Investment Guarantee Agency—MIGA

Address: 1818 H Street, NW, Washington, DC 20433, USA.

Telephone: (202) 473-6163; **fax:** (202) 522-2630; **internet:** www.miga.org.

MIGA was founded in 1988 as an affiliate of the World Bank. Its mandate is to encourage the flow of foreign direct investment to, and among, developing member countries, through the provision of political risk insurance and investment marketing services to foreign investors and host governments, respectively.

MEMBERS

At March 2002 MIGA had 154 member countries. Membership is open to all countries that are members of the World Bank.

Organization

(March 2002)

MIGA is legally and financially separate from the World Bank. It is supervised by a Council of Governors (comprising one Governor and one Alternate of each member country) and an elected Board of Directors (of no less than 12 members).

President: JAMES D. WOLFENSOHN (USA).

Executive Vice-President: MOTOMICHI IKAWA (Japan).

Activities

The convention establishing MIGA took effect in April 1988. Authorized capital was US $1,082m. In April 1998 the Board of Directors approved an increase in the Agency's capital base. A grant of $150m. was transferred from the IBRD as part of the package, while the capital increase (totalling $700m. callable capital and $150m. paid-in capital) was approved by MIGA's Council of Governors in April 1999. A three-year subscription period then commenced, covering the period April 1999–March 2002. At 30 June 2001 total subscriptions to the capital stock amounted to $1,438m., of which $279m. was paid-in.

MIGA guarantees eligible investments against losses resulting from non-commercial risks, under four main categories:

(i) transfer risk resulting from host government restrictions on currency conversion and transfer;
(ii) risk of loss resulting from legislative or administrative actions of the host government;
(iii) repudiation by the host government of contracts with investors in cases in which the investor has no access to a competent forum;
(iv) the risk of armed conflict and civil unrest.

Before guaranteeing any investment, MIGA must ensure that it is commercially viable, contributes to the development process and is not harmful to the environment. During the fiscal year 1998/99 MIGA and IFC appointed the first Compliance Advisor and Ombudsman to consider the concerns of local communities directly affected by MIGA or IFC sponsored projects. In February 1999 the Board of Directors approved an increase in the amount of political risk insurance available for each project, from US $75m. to $200m.

During the year ending 30 June 2001 MIGA issued 66 investment insurance contracts for 46 projects in 28 countries with a value of US $2,000m., compared with 53 contracts valued at $1,605m. in 1999/2000. The amount of direct investment associated with the contracts totalled approximately $5,200m. in 2000/01 (compared with $5,450m. in the previous year), bringing the total estimate investment facilitated since 1988 to $41,200m.

MIGA administers two investment guarantee trust funds, for Bosnia and Herzogovina and for the West Bank and Gaza Strip, to underwrite investment in post-conflict reconstruction activities.

MIGA also provides policy and advisory services to promote foreign investment in developing countries and in transitional economies, and to disseminate information on investment opportunities. In October 1995 MIGA established a new network on investment opportunities, which connected investment promotion agencies (IPAs) throughout the world on an electronic information network. The so-called IPA*net* aimed to encourage further investments among developing countries, to provide access to comprehensive information on investment laws and conditions and to strengthen links between governmental, business and financial associations and investors. A new version of IPA*net* was launched in 1997 (and can be accessed at www.ipanet.net). In June 1998 MIGA initiated a new internet-based facility, 'PrivatizationLink', to provide information on investment opportunities resulting from the privatization of industries in emerging economies. In October 2000 a specialized facility within the service was established to facilitate investment in Russia (russia.privatizationlink.com). During 2000/01 an office was established in Paris, France, to promote and co-ordinate European investment in developing countries, in particular in Africa and Eastern Europe.

Publications

Annual Report.

Investment Promotion Quarterly (electronic news update).

MIGA News (quarterly).

International Civil Aviation Organization—ICAO

Address: 999 University St, Montreal, QC H3C 5H7, Canada.

Telephone: (514) 954-8219; **fax:** (514) 954-6077; **e-mail:** icaohq@icao.int; **internet:** www.icao.int.

The Convention on International Civil Aviation was signed in Chicago in 1944. As a result, ICAO was founded in 1947 to develop the techniques of international air navigation and to help in the planning and improvement of international air transport.

MEMBERS

187 members: see Table on pp. 211–213.

Organization

(March 2002)

ASSEMBLY

Composed of representatives of all member states, the Assembly is the organization's legislative body and meets at least once every three years. It reviews the work of the organization, sets out the work programme for the next three years, approves the budget and determines members' contributions. The 33rd Assembly was held in September/October 2001.

COUNCIL

Composed of representatives of 33 member states, elected by the Assembly. It is the executive body, and establishes and supervises subsidiary technical committees and makes recommendations to member governments; meets in virtually continuous session; elects the President, appoints the Secretary-General, and administers the finances of the organization. The Council is assisted by the Air Navigation Commission (on technical matters), the Air Transport Committee (on economic matters), the Committee on Joint Support of Air Navigation Services and the Finance Committee. The functions of the Council are:

(i) to adopt international standards and recommended practices and incorporate them as annexes to the Convention on International Civil Aviation;

(ii) to arbitrate between member states on matters concerning aviation and implementation of the Convention;

(iii) to investigate any situation which presents avoidable obstacles to development of international air navigation;

(iv) to take whatever steps are necessary to maintain safety and regularity of operation of international air transport;

(v) to provide technical assistance to the developing countries under the UN Development Programme and other assistance programmes.

President of the Council: Dr ASSAD KOTAITE (Lebanon).

SECRETARIAT

The Secretariat, headed by a Secretary-General, is divided into five main divisions: the Air Navigation Bureau, the Air Transport Bureau, The Technical Co-operation Bureau, the Legal Bureau, and the Bureau of Administration and Services.

Secretary-General: RENATO CLAUDIO COSTA PEREIRA (Brazil).

REGIONAL OFFICES

Asia and Pacific: 252/1 Vipavadee Rangsit Rd, Ladyao, Chatuchak, POB 11, Bangkok 10900, Thailand.

Eastern and Southern Africa: Limuru Rd, Gigiri, POB 46294, Nairobi, Kenya.

Europe: 3 bis, Villa Emile-Bergerat, 92522 Neuilly-sur-Seine Cédex, France.

Middle East: Egyptian Civil Aviation Complex, Cairo Airport Rd, Cairo, Egypt.

North America, Central America and the Caribbean: Apdo Postal 5-377, CP 11590, México 5, DF, Mexico.

South America: Apdo 4127, Lima 100, Peru.

Western and Central Africa: 15 blvd de la République, BP 2356, Dakar, Senegal.

Activities

ICAO aims to ensure the safe and orderly growth of civil aviation; to encourage skills in aircraft design and operation; to improve airways, airports and air navigation; to prevent the waste of resources in unreasonable competition; to safeguard the rights of each contracting party to operate international air transport; and to prevent discriminatory practices. ICAO collects and publishes statistics relating to civil aviation. In the late 1990s ICAO implemented a programme to address potential malfunctions, resulting from the date change at the start of the new century, of systems affecting the safety, regularity and efficiency of international civil aviation operations; this entailed the harmonization of regional contingency plans and the development of an extensive inventory of air traffic systems and aviation facilities. In February 2002 a high-level ministerial conference organized by ICAO endorsed a plan of action aimed at strengthening aviation security (see below).

SAFETY AND SECURITY

ICAO aims to enhance all aspects of air safety and security. In 1998 a Global Aviation Safety Plan was initiated to promote new safety measures. A Programme for the Prevention of Controlled Flights into Terrain continued to be implemented. ICAO assists member countries to develop appropriate educational and training activities. It also supports programmes to assist the victims of aircraft accidents. The 32nd Assembly, held in September/October 1998, endorsed the establishment of a Universal Safety Oversight Programme, to provide for mandatory, systematic and harmonized safety audits regularly to be undertaken in member states. The Programme became operational on 1 January 1999 with the aim of auditing all member states over an initial three-year period. In October 1998 a protocol to the Chicago Convention, prohibiting the use of weapons against civil aircraft in flight, entered into effect, having been adopted in 1984 following an attack on a Korean Airlines passenger flight. In 2000 ICAO developed model legislation to cover offences committed on board aircraft by unruly passengers (other than hijacking, sabotage etc., which are already governed by international legislation). Following the major terrorist attacks perpetrated against targets in the USA in September 2001, involving the use of hijacked aircraft as weapons of mass destruction, the 33rd Assembly—held in September/October—approved the staging of a high-level ministerial conference to discuss preventing, combating and eradicating acts of terrorism involving civil aviation. The conference, convened under ICAO auspices in February 2002, endorsed a global Aviation Security Plan of Action and reaffirmed the responsibility of states to ensure aviation security on their territories. The plan was to provide for continued implementation of the Universal Safety Oversight Programme until the end of 2004; development of an effective global response to emerging threats; strengthened security-related provisions of the Convention on International Civil Aviation; and enhanced co-ordination of regional and sub-regional audit programmes. It was envisaged that the ICAO Council would adopt the plan by mid-June, and that its implementation would commence immediately thereafter.

NAVIGATION

ICAO projects relating to navigation have included automated data interchange systems, all-weather navigation, obstacle clearances and the use of space technology in air navigation. In May 1998 an international conference was held in Rio de Janeiro, Brazil, to consider implementation of the Communications, Navigation, Surveillance, and Air Traffic Management (CNS/ATM) systems. The conference urged greater financing and co-operation between states to ensure that the CNS/ATM becomes the basis of a global ATM system. An Air Traffic Management Operational Concept Panel, which was to develop standards and recommend procedures for the development of an integrated ATM system, was convened for the first time in March/April 1999. In October 1998 the Assembly adopted a Charter on the Rights and Obligations of States relating to Global Navigation Satellite Systems (GNSS) to serve as an interim framework on the GNSS. A long-term legal framework on principles governing the GNSS, including a new international convention, remained under consideration.

ENVIRONMENT

International standards and guide-lines for noise certification of aircraft and international provisions for the regulation of aircraft engine emissions have been adopted and published in Annex 16 to the Chicago Convention. However, these remain under consideration. ICAO was recognized in the Kyoto Protocol to the Framework Convention on Climate Change as the global body through which industrialized nations were to pursue the limitation or reduction of so-called greenhouse gas emissions from international aviation. In 1998 ICAO's Committee on Aviation Environmental Protection recommended a reduction of 16% in the permissible levels of nitrogen oxides emitted by aircraft engines. The new limits, to be applicable to new engine designs from 2003, were adopted by the ICAO Council in early 1999. In January 2001 the Committee recommended several measures for review by the Council concerning aircraft noise mitigation; the proposals included a new noise standard, set at 10 decibels lower than the existing one, for new engine designs from 2006, and new take-off noise abatement procedures.

ICAO SPECIFICATIONS

These are contained in annexes to the Chicago Convention, and in three sets of Procedures for Air Navigation Services (PANS Documents). The specifications are periodically revised in keeping with developments in technology and changing requirements. The 18 annexes to the Convention include personnel licensing, rules relating to the conduct of flights, meteorological services, aeronautical charts, air/ground communications, safety specifications, identification, air-traffic control, rescue services, environmental protection, security and the transporting of dangerous goods. Technical Manuals and Circulars are issued to facilitate implementation.

ICAO REGIONAL PLANS

These set out the technical requirements for air navigation facilities in the nine ICAO regions; Regional Offices offer assistance (see addresses above). Because of growth in air traffic and changes in the pattern of air routes, the Plans are periodically amended. ICAO maintains a structure of Planning and Implementation Regional Groups.

TECHNICAL CO-OPERATION

ICAO's Technical Co-operation Bureau promotes the implementation of ICAO Standards and Recommended Practices, including the CNS/ATM and Safety Oversight Programmes, and assists developing countries in the execution of various projects, financed by UNDP and other sources.

ICAO works in close co-operation with other UN bodies, such as the World Meteorological Organization, the International Telecommunication Union, the Universal Postal Union, the World Health Organization and the International Maritime Organization. Non-governmental organizations which also participate in ICAO's work include the International Air Transport Association (q.v.), the Airports Council International (q.v.), the International Federation of Air Line Pilots' Associations (q.v.), and the International Council of Aircraft Owner and Pilot Associations.

Finance

ICAO is financed mainly by contributions from member states; the 33nd Session of the Assembly, held in September/October 2001, approved budget allocations of US $56.7m. for 2002, $57.6m. for 2003 and $60.5m. for 2004.

Publications

Aircraft Accident Digest.

Annual Civil Aviation Report.

Civil Aviation Statistics of the World (annually).

ICAO Journal (10 a year, in English, French and Spanish; quarterly digest in Russian).

Lexicon of Terms.

Regional Air Navigation Plans.

Transition (CNS/ATM newsletter, quarterly).

Conventions, agreements, rules of procedures, regulations, technical publications and manuals.

International Fund for Agricultural Development—IFAD

Address: Via del Serafico 107, 00142 Rome, Italy.

Telephone: (06) 54591; **fax:** (06) 5043463; **e-mail:** ifad@ifad.org; **internet:** www.ifad.org.

IFAD was established in 1977, following a decision by the 1974 UN World Food Conference, with a mandate to combat hunger and eradicate poverty on a sustainable basis in the low-income, food-deficit regions of the world. Funding operations began in January 1978.

MEMBERS

161 members: see Table on pp. 211–213.

Organization

(March 2002)

GOVERNING COUNCIL

Each member state is represented in the Governing Council (the Fund's highest authority) by a Governor and an Alternate. Sessions are held annually with special sessions as required. The Governing Council elects the President of the Fund (who also chairs the Executive Board) by a two-thirds majority for a four-year term. The President is eligible for re-election.

EXECUTIVE BOARD

Consists of 18 members and 18 alternates, elected by the Governing Council, who serve for three years. The Executive Board is responsible for the conduct and general operation of IFAD and approves loans and grants for projects; it holds three regular sessions each year.

Following agreement on the fourth replenishment of the Fund's resources in February 1997, the governance structure of the Fund was amended. Former Category I countries (i.e. industrialized donor countries) were reclassified as List A countries and were awarded a greater share of the 1,800 votes in the Governing Council and Executive Board, in order to reflect their financial contributions to the Fund. Former Category II countries (petroleum-exporting developing donor countries) were reclassified as List B countries, while recipient developing countries, formally Category III countries, were termed as List C countries, and divided into three regional Sub-Lists. Where previously each category was ensured equal representation on the Executive Board, the new allocation of seats was as follows: eight List A countries, four List B, and two of each Sub-List C group of countries.

President and Chairman of Executive Board: LENNART BÅGE (Sweden).

Vice-President: JOHN WESTLEY (USA).

DEPARTMENTS

IFAD has three main administrative departments: the Economic Policy and Resource Strategy Department; the Programme Management Department (with five regional Divisions and a Technical Advisory Division); and the Management and Personnel Services Department (including Office of the Secretary, Management Information Systems, Personnel Division, and Administrative Services). At June 2001 IFAD had 290 regular staff.

Activities

The Fund's objective is to mobilize additional resources to be made available on concessionary terms for agricultural development in developing member states. IFAD provides financing primarily for projects designed to improve food production systems and to strengthen related policies, services and institutions. In allocating resources IFAD is guided by: the need to increase food production in the poorest food-deficit countries; the potential for increasing food production in other developing countries; and the importance of improving the nutrition, health and education of the poorest people in developing countries, i.e. small-scale farmers, artisanal fishermen, nomadic pastoralists, indigenous populations, rural women, and the rural landless. All projects emphasize the participation of beneficiaries in development initiatives, both at the local and national level. IFAD is a leading repository in the world of knowledge, resources and expertise in the field of rural hunger and poverty alleviation. Through its technical assistance grants, IFAD aims to promote research and capacity-building in the agricultural sector, as well as the development of technologies to increase production and alleviate rural poverty. In recent years IFAD has been increasingly involved in promoting the use of communication technology to facilitate the exchange of information and experience among rural communities, specialized institutions and organizations and IFAD-sponsored projects. IFAD is committed to achieving the so-called Millennium Goal, pledged by governments attending a special session of the UN General Assembly in September 2000, of reducing by 50% the proportion of people living in extreme poverty by 2015.

IFAD is empowered to make both grants and loans. Grants are limited to 7.5% of the resources committed in any one financial year. Loans are available on highly concessionary, intermediate and ordinary terms. Highly concessionary loans carry no interest but have an annual service charge of 0.75% and a repayment period of 40 years, including a 10-year grace period. Intermediate term loans are subject to a variable interest charge, equivalent to 50% of the interest rate charged on World Bank loans, and are repaid over 20 years. Ordinary loans carry a variable interest charge equal to that charged by the World Bank, and are repaid over 15–18 years. Highly concessionary loans form about two-thirds of the total lent annually by IFAD. To avoid duplication of work, the administration of loans, for the purposes of disbursements and supervision of project implementation, is entrusted to competent international financial institutions, with the Fund retaining an active interest. In order to increase the impact of its lending resources on food production, the Fund seeks as much as possible to attract other external donors and beneficiary governments as co-financiers of its projects.

At the end of 2000 total IFAD loans approved since 1978 amounted to US $6,900.2m. for 578 projects. During the same period the Fund approved 1,457 research and technical assistance grants, at a cost of $387.9m. In 2000 IFAD approved $409.0m. for 27 projects, as follows: $156.5m. for 12 projects in sub-Saharan Africa, (or 38.2% of the total committed in that year), $127.5m. for six operations in Asia and the Pacific (31.2%), $64.0m. for four projects in Latin America and the Caribbean (15.7%) and $60.9m. for five projects in the Near East and North Africa (14.9%). Technical assistance grants amounting to $32.8m. (for research, training and project preparation and development), were awarded, bringing the total financial assistance approved in 2000 to $441.8m., compared with $462.3m. in 1999.

IFAD's development projects usually include a number of components, such as infrastructure (e.g. improvement of water supplies, small-scale irrigation and road construction); input supply (e.g. improved seeds, fertilizers and pesticides); institutional support (e.g. research, training and extension services); and producer incentives (e.g. pricing and marketing improvements). IFAD also attempts to enable the landless to acquire income-generating assets: by increasing the provision of credit for the rural poor, it seeks to free them from dependence on the capital market and to generate productive activities.

The Fund supports projects that are concerned with environmental conservation, in an effort to alleviate poverty that results from the deterioration of natural resources. In addition, it extends environmental assessment grants to review the environmental consequences of projects under preparation.

In addition to its regular efforts to identify projects and programmes, IFAD organizes special programming missions to certain selected countries to undertake a comprehensive review of the constraints affecting the rural poor, and to help countries to design strategies for the removal of these constraints. In general, projects based on the recommendations of these missions tend to focus on institutional improvements at the national and local level to direct inputs and services to small farmers and the landless rural poor. Monitoring and evaluation missions are also sent to check the progress of projects.

In October 1997 IFAD was appointed to administer the Global Mechanism of the Convention to Combat Desertification in those Countries Experiencing Drought and Desertification, particularly in Africa, which entered into force in December 1996. The Mechanism was envisaged as a means of mobilizing and channelling resources for implementation of the Convention. A series of collaborative institutional arrangements were to be concluded between IFAD, UNDP and the World Bank in order to facilitate the effective functioning of the Mechanism.

In February 1998 IFAD inaugurated a new Trust Fund to complement the multilateral debt initiative for Heavily Indebted Poor Countries (HIPCs—see World Bank p. 154). The Fund was intended to assist IFAD's poorest members deemed to be eligible under the initiative to channel resources from debt repayments to communities in need. In February 2000 the Governing Council approved full participation by IFAD in the enhanced HIPC debt initiative agreed by the World Bank and IMF in September 1999.

In November 1995 IFAD organized a Conference on Hunger and Poverty, which was held in Brussels, Belgium, together with the World Bank, the European Commission, FAO, WFP and several European governments. The conference was attended by representatives from some 300 non-governmental organizations, and approved a programme of action to combat hunger and poverty. During 1998 the Executive Board endorsed a policy framework for the Fund's provision of assistance in post-conflict situations, with the aim of achieving a continuum from emergency relief to a secure basis from which to pursue sustainable development. In July 2001 IFAD and UNAIDS signed a memorandum of understanding on developing a co-operation agreement. A meeting of technical experts from IFAD, FAO, WFP and UNAIDS, held in December, addressed means of mitigating the impact of HIV/AIDS on food security and rural livelihoods in affected regions.

During the late 1990s IFAD established several partnerships within the agribusiness sector, with a view to improving performance at project level, broadening access to capital markets, and encouraging the advancement of new technologies.

Finance

In accordance with the Articles of Agreement establishing IFAD, the Governing Council periodically undertakes a review of the adequacy of resources available to the Fund and may request members to make additional contributions. The target for the fifth replenishment of IFAD funds, covering the period 2000–02, amounted to US $460m. The provisional budget for administrative expenses for 2001 amounted to $53.6m.

Publications

Annual Report.

IFAD Update (2 a year).

Rural Poverty Report (annually).

Staff Working Papers (series).

International Labour Organization—ILO

Address: 4 route des Morillons, 1211 Geneva 22, Switzerland.

Telephone: (22) 7996111; **fax:** (22) 7988685; **e-mail:** ilo@ilo.org; **internet:** www.ilo.org.

ILO was founded in 1919 to work for social justice as a basis for lasting peace. It carries out this mandate by promoting decent living standards, satisfactory conditions of work and pay and adequate employment opportunities. Methods of action include the creation of international labour standards; the provision of technical co-operation services; and research and publications on social and labour matters. In 1946 ILO became a specialized agency associated with the UN. It was awarded the Nobel Peace Prize in 1969. ILO's tripartite structure gives representation to employers' and workers' organizations alongside governments.

MEMBERS

175 members: see Table on pp. 211–213.

Organization

(March 2002)

INTERNATIONAL LABOUR CONFERENCE

The supreme deliberative body of ILO, the Conference meets annually in Geneva, with a session devoted to maritime questions when necessary; it is attended by about 2,000 delegates, advisers and observers. National delegations are composed of two government delegates, one employers' delegate and one workers' delegate. Non-governmental delegates can speak and vote independently of the views of their national government. The conference elects the Governing Body and adopts International Labour Conventions and Recommendations. Every two years the Conference adopts the ILO Budget.

The President and Vice-Presidents hold office for the term of the Conference only.

GOVERNING BODY

ILO's executive council meets three times a year in Geneva to decide policy and programmes. It is composed of 28 government members, 14 employers' members and 14 workers' members. Ten seats are reserved for 'states of chief industrial importance': Brazil, the People's Republic of China, France, Germany, India, Italy, Japan, Russia, the United Kingdom and the USA. The remaining 18 are elected from other countries every three years. Employers' and workers' members are elected as individuals, not as national candidates.

Among the Committees formed by the Governing Body are: the Committee on Freedom of Association; the Programme, Financial and Administrative Committee; the Building Sub-Committee; the Committee on Legal Issues and International Labour Standards; the Sub-Committee on Multinational Enterprises; the Working Party on Policy regarding the Revision of Standards; the Committee on Employment and Social Policy; the Committee on Sectoral and Technical Meetings and Related Issues; the Committee on Technical Co-operation; and the Working Party on the Social Dimensions of the Liberalization of International Trade.

Chairman (2001–02): ALAIN LUDOVIC TOU (Burkina Faso).

Employers' Vice-Chairman: DANIEL FUNES DE RIOJA (Argentina).

Workers' Vice-Chairman: WILLIAM BRETT (United Kingdom).

INTERNATIONAL LABOUR OFFICE

The International Labour Office is ILO's secretariat, operational headquarters and publishing house. It is staffed in Geneva and in the field by about 2,250 people of some 120 nationalities. Operations are decentralized to regional, area and branch offices in nearly 40 countries.

Director-General: JUAN O. SOMAVÍA (Chile).

REGIONAL OFFICES

Regional Office for Africa: BP 3960, Abidjan 01, Côte d'Ivoire.

Regional Office for the Americas: Apdo Postal 3638, Lima 1, Peru.

Regional Office for Arab States: POB 11-4088, Beirut, Lebanon.

Regional Office for Asia and the Pacific: POB 2-349, Bangkok 10200, Thailand.

Activities

ILO identified the following four principal themes as strategic objectives for its 2002–03 work programme: to promote and realize standards and fundamental principles and rights at work; to create greater opportunities for women and men to secure decent employment and income; to enhance the coverage and effectiveness of social protection for all; and to strengthen tripartism and social dialogue.

STANDARDS AND FUNDAMENTAL PRINCIPLES AND RIGHTS AT WORK

One of ILO's primary functions is the adoption by the International Labour Conference of conventions and recommendations setting minimum labour standards. Through ratification by member states, conventions create binding obligations to put their provisions into effect. Recommendations provide guidance as to policy and practice. At June 2001 a total of 184 conventions and 192 recommendations had been adopted, ranging over a wide field of social and labour matters, based on the following principles: freedom of association, the abolition of forced and child labour, and the elimination of discrimination in employment promotion, training and the protection of workers. Together they form the International Labour Code. By January 2002 more than 7,000 ratifications of the conventions had been registered by member states. The Committee of Experts on the Application of Conventions and Recommendations and the Conference Committee on the Application of Standards monitor the adoption of international labour standards. In June 1998 a Declaration on Fundamental Principles and Rights at Work, establishing seven fundamental labour standards, was adopted by the Conference. All member states were obliged to observe the four principles upon which these standards were based (see above), whether or not they had ratified the corresponding international conventions.

From 1996 ILO resolved to strengthen its efforts, working closely with UNICEF, to encourage member states to ratify and to implement relevant international standards on child labour. In June 1999 the International Labour Conference adopted the Worst Forms of Child Labour Convention; by February 2002 this had been ratified by 116 states and ILO was preparing for its implementation. The Organization helped to organize an International Conference on Child Labour, convened in The Hague, Netherlands, in February 2002. By late 2001 some 90 countries were taking part in ILO's International Programme for the Elimination of Child Labour (IPEC, established in 1992), with emphasis placed on the elimination of the most severe forms of labour such as hazardous working conditions and occupations, child prostitution and trafficking of children. In addition, IPEC gives special attention to children who are particularly vulnerable, for example those under 12 years of age.

In 2000 the Global Compact, an initiative of the UN Secretary-General, was inaugurated; this comprised leaders in the fields of business, labour and civil society who undertook to promote human rights, the fundamental principles of ILO, and protection of the environment.

DECENT EMPLOYMENT AND INCOME

ILO aims to monitor, examine and report on the situation and trends in employment throughout the world, and considers the effects on employment and social justice of economic trade, investment and related phenomena. A programme on crisis response and reconstruction addresses the effect on employment of armed conflicts, natural disasters, social movements or political transitions, and financial and economic disruptions. The impact on employment and related social issues of the financial crisis that affected several Asian economies from mid-1997 was of particular concern to ILO. In 1998 ILO estimated that some 1,000m. workers, or one-third of the world's labour force, were unemployed or underemployed.

ILO's programme sector on skills, knowledge and employability supports governments in structuring policies for improved investment in learning and training for enhanced employability, productivity and social inclusion. The programme focuses on promoting access to training and decent work for specific groups, such as youths, the disabled, and workers in the informal economy, and on protecting the rights of the elderly. The job creation and enterprise development programme aims to assist governments, employers, workers and other related groups with fostering a successful business environment, for example through the identification and implementation of appropriate policies, legal frameworks and management strategies, the promotion of access to business development and training services, and the promotion of local economic development programmes. The Tripartite Declaration of Principles concerning Multinational Enterprises and Social Policy, adopted in 1977 and amended in 2000, provides international guide-lines—agreed by governments and employers' and workers' organizations— on investment policy and practice. ILO's gender promotion programme aims to promote effective gender mainstreaming and the creation of more and better jobs for women and men. The impact of current global financial and economic trends on employment creation, poverty alleviation and social exclusion are addressed by ILO's social finance programme. In February 2002 ILO established a World Commission on the Social Dimension of Globalization to consider means of utilizing economic globalization to stimulate economic growth and reduce poverty.

ILO maintains technical relations with the IMF, the World Bank, OECD, the WTO and other international organizations on global economic issues, international and national strategies for employment, structural adjustment, and labour market and training policies. A number of employment policy reviews have been carried out by ILO within the framework of the UN Administrative Committee on Co-ordination Task Force on Full Employment and Sustainable Livelihoods.

SOCIAL PROTECTION FOR ALL

Access to an adequate level of social protection is recognized in ILO's 1944 Declaration of Philadelphia, as well as in a number of international labour standards, as a basic right of all individuals. ILO aims to enable countries to extend social protection to all groups in society and to improve working conditions and safety at work. The fundamental premise of ILO's programme sector on socio-economic security is that basic security for all is essential for productive work and human dignity in the future global economy. The achievement of basic security is deemed to entail the attainment of basic humanitarian needs, including universal access to health services and a decent level of education. The programme aims to address the following concerns: what constitutes socio-economic security and insecurity in member countries; identifying the sources of such insecurity; and identifying economic, labour and social policies that could improve socio-economic security while promoting sustainable economic growth. The programme focuses on the following dimensions of work-based security: security in the labour market (the provision of adequate employment opportunities); employment security (for example, protection against dismissal); occupational security (the opportunity to develop a career); work security (protection against accidents, illness and stress at work); skill reproduction security; income security; and representation security (the right to collective representation in the labour market, through independent trade unions and employers associations, etc.). ILO's Social Security Policy and Development Branch assists member states and constituents in the design, reform and implementation of social security policies based on the principles embodied in international labour standards, with a special focus on developing strategies to extend social security coverage. The Branch provides general research and analysis of social security issues; extends technical assistance to member states for designing, reforming and expanding social security schemes; provides services to enable community-based organizations to develop their own social security systems; promotes and oversees the implementation of ILO standards on social security; develops training programmes and materials; and disseminates information. The Financial, Actuarial and Statistical Branch assists with the long-term financial planning of social protection systems.

ILO's Global Programme on Safety, Health and the Environment aims to protect workers in hazardous occupations (e.g. agriculture, mining and construction); to provide protection to vulnerable groups of workers outside the scope of normal protection measures; to improve the capacity of governments and employers' and workers' organizations to address workers' well-being, extend the scope of occupational health care, etc.; and to ensure that policy-makers recognize and document the social and economic impact of implementing measures that enhance workers' protection. ILO's Conditions of Work Branch conducts research and provides advocacy, training and technical co-operation to governments and employers' and workers' organizations. The International Labour Migration Branch focuses on protecting the rights, and promoting the integration, of migrant workers, forging international consensus on the management of migration, and furthering knowledge of international migration. ILO's Global Programme on HIV/AIDS and the World of Work, formally established in November 2000, issued a code of practice in May 2001. In October ILO became the eighth co-sponsor of the Joint UN Programme on HIV/AIDS (UNAIDS), which was established on 1 January 1996 by UNICEF, UNDP, UNFPA, UNESCO, WHO and the World Bank, with participation by UNDCP from 1999.

TRIPARTISM AND SOCIAL DIALOGUE

This area was identified as one of the four strategic objectives in order to concentrate and reinforce ILO's support for strengthening the process of tripartism, the role and activities of its tripartite constituents (i.e. governments, employers and workers' organizations), and, in particular, their capacity to engage in and to promote the use of social dialogue. ILO recognizes that the enactment of labour laws, and ensuring their effective enforcement, collective bargaining and other forms of co-operation are important means of promoting social justice. It aims to assist governments and employers' and workers' organizations to establish sound labour relations, to adapt labour laws to meet changing economic and social needs, and to improve labour administration.

INTERNATIONAL LABOUR CONFERENCE

88th Session: May/June 2000. Adopted the Maternity Protection Convention, 2000 (No 183), requiring signatory states to expand maternity protection to cover more categories of employment, including the informal sector; to extend statutory maternity leave from 12 to 14 weeks; to guarantee the right to leave from work prior to and after childbirth in cases of related complications or illness; to reimburse employers in respect of maternity leave through compulsory social insurance schemes, public funds or in another manner determined by national law or practice; and to permit short daily breaks from work for the purpose of breast-feeding. Held a special high-level meeting on the impact of HIV/AIDS on work, productivity and development, and discussed the social consequences of globalization. Adopted an unprecedented resolution threatening the imposition of punitive measures against Myanmar if it was still deemed to be contravening the Forced Labour Convention at 30 November 2000. (The sanctions were subsequently imposed.) Held a first discussion on drafting a new standard concerning health and safety in agriculture.

89th Session: June 2001. Adopted a Convention and Recommendation on Agricultural Safety and Health. (It is estimated that about one-half of occupational fatalities annually occur in the agricultural sector, primarily as a result of exposure to pesticides and other toxins or accidents with machinery.) The Director-General presented a report entitled 'Reducing the Decent Work Deficit', emphasizing the need to implement the Organization's agenda on decent work at policy level. Determined to send a high level team to evaluate the situation in Myanmar, welcoming the Myanmar Government's decision to co-operate with ILO by promising freedom of movement, access to and protection of witnesses. Considered a global report on forced labour and examined a report by the Director-General on the condition of workers in the Occupied Territories.

MEETINGS

Meetings held during 2001, in addition to the regular Governing Body sessions, included: the Tripartite Meeting on Human Resources Development, Employment and Globalization in the Hotel, Catering and Tourism Sector; Meeting of Experts on ILO Guide-lines on Occupational Safety and Health Management Systems; Tripartite Meeting of Experts on HIV/AIDS and the World of Work; Tripartite Meeting on the Social and Labour Dimensions of the Forestry and Wood Industries on the Move; International Symposium to Strengthen Workers' Participation in the UN System and Impact on Bretton Woods Institutions; Tripartite Meeting of Experts on the Management of Disability at the Workplace; and the Tripartite Meeting on the Construction Industry in the 21st Century.

INTERNATIONAL INSTITUTE FOR LABOUR STUDIES

Established in 1960 and based at ILO's Geneva headquarters, the Institute promotes the study and discussion of policy issues of concern to ILO and its constituents, i.e. government, employers and workers. The core theme of the Institute's activities is the interaction between labour institutions, development and civil society in a global economy. It identifies emerging social and labour issues by developing new areas for research and action, and encourages dialogue on social policy between the tripartite constituency of ILO and the international academic community and other experts. The Institute maintains research networks, conducts courses, seminars and social policy forums, and supports internships and visiting scholar and internship programmes.

INTERNATIONAL TRAINING CENTRE OF ILO

Address: Corso Unità d'Italia 125, 10127 Turin, Italy.

The Centre became operational in 1965. The ILO Director-General is Chairman of the Board of the Centre. It provides programmes for directors in charge of technical and vocational institutions, training officers, senior and middle-level managers in private and public enterprises, trade union leaders, and technicians, primarily from the developing regions of the world. Since 1991 the Centre has been increasingly used by UN agencies to provide training for improving the management of development and for building national capacities to sustain development programmes.

Finance

The proposed regular budget for the two years 2002–03 was US $472.5m.

Publications

(in English, French and Spanish unless otherwise indicated)

Bulletin of Labour Statistics (quarterly).

International Labour Review (quarterly).

International studies, surveys, works of practical guidance or reference on questions of social policy, manpower, industrial relations, working conditions, social security, training, management development, etc.

Key Indicators of the Labour Market.

Labour Law Documents (selected labour and social security laws and regulations; 3 a year).

Official Bulletin (3 a year).

Reports for the annual sessions of the International Labour Conference, etc. (also in Arabic, Chinese and Russian).

World Employment Report (every 2 years).

World Labour Report (every 2 years).

World of Work (magazine issued in several languages; 5 a year).

Yearbook of Labour Statistics.

Also maintains a database on international labour standards, ILOLEX, and a database on national labour law, NATLEX, in electronic form.

Declaration concerning the aims and purpose of the International Labour Organization (Philadelphia Declaration)

(10 May 1944)

I. The Conference reaffirms the fundamental principles on which the Organization is based and, in particular, that:

(a) labour is not a commodity;
(b) freedom of expression and of association are essential to sustained progress;
(c) poverty anywhere constitutes a danger to prosperity everywhere;
(d) the war against want requires to be carried on with unrelenting vigour within each nation, and by continuous and concerted international effort in which the representatives of workers and employers, enjoying equal status with those of governments, join with them in free discussion and democratic decision with a view to the promotion of the common welfare.

II. Believing that experience has fully demonstrated the truth of the statement in the Constitution of the International Labour Organization that lasting peace can be established only if it is based on social justice, the Conference affirms that:

(a) all human beings, irrespective of race, creed or sex, have the right to pursue both their material well-being and their spiritual development in conditions of freedom and dignity, of economic security and equal opportunity;
(b) the attainment of the conditions in which this shall be possible must constitute the central aim of national and international policy;
(c) all national and international policies and measures, in particular those of an economic and financial character, should be judged in this light and accepted only in so far as they may be held to promote and not to hinder the achievement of this fundamental objective;
(d) it is a responsibility of the International Labour Organization to examine and consider all international economic and financial policies and measures in the light of this fundamental objective;
(e) in discharging the tasks entrusted to it the International Labour Organization, having considered all relevant economic and financial factors, may include in its decisions and recommendations any provisions which it considers appropriate.

III. The Conference recognizes the solemn obligation of the International Labour Organization to further among the nations of the world programmes which will achieve:

(a) full employment and the raising of standards of living;
(b) the employment of workers in the occupations in which they can have the satisfaction of giving the fullest measure of their skill and attainments and make their greatest contribution to the common well-being;
(c) the provision, as a means to the attainment of this end and under adequate guarantees for all concerned, of facilities for training and the transfer of labour, including migration for employment and settlement;
(d) policies in regard to wages and earnings, hours and other conditions of work calculated to ensure a just share of the fruits of progress to all, and a minimum living wage to all employed and in need of such protection;
(e) the effective recognition of the right of collective bargaining, the co-operation of management and labour in the continuous improvement of productive efficiency, and the collaboration of workers and employers in the preparation and application of social and economic measures;
(f) the extension of social security measures to provide a basic income to all in need of such protection and comprehensive medical care;
(g) adequate protection for the life and health of workers in all occupations;
(h) provision for child welfare and maternity protection;
(i) the provision of adequate nutrition, housing and facilities for recreation and culture;
(j) the assurance of equality of educational and vocational opportunity.

IV. Confident that the fuller and broader utilization of the world's productive resources necessary for the achievement of the objectives set forth in this Declaration can be secured by effective international and national action, including measures to expand production and consumption, to avoid severe economic fluctuations to promote the economic and social advancement of the less developed regions of the world, to assure greater stability in world prices of primary products, and to promote a high and steady volume of international trade, the Conference pledges the full co-operation of the International Labour Organization with such international bodies as may be entrusted with a share of the responsibility for this great task and for the promotion of the health, education and well-being of all peoples.

V. The conference affirms that the principles set forth in this Declaration are fully applicable to all peoples everywhere and that, while the manner of their application must be determined with due regard to the stage of social and economic development reached by each people, their progressive application to peoples who are still dependent, as well as to those who have already achieved self-government, is a matter of concern to the whole civilized world.

International Maritime Organization—IMO

Address: 4 Albert Embankment, London, SE1 7SR, United Kingdom.

Telephone: (20) 7735-7611; **fax:** (20) 7587-3210; **e-mail:** info@imo.org; **internet:** www.imo.org.

The Inter-Governmental Maritime Consultative Organization (IMCO) began operations in 1959, as a specialized agency of the UN to facilitate co-operation among governments on technical matters affecting international shipping. Its main functions are the achievement of safe and efficient navigation, and the control of pollution caused by ships and craft operating in the marine environment. IMCO became IMO in 1982.

MEMBERS

160 members and two associate members: see Table on pp. 211–213.

Organization

(March 2002)

ASSEMBLY

The Assembly consists of delegates from all member countries, who each have one vote. Associate members and observers from other governments and the international agencies are also present. Regular sessions are held every two years. The Assembly is responsible for the election of members to the Council and approves the appointment of the Secretary-General of the Secretariat. It considers reports from all subsidiary bodies and decides the action to be taken on them; it votes the agency's budget and determines the work programme and financial policy. The 22nd regular session of the Assembly was held in London in November 2001.

The Assembly also recommends to members measures to promote maritime safety and to prevent and control maritime pollution from ships.

COUNCIL

The Council is the governing body of the Organization between the biennial sessions of the Assembly. Its members, representatives of 32 states, are elected by the Assembly for a term of two years. (With effect from November 2002 the Council was to comprise representatives of 40 states.) The Council appoints the Secretary-General; transmits reports by the subsidiary bodies, including the Maritime Safety Committee, to the Assembly, and reports on the work of the Organization generally; submits budget estimates and financial statements with comments and recommendations to the Assembly. The Council normally meets twice a year.

Facilitation Committee: Constituted by the Council in May 1972 as a subsidiary body, this Committee deals with measures to facilitate maritime travel and transport and matters arising from the 1965 Facilitation Convention. Membership is open to all IMO member states.

MARITIME SAFETY COMMITTEE

The Maritime Safety Committee is open to all IMO members. The Committee meets at least once a year and submits proposals to the Assembly on technical matters affecting the safety of shipping.

Sub-Committees:

Bulk Liquids and Gases*.
Carriage of Dangerous Goods, Solid Cargoes and Containers.
Fire Protection.
Flag State Implementation*.
Radiocommunications and Search and Rescue.
Safety of Navigation.
Ship Design and Equipment.
Stability and Load Lines and Fishing Vessel Safety.
Standards of Training and Watchkeeping.

* Also sub-committees of the Marine Environment Protection Committee.

LEGAL COMMITTEE

Established by the Council in June 1967 to deal initially with problems connected with the loss of the tanker *Torrey Canyon*, and subsequently with any legal problems laid before IMO. Membership open to all IMO member states.

MARINE ENVIRONMENT PROTECTION COMMITTEE

Established by the eighth Assembly (1973) to co-ordinate IMO's work on the prevention and control of marine pollution from ships, and to assist IMO in its consultations with other UN bodies, and with international organizations and expert bodies in the field of marine pollution. Membership is open to all IMO members.

TECHNICAL CO-OPERATION COMMITTEE

Constituted by the Council in May 1972, this Committee evaluates the implementation of UN Development Programme projects for which IMO is the executing agency, and generally reviews IMO's technical assistance programmes. Its membership is open to all IMO member states.

SECRETARIAT

The Secretariat consists of the Secretary-General and a staff appointed by the Secretary-General and recruited on as wide a geographical basis as possible.

Secretary-General: WILLIAM A. O'NEIL (Canada).

Divisions of the Secretariat:

Administrative
Conference
Legal Affairs and External Relations
Marine Environment
Maritime Safety
Technical Co-operation

Activities

In addition to the work of its committees and sub-committees, the organization works in connection with the following Conventions, of which it is the depository:

Convention on Facilitation of International Maritime Traffic, 1965. Came into force in March 1967.

International Convention on Load Lines, 1966. Came into force in July 1968.

International Convention on Tonnage Measurement of Ships, 1969. Convention embodies a universal system for measuring ships' tonnage. Came into force in 1982.

International Convention relating to Intervention on the High Seas in Cases of Oil Pollution Casualties, 1969. Came into force in May 1975. A Protocol adopted in 1973 came into force in 1983.

International Convention on Civil Liability for Oil Pollution Damage, 1969. Came into force in June 1975.

Intenational Convention on the Establishment of an International Fund for Compensation for Oil Pollution Damage, 1971. Came into force in October 1978.

Convention relating to Civil Liability in the Field of Maritime Carriage of Nuclear Material, 1971. Came into force in 1975.

Special Trade Passenger Ships Agreement, 1971. Came into force in 1974.

Convention on the International Regulations for Preventing Collisions at Sea, 1972. Came into force in July 1977.

Convention on the Prevention of Marine Pollution by Dumping of Wastes and Other Matter, 1972. Came into force in August 1975. Extended to include a ban on low-level nuclear waste in November 1993; came into force in February 1994.

International Convention for Safe Containers, 1972. Came into force in September 1977.

International Convention for the Prevention of Pollution from Ships, 1973 (as modified by the Protocol of 1978). Came into force in October 1983. Extended to include regulations to prevent air pollution in September 1997; amendments will come into force 12 months after 15 countries whose combined fishing fleets constitute 50% of the world's merchant fleet have become parties thereto.

International Convention on Safety of Life at Sea, 1974. Came into force in May 1980. A Protocol drawn up in 1978 came into force in May 1981. Numerous extensions and amendments.

Athens Convention relating to the Carriage of Passengers and their Luggage by Sea, 1974. Came into force in April 1987.

Convention on the International Maritime Satellite Organization, 1976. Came into force in July 1979.

Convention on Limitation of Liability for Maritime Claims, 1976. Came into force in December 1986.

International Convention for the Safety of Fishing Vessels, Torremolinos, 1977. Will come into force 12 months after 15 countries whose combined fishing fleets constitute 50% of world fishing fleets of 24 metres in length and over have become parties thereto.

International Convention on Standards of Training, Certification and Watchkeeping for Seafarers, 1978. Came into force in April 1984; restructured by amendments that entered into force in February 1997.

International Convention on Maritime Search and Rescue, 1979. Came into force in June 1985.

Paris Memorandum of Understanding on Port State Control, 1982.

International Convention for the Suppression of Unlawful Acts against the Safety of International Shipping, 1988. Came into force in March 1992.

Protocol for the Suppression of Unlawful Acts against the Safety of Fixed Platform located on the Continental Shelf, 1988. Came into force in March 1992.

International Convention on Salvage, 1989. Came into force in July 1996.

International Convention on Oil Pollution, Preparedness, Response and Co-operation, 1990. Came into force on 13 May 1995.

International Convention on Liability and Compensation for Damage in Connection with the Carriage of Hazardous and Noxious Substances by Sea, 1996. Will come into force 18 months after 12 states of which four have not less than 2m. units of gross tonnage have become parties thereto.

International Convention on Civil Liability for Bunker Oil Pollution Damage, 2001.

Convention on Control of Harmful Anti-fouling Systems on Ships, 2001. Will enter into force 12 months after 25 states representing 25% of the world's merchant shipping tonnage have become parties thereto.

ASSOCIATED INSTITUTES

IMO Maritime Law Institute—IMLI: POB 31, Msida, MSD 01, Malta; tel. 319343; fax 343092; e-mail imli@maltanet.net; internet www.imli.org; provides training for maritime lawyers. Dir Prof. DAVID ATTARD.

International Maritime Academy—IMA: via E. Weiss 15, 34127 Trieste, Italy; tel. (40) 350829; fax (40) 350322; e-mail imoima@imoima.org; internet www.imoima.org; provides post-graduate training for seafarers and onshore staff employed in maritime-related fields; Dir PIETRO MARIN.

Regional Marine Pollution Emergency Response Centre for the Mediterranean Sea—REMPEC: Manoel Island, GZR 03, Malta; tel. 337296; fax 339951; e-mail rempec@waldonet.mt; internet www.rempec.org; f. 1976 as the Regional Oil Combating Centre for the Mediterranean Sea. Administered by IMO in conjunction with the Regional Seas Programme of the UN Environment Programme. Aims to develop measures to combat pollution in the Mediterranean. Dir ROBERTO PATRUNO.

World Maritime University—WMU: POB 500, Citadellsvägen 29, 201 24 Malmö, Sweden; tel. (40) 356300; fax (40) 128442; e-mail info@wmu.se; internet www.wmu.se; f. by IMO in 1983. Offers postgraduate courses in various maritime disciplines, mainly for students from developing countries. Rector K. LAUBSTEIN. Publs *WMU Newsletter*, *WMU Handbook*.

Finance

Contributions are received from the member states. The budget appropriation for the two years 2002–03 amounted to £39.5m.

Publications

IMO News (quarterly).

Numerous specialized publications, including international conventions of which IMO is depositary.

International Monetary Fund—IMF

Address: 700 19th St, NW, Washington, DC 20431, USA.

Telephone: (202) 623-7300; **fax:** (202) 623-6220; **e-mail:** publicaffairs@imf.org; **internet:** www.imf.org.

The IMF was established at the same time as the World Bank in December 1945, to promote international monetary co-operation, to facilitate the expansion and balanced growth of international trade and to promote stability in foreign exchange.

MEMBERS

183 members: see Table on pp. 211–213.

Organization

(March 2002)

Managing Director: HORST KÖHLER (Germany).

First Deputy Managing Director: ANNE KRUEGER (USA).

Deputy Managing Directors: SHIGEMITSU SUGISAKI (Japan); EDUARDO ANINAT (Chile).

BOARD OF GOVERNORS

The highest authority of the Fund is exercised by the Board of Governors, on which each member country is represented by a Governor and an Alternate Governor. The Board normally meets once a year. The Board of Governors has delegated many of its powers to the Executive Directors. However, the conditions governing the admission of new members, adjustment of quotas and the election of Executive Directors, as well as certain other important powers, remain the sole responsibility of the Board of Governors. The voting power of each member on the Board of Governors is related to its quota in the Fund (see p. 175).

In September 1999 the Board of Governors adopted a resolution to transform the Interim Committee of the Board of Governors (established 1974) into the International Monetary and Financial Committee (IMFC). The IMFC, which held its inaugural meeting in April 2000, comprises 24 members, representing the same countries or groups of countries as those on the Board of Executive Directors (see below). It advises and reports to the Board on matters relating to the management and adaptation of the international monetary and financial system, sudden disturbances that might threaten the system and proposals to amend the Articles of Agreement, but has no decision-making authority.

The Development Committee (the Joint Ministerial Committee of the Boards of Governors of the World Bank and the IMF on the Transfer of Real Resources to Developing Countries, created in 1974, with a structure similar to that of the IMFC) reviews development policy issues and financing requirements.

BOARD OF EXECUTIVE DIRECTORS

The 24-member Board of Executive Directors, responsible for the day-to-day operations of the Fund, is in continuous session in Washington, under the chairmanship of the Fund's Managing Director or Deputy Managing Directors. The USA, the United Kingdom, Germany, France and Japan each appoint one Executive Director. There is also one Executive Director each from the People's Republic of China, Russia and Saudi Arabia, while the remainder are elected by groups of the remaining countries. As in the Board of Governors, the voting power of each member is related to its quota in the Fund, but in practice the Executive Directors normally operate by consensus.

The Managing Director of the Fund serves as head of its staff, which is organized into departments by function and area. At 31 December 2000 the Fund staff employed 2,455 staff members (with a further 380 additional authorized staff positions) from 133 countries. In mid-1994 two new positions of Deputy Managing Director were created, bringing the total to three. This major structural development was approved by the Executive Board and reflected the increase in reponsibilities of that position, owing to the IMF's greatly enlarged membership.

Activities

The purposes of the IMF, as defined in the Articles of Agreement, are:

(i) To promote international monetary co-operation through a permanent institution which provides the machinery for consultation and collaboration on monetary problems.

(ii) To facilitate the expansion and balanced growth of international trade, and to contribute thereby to the promotion and maintenance of high levels of employment and real income and to the development of members' productive resources.

(iii) To promote exchange stability, to maintain orderly exchange arrangements among members, and to avoid competitive exchange depreciation.

(iv) To assist in the establishment of a multilateral system of payments in respect of current transactions between members and in the elimination of foreign exchange restrictions which hamper the growth of trade.

(v) To give confidence to members by making the general resources of the Fund temporarily available to them, under adequate safeguards, thus providing them with the opportunity to correct maladjustments in their balance of payments, without resorting to measures destructive of national or international prosperity.

(vi) In accordance with the above, to shorten the duration of and lessen the degree of disequilibrium in the international balances of payments of members.

In joining the Fund, each country agrees to co-operate with the above objectives. In accordance with its objective of facilitating the expansion of international trade, the IMF encourages its members to accept the obligations of Article VIII, Sections two, three and four, of the Articles of Agreement. Members that accept Article VIII undertake to refrain from imposing restrictions on the making of payments and transfers for current international transactions and from engaging in discriminatory currency arrangements or multiple currency practices without IMF approval. By January 2002 151 members had accepted Article VIII status.

The financial crises of the late 1990s, notably in several Asian countries, Brazil and Russia, contributed to widespread discussions concerning the strengthening of the international monetary system. In April 1998 the Executive Board identified the following fundamental aspects of the debate: reinforcing international and domestic financial systems; strengthening IMF surveillance; promoting greater availability and transparency of information regarding member countries' economic data and policies; emphasizing the central role of the IMF in crisis management; and establishing effective procedures to involve the private sector in forestalling or resolving financial crises. During 1999/2000 the Fund implemented several measures in connection with its ongoing efforts to appraise and reinforce the global financial architecture, including, in March 2000, the adoption by the Executive Board of a strengthened framework to safeguard the use of IMF resources. During 2000 the Fund established the IMF Center, in Washington, DC, which aimed to promote awareness and understanding of its activities. In September the Fund's new Managing Director announced his intention to focus and streamline the principals of conditionality (which links Fund financing with the implementation of specific economic policies by the recipient countries) in order to strengthen the concept of national ownership and as part of the wider reform of the international financial system. The issue remained under discussion by the Executive Board, and was to be open to public comment. In 2000/01 the Fund established an International Capital Markets Department to improve its understanding of financial markets and a separate Consultative Group on capital markets to serve as a forum for regular dialogue between the Fund and representatives of the private sector.

In early 2002 a position of Director for Special Operations was created to enhance the Fund's ability to respond to critical situations affecting member countries. In February the newly-appointed Director immediately assumed leadership of the staff team working with the authorities in Argentina to help that country to overcome its extreme economic and social difficulties.

SURVEILLANCE

Under its Articles of Agreement, the Fund is mandated to oversee the effective functioning of the international monetary system. Accordingly, the Fund aims to exercise firm surveillance over the exchange rate policies of member states and to assess whether a country's economic situation and policies are consistent with the objectives of sustainable development and domestic and external stability. The Fund's main tools of surveillance are regular, bilateral consultations with member countries conducted in accordance with Article IV of the Articles of Agreement, which cover fiscal and monetary policies, balance of payments and external debt developments, as well as policies that affect the economic performance of a country, such as the labour market, social and environmental issues and good governance, and aspects of the country's capital accounts, and finance and banking sectors. In April 1997, in an effort to improve the value of surveillance by means of increased transparency, the Executive Board agreed to the voluntary issue of Press Information Notices (PINs) (on the internet and in *IMF Economic Reviews*), following each member's Article IV consultation with the Board, to those member countries wishing to make public the Fund's views. Other background papers providing information on and analysis of economic developments in individual countries continued to be made available. In addition, World Economic Outlook discussions are held, normally twice a year, by the Executive Board to assess policy implications from a multilateral perspective and to monitor global developments.

The rapid decline in the value of the Mexican peso in late 1994 and the financial crisis in Asia, which became apparent in mid-1997, focused attention on the importance of IMF surveillance of the economies and financial policies of member states and prompted the Fund to enhance the effectiveness of its surveillance and to encourage the full and timely provision of data by member countries in order to maintain fiscal transparency. In April 1996 the IMF established the Special Data Dissemination Standard (SDDS), which was intended to improve access to reliable economic statistical information for member countries that have, or are seeking, access to international capital markets. In March 1999 the IMF undertook to strengthen the Standard by the introduction of a new reserves data template. By September 2001 49 countries had subscribed to the Standard. In December 1997 the Executive Board approved a new General Data Dissemination System (GDDS), to encourage all member countries to improve the production and dissemination of core economic data. The operational phase of the GDDS commenced in May 2000. The Fund maintains a Dissemination Standards Bulletin Board (accessible at dsbb.imf.org), which aims to ensure that information on SDDS subscribing countries is widely available.

In April 1998 the then Interim Committee adopted a voluntary Code of Good Practices on Fiscal Transparency: Declaration of Principles, which aimed to increase the quality and promptness of official reports on economic indicators, and in September 1999 it adopted a Code of Good Practices on Transparency in Monetary and Financial Policies: Declaration of Principles. The IMF and World Bank jointly established a Financial Sector Assessment Programme (FSAP) in May 1999, initially as a pilot project, which aimed to promote greater global financial security through the preparation of confidential detailed evaluations of the financial sectors of individual countries. Assessments were undertaken of 12 industrialized countries, emerging market economies and developing countries. During 2000 the FSAP was extended to cover a further 24 countries. It remained under regular review by the Boards of Governors of the Fund and World Bank. As part of the FSAP, Fund staff may conclude a Financial System Stability Assessment (FSSA), addressing issues relating to macroeconomic stability and the strength of a country's financial system. A separate component of the FSAP are Reports on the Observance of Standards and Codes, which are compiled after an assessment of a country's implementation and observance of internationally recognized financial standards. In March 2000 the IMF Executive Board adopted a strengthened framework to safeguard the use of IMF resources. All member countries making use of Fund resources were to be required to publish annual central bank statements audited in accordance with internationally accepted standards. It was also agreed that any instance of intentional misreporting of information by a member country should be publicized. In the following month the Executive Board approved the establishment of an Independent Evaluation Office to conduct objective evaluations of IMF policy and operations. In August the Executive Board adopted a Code of Conduct to guide its activities.

In April 2001 the Executive Board agreed on measures to enhance international efforts to counter money-laundering, in particular through the Fund's ongoing financial supervision activities and its programme of assessment of offshore financial centres. In November the IMFC, in response to the terrorist attacks against targets in the USA, which had occurred in September, resolved, *inter alia*, to strengthen the Fund's focus on surveillance, and, in particular, to extend measures to counter money-laundering to include the funds of terrorist organizations. It determined to accelerate efforts to assess offshore centres and to provide technical support to enable poorer countries to meet international financial standards.

SPECIAL DRAWING RIGHTS

The special drawing right (SDR) was introduced in 1970 as a substitute for gold in international payments, and was intended eventually to become the principal reserve asset in the international monetary system. SDRs are allocated to members in proportion to their quotas. The IMF has allocated a total of SDR 21,433m. since the SDR was created in 1970. In October 1996 the Executive Board agreed to a new allocation of SDRs in order to achieve their equitable distribution among member states (i.e. all members would have an equal number of SDRs relative to the size of their quotas). In particular, this was deemed necessary since 38 countries that had joined the Fund since the last allocation of SDRs in 1981 had not yet received any of the units of account. In September 1997 at the annual meeting of the Executive Board, a resolution approving a special allocation of SDR 21,400m. was passed, in order to ensure an SDR to quota ratio of 29.32%, for all member countries. The resolution was to come into effect following its acceptance by 60% of member countries, having 85% of the total voting power.

From 1974 to 1980 the SDR was valued on the basis of the market exchange rate for a basket of 16 currencies, belonging to the members with the largest exports of goods and services; since 1981 it has been based on the currencies of the five largest exporters (France, Germany, Japan, the United Kingdom and the USA), although the list of currencies and the weight of each

BOARD OF EXECUTIVE DIRECTORS (March 2002)

Director	Casting Votes of	Total Votes	%
Appointed:			
RANDAL QUARLES	USA	371,743	17.16
KEN YAGI	Japan	133,378	6.16
KARLHEINZ BISCHOFBERGER	Germany	130,332	6.02
PIERRE DUQUESNE	France	107,635	4.97
TOM SCHOLAR	United Kingdom	107,635	4.97
Elected:			
WILLY KIEKENS (Belgium)	Austria, Belarus, Belgium, Czech Republic, Hungary, Kazakhstan, Luxembourg, Slovakia, Slovenia, Turkey	111,696	5.16
J. DE BEAUFORT WIJNHOLDS (Netherlands)	Armenia, Bosnia and Herzegovina, Bulgaria, Croatia, Cyprus, Georgia, Israel, the former Yugoslav republic of Macedonia, Moldova, Netherlands, Romania, Ukraine	105,412	4.87
FERNANDO VARELA (Spain)	Costa Rica, El Salvador, Guatemala, Honduras, Mexico, Nicaragua, Spain, Venezuela	92,989	4.29
PIER CARLO PADOAN (Italy)	Albania, Greece, Italy, Malta, Portugal, San Marino	90,636	4.18
IAN E. BENNETT (Canada)	Antigua and Barbuda, Bahamas, Barbados, Belize, Canada, Dominica, Grenada, Ireland, Jamaica, Saint Christopher and Nevis, Saint Lucia, Saint Vincent and the Grenadines	80,636	3.72
ÓLAFUR ÍSLEIFSSON (Iceland)	Denmark, Estonia, Finland, Iceland, Latvia, Lithuania, Norway, Sweden	76,276	3.52
MICHAEL J. CALLAGHAN (Australia)	Australia, Kiribati, Republic of Korea, Marshall Islands, Federated States of Micronesia, Mongolia, New Zealand, Palau, Papua New Guinea, Philippines, Samoa, Seychelles, Solomon Islands, Vanuatu	72,413	3.34
SULAIMAN M. AL-TURKI	Saudi Arabia	70,105	3.24
CYRUS RUSTOMJEE (South Africa)	Angola, Botswana, Burundi, Eritrea, Ethiopia, The Gambia, Kenya, Lesotho, Liberia, Malawi, Mozambique, Namibia, Nigeria, Sierra Leone, South Africa, Sudan, Swaziland, Tanzania, Uganda, Zambia, Zimbabwe	69,968	3.23
DONO ISKANDAR DJOJOSUBROTO (Indonesia)	Brunei, Cambodia, Fiji, Indonesia, Laos, Malaysia, Myanmar, Nepal, Singapore, Thailand, Tonga, Viet Nam	68,367	3.16
A. SHAKOUR SHAALAN (Egypt)	Bahrain, Egypt, Iraq, Jordan, Kuwait, Lebanon, Libya, Maldives, Oman, Qatar, Syria, United Arab Emirates, Yemen	64,008	2.95
WEI BENHUA	People's Republic of China	63,942	2.95
ALEKSEI V. MOZHIN	Russia	59,704	2.76
ROBERTO F. CIPPA (Switzerland)	Azerbaijan, Kyrgyzstan, Poland, Switzerland, Tajikistan, Turkmenistan, Uzbekistan	56,900	2.63
MURILO PORTUGAL (Brazil)	Brazil, Colombia, Dominican Republic, Ecuador, Guyana, Haiti, Panama, Suriname, Trinidad and Tobago	53,422	2.47
VIJAY L. KELKAR (India)	Bangladesh, Bhutan, India, Sri Lanka	52,112	2.41
ABBAS MIRAKHOR (Iran)	Algeria, Ghana, Iran, Morocco, Pakistan, Tunisia	51,793	2.39
A. GUILLERMO ZOCCALI (Argentina)	Argentina, Bolivia, Chile, Paraguay, Peru, Uruguay	43,395	2.00
ALEXANDRE BARRO CHAMBRIER (Gabon)	Benin, Burkina Faso, Cameroon, Cape Verde, Central African Republic, Chad, Comoros, Republic of the Congo, Côte d'Ivoire, Djibouti, Equatorial Guinea, Gabon, Guinea, Guinea-Bissau, Madagascar, Mali, Mauritania, Mauritius, Niger, Rwanda, São Tomé and Príncipe, Senegal, Togo	25,169	1.16

Note: At 5 March 2002 member countries' votes totalled 2,166,739, while votes in the Board of Executive Directors totalled 2,159,666. The latter total does not include the votes of Afghanistan, Somalia and the Federal Republic of Yugoslavia, which did not participate in the 2000 election of Executive Directors; it also excludes the votes of the Democratic Republic of the Congo, whose voting rights were suspended with effect from 2 June 1994.

in the SDR valuation basket is revised every five years. In January 1999 the IMF incorporated the new currency of the European Economic and Monetary Union, the euro, into the valuation basket; it replaced the French and German currencies, on the basis of their conversion rates with the euro as agreed by the EU. From 1 January 2001 the relative weights assigned to the currencies in the valuation basket were redistributed. The value of the SDR averaged US $1.27304 during 2001, and at 5 March 2002 stood at $1.24539.

The Second Amendment to the Articles of Agreement (1978) altered and expanded the possible uses of the SDR in transactions with other participants. These 'prescribed holders' of the SDRs have the same degree of freedom as Fund members to buy and sell SDRs and to receive or use them in loans, pledges, swaps, donations or settlement of financial obligations. In 2000/01 there were 16 'prescribed holders': the African Development Bank and the African Development Fund, the Arab Monetary Fund, the Asian Development Bank, the Bank of Central African States, the Bank for International Settlements, the Central Bank of West African States, the East African Development Bank, the Eastern Caribbean Central Bank, the European Central Bank, the International Bank for Reconstruction and Development and the International Development Association, the International Fund for Agricultural Development, the Islamic Development Bank, the Latin American Reserve Fund and the Nordic Investment Bank.

QUOTAS

Each member is assigned a quota related to its national income, monetary reserves, trade balance and other economic indicators. A member's subscription is equal to its quota and is payable partly in SDRs and partly in its own currency. The quota determines a member's voting power, which is based on one vote for each SDR 100,000 of its quota *plus* the 250 votes to which each member is entitled. A member's quota also determines its access to the financial resources of the IMF, and its allocation of SDRs.

Quotas are reviewed at intervals of not more than five years, to take into account the state of the world economy and members' different rates of development. Special increases, separate to the general review, may be made in exceptional circumstances. These have been approved by the Fund for the People's Republic of China in 1980 and 2001, for Saudi Arabia in 1981, and for Cambodia in 1984. In June 1990 the Board of Governors authorized proposals for a Ninth General Review of quotas. Total quotas were to be increased by roughly 50% (depending on various factors). At the same time the Board of Governors stipulated that the quota increase could occur only after the Third Amendment of the IMF's Articles of Agreement had come into effect. The amendment provides for the suspension of voting and other related rights of members that do not fulfil their obligations under the Articles. By September 1992 the necessary proportion of IMF members had accepted the amendment, and it entered into force in November. The Tenth General Review of quotas was concluded in December 1994, with the Board recommending no further increase in quotas. However, the Board resolved to monitor closely the Fund's liquidity. In October 1996 the Fund's Managing Director advocated an increase in quotas under the latest review of at least two-thirds in the light of the IMF's reduced liquidity position. (The IMF had extended unprecedentedly large amounts in stand-by arrangements during the period 1995–96, notably to Mexico and Russia.) In January 1998 the Board of Governors adopted a resolution in support of an increase in quotas of 45%, subject to approval by member states constituting 85% of total quotas (as at December 1997). Sufficient consent had been granted by January 1999 to enable the Eleventh General Review of Quotas to enter into effect. At 5 March 2002 total quotas in the Fund amounted to SDR 212,414.9m.

RESOURCES

Members' subscriptions form the basic resource of the IMF. They are supplemented by borrowing. Under the General Arrangements to Borrow (GAB), established in 1962, the 'Group of Ten' industrialized nations (G-10—Belgium, Canada, France, Germany, Italy, Japan, the Netherlands, Sweden, the United Kingdom and the USA) and Switzerland (which became a member of the IMF in May 1992 but which had been a full participant in the GAB from April 1984) undertake to lend the Fund as much as SDR 17,000m. in their own currencies, to assist in fulfilling the balance-of-payments requirements of any member of the group, or in response to requests to the Fund from countries with balance-of-payments problems that could threaten the stability of the international monetary system. In 1983 the Fund entered into an agreement with Saudi Arabia, in association with the GAB, making available SDR 1,500m., and other borrowing arrangements were completed in 1984 with the Bank for International Settlements, the Saudi Arabian Monetary Agency, Belgium and Japan, making available a further SDR 6,000m. In 1986 another borrowing arrangement with Japan made available SDR 3,000m. In May 1996 GAB participants concluded an agreement in principle to expand the resources available for borrowing to SDR 34,000m., by securing the support of 25 countries with the financial capacity to support the international monetary system. The so-called New Arrangements to Borrow (NAB) was approved by the Executive Board in January 1997. It was to enter into force, for an initial five-year period, as soon as the five largest potential creditors participating in NAB had approved the initiative and the total credit arrangement of participants endorsing the scheme had reached at least SDR 28,900m. While the GAB credit arrangement was to remain in effect, the NAB was expected to be the first facility to be activated in the event of the Fund's requiring supplementary resources. In July 1998 the GAB was activated for the first time in more than 20 years in order to provide funds of up to US $6,300m. in support of an IMF emergency assistance package for Russia (the first time the GAB had been used for a non-participant). The NAB became effective in November, and was used for the first time as part of an extensive programme of support for Brazil, which was adopted by the IMF in early December.

DRAWING ARRANGEMENTS

Exchange transactions within the Fund take the form of members' purchases (i.e. drawings) from the Fund of the currencies of other members for the equivalent amounts of their own currencies. Fund resources are available to eligible members on an essentially short-term and revolving basis to provide members with temporary assistance to contribute to the solution of their payments problems. Before making a purchase, a member must show that its balance of payments or reserve position makes the purchase necessary. Apart from this requirement, reserve tranche purchases (i.e. purchases that do not bring the Fund's holdings of the member's currency to a level above its quota) are permitted unconditionally.

With further purchases, however, the Fund's policy of 'conditionality' means that a member requesting assistance must agree to adjust its economic policies, as stipulated by the IMF. All requests other than for use of the reserve tranche are examined by the Executive Board to determine whether the proposed use would be consistent with the Fund's policies, and a member must discuss its proposed adjustment programme (including fiscal, monetary, exchange and trade policies) with IMF staff. Purchases outside the reserve tranche are made in four credit tranches, each equivalent to 25% of the member's quota; a member must reverse the transaction by repurchasing its own currency (with SDRs or currencies specified by the Fund) within a specified time. A credit tranche purchase is usually made under a 'Stand-by Arrangement' with the Fund, or under the Extended Fund Facility. A Stand-by Arrangement is normally of one or two years' duration, and the amount is made available in instalments, subject to the member's observance of 'performance criteria'; repurchases must be made within three-and-a-quarter to five years. An Extended Arrangement is normally of three years' duration, and the member must submit detailed economic programmes and progress reports for each year; repurchases must be made within four-and-a-half to 10 years. A member whose payments imbalance is large in relation to its quota may make use of temporary facilities established by the Fund using borrowed resources, namely the 'enlarged access policy' established in 1981, which helps to finance Stand-by and Extended Arrangements for such a member, up to a limit of between 90% and 110% of the member's quota annually. Repurchases are made within three-and-a-half to seven years. In October 1994 the Executive Board approved a temporary increase in members' access to IMF resources, on the basis of a recommendation by the Interim Committee. The annual access limit under IMF regular tranche drawings, Stand-by Arrangements and Extended Fund Facility credits was increased from 68% to 100% of a member's quota, with the cumulative access limit remaining at 300% of quota. The arrangements were extended, on a temporary basis, in November 1997.

In addition, special-purpose arrangements have been introduced, all of which are subject to the member's co-operation with the Fund to find an appropriate solution to its difficulties. During late 1999 the Fund undertook a review of its non-concessional lending facilities. The Buffer Stock Financing Facility (BSFF), established in 1969 in order to enable members to pay their contributions to the buffer stocks which were intended to stabilize markets for primary commodities, was abolished in January 2000, having last been used in 1984. In January 2000 the Executive Board also resolved to eliminate the contingency component of the former Compensatory and Contingency Financing Facility, established in 1988, reforming it as the Compensatory Financing Facility (CCF). The CCF provides compensation to members whose export earnings are reduced as a result of circumstances beyond their control, or which are affected by excess costs of cereal imports. In December 1997 the Executive Board established a new Supplemental Reserve Facility (SRF) to provide short-term assistance to members experiencing exceptional balance-of-payments difficulties resulting from a sudden loss of market confidence. Repayments were to be made within one to one-and-a-half years of the purchase, unless otherwise extended by the Board. The SRF was activated immediately to provide SDR 9,950m. to the Republic of Korea, as part of a Stand-by Arrangement amounting to SDR 15,550m., the largest amount ever committed by the Fund. (With additional financing from governments and international institutions, the total assistance 'package' for the Republic of Korea reached an estimated $57,000m.) In July 1998 SDR 4,000m. was made available to Russia under the SRF and, in December, some SDR 9,100m. was extended to Brazil under the SRF as part of a new Stand-by Arrangement. In January 2001 some SDR 2,100m. in SRF resources were approved for Argentina as part of an SDR 5,187m. Stand-by Arrangement augmentation. (In January 2002 the Executive Board approved an extension of one year for Argentina's SRF repayments.) In April 1999 an additional facility, the Contingent Credit Lines (CCL), was established to provide short-term financing on similar terms to the SRF in order to prevent more stable economies being affected by adverse international financial developments and to maintain investor confidence. Under the CCL member countries were to have short-term access to up to 500% of their quota, subject to meeting various economic criteria stipulated by the Fund. No funds under the CCL were committed in 2000/01.

In October 1995 the Interim Committee of the Board of Governors endorsed recent decisions of the Executive Board to strengthen IMF financial support to members requiring exceptional assistance. An Emergency Financing Mechanism was established to enable the IMF to respond swiftly to potential or actual financial crises, while additional funds were made available for short-term currency stabilization. (The Mechanism was activated for the first time in July 1997, in response to a request by the Philippines Government to reinforce the country's international reserves, and was subsequently used during that year to assist Thailand, Indonesia and the Republic of Korea, and, in July 1998, Russia.) Emergency assistance was also to be available to countries in a post-conflict situation, in addition to existing arrangements for countries having been affected by natural disasters, to facilitate the rehabilitation of their economies and to improve their eligibility for further IMF concessionary arrangements. During 2000/01 the IMF extended emergency post-conflict assistance totalling SDR 138m. to the Republic of Congo, Sierra Leone and the Federal Republic of Yugoslavia.

In November 1999 the Fund's existing facility to provide balance-of-payments assistance on concessionary terms to low-income member countries, the Enhanced Structural Adjustment Facility, was reformulated as the Poverty Reduction and Growth Facility (PRGF), with greater emphasis on poverty reduction and sustainable development as key elements of growth-orientated economic strategies. Assistance under the PRGF (for which 77 countries were deemed eligible) was to be carefully matched to specific national requirements. Prior to drawing on the facility each recipient country was, in collaboration with representatives of civil society, non-governmental organizations and bilateral and multilateral institutions, to develop a national poverty reduction strategy, which was to be presented in a Poverty Reduction Strategy Paper (PRSP). PRGF loans carry an interest rate of 0.5% per year and are repayable over 10 years, with a five-and-a-half-year grace period; each eligible country is normally permitted to borrow up to 140% of its quota (in exceptional circumstances the maximum access can be raised to 185%). A PGRF Trust replaced the former ESAF Trust.

The PRGF supports, through long-maturity loans and grants, IMF participation in a joint initiative, with the World Bank, to provide exceptional assistance to heavily indebted poor countries (HIPCs), in order to help them to achieve a sustainable level of debt management. The initiative was formally approved at the September 1996 meeting of the Interim Committee, having received the support of the 'Paris Club' of official creditors, which agreed to increase the relief on official debt from 67% to 80%. In all, 41 HIPCs were identified, of which 33 were in sub-Saharan Africa. In April 1997 Uganda was approved as the first beneficiary of the initiative (see World Bank, p. 154). Resources for the HIPC initiative are channelled through the PRGF Trust. In early 1999 the IMF and World Bank initiated a comprehensive review of the HIPC scheme, in order to consider modifications of the initiative and to strengthen the link between debt relief and poverty reduction. A consensus emerged among the financial institutions and leading industralized nations to enhance the scheme, in order to make it available to more countries, and to accelerate the process of providing debt relief. In September the IMF Board of Governors expressed its commitment to undertaking an off-market transaction of a percentage of the Fund's gold reserves (i.e. a sale, at market prices, to central banks of member countries with repayment obligations to the Fund, which were then to be made in gold), as part of the funding arrangements of the enhanced HIPC scheme; this was undertaken during the period December 1999–April 2000. Under the enhanced initiative it was agreed that countries seeking debt relief should first formulate, and successfully implement for at least one year, a national poverty reduction strategy (see above). In May 2000 Uganda became the first country to qualify for full debt relief under the enhanced scheme. By 1 March 2002 26 eligible countries had reached their decision points (including Cote d'Ivoire reached under the original scheme) for which the Fund had committed SDR 1,472m.

During 2000/01 the IMF approved funding commitments for new arrangements amounting to SDR 14,333m., compared with SDR 22,929m. in the previous year. Of the total amount, SDR 13,093m. was committed under nine new Stand-by Arrangements and the augmentation of two already in place (for Turkey and Argentina); one new Extended Arrangement, amounting to SDR 24m. was approved, while an Extended Arrangement for Yemen was reduced by SDR 37m. Some 37 PRGF arrangements were approved in 2000/01, amounting to SDR 630m. During 2000/01 members' purchases from the general resources account amounted to SDR 9,599m., compared with SDR 6,377m. in the previous year, with the main users of IMF resources being Mexico, the Republic of Korea and Russia. Outstanding IMF credit at 30 April 2001 totalled SDR 48,691m., compared with SDR 50,370m. as at the previous year.

TECHNICAL ASSISTANCE

Technical assistance is provided by special missions or resident representatives who advise members on every aspect of economic management, while more specialized assistance is provided by the IMF's various departments. In 2000/01 the IMFC determined that technical assistance should be central to IMF's work in crisis prevention and management, in capacity-building for low-income countries, and in restoring macroeconomic stability in countries following a financial crisis. Technical assistance activities subsequently underwent a process of review and reorganization to align them more closely with IMF policy priorities and other initiatives, for example the Financial Stability Assessment Programme. The majority of technical assistance is provided by the Departments of Monetary and Exchange Affairs, of Fiscal Affairs and of Statistics, and by the IMF Institute. The Institute, founded in 1964, trains officials from member countries in financial analysis and policy, balance-of-payments methodology and public finance; it also gives assistance to national and regional training centres. In May 1998 an IMF—Singapore Regional Training Institute (an affiliate of the IMF Institute) was inaugurated, in collaboration with the Singaporean Government, in order to provide training for officials from the Asia-Pacific region. The IMF is a co-sponsor, with UNDP and the Japan administered account, of the Joint Vienna Institute, which was opened in the Austrian capital in October 1992 and which trains officials from former centrally-planned economies in various aspects of economic management and public administration. In January 1999 the IMF, in co-operation with the African Development Bank and the World Bank, announced the establishment of a Joint Africa Institute, in Abidjan, Côte d'Ivoire, which was to offer training to officials from African countries from the second half of the year. The IMF Institute also co-operates with other established regional training centres and institutes in order to refine its delivery of technical assistance and training services. During 2000/01 the Institute established a new training programme with government officials in the People's Republic of China and agreed to establish a regional training centre in Brazil.

Publications

Annual Report.

Balance of Payments Statistics Yearbook.

Direction of Trade Statistics (quarterly and annually).

Emerging Market Financing (quarterly).

Finance and Development (quarterly, published jointly with the World Bank).

Government Finance Statistics Yearbook.

IMF Economic Reviews (3 a year).

IMF Survey (2 a month).

International Capital Markets: Developments, Prospects and Key Policy Issues.

International Financial Statistics (monthly and annually, also on CD-ROM).

Joint BIS-IMF-OECD-World Bank Statistics on External Debt (quarterly).

Staff Papers (quarterly).

World Economic Outlook (2 a year).

Occasional papers, economic and financial surveys, pamphlets, booklets.

Statistics

QUOTAS (SDR million)

	5 March 2002
Afghanistan*	(161.9) 120.4
Albania	48.7
Algeria	1,254.7
Angola	286.3
Antigua and Barbuda	13.5
Argentina	2,117.1
Armenia	92.0
Australia	3,236.4
Austria	1,872.3
Azerbaijan	160.9
Bahamas	130.3
Bahrain	135.0
Bangladesh	533.3
Barbados	67.5
Belarus	386.4
Belgium	4,605.2
Belize	18.8
Benin	61.9
Bhutan	6.3
Bolivia	171.5
Bosnia and Herzegovina	169.1
Botswana	63.0
Brazil	3,036.1
Brunei†	(215.2) 150.0
Bulgaria	640.2
Burkina Faso	60.2
Burundi	77.0
Cambodia	87.5
Cameroon	185.7
Canada	6,369.2
Cape Verde	9.6
Central African Republic	55.7
Chad	56.0
Chile	856.1
China, People's Republic	6,369.2
Colombia	774.0
Comoros	8.9
Congo, Democratic Republic*	(533.0) 291.0
Congo, Republic	84.6
Costa Rica	164.1
Côte d'Ivoire	325.2
Croatia	365.1
Cyprus	139.6
Czech Republic	819.3
Denmark	1,642.8
Djibouti	15.9
Dominica	8.2
Dominican Republic	218.9
Ecuador	302.3
Egypt	943.7
El Salvador	171.3
Equatorial Guinea	32.6
Eritrea	15.9
Estonia	65.2
Ethiopia	133.7

— continued	5 March 2002
Fiji	70.3
Finland	1,263.8
France	10,738.5
Gabon	154.3
The Gambia	31.1
Georgia	150.3
Germany	13,008.2
Ghana	369.0
Greece	823.0
Grenada	11.7
Guatemala	210.2
Guinea	107.1
Guinea-Bissau	14.2
Guyana	90.9
Haiti†	(81.9) 60.7
Honduras	129.5
Hungary	1,038.4
Iceland	117.6
India	4,158.2
Indonesia	2,079.3
Iran	1,497.2
Iraq*	(1,188.4) 504.0
Ireland	838.4
Israel	928.2
Italy	7,055.5
Jamaica	273.5
Japan	13,312.8
Jordan	170.5
Kazakhstan	365.7
Kenya	271.4
Kiribati	5.6
Korea, Republic	1,633.6
Kuwait	1,381.1
Kyrgyzstan	88.8
Laos†	52.9
Latvia	126.8
Lebanon	203.0
Lesotho	34.9
Liberia*	(129.2) 71.3
Libya	1,123.7
Lithuania	144.2
Luxembourg	279.1
Macedonia, former Yugoslav republic	68.9
Madagascar	122.2
Malawi	69.4
Malaysia	1,486.6
Maldives	8.2
Mali	93.3
Malta	102.0
Marshall Islands†	(3.5) 2.5
Mauritania	64.4
Mauritius	101.6
Mexico	2,585.8
Micronesia, Federated States	5.1
Moldova	123.2
Mongolia	51.1
Morocco	588.2
Mozambique	113.6
Myanmar	258.4
Namibia	136.5
Nepal	71.3
Netherlands	5,162.4
New Zealand	894.6
Nicaragua	130.0
Niger	65.8
Nigeria	1,753.2
Norway	1,671.7
Oman	194.0
Pakistan	1,033.7
Palau	3.1
Panama	206.6

— *continued*	5 March 2002
Papua New Guinea	131.6
Paraguay	99.9
Peru	638.4
Philippines	879.9
Poland	1,369.0
Portugal	867.4
Qatar	263.8
Romania	1,030.2
Russia	5,945.4
Rwanda	80.1
Saint Christopher and Nevis	8.9
Saint Lucia	15.3
Saint Vincent and the Grenadines	8.3
Samoa	11.6
San Marino	17.0
São Tomé and Príncipe	7.4
Saudi Arabia	6,985.5
Senegal	161.8
Seychelles	8.8
Sierra Leone	103.7
Singapore	862.5
Slovakia	357.5
Slovenia	231.7
Solomon Islands	10.4
Somalia*	(81.7) 44.2
South Africa	1,868.5
Spain	3,048.9
Sri Lanka	413.4
Sudan*	(315.1) 169.7
Suriname	92.1
Swaziland	50.7
Sweden	2,395.5
Switzerland	3,458.5
Syria	293.6
Tajikistan	87.0
Tanzania	198.9
Thailand	1,081.9
Togo	73.4
Tonga	6.9
Trinidad and Tobago	335.6
Tunisia	286.5
Turkey	964.0
Turkmenistan	75.2
Uganda	180.5
Ukraine	1,372.0
United Arab Emirates	611.7
United Kingdom	10,738.5
USA	37,149.3
Uruguay	306.5
Uzbekistan	275.6
Vanuatu	17.0
Venezuela	2,659.1
Viet Nam	329.1
Yemen	243.5
Yugoslavia, Federal Republic	467.7
Zambia	489.1
Zimbabwe	353.4

* At 5 March 2002 these members had overdue obligations and were therefore ineligible to consent to the increase in quotas under the Eleventh General Review (which came into effect in January 1999). The figures listed are those determined under previous reviews, while the figures in parentheses are the proposed Eleventh General Review quotas.

† At 5 March 2002 these members had not yet consented to their increased quotas under the Eleventh General Review. The proposed quotas are those in parentheses.

FINANCIAL ACTIVITIES (SDR million, year ending 30 April)

Type of Transaction	1996	1997	1998	1999	2000	2001
Total disbursements	12,347	5,644	20,973	24,897	6,890	10,229
Purchases by facility (General Resources Account)*	10,870	4,939	20,000	24,071	6,377	9,599†
Loans under SAF/PRGF arrangements	1,477	705	973	826	513	630
Repurchases and repayments	7,100	7,196	4,385	11,092	23,627	11,831
Repurchases	6,698	6,668	3,789	10,465	22,993	11,831
Trust Fund and SAF/PRGF loan repayments	402	529	596	627	634	588
Total outstanding credit provided by Fund (end of year)	42,040	40,488	56,026	67,175	50,370	48,691
Of which:						
General Resources Account	36,268	34,539	49,701	60,651	43,968	42,219
SAF Arrangements	1,208	954	730	565	456	432
PRGF Arrangements‡	4,469	4,904	5,505	5,870	5,857	5,951
Trust Fund	95	90	90	89	89	89

* Including reserve tranche purchases.

† Comprising (in SDR million): 106 in reserve tranche purchases, 4,395 in Stand-by Arrangements and credit tranche purchases, 1,013 under the Extended Fund Facility, and 4,085 under the Supplemental Reserve Facility.

‡ Including Saudi Fund for Development associated loans.

Source: *International Monetary Fund Annual Report 2001.*

International Telecommunication Union—ITU

Address: Place des Nations, 1211 Geneva 20, Switzerland.

Telephone: (22) 7305111; **fax:** (22) 7337256; **e-mail:** itumail @itu.int; **internet:** www.itu.int.

Founded in 1865, ITU became a specialized agency of the UN in 1947. It acts *inter alia* to encourage world co-operation for the improvement and national use of telecommunications to promote technical development, to harmonize national policies in the field, and to promote the extension of telecommunications throughout the world.

MEMBERS

189 member states: see Table on pp. 211-213. More than 650 scientific and technical companies, public and private operators, broadcasters and other organizations are also ITU members.

Organization

(March 2002)

PLENIPOTENTIARY CONFERENCE

The supreme organ of ITU; normally meets every four years. The main tasks of the Conference are to elect ITU's leadership, establish policies, revise the Constitution and Convention (see below) and approve limits on budgetary spending.

WORLD CONFERENCES ON INTERNATIONAL TELECOMMUNICATIONS

The World Conferences on International Telecommunications are held at the request of members and after approval by the Plenipotentiary Conference. The World Conferences are authorized to review and revise the regulations applying to the provision and operation of international telecommunications services. As part of the 1993 restructuring of ITU, separate Conferences were to be held by three sectors (see below): Radiocommunication Conferences (to be held every two or three years); Telecommunication Standardization Assemblies (to be held every four years or at the request of one-quarter of ITU members); and Telecommunication Development Conferences (to be held every four years).

ITU COUNCIL

The Council meets annually in Geneva and is composed of 46 members elected by the Plenipotentiary Conference.

The Council ensures the efficient co-ordination and implementation of the work of the Union in all matters of policy, administration and finance, in the interval between Plenipotentiary Conferences, and approves the annual budget.

GENERAL SECRETARIAT

The Secretary-General is elected by the Plenipotentiary Conference, and is responsible to it for the Secretariat's work, and for the Union's administrative and financial services. The Secretariat's staff totals about 790, representing 83 nationalities; the official and working languages are Arabic, Chinese, English, French, Russian and Spanish.

Secretary-General: YOSHIO UTSUMI (Japan).

Deputy Secretary-General: ROBERTO BLOIS MONTES DE SOUZA (Brazil).

Constitution and Convention

Between 1865 and 1992 each Plenipotentiary Conference adopted a new Convention of ITU. At the Additional Plenipotentiary Conference held in December 1992, in Geneva, Switzerland, a new Constitution and Convention were signed. They were partially amended by the following two Plenipotentiary Conferences held in Kyoto, Japan, in 1994, and Minneapolis, USA, in 1998. The Constitution contains the fundamental provisions of ITU, whereas the Convention contains other provisions which complement those of the Constitution and which, by their nature, require periodic revision.

The Constitution establishes the purposes and structure of the Union, contains the general provisions relating to telecommunications and special provisions for radio, and deals with relations with the UN and other organizations. The Convention establishes the functioning of the Union and the three sectors, and contains the general provisions regarding conferences and assemblies. Both instruments are further complemented by the administrative regulations listed below.

INTERNATIONAL TELECOMMUNICATIONS REGULATIONS

The International Telecommunications Regulations were adopted in 1988 and entered into force in 1990. They establish the general principles relating to the provision and operation of international telecommunication services offered to the public. They also establish rules applicable to administrations and recognized private operating agencies. Their provisions are applied to both wire and wireless telegraph and telephone communications in so far as the Radio Regulations do not provide otherwise.

RADIO REGULATIONS

The Radio Regulations, which first appeared in 1906, include general rules for the assignment and use of frequencies and the associated orbital positions for space stations. They include a Table of Frequency Allocations (governing the use of radio frequency bands between 9 kHz and 400 GHz) for the various radio services (*inter alia* radio broadcasting, television, radio astronomy, navigation aids, point-to-point service, maritime mobile, amateur).

The 1979 World Administrative Radio Conference undertook a complete revision of the radio spectrum allocation. Partial revisions were also made by subsequent world and regional administrative radio conferences, particularly with reference to space radiocommunications, using satellites. The last revision of the Radio Regulations was signed in İstanbul, Turkey, in 2000.

Activities

In December 1992 an Additional Plenipotentiary Conference was held in Geneva, Switzerland, which agreed on reforms to the structure and functioning of ITU. As a result, ITU comprised three sectors corresponding to its main functions: standardization; radiocommunication; and development. Separate sector conferences were to be held. In October 1994 the ordinary Plenipotentiary Conference, held in Kyoto, Japan, adopted ITU's first strategic plan. A second strategic plan, for the period 1999–2003, was adopted by the conference, convened in Minneapolis, USA, in October/November 1998. The plan recognized new trends and developments in the world telecommunication environment, such as globalization, liberalization, and greater competition, assessed their implications for ITU, and proposed new strategies and priorities to enable ITU to function effectively. The conference approved the active involvement of ITU in governance issues relating to the internet, and recommended that a World Summit on the Information Society be convened, given the rapid developments in that field. Accordingly, the ITU is undertaking a lead role in organizing the summit, which was scheduled to be held in two phases: the first to take place in Geneva in 2003, and the second in Tunisia in 2005.

RADIOCOMMUNICATION SECTOR

The role of the sector is to ensure an equitable and efficient use of the radio-frequency spectrum by all radiocommunication services, to conduct studies, and to adopt recommendations on sector issues. The Radio Regulations are reviewed and revised by the World Radiocommunition Conferences. The technical work on issues to be considered by the conferences is conducted by Radiocommunication Assemblies, on the basis of recommendations made by Study Groups. These groups of experts study technical questions relating to radiocommunications, according to a study programme formulated by the Assemblies. The Assemblies may approve, modify or reject any recommendations of the Study Groups, and are authorized to establish new groups and to abolish others. The procedural rules used in the application of the Radio Regulations were to be considered by a Radio Regulations Board, which may also perform duties relating to the allocation and use of frequencies and consider cases of interference. The sector administers ITU's 'International Mobile Telecommunication-2000' initiative relating to third generation (3G) mobile communication systems, which aims to provide wireless access to the global telecommunication infrastructure through satellite and terrestrial systems. The 1998 Plenipotentiary Conference resolved to establish a working group open to sector members to prepare recommendations concerning the submission and processing of charges of satellite networking filings.

The administrative work of the sector is the responsibility of the Radiocommunication Bureau, which is headed by an elected Director. The Bureau co-ordinates the work of Study Groups, provides administrative support for the Radio Regulations Board, and works alongside the General Secretariat to prepare conferences and to provide relevant assistance to developing countries. The Director is assisted by an Advisory Group.

Director: ROBERT W. JONES (Canada).

TELECOMMUNICATION STANDARDIZATION SECTOR

The sector was established to study technical, operational and tariff issues in order to standardize telecommunications throughout the world. The sector's conferences consider draft standards, referred to as Recommendations, which, if approved, establish ITU guide-lines to guarantee the effective provision of telecommunication services. According to the priority given to different issues concerning draft standards, the conferences may maintain, establish or abolish Study Groups. Recommendations may be approved outside of the four-year interval between conferences if a Study Group concludes such action to be urgent. According to the 1999–2003 strategic plan, one of the priorities for the sector was to be the formulation of recommendations relating to Internet Protocol-based networks, as well as more general recommendations to keep pace with the rapid technological developments and expansion of market demand. A World Telecommunication Standardization Assembly was held in Montréal, Canada, in September/October 2000, to approve settlement rates for international connections. The meeting also approved the establishment of a management board to oversee the implementation of 3G mobile services. In June 1999 an ITU Study Group recommended implementing a scaled system of accounting rates based on telephone densities.

Preparations for conferences and other meetings of the sector are made by the Telecommunication Standardization Bureau (ITU-T). It administers the application of conference decisions, as well as relevant provisions of the International Telecommunications Regulations. The ITU-T is headed by an elected Director, who is assisted by an Advisory Group. The Director reports to conferences and to the ITU Council on the activities of the sector.

Director: HOULIN ZHAO (People's Republic of China).

TELECOMMUNICATION DEVELOPMENT SECTOR

The sector's objectives are to facilitate and enhance telecommunications development by offering, organizing and co-ordinating technical co-operation and assistance activities, to promote the development of telecommunication networks and services in developing countries, to facilitate the transfer of appropriate technologies and the use of resources, and to provide advice on issues specific to telecommunications. The sector implements projects under the UN development system or other funding arrangements.

The sector holds conferences regularly to encourage international co-operation in the development of telecommunications, and to determine strategies for development. Conferences consider the result of work undertaken by Study Groups on issues of benefit to developing countries, including development policy, finance, network planning and operation of services. The 1999–2003 strategic plan emphasized the need for the sector to enhance collaboration with the private sector and relevant organizations, especially at regional and sub-regional levels, and to promote new and more effective partnership arrangements in and between the public and private sectors.

The administrative work of the sector is conducted by the Telecommunication Development Bureau, which may also study specific problems presented by a member state. The Director of the Bureau reports to conferences and the ITU Council, and is assisted by an Advisory Board.

Director: HAMEDOUN I. TOURÉ (Mali).

INFORMATION

ITU issues numerous technical and statistical publications (see below) and maintains a library and archives. It also offers the use of an on-line computer-based telecom information exchange service (TIES), which provides access to ITU databases, document exchange, and other telecommunication information.

Finance

The 1998 Plenipotentiary Conference approved a maximum budget of 333.6m. Swiss francs for the two-year period 2002–03.

Publications

List of Publications (2 a year).

Telecommunication Journal (monthly in English, French and Spanish).

World Telecommunication Development Report.

Conventions, statistics, regulations, technical documents and manuals, conference documents.

United Nations Educational, Scientific and Cultural Organization—UNESCO

Address: 7 place de Fontenoy, 75352 Paris 07 SP, France.

Telephone: 1-45-68-10-00; **fax:** 1-45-67-16-90; **e-mail** scg@unesco.org; **internet:** www.unesco.org.

UNESCO was established in 1946 'for the purpose of advancing, through the educational, scientific and cultural relations of the peoples of the world, the objectives of international peace and the common welfare of mankind'.

MEMBERS

188 members, and six associate members: see Table on pp. 211–213.

Organization

(March 2002)

GENERAL CONFERENCE

The supreme governing body of the Organization, the Conference meets in ordinary session once in two years and is composed of representatives of the member states.

EXECUTIVE BOARD

The Board, comprising 58 members, prepares the programme to be submitted to the Conference and supervises its execution; it meets twice or sometimes three times a year.

SECRETARIAT

Director-General: KOICHIRO MATSUURA (Japan).

CO-OPERATING BODIES

In accordance with UNESCO's constitution, national Commissions have been set up in most member states. These help to integrate work within the member states and the work of UNESCO.

PRINCIPAL REGIONAL OFFICES

Africa

Regional Office for Education in Africa: 12 ave Roume, BP 3311, Dakar, Senegal; tel. 823-50-82; fax 823-83-93; e-mail uhdak@unesco.org; Dir P. OBANYA.

Regional Office for Science and Technology for Africa: POB 30592, Nairobi, Kenya; tel. (2) 621234; fax (2) 215991; e-mail nairobi@unesco.org; internet www.unesco-nairobi.unon.org; f. 1965 to execute UNESCO's regional science programme, and to assist in the planning and execution of national programmes. Dir P. B. VITTA.

Arab States

Regional Office for Education in the Arab States: POB 5244, ave Cité Sportive, Beirut, Lebanon; tel. (1) 850075; fax (1) 824854; e-mail uhbei@unesco.org; internet www.unesco.org.lb; Dir V. BILLEH.

Regional Office for Science and Technology in the Arab States—ROSTAS: 8 Abdel Rahman Fahmy St, Garden City, Cairo 11511, Egypt; tel. (2) 7945599; fax (2) 78945296; e-mail cairo@unesco.org; internet www.unesco-cairo.org; also covers informatics; Dir Dr MOHAMED EL-DEEK.

Regional Office for Social and Human Sciences in the Arab Region: POB 363, 12 rue de Rhodes-Notre Dame, 1002 Tunis, Tunisia; tel. (1) 790947; fax (1) 791588; e-mail tunis@unesco.org; liaison office with the Arab League Educational, Cultural and Scientific Organization; Dir FRANCISCO CARRILLO-MONTESINOS.

Asia and the Pacific

Principal Regional Office for Asia and the Pacific: 920 Sukhumvit Rd, POB 967, Bangkok 10110, Thailand; tel. (2) 391-0577; fax (2) 391-0866; e-mail uhbgk@unesco-proap.org; internet www.unescobkk.org; Dir SHELDON SCHAEFFER.

Regional Office for Book Development in Asia and the Pacific: POB 2034, Islamabad 44000, Pakistan; tel. (51) 2813308; fax (51) 2825341; e-mail unesco@isb.compol.com; Dir M. M. KASEJU.

Regional Office for Science and Technology for South-East Asia: UN Building (2nd Floor), Jalan M. H. Thamrin 14, Tromol Pos 1273/JKT, Jakarta 10002, Indonesia; tel. (21) 3141308; fax (21) 3150382; e-mail uhjak@unesco.org; internet www.unesco.or.id; Dir Prof. STEPHEN HILL.

Europe and North America

European Centre for Higher Education (CEPES): Str. Stirbei Vodă 39, 70732 Bucharest, Romania; tel. (1) 3159956; fax (1) 3123567; e-mail cepes@cepes.ro; internet www.cepes.ro; Dir JAN SADLAK.

Regional Office for Science and Technology for Europe: Palazzo Loredan degli Ambasciatori, 1262/A Dorsoduro, 30123 Venice, Italy; tel. (041) 522-5535; fax (041) 528-9995; e-mail roste@unesco.org; Dir Prof. PIERRE LASSERRE.

Latin America and the Caribbean

Caribbean Network of Educational Innovation for Development: POB 423, Bridgetown, St Michael, Barbados; tel. 4274771; fax 4360094; e-mail uhbri@unesco.org; Head of Office R. COLLEEN WINTER-BRAITHWAITE.

Regional Centre for Higher Education in Latin America and the Caribbean (CRESALC): Ave Los Chorros, c/c Calle Acueducto, Edif. Asovincar, Altos de Sebucan, Apdo 68394, Caracas 1062 A, Venezuela; tel. (2) 286-0721; fax (2) 286-2039; e-mail uhcar@unesco.org; Dir L. YARZABAL.

Regional Office for Culture in Latin America and the Caribbean: Apdo 4158, Havana 4, Cuba; tel. (7) 32-7741; fax (7) 33-3144; e-mail uhldo@unesco.org; Dir GLORIA LÓPEZ MORALES.

Regional Office for Education in Latin America and the Caribbean: Calle Enrique Delpiano 2058, Plaza Pedro de Valdivia, Casilla 3187, Santiago, Chile; tel. (2) 2049032; fax (2) 2091875; e-mail uhstg@unesco.org; Dir A. MACHADO PINHEIRO.

Regional Office for Science and Technology for Latin America and the Caribbean: Avda Brasil 2697, 4° Casilla 859, 11300 Montevideo, Uruguay; tel. (2) 7072023; fax (2) 7072140; e-mail orcyt@unesco.org.uy; internet www.unesco.org.uy; Dir MIGUEL ANGEL ENRIQUES.

Activities

In November 2001 the General Conference approved a medium-term strategy to guide UNESCO during the period 2002–07. The Conference adopted a new unifying theme for the organization: 'UNESCO contributing to peace and human development in an era of globalization through education, the sciences, culture and communication'. UNESCO's central mission as defined under the strategy was to contribute to peace and human development in the globalized world through its four programme domains (Education, Natural and Social and Human Sciences, Culture, and Communication and Information), incorporating the following three principal dimensions: developing universal principles and norms to meet emerging challenges and protect the 'common public good'; promoting pluralism and diversity; and promoting empowerment and participation in the emerging knowledge society through equitable access, capacity-building and knowledge-sharing. Programme activities were to be focused particularly on supporting disadvantaged and excluded groups or geographic regions. The organization aimed to decentralize its operations in order to ensure more country-driven programming.

UNESCO's overall work programme for 2002–03 comprised the following major programmes: education; natural sciences; social and human sciences; culture; and communication and information. Basic education; fresh water resources and ecosystems; the ethics of science and technology; diversity, intercultural pluralism and dialogue; and universal access to information, especially in the public domain, were designated as the priority themes. The work programme incorporated two transdisciplinary projects—eradication of poverty, especially extreme poverty; and the contribution of information and communication technologies to the development of education, science and culture and the construction of a knowledge society. UNESCO aims to promote a culture of peace. The UN General Assembly designated UNESCO as the lead agency for co-ordinating the International Decade for a Culture of Peace and Non-Violence for the Children of the World (2001–10), with a focus on education. In the implementation of all its activities UNESCO aims to contribute to achieving the UN Millennium Goal of halving levels of extreme poverty by 2015.

EDUCATION

Since its establishment UNESCO has devoted itself to promoting education in accordance with principles based on democracy and respect for human rights.

In March 1990 UNESCO, with other UN agencies, sponsored the World Conference on Education for All. 'Education for All' was subsequently adopted as a guiding principle of UNESCO's contribution to development. UNESCO advocates 'Literacy for All' as a key component of 'Education for All', regarding literacy as essential to basic education and to social and human development. In April 2000 several UN agencies, including UNESCO and UNICEF, and other partners sponsored the World Education Forum, held in Dakar, Senegal, to assess international progress in achieving the goal of 'Education for All' and to adopt a strategy for further action (the 'Dakar Framework'), with the aim of ensuring universal basic education by 2015. The Forum launched the Global Initiative for Education for All. The Dakar Framework emphasized the role of improved access to education in the reduction of poverty and in diminishing inequalities within and between societies. UNESCO was appointed as the lead agency in the implementation of the Framework. UNESCO's role in pursuing the goals of the Dakar Forum was to focus on co-ordination, advocacy, mobilization of resources, and information-sharing at international, regional and national levels. It was to oversee national policy reforms, with a particular focus on the integration of 'Education for All' objectives into national education plans, which were to be produced by all member countries by 2002. UNESCO's work programme on Education for 2002–03 aimed to promote an effective follow-up to the Forum and comprised the following two main components: Basic Education for All: Meeting the Commitments of the Dakar World Education Forum; and Building Knowledge Societies through Quality Education and a Renewal of Education Systems. 'Basic Education for All', signifying the promotion of access to learning opportunities throughout the lives of all individuals, including the most disadvantaged, was designated as the principal theme of the programme and was deemed to require urgent action. The second part of the strategy was to improve the quality of educational provision and renew and diversify education systems, with a view to ensuring that educational needs at all levels were met. This component included updating curricular programmes in secondary education, strengthening science and technology activities and ensuring equal access to education for girls and women. (UNESCO supports the UN Girls' Education Initiative, established following the Dakar Forum.) The work programme emphasized the importance of knowledge, information and communication in the increasingly globalized world, and the significance of education as a means of empowerment for the poor and of enhancing basic quality of life.

In December 1993 the heads of government of nine highly-populated developing countries (Bangladesh, Brazil, the People's Republic of China, Egypt, India, Indonesia, Mexico, Nigeria and Pakistan), meeting in Delhi, India, agreed to co-operate, with the objective of achieving comprehensive primary education for all children and of expanding further learning opportunities for children and adults. By September 1999 all of the so-called 'E-9' (or Education-9) countries had officially signed the 'Delhi Declaration' issued by the meeting. An evaluation of the 'E-9' initiative was to be conducted during the period of UNESCO's 2002–03 work programme.

Within the UN system, UNESCO is responsible for providing technical assistance and educational services in the context of emergency situations. This includes providing education to refugees and displaced persons, as well as assistance for the rehabilitation of national education systems. In Palestine, UNESCO collaborates with UNRWA (q.v.) to assist with the training of teachers, educational planning and rehabilitation of schools.

UNESCO is concerned with improving the quality, relevance and efficiency of higher education. It assists member states in reforming their national systems, organizes high-level conferences for Ministers of Education and other decision-makers, and disseminates research papers. A World Conference on Higher Education was convened in October 1998 in Paris, France. The Conference adopted a World Declaration on Higher Education for the 21st Century, incorporating proposals to reform higher education, with emphasis on access to education, and educating for individual development and active participation in society. The Conference also approved a framework for Priority Action for Change and Development of Higher Education, which comprised guide-lines for governments and institutions to meet the objectives of greater accessibility, as well as improved standards and relevancy of higher education.

The International Institute for Educational Planning and the International Bureau of Education (see below) undertake training, research and the exchange of information on aspects of education. A UNESCO Institute for Education, based in Hamburg, Germany, researches literacy activities and the evolution of adult learning systems. UNESCO aims to promote the use of new information and communication technologies in the expansion of learning opportunities. A joint UNESCO/ILO committee of experts has been established to consider strategies for enhancing the status of the teaching profession.

The April 2000 World Education Forum recognized the global HIV/AIDS pandemic to be a significant challenge to the attainment of 'Education for All'. UNESCO, as a co-sponsor of UNAIDS, takes an active role in promoting formal and non-formal preventive health education.

NATURAL SCIENCES

In November 1999 the General Conference endorsed a Declaration on Science and the Use of Scientific Knowledge and an agenda for action, which had been adopted at the World Conference on Science, held in June/July 1999, in Budapest, Hungary. UNESCO was to co-ordinate the follow-up to the conference and, in conjunction with the International Council for Science (q.v.), to promote initiatives in international scientific partnership. The following were identified as priority areas of UNESCO's work programme on Natural Sciences for 2002–03: Science and Technology: Capacity-building and Management; and Sciences, Environment and Sustainable Development. Water Security in the 21st Century was designated as the principal theme, involving addressing threats to water resources and their associated ecosystems. UNESCO was to be the lead UN agency involved in the preparation of the first *World Water Development Report*, due to be issued in 2003. The Science and Technology component of the programme focused on the follow-up of the World Conference on Science, involving the elaboration of national policies on science and technology; strengthening science education; improving university teaching and enhancing national research capacities; and reinforcing international co-operation in mathematics, physics, chemistry, biology, biotechnology and the engineering sciences. UNESCO aims to contribute to bridging the divide between community-held traditional knowledge and scientific knowledge.

UNESCO aims to improve the level of university teaching of the basic sciences through training courses, establishing national and regional networks and centres of excellence, and fostering co-operative research. In carrying out its mission, UNESCO relies on partnerships with non-governmental organizations and the world scientific communities. With the International Council of Scientific Unions and the Third World Academy of Sciences, UNESCO operates a short-term fellowship programme in the basic sciences and an exchange programme of visiting lecturers. In September 1996 UNESCO initiated a 10-year World Solar

Programme, which aimed to promote the application of solar energy and to increase research, development and public awareness of all forms of ecologically-sustainable energy use.

UNESCO has over the years established various forms of intergovernmental co-operation concerned with the environmental sciences and research on natural resources, in order to support the recommendations of the June 1992 UN Conference on Environment and Development and, in particular, the implementation of 'Agenda 21' to promote sustainable development. The International Geological Correlation Programme, undertaken jointly with the International Union of Geological Sciences, aims to improve and facilitate global research of geological processes. In the context of the International Decade for Natural Disaster Reduction (declared in 1990), UNESCO conducted scientific studies of natural hazards and means of mitigating their effects and organized several disaster-related workshops. The International Hydrological Programme considers scientific aspects of water resources assessment and management; and the Intergovernmental Oceanographic Commission (IOC, q.v.) focuses on issues relating to oceans, shorelines and marine resources, in particular the role of the ocean in climate and global systems. The IOC has been actively involved in the establishment of a Global Coral Reef Monitoring Network and is developing a Global Ocean Observing System. An initiative on Environment and Development in Coastal Regions and in Small Islands is concerned with ensuring environmentally-sound and sustainable development by strengthening management of the following key areas: freshwater resources; the mitigation of coastline instability; biological diversity; and coastal ecosystem productivity. UNESCO hosts the secretariat of the World Water Assessment Programme on freshwater resources.

UNESCO's Man and the Biosphere Programme supports a world-wide network of biosphere reserves (comprising 411 sites in 94 countries in September 2001), which aim to promote environmental conservation and research, education and training in biodiversity and problems of land use (including the fertility of tropical soils and the cultivation of sacred sites). Following the signing of the Convention to Combat Desertification in October 1994, UNESCO initiated an International Programme for Arid Land Crops, based on a network of existing institutions, to assist implementation of the Convention.

Abdus Salam International Centre for Theoretical Physics: based in Trieste, Italy, the Centre brings together scientists from the developed and developing countries. With support from the Italian Government, the Centre has been operated jointly by the IAEA and UNESCO since 1970. At the end of 1995 administrative responsibility for the Centre was transferred to UNESCO, although IAEA remained a partner in the operations of the Centre. Each year it offers seminars followed by a research workshop, as well as short topical seminars, training courses, symposia and panels. Independent research is also carried out. The programme concentrates on condensed matter physics, high-energy physics, mathematics, physics of weather and climate, structure and nonlinear dynamics of the earth, and microprocessors; Dir Prof. MIGUEL A. VIRASORO (Argentina).

SOCIAL AND HUMAN SCIENCES

UNESCO is mandated to contribute to the world-wide development of the social and human sciences and philosophy, which it regards as of great importance in policy-making and maintaining ethical vigilance. The structure of UNESCO's Social and Human Sciences programme takes into account both an ethical and standard-setting dimension, and research, policy-making, action in the field and future-oriented activities. UNESCO's work programme for 2002–03 on Social and Human Sciences comprised three main components: The Ethics of Science and Technology; Promotion of Human Rights, Peace and Democratic Principles; and Improvement of Policies Relating to Social Transformations and Promotion of Anticipation and Prospective Studies. Each of these involved the practical application to contemporary challenges of concepts and methods derived from the fields of social and human sciences and philosophy. The priority Ethics of Science and Technology element aimed to reinforce UNESCO's role as an intellectual forum for ethical reflection on challenges related to the advance of science and technology; oversee the follow-up of the Universal Declaration on the Human Genome and Human Rights (see below); promote education in science and technology; ensure UNESCO's role in promoting good practices through encouraging the inclusion of ethical guiding principles in policy formulation and reinforcing international networks; and to promote international co-operation in human sciences and philosophy. The Social and Human Sciences programme had the main intellectual and conceptual responsibility for the transdisciplinary theme 'eradication of poverty, especially extreme poverty'.

UNESCO aims to promote and protect human rights and acts as an interdisciplinary, multicultural and pluralistic forum for reflection on issues relating to the ethical dimension of scientific advances, for example in biogenetics, new technology, and medicine. In May 1997 the International Bioethics Committee, a group of 36 specialists who meet under UNESCO auspices, approved a draft version of a Universal Declaration on the Human Genome and Human Rights, in an attempt to provide ethical guide-lines for developments in human genetics. The Declaration, which identified some 100,000 hereditary genes as 'common heritage', was adopted by the UNESCO General Conference in November and committed states to promoting the dissemination of relevant scientific knowledge and co-operating in genome research. The November Conference also resolved to establish an 18-member World Commission on the Ethics of Scientific Knowledge and Technology (COMEST) to serve as a forum for the exchange of information and ideas and to promote dialogue between scientific communities, decision-makers and the public. UNESCO hosts the secretariat of COMEST. COMEST met for the first time in April 1999 in Oslo, Norway. Its second meeting, which took place in December 2001 in Berlin, Germany, focused on the ethics of energy, fresh water and outer space.

In 1994 UNESCO initiated an international social science research programme, the Management of Social Transformations (MOST), to promote capacity-building in social planning at all levels of decision-making. UNESCO sponsors several research fellowships in the social sciences. In other activities UNESCO promotes the rehabilitation of underprivileged urban areas, the research of socio-cultural factors affecting demographic change, and the study of family issues.

UNESCO aims to assist the building and consolidation of peaceful and democratic societies. An international network of institutions and centres involved in research on conflict resolution is being established to support the promotion of peace. Other training, workshop and research activities have been undertaken in countries that have suffered conflict. The Associated Schools Project (ASPnet—comprising more than 6,700 institutions in 166 countries in 2001) has, for nearly 50 years, promoted the principles of peace, human rights, democracy and international co-operation through education. An International Youth Clearing House and Information Service (INFOYOUTH) aims to increase and consolidate the information available on the situation of young people in society, and to heighten awareness of their needs, aspirations and potential among public and private decision-makers. UNESCO also focuses on the educational and cultural dimensions of physical education and sport and their capacity to preserve and improve health. Fundamental to UNESCO's mission is the rejection of all forms of discrimination. It disseminates scientific information aimed at combating racial prejudice, works to improve the status of women and their access to education, and promotes equality between men and women.

CULTURE

In undertaking efforts to preserve the world's cultural and natural heritage UNESCO has attempted to emphasize the link between culture and development. In November 2001 the General Conference adopted the UNESCO Universal Declaration on Cultural Diversity, which affirmed the importance of intercultural dialogue in establishing a climate of peace. The work programme on Culture for 2002–03 included the following interrelated components: Reinforcing Normative Action in the Field of Culture; Protecting Cultural Diversity and Promoting Cultural Pluralism and Intercultural Dialogue; and Strengthening Links between

Culture and Development. The focus was to be on all aspects of cultural heritage, and on the encouragement of cultural diversity and dialogue between cultures and civilizations. Under the 2002–03 programme UNESCO aimed to launch the Global Alliance on Cultural Diversity, a six-year initiative to promote partnerships between governments, non-governmental bodies and the private sector, with a view to supporting cultural diversity through the strengthening of cultural industries and the prevention of cultural piracy.

UNESCO's World Heritage Programme, inaugurated in 1978, aims to protect historic sites and natural landmarks of outstanding universal significance, in accordance with the 1972 UNESCO Convention Concerning the Protection of the World Cultural and Natural Heritage, by providing financial aid for restoration, technical assistance, training and management planning. By December 2001 the 'World Heritage List' comprised 721 sites in 124 countries, of which 554 had cultural significance, 144 were natural landmarks, and 23 were of 'mixed' importance. Examples include: the Great Barrier Reef in Australia, the Galapagos Islands (Ecuador), Chartres Cathedral (France), the Taj Mahal at Agra (India), Auschwitz concentration camp (Poland), the historic sanctuary of Machu Picchu (Peru), Robben Island (South Africa), the Serengeti National Park (Tanzania), and the archaeological site of Troy (Turkey). UNESCO also maintains a 'List of World Heritage in Danger', comprising 31 sites at December 2001, in order to attract international attention to sites particularly at risk from the environment or human activities. In 1992 a World Heritage Centre was established to enable rapid mobilization of international technical assistance for the preservation of cultural sites. Through the World Heritage Information Network (WHIN), a world-wide network of more than 800 information providers, UNESCO promotes global awareness and information exchange. In addition, UNESCO supports efforts for the collection and safeguarding of humanity's non-material 'intangible' heritage, including oral traditions, music, dance and medicine. In May 2001 UNESCO awarded the title of 'Masterpieces of the Oral and Intangible Heritage of Humanity' to 19 cultural spaces (i.e. physical or temporal spaces hosting recurrent cultural events) and popular forms of expression deemed to be of outstanding value. In co-operation with the International Council for Philosophy and Humanistic Studies, UNESCO is compiling a directory of endangered languages. In early 2001 UNESCO condemned an edict by the fundamentalist Islamist Taliban regime in Afghanistan ordering the destruction of all statues in that country which, owing to their representation of human likenesses, were regarded as non-Islamic. In March UNESCO protested strongly against the reported destruction by order of the Taliban of two ancient monuments of Buddha at Bamiyan. The formulation of a Declaration against the Intentional Destruction of Cultural Heritage was authorized by the General Conference in November of that year. In addition, the November General Conference adopted the Convention on the Protection of the Underwater Cultural Heritage, covering the protection from commercial exploitation of shipwrecks, submerged historical sites, etc., situated in the territorial waters of signatory states. UNESCO also administers the 1954 Hague Convention on the Protection of Cultural Property in the Event of Armed Conflict and the 1970 Convention on the Means of Prohibiting and Preventing the Illicit Import, Export and Transfer of Ownership of Cultural Property.

UNESCO encourages the translation and publication of literary works, publishes albums of art, and produces records, audiovisual programmes and travelling art exhibitions. It supports the development of book publishing and distribution, including the free flow of books and educational material across borders, and the training of editors and managers in publishing. UNESCO is active in preparing and encouraging the enforcement of international legislation on copyright.

In December 1992 UNESCO established the World Commission on Culture and Development, to strengthen links between culture and development and to prepare a report on the issue. The first World Conference on Culture and Development was held in June 1999, in Havana, Cuba. Within the context of the UN's World Decade for Cultural Development (1988–97) UNESCO launched the Silk Roads Project, as a multi-disciplinary study of the interactions among cultures and civilizations along the routes linking Asia and Europe, and established an International Fund for the Promotion of Culture, awarding two annual prizes for music and the promotion of arts. In April 1999 UNESCO celebrated the completion of a major international project, the *General History of Africa*.

COMMUNICATION AND INFORMATION

In 2001 UNESCO introduced a major programme, 'Information for All', as the principal policy-guiding framework for the Communication and Information sector. The organization works towards establishing an open, non-exclusive knowledge society based on information-sharing and incorporating the socio-cultural and ethical dimensions of sustainable development. It promotes the free flow of, and universal access to information, knowledge, data and best practices, through the development of communications infrastructures, the elimination of impediments to freedom of expression, and the promotion of the right to information; through encouraging international co-operation in maintaining libraries and archives; and through efforts to harness informatics for development purposes and strengthen member states' capacities in this field. Activities include assistance with the development of legislation and training programmes in countries where independent and pluralistic media are emerging; assistance in the monitoring of media independence, pluralism and diversity; promotion of exchange programmes and study tours; and improving access and opportunities for women in the media. UNESCO recognizes that the so-called global 'digital divide', in addition to other developmental differences between countries, generates exclusion and marginalization, and that increased participation in the democratic process can be attained through strengthening national communication and information capacities. UNESCO promotes the upholding of human rights in the use of cyberspace. The organization was to participate in the World Summit on the Information Society, scheduled to take place in Geneva, Switzerland, in December 2003. The work programme on Communication and Information for 2002–03 comprised the following components: Promoting Equitable Access to Information and Knowledge Especially in the Public Domain; and Promoting Freedom of Expression and Strengthening Communication Capacities. During 2002–03 UNESCO was to evaluate its interactive internet-based WebWorld Portal, which aims to provide global communication and information services at all levels of society. UNESCO's Memory of the World project aims to preserve in digital form, and thereby to promote wide access to, the world's documentary heritage.

In regions affected by conflict UNESCO supports efforts to establish and maintain an independent media service. This strategy is largely implemented through an International Programme for the Development of Communication (IPDC—see below). In Cambodia, Haiti and Mozambique UNESCO participated in the restructuring of the media in the context of national reconciliation and in Bosnia and Herzegovina it assisted in the development of independent media. In December 1998 the Israeli–Palestinian Media Forum was established, to foster professional co-operation between Israeli and Palestinian journalists. IPDC provides support to communication and media development projects in the developing world, including the establishment of news agencies and newspapers and training editorial and technical staff. Since its establishment in 1982 IPDC, has provided around US $85m. to finance some 900 projects.

In March 1997 the first International Congress on Ethical, Legal and Societal Aspects of Digital Information ('InfoEthics') was held in Monte Carlo, Monaco. At the second 'InfoEthics' Congress, held in October 1998, experts discussed issues concerning privacy, confidentiality and security in the electronic transfer of information. UNESCO maintains an Observatory on the Information Society, which provides up-to-date information on the development of new information and communications technologies, analyses of major trends, and aims to raise awareness of related ethical, legal and societal issues. A UNESCO Institute for Information Technologies in Education was established in Moscow, Russia in 1998. In 2001 the UNESCO Institute for Statistics was established in Montréal, Canada.

Finance

UNESCO's activities are funded through a regular budget provided by contributions from member states and extrabudgetary funds from other sources, particularly UNDP, the World Bank, regional banks and other bilateral Funds-in-Trust arrangements. UNESCO co-operates with many other UN agencies and international non-governmental organizations.

UNESCO's Regular Programme budget for the two years 2002–03 was US $544.4m., the same as for the previous biennium. Extrabudgetary funds for 2002–03 were estimated at $320m.

Publications

(mostly in English, French and Spanish editions; Arabic, Chinese and Russian versions are also available in many cases)

Copyright Bulletin (quarterly).

International Review of Education (quarterly).

International Social Science Journal (quarterly).

Museum International (quarterly).

Nature and Resources (quarterly).

Prospects (quarterly review on education).

UNESCO Courier (monthly, in 27 languages).

UNESCO Sources (monthly).

UNESCO Statistical Yearbook.

World Communication Report.

World Educational Report (every 2 years).

World Heritage Review (quarterly).

World Information Report.

World Science Report (every 2 years).

Books, databases, video and radio documentaries, statistics, scientific maps and atlases.

INTERGOVERNMENTAL COMMITTEE FOR PHYSICAL EDUCATION AND SPORT

Address: 7 place de Fontenoy, 75352 Paris, France.

Established by UNESCO in 1978 to serve as a permanent intergovernmental body in the field of physical education and sport.

The Committee is composed of 30 representatives of member states of UNESCO, elected by the General Conference.

Among its many activities aimed at further development of physical education and sport throughout the world, the Committee is responsible for supervising the planning and implementation of UNESCO's programme of activities in physical education and sport, promoting international co-operation in this area and facilitating the adoption and implementation of an International Charter of physical education and sport.

INTERNATIONAL BUREAU OF EDUCATION—IBE

Address: POB 199, 1211 Geneva 20, Switzerland.

Telephone: (22) 9177800; **fax:** (22) 9177801; **e-mail:** doc.centre@ibe.unesco.org; **internet:** www.ibe.unesco.org.

Founded in 1925, the IBE became an intergovernmental organization in 1929 and was incorporated into UNESCO in 1969. The Bureau's fundamental mission is to deal with matters concerning educational content, methods, and teaching/learning strategies. In addition, the IBE, as an observatory of educational trends and innovations, has assumed responsibilities in the field of educational information. It publishes a quarterly review of education and a newsletter, in addition to various monographs and reference works. The Council of the IBE is composed of representatives of 28 member states of UNESCO, designated by the General Conference. The International Conference on Education is held periodically.

Director: CECILIA BRASLAVSKY (Argentina).

INTERNATIONAL INSTITUTE FOR EDUCATIONAL PLANNING—IIEP

Address: 7–9 rue Eugène Delacroix, 75116 Paris, France.

Telephone: 1-45-03-77-00; **fax:** 1-40-72-83-66; **e-mail:** information@iiep.unesco.org; **internet:** www.unesco.org/iiep.

The Institute was established by UNESCO in 1963 to serve as a world centre for advanced training and research in educational planning. Its purpose is to help all member states of UNESCO in their social and economic development efforts, by enlarging the fund of knowledge about educational planning and the supply of competent experts in this field.

Legally and administratively a part of UNESCO, the Institute is autonomous, and its policies and programme are controlled by its own Governing Board, under special statutes voted by the General Conference of UNESCO.

A satellite office of the IIEP was opened in Buenos Aires, Argentina, in June 1998.

Director: GUDMUND HERNES (Norway).

INSTITUTE FOR INFORMATION TECHNOLOGIES IN EDUCATION

Address: 8 Kedrova St, 117292 Moscow, Russia.

Telephone: (95) 1292990; **fax:** (95) 1291225; **e-mail:** info@iite.ru; **internet:** www.iite.ru/iite/index.

The Institute aims to formulate policies regarding the development of, and to support and monitor the use of, information and communication technologies in education. The Institute also conducts research and organizes training programmes.

Director: VLADIMIR KINELEV.

UNESCO INSTITUTE FOR STATISTICS

Address: 5255 ave Decelles, 7th Floor, Montréal, QC, H3T 2BA, Canada.

Telephone: (514) 3436880; **fax:** (514) 3436882; **e-mail:** uis@unesco.org; **internet:** www.uis.unesco.org.

The Institute for Statistics, established in 2001, collects and analyzes national statistics on education, science, technology, culture and communications.

Director: DENISE LIEVESLEY.

United Nations Industrial Development Organization—UNIDO

Address: Vienna International Centre, POB 300, A-1400 Vienna, Austria.

Telephone: (1) 26026; **fax:** (1) 2692669; **e-mail:** unido@unido.org; **internet:** www.unido.org.

UNIDO began operations in 1967, as an autonomous organization within the UN Secretariat, and became a specialized agency of the UN in 1985. UNIDO's objective is to promote sustainable industrial development in developing nations and states with economies in transition. It aims to assist such countries to integrate fully into the global economic system by mobilizing knowledge, skills, information and technology to promote productive employment, competitive economies and sound environment.

MEMBERS

169 members: see Table on pp. 211–213.

Organization

(March 2002)

GENERAL CONFERENCE

The General Conference, which consists of representatives of all member states, meets once every two years. It is the chief policy-making organ of the Organization, and reviews UNIDO's policy concepts, strategies on industrial development and budget. The ninth General Conference was held in Vienna, Austria, in December 2001.

INDUSTRIAL DEVELOPMENT BOARD

The Board consists of 53 members elected by the General Conference for a four-year period. It reviews the implementation of the approved work programme, the regular and operational budgets and other General Conference decisions, and, every four years, recommends a candidate for the post of Director-General to the General Conference for appointment.

PROGRAMME AND BUDGET COMMITTEE

The Committee, consisting of 27 members elected by the General Conference for a two-year term, assists the Industrial Development Board in preparing work programmes and budgets.

SECRETARIAT

The Secretariat comprises the office of the Director-General and three divisions, each headed by a Managing Director: Investment Promotion and Institutional Capacity Building; Sectoral Support and Environmental Sustainability; and Field Operations and Administration. In 2001 the Secretariat comprised 553 staff members.

Director-General: CARLOS ALFREDO MAGARIÑOS (Argentina).

FIELD REPRESENTATION

In August 2001 UNIDO had field offices in 35 developing countries.

Activities

In its efforts to promote the advancement and integration of industry, UNIDO fulfils two core functions. Firstly, as a global forum, it generates and disseminates knowledge relating to industrial matters and provides a platform for policy- and decision-makers to enhance co-operation, establish dialogue and develop partnerships to address effectively challenges to sustainable industrialization. Secondly, as a technical co-operation agency, UNIDO designs and implements programmes to support national industrial development efforts. It also offers specialized support for programme development. The two core functions are complementary and mutually supportive: policy-makers benefit from experience gained in technical co-operation projects, while, by helping to define priorities, the Organization's analytical work identifies where technical co-operation will have greatest impact.

UNIDO's services are designed to be easily integrated into country-specific packages, and local ownership ensures a custom-made approach. The comprehensive services provided by UNIDO cover:

(i) Industrial governance;
(ii) Promotion of investment and technology;
(iii) Quality infrastructure and productivity;
(iv) Private-sector development;
(v) The Montreal Protocol;
(vi) Industrial development and the Kyoto Protocol;
(vii) Environmental management.
(viii) Support for agro-industry production.

Between 1993 and 1998 UNIDO implemented a major restructuring programme in order to respond to changes in the global economy and industrial development. The seventh session of the General Conference, held in December 1997, endorsed a Business Plan on the Future Role and Functions of UNIDO, which regrouped the Organization's activities into two main areas—Strengthening of industrial capacities, and Cleaner and sustainable industrial development. According to the Plan, activities were to be concentrated in support of the development and mainstreaming of SMEs (identified as the principal means for achieving equitable and sustainable industrial development), in support of agro-based industries and their integration into national industrial structures, and in least-developed countries, in particular in Africa, with emphasis on service provision at regional and sub-regional level. In December 1999, at its eighth session, the General Conference approved funding arrangements for a new strategy of developing integrated industrial service packages designed specifically for individual countries. (Some 44 of these were being implemented in early 2002.)

In 2000 UNIDO's investment promotion and institutional capacity-building activities delivered US $24.6m. in technical co-operation to developing countries and economies in transition in seven priority areas: industrial policy forumulation and implementation; statistics and information networks; metrology, standardization, certification and accreditation; continuous improvement and quality management; investment and technology promotion; policy framework for small and medium-sized enterprises (SMEs); policy for women's entrepreneurship and entrepreneurship development. UNIDO has extended its networking with the private sector while assisting developing countries and economies in transition with capacity-building for sustained industrial growth. Promotion of business partnerships, for example, has been strengthened through the Organization's world-wide network of investment and technology promotion offices, investment promotion units, and subcontracting and partnership exchanges, as well as through the Asia-Africa Investment and Technology Promotion Centre. UNIDO has pursued efforts to overcome the so-called 'digital divide' between and within countries. The Organization has helped to develop electronic and mobile business for SMEs in developing countries and economies in transition. It has also launched an internet-based electronic platform, UNIDO Exchange, for sharing intelligence and fostering business partnerships.

Through strategic alliances with international certification and standards organizations UNIDO is assisting enterprises in developing countries to overcome technical barriers while improving product quality and access to international markets. UNIDO's industrial business development services—such as business incubators, rural entrepreneurship development and SME cluster development—for SME support institutions are aimed at enabling SMEs to play a key role in economic growth.

UNIDO provides advice to governmental agencies and industrial institutions to improve the management of human resources. The Organization also undertakes training projects to develop human resources in specific industries, and aims to encourage the full participation of women in economic progress through gender awareness programmes and practical training to improve women's access to employment and business opportunities.

As a result of the reforms introduced in the 1990s, UNIDO shifted its programming modality from a project-based framework to one with a national scope. Emphasis was given to industrialization in Africa, owing to the prevalence of 'least developed countries' there and the necessity to reduce regional inequalities in view of increasing globalization. Such national integrated industrial development programmes emphasize capacity-building for the enhancement of industrial competitiveness and private-sector development, which is regarded as a major priority for the transformation of African economies. The basic philosophy has been to identify, jointly with key stakeholders in major industrial sub-sectors, the basic tools required to determine their national industrial development needs and priorities. This process has facilitated the definition and establishment of comprehensive national medium-term and long-term industrial development agenda. By 2001 national programmes, valued at an estimated US \$151.3m., had been developed for 18 African countries. UNIDO formally inaugurated the Alliance for Africa's Industrialization, which constituted the industrial sector element of the UN System-wide Special Initiative on Africa, in 1996. This aimed to promote development of the continent's natural resources, strengthen labour resources and build government capacities in order to exploit new global markets, in particular in the agro-industrial sector. The Organization supported the Conference on Industrial Partnership and Investment in Africa, held in October 1999 in Dakar, Senegal, which aimed to provide a forum for developing industrial partnerships and promote industrial development. UNIDO was to be responsible for the technical implementation of a regional programme on quality management and standardization, covering the member countries of the Union économique et monétaire ouest-africaine—UEMOA, q.v.), to be undertaken in collaboration with the European Union, that was approved in 2000. In addition, a technical support programme to improve the level of fish exports has been approved.

UNIDO is increasingly involved in general environmental projects. As one of the four implementing agencies of the Multilateral Fund for the Implementation of the Montreal Protocol, UNIDO assists developing countries in efforts gradually to reduce the use of ozone-depleting substances. It is also involved in implementing the Kyoto Protocol of the Framework Convention on Climate Change (relating to greenhouse gas emissions) in old factories world-wide. In 1994 UNIDO and UNEP launched the National Cleaner Production Centres Programme; by January 2001 19 Centres had been established world-wide.

UNIDO also supports collaborative efforts between countries with complementary experience or resources in specific sectors. The investment and technology promotion network publicizes investment opportunities, provides information to investors and promotes business contacts between industrialized and developing countries and economies in transition. UNIDO is increasingly working to achieve investment promotion and transfer of technology and knowledge among developing countries. The Organization has developed several databases, including the Biosafety Information Network Advisory Service (BINAS), the Business Environment Strategic Toolkit (BEST), Industrial Development Abstracts (IDA, providing information on technical co-operation), and the International Referral System on Sources of Information (IRS).

UNIDO established and operates the International Centre for Science and High Technology, based in Trieste (Italy); the International Centre for Advancement of Manufacturing Technology in Bangalore (India); the Centre for the Application of Solar Energy in Perth (Australia); the International Centre of Medicine Biotechnology in Obolensk (Russia); and the International Materials Assessment and Application Centre in Rio de Janeiro (Brazil).

Finance

The regular budget for the two years 2002–03 amounted to €133.7m., financed by assessed contributionss payable by member states. There was an operational budget of some €22.0m. for the same period, financed from the reinbursement of support costs pertaining to technical co-operation and other services for the same period. UNIDO's technical co-operation expenditure amounted to €193.5m. In 2000 allocations were received from UNDP, the Multilateral Fund for the Implementation of the Montreal Protocol on Substances that Deplete the Ozone Layer, the Global Environment Facility, and the Common Fund for Commodities. In addition, voluntary contributions were received from 25 member states. The Industrial Development Fund is used by UNIDO to finance development projects that fall outside the usual systems of multilateral funding.

Publications

African Industry 2000: The Challenge of Going Global.

Annual Report.

Industry for Growth into the New Millennium.

International Yearbook of Industrial Statistics (annually).

Manual for the Evaluation of Industrial Projects.

Manual for Small Industrial Businesses.

UNIDOScope (monthly, electronic newsletter).

Using Statistics for Process Control and Improvement: An Introduction to Basic Concepts and Techniques.

World Industrial Development Report.

World Information Directory of Industrial Technology and Investment Support Services.

Several other manuals; guide-lines; numerous working papers and reports.

Universal Postal Union—UPU

Address: Weltpoststr. 4, 3000 Berne 15, Switzerland.

Telephone: (31) 3503111; **fax:** (31) 3503110; **e-mail:** info@upu.int; **internet:** www.upu.int.

The General Postal Union was founded by the Treaty of Berne (1874), beginning operations in July 1875. Three years later its name was changed to the Universal Postal Union. In 1948 the UPU became a specialized agency of the UN.

MEMBERS

189 members: see Table on pp. 211–213.

Organization

(March 2002)

CONGRESS

The supreme body of the Union is the Universal Postal Congress, which meets, in principle, every five years. Congress focuses on general principles and broad policy issues. It is responsible for the Constitution (the basic act of the Union), the General Regulations (which contain provisions relating to the application of the Constitution and the operation of the Union), changes in the provision of the Universal Postal Convention, approval of the strategic plan and budget parameters, formulation of overall policy on technical co-operation and for elections and appointments. Amendments to the Constitution are recorded in Additional Protocols, of which there are currently six. The 22nd Congress was held in Beijing, People's Republic of China, in August/September 1999; the 23rd Congress was to be held in Abidjan, Côte d'Ivoire in September/October 2004.

COUNCIL OF ADMINISTRATION

The Council, created by the Seoul Congress, 1994, to replace the former Executive Council, meets annually at Berne. It is composed of a Chairman and representatives of 40 member countries of the Union elected by Congress on the basis of an equitable geographical distribution. It is responsible for supervising the affairs of the Union between Congresses. The Council also considers policies that may affect other sectors, such as standardization and quality of service, provides a forum for considering the implications of governmental policies with respect to competition, deregulation, and trade-in-service issues for international postal services, and considers intergovernmental aspects of technical co-operation. The Council approves the Union's budget, supervises the activities of the International Bureau and takes decisions regarding UPU contacts with other international agencies and bodies. It is also responsible for promoting and co-ordinating all aspects of technical assistance among member countries. In October 2001, on the recommendation of a high-level group established by the 1999 Beijing Congress to consider the future development of the UPU, the Council approved the establishment of a consultative committee representing external stakeholders in postal systems. This was to be formally established following the 2004 Abidjan Congress.

POSTAL OPERATIONS COUNCIL (POC)

As the technical organ of the UPU, the Council, which holds annual sessions and comprises 40 elected member countries, is responsible for the operational, economic and commercial aspects of international postal services. The POC has the authority to amend and enact the Detailed Regulations of the Universal Postal Convention, on the basis of decisions made at Congress. It promotes the studies undertaken by some postal services and the introduction of new postal products. It also prepares and issues recommendations for member countries concerning uniform standards of practice for technological, operational or other processes within its competence. The POC aims to assist national postal services to modernize postal products, including letter and parcel post, financial services and expedited mail services.

INTERNATIONAL BUREAU

The day-to-day administrative work of UPU is executed through the International Bureau, which provides secretariat and support facilities for the UPU's bodies. It serves as an instrument of liaison, information and consultation for the postal administration of the member countries and promotes technical co-operation among Union members. It also acts as a clearing house for the settlement of accounts between postal administrations for inter-administration charges related to the exchange of postal items and international reply coupons. The Bureau supports the technical assistance programmes of the UPU and serves as an intermediary between the UPU, the UN, its agencies and other international organizations, customer organizations and private delivery services. Increasingly the Bureau has assumed a greater role in certain areas of postal administration, for example, the application of Electronic Data Interchange (EDI) technology and the monitoring of quality of postal services world-wide.

Director-General of the International Bureau: THOMAS E. LEAVEY (USA).

Activities

The essential principles of the Union are the following:

(i) to develop social, cultural and commercial communication between people through the efficient operation of the postal services;

(ii) to guarantee freedom of transit and free circulation of postal items;

(iii) to ensure the organization, development and modernization of the postal services;

(iv) to promote and participate in postal technical assistance between member countries;

(v) to ensure the interoperability of postal networks by implementing a suitable policy of standardization;

(vi) to meet the changing needs of customers; and

(vii) to improve the quality of service.

In addition to the Constitution and the General Regulations, the Universal Postal Convention is also a compulsory Act of the UPU (binding on all member countries), in view of its importance in the postal field and historical value. The Convention and its Detailed Regulations contain the common rules applicable to the international postal service and provisions concerning letter- and parcel- post. The Detailed Regulations are agreements concluded by the national postal administrations elected by Congress to the POC. The POC is empowered to revise and enact these, taking into account decisions made at Congress.

The Postal Payment Services Agreement and its Regulations, adopted by the 1999 Beijing Congress to replace the former Money Orders, Giro and Cash-on-Delivery Agreements, is an optional arrangement. Not all member countries have acceded to this Agreement.

Finance

The 1999 Beijing Congress agreed to replace the Union's annual budget with a biennial budget from 2001. The approved budget for 2001–02 amounted to 71.4m. Swiss francs. All of the UPU's regular budget expenses are financed by member countries, based on a contribution class system. Members are listed in 11 classes, establishing the proportion that they should pay.

Publications

Postal Statistics.

Union Postale (quarterly, in French, German, English, Arabic, Chinese, Spanish and Russian).

Other UPU publications are listed in *Liste des publications du Bureau international*; all are in French and English, some also in Arabic and Spanish.

World Health Organization—WHO

Address: Ave Appia 20, 1211 Geneva 27, Switzerland.

Telephone: (22) 7912111; **fax:** (22) 7913111; **e-mail:** info@who.int; **internet:** www.who.int.

WHO, established in 1948, is the lead agency within the UN system concerned with the protection and improvement of public health.

MEMBERS

191 members and two associate members: see Table on pp. 211–213.

Organization

(March 2002)

WORLD HEALTH ASSEMBLY

The Assembly meets in Geneva, once a year; it is responsible for policy making and the biennial programme and budget; appoints the Director-General, admits new members and reviews budget contributions.

EXECUTIVE BOARD

The Board is composed of 32 health experts designated by, but not representing, their governments; they serve for three years, and the World Health Assembly elects 10–12 member states each year to the Board. It meets at least twice a year to review the Director-General's programme, which it forwards to the Assembly with any recommendations that seem necessary. It advises on questions referred to it by the Assembly and is responsible for putting into effect the decisions and policies of the Assembly. It is also empowered to take emergency measures in case of epidemics or disasters.

Chairman: MYRIAM ABEL (Vanuatu).

SECRETARIAT

Director-General: Dr GRO HARLEM BRUNDTLAND (Norway).

Executive Directors: Dr ANARFI ASAMOA-BAAH (Ghana) (External Relations and Governing Bodies), MARYAN BAQUEROT (General Management), Dr DAVID L. HEYMANN (USA) (Communicable Diseases), Dr CHRISTOPHER MURRAY (Evidence and Information for Policy), Dr DAVID NABARRO (United Kingdom) (Office of the Director-General), Dr YASUHIRO SUZUKI (Japan) (Health Technology and Pharmaceuticals), Dr TOMRIS TÜRMEN (Turkey) (Family and Community Health), Dr DEREK YACH (South Africa) (Non-communicable Diseases and Mental Health).

At March 2002 the post of Executive Director for Sustainable Development and Healthy Environments remained vacant.

REGIONAL OFFICES

Each of WHO's six geographical regions has its own organization consisting of a regional committee representing the member states and associate members in the region concerned, and a regional office staffed by experts in various fields of health.

Africa: (temporary office) Parirenyatwa Hospital, Mazoe St, POB BE 773, Belvedere, Harare, Zimbabwe; tel. (4) 707493; fax (4) 700742; e-mail regafro@whoafr.org; internet www.whoafr.org; Dir Dr EBRAHIM MALICK SAMBA (The Gambia).

Americas: Pan-American Sanitary Bureau, 525 23rd St, NW, Washington, DC 20037, USA; tel. (202) 974-3000; fax (202) 974-3663; e-mail postmaster@paho.org; internet www.paho.org; Dir Sir GEORGE ALLEYNE (Barbados).

Eastern Mediterranean: WHO Post Office, Abdul Razzak al Sanhouri St, Cairo (Nasr City) 11371, Egypt; tel. (2) 6702535; fax (2) 6702492; e-mail emro@who.sci.eg; internet www.who.sci.eg; Dir Dr HUSSEIN ABDUL-RAZZAQ GEZAIRY.

Europe: 8 Scherfigsvej, 2100 Copenhagen Ø, Denmark; tel. (1) 39-17-17-17; fax (1) 39-17-18-18; e-mail webmaster@who.dk; internet www.who.dk; Dir Dr MARC DANZON (France).

South-East Asia: World Health House, Indraprastha Estate, Mahatma Gandhi Rd, New Delhi 110 002, India; tel. (11) 3370804; fax (11) 3379507; e-mail pandeyh@whosea.org; internet w3.whosea.org; Dir Dr UTON MUCHTAR RAFEI (Indonesia).

Western Pacific: POB 2932, Manila 1000, Philippines; tel. (2) 5288001; fax (2) 5211036; e-mail postmaster@who.org.ph; internet www.wpro.who.int; Dir Dr SHIGERU OMI (Japan).

Activities

WHO's objective is stated in the constitution as 'the attainment by all peoples of the highest possible level of health'. 'Health' is defined as 'a state of complete physical, mental and social well-being and not merely the absence of disease and infirmity'. In November 2001 WHO issued the International Classification of Functioning, Disability and Health (ICF) to act as an international standard and guide-lines for determining health and disability.

It acts as the central authority directing international health work, and establishes relations with professional groups and government health authorities on that basis.

It provides, on request from member states, technical and policy assistance in support of programmes to promote health, prevent and control health problems, control or eradicate disease, train health workers best suited to local needs and strengthen national health systems. Aid is provided in emergencies and natural disasters.

A global programme of collaborative research and exchange of scientific information is carried out in co-operation with about 1,200 national institutions. Particular stress is laid on the widespread communicable diseases of the tropics, and the countries directly concerned are assisted in developing their research capabilities.

It keeps communicable and non-communicable diseases and other health problems under constant surveillance, promotes the exchange of prompt and accurate information and of notification of outbreaks of diseases, and administers the International Health Regulations. It sets standards for the quality control of drugs, vaccines and other substances affecting health.

It collects and disseminates health data and carries out statistical analyses and comparative studies in such diseases as cancer, heart disease and mental illness.

It receives reports on drugs observed to have shown adverse reactions in any country, and transmits the information to other member states.

It promotes improved environmental conditions, including housing, sanitation and working conditions. All available information on effects on human health of the pollutants in the environment is critically reviewed and published.

Co-operation among scientists and professional groups is encouraged. The organization negotiates and sustains national and global partnerships. It may propose international conventions and agreements, and develops and promotes international norms and standards. The organization promotes the development and testing of new technologies, tools and guide-lines. It assists in developing an informed public opinion on matters of health.

HEALTH FOR ALL

WHO's first global strategy for pursing 'Health for all' was adopted in May 1981 by the 34th World Health Assembly. The objective of 'Health for all' was identified as the attainment by all citizens of the world of a level of health that would permit them to lead a socially and economically productive life, requiring fair distribution of available resources, universal access to essential health care, and the promotion of preventive health care. In May 1998 the 51st World Health Assembly renewed the initiative, adopting a global strategy in support of 'Health for all in the 21st century', to be effected through regional and national health policies. The new approach was to build on the primary health care approach of the initial strategy, but was to strengthen the emphasis on quality of life, equity in health and access to health services. The following have been identified as minimum requirements of 'Health for All':

Safe water in the home or within 15 minutes' walking distance, and adequate sanitary facilities in the home or immediate vicinity;

Immunization against diphtheria, pertussis (whooping cough), tetanus, poliomyelitis, measles and tuberculosis;

Local health care, including availability of essential drugs, within one hour's travel;

Trained personnel to attend childbirth, and to care for pregnant mothers and children up to at least one year old.

In July 1998 Dr Gro Harlem Brundtland officially took office as the new Director-General of WHO. She immediately announced an extensive reform of the organization, including restructuring the WHO technical programmes into nine groups, or 'clusters', each headed by an Executive Director. The groups are as follows: Communicable Diseases; Non-communicable Diseases and Mental Health; Family and Community Health; Sustainable Development and Healthy Environments; Health Technology and Pharmaceuticals; Evidence and Information for Policy; External affairs and Governing Bodies; General Management; and Office of the Director-General (including audit, oversight and legal activities). In 2000 WHO adopted a new corporate strategy, entailing a stronger focus on performance and programme delivery through standardized plans of action, and increased consistency and efficiency throughout the organization.

The Tenth General Programme of Work, for the period 2002–05, defined a policy framework for pursuing the principal objectives of building healthy populations and combating ill health. The Programme took into account: increasing understanding of the social, economic, political and cultural factors involved in achieving better health and the role played by better health in poverty reduction; the increasing complexity of health systems; the importance of safeguarding health as a component of humanitarian action; and the need for greater co-ordination among development organizations. It incorporated four interrelated strategic directions: lessening excess mortality, morbidity and disability, especially in poor and marginalized populations; promoting healthy lifestyles and reducing risk factors to human health arising from environmental, economic, social and behavioural causes; developing equitable and financially fair health systems; and establishing an enabling policy and an institutional environment for the health sector and promoting an effective health dimension to social, economic, environmental and development policy.

COMMUNICABLE DISEASES

WHO identifies infectious and parasitic communicable diseases as a major obstacle to social and economic progress, particularly in developing countries, where, in addition to disabilities and loss of productivity and household earnings, they cause nearly one-half of all deaths. Emerging and re-emerging diseases, those likely to cause epidemics, increasing incidence of zoonoses (diseases passed from animals to humans either directly or by insects) attributable to environmental changes, outbreaks of unknown etiology, and the undermining of some drug therapies by the spread of antimicrobial resistance are main areas of concern. In recent years WHO has noted the global spread of communicable diseases through international travel, voluntary human migration and involuntary population displacement.

WHO's Communicable Diseases group works to reduce the impact of infectious diseases world-wide through surveillance and response; prevention, control and eradication strategies; and research and product development. Combating malaria and tuberculosis (TB) are organization-wide priorities and, as such, are supported not only by their own areas of work but also by activities undertaken in other areas. The group seeks to identify new technologies and tools, and to foster national development through strengthening health services and the better use of existing tools. It aims to strengthen global monitoring of important communicable disease problems. The group advocates a functional approach to disease control. It aims to create consensus and consolidate partnerships around targeted diseases and collaborates with other groups at all stages to provide an integrated response. In April 2000 WHO and several partner institutions in epidemic surveillance established a Global Outbreak Alert and Response Network. Through the Network WHO aims to maintain constant vigilance regarding outbreaks of disease and to link world-wide expertise to provide an immediate response capability. A Global Fund to Fight AIDS, TB and Malaria was established, with WHO participation, in 2001 (see below).

A Ministerial Conference on Malaria, organized by WHO, was held in October 1992, attended by representatives from 102 member countries. The Conference adopted a plan of action for the 1990s for the control of the disease, which kills an estimated 1m. people every year and affects a further 300m.–500m. Some 90% of all cases are in sub-Saharan Africa. WHO assists countries where malaria is endemic to prepare national plans of action for malaria control in accordance with its Global Malaria Control Strategy, which emphasizes strengthening local capabilities, for example through training, for effective health control. In July 1998 WHO declared the control of malaria a priority concern, and in October the organization formally launched the 'Roll Back Malaria' programme, in conjunction with UNICEF, the World Bank and UNDP, which aimed to halve the prevalence of malaria by 2010. Emphasis was to be placed on strengthening local health systems and on the promotion of inexpensive preventive measures, including the use of bednets treated with insecticides. The global Roll Back Malaria partnership, linking governments, development agencies, and other parties, aims to mobilize resources and support for controlling the disease. WHO, with several private- and public-sector partners, supports the development of more effective anti-malaria drugs and vaccines through the 'Medicines for Malaria' venture.

In 1995 WHO established a Global Tuberculosis Programme to address the challenges of the TB epidemic, which had been declared a global emergency by the Organization in 1993. According to WHO estimates, one-third of the world's population carries the TB bacillus, and 2m.–3m. people die from the disease each year. WHO provides technical support to all member countries, with special attention given to those with high TB prevalence, to establish effective national tuberculosis control programmes. WHO's strategy for TB control includes the use of DOTS (direct observation treatment, short-course), standardized treatment guide-lines, and result accountability through routine evaluation of treatment outcomes. Simultaneously, WHO is encouraging research with the aim of further disseminating DOTS, adapting DOTS for wider use, developing new tools for prevention, diagnosis and treatment, and containing new threats such as the HIV/TB co-epidemic. In March 1999 WHO announced the launch of a new initiative, 'Stop TB', in partnership with the World Bank, the US Government and a coalition of non-governmental organizations, which aimed to promote DOTS to ensure its use in 85% of cases by 2005 (compared with around one-quarter in 1999). However, inadequate control of DOTS in some areas, leading to partial and inconsistent treatments, has resulted in the development of drug-resistant and, often, incurable strains of the disease. The incidence of so-called multidrug-resistant TB (MDR-TB) strains, that are unresponsive to the two main anti-TB drugs, has risen in recent years. During 2001 WHO was developing and testing DOTS-Plus, a strategy for controlling the spread of MDR-TB in areas of high prevalence. In 2001 WHO estimated that more than 8m. new cases of TB were occurring world-wide each year, of which the largest concentration was in south-east Asia. It envisaged a substantial increase in new cases by 2005, mainly owing to the severity of the HIV/TB co-epidemic. TB is the principal cause of death for people infected with the HIV virus. In March 2001 the Global TB Drug Facility was launched under the 'Stop TB' initiative; this aimed to increase access to high-quality anti-TB drugs for sufferers in developing countries. In October the 'Stop TB' partnership announced a Global Plan to Stop TB, which envisaged the expansion of access to DOTS; the advancement of MDR-TB prevention measures; the development of anti-TB drugs entailing a shorter treatment period; and the implementation of new strategies for treating people with HIV and TB.

One of WHO's major achievements was the eradication of smallpox. Following a massive international campaign of vaccination and surveillance (begun in 1958 and intensified in 1967), the last case was detected in 1977 and the eradication of the disease was declared in 1980. In May 1996 the World Health Assembly resolved that, pending a final endorsement, all remaining stocks of the smallpox virus were to be destroyed on 30 June 1999, although 500,000 doses of smallpox vaccine were to remain, along with a supply of the smallpox vaccine seed virus, in order to ensure that a further supply of the vaccine could be made available if required. In May 1999, however, the Assembly authorized a temporary retention of stocks of the virus until 2002. In late 2001, in response to fears that illegally-held virus stocks could be used in acts of biological terrorism (see below), WHO reassembled a team of technical experts on smallpox.

In 1988 the World Health Assembly declared its commitment to the eradication of poliomyelitis by the end of 2000 and launched the Global Polio Eradication Initiative. In August 1996 WHO, UNICEF and Rotary International, together with other national and international partners, initiated a campaign to 'Kick Polio out of Africa', with the aim of immunizing more than 100m. children in 46 countries against the disease over a three-year period. By the end of 1999 the number of reported polio cases world-wide had declined to some 7,000, from 35,000 in 1988 (the actual number of cases in 1988 was estimated at around 350,000). At the end of 2000 20 countries were still known or suspected of being polio endemic; of these, 16 were in Africa and four in Asia. In 2000 WHO adopted a strategic plan for the eradication of polio covering the period 2001–05, which envisaged the effective use of National Immunization Days (NIDs) to secure global interruption of polio transmission by the end of 2002, with a view to achieving certification of the global eradication of polio by the end of 2005. (In conflict zones so-called 'days of tranquility' have been negotiated to facilitate the implementation of NIDs.) Meanwhile, routine immunization services were to be strengthened.

The Onchocerciasis Control Programme in West Africa (OCP) was initiated in 1974 to eliminate onchocerciasis, which can cause blindness, as a major public health problem and an impediment to socio-economic development in 11 countries of the region.

In January 1996 a new initiative, the African Programme for Onchocerciasis Control (APOC), covering 19 countries outside West Africa, became operational, with funding co-ordinated by the World Bank and with WHO as the executing agency. In December 1994 WHO announced that the OCP was to be terminated by the end of 2002, by which time it was estimated that 40m. people would have been protected from the disease and 600,000 people prevented from blindness. In May 1999 WHO reported that the OCP, based in Ouagadougou, Burkina Faso, was to be transformed into a Multi-disease Surveillance Centre. The Onchocerciasis Elimination Programme in the Americas (OEPA), launched in 1992, co-ordinates work to control the disease in six endemic countries of Latin America. In January 1998 a new 20-year programme to eliminate lymphatic filariasis was initiated, with substantial funding and support from two major pharmaceutical companies, and in collaboration with the World Bank, the Arab Fund for Economic and Social Development and the governments of Japan, the United Kingdom and the USA. A regional intergovernmental commission is implementing a programme to eliminate South American trypanosomiasis ('Chagas disease', which causes the deaths of some 45,000 people each year and infects a further 16m.–18m.) from the Southern Cone region of Latin America; it is hoped that this goal will be achieved by 2010. The countries of the Andean region of Latin America initiated a plan for the elimination of transmission of Chagas disease in February 1997; a similar plan was launched by Central American governments in October.

WHO is committed to the elimination of leprosy (the reductionn of the prevalence of leprosy to less than one case per 10,000 population). The use of a highly effective combination of three drugs (known as multi-drug therapy—MDT) resulted in a reduction in the number of leprosy cases world-wide from 10m.–12m. in 1988 to 597,000 in 2000. The number of countries having more than one case of leprosy per 10,000 had declined to from to 15 by 2000, compared with 122 in 1985. In 2000 the world-wide leprosy prevalence rate stood at 1.4 cases per 10,000 people, although the rate in the 11 most endemic countries was 4.5 cases per 10,000. India has more than one-half of all active leprosy cases. The Global Alliance for the Elimination of Leprosy, launched in November 1999 by WHO, in collaboration with governments of affected countries and several private partners, including a major pharmaceutical company, aims to bring about the eradication of the disease by the end of 2005, through the continued use of MDT treatment. In July 1998 the Director-General of WHO and representatives of more than 20 countries, meeting in Yamoussoukro, Côte d'Ivoire, signed a declaration on the control of another mycobacterial disease, Buruli ulcer.

The Special Programme for Research and Training in Tropical Diseases, established in 1975 and sponsored jointly by WHO, UNDP and the World Bank, as well as by contributions from donor countries, involves a world-wide network of some 5,000 scientists working on the development and application of vaccines, new drugs, diagnostic kits and preventive measures, and an applied field research on practical community issues affecting the target diseases.

The objective of providing immunization for all children by 1990 was adopted by the World Health Assembly in 1977. Six diseases (measles, whooping cough, tetanus, poliomyelitis, tuberculosis and diphtheria) became the target of the Expanded Programme on Immunization (EPI), in which WHO, UNICEF and many other organizations collaborated. As a result of massive international and national efforts, the global immunization coverage increased from 20% in the early 1980s to the targeted rate of 80% by the end of 1990. This coverage signified that more than 100m. children in the developing world under the age of one had been successfully vaccinated against the targeted diseases, the lives of about 3m. children had been saved every year, and 500,000 annual cases of paralysis as a result of polio had been prevented. In 1992 the Assembly resolved to reach a new target of 90% immunization coverage with the six EPI vaccines; to introduce hepatitis B as a seventh vaccine (with the aim of an 80% reduction in the incidence of the disease in children by 2001); and to introduce the yellow fever vaccine in areas where it occurs endemically.

In June 2000 WHO released a report entitled 'Overcoming Antimicrobial Resistance', in which it warned that the misuse of antibiotics could render some common infectious illnesses unresponsive to treatment. At that time WHO issued guide-lines which aimed to mitigate the risks associated with the use of antimicrobials in livestock reared for human consumption.

NON-COMMUNICABLE DISEASES AND MENTAL HEALTH

The new Non-communicable Diseases and Mental Health group, formed in 2000 by the amalgamation of the former Non-communicable Diseases group and Social Change and Mental Health group, comprises departments for the surveillance, prevention and management of uninfectious diseases, such as those arising from an unhealthy diet, and departments for health promotion, disability, injury prevention and rehabilitation, mental health and substance abuse. Surveillance, prevention and management of non-communicable diseases, tobacco, and mental health are organization-wide priorities.

Tobacco use, unhealthy diet and physical inactivity are regarded as common, preventable risk factors for the four most prominent non-communicable diseases: cardiovascular diseases, cancer, chronic respiratory disease and diabetes. WHO aims to monitor the global epidemiological situation of non-communicable diseases, to co-ordinate multinational research activities concerned with prevention and care, and to analyse determining factors such as gender and poverty. In mid-1998 the organization adopted a resolution on measures to be taken to combat non-communicable diseases; their prevalence was anticipated to increase, particularly in developing countries, owing to rising life expectancy and changes in lifestyles. For example, between 1995 and 2025 the number of adults affected by diabetes was projected to increase from 135m. to 300m. In February 1999 WHO initiated a new programme, 'Vision 2020: the Right to Sight', which aimed to eliminate avoidable blindness (estimated to be as much as 80% of all cases) by 2020. Blindness was otherwise predicted to increase by as much as twofold, owing to the increased longevity of the global population.

WHO's programmes for diabetes mellitus, chronic rheumatic diseases and asthma assist with the development of national initiatives, based upon goals and targets for the improvement of early detection, care and reduction of long-term complications. WHO's cardiovascular diseases programme aims to prevent and control the major cardiovascular diseases, which are responsible for more than 14m. deaths each year. It is estimated that one-third of these deaths could have been prevented with existing scientific knowledge The programme on cancer control is concerned with the prevention of cancer, improving its detection and cure and ensuring care of all cancer patients in need. In 1998 a five-year programme to improve cancer care in developing countries was established, sponsored by private enterprises.

The WHO Human Genetics Programme manages genetic approaches for the prevention and control of common hereditary diseases and of those with a genetic predisposition representing a major health importance. The Programme also concentrates on the further development of genetic approaches suitable for incorporation into health care systems, as well as developing a network of international collaborating programmes.

WHO works to assess the impact of injuries, violence and sensory impairments on health, and formulates guide-lines and protocols for the prevention and management of mental problems. The health promotion division promotes decentralized and community-based health programmes and is concerned with developing new approaches to population ageing and encouraging healthy life-styles and self-care. It also seeks to relieve the negative impact of social changes such as urbanization, migration and changes in family structure upon health. WHO advocates a multi-sectoral approach—involving public health, legal and educational systems—to the prevention of injuries, which represent 16% of the global burden of disease. It aims to support governments in developing suitable strategies to prevent and mitigate the consequences of violence, unintentional injury and disability. Several health promotion projects have been undertaken, in collaboration between WHO regional and country offices and other relevant organizations, including: the Global School Health Initiative, to bridge the sectors of health and education and to promote the health of school-age children; the Global Strategy for Occupational Health, to promote the health of the working population and the control of occupational health risks; Community-based Rehabilitation, aimed at providing a more enabling environment for people with disabilities; and a communication strategy to provide training and support for health communications personnel and initiatives. In 2000 WHO, UNESCO, the World Bank and UNICEF adopted the joint Focusing Resources for Effective School Health (FRESH Start) approach to promoting life skills among adolescents.

In July 1997 the fourth International Conference on Health Promotion (ICHP) was held in Jakarta, Indonesia, where a declaration on 'Health Promotion into the 21st Century' was agreed. The fifth ICHP was convened in June 2000, in Mexico City, Mexico.

Mental health problems, which include unipolar and bipolar affective disorders, psychosis, epilepsy, dementia, Parkinson's disease, multiple sclerosis, drug and alcohol dependency, and neuropsychiatric disorders such as post-traumatic stress disorder, obsessive compulsive disorder and panic disorder, have been identified by WHO as significant global health problems. Although, overall, physical health has improved, mental, behavioural and social health problems are increasing, owing to extended life expectancy and improved child mortality rates, and factors such as war and poverty. WHO aims to address mental problems by increasing awareness of mental health issues and promoting improved mental health services and primary care.

The Substance Abuse department is concerned with problems of alcohol, drugs and other substance abuse. Within its Programme on Substance Abuse (PSA), which was established in 1990 in response to the global increase in substance abuse, WHO provides technical support to assist countries in formulating policies with regard to the prevention and reduction of the health and social effects of psychoactive substance abuse. PSA's sphere of activity includes epidemiological surveillance and risk assessment, advocacy and the dissemination of information, strengthening national and regional prevention and health promotion techniques and strategies, the development of cost-effective treatment and rehabilitation approaches, and also encompasses regulatory activities as required under the international drugs-control treaties in force.

The Tobacco or Health Programme aims to reduce the use of tobacco, by educating tobacco-users and preventing young people from adopting the habit. In 1996 WHO published its first report on the tobacco situation world-wide. According to WHO, about one-third of the world's population aged over 15 years smoke tobacco, which causes approximately 3.5m. deaths each year (through lung cancer, heart disease, chronic bronchitis and other effects). In 1998 the 'Tobacco Free Initiative', a major global anti-smoking campaign, was established. In May 1999 the World Health Assembly endorsed the formulation of a Framework Convention on Tobacco Control (FCTC) to help to combat the increase in tobacco use (although a number of tobacco growers expressed concerns about the effect of the convention on their livelihoods). It was envisaged that the Framework Convention would be adopted in 2003. The greatest increase in tobacco use was forecast to occur in developing countries.

FAMILY AND COMMUNITY HEALTH

WHO's Family and Community Health group addresses the following areas of work: child and adolescent health, research and programme development in reproductive health, making pregnancy safer, women's health, and HIV/AIDS. Making pregnancy safer and HIV/AIDS are organization-wide priorities. The group's aim is to improve access to sustainable health care for all by strengthening health systems and fostering individual, family and community development. Activities include newborn care; child health, including promoting and protecting the health and development of the child through such approaches as promotion of breast-feeding and use of the mother-baby package, as well as care of the sick child, including diarrhoeal and acute respiratory disease control, and support to women and children in difficult circumstances; the promotion of safe motherhood and maternal health; adolescent health, including the promotion and development of young people and the prevention of specific health problems; women, health and development, including addressing issues of gender, sexual violence, and harmful traditional practices; and human reproduction, including research related to contraceptive technologies and effective methods. In addition, WHO aims to provide technical leadership and co-ordination on reproductive health and to support countries in their efforts to ensure that people: experience healthy sexual development and maturation; have the capacity for healthy, equitable and responsible relationships; can achieve their reproductive intentions safely and healthily; avoid illnesses, diseases and injury related to sexuality and reproduction; and receive appropriate counselling, care and rehabilitation for diseases and conditions related to sexuality and reproduction.

In September 1997 WHO, in collaboration with UNICEF, formally launched a programme advocating the Integrated Management of Childhood Illness (IMCI), following successful regional trials in more than 20 developing countries during 1996–97. IMCI recognizes that pneumonia, diarrhoea, measles, malaria and malnutrition cause some 70% of the approximately 11m. childhood deaths each year, and recommends screening sick children for all five conditions, to obtain a more accurate diagnosis than may be achieved from the results of a single assessment. WHO's Division of Diarrhoeal and Acute Respiratory Disease Control encourages national programmes aimed at reducing childhood deaths as a result of diarrhoea, particularly through the use of oral rehydration therapy and preventive measures. The Division is also seeking to reduce deaths from pneumonia in infants through the use of a simple case-management strategy involving the recognition of danger signs and treatment with an appropriate antibiotic.

The HIV/AIDS epidemic represents a major threat to human well-being and socio-economic progress. Some 95% of those known to be infected with HIV/AIDS live in developing countries, and AIDS-related illnesses are the leading cause of death in sub-Saharan Africa. At December 2001 an estimated 40m. adults and children world-wide were living with HIV/AIDS, of whom 5m. were newly infected during that year. By the end of 2000 21.8m. people, including 4.3m. children, had died of AIDS-related illnesses since the start of the epidemic. WHO's Global Programme on AIDS, initiated in 1987, was concluded in December 1995. A Joint UN Programme on HIV/AIDS (UNAIDS) became operational on 1 January 1996, sponsored by WHO, the World Bank, UNICEF, UNDP, UNESCO and UNFPA. (The UN International Drug Control Programme became the seventh sponsoring agency of UNAIDS in 1999, and in 2001 ILO became the eighth sponsor.) The UNAIDS secretariat is based at WHO headquarters. WHO established an Office of HIV/AIDS and Sexually-Transmitted Diseases in order to ensure the continuity of its global response to the problem, which included support for national control and education plans, improving the safety of blood supplies and improving the care and support of AIDS patients. In addition, the Office was to liaise with UNAIDS and to make available WHO's research and technical expertise. Sufferers of HIV/AIDS in developing countries have often failed to receive advanced antiretroviral (ARV) treatments that are widely available in industrialized countries, owing to their high cost. In May 2000 the World Health Assembly adopted a resolution urging WHO member states to improve access to the prevention and treatment of HIV-related illnesses and to increase the availability and affordability of drugs. WHO, with UNAIDS, UNICEF, UNFPA, the World Bank, and major pharmaceutical companies, participates in the 'Accelerating Access' initiative, which aims to expand access to care, support and ARVs for people with HIV/AIDS. A WHO-UNAIDS HIV Vaccine Initiative was launched in 2000. In July 2001 a meeting of the Group of Seven industrialized nations and Russia (G-8), convened in Genoa, Italy, announced the formation of a new Global Fund to Fight AIDS, TB and Malaria (as previously proposed by the UN Secretary-General and recommended by the World Health Assembly). The Fund, a partnership between governments, UN bodies (including WHO) and other agencies, and private-sector interests, aimed to disburse US $700–$800m. in grants during 2002, thereby increasing annual global expenditure on combating those diseases by about 50%. WHO supports governments in developing effective health-sector responses to the HIV/AIDS epidemic through enhancing the planning and managerial capabilities, implementation capacity, and resources of health systems.

By the late 1990s many countries had failed significantly to reduce inequalities in healthcare, to improve the health of poor and disadvantaged people or to improve the sustainability of health systems, owing to weak national health systems and the insufficient use of evidence-based, cost-effective treatment methods. In addition, there was a lack of systems to monitor improvements in health services and to determine overall changes in health. The Family and Community Health group, therefore, aims to address these problems and works to ensure that treatment concerning children, adolescents and women, and reproductive health, HIV/AIDS and other sexually transmitted infections, is effectively provided. WHO assists countries to expand and improve the functioning of their health infrastructure in order to ensure wider access to care, hospital services and health education. It works with countries to ensure continuity and quality of care at all levels, by well-trained health personnel.

In March 1996 WHO's Centre for Health Development opened at Kobe, Japan. The Centre was to research health developments and other determinants to strengthen policy decision-making within the health sector.

SUSTAINABLE DEVELOPMENT AND HEALTHY ENVIRONMENTS

The Sustainable Development and Healthy Environments group focuses on the following areas of work: health in sustainable development; nutrition; health and environment; food safety; and emergency preparedness and response. Food safety is an organization-wide priority.

WHO promotes recognition of good health status as one of the most important assets of the poor. The Sustainable Development and Healthy Environment group seeks to monitor the advantages and disadvantages for health, nutrition, environment and development arising from the process of globalization (i.e. increased global flows of capital, goods and services, people, and knowledge); to integrate the issue of health into poverty reduction programmes; and to promote human rights and equality. Adequate and safe food and nutrition is a priority programme area. WHO collaborates with FAO, the World Food Programme, UNICEF and other UN agencies in pursuing its objectives relating to nutrition and food safety. An estimated 780m. people worldwide cannot meet basic needs for energy and protein, more than 2,000m. people lack essential vitamins and minerals, and 170m. children are estimated to be malnourished. In December 1992 WHO and FAO hosted an international conference on nutrition, at which a World Declaration and Plan of Action on Nutrition was adopted to make the fight against malnutrition a development priority. Following the conference, WHO promoted the elaboration and implementation of national plans of action on nutrition. WHO aims to support the enhancement of member states' capabilities in dealing with their nutrition situations, and addressing scientific issues related to preventing, managing and monitoring protein-energy malnutrition; micronutrient malnutrition, including iodine deficiency disorders, vitamin A deficiency, and nutritional anaemia; and diet-related conditions and non-communicable diseases such as obesity (increasingly affecting children, adolescents and adults, mainly in industrialized countries), cancer and heart disease. In 1990 the World Health Assembly resolved to eliminate iodine deficiency (causing mental retardation); a strategy of universal salt iodization was launched in 1993. In collaboration with other international agencies, WHO is implementing a comprehensive strategy for promoting appropriate infant, young child and maternal nutrition, and for dealing effectively with nutritional emergencies in large populations. Areas of emphasis include promoting health-care practices that enhance successful breast-feeding; appropriate complementary feeding; refining the use and interpretation of body measurements for assessing nutritional status; relevant information, education and training; and action to give effect to the International Code of Marketing of Breast-milk Substitutes. The food safety programme aims to protect human health against risks associated with biological and chemical contaminants and additives in food. With FAO, WHO establishes food standards (through the work of the Codex Alimentarius Commission and its subsidiary committees) and evaluates food additives, pesticide residues and other contaminants and their implications for health. The programme provides expert advice on such issues as food-borne pathogens (e.g. listeria), production methods (e.g. aquaculture) and food biotechnology (e.g. genetic modification). In January 2001 a joint team of FAO and WHO experts issued a report concerning the allergenicity of foods derived from biotechnology (i.e. genetically modified—GM foods). The Codex Alimentarius Commission adopted the first global principles for assessing the safety of GM foods in July.

WHO's programme area on environment and health undertakes a wide range of initiatives to tackle the increasing threats to health and well-being from a changing environment, especially in relation to air pollution, water quality, sanitation, protection against radiation, management of hazardous waste, chemical safety and housing hygiene. Some 1,100m. people world-wide have no access to clean drinking water, while a further 2,400m. people are denied suitable sanitation systems. WHO helped launch the Water Supply and Sanitation Council in 1990 and regularly updates its *Guidelines for Drinking Water Quality*. In rural areas, the emphasis continues to be on the provision and maintenance of safe and sufficient water supplies and adequate sanitation, the health aspects of rural housing, vector control in water resource management, and the safe use of agrochemicals. In urban areas, assistance is provided to identify local environmental health priorities and to improve municipal governments' ability to deal with environmental conditions and health problems in an integrated manner; promotion of the 'Healthy City' approach is a major component of the Programme. Other Programme activities include environmental health information development and management, human resources development, environmental health planning methods, research and work on problems relating to global environment change, such as UV-radiation. A report considering the implications of climate change on human health, prepared jointly by WHO, WMO and UNEP, was published in July 1996. The WHO Global Strategy for Health and Environment, developed in response to the WHO Commission on Health and Environment which reported to the UN Conference on Environment and Development in June 1992, provides the framework for programme activities. In December 2001 WHO published a report on the relationship between macroeconomics and health.

WHO's work in the promotion of chemical safety is undertaken in collaboration with ILO and UNEP through the International Programme on Chemical Safety (IPCS), the Central Unit for which is located in WHO. The Programme provides internationally-evaluated scientific information on chemicals, promotes the use of such information in national programmes, assists member states in establishment of their own chemical safety measures and programmes, and helps them strengthen their capabilities in chemical emergency preparedness and response and in chemical risk reduction. In 1995 an Inter-organization Programme for the Social Management of Chemicals was established by UNEP, ILO, FAO, WHO, UNIDO and OECD, in order to strengthen international co-operation in the field of chemical safety. In 1998 WHO led an international assessment of the health risk from bendocine disruptors (chemicals which disrupt hormonal activities). In January 2001 WHO sent a team of experts to Kosovo and Metohija (Federal Republic of Yugoslavia—FRY) to assess the potential impact on the health of the local population of exposure to depleted uranium, which had been used by NATO in ammunition during its aerial offensive against the FRY in 1999.

Following the major terrorist attacks perpetrated against targets in the USA in September 2001, WHO focused renewed attention on the potential deliberate use of infectious diseases, such as anthrax and smallpox, or of chemical agents, in acts of biological or chemical terrorism. In September 2001 WHO issued draft guide-lines entitled 'Health Aspects of Biological and Chemical Weapons.'

Within the UN system, WHO's Division of Emergency Preparedness and Response co-ordinates the international response to emergencies and natural disasters in the health field, in close co-operation with other agencies and within the framework set out by the UN's Office for the Co-ordination of Humanitarian Affairs. In this context, WHO provides expert advice on epidemiological surveillance, control of communicable diseases, public health information and health emergency training. Its emergency preparedness activities include co-ordination, policy-making and planning, awareness-building, technical advice, training, publication of standards and guide-lines, and research. Its emergency relief activities include organizational support, the provision of emergency drugs and supplies and conducting technical emergency assessment missions. The Division's objective is to strengthen the national capacity of member states to reduce the adverse health consequences of disasters. In responding to emergency situations, WHO always tries to develop projects and activities that will assist the national authorities concerned in rebuilding or strengthening their own capacity to handle the impact of such situations In May 2001 WHO participated with governments and other international agencies in a joint exercise to evaluate national and international procedures for responding to a nuclear emergency.

HEALTH TECHNOLOGY AND PHARMACEUTICALS

WHO's Health Technology and Pharmaceuticals group, made up of the departments of essential drugs and other medicines, vaccines and other biologicals, and blood safety and clinical technology, covers the following areas of work: essential medicines—access, quality and rational use; immunization and vaccine development; and world-wide co-operation on blood safety and clinical technology. Blood safety and clinical technology are an organization-wide priority.

The Department of Essential Drugs and Other Medicines promotes public health through the development of national drugs policies and global guide-lines and through collaboration with member countries to promote access to essential drugs, the rational use of medicines and compliance with international drug-control requirements. The department comprises four teams: Policy Access and Rational Use; the Drug Action Programme; Quality, Safety and the Regulation of Medicines; and Traditional Medicine.

The Department of Vaccines and Other Biologicals undertakes activities related to quality assurance and safety of biologicals; vaccine development; vaccine assessment and monitoring; access to technologies; and the development of policies and strategies aimed at maximizing the use of vaccines.

The Policy Access and Rational Use team and the Drug Action Programme assist in the development and implementation by member states of pharmaceutical policies, in ensuring a supply of essential drugs of good quality at low cost, and in the rational use of drugs. Other activities include global and national operational research in the pharmaceutical sector, and the development of technical tools for problem solving, management and evaluation. The Policy Access and Rational Use team also has a strong advocacy and information role, promulgated through a periodical, the *Essential Drugs Monitor*, an extensive range of technical publications, and an information dissemination programme targeting developing countries.

The Quality, Safety and Regulation of Medicines team supports national drug-regulatory authorities and drug-procurement agencies and facilitates international pharmaceutical trade through the exchange of technical information and the harmonization of internationally respected norms and standards. In particular, it publishes the *International Pharmacopoeia*, the *Consultative List of International Nonproprietary Names for Pharmaceutical Substances*, and annual and biennial reports of Expert Committees responsible for determining relevant international standards for the manufacture and specification of pharmaceutical and biological products in international commerce. It provides information on the safety and efficacy of drugs, with particular regard to counterfeit and substandard projects, to health agencies and providers of health care, and it maintains the pharmaceuticals section of the UN *Consolidated List of Products whose Consumption and/or Sale have been Banned, Withdrawn, Severely Restricted or Not Approved by Governments*. The *WHO Model List of Essential Drugs* is updated about every two years and is complemented by corresponding model prescribing information; the 11th *Model List* was published in 1999 and identified 306 essential drugs.

The Traditional Medicine team encourages and supports member states in the integration of traditional medicine into national health-care systems and in the appropriate use of traditional medicine, in particular through the provision of technical guide-lines, standards and methodologies.

In January 1999 the Executive Board adopted a resolution on WHO's Revised Drug Strategy which placed emphasis on the inequalities of access to pharmaceuticals, and also covered specific aspects of drugs policy, quality assurance, drug promotion, drug donation, independent drug information and rational drug use. Plans of action involving co-operation with member states and other international organizations were to be developed to monitor and analyse the pharmaceutical and public health implications of international agreements, including trade agreements. In April 2001 experts from WHO and the World Trade Organization participated in a workshop to address ways of lowering the cost of medicines in less developed countries. In the following month the World Health Assembly adopted a resolution urging member states to promote equitable access to essential drugs, noting that this was denied to about one-third of the world's population. WHO participates with other partners in the 'Accelerating Access' initiative, which aims to expand access to antiretroviral drugs for people with HIV/AIDS (see above).

WHO reports that 2m. children die each year of diseases for which common vaccines exist. In September 1991 the Children's Vaccine Initiative (CVI) was launched, jointly sponsored by the Rockefeller Foundation, UNDP, UNICEF, the World Bank and WHO, to facilitate the development and provision of children's vaccines. The CVI has as its ultimate goal the development of a single oral immunization shortly after birth that will protect against all major childhood diseases. An International Vaccine Institute was established in Seoul, Republic of Korea, as part of the CVI, to provide scientific and technical services for the production of vaccines for developing countries. In September 1996 WHO, jointly with UNICEF, published a comprehensive survey, entitled *State of the World's Vaccines and Immunization*. In 1999 WHO, UNICEF, the World Bank and a number of public- and private-sector partners formed the Global Alliance for Vaccines and Immunization (GAVI), which aimed to expand the provision of existing vaccines and to accelerate the development and introduction of new vaccines and technologies, with the ultimate goal of protecting children of all nations and from all socio-economic backgrounds against vaccine-preventable diseases.

WHO supports states in ensuring access to safe blood, blood products, transfusions, injections, and health-care technologies.

EVIDENCE AND INFORMATION FOR HEALTH POLICY

The Evidence and Information for Health Policy group addresses the following areas of work: evidence for health policy; health information management and dissemination; and research policy and promotion and organization of health systems. Through the generation and dissemination of evidence the Evidence and Information for Health Policy group aims to assist policy-makers assess health needs, choose intervention strategies, design policy and monitor performance, and thereby improve the performance of national health systems. The group also supports international and national dialogue on health policy.

In July WHO and six leading medical publishers announced an initiative to enable relevant authorities in developing countries to access nearly 1,000 biomedical journals through the internet at no or greatly reduced cost, in order to improve the world-wide circulation of scientific information.

HEALTH DAYS

World Health Day is observed on 7 April every year, and is used to promote awareness of a particular health topic ('Benefits of Physical Activity', in 2002). World Leprosy Day is held every year on 30 January, World TB Day on 24 March, World No Tobacco Day on 31 May, World Heart Day on 24 September, World Mental Health Day on 10 October, World Diabetes Day, in association with the International Diabetes Federation, on 14 November, World AIDS Day on 1 December, and World Asthma Day on 11 December.

ASSOCIATED AGENCY

International Agency for Research on Cancer: 150 Cours Albert Thomas, 69372 Lyon Cédex 08, France; tel. 4-72-73-85-67; fax 4-72-73-85-75; e-mail gaudin@iarc.fr. Established in 1965 as a self-governing body within the framework of WHO, the Agency organizes international research on cancer. It has its own laboratories and runs a programme of research on the environmental factors causing cancer. Members: Argentina, Australia, Belgium, Brazil, Canada, Denmark, Finland, France, Germany, Italy, Japan, Netherlands, Norway, Sweden, Switzerland, United Kingdom, USA. Dir Dr PAUL KLEIHUES (Germany).

Finance

WHO's regular budget is provided by assessment of member states and associate members. An additional fund for specific projects is provided by voluntary contributions from members and other sources, including UNDP and UNFPA.

A regular budget of US $842.7m. was proposed for the two years 2002–03, the same as for the previous biennium.

WHO budget appropriations by region, 2002–03

Region	Amount ('000 US dollars)	% of total budget
Africa	186,472	22.13
Americas	74,682	8.86
South-East Asia	93,022	11.04
Europe	52,771	6.26
Eastern Mediterranean	83,390	9.90
Western Pacific	73,262	8.69
Headquarters	279,055	33.12
Total	842,654	100.00

Publications

Bulletin of WHO (monthly).

Environmental Health Criteria.

International Digest of Health Legislation (quarterly).

International Classification of Functioning, Disability and Health—ICF.

International Statistical Classification of Diseases and Related Health Problems, Tenth Revision, 1992–1994 (versions in 37 languages).

Model List of Essential Drugs (biennially).

Weekly Epidemiological Record.

WHO Drug Information (quarterly).

World Health Report (annually).

World Health Statistics Annual.

Technical report series; catalogues of specific scientific, technical and medical fields available.

World Intellectual Property Organization—WIPO

Address: 34 chemin des Colombettes, 1211 Geneva 20, Switzerland.

Telephone: (22) 3389111; **fax:** (22) 7335428; **e-mail:** wipo.mail@wipo.int; **internet:** www.wipo.int.

WIPO was established by a Convention signed in Stockholm in 1967, which came into force in 1970. It became a specialized agency of the UN in December 1974.

MEMBERS

178 members: see Table on pp. 211–213.

Organization

(March 2002)

GENERAL ASSEMBLY

The General Assembly is one of the three WIPO governing bodies, and is composed of all states that are party to the WIPO Convention and that are also members of any of the WIPO-administered Unions (see below). In February 2002 the Assembly comprised 166 members. The Assembly meets in ordinary session once every two years to agree on programmes and budgets. It elects the Director-General, who is the executive head of WIPO.

CONFERENCE

All member states are represented in the Conference, which meets in ordinary session once every two years to adopt budgets and programmes.

CO-ORDINATION COMMITTEE

Countries belonging to the Committee are elected from among the member states of WIPO, the Paris and Berne Unions, and, *ex officio*, Switzerland. At February 2002 there were 79 members of the Committee, including four *ad hoc* members and Switzerland. It meets in ordinary session once a year.

INTERNATIONAL BUREAU

The International Bureau, as WIPO's secretariat, prepares the meetings of the various bodies of WIPO and the Unions, mainly through the provision of reports and working documents. It organizes the meetings, and sees that the decisions are communicated to all concerned, and, as far as possible, that they are carried out.

The International Bureau implements projects and initiates new ones to promote international co-operation in the field of intellectual property. It acts as an information service and publishes reviews. It is also the depositary of most of the treaties administered by WIPO.

Director-General: Dr Kamil Idris (Sudan).

More than 160 non-governmental organizations have observer status at WIPO. There are two advisory bodies: the Policy Advisory Commission (comprising eminent politicians, diplomats, lawyers and public officials) and the Industry Advisory Commission (comprising senior business representatives).

Activities

WIPO is responsible for promoting the protection of intellectual property throughout the world. Intellectual property comprises two principal branches: industrial property (patents and other rights in technological inventions, rights in trademarks, industrial designs, appellations of origin, etc.) and copyright and neighbouring rights (in literary, musical, artistic, photographic and audiovisual works).

WIPO administers and encourages member states to sign and enforce international treaties relating to the protection of intellectual property, of which the most fundamental are the Paris Convention for the Protection of Industrial Property (1883), the Berne Convention for the Protection of Literary and Artistic Works (1886), and the Patent Co-operation Treaty (PCT). WIPO's main areas of activity are progressive development of international intellectual property law, global protection systems and services, and co-operation for development. The organization seeks to harmonize national intellectual property legislation and procedures, provide services for international applications for industrial property rights, exchange information on intellectual property, provide training and legal and technical assistance to developing countries, facilitate the resolution of private intellectual property disputes, and develop the use of information technology for storing, accessing and using valuable intellectual property information. The rapid advancement of digital communications networks has posed challenges regarding the protection and enforcement of intellectual property rights. WIPO has undertaken a range of initiatives to address the implications for copyright and industrial property law, and for electronic commerce transcending national jurisdictions. In 1998 WIPO established the Electronic Commerce Section to co-ordinate programmes and activities relating to the intellectual property aspects of electronic commerce. In September 1999 WIPO organized the first International Conference on Electronic Commerce and Intellectual Property. The second International Conference on Electronic Commerce and Intellectual Property was held in September 2001.

In view of advances in technology and economic globalization WIPO has focused increasingly in recent years on the relationship between intellectual property and issues such as traditional knowledge, biological diversity, environmental protection and human rights. In 1998–99 WIPO prepared the first ever report on the intellectual property concerns of holders of traditional knowledge. In April 2000 the organization convened its first Meeting on Intellectual Property and Genetic Resources. A WIPO Intergovernmental Committee on Intellectual Property and Genetic Resources, Traditional Knowledge and Folklore was established in September.

PROGRESSIVE DEVELOPMENT OF INTERNATIONAL PROPERTY LAW

One of WIPO's major activities is the progressive development and application of international norms and standards. The organization prepares new treaties and undertakes the revision of the existing treaties that it administers. WIPO administers international classifications established by treaties and relating to inventions, marks and industrial designs: periodically it reviews these to ensure their improvement in terms of coverage and precision. WIPO also carries out studies on issues in the field of intellectual property that could be the subject of model laws or guidelines for implementation at national or international levels. The organization is increasingly active in harmonizing and simplifying procedures in order to make the registration of intellectual property more easily accessible. WIPO aims to keep pace with rapid developments in the intellectual property domain. Standing committees have been formed by member states to examine questions of substantive law or harmonization in the organization's main fields of activity and to ensure that the interests of member states are addressed promptly.

CO-OPERATION FOR DEVELOPMENT

WIPO aims to modernize national intellectual property systems. It offers assistance to increase the capabilities of developing countries to benefit from the international intellectual property framework, with a view to promoting the optimal use of human and other resources and thereby contributing to national prosperity. WIPO supports governments with intellectual property-related institution-building, human resources development, and preparation and implementation of legislation. The WIPO Worldwide Academy, created in 1998, undertakes training, teaching and research on intellectual property matters, focusing particularly on developing countries. The Academy maintains a Distance Learning Centre using on-line facilities, digital multimedia technology and video conferencing. WIPO's Information and Documentation Centre holds extensive reference materials. In January 2001 WIPO launched WIPONET, a global digital network of intellectual property information capable of transmitting confidential data. The organization is also implementing the Intellectual Property Digital Libraries database project and maintains the WIPO Collection of Laws for Electronic Access (CLEA) multi-lingual database.

WIPO advises countries on obligations under the World Trade Organization's agreement on Trade-Related Aspects of Intellectual Property Rights (TRIPS). The two organizations are undertaking a joint technical co-operation initiative to assist least-developed countries to harmonize their national legislative and administrative structures in compliance with the TRIPS accord by 1 January 2006.

A new programme focusing on the intellectual property concerns of small- and medium-sized enterprises was approved by the WIPO General Assembly in September 2000.

GLOBAL PROTECTION SYSTEMS AND SERVICES

WIPO administers a small number of treaties, covering inventions (patents), trademarks and industrial designs, under which one international registration or filing has effect in any of the relevant signatory states. The services provided by WIPO under such treaties simplify the registration process and reduce the cost of making individual applications or filings in each country in which protection for a given intellectual property right is sought. The most widely used of these treaties is the PCT, under which a single international patent application is valid in all signatory countries selected by the applicant. The PCT system has expanded rapidly in recent years. Through its Information Management for the PCT (IMPACT) project WIPO aims to automate fully the operations of the PCT. The corresponding treaties concerning the international registration of trademarks and industrial designs are, respectively, the Madrid Agreement (and its Protocol), and the Hague Agreement.

WIPO maintains the following international registration services:

International registration of trademarks: operating since 1893; during 2000 there were nearly 29,900 registrations and renewals of trademarks; publ. *WIPO Gazette of International Marks* (monthly).

International deposit of industrial designs: operating since 1928; during 2000 approximately 7,300 deposits, renewals and prolongations of industrial designs were made; publ. *International Designs Bulletin* (monthly).

International applications for patents: operating since 1978; during 2000 90,948 record copies of international applications for patents under the PCT were received.

WIPO also maintains the WIPO Arbitration and Mediation Centre, which became operational on 1 October 1994, to facilitate the settlement of intellectual property disputes between private parties. The Centre also organizes arbitrator and mediator workshops and assists in the development of WIPO model contract clauses and industry-specific resolution schemes. The Centre operates a Domain Name Dispute Resolution Service, which plays a leading role in reviewing cases of conflict between trademarks and internet domain names, in accordance with the Uniform Domain Name Dispute Resolution Policy that was, on WIPO's recommendation, adopted by the Internet Corporation for Assigned Names and Numbers (ICANN, q.v.) in October 1999. In 2001 1,506 cases concerning disputes over generic top-level domains were filed with the Centre. WIPO's first Internet Domain Name Process, a series of international consultations, undertaken in 1999, issued several recommendations for controlling the abuse of trademarks on the internet. A second Internet Domain Name Process, completed in 2001, addressed the improper registration of other identifiers, including standard non-proprietary names for pharmaceutical substances, names and acronyms of intergovernmental organizations, geographical indications and terms, and trade names.

PARIS AND BERNE CONVENTIONS

International Union for the Protection of Industrial Property (Paris Convention): the treaty was signed in Paris in 1883, and last revised in 1967; there were 159 members of the Union's Assembly at February 2002 and three parties to the Convention that were not Assembly members. Member states must accord to nationals and residents of other member states the same advantages under their laws relating to the protection of inventions, trademarks and other subjects of industrial property as they accord to their own nationals.

International Union for the Protection of Literary and Artistic Works (Berne Union): the treaty was signed in Berne in 1886 and last revised in 1971; there were 145 members of the Union's Assembly at February 2002 and three parties to the Convention that were not Assembly members. Members of the Union's Assembly must accord the same protection to the copyright of nationals of other member states as to their own. The treaty also prescribes minimum standards of protection, for example, that copyright protection generally continues throughout the author's life and for 50 years after. It includes special provision for the developing countries.

OTHER AGREEMENTS

(Status at January 2002, unless otherwise indicated)

International Protection of Industrial Property:

Madrid Agreement of 14 April 1891, for the Repression of False or Deceptive Indications of Source on Goods; 33 states party to the Agreement.

Madrid Agreement of 14 April 1891, Concerning the International Registration of Marks; 52 states party to the Agreement.

The Hague Agreement of 6 November 1925, Concerning the International Deposit of Industrial Designs; 29 states party to the Agreement.

Nice Agreement of 15 June 1957, Concerning the International Classification of Goods and Services for the Purposes of the Registration of Marks; 69 states party to the Agreement.

Lisbon Agreement of 31 October 1958, for the Protection of Appellations of Origin and their International Registration; 20 states party to the Agreement.

Locarno Agreement of 8 October 1968, Establishing an International Classification for Industrial Designs; 40 states party to the Agreement.

Patent Co-operation Treaty of 19 June 1970 (PCT); 115 states party to the Treaty.

Strasbourg Agreement of 24 March 1971, Concerning the International Patent Classification (IPC); 52 states party to the Agreement.

Vienna Agreement of 12 June 1973, Establishing an International Classification of the Figurative Elements of Marks; 19 states party to the Agreement.

Budapest Treaty of 28 April 1977, on the International Recognition of the Deposit of Micro-organisms for the Purposes of Patent Procedure; 54 states party to the Treaty.

Nairobi Treaty of 26 September 1981, on the Protection of the Olympic Symbol; 40 states party to the Treaty.

Trademark Law Treaty of 27 October 1994; 27 states party to the Treaty.

Protocol Relating to the Madrid Agreement Concerning the International Registration of Marks, signed on 28 June 1989; 55 contracting states.

Geneva Act of the Hague Agreement Concerning the International Registration of Industrial Designs, 1999; not yet entered into force.

Patent Law Treaty, 2000; not yet entered into force.

Copyright and Special International Protection of the Rights of Performers, Producers of Phonograms and Broadcasting Organizations ('Neighbouring Rights'):

Rome Convention, 26 October 1961, for the Protection of Performers, Producers of Phonograms and Broadcasting Organizations; 68 states party to the Convention.

Geneva Convention, 29 October 1971, for the Protection of Producers of Phonograms against Unauthorized Duplication of their Phonograms; 67 states party to the Convention.

Brussels Convention, 21 May 1974, Relating to the Distribution of Programme-carrying Signals Transmitted by Satellite; 24 states party to the Convention.

Treaty on the International Registration of Audiovisual Works, 1989; 13 states party to the Treaty.

Performances and Phonograms Treaty, 1996; scheduled to enter into force 20 May 2002.

Copyright Treaty, 1996; 30 states party to the Treaty (at 6 March 2002).

Finance

The proposed budget for the two years 2002–03 amounted to 678m. Swiss francs, compared with a revised budget of 566m. Swiss francs in 2000–01.

Publications

Annual Report.

Les appellations d'origine (irregular, in French).

Essential Elements of Intellectual Property (CD-Rom).

Industrial Property and Copyright (monthly in English and French; bimonthly in Spanish).

Intellectual Property in Asia and the Pacific (quarterly in English).

International Designs Bulletin (monthly in English and French, also on CD-Rom).

Newsletter (irregular in Arabic, English, French, Portuguese, Russian and Spanish).

PCT Gazette (weekly in English and French).

PCT Newsletter (monthly in English).

WIPO Gazette of International Marks (monthly, in English and French, also on CD-Rom).

A collection of industrial property and copyright laws and treaties; a selection of publications related to intellectual property.

World Meteorological Organization—WMO

Address: 7 bis, ave de la Paix, CP 2300, 1211 Geneva 2, Switzerland.

Telephone: (22) 7308111; **fax:** (22) 7308181; **e-mail:** ipa@wmo.ch; **internet:** www.wmo.ch.

The WMO was established in 1950 and was recognized as a Specialized Agency of the UN in 1951, operating in the fields of meteorology, climatology, operational hydrology and related fields, as well as their applications.

MEMBERS

185 members: see Table on pp. 211–213.

Organization

(March 2002)

WORLD METEOROLOGICAL CONGRESS

The supreme body of the Organization, the Congress, is convened every four years and represents all members; it adopts regulations, and determines policy, programme and budget. Thirteenth Congress: May 1999.

EXECUTIVE COUNCIL

The Council has 36 members and meets at least yearly to prepare studies and recommendations for the Congress; it supervises the implementation of Congress resolutions and regulations, informs members on technical matters and offers advice.

SECRETARIAT

The secretariat acts as an administrative, documentary and information centre; undertakes special technical studies; produces publications; organizes meetings of WMO constituent bodies; acts as a link between the meteorological and hydrometeorological services of the world, and provides information for the general public.

Secretary-General: Prof. G. O. P. OBASI (Nigeria).

REGIONAL ASSOCIATIONS

Members are grouped in six Regional Associations (Africa, Asia, Europe, North and Central America, South America and South-West Pacific), whose task is to co-ordinate meteorological activity within their regions and to examine questions referred to them by the Executive Council. Sessions are held at least once every four years.

TECHNICAL COMMISSIONS

The Technical Commissions are composed of experts nominated by the members of the Organization. Sessions are held at least once every four years. The Commissions cover the following areas: Basic Systems; Climatology; Instruments and Methods of Observation; Atmospheric Sciences; Aeronautical Meteorology; Agricultural Meteorology; Hydrology; Marine Meteorology.

Activities

WORLD WEATHER WATCH PROGRAMME

Combining facilities and services provided by the members, the Programme's primary purpose is to make available meteorological and related geophysical and environmental information enabling them to maintain efficient meteorological services. Facilities in regions outside any national territory (outer space, ocean areas and Antarctica) are maintained by members on a voluntary basis.

Antarctic Activities: co-ordinate WMO activities related to the Antarctic, in particular the surface and upper-air observing programme, plan the regular exchange of observational data and products needed for operational and research purposes, study problems related to instruments and methods of observation peculiar to the Antarctic, and develop appropriate regional coding practices. Contacts are maintained with scientific bodies dealing with Antarctic research and with other international organizations on aspects of Antarctic meteorology.

Data Management: This aspect of the Programme monitors the integration of the different components of the World Weather Watch (WWW) Programme, with the intention of increasing the efficiency of, in particular, the Global Observing System, the Global Data Processing System and the Global Telecommunication System. The Data Management component of the WWW Programme develops data handling procedures and standards for enhanced forms of data representation, in order to aid member countries in processing large volumes of meteorological data. It also supports the co-ordinated transfer of expertise and technology to developing countries.

Emergency Response Activities: assist national meteorological services to respond effectively to man-made environmental emergencies, particularly nuclear accidents, through the development, co-ordination and implementation of WMO/IAEA established procedures and response mechanisms for the provision and exchange of observational data and specialized transport model products.

Global Data Processing System: consists of World Meteorological Centres (WMCs) in Melbourne (Australia), Moscow (Russia) and Washington, DC (USA), 40 Regional/Specialized Meteorological Centres (RSMCs) and 187 National Meteorological Centres. The WMCs and RSMCs provide analyses, forecasts and warnings for exchange on the Global Telecommunications System. Some centres concentrate on the monitoring and forecasting of environmental quality and special weather phenomena, such as tropical cyclones, monsoons, droughts, etc., which have a major impact on human safety and national economies. These analyses and forecasts are designed to assist the members in making local and specialized forecasts.

Global Observing System: Simultaneous observations are made at more than 10,000 land stations. Meteorological information is also received from 3,000 aircraft, 7,000 ships, 600 drifting buoys, and nine polar orbiting and six geostationary meteorological satellites. About 160 members operate some 1,300 ground stations equipped to receive picture transmissions from geostationary and polar-orbiting satellites.

Global Telecommunication System: provides telecommunication services for the rapid collection and exchange of meteorological information and related data; consists of (a) the Main Telecommunication Network (MTN), (b) six Regional Meteorological Telecommunication networks, and (c) the national telecommunication networks. The system operates through 183 National Meteorological Centres, 29 Regional Telecommunications Hubs and the three WMCs.

Instruments and Methods of Observation Programme: promotes the world-wide standardization of meteorological and geophysical instruments and methods of observation and measurement to meet agreed accuracy requirements. It provides related guidance material and training assistance in the use and maintenance of the instruments.

System Support Activity: provides guidance and support to members in the planning, establishment and operation of the WWW. It includes training, technical co-operation support, system and methodology support, operational WWW evaluations, advanced technology support, an operations information service, and the WWW referral catalogue.

Tropical Cyclone Programme: established in response to UN General Assembly Resolution 2733 (XXV), aims at the development of national and regionally co-ordinated systems to ensure that the loss of life and damage caused by tropical cyclones and associated floods, landslides and storm surges are reduced to a minimum. The programme supports the transfer of technology, and includes five regional tropical cyclone bodies covering more than 60 countries, to improve warning systems and for collaboration with other international organizations in activities related to disaster mitigation.

WORLD CLIMATE PROGRAMME

Adopted by the Eighth World Meteorological Congress (1979), the World Climate Programme (WCP) comprises the following components: World Climate Data and Monitoring Programme (WCDMP), World Climate Applications and Services Programme (WCASP), World Climate Impact Assessment and Response Strategies Programme (WCIRP), World Climate Research Programme (WCRP). The WCP is supported by the Global Climate Observing System (GCOS), which provides comprehensive observation of the global climate system, involving a multi-disciplinary range of atmospheric, oceanic, hydrologic, cyrospheric and biotic properties and processes. In 1997/98 the GCOS was particularly active in monitoring the impact of the El Niño weather phenomenon on the climate system. The objectives of the WCP are: to use existing climate information to improve economic and social planning; to improve the understanding of climate processes through research, so as to determine the predictability of climate and the extent of man's influence on it; and to detect and warn governments of impending climate variations or changes, either natural or man-made, which may significantly affect critical human activities.

Co-ordination of the overall Programme is the responsibility of the WMO, along with direct management of the WCDMP and WCASP. The UN Environment Programme (UNEP, q.v.) has accepted responsibility for the WCIRP, while the WCRP is jointly administered by WMO, the International Council of Scientific Unions (ICSU, q.v.) and UNESCO's Intergovernmental Oceanographic Commission. Other organizations involved in the Programme include FAO, WHO, and the Consultative Group on International Agricultural Research (CGIAR). The WCP Co-ordinating Committee co-ordinates the activities of the four components of the Programme and liaises with other international bodies concerned with climate. In addition, the WCP supports the WMO/UNEP Intergovernmental Panel on Climate Change and the implementation of international agreements, such as the UN Framework Convention on Climate Change (see below).

World Climate Applications and Services Programme (WCASP): promotes applications of climate knowledge in the areas of food production, water, energy (especially solar and wind energy), urban planning and building, human health, transport, tourism and recreation.

World Climate Data and Monitoring Programme (WCDMP): aims to make available reliable climate data for detecting and monitoring climate change for both practical applications and research purposes. The major projects are: the Climate Change Detection Project (CCDP); development of climate data bases; computer systems for climate data management (CLICOM); the World Data and Information Referral Service (INFOCLIMA); the Climate Monitoring System; and the Data Rescue (DARE) project.

World Climate Impact Assessment and Response Strategies Programme (WCIRP): aims to make reliable estimates of the socio-economic impact of climate changes, and to assist in forming national policies accordingly. It concentrates on: study of the impact of climate variations on national food systems; assessment of the impact of man's activities on the climate, especially through increasing the amount of carbon dioxide and other radiatively active gases in the atmosphere; and developing the methodology of climate impact assessments.

World Climate Research Programme (WCRP): organized jointly with the Intergovernmental Oceanographic Commission of UNESCO and the ICSU, to determine to what extent climate can be predicted, and the extent of man's influence on climate. Its three specific objectives are: establishing the physical basis for weather predictions over time ranges of one to two months; understanding and predicting the variability of the global climate over periods of several years; and studying the long-term variations and the response of climate to natural or man-made influence over periods of several decades. Studies include: changes in the atmosphere caused by emissions of carbon dioxide, aerosols and other gases; the effect of cloudiness on the radiation balance; the effect of ground water storage and vegetation on evaporation; the Arctic and Antarctic climate process; and the effects of oceanic circulation changes on the global atmosphere. The 10-year Tropical Ocean and Global Atmosphere Project, which ended in 1994, developed forecasting techniques used to monitor the climate phenomenon, El Niño, in 1997–98.

ATMOSPHERIC RESEARCH AND ENVIRONMENT PROGRAMME

This major programme aims to help members to implement research projects; to disseminate relevant scientific information; to draw the attention of members to outstanding research problems of major importance, such as atmospheric composition and environment changes; and to encourage and help members to incorporate the results of research into operational forecasting or other appropriate techniques, particularly when such changes of procedure require international co-ordination and agreement.

Global Atmosphere Watch (GAW): This is a world-wide system that integrates most monitoring and research activities involving the measurement of atmospheric composition, and is intended to serve as an early warning system to detect further changes in atmospheric concentrations of 'greenhouse' gases, changes in the ozone layer and in long-range transport of pollutants, including acidity and toxicity of rain, as well as the atmospheric burden of aerosols. The instruments of these globally standardized observations and related research are a set of 22 global stations in remote areas and, in order to address regional effects, some 200 regional stations measuring specific atmospheric chemistry parameters, such as ozone and acid deposition. GAW is the main contributor of data on chemical composition and physical characteristics of the atmosphere to the GCOS. Through GAW, WMO has collaborated with the UN Economic Commission for Europe (ECE) and has been responsible for the meteorological part of the Monitoring and Evaluation of the Long-range Transmission of Air Pollutants in Europe. In this respect, WMO has arranged for the establishment of two Meteorological Synthesizing Centres (Oslo, Norway, and Moscow, Russia) which provide daily analysis of the transport of pollution over Europe. GAW also gives attention to atmospheric chemistry studies, prepares scientific assessments and encourages integrated environmental monitoring. Quality Assurance Science Activities Centres have been established to ensure an overall level of quality in GAW. Atmospheric composition information is maintained by and available through a series of six GAW World Data Centres. GAW operates the GAW Urban Environment Meteorological Research Programme (GURME), which assists National Meteorological and Hydrological Services (NMHSs) in dealing with regional and urban pollution monitoring forecasting, through the provision of guide-lines and information on the requisite measuring and modelling infrastructures, and by bringing together NMHSs, regional and city administrations and health authorities. GURME is being developed in co-operation with the World Health Organization.

Physics and Chemistry of Clouds and Weather Modification Research Programme: encourages scientific research on cloud physics and chemistry, with special emphasis on interaction between clouds and atmospheric chemistry, as well as weather modification such as precipitation enhancement ('rain-making') and hail suppression. It provides information on world-wide weather modification projects, and guidance in the design and evaluation of experiments. It also studies the chemistry of clouds and their role in the transport, transformation and dispersion of pollution.

Tropical Meteorology Research Programme: aims at the promotion and co-ordination of members' research efforts into such important problems as monsoons, tropical cyclones, meteorological aspects of droughts in the arid zones of the tropics, rain-producing tropical weather systems, and the interaction between tropical and mid-latitude weather systems. This should lead to a better understanding of tropical systems and forecasting, and thus be of economic benefit to tropical countries.

Weather Prediction Research Programmes: The programmes assist members in exchanging the results of research on weather prediction and long-range forecasting by means of international conferences and technical reports and progress reports on numerical weather prediction, in order to improve members' weather services. The Programme on Very Short- and Short-range Weather Prediction Research is designed to promote and co-ordinate research activities by members, with a view to improving forecast accuracy over a period extending to three or four days. The Programme on Medium- and Long-range Weather Prediction Research is aimed at the improvement and better co-ordination of members' research activities in weather prediction beyond day four, including monthly and seasonal forecasting.

World Weather Research Programme: Promotes the development and application of improved weather forecasting techniques. The Programme is primarily concerned with forecasting weather events that have the potential to cause considerable socio-economic dislocation. Advances in forecasting capability are pursued through a combination of improved scientific understanding (gained through field experiments and research), forecast technique development, the demonstration of new forecasting capabilities, and the transfer of these advances to all NMHSs in conjunction with related training.

APPLICATIONS OF METEOROLOGY PROGRAMME

Public Weather Services Programme: assists members in providing reliable and effective weather and related services for the benefit of the public. The main objectives of the programme are: to strengthen members' capabilities to meet the needs of the community through the provision of comprehensive weather and related services, with particular emphasis on public safety and welfare; and to foster a better understanding by the public of the capabilities of national meteorological services and how best to use their services.

Agricultural Meteorology Programme: the study of weather and climate as they affect agriculture and forestry, the selection of crops and their protection from disease and deterioration in storage, soil conservation, phenology and physiology of crops and productivity and health of farm animals; the Commission for Agricultural Meteorology supervises the applications projects and also advises the Secretary-General in his efforts to co-ordinate activities in support of food production. There are also special activities in agrometeorology to monitor and combat drought and desertification, to apply climate and real-time weather information in agricultural planning and operations, and to help improve the efficiency of the use of human labour, land, water and energy in agriculture; close co-operation is maintained with FAO, centres of CGIAR and UNEP.

Aeronautical Meteorology Programme: to provide operational meteorological information required for safe, regular and efficient air navigation, as well as meteorological assistance to non-real-time activities of the aviation industry. The objective is to ensure the world-wide provision of cost-effective and responsive meteorological services, in support of safe, regular and efficient aviation operations. The programme is implemented at global, regional and national levels by the Commission for Aeronautical Meteorology (CAeM) playing a major role, taking into account relevant meteorological developments in science and technology, studying aeronautical requirements for meteorological services, promoting international standardization of methods, procedures and techniques, and considering requirements for basic and climatological data as well as aeronautical requirements for meteorological observations and specialized instruments and enhanced understanding and awareness of the impact of aviation on the environment. Activities under this programme are carried out, where relevant, with the International Civil Aviation Organization (ICAO, q.v.) and in collaboration with users of services provided to aviation.

Marine Meteorology and Associated Oceanographic Activities Programme: operational monitoring of the oceans and the maritime atmosphere; collection, exchange, archival recording and management of marine data; processing of marine data, and the provision of marine meteorological and oceanographic services in support of the safety of life and property at sea and of the efficient and economic operation of all sea-based activities. The joint WMO/Intergovernmental Oceanographic Commission (IOC) Technical Commission for Oceanography and Marine Meteorology (JCOMM) has broad responsibilities in the overall management of the programme. Many programme elements are undertaken jointly with the IOC, within the context of JCOMM, and also of the Global Ocean Observing System (GOOS). Close co-operation also occurs with the International Maritime Organization (IMO, q.v.), as well as with other bodies both within and outside the UN system.

HYDROLOGY AND WATER RESOURCES PROGRAMME

The overall objective of this major programme is to apply hydrology to meet the needs of sustainable development and use of water and related resources; for the mitigation of water-related disasters; and to ensure effective environment management at national and international levels. The Programme consists of the following mutually supporting component programmes:

Programme on Basic Systems in Hydrology (BSH): provides the basis and framework for the majority of the scientific and technical aspects of WMO activities in hydrology and water resources. The BSH covers the collection, transmission and storage of data, the implementation of the Hydrological Operational Multipurpose System (HOMS), and the development of the World Hydrological Cycle Observing System (WHYCOS).

Programme on Forecasting and Applications in Hydrology (FAH): covers aspects of the Hydrology and Water Resources Programme relating to hydrological modelling and forecasting, and to the application of hydrology in studies of global change. The FAH organizes activities in support of water resources development and management, and hazard mitigation, and conducts studies on climate change and environmental protection. The Programme is linked to the World Climate and Tropical Cyclone programmes.

Programme on Sustainable Development of Water Resources (SDW): encourages the full participation of hydrological services in national planning and in the implementation of actions consequent to the relevant recommendations of the United Nations Conference on Environment and Development (UNCED, held in Rio de Janeiro, Brazil, in 1992), and of its review conference in 1997.

Programme on Capacity Building in Hydrology and Water Resources (CBH): provides a framework under which National Hydrological Services (NHSs) can request advice and assistance. Supports NHSs' capacity-building efforts.

Programme on Water-related Issues (WRI): maintains WMO's important role in international activities relating to water resource assessment and hydrological forecasting. A major aspect of this component programme is the Organization's collaboration with other UN agencies. In addition, the WRI involves joint activities with international river basin commissions and with scientific and technical non-governmental organizations.

Specific suppport for the transfer of operational technology is provided through the Hydrological Operational Multipurpose System (HOMS).

Other WMO programmes contain hydrological elements, which are closely co-ordinated with the Hydrology and Water Resources Programme. These include the Tropical Cyclone Programme, the World Climate Programme, and the Global Energy and Water Budget Experiment of the World Climate Research Programme.

EDUCATION AND TRAINING PROGRAMME

The overall objective of this programme is to assist members in developing adequately trained staff to meet their responsibilities for providing meteorological and hydrological information services.

Activities include surveys of the training requirements of member states, the development of appropriate training programmes, the monitoring and improvement of the network of WMO Regional Meteorological Training Centres, the organization of training courses, seminars and conferences and the preparation of training materials. The Programme also arranges individual training programmes and the provision of fellowships. There are about 500 trainees in any one year. About 300 fellowships are awarded annually. Advice is given on training materials, resources and expertise between members. A Panel of Experts on Education and Training was set up by the Executive Council to serve as an advisory body on all aspects of technical and scientific education and of training in meteorology and operational hydrology.

TECHNICAL CO-OPERATION PROGRAMME

The objective of the WMO Technical Co-operation Programme is to assist developing countries in improving their meteorological and hydrological services so that they can serve the needs of their people more effectively. This is through improving, *inter alia*, their early warning systems for severe weather; their agricultural-meteorological services, to assist in more reliable and fruitful food production; and the assessment of climatological factors for economic planning. At a regional level the Programme concentrates on disaster prevention and mitigation. In 2000 the cost of the assistance to developing countries, administered or arranged by the Technical Co-operation Programme, was US $16.6m.

United Nations Development Programme (UNDP): WMO provides assistance in the development of national meteorological and hydrological services, in the application of meteorological and hydrological data to national economic development, and in the training of personnel. Assistance in the form of expert missions, fellowships and equipment was provided to 18 countries in 2000 at a cost of US $2.6m., financed by UNDP.

Voluntary Co-operation Programme (VCP): WMO assists members in implementing the World Weather Watch Programme to develop an integrated observing and forecasting system. Member governments contribute equipment, services and fellowships for training, in addition to cash donations. During 2000 167 projects in 778 countries received support under the VCP, while 124 short-term and 78 long-term fellowships were being implemented in the framework of the programme. Contributions to the VCP totalled US $8.4m. in 2000.

WMO also carries out assistance projects under Trust Fund arrangements, financed by national authorities, either for activities in their own country or in a beneficiary country and managed by UNDP, the World Bank and UNEP. Such arrangements provided one-third of total Programme funds in 2000.

Financial support from WMO's regular budget for fellowships, group training, technical conferences and study tours amounted to US $800,000 in 2000.

CO-OPERATION WITH OTHER BODIES

As a Specialized Agency of the UN, WMO is actively involved in the activities of the UN system. In addition, WMO has concluded a number of formal agreements and working arrangements with international organizations both within and outside the UN system, at the intergovernmental and non-governmental level. As a result, WMO participates in major international conferences convened under the auspices of the UN or other organizations.

Intergovernmental Panel on Climate Change (IPCC): established in 1988 by WMO and UNEP; comprises some 3,000 scientists as well as other experts and representatives of all UN member governments. Approximately every five years the IPCC assesses all available scientific, technical and socio-economic information on anthropogenic climate change. IPCC provides, on request, scientific, technical and socio-economic advice to the parties to the Conference of the Parties to the UN Framework Convention on Climate Change (UNFCCC) and to its subsidiary bodies, and compiles reports on specialized topics, such as *Aviation and the Global Atmosphere* and *Regional Impacts of Climate Change*. The IPCC informs and guides, but does not prescribe, policy. In December 1995 the IPCC presented evidence to 120 governments, demonstrating 'a discernible human influence on global climate'. In 2001 the Panel issued its *Third Assessment Report*, in which it confirmed this finding and presented new and strengthened evidence attributing most global climate warming over the past 50 years to human activities.

Secretariat of the UN Framework Convention on Climate Change: Haus Carstanjen, Martin-Luther-King-Strasse 8, 53175 Bonn, Germany; tel. (228) 815-1000; fax (228) 815-1999; e-mail secretariat@unfccc.int; internet unfccc.int. WMO and UNEP worked together to formulate the Convention, in response to the first report of the IPCC, issued in August 1990, which predicted an increase in the concentration of 'greenhouse' gases (i.e. carbon dioxide and other gases that have a warming effect on the atmosphere) owing to human activity. The UNFCCC was signed in May 1992 and formally adopted at the UN Conference on Environment and Development, held in June. It entered into force in March 1994. It commited countries to submitting reports on measures being taken to reduce the emission of greenhouse gases and recommended stabilizing these emissions at 1990 levels by 2000; however, this was not legally-binding. In July 1996, at the second session of the Conference of the Parties (COP) of the Convention, representatives of developed countries declared their willingness to commit to legally-binding objectives for emission limitations in a specified timetable. Multilateral negotiations ensued to formulate a mandatory treaty on greenhouse gas emissions. At the third COP, held in Kyoto, Japan, in December 1997, 38 industrial nations endorsed mandatory reductions of emissions of the six most harmful gases by an average of 5.2% from 1990 levels, between 2008 and 2012. The so-called Kyoto Protocol was to enter into force on being ratified by countries representing 55% of the world's carbon dioxide emissions in 1990. Many of the Protocol's operational details, however, remained to be determined. The fourth COP, convened in Buenos Aires, Argentina, in November 1998, adopted a plan of action to promote implementation of the UNFCCC and to finalize the operational details of the Kyoto Protocol. These included the Clean Development Mechanism, by which industrialized countries may obtain credits towards achieving their reduction targets by assisting developing countries to implement emission-reducing measures, and a system of trading emission quotas. The fifth COP, held in Bonn, Germany, in October/November 1999, and the first session of the sixth COP, convened in The Hague, Netherlands, in November 2000, failed to reach agreement on the implementation of the Buenos Aires plan of action, owing to a lack of consensus on several technical matters, including the formulation of an effective mechanism for ascertaining compliance under the Kyoto Protocol, and adequately defining a provision of the Protocol under which industrialized countries may obtain credits towards achieving their reduction targets in respect of the absorption of emissions resulting from activities in the so-called land-use, land-use change and forestry (LULUCF) sector. Further, informal, talks were held in Ottawa, Canada, in early December. Agreement on implementing the Buenos Aires action plan was finally achieved at the second session of the sixth COP, held in Bonn in July 2001. The seventh COP, convened in Marrakech, Morocco, in October/November, formally adopted the decisions reached in July, and elected 15 members to the Executive Board of the Clean Development Mechanism. In March the USA (the most prolific national producer of harmful gas emissions) announced that it would not ratify the Kyoto Protocol.

INTERNATIONAL DAY

World Meteorological Day is observed every year on 23 March. The theme in 2002 was 'Reducing Vulnerability to Weather and Climate Extremes'.

Finance

WMO is financed by contributions from members on a proportional scale of assessment. The assessed regular budget for the four years 2000–03 was 248.8m. Swiss francs; additional expenditure of 3.5m. Swiss francs was also authorized to be used for high priority activities. Outside this budget, WMO implements a number of projects as executing agency for UNDP or else under trust-fund arrangements.

Publications

Annual Report.

Statements on the Status of the Global Climate.

WMO Bulletin (quarterly in English, French, Russian and Spanish).

Reports, technical regulations, manuals and notes and training publications.

United Nations Framework Convention on Climate Change

(9 May 1992)

The Parties to this Convention,

Acknowledging that change in the Earth's climate and its adverse effect are a common concern of humankind,

Concerned that human activities have been substantially increasing the atmospheric concentrations of greenhouse gases, that these increases enhance the natural greenhouse effect, and that this will result on average in an additional warming of the Earth's surface and atmosphere and may adversely affect natural ecosystems and humankind,

Noting that the largest share of historical and current global emissions of greenhouse gases has originated in developed countries, that per capita emissions in developing countries are still relatively low and that the share of global emissions originating in developing countries will grow to meet their social and development needs,

Aware of the role and importance in terrestrial and marine ecosystems of sinks and reservoirs of greenhouse gases,

Noting that there are many uncertainties in predictions of climate change, particularly with regard to the timing, magnitude and regional patterns thereof,

Acknowledging that the global nature of climate change calls for the widest possible co-operation by all countries and their participation in an effective and appropriate international response, in accordance with their common but differentiated responsibilities and respective capabilities and their social and economic conditions,

Recalling the pertinent provisions of the Declaration of the United Nations Conference on the Human Environment, adopted at Stockholm on 16 June 1972,

Recalling also that States have, in accordance with the Charter of the United Nations and the principles of international law, the sovereign right to exploit their own resources pursuant to their own environmental and developmental policies, and the responsibility to ensure that activities within their jurisdiction or control do not cause damage to the environment of other States or of areas beyond the limits of national jurisdiction,

Reaffirming the principle of sovereignty of States in international co-operation to address climate change,

Recognizing that States should enact effective environmental legislation, that environmental standards, management objectives and priorities should reflect the environmental and developmental context to which they apply, and that standards applied by some countries may be inappropriate and of unwarranted economic and social cost to other countries, in particular developing countries,

Recalling the provisions of the General Assembly . . . on the United Nations Conference on Environment and Development, and . . . on protection of global climate for present and future generations of mankind,

Recalling also the provisions of the General Assembly . . . on the possible adverse effects of sea-level rise on islands and coastal areas, particularly low-lying coastal areas, and . . . on the implementation of the Plan of Action to Combat Desertification,

Recalling further the Vienna Convention for the Protection of the Ozone Layer, 1985, and the Montreal Protocol on Substances that Deplete the Ozone Layer, 1987, as adjusted and amended on 29 June 1990,

Noting the Ministerial Declaration of the Second World Climate Conference adopted on 7 November 1990,

Conscious of the valuable analytical work being conducted by many States on climate change and of the important contributions of the World Meteorological Organization, the United Nations Environment Programme and other organs, organizations and bodies of the United Nations system, as well as other international and intergovernmental bodies, to the exchange of results of scientific research and the co-ordination of research,

Recognizing that steps required to understand and address climate change will be environmentally, socially and economically most effective if they are based on relevant scientific, technical and economic considerations and continually re-evaluated in the light of new findings in these areas,

Recognizing that various actions to address climate change can be justified economically in their own right and can also help in solving other environmental problems,

Recognizing also the need for developed countries to take immediate action in a flexible manner on the basis of clear priorities, as a first step towards comprehensive response strategies at the global, national and, where agreed, regional levels that take into account all greenhouse gases, with due consideration of their relative contributions to the enhancement of the greenhouse effect,

Recognizing further that low-lying and other small island countries, countries with low-lying coastal, arid and semi-arid areas or areas liable to floods, drought and desertification, and developing countries with fragile mountainous ecosystems are particularly vulnerable to the adverse effects of climate change,

Recognizing the special difficulties of those countries, especially developing countries, whose economies are particularly dependent on fossil fuel production, use and exportation, as a consequence of action taken on limiting greenhouse gas emissions,

Affirming that responses to climate change should be co-ordinated with social and economic development in an integrated manner with a view to avoiding adverse impacts on the latter, taking into full account the legitimate priority needs of developing countries for the achievement of sustained economic growth and the eradication of poverty,

Recognizing that all countries, especially developing countries, need access to resources required to achieve sustainable social and economic development and that, in order for developing countries to progress towards that goal, their energy consumption will need to grow, taking into account the possibilities for achieving greater energy efficiency and for controlling greenhouse gas emissions in general, including through the application of new technologies on terms which make such an application economically and socially beneficial,

Determined to protect the climate system for present and further generations,

Have agreed as follows:

Article 1

For the purposes of this Convention:

1. "Adverse effects of climate change" means changes in the physical environment or biota resulting from climate change which have significant deleterious effects on the composition, resilience or productivity of natural and managed ecosystems or on the operation of socio-economic systems or on human health and welfare.

2. "Climate change" means a change of climate which is attributed directly or indirectly to human activity that alters the composition of the global atmosphere and which is in addition to natural climate variability observed over comparable time periods.

3. "Climate system" means the totality of the atmosphere, hydrosphere, biosphere and geosphere and their interactions.

4. "Emissions" means the release of greenhouse gases and/or their precursors into the atmosphere over a specified area and period of time.

5. "Greenhouse gases" means those gaseous constituents of the atmosphere, both natural and anthropogenic, that absorb and re-emit infrared radiation.

6. "Regional economic integration organization" means an organization constituted by sovereign States of a given region which has competence in respect of matters governed by this Convention or its protocols and has been duly authorized, in accordance with its internal procedures, to sign, ratify, accept, approve or accede to the instruments concerned.

7. "Reservoir" means a component or components of the climate system where a greenhouse gas or a precursor of a greenhouse gas is stored.

8. "Sink" means any process, activity or mechanism which removes a greenhouse gas, an aerosol or a precursor of a greenhouse gas from the atmosphere.

9. "Source" means any process or activity which releases a greenhouse gas, an aerosol or a precursor of a greenhouse gas into the atmosphere.

Article 2

The ultimate objective of this Convention and any related legal instruments that the Conference of the Parties may adopt is to achieve, in accordance with the relevant provisions of the Convention, stabilization of greenhouse gas concentrations in the atmosphere at a level that would prevent dangerous anthropogenic interference with the climate system. Such a level should be achieved within a time-frame sufficient to allow ecosystems to adapt naturally to climate change, to ensure that food production is not threatened and to enable economic development to proceed in a sustainable manner.

Article 3

In their actions to achieve the objective of the Convention and to implement its provisions, the Parties shall be guided, *inter alia*, by the following:

1. The Parties should protect the climate system for the benefit of present and future generations of humankind, on the basis of equity and in accordance with their common but differentiated responsibilities and respective capabilities. Accordingly, the developed country Parties should take the lead in combating climate change and the adverse effects thereof.

2. The specific needs and special circumstances of developing country Parties, especially those that are particularly vulnerable to the adverse effects of climate change, and of those Parties, especially developing country Parties, that would have to bear a disproportionate or abnormal burden under the Convention, should be given full consideration.

3. The Parties should take precautionary measures to anticipate, prevent or minimize the causes of climate change and mitigate its adverse effects. Where there are threats of serious or irreversible damage, lack of full scientific certainty should not be used as a reason for postponing such measures, taking into account that policies and measures to deal with climate change should be cost-effective so as to ensure global benefits at the lowest possible cost. To achieve this, such policies and measures should take into account different socio-economic contexts, be comprehensive, cover all relevant sources, sinks and reservoirs of greenhouse gases and adaptation, and comprise all economic sectors. Efforts to address climate change may be carried out co-operatively by interested Parties.

4. The Parties have a right to, and should, promote sustainable development. Policies and measures to protect the climate system against human-induced change should be appropriate for the specific conditions of each Party and should be integrated with national development programmes, taking into account that economic development is essential for adopting measures to address climate change.

5. The Parties should co-operate to promote a supportive and open international economic system that would lead to sustainable economic growth and development in all Parties, particularly developing country Parties, thus enabling them better to address the problems of climate change. Measures taken to combat climate change, including unilateral ones, should not constitute a means of arbitrary or unjustifiable discrimination or a disguised restriction on international trade.

Article 4

1. All Parties, taking into account their common but differentiated responsibilities and their specific national and regional development priorities, objectives and circumstances, shall:

(a) Develop, periodically update, publish and make available to the Conference of the Parties, in accordance with Article 12, national inventories of anthropogenic emissions by sources and removals by sinks of all greenhouse gases not controlled by the Montreal Protocol, using comparable methodologies to be agreed upon by the Conference of the Parties;

(b) Formulate, implement, publish and regularly update national and, where appropriate, regional programmes containing measures to mitigate climate change by addressing anthropogenic emissions by sources and removals by sinks of all greenhouse gases not controlled by the Montreal Protocol, and measures to facilitate adequate adaptation to climate change;

(c) Promote and co-operate in the development, application and diffusion, including transfer, of technologies, practices and processes that control, reduce or prevent anthropogenic emissions of greenhouse gases not controlled by the Montreal Protocol in all relevant sectors, including the energy, transport, industry, agriculture, forestry and waste management sectors;

(d) Promote sustainable management, and promote and co-operate in the conservation and enhancement, as appropriate, of sinks and reservoirs of all greenhouses gases not controlled by the Montreal Protocol, including biomass, forests and oceans as well as other terrestrial, coastal and marine ecosystems;

(e) Co-operate in preparing for adaptation to the impacts of climate change; develop and elaborate appropriate and integrated plans for coastal zone management, water resources and agriculture, and for the protection and rehabilitation of areas, particularly in Africa, affected by drought and desertification, as well as floods;

(f) Take climate change considerations into account, to the extent feasible, in their relevant social, economic and environmental policies and actions, and employ appropriate methods, for example impact assessments, formulated and determined nationally, with a view to minimizing adverse effects on the economy, on public health and on the quality of the environment, of projects or measures undertaken by them to mitigate or adapt to climate change;

(g) Promote and co-operate in scientific, technological, technical, socio-economic and other research, systematic observation and development of data archives related to the climate system and intended to further the understanding and to reduce or eliminate the remaining uncertainties regarding the causes, effects, magnitude and timing of climate change and the economic and social consequences of various response strategies;

(h) Promote and co-operate in the full, open and prompt exchange of relevant scientific, technological, technical, socio-economic and legal information related to the climate system and climate change, and to the economic and social consequences of various response strategies;

(i) Promote and co-operate in education, training and public awareness related to climate change and encourage the widest participation in this process, including that of non-governmental organizations; and

(j) Communicate to the Conference of the Parties information related to implementation, in accordance with Article 12.

2. The developed country Parties and other Parties included in Annex I commit themselves specifically as provided for in the following:

(a) Each of these Parties shall adopt national policies and take corresponding measures on the mitigation of climate change, by limiting its anthropogenic emissions of greenhouse gases and protecting and enhancing its greenhouse gas sinks and reservoirs. These policies and measures will demonstrate that developed countries are taking the lead in modifying longer-term trends in anthropogenic emissions consistent with the objective of the Convention, recognizing that the return by the end of the present decade to earlier levels of anthropogenic emissions of carbon dioxide and other greenhouse gases not controlled by the Montreal Protocol would contribute to such modification, and taking into account the differences in these Parties' starting points and approaches, economic structures and resource bases, the need to maintain strong and sustainable economic growth, available technologies and other individual circumstances, as well as the need for equitable and appropriate contributions by each of these Parties to the global effort regarding that objective. These Parties may implement such policies and measures jointly with other Parties and may assist other Parties in contributing to the achievement of the objective of the Convention and, in particular, that of this sub-paragraph;

(b) In order to promote progress to this end, each of these Parties shall communicate, within six months of the entry into force of the Convention and periodically thereafter, and in accordance with Article 12, detailed information on its policies and measures referred to in sub-paragraph (a) above, as well as on its resulting projected anthropogenic emissions by sources and removals by sinks of greenhouse gases not controlled by the Montreal Protocol for the period referred to in sub-paragraph (a), with the aim of returning individually or jointly to their 1990 levels these anthropogenic emissions of carbon dioxide and other greenhouse gases not controlled by the Montreal Protocol. This information will be reviewed by the Conference of the Parties, at its first session and periodically thereafter, in accordance with Article 7;

(c) Calculations of emissions by sources and removals by sinks of greenhouse gases for the purposes of sub-paragraph (b) above should take into account the best available scientific knowledge, including of the effective capacity of sinks and the respective contributions of such gases to climate change. The Conference of the Parties shall consider and agree on methodologies for these calculations at its first session and review them regularly thereafter;

(d) The Conference of the Parties shall, at its first session, review the adequacy of sub-paragraphs (a) and (b) above. Such review shall be carried out in the light of the best available scientific information and assessment on climate change and its impacts, as well as relevant technical, social and economic information. Based on this review, the Conference of the Parties shall take appropriate action, which may include the adoption of amendments to the commitments in sub-paragraphs (a) and (b) above. The Conference of the Parties, at its first session, shall also take decisions regarding criteria for joint implementation as indicated in sub-paragraph (a) above. A second review of sub-paragraphs (a) and (b) shall take place not later than 31 December 1998, and thereafter at regular intervals determined by the Conference of the Parties, until the objective of the Convention is met;

(e) Each of these Parties shall;

(i) Co-ordinate as appropriate with other such Parties, relevant economic and administrative instruments developed to achieve the objective of the Convention; and

(ii) Identify and periodically review its own policies and practices which encourage activities that lead to greater levels of anthropogenic emissions of greenhouse gases not controlled by the Montreal Protocol than would otherwise occur;

(f) The Conference of the Parties shall review, not later than 31 December 1998, available information with a view to taking decisions regarding such amendments to the lists in Annexes I and II as may be appropriate, with the approval of the Party concerned;

(g) Any Party not included in Annex I may, in its instrument of ratification, acceptance, approval or accession, or at any time thereafter, notify the Depositary that it intends to be bound by sub-paragraphs (a) and (b) above. The Depositary shall inform the other signatories and Parties of any such notification.

3. The developed country Parties and other developed Parties included in Annex II shall provide new and additional financial resources to meet the agreed full costs incurred by developing country Parties in complying with their obligations under Article 12, paragraph 1. They shall also provide such financial resources, including for the transfer of technology, needed by the developing country Parties to meet the agreed full incremental costs of implementing measures that are covered by paragraph 1 of this Article and that are agreed between a developing country Party and the international entity or entities referred to in Article 11, in accordance with that Article. The implementation of these commitments shall take into account the need for adequacy and predictability in the flow of funds and the importance of appropriate burden-sharing among the developed country Parties.

4. The developed country Parties and other developed Parties included in Annex II shall also assist the developing country Parties that are particularly vulnerable to the adverse effects of climate change in meeting costs of adaptation to those adverse effects.

5. The developed country Parties and other developed Parties included in Annex II shall take all practicable steps to promote, facilitate and finance, as appropriate, the transfer of, or access to, environmentally sound technologies and know-how to other Parties, particularly developing country Parties, to enable them to implement the provisions of the Convention. In this process, the developed country Parties shall support the development and enhancement of endogenous capacities and technologies of developing country Parties. Other Parties and organizations in a position to do so may also assist in facilitating the transfer of such technologies.

6. In the implementation of their commitments under paragraph 2 above, a certain degree of flexibility shall be allowed by the Conference of the Parties to the Parties included in Annex I undergoing the process of transition to a market economy, in order to enhance the ability of these Parties to address climate change, including with regard to the historical level of anthropo-

genic emissions of greenhouse gases not controlled by the Montreal Protocol chosen as a reference.

7. The extent to which developing country Parties will effectively implement their commitments under the Convention will depend on the effective implementation by developed country Parties of their commitments under the Convention related to financial resources and transfer of technology and will take fully into account that economic and social development and poverty eradication are the first and overriding priorities of the developing country Parties.

8. In the implementation of the commitments in this Article, the Parties shall give full consideration to what actions are necessary under the Convention, including actions related to funding, insurance and the transfer of technology, to meet the specific needs and concerns of developing country Parties arising from the adverse effects of climate change and/or the impact of the implementation of response measures, especially on:

(a) Small island countries;

(b) Countries with low-lying coastal areas;

(c) Countries with arid and semi-arid areas, forested areas and areas liable to forest decay;

(d) Countries with areas prone to natural disasters;

(e) Countries with areas liable to drought and desertification;

(f) Countries with areas of high urban atmospheric pollution;

(g) Countries with areas with fragile ecosystems, including mountainous ecosystems;

(h) Countries whose economies are highly dependent on income generated from the production, processing and export, and/or on consumption of fossil fuels and associated energy-intensive products; and

(i) Land-locked and transit countries.

Further, the Conference of the Parties may take actions, as appropriate, with respect to this paragraph.

9. The Parties shall take full account of the specific needs and special situations of the least developed countries in their actions with regard to funding and transfer of technology.

10. The Parties shall, in accordance with Article 10, take into consideration in the implementation of the commitments of the Convention the situation of Parties, particularly developing country Parties, with economies that are vulnerable to the adverse effects of the implementation of measures to respond to climate change. This applies notably to Parties with economies that are highly dependent on income generated from the production, processing and export, and/or consumption of fossil fuels and associated energy-intensive products and/or the use of fossil fuels for which such Parties have serious difficulties in switching to alternatives.

Article 5

In carrying out their commitments under Article 4, paragraph 1(g), the Parties shall:

(a) Support and further develop, as appropriate, international and intergovernmental programmes and networks or organizations aimed at defining, conducting, assessing and financing research, data collection and systematic observation, taking into account the need to minimize duplication of effort;

(b) Support international and intergovernmental efforts to strengthen systematic observation and national scientific and technical research capacities and capabilities, particularly in developing countries, and to promote access to, and the exchange of, data and analyses thereof obtained from areas beyond national jurisdiction; and

(c) Take into account the particular concerns and needs of developing countries and co-operate in improving their endogenous capacities and capabilities to participate in the efforts referred to in sub-paragraphs (a) and (b) above.

Article 6

In carrying out their commitments under Article 4, paragraph 1(i), the Parties shall:

(a) Promote and facilitate at the national and, as appropriate, sub-regional and regional levels, and in accordance with national laws and regulations, and within their respective capacities:

(i) The development and implementation of educational and public awareness programmes on climate change and its effects;

(ii) Public access to information on climate change and its effects;

(iii) Public participation in addressing climate change and its effects and developing adequate responses; and

(iv) Training of scientific, technical and managerial personnel.

(b) Co-operate in and promote, at the international level, and, where appropriate, using existing bodies:

(i) The development and exchange of educational and public awareness material on climate change and its effects; and

(ii) The development and implementation of education and training programmes, including the strengthening of national institutions and the exchange or secondment of personnel to train experts in this field, in particular for developing countries.

Article 7

1. A Conference of the Parties is hereby established.

2. The Conference of the Parties, as the supreme body of this Convention, shall keep under regular review the implementation of the Convention and any related legal instruments that the Conference of the Parties may adopt, and shall make, within its mandate, the decisions necessary to promote the effective implementation of the Convention. To this end, it shall:

(a) Periodically examine the obligations of the Parties and the institutional arrangements under the Convention, in the light of the objective of the Convention, the experience gained in its implementation and the evolution of scientific and technological knowledge;

(b) Promote and facilitate the exchange of information on measures adopted by the Parties to address climate change and its effects, taking into account the differing circumstances, responsibilities and capabilities of the Parties and their respective commitments under the Convention;

(c) Facilitate, at the request of two or more Parties, the co-ordination of measures adopted by them to address climate change and its effects, taking into account the differing circumstances, responsibilities and capabilities of the Parties and their respective commitments under the Convention;

(d) Promote and guide, in accordance with the objective and provisions of the Convention, the development and periodic refinement of comparable methodologies, to be agreed on by the Conference of the Parties, *inter alia,* for preparing inventories of greenhouse gas emissions by sources and removals by sinks, and for evaluating the effectiveness of measures to limit the emissions and enhance the removals of these gases;

(e) Assess, on the basis of all information made available to it in accordance with the provisions of the Convention, the implementation of the Convention by the Parties, the overall effects of the measures taken pursuant to the Convention, in particular environmental, economic and social effects as well as their cumulative impacts and the extent to which progress towards the objective of the Convention is being achieved;

(f) Consider and adopt regular reports on the implementation of the Convention and ensure their publication;

(g) Make recommendations on any matters necessary for the implementation of the Convention;

(h) Seek to mobilize financial resources . . .;

(i) Establish such subsidiary bodies as are deemed necessary for the implementation of the Convention;

(j) Review reports submitted by its subsidiary bodies and provide guidance to them;

(k) Agree upon and adopt, by consensus, rules of procedure and financial rules for itself and for any subsidiary bodies;

(l) Seek and utilize, where appropriate, the services and co-operation of, and information provided by, competent international organizations and intergovernmental and non-governmental bodies; and

(m) Exercise such other functions as are required for the achievement of the objective of the Convention as well as all other functions assigned to it under the Convention.

3. The Conference of the Parties shall, at its first session, adopt its own rules of procedure as well as those of the subsidiary bodies established by the Convention, which shall include decision-making procedures for matters not already covered by decision-making procedures stipulated in the Convention. Such procedures may include specified majorities required for the adoption of particular decisions.

4. The first session of the Conference of the Parties shall be convened by the interim secretariat referred to in Article 21 and shall take place not later than one year after the date of entry into force of the Convention. Thereafter, ordinary sessions of the Conference of the Parties shall be held every year unless otherwise decided by the Conference of the Parties.

5. Extraordinary sessions of the Conference of the Parties shall be held at such other times as may be deemed necessary by the Conference, or at the written request of any Party, provided that, within six months of the request being communicated to the Parties by the secretariat, it is supported by at least one-third of the Parties.

6. The United Nations, its specialized agencies and the International Atomic Energy Agency, as well as any State member thereof or observers thereto not Party to the Convention, may be represented at sessions of the Conference of the Parties as observers. Any body or agency, whether national or international, governmental or non-governmental, which is qualified in matters covered by the Convention, and which has informed the secretariat of its wish to be represented at a session of the Conference of the Parties as an observer, may be so admitted unless at least one-third of the Parties present object. The admission and participation of observers shall be subject to the rules of procedures adopted by the Conference of the Parties.

Article 8

1. A secretariat is hereby established.

2. The functions of the secretariat shall be:

(a) To make arrangements for sessions of the Conference of the Parties and its subsidiary bodies established under the Convention and to provide them with services as required;

(b) To compile and transmit reports submitted to it;

(c) To facilitate assistance to the Parties, particularly developing country Parties, on request, in the compilation and communication of information required in accordance with the provisions of the Convention;

(d) To prepare reports on its activities and present them to the Conference of the Parties;

(e) To ensure the necessary co-ordination with the secretariats of other relevant international bodies;

(f) To enter, under the overall guidance of the Conference of the Parties, into such administrative and contractual arrangements as may be required for the effective discharge of its functions; and

(g) To perform the other secretariat functions specified in the Convention and in any of its protocols and such other functions as may be determined by the Conference of the Parties.

3. The Conference of the Parties, at its first session, shall designate a permanent secretariat and make arrangements for its functioning.

Article 9

1. A subsidiary body for scientific and technological advice is hereby established to provide the Conference of the Parties and, as appropriate, its other subsidiary bodies with timely information and advice on scientific and technological matters relating to the Convention. This body shall be open to participation by all Parties and shall be multidisciplinary. It shall comprise government representatives competent in the relevant field of expertise. It shall report regularly to the Conference of the Parties on all aspects of its work.

2. Under the guidance of the Conference of the Parties, and drawing upon existing competent international bodies, this body shall:

(a) Provide assessments of the state of scientific knowledge relating to climate change and its effects;

(b) Prepare scientific assessments on the effects of measures taken in the implementation of the Convention;

(c) Identify innovative, efficient and state-of-the-art technologies and know-how and advise on the ways and means of promoting development and/or transferring such technologies;

(d) Provide advice on scientific programmes, international co-operation in research and development related to climate change, as well as on ways and means of supporting endogenous capacity-building in developing countries; and

(e) Respond to scientific, technological and methodological questions that the Conference of the Parties and its subsidiary bodies may put to the body.

3. The functions and terms of reference of this body may be further elaborated by the Conference of the Parties.

Article 10

1. A subsidiary body for implementation is hereby established to assist the Conference of the Parties in the assessment and review of the effective implementation of the Convention. This body shall be open to participation by all Parties and comprise government representatives who are experts on matters related to climate change. It shall report regularly to the Conference of the Parties on all aspects of its work.

2. Under the guidance of the Conference of the Parties, this body shall:

(a) Consider the information communicated in accordance with Article 12, paragraph 1, to assess the overall aggregated effect of the steps taken by the Parties in the light of the latest scientific assessments concerning climate change;

(b) Consider the information communicated in accordance with Article 12, paragraph 2, in order to assist the Conference of the Parties in carrying out the reviews required by Article 4, paragraph 2(d); and

(c) Assist the Conference of the Parties, as appropriate, in the preparation and implementation of its decisions.

Article 11

1. A mechanism for the provision of financial resources on a grant or concessional basis, including for the transfer of technology, is hereby defined. It shall function under the guidance of and be accountable to the Conference of the Parties, which shall decide on its policies, programme priorities and eligibility criteria related to this Convention. Its operation shall be entrusted to one or more existing international entities.

2. The financial mechanism shall have an equitable and balanced representation of all Parties within a transparent system of governance.

3. The Conference of the Parties and the entity or entities entrusted with the operation of the financial mechanism shall agree upon arrangements to give effect to the above paragraphs, which shall include the following:

(a) Modalities to ensure that the funded projects to address climate change are in conformity with the policies, programme priorities and eligibility criteria established by the Conference of the Parties;

(b) Modalities by which a particular funding decision may be reconsidered in light of these policies, programme priorities and eligibility criteria;

(c) Provision by the entity or entities of regular reports to the Conference of the Parties on its funding operations, which is consistent with the requirement for accountability set out in paragraph 1 above; and

(d) Determination in a predictable and identifiable manner of the amount of funding necessary and available for the implementation of this Convention and the conditions under which that amount shall be periodically reviewed.

4. The Conference of the Parties shall make arrangements to implement the above-mentioned provisions at its first session, reviewing and taking into account the interim arrangements referred to in Article 21, paragraph 3, and shall decide whether these interim arrangements shall be maintained. Within four years thereafter, the Conference of the Parties shall review the financial mechanism and take appropriate measures.

5. The developed country Parties may also provide, and developing country Parties avail themselves of financial resources related to the implementation of the Convention through bilateral, regional and other multilateral channels.

Article 12

1. In accordance with Article 4, paragraph 1, each Party shall communicate to the Conference of the Parties, through the secretariat, the following elements of information:

(a) A national inventory of anthropogenic emissions by sources and removals by sinks of all greenhouse gases not controlled by the Montreal Protocol, to the extent its capacities permit, using comparable methodologies to be promoted and agreed upon by the Conference of the Parties;

(b) A general description of steps taken or envisaged by the Party to implement the Convention; and

(c) Any other information that the Party considers relevant to the achievement of the objective of the Convention and suitable for inclusion in its communication, including, if feasible, material relevant for calculations of global emission trends.

2. Each developed country Party and each other Party included in Annex I shall incorporate in its communication the following elements of information:

(a) A detailed description of the policies and measures that it has adopted to implement its commitment under Article 4, paragraphs 2(a) and 2(b); and

(b) A specific estimate of the effects that [those] policies and measures will have on anthropogenic emissions by its sources and removals by its sinks of greenhouse gases during the period referred to in Article 4, paragraph 2(a).

3. In addition, each developed country Party and each other developed Party included in Annex II shall incorporate details of measures taken in accordance with Article 4, paragraphs 3, 4 and 5.

4. Developing country Parties may, on a voluntary basis, propose projects for financing, including specific technologies, materials, equipment, techniques or practices that would be needed to implement such projects, along with, if possible, an estimate of all incremental costs, of the reductions of emissions and increments of removals of greenhouse gases, as well as an estimate of the consequent benefits.

5. Each developed country Party and each other Party included in Annex I shall make its initial communication within six months of the entry into force of the Convention for that Party. Each Party not so listed shall make its initial communication within three years of the entry into force of the Convention for that Party, or of the availability of financial resources in accordance with Article 4, paragraph 3. Parties that are least developed countries may make their initial communication at their discretion. The frequency of subsequent communications by all Parties shall be determined by the Conference of the Parties, taking into account the differentiated timetable set by this paragraph.

6. Information communicated by Parties under this Article shall be transmitted by the secretariat as soon as possible to the Conference of the Parties and to any subsidiary bodies concerned. If necessary, the procedures for the communication of information may be further considered by the Conference of the Parties.

7. From its first session, the Conference of the Parties shall arrange for the provision to developing country Parties of technical and financial support, on request, in compiling and communicating information under this Article, as well as in identifying the technical and financial needs associated with proposed projects and response measures under Article 4. Such support may be provided by other parties, by competent international organizations and by the secretariat, as appropriate.

8. Any group of Parties may, subject to guidelines adopted by the Conference of the Parties, and to prior notification to the Conference of the Parties, make a joint communication in fulfilment of their obligations under this Article, provided that such a communication includes information on the fulfilment by each of these Parties of its individual obligations under the Convention.

9. Information received by the secretariat that is designated by a Party as confidential, in accordance with criteria to be established by the Conference of the Parties, shall be aggregated by the secretariat to protect its confidentiality before being made available to any of the bodies involved in the communication and review of information.

10. Subject to paragraph 9 above, and without prejudice to the ability of any Party to make public its communication at any time, the secretariat shall make communications by Parties under this Article publicly available at the time they are submitted to the Conference of the Parties.

Article 13

The Conference of the Parties shall, at its first session, consider the establishment of a multilateral consultative process, available to Parties on their request, for the resolution of questions regarding the implementation of the Convention.

Article 14

1. In the event of a dispute between any two or more Parties concerning the interpretation or application of the Convention, the Parties concerned shall seek a settlement of the dispute through negotiation or any other peaceful means of their own choice.

2. When ratifying, accepting, approving or acceding to the Convention, or at any time thereafter, a Party which is not a regional economic integration organization may declare in a written instrument submitted to the Depositary that, in respect of any dispute concerning the interpretation or application of the Convention, it recognizes as compulsory *ipso facto* and without special agreement, in relation to any Party accepting the same obligation:

(a) Submission of the dispute to the International Court of Justice, and/or

(b) Arbitration in accordance with procedures to be adopted by the Conference of the Parties as soon as practicable, in an annex on arbitration.

A Party which is a regional economic integration organization may make a declaration with like effect in relation to arbitration in accordance with the procedures referred to in sub-paragraph (b) above.

3. A declaration made under paragraph 2 above shall remain in force until it expires in accordance with its terms or until three months after written notice of its revocation has been deposited with the Depositary.

4. A new declaration, a notice of revocation or the expiry of a declaration shall not in any way affect proceedings pending before the International Court of Justice or the arbitral tribunal, unless the parties to the dispute otherwise agree.

5. Subject to the operation of paragraph 2 above, if after 12 months following notification by one Party to another that a dispute exists between them, the Parties concerned have not been able to settle their dispute through the means mentioned in paragraph 1 above, the dispute shall be submitted, at the request of any of the parties to the dispute, to conciliation.

6. A conciliation commission shall be created upon the request of one of the parties to the dispute. The commission shall be composed of an equal number of members appointed by each party concerned and a chairman chosen jointly by the members appointed by each party. The commission shall render a recommendatory award, which the parties shall consider in good faith . . .

7. Additional procedures relating to conciliation shall be adopted by the Conference of the Parties, as soon as practicable, in an annex on conciliation.

Article 15

1. Any Party may propose amendments to the Convention.

2. Amendments to the Convention shall be adopted at an ordinary session of the Conference of the Parties. The text of any proposed amendment to the Convention shall be communicated to the Parties by the secretariat at least six months before the meeting at which it is proposed for adoption. The secretariat shall also communicate proposed amendments to the signatories to the Convention and, for information, to the Depositary [the Secretary-General of the UN].

3. The Parties shall make every effort to reach agreement on any proposed amendment to the Convention by consensus. If all efforts at consensus have been exhausted, and no agreement reached, the amendment shall as a last resort be adopted by a three-fourths majority vote of the Parties present and voting at the meeting. The adopted amendment shall be communicated by the secretariat to the Depositary, who shall circulate it to all Parties for their acceptance.

4. Instruments of acceptance in respect of an amendment shall be deposited with the Depositary. An amendment adopted in accordance with paragraph 3 above shall enter into force for those Parties having accepted it on the ninetieth day after the date of receipt by the Depositary of an instrument of acceptance by at least three-fourths of the Parties to the Convention.

5. The amendment shall enter into force for any other Party on the ninetieth day after the date on which that Party deposits with the Depositary its instrument of acceptance of the said amendment . . .

Article 16

1. Annexes to the Convention shall form an integral part thereof and, unless otherwise expressly provided, a reference to the Convention constitutes at the same time a reference to any annexes thereto. Without prejudice to the provisions of Article 14, paragraphs 2(b) and 7, such annexes shall be restricted to lists, forms and any other material of a descriptive nature that is of a scientific, technical, procedural or administrative character.

2. Annexes to the Convention shall be proposed and adopted in accordance with the procedure set forth in Article 15, paragraphs 2, 3 and 4.

3. An annex that has been adopted in accordance with paragraph 2 above shall enter into force for all Parties to the Convention six months after the date of the communication by the Depositary to such Parties of the adoption of the annex, except for those Parties that have notified the Depositary, in writing, within that period of their non-acceptance of the annex. The annex shall enter into force for Parties which withdraw their notification of non-acceptance on the ninetieth day after the date on which withdrawal of such notification has been received by the Depositary.

4. The proposal, adoption and entry into force of amendments to annexes to the Convention shall be subject to the same procedure as that for the proposal, adoption and entry into force of annexes to the Convention in accordance with paragraphs 2 and 3 above.

5. If the adoption of an annex or an amendment to an annex involves an amendment to the Convention, that annex or amendment to an annex shall not enter into force until such time as the amendment to the Convention enters into force.

Article 17

1. The Conference of the Parties may, at any ordinary session, adopt protocols to the Convention.

2. The text of any proposed protocol shall be communicated to the Parties by the secretariat at least six months before such a session.

3. The requirements for the entry into force of any protocol shall be established by that instrument.

4. Only Parties to the Convention may be Parties to a protocol.

5. Decisions under any protocol shall be taken only by the Parties to the protocol concerned.

Articles 18-26

(Voting, ratification, withdrawal and other general provisions.)

ANNEX I

Australia	Japan
Austria	Latvia*
Belarus*	Lithuania*
Belgium	Luxembourg
Bulgaria*	Netherlands
Canada	New Zealand
Czechoslovakia*†	Norway
Denmark	Poland*
European Economic Community	Portugal
	Romania*
Estonia*	Russian Federation*
Finland	Spain
France	Sweden
Germany	Switzerland
Greece	Turkey
Hungary*	Ukraine*
Iceland	United Kingdom
Ireland	United States of America
Italy	

* Countries that are undergoing the process of transition to a market economy.

† Czechoslovakia was succeeded by the Czech Republic and Slovakia from 31 December 1992.

ANNEX II

Australia	Italy
Austria	Japan
Belgium	Luxembourg
Canada	Netherlands
Denmark	New Zealand
European Economic Community	Norway
	Portugal
Finland	Spain
France	Sweden
Germany	Switzerland
Greece	Turkey
Iceland	United Kingdom
Ireland	United States of America

Kyoto Protocol to the United Nations Framework Convention on Climate Change

(11 December 1997)

The Parties to this Protocol,

Being Parties to the United Nations Framework Convention on Climate Change, hereinafter referred to as "the Convention",

In pursuit of the ultimate objective of the Convention as stated in its Article 2,

Recalling the provisions of the Convention,

Being guided by Article 3 of the Convention,

Pursuant to the Berlin Mandate adopted by decision 1/CP.1 of the Conference of the Parties to the Convention at its first session,

Have agreed as follows:

Article 1

(Definitions)

Article 2

1. Each Party included in Annex I, in achieving its quantified emission limitation and reduction commitments under Article 3, in order to promote sustainable development, shall:

(a) Implement and/or further elaborate policies and measures in accordance with its national circumstances, such as:

(i) Enhancement of energy efficiency in relevant sectors of the national economy;

(ii) Protection and enhancement of sinks and reservoirs of greenhouse gases not controlled by the Montreal Protocol, taking into account its commitments under relevant international environmental agreements; promotion of sustainable forest management practices, afforestation and reforestation;

(iii) Promotion of sustainable forms of agriculture in light of climate change considerations;

(iv) Research on, and promotion, development and increased use of, new and renewable forms of energy, of carbon dioxide sequestration technologies and of advanced and innovative environmentally sound technologies;

(v) Progressive reduction or phasing out of market imperfections, fiscal incentives, tax and duty exemptions and subsidies in all greenhouse gas emitting sectors that run counter to the objective of the Convention and application of market instruments;

(vi) Encouragement of appropriate reforms in relevant sectors aimed at promoting policies and measures which limit or reduce emissions of greenhouse gases not controlled by the Montreal Protocol;

(vii) Measures to limit and/or reduce emissions of greenhouse gases not controlled by the Montreal Protocol in the transport sector;

(viii) Limitation and/or reduction of methane emissions through recovery and use in waste management, as well as in the production, transport and distribution of energy;

(b) Co-operate with other such Parties to enhance the individual and combined effectiveness of their policies and measures adopted under this Article, pursuant to Article 4, paragraph 2(e)(i), of the Convention. To this end, these Parties shall take steps to share their experience and exchange information on such policies and measures, including developing ways of improving their comparability, transparency and effectiveness. The Conference of the Parties serving as the meeting of the Parties to this Protocol shall, at its first session or as soon as practicable thereafter, consider ways to facilitate such co-operation, taking into account all relevant information.

2. The Parties included in Annex I shall pursue limitation or reduction of emissions of greenhouse gases not controlled by the Montreal Protocol from aviation and marine bunker fuels, working through the International Civil Aviation Organization and the International Maritime Organization, respectively.

3. The Parties included in Annex I shall strive to implement policies and measures under this Article in such a way as to minimize adverse effects, including the adverse effects of climate change, effects on international trade, and social, environmental and economic impacts on other Parties, especially developing country Parties and in particular those identified in Article 4, paragraphs 8 and 9, of the Convention, taking into account Article 3 of the Convention. The Conference of the Parties serving as the meeting of the Parties to this Protocol may take further actions, as appropriate, to promote the implementation of the provisions of this paragraph.

4. The Conference of the Parties . . ., if it decides that it would be beneficial to co-ordinate any of the policies and measures in paragraph 1(a) above, taking into account different national circumstances and potential effects, shall consider ways and means to elaborate the co-ordination of such policies and measures.

Article 3

1. The Parties included in Annex I shall, individually or jointly, ensure that their aggregate anthropogenic carbon dioxide equivalent emissions of the greenhouse gases listed in Annex A do not exceed their assigned amounts, calculated pursuant to their qualified emission limitation and reduction commitments inscribed in Annex B and in accordance with the provisions of this Article, with a view to reducing their overall emissions of such gases by at least 5 per cent below 1990 levels in the commitment period 2008 to 2012.

2. Each Party included in Annex I shall, by 2005, have made demonstrable progress in achieving its commitments under this Protocol.

3. The net changes in greenhouse gas emissions by sources and removals by sinks resulting from direct human-induced land-use change and forestry activities, limited to afforestation, reforestation and deforestation since 1990, measured as verifiable changes in carbon stocks in each commitment period, shall be used to meet the commitments under this Article of each Party included in Annex I. The greenhouse gas emissions by sources and removals by sinks associated with those activities shall be reported in a transparent and verifiable manner and reviewed in accordance with Articles 7 and 8.

4. Prior to the first session of the Conference of the Parties serving as the meeting of the Parties to this Protocol, each Party included in Annex I shall provide, for consideration by the Subsidiary Body for Scientific and Technological Advice, data to establish its level of carbon stocks in 1990 and to enable an estimate to be made of its changes in carbon stocks in subsequent years. The Conference of the Parties . . . shall, at its first session or as soon as practicable thereafter, decide upon modalities, rules and guidelines as to how, and which, additional human-induced activities related to changes in greenhouse gas emissions by sources and removals by sinks in the agricultural soils and the land-use change and forestry categories shall be added to, or subtracted from, the assigned amounts for Parties included in Annex I, taking into account uncertainties, transparency in reporting, verifiability, the methodological work of the Intergovernmental Panel on Climate Change (IPCC), the advice provided by the Subsidiary Body for Scientific and Technological Advice in accordance with Article 5 and the decisions of the Conference of the Parties. Such a decision shall apply in the second and subsequent commitment periods. A Party may choose to apply such a decision on these additional human-induced activities for its first commitment period, provided that these activities have taken place since 1990.

5. The Parties included in Annex I undergoing the process of transition to a market economy whose base year or period was established pursuant to decision 9/CP.2 of the Conference of the Parties at its second session shall use that base year or period for the implementation of their commitments under this Article. Any other Party included in Annex I undergoing the process of transition to a market economy which has not yet submitted its first national communication under Article 12 of the Convention may also notify the Conference of the Parties . . . that it intends to use an historical base year or period other than 1990 for the implementation of its commitments under this Article. The Conference of the Parties . . . shall decide on the acceptance of such notification.

6. Taking into account Article 4, paragraph 6, of the Convention, in the implementation of their commitments under this Protocol other than those under this Article, a certain degree of flexibility shall be allowed by the Conference of the Parties . . . to the Parties included in Annex I undergoing the process of transition to a market economy.

7. In the first quantified emission limitation and reduction commitment period, from 2008 to 2012, the assigned amount for each Party included in Annex I shall be equal to the percentage inscribed for it in Annex B of its aggregate anthropogenic carbon dioxide equivalent emissions of the greenhouse gases listed in Annex A in 1990, or the base year or period determined in accordance with paragraph 5 above, multiplied by five. Those Parties included in Annex I for whom land-use change and forestry constituted a net source of greenhouse gas emissions in 1990 shall include in their 1990 emissions base year or period the aggregate anthropogenic carbon dioxide equivalent emissions by sources minus removals by sinks in 1990 from land-use change for the purposes of calculating their assigned amount.

8. Any Party included in Annex I may use 1995 as its base year for hydrofluorocarbons, perfluorocarbons and sulphur hexafluoride, for the purposes of the calculation referred to in paragraph 7 above.

9. Commitments for subsequent periods for Parties included in Annex I shall be established in amendments to Annex B to this Protocol, which shall be adopted in accordance with the provisions of Article 21, paragraph 7. The Conference of the Parties serving as the meeting of the Parties to this Protocol shall initiate the consideration of such commitments at least seven years before the end of the first commitment period referred to in paragraph 1 above.

10. Any emission reduction units, or any part of an assigned amount, which a Party acquires from another Party in accordance with the provisions of Article 6 or Article 17 shall be added to the assigned amount for the acquiring Party.

11. Any emission reduction units, or any part of an assigned amount, which a Party transfers to another Party in accordance with the provisions of Article 6 or of Article 17 shall be subtracted from the assigned amount for the transferring Party.

12. Any certified emission reductions which a Party acquires from another Party in accordance with the provisions of Article 12 shall be added to the assigned amount for the acquiring Party.

13. If the emissions of a Party included in Annex I in a commitment period are less than its assigned amount under this Article, this difference shall, on request of that Party, be added to the assigned amount for that Party for subsequent commitment periods.

14. Each Party included in Annex I shall strive to implement the commitments mentioned in paragraph 1 above in such a way as to minimize adverse social, environmental and economic impacts on developing country Parties, particularly those identified in Article 4, paragraphs 8 and 9, for the Convention. In line with relevant decisions . . . on the implementation of those paragraphs, the Conference of the Parties . . . shall, at its first session, consider what actions are necessary to minimize the

adverse effects of climate change and/or the impacts of response measures on Parties referred to in those paragraphs. Among the issues to be considered shall be the establishment of funding, insurance and transfer of technology.

Article 4

1. Any Parties included in Annex I that have reached an agreement to fulfil their commitments under Article 3 jointly, shall be deemed to have met those commitments provided that their total combined aggregate anthropogenic carbon dioxide equivalent emissions of the greenhouse gases listed in Annex A do not exceed their assigned amounts calculated pursuant to their quantified emission limitation and reduction commitments inscribed in Annex B and in accordance with the provisions of Article 3. The respective emission level allocated to each of the Parties to the agreement shall be set out in that agreement.

2. The Parties to any such agreement shall notify the secretariat of the terms of the agreement on the date of deposit of their instruments of ratification, acceptance or approval of this Protocol, or accession thereto. The secretariat shall in turn inform the Parties and signatories to the Convention of the terms of the agreement.

3. Any such agreement shall remain in operation for the duration of the commitment period specified in Article 3, paragraph 7.

4. If Parties acting jointly do so in the framework of, and together with, a regional economic integration organization, any alteration in the composition of the organization after adoption of this Protocol shall not affect existing commitments under this Protocol. Any alteration in the composition of the organization shall only apply for the purposes of those commitments under Article 3 that are adopted subsequent to that alteration.

5. In the event of failure by the Parties to such an agreement to achieve their total combined level of emission reductions, each Party to that agreement shall be responsible for its own level of emissions set out in the agreement.

6. If Parties acting jointly do so in the framework of, and together with, a regional economic integration organization which is itself a Party to this Protocol, each member State of that regional economic integration organization individually, and together with the regional economic integration organization acting in accordance with Article 24, shall, in the event of failure to achieve the total combined level of emission reductions, be responsible for its level of emissions as notified in accordance with this Article.

Article 5

1. Each Party included in Annex I shall have in place, no later than one year prior to the start of the first commitment period, a national system for the estimation of anthropogenic emissions by sources and removals by sinks of all greenhouse gases not controlled by the Montreal Protocol. Guidelines for such national systems, which shall incorporate the methodologies specified in paragraph 2 below, shall be decided upon by the Conference of the Parties . . .

2. Methodologies for estimating anthropogenic emissions by sources and removals by sinks of all greenhouse gases not controlled by the Montreal Protocol shall be those accepted by the IPCC and agreed upon by the Conference of the Parties at its third session. Where such methodologies are not used, appropriate adjustments shall be applied according to methodologies agreed upon by the Conference of the Parties. Based on the work of, *inter alia*, the IPCC and advice provided by the Subsidiary Body for Scientific and Technological Advice, the Conference of the Parties shall regularly review and, as appropriate, revise such methodologies and adjustments, taking fully into account any relevant decisions by the Conference of the Parties. Any revision to methodologies or adjustments shall be used only for the purposes of ascertaining compliance with commitments under Article 3 in respect of any commitment period adopted subsequent to that revision.

3. The global warming potentials used to calculate the carbon dioxide equivalence of anthropogenic emissions by sources and removals by sinks of greenhouse gases listed in Annex A shall be those accepted by the IPCC and agreed upon by the Conference of the Parties at its third session. Based on the work of, *inter alia*, the IPCC and advice provided by the Subsidiary Body for Scientific and Technological Advice, the Conference of the Parties . . . shall regularly review and, as appropriate, revise the global warming potential of each such greenhouse gas . . .

Article 6

1. For the purpose of meeting its commitments under Article 3, any Party included in Annex I may transfer to, or acquire from, any other such Party emission reduction units resulting from projects aimed at reducing anthropogenic emissions by sources or enhancing anthropogenic removals by sinks of greenhouse gases in any sector of the economy, provided that:

(a) Any such project has the approval of the Parties involved;

(b) Any such project provides a reduction in emissions by sources, or an enhancement of removals by sinks, that is additional to any that would otherwise occur;

(c) It does not acquire any emission reduction units if it is not in compliance with its obligations under Articles 5 and 7; and

(d) The acquisition of emission reduction units shall be supplemental to domestic actions for the purposes of meeting commitments under Article 3.

2. The Conference of the Parties serving as the meeting of the Parties to this Protocol may, at its first session or as soon as practicable thereafter, further elaborate guidelines for the implementation of this Article, including for verification and reporting.

3. A Party included in Annex I may authorize legal entities to participate, under its responsibility, in actions leading to the generation, transfer or acquisition under this Article of emission reduction units.

4. If a question of implementation by a Party included in Annex I of the requirements referred to in this Article is identified in accordance with the relevant provisions of Article 8, transfers and acquisitions of emission reduction units may continue to be made after the question has been identified, provided that any such units may not be used by a Party to meet its commitments under Article 3 until any issue of compliance is resolved.

Article 7

1. Each Party included in Annex I shall incorporate in its annual inventory of anthropogenic emissions by sources and removals by sinks of greenhouse gases not controlled by the Montreal Protocol, submitted in accordance with the relevant decisions of the Conference of the Parties, the necessary supplementary information for the purposes of ensuring compliance with Article 3, to be determined in accordance with paragraph 4 below.

2. Each Party included in Annex I shall incorporate in its national communication, submitted under Article 12 of the Convention, the supplementary information necessary to demonstrate compliance with its commitments under this Protocol, to be determined in accordance with paragraph 4 below.

3. Each Party included in Annex I shall submit the information required under paragraph 1 above annually, beginning with the first inventory due under the Convention for the first year of the commitment period after this Protocol has entered into force for that Party. Each such Party shall submit the information required under paragraph 2 above as part of the first national communication due under the Convention after this Protocol has entered into force and after the adoption of guidelines as provided for in paragraph 4 below. The frequency of subsequent submission of information required under this Article shall be determined by the Conference of the Parties serving as the meeting of the Parties to this Protocol, taking into account any timetable for the submission of national communications decided upon by the Conference of the Parties.

4. The Conference of the Parties serving as the meeting of the Parties to this Protocol shall adopt at its first session, and review periodically thereafter, guidelines of the preparation of the information required under this Article, taking into account guidelines for the preparation of national communications by Parties included in Annex I adopted by the Conference of the Parties. The Conference of the Parties serving as the meeting of the Parties to this Protocol shall also, prior to the first commitment period, decide upon modalities for the accounting of assigned amounts.

Article 8

1. The information submitted under Article 7 by each Party included in Annex I shall be reviewed by expert review teams . . . as part of the annual compilation and accounting of emissions inventories and assigned amounts . . . [and] as part of the review of communications.

2. Expert review teams shall be co-ordinated by the secretariat and shall be composed of experts selected from those nominated by Parties to the Convention and, as appropriate, by intergovernmental organizations, in accordance with guidance provided for this purpose by the Conference of the Parties.

3. The review process shall provide a thorough and comprehensive technical assessment of all aspects of the implementation by a Party of this Protocol. The export review teams shall prepare a report . . . assessing the implementation of the commitments of the Party and identifying any potential problems in, and factors influencing, the fulfilment of commitments. Such reports shall be circulated by the secretariat to all Parties to the Convention. The secretariat shall list those questions of implementation indicated in such reports for further consideration by the Conference of the Parties . . .

4. The Conference of the Parties . . . shall adopt at its first session, and review periodically thereafter, guidelines for the review of implementation of this Protocol by expert review teams taking into account the relevant decisions of the Conference of the Parties.

Article 9

1. The Conference of the Parties . . . shall periodically review this Protocol in the light of the best available scientific information and assessments on climate change and its impacts, as well as relevant technical, social and economic information . . .

2. The first review shall take place at the second session of the Conference of the Parties serving as the meeting of the Parties to this Protocol. Further reviews shall take place at regular intervals and in a timely manner.

Article 10

All Parties, taking into account their common but differentiated responsibilities and their specific national and regional development priorities, objectives and circumstances, without introducing any new commitments for Parties not included in Annex I, but reaffirming existing commitments under Article 4, paragraph 1, of the Convention, and continuing to advance the implementation of these commitments in order to achieve sustainable development, taking into account Article 4, paragraphs 3, 5 and 7, of the Convention, shall:

(a) Formulate, where relevant and to the extent possible, cost-effective national and, where appropriate, regional programmes to improve the quality of local emission factors, activity data and/or models which reflect the socio-economic conditions of each Party for the preparation and periodic updating of national inventories of anthropogenic emissions by sources and removals by sinks of all greenhouse gases not controlled by the Montreal Protocol, using comparable methodologies to be agreed upon by the Conference of the Parties, and consistent with the guidelines for the preparation of national communications adopted by the Conference of the Parties;

(b) Formulate, implement, publish and regularly update national and, where appropriate, regional programmes containing measures to mitigate climate change and measures to facilitate adequate adaptation to climate change:

(i) Such programme would, *inter alia*, concern the energy, transport and industry sectors as well as agriculture, forestry and waste management. Furthermore, adaptation technologies and methods for improving spatial planning would improve adaptation to climate change; and

(ii) Parties included in Annex I shall submit information on action under this Protocol, including national programmes, in accordance with Article 7; and other Parties shall seek to include in their national communications, as appropriate, information on programmes which contain measures that the Party believes contribute to addressing climate change and its adverse impacts, including the abatement of increases in greenhouse gas emissions, and enhancement of and removals by sinks, capacity building and adaptation measures;

(c) Co-operate in the promotion of effective modalities for the development, application and diffusion of, and take all practicable steps to promote, facilitate and finance, as appropriate, the transfer of, or access to, environmentally sound technologies, know-how, practices and processes pertinent to climate change, in particular to developing countries, including the formulation of policies and programmes for the effective transfer of environmentally sound technologies that are publicly owned or in the public domain and the creation of an enabling environment for the private sector, to promote and enhance the transfer of, and access to, environmentally sound technologies;

(d) Co-operate in scientific and technical research and promote the maintenance and the development of systematic observation systems and development of data archives to reduce uncertainties related to the climate system, the adverse impacts of climate change and the economic and social consequences of various response strategies, and promote the development and strengthening of endogenous capacities and capabilities to participate in international and intergovernmental efforts, programmes and networks on research and systematic observation, taking into account Article 5 of the Convention;

(e) Co-operate in and promote at the international level, and, where appropriate, using existing bodies, the development and implementation of education and training programmes, including the strengthening of national capacity building, in particular human and institutional capacities and the exchange or secondment of personnel to train experts in this field, in particular for developing countries, and facilitate at the national level public awareness of, and public access to information on, climate change. Suitable modalities should be developed to implement these activities through the relevant bodies of the Convention, taking into account Article 6 of the Convention;

(f) Include in their national communications information on programmes and activities undertaken pursuant to this Article in accordance with relevant decisions of the Conference of the Parties; and

(g) Give full consideration, in implementing the commitments under this Article, to Article 4, paragraph 8, of the Convention.

Article 11

2. . . . The developed country Parties and other developed Parties included in Annex II to the Convention shall:

(a) Provide new and additional financial resources to meet the agreed full costs incurred by developing country Parties in advancing the implementation of existing commitments under Article 4, paragraph 1(a) . . .; and

(b) Also provide such financial resources, including for the transfer of technology, needed by the developing country Parties to meet the agreed full incremental costs of advancing the implementation of existing commitments under Article 4, paragraph 1, of the Convention that are covered by Article 10 and that are agreed between a developing country Party and the international entity or entities referred to in Article 11 of the Convention, in accordance with that Article. The implementation of these existing commitments shall take into account the need for adequacy and predictability in the flow of funds and the importance of appropriate burden-sharing among developed country Parties. The guidance to the entity or entities entrusted with the operation of the financial mechanism of the Convention in relevant decisions of the Conference of the Parties, including those agreed before the adoption of this Protocol, shall apply *mutatis mutandis* to the provisions of this paragraph.

3. The developed country Parties and other developed Parties in Annex II to the Convention may also provide, and developing country Parties avail themselves of, financial resources for the implementation of Article 10, through bilateral, regional and other multilateral channels.

Article 12

1. A clean development mechanism is hereby defined.

2. The purpose of the clean development mechanism shall be to assist Parties not included in Annex I in achieving sustainable development and in contributing to the ultimate objective of the Convention, and to assist Parties included in Annex I in achieving

compliance with their quantified emission limitation and reduction commitments under Article 3.

3. Under the clean development mechanism:

(a) Parties not included in Annex I will benefit from project activities resulting in certified emission reductions; and

(b) Parties included in Annex I may use the certified emission reductions accruing from such project activities to contribute to compliance with part of their quantified emission limitation and reduction commitments under Article 3, as determined by the Conference of the Parties serving as the meeting of the Parties to this Protocol.

4. The clean development mechanism shall be subject to the authority and guidance of the Conference of the Parties serving as the meeting of the Parties to this Protocol and be supervised by an executive board of the clean development mechanism.

5. Emission reductions resulting from each project activity shall be certified by operational entities to be designated by the Conference of the Parties serving as the meeting of the Parties to this Protocol, on the basis of:

(a) Voluntary participation approved by each Party involved;

(b) Real, measurable, and long-term benefits related to the mitigation of climate change; and

(c) Reductions in emissions that are additional to any that would occur in the absence of the certified project activity.

6. The clean development mechanism shall assist in arranging funding of certified project activities as necessary.

7. The Conference of the Parties . . . shall elaborate modalities and procedures with the objective of ensuring transparency, efficiency and accountability through independent auditing and verification of project activities.

8. The Conference of the Parties . . . shall ensure that a share of the proceeds from certified project activities is used to cover administrative expenses as well as to assist developing country Parties that are particularly vulnerable to the adverse effects of climate change to meet the costs of adaptation.

9. Participation under the clean development mechanism, including in activities mentioned in paragraph 3(a) above and in the acquisition of certified emission reductions, may involve private and/or public entities, and is to be subject to whatever guidance may be provided by the executive board of the clean development mechanism.

10. Certified emission reductions obtained during the period from the year 2000 up to the beginning of the first commitment period can be used to assist in achieving compliance in the first commitment period.

Article 13

1. The Conference of the Parties, the supreme body of the Convention, shall serve as the meeting of the Parties to this Protocol.

2. Parties to the Convention that are not Parties to this Protocol may participate as observers in the proceedings of any session of the Conference of the Parties serving as the meeting of the Parties to this Protocol . . . Decisions under this Protocol shall be taken only by those that are Parties to this Protocol . . .

Article 14

1. The secretariat established by Article 8 of the Convention shall serve as the secretariat of this Protocol.

2. Article 8, paragraph 2, of the Convention on the functions of the secretariat, and Article 8, paragraph 3, of the Convention on arrangements made for the functioning of the secretariat, shall apply *mutatis mutandis* to this Protocol. The secretariat shall, in addition, exercise the functions assigned to it under this Protocol.

Article 15

1. The Subsidiary Body for Scientific and Technological Advice and the Subsidiary Body for Implementation established by Articles 9 and 10 of the Convention shall serve as, respectively, the Subsidiary Body for Scientific and Technological Advice and the Subsidiary Body for Implementation of this Protocol. The provisions relating to the functioning of these two bodies under the Convention shall apply *mutatis mutandis* to this Protocol. Sessions of the meetings of the Subsidiary Body for Scientific and Technological Advice and the Subsidiary Body for Implementation of this Protocol shall be held in conjunction with the meetings of, respectively, the Subsidiary Body for Scientific and Technological Advice and the Subsidiary Body for Implementation of the Convention.

2. Parties to the Convention that are not Parties to this Protocol may participate as observers in the proceedings of any session of the subsidiary bodies. When the subsidiary bodies serve as the subsidiary bodies of this Protocol, decisions under this Protocol shall be taken only by those that are Parties to this Protocol . . .

Article 16

The Conference of the Parties . . . shall, as soon as praticable, consider the application to this Protocol of, and modify as appropriate, the multilateral consultative process referred to in Article 13 of the Convention, in the light of any relevant decisions that may be taken by the Conference of the Parties. Any multilateral consultative process that may be applied to this Protocol shall operate without prejudice to the procedures and mechanisms established in accordance with Article 18.

Article 17

The Conference of the Parties shall define the relevant principles, modalities, rules and guidelines, in particular for verification, reporting and accountability for emissions trading. The Parties included in Annex B may participate in emissions trading for the purposes of fulfilling their commitments under Article 3. Any such trading shall be supplemental to domestic actions for the purpose of meeting quantified emission limitation and reduction commitments under that Article.

Article 18

The Conference of the Parties serving as the meeting of the Parties to this Protocol shall, at its first session, approve appropriate and effective procedures and mechanisms to determine and to address cases of non-compliance with the provisions of this Protocol, including through the development of an indicative list of consequences, taking into account the cause, type, degree and frequency of non-compliance. Any procedures and mechanisms under this Article entailing binding consequences shall be adopted by means of an amendment to this Protocol.

Article 19

The provisions of Article 14 of the Convention on settlement of disputes shall apply *mutatis mutandis* to this Protocol.

Article 20

(Amendments.)

Article 21

(Annexes.)

Articles 22-28

(Voting, ratification, reservations, etc.)

ANNEX A

Greenhouse gases
Carbon dioxide (CO_2)
Methane (CH_4)
Nitrous oxide (N_2O)
Hydrofluorocarbons (HFCs)
Perfluorocarbons (PFCs)
Sulphur hexafloride (SF_6)

Sectors/source categories
Energy
Fuel combustion
Energy industries
Manufacturing industries and construction
Transport
Other sectors
Other
Fugitive emissions from fuels
Solid fuels
Oil and natural gas
Other
Industrial processes
Mineral products
Chemical industry
Metal production
Other production
Production of halocarbons and sulphur hexafluoride
Consumption of halocarbons and sulphur hexafluoride
Other
Solvent and other product use
Agriculture
Enteric fermentation
Manure management
Rice cultivation
Agricultural soils
Prescribed burning of savannahs
Field burning of agricultural residues
Other
Waste
Solid waste disposal on land
Wastewater handling
Waste incineration
Other

ANNEX B

Party quantified emission limitation or reduction commitment
(percentage of base year or period)

Australia 108
Austria 92
Belgium 92
Bulgaria* 92
Canada 94
Croatia* 95
Czech Republic* 92
Denmark 92
Estonia* 92
European Community 92
Finland 92
France 92
Germany 92
Greece 92
Hungary* 94
Iceland 110
Ireland 92
Italy 92
Japan 94
Latvia* 92
Liechtenstein 92
Lithuania* 92
Luxembourg 92
Monaco 92
Netherlands 92
New Zealand 100
Norway 101
Poland* 94
Portugal 92
Romania* 92
Russian Federation* 100
Slovakia* 92
Slovenia* 92
Spain 92
Sweden 92
Switzerland 92
Ukraine* 100
United Kingdom 92
United States of America 93

* Countries that are undergoing the process of transition to a market economy.

Membership of the United Nations and its Specialized Agencies

(at March 2002)

	UN	IAEA	IBRD	IDA	IFC	IMF	FAO[1]	IFAD[2]	IMO[3]	ICAO[4]	ILO	ITU[5]	UNESCO[6]	UNIDO	UPU[7]	WHO[8]	WMO[9]	WIPO
Afghanistan	x	x	x	x	x	x	x	x		x	x	x	x	x	x	x	x	
Albania	x	x	x	x	x	x	x	x	x	x	x	x	x	x	x	x	x	x
Algeria	x	x	x	x	x	x	x	x	x	x	x	x	x	x	x	x	x	x
Andorra	x									x		x	x			x		x
Angola	x	x	x	x	x	x	x	x	x	x	x	x	x	x	x	x	x	x
Antigua and Barbuda	x		x		x	x	x	x	x	x	x	x	x		x	x	x	x
Argentina	x	x	x	x	x	x	x	x	x	x	x	x	x	x	x	x	x	x
Armenia	x	x	x	x	x	x	x	x		x	x	x	x	x	x	x	x	x
Australia	x	x	x	x	x	x	x	x	x	x	x	x	x		x	x	x	x
Austria	x	x	x	x	x	x	x	x	x	x	x	x	x	x	x	x	x	x
Azerbaijan	x	x	x	x	x	x	x	x	x	x	x	x	x	x	x	x	x	x
Bahamas	x		x		x	x	x		x	x	x	x	x	x	x	x	x	x
Bahrain	x		x		x	x	x		x	x	x	x	x	x	x	x	x	x
Bangladesh	x	x	x	x	x	x	x	x	x	x	x	x	x	x	x	x	x	x
Barbados	x		x	x	x	x	x	x	x	x	x	x	x	x	x	x	x	x
Belarus	x	x	x		x	x				x	x	x	x	x	x	x	x	x
Belgium	x	x	x	x	x	x	x	x	x	x	x	x	x	x	x	x	x	x
Belize	x		x	x	x	x	x	x	x	x	x	x	x	x	x	x	x	x
Benin	x	x	x	x	x	x	x	x	x	x	x	x	x	x	x	x	x	x
Bhutan	x		x	x		x	x	x		x		x	x	x	x	x		x
Bolivia	x	x	x	x	x	x	x	x	x	x	x	x	x	x	x	x	x	x
Bosnia and Herzegovina	x	x	x	x	x	x	x	x	x	x	x	x	x	x	x	x	x	x
Botswana	x		x	x	x	x	x	x		x	x	x	x	x	x	x	x	x
Brazil	x	x	x	x	x	x	x	x	x	x	x	x	x	x	x	x	x	x
Brunei	x		x			x			x	x		x			x	x	x	x
Bulgaria	x	x	x		x	x	x		x	x	x	x	x	x	x	x	x	x
Burkina Faso	x	x	x	x	x	x	x	x		x	x	x	x	x	x	x	x	x
Burundi	x		x	x	x	x	x	x		x	x	x	x	x	x	x	x	x
Cambodia	x	x	x	x	x	x	x	x	x	x	x	x	x	x	x	x	x	x
Cameroon	x	x	x	x	x	x	x	x	x	x	x	x	x	x	x	x	x	x
Canada	x	x	x	x	x	x	x	x	x	x	x	x	x		x	x	x	x
Cape Verde	x		x	x	x	x	x	x	x	x	x	x	x	x	x	x	x	x
Central African Republic	x	x	x	x	x	x	x	x		x	x	x	x	x	x	x	x	x
Chad	x		x	x	x	x	x	x		x	x	x	x	x	x	x	x	x
Chile	x	x	x	x	x	x	x	x	x	x	x	x	x	x	x	x	x	x
China, People's Republic	x	x	x	x	x	x	x	x	x	x	x	x	x	x	x	x	x	x
Colombia	x	x	x	x	x	x	x	x	x	x	x	x	x	x	x	x	x	x
Comoros	x		x	x	x	x	x	x	x	x	x	x	x	x	x	x	x	
Congo, Democratic Republic	x	x	x	x	x	x	x	x	x	x	x	x	x	x	x	x	x	x
Congo, Republic	x		x	x	x	x	x	x	x	x	x	x	x	x	x	x	x	x
Costa Rica	x	x	x	x	x	x	x	x	x	x	x	x	x	x	x	x	x	x
Côte d'Ivoire	x	x	x	x	x	x	x	x	x	x	x	x	x	x	x	x	x	x
Croatia	x	x	x	x	x	x	x	x	x	x	x	x	x	x	x	x	x	x
Cuba	x	x					x	x	x	x	x	x	x	x	x	x	x	x
Cyprus	x	x	x	x	x	x	x	x	x	x	x	x	x	x	x	x	x	x
Czech Republic	x	x	x	x	x	x	x		x	x	x	x	x	x	x	x	x	x
Denmark	x	x	x	x	x	x	x	x	x	x	x	x	x	x	x	x	x	x
Djibouti	x		x	x	x	x	x	x	x	x	x	x	x	x	x	x	x	
Dominica	x		x	x	x	x	x	x	x		x	x	x	x	x	x	x	x
Dominican Republic	x	x	x	x	x	x	x	x	x	x	x	x	x	x	x	x	x	x
Ecuador	x	x	x	x	x	x	x	x	x	x	x	x	x	x	x	x	x	x
Egypt	x	x	x	x	x	x	x	x	x	x	x	x	x	x	x	x	x	x
El Salvador	x	x	x	x	x	x	x	x	x	x	x	x	x	x	x	x	x	x
Equatorial Guinea	x		x	x	x	x	x	x	x	x	x	x	x	x	x	x		x
Eritrea	x		x	x	x	x	x	x	x	x	x	x	x	x	x	x	x	x
Estonia	x	x	x		x	x	x		x	x	x	x	x		x	x	x	x
Ethiopia	x	x	x	x	x	x	x	x	x	x	x	x	x	x	x	x	x	x
Fiji	x		x	x	x	x	x	x	x	x	x	x	x	x	x	x	x	x
Finland	x	x	x	x	x	x	x	x	x	x	x	x	x	x	x	x	x	x
France	x	x	x	x	x	x	x	x	x	x	x	x	x	x	x	x	x	x
Gabon	x	x	x	x	x	x	x	x	x	x	x	x	x	x	x	x	x	x
The Gambia	x		x	x	x	x	x	x	x	x	x	x	x	x	x	x	x	x

continued

	UN	IAEA	IBRD	IDA	IFC	IMF	FAO[1]	IFAD[2]	IMO[3]	ICAO[4]	ILO	ITU[5]	UNESCO[6]	UNIDO	UPU[7]	WHO[8]	WMO[9]	WIPO
Georgia	x	x	x	x	x	x	x	x	x	x	x	x	x	x	x	x	x	x
Germany	x	x	x	x	x	x	x	x	x	x	x	x	x	x	x	x	x	x
Ghana	x	x	x	x	x	x	x	x	x	x	x	x	x	x	x	x	x	x
Greece	x	x	x	x	x	x	x	x	x	x	x	x	x	x	x	x	x	x
Grenada	x		x	x	x	x	x	x	x	x	x	x	x	x	x	x		x
Guatemala	x	x	x	x	x	x	x	x	x	x	x	x	x	x	x	x	x	x
Guinea	x		x	x	x	x	x	x	x	x	x	x	x	x	x	x	x	x
Guinea-Bissau	x		x	x	x	x	x	x	x	x	x	x	x	x	x	x	x	x
Guyana	x		x	x	x	x	x	x	x	x	x	x	x	x	x	x	x	x
Haiti	x	x	x	x	x	x	x	x	x	x	x	x	x	x	x	x	x	x
Honduras	x	x	x	x	x	x	x	x	x	x	x	x	x	x	x	x	x	x
Hungary	x	x	x	x	x	x	x		x	x	x	x	x	x	x	x	x	x
Iceland	x	x	x	x	x	x	x		x	x	x	x	x		x	x	x	x
India	x	x	x	x	x	x	x	x	x	x	x	x	x	x	x	x	x	x
Indonesia	x	x	x	x	x	x	x	x	x	x	x	x	x	x	x	x	x	x
Iran	x	x	x	x	x	x	x	x	x	x	x	x	x	x	x	x	x	x
Iraq	x	x	x	x	x	x	x	x	x	x	x	x	x	x	x	x	x	x
Ireland	x	x	x	x	x	x	x	x	x	x	x	x	x	x	x	x	x	x
Israel	x	x	x	x	x	x	x	x	x	x	x	x	x	x	x	x	x	x
Italy	x	x	x	x	x	x	x	x	x	x	x	x	x	x	x	x	x	x
Jamaica	x	x	x		x	x	x	x	x	x	x	x	x	x	x	x	x	x
Japan	x	x	x	x	x	x	x	x	x	x	x	x	x	x	x	x	x	x
Jordan	x	x	x	x	x	x	x	x	x	x	x	x	x	x	x	x	x	x
Kazakhstan	x	x	x	x	x	x	x	x	x	x	x	x	x	x	x	x	x	x
Kenya	x	x	x	x	x	x	x	x	x	x	x	x	x	x	x	x	x	x
Kiribati	x		x	x	x	x	x			x		x	x		x	x		
Korea, Democratic People's Republic	x						x	x	x	x		x	x	x	x	x	x	x
Korea, Republic	x	x	x	x	x	x	x	x	x	x	x	x	x	x	x	x	x	x
Kuwait	x	x	x	x	x	x	x	x	x	x	x	x	x	x	x	x	x	x
Kyrgyzstan	x		x	x	x	x	x	x		x	x	x	x	x	x	x	x	x
Laos	x		x	x	x	x	x	x		x	x	x	x	x	x	x	x	x
Latvia	x	x	x	x	x	x	x		x	x	x	x	x		x	x	x	x
Lebanon	x	x	x	x	x	x	x	x	x	x	x	x	x	x	x	x	x	x
Lesotho	x		x	x	x	x	x	x		x	x	x	x	x	x	x	x	x
Liberia	x	x	x	x	x	x	x	x	x	x	x	x	x	x	x	x	x	x
Libya	x	x	x	x	x	x	x	x	x	x	x	x	x	x	x	x	x	x
Liechtenstein	x	x										x			x	x		x
Lithuania	x	x	x		x	x	x		x	x	x	x	x	x	x	x	x	x
Luxembourg	x	x	x	x	x	x	x	x	x	x	x	x	x	x	x	x	x	x
Macedonia, former Yugoslav republic	x		x	x	x	x	x	x	x	x	x	x	x	x	x	x	x	x
Madagascar	x	x	x	x	x	x	x	x	x	x	x	x	x	x	x	x	x	x
Malawi	x		x	x	x	x	x	x	x	x	x	x	x	x	x	x	x	x
Malaysia	x	x	x	x	x	x	x	x	x	x	x	x	x	x	x	x	x	x
Maldives	x		x	x	x	x	x	x	x	x		x	x	x	x	x	x	
Mali	x	x	x	x	x	x	x	x		x	x	x	x	x	x	x	x	x
Malta	x	x	x			x	x	x	x	x	x	x	x	x	x	x	x	x
Marshall Islands	x	x	x	x	x	x	x		x	x		x	x			x		
Mauritania	x		x	x	x	x	x	x	x	x	x	x	x	x	x	x	x	x
Mauritius	x	x	x	x	x	x	x	x	x	x	x	x	x	x	x	x	x	x
Mexico	x	x	x	x	x	x	x	x	x	x	x	x	x	x	x	x	x	x
Micronesia, Federated States of	x		x	x	x	x				x		x	x			x	x	
Moldova	x	x	x	x	x	x	x	x	x	x	x	x	x	x	x	x	x	x
Monaco	x	x					x		x	x		x	x		x	x	x	x
Mongolia	x	x	x	x	x	x	x	x	x	x	x	x	x	x	x	x	x	x
Morocco	x	x	x	x	x	x	x	x	x	x	x	x	x	x	x	x	x	x
Mozambique	x		x	x	x	x	x	x	x	x	x	x	x	x	x	x	x	x
Myanmar	x	x	x	x	x	x	x	x	x	x	x	x	x	x	x	x	x	x
Namibia	x		x		x	x	x	x	x	x	x	x	x	x	x	x	x	x
Nauru	x						x			x		x	x		x	x		
Nepal	x		x	x	x	x	x	x	x	x	x	x	x	x	x	x	x	x
Netherlands	x	x	x	x	x	x	x	x	x	x	x	x	x	x	x	x	x	x
New Zealand	x	x	x	x	x	x	x	x	x	x	x	x	x	x	x	x	x	x
Nicaragua	x	x	x	x	x	x	x	x	x	x	x	x	x	x	x	x	x	x
Niger	x	x	x	x	x	x	x	x		x	x	x	x	x	x	x	x	x
Nigeria	x	x	x	x	x	x	x	x	x	x	x	x	x	x	x	x	x	x
Norway	x	x	x	x	x	x	x	x	x	x	x	x	x	x	x	x	x	x
Oman	x		x	x	x	x	x	x	x	x	x	x	x	x	x	x	x	x
Pakistan	x	x	x	x	x	x	x	x	x	x	x	x	x	x	x	x	x	x
Palau	x		x	x	x	x	x		x	x			x			x		

continued

	UN	IAEA	IBRD	IDA	IFC	IMF	FAO[1]	IFAD[2]	IMO[3]	ICAO[4]	ILO	ITU[5]	UNESCO[6]	UNIDO	UPU[7]	WHO[8]	WMO[9]	WIPO
Panama	x	x	x	x	x	x	x	x	x	x	x	x	x	x	x	x	x	x
Papua New Guinea	x		x	x	x	x	x	x	x	x	x	x	x	x	x	x	x	x
Paraguay	x	x	x	x	x	x	x	x	x	x	x	x	x	x	x	x	x	x
Peru	x	x	x	x	x	x	x	x	x	x	x	x	x	x	x	x	x	x
Philippines	x	x	x	x	x	x	x	x	x	x	x	x	x	x	x	x	x	x
Poland	x	x	x	x	x	x	x		x	x	x	x	x	x	x	x	x	x
Portugal	x	x	x	x	x	x	x	x	x	x	x	x	x	x	x	x	x	x
Qatar	x	x	x			x	x	x	x	x	x	x	x	x	x	x	x	x
Romania	x	x	x		x	x	x	x	x	x	x	x	x	x	x	x	x	x
Russia	x	x	x	x	x	x			x	x	x	x	x	x	x	x	x	x
Rwanda	x		x	x	x	x	x	x		x	x	x	x	x	x	x	x	x
Saint Christopher and Nevis	x		x	x	x	x	x	x	x		x		x	x	x	x		x
Saint Lucia	x		x	x	x	x	x	x	x	x	x	x	x	x	x	x	x	x
Saint Vincent and the Grenadines	x		x	x		x	x	x	x	x	x	x	x	x	x	x		x
Samoa	x		x	x	x	x	x	x	x	x		x	x		x	x	x	x
San Marino	x		x			x	x			x	x	x	x		x	x		x
São Tomé and Príncipe	x		x	x		x	x	x	x	x	x	x	x	x	x	x	x	x
Saudi Arabia	x	x	x	x	x	x	x	x	x	x	x	x	x	x	x	x	x	x
Senegal	x	x	x	x	x	x	x	x	x	x	x	x	x	x	x	x	x	x
Seychelles	x		x		x	x	x	x		x	x	x	x	x	x	x	x	x
Sierra Leone	x	x	x	x	x	x	x	x	x	x	x	x	x	x	x	x	x	x
Singapore	x	x	x		x	x			x	x	x	x			x	x	x	x
Slovakia	x	x	x	x	x	x	x		x	x	x	x	x	x	x	x	x	x
Slovenia	x	x	x	x	x	x	x		x	x	x	x	x	x	x	x	x	x
Solomon Islands	x		x	x	x	x	x	x	x	x	x	x	x		x	x	x	
Somalia	x		x	x	x	x	x	x	x	x	x	x	x	x	x	x	x	x
South Africa	x	x	x	x	x	x	x	x	x	x	x	x	x	x	x	x	x	x
Spain	x	x	x	x	x	x	x	x	x	x	x	x	x	x	x	x	x	x
Sri Lanka	x	x	x	x	x	x	x	x	x	x	x	x	x	x	x	x	x	x
Sudan	x	x	x	x	x	x	x	x	x	x	x	x	x	x	x	x	x	x
Suriname	x		x			x	x	x	x	x	x	x	x	x	x	x	x	x
Swaziland	x		x	x	x	x	x	x		x	x	x	x	x	x	x	x	x
Sweden	x	x	x	x	x	x	x	x	x	x	x	x	x	x	x	x	x	x
Switzerland		x	x	x	x	x	x	x	x	x	x	x	x	x	x	x	x	x
Syria	x	x	x	x	x	x	x	x	x	x	x	x	x	x	x	x	x	
Tajikistan	x	x	x	x	x	x	x	x		x	x	x	x	x	x	x	x	x
Tanzania	x	x	x	x	x	x	x	x	x	x	x	x	x	x	x	x	x	x
Thailand	x	x	x	x	x	x	x	x	x	x	x	x	x	x	x	x	x	x
Togo	x		x	x	x	x	x	x	x	x	x	x	x	x	x	x	x	x
Tonga	x		x	x	x	x	x	x	x	x		x	x	x	x	x	x	x
Trinidad and Tobago	x		x	x	x	x	x	x	x	x	x	x	x	x	x	x	x	x
Tunisia	x	x	x	x	x	x	x	x	x	x	x	x	x	x	x	x	x	x
Turkey	x	x	x	x	x	x	x	x	x	x	x	x	x	x	x	x	x	x
Turkmenistan	x		x		x	x	x		x	x	x	x	x	x	x	x	x	x
Tuvalu	x											x	x		x	x		
Uganda	x	x	x	x	x	x	x	x		x	x	x	x	x	x	x	x	x
Ukraine	x	x	x		x	x			x	x	x	x	x	x	x	x	x	x
United Arab Emirates	x	x	x	x	x	x	x	x	x	x	x	x	x	x	x	x	x	x
United Kingdom	x	x	x	x	x	x	x	x	x	x	x	x	x	x	x	x	x	x
USA	x	x	x	x	x	x	x	x	x	x	x	x			x	x	x	x
Uruguay	x	x	x		x	x	x	x	x	x	x	x	x	x	x	x	x	x
Uzbekistan	x	x	x	x	x	x	x			x	x	x	x	x	x	x	x	x
Vanuatu	x		x	x	x	x	x		x	x		x	x	x	x	x	x	
Vatican City		x										x			x			x
Venezuela	x	x	x		x	x	x	x	x	x	x	x	x	x	x	x	x	x
Viet Nam	x	x	x	x	x	x	x	x	x	x	x	x	x	x	x	x	x	x
Yemen	x	x	x	x	x	x	x	x	x	x	x	x	x	x	x	x	x	x
Yugoslavia, Federal Republic	x	x	x	x	x	x	x	x	x	x	x	x	x	x	x	x	x	x
Zambia	x	x	x	x	x	x	x	x		x	x	x	x	x	x	x	x	x
Zimbabwe	x	x	x	x	x	x	x	x	x	x	x	x	x	x	x	x	x	x

[1] The Cook Islands, Niue and the European Union are members of FAO.
[2] The Cook Islands is a member of IFAD.
[3] Hong Kong and Macau are associate members of IMO.
[4] The Cook Islands is a member of ICAO.
[5] Members also include British Overseas Territories, French Overseas Territories and United States Territories.
[6] The Cook Islands and Niue are members of UNESCO; Aruba, the British Virgin Islands, the Cayman Islands, Macau and the Netherlands Antilles are associate members.
[7] Members also include British Overseas Territories and the Netherlands Antilles and Aruba.
[8] The Cook Islands and Niue are members of WHO; Puerto Rico and Tokelau are associate members.
[9] Members also include British Caribbean Territories, the Cook Islands, French Polynesia, Hong Kong, Macau, the Netherlands Antilles and Aruba, New Caledonia and Niue.

PART THREE

Major Non-UN Organizations

AFRICAN DEVELOPMENT BANK—ADB

Address: rue Joseph Anoma, 01 BP 1387, Abidjan 01, Côte d'Ivoire.

Telephone: 20-20-44-44; **fax:** 20-20-40-06; **e-mail:** comuadb@afdb.org; **internet:** www.afdb.org.

Established in 1964, the Bank began operations in July 1966, with the aim of financing economic and social development in African countries.

AFRICAN MEMBERS

Algeria	Equatorial Guinea	Namibia
Angola	Eritrea	Niger
Benin	Ethiopia	Nigeria
Botswana	Gabon	Rwanda
Burkina Faso	The Gambia	São Tomé and Príncipe
Burundi	Ghana	Senegal
Cameroon	Guinea	Seychelles
Cape Verde	Guinea-Bissau	Sierra Leone
Central African Republic	Kenya	Somalia
Chad	Lesotho	South Africa
Comoros	Liberia	Sudan
Congo, Democratic Republic	Libya	Swaziland
Congo, Republic	Madagascar	Tanzania
Côte d'Ivoire	Malawi	Togo
Djibouti	Mali	Tunisia
Egypt	Mauritania	Uganda
	Mauritius	Zambia
	Morocco	Zimbabwe
	Mozambique	

There are also 24 non-African members.

Organization

(April 2002)

BOARD OF GOVERNORS

The highest policy-making body of the Bank. Each member country nominates one Governor, usually its Minister of Finance and Economic Affairs, and an alternate Governor or the Governor of its Central Bank. The Board meets once a year. It elects the Board of Directors and the President.

BOARD OF DIRECTORS

The Board consists of 18 members (of whom six are non-African), elected by the Board of Governors for a term of three years, renewable once; it is responsible for the general operations of the Bank. The Board meets on a weekly basis.

OFFICERS

The President is responsible for the organization and the day-to-day operations of the Bank under guidance of the Board of Directors. The President is elected for a five-year term and serves as the Chairman of the Board of Directors. In 2000 the Bank initiated a process of organizational restructuring as part of a new Bank Vision, approved by the Board of Governors in the previous year. The objectives of the reorganization were to give greater priority to client needs, strategically oriented planning, and human resources management. A new structure was introduced on 1 January 2002. Accordingly, the number of Vice-Presidents was increased from three to five, responsible for Planning, Policy and Research; Corporate Management; Operations, Central and West Regions; Operations, North, East and South Regions; and Finance.

Executive President and Chairman of Board of Directors: OMAR KABBAJ (Morocco).

Secretary-General: PHILIBERT AFRIKA (Rwanda).

FINANCIAL STRUCTURE

The ADB Group of development financing institutions comprises the African Development Fund (ADF) and the Nigeria Trust Fund (NTF), which provide concessionary loans, and the African Development Bank itself. The group uses a unit of account (UA), which, at April 2001, was valued at US $1.2063.

The capital stock of the Bank was at first exclusively open for subscription by African countries, with each member's subscription consisting of an equal number of paid-up and callable shares. In 1978, however, the Governors agreed to open the capital stock of the Bank to subscription by non-regional states on the basis of nine principles aimed at maintaining the African character of the institution. The decision was finally ratified in May 1982, and the participation of non-regional countries became effective on 30 December. It was agreed that African members should still hold two-thirds of the share capital, that all loan operations should be restricted to African members, and that the Bank's President should always be an African national. In May 1998 the Board of Governors approved an increase in capital of 35%, and resolved that the non-African members' share of the capital be increased from 33.3% to 40%. In 2000 the ADB's authorized capital was US $28,495m. At the end of 2000 subscribed capital was $26,772m. (of which the paid-up portion was $2,628m.).

Activities

At the end of 2000 total loan and grant approvals by the ADB Group since the beginning of its operations amounted to US $39,116m. Of that amount agriculture received the largest proportion of assistance (19.3%), while transport received 16.3%, multi-sector activities 14.4%, and finance 12.8%. In 2000 the group approved 143 loans and grants amounting to $2,585m., compared with $1,764m. for 92 loans and grants in the previous year.

A new credit policy, adopted in May 1995, effectively disqualified 39 low-income regional members, deemed to be non-creditworthy, from receiving non-concessional ADB financing, in an attempt to reduce the accumulation of arrears. The ADB Group estimated that its capital requirements for the period 1997–2001 would amount to US $46,500m. to allow for greater flexibility in its lending. In September 1997 the Bank established a Supplementary Financing Mechanism, to provide countries eligible for ADF funds with quick-disbursing resources to meet interest payments on outstanding Bank debt. The Bank allocated UA 222m. for the mechanism, which became operational in March 1998.

The ADB contributed funds for the establishment in 1986 of the Africa Project Development Facility, which assists the private sector in Africa by providing advisory services and finance for entrepreneurs: it is managed by the International Finance Corporation (IFC—see p. 160). In 1989 the ADB, in co-ordination with IFC and UNDP, created the African Management Services Company (AMSCo) which provides management support and training to private companies in Africa. The Bank is one of three multilateral donors, with the World Bank and UNDP, supporting the African Capacity Building Foundation (q.v.), which was established in 1991 to strengthen and develop institutional and human capacity in support of sustainable development activities.

The Bank also provides technical assistance to regional member countries in the form of experts' services, pre-investment feasibility studies, and staff training; much of this assistance is financed through bilateral aid funds contributed by non-African member states. The Bank's African Development Institute provides training for officials of regional member countries in order to enhance the management of Bank-financed projects and, more broadly, to strengthen national capacities for promoting sustainable development. In 1990 the ADB established the African Business Round Table (ABR), which is composed of the chief executives of Africa's leading corporations. The ABR aims to strengthen Africa's private sector, promote intra-African trade and investment, and attract foreign investment to Africa. The ABR is chaired by the ADB's Executive President. At its fourth annual meeting, held in Arusha, Tanzania, in March 1994, the ABR resolved to establish an African Investment Bank, in co-operation with the ADB, which was to provide financial services to African companies. In November 1999 a Joint Africa Institute, which had been established by the Bank, the World Bank and the IMF, was formally inaugurated in Abidjan, Côte d'Ivoire. The Institute aimed to enhance training opportunities in economic policy and management and to strengthen capacity-building in the region.

In 1990 a Memorandum of Understanding (MOU) for the Reinforcement of Co-operation between the Organization of African Unity (OAU—q.v.), the UN's Economic Commission for Africa (q.v.) and the ADB was signed by the three organizations. A joint secretariat supports co-operation activities between the organizations. In 1999 a Co-operation Agreement was formally concluded between the Bank and the Common Market for Eastern and Southern Africa (COMESA, q.v.). In March 2000 the Bank signed an MOU on its strategic partnership with the World Bank. Other MOUs were signed during that year with the United Nations Industrial Development Organization, the World Food Programme, and the Arab Maghreb Union. Since 1996 the Bank has collaborated closely with international partners, in particular the World Bank, in efforts to address the problems of heavily indebted poor countries (HIPCs) (see World Bank, p. 154). Following the introduction of an enhanced framework for the initiative, extending the number of eligible African countries from 25 to 31, the Bank has been actively involved in the preparation of Poverty Reduction Strategy Papers, that provide national frameworks for poverty reduction programmes. At 31 December 2000 the Bank had approved US $635.8m. (in 1999 net present value terms) to 10 countries under the enhanced HIPC initiative.

Summary of Bank Group Activities (US $ million)

	1999	2000	Cumulative total*
ADB loans			
Number	22	38	832
Amount approved	1,082.56	1,098.99	24,054.71
Disbursements	700.62	535.42	16,098.25
ADF loans and grants			
Number	70	102	1,577
Amount approved	681.93	1,472.17	114,726.70
Disbursements	504.94	352.99	9,093.46
NTF loans			
Number	—	3	61
Amount approved	—	13.92	334.19
Disbursements	10.27	8.28	235.79
Group total			
Number	92	143	2,470
Amount approved	1,764.49	2,585.08	39,115.59
Disbursements	1,215.83	896.68	25,427.49

* Since the initial operations of the three institutions (1967 for ADB, 1974 for ADF and 1976 for NTF).

Source: *Annual Report 2000.*

AFRICAN DEVELOPMENT BANK (ADB)

The Bank makes loans at a variable rate of interest, which is adjusted twice a year, plus a commitment fee of 0.75%. Loan approvals amounted to US $1,099.0m. for 38 loans in 2000. Since October 1997 new fixed and floating rate loans have also been made available.

AFRICAN DEVELOPMENT FUND (ADF)

The Fund commenced operations in 1974. It grants interest-free loans to low-income African countries for projects with repayment over 50 years (including a 10-year grace period) and with a service charge of 0.75% per annum. Grants for project feasibility studies are made to the poorest countries.

In 1991 a sixth replenishment of the Fund's resources amounting to US $3,340m. was approved for 1991–93. Negotiations for the seventh replenishment of the Fund's resources commenced in May 1993. However, in May 1994, donor countries withheld any new funds owing to dissatisfaction with the Bank's governance. In May 1996, following the implementation of various institutional reforms to strengthen the Bank's financial management and decision-making capabilities and to reduce its administrative costs, an agreement was concluded on the seventh replenishment of the ADF. Donor countries pledged some $2,690m. for the period 1996–98. An additional allocation of $420m. was endorsed at a special donors' meeting held in Osaka, Japan, in June. The ADF aimed to offer concessional assistance to 42 African countries over the period 1996–98. The seventh replenishment provided for the establishment of an ADF Microfinance Initiative (AMINA), initially for a two-year period, to support small-scale capacity-building projects. In January 1999 negotiations on the eighth replenishment of the Fund were concluded with an agreement to provide additional resources amounting to $3,437m. The replenishment was approved by the Board of Governors in May, and came into effect in December.

In 2000 102 ADF loans and grants were approved amounting to US $1,472.2m.

Group Loan and Grant Approvals by Country
(millions of UA)

Country	1999	2000	Cumulative total*
Algeria	157.46	89.25	1,739.92
Angola	—	—	294.14
Benin	12.27	27.34	304.86
Botswana	—	2.78	327.71
Burkina Faso	10.00	10.96	315.85
Burundi	—	0.37	276.33
Cameroon	21.95	26.46	603.82
Cape Verde	0.13	5.74	153.96
Central African Republic	—	—	139.39
Chad	21.10	12.00	305.63
Comoros	—	—	64.74
Congo, Democratic Republic	—	—	936.20
Congo, Republic	—	—	278.18
Côte d'Ivoire	32.67	28.66	1,060.21
Djibouti	—	0.81	91.76
Egypt	53.55	—	1,488.23
Equatorial Guinea	—	—	67.19
Eritrea	—	2.30	39.90
Ethiopia	—	4.08	1,048.35
Gabon	—	—	596.81
Gambia	5.65	12.91	188.31
Ghana	16.16	40.75	628.22
Guinea	—	22.86	480.04
Guinea Bissau	—	0.38	157.64
Kenya	15.50	28.62	554.91
Lesotho	6.05	11.74	277.59
Liberia	0.37	—	153.62
Madagascar	26.10	22.89	424.90
Malawi	24.24	11.73	521.85
Mali	21.94	20.75	432.16
Mauritania	23.02	1.80	265.06
Mauritius	—	14.87	166.82
Morocco	19.60	79.87	2,789.95
Mozambique	37.25	118.56	754.77
Namibia	7.10	—	62.13
Niger	—	—	210.50
Nigeria	36.51	43.40	1,982.78
Rwanda	—	19.87	298.69
São Tomé and Príncipe	4.20	—	93.78
Senegal	24.75	30.00	463.89
Seychelles	7.09	—	89.49
Sierra Leone	9.21	0.39	168.35
Somalia	—	—	150.40
South Africa	82.59	75.76	272.55
Sudan	0.35	0.37	350.52
Swaziland	11.11	—	200.04
Tanzania	28.15	7.71	642.93
Togo	12.18	—	170.68
Tunisia	262.97	115.28	2,534.84
Uganda	32.54	82.77	640.89
Zambia	33.77	31.65	604.20
Zimbabwe	118.23	0.37	726.53
Total	1,175.76	1,006.47	27,592.59

* Since the initial operation of the three institutions (1967 for ADB, 1974 for ADF and 1976 for NTF).

NIGERIA TRUST FUND (NTF)

The Agreement establishing the Nigeria Trust Fund was signed in February 1976 by the Bank and the Government of Nigeria. The Fund is administered by the Bank and its loans are granted for up to 25 years, including grace periods of up to five years, and carry 0.75% commission charges and 4% interest charges. The loans are intended to provide financing for projects in co-operation with other lending institutions. The Fund also aims to promote the private sector and trade between African countries by providing information on African and international financial institutions able to finance African trade.

During 1999 negotiations on a revised Agreement and replenishment of the Fund's resources were undertaken. Three loans were approved during 2000 amounting to US $13.9m.

ASSOCIATED INSTITUTIONS

The ADB actively participated in the establishment of five associated institutions:

Africa Reinsurance Corporation—Africa-Re: Reinsurance House, 46 Marina, PMB 12765, Lagos, Nigeria; tel. (1) 2663323; fax (1) 2668802; e-mail africare@hyperia.com; f. 1977; started operations in 1978; its purpose is to foster the development of the insurance and reinsurance industry in Africa and to promote the growth of national and regional underwriting capacities; auth. cap. US $50m., of which the ADB holds 10%. There are 12 directors, one appointed by the Bank. Mems: 41 countries, the ADB, and some 90 insurance and reinsurance cos. Man. Dir BAKARY KAMARA.

African Export-Import Bank—Afreximbank: POB 404 Gezira, Cairo 11568; World Trade Centre Bldg, 1191 Corniche el-Nil, Cairo 11221, Egypt; tel. (2) 5780282; fax (2) 5780277; e-mail mail@afreximbank.com; internet www.afreximbank.com; f. 1993; aims to increase the volume of African exports and to expand intra-African trade by financing exporters and importers directly and indirectly through trade finance institutions, such as commercial banks; auth. cap. US $750m.; paid-up cap. $145.7m. (Dec. 1999). Pres. CHRISTOPHER C. EDORDU; Exec. Vice-Pres. JEAN-LOUIS EKRA. Publ. *Annual Report.*

Association of African Development Finance Institutions—AADFI: Immeuble AIAFD, blvd Latrille, rue J61, Cocody Deux Plateaux, Abidjan 04, Côte d'Ivoire; tel. 22-52-33-89; fax 22-52-25-84; e-mail adfi@aviso.ci; f. 1975; aims to promote co-operation among financial institutions in the region in matters relating to economic and social development, research, project design, financing and the exchange of information. Mems: 92 in 43 African and non-African countries. Pres. GERSHOM MUMBA; Sec.-Gen. J. A. AMIHERE (acting).

Shelter-Afrique (Société pour l'habitat et le logement territorial en Afrique): Longonot Rd, POB 41479, Nairobi, Kenya; tel. (2) 722305; fax (2) 722024; e-mail info@shelterafrique.co.ke; f. 1982 to finance housing in ADB mem. countries. Share cap. is US $300m., held by 40 African countries, the ADB, Africa-Re and the Commonwealth Development Corpn; Chair. Paul M. N'KOUE-N'KONGO; Man. Dir P. M'BAYE.

Société Internationale Financière pour les Investissements et le Développement en Afrique—SIFIDA: 22 rue François-Perréard, BP 310, 1225 Chêne-Bourg/Geneva, Switzerland; tel. (22) 8692000; fax (22) 8692001; e-mail headoffice@sifida.com; internet www.sifida.com; f. 1970 by 120 financial and industrial institutions, including the ADB and the IFC. Following a restructuring at the end of 1995, the main shareholders are the Banque Nationale de Paris (BNP), SFOM (itself owned by BNP and Dresdner Bank) and the six banking affiliates of BNP/SFOM in West and Central Africa. SIFIDA is active in the fields of project and trade finance in Africa and also provides financial advisory services, notably in the context of privatizations and debt conversion; auth. cap. US $75m., subscribed cap. $12.5m. Chair. VIVIEN LÉVY-GARBOUA; Man. Dir PHILIPPE SÉCHAUD. Publ. *African Banking Directory* (annually).

Publications

Annual Report.

ADB Business Bulletin (10 a year).

ADB Statistical Pocketbook.

ADB Today (every 2 months).

African Development Report (annually).

African Development Review.

Annual Procurement Report.

Basic Information (annually).

Economic Research Papers.

Quarterly Operational Summary.

Summaries of operations in each member country and various background documents.

ANDEAN COMMUNITY OF NATIONS

(COMUNIDAD ANDINA DE NACIONES—CAN)

Address: Avda Paseo de la República 3895, San Isidro, Lima 27; Apdo 18-1177, Lima 18, Peru.

Telephone: (1) 4111400; **fax:** (1) 2213329; **e-mail:** contacto@comunidadandina.org; **internet:** www.comunidadandina.org.

The organization was established in 1969 as the Acuerdo de Cartagena (the Cartagena Agreement), also referred to as the Grupo Andino (Andean Group) or the Pacto Andino (Andean Pact). In March 1996 member countries signed a Reform Protocol of the Cartagena Agreement, in accordance with which the Andean Group was superseded in August 1997 by the Andean Community of Nations (CAN, generally referred to as the Andean Community). The Andean Community was to promote greater economic, commercial and political integration under a new Andean Integration System (Sistema Andino de Integración), comprising the organization's bodies and institutions. The Community covers an area of 4,710,000 sq km, with some 113m. inhabitants.

MEMBERS

Bolivia Colombia Ecuador Peru Venezuela

Note: Chile withdrew from the Andean Group in 1976. Panama has observer status with the Community.

Organization

(April 2002)

ANDEAN PRESIDENTIAL COUNCIL

The presidential summits, which had been held annually since 1989, were formalized under the 1996 Reform Protocol of the Cartagena Agreement as the Andean Presidential Council. The Council is the highest-level body of the Andean Integration System, and provides the political leadership of the Community.

COMMISSION

The Commission consists of a plenipotentiary representative from each member country, with each country holding the presidency in turn. The Commission is the main policy-making organ of the Andean Community, and is responsible for co-ordinating Andean trade policy.

COUNCIL OF FOREIGN MINISTERS

The Council of Foreign Ministers meets annually or whenever it is considered necessary, to formulate common external policy and to co-ordinate the process of integration.

GENERAL SECRETARIAT

The General Secretariat (formerly the Junta) is the body charged with implementation of all guide-lines and decisions issued by the bodies listed above. It submits proposals to the Commission for facilitating the fulfilment of the Community's objectives. Members are appointed for a three-year term. They supervise technical officials assigned to the following Departments: External Relations, Agricultural Development, Press Office, Economic Policy, Physical Integration, Programme of Assistance to Bolivia, Industrial Development, Programme Planning, Legal Affairs, Technology. Under the reforms agreed in March 1996 the Secretary-General is elected by the Council of Foreign Ministers and has enhanced powers to adjudicate in disputes arising between member states. In August 1997 it assumed the functions of the Board of the Cartagena Agreement.

Secretary-General: SEBASTIÁN ALEGRETT (Venezuela).

PARLIAMENT

Parlamento Andino: Carrera 7ª, No. 13–58, Of. 401, Santafé de Bogotá, Colombia; tel. (1) 284-4191; fax (1) 284-3270; e-mail pandino@cable.net.co; internet www.parlamentoandino.org; f. 1979; comprises five members from each country, and meets in each capital city in turn; makes recommendations on regional policy. In April 1997 a new protocol was adopted which provided for the election of members by direct and universal voting. In November 1998 Venezuela put the new voting mechanism into practice; the remaining Community countries were expected to complete the process by 2007. Sec.-Gen. Dr RUBÉN VÉLEZ NÚÑEZ.

COURT OF JUSTICE

Tribunal de Justicia de la Comunidad Andina: Calle Roca 450, Quito, Ecuador; tel. (2) 529998; fax (2) 565007; e-mail tjca@impsat.net.ec; internet www.altesa.net/tribunal; f. 1979, began operating in 1984; a protocol approved in May 1996 (which came into force in August 1999) modified the Court's functions; its main responsibilities are to resolve disputes among member countries and interpret community legislation. It comprises five judges, one from each member country, appointed for a renewable period of six years. The Presidency is assumed annually by each judge in turn.

Activities

In May 1979, at Cartagena, Colombia, the Presidents of the five member countries signed the 'Mandate of Cartagena', which envisaged greater economic and political co-operation, including the establishment of more sub-regional development programmes (especially in industry). In May 1989 the Group undertook to revitalize the process of Andean integration, by withdrawing measures that obstructed the programme of trade liberalization, and by complying with tariff reductions that had already been agreed upon. In May 1991, in Caracas, Venezuela, a summit meeting of the Andean Group agreed the framework for the establishment of a free-trade area on 1 January 1992 (achieved in February 1993) and for an eventual Andean common market (see below, under Trade).

In March 1996 heads of state, meeting in Trujillo, Peru, affirmed member countries' commitment to combating drugs trafficking and, indirectly, condemned the decision of the USA to 'decertify' the Colombian anti-narcotics campaign (and thus to suspend financial assistance to that country). At the same meeting, member countries agreed to a substantial restructuring of the Andean Group. The heads of state signed the Reform Protocol of the Cartagena Agreement, providing for the establishment of the Andean Community of Nations, which was to have more ambitious economic and political objectives than the Group. Consequently, in August 1997 the Andean Community was inaugurated, and the Group's Junta was replaced by a new General Secretariat, headed by a Secretary-General with enhanced executive and decision-making powers. The initiation of these reforms was designed to accelerate harmonization in economic matters, particularly the achievement of a common external tariff. In September 1996 the Group agreed to negotiate a free-trade agreement with the Mercado Común del Sur (Mercosur—see p. 502). (Disunity among the Andean nations had been evident in June, when Bolivia had agreed to enter into free-trade negotiations with Mercosur on a unilateral basis, thus becoming an associate member of that grouping.) In April 1997 the Peruvian Government announced its intention to withdraw from the Cartagena Agreement, owing to disagreements about the terms of Peru's full integration into the Community's trading system. Later in that month the heads of state of the four other members attended a summit meeting, in Sucre, Bolivia, and reiterated their commitment to strengthening regional integration. A high-level group of representatives was established to pursue negotiations with Peru regarding its future relationship with the Community (agreement was reached in June—see below). In April 2001 Venezuela announced that it intended to apply for membership of Mercosur (while retaining its membership of the Community).

At the 13th presidential summit, held in Valencia, Venezuela, in June 2001, heads of state adopted an Andean Co-operation Plan for the Control of Illegal Drugs and Related Offences, which was to promote a united approach to combating these problems. An executive committee was to be established under the accord to oversee implementation of an action plan. It was also agreed that an Andean passport system should enter into effect no later than December 2005. In January 2002 a special Andean presidential summit, held in Santa Cruz, Bolivia, reiterated the objective of creating a common market and renewing efforts to strengthen sub-regional integration, including the adoption of a common agricultural policy and the standardization of macro-economic policies.

TRADE

Trade within the group increased by about 37% annually between 1978 and 1980. A council for customs affairs met for the first time in January 1982, aiming to harmonize national legislation within the group. In December 1984 the member states launched a common currency, the Andean peso, aiming to reduce dependence on the US dollar and to increase regional trade. The new currency was to be backed by special contributions to the Fondo Andino de Reservas (now the Fondo Latinoamericano de Reservas) amounting to US $80m., and was to be 'pegged' to the US dollar, taking the form of financial drafts rather than notes and coins. In May 1986 a formula for trade among member countries was agreed, in order to restrict the number of products exempted from trade liberalization measures to 40 'sensitive' products.

The 'Caracas Declaration' of May 1991 provided for the establishment of an Andean free-trade area, which entered into effect (excluding Peru—see below) in February 1993. Heads of state also agreed in May 1991 to create a common external tariff (CET), to standardize member countries' trade barriers in their dealings with the rest of the world, and envisaged the eventual creation of an Andean common market. In December heads of state defined four main levels of external tariffs (between 5% and 20%). The conclusion of negotiations, however, was subsequently delayed, notably by Ecuador's request for numerous exceptions and by a deterioration in relations between Peru and Venezuela during 1992 (following the suspension of the Peruvian Constitution in April), which halted progress completely. In August the Group approved a request by Peru for the suspension of its rights and obligations under the Pact, thereby enabling the other members to proceed with negotiations on the CET. Peru was readmitted as a full member of the Group in 1994, but participated only as an observer in the ongoing negotiations.

In November 1994 ministers of trade and integration, meeting in Quito, Ecuador, concluded a final agreement on a four-tier structure of external tariffs (although Bolivia was to retain a two-level system). The CET agreement, which came into effect in February 1995, covered 90% of the region's imports (the remainder to be incorporated by 1999, later extended to June 2000), which were to be subject to the following tariff bands: 5% for raw materials; 10%–15% for semi-manufactured goods; and 20% for finished products. In order to reach an agreement, special treatment and exemptions were granted, while Peru, initially, was to remain a 'non-active' member of the accord: Bolivia was to maintain external tariffs of 5% and 10%, Ecuador was permitted to apply the lowest rate of 5% to 990 items and was granted an initial exemption from tariffs on 400 items, while Colombia and Venezuela were granted 230 items to be subject to special treatment for four years. In June 1997 an agreement was concluded to ensure Peru's continued membership of the Community, which provided for that country's integration into the free-trade area. The Peruvian Government determined to eliminate customs duties on some 2,500 products with immediate effect, and it was agreed that the process be completed by 2005. However, negotiations were to continue with regard to the replacement of Peru's single tariff on products from outside the region with the Community's scale of external duties.

In May 1999 the Community adopted a policy on border integration and development to prepare the border regions of member countries for the envisaged free circulation of people, goods, capital and services, while consolidating sub-regional security. Community heads of state, meeting in January 2002 at a special Andean presidential summit, agreed to consolidate and improve the free-trade zone by mid-2002 and apply a new common external tariff (with four levels, ranging from 0%–20%) by December 2003. To facilitate this process a common agricultural policy was to be adopted, and macroeconomic policies were to be harmonized.

EXTERNAL RELATIONS

In September 1995 heads of state of member countries identified the formulation of common positions on foreign relations as an important part of the process of relaunching the integration initiative. A Protocol Amending the Cartagena Agreement was signed in June 1997 to confirm the formulation of a common foreign policy. During 1998 the General Secretariat held consultations with government experts, academics, representatives of the private sector and other interested parties to help formulate a document on guide-lines for a common foreign policy. The guidelines, establishing the principles, objectives and mechanisms of a common foreign policy, were approved by the Council of Foreign Ministers in 1999. Councils on Trade and Investment between the Andean Community and the USA, and between the Community and Canada, have been established to strengthen bilateral trading relations. At the special Andean presidential summit in January 2002, members reiterated their intention to appeal to the US Congress to renew and extend the Andean Trade Preferences Act, which expired in December 2001. The Group has also sought to strengthen relations with the European Union, and a co-operation agreement was signed between the two blocs in April 1993. A Euro-Andean Forum is held periodically to promote mutual co-operation, trade and investment. In February 1998 the Community signed a co-operation and technical assistance agreement with the EU in order to combat drugs trafficking. In March 2000 the Community concluded an agreement to establish a political consultation and co-operation mechanism with the People's Republic of China.

In April 1998, at the 10th Andean presidential summit, an agreement was signed with Panama establishing a framework for negotiations providing for the conclusion of a free-trade accord by the end of 1998 and for Panama's eventual associate membership of the Community. Also in April 1998 the Community signed a framework agreement with Mercosur on the establishment of a free-trade accord. Although negotiations between the Community and Mercosur were subsequently delayed, bilateral agreements between the countries of the two groupings were extended. A preferential tariff agreement was concluded between Brazil and the Community in July 1999; the accord entered into effect, for a period of two years, in August. In August 2000 a preferential tariff agreement concluded with Argentina entered into force. The Community commenced negotiations on drafting a preferential tariff agreement with (jointly) El Salvador, Guatemala and Honduras in March of that year. In September leaders of the Community and Mercosur, meeting at a summit of Latin American heads of state, determined to relaunch negotiations, with a view to establishing a free-trade area by 1 January 2002. In July 2001 ministers of foreign affairs of the two groupings approved the establishment of a formal mechanism for political dialogue and co-ordination in order to facilitate negotiations and to enhance economic and social integration. At the special presidential summit in January 2002, heads of state reiterated their intention to establish the free-trade area by June of that year.

In March 1998 ministers of trade from 34 countries, meeting in San José, Costa Rica, concluded an agreement on the structure of negotiations for the establishment of a Free Trade Area of the Americas (FTAA). The process was formally initiated by heads of state, meeting in Santiago, Chile, in the following month. The Community negotiated as a bloc to obtain chairmanship of three of the nine negotiating groups: on market access (Colombia), on competition policy (Peru), and on intellectual property (Venezuela). The Community insisted that the final declaration issued by the meeting include recognition that the varying levels of development of the participating countries should be taken into consideration throughout the negotiating process.

In August 1999 the Secretary-General of the Community visited Guyana in order to promote bilateral trading opportunities and to strengthen relations with the Caribbean Community. The Community held a meeting on trade relations with the Caribbean Community during 2000.

INDUSTRY

Negotiations began in 1970 for the formulation of joint industrial programmes, particularly in the petrochemicals, metal-working and motor vehicle sectors, but disagreements over the allocation of different plants, and the choice of foreign manufacturers for co-operation, prevented progress and by 1984 the more ambitious schemes had been abandoned. Instead, emphasis was to be placed on assisting small and medium-sized industries, particularly in the agro-industrial and electronics sectors, in co-operation with national industrial organizations.

An Andean Agricultural Development Programme was formulated in 1976 within which 22 resolutions aimed at integrating the Andean agricultural sector were approved. In 1984 the Andean Food Security System was created to develop the agrarian sector, replace imports progressively with local produce, and improve rural living conditions. In April 1998 the Presidential Council instructed the Commission, together with ministers of agriculture, to formulate an Andean Common Agricultural Policy, including measures to harmonize trade policy instruments and legislation on animal and plant health. The 12th Andean presidential summit, held in June 2000, authorized the adoption of the concluded Policy and the enforcement of a plan of action for its implementation. In January 2002, at the special Andean presidential summit, it was agreed that all countries in the bloc would adopt price stabilization mechanisms for agricultural products.

In May 1987 member countries signed the Quito Protocol, modifying the Cartagena Agreement, to amend the strict rules that had formerly been imposed on foreign investors in the region. The Protocol entered into force in May 1988. Accordingly, each government was to decide which sectors were to be closed to foreign participation, and the period within which foreign investors must transfer a majority shareholding to local investors was extended to 30 years (37 years in Bolivia and Ecuador). In March 1991 the Protocol was amended, with the aim of further liberalizing foreign investment and stimulating an inflow of foreign capital and technology. External and regional investors were to be permitted to repatriate their profits (in accordance with the laws of the country concerned) and there was no stipulation that a majority share-holding must eventually be transferred to local investors. A further directive, adopted in March, covered the formation of 'Empresas Multinacionales Andinas' (multinational enterprises) in order to ensure that at least two member countries have a shareholding of 15% or more of the capital, including the country where the enterprise was to be based. These enterprises were entitled to participate in sectors otherwise reserved for national enterprises, subject to the same conditions as national enterprises in terms of taxation and export regulations, and to gain access to the markets of all member countries.

In November 1988 member states established a bank, the Banco Intermunicipal Andino, which was to finance public works.

In May 1995 the Group initiated a programme to promote the use of cheap and efficient energy sources and greater co-operation in the energy sector. The programme planned to develop a regional electricity grid.

In September 1999 Colombia, Ecuador and Venezuela signed an accord to facilitate the production and sale of vehicles within the region. The agreement became effective in January 2000, with a duration of 10 years.

TRANSPORT AND COMMUNICATIONS

The Andean Community has pursued efforts to improve infrastructure throughout the region. In 1983 the Commission formulated a plan to assist land-locked Bolivia, particularly through improving roads connecting it with neighbouring countries and the Pacific Ocean. An 'open skies' agreement, giving airlines of member states equal rights to airspace and airport facilities within the grouping, was signed in May 1991. In June 1998 the Commission approved the establishment of an Andean Commission of Land Transportation Authorities, which was to oversee the operation and development of land transportation services. Similarly, an Andean Committee of Water Transportation Authorities has been established to ensure compliance with Community regulations regarding ocean transportation activities. The Community aims to facilitate the movement of goods throughout the region by the use of different modes of transport ('multimodal transport') and to guarantee operational standards. It also intends to harmonize Community transport regulations and standards with those of Mercosur countries.

In August 1996 a regulatory framework was approved for the development of a commercial Andean satellite system. In December 1997 the General Secretariat approved regulations for granting authorization for the use of the system; the Commission subsequently granted the first Community authorization to an Andean multinational enterprise (Andesat), comprising 48 companies from all five member states. The system was expected to be fully operational from mid-2002. In 1994 the Community initiated efforts to establish digital technology infrastructure throughout the Community: the resulting Andean Digital Corridor comprises ground, underwater and satellite routes providing a series of cross-border interconnections between the member countries. The Andean Internet System, which aims to provide internet protocol-based services throughout the Community, was operational in Colombia, Ecuador and Venezuela in 2000, and was due to be extended to all five member countries. In May 1999 the Andean Committee of Telecommunications Authorities agreed to remove all restrictions to free trade in telecommunications services (excluding sound broadcasting and television) by 1 January 2002. The Committee also determined to formulate provisions on interconnection and the safeguarding of free competition and principles of transparency within the sector.

Asociación de Empresas de Telecomunicaciones de la Comunidad Andina—ASETA: Calle La Pradera 510 y San Salvador, Casilla 17-1106042, Quito, Ecuador; tel. (2) 563-812; fax (2) 562-499; e-mail info@aseta.org; internet www.aseta.org; f. 1974; co-ordinates improvements in national telecommunications services, in order to contribute to the further integration of the countries of the Andean Community. Sec.-Gen. MARCELO LÓPEZ ARJONA.

SOCIAL INTEGRATION

Several formal agreements and institutions have been established within the framework of the grouping to enhance social development and welfare (see below). The Community aims to incorporate these bodies into the process of enhanced integration and to promote greater involvement of representatives of civil society. In May 1999 the 11th Andean presidential summit adopted a 'multidimensional social agenda' focusing on job creation and on improvements in the fields of education, health and housing throughout the Community. In June 2000 the 12th presidential summit instructed the Andean institutions to prepare individual programmes aimed at consolidating implementation of the Community's integration programme and advancing the development of the social agenda. At a special presidential summit in January 2002, corresponding ministers were directed to meet during the first half of the year to develop a Community strategy to complement national efforts in this area. The heads of state also accepted an invitation by Peruvian President Alejandro Toledo to convene a conference of Community ministers of defence and of foreign affairs in Peru, in April, to consider a proposal to reduce defence expenditures, in order to assign more resources to poverty-reduction initiatives.

INSTITUTIONS

Consejo Consultivo Empresarial Andino (Andean Business Advisory Council): Paseo de la República 3895, Lima, Peru; tel. (1) 4111400; fax (1) 2213329; e-mail rsuarez@comunidadandina.org; first meeting held in November 1998; an advisory institution within the framework of the Sistema Andino de Integración; comprises elected representatives of business organizations; advises Community ministers and officials on integration activities affecting the business sector.

Consejo Consultivo Laboral Andino (Andean Labour Advisory Council): Central Obrera Boliviana, Calle Pisagua 618, La Paz, Bolivia; tel. & fax (2) 28-0420; an advisory institution within the framework of the Sistema Andino de Integración; comprises elected representatives of labour organizations; advises Community ministers and officers on related labour issues.

Convenio Andrés Bello (Andrés Bello Agreement): Paralela Autopista Norte, Avda 13 85–60, Santafé de Bogotá, Colombia; tel. (1) 6301639; fax (1) 6100139; e-mail ecobello@col1.telecom.com.co; internet www.cab.int.co; f. 1970, modified in 1990; aims to promote integration in the educational, technical and cultural sectors. Mems: Bolivia, Chile, Colombia, Cuba, Ecuador, Panama, Peru, Spain, Venezuela.

Convenio Hipólito Unanue (Hipólito Unanue Agreement): Edif. Cartagena, Paseo de la República 3832, 3°, Lima, Peru; tel. (1) 4226862; fax (1) 4409285; e-mail postmaster@conhu.org.pe; internet www.conhu.org.pe; f. 1971 on the occasion of the first meeting of Andean ministers of health; aims to enhance the development of health services, and to promote regional co-ordination in areas such as environmental health, disaster preparedness and the prevention and control of drug abuse.

Convenio Simón Rodríguez (Simón Rodríguez Agreement): Paseo de la República 3895, esq. Aramburú, San Isidro, Lima 27, Peru; tel. (1) 4111400; fax (1) 2213329; promotes a convergence of social and labour conditions throughout the Community, for example, working hours and conditions, employment and social security policies, and to promote the participation of workers and employers in the sub-regional integration process.

Corporación Andina de Fomento—CAF (Andean Development Corporation): Torre CAF, Avda Luis Roche, Altamira, Apdo 5086, Caracas, Venezuela; tel. (2) 2092111; fax (2) 28457544; e-mail sede@caf.com; internet www.caf.com; f. 1968, began operations in 1970; aims to encourage the integration of the Andean countries by specialization and an equitable distribution of investments. It conducts research to identify investment opportunities, and prepares the resulting investment projects; gives technical and financial assistance; and attracts internal and external credit. Auth. cap. US $3,000m., subscribed or underwritten by the governments of member countries, or by public, semi-public and private-sector institutions authorized by those governments. The Board of Directors comprises representatives of each country at ministerial level. Mems: the Andean Community, Argentina, Brazil, Chile, Jamaica, Mexico, Panama, Paraguay, Spain, Trinidad and Tobago, and 22 private banks in the Andean region. Exec. Pres. ENRIQUE GARCÍA RODRÍGUEZ (Bolivia).

Fondo Latinoamericano de Reservas—FLAR (Latin American Reserve Fund): Edif. Banco de Occidente, Carrera 13, No. 27–47, 10°, Santafé de Bogotá, Colombia; tel. (1) 2858511; fax (1) 2881117; e-mail agamarra@bloomberg.net; internet www.flar.net; f. 1978 as the Fondo Andino de Reservas to support the balance of payments of member countries, provide credit, guarantee loans, and contribute to the harmonization of monetary and financial policies; adopted present name in 1991, in order to allow the admission of other Latin American countries. In 1992 the Fund began extending credit lines to commercial for export financing. It is administered by an Assembly of the ministers of finance and economy of the member countries, and a Board of Directors comprising the Presidents of the central banks of the member states. In October 1995 it was agreed to expand the Fund's capital from US $800m. to $1,000m.; the increase became effective on 30 June 1997. Exec. Pres. ROBERTO GUARNIERI (Venezuela); Sec.-Gen. BORIS HERNÁNDEZ (Colombia).

Universidad Andina Simón Bolívar (Simón Bolívar Andean University): Calle Real Audiencia 73, Casilla 608-33, Sucre, Bolivia; tel. (64) 60265; fax (64) 60833; e-mail uasb@uasb.edu.bo; internet www.uasb.edu.bo; f. 1985; institution for post-graduate study and research; promotes co-operation between other universities in the Andean region; branches in Quito (Ecuador), La Paz (Bolivia), Caracas (Venezuela) and Cali (Colombia). Pres. JULIO GARRET AILLON.

Publications

Gaceta Oficial del Acuerdo de Cartagena.

Trade and Investment Guide.

Reports, working papers.

ARAB FUND FOR ECONOMIC AND SOCIAL DEVELOPMENT—AFESD

Address: POB 21923, Safat, 13080 Kuwait.

Telephone: 4844500; **fax:** 4815760; **e-mail:** hq@arabfund.org; **internet:** www.arabfund.org.

Established in 1968 by the Economic Council of the Arab League, the Fund began its operations in 1974. It participates in the financing of economic and social development projects in the Arab states.

MEMBERSHIP

Twenty-one members (see table of subscriptions below).

Organization

(April 2002)

BOARD OF GOVERNORS

The Board of Governors consists of a Governor and an Alternate Governor appointed by each member of the Fund. The Board of Governors is considered as the General Assembly of the Fund, and has all powers.

BOARD OF DIRECTORS

The Board of Directors is composed of eight Directors elected by the Board of Governors from among Arab citizens of recognized experience and competence. They are elected for a renewable term of two years.

The Board of Directors is charged with all the activities of the Fund and exercises the powers delegated to it by the Board of Governors.

Director-General and Chairman of the Board of Directors: ABDLATIF YOUSUF AL-HAMAD.

FINANCIAL STRUCTURE

In 1982 the authorized capital was increased from 400m. Kuwaiti dinars (KD) to KD 800m., divided into 80,000 shares having a value of KD 10,000 each. At the end of 2000 paid-up capital was KD 663.04m.

SUBSCRIPTIONS (KD million, December 2000)*

Algeria	64.78	Oman	17.28
Bahrain	2.16	Palestine	1.10
Djibouti	0.02	Qatar	6.75
Egypt	40.50	Saudi Arabia	159.07
Iraq	31.76	Somalia	0.21
Jordan	17.30	Sudan	11.06
Kuwait	169.70	Syria	24.00
Lebanon	2.00	Tunisia	6.16
Libya	59.85	United Arab Emirates	28.00
Mauritania	0.82	Yemen	4.52
Morocco	16.00		
		Total	663.04

* 100 Kuwaiti dinars = US $327.4 (December 2000).

LOANS BY MEMBER, 2000

Member	Project	Amount (KD million)
Algeria	Modernization of electric grid	30.0
	Development of social housing in the Central Region	35.0
Djibouti	Modernization of the port of Djibouti (phase IV)	3.0
	Social housing	5.0
Egypt	Rehabilitation and upgrading of locomotives and workshops of the Egyptian National Railroads Authority	16.0
Jordan	Al-Wehda dam	35.0
Lebanon	Interconnection of the Lebanese and Syrian electric grids	8.0
Libya	Development credit	25.0
Morocco	Afourer pumped storage hydro-electric plant	25.0
Oman	Rimal Ash-Sharqiya water distribution system	9.5
	Messerrat water conveyance system	11.0
Sudan	Highway improvements	23.0
	Rossaires dam	12.0
Tunisia	Development of industrial parks	14.0
	El-Kebir and El-Maoula dams	28.0
Total		279.5

Activities

Pursuant to the Agreement Establishing the Fund (as amended in 1997 by the Board of Governors), the purpose of the Fund is to contribute to the financing of economic and social development projects in the Arab states and countries by:

1. Financing economic development projects of an investment character by means of loans granted on concessionary terms to governments and public enterprises and corporations, giving preference to projects which are vital to the Arab entity, as well as to joint Arab projects.

2. Financing private sector projects in member states by providing all forms of loans and guarantees to corporations and enterprises (possessing juridical personality), participating in their equity capital, and providing other forms of financing and the requisite financial, technical and advisory services, in accordance with such regulations and subject to such conditions as may be prescribed by the Board of Directors.

3. Forming or participating in the equity capital of corporations possessing juridical personality, for the implementation and financing of private sector projects in member states, including the provision and financing of technical, advisory and financial services.

4. Establishing and administering special funds with aims compatible with those of the Fund and with resources provided by the Fund or other sources.

5. Encouraging, directly or indirectly, the investment of public and private capital in a manner conducive to the development and growth of the Arab economy.

6. Providing expertise and technical assistance in the various fields of economic development.

The Fund co-operates with other Arab organizations such as the Arab Monetary Fund, the League of Arab States and OAPEC

LOANS BY SECTOR, 2000

Sector	Amount (KD million)	%
Agriculture and rural development	75.0	26.8
Energy and electricity	63.0	22.6
Industry and mining	39.0	14.0
Transport and telecommunications	42.0	15.0
Water and sewerage	20.5	7.3
Other	40.0	14.3
Total	279.5	100.0

in preparing regional studies and conferences, for example in the areas of human resource development, demographic research and private sector financing of infrastructure projects. It also acts as the secretariat of the Co-ordination Group of Arab National and Regional Development Institutions. These organizations also work together to produce a *Unified Arab Economic Report*, which considers economic and social developments in the Arab states.

During 2000 the Fund approved 15 loans, totalling KD 279.5m., for projects in 10 member countries. At the end of that year total lending since 1974 amounted to KD 3,573.7m., which helped to finance 333 projects in 17 Arab countries.

The total number of technical assistance grants provided by the end of 2000 was 650, with a value of KD 84.1m. During 2000 the Fund extended 41 new grants, totalling KD 13.0m., of which 46% was to support institution building and reconstruction in south Lebanon and Palestinian controlled areas, 34% for other institutional support and training, 10% for general studies, research, seminars and conferences, and 10% for feasibility studies and project preparation.

In December 1997 AFESD initiated an Arab Fund Fellowships Programme, which aimed to provide grants to Arab academics to conduct university teaching or advanced research.

ARAB MONETARY FUND

Address: Arab Monetary Fund Bldg, Corniche Rd, POB 2818, Abu Dhabi, United Arab Emirates.

Telephone: (2) 215000; **fax:** (2) 326454; **e-mail:** centralmail@amfad.org.ae; **internet:** www.amf.org.ae.

The Agreement establishing the Arab Monetary Fund was approved by the Economic Council of Arab States in Rabat, Morocco, in April 1976 and entered into force on 2 February 1977.

MEMBERS

Algeria	Oman
Bahrain	Palestine
Djibouti	Qatar
Egypt	Saudi Arabia
Iraq*	Somalia*
Jordan	Sudan*
Kuwait	Syria
Lebanon	Tunisia
Libya	United Arab Emirates
Mauritania	Yemen
Morocco	

* From July 1993 loans to Iraq, Somalia and Sudan were suspended as a result of their failure to repay debts to the Fund totalling US $603m. By the end of 1998 the arrears amounted to AAD 197.3m. (or some $833.4m.). Sudan was readmitted in April 2000, having settled arrears of $214m.

Organization

(April 2002)

BOARD OF GOVERNORS

The Board of Governors is the highest authority of the Arab Monetary Fund. It formulates policies on Arab economic integration and liberalization of trade among member states. With certain exceptions, it may delegate to the Board of Executive Directors some of its powers. The Board of Governors is composed of a governor and a deputy governor appointed by each member state for a term of five years. It meets at least once a year; meetings may also be convened at the request of half the members, or of members holding half of the total voting power.

BOARD OF EXECUTIVE DIRECTORS

The Board of Executive Directors exercises all powers vested in it by the Board of Governors and may delegate to the Director-General such powers as it deems fit. It is composed of the Director-General and eight non-resident directors elected by the Board of Governors. Each director holds office for three years and may be re-elected.

DIRECTOR-GENERAL

The Director-General of the Fund is appointed by the Board of Governors for a renewable five-year term, and serves as Chairman of the Board of Executive Directors.

The Director-General supervises a Committee on Loans and a Committee on Investments to make recommendations on loan and investment policies to the Board of Executive Directors, and is required to submit an Annual Report to the Board of Governors.

Director-General and Chairman of the Board of Executive Directors: Dr JASSIM ABDULLAH AL-MANNAI.

FINANCE

The Arab Accounting Dinar (AAD) is a unit of account equivalent to three IMF Special Drawing Rights. (The average value of the SDR in 2000 was US $1.27304.)

Each member paid, in convertible currencies, 5% of the value of its shares at the time of its ratification of the Agreement and another 20% when the Agreement entered into force. In addition, each member paid 2% of the value of its shares in its national currency regardless of whether it is convertible. The second 25% of the capital was to be subscribed by the end of September 1979, bringing the total paid-up capital in convertible currencies to AAD 131.5m. An increase in requests for loans led to a resolution by the Board of Governors in April 1981, giving members the option of paying the balance of their subscribed capital. This payment became obligatory in July 1981, when total approved loans exceeded 50% of the already paid-up capital in convertible currencies. In April 1983 the authorized capital of the Fund was increased from AAD 288m. to AAD 600m. The new capital stock comprised 12,000 shares, each having the value of AAD 50,000. At the end of 2000 total paid-up capital was AAD 324.1m.

CAPITAL SUBSCRIPTIONS
(million Arab Accounting Dinars, 31 December 2000)

Member	Paid-up capital
Algeria	42.40
Bahrain	5.00
Djibouti	0.25
Egypt	32.00
Iraq	42.40
Jordan	5.40
Kuwait	32.00
Lebanon	5.00
Libya	13.44
Mauritania	5.00
Morocco	15.00
Oman	5.00
Palestine	2.16
Qatar	10.00
Saudi Arabia	48.40
Somalia	4.00
Sudan	10.00
Syria	7.20
Tunisia	7.00
United Arab Emirates	19.20
Yemen	15.40
Total	324.09*

* Excluding Palestine's share, which was deferred by a Board of Governors' resolution in 1978.

Activities

The creation of the Arab Monetary Fund was seen as a step towards the goal of Arab economic integration. It assists member states in balance of payments difficulties, and also has a broad range of aims.

The Articles of Agreement define the Fund's aims as follows:

(*a*) to correct disequilibria in the balance of payments of member states;

(*b*) to promote the stability of exchange rates among Arab currencies, to render them mutually convertible, and to eliminate restrictions on current payments between member states;

(*c*) to establish policies and modes of monetary co-operation to accelerate Arab economic integration and economic development in the member states;

(*d*) to tender advice on the investment of member states' financial resources in foreign markets, whenever called upon to do so;

(*e*) to promote the development of Arab financial markets;

(*f*) to promote the use of the Arab dinar as a unit of account and to pave the way for the creation of a unified Arab currency;

(*g*) to co-ordinate the positions of member states in dealing with international monetary and economic problems; and (*h*) to provide a mechanism for the settlement of current payments between member states in order to promote trade among them.

The Arab Monetary Fund functions both as a fund and a bank. It is empowered:

(*a*) to provide short- and medium-term loans to finance balance of payments deficits of member states;

(*b*) to issue guarantees to member states to strengthen their borrowing capabilities;

(*c*) to act as intermediary in the issuance of loans in Arab and international markets for the account of member states and under their guarantees;

(*d*) to co-ordinate the monetary policies of member states;

(*e*) to manage any funds placed under its charge by member states;

(*f*) to hold periodic consultations with member states on their economic conditions; and

(*g*) to provide technical assistance to banking and monetary institutions in member states.

Loans are intended to finance an overall balance of payments deficit and a member may draw up to 75% of its paid-up subscription, in convertible currencies, for this purpose unconditionally (automatic loans). A member may, however, obtain loans in excess of this limit, subject to agreement with the Fund on a programme aimed at reducing its balance of payments deficit (ordinary and extended loans, equivalent to 175% and 250% of its quota respectively). From 1981 a country receiving no extended loans was entitled to a loan under the Inter-Arab Trade Facility (discontinued in 1989) of up to 100% of its quota. In addition, a member has the right to borrow up to 50% of its paid-up capital in order to cope with an unexpected deficit in its balance of payments resulting from a decrease in its exports of goods and services or a large increase in its imports of agricultural products following a poor harvest (compensatory loans).

Automatic and compensatory loans are repayable within three years, while ordinary and extended loans are repayable within

LOANS APPROVED, 1978–2000

Type of loan	Number of loans	Amount (AAD '000)
Automatic	55	266,625
Ordinary	11	104,566
Compensatory	12	79,885
Extended	19	223,451
Structural Adjustment Facility	7	88,332
Inter-Arab Trade Facility (cancelled in 1989)	11	64,730
Total	115	827,589

five and seven years respectively. Loans are granted at concessionary and uniform rates of interest which increase with the length of the period of the loan. In 1988 the Fund's executive directors agreed to modify their policy on lending, placing an emphasis on the correction of economic imbalances in recipient countries. In 1996 the Fund established the Structural Adjustment Facility, providing up to 75% of a member's paid-up subscription. This may include a technical assistance component comprising a grant of up to 2% of the total loan.

Over the period 1978–2000 the Fund extended 115 loans amounting to AAD 827.6m. During 2000 the Fund approved

LOANS APPROVED, 2000

Borrower	Type of loan	Amount (AAD million)
Djibouti	Extended	0.245
Egypt	Structural Adjustment Facility	23.152
Lebanon	Structural Adjustment Facility	3.602
Mauritania	Extended	4.000
Morocco	Compensatory	7.400
Total		38.399

five loans, amounting to AAD 38.4m., while loan disbursements amounted to AAD 47.2m.

The Fund's technical assistance activities are extended through either the provision of experts to the country concerned or in the form of specialized training of officials of member countries. In view of the increased importance of this type of assistance, the Fund established, in 1988, the Economic Policy Institute (EPI) which offers regular training courses and specialized seminars for middle-level and senior staff, respectively, of financial and monetary institutions of the Arab countries. On 1 April 1999 the Fund signed a memorandum of understanding with the International Monetary Fund to establish a joint regional training programme. During 2000 eight training courses and one workshop were organized by the EPI under this joint programme.

TRADE PROMOTION

Arab Trade Financing Program—ATFP: POB 26799, Arab Monetary Fund Bldg, 7th Floor, Corniche Rd, Abu Dhabi, United Arab Emirates; tel. (2) 6316999; fax (2) 6316793; e-mail atfphq@atfp.org.ae; internet www.atfp.org.ae; f. 1989 to develop and promote trade between Arab countries and to enhance the competitive ability of Arab exporters; operates by extending lines of credit to Arab exporters and importers through national agencies (some 121 agencies designated by the monetary authorities of 18 Arab countries at early 2001). The Arab Monetary Fund provided 50% of ATFP's authorized capital of US $500m.; participation was also invited from private and official Arab financial institutions and joint Arab/foreign institutions. ATFP administers the Inter-Arab Trade Information Network (IATIN), and organizes Buyers-Sellers meetings to promote Arab goods. Chair. and Chief Exec. Dr JASSIM ABDULLAH AL-MANNAI. Publs *Annual Report* (Arabic and English), *IATIN Quarterly Bulletin* (Arabic).

Publications

Annual Report.

AMDB Bulletin (quarterly).

Arab Countries: Economic Indicators (annually).

Balance of Payments and External Public Debt of Arab Countries (annually).

Foreign Trade of Arab Countries (annually).

Joint Arab Economic Report (annually).

Money and Credit in Arab Countries.

National Accounts of Arab Countries (annually).

Reports on commodity structure (by value and quantity) of member countries' imports from and exports to other Arab countries; other studies on economic, social, management and fiscal issues.

ASIA-PACIFIC ECONOMIC CO-OPERATION—APEC

Address: 438 Alexandra Rd, 14th Floor, Alexandra Point, Singapore 119958.

Telephone: 62761880; **fax:** 62761775; **e-mail:** info@mail.apecsec.org.sg; **internet:** www.apecsec.org.sg.

Asia-Pacific Economic Co-operation (APEC) was initiated in November 1989, in Canberra, Australia, as an informal consultative forum. Its aim is to promote multilateral economic co-operation on issues of trade and investment.

MEMBERS

Australia	Japan	Philippines
Brunei	Korea, Republic	Russia
Canada	Malaysia	Singapore
Chile	Mexico	Taiwan*
China, People's Republic	New Zealand	Thailand
Hong Kong	Papua New Guinea	USA
Indonesia	Peru	Viet Nam

* Admitted as Chinese Taipei.

Organization

(April 2002)

ECONOMIC LEADERS' MEETINGS

The first meeting of APEC heads of government was convened in November 1993, in Seattle, USA. Subsequently, each annual meeting of APEC ministers of foreign affairs and of economic affairs has been followed by an informal gathering of the leaders of the APEC economies, at which the policy objectives of the grouping are discussed and defined. The 2001 meeting was held in mid-October in Shanghai, the People's Republic of China; the 10th Leaders' Meeting was scheduled to be held in Mexico, in October 2002.

MINISTERIAL MEETINGS

APEC ministers of foreign affairs and ministers of economic affairs meet annually. These meetings are hosted by the APEC Chair, which rotates each year, although it was agreed, in 1989, that alternate Ministerial Meetings were to be convened in an ASEAN member country. A Senior Officials' Meeting (SOM) convenes regularly between Ministerial Meetings to co-ordinate and administer the budgets and work programmes of APEC's committees and working groups. Other meetings of ministers are held on a regular basis to enhance co-operation in specific areas.

SECRETARIAT

In 1992 the Ministerial Meeting, held in Bangkok, Thailand, agreed to establish a permanent secretariat to support APEC activities, and approved an annual budget of US $2m. The Secretariat became operational in February 1993. The Executive Director is appointed from the member economy chairing the group and serves a one-year term. A Deputy Executive Director is appointed by the member economy designated to chair APEC in the following year.

Executive Director: ALEJANDRO DE LA PEÑA NAVARRETE (Mexico).

Deputy Executive Director: PIAMSAK MILINTACHINDA (Thailand).

COMMITTEES AND GROUPS

Budget and Management Committee—BMC: f. 1993 as Budget and Administrative Committee, present name adopted 1998; advises APEC senior officials on budgetary, administrative and managerial issues. The Committee reviews the operational budgets of APEC committees and groups, evaluates their effectiveness and conducts assessments of group projects.

Committee on Trade and Investment—CTI: f. 1993 on the basis of a Declaration signed by ministers meeting in Seattle, USA, in order to facilitate the expansion of trade and the development of a liberalized environment for investment among member countries. The CTI undertakes initiatives to improve the flow of goods, services and technology in the region. In May 1997 an APEC Tariff Database was inaugurated, with sponsorship from the private sector. A new Market Access Group was established in 1998 to administer CTI activities concerned with non-tariff measures. In 2001 the CTI finalized a set of non-binding Principles on Trade Facilitation. The development of the nine principles was intended to help eliminate procedural and administrative impediments to trade and to increase trading opportunities.

Economic Committee—EC: f. 1994 following an agreement, in November, to transform the existing *ad hoc* group on economic trends and issues into a formal committee. The Committee aims to enhance APEC's capacity to analyse economic trends and to research and report on issues affecting economic and technical co-operation in the region. In addition, the Committee is considering the environmental and development implications of expanding population and economic growth.

Sub-Committee on Economic and Technical Co-operation—ESC: f. 1998 to assist the SOM with the co-ordination of APEC's economic and technical co-operation programme (ECOTECH). The ESC monitors and evaluates project implementation and also supervises the work of the Group on Economic Infrastructure (GEI), which carries out projects designed to strengthen economic and technical co-operation in infrastructure. The ESC co-ordinated the development of APEC's Human-Capacity Building Strategy in 2001.

In addition, the following Working Groups promote and co-ordinate practical co-operation between member countries in different activities: Agricultural technical co-operation; Energy; Fisheries; Human resources development; Industrial science and technology; Marine resource conservation; Small and medium enterprises (SMEs); Telecommunications and Information; Tourism; Trade promotion; and Transportation. (See below for more detailed information.)

ADVISORY COUNCIL

APEC Business Advisory Council—ABAC: Equitable Card Center Bldg, 8th Floor, 203 Salcedo St, Legaspi Village, Makati City 1229, Philippines; tel. (2) 8436001; fax (2) 8454832; e-mail abacsec@pfgc.ph; internet www.abaconline.org; an agreement to establish ABAC, comprising up to three senior representatives of the private sector from each APEC member economy, was concluded at the Ministerial Meeting held in November 1995. ABAC was mandated to advise member states on the implementation of APEC's Action Agenda and on other business matters, and to provide business-related information to APEC fora. ABAC meets three or four times each year and holds a dialogue with APEC economic leaders prior to their annual informal meeting. ABAC's first meeting, convened in June 1996 in Manila, the Philippines, resolved to accelerate the liberalization of regional trade. In 1998 ABAC focused on measures to alleviate the effects of the financial crisis in Asia, in particular, by enhancing confidence in the private sector, as well as efforts to support SMEs, to develop electronic commerce in the region and to advise on APEC Individual Action Plans (IAPs, see below). In 2000 ABAC addressed the relevance of APEC to the challenges of globalization and, in its annual report to APEC leaders, issued several recommendations, including support for a new round of multilateral trade negotiations; enhancement of the IAP process, with increased implementation of electronic IAPs (e-IAPS); implementation of a proposed food system for member states; the establishment of an APEC Institute of Directors Forum; and the adoption of a regulatory framework conducive to the development of e-commerce. In 2001 ABAC concentrated on the challenges posed by globalization; the impact on APEC members of the global economic slowdown; and capacity-building in financial systems. ABAC's declared theme for 2002 is Sharing Development to Reinforce Global Security. At a meeting in February 2002 the Council considered the relationship between global security and its work to facilitate trade and investment flows. Chair. JAVIER PRIETO DE LA FUENTE (Mexico).

Activities

APEC was initiated in 1989 as a forum for informal discussion between the then six ASEAN members and their six dialogue partners in the Pacific, and, in particular, to promote trade liberalization in the Uruguay Round of negotiations, which were being conducted under the General Agreement on Tariffs and Trade (GATT). The Seoul Declaration, adopted by ministers meeting in the Republic of Korea in November 1991, defined the objectives of APEC (see below).

ASEAN countries were initially reluctant to support any more formal structure of the forum, or to admit new members, owing to concerns that it would undermine ASEAN's standing as a regional grouping and be dominated by powerful non-ASEAN economies. In August 1991 it was agreed to extend membership to the People's Republic of China, Hong Kong and Taiwan (subject to conditions imposed by the People's Republic of China, including that a Taiwanese official of no higher than vice-ministerial level should attend the annual meeting of ministers of foreign affairs). Mexico and Papua New Guinea acceded to the organization in November 1993, and Chile joined in November 1994. The summit meeting held in November 1997 agreed that Peru, Russia and Viet Nam should be admitted to APEC at the 1998 meeting, but imposed a 10-year moratorium on further expansion of the grouping.

In September 1992 APEC ministers agreed to establish a permanent secretariat. In addition, the meeting created an 11-member non-governmental Eminent Persons Group (EPG), which was to assess trade patterns within the region and propose measures to promote co-operation. At the Ministerial Meeting in Seattle, USA, in November 1993, members agreed on a framework for expanding trade and investment among member countries, and to establish a permanent committee (the CTI, see above) to pursue these objectives.

In August 1994 the EPG proposed the following timetable for the liberalization of all trade across the Asia-Pacific region: negotiations for the elimination of trade barriers were to commence in 2000 and be completed within 10 years in developed countries, 15 years in newly-industrialized economies and by 2020 in developing countries. Trade concessions could then be extended on a reciprocal basis to non-members in order to encourage world-wide trade liberalization, rather than isolate APEC as a unique trading bloc. In November 1994 the meeting of APEC heads of government adopted the Bogor Declaration of Common Resolve, which endorsed the EPG's timetable for free and open trade and investment in the region by the year 2020. Other issues incorporated into the Declaration included the implementation of GATT commitments in full and strengthening the multilateral trading system through the forthcoming establishment of the World Trade Organization (WTO), intensifying development co-operation in the Asia-Pacific region and expanding and accelerating trade and investment programmes.

During 1995 meetings of APEC officials and other efforts to substantiate the trade liberalization agreement revealed certain differences among members regarding the timetable and means of implementing the measures, which were to be agreed upon at the 1995 Economic Leaders' Meeting. The principal concern, expressed notably by the USA, focused on whether tariff reductions were to be achieved by individual trade liberalization plans or based on some reciprocal or common approach. In August the EPG issued a report, to be considered at the November Leaders' Meeting, which advocated acceleration of tariff reductions and other trade liberalization measures agreed under GATT; the establishment of a dispute mediation service to reduce and settle regional trade conflicts; and a review of new trade groupings within the APEC region. Further proposals for the implementation of the Bogor Declaration objectives were presented, in September, by the Pacific Business Forum, comprising APEC business representatives. The recommendations included harmonization of product quality, the establishment of one-stop investment agencies in each APEC country, training and technology transfers and the implementation of visa-free business travel by 1999. In November 1995 the Ministerial Meeting decided to dismantle the EPG, and to establish an APEC Business Advisory Council (ABAC), consisting of private-sector representatives.

In November 1995 APEC heads of government, meeting in Osaka, Japan, adopted an Action Agenda as a framework to achieve the commitments of the Bogor Declaration. Part One of the Agenda identified action areas for the liberalization of trade and investment and the facilitation of business, for example, customs procedures, rules of origin and non-tariff barriers. It incorporated agreements that the process was to be comprehensive, consistent with WTO commitments, comparable among all APEC economies and non-discriminatory. Each member economy was to ensure the transparency of its laws, regulations and procedures affecting the flow of goods, services and capital among APEC economies and to refrain from implementing any trade protection measures. A second part of the Agenda was to provide a framework for further economic and technical co-operation between APEC members in areas such as energy, transport, infrastructure, SMEs and agricultural technology. In order to resolve a disagreement concerning the inclusion of agricultural products in the trade liberalization process, a provision for flexibility was incorporated into the Agenda, taking into account diverse circumstances and different levels of development in APEC member economies. Liberalization measures were to be implemented from January 1997 (i.e. three years earlier than previously agreed) and were to be subject to annual reviews. A Trade and Investment Liberalization and Facilitation Special Account was established to finance projects in support of the implementation of the Osaka Action Agenda. In May 1996 APEC senior officials met in Cebu, the Philippines, to review Individual Action Plans—IAPs, annual reports submitted by each member state on progress in the implementation of trade liberalization measures—and to achieve some coherent approach to tariff liberalization prior to the Leaders' Meeting in November.

In November 1996 the Economic Leaders' Meeting, held in Subic Bay, the Philippines, approved the Manila Action Plan for APEC (MAPA), which had been formulated at the preceding Ministerial Meeting, held in Manila. MAPA incorporated the IAPs and other collective measures aimed at achieving the trade liberalization and co-operation objectives of the Bogor Declaration, as well as the joint activities specified in the second part of the Osaka Agenda. Heads of government also endorsed a US proposal to eliminate tariffs and other barriers to trade in information technology products by 2000 and determined to support efforts to conclude an agreement to this effect at the forthcoming WTO conference; however, they insisted on the provision of an element of flexibility in achieving trade liberalization in this sector.

The 1997 Economic Leaders' Meeting, held in Vancouver, Canada, in November, was dominated by concern at the financial instability that had affected several Asian economies during 1997. The final declaration of the summit meeting endorsed a framework of measures that had been agreed by APEC deputy ministers of finance and central bank governors at an emergency meeting convened in the previous week in Manila, the Philippines (the so-called Manila Framework for Enhanced Asian Regional Co-operation to Promote Financial Stability). The meeting, attended by representatives of the IMF, the World Bank and the Asian Development Bank, committed all member economies receiving IMF assistance to undertake specified economic and financial reforms, and supported the establishment of a separate Asian funding facility to supplement international financial assistance (although this was later rejected by the IMF). APEC ministers of finance and governors of central banks were urged to accelerate efforts for the development of the region's financial and capital markets and to liberalize capital flows in the region. Measures were to include strengthening financial market supervision and clearing and settlement infrastructure, the reform of pension systems, and promoting co-operation among export credit agencies and financing institutions. The principal item on the Vancouver summit agenda was an initiative to enhance trade liberalization, which, the grouping insisted, should not be undermined by the financial instability in Asia. The following 15 economic sectors were identified for 'early voluntary sectoral liberalization' ('EVSL'): environmental goods and services; fish and fish products; forest products; medical equipment and instruments; toys; energy; chemicals; gems and jewellery; telecommunications; oilseeds and oilseed products; food; natural and synthetic rubber; fertilizers; automobiles; and civil aircraft. The implementation of EVSL was to encompass market opening, trade facilitation, and economic and technical co-operation activities. The heads of government subsequently requested the authorities in each member state to formulate details of tariff reductions in these sectors by mid-1998, with a view to implementing the measures in 1999. (In June 1998, however, ministers of trade, meeting in Malaysia, failed to conclude an agreement on early tariff reductions, in part owing to Japan's reluctance to liberalize trade in fish and forest products.) In Vancouver APEC Economic Leaders also declared their support for an agreement to liberalize financial services (which was successfully negotiated under the auspices of the WTO in December 1997) and for the objective of reducing the emission of 'greenhouse gases', which was under consideration at a global conference, held in Kyoto, Japan, in December (resulting in the adoption of the Kyoto Protocol to the UN Framework Convention on Climate Change).

In May 1998 APEC finance ministers met in Canada to consider the ongoing financial and economic crisis in Asia and to review progress in implementing efforts to alleviate the difficulties experienced by several member economies. The ministers agreed to pursue activities in the following three priority areas: capital market development, capital account liberalization and strengthening financial systems (including corporate governance). The region's economic difficulties remained the principal topic of discussion at the Economic Leaders' Meeting held in Kuala Lumpur, Malaysia, in November. A final declaration reiterated their commitment to co-operation in pursuit of sustainable economic recovery and growth, in particular through the restructuring of financial and corporate sectors, promoting and facilitating private-sector capital flows, and efforts to strengthen the global financial system. The meeting endorsed a proposal of ABAC to establish a partnership for equitable growth, with the aim of enhancing business involvement in APEC's programme of economic and technical co-operation. Other initiatives approved included an Agenda of APEC Science and Technology Industry Co-operation into the 21st Century (for which the People's Republic of China announced it was to establish a special fund), and an Action Programme on Skills and Development in APEC. Japan's persisting opposition to a reduction of tariffs in the fish and forestry sectors again prevented the conclusion of tariff negotiations under the EVSL scheme, and it was therefore agreed that responsibility for managing the tariff reduction element of the initiative should be transferred to the WTO. The meeting was divided by political differences regarding human rights, and in particular, the treatment by the Malaysian authorities of the imprisoned former Deputy Prime Minister, Anwar Ibrahim. A declaration of support for the democratic reform movement in Malaysia by the US representative, Vice-President Gore, dominated discussions at the start of the summit meeting and provoked a formal complaint from the Malaysian Government.

In September 1999 political dialogue regarding the civil conflict in East Timor dominated the start of the annual meetings of the grouping, held in Auckland, New Zealand, although the issue remained separate from the official agenda. Ministers of foreign affairs, convened in emergency session, declared their support for the establishment of a multinational force, under UN auspices, to restore peace in the territory and determined to provide humanitarian and technical assistance to facilitate the process of reconstruction and rehabilitation. The Economic Leaders' Meeting considered measures to sustain the economic recovery in Asia and endorsed the APEC Principles to Enhance Competition and Regulatory Reform (for example, transparency, accountability, non-discrimination) as a framework to strengthen APEC markets and to enable further integration and implementation of the IAPs. The meeting endorsed a report prepared during the year by an *ad hoc* task force concerning an ABAC proposal for the development of an APEC food system. Also under discussion was the forthcoming round of multilateral trade negotiations, to be initiated by the WTO. The heads of government proposed the objective of completing a single package of trade agreements within three years and endorsed the abolition of export subsidies for agricultural products. The meeting determined to support the efforts of the People's Republic of China, Russia, Taiwan and Viet Nam to accede to WTO membership.

The Economic Leaders' Meeting for 2000, held in Brunei in November, noted the generally strong recovery from the Asian economic crisis of 1997–98 and reiterated support for APEC's goals. The heads of government urged that an agenda for the now-stalled round of multilateral trade negotiations should be formulated without further delay. The meeting endorsed a plan of action to promote the utilization of advances in information and communications technologies in member economies, for the benefit of all citizens. It adopted the aim of tripling the number of people in the region with access to the internet by 2005, and determined to co-operate with business and education sector interests to attract investment and expertise in the pursuit of this goal. A proposal that the Democratic People's Republic of Korea be permitted to participate in APEC working groups was approved at the meeting.

The 2001 Economic Leaders' Meeting, held in mid-October, in Shanghai, the People's Republic of China, condemned the terrorist attacks against targets in the USA of the previous month and resolved to take action to combat the threat of international terrorism. The heads of state declared terrorism to be a direct challenge to APEC's vision of free, open and prosperous economies, and concluded that the threat made the continuing move to free trade, with its aim of bolstering economies, increasing prosperity and encouraging integration, even more of a priority. The meeting stressed the importance of sharing the benefits of globalization. The leaders also expressed their determination to address the effects on APEC countries of the prevailing global economic downturn. They noted that the reforms carried out after the 1997–98 financial crisis had strengthened APEC economies, and advocated timely policy actions in the coming year to rebuild confidence and boost growth. Human capacity-building was a central theme. The heads of state committed support to the launch of the next round of WTO multilateral trade negotiations and applauded the recent successful conclusion of negotiations on WTO membership for the People's Republic of China. The meeting adopted the Shanghai Accord, which identified development goals for APEC during its second decade and clarified measures for achieving the Bogor goals within the agreed timetable. Among other initiatives, the Accord suggested broadening and updating the Osaka Action Agenda to reflect developments in the new economy. The meeting also outlined the e-APEC Strategy developed by the e-APEC Task Force established after the Brunei Economic Leaders' meeting. Considering issues of entrepreneurship, structural and regulatory reform, competition, intellectual property rights and information security, the strategy aimed to facilitate technological development in the region.

WORKING GROUPS

APEC's structure of working groups aims to promote practical and technical co-operation in specific areas, and to help implement individual and collective action plans in response to the directives of the Economic Leaders. APEC recognizes sustainable development as a key issue cross-cutting all forum activities. In 1997 APEC leaders declared their commitment to the integration of women into the mainstream of APEC activities.

Agricultural Technical Co-operation: Formally established as an APEC Expert's Group in 1996, and incorporated into the system of working groups in 2000. The group aims to enhance the role of agriculture in the economic growth of the region and to promote co-operation in the following areas: conservation and utilization of plant and animal genetic resources; research, development and extension of agricultural biotechnology; processing, marketing, distribution and consumption of agricultural products; plant and animal quarantine and pest management; development of an agricultural finance system; sustainable agriculture; and agricultural technology transfer and training. The group has primary responsibility for undertaking recommendations connected with the implementation of the proposed APEC food system. In 2001 the group conducted projects on human resource development in post-harvest technology and on capacity-building, safety assessment and communication in biotechnology.

Energy: Responsible for the development of the energy component of the 1995 Action Agenda. APEC ministers responsible for energy convened for the first time in 1996 to discuss major energy challenges confronting the region and to provide guidance for the working group. The group's main objectives were determined as: the enhancement of regional energy security and improvement of the fuel supply market for the power sector; the development and implementation of programmes of work promoting the adoption of environmentally sound energy technologies and promoting private-sector investment in regional power infrastructure; the development of energy efficiency guide-lines; and the standardization of testing facilities and results. In March 1999 the group resolved to establish a business network to improve relations and communications with the private sector. The first meeting of the network took place in April. In October 1998 APEC energy ministers, meeting in Okinawa, Japan, emphasized the role of the energy sector in stimulating economic activity and stressed the need to develop infrastructure, improve energy efficiency and accelerate the development of natural gas reserves. In May 2000 ministers meeting in San Diego, USA, launched the APEC 21st Century Renewable Energy Initiative, which aims to encourage co-operation in and advance the utilization of renewable energy technologies, envisaging the establishment of a Private Sector Renewable Energy Forum.

Fisheries: Aims to maximize the economic benefits and sustainability of fisheries resources for all APEC members. Recent concerns include food safety, the quality of fish products and resource management. In 1996 the group initiated a four-year study on trade and investment liberalization in the sector, in the areas of tariffs, non-tariff barriers and investment measures and subsidies. In 1997 the group organized two technical workshops on seafood inspection systems, and conducted a workshop addressing destructive fishing techniques. The first APEC Aquaculture Forum, which considered the sustainable development of aquaculture in the region and the development of new markets for APEC fish products, was held in Taipei, Taiwan, in June 1998. In May 1999 new guide-lines were adopted to encourage the participation of the private sector in the activities of the working group. The group's first business forum was convened in July 2000.

Human Resources Development: Comprises three networks promoting co-operation in different areas of human resources, training and education: the Capacity Building Network, with a focus on human capacity building, including management and technical skills development and corporate governance; the Education Network, promoting effective learning systems and supporting the role of education in advancing individual, social and economic development; and the Labour and Social Protection Network, concerned with promoting social integration through the strengthening of labour markets, the development of labour market information and policy, and improvements in working conditions and social safety net frameworks. The working group undertakes activities through these networks to implement ministerial and leaders' directives, as well as the 'Medium Term Strategic Priorities', which were formulated in January 1997. A voluntary network of APEC Study Centers links higher education and research institutions in member economies. In January 1998 the working group established a Task Force on the Human Resource and Social Impacts of the Financial Crisis. Private-sector participation in the working group has been strengthened by the establishment of a network of APEC senior executives responsible for human resources management. Recent activities have included programmes on information technology in the learning society; the implementation of standards and accreditation in supply chain management; and child labour.

Industrial Science and Technology: Aims to contribute to sustainable development in the region, improve the availability of information, enhance human resources development in the sector, improve the business climate, promote policy dialogue and review and facilitate networks and partnerships. Accordingly, the group has helped to establish an APEC Virtual Centre for Environmental Technology Exchange in Japan; a Science and Technology Industrial Parks Network; an International Molecular Biology Network for the APEC Region; an APEC Centre for Technology Foresight, based in Thailand; and the APEC Science and Technology Web, an online database. In 2001 the group worked on developing a Strategy to Combat HIV/AIDS and Other Infectious Diseases, as requested by the Economic Leaders' meeting in 2000. A dialogue on the subject was initiated with the World Health Organization.

Marine Resource Conservation: Promotes initiatives within APEC to protect the marine environment and its resources. In 1996 a five-year project was initiated for the management of red tide and harmful algal blooms in the APEC region. An APEC Action Plan for Sustainability of the Marine Environment was adopted by ministers responsible for the environment, meeting in June 1997. The Plan aimed to promote regional co-operation, an integrated approach to coastal management, the prevention, reduction and control of marine pollution, and sustainable development.. Efforts were also being undertaken to establish an Ocean Research Network of centres of excellence in the Pacific. In December 1997 the group organized a workshop, in Hong Kong, on the impact of destructive fishing practices on the marine environment. A workshop was held in Australia, in April 1998, on preventing maritime accidents and pollution in the Pacific region. In April 1999 the group organized a training course, held in Hong Kong, on the satellite remote sensing of algal blooms. Strategies to encourage private-sector participation in promoting the sustainable management of marine resources were endorsed by the group in June 2000. Four main themes were identified for the Action Plan in the 21st century: balancing coastal development and resource protection; ensuring sustainable fisheries and aquaculture; understanding and observing the oceans and seas; and promoting economic and technical co-operation in oceans management.

Small and Medium Enterprises: The group was established in 1995, as the Ad Hoc Policy Level Group on Small and Medium Enterprises, with a temporary mandate to oversee all APEC activities relating to SMEs. It supported the establishment of an APEC Centre for Technical Exchange and Training for Small and Medium Enterprises, which was inaugurated at Los Baños, near Manila, the Philippines, in September 1996. A five-year action plan for SMEs was endorsed in 1998. The group was resdesignated as a working group, with permanent status, in 2000. In 2000 and 2001 the group considered issues relating to globalization, innovation, human resource development, information technology and e-commerce, financing, and the forming of strategic alliances with other SMEs and larger firms.

Telecommunications and Information: Incorporates four steering groups concerned with different aspects of the development and liberalization of the sector—Liberalization; Business facilitation; Development co-operation; and Human resource development. Activities are guided by directives of ministers responsible for telecommunications, who first met in 1995, in the Republic of Korea, and adopted a Seoul Declaration on Asia Pacific Information Infrastructure (APII). The second ministerial meeting, held in Gold Coast, Australia, in September 1996, adopted more detailed proposals for liberalization of the sector in member economies. In June 1998 ministers, meeting in Singapore, agreed to remove technical barriers to trade in telecommunications equipment (although Chile and New Zealand declined to sign up to the arrangement). At their fourth meeting, convened in May 2000 in Cancún, Mexico, telecommunications ministers approved a programme of action that included measures to bridge the 'digital divide' between developed and developing member economies, and adopted the APEC Principles on International Charging Arrangements for Internet Services and the APEC Principles of Interconnection.

Tourism: Established in 1991, with the aim of promoting the long-term sustainability of the tourism industry, in both environmental and social terms. The group administers a Tourism Information Network and an APEC Centre for Sustainable Tourism. In 1998 the group initiated a project to assess the impact of the Asian financial crisis on regional tourism and to identify strategies to counter any negative effects. The first meeting of APEC ministers of tourism, held in the Republic of Korea in July 2000, adopted the Seoul Declaration on the APEC Tourism Charter. The group's work plan is based on four policy goals inherent in the Seoul Declaration, namely, the removal of impediments to tourism business and investment; increased mobility of visitors and increased demand for tourism goods and services; sustainable management of tourism; and enhanced recognition of tourism as a vehicle for economic and social development. At a meeting of the working group in April 2001, APEC and the Pacific Asia Travel Association (PATA) adopted a Code for Sustainable Tourism. The Code is designed for adoption and implementation by a variety of tourism companies and government agencies. It urges members to conserve the natural environment, ecosystems and biodiversity; respect local traditions and cultures; conserve energy; reduce pollution and waste; and ensure that regular environmental audits are carried out. In November 2001 the working group considered the impact on tourism of the September terrorist attacks on the USA. The group noted that while the short-term negative effects could be substantial, a return to the long-term growth path was expected in 2002. The group advocated work to improve the quality and timeliness of tourism data, to enable accurate assessment of the situation.

Trade Promotion: Aims to promote trade, as a key aspect of regional economic co-operation, through activities to enhance trade financing, skills and training, information and networking (for example, through the establishment of APEC Net, providing information to the business community via the internet, accessible at www.apecnet.org.sg), and co-operation with the private sector and public agencies, including trade promotion organizations. Organizes an APEC International Trade Fair, the fourth of which was held in Jakarta, Indonesia, in October 2000.

Transportation: Undertakes initiatives to enhance the efficiency and safety of the regional transportation system, in order to facilitate the development of trade. The working group focuses on three main areas: improving the competitiveness of the transportation industry; promoting a safe and environmentally-sound regional transportation system; and human resources development, including training, research and education. The group has published surveys, directories and manuals on all types of transportation systems, and has compiled an inventory on regional co-operation on oil spills preparedness and response arrangements. A Road Transportation Harmonization Project aims to provide the basis for common standards in the automotive industry in the Asia-Pacific region. The group has established an internet database on ports and the internet-based Virtual Centre for Transportation Research, Development and Education. It plans to develop a regional action plan on the implementation of Global Navigation Satellite Systems, in consultation with the relevant international bodies.

Publications

ABAC Report to APEC Leaders (annually).

APEC Economic Outlook (annually).

APEC Economies Beyond the Asian Crisis.

APEC Energy Handbook (annually).

APEC Energy Statistics (annually).

Foreign Direct Investment and APEC Economic Integration (irregular).

Guide to the Investment Regimes of the APEC Member Economies.

Key APEC Documents (annually).

The State of Economic and Technical Co-operation in APEC.

Towards Knowledge-based Economies in APEC.

Trade and Investment Liberalization in APEC.

Working group reports, regional directories, other irregular surveys.

Seoul Declaration

(14 November 1991)

OBJECTIVES

Representatives of Australia, Brunei, Canada, the People's Republic of China, Hong Kong, Indonesia, Japan, the Republic of Korea, Malaysia, New Zealand, the Philippines, Singapore, Taiwan, Thailand and the USA, meeting in Seoul, the Republic of Korea, from 12 to 14 November 1991 at ministerial level,

Recognizing that the dynamic growth of economies in the Asia-Pacific region has brought with it growing economic interdependence and strong common interests in maintaining the region's economic dynamism;

Conscious of the vital interests shared by the Asia-Pacific economies in the expansion of free trade and investment, both at the regional and global level, and of the dangers inherent in protectionism;

Recognizing that the healthy and balanced development of economic interdependence within the Asia-Pacific region based upon openness and a spirit of partnership is essential for the prosperity, stability and progress of the entire region;

Convinced that closer co-operation is needed to utilize more effectively human and natural resources of the Asia-Pacific region so as to attain sustainable growth of its economies, while reducing economic disparities among them, and improve the economic and social well-being of its peoples;

Recalling the productive outcome of their two previous meetings held in Canberra, Australia, during 5–7 November 1989 and in Singapore, during 29–31 July 1990, the basic principles for Asia-Pacific Economic Co-operation which emerged therefrom, and the process of consultations and co-operation evolving among the participating Asia-Pacific economies;

Acknowledging the important contribution made by the Association of South-East Asian Nations (ASEAN) and the pioneering role played by the Pacific Economic Co-operation Conference (PECC) in fostering closer regional links and dialogue;

Recognizing the important role played by the GATT in fostering a healthy and open multilateral trading system, in reducing barriers to trade and in eliminating discriminatory treatment in international commerce;

Believing that Asia-Pacific Economic Co-operation should serve as an exemplary model of open regional co-operation;

Do hereby declare as follows:

1. The objectives of Asia-Pacific Economic Co-operation (hereinafter referred to as APEC) will be:

(a) to sustain the growth and development of the region for the common good of its peoples and, in this way, to contribute to the growth and development of the world economy;

(b) to enhance the positive gains, both for the region and the world economy, resulting from increasing economic interdependence, including by encouraging the flow of goods, services, capital and technology;

(c) to develop and strengthen the open multilateral trading system in the interest of Asia-Pacific and all other economies;

(d) to reduce barriers to trade in goods and services and investment among participants in a manner consistent with GATT principles, where applicable, and without detriment to other economies.

SCOPE OF ACTIVITY

2. APEC will focus on those economic areas where there is scope to advance common interests and achieve mutual benefits, including through:

(a) exchange of information and consultation on policies and developments relevant to the common efforts of APEC economies to sustain growth, promote adjustment and reduceeconomic disparities;

(b) development of strategies to reduce impediments to the flow of goods and services and investment world-wide and within the region;

(c) promotion of regional trade, investment, financial resource flows, human resources development, technology transfer, industrial co-operation and infrastructure development;

(d) co-operation in specific sectors such as energy, environment, fisheries, tourism, transportation and telecommunications.

3. In each of these fields, APEC will seek:

(a) to improve the identification and definition of the region's common interests and where appropriate, to project these interests in multilateral forums such as the GATT;

(b) to improve the understanding of the policy concerns, interests and experiences of economic partners, particularly of their international implications, and to help promote consistency in policy-making in appropriate areas;

(c) to develop practical programmes of economic co-operation to contribute to economic dynamism and improved living standards throughout the region;

(d) to enhance and promote the role of the private sector and the application of free market principles in maximizing the benefits of regional co-operation.

MODE OF OPERATION

4. Co-operation will be based on:

(a) the principle of mutual benefit, taking into account differences in the stages of economic development and in the sociopolitical systems, and giving due consideration to the needs of developing economies; and

(b) a commitment to open dialogue and consensus-building, with equal respect for the views of all participants.

5. APEC will operate through a process of consultation and exchange of views among high-level representatives of APEC economies, drawing upon research, analysis and policy ideas contributed by participating economies and other relevant organizations including the ASEAN and the South Pacific Forum(SPF) Secretariats and the PECC.

6. Recognizing the important contribution of the private sector to the dynamism of APEC economies, APEC welcomes and encourages active private-sector participation in appropriate APEC activities.

PARTICIPATION

7. Participation in APEC will be open, in principle, to those economies in the Asia-Pacific region which:

(a) have strong economic linkages in the Asia-Pacific region; and

(b) accept the objectives and principles of APEC as embodied in this Declaration.

8. Decisions regarding future participation in APEC will be made on the basis of a consensus of all existing participants.

9. Non-participant economies or organizations may be invited to the meetings of APEC upon such terms and conditions as may be determined by all existing participants.

ORGANIZATION

10. A ministerial meeting of APEC participants will be held annually to determine the direction and nature of APEC activities within the framework of this Declaration and decide on arrangements for implementation. Participants who wish to host ministerial meetings will have the opportunity to do so, with the host in each case providing the chairman of the meeting.

11. Additional ministerial meetings may be convened as necessary to deal with specific issues of common interest.

12. Responsibility for developing the APEC process in accord with the decisions of the ministerial meetings and the work programme determined at those meetings will lie with a senior officials' meeting of representatives from each participant. The senior officials' meeting will be chaired by a representative of the host of the subsequent annual ministerial meeting, and will make necessary preparations for that meeting.

13. Each project on the work programme will be pursued by a working group composed of representatives from participants, co-ordinated by one or more participants. The working groups will identify specific areas of co-operation and policy options relating to each project.

THE FUTURE OF APEC

14. Recognizing the ongoing and dynamic nature of the APEC process, APEC will retain the flexibility to evolve in line with the changes in regional economic circumstances and the global economic environment, and in response to the economic policy challenges facing the Asia-Pacific region.

ASIAN DEVELOPMENT BANK—ADB

Address: 6 ADB Ave, Mandaluyong City, 0401 Metro Manila, Philippines; POB 789, 0980 Manila, Philippines.

Telephone: (2) 6324444; **fax:** (2) 6362444; **e-mail:** information@adb.org; **internet:** www.adb.org.

The ADB commenced operations in December 1966. The Bank's principal functions are to provide loans and equity investments for the economic and social advancement of its developing member countries, to give technical assistance for the preparation and implementation of development projects and programmes and advisory services, to promote investment of public and private capital for development purposes, and to respond to requests from developing member countries for assistance in the co-ordination of their development policies and plans.

MEMBERS

There are 43 member countries and territories within the ESCAP region and 16 others (see list of subscriptions below).

Organization

(April 2002)

BOARD OF GOVERNORS

All powers of the Bank are vested in the Board, which may delegate its powers to the Board of Directors except in such matters as admission of new members, changes in the Bank's authorized capital stock, election of Directors and President, and amendment of the Charter. One Governor and one Alternate Governor are appointed by each member country. The Board meets at least once a year.

BOARD OF DIRECTORS

The Board of Directors is responsible for general direction of operations and exercises all powers delegated by the Board of Governors, which elects it. Of the 12 Directors, eight represent constituency groups of member countries within the ESCAP region (with about 65% of the voting power) and four represent the rest of the member countries. Each Director serves for two years and may be re-elected.

Three specialized committees (the Audit Committee, the Budget Review Committee and the Inspection Committee), each comprising six members, assist the Board of Directors in exercising its authority with regard to supervising the Bank's financial statements, approving the administrative budget, and reviewing and approving policy documents and assistance operations.

The President of the Bank, though not a Director, is Chairman of the Board.

Chairman of Board of Directors and President: TADAO CHINO (Japan).

Vice-Presidents: JOSEPH B. EICHENBERGER (USA); JOHN LINTJER (Netherlands); MYOUNG-HO SHIN (Republic of Korea).

ADMINISTRATION

The Bank had 2,058 staff at 31 December 2000.

On 1 January 2002 the Bank implemented a new organizational structure, which had been under review in 2001. The reorganization aimed to strengthen the Bank's country and sub-regional focus, as well as its capacity for poverty reduction and implementing its long-term strategic framework. Five regional departments cover East and Central Asia, the Mekong, the Pacific, South Asia, and South East Asia. Other departments and offices include Private Sector Operations, Central Operations Services, Regional and Sustainable Development, Strategy and Policy, Cofinancing Operations, and Economics and Research, as well as other administrative units.

There are Bank Resident Missions in Bangladesh, Cambodia, the People's Republic of China, India, Indonesia, Kazakhstan, Kyrgyzstan, Laos, Mongolia, Nepal, Pakistan, Sri Lanka, Uzbekistan and Viet Nam, all of which report to the head of the regional department. In addition, there is a country office in the Philippines, an Extended Mission in Papua New Guinea, a Special Liaison Office in East Timor, and a South Pacific Regional Mission, based in Vanuatu. Representative Offices are located in Tokyo, Japan, Frankfurt am Main, Germany (for Europe), and Washington, DC, USA (for North America).

Secretary: BINDU N. LOHANI.

General Counsel: GERALD A. SUMIDA.

INSTITUTE

ADB Institute—ADBI: Kasumigaseki Bldg, 8th Floor, 2–5 Kasumigaseki 3-chome, Chiyoda-ku, Tokyo 100-6008, Japan; tel. (3) 3593-5500; fax (3) 3593-5571; e-mail webmaster@adbi.org; internet www.adbi.org; f. 1997 as a subsidiary body of the ADB to research and analyse long-term development issues and to disseminate development practices through training and other capacity-building activities. Dean MASARU YOSHITOMI (Japan).

FINANCIAL STRUCTURE

The Bank's ordinary capital resources (which are used for loans to the more advanced developing member countries) are held and used entirely separately from its Special Funds resources (see below). A fourth General Capital Increase (GCI IV), amounting to US $26,318m. (or some 100%), was authorized in May 1994. At the final deadline for subscription to GCI IV, on 30 September 1996, 55 member countries had subscribed shares amounting to $24,675.4m.

At 31 December 2000 the position of subscriptions to the capital stock was as follows: authorized US $45,485m.; subscribed $45,271m.

The Bank also borrows funds from the world capital markets. Total borrowings during 2000 amounted to US $1,692.6m. (compared with $5,186m. in 1999). At 31 December 2000 total outstanding borrowings amounted to $25,367.2m.

In July 1986 the Bank abolished the system of fixed lending rates, under which ordinary operations loans had carried interest rates fixed at the time of loan commitment for the entire life of the loan. Under the new system the lending rate is adjusted every six months, to take into account changing conditions in international financial markets.

SPECIAL FUNDS

The Asian Development Fund (ADF) was established in 1974 in order to provide a systematic mechanism for mobilizing and administering resources for the Bank to lend on concessionary terms to the least-developed member countries. In 1998 the Bank revised the terms of ADF. Since 1 January 1999 all new project loans are repayable within 32 years, including an eight-year grace period, while quick-disbursing programme loans have a 24-year maturity, also including an eight-year grace period. The previous annual service charge was redesignated as an interest charge, including a portion to cover administrative expenses. The new interest charges on all loans are 1%–1.5% per annum. At 31 December 2000 total ADF loans approved amounted to US $24,353m. for 871 loans, while cumulative disbursements from ADF resources totalled $16,528m.

Successive replenishments of the Fund's resources amounted to $809m. for the period 1976–78, $2,150m. for 1979–82, $3,214m. for 1983–86, $3,600m. for 1987–90, $4,200m. for 1992–95, and $6,300m. for 1997–2000. In September 2000 25 donor countries pledged $2,910m. towards the ADF's seventh replenishment (ADF VII), which totalled $5,650m. to provide resources for the period 2001–04; repayments of earlier ADF loans were to provide the remaining $2,740m.

The Bank provides technical assistance grants from its Technical Assistance Special Fund (TASF). By the end of 2000, the Fund's total resources amounted to US $899.5m., of which $784.0m. had been utilized or committed. The Japan Special Fund (JSF) was established in 1988 to provide finance for technical assistance by means of grants, in both the public and private sectors. The JSF aims to help developing member countries restructure their economies, enhance the opportunities for attracting new investment, and recycle funds. The Japanese Government had committed a total of 90,600m. yen (equivalent to some $783m.) to the JSF by the end of 2000 (of which $732m. had been utilized). In March 1999 an Asian Currency Crisis Support Facility (ACCSF) was established, for a three-year period, as an independent component of the JSF to provide additional technical assistance, interest payment assistance and guarantees to countries most affected by financial instability, i.e. Indonesia, Republic of Korea, Malaysia, Philippines and Thailand. At the end of 2000 the Japanese Government, as the sole financier of the fund, had contributed 27,500m. yen (some $241m.) to the new Facility. The Japanese Government also funds the Japan Scholarship Program, under which 1,164 scholarships had been awarded to recipients from 33 member countries between 1988 and 2000, and the ADB Institute Special Fund, which was established to finance the initial operations of the new Institute (see above). By 31 December 2000 cumulative commitments to the Special Fund amounted to 5,300m. yen (or $43m.). In May 2000 the Japan Fund for Poverty Reduction was established, with an initial contribution of 10,000m. yen (approximately $92.6m.) from the Japanese Government, to support ADB-financed poverty reduction and social development activities.

Activities

Loans by the ADB are usually aimed at specific projects. In responding to requests from member governments for loans, the Bank's staff assesses the financial and economic viability of projects and the way in which they fit into the economic framework and priorities of development of the country concerned. In 1987 the Bank adopted a policy of lending in support of programmes of sectoral adjustment, not limited to specific projects; such loans were not to exceed 15% of total Bank public sector lending. In 1999 the Board of Directors increased the ceiling on programme lending to 20% of the annual total. In 1985 the Bank decided to expand its assistance to the private sector, hitherto comprising loans to development finance institutions, under government guarantee, for lending to small and medium-sized enterprises; a programme was formulated for direct financial assistance, in the form of equity and loans without government guarantee, to private enterprises. In addition, the Bank was to increase its support for financial institutions and capital markets and, where appropriate, give assistance for the privatization of public sector enterprises. In 1992 a Social Dimensions Unit was established as part of the central administrative structure of the Bank, which contributed to the Bank's increasing awareness of the importance of social aspects of development as essential components of sustainable economic growth. During the early 1990s the Bank also aimed to expand its role as project financier by providing assistance for policy formulation and review and promoting regional co-operation, while placing greater emphasis on individual country requirements.

Under the Bank's Medium-Term Strategic Framework for the period 1995–98 the following concerns were identified as strategic development objectives: promoting economic growth; reducing poverty; supporting human development; improving the status of women; and protecting the environment. Accordingly, the Bank resolved to promote sound development management, by integrating into its operations and projects the promotion of governance issues, such as capacity-building, legal frameworks and openness of information. During 1995 the Bank introduced other specific policy initiatives including a new co-financing and guarantee policy to extend the use of guarantees and to provide greater assistance to co-financiers in order to mobilize more effectively private resources for development projects; a commitment to assess development projects for their impact on the local population and to avoid all involuntary resettlement where possible; the establishment of a formal procedure for grievances, under which the Board may authorize an inspection of a project, by an independent panel of experts, at the request of the affected community or group; and a policy to place greater emphasis on the development of the private sector, through the Bank's lending commitments and technical assistance activities. During 1997 the Bank attempted to refine its policy on good governance by emphasizing the following two objectives: assisting the gov-

SUBSCRIPTIONS AND VOTING POWER*
(31 December 2000)

Country	Subscribed capital (% of total)	Voting power (% of total)
Regional:		
Afghanistan	0.034	0.366
Australia	5.892	5.053
Azerbaijan	0.453	0.701
Bangladesh	1.040	1.171
Bhutan	0.006	0.344
Cambodia	0.050	0.379
China, People's Republic	6.562	5.588
Cook Islands	0.003	0.341
Fiji	0.069	0.394
Hong Kong	0.555	0.783
India	6.447	5.497
Indonesia	5.546	4.776
Japan	15.893	13.053
Kazakhstan	0.821	0.996
Kiribati	0.004	0.342
Korea, Republic	5.130	4.443
Kyrgyzstan	0.305	0.583
Laos	0.014	0.350
Malaysia	2.773	2.557
Maldives	0.004	0.342
Marshall Islands	0.003	0.341
Micronesia, Federated States	0.004	0.342
Mongolia	0.015	0.351
Myanmar	0.555	0.783
Nauru	0.004	0.342
Nepal	0.150	0.459
New Zealand	1.564	1.590
Pakistan	2.218	2.114
Papua New Guinea	0.096	0.415
Philippines	2.426	2.280
Samoa	0.003	0.342
Singapore	0.347	0.616
Solomon Islands	0.007	0.344
Sri Lanka	0.591	0.811
Taiwan	1.109	1.226
Tajikistan	0.292	0.572
Thailand	1.386	1.448
Tonga	0.004	0.342
Turkmenistan	0.258	0.545
Tuvalu	0.001	0.340
Uzbekistan	0.686	0.888
Vanuatu	0.007	0.344
Viet Nam	0.348	0.617
Sub-total	63.674	65.515
Non-regional:		
Austria	0.347	0.616
Belgium	0.347	0.616
Canada	5.327	4.600
Denmark	0.347	0.616
Finland	0.347	0.616
France	2.370	2.235
Germany	4.405	3.863
Italy	1.840	1.811
Netherlands	1.045	1.175
Norway	0.347	0.616
Spain	0.347	0.616
Sweden	0.347	0.616
Switzerland	0.594	0.814
Turkey	0.347	0.616
United Kingdom	2.080	2.003
USA	15.893	13.053
Sub-total	36.326	34.485
Total	100.000	100.000

ernments of developing countries to create conditions conducive to private-sector investment, for example through public-sector management reforms; and assisting those governments to identify and secure large-scale and long-term funding, for example through the establishment of joint public-private ventures and the formulation of legal frameworks. In 1998 the Bank approved a new anticorruption strategy.

The currency instability and ensuing financial crises affecting many Asian economies in the second half of 1997 and in 1998 prompted the Bank to reflect on its role in the region. The Bank resolved to strengthen its activities as a broad-based development institution, rather than solely as a project financier, through lending policies, dialogue, co-financing and technical assistance. A Task Force on Financial Sector Reform was established to review the causes and effects of the regional financial crisis. The Task Force identified the Bank's initial priorities as being to accelerate banking and capital market reforms in member countries, to promote market efficiency in the financial, trade and industrial sectors, to promote good governance and sound corporate management, and to alleviate the social impact of structural adjustments. In mid-1999 the Bank approved a technical assistance grant to establish an internet-based Asian Recovery Information Centre, within a new Regional Monitoring Unit, which aimed to facilitate access to information regarding the economic and social impact of the Asian financial crisis, analyses of economic needs of countries, reform programmes and monitoring of the economic recovery process. In November the Board of Directors approved a new overall strategy objective of poverty reduction, which was to be the principal consideration for all future Bank lending, project financing and technical assistance. The strategy incorporated key aims of supporting sustainable, grass-roots based economic growth, social development and good governance. The Board also approved a health sector policy, to concentrate resources on basic primary healthcare, and initiated reviews of the Bank's private sector strategy and the efficiency of resident missions. During 2000 the Bank began to refocus its country strategies, projects and lending targets to complement the poverty reduction strategy. In addition, it initiated a process of wide-ranging discussions to formulate a long-term strategic framework for the next 15 years, based on the target of reducing by 50% the incidence of extreme poverty by 2015.

In 2000 the Bank approved 90 loans in 74 projects amounting to US $5,840.4m. (compared with $4,978.6m. for 66 loans in 52 projects in 1999). Loans from ordinary capital resources in 2000 totalled $4,257.9m., while loans from the ADF amounted to $1,592.5m. Private-sector operations approved amounted to $234.2m., which included direct loans without government guarantee of $156.0m. and equity investments of $78.2m. The largest proportion of assistance, amounting to some 24% of total lending, was allocated to social infrastructure projects, including water supply and sanitation, education, and housing. Disbursements of loans during 2000 amounted to $4,019.1m., bringing cumulative disbursements to a total of $58,294.1m.

In 2000 grants approved for technical assistance (e.g. project preparation, consultant services and training) amounted to US $172.0m. for 306 projects, with $77.7m. deriving from the Bank's ordinary resources and the TASF, $77.1m. from the JSF, $7.6m. from the newly-established ACCSF, and $9.6m. from bilateral and multilateral sources. The Bank's Operations Evaluation Office prepares reports on completed projects, in order to assess achievements and problems. In 1997 the Bank adopted several new initiatives to evaluate and classify project performance and to assess the impact on development of individual projects. In April 2000 the Bank announced that, from 2001, some new loans would be denominated in local currencies, in order to ease the repayment burden on recipient economies.

The Bank co-operates with other international organizations active in the region, particularly the World Bank group, the IMF, UNDP and APEC, and participates in meetings of aid donors for developing member countries. In early 2002 the Bank worked with the World Bank and UNDP to assess the needs of the interim administration in Afghanistan, in preparation for an International Conference on Reconstruction Assistance to Afghanistan, held in late January, in Tokyo. The Bank pledged to work with its member governments to provide highly concessional grants and loans of some US $500m., with a particular focus on road reconstruction, basic education, and agricultural irrigation rehabilitation. In 1996 the Bank signed a memorandum of understanding with the UN Industrial Development Organization (UNIDO), in order to strengthen co-operation between the two organizations. A new policy concerning co-operation with non-governmental organizations (NGOs) was approved by the Bank in 1998. During 2000 64% of the public sector projects were prepared with NGO involvement.

Finance

Internal administrative expenses amounted to US $204.9m. in 2000, and were projected to total $226.9m. in 2001.

Publications

ADB Business Opportunities (monthly).

ADB Institute Newsletter.

ADB Review (6 a year).

Annual Report.

Asian Development Outlook (annually).

Asian Development Review (2 a year).

Basic Statistics (annually).

Key Indicators of Developing Asian and Pacific Countries (annually).

Law and Policy Reform Bulletin (annually).

Loan Disbursement Handbook.

Studies and technical assistance reports, information brochures, guide-lines, sample bidding documents, staff papers.

Statistics

BANK ACTIVITIES BY SECTOR

	Loan Approvals (US $ million)		
	2000		1968–2000
Sector	Amount	%	%
Agriculture and natural resources	1,051.20	17.97	18.72
Energy	1,141.60	19.51	21.36
Finance	185.40	3.17	14.76
Industry and non-fuel minerals	350.00	5.98	3.57
Social infrastructure	1,400.16	23.93	16.69
Transport and communications	1,344.20	22.98	19.47
Multi-sector and others	377.82	6.46	5.21
Total	5,850.38	100.00	100.00

LENDING ACTIVITIES BY COUNTRY (US $ million)

	Loans approved in 2000		
Country	Ordinary Capital	ADF	Total
Bangladesh	72.00	203.10	275.10
Bhutan	—	19.60	19.60
Cambodia	—	0	109.60
China, People's Republic	872.30	—	872.30
India	1,330.00	—	1,330.00
Indonesia	635.00	165.00	800.00
Kyrgyzstan	—	61.00	61.00
Laos	—	60.50	60.50
Marshall Islands	—	6.82	6.82
Micronesia, Federated States	—	8.02	8.02
Mongolia	—	41.90	41.90
Nepal	—	173.30	173.30
Pakistan	450.00	257.00	707.00
Papua New Guinea	20.60	24.94	45.54
Philippines	515.00	—	515.00
Samoa	—	10.50	10.50
Solomon Islands	—	10.00	10.00
Sri Lanka	41.00	193.70	234.70
Tajikistan	—	54.00	54.00
Uzbekistan	177.00	—	177.00
Viet Nam	35.00	188.50	223.50
Regional	65.00	5.00	70.00
Total	4,257.90	1,592.48	5,850.38

LENDING ACTIVITIES (in %)

	1993–97		1998–2000	
Country	Ordinary Capital	ADF	Ordinary Capital	ADF
Bangladesh	0.2	21.0	1.3	17.5
Bhutan	—	0.3	—	1.0
Cambodia	—	2.5	—	5.4
China, People's Republic	23.4	—	25.3	—
Cook Islands	—	0.2	—	—
Fiji	0.2	—	—	—
India	13.0	—	16.8	—
Indonesia	22.2	3.7	26.5	4.5
Kazakhstan	1.6	0.8	0.3	—
Kiribati	—	—	—	0.3
Korea, Republic	18.4	—	—	—
Kyrgyzstan	—	3.5	—	5.4
Laos	—	5.8	—	2.9
Malaysia	0.9	—	—	—
Maldives	—	0.2	—	0.4
Marshall Islands	—	0.5	—	0.4
Micronesia, Federated States	—	0.5	—	0.2
Mongolia	—	4.8	—	2.5
Nauru	—	—	0.0	—
Nepal	0.2	5.2	—	9.0
Pakistan	4.1	20.5	5.8	9.7
Papua New Guinea	0.2	0.6	0.9	1.2
Philippines	6.7	3.1	11.0	0.2
Samoa	—	0.0	—	0.5
Solomon Islands	—	0.0	—	1.0
Sri Lanka	0.0	7.8	0.6	14.5
Tajikistan	—	—	—	2.7
Thailand	8.5	—	7.6	—
Tonga	—	0.2	—	—
Tuvalu	—	—	—	0.1
Uzbekistan	0.3	0.3	2.3	—
Vanuatu	—	0.1	—	0.6
Viet Nam	0.1	18.2	0.6	14.5
Regional	—	—	1.0	5.5
Total	100.0	100.0	100.0	100.0
Value (US $ million)	21,853.8	7,139.5	13,161.3	3,650.1

Source: *ADB Annual Report 2000.*

ASSOCIATION OF SOUTH EAST ASIAN NATIONS—ASEAN

Address: 70A Jalan Sisingamangaraja, POB 2072, Jakarta 12110, Indonesia.

Telephone: (21) 7262991; **fax:** (21) 7398234; **e-mail:** public @asean.or.id; **internet:** www.aseansec.org.

ASEAN was established in August 1967 in Bangkok, Thailand, to accelerate economic progress and to increase the stability of the South-East Asian region.

MEMBERS

Brunei	Malaysia	Singapore
Cambodia	Myanmar	Thailand
Indonesia	Philippines	Viet Nam
Laos		

Organization

(April 2002)

SUMMIT MEETING

The highest authority of ASEAN, bringing together the heads of government of member countries. The first meeting was held in Bali, Indonesia, in February 1976. In 1992 it was agreed that summit meetings were to be held every three years, with an informal gathering of heads of government convened at least once in the intervening period. The 30th anniversary of the founding of ASEAN was commemorated at an informal summit meeting held in Kuala Lumpur, Malaysia, in December 1997. The sixth summit meeting was convened in Hanoi, Viet Nam, in December 1998 and informal summit meetings were held in Manila, Philippines, in November 1999 and in Singapore, in November 2000. The seventh summit meeting took place in Bandar Seri Begawan, Brunei, in November 2001.

MINISTERIAL MEETINGS

The ASEAN Ministerial Meeting (AMM), comprising ministers of foreign affairs of member states, meets annually, in each member country in turn, to formulate policy guide-lines and to co-ordinate ASEAN activities. These meetings are followed by 'post-ministerial conferences' (PMCs), where ASEAN ministers of foreign affairs meet with their counterparts from countries that are 'dialogue partners' as well as with ministers from other countries. Ministers of economic affairs also meet once a year, to direct ASEAN economic co-operation. Joint Ministerial Meetings, consisting of ministers of foreign affairs and of economic affairs are convened prior to a summit meeting, and may be held at the request of either group of ministers. Other ministers meet regularly to promote co-operation in different sectors.

STANDING COMMITTEE

The Standing Committee normally meets every two months. It consists of the minister of foreign affairs of the host country and ambassadors of the other members accredited to the host country.

SECRETARIATS

A permanent secretariat was established in Jakarta, Indonesia, in 1976 to form a central co-ordinating body. The Secretariat comprises four bureaux relating to: Programme Co-ordination and External Relations; Trade, Industry and Services; Investment, Finance and Surveillance; and Economic and Functional Co-operation. The Secretary-General holds office for a five-year term, and is assisted by two Deputy Secretaries-General. In each member country day-to-day work is co-ordinated by an ASEAN National Secretariat.

Secretary-General: RODOLFO CERTEZA SEVERINO (Philippines).

Deputy Secretaries-General: TRAN DUC MINH (Viet Nam), AHMAD MOKHTAR SELAT (Malaysia).

COMMITTEES AND SENIOR OFFICIALS' MEETINGS

Ministerial meetings are serviced by 29 committees of senior officials, supported by 122 technical working groups. There is a network of subsidiary technical bodies comprising sub-committees, expert groups, *ad hoc* working groups and working parties.

To support the conduct of relations with other countries and international organizations, ASEAN committees (composed of heads of diplomatic missions) have been established in 14 foreign capitals: those of Australia, Belgium, Canada, the People's Republic of China, France, India, Japan, the Republic of Korea, New Zealand, Pakistan, Russia, Switzerland, the United Kingdom and the USA. There is also an ASEAN committee in New York (USA).

Activities

ASEAN was established in 1967 with the signing of the ASEAN Declaration, otherwise known as the Bangkok Declaration, by the ministers of foreign affairs of Indonesia, Malaysia, the Philippines, Singapore and Thailand. Brunei joined the organization in January 1984, shortly after attaining independence. Viet Nam was admitted as the seventh member of ASEAN in July 1995. Laos and Myanmar joined in July 1997 and Cambodia was formally admitted in April 1999, fulfilling the organization's ambition to incorporate all 10 countries in the sub-region.

TRADE AND ECONOMIC CO-OPERATION

A Basic Agreement on the Establishment of ASEAN Preferential Trade Arrangements was concluded in 1977, but by mid-1987 the system covered only about 5% of trade between member states, since individual countries were permitted to exclude any 'sensitive' products from preferential import tariffs. In December 1987 the meeting of ASEAN heads of government resolved to reduce such exclusions to a maximum of 10% of the number of items traded and to a maximum of 50% of the value of trade, over the next five years (seven years for Indonesia and the Philippines).

In January 1992 heads of government, meeting in Singapore, signed an agreement to create an 'ASEAN Free Trade Area' (AFTA) by 2008. In accordance with the agreement, a common effective preferential tariff (CEPT) scheme came into effect in January 1993. The CEPT covered all manufactured products, including capital goods, and processed agricultural products (which together accounted for two-thirds of intra-ASEAN trade), but was to exclude unprocessed agricultural products. Tariffs were to be reduced to a maximum of 20% within a period of five to eight years and to 0%–5% during the subsequent seven to 10 years. Fifteen categories were designated for accelerated tariff reduction, including vegetable oils, rubber products, textiles, cement and pharmaceuticals. Member states were, however, still to be permitted exclusion for certain 'sensitive' products. In October 1993 ASEAN trade ministers agreed to modify the CEPT, with only Malaysia and Singapore having adhered to the original tariff reduction schedule. The new AFTA programme, under which all member countries except Brunei were scheduled to begin tariff reductions from 1 January 1994, substantially enlarged the number of products to be included in the tariff-reduction process and reduced the list of products eligible for protection. In September 1994 ASEAN ministers of economic affairs agreed to accelerate the implementation of AFTA: tariffs were to be reduced to 0%–5% within seven to 10 years, or within five to eight years for products designated for accelerated tariff cuts. In July 1995 Viet Nam was admitted as a member of ASEAN and was granted until 2006 to implement the AFTA trade agreements (this deadline was subsequently advanced to 2003). In December 1995 heads of government, at a meeting convened in Bangkok, agreed to maintain the objective of achieving AFTA by 2003, while pursuing efforts to eliminate or reduce tariffs to less than 5% on the majority of products by 2000. Liberalization was to be extended to certain service industries, including banking, telecommunications and tourism. In July 1997 Laos and Myanmar became members of ASEAN and were granted a 10-year period, from 1 January 1998, to comply with the AFTA schedule. (This deadline was subsequently advanced to 2005.)

In December 1998, meeting in Hanoi, Viet Nam, heads of government approved a Statement on Bold Measures, detailing ASEAN's strategies to deal with the economic crisis that had prevailed in the region since late 1997. These included incentives to attract investors, for example a three-year exemption on corporate taxation, accelerated implementation of the ASEAN Investment Area (AIA, see below), and advancing the AFTA deadline, for the original six members, to 2002, with some 85% of products to be covered by the arrangements by 2000, and 90% by 2001. It was envisaged that the original six members and the new members would achieve the elimination of all tariffs by 2015 and 2018, respectively. The Hanoi Plan of Action, which was also adopted at the meeting as a framework for the development of the organization over the period 1999–2004, incorporated a series of measures aimed at strengthening macroeconomic and financial co-operation and enhancing economic integration. In April 1999 Cambodia, on being admitted as a full member of ASEAN, signed an agreement to implement the tariff reduction programme over a 10-year period, commencing 1 January 2000. Cambodia also signed a declaration endorsing the commitments of the 1998 Statement on Bold Measures. In May 2000 Malaysia was granted a special exemption to postpone implementing tariff reductions on motor vehicles for two years from 1 January 2003. In November 2000 a protocol was approved permitting further temporary exclusion of products from the CEPT scheme for countries experiencing economic difficulties. In September 2001 ASEAN ministers of economic affairs reviewed progress in the completion of the free trade area and the AIA, and reported that the grouping's six original members had achieved the objective of reducing to less than 5% (specifically, reaching a level of 3.2%) trade restrictions on 90% of products.

To complement AFTA in facilitating intra-ASEAN trade, member countries are committed to the removal of non-tariff barriers (such as quotas), the harmonization of standards and conformance measures, and the simplification and harmonization of customs procedures. In June 1996 the Working Group on Customs Procedures completed a draft legal framework for regional co-operation, designed to simplify and harmonize customs procedures, legislation and product classification. The agreement was signed in March 1997 at the inaugural meeting of ASEAN finance ministers. (Laos and Myanmar signed the customs agreement in July 1997 and Cambodia assented to it in April 1999.) In 2001 ASEAN finalized its system of harmonized tariff nomenclature. Implementation began in 2002, with training on the new system to be given to public- and private-sector officials over the course of the year.

At the seventh summit meeting, held in Brunei, in November 2001 heads of government noted the challenges posed by the severe global economic slowdown, at a time when ASEAN countries were beginning to emerge from the 1997–98 crisis. Members discussed moving beyond the group's existing free-trade and investment commitments by deepening market liberalization. Specifically, it was proposed that negotiations on the liberalization of intra-ASEAN trade in services be accelerated. The third round of negotiations on liberalizing trade in services began at the end of 2001; it was scheduled to be completed by 2004. Members also agreed to start negotiations on mutual recognition arrangements for professional services. The summit meeting stated that tariff preferences would be extended to ASEAN's newer members from January 2002, under the ASEAN Integration System of Preferences (AISP), thus allowing Cambodia, Laos, Myanmar and Viet Nam tariff-free access to the more developed ASEAN markets earlier than the previously agreed target date of 2010.

In 1991 ASEAN ministers discussed a proposal of the Malaysian Government for the formation of an economic grouping, to be composed of ASEAN members, the People's Republic of China, Hong Kong, Japan, the Republic of Korea and Taiwan. In July 1993 ASEAN ministers of foreign affairs agreed a compromise, whereby the grouping was to be a caucus within APEC, although it was to be co-ordinated by ASEAN's meeting of economy ministers. In July 1994 ministers of foreign affairs of nine prospective members of the group held their first informal collective meeting; however, no progress was made towards forming the proposed East Asia Economic Caucus. There was renewed speculation on the formation of an East Asian grouping following the onset of the Asian financial crisis of the late 1990s. At an informal meeting of leaders of ASEAN countries, China, Japan and the Republic of Korea, held in November 1999, all parties (designating themselves 'ASEAN + 3') issued a Joint Statement on East Asian Co-operation, in which they agreed to strengthen regional unity and addressed the long-term possibility of establishing an East Asian common market and currency. Meeting in May 2000, in Chiang Mai, Thailand, ASEAN + 3 ministers of economic affairs proposed the establishment of an enhanced currency-swap mechanism, enabling countries to draw on liquidity support to defend their economies during balance-of-payments difficulties or speculative currency attacks and to prevent future financial crises. In July ASEAN + 3 ministers of foreign affairs convened an inaugural formal summit in Bangkok, Thailand, and in October ASEAN + 3 economic affairs ministers agreed to hold their hitherto twice-yearly informal meetings on an institutionalized basis. In November an informal meeting of ASEAN +3 leaders approved further co-operation in various sectors and initiated a feasibility study into a proposal to establish a regional free trade area. In May 2001 ASEAN + 3 ministers of economic affairs endorsed a series of projects for co-operation in information technology, environment, small and medium-sized enterprises, Mekong Basin development, and harmonization of standards. In the same month the so-called Chiang Mai initiative on currency-swap arrangements was formally approved by ASEAN + 3 finance ministers. The fifth summit of the ASEAN + 3 leaders was held alongside the seventh ASEAN summit in November 2001. It was proposed to establish an ASEAN + 3 secretariat. In October 2001 ASEAN + 3 agriculture and forestry ministers met for the first time, and discussed issues of poverty alleviation, food security, agricultural research and human resource development. The first meeting of ASEAN + 3 tourism ministers was held in January 2002.

INDUSTRY

The ASEAN-Chambers of Commerce and Industry (CCI) aims to enhance ASEAN economic and industrial co-operation and the participation in these activities of the private sector. In March 1996 a permanent ASEAN-CCI secretariat became operational at the ASEAN Secretariat. The first AIA Council-Business Sector Forum was convened in September 2001, with the aim of developing alliances between the public and private sectors. The seventh ASEAN summit in November resolved to encourage the private sector to convene a regular ASEAN Business Summit. It was also agreed to set up an ASEAN Business Advisory Council.

The ASEAN Industrial Co-operation (AICO) scheme, initiated in 1996, encourages companies in the ASEAN region to undertake joint manufacturing activities. Products derived from an AICO arrangement benefit immediately from a preferential tariff rate of 0%–5%. The AICO scheme superseded the ASEAN industrial joint venture scheme, established in 1983. The attractiveness of the scheme is expected slowly to diminish as ASEAN moves towards the full implementation of the CEPT scheme. ASEAN has initiated studies of new methods of industrial co-operation within the grouping, with the aim of achieving further integration.

The ASEAN Consultative Committee on Standards and Quality (ACCSQ) aims to promote the understanding and implementation of quality concepts, considered to be important in strengthening the economic development of a member state and in helping to eliminate trade barriers. ACCSQ comprises three working groups: standards and information; conformance and assessment; and testing and calibration. In September 1994 an *ad hoc* Working Group on Intellectual Property Co-operation was established, with a mandate to formulate a framework agreement on intellectual property co-operation and to strengthen ASEAN activities in intellectual property protection. ASEAN aims to establish, by 2004, a regional electronic database, to strengthen the administration of intellectual property. ASEAN is also developing a Regulatory Trademark Filing System, as a first step towards the creation of an ASEAN Trademark System.

In 1988 the ASEAN Fund was established, with capital of US $150m., to provide finance for portfolio investments in ASEAN countries, in particular for small and medium-sized enterprises (SMEs). The Hanoi Plan of Action, which was adopted by ASEAN heads of state in December 1998, incorporated a series of initiatives to enhance the development of SMEs, including training and technical assistance, co-operation activities and greater access to information.

FINANCE, BANKING AND INVESTMENT

In 1987 heads of government agreed to accelerate regional financial co-operation, to support intra-ASEAN trade and investment. They adopted measures to increase the role of ASEAN currencies in regional trade, to assist negotiations on the avoidance of double taxation, and to improve the efficiency of tax and customs administrators. An ASEAN Reinsurance Corporation was established in 1988, with initial authorized capital of US $10m. In December 1995 the summit meeting proposed the establishment of an ASEAN Investment Area (AIA). Other measures to attract greater financial resource flows in the region, including an ASEAN Plan of Action for the Promotion of Foreign Direct Investment and Intra-ASEAN Investment, were implemented during 1996.

In February 1997 ASEAN central bank governors agreed to strengthen efforts to combat currency speculation through the established network of foreign-exchange repurchase agreements. However, from mid-1997 several Asian currencies were undermined by speculative activities. Subsequent unsuccessful attempts to support the foreign-exchange rates contributed to a collapse in the value of financial markets in some countries and to a reversal of the region's economic growth, at least in the short term, while governments undertook macro-economic structural reforms. In early December ASEAN ministers of finance, meeting in Malaysia, agreed to liberalize markets for financial services and to strengthen surveillance of member country economies, to help prevent further deterioration of the regional economy. The ministers also endorsed a proposal for the establishment of an Asian funding facility to provide emergency assistance in support of international credit and structural reform programmes. At the informal summit meeting held later in December, ASEAN leaders issued a joint statement in which they expressed the need for mutual support to counter the region's financial crisis and urged greater international assistance to help overcome the situation and address the underlying problems. The heads of government also resolved to accelerate the implementation of the AIA.

In July 1998 the ASEAN Ministerial Meeting endorsed the decisions of finance ministers, taken in February, to promote greater use of regional currencies for trade payments and to establish an economic surveillance mechanism. In October ministers of economic affairs, meeting in Manila, the Philippines, signed a framework agreement on the AIA, which was expected to provide for equal treatment of domestic and other ASEAN direct investment proposals within the grouping by 2010, and of all foreign investors by 2020. The meeting also confirmed that the proposed ASEAN Surveillance Process (ASP), to monitor the economic stability and financial systems of member states, would be implemented with immediate effect, and would require the voluntary submission of economic information by all members to a monitoring committee, to be based in Jakarta, Indonesia. The ASP and the framework agreement on the AIA were incorporated into the Hanoi Plan of Action, adopted by heads of state in December 1998. The December summit meeting also resolved to accelerate reforms, particularly in the banking and financial sectors, in order to strengthen the region's economies, and to promote the liberalization of the financial services sector.

In March 1999 ASEAN ministers of trade and industry, meeting in Phuket, Thailand, as the AIA Council, agreed to open their manufacturing, agriculture, fisheries, forestry and mining industries to foreign investment. Investment restrictions affecting those industries were to be eliminated by 2003 in most cases, although Laos and Viet Nam were granted until 2010 to eliminate restrictions. In addition, ministers adopted a number of measures to encourage investment in the region, including access to three-year corporate income-tax exemptions, and tax allowances of 30% for investors. The AIA agreement formally entered into force in June 1999, having been ratified by all member countries. Under the agreement, member countries submitted individual action plans for 2000–04, noting specific action to be taken in the areas of investment promotion, facilitation and liberalization. In September 2001 ministers agreed to accelerate the full realization of the AIA for non-ASEAN investors in manufacturing, agriculture, forestry, fishing and mining sectors. The date for full implementation was advanced to 2010 for the original six ASEAN members and to 2015 for the newer members.

In November 2001 ASEAN heads of state considered the difficulties facing member countries as a result of the global economic and political uncertainties following the terrorist attacks on the USA in September. The summit meeting noted the recent decline in foreign direct investment and the erosion of the region's competitiveness. Short-term priorities were stated to be the stimulation of economies to lessen the impact of reduced external demand, and the adoption of appropriate fiscal and monetary policies, together with a renewed commitment to structural reform.

SECURITY

In 1971 ASEAN members endorsed a declaration envisaging the establishment of a Zone of Peace, Freedom and Neutrality (ZOPFAN) in the South-East Asian region. This objective was incorporated in the Declaration of ASEAN Concord, which was adopted at the first summit meeting of the organization, held in Bali, Indonesia, in February 1976. (The Declaration also issued guide-lines for co-operation in economic development and the promotion of social justice and welfare.) Also in February 1976 a Treaty of Amity and Co-operation was signed by heads of state, establishing principles of mutual respect for the independence and sovereignty of all nations, non-interference in the internal affairs of one another and settlement of disputes by peaceful means. The Treaty was amended in December 1987 by a protocol providing for the accession of Papua New Guinea and other non-member countries in the region; it was reinforced by a second protocol, signed in July 1998.

In December 1995 ASEAN heads of government, meeting in Bangkok, signed a treaty establishing a South-East Asia Nuclear-Weapon Free Zone (SEANWFZ). The treaty was also signed by Cambodia, Myanmar and Laos. It was extended to cover the offshore economic exclusion zones of each country. On ratification by all parties, the Treaty was to prohibit the manufacture or storage of nuclear weapons within the region. Individual signatories were to decide whether to allow port visits or transportation of nuclear weapons by foreign powers through territorial waters. The Treaty entered into force on 27 March 1997. ASEAN senior officials were mandated to oversee implementation of the Treaty, pending the establishment of a permanent monitoring committee. In July 1999 the People's Republic of China and India agreed to observe the terms of the SEANWFZ.

In January 1992 ASEAN leaders agreed that there should be greater co-operation on security matters within the grouping, and that ASEAN's post-ministerial conferences (PMCs) should be used as a forum for discussion of questions relating to security with dialogue partners and other countries. In July 1992 the ASEAN Ministerial Meeting issued a statement calling for a peaceful resolution of the dispute concerning the strategically significant Spratly Islands in the South China Sea, which are claimed, wholly or partly, by the People's Republic of China, Viet Nam, Taiwan, Brunei, Malaysia and the Philippines. (In February China had introduced legislation that defined the Spratly Islands as belonging to its territorial waters.) The ministers proposed a code of international conduct for the South China Sea, to be based on the principles contained in ASEAN's Treaty of Amity and Co-operation. Tensions in the region heightened in early 1995, owing to Chinese occupation of part of the disputed territory. Viet Nam's accession to ASEAN in July 1995, bringing all the Spratly Islands claimants except China and Taiwan into the grouping, was expected to strengthen ASEAN's position of negotiating a multilateral settlement on the islands. In mid-1999 ASEAN established a special committee to formulate a code of conduct to be observed by all claimants to the Spratly Islands. Proposals under consideration were a ban on the building of all new structures, which had been the cause of escalating tensions in 1998, and a declaration rejecting the use of force to resolve disputes. A draft code of conduct was approved in November 1999. China, insisting that it would adopt the proposed code only as a set of guide-lines and not as a legally-binding document, resolved not to strengthen its presence on the islands. In 2000 and 2001 it participated in discussions with ASEAN officials concerning the document.

In July 1997 ASEAN ministers of foreign affairs reiterated their commitment to the principle of non-interference in the internal affairs of other countries. However, the group's efforts in Cambodia (see below) marked a significant shift in diplomatic policy towards one of 'constructive intervention', which had been proposed by Malaysia's Deputy Prime Minister in recognition of the increasing interdependence of the region. At the Ministerial Meeting in July 1998 Thailand's Minister of Foreign Affairs, supported by his Philippine counterpart, proposed that the grouping formally adopt a policy of 'flexible engagement'. The proposal, based partly on concerns that the continued restrictions imposed by the Myanma authorities on dissident political activists was damaging ASEAN relations with its dialogue partners, was to provide for the discussion of the affairs of other member states when they have an impact on neighbouring countries. While rejecting the proposal, other ASEAN ministers agreed to pursue a more limited version, referred to as 'enhanced interaction', and to maintain open dialogue within the grouping. In September 1999 the unrest prompted by the popular referendum on the future of East Timor and the resulting humanitarian crisis highlighted the unwillingness of some ASEAN member states to intervene in other member countries and undermined the political unity of the grouping. A compromise agreement, enabling countries to act on an individual basis rather than as representatives of ASEAN, was formulated prior to an emergency meeting of ministers of foreign affairs, held during the APEC meetings in Auckland, New Zealand. Malaysia, the Philippines, Singapore and Thailand declared their support for the establishment of a multinational force to restore peace in East Timor and committed troops to participate in the Australian-led operation. Myanmar and Viet Nam, however, remained opposed to intervention in the territory. At their informal summit in November 1999 heads of state approved the establishment of an ASEAN Troika, with a view to providing a rapid response mechanism in the event of a regional crisis. The Troika, which was to be constituted as an *ad hoc* body comprising the foreign ministers of the Association's current, previous and future chairmanship, was to present recommendations to the meeting of foreign ministers.

In June 1999 the first ministerial meeting to consider issues relating to transnational crime was convened. Regular meetings of senior officials and ministers were subsequently held. The third ministerial meeting, in October 2001, considered initiatives to combat transnational crime, which was defined as including terrorism, trafficking in drugs, arms and people, money-laundering, cyber-crime, piracy and economic crime.

On 12 September 2001 ASEAN issued a ministerial statement on international terrorism, condemning the attacks of the previous day in the USA and urging greater international co-operation to counter terrorism. The seventh summit meeting in November issued a Declaration on a Joint Action to Combat Terrorism. This condemned the September attacks, stated that terrorism was a direct challenge to ASEAN's aims, and affirmed the grouping's commitment to strong measures to counter terrorism. The summit encouraged member countries to sign (or ratify) the International Convention for the Suppression of Financing of Terrorism, to strengthen national mechanisms against terrorism, and to work to deepen co-operation, particularly in the area of intelligence exchange; international conventions to combat terrorism would be studied to see if they could be integrated into the ASEAN structure, while the possibility of developing a regional anti-terrorism convention was discussed. The summit noted the need to strengthen security co-operation to restore investor confidence. In its Declaration and other notes, the summit explicitly rejected any attempt to link terrorism with religion or race, and expressed concern for the sufferings of innocent Afghanis during the US military action against the Taliban authorities in Afghanistan. The summit's final Declaration was worded so as to avoid any mention of the US action, to which Muslim ASEAN states such as Malaysia and Indonesia were strongly opposed. Several ASEAN countries offered to assist in peace-keeping and reconstruction in Afghanistan, following the removal of the Taliban and establishment of an interim authority.

ASEAN Regional Forum (ARF): In July 1993 the meeting of ASEAN ministers of foreign affairs sanctioned the establishment of a forum to discuss and promote co-operation on security issues within the region, and, in particular, to ensure the involvement of the People's Republic of China in regional dialogue. The ARF was informally initiated during that year's PMC, comprising the ASEAN countries, its dialogue partners (at that time—Australia, Canada, the EC, Japan, the Republic of Korea, New Zealand and the USA), and the People's Republic of China, Laos, Papua New Guinea, Russia and Viet Nam. The first formal meeting of the ARF was conducted in July 1994, following the Ministerial Meeting held in Bangkok, Thailand, and it was agreed that the ARF would be convened on an annual basis. The 1995 meeting, held in Brunei, in August, attempted to define a framework for the future of the Forum. It was perceived as evolving through three stages: the promotion of confidence-building (including disaster relief and peace-keeping activities); the development of preventive diplomacy; and the elaboration of approaches to conflict. The 19 ministers of foreign affairs attending the meeting (Cambodia participated for the first time) recognized that the ARF was still in the initial stage of implementing confidence-building measures. The ministers, having conceded to a request by China not to discuss explicitly the Spratly Islands, expressed concern at overlapping sovereignty claims in the region. In a further statement, the ministers urged an 'immediate end' to the testing of nuclear weapons, then being undertaken by the French Government in the South Pacific region. The third ARF, convened in July 1996, which was attended for the first time by India and Myanmar, agreed a set of criteria and guiding principles for the future expansion of the grouping. In particular, it was decided that the ARF would only admit as participants countries that had a direct influence on the peace and security of the East Asia and Pacific region. The meeting supported the efforts of all claimants to territories in the South China Sea to resolve disputes in accordance with international law, and recognized the importance of ending all testing of nuclear weapons in the region. The ARF held in July 1997 reviewed progress made in developing the first two 'tracks' of the ARF process, through the structure of inter-sessional working groups and meetings. The Forum's consideration of security issues in the region was dominated by concern at the political situation in Cambodia; support was expressed for ASEAN mediation to restore stability within that country. Myanmar and Laos attended the ARF for the first time. Mongolia was admitted into the ARF at its meeting in July 1998. India rejected a proposal that Pakistan attend the meeting to discuss issues relating to both countries' testing of nuclear weapons. The meeting ultimately condemned the testing of nuclear weapons in the region, but declined to criticize specifically India and Pakistan. In July 1999 the ARF warned the Democratic People's Republic of Korea (DPRK) not to conduct any further testing of missiles over the Pacific. At the seventh meeting of the ARF, convened in Bangkok, Thailand, in July 2000, the DPRK was admitted to the Forum. The meeting considered the positive effects and challenges of globalization, including the possibilities for greater economic interdependence and for a growth in transnational crime. The eighth ARF meeting in July 2001 in Hanoi, Viet Nam, pursued these themes, and also discussed the widening development gap between nations. Since 2000 the ARF has published the *Annual Security Outlook*.

EXTERNAL RELATIONS

ASEAN's external relations have been pursued through a dialogue system, initially with the objective of promoting co-operation in economic areas with key trading partners. The system has been expanded in recent years to encompass regional security concerns and co-operation in other areas, such as the environment. The ARF (see above) emerged from the dialogue system, and more recently the formalized discussions of ASEAN with Japan, China and the Republic of Korea has evolved as a separate process with its own strategic agenda.

European Union: In March 1980 a co-operation agreement was signed between ASEAN and the European Community (EC, as the EU was known prior to its restructuring on 1 November 1993), which provided for the strengthening of existing trade links and increased co-operation in the scientific and agricultural spheres. A Joint Co-operation Committee met in November (and annually thereafter). An ASEAN-EC Business Council was launched in December 1983, and three European Business Information Councils have since been established, in Malaysia, the Philippines and Thailand, to promote private-sector co-operation. The first meeting of ministers of economic affairs from ASEAN and EC member countries took place in October 1985. In December 1990 the Community adopted new guide-lines on development co-operation, with an increase in assistance to Asia, and a change in the type of aid given to ASEAN members, emphasizing training, science and technology and venture capital, rather than assistance for rural development. In October 1992 the EC and ASEAN agreed to promote further trade between the regions, as well as bilateral investment, and made a joint declaration in support of human rights. An EU-ASEAN Junior Managers Exchange Programme was initiated in November 1996, as part of efforts to promote co-operation and understanding between the industrial and business sectors in both regions. An ASEAN-EU Business Network was established in Brussels in 2001, to develop political and commercial contacts between the two sides.

In May 1995 ASEAN and EU senior officials endorsed an initiative to strengthen relations between the two economic regions within the framework of an Asia-Europe Meeting of heads of government (ASEM). The first ASEM was convened in Bangkok, Thailand, in March 1996, at which leaders approved a new Asia-Europe Partnership for Greater Growth (see EU, p. 357). The second ASEM summit meeting, held in April 1998, focused heavily on economic concerns. In February 1997 ministers of foreign affairs of countries participating in ASEM met in Singapore. Despite ongoing differences regarding human rights issues, in particular concerning ASEAN's granting of full membership status to Myanmar and the situation in East Timor (which precluded the conclusion of a new co-operation agreement), the Ministerial Meeting issued a final joint declaration, committing both sides to strengthening co-operation and dialogue on economic, international and bilateral trade, security and social issues. A protocol to the 1980 co-operation agreement was signed, enabling the participation of Viet Nam in the dialogue process. In November 1997 a session of the Joint Co-operation Committee was postponed and later cancelled, owing to a dispute concerning objections by the EU to the participation of Myanmar. A compromise agreement, allowing Myanma officials to attend meetings as 'silent' observers, was concluded in November 1998. However, a meeting of the Joint Co-operation Committee, scheduled to take place in January 1999, was again cancelled, owing to controversy over perceived discrimination by the EU against Myanmar's status. The meeting was finally convened in Bangkok, Thailand, in late May. In December 2000 an ASEAN-EU Ministerial Meeting was held in Vientiane, Laos. Both sides agreed to pursue dialogue and co-operation and issued a joint declaration that accorded support for the efforts of the UN Secretary-General's special envoy towards restoring political dialogue in Myanmar. Myanmar agreed to permit an EU delegation to visit the country, and opposition leaders, in early 2001. In September 2001 the Joint Co-operation Committee met for the first time since 1999 and resolved to strengthen policy dialogue, in particular in areas fostering regional integration. Four new EC delegations were to be established—in Cambodia, Laos, Myanmar and Singapore.

People's Republic of China: Efforts to develop consultative relations between ASEAN and China were initiated in 1993. Joint Committees on economic and trade co-operation and on scientific and technological co-operation were subsequently established. The first formal consultations between senior officials of the two sides were held in April 1995. In July 1996, in spite of ASEAN's continued concern at China's territorial claims to the Spratly Islands in the South China Sea, China was admitted to the PMC as a full dialogue partner. In February 1997 a Joint Co-operation Committee was established to co-ordinate the China-ASEAN dialogue and all aspects of relations between the two sides. Relations were further strengthened by the decision to form a joint business council to promote bilateral trade and investment. China participated in the informal summit meeting held in December, at the end of which both sides issued a joint statement affirming their commitment to resolving regional disputes through peaceful means. A second meeting of the Joint Co-operation Committee was held in March 1999. China was a participant in the first official ASEAN + 3 meeting of foreign ministers, which was convened in July 2000 (see above). An ASEAN-China Experts Group was established in November, to consider future economic co-operation and free trade opportunities. The Group held its first meeting in April 2001 and proposed a Framework on Economic Co-operation and the establishment of an ASEAN-China free-trade area within 10 years (with differential treatment and flexibility for newer ASEAN members). Both proposals were endorsed at the seventh ASEAN summit meeting in November 2001. The free-trade area would have a potential market of around 1,700m. people. China also agreed to grant preferential tariff treatment for some goods from Cambodia, Laos and Myanmar.

Japan: The ASEAN-Japan Forum was established in 1977 to discuss matters of mutual concern in trade, investment, technology transfer and development assistance. The first ever meeting between ASEAN economic ministers and the Japanese Minister of International Trade and Industry was held in October 1992. At this meeting, and subsequently, ASEAN requested Japan to increase its investment in member countries and to make Japanese markets more accessible to ASEAN products, in order to reduce the trade deficit with Japan. Japan agreed to extend ASEAN's privileges under its generalized system of tariffs until 2001. Since 1993 ASEAN-Japanese development and cultural co-operation has expanded under schemes including the Inter-ASEAN Technical Exchange Programme, the Japan-ASEAN Co-operation Promotion Programme and the ASEAN-Japan Friendship Programme. In December 1997 Japan, attending the informal summit meeting in Malaysia, agreed to improve market access for ASEAN products and to provide training opportunities for more than 20,000 young people in order to help develop local economies. In December 1998 ASEAN heads of government welcomed a Japanese initiative, announced in October, to allocate US $30,000m. to promote economic recovery in the region. At the same time the Japanese Prime Minister announced a further package of $5,000m. to be made available as concessionary loans for infrastructure projects. In mid-2000 a new Japan-ASEAN General Exchange Fund (JAGEF) was established to promote and facilitate the transfer of technology, investment and personnel. In November 1999 Japan, along with the People's Republic of China and the Republic of Korea, attending an informal summit meeting of ASEAN, agreed to strengthen economic and political co-operation with the ASEAN countries, to enhance political and security dialogue, and to implement joint infrastructure and social projects. Japan participated in the first official ASEAN + 3 meeting of foreign ministers, which was convened in July 2000. An ASEAN-Japan Experts Group, similar to that for China, was to be established to consider how economic relations between the two sides can be strengthened. In recent years Japan has provided information technology (IT) support to ASEAN countries, and has offered assistance in environmental and health matters and for educational training and human resource development (particularly in engineering).

Australia and New Zealand: Under the ASEAN-Australia Development (formerly Economic) Co-operation Programme, Australia gives financial support for ASEAN activities. A fourth phase of the Programme was initiated in April 1999, with assistance amounting to $A45m. Co-operation relations with New Zealand are based on the Inter-Institutional Linkages Programme and the Trade and Investment Promotion Programme, which mainly provide assistance in forestry development, dairy technology, veterinary management and legal aid training. An ASEAN-New Zealand Joint Management Committee was established in November 1993, to oversee the implementation of co-operation projects. New Zealand's English Language Training for Officials Programme is among the most important of these projects. In September 2001 ASEAN ministers of economic affairs signed a Framework for Closer Economic Partnership (CEP) with their counterparts from Australia and New Zealand (the Closer Economic Relations—CER—countries), and agreed to establish a Business Council to involve the business communities of all countries in the CEP. The CEP was perceived as a first step towards the creation of a free-trade area between ASEAN and CER countries. The establishment of such an area would strengthen the grouping's bargaining position regionally and multilaterally, and bring benefits such as increased foreign direct investment and the possible relocation of industry.

Other countries: The USA gives assistance for the development of small and medium-sized businesses and other projects, and supports a Center for Technology Exchange. In 1990 ASEAN and the USA established an ASEAN-US Joint Working Group, whose purpose is to review ASEAN's economic relations with the USA and to identify measures by which economic links could be strengthened. In recent years, dialogue has increasingly focused on political and security issues. ASEAN-Canadian co-operation projects include fisheries technology, the telecommunications industry, use of solar energy, and a forest seed centre. A Working Group on the Revitalization of ASEAN-Canada relations met in February 1999. At a meeting in Bangkok in July 2000, the two sides agreed to explore less formal avenues for project implementation.

In July 1991 the Republic of Korea was accepted as a 'dialogue partner' in ASEAN, and in December a joint ASEAN-Korea Chamber of Commerce was established. In 1995 co-operation projects on human resources development, science and technology, agricultural development and trade and investment policies were implemented. The Republic of Korea participated in ASEAN's informal summit meetings in December 1997 and November 1999 (see above), and took part in the first official ASEAN + 3 meeting of foreign ministers, convened in July 2000. The Republic's assistance in the field of information technology (IT) has become particularly valuable in recent years. In March 2001, in a sign of developing co-operation, ASEAN and the Republic of Korea exchanged views on political and security issues in the region for the first time. The ASEAN-Korea Work Programme for 2001–03 covers, among other areas, the environment, transport, science and technology and cultural sectors.

In July 1993 both India and Pakistan were accepted as sectoral partners, providing for their participation in ASEAN meetings in sectors such as trade, transport and communications and tourism. An ASEAN-India Business Council was established, and met for the first time, in New Delhi, in February 1995. In December 1995 the ASEAN summit meeting agreed to enhance India's status to that of a full dialogue partner; India was formally admitted to the PMC in July 1996. At a meeting of the ASEAN-India Working Group in March 2001 the two sides agreed to pursue co-operation in new areas, such as health and pharmaceuticals, social security and rural development. The fourth meeting of the ASEAN-India Joint Co-operation Committee in January 2002 agreed to strengthen co-operation in these areas and others, including technology. An investment summit with India was scheduled to be held in September 2002; a full ASEAN-India summit is also due in that year. An ASEAN-Pakistan Joint Business Council met for the first time in February 2000. In early 2001 both sides agreed to co-operate in projects relating to new and renewable energy resources, IT, agricultural research and transport and communications.

In March 2000 the first ASEAN-Russia business forum opened in Kuala Lumpur, Malaysia. East Timor was granted observer status at the AMM which took place in July, amid speculation that it might be admitted to ASEAN following the attainment of full independence.

Indo-China: In July 1992 Viet Nam and Laos signed ASEAN's Treaty on Amity and Co-operation and subsequently participated in ASEAN meetings and committees as observers. Viet Nam was admitted as a full member of ASEAN in July 1995. In July 1994 an official delegation from Myanmar attended the annual Ministerial Meeting, having been invited by the host Thai Government on the basis of ASEAN's policy of pursuing limited 'constructive engagement' with Myanmar in order to encourage democracy in that country. In July 1995 Myanmar signed ASEAN's Treaty on Amity and Co-operation. In July 1996 ASEAN granted Myanmar observer status and admitted it to the ARF, despite the expression of strong reservations by (among others) the Governments of Australia, Canada and the USA owing to the human rights situation in Myanmar. In November ASEAN heads of government, attending an informal summit meeting in Jakarta, Indonesia, agreed to admit Myanmar as a full member of the grouping at the same time as Cambodia and Laos. While Cambodia's membership was postponed, Laos and Myanmar were admitted to ASEAN in July 1997.

Cambodia was accorded observer status in July 1995. Subsequent co-operation focused on issues relating to Cambodia's future admission to the grouping as a full member. In May 1997 ASEAN ministers of foreign affairs confirmed that Cambodia, together with Laos and Myanmar, was to be admitted to the grouping in July of that year. In mid-July, however, Cambodia's membership was postponed owing to the deposition of Prince Ranariddh, and the resulting civil unrest. Later in that month Cambodia's *de facto* leader, Second Prime Minister Hun Sen, agreed to ASEAN's pursuit of a mediation role in restoring stability in the country and in preparing for democratic elections. In early August the ministers of foreign affairs of Indonesia, the Philippines and Thailand, representing ASEAN, met Hun Sen to confirm these objectives. A team of ASEAN observers joined an international monitoring mission to supervise the election held in Cambodia in July 1998. International approval of the conduct of the election, and consequently of Hun Sen's victory, prompted ASEAN to agree to reconsider Cambodia's admission into the Association. In December, following the establishment of a coalition administration in Cambodia, the country was welcomed, by the Vietnamese Government, as the 10th member of ASEAN, despite an earlier meeting of ministers of foreign affairs failing to reach a consensus decision. Its formal admission took place on 30 April 1999.

In June 1996 ministers of ASEAN countries, and of the People's Republic of China, Cambodia, Laos and Myanmar adopted a framework for ASEAN-Mekong Basin Development Co-operation. The initiative aimed to strengthen the region's cohesiveness, with greater co-operation on issues such as drugs-trafficking, labour migration and terrorism, and to facilitate the process of future expansion of ASEAN. Groups of experts and senior officials were to be convened to consider funding issues and proposals to link the two regions, including a gas pipeline network, rail links and the establishment of a common time zone. In December 1996 the working group on rail links appointed a team of consultants to conduct a feasibility study of the proposals. The completed study was presented at the second ministerial conference on ASEAN-Mekong Basin Development Co-operation, convened in Hanoi, Viet Nam, in July 2000. At the November 2001 summit China pledged US $5m. to assist with navigation along the upper stretches of the Mekong River, while other means by which China could increase its investment in the Mekong Basin area were considered. At the meeting the Republic of Korea was invited to become a core member of the grouping. Other growth regions sponsored by ASEAN include the Brunei, Indonesia, Malaysia, Philippines, East ASEAN Growth Area (BIMP-EAGA), the Indonesia, Malaysia, Singapore Growth Triangle (IMS-GT), the Indonesia, Malaysia, Thailand Growth Triangle (IMT-GT), and the West-East Corridor within the Mekong Basin Development initiative.

AGRICULTURE, FISHERIES AND FORESTRY

In October 1983 a ministerial agreement on fisheries co-operation was concluded, providing for the joint management of fish resources, the sharing of technology, and co-operation in marketing. In July 1994 a Conference on Fisheries Management and Development Strategies in the ASEAN region, held in Bangkok, Thailand, resolved to enhance fish production through the introduction of new technologies, aquaculture development, improvements of product quality and greater involvement by the private sector.

Co-operation in forestry is focused on joint projects, funded by ASEAN's dialogue partners, which include a Forest Tree Seed Centre, an Institute of Forest Management and the ASEAN Timber Technology Centre. In April 1995 representatives of the ASEAN Secretariat and private-sector groups met to co-ordinate the implementation of a scheme to promote the export of ASEAN agricultural and forestry products. In recent years ASEAN has urged member countries to take action to prevent illegal logging in order to prevent the further degradation of forest resources.

ASEAN holds an emergency rice reserve, amounting to 87,000 metric tons, as part of its efforts to ensure food security in the region. There is an established ASEAN programme of training and study exchanges for farm workers, agricultural experts and members of agricultural co-operatives. During 1998 ASEAN was particularly concerned with the impact of the region's economic crisis on the agricultural sector, and the possible effects of climatic change. In September ministers of agriculture and forestry, meeting in Hanoi, Viet Nam, endorsed a Strategic Plan of Action on ASEAN Co-operation in Food, Agriculture and Forestry for 1999–2004. The Plan focused on programmes and activities aimed at enhancing food security, the international competitiveness of ASEAN food, agriculture and forestry products, promoting the sustainable use and conservation of natural resources, encouraging greater involvement by the private sector in the food and agricultural industry, and strengthening joint approaches on international and regional issues. An ASEAN Task Force has been formed to harmonize regulations on agricultural products derived from biotechnology. In December 1998 heads of state resolved to establish an ASEAN Food Security Information Service to enhance the capacity of member states to forecast and manage food supplies. In 1999 agriculture ministers endorsed guide-lines on assessing risk from genetically modified organisms (GMOs) in agriculture, to ensure a common approach. In 2001 work was undertaken to increase public and professional awareness of GMO issues, through workshops and studies.

MINERALS AND ENERGY

The ASEAN Centre for Energy (ACE), based in Jakarta, Indonesia, provides an energy information network, promotes the establishment of interconnecting energy structures among ASEAN member countries, supports the development of renewable energy resources and encourages co-operation in energy efficiency and conservation. An ASEAN energy business forum is held annually and attended by representatives of the energy industry in the private and public sectors. Efforts to establish an ASEAN electricity grid were initiated in 1990. An ASEAN Interconnection Masterplan Study Working Group was established in April 2000 to formulate a study on the power grid. In November 1999 a Trans-ASEAN Gas Pipeline Task Force was established, and a masterplan study for a regional gas pipeline project was initiated. ASEAN has forged partnerships with the EU and Japan in the field of energy, under the ASEAN Plan of Action for Energy Co-operation, running from 1999–2004.

A Framework of Co-operation in Minerals was adopted by an ASEAN working group of experts in August 1993. The group has also developed a programme of action for ASEAN co-operation in the development and utilization of industrial minerals, to promote the exploration and development of mineral resources, the transfer of mining technology and expertise, and the participation of the private sector in industrial mineral production. The programme of action is implemented by an ASEAN Regional Development Centre for Mineral Resources, which also conducts workshops and training programmes relating to the sector.

TRANSPORT AND COMMUNICATIONS

ASEAN aims to promote greater co-operation in the transport and communications sector, and in particular, to develop multi-modal transport; to harmonize road transport laws and regulations; to improve air space management; to develop ASEAN legislation for the carriage of dangerous goods and waste by land and sea; and to achieve interoperability and interconnectivity in telecommunications. The summit meeting of December 1998 agreed to work to develop a trans-ASEAN transportation network by 2000, comprising principal routes for the movement of goods and people. (The deadline for the full implementation of the agreement was subsequently moved to the end of 2000.) In September 1999 ASEAN ministers of transport and communications resolved to establish working groups to strengthen co-operation within the sector and adopted a programme of action for development of the sector in 1999–2004. By September 2001, under the action programme, a harmonized road route numbering system had been completed, a road safety implementation work plan agreed, and two pilot courses, on port management and traffic engineering and safety, had been adopted. A Framework Agreement on Facilitation of Goods in Transport entered into force in October 2000.

ASEAN is seeking to develop a Competitive Air Services Policy, possibly as a first step towards the creation of an ASEAN Open Skies Policy. The sixth meeting of transport ministers in September 2000 agreed to embark on a study to formulate maritime shipping policy, to cover, *inter alia*, issues of transshipment, the competitiveness of ports, liberalization, and the integration of maritime shipping into the overall transport system. The seventh ministerial meeting took place in October 2001, in Kuala Lumpur, Malaysia. Ministers approved the third package of commitments for the air and transport sectors under the ASEAN framework agreement on services (according to which member countries were to liberalize the selling and marketing of air and maritime transport services. The summit meeting held in November 2001 reaffirmed the large-scale Singapore–Kunming rail link as a priority transport project. Emphasis was also put on smaller-scale (and cheaper) projects in 2001.

In October 1999 an e-ASEAN initiative was launched, aiming to promote and co-ordinate electronic commerce and internet utilization. In November 2000 the informal meeting of ASEAN heads of government approved an e-ASEAN Framework Agreement to further the aims of the initiative. The Agreement incorporated commitments to develop and strengthen ASEAN's information infrastructure, in order to provide for universal and affordable access to communications services. Tariff reduction on IT products was to be accelerated, with the aim of eliminating all tariffs in the sector by 2010. In July 2001 ministers of foreign affairs discussed measures for the economic liberalization of IT products and for developing IT capabilities in poorer member countries. In the same month the first meeting of ASEAN ministers responsible for telecommunications was held, in Kuala Lumpur, Malaysia, during which a Ministerial Understanding on ASEAN co-operation in telecommunications and IT was signed. In September ASEAN ministers of economic affairs approved a list of information and communications technology products eligible for the elimination of duties under the e-ASEAN Framework Agreement. This was to take place in three annual tranches, commencing in 2003 for the six original members of ASEAN and in 2008 for the newer member countries. During 2001 ASEAN continued to develop a reference framework for e-commerce legislation; it aimed to have e-commerce legislation in place in all member states by 2003.

SCIENCE AND TECHNOLOGY

Through its sub-committees and the implementation of regional projects, ASEAN's Committee on Science and Technology (COST) supports co-operation in food science and technology, meteorology and geophysics, microelectronics and IT, biotechnology, non-conventional energy research, materials science and technology, space technology applications, science and technology infrastructure and resources development, and marine science. There is an ASEAN Science Fund, used to finance policy studies in science and technology and to support information exchange and dissemination.

The Hanoi Plan of Action, adopted in December 1998, envisaged a series of measures aimed at promoting development in the fields of science and technology, including the establishment of networks of science and technology centres of excellence and academic institutions, the creation of a technology scan mechanism, the promotion of public- and private-sector co-operation in scientific and technological (particularly IT) activities, and an increase in research on strategic technologies. In September 2001 the ASEAN Ministerial Meeting on Science and Technology, convened for its first meeting since 1998, approved a new framework for implementation of ASEAN's Plan of Action on Science and Technology during the period 2001–04. The Plan aimed to help less developed member countries become competitive in the sector and integrate into regional co-operation activities. The meeting coincided with the sixth ASEAN Science and Technology Week, during which seminars and technical conferences were held, focusing on the theme Science and Technology: Enhancing the Quality of Life.

ENVIRONMENT

A ministerial meeting on the environment in April 1994 approved an ASEAN Strategic Plan of Action on the Environment for 1994–98. The Plan established long-term objectives on environmental quality and standards for the ASEAN region, aiming to enhance joint action in addressing environmental concerns. At the same time, ministers adopted standards for air quality and river water to be achieved by all ASEAN member countries by 2010. In June 1995 ministers agreed to co-operate to counter the problems of transboundary pollution.

In December 1997 ASEAN heads of state endorsed a Regional Haze Action Plan to address the environmental problems resulting from forest fires, which had afflicted several countries in the region throughout that year. A Haze Technical Task Force undertook to implement the plan in 1998, with assistance from the UN Environment Programme. In March ministers of the environment requested international financial assistance to help mitigate the dangers of forest fires in Indonesia, which had suffered an estimated US $1,000m. in damage in 1997. Sub-regional fire-fighting arrangement working groups for Sumatra and Borneo were established in April 1998 and in May the Task Force organized a regional workshop to strengthen ASEAN capacity to prevent and alleviate the haze caused by the extensive fires. A pilot project of aerial surveillance of the areas in the region most at risk of forest fires was initiated in July. In December heads of government resolved to establish an ASEAN Regional Research and Training Centre for Land and Forest Fire Management by 2004. An agreement on Transboundary Haze Pollution, covering monitoring, assessment and prevention of haze and fires, and action (including migration) in case of disaster, was presented to the ASEAN summit in November 2001. The ASEAN Specialized Meteorological Centre (ASMC) based in Singapore, plays a primary role in long-range climatological forecasting, early detection and monitoring of fires and haze.

In April 2000 ministers adopted a Strategic Plan of Action on the Environment for 1999–2004. Activities under the Plan focus on issues of coastal and marine erosion, nature conservation and biodiversity, the implementation of multilateral environmental agreements, and forest fires and haze. Other ASEAN environmental objectives include the implementation of a water conservation programme and the formation and adoption of an ASEAN protocol on access to genetic resources. The ASEAN Environment Year in 2000 (with the theme Our Heritage—Our Future) aimed to raise awareness of issues, promote private-sector partnerships and stimulate regional activities. An ASEAN Regional Centre for Biodiversity Conservation (ARCBC) was established in February 1999. It held several workshops in 2000 and 2001, on issues including genetically modified organisms (GMOs), access to genetic resources and data sharing. In May 2001 environment ministers launched the ASEAN Environment Education Action Plan (AEEAP), with the aim of making citizens 'environmentally literate', and willing and able to participate in sustainable regional development.

SOCIAL DEVELOPMENT

ASEAN concerns in social development include youth development, the role of women, health and nutrition, education, labour affairs and disaster management. In December 1993 ASEAN ministers responsible for social affairs adopted a Plan of Action for Children, which provided a framework for regional co-operation for the survival, protection and development of children in member countries.

The seventh ASEAN summit meeting, held in November 2001, declared work on combating HIV and AIDS to be a priority. The second phase of a work programme to combat AIDS and provide help for sufferers was endorsed at the meeting. Heads of government expressed their readiness to commit the necessary resources for prevention and care, and to attempt to obtain access to cheaper drugs. More than 1.5m. people in South-East Asia were known to be infected with the HIV virus. An ASEAN task force on AIDS has been operational since March 1993.

ASEAN supports efforts to combat drug abuse and illegal drugs-trafficking. It aims to promote education and drug-awareness campaigns throughout the region, and administers a project to strengthen the training of personnel involved in combating drug abuse. In October 1994 a meeting of ASEAN Senior Officials on Drug Matters approved a three-year plan of action on drug abuse, providing a framework for co-operation in four priority areas: preventive drug education; treatment and rehabilitation; law enforcement; and research. In July 1998 ASEAN ministers of foreign affairs signed a Joint Declaration for a Drug-Free ASEAN, which envisaged greater co-operation among member states, in particular in information exchange, educational resources and legal procedures, in order to eliminate the illicit production, processing and trafficking of narcotic substances by 2020. (This deadline was subsequently advanced to 2015.)

In January 1992 the ASEAN summit meeting resolved to establish an ASEAN University Network (AUN) to hasten the development of a regional identity. A draft AUN Charter and Agreement were adopted in 1995. The Network aims to strengthen co-operation within the grouping, develop academic and professional human resources and transmit information and knowledge. The 17 universities linked in the network carry out collaborative studies and research programmes. At the seventh ASEAN summit in November 2001 heads of government agreed to establish the first ASEAN University, in Malaysia.

In December 1998 ASEAN leaders approved a series of measures aimed at mitigating the social impact of the financial and economic crises that had affected many countries in the region. Plans of Action were formulated on issues of rural development and poverty eradication, while Social Safety Nets, which aimed to protect the most vulnerable members of society, were approved. The summit meeting emphasized the need to promote job generation as a key element of strategies for economic recovery and growth. In November 2000 heads of government endorsed an Initiative for ASEAN Integration, which aimed to reduce economic disparities within the region through effective co-operation, in particular, in training and other educational opportunities. The fourth meeting of ministers of social welfare in August 2001 noted the need for a holistic approach to social problems, integrating social and economic development. The summit meeting in November considered the widening development gap between ASEAN members and concluded that bridging this gap was a priority, particularly with respect to developing human resources and infrastructure and providing access to IT.

TOURISM

National Tourist Organizations from ASEAN countries meet regularly to assist in co-ordinating the region's tourist industry, and a Tourism Forum is held annually to promote the sector. The first formal meeting of ASEAN ministers of tourism was held in January 1998, in Cebu, the Philippines. The meeting adopted a Plan of Action on ASEAN Co-operation in Tourism, which aimed to promote intra-ASEAN travel, greater investment in the sector, joint marketing of the region as a single tourist destination and environmentally sustainable tourism. The second meeting of ASEAN ministers of tourism was held in Singapore in January 1999. Ministers agreed to appoint country co-ordinators to implement various initiatives, including the designation of 2002 as 'Visit ASEAN Millennium Year'; research to promote the region as a tourist destination in the 21st century, and to develop a cruise-ship industry; and the establishment of a network of ASEAN Tourism Training Centres to develop new skills and technologies in the tourism industry by 2001. The third meeting of tourism ministers, held in Bangkok, Thailand, in January 2000, agreed to reformulate the Visit ASEAN Millennium Year initiative as a long-term Visit ASEAN programme. This was formally launched in January 2001 at the fourth ministerial meeting. The first phase of the programme, implemented in 2001, promoted brand awareness through an intense marketing effort; the second phase, initiated at the fifth ministers' meeting, held in Yogyakarta, Indonesia, in January 2002, was to direct campaigns towards end-consumers. Ministers urged member states to abolish all fiscal and non-fiscal travel barriers, to encourage tourism, including intra-ASEAN travel. A seminar on sustainable tourism was held in Malaysia in October 2001.

CULTURE AND INFORMATION

Regular workshops and festivals are held in visual and performing arts, youth music, radio, television and films, and print and interpersonal media. In addition, ASEAN administers a News Exchange and provides support for the training of editors, journalists and information officers. In 2000 ASEAN adopted new cultural strategies, with the aims of raising awareness of the grouping's objectives and achievements, both regionally and internationally. The strategies included: producing ASEAN cultural and historical educational materials; promoting cultural exchanges (especially for young people); and achieving greater exposure of ASEAN cultural activities and issues in the mass media. It was agreed to work towards the creation of an ASEAN Cultural Heritage Network, for use by professionals and the public, by 2002. An ASEAN Youth Camp, with the theme Trail of Unity, was held in Malaysia in June 2001.

In July 1997 ASEAN ministers of foreign affairs endorsed the establishment of an ASEAN Foundation to promote awareness of the organization and greater participation in its activities; this was inaugurated in July 1998 and is based at the ASEAN secretariat building (www.aseanfoundation.org). The Foundation's work programme for 2000–03 has four major goals: promotion of awareness of ASEAN activities; reinforcement of ASEAN solidarity; promotion of development co-operation in poverty alleviation and related issues; and organizational development.

Publications

Annual Report.

AFTA Brochure.

ASEAN Investment Report (annually).

ASEAN State of the Environment Report (1st report: 1997; 2nd report: 2000).

ASEAN Update (6 a year).

Business ASEAN (6 a year).

Public Information Series, Briefing Papers, Documents Series, educational materials.

The ASEAN Declaration (Bangkok Declaration)

(8 August 1967)

The Presidium Minister for Political Affairs/Minister for Foreign Affairs of Indonesia, the Deputy Prime Minister of Malaysia, the Secretary of Foreign Affairs of the Philippines, the Minister for Foreign Affairs of Singapore and the Minister of Foreign Affairs of Thailand:

Mindful of the existence of mutual interests and common problems among countries of South-East Asia and convinced of the need to strengthen further the existing bonds of regional solidarity and co-operation;

Desiring to establish a firm foundation for common action to promote regional co-operation in South-East Asia in the spirit of equality and partnership and thereby contribute towards peace, progress and prosperity in the region;

Conscious that in an increasingly interdependent world, the cherished ideals of peace, freedom, social justice and economic well-being are best attained by fostering good understanding, good neighbourliness and meaningful co-operation among the countries of the region already bound together by ties of history and culture;

Considering that the countries of South-East Asia share a primary responsibility for strengthening the economic and social stabilility of the region and ensuring their peaceful and progressive national development, and that they are determined to ensure their stability and security from external interference in any form or manifestation in order to preserve their national identities in accordance with the ideals and aspirations of their peoples;

Affirming that all foreign bases are temporary and remain only with the expressed concurrence of the countries concerned and are not intended to be used directly or indirectly to subvert the national independence and freedom of States in the area or prejudice the orderly processes of their national development;

Do hereby declare:

First, the establishment of an Association for Regional Co-operation among the countries of South-East Asia to be known as the Association of South-East Asian Nations (ASEAN).

Second, that the aims and purposes of the Association shall be:

1. To accelerate the economic growth, social progress and cultural development in the region through joint endeavours in the spirit of equality and partnership in order to strengthen the foundation for a prosperous and peaceful community of South-East Asian Nations;
2. To promote regional peace and stability through abiding respect for justice and the rule of law in the relationship among countries of the region and adherence to the principles of the United Nations Charter;
3. To promote active collaboration and mutual assistance on matters of common interest in the economic, social, cultural, technical, scientific and administrative fields;
4. To provide assistance to each other in the form of training and research facilities in the educational, professional, technical and administrative spheres;
5. To collaborate more effectively for the greater utilization of their agriculture and industries, the expansion of their trade, including the study of the problems of international commodity trade, the improvement of their transportation and communications facilities and the raising of the living standards of their peoples;
6. To promote South-East Asian studies;
7. To maintain close and beneficial co-operation with existing international and regional organizations with similar aims and purposes, and explore all avenues for even closer co-operation among themselves.

Third, that to carry out these aims and purposes, the following machinery shall be established:

(a) Annual Meeting of Foreign Ministers, which shall be by rotation and referred to as ASEAN Ministerial Meeting. Special Meetings of Foreign Ministers may be convened as required.

(b) A Standing committee, under the chairmanship of the Foreign Minister of the host country or his representative and having as its members the accredited Ambassadors of the other member countries, to carry on the work of the Association in between Meetings of Foreign Ministers.

(c) *Ad-hoc* Committees and Permanent Committees of specialists and officials on specific subjects.

(d) A National Secretariat in each member country to carry out the work of the Association on behalf of that country and to service the Annual or Special Meetings of Foreign Ministers, the Standing Committee and such other committees as may hereafter be established.

Fourth, that the Association is open for participation to all States in the South-East Asian Region subscribing to the aforementioned aims, principles and purposes.

Fifth, that the Association represents the collective will of the nations of South-East Asia to bind themselves together in friendship and co-operation and, through joint efforts and sacrifices, secure for their peoples and for posterity the blessings of peace, freedom and prosperity.

Treaty of Amity and Co-operation in South-East Asia

(24 February 1976)

The High Contracting Parties:

Conscious of the existing ties of history, geography and culture, which have bound their peoples together;

Anxious to promote regional peace and stability through abiding respect for justice and the rule of law and enhancing regional resilience in their relations;

Desiring to enhance peace, friendship and mutual co-operation on matters affecting South-East Asia consistent with the spirit and principles of the Charter of the United Nations, the Ten Principles adopted by the Asian-African Conference in Bandung on 25 April 1955, the Declaration of the Association of South-East Asian Nations signed in Bangkok on 8 August 1967, and the Declaration signed in Kuala Lumpur on 27 November 1971;

Convinced that the settlement of differences or disputes between their countries should be regulated by rational, effective and sufficiently flexible procedures, avoiding negative attitudes which might endanger or hinder co-operation;

Believing in the need for co-operation with all peace-loving nations, both within and outside South-East Asia, in the furtherance of world peace, stability and harmony;

Solemnly agree to enter into a Treaty of Amity and Co-operation as follows:

I. PURPOSE AND PRINCIPLES

Article 1

The purpose of this Treaty is to promote perpetual peace, everlasting amity and co-operation among their peoples which would contribute to their strength, solidarity and closer relationship.

Article 2

In their relations with one another, the High Contracting Parties shall be guided by the following fundamental principles:

(a) Mutual respect for the independence, sovereignty, equality, territorial integrity and national identity of all nations;

(b) The right of every State to lead its national existence free from external interference, subversion or coercion;

(c) Non-interference in the internal affairs of one another;

(d) Settlement of differences or disputes by peaceful means;
(e) Renunciation of the threat or use of force;
(f) Effective co-operation among themselves.

II. AMITY

Article 3
In pursuance of the purpose of this Treaty the High Contracting Parties shall endeavour to develop and strengthen the traditional, cultural and historical ties of friendship, good neighbourliness and co-operation which bind them together and shall fulfill in good faith the obligations assumed under this Treaty. In order to promote closer understanding among them, the High Contracting Parties shall encourage and facilitate contract and intercourse among their peoples.

III. CO-OPERATION

Article 4
The High Contracting Parties shall promote active co-operation in the economic, social, technical, scientific and administrative fields as well as in matters of common ideals and aspirations of international peace and stability in the region and all other matters of common interest.

Article 5
Pursuant to Article 4 the High Contracting Parties shall exert their maximum efforts multilaterally as well as bilaterally on the basis of equality, non-discrimination and mutual benefit.

Article 6
The High Contracting Parties shall collaborate for the acceleration of the economic growth in the region in order to strengthen the foundation for a prosperous and peaceful community of nations in South-East Asia. To this end, they shall promote the greater utilization of their agricultural and industries, the expansion of their trade and the improvement of their economic infrastructure for the mutual benefit of their peoples. In this regard, they shall continue to explore all avenues for close and beneficial co-operation with other States as well as international and regional organizations outside the region.

Article 7
The High Contracting Parties, in order to achieve social justice and to raise the standards of living of the peoples of the region, shall intensify economic co-operation. For this purpose, they shall adopt appropriate regional strategies for economic development and mutual assistance.

Article 8
The High Contracting Parties shall strive to achieve the closest co-operation on the widest scale and shall seek to provide assistance to one another in the form of training and research facilities in the social, cultural, technical, scientific and administrative fields.

Article 9
The High Contracting Parties shall endeavour to foster co-operation in the furtherance of the cause of peace, harmony, and stability in the region. To this end, the High Contracting Parties shall maintain regular contacts and consultations with one another on international and regional matters with a view to co-ordinating their views and policies.

Article 10
Each High Contracting Party shall not in any manner or form participate in any activity which shall constitute a threat to the political and economic stability, sovereignty, or territorial integrity of another High Contracting Party.

Article 11
The High Contracting Parties shall endeavour to strengthen their respective national resilience in their political, economic, socio-cultural as well as security fields in conformity with their respective ideals and aspirations, free from external interference as well as internal subversive activities in order to preserve their respective national identities.

Article 12
The High Contracting Parties in their efforts to achieve regional prosperity and security, shall endeavour to co-operate in all fields for the promotion of regional resilience, based on the principles of self-confidence, self-reliance, mutual respect, co-operation of solidarity which will constitute the foundation for a strong and viable community of nations in South-East Asia.

IV. PACIFIC SETTLEMENT OF DISPUTES

Article 13
The High Contracting Parties shall have the determination and good faith to prevent disputes from arising. In the case of disputes on matters directly affecting them, the High Contracting Parties shall refrain from the threat or use of force and shall at all times settle such disputes among themselves through friendly negotiations.

Article 14
To settle disputes through regional processes, the High Contracting Parties shall constitute, as a continuing body, a High Council comprising a Representative at ministerial level from each of the High Contracting Parties to take cognizance of the existence of disputes or situations likely to disturb regional peace and harmony.

Article 15
In the event no solution is reached through direct negotiations, the High Council shall take cognizance of the dispute or the situation and shall recommend to the parties in dispute appropriate means of settlement such as good offices, mediation, inquiry or conciliation. The High Council may, however, offer its good offices, or upon agreement of the parties in dispute, constitute itself into a committee of mediation, inquiry or conciliation. When deemed necessary, the High Council shall recommend appropriate measures for the prevention of a deterioration of the dispute of the situation.

Article 16
The foregoing provision of this Chapter shall not apply to a dispute unless all the parties to the dispute agree to their application to that dispute. However, this shall not preclude the other High Contracting Parties not party to the dispute from offering all possible assistance to settle the said dispute. Parties to the dispute should be well disposed towards such offers of assistance.

Article 17
Nothing in this Treaty shall preclude recourse to the modes of peaceful settlement contained in Article 33(1) of the Charter of the United Nations. The High Contracting Parties which are parties to a dispute should be encouraged to take initiatives to solve it by friendly negotiations before resorting to the other procedures provided for in the Charter of the United Nations.

V. GENERAL PROVISIONS

(Articles 18–20)

Declaration of ASEAN Concord

(24 February 1976)

The President of the Republic of Indonesia, the Prime Minister of Malaysia, the President of the Republic of the Philippines, the Prime Minister of the Republic of Singapore and the Prime Minister of the Kingdom of Thailand:

Reaffirm their commitment to the Declarations of Bandung, Bangkok and Kuala Lumpur, and the Charter of the United Nations;

Endeavour to promote peace, progress, prosperity and the welfare of the peoples of member states;

Undertake to consolidate the achievements of ASEAN and expand ASEAN co-operation in the economic, social, cultural and political fields;

Do hereby declare:

ASEAN co-operation shall take into account, among others, the following objectives and principles in the pursuit of political stability:

1. The stability of each member state and of the ASEAN region is an essential contribution to international peace and security. Each member state resolves to eliminate threats posed by subversion to its stability, thus strengthening national and ASEAN resilience.
2. Member states, individually and collectively, shall take active steps for the early establishment of the Zone of Peace, Freedom and Neutrality.
3. The elimination of poverty, hunger, disease and illiteracy is a primary concern of member states. They shall therefore intensify co-operation in economic and social development, with particular

emphasis on the promotion of social justice and on the improvement of the living standards of their peoples.

4. Natural disasters and other major calamities can retard the pace of development of member states. They shall extend, within their capabilities, assistance for relief of member states in distress.

5. Member states shall take co-operative action in their national and regional development programmes, utilizing as far as possible the resources available in the ASEAN region to broaden the complementarity of their respective economies.

6. Member states, in the spirit of ASEAN solidarity, shall rely exclusively on peaceful processes in the settlement of intra-regional differences.

7. Member states shall strive, individually and collectively, to create conditions conducive to the promotion of peaceful co-operation among the nations of South-East Asia on the basis of mutual respect and mutual benefit.

8. Member states shall vigorously develop an awareness of regional identity and exert all efforts to create a strong ASEAN community, respected by all and respecting all nations on the basis of mutually advantageous relationships, and in accordance with the principles of self-determination, sovereign equality and non-interference in the internal affairs of nations.

And do hereby adopt

The following programme of action as a framework for ASEAN co-operation.

A. POLITICAL

1. Meeting of the Heads of Government of the member states as and when necessary.

2. Signing of the Treaty of Amity and Co-operation in South-East Asia.

3. Settlement of intra-regional disputes by peaceful means as soon as possible.

4. Immediate consideration of initial steps towards recognition of and respect for the Zone of Peace, Freedom and Neutrality wherever possible.

5. Improvement of ASEAN machinery to strengthen political co-operation.

6. Study on how to develop judicial co-operation including the possibility of an ASEAN Extradition Treaty.

7. Strengthening of political solidarity by promoting the harmonization of views, co-ordinating position and, where possible and desirable, taking common actions.

B. ECONOMIC

1. Co-operation on Basic Commodities, particularly Food and Energy.

(i) Member states shall assist each other by according priority to the supply of the individual country's needs in critical circumstances, and priority to the acquisition of exports from member states, in respect of basic commodities, particularly food and energy.

(ii) Member states shall also intensify co-operation in the production of basic commodities, particularly food and energy, in the individual member states of the region.

2. Industrial Co-operation.

(i) Member states shall co-operate to establish large-scale ASEAN industrial plants particularly to meet regional requirements of essential commodities.

(ii) Priority shall be given to projects which utilize the available materials in the member states, contribute to the increase of food production, increase foreign exchange earnings or save foreign exchange and create employment.

3. Co-operation in Trade.

(i) Member states shall co-operate in the fields of trade in order to promote development and growth of new production and trade and to improve the trade structures of individual states and among countries of ASEAN conducive to further development and to safeguard and increase their foreign exchange earnings and reserves.

(ii) Member states shall progress towards the establishment of preferential trading arrangements as a long-term objective on a basis deemed to be at any particular time appropriate through rounds of negotiations subject to the unanimous agreement of member states.

(iii) The expansion of trade among member states shall be facilitated through co-operation on basic commodities, particularly in food and energy and through co-operation in ASEAN industrial projects.

(iv) Member states shall accelerate joint efforts to improve access to markets outside ASEAN for their raw material and finished products by seeking the elimination of all trade barriers in those markets, developing new usage for these products and in adopting common approaches and actions in dealing with regional groupings and individual economic powers.

(v) Such efforts shall also lead to co-operation in the field of technology and production methods in order to increase the production and to improve the quality of export products, as well as to develop new export products with a view to diversifying exports.

4. Joint Approach to International Commodity Problems and Other World Economic Problems.

(i) The principle of ASEAN co-operation on trade shall also be reflected on a priority basis in joint approaches to international commodity problems and other world economic problems, such as the reform of international trading systems, the reform of the international monetary system and the transfer of real resources, at the United Nations and other relevant multilateral fora, with a view to contributing to the establishment of the New International Economic Order.

(ii) Member states shall give priority to the stabilization and increase of export earnings of those commodities produced and exported by them through commodity agreements including bufferstock schemes and other means.

5. Machinery for Economic Co-operation. Ministerial meetings on economic matters shall be held regularly or as deemed necessary in order to:

(i) formulate recommendations for the consideration of Governments of member states for the strengthening of ASEAN economic co-operation;

(ii) review the co-ordination and implementation of agreed ASEAN programmes and projects on economic co-operation;

(iii) exchange views and consult on national development plans and policies as a step towards harmonizing regional development; and

(iv) perform such other relevant functions as agreed upon by the member Governments.

C. SOCIAL

1. Co-operation in the field of social development, with emphasis on the well-being of the low-income group and of the rural population, through the expansion of opportunities for productive employment with fair remuneration.

2. Support for the active involvement of all sectors and levels of the ASEAN communities, particularly the women and youth, in development efforts.

3. Intensification and expansion of existing co-operation in meeting the problems of population growth in the ASEAN region, and where possible, formulation of new strategies in collaboration with appropriate international agencies.

4. Intensification of co-operation among member states as well as with the relevant international bodies in the prevention and eradication of the abuse of narcotics and the illegal trafficking of drugs.

D. CULTURAL AND INFORMATION

1. Introduction of the study of ASEAN, its member states and their national languages as part of the curricula of schools and other institutions of learning in the member states.

2. Support of ASEAN scholars, writers, artists and mass media representatives to enable them to play an active role in fostering a sense of regional identity and fellowship.
3. Promotion of South-East Asian studies through closer collaboration among national institutes.

E. SECURITY

Continuation of co-operation on a non-ASEAN basis between the member states in security matters in accordance with their mutual needs and interests.

F. IMPROVEMENT OF ASEAN MACHINERY

1. Signing of the Agreement on the Establishment of the ASEAN Secretariat.
2. Regular review of the ASEAN organizational structure with a view to improving its effectiveness.
3. Study of the desirability of a new constitutional framework for ASEAN.

BANK FOR INTERNATIONAL SETTLEMENTS—BIS

Address: Centralbahnplatz 2, 4052 Basel, Switzerland.

Telephone: (61) 2808080; **fax:** (61) 2809100; **e-mail:** emailmaster@bis.org; **internet:** www.bis.org.

The Bank for International Settlements was founded pursuant to the Hague Agreements of 1930 to promote co-operation among national central banks and to provide additional facilities for international financial operations.

Organization

(April 2002)

GENERAL MEETING

The General Meeting is held annually in June and is attended by representatives of the central banks of countries in which shares have been subscribed. At March 2002 the central banks of the following authorities were entitled to attend and vote at General Meetings of the BIS: Argentina, Australia, Austria, Belgium, Bosnia and Herzegovina, Brazil, Bulgaria, Canada, the People's Republic of China, Croatia, the Czech Republic, Denmark, Estonia, Finland, France, Germany, Greece, Hong Kong, Hungary, Iceland, India, Ireland, Italy, Japan, the Republic of Korea, Latvia, Lithuania, the former Yugoslav republic of Macedonia, Malaysia, Mexico, the Netherlands, Norway, Poland, Portugal, Romania, Russia, Saudi Arabia, Singapore, Slovakia, Slovenia, South Africa, Spain, Sweden, Switzerland, Thailand, Turkey, the United Kingdom and the USA. The European Central Bank became a shareholder in December 1999.

BOARD OF DIRECTORS

The Board of Directors is responsible for the conduct of the Bank's operations at the highest level, and comprises the Governors in office of the central banks of Belgium, France, Germany, Italy, the United Kingdom and the USA, each of whom appoints another member of the same nationality. The statutes also provide for the election to the Board of not more than nine Governors of other member central banks: those of Canada, Japan, the Netherlands, Sweden and Switzerland are elected members of the Board.

Chairman of the Board and President of the Bank: NOUT WELLINK (Netherlands).

MANAGEMENT

The Bank has a staff of about 500 employees, from 35 countries. In July 1998 the BIS inaugurated its first overseas administrative unit, the Representative Office for Asia and the Pacific, which was based in Hong Kong. In November 2001 an agreement was concluded to open a Representative Office for the Americas in Mexico City, Mexico.

General Manager: ANDREW CROCKETT (United Kingdom).

Activities

The BIS is an international financial institution whose role is to promote international monetary and financial co-operation, and to fulfil the function of a 'central banks' bank'. Although it has the legal form of a company limited by shares, it is an international organization governed by international law, and enjoys special privileges and immunities in keeping with its role (a Headquarters Agreement was concluded with Switzerland in 1987). The participating central banks were originally given the option of subscribing the shares themselves or arranging for their subscription in their own countries: thus the BIS also has some private shareholders, but they have no right of participation in the General Meeting. Some 86% of the total share capital is in the hands of central banks and 14% is held by private shareholders. In January 2001 an extraordinary general meeting amended the Bank's statutes to restrict ownership to central banks. Accordingly, all shares held by private shareholders were to be repurchased at a specified rate of compensation.

FINANCE

The authorized capital of the Bank is 1,500m. gold francs, divided into 600,000 shares of 2,500 gold francs each.

Statement of Account*

(In millions of gold francs; units of 0.29032258 . . . gram of fine gold—Art. 4 of the Statutes; 31 March 2001)

Assets		%
Gold (bars)	2,195.3	2.89
Cash on hand and on sight a/c with banks	20.3	0.03
Treasury bills	4,597.8	6.05
Time deposits and advances	46,122.2	60.64
Securities at term	22,221.5	29.22
Miscellaneous	896.9	1.18
Total	76,054.0	100.00

Liabilities		%
Authorized cap.: 1,500,000,000		
Issued cap.: 1,292,912,500 viz. 529,165 shares of which 25% paid up	330.7	0.43
Reserves	3,134.7	4.12
Deposits (gold)	2,842.3	3.74
Deposits (currencies)	67,274.8	88.46
Miscellaneous	2,422.9	3.19
Dividend payable on 1 July	48.6	0.06
Total	76,054.0	100.0

* Assets and liabilities in US dollars are converted at a fixed rate of US $208 per fine ounce of gold (equivalent to 1 gold franc = $1.94149 . . .) and all other items in currencies on the basis of market rates against the US dollar.

BANKING OPERATIONS

The BIS assists central banks in managing and investing their monetary reserves: in 2001 some 120 international financial institutions and central banks from all over the world had deposits with the BIS, representing around 7% of world foreign exchange reserves.

The BIS uses the funds deposited with it partly for lending to central banks. Its credit transactions may take the form of swaps against gold; covered credits secured by means of a pledge of gold or marketable short-term securities; credits against gold or currency deposits of the same amount and for the same duration held with the BIS; unsecured credits in the form of advances or deposits; or standby credits, which in individual instances are backed by guarantees given by member central banks. In addition, the Bank undertakes operations in foreign exchange and in gold, both with central banks and with the markets.

In 1982, faced with the increasingly critical debt situation of some Latin American countries and the resultant threat to the viability of the international financial system, the BIS granted comparatively large-scale loans to central banks that did not number among its shareholders: the central banks of Argentina, Brazil and Mexico were granted bridging loans pending the disbursement of balance-of-payments credits extended by the IMF. These facilities amounted to almost US $3,000m., all of which had been repaid by the end of 1983. The Bank subsequently made similar loans, but with decreasing frequency. Since 1990 the BIS has contributed funds to bridging facilities arranged for the central banks of Venezuela, Guyana, Hungary, Romania, the former Yugoslav republic of Macedonia, Mexico (in 1995) and Thailand (in August 1997). Within the framework of an international financial programme, approved in support of the Brazilian economy in late 1998, the Bank was to co-ordinate a credit facility of up to $13,280m. in favour of the Banco Central do Brasil. Funds were provided with the backing or guarantee of 19 central banks; the load was repaid in full in April 2000.

The BIS also engages in traditional types of investment: funds not required for lending to central banks are placed in the market as deposits with commercial banks and purchases of short-term negotiable paper, including Treasury bills. Such operations constitute a major part of the Bank's business.

Because the central banks' monetary reserves must be available at short notice, they can only be placed with the BIS at short term, for fixed periods and with clearly defined repayment terms. The BIS has to match its assets to the maturity structure and nature of its commitments, and must therefore conduct its business with special regard to maintaining a high degree of liquidity.

The Bank's operations must be in conformity with the monetary policy of the central banks of the countries concerned. It is not permitted to make advances to governments or to open current accounts in their name. Real estate transactions are also excluded.

INTERNATIONAL MONETARY CO-OPERATION

Governors of central banks meet for regular discussions at the BIS to co-ordinate international monetary policy and ensure orderly conditions on the international financial markets. There is close co-operation with the IMF and the World Bank. The BIS participates in meetings of the so-called Group of 10 (G-10) industrialized nations (see IMF p. 173), which has been a major forum for discussion of international monetary issues since its establishment in 1962. Governors of central banks of the G-10 countries convene for regular Basle Monthly Meetings. In 1971 a Standing Committee of the G-10 central banks was established at the BIS to consider aspects of the development of Euro-currency markets. In February 1999 the G-10 renamed the body the Committee on the Global Financial System, and approved a revised mandate to undertake systematic short-term monitoring of global financial system conditions; longer-term analysis of the functioning of financial markets; and the articulation of policy recommendations aimed at improving market functioning and promoting stability. The Committee was to meet four times a year.

In 1974 the Governors of central banks of the G-10 set up the Basle Committee on Banking Supervision (whose secretariat is provided by the BIS) to co-ordinate banking supervision at the international level. The Committee pools information on banking supervisory regulations and surveillance systems, including the supervision of banks' foreign currency business, identifies possible danger areas and proposes measures to safeguard the banks' solvency and liquidity. An International Conference of Banking Supervisors is held every two years. In 1997 the Committee published new guide-lines, entitled Core Principles for Effective Banking Supervision, that were intended to provide a comprehensive set of standards to ensure sound banking. In 1998 the Committee was concerned with the development and implementation of the Core Principles, particularly given the ongoing financial and economic crisis affecting several Asian countries and instability of other major economies. In January 2001 the Committee issued preliminary proposals on capital adequacy rules; a new regime was scheduled to come into effect in 2004. A Financial Stability Institute was established in 1998, jointly by the BIS and Basle Committee, to enhance the capacity of central banks and supervisory bodies to implement aspects of the Core Principles, through the provision of training programmes and other policy workshops.

In February 1999 ministers of finance and governors of the central banks of the Group of Seven (G-7) industrialized nations approved the establishment of a Financial Stability Forum to strengthen co-operation among the world's largest economies and economic bodies, to improve the monitoring of international finance and to prevent a recurrence of the economic crises of 1997 and 1998. The General Manager of the BIS was appointed to chair the Forum for an initial three-year term. The first meeting of the Forum, comprising representatives of G-7 ministries of finance and central banks, and of international financial institutions and regulatory bodies, took place at the headquarters of the IMF in Washington, DC, USA, in April 1999. Three working groups were established to study aspects of highly leveraged, or unregulated, institutions, offshore financial centres, and short-term capital flows. In November the Forum constituted additional groups to review deposit insurance schemes and to consider measures to promote implementation of international standards. In March 2001 the Forum convened for its seventh meeting and considered, *inter alia,* measures to combat the financing of terrorism and the progress of offshore financial centres in strengthening their supervisory, regulatory and other practices.

The Bank organizes and provides the secretariat for periodic meetings of experts, such as the Group of Computer Experts, the Committee on Payment and Settlement Systems, the Group of Experts on Monetary and Economic Data Bank Questions, which aims to develop a data bank service for the G-10 central banks and the BIS, and the Committee of Experts on Gold and Foreign Exchange, which monitors financial market developments.

Since January 1998 the BIS has hosted the secretariat of the International Association of Insurance Supervisors, which aims to promote co-operation within the insurance industry with regard to effective supervision and the development of domestic insurance markets.

RESEARCH

The Bank's Monetary and Economic Department conducts research, particularly into monetary and financial questions; collects and publishes data on securities markets and international banking developments; and organizes a data bank for central banks. The BIS Annual Report provides an independent analysis of monetary and economic developments. Statistics on international banking and on external indebtedness are also published regularly.

AGENCY AND TRUSTEE FUNCTIONS

Throughout its history the BIS has undertaken various duties as Trustee Fiscal Agent or Depository with regard to international loan agreements. From October 1986 the BIS performed the functions of Agent for the private European Currency Unit (ECU) clearing and settlement system, in accordance with the provisions of successive agreements concluded between the then ECU Banking Association (now Euro Banking Association—EBA), based in Paris, and the BIS. This arrangement was terminated following the introduction of the euro on 1 January 1999, when the ECU clearing system was replaced by a new euro clearing system of the EBA. At that time 62 banks had been granted the status of clearing bank by the EBA.

In April 1994 the BIS assumed new functions in connection with the rescheduling of Brazil's external debt, which had been agreed by the Brazilian Government in November 1993. In accordance with two collateral pledge agreements, the BIS acts in the capacity of Collateral Agent to hold and invest collateral for the benefit of the holders of certain US dollar-denominated bonds, maturing in 15 or 30 years, which have been issued by Brazil under the rescheduling arrangements. The Bank acts in a similar capacity for Peru, in accordance with external debt agreements concluded in November 1996 and a collateral agreement signed with the BIS in March 1997, and for Côte d'Ivoire, under a restructuring agreement signed in May 1997 and collateral agreement signed in March 1998.

Publications

Annual Report (in English, French, German and Italian).

The BIS Consolidated International Banking Statistics (every 6 months).

BIS Papers (series).

Central Bank Survey of Foreign Exchange and Derivatives Market Activity (3 a year).

Joint BIS-IMF-OECD-World Bank Statistics on External Debt (quarterly).

Quarterly Review: International Banking and Financial Market Developments (English, French, German and Italian).

Regular OTC Derivatives Market Statistics (every 6 months).

CARIBBEAN COMMUNITY AND COMMON MARKET—CARICOM

Address: Bank of Guyana Building, POB 10827, Georgetown, Guyana.

Telephone: (2) 69281; **fax:** (2) 67816; **e-mail:** carisec3@caricom.org; **internet:** www.caricom.org.

CARICOM was formed in 1973 by the Treaty of Chaguaramas, signed in Trinidad, as a movement towards unity in the Caribbean; it replaced the Caribbean Free Trade Association (CARIFTA), founded in 1965. A revision of the Treaty of Chaguaramas (by means of nine separate Protocols) was undertaken in the 1990s, to institute greater regional integration and to establish a single Caribbean market and economy.

MEMBERS

Anguilla*	Jamaica
Antigua and Barbuda	Montserrat
Bahamas†	Saint Christopher and Nevis
Barbados	Saint Lucia
Belize	Saint Vincent and the Grenadines
British Virgin Islands*	Suriname
Dominica	Trinidad and Tobago
Grenada	Turks and Caicos Islands*
Guyana	

* The British Virgin Islands and the Turks and Caicos Islands were granted associate membership in 1991; Anguilla's application for associate membership was approved in July 1998 and formally implemented in July 1999.

† The Bahamas is a member of the Community but not the Common Market.

Note: Haiti was accepted as a full member of the Community in July 1997, although the final terms and conditions of its accession had yet to be concluded; it was invited to participate in the deliberations of all the organs and bodies of the Community in the interim. The terms for Haiti's accession were agreed in July 1999 and required ratification by that country's parliament. Aruba, Bermuda, the Cayman Islands, Colombia, the Dominican Republic, Mexico, the Netherlands Antilles, Puerto Rico and Venezuela have observer status with the Community.

Organization

(April 2002)

HEADS OF GOVERNMENT CONFERENCE AND BUREAU

The Conference is the final authority of the Community and determines policy. It is responsible for the conclusion of treaties on behalf of the Community and for entering into relationships between the Community and international organizations and states. Decisions of the Conference are generally taken unanimously. Heads of government meet annually, although intersessional meetings may be convened.

At a special meeting of the Conference, held in Trinidad and Tobago in October 1992, participants decided to establish a Heads of Government Bureau, with the capacity to initiate proposals, to update consensus and to secure the implementation of CARICOM decisions. The Bureau became operational in December, comprising the Chairman of the Conference, as Chairman, as well as the incoming and outgoing Chairmen of the Conference, and the Secretary-General of the Conference, in the capacity of Chief Executive Officer.

COMMUNITY COUNCIL OF MINISTERS

In October 1992 CARICOM heads of government agreed that a Caribbean Community Council of Ministers should be established to replace the existing Common Market Council of Ministers as the second highest organ of the Community. Protocol I amending the Treaty of Chaguaramas, to restructure the organs and institutions of the Community, was formally adopted at a meeting of CARICOM heads of government in February 1997 and was signed by all member states in July. The inaugural meeting of the Community Council of Ministers was held in Nassau, the Bahamas, in February 1998. The Council consists of ministers responsible for community affairs, as well as other government ministers designated by member states, and is responsible for the development of the Community's strategic planning and co-ordination in the areas of economic integration, functional co-operation and external relations.

MINISTERIAL COUNCILS

The principal organs of the Community are assisted in their functions by the following bodies, established under Protocol I amending the Treaty of Chaguaramas: the Council for Trade and Economic Development (COTED); the Council for Foreign and Community Relations (COFCOR); the Council for Human and Social Development (COHSOD); and the Council for Finance and Planning (COFAP). The Councils are responsible for formulating policies, promoting their implementation and supervising co-operation in the relevant areas.

SECRETARIAT

The Secretariat is the main administrative body of the Caribbean Community. The functions of the Secretariat are: to service meetings of the Community and of its Committees; to take appropriate follow-up action on decisions made at such meetings; to carry out studies on questions of economic and functional co-operation relating to the region as a whole; to provide services to member states at their request in respect of matters relating to the achievement of the objectives of the Community.

Secretary-General: EDWIN W. CARRINGTON (Trinidad and Tobago).

Deputy Secretary-General: Dr CARLA BARNETT (Belize).

Activities

REGIONAL INTEGRATION

In 1989 CARICOM heads of government established the 15-member West Indian Commission to study regional political and economic integration. The Commission's final report, submitted in July 1992, recommended that CARICOM should remain a community of sovereign states (rather than a federation), but should strengthen the integration process and expand to include the wider Caribbean region. It recommended the formation of an Association of Caribbean States (ACS), to include all the countries within and surrounding the Caribbean Basin (see p. 530). In November 1997 the Secretaries-General of CARICOM and the ACS signed a Co-operation Agreement to formalize the reciprocal procedures through which the organizations work to enhance and facilitate regional integration.The Heads of Government Conference that was held in October 1992 established an Inter-Governmental Task Force, which was to undertake preparations for a reorientation of CARICOM. In February 1993 it presented a draft Charter of Civil Society for the Community, which set out principles in the areas of democracy, government, parliament, freedom of the press and human rights. The Charter was signed by Community heads of government in February 1997. Suriname was admitted to the organization in July 1995. In July 1997 the Heads of Government Conference agreed to admit Haiti as a member, although the terms and conditions of its accession to the organization had yet to be negotiated. These were finalized in July 1999. In July 2001 the CARICOM Secretary-General formally inaugurated a CARICOM Office in Haiti, which aimed to provide technical assistance in preparation of Haiti's accession to the Community. In January 2002 a CARICOM special mission visited Haiti, following an escalation of the political violence which had started in the previous month. Ministers of foreign affairs emphasized the need for international aid for Haiti when they met their US counterpart in February.

In August 1998 CARICOM and the Dominican Republic signed a free-trade accord, covering trade in goods and services, technical barriers to trade, government procurement, and sanitary and phytosanitary measures and standards. A protocol to the agreement was signed in April 2000, following the resolution of differences concerning exempted items. The accord was ratified by the Dominican Republic in February 2001 and entered partially into force on 1 December (except in Guyana, Suriname and the Bahamas).

In July 1999 CARICOM heads of government endorsed proposals to establish a Caribbean Court of Justice, which, it was provisionally agreed, would be located in Port of Spain, Trinidad and Tobago. The Court was intended to replace the Judicial Committee of the Privy Council as the Court of Final Appeal for those countries recognizing its jurisdiction, and was also to adjudicate on trade disputes and on the interpretation of the CARICOM Treaty. An agreement establishing the Court was formally signed by 10 member countries in February 2001.

In November 2001 the CARICOM Secretary-General formally inaugurated a Caribbean Regional Technical Assistance Centre (CARTAC), in Barbados. The Centre was intended to provide technical advice and training to officials from member countries and the Dominican Republic in support of the region's development, with particular focus on fiscal management, financial sector supervision and regulation, and the compilation of statistics. The IMF was to manage the Centre's operations, while UNDP was to provide administrative and logistical support.

CO-ORDINATION OF FOREIGN POLICY

The co-ordination of foreign policies of member states is listed as one of the main objectives of the Community in its founding treaty. Activities include: strengthening of member states' position in international organizations; joint diplomatic action on issues of particular interest to the Caribbean; joint co-operation arrangements with third countries and organizations; and the negotiation of free-trade agreements with third countries and other regional groupings. This last area of activity has assumed increasing importance since the agreement in 1994 by almost all the governments of countries in the Americas to establish a 'Free Trade Area of the Americas' (FTAA) by 2005. In April 1997 CARICOM inaugurated a Regional Negotiating Machinery body to co-ordinate and strengthen the region's presence at external economic negotiations. The main focus of activities has been the establishment of the FTAA, ACP relations with the EU, and multilateral trade negotiations under the WTO.

In July 1991 Venezuela applied for membership of CARICOM, and offered a non-reciprocal free-trade agreement for CARICOM exports to Venezuela, over an initial five-year period. In October 1993 the newly-established Group of Three (Colombia, Mexico and Venezuela) signed joint agreements with CARICOM and Suriname on combating drugs-trafficking and environmental protection. In June 1994 CARICOM and Colombia concluded an agreement on trade, economic and technical co-operation, which, *inter alia*, gives special treatment to the least-developed CARICOM countries. CARICOM has observer status in the Latin American Rio Group (see p. 545).

In 1992 Cuba applied for observer status within CARICOM, and in July 1993 a joint commission was inaugurated to establish closer ties between CARICOM and Cuba and to provide a mechanism for regular dialogue. In July 1997 the heads of government agreed to pursue consideration of a free-trade accord between the Community and Cuba. A Trade and Economic Agreement was signed by the two sides in July 2000, and a CARICOM office was established in Cuba, in February 2001. In February 1992 ministers of foreign affairs from CARICOM and Central American states met to discuss future co-operation, in view of the imminent conclusion of the North American Free Trade Agreement (NAFTA, see p. 427) between the USA, Canada and Mexico. It was agreed that a consultative forum would be established to discuss the possible formation of a Caribbean and Central American free-trade zone. In October 1993 CARICOM declared its support for NAFTA, but requested a 'grace period', during which the region's exports would have parity with Mexican products, and in March 1994 requested that it should be considered for early entry into NAFTA. In July 1996 the heads of government expressed strong concern over the complaint lodged with the World Trade Organization (WTO) by the USA, Ecuador, Guatemala and Honduras regarding the European Union's import regime on bananas, which gives preferential access to bananas from the ACP countries (see the EU, p. 361). CARICOM requested the US Government to withdraw its complaint and to negotiate a settlement. Nevertheless, WTO panel hearings on the complaint were initiated in September. Banana producers from the ACP countries were granted third-party status, at the insistence of the Eastern Caribbean ambassador to the EU, Edwin Laurent. In December a special meeting of the Heads of Government Conference was convened, in Barbados, in order to formulate a common position on relations with the USA, in particular with respect to measures to combat illegal drugs-trafficking, following reports that the US Government was planning to impose punitive measures against certain regional authorities, owing to their perceived failure to implement effective controls on illicit drugs.

In May 1997 CARICOM heads of government met the US President, Bill Clinton, to discuss issues of mutual concern. A partnership for prosperity and security was established at the meeting, and arrangements were instituted for annual consultations between the ministers of foreign affairs of CARICOM countries and the US Secretary of State. However, the Community failed to secure a commitment by the USA to grant the region's exports 'NAFTA-parity' status, or to guarantee concessions to the region's banana industry, following a temporary ruling of the WTO, issued in March, upholding the US trade complaint. The WTO ruling was confirmed in May and endorsed by the WTO dispute settlement body in September. The USA's opposition to a new EU banana policy (which was to terminate the import licensing system, extending import quotas to 'dollar' producers, while maintaining a limited duty-free quota for Caribbean producers) was strongly criticized by CARICOM leaders, meeting in July 1998. In March 1999 the Inter-Sessional meeting of the Conference of Heads of Government issued a statement condemning the imposition by the USA of sanctions against a number of EU imports, in protest at the revised EU banana regime, and the consequences of this action on Caribbean economies, and agreed to review its co-operation with the USA under the partnership for prosperity and security.

During 1998 CARICOM was particularly concerned by the movement within Nevis to secede from its federation with Saint Christopher. In July heads of government agreed to dispatch a mediation team to the country (postponed until September). The Heads of Government Conference held in March 1999 welcomed the establishment of a Constitutional Task Force by the local authorities to prepare a draft constitution, on the basis of recommendations of a previous constitutional commission and the outcome of a series of public meetings. In July 1998 heads of government expressed concern at the hostility between the Government and opposition groupings in Guyana. The two sides signed an agreement, under CARICOM auspices, and in September a CARICOM mediation mission visited Guyana to promote further dialogue. CARICOM has declared its support for Guyana in its territorial disputes with Venezuela and Suriname. In June 2000 CARICOM initiated negotiations following Suriname's removal of petroleum drilling equipment from Guyanan territorial waters. In March 2000 heads of government issued a statement supporting the territorial integrity and security of Belize in that country's ongoing border dispute with Guatemala. CARICOM subsequently urged both countries to implement the provisions of an agreement signed in November. In December 2001 a CARICOM mission observed a general election in Trinidad and Tobago. Following an inconclusive outcome to the election, a delegation from CARICOM visited that country in late January 2002.

In July 2000 the Heads of Government meeting issued a statement strongly opposing the OECD Harmful Tax Initiative, under which punitive measures had been threatened against 35 countries, including CARICOM member states, if they failed to tighten taxation legislation. The meeting also condemned a separate list, issued by the OECD's Financial Action Task Force on Money Laundering (FATF, see p. 536), which identified 15 countries, including five Caribbean states, of failing to counter effectively international money-laundering. The statement reaffirmed CARICOM's commitment to fighting financial crimes and support for any necessary reform of supervisory practices or legislation, but insisted that national taxation jurisdictions, and specifically competitive regimes designed to attract offshore business, was not a matter for OECD concern. CARICOM remained actively involved in efforts to counter the scheme, and in April 2001 presented its case to the US President. In September the FATF issued a revised list of 19 'unco-operative jurisdictions', including Dominica, Grenada, St Christopher and Nevis and St Vincent and the Grenadines. In early 2002 most Caribbean states concluded a provisional agreement with the OECD to work to improve the transparency and supervision of offshore sectors, in advance of a deadline of 28 February.

In February 2002 the first meeting of heads of state and of government of CARICOM and the Central American Integration System convened in Belize City. The meeting aimed to strengthen co-operation between the groupings, in particular in international negotiations, efforts to counter transnational organized crime, and support for the regions' economies.

ECONOMIC CO-OPERATION

The Caribbean Community's main field of activity is economic integration, by means of a Caribbean Common Market which replaced the former Caribbean Free Trade Association. The Secretariat and the Caribbean Development Bank undertake research on the best means of facing economic difficulties, and meetings of the Chief Executives of commercial banks and of central bank officials are also held with the aim of strengthening regional co-operation. In October 1998 the CARICOM Bureau requested an urgent assessment of the impact on the region of the financial and economic instability apparent in several major economies.

During the 1980s the economic difficulties of member states hindered the development of intra-regional trade. At the annual Conference held in June/July 1987, the heads of government agreed to dismantle all obstacles to trade within CARICOM by October 1988. This was implemented as planned, but included a three-year period of protection for 17 products from the member countries of the Organisation of Eastern Caribbean States (OECS, see p. 533).

In July 1984 heads of government agreed to establish a common external tariff (CET) on certain products, in order to protect domestic industries, although implementation of the CET was considerably delayed (see below). They also urged the necessity of structural adjustment in the economies of the region, including measures to expand production and reduce imports. In 1989 the Conference of Heads of Government agreed to implement, by July 1993, a series of measures to encourage the creation of a single Caribbean market. These included the establishment of a CARICOM Industrial Programming Scheme; the inauguration of the CARICOM Enterprise Regime; abolition of passport requirements for CARICOM nationals travelling within the region; full implementation of the rules of origin and the revised scheme for the harmonization of fiscal incentives; free movement of skilled workers; removal of all remaining regional barriers to trade; establishment of a regional system of air and sea transport; and the introduction of a scheme for regional capital movement. A CARICOM Export Development Council, established in November 1989, undertook a three-year export development project to stimulate trade within CARICOM and to promote exports outside the region.

In August 1990 CARICOM heads of government mandated the governors of CARICOM members' central banks to begin a study of the means to achieve a monetary union within CARICOM; they also institutionalized meetings of CARICOM ministers of finance and senior finance officials, to take place twice a year.

The initial deadline of 1 January 1991 for the establishment of a CET was not achieved, and in July a new deadline of 1 October was set for those members which had not complied—Antigua and Barbuda, Belize, Montserrat, Saint Christopher and Nevis and Saint Lucia, whose governments feared that the tariff would cause an increase in the rate of inflation and damage domestic industries. This deadline was later (again unsuccessfully) extended to February 1992. The tariff, which imposed a maximum level of duty of 45% on imports, was also criticized by the World Bank, the IMF and the US Government as being likely to reduce the region's competitiveness. At a special meeting, held in October 1992, CARICOM heads of government agreed to reduce the maximum level of tariffs to between 30% and 35%, to be in effect by 30 June 1993 (the level was to be further lowered, to 25%–30% by 1995). The Bahamas, however, was not party to these trading arrangements (since it is a member of the Community but not of the Common Market), and Belize was granted an extension for the implementation of the new tariff levels. At the Heads of Government Conference, held in July 1995 in Guyana, Suriname was admitted as a full member of CARICOM and acceded to the treaty establishing the Common Market. It was granted until 1 January 1996 for implementation of the tariff reductions.

The 1995 Heads of Government Conference approved additional measures to promote the single market. The free movement of skilled workers (mainly graduates from recognized regional institutions) was to be permitted from 1 January 1996. At the same time an agreement on the mutual protection and provision of social security benefits was to enter into force. In July 1996 the heads of government decided that CARICOM ministers of finance, central bank governors and planning agencies should meet more frequently to address single market issues and agreed to extend the provisions of free movement to sports people, musicians and others working in the arts and media.

In July 1997 the heads of government, meeting in Montego Bay, Jamaica, agreed to accelerate economic integration, with the aim of completing a single market by 1999. At the meeting 11 member states signed Protocol II amending the Treaty of Chaguaramas, which constituted a central element of a CARICOM Single Market and Economy (CSME), providing for the right to establish enterprises, the provision of services and the free movement of capital and labour throughout participating countries. A regional collaborative network was established to promote the CSME. In November 2000 a special consultation on the single market and economy was held in Barbados, involving CARICOM and government officials, academics, and representatives of the private sector, labour organizations, the media, and other regional groupings. In February 2001 heads of government agreed to establish a new high-level sub-committee to accelerate the establishment of the CSME and to promote its objectives. The sub-committee was to be supported by a Technical Advisory Council, comprising representatives of the public and private sectors. By June all member states had signed and declared the provisional application of Protocol II, which had received two ratifications. At that time eight countries had completed the fourth phase of the CET.

In July 1998, at the meeting of heads of government, held in Saint Lucia, an agreement was signed with the Insurance Company of the West Indies to accelerate the establishment of a Caribbean Investment Fund, which was to mobilize foreign currency from extra-regional capital markets for investment in new or existing enterprises in the region. Some 60% of all funds generated were to be used by CARICOM countries and the remainder by non-CARICOM members of the ACS.

CRIME AND SECURITY

In December 1996 CARICOM heads of government determined to strengthen comprehensive co-operation and technical assistance to combat illegal drugs-trafficking. The Conference decided to establish a Caribbean Security Task Force to help formulate a single regional agreement on maritime interdiction, incorporating agreements already concluded by individual members. A Regional Drugs Control Programme at the CARICOM Secretariat aims to co-ordinate regional initiatives with the overall objective of reducing the demand and supply of illegal substances. In July 2001 the Prime Minister of Antigua and Barbuda, Lester Bird, proposed the establishment of a rapid response unit to deal with drugs-related and other serious crimes. Heads of government agreed, instead, to establish a task force to be responsible for producing recommendations for a forthcoming meeting of national security advisers. In October, heads of government convened an emergency meeting in Nassau, the Bahamas, to consider the impact of the terrorist attacks against the USA which had occurred in September. The meeting determined to convene immediately the so-called Task Force on Crime and Security in order to implement new policy directives. It was agreed to enhance co-ordination and collaboration of security services throughout the region, in particular in intelligence gathering, analysis and sharing in relation to crime, illicit drugs and terrorism, and to strengthen security at airports, seaports and borders.

INDUSTRY AND ENERGY

CARICOM aims to promote the development of joint ventures in exporting industries (particularly the woodwork, furniture, ceramics and foundry industries) through an agreement (reached in 1989) on an industrial programming scheme. CARICOM's Export Development Council gives training and consultancy services to regional manufacturers. Regional manufacturers' exhibitions (CARIMEX) are held every three years. The Caribbean Trade Information System (CARTIS) comprises computer databases covering country and product profiles, trade statistics, trade opportunities, institutions and bibliographical information; it links the national trade centres of CARICOM members. A protocol relating to the CARICOM Industrial Programming Scheme (CIPS), approved in 1988, is the Community's instrument for promoting the co-operative development of industry in the region. Protocol III amending the Treaty of Chaguaramas, with respect to industrial policy, was opened for signature in July 1998. At June 2001 it had been signed by 13 member states, provisionally applied by 12, and ratified by one.

The Secretariat has established a national standards bureau in each member country to harmonize technical standards, and supervises the metrication of weights and measures. In 1999 members agreed to establish a new CARICOM Regional Organization of Standards and Quality (CROSQ) to develop common regional standards and resolve disputes. CROSQ, to be located in Barbados, was not yet operational in early 2002.

The CARICOM Alternative Energy Systems Project provides training, assesses energy needs and conducts energy audits. Efforts in regional energy development are directed at the collection and analysis of data for national energy policy documents.

TRANSPORT, COMMUNICATIONS AND TOURISM

A Caribbean Confederation of Shippers' Councils represents the interests of regional exporters and importers. In July 1990 the Caribbean Telecommunications Union was established to oversee developments in regional telecommunications.

In 1988 a Consultative Committee on Caribbean Regional Information Systems (CCCRIS) was established to evaluate and monitor the functioning of existing information systems and to seek to co-ordinate and advise on the establishment of new systems.

A Summit of Heads of Government on Tourism, Trade and Transportation was held in Trinidad and Tobago, in August 1995, to which all members of the ACS and regional tourism organizations were invited. In 1997 CARICOM heads of government considered a number of proposals relating to air transportation, tourism, human resource development and capital investment, which had been identified by Community ministers of tourism as critical issues in the sustainable development of the tourist industry. The heads of government requested ministers to meet regularly to develop tourism policies, and in particular to undertake an in-depth study of human resource development issues in early 1998. A new fund to help train young people from the region in aspects of the tourist industry was inaugurated in July 1997, in memory of the former Prime Minister of Jamaica, Michael Manley. A regional summit on tourism, in recognition of the importance of the industry to the economic development of the region, was held in the Bahamas, in December 2001.

A Multilateral Agreement Concerning the Operations of Air Services within the Caribbean Community entered into force in November 1998, providing a formal framework for the regulation of the air transport industry and enabling CARICOM-owned and -controlled airlines to operate freely within the region. In July 1999 heads of government signed Protocol VI amending the Treaty of Chaguaramas providing for a common transportation policy, with harmonized standards and practices, which was to be an integral component of the development of a single market and economy. In November 2001 representatives of national civil aviation authorities signed a memorandum of understanding, providing for the establishment of a regional body, with the aim of promoting the development of a Regional Aviation Oversight Safety System.

AGRICULTURE

In 1985 the New Marketing Arrangements for Primary Agricultural Products and Livestock were instituted, with the aim of increasing the flow of agricultural commodities within the region. A computer-based Caribbean Agricultural Marketing Information System was initiated in 1987.

At the CARICOM summit meeting in July 1996 it was agreed to undertake wide-ranging measures in order to modernize the agricultural sector and to increase the international competitiveness of Caribbean agricultural produce. The CARICOM Secretariat was to support national programmes with assistance in policy formulation, human resource development and the promotion of research and technology development in the areas of productivity, marketing, agri-business and water resources management. During 1997 CARICOM Governments continued to lobby against a complaint lodged at the WTO with regard to the EU's banana import regime (offering favourable conditions to ACP producers—see above) and to generate awareness of the economic and social importance of the banana industry to the region. Protocol V amending the Treaty of Chaguaramas, which was concerned with agricultural policy, was opened for signature by heads of government in July 1998. At June 2001 it had been signed and provisionally applied by 13 member states, and ratified by one (Guyana).

HEALTH AND EDUCATION

In 1986 CARICOM and the Pan-American Health Organization launched 'Caribbean Co-operation in Health' with projects to be undertaken in six main areas: environmental protection, including the control of disease-bearing pests; development of human resources; chronic non-communicable diseases and accidents; strengthening health systems; food and nutrition; maternal and child health care; and population activities. In 2001 CARICOM co-ordinated a new regional partnership to reduce the spread and impact of HIV and AIDS in member countries. All countries were to prepare national strategic plans to facilitate access to funding to combat the problem. A meeting of the partnership was convened in November. A Caribbean Environmental Health Institute (see below) aims to promote collaboration among member states in all areas of environmental management and human health. In July 2001 heads of government, meeting in the Bahamas, issued the Nassau Declaration on Health, advocating greater regional strategic co-ordination and planning in the health sector, institutional reform, and increased resources.

CARICOM educational programmes have included the improvement of reading in schools through assistance for teacher-training; and ensuring the availability of low-cost educational material throughout the region. In July 1997 CARICOM heads of government adopted the recommendations of a ministerial committee, which identified priority measures for implementation in the education sector. These included the objective of achieving universal, quality secondary education and the enrolment of 15% of post-secondary students in tertiary education by 2005, as well as improved training in foreign languages and science and technology. From the late 1990s youth activities have been increasingly emphasized by the Community. These have included new programmes for disadvantaged youths, a mechanism for youth exchange and the convening of a Caribbean Youth Parliament.

EMERGENCY ASSISTANCE

A Caribbean Disaster Emergency Response Agency (CDERA) was established in 1991 to co-ordinate immediate disaster relief, primarily in the event of hurricanes. During 1997 CARICOM Governments remained actively concerned with the situation in Montserrat, which had suffered a series of massive volcanic eruptions. At the Heads of Government Conference in July, the Community pledged humanitarian, economic and technical assistance and resolved to help mobilize external assistance from regional and international donor countries and institutions. In March 1998 CARICOM heads of government agreed to establish a team, comprising representatives of the CARICOM Secretariat, CDERA and the Caribbean Development Bank, to assist the Montserrat Government in formulating programmes to provide a secure future for the island. In November the Community determined to support the countries of Central America in their reconstruction and rehabilitation efforts following the devastation caused by 'Hurricane Mitch', and to co-ordinate the provision of immediate humanitarian assistance by CARICOM member countries.

INSTITUTIONS

The following are among the institutions formally established within the framework of CARICOM.

Assembly of Caribbean Community Parliamentarians: c/o CARICOM Secretariat; an intergovernmental agreement on the establishment of a regional parliament entered into force in August 1994; inaugural meeting held in Barbados, in May 1996. Comprises up to four representatives of the parliaments of each member country, and up to two of each associate member. It aims to provide a forum for wider community involvement in the process of integration and for enhanced deliberation on CARICOM affairs; authorized to issue recommendations for the Conference of Heads of Government and to adopt resolutions on any matter arising under the Treaty of Chaguaramas.

Caribbean Agricultural Research and Development Institute—CARDI: UWI Campus, St Augustine, Trinidad and Tobago; tel. 645-1205; fax 645-1208; e-mail infocentre@cardi.org; internet www.cardi.org; f. 1975; aims to contribute to the competitiveness and sustainability of Caribbean agriculture by generating and transferring new and appropriate technologies and by developing effective partnerships with regional and international entities. Exec. Dir Dr COMPTON PAUL. Publs *CARDI Weekly*, *Procicaribe News*, *CARDI Annual Report*, Technical bulletin series.

Caribbean Centre for Development Administration—CARICAD: ICB Bldg, Roebuck St, St Michael, Barbados; tel. 4278535; fax 4361709; e-mail caricad@caribsurf.com; f. 1980; aims to assist governments in the reform of the public sector and to strengthen their managerial capacities for public administration; promotes the involvement of the private sector, non-governmental organizations and other bodies in all decision-making processes. Exec. Dir Dr P. I. GOMES.

Caribbean Disaster Emergency Response Agency—CDERA: The Garrison, St Michael, Barbados; tel. 436-9651; fax 437-7649; e-mail cdera@caribsurf.com; internet www.cdera.org; f. 1991. For activities, see Emergency Assistance above. Regional Co-ordinator JEREMY COLLYMORE.

Caribbean Environmental Health Institute—CEHI: POB 1111, The Morne, Castries, St Lucia; tel. 4522501; fax 4532721; e-mail cehi@candw.lc; internet www.cehi.org.lc; f. 1980 (began operations in 1982); provides technical and advisory services to member states in formulating environmental health policy legislation and in all areas of environmental management (for example, solid waste management, water supplies, beach and air pollution, and pesticides control); promotes, collates and disseminates relevant research; conducts courses, seminars and workshops throughout the region. Exec. Dir VINCENT SWEENEY.

Caribbean Food and Nutrition Institute: UWI Campus, St Augustine, Trinidad and Tobago; tel. 662-7025; fax 662-5511; f. 1967 to serve the governments and people of the region and to act as a catalyst among persons and organizations concerned with food and nutrition through research and field investigations, training in nutrition, dissemination of information, advisory services and production of educational material. Mems: all English-speaking Caribbean territories, including the mainland countries of Belize and Guyana. Dir Dr FITZROY HENRY. Publs *Cajanus* (quarterly), *Nyam News* (monthly), *Nutrient-Cost Tables* (quarterly), educational material.

Caribbean Food Corporation—CFC: 30 Queen's Park West, Post Office Bag 264B, Port of Spain, Trinidad and Tobago; tel. 622-5827; fax 622-4430; e-mail cfc@trinidad-net; f. 1976 (began operations in 1979); implements joint-venture projects with investors from the private and public sectors to enhance regional food self-sufficiency and reduce the need for food imports. Man. Dir E. C. CLYDE PARRIS.

Caribbean Meteorological Organization—CMO: POB 461, Port of Spain, Trinidad and Tobago; tel. 624-4481; fax 623-3634; e-mail hqcmo@tstt.net.tt; f. 1951 to co-ordinate regional activities in meteorology, operational hydrology and allied sciences; became an associate institution of CARICOM in 1983. Comprises a headquarters unit, a Council of Government Ministers, the Caribbean Meteorological Foundation and the Caribbean Institute for Meteorology and Hydrology, located in Barbados. Mems: govts of 16 countries and territories represented by the National Meteorological and Hydro-meteorological Services. Co-ordinating Dir T. W. SUTHERLAND.

ASSOCIATE INSTITUTIONS

Caribbean Development Bank: POB 408, Wildey, St Michael, Barbados; tel. 431-1600; fax 426-7269; e-mail info@caribank.org; internet www.caribank.org; f. 1969 to stimulate regional economic growth through support for agriculture, industry, transport and other infrastructure, tourism, housing and education; subscribed cap. US $687.2m. (Dec. 1999). In 1999 net approvals totalled $146.6m. for 16 projects; at the end of 1999 cumulative grant and loan disbursements totalled $1,275.0m. The Special Development Fund was replenished in 1996. Mems: CARICOM states, and Canada, Cayman Islands, the People's Republic of China, Colombia, France, Germany, Italy, Mexico, United Kingdom, Venezuela. Pres. Prof. COMPTON BOURNE.

Caribbean Law Institute: University of the West Indies, Cave Hill Campus, POB 64, Bridgetown, Barbados; tel. 417-4560; fax 417-4138.

Other Associate Institutions of CARICOM, in accordance with its constitution, are the University of Guyana and the University of the West Indies.

Publications

Annual Report.

Caribbean Trade and Investment Report.

Caribbean View (every 2 months).

Statistics — News and Views (2 a year).

CENTRAL AMERICAN INTEGRATION SYSTEM

(SISTEMA DE LA INTEGRACIÓN CENTROAMERICANA—SICA)

Address: blvd Orden de Malta 470, Santa Elena, Antiguo Cuscatlán, San Salvador, El Salvador.

Telephone: 289-6131; **fax:** 289-6124; **e-mail:** sgsica@sgsica.org; **internet:** www.sgsica.org.

Founded in December 1991, when the heads of state of six Central American countries signed the Protocol of Tegucigalpa to the agreement establishing the Organization of Central American States (f. 1951), creating a new framework for regional integration. A General Secretariat of the Sistema de la Integración Centroamericana (SICA) was inaugurated in February 1993 to co-ordinate the process of political, economic, social cultural and environmental integration and to promote democracy and respect for human rights throughout the region.

MEMBERS

Belize	Guatemala	Nicaragua
Costa Rica	Honduras	Panama
El Salvador		

OBSERVERS

Dominican Republic	Taiwan

Organization

(April 2002)

SUMMIT MEETINGS

The meetings of heads of state of member countries serve as the supreme decision-making organ of SICA.

COUNCIL OF MINISTERS

Ministers of Foreign Affairs of member states meet regularly to provide policy direction for the process of integration.

CONSULTATIVE COMMITTEE

The Committee comprises representatives of business organizations, trade unions, academic institutions and other federations concerned with the process of integration in the region. It is an integral element of the integration system and assists the Secretary-General in determining the policies of the organization.

President: RICARDO SOL.

GENERAL SECRETARIAT

The General Secretariat of SICA was established in February 1993 to co-ordinate the process of enhanced regional integration. It comprises the following divisions: inter-institutional relations; research and co-operation; legal and political affairs; economic affairs; and communications and information.

In September 1997 Central American Common Market (CACM) heads of state, meeting in the Nicaraguan capital, signed the Managua Declaration in support of further regional integration and the establishment of a political union. A commission was to be established to consider all aspects of the policy and to formulate a timetable for the integration process. In February 1998 SICA heads of state resolved to establish a Unified General Secretariat to integrate the institutional aspects of SICA (see below) in a single office, to be located in San Salvador. The process was ongoing in 2002.

Secretary-General: Dr OSCAR ALFREDO SANTAMARÍA.

SPECIALIZED TECHNICAL SECRETARIATS

Secretaría Ejecutiva de la Comisión Centroamericana de Ambiente y Desarrollo—SE-CCAD: blvd Orden de Malta 470, Santa Elena, Antiguo Cuscatlán, San Salvador, El Salvador; tel. 289-6131; fax 289-6124; internet www.ccad.sgsica.org; f. 1989 to enhance collaboration in the promotion of sustainable development and environmental protection. Exec. Sec. MAURICIO CASTRO.

Secretaría General de la Coordinación Educativa y Cultural Centroamericana—SG-CECC: 175m. norte de la esquina oeste del ICE, Sabana Norte, San José, Costa Rica; tel. 232-3783; fax 231-2366; e-mail info@sieca.org.gt; f. 1982; promotes development of regional programmes in the fields of education and culture. Sec.-Gen. MARVIN HERRERA ARAYA.

Secretaría Permanente del Tratado General de Integración Económica Centroamericana—SIECA: 4A Avda 10–25, Zona 14, Apdo 1237, 01901 Guatemala City, Guatemala; tel. (2) 333-4617; fax (2) 368-1071; e-mail info@sieca.org.gt; internet www.sieca.org.gt; f. 1960 to assist the process of economic integration and the creation of a Central American Common Market (CACM—established by the organization of Central American States under the General Treaty of Central American Economic Integration, signed in December 1960 and ratified by Costa Rica, Guatemala, El Salvador, Honduras and Nicaragua in September 1963). Supervises the correct implementation of the legal instruments of economic integration, carries out relevant studies at the request of the CACM, and arranges meetings. There are departments covering the working of the CACM; negotiations and external trade policy; external co-operation; systems and statistics; finance and administration. There is also a unit for co-operation with the private sector and finance institutions, and a legal consultative committee; Sec.-Gen. RÓGER HAROLDO RODAS MELARA. Publs *Anuario Estadístico Centroamericano de Comercio Exterior, Carta Informativa* (monthly), *Cuadernos de la SIECA* (2 a year), *Estadísticas Macroeconómicas de Centroamérica* (annually), *Series Estadísticas Seleccionadas de Centroamérica* (annually).

Secretaría Técnica del Consejo de Integración Social—SISCA: blvd Orden de Malta 470, Santa Elena, Antiguo Cuscatlán, San Salvador, El Salvador; tel. 289-6131; fax 289-6124; e-mail hmorgado@sgsica.org.sv; f. 1995; Dir-Gen. Dr HUGO MORGADO.

OTHER SPECIALIZED SECRETARIATS

Secretaría de Integración Turística Centroamericana—SITCA: blvd Orden de Malta 470, Santa Elena, Antiguo Cuscatlán, San Salvador, El Salvador; tel. 289-6131; fax 289-6124; e-mail econtreras@sgsica.org.sv; f. 1965 to develop regional tourism activities; Sec.-Gen. EDGARDO CONTRERAS SCHNEIDER.

Secretaría del Consejo Agropecuario Centroamericano—SCAC: Sede del IICA, Apdo Postal 55-2200 Coronado, San José, Costa Rica; tel. 216-0303; fax 216-0285; e-mail rguillen@iica.ac.cr; f. 1991 to determine and co-ordinate regional policies and programmes relating to agriculture and agroindustry. Sec-Gen. RÓGER GUILLÉN BUSTOS.

Secretaría Ejecutiva del Consejo Monetario Centroamericano—CMCA (Central American Monetary Council): Ofiplaza del Este, Edif. C, 75m. oeste de la Rotonda la Bandera, San Pedro Montes de Oca, Apdo Postal 5438, 1000 San José, Costa Rica; tel. 280-9522; fax 280-9511; e-mail secma@sol.racsa.co.cr; internet www.cmca.or.ca; f. 1964 by the presidents of Central American central banks, to co-ordinate monetary policies. Exec. Sec. MIGUEL ALEMÁN. Publs *Boletín Estadístico* (annually), *Informe Económico* (annually).

Secretaría Ejecutiva de la Comisión Centroamericana de Transporte Marítimo—COCATRAM: Cine Cabrera 2c. arriba y 2½ al sur, Apdo 2423, Managua, Nicaragua; tel. (2) 222754; fax (2) 222759; e-mail cocatram@ibw.com.ni; f. 1981; Exec. Sec. ALFONSO BREUILLET.

PARLIAMENT

Address: 12A Avda 33-04, Zona 5, Guatemala City, Guatemala.

Telephone: (2) 339-0466; **fax:** (2) 334-6670; **e-mail:** parlacensv@sgsica.org.gt; **internet:** www.parlacen.org.gt.

Officially inaugurated in 1991. Comprises representatives of El Salvador, Guatemala, Honduras, Nicaragua and Panama. In February 1998 heads of state of member countries resolved to limit the number of deputies to 10–15 from each country.

President: RODRIGO SAMAYOA RIVAS (El Salvador).

COURT OF JUSTICE

Address: Kilómetro 17½ Carretera Norte, contiguo a la TANIC, Managua, Nicaragua.

Telephone: 233-2128; **fax:** 233-2135; **e-mail:** cortecen@tmx.com.ni; **internet:** www.ccj.org.ni.

Tribunal authorized to consider disputes relating to treaties agreed within the regional integration system. In February 1998 Central American heads of state agreed to limit the number of magistrates in the Court to one per country.

President: Dr ADOLFO LEÓN GÓMEZ.

AD HOC INTERGOVERNMENTAL SECRETARIATS

Comisión de Ciencia y Tecnología de Centroamérica y Panamá (Commission for Science and Technology in Central America and Panama): Col. Palmira, Avda República de Brasil 2231, Apdo 4458, Tegucigalpa, Honduras; tel. and fax 232-5669; f. 1976; Pres. GERARDO ZEPEDA.

Consejo Centroamericano de Instituciones de Seguridad Social—COCISS: Caja de Seguridad Social, Panamá, Panama; tel. 261-7264; f. 1992; Pres. Dr MARIANELA MORALES.

Consejo del Istmo Centroamericano de Deportes y Recreación: Apdo Postal 5.009, 1000 San José, Costa Rica; tel. 257-8770; fax 222-5003; f. 1992; Pres. HILDA GONZÁLEZ.

Secretaría Ejecutiva del Consejo Centroamericana de Vivienda y Asentamientos Humanos (Central American Council on Housing and Human Settlements): Avda la Paz 244, Tegucigalpa, Honduras; tel. 236-5804; fax 236-6560; f. 1992; Dir Dr CONCEPCIÓN RAMOS.

Secretaría Ejecutiva del Consejo de Electrificación de América Central: Apdo Postal 10032, San José, Costa Rica; tel. 220-7562; fax 220-8232; e-mail ceac@ns.ice.go.cr; f. 1985; Dir LUIS BUJÁN.

OTHER REGIONAL INSTITUTIONS

Finance

Banco Centroamericano de Integración Económica—BCIE (Central American Bank for Economic Integration): Blvd Suyapa, Contigua a Banco de Honduras, Apdo 772, Tegucigalpa, Honduras; tel. 228-2182; fax 228-2183; e-mail webmail-hn@bcie.org; internet www.bcie.hn; f. 1961 to promote the economic integration and balanced economic development of member countries; finances public and private development projects, particularly those related to industrialization and infrastructure. By June 1993 cumulative lending amounted to US $3,217m., mainly for roads, hydroelectricity projects, housing and telecommunications. Auth. cap. $2,000m. Regional mems: Costa Rica, El Salvador, Guatemala, Honduras, Nicaragua; Non-regional mems: Argentina, the People's Republic of China, Colombia, Mexico. Pres. PABLO SCHNEIDER. Publs *Annual Report, Revista de la Integración y el Desarrollo de Centroamérica.*

Public Administration

Centro de Coordinación para la Prevención de Desastres Naturales en América Central—CEPREDENAC: Llanos de Curundo, Edif. 1996B, Panamá, Panama; tel. 3160065; fax 3160074; e-mail secretaria@cepredenac.org; internet www.cepredenac.org; Dir JORGE AYALA MARROQUÍN.

Comisión Centroamericana Permanente para la Erradicación de la Producción, Tráfico, Consumo y Uso Ilícitos de Estupefacientes y Sustancias Psicotrópicas y Delitos Conexos—CCP: Edif. de Comisiones, 1°, Tegucigalpa, Honduras; tel. 237-0568; fax 238-3960. Pres. Dr CARLOS SOSA COELLO.

Instituto Centroamericano de Administración Pública—ICAP (Central American Institute of Public Administration): Apdo Postal 10.025, 1000 San José, Costa Rica; tel. 234-1011; fax 225-2049; e-mail icapcr@sol.racsa.co.cr; internet www.icap.ac.cr; f. 1954 by the five Central American Republics and the United Nations, with later participation by Panama. The Institute aims to train the region's public servants, provide technical assistance and carry out research leading to reforms in public administration. Dir Dr HUGO ZELAYA CÁLIX.

Secretaría Ejecutiva de la Comisión Regional de Recursos Hidráulicos—SE-CRRH: Apdo Postal 21-2300, Curridabat, San José, Costa Rica; tel. 231-5791; fax 296-0047; e-mail crrhcr@sol.racsa.co.cr; f. 1966. Mems: Belize, Costa Rica, El Salvador, Guatemala, Honduras, Nicaragua, Panama; Exec. Dir MAX CAMPOS O.

Education and Health

Comité Coordinador Regional de Instituciones de Agua Potable y Saneamiento de Centroamérica, Panamá y República Dominicana—CAPRE: De la casa Italia, 100m. al sur y 100 al este, diagonal a farmacia Umaña, Barrio Francisco Peralta, San Pedro de Montes de OCA, San José, Costa Rica; tel. 280-4460; fax 280-4414; e-mail capregtz@sol.racsa.co.cr; f. 1979; Dir LILIANA ARCE UMAÑA.

Consejo Superior Universitario Centroamericano—CSUCA (Central American University Council): Apdo Postal 372060, Ciudad Universitaria Rodrigo Facio, San Pedro de Montes de Oca, de Autos San Pedro, 100 mts al norte, mano derecha casa blanca, 2060 San José, Costa Rica; tel. 225-2744; fax 234-0071; e-mail rsol@cariari.ucr.ac.cr; internet www.csuca.ac.cr; f. 1948 to guarantee academic, administrative and economic autonomy for universities and to encourage regional integration of higher education; maintains libraries and documentation centres; Council of 32 mems. Mems: 16 universities, in Belize, Costa Rica (four), El Salvador, Guatemala, Honduras (two), Nicaragua (four) and Panama (three). Sec.-Gen. Dr RICARDO SOL ARRIAZA (El Salvador). Publs *Estudios Sociales Centroamericanos* (quarterly), *Cuadernos de Investigación* (monthly), *Carta Informativa de la Secretaría General* (monthly).

Instituto de Nutrición de Centroamérica y Panamá—INCAP (Institute of Nutrition of Central America and Panama): Apdo 1188, Carretera Roosevelt, Zona 11, 01901 Guatemala City, Guatemala; tel. (2) 4723762; fax (2) 4736529; e-mail hdelgado@incap.org.gt; f. 1949 to promote the development of nutritional sciences and their application and to strengthen the technical capacity of member countries to reach food and nutrition security; provides training and technical assistance for nutrition education and planning; conducts applied research; disseminates information. Maintains library (including about 600 periodicals). Administered by the Pan American Health Organization (PAHO) and the World Health Organization. Mems: CACM mems and Belize and Panama. Dir Dr HERNÁN L. DELGADO. Publ. *Annual Report.*

Organismo Internacional Regional de Sanidad Agropecuaria—OIRSA (International Regional Organization of Plant Protection and Animal Health): 14 Avda Las Camelias, Col San Francisco, Apdo 61, San Salvador, El Salvador; tel. 263-1123; fax 279-0189; e-mail orgoirsa@gbm.net; internet www.ns1.oirsa.org.sv; f. 1953 for the prevention of the introduction of animal and plant pests and diseases unknown in the region; research, control and eradication programmes of the principal pests present in agriculture; technical assistance and advice to the ministries of agriculture and livestock of member countries; education and qualification of personnel. Mems: Belize, Costa Rica, Dominican Republic, El Salvador, Guatemala, Honduras, Mexico, Nicaragua, Panama. Exec. Dir Dr CELIO HUMBERTO BARRETO.

Transport and Communications

Comisión Técnica de Telecomunicaciones—COMTELCA (Technical Commission for Telecommunications): Col. Palmira, Edif. Alpha, 608 Avda Brasil, Apdo 1793, Tegucigalpa, Honduras; tel. 220-6666; fax 220-1197; e-mail hectorrm@comtelca.hn; internet www.comtelca.hn; f. 1966 to co-ordinate and improve the regional telecommunications network. Dir-Gen. HÉCTOR LEONEL RODRÍGUEZ MILLA.

Corporación Centroamericana de Servicios de Navegación Aérea—COCESNA (Central American Air Navigation Service Corporation): Apdo 660, Aeropuerto de Toncontín, Tegucigalpa, Honduras; tel. 233-1143; fax 233-1219; e-mail gergral@

cocesna.hn; f. 1960; offers radar air traffic control services, aeronautical telecommunications services, flight inspections and radio assistance services for air navigation; administers the Central American Aeronautical School. Gen. Man. EDUARDO JOSÉ MARÍN.

Activities

In June 1990 the presidents of the Central American Common Market (CACM) countries (Costa Rica, El Salvador, Guatemala, Honduras and Nicaragua) signed a declaration welcoming peace initiatives in El Salvador, Guatemala and Nicaragua, and appealing for a revitalization of CACM, as a means of promoting lasting peace in the region. In December the presidents committed themselves to the creation of an effective common market, proposing the opening of negotiations on a comprehensive regional customs and tariffs policy by March 1991, and the introduction of a regional 'anti-dumping' code by December 1991. They requested the support of multilateral lending institutions through investment in regional development, and the cancellation or rescheduling of member countries' debts. In December 1991 the heads of state of the five CACM countries and Panama signed the Protocol of Tegucigalpa, and in February 1993 the General Secretariat of SICA was inaugurated to co-ordinate the integration process in the region.

In February 1993 the European Community (EC) signed a new framework co-operation agreement with the CACM member states extending the programme of economic assistance and political dialogue initiated in 1984; a further co-operation agreement with the European Union (as the EC had become) was signed in early 1996.

In October 1993 the presidents of the CACM countries and Panama signed a protocol to the 1960 General Treaty, committing themselves to full economic integration in the region (with a common external tariff of 20% for finished products and 5% for raw materials and capital goods) and creating conditions for increased free trade. The countries agreed to accelerate the removal of internal non-tariff barriers, but no deadline was set. Full implementation of the protocol was to be 'voluntary and gradual', owing to objections on the part of Costa Rica and Panama. In May 1994, however, Costa Rica committed itself to full participation in the protocol. In March 1995 a meeting of the Central American Monetary Council discussed and endorsed a reduction in the tariff levels from 20% to 15% and from 5% to 1%. However, efforts to adopt this as a common policy were hindered by the implementation of these tariff levels by El Salvador on a unilateral basis, from 1 April, and the subsequent modifications by Guatemala and Costa Rica of their external tariffs.

In May 1997 the heads of state of CACM member countries, together with the Prime Minister of Belize, conferred with the US President, Bill Clinton, in San José, Costa Rica. The leaders resolved to establish a Trade and Investment Council to promote trade relations; however, Clinton failed to endorse a request from CACM members that their products receive preferential access to US markets, on similar terms to those from Mexico agreed under the NAFTA accord. During the 1990s the Central American Governments pursued negotiations to conclude free-trade agreements with Mexico, Panama and the members of the Caribbean Community and Common Market (CARICOM). Nicaragua signed a bilateral accord with Mexico in December (Costa Rica already having done so in 1994). El Salvador, Guatemala and Honduras jointly concluded a free-trade arrangement with Mexico in May 2000; this was to enter into effect in January 2001. In November 1997, at a special summit meeting of CACM heads of state, an agreement was reached with the President of the Dominican Republic to initiate a gradual process of incorporating that country into the process of Central American integration, with the aim of promoting sustainable development throughout the region. The first sectors for increased co-operation between the two sides were to be tourism, health, investment promotion and air transport. A free-trade accord with the Dominican Republic was concluded in April 1998, and formally signed in November.

In November 1998 Central American heads of state held an emergency summit meeting to consider the devastation in the region caused by 'Hurricane Mitch'. The Presidents urged international creditors to write off the region's estimated debts of US $16,000m. to assist in the economic recovery of the countries worst-affected. They also reiterated requests for preferential treatment for the region's exports within the NAFTA framework. In October 1999 the heads of state adopted a strategic framework for the period 2000–04 to strengthen the capacity for the physical, social, economic and environmental infrastructure of Central American countries to withstand the impact of natural disasters. In particular, programmes for the integrated management and conservation of water resources, and for the prevention of forest fires were to be implemented. In June 2001 the heads of state agreed to activate a plan to strengthen communications infrastructure, and to develop a single power grid in the region. During 2001, however, the integration process was undermined by ongoing border disputes between Guatemala and Belize, and between Honduras and Nicaragua.

In April 2001 Costa Rica concluded a free-trade accord with Canada; the other four CACM countries commenced negotiations with Canada in November with the aim of reaching a similar agreement. In late February 2002 heads of state of SICA countries convened an extraordinary summit meeting in Managua, Nicaragua, at which they resolved to implement measures to further the political and economic integration of the region. The leaders determined to pursue initial proposals for a free-trade pact with the USA during the visit to the region of US President George W. Bush in the following month, and, more generally, to strengthen trading relations with the European Union. They also pledged to resolve all regional conflicts by peaceful means. Earlier in February the first meeting of heads of state or government of SICA and CARICOM countries took place in Belize, with the aim of strengthening political and economic relations between the two groupings. The meeting agreed to work towards concluding common negotiating positions, for example in respect of the FTAA and World Trade Organization.

COMMON MARKET FOR EASTERN AND SOUTHERN AFRICA—COMESA

Address: COMESA Centre, Ben Bella Rd, POB 30051, 101101 Lusaka, Zambia.

Telephone: (1) 229726; **fax:** (1) 225107; **e-mail:** comesa@comesa.int; **internet:** www.comesa.int.

The COMESA treaty was signed by member states of the Preferential Trade Area for Eastern and Southern Africa (PTA) in November 1993. COMESA formally succeeded the PTA in December 1994. COMESA aims to promote regional economic and social development.

MEMBERS

Angola	Malawi
Burundi	Mauritius
Comoros	Namibia
Congo, Democratic Republic	Rwanda
Djibouti	Seychelles
Egypt	Sudan
Eritrea	Swaziland
Ethiopia	Uganda
Kenya	Zambia
Madagascar	Zimbabwe

Organization

(April 2002)

AUTHORITY

The Authority of the Common Market is the supreme policy organ of COMESA, comprising heads of state or of government of member countries. The inaugural meeting of the Authority took place in Lilongwe, Malawi, in December 1994. The sixth summit meeting was held in Cairo, Egypt, in May 2001.

COUNCIL OF MINISTERS

Each member government appoints a minister to participate in the Council. The Council monitors COMESA activities, including supervision of the Secretariat, recommends policy direction and development, and reports to the Authority.

A Committee of Governors of Central Banks advises the Authority and the Council of Ministers on monetary and financial matters.

COURT OF JUSTICE

The inaugural session of the COMESA Court of Justice was held in March 2001. The sub-regional Court is vested with the authority to settle disputes between member states and to adjudicate on matters concerning the interpretation of the COMESA treaty. The Court is composed of seven judges, who serve terms of five years' duration.

President: Akilano Molade Akiwumi (Kenya).

SECRETARIAT

COMESA's Secretariat comprises the following divisions: Trade, customs and monetary harmonization; Investment promotion and private sector development; Infrastructure development; and Information and networking. The COMESA/SADC task force operates from the secretariats of both organizations.

Secretary-General: J. E. O. (Erastus) Mwencha (Kenya).

Activities

COMESA aims to promote economic and social progress in member states. Since its establishment in 1994 COMESA has pursued efforts to strengthen the process of regional economic integration that was initiated under the PTA, in order to help member states achieve sustainable economic growth. In May 1999 COMESA established a Free Trade Area Committee to facilitate and co-ordinate preparations for the establishment of the common market envisaged under the COMESA treaty. An extraordinary summit of COMESA heads of state or government, held in October 2000, established the free-trade area, with nine initial members: Djibouti, Egypt, Kenya, Madagascar, Malawi, Mauritius, Sudan, Zambia and Zimbabwe. The final deadline for all states to join was 30 April 2002. Trading practices within the free-trade area were fully liberalized, including the elimination of non-tariff barriers, thereby enabling the free internal movement of goods, services and capital. It was envisaged that a regional customs union would be established by December 2004, with a common external tariff set at 0%, 5%, 15% and 30% for, respectively, capital goods, raw materials, intermediate goods and final goods. In 2002 a COMESA Fund was under development, in order to assist member states address structural imbalances in their economies. COMESA also plans to form an economic community (entailing monetary union and the free movement of people between member states) by 2014. COMESA aims to formulate a common investment procedure to promote domestic, cross-border and direct foreign investment by ensuring the free movement of capital, services and labour. Heads of regional investment agencies, meeting in August 2000, developed a plan of action for the creation of a common investment agency to facilitate the establishment of a common investment area, in accordance with recommendations by the Authority. The development of a protocol to the COMESA treaty on the Free Movement of Persons, Labour, Services, the Right of Establishment and Residence is under way. In October 2001 COMESA concluded a Trade and Investment Framework Agreement with the USA.

A clearing house (based in Harare, Zimbabwe) dealing with credit arrangements and balance of payments issues became operational under the PTA in 1984 in order to facilitate intra-regional trade. The clearing house remained an integral part of the COMESA infrastructure, although its role was diminished by the liberalization of foreign exchange markets in the majority of member countries. The fourth COMESA business forum proposed that the Clearing House should be reformed to facilitate money transfers without the use of foreign currency. In April 1997 the Authority approved the introduction of the COMESA dollar (CMD) to replace the UAPTA (introduced by the PTA). The CMD was to be equivalent to the value of the US currency. An Automated System of Customs Data (ASYCUDA) has been established to facilitate customs administration in all COMESA member states. Through support for capacity-building activities and the establishment of other specialized institutions (see below) COMESA aims to reinforce its objectives of regional integration. In August 2001 COMESA officially inaugurated the African Trade Insurance Agency (ATI), based in Nairobi, Kenya, with Burundi, Kenya, Malawi, Rwanda, Tanzania, Uganda and Zambia as initial members. The ATI underwrites political risk cover for trade and investment activities throughout the region.

Co-operation programmes have been implemented by COMESA in the industrial, agricultural, energy and transport and communications sectors. A regional food security programme aimed to ensure continuous adequate food supplies. In 1997 COMESA Heads of State advocated that the food sector be supported by the immediate implementation of an irrigation action plan for the region. The organization also supports the establishment of common agricultural standards and phytosanitary regulations throughout the region in order to stimulate trade in food crops. Other initiatives include a road customs declaration document, a regional customs bond guarantee scheme, and schemes for third party motor vehicle insurance and regional travellers cheques. A Trade Information Network co-ordinates information on the production and marketing of goods manufactured and traded in the region. COMESA is implementing the new COMESA Information Network, which aims to develop the utilization by member states of advanced information and communication technologies. A COMESA Telecommunications Company (COMTEL) was registered in May 2000. The first COMESA trade fair was held in Nairobi, Kenya, in May 1999.

The first COMESA economic forum was held in Cairo, Egypt, in February 2000. The fourth COMESA business forum took place in Cairo, Egypt, in May 2001.

In May 1999 the COMESA Authority resolved to establish a Committee on Peace and Security comprising ministers of foreign affairs from member states. It was envisaged that the Committee would convene at least once a year to address matters concerning regional stability. (Instability in certain member states was regarded as a potential threat to the successful implementation of the FTA.) The Committee met for the first time in 2000.

Since COMESA's establishment there have been concerns on the part of member states, as well as other regional non-member countries, in particular South Africa, of adverse rivalry between COMESA and the Southern African Development Community (SADC, q.v.) and of a duplication of roles. In 1997 Lesotho and Mozambique terminated their membership of COMESA owing to concerns that their continued participation in the organization was incompatible with their SADC membership. Tanzania withdrew from COMESA in September 2000, reportedly also in view of its dual commitment to that organization and to the SADC. The summit meeting of COMESA heads of state held in May of that year expressed support for an ongoing programme of co-operation by the secretariats of COMESA and the SADC aimed at reducing the duplication of roles between the two organizations, and urged further mutual collaboration. A co-ordinating COMESA/SADC task force was established in 2001. In 2002 COMESA was co-operating with other sub-regional organizations to finalize a common position on co-operation between African ACP countries and the EU under the Cotonou Agreement (concluded in June 2000, q.v.).

COMESA INSTITUTIONS

African Trade Insurance Agency (ATI): based in Nairobi, Kenya; f. 2001; Man. Dir BERNARD DE HALDERANG.

COMESA Association of Commercial Banks: 12 Victoria Ave, Unit House (GF), Private Bag 271, Blantyre, Malawi; tel. (4) 621503; fax (4) 621204; e-mail initereka@malawi.net; aims to strengthen co-operation between banks in the region; organizes training activities; conducts studies to harmonize banking laws and operations; initiated a project to combat bank fraud and money laundering in December 2000. Mems: commercial banking orgs in Burundi, Ethiopia, Malawi, Rwanda, Sudan, Uganda.

COMESA Leather and Leather Products Institute—LLPI: POB 5538, Addis Ababa, Ethiopia; tel (1) 510361; fax (1) 512799; e-mail comesa.llpi@telecom.net.et; f. 1990 as the PTA Leather Institute. Mems: Govts of 16 COMESA mem. states; Dir Dr ROBERT ARUNGA.

COMESA Metallurgical Industries Association (COMESAMIA): Kampala, Uganda; f. 1999; aims to advance capabilities in the production, processing and marketing of metals and allied engineering products, and to develop co-operation and networking in the sector.

Compagnie de réassurance de la Zone d'échanges préférentiels—ZEP-RE (PTA Reinsurance Co): Anniversary Towers, University Way, POB 42769, Nairobi, Kenya; tel. (2) 212792; fax (2) 224102; e-mail mail@zep-re.com; internet www.zep-re.com; f. 1992 (began operations on 1 January 1993); provides local reinsurance services and training to personnel in the insurance industry; auth. cap. CMD 27.3m.; Man. Dir S. M. LUBASI.

Eastern and Southern African Trade and Development Bank: NSSF Bldg, 23rd Floor, Bishop's Rd, POB 48596, Nairobi, Kenya; tel. (2) 712260; fax (2) 711510; e-mail infoserv@ptabank.co.ke; internet www.ptabank.co.ke; f. 1983 as PTA Development Bank; aims to mobilize resources and finance COMESA activities to foster regional integration; promotes investment and co-financing within the region; shareholders 16 COMESA mem. states and the African Development Bank; cumulative project approvals totalled CMD 181.9m. at Dec. 2000; cap. p.u. CMD 67.4m. (Dec. 2000); Pres. Dr MICHAEL GONDWE; Dir Dr BWALYA K. E. NG'ANDU.

Federation of National Associations of Women in Business —FEMCOM: c/o COMESA Secretariat; f. 1993 to provide links between female business executives throughout the region and to promote greater awareness of relevant issues at policy level. FEMCOM was to be supported by a Revolving Fund for Women in Business.

Finance

COMESA is financed by member states. In April 1997 COMESA heads of state concluded that the organization's activities were being undermined by lack of resources, and determined to expel countries which fail to pay membership dues over a five-year period.

Publications

Annual Report of the Council of Ministers.

Asycuda Newsletter.

COMESA Journal.

COMESA Trade Directory (annually).

COMESA Trade Information Newsletter (monthly).

Demand/supply surveys, catalogues and reports.

THE COMMONWEALTH

Address: Commonwealth Secretariat, Marlborough House, Pall Mall, London, SW1Y 5HX, United Kingdom.

Telephone: (20) 7839-3411; **fax:** (20) 7930-0827; **e-mail:** info@commonwealth.int; **internet:** www.thecommonwealth.org.

The Commonwealth is a voluntary association of 54 independent states, comprising about one-quarter of the world's population. It includes the United Kingdom and most of its former dependencies, and former dependencies of Australia and New Zealand (themselves Commonwealth countries).

The evolution of the Commonwealth began with the introduction of self-government in Canada in the 1840s; Australia, New Zealand and South Africa became independent before the First World War. At the Imperial Conference of 1926 the United Kingdom and the Dominions, as they were then called, were described as 'autonomous communities within the British Empire, equal in status', and this change was enacted into law by the Statute of Westminster, in 1931.

The modern Commonwealth began with the entry of India and Pakistan in 1947, and of Sri Lanka (then Ceylon) in 1948. In 1949, when India decided to become a republic, the Commonwealth Heads of Government agreed to replace allegiance to the British Crown with recognition of the British monarch as Head of the Commonwealth, as a condition of membership. This was a precedent for a number of other members (see Heads of State and Heads of Government, below).

MEMBERS*

Antigua and Barbuda
Australia
Bahamas
Bangladesh
Barbados
Belize
Botswana
Brunei
Cameroon
Canada
Cyprus
Dominica
Fiji
The Gambia
Ghana
Grenada
Guyana
India
Jamaica
Kenya
Kiribati
Lesotho
Malawi
Malaysia
Maldives
Malta
Mauritius
Mozambique
Namibia
Nauru
New Zealand
Nigeria
Pakistan
Papua New Guinea
Saint Christopher and Nevis
Saint Lucia
Saint Vincent and the Grenadines
Samoa
Seychelles
Sierra Leone
Singapore
Solomon Islands
South Africa
Sri Lanka
Swaziland
Tanzania
Tonga
Trinidad and Tobago
Tuvalu
Uganda
United Kingdom
Vanuatu
Zambia
Zimbabwe

* Ireland, South Africa and Pakistan withdrew from the Commonwealth in 1949, 1961 and 1972 respectively. In October 1987 Fiji's membership was declared to have lapsed (following the proclamation of a republic there). It was readmitted in October 1997, but was suspended from participation in meetings of the Commonwealth in June 2000. Fiji was formally readmitted to Commonwealth meetings in December 2001 following the staging of free and fair legislative elections in August/September. Pakistan rejoined the Commonwealth in October 1989; however, it was suspended from participation in meetings in October 1999. South Africa rejoined in June 1994. Nigeria's membership was suspended in November 1995; it formally resumed membership in May 1999, when a new civilian government was inaugurated. Tuvalu, previously a special member of the Commonwealth with the right to participate in all activities except full Meetings of Heads of Government, became a full member of the Commonwealth in September 2000. In March 2002 Zimbabwe was suspended from meetings of the Commonwealth for one year.

Dependencies and Associated States

Australia:
- Ashmore and Cartier Islands
- Australian Antarctic Territory
- Christmas Island
- Cocos (Keeling) Islands
- Coral Sea Islands Territory
- Heard Island and the McDonald Islands
- Norfolk Island

New Zealand:
- Cook Islands
- Niue
- Ross Dependency
- Tokelau

United Kingdom:
- Anguilla
- Bermuda
- British Antarctic Territory
- British Indian Ocean Territory
- British Virgin Islands
- Cayman Islands
- Channel Islands
- Falkland Islands
- Gibraltar
- Isle of Man
- Montserrat
- Pitcairn Islands
- St Helena
  - Ascension
  - Tristan da Cunha
- South Georgia and the South Sandwich Islands
- Turks and Caicos Islands

HEADS OF STATE AND HEADS OF GOVERNMENT

At April 2002 21 member countries were monarchies and 33 were republics. All Commonwealth countries accept Queen Elizabeth II as the symbol of the free association of the independent member nations and as such the Head of the Commonwealth. Of the 33 republics, the offices of Head of State and Head of Government were combined in 22: Botswana, Cameroon, Cyprus, The Gambia, Ghana, Guyana, Kenya, Kiribati, Malawi, Maldives, Mozambique, Namibia, Nauru, Nigeria, Seychelles, Sierra Leone, South Africa, Sri Lanka, Tanzania, Uganda, Zambia and Zimbabwe. The two offices were separated in the remaining 11: Bangladesh, Dominica, Fiji, India, Malta, Mauritius, Pakistan, Samoa, Singapore, Trinidad and Tobago and Vanuatu.

Of the monarchies, the Queen is Head of State of the United Kingdom and of 15 others, in each of which she is represented by a Governor-General: Antigua and Barbuda, Australia, the Bahamas, Barbados, Belize, Canada, Grenada, Jamaica, New Zealand, Papua New Guinea, Saint Christopher and Nevis, Saint Lucia, Saint Vincent and the Grenadines, Solomon Islands and Tuvalu. Brunei, Lesotho, Malaysia, Swaziland and Tonga are also monarchies, where the traditional monarch is Head of State.

The Governors-General are appointed by the Queen on the advice of the Prime Ministers of the country concerned. They are wholly independent of the Government of the United Kingdom.

HIGH COMMISSIONERS

Governments of member countries are represented in other Commonwealth countries by High Commissioners, who have a status equivalent to that of Ambassadors.

Organization

(April 2002)

The Commonwealth is not a federation: there is no central government nor are there any rigid contractual obligations such as bind members of the United Nations.

The Commonwealth has no written constitution but its members subscribe to the ideals of the Declaration of Commonwealth Principles unanimously approved by a meeting of heads of government in Singapore in 1971. Members also approved the 1977 statement on apartheid in sport (the Gleneagles Agreement); the 1979 Lusaka Declaration on Racism and Racial Prejudice; the 1981 Melbourne Declaration on relations between developed and developing countries; the 1983 New Delhi Statement on Economic Action; the 1983 Goa Declaration on International Security; the 1985 Nassau Declaration on World Order; the Commonwealth Accord on Southern Africa (1985); the 1987 Vancouver Declaration on World Trade; the Okanagan Statement and Programme of Action on Southern Africa (1987); the Langkawi Declaration on the Environment (1989); the Kuala Lumpur Statement on Southern Africa (1989); the Harare Commonwealth

Declaration (1991); the Ottawa Declaration on Women and Structural Adjustment (1991); the Limassol Statement on the Uruguay Round of multilateral trade negotiations (1993); the Millbrook Commonwealth Action Programme on the Harare Declaration (1995); the Edinburgh Commonwealth Economic Declaration (1997); the Fancourt Commonwealth Declaration on Globalization and People-centred Development (1999); and the Coolum Declaration on the Commonwealth in the 21st Century: Continuity and Renewal (2002).

MEETINGS OF HEADS OF GOVERNMENT

Meetings are private and informal and operate not by voting but by consensus. The emphasis is on consultation and exchange of views for co-operation. A communiqué is issued at the end of every meeting. Meetings are held every two years in different capitals in the Commonwealth. The 1999 meeting was held in Durban, South Africa, in November. The next meeting was held in Brisbane, Australia, in March 2002. (It was originally scheduled to be held in October 2001, but was postponed in view of the international political crisis that followed major terrorist attacks on the USA in September.)

OTHER CONSULTATIONS

Meetings at ministerial and official level are also held regularly. Since 1959 finance ministers have met in a Commonwealth country in the week prior to the annual meetings of the IMF and the World Bank. Meetings on education, legal, women's and youth affairs are held at ministerial level every three years. Ministers of health hold annual meetings, with major meetings every three years, and ministers of agriculture meet every two years. Ministers of trade, labour and employment, industry, science and the environment also hold periodic meetings.

Senior officials—cabinet secretaries, permanent secretaries to heads of government and others—meet regularly in the year between meetings of heads of government to provide continuity and to exchange views on various developments.

In November 1999 the heads of government meeting established a 10-member Commonwealth High Level Review Group to review the role and activities of the Commonwealth. In 2000 the Group initiated a programme of consultations to proceed with its mandate and established a working group of experts to consider the Commonwealth's role in supporting information technology capabilities in member countries.

COMMONWEALTH SECRETARIAT

The Secretariat, established by Commonwealth heads of government in 1965, operates as an international organization at the service of all Commonwealth countries. It organizes consultations between governments and runs programmes of co-operation. Meetings of heads of government, ministers and senior officials decide these programmes and provide overall direction.

The Secretariat is headed by a secretary-general (elected by heads of government), assisted by three deputy secretaries-general. One deputy is responsible for political affairs, one for economic and social affairs, and one for development co-operation (including the Commonwealth Fund for Technical Co-operation—see below). The Secretariat comprises 12 Divisions in the fields of political affairs; legal and constitutional affairs; information and public affairs; administration; economic affairs; human resource development; gender and youth affairs; science and technology; economic and legal advisory services; export and industrial development; management and training services; and general technical assistance services. It also includes a non-governmental organizations desk and a unit for strategic planning and evaluation.

In 2000 the Secretariat adopted the following as its guiding mission: working for all people of the Commonwealth as a force for democracy and good governance, as a platform for global consensus-building, and as a source of practical assistance for sustainable development.

Secretary-General: DONALD (DON) C. MCKINNON (New Zealand).

Deputy Secretary-General (Political): FLORENCE MUGASHA (Uganda) (from 1 May 2002).

Deputy Secretary-General (Economic and Social): Dame VERONICA SUTHERLAND (United Kingdom).

Deputy Secretary-General (Development Co-operation): WINSTON A. COX (Barbados).

Activities

INTERNATIONAL AFFAIRS

In October 1991 heads of government, meeting in Harare, Zimbabwe, issued the Harare Commonwealth Declaration, in which they reaffirmed their commitment to the Commonwealth Principles declared in 1971, and stressed the need to promote sustainable development and the alleviation of poverty. The Declaration placed emphasis on the promotion of democracy and respect for human rights and resolved to strengthen the Commonwealth's capacity to assist countries in entrenching democratic practices. The meeting also welcomed the political reforms introduced by the South African Government to end the system of apartheid and urged all South African political parties to commence negotiations on a new constitution as soon as possible. The meeting endorsed measures on the phased removal of punitive measures against South Africa. In December a group of six eminent Commonwealth citizens was dispatched to observe multi-party negotiations on the future of South Africa and to assist the process where possible. In October 1992, in a fresh attempt to assist the South African peace process, a Commonwealth team of 18 observers was sent to monitor political violence in the country. A second phase of the Commonwealth Mission to South Africa (COMSA) began in February 1993, comprising 10 observers with backgrounds in policing, the law, politics and public life. COMSA issued a report in May in which it urged a concerted effort to build a culture of political tolerance in South Africa. In a report on its third phase, issued in December, COMSA appealed strongly to all political parties to participate in the transitional arrangements leading to democratic elections. In October the Commonwealth heads of government, meeting in Limassol, Cyprus, agreed that a democratic and non-racial South Africa would be invited to join the organization. They endorsed the removal of all economic sanctions against South Africa, but agreed to retain the arms embargo until a post-apartheid, democratic government had been established.

In November 1995 Commonwealth heads of government, convened in New Zealand, formulated and adopted the Millbrook Commonwealth Action Programme on the Harare Declaration, to promote adherence by member countries to the fundamental principles of democracy and human rights (as proclaimed in the 1991 Declaration). The Programme incorporated a framework of measures to be pursued in support of democratic processes and institutions, and actions to be taken in response to violations of the Harare Declaration principles, in particular the unlawful removal of a democratically-elected government. A Commonwealth Ministerial Action Group on the Harare Declaration (CMAG) was to be established to implement this process and to assist the member country involved to comply with the Harare principles. On the basis of this Programme, the leaders suspended Nigeria from the Commonwealth with immediate effect, following the execution by that country's military Government of nine environmental and human rights protesters and a series of other violations of human rights. The meeting determined to expel Nigeria from the Commonwealth if no 'demonstrable progress' had been made towards the establishment of a democratic authority by the time of the next summit meeting. In addition, the Programme formulated measures to promote sustainable development in member countries, which was considered to be an important element in sustaining democracy, and to facilitate consensus-building within the international community. Earlier in the meeting a statement was issued declaring the 'overwhelming majority' of Commonwealth governments to be opposed to nuclear-testing programmes being undertaken in the South Pacific region. However, in view of events in Nigeria, the issue of nuclear testing and disagreement among member countries did not assume the significance anticipated.

In December 1995 CMAG convened for its inaugural meeting in London. The Group, comprising the ministers of foreign affairs of Canada, Ghana, Jamaica, Malaysia, New Zealand, South Africa, the United Kingdom and Zimbabwe, commenced by considering efforts to restore democratic government in the three Commonwealth countries under military regimes, i.e. The Gambia, Nigeria and Sierra Leone. At the second meeting of the Group, in April 1996, ministers commended the conduct of presidential and parliamentary elections in Sierra Leone and the announcement by The Gambia's military leaders to proceed with a transition to civilian rule. In June a three-member CMAG delegation visited The Gambia to reaffirm Commonwealth support of the transition process in that country and to identify possible areas of further Commonwealth assistance. In August the Gambian authorities issued a decree removing the ban on political activities and parties, although shortly afterwards prohibited certain parties and candidates involved in political life prior to the military take-over from contesting the elections. CMAG recommended that in such circumstances there should be no Commonwealth observers sent to either the presidential or parliamentary elections, which were held in September 1996 and January 1997 respectively. Following the restoration of a civilian Government in early 1997, CMAG requested the Commonwealth Secretary-General to extend technical assistance to The Gambia in order to consolidate the democratic transition process. In April 1996 it was noted that the human rights situation in Nigeria had continued to deteriorate. CMAG, having pursued unsuccessful efforts to initiate dialogue with the Nigerian authorities, outlined a series of punitive and restrictive measures (including visa restrictions on members of the administration, a cessation of sporting contacts and an embargo on the export of armaments) that it would recommend for collective Commonwealth action in order to exert further pressure for reform in Nigeria. Following a meeting of a high-level delegation of the Nigerian Government and CMAG in June, the Group agreed to postpone the implementation of the sanctions, pending progress on the dialogue. (Canada, however, determined, unilaterally, to impose the measures with immediate effect; the United Kingdom did so in accordance with a decision of the European Union to implement limited sanctions against Nigeria.) A proposed CMAG mission to Nigeria was postponed in August, owing to restrictions imposed by the military authorities on access to political detainees and other civilian activists in that country. In September the Group agreed to proceed with the visit and to delay further a decision on the implementation of sanction measures. CMAG, without the participation of the representative of the Canadian Government, undertook its ministerial mission in November. In July 1997 the Group reiterated the Commonwealth Secretary-General's condemnation of a military coup in Sierra Leone in May, and decided to suspend that country's participation in meetings of the Commonwealth pending the restoration of a democratic government.

In October 1997 Commonwealth heads of government, meeting in Edinburgh, the United Kingdom, endorsed CMAG's recommendation that the imposition of sanctions against Nigeria be held in abeyance pending the scheduled completion of a transition programme towards democracy by October 1998. It was also agreed that CMAG be formally constituted as a permanent organ to investigate abuses of human rights throughout the Commonwealth. Jamaica and South Africa were to be replaced as members of CMAG by Barbados and Botswana, respectively.

In March 1998 CMAG, at its ninth meeting, commended the efforts of ECOWAS in restoring the democratically-elected Government of President Ahmed Tejan Kabbah in Sierra Leone, and agreed to remove all restrictions on Sierra Leone's participation in Commonwealth activities. Later in that month, a representative mission of CMAG visited Sierra Leone to express its support for Kabbah's administration and to consider the country's needs in its process of reconstruction. At the CMAG meeting held in October members agreed that Sierra Leone should no longer be considered under the Group's mandate; however, they urged the Secretary-General to continue to assist that country in the process of national reconciliation and to facilitate negotiations with opposition forces to ensure a lasting cease-fire. A Special Envoy of the Secretary-General co-operates with the UN, ECOWAS and the OAU in monitoring the implementation of the Sierra Leone peace process, and the Commonwealth has supported the rebuilding of the Sierra Leone police force. In September 2001 CMAG recommended that Sierra Leone be removed from its remit, but that the Secretary-General should continue to monitor developments there.

In April 1998 the Nigerian military leader, Gen. Sani Abacha, confirmed his intention to conduct a presidential election in August, but indicated that, following an agreement with other political organizations, he was to be the sole candidate. In June, however, Abacha died suddenly. His successor, Gen. Abdulsalam Abubakar, immediately released several prominent political prisoners, and in early July agreed to meet with the Secretaries-General of the UN and the Commonwealth to discuss the release of the imprisoned opposition leader, Chief Moshood Abiola. Abubakar also confirmed his intention to abide by the programme for transition to civilian rule by October. In mid-July, however, shortly before he was to have been liberated, Abiola died. The Commonwealth Secretary-General subsequently endorsed a new transition programme, which provided for the election of a civilian leader in May 1999. In October 1998 CMAG, convened for its 10th formal meeting, acknowledged Abubakar's efforts towards restoring a democratic government and recommended that member states begin to remove sanctions against Nigeria and that it resume participation in certain Commonwealth activities. The Commonwealth Secretary-General subsequently announced a programme of technical assistance to support Nigeria in the planning and conduct of democratic elections. Staff teams from the Commonwealth Secretariat observed local government, and state and governorship elections, held in December and in January 1999, respectively. A 23-member Commonwealth Observer Group was also dispatched to Nigeria to monitor preparations and conduct of legislative and presidential elections, held in late February. While the Group reported several deficiencies and irregularities in the conduct of the polling, it confirmed that, in general, the conditions had existed for free and fair elections and that the elections were a legitimate basis for the transition of power to a democratic, civilian government. In April CMAG voted to readmit Nigeria to full membership on 29 May, upon the installation of the new civilian administration.

In 1999 the Commonwealth Secretary-General appointed a Special Envoy to broker an agreement in order to end a civil dispute in Honiara, Solomon Islands. An accord was signed in late June, and it was envisaged that the Commonwealth would monitor its implementation. In October a Commonwealth Multinational Police Peace Monitoring Group was stationed in Solomon Islands; this was renamed the Commonwealth Multinational Police Assistance Group in February 2000. Following further internal unrest, however, the Group was disbanded. In June CMAG determined to send a new mission to Solomon Islands in order to facilitate negotiations between the opposing parties, to convey the Commonwealth's concern and to offer assistance. The Commonwealth welcomed the peace accord concluded in Solomon Islands in October, and extended its support to the International Peace Monitoring Team which was established to oversee implementation of the peace accords. CMAG welcomed the conduct of parliamentary elections held in Solomon Islands in December 2001. In June 1999 an agreement was concluded between opposing political groups in Zanzibar, having been facilitated by the good offices of the Secretary-General; however, this was only partially implemented.

In mid-October 1999 a special meeting of CMAG was convened to consider the overthrow of the democratically-elected Government in Pakistan in a military coup. The meeting condemned the action as a violation of Commonwealth principles and urged the new authorities to declare a timetable for the return to democratic rule. CMAG also resolved to send a four-member delegation, comprising the ministers of foreign affairs of Barbados, Canada, Ghana and Malaysia, to discuss this future course of action with the military regime. Pakistan was suspended from participation in meetings of the Commonwealth with immediate effect. The suspension, pending the restoration of a democratic government, was endorsed by heads of government, meeting in November, who requested that CMAG keep the situation in Pakistan under review. At the meeting, held in Durban, South Africa, CMAG was reconstituted to comprise the ministers of foreign affairs of Australia, Bangladesh, Barbados, Botswana, Canada, Malaysia, Nigeria and the United Kingdom. It was agreed that no country would serve for more than two consecutive two-year terms. CMAG was requested to remain actively involved in the post-conflict development and rehabilitation of Sierra Leone and the process of consolidating peace. In addition, it was urged to monitor persistent violations of the Harare Declaration principles in all countries. Heads of government also agreed to establish a new ministerial group on Guyana and to reconvene a ministerial committee on Belize, in order to facilitate dialogue in ongoing territorial disputes with neighbouring countries.

In June 2000, following the overthrow in May of the Fijian Government by a group of armed civilians, and the subsequent illegal detention of members of the elected administration, CMAG suspended Fiji's participation in meetings of the Commonwealth pending the restoration of democratic rule. In September, upon the request of CMAG, the Secretary-General appointed a Special Envoy to support efforts towards political dialogue and a return to democratic rule in Fiji. The Special Envoy under took his first visit in December. In December 2001, following the staging of democratic legislative elections in August/September, Fiji was readmitted to Commonwealth meetings on the recommendation of CMAG.

In March 2001 CMAG resolved to send a ministerial mission to Zimbabwe, in order to relay to the government the Commonwealth's concerns at the ongoing violence and abuses of human rights in that country, as well as to discuss the conduct of parliamentary elections and extend technical assistance. The mission was rejected by the Zimbabwean Government. In September, under the auspices of CMAG, the Zimbabwe Government signed the Abuja Agreement, which provided for the cessation of illegal occupations of white-owned farms and the resumption of the rule of law, in return for financial assistance to support the ongoing process of land reform in that country. In January 2002 CMAG expressed strong concern at the continuing violence and political intimidation in Zimbabwe. Commonwealth observers arrived in Zimbabwe from early February to monitor the presidential election scheduled to be held there during March. The summit of Commonwealth heads of government held in early March (see below) also expressed concern at the situation in Zimababwe, and mandated a Commonwealth Chairperson's Committee on Zimbabwe to determine appropriate action should the forthcoming presidential election be found not to have been conducted freely and fairly. Following the publication by the observer team of an unfavourable report on the conduct of the election, the Committee decided to suspend Zimbabwe from meetings of the Commonwealth for one year.

In September 2001 it was announced that the next meeting of Commonwealth heads of government, originally scheduled to be held in early October, in Brisbane, Australia, would be postponed in view of the international political crisis that followed major terrorist attacks perpetrated against targets in the USA in early September. The meeting was eventually convened in March 2002, in Brisbane. It adopted the Coolum Declaration on the Commonwealth in the 21st Century: Continuity and Renewal, which reiterated commitment to the organization's principles and values. Leaders at the meeting condemned all forms of terrorism; welcomed the Millennium Goals of the UN General Assembly; called on the Secretary-General to constitute a high-level expert group on implementing the objectives of the Fancourt Declaration; pledged continued support for small states; and urged renewed efforts to combat the spread of HIV/AIDS. The meeting adopted a report on the future of the Commonwealth drafted by the High Level Review Group. The document recommended strengthening the Commonwealth's role in conflict prevention and resolution and support of democratic practices; enhancing the good offices role of the Secretary-General; better promoting member states' economic and development needs; strengthening the organization's role in facilitating member states' access to international assistance; and promoting increased access to modern information and communications technologies.

Political Affairs Division: assists consultation among member governments on international and Commonwealth matters of common interest. In association with host governments, it organizes the meetings of heads of government and senior officials. The Division services committees and special groups set up by heads of government dealing with political matters. The Secretariat has observer status at the United Nations, and the Division manages a joint office in New York to enable small states, which would otherwise be unable to afford facilities there, to maintain a presence at the United Nations. The Division monitors political developments in the Commonwealth and international progress in such matters as disarmament, the concerns of small states, dismantling of apartheid and the Law of the Sea. It also undertakes research on matters of common interest to member governments, and reports back to them. The Division is involved in diplomatic training and consular co-operation.

In 1990 Commonwealth heads of government mandated the Division to support the promotion of democracy by monitoring the preparations for and conduct of parliamentary, presidential or other elections in member countries at the request of national governments. By the end of 2000 the Commonwealth had dispatched more than 30 electoral missions in accordance with this mandate.

A new expert group on good governance and the elimination of corruption in economic management convened for its first meeting in May 1998. In November 1999 Commonwealth heads of government endorsed a Framework for Principles for Promoting Good Governance and Combating Corruption, which had been drafted by the group.

LAW

Legal and Constitutional Affairs Division: promotes and facilitates co-operation and the exchange of information among member governments on legal matters. It administers, jointly with the Commonwealth of Learning, a distance training programme for legislative draftsmen and assists governments to reform national laws to meet the obligations of international conventions. The Division organizes the triennial meeting of ministers, Attorneys General and senior ministry officials concerned with the legal systems in Commonwealth countries. It has also initiated four Commonwealth schemes for co-operation on extradition, the protection of material cultural heritage, mutual assistance in criminal matters and the transfer of convicted offenders within the Commonwealth. It liaises with the Commonwealth Magistrates' and Judges' Association, the Commonwealth Legal Education Association, the Commonwealth Lawyers' Association (with which it helps to prepare the triennial Commonwealth Law Conference for the practising profession), the Commonwealth Association of Legislative Counsel, and with other international non-governmental organizations. The Division provides in-house legal advice for the Secretariat. The quarterly *Commonwealth Law Bulletin* reports on legal developments in and beyond the Commonwealth.

The Division's Commercial Crime Unit assists member countries to combat financial and organized crime, in particular transborder criminal activities, and promotes the exchange of information regarding national and international efforts to combat serious commercial crime through a quarterly publication, *Commonwealth Legal Assistance News,* and the *Crimewatch* bulletin. A Human Rights Unit aims to assist governments to strengthen national institutions and other mechanisms for the protection for human rights. It also organizes training workshops and promotes the exchange of relevant information among member countries.

ECONOMIC CO-OPERATION

In October 1997 Commonwealth heads of government, meeting in Edinburgh, the United Kingdom, signed an Economic Declaration that focused on issues relating to global trade, investment and development and committed all member countries to free-market economic principles. The Declaration also incorporated a provision for the establishment of a Trade and Investment Access Facility within the Secretariat in order to assist developing member states in the process of international trade liberalization and promote intra-Commonwealth trade.

In May 1998 the Commonwealth Secretary-General appealed to the Group of Eight industrialized nations to accelerate and expand the initiative to ease the debt burden of the most heavily indebted poor countries (HIPCs) (see World Bank and IMF). However, the Group failed to endorse the so-called 'Mauritius Mandate', adopted by Commonwealth finance ministers, meeting in Mauritius, in September 1997, which stipulated that by 2000 all eligible HIPCs should have in progress measures to reduce their external debt. In October 1998 Commonwealth finance ministers, convened in Ottawa, Canada, reiterated their appeal to international financial institutions to accelerate the HIPC initiative. The meeting also issued a Commonwealth Statement on the global economic crisis and endorsed several proposals to help to counter the difficulties experienced by several countries. These measures included a mechanism to enable countries to suspend payments on all short-term financial obligations at a time of emergency without defaulting, assistance to governments to attract private capital and to manage capital market volatility, and the development of international codes of conduct regarding financial and monetary policies and corporate governance. In March 1999 the Commonwealth Secretariat hosted a joint IMF-World Bank conference to review the HIPC scheme and initiate a process of reform. In November Commonwealth heads of government, meeting in South Africa, declared their support for measures undertaken by the World Bank and IMF to enhance the HIPC initiative. At the end of an informal retreat the leaders adopted the Fancourt Commonwealth Declaration on Globalization and People-Centred Development, which emphasized the need for a more equitable spread of wealth generated by the process of globalization, and expressed a renewed commitment to the elimination of all forms of discrimination, the promotion of people-centred development and capacity-building, and efforts to ensure developing countries benefit from future multilateral trade liberalization measures.

In February 1998 the Commonwealth Secretariat hosted the first Inter-Governmental Organizations Meeting to promote co-operation between small island states and the formulation of a unified policy approach to international fora. A second meeting was convened in March 2001, where discussions focused on the forthcoming WTO ministerial meeting and the OECD's harmful tax competition initiative. In September 2000 Commonwealth finance ministers, meeting in Malta, reviewed the OECD initiative and agreed that the measures, affecting many member countries with offshore financial centres, should not be imposed on governments. The ministers mandated the involvement of the Commonwealth Secretariat in efforts to resolve the dispute; a joint working group was subsequently established by the Secretariat with the OECD.

The first meeting of governors of central banks from Commonwealth countries was held in June 2001 in London, United Kingdom.

Economic Affairs Division: organizes and services the annual meetings of Commonwealth ministers of finance and the ministerial group on small states and assists in servicing the biennial meetings of heads of government and periodic meetings of environment ministers. It engages in research and analysis on economic issues of interest to member governments and organizes seminars and conferences of government officials and experts. The Division undertook a major programme of technical assistance to enable developing Commonwealth countries to participate in the Uruguay Round of multilateral trade negotiations and has assisted the African, Caribbean and Pacific (ACP) group of countries in their trade negotiations with the European Union. It continues to help developing countries to strengthen their links with international capital markets and foreign investors. The Division also services groups of experts on economic affairs that have been commissioned by governments to report on, among other things, protectionism; obstacles to the North-South negotiating process; reform of the international financial and trading system; the debt crisis; management of technological change; the special needs of small states; the impact of change on the development process; environmental issues; women and structural adjustment; and youth unemployment. A Commonwealth Secretariat Debt Recording and Management System has been developed by the Economic and Legal Advisory Services Division, which operates the system for the benefit of member countries and concerned organizations. The Economic Affairs Division co-ordinates the Secretariat's environmental work and manages the Iwokrama International Centre for Rainforest Conservation and Development.

The Division played a catalytic role in the establishment of a Commonwealth Equity Fund, initiated in September 1990, to allow developing member countries to improve their access to private institutional investment, and promoted a Caribbean Investment Fund. The Division supported the establishment of a Commonwealth Private Investment Initiative (CPII) to mobilize capital, on a regional basis, for investment in newly-privatized companies and in small and medium-sized businesses in the private sector. The first regional fund under the CPII was launched in July 1996. The Commonwealth Africa Investment Fund (Comafin), was to be managed by the United Kingdom's official development institution, the Commonwealth Development Corporation, to assist businesses in 19 countries in sub-Saharan Africa, with initial resources of US $63.5m. In August 1997 a fund for the Pacific Islands was launched, with an initial capital of $15.0m. A $200m. South Asia Regional Fund was established at the Heads of Government Meeting in October. In October 1998 a fund for the Caribbean states was inaugurated, at a meeting of Commonwealth finance ministers. The 2001 summit of Commonwealth heads of government authorized the establishment of a new fund for Africa.

HUMAN RESOURCES

Human Resource Development Division: consists of two departments concerned with education and health. The Division co-operates with member countries in devising strategies for human resource development.

The **Education Department** arranges specialist seminars, workshops and co-operative projects, and commissions studies in areas identified by ministers of education, whose three-yearly meetings it also services. Its present areas of emphasis include improving the quality of and access to basic education; strengthening the culture of science, technology and mathematics education in formal and non-formal areas of education; improving the quality of management in institutions of higher learning and basic education; improving the performance of teachers; strengthening examination assessment systems; and promoting the movement of students between Commonwealth countries. The Department also promotes multi-sectoral strategies to be incorporated in the development of human resources. Emphasis is placed on ensuring a gender balance, the appropriate use of technology, promoting good governance, addressing the problems of scale particular to smaller member countries, and encouraging collaboration between governments, the private sector and other non-governmental organizations.

The **Health Department** organizes ministerial, technical and expert group meetings and workshops, to promote co-operation on health matters, and the exchange of health information and expertise. The Department commissions relevant studies and provides professional and technical advice to member countries and to the Secretariat. It also supports the work of regional health organizations and promotes health for all people in Commonwealth countries.

Gender and Youth Affairs Division: consists of the Gender Affairs Department and the Commonwealth Youth Affairs Department.

The **Gender Affairs Department** is responsible for the implementation of the 1995 Commonwealth Plan of Action on Gender and Development, which was endorsed by the Heads of Government in order to achieve gender equality in the Commonwealth. The main objective of the Plan is to ensure that gender is incorporated into all policies, programmes, structures and procedures of member states and of the Commonwealth Secretariat. A further gender equality plan, 'Advancing the Commonwealth Agenda in the New Millennium', covers the period 2000–05. The Department is also addressing specific concerns such as the integration of gender issues into national budgetary processes, increasing the participation of women in politics and conflict prevention and resolution (with the objective of raising the level of female participation to 30%), and the promotion of human rights, including the elimination of violence against women and girls.

The **Youth Affairs Department** administers the Commonwealth Youth Programme (CYP), funded through separate voluntary contributions from governments, which seeks to promote the involvement of young people in the economic and social development of their countries. The CYP was awarded a budget of £2.2m. for 2000/01. It provides policy advice for governments and operates regional training programmes for youth workers and policy-makers through its centres in Africa, Asia, the Caribbean and the Pacific. It conducts a Youth Study Fellowship scheme, a Youth Project Fund, a Youth Exchange Programme (in the Caribbean), and a Youth Service Awards Scheme, holds conferences and seminars, carries out research and disseminates information. In May 1995 a Commonwealth Youth Credit Initiative was launched, in order to provide funds, training and advice to young entrepreneurs. In May 1998 a Commonwealth ministerial meeting, held in Kuala Lumpur, Malaysia, approved a new Plan of Action on Youth Empowerment to the Year 2005. In March 2002 Commonwealth heads of government approved the Youth for the Future initiative concerning technology and skills development and promoting youth enterprise.

SCIENCE

Science and Technology Division: is partially funded and governed by the Commonwealth Science Council, consisting of 35 member governments, which aims to enhance the scientific and technological capabilities of member countries, through co-operative research, training and the exchange of information. Current priority areas of work are concerned with the promotion of sustainable development and cover biological diversity and genetic resources, water resources, and renewable energy.

TECHNICAL CO-OPERATION

Commonwealth Fund for Technical Co-operation (CFTC): f. 1971 to facilitate the exchange of skills between member countries and to promote economic and social development. It is administered by the Commonwealth Secretariat and financed by voluntary subscriptions from member governments. The CFTC responds to requests from member governments for technical assistance, such as the provision of experts for short- or medium-term projects, advice on economic or legal matters, in particular in the areas of natural resources management and public-sector reform, and training programmes. Since 1995 the CFTC has operated a volunteer scheme, the Commonwealth Service Abroad Programme, for senior professionals willing to undertake short-term assignments. The CFTC also administers the Langkawi awards for the study of environmental issues, which is funded by the Canadian Government. The CFTC budget for 2000–01 amounted to £20.5m.

CFTC activities are implemented by the following divisions:

Economic and Legal Advisory Services Division: serves as an in-house consultancy, offering advice to governments on macroeconomic and financial management, capital market and private-sector development, debt management, the development of natural resources, and the negotiation of maritime boundaries and fisheries access agreements;

Export and Industrial Development Division: advises on all aspects of export marketing and the development of tourism, industry, small businesses and enterprises. Includes an Agricultural Development Unit, which provides technical assistance in agriculture and renewable resources;

General Technical Assistance Services Division: provides short- and long-term experts in all fields of development;

Management and Training Services Division: provides integrated packages of consultancy and training to enhance skills in areas such as public sector reform and the restructuring of enterprises, and arranges specific country and overseas training programmes.

The Secretariat also includes an Administration Division, a Strategic Planning and Evaluation Unit, and an Information and Public Affairs Division, which produces information publications, and radio and television programmes, about Commonwealth co-operation and consultation activities.

Finance

The Secretariat's budget for 2000/01 was £11.0m. Member governments meet the cost of the Secretariat through subscriptions on a scale related to income and population.

Publications

Commonwealth Currents (quarterly).

Commonwealth Law Bulletin (2 a year).

Commonwealth Organisations (directory).

In Common (quarterly newsletter of the Youth Programme).

International Development Policies (quarterly).

Link In to Gender and Development (annually).

Report of the Commonwealth Secretary-General (every 2 years).

The Commonwealth Yearbook.

Numerous reports, studies and papers (catalogue available).

Commonwealth Organizations

(In the United Kingdom, unless otherwise stated.)

PRINCIPAL BODIES

Commonwealth Foundation: Marlborough House, Pall Mall, London, SW1Y 5HY; tel. (20) 7930-3783; fax (20) 7839-8157; e-mail geninfo@commonwealth.int; internet www.commonwealthfoundation.com; f. 1966; intergovernmental body promoting people-to-people interaction, and collaboration within the non-governmental sector of the Commonwealth; supports non-governmental organizations, professional associations and Commonwealth arts and culture. Awards an annual Commonwealth Writers' Prize. Funds are provided by Commonwealth govts. Chair. GRACA MACHEL (Mozambique); Dir COLIN BELL (United Kingdom). Publ. *Common Path* (quarterly).

The Commonwealth of Learning (COL): 1285 West Broadway, Suite 600, Vancouver, BC V6H 3X8, Canada; tel. (604) 775-8200; fax (604) 775-8210; e-mail info@col.org; internet www.col.org; f. 1987 by Commonwealth Heads of Government to promote the devt and sharing of distance education and open learning resources, including materials, expertise and technologies, throughout the Commonwealth and in other countries; implements and assists with national and regional educational programmes; acts as consultant to international agencies and national governments; conducts seminars and studies on specific educational needs. COL is financed by Commonwealth governments on a voluntary basis; in 1999 heads of government endorsed an annual core budget for COL of US $9m. Pres. and CEO Dato' Prof. GAJARAJ DHANARAJAN (Malaysia). Publs *Connections, EdTech News.*

The following represents a selection of other Commonwealth organizations:

AGRICULTURE AND FORESTRY

Commonwealth Forestry Association: , 6–8 South Parks Rd, Oxford, OX1 3UB; tel. (1865) 271037; fax (1865) 275074; e-mail cfa_ox@hotmail.com; f. 1921; produces, collects and circulates information relating to world forestry and promotes good management, use and conservation of forests and forest lands throughout the world. Mems: 1,000. Chair. Prof. JULIAN EVANS. Publs *International Forestry Review* (quarterly), *Commonwealth Forestry News* (quarterly), *Commonwealth Forestry Handbook* (irregular).

Standing Committee on Commonwealth Forestry: Forestry Commission, 231 Corstorphine Rd, Edinburgh, EH12 7AT; tel. (131) 314-6137; fax (131) 334-0442; e-mail libby.jones@forestry.gsi.gov.uk; f. 1923 to provide continuity between Confs, and to provide a forum for discussion on any forestry matters of common interest to mem. govts which may be brought to the Cttee's notice by any member country or organization; 54 mems. 1997 Conference: Victoria Falls, Zimbabwe; 2005 Conference: Sri Lanka. Sec. LIBBY JONES. Publ. *Newsletter* (quarterly).

COMMONWEALTH STUDIES

Institute of Commonwealth Studies: 28 Russell Sq., London, WC1B 5DS; tel. (20) 7862-8844; fax (20) 7862-8820; e-mail ics@sas.ac.uk; internet www.sas.ac.uk/commonwealthstudies/; f. 1949 to promote advanced study of the Commonwealth; provides a library and meeting place for postgraduate students and academic staff engaged in research in this field; offers postgraduate teaching. Dir Prof. PAT CAPLAN. Publs *Annual Report, Collected Seminar Papers, Newsletter, Theses in Progress in Commonwealth Studies.*

COMMUNICATIONS

Commonwealth Telecommunications Organization: Clareville House, 26–27 Oxendon St, London, SW1Y 4EL; tel. (20) 7930-5516; fax (20) 7930-4248; e-mail info@cto.int; internet www.cto.int; f. 1967; aims to enhance the development of telecommunications in Commonwealth countries and contribute to the communications infrastructure required for economic and social devt, through a devt and training programme. Exec. Dir Dr DAVID SOUTER. Publ. *CTO Briefing* (3 a year).

EDUCATION AND CULTURE

Association of Commonwealth Universities (ACU): John Foster House, 36 Gordon Sq., London, WC1H 0PF; tel. (20) 7380-6700; fax (20) 7387-2655; e-mail info@acu.ac.uk; internet www.acu.ac.uk; f. 1913; organizes major meetings of Commonwealth universities and their representatives; publishes factual information about Commonwealth universities and access to them; acts as a liaison office and general information centre and provides a recruitment advertising and publicity service; hosts a management consultancy service; supplies secretariats for the Commonwealth Scholarship Comm., the Marshall Aid Commemoration Comm. and the Commonwealth Universities Study Abroad Consortium; administers various other fellowship and scholarship programmes. Mems: 480 universities in 36 Commonwealth countries or regions. Sec.-Gen. Prof. MICHAEL GIBBONS. Publs include: *Commonwealth Universities Yearbook, ACU Bulletin* (5 a year), *Report of the Council of the ACU* (annually), *Awards for University Teachers and Research Workers, Awards for Postgraduate Study at Commonwealth Universities, Awards for First Degree Study at Commonwealth Universities, Awards for University Administrators and Librarians, Who's Who of Executive Heads: Vice-Chancellors, Presidents, Principals and Rectors,* Student Information Papers (study abroad series).

Commonwealth Association for Education in Journalism and Communication—CAEJC: c/o Faculty of Law, University of Western Ontario, London, ON N6A 3K7, Canada; tel. (519) 6613348; fax (519) 6613790; e-mail caejc@julian.uwo.ca; f. 1985; aims to foster high standards of journalism and communication education and research in Commonwealth countries and to promote co-operation among institutions and professions. c. 700 mems in 32 Commonwealth countries. Pres. Prof. SYED ARABI IDID (Malaysia); Sec. Prof. ROBERT MARTIN (Canada). Publ. *CAEJAC Journal* (annually).

Commonwealth Association of Science, Technology and Mathematics Educators—CASTME: c/o Education Dept, Human Resource Development Division, Commonwealth Secretariat, Marlborough House, Pall Mall, London, SW1Y 5HX; tel. (20) 7747-6282; fax (20) 7747-6287; e-mail v.goel@commonwealth.int; f. 1974; special emphasis is given to the social significance of education in these subjects. Organizes an Awards Scheme to promote effective teaching and learning in these subjects, and biennial regional seminars. Pres. Sir HERMANN BONDI; Hon. Sec. Dr VED GOEL. Publ. *CASTME Journal* (quarterly).

Commonwealth Council for Educational Administration and Management: c/o International Educational Leadership Centre, School of Management, Lincoln University Campus, Brayford Pool, Lincoln, LN6 7TS; tel. (1522) 886071; fax (1522) 886023; e-mail athody@lincoln.ac.uk; f. 1970; aims to foster quality in professional development and links among educational administrators; holds nat. and regional confs, as well as visits and seminars. Mems: 24 affiliated groups representing 3,000 persons. Pres. Prof. ANGELA THODY; Sec. GERALDINE BRISTOW. Publs *Managing Education Matters* (2 a year), *International Studies in Educational Administration* (2 a year).

Commonwealth Institute: 230 Kensington High St, London, W8 6NQ; tel. (20) 7603-4535; fax (20) 7602-7374; e-mail info@commonwealth.org.uk; internet www.commonwealth.org.uk; f. 1893 as the Imperial Institute; restructured as an independent pan-Commonwealth agency Jan. 2000; governed by a Bd of Trustees elected by the Bd of Governors; Commonwealth High Commissioners to the United Kingdom act as ex-officio Governors; the Inst. houses a Commonwealth Resource and Literature Library and a Conference and Events Centre; supplies educational resource materials and training throughout the United Kingdom; provides internet services to the Commonwealth; operates as an arts and conference centre, running a Commonwealth-based cultural programme; a new five-year strategic plan, entitled 'Commonwealth 21', was inaugurated in 1998. Chair. DAVID A. THOMPSON; Chief Exec. DAVID FRENCH. Publ. *Annual Review.*

League for the Exchange of Commonwealth Teachers: 7 Lion Yard, Tremadoc Rd, London, SW4 7NQ; tel. (20) 7498-1101; fax (20) 7720-5403; e-mail lectcom_exchange@compuserve.com; internet www.lect.org.uk; f. 1901; promotes educational exchanges between teachers in Australia, the Bahamas, Barbados, Bermuda, Canada, Guyana, India, Jamaica, Kenya, Malawi, New Zealand, Pakistan, South Africa and Trinidad and Tobago. Dir ANNA TOMLINSON. Publs *Annual Report, Exchange Teacher* (annually).

HEALTH

Commonwealth Medical Association: BMA House, Tavistock Sq., London, WC1H 9JP; tel. (20) 7272-8492; fax (20) 7272-1663; e-mail office@commat.org; internet www.commat.org; f. 1962 for the exchange of information; provision of tech. co-operation and advice; formulation and maintenance of a code of ethics; provision of continuing medical education; devt and promotion of health education programmes; and liaison with WHO and the UN on health issues; meetings of its Council are held every three years. Mems: medical asscns in Commonwealth countries. Sec. Dr JANE RICHARDS.

Commonwealth Pharmaceutical Association: 1 Lambeth High St, London, SE1 7JN; tel. (20) 7572-2364 ; fax (20) 7572-2508; e-mail bfalconbridge@rpsgb.org.uk; f. 1970 to promote the interests of pharmaceutical sciences and the profession of pharmacy in the Commonwealth; to maintain high professional standards, encourage links between members and the creation of nat. asscns; and to facilitate the dissemination of information. Holds confs (every four years) and regional meetings. Mems: 39 pharmaceutical asscns. Sec. TONY MOFFAT. Publ. *Quarterly Newsletter.*

Commonwealth Society for the Deaf: 34 Buckingham Palace Rd, London, SW1W 0RE; tel. (20) 7233-5700; fax (20) 7233-5800; e-mail sound.seekers@btinternet.com; internet www.sound-seekers.org.uk; promotes the health, education and general welfare of the deaf in developing Commonwealth countries; encourages and assists the development of educational facilities, the training of teachers of the deaf, and the provision of support for parents of deaf children; organizes visits by volunteer specialists to developing countries; provides audiological equipment and organizes the training of audiological maintenance technicians; conducts research into the causes and prevention of deafness. CEO Brig. J. A. DAVIS. Publ. *Annual Report.*

Sight Savers International (Royal Commonwealth Society for the Blind): Grosvenor Hall, Bolnore Rd, Haywards Heath, West Sussex, RH16 4BX; tel. (1444) 446600; fax (1444) 446688; e-mail generalinformation@sightsavers.org; internet www.sightsavers.org; f. 1950 to prevent blindness and restore sight in developing countries, and to provide education and community-based training for incurably blind people; operates in collaboration with local partners, with high priority given to training local staff; Chair. SIR JOHN COLES; Dir RICHARD PORTER. Publ. *Sight Savers News.*

INFORMATION AND THE MEDIA

Commonwealth Broadcasting Association: 17 Fleet St, London, EC4Y 1AA; tel. (20) 7583-5550; fax (20) 7583-5549; e-mail cba@cba.org.uk; internet www.cba.org.uk; f. 1945; gen. confs are held every two years (2002: Manchester, United Kingdom). Mems: 97 in 57 countries. Acting Pres. GEORGE VALARINO; Sec.-Gen. ELIZABETH SMITH. Publs *Commonwealth Broadcaster* (quarterly), *Commonwealth Broadcaster Directory* (annually).

Commonwealth Institute: see under Education.

Commonwealth Journalists Association: 17 Nottingham St, London, W1M 3RD; tel. (20) 7486-3844; fax (20) 7486-3822; e-mail ian.cjalon@virgin.net; internet www.ozemail.com.au/~pwessels/cja.html; f. 1978 to promote co-operation between journalists in Commonwealth countries, organize training facilities and confs, and foster understanding among Commonwealth peoples. Pres. MURRAY BURT; Exec. Dir IAN GILLHAM.

Commonwealth Press Union (Asscn of Commonwealth Newspapers, News Agencies and Periodicals): 17 Fleet St, London, EC4Y 1AA; tel. (20) 7583-7733; fax (20) 7583-6868; e-mail 106156.3331@compuserve.com; f. 1950; promotes the welfare of the Commonwealth press; provides training for journalists and organizes biennial confs. Mems: c. 1,000 newspapers, news agencies, periodicals in 42 Commonwealth countries. Dir ROBIN MACKICHAN. Publs *CPU News, Annual Report.*

LAW

Commonwealth Lawyers' Association: c/o The Law Society, 114 Chancery Lane, London, WC2A 1PL; tel. (20) 7320-5911; fax (20) 7831-0057; e-mail cla@lawsociety.org.uk; internet www.commonwealthlawyers.com; f. 1983 (fmrly the Commonwealth Legal Bureau); seeks to maintain and promote the rule of law throughout the Commonwealth, by ensuring that the people of the Commonwealth are served by an independent and efficient legal profession; upholds professional standards and promotes the availability of legal services; assists in organizing the triennial Commonwealth law confs. Pres. (1999–2003) CYRUS DAS; Exec. Sec. CHRISTINE AMOH. Publs *The Commonwealth Lawyer, Clarion.*

Commonwealth Legal Advisory Service: c/o British Institute of International and Comparative Law, Charles Clore House, 17 Russell Sq., London, WC1B 5JP; tel. (20) 7862-5151; fax (20) 7862-5152; e-mail info@biicl.org; financed by the British Institute and by contributions from Commonwealth govts; provides research facilities for Commonwealth govts and law reform commissions.

Commonwealth Legal Education Association: c/o Legal and Constitutional Affairs Division, Commonwealth Secretariat, Marlborough House, Pall Mall, London, SW1Y 5HX; tel. (20) 7747-6415; fax (20) 7747-6406; e-mail clea@commonwealth.int; internet www.clea.org.uk; f. 1971 to promote contacts and exchanges and to provide information regarding legal education. Gen. Sec. JOHN HATCHARD. Publs *Commonwealth Legal Education Association Newsletter* (3 a year), *Directory of Commonwealth Law Schools* (every 2 years).

Commonwealth Magistrates' and Judges' Association: Uganda House, 58/59 Trafalgar Sq., London, WC2N 5DX; tel. (20) 7976-1007; fax (20) 7976-2395; e-mail info@cmja.org; internet www.cmja.org; f. 1970 to advance the administration of the law by promoting the independence of the judiciary, to further education in law and crime prevention and to disseminate information; confs and study tours; corporate membership for asscns of the judiciary or courts of limited jurisdiction; assoc. membership for individuals. Pres. DAVID ARMATI; Sec.-Gen. Dr KAREN BREWER. Publ. *Commonwealth Judicial Journal* (2 a year).

PARLIAMENTARY AFFAIRS

Commonwealth Parliamentary Association: Westminster House, Suite 700, 7 Millbank, London, SW1P 3JA; tel. (20) 7799-1460; fax (20) 7222-6073; e-mail hq.sec@comparlhq.org.uk; internet www.comparlhq.org.uk; f. 1911 to promote understanding and co-operation between Commonwealth parliamentarians; organization: Exec. Cttee of 32 MPs responsible to annual Gen. Assembly; 148 brs throughout the Commonwealth; holds annual Commonwealth Parliamentary Confs and seminars; also regional confs and seminars; Sec.-Gen. ARTHUR DONAHOE. Publ. *The Parliamentarian* (quarterly).

PROFESSIONAL AND INDUSTRIAL RELATIONS

Commonwealth Association of Architects: 66 Portland Pl., London, W1N 4AD; tel. (20) 7490-3024; fax (20) 7253-2592; e-mail caa@gharchitects.demon.co.uk; internet www.archexchange.org; f. 1964; an asscn of 38 socs of architects in various Commonwealth countries. Objects: to facilitate the reciprocal recognition of professional qualifications; to provide a clearing house for information on architectural practice, and to encourage collaboration. Plenary confs every three years; regional confs are also held. Exec. Dir TONY GODWIN. Publs *Handbook, Objectives and Procedures: CAA Schools Visiting Boards, Architectural Education in the Commonwealth* (annotated bibliography of research), *CAA Newsnet* (2 a year), a survey and list of schools of architecture.

Commonwealth Association for Public Administration and Management—CAPAM: 1075 Bay St, Suite 402, Toronto, ON M5S 2B1, Canada; tel. (416) 920-3337; fax (416) 920-6574; e-mail capam@capam.ca; internet www.capam.comnet.mt/; f. 1994; aims to promote sound management of the public sector in Commonwealth countries and to assist those countries undergoing political or financial reforms. An international awards programme to reward innovation within the public sector was introduced in 1997, and is awarded every 2 years. Pres. Sir Richard Mottram (United Kingdom); Exec. Dir ART STEVENSON (Canada).

Commonwealth Trade Union Council: Congress House, 23–28 Great Russell St, London, WC1B 3LS; tel. (20) 7467-1301; fax (20) 7436-0301; e-mail info@commonwealthtuc.org; internet www.commonwealthtuc.org; f. 1979; links trade union national centres (representing more than 30m. trade union mems) throughout the Commonwealth; promotes the application of democratic principles and core labour standards, works closely with other international trade union orgs. Dir ANNIE WATSON. Publ. *Annual Report.*

SCIENCE AND TECHNOLOGY

Commonwealth Engineers' Council: c/o Institution of Civil Engineers, One Great George St, London, SW1P 3AA; tel. (20) 7222-7722; fax (20) 7222-7500; e-mail international@ice.org.uk; f. 1946; the Council meets every two years to provide an opportunity for engineering institutions of Commonwealth countries to exchange views on collaboration; there is a standing cttee on engineering education and training; organizes seminars on related topics. Sec. J. A. WHITWELL.

Commonwealth Geological Surveys Forum: c/o Commonwealth Science Council, CSC Earth Sciences Programme, Marlborough House, Pall Mall, London, SW1Y 5HX; tel. (20) 7839-3411; fax (20) 7839-6174; e-mail comsci@gn.apc.org; f. 1948 to promote collaboration in geological, geochemical, geophysical and remote sensing techniques and the exchange of information. Geological Programme Officer Dr SIYAN MALOMO.

SPORT

Commonwealth Games Federation: Walkden House, 3–10 Melton St, London, NW1 2EB; tel. (20) 7383-5596; fax (20) 7383-5506; e-mail commonwealthgamesfederation@abtinternet.com; internet www.commonwealthgames-fed.org; the Games were first held in 1930 and are now held every four years; participation is limited to competitors representing the mem. countries of the Commonwealth; to be held in Manchester, United Kingdom, in 2002. Mems: 72 affiliated bodies. Pres. HRH The Earl of WESSEX; Chair. MICHAEL FENNELL.

YOUTH

Commonwealth Youth Exchange Council: 7 Lion Yard, Tremadoc Rd, London, SW4 7NQ; tel. (20) 7498-6151; fax (20) 7720-5403; e-mail mail@cyec.demon.co.uk; f. 1970; promotes contact between groups of young people of the United Kingdom and other Commonwealth countries by means of educational exchange visits, provides information for organizers and allocates grants; 224 mem. orgs. Dir V. S. G. CRAGGS. Publs *Contact* (handbook), *Exchange* (newsletter), *Safety and Welfare* (guidelines for Commonwealth Youth Exchange groups).

Duke of Edinburgh's Award International Association: Award House, 7-11 St Matthew St, London, SW1P 2JT; tel. (20) 7222-4242; fax (20) 7222-4141; e-mail sect@intaward.org; internet www.intaward.org; f. 1956; offers a programme of leisure activities for young people, comprising Service, Expeditions, Physical Recreation, and Skills; operates in more than 60 countries (not confined to the Commonwealth). International Sec.-Gen. PAUL ARENGO-JONES. Publs *Award World* (2 a year), *Annual Report*, handbooks and guides.

MISCELLANEOUS

British Commonwealth Ex-Services League: 48 Pall Mall, London, SW1Y 5JG; tel. (20) 7973-7263; fax (20) 7973-7308; links the ex-service orgs in the Commonwealth, assists ex-servicemen of the Crown and their dependants who are resident abroad; holds triennial confs. Grand Pres. HRH The Duke of EDINBURGH; Sec.-Gen. Col BRIAN NICHOLSON. Publ. *Annual Report.*

Commonwealth Countries League: 14 Thistleworth Close, Isleworth, Middlesex, TW7 4QQ; tel. (20) 8737-3572; fax (20) 8568-2495; f. 1925 to secure equal opportunities and status between men and women in the Commonwealth, to act as a link between Commonwealth women's orgs, and to promote and finance secondary education of disadvantaged girls of high ability in their own countries, through the CCL Educational Fund; holds meetings with speakers and an annual Conf., organizes the annual Commonwealth Fair for fund-raising; individual mems and affiliated socs in the Commonwealth. Sec.-Gen. SHEILA O'REILLY. Publ. *CCL Newsletter* (3 a year).

Commonwealth War Graves Commission: 2 Marlow Rd, Maidenhead, Berks, SL6 7DX; tel. (1628) 634221; fax (1628) 771208; e-mail general.enq@cwgc.org; casualty and cemetery enquiries casualty.enq@cwgc.org; internet www.cwgc.org; f. 1917 (as Imperial War Graves Commission); responsible for the commemoration in perpetuity of the 1.7m. members of the Commonwealth Forces who died during the wars of 1914–18 and 1939–45; provides for the marking and maintenance of war graves and memorials at some 23,000 locations in 150 countries. Mems: Australia, Canada, India, New Zealand, South Africa, United Kingdom. Pres. HRH The Duke of KENT; Dir-Gen. R. KELLAWAY.

Joint Commonwealth Societies' Council: c/o Royal Commonwealth Society, 18 Northumberland Ave, London, WC2N 5BJ; tel. (20) 7930-6733; fax (20) 7930-9705; e-mail jcsc@rcsint.org; internet www.commonwealthday.com; f. 1947; provides a forum for the exchange of information regarding activities of mem. orgs which promote understanding among countries of the Commonwealth; co-ordinates the distribution of the Commonwealth Day message by Queen Elizabeth, organizes the observance of the Commonwealth Day and produces educational materials relating to the occasion; mems: 16 unofficial Commonwealth orgs and four official bodies. Chair. Sir PETER MARSHALL; Sec. N. J. HERCULES.

Royal Commonwealth Society: 18 Northumberland Ave, London, WC2N 5BJ; tel. (20) 7930-6733; fax (20) 7930-9705; e-mail info@rcsint.org; internet www.rcsint.org; f. 1868; to promote international understanding of the Commonwealth and its people; organizes meetings and seminars on topical issues, and cultural and social events; library housed by Cambridge University Library. Chair. Sir MICHAEL MCWILLIAM; Dir STUART MOLE. Publs *Annual Report, Newsletter* (3 a year), conference reports.

Royal Over-Seas League: Over-Seas House, Park Place, St James's St, London, SW1A 1LR; tel. (20) 7408-0214; fax (20) 7499-6738; internet www.rost.org.uk; f. 1910 to promote friendship and understanding in the Commonwealth; club houses in London and Edinburgh; membership is open to all British subjects and Commonwealth citizens. Chair. Sir GEOFFREY ELLERTON; Dir-Gen. ROBERT F. NEWELL. Publ. *Overseas* (quarterly).

The Victoria League for Commonwealth Friendship: 55 Leinster Sq., London, W2 4PW; tel. (20) 7243-2633; fax (20) 7229-2994; f. 1901; aims to further personal friendship among Commonwealth peoples and to provide hospitality for visitors; maintains Student House, providing accommodation for students from Commonwealth countries; has brs elsewhere in the UK and abroad. Chair. COLIN WEBBER; Gen. Sec. JOHN ALLAN. Publ. *Annual Report.*

Declaration of Commonwealth Principles

(Agreed by the Commonwealth Heads of Government Meeting at Singapore, 22 January 1971.)

The Commonwealth of Nations is a voluntary association of independent sovereign states, each responsible for its own policies, consulting and co-operating in the common interests of their peoples and in the promotion of international understanding and world peace.

Members of the Commonwealth come from territories in the six continents and five oceans, include peoples of different races, languages and religions, and display every stage of economic development from poor developing nations to wealthy industrialized nations. They encompass a rich variety of cultures, traditions and institutions.

Membership of the Commonwealth is compatible with the freedom of member-governments to be non-aligned or to belong to any other grouping, association or alliance. Within this diversity all members of the Commonwealth hold certain principles in common. It is by pursuing these principles that the Commonwealth can continue to influence international society for the benefit of mankind.

We believe that international peace and order are essential to the security and prosperity of mankind; we therefore support the United Nations and seek to strengthen its influence for peace in the world, and its efforts to remove the causes of tension between nations.

We believe in the liberty of the individual, in equal rights for all citizens regardless of race, colour, creed or political belief, and in their inalienable right to participate by means of free and democratic political processes in framing the society in which they live. We therefore strive to promote in each of our countries those representative institutions and guarantees for personal freedom under the law that are our common heritage.

We recognize racial prejudice as a dangerous sickness threatening the healthy development of the human race and racial discrimination as an unmitigated evil of society. Each of us will vigorously combat this evil within our own nation.

No country will afford to regimes which practise racial discrimination assistance which in its own judgment directly contributes to the pursuit or consolidation of this evil policy. We oppose all forms of colonial domination and racial oppression and are committed to the principles of human dignity and equality.

We will therefore use all our efforts to foster human equality and dignity everywhere, and to further the principles of self-determination and non-racialism.

We believe that the wide disparities in wealth now existing between different sections of mankind are too great to be tolerated. They also create world tensions. Our aim is their progressive removal. We therefore seek to use our efforts to overcome poverty, ignorance and disease, in raising standards of life and achieving a more equitable international society.

To this end our aim is to achieve the freest possible flow of international trade on terms fair and equitable to all, taking into account the special requirements of the developing countries, and to encourage the flow of adequate resources, including governmental and private resources, to the developing countries, bearing in mind the importance of doing this in a true spirit of partnership and of establishing for this purpose in the developing countries conditions which are conducive to sustained investment and growth.

We believe that international co-operation is essential to remove the causes of war, promote tolerance, combat injustice, and secure development among the peoples of the world. We are convinced that the Commonwealth is one of the most fruitful associations for these purposes.

In pursuing these principles the members of the Commonwealth believe that they can provide a constructive example of the multi-national approach which is vital to peace and progress in the modern world. The association is based on consultation, discussion and co-operation.

In rejecting coercion as an instrument of policy they recognize that the security of each member state from external aggression is a matter of concern to all members. It provides many channels for continuing exchanges of knowledge and views on professional, cultural, economic, legal and political issues among member states.

These relationships we intend to foster and extend, for we believe that our multi-national association can expand human understanding and understanding among nations, assist in the elimination of discrimination based on differences of race, colour or creed, maintain and strengthen personal liberty, contribute to the enrichment of life for all, and provide a powerful influence for peace among nations.

The Lusaka Declaration on Racism and Racial Prejudice

The Declaration, adopted by Heads of Government in 1979, includes the following statements:

United in our desire to rid the world of the evils of racism and racial prejudice, we proclaim our faith in the inherent dignity and worth of the human person and declare that:

(i) the peoples of the Commonwealth have the right to live freely in dignity and equality, without any distinction or exclusion based on race, colour, sex, descent, or national or ethnic origin;

(ii) while everyone is free to retain diversity in his or her culture and lifestyle this diversity does not justify the perpetuation of racial prejudice or racially discriminatory practices;

(iii) everyone has the right to equality before the law and equal justice under the law; and

(iv) everyone has the right to effective remedies and protection against any form of discrimination based on the grounds of race, colour, sex, descent, or national or ethnic origin.

We reject as inhuman and intolerable all policies designed to perpetuate apartheid, racial segregation or other policies based on theories that racial groups are or may be inherently superior or inferior.

We reaffirm that it is the duty of all the peoples of the Commonwealth to work together for the total eradication of the infamous policy of apartheid which is internationally recognized as a crime against the conscience and dignity of mankind and the very existence of which is an affront to humanity.

We agree that everyone has the right to protection against acts of incitement to racial hatred and discrimination, whether committed by individuals, groups or other organizations. . . .

Inspired by the principles of freedom and equality which characterise our association, we accept the solemn duty of working together to eliminate racism and racial prejudice. This duty involves the acceptance of the principle that positive measures may be required to advance the elimination of racism, including assistance to those struggling to rid themselves and their environment of the practice.

Being aware that legislation alone cannot eliminate racism and racial prejudice, we endorse the need to initiate public information and education policies designed to promote understanding, tolerance, respect and friendship among peoples and racial groups. . . .

We note that racism and racial prejudice, wherever they occur, are significant factors contributing to tension between nations and thus inhibit peaceful progress and development. We believe that the goal of the eradication of racism stands as a critical priority for governments of the Commonwealth committed as they are to the promotion of the ideals of peaceful and happy lives for their people.

Harare Commonwealth Declaration

The following are the major points of the Declaration adopted by Heads of Government at the meeting held in Harare, Zimbabwe, in 1991:

Having reaffirmed the principles to which the Commonwealth is committed, and reviewed the problems and challenges which the world, and the Commonwealth as part of it, face, we pledge the Commonwealth and our countries to work with renewed vigour, concentrating especially in the following areas: the protection and promotion of the fundamental political values of the Commonwealth; equality for women, so that they may exercise their full and equal rights; provision of universal access to education for the population of our countries; continuing action to bring about the end of apartheid and the establishment of a free, democratic, non-racial and prosperous South Africa; the promotion of sustainable development and the alleviation of poverty in the countries of the Commonwealth; extending the benefits of development within a framework of respect for human rights; the protection of the environment through respect for the principles of sustainable development which we enunciated at Langkawi; action to combat drugs trafficking and abuse and communicable diseases; help for small Commonwealth states in tackling their particular economic and security problems; and support of the United Nations and other international institutions in the world's search for peace, disarmament and effective arms control; and in the promotion of international consensus on major global political, economic and social issues.

To give weight and effectiveness to our commitments we intend to focus and improve Commonwealth co-operation in these areas. This would include strengthening the capacity of the Commonwealth to respond to requests from members for assistance in entrenching the practices of democracy, accountable administration and the rule of law.

In reaffirming the principles of the Commonwealth and in committing ourselves to pursue them in policy and action in response to the challenges of the 1990s, in areas where we believe that the Commonwealth has a distinctive contribution to offer, we the Heads of Government express our determination to renew and enhance the value and importance of the Commonwealth as an institution which can and should strengthen and enrich the lives not only of its own members and their peoples but also of the wider community of peoples of which they are a part.

THE COMMONWEALTH OF INDEPENDENT STATES—CIS

Address: 220000 Minsk, Kirava 17, Belarus.
Telephone: (172) 22-35-17; **fax:** (172) 27-23-39; **e-mail:** postmaster@www.cis.minsk.by; **internet:** www.cis.minsk.by.

The Commonwealth of Independent States is a voluntary association of 12 (originally 11) states, established at the time of the collapse of the USSR in December 1991.

MEMBERS

Armenia	Moldova
Azerbaijan	Russia
Belarus	Tajikistan
Georgia	Turkmenistan
Kazakhstan	Ukraine
Kyrgyzstan	Uzbekistan

Note: Azerbaijan signed the Alma-Ata Declaration (see below), but in October 1992 the Azerbaijan legislature voted against ratification of the foundation documents by which the Commonwealth of Independent States had been established in December 1991. Azerbaijan formally became a member of the CIS in September 1993, after the legislature voted in favour of membership. Georgia was admitted to the CIS in December 1993.

Organization

(April 2002)

COUNCIL OF HEADS OF STATE

This is the supreme body of the CIS, on which all the member states of the Commonwealth are represented at the level of head of state, for discussion of issues relating to the co-ordination of Commonwealth activities and the development of the Minsk Agreement. Decisions of the Council are taken by common consent, with each state having equal voting rights. The Council meets at least twice a year. An extraordinary meeting may be convened on the initiative of the majority of Commonwealth heads of state.

COUNCIL OF HEADS OF GOVERNMENT

This Council convenes for meetings at least once every three months; an extraordinary sitting may be convened on the initiative of a majority of Commonwealth heads of government. The two Councils may discuss and take necessary decisions on important domestic and external issues, and may hold joint sittings.

Working and auxiliary bodies, composed of authorized representatives of the participating states, may be set up on a permanent or interim basis on the decision of the Council of Heads of State and the Council of Heads of Government.

CIS EXECUTIVE COMMITTEE

The Executive Committee was established by the Council of Heads of State in April 1999 to supersede the existing Secretariat, the Inter-state Economic Committee and other working bodies and committees, in order to improve the efficient functioning of the organization. The Executive Committee co-operates closely with other CIS bodies including the councils of foreign ministers and defence ministers; the Economic Council; Council of Border Troops Commanders; the Collective Security Council; the Secretariat of the Council of the Inter-parliamentary Assembly; and the Inter-state Committee for Statistics.

Executive Secretary and Chairman of the Executive Committee: YURII YAROV.

Activities

On 8 December 1991 the heads of state of Belarus, Russia and Ukraine signed the Minsk Agreement, providing for the establishment of a Commonwealth of Independent States. Formal recognition of the dissolution of the USSR was incorporated in a second treaty (the Alma-Ata Declaration), signed by 11 heads of state in the then Kazakh capital, Alma-Ata (Almaty), later in that month.

In March 1992 a meeting of the CIS Council of Heads of Government decided to establish a commission to examine the resolution that 'all CIS member states are the legal successors of the rights and obligations of the former Soviet Union'. Documents relating to the legal succession of the Soviet Union were signed at a meeting of Heads of State in July. In April an agreement establishing an Inter-parliamentary Assembly (IPA), signed by Armenia, Belarus, Kazakhstan, Kyrgyzstan, Russia, Tajikistan and Uzbekistan, was published. The first Assembly was held in Bishkek, Kyrgyzstan, in September, attended by delegates from all these countries, with the exception of Uzbekistan.

A CIS Charter was formulated at the meeting of the heads of state in Minsk, Belarus, in January 1993. The Charter, providing for a defence alliance, an inter-state court and an economic co-ordination committee, was to serve as a framework for closer co-operation and was signed by all of the members except Moldova, Turkmenistan and Ukraine.

In May 1994 the CIS and UNCTAD signed a co-operation accord. A similar agreement was concluded with the UN Economic Commission for Europe in June 1996. Working contacts have also been established with ILO, UNHCR, WHO and the European Union. In June 1998 the IPA approved a decision to sign the European Social Charter (see Council of Europe); a declaration of co-operation between the Assembly and the OSCE Parliamentary Assembly (q.v.) was also signed.

In November 1995, at the Council of Heads of Government meeting, Russia expressed concern at the level of non-payment of debts by CIS members, which, it said, was hindering further integration. At the meeting of the Council in April 1996 a long-term plan for the integrated development of the CIS, incorporating measures for further socio-economic, military and political co-operation, was approved.

In March 1997 the then Russian President, Boris Yeltsin, admitted that the CIS institutional structure had failed to ameliorate the severe economic situation of certain member states. Nevertheless, support for the CIS as an institution was reaffirmed by the participants during the meeting. At the heads of state meeting held in Chişinău, Moldova, in October, Russia was reportedly criticized by the other country delegations for failing to implement CIS agreements, for hindering development of the organization and for failing to resolve regional conflicts. Russia, for its part, urged all member states to participate more actively in defining, adopting and implementing CIS policies. Meeting in April 1998 heads of state emphasized the necessity of improving the activities of the CIS and of reforming its bureaucratic structure. Reform of the CIS was also the main item on the agenda of the eleventh IPA, held in June. It was agreed that an essentially new institution needed to be created, taking into account the relations between the states in a new way. In the same month the first plenary meeting of a special forum, convened to address issues of restructuring the CIS, was held. Working groups were to be established to co-ordinate proposals and draft documents. However, in October reform proposals drawn up by 'experienced specialists' and presented by the Executive Secretary were unanimously rejected as inadequate by the 12 member states. In March 1999 Boris Yeltsin, acting as Chairman of the Council of Heads of State, dismissed the then Executive Secretary, Boris Berezovskii, owing to alleged misconduct and neglect of duties. The decision was endorsed by the Council of Heads of Government meeting in early April. The Council also adopted guide-lines for restructuring the CIS and for the future development of the organization. Economic co-operation was to be a priority area of activity, and in particular, the establishment of a free-trade zone. Vladimir Putin, then acting President of the Russian Federation, was elected as the new Chairman of the Council of Heads of State at a CIS summit held in Moscow in January 2000. Meeting in June, a summit of the Councils of Heads of State and Government issued a declaration concerning the maintenance of strategic stability, approved a plan and schedule for pursuing economic integration, and adopted a programme for combating international terrorism (perceived to be a significant threat in Central Asia) during 2000–03. The Council of Heads of Government approved a programme of action to guide the organization's activities until 2005. In December the CIS summit authorized the establishment of an anti-terrorism centre (see Regional Security). An informal CIS 10-year 'jubilee' summit, convened in November 2001, adopted a statement identifying the collective pursuit of stable socio-economic development and integration on a global level as the organization's principal objective.

Member states of the CIS have formed alliances of various kinds among themselves, thereby potentially undermining the unity of the Commonwealth. In March 1996 Belarus, Kazakhstan, Kyrgyzstan and the Russian Federation signed the Quadripartite Treaty for greater integration. This envisaged the establishment of a 'New Union', based, initially on a common market and customs union, and was to be open to all CIS members and the Baltic states. Consequently these countries (with Tajikistan) became founding members of the Eurasian Economic Community, inaugurated in October 2001. In April 1996 Belarus and Russia signed the Treaty on the Formation of a Community of Sovereign Republics (CSR), which provided for extensive economic, political and military co-operation. In April 1997 the two countries signed a further Treaty of Union and, in addition, initialled the Charter of the Union, which detailed the procedures and institutions designed to develop a common infrastructure, a single currency and a joint defence policy within the CSR, with the eventual aim of 'voluntary unification of the member states'. The Charter was signed in May and ratified by the respective legislatures the following month. The Union's Parliamentary Assembly, comprising 36 members from the legislature of each country, convened in official session for the first time shortly afterwards. Azerbaijan, Georgia, Moldova and Ukraine co-operated increasingly during the late 1990s as the so-called GUAM Group, which envisaged implementing joint economic and transportation initiatives and establishing a sub-regional free-trade zone. In October 1997 the GUAM countries agreed collectively to establish a Eurasian Trans-Caucasus transportation corridor. Uzbekistan joined in April 1999, creating GUUAM (q.v.). The group agreed in September 2000 to convene regular annual summits of member countries' heads of state and to organize meetings of ministers of foreign affairs at least twice a year. Russia, Armenia, Azerbaijan and Georgia convene regular meetings as the 'Caucasian Group of Four'.

ECONOMIC AFFAIRS

At a meeting of the Council of Heads of Government in March 1992 agreement was reached on repayment of the foreign debt of the former USSR. Agreements were also signed on pensions, joint tax policy and the servicing of internal debt. In May an accord on repayment of inter-state debt and the issue of balance-of-payments statements was adopted by the heads of government, meeting in Tashkent, Uzbekistan. In July it was decided to establish an economic court in Minsk.

The CIS Charter, formulated in January 1993 and signed by seven of the 10 member countries, provided for the establishment of an economic co-ordination committee. In February, at a meeting of the heads of foreign economic departments, a foreign economic council was formed. In May all member states, with the exception of Turkmenistan, adopted a declaration of support for increased economic union and, in September, agreement was reached by all states except Ukraine and Turkmenistan on a framework for economic union, including the gradual removal of tariffs and creation of a currency union. Turkmenistan was subsequently admitted as a full member of the economic union in December 1993 and Ukraine as an associate member in April 1994.

At the Council of Heads of Government meeting in September 1994 all member states, except Turkmenistan, agreed to establish an Inter-state Economic Committee to implement economic treaties adopted within the context of an economic union. The establishment of a payments union to improve the settlement of accounts was also agreed. In April 1998 CIS heads of state resolved to incorporate the functions of the Inter-state Economic Committee, along with those of other working bodies and sectional committees, into a new CIS Executive Committee.

In October 1997 seven heads of government signed a document on implementing the 'concept for the integrated economic development of the CIS'. The development of economic co-operation between the member states was a priority task of the special forum on reform held in June 1998. In the same month an economic forum, held in St Petersburg, Russia, acknowledged the severe economic conditions prevailing in certain CIS states.

Guide-lines adopted by the Council of Heads of State in April 1999 concerning the future development of the CIS identified economic co-operation and the establishment of a free-trade zone (see Trade) as priority areas for action. The plan of action for the development of the CIS until 2005, adopted by the Council of Heads of Government in June 2000, outlined medium-term economic co-operation measures, including the formulation of intergovernmental accords to provide the legal basis for the free movement of services, capital, people, etc.; the development of private business and markets; and joint participation in the implementation of major economic projects.

TRADE

Agreement was reached on the free movement of goods between republics at a meeting of the Council of Heads of State in February 1992, and in April 1994 an agreement on the creation of a CIS free-trade zone (envisaged as the first stage of economic union) was concluded. In July a council of the heads of customs committees, meeting in Moscow, approved a draft framework for customs legislation in CIS countries, to facilitate the establishment of a free-trade zone. The framework was approved by all the participants, with the exception of Turkmenistan. In April 1999 CIS heads of state signed a protocol to the 1994 free-trade area accord, which aimed to accelerate co-operation. In June 2000 the Council of Heads of State adopted a plan and schedule for the implementation of priority measures related to the establishment of the free-trade zone.

At the first session of the Inter-state Economic Committee in November 1994 draft legislation regarding a customs union was approved. In March 1998 Russia, Belarus, Kazakhstan and Kyrgyzstan signed an agreement establishing a customs union, which was to be implemented in two stages: firstly, the removal of trade restrictions and the unification of trade and customs regulations; followed by the integration of economic, monetary and trade policies (see above). The development of a customs union and the strengthening of intra-CIS trade were objectives endorsed by all participants, with the exception of Georgia, at the Council of Heads of Government meeting held in March 1997. In February 1999 Tajikistan signed the 1998 agreement to become the fifth member of the customs union. In October 1999 the heads of state of the five member states of the customs union reiterated their political determination to implement the customs union and approved a programme to harmonize national legislation to create a single economic space. In May 2000 the heads of state announced their intention to raise the status of the customs union to that of an inter-state economic organization, and, in October, the leaders signed a treaty establishing the Eurasian Economic Community. Under the new structure member states aimed to formulate a unified foreign economic policy, and collectively to pursue the creation of the planned single economic space. In the following month the five member governments signed an agreement enabling visa-free travel within the new Community. (Earlier in 2000 Russia had withdrawn from a CIS-wide visa-free travel arrangement agreed in 1992.) In December 2000 member states of the Community adopted several documents aimed at facilitating economic co-operation. The Eurasian Economic Community, governed by an inter-state council based in Astana, Kazakhstan, was formally inaugurated in October 2001.

The CIS maintains a 'loose co-ordination' on issues related to applications by member states to join the WTO.

BANKING AND FINANCE

In February 1992 CIS heads of state agreed to retain the rouble as the common currency for trade between the republics. However, in July 1993, in an attempt to control inflation, notes printed before 1993 were withdrawn from circulation and no new ones were issued until January 1994. Despite various agreements to recreate the 'rouble zone', including a protocol agreement signed in September 1993 by six states, it effectively remained confined to Tajikistan, which joined in January 1994, and Belarus, which joined in April. Both those countries proceeded to introduce national currencies in May 1995. In January 1993, at the signing of the CIS Charter, all 10 member countries endorsed the establishment of an inter-state bank to facilitate payments between the republics and to co-ordinate monetary-credit policy. Russia was to hold 50% of shares in the bank, but decisions were to be made only with a two-thirds majority approval. In December 2000, in accordance with the CSR and Treaty of Union (see above), the Presidents of Belarus and Russia signed an agreement providing for the adoption by Belarus of the Russian currency from 1 January 2005, and for the introduction of a new joint Union currency by 1 January 2008.

DEFENCE

An Agreement on Armed Forces and Border Troops was concluded on 30 December 1991, at the same time as the Agreement on Strategic Forces. This confirmed the right of member states to set up their own armed forces and appointed Commanders-in-Chief of the Armed Forces and of the Border Troops, who were to elaborate joint security procedures. In February 1992 an agreement was signed stipulating that the commander of the strategic forces was subordinate to the Council of Heads of States. Eight states agreed on a unified command for general-purpose (i.e. non-strategic) armed forces for a transitional period of two years. Azerbaijan, Moldova and Ukraine resolved to establish independent armed forces.

In January 1992 Commissions on the Black Sea Fleet (control of which was disputed by Russia and Ukraine) and the Caspian Flotilla (the former Soviet naval forces on the Caspian Sea) were established. The defence and stability of CIS external borders and the status of strategic and nuclear forces were among topics discussed at the meeting of heads of state and of government, in Bishkek, in October. The formation of a defence alliance was provided for in the CIS Charter formulated in January 1993 and signed by seven of the 10 member countries; a proposal by Russia to assume control of all nuclear weapons in the former USSR was rejected at the same time.

In June 1993 CIS defence ministers agreed to abolish CIS joint military command and to abandon efforts to maintain a unified defence structure. The existing CIS command was to be replaced, on a provisional basis, by a 'joint staff for co-ordinating military co-operation between the states of the Commonwealth'. It was widely reported that Russia had encouraged the decision to abolish the joint command, owing to concerns at the projected cost of a CIS joint military structure and support within Russia's military leadership of bilateral military agreements with the country's neighbours. In December the Council of Defence Ministers agreed to establish a secretariat to co-ordinate military co-operation as a replacement to the joint military command. In November 1995 the Council of Defence Ministers authorized the establishment of a Joint Air Defence System, to be co-ordinated largely by Russia. A CIS combat duty system was to be created in 1999–2005. Russia and Belarus are also developing a joint air-defence unit in the context of the CSR (see above).

In September 1996 the first meeting of the inter-state commission for military economic co-operation was held; a draft agreement on the export of military projects and services to third countries was approved. The basic principles of a programme for greater military and technical co-operation were approved by the Council of Defence Ministers in March 1997. In April 1998 the Council proposed drawing up a draft programme for military and technical co-operation between member countries and also discussed procedures advising on the use and maintenance of armaments and military hardware. Draft proposals relating to information security for the military were approved by the Council in December. It was remarked that the inadequate funding of the Council was impeding co-operation. In May 2001 a draft plan for military co-operation until 2005 was agreed.

In August 1996 the Council of Defence Ministers condemned what it described as the political, economic and military threat implied in any expansion of NATO (q.v.). The statement was not signed by Ukraine. The eighth plenary session of the IPA, held in November, urged NATO countries to abandon plans for the organization's expansion. Strategic co-operation between NATO and CIS member states increased from the mid-1990s, particularly with Russia and Ukraine. In the late 1990s the USA established bilateral military assistance programmes for Azerbaijan, Georgia, and Uzbekistan. Uzbekistan and other central Asian CIS states played a support role in the US-led action initiated in late 2001 against the then Taliban-held areas of Afghanistan (see below).

REGIONAL SECURITY

At a meeting of heads of government in March 1992 agreements on settling inter-state conflicts were signed by all participating states (except Turkmenistan). At the same meeting an agreement on the status of border troops was signed by five states. In May a five-year Collective Security Agreement was signed. In July further documents were signed on collective security and it was agreed to establish joint peacemaking forces to intervene in CIS disputes. In April 1999 Armenia, Belarus, Kazakhstan, Kyrgyzstan, Russia and Tajikistan signed a protocol to extend the Collective Security Agreement for a further five-year period.

In September 1993 the Council of Heads of State agreed to establish a Bureau of Organized Crime, to be based in Moscow. A meeting of the Council of Border Troop Commanders in January 1994 prepared a report on the issue of illegal migration and drug trade across the extenal borders of the CIS; Moldova, Georgia and Tajikistan did not attend. A programme to counter organized crime within the CIS was approved by heads of government, meeting in Moscow, in April 1996. In March 2001 CIS interior ministers agreed to strengthen co-operation in combating transnational organized crime, in view of reportedly mounting levels of illicit drugs-trafficking in the region.

In February 1995 a non-binding memorandum on maintaining peace and stability was adopted by heads of state, meeting in Almaty. Signatories were to refrain from applying military, political, economic or other pressure on another member country, to seek the peaceful resolution of border or territorial disputes and not to support or assist separatist movements active in other member countries. In April 1998 the Council of Defence Ministers approved a draft document proposing that coalition forces be provided with technical equipment to enhance collective security.

In June 1998, at a session of the Council of Border Troop Commanders, some 33 documents were signed relating to border co-operation. A framework protocol on the formation and expedient use of a border troops reserve in critical situations was discussed and signed by several participants. A register of work in scientific and engineering research carried out in CIS countries in the interests of border troops was also adopted.

In June 1998 CIS interior ministers, meeting in Tashkent, Uzbekistan, adopted a number of co-operation agreements, including a framework for the exchange of information between CIS law-enforcement agencies; it was also decided to maintain contact with Interpol.

An emergency meeting of heads of state in October 1996 discussed the ongoing conflict in nearby Afghanistan and the consequent threat to regional security. The participants requested the UN Security Council to adopt measures to resolve the situation. The IPA subsequently reiterated the call for a cessation of hostilities in that country. In May 2000 the six signatory states to the Collective Security Agreement pledged to strengthen military co-operation in view of the perceived threat to their security from the Taliban regime in Afghanistan. It was reported that a mechanism had been approved that would enable parties to the Agreement to purchase arms from Russia at special rates. In October the parties to the Collective Security Agreement signed an agreement on the Status of Forces and Means of Collective Security Systems, establishing a joint rapid deployment function. The so-called CIS Collective Rapid Reaction Force was to be assembled to combat insurgencies, with particular reference to trans-border terrorism from Afghanistan, and also to deter trans-border illegal drugs trafficking (see above). In September 2001 a CIS anti-terrorism centre was established in Bishket, Kyrgyzstan. The centre was to co-ordinate counter-terrorism activities and to compile a database of international terrorist organizations operating in member states. In October 2001, in response to the major terrorist attacks perpetrated in September against targets in the USA—allegedly co-ordinated by Afghanistan-based militant fundamentalist Islamist leader Osama bin Laden—the parties to the Collective Security Treaty adopted a new anti-terrorism plan. In November the head of the co-ordinating Collective Security Council identified combating international terrorism as the main focus of the Collective Security Agreement at that time. The signatory countries to the Collective Security Agreement participate in regular so-called 'CIS Southern Shield' joint military exercises.

The formation of a new regional security organization, the Central Asian Co-operation Pact, was announced in February 2002 by Kazakhstan, Kyrgyzstan, Tajikistan and Uzbekistan.

The fourth plenary session of the IPA in March 1994 established a commission for the resolution of the conflicts in the secessionist regions of Nagornyi Karabakh (Azerbaijan) and Abkhazia (Georgia) and endorsed the use of CIS peace-keeping forces. In the following month Russia agreed to send peace-keeping forces to Georgia, and the dispatch of peace-keeping forces was approved by the Council of Defence Ministers in October. The subsequent session of the IPA in October adopted a resolution to send groups of military observers to Abkhazia and to Moldova. The inter-parliamentary commission on the conflict between Abkhazia and Georgia proposed initiating direct negotiations with the two sides in order to reach a peaceful settlement.

In December 1994 the Council of Defence Ministers enlarged the mandate of the commander of the CIS collective peace-keeping forces in Tajikistan: when necessary CIS military contingents were permitted to engage in combat operations without the prior consent of individual governments. At the Heads of State meeting in Moscow in January 1996 Georgia's proposal to impose sanctions against Abkhazia was approved, in an attempt to achieve a resolution of the conflict. Provisions on arrangements relating to collective peace-keeping operations were approved at the meeting; the training of military and civilian personnel for these operations was to commence in October. In March 1997 the Council of Defence Ministers agreed to extend the peace-keeping mandates for CIS forces in Tajiskistan and Abkhazia (following much disagreement, the peace-keepers' mandate in Abkhazia was further renewed in October). At a meeting of the Council in January 1998 a request from Georgia that the CIS carry out its decisions to settle the conflict with Abkhazia was added to the agenda. The Council discussed the promotion of military co-operation and the improvement of peace-making activities, and declared that there was progress in the formation of the collective security system, although the situation in the North Caucasus remained tense. In April President Yeltsin requested that the Armenian and Azerbaijani presidents sign a document to end the conflict in Nagornyi Karabakh; the two subsequently issued a statement expressing their support for a political settlement of the conflict. A document proposing a settlement of the conflict in Abkhazia was also drawn up, but the resolutions adopted were not accepted by Abkhazia. Against the wishes of the Abkhazian authorities, the mandate for the CIS troops in the region was extended to cover the whole of the Gali district. The mandate expired in July 1998, but the forces remained in the region while its renewal was debated. In April 1999 the Council of Heads of State agreed to a retrospective extension of the operation's mandate; the mandate has subsequently continued to be renewed at six-monthly intervals. The mandate of the CIS peace-keeping operation in Tajikistan was terminated in June 2000. In February 2001 it was reported that regulations had been drafted for the inistitution of a CIS Special Envoy for the Settlement of Conflicts.

LEGISLATIVE CO-OPERATION

An agreement on legislative co-operation was signed at an Inter-Parliamentary Conference in January 1992; joint commissions were established to co-ordinate action on economy, law, pensions, housing, energy and ecology. The CIS Charter, formulated in January 1993, provided for the establishment of an inter-state court. In October 1994 a Convention on the rights of minorities was adopted at the meeting of the Heads of State. In May 1995, at the sixth plenary session of the IPA, several acts to improve co-ordination of legislation were approved, relating to migration of labour, consumer rights, and the rights of prisoners of war.

The creation of a Council of Ministers of Internal Affairs was approved at the Heads of State meeting in January 1996; the Council was to promote co-operation between the law-enforcement bodies of member states. At the 10th plenary session of the IPA in December 1997 14 laws, relating to banking and financial services, education, ecology and charity were adopted. At the IPA session held in June 1998 10 model laws relating to social issues were approved, including a law on obligatory social insurance against production accidents and occupational diseases, and on the general principles of regulating refugee problems.

OTHER ACTIVITIES

The CIS has held a number of discussions relating to the environment. In July 1992 agreements were concluded to establish an Inter-state Ecological Council. It was also agreed in that month to establish an Inter-state Television and Radio Company (ITRC). In February 1995 the IPA established a Council of Heads of News Agencies, in order to promote the concept of a single information area.

A Petroleum and Gas Council was created at a Heads of Government meeting in March 1993, to guarantee energy supplies and to invest in the Siberian petroleum industry. The Council was to have a secretariat based in Tyumen, Siberia. In the field of civil aviation, the inter-state economic committee agreed in February 1997 to establish an Aviation Alliance to promote co-operation between the countries' civil aviation industries.

The Minsk Agreement

(8 December 1991)

PREAMBLE

We, the Republic of Belarus, the Russian Federation and the Republic of Ukraine, as founder states of the Union of Soviet Socialist Republics (USSR), which signed the 1922 Union Treaty, further described as the high contracting parties, conclude that the USSR has ceased to exist as a subject of international law and a geopolitical reality.

Taking as our basis the historic community of our peoples and the ties which have been established between them, taking into account the bilateral treaties concluded between the high contracting parties;

striving to build democratic law-governed states; intending to develop our relations on the basis of mutual recognition and respect for state sovereignty, the inalienable right to self-determination, the principles of equality and non-interference in internal affairs, repudiation of the use of force and of economic or any other methods of coercion, settlement of contentious problems by means of mediation and other generally-recognized principles and norms of international law;

considering that further development and strengthening of relations of friendship, good-neighbourliness and mutually beneficial co-operation between our states correspond to the vital national interests of their peoples and serve the cause of peace and security;

confirming our adherence to the goals and principles of the United Nations Charter, the Helsinki Final Act and other documents of the Conference on Security and Co-operation in Europe;

and committing ourselves to observe the generally recognized internal norms on human rights and the rights of peoples, we have agreed the following:

Article 1

The high contracting parties form the Commonwealth of Independent States.

Article 2

The high contracting parties guarantee their citizens equal rights and freedoms regardless of nationality or other distinctions. Each of the high contracting parties guarantees the citizens of the other parties, and also persons without citizenship that live on its territory, civil, political, social, economic and cultural rights and freedoms in accordance with generally recognized international norms of human rights, regardless of national allegiance or other distinctions.

Article 3

The high contracting parties, desiring to promote the expression, preservation and development of the ethnic, cultural, linguistic and religious individuality of the national minorities resident on their territories, and that of the unique ethno-cultural regions that have come into being, take them under their protection.

Article 4

The high contracting parties will develop the equal and mutually beneficial co-operation of their peoples and states in the spheres of politics, the economy, culture, education, public health, protection of the environment, science and trade and in the humanitarian and other spheres, will promote the broad exchange of information and will conscientiously and unconditionally observe reciprocal obligations.

The parties consider it a necessity to conclude agreements on co-operation in the above spheres.

Article 5
The high contracting parties recognize and respect one another's territorial integrity and the inviolability of existing borders within the Commonwealth.

They guarantee openness of borders, freedom of movement for citizens and of transmission of information within the Commonwealth.

Article 6
The member states of the Commonwealth will co-operate in safeguarding international peace and security and in implementing effective measures for reducing weapons and military spending. They seek the elimination of all nuclear weapons and universal total disarmament under strict international control.

The parties will respect one another's aspiration to attain the status of a non-nuclear zone and a neutral state.

The member states of the Commonwealth will preserve and maintain under united command a common military-strategic space, including unified control over nuclear weapons, the procedure for implementing which is regulated by a special agreement.

They also jointly guarantee the necessary conditions for the stationing and functioning of and for material and social provision for the strategic armed forces. The parties contract to pursue a harmonized policy on questions of social protection and pension provision for members of the services and their families.

Article 7
The high contracting parties recognize that within the sphere of their activities, implemented on the equal basis through the common co-ordinating institutions of the Commonwealth, will be the following:

co-operation in the sphere of foreign policy;

co-operation in forming and developing the united economic area, the common European and Eurasian markets, in the area of customs policy;

co-operation in developing transport and communication systems;

co-operation in preservation of the environment, and participation in creating a comprehensive international system of ecological safety;

migration policy issues;

and fighting organized crime.

Article 8
The parties realize the planetary character of the Chernobyl catastrophe and pledge themselves to unite and co-ordinate their efforts in minimizing and overcoming its consequences.

To these ends they have decided to conclude a special agreement which will take consideration of the gravity of the consequences of this catastrophe.

Article 9
The disputes regarding interpretation and application of the norms of this agreement are to be solved by way of negotiations between the appropriate bodies, and, when necessary, at the level of heads of the governments and states.

Article 10
Each of the high contracting parties reserves the right to suspend the validity of the present agreement or individual articles thereof, after informing the parties to the agreement of this a year in advance.

The clauses of the present agreement may be addended to or amended with the common consent of the high contracting parties.

Article 11
From the moment that the present agreement is signed, the norms of third states, including the former USSR, are not permitted to be implemented on the territories of the signatory states.

Article 12
The high contracting parties guarantee the fulfilment of the international obligations binding upon them from the treaties and agreements of the former USSR.

Article 13
The present agreement does not affect the obligations of the high contracting parties in regard to third states.

The present agreement is open for all member states of the former USSR to join, and also for other states which share the goals and principles of the present agreement.

Article 14
The city of Minsk is the official location of the co-ordinating bodies of the Commonwealth.

The activities of bodies of the former USSR are discontinued on the territories of the member states of the Commonwealth.

The Alma-Ata Declaration

(21 December 1991)

PREAMBLE

The independent states:

The Republic of Armenia, the Republic of Azerbaijan, the Republic of Belarus, the Republic of Kazakhstan, the Republic of Kyrgyzstan, the Republic of Moldova, the Russian Federation, the Republic of Tajikistan, the Republic of Turkmenistan, the Republic of Ukraine and the Republic of Uzbekistan;

seeking to build democratic law-governed states, the relations between which will develop on the basis of mutual recognition and respect for state sovereignty and sovereign equality, the inalienable right to self-determination, principles of equality and non-interference in the internal affairs, the rejection of the use of force, the threat of force and economic and any other methods of pressure, a peaceful settlement of disputes, respect for human rights and freedoms, including the rights of national minorities, a conscientious fulfilment of commitments and other generally recognized principles and standards of international law;

recognizing and respecting each other's territorial integrity and the inviolability of the existing borders;

believing that the strengthening of the relations of friendship, good neighbourliness and mutually advantageous co-operation, which has deep historic roots, meets the basic interests of nations and promotes the cause of peace and security;

being aware of their responsibility for the preservation of civilian peace and inter-ethnic accord;

being loyal to the objectives and principles of the agreement on the creation of the Commonwealth of Independent States;

are making the following statement:

THE DECLARATION

Co-operation between members of the Commonwealth will be carried out in accordance with the principle of equality through co-ordinating institutions formed on a parity basis and operating in the way established by the agreements between members of the Commonwealth, which is neither a state, nor a super-state structure.

In order to ensure international strategic stability and security, allied command of the military-strategic forces and a single control over nuclear weapons will be preserved, the sides will respect each other's desire to attain the status of a non-nuclear and (or) neutral state.

The Commonwealth of Independent States is open, with the agreement of all its participants, to the states—members of the former USSR, as well as other states—sharing the goals and principles of the Commonwealth.

The allegiance to co-operation in the formation and development of the common economic space, and all-European and Eurasian markets, is being confirmed.

With the formation of the Commonwealth of Independent States, the USSR ceases to exist. Member states of the Commonwealth guarantee, in accordance with their constitutional procedures, the fulfilment of international obligations, stemming from the treaties and agreements of the former USSR.

Member states of the Commonwealth pledge to observe strictly the principles of this declaration.

Agreement on Strategic Forces

(30 December 1991)

Guided by the necessity for a co-ordinated and organized solution to issues in the sphere of the control of the strategic forces and the single control over nuclear weapons, the Republic of Armenia, the Republic of Azerbaijan, the Republic of Belarus, the Republic of Kazakhstan, the Republic of Kyrgyzstan, the Republic of Moldova, the Russian Federation, the Republic of Tajikistan, the Republic of Turkmenistan, the Republic of Ukraine and the Republic of Uzbekistan, subsequently referred to as 'the member states of the Commonwealth', have agreed on the following:

Article 1

The term 'strategic forces' means: groupings, formations, units, institutions, the military training institutes for the strategic missile troops, for the air force, for the navy and for the air defences; the directorates of the Space Command and of the airborne troops, and of strategic and operational intelligence, and the nuclear technical units and also the forces, equipment and other military facilities designed for the control and maintenance of the strategic forces of the former USSR (the schedule is to be determined for each state participating in the Commonwealth in a separate protocol).

Article 2

The member states of the Commonwealth undertake to observe the international treaties of the former USSR, to pursue a co-ordinated policy in the area of international security, disarmament and arms control, and to participate in the preparation and implementation of programmes for reductions in arms and armed forces. The member states of the Commonwealth are immediately entering into negotiations with one another and also with other states which were formerly part of the USSR, but which have not joined the Commonwealth, with the aim of ensuring guarantees and developing mechanisms for implementing the aforementioned treaties.

Article 3

The member states of the Commonwealth recognize the need for joint command of strategic forces and for maintaining unified control of nuclear weapons, and other types of weapons of mass destruction, of the armed forces of the former USSR.

Article 4

Until the complete elimination of nuclear weapons, the decision on the need for their use is taken by the President of the Russian Federation in agreement with the heads of the Republic of Belarus, the Republic of Kazakhstan and the Republic of Ukraine, and in consultation with the heads of the other member states of the Commonwealth.

Until their destruction in full, nuclear weapons located on the territory of the Republic of Ukraine shall be under the control of the Combined Strategic Forces Command, with the aim that they not be used and be dismantled by the end of 1994, including tactical nuclear weapons by 1 July 1992.

The process of destruction of nuclear weapons located on the territory of the Republic of Belarus and the Republic of Ukraine shall take place with the participation of the Republic of Belarus, the Russian Federation and the Republic of Ukraine under the joint control of the Commonwealth states.

Article 5

The status of strategic forces and the procedure for service in them shall be defined in a special agreement.

Article 6

This agreement shall enter into force from the moment of its signing and shall be terminated by decision of the signatory states or the Council of Heads of State of the Commonwealth.

This agreement shall cease to apply to a signatory state from whose territory strategic forces or nuclear weapons are withdrawn.

Note: The last nuclear warheads were removed from Kazakhstan in April 1995, from Belarus in March 1996 and from Ukraine in May–June 1996. All strategic offensive arms in Belarus and Kazakhstan have been destroyed, and those in Ukraine are being eliminated.

CO-OPERATION COUNCIL FOR THE ARAB STATES OF THE GULF

Address: POB 7153, Riyadh 11462, Saudi Arabia.

Telephone: (1) 482-7777; **fax:** (1) 482-9089; **internet:** www.gcc-sg.org.

More generally known as the Gulf Co-operation Council (GCC), the organization was established on 25 May 1981 by six Arab states.

MEMBERS

Bahrain	Oman	Saudi Arabia
Kuwait	Qatar	United Arab Emirates

Organization

(April 2002)

SUPREME COUNCIL

The Supreme Council is the highest authority of the GCC. It comprises the heads of member states and meets annually in ordinary session, and in emergency session if demanded by two or more members. The Council also convenes an annual consultative meeting. The Presidency of the Council is undertaken by each state in turn, in alphabetical order. The Supreme Council draws up the overall policy of the organization; it discusses recommendations and laws presented to it by the Ministerial Council and the Secretariat General in preparation for endorsement. The GCC's charter provides for the creation of a commission for the settlement of disputes between member states, to be attached to and appointed by the Supreme Council. The Supreme Council convenes a commission for the settlement of disputes on an *ad hoc* basis to address altercations between member states as they arise.

MINISTERIAL COUNCIL

The Ministerial Council consists of the foreign ministers of member states (or other ministers acting on their behalf), meeting every three months, and in emergency session if demanded by two or more members. It prepares for the meetings of the Supreme Council, and draws up policies, recommendations, studies and projects aimed at developing co-operation and co-ordination among member states in various spheres.

CONSULTATIVE COMMISSION

The Consultative Commission comprising 30 members (five from each member state) nominated for a three-year period, acts as an advisory body, considering matters referred to it by the Supreme Council.

SECRETARIAT GENERAL

The Secretariat assists member states in implementing recommendations by the Supreme and Ministerial Councils, and prepares reports and studies, budgets and accounts. The Secretary-General is appointed by the Supreme Council for a three-year term renewable once. In March 1996 the Ministerial Council approved a proposal that, in future, the position of Secretary-General be rotated among member states, in order to ensure equal representation. Assistant Secretary-Generals are appointed by the Ministerial Council upon the recommendation of the Secretary General. The Secretariat comprises the following divisions and departments: political affairs; economic affairs; military affairs; human and environmental affairs; the Office of the Secretary-General, Finance and Administrative Affairs; a patent bureau; an administrative development unit; an internal auditing unit; an information centre; and a telecommunications bureau (based in Bahrain). All member states contribute in equal proportions towards the budget of the Secretariat.

Secretary-General: ABDUL RAHMAN IBN HAMAD AL-ATTIYA (Qatar).

Assistant Secretary-General for Political Affairs: Dr HAMAD ALI AS-SULAYTI (Bahrain).

Assistant Secretary-General for Economic Affairs: AJLAN BEN ALI AL-KUWARI (Qatar).

Assistant Secretary-General for Military Affairs: Maj.-Gen. ALI IBN SALEM AL MUAMARI (Oman).

Note: In December 2001 the Supreme Council authorized the establishment of a Supreme Defence Council. This was to be composed of defence ministers meeting on an annual basis to consider security matters and supervise the implementation of the organization's joint defence pact.

Activities

The GCC was established following a series of meetings of foreign ministers of the states concerned, culminating in an agreement on the basic details of its charter on 10 March 1981. The Charter was signed by the six heads of state on 25 May. It describes the organization as providing 'the means for realizing co-ordination, integration and co-operation' in all economic, social and cultural affairs.

ECONOMIC CO-OPERATION

In November 1981 GCC ministers drew up a 'unified economic agreement' covering freedom of movement of people and capital, the abolition of customs duties, technical co-operation, harmonization of banking regulations and financial and monetary co-ordination. At the same time GCC heads of state approved the formation of a Gulf Investment Corporation, to be based in Kuwait (see below). In March 1983 customs duties on domestic products of the Gulf states were abolished, and new regulations allowing free movement of workers and vehicles between member states were also introduced. A common minimum customs levy (of between 4% and 20%) on foreign imports was imposed in 1986. In February 1987 the governors of the member states' central banks agreed in principle to co-ordinate their rates of exchange, and this was approved by the Supreme Council in November. It was subsequently agreed to link the Gulf currencies to a 'basket' of other currencies. In April 1993 the Gulf central bank governors decided to allow Kuwait's currency to become part of the GCC monetary system that was established following Iraq's invasion of Kuwait in order to defend the Gulf currencies. In May 1992 GCC trade ministers announced the objective of establishing a GCC common market. Meeting in September GCC ministers reached agreement on the application of a unified system of tariffs by March 1993. A meeting of the Supreme Council, held in December 1992, however, decided to mandate GCC officials to formulate a plan for the introduction of common external tariffs, to be presented to the Council in December 1993. Only the tax on tobacco products was to be standardized from March 1993, at a rate of 50% (later increased to 70%). In April 1994 ministers of finance agreed to pursue a gradual approach to the unification of tariffs. A technical committee, which had been constituted to consider aspects of establishing a customs union, met for the first time in June 1998. In December the Supreme Council requested that ministers of finance should promptly secure an agreement on a unified customs tariff in order to accelerate the inauguration of the proposed customs union. In November 1999 the Supreme Council concluded an agreement to establish the customs union by 1 March 2005. However, in December 2002 the Supreme Council, meeting in Muscat, Oman, adopted a new agreement on regional economic union ('Economic Agreement Between the Arab GCC States'), which superseded the 1981 'unified economic agreement'. The new accord brought forward the establishment of the proposed customs union to 1 January 2003 (to coincide with the entry into force of the World Trade Agreement) and provided for a standard tariff level of 5% for foreign imports (with the exception of 53 essential commodities previously exempted by the Supreme Council). The agreement also provided for the introduction, by 1 January 2010, of a GCC single currency, linked to the US dollar (with all member states' national currencies to be pegged to the US currency by the end of 2002). The necessary economic performance measures for monetary union were to be established by the end of 2005. The Supreme Council also authorized the creation of a new independent authority for overseeing the unification of specifications and standards throughout member states.

In April 1993 GCC central bank governors agreed to establish a joint banking supervisory committee, in order to devise rules for GCC banks to operate in other member states. In December 1997 GCC heads of state authorized guide-lines to this effect. These were to apply only to banks established at least 10 years previously with a share capital of more than US $100m.

TRADE AND INDUSTRY

In 1982 a ministerial committee was formed to co-ordinate trade policies and development in the region. Technical subcommittees were established to oversee a strategic food reserve for the member states, and joint trade exhibitions (which were generally held every year until responsibility was transferred to the private sector in 1996). In November 1986 the Supreme Council approved a measure whereby citizens of GCC member states were enabled to undertake certain retail trade activities in any other member state, with effect from 1 March 1987. In September 2000 GCC ministers of commerce agreed to establish a technical committee to promote the development of electronic commerce and trade among member states.

In 1976 the GCC member states formed the Gulf Organization for Industrial Consulting (q.v.), based in Doha, Qatar, which promotes regional industrial development. In 1985 the Supreme Council endorsed a common industrial strategy for the Gulf states. It approved regulations stipulating that priority should be given to imports of GCC industrial products, and permitting GCC investors to obtain loans from GCC industrial development banks. In November 1986 resolutions were adopted on the protection of industrial products, and on the co-ordination of industrial projects, in order to avoid duplication. In 1989 the Ministerial Council approved the Unified GCC Foreign Capital Investment Regulations, which aimed to attract foreign investment and to co-ordinate investments amongst GCC countries. Further guidelines to promote foreign investment in the region were formulated during 1997. In December 1999 the Supreme Council amended the conditions determining rules of origin on industrial products in order to promote direct investment and intra-Community trade. In December 1992 the Supreme Council endorsed Patent Regulations for GCC member states to facilitate regional scientific and technological research. A GCC Patent Office for the protection of intellectual property in the region, was established in 1998.

In December 1998 the Supreme Council approved a long-term strategy for regional development, covering the period 2000–25, which had been formulated by GCC ministers of planning. The strategy aimed to achieve integrated, sustainable development in all member states and the co-ordination of national development plans. The Supreme Council also approved a framework Gulf population strategy formulated by the ministers of planning. In December 2000 the Supreme Council agreed gradually to limit, by means of the imposition of quotas and deterrent taxation measures, the numbers of foreign workers admitted to member states, in order to redress the current demographic imbalance resulting from the large foreign population resident in the region (believed to comprise more than one-third of the overall population). Unified procedures and measures for facilitating the intra-regional movement of people and commercial traffic were adopted by the Supreme Council in December 2001, as well as unified standards in the areas of education and healthcare.

AGRICULTURE

A unified agricultural policy for GCC countries was endorsed by the Supreme Council in November 1985. Co-operation in the agricultural sector extends to consideration of the water resources in the region. Between 1983 and 1990 ministers also approved proposals for harmonizing legislation relating to water conservation, veterinary vaccines, insecticides, fertilizers, fisheries and seeds. A permanent committee on fisheries aims to co-ordinate national fisheries policies, to establish designated fishing periods and to undertake surveys of the fishing potential in the Arabian (Persian) Gulf. In February 2001 GCC ministers responsible for water and electricity determined to formulate a common water policy for the region, which experiences annual shortfalls of water. Unified agricultural quarantine laws were adopted by the Supreme Council in December 2001.

TRANSPORT, COMMUNICATIONS AND INFORMATION

During 1985 feasibility studies were undertaken on new rail and road links between member states, and on the establishment of a joint coastal transport company. A scheme to build a 1,700-km railway to link all the member states and Iraq (and thereby the European railway network) was postponed, owing to its high estimated cost. In November 1993 ministers agreed to request assistance from the International Telecommunication Union on the establishment of a joint telecommunications network, which had been approved by ministers in 1986. The region's telecommunications systems were to be integrated through underwater fibre-optic cables and a satellite-based mobile telephone network. In the mid-1990s GCC ministers of information began convening on a regular basis with a view to formulating a joint external information policy. In November 1997 GCC interior ministers approved a simplified passport system to facilitate travel between member countries.

ENERGY

In 1982 a ministerial committee was established to co-ordinate hydrocarbons policies and prices. Ministers adopted a petroleum security plan to safeguard individual members against a halt in their production, to form a stockpile of petroleum products, and to organize a boycott of any non-member country when appropriate. In December 1987 the Supreme Council adopted a plan whereby a member state whose petroleum production was disrupted could 'borrow' petroleum from other members, in order to fulfil its export obligations. GCC petroleum ministers hold occasional co-ordination meetings to discuss the agenda and policies of OPEC (q.v.), to which all six member states belong.

During the early 1990s proposals were formulated to integrate the electricity networks of the six member countries. In the first stage of the plan the networks of Saudi Arabia, Bahrain, Kuwait and Qatar would be integrated; those of the United Arab Emirates (UAE) and Oman would be interconnected and finally linked to the others in the second stage. In December 1997 GCC heads of state declared that work should commence on the first stage of the plan, under the management of an independent authority. The estimated cost of the project was more than US $6,000m. However, it was agreed not to invite private developers to participate in construction of the grid, but that the first phase of the project be financed by member states (to contribute 35% of the estimated $2,000m. required), and by loans from commercial banking and international monetary institutions. The Gulf Council Interconnection Authority was established in 1999, with its headquarters in Dammam, Saudi Arabia.

CULTURAL CO-OPERATION

The GCC Folklore Centre, based in Doha, Qatar, was established in 1983 to collect, document and classify the regional cultural heritage, publish research, sponsor and protect regional folklore, provide a database on Gulf folklore, and to promote traditional culture through education.

REGIONAL SECURITY

Although no mention of defence or security was made in the original charter, the summit meeting which ratified the charter also issued a statement rejecting any foreign military presence in the region. The Supreme Council meeting in November 1981 agreed to include defence co-operation in the activities of the organization: as a result, defence ministers met in January 1982 to discuss a common security policy, including a joint air defence system and standardization of weapons. In November 1984 member states agreed to form the Peninsula Shield Force for rapid deployment against external aggression, comprising units from the armed forces of each country under a central command to be based in north-eastern Saudi Arabia.

In October 1987 (following an Iranian missile attack on Kuwait, which supported Iraq in its war against Iran) GCC ministers of foreign affairs issued a statement declaring that aggression against one member state was regarded as aggression against them all. In December the Supreme Council approved a joint pact on regional co-operation in matters of security. In August 1990 the Ministerial Council condemned Iraq's invasion of Kuwait as a violation of sovereignty, and demanded the withdrawal of all Iraqi troops from Kuwait. The Peninsula Shield Force was not sufficiently developed to be deployed in defence of Kuwait. During the crisis and the ensuing war between Iraq and a multinational force which took place in January and February 1991, the GCC developed closer links with Egypt and Syria, which, together with Saudi Arabia, played the most active role among the Arab countries in the anti-Iraqi alliance. In March the six GCC nations, Egypt and Syria formulated the 'Declaration of Damascus', which announced plans to establish a regional peace-keeping force. The Declaration also urged the abolition of all weapons of mass destruction in the area, and recommended the resolution of the Palestinian question by an international conference. In June Egypt and Syria, whose troops were to have formed the largest proportion of the proposed peace-keeping force, announced their withdrawal from the project, reportedly as a result of disagreements with the GCC concerning the composition of the force and the remuneration involved. A meeting of ministers of foreign affairs of the eight countries took place in July, but agreed only to provide mutual military assistance when necessary. In September 1992 the signatories of the Damascus Declaration adopted a joint statement on regional questions, including the Middle East peace process and the dispute between the UAE and Iran (see below), but rejected an Egyptian proposal to establish a series of rapid deployment forces which could be called upon to defend the interests of any of the eight countries. A meeting of GCC ministers of defence in November agreed to maintain the Peninsula Shield Force. In November 1993 GCC ministers of defence approved a proposal for the significant expansion of the Force and for the incorporation of air and naval units. Ministers also agreed to strengthen the defence of the region by developing joint surveillance and early warning systems. A GCC military committee was established, and convened for the first time in April 1994, to discuss the implementation of the proposals. However, the expansion of the Peninsula Shield Force was not implemented. Joint military training exercises were conducted by troops from five GCC states (excluding Qatar) in northern Kuwait in March 1996. In December 1997 the Supreme Council approved plans for linking the region's military telecommunications networks and establishing a common early warning system. In December 2000 GCC leaders adopted a joint defence pact aimed at enhancing the grouping's defence capability. The pact formally committed member states to defending any other member state from external attack, envisaging the expansion of the Peninsula Shield Force from 5,000 to 22,000 troops and the creation of a new rapid deployment function within the Force. In March 2001 the GCC member states inaugurated the first phase of the long-envisaged joint air defence system. In December GCC heads of state authorized the establishment of a supreme defence council, comprising member states' ministers of defence, to address security-related matters and supervise the implementation of the joint defence pact. The council was to convene on an annual basis.

In 1992 Iran extended its authority over the island of Abu Musa, which it had administered under a joint arrangement with the UAE since 1971. In September 1992 the GCC Ministerial Council condemned Iran's continued occupation of the island and efforts to consolidate its presence, and reiterated support of UAE sovereignty over Abu Musa, as well as the largely uninhabited Greater and Lesser Tunb islands (also claimed by Iran). All three islands are situated at the approach to the Strait of Hormuz, through which petroleum exports are transported. In December 1994 the GCC supported the UAE's request that the dispute be referred to the International Court of Justice.

In September 1992 a rift within the GCC was caused by an incident on the disputed border between Saudi Arabia and Qatar. Qatar's threat to boycott a meeting of the Supreme Council in December was allayed at the last minute as a result of mediation efforts by the Egyptian President. At the meeting, which was held in UAE, Qatar and Saudi Arabia agreed to establish a joint technical committee to demarcate the disputed border. In November 1994 a security agreement, to counter regional crime and terrorism, was concluded by GCC states. The pact, however, was not signed by Kuwait, which claimed that a clause concerning the extradition of offenders was in contravention of its constitution; Qatar did not attend the meeting, held in Riyadh, owing to its ongoing dispute with Saudi Arabia. The resolution of border disputes was the principal concern of GCC heads of state when they convened for their annual meeting in the following month, in Bahrain. In April 1995 GCC interior ministers convened to discuss ongoing civil unrest in Bahrain; the ministers collectively supported measures adopted by the Bahraini Government to secure political and civil stability. The continuing unrest in Bahrain and the involvement of the Iranian Government in Bahraini domestic affairs remained issues of concern for the GCC in the mid-1990s.

During 1995 the deterioration of relations between Qatar and other GCC states threatened to undermine the Council's solidarity. In December Qatar publicly displayed its dissatisfaction at the appointment, without a consensus agreement, of Saudi Arabia's nominee as the new Secretary-General by failing to attend the final session of the Supreme Council, held in Muscat, Oman. However, at a meeting of ministers of foreign affairs in March 1996, Qatar endorsed the new Secretary-General, following an agreement on future appointment procedures, and reasserted its commitment to the organization. In June Saudi Arabia and Qatar agreed to reactivate the joint technical committee in order to finalize the demarcation of their mutual border: border maps drafted by the committee were approved by both sides in December 1999. In December 1996 Qatar hosted the annual GCC summit meeting; however, Bahrain refused to attend, owing to Qatar's 'unfriendly attitude' and a long-standing dispute between the two countries (referred by Qatar to the International Court of Justice—ICJ in 1991) concerning the sovereignty of the Hawar islands, and of other islands, maritime and border areas. The issue dominated the meeting, which agreed to establish a four-member committee to resolve the conflicting sovereignty claims. In January 1997 the ministers of foreign affairs of Kuwait, Oman, Saudi Arabia and the UAE, meeting in Riyadh, formulated a seven-point memorandum of understanding to ease tensions between Bahrain and Qatar. The two countries refused to sign the agreement; however, in March both sides announced their intention to establish diplomatic relations at ambassadorial level. In March 2001 the ICJ ruled on the dispute between Bahrain and Qatar concerning the sovereignty of the Hawar Islands and other territorial boundaries, awarding Bahrain sovereignty of the Hawar islands, while supporting Qatar's sovereignty over other disputed territories. The GCC welcomed the judgement, which was accepted by the Governments of both countries.

In May 1997 the Ministerial Council, meeting in Riyadh, expressed concern at Turkey's cross-border military operation in northern Iraq and urged a withdrawal of Turkish troops from Iraqi territory. In December the Supreme Council reaffirmed the need to ensure the sovereignty and territorial integrity of Iraq. At the same time, however, the Council expressed concern at the escalation of tensions in the region, owing to Iraq's failure to co-operate with the UN Special Commission (UNSCOM). The Council also noted the opportunity to strengthen relations with Iran, in view of political developments in that country. In February 1998 the US Defense Secretary visited each of the GCC countries in order to generate regional support for any punitive military action against Iraq, given that country's obstruction of UN weapons inspectors. Kuwait was the only country to declare its support for the use of force (and to permit the use of its bases in military operations against Iraq), while other member states urged a diplomatic solution to the crisis. Qatar pursued a diplomatic initiative to negotiate directly with the Iraqi authorities, and during February, the Qatari Minister of Foreign Affairs became the most senior GCC government official to visit Iraq since 1990. The GCC supported an agreement concluded between the UN Secretary-General and the Iraqi authorities at the end of February 1998, and urged Iraq to co-operate with UNSCOM in order to secure an end to the problem and a removal of the international embargo against the country. This position has subsequently been reiterated by the Supreme Council. (In December 1999 UNSCOM was replaced by a new arms inspection body, the UN Monitoring, Verification and Inspection Commission—UNMOVIC.) In December 2000 Kuwait and Saudi Arabia rejected a proposal by the Qatari

Government, supported by the UAE, that the GCC should soften its policy on Iraq and demand the immediate removal of the international embargo against that country. During that month the Supreme Council determined to establish a committee with the function of touring Arab states to explain the GCC's Iraq policy. The GCC welcomed the resumption of dialogue between Iraq and the UN in early 2002.

The GCC has condemned repeated military exercises conducted by Iran in the waters around the disputed islands of Abu Musa and Greater and Lesser Tunb as a threat to regional security and a violation of the UAE's sovereignty. Nevertheless, member countries have pursued efforts to strengthen relations with Iran. In May 1999 President Khatami undertook a state visit to Qatar, Saudi Arabia and Syria, prompting concern on the part of the UAE that its support within the GCC and the solidarity of the grouping were being undermined. In June a meeting of GCC ministers of foreign affairs was adjourned, owing to reported disagreements between Saudi Arabia and the UAE. Diplomatic efforts secured commitments, issued by both countries later in that month, to co-operate fully within the GCC. In early July the Ministerial Council reasserted GCC support of the UAE's sovereignty claim over the three disputed islands and determined to establish a committee, comprising the ministers of foreign affairs of Oman, Qatar and Saudi Arabia and the GCC Secretary-General, to resolve the dispute. In December the Supreme Council extended the mandate of the committee to establish a mechanism for direct negotiations between UAE and Iran. Iran, however, refused to co-operate with the committee; consequently, the committee's mandate was terminated in January 2001. In March the Ministerial Council demanded that Iran cease the construction of buildings for settlement on the disputed islands, and reiterated its support for the UAE's sovereignty claim.

EXTERNAL RELATIONS

In June 1988 an agreement was signed by GCC and European Community (EC) ministers on economic co-operation; this took effect from January 1990. Under the accord a joint ministerial council (meeting on an annual basis) was established, and working groups were subsequently created to promote co-operation in several specific areas, including business, energy, the environment and industry. In October 1990 GCC and EC ministers of foreign affairs commenced negotiations on formulating a free-trade agreement. In October 1995 a conference was held in Muscat, Oman, which aimed to strengthen economic co-operation between European Union (EU, as the restructured EC was now known) and GCC member states, and to promote investment in both regions. GCC heads of state, meeting in December 1997, condemned statements issued by the European Parliament, as well as by other organizations, regarding human rights issues in member states and insisted they amounted to interference in GCC judicial systems. In December 2001 the GCC Supreme Council agreed to establish a customs union—a precondition of the proposed GCC-EU free-trade agreement—by 1 January 2003 (see above). Free-trade negotiations were continuing in 2002.

In September 1994 GCC ministers of foreign affairs decided to end the secondary and tertiary embargo on trade with Israel. In February 1995 a ministerial meeting of signatories of the Damascus Declaration adopted a common stand, criticizing Israel for its refusal to renew the nuclear non-proliferation treaty. In December 1996 the foreign ministers of the Damascus Declaration states, convened in Cairo, requested the USA to exert financial pressure on Israel to halt the construction of settlements on occupied Arab territory. In December 2001 GCC heads of state issued a statement holding Israeli government policy responsible for the escalating crisis in the Palestinian territories. The Council of Ministers declared its support in March 2002 for a Saudi-proposed initiative aimed at achieving a peaceful resolution of the crisis. In early April the GCC Secretary-General condemned Israeli aggression and urged Israel immediately to withdraw from Palestinian cities, in accordance with a resolution adopted by the UN Security Council at the end of March.

In June 1997 ministers of foreign affairs of the Damascus Declaration states agreed to pursue efforts to establish a free-trade zone throughout the region, which they envisaged as the nucleus of a future Arab common market. (Meanwhile, the League of Arab States (q.v.) has also initiated efforts to create a Greater Arab Free Trade Area.)

The GCC-USA Economic Dialogue, which commenced in 1985, convenes periodically as a government forum to promote co-operation between the GCC economies and the USA. Since the late 1990s private-sector interests have been increasingly represented at sessions of the Dialogue. It was announced in March 2001 that a business forum was to be established under the auspices of the Dialogue, to act as a permanent means of facilitating trade and investment between the GCC countries and the USA.

The GCC Secretary-General denounced the major terrorist attacks that were perpetrated in September 2001 against targets in the USA. Meeting in an emergency session in mid-September, in Riyadh, Saudi Arabia, GCC foreign ministers agreed to support the aims of the developing international coalition against terrorism. Meanwhile, however, member states urged parallel international resolve to halt action by the Israeli security forces against Palestinians. In December the Supreme Council declared the organization's total co-operation with the anti-terrorism coalition.

INVESTMENT CORPORATION

Gulf Investment Corporation (GIC): Joint Banking Center, Kuwait Real Estate Bldg, POB 3402, Safat 13035, Kuwait; tel. 2431911; fax 2448894; e-mail gic@gic.com.kw; f. 1983 by the six member states of the GCC, each contributing US $350m. of the total capital of $2,100m.; total assets $19,500m. (1999); investment chiefly in the Gulf region, financing industrial projects (including pharmaceuticals, chemicals, steel wire, aircraft engineering, aluminium, dairy produce and chicken-breeding). GIC provides merchant banking and financial advisory services, and in 1992 was appointed to advise the Kuwaiti Government on a programme of privatization. Chair. IBRAHIM ABDUL-KARIM; Gen. Man. HISHAM A. RAZZUQI. Publ. *The GIC Gazetteer* (annually).

Gulf International Bank: POB 1017, Al-Dowali Bldg, 3 Palace Ave, Manama 317, Bahrain; tel. 534000; fax 522633; e-mail info@gib.com.bh; internet www.gibonline.com; f. 1976 by the six GCC states and Iraq; became a wholly-owned subsidiary of the GIC (without Iraqi shareholdings) in 1991; in April 1999 a merger with Saudi Investment Bank was concluded; cap. US $1,000m., dep. $11,414m., total assets $15,119.5m. (Dec. 2000). Chair. EBRAHIM AL-KHALIFA.

Publications

GCC News (monthly).

At-Ta'awun (periodical).

COUNCIL OF ARAB ECONOMIC UNITY

Address: 1191 Corniche en-Nil, 12th Floor, POB 1, Mohammed Fareed, Cairo, Egypt.

Telephone: (2) 5755321; **fax:** (2) 5754090.

Established in 1957 by the Economic Council of the League of Arab States (q.v.). The first meeting of the Council was held in 1964.

MEMBERS

Egypt	Palestine
Iraq	Somalia
Jordan	Sudan
Libya	Syria
Mauritania	Yemen

Organization

(April 2002)

COUNCIL

The Council consists of representatives of member states, usually ministers of economy, finance and trade. It meets twice a year; meetings are chaired by the representative of each country for one year.

GENERAL SECRETARIAT

Entrusted with the implementation of the Council's decisions and with proposing work plans, including efforts to encourage participation by member states in the Arab Economic Unity Agreement. The Secretariat also compiles statistics, conducts research and publishes studies on Arab economic problems and on the effects of major world economic trends.

General Secretary: Dr AHMED GOWEILI (Egypt).

COMMITTEES

There are seven standing committees: preparatory, follow-up and Arab Common Market development; Permanent Delegates; budget; economic planning; fiscal and monetary matters; customs and trade planning and co-ordination; statistics. There are also seven *ad hoc* committees, including meetings of experts on tariffs, trade promotion and trade legislation.

Activities

The Council undertakes to co-ordinate measures leading to a customs union subject to a unified administration; conduct market and commodity studies; assist with the unification of statistical terminology and methods of data collection; conduct studies for the formation of new joint Arab companies and federations; and to formulate specific programmes for agricultural and industrial co-ordination and for improving road and railway networks.

ARAB COMMON MARKET

Based on a resolution passed by the Council in August 1964; its implementation was to be supervised by the Council. Customs duties and other taxes on trade between the member countries were to be eliminated in stages prior to the adoption of a full customs union, and ultimately all restrictions on trade between the member countries, including quotas, and restrictions on residence, employment and transport, were to be abolished. In practice little progress was achieved in the development of an Arab common market during 1964–2000. However, efforts towards liberalizing intra-Arab trade were intensified in 2001. A meeting of Council ministers of economy and trade convened in Baghdad, Iraq, in June, issued the 'Baghdad Declaration' on establishing an, initially, quadripartite free-trade area comprising Egypt, Iraq, Libya and Syria; future participation by other member states was urged by the Council's General Secretary. The initiative was envisaged as a cornerstone of the Greater Arab Free Trade Area—GAFTA (q.v.), which was being implemented by the Arab League. The meeting also approved an executive programme for developing the common market and a 10-year strategy for joint Arab economic action, determined to establish a compensation fund to support the integration of the least developed Arab states into the regional economy, and agreed to provide technical assistance for Arab states aiming to join the WTO. It was reported in late 2001 that the Palestine National Authority had also applied to join the free-trade area, and that consideration of its application would delay the zone's entry into force. In May Egypt, Jordan, Morocco and Tunisia, meeting in Agadir, Morocco, had agreed to establish the Mediterranean Arab Free Trade Area (MAFTA) as a cornerstone of a planned larger Arab-Mediterranean free trade area. In early 2002 the Council was considering a draft general framework for Arab economic action in the areas of investment, technology, trade and joint ventures (see below) covering the next 20 years.

JOINT VENTURES

A number of multilateral organizations in industry and agriculture have been formed on the principle that faster development and economies of scale may be achieved by combining the efforts of member states. In industries that are new to the member countries, Arab Joint Companies are formed, while existing industries are co-ordinated by the setting up of Arab Specialized Unions. The unions are for closer co-operation on problems of production and marketing, and to help companies deal as a group in international markets. The companies are intended to be self-supporting on a purely commercial basis; they may issue shares to citizens of the participating countries. The joint ventures are:

Arab Joint Companies:

Arab Company for Drug Industries and Medical Appliances: POB 925161, Amman, Jordan; tel. (6) 5821618; fax (6) 5821649; e-mail acdima@go.com.jo; f. 1976.

Arab Company for Electronic Commerce.

Arab Company for Industrial Investment: POB 3385, Alwiyah, Baghdad, Iraq; tel. 718-9215; fax 718-0710.

Arab Company for Livestock Development: POB 5305, Damascus, Syria; tel. 666037.

Arab Mining Company: POB 20198, Amman, Jordan; tel. (6) 5663148; fax (6) 5684114; e-mail armico@go.com.jo; f. 1974.

Specialized Arab Unions and Federations:

Arab Co-operative Federation: POB 57640, Baghdad, Iraq; tel. (1) 888-8121; f. 1985.

Arab Federation for Paper, Printing and Packaging Industries: POB 5456, Baghdad, Iraq; tel. (1) 887-2384; fax (1) 886-9639; f. 1977; 250 mems.

Arab Federation for Information Technology.

Arab Federation of Chemical Fertilizers Producers: Cairo, Egypt; f. 1976.

Arab Federation of Engineering Industries: POB 509, Baghdad, Iraq; tel. (1) 776-1101.

Arab Federation of Shipping: POB 1161, Baghdad, Iraq; tel. (1) 717-4540; fax (1) 717-7243; f. 1979; 22 mems.

Arab Federation of Leather Industries: POB 2188, Damascus, Syria; f. 1978.

Arab Federation of Textile Industries: POB 620, Damascus, Syria.

Arab Federation of Travel Agents: POB 7090, Amman, Jordan.

Arab Seaports Federation: Alexandria, Egypt; f. 1977.

Arab Sugar Federation: POB 195, Khartoum, Sudan; f. 1977.

Arab Union for Cement and Building Materials: POB 9015, Damascus, Syria; tel. (11) 6118598; fax (11) 6111318; e-mail aucbm@net.sy; internet www.aucbm.org; f. 1977; 22 mem. countries, 100 mem. cos.

Arab Union for Information Technology.

Arab Union of Fish Producers: POB 15064, Baghdad, Iraq; tel. (1) 551-1261; f. 1976.

Arab Union of Food Industries: POB 13025, Baghdad, Iraq; f. 1976.

Arab Union of Hotels and Tourism: Beirut, Lebanon; f. 1994.

Arab Union of Land Transport: POB 926324, Amman 11110, Jordan; tel. (6) 5663153; fax (6) 5664232; f. 1978.

Arab Union of the Manufacturers of Pharmaceuticals and Medical Appliances: POB 81150, Amman 11181, Jordan; tel. (6) 4654306; fax (6) 4648141; f. 1986.

Arab Union of Railways: POB 6599, Aleppo, Syria; tel. (21) 220302; f. 1979.

General Arab Insurance Federation: POB 611, 11511 Cairo, Egypt; tel. (2) 5743177; fax (2) 5762310; f. 1964.

General Union of Arab Agricultural Workers and Co-operatives: Tripoli, Libya; f. 1993.

Union of Arab Contractors: Cairo, Egypt; f. 1995.

Union of Arab Investors: Cairo, Egypt; f. 1995.

Publications

Annual Bulletin for Arab Countries' Foreign Trade Statistics.

Annual Bulletin for Official Exchange Rates of Arab Currencies.

Arab Economic Unity Bulletin (2 a year).

Demographic Yearbook for Arab Countries.

Economic Report of the General Secretary (2 a year).

Guide to Studies prepared by Secretariat.

Progress Report (2 a year).

Statistical Yearbook for Arab Countries.

Yearbook for Intra-Arab Trade Statistics.

Yearbook of National Accounts for Arab Countries.

COUNCIL OF BALTIC SEA STATES—CBSS

Address: Strömsberg, POB 2010, 103 11 Stockhölm, Sweden.

Telephone: (8) 440-19-20; **fax:** (8) 440-19-44; **e-mail:** cbss@cbss.st; **internet:** www.cbss.st.

The Council of Baltic Sea States (CBSS) was established in 1992 to intensify co-operation between member states.

MEMBERS

Denmark	Iceland	Poland
Estonia	Latvia	Russia
Finland	Lithuania	Sweden
Germany	Norway	

The European Commission also has full membership status.

Organization

(April 2002)

PRESIDENCY

The presidency is occupied by member states for one year, on a rotating basis. Summit meetings of heads of government are convened every two years. The last summit meeting was held in Kolding, Denmark, in April 2000, and the next summit is scheduled to be held in St Petersburg, Russia, in June 2002.

COUNCIL

The Council comprises the ministers of foreign affairs of each member state and a representative of the European Commission. The Council meets annually and aims to serve as a forum for guidance, direction of work and overall co-ordination among participating states. The minister of foreign affairs of the presiding country acts as Chairman of the Council and is responsible for co-ordinating the Council's activities between ministerial sessions, with assistance from the Committee of Senior Officials. (Other ministers also convene periodically, on an *ad hoc* basis by their own decision.)

COMMITTEE OF SENIOR OFFICIALS—CSO

The Committee consists of senior officials of the ministries of foreign affairs of the member states and of the European Commission. It serves as a discussion forum for matters relating to the work of the Council and undertakes inter-sessional activities. The Chairman of the Committee, from the same country serving as President of the CBSS, meets regularly with the previous and future Chairmen. The so-called Troika aims to maintain information co-operation, promote better exchange of information, and ensure more effective decision-making.

SECRETARIAT

In October 1998 the presidency inaugurated a permanent secretariat in Stockholm. The tasks of the secretariat include the preparation of summit meetings, annual sessions of ministers of foreign affairs, and other meetings of high-level officials and experts, the provision of technical support to the presidency regarding the implementation of plans, maintaining contacts with other sub-regional organizations, and strengthening awareness of the Council and its activities.

Secretary-General: JACEK STAROSCIAK (Poland).

COMMISSIONER ON DEMOCRATIC DEVELOPMENT

Address: Amagertorv 14², POB 1165, 1010 Copenhagen K, Denmark.

Telephone: 33-91-22-88; **fax:** 33-91-22-96; **e-mail:** mail@cbsscommissioner.org; **internet:** www.cbss-commissioner.org.

The ministerial session held in May 1994 agreed to appoint an independent Commissioner on democratic institutions and human rights to serve a three-year term of office, from October of that year. In July 1997, at the sixth ministerial session held in Riga, Latvia, the Commissioner's term of office was extended by a further three years. The ninth ministerial session, held in Bergen, Norway, in June 2000, renewed the Commissioner's mandate until September 2003. The Commissioner is based in Copenhagen, Denmark.

Commissioner on Democratic Development: HELLE DEGN (Denmark).

Activities

The CBSS was established in March 1992 as a forum to enhance and strengthen co-operation between countries in the Baltic Sea region. At a meeting of the Council in Kalmar, Sweden, in July 1996, ministers adopted an Action Programme as a guide-line for CBSS activities. The main programme areas covered stable and participatory political development; economic integration and prosperity; and protection of the environment. The third summit meeting of CBSS heads of government, held at Kolding, Denmark, in April 2000, recommended a restructuring of the organization to consolidate regional intergovernmental, multilateral co-operation in all sectors. In June the ninth meeting of the CBSS Council approved the summit's recommendations. The 10th ministerial session, held in Hamburg, Germany, in June 2001, adopted a set of guide-lines regarding the strengthening of the CBSS.

At the first Baltic Sea States summit, held in Visby, Sweden, in May 1996, heads of government agreed to establish a Task Force on organized crime to counter drugs-trafficking, strengthen judicial co-operation, increase the dissemination of information, impose regional crime-prevention measures, improve border controls and provide training. In January 1998 the second summit meeting, convened in Riga, Latvia, agreed to extend the mandate of the Task Force until the end of 2000 and to enhance co-operation in the areas of civic security and border control. In April 2000 the third Baltic Sea States summit prolonged the Task Force's mandate further, until the end of 2004. The 2000 summit also authorized the establishment of a Task Force on Communicable Disease Control (TFCDC).

The Council has founded a number of working groups, comprising experts in specific fields, which aim to report on and recommend action on issues of concern to the Council. In early 2002 there were three groups working under the auspices of the CSO: the working group on assistance to democratic institutions, based in Riga, Latvia; the working group on economic co-operation, based in Bonn, Germany; and the working group on nuclear and radiation safety, based in Helsinki, Finland. The Swedish Special Group originated as a working group with a mandate to support the elimination of the sexual exploitation of children for commercial purposes in the Baltic Sea region. The Group helped to organize a conference on the subject held in Tallinn, Estonia, in September 1998.

A Baltic Business Advisory Council was estabished in 1996. In July 1998 ministers of trade of member states met in Vilnius, Lithuania, to discuss the development of small and medium-sized enterprises. Ministers agreed to strengthen links between member states, to implement measures to increase access to information in the region and to improve procedures for commercial border crossings.

In January 2001 the CBSS Council agreed to establish a secretariat to implement Baltic 21, the regional variant (adopted by the CBSS in 1998) of 'Agenda 21', the programme of action agreed by the UN Conference on Environment and Development, held in Rio de Janeiro, Brazil, in June 1992. Baltic 21 comprised a programme of 30 projects throughout the region, which aim to promote sustainable development in the agriculture, forestry and fisheries, energy, industry, tourism, transport, and spatial planning sectors. The Baltic Sea Region Energy Co-operation (BASREC) has its own secretariat function and council of senior energy officials, administered by the CBSS secretariat. BASREC also has *ad hoc* groups on electricity markets, gas markets, energy efficiency and climate change.

Finance

Contributions of the governments of Council's 11 member states finance the Secretariat and the Commissioner on Democratic Development. Ongoing activities and co-operation projects are funded through voluntary contributions from member states on the basis of special contribution schemes.

Publication

Newsletter (monthly).

THE COUNCIL OF EUROPE

Address: 67075 Strasbourg Cedex, France.

Telephone: 3-88-41-20-00; **fax:** 3-88-41-27-81; **e-mail:** pointi@coe.int; **internet:** www.coe.int.

The Council was founded in May 1949 to achieve a greater unity between its members, to facilitate their social progress and to uphold the principles of parliamentary democracy, respect for human rights and the rule of law. Membership has risen from the original 10 to 43.

MEMBERS*

Albania	Liechtenstein
Andorra	Lithuania
Armenia	Luxembourg
Austria	Macedonia, former Yugoslav republic
Azerbaijan	Malta
Belgium	Moldova
Bulgaria	Netherlands
Croatia	Norway
Cyprus	Poland
Czech Republic	Portugal
Denmark	Romania
Estonia	Russia
Finland	San Marino
France	Slovakia
Georgia	Slovenia
Germany	Spain
Greece	Sweden
Hungary	Switzerland
Iceland	Turkey
Ireland	Ukraine
Italy	United Kingdom
Latvia	

* The Holy See, Canada, Japan, Mexico and the USA have observer status with the organization. Bosnia and Herzegovina and the Federal Republic of Yugoslavia have been granted special guest status at the Parliamentary Assembly; Canada, Israel and Mexico have observer status with the Parliamentary Assembly. On 20 March 2002 the Committee of Ministers invited Bosnia and Herzegovina to accede to full membership of the Council.

Organization

(April 2002)

COMMITTEE OF MINISTERS

The Committee consists of the ministers of foreign affairs of all member states (or their deputies); it decides with binding effect all matters of internal organization, makes recommendations to governments and draws up conventions and agreements; it also discusses matters of political concern, such as European co-operation, compliance with member states' commitments, in particular concerning the protection of human rights, and considers possible co-ordination with other institutions, such as the European Union (EU) and the Organization for Security and Co-operation in Europe (OSCE). The Committee usually meets in May and November each year.

CONFERENCES OF SPECIALIZED MINISTERS

There are 19 Conferences of specialized ministers, meeting regularly for intergovernmental co-operation in various fields.

PARLIAMENTARY ASSEMBLY

President: PETER SCHIEDER (Austria).

Chairman of the Socialist Group: TERRY DAVIS (United Kingdom).

Chairman of the Group of the European People's Party: RENÉ VAN DER LINDEN (Netherlands).

Chairman of the European Democratic (Conservative) Group: DAVID ATKINSON (United Kingdom).

Chairman of the Liberal Democratic and Reformers' Group: MÁTYÁS EÖRSI (Hungary).

Chairman of the Unified European Left Group: JAAKKO LAAKSO (Finland).

Members are elected or appointed by their national parliaments from among the members thereof; political parties in each delegation follow the proportion of their strength in the national parliament. Members do not represent their governments; they speak on their own behalf. At March 2002 the Assembly had 301 members (and 301 substitutes): 18 each for France, Germany, Italy, Russia and the United Kingdom; 12 each for Poland, Spain, Turkey and Ukraine; 10 for Romania; seven each for Belgium, the Czech Republic, Greece, Hungary, the Netherlands and Portugal; six each for Austria, Azerbaijan, Bulgaria, Sweden and Switzerland; five each for Croatia, Denmark, Finland, Georgia, Moldova, Norway and Slovakia; four each for Albania, Armenia, Ireland and Lithuania; three each for Cyprus, Estonia, Iceland, Latvia, Luxembourg, the former Yugoslav republic of Macedonia, Malta and Slovenia; and two each for Andorra, Liechtenstein and San Marino. Israel, Canada and Mexico have permanent observer status, while Belarus, Bosnia and Herzegovina and the Federal Republic of Yugoslavia have been granted special 'guest status'. (Belarus's special status was suspended in January 1997.)

The Assembly meets in ordinary session once a year. The session is divided into four parts, held in the last full week of January, April, June and September. The Assembly submits Recommendations to the Committee of Ministers, passes Resolutions, and discusses reports on any matters of common European interest. It is also a consultative body to the Committee of Ministers, and elects the Secretary-General, the Deputy Secretary-General, the Secretary-General of the Assembly, the Council's Commissioner for Human Rights, and the members of the European Court of Human Rights.

Standing Committee: Represents the Assembly when it is not in session, and may adopt Recommendations to the Committee of Ministers and Resolutions on behalf of the Assembly. Consists of the President, Vice-Presidents, Chairmen of the Political Groups, Chairmen of the Ordinary Committees and Chairmen of national delegations. Meets usually three times a year.

Ordinary Committees: political; economic and development; social, health and family affairs; legal and human rights; culture, science and education; environment and agriculture; migration, refugees and demography; rules of procedure and immunities; monitoring; equal opportunities; honouring of obligations and commitments by member states of the Council of Europe.

CONGRESS OF LOCAL AND REGIONAL AUTHORITIES OF EUROPE—CLRAE

The Congress was established in 1994, incorporating the former Standing Conference of Local and Regional Authorities, in order to protect and promote the political, administrative and financial autonomy of local and regional European authorities by encouraging central governments to develop effective local democracy. The Congress comprises two chambers—a Chamber of Local Authorities and a Chamber of Regions—with a total membership of 301 elected representatives (and 301 elected substitutes). Annual sessions are mainly concerned with local government matters, regional planning, protection of the environment, town and country planning, and social and cultural affairs. A Standing Committee, drawn from all national delegations, meets between plenary sessions of the Congress. Four Statutory Committees (Institutional; Sustainable Development; Social Cohesion; Culture and Education) meet twice a year in order to prepare texts for adoption by the Congress.

The Congress advises the Council's Committee of Ministers and the Parliamentary Assembly on all aspects of local and regional policy and co-operates with other national and international organizations representing local government. The Congress monitors implementation of the European Charter of Local Self-Government, which was opened for signature in 1985 and provides common standards for effective local democracy. Other legislative guide-lines for the activities of local authorities and the promotion of democracy at local level include the 1980 European Outline Convention on Transfrontier Co-operation, and its Additional Protocol which was opened for signature in 1995, a Convention on the Participation of Foreigners in Public Life at Local Level (1992), and the European Charter for Regional or Minority Languages (1992). In addition, the European Urban Charter defines citizens' rights in European towns and cities, for example in the areas of transport, urban architecture, pollution and security.

President: LLIBERT CUATRECASAS (Spain).

SECRETARIAT

Secretary-General: Dr WALTER SCHWIMMER (Austria).

Deputy Secretary-General: HANS CHRISTIAN KRÜGER (Germany).

Secretary-General of the Parliamentary Assembly: BRUNO HALLER (France).

Activities

In an effort to harmonize national laws, to put the citizens of member countries on an equal footing and to pool certain resources and facilities, the Council has concluded a number of conventions and agreements covering particular aspects of European co-operation. Since 1989 the Council has undertaken to increase co-operation with all countries of the former Eastern bloc and to facilitate their accession to the organization. In October 1997 heads of state or government of member countries convened for only the second time (the first meeting took place in Vienna, in October 1993—see below) with the aim of formulating a new social model to consolidate democracy throughout Europe. The meeting endorsed a Final Declaration and an Action Plan, which established priority areas for future Council activities, including fostering social cohesion; protecting civilian security; promoting human rights; enhancing joint measures to counter cross-border illegal trafficking; and strengthening democracy through education and other cultural activities. In addition, the meeting generated renewed political commitment to the Programme of Action against Corruption, which has become a key element of Council activities.

HUMAN RIGHTS

The promotion and development of human rights is one of the major tasks of the Council of Europe. The European Convention for the Protection of Human Rights and Fundamental Freedoms (European Convention on Human Rights) was opened for signature in 1950. The Steering Committee for Human Rights is responsible for inter-governmental co-operation in the field of human rights and fundamental freedoms; it works to strengthen the effectiveness of systems for protecting human rights, to identify potential threats and challenges to human rights, and to encourage education and provide information on the subject. The Committee has been responsible for the elaboration of several conventions and other legal instruments including most recently Protocol (No. 12) of the European Convention on Human Rights, adopted in June 2000, which enforces a general prohibition of discrimination.

The Committee was responsible for the preparation of the European Ministerial Conference on Human Rights, held in Rome in November 2000, which commemorated the 50th anniversary of the adoption of the European Convention on Human Rights. Delegates addressed issues such as the protection of human rights during armed conflicts and in situations of national crisis; the abolition of the death penalty during times of war, etc.

At the Council's first meeting of heads of state and of government, held in Vienna, Austria, in October 1993, members agreed to draw up a new Protocol to the European Convention on Human Rights to establish cultural rights of minorities and to draw up a new Framework Convention for the protection of national minorities. (Work on the Additional Protocol, however, was suspended in 1996.) The Framework Convention was adopted by the Council's Committee of Ministers in November 1994 and opened for signature on 1 February 1995. It entered into force on 1 February 1998 as the first ever legally-binding instrument devoted to the general protection of national minorities. In addition, the Convention obliged all parties to implement domestic legislation and programmes to fulfil the objectives of the instrument and to submit regular reports, to an 18-member Advisory Committee, on their implementation of the Convention. At 31 October 2001 the Framework Convention had been ratified by 39 states.

The 1993 Vienna summit meeting also agreed to restructure the control mechanism for the protection of human rights, mainly the procedure for the consideration of cases, in order to reduce the length of time before a case is concluded. As a result, Protocol (No. 11) to the European Convention on Human Rights was opened for signature by member states in May 1994. The then existing institutions (i.e. the European Commission of Human Rights and the European Court of Human Rights) were consequently replaced in November 1998 (when Protocol No. 11 entered into force) by a single Court, working on a full-time basis.

The second summit meeting of the Council's heads of state and government, held in Strasbourg, France, in October 1997, welcomed a proposal to institute a Council of Europe Commissioner for Human Rights to promote respect for human rights in member states; this office was established by a resolution of the Council's Committee of Ministers in May 1999.

Commissioner for Human Rights: ALVARO GIL-ROBLES (Spain).

European Court of Human Rights

The Court has compulsory jurisdiction and is competent to consider complaints lodged by states party to the European Convention and by individuals, groups of individuals or non-governmental organizations claiming to be victims of breaches of the Convention's guarantees. The Court comprises one judge for each contracting state (i.e. 41 in January 2002). The Court sits in three-member Committees, empowered to declare applications inadmissible in the event of unanimity and where no further examination is necessary, seven-member Chambers, and a 17-member Grand Chamber. Chamber judgments become final three months after delivery, during which period parties may request a rehearing before the Grand Chamber, subject to acceptance by a panel of five judges. Grand Chamber judgments are final. At January 2002 18,383 applications were pending before the Court.

President: LUZIUS WILDHABER (Switzerland).

Registrar: PAUL MAHONEY (United Kingdom).

European Committee for the Prevention of Torture and Inhuman or Degrading Treatment or Punishment—CPT

The Committee was established under the 1987 Convention for the Prevention of Torture as an integral part of the Council of Europe's system for the protection of human rights. The Committee, comprising independent experts, aims to examine the treatment of persons deprived of their liberty with a view to strengthening, if necessary, the protection of such persons from torture and from inhuman or degrading treatment or punishment. It conducts periodic visits to police stations, prisons, detention centres, and all other sites where persons are deprived of their liberty by a public authority, in all states parties to the Convention, and may also undertake *ad hoc* visits when the Committee considers them necessary. By January 2002 the Committee had undertaken 87 periodic visits and 40 *ad hoc* visits. After each visit the Committee drafts a report of its findings and any further advice or recommendations, based on dialogue and co-operation.

President: SILVIA CASALE (United Kingdom).

European Social Charter

The European Social Charter, in force since 1965, is the counterpart of the European Convention on Human Rights, in the field of protection of economic and social rights. A revised Charter, which amended existing guarantees and incorporated new rights, was opened for signature in May 1996, and entered into force on 1 July 1999. By January 2002 all 43 member states had signed the Charter, of which 30 had ratified it. Rights covered under the Charter include conditions of employment (such as the prohibition on the employment of children, non-discrimination in employment, the right to decent working conditions and a fair remuneration, and trade union rights), and of social cohesion (such as the right to social security and assistance, and the rights of families, migrants and elderly persons to legal, social and economic protection). A supervisory procedure is in place to monitor the practical application of the rights guaranteed. The European Committee of Social Rights, composed of 12 independent experts, undertakes a legal assessment of national legislation, regulations and practices within the context of the Charter. Having taken into account social, economic and other policy considerations, the Committee of Ministers may then, on the basis of decisions prepared by a Governmental Committee (composed of representatives of each Contracting Party) issue recommendations to the state concerned, inviting it to change its legislation or practice in accordance with the Charter's requirements. An Additional Protocol (1995), providing for a system of collective complaints, entered into force on 1 July 1998 and permits trade unions, employers' organizations and NGOs to lodge complaints against perceived contraventions of the Charter.

President of the European Committee of Social Rights: STEIN EVJU (Norway).

RACISM AND INTOLERANCE

In October 1993 heads of state and of government, meeting in Vienna, resolved to reinforce a policy to combat all forms of intolerance, in response to the increasing incidence of racial hostility and intolerance towards minorities in European societies. A European Commission against Racism and Intolerance (ECRI) was established by the summit meeting to analyse and assess the effectiveness of legal, policy and other measures taken by member states to combat these problems. It became operational in March 1996. Members of ECRI are designated by governments on the basis of their recognized expertise in the field, although participate in the Commission in an independent capacity. ECRI undertakes activities in three programme areas: country-by-country approach; work on general themes; and ECRI and civil society. In the first area of activity, ECRI analyses the situation regarding racism and intolerance in each of the member states, in order to advise governments on measures to combat these problems. In December 1998 ECRI completed a first round of reports for all Council members. A follow-up series of reports were prepared during the four-year period 1999–2002. ECRI's work on general themes includes the preparation of policy recommendations and guide-lines on issues of importance to combating racism and intolerance. ECRI also collects and disseminates examples of good practices relating to these issues. Under the third programme area ECRI aims to disseminate information and raise awareness of the problems of racism and intolerance among the general public.

A Committee on the Rehabilitation and Integration of People with Disabilities supports co-operation between member states in this field and undertakes studies in order to promote legislative and administrative action.

MEDIA AND COMMUNICATIONS

Article 10 of the European Convention on Human Rights (freedom of expression and information) forms the basis for the Council of Europe's mass media activities. Implementation of the Council of Europe's work programme concerning the media is undertaken by the Steering Committee on the Mass Media (CDMM), which comprises senior government officials and representatives of professional organizations, meeting in plenary session twice a year. The CDMM is mandated to devise concerted European policy measures and appropriate legal instruments. Its underlying aims are to further freedom of expression and information in a pluralistic democracy, and to promote the free flow of information and ideas. The CDMM is assisted by various specialist groups and committees. Policy and legal instruments have been developed on subjects including: exclusivity rights; media concentrations and transparency of media ownership; protection of journalists in situations of conflict and tension; independence of public-service broadcasting, protection of rights holders; legal protection of encrypted television services; media and elections; protection of journalists' sources of information; and the independence and functions of broadcasting regulatory authorities. These policy and legal instruments (mainly in the form on non-binding recommendations addressed to member governments) are complemented by the publication of studies, analyses and seminar proceedings on topics of media law and policy. The CDMM has also prepared a number of international binding legal instruments, including the European Convention on Transfrontier Television (adopted in 1989 and ratified by 23 countries by 31 December 2001), the European Convention on the legal protection of services based on or consisting of conditional access (signed by five countries at the end of 2001), and the European Convention relating to questions on copyright law and other rights in the context of transfrontier broadcasting by satellite (ratified by two countries and signed by seven other member states and the European Community at the end of 2001). CDMM areas of activity in 2001 included: self-regulation of internet services; credibility of information disseminated online; media and privacy; and the regulation of digital broadcasting services.

SOCIAL COHESION

In June 1998, the Committee of Ministers established the European Committee for Social Cohesion (CDCS). The CDCS has the following responsibilities: to co-ordinate, guide and stimulate co-operation between member States with a view to promoting social cohesion in Europe, to develop and promote integrated, multidisciplinary responses to social issues, and to promote the social standards embodied in the European Social Charter and other Council of European instruments, including the European Code of Social Security. The CDCS is also responsible for executing the terms of reference of the European Code of Social Security, the European Convention on Social Security and the European Agreement on 'au pair' Placement. The CDCS has agreed on policy guide-lines on access to employment, housing and social protection. It supervises a programme of work on families and children.

The European Code of Social Security and its Protocol entered into force in 1968; by March 2002 the Code and Protocol had been ratified by Belgium, Germany, Luxembourg, the Netherlands, Norway, Portugal and Sweden, while the Code alone had, additionally, been ratified by Cyprus, the Czech Republic, Denmark, France, Greece, Ireland, Italy, Spain, Switzerland, Turkey and the United Kingdom. These instruments set minimum standards for medical care and the following benefits: sickness, old-age, unemployment, employment injury, family, maternity, invalidity and survivor's benefit. A revision of these instruments, aiming to provide higher standards and greater flexibility, was completed for signature in 1990 and had been signed by 14 states at March 2002.

The European Convention on Social Security, in force since 1977, now applies in Austria, Belgium, Italy, Luxembourg, the Netherlands, Portugal, Spain and Turkey; most of the provisions apply automatically, while others are subject to the conclusion of additional multilateral or bilateral agreements. The Convention is concerned with establishing the following four fundamental principles of international law on social security: equality of treatment, unity of applicable legislation, conservation of rights accrued or in course of acquisition, and payment of benefits abroad. In 1994 a Protocol to the Convention, providing for the enlargement of the personal scope of the Convention, was opened for signature. By March 2002 it had been signed by Austria, Greece, Luxembourg and Portugal.

HEALTH

Through a series of expert committees, the Council aims to ensure constant co-operation in Europe in a variety of health-related fields, with particular emphasis on patients' rights, for example: equity in access to health care, quality assurance, health services for institutionalized populations (prisoners, elderly in homes), discrimination resulting from health status and education for health. These efforts are supplemented by the training of health personnel.

Improvement of blood transfusion safety and availability of blood and blood derivatives has been ensured through European Agreements and guide-lines. Advances in this field and in organ transplantation are continuously assessed by expert committees.

Eighteen states co-operate in a Partial Agreement to protect the consumer from potential health risks connected with commonplace or domestic activities. The committees of experts of the Public Health Committee provide the scientific base for national and international regulations regarding products which have a direct or indirect impact on the human food chain, pesticides, pharmaceuticals and cosmetics.

In the co-operation group to combat drug abuse and illicit drugs trafficking (Pompidou Group), 34 states work together, through meetings of ministers, officials and experts, to counteract drug abuse. The Group follows a multidisciplinary approach embracing in particular legislation, law enforcement, prevention, treatment, rehabilitation and data collection.

The Convention on the Elaboration of a European Pharmacopoeia (establishing legally binding standards for medicinal substances, auxiliary substances, pharmaceutical preparations, vaccines for human and vetinary use and other articles) entered into force in eight signatory states in May 1974: in March 2002 29 states and the European Union were parties to the Convention. WHO and 15 European and non-European states participate as observers in the sessions of the European Pharmacopoeia Commission. In 1994 a procedure on certification of suitability to the European Pharmacopoeia monographs for manufacturers of substances for pharmaceutical use was established. In 2001 almost 300 certificates had been granted. A network of official control laboratories for human and veterinary medicines was established in 1995, open to all signatory countries to the Convention and observers at the Pharmacopoeia Commission. The fourth edition of the European Pharmacopoeia (published in early 2001) includes some 1,800 harmonized European standards, or 'monographs', 300 general methods of analysis and 1,000 reagents.

In April 1997 the first international convention on biomedicine was opened for signature at a meeting of health ministers of member states, in Oviedo, Spain. The so-called Convention for the Protection of Human Rights and the Dignity of Human Beings with Respect to the Applications of Biology and Medicine incorporated provisions on scientific research, the principle of informed patient consent, organ and tissue transplants and the prohibition of financial gain and disposal of a part of the human body. It entered into force on 1 November 1999 (see below).

POPULATION AND MIGRATION

The European Convention on the Legal Status of Migrant Workers, in force since 1983, has been ratified by France, Italy, the Netherlands, Norway, Portugal, Spain, Sweden and Turkey. The Convention is based on the principle of equality of treatment for migrant workers and the nationals of the host country as to housing, working conditions, and social security. The Convention also upholds the principle of the right to family reunion. An international consultative committee, representing the parties to the Convention, monitors the application of the Convention.

In 1996 the European Committee on Migration concluded work on a project entitled 'The Integration of Immigrants: Towards Equal Opportunities' was concluded and the results were presented at the sixth conference of European ministers responsible for migration affairs, held in Warsaw, Poland. At the conference a new project, entitled 'Tensions and Tolerance: Building better integrated communities across Europe' was initiated; it was concluded in 1999. The Committee was responsible for activities concerning Roma/Gypsies in Europe, in co-ordination with other relevant Council of Europe bodies. The Committee is also jointly responsible, with the *ad hoc* Committee of Experts on the legal aspects of territorial asylum, refugees and stateless persons, for the examination of migration issues arising at the pan-European level.

The European Population Committee, an intergovernmental committee of scientists and government officials responsible for population matters, monitors and analyses population trends throughout Europe and informs governments, research centres and the public of demographic developments and their impact on policy decisions. It compiles an annual statistical review of demographic developments (covering 46 European states) and publishes the results of studies on population issues, such as *Fertility and new types of households and family formation in Europe* (2001), and *Trends in mortality and differential mortality in Europe* (2001). Future publications were to include studies on the demographic characteristics of immigrant populations, the demographic consequences of economic transition in the countries of central and eastern Europe, and social exclusion.

COUNCIL OF EUROPE DEVELOPMENT BANK

The Council of Europe Development Bank was created in 1956 (initially as the Resettlement Fund, and later as the Council of Europe Social Development Fund, renamed in November 1999). Its primary aim is to finance projects to benefit refugees, migrants and displaced persons, and victims of natural or ecological disasters. As a secondary objective, it also funds social projects involving job creation, vocational training, social housing, education, health, the protection of the environment, and the protection and rehabilitation of the historic heritage. The Bank provides approximately €1,000m. in loans each year for projects in 35 European countries (the Bank's shareholders). At October 2001 the Bank's capital amounted to €3,003.8m.

EQUALITY BETWEEN WOMEN AND MEN

The Steering Committee for Equality between Women and Men (CDEG—an intergovernmental committee of experts) is responsible for encouraging action at both national and Council of Europe level to promote equality of rights and opportunities between the two sexes. Assisted by various specialist groups and committees, the CDEG is mandated to establish analyses, studies and evaluations, to examine national policies and experiences, to work out concerted policy strategies and measures for implementing equality and, as necessary, to prepare appropriate legal and other instruments. It is also responsible for preparing the European Ministerial Conferences on Equality between Women and Men. The main areas of CDEG activities are the comprehensive inclusion of the rights of women (for example, combating violence against women) within the context of human rights; the issue of equality and democracy, including the promotion of the participation of women in political and public life; projects aimed at studying the specific equality problems related to cultural diversity, migration and minorities; positive action in the field of equality between men and women and the mainstreaming of equality into all policies and programmes at all levels of society. In October 1998 the Committee of Ministers adopted a recommendation to member states on gender mainstreaming and in May 2000 adopted a recommendation on action against and trafficking in human beings for the purpose of sexual exploitation.

LEGAL MATTERS

The European Committee on Legal Co-operation develops co-operation between member states in the field of law, with the objective of harmonizing and modernizing public and private law, including administrative law and the law relating to the judiciary. The Committee is responsible for expert groups which consider issues relating to administrative law, efficiency of justice, family law, nationality, information technology and data protection.

Numerous conventions and Recommendations have been adopted, and followed up by appropriate committees or groups of experts, on matters which include: efficiency of justice, nationality, legal aid, rights of children, data protection, information technology, children born out of wedlock, animal protection, adoption, information on foreign law, and the legal status of non-governmental organizations. In addition, a new draft Convention on contact concerning children has been formulated.

In November 1999 the Convention for the Protection of Human Rights and the Dignity of Human Beings with Respect to the Applications of Biology and Medicine (Convention on Human Rights and Biomedicine) entered into force, as the first internationally-binding legal text to protect people against the misuse of biological and medical advances. It aimed to preserve human dignity and identify, rights and freedoms, through a series of principles and rules. Additional protocols aimed to develop the Convention's general provisions by means of specialized texts. A Protocol prohibiting the medical cloning of human beings was approved by Council heads of state and government in October 1997 and entered into force on 1 March 2001. A Protocol on the transplantation of human organs and tissue opened for signature in January 2002. At that time work was ongoing to draft protocols relating to biomedical research, protection of the human embryo and foetus, and genetics. A draft Recommendation on xenotransplantation was nearing completion.

In 2001 an Additional Protocol to the Convention for the protection of individuals with regard to automatic processing of personal data was adopted. The Protocol, which opened for signature in November, concerned supervisory authorities and transborder data flows. By the end of April 2002 it had been signed by 17 states, and ratified by one (Sweden).

The Consultative Council of European Judges has prepared a framework global action plan for judges in Europe. In addition, it has contributed to the implementation of this programme by the adoption of opinions on standards concerning the independence of the judiciary and the irremovability of judges, and on the funding and management of courts.

A Committee of Legal Advisors on Public and International Law (CAHDI), comprising the legal advisors of ministers of foreign affairs of member states and of several observer states, is authorized by the Committee of Ministers to examine questions of public international law, and to exchange and, if appropriate, to co-ordinate the views of member states. Recent activities of the CAHDI include the preparation of a Recommendation on reactions to inadmissible reservations to international treaties, and publication of reports on a pilot project relating to state practice with regard to state succession and recognition in the period 1989-94, and on expression of consent of states to be bound by a treaty. In 2002 the CAHDI was conducting research into the practice of states with regard to state immunity.

An *ad hoc* Committee of Experts on the Legal Aspects of Territorial Asylum, Refugees and Stateless Persons (CAHAR) proposes solutions to practical and legal problems relating to its area of expertise, formulates appropriate legal instruments, reviews relevant national and international developments and adopts Recommendations. The CAHAR has adopted a series of opinions for the Committee of Ministers on the situation of refugees and displaced persons in the CIS, on access to asylum by EU citizens, and on the human rights of refugees and asylum-seekers in Europe. It works closely with other international bodies, in particular UNHCR and the Council's Parliamentary Assembly.

With regard to crime, expert committees and groups operating under the authority of the European Committee on Crime Problems have prepared conventions on such matters as extradition, mutual assistance, recognition and enforcement of foreign judgments, the transfer of proceedings, the suppression of terrorism, the transfer of prisoners, the compensation to be paid to victims of violent crime, money-laundering, confiscation of the proceeds from crime, cybercrime and corruption. In 2001 Recommendations were adopted relating to organized crime, police ethics, and the protection of children against sexual exploitation. In October the 24th Conference of European Ministers of Justice was held, in Moscow, Russia. The meeting adopted resolutions on combating international terrorism, the implementation of long-term sentences, and the effective enforcement of judicial decisions. In November a Convention on Cybercrime was opened for signature.

A new monitoring body, the Group of States against Corruption (GRECO), became operational in May 1999, on the basis of an agreement concluded in the previous year. By January 2002 GRECO had 33 members, including two (Bosnia and Herzegovina, and the USA) which are not members of the Council of Europe. A Civil Law Convention against Corruption was opened for signature in November 1999. In May 2000 a Recommendation on codes of conduct for public officials was adopted by the Committee of Ministers.

A Criminological Scientific Council, composed of specialists in law, psychology, sociology and related sciences, advises the Committee and organizes criminological research conferences and colloquia. A Council for Penological Co-operation organizes regular high-level conferences of directors of prison administration and is responsible for collating statistical information on detention and community sanctions in Europe. The Council prepared the European Prison Rules in 1987 and the European Rules on Community Sanctions (alternatives to imprisonment) in 1992.

In May 1990 the Committee of Ministers adopted a Partial Agreement to establish the European Commission for Democracy through Law, to be based in Venice, Italy. The so-called Venice Commission (comprising 43 member states, at early 2002) is composed of independent legal and political experts, mainly senior academics, supreme or consitutional court judges, members of national parliaments, and senior public officers. Its main activity is constitutional assistance and may supply opinions upon request, made through the Committee of Ministers, by the Parliamentary Assembly, the Secretary-General or any member states of the Council of Europe. Other states and international organizations may request opinions with the consent of the Committee of Ministers. The Commission is active throughout the constitutional domain, and has worked on issues including legislation on constitutional courts and national minorities, electoral law and other legislation with implications for national democratic institutions. The Commission disseminates its work through the UniDem (University for Democracy) programme of seminars, the CODICES database, and the *Bulletin of Constitutional Case-Law*.

The promotion of local and regional democracy and of transfrontier co-operation constitutes a major aim of the Council's intergovernmental programme of activities. The Steering Committee on Local and Regional Democracy (CDLR) serves as a forum for representatives of member states to exchange information and pursue co-operation in order to promote the decentralization of powers, in accordance with the European Charter on Local Self-Government. The CDLR's principal objective is to improve the legal, institutional and financial framework of local democracy and to encourage citizen participation in local and regional communities. In December 2001 the Committee of Ministers adopted a Recommendation on citizens' participation in public life at local level, drafted on the basis of the work conducted by the CDLR. The CDLR publishes comparative studies and national reports, and aims to identify guide-lines for the effective implementation of the principles of subsidiarity and solidarity. Its work also constitutes a basis for the provision of aid to central and eastern European countries in the field of local democracy.The CDLR is responsible for the preparation and follow-up of Conferences of Ministers responsible for local and regional government. The 13th Conference was scheduled to be held in Helsinki, Iceland, in June 2002 on the theme of regionalization.

The policy of the Council of Europe on transfrontier co-operation between territorial communities or authorities is implemented through two committees. The Committee of Experts on Transfrontier Co-operation (LR -CT), working under the supervision of the CDLR, aims to monitor the implementation of the European Outline Convention on Transfrontier Co-operation between Territorial Communities or Authorities; to make proposals for the elimination of obstacles, in particular of a legal nature, to transfrontier and interterritorial co-operation; and to compile 'best practice' examples of transfrontier co-operation in various fields of activity. In 2001 the Committee prepared a draft recommendation on the mutual aid and assistance between central and local authorities in the event of disasters affecting frontier areas. A Committee of Advisers for the development of transfrontier co-operation in central and eastern Europe is composed of six members appointed or elected by the Secretary-General, the Committee of Ministers and the Congress of Local and Regional Authorities of Europe. Its task is to guide the promotion of transfrontier co-operation in central and eastern European countries, with a view to fostering good neighbourly relations between the frontier populations, especially in particularly sensitive regions. Its programme comprises: conferences and colloquies designed to raise awareness on the Outline Convention; meetings in border regions between representatives of local communities with a view to strengthening mutual trust; and legal assistance to, and restricted meetings with, national and local representatives responsible for preparing the legal texts for ratification and/or implementation of the Outline Convention. The priority areas which had been outlined by the Committee of Advisers include South-East Europe, northern Europe around the Baltic Sea, the external frontiers of an enlarged European Union, and the Caucasus.

EDUCATION, CULTURE AND HERITAGE

The European Cultural Convention covers education, culture, heritage, sport and youth. Programmes on education, higher education, culture and cultural heritage are managed by the Council for Cultural Co-operation, assisted by four specialized committees.

The education programme consists of projects on 'Education for democratic citizenship', 'Learning and teaching about the history of Europe in the 20th century', 'Language policies for a multilingual and multicultural Europe', and 'Education strategies for social cohesion and democratic security'. Other activities include: the annual European Schools Day Competition, organized in co-operation with the EU; the In-service Educational Staff Training Programme; the Network for School Links and Exchanges; and the European Secondary School Students Exchange Programme. The Council's main contribution in the field of higher education is its activity on the recognition of qualifications and mobility of students and staff. The Council of Europe/UNESCO Convention on the Recognition of Qualifications Concerning Higher Education in the European Region was adopted in 1997 and entered into force on 1 February 1999. Practical recognition work is conducted within the framework of a European Network of National Information Centres (ENIC) network on academic recognition and mobility. Other activities include a legislative reform programme; lifelong learning for equity and social cohesion; universities as sites of citizenship and civic responsibility; and techical co-operation and assistance to South-East Europe, in particular Bosnia and Herzegovina and Kosovo and Metohija.

In December 2000 the Committee of Ministers adopted a Declaration on Cultural Diversity, formulated in consultation with other organizations (including the European Union and UNESCO), which created a framework for developing a European approach to valuing cultural diversity. A European Charter for Regional or Minority languages entered into force in 1998, with the aim of protecting regional or minority languages as a threatened aspect of Europe's cultural heritage. It was intended to promote the use in private and public life of languages traditionally used within a state's territory. The Charter provides for a monitoring system enabling states, the Council of Europe and individuals to follow and observe its implementation.

In the field of cultural policy, a series of surveys of national policies have been conducted. Since 1998 this series has been complemented by 'transversal' policy reviews, for example on national cultural institutions and on cultural policy and cultural diversity. A Research and Development Unit for cultural policies became operational in 1997 with responsibility for the improvement, accuracy and circulation of information concerning European cultural policies. Guide-lines have been formulated on library legislation and policy in Europe, and in early 2000 work was ongoing on the preparation of guide-lines on book development and electronic publishing, and on a European policy on access to archives. Two main archive projects were being undertaken at early 2000—the computerization of the Komintern Archives in Moscow, Russia, and the reconstitution of archival sources relating to Polish history. In 1998 the Council initiated a new four-year assistance programme to support cultural development in South-East Europe (the MOSAIC project). A similar plan, the STAGE project, for countries of the Caucasus became operational in 2000.

The European Convention on Cinematographic Co-production was opened for signature in October 1992. The Eurimages support fund helps to finance co-production of films. Conventions for the Protection of the Architectural Heritage and the Protection of the Archaeological Heritage provide a legal framework for European co-operation in these areas. The Cultural Heritage Committee promotes discussion on measures relating to heritage and consolidating democracy in Europe, the formulation of strategies for sustainable development, and on national experience and policies concerning conservation and enhancement of the European cultural heritage. In September 1999 a new campaign was inaugurated to promote co-operation and to generate awareness of the common heritage of Europe. In 1996 the European Conference of Ministers responsible for cultural heritage resolved to establish a network for the dissemination of information, using the electronic media, on heritage policies in states party to the European Cultural Convention. The network was initiated as a pilot scheme, covering six countries, in 1999. It was being developed by the European Foundation for Heritage Skills, which aimed to develop practical co-operation among professionals of all European countries.

YOUTH

In 1972 the Council of Europe established the European Youth Centre (EYC) in Strasbourg. A second residential centre was created in Budapest in 1995. The centres, run with and by international non-governmental youth organizations representing a wide range of interests, provide about 50 residential courses a year (study sessions, training courses, symposia). A notable feature of the EYC is its decision-making structure, by which decisions on its programme and general policy matters are taken by a Programming Committee composed of an equal number of youth organizations and government representatives.

The European Youth Foundation (EYF) aims to provide financial assistance to European activities of non-governmental youth organizations and began operations in 1973. Since that time more than 380 organizations have received financial aid for carrying out international activities, while more than 210,000 young people have participated in meetings supported by the Foundation. The European Steering Committee for Intergovernmental Co-operation in the Youth Field conducts research in youth-related matters and prepares for ministerial conferences.

SPORT

The Committee for the Development of Sport, founded in November 1977, administers the Sports Fund. Its activities concentrate on the implementation of the European Sports Charter; the role of sport in society (e.g. medical, political, ethical and educational aspects); the provision of assistance in sports reform to new member states in central and eastern Europe; and the practice of sport (activities, special projects, etc.). The Committee is also responsible for preparing the conference of European ministers responsible for sport. In 1985 the Committee of Ministers adopted the European Convention on Spectator Violence and Misbehaviour at Sports Events. A Charter on Sport for Disabled Persons was adopted in 1986, an Anti-Doping Convention in 1989, and a Code of Sports Ethics in 1992. During the period 1996–2000 the Committee for the Development of Sport implemented an Action Plan for Bosnia and Herzegovina, entitled 'Rehabilitation through Sport'.

ENVIRONMENT AND SUSTAINABLE DEVELOPMENT

In 1995 a pan-European biological and landscape diversity strategy, formulated by the Committee of Ministers, was endorsed at a ministerial conference of the UN Economic Commission for Europe, which was held in Sofia, Bulgaria. The strategy was to be implemented jointly by the Council of Europe and UNEP, in close co-operation with the European Community. In particular, it provided for implementation of the Convention on Biological Diversity.

At March 2002 45 states and the European Community had ratified a Convention on the Conservation of European Wildlife and Natural Habitats, which entered into force in June 1982 and gives total protection to 693 species of plants, 89 mammals, 294 birds, 43 reptiles, 21 amphibians, 115 freshwater fishes, 113 invertebrates and their habitats. The Convention established a network of protected areas known as the 'Emerald Network'. The Council's NATUROPA Centre provides information and documentation on the environment, through periodicals and campaigns. The Council awards the European Diploma for protection of sites of European significance, supervises a network of biogenetic reserves, and co-ordinates conservation action for threatened animals and plants.

Regional disparities constitute a major obstacle to the process of European integration. Conferences of ministers of regional planning are held to discuss these issues. In 2000 they adopted guiding principles for sustainable development of the European continent.

EXTERNAL RELATIONS

Agreements providing for co-operation and exchange of documents and observers have been concluded with the United Nations and its agencies, and with most of the European intergovernmental organizations and the Organization of American States. Particularly close relations exist with the EU, OECD, and the OSCE. Relations with non-member states, other organizations and non-governmental organizations are co-ordinated by the Directorate General of Political Affairs.

Israel, Canada and Mexico are represented in the Parliamentary Assembly by observer delegations, and certain European and other non-member countries participate in or send observers to certain meetings of technical committees and specialized conferences at intergovernmental level. Full observer status with the Council was granted to the USA in 1995, to Canada and Japan in 1996 and to Mexico in 1999. The Holy See has had a similar status since 1970.

The European Centre for Global Interdependence and Solidarity (the 'North–South Centre') was established in Lisbon, Portugal, in 1990, in order to provide a framework for European co-operation in this area and to promote pluralist democracy and respect for human rights. The Centre is co-managed by parliamentarians, governments, non-governmental organizations and local and regional authorities. Its activities are divided into three programmes: public information and media relations; education and training for global interdependence; and dialogue for global partnership. The Centre organizes workshops, seminars and training courses on global interdependence and convenes international colloquies on human rights.

During the early 1990s the Council of Europe established a structure of programmes to assist the process of democratic reform in central and eastern European countries that had formerly been under communist rule. In October 1997 the meeting of heads of state or of government of Council members agreed to extend the programmes as the means by which all states are assisted to meet their undertakings as members of the Council. These specific co-operation programmes were mainly concerned with the development of the rule of law; the protection and promotion of human rights; and strengthening local democracy. A scheme of Democratic Leadership Programmes has also been established for the training of political leaders. Within the framework of the co-operation programme 20 information and documentation centres have been established in 15 countries of Central and Eastern Europe. A secretariat representation to co-ordinate the Council's contribution to the UN operation in Kosovo was established in Priština (the capital of Kosovo and Metohija), in mid-1999.

In March 2002 the Council's Parliamentary Assembly organized, jointly with the Inter-parliamentary Assembly of the CIS, a conference on combating terrorism. The meeting, held in St Petersburg, Russia, aimed to provide support for the global campaign against the terrorism.

Finance

The budget is financed by contributions from members on a proportional scale of assessment (using population and gross domestic product as common indicators). The 2002 budget totalled €169m.

Publications

Activities and achievements (in 17 languages).

Activities Report (in French and English).

Annual Report of the Council for Cultural Co-operation.

The Bulletin (newsletter of the CLRAE, 3 a year).

Europa40plus (electronic newsletter, monthly, in English and French).

European Cultural Diary (annually).

European Heritage (2 a year, in English, French and German).

The Europeans (electronic bulletin of the Parliamentary Assembly).

Naturopa (3 a year, in 15 languages).

Official Gazette of the Council of Europe (monthly, in English and French).

Sports Information Bulletin (quarterly).

Strategy Bulletin (6 a year, in 5 languages).

European Social Charter

(4 November 1950; text as revised 3 May 1996)

PREAMBLE

The governments signatory hereto, being members of the Council of Europe,

Considering that the aim of the Council of Europe is the achievement of greater unity between its members for the purpose of safeguarding and realising the ideals and principles which are their common heritage and of facilitating their economic and social progress, in particular by the maintenance and further realisation of human rights and fundamental freedoms;

Considering that in the European Convention for the Protection of Human Rights and Fundamental Freedoms signed at Rome on 4 November 1950, and the Protocols thereto, the member States of the Council of Europe agreed to secure to their populations the civil and political rights and freedoms therein specified;

Considering that in the European Social Charter opened for signature in Turin on 18 October 1961 and the Protocols thereto, the member States of the Council of Europe agreed to secure to their populations the social rights specified therein in order to improve their standard of living and their social well-being;

Recalling that the Ministerial Conference on Human Rights held in Rome on 5 November 1990 stressed the need, on the one hand, to preserve the indivisible nature of all human rights, be they civil, political, economic, social or cultural and, on the other hand, to give the European Social Charter fresh impetus;

Resolved, as was decided during the Ministerial Conference held in Turin on 21 and 22 October 1991, to update and adapt the substantive contents of the Charter in order to take account in particular of the fundamental social changes which have occurred since the text was adopted;

Recognising the advantage of embodying in a Revised Charter, designed progressively to take the place of the European Social Charter, the rights guaranteed by the Charter as amended, the rights guaranteed by the Additional Protocol of 1988 and to add new rights,

Have agreed as follows;

PART I

The Parties accept as the aim of their policy, to be pursued by all appropriate means both national and international in character, the attainment of conditions in which the following rights and principles may be effectively realised:

1. Everyone shall have the opportunity to earn his living in an occupation freely entered upon.

2. All workers have the right to just conditions of work.

3. All workers have the right to safe and healthy working conditions.

4. All workers have the right to a fair remuneration sufficient for a decent standard of living for themselves and their families.

5. All workers and employers have the right to freedom of association in national or international organizations for the protection of their economic and social interests.

6. All workers and employers have the right to bargain collectively.

7. Children and young persons have the right to a special protection against the physical and moral hazards to which they are exposed.

8. Employed women, in case of maternity, have the right to a special protection.

9. Everyone has the right to appropriate facilities for vocational guidance with a view to helping him choose an occupation suited to his personal aptitude and interests.

10. Everyone has the right to appropriate facilities for vocational training.

11. Everyone has the right to benefit from any measures enabling him to enjoy the highest possible standard of health attainable.

12. All workers and their dependents have the right to social security.

13. Anyone without adequate resources has the right to social and medical assistance.

14. Everyone has the right to benefit from social welfare services.

15. Disabled persons have the right to independence, social integration and participation in the life of the community.

16. The family as a fundamental unit of society has the right to appropriate social, legal and economic protection to ensure its full development.

17. Children and young persons have the right to appropriate social, legal and economic protection.

18. The nationals of any one of the Parties have the right to engage in any gainful occupation in the territory of any one of the others on a footing of equality with the nationals of the latter, subject to restrictions based on cogent economic or social reasons.

19. Migrant workers who are nationals of a Party and their families have the right to protection and assistance in the territory of any other Party.

20. All workers have the right to equal opportunities and equal treatment in matters of employment and occupation without discrimination on the grounds of sex.

21. Workers have the right to be informed and to be consulted within the undertaking.

22. Workers have the right to take part in the determination and improvement of the working conditions and working environment in the undertaking.

23. Every elderly person has the right to social protection.

24. All workers have the right to protection in cases of termination of employment.

25. All workers have the right to protection of their claims in the event of the insolvency of their employer.

26. All workers have the right to dignity at work.

27. All persons with family responsibilities and who are engaged or wish to engage in employment have a right to do so without being subject to discrimination and as far as possible without conflict between their employment and family responsibilities.

28. Workers' representatives in undertakings have the right to protection against acts prejudicial to them and should be afforded appropriate facilities to carry out their functions.

29. All workers have the right to be informed and consulted in collective redundancy procedures.

30. Everyone has the right to protection against poverty and social exclusion.

31. Everyone has the right to housing.

PART II

The Parties undertake, as provided for in Part III, to consider themselves bound by the obligations laid down in the following articles and paragraphs.

Article 1. The right to work.

With a view to ensuring the effective exercise of the right to work, the Parties undertake:

1. to accept as one of their primary aims and responsibilities the achievement and maintenance of as high and stable a level of employment as possible, with a view to the attainment of full employment;

2. to protect effectively the right of the worker to earn his living in an occupation freely entered upon;

3. to establish or maintain free employment services for all workers;

4. to provide or promote appropriate vocational guidance, training and rehabilitation.

Article 2. The right to just conditions of work.

With a view to ensuring the effective exercise of the right to just conditions of work, the Parties undertake:

1. to provide for reasonable daily and weekly working hours, the working week to be progressively reduced to the extent that the increase of productivity and other relevant factors permit;

2. to provide for public holidays with pay;

3. to provide for a minimum of four weeks' annual holiday with pay;

4. to eliminate risks in inherently dangerous or unhealthy occupations, and where it has not yet been possible to eliminate or reduce sufficiently these risks, to provide for either a reduction of working hours or additional paid holidays for workers engaged in such occupations;

5. to ensure a weekly rest period which shall, as far as possible, coincide with the day recognised by tradition or custom in the country or region concerned as a day of rest;

6. to ensure that workers are informed in written form, as soon as possible, and in any event not later than two months after the date of commencing their employment, of the essential aspects of the contract or employment relationship;

7. to ensure that workers performing night work benefit from measures which take account of the special nature of the work.

Article 3. The right to safe and healthy working conditions.

With a view to ensuring the effective exercise of the right to safe and healthy working conditions, the Parties undertake, in consultation with employers' and workers' organizations:

1. to formulate, implement and periodically review a coherent national policy on occupational safety, occupational health and the working environment. The primary aim of this policy shall be to improve occupational safety and health and to prevent accidents and injury to health arising out of, linked with or occurring in the course of work, particularly by minimising the causes of hazards inherent in the working environment;

2. to issue safety and health regulations;

3. to provide for the enforcement of such regulations by measures of supervision;

4. to promote the progressive development of occupational health services for all workers with essentially preventive and advisory functions.

Article 4. The right to a fair remuneration.

With a view to ensuring the effective exercise of the right to a fair remuneration, the Parties undertake:

1. to recognize the right of workers to a remuneration such as will give them and their families a decent standard of living;

2. to recognize the right of workers to an increased rate of remuneration for overtime work, subject to exceptions in particular cases;

3. to recognize the right of men and women workers to equal pay for work of equal value;

4. to recognize the right of all workers to a reasonable period of notice for termination of employment;

5. to permit deductions from wages only under conditions and to the extent prescribed by national laws or regulations or fixed by collective agreements or arbitration awards.

The exercise of these rights shall be achieved by freely concluded collective agreements, by statutory wage-fixing machinery, or by other means appropriate to national conditions.

Article 5. The right to organize.

With a review to ensuring or promoting the freedom of workers and employers to form local, national or international organizations for the protection of their economic and social interests and to join those organizations, the Parties undertake that national law shall not be such as to impair, nor shall it be so applied as to impair, this freedom. The extent to which the guarantees provided for in this article shall apply to the police shall be determined by national laws or regulations. The principle governing the application to the members of the armed forces of these guarantees and the extent to which they shall apply to persons in this category shall equally be determined by national laws or regulations.

Article 6. The right to bargain collectively.

With a view to ensuring the effective exercise of the right to bargain collectively, the Parties undertake:

1. to promote joint consultation between workers and employers;

2. to promote, where necessary and appropriate, machinery for voluntary negotiations between employers or employers' organizations and workers' organizations, with a view to the regulation of terms and conditions of employment by means of collective agreements;

3. to promote the establishment and use of appropriate machinery for conciliation and voluntary arbitration for the settlement of labour disputes;

and recognize:

4. the right of workers and employers to collective action in cases of conflicts of interest, including the right to strike, subject to obligations that might arise out of collective agreements previously entered into.

Article 7. The right of children and young persons to protection.

With a view to ensuring the effective exercise of the right of children and young persons to protection, the Parties undertake:

1. to provide that the minimum age of admission to employment shall be 15 years, subject to exceptions for children employed in prescribed light work without harm to their health, morals or education;

2. to provide that the minimum age of admission to employment shall be 18 years with respect to prescribed occupations regarded as dangerous or unhealthy;

3. to provide that persons who are still subject to compulsory education shall not be employed in such work as would deprive them of the full benefit of their education;

4. to provide that the working hours of persons under 18 years of age shall be limited in accordance with the needs of their development, and particularly with their need for vocational training;

5. to recognize the right of young workers and apprentices to a fair wage or other appropriate allowances;

6. to provide that the time spent by young persons in vocational training during the normal working hours with the consent of the employer shall be treated as forming part of the working day;

7. to provide that employed persons of under 18 years of age shall be entitled to a minimum of four weeks' annual holiday with pay;

8. to provide that persons under 18 years of age shall not be employed in night work with the exception of certain occupations provided for by national laws or regulations;

9. to provide that persons under 18 years of age employed in occupations prescribed by national laws or regulations shall be subject to regular medical control;

10. to ensure special protection against physical and moral dangers to which children and young persons are exposed, and particularly against those resulting directly or indirectly from their work.

Article 8. The right of employed women to protection of maternity.

With a view to ensuring the effective exercise of the right of employed women to the protection of maternity, the Parties undertake:

1. to provide either by paid leave, by adequate social security benefits or by benefits from public funds for employed women to take leave before and after childbirth up to a total of at least fourteen weeks;

2. to consider it as unlawful for an employer to give a women notice of dismissal during the period from the time she notifies her employer that she is pregnant until the end of her maternity leave, or to give her notice of dismissal at such a time that the notice would expire during such a period;

3. to provide that mothers who are nursing their infants shall be entitled to sufficient time off for this purpose;

4. to regulate the employment in night work of pregnant women, women who have recently given birth and women nursing their infants;

5. to prohibit the employment of pregnant women, women who have recently given birth or who are nursing their infants in underground mining and all other work which is unsuitable by reason of its dangerous, unhealthy or arduous nature and to take appropriate measures to protect the employment rights of these women.

Article 9. The right to vocational guidance.

With a view to ensuring the effective exercise of the right to vocational guidance, the Parties undertake to provide or promote, as necessary, a service which will assist all persons, including the handicapped, to solve problems related to occupational choice and progress, with due regard to the individual's characteristics and their relation to occupational opportunity: this assistance should be available free of charge, both to young persons, including schoolchildren, and to adults.

Article 10. The right to vocational training.

With a view to ensuring the effective exercise of the right to vocational training, the Parties undertake:

1. to provide or promote, as necessary, the technical and vocational training of all persons, including the handicapped, in consultation with employers' and workers' organizations, and to grant facilities for access to higher technical and university education, based solely on individual aptitude;

2. to provide or promote a system of apprenticeship and other systematic arrangements for training young boys and girls in their various employments;

3. to provide or promote, as necessary:

(a) adequate and readily available training facilities for adult workers;

(b) special facilities for the retraining of adult workers needed as a result of technological development or new trends in employment;

4. to provide or promote, as necessary, special measures for the retraining and reintegration of the long-term unemployed;

5. to encourage the full utilisation of the facilities provided by appropriate measures such as:

(a) reducing or abolishing any fees or charges;

(b) granting financial assistance in appropriate cases;

(c) including in the normal working hours time spent on supplementary training taken by the worker, at the request of his employer, during employment;

(d) ensuring, through adequate supervision, in consultation with the employers' and workers' organizations, the efficiency of apprenticeship and other training arrangements for young workers, and the adequate protection of young workers generally.

Article 11. The right to protection of health.

With a view to ensuring the effective exercise of the right to protection of health, the Parties undertake, either directly or in co-operation with public or private organizations, to take appropriate measures designed *inter alia*:

1. to remove as far as possible the causes of ill-health;

2. to provide advisory and educational facilities for the promotion of health and the encouragement of individual responsibility in matters of health;

3. to prevent as far as possible epidemic, endemic and other diseases, as well as accidents.

Article 12. The right to social security.

With a view to ensuring the effective exercise of the right to social security, the Parties undertake:

1. to establish or maintain a system of social security;

2. to maintain the social security system at a satisfactory level at least equal to that necessary for the ratification of the European Code of Social Security;

3. to endeavour to raise progressively the system of social security to a higher level;

4. to take steps, by the conclusion of appropriate bilateral and multilateral agreements or by other means, and subject to the conditions laid down in such agreements, in order to ensure:

(a) equal treatment with their own nationals of the nationals of other Parties in respect of social security rights, including the retention of benefits arising out of social security legislation, whatever movements the persons protected may undertake between the territories of the Parties;

(b) the granting, maintenance and resumption of social security rights by such means as the accumulation of insurance or employment periods completed under the legislation of each of the Parties.

Article 13. The right to social and medical assistance.

With a view to ensuring the effective exercise of the right to social and medical assistance, the Parties undertake:

1. to ensure that any person who is without adequate resources and who is unable to secure such resources either by his own efforts or from other sources, in particular by benefits under a social security scheme, be granted adequate assistance, and, in case of sickness, the care necessitated by his condition;

2. to ensure that persons receiving such assistance shall not, for that reason, suffer from a diminution of their political or social rights;

3. to provide that everyone may receive by appropriate public or private services such advice and personal help as may be required to prevent, to remove, or to alleviate personal or family want;

4. to apply the provisons referred to in paragraphs 1, 2 and 3 of this article on an equal footing with their nationals to nationals of other Parties lawfully within their territories, in accordance with their obligations under the European Convention on Social and Medical Assistance, signed at Paris on 11 December 1953.

Article 14. The right to benefit from social welfare services.

With a view to ensuring the effective exercise of the right to benefit from social welfare services, the Parties undertake:

1. to promote or provide services which, by using methods of social work, would contribute to the welfare and development of both individuals and groups in the community, and to their adjustment to the social environment;

2. to encourage the participation of individuals and voluntary or other organizations in the establishment and maintenance of such services.

Article 15. The right of persons with disabilities to independence, social integration and participation in the life of the community.

With a view to ensuring to persons with disabilities, irrespective of age and the nature and origin of their disabilities, the effective exercise of the right to independence, social integration and participation in the life of the community, the Parties undertake, in particular:

1. to take the necessary measures to provide persons with disabilities with guidance, education and vocational training in the framework of general schemes wherever possible or, where this is not possible, through specialized bodies, public or private;

2. to promote their access to employment through all measures tending to encourage employers to hire and keep in employment persons with disabilities in the ordinary working environment and to adjust the working conditions to the needs of the disabled or, where this is not possible by reason of the disability, by arranging for or creating sheltered employment according to the level of disability. In certain cases, such measures may require recourse to specialized placement and support services;

3. to promote their full social integration and participation in the life of the community in particular through measures, including technical aids, aiming to overcome barriers to communication and mobility and enabling access to transport, housing, cultural activities and leisure.

Article 16. The right of the family to social, legal and economic protection.

With a view to ensuring the necessary conditions for the full development of the family, which is a fundamental unit of society, the Parties undertake to promote the economic, legal and social protection of family life by such means as social and family benefits, fiscal arrangements, provision of family housing, benefits for the newly married and other appropriate means.

Article 17. The right of children and young persons to social, legal and economic protection.

With a view to ensuring the effective exercise of the right of children and young persons to grow up in an environment which encourages the full development of their personality and of their physical and mental capacities, the Parties undertake, either directly or in co-operation with public and private organizations, to take all appropriate and necessary measures designed:

1. (a) to ensure that children and young persons, taking account of the rights and duties of their parents, have the care, the assistance, the education and the training they need, in particular by providing for the establishment or maintenance of institutions and services sufficient and adequate for this purpose;

   (b) to protect children and young persons against negligence, violence or exploitation;

   (c) to provide protection and special aid from the state for children and young persons temporarily or definitively deprived of their family's support;

2. to provide to children and young persons a free primary and secondary education as well as to encourage regular attendance at schools.

Article 18. The right to engage in a gainful occupation in the territory of other Parties.

With a view to ensuring the effective exercise of the right to engage in a gainful occupation in the territory of any other Party, the Parties undertake:

1. to apply existing regulations in a spirit of liberality;

2. to simplify existing formalities and to reduce or abolish chancery dues and other charges payable by foreign workers or their employers;

3. to liberalize, individually or collectively, regulations governing the employment of foreign workers;

and recognize:

4. the right of their nationals to leave the country to engage in a gainful occupation in the territories of the other Parties.

Article 19. The right of migrant workers and their families to protection and assistance.

With a view to ensuring the effective exercise of the right of migrant workers and their families to protection and assistance in the territory of any other Party, the Parties undertake:

1. to maintain or to satisfy themselves that there are maintained adequate and free services to assist such workers, particularly in obtaining accurate information, and to take all appropriate steps, so far as national laws and regulations permit, against misleading propaganda relating to emigration and immigration;

2. to adopt appropriate measures within their own jurisdiction to facilitate the departure, journey and reception of such workers and their families, and to provide, within their own jurisdiction, appropriate services for health, medical attention and good hygienic conditions during the journey;

3. to promote co-operation, as appropriate, between social services, public and private, in emigration and immigration countries;

4. to secure for such workers lawfully within their territories, insofar as such matters are regulated by law or regulations or are subject to the control of administrative authorities, treatment not less favourable than that of their own nationals in respect of the following matters:

   (a) remuneration and other employment and working conditions;

   (b) membership of trade unions and enjoyment of the benefits of collective bargaining;

   (c) accommodation;

5. to secure for such workers lawfully within their territories treatment not less favourable than that of their own nationals with regard to employment taxes, dues or contributions payable in respect of employed persons;

6. to facilitate as far as possible the reunion of the family of a foreign worker permitted to establish himself in the territory;

7. to secure for such workers lawfully within their territories treatment not less favourable than that of their own nationals in respect of legal proceedings relating to matters referred to in this article;

8. to secure that such workers lawfully residing within their territories are not expelled unless they endanger national security or offend against public interest or morality;

9. to permit, within legal limits, the transfer of such parts of the earnings and savings of such workers as they may desire;

10. to extend the protection and assistance provided for in this article to self-employed migrants insofar as such measures apply;

11. to promote and facilitate the teaching of the national language of the receiving state or, if there are several, one of these languages, to migrant workers and members of their families.

12. to promote and facilitate, as far as practicable, the teaching of the migrant worker's mother tongue to the children of the migrant worker.

Article 20. The right to equal opportunities and equal treatment in matters of employment and occupation without discrimination on the grounds of sex.

With a view to ensuring the effective exercise of the right to equal opportunities and equal treatment in matters of employment and occupation without discrimination on the grounds of sex, the Parties undertake to recognize that right and to take appropriate measures to ensure or promote its application in the following fields:

(a) access to employment, protection against dismissal and occupational reintegration;

(b) vocational guidance, training, retraining and rehabilitation;

(c) terms of employment and working conditions, including remuneration;

(d) career development, including promotion.

Article 21. The right to information and consultation.

With a view to ensuring the effective exercise of the right of workers to be informed and consulted within the undertaking, the Parties undertake to adopt or encourage measures enabling workers or their representatives, in accordance with national legislation and practice:

(a) to be informed regularly or at the appropriate time and in a comprehensible way about the economic and financial situation of the undertaking employing them, on the understanding that the disclosure of certain information which could be prejudicial to the undertaking may be refused or subject to confidentiality; and

(b) to be consulted in good time on proposed decisions which could substantially affect the interests of workers, particularly on those decisions which could have an important impact on the employment situation in the undertaking.

Article 22. The right to take part in the determination and improvement of the working conditions and working environment.

With a view to ensuring the effective exercise of the right of workers to take part in the determination and improvement of the working conditions and working environment in the undertaking, the Parties undertake to adopt or encourage measures enabling workers or their representatives, in accordance with national legislation and practice, to contribute:

(a) to the determination and the improvement of the working conditions, work organization and working environment;

(b) to the protection of health and safety within the undertaking;

(c) to the organisation of social and socio-cultural services and facilities within the undertaking;

(d) to the supervision of the observance of regulations on these matters.

Article 23. The right of elderly persons to social protection.

With a view to ensuring the effective exercise of the right of elderly persons to social protection, the Parties undertake to adopt or encourage, either directly or in co-operation with public or private organizations, appropriate measures designed in particular:

1. to enable elderly persons to remain full members of society for as long as possible, by means of:

(a) adequate resources enabling them to lead a decent life and play an active part in public, social and cultural life;

(b) provision of information about services and facilities available for elderly persons and their opportunities to make use of them;

2. to enable elderly persons to choose their life-style freely and to lead independent lives in their familiar surroundings for as long as they wish and are able, by means of:

(a) provision of housing suited to their needs and their state of health or of adequate support for adapting their housing;

(b) the health care and the services necessitated by their state;

3. to guarantee elderly persons living in institutions appropriate support, while respecting their privacy, and participation in decisions concerning living conditions in the institution.

Article 24. The right to protection in cases of termination of employment.

With a view to ensuring the effective exercise of the right of workers to protection in cases of termination of employment, the Parties undertake to recognize:

(a) the right of all workers not to have their employment terminated without valid reasons for such termination connected with their capacity or conduct or based on the operational requirements of the undertaking, establishment or service;

(b) the right of workers whose employment is terminated without a valid reason to adequate compensation or other appropriate relief.

To this end the Parties undertake to ensure that a worker who considers that his employment has been terminated without a valid reason shall have the right to appeal to an impartial body.

Article 25. The right of workers to the protection of their claims in the event of the insolvency of their employer.

With a view to ensuring the effective exercise of the right of workers to the protection of their claims in the event of the insolvency of their employer, the Parties undertake to provide that workers' claims arising from contracts of employment or employment relationships be guaranteed by a guarantee institution or by any other effective form of protection.

Article 26. The right to dignity at work.

With a view to ensuring the effective exercise of the right of all workers to protection of their dignity at work, the Parties undertake, in consultation with employers' and workers' organizations:

1. to promote awareness, information and prevention of sexual harassment in the workplace or in relation to work and to take all appropriate measures to protect workers from such conduct;

2. to promote awareness, information and prevention of recurrent reprehensible or distinctly negative and offensive actions directed against individual workers in the workplace or in relation to work and to take all appropriate measures to protect workers from such conduct.

Article 27. The right of workers with family responsibilities to equal opportunities and equal treatment.

With a view to ensuring the exercise of the right to equality of opportunity and treatment for men and women workers with family responsibilities and between such workers and other workers, the Parties undertake:

1. to take appropriate measures:

(a) to enable workers with family responsibilities to enter and remain in employment, as well as to re-enter employment after an absence due to those responsibilities, including measures in the field of vocational guidance and training;

(b) to take account of their needs in terms of conditions of employment and social security;

(c) to develop or promote services, public or private, in particular child daycare services and other childcare arrangements;

2. to provide a possibility for either parent to obtain, during a period after maternity leave, parental leave to take care of a child, the duration and conditions of which should be determined by national legislation, collective agreements or practice;

3. to ensure that family responsibilities shall not, as such, constitute a valid reason for termination of employment.

Article 28. The right of workers' representatives to protection in the undertaking and facilities to be accorded to them.

With a view to ensuring the effective exercise of the right of workers' representatives to carry out their functions, the Parties undertake to ensure that in the undertaking:

(a) they enjoy effective protection against acts prejudicial to them, including dismissal, based on their status or activities as workers' representatives within the undertaking;

(b) they are afforded such facilities as may be appropriate in order to enable them to carry out their functions promptly and efficiently, account being taken of the industrial relations system of the country and the needs, size and capabilities of the undertaking concerned.

Article 29. The right to information and consultation in collective redundancy procedures.

With a view to ensuring the effective exercise of the right of workers to be informed and consulted in situations of collective redundancies, the Parties undertake to ensure that employers shall inform and consult workers' representatives, in good time prior to such collective redundancies, on ways and means of avoiding collective redundancies or limiting their occurrence and mitigating their consequences, for example by recourse to accompanying social measures aimed, in particular, at aid for the redeployment or retraining of the workers concerned.

Article 30. The right to protection against poverty and social exclusion.

With a view to ensuring the effective exercise of the right to protection against poverty and social exclusion, the Parties undertake:

(a) to take measures within the framework of an overall and co-ordinated approach to promote the effective access of persons who live or risk living in a situation of social exclusion or poverty, as well as their families, to, in particular, employment, housing, training, education, culture and social and medical assistance;

(b) to review these measures with a view to their adaptation if necessary.

Article 31. The right to housing.

With a view to ensuring the effective exercise of the right to housing, the Parties undertake to take measures designed:

1. to promote access to housing of an adequate standard;

2. to prevent and reduce homelessness with a view to its gradual elimination;

3. to make the price of housing accessible to those without adequate resources.

PART III

Article A. Undertakings.

1. Subject to the provisions of Article B below, each of the Parties undertakes:

(a) to consider Part I of this Charter as a declaration of the aims which it will pursue by all appropriate means, as stated in the introductory paragraph of that part;

(b) to consider itself bound by at least six of the following nine articles of Part II of this Charter: Articles 1, 5, 6, 7, 12 13, 16, 19 and 20;

(c) to consider itself bound by an additional number of articles or numbered paragraphs of Part II of the Charter which it may select, provided that the total number of articles or numbered paragraphs by which it is bound is not less than sixteen articles or sixty-three numbered paragraphs.

2. The articles or paragraphs selected in accordance with sub-paragraphs b and c of paragraph 1 of this article shall be notified to the Secretary-General of the Council of Europe at the time when the instrument of ratification, acceptance or approval is deposited.

3. Any Party may, at a later date, declare by notification addressed to the Secretary-General that it considers itself bound by any articles or any numbered paragraphs of Part II of the Charter which it has not already accepted under the terms of paragraph 1 of this article. Such undertakings subsequently given shall be deemed to be an integral part of the ratification, acceptance or approval and shall have the same effect as from the first day of the month following the expiration of a period of one month after the date of the notification.

4. Each Party shall maintain a system of labour inspection appropriate to national conditions.

Article B. Links with the European Social Charter and the 1988 Additional Protocol.

No Contracting Party to the European Social Charter or Party to the Additional Protocol of 5 May 1988 may ratify, accept or approve this Charter without considering itself bound by at least the provisions corresponding to the provisions of the European Social Charter and, where appropriate, of the Additional Protocol, to which it was bound.

Acceptance of the obligations of any provision of this Charter shall, from the date of entry into force of those obligations for the Party concerned, result in the corresponding provision of the European Social Charter and, where appropriate, of its Additional Protocol of 1988 ceasing to apply to the Party concerned in the event of that Party being bound by the first of those instruments or by both instruments.

PART IV

Article C. Supervision of the implementation of the undertakings contained in this Charter.

The implementation of the legal obligations contained in this Charter shall be submitted to the same supervision as the European Social Charter.

Article D. Collective complaints.

1. The provisions of the Additional Protocol to the European Social Charter providing for a system of collective complaints shall apply to the undertakings given in this Charter for the States which have ratified the said Protocol.

2. Any State which is not bound by the Additional Protocol to the European Social Charter providing for a system of collective complaints may when depositing its instrument of ratification, acceptance or approval of this Charter or at any time thereafter, declare by notification addressed to the Secretary-General of the Council of Europe, that it accepts the supervision of its obligations under this Charter following the procedure provided for in the said Protocol.

PART V

Article E. Non-discrimination.

The enjoyment of the rights set forth in this Charter shall be secured without discrimination on any ground such as race, colour, sex, language, religion, political or other opinion, national extraction or social origin, health, association with a national minority, birth or other status.

Article F. Derogations in time of war or public emergency.

1. In time of war or other public emergency threatening the life of the nation any Party may take measures derogating from its obligations under this Charter to the extent strictly required by the exigencies of the situation, provided that such measures are not inconsistent with its other obligations under international law.

2. Any Party which has availed itself of this right of derogation shall, within a reasonable lapse of time, keep the Secretary-General of the Council of Europe fully informed of the measures taken and of the reasons therefor. It shall likewise inform the Secretary-General when such measures have ceased to operate and the provisions of the Charter which it has accepted are again being fully executed.

Article G. Restrictions.

1. The rights and principles set forth in Part I when effectively realised, and their effective exercise as provided for in Part II, shall not be subject to any restrictions or limitations not specified in those parts, except such as are prescribed by law and are necessary in a democratic society for the protection of the rights and freedoms of others or for the protection of public interest, national security, public health, or morals.

2. The restrictions permitted under this Charter to the rights and obligations set forth herein shall not be applied for any purpose other than that for which they have been prescribed.

Article H. Relations between the Charter and domestic law or international agreements.

The provisions of this Charter shall not prejudice the provisions of domestic law or of any bilateral or multilateral treaties, conventions or agreements which are already in force, or may come into force, under which more favourable treatment would be accorded to the persons protected.

Article I. Implementation of the undertakings given.

1. Without prejudice to the methods of implementation foreseen in these articles the relevant provisions of Articles 1 to 31 of Part II of this Charter shall be implemented by:

(a) laws or regulations;

(b) agreements between employers or employers' organizations and workers' organizations;

(c) combination of those two methods;

(d) other appropriate means.

2. Compliance with the undertakings deriving from the provisions of paragraphs 1, 2, 3, 4, 5 and 7 of Article 2, paragraphs 4, 6 and 7 of Article 7, paragraphs 1, 2, 3 and 5 of Article 10 and Articles 21 and 22 of Part II of this Charter shall be regarded as effective if the provisions are applied, in accordance with paragraph 1 of this article, to the great majority of the workers concerned.

(Article J. Amendments.)

PART VI

(Articles K–O. General provisions.)

APPENDIX

Note: In accordance with Article N of the Charter, the Appendix forms an integral part of the revised document.

Scope of the Revised European Social Charter in terms of persons protected.

1. Without prejudice to Article 12, paragraph 4, and Article 13, paragraph 4, the persons covered by Articles 1 to 17 and 20 to

31 include foreigners only in so far as they are nationals of other Parties lawfully resident or working regularly within the territory of the Party concerned, subject to the understanding that these articles are to be interpreted in the light of the provisions of Articles 18 and 19. This interpretation would not prejudice the extension of similar facilities to other persons by any of the Parties.

2. Each Party will grant to refugees as defined in the Convention relating to the Status of Refugees, signed in Geneva on 28 July 1951 and in the Protocol of 31 January 1967, and lawfully staying in its territory, treatment as favourable as possible, and in any case not less favourable than under the obligations accepted by the Party under the said convention and under any other existing international instruments applicable to those refugees.

3. Each Party will grant to stateless persons as defined in the Convention on the Status of Stateless Persons done in New York on 28 September 1954 and lawfully staying in its territory, treatment as favourable as possible and in any case not less favourable than under the obligations accepted by the Party under the said instrument and under any other existing international instruments applicable to those stateless persons . . .

Part II

Article 1, paragraph 2.

This provision shall not be interpreted as prohibiting or authorizing any union security clause or practice.

Article 2, paragraph 6.

Parties may provide that this provision shall not apply:

(a) to workers having a contract or employment relationship with a total duration not exceeding one month and/or with a working week not exceeding eight hours;

(b) where the contract or employment relationship is of a casual and/or specific nature, provided, in these cases, that its non-application is justified by objective considerations.

Article 3, paragraph 4.

It is understood that for the purposes of this provision the functions, organization and conditions of operation of these services shall be determined by national laws or regulations, collective agreements or other means appropriate to national conditions.

Article 4, paragraph 4.

This provision shall be so understood as not to prohibit immediate dismissal for any serious offence.

Article 4, paragraph 5.

It is understood that a Party may give the undertaking required in this paragraph if the great majority of workers are not permitted to suffer deductions from wages either by law or through collective agreements or arbitration awards, the exceptions being those persons not so covered.

Article 6, paragraph 4.

It is understood that each Party may, insofar as it is concerned, regulate the exercise of the right to strike by law, provided that any further restriction that this might place on the right can be justified under the terms of Article G.

Article 7, paragraph 2.

This provision does not prevent Parties from providing in their legislation that young persons not having reached the minimum age laid down may perform work insofar as it is absolutely necessary for their vocational training where such work is carried out in accordance with conditions prescribed by the competent authority and measures are taken to protect the health and safety of these young persons.

Article 7, paragraph 8.

It is understood that a Party may give the undertaking required in this paragraph if it fulfils the spirit of the undertaking by providing by law that the great majority of persons under eighteen years of age shall not be employed in night work.

Article 8, paragraph 2.

This provision shall not be interpreted as laying down an absolute prohibition. Exceptions could be made, for instance, in the following cases:

(a) if an employed woman has been guilty of misconduct which justifies breaking off the employment relationship;

(b) if the undertaking concerned ceases to operate;

(c) if the period prescribed in the employment contract has expired.

Article 12, paragraph 4.

The words 'and subject to the conditions laid down in such agreements' in the introduction to this paragraph are taken to imply *inter alia* that with regard to benefits which are available independently of any insurance contribution, a Party may require the completion of a prescribed period of residence before granting such benefits to nationals of other Parties.

Article 13, paragraph 4.

Governments not Parties to the European Convention on Social and Medical Assistance may ratify the Charter in respect of this paragraph provided that they grant to nationals of other Parties a treatment which is in conformity with the provisions of the said convention.

Article 16.

It is understood that the protection afforded in this provision covers single-parent families.

Article 17.

It is understood that this provision covers all persons below the age of 18 years, unless under the law applicable to the child majority is attained earlier, without prejudice to the other specific provisions provided by the Charter, particularly Article 7.

This does not imply an obligation to provide compulsory education up to the above-mentioned age.

Article 19, paragraph 6.

For the purpose of applying this provision, the term 'family of a foreign worker' is understood to mean at least the worker's spouse and unmarried children, as long as the latter are considered to be minors by the receiving State and are dependent on the migrant worker.

Article 20.

1. It is understood that social security matters, as well as other provisions relating to unemployment benefit, old age benefit and survivor's benefit, may be excluded from the scope of this article.

2. Provisions concerning the protection of women, particularly as regards pregnancy, confinement and the post-natal period, shall not be deemed to be discrimination as referred to in this article.

3. This article shall not prevent the adoption of specific measures aimed at removing *de facto* inequalities.

4. Occupational activities which, by reason of their nature or the context in which they are carried out, can be entrusted only to persons of a particular sex may be excluded from the scope of this article or some of its provisions. This provision is not to be interpreted as requiring the Parties to embody in laws or regulations a list of occupations which, by reason of their nature or the context in which they are carried out, may be reserved to persons of a particular sex.

Article 21 and 22.

1. For the purpose of the application of these articles, the term 'workers' representatives' means persons who are recognized as such under national legislation or practice.

2. The terms 'national legislation and practice' embrace as the case may be, in addition to laws and regulations, collective agreements, other agreements between employers and workers' representatives, customs as well as relevant case law.

3. For the purpose of the application of these articles, the term 'undertaking' is understood as referring to a set of tangible and intangible components, with or without legal personality, formed to produce goods or provide services for financial gain and with power to determine its own market policy.

4. It is understood that religious communities and their institutions may be excluded from the application of these articles, even if these institutions are 'undertakings' within the meaning of paragraph 3. Establishments pursuing activities which are inspired by certain ideals or guided by certain moral concepts, ideals and concepts which are protected by national legislation, may be excluded from the application of these articles to such an extent as is necessary to protect the orientation of the undertaking.

5. It is understood that where in a state the rights set out in these articles are exercised in the various establishments of the

undertaking, the Party concerned is to be considered as fulfilling the obligations deriving from these provisions.

6. The Parties may exclude from the field of application of these articles, those undertakings employing less than a certain number of workers, to be determined by national legislation or practice.

Article 22.

1. This provision affects neither the powers and obligations of states as regards the adoption of health and safety regulations for workplaces, nor the powers and responsibilities of the bodies in charge of monitoring their application.

2. The terms 'social and socio-cultural services and facilities' are understood as referring to the social and/or cultural facilities for workers provided by some undertakings such as welfare assistance, sports fields, rooms for nursing mothers, libraries, children's holiday camps, etc.

Article 23, paragraph 1.

For the purpose of the application of this paragraph, the term 'for as long as possible' refers to the elderly person's physical, psychological and intellectual capacities.

Article 24.

1. It is understood that for the purposes of this article the terms 'termination of employment' and 'terminated' mean termination of employment at the initiative of the employer.

2. It is understood that this article covers all workers but that a Party may exclude from some or all of its protection the following categories of employed persons:

(a) workers engaged under a contract of employment for a specified period of time or a specified task;

(b) workers undergoing a period of probation or a qualifying period of employment, provided that this is determined in advance and is of a reasonable duration;

(c) workers engaged on a casual basis for a short period.

3. For the purpose of this article the following, in particular, shall not constitute valid reasons for termination of employment:

(a) trade union membership or participation in union activities outside working hours, or, with the consent of the employer, within working hours;

(b) seeking office as, acting or having acted in the capacity of a workers' representative;

(c) the filing of a complaint or the participation in proceedings against an employer involving alleged violation of laws or regulations or recourse to competent administrative authorities;

(d) race, colour, sex, marital status, family responsibilities, pregnancy, religion, political opinion, national extraction or social origin;

(e) maternity or parental leave;

(f) temporary absence from work due to illness or injury.

4. It is understood that compensation or other appropriate relief in case of termination of employment without valid reasons shall be determined by national laws or regulations, collective agreements or other means appropriate to national conditions.

Article 25.

1. It is understood that the competent national authority may, by way of exemption and after consulting organizations of employers and workers, exclude certain categories of workers from the protection provided in this provision by reason of the special nature of their employment relationship.

2. it is understood that the definition of the term 'insolvency' must be determined by national law and practice.

3. The workers' claims covered by this provision shall include at least:

(a) the workers' claims for wages relating to a prescribed period, which shall not be less than three months under a privilege system and eight weeks under a guarantee system, prior to the insolvency or to the termination of employment;

(b) the workers' claims for holiday pay due as a result of work performed during the year in which the insolvency or the termination of employment occurred;

(c) the workers' claims for amounts due in respect of other types of paid absence relating to a prescribed period, which shall not be less than three months under a privilege system and eight weeks under a guarantee system, prior to the insolvency or the termination of the employment.

4. National laws or regulations may limit the protection of workers' claims to a prescribed amount, which shall be of a socially acceptable level.

Article 26.

It is understood that this article does not require that legislation be enacted by the Parties.

It is understood that paragraph 2 does not cover sexual harassment.

Article 27.

It is understood that this article applies to men and women workers with family responsibilities in relation to their dependent children as well as in relation to other members of their immediate family who clearly need their care or support where such responsibilities restrict their possibilities of preparing for, entering, participating in or advancing in economic activity. The terms 'dependent children' and 'other members of their immediate family who clearly need their care and support' mean persons defined as such by the national legislation of the Party concerned.

Article 28 and 29.

For the purpose of the application of this article, the term 'workers' representatives' means persons who are recognized as such under national legislation or practice.

Part III

It is understood that the Charter contains legal obligations of an international character, the application of which is submitted solely to the supervision provided for in Part IV thereof.

Part V

Article E.

A differential treatment based on an objective and reasonable justification shall not be deemed discriminatory.

Article F.

The terms 'in time of war or other public emergency' shall be so understood as to cover also the threat of war.

Article I.

It is understood that workers excluded in accordance with the appendix to Articles 21 and 22 are not taken into account in establishing the number of workers concerned.

Article J.

The term 'amendment' shall be extended so as to cover also the addition of new articles to the Charter.

Convention for Protection of Human Rights and Fundamental Freedoms (European Convention on Human Rights)

(4 November 1950)

Note: The text of the Convention has been amended according to the provisions of Protocol II, which entered into force on 1 November 1998 and replaced all previous protocols.

The governments signatory hereto, being members of the Council of Europe,

Considering the Universal Declaration of Human Rights proclaimed by the General Assembly of the United Nations on 10 December 1948;

Considering that this Declaration aims at securing the universal and effective recognition and observance of the Rights therein declared;

Considering that the aim of the Council of Europe is the achievement of greater unity between its members and that one of the methods by which that aim is to be pursued is the maintenance and further realisation of human rights and fundamental freedoms;

Reaffirming their profound belief in those fundamental freedoms which are the foundation of justice and peace in the world and are best maintained on the one hand by an effective political democracy and on the other by a common understanding and observance of the human rights upon which they depend;

Being resolved, as the governments of European countries which are like-minded and have a common heritage of political traditions, ideals, freedom and the rule of law, to take the first steps for the collective enforcement of certain of the rights stated in the Universal Declaration,

Have agreed as follows:

Article 1. Obligation to respect human rights.

The High Contracting Parties shall secure to everyone within their jurisdiction the rights and freedoms defined in Section I of this Convention.

I. RIGHTS AND FREEDOMS

Article 2. Right to life.

1. Everyone's right to life shall be protected by law. No one shall be deprived of his life intentionally save in the execution of a sentence of a court following his conviction of a crime for which this penalty is provided by law.

2. Deprivation of life shall not be regarded as inflicted in contravention of this article when it results from the use of force which is no more than absolutely necessary:

(a) in defence of any person from unlawful violence;

(b) in order to effect a lawful arrest or to prevent the escape of a person lawfully detained;

(c) in action lawfully taken for the purpose of quelling a riot or insurrection.

Article 3. Prohibition of torture.

No one shall be subjected to torture or to inhuman or degrading treatment or punishment.

Article 4. Prohibition of slavery and forced labour.

1. No one shall be held in slavery or servitude.

2. No one shall be required to perform forced or compulsory labour.

3. For the purpose of this article the term 'forced or compulsory labour' shall not include:

(a) any work required to be done in the ordinary course of detention imposed according to the provisions of Article 5 of this Convention or during conditional release from such detention;

(b) any service of a military character or, in case of conscientious objectors in countries where they are recognized, service exacted instead of compulsory military service;

(c) any service exacted in case of an emergency or calamity threatening the life or well-being of the community;

(d) any work or service which forms part of normal civic obligations.

Article 5. Right to liberty and security.

1. Everyone has the right to liberty and security of person. No one shall be deprived of his liberty save in the following cases and in accordance with a procedure prescribed by law:

(a) the lawful detention of a person after conviction by a competent court;

(b) the lawful arrest or detention of a person for non-compliance with the lawful order of a court or in order to secure the fulfilment of any obligation prescribed by law;

(c) the lawful arrest or detention of a person effected for the purpose of bringing him before the competent legal authority on reasonable suspicion of having committed an offence or when it is reasonably considered necessary to prevent his committing an offence or fleeing after having done so;

(d) the detention of a minor by lawful order for the purpose of educational supervision or his lawful detention for the purpose of bringing him before the competent legal authority;

(e) the lawful detention of persons for the prevention of the spreading of infectious diseases, of persons of unsound mind, alcoholics or drug addicts or vagrants;

(f) the lawful arrest or detention of a person to prevent his effecting an unauthorized entry into the country or of a person against whom action is being taken with a view to deportation or extradition.

2. Everyone who is arrested shall be informed promptly, in a language which he understands, of the reasons for his arrest and of any charge against him.

3. Everyone arrested or detained in accordance with the provisions of paragraph 1.c of this article shall be brought promptly before a judge or other officer authorized by law to exercise judicial power and shall be entitled to trial within a reasonable time or to release pending trial. Release may be conditioned by guarantees to appear for trial.

4. Everyone who is deprived of his liberty by arrest or detention shall be entitled to take proceedings by which the lawfulness of his detention shall be decided speedily by a court and his release ordered if the detention is not lawful.

5. Everyone who has been the victim of arrest or detention in contravention of the provisions of this article shall have an enforceable right to compensation.

Article 6. Right to a fair trial.

1. In the determination of his civil rights and obligations or of any criminal charge against him, everyone is entitled to a fair and public hearing within a reasonable time by an independent and impartial tribunal established by law. Judgment shall be pronounced publicly but the press and public may be excluded from all or part of the trial in the interests of morals, public order or national security in a democratic society, where the interests of juveniles or the protection of the private life of the parties so require, or to the extent strictly necessary in the opinion of the court in special circumstances where publicity would prejudice the interests of justice.

2. Everyone charged with a criminal offence shall be presumed innocent until proved guilty according to law.

3. Everyone charged with a criminal offence has the following minimum rights:

(a) to be informed promptly, in a language which he understands and in detail, of the nature and cause of the accusation against him;

(b) to have adequate time and facilities for the preparation of his defence;

(c) to defend himself in person or through legal assistance of his own choosing or, if he has not sufficient means to pay for legal assistance, to be given it free when the interests of justice so require;

(d) to examine or have examined witnesses against him and to obtain the attendance and examination of witnesses on his behalf under the same conditions as witnesses against him;

(e) to have the free assistance of an interpreter if he cannot understand or speak the language used in court.

Article 7. No punishment without law.

1. No one shall be held guilty of any criminal offence on account of any act or omission which did not constitute a criminal offence under national or international law at the time when it was committed. Nor shall a heavier penalty be imposed than the one that was applicable at the time the criminal offence was committed.

2. This article shall not prejudice the trial and punishment of any person for any act or omission which, at the time when it was committed, was criminal according to the general principles of law recognized by civilized nations.

Article 8. Right to respect for private and family life.

1. Everyone has the right to respect for his private and family life, his home and his correspondence.

2. There shall be no interference by a public authority with the exercise of this right except such as is in accordance with the law and is necessary in a democratic society in the interests of national security, public safety or the economic well-being of the country, for the prevention of disorder or crime, for the protection of health or morals, or for the protection of the rights and freedoms of others.

Article 9. Freedom of thought, conscience and religion.

1. Everyone has the right to freedom of thought, conscience and religion; this right includes freedom to change his religion or belief and freedom, either alone or in community with others and in public or private, to manifest his religion or belief, in worship, teaching, practice and observance.

2. Freedom to manifest one's religion or beliefs shall be subject only to such limitations as are prescribed by law and are necessary in a democratic society in the interests of public safety, for the protection of public order, health or morals, or for the protection of the rights and freedoms of others.

Article 10. Freedom of expression.

1. Everyone has the right to freedom of expression. This right shall include freedom to hold opinions and to receive and impart information and ideas without interference by public authority and regardless of frontiers. This article shall not prevent States from requiring the licensing of broadcasting, television or cinema enterprises.

2. The exercise of these freedoms, since it carries with it duties and responsibilities, may be subject to such formalities, conditions, restrictions or penalties as are prescribed by law and are necessary in a democratic society, in the interests of national security, territorial integrity or public safety, for the prevention of disorder or crime, for the protection of health or morals, for the protection of the reputation or rights of others, for preventing the disclosure of information received in confidence, or for maintaining the authority and impartiality of the judiciary.

Article 11. Freedom of assembly and association.

1. Everyone has the right to freedom of peaceful assembly and to freedom of association with others, including the right to form and to join trade unions for the protection of his interests.

2. No restrictions shall be placed on the exercise of these rights other than such as are prescribed by law and are necessary in a democratic society in the interests of national security or public safety, for the prevention of disorder or crime, for the protection of health or morals or for the protection of the rights and freedoms of others. This article shall not prevent the imposition of lawful restrictions on the exercise of these rights by members of the armed forces, of the police or of the administration of the State.

Article 12. Right to marry.

Men and women of marriageable age have the right to marry and to found a family, according to the national laws governing the exercise of this right.

Article 13. Right to an effective remedy.

Everyone whose rights and freedoms as set forth in this Convention are violated shall have an effective remedy before a national authority notwithstanding that the violation has been committed by persons acting in an official capacity.

Article 14. Prohibition of discrimination.

The enjoyment of the rights and freedoms set forth in this Convention shall be secured without discrimination on any ground such as sex, race, colour, language, religion, political or other opinion, national or social origin, association with a national minority, property, birth or other status.

Article 15. Derogation in time of emergency.

1. In time of war or other public emergency threatening the life of the nation any High Contracting Party may take measures derogating from its obligations under this Convention to the extent strictly required by the exigencies of the situation, provided that such measures are not inconsistent with its other obligations under international law.

2. No derogation from Article 2, except in respect of deaths resulting from lawful acts of war, or from Articles 3, 4 (paragraph 1) and 7 shall be made under this provision.

3. Any High Contracting Party availing itself of this right of derogation shall keep the Secretary-General of the Council of Europe fully informed of the measures which it has taken and the reasons therefor. It shall also inform the Secretary-General of the Council of Europe when such measures have ceased to operate and the provisions of the Convention are again being fully executed.

Article 16. Restrictions on political activity of aliens.

Nothing in Articles 10, 11 and 14 shall be regarded as preventing the High Contracting Parties from imposing restrictions on the political activity of aliens.

Article 17. Prohibition of abuse of rights.

Nothing in this Convention may be interpreted as implying for any State, group or person any right to engage in any activity or perform any act aimed at the destruction of any of the rights and freedoms set forth herein or at their limitation to a greater extent than is provided for in the Convention.

Article 18. Limitation on use of restrictions on rights.

The restrictions permitted under this Convention to the said rights and freedoms shall not be applied for any purpose other than those for which they have been prescribed.

II. EUROPEAN COURT OF HUMAN RIGHTS

Article 19. Establishment of the Court.

To ensure the observance of the engagements undertaken by the High Contracting Parties in the Convention and the Protocols thereto, there shall be set up a European Court of Human Rights, hereinafter referred to as 'the Court'. It shall function on a permanent basis.

Article 20. Number of judges.

The Court shall consist of a number of judges equal to that of the High Contracting Parties.

Article 21. Criteria for office.

1. The judges shall be of high moral character and must either possess the qualifications required for appointment to high judicial officer or be jurisconsults of recognized competence.

2. The judges shall sit on the Court in their individual capacity.

3. During their term of office the judges shall not engage in any activity which is incompatible with their independence, impartiality or with the demands of a full-time office; all questions arising from the application of this paragraph shall be decided by the Court.

Article 22. Election of judges.

1. The judges shall be elected by the Parliamentary Assembly with respect to each High Contracting Party by a majority of votes cast from a list of three candidates nominated by the High Contracting Party.

2. The same procedure shall be followed to complete the Court in the event of the accession of new High Contracting Parties and in filling casual vacancies.

Article 23. Terms of office.

1. The judges shall be elected for a period of six years. They may be re-elected. However, the terms of office of one-half of the judges elected at the first election shall expire at the end of three years.

2. The judges whose terms of office are to expire at the end of the initial period of three years shall be chosen by lot by the Secretary-General of the Council of Europe immediately after their election.

3. In order to ensure that, as far as possible, the terms of office of one-half of the judges are renewed every three years, the Parliamentary Assembly may decide, before proceeding to any subsequent election, that the term or terms of office of one or more judges to be elected shall be for a period other than six years but not more than nine and not less than three years.

4. In cases where more than one term of office is involved and where the Parliamentary Assembly applies the preceding paragraph, the allocation of the terms of office shall be effected by a drawing of lots by the Secretary-General of the Council of Europe immediately after the election.

5. A judge elected to replace a judge whose term of office has not expired shall hold office for the remainder of his predecessor's term.

6. The terms of office of judges shall expire when they reach the age of 70.

7. The judges shall hold office until replaced. They shall, however, continue to deal with such cases as they already have under consideration.

Article 24. Dismissal.

No judge may be dismissed from his office unless the other judges decide by a majority of two-thirds that he has ceased to fulfil the required conditions.

Article 25. Registry and legal secretaries.

The Court shall have a registry, the functions and organization of which shall be laid down in the rules of the Court. The Court shall be assisted by legal secretaries.

Article 26. Plenary Court.

The plenary Court shall

(a) elect its President and one or two Vice-Presidents for a period of three years; they may be re-elected;

(b) set up Chambers, constituted for a fixed period of time;

(c) elect the Presidents of the Chambers of the Court; they may be re-elected;

(d) adopt the rules of the Court, and

(e) elect the Registrar and one or more Deputy Registrars.

Article 27. Committees, Chambers and Grand Chamber.

1. To consider cases brought before it, the Court shall sit in committees of three judges, in Chambers of seven judges and in a Grand Chamber of seventeen judges. The Court's Chambers shall set up committees for a fixed period of time.

2. There shall sit as an *ex officio* member of the Chamber and the Grand Chamber the judge elected in respect of the State Party concerned or, if there is none or if he is unable to sit, a person of its choice who shall sit in the capacity of judge.

3. The Grand Chamber shall also include the President of the Court, the Vice-Presidents, the Presidents of the Chambers and other judges chosen in accordance with the rules of the Court. When a case is referred to the Grand Chamber under Article 43, no judge from the Chamber which rendered the judgment shall sit in the Grand Chamber, with the exception of the President of the Chamber and the judge who sat in respect of the State Party concerned.

Article 28. Declarations of inadmissibility by committees.

A committee may, by a unanimous vote, declare inadmissible or strike out of its list of cases an application submitted under Article 34 where such a decision can be taken without further examination. The decision shall be final.

Article 29. Decisions by Chambers on admissibility and merits.

1. If no decision is taken under Article 28, a Chamber shall decide on the admissibility and merits of individual applications submitted under Article 34.

2. A Chamber shall decide on the admissibility and merits of inter-State applications submitted under Article 33.

3. The decision on admissibility shall be taken separately unless the Court, in exceptional cases, decides otherwise.

Article 30. Relinquishment of jurisdiction to the Grand Chamber.

Where a case pending before a Chamber raises a serious question affecting the interpretation of the Convention or the protocols thereto, or where the resolution of a question before the Chamber might have a result inconsistent with a judgment previously delivered by the Court, the Chamber may, at any time before it has rendered its judgment, relinquish jurisdiction in favour of the Grand Chamber, unless one of the parties to the case objects.

Article 31. Powers of the Grand Chamber.

The Grand Chamber shall

(a) determine applications submitted either under Article 33 or Article 34 when a Chamber has relinquished jurisdiction under Article 30 or when the case has been referred to it under Article 43; and

(b) consider requests for advisory opinions submitted under Article 47.

Article 32. Jurisdiction of the Court.

1. The jurisdiction of the Court shall extend to all matters concerning the interpretation and application of the Convention and the protocols thereto which are referred to it as provided in Articles 33, 34 and 47.

2. In the event of dispute as to whether the Court has jurisdiction, the Court shall decide.

Article 33. Inter-State cases.

Any High Contracting Party may refer to the Court any alleged breach of the provisions of the Convention and the protocols thereto by another High Contracting Party.

Article 34. Individual applications.

The Court may receive applications from any person, non-governmental organization or group of individuals claiming to be the victim of a violation by one of the High Contracting Parties of the rights set forth in the Convention or the protocols thereto. The High Contracting Parties undertake not to hinder in any way the effective exercise of this right.

Article 35. Admissibility criteria.

1. The Court may only deal with the matter after all domestic remedies have been exhausted, according to the generally recognized rules of international law, and within a period of six months from the date on which the final decision was taken.

2. The Court shall not deal with any application submitted under Article 34 that

(a) is anonymous; or

(b) is substantially the same as a matter that has already been examined by the Court or has already been submitted to another procedure of international investigation or settlement and contains no relevant new information.

3. The Court shall declare inadmissible any individual application submitted under Article 34 which it considers incompatible with the provisions of the Convention or the protocols thereto, manifestly ill-founded, or an abuse of the right of application.

4. The Court shall reject any application which it considers inadmissible under this Article. It may do so at any stage of the proceedings.

Article 36. Third party intervention.

1. In all cases before a Chamber of the Grand Chamber, a High Contracting Party one of whose nationals is an applicant shall have the right to submit written comments and to take part in hearings.

2. The President of the Court may, in the interest of the proper administration of justice, invite any High Contracting Party which is not a party to the proceedings or any person concerned who is not the applicant to submit written comments or take part in hearings.

Article 37. Striking out applications.

1. The Court may at any stage of the proceedings decide to strike an application out of its list of cases where the circumstances lead to the conclusion that

(a) the applicant does not intend to pursue his application; or

(b) the matter has been resolved; or

(c) for any other reason established by the Court, it is no longer justified to continue the examination of the application.

However, the Court shall continue the examination of the application if respect for human rights as defined in the Convention and the protocols thereto so requires.

2. The Court may decide to restore an application to its list of cases if it considers that the circumstances justify such a course.

Article 38. Examination of the case and friendly settlement proceedings.

1. If the Court declares the application admissible, it shall

(a) pursue the examination of the case, together with the representatives of the parties, and if need be, undertake an investigation, for the effective conduct of which the States concerned shall furnish all necessary facilities;

(b) place itself at the disposal of the parties concerned with a view to securing a friendly settlement of the matter on the basis of respect for human rights as defined in the Convention and the protocols thereto.

2. Proceedings conducted under paragraph 1(b) shall be confidential.

Article 39. Finding of a friendly settlement.

If a friendly settlement is effected, the Court shall strike the case out of its list by means of a decision which shall be confined to a brief statement of the facts and of the solution reached.

Article 40. Public hearings and access to documents.

1. Hearings shall be in public unless the Court in exceptional circumstances decides otherwise.

2. Documents deposited with the Registrar shall be accessible to the public unless the President of the Court decides otherwise.

Article 41. Just satisfaction.

If the Court finds that there has been a violation of the Convention or the protocols thereto, and if the internal law of the High Contracting Party concerned allows only partial reparation to be made, the Court shall, if necessary, afford just satisfaction to the injured party.

Article 42. Judgments of Chambers.

Judgments of Chambers shall become final in accordance with the provisions of Article 44, paragraph 2.

Article 43. Referral to the Grand Chamber.

1. Within a period of three months from the date of the judgment of the Chamber, any party to the case may, in exceptional cases, request that the case be referred to the Grand Chamber.

2. A panel of five judges of the Grand Chamber shall accept the request if the case raises a serious question affecting the interpretation or application of the Convention or the protocols thereto, or a serious issue of general importance.

3. If the panel accepts the request, the Grand Chamber shall decide the case by means of a judgment.

Article 44. Final judgments.

1. The judgment of the Grand Chamber shall be final.

2. The judgment of a Chamber shall become final

(a) when the parties declare that they will not request that the case be referred to the Grand Chamber; or

(b) three months after the date of the judgment, if reference of the case to the Grand Chamber has not been requested; or

(c) when the panel of the Grand Chamber rejects the request to refer under Article 43.

3. The final judgment shall be published.

Article 45. Reasons for judgments and decisions.

1. Reasons shall be given for judgments as well as for decisions declaring applications admissible or inadmissible.

2. If a judgment does not represent, in whole or in part, the unanimous opinion of the judges, any judge shall be entitled to deliver a separate opinion.

Article 46. Binding force and execution of judgments.

1. The High Contracting Parties undertake to abide by the final judgment of the Court in any case to which they are parties.

2. The final judgment of the Court shall be transmitted to the Committee of Ministers, which shall supervise its execution.

Article 47. Advisory opinions.

1. The Court may, at the request of the Committee of Ministers, give advisory opinions on legal questions concerning the interpretation of the Convention and the protocols thereto.

2. Such opinions shall not deal with any question relating to the content or scope of the rights or freedoms defined in Section I of the Convention and the protocols thereto, or with any other question which the Court or the Committee of Ministers might have to consider in consequence of any such proceedings as could be instituted in accordance with the Convention.

3. Decision of the Committee of Ministers to request an advisory opinion of the Court shall require a majority vote of the representatives entitled to sit on the Committee.

Article 48. Advisory jurisdiction of the Court.

The Court shall decide whether a request for an advisory opinion submitted by the Committee of Ministers is within its competence as defined in Article 47.

Article 49. Reasons for advisory opinions.

1. Reasons shall be given for advisory opinions of the Court.

2. If the advisory opinion does not represent, in whole or in part, the unanimous opinion of the judges, any judge shall be entitled to deliver a separate opinion.

3. Advisory opinions of the Court shall be communicated to the Committee of Ministers.

Article 50. Expenditure on the Court.

The expenditure on the Court shall be borne by the Council of Europe.

Article 51. Privileges and immunities of judges.

The judges shall be entitled, during the exercise of their functions, to the privileges and immunities provided for in Article 40 of the Statute of the Council of Europe and in the agreements made thereunder.

III. MISCELLANEOUS PROVISIONS

Article 52. Inquiries by the Secretary-General.

On receipt of a request from the Secretary-General of the Council of Europe any High Contracting Party shall furnish an explanation of the manner in which its internal law ensures the effective implementation of any of the provisions of the Convention.

Article 53. Safeguard for existing human rights.

Nothing in this Convention shall be construed as limiting or derogating from any of the human rights and fundamental freedoms which may be ensured under the laws of any High Contracting Party or under any other agreement to which it is a Party.

Article 54. Powers of the Committee of Ministers.

Nothing in this Convention shall prejudice the powers conferred on the Committee of Ministers by the Statute of the Council of Europe.

Article 55. Exclusion of other means of dispute settlement.

The High Contracting Parties agree that, except by special agreement, they will not avail themselves of treaties, conventions or declarations in force between them for the purpose of submitting, by way of petition, a dispute arising out of the interpretation or application of this Convention to a means of settlement other than those provided for in this Convention.

Article 56. Territorial application.

1. Any State may at the time of its ratification or at any time thereafter declare by notification addressed to the Secretary-General of the Council of Europe that the present Convention shall, subject to paragraph 4 of this Article, extend to all or any of the territories for whose international relations it is responsible.

2. The Convention shall extend to the territory or territories named in the notification as from the thirtieth day after the receipt of this notification by the Secretary-General of the Council of Europe.

3. The provisions of this Convention shall be applied in such territories with due regard, however, to local requirements.

4. Any State which has made a declaration in accordance with paragraph 1 of this article may at any time thereafter declare on behalf of one or more of the territories to which the declaration relates that it accepts the competence of the Court to receive applications from individuals, non-governmental organizations or groups of individuals as provided by Article 34 of the Convention.

(Article 57. Reservations.)

(Article 58. Denunciation.)

(Article 59. Signature and ratification.)

ECONOMIC COMMUNITY OF WEST AFRICAN STATES—ECOWAS

Address: ECOWAS Secretariat and Conference Centre, 60 Yakubu Gowon Crescent, Asokoro, Abuja, Nigeria.

Telephone: (9) 3147647; **fax:** (9) 3147646; **e-mail:** info@ecowasmail.net; **internet:** www.ecowas.int.

The Treaty of Lagos, establishing ECOWAS, was signed in May 1975 by 15 states, with the object of promoting trade, co-operation and self-reliance in West Africa. Outstanding protocols bringing certain key features of the Treaty into effect were ratified in November 1976. Cape Verde joined in 1977. A revised ECOWAS treaty, designed to accelerate economic integration and to increase political co-operation, was signed in July 1993.

MEMBERS

Benin	Ghana	Niger
Burkina Faso	Guinea	Nigeria
Cape Verde	Guinea-Bissau	Senegal
Côte d'Ivoire	Liberia	Sierra Leone
The Gambia	Mali	Togo

Organization

(April 2002)

AUTHORITY OF HEADS OF STATE AND GOVERNMENT

The Authority is the supreme decision-making organ of the Community, with responsibility for its general development and realization of its objectives. The Chairman is drawn from the member states in turn. In August 1997 ECOWAS heads of state decided that the Authority (previously convened on an annual basis) should meet twice each year to enhance monitoring and co-ordination of the Community's activities.

COUNCIL OF MINISTERS

The Council consists of two representatives from each member country; a chairman is drawn from each country in turn. It meets at least twice a year, and is responsible for the running of the Community.

EXECUTIVE SECRETARIAT

The Executive Secretary is elected for a four-year term, which may be renewed once only.

Executive Secretary: MOHAMED IBN CHAMBAS (Ghana).

SPECIALIZED TECHNICAL COMMISSIONS

There are eight commissions, comprising representatives of each member state, which prepare Community projects and programmes in the following areas:

(i) Food and Agriculture;

(ii) Industry, Science and Technology, and Energy;

(iii) Environment and Natural Resources;

(iv) Transport, Communications, and Tourism;

(v) Trade, Customs, Taxation, Statistics, and Money and Payments;

(vi) Political, Judicial and Legal Affairs, Regional Security, and Integration;

(vii) Human Resources, Information, and Social and Cultural Affairs; and

(viii) Administration and Finance.

ECOWAS PARLIAMENT

The inaugural session of the 120-member ECOWAS Parliament, based in Abuja, Nigeria, was held in November 2000. Members of the Parliament are elected for five-year terms. Each ECOWAS member state is allocated a minimum of five seats; the distribution of the remaining 45 seats is proportionate to the relative sizes of member states' populations. There is a co-ordinating administrative bureau, comprising a speaker, elected for a five-year term of office, and other elected officials. There are 13 technical committees covering the Parliament's areas of activity, including defence and security, economics and finance, energy, environment and natural resources, foreign affairs, human rights, laws and regulations, rural development, transport and communications, and women's and children's affairs.

Speaker: Prof. ALI NOUHOUM DIALLO (Mali).

ECOWAS COURT OF JUSTICE

The Court of Justice, established in January 2001, is based in Abuja, Nigeria, and comprises seven judges who serve a five-year renewable term of office.

Chief Justice: HASSINE DONLI (Nigeria).

ECOWAS FUND FOR CO-OPERATION, COMPENSATION AND DEVELOPMENT

Address: BP 2704, blvd du 13 Janvier, Lomé, Togo.

Telephone: 216864; **fax:** 218684; **e-mail:** info-fund@ecowasmail.net; **internet:** www.ecowas-fund.org.

The Fund is administered by a Board of Directors. The chief executive of the Fund is the Managing Director, who holds office for a renewable term of four years. There is a staff of 100. The authorized cap. of the Fund is US $500m.; paid-up cap. totalled $84m. in 2000. In 1988 agreements were reached with the African Development Bank and the Islamic Development Bank on the co-financing of projects and joint training of staff. Efforts have been initiated to enhance the Fund's financial resources, by opening its capital to non-regional participants. At a summit of ECOWAS heads of state and government in December 1999 it was announced that the Fund was to be converted into the ECOWAS Investment and Development Bank, which was to have two divisions, a Regional Investment Bank and a Regional Development Fund. The ECOWAS summit held in December 2001 urged that the protocol on establishing the Investment and Development Bank be ratified during 2002.

Managing Director: DRABO D. BARTHELAMY (acting).

Activities

ECOWAS aims to promote co-operation and development in economic, social and cultural activity, particularly in the fields for which specialized technical commissions (see above) are appointed, to raise the standard of living of the people of the member countries, increase and maintain economic stability, improve relations among member countries and contribute to the progress and development of Africa. ECOWAS is committed to abolishing all obstacles to the free movement of people, services and capital, and to promoting: harmonization of agricultural policies; common projects in marketing, research and the agriculturally-based industries; joint development of economic and industrial policies and elimination of disparities in levels of development; and common monetary policies. The ECOWAS treaty provides for compensation for states whose import duties are reduced through trade liberalization and contains a clause permitting safeguard measures in favour of any country affected by economic disturbances through the application of the treaty.

Initial slow progress in achieving many of ECOWAS' aims was attributed to the reluctance of some governments to implement policies at the national level, their failure to provide the agreed financial resources, and the absence of national links with the Secretariat; to the high cost of compensating loss of customs revenue; and to the existence of numerous other intergovernmental organizations in the region (in particular the Union économique et monétaire ouest-africaine—UEMOA, q.v., which replaced the francophone Communauté économique de l'Afrique de l'ouest in 1994). In respect of the latter obstacle to progress, however, ECOWAS and UEMOA resolved in February 2000 to create a single monetary zone (see below). In October ECOWAS and the European Union (EU) held their first joint high-level meeting, at which the EU pledged financial support for ECOWAS' economic integration programme, and, in April 2001 it was announced that the IMF (q.v.) had agreed to provide technical assistance for the programme.

A revised treaty for the Community was drawn up by an ECOWAS Committee of Eminent Persons in 1991–92, and was signed at the ECOWAS summit conference that took place in Cotonou, Benin, in July 1993. The treaty, which was to extend economic and political co-operation among member states, designated the achievement of a common market and a single currency as economic objectives, while in the political sphere it envisaged the establishment of an ECOWAS parliament, an economic and social council, and an ECOWAS court of justice to enforce Community decisions. The treaty also formally assigned the Community with the responsibility of preventing and settling regional conflicts. At a summit meeting held in Abuja, Nigeria, in August 1994, ECOWAS heads of state and government signed a protocol agreement for the establishment of a regional parliament. The meeting also adopted a Convention on Extradition of non-political offenders. The new ECOWAS treaty entered into effect in August 1995, having received the required number of ratifications. A draft protocol providing for the creation of a mechanism for the prevention, management and settlement of conflicts, and for the maintenance of peace in the region, was approved by ECOWAS heads of state and government in December 1999. The protocol establishing the ECOWAS Parliament came into effect in March 2000. The inaugural session of the Parliament was held in Abuja, Nigeria, in November, and in January 2001 the seven judges of the ECOWAS Court of Justice were sworn in. At December 2000 the revised ECOWAS treaty had been ratified by 13 member states (all but Cape Verde, Guinea Bissau and Mauritania; Mauritania left the grouping at the end of that month).

TRADE AND MONETARY UNION

Under the founding ECOWAS treaty elimination of tariffs and other obstructions to trade among member states, and the establishment of a common external tariff, were planned over a transitional period of 15 years, from 1975. At the 1978 Conference of Heads of State and Government it was decided that from May 1979 no member state might increase its customs tariff on goods from another member. This was regarded as the first step towards the abolition of customs duties within the Community. During the first two years import duties on intra-community trade were to be maintained, and then eliminated in phases over the next eight years. Quotas and other restrictions of equivalent effect were to be abolished in the first 10 years. It was envisaged that in the remaining five years all differences between external customs tariffs would be abolished.

In 1980 ECOWAS heads of state and government decided to establish a free-trade area for unprocessed agricultural products and handicrafts from May 1981. Tariffs on industrial products made by specified community enterprises were also to be abolished from that date, but implementation was delayed by difficulties in defining the enterprises. From 1 January 1990 tariffs were eliminated on 25 listed items manufactured in ECOWAS member states. Over the ensuing decade, tariffs on other industrial products were to be eliminated as follows: the 'most-developed' countries of ECOWAS (Côte d'Ivoire, Ghana, Nigeria and Senegal) were to abolish tariffs on 'priority' products within four years and on 'non-priority' products within six years; the second group (Benin, Guinea, Liberia, Sierra Leone and Togo) were to abolish tariffs on 'priority' products within six years, and on 'non-priority' products within eight years; and the 'least-developed' members (Burkina Faso, Cape Verde, The Gambia, Guinea-Bissau, Mali and Niger) were to abolish tariffs on 'priority' products within eight years and on 'non-priority' products within 10 years. By December 2000 only Benin had removed tariffs on all industrial products. By mid-2001 an estimated 1,360 products had been approved under the trade liberalization scheme.

In 1990 ECOWAS heads of state and government agreed to adopt measures that would create a single monetary zone and remove barriers to trade in goods that originated in the Community. ECOWAS regards monetary union as necessary to encourage investment in the region, since it would greatly facilitate capital transactions with foreign countries. In September 1992 it was announced that, as part of efforts to enhance monetary co-operation and financial harmonization in the region, the West African Clearing House was to be restructured as the West African Monetary Agency (WAMA, see p. 537). As a specialized agency of ECOWAS, WAMA was to be responsible for administering an ECOWAS exchange rate system (EERS) and for establishing the single monetary zone. A credit guarantee scheme and travellers' cheque system were to be established in association with the EERS. The agreement founding WAMA was signed by the Governors of the central banks of ECOWAS member states, meeting in Banjul, The Gambia, in March 1996. In July the Authority agreed to impose a common value-added tax (VAT) on consumer goods, in order to rationalize indirect taxation and to stimulate greater intra-Community trade. In August 1997 ECOWAS heads of state and government appointed an *ad hoc* monitoring committee to promote and oversee the implementation of trade liberalization measures and the establishment of a single monetary zone by 2000. (This deadline was subsequently revised to 1 January 2004.) The meeting also authorized the introduction of the regional travellers' cheque scheme. In March 1998 senior customs officials of ECOWAS countries agreed to harmonize customs policies and administrations, in order to facilitate intra-Community trade, and to pursue the objective of establishing a common external tariff by 2000. (This deadline was not met. The ECOWAS Authority summit held in December 2000 in Bamako, Mali, determined that the harmonization of member countries' tariff structures should be accelerated to facilitate the implementation of the planned customs union.) In October 1998 the travellers' cheque scheme was formally inaugurated at a meeting of ECOWAS heads of state. The cheques were to be issued by WAMA in denominations of a West African Unit of Account and convertible into each local currency at the rate of one Special Drawing Right (SDR—see IMF p. 171). The cheques entered into circulation on 1 July 1999. In December 1999 the ECOWAS Authority determined to pursue a 'Fast Track Approach' to economic integration, involving a two-track implementation of related measures. In April 2000 seven, predominantly anglophone, ECOWAS member states—Cape Verde, Gambia, Ghana, Guinea, Liberia, Nigeria and Sierra Leone—issued the 'Accra Declaration', in which they agreed to establish by 1 January 2003 a second West African monetary union to coexist alongside UEMOA, which unites eight, mainly francophone, ECOWAS member states. As preconditions for adopting a single currency and common monetary and exchange rate policy, the member states of the second West African monetary union were to attain a number of convergence criteria, including: a satisfactory level of price stability; sustainable budget deficits; a reduction in inflation; and the maintenance of an adequate level of foreign exchange reserves. The two complementary monetary unions were expected to harmonize their economic programmes, with a view to effecting a merger prior to the planned creation of a single West African Monetary Zone (WAMZ) in 2004. The proposed merger of the two monetary unions was outlined in an action plan adopted by ECOWAS and UEMOA in February 2000. The ECOWAS Authority summit in December approved the establishment of a West African Monetary Institute to prepare for the formation of a West African Central Bank. In December 2001 the Authority determined that the currency of the second West African monetary union would be known as the 'eco' and authorized the establishment—scheduled for April 2002— of an exchange rate mechanism.

In December 1992 ECOWAS ministers agreed on the institutionalization of an ECOWAS trade fair, in order to promote trade liberalization and intra-Community trade. The first trade fair, which was held in Dakar, Senegal, in May/June 1995, was attended by some 400 private businesses from member states. A second trade fair was staged in Accra, Ghana, in March 1999.

TRAVEL, TRANSPORT AND COMMUNICATIONS

In 1979 ECOWAS heads of state signed a Protocol relating to free circulation of the region's citizens and to rights of residence and establishment of commercial enterprises. The first provision (the right of entry without a visa) came into force in 1980. An optional ECOWAS travel certificate, valid for travel within the

Community in place of a national passport, was established in July 1985. The second provision of the 1979 Protocol, allowing unlimited rights of residence, was signed in 1986 (although Nigeria indicated that unskilled workers and certain categories of professionals would not be allowed to stay for an indefinite period) and came into force in 1989. The third provision, concerning the right to establish a commercial enterprise in another member state was signed in 1990. In July 1992 the ECOWAS Authority formulated a Minimum Agenda for Action for the implementation of Community agreements regarding the free movement of goods and people, for example the removal of non-tariff barriers, the simplification of customs and transit procedures and a reduction in the number of control posts on international roads. By mid-1996 the ECOWAS summit meeting observed that few measures had been adopted by member states to implement the Minimum Agenda, and emphasized that it remained a central element of the Community's integration process. In April 1997 Gambian and Senegalese finance and trade officials concluded an agreement on measures to facilitate the export of goods via Senegal to neighbouring countries, in accordance with ECOWAS protocols relating to inter-state road transit arrangements. An Inter-state Road Transit Authority has been established. A Brown Card scheme provides recognized third-party liability insurance throughout the region. In October 2001 an ECOWAS passport was reported to be ready for issuance; the ECOWAS travel certificate was to remain in operation, while national passports were to be gradually eliminated over a period of five years.

In February 1996 ECOWAS and several private-sector partners established ECOAir Ltd, based in Abuja, Nigeria, which was to develop a regional airline. It was envisaged that ECOAir would become operative in 2002. The establishment of a regional shipping company, ECOMARINE, is also planned.

In August 1996 the initial phase of a programme to improve regional telecommunications was reported to have been completed. Some US $35m. had been granted for project financing in eight ECOWAS countries. A second phase of the programme (INTELCOM II), which aimed to modernize and expand the region's telecommunications services, was initiated by ECOWAS heads of state in August 1997. A West African Telecommunications Regulators' Association was established, under the auspices of ECOWAS, in September 2000.

A programme for the development of an integrated regional road network was adopted in 1980. Under the programme, two major trans-regional roads were to be completed: the Trans-Coastal Highway, linking Lagos, Nigeria, with Nouackchott, Mauritania (4,767 km); and the Trans-Sahelian Highway, linking Dakar, Senegal, with N'Djamena, Chad (4,633 km). By the end of 2000 about 83% of the trans-coastal route was reportedly complete, and about 87% of the trans-Sahelian route.

ECONOMIC AND INDUSTRIAL DEVELOPMENT

In November 1984 ECOWAS heads of state and government approved the establishment of a private regional investment bank, to be known as Ecobank Transnational Inc. The bank, which was based in Lomé, Togo, opened in March 1988. ECOWAS has a 10% share in the bank. By the end of 2000 Ecobank affiliates were operating in 11 member countries.

The West African Industrial Forum, sponsored by ECOWAS, is held every two years to promote regional industrial investment. Community ministers of industry are implementing an action plan on the formulation of a West African Industrial Master Plan identifying strategies for stimulating regional economic development and attracting external investment.

In September 1995 Nigeria, Ghana, Togo and Benin resolved to develop a gas pipeline to connect Nigerian gas supplies to the other countries. In August 1999 the participating countries, together with two petroleum companies operating in Nigeria, signed an agreement on the financing and construction of the pipeline, which was expected to become operational in 2002. During 2000 a Community initiative to connect the electricity supply networks throughout the region was under consideration. The implementation of a planned energy exchange scheme, known as the West African Power Pool Project, is envisaged as a means of efficiently utilizing the region's hydro-electricity and thermal power capabilities by transferring power from surplus producers to countries unable to meet their energy requirements. ECOWAS is developing an initiative aimed at promoting the use of renewable energy resources.

REGIONAL SECURITY

In 1990 a Standing Mediation Committee was formed to mediate disputes between member states. Member states reaffirmed their commitment to refrain from aggression against one another at a summit conference in 1991. The revised ECOWAS treaty, signed in July 1993, incorporates a separate provision for regional security, requiring member states to work towards the maintenance of peace, stability and security.

In December 1997 an extraordinary meeting of ECOWAS heads of state and government was convened in Lomé, Togo, to consider the future stability and security of the region. It was agreed that a permanent mechanism be established for conflict prevention and the maintenance of peace. ECOWAS leaders also reaffirmed their commitment to pursuing dialogue to prevent conflicts, co-operating in the early deployment of peace-keeping forces and implementing measures to counter trans-border crime and the illegal trafficking of armaments and drugs. At the meeting ECOWAS leaders acknowledged ECOMOG's role in restoring constitutional order in Liberia and expressed their appreciation of the force's current efforts in Sierra Leone (see below). In March 1998 ECOWAS ministers of foreign affairs, meeting in Yamoussoukro, Côte d'Ivoire, resolved that ECOMOG should become the region's permanent peace-keeping force, and upheld the decision of heads of state regarding the establishment of a new body, which should be used to observe, analyse and monitor the security situation in the West African region. Ministers agreed to undertake a redefinition of the command structure within the organization in order to strengthen decision-making and the legal status of the ECOMOG force.

In July 1998 ECOWAS ministers of defence and of security adopted a draft mechanism for conflict management, peace-keeping and security, which provided for ECOWAS intervention in the internal affairs of member states, where a conflict or military uprising threatened the region's security. In October the ECOWAS Authority determined to implement a renewable three-year ban on the import, export or manufacture of small armaments in order to enhance the security of the sub-region. (The ban was renewed for a further three years in July 2001.) The Authority also issued a declaration on the control and prevention of drug abuse, agreeing to allocate US $150,000 to establish an Eco-Drug Fund to finance regional activities in countering substance abuse.

The summit meeting of ECOWAS heads of state and government held in December 1999 in Lomé, Togo, approved a draft protocol to the organization's treaty, providing for the establishment of a Permanent Mechanism for the Prevention, Management and Settlement of Conflicts and the Maintenance of Peace in the Region, as envisaged at their conference in December 1997, and for the creation in connection with the Mechanism of a Mediation and Security Council, to comprise representatives of 10 member states, elected for two-year terms. The Mediation and Security Council was to be supported by an advisory Council of Elders, comprising 32 eminent statesmen from the region. ECOMOG was to be transformed from an *ad hoc* cease-fire monitoring group into a permanent standby force available for immediate deployment to avert emerging conflicts in the region.

In early 2002 ECOWAS, with assistance from the USA, was developing an early warning system for monitoring threats to regional security.

Peace-keeping operations

In August 1990 an ECOWAS Cease-fire Monitoring Group (ECOMOG—initially comprising about 4,000 troops from The Gambia, Ghana, Guinea, Nigeria and Sierra Leone) was dispatched to Liberia in an attempt to enforce a cease-fire between conflicting factions there, to restore public order, and to establish an interim government, until elections could be held. In November a temporary cease-fire was agreed by the protagonists in Liberia, and an interim president was installed by ECOMOG. Following the signature of a new cease-fire agreement a national conference, organized by ECOWAS in March 1991, established a temporary government, pending elections to be held in early 1992. In June 1991 ECOWAS established a committee (initially comprising representatives of five member states, later expanded to nine) to co-ordinate the peace negotiations. In September, at a meeting in Yamoussoukro, Côte d'Ivoire, held under the aegis of the ECOWAS committee, two of the rival factions in Liberia agreed to encamp their troops in designated areas and to disarm under ECOMOG supervision. During the period preceding the proposed elections, ECOMOG was to occupy Liberian air and sea ports, and create a 'buffer zone' along the country's border with Sierra Leone. By September 1992, however, ECOMOG had been unable either to effect the disarmament of two of the principal military factions, the National Patriotic Front of Liberia (NPFL) and the United Liberation Movement of Liberia for Democracy (ULIMO), or to occupy positions in substantial areas of the country, as a result of resistance on the part of the NPFL. The proposed elections were consequently postponed indefinitely.

In October 1992 ECOMOG began offensive action against NPFL positions, with a campaign of aerial bombardment. In November ECOWAS imposed a land, sea and air blockade on the NPFL's territory, in response to the Front's refusal to comply with the Yamoussoukro accord of October 1991. In April 1993 ECOMOG announced that the disarmament of ULIMO had been completed, amid widespread accusations that ECOMOG had supported ULIMO against the NPFL, and was no longer a neutral force. An ECOWAS-brokered cease-fire agreement was signed in Cotonou, Benin, in July, and took effect on 1 August. In September a UN observer mission (UNOMIL) was established in Liberia to work alongside ECOMOG in monitoring the process of disarming troops, as well as to verify the impartiality of ECOMOG.

In September 1994 leaders of Liberia's main military factions, having negotiated with representatives of ECOWAS, the Organization of African Unity (OAU, q.v.) and the UN, signed an amendment to the Cotonou accord in Akosombo, Ghana. This provided for a new five-member Council of State, in the context of a cease-fire, as a replacement to the expired interim executive authority, and established a new timetable for democratic elections. In early 1995 negotiations to secure a peace settlement, conducted under ECOWAS auspices, collapsed, owing to disagreement on the composition of the new Council of State. In May, in an attempt to ease the political deadlock, ECOWAS heads of state and of government met leaders of the six main warring factions. Under continuing pressure from the international community, the leaders of the Liberian factions signed a new peace accord, in Abuja, Nigeria, in August. This political development led to renewed efforts on the part of ECOWAS countries to strengthen ECOMOG, and by October Burkina Faso, Nigeria, Ghana and Guinea had pledged troop contributions to increase the force strength from 7,268 to 12,000. In accordance with the peace agreement, ECOMOG forces, with UNOMIL, were to be deployed throughout Liberia and along its borders to prevent the flow of arms into the country and to monitor the disarmament of the warring parties. In December an attack on ECOMOG troops, by a dissident ULIMO faction (ULIMO–J), disrupted the deployment of the multinational forces and the disarmament process, which was scheduled to commence in mid-January 1996. At least 16 members of the peace-keeping force were killed in the fighting that ensued. Clashes between ECOMOG and the ULIMO–J forces continued in the west of the country in late December 1995 and early January 1996, during which time 130 Nigerian members of ECOMOG were held hostage. In April, following a series of violations of the cease-fire, serious hostilities erupted in the Liberian capital, Monrovia, between government forces and dissident troops. An initial agreement to end the fighting, negotiated under ECOWAS auspices, was unsuccessful; however, it secured the release of several civilians and soldiers who had been taken hostage during the civil disruption. Later in April a further cease-fire agreement was concluded, under the aegis of the US Government, the UN and ECOWAS. In May ministers of foreign affairs of the countries constituting the ECOWAS Committee of Nine advocated that all armed factions be withdrawn from Monrovia and that ECOMOG troops be deployed throughout the capital in order to re-establish the city's 'safe-haven' status. According to the Committee's demands, all property, armaments and equipment seized unlawfully from civilians, ECOMOG and other international organizations during the fighting were to be returned, while efforts to disarm the warring factions and to pursue the restoration of democracy in the country were to be resumed. At the end of May the deployment of ECOMOG troops was initiated. In August a new cease-fire accord was signed by the leaders of the principal factions in Liberia, which envisaged the completion of the disarmament process by the end of January 1997, with elections to be held in May. The disarmament process began in November 1996, and by the end of January 1997 ECOMOG confirmed that 23,000 of the targeted 30,000–35,000 soldiers had been disarmed. The deadline for disarmament was extended by seven days, during which time a further 1,500 soldiers were reported to have been disarmed. However, vigilante attacks by remaining armed faction fighters persisted. The Committee of Nine announced in February that presidential and legislative elections would be held in May, later revising the election schedule to mid-July. ECOMOG was to withdraw from Liberia six months after the election date, until which time it had proposed to offer security for the incoming government and to provide training for a new unified Liberian army. The Committee also agreed, in consultation with the Council of State, to replace the existing Electoral Commission with a new Commission comprising seven members, to reflect all aspects of Liberian society. The Chairman would be selected from among the seven, in consultation with ECOWAS, which along with the UN and the OAU, would act as a 'technical adviser' to the Commission. ECOMOG deployed additional troops, who were joined by other international observers in ensuring that the elections were conducted in the necessary conditions of security. In August, following the inauguration of Charles Taylor (formerly leader of the NPFL) as Liberia's democratically-elected President, ECOWAS heads of state agreed that the ECOMOG force in Liberia was to be reconstituted and would henceforth assist in the process of national reconstruction, including the restructuring of the armed and security forces, and the maintenance of security; it was further envisaged that ECOMOG's mandate (officially due to expire in February 1998) would be extended in agreement with the Liberian Government. A Status of Forces Agreement, which defined ECOMOG's post-conflict responsibilities (i.e. capacity-building and maintenance of security) and imposed conditions on the peace-keeping forces remaining in the country, was signed by the Liberian Government and ECOWAS in June 1998. Relations with the Taylor administration, however, deteriorated, owing to accusations that ECOMOG was providing assistance to opposition groupings. The tense political situation, therefore, and the need for greater resources in Sierra Leone, resulted in ECOMOG transferring its headquarters from Monrovia to Freetown in Sierra Leone. The transfer was reported to have been completed by October, with just two ECOMOG battalions remaining in Liberia. The ECOMOG mission in Liberia was effectively terminated in October 1999 when the final declared stocks of rebel armaments were destroyed. In April 2001 the ECOWAS Authority determined to send a Mediation and Security Council mission to Liberia to monitor compliance with a resolution of the UN Security Council imposing sanctions on the Liberian regime. A Liberian National Reconciliation Forum was to be staged in July 2002, in Monrovia, under ECOWAS auspices.

In August 1999 a regional meeting was convened, under ECOWAS auspices, to attempt to defuse escalating tensions between Liberia and Guinea following an incursion into northern Liberia by Guinean rebel forces earlier in that month. In September representatives of eight member countries determined to establish a monitoring body to supervise the border region between Guinea, Liberia and Sierra Leone. Insecurity in the area escalated in the latter part of 2000, particularly in southern Guinea, which was increasingly subjected to insurgencies by Sierra Leonean RUF rebels, combated forcefully by Guinean troops, and prompting massive displacement of and severe hardship for the local population, which included significant numbers of refugees who had fled unrest in Liberia and Sierra Leone. Relations between the three countries deteriorated swiftly, amidst mutual accusations and counter-accusations concerning the provision of external support for dissidents in their respective territories. Allegations that the RUF rebels were supported by the Liberian authorities were the subject of a report issued by an independent UN panel of experts in December. During that month the ECOWAS Authority approved the deployment of a 1,700-strong ECOMOG interposition force to act as a buffer in the Guinea-Liberia-Sierra Leone border region, in order to deter the rebel activity and thereby alleviate the ongoing humanitarian crisis. (In early October the grouping's newly-formed Mediation and Security Council had authorized the deployment of a military observer mission to the area.) Meanwhile, the governments of the three (Mano River Union, q.v.) countries agreed to disarm rebel groups and to prevent these from entering neighbouring countries from their territories. However, the political crisis subsequently intensified, amid mutual expulsions of diplomatic personnel. In April 2001, by which time the presidents of Guinea and Liberia had still not signed the Status of Force Agreement necessary to enable the deployment of the proposed ECOMOG interposition force, the ECOWAS Authority agreed to postpone the deployment indefinitely. In that month an ECOWAS committee, comprising the presidents of Mali, Nigeria and Togo, was established to mediate a resolution to the crisis. From August ministers of foreign affairs and defence from the three Mano River Union countries held a series of meetings to address the situation. The deployment of the ECOMOG interposition force remained suspended.

In May 1997 the democratically-elected Sierra Leonean leader, President Ahmed Tejan Kabbah, was overthrown by a military coup involving officers of the national army and RUF rebels. Nigerian forces based in Sierra Leone as part of a bilateral defence pact attempted to restore constitutional order. Their numbers were strengthened by the arrival of more than 700 Nigerian soldiers and two naval vessels which had been serving under the ECOMOG mandate in neighbouring Liberia. At the end of June ECOWAS ministers of foreign affairs, convened in Conakry, Guinea, agreed to pursue the objective of restoring a democratic government in Sierra Leone through dialogue and the imposition of economic sanctions. In July a five-member ECOWAS committee, comprising the foreign ministers of Côte d'Ivoire, Ghana, Guinea, Liberia and Nigeria, together with representatives of the OAU, negotiated an agreement with the so-called Armed Forces Revolutionary Council (AFRC) in Sierra Leone to establish an immediate cease-fire and to pursue efforts towards the restoration of constitutional order. In August ECOWAS heads of state reaffirmed the Community's condemnation of the removal of President Kabbah and officially endorsed a series of punitive measures against the AFRC authorities in order to accelerate the restoration of democratic government. The meeting mandated ECOMOG to maintain and monitor the cease-fire and to prevent all goods, excepting essential humanitarian supplies, from entering that country. It was also agreed that the committee on Sierra Leone include Liberia and be convened at the level of heads of state. In October the UN Security Council imposed an embargo on the sale or supply of armaments to Sierra Leone and authorized ECOWAS to ensure implementation of these measures. ECOMOG conducted a number of attacks against commercial and military targets, with the aim of upholding the international sanctions, and clashes occurred between ECOMOG troops and AFRC/RUF soldiers, in particular around the area of Freetown's Lungi international airport which had been seized by ECOMOG. Despite the escalation in hostilities, the ECOWAS Committee of Five pursued negotiations with the military authorities, and at the end of October both sides signed a peace agreement, in Conakry, Guinea, providing for an immediate end to all fighting and the reinstatement of Kabbah's Government by April 1998; all combatants were to be disarmed and demobilized under the supervision of a disarmament committee comprising representatives of ECOMOG, the military authorities and local forces loyal to President Kabbah. In November 1997, however, the peace process was undermined by reports that ECOMOG forces had violated the cease-fire agreement following a series of air raids on Freetown, which ECOMOG claimed to have been in retaliation for attacks by AFRC/RUF-operated anti-aircraft equipment, and a demand by the AFRC authorities that the Nigerian contingent of ECOMOG leave the country. In mid-February 1998, following a series of offensive attacks against forces loyal to the military authorities, ECOMOG assumed control of Freetown and arrested several members of the AFRC/RUC regime. Some 50 AFRC officials were arrested by troops serving under ECOMOG on arrival at James Spriggs Payne Airport in Liberia, prompting protests from the Liberian Government at the Nigerian military intervention. An 11-member supervisory task force, which included the ECOMOG Commander, was established in Sierra Leone to maintain order, pending Kabbah's return from exile. ECOMOG troops subsequently also monitored the removal of the embargo against the use of the airport and port facilities in Freetown. Kabbah returned to Sierra Leone in March and installed a new administration. It was agreed that ECOMOG forces were to remain in the country in order to ensure the full restoration of peace and security, to assist in the restructuring of the armed forces and to help to resolve the problems of the substantial numbers of refugees and internally displaced persons. In early May ECOWAS Chiefs of Staff, meeting in Accra, Ghana, urged member states to provide more troops and logistical support to strengthen the ECOMOG force in Sierra Leone (at that time numbering some 10,000 troops), which was still involved in ongoing clashes with remaining rebel soldiers in eastern regions of the country. The UN established an Observer Mission in Sierra Leone (UNOMSIL) in July, which was to monitor the cease-fire, mainly in areas secured by ECOMOG troops. In October ECOMOG transferred its headquarters to Freetown, in order, partly, to reinforce its presence in the country. In January 1999 rebel soldiers attacked the capital and engaged in heavy fighting with ECOMOG forces, amid reports that the Liberian Government was supporting the rebels. Nigeria dispatched several thousand additional troops to counter the rebel advance and to secure the border with Liberia. In February, however, once ECOMOG had regained control of Freetown, the Nigerian Government expressed its desire to withdraw all its troops from the peace-keeping force by May, owing to financial restraints. Efforts to negotiate a peace settlement were initiated, with the Chairman of ECOWAS at that time, President Gnassingbe EyadE ma of Togo, actively involved in mediation between the opposing groups, despite persisting reports of fighting between ECOMOG and rebel soldiers in areas east of the capital. A cease-fire agreement was concluded in May, and a political settlement was signed, by Kabbah and the RUF leader, in Lomé, Togo, in July. ECOMOG's mandate in Sierra Leone was adapted to support the consolidation of peace in that country and national reconstruction. In October UNOMSIL was replaced by the UN Mission in Sierra Leone (UNAMSIL), which was to assist with the implementation of the Lomé accord and to assume many of the functions then being performed by ECOMOG, including the provision of security at Lungi international airport and at other key installations, buildings and government institutions in the Freetown area. In consequence the ECOMOG contingent was withdrawn in April 2000. However, following a resurgence of RUF violence in April and May, when as many as 500 members of UNAMSIL (which had not been deployed to full strength) were captured by the rebels, ECOWAS heads of government agreed to reinforce the UN peace-keeping operation with some 3,000 regional troops. A UN Security Council mission to Sierra Leone in September recommended the establishment of a mechanism to co-ordinate the formulation and implementation by the UN, ECOWAS, the Sierra Leone Government and other parties of a unified strategy to resolve the insecurity in Sierra Leone. A new cease-fire accord was agreed by the Sierra Leone Government and the RUF in November, in Abuja, Nigeria. In April 2001 representatives of the Mediation and Security Council were dispatched to Liberia to monitor, jointly with a UN delegation, the Liberian Government's compliance with a UN Security Council Resolution aimed at ending support for and eradicating RUF activity in that country, and at terminating illicit trading there in Sierra Leonean diamonds.

In July 1998 ECOWAS ministers of defence and of foreign affairs met to consider the political unrest in Guinea-Bissau, following an unsuccessful attempt by rebel soldiers, in June, to overthrow the Government of President João Vieira, and urged both sides to co-operate in negotiating a settlement. An ECOWAS Committee of Seven on Guinea-Bissau (comprising the ministers of foreign affairs of Burkina Faso, Côte d'Ivoire, The Gambia, Ghana, Guinea, Nigeria and Senegal) was established and met for the first time in August. In late August, following mediation by ECOWAS representatives and a contact group of the Comunidade dos Países de Língua Portuguesa (CPLP, q.v.), which had secured an initial cease-fire, an agreement was signed by the conflicting parties providing for an end to hostilities, the reopening of the international airport to facilitate the provision of humanitarian supplies, and for independent supervision of the cease-fire agreement. ECOWAS subsequently held discussions with the CPLP in order to co-ordinate efforts to secure peace in Guinea-Bissau. In late October ECOWAS heads of state endorsed the deployment of ECOMOG forces in Guinea-Bissau. On 1 November the two sides in the dispute, meeting in Abuja, Nigeria, signed a peace accord under ECOWAS auspices, which reinforced the August cease-fire and incorporated an agreement to establish a government of national unity. ECOMOG forces were to replace all foreign troops, mainly Senegalese, currently in Guinea-Bissau, supervise the security of the border region between those two countries, and enable humanitarian organizations to have free access to those needing assistance. In addition ECOMOG was to be responsible for monitoring the conduct of presidential and legislative elections, scheduled to be held in 1999. In early February President Vieira and the rebel leader Gen. Manè signed a cease-fire accord, under ECOWAS auspices. A new Government of National Unity was established later in that month and an ECOMOG Interposition Force began to be dispatched to Guinea-Bissau. In early May, however, President Vieira was ousted by the rebel forces. Meeting later in that month, in Lomé, Togo, ECOWAS ministers of foreign affairs condemned the overthrow of Vieira. They resolved to withdraw the ECOMOG contingent, at that time numbering 600 troops from Benin, Gabon, Niger and Togo, owing to the political developments and lack of finances. By early June all ECOMOG troops had left Guinea-Bissau.

ECOWAS supported the establishment by the OAU in July 2000 of a committee, comprising the foreign ministers of 10 OAU member countries, which was mandated to address the ongoing political crisis in Côte d'Ivoire.

In May 2000 the ECOWAS Authority authorized the initiation of an inquiry into the link between illicit trading in diamonds and ongoing rebel activity in the region, with a particular focus on Liberia and Sierra Leone.

ENVIRONMENTAL PROTECTION

ECOWAS promotes implementation of the UN Convention on Desertification Control and supports programmes initiated at national and sub-regional level within the framework of the treaty. Together with the Permanent Inter-State Committee on Drought Control in the Sahel (CILSS, q.v.). ECOWAS has been designated as a project leader for implementing the Convention in West Africa. Other environmental initiatives include a regional meteorological project to enhance meteorological activities and applications, and in particular to contribute to food security and natural resource management in the sub-region. ECOWAS pilot schemes have formed the basis of integrated control projects for the control of floating weeds in five water basins in West Africa, which had hindered the development of the local fishery sectors. A rural water supply programme aims to ensure adequate water for rural dwellers in order to improve their living standards. The first phase of the project focused on schemes to develop village and pastoral water points in Burkina Faso, Guinea, Mali, Niger and Senegal, with funds from various multilateral donors.

AGRICULTURE AND FISHING

In November 1995 an agro-industrial forum, jointly organized by ECOWAS and the EU, was held in Dakar, Senegal. The forum aimed to facilitate co-operation between companies in the two regions, to develop the agro-industrial sector in West Africa and to promote business opportunities.

In February 2001 ECOWAS ministers of agriculture adopted an action plan for the formulation of a common agricultural policy, as envisaged under the ECOWAS treaty. The Community enforces a transhumance certification scheme for facilitating the monitoring of animal movement and animal health surveillance and protection in the sub-region.

SOCIAL PROGRAMME

Four organizations have been established within ECOWAS by the Executive Secretariat: the Organization of Trade Unions of West Africa, which held its first meeting in 1984; the West African Youth Association; the West African Universities' Association; and the West Africa Women's Association (whose statutes were approved by a meeting of ministers of social affairs in May 1987). Regional sports competitions are held annually. The West African Health Organization (WAHO) was established in 2000 by merger of the West African Health Community and the Organization for Co-ordination and Co-operation in the Struggle against Endemic Diseases. In December 2001 the ECOWAS summit of heads of state and government adopted a plan of action aimed at combating trafficking in human beings and authorized the establishment of an ECOWAS Criminal Intelligence Bureau.

INFORMATION AND MEDIA

In March 1990 ECOWAS ministers of information formulated a policy on the dissemination of information about ECOWAS throughout the region and the appraisal of attitudes of its population towards the Community. The ministers established a new information commission. In November 1991 a conference on press communication and African integration, organized by ECOWAS, recommended the creation of an ECOWAS press card, judicial safeguards to protect journalists, training programmes for journalists and the establishment of a regional documentation centre and data bank. In November 1994 the commission of social and cultural affairs, meeting in Lagos, Nigeria, endorsed a series of measures to promote west African integration. These included special radio, television and newspaper features, sporting events and other competitions or rallies. In December 2000 the Council of Ministers approved a new policy on the dissemination of information about the Community's activities.

SPECIALIZED AGENCIES

West African Monetary Agency: 11–13 ECOWAS St, PMB 218, Freetown, Sierra Leone; tel. 224485; fax 223943; e-mail wama@sierratel.sl; f. 1975 as West African Clearing House; administers transactions between its 10 member central banks in order to promote sub-regional trade and monetary co-operation; administers ECOWAS travellers' cheques scheme. Mems: Banque Centrale des Etats de l'Afrique de l'Ouest (serving Benin, Burkina Faso, Côte d'Ivoire, Guinea-Bissau, Mali, Niger, Senegal, Togo) and the central banks of Cape Verde, The Gambia, Ghana, Guinea, Liberia, Mauritania, Nigeria and Sierra Leone. Dir-Gen. ANTOINE M. F. NDIAYE (Senegal). Publ. *Annual Report.*

West African Monetary Institute: Premier Towers, 8th/9th Floors, Cantonments 75, Accra, Ghana; tel. (21) 676-901; fax (21) 676-903; e-mail info@wami-imao.org; internet www.ecowas.int/wami-imao/; f. by the ECOWAS Authority summit in December 2000 to prepare for the establishment of a West African Central Bank; Dir-Gen. Dr MICHAEL OLUFEMI OJO.

West African Health Organization (WAHO): BP 153 Bobo-Dioulasso 01, Burkina Faso; tel (226) 975772; fax (226) 975772; e-mail wahooas@fasonet.bf; f. 2000 by merger of the West African Health Community (f. 1978) and the Organization for Co-ordination and Co-operation in the Struggle against Endemic Diseases (f. 1960); aims to harmonize member states' health policies and to promote research, training, the sharing of resources and diffusion of information; Dir-Gen. Dr KABBA T. JOINER. Publ. *Bulletin Bibliographique* (quarterly).

Finance

ECOWAS is financed by contributions from member states, although there is a poor record of punctual payment of dues, which has hampered the work of the Secretariat. Arrears in contributions to the Secretariat were reported to total US $37m. at September 2000. Under the revised treaty, ECOWAS was to receive revenue from a community tax, based on the total value of imports from member countries. In July 1996 the summit meeting approved a protocol on a community levy, providing for the imposition of a 0.5% tax on the value of imports from a third country. In August 1997 the Authority of Heads of State and Government determined that the community levy should replace budgetary contributions as the organization's principal source of finance. The protocol came into force in January 2000, having been ratified by nine member states. By December the protocol had been ratified by 11 member states, and was being implemented by six of these, as well as by two states (Benin and Senegal) which were applying the protocol prior to ratifying it.

The provisional budget for 2001 amounted to approximately US $9m.

Publications

Annual Report.

Contact.

ECOWAS National Accounts.

ECOWAS News.

West African Bulletin.

ECONOMIC CO-OPERATION ORGANIZATION—ECO

Address: 1 Golbou Alley, Kamranieh St, POB 14155-6176, Tehran, Iran.

Telephone: (21) 2831733; **fax:** (21) 2831732; **e-mail:** registry@ecosecretariat.org; **internet:** www.ecosecretariat.org.

The Economic Co-operation Organization (ECO) was established in 1985 as the successor to the Regional Co-operation for Development, founded in 1964.

MEMBERS

Afghanistan	Kyrgyzstan	Turkey
Azerbaijan	Pakistan	Turkmenistan
Iran	Tajikistan	Uzbekistan
Kazakhstan		

The 'Turkish Republic of Northern Cyprus' has been granted special guest status.

Organization

(March 2002)

SUMMIT MEETING

The first summit meeting of heads of state and of government of member countries was held in Tehran in February 1992. Summit meetings are held at least once every two years. The sixth summit meeting was convened in Tehran in June 2000.

COUNCIL OF MINISTERS

The Council of Ministers, comprising ministers of foreign affairs of member states, is the principal policy- and decision-making body of ECO. It meets at least once a year.

COUNCIL OF PERMANENT REPRESENTATIVES

Permanent representatives or Ambassadors of member countries accredited to Iran meet regularly to formulate policy for consideration by the Council of Ministers and to promote implementation of decisions reached at ministerial or summit level.

REGIONAL PLANNING COUNCIL

The Council, comprising senior planning officials or other representatives of member states, meets at least once a year. It is responsible for reviewing programmes of activity and evaluating results achieved, and for proposing future plans of action to the Council of Ministers.

SECRETARIAT

The Secretariat is headed by a Secretary-General, who is supported by two Deputy Secretaries-General. The following Directorates administer and co-ordinate the main areas of ECO activities: Trade and investment; Transport and communications; Energy, minerals and environment; Industry and agriculture (to be renamed Human Development); Project research; and Economic research and statistics.

Secretary-General: Dr ABDULRAHIM GAVAHI (Iran).

Activities

The Regional Co-operation for Development (RCD) was established in 1964 as a tripartite arrangement between Iran, Pakistan and Turkey, which aimed to promote economic co-operation between member states. ECO replaced the RCD in 1985, and seven additional members were admitted to the Organization in November 1992. The main areas of co-operation are transport (including the building of road and rail links), telecommunications and post, trade and investment, energy (including the interconnection of power grids in the region), minerals, environmental issues, industry, and agriculture. ECO priorities and objectives for each sector are defined in the Quetta Plan of Action and the İstanbul Declaration; an Almaty Outline Plan, which was adopted in 1993, is specifically concerned with the development of regional transport and communication infrastructure.

In 1990 an ECO College of Insurance was inaugurated. A joint Chamber of Commerce and Industry was established in 1993. The third ECO summit meeting, held in Islamabad, Pakistan, in March 1995, concluded formal agreements on the establishment of several other regional institutes and agencies: an ECO Trade and Development Bank, in İstanbul, Turkey (with main branches in Tehran, Iran, and Islamabad, Pakistan), a joint shipping company, airline, and an ECO Cultural Institute, all to be based in Iran, and an ECO Reinsurance Company and an ECO Science Foundation, with headquarters in Pakistan. In addition, heads of state and of government endorsed the creation of an ECO eminent persons group and signed the following two agreements in order to enhance and facilitate trade throughout the region: the Transit Trade Agreement (which entered into force in December 1997) and the Agreement on the Simplification of Visa Procedures for Businessmen of ECO Countries (which came into effect in March 1998). The sixth ECO summit meeting, held in June 2000 in Tehran, urged the completion of the necessary formalities for the creation of the planned ECO Trade and Development Bank and ECO Reinsurance Company. In May 2001 the Council of Ministers agreed to terminate the ECO airline project, owing to its unsustainable cost, and to replace it with a framework agreement on co-operation in the field of air transport.

In September 1996, at an extraordinary meeting of the ECO Council of Ministers, held in Izmir, Turkey, member countries signed a revised Treaty of Izmir, the Organization's fundamental charter. An extraordinary summit meeting, held in Ashgabat, Turkmenistan, in May 1997, adopted the Ashgabat Declaration, emphasizing the importance of the development of the transport and communications infrastructure and the network of transnational petroleum and gas pipelines through bilateral and regional arrangements in the ECO area. In May 1998, at the fifth summit meeting, held in Almaty, Kazakhstan, ECO heads of state and of government signed a Transit Transport Framework Agreement and a memorandum of understanding to help combat the cross-border trafficking of illegal goods. The meeting also agreed to establish an ECO Educational Institute in Ankara, Turkey. In June 2000 the sixth ECO summit encouraged member states to participate in the development of information and communication technologies through the establishment of a database of regional educational and training institutions specializing in that field. The ECO heads of state and government also reconfirmed their commitment to the Ashgabat Declaration. In December 2001 ECO organized its first workshop on energy conservation and efficiency in Ankara.

Convening in conference for the first time in early March 2000, ECO ministers of trade signed a Framework Agreement on ECO Trade Co-operation (ECOFAT), which established a basis for the expansion of intra-regional trade. The Framework Agreement envisaged the eventual adoption of an ECO Trade Agreement (ECOTA), providing for the gradual elimination of regional tariff and non-tariff barriers between member states. ECO and the International Trade Centre are jointly implementing a project on expanding intra-ECO trade. In November the first meeting of ECO ministers responsible for energy and petroleum, convened in Islamabad, adopted a plan of action for regional co-operation on energy and petroleum matters over the period 2001–05.

ECO staged its third trade fair in Bandar Anzali, Iran, in July 1998. The fourth fair was to be held in Karachi, Pakistan, in

April/May 2002. The Organization maintains ECO TradeNet, an internet-based repository of regional trade information. ECO has co-operation agreements with several UN agencies and other international organizations in development-related activities. An ECO-UN International Drug Control Programme (UNDCP) Project on Drug Control and Co-ordination Unit commenced operations in Tehran in July 1999. ECO has been granted observer status at the UN, OIC and WTO.

Finance

Member states contribute to a centralized administrative budget.

Publication

ECO Annual Economic Report.
ECO News Bulletin (3 a year).

EUROPEAN BANK FOR RECONSTRUCTION AND DEVELOPMENT—EBRD

Address: One Exchange Square, 175 Bishopsgate, London, EC2A 2EH, United Kingdom.

Telephone: (20) 7338-6000; **fax:** (20) 7338-6100; **internet:** www.ebrd.com.

The EBRD was founded in May 1990 and inaugurated in April 1991. Its object is to contribute to the progress and the economic reconstruction of the countries of central and eastern Europe which undertake to respect and put into practice the principles of multi-party democracy, pluralism, the rule of law, respect for human rights and a market economy.

MEMBERS

Countries of Operations:

Albania	Macedonia, former Yugoslav republic
Armenia	Moldova
Azerbaijan	Mongolia
Belarus	Poland
Bosnia and Herzegovina	Romania
Bulgaria	Russia
Croatia	Slovakia
Czech Republic	Slovenia
Estonia	Tajikistan
Georgia	Turkmenistan
Hungary	Ukraine
Kazakhstan	Uzbekistan
Kyrgyzstan	Yugoslavia
Latvia	
Lithuania	

EU members*:

Austria	Italy
Belgium	Luxembourg
Denmark	Netherlands
Finland	Portugal
France	Spain
Germany	Sweden
Greece	United Kingdom
Ireland	

EFTA members:

Iceland	Norway
Liechtenstein	Switzerland

Other countries:

Australia	Malta
Canada	Mexico
Cyprus	Mongolia
Egypt	Morocco
Israel	New Zealand
Japan	Turkey
Republic of Korea	USA

* The European Community and the European Investment Bank are also shareholder members in their own right.

Organization

(April 2002)

BOARD OF GOVERNORS

The Board of Governors, to which each member appoints a Governor and an alternate, is the highest authority of the EBRD.

BOARD OF DIRECTORS

The Board is responsible for the organization and operations of the EBRD. The Governors elect 23 directors for a three-year term and a President for a term of four years. Vice-Presidents are appointed by the Board on the recommendation of the President.

ADMINISTRATION

The EBRD's operations are conducted by its Banking Department, headed by the First Vice-President. The other departments are: Finance; Personnel and Administration; Evaluation, Operational and Environmental Support; Internal Audit; Communications; and Offices of the Secretary-General, the General Counsel and the Chief Economist. A structure of country teams, industry teams and operations support units oversee the implementation of projects. The EBRD has 30 Resident Offices or other offices in all of its countries of operations. There were some 862 regular staff at the end of 2000.

President: JEAN LEMIERRE (France).

First Vice-President: NOREEN DOYLE (USA).

Activities

In April 1996 EBRD shareholders, meeting in Sofia, Bulgaria, agreed to increase the Bank's capital from ECU 10,000m. to ECU 20,000m., to enable the Bank to continue, and to enhance, its lending programme (the ECU was replaced by the euro, with an equivalent value, from 1 January 1999). It was agreed that 22.5% of the ECU 10,000m. of new resources, was to be paid-up, with the remainder as 'callable' shares. Contributions were to be paid over a 13-year period from April 1998. By 31 December 2000 all but three members had subscribed to the capital increase.

The Bank aims to assist the transition of the economies of central and eastern European countries towards a market economy system, and to encourage private enterprise. The Agreement establishing the EBRD specifies that 60% of its lending should be for the private sector, and that its operations do not displace commercial sources of finance. The Bank helps the beneficiaries to undertake structural and sectoral reforms, including the dismantling of monopolies, decentralization, and privatization of state enterprises, to enable these countries to become fully integrated in the international economy. To this end, the Bank promotes the establishment and improvement of activities of a productive, competitive and private nature, particularly small and medium-sized enterprises (SMEs), and works to strengthen financial institutions. It mobilizes national and foreign capital, together with experienced management teams, and helps to develop an appropriate legal framework to support a market-orientated economy. The Bank provides extensive financial services, including loans, equity and guarantees. The EBRD's founding Agreement specifies that all operations are to be undertaken in the context of promoting environmentally sound and sustainable development. It undertakes environmental audits and impact assessments in areas of particular concern, which enable the Bank to incorporate environmental action plans into any project approved for funding. An Environment Advisory Council assists with the development of policy and strategy in this area.

In the year ending 31 December 2000 the EBRD approved 95 operations, involving funds of €2,673m., compared with €2,162m. for 88 operations in the previous year. During 2000 29% of all project financing committed was allocated to the financial sector, in order to support the development and restructuring of sound financial institutions and to make more funds available, through banks and local intermediaries, for small-scale private enterprises. A similar proportion of funds was committed to projects in the industry and commerce sector, of which almost one-half was for agribusiness.

The economic crisis in Russia, in August 1998, undermined the viability of many proposed projects and adversely affected the Bank's large portfolio of Russian investments. In March 1999, partly in response to the region's economic difficulties, the Board of Directors approved a new medium-term strategy for 2000–03, which focused on advancing the process of transition. Key aspects of the strategy were to develop a sound financial sector and investment climate in its countries of operations; to provide leadership for the development of SMEs; to promote infrastructure development; and to ensure a balanced and focused project portfolio. In September a specific strategy to promote SMEs, through an expanded level of financing, an improved investment climate and the development of new support networks, was approved by the Board. In April 1999 the Bank and the European Commission launched a new SME Finance Facility, with committed funds of €125m., to provide equity and loan financing for SMEs in countries seeking accession to the EU. A Trade Facilitation Programme, which extends bank guarantees in order to promote trading capabilities in the region, was expanded during 1999. By the end of 2000 46 issuing banks in 20 countries were participating in the Programme. During 1999 the Bank participated in international efforts to secure economic and political stability in the Balkans, following the conflict in Kosovo. Subsequently the Bank has promoted the objectives of the Stability Pact for South-Eastern Europe by expanding its commitments in the region and by taking a lead role among international financial institutions in promoting private sector development.

A high priority is given to attracting external finance for Bank-sponsored projects, in particular in countries at advanced stages of transition, from government agencies, international financial institutions, commercial banks and export credit agencies. In 2000 those sources provided co-financing funds amounting to €1,365m. The EBRD's Technical Co-operation Funds Programme (TCFP) aims to facilitate access to the Bank's capital resources for countries of operations by providing support for project preparation, project implementation and institutional development. In 2000 the EBRD committed €67.7m. to finance 295 consultancy assignments under the TCFP, bringing the total amount committed since 1991 to €659.0m. for 2,651 assignments. Resources for technical co-operation originate from regular TCFP contributions, specific agreements and contributions to Special Funds. The Baltic Investment Programme, which is administered by Nordic countries, consists of two special funds to co-finance investment and technical assistance projects in the private sectors of Baltic states. The Funds are open to contributions from all EBRD member states. The Russia Small Business Special Funds, established in October 1993, support local SMEs through similar investment and technical co-operation activities. Other financing mechanisms that the EBRD uses to address the needs of the region include Regional Venture Funds, which invest equity in privatized companies, in particular in Russia, and provide relevant management assistance, and the Central European Agency Lines, which disburse lines of credit to small-scale projects through local intermediaries. A TurnAround Management Programme (TAM) provides practical assistance to senior managers of industrial enterprises to facilitate the expansion of businesses in a market economy. A Business Advisory Services programme complements TAM by undertaking projects to improve competitiveness, strategic planning, marketing and financial management in SMEs.

The Bank administers a Nuclear Safety Account (NSA), which was established in 1993 to fund a multilateral programme of action for the improvement of safety in nuclear power plants of the former eastern bloc. At the end of 2000 14 countries and the European Community had pledged funds amounting to some €261m. to the NSA. At that time short-term projects to improve safety at plants in Bulgaria, Lithuania, Russia and Ukraine had been completed.

In 1997 the G-7, together with the European Community and Ukraine, endorsed the creation of a supplemental multilateral funding mechanism to assist Ukraine in repairing the protective sarcophagus covering the faulty Chornobyl (Chernobyl) reactor, under the Chornobyl Unit 4 Shelter Implementation Plan (SIP). The EBRD's Board of Directors approved the participation of the Bank in September 1997. The rules of the so-called Chornobyl Shelter Fund, which the EBRD was to administer, were approved in November and the Fund became operational in the following month. In 1995 the G-7 requested that the Bank fund the completion of two new nuclear reactors in Ukraine, to provide alternative energy sources to the Chornobyl power-station, which, it was agreed, was to shut down in December 2000. A study questioning the financial viability of the proposed reactors threatened funding in early 1997; a second survey, carried out by the EBRD, pronounced the plan viable, although environmental groups continued to dispute the proposals. In July 2000 donor countries committed additional funds to the SIP, raising the total pledged to €766m. In December the Chornobyl power station was closed. The NSA is financing the construction of two major pre-decommissioning facilities in Ukraine, which were scheduled to be completed in 2003. In June 2000 the Bank approved the establishment of three International Decommissioning Support Funds, to assist the governments of Bulgaria, Lithuania and Slovakia in their commitments to close certain reactors.

Publications

Annual Report.

Environments in Transition (2 a year).

Transition Report (annually).

PROJECT FINANCING COMMITTED BY SECTOR

	2000		Cumulative to 31 Dec. 2000	
	Number	Amount (€ million)	Number	Amount (€ million)
Financial institutions				
Bank equity	7	73	73	831
Bank lending	7	302	105	2,546
Equity funds	9	263	59	1,014
Non-bank financial institutions	4	70	19	142
Small business finance	4	80	13	303
Industry and commerce				
Agribusiness	16	352	73	1,210
Natural resources	4	228	32	1,359
Property, tourism and shipping*	4	70	40	684
Telecommunications, informatics and media	3	125	47	1,494
Infrastructure				
Energy efficiency	1	17	7	188
Municipal and environmental infrastructure	8	211	29	822
Power and energy	7	267	36	1,512
Transport	5	216	64	2,248
General industry				
General industry	17	400	111	2,200
Total	95	2,673	708	16,553

* Excluding equity funds.

PROJECT FINANCING COMMITTED BY COUNTRY

	2000		Cumulative to 31 Dec. 2000	
	Number	Amount (€ million)	Number	Amount (€ million)
Albania	1	2	13	105
Armenia	2	44	5	133
Azerbaijan	1	82	11	359
Belarus	0	2	6	173
Bosnia and Herzegovina	3	61	12	145
Bulgaria	7	116	31	482
Croatia	5	153	29	728
Czech Republic	2	51	33	793
Estonia	3	57	37	360
Georgia	1	38	13	226
Hungary	1	13	57	1,204
Kazakhstan	3	127	14	655
Kyrgyzstan	1	1	12	177
Latvia	2	49	22	293
Lithuania	4	108	22	378
Macedonia, former Yugoslav republic	2	65	13	241
Moldova	4	43	16	193
Poland	17	566	96	1,978
Romania	4	126	50	1,677
Russia	18	579	106	3,406
Slovakia	1	18	23	552
Slovenia	2	20	22	361
Tajikistan	0	0	4	17
Turkmenistan	0	2	4	169
Ukraine	10	293	40	1,171
Uzbekistan	2	57	15	580
Total	95	2,673	708	16,553

Note: Operations may be counted as fractional numbers if multiple sub-loans are grouped under one framework agreement.
Source: EBRD, *Annual Report 2000.*

EUROPEAN FREE TRADE ASSOCIATION—EFTA

Address (secretariat headquarters): 9-11 rue de Varembé, 1211 Geneva 20, Switzerland.

Telephone: (22) 7491111; **fax:** (22) 7339291; **e-mail:** efta-mailbox@efta.int; **internet:** www.efta.int.

Established in 1960, EFTA aimed to bring about free trade in industrial goods and to contribute to the liberalization and expansion of world trade. EFTA now serves as the structure through which three of its members participate in the European Economic Area (EEA), together with the 15 member states of the European Union (q.v.).

MEMBERS

Iceland	Norway
Liechtenstein	Switzerland

Three founder members subsequently left EFTA and joined the European Community (EC): Denmark (1973), the United Kingdom (1973) and Portugal (1986). Finland, formerly an associate member of EFTA, became a full member on 1 January 1986. Liechtenstein joined EFTA as a full member in September 1991, having hitherto had associate status through its customs union with Switzerland. Austria, Sweden (both founder members) and Finland left the Association on 31 December 1994 to become members of the European Union (as the EC had been restyled).

Organization

(April 2002)

EFTA COUNCIL

The Council is EFTA's governing body. The Chair is held for six months by each country in turn. The Council's decisions are binding on member states and must be unanimous. The Council is assisted by a substructure of committees and working groups.

EFTA STANDING COMMITTEES

Board of Auditors.

Budget Committee.

Committee of Members of Parliament of the EFTA Countries.

Committee of Origin and Customs Experts.

Committee on Technical Barriers to Trade.

Committee on Third Country Relations.

Committee of Trade Experts.

Consultative Committee.

Economic Committee.

Steering Committee of the Portuguese Fund.

MATTERS RELATED TO THE EEA

The treaty establishing the EEA, which entered into force in 1994, provided for an institutional structure to enhance its operations. An EEA Council, comprising ministers of all signatory countries, provides policy direction, while a Joint Committee, comprising representatives of the EFTA states in the EEA, the European Commission and EU member states, is responsible for the day-to-day management of EEA matters. A Standing Committee serves as the forum of consultation within EFTA, consisting of representatives from Iceland, Liechtenstein and Norway and observers from Switzerland. It is assisted by five Subcommittees (for free movement of goods; free movement of capital and services; free movement of persons; flanking and horizontal policies; and legal and institutional matters) and a number of Working Groups. An independent EFTA Surveillance Authority and an EFTA Court have also been established to provide judicial control.

SECRETARIAT

The secretariat headquarters, in Geneva, Switzerland, provides support to the EFTA Council and on third country relations, as well as servicing the operation of certain conventions and schemes. About one-third of secretariat staff are deployed at headquarters. A secretariat division based in Brussels, Belgium, and employing most of the remaining staff, assists member states on EEA matters. The Office of the Statistical Adviser is based in Luxembourg, and a Customs Officer is based in Paris, France.

Address (Brussels division): 74 rue de Trèves, 1040 Brussels, Belgium.

Telephone: (2) 286-17-11; **fax:** (2) 286-17-50.

Secretary-General: WILLIAM ROSSIER (Switzerland).

Activities

The creation of a single market including all the countries in Western Europe was the ultimate objective of EFTA when it was created in 1960. Member states were, however, not ready or able to accept the far-reaching political and economic implications of joining the EC, which was established in 1958. EFTA's first target, the creation of free trade in industrial goods between its members, was achieved by the end of 1966. By 1991 tariffs or import duties had been removed on all imports except agricultural products.

THE EEA

In 1972 EFTA member states signed bilateral agreements with the EC, which established free trade in most industrial goods between them from 1 July 1977. The last restrictions on free industrial trade were abolished from 1 January 1984. In April of that year ministers from all EFTA and EC member countries agreed on general guidelines for developing the EFTA-EC relationship. Their Declaration (known as the Luxembourg Declaration) recommended intensified efforts to improve the free circulation of industrial products between their countries, and closer co-operation beyond the framework of the free-trade agreements, in fields such as education, the environment, social policy, and research and development. In March 1989 the EFTA heads of government issued a declaration reaffirming their commitment to establish a European Economic Area (EEA), consisting of all the member states of EFTA and the EC. Formal negotiations on the establishment of the EEA commenced in June 1990, and the Agreement was signed in Oporto, Portugal, in May 1992. In December a Swiss referendum voted to oppose ratification of the EEA treaty. The ministers of trade of the remaining 18 member countries, however, signed an adjustment protocol in March 1993, allowing the EEA to be established without Switzerland. The EEA entered into force on 1 January 1994. Liechtenstein joined the EEA on 1 May 1995, having amended its customs union agreement and secured the support of the majority of its population in a national referendum. The EEA Agreement provided for the removal of all restrictions on the movement of goods, persons, services and capital within the area, effectively extending the internal market of the EU to the three EFTA countries within the EEA. In addition, the Agreement provided for co-operation in areas such as the environment, social policy, education and training, tourism, culture, consumer protection and small and medium-sized enterprises. To maintain homogeneity within the EEA, the Agreement is amended on a continuous basis to ensure that relevant EU legislation is extended to the EFTA EEA grouping.

THIRD COUNTRY RELATIONS

In recent years EFTA has developed 'third country relations' with a growing network of partners. From an initial focus on states in the Balkans and Mediterranean areas, EFTA is currently in the process of extending the geographical scope of its third country relations. The proposed free-trade agreement that was the focus of negotiations entered into by EFTA and Canada in 1998 (see list below), at Canada's behest, was envisaged as the basis for establishing a transatlantic free-trade area. EFTA subsequently engaged in negotiations with other countries, and regional and sub-regional groupings, from beyond Europe and the Mediterranean. The free-trade agreement concluded with Mexico in 2001 was the most comprehensive developed to date, covering areas including services and investment and public procurement.

EFTA has concluded free-trade agreements with: Turkey (in December 1991); with Czechoslovakia (March 1992) (with protocols on succession with the Czech Republic and Slovakia in April 1993); with Israel (September 1992); with Poland and Romania (December 1992); with Bulgaria and Hungary (March 1993); with Slovenia (July 1995); with Estonia, Latvia and Lithuania (December 1995); with Morocco (which was granted a 12-year transitional period to phase out customs duties) (June 1997); with the Palestinian National Authority (November 1998); with the former Yugoslav Republic of Macedonia (June 2000); and with Mexico (July 2001). In addition, declarations on co-operation (with a view to securing a free-trade agreement) are in force with: Albania (signed in December 1992); with Egypt and Tunisia (December 1995); with Jordan and Lebanon (June 1997); with Croatia, Ukraine and the Co-operation Council for the Arab States of the Gulf (June 2000); and with Yugoslavia and Mercosur (the latter a declaration on trade and investment co-operation) (December 2000). Formal negotiations on instigating a free-trade agreement were initiated with Cyprus in March 1998, with Canada in October 1998, with Chile in December 2000, and with Singapore in July 2001. Exploratory contact has been established with ASEAN, Algeria and South Africa.

Although Portugal withdrew from EFTA in 1985, EFTA decided to maintain an industrial development fund (established in 1976) for that country, for the 25-year period originally foreseen.

Finance

Net budget for 2001: 20.1m. Swiss francs.

Publications

EFTA Annual Report.

EFTA Bulletin.

EFTA Traders' ABC (CD-Rom).

Factsheets, legal documents.

EUROPEAN SPACE AGENCY—ESA

Address: 8–10 rue Mario Nikis, 75738 Paris Cédex 15, France.

Telephone: 1-53-69-76-54; **fax:** 1-53-69-75-60; **e-mail:** mailcom@esa.int; **internet:** www.esa.int.

ESA was established in 1975 to provide for, and to promote, European co-operation in space research and technology, and their applications, for exclusively peaceful purposes. It replaced the European Space Research Organisation (ESRO) and the European Launcher Development Organisation (both founded in 1962).

MEMBERS*

Austria	Netherlands
Belgium	Norway
Denmark	Portugal
Finland	Spain
France	Sweden
Germany	Switzerland
Ireland	United Kingdom
Italy	

* Canada has signed an agreement for close co-operation with ESA, including representation on the ESA Council.

Organization

(April 2002)

Director-General: ANTONIO RODOTÀ (Italy).

COUNCIL

The Council is composed of representatives of all member states. It is responsible for formulating policy and meets at ministerial or delegate level.

PROGRAMME BOARDS AND COMMITTEES

The Council is assisted in its work by six specialized Programme Boards, which oversee the management of the following ESA activities: Communication Satellite Programmes; Satellite Navigation; Earth Observation; Microgravity; Ariane Launcher; and Manned Spaceflight. The other principal bodies of the ESA administrative structure are the Committees for Administration and Finance, Industrial Policy, Science Programme and International Relations.

ESA CENTRES

European Space Research and Technology Centre—ESTEC: Noordwijk, Netherlands. ESA's principal technical establishment, at which the majority of project teams are based, together with the space science department and the technological research and support engineers; provides the appropriate testing and laboratory facilities.

European Space Operations Centre—ESOC: Darmstadt, Germany. Responsible for all satellite operations and the corresponding ground facilities and communications networks.

European Space Research Institute—ESRIN: Frascati, Italy. Responsible for the corporate exploitation of Earth observation data from space.

European Astronaut Centre—EAC: Porz-Wahn, Germany. Co-ordinates all European astronaut activities, including the training of astronauts. In 1996 the Centre began to develop computer-based training courses for the ESA aspects of the International Space Station.

ESA also helps to maintain the Space Centre at Kourou, French Guyana, which is used for the Ariane launchers.

ESA had a total of some 1,700 permanent staff at March 2002.

Activities

ESA's tasks are to define and put into effect a long-term European space policy of scientific research and technological development and to encourage all members to co-ordinate their national programmes with those of ESA to ensure that Europe maintains a competitive position in the field of space technology. ESA's basic activities cover studies on future projects, technological research, shared technical investments, information systems and training programmes. These, and the science programme, are mandatory activities to which all members must contribute; other programmes are optional and members may determine their own level of participation. In November 2000 the ESA Council and the Council of the European Union adopted parallel resolutions endorsing a European strategy for space. The strategy, which had been jointly prepared in 1999 and was entitled *Europe and Space: A New Chapter*, aimed to strengthen the foundation for European space activities; advance scientific knowledge; and to use the technical capabilities developed in connection with space activities to secure wider economic and social benefits.

ESA is committed to pursuing international co-operation to achieve its objectives of developing the peaceful applications of space technology. ESA works closely with both the US National Aeronautics and Space Administration (NASA) and the Russian Space Agency. In recent years it has developed a co-operative relationship with Japan, in particular in data relay satellites and the exchange of materials for the International Space Station. ESA has also concluded co-operation agreements with the Czech Republic, Greece, Hungary, Poland and Romania, providing for technical training and joint projects in the fields of space science, Earth observation and telecommunications. ESA assists other developing and transitional countries to expand their space activities. It works closely with other international organizations, in particular the European Union and EUMETSAT (q.v.). ESA has observer status with the UN Committee on the Peaceful Uses of Outer Space and co-operates closely with the UN's Office of Outer Space Affairs, in particular through the organization of a training and fellowship programme.

SCIENCE

The first European scientific space programmes were undertaken under the aegis of ESRO, which launched seven satellites during 1968–72. The science programmes are mandatory activities of the Agency and form the basis of co-operation between member states. The first astronomical satellite (COS–B) was launched by ESA in August 1975. By March 2002 ESA had launched 17 scientific satellites and probes, among the most successful being the Giotto probe, launched in 1985 to study the composition of Halley's comet and reactivated in 1990 to observe the Grigg-Skjellerup comet in July 1992, and Hipparcos, which, between 1989 and 1993, determined the precise astronomic positions and distances of more than 1m. stars. In November 1995 ESA launched the Infrared Space Observatory, which has successfully conducted pre-planned scientific studies providing data on galaxy and star formation and on interstellar matter. ESA is collaborating with NASA in the Ulysses space project (a solar polar mission), the Solar and Helispheric Observatory (SOHO), launched in 1995 to study the internal structure of the sun, and the Hubble Space Telescope. In October 1997 the Huygens space probe was launched under the framework of a joint NASA–ESA project (the Cassini/Huygens mission) to study the planet Saturn and its largest moon, Titan. In December 1999 the X-Ray Multimirror Mission (XMM–Newton) was launched from Kourou, French Guyana. It was envisaged that XMM–Newton, the most powerful x-ray telescope ever placed in orbit, would investigate the origin of galaxies, the formation of black holes, etc. Four cluster satellites, launched from Baikonur, Russia, in July/August 2000, were, in association with SOHO, to explore the interaction between the Earth's magnetic field and electrically-charged particles transported on the solar wind.

ESA's space missions are an integral part of its long-term science programme, Horizon 2000, which was initiated in 1984. In 1994 a new set of missions was defined, to enable the inclusion of projects using new technologies and participation in future international space activities, which formed the Horizon 2000 Plus extension covering the period 2005–16. Together they are called Horizons 2000.

The main projects being developed under the science programme in 2002 included the International Gamma-Ray Astrophysical Laboratory (Integral), scheduled to be launched in October 2002; the Rosetta spacecraft, which was to research Comet 46 P/Wirtanen and was due to be launched in early 2003; the Mars Express spacecraft, which aimed to map and search for water on Mars, and was to be launched in 2003; and the Herschel Space Observatory, which was to investigate the formation of stars and galaxies, and was to be launched in 2007.

OBSERVATION OF THE EARTH AND ITS ENVIRONMENT

ESA has contributed to the understanding and monitoring of the Earth's environment through its satellite projects. Since 1977 ESA has launched seven Meteosat spacecraft into geosynchronous orbit, which have provided continuous meteorological data, mainly for the purposes of weather forecasting. The Meteosat systems are financed and owned by EUMETSAT, but were operated by ESA until December 1995. ESA and EUMETSAT have collaborated on the development of a successor to the Meteosat weather satellites (Meteosat Second Generation) to provide enhanced geostationary data coverage. The first satellite was to be launched in 2002. ESA and EUMETSAT have also begun development of the METOP/EPS (EUMETSAT Polar System) programme, to provide observations from polar orbit. The first METOP satellite was scheduled for launch in 2003.

In 1991 ESA launched the ERS–1 satellite, which carried sophisticated instruments to measure the Earth's surface and its atmosphere. A second ERS satellite was launched in April 1995 with the specific purpose of measuring the stratospheric and tropospheric ozone. ENVISAT, the largest and most advanced European-built observation satellite, was launched in February 2002 from Kourou, French Guyana. ENVISAT aims to provide a detailed assessment of the impact of human activities on the Earth's atmosphere, and land and coastal processes, and to monitor exceptional natural events, such as volcanic eruptions.

In June 1998 the ESA Council approved the initiation of activities related to the Living Planet Programme, designed to increase understanding of environmental issues. In May 1999 the Council committed funds for a research mission, Cryosat, to be undertaken, in order to study the impact of global warming on polar ice caps. Cryosat was due to be launched in 2003. Future missions also include the Gravity Field and Steady-State Ocean Circulation Explorer (GOCE), scheduled to be launched in 2005; the GOCE mission was to use a unique measurement technique to recover geodetic precision data on the Earth's gravity field.

TELECOMMUNICATIONS

ESA commenced the development of communications satellites in 1968. These have since become the largest markets for space use and have transformed global communications, with more than 100 satellites circling the Earth for the purposes of telecommunications. The main series of operational satellites developed by ESA are the European Communications Satellites (ECS), based on the original orbital test satellite and used by EUTELSAT, and the Maritime Communications Satellites (MARECS), which have been leased for operations to INMARSAT (q.v.).

In 1989 ESA launched an experimental civilian telecommunications satellite, Olympus, to develop and demonstrate new broadcasting services. An Advanced Relay and Technology Mission Satellite (ARTEMIS) has been developed by ESA to test and operate new telecommunications techniques, and in particular to enable the relay of information directly between satellites. ARTEMIS was launched in July 2001. In 1998 ESA, together with the EU and EUROCONTROL (q.v.), continued to implement a satellite-based navigation system to be used for civilian aircraft and maritime services, similar to the two existing systems operational for military use. ESA was also working with the EU and representatives of the private sector to enhance the region's role in the development of electronic media infrastructure to meet the expanding global demand. In May 1999 the Council approved funding for a satellite multimedia programme, Artes 3, which aimed to support the development of satellite systems and services for delivering information through high-speed internet access.

LAUNCHERS

In 1973 several European Governments adopted a programme to ensure that the future ESA had independent access to space, and determined to co-ordinate knowledge gained through national programmes to develop a space launcher. The resulting Ariane rocket was first launched in December 1979. The project, which incorporated four different launchers during the 1980s, subsequently became an essential element of ESA's programme activities and, furthermore, developed a successful commercial role in placing satellites into orbit. From 1985 ESA worked to develop Ariane–5, which was to be the prototype for future launchers. The third and final qualification flight took place in October 1998. Ariane–5 successfully completed its first year of service in 2000. Ariane–5 was to be upgraded by 2005 to enable it to lift into geostationary orbit a payload of 11m. metric tons (compared with the current limit of 6.5m. tons). In December 2000 the ESA Council approved the Vega Small Launcher Development programme and the P80 Advanced Solid Propulsion Stage Demonstrator programme. The Vega programme was to support small payloads of up to 1,500 kg for polar earth orbit missions at 700 km. The first Vega launch was due to take place in 2005.

MANNED SPACEFLIGHT AND MICROGRAVITY

European astronauts and scientists have gained access to space through Spacelab, which ESA developed and contributed as part of the US Space Shuttle Programme, and through joint missions on the Russian space station, Mir. The Spacelab project enabled ESA to conduct research in life and material sciences under microgravity conditions. ESA has an ongoing programme of research in microgravity, and in 1997 initiated a new project to develop the facilities required for microgravity experiments to be conducted on the Columbus Laboratory module of the International Space Station (ISS). ESA is a partner in the ISS, which was initiated by the US Government in 1984, and was subsequently developed as a joint project between five partners—Canada, Europe, Japan, Russia and the USA. ESA's main contributions to the ISS are the Columbus Laboratory (due to be launched in 2004); and the Automated Transfer Vehicle—ATV (due to be launched by Ariane–5, with the first flight scheduled for 2003), which is to provide logistical support to the Space Station. ESA is also co-operating with NASA on developing a prototype Crew Return Vehicle (CRV), known as the X-38.

NAVIGATION

ESA and the European Commission are collaborating to design and develop a European satellite and navigation system, *Galileo*. The project will consist of about 30 satellites, a global network of tracking stations, and central control facilities in Europe. It represents Europe's contribution to the second stage of the Global Navigation Satellite System, which aims to use the *Galileo*, (American) GPS and (Russian) GLONASS systems to provide an integrated satellite navigation service of unprecedented accuracy and global coverage under civilian control. The satellites are due to be launched between 2005 and 2008. An initial *Galileo* service will be available from 2006.

Finance

All member states contribute to ESA's mandatory programme activities, on a scale based on their national income, and are free to decide on their level of commitment in optional programmes, such as telecommunications, the Ariane project and future space station and platform projects. The 2001 budget totalled about €2,800m., including €637m. (22.8%) for manned spaceflight, €593m. (21.2%) for launchers; €459m. (16.4%) for Earth observation programmes, and €363m. (13.0%) for the science programme.

Publications

ESA Annual Report.

ECSL News (quarterly).

ESA Bulletin (quarterly).
Earth Observation Quarterly.
Microgravity News (3 a year).
Preparing for the Future (quarterly).
Reaching for the Skies (quarterly).

Scientific and technical reports, brochures, training manuals, conference proceedings.

THE EUROPEAN UNION—EU

No final decision has been made on a headquarters for the Union. Meetings of the principal organs take place in Brussels, Luxembourg and Strasbourg.

The European Coal and Steel Community (ECSC) was created by a treaty signed in Paris on 18 April 1951 (effective from 25 July 1952) to pool the coal and steel production of the six original members (see below). It was seen as a first step towards a united Europe. The European Economic Community (EEC) and European Atomic Energy Community (Euratom) were established by separate treaties signed in Rome on 25 March 1957 (effective from 1 January 1958), the former to create a common market and to approximate economic policies, the latter to promote growth in nuclear industries. The common institutions of the three Communities were established by a treaty signed in Brussels on 8 April 1965 (effective from 1 July 1967).

The EEC was formally changed to the European Community (EC) under the Treaty on European Union (effective from 1 November 1993), although in practice the term EC had been used for several years to describe the three Communities together. The new Treaty established a European Union (EU), which introduced citizenship thereof and aimed to increase intergovernmental co-operation in economic and monetary affairs; to establish a common foreign and security policy; and to introduce co-operation in justice and home affairs. The EU was placed under the supervision of the European Council (comprising Heads of State or Government of member countries), while the EC continued to exist, having competence in matters relating to the Treaty of Rome and its amendments.

MEMBERS

Austria	Germany*	Netherlands*
Belgium*	Greece	Portugal
Denmark	Ireland	Spain
Finland	Italy*	Sweden
France*	Luxembourg*	United Kingdom

* Original members. Denmark, Ireland and the United Kingdom joined on 1 January 1973, and Greece on 1 January 1981. In a referendum held in February 1982, the inhabitants of Greenland voted to end their membership of the Community, entered into when under full Danish rule. Greenland's withdrawal took effect from 1 February 1985. Portugal and Spain became members on 1 January 1986. Following the reunification of Germany in October 1990, the former German Democratic Republic immediately became part of the Community, although a transitional period was to be allowed before certain Community legislation took effect there. Austria, Finland and Sweden became members on 1 January 1995.

PERMANENT REPRESENTATIVES OF MEMBER STATES

Austria: 30 ave de Cortenbergh, 1040 Brussels; tel. (2) 234-53-00; fax (2) 235-63-00; e-mail austria.press@pophost.eunet.be; GREGOR WOSCHNAGG.

Belgium: Rond-point Schuman 6, 1040 Brussels; tel. (2) 233-21-11; fax (2) 231-10-75; e-mail belgoeurop@skynet.be; FRANS VAN DAELE.

Denmark: 73 rue d'Arlon, 1040 Brussels; tel. (2) 233-08-11; fax (2) 230-93-84; e-mail brurep@um.dk; POUL SKYTTE CHRISTOFFERSEN.

Finland: 100 rue de Trèves, 1040 Brussels; tel. (2) 287-84-11; fax (2) 287-84-00; EIKKA KOSONEN.

France: 14 place de Louvain, 1000 Brussels; tel. (2) 229-82-11; fax (2) 229-82-82; e-mail firstname.lastname@diplomatie.fr; internet www.rpfrance.org; PIERRE VIMONT.

Germany: 19–21 rue J. de Lalaing, 1040 Brussels; tel. (2) 238-18-11; fax (2) 238-19-78; Dr WILHELM SCHÖNFELDER.

Greece: 25 rue Montoyer, 1000 Brussels; tel. (2) 551-56-11; fax (2) 551-56-51; e-mail mea.bruxelles@rp-grece.be; ARISTIDE AGATHOCLES.

Ireland: 89–93 rue Froissart, 1040 Brussels; tel. (2) 230-85-80; fax (2) 230-32-03; e-mail reppermirl@online.be; DENIS O'LEARY.

Italy: 9-11 rue du Marteau, 1000 Brussels; tel. (2) 220-04-11; fax (2) 219-34-49; e-mail rpue@rpue.it; internet www.rpue.it; UMBERTO VATTANI.

Luxembourg: 75 ave de Cortenbergh, 1000 Brussels; tel. (2) 737-56-00; fax (2) 737-56-10; e-mail secretariat@rpue.etat.lu; NICOLAS SCHMIT.

Netherlands: 48 ave Herrmann Debroux, 1160 Brussels; tel. (2) 679-15-11; fax (2) 679-17-75; Dr BERNHARD R. BOT.

Portugal: 12 ave de Cortenbergh, 1040 Brussels; tel. (2) 286-42-00; fax (2) 231-00-26; e-mail reper@reper.portugal.be; VASCO VALENTE.

Spain: 52 blvd du Régent, 1000 Brussels; tel. (2) 509-86-11; fax (2) 511-19-40; FRANCISCO JAVIER CONDE DE SARO.

Sweden: 30 square de Meeûs, 1000 Brussels; tel. (2) 289-56-11; fax (2) 289-56-00; e-mail representationen.bryssel@foreign.ministry.se; GUNNAR LUND.

United Kingdom: 10 ave D'Auderghem, 1040 Brussels; tel. (2) 287-82-11; fax (2) 287-83-98; internet ukrep.fco.gov.uk; Sir NIGEL SHEINWALD.

PERMANENT MISSIONS TO THE EUROPEAN UNION, WITH AMBASSADORS

(April 2002)

Afghanistan: 32 ave Raphaël, 75016 Paris, France; tel. 1-45-25-05-29; fax 1-45-24-46-87; Chargé d'affaires a.i.: MEHRABODIN MASSTAN.

Albania: 42 rue Alphonse Hottat, 1050 Brussels; tel. (2) 640-35-44; fax (2) 640-31-77; e-mail amba.brux@skynet.be; FERIT HOXHA.

Algeria: 209 ave Molière, 1050 Brussels; tel. (2) 343-50-78; fax (2) 343-51-68; MUHAMMAD LAMARI.

Andorra: 10 rue de la Montagne, 1000 Brussels; tel. (2) 513-28-06; fax (2) 513-07-41; e-mail meritxell.mateûdorra.be.be; MERITXELL MATEU I PI.

Angola: 182 rue Franz Merjay, 1180 Brussels; tel. (2) 346-18-80; fax (2) 344-08-94; JOSÉ GUERREIRO ALVES PRIMO.

Antigua and Barbuda: 100 rue des Aduatiques, 1040 Brussels; tel. (2) 733-43-28; fax (2) 735-72-37; e-mail ecs.embassies@skynet.be; EDWIN P. J. LAURENT.

Argentina: 225 ave Louise (7e étage), Boîte 2, 1050 Brussels; tel. (2) 648-93-71; fax (2) 648-08-04; JUAN JOSÉ URANGA.

Armenia: 157 rue Franz Merjay, 1060 Brussels; tel. and fax (2) 346-56-67; V. CHITECHIAN.

Australia: 6–8 rue Guimard, 1040 Brussels; tel. (2) 286-05-00; fax (2) 230-68-02; e-mail pub.affs.brussels@dfat.gov.au; internet www.austemb.be; JOANNA HEWITT.

Bahamas: 10 Chesterfield St, London, W1J 5JL, United Kingdom; tel. (20) 7408-4488; fax (20) 7499-9937; e-mail information@bahamashclondon.net; BASIL G. O'BRIEN.

Bangladesh: 29–31 rue Jacques Jordaens, 1000 Brussels; tel. (2) 640-55-00; fax (2) 646-59-98; MUHAMMAD ZAMIR.

Barbados: 100 ave F. D. Roosevelt, 1050 Brussels; tel. (2) 732-17-37; fax (2) 732-32-66; e-mail embar@pophost.eunet.be; internet www.foreign.barbadosgov.org; MICHAEL I. KING.

Belize: 100 rue des Aduatiques, 1040 Brussels; tel. (2) 732-62-04; fax (2) 732-62-46; e-mail ecs.embassies@skynet.be; EDWIN P. J. LAURENT.

Benin: 5 ave de l'Observatoire, 1180 Brussels; tel. (2) 375-06-74; fax (2) 375-83-26; ABOUDOU SALIOU.

Bhutan: 17–19 chemin du Champ d'Anier, 1209 Geneva, Switzerland; tel. (22) 7990890; fax (22) 7990899; e-mail mission.bhutan.ties.itu.int; BAP KESANG.

Bolivia: 176 ave Louise, Boîte 6, 1050 Brussels; tel. (2) 627-00-10; fax (2) 647-47-82; e-mail embolbrus@arcadis.be; ARTURO LIEBERS BALDIVIESO.

Bosnia and Herzegovina: 9 rue Paul Lauters, 1000 Brussels; tel. (2) 644-00-47; fax (2) 644-16-98; e-mail mission.bih.brussels@euronet.be; VITOMIR MILES RAGUZ.

Botswana: 169 ave de Tervueren, 1150 Brussels; tel. (2) 735-20-70; fax (2) 735-63-18; SASALA CHASALA GEORGE.

Brazil: 30 ave F.D. Roosevelt, 1050 Brussels; tel. (2) 640-20-40; fax (2) 648-80-40; e-mail braseuropa@compuserve.com; JORIO DAUSTER MAGALHÃES E SILVA.

Brunei: 238 ave F. D. Roosevelt, 1050 Brussels; tel. (2) 675-08-78; fax (2) 672-93-58; e-mail kedutaan-brunei.brussels@skynet.be; Pengiran MASHOR AHMAD.

Bulgaria: 7 ave Moscicki, 1180 Brussels; tel. (2) 374-84-68; fax (2) 374-91-88; e-mail missionlog@village.eunet.be; ANTOINETTE PRIMATAROVA.

Burkina Faso: 16 place Guy d'Arezzo, 1180 Brussels; tel. (2) 345-99-12; fax (2) 345-06-12; e-mail ambassade.burkina@skynet.be; KADRÉ DÉSIRÉ OUÉDRAOGO.

Burundi: 46 square Marie-Louise, 1040 Brussels; tel. (2) 230-45-35; fax (2) 230-78-83; e-mail ambassade.burundi@skynet.be; internet www.burundi.gov.bi; LÉONIDAS NDORICIMPA.

Cameroon: 131–133 ave Brugmann, 1190 Brussels; tel. (2) 345-18-70; fax (2) 344-57-35; ISABELLE BASSONG.

Canada: 2 ave de Tervueren, 1040 Brussels; tel. (2) 741-06-60; fax (2) 741-06-29; internet www.dfait-maeci.gc.ca/eu-mission; JAMES BARTLEMAN.

Cape Verde: 29 ave Jeanne, 1050 Brussels; tel. (2) 643-62-70; fax (2) 646-33-85; e-mail emb.caboverde@skynet.be; FERNANDO WAHNON FERREIRA.

Central African Republic: 416 blvd Lambermont, 1030 Brussels; tel. (2) 242-28-80; fax (2) 215-13-11; ARMAND GUY ZOUNGUERE-SOKAMBI.

Chad: 52 blvd Lambermont, 1030 Brussels; tel. (2) 215-19-75; fax (2) 216-35-26; ABDERAHIM YACOUB N'DAIYE.

Chile: 13 blvd St Michel, 1040 Brussels; tel. (2) 743-36-60; fax (2) 736-49-94; e-mail misue@misionchile-ue.org; ALBERTO VAN KLAVEREN.

China, People's Republic: 443–445 ave de Tervueren, 1150 Brussels; tel. (2) 771-33-09; fax (2) 779-28-95; SONG MINGJIANG.

Colombia: 96A ave F.D. Roosevelt, 1050 Brussels; tel. (2) 649-56-79; fax (2) 646-54-91; e-mail colombia@emcolbru.org; ROBERT ARENAS BONILLA.

Comoros: 27 chemin des Pins, 1180 Brussels; tel. (2) 218-41-43; fax (2) 218-69-84; e-mail ambassade.comores@skynet.be; AMOÏSS ASSOUMANI.

Congo, Democratic Republic: 30 rue Marie de Bourgogne, 1040 Brussels; tel. (2) 513-66-10; fax (2) 514-04-03; JUSTINE M'POYO-KASA VUBU.

Congo, Republic: 16–18 ave F. D. Roosevelt, 1050 Brussels; tel. (2) 648-38-56; fax (2) 648-42-13; JACQUES OBIA.

Costa Rica: 489 ave Louise (4e étage), 1050 Brussels; tel. (2) 640-55-41; fax (2) 648-31-92; e-mail embcrbel@infonie.be; MARIO FERNÁNDEZ-SILVA.

Côte d'Ivoire: 234 ave F. D. Roosevelt, 1050 Brussels; tel. (2) 672-95-77; fax (2) 672-04-91; ANET N'ZI NANAN KOLIABO.

Croatia: 50 ave des Arts, Boîte 14, 1000 Brussels; tel. (2) 500-09-20; fax (2) 512-03-38; ŽELJKO MATIĆ.

Cuba: 77 rue Robert Jones, 1180 Brussels; tel. (2) 343-00-20; fax (2) 344-96-91; RENÉ MUJICA CANTELAR.

Cyprus: 2 square Ambiorix, 1000 Brussels; tel. (2) 735-35-10; fax (2) 735-45-52; e-mail cyprus.embassy@skynet.be; K. KORNELIOU.

Czech Republic: 15 rue Caroly, 1050 Brussels; tel. (2) 213-01-11; fax (2) 213-01-85; e-mail eu.brussels@embassy.mzv.cz; LIBOR SECKA.

Djibouti: 26 rue Emile-Menier, 75116 Paris, France; tel. 1-47-27-49-22; fax 1-45-53-52-53; OMAR MOUINE ROBLEH.

Dominica: 100 rue des Aduatiques, 1040 Brussels; tel. (2) 733-43-28; fax (2) 735-72-37; e-mail ecs.embassies@skynet.be; EDWIN P. J. LAURENT.

Dominican Republic: 12 ave Bel Air, 1180 Brussels; tel. (2) 346-49-35; fax (2) 346-51-52; CLARA JOSELYN QUIÑONES RODRÍGUEZ.

Ecuador: 363 ave Louise, 1050 Brussels; tel. (2) 644-30-50; fax (2) 644-28-13; ALFREDO PINOARGOTE CEVALLOS.

Egypt: 44 ave Léo Errera, 1180 Brussels; tel. (2) 345-52-53; fax (2) 343-65-33; MUHAMMAD CHABANE.

El Salvador: 171 ave de Tervueren, 1150 Brussels; tel. (2) 733-04-85; fax (2) 735-02-11; JOAQUÍN RODEZNA MUNGUIA.

Equatorial Guinea: 17 ave Jupiter, 1190 Brussels; tel. (2) 346-25-09; fax (2) 346-33-09; e-mail guineaecuatorial.brux@skynet.be; MARI-CRUZ EVONA ANDEME.

Eritrea: 15–17 ave de Wolvendael, 1180 Brussels; tel. (2) 374-44-34; fax (2) 372-07-30; e-mail eebb@pophost.eunet.be; ANDEBRHAN WELDEGIORGIS.

Estonia: 1–3 rue Marie-Thérèse, 1000 Brussels; tel. (2) 227-39-10; fax (2) 227-39-25; e-mail eu.all@eu.estemb.be; PRIIT KOLBRE.

Ethiopia: 231 ave de Tervueren, Brussels; tel. (2) 771-32-94; fax (2) 771-49-14; PETER GABRIEL ROBLEH.

Fiji: 66 ave de Cortenbergh (7e étage), Boîte 7, 1000 Brussels; tel. (2) 736-90-50; fax (2) 736-14-58; ISIKELI ULUINAIRAI MATAITOGA.

Gabon: 112 ave Winston Churchill, 1180 Brussels; tel. (2) 340-62-10; fax (2) 346-46-69; e-mail bs.175335@skynet.be; JEAN-ROBERT GOULONGANA.

The Gambia: 126 ave F. D. Roosevelt, 1050 Brussels; tel. (2) 640-10-49; fax (2) 646-32-77; e-mail gambianmission@hotmail.com; ALICU M. NGUM.

Georgia: 15 rue Vergote, 1030 Brussels; tel. (2) 732-85-50; fax (2) 732-85-47; e-mail geoemb.bru@skynet.be; ZURAB ABACHIDZE.

Ghana: 7 blvd Gén. Wahis, 1030 Brussels; tel. (2) 705-82-20; fax (2) 705-66-53; e-mail head@ghembassy.arc.be; KOBINA WUDU.

Grenada: 123 rue de Laeken, 1000 Brussels; tel. (2) 223-73-03; fax (2) 223-73-07; FABIAN A. REDHEAD.

Guatemala: 185 ave Winston Churchill, 1180 Brussels; tel. (2) 345-90-58; fax (2) 344-64-99; e-mail obguab@infoboard.be; EDMOND MULET LESIEUR.

Guinea: 75 ave Roger Vandendriessche, 1150 Brussels; tel. (2) 771-01-26; fax (2) 762-60-36; MAMADOU BOBO CAMARA.

Guinea-Bissau: 70 ave F. D. Roosevelt, 1050 Brussels; tel. (2) 647-08-90; fax (2) 640-43-12; Chargé d'affaires a.i.: JOSE FONSECA.

Guyana: 12 ave du Brésil, 1000 Brussels; tel. (2) 675-62-16; fax (2) 675-55-98; e-mail embassy.guyana@skynet.be; HAVELOCK R. H. BREWSTER.

Haiti: 139 Chaussée de Charleroi, 1060 Brussels; tel. (2) 649-73-81; fax (2) 640-60-80; e-mail amb.haiti.bel@skynet.be; YOLETTE AZOR-CHARLES.

Holy See: 5–9 ave des Franciscains, 1150 Brussels; tel. (2) 762-20-05; fax (2) 762-20-32; Apostolic Nuncio: Most Rev. PIER LUIGI CELATA, Titular Archbishop of Doclea.

Honduras: 3 ave des Gaulois (5e étage), 1040 Brussels; tel. (2) 734-00-00; fax (2) 735-26-26; IVÁN ROMERO MARTÍNEZ.

Hungary: 44 ave du Vert Chasseur, 1180 Brussels; tel. (2) 379-09-00; fax (2) 372-07-84; e-mail titkarsag@humisbeu.be; internet www.humiseu.be; ENDRE JUHÁSZ.

Iceland: 74 rue de Trèves, 1040 Brussels; tel. (2) 286-17-00; fax (2) 286-17-70; e-mail icemb.brussel@utn.stjr.is; internet www.iceland.org/be; GUNNAR SNORRI GUNNARSSON.

India: 217 chaussée de Vleurgat, 1050 Brussels; tel. (2) 640-91-40; fax (2) 648-96-38; e-mail eoibru@mail.skynet.be; C. DASGUPTA.

Indonesia: 38 blvd de la Woluwe, 1200 Brussels; tel. (2) 779-09-15; fax (2) 772-82-10; POEDJI KOENTARSO.

Iran: 415 ave de Tervueren, 1150 Brussels; tel. (2) 762-37-45; fax (2) 762-39-15; e-mail eiri.bxl@skynet.be; ABOLGHASEM DELFI.

Iraq: 23 ave des Aubépines, 1180 Brussels; tel. (2) 374-59-92; fax (2) 374-76-15; e-mail ambassade.irak@skynet.be; Chargé d'affaires a.i.: DR RIADH AL-WEYESAHDI S. HAMOUDI.

Israel: 40 ave de l'Observatoire, 1180 Brussels; tel. (2) 373-55-00; fax (2) 373-56-17; HARRY KNEY-TAL.

Jamaica: 2 ave Palmerston, 1000 Brussels; tel. (2) 230-11-70; fax (2) 230-37-09; e-mail emb.jam.brussels@skynet.be; DOUGLAS ANTHONY CLIVE SAUNDERS.

Japan: 5–6 Sq. de Meeûs, 1000 Brussels; tel. (2) 500-77-11; fax (2) 513-32-41; e-mail inf@jmission-eu-be; internet www.jmission-eu.be; TAKAYUKI KIMURA.

Jordan: 104 ave F. D. Roosevelt, 1050 Brussels; tel. (2) 640-77-55; fax (2) 640-27-96; Dr UMAYYA TOUKAN.

Kazakhstan: 30 ave Van Bever, 1180 Brussels; tel. (2) 374-95-62; fax (2) 374-50-91; AKHMETZHAN S. YESIMOV.

Kenya: 208 ave Winston Churchill, 1180 Brussels; tel. (2) 340-10-40; fax (2) 340-10-50; e-mail kenbrussels@hotmail.com; PETER OLE NKURAIYIA.

Kiribati: c/o Ministry of Foreign Affairs, POB 68, Bairiki, Tarawa; tel. 21342; fax 21466.

Korea, Republic: 173–175 chaussée de la Hulpe, 1170 Brussels; tel. (2) 675-57-77; fax (2) 675-52-21; LEE JAI CHUN.

Kuwait: 43 ave F. D. Roosevelt, 1050 Brussels; tel. (2) 647-79-50; fax (2) 646-12-98; e-mail embassy.kwt@euronet.be; ABDULAZEEZ A. AL-SHARIKH.

Kyrgyzstan: 133 rue Tenbosch, 1050 Brussels; tel. (2) 534-63-99; fax (2) 534-23-25; CHINGIZ TOREKULOVICH AITMATOV.

Laos: 74 ave Raymond Poincaré, 75116 Paris, France; tel. 1-45-53-02-98; fax 1-47-57-27-89; KHAMPHAN SIMMALAVONG.

Latvia: 39–41 rue d'Arlon, Boîte 6, 1000 Brussels; tel. (2) 282-03-60; fax (2) 282-03-69; e-mail missioneu@mfa.gov.lv; ANDRIS PIEBALGS.

Lebanon: 2 rue Guillaume Stocq, 1050 Brussels; tel. (2) 645-77-60; fax (2) 645-77-69; FAWZI FAWAZ.

Lesotho: 45 blvd Général Wahis, 1030 Brussels; tel. (2) 705-39-76; fax (2) 705-67-79; e-mail lesothobruemb@skynet.be; R. V. LECHESA.

Liberia: 50 ave du Château, 1081 Brussels; tel. (2) 414-73-17; fax (2) 411-09-12; Dr CECIL T. O. BRANDY.

Libya: 28 ave Victoria, 1050 Brussels; tel. (2) 649-21-12; HAMED AHMED ELHOUDERI.

Liechtenstein: 1 Place du Congrès, 1000 Brussels; tel. (2) 229-39-00; fax (2) 219-35-45; e-mail ambassade.liechtenstein@bbru.llv.li; Prince NIKOLAUS VON LIECHTENSTEIN.

Lithuania: 51 ave des Cinq Bonniers, 1150 Brussels; tel. (2) 771-01-40; fax (2) 771-45-97; ROMUALDAS KOLONAITIS.

Macedonia, former Yugoslav republic: 128 ave de Tervueren, 1150 Brussels; tel. (2) 732-91-08; fax (2) 732-91-11; SASKO STEFKOV.

Madagascar: 297 ave de Tervueren, 1150 Brussels; tel. (2) 770-17-26; fax (2) 772-37-31; e-mail pierre.rabarivola@ambassademadagascar.be; internet www.ambassademadagascar.be; DR PIERRE RABARIVOLA.

Malawi: 15 rue de la Loi, 1040 Brussels; tel. (2) 231-09-80; fax (2) 231-10-66; JULIE NANYONI MPHANDE.

Malaysia: 414A ave de Tervueren, 1150 Brussels; tel. (2) 776-03-40; fax (2) 762-67-67; e-mail embassy.malaysia@euronet.be; Dato' M. M. SATHIAH.

Maldives: 212 East 47th St, Apt 15B, New York, NY 10017, USA; tel. (212) 688-0776.

Mali: 487 ave Molière, 1050 Brussels; tel. (2) 345-74-32; fax (2) 344-57-00; AHMED MOHAMED AG HAMANI.

Malta: 44 rue Jules Lejeune, 1050 Brussels; tel. (2) 343-01-95; fax (2) 343-01-06; VICTOR CAMILLERI.

Mauritania: 6 ave de la Colombie, 1050 Brussels; tel. (2) 672-47-47; fax (2) 672-20-51; BOULLAH OULD MOGUEYE.

Mauritius: 68 rue des Bollandistes, 1040 Brussels; tel. (2) 733-99-88; fax (2) 734-40-21; e-mail ambmaur@skynet.be; S. GUNESSEE.

Mexico: 94 ave F.D. Roosevelt, 1050 Brussels; tel. (2) 629-07-11; fax (2) 644-08-19; e-mail mex-ue@pophost.eunet.be; PORFIRIO MUÑOZ-LEDO Y LAZO DE LA VEGA.

Mongolia: 18 ave Besme, 1190 Brussels; tel. (2) 344-69-74; fax (2) 344-32-15; e-mail brussels.mn.embassy@chello.be; SODOV ONON.

Morocco: 275 ave Louise, 1050 Brussels; tel. (2) 736-11-00; fax (2) 734-64-68; e-mail sifamabruxe@infoboard.be; Chargé d'affaires a.i.: AICHA BELARBI SAUBRY.

Mozambique: 97 blvd Saint-Michel, 1040 Brussels; tel. (2) 736-25-64; fax (2) 735-62-07; e-mail embamoc.bru@skynet.be; ÁLVARO MANUEL TRINIDADE DA SILVA.

Myanmar: Schumannstrasse 112, 53113 Bonn, Germany; tel. (228) 210091; fax (228) 219316; U TUN NGWE.

Namibia: 454 ave de Tervueren, 1150 Brussels; tel. (2) 771-14-10; fax (2) 771-96-89; e-mail nam.emb@brutele.be; Dr ZEDEKIA JOSEF NGAVIRUE.

Nepal: 68 ave Winston Churchill, 1180 Brussels; tel. (2) 346-26-58; fax (2) 344-13-61; e-mail rne.bru@skynet.be; KEDAR BHAKTA SHRESTHA.

New Zealand: 1 square de Meeus, 1000 Brussels; tel. (2) 512-10-40; fax (2) 513-48-56; e-mail nzemb.brussels@skynet.be; DELL HIGGIE.

Nicaragua: 55 ave de Wolvendael, 1180 Brussels; tel. (2) 375-64-34; fax (2) 375-71-88; ALVARO PORTA BERMÚDEZ.

Niger: 78 ave F. D. Roosevelt, 1050 Brussels; tel. (2) 648-61-40; fax (2) 648-27-84; HOUSSEINI ABDOU-SALEYE.

Nigeria: 288 ave de Tervueren, 1150 Brussels; tel. (2) 762-52-00; fax (2) 762-37-63; GABRIEL SAM AKUNWAFOR.

Norway: 17 rue Archimède, 1000 Brussels; tel. (2) 234-11-11; fax (2) 234-11-50; EINAR M. BULL.

Oman: 50 ave d'Iéna, 75116 Paris, France; tel. 1-47-23-01-63; fax 1-47-23-77-10; MUHAMMAD BIN SULTAN AL-BUSAIDI.

Pakistan: 57 ave Delleur, 1170 Brussels; tel. (2) 673-80-07; fax (2) 675-83-94; e-mail parepbru_econ@infoboard.be; SAIDULLA KHAN DEHLAVI.

Panama: 390–392 ave Louise, 1050 Brussels; tel. (2) 649-07-29; fax (2) 648-92-16; e-mail panama@antrasite.be; Chargé d'affaires a.i.: ELENA BARLETTA DE NOTTEBOHM.

Papua New Guinea: 430 ave de Tervueren, 1150 Brussels; tel. (2) 779-08-26; fax (2) 772-70-88; GABRIEL KOIBA PEPSON.

Paraguay: 475 ave Louise (12e étage), 1050 Brussels; tel. (2) 649-90-55; fax (2) 647-42-48; MANUEL MARÍA CÁCERES.

Peru: 179 ave de Tervueren, 1150 Brussels; tel. (2) 733-33-19; fax (2) 733-48-19; e-mail comunicaciones@embassy-of-peru.be; JOSÉ URRUTIA.

Philippines: 297 ave Molière, 1050 Brussels; tel. (2) 340-33-77; fax (2) 345-64-25; e-mail pleu.pe@skynet.be; internet www.philembassy.be; CLEMENCIO F. MONTESA.

Poland: 282–284 ave de Tervueren, 1150 Brussels; tel. (2) 777-72-00; fax (2) 777-72-97; e-mail 101642.2616@compuserve.com; JAN TRUSZCZYNSKI.

Qatar: 71 ave F. D. Roosevelt, 1050 Brussels; tel. (2) 640-29-00; fax (2) 648-40-78; e-mail qatar@infonie.be; Chargé d'affaires a.i.: MOHAMED AL-HAIYKI.

Romania: 107 rue Gabrielle, 1180 Brussels; tel. (2) 344-41-45; fax (2) 344-24-79; e-mail rommis@pophost.eunet.be; L. COMANESCU.

Russia: 56 ave Louis Lepoutre, 1060 Brussels; tel. (2) 343-03-39; fax (2) 346-24-53; e-mail misrusce@interpac.be; VASILII LIKHACHEN.

Rwanda: 1 ave des Fleurs, 1150 Brussels; tel. (2) 763-07-02; fax (2) 763-07-53; e-mail ambarwanda.@skynet.be; internet www.ambarwanda.be; MANZI BAKURAMURZA.

Saint Christopher and Nevis: 42 rue de Livourne, 1000 Brussels; tel. (2) 534-26-11; fax (2) 539-40-09; e-mail ecs.embassies@skynet.be; EDWIN P. J. LAURENT.

Saint Lucia: 42 rue de Livourne, 1000 Brussels; tel. (2) 534-26-11; fax (2) 539-40-09; e-mail ecs.embassies@skynet.be; EDWIN P. J. LAURENT.

Saint Vincent and the Grenadines: 42 rue de Livourne, 1000 Brussels; tel. (2) 534-26-11; fax (2) 539-40-09; e-mail ecs.embassies@skynet.be; EDWIN P. J. LAURENT.

Samoa: 123 ave F. D. Roosevelt, Boîte 14, 1050 Brussels; tel. (2) 660-84-54; fax (2) 675-03-36; e-mail samoa.emb.bxl@skynet.be; TAUILIILI UILI MEREDITH.

San Marino: 62 ave F.D. Roosevelt, 1050 Brussels; tel. (2) 644-22-24; fax (2) 644-20-57; SAVINA ZAFFERANI.

São Tomé and Príncipe: 175 ave de Tervueren, 1150 Brussels; tel. and fax (2) 734-88-15; e-mail ambassade.sao.tome@skynet.be; Chargé d'affaires a.i.: ARMINDO DE BRITO FERNANDES.

Saudi Arabia: 45 ave F. D. Roosevelt, 1050 Brussels; tel. (2) 649-20-44; fax (2) 647-24-92; NASSIR AL-ALASSAF.

Senegal: 196 ave F. D. Roosevelt, 1050 Brussels; tel. (2) 673-00-97; fax (2) 675-04-60; SALIOU CISSE.

Seychelles: 51 ave Mozart, 75016 Paris, France; tel. 1-42-30-57-47; fax 1-42-30-57-40; e-mail ambsey@aol.com; CALLIXTE FRANÇOIS-XAVIER D'OFFAY.

Sierra Leone: 410 ave de Tervueren, 1150 Brussels; tel. (2) 771-00-53; fax (2) 771-82-30; FODE M. DABOR .

Singapore: 198 ave F. D. Roosevelt, 1050 Brussels; tel. (2) 660-29-79; fax (2) 660-86-85; e-mail amb.eu@singembbru.be; A. SELVERAJAH.

Slovakia: 79 ave Cortenbergh, 1000 Brussels; tel. (2) 743-68-11; fax (2) 743-68-88; e-mail slovakmission@pmsreu.be; JURAJ MIGAS.

Slovenia: 30 ave Marnix, 1000 Brussels; tel. (2) 512-44-66; fax (2) 512-09-97; e-mail mission.bruxelles@mzz-dkp.sigor.si; MARKO KRANJEC.

Solomon Islands: 13 ave de L'Yser, Boîte 3, 1040 Brussels; tel. (2) 732-70-85; fax (2) 732-68-85; ROBERT SISILO.

Somalia: 26 rue Dumont d'Urville, 75116 Paris, France; tel. 1-45-00-76-51; (vacant).

South Africa: 26 rue de la Loi, Boîtes 7–8, 1040 Brussels; tel. (2) 285-44-00; fax (2) 285-44-87; e-mail embassy.southafrica@belgium.online.be; (vacant).

Sri Lanka: 27 rue Jules Lejeune, 1050 Brussels; tel. (2) 344-53-94; fax (2) 344-67-37; e-mail sri.lanka@euronet.be; N. NAVARATNARAJAH.

Sudan: 124 ave F. D. Roosevelt, 1050 Brussels; tel. (2) 647-51-59; fax (2) 648-34-99; GALAL HASSAN ATABANI.

Suriname: 379 ave Louise, 1050 Brussels; tel. (2) 640-11-72; fax (2) 646-39-62; e-mail sur.amb.bru@online.be; Chargé d'affaires a.i.: JANE R. NANHU.

Swaziland: 188 ave Winston Churchill, 1180 Brussels; tel. (2) 347-47-71; fax (2) 347-46-23; Dr THEMBAYENA ANNASTASIA DLAMINI.

Switzerland: 1 place du Luxembourg, Boîte 9, 1050 Brussels; tel. (2) 286-13-11; fax (2) 230-45-09; e-mail vertretung@brm.rep.admin.ch; DANTE MARTINELLI.

Syria: 3 ave F. D. Roosevelt, 1050 Brussels; tel. (2) 648-01-35; fax (2) 646-40-18; (vacant).

Tanzania: 363 ave Louise (7e étage), 1050 Brussels; tel. (2) 640-65-00; fax (2) 646-80-26; ALI ABEID AMAN KARUME.

Thailand: 2 square du Val de la Cambre, 1050 Brussels; tel. (2) 640-68-10; fax (2) 648-30-66; e-mail thaibxl@pophost.eunet.be; internet www.waw.be/rte-be; SURAPONG POSAYANOND.

Togo: 264 ave de Tervueren, 1150 Brussels; tel. (2) 770-17-91; fax (2) 771-50-75; ELIOTT LATEVI-ATCHO LAWSON.

Tonga: 36 Molyneux St, London, W1H 6AB, United Kingdom; tel. (20) 7724-5828; fax (20) 7723-9074; e-mail tongahicommission@btinternet.com; 'AKOSITA FINEANGANOFO.

Trinidad and Tobago: 14 ave de la Faisanderie, 1150 Brussels; tel. (2) 762-94-15; fax (2) 772-27-83; e-mail information@ttm.eunet.be; Chargé d'affaires a. i.: S. N. GORDON.

Tunisia: 278 ave de Tervueren, 1150 Brussels; tel. (2) 771-73-95; fax (2) 771-94-33; TAHAR SIOUD.

Turkey: 4 rue Montoyer, 1000 Brussels; tel. (2) 513-28-36; fax (2) 511-0450; e-mail turkdelegeu@euronet.be; NIHAT AKYOL.

Tuvalu: c/o Prime Minister's Office, Vaiaku, Funafuti, Tuvalu.

Uganda: 317 ave de Tervueren, 1150 Brussels; tel. (2) 762-58-25; fax (2) 763-04-38; e-mail ugembrus@brutele.be; KAMIMA NTAMBI.

Ukraine: 7 rue Guimard, 1040 Brussels; tel. (2) 511-46-09; fax (2) 512-40-45; ROMAN SHPEK.

United Arab Emirates: 73 ave F. D. Roosevelt, 1050 Brussels; tel. (2) 640-60-00; fax (2) 646-24-73; e-mail emirates.bxl@infonie.be; ABDEL HADI ABDEL WAHID AL-KHAJA.

USA: 40 blvd du Régent, Boîte 3, 1000 Brussels; tel. (2) 500-27-74; fax (2) 512-57-20; e-mail useu@usinfo.be; internet www.useu.be; ROCKWELL A. SCHNABEL.

Uruguay: 22 ave F. D. Roosevelt, 1050 Brussels; tel (2) 640-11-69; fax (2) 648-29-09; e-mail uruemb@euronet.be; GUILLERMO VALLES.

Vanuatu: c/o Prime Minister's Office, POB 110, Port Vila, Vanuatu.

Venezuela: 10 ave F. D. Roosevelt, 1050 Brussels; tel. (2) 639-03-40; fax (2) 647-88-20; LUIS XAVIER GRISANTI.

Viet Nam: 130 ave de la Floride, 1180 Brussels; tel. (2) 374-91-33; fax (2) 374-93-76; HUYNH ANH DZUNG.

Yemen: 114 ave F. D. Roosevelt, 1050 Brussels; tel. (2) 646-52-90; fax (2) 646-29-11; GAZEM A. K. AL-AGHBARI.

Yugoslavia: 11 ave Emile Demot, 1000 Brussels; tel. (2) 649-83-65; fax (2) 649-08-78; DRAGOSLAV JOVANOVIĆ.

Zambia: 469 ave Molière, 1060 Brussels; tel. (2) 343-56-49; fax (2) 347-43-33; GRIFFINKAFWIMBI NYIRONGO.

Zimbabwe: 11 square Joséphine Charlotte, 1200 Brussels; tel. (2) 762-58-08; fax (2) 762-96-05; SIMBARASHE S. MUMBENGEGWI.

Union Institutions

Originally each of the Communities had its own Commission (High Authority in the case of the ECSC) and Council, but a treaty transferring the powers of these bodies to a single Commission and a single Council came into effect in 1967.

EUROPEAN COMMISSION

Address: 200 rue de la Loi, 1049 Brussels, Belgium.

Telephone: (2) 299-11-11; **fax:** (2) 295-01-38; **internet:** www.europa.eu.int/comm/index.htm.

MEMBERS OF THE COMMISSION

(with their responsibilities: April 2002)

President: ROMANO PRODI (Italy): Secretariat General; Forward Studies Unit; Legal Service; Media and Communication.

Vice-Presidents:

NEIL KINNOCK (United Kingdom): Administrative reform; Personnel and administration; Linguistic services; Protocol and security; Internal Audit Service.

LOYOLA DE PALACIO (Spain): Relations with the European Parliament; Relations with the Committee of the Regions, the Economic and Social Committee, and the Ombudsman; Transport, including trans-European networks; Energy.

Other Members:

MARIO MONTI (Italy): Competition.

FRANZ FISCHLER (Austria): Agriculture; Rural development; Fisheries.

ERKKI LIIKANEN (Finland): Enterprise; Competitiveness; Innovation; Information Society.

FRITS BOLKESTEIN (Netherlands): Internal market; Financial services; Customs; Taxation.

PHILIPPE BUSQUIN (Belgium): Science, research and development; Joint Research Centre.

PEDRO SOLBES MIRA (Spain): Economic and financial affairs; Monetary matters; Statistical office.

POUL NIELSON (Denmark): Development aid and co-operation; Humanitarian Aid office.

GÜNTER VERHEUGEN (Germany): Enlargement process, including the pre-accession strategy.

CHRISTOPHER PATTEN (United Kingdom): External relations; Common foreign and security policy; Delegations to non-member countries; Common service for external relations.

PASCAL LAMY (France): Trade policy and instruments of trade policy.

DAVID BYRNE (Ireland): Public health; Consumer protection.

MICHEL BARNIER (France): Regional policy; Cohesion fund; Intergovernmental Conference.

VIVIANE REDING (Luxembourg): Citizens' Europe; Transparency; Education and culture; Publications office.

MICHAELE SCHREYER (Germany): Budget; Financial control; Fraud prevention.

MARGOT WALLSTRÖM (Sweden): Environment; Nuclear safety.

ANTÓNIO VITORINO (Portugal): Freedom, security and justice.

ANNA DIAMANTOPOULOU (Greece): Employment and social affairs; Equal opportunities.

The functions of the Commission are fourfold: to ensure the application of the provisions of the Treaties and of the provisions enacted by the institutions of the Communities in pursuance thereof; to formulate recommendations or opinions in matters which are the subject of the Treaties, where the latter expressly so provides or where the Commission considers it necessary; to dispose, under the conditions laid down in the Treaties, of a power of decision of its own and to participate in the preparation of acts of the Council of the European Union and of the European Parliament; and to exercise the competence conferred on it by the Council of the European Union for the implementation of the rules laid down by the latter.

The Commission may not include more than two members having the nationality of the same state; the number of members of the Commission may be amended by a unanimous vote of the Council of the European Union. In the performance of their duties, the members of the Commission are forbidden to seek or accept instructions from any Government or other body, or to engage in any other paid or unpaid professional activity.

The members of the Commission are nominated by the Governments of the member states acting in common agreement normally for a renewable term of five years. From January 1995, under the terms of the Treaty on European Union, the nominated President and other members of the Commission must be approved as a body by the European Parliament before they can take office. Once approved, the Commission may nominate one or two of its members as Vice-President. Any member of the Commission, if he or she no longer fulfils the conditions required for the performance of his or her duties, or commits a serious offence, may be declared removed from office by the Court of Justice. The Court may furthermore, on the petition of the Council of the European Union or of the Commission itself, provisionally suspend any member of the Commission from his or her duties. The European Parliament has the authority to dismiss the entire Commission.

In January 1999 Commissioners accused of mismanagement and corruption retained their positions following a vote of censure by Parliament. However, Parliament proceeded to appoint a five-member Committee of Independent Experts to investigate allegations of fraud, mismanagement and nepotism within the Commission. In early March two new codes of conduct for Commissioners were announced. On 15 March the Committee published a report that criticized the Commission's failure to control the administration and to take responsibility for the budget and other measures implemented by each department. The report also identified individual Commissioners as guilty of nepotism and mismanagement and proposed the establishment of a new independent unit to investigate fraud. As a consequence of the report the Commission agreed, collectively, to resign, although Commissioners were to retain their positions, and exercise limited duties, until their successors were appointed. In late March EU heads of state and of government nominated Romano Prodi, the former Italian Prime Minister, as the next President of the Commission. His appointment was endorsed by the outgoing Parliament in early May, but it required formal ratification by the newly-constituted Parliament, which was scheduled to convene for the first time in July, following elections in June. Prodi's appointment, and the team of Commissioners that he had appointed in the interim, were duly ratified by Parliament in September. However, Parliament made ratification subject to conditions, forming the foundation of a future inter-institutional agreement between itself and the Commission: while it did not lose any of its powers, the Commission undertook to be more open in its future dealings with the Parliament. In February 2000 Prodi issued a mission statement proposing a radical restructuring of the EU's system of governance, including a redistribution of responsibilities between EU, national, regional and local authorities.

ADMINISTRATION

Offices are at the address of the European Commission (see above) unless otherwise stated.

GENERAL SERVICES

Secretariat-General of the Commission: Sec.-Gen. DAVID O'SULLIVAN.

Statistical Office (EUROSTAT): Bâtiment Jean Monnet, rue Alcide de Gasperi, 2920 Luxembourg; tel. 4301-33-107; fax 4301-33-015; e-mail media.support@eurostat.cec.be; internet europa.eu.int/eurostat.html; Dir-Gen. YVES FRANCHET.

Press and Communication: Dir JONATHAN FAULL.

Office for Official Publications of the European Union (EUR-OP): 2 rue Mercier, 2985 Luxembourg; tel. 2929-1; fax 2929-44619; e-mail europ@opoce.cec.be; internet eur-op.eu.int; Dir-Gen. THOMAS L. CRANFIELD.

European Anti-fraud Office: Dir-Gen. FRANZ-HERMANN BRUENER.

POLICIES

Agriculture: Dir-Gen. JOSÉ MANUEL SILVA RODRÍGUEZ.

Competition: Dir-Gen. ALEXANDER SCHAUB.

Economics and Financial Affairs: Dir-Gen. KLAUS REGLING.

Education and Culture: Dir-Gen. NIKOLAUS VAN DER PAS.

Employment and Social Affairs: Dir-Gen. ODILE QUINTIN.

Energy and Transport: Dir-Gen. FRANÇOIS LAMOUREUX.

Enterprise: Dir-Gen. FABIO COLASANTI.

Environment: Dir-Gen. JEAN-FRANÇOIS VERSTRYNGE (acting).

Fisheries: Dir-Gen. STEFFEN SMIDT.

Health and Consumer Protection: Dir-Gen. ROBERT COLEMAN.

Information Society: Dir-Gen. ROBERT VERRUE.

Internal Market: Dir-Gen. JOHN F. MOGG.

Joint Research Centre: Dir-Gen. FINBARR MCSWEENEY.

Justice and Home Affairs: Dir-Gen. ADRIAN FORTESCUE.

Regional Policy: Dir-Gen. GUY CRAUSER.

Research: Dir-Gen. ACHILLEAS MITSOS.

Taxation and Customs Union: Dir-Gen. MICHEL VANDEN ABEELE.

EXTERNAL RELATIONS

Common Service for External Relations: Dir-Gen. DANIELA TRAMACERE.

Development: Dir-Gen. JACOBUS RICHELLE.

Enlargement: Dir-Gen. ENEKO LANDÁBURU ILLARRAMENDI.

EuropeAid - Co-operation Office: Dir-Gen. GIORGIO BONACCI.

External Relations: Dir-Gen. GUY LEGRAS.

European Community Humanitarian Office (ECHO): Dir COSTANZA ADINOLFI.

Trade: Dir-Gen. MOGENS PETER CARL.

INTERNAL SERVICES

Budget: Dir-Gen. JEAN-PAUL MINGASSON.

Financial Control: Dir-Gen. EDITH KITZMANTEL.

Joint Interpreting and Conference Service: Head of Service MARCO BENEDETTI.

Legal Service: Dir-Gen. MICHEL PETITE.

Personnel and Administration: Dir-Gen. HORST REICHENBACH.

Translation Service: Dir-Gen. BRIAN MCCLUSKEY (acting).

THE EUROPEAN COUNCIL

The heads of state or of government of the member countries meet at least twice a year, in the member state which currently exercises the presidency of the Council of the European Union, or in Brussels.

Until 1975 summit meetings were held less frequently, on an *ad hoc* basis, usually to adopt major policy decisions regarding the future development of the Community. In answer to the evident need for more frequent consultation at the highest level, it was decided at the summit meeting in Paris, in December 1974, to hold the meetings on a regular basis, under the rubric of the European Council. There was no provision made for the existence of the European Council in the Treaty of Rome, but its position was acknowledged and regularized in the Single European Act (1987). Its role was further strengthened in the Treaty on European Union, which entered into force on 1 November 1993. As a result of the Treaty, the European Council became directly responsible for common policies within the fields of Common Foreign and Security Policy and Justice and Home Affairs.

COUNCIL OF THE EUROPEAN UNION

The Council of the European Union (until 1994 known formally as the Council of Ministers of the European Community and still frequently referred to as the Council of Ministers) is the only institution that directly represents the member states. It is the Community's principal decision-making body, acting on proposals made by the Commission, and is responsible for ensuring the co-ordination of the general economic policies of the member states and for taking the decisions necessary to implement the Treaties. The Council is composed of representatives of the member states, each Government delegating to it one of its members, according to the subject to be discussed. These meetings are generally referred to as the Agriculture Council, Telecommunications Council, etc. The Foreign Affairs, Economics and Finance ('ECOFIN') and Agriculture Councils normally meet once a month. The office of President is exercised for a term of six months by each member of the Council in rotation (January–June 2002: Spain; July–December: Denmark). Meetings of the Council are convened and chaired by the President, acting on his or her own initiative or at the request of a member or of the Commission.

The Treaty of Rome prescribed three types of voting: simple majority, qualified majority and unanimity. The votes of its members are weighted as follows: France, Germany, Italy and the United Kingdom 10; Spain 8; Belgium, Greece, the Netherlands and Portugal 5; Austria and Sweden 4; Denmark, Finland and Ireland 3; Luxembourg 2. Out of a total number of votes of 87, 62 are required for a qualified majority decision, making 26 votes sufficient for a blocking minority. During negotiations for enlargement of the EU, an agreement was reached, in March 1994, on new rules regulating voting procedures in the expanded Council, in response to concerns on the part of Spain and the United Kingdom that their individual influence would be diminished. Under the 'Ioannina compromise' (named after the Greek town where the agreement was concluded) 23–25 opposing votes were to be sufficient to continue debate of legislation for a 'reasonable period' until a consensus decision is reached. Amendments to the Treaty of Rome (the Single European Act), effective from July 1987, restricted the right of 'veto', and were expected to accelerate the development of a genuine common market: they allowed proposals relating to the dismantling of barriers to the free movement of goods, persons, services and capital to be approved by a majority vote in the Council, rather than by a unanimous vote. Unanimity would still be required, however, for certain areas, including harmonization of indirect taxes, legislation on health and safety, veterinary controls, and environmental protection; individual states would also retain control over immigration rules, prevention of terrorism and drugs-trafficking. The Treaty of Amsterdam, which came into force on 1 May 1999, extended the use of qualified majority voting to limited policy areas.

The Single European Act introduced a 'co-operation procedure' whereby a proposal adopted by a qualified majority in the Council must be submitted to the European Parliament for approval: if the Parliament rejects the Council's common position, unanimity shall be required for the Council to act on a second reading, and if the Parliament suggests amendments, the Commission must re-examine the proposal and forward it to the Council again. A 'co-decision procedure' was introduced in 1993 by the Treaty on European Union. The procedure allows a proposal to be submitted for a third reading by a so-called 'Conciliation Committee', composed equally of Council representatives and members of the European Parliament. The Treaty of Amsterdam was to simplify the co-decision procedure, and extend it to matters previously resolved under the co-operation procedure, although the latter was to remain in place for matters concerning economic and monetary union.

Under the Treaty of Amsterdam, the Secretary-General of the Council was also to take the role of 'High Representative', responsible for the co-ordination of common foreign and security policy. The Secretary-General was to be supported by a policy planning and early warning unit. In June 1999 Javier Solana Madariaga, at that time Secretary-General of NATO, was designated as the first Secretary-General of the Council.

The Treaty of Nice, initialled in February 2001, addresses institutional issues that remained outstanding under the Treaty of Amsterdam and which had to be settled before the enlargement of the EU from 2003, and various other issues not directly connected with enlargement. The main focus of the Treaty is the establishment of principles governing the new distribution of seats in the European Parliament, the new composition of the Commission and a new definition of qualified majority voting within the European Council. It stipulates that, with effect from the appointment of the next European Commission, in January 2005, the five largest member states (France, Germany, Italy, Spain and the United Kingdom) will lose their present right each to nominate two Commissioners. Instead, all member states will be entitled to nominate one member of the Commission, which may be enlarged to an upper limit of 26 Commissioners. Were the number of EU member states to expand beyond 26, the Council would set a limit on Commission membership, at 26 Commissioners or fewer, to be appointed on a rotational basis. The powers of the President of the Commission were to be enhanced. The new weighting system for existing members' votes within the European Council, effective from 1 January 2005, was designated as follows: France, Germany, Italy and the United Kingdom 29; Spain 27; Netherlands 13; Greece, Belgium and Portugal 12; Sweden and Austria 10; Denmark, Finland and Ireland 7; Luxembourg 4. Of the total number of 237 votes (based on the current 15 member states), a majority of 169 (71.3%) would be required for the adoption of a decision by the Council. The number of weighted votes needed for the adoption of a decision (referred to as the 'qualified majority threshold') was to be reassessed on the accession of each new member state. Qualified majority voting was to be applied to 30 additional policy areas that were presently subject to national vetos. The Treaty also provides for a major reform of the EU's legal system, and for changes to the rules on decision-making within the European Central Bank and the European Investment Bank. Under the terms of the Treaty some alterations are made to the EU's common foreign and security policy, mainly entailing an increased role for the EU in crisis prevention and conflict management activities. In December 2000 EU heads of state or government reached agreement on the development of a regional military rapid response capability (the so-called Rapid Reaction Force—RRF). During that month EU leaders also signed a European Charter of Fundamental Rights; this was not incorporated into the Treaty of Nice, however, and so was not to be legally binding in member states. The Treaty of Nice requires ratification by member states' legislatures or approval by national popular referendums prior to its entry into force.

PERMANENT REPRESENTATIVES

Preparation and co-ordination of the Council's work is entrusted to a Committee of Permanent Representatives (COREPER), meeting in Brussels, consisting of the ambassadors of the member countries to the Union. A staff of national civil servants assists each ambassador.

GENERAL SECRETARIAT

Address: Justus Lipsius Bldg, 175 rue de la Loi, 1048 Brussels, Belgium.

Telephone: (2) 285-61-11; **fax:** (2) 285-73-97; **e-mail:** public.relations@consilium.eu.int; **internet:** ue.eu.int.

Secretary-General and High Representative: JAVIER SOLANA MADARIAGA.

Deputy Secretary-General: PIERRE DE BOISSEAU.

Secretary-General's Private Office: Dir and Head of Cabinet ALBERTO NAVARRO GONZÁLEZ.

Legal Service: Dir-Gen. (Juriconsult of the Council) JEAN-CLAUDE PIRIS.

Directorates-General:

A (Administration and Protocol): Dir-Gen. VITTORIO GIFFO.

B (Agriculture and Fisheries): Dir-Gen. ÁNGEL BOIXAREU CARRERA .

C (Internal Market, Customs Union, Industrial Policy, Telecommunications, Information Society, Research, Energy and Transport): Dir-Gen. KLAUS GRETSCHMANN.

E* (External Economic Relations and Common Foreign and Security Policy): Dirs-Gen. BRIAN L. CROWE, CORNELIS STEKELENBURG.

F (Press and Communications): Deputy Dir-Gen. HANS BRUNMAYR.

G (Economic and Financial Affairs and European Monetary Union—EMU): Dir-Gen. SIXTEN KORKMAN.

H (Justice and Home Affairs): Dir-Gen. CHARLES ELSEN.

I (Environmental and Consumer Protection, Civil Protection, Health, Foodstuffs Legislation, Drug Addiction, AIDS Education and Youth, Culture and Audio-visual Media): Dir-Gen. KERSTIN NIBLAEUS.

*Directorate-General D no longer exists.

EUROPEAN PARLIAMENT

Address: Centre Européen, Plateau du Kirchberg, BP 1601, 2929 Luxembourg.

Telephone: 4300-1; **fax:** 4300-29494; **internet:** www.europarl .eu.int.

PRESIDENT AND MEMBERS
(April 2002)

President: PAT COX (Ireland).

Members: 626 members, apportioned as follows: Germany 99 members; France, Italy and the United Kingdom 87 members each; Spain 64; the Netherlands 31; Belgium, Greece and Portugal 25 each; Sweden 22; Austria 21; Denmark and Finland 16 each; Ireland 15; Luxembourg 6. Members are elected for a five-year term by direct universal suffrage by the citizens of the member states. Members sit in the Chamber in political, not national, groups.

The tasks of the European Parliament are: amending legislation, scrutinizing the Union budget and exercising a measure of democratic control over the executive organs of the European Communities, the Commission and the Council. It has the power to dismiss the Commission by a vote of censure (see above). Increases in parliamentary powers have been brought about through amendments to the Treaty of Rome. The Single European Act, which entered into force on 1 July 1987, introduced, in certain circumstances where the Council normally adopts legislation through majority voting, a co-operation procedure involving a second parliamentary reading, enabling Parliament to amend legislation. Community agreements with third countries require parliamentary approval. The Treaty on European Union, which came into force in November 1993, introduced the co-decision procedure, permitting a third parliamentary reading (see Council of the European Union, above). The Treaty also gives Parliament the right to veto legislation, and allows Parliament a vote of approval for a new Commission. Parliament appoints the European Ombudsman, who investigates reports of maladministration in Community institutions. The Treaty of Amsterdam, which entered into force in May 1999, expanded and simplified Parliament's legislative role.

Political Groupings

	Distribution of seats (April 2002)
Group of the European People's Party	233
Party of European Socialists	179
Group of the European Liberal, Democrat and Reform Party	53
Green/European Free Alliance	45
Confederal Group of the European United Left/ Nordic Green Left	44
Union for a Europe of the Nations	22
Group for a Europe of Democracies and Diversities	18
Non-attached	32
Total	626

Parliament has an annual session, divided into about 12 one-week meetings, normally held in Strasbourg, France. The session opens with the March meeting. Committees and political group meetings and additional sittings of Parliament are held in Brussels.

The budgetary powers of Parliament (which, with the Council, forms the Budgetary Authority of the Communities) were increased to their present status by a treaty of 22 July 1975. Under this treaty, it can amend non-agricultural spending and reject the draft budget, acting by a majority of its members and two-thirds of the votes cast.

Parliament is run by a Bureau comprising the President, 14 Vice-Presidents elected from its members by secret ballot to serve for two-and-a-half years, and the five members of the College of Quaestors. Elections to the Bureau took place most recently in June 1999. The Conference of Presidents is the political governing body of Parliament, with responsibility for formulating the agenda for plenary sessions and the timetable for the work of parliamentary bodies, and for establishing the terms of reference and the size of committees and delegations. It comprises the President of Parliament and Chairmen of the political groupings.

There are Standing Parliamentary Committees on Foreign Affairs, Human Rights, Common Security, and Defence Policy; Agriculture and Rural Development; Budgets; Budgetary Control; Economic and Monetary Affairs; Legal Affairs and the Internal Market; Industry, External Trade, Research and Energy; Employment and Social Affairs; Public Health and Consumer Policy; Culture, Youth, Education, the Media and Sport; Development and Co-operation; Fisheries; Constitutional Affairs; Petitions; and Women's Rights and Equal Opportunities.

The first direct elections to the European Parliament took place in June 1979, and Parliament met for the first time in July. The second elections were held in June 1984 (with separate elections held in Portugal and Spain in 1987, following the accession of these two countries to the Community), the third in June 1989, the fourth in June 1994. Direct elections to the European Parliament were held in Sweden in September 1995, and in Austria and Finland in October 1996. The fifth European Parliament was elected in June 1999.

EUROPEAN OMBUDSMAN

Address: ave du President Robert Schuman 1, BP 403, 67001 Strasbourg Cedex, France.

Telephone: 3-88-17-40-01; **fax:** 3-88-17-90-62; **e-mail:** euro-ombudsman@europarl.eu.int; **internet:** www.euro-ombudsman .eu.int.

The position was created by the Treaty on European Union, and the first Ombudsman took office in July 1995. The Ombudsman is appointed by the European Parliament for a renewable five-year term. He is authorized to receive complaints regarding maladministration in Community institutions and bodies (except in the Court of Justice and Court of First Instance), to make recommendations, and to refer any matters to the Parliament.

European Ombudsman: JACOB SÖDERMAN.

COURT OF JUSTICE OF THE EUROPEAN COMMUNITIES

Address: Palais de la Cour de Justice, blvd Konrad Adenauer, Kirchberg, 2925 Luxembourg.

Telephone: 4303-1; **fax:** 4303-2600; **internet:** www.curia .eu.int.

The task of the Court of Justice is to ensure the observance of law in the interpretation and application of the Treaties setting up the three Communities. The 15 Judges and the eight Advocates General are appointed for renewable six-year terms by the Governments of the member states. The President of the Court is elected by the Judges from among their number for a renewable term of three years. The majority of cases are dealt with by one of the six chambers, each of which consists of a President of Chamber and two or four Judges. The Court may sit in plenary session in cases of particular importance or when a member state or Community institution that is a party to the proceedings so requests. The Court has jurisdiction to award damages. It may review the legality of acts (other than recommendations or opinions) of the Council, the Commission or the European Central Bank, of acts adopted jointly by the European Parliament and the Council and of Acts adopted by Parliament and intended to produce legal effects *vis-à-vis* third parties. It is also competent to give judgment on actions by a member state, the Council or the Commission on grounds of lack of competence, of infringement of an essential procedural requirement, of infringement of a Treaty or of any legal rule relating to its application, or of misuse of power. The Court of Justice may hear appeals, on a point of law only, from the Court of First Instance.

The Court is also empowered to hear certain other cases concerning the contractual and non-contractual liability of the Communities and disputes between member states in connection with the objects of the Treaties. It also gives preliminary rulings at the request of national courts on the interpretation of the Treaties, of Union legislation, and of the Brussels Convention on Jurisdiction and the Enforcement of Judgments in Civil and Commercial Matters. During 2000 463 new cases were completed, of which 74 were appeals, while 803 cases were pending.

Composition of the Court (in order of precedence, as at April 2002):

GIL CARLOS RODRÍGUEZ IGLESIAS (Spain), President of the Court of Justice.

PETER JANN (Austria), President of the First and Fifth Chambers.

SIEGBERT ALBER (Germany), First Advocate General.

FIDELMA O'KELLY MACKEN (Ireland), President of the Third and Sixth Chambers.

NINON COLNERIC (Germany), President of the Second Chamber.

STIG VON BAHR (Sweden), President of the Fourth Chamber.

FRANCIS JACOBS (United Kingdom), Advocate General.

CLAUS CHRISTIAN GULMANN (Denmark), Judge.

DAVID ALEXANDER OGILVY EDWARD (United Kingdom), Judge.

ANTONIO MARIO LA PERGOLA (Italy), Judge.

JEAN-PIERRE PUISSOCHET (France), Judge.

PHILIPPE LÉGER (France), Advocate General.

DÁMASO RUIZ-JARABO COLOMER (Spain), Advocate General.

MELCHIOR WATHELET (Belgium), Judge.

ROMAIN SCHINTGEN (Luxembourg), Judge.

JEAN MISCHO (Luxembourg), Advocate General.

VASSILIOS SKOURIS (Greece), Judge.

ANTONIO TIZZANO (Italy), Advocate General.

JOSÉ NARCISO DA CUNHA RODRIGUES (Portugal), Judge.

CHRISTIAAN WILLEM ANTON TIMMERMANS (Netherlands), Judge.

LEENDERT A. GEELHOED (Netherlands), Advocate General.

CHRISTINE STIX-HACKL (Austria), Advocate General.

ALLAN ROSAS (Finland), Judge.

ROGER GRASS (France), Registrar.

COURT OF FIRST INSTANCE OF THE EUROPEAN COMMUNITIES

Address: blvd Konrad Adenauer, 2925 Luxembourg.

Telephone: 4303-1; **fax:** 4303-2100; **internet:** www.curia .eu.int.

By a decision of 24 October 1988, as amended by decisions of 8 June 1993 and 7 March 1994, the European Council, exercising powers conferred upon it by the Single European Act, established a Court of First Instance with jurisdiction to hear and determine cases brought by natural or legal persons and which had hitherto been dealt with by the Court of Justice. During 2000 the Court considered 258 cases, while 661 were pending.

Composition of the Court of First Instance (in order of precedence, as at April 2002):

BO VESTERDORF (Denmark), President of the Court of First Instance.

RUI MANUEL GENS DE MOURA RAMOS (Portugal), President of Chamber.

JOHN D. COOKE (Ireland), President of Chamber.

MARC JAEGER (Luxembourg), President of Chamber.

MIHALIS VILARAS (Greece), President of Chamber.

RAFAEL GARCÍA-VALDECASAS Y FERNÁNDEZ (Spain), Judge.

KOENRAAD LENAERTS (Belgium), Judge.

VIRPI E. TIILI (Finland), Judge.

PERNILLA LINDH (Sweden), Judge.

JOSEF AZIZI (Austria), Judge.

JÖRG PIRRUNG (Germany), Judge.

PAOLO MENGOZZI (Italy), Judge.

ARJEN W. H. MEIJ (Netherlands), Judge.

NICHOLAS JAMES FORWOOD (United Kingdom), Judge.

HUBERT LEGAL (France), Judge.

HANS JUNG (Germany), Registrar.

COURT OF AUDITORS OF THE EUROPEAN COMMUNITIES

Address: 12 rue Alcide De Gasperi, 1615 Luxembourg.

Telephone: 4398-45410; **fax:** 4398-46430; **e-mail:** euraud@ eca.eu.int; **internet:** www.eca.eu.int.

The Court of Auditors was created by the Treaty of Brussels, which was signed on 22 July 1975, and commenced its duties in late 1977. It was given the status of an institution on a par with the Commission, the Council, the Court of Justice and the Parliament by the Treaty on European Union. It is the institution responsible for the external audit of the resources managed by the three Communities and the European Union. It consists of 15 members who are appointed for six-year terms by unanimous decision of the Council of the European Union, after consultation with the European Parliament. The members elect the President from among their number for a term of three years.

The Court is organized and acts as a collegiate body. It adopts its decisions by a majority of its members. Each member, however, has a direct responsibility for the audit of certain sectors of Union activities.

The Court examines the accounts of all expenditure and revenue of the European Communities and of any body created by them in so far as the relevant constituent instrument does not preclude such examination. It examines whether all revenue has been received and all expenditure incurred in a lawful and regular manner and whether the financial management has been sound. The audit is based on records, and if necessary is performed directly in the institutions of the Communities, in the member states and in other countries. In the member states the audit is carried out in co-operation with the national audit bodies. The Court of Auditors draws up an annual report after the close of each financial year. The Court provides the Parliament and the Council with a statement of assurance as to the reliability of the accounts, and the legality and regularity of the underlying transactions. It may also, at any time, submit observations on specific questions (usually in the form of special reports) and deliver opinions at the request of one of the institutions of the Communities. It assists the European Parliament and the Council in exercising their powers of control over the implementation of the budget, in particular in the framework of the annual discharge procedure, and gives its prior opinion on the financial regulations, on the methods and procedure whereby the budgetary revenue is made available to the Commission, and on the formulation of rules concerning the responsibility of authorizing officers and accounting officers and concerning appropriate arrangements for inspection.

President: JUAN MANUEL FABRA VALLÉS (Spain).

Audit Group I: JEAN-FRANÇOIS BERNICOT, HEDDA VON WEDEL, DAVID BOSTOCK.

Audit Group II: GIORGIO CLEMENTE, JØRGEN MOHR, FRANÇOIS COLLING, LARS TOBISSON.

Audit Group III: HUBERT WEBER, MAARTEN ENGWIRDA, ROBERT REYNDERS.

Audit Group IV: AUNUS SALMI, MORTEN LOUIS LEVYSOHN, IOANNIS SARMAS.

Audit Development and Reports (ADAR) Group: MÁIRE GEOGHEGAN-QUINN, VITOR MANUEL DA SILVA CADEIRA.

Secretary-General: MICHEL HERVÉ.

EUROPEAN CENTRAL BANK

Address: 60066 Frankfurt am Main, Kaiserstr. 29, Postfach 160319, Germany.

Telephone: (69) 13440; **fax:** (69) 13446000; **internet:** www.ecb.int.

The European Central Bank (ECB) was formally established on 1 June 1998, replacing the European Monetary Institute, which had been operational since January 1994. The Bank has the authority to issue the single currency, the euro, which replaced the European Currency Unit (ECU) on 1 January 1999, at the beginning of Stage III of Economic and Monetary Union (EMU), in accordance with the provisions of the Treaty on European Union ('the Maastricht Treaty'). The Bank's leadership is provided by a six-member executive board, appointed for a non-renewable term of eight years (it should be noted that the Statute of the European System of Central Banks—ESCB—provides for a system of staggered appointments to the first executive board for members other than the President in order to ensure continuity), which is responsible for the preparation of meetings of the governing council, the implementation of monetary policy in accordance with the guide-lines and decisions laid down by the governing council and for the current business of the ECB. The ECB and the national central banks of EU member states together comprise the ESCB. The governing council of the ESCB, which consists of ECB executive board members and the governors of central banks of countries participating in EMU, meets twice a month. The general council comprises the President, the Vice-President and the governors of the central banks of all EU member states.

President: WILLEM (WIM) F. DUISENBERG (Netherlands).

Vice-President: (from May 2002) LUCAS PAPADEMOS (Greece).

Executive Board: SIRKKA HÄMÄLÄINEN (Finland), OTMAR ISSING (Germany), TOMMASO PADOA-SCHIOPPA (Italy), EUGENIO DOMINGO SOLANS (Spain).

EUROPEAN INVESTMENT BANK

Address: 100 blvd Konrad Adenauer, 2950 Luxembourg.

Telephone: 4379-1; **fax:** 4377-04; **e-mail:** info@eib.org; **internet:** www.eib.org.

The European Investment Bank (EIB) was created in 1958 by the six founder member states of the European Economic Community. In June 1998 the Board of Governors agreed to increase subscribed capital to €100,000m., from January 1999. Capital structure at 31 December 2000 was as follows: France, Germany, Italy and the United Kingdom 17.8% each; Spain 6.5%; Belgium and the Netherlands 4.9% each; Sweden 3.3%; Denmark 2.5%; Austria 2.4%; Finland 1.4%; Greece 1.3%; Portugal 0.9%; Ireland 0.6%; Luxembourg 0.1%. The bulk of the EIB's resources comes from borrowings, principally public bond issues or private placements on capital markets inside and outside the Union. In 2001 the Bank raised €32,172m. in resources, of which 89% was in Community currencies.

The EIB's principal task, defined by the Treaty of Rome, is to work on a non-profit basis, making or guaranteeing loans for investment projects which contribute to the balanced and steady development of EU member states. Throughout the Bank's history, priority has been given to financing investment projects which further regional development within the Community. The EIB also finances projects that improve communications, protect and improve the environment, promote urban development, strengthen the competitive position of industry and encourage industrial integration within the Union, support the activities of small and medium-sized enterprises (SMEs), and help ensure the security of energy supplies. The EIB also provides finance for developing countries in Africa, the Caribbean and the Pacific, under the terms of the Lomé Convention (q.v.); for countries in the Mediterranean region, under co-operation agreements; and for Accession countries in central and eastern Europe.

In 2001 total financing contracts signed by the EIB, both inside and outside the European Union, amounted to €36,766m., compared with €36,033m. in 2000, bringing cumulative operations to €159,340m. since 1997.

The Board of Governors of the EIB, which usually meets only once a year, lays down general directives on credit policy, approves the annual report and accounts and decides on capital increases. The Board of Directors has sole power to take decisions in respect of loans, guarantees and borrowings. Its members are appointed by the Governors for a renewable five-year term following nomination by the member states. The Bank's President presides over meetings of the Board of Directors. The day-to-day management of operations is the responsibility of the Management Committee, which is the EIB's collegiate executive body and recommends decisions to the Board of Directors. It comprises the President and seven Vice-Presidents, nominated for six-year terms by the Board of Directors and approved by the Board of Governors. The Audit Committee, which reports to the Board of Governors regarding the management of operations and the maintenance

FINANCE CONTRACTS SIGNED

	2001		1997–2001	
Recipient	Amount (€ million)	%	Amount (€ million)	%
Austria	820	2.6	3,045	2.2
Belgium	365	1.2	3,091	2.3
Denmark	1,172	3.8	4,536	3.3
Finland	695	2.2	2,668	2.0
France	3,825	12.3	16,908	12.4
Germany	6,017	19.3	26,045	19.1
Greece	1,658	5.3	6,271	4.6
Ireland	525	1.7	1,454	1.1
Italy	5,488	17.6	22,901	16.8
Luxembourg	10	0.0	511	0.4
Netherlands	787	2.5	2,156	1.6
Portugal	1,799	5.8	8,098	5.9
Spain	4,559	14.6	18,592	13.6
Sweden	953	3.1	3,695	2.7
United Kingdom	2,337	7.5	15,626	11.4
Other*	174	0.6	1,058	0.8
EU total	31,184	100.0	136,655	100.0
Euro-Mediterranean Partnership countries	1,401	25.1	5,366	23.7
ACP-Overseas countries and territories	520	9.3	1,896	8.4
South Africa	150	2.7	776	3.4
Latin America and Asia	543	9.7	2,124	9.4
Balkans	319	5.7	625	2.8
Accession countries	2,659	47.6	11,898	52.4
Non-EU total	5,592	100.0	22,685	100.0
Total	36,776	—	159,340	—

* Projects with a European dimension located outside the member states.

of the Bank's accounts, is an independent body comprising three members who are appointed by the Board of Governors for a renewable three-year term.

Board of Governors: One minister (usually the minister of finance) from each member state.

Board of Directors: Twenty-five directors and 13 alternates (senior officials from finance or economic ministries, public-sector banks or credit institutions), appointed for a renewable five-year term, of whom 24 and 12 respectively are nominated by the member states; one director and one alternate are nominated by the Commission of the European Communities.

Management Committee:

President: PHILIPPE MAYSTADT.

Vice-Presidents: WOLFGANG ROTH, MASSIMO PONZELLINI, EWALD NOWOTNY, FRANCIS MAYER, PETER SEDGWICK, ISABEL MARTÍN CASTELLÁ, MICHAEL G. TUTTY.

ECONOMIC AND SOCIAL COMMITTEE

Address: 2 rue Ravenstein, 1000 Brussels.

Telephone: (2) 546-90-11; **fax:** (2) 513-48-93; **internet:** www.esc.eu.int.

The Committee is advisory and is consulted by the Council of the European Union or by the European Commission, particularly with regard to agriculture, free movement of workers, harmonization of laws and transport, as well as legislation adopted under the Euratom Treaty. In certain cases consultation of the Committee by the Commission or the Council is mandatory. In addition, the Committee has the power to deliver opinions on its own initiative.

The Committee has 222 members: 24 each from France, Germany, Italy and the United Kingdom, 21 from Spain, 12 each from Austria, Belgium, Greece, the Netherlands, Portugal and Sweden, nine from Denmark, Finland and Ireland, and six from Luxembourg. One-third represents employers, one-third employees, and one-third various interest groups (e.g. agriculture, small enterprises, consumers). The Committee is appointed for a renewable term of four years by the unanimous vote of the Council of the European Union. Members are nominated by their governments, but are appointed in their personal capacity and are not bound by any mandatory instructions. The Committee is served by a permanent and independent General Secretariat, headed by the Secretary-General.

President: GöKE DANIEL FRERICHS (Germany).

Vice-Presidents: GIOVANNI VINAY (Italy), JOHN SIMPSON (United Kingdom).

Secretary-General: PATRICK VENTURINI.

COMMITTEE OF THE REGIONS

Address: rue Montoyer 92-102, 1000 Brussels.

Telephone: (2) 282-22-11; **fax:** (2) 282-23-25; **internet:** www.cor.eu.int.

The Treaty on European Union provided for a committee to be established, with advisory status, comprising representatives of regional and local bodies throughout the EU. The first meeting of the Committee was held in March 1994. It may be consulted on EU proposals concerning economic and social cohesion, trans-European networks, public health, education and culture, and may issue an opinion on any issue with regional implications. The Committee meets in plenary session five times a year.

The number of members of the Committee is equal to that of the Economic and Social Committee (see above). Members are appointed for a renewable term of four years by the Council, acting unanimously on the proposals from the respective member states. The Committee elects its principal officers from among its members for a two-year term.

President: Sir ALBERT BORE (United Kingdom).

First Vice-President: EDUARDO ZAPLANA HERNÁNDEZ-SORO.

OTHER BODIES

EUROPEAN INVESTMENT FUND—EIF

Address: 43 ave J. F. Kennedy, 2968 Luxembourg.

Telephone: 4266-881; **fax:** 4266-88200; **e-mail:** info@eif.org; **internet:** www.eif.org.

The European Investment Fund was founded in 1994 as a specialized financial institution to support the growth of small and medium-sized enterprises (SMEs). Its operations are focused on the provision of venture capital, through investment in funds that support SMEs, and on guarantee activities to facilitate access to finance for SMEs. In all its activities the Fund aims to maintain a commercial approach to investment, and to apply risk-sharing principles. Since 1998 the Fund has managed the European Technology Faculty (ETF) −Start-Up, and the SME Guarantee Facility. A new legal framework for these operations, under the Multiannual Programme (MAP) for enterprise and entrepreneurship was approved in December 2001, with a budget of €317m. During 2001 the Fund signed €958m. for 39 guarantee operations and €800m. for 57 investments in venture capital funds. Authorized capital totals €2,000m., held by the European Investment Bank (60.75%), the European Commission (30.00%), and other European banks and financial institutions (9.25%).

Chief Executive: WALTER CERNOIA.

ECSC CONSULTATIVE COMMITTEE

Address: Bâtiment Jean Monnet, 2920 Luxembourg.

Telephone: 4301-32846; **fax:** 4301-34455.

The Committee is advisory and is attached to the Commission. It advises the Commission on matters relating to the coal and steel industries of the Union. Its members are appointed by the Council of the European Union for two years and are not bound by any mandate from the organizations that designated them in the first place.

There are 108 members representing, in equal proportions, producers, workers and consumers and dealers in the coal and steel industries.

President: ENRICO GIBELLIERI (Italy).

OTHER ADVISORY COMMITTEES

There are advisory committees dealing with all aspects of EU policy. Consultation with some committees is compulsory in the procedure for drafting EC legislation.

In addition to the consultative bodies listed above there are several hundred special interest groups representing every type of interest within the Union. All these hold unofficial talks with the Commission.

AGENCIES

Community Plant Variety Office: POB 2141, 49021 Angers Cedex 2; 3 blvd Foch, 49100 Angers, France; tel. 2-41-25-64-00; fax 2-41-25-64-10; e-mail cpvo@cpvo.eu.int; internet www.cpvo.eu.int.

Began operations in April 1995, with responsibility for granting intellectual property rights for plant varieties. Supervised by an Administrative Council, and managed by a President, appointed by the Council of the European Union. A Board of Appeal has been established to consider appeals against certain technical decisions taken by the Office.

President: BARTELD P. KIEWIET.

European Agency for Reconstruction: POB 10177, 54626 Thessaloniki; Egnatia 4, 54626 Thessaloniki, Greece; tel. (31) 505120; fax (31) 5051172; e-mail info@ear.eu.int; internet www.ear.eu.int.

Established in February 2000 (upon a Council regulation of November 1999) to assume responsibilities of the European Commission's Task Force for the Reconstruction of Kosovo (which had become operational in July 1999 following the end of hostilities in the southern Serbian province of Kosovo and Metohija). The Agency's mandate is to prepare and implement reconstruction and refugee return programmes for Kosovo, as well as for other parts of the Federal Republic of Yugoslavia. In December 2001 the Agency assumed responsibility for the EU's main assistance programmes in the former Yugoslav republic of Macedonia.

Director: HUGUES MINGARELLI.

European Agency for Safety and Health at Work: Gran Vía 33, 48009 Bilbao, Spain; tel. (94) 479-43-60; fax (94) 479-43-83; e-mail information@osha.eu.int; internet www.osha.eu.int.

Began operations in 1996. Aims to encourage improvements in the working environment, and to make available all necessary technical, scientific and economic information for use in the field of health and safety at work. A 48-member Administrative Board comprising representatives from each member state's government, employers' and workers' organizations, and three representatives from the European Commission, adopts the Agency's work programme and other strategic decisions of the Agency, and appoints the Director. The Agency supports a network of Focal Points in each member state.

Director: HANS-HORST KONKOLEWSKY.

European Agency for the Evaluation of Medicinal Products—EMEA: 7 Westferry Circus, Canary Wharf, London, E14 4HB, United Kingdom; tel. (20) 7418-8400; fax (20) 7418-8416; e-mail mail@emea.eudra.org; internet www.emea.eu.int.

Established in 1993 for the authorization and supervision of medicinal products for human and veterinary use. In 2000 the Agency's proposed budget was €50.36m.

Chairman of the Management Board: KEITH JONES (United Kingdom).

Chairman of the Scientific Committee for Proprietary Medicinal Products (CPMP): DR DANIEL BRASSEUR.

Chairman of the Scientific Committee for Veterinary Medicinal Products (CVMP): Dr STEVE DEAN.

Executive Director: THOMAS LÖNNGREN.

European Centre for the Development of Vocational Training—CEDEFOP: POB 22427, Thessaloniki; Europe 123, 57001 Thessaloniki, Greece; tel. (31) 490111; fax (31) 490102; e-mail info@cedefop.eu.int.

Assist policy-makers and other officials in member states and partner organizations in issues relating to vocational training policies, and assists the European Commission in the development of these policies. Manages a European Training Village internet site.

Director: JOHAN VAN RENS (Netherlands).

European Environment Agency—EEA: 6 Kongens Nytorv, 1050 Copenhagen K, Denmark; tel. 33-36-71-00; fax 33-36-71-99; e-mail eea@eea.eu.int; internet www.eea.eu.int.

Became operational in 1994, having been approved in 1990, to gather and supply information to assist the implementation of Community policy on environmental protection and improvement. In 1999 the Agency's budget amounted to €18.2m. The Agency publishes a report on the state of the environment every three years.

Chairman of the Management Board: KEES ZOETMAN (Netherlands).

Chairman of the Scientific Committee: Prof. BEDRICH MOLDAN.

Executive Director: DOMINGO JIMÉNEZ-BELTRÁN (Spain).

European Foundation for the Improvement of Living and Working Conditions: Wyattville Rd, Loughlinstown, Shankill, Co Dublin, Ireland; tel. (1) 204-3100; fax (1) 282-6456; e-mail postmaster@eurofound.ie; internet www.eurofound.eu.int.

Established in 1975 to develop strategies for the medium- and long-term improvement of living and working conditions. The Foundation publishes a regular newsletter.

Chairman of the Administrative Board: MARC BOISEL.

Director: RAYMOND-PIERRE BODIN.

European Monitoring Centre for Drugs and Drug Addiction (EMCDDA): Palacete Mascarenhas, Rua da Cruz de Sta. Apolónia 23–25, 1149 Lisbon, Portugal; tel. (1) 21811-30-00; fax (1) 21811-17-11; e-mail info@emcdda.org; internet www.emcdda.org.

Became fully operational at the end of 1995, with the aim of providing member states with objective, reliable and comparable information on drugs and drug addiction in order to assist in combatting the problem. The Centre co-operates with other European and international organizations and non-Community countries. The Centre publishes an *Annual Report on the State of the Drugs Problem in Europe*. A newsletter, *Drugnet Europe*, is published every two months.

Chairman of the Management Board: MIKE TRACE (Germany).

Executive Director: GEORGES ESTIEVENART (France).

European Monitoring Centre on Racism and Xenophobia: Rahlgasse 3. 1060 Vienna, Austria; tel. (1) 580300; fax (1) 5803099; e-mail office@eumc.eu.int; internet www.eumc.eu.int.

Established by a decision of the European Council in June 1997, and began operations in July 1998. Aims to review issues relating to racism, xenophobia and anti-semitism and to promote best practices to combat the problem. Working to establish a European Information Network on Racism and Xenophobic (RAXEN).

Chairman of Executive Board: ROBERT PURKISS (United Kingdom).

Director: Dr BEATE WINKLER.

European Training Foundation (ETF): Villa Gualino, Viale Settimio Severo 65, 10133 Turin, Italy; tel. (011) 630-22-22; fax (011) 630-22-00; e-mail info@etf.eu.int; internet www.etf.eu.int.

Established in 1995 with the aim of contributing to the development of the vocational training systems of designated central and eastern European countries. In 1998 the Foundation's responsibilities were extended to include certain non-member Mediterranean countries.

Director: PETER G. M. DE ROOIJ.

Office for Harmonization in the Internal Market (Trade Marks and Designs) (OHIM): Avda de Europa 4, 03080 Alicante, Spain; tel. (96) 513-91-00; fax (96) 513-91-73; e-mail information@oami.eu.int; internet www.oami.eu.int.

Established in 1993 to promote and control trade marks and designs throughout the European Union.

Chairman of the Administrative Board: CARL-ANDERS IFVARSSON.

Chairman of the Budget Committee: PETER LAWRENCE.

President: WUBBO DE BOER.

Translation Centre for the Bodies of the European Union: Bâtiment Nouvel Hémicycle, 1 rue de Fort Thungen, 1499 Luxembourg; tel. 4217-11200; fax 4217-11220; e-mail cdt@eu.int; internet www.cdt.eu.int.

Established in 1994 to meet the transition needs of other decentralized Community agencies.

Director: FRANCISCO DE VICENTE.

Activities of the Community

AGRICULTURE

Co-operation in the Community has traditionally been at its most highly organized in the area of agriculture. The objectives of the Common Agricultural Policy (CAP) are described in the Treaty of Rome. The markets for agricultural products have been progressively organized following three basic principles: (i) unity of the market (products must be able to circulate freely within the Community and markets must be organized according to common rules); (ii) Community preference (products must be protected from low-cost imports and from fluctuations on the world market); (iii) common financial responsibility: the European Agricultural Guidance and Guarantee Fund (EAGGF) finances, through its Guarantee Section, all public expenditure intervention, storage costs, marketing subsidies and export rebates.

Agricultural prices are, in theory, fixed each year at a common level for the Community as a whole, taking into account the rate of inflation and the need to discourage surplus production of certain commodities. Export subsidies are paid to enable farmers to sell produce at the lower world market prices without loss. These subsidies account for some 50% of agricultural spending. When market prices of certain cereals, sugar, some fruits and vegetables, dairy produce and meat fall below a designated level the Community intervenes, and buys a certain quantity which is then stored until prices recover. During the 1980s expanding production led to food surpluses, costly to maintain, particularly in dairy produce, beef, cereals and wine, and to the destruction of large quantities of fruit and vegetables.

Agriculture is by far the largest item on the Community budget, accounting for about two-thirds of annual expenditure, mainly for supporting prices through the EAGGF Guarantee Section (appropriations for which amounted to €44,505m., or 45% of total commitment appropriations, in 2002). A system of 'stabilizers' was introduced in February 1988, imposing an upper limit on the production of certain products. Any over-production would result in a decrease in the guaranteed intervention price for the following year. Similar 'stabilizers' were later imposed on production of oilseeds, protein feed crops, wine, sugar, fruit and vegetables, tobacco, olive oil, cotton and mutton.

In 1990 the CAP was criticized during the 'Uruguay Round' of negotiations on the General Agreement on Tariffs and Trade (GATT, see World Trade Organization—WTO). The US Government demanded massive reductions in the EC's agricultural and export subsidies, on the grounds that they disrupted world markets. In November Community ministers of agriculture agreed to accept proposals by the Commission for a reduction of 30% in agricultural subsidies over a 10-year period. In 1990 increasing surpluses of cereals, beef and dairy products were again reported, and a decline in international wheat prices increased the cost to the Community of exporting surplus wheat. In May 1992, on the basis of proposals made by the Commission in 1991, ministers adopted a number of reforms, which aimed to transfer the Community's agricultural support from upholding prices to maintaining farmers' incomes, thereby removing the incentive to over-produce. Intervention prices were reduced by 29% for cereals, 15% for beef and poultry and 5% for dairy products. Farmers were to be compensated for the price reductions by receiving additional grants, which, in the case of crops, took the form of a subsidy per hectare of land planted. To qualify for these subsidies, arable farmers (except for those with the smallest farms) were to be obliged to remove 15% of their land from cultivation (the 'set-aside' scheme). Incentives were to be given for alternative uses of the withdrawn land (e.g. forestry). The reform reduced prices payable for cereals to the level of those prevailing in the international market.

In May 1992 the US Government threatened to impose a large increase in import tariffs on European products, in retaliation against subsidies paid by the EC to oilseed producers, which, the US Government claimed, led to unfair competition for US exports of soya beans. In November, however, agreement was reached between the USA and the European Commission: the USA agreed that limits should be imposed on the area of EC land on which cultivation of oilseed was permitted. The USA also agreed to accept a reduction of 21% in the volume and 36% in the value of the EC's subsidized exports of farm produce, over a six-year period (the amounts being based on average production during 1986–90). These agreements formed the basis of the GATT agricultural accord, which was concluded as part of the Uruguay Round trade agreement in mid-December 1993.

The Commission estimated that between September 1992 and the end of July 1993, as a result of the turmoil in the exchange-rate mechanism (see under Economic Co-operation), an extra ECU 1,500m. was spent in price-support payments to farmers. In February 1995 ministers adopted a new agrimonetary regime, which limited the amount of compensation paid to farmers as a result of currency fluctuations. Further amendments, introduced in June, abandoned the existing common exchange rate, used to calculate compensation payments, and introduced two rates: one for currencies linked to the Deutsche Mark and one for all other EU currencies. Attempts by some member states to reform the system further were unsuccessful, and in October ministers agreed that national governments would be permitted to compensate farmers who had suffered loss of income as a result of currency fluctuations. In June 1997 it was reported that cereal farmers had been over-compensated by some ECU 8,500m. over the previous four years as a result of inaccurate price-reduction forecasts. The Commission is allowed to recover from member states sums that they have paid out under the CAP without sufficient guarantees of legitimacy or without adequate regard to control and verification. In May 1998 the Commission announced that it was to recover ECU 308m. paid to member states in 1994; in February 1999 the Commission decided to recover a further €493m., mainly relating to spending in 1995.

In June 1995 the guaranteed intervention price for beef was decreased by 5% and that for cereals by 7.5%. In September ministers agreed to reduce the level of compulsory 'set-aside' for 1996/97 to 10%, in response to much lower food surpluses in the EU and high world prices for cereal crops. In July 1996 agriculture ministers agreed on a further reduction in the 'set-aside' rate for cereals to 5%. Fruit and vegetable production subsidies were fixed at no more than 4% of the value of total marketed production, rising to 4.5% in 1999. The aim was to improve competitiveness in the European market and avoid the widespread destruction of surplus fruit and vegetables that had taken place in previous years.

In March 1998 the Commission outlined firm proposals for reform of the CAP as part of its 'Agenda 2000', concerning the enlargement of the EU and the Community's budget for 2000–06, published in July 1997. The plans envisaged imposing limits on subsidies and reductions of up to 30% in guaranteed prices, to allow compliance with WTO rules. In June 1998 the Commission adopted proposals to introduce new agrimonetary arrangements for a period of three years from January 1999, owing to the launch of the euro. The arrangements were to compensate farmers in those EU member states not participating in the process of economic and monetary union (EMU) for currency fluctuations until 2002. Farmers in countries taking part in EMU were also to be compensated for reductions in prices and aid payments resulting from the abolition of currency differentials. In 2000, as a result of the appreciation of the currencies in Denmark, Sweden and the United Kingdom, agrimonetary measures were fixed to compensate these countries for the reduction in certain direct payments converted into national currencies.

In March 1999 EU ministers of agriculture reached a compromise agreement on reform of the CAP, which proposed reductions of up to 20% in guaranteed prices and increases in milk quotas from 2003/04. The plans were approved by heads of state and of government later that month, although they were modified to include less dramatic reductions in the guaranteed prices for cereals and to delay reforms to the dairy sector until 2005/06. According to the final agreement on the reforms, guaranteed prices for cereals were to be reduced by 7.5% in both 2000 and 2001 and the 'set-aside' rate was to be fixed at 10% until 2006. Guaranteed prices for beef were to be abolished and the 'basic price' offered for the meat was to decrease by a total of 20% over a three-year period from 2000 (more far-reaching reform for the beef sector was later proposed, as a result of the BSE crisis—see below). Direct annual payments to farmers were to be increased, thereby compensating farmers for the reductions in guaranteed prices and removing incentives for over-production. A proposed limit on payments made to farmers, which aimed at preventing large-scale producers from receiving excessive compensation, failed to win approval. The CAP budget was expected to stabilize at some €4,500m. until 2006, although some officials expressed concern that the reforms were not sufficiently far-reaching to achieve this aim.

In 2000 the CAP reforms under Agenda 2000 relating to arable crops, beef and veal, milk and milk products, financing and rural development, were adopted. As a result of the reforms, the annual price-setting exercise in 2000 involved just six sectors: pig meat, sugar, silkworms, sheep meat, goat meat, and monthly increases for cereal and rice, on a multi-annual basis. For sugar, prices and amounts were set only until the end of the 2000/01 marketing year, when the production quota regime was due to expire. In April 2000, in the wake of sharper cyclical price movements on the market for pig meat, the Commission proposed introducing a regulatory fund into the market organization. This would aim to stabilize incomes, by collecting revenue when the situation was favourable and making payments in more difficult times.

Throughout 2000 the Commission held meetings with working parties and advisory committees (including consumer groupings) on the future development of the CAP. The process of simplifying agricultural legislation continued, notably through the streamlining of the import and export licensing procedures. In December the varying procedures on the promotion of agricultural products in the internal market were replaced by one harmonized system. In January 2000 the Commission adopted a communication on the integration of environmental concerns into the CAP, formulated as part of the environmental integration strategy approved by the European Council, meeting in Helsinki. Additional payments to farmers who adopt extra environmental protection measures were under consideration.

A further element of reform is the enlargement of the CAP to encompass the wider rural population. The policy of rural development under the CAP (described as the 'second pillar' of the CAP in Agenda 2000) aims to restore and increase the competitiveness of rural areas, through supporting employment, diversification and population growth. In addition, producers are to be rewarded for the preservation of rural heritage. Specifically, the policy will provide funds for the modernization of agricultural holdings, for establishing young farmers, for training and for early retirement. Forestry is recognized as an integral part of rural development (previous treaties on the EU made no provision for a comprehensive common forestry policy). During 1999 and 2000 member states developed rural development programmes for 2000–06. In June 2000 the Commission began the process of approval of these schemes, to which annual expenditure of €4,300m. had been committed. In late 2000 rural development programmes for a number of applicant countries were also adopted. These are drawn up under the EU's Special Accession Programme for Agriculture and Rural Development (SAPARD), which aims to help candidate countries manage structural adjustment in their agricultural sectors. Pre-accession aid of €520m per year is provided under SAPARD for 2000-06.

The EU has adopted a number of measures on the safety of agricultural produce. In 1986 the first case of bovine spongiform encephalopathy (BSE) in UK cattle was noted. The use of meat and bone meal (MBM) in animal feed was identified as being responsible for the disease, which causes the brain tissue of cattle to degenerate, and was banned for use in cattle feed in 1988. The use of certain cuts of offal in human foodstuffs was prohibited in the United Kingdom in the following year. In July 1994 strict controls on carcass beef trade were imposed, with the time-scale for the prohibition of exports from diseased herds extended from two to six years. The agreement temporarily resolved a dispute between the United Kingdom and Germany, which had attempted to impose a unilateral ban on UK beef exports, provoking that country to seek a judicial ruling on the action by the European Court of Justice. New fears about possible links between BSE and Creutzfeldt-Jakob disease (CJD), which affects humans, led to a collapse in consumer confidence in the European beef market in early 1996. In March the Commission accepted that member countries could unilaterally stop imports of UK beef on health grounds, pending a decision by a committee of scientific and veterinary experts from all member states. At the end of the month the Commission agreed a full ban on exports from the United Kingdom of live cattle, beef and beef products. In 1996 the UK Government proposed a programme of selective slaughter and the implementation of new national legislation to ensure that meat and bonemeal were excluded from the manufacture of animal feeds. However, the planned cull was later abandoned, with the country proposing instead a much smaller slaughter scheme. In July the European Court of Justice rejected the UK Government's application for the beef export ban to be suspended. At the end of 1996 the Commission was estimated to have spent some ECU 1,500m., including ECU 850m. as compensation paid to beef farmers, on dealing with the consequences of the BSE crisis.

In December 1996 the UK Government yielded to the European Commission's demand for a more substantial cull. The Commission also stated that the United Kingdom was to submit plans for a certified BSE-free herd scheme, to provide computerized evidence that cattle herds had had no contact with other animals infected with BSE, before a phased removal of the export embargo could begin. In June 1997 the United Kingdom's plans for monitoring and preventing BSE were judged by the Commission to be inadequate. In July the United Kingdom was reported by the Commission to have engaged in the illegal export of beef, while in late June the Commission commenced infringement proceedings against 10 EU countries accused of evading the full implementation of hygiene procedures for the eradication of BSE. In July agriculture ministers voted to introduce a complete ban on the use for any purpose of 'specified risk materials' (SRMs—i.e. those most likely to carry BSE) from cattle, sheep and goats. The introduction of the ban was postponed until January 1999, as a result of opposition from a number of EU member states, particularly Germany, as well as the USA.

In May 1998 the Commission agreed to ease the export ban on UK beef, to allow the export of deboned beef from Northern Irish herds certified as BSE-free for eight years, from June. In November the Agriculture Council fully endorsed the United Kingdom's Date-based Export Scheme, which permitted the export of deboned beef produced from animals born after August 1996 and tracked by an official monitoring system. In October 1998 Portugal was banned from exporting beef and live cattle, following a two-fold increase in reported cases of BSE in the country. The ban on Portuguese beef exports was originally supposed to expire after nine months, but restrictions only began to be removed in March 2001.

In July 1999 the United Kingdom was deemed to have met all of the conditions pertaining to the lifting of the ban on its beef exports; the European Commission announced that exports would be permitted to resume from 1 August. However, the French Government, with some support from Germany, remained unconvinced that UK beef presented no threat to consumers. In January 2000 the Commission commenced legal action against the French Government over its continued unilateral ban on imports of UK beef. In December 2001 the European Court of Justice ruled in favour of the EU and ordered France to lift its ban. The Commission also started legal action against Germany in February 2000, but abandoned this the following month when Germany agreed to revoke the ban.

In June 2000 a new surveillance system to improve the detection of BSE was introduced. In the following month the EU established a system for identifying and registering bovine animals and for labelling beef and beef products. The aim was to introduce, from September, a compulsory beef-labelling system making beef traceable 'from stable to table'. (The rules were further tightened in January 2002, to oblige producers to indicate precisely where animals had been born and reared.) In November 2000 the EU decided to convene a group of experts responsible for reviewing research into BSE and CJD.

In December 2000, as an emergency measure to boost confidence in European beef, agriculture ministers determined to ban from the regional food chain (with effect from 1 January 2001) all cattle aged more than 30 months, unless these had been tested and proven not to be infected with the disease. The age limit was lowered to 24 months in June 2001. Also in June the EU set out further rules on the use of animal materials excluded from the human food chain. The ban on the use of MBM in feed for pigs and poultry, first adopted in January, was extended.

While EU beef consumption increased in 2001, the imbalance between supply and demand continued to cause concern. In April a special purchase scheme for beef was introduced, as part of a seven-point plan to ease the pressures on the sector. The scheme was extended in December. In June the Council agreed on the need for reform of the entire beef and veal sector, proposing an increase in the ceiling for intervention from 350,000 to 500,000 tonnes.

By January 2001 incidences of BSE infection had been reported in 11 of the 15 member countries (with the number of confirmed cases in France and Ireland increasing significantly in 2000). The BSE epidemic in the United Kingdom had eased progressively since its peak in 1993, but in early 2001 around 30 suspected cases were still being reported every week. In December EU vets and scientists reported that they believed the incidence of BSE in UK cattle to be far higher than official figures indicated. By September 2001 the total official number of cases of BSE in the EU stood at 181,946, of which 180,019 had occurred in the United Kingdom.

Following an outbreak of foot-and-mouth disease on farms in the United Kingdom in February 2001, the EU imposed a temporary ban on imports of UK livestock products. Three days after the first cases were reported, all movement of susceptible livestock in the United Kingdom was stopped. The culling of sheep imported from the United Kingdom to other member states began in February. An EU-wide ban on assembly points and markets for all potentially affected species was imposed (with exceptions for direct transport to slaughter-houses and other farms) and measures were adopted requiring the disinfection of vehicles travelling from the United Kingdom to other member states. Cases of foot-and-mouth disease were also noted in the

Netherlands, France and Ireland. These three countries were declared free of the disease in September. During the outbreak, the USA and other third countries imposed import restrictions on fresh meat and livestock from the EU. As the outbreak waned, the EU announced that its policy on vaccination (currently used only as a temporary emergency measure on animals awaiting slaughter and destruction, rather than pre-emptively, to prevent infection) would be reviewed. In January 2002 the United Kingdom regained 'clear' status, without recourse to vaccination.

In April 1999 a dispute arose between the EU and the USA after the EU announced plans to ban all imports of US beef, as a result of traces of growth hormones found in imported meat that was supposed to be hormone-free. In May the EU informed the WTO that it would not be able to lift its ban on US hormone-treated beef by 13 May 1999, as the WTO had ordered that it should. The USA subsequently imposed sanctions, and the dispute persisted throughout 2000 and 2001.

In June 1999 the USA impounded all imports of European pork and poultry, because of the possibility that these might have been contaminated by a carcinogen, dioxin, extremely high levels of which had been discovered in some Belgian supplies of animal feedstuffs. The European Commission had already prohibited the sale of some Belgian food products. In 2000, following the successful completion in Belgium of a programme to detect dioxins on farms and in produce, the Commission lifted the restrictions on Belgium. As part of ongoing efforts to tighten controls relating to animal health, the Commission adopted a proposal for a directive on measures to control classical swine fever in 2000. In June 2001 random testing for transmissible spongiform encephalopathies (TSEs, including scrapie) was introduced for sheep and goats.

The EU has also adopted a number of protective measures to prevent the introduction of organisms harmful to plants and plant products. In 2000 the Commission adopted four directives determining the maximum levels of pesticide residues permitted in products of plant origin. In mid-2001, noting consumer interest in organic products, the Council invited discussion towards a future action plan to promote organic food and farming. By the end of 2000 there were 541 registered names (protected geographical indications—PGI—and protected designations of origin—PDO) of agricultural products and foodstuffs in the EU.

The EU's Food and Veterinary Office was established in April 1997 to ensure that the laws on food safety, animal health and welfare and plant health are applied in all member states. The office carries out audits and checks on food safety in member states and in third countries exporting agricultural produce to the EU. A new food policy was laid out in a White Paper on food safety in January 2000. The policy aims to streamline legislation, improve controls and increase the capability of the scientific advice system. A European Food Safety Authority (EFSA) was scheduled to be set up in 2002 to provide independent scientific advice and support and to give the public information on food risks. It will have no regulatory or judicial power, but will co-operate closely with similar bodies in the member states.

In April 2000 a team of EU experts was set up to provide advice on issues concerning genetically-modified (GM) crops and food products. A draft directive regulating the planting, testing and sale of GM products was approved by the European Parliament in February 2001. Among other provisions, this requires a risk assessment to be carried out for each GM organism (GMO), and the creation of a public register of all GMOs released for trial and for commercial purposes. Additional rules on the labelling and tracing of GM foods were drafted in 2001. When approved, the EU envisaged that these would be sufficiently stringent to allow the issue of marketing permits for new GM products. The planned European Food Safety Authority was to carry out risk assessments and participate in the authorization process.

In June 1995 the Agriculture Council agreed to new rules on the welfare of livestock during transport. The agreement, which came into effect in 1996, limited transport of livestock to a maximum of eight hours in any 24-hour period, and stipulated higher standards for their accommodation and care while in transit. In January 1996 the Commission proposed a ban on veal crates, which was to come into effect from January 1998. In April 2001 the Commission adopted new rules for long-distance animal transport, setting out the required standards of ventilation, temperature and humidity control. Under the regulations, lorries carrying animals must be equipped with a monitoring and warning system. In June 1999 EU agriculture ministers agreed to end battery egg production within the EU by 2012; in December 2000 a regulation was adopted requiring EU producers to indicate the rearing method on eggs and egg-packaging.

FISHERIES

The Common Fisheries Policy (CFP) came into effect in January 1983 after seven years of negotiations, particularly concerning the problem of access to fishing-grounds. In 1973 a 10-year agreement had been reached, whereby member states could have exclusive access to waters up to six nautical miles (11.1 km) or, in some cases, 12 miles from their shores; 'historic rights' were reserved in certain cases for foreign fishermen who had traditionally fished within a country's waters. In 1977 the Community set up a 200-mile (370-km) fishing zone around its coastline (excluding the Mediterranean) within which all members would have access to fishing. The 1983 agreement confirmed the 200-mile zone and allowed exclusive national zones of six miles with access between six and 12 miles from the shore for other countries according to specified historic rights. Rules furthering conservation (e.g. standards for fishing tackle) were imposed under the policy, with checks by a Community fisheries inspectorate. Total allowable catches (TACs) are fixed annually by species, divided into national quotas under the renewable Multiannual Guidance Programme (MAGP). The Commission monitors compliance with the quotas and TACs and with technical measures in Community and some international waters. Non-compliance resulted in the closure of 39 fisheries in 2000.

In 1990 it was reported that stocks of certain species of fish in EC waters had seriously diminished. Consequently a reduction in quotas was agreed, together with the imposition of a compulsory eight-day period in each month during which fishermen in certain areas (chiefly the North Sea) would stay in port, with exemptions for fishermen using nets with larger meshes that would allow immature fish to escape. In 1992 the compulsory non-fishing period was increased to 135 days between February and December (with similar exemptions).

In December 1992 EC ministers agreed to extend the CFP for a further 10-year period. Two years later ministers concluded a final agreement on the revised CFP, allowing Spain and Portugal to be integrated into the policy by 1 January 1996. A compromise accord was reached regarding access to waters around Ireland and off south-west Great Britain (referred to as the 'Irish box'), by means of which up to 40 Spanish vessels were granted access to 80,000 sq miles of the 90,000 sq mile area. However, the accord was strongly opposed by Irish and UK fishermen. In April 1995 seven Spanish vessels were seized by the Irish navy, allegedly for fishing illegally in the Irish Sea. In October fisheries ministers agreed a regime to control fishing in the 'Irish box', introducing stricter controls and instituting new surveillance measures.

The organization of fish marketing involves common rules on quality and packing and a system of guide prices established annually by the Council. Fish are withdrawn from the market if prices fall too far below the guide price, and compensation may then be paid to the fishermen. Export subsidies are paid to enable the export of fish onto the lower-priced world market and import levies are imposed to prevent competition from low-priced imports. A new import regime took effect from May 1993. This enables regional fishermens' associations to increase prices to a maximum of 10% over the Community's reference price, although this applies to both EU and imported fish. In September 2001 the EU proposed extending until the end of 2002 a scheme providing compensation for the costs of marketing fisheries products in the EU's most remote areas.

Initially, structural assistance actions for fisheries were financed by the EAGGF. Following the reform of the structural funds in 1993, a separate fund, the Financial Instrument for Fisheries Guidance (FIFG), was set up, with a budget of €2,700m. for 1994–99. The instrument's principal responsibilities include the decommissioning of vessels and the creation, with foreign investors, of joint ventures designed to reduce the fishing effort in EU waters. The fund also supports the building and modernizing of vessels, developments in the aquaculture sector and the creation of protected coastal areas. In addition, it finances contributions to redundancy payments. In 2001 the EU considered proposals to modify the FIFG regulation with reference to fishing under flags of convenience, which had become an increasing concern. The proposals would prevent states from granting public aid for the transfer of vessels to third countries that have been identified as fishing in a manner threatening the effectiveness of conservation measures.

The proposals put forward in May 1996 by the European Commission for the fourth MAGP, covering 1997–2002, envisaged catch reductions of up to 40% for species most at risk, and set targets and detailed rules for restructuring fishing fleets in the EU. The draft MAGP IV failed to gain approval at the meeting of fisheries ministers held in November 1996. The UK Government, in October, insisted that it would not accept additional limits on catches without action to stop quota-hopping, in which UK-registered boats are bought by operators in other EU countries (mainly Spain and the Netherlands), which are thus able to gain part of the UK fishing quotas. (In mid-1998 the UK Government received approval from the Commission to introduce new licensing conditions from 1 January 1999 that would compel the owners of boats involved in 'quota-hopping' to establish economic links with the United Kingdom.) In April 1997, following a number of concessions by the Commission, ministers approved MAGP IV. The programme fixed catch reductions at 30% for species most at risk and at 20% for other over-fished species. In December 1996 ministers agreed upon the establishment of a satellite monitoring system, which was to be used to verify the fishing activities of boats greater than 20 m in length. The new system was introduced from 1 June 1998. In July it was agreed that funds of €39.4m. would be made available for monitoring activities, including the purchase of inspection boats and the provision of onshore centres for the management of satellite-monitoring activities.

In June 1998 the Council overcame long-standing objections from a number of member states and adopted a ban on the use of drift nets in the Atlantic Ocean and the Mediterranean Sea, in an attempt to prevent the unnecessary deaths of marine life such as dolphins and sharks. The ban, introduced in January 2002, partially implemented a 1992 UN resolution demanding a complete cessation of drift-net fishing. A series of compensatory measures aims to rectify any short-term detrimental impact on EU fishing fleets.

A meeting of the European Council in Helsinki, in December 1999, requested the Fisheries Council to formulate a strategy for the integration of environmental issues into the CFP. It was agreed that the CFP should adopt the principles of the EU's environmental policy, including recognizing the precedence of preventative action, the need to rectify environmental damage at source and the economic responsibility of the 'authors' of environmental damage. In March 2001 the Commission adopted a series of action plans designed to integrate the protection of biodiversity into fisheries policies, building on the Community biodiversity strategy presented in 1998.

In December 1999 fisheries ministers agreed to implement a reduction of almost 40% in the total EU catch in 2000, with the principal objective of saving stocks in the North and Irish Seas. For some species these had been scientifically assessed as dangerously low. The Commission had demanded an even more severe reduction, including a total ban on fishing for cod in these areas. In December 2000 fisheries ministers adopted a further significant reduction in the EU catch for 2001, including a 45% cut in the total permissible catch of North Sea cod.

With concern over stocks continuing to mount, an emergency 11-week ban on deep-sea cod fishing over 40,000 sq miles of the North Sea was introduced in February 2001. In March similar emergency measures for the west of Scotland entered into effect, while emergency measures for the northern hake catch were adopted in June. Measures for the Irish Sea had been instituted in 2000. In December 2001 the Fisheries Council fixed TACs for 2002, incorporating further substantial reductions, with the aim of achieving 'biologically acceptable' levels of stocks. Among the measures agreed was a 22% cut in the haddock catch from the Irish Sea. It was agreed to extend MAGP IV until June 2002. In the same month the Commission presented its long-term recovery plans for cod and hake. Under the plans, the Commission proposed establishing a procedure for setting TACs so as to achieve a significant increase in mature fish stocks, with limits on the fishing effort fixed in accordance with the TACs. The plans also provided for the temporary closure of areas where endangered species have congregated, and allowed for more generous EU aid for the decommissioning of vessels (aid for the modernization of vessels, which tends to increase the fishing catch, was to be reduced). The Commission proposed catch limits for deep-water fish stocks (including blue ling, red seabream and black scabbardfish) for the first time in December.

In April 2001 a Green Paper on the future of the CFP was presented. The paper stated that a balance between fishing effort and resources must be reached, to achieve a sustainable future for the industry. It concluded that a 'thorough and urgent reform' was needed. Proposals included the imposition of a multi-annual strategy for TAC and quota management; the development of a new fleet policy; measures to enhance the EU's profile in regional fisheries organizations; and the creation of an EU-wide joint inspection structure.

Agreements have been signed with other countries (Norway, Sweden, Canada and the USA) allowing reciprocal fishing rights and other advantages, and with some African countries that receive assistance in strengthening their fishing industries in return for allowing EU boats to fish in their waters. Following the withdrawal of Greenland from the Community in February 1985, Community vessels retained fishing rights in Greenland waters, in exchange for financial compensation. In 1992 fisheries agreements with Estonia, Latvia, Lithuania and Argentina were initialled; and in 1993 an agreement was reached with Mauritania to benefit Spanish fishermen in the Canary Islands. Under a four-year agreement signed with Morocco in November 1995, the size of catches by EU vessels fishing in Moroccan waters was reduced by 20%–40% for various species, and the EU provided financial compensation to Morocco amounting to ECU 355m. Morocco decided that it would not renew the fishing agreement with the EU in 1999, and the accord became void at the end of November. More than 400 ships and 4,300 fishermen left Moroccan waters. As negotiations over a new agreement stalled, the EU planned a conversion operation to help those fishermen find other work or take early retirement, and to encourage the economic diversification of the affected areas. In November 2001 the Commission agreed an aid package of €197m. to convert the Spanish and Portuguese fleets that fished Moroccan waters, including €63m. for social measures to aid the crews of the boats.

RESEARCH AND TECHNOLOGY

In the amendments to the Treaty of Rome, effective from July 1987, a section on research and technology was included for the first time, defining the extent of Community co-operation in this area. Most of the funds allocated to research and technology are granted to companies or institutions that apply to participate in EU research programmes. In March 1996 task forces established by the Commission presented a report identifying priority topics for European research: the car of tomorrow; educational software and multimedia; new generation aircraft; vaccines and viral diseases; trains and railway systems of the future; intermodal transport; maritime systems; and the environment, with a particular focus on water resources. The fifth framework programme, covering the period 1999–2002, was proposed by the Commission in April 1997. With a budget of €14,960m., it concentrated on four main areas: preservation of the ecosystem; the management of living resources; the development of the 'information society'; and issues of competitive and sustainable growth. Like previous framework programmes, it aimed to improve the dissemination of research and development findings and strengthen the capacity of the EU for research. In July 1998 the Commission proposed that the 11 candidate countries for EU membership should have the opportunity to contribute to the fifth framework programme.

Projects launched under the fifth framework programme in 2000 included measures to stimulate the use of large-capacity electronic networks by scientific communities; genomics projects; activities in nanotechnologies; and action to combat major illnesses. Efforts were made to increase the interconnection of networks; a consortium was awarded €80m. to put in place a trans-European internet 'backbone' connecting 30 countries for research purposes. In January 2000 the Commission launched an initiative to establish a European Research Area (ERA). The aim was to promote the more effective use of scientific resources within a single area, in order to enhance the EU's competitiveness and create jobs. ERA will provide venture capital and tax breaks for research and high-technology start-up companies.

The creation of ERA will be supported through the sixth framework programme, discussions on which began in mid-2001. It was agreed that the new programme's focus should be limited to projects of particular European importance. The proposed priority research areas are genomics and biotechnology; information society technologies; nanotechnologies, intelligent materials and new production processes; aeronautics and space; food safety and health risks; sustainable development and global change; and citizens and governance. The programme aims to set up 'networks of excellence' to integrate research capacities in Europe. It has a proposed budget of €17,500m.

The European Strategic Programme for Research and Development in Information Technology (ESPRIT) was inaugurated in 1984 and concentrated on five key areas: advanced microelectronics; software technology; advanced information processing; office automation; and computer integrated manufacturing. The programme was financed half by the EU and half by the participating research institutes, universities and industrial companies. ESPRIT was integrated into the EU's Information Society Technologies (IST) initiative under the fifth framework programme. The IST initiative is designed to accelerate the emergence of an information society in Europe by promoting the development of high-quality, affordable services.

In July 1997 the European Parliament approved the Life Patent Directive, a proposal aiming to harmonize European rules on gene patenting in order to promote research into genetic diseases, despite objections over the ethical implications. In December 2000 the EU agreed to establish a parliamentary committee to examine new developments in human genetics. In late 2001 the Commission set up a website to encourage debate on stem cell research, aiming to create a dialogue between experts and the public. The EU is also participating actively in the international human genome project, which seeks to characterize the genomes of humans and other organisms, through mapping and sequencing of their DNA.

The EU is making efforts to integrate space science into its research activities, and is increasingly collaborating with the European Space Agency (ESA). In November 2000 the EU and ESA adopted a joint European strategy for space. In March 2002 the EU approved the development of the 'Galileo' civil satellite navigation and positioning system. Start-up costs are projected at €3,250m.; the system will require €220m. a year for maintenance from 2008.

In February 2000 the European Parliament called for action to be taken to combat the under-representation of women in science. In June the Commission began an assessment of the gender balance in the specific projects carried out under the fifth framework programme. The Commission is working towards a target of 40% participation by women at all levels in the implementation and management of research programmes.

Following a further reorganization in September 2001, the Community's own Joint Research Centre (JRC) comprises six institutes, based at Ispra (Italy), Geel (Belgium), Karlsruhe (Germany), Seville (Spain) and Petten (Netherlands). In 2000 the JRC restructured its work around four areas: safety of food and chemicals; the environment; the dependability of information systems and services; and nuclear safety and safeguards. In particular, it prioritized work on genetically-modified organisms. Nuclear work accounted for about 27% of total JRC activities in 2000, with the share accounted for by non-nuclear work increasing. The JRC also provides technical assistance to applicant countries. Proposed funding for the JRC under the fifth framework programme amounted to €815m. The new Science Strategy Directorate, based in Brussels, serves as a link between the JRC institutes and European policymakers.

The EU also co-operates with non-member countries (particularly EFTA states) in bilateral research projects. The Commission and 19 European countries (including the members of the EU as individuals) participate in the 'Eureka' programme of research in advanced technology, which was relaunched in 1999. The programme, focusing on robotics, engineering, IT and environmental science, allows resources to be pooled and promotes collaboration. In 2000 Croatia, Israel and Latvia joined Eureka. In addition, the Community research and development information service ('Cordis') disseminates findings in this field, with eight databases, while the 'Value' programme funds the publication and dissemination of technical reports from specific research projects. In 1994 a European Technology Assessment Network (ETAN) was developed to improve the dissemination of technological research findings; under the fifth framework programme this was replaced by the Strategic Analysis of Specific Political Issues (Strata) programme, which sets up groups of experts and works to develop networks.

ENERGY

The treaty establishing the European Atomic Energy Community ('Euratom') came into force on 1 January 1958. This was designed to encourage the growth of the nuclear energy industry in the Community by conducting research, providing access to information, supplying nuclear fuels, building reactors and establishing common laws and procedures. A common market for nuclear materials was introduced in 1959 and there is a common insurance scheme against nuclear risks. In 1977 the Commission began granting loans on behalf of Euratom to finance investment in nuclear power stations and the enrichment of fissile materials. An agreement with the International Atomic Energy Authority entered into force in 1977, to facilitate co-operation in research on nuclear safeguards and controls. The EU's Joint Research Centre (JRC, see under Research and Technology) conducts research on nuclear safety and the management of radioactive waste. The fifth framework programme for research and technological development (1998–2002; see under Research and Technology) allocated €1,260m. for Euratom research projects.

The Joint European Torus (JET) is an experimental thermonuclear machine designed to pioneer new processes of nuclear fusion, using the 'Tokamak' system of magnetic confinement to heat gases to very high temperatures and bring about the fusion of tritium and deuterium nuclei. Switzerland is also a member of the JET project. Since 1974 work has been proceeding at Culham in the United Kingdom, and the project was formally inaugurated in April 1984. In 1991 JET became the first fusion facility in the world to achieve significant production of controlled fusion power. In 1988 work began with representatives of Japan, the former USSR and the USA on the joint design of an International Thermonuclear Experimental Reactor (ITER), based on JET. The aim of ITER was to demonstrate the scientific and technical capacities of fusion energy for peaceful purposes. The European Fusion Development Agreement (EFDA), which entered into force in January 1999, and a new JET implementing agreement, which came into force in January 2000, provided the framework for the collective use of the JET facilities until at least the end of 2002.

Legislation on the completion of the 'internal energy market', adopted in 1990, aimed to encourage the sale of electricity and gas across national borders in the Community by opening national networks to foreign supplies, obliging suppliers to publish their prices and co-ordinating investment in energy. Energy ministers reached agreement in June 1996 on rules for the progressive liberalization of the electricity market. Twenty-five per cent of the market was to be opened up from mid-February 1999, rising to 33% by 2003. Belgium and Ireland were to implement the agreement in 2000, while Greece would be exempt until 2001. In November 1999 the Commission commenced legal action against France and Luxembourg for failure to meet the February deadline for opening their electricity markets. In December 1997 the Council agreed rules to allow the gas market to be opened up in three stages, over a 10-year period. The staged scheme allowed the largest gas suppliers to receive temporary exemptions from trade liberalization if the presence of competitors caused demand for supplies to drop below the amount that the distributor was contracted to purchase in the long term.

In 2001 the Commission amended the timetable for liberalizing the electricity and gas markets: by 2003 all non-domestic consumers were to have the freedom to choose their electricity supplier; by 2004 non-domestic consumers were to have the freedom to choose their gas supplier; and by 2005 all consumers, domestic and non-domestic, would be able to choose both suppliers. The Commission further proposed that the management of transmission and distribution grids should be legally separated from production and sales activities (except for small-scale distribution companies). It was suggested that network access tariffs should be published and approved by national regulators before entering into force, and that a regulator should be established for each member state. To create a genuine single market, the Commission proposed adopting rules on tariff-setting across borders, developing a European infrastructure plan for electricity and gas, and negotiating reciprocal agreements on the opening of electricity markets with the EU's neighbours. In December the Commission adopted a package of energy infrastructure development measures.

The Commission has consistently urged the formation of an effective overall energy policy. The five-year 'SAVE' programme, introduced in 1991, emphasized the improvement of energy efficiency, reduction of the energy consumption of vehicles and the use of renewable energy. A second five-year programme, SAVE II, was initiated in 1995, covering 1996–2000. This aimed to continue the work of the first programme and to establish energy efficiency as a criterion for all EU projects. In February 2002 SAVE was integrated into the 'Energy, Environment and Sustainable Development—EESD' thematic programme initiated under the fifth framework programme for 1998–2002. The 'Carnot' programme, which promotes the use of clean technologies for solid fuels, and the ETAP multi-annual programme of studies and forecasts in the energy sector, are also integrated into the fifth framework programme. A total of 163 new energy projects were launched under the framework programme in 2000.

In 1990 the Council established the ALTENER programme, which aimed to increase the contribution of renewable energy sources (RES), such as wind, solar, biomass and small-scale hydropower, within the Community. The programme finished at the end of 1997, having supported 278 projects since 1993, at a cost of ECU 26.9m. A replacement programme for 1998–2002, ALTENER II, was allocated a budget of €77m. A Green Paper on ways of promoting RES in the EU was issued in November 1996. These sources provided less than 6% of the total energy produced in the EU at that time. In May 1998, following the publication of a report by the Commission in late 1997, the Council committed the EU to increasing the use of RES to 12% by 2010. The Campaign for Take-Off, initiated after the 1997 report, set out a framework for action, with four main objectives: developing 1m. photovoltaic systems; establishing wind-farm-generating capacity of 10,000 MW; reaching 10,000 MW (thermal) of biomass installation; and integrating RES to meet the total electricity requirements of 100 communities. The Renewable Energy Partnership scheme works to involve public and private partners in the campaign. In May 2000 the EU set out a fourfold strategy on the promotion of electricity from RES in the internal energy market, based on the 1997 report: member states were to set and comply with national targets for the future consumption of energy from RES, consistent with the commitments entered into under the Kyoto protocol (see under Environment Policy), and to introduce a system for certifying the origin of electricity from RES; operators of transmission and district networks were to be encouraged to give priority to RES electricity; and measures were to be taken to establish a harmonized support system for RES producers. In December an action plan on energy efficiency was adopted, setting out measures to integrate energy efficiency into other EU policies and programmes. In January 2000 the Commission submitted a proposal for an EU energy-efficiency labelling programme for office and communications technical equipment: under the proposal equipment meeting certain standards would carry the Energy Star logo.

The Synergy II programme governs the EU's general energy relations with third countries and is the international co-operation component of the fifth framework programme. Energy ministers from the EU member states and 12 Mediterranean countries agreed at a meeting held in June 1996 in Trieste, Italy, to develop a Euro-Mediterranean gas and electricity network. The first Euro-Med Energy Forum was held in May 1997, and an action plan to develop the network was adopted at a Euro-Med conference of energy ministers in May 1998. In 1997 a programme for the Optimal Use of Energy Resources in Latin America (ALURE) began the implementation of projects in that region. In 1997 the Community agreed to help a number of eastern European countries to overcome energy problems by means of the Interstate Oil and Gas to Europe programme (INOGATE). This programme, which was to receive €50m. over a five-year period, aimed to improve energy flows in eastern Europe and to increase the access of newly independent countries to European markets. INOGATE forms part of the TACIS programme (see under External Relations).

The EU also promotes trans-European energy networks (TENs, see under Transport Policy), with the aim of improving the operation of the internal energy market and reinforcing the security of supplies. In 2001 90 projects of common interest for electricity and gas TENS had been identified. These included linking isolated networks; developing interconnections between member states and with third countries; introducing natural gas to new regions; and increasing the capacity for the transmission, reception and storage of natural gas.

In a communication in September 2000 the Commission set out the broad lines of a new EU strategy on nuclear safety in central and eastern Europe and the former Soviet states. The strategy entailed supporting those countries in their efforts to improve operating safety, strengthening their regulatory frameworks, and closing reactors that could not be upgraded to an acceptable standard. The SURE programme of action under the fifth framework programme aims to improve safety and co-operation in the nuclear sector with countries participating in the TACIS programme. In December 2000, in accordance with its commitments, the Commission approved a grant of €25m. from the TACIS budget for 2000 for the closure of the Chernobyl (Chornobyl) nuclear power station in Ukraine, to cover part of the cost of the resulting temporary power shortfall. A Euratom loan of €558m. was granted for completion of the replacement reactors. In November 1999 the Commission indicated the need to strengthen the EU's 'Northern Dimension' energy policy (covering Scandinavia, the Baltic states and northwest Russia.)

In November 2000 the Commission adopted a Green Paper on the security of energy supply, which was aimed at launching a broad debate on the role of each energy source, with regard to the security of supply, sustainable development, questions of enlargement, and action needed to combat climate change. Security of supply is of vital importance as the EU currently meets 50% of its energy requirements through imports. In October 2000, in response to a sharp rise in petroleum prices, the Commission issued a communication emphasizing the importance of dialogue between the major producer and consumer countries and the need to adjust priorities with a view to maintaining prices at a stable level.

INDUSTRY, ENTERPRISE AND BUSINESS POLICY

Industrial co-operation was the earliest activity of the Community. The treaty establishing the European Coal and Steel Community (ECSC) came into force in July 1952, and by the end of 1954 nearly all barriers to trade in coal, coke, steel, pig-iron and scrap iron had been removed. The ECSC treaty was due to expire in July 2002, and in 1991 the Council agreed that, by that date, the provisions of the ECSC treaty should be incorporated in the EEC treaty, on the grounds that it was no longer appropriate to treat the coal and steel sectors separately.

In the late 1970s and 1980s measures were adopted to restructure the steel industry in response to a dramatic reduction in world demand for steel. These included production capacity quotas and a reduction of state subsidies. In November 1992 the Commission announced a three-year emergency programme to further restructure the industry, following a reduction of 30% in steel prices over the previous two years. In December 1993 ministers approved aid totalling ECU 7,000m. to achieve a further reduction in annual capacity at a number of state-owned steel plants. The industry failed to achieve the required reduction in capacity of 19m. metric tons, and in October 1994 the Commission decided to abandon the restructuring plan, although the social measures, which allocated ECU 240m. to compensate for job losses, were to be maintained. Output of crude steel totalled 156m. tons in 1995, reversing the downward trend of previous years. In December 1996 the Commission adopted a new code on steel aid, for the period 1997–2002. The new code stipulated the conditions under which member states could grant aid to steel companies, namely for research and development, environmental protection, and for full or partial closures of capacity. In October 1997 the Commission announced plans to finance, using ECSC reserves, research of benefit to the coal and steel industries amounting to some ECU 40m. each year, after the expiry of the

ECSC Treaty in 2002. In 2000 total EU steel production was estimated at 163m. tons. In December the Commission adopted a draft forward programme for steel for 2001, aimed at strengthening the EU's competitive position in this sector.

The European textile and clothing industry has been seriously affected by overseas competition over an extended period. The Community participates in the Multi-fibre Arrangement (MFA, see WTO), to limit imports from low-cost suppliers overseas. A proposal by the Commission in October 1996 to accelerate liberalization of the textiles and clothing market in the EU provoked anger among industry leaders in member states, because no reciprocal concessions, in the form of removal of trade barriers, were being obtained from the major textile-exporting countries in other parts of the world. The Commission planned to include several 'sensitive' categories in the second stage of the phasing-out of trade barriers under the MFA, which was to start in January 1998. These categories included woollen yarns and fabrics, gloves, and synthetic ropes. A proposal by the Commission to impose duties of between 3% and 36% on imports of unfinished cotton fabrics, to counter alleged 'dumping' by several developing countries, was opposed by a majority of EU member states. The proposal aimed to help weaving industries (mainly in France and Italy), which had been adversely affected by the developing countries' practice of sharply undercutting their prices. Duties were provisionally introduced, for a period of six months, in late 1996. In March 1998 provisional duties of between 14% and 32.5% were imposed on imports of unbleached cotton from six countries, despite opposition by nine EU member states. Ministers of foreign affairs voted to remove duties in October. An action plan for the industry was drawn up in 1997. This was designed to improve competitiveness, facilitate structural adjustment in the industry and improve conditions of employment and training. In December 2000 the Commission published a report on the implementation of the plan, noting that there was still insufficient investment in research and innovation. The 2000 report established future priorities for the sector, focusing on preparations for the enlargement of the EU and systems for co-operation in the 'new economy'.

Production in EU member states' shipyards has fallen drastically since the 1970s, mainly as a result of competition from shipbuilders in the Far East. In the first half of the 1980s a Council directive allowed for subsidies to help reorganize the shipbuilding industry and to increase efficiency, but subsequently, rigorous curbs on state aid to the industry were introduced. The permitted maximum percentage of state aid for shipbuilding was reduced from 28% of the value of each vessel in 1987 to 9% in 1992. In July 1994 the EU signed an accord with Japan, the USA, the Republic of Korea and the Nordic countries to end subsidies to the shipbuilding industry from 1996, subject to ratification by member states. However, subsidies available in several EU countries in 1996 were higher than the official ceiling, and state aid was also given for industrial restructuring (for example, for modernization of east German shipyards) and for rescuing state-owned yards in difficulties (as in Spain). In October 1997 the Commission proposed to maintain state aid until the end of 2000; it was eventually phased out in early 2001. In May 2000 the Commission adopted a report on the state of world shipbuilding. It concluded that, in the absence of an international agreement, the market was facing a serious crisis, owing to the extremely low prices offered by South Korean shipyards. In May 2001 the EU agreed to launch WTO procedures against South Korea, if no progress had been made in negotiations. The Commission proposed a 'temporary defensive mechanism' of state subsidies for 2002 to boost the industry while the case was argued at the WTO; however, member states failed to support this. In September the EU and South Korea reached an agreement in principle on pricing for cargo ships.

The Commission has made a number of proposals for the development of the information technology (IT) industry in Europe, particularly in view of the superiority of Japan and the USA in the market for advanced electronic circuits. Under the fifth framework programme for 1998–2002, several of the EU's IT programmes were integrated into an overall Information Society Technologies (IST) programme (see under Research and Technology), designed to facilitate the development of IT in Europe. Various other initiatives to promote e-commerce and IT to businesses are under way (see under Telecommunications and Information Technology).

Harmonization of national company law to form a common legal structure within the Community has led to the adoption of directives on disclosure of information, company capital, internal mergers, the accounts of companies and of financial institutions, the division of companies, the qualification of auditors, single-member private limited companies, mergers, take-over bids and the formation of joint ventures. The Community Patent Convention was signed in 1975. In June 1997 the Commission published a consultative document containing proposals to simplify the European patent system through the introduction of a unitary Community patent, which would remove the need to file patent applications with individual member states. The Commission hoped to have the patent in place by the end of 2001, but disagreements between member states resulted in this deadline being missed. Once established, the patent was to be issued by the European Patent Office (EPO), based in Munich. An Office for Harmonization in the Internal Market (OHIM), based in Alicante, Spain, was established in December 1993, and is responsible for the registration of Community trade-marks and for ensuring that these receive uniform protection throughout the EU. Numerous directives have been adopted on the technical harmonization and standardization of products (e.g. on safety devices in motor vehicles, labelling of foodstuffs and of dangerous substances, and classification of medicines).

The liberalization of Community public procurement has played an important role in the establishment of the internal market. A directive on public supplies contracts (effective from January 1989, or from March 1992 in Greece, Portugal and Spain) stipulated that major purchases of supplies by public authorities should be offered for tender throughout the community. Public contracts for construction or civil engineering works in excess of ECU 5m. were to be offered for tender throughout the EC from July 1990 (March 1992 for Greece, Portugal and Spain). From January 1993 the liberalization of procurement was extended to include public utilities in the previously excluded sectors of energy, transport, drinking-water and telecommunications. In mid-1998 business leaders proposed introducing independent ombudsmen to monitor the operation of public procurement throughout the EU and to verify its compliance with competition rules. An action plan was adopted in 1998for revitalizing public procurement policy. In particular, it aimed to make contract award procedures clearer and more flexible. In April and May 2000 measures were taken to simplify and modernize the legal framework for awarding public contracts, building on the proposals of the action plan. The revisions took into account the liberalization of the telecommunications sector and the transition to the 'new economy'. The Commission has launched the Système d'information pour les marchés publics (SIMAP) programme, which gives information on rules, procedures and opportunities in the public procurement market. SIMAP aims to encourage the optimum use of IT in public procurement; the March 2000 Lisbon summit set the goal of bringing EU and government procurement fully online by 2003.

In October 2001 the Commission presented a strategy for company taxation in the EU, suggesting the introduction of a single consolidated tax base, to eliminate the large variations in effective company tax rates across the EU. The Commission noted that a new approach was needed, in view of increasing globalization and economic integration in the internal market as well as developments such as economic and monetary union (EMU, see under Economic Co-operation). In that month the European Council also adopted two legislative instruments enabling companies to form a European Company (known as a Societas Europaea—SE). A vital element of the internal market, the legislation gave companies operating in more than one member state the option of establishing themselves as single companies, thereby able to function throughout the EU under one set of rules and through a unified management system; companies might be merged to establish an SE. The legislation was aimed at making cross-border enterprise management more flexible and less bureaucratic, and at helping to improve competitiveness.

The Business Co-operation Centre, established in 1973, supplies information to businesses and introduces firms from 70 different countries wishing to co-operate or form links. The

Business Co-operation Network (BC-Net) links enterprises, both public and private, which wish to form alliances with others (e.g. licensing agreements), on a confidential basis. The Business Environment Simplification Task Force was established in September 1997 to consider ways of improving legislation and of removing hindrances to the development of businesses, especially small and medium-sized enterprises (SMEs). It presented its report in 1998; the subsequent action plan, designed to improve the overall environment for business, was endorsed in April 1999.

In September 1995 a Commission report outlined proposals to improve the business environment for SMEs in particular, by improving fiscal policies and access to finance, and introducing measures aimed at reducing delays in payments and lowering the costs of international transactions. In March 1996 the Commission agreed new guide-lines for state aid to SMEs. Aid for the acquisition of patent rights, licences, expertise, etc., was to be allowed at the same level as that for tangible investment. In July 1997 the I-TEC scheme was inaugurated, with a budget of ECU 7.5m., to encourage SMEs to invest in new technology. By mid-1998 I-TEC had facilitated investments amounting to over ECU 250m. A Charter for Small Enterprises, approved in June 2000, aimed to support SMEs in areas such as education and training, the development of regulations, and taxation and financial matters, and to increase representation of the interests of small businesses at national and EU level. In October 2001 SMEs comprised 98% of all EU enterprises and employed almost 75m. people. The EU has repeatedly stated that it views small businesses as a vital source of economic growth and employment creation; in December 2001 the Commission appointed an 'SME Envoy' to act as a representative for, and a contact with, SMEs.

The European Investment Bank (see p. 329) provides finance for small businesses by means of 'global loans' to financial intermediaries. A mechanism providing small businesses with subsidized loans was approved by ministers in April 1992. In 2001, noting that SMEs were gradually switching from loan finance to other instruments, including equity, the EU began an initiative to develop European venture capital markets.

A network of 39 Euro Info Centres (EICs), aimed particularly at small businesses, began work in 1987. A total of 270 EICs and 11 Euro Info Correspondence Centres were in operation in 2000. The EU's other information services for business include the Community Research and Development Information Service (Cordis, see under Research and Technology) and the internet-based Dialogue with Business, which brings together advice and data from various sources.

Meeting in Lisbon, in March 2000, the European Council set the EU the new strategic goal of transforming itself into the most competitive and dynamic economy in the world over the following decade. In January 2000 the EU's Directorate-Generals for Industry and SMEs and for Innovation were transformed into one Directorate-General for Enterprise Policy. The Commission subsequently adopted a multiannual programme on enterprise and entrepreneurship covering the period 2001–05, aimed particularly at SMEs. It was noted that business start-ups should be made easier and the cost of doing business in Europe lowered. Stronger measures were proposed for the protection of intellectual property rights (IPRs), and the harmonization of legislation on IPRs was advocated (differences between national laws in this respect could constitute protectionist barriers to the EU's principle of free movement of goods and services). The programme's overall objective was to create a dynamic, sustainable, innovation-based environment for EU businesses and to develop a climate of confidence among investors.

In order to analyse the EU's performance, the Commission has established innovation and enterprise policy scoreboards; these involve a set of performance indicators that serve as a benchmark for evaluating progress. In October 2001 the innovation scoreboard, in an assessment of Europe's fitness for the 'knowledge economy', concluded that the EU as a whole was not keeping pace with the USA and Japan. Major concerns included the relatively weak investment by businesses in research and development (R&D) and the low level of patenting activity. However, the scoreboard's assessment indicated that overall innovation was improving.

Through its joint European venture programme, the EU backs the establishment of joint ventures between enterprises from at least two member states. The European Business Angels Network (EBAN) provides a means of introduction between SMEs and investors and encourages the exchange of expertise. The Commission also promotes inter-industry co-operation between enterprises in the EU and in third countries through the Euro-Med Industrial Co-operation working party, the Transatlantic Business Dialogue (TABD), the EU-Japan Centre for Industrial Co-operation, and the Mercosur-Europe Business Forum (MEBF). An EU-Russia Round Table on industry was held in October 2000.

COMPETITION POLICY

The Treaty of Rome establishing the European Economic Community provided for the creation of a common market based on the free movement of goods, persons, services and capital. The EU's competition policy aims to guarantee the unity of this internal market, by providing access to a range of high-quality goods and services, at competitive prices. It seeks to prevent anti-competitive practices by companies or national authorities, and to outlaw monopolization, protective agreements and abuses of dominant positions. Overall, it aims to create a climate favourable to innovation, while protecting the interests of consumers.

The Commission has wide investigative powers in the area of competition policy. It may act on its own initiative, or after a complaint from a member state, firm or individual, or after being notified of agreements or planned state aid. Before taking a decision, the Commission organizes hearings; its decisions can be challenged before the Court of First Instance and the Court of Justice, or in national courts. In 2000 the Commission recommended measures to strengthen its investigative powers.

State aid—which ranges from discrimination in favour of public enterprises to the granting of aid to private-sector companies—is contrary to the principles of competition policy. The EU does not attempt to ban state aid completely, but encourages a reduction in its overall level and works to ensure that all aid granted is compatible with the principles of the common market. The procedural rules on state aid were consolidated and clarified in a regulation in 1999. There are several exemptions, notably regarding the provision of aid to small and medium-sized enterprises (SMEs) and for training. The EU has drawn up 'regional aid maps' designed to concentrate aid in those regions with the most severe development problems. In 2000 the Commission received 869 notifications of new or amended aid schemes and registered 133 cases of unnotified schemes. It raised no objections in 623 cases; in the others it carried out investigations. The overall level of state aid granted for 1996–98 fell by 11% compared with the level for 1994–96.

The Treaty of Rome prohibits agreements and concerted practices between firms resulting in the prevention, restriction or distortion of competition within the common market. This ban applies both to horizontal agreements (between firms at the same stage of the production process) and vertical agreements (between firms at different stages). The type of agreements and practices that are prohibited include: price-fixing; imposing conditions on sale; seeking to isolate market segments; imposing production or delivery quotas; agreements on investments; establishing joint sales offices; market-sharing agreements; creating exclusive collective markets; agreements leading to discrimination against other trading parties; collective boycotting; and voluntary restraints on competitive behaviour. Certain types of co-operation considered as positive, such as agreements promoting technical and economic progress, may be exempt.

In addition, mergers that would significantly impede competition in the common market are banned. The Commission examines prospective mergers in order to decide whether they are compatible with competition principles. In July 1996 the Commission proposed an extension of its authority for overseeing merger operations to include smaller mergers and joint ventures overseen by national regulators. The Commission planned to have authority over operations involving companies with combined global turnover of more than €2,000m. and turnover within the EU of €150m.; however, the proposal was widely opposed. In 2000 the Commission adopted a simplified procedure for investigating mergers, acquisitions and joint ventures that did not pose any competition problems. In December 2000 the Commission adopted a communication setting out EU guide-lines on merger control, with the aim of making the process more predictable for all parties.

In 2000 the EU received 345 notifications under the merger regulation. All mergers are subject to various conditions. In July 2001 the EU blocked a merger between two US companies for the first time on the grounds that EU companies would be adversely affected.

The Commission is attempting to abolish monopolies in the networks supplying basic services to member states. In December 1997 the Council adopted a directive on postal services, defining the level of service to be provided throughout the EU and establishing a timetable for the liberalization of services. Liberalization is also being pursued in the gas and electricity, telecommunications and transport sectors (see relevant sections for more information). In addition, efforts are being made to integrate aspects of environment policy and issues of sustainable development into competition policy. In return, competition law must be respected when environmental initiatives are put into place.

In April 1999 reforms to competition policy were proposed in a White Paper presented by the Commission. The reforms aim to transfer responsibility for much of the routine enforcement of EU competition rules to national authorities and courts. Under the proposals companies would have to notify the EU's competition watchdog only of mergers and acquisitions, but not of other agreements, thereby freeing the Commission from the need to process every deal. The European Parliament began to debate the reforms in January 2000.

The international affairs unit of the Directorate-General for Competition co-operates with foreign competition authorities (particularly in the USA) and promotes competition instruments in applicant countries, where it also provides technical assistance. The unit works within the framework of international organizations such as the WTO, the Organisation for Economic Co-operation and Development (OECD) and the United Nations Conference on Trade and Development (UNCTAD).

TELECOMMUNICATIONS AND INFORMATION TECHNOLOGY

In 1990 proposals were adopted by the Council on the co-ordinated introduction of a European public paging system and of cellular digital land-based mobile communications. In 1991 the Council adopted a directive requiring member states to liberalize their rules on the supply of telecommunications terminal equipment, thus ending the monopolies of national telecommunications authorities. In the same year the Council adopted a plan for the gradual introduction of a competitive market in satellite communications. In October 1995 the Commission adopted a directive liberalizing the use of cable telecommunications, requiring member states to permit a wide range of services, in addition to television broadcasts, on such networks. The EU market for mobile telephone networks was opened to full competition as a result of a directive adopted by the Commission in January 1996, according to which member states were to abolish all exclusive and special rights in this area, and establish open and fair licensing procedures for digital services. The telecommunications market was to be fully deregulated by 1998, although extensions to the deregulation schedule were agreed for a number of member states. In October 1997 the Commission announced plans to commence legal proceedings against those member states that had not yet adopted the legislation necessary to permit the liberalization of the telecommunications market. Spain agreed to bring forward the full deregulation of its telecommunications market from January 2003 to 1998, which meant that all the major EU telecommunications markets were open to competition from 1998. In March 2000 the EU resolved that telecommunications markets throughout the Community should be fully liberalized and integrated by 2002.

In July 1998 the Commission identified 14 cases of unfair pricing after commencing an investigation into the charges imposed by telecommunications companies for interconnection between fixed and mobile telephone networks. In December the Commission suspended some of its investigations, after a number of companies introduced price reductions. In February 2000 the Commission requested that national competition authorities, telecommunications regulators, mobile network operators and service providers give information on conditions and price structures for national and international mobile services. The EU has registered concern at the lack of competition in the mobile market.

In July 2000 a comprehensive reform of the regulatory framework for telecommunications—the so-called 'telecoms package'—was launched. The reform aimed to update EU regulations to take account of changes in the telecommunications, media and information technology (IT) sectors. Noting the continuing convergence of these sectors, the Commission aimed to develop a single regulatory framework for all transmission networks and associated services, in order to exploit the full potential for growth, competition and job creation. The Commission recommended, as a priority, introducing a regulation on unbundled access to the local loop (the final connection of telephone wires into the home). The lack of competition in this part of the network was considered a significant obstacle to the widespread provision of low-cost internet access. The regulation obliged incumbent operators to permit shared and full access to the local loop by the end of 2000. (In December 2001 the Commission initiated infringement procedures against Greece, Portugal and Germany for failure to ensure this.) The EU has also made efforts to increase broadband use, which provides faster access to the internet. The Commission is working to develop a policy framework for so-called third-generation (3G) mobile communications within the EU, including an agreement on a regulatory framework for broadband networks. In December 2001 Parliament voted to adopt a compromise telecoms package. This gives the Commission powers to oversee national regulatory regimes and, in some cases, to overrule national regulatory authorities. It is designed to reduce the dominant market position of monopolies and to open the market to competition. The package includes a framework directive and three specific directives (covering issues of authorization, access and interconnection, universal service and users' rights) and measures to ensure harmonized conditions in radio spectrum policy.

The EU is undertaking efforts to make the internet more user-friendly, with targeted online services, technical support and information technology training for those at risk of 'digital exclusion'. A high-level group on Employment and the Social Dimension of the Information Society (ESDIS) was established in 1998 to focus on promoting digital inclusion. At the European Council meeting held in January 2000, referred to as the 'dot.com summit', the Commission agreed to put all remaining e-commerce legislation in place by the end of the year. The Lisbon European Council meeting in March 2000 set the EU a new strategic goal of transforming itself into the most competitive and dynamic knowledge-based economy in the world. The Commission presented the Council with a draft action plan entitled 'e-Europe 2002: an information society for all'. Priority actions under the plan include developing cheaper internet access; establishing online healthcare and government services; updating schools' networks; training all teachers in internet use; developing a faster internet for use by researchers and students; promoting the use of smart cards for secure electronic access; providing internet access to basic public services by 2003; and encouraging participation by the disabled. Internet access for all schoolchildren in the Community was to be achieved by 2001. The EU aims to ensure that the movement into the digital age is socially inclusive and serves to build consumer trust. In December 2000 the Commission's programme on European digital content was adopted. Recognizing that a large proportion of the material on the internet originated in the USA, this sought to develop the regional potential in this area. In June 2001 a communication on the security of electronic networks and information systems was adopted, considering problems and possible solutions. The '.eu' domain name was formally agreed by EU ministries in June 2001, giving a European identity for providers of services and information.

The EU maintains several information society programmes. The Community's overall Information Society Technologies (IST) programme (see under Research and Technology) is designed to accelerate the emergence of an information society and promotes the development of high-quality, efficient, affordable services. The Interchange of Data between Administrations (IDA) initiative supports the rapid electronic exchange of information between EU administrations. The Safer Internet action plan for 1999–2002, with a budget of €25m, aimed to create a more secure internet environment, in part through the development of filtering and rating systems.

In 1992 a White Paper proposed the establishment of trans-European networks (TENs) in telecommunications, energy and transport (see under those sections), in order to improve infrastructure and assist in the development of the common market. Following the liberalization of the telecommunications market in 1998, efforts in this area were concentrated on support for the development of broadband networks and multimedia applications.

TRANSPORT POLICY

The establishment of a common transport policy is stipulated in the Treaty of Rome, with the aim of gradually standardizing the national regulations that hinder the free movement of traffic within the Community, such as the varying safety and licensing rules, diverse restrictions on the size of lorries, and frontier-crossing formalities. A White Paper in 1992 set out a common transport policy for the EU. The paper proposed the establishment of trans-European networks (TENs) to improve transport, telecommunications and energy infrastructure throughout the Community, as well as the integration of transport systems and measures to protect the environment and improve safety. An action programme for 1995–2000 set out initiatives in three basic areas: developing integrated transport systems based on advanced technologies; improving the functioning of the single market through transport policy; and improving transport links between the EU and third countries. A new action plan based on this was adopted for 1998–2004. Significant progress has been made, through harmonization and liberalization, towards the achievement of a single transport market.

The overall aim of the EU's TENs policy, which included so-called intelligent transport systems, was to unite the 15 national networks into a single European network, by eliminating bottlenecks and adding missing links. The 2000–06 budget for the 14 TENs projects totalled €4,600m., funded in part by the European Regional Development Fund, the European Investment Bank and the European Investment Fund. In addition, efforts are being made to increase the private-sector involvement financing TENs, through the development of public-private partnerships (PPPs). The majority of the financial backing, however, is provided by individual member states. In April 1997 plans were announced to extend the TENs scheme into central and eastern Europe. A project to develop a motorway providing a Berlin–Kiev link began in May, aided by a grant of ECU 68m. from the PHARE programme.

In recent years the EU has focused on integrating environmental issues and questions of sustainable development into transport policy. In July 1998 the Commission proposed linking the cost of using air services, ports, railways and roads to the social costs incurred by each means of travel. In September 2001 the Commission adopted a White Paper on Transport Policy for 2010. This set out a framework designed to accommodate the forecast strong growth in demand for transport, on a sustainable basis. The new policy aimed to shift the balance between modes of transport by 2010, by revitalizing railways, promoting maritime and inland waterway transport systems, and by linking up different kinds of transport. The paper proposed an action plan and a strategy designed gradually to break the link between economic and transport growth, with the aim of reducing pressure on the environment and relieving congestion.

In 1986 transport ministers agreed on a system of Community-wide permits for commercial vehicles, to facilitate the crossing of frontiers, and in 1993 they agreed on measures concerning road haulage. A common tax system for trucks using EC roads was to lead to the full liberalization of road 'cabotage' (whereby road hauliers may provide services in the domestic market of another member state) by 1998. In May 1998 transport ministers approved legislation compelling member governments to clear serious obstructions, such as truck blockades, that hinder the free movement of goods. The White Paper on Transport Policy adopted in September 2001 proposed the harmonization of petrol taxes across the EU.

In 1991 directives were adopted by the Council on the compulsory use of safety belts in vehicles weighing less than 3.5 metric tons. Further regulations applying to minibuses and coaches were to be introduced, following approval by the Commission in mid-1996. In June 2000 the Commission issued a communication setting out measures to improve the safety and efficiency of road transport and to ensure fair competition. These included road traffic monitoring, the regulation of employed drivers' working time, and regularity of employment conditions. Work on the problem of drink-driving and impairment due to the use of drugs and medications was ongoing.

In the late 1980s ministers of transport approved measures to contribute to the liberalization of air transport within the Community. In 1990 ministers agreed to make further reductions in guaranteed quotas for a country's airlines on routes to another country, and to liberalize air cargo services. In 1992 they approved an 'open skies' arrangement that would allow any EC airline to operate domestic flights within another member state (with effect from 1 April 1997). In June 1996 the ministers of transport approved a limited mandate for the Commission to negotiate an 'open skies' agreement with the USA, under which a common EU–US aviation area would be created. However, the USA wished to negotiate on the basis of a full mandate. In October 1998 ministers failed to award a full mandate to the Commission. In November the Commission filed a case with the European Court of Justice, accusing eight member countries that had reached bilateral 'open skies' agreements with the USA of distorting competition to the disadvantage of EU airlines. The Commission also initiated legal action against agreements made with the USA by Iceland, Norway and Switzerland. In 2001 the EU stated that if the Court of Justice ruled in its favour, it would seek to build on the existing agreements, rather than to abolish them.

In July 1994, despite the recommendations of a 'Committee of Wise Men' for tighter controls on subsidies awarded to airlines, as part of efforts to increase competitiveness within the industry, the Commission approved substantial subsidies that had been granted by the French and Greek governments to their respective national airlines. Subsequently, the Commission specified that state assistance could be granted to airlines 'in exceptional, unforeseen circumstances, outside the control of the company'. In June 1998 the European Court of Justice declared the subsidies awarded by the French Government illegal. However, in the following month the Commission stated that the subsidies were valid, as they had been accompanied by restructuring measures and certain competition guarantees. Following the major terrorist attacks perpetrated against targets in the USA in September 2001, and the consequent difficulties suffered by the air transport sector, the EU ruled that a degree of aid or compensation was permissible, but stressed that this must not lead to distortion of competition. The Commission approved a one-month loan to the Belgian national airline, Sabena (which subsequently collapsed), and agreed to compensate airlines for revenues lost in the immediate aftermath of the attacks. However, further subsidies were refused.

In early 1999 a dispute arose between the EU and the USA over the introduction of new EU legislation to curb aircraft noise. Initially, the EU proposed to prevent aircraft fitted with hush kits from flying in the EU after 1 April 2002 unless they were already operating there before 1 April 1999 (aircraft fitted with hush kits create more noise than newer aircraft, use more fuel and cause more pollution). The legislation was subsequently amended to avert the threat of a temporary boycott of some European flights by the US authorities, but the dispute persisted. The USA lodged an official complaint with the International Civil Aviation Organisation in March 2000.

In September 2000 the Commission adopted a proposal for a regulation creating a European Aviation Safety Agency (EASA). The EASA was to cover all aircraft registered in member states, unless agreed otherwise. The Commission has also formulated ground rules for enquiries into civil air incidents and has issued proposals for assessing the safety of aircraft registered outside the EU. In October 2001 the Commission proposed establishing common rules in the field of civil aviation safety, to strengthen public confidence in air transport following the terrorist attacks on the USA. Issues addressed included securing cockpits, improving air-ground communications and using video cameras in aircraft. Member states also agreed to incorporate into Community law co-operation arrangements on security measures. These measures covered control of access to sensitive areas of airports and aircraft, control of passengers and hand luggage, control and monitoring of hold luggage, and training of ground staff.

In December 1999 the Commission presented a communication on streamlining air-traffic control to create a Single European Sky. Based on several lines of action, proposals include the joint management of airspace; the establishment of a strong EU regulator; and the gradual integration of civilian and military air traffic management. The overall aim was to restructure the EU's airspace on the basis of traffic, rather than national frontiers.

In 1986 progress was made towards the establishment of a common maritime transport policy, with the adoption of regulations on unfair pricing practices, safeguard of access to cargoes, application of competition rules and the eventual elimination of unilateral cargo reservation and discriminatory cargo-sharing arrangements. In December 1990 the Council approved, in principle, the freedom for shipping companies to provide maritime transport anywhere within the Community. Cabotage by sea began to be phased in from January 1993. The introduction of cabotage, and the need to improve conditions, resulted in the adoption of measures relating to competition policy, the prevention of unfair pricing practices, standards for ships engaged in transport of dangerous goods, and working conditions. The conditions governing admission to the occupation were also defined. Cabotage was introduced in the inland waterway transport sector in 1993. The inland waterways market was liberalized by January 2000, although obstacles to the functioning of the single market subsequently persisted, including differing technical regulations among member states and numerous bilateral agreements.

In March 2000 the Commission adopted a communication on the safety of the seaborne oil trade. It proposed the introduction of a first package of short-term measures to strengthen controls, including the right to refuse access to substandard ships, more stringent inspections and a generalization of the ban on single-hull oil tankers. In May the Commission adopted a proposal to harmonize procedures between bulk carriers and terminals, in order to reduce the risk of accidents caused by incorrect loading and unloading. In the same month the Commission signed a memorandum of understanding with several countries on the establishment of the Equasis database, intended to provide information on the safety and quality of ships. The Commission adopted a report in September advocating the establishment of a Community maritime traffic monitoring, control and information system; a European oil pollution compensation fund (COPE); and a European Maritime Safety Agency. In December the Commission set out a second package of safety measures, together with legislative proposals relating to the establishment of these bodies. Broad agreement was reached on the first package, and the EU agreed to accelerate the phasing in of double-hull tankers. The compatibility with international maritime legislation of some of the second package of measures was, however, questioned.

In September 2000 a proposal for a directive on port reception facilities for ship-generated waste and cargo residues was adopted. Ports were to be required to draft plans for the management and collection of such waste and to provide ships with an efficient service at reasonable cost, to remove the incentive for dumping at sea. The directive stipulated penalties for non-compliance.

In April 1998 the Commission published a report on railway policy, with the aim of achieving greater harmonization, the regulation of state subsidies and the progressive liberalization of the rail freight market. The Commission proposed the immediate liberalization of 5% of the market, increasing to 15% after five years and to 25% after 10 years. In October 1999 EU transport ministers concluded an agreement that was regarded as a precursor to the full liberalization of the rail-freight market. The agreement provided for the extension of access to a planned Trans-European Rail Freight Network (TERFN, covering some 50,000 km), with a charging system designed to ensure optimum competitiveness.

In December 2000 the EU adopted the first 'Railway Package'. This aimed to open up the TERFN to international goods services by 2003, and to open the rest of the network by 2008. Following the presentation of the White Paper on Transport Policy for 2010, the Commission made more radical proposals to revitalize the railways in its second Railway Package, adopted in January 2002. Under the framework of the second package, the EU aimed to open up the entire network, including national networks, by 2006. Other measures included developing a common approach to rail safety; bolstering principles of interoperability; and setting up a European Railway Agency. Rail transport's share of the total freight market declined from 21% in 1970 to 8% by the end of 2001. The EU aims also to liberalize progressively passenger rail services.

The PACT (pilot action for combined transport) scheme was instigated in 1992 and had funded 65 combined transport projects (where goods are moved by at least two forms of transport without unloading) on 22 routes by July 1996, when the Commission approved plans to extend the programme from 1997 to 2001, with an additional budget of €35m. The successor programme to PACT, 'Marco Polo', was scheduled to be operational by 2003. This was to have an increased focus on international projects.

JUSTICE AND HOME AFFAIRS

Under the Treaty on European Union, EU member states undertook to co-operate in the areas of justice and home affairs, particularly in relation to the free movement of people between member states. Issues of common interest were defined as asylum policy; border controls; immigration; drug addiction; fraud; judicial co-operation in civil and criminal matters; customs co-operation; and police co-operation for the purposes of combating terrorism, drugs-trafficking and other serious forms of international crime. The EU's current action plan for justice and home affairs covers the period 2000–04. In view of the sensitivity of many of the issues involved in this sphere, the EU affords great weight to the positions and opinions of individual states. There tends to be a greater degree of flexibility than in other areas, and requirements are frequently less stringent.

A European Police Office (Europol), facilitating the exchange of information between police forces, operates from The Hague, Netherlands. A special Europol unit dealing with the trafficking of illicit drugs and nuclear and radioactive materials began work in 1994. Europol's mandate has been extended to cover illegal immigrants, stolen vehicles, paedophilia and terrorist activities, and, since November 2000, money-laundering. Europol had a budget of €48.5m. for 2002.

In 2001, following increasingly disruptive and violent protests by anti-globalization and anti-capitalist demonstrators at a number of high-level global summits, the EU considered means of intensifying police co-operation around the location of summit meetings. Proposed measures included the temporary closure of borders and preventing suspected protesters from travelling.

The EU convention on extradition, signed by ministers of justice in September 1996 prior to ratification by national governments, simplified and accelerated procedures in this area, reduced the number of cases where extradition could be refused, and made it easier to extradite members of criminal organizations. In November 1997 the Commission proposed an extension to European law to allow civil and commercial judgments made in the courts of member states to be enforced throughout the whole of the EU. A regulation on the mutual recognition and enforcement of such judgements was to come into force in March 2001 across the EU, with the exception of Denmark. The EU recognizes that some harmonization of legal standards may be required for mutual recognition to be effective. In 2000 a convention on mutual assistance in criminal matters was adopted. This contained provisions on a number of specific forms of mutual assistance (such as criminal hearings by video and telephone conference and cross-border investigations). In 2001 discussions were held on extra-judicial means of settling disputes in civil and commercial matters.

The Grotius-Civil programme of incentives and exchanges for legal practitioners was established in 1996. It was designed to aid judicial co-operation between member states by improving reciprocal knowledge of legal and judicial systems. The successor programme, Grotius II, focused on general and criminal law. The establishment of a European legal training network for judges has also been proposed. In addition, the EU aims to establish a 'Eurojust' unit, composed of prosecutors, magistrates and police officers from member states, to help co-ordinate prosecutions and support investigations into incidences of serious organized crime. In December 2000 it was decided to establish a provisional judicial co-operation unit (Pro-Eurojust), pending the entry into operation of Eurojust. A European Police College (CEPOL) has also been created to train senior members of Community police departments, as well as officers from the central and eastern European states. CEPOL consists of a network of existing national training institutes; a permanent institution may eventually be created.

In March 2000 an action programme entitled 'The prevention and control of organized crime: a European strategy' was adopted.

A European crime prevention network was formally established in May 2001. There are also agreements within the EU on co-operation between financial intelligence units and between police forces for the purposes of combating child pornography. In addition, the EU has a common strategy designed to help Russia combat organized crime. The EU runs the FALCONE programme—a series of incentives, training opportunities and exchanges for those responsible for the fight against organized crime in individual member states. The STOP (sexual treatment of persons) programme operates a similar system for those responsible for combating trade in humans and the sexual exploitation of children. The EU has focused recent efforts on preventing child pornography on the internet. In September 2001 member states harmonized their definitions of human trafficking and set common minimum jail sentences. In June 2000 an action plan was approved on combating usage of and trafficking illicit drugs. The plan, covering the period 2000–04, identified a range of measures to be implemented. The European Monitoring Centre for Drugs and Drug Addiction (EMCDDA) is based in Lisbon, Portugal. In September 2000 Norway became the first non-EU state to be admitted to EMCDDA. The EU is working with other third countries to tackle issues of drugs demand and supply.

The EU's draft Charter of Fundamental Rights, signed in December 2000, outlines the rights and freedoms recognized by the EU. It includes civil, political, economic and social rights, with each based on a previous charter, convention, treaty or jurisprudence. The charter may be used to challenge decisions taken by the Community institutions and by member states when implementing EU law.

The Justice and Home Affairs Council held an emergency meeting in September 2001 following the terrorist attacks on the USA. It determined a number of measures to be taken to improve security in the Community. First, the Council sought to reach a common definition of acts of terrorism, and to establish higher penalties for such acts. The new definition includeed cyber and environmental attacks. The Council decided that, for the perpetrators of terrorist attacks, as well as those involved in other serious crimes (including trafficking in arms, people and drugs and money-laundering), the process of extradition would ultimately be replaced by a procedure for hand-over based on a European arrest warrant. In the meantime, member states were urged to take the necessary steps to allow the existing conventions on extradition to enter into force. The member states reached agreement on the arrest warrant in December; under the agreement, covering 32 serious offences, EU countries may no longer refuse to extradite their own nationals. The warrant was scheduled to come into force in January 2004. The Council also determined to accelerate the implementation of the convention on mutual assistance in criminal matters and to establish a joint investigation team. Member states were encouraged to ratify the convention on combating the financing of terrorism and to exercise greater rigour in the issuing of travel documents. The heads of the security and intelligence services of member states met in October, in the first EU-wide meeting of this kind, to discuss the co-ordinated action to be taken to curb terrorism. They were to meet in regular sessions thereafter. A team of counter-terrorist specialists, established within Europol, was to produce an assessment of terrorist threats to EU states, indicating the likely nature and location of any such attacks. Rapid links were being forged with US counterparts—in December Europol signed a co-operation agreement on the exchange of strategic information (excluding personal data) with the USA. The heads of the EU's anti-terrorist units also held a meeting following the September attacks, to discuss issues such as joint training exercises, equipment sharing, the joint procurement of equipment and possible joint operations. Prior to these emergency meetings, intelligence and security information had been shared bilaterally and on a small scale, impeding Europol's effectiveness.

Measures related to the abolition of customs formalities at intra-community frontiers were completed by mid-1991, and entered into force in January 1993. However, disagreements remained among member governments concerning the free movement of persons: discussions continued in 1992 on the abuse of open frontiers by organized crime, particularly for drugs-trafficking; on extradition procedures; and on rules of asylum and immigration. In June 1990 Belgium, France, Germany, Luxembourg and the Netherlands, meeting in Schengen, Luxembourg, signed a convention to implement an earlier agreement (concluded in 1985 at the same location), abolishing frontier controls on the free movement of persons from 1993. Delay in the establishment of the Schengen Information System (SIS), providing a computer network on criminals and illegal immigrants for use by the police forces of signatory states, resulted in the postponement of the implementation of the new agreement. Seven countries (Belgium, France, Germany, Luxembourg, the Netherlands, Portugal and Spain) agreed to implement the agreement with effect from March 1995. Frontier controls at airports on those travelling between the seven countries were dismantled during a three-month transition period, which ended on 1 July 1995. However, after that date the French government announced that it would retain land-border controls for a further six months, claiming that drugs-trafficking and illegal immigration had increased as a result of the agreement. In March 1996 France decided to lift its border controls with Spain and Germany while maintaining controls on borders with the Benelux countries, mainly owing to fears concerning the transportation of illicit drugs from the Netherlands via Belgium and Luxembourg. Italy joined the 'Schengen Group' in October 1997, and Austria in December. Border controls for both countries were removed in 1998. Denmark, Finland and Sweden (and non-EU members Norway and Iceland) were admitted as observers of the accord from 1 May 1996. The latter agreement was framed in such a way as to enable the first three countries to accede to the Schengen agreement in the future without adversely affecting the border-free zone provided by the Nordic Passport Union. In April 1998 Sweden voted to join the 'Schengen Group'. Denmark and Finland were also reported to be making preparations for membership. In March 1999 signatories of the Schengen accords on visa-free border crossings began to waive visa requirements with Estonia, Latvia and Lithuania. The Treaty of Amsterdam, which came into effect on 1 May 1999, incorporated the so-called Schengen *'acquis'* (comprising the 1985 agreement, 1990 convention and additional accession protocols and executive decisions), in order to integrate it into the framework of the EU. The Treaty permitted the United Kingdom and Ireland to maintain permanent jurisdiction over their borders and rules of asylum and immigration. Countries acceding to the EU after 2000 were automatically to adhere to the Schengen arrangements. The Schengen agreement came into force in the Nordic states in March 2001.

The EC defined objectives on the subject of asylum that were to be met within five years of the Amsterdam Treaty entering into force. These included: establishing criteria and mechanisms for determining which member state was responsible for considering an asylum application; setting minimum standards for the reception of asylum seekers (covering issues of residence and freedom of movement, financial and material assistance, work, healthcare, family unity and schooling of minors, among others); establishing rules for the temporary protection of refugees; setting minimum standards for conditions to obtain refugee statues and for having this withdrawn; determining measures to be taken against illegal immigration, including the use of repatriation; and formulating rulings relating to other third country nationals. The need to develop a common policy on immigration was expressed more strongly in the late 1990s, with the number of immigrants forecast to increase in coming years.

In November 2000 the Commission adopted a communication outlining a common asylum procedure and providing for a uniform status, valid throughout the EU, for persons granted asylum. Efforts towards a full harmonization of the rules on immigration continued. In March 2001 a common list of countries whose citizens required visas to enter the EU was finally adopted. In January 2002 the visa requirement for Romanian nationals crossing EU borders was removed. The EU has also developed the so-called 'Eurodac' database for co-ordinating information on the movements of asylum-seekers; Eurodac allows for the comparison of fingerprints of refugees. In September 2001 the Commission launched a directive establishing a common European definition of a refugee, aimed at curtailing so-called 'asylum shopping' (in which a person moves from one state to another until reaching one prepared to give protection). The EU was also seeking to develop common repatriation procedures for unsuccessful claimants. (Under current arrangements refugees may simply be repatriated to the EU state from which they arrived.)

The European Refugee Fund, with funds of €216m. for 2000–04, was established in September 2000. It aims to support the efforts of member states to receive refugees and, with a reserve of €10m., allows emergency measures to be taken in the event of a sudden, mass influx. The Odysseus programme of training, exchange and co-operation assists officials working in the field of asylum and immigration. A high-level working group on asylum and migration was set up in December 1998. It implements action plans in the main source countries for immigration to western Europe (Afghanistan and the surrounding region; Iraq; Morocco; Somalia; Sri Lanka; and Albania and Kosovo). In 2000 and 2001 there was particular concern at the level of illegal immigration from the West Balkans; the establishment of a network of national immigration liaison offices was planned in that region to help control illegal immigration flows. In 2000 the EU and China agreed to co-operate to combat the illegal immigration network from China.

In July 2001, noting the problems likely to arise in the future from labour shortages and ageing populations in EU countries, the Commission proposed the introduction of a 'green card' system. If adopted, this would consider age, profession and language skills, in order to help regulate legal immigration and fill gaps in the labour market.

EDUCATION, CULTURE AND BROADCASTING

The Treaty of Rome, although not covering education directly, gave the Community the role of establishing general principles for implementing a common vocational training policy. The Treaty on European Union urged greater co-operation on education policy, including encouraging exchanges and mobility for students and teachers, distance learning and the development of European studies. In July 2000 the EU's Economic and Social Committee adopted a report on education in Europe. The Committee considered the development of a more integrated education strategy for Europe and advocated the study of new approaches to schooling, including differing structures and wider objectives, more diverse fields of learning and greater use of modern technologies.

The postgraduate European University Institute was founded in Florence in 1972, with departments of history, economics, law, and political and social sciences, together with a European Policy Unit and a European Culture Research Centre. In 2000 there were some 450 research students. In April 1998 202 research and teaching projects were approved for EU universities, including the establishment of 25 Jean Monnet European Centres of Excellence. The Jean Monnet project also finances the establishment of Jean Monnet chairs at universities; there were 486 such chairs in 2000.

In September 1980 an educational information network, 'Eurydice', began operations, with a central unit in Brussels and national units providing data on the widely varying systems of education within member states. In 1987 the Council adopted a European Action Scheme for the Mobility of University Students ('Erasmus'). The scheme was expanded to include EFTA member states from 1992. The 'Lingua' programme promoted the teaching of foreign languages in the Community. From 1 January 1995 the Erasmus and Lingua schemes were incorporated into a new Community programme, 'Socrates', with a budget of ECU 850m for 1995–99. In 2000, under Erasmus, financial assistance was given to 1,814 higher education establishments and to 122 projects to develop joint syllabuses. Some 229,000 students and 45,000 teachers participated in educational exchanges. In addition to Erasmus, Socrates incorporates the Comenius strand (which financed 2,738 school partnerships in 2000); the Gruntvig strand (which deals with adult education and gave aid to 76 projects in 2000); and the Minerva strand (for open and distance learning, which supported 70 projects). The second phase of Socrates runs from 2000–06, with a budget of €1,850m. It is prioritizing the learning of EU languages (2001 was nominated the European Year of Languages); the promotion of mobility in education; innovation in educational practices; and life-long learning. The EU also co-operates with Canada and the USA in projects relating to higher education and training.

The Trans-European Mobility Programme for University Studies (TEMPUS) was launched in 1990 to foster co-operation between institutions of higher education and their counterparts in central and eastern Europe, as part of the wider aid programme to those countries. Under the second phase of the scheme (TEMPUS II) for 1994–98, the former Soviet republics were eligible to participate. TEMPUS III covers 2000–06. Under this third phase, the programme has widened its remit to cover certain non-academic institutions. The European Training Foundation, based in Turin, supports TEMPUS projects as part of its general assistance for the development of vocational training in EU partner countries. The Foundation deals with those countries eligible to participate in the EU's Phare, CARDS, TACIS and MEDA programmes (see under External Relations).

In 1975 a European Centre for the Development of Vocational Training (CEDEFOP) was established in Berlin, Germany. The centre relocated to Thessaloniki, Greece, in 1995. The priority areas for the centre in 2000–03 included promoting key skills and lifelong learning; developing new ways of learning; and supporting employment and competitiveness. Between 1995 and 1999 the Leonardo da Vinci programme for vocational training supported more than 3,000 projects, with a budget of ECU 620m.. The second phase of the programme (2000–06) had a budget of €1,150m. In January 2000 the 1999 decision on the promotion of European pathways for work-linked training, including apprenticeship, came into force. This involved the introduction of the new EU 'Europass Training' document, which attests to periods of training completed in another member state.

In April 2000 the EU's 'Youth' community action programme for 2000–06 was adopted, with a budget of €520m. This incorporated all the previous youth programmes and related activities, including Youth for Europe, which covered the period 1995–99, and the European Voluntary Service (EVS) programmes. The overall objective of the new programme was to help young people contribute to the building of Europe and to foster a spirit of initiative. Around 7,000 projects were financed under the programme in 2000. From the outset Youth included applicant countries. The new Socrates, Leonardo da Vinci and Youth programmes were officially launched in March 2000. Together, they aimed to halve, by 2010, the number of people aged 18–24 who had completed only the first part of secondary education; promote life-long learning; encourage electronic learning; develop a European certificate of competence in information technology (IT); and promote mobility.

In May 2000 the Commission adopted an initiative entitled 'e-Learning: designing tomorrow's education' as part of its overall 'e-Europe' action plan (see under Telecommunications and Information Technology). One of the main objectives of the e-Europe programme was to encourage the use of the internet in schools and universities. A Commission report in January 2000 considered the use of IT in schools and the possibilities for development. The report noted problems such as the rapid obsolescence of technical equipment, the need for lower costs and greater reliability in internet use, and the need for training, particularly at secondary level.

The Commission organizes the annual so-called 'Netd@ys' Europe, aimed at exchanging and disseminating experience in the use of new media, especially the internet, as a teaching, learning and cultural resource. Non-member countries are involved in the initiative, which is held over the course of one week. The 2000 Netd@ys concentrated on the changing role of teachers and trainers, and the capacity of new technologies to improve quality of life, especially for people in isolated areas.

The EU's Culture 2000 framework programme, with a budget of €167m., replaced the Raphael, Kaleidoscope and Ariane programmes. The new framework programme, ending in 2004, was to focus on the following themes: legislation of benefit to cultural projects; the cultural aspects of existing support policies; and the incorporation of culture into the field of external relations. Culture 2000 supported 200 projects in 27 countries (including applicant countries) in 2001.

The European City of Culture initiative was launched in 1985 (it was renamed the Cultural Capital of Europe initiative in 1999). Member states designate cities, which receive a subsidy from the Commission. In 2001 Porto (Portugal) and Rotterdam (Netherlands) were nominated. As part of the so-called Cardiff process of integration of environmental and sustainable development issues (see under Environment Policy), the Commission is bound to make efforts to preserve cultural heritage in the formulation of other policies. At the end of 1999 a Commission support plan to combat doping in sport was adopted. Funds of €5m. were allocated to this for 2000. In October the Commission, with France, organized a European sports forum.

In 1989 ministers of foreign affairs adopted a directive (television without frontiers) establishing minimum standards for television programmes to be broadcast freely throughout the Community: limits were placed on the amount of time devoted to advertisements, a majority of programmes broadcast were to be from the Community, where practicable, and governments were allowed to forbid the transmission of programmes considered morally harmful. The 'Media' programme was introduced in 1991 to provide financial support to the television and film industry. 'Media II', covering 1996–2000, was followed by Media Plus, covering 2001–05, with a budget of €400m. Media Plus was to take account of the new regulatory environment (see under Telecommunications and Information Technology), and aimed to encourage the development, distribution and marketing of European audiovisual material.

The Commission presented a Green Paper in December 1997 on the convergence of the telecommunications, media and IT sectors. It proposed increased self-regulation in these sectors; separate regulatory approaches for the transport of electrical signals and for content; more effective protection of freedom of expression and authors' rights; and improved protection of minors. In 1999 the Commission adopted principles and guidelines for audiovisual policy in view of increasing digitalization. It noted that digital technologies were allowing an enormous increase in the amount of audiovisual content available and permitting a wide range of new operators. As rapid growth was expected to continue, these changes were likely to require the adaptation of the regulatory framework and support mechanisms. The 1999 communication proposed a timetable for discussion and action, noting the need for the sector to remain competitive and for the promotion of cultural and linguistic diversity.

SOCIAL POLICY

The Single European Act, which entered into force in 1987, added to the original Treaty of Rome articles that emphasized the need for 'economic and social cohesion' in the Community, i.e. the reduction of disparities between the various regions. This was to be achieved principally through the existing 'structural funds'—the European Regional Development Fund, the European Social Fund, and the Guidance Section of the European Agricultural Guidance and Guarantee Fund (EAGGF—for details of these funds, as well as the Cohesion Fund, which became operational in 1993, see p. 363). In 1988 the Council declared that Community operations through the structural funds, the European Investment Bank (EIB) and other financial instruments should have five priority objectives: (i) promoting the development and structural adjustment of the less-developed regions (where gross domestic product per head is less than 75% of the Community average); (ii) converting the regions, frontier regions or parts of regions seriously affected by industrial decline; (iii) combating long-term unemployment among people above the age of 25; (iv) providing employment for young people (aged under 25); and (v) with a view to the reform of the common agricultural policy (CAP), speeding up the adjustment of agricultural structures and promoting the development of rural areas. 'Agenda 2000', concerning the Community's budget after 2000, which was published in July 1997, envisaged a reform of the structural funds. Political agreement on 'Agenda 2000' was reached in March 1999.

In 1989 the Commission proposed a Charter on the Fundamental Social Rights of Workers (Social Charter), covering freedom of movement, fair remuneration, improvement of working conditions, the right to social security, freedom of association and collective wage agreements, the development of participation by workers in management, and sexual equality. The Charter was approved by the heads of government of all Community member states, except the United Kingdom, in December. On the insistence of the United Kingdom, the chapter on social affairs of the Treaty on European Union, negotiated in December 1991, was omitted from the Treaty to form a separate protocol.

In September 1994 ministers adopted the first directive to be approved under the Social Charter, concerning the establishment of mandatory works councils in multinational companies. After lengthy negotiations, it was agreed that the legislation was to apply to companies employing more than 1,000 people, of whom 150 worked in at least two EU member states. The United Kingdom was excluded from the directive; however, UK companies operating in other European countries were to participate in the scheme (although without counting UK-based employees towards the applicability thresholds). The directive came into force in September 1996. In April 1996 the Commission proposed that part-time, fixed-term and temporary employees should receive comparable treatment to permanent, full-time employees. A directive ensuring equal treatment for part-time employees was adopted by the Council in December 1997. A directive on parental leave, the second directive to be adopted under the Social Charter, provided for a statutory minimum of three months' unpaid leave to allow parents to care for young children, and was adopted in June 1996.

In May 1997 the new United Kingdom Government approved the Social Charter, which was to be incorporated into the Treaty of Amsterdam. The Treaty, which entered into force in May 1999, included a new chapter on employment. In December 1999 the Council adopted amendments extending the two directives adopted under the Charter to include the United Kingdom. In November 1998 the Commission proposed a directive compelling companies employing more than 50 staff to consult workers about decisions likely to cause significant organizational or contractual changes. In June 2001, after significant opposition from the United Kingdom, agreement was reached on an amended proposal, under which the directive would be implemented gradually and the United Kingdom granted an exemption from the legislation for seven years. In October the European Parliament rejected this transitional arrangement, and negotiations resumed.

The Treaty of Amsterdam authorized the European Council to take action against all types of discrimination. Several directives and programmes on gender equality and equal opportunities have been approved and the Commission has initiated legal proceedings against a number of member states before the European Court of Justice for infringements. In 1991–95 the third Community action programme on the promotion of equal opportunities for women was undertaken. This aimed to bring about equal treatment for men and women in occupational social schemes (e.g. sick pay and pensions) and in self-employed occupations, including agriculture, and to develop legislation on parental leave. The first EU meeting on female employment was held in Belfast, UK, in May 1998. A fourth equal opportunities action programme, with a budget of €30m. for 1996–2000, aimed to ensure that the issue of gender equality was integrated ('mainstreamed') into all relevant policy issues. In June 2000 the Commission presented a framework strategy on gender equality for 2001–05, aimed at altering roles and eliminating stereotypes. A directive agreed in June 2001 brought together case law and other directives on non-discrimination in employment and vocational training. The directive increased protection for women returning to work after maternity leave and for men on paternity leave (where this exists) and tightened the rules on sexual harassment. In June 2000 the Council adopted a directive implementing the principle of equal treatment regardless of racial or ethnic origin in employment, education, social security, healthcare and access to goods and services. This was followed in November by a directive establishing a framework for equal treatment regardless of religion or belief, disability, age or sexual orientation. The European Monitoring Centre on Racism and Xenophobia, created in 1997, was inaugurated in April 2000. It is based in Vienna and maintains an information network and database.

Numerous directives on health and safety in the workplace have been adopted by the Community. The creation of a Major Accident Hazards Bureau (MAHB) was announced by the Commission in February 1996. Based at the Joint Research Centre at Ispra in Italy, its purpose is to help prevent industrial accidents in the EU. There is also a European Agency for Health and Safety at Work, located in Bilbao, Spain. The EU's 1996–2000 programme on health and safety at work sought to reduce work accidents and occupational diseases to a minimum level, focusing on the provision of information and the enforcement of legislation. In June 2000 the Commission drafted a list of exposure limits for chemicals at work. In September a directive on protection from exposure to biological agents was adopted, incorporating guidelines for pregnant women and new mothers.

In June 1993 the Working Time directive was approved, restricting the working week to 48 hours, except where overtime arrangements are agreed with trade unions. In October ministers adopted further legislation limiting the number of hours worked by young people. The United Kingdom secured a dispensation to delay implementation of these measures for four years. The Working Time directive, which also prescribed minimum rest periods and a minimum of four weeks' paid holiday a year, had to be implemented by late November 1996. Certain categories of employee were exempt from the maximum 48-hour week rule, including those in the transport sector, fishermen and junior hospital doctors. In April 2000 a Conciliation Committee comprising MEPs and the Council of Ministers reached agreement on extending the directive to cover most excluded workers (further talks were held on extending the directive to workers in the road transport sector). The extension was to be phased in under transitional arrangements and could, for example, take 12 years to apply to junior doctors.

The European Foundation for the Improvement of Living and Working Conditions (Dublin), established in 1975, undertakes four-year research programmes. It established six priority areas for 1997–2000: employment; sustainable development; equal opportunities; social cohesion; health and well-being; and participation. The European Work Organisation Network also considers questions relating to the quality of working life. It has stressed the importance of organizational innovation to allow businesses to adapt to change.

The European Confidence Pact for Employment was launched by the Commission in January 1996 as a comprehensive strategy to combat unemployment, involving a common approach by public authorities, employers and employees. An employment body, EURES, launched in November 1994, operates as a network of 450 advisers with access to two European databases listing job vacancies in the EU and in Norway and Iceland. During 1996–97 EURES assisted more than 1m. people. (Its website can be accessed at europa.eu.int/jobs/eures.) In November 1998 the Commission proposed that national public employment services should have greater involvement with EURES.

An employment summit was held in Luxembourg in November 1997. The conference focused on four themes: employability, entrepreneurship, equal opportunities and adaptability, and committed member governments to providing training or work placements for unemployed young people within six months, and for the long-term unemployed within 12 months. Member states also agreed to reduce taxation on labour-intensive service industries from 1 July 1998 and to produce national action plans for employment. Under the European employment strategy, initiated in 1997, an employment package is presented each year. The package contains reports on member states' performances, individual recommendations and policy guidelines for the future. In 2000 some 3m. jobs were created under the employment strategy. The overall EU employment rate averaged 63.3% in 2000. In March 2001 a meeting of the European Council in Stockholm established a target employment rate of 67% by 2005 (57% for women) and of 50% for older workers (aged 55–64) by 2010, when the target for full employment was 70%. The EU aims to ensure that the development of the information society increases employment opportunities.

In March 2000 the Commission adopted a communication entitled 'Building an inclusive Europe', which discussed methods of combating poverty and social exclusion. In June the Commission adopted a new Agenda for Social Policy for 2000–05. This aimed to modernize the overall European social model, in order to address the challenges resulting from changes in employment, the development of the knowledge-based economy, the forthcoming enlargement of the EU, and issues related to globalization. The new strategy is geared towards integrating economic, social and employment policies. A European Social Protection Committee was also established in June. In 2001 the Committee considered the best means of developing safe and sustainable pensions, given the problems entailed by the ageing of the EU's populations. In addition, the EU runs MISSOC—the Mutual Information System on Social Protection in EU member states and the European Economic Area.

EU activities relating to disability include the HELIOS programme for disabled people, which focuses on mobility, integration and independence, and the Technology Initiative for Disabled and Elderly people (TIDE), which aims to develop technologies to improve the living conditions of these groups.

CONSUMER PROTECTION AND HEALTH

The Community's second consumer protection programme was approved by the Council in 1981, based on the principles of the first programme: protection of health and safety; standardization of rules for food additives and packaging; rules for machines and equipment; and authorization procedures for new products. The programme also included measures for monitoring the quality and durability of products and for improving after-sales services, legal remedies for unsatisfactory goods and services, and action to promote consumer associations. In 1993 a three-year action plan was inaugurated, with the aim of strengthening consumer power in the single market. The Community's plan for 1997–98 aimed to protect consumer interests in the supply of public utilities; improve confidence in foodstuffs; strengthen consumer representation; and develop consumer policies in central and eastern Europe. A new framework programme was adopted for 1999–2003, with a budget of €112.5m. This and an action plan for consumer policy were the central elements of the EU's strategy to place consumer protection at the heart of overall policy development.

In November 1996 ministers approved a Commission directive enabling a consumer body in one member state to take action in another in connection with breaches of certain EU laws, such as those on consumer credit, package holidays and misleading advertising. In April 1998 the Council agreed to introduce two-year guarantees on consumer goods purchased in any EU country. In April 2000 the Council adopted a resolution encouraging the out-of-court settlement of consumer disputes. A cross-border out-of-court complaints network for financial services, FIN-NET, was launched in February 2001.

In 2000 the EU granted €4.7m. for the funding of 36 consumer information and education projects, while €1.6m. was given to European consumer organizations. A new consumer committee was established in May 2000, to serve for three years. A network of European consumer information and advice centers—Euroguichets—distributes information on legislation, and an internet-based consumer assistance service is also in operation.

In April 1997 Denmark raised concerns about possible risks to children's health from phthalates (chemicals used to soften PVC) in childcare articles and toys. Precautionary measures were imposed by eight individual states in mid-1998. In December 1999 the Commission adopted a temporary emergency decision banning the articles, under a 1992 directive on product safety. The ban was extended in 2000, pending further scientific tests.

In February 1997 the Commission extended the function of its directorate-general on consumer policy to incorporate consumer health protection. This decision (which followed widespread consumer concerns regarding the BSE crisis), was designed to ensure that sufficient importance was given to food safety. In November a Scientific Steering Committee was established to provide advice on consumer health issues. Eight sectoral steering committees were formed at the same time, covering a range of public health and consumer protection issues. Five of the committees were devoted to food safety, one to cosmetic and non-food products, one to medicinal products and medical devices, and one to issues of toxicity and the environment. In July 1998 an Institute for Health and Consumer Protection, attached to the Commission's Joint Research Centre, was established to improve research in this field.

In January 2000 the Commission adopted a White Paper on food safety, proposing a comprehensive, integrated approach covering foodstuffs from 'farm to table'. The paper envisaged a programme of measures, including legislation on the responsibilities of food and feedstuff manufacturers and the traceability of products. Stringent rules and appropriate checks at all stages of the production chain were to be introduced and the importance of clear labelling was emphasized. The paper also formally proposed the creation of an independent European Food Safety Authority (EFSA), which was to be set up in 2002. Composed of independent experts, EFSA's tasks were to include the collection and dissemination of scientific information, risk assessment and crisis management.

The European Council's 2000 directive on the labelling, presentation and advertizing of foodstuffs aimed to ensure that essential, objective information was given to consumers. The White Paper on food safety proposed that certain substances recognized scientifically as being sources of allergies should be included in lists of ingredients on labels. From October 1999 food products labelled as 'GM-free' in the EU were permitted to contain up to 1% of GM material. In July 2001 the Commission developed its rules on the labelling and tracing of GM organisms (GMOs, see Agriculture).

In May 2000 the Commission adopted a communication on the EU's overall health strategy, together with a proposal for a plan of action in the field of public health. The plan had three priorities: the introduction of a comprehensive information system; the development of a mechanism to respond rapidly to health threats; and promotion and prevention measures. A European health forum was to be established to allow all interested parties to contribute to the development of policy. In June 2000 a public health action programme for 2001–06 was proposed, with funding of €300m. This was ultimately to replace the eight sectoral programmes.

Various epidemiological surveillance systems are in operation, covering major communicable diseases. An early warning and response system to help member states deal with outbreaks of diseases was in place by the end of 2000. The EU implements a number of individual action plans, including one to combat cancer: 41 new projects were adopted under this in 2000. In 2000 funding was also granted to the prevention and treatment of drug dependence (€5.3m), pollution-related diseases (€1.8m.), rare diseases (€1.2m), HIV/AIDS and other communicable diseases (€10.9m.), and to health promotion, information, education and training (€3.8m.), health monitoring (€3.6m.) and injury prevention (€2.6m.). Under the Treaty on European Union, the EU assumed responsibility for the problem of drug addiction; a European Monitoring Centre for Drugs and Drug Addiction (EMCDDA, see under Justice and Home Affairs) was established in Lisbon, Portugal, in 1995.

ENVIRONMENT POLICY

Environmental action by the EU was initiated in 1972. Four successive action programmes were complemented by a variety of legislation, including regulations on air and water pollution (e.g. 'acid rain', pollution by fertilizers and pesticides, and emissions from vehicles), directives on the transport of hazardous waste across national boundaries, measures on waste treatment, noise abatement and the protection of natural resources, and legislation to guarantee freedom of access to information on the environment held by public authorities. The Maastricht Treaty on European Union, which entered into force in November 1993, gave environmental action policy status, and the Treaty of Amsterdam identified sustainable development as one of the Community's overall aims.

The Community's fifth environmental action programme (1993–2000), entitled 'Towards Sustainability', aimed to address the root causes of environmental degradation, by raising public awareness and working to change the behaviour of authorities, enterprises and the general public. The programme focused on anticipating, as well as addressing, environmental problems. A 1998 communication on the so-called 'Cardiff Process' of integrating environmental considerations into all EU policies confirmed this programme's broad approach. The Commission recognized that full integration was a long-term aim. For the short term, it identified two priority objectives: the fulfillment of the environmental measures contained in the Agenda 2000 action programme (relating for example to the reform of the Common Agricultural Policy and to EU enlargement), and the implementation of the Kyoto Protocol (see below).

The EU's sixth environmental action programme, covering 2001–10, emphasized the continuing importance of the integration of environmental considerations into other EU policies, and was to focus on the health-related aspects of environmental issues. It aimed to maintain the EU's leadership role in international fora. Long-term targets for 2010 included benchmarks for the stabilization of global temperature change and carbon dioxide concentrations; the gradual withdrawal of fossil fuel subsidies; reversing the loss of biodiversity; and the derivation of 12% of total energy use from renewable energy sources.

The Community's programme of research and technological development on the environment, carried out on a shared-cost basis by various scientific institutions, covers the economic and social aspects of environmental issues and the EU's participation in global change programmes. The programme is open to all European countries. A separate programme covers research in marine science and technology. In 1990 the EC established the European Environment Agency (EEA, see p. 331) to monitor environmental issues and provide advice. The agency, which became operational in November 1994, also provides targeted information to policymakers and the public and disseminates comparable environmental data. In August 2001 Bulgaria, Latvia, Lithuania, Slovenia, Slovakia, Malta and Cyprus joined the EEA—the first time an EU agency accepted candidate countries as full members. Negotiations on permitting Switzerland to attend as an observer were completed in 2000.

In 1996 the LIFE programme was established as a financial instrument to promote the development and implementation of environmental policy. LIFE funds priority activities in EU member states and provides technical assistance to countries in central and eastern Europe and the Mediterranean. The LIFE programme entered its third phase, covering 2000–04, in July 2000. The programme (with a total budget of €640m.) is subdivided into LIFE-Environment (addressing the further development of environmental policy and receiving 47% of funds); LIFE-Nature (managing conservation of wild birds and natural habitats and also receiving 47% of funds); and LIFE-Third countries (contributing to the development of environmental policy and action programmes in third countries, with 6% of funds). In view of the impending enlargement of the EU the poor state of the environment in some central and eastern European countries has become a pressing issue.

In 1985 the Community (and a number of individual member states) ratified the Vienna Convention for the Protection of the Ozone Layer, and in 1987 the Community signed a protocol to the treaty, controlling the production of chlorofluorocarbons. In 1990 ministers of the environment undertook to ban the production of chlorofluorocarbons by mid-1997; the introduction of the ban was later brought forward to 1996. In July 1998 the Commission proposed committing EU countries to the progressive elimination of remaining ozone-depleting substances, by introducing a ban on the sale and use of CFCs and imposing production limits on HCFCs, which were originally introduced to replace CFCs. In 1990 ministers agreed to stabilize emissions of carbon dioxide, believed to be responsible for 'global warming', at 1990 levels by 2000 (2005 for the United Kingdom). In December 1997, at the third conference of parties to the UN Framework Convention on Climate Change (UNFCCC), agreement was reached on the Kyoto Protocol, under which emissions of six greenhouse gases were to be reduced by 8% between 2008 and 2012, in comparison with 1990 levels. In June 1998 ministers of the environment agreed upon individual emission targets for each EU member state. The agreement allows a number of less industrialized countries to increase their gas emissions.

In March 2000 the Commission noted that emissions were actually rising in relation to 1990 levels. In that month the Commission adopted a Green Paper on the trading of greenhouse gas emissions within the EU, exploring the role that such a scheme could play in the fulfilment of the Kyoto commitments. At the same time, the European Climate Change Programme (ECCP) was adopted. This outlined the strategy needed to meet commitments under the Kyoto Protocol and aimed to incorporate climate-change concerns into various EU policies. Six working groups were established under the programme, covering energy supply; energy consumption; transport; industry; research; and the mechanisms of the Kyoto Protocol. In January 2000 the EU's Theseo 2000-Solve experiment was launched; this was the largest experiment ever undertaken to study the ozone layer above northern Europe.

In June 1996 the Commission agreed a strategy, drawn up in collaboration with the European petroleum and car industries, for reducing harmful emissions from road vehicles by between 60% and 70% by 2010. In late June 1998 EU member states reached an 'auto-oil' agreement to reduce air pollution. The agreement committed member states to the progressive elimination of leaded petrol by 2000 (with limited exemptions until 2005). From 2000 petrol-powered road vehicles were to be fitted with 'on-board diagnostic' (OBD) systems to monitor emissions. Diesel vehicles were to be installed with OBD systems by 2005.

In July the Commission announced plans to decrease pollution from nuclear power stations by reducing emissions of sulphur dioxides, nitrogen oxides and dust by one-half. The auto-oil agreement entered a second phase—auto-oil II—in 1997, terminating in 2000. It forecast and assessed likely trends in emissions and air quality and established a framework to determine options for reducing emissions. Following a review in December 2000, it was agreed to launch a Clean Air for Europe (CAFE) programme. Continuing the auto-oil principles, this aimed to develop an air-quality policy covering all emissions sources by 2004.

In September 2000 the EU adopted a directive on end-of-life vehicles (ELVs), containing measures for the collection, treatment, recovery and disposal of such waste. The ruling forces manufacturers to pay for the disposal of new cars from July 2002 and of old cars from January 2007. The directive set recycling and recovery targets, restricted the use of heavy metals in new cars from 2003, and specified that ELVs might only be dismantled by authorized agencies. In June 2000 the Commission adopted two proposals on the management of waste from electronic and electrical equipment. The EU aimed to implement a directive in this field by 2004, making manufacturers of such equipment similarly responsible for the disposal of used goods.

An action programme for the protection and management of groundwater resources was adopted by the Commission in July 1997. Member states were asked to prepare national prorammes to identify, map and protect groundwater resources. In December 2000 a framework for action in water policy, designed to increase protection for all water resources, entered into force.

A regulation revising EU laws on trade in wild animals and plants was adopted by ministers of the environment in December 1996. This aimed to tighten controls and improve the enforcement of restrictions on trade in endangered species. In mid-1999 the EU reportedly threatened to withhold structural fund payments from certain member states if they did not implement the Community's habitats directive and establish protected environmental areas and nature reserves.

The voluntary Eco-Management and Audit Scheme (EMAS) was launched in April 1995. Under the scheme, participating industrial companies undergo an independent audit of their environmental performance. In addition, the EU awards 'eco-labels' for products that limit harmful effects on the environment (excluding foodstuffs, drinks and pharmaceutical products, among others). The criteria to be met are set by the EU Eco-Labelling Board (EUEB).

SECURITY AND DEFENCE

Under the Single European Act, which came into force on 1 July 1987 (amending the Treaty of Rome), it was formally stipulated for the first time that member states should inform and consult each other on foreign policy matters (as was already, in practice, often the case).

The Maastricht Treaty on European Union, which came into force on 1 November 1993, provided for joint action by member governments in matters of common foreign and security policy (CFSP), and envisaged the eventual formation of a European security and defence policy (ESDP), with the possibility of a common defence force. The Western European Union (WEU, q.v.), to which all EU members except Denmark, Greece and Ireland belong, was to be developed as the 'defence component' of the Union, but member states' existing commitments to NATO were to be honoured. The CFSP is the province of the EU (as opposed to the EC), and decisions in this field are made by the European Council and the Council of the European Union.

The Treaty of Amsterdam, which entered into force in May 1999, aimed to strengthen the concept of a CFSP within the Union and incorporated a process of common strategies to co-ordinate external relations with a third party. Under the Amsterdam Treaty, WEU was to provide the EU with access to operational capability for undertaking the so-called 'Petersberg tasks' relating to crisis management, including humanitarian, peace-keeping and peace-making operations. Accordingly, a High Representative, responsible for the co-ordination of the CFSP, was to be appointed to represent the EU at international meetings. In late March representatives of the Commission and NATO held a joint meeting, for the first time, to discuss the conflict in the southern Serbian province of Kosovo. In April a meeting of NATO heads of state and government determined that NATO's equipment, personnel and infrastructure would be available to any future EU military operation. In June the European Council, meeting in Cologne, determined to strengthen the ESDP, and initiated a process of assuming direct responsibility for the Petersberg tasks, which were placed at the core of the ESDP process. In October 1999 Javier Solana, hitherto Secretary-General of NATO, was appointed as Secretary-General of the Council of the European Union and as the EU's High Representative. In the following month he also became the Secretary-General of WEU, providing for a very high degree of co-operation between the two organizations. The process of transferring the crisis-management responsibilities of WEU to the EU was finalized by July 2001.

The June 1999 Cologne meeting of the European Council stated that the EU must have a capacity for autonomous action, without prejudice to actions by NATO and acknowledging the supreme prerogatives of the UN Security Council. In December 1999, following consultation with NATO, the European Council, meeting in Helsinki, adopted the European Defence Initiative, comprising the following goals: by 2003 the EU should be able to deploy within 60 days and for a period of up to one year a rapid reaction force, comprising up to 60,000 national troops from member states capable of implementing the full range of Petersberg tasks. The force was to be militarily self-sustaining, with all services and support provided, and was to include smaller, rapid response elements. In November EU member states took part in a Capabilities Commitment Conference to assess the need to upgrade assets. The Council stressed the need to work on measures in the field of command and control, intelligence and strategic transport. In late 2001 defence ministers acknowledged that certain military capabilities, including strategic airlift, would not be available until 2006. Nevertheless, in December 2001 the EU announced that the force was, theoretically, ready, although only as yet capable of undertaking small-scale crisis management tasks.

In December 1999 the Helsinki meeting of the European Council proposed the establishment of three permanent military institutions: a Political and Security Committee (PSC), a Military Body and a Military Staff. In February 2000 the EU set up an interim PSC and an interim Military Body. When fully established, the PSC was to monitor the international situation, help define policies and assess their implementation, encourage dialogue and, under the auspices of the Council, take responsibility for the political direction of capability development. In the event of a crisis situation, it was to oversee the strategic direction of any military response, propose political objectives and supervise their enactment. The Military Body was to give military advice to the PSC, and was tol comprise the chiefs of defence of member states, represented by military delegates. It was to serve as a forum for military consultation and co-operation and was to deal with risk assessment, the development of crisis management and military relations with non-EU European NATO members, accession countries, and NATO itself. Meanwhile, the Military Staff, comprising experts seconded by the member states, was to provide the EU with an early-warning capability, and would conduct assessments of situations, take responsibility for strategic planning for the Petersberg tasks and implement the Military Body's policies. A range of exercises was planned to test all these structures. Permanent arrangements have been agreed for EU–NATO consultation and co-operation in this area.

In June 2001 the European Council approved a programme on the prevention of violent conflicts. Its priorities included efforts to improve the EU's early-warning mechanisms; measures to improve capability and to develop a coherent relationship between policy and action; and building partnerships, with targeted international co-operation. In 2001 the Commission proposed a systematic integration of the objective of conflict prevention into all EU external aid programmes.

In June 2000 the EU established a civilian crisis management committee. The Feira meeting of the European Council in that month defined four priority areas for civilian crisis management: developing the role of the police; strengthening the rule of law; strengthening civilian administrations; and improving civil protection. As part of the general rapid reaction force (see above), the EU aimed to be able to deploy up to 5,000 police officers for international missions by 2003. In February 2001 the Council adopted a regulation creating a rapid reaction mechanism (RRM) to improve the EU's civilian capacity to respond to crises. The mechanism bypasses cumbersome decision-making processes, to enable civilian experts in fields such as mine clearance, customs, police training, election-monitoring, institution-building, media support, rehabilitation and mediation to be mobilized speedily. The RRM was granted funds of €25m. for 2002.

Under the European code of conduct on arms exports the EU publishes an annual report on defence exports based on confidential information provided by each member state. EU member states must withhold export licences to countries where it is deemed that arms sales might lead to political repression or external aggression. The Community funds projects aimed at the collection and destruction of weapons in countries emerging from conflict. The EU is strongly committed to nuclear non-proliferation. Under its programme of co-operation with Russia, it works to dismantle or destroy nuclear, chemical and biological weapons and weapons of mass destruction.

FINANCIAL SERVICES AND CAPITAL MOVEMENTS

Freedom of capital movement and the creation of a uniform financial area were regarded as vital for the completion of the EU's internal market by 1992. In 1987, as part of the liberalization of the flow of capital, a Council directive came into force whereby member states were obliged to remove restrictions on three categories of transactions: long-term credits related to commercial transactions; acquisition of securities; and the admission of securities to capital markets. In June 1988 the Council of Ministers approved a directive whereby all restrictions on capital movements (financial loans and credits, current and deposit account operations, transactions in securities and other instruments normally dealt in on the money market) were to be removed by 1 July 1990. A number of countries were permitted to exercise certain restrictions until the end of 1992, and further extensions were then granted to Portugal and Greece. With the entry into force of the Maastricht Treaty in November 1993, the principle of full freedom of capital movements was incorporated into the structure of the EU.

The EU worked to develop a single market in financial services throughout the 1990s. In October 1998 the Commission drew up a framework for action in the financial services sector. This noted that investors should be free to invest their assets without legal, administrative or information barriers, and proposed that this could be achieved through the further harmonization of accounting rules; by eliminating restrictions on investments by supplementary pension and life-assurance funds; by developing a level playing field for similar financial products; and by harmonizing the prudential and tax aspects of the EU's regulatory framework. The communication was followed by a Financial Services Action Plan (FSAP) in May 1999, with three strategic objectives: to establish a single market in wholesale financial services; to make retail markets open and secure; and to strengthen the rules on prudential supervision, to keep pace with new sources of financial risk. The prudential supervision of financial conglomerates (entities offering a range of financial services in areas such as banking, insurance and securities), which are developing rapidly, has been identified as an area of particular importance. Individual targets included removing the outstanding barriers to raising capital within the EU; creating a coherent legal framework for supplementary pension funds; and providing greater legal certainty in cross-border securities trading. In line with the FSAP, directives were issued in 2001 co-ordinating the conditions for the admission of securities to official stock-exchange listings.

The EU initially aimed to meet its targets under the FSAP by 2005. In November 2000, however, it noted that at the current rate of progress, the FSAP would not be completed by that date. In February 2001 the Commission asked for political support from the Council for the creation of a European securities committee and a regulatory securities committee. The Stockholm meeting of the European Council in March urged member states to make further efforts to have an integrated securities market operational by the end of 2003. It noted that this work was complemented by the implementation of the risk capital action plan, which aimed to develop a well-functioning risk capital market by 2003.

In July 2001 progress towards the creation of a single financial market was impeded by the European Parliament's rejection of a proposed takeover directive that had been under negotiation for 12 years. The directive had aimed to ensure that shareholders were treated in the same way throughout the EU after takeover bids, and had sought to create a single Community framework governing takeovers.

A directive on Community banking, adopted in 1977, laid down common prudential criteria for the establishment and operation of banks in member states. A second banking directive, adopted in 1989, aimed to create a single community licence for banking, thereby permitting a bank established in one member country to open branches in any other. The directive entered into force on 1 January 1993. Related measures were subsequently adopted, with the aim of ensuring the capital adequacy of credit institutions and the prevention of 'money-laundering' by criminals. In September 1993 ministers approved a directive on a bank deposit scheme to protect account-holders: banks were to be obliged to raise protection to 90% on the first ECU 20,000 in an account from 1 January 1995. These directives were consolidated into one overall banking directive in March 2000. Non-bank institutions may be granted a 'European passport' once they have complied with the principles laid down in the EU's first banking directive on the mutual recognition of licences, prudential supervision and supervision by the home member state. Non-bank institutions must also comply with the directive on money-laundering.

In September 2000 a directive was issued governing the actions of non-bank institutions with regard to the issuance of 'electronic money' (money stored on an electronic device, for example, a chip card or in a computer memory). The directive authorized non-bank institutions to issue electronic money on a non-professional basis, with the aim of promoting a level playing field with other credit institutions. Other regulations oblige the institutions to redeem electronic money at par value in coins and bank notes, or by transfer without charge.

In May 2001 a directive on the reorganization and winding up of failed credit institutions with branches in more than one member state was agreed; it was to enter into force in May 2004. The directive recognizes the principle of home country control and requires certain information to be given to creditors. It also enforces co-operation between supervisory authorities.

In 1992 the third insurance co-ordination directives, relating to life assurance and non-life insurance, were adopted, creating a framework for an integrated Community insurance market. The directives provide greater access for insurance companies and customers to the European market, guarantee greater protection for purchasers of life assurance policies and prohibit substantive control of rates. The directives came into effect on 1 July 1994. Community legislation also covers motor-vehicle liability insurance and legal protection insurance. The EU's insurance committee works to improve co-operation with national supervisory authorities.

In May 1993 ministers adopted a directive on investment services, which (with effect from 1 January 1996) allowed credit institutions to offer investment services in any member state, on the basis of a licence held in one state. The 1999 FSAP aimed to achieve the further convergence of national approaches to investment, in order to increase the effectiveness of the 1993 directive.

In late 1999 the Commission put forward proposals to remove tax barriers and investment restrictions affecting cross-border pension schemes. At present, variations among member states in the tax liability of contributions to supplementary pension schemes obstruct the transfer of pension rights from one state to another, contradicting the Treaty of Rome's principles of free movement. In October 2000 a specific legal framework for institutions for occupational retirement provision (IORPs) was proposed. This seeks to abolish barriers to investment by pension funds and would permit the cross-border management of IORP pension schemes, with mutual recognition of the supervisory methods in force.

In November 1997 the Commission adopted proposals to co-ordinate tax policy among member states. The measures, including a code of conduct on corporate taxation, aimed to simplify the transfer of royalty and interest payments between member states and to prevent the withholding of taxes. In February 1999 Parliament endorsed a proposal by the Commission to harmonize taxation further, through the co-ordination of savings taxes. In November 2000 finance ministers agreed on a proposed 'tax savings' directive. This set out rules on the exchange of information on savings accounts of individuals resident in one EU country and receiving interest in another. Ministers agreed that for a seven-year transitional period member states must either exchange information on the savings income of non-residents or apply a withholding tax. Standards would be in place for the full exchange of information when the transitional period expired. Agreement on the issue was reached in July 2001. However, in December Austria, Luxembourg and Belgium abandoned the agreement, insisting that they would only comply if other 'tax havens' in Europe, such as Monaco, Liechtenstein and Switzerland, were compelled to amend their banking secrecy laws.

Two other proposed directives were issued in November 2000, the first relating to interest and royalties and the second concerning the code of conduct for business taxation. Together with the tax savings directive, these are known as the 'EU tax package'. The Council aimed to reach agreement on the tax package by the end of 2002.

The EU's action plan on combating fraud in financial services covers the period 2001–03. The May 2000 convention on mutual assistance in criminal matters (see under Justice and Home Affairs) commits member states to co-operation in combating economic and financial crime. In May 2001 the Council adopted a framework decision on preventing fraud and counterfeiting in non-cash means of payment, recognizing this as a criminal offence. Following the terrorist attacks on the USA in September 2001, the EU attempted to accelerate the adoption of the convention combating the financing of terrorism, and began work on a new directive on 'freezing' assets or evidence related to terrorist crimes.

In January 2001 the Commission launched a complaints network for out-of-court settlements in the financial sector (FIN-NET), to help consumers find amicable solutions in cases where the supplier is in another member state. In September the EU agreed harmonized rules on the cross-border distance-selling of financial services.

ECONOMIC CO-OPERATION

A review of the economic situation is presented annually by the Commission, analysing recent developments and short- and medium-term prospects. Economic policy guide-lines for the following year are adopted annually by the Council.

The following objectives for the end of 1973 were agreed by the Council in 1971, as the first of three stages towards European economic and monetary union:

> the narrowing of exchange-rate margins to 2.25%; creation of a medium-term pool of reserves; co-ordination of short- and medium-term economic and budgetary policies; a joint position on international monetary issues; harmonization of taxes; creation of the European Monetary Co-operation Fund (EMCF); and creation of the European Regional Development Fund.

The narrowing of exchange margins (the 'snake') came into effect in 1972; but Denmark, France, Ireland, Italy and the United Kingdom later floated their currencies, with only Denmark permanently returning to the arrangement. Sweden and Norway also linked their currencies to the 'snake', but Sweden withdrew from the arrangement in August 1977, and Norway withdrew in December 1978.

The European Monetary System (EMS) came into force in March 1979, with the aim of creating closer monetary co-operation, leading to a zone of monetary stability in Europe, principally through an exchange-rate mechanism (ERM), supervised by the ministries of finance and the central banks of member states. Not all Community members participated in the ERM: Greece did not join, Spain joined only in June 1989, the United Kingdom in October 1990 and Portugal in April 1992. To prevent wide fluctuations in the value of members' currencies against each other, the ERM fixed for each currency a central rate in European Currency Units (ECUs, see below), based on a 'basket' of national currencies; a reference rate in relation to other currencies was fixed for each currency, with established fluctuation margins (until July 1993, 6% for the Portuguese escudo and the Spanish peseta, 2.25% for others). Central banks of the participating states intervened by buying or selling currencies when the agreed margin was likely to be exceeded. Each member placed 20% of its gold reserves and dollar reserves, respectively, into the EMCF, and received a supply of ECUs to regulate central bank interventions. Short- and medium-term credit facilities were given to support the balance of payments of member countries. The EMS was initially put under strain by the wide fluctuations in the exchange rates of non-Community currencies and by the differences in economic development among members, which led to nine realignments of currencies in 1979–83. Subsequently, greater stability was achieved, with only two realignments of currencies between 1984 and 1988. In September 1992, however, with great pressure on currency markets, the Italian and Spanish currencies were devalued by 7% and 5% respectively within the ERM and Italian and British membership was suspended; in November the Portuguese and Spanish currencies were both devalued by 6% within the ERM. In May 1993 the Spanish and Portuguese currencies were further devalued (by 8% and 6.5%, respectively). In late July, as a result of intensive currency speculation on European financial markets (forcing the weaker currencies to the very edge of their permitted margins), the ERM almost collapsed. In response to the crisis, EC finance ministers decided to widen the fluctuation margins allowed for each currency to 15%, except in the cases of Germany and the Netherlands, which agreed to maintain their currencies within the original 2.25% limits. The 15% margins were regarded as allowing for so much fluctuation in exchange rates as to represent a virtual suspension of the ERM; however, some countries, notably France and Belgium, expressed determination to adhere as far as possible to the original 'bands' in order to fulfil the conditions for eventual monetary union. In practice, during 1994, most currencies remained within the former 2.25% and 6% bands. Austria became a member of the EMS in January 1995, and its currency was subject to ERM conditions. While Sweden decided to remain outside the EMS, Finland joined in October 1996. In November the Italian lira was readmitted to the ERM.

In September 1988 a committee (chaired by Jacques Delors, then President of the European Commission, and comprising the governors of member countries' central banks, representatives of the European Commission and outside experts) was established to discuss European monetary union. The resulting 'Delors plan' was presented to heads of government in June 1989, who agreed to begin the first stage of the process of monetary union—the drafting of a treaty on the subject—in 1990. The Intergovernmental Conference on Economic and Monetary Union was initiated in December 1990, and continued to work (in parallel with the Intergovernmental Conference on Political Union) throughout 1991. The Intergovernmental Conference was responsible for the drafting of the economic and monetary provisions of the Treaty on European Union, which was agreed by the European Council in December 1991 and which came into force on 1 November 1993. The principal feature of the Treaty's provisions on economic and monetary union (EMU) was the gradual introduction of a single currency, to be administered by a single central bank. During the remainder of Stage I, member states were to adopt programmes for the 'convergence' of their economies and ensure the complete liberalization of capital movements. Stage II began on 1 January 1994, and included the establishment of a European Monetary Institute (EMI), replacing the EMCF and comprising governors of central banks and a president appointed by heads of government. Heads of government were to decide, not later than 31 December 1996, whether a majority of member states fulfilled the necessary conditions for the adoption of a single currency: if so, they were to establish a date for the beginning of Stage III. If no date had been set by the end of 1997, Stage III was to begin on 1 January 1999, and was to be confined to those members that did fulfil the necessary conditions. After the establishment of a starting date for Stage III, the European Central Bank (ECB) and a European System of Central Banks were to be set up to replace the EMI. During Stage III, exchange rates were to be irrevocably fixed, and a single currency introduced. Member states that had not fulfilled the necessary conditions for the adoption of a single currency would be exempt from participating. The United Kingdom was to be allowed to make a later, separate decision on whether to proceed to Stage III, while Denmark reserved the right to submit its participation in Stage III to a referendum. The near-collapse of the ERM in July 1993 cast serious doubts on the agreed timetable for monetary union, although in October the EC heads of government reaffirmed their commitment to the objective.

In December 1995 the European Council, meeting in Madrid, confirmed that Stage III of Economic and Monetary Union was to begin on 1 January 1999. The economic conditions for member states wishing to enter Stage III (including an annual budget deficit of no more than 3% of annual gross domestic product—GDP—and total public debt of no more than 60% of annual GDP) were also confirmed. The meeting decided that the proposed single currency would be officially known as the 'euro'. Participants in EMU were to be selected in early 1998, on the basis of economic performance during 1997. In October 1996 the Commission issued a draft regulation on a proposed 'stability pact', intended to ensure that member countries maintained strict budgetary discipline during Stage III of monetary union. Another draft regulation formed the legal framework for the euro, confirming that it would be the single currency of participating countries from 1 January 1999. During a transitional period of up to three years, national currencies would remain in circulation, having equivalent legal status to the euro. The communication outlined the main features of a new ERM, which would act as a 'waiting room' for countries preparing to join the single currency. Member countries remaining outside the monetary system, whether or not by choice, would still be part of the single market.

Although all 15 members of the EU endorsed the principle of monetary union, with France and Germany the most ardent supporters, certain countries were known to have political doubts about joining. In October 1997 both the United Kingdom and Sweden confirmed that they would not participate in EMU from 1999. Denmark was also to remain outside the single currency.

Technical preparations for the euro were confirmed during a meeting of the European Council in Dublin in December 1996. The heads of government endorsed the new ERM and the legal framework for the euro and agreed to the proposed 'stability pact'. In June the European Council, meeting in Amsterdam, reached final agreement on the content of the 'stability pact', which included a resolution on growth. In March 1998 the Commission and the European Investment Bank (EIB) published reports on the progress made by member states towards the fulfilment of convergence criteria. The Commission concluded that Greece alone failed to satisfy the necessary conditions. However, the EIB warned that Italy and Belgium, with public-debt ratios of over 100% of GDP, had made insufficient progress towards the reduction of debt levels. In March Greece was admitted to the ERM, causing a 14% devaluation of its national currency. In early May 1998 heads of state and of government confirmed that Greece failed to fulfil the conditions required for the adoption of a single currency from 1999, and that 11 countries would take part in Stage III of EMU. After substantial debate, the European Council agreed to appoint Willem (Wim) Duisenberg, governor of the central bank of the Netherlands, as the President of the new ECB. Duisenberg was to be succeeded by Jean-Claude Trichet, governor of the French central bank, before the end of the usual eight-year term. The Vice-President and the remaining four members of the ECB's executive board were also appointed. The meeting agreed that existing ERM central rates were to be used to determine the final rates of exchange between national currencies and the euro, which would be adopted on 1 January 1999. The ECB, which was established on 1 June 1998 and ceremonially launched on 30 June, was to be accountable to a European Forum, comprising members of the European Parliament (MEPs) and chairmen of the finance committees of the national parliaments of EU member countries. Euro-XI, an informal grouping of the ministers of finance of member states participating in EMU, met for the first time in June 1998. The euro was to be represented at an international level by a delegation involving the Council of Ministers, the Commission and the ECB.

In September 1998 Sweden and the United Kingdom came under pressure to join the successor to the ERM, ERM2, launched on 1 January 1999, as a precondition of future participation in EMU. In October 1998 ministers discussed Greece's convergence programme for 1998–2001; this sought to allow Greece to join the single currency from 1 January 2001. On 31 December 1998 the ECOFIN Council adopted the conversion rates for the national currencies of the countries participating in the single currency. The euro was formally launched on 1 January 1999. Both Greece and Denmark joined ERM2. In September 2000 some 53% of Danish voters participating in a national referendum rejected the adoption of the euro. On 1 January 2001 Greece became the twelfth EU member state to adopt the euro, in the first enlargement of the euro area since its inception.

The euro

With the creation of the European Monetary System (EMS), a new monetary unit, the European Currency Unit (ECU), was adopted. Its value and composition were identical to those of the European Unit of Account (EUA) already used in the administrative fields of the Community. The ECU was a composite monetary unit, in which the relative value of each currency was determined by the gross national product and the volume of trade of each country.

The ECU, which was assigned the function of the unit of account used by the European Monetary Co-operation Fund (EMCF), was also used as the denominator for the exchange-rate mechanism (ERM); as the denominator for operations in both the intervention and the credit mechanisms; and as a means of settlement between monetary authorities of the European Community. From April 1979 the ECU was also used as the unit of account for the purposes of the Common Agricultural Policy (CAP). From 1981 it replaced the EUA in the general budget of the Community; the activities of the European Development Fund (EDF) under the Lomé Convention; the balance sheets and loan operations of the European Investment Bank (EIB); and the activities of the European Coal and Steel Community (ECSC). In June 1985 measures were adopted by the governors of the Community's central banks, aiming to strengthen the EMS by expanding the use of the ECU, for example, by allowing international monetary institutions and the central banks of non-member countries to become 'other holders' of ECUs.

In June 1989 it was announced that, with effect from 20 September, the Portuguese and Spanish currencies were to be included in the composition of the ECU. From that date the amounts of the national currencies included in the composition of the ECU were 'weighted' as follows (in percentages): Belgian franc 7.6; Danish krone 2.5; French franc 19.0; Deutsche Mark 30.1; Greek drachma 0.8; Irish pound 1.1; Italian lira 10.2; Luxembourg franc 0.3; Netherlands guilder 9.4; Portuguese escudo 0.8; Spanish peseta 5.3; and the United Kingdom pound sterling 13.0. The composition of the ECU 'basket' of currencies was 'frozen' with the entry into force of the Treaty on European Union on 1 November 1993. This was not affected by the accession to the EU of Austria, Finland and Sweden; consequently those countries' currencies were not represented in the ECU 'basket'.

As part of Stage III of the process of economic and monetary union (EMU), the ECU was replaced by a single currency, the euro (€), on 1 January 1999, at a conversion rate of 1:1.

Designs for the euro bank notes, and the symbol for the single currency, were presented by the EMI in December 1996; designs for the euro coins were presented in June 1997. The notes and coins were to enter into circulation in 2002, when the euro would gradually replace the national currencies of participating countries. EU finance ministers subsequently agreed that national currencies should be replaced by the euro during the first two months of 2002. In May 1998 the French Government began minting the new euro coins. Changes to the specifications of euro coins were proposed in July, to aid the identification of 10- and 50-cent coins by the visually impaired and by vending machines.

In April 1998 ministers agreed that banks should make no charge for the conversion of accounts or payments of national currency into euros, during a transitional period. In July agreement was reached with trade and consumer groups to establish a voluntary scheme allowing retailers to display prices in euros and to accept payments made in euros without imposing any additional charges. Retailers taking part in the scheme were to display a logo to show their compliance with a code of practice on the single currency.

In July 1998 the Commission proposed measures to combat the counterfeiting of euros. In October the ECB agreed to introduce an analysis centre for counterfeit currency, with a database accessible to national central banks. The EU encouraged each member state to establish its own coin analysis centre. Efforts were undertaken to increase co-operation in combating money-laundering during the late 1990s.

A payments settlement system, known as Target (Trans-European Automated Real-time Gross Settlement Express Transfer), was introduced for countries participating in EMU on 4 January

1999. By 2001 Target was processing some 4m. domestic and cross-border payments each month.

On 1 January 2002 the euro entered into circulation in the 12 participating countries. By the end of February the former national currencies of all the participating countries had been withdrawn.

The euro's value in national currencies is calculated and published daily. By mid-1999 the value of the euro had declined by some 12% against the US dollar compared with its value on introduction. Its decline was attributed to the relatively high degree of economic growth taking place in the USA compared with rates in the euro zone. Signs of economic recovery, especially in Germany, led to the strengthening of the euro against the US dollar in the second half of 1999. However, this renewal of confidence was not sustained and the euro dropped below parity level with the dollar in December. The ECB raised interest rates four times during the six months to May 2000, in an attempt to combat the failure in confidence. In September 2000 the monetary authorities of the USA and Japan, concerned about the impact of the weakness of the euro on the world economy, intervened jointly with the ECB in exchange markets. In November 2000 the currency reached its lowest recorded level. The euro rallied briefly in early 2001, but by June its value was declining once again. The ECB lowered interest rates four times during 2001 (including in September, as part of a joint effort by central banks to counteract the economic effects of the terrorist attacks on the USA). By November the currency had lost about one-fifth of its value against the US dollar since its launch in 1999.

Immediately following the introduction of the euro in the 12 participating countries in January 2002, its value rose significantly; it stood at €1 = US $0.87 at 5 February.

In March 2000 Belgium, France and the Netherlands announced the pending merger of their stock exchanges, to form a joint exchange, EURONEXT, with a view to facilitating cross-border euro commerce. This was achieved in September. Once fully operative, EURONEXT was to be the first fully integrated cross-border European market for equities, bonds, derivatives and commodities.

External Relations

The EU has diplomatic relations in its own right with many countries, and with international organizations, and participates as a body in international conferences on trade and development, such as the 'Uruguay Round' of trade negotiations, under the General Agreement on Tariffs and Trade (GATT—see WTO, p. 513), and the 'Doha Round' launched by WTO in November 2001. It has observer status at the United Nations. Agreements have been signed with numerous countries and groups of countries, allowing for co-operation in trade and other matters. Association agreements were initially signed between the EC and other European countries for the purpose of customs union or possible accession. After the decline of Communism in eastern Europe in 1989, it was decided that the new states, many of which expressed a desire to become full members of the EC, should be offered association status in the first instance. The resulting agreements are known as 'Europe Agreements'. Co-operation agreements are less comprehensive, and seek to facilitate economic co-operation with both European and non-European countries. Prior to 1989 they represented the preferred form of relationship with eastern European countries. Within the framework of the Stabilization and Association Process the EU is negotiating Stabilization and Association Agreements with Balkans countries, with the long-term goal of admitting them as members. In addition several Euro-Mediterranean association agreements have been concluded. The Union is a party to various international conventions (in some of these to the exclusion of the individual member states).

CENTRAL AND EASTERN EUROPE

During the late 1980s the extensive political changes and reforms in eastern European countries led to a strengthening of links with the EC. Agreements on trade and economic co-operation were concluded with Hungary (1988), Poland (1989), the USSR (1989), Czechoslovakia (1988—on trade only—and 1990), Bulgaria (1990), the German Democratic Republic (GDR—1990) and Romania (1990). In July 1989 the EC was entrusted with the co-ordination of aid from member states of the Organisation for Economic Co-operation and Development (OECD, q.v.) to Hungary and Poland ('Operation PHARE'—Poland/Hungary Aid for Restructuring of Economies): this programme was subsequently extended to include Albania, Bulgaria, the Czech Republic, Slovakia, Romania and the Baltic states (Estonia, Latvia and Lithuania). Community heads of government agreed in December 1989 to establish a European Bank for Reconstruction and Development (EBRD, q.v.), with participation by member states of the OECD and the Council for Mutual Economic Assistance, to promote investment in eastern Europe; the EBRD began operations in April 1991. In June 1995 the European Council agreed to provide total funding under the PHARE programme of ECU 6,693m. to central and eastern European countries for the period 1995–99.

'Europe Agreements' between the EC and Czechoslovakia, Hungary and Poland were signed in December 1991, with the aim of establishing a free-trade area within 10 years and developing political co-operation. In April 1994 Hungary and Poland submitted formal applications for EU membership. The Czech Republic applied formally in January 1996. In June 1991 the EC established diplomatic relations with Albania, and in May 1992 an agreement on trade and co-operation was signed. Europe Agreements were initialled with Romania in October, and with Bulgaria in March 1993. In June 1995 Romania formally applied for EU membership, followed by Bulgaria in December. In June 1993 the European Council approved measures to accelerate the opening of EC markets to goods from central and eastern European countries, with customs duties on many industrial items to be removed by the end of 1994. In September 1993 a co-operation agreement with Slovenia came into force; a Europe Agreement was signed in 1996, and Slovenia then formally applied for EU membership. An interim agreement, implementing the measures approved in June 1993, entered into force on 1 January 1997, providing for the gradual establishment of a free-trade area during a transitional period of six years. In December 2000 a preferential trade regime with the EU entered into effect in the region.

Trade and co-operation agreements with the three Baltic states were signed in May 1992. In July 1994 free-trade agreements with these countries were finalized by the EU, coming into effect on 1 January 1995. The EU concluded Europe Agreements with the Baltic states in June 1995. In October 1995 Latvia submitted a formal application for EU membership. Formal applications by Estonia and Lithuania were submitted in December.

In 1991 the EC established the Technical Assistance to the Commonwealth of Independent States (TACIS) programme, to promote the development of successful market economies and foster democracy in the countries of the former USSR through the provision of expertise and training. (TACIS initially extended assistance to the Baltic states. In 1992, however, these became eligible for assistance under PHARE and withdrew from TACIS.) The TACIS/EBRD Bangkok Facility provides EU financing to assist in the preparation for, and implementation of, EBRD investment in the CIS region. In 1994 Mongolia also became eligible for TACIS assistance. The TACIS programme's budget for 2000–06 was €3,138m.

In 1992 EU heads of government decided to replace the agreement on trade and economic co-operation that had been concluded with the USSR in 1989 with new Partnership and Co-operation Agreements (PCAs), providing a framework for closer political, cultural and economic relations between the EU and the former republics of the USSR. The PCAs are preceded by preliminary Interim Agreements. An Interim Agreement with Russia on trade concessions came into effect in February 1996, giving EU exporters improved access to the Russian market for specific products, and at the same time abolishing quantitative restrictions on some Russian exports to the EU. In December 1997 a PCA with Russia entered into force. The first meeting of the Co-operation Council for the EU–Russia PCA took place in January 1998, and, in July, an EU–Russia Space Dialogue was established. In June 1999 the EU adopted a Common Strategy on Russia. This aimed to promote the consolidation of democracy and rule of law in the country; the integration of Russia into the common European economic and social space; and regional stability and security. At the sixth EU–Russia summit in October 2000 the two sides agreed to initiate a regular energy dialogue, with the aim of establishing an EU–Russia Energy Partnership.

The EU's 'Northern Dimension' programme, covering Scandinavia, the Baltic states and northwest Russia, aims to address the specific challenges of these areas and to encourage co-operation with external states. The Northern Dimension programme operates within the framework of the EU–Russia PCA and the TACIS programme, as well as other agreements and financial instruments.

In February 1994 the EU Council of Ministers agreed to pursue closer economic and political relations with Ukraine, following an agreement by that country to renounce control of nuclear weapons on its territory. A PCA was signed by the two sides in June. In December EU ministers of finance approved a loan totalling ECU 85m., conditional on Ukraine's implementation of a strategy to close the Chernobyl (Chornobyl) nuclear power plant. An Interim Trade Agreement with Ukraine came into force in February 1996; this was replaced by a PCA in March 1998. In December 1999 the EU adopted a Common Strategy on Ukraine, aimed at developing a strategic partnership on the basis of the PCA. The Chernobyl plant closed in December 2000. The EU has provided funding to cover the interim period prior to the completion of two new reactors (supported by the EBRD and the European Atomic Energy Community—Euratom) to replace the plant's generating capacity. The EU has also been involved in social regeneration projects in the Chernobyl area. An Interim Agreement with Belarus was signed in March 1996. However, in February 1997 the EU suspended negotiations for the conclusion of the Interim Agreement and for a PCA in view of serious reverses to the development of democracy in that country. EU technical assistance programmes were suspended, with the exception of aid programmes and those considered directly beneficial to the democratic process. Relations deteriorated further in June 1998, when the EU withdrew its ambassadors to Belarus after three EU diplomats were denied access to their residential compound by the state authorities; the ambassadors returned to Belarus in mid-January 1999. In 1999 the EU announced that the punitive measures would be withdrawn gradually upon the attainment of certain benchmarks. In 2000 the EU criticized the Belarus Government for failing to accept its recommendations on the conduct of legislative elections held in October. By July 1999 PCAs had entered into force with all the CIS states except for Belarus, Tajikistan and Turkmenistan.

In May 1994 a Conference on Stability in Europe was convened in Paris to discuss the prevention of ethnic and territorial conflicts in central and eastern Europe. In particular, the conference sought to secure bilateral 'good-neighbour' accords between nine European countries that were regarded as potential future members of the EU (Bulgaria, the Czech Republic, Estonia, Hungary, Latvia, Lithuania, Poland, Romania and Slovakia). These countries, together with EU member states and other European countries (including Belarus, Moldova, Russia and Ukraine), signed a 'Stability Pact' in Paris in March 1995.

In July 1997 the European Commission published a report entitled 'Agenda 2000', which presented the Commission's new 'reinforced pre-accession strategy', uniting all the existing forms of support, including PHARE, into a single 'Accession Partnership' (AP) programme for each country. The APs, approved by the Commission in March 1998, were designed to support each country's preparations for accession by identifying priority areas and providing financial assistance. Each AP was complemented by a 'National Programme for the Adoption of the Acquis' (NPAA). (The acquis communautaire is the entire body of legislation of the European Community.) In 2000 the EU's PHARE and other schemes for the then five countries with SAAs (see below) were streamlined into the CARDS (Community Assistance for Reconstruction, Democratization and Stabilization) programme, now the EU's main channel for financial and technical assistance to the countries of South-Eastern Europe. A total of €4,650m. was allocated under CARDS for 2000–06.

Concurrently with Agenda 2000 the Commission published 'Opinions' on the application for membership of each of the candidate countries. It proposed that accession negotiations should commence with the Czech Republic, Estonia, Hungary, Poland and Slovenia. It was recommended that discussions with Bulgaria, Latvia, Lithuania, Romania and Slovakia be deferred, owing to the need for further economic or democratic reform in those countries. The report acknowledged that it was necessary for the EU to be restructured in order to ensure its successful operation following expansion. Accession negotiations at ministerial level commenced on 10 November 1998 with the first group of applicant countries. In December 1999 it was agreed to initiate accession negotiations with Bulgaria, Latvia, Lithuania, Romania and Slovakia; these commenced in February 2000. In June the European Council announced that it envisaged opening negotiations on all areas covered by the acquis communautaire with Bulgaria, Latvia, Lithuania, Romania and Slovakia in 2001. The Commission has set the end of 2002 as the earliest date for the entry of new members. Two Eastern European programmes designed to aid candidate countries in their efforts towards accession began in 2000. The Special Accession Programme for Agriculture and Rural Development (SAPARD) aims to help candidate countries manage the problems of structural adjustment in their agricultural sectors. It has an annual budget of €250m.The Instrument for Structural Policies for Preaccession (ISPA) has a budget for 2000–06 of €1,040m. Funds are available for infrastructure projects in the environment and transport sectors of candidate countries.

Following the introduction on 1 July 1990 of monetary, economic and social union between the Federal Republic of Germany and the GDR, and the formal integration of the two countries on 3 October, Community legislation was introduced within the former GDR over a transitional period.

A co-operation agreement was signed with Yugoslavia in 1980 (but not ratified until April 1983), allowing tariff-free imports and Community loans. New financial protocols were signed in 1987 and 1991. However, EC aid was suspended in July 1991, following the declarations of independence by the Yugoslav republics of Croatia and Slovenia, and the subsequent outbreak of civil conflict. Efforts were made in the ensuing months by EC ministers of foreign affairs to negotiate a peaceful settlement between the Croatian and Serbian factions, and a team of EC observers was maintained in Yugoslavia from July onwards, to monitor successive cease-fire agreements. In October the EC proposed a plan for an association of independent states, to replace the Yugoslav federation: this was accepted by all the Yugoslav republics except Serbia, which demanded a redefining of boundaries to accommodate within Serbia all predominantly Serbian areas. In November the application of the Community's co-operation agreements with Yugoslavia was suspended (with exemptions for the republics which co-operated in the peace negotiations). In January 1992 the Community granted diplomatic recognition to the former Yugoslav republics of Croatia and Slovenia, and in April it recognized Bosnia and Herzegovina, while withholding recognition from Macedonia (owing to pressure from the Greek Government, which feared that the existence of an independent Macedonia would imply a claim on the Greek province of the same name). In May EC ambassadors were withdrawn from Belgrade, in protest at Serbia's support for aggression by Bosnian Serbs against other ethnic groups in Bosnia and Herzegovina, and in the same month the Community imposed a trade embargo on Serbia and Montenegro.

New proposals for a settlement of the Bosnian conflict, submitted by EC and UN mediators in 1993, were accepted by the Bosnian Croats and by the Bosnian Government in March, but rejected by the Bosnian Serbs. In June the European Council pledged more rigorous enforcement of sanctions against Serbia. In July, at UN/EC talks in Geneva, all three parties to the Bosnian war agreed on a plan to divide Bosnia and Herzegovina into three separate republics; however, the Bosnian Government rejected the proposals for the share of territory to be allotted to the Muslims.

In April 1994, following a request from EU ministers of foreign affairs, a Contact Group, consisting of France, Germany, the United Kingdom, the USA and Russia, was initiated to undertake peace negotiations. The following month ministers of foreign affairs of the USA, Russia and the EU (represented by five member states) jointly endorsed a proposal to divide Bosnia and Herzegovina in proportions of 49% to the Bosnian Serbs and 51% to the newly-established Federation of Muslims and Croats. The proposal was rejected by the Bosnian Serb assembly in July and had to be abandoned after the Muslim-Croat Federation withdrew its support subsequent to the Bosnian Serb vote. In July the EU formally assumed political control of Mostar, a town in southern Bosnia and Herzegovina, in order to restore the city's administrative infrastructure and secure peace.

Despite some criticism of US policy towards the former Yugoslavia, in September 1995 the EU supported US-led negotiations in Geneva to devise a plan to end the conflict in Bosnia and Herzegovina. The plan closely resembled the previous proposals of the Contact Group: two self-governing entities were to be created within Bosnia and Herzegovina, with 51% of territory being allocated to the Muslim-Croat Federation, and 49% to Bosnian Serbs. The proposals were finally agreed after negotiations in Dayton, USA, in November 1995, and an accord was signed in Paris in December. During 1991–2000 Bosnia and Herzegovina received a total of €1,032m. in assistance from the EU. The European Community Humanitarian Office (ECHO) programme for that country was phased out in 2000; under the new CARDS programme, the country was to receive €105m. in 2001. In 2000 the EU published a 'road map' for Bosnia and Herzegovina, outlining measures that must be undertaken by the Government prior to the initiation of a feasibility study on the formulation of a Stabilization and Association Agreement (SAA). An EU consultative task force (CTF) is in operation in that country, with the aim of developing a legal and regulatory framework compatible with that of the EU.

Negotiations towards a trade and co-operation agreement with Croatia began in June 1995, but talks were suspended in early August, following Croatia's military offensive in the Krajina region, which was strongly criticized by the EU. A CTF was established in Croatia in February 2000. An SAA with Croatia entered into force in October 2001.

In January 1996 the EU announced its intention to recognize Yugoslavia (Serbia and Montenegro), despite the opposition of the USA. During 1996–99 the EU allocated ECU 1,000m. for the repatriation of refugees, restructuring the economy and technical assistance, in addition to ECU 1,000m. in humanitarian aid provided since the beginning of the conflict in the former Yugoslavia.

In December 1993 six member states of the EU formally recognized the former Yugoslav republic of Macedonia (FYRM) as an independent state, but in February 1994 Greece imposed a commercial embargo against the FYRM, on the grounds that the use of the name and symbols (e.g. on the state flag) of 'Macedonia' was a threat to Greek national security. In March, however, ministers of foreign affairs of the EU decided that the embargo was in contravention of EU law, and in April the Commission commenced legal proceedings in the European Court of Justice against Greece. In September 1995 Greece and the FYRM began a process of normalizing relations, after the FYRM agreed to change the design of its state flag. In October Greece ended its economic blockade of the FYRM. A trade and co-operation agreement with the FYRM entered into force in January 1998. From March 2001 insecurity prevailed in the FYRM, owing to an insurgency by ethnic Albanian rebels. The EU undertook diplomatic efforts in pursuit of a settlement to the conflict and committed funds for reconstruction and rehabilitation. In April an SAA was signed with the FYRM. At the same time, an interim agreement was adopted, allowing for trade-related matters of the SAA to enter into effect in June, without the need for formal ratification by the national parliaments of the EU member states. (The SAA provided for the EU to open its markets to 95% of exports from the FYRM.) However, the the Macedonian Government was informed that it would be required to deliver concessions to the ethnic Albanian minority population prior to entering into the agreement. Under the CARDS programme the FRYM was to receive €42.50m. in 2001. It was to receive €96.57m. under the ECHO programme, which was being gradually phased out

In March 1997 the EU sent two advisory delegations to Albania to help to restore order after violent unrest and political instability erupted in that country. A request by the Albanian Government for the deployment of EU peace-keeping troops was refused, but it was announced in early April that the EU was to provide humanitarian aid of some ECU 2m., to be used for emergency relief. During 1991–2000 a total of €1,021m. was granted to Albania. In June 2001 the European Council invited the Commission to present draft negotiation directives for an SAA with Albania.

In 1998 the escalation of violence in Kosovo and Metohija (Federal Republic of Yugoslavia), between Serbs and the ethnic Albanian majority, prompted the imposition of sanctions by EU ministers of foreign affairs. In March ministers agreed to impose an arms embargo, to halt export credit guarantees to Yugoslavia and to restrict visas for Serbian officials. A ban on new investment in the region was imposed in June. In the same month military observers from the EU, Russia and the USA were deployed to Kosovo. In September the EU agreed to deny JAT, the Yugoslav airline, landing rights in EU countries. During the following month the Yugoslav Government allowed a team of international experts to investigate atrocities in the region, under an EU mandate. Several EU countries participated in the NATO military offensive against Yugoslavia, which was initiated in March 1999 owing to the continued repression of ethnic Albanians in Kosovo by Serbian forces. Ministers approved a new series of punitive measures in April, including an embargo on the sale or supply of petroleum to the Yugoslav authorities and an extension of a travel ban on Serbian official and business executives. Humanitarian assistance was extended to provide relief for the substantial numbers of refugees who fled Kosovo amid the escalating violence, in particular to assist the Governments of Albania and the FYRM.

In September 1999 EU foreign ministers agreed to ease sanctions in force against Kosovo and Montenegro. In October the EU began to implement an 'Energy for Democracy' initiative, with the objective of supplying some €5m.-worth of heating oil to Serbian towns controlled by groups in opposition to the then Yugoslav President Slobodan Milošević. In February 2000 the EU suspended its ban on the Yugoslav national airline. However, the restrictions on visas for Serbian officials were reinforced. Kosovo received a total of €474.7m. under EU programmes in 2000 and the EU remained the largest financial contributor to the province in 2001. In February 2001 the EU warned that aid for the region would be reduced if ethnic Albanian separatists continued to launch cross-border attacks against security forces in southern Serbia.

In May 2000 the EU agreed an emergency aid package to support Montenegro against destabilization by Serbia. Following the election of a new FRY administration in late 2000 the EU immediately withdrew all remaining sanctions, with the exception of those directed against Milošević and his associates, and pledged financial support of €200m. The FRY was welcomed as a full participant in the stabilization and association process (see Stability Pact, below). It was announced that a CTF would be set up when conditions permitted. The EU insisted that the FRY must co-operate fully with the International Criminal Tribunal for the Former Yugoslavia (ICTY, q.v.). Following the arrest of Milošević by the FRY authorities in April 2001, the first part of the EU's aid package for that year (amounting to €240m.) was released.

At a Balkan summit convened in Zagreb, Croatia, in November 2000, the EU pledged €4,650m. for reconstruction aid to the region over the period 2000–06.

In June 1999 the EU, in conjunction with the Group of Seven industrialized nations and Russia (the G-8), regional governments and other organizations concerned with the stability of the region, launched the Stability Pact for South-Eastern Europe, which was placed under the auspices of the OSCE. For its part, the EU proposed to offer customized SAAs (see above) to Albania, Bosnia, Croatia, Macedonia and, eventually, the FRY, provided that they fulfilled certain conditions. (The FRY was excluded from the Pact until October 2000, following the staging there of democratic presidential elections.) Since the establishment of the Pact, heads of state and government of the South-East European countries have met regularly in the framework of the South East Europe Co-operation Process (SEECP). At the Stability Pact's first regional funding conference, held in March 2000, a 'quick start package', comprising 244 projects, was announced; by June 2001 some 201 projects were under way.

OTHER EUROPEAN COUNTRIES

The members of the European Free Trade Association (EFTA) concluded bilateral free trade agreements with the EEC and the ECSC during the 1970s. On 1 January 1984 the last tariff barriers were eliminated, thus establishing full free trade for industrial products between the Community and EFTA members. Some EFTA members subsequently applied for membership of the EC: Austria in 1989, Sweden in 1991, and Finland, Switzerland and Norway in 1992. Formal negotiations on the creation of a

'European Economic Area' (EEA), a single market for goods, services, capital and labour among EC and EFTA members, began in June 1990, and were concluded in October 1991. The agreement was signed in May 1992 (after a delay caused by a ruling of the Court of Justice of the EC that a proposed joint EC-EFTA court, for adjudication in disputes, was incompatible with the Treaty of Rome; EFTA members then agreed to concede jurisdiction to the Court of Justice on cases of competition involving both EC and EFTA members, and to establish a special joint committee for other disputes). In a referendum in December Swiss voters rejected ratification of the agreement, and the remaining 18 countries signed an adjustment protocol in March 1993, allowing the EEA to be established without Switzerland (which was to have observer status). The EEA entered into force on 1 January 1994. Formal negotiations on the accession to the EU of Austria, Finland and Sweden began on 1 February, and those on Norway's membership started on 1 April. Negotiations were concluded with Austria, Finland and Sweden on 1 March 1994, and with Norway on 16 March, having been delayed by issues concerning the fisheries sector. Heads of government of the four countries signed treaties of accession to the EU in June, which were to come into effect from 1995, subject to approval by a national referendum in each country. Accession to the EU was endorsed by the electorates of Austria, Finland and Sweden in June, October and November respectively. Norway's accession was rejected by a referendum conducted at the end of November. Austria, Finland and Sweden became members of the EU on 1 January 1995. Liechtenstein, which became a full member of EFTA in September 1991, joined the EEA on 1 May 1995. Negotiations conducted with Switzerland since 1992 on the formulation of a new bilateral economic arrangement proceeded slowly. The main obstacles to an agreement concerned Switzerland's work permit quotas for EU citizens, and the weight limit on trucks passing through its territory. In December 1996 it was reported that Switzerland had agreed to phase out the use of work permit quotas within six years of a treaty being signed. In early December 1998 political agreement was reached with Switzerland to abolish the weight limit and instead impose road-haulage charges on trucks weighing 40 metric tons or more. Later in that month an interim trade agreement was concluded.

A trade agreement with Andorra entered into force on 1 January 1991, establishing a customs union for industrial products, and allowing duty-free access to the EC for certain Andorran agricultural products. In January 1998 negotiations on a co-operation agreement with Andorra were finalized. However, the agreement remains to be adopted. Negotiations on a trade agreement with San Marino were concluded in December 1991.

THE MIDDLE EAST AND THE MEDITERRANEAN

A scheme to negotiate a series of parallel trade and co-operation agreements encompassing almost all of the non-member states on the coast of the Mediterranean was formulated by the EC in 1972. Association agreements, intended to lead to customs union or the eventual full accession of the country concerned, had been signed with Greece (which eventually became a member of the Community in 1981) in 1962, Turkey in 1964 and Malta in 1971; a fourth agreement was signed with Cyprus in 1972. These established free access to the Community market for most industrial products and tariff reductions for most agricultural products. Annexed were financial protocols under which the Community was to provide concessional finance. During the 1970s a series of agreements covering trade and economic co-operation were concluded with the Arab Mediterranean countries and Israel, all establishing free access to EC markets for most industrial products, either immediately or shortly afterwards. Access for agricultural products was facilitated, although some tariffs remained. In 1982 the Commission formulated an integrated plan for the development of its own Mediterranean regions and recommended the adoption of a new policy towards the non-Community countries of the Mediterranean. This was to include greater efforts towards diversifying agriculture, in order to avoid surpluses of items such as citrus fruits, olive oil and wine (which the Mediterranean countries all wished to export to the Community) and to reduce these countries' dependence on imported food. From 1 January 1993 the majority of agricultural exports from Mediterranean non-Community countries were granted exemption from customs duties.

In June 1995 the European Council endorsed a proposal by the Commission to reform and strengthen the Mediterranean policy of the EU. The initiative envisaged the eventual establishment of a Euro-Mediterranean Economic Area (EMEA), to be prereceded by a gradual liberalization of trade within the region through bilateral and regional free-trade arrangements, and the adoption of financial and technical measures to support the implementation of structural reforms in Mediterranean partner countries. In November 1995 a conference of foreign affairs ministers of the EU member states, 11 Mediterranean non-member countries (excluding Libya) and the Palestinian authorities was convened in Barcelona, Spain. The conference endorsed the agreement on the EMEA and resolved to establish a permanent Euro-Mediterranean ministerial dialogue. It issued the 'Barcelona Declaration', endorsing commitments to uphold democratic principles and to pursue greater co-operation in the control of international crime, drugs-trafficking and illegal migration. The Declaration set the objective of establishing a Euro-Mediterranean free-trade area by 2010. The process of co-operation and dialogue under this agreement became known as the Euro-Mediterranean Partnership (or 'Barcelona Process'). In September 1998 the Commission proposed measures to extend the single market to the Mediterranean countries and sought to formulate common rules on customs and taxation, free movement of goods, public procurement, intellectual property, financial services, data protection and accounting.

In April 1997 the second Euro-Mediterranean Conference of ministers of foreign affairs was held, in Malta, to review implementation of the partnership strategy. Euro-Mediterranean foreign ministers convened for a third conference in April 1999, in Stuttgart, Germany. The Stuttgart conference agreed that Libya could eventually become a partner in the process, following the removal of UN sanctions on that country and acceptance of the full terms of the Barcelona Declaration. Libya subsequently attended some meetings as an observer. A fourth conference, convened in November 2000, in Marseilles, France, focused on the adoption of a new common strategy for the Mediterranean, aimed at strengthening the Barcelona Process. With economic, financial, social and cultural components, the new approach involved increased political dialogue with partnership countries as well as further efforts to improve security, democracy and human rights. A fifth conference of foreign ministers was scheduled to be held in 2002.

The EU's primary financial instrument for the implementation of the Euro-Mediterranean Partnership has been the MEDA programme, providing support for the reform of economic and social structures within partnership countries. The legal basis of the MEDA programme was the MEDA Regulation, adopted in July 1996. Financial aid commitments under MEDA I (covering 1995–99) amounted to ECU 3,400m. In 1999 the MEDA Regulation was reviewed and revised. The amended programme was named MEDA II. Covering the period 2000–06, MEDA II was granted a budget of €5,350m.

The first Euro-Mediterranean Energy Forum was convened in May 1997 and a second Energy Forum was held in May 1998; a number of other sectoral conferences have been organized. The inaugural meeting of a Euro-Mediterranean Parliamentary Forum was convened in Brussels in October 1998. The second meeting of the Forum took place in Brussels in February 2001. (The meeting will now be held annually.) The first Euro-Mediterranean ministerial meeting on trade was convened in May 2001; ministers have agreed to hold regular meetings within this framework.

In 1987 Turkey applied for membership of the EC. In 1989 the European Commission stated that, for formal negotiations on Turkish membership to take place, it would be necessary for Turkey to restructure its economy, improve its observance of human rights, and harmonize its relations with Greece. Negotiations in early 1995 to conclude a customs union agreement with Turkey were obstructed by the opposition of Greece. In early March, however, Greece removed its veto on the customs union, having received assurance on the accession of Cyprus to the EU. Ratification of the agreement by the European Parliament was delayed until mid-December, owing to concern over issues of human rights, in particular the policies of the Turkish Government towards the country's Kurdish population. Under the agreement, Turkey was to receive some ECU 1,400m. in grants and loans in 1995–99. In July 1990 Cyprus and Malta made formal applications to join the Community. In June 1993 the European Commission approved the eligibility of both countries to join the Community, but in November 1996 Malta's new Government announced its intention to 'freeze' its application. In September 1998, following the return to power of a Nationalist government, Malta renewed its membership application. In February 1999 the Commission recommended the initiation of membership negotiations; these commenced in February 2000. In 1996 and 1997 the EU, along with the USA, took part in extensive diplomatic activity to facilitate Cyprus' accession as a single entity. In March 1997 Turkey received assurances that its application for membership would be considered on equal terms with that of any other country. However, in July the Commission's report 'Agenda 2000' recommended that accession negotiations should begin with the (Greek) Cypriot Government, while talks with Turkey were to be postponed indefinitely. In December ministers of foreign affairs, meeting in Luxembourg, endorsed the report's proposals. Detailed accession talks with Cyprus began in November 1998, and were expected to be completed in 2002. From August 1999, when a devastating earthquake struck north-western Turkey, a *rapprochement* began to take place between Greece and Turkey. Greece lifted its longstanding veto on disbursements of aid to Turkey and the EU made a loan of €600m. to the Turkish government to assist reconstruction. This improvement in relations culminated, at the Helsinki summit meeting of EU leaders in December, in a formal invitation to Turkey to present its candidacy for EU membership. In May 2001 the European Court of Human Rights ruled that Turkey had violated human rights legislation on 14 counts relating to its invasion of northern Cyprus in 1974 and the subsequent treatment of Greek Cypriots, prompting fears that EU–Turkey relations could deteriorate once again.

Co-operation agreements concluded in the 1970s with the Maghreb countries (Algeria, Morocco and Tunisia), the Mashreq countries (Egypt, Jordan, Lebanon and Syria) and Israel covered free access to the Community market for industrial products, customs preferences for certain agricultural products, and financial aid in the form of grants and loans from the European Investment Bank. A co-operation agreement negotiated with the Republic of Yemen was non-preferential. In June 1992 the EC approved a proposal to conclude new bilateral agreements with the Maghreb countries, incorporating the following components: political dialogue; financial, economic, technical and cultural co-operation; and the eventual establishment of a free-trade area. A Euro-Mediterranean Association Agreement with Tunisia was signed in July 1995 and entered into force in March 1998. A similar agreement with Morocco entered into force in March 2000. (In July 1987 Morocco applied to join the Community, but its application was rejected on the grounds that it is not a European country.) The EU's relations with Algeria have been affected by political and civil instability in that country and by concerns regarding the Government's respect for human rights and democratic principles. In March 1997 negotiations were initiated between the European Commission and representatives of the Algerian government on a Euro-Mediterranean Association Agreement that would incorporate political commitments relating to democracy and human rights; this was signed in December 2001. A Euro-Mediterranean Association Agreement with Egypt was signed in June. In May of that year, Egypt, together with Jordan, Tunisia and Morocco, issued the Agadir Declaration, providing for the establishment of a free-trade area, as a cornerstone of the planned Euro-Mediterranean free-trade area. Negotiations for the conclusion of an association agreement with Syria were initiated in July 1996, although formal authorization to the European Commission to conclude an association agreement was only granted by EU heads of government in December 1997. Negotiations on the agreement were ongoing in 2002. Negotiations on an association agreement with Jordan were formally concluded in November 1997; this was expected to enter into force in 2002. A similar agreement with Lebanon was signed in January 2002.

In January 1989 the EC and Israel eliminated the last tariff barriers to full free trade for industrial products. A Euro-Mediterranean Association Agreement with Israel was signed in 1995, providing further trade concessions and establishing an institutional political dialogue between the two parties. The agreement entered into force in June 2000. Following the signing of the September 1993 Israeli-Palestine Liberation Organization (PLO) peace agreement, the EC committed substantial funds in humanitarian assistance for the Palestinians. In November 1996 the EU appointed a special envoy to the Middle East with responsibility for promoting a peaceful settlement. A Euro-Mediterranean Interim Association Agreement on Trade and Co-operation was signed with the PLO in January 1997 and entered into force in July. The agreement confirmed existing trade concessions offered to the Palestinians since 1986 and provided for free trade to be introduced during an initial five-year period. In April 1998 the EU and the Palestinian National Authority (PNA) signed a security co-operation agreement, which provided for regular meetings to promote joint efforts on security issues, in particular in combating terrorism. The EU approved an assistance programme for the Palestinians in November totalling ECU 500m.; this was to cover the period 1999–2003. In March 1999 EU heads of state and government urged Israel to fulfil within one year the 'unqualified Palestinian right' to independence. Israel was strongly critical of what it perceived as an ultimatum and stated that the EU had reduced its scope as a mediator in the Middle East peace process. In April the European Parliament demanded an investigation into the handling of Commission funds to Palestinian-controlled areas of the West Bank and Gaza. At that time the EU was reported to be the largest donor to the PNA. The escalation of violence between Israel and the Palestinians from September 2000 resulted in a significant deterioration of EU–Israel relations. In view of the economic difficulties that ensued for the PNA, the EU granted emergency loans to cover the Authority's operational costs.

A new co-operation agreement with Yemen, incorporating a political element (i.e. commitments to democratic principles and respect for human rights), and providing for 'most favoured nation' treatment, entered into force in July 1998.

Talks were held with Iran in April 1992 on the establishment of a co-operation accord. In December the Council of Ministers recommended that a 'critical dialogue' be undertaken with Iran, owing to the country's significance to regional security. In April 1997 the 'critical dialogue' was suspended and ambassadors were recalled from Iran, following a German court ruling that found the Iranian authorities responsible for ordering the murder of four Kurdish dissidents in Berlin in 1992. Later that month ministers of foreign affairs resolved to restore diplomatic relations with Iran, in order to protect the strong trading partnership. However, diplomatic relations were not resumed until November, as EU ministers reversed their decision to return diplomats to Tehran, owing to the Iranian Government's reluctance to readmit the German and Dutch ambassadors. In February 1998 EU ministers of foreign affairs removed the ban on high-level contacts with Iran, in an attempt to strengthen dialogue with that country. In August 1999 the Iranian ministry of foreign affairs acknowledged an improvement in EU-Iranian relations since the election of Dr Sayed Muhammad Khatami as President. In November 2000 an EU–Iran working group on trade and investment met for the first time. The Commission adopted a communication on developing closer relations with Iran in February 2001; it was hoped that this would accelerate progress towards concluding a trade and co-operation agreement. The EU welcomed Dr Khatami's re-election to the presidency in June.

An co-operation agreement between the EC and the countries of the Gulf Co-operation Council (GCC), which entered into force in January 1990, provided for co-operation in industry, energy, technology and other fields. Negotiations on a full free-trade pact began in October 1990, but it was expected that any agreement would involve transition periods of some 12 years for the reduction of European tariffs on 'sensitive products' (i.e. petrochemicals). In November 1999 the GCC Supreme Council agreed to establish a customs union (a precondition of the proposed EU-GCC free-trade agreement) by March 2005. Free-trade negotiations were continuing in 2002.

Contacts with the Arab world in general take place within the framework of the 'Euro-Arab Dialogue', established in 1973 to provide a forum for discussion of economic issues through working groups on specific topics. Following a decision in 1989 to reactivate the Dialogue, meetings were suspended in 1990 as a result of Iraq's invasion of Kuwait. In April 1992 senior EC and Arab officials agreed to resume the process.

LATIN AMERICA

A non-preferential trade agreement was signed with Uruguay in 1974, and economic and commercial co-operation agreements with Mexico in 1975 and Brazil in 1980. A five-year co-operation agreement with the members of the Central American Common Market and with Panama entered into force in 1987, as did a similar agreement with the member countries (see below) of the Andean Group (now the Andean Community). Co-operation agreements were signed with Argentina and Chile in 1990, and in that year tariff preferences were approved for Bolivia, Colombia, Ecuador and Peru, in support of those countries' efforts to combat drugs-trafficking. In May 1992 an interinstitutional co-operation agreement was signed with the Southern Common Market (Mercosur); in the following month the EC and the member states of the Andean Group (Bolivia, Colombia, Ecuador, Peru and Venezuela) initialled a new co-operation agreement, which was to broaden the scope of economic and development co-operation and enhance trade relations, and a new co-operation agreement was signed with Brazil. In July 1993 the EC introduced a tariff regime to limit the import of bananas from Latin America, in order to protect the banana-producing countries of the ACP group, then linked to the EC by the Lomé Convention (see below). In June 1995 a Commission communication advocated greater economic co-operation with Cuba. This policy was strongly supported by a resolution of the European Parliament in January 1996, but was criticized by the US Government, which continued to maintain an economic embargo against Cuba. In April 2000 Cuba rejected the Cotonou Agreement (see below), following criticism by some European governments of its human rights record.

In October 1995 the EU announced its intention to forge closer links with Latin America during 1996–2000, by means of strengthened political ties, an increase in economic integration and free trade, and co-operation in other areas. In April 1997 the EU extended further trade benefits to the countries of the Andean Community. In July the EU and Mexico concluded an Economic Partnership, Political Co-operation and Co-operation Agreement and an interim agreement on trade. The accords were signed in December. The main part of the interim agreement entered into effect in July 2000 and the co-operation agreement entered into force in October. In November 1998 formal negotiations were commenced with Mexico, towards a more extensive free-trade agreement, which was to cover economic co-operation, drugs-trafficking and human rights issues. In November 1999 the EU and Mexico concluded a free-trade agreement which, on implementation, was to lead to the removal of all tariffs on bilateral trade in industrial products by 2007. The first summit meeting of all EU and Latin American heads of state or government was held in Rio de Janeiro, Brazil, in June 1999.

In June 1996 the EU and Chile signed a framework agreement on political and economic co-operation, which provided for a process of bilateral trade liberalization, as well as co-operation in other industrial and financial areas. An EU-Chile Joint Council was established. In November 1999 the EU and Chile commenced practical negotiations on developing closer political and economic co-operation, within the framework of the proposed EU-Mercosur/Chile association agreement (see below).

The first ministerial conference between the EC and the then 11 Latin American states of the Rio Group took place in April 1991; thereafter high-level joint ministerial meetings have been held on a regular basis. In late December 1994 the EU and Mercosur signed a joint declaration that aimed to promote trade liberalization and greater political co-operation. In September 1995, at a meeting in Montevideo, Uruguay, a framework agreement on the establishment of a free-trade regime between the two organizations was initialled. The agreement was formally signed in December. In July 1998 the Commission voted to commence negotiations towards an interregional association agreement with Mercosur and Chile, which would strengthen existing co-operation agreements. Negotiations were initiated in April 2000.

In February 2001 the European Parliament adopted a resolution opposing Plan Colombia, a US-backed initiative which aimed to combat the Colombian illegal narcotics trade through measures that included military-supported aerial crop spraying to destroy coca production; the Plan had reportedly resulted in the forced displacement of some farming communities. The Parliament urged support for the ongoing peace process in Colombia and for the adoption of structural reforms in that country as the preferred means of addressing the drugs problem. In April the EU announced an €30m. aid package designed to support the peace process. (In July the USA proposed the inauguration of a new Andean Regional Initiative, which shifted emphasis from the military-backed focus of Plan Colombia to the region-wide promotion of democracy and development.)

ASIA AND AUSTRALASIA

Relations between the EU and ASEAN (q.v.) are based on the Co-operation Agreement of 1980. Under this agreement, joint committee meetings are held approximately every 18 months. There are also regular ministerial meetings and post-ministerial conferences. In addition, the EU is a member of the ASEAN Regional Forum (ARF), a security grouping designed to promote peace and stability, established in 1994. In December of that year the European Council endorsed a new strategy for Asia, which recognized the region's increasing economic and political importance and pledged to strengthen bilateral and regional dialogue. The strategy aimed to enhance the development of trade and investment, promote peace and security, and assist the less-developed countries in Asia. In May 1995 ASEAN and EU senior officials endorsed an initiative to convene an Asia-Europe Meeting of heads of government (ASEM). The first Asia-Europe meeting (ASEM) was held in March 1996 in Bangkok, Thailand. It was agreed to launch an Asia-Europe Partnership for Greater Growth, in order to expand trade, investment and technology transfer. An Asia-Business Forum was to be formed, as well as an Asia-Europe Foundation in Singapore to promote educational and cultural exchanges. The EU-Republic of Korea Framework Agreement was initialled, and Malaysia was appointed to oversee the building of an integrated Asian electric rail network to link Singapore to Europe via China. The second ASEM summit, convened in the United Kingdom in April 1998, was dominated by economic and financial concerns, and both sides' declared intention to prevent a return to protectionist trading policies. A special statement, issued at the end of the meeting, identified the need for economic reform in individual countries and for a reinforcement of international financial institutions. The meeting established an ASEM Trust Fund, under the auspices of the World Bank, to alleviate the social impact of the financial crisis. Other initiatives adopted by ASEM were an Asia-Europe Co-operation Framework to co-ordinate political, economic and financial co-operation, a Trade Facilitation Action Plan, and an Investment Promotion Action Plan, which incorporated a new Investment Experts Group. The meeting resolved to promote efforts to strengthen relations in all areas, and to establish a series of working bodies to promote specific areas of co-operation; however it was decided not to establish a permanent secretariat for the ASEM arrangement. ASEM heads of government convened for the third time in Seoul, Republic of Korea, in October 2000. ASEM III welcomed the ongoing *rapprochement* between the two Korean nations, declared a commitment to the promotion of human rights, and endorsed several initiatives related to globalization and information technology, including an Initiative to Address the Digital Divide and the creation of a Trans-Eurasia Information Network. Initiatives aimed at combating money-laundering, corruption and transnational crime were also adopted. The meeting established a new Asia-Europe Co-operation Framework (AECF), identifying ASEM's principles and priorities for the next 10 years. ASEM IV was scheduled to take place in Copenhagen, Denmark, in September 2002.

In early September 2001 the EU adopted a new Communication on relations with Asia for the coming decade. Representing an updating of the 1994 strategy, this focused on strengthened partnership, particularly in the areas of politics, security, trade and investment. It aimed to reduce poverty and to promote democracy, good governance and the rule of law throughout the region. Partnerships and alliances on global issues were to be forged. A fundamental aim was to strengthen the EU's presence in Asia, promoting mutual awareness and knowledge on both sides. To this end, the EU established a scholarship scheme in the People's Republic of China and increased the number of EU delegation offices in the region.

Bilateral non-preferential co-operation agreements were signed with Bangladesh, India, Pakistan and Sri Lanka between 1973 and 1976. A further agreement with India, extended to include co-operation in trade, industry, energy, science and finance, came into force in December 1981. A third agreement, which entered into effect in August 1994, included commitments to develop co-operation between the two sides and improve market access, as well as for the observance of human rights and democratic principles. The first EU–India summit meeting was held in Lisbon in June 2000. A new and extended agreement with Pakistan on commercial and economic co-operation entered into force in May 1986; in May 1992 an agreement was signed on measures to stimulate private investment in Pakistan. A new accord with Sri Lanka, designed to promote co-operation in areas such as trade, investment and protection of the environment, entered into force in April 1995. A similar agreement with Nepal entered into force in June 1996. These co-operation agreements, which incorporated provisions for respect for human rights and democratic principles, did not include a financial protocol. In July 1996 EU Governments authorized the European Commission to conclude similar agreements with Bangladesh and Pakistan. A draft co-operation agreement was initialled with Pakistan in April 1998. However, following the October 1999 military coup in Pakistan, the agreement was suspended. Political dialogue with Pakistan recommenced on an *ad hoc* basis in November 2000, and the co-operation agreement was signed in November 2001. The new co-operation accord with Bangladesh was signed in May 2000 and came into force in March 2001.

A trade agreement was signed with the People's Republic of China (PRC) in 1978, and renewed in May 1985. In June 1989, following the violent repression of the Chinese pro-democracy movement by the PRC Government, the EC imposed economic sanctions on that country. In October 1990 it was decided that relations with the PRC should be 'progressively normalized'. In November 1994 a China-Europe International Business School was initiated in Shanghai. The EU has supported the PRC's increased involvement in the international community and, in particular, supported its application for membership of the WTO (eventually approved in 2001, see below). In October 1997 senior EU representatives signed a memorandum of understanding with the PRC on future co-operation. The first EU-PRC meeting of heads of government was convened in April 1998. In November the President of the Commission made an official visit to the PRC and urged that country to remove trade restrictions imposed on European products. In the same month the EU and Hong Kong signed a co-operation agreement to combat drugs-trafficking and copyright piracy. The agreement was the first international accord to be signed by the territory since its reversion to Chinese sovereignty in July 1997. At the second Asia-Europe meeting (ASEM, see below) of foreign ministers in March 1999 criticism of the PRC's human rights record was rejected by the Chinese minister of foreign affairs. A bilateral trade agreement between the EU and the PRC was concluded in May 2000, removing a major barrier to the PRC's accession to the WTO; this was approved in November 2001. A third EU–PRC summit meeting was held in Beijing in October 2000. At the fourth summit, convened in September 2001, the two sides agreed to strengthen and widen political dialogue and to continue discussions on human rights issues. Negotiations on an EU-PRC maritime transport agreement were also formally opened in September.

In October 1997 the EU and the Republic of Korea signed an agreement regarding a reciprocal opening of markets for telecommunications equipment, following a protracted dispute, which had led the EU to lodge a complaint with the WTO. In September 1997, however, the Commission submitted a further complaint to the WTO, accusing the Republic of Korea of tax discrimination against European spirits exporters. In the same month the EU joined the Korean Peninsular Energy Development Organization, an initiative to increase nuclear safety and reduce the risk of nuclear proliferation from the energy programme of the Democratic People's Republic of Korea (DPRK). In September 1999, for the first time ever, ministerial-level discussions took place between the EU and the DPRK at the United Nations General Assembly. In May 2001 the EU announced that it was to establish diplomatic relations with the DPRK.

In June 1992 the EC signed trade and co-operation agreements with Mongolia and Macao, with respect for democracy and human rights forming the basis of envisaged co-operation. A co-operation accord was formally signed with Viet Nam in July 1995, under which the EU agreed to increase quotas for Vietnamese textile products, to support the country's efforts to join the WTO and to provide aid for environmental and public management projects. The agreement, which entered into force on 1 June 1996, incorporated a commitment by Viet Nam to guarantee human rights and a procedure for the gradual repatriation of some 40,000 Vietnamese refugees from Germany, who had lost their legal status after German reunification. A permanent EU mission to Viet Nam was established in February 1996. In July 1996 a European Business Information Centre was opened in Malaysia, with the object of promoting trade. In October the EU imposed strict limits on entry visas for Myanmar officials, because of Myanmar's refusal to allow the Commission to send a mission to investigate allegations of forced labour. In March 1997 EU ministers of foreign affairs agreed to revoke Myanmar's special trade privileges under the Generalized System of Preferences (GSP). In November a meeting of EU and ASEAN officials was postponed, owing to Myanmar's insistence (then as a full member of the ASEAN grouping) that it should attend with full observer status. After several further delays, the meeting was finally convened, with Myanmar as a 'silent' observer, in late May 1999. The EU has successively extended its ban on arms exports to Myanmar and its prohibition on the issuing of visas, most recently until April 2002. Non-preferential co-operation agreements were signed with Laos and Cambodia in April 1997. The agreement with Laos entered into force on 1 December; the agreement with Cambodia was postponed owing to adverse political developments in that country. In 1998 the EU provided financial assistance to support preparations for a general election in Cambodia, and dispatched observers to monitor the election, which was held in July. In September 1999 the EU briefly imposed an arms embargo against Indonesia, which was at that time refusing to permit the deployment of an international peace-keeping force in East Timor.

Textiles exports by Asian countries have caused concern in the EU, owing to the depressed state of its textiles industry. In 1982 bilateral negotiations were held under the Multi-fibre Arrangement (MFA, see WTO) with Asian producers, notably Hong Kong, the Republic of Korea and Macau. Agreements were eventually reached involving reductions in clothing quotas and 'anti-surge' clauses to prevent flooding of European markets. In 1986 new bilateral negotiations were held and agreements were reached with the principal Asian textile exporters, for the period 1987–91 (later extended to December 1993, when the 'Uruguay Round' of GATT negotiations was finally concluded): in most cases a slight increase in quotas was permitted. Under the conclusions of the Uruguay Round, the MFA was to be progressively eliminated over a 10-year period. In January 1995 bilateral textiles agreements, signed by the EU with India, Pakistan and the PRC, specified certain trade liberalization measures to be undertaken, including an increase of the PRC's silk export quota to 38,000 metric tons and a removal of trade barriers on small-business and handloom textile products from India, while including commitments from the Asian countries for greater efforts to combat textile and design fraud.

Numerous discussions have been held since 1981 on the Community's increasing trade deficit with Japan, and on the failure of the Japanese market to accept more European exports. In July 1991 the heads of government of Japan and of the EC signed a joint declaration on closer co-operation in both economic and political matters. In the same month an agreement was reached on limiting exports of Japanese cars to the EC until the end of 1999. The agreement did not include vehicles produced in Europe by Japanese companies. The Vulcanus programme, launched in June 1995 by the European Commission and the Japanese Ministry of International Trade and Industry, aimed to foster links with Japan through the hosting of Japanese advanced students by European companies. The European office of the EU-Japan Industrial Co-operation Centre was opened in Brussels in June 1996; the Centre, which was established in 1987 as a joint venture between the Japanese Government and the European Commission, sought to boost industrial co-operation between the EU and Japan and foster business contacts between companies and universities. In October 1996 the WTO upheld a long-standing complaint brought by the EU that Japanese taxes on alcoholic spirits discriminated against certain European products. In January 1998 an EU-Japan summit meeting was held, followed by a meeting at ministerial level in October. Subsequent summits (the ninth was held in July 2000) have aimed to strengthen dialogue.

In Feburary 2000, in support of a UN Security Council Resolution to that effect, the European Council adopted a regulation prohibiting flights in EU airspace by airlines controlled by the Afghan Taliban, and freezing Taliban funds and other financial resources. The EU also adopted resolutions expressing concern at the nature of the Taliban regime and at the situation then prevailing in Afghanistan. In 2001 ECHO allocated €54.7m. in assistance for that country.

In 2000 the EU contributed €19m. to a Trust Fund established by the World Bank to finance reconstruction activities in East Timor. In December the EU hosted the third multilateral conference of donors to the territory.

Regular consultations are held with Australia at ministerial level. In January 1996 the Commission proposed a framework agreement to formalize the EU's trade and political relationship with that country. However, in September negotiations were suspended, following the Australian Government's objections to the human rights clause contained in all EU international agreements. In June 1997 a joint declaration was signed, committing both sides to greater political, cultural and economic co-operation. Despite intensive negotiations between the EU and the New Zealand Government in 1996, no conclusion was reached regarding import duties. In March 1997 New Zealand took the case to the WTO, which later ruled against the EU. A joint declaration detailing areas of co-operation and establishing a consultative framework to facilitate the development of these was signed in May 1999. Mutual recognition agreements were also signed with Australia and New Zealand in 1999, with the aim of facilitating bilateral trade in industrial products.

CANADA AND THE USA

A framework agreement for commercial and economic co-operation between the Community and Canada was signed in Ottawa in 1976. It was superseded in 1990 by a Declaration on EC-Canada Relations. In 1995 relations with Canada were strained as a result of a dispute regarding fishing rights in the north-west Atlantic Ocean. An agreement on a new division of quotas between EU and Canadian fishermen was concluded in April (see above under Fisheries). In February 1996 the Commission proposed closer ties with Canada, and an action plan including early warning to avoid trade disputes, elimination of trade barriers, and promotion of business contacts. An action plan and joint political declaration were signed in December. In 1996 and 1997 negotiations took place over the use of leg-hold traps in the Canadian hunting and fur industry. In July 1997 an agreement was reached, limiting their use.

A number of specific agreements have been concluded between the Community and the USA: a co-operation agreement on the peaceful use of atomic energy entered into force in 1959, and agreements on environmental matters and on fisheries came into force in 1974 and 1984 respectively. Additional agreements provide for co-operation in other fields of scientific research and development, while bilateral contacts take place in many areas not covered by a formal agreement.

The USA has frequently criticized the Common Agricultural Policy, which it sees as creating unfair competition for American exports by its system of export refunds and preferential agreements. A similar criticism has been levelled at Community subsidies to the steel industry. In October 1985 and September 1986 agreements were reached on Community exports of steel to the USA until September 1989 (subsequently extended until March 1992). In January 1993 the USA announced the imposition of substantial duties on imports of steel from 19 countries, including seven EC member states, as an 'anti-dumping' measure. Meanwhile, a further trade dispute emerged between the EC and the USA regarding the liberalization of public procurement of services (e.g. telecommunications, transport and power). In early December the EC and the USA undertook intensive trade negotiations, which facilitated the conclusion of GATT's Uruguay Round of talks by the deadline of 15 December.

A 'Transatlantic Declaration' on EC-US relations was agreed in November 1990: the two parties agreed to consult each other on important matters of common interest, and to increase formal contacts. A new Trans-Atlantic Agenda for EU-US relations was signed by the US President and the Presidents of the European Commission and European Council at a meeting in Madrid, Spain, in December 1995. In October 1996 EU ministers of foreign affairs agreed to pursue in the WTO a complaint regarding the effects on European businesses of the USA's trade embargo against Cuba, formulated in the Helms-Burton Act. In April 1997 the EU and the USA approved a temporary resolution of the Helms-Burton dispute, whereby the US Administration was to limit the application of sanctions in return for a formal suspension of the WTO case. In mid-1996 the US Congress had adopted legislation imposing an additional trade embargo (threatening sanctions against any foreign company investing more than US $40m. in energy projects in a number of prescribed states, including Iran and Libya), the presence of which further complicated the EU-US debate in September 1997, when a French petroleum company, Total, provoked US anger, owing to its proposed investment in an Iranian natural gas project. In May 1998 an EU-USA summit meeting reached agreement on a 'Trans-Atlantic Economic Partnership' (TEP), to remove technical trade barriers, eliminate industrial tariffs, establish a free-trade area in services, and further liberalize measures relating to government procurement, intellectual property and investment. The agricultural and audio-visual sectors were to be excluded from the agreement. Initial objections from France were overcome when the EU and the USA reached a resolution to the dispute on sanctions legislation. The USA agreed to exempt European companies from the trade embargo on Iran and Libya, and to seek congressional approval for an indefinite waiver for the Helms-Burton Act, thereby removing the threat of sanctions from Total. The EU had allowed the WTO case to lapse in April, but it warned that a new WTO panel would be established if the USA took action against European companies trading with Cuba. In return, the EU agreed to increase co-operation in combating terrorism and the proliferation of weapons of mass destruction and to discourage investment in expropriated property. Following approval by the Council in November, it was agreed that implementation of the TEP would begin in advance of an EU-USA summit meeting in December. The EU-USA summit meeting held in June 1999 issued the 'Bonn Declaration', pledging a 'full and equal partnership' in economic, political and security matters.

In July 1997 the EU became involved in intensive negotiations with the US aircraft company, Boeing, over fears that its planned merger with McDonnell Douglas would harm European interests. In late July the EU approved the merger, after Boeing accepted concessions including an agreement to dispense with exclusivity clauses for 20-year supply contracts and to maintain McDonnell Douglas as a separate company for a period of 10 years. In June the EU and the USA agreed to introduce a mutual recognition agreement, which was to enable goods (including medicines, pharmaceutical products, telecommunications equipment and electrical apparatus) undergoing tests in Europe to be marketed in the USA or Canada without the need for further testing. In May 1997 the WTO upheld a US complaint against the EU's ban on imports of hormone-treated beef, which had led to a retaliatory US ban on meat imports from the EU. Negotiations took place in 1998 regarding the enforcement of European meat hygiene regulations (see under Agriculture), the reform of the EU's banana import regime (see Lomé Convention, below) and the application of a data protection law, which empowers national regulators to stop the transfer of personal information to countries judged to have inadequate data protection arrangements (including the USA). In July the Commission submitted a complaint to the WTO regarding tax exemptions granted to US companies exporting goods via subsidiaries established in tax-free countries (foreign sales corporations). Agreement on the banana dispute was eventually reached in May 2001. In early March 2002 the EU protested strongly against, and determined to launch a complaint at the WTO regarding, a US decision to stringently restrict steel imports from the rest of the world.

GENERALIZED PREFERENCES

In July 1971 the Community introduced a system of generalized tariff preferences (GSP) in favour of developing countries, ensuring duty-free entry to the EC of all otherwise dutiable manufactured and semi-manufactured industrial products, including textiles—but subject in certain circumstances to preferential limits. Preferences, usually in the form of a tariff reduction, are also offered on some agricultural products. In 1980 the Council agreed to the extension of the scheme for a second decade (1981–90): at the same time it adopted an operational framework for industrial products, which gives individual preferential limits based on the degree of competitiveness of the developing country concerned. From the end of 1990 an interim scheme was in operation, pending the introduction of a revised scheme based on the outcome of the 'Uruguay Round' of GATT negotiations on international trade (which were finally concluded in December 1993). Since 1977 the Community has progressively liberalized GSP access for the least-developed countries by according them duty-free entry on all products and by exempting them from virtually all preferential limits. In 1992–93 the GSP was extended to Albania, the Baltic states, the CIS and Georgia; in September 1994 it was extended to South Africa.

In December 1994 the European Council adopted a revised GSP to operate during 1995–98. It provided additional trade benefits to encourage the introduction by governments of environmentally sound policies and of internationally-recognized labour standards. Conversely, a country's preferential entitlement could be withdrawn, for example, if it permitted forced labour. Under the new scheme preferential tariffs amounted to 85% of the common customs duty for very sensitive products (for example, most textile products), and 70% or 35% for products classified as sensitive (for example, chemicals, electrical goods). The common customs duty was suspended for non-sensitive products (for example, paper, books, cosmetics). In accordance with the EU's foreign policy objective of focusing on the development of the world's poorest countries, duties were eliminated in their entirety for 49 least-developed countries. Duties were also suspended for a further five Latin American countries, conditional on the implementation of campaigns against the production and trade of illegal drugs.

A new GSP for 1999–2001 largely extended the existing scheme unchanged. The next GSP regulation, for 2002–04, was revised to expand product coverage and improve preferential margins.

AID TO DEVELOPING AND NON-EU COUNTRIES

The main channels for Community aid to developing countries are the Cotonou Agreement (see below) and the Mediterranean Financial Protocols, but technical and financial aid, and assistance for refugees, training, trade promotion and co-operation in industry, energy, science and technology is also provided to about 30 countries in Asia and Latin America. The EC International Investment Partners facility, established in 1988, promotes private-sector investment in Asian, Latin American and Mediterranean countries, especially in the form of joint ventures. The European Community Humanitarian Office (ECHO) was established in 1991 with a mandate to co-ordinate emergency aid provided by the Community and became fully operational in early 1993. ECHO finances operations conducted by non-governmental organizations and international agencies, with which it works in partnership. In 2000 the EU provided humanitarian aid worth €491.8m., of which 35% was allocated to ACP countries, 20% to the former Yugoslavia, 16% to Asia and 10% to the Middle East and North Africa. In April 1999 ECHO signed a framework partnership agreement with the International Federation of Red Cross and Red Crescent Societies to promote effective co-operation in the provision of humanitarian assistance.

EU-ACP PARTNERSHIP

From 1976 to February 2000 the principal means of co-operation between the Community and developing countries were the Lomé Conventions, concluded by the EU and African, Caribbean and Pacific (ACP) countries. The First Lomé Convention (Lomé I), which was concluded at Lomé, Togo, in February 1975 and came into force on 1 April 1976, replaced the Yaoundé Conventions and the Arusha Agreement. Lomé I was designed to provide a new framework of co-operation, taking into account the varying needs of developing African, Caribbean and Pacific (ACP) countries. The Second Lomé Convention entered into force on 1 January 1981. The Third Lomé Convention came into force on 1 March 1985 (trade provisions) and 1 May 1986 (aid). The Fourth Lomé Convention, which had a 10-year commitment period, was signed in December 1989: its trade provisions entered into force on 1 March 1990, and the remainder entered into force in September 1991. In June 2000, meeting in Cotonou, Benin, EU and ACP heads of state and government concluded a new 20-year partnership accord with 77 ACP states. The so-called Cotonou Agreement was to enter into effect once it had been ratified by the European Parliament and by the ACP national legislatures. By February 2002 38 ACP countries and four EU member states had ratified the Agreement.

ACP-EU Institutions

Council of Ministers: one minister from each signatory state; one co-chairman from each of the two groups; meets annually.

Committee of Ambassadors: one ambassador from each signatory state; chairmanship alternates between the two groups; meets at least every six months.

Joint Assembly: EU and ACP are equally represented; attended by parliamentary delegates from each of the ACP countries and an equal number of members of the European Parliament; one co-chairman from each of the two groups; meets twice a year.

Secretariat of the ACP-EU Council of Ministers: 175 rue de la Loi, 1048 Brussels; tel. (2) 285-61-11; fax (2) 285-74-58.

Centre for the Development of Industry (CDI): 52 ave Herrmann Debroux, 1160 Brussels, Belgium; tel. (2) 679-18-11; fax (2) 675-26-03; e-mail director@cdi.be; internet www.cdi.be; f. 1977 to encourage and support the creation, expansion and restructuring of industrial companies (mainly in the fields of manufacturing and agro-industry) in the ACP states by promoting co-operation between ACP and European companies, in the form of financial, technical or commercial partnership, management contracts, licensing or franchise agreements, sub-contracts, etc.; Dir FERNANDO MATOS ROSA.

Technical Centre for Agricultural and Rural Co-operation: Postbus 380, 6700 AJ Wageningen, Netherlands; tel. (317) 467100; fax (317) 460067; e-mail cta@cta.nl; internet www.agricta.org; f. 1983 to provide ACP states with better access to information, research, training and innovations in agricultural development and extension; Dir CARL B. GREENIDGE.

ACP Institutions

ACP Council of Ministers.

ACP Committee of Ambassadors.

ACP Secretariat: ACP House, 451 ave Georges Henri, Brussels, Belgium; tel. (2) 743-06-00; fax (2) 735-55-73; e-mail info@acpsec.org; internet www.acpsec.org; Sec.-Gen. JEAN-ROBERT GOULONGANA (Gabon).

The ACP States (at July 2000)

Angola	Eritrea
Antigua and Barbuda	Ethiopia
Bahamas	Fiji
Barbados	Gabon
Belize	The Gambia
Benin	Ghana
Botswana	Grenada
Burkina Faso	Guinea
Burundi	Guinea-Bissau
Cameroon	Guyana
Cape Verde	Haiti
Central African Republic	Jamaica
Chad	Kenya
Comoros	Kiribati
Congo, Democratic Republic	Lesotho
Congo, Republic	Liberia
Cook Islands	Madagascar
Côte d'Ivoire	Malawi
Djibouti	Mali
Dominica	Marshall Islands
Dominican Republic	Mauritania
Equatorial Guinea	Mauritius

Federated States of Micronesia	Seychelles
Mozambique	Sierra Leone
Namibia	Solomon Islands
Nauru	Somalia
Niger	South Africa
Nigeria	Sudan
Niue	Suriname
Palau	Swaziland
Papua New Guinea	Tanzania
Rwanda	Togo
Saint Christopher and Nevis	Tonga
Saint Lucia	Trinidad and Tobago
Saint Vincent and the Grenadines	Tuvalu
Samoa	Uganda
São Tomé and Príncipe	Vanuatu
Senegal	Western Samoa
	Zambia
	Zimbabwe

Under Lomé I, the Community committed ECU 3,052.4m. for aid and investment in developing countries, through the European Development Fund (EDF) and the European Investment Bank (EIB). Provision was made for over 99% of ACP (mainly agricultural) exports to enter the EC market duty free, while certain products which compete directly with Community agriculture, such as sugar, were given preferential treatment but not free access. The Stabex (Stabilization of Export Earnings) scheme was designed to help developing countries to withstand fluctuations in the price of their agricultural products, by paying compensation for reduced export earnings.

The Second Lomé Convention (1981–85) envisaged Community expenditure of ECU 5,530m.: it extended some of the provisions of Lomé I, and introduced new fields of co-operation, including a scheme (Sysmin) to safeguard exports of mineral products.

Lomé III made commitments of ECU 8,500m., including loans of ECU 1,100m. from the EIB. Innovations included an emphasis on agriculture and fisheries, and measures to combat desertification; assistance for rehabilitating existing industries or sectoral improvements; improvements in the efficiency of the Stabex system (now covering a list of 48 agricultural products) and of Sysmin; simplification of the rules of origin of products; the promotion of private investment; co-operation in transport and communications; cultural and social co-operation; restructuring of emergency aid, and more efficient procedures for technical and financial assistance.

The Fourth Lomé Convention was to cover the period 1990–99 (subsequently extended to February 2000). The budget for financial and technical co-operation for 1990–95 amounted to ECU 12,000m., of which ECU 10,800m. was from the EDF (including ECU 1,500m. for Stabex and ECU 480m. for Sysmin) and ECU 1,200m. from the EIB. The budget for the second five years was ECU 14,625m., of which ECU 12,967m. was from the EDF, and ECU 1,658m. from the EIB. Under Lomé IV, the obligation of most of the ACP states to contribute to the replenishment of STABEX resources, including the repayment of transfers made under the first three Conventions, was removed. In addition, special loans made to ACP member countries were to be cancelled, except in the case of profit-orientated businesses. Other innovations included the provision of assistance for structural adjustment programmes (amounting to ECU 1,150m.); increased support for the private sector, environmental protection, and control of growth in population; and measures to avoid increasing the recipient countries' indebtedness (e.g. by providing Stabex and Sysmin assistance in the form of grants, rather than loans).

On 1 July 1993 the EC introduced a regime covering the import of bananas into the Community. This was designed to protect the banana industries of ACP countries (mostly in the Caribbean), which were threatened by the availability of cheaper bananas, produced by countries in Latin America. The new regime guaranteed 30% of the European market to ACP producers, and established an annual quota of 2m. metric tons for bananas imported from Latin America, which would incur a uniform duty of 20%, while imports above this level were to be subject to a tariff of ECU 850 per ton. In February 1994 a dispute panel of GATT upheld a complaint, brought by five Latin American countries, that the EU banana import regime was in contravention of free-trade principles. An agreement was reached in March, under which the EU increased the annual quota for Latin American banana imports to 2.1m. tons with effect from October 1994, and to 2.2m. tons in 1995. However, in 1995 the USA, supported by Guatemala, Honduras and Mexico (and subsequently by Ecuador), filed a complaint with the WTO against the EU's banana regime. In May 1997 the WTO concluded that the EU banana import regime violated 19 free-trade regulations. The EU appealed against the ruling in July, but in September the WTO's dispute settlement body endorsed the original verdict. However, the allocation of preferential tariffs to ACP producers, covered by a waiver since late 1994, was upheld. In October 1997 the EU agreed to amend its banana import regime to comply with the WTO ruling. An arbitration report, published in January 1998, compelled the EU to implement changes by 1 January 1999. In June 1998 EU ministers of agriculture approved a reform of the import regime, providing for two separate quota systems, granting Latin American producers greater access to the European market, with a quota of 2.53m. tons (at a tariff of ECU 75 per ton), while ACP countries would have a quota of 857,000 tons (tariff-free). The quota systems, which were to apply from 1 January 1999, were approved by the Commission in October. However, in November the USA proposed the imposition of duties of 100% on a number of European imports, in protest at the reform, which it continued to regard as discriminatory and incompatible with WTO provisions. In February 1999 the EU requested that a WTO panel be established to investigate the validity of the clause of the US Trade Act that permitted the imposition of retaliatory sanctions (considered by the EU to be in breach of the WTO dispute settlement procedure). In March, however, the USA imposed provisional measures against a diverse range of EU products, prompting the EU to issue a complaint with the WTO. In April an arbitration panel of the WTO confirmed that the EU had failed to conform its banana regime with WTO rules and formally authorized the USA to impose trade sanctions, valued at US $191.4m. In November the Commission proposed a radical reform of the EU's banana regime, involving the gradual dismantling of the existing quota system and its replacement with a tariff system that would open the banana market to other competitors. However, US trade representatives indicated that the USA would find the reforms unacceptable. A satisfactory accord, involving the adoption by the EU of a new system of licences and quotas to cover the period 2001–06 and the introduction of a new tariff-only system from 2006, was eventually reached by the EU and USA in April 2001, subject to approval by EU member states; the USA consequently agreed to suspend its punitive trade sanctions.

In September 1993 the Community announced plans to revise and strengthen its relations with the ACP countries under the Lomé Convention. In May 1994 representatives of EU member states and ACP countries initiated the mid-term review of Lomé IV. The Community reiterated its intention to maintain the Convention as an aid instrument but emphasized that stricter conditions relating to the awarding of aid would be imposed, based on standards of human rights, human resource development and environmental protection. However, negotiations between EU and ACP states were adjourned in February 1995, owing to disagreements among EU states concerning reimbursement of the EDF in the period 1995–2000. In June the European Council agreed to provide ECU 14,625m. for the second phase of Lomé IV, of which ECU 12,967m. was to be allocated from the EDF and ECU 1,658m. in loans from the EIB. Agreement was also reached on revision of the 'country-of-origin' rules for manufactured goods, a new protocol on the sustainable management of forest resources and a joint declaration on support for the banana industry. The agreement was subsequently endorsed by an EU-ACP ministerial group, and the revised Convention was signed in November, in Mauritius. In March 1997 the Commission proposed granting debt relief assistance of ECU 25m. each year for the period 1997–2000 to the 11 heavily-indebted poor countries (as identified by the World Bank and the IMF) forming part of the ACP group. Funding was to be used to support international efforts to reduce debt and encourage the economic prospects of such countries. In May 2001 the EU announced that it would cancel all outstanding debts arising from its trade accords with former colonies of member states. It was believed that the loans made under the Lomé Conventions could be as high as US $200m.

In June 1995 negotiations opened with a view to concluding a wide-ranging trade and co-operation agreement with South Africa, including the eventual creation of a free-trade area (FTA). The accord was approved by heads of state and of government in March 1999, after agreement was reached to eliminate progressively, over a 12-year period, the use of the terms 'port' and 'sherry' to describe South African fortified wines. The accord provided for the removal of duties from about 99% of South Africa's industrial exports and some 75% of its agricultural products within 10 years, while South Africa was to liberalize its market for some 86% of EU industrial goods (with protection for the motor vehicle and textiles industries), within a 12-year period. The accord also introduced increased development assistance for South Africa after 1999. Implementation of the accord was delayed in January 2000 after some member states refused to ratify it unless South Africa also agreed to abandon the use of names such as 'ouzo' and 'grappa'. A duty-free quota for exports of South African wine was suspended pending a resolution. The dispute was eventually resolved in February. In March 1997 the Commission approved a Special Protocol for South Africa's accession to the Lomé Convention, and in April South Africa attained partial membership. Full membership was withheld, as South Africa was not regarded as, in all respects, a developing country, and was therefore not entitled to aid provisions. A special provision was introduced into the revised Lomé Convention to allow Somalia to accede, should constitutional government be established in that country prior to the expiry of the Convention.

Intensive debate took place from 1995 on the future of relations between the ACP states and the EU, in view of the increasingly global nature of the EU's foreign policies, and particular the growing emphasis it was placing on relations with central and eastern Europe and countries of the Mediterranean rim. In November 1996 the Commission published a consultative document to consider the options for future ACP-EU relations. The document focused on the areas of trade, aid and politics, and included proposals to encourage competitiveness, to support private-sector investment and to enhance democracy. The report suggested abolishing or restructuring Stabex and Sysmin, and considered altering the grouping of the ACP states for the purpose of implementing economic agreements. The ultimate aim of the document was to foster conditions in which the EU and the ACP countries could co-exist as equal partners. In November 1997 the first summit of heads of state of ACP countries was held in Libreville, Gabon. The ACP council of ministers prepared a mandate for negotiations towards a renewed Lomé Convention, which was approved by the Commission in January 1998. The Joint Assembly of ACP ministers, meeting in Mauritius in April, and the ACP-EU Council of Ministers, meeting in Barbados in May, discussed proposals for future ACP-EU relations after the expiry of Lomé IV. The ACP states emphasized that they should be regarded as a single entity, with recognition for the individual requirements of each region, and that any renewed partnership should continue to support the elimination of poverty as its main objective. In late June EU ministers of foreign affairs approved preliminary directives for the negotiation of a new partnership agreement. The ministers agreed to allow Cuba to participate in the negotiations, with observer status, but emphasized that their decision would have no influence on any future accession discussions should Cuba wish to join the Lomé Convention. In November Cuba formally applied for full membership. Formal negotiations on the conclusion of a successor agreement to the Lomé Convention were initiated at the end of September and were concluded in February 2000: the new partnership accord was signed by ACP and EU heads of state and government in June of that year in Cotonou, Benin. The so-called Cotonou Agreement was to enter into effect following ratification by the European Parliament and the ACP national legislatures, and was to cover the period 2000–20. It comprised the following main elements: increased political co-operation; the enhanced participation of civil society in ACP–EC partnership affairs; a strong focus on the reduction of poverty (addressing the economic and technical marginalization of developing nations was a primary concern); reform of the existing structures for financial co-operation; and a new framework for economic and trade co-operation. Under the provisions of the new accord, the EU was to negotiate free-trade arrangements (replacing the previous non-reciprocal trade preferences) with the most developed ACP countries during 2000–08; these would be structured around a system of regional free-trade zones, and would be designed to ensure full compatibility with WTO provisions. Once in force, the agreements would be subject to revision every five years. An assessment to be conducted in 2004 would identify those mid-ranking ACP nations also capable of entering into such free-trade deals. Meanwhile, the least-developed ACP nations were to benefit from an EU initiative to allow free access for most of their products by 2005. The preferential agreements currently in force would be retained initially (phase I), in view of a waiver granted by the WTO; thereafter ACP–EU trade was to be gradually liberalized over a period of 12–15 years (phase II). It was envisaged that Stabex and Sysmin would be eliminated gradually.

The first meeting of the ACP–EU Joint Parliamentary Assembly following the signing of the Cotonou Agreement was held in Brussels in October 2000. In total, the EU provided €3,612m. in financing for ACP countries in 2000. The EDF had funds of €13,500m. to cover the first five years of operation of the Cotonou Agreement. In February 2001 the EU agreed to phase out trade barriers on imports of everything but military weapons from the world's 48 least developed countries, 39 of which were in the ACP group. Duties on sugar, rice, bananas and some other products were to remain until 2009.

Finance

THE COMMUNITY BUDGET

The general budget of the European Union covers all EEC and Euratom expenditure and the administrative expenditure of the ECSC. The Commission is responsible for implementing the budget. (The ECSC, like the EIB, has its own resources and conducts its own financial operations.) Under the Council decision of 24 June 1988 all revenue (except that expressly designated for supplementary research and technological development programmes) is used without distinction to finance all expenditure, and all budget expenditure must be covered in full by the revenue entered in the budget. Any amendment of this decision requires the unanimous approval of the Council and must be ratified by the member states. The Treaty of Rome requires member states to release funds to cover the appropriations entered in the budget.

Each Community institution draws up estimates of its expenditure, and sends them to the Commission before 1 July of the year preceding the financial year (1 January–31 December) in question. The Commission consolidates these estimates in a preliminary draft budget, which it sends to the Council by 1 September. Expenditure is divided into two categories: that necessarily resulting from the Treaties (compulsory expenditure) and other (non-compulsory) expenditure. The draft budget must be approved by a qualified majority in the Council, and presented to Parliament by 5 October. Parliament may propose modifications to compulsory expenditure, and may (within the limits of the 'maximum rate of increase', dependent on growth of member states' gross national product—GNP—and budgets) amend non-compulsory expenditure. The budget must normally be declared finally adopted 75 days after the draft is presented to Parliament. If the budget has not been adopted by the beginning of the financial year, monthly expenditure may amount to one-twelfth of the appropriations adopted for the previous year's budget. The Commission may (even late in the year during which the budget is being executed) revise estimates of revenue and expenditure, by presenting supplementary and/or amending budgets.

Expenditure under the general budget is financed by 'own resources', comprising agricultural duties (on imports of agricultural produce from non-member states), customs duties, application of value-added tax (VAT) on goods and services, and (since 1988) a levy based on the GNP of member states. Member states are obliged to collect 'own resources' on the Community's behalf. From May 1985 arrangements were introduced for the correction of budgetary imbalances, as a result of which the United Kingdom received compensation in the form of reductions in VAT payments. In 1988 it was decided by the Community's heads of government to set a maximum amount for 'own resources' that might be called up in any one year.

The general budget contains the expenditures of the six main Community institutions—the Commission, the Council, Parliament, the Court of Justice, the Court of Auditors, and the Economic and Social Committee and the Committee of the Regions—of which Commission expenditure (covering administrative costs and expenditure on operations) forms the largest proportion. The Common Agricultural Policy accounts for about 50% of total expenditure, principally in agricultural guarantees. In 1988 it was decided (as part of a system of budgetary discipline agreed by the Council) that the rate of increase in spending on agricultural guarantees between 1988 and a given year was not to exceed 74% of the growth rate of Community GNP during the same period. In December 1992 it was agreed to increase the upper limit on Community expenditure from 1.2% of the EC's combined GNP to 1.27% in 1999. 'Agenda 2000', concerning financial arrangements for the period 2000–2006, proposed maintaining the limit at 1.27% from 2000. In December 1994, taking into account the enlargement of the EU to 15 countries (from 1 January 1995) it was agreed to set a level of maximum expenditure at ECU 75,500m. in 1995, increasing to ECU 87,000m. in 1999, at constant 1992 prices. Agenda 2000 proposed that maximum annual expenditure would increase to €104,600m. at 1999 prices, by 2006.

The general budget for 2002, adopted in December 2001, allocated €98,635m. in total commitment appropriations, of which €5.2m.were for administration, €44.3m. for agriculture, € 33.8m. for structural operations, €6.6m. for internal policies, €4.8m. for external action, and €3.3m. for pre-accession assistance.

STRUCTURAL FUNDS

The Community's 'structural funds' comprise the Guidance Section of the European Agricultural Guidance and Guarantee Fund, the European Regional Development Fund, the European Social Fund and the Cohesion Fund. There is also a financial instrument for fisheries guidance, commitments for which amounted to ECU 308.2m. in 1997. In accordance with the Single European Act (1987), reforms of the Community's structural funds were adopted by the Council with effect from 1 January 1989, with the aim of more accurate identification of priority targets, and greater selectivity to enable action to be concentrated in the least-favoured regions (see Social Policy, p. 196). In December 1992 it was agreed that total 'structural' expenditure would be increased to ECU 30,000m. per year by 1999, at constant 1992 prices. 'Agenda 2000', which was approved by the Council in March 1999, provided for the reform of the structural funds to make available some €213,000m. for 2000–2006, at 1999 prices.

Cohesion Fund

The Treaty on European Union and its protocol on economic and social cohesion provided for the establishment of a 'cohesion fund', which began operating on 1 April 1993, with a budget of ECU 1,500m. for the first year. This was to subsidize projects in the fields of the environment and trans-European energy and communications networks in member states with a per caput GNP of less than 90% of the Community average (in practice, this was to mean Greece, Ireland, Portugal and Spain). Commitments under the fund in the budget appropriations for 2002 amounted to €2,789m. The fund's total budget for the period 2000–06 was €18,000m.

European Agricultural Guidance and Guarantee Fund (EAGGF)—Guidance Section

Created in 1962, the European Agricultural Guidance and Guarantee Fund is administered by the Commission. The Guidance section covers expenditure on Community aid for projects to improve farming conditions in the member states. It includes aid for poor rural areas and the structural adjustment of rural areas, particularly in the context of the reform of the common agricultural policy (CAP). This aid is usually granted in the form of financial contributions to programmes also supported by the member governments themselves.

European Regional Development Fund—ERDF

Payments began in 1975. The Fund is intended to compensate for the unequal rate of development in different regions of the Community, by encouraging investment and improving infrastructure in 'problem regions'.

European Social Fund

Internet: europa.eu.int/comm/dgo5/esf/en/index.htm.

The Fund (established in 1960) provides resources with the aim of combating long-term unemployment and facilitating the integration into the labour market of young people and the socially disadvantaged. It also supports schemes to help workers to adapt to industrial changes. The fund's total budget for the period 1994–99 was ECU 47,000m.

Publications*

Bulletin of the European Union (10 a year).

The Courier (every 2 months, on ACP-EU affairs).

European Economy (every 6 months, with supplements).

European Voice (weekly).

General Report on the Activities of the European Union (annually).

Official Journal of the European Communities.

Publications of the European Communities (quarterly).

EUR-Lex Website (treaties, legislation and judgments, europa.eu.int/eur-lex/en/index.html).

Information sheets, background reports and statistical documents.

* Most publications are available in all the official languages of the Union. They are obtainable from the Office for Official Publications of the European Communities, 2 rue Mercier, 2985 Luxembourg; tel. 29291; fax 495719; e-mail europ@opoce.cec.be; internet eur-op.eu.int.

Summary of the Treaty establishing the European Coal and Steel Community (Treaty of Paris)

(effective from 25 July 1952; as amended by subsequent treaties, including the Merger Treaty, the Treaty on European Union and the Treaty of Amsterdam)

Note: The Treaty establishing the European Coal and Steel Community was due to expire in July 2002, and in 1991 the Council of Ministers agreed that, by that date, the provisions of the Treaty should be incorporated in the Treaty establishing the European Economic Community (the Treaty of Rome), on the grounds that it was no longer appropriate to treat the coal and steel sectors separately.

TITLE I: THE EUROPEAN COAL AND STEEL COMMUNITY

Articles 1–6

By this Treaty, the High Contracting Parties establish among themselves a European Coal and Steel Community, founded upon a common market, common objectives and common institutions. The European Coal and Steel Community shall have as its task to contribute, in harmony with the general economy of the Member States and through the establishment of a common market as provided in this Treaty, to economic expansion, growth of employment and a rising standard of living in the Member States. The Community shall bring about conditions which will of themselves ensure the most rational distribution of production at the highest possible level of productivity, while safeguarding continuity of employment and taking care not to provoke fundamental and persistent disturbances in the economies of Member States.

The institutions of the Community shall, within the limits of their respective powers, in the common interest:

(a) ensure an orderly supply to the common market, taking into account the needs of third countries;
(b) ensure that all comparably placed consumers in the common market have equal access to the sources of production;
(c) ensure the establishment of the lowest prices under such conditions that these prices do not result in higher prices charged by the same undertakings in other transactions or in a higher general price level at another time, while allowing necessary amortization and normal return on invested capital;
(d) ensure the maintenance of conditions which will encourage undertakings to expand and improve their production potential and to promote a policy of using natural resources rationally and avoiding their unconsidered exhaustion;
(e) promote improved working conditions and an improvedstandard of living for the workers in each of the industries for which it is responsible, so as to make possible their harmonization while the improvement is being maintained;
(f) promote the growth of international trade and ensure that equitable limits are observed in export pricing;
(g) promote the orderly expansion and modernization of production, and the improvement of quality, with no protection against competing industries that is not justified by improper action on their part or in their favour.

The following are recognized as incompatible with the common market for coal and steel and shall accordingly be prohibited within the Community, as provided in this Treaty:

(a) import and export duties, or charges having equivalent effect, and quantitative restrictions on the movement of products;
(b) measures or practices which discriminate between producers, between purchasers or between consumers, especially in prices and delivery terms or transport rates and conditions, and measures or practices which interfere with the purchaser's free choice of supplier;
(c) subsidies or aids granted by States, or special charges imposed by States, in any form whatsoever;
(d) restrictive practices which tend towards the sharing or exploiting of markets.

TITLE II: THE INSTITUTIONS OF THE COMMUNITY

Articles 7–45

The institutions of the Community shall be:

a Commission,
a European Parliament,
a Council,
a Court of Justice,
a Court of Auditors.

The Commission shall be assisted by a Consultative Committee.

In order to carry out the tasks assigned to it the Commission shall, in accordance with the provisions of this Treaty, take decisions, make recommendations or deliver opinions. Decisions shall be binding in their entirety. Recommendations shall be binding as to the aims to be pursued but shall leave the choice of the appropriate methods for achieving these aims to those to whom the recommendations are addressed. Opinions shall have no binding force.

TITLE III: ECONOMIC AND SOCIAL PROVISIONS

General Provisions

Articles 46–48

To provide guidance, in line with the tasks assigned to the Community, on the course of action to be followed by all concerned, and to determine its own course of action, in accordance with the provisions of this Treaty, the Commission shall, in consultation:

1. conduct a continuous study of market and price trends;
2. periodically draw up programmes indicating foreseeable developments in production, consumption, exports and imports;
3. periodically lay down general objectives for modernization, long-term planning of manufacture and expansion of productive capacity;
4. take part, at the request of the Governments concerned, in studying the possibilities for re-employing, in existing industries or through the creation of new activities, workers made redundant by market developments or technical changes;
5. obtain the information it requires to assess the possibilities for improving working conditions and living standards for workers in the industries within its province, and the threats to those standards.

Financial Provisions

Articles 49–53

The Commission is empowered to procure the funds it requires to carry out its tasks by imposing levies on the production of coal and steel and by contracting loans. It may receive gifts. The levies shall be assessed annually on the various products according to their average value; the rate thereof shall not, however, exceed 1% unless previously authorized by the Council, acting by a two-thirds majority. The mode of assessment and collection shall be determined by a general decision of the Commission taken after consulting the Council; cumulative imposition shall be avoided as far as possible.

Investment and Financial Aid

Articles 54–56

The Commission may facilitate the carrying out of investment programmes by granting loans to undertakings or by guaranteeing other loans which they may contract. It shall promote technical and economic research relating to the production and increased use of coal and steel and to occupational safety in the coal and steel industries. To this end it shall organize all appropriate contacts among existing research bodies.

If the introduction, within the framework of the general objectives of the Commission, of new technical processes or equipment should lead to an exceptionally large reduction in labour requirements in the coal or the steel industry, making it particularly difficult in one or more areas to re-employ redundant workers, the Commission, on application by the Governments concerned:

(a) shall obtain the opinion of the Consultative Committee;
(b) may facilitate, either in the industries within its jurisdiction or, with the assent of the Council, in any other industry, the financing of such programmes as it may approve for the creation of new and economically sound activities capable of reabsorbing the redundant workers into productive employment;
(c) shall provide: non-repayable aid towards the payment of tide-over allowances to workers, the payment of resettlement allowances to workers, the financing of vocational retraining for workers having to change their employment.

Production

Articles 57–59

In the sphere of production, the Commission shall give preference to the indirect means of action at its disposal, such as co-operation with Governments to regularize or influence general consumption, particularly that of the public services, and intervention in regard to prices and commercial policy as provided for in this Treaty.

In the event of a decline in demand, if the Commission considers that the Community is confronted with a period of manifest crisis and that the means of action provided for above are not sufficient to deal with this, it shall, after consulting the Consultative Committee and with the assent of the Council, establish a system of production quotas.

The Commission may impose fines upon undertakings which do not comply with decisions taken by it.

Prices

Articles 60–64

Pricing practices contrary to the Articles of this Treaty shall be prohibited, in particular:

unfair competitive practices, especially purely temporary or purely local price reductions tending towards the acquisition of a monopoly position within the common market;

discriminatory practices involving, within the common market, the application by a seller of dissimilar conditions to comparable transactions, especially on the grounds of the nationality of the buyer.

The Commission may, for one or more of the products within its jurisdiction:

(a) fix maximum prices within the common market, if it finds that such a decision is necessary to attain the objectives set out in this Treaty;

(b) fix minimum prices within the common market, if it finds that a manifest crisis exists or is imminent and that such a decision is necessary to attain the objectives of the Treaty.

(c) fix, by methods appropriate to the nature of the export markets, minimum or maximum export prices.

Agreements and Concentrations

Articles 65–66

All agreements between undertakings, decisions by associations of undertakings and concerted practices tending directly or indirectly to prevent, restrict or distort normal competition within the common market shall be prohibited, and in particular those tending to fix or determine prices, to restrict or control production, technical development or investment, and to share markets, products, customers or sources of supply. However, the Commission shall authorize specialization agreements or joint-buying or joint-selling agreements in respect of particular products if it finds that:

(a) such specialization or such joint-buying or -selling will make for substantial improvement in the production or distribution of those products;

(b) the agreement in question is essential in order to achieve these results and is not more restrictive than is necessary for that purpose; and

(c) the agreement is not liable to give the undertakings concerned the power to determine the prices, or to control or restrict the production or marketing, of a substantial part of the products in question within the common market, or to shield them against effective competition from other undertakings within the common market.

If the Commission finds that public or private undertakings which, in law or in fact, hold or acquire in the market for one of the products within its jurisdiction a dominant position shielding them against effective competition in a substantial part of the common market are using that position for purposes contrary to the objectives of the Treaty, it shall make to them such recommendations as may be appropriate to prevent the position from being so used. If these recommendations are not implemented satisfactorily within a reasonable time, the Commission shall, by decisions taken in consultation with the Government concerned, determine the prices and conditions of sale to be applied by the undertaking in question or draw up production or delivery programmes with which it must comply, subject to liability to the penalties provided for in this Treaty.

Interference with Conditions of Competition

Article 67

Any action by a Member State which is liable to have appreciable repercussions on conditions of competition in the coal or the steel industry shall be brought to the knowledge of the Commission by the Government concerned. If the action taken by that State is having harmful effects on the coal or steel undertakings within the jurisdiction of that State, the Commission may authorize it to grant aid to these undertakings. If the action taken by that State is having harmful effects on the coal or steel undertakings within the jurisdiction of other Member States, the Commission shall make a recommendation to that State with a view to remedying these effects by such measures as that State may consider most compatible with its own economic equilibrium.

Wages and Movement of Workers

Articles 68–69

The methods used for fixing wages and welfare benefits in the several Member States shall not, in the case of the coal and steel industries, be affected by this Treaty, subject to provisions.

Member States undertake to remove any restriction based on nationality upon the employment in the coal and steel industries of workers who are nationals of Member States and have recognized qualifications in a coalmining or steelmaking occupation, subject to the limitations imposed by the basic requirements of health and public policy. They shall prohibit any discrimination in remuneration and working conditions between nationals and immigrant workers.

Transport

Article 70

It is recognized that the establishment of the common market necessitates the application of such rates and conditions for the carriage of coal and steel as will afford comparable price conditions to comparably placed consumers. Any discrimination in rates and conditions of carriage of every kind which is based on the country of origin or destination of products shall be prohibited in traffic between Member States.

Commercial Policy

Articles 71–75

The powers of the Governments of Member States in matters of commercial policy shall not be affected by this Treaty, save as otherwise provided therein. The powers conferred on the Community by this Treaty in matters of commercial policy towards third countries may not exceed those accorded to Member States under international agreements to which they are parties. The Governments of Member States shall afford each other such mutual assistance as is necessary to implement measures recognized by the Commission as being in accordance with this Treaty and with existing international agreements.

Minimum rates below which Member States undertake not to lower their customs duties on coal and steel as against third countries, and maximum rates above which they undertake not to raise them, may be fixed by decision of the Council acting on a proposal from the Commission.

TITLE IV: GENERAL PROVISIONS

Articles 76–100

The Community shall enjoy in the territories of the Member States such privileges and immunities as are necessary for the performance of its tasks, under the conditions laid down in the Protocol annexed to this Treaty on the privileges and immunities of the European Communities.

The financial year shall run from 1 January to 31 December. Each institution of the Community shall, before 1 July, draw up estimates of its administrative expenditure. The Commission shall consolidate these estimates in a preliminary draft administrative budget.

This Treaty shall apply to the European territories of the High Contracting Parties. It shall also apply to European territories for whose external relations a signatory State is responsible, subject to certain exceptions stipulated in Treaties of Accession of new Member States. Each High Contracting Party undertakes to extend to the other Member States the preferential treatment which it enjoys with respect to coal and steel in the non-European territories under its jurisdiction.

The establishment of the Community shall in no way prejudice the system of ownership of the undertakings to which this Treaty applies.

Member States undertake to take all appropriate measures, whether general or particular, to ensure fulfilment of the obligations resulting from decisions and recommendations of the institutions of the Community and to facilitate the performance of the Community's tasks.

Officials of the Commission entrusted by it with tasks of inspection shall enjoy in the territories of Member States, to the full extent required for the performance of their duties, such rights and powers as are granted by the laws of these States to their own revenue officials.

If a State has not fulfilled its obligation under this Treaty by the time limit set by the Commission, or if it brings an action which is dismissed, the Commission may, with the assent of the Council acting by a two-thirds majority:

(a) suspend the payment of any sums which it may be liable to pay to the State in question under this Treaty;

(b) take measures, or authorize the other Member States to take measures, in order to correct the effects of the infringement of the obligation.

Decisions of the Commission which impose a pecuniary obligation shall be enforceable.

Where a decision has been taken to suspend the voting rights of the representative of the government of a Member State in accordance with Article F.1 (2) of the Treaty on European Union, these voting rights shall also be suspended with regard to this Treaty.

This Treaty shall expire on 23 July 2002.

Summary of the Treaty establishing the European Atomic Energy Community (Treaty of Rome)

(Effective from 1 January 1958; as amended by subsequent treaties, including the Merger Treaty, the Treaty on European Union and the Treaty of Amsterdam)

TITLE I: THE TASKS OF THE COMMUNITY

Articles 1–3

By this Treaty the High Contracting Parties establish among themselves a European Atomic Energy Community (Euratom). It shall be the task of the Community to contribute to the raising of the standard of living in the Member States and to the development of relations with the other countries by creating the conditions necessary for the speedy establishment and growth of nuclear industries. In order to perform its task, the Community shall, as provided in this Treaty:

(a) promote research and ensure the dissemination of technical information;

(b) establish uniform safety standards to protect the health of workers and of the general public and ensure that they are applied;

(c) facilitate investment and ensure, particularly by encouraging ventures on the part of undertakings, the establishment of the basic installations necessary for the development of nuclear energy in the Community;

(d) ensure that all users in the Community receive a regular and equitable supply of ores and nuclear fuels;

(e) make certain, by appropriate supervision, that nuclear materials are not diverted to purposes other than those for which they are intended;

(f) exercise the right of ownership conferred upon it with respect to special fissile materials;

(g) ensure wide commercial outlets and access to the best technical facilities by the creation of a common market in specialized materials and equipment, by the free movement of capital for investment in the field of nuclear energy and by freedom of employment for specialists within the Community;

(h) establish with other countries and international organizations such relations as will foster progress in the peaceful uses of nuclear energy.

The tasks entrusted to the Community shall be carried out by the following institutions:

a European Parliament,
a Council,
a Commission,
a Court of Justice,
a Court of Auditors.

The Council and the Commission shall be assisted by an Economic and Social Committee acting in an advisory capacity.

TITLE II: PROVISIONS FOR THE ENCOURAGEMENT OF PROGRESS IN THE FIELD OF NUCLEAR ENERGY

Promotion of Research

Articles 4–11

The Commission shall be responsible for promoting and facilitating nuclear research in the Member States and for complementing it by carrying out a Community research and training programme. To encourage the carrying out of research programmes communicated to it the Commission may:

(a) provide financial assistance within the framework of research contracts, without, however, offering subsidies;

(b) supply, either free of charge or against payment, for carrying out such programmes, any source materials or special fissile materials which it has available;

(c) place installations, equipment or expert assistance at the disposal of Member States, persons or undertakings, either free of charge or against payment;

(d) promote joint financing by the Member States, persons or undertakings concerned.

After consulting the Scientific and Technical Committee, the Commission shall establish a Joint Nuclear Research Centre. The Centre shall ensure that a uniform nuclear terminology and a standard system of measurements are established.

Dissemination of Information

Articles 12–29

Information over which the Community has power of disposal

Member States, persons or undertakings shall have the right, on application to the Commission, to obtain non-exclusive licences under patents, provisionally protected patent rights, utility models or patent applications owned by the Community, where they are able to make effective use of the inventions covered thereby. Under the same conditions, the Commission shall grant sub-licences under patents, provisionally protected patent rights, utility models or patent applications, where the Community holds contractual licences conferring power to do so.

Security provisions

Information which the Community acquires as a result of carrying out its research programme, and the disclosure of which is liable to harm the defence interests of one or more Member States, shall be subject to a security system in accordance with the provisions of this Treaty.

Health and Safety

Articles 30–39

Basic standards shall be laid down within the Community for the protection of the health of workers and the general public against the dangers arising from ionizing radiations. Each Member State shall lay down the appropriate provisions, whether by legislation, regulation or administrative action, to ensure compliance with the basic standards which have been established and shall take the necessary measures with regard to teaching, education and vocational training; shall establish the facilities necessary to carry out continuous monitoring of the level of radioactivity in the air, water and soil and to ensure compliance with the basic standards; and shall provide the Commission with such general data relating to any plan for the disposal of radioactive waste in whatever form as will make it possible to determine whether the implementation of such plan is liable to result in the radioactive contamination of the water, soil or airspace of another Member State.

Investment

Articles 40–44

In order to stimulate action by persons and undertakings and to facilitate co-ordinated development of their investment in the nuclear field, the Commission shall periodically publish illustrative programmes indicating in particular nuclear energy production targets and all the types of investment required for their attainment.

Joint Undertakings

Articles 45–51

Undertakings which are of fundamental importance to the development of the nuclear industry in the Community may be established as Joint Undertakings. Every project for establishing a Joint Undertaking, whether originating from the Commission, a Member State or any other quarter, shall be the subject of an inquiry by the Commission, and shall be established by Council decision.

Supplies

Articles 52–76

The supply of ores, source materials and special fissile materials shall be ensured, in accordance with the provisions of this Treaty, by means of a common supply policy on the principle of equal access to sources of supply. For this purpose all practices designed to secure a privileged position for certain users shall be prohibited, and an Agency is hereby established; it shall have a right of option on ores, source materials and special fissile materials produced in the territories of Member States and an exclusive right to conclude contracts relating to the supply of ores, source materials and special fissile materials coming from inside the Community or from outside.

The Agency

The Agency shall be under the supervision of the Commission, which shall issue directives to it, possess a right of veto over its decisions and appoint its Director-General and Deputy Director-General. The Member States shall be responsible for ensuring that the Agency may operate freely in their territories.

Ores, source materials and special fissile materials coming from inside the Community

Special fissile materials may be exported only through the Agency. Potential users shall periodically inform the Agency of the supplies they require, specifying the quantities, the physical and chemical nature, the place of origin, the intended use, delivery dates and price terms, which are to form the terms and conditions of the supply contract which they wish to conclude. Similarly, producers shall inform the Agency of offers which they are able to make, stating all the specifications, and in particular the duration of contracts, required to enable their production programmes to be drawn up. The Agency shall inform all potential users of the offers and of the volume of applications which it has received, and when the Agency has received all such orders, it shall make known the terms on which it can meet them. If the Agency cannot meet in their entirety all the orders received, it shall share out the supplies proportionately among the orders relating to each offer. Agency rules, which shall require approval by the Commission, shall determine the manner in which demand is to be balanced against supply.

Ores, source materials and special fissile materials coming from outside the Community

The Agency, acting where appropriate within the framework of agreements concluded between the Community and a third State or an international organization, shall, subject to the exceptions provided for in this Treaty, have the exclusive right to enter into agreements or contracts whose principal aim is the supply of ores, source materials or special fissile materials coming from outside the Community.

Prices

Save where exceptions are provided for in this Treaty, prices shall be determined as a result of balancing supply against demand. Pricing practices designed to secure a privileged position for certain users in violation of the principle of equal access laid down in the provisions of this Chapter shall be prohibited. The Council may fix prices.

Provisions relating to supply policy

The Commission may give financial support to prospecting programmes in the territories of Member States. If, although the prospects for extraction appear economically justified on a long-term basis, prospecting activities and the expansion of mining operations continue to be markedly inadequate, the Member State concerned shall, for as long as it has failed to remedy this situation, be deemed to have waived, both for itself and for its nationals, the right of equal access to other sources of supply within the Community.

Safeguards

Articles 77–85

The Commission shall satisfy itself that, in the territories of Member States,

(a) ores, source materials and special fissile materials are not diverted from their intended uses as declared by the users;

(b) the provisions relating to supply and any particular safeguarding obligations assumed by the Community under an agreement concluded with a third State or an international organization are complied with.

The Commission may send inspectors into the territories of Member States, who shall at all times have access to all places and data and to all persons who, by reason of their occupation, deal with materials, equipment or installations. In the event of an infringement on the part of persons or undertakings of the obligations imposed on them by these conditions, the Commission may impose sanctions on such persons or undertakings. Decisions taken by the Commission shall be enforceable.

Property Ownership

Articles 86–91

Special fissile materials shall be the property of the Community, and Member States, persons or undertakings shall have the unlimited right of use and consumption of special fissile materials which have properly come into their possession.

The Nuclear Common Market

Articles 92–100

Member States shall prohibit between themselves all customs duties on imports and exports or charges having equivalent effect, and all quantitative restrictions on imports and exports for the goods and products covered by this Treaty. Non-European territories under the jurisdiction of a Member State may, however, continue to levy import and export duties or charges having equivalent effect where they are of an exclusively fiscal nature. The rates of such duties and charges and the system governing them shall not give rise to any discrimination between that State and the other Member States.

The Member States shall abolish all restrictions based on nationality affecting the right of nationals of any Member State to take skilled employment in the field of nuclear energy, subject to the limitations resulting from the basic requirements of public policy, public security or public health.

External Relations

Articles 101–106

The Community may, within the limits of its powers and jurisdiction, enter into obligations by concluding agreements or contracts with a third State, an international organization or a national of a third State. No person or undertaking concluding or renewing an agreement or contract with a third State, an international organization or a national of a third State after 1 January 1958 or, for acceding States, after the date of their accession, may invoke that agreement or contract in order to evade the obligations imposed by this Treaty.

TITLE III: PROVISIONS GOVERNING THE INSTITUTIONS

Articles 107–160

The Council and the Commission shall consult each other and shall settle by common accord their methods of co-operation. The Commission shall adopt its rules of procedure so as to ensure that both it and its departments operate in accordance with the provisions of this Treaty. It shall ensure that these rules are published.

Provisions Common to Several Institutions

Articles 161–164

In order to carry out their task the Council and the Commission shall, in accordance with the provisions of this Treaty, make regulations, issue directives, take decisions, make recommendations or deliver opinions. A regulation shall have general application. It shall be binding in its entirety and directly applicable in all Member States. A directive shall be binding, as to the result to be achieved, upon each Member State to which it is addressed, but shall leave to the national authorities the choice of form and methods. A decision shall be binding in its entirety upon those to whom it is addressed. Recommendations and opinions shall have no binding force.

The Economic and Social Committee

Articles 165–170

An Economic and Social Committee is hereby established. It shall have advisory status. The committee shall consist of representatives of the various categories of economic and social activity. The Committee may be consulted by the European Parliament.

TITLE IV: FINANCIAL PROVISIONS

Articles 171–183

Estimates shall be drawn up for each financial year of all revenue and expenditure of the Community, other than those of the Agency and the Joint Undertakings, and such revenue and expenditure shall be shown either in the operating budget or in the research and investment budget. The revenue and expenditure shown in each budget shall be in balance. The revenue and expenditure of the Agency, which shall operate in accordance with commercial principles, shall be budgeted for in a special account. Without prejudice to other revenue, the budget shall be financed wholly from own resources.

TITLE V: GENERAL PROVISIONS

Articles 184–208

In each of the Member States, the Community shall enjoy the most extensive legal capacity accorded to legal persons under their laws; it may, in particular, acquire or dispose of movable and immovable property and may be a party to legal proceedings. To this end, the Community shall be represented by the Commission.

The officials and other servants of the European Coal and Steel Community, the European Economic Community and the European Atomic Energy Community shall, at the date of entry into force of this Treaty, become officials and other servants of the European Communities and form part of the single administration of these Communities.

The European Communities shall enjoy in the territories of the Member States such privileges and immunities as are necessary for the performance of their tasks, under the conditions laid down in the Protocol annexed to this Treaty. The same shall apply to the European Investment Bank.

Member States shall take all appropriate measures, whether general or particular, to ensure fulfilment of the obligations arising out of this Treaty or resulting from action taken by the institutions of the Community. They shall facilitate the achievement of the Community's tasks. They shall abstain from any measure which could jeopardize the attainment of the objectives of this Treaty. The institutions of the Community, the Agency and the Joint Undertakings shall, in applying this Treaty, comply with the conditions of access to ores, source materials and special fissile materials laid down in national rules and regulations made for reasons of public policy or public health.

Save as otherwise provided, this Treaty shall apply to the European territories of Member States and to non-European territories under their jurisdiction. It shall also apply to the European territories for whose external relations a Member State is responsible, subject to certain exceptions stipulated in Treaties of Accession of new Member States.

It shall be for the Commission to ensure the maintenance of all appropriate relations with the organs of the United Nations, of its specialized agencies and of the World Trade Organization; it shall also maintain such relations as are appropriate with all international organizations. The Community shall establish all appropriate forms of co-operation with the Council of Europe, and shall establish close co-operation with the Organisation for Economic Co-operation and Development, the details to be determined by common accord. The provisions of this Treaty shall not preclude the existence or completion of regional unions between Belgium and Luxembourg, or between Belgium, Luxembourg and the Netherlands, to the extent that the objectives of these regional unions are not attained by application of this Treaty.

Where a decision has been taken to suspend the voting rights of the representative of the government of a Member State in accordance with Article 7 (2) of the Treaty on European Union, these voting rights shall also be suspended with regard to this Treaty.

The Community may conclude with one or more States or international organizations agreements establishing an association involving reciprocal rights and obligations, common action and special procedures. These agreements shall be concluded by the Council, acting unanimously after consulting the European Parliament.

This Treaty is concluded for an unlimited period.

Summary of the Treaty establishing the European Economic Community (Treaty of Rome)

(effective from 1 January 1958; as amended by subsequent treaties, including the Merger Treaty, the Single European Act, the Treaty on European Union and the Treaty of Amsterdam)

Note: The Treaty of Amsterdam, as well as providing in its Part One for substantive amendments to the Treaty of Rome, in its Part Two amended the Treaty and its annexes and protocols, for the purpose of deleting lapsed provisions of the Treaty and adapting in consequence the text of certain of its provisions. It also renumbered the Articles of the Treaty to take into account those Articles which had been inserted or had lapsed.

The first paragraphs of Article 8 of the Treaty on European Union read as follows:

The Treaty establishing the European Economic Community shall be amended in accordance with the provisions of this Article, in order to establish a European Community.

Throughout the Treaty: The term 'European Economic Community' shall be replaced by the term 'European Community'.

PART ONE: PRINCIPLES

Articles 1–16

The Community shall have as its task, by establishing a common market and an economic and monetary union and by implementing the common policies or activities referred to in Articles 3 and 4, to promote throughout the Community a harmonious, balanced and sustainable development of economic activities, a high level of employment and of social protection, equality between men and women, sustainable and non-inflationary growth, a high degree of competitiveness and convergence of economic performance, a high level of protection and improvement of the quality of the environment, the raising of the standard of living and quality of life, and economic and social cohesion and solidarity among Member States. With these aims in view, the activities of the Community will include:

(a) the prohibition between Member States of customs duties and of quantitative restrictions in regard to the importation and exportation of goods, as well as of all other measures with equivalent effect;
(b) a common commercial policy;
(c) an internal market characterized by the abolition, as between Member States, of obstacles to the free movement of goods, persons, services and capital;
(d) measures concerning the entry and movement of persons as provided for in Title IV;
(e) a common policy in the sphere of agriculture and fisheries;
(f) a common policy in the sphere of transport;
(g) a system ensuring that competition in the internal market is not distorted;
(h) the approximation of the laws of Member States to the extent required for the functioning of the common market;
(i) the promotion of co-ordination between employment policies of the Member States with a view to enhancing their effectiveness by developing a co-ordinated strategy for employment;
(j) a policy in the social sphere comprising a European Social Fund;
(k) the strengthening of economic and social cohesion;
(l) a policy in the sphere of the environment;
(m) the strengthening of the competitiveness of Community industry;
(n) the promotion of research and technological development;
(o) encouragement for the establishment and development of trans-European networks;
(p) a contribution to the attainment of a high level of health protection;
(q) a contribution to education and training of quality and to the flowering of the cultures of the Member States;
(r) a policy in the sphere of development co-operation;
(s) the association of the overseas countries and territories in order to increase trade and promote jointly economic and social development;
(t) a contribution to the strengthening of consumer protection; and
(u) measures in the spheres of energy, civil protection and tourism.

In all the activities referred to in this Article, the Community shall aim to eliminate inequalities, and to promote equality, between men and women.

Environmental protection requirements must be integrated into the definition and implementation of the Community policies and activities referred to in Article 3, in particular with a view to promoting sustainable development.

Member States which intend to establish closer co-operation between themselves may be authorized, subject to Articles 43 and 44 of the Treaty on European Union, to make use of the institutions, procedures and mechanisms laid down by this Treaty.

The activities of the Member States and the Community shall include the adoption of an economic policy which is based on the close co-ordination of Member States' economic policies, on the internal market and on the definition of common objectives, and conducted in accordance with the principle of an open market economy with free competition. These activities shall include the irrevocable fixing of exchange rates leading to the introduction of a single currency, the ECU, and the definition and conduct of a single monetary policy and exchange-rate policy the primary objective of both of which shall be to maintain price stability and, without prejudice to this objective, to support the general economic policies in the Community, in accordance with the principle of an open market economy with free competition. These activities of the Member States and the Community shall entail compliance with the following guiding principles: stable prices, sound public finances and monetary conditions and a sustainable balance of payments.

The Community shall act within the limits of the powers conferred upon it by this Treaty and of the objectives assigned to it therein.

In areas which do not fall within its exclusive competence, the Community shall take action, in accordance with the principle of subsidiarity, only if and in so far as the objectives of the proposed action cannot be sufficiently achieved by the Member States and can therefore, by reason of the scale or effects of the proposed action, be better achieved by the Community.

Any action by the Community shall not go beyond what is necessary to achieve the objectives of this Treaty.

The tasks entrusted to the Community shall be carried out by the following institutions: a European Parliament; a Council; a Commission; a Court of Justice; a Court of Auditors. A European System of Central Banks (ESCB) and a European Central Bank (ECB) shall be established. A European Investment Bank is hereby established.

The Council, acting unanimously on a proposal from the Commission and after consulting the European Parliament, may take appropriate action to combat discrimination based on sex, racial or ethnic origin, religion or belief, disability, age or sexual orientation.

The Community shall adopt measures with the aim of progressively establishing the internal market over a period expiring on 31 December 1992.

PART TWO: CITIZENSHIP OF THE UNION

Articles 17–22

Citizenship of the Union is hereby established. Every person holding the nationality of a Member State shall be a citizen of the Union. Citizenship of the Union shall complement and not replace national citizenship. Every citizen of the Union shall have the right to move and reside freely within the territory of the Member States, subject to the limitations and conditions laid down in this Treaty and by the measures adopted to give it effect. Every citizen of the Union residing in a Member State of which he is not a national shall have the right to vote and to stand as a candidate at municipal elections and elections to the European Parliament in the Member State in which he resides, under the same conditions as nationals of that State. Every citizen of the Union shall, in the territory of a third country in which the Member State of which he is a national is not represented, be entitled to protection by the diplomatic or consular authorities of any Member State, on the same conditions as the nationals of that State.

PART THREE: COMMUNITY POLICIES

Title I: Free Movement of Goods

The Customs Union

Articles 23–27

Customs duties on imports and exports and charges having equivalent effect shall be prohibited between Member States. This prohibition shall also apply to customs duties of a fiscal nature.

Common Customs Tariff duties shall be fixed by the Council acting by a qualified majority on a proposal from the Commission.

Prohibition of Quantitative Restrictions between Member States

Articles 28–31

Quantitative restrictions on imports and all measures having equivalent effect shall be prohibited between Member States. Quantitative restrictions on exports, and all measures having equivalent effect, shall be prohibited between Member States. These provisions shall not be an obstacle to prohibitions or restrictions in respect of importation, exportation or transit which are justified on grounds of public morality, health or safety, the protection of human or animal life or health, the preservation of plant life, the protection of national treasures of artistic, historic or archaeological value or the protection of industrial and commercial property. Such prohibitions or restrictions shall not, however, constitute either a means of arbitrary discrimination or a disguised restriction on trade between Member States. Member States shall adjust any state monopolies of a commercial character in such a manner as will ensure the exclusion of all discrimination between the nationals of Member States in regard to conditions of supply and marketing of goods. These provisions shall apply to any body by means of which a Member State shall *de jure* or *de facto,* either directly or indirectly, control or appreciably influence importation or exportation between Member States, and also to monopolies assigned by the state. In the case of a commercial monopoly which is accompanied by regulations designed to facilitate the marketing or the valorization of agricultural products, it should be ensured that in the application of these provisions equivalent guarantees are provided in respect of the employment and standard of living of the producers concerned.

Title II: Agriculture

Articles 32–38

The common market shall extend to agriculture and trade in agricultural products. The common agricultural policy shall have as its objectives:

(a) the increase of agricultural productivity by developing technical progress and by ensuring the rational development of agricultural production and the optimum utilization of the factors of production, particularly labour;
(b) the ensurance thereby of a fair standard of living for the agricultural population;
(c) the stabilization of markets;
(d) regular supplies;
(e) reasonable prices in supplies to consumers.

Due account must be taken of the particular character of agricultural activities, arising from the social structure of agriculture and from structural and natural disparities between the various agricultural regions; of the need to make the appropriate adjustments gradually; and of the fact that in Member States agriculture constitutes a sector which is closely linked with the economy as a whole. In order to attain the objectives of a common agricultural policy, a common organization of agricultural markets shall be effected.

Title III: Free Movement of Persons, Services and Capital

Workers

Articles 39–42

The free movement of workers shall be ensured within the Community, involving the abolition of any discrimination based on nationality between workers of the Member States as regards employment, remuneration and other working conditions. This shall include the right to accept offers of employment actually made, to move about freely for this purpose within the territory of the Member States, to stay in any Member State in order to carry on an employment in conformity with the legislative and administrative provisions governing the employment of the workers of that State, and to live, on conditions which shall be the subject of implementing regulations laid down by the Commission, in the territory of a Member State after having been employed there. (These provisions do not apply to employment in the public administration.)

In the field of social security, the Council shall adopt the measures necessary to effect the free movement of workers. To this end, it shall make arrangements to secure for migrant workers and their dependants aggregation, for the purpose of acquiring and retaining the right to benefit and of calculating the amount of benefit, of all periods taken into account under the laws of the several countries; and payment of benefits to persons resident in the territories of Member States.

Right of Establishment

Articles 43–48

Restrictions on the freedom of establishment of nationals of a Member State in the territory of another Member State shall be prohibited, nor may any new restrictions of a similar character be introduced. Such prohibition shall also extend to restrictions on the setting-up of agencies, branches or subsidiaries. Freedom of establishment shall include the right to engage in and carry on non-wage-earning activities and also to set up and manage enterprises and companies under the conditions laid down by the law of the country of establishment for its own nationals, subject to the provisions of this Treaty relating to capital.

Services

Articles 49–55

Restrictions on the free supply of services within the Community shall be prohibited in respect of nationals of Member States who are established in a state of the Community other than that of the person to whom the services are supplied; no new restrictions of a similar character may be introduced.

The Council, acting by a qualified majority on a proposal of the Commission, may extend the benefit of these provisions to cover services supplied by nationals of any third country who are established within the Community.

Particular services involved are activities of an industrial or artisan character and those of the liberal professions.

Capital

Articles 56–60

Within the framework of the provisions set out in this Chapter, all restrictions on the movement of capital between Member States and between Member States and third countries shall be prohibited.

Title IV: Visas, Asylum, Immigration and Other Policies Related to Free Movement of Persons

Articles 61–69

In order to establish progressively an area of freedom, security and justice, the Council shall adopt within a period of five years after the entry into force of the Treaty of Amsterdam, measures aimed at ensuring the free movement of persons, in conjunction with directly related flanking measures with respect to external border controls, asylum and immigration, and measures to prevent and combat crime; other measures in the fields of asylum, immigration and safeguarding the rights of nationals of third countries; measures in the field of judicial co-operation in civil matters; appropriate measures to encourage and strengthen administrative co-operation; and measures in the field of police and judicial co-operation in criminal matters aimed at a high level of security by preventing and combating crime with the Union.

The Council shall, within a period of five years after the entry into force of the Treaty of Amsterdam, adopt measures with a view to ensuring the absence of any controls on the persons, be they citizens of the Union or nationals of third countries, when crossing internal borders; and measures on the crossing of the external borders of the Member States.

The Council shall, within a period of five years after the entry into force of the Treaty of Amsterdam, adopt measures on asylum, in accordance with the Geneva Convention of 28 July 1951 and the Protocol of 31 January 1967 relating to the status of refugees and other relevant treaties; measures on refugees and displaced persons who cannot return to their country of origin or who otherwise need international protection; measures on immigration policy; and measures defining the rights and conditions under which nationals of third countries who are legally resident in a Member State may reside in other Member States.

The application of this Title shall be subject to the provisions of the Protocol on the position of the United Kingdom and Ireland and to the Protocol on the position of Denmark.

Title V: Transport

Articles 70–80

With a view to establishing a common transport policy, the Council of Ministers shall, acting in accordance with the procedure referred to in Article 251 and after consulting the Economic and Social Committee and the Committee of the Regions, lay down common rules applicable to international transport to or from the territory of a Member State or passing across the territory of one or more Member States, conditions under which non-resident carriers may operate transport services within a Member State, measures to improve transport safety and any other appropriate provisions. Until these have been enacted and unless the Council of Ministers gives its unanimous consent, no Member State shall apply the various provisions governing this subject on 1 January 1958 or, for acceding States, the date of their accession in such a way as to make them less favourable, in their direct or indirect effect, for carriers of other Member States by comparison with its own national carriers.

Any discrimination which consists in the application by a carrier, in respect of the same goods conveyed in the same circumstances, of transport rates and conditions which differ on the ground of the country of origin or destination of the goods carried, shall be abolished in the traffic of the Community.

A Committee with consultative status, composed of experts appointed by the Governments of the Member States, shall be established and attached to the Commission, without prejudice to the powers of the Economic and Social Committee.

Title VI: Common Rules on Competition, Taxation and Approximation of Laws

Rules on Competition

Articles 81–89

Rules applying to undertakings:

The following practices by enterprises are prohibited: the direct or indirect fixing of purchase or selling prices or of any other trading conditions; the limitation of control of production, markets, technical development of investment; market-sharing or the sharing of sources of supply; the application to parties to transactions of unequal terms in respect of equivalent supplies, thereby placing them at a competitive disadvantage; the subjection of the conclusion of a contract to the acceptance by a party of additional supplies which, either by their nature or according to commercial usage, have no connection with the subject of such contract. The provisions may be declared inapplicable if the agreements neither impose on the enterprises concerned any restrictions not indispensable to the attainment of improved production, distribution or technical progress, nor enable enterprises to eliminate competition in respect of a substantial proportion of the goods concerned.

Aids granted by States:

Any aid granted by a Member State or granted by means of State resources which is contrary to the purposes of the Treaty is forbidden. The following shall be deemed to be compatible with the common market:

(a) aids of a social character granted without discrimination to individual consumers;

(b) aids intended to remedy damage caused by natural calamities or other extraordinary events;

(c) aids granted to the economy of certain regions of the Federal German Republic affected by the division of Germany, to the extent that they are necessary to compensate for the economic disadvantages caused by the division.

The following may be deemed to be compatible with the common market:

(a) aids intended to promote the economic development of regions where the standard of living is abnormally low or where there exists serious underemployment;

(b) aids intended to promote the execution of important projects of common European interest or to remedy a serious economic disturbance of the economy of a Member State;

(c) aids intended to facilitate the development of certain activities or of certain economic regions, provided that such aids do not change trading conditions to such a degree as would be contrary to the common interest;

(d) aid to promote culture and heritage conservation where such aid does not affect trading conditions and competition in the Community to an extent that is contrary to the common interest;

(e) such other categories of aids as may be specified by a decision of the Council of Ministers acting on a proposal of the Commission.

The Commission is charged to examine constantly all systems of aids existing in the Member States, and may require any Member State to abolish or modify any aid which it finds to be in conflict with the principles of the common market.

Tax Provisions

Articles 90–93

A Member State shall not impose, directly or indirectly, on the products of other Member States, any internal charges of any kind in excess of those applied directly or indirectly to like domestic products. Furthermore, a Member State shall not impose on the product of other Member States any internal charges of such a nature as to afford indirect protection to other productions. Products exported to any Member State may not benefit from any drawback on internal charges in excess of those charges imposed directly or indirectly on them.

Approximation of Laws

Articles 94–97

The Council shall, acting unanimously on a proposal of the Commission and after consulting the European Parliament and the Economic and Social Committee, issue directives for the approximation of such laws, regulations or administrative provisions of the Member States as directly affect the establishment or functioning of the common market.

Where the Commission finds that a difference between the provisions laid down by law, regulation or administrative action in Member States is distorting the conditions of competition in the common market and that the resultant distortion needs to be eliminated, it shall consult the Member States concerned. If such consultation does not result in an agreement, the Council shall, on a proposal from the Commission, acting by a qualified majority, issue the necessary directives.

Title VII: Economic and Monetary Policy

Economic Policy

Articles 98–104

Member States shall conduct their economic policies with a view to contributing to the achievement of the objectives of the Community. The Member States and the Community shall act in accordance with the principle of an open market economy with free competition, favouring an efficient allocation of resources.

Member States shall regard their economic policies as a matter of common concern and shall co-ordinate them within the Council. The Council shall, acting by a qualified majority on a recommendation from the Commission, formulate a draft for the broad guidelines of the economic policies of the Member States and of the Community, and shall report its findings to the European Council; the European Council shall discuss a conclusion on the broad guidelines of the economic policies of the Member States and of the Community; on the basis of this conclusion, the Council shall, acting by a qualified majority, adopt a recommendation setting out these broad guidelines. In order to ensure closer co-ordination of economic policies and sustained convergence of the economic performances of the Member States, the Council shall, on the basis of reports submitted by the Commission, monitor economic developments in each of the Member States and in the Community as well as the consistency of economic policies, and regularly carry out an overall assessment. Where it is established that the economic policies of a Member State are not consistent with the broad guidelines referred to above or that they risk jeopardizing the proper functioning of economic and monetary union, the Council may, acting by a qualified majority on a recommendation from the Commission, make the necessary recommendations to the Member State concerned.

The Council may, acting unanimously on a proposal from the Commission, decide upon the measures appropriate to the economic situation, in particular if severe difficulties arise in the supply of certain products. Where a Member State is in difficulties or is seriously threatened with severe difficulties caused by exceptional occurrences beyond its control, the Council may, acting unanimously on a proposal from the Commission, grant, under certain conditions, Community financial assistance to the

Member State concerned. Where the severe difficulties are caused by natural disasters, the Council shall act by qualified majority.

Overdraft facilities or any other type of credit facility with the ECB or with the central banks of the Member States in favour of Community institutions or bodies, central governments, regional, local or other public authorities, other bodies governed by public law, or public undertakings of Member States shall be prohibited, as shall the purchase directly from them by the ECB or national central banks of debt instruments. This shall not apply to publicly owned credit institutions which, in the context of the supply of reserves by central banks, shall be given the same treatment by national central banks and the ECB as private credit institutions.

Any measure, not based on prudential considerations, establishing privileged access by Community institutions or bodies, central governments, regional, local or other public authorities, other bodies governed by public law, or public undertakings of Member States to financial institutions shall be prohibited.

The Community shall not be liable for or assume the commitments of central governments, regional, local or other public authorities, other bodies governed by public law, or public undertakings of any Member State, without prejudice to mutual financial guarantees for the joint execution of a specific project. A Member State shall not be liable for or assume the commitments of central governments, regional, local or other public authorities, other bodies governed by public law or public undertakings of another Member State, without prejudice to mutual financial guarantees for the joint execution of a specific project.

Member States shall avoid excessive government deficits. The Commission shall monitor the development of the budgetary situation and of the stock of government debt in the Member States with a view to identifying gross errors. Where the existence of an excessive deficit is decided by the Council, acting by a qualified majority on a recommendation from the Commission, the Council shall make recommendations to the Member State concerned with a view to bringing that situation to an end within a given period. If a Member State persists in failing to put into practice the recommendations of the Council, the Council may decide to give notice to the Member State to take, within a specified time-limit, measures for the deficit reduction which is judged necessary by the Council in order to remedy the situation. As long as a Member State fails to comply with a decision taken in accordance with the above, the Council may decide to apply or, as the case may be, intensify one or more of the following measures: to require the Member State concerned to publish additional information, to be specified by the Council, before issuing bonds and securities; to invite the European Investment Bank to reconsider its lending policy towards the Member State concerned; to require the Member State concerned to make a non-interest-bearing deposit of an appropriate size with the Community until the excessive deficit has, in the view of the Council, been corrected; to impose fines of an appropriate size.

Monetary Policy

Articles 105–111

The primary objective of the European System of Central Banks (ESCB) shall be to maintain price stability. Without prejudice to the objective of price stability, the ESCB shall support the general economic policies in the Community with a view to contributing to the achievement of the objectives of the Community. The ESCB shall act in accordance with the principle of an open market economy with free competition, favouring an efficient allocation of resources, and in compliance with the principles set out in the Treaty. The basic tasks to be carried out through the ESCB shall be to define and implement the monetary policy of the Community, to conduct foreign-exchange operations, to hold and manage the official foreign reserves of the Member States and to promote the smooth operation of payment systems.

The ECB shall have the exclusive right to authorize the issue of banknotes within the Community. The ECB and the national central banks may issue such notes. Member States may issue coins subject to approval by the ECB of the volume of the issue.

In order to carry out the tasks entrusted to the ESCB, the ECB shall make regulations, take decisions, made recommendations and deliver opinions.

Institutional Provisions

Articles 112–115

In order to promote co-ordination of the policies of Member States to the full extent needed for the functioning of the internal market, a Monetary Committee with advisory status is hereby set up to keep under review the monetary and financial situation of the Member States and of the Community and the general payments system of the Member States and to report regularly thereon to the Council and to the Commission; to deliver opinions at the request of the Council or of the Commission, or on its own initiative for submission to those institutions; and to examine, at least once a year, the situation regarding the movement of capital and the freedom of payments, as they result from the application of this Treaty and of measures adopted by the Council. The Member States and the Commission shall each appoint two members of the Monetary Committee. At the start of the third stage, an Economic and Financial Committee shall be set up; the Monetary Committee shall be dissolved.

Transitional Provisions

Articles 116–124

The second stage for achieving economic and monetary union shall begin on 1 January 1994. Each Member State shall adopt, if necessary, multiannual programmes intended to ensure the lasting convergence necessary for the achievement of economic and monetary union, in particular with regard to price stability and sound public finances. Each Member State shall endeavour to avoid excessive government deficits, and shall, as appropriate, start the process leading to the independence of its central bank.

A European Monetary Institute (EMI) shall be established to strengthen co-operation between the national central banks; strengthen the co-ordination of monetary policies of the Member States, with the aim of ensuring price stability; monitor the functioning of the European Monetary System; hold consultations concerning issues falling within the competence of the national central banks and affecting the stability of financial institutions and markets; take over the tasks of the European Monetary Co-operation Fund, which shall be dissolved; and facilitate the use of the ECU and oversee its development, including the smooth functioning of the ECU clearing system. For the preparation of the third stage, the EMI shall prepare the instruments and the procedures necessary for carrying out a single monetary policy in the third stage; promote the harmonization, where necessary, of the rules and practices governing the collection, compilation and distribution of statistics in the areas within its field of competence; prepare the rules for operations to be undertaken by the national central banks within the framework of the ESCB; promote the efficiency of cross-border payments; and supervise the technical preparation of ECU banknotes.

The EMI may formulate opinions or recommendations; submit opinions or recommendations to governments and to the Council; and make recommendations to the monetary authorities of the Member States.

From the start of the third stage, the value of the ECU shall be irrevocably fixed in accordance with this Treaty.

Where a Member State is in difficulties or is seriously threatened with difficulties as regards its balance of payments, and where such difficulties are liable in particular to jeopardize the functioning of the common market or the progressive implementation of the common commercial policy, the Commission shall immediately investigate the position of the State in question and the action which, making use of all the means at its disposal, that State has taken or may take in accordance with the provisions of this Treaty. The Commission shall state what measures it recommends the State concerned to take.

The Commission and the EMI shall report to the Council on the progress made in the fulfilment by the Member States of their obligations regarding the achievement of economic and monetary union. The reports shall examine the achievement of a high degree of sustainable convergence. Taking due account of the reports and the opinion of the European Parliament, the Council, meeting in the composition of Heads of State or Government, shall, acting by a qualified majority, not later than 31 December 1996 decide whether a majority of the Member

States fulfil the necessary conditions for the adoption of a single currency; decide whether it is appropriate for the Community to enter the third stage; and if so set the date for the beginning of the third stage.

If the Council has confirmed which Member States fulfil the necessary conditions for the adoption of a single currency, those Member States which do not fulfil the conditions shall have a derogation.

At the starting date of the third stage, the Council shall, acting with the unanimity of the Member States without a derogation, on a proposal from the Commission and after consulting the ECB, adopt the conversion rates at which their currencies shall be irrevocably fixed and at which irrevocably fixed rate the ECU shall be substituted for these currencies, and the ECU will become a currency in its own right.

Title VIII: Employment

Articles 125–130

Member States and the Community shall work towards developing a co-ordinated strategy for employment and particularly for promoting a skilled, trained and adaptable workforce and labour markets responsive to economic change.

The European Council shall each year consider the employment situation in the Community and adopt conclusions thereon, on the basis of a joint annual report by the Council and the Commission. On the basis of the conclusions of the European Council, the Council, acting by a qualified majority on a proposal from the Commission and after consulting the European Parliament, the Economic and Social Committee, the Committee of the Regions and the Employment Committee referred to in Article 130, shall each year draw up guidelines which the Member States shall take into account in their employment policies.

The Council, after consulting the European Parliament, shall establish an Employment Committee with advisory status to promote co-ordination between Member States on employment and labour market policies. Each Member State and the Commission shall appoint two members of the Committee.

Title IX: Common Commercial Policy

Articles 131–134

The common commercial policy shall be based on uniform principles, particularly in regard to changes in tariff rates, the conclusion of tariff and trade agreements, the achievement of uniformity in measures of liberalization, export policy and measures to protect trade such as those to be taken in the event of dumping or subsidies. Where agreements with one or more States or international organizations need to be negotiated, the Commission shall make recommendations to the Council, which shall authorize the Commission to open the necessary negotiations.

In order to ensure that the execution of measures of commercial policy taken in accordance with this Treaty by any Member State is not obstructed by deflection of trade, or where differences between such measures lead to economic difficulties in one or more Member States, the Commission shall recommend the methods for the requisite co-operation between Member States. Failing this, the Commission may authorize Member States to take the necessary protective measures.

Title X: Customs Co-operation

Article 135

Within the scope of application of this Treaty, the Council shall take measures in order to strengthen customs co-operation between Member States and between the latter and the Commission. These measures shall not concern the application of national criminal law or the national administration of justice.

Title XI: Social Policy, Education, Vocational Training and Youth

Social provisions

Articles 136–145

The Community and the Member States, having in mind fundamental social rights such as those set out in the European Social Charter signed at Turin on 18 October 1961 and in the 1989 Community Charter of the Fundamental Social Rights of Workers, shall have as their objectives the promotion of employment, improved living and working conditions, so as to make possible their harmonization while the improvement is being maintained, proper social protection, dialogue between management and labour, the development of human resources with a view to lasting high employment and the combating of exclusion. To this end the Community and the Member States shall implement measures which take account of the diverse forms of national practices, in particular in the field of contractual relations, and the need to maintain the competitiveness of the Community economy.

The Commission shall have the task of promoting the consultation of management and labour at Community level and shall take any relevant measure to facilitate their dialogue by ensuring balanced support for the parties.

Each Member State shall ensure that the principle of equal pay for male and female workers for equal work or work of equal value is applied. With a view to ensuring full equality in practice between men and women in working life, the principle of equal treatment shall not prevent any Member State from maintaining or adopting measures providing for specific advantages in order to make it easier for the under-represented sex to pursue a vocational activity or to prevent or compensate for disadvantages in professional careers.

The European Social Fund

Articles 146–148

In order to improve employment opportunities for workers in the internal market and to contribute thereby to raising the standard of living, a European Social Fund is hereby established; it shall have the task of rendering the employment of workers easier and of increasing their geographical and occupational mobility within the Community, and to facilitate their adaptation to industrial changes and to changes in production systems, in particular through vocational training and retraining. The Fund shall be administered by the Commission. The Council, acting in accordance with the procedure referred to in Article 251 and after consulting the Economic and Social Committee and the Committee of the Regions, shall adopt implementing decisions relating to the European Social Fund.

Education, Vocational Training and Youth

Articles 149–150

The Community shall contribute to the development of quality education by encouraging co-operation between Member States and, if necessary, by supporting and supplementing their action. The Community shall implement a vocational training policy which shall support and supplement the action of the Member States.

Title XII: Culture

Article 151

The Community shall contribute to the flowering of the cultures of the Member States, while respecting their national and regional diversity and at the same time bringing the common cultural heritage to the fore. The Community shall take cultural aspects into account in its action under other provisions of this Treaty, in particular in order to respect and to promote the diversity of its cultures.

Title XIII: Public Health

Article 152

A high level of human health protection shall be ensured in the definition and implementation of all Community policies and activities. Community action, which shall complement national policies, shall be directed towards improving public health, preventing human illness and diseases, and obviating sources of danger to human health. Such action shall cover the fight against the major health scourges, by promoting research into their causes, their transmission and their prevention, as well as health information and education. The Community shall complement the Member States' action in reducing drugs-related health damage, including information and prevention. The Community and the Member States shall foster co-operation with third countries and the competent international organizations in the sphere of public health. Community action in the field of public health shall fully respect the responsibilities of the Member States for the organization and delivery of health services and medical care.

Title XIV: Consumer Protection

Article 153

In order to promote the interests of consumers and to ensure a high level of consumer protection, the Community shall contribute to protecting the health, safety and economic interests of consumers, as well as to promoting their right to information, education and to organize themselves in order to safeguard their interests.

Title XV: Trans-European Networks

Articles 154–156

The Community shall contribute to the establishment and development of trans-European networks in the areas of transport, telecommunications and energy infrastructures. Action by the Community shall aim at promoting the interconnection and interoperability of national networks as well as access to such networks. It shall take account in particular of the need to link island, landlocked and peripheral regions with the central regions of the Community.

Title XVI: Industry

Article 157

The Community and the Member States shall ensure that the conditions necessary for the competitiveness of the Community's industry exist. Their action shall be aimed at speeding up the adjustment of industry to structural changes; encouraging an environment favourable to initiative and the development of undertakings throughout the Community, particularly small and medium-sized undertakings; encouraging an environment favourable to co-operation between undertakings; and fostering better exploitation of the industrial potential of policies of innovation, research and technological development. The Member States shall consult each other in liaison with the Commission and, where necessary, shall co-ordinate their action.

Title XVII: Economic and Social Cohesion

Articles 158–162

The Community shall develop and pursue its actions leading to the strengthening of its economic and social cohesion. In particular, the Community shall aim at reducing disparities between the levels of development of the various regions and the backwardness of the least favoured regions or islands, including rural areas.

Implementing decisions relating to the European Regional Development Fund shall be taken by the Council, acting in accordance with the procedure referred to in Article 251 and after consulting the Economic and Social Committee and the Committee of the Regions.

Title XVIII: Research and Technological Development

Articles 163–173

The Community shall have the objective of strengthening the scientific and technological bases of Community industry and encouraging it to become more competitive at international level. The Community shall carry out the following activities, complementing the activities carried out in the Member States: implementation of research, technological development and demonstration programmes, by promoting co-operation with and between undertakings, research centres and universities; promotion of co-operation in the field of Community research, technological development and demonstration with third countries and international organizations; dissemination and optimization of the results of activities in Community research, technological development and demonstration; stimulation of the training and mobility of researchers in the Community.

A multiannual framework programme shall be adopted by the Council.

Title XIX: Environment

Articles 174–176

Community policy on the environment shall aim at a high level of protection taking into account the diversity of situations in the various regions of the Community. It shall be based on the precautionary principle and on the principles that preventive action should be taken, that environmental damage should as a priority be rectified at source and that the polluter should pay. In this context, harmonization measures answering environmental protection requirements shall include, where appropriate, a safeguard clause allowing Member States to take provisional measures, for non-economic environmental reasons, subject to a Community inspection procedure.

Title XX: Development Co-operation

Articles 177–181

Community policy in the sphere of development co-operation, which shall be complementary to the policies pursued by the Member States, shall foster the sustainable economic and social development of the developing countries, and more particularly the most disadvantaged among them; the smooth and gradual integration of the developing countries into the world economy; and the campaign against poverty in the developing countries. Community policy in this area shall contribute to the general objective of developing and consolidating democracy and the rule of law, and to that of respecting human rights and fundamental freedoms. The community and the Member States shall comply with the commitments and take account of the objectives they have approved in the context of the United Nations and other competent international organizations.

The Community and the Member States shall co-ordinate their policies on development co-operation and shall consult each other on their aid programmes, including in international organizations and during international conferences. They may undertake joint action. Member States shall contribute if necessary to the implementation of Community aid programmes.

PART FOUR: ASSOCIATION OF THE OVERSEAS COUNTRIES AND TERRITORIES

Articles 182–188

The Member States agree to bring into association with the Community the non-European countries and territories which have special relations with Denmark, France, the Netherlands and the United Kingdom in order to promote the economic and social development of these countries and territories and to establish close economic relations between them and the Community as a whole. Association shall serve primarily to further the interests and prosperity of the inhabitants of these countries and territories in order to lead them to the economic, social and cultural development to which they aspire.

Member States shall, in their commercial exchanges with the countries and territories, apply the same rules which they apply among themselves pursuant to the Treaty. Each country or territory shall apply to its commercial exchanges with Member States and with other countries and territories the same rules which it applies in respect of the European States with which it has special relations. Member States shall contribute to the investments required by the progressive development of these countries and territories.

Customs duties on trade between Member States and the countries and territories are to be prohibited according to the same timetable as for trade between the Member States themselves. The countries and territories may, however, levy customs duties which correspond to the needs of their development and to the requirements of their industrialization or which, being of a fiscal nature, have the object of contributing to their budgets.

PART FIVE: INSTITUTIONS OF THE COMMUNITY

Title I: Provisions Governing the Institutions

Articles 189–267

In order to carry out their task and in accordance with the provisions of this Treaty, the European Parliament acting jointly with the Council, the Council and the Commission shall make regulations and issue directives, take decisions, make recommendations or deliver opinions. A regulation shall have general application. It shall be binding in its entirety and directly applicable in all Member States. A directive shall be binding, as to the result to be achieved, upon each Member State to which it is addressed, but shall leave to the national authorities the choice of form and methods. A decision shall be binding in its entirety upon those to whom it is addressed. Recommendations and opinions shall have no binding force.

Where reference is made in this Treaty to this Article [Article 251] for the adoption of an act, the following procedure shall apply. The Commission shall submit a proposal to the European Parliament and the Council. The Council, acting by a qualified majority after obtaining the opinion of the European Parliament:

if it approves all the amendments contained in the European Parliament's opinion, may adopt the proposed act thus amended;

if the European Parliament does not propose any amendments, may adopt the proposed act;

shall otherwise adopt a common position and communicate it to the European Parliament. The Commission shall inform the European Parliament fully of its position.

If, within three months of such communication, the European Parliament:

(a) approves the common position or has not taken a decision, the act in question shall be deemed to have been adopted in accordance with that common position;
(b) rejects, by an absolute majority of its component members, the common position, the proposed act shall be deemed not to have been adopted;
(c) proposes amendments to the common position by an absolute majority of its component members, the amended text shall be forwarded to the Council and to the Commission, which shall deliver an opinion on those amendments.

If, within three months of the matter being referred to it, the Council, acting by a qualified majority, approves all the amendments of the European Parliament, the act shall be deemed to have been adopted in the form of the common position; however, the Council shall act unanimously on the amendments on which the Commission has delivered a negative opinion. If the Council does not approve all the amendments, the President of the Council, in agreement with the President of the European Parliament, shall within six weeks convene a meeting of the Conciliation Committee. If, within six weeks of its being convened, the Conciliation Committee approves a joint text, the European Parliament, acting by an absolute majority of the votes cast, and the Council, acting by a qualified majority, shall each have a period of six weeks in which to adopt the act in accordance with the joint text. If either of the two institutions fails to approve the proposed act, it shall be deemed not to have been adopted. Where the Conciliation Committee does not approve a joint text, the proposed act shall be deemed not to have been adopted.

Title II: Financial Provisions

Articles 268–280

All items of revenue and expenditure of the Community, including those relating to the European Social Fund, shall be included in estimates to be drawn up for each financial year and shall be shown in the budget. Administrative expenditure occasioned for the institutions by the provisions of the Treaty on European Union relating to common foreign and security policy and to co-operation in the fields of justice and home affairs shall be charged to the budget. The operational expenditure occasioned by the implementation of the said provisions may, under the conditions referred to therein, be charged to the budget. The revenue and expenditure shown in the budget shall be in balance.

Without prejudice to other revenue, the budget shall be financed wholly from own resources.

The Commission shall implement the budget, in accordance with the provisions of the regulations made pursuant to Article 279, on its own responsibility and within the limits of the appropriations, having regard to the principles of sound financial management. Member States shall co-operate with the Commission to ensure that the appropriations are used in accordance with the principles of sound financial management.

The Council, acting unanimously on a proposal from the Commission and after consulting the European Parliament and obtaining the opinion of the Court of Auditors, shall:

(a) make Financial Regulations specifying in particular the procedure to be adopted for establishing and implementing the budget and for presenting and auditing accounts;
(b) determine the methods and procedure whereby the budget revenue provided under the arrangements relating to the Community's own resources shall be made available to the Commission, and determine the measures to be applied, if need be, to meet cash requirements; and
(c) lay down rules concerning the responsibility of financial controllers, authorizing officers and accounting officers, and concerning appropriate arrangements for inspection.

The Community and the Member States shall counter fraud and any other illegal activities affecting the financial interests of the Community.

PART SIX: GENERAL AND FINAL PROVISIONS

Articles 281–312

Member States shall, in so far as is necessary, engage in negotiations with each other with a view to ensuring for the benefit of their nationals:

(a) the protection of persons as well as the enjoyment of protection of rights under the conditions granted by each State to its own nationals;
(b) the elimination of double taxation within the Community;
(c) the mutual recognition of companies, the maintenance of their legal personality in cases where the registered office is transferred from one country to another, and the possibility for companies subject to the municipal law of different Member States to form mergers; and
(d) the simplification of the formalities governing the reciprocal recognition and execution of judicial decisions and arbitral awards.

Within a period of three years after the date of the entry into force of the Treaty, Member States shall treat nationals of other Member States in the same manner, as regards financial participation by such nationals in the capital of companies, as they treat their own nationals, without prejudice to the application of the other provisions of the Treaty.

The Treaty shall in no way prejudice the system existing in Member States in respect of property.

The provisions of the Treaty shall not detract from the following rules:

(a) no Member State shall be obliged to supply information the disclosure of which it considers contrary to the essential interests of its security;
(b) any Member State may take the measures which it considers necessary for the protection of the essential interests of its security, and which are connected with the production of or the trade in arms, ammunition and war material; such measures shall not, however, prejudice conditions of competition in the common market in respect of products not intended for specifically military purposes.

The list of products to which (b) applies shall be determined by the Council in the course of the first year after the date of entry into force of the Treaty. The list may be subsequently amended by the unanimous vote of the Council on a proposal of the Commission.

Member States shall consult one another for the purpose of enacting in common the necessary provisions to prevent the functioning of the common market from being affected by measures which a Member State may be called upon to take in case of serious internal disturbances affecting public order, in case of war or in order to carry out undertakings into which it has entered for the purpose of maintaining peace and international security.

Where this Treaty provides for the conclusion of agreements between the Community and one or more States or international organizations, the Commission shall make recommendations to the Council, which shall authorize the Commission to open the necessary negotiations. The Commission shall conduct these negotiations in consultation with special committees appointed by the Council to assist it in this task and within the framework of such directives as the Council may issue to it. The agreements shall be concluded by the Council, after consulting the European Parliament, acting by a qualified majority on a proposal from the Commission. The Council shall act unanimously when the agreement covers a field for which unanimity is required.

The provisions of the Treaty shall not affect those of the Treaty establishing the European Coal and Steel Community, nor those of the Treaty establishing the European Atomic Energy Community; nor shall they be an obstacle to the existence or completion of regional unions between Belgium and Luxembourg, and between Belgium, Luxembourg and the Netherlands, in so far as the objectives of these regional unions are not achieved by the application of this Treaty.

Where a decision has been taken to suspend the voting rights of the representative of the government of a Member State in accordance with Article 7 (2) of the Treaty on European Union, these voting rights shall also be suspended with regard to this Treaty.

The Community may conclude with one or more States or international organizations agreements establishing an association involving reciprocal rights and obligations, common action and special procedures.

The Treaty is concluded for an unlimited period.

The Single European Act (SEA)

On 1 July 1987 amendments to the Treaties of Paris and Rome, in the form of the Single European Act (SEA), came into effect, following ratification by all the Member States. The Act contained provisions which aimed to complete by 31 December 1992 the creation of a single Community market—'an area without internal frontiers in which the free movement of goods, persons, services and capital is ensured'. Other provisions increased Community co-operation in research and technology, social policy (particularly the improvement of working conditions), economic and social cohesion (reduction of disparities between regions), environmental protection, creation of economic and monetary union, and foreign policy. It allowed the Council of Ministers to take decisions by a qualified majority vote on matters which previously, under the Treaty of Rome, had required unanimity; this applied principally to matters relating to the establishment of the internal market. The Act increased the powers of the European Parliament to delay and amend legislation, by introducing a new co-operation procedure for major decisions concerned with the completion of the internal market, although the Council retained final decision-making powers. The Act provided for the establishment of the Court of First Instance. The Act also provided for the establishment of a secretariat for European political co-operation on matters of foreign policy.

Summary of the Treaty on European Union (Maastricht Treaty)

(effective from 1 November 1993; as amended by the Treaty of Amsterdam)

Note: At the meeting of the European Council in December 1992, it was agreed that Denmark was to be exempted from certain central provisions of the Treaty, including those regarding monetary union, European citizenship and defence (subject to approval by a second Danish referendum, which ratified the Treaty in May 1993).

A protocol to the Treaty was approved and a separate agreement signed by all Member States except the United Kingdom on social policy, based on the Charter of Fundamental Social Rights (the Social Charter) of 1989.

TITLE I: COMMON PROVISIONS

Article 1

By this Treaty, the High Contracting Parties establish among themselves a European Union, hereinafter called 'the Union'.

This Treaty marks a new stage in the process of creating an ever closer union among the peoples of Europe, in which decisions are taken as openly as possible and as closely as possible to the citizen.

The Union shall be founded on the European Communities, supplemented by the policies and forms of co-operation established by this Treaty. Its task shall be to organize, in a manner demonstrating consistency and solidarity, relations between the Member States and between their peoples.

Article 2

The Union shall set itself the following objectives:

to promote economic and social progress and a high level of employment and to achieve balanced and sustainable development, in particular through the creation of an area without internal frontiers, through the strengthening of economic and social cohesion and through the establishment of economic and monetary union, ultimately including a single currency in accordance with the provisions of this Treaty;

to assert its identity on the international scene, in particular through the implementation of a common foreign and security policy including the progressive framing of a common defence policy, which might lead to a common defence;

to strengthen the protection of the rights and interests of the nationals of its Member States through the introduction of a citizenship of the Union;

to maintain and develop the Union as an area of freedom, security and justice, in which the free movement of persons is assured in conjunction with appropriate measures with respect to external border controls, asylum, immigration and the prevention and combating of crime;

to maintain in full the *acquis communautaire* and build on it with a view to considering to what extent the policies and forms of co-operation introduced by this Treaty may need to be revised with the aim of ensuring the effectiveness of the mechanisms and the institutions of the Community.

The objectives of the Union shall be achieved as provided in this Treaty and in accordance with the conditions and the timetable set out therein while respecting the principle of subsidiarity as defined in Article 3b of the Treaty establishing the European Community.

Article 3

The Union shall be served by a single institutional framework which shall ensure the consistency and the continuity of the activities carried out in order to attain its objectives while respecting and building upon the *acquis communautaire.*

The Union shall in particular ensure the consistency of its external activities as a whole in the context of its external relations, security, economic and development policies. The Council and the Commission shall be responsible for ensuring such consistency and shall co-operate to this end. They shall ensure the implementation of these policies, each in accordance with its respective powers.

Article 4

The European Council shall provide the Union with the necessary impetus for its development and shall define the general political guidelines thereof.

The European Council shall bring together the Heads of State or Government of the Member States and the President of the Commission. They shall be assisted by the Ministers for Foreign Affairs of the Member States and by a Member of the Commission. The European Council shall meet at least twice a year, under the chairmanship of the Head of State or Government of the Member State which holds the Presidency of the Council.

The European Council shall submit to the European Parliament a report after each of its meetings and a yearly written report on the progress achieved by the Union.

Article 5

The European Parliament, the Council, the Commission, the Court of Justice and the Court of Auditors shall exercise their powers under the conditions and for the purposes provided for, on the one hand, by the provisions of the Treaties establishing the European Communities and of the subsequent Treaties and Acts modifying and supplementing them and, on the other hand, by the other provisions of this Treaty.

Article 6

1. The Union is founded on the principles of liberty, democracy, respect for human rights and fundamental freedoms, and the rule of law, principles which are common to the Member States.

2. The Union shall respect fundamental rights, as guaranteed by the European Convention for the Protection of Human Rights and Fundamental Freedoms signed in Rome on 4 November 1950 and as they result from the constitutional traditions common to the Member States, as general principles of Community law.
3. The Union shall respect the national identities of its Member States.
4. The Union shall provide itself with the means necessary to attain its objectives and carry through its policies.

Article 7

1. The Council, meeting in the composition of the Heads of State or Government and acting by unanimity on a proposal by one-third of the Member States or by the Commission and after obtaining the assent of the European Parliament, may determine the existence of a serious and persistent breach by a Member State of principles mentioned in Article 6 (1).
2. The Council, acting by a qualified majority, may decide to suspend certain of the rights deriving from the application of this Treaty to the Member State in question.

TITLE II: PROVISIONS AMENDING THE TREATY ESTABLISHING THE EUROPEAN ECONOMIC COMMUNITY WITH A VIEW TO ESTABLISHING THE EUROPEAN COMMUNITY

Article 8

The Treaty establishing the European Economic Community shall be amended in accordance with the provisions of this Article, in order to establish a European Community.

Throughout the Treaty: The term 'European Economic Community' shall be replaced by the term 'European Community'.

TITLE III: PROVISIONS AMENDING THE TREATY ESTABLISHING THE EUROPEAN COAL AND STEEL COMMUNITY

Article 9

The Treaty establishing the European Coal and Steel Community shall be amended in accordance with the provisions of this Article.

TITLE IV: PROVISIONS AMENDING THE TREATY ESTABLISHING THE EUROPEAN ATOMIC ENERGY COMMUNITY

Article 10

The Treaty establishing the European Atomic Energy Community shall be amended in accordance with the provisions of this Article.

TITLE V: PROVISIONS ON A COMMON FOREIGN AND SECURITY POLICY

Articles 11–28

The Union shall define and implement a common foreign and security policy covering all areas of foreign and security policy. The objectives of this policy shall be: to safeguard the common values, fundamental interests, independence and integrity of the Union in conformity with the principles of the United Nations Charter; to strengthen the security of the Union in all ways; to preserve peace and strengthen international security, in accordance with the principles of the United Nations Charter, as well as the principles of the Helsinki Final Act and the objectives of the Paris Charter, including those on external borders; to promote international co-operation; to develop and consolidate democracy and the rule of law, and respect for human rights and fundamental freedoms. The Member States shall support the Union's external and security policy actively and unreservedly in a spirit of loyalty and mutual solidarity. They shall refrain from any action which is contrary to the interests of the Union or likely to impair its effectiveness as a cohesive force in international relations.

The Union shall pursue its objectives by defining the principles of and general guidelines for the common foreign and security policy; deciding on common strategies; adopting joint actions; adopting common positions; strengthening systematic co-operation between Member States in the conduct of policy.

The European Council shall define the principles of and general guidelines for the common and security policy, including for matters with defence implications. The Council shall ensure the unity, consistency and effectiveness of action by the Union.

The Council shall adopt common positions, which shall define the approach of the Union to a particular matter of a geographical or thematic nature. Member States shall ensure that their national policies conform to the common positions.

The common foreign and security policy shall include all questions relating to the security of the Union, including the progressive framing of a common defence policy, which might lead to a common defence, should the European Council so decide. The Western European Union (WEU) is an integral part of the development of the Union providing the Union with access to an operational capability. The Union shall accordingly foster closer institutional relations with the WEU with a view to the possibility of the integration of the WEU into the Union, should the European Council so decide. The progressive framing of a common defence policy will be supported, as Member States consider appropriate, by co-operation between them in the field of armaments. Questions referred to shall include humanitarian and rescue tasks, peace-keeping tasks and tasks of combat forces in crisis managment, including peace-making. The provisions of this Article shall not prevent the development of closer co-operation between two or more Member States on a bilateral level.

The Presidency shall represent the Union in matters coming within the common foreign and security policy.

Member States shall co-ordinate their action in international organizations and at international conferences.

The diplomatic and consular missions of the Member States and the Commission Delegations in third countries and international conferences, and their representations to international organizations, shall co-operate in ensuring that the common positions and joint actions adopted by the Council are complied with and implemented.

The Presidency shall consult the European Parliament and shall ensure that the views of the European Parliament are duly taken into consideration.

Decisions under this Title shall be taken by the Council acting unanimously. Abstentions by members present in person or represented shall not prevent the adoption of such decisions.

A Political Committee shall monitor the international situation in the areas covered by the common foreign and security policy and contribute to the definition of policies by delivering opinions to the Council. It shall also monitor the implementation of agreed policies.

TITLE VI: PROVISIONS ON POLICE AND JUDICIAL CO-OPERATION IN CRIMINAL MATTERS

Article 29

Without prejudice to the powers of the European Community, the Union's objective shall be to provide citizens with a high level of safety within an area of freedom, security and justice by developing common action among the Member States in the fields of police and judicial co-operation in criminal matters and by preventing and combating racism and xenophobia. That objective shall be achieved by preventing and combating crime, organized or otherwise, in particular terrorism, trafficking in persons and offences against children, illicit drug trafficking and illicit arms trafficking, corruption and fraud, through:

closer co-operation between police forces, customs authorities and other competent authorities in the Member States, both directly and through the European Police Office (Europol);

closer co-operation between judicial and other competent authorities of the Member States;

approximation, where necessary, of rules on criminal matters in the Member States.

Article 30

Common action in the field of police co-operation shall include:

(a) operational co-operation between the competent authorities, including the police, customs and other specialized law enforcement services of the Member States in relation to the prevention, detection and investigation of criminal offences;
(b) the collection, storage, processing, analysis and exchange of relevant information, in particular through Europol;
(c) co-operation and joint initiatives in training, the exchange of liaison officers, secondments, the use of equipment, and forensic research;
(d) the common evaluation of particular investigative techniques in relation to the detection of serious forms of organized crime.

The Council shall promote co-operation through Europol.

Article 31

Common action on judicial co-operation in criminal matters shall include facilitating and accelerating co-operation between competent ministries and judicial or equivalent authorities of the Member States in relation to proceedings and the enforcement of decisions; facilitating extradition between Member States; ensuring compatibility in rules applicable in the Member States, as may be necessary to improve such co-operation; preventing conflicts of jurisdiction between Member States; progressively adopting measures establishing minimum rules relating to the constituent elements of criminal acts and to penalties in the fields of organized crime, terrorism and illicit drug trafficking.

Article 34

Member States shall inform and consult one another within the Council with a view to co-ordinating their action.

Article 35

The Court of Justice of the European Communities shall have jurisdiction to give preliminary rulings on the validity and interpretation of framework decisions and decisions, on the interpretation of conventions and on the validity and interpretation of the measures implementing them.

Article 39

The Council shall consult the European Parliament before adopting any measures referred to in subsections of Article 34. The Presidency and the Commission shall regularly inform the European Parliament of discussions in the areas covered by this Title. The European Parliament may ask questions of the Council or make recommendations to it.

TITLE VII: PROVISIONS ON CLOSER CO-OPERATION

Article 43

Member States which intend to establish closer co-operation between themselves may make use of the institutions, procedures and mechanisms laid down by this Treaty and the Treaty establishing the European Community.

TITLE VIII: FINAL PROVISIONS

Articles 46–53

Any European State which respects the principles set out in Article 7 may apply to become a member of the Union.

This Treaty is concluded for an unlimited period.

Summary of the Treaty of Amsterdam

(amending the Treaty on European Union, the Treaties Establishing the European Communities and Certain Related Acts—effective from 1 May 1999)

Note: Following the decision of the Government of the United Kingdom to subscribe to the Charter of Fundamental Social Rights (the Social Charter) of 1989 with effect from May 1997, the Treaty incorporated the protocol based on the Charter (by amending the Treaty of Rome establishing the European Economic Community).

A Protocol to the Treaty also incorporated the Schengen *acquis* on the freedom of movement of persons across internal European Union boundaries in order to integrate it into the framework of the European Union. The *acquis* includes the Schengen Agreement, signed on 14 June 1985 between the Governments of the States of the Benelux Economic Union, the Federal Republic of Germany and France; the Convention, signed in Schengen on 19 June 1990 between Belgium, the Federal Republic of Germany, France, Luxembourg and the Netherlands; the Accession Protocols and Agreements to the 1985 Agreement and the 1990 Implementation Convention with Italy, Spain and Portugal, Greece, Austria, Denmark, Finland and Sweden; and decisions and declarations adopted by the Executive Committee established by the Implementation Convention, as well as acts adopted for the implementation of the Convention by the organs upon which the Executive Committee has conferred decision-making powers.

PART ONE: SUBSTANTIVE AMENDMENTS

Article 1

The Treaty on European Union shall be amended in accordance with the provisions of this Article.

Article 2

The Treaty establishing the European Community shall be amended in accordance with the provisions of this Article.

Article 3

The Treaty establishing the European Coal and Steel Community shall be amended in accordance with the provisions of this Article.

Article 4

The Treaty establishing the European Atomic Energy Community shall be amended in accordance with the provisions of this Article.

Article 5

The Act concerning the election of the representatives of the European Parliament by direct universal suffrage annexed to the Council Decision of 20 September 1976 shall be amended in accordance with the provisions of this Article.

In Article 2, the following paragraph shall be added:

> In the event of amendments to this Article, the number of representatives elected in each Member State must ensure appropriate representation for the peoples of the States brought together in the Community.

Article 7 (2) shall be replaced by the following:

> Pending the entry into force of a uniform electoral procedure or a procedure based on common principles and subject to the other provisions of this Act, the electoral procedure shall be governed in each Member State by its national provisions.

PART TWO: SIMPLIFICATION

(Articles 6–11)

Article 6

The Treaty establishing the European Community, including the annexes and protocols thereto, shall be amended in accordance with the provisions of this Article for the purpose of deleting lapsed provisions of the Treaty and adapting in consequence the text of certain of its provisions.

Article 7

The Treaty establishing the European Coal and Steel Community, including the annexes, protocols and other acts annexed thereto, shall be amended in accordance with the provisions of this Article for the purpose of deleting lapsed provisions of the Treaty and adapting in consequence the text of certain of its provisions.

Article 8

The Treaty establishing the European Atomic Energy Community, including the annexes and protocols thereto, shall be amended in accordance with the provisions of this Article for the purpose of deleting lapsed provisions of the Treaty and adapting in consequence the text of certain of its provisions.

Article 9

The Convention of 25 March 1957 on certain institutions common to the European Communities and the Treaty of 8 April 1965 establishing a Single Council and a Single Commission of the European Communities shall be repealed. This is with the exception of the Protocol of 8 April 1965 on the privileges and immunities of the European Communities, to which is added an Article 23, applying the Protocol to the European Central Bank, to the members of its organs and to its staff.

The powers conferred on the European Parliament, the Council, the Commission, the Court of Justice and the Court of Auditors by the Treaty establishing the European Community, the Treaty establishing the European Coal and Steel Community and the Treaty establishing the European Atomic Energy Community shall be exercised by the single institutions under the conditions laid down respectively by the said Treaties and this Article.

The functions conferred on the Economic and Social Committee by the Treaty establishing the European Community and the Treaty establishing the European Atomic Energy Community shall be exercised by a single committee.

The European Communities shall enjoy in the territories of the Member States such privileges and immunities as are necessary for the performance of their tasks. The position shall be the same as regards the European Central Bank, the European Monetary Institute and the European Investment Bank.

Article 10

The repeal or deletion of lapsed provisions of the Treaty establishing the European Community, the Treaty establishing the European Coal and Steel Community and the Treaty establishing the European Atomic Energy Community and the adaptation of certain of their provisions shall not bring about any change in the legal effects of the provisions of those Treaties.

PART THREE: GENERAL AND FINAL PROVISIONS

(Articles 12–15.)

Article 12

The articles, titles and sections of the Treaty on European Union and of the Treaty establishing the European Community, as amended by the provisions of this Treaty, shall be renumbered in accordance with the tables of equivalences set out in the Annex to this Treaty.

Article 13

This Treaty is concluded for an unlimited period.

Article 14

This Treaty shall be ratified by the High Contracting Parties in accordance with their respective constitutional requirements. This Treaty shall enter into force on the first day of the second month following that in which the instrument of ratification is deposited by the last signatory State to fulfil that formality.

Other Treaties

The following additional treaties have been signed by Member States of the European Union:

Treaty Instituting a Single Council and a Single Commission of the European Communities: signed in Brussels on 8 April 1965 by the six original members. This Treaty was repealed by the Treaty of Amsterdam.

Treaty Modifying Certain Budgetary Arrangements of the European Communities and of the Treaty Instituting a Single Council and a Single Commission of the European Communities: signed in Luxembourg on 22 April 1970 by the six original members.

Treaty Concerning the Accession of the Kingdom of Denmark, Ireland, the Kingdom of Norway and the United Kingdom of Great Britain and Northern Ireland to the European Economic Community and the European Atomic Energy Community: signed in Brussels on 22 January 1972 (amended on 1 January 1973, owing to the non-accession of Norway).

Treaty of Accession of the Hellenic Republic to the European Economic Community and to the European Atomic Energy Community: signed in Athens on 28 May 1979.

Treaty of Accession of the Portuguese Republic and the Kingdom of Spain to the European Economic Community and to the European Atomic Energy Community: signed in Lisbon and Madrid on 12 June 1985.

Note: Accession of new members to the European Coal and Steel Community was enacted separately, by a Decision of the European Council.

Treaty Concerning the Accession of the Kingdom of Norway, the Republic of Austria, the Republic of Finland and the Kingdom of Sweden to the European Union: signed in Corfu on 24 June 1994 (amended on 1 January 1995, owing to the non-accession of Norway).

On 26 February 2001 EU ministers of foreign affairs signed the Treaty of Nice (see p. 326). On entering into force (following ratification by member states' national legislatures or approval by national popular referendums) the Treaty of Nice was to amend previous treaties in order to enable the proposed enlargement of the European Union.

THE FRANC ZONE

Address: Direction Générale des Services Etrangers (Service de la Zone Franc), Banque de France, 39 rue Croix-des-Petits-Champs, 75049, Paris Cédex 01, France.

Telephone: 1-42-92-31-46; **fax:** 1-42-92-39-88.

MEMBERS*

Benin	Equatorial Guinea
Burkina Faso	French Overseas Territories
Cameroon	Gabon
Central African Republic	Guinea-Bissau
Chad	Mali
The Comoros	Niger
Republic of the Congo	Senegal
Côte d'Ivoire	Togo

* The following states withdrew from the Franc Zone during the period 1958–73: Guinea, Tunisia, Morocco, Algeria, Mauritania and Madagascar. Equatorial Guinea (formerly a Spanish territory, joined the Franc Zone in January 1985, and Guinea-Bissau, a former Portuguese territory, joined in May 1997. Prior to 1 January 2002, when the transition to a single European currency (euro) was finalized (see below), the Franc Zone also included Metropolitan France; the French Overseas Collectivités Territoriales (Mayotte and St Pierre and Miquelon); and the French Overseas Departments. The French Overseas Territories— New Caledonia, French Polynesia and the Wallis and Futuna Islands—continued to use the franc CFP (franc des Comptoirs français du Pacifique, 'French Pacific franc') following the transition to the euro.

The Franc Zone operates on the basis of agreements concluded between France and each group of member countries, and the Comoros. The currencies in the Franc Zone were formerly linked with the French franc at a fixed rate of exchange. However, following the introduction of the euro (European single currency) in January 1999, within the framework of European economic and monetary union, in which France was a participant, the Franc Zone currencies were effectively linked at fixed parity to the euro (i.e. parity was based on the fixed conversion rate for the French franc and the euro). From 1 January 2002, when European economic and monetary union was finalized and the French franc withdrawn from circulation, the franc CFA, Comoros franc and franc CFP became officially pegged to the euro, at a fixed rate of exchange. (In accordance with Protocol 13 on France, appended to the 1993 Maastricht Treaty on European Union, France was permitted to continue issuing currencies in its Overseas Territories—i.e. the franc CFP—following the completion of European economic and monetary union.) All the convertability arrangements previously concluded between France and the Franc Zone remained in force. Therefore Franc Zone currencies are freely convertible into euros, at the fixed exchange rate, guaranteed by the French Treasury. Each group of member countries, and the Comoros, has its own central issuing bank, with overdraft facilities provided by the French Treasury. (The issuing authority for the French Overseas Territories is the Institut d'émission d'outre-mer, based in Paris.) Monetary reserves are held mainly in the form of euros. The Banque centrale des états de l'Afrique de l'ouest—BCEAO and the Banque des états de l'Afrique centrale—BEAC are authorized to hold up to 35% of their foreign exchange holdings in currencies other than the euro.

The Comoros, formerly a French Overseas Territory, did not join the Franc Zone following its unilateral declaration of independence in 1975. However, the franc CFA was used as the currency of the new state and the Institut d'émission des Comores continued to function as a Franc Zone organization. In 1976 the Comoros formally assumed membership. In July 1981 the Banque centrale des Comores replaced the Institut d'émission des Comores, establishing its own currency, the Comoros franc.

Apart from Guinea and Mauritania, all of the countries that formerly comprised French West and Equatorial Africa are members of the Franc Zone. The former West and Equatorial African territories are still grouped within the two currency areas that existed before independence, each group having its own variant on the CFA, issued by a central bank: the franc de la Communauté Financière d'Afrique ('franc CFA de l'Ouest'), issued by the BCEAO, and the franc Coopération financière en Afrique centrale ('franc CFA central'), issued by the BEAC.

During the late 1980s and early 1990s the economies of the African Franc Zone countries were adversely affected by increasing foreign debt and by a decline in the prices paid for their principal export commodities. The French Government, however, refused to devalue the franc CFA, as recommended by the IMF. In 1990 the Franc Zone governments agreed to develop economic union, with integrated public finances and common commercial legislation. In April 1992, at a meeting of Franc Zone ministers, a treaty on the insurance industry was adopted, providing for the establishment of a regulatory body for the industry, the Conférence Intrafricaine des Marchés d'Assurances (CIMA), and for the creation of a council of Franc Zone ministers responsible for the insurance industry, with its secretariat in Libreville, Gabon. (A code of conduct for members of CIMA entered into force in February 1995.) At the meeting held in April 1992 ministers also agreed that a further council of ministers was to be created with the task of monitoring the social security systems in Franc Zone countries. A programme drawn up by Franc Zone finance ministers concerning the harmonization of commercial legislation in member states through the establishment of l'Organisation pour l'Harmonisation du Droit des Affaires en Afrique (OHADA) was approved by the Franco-African summit in October. A treaty to align corporate and investment regulations was signed by 11 member countries at the annual meeting with France in October 1993.

In August 1993, in view of financial turmoil related to the continuing weakness of the French franc and the abandonment of the European exchange rate mechanism, the BCEAO and the BEAC determined to suspend repurchasing of francs CFA outside the Franc Zone. Effectively this signified the temporary withdrawal of guaranteed convertibility of the franc CFA with the French franc. Devaluations of the franc CFA and the Comoros franc (by 50% and 33.3%, respectively) were implemented in January 1994. Following the devaluation the CFA countries embarked on programmes of economic adjustment, including restrictive fiscal and wage policies and other monetary, structural and social measures, designed to stimulate growth and to ensure eligibility for development assistance from international financial institutions. France established a special development fund of FFr 300m. to alleviate the immediate social consequences of the devaluation, and announced substantial debt cancellations. In April the French Government announced assistance amounting to FFr 10,000m. over three years to Franc Zone countries undertaking structural adjustment programmes. The IMF, which had strongly advocated a devaluation of the franc CFA, and the World Bank approved immediate soft-credit loans, technical assistance and cancellations or rescheduling of debts. In June 1994 heads of state (or representatives) of African Franc Zone countries convened in Libreville, Gabon, to review the effects of the currency realignment. The final communiqué of the meeting urged further international support for the countries' economic development efforts. In April 1995 Franc Zone finance ministers, meeting in Paris, recognized the positive impact of the devaluation on agricultural export sectors, in particular in west African countries. In September the Franc Zone member countries and the French Government agreed to establish a research and training institution, Afristat, which was to support national statistical organizations in order to strengthen economic management capabilities in participating states. Subsequently the IMF and the World Bank continued to support economic development efforts in the Franc Zone. France provides debt relief to Franc Zone member states eligible under the World Bank's HIPC initiative (q.v.).

In February 2000 UEMOA and ECOWAS (q.v) adopted an action plan for the proposed creation, by 1 January 2004, of a single West African Monetary Zone and consequent replacement of the franc Communauté financiere africaine by a single West African currency (see below).

CURRENCIES OF THE FRANC ZONE

1 franc CFA = €0.00152. CFA stands for Communauté financière africaine in the West African area and for Coopération financière en Afrique centrale in the Central African area. Used in the monetary areas of West and Central Africa respectively.

1 Comoros franc = €0.00201. Used in the Comoros, where it replaced the franc CFA in 1981.

1 franc CFP = €0.00839. CFP stands for Comptoirs français du Pacifique. Used in New Caledonia, French Polynesia and the Wallis and Futuna Islands.

WEST AFRICA

Union économique et monétaire ouest-africaine—UEMOA: BP 543, Ouagadougou, Burkina Faso; tel. 31-88-73; fax 31-88-72; e-mail commission@uemoa.bf; internet www.uemoa.int; f.1994; replaced the Communauté économique de l'Afrique de l'ouest–CEAO; promotes regional monetary and economic convergence, and envisages the eventual creation of a sub-regional common market. A preferential tariff scheme, eliminating duties on most local products and reducing by 30% import duties on many Union-produced industrial goods, became operational on 1 July 1996; in addition, from 1 July, a community solidarity tax of 0.5% was imposed on all goods from third countries sold within the Union, in order to strengthen UEMOA's capacity to promote economic integration. (This was increased to 1% in December 1999.) In June 1997 UEMOA heads of state and government agreed to reduce import duties on industrial products originating in the Union by a further 30%. An inter-parliamentary committee, recognized as the predecessor of a UEMOA legislature, was inaugurated in Mali in March 1998. In September Côte d'Ivoire's stock exchange was transformed into the Bourse regionale des valeurs mobilières, a regional stock exchange serving the Union, in order to further economic integration. In August 1999 an inter-parliamentary committee, recognized as the predecessor of a UEMOA legislature, adopted a draft treaty on the establishment of a UEMOA parliament. On 1 January 2000 internal tariffs were eliminated on all local products (including industrial goods) and a joint external tariff system, reportedly in five bands of between 0% and 20%, was imposed on goods deriving from outside the new customs union. Guinea-Bissau was excluded from the arrangement owing to its unstable political situation. The UEMOA member countries also belong to ECOWAS and, in accordance with an action plan adopted by the two organizations in February 2000, aim to harmonize UEMOA's economic programme with that of a planned second West African monetary union, scheduled to be established in January 2003 by the remaining—mainly anglophone—ECOWAS member states. A merger of the two complementary monetary unions is then envisaged, to enable the creation in January 2004 of the West African Monetary Zone and the replacement of the franc Communauté financière africaine by a new single West African currency. Mems: Benin, Burkina Faso, Côte d'Ivoire, Guinea-Bissau, Mali, Niger, Senegal and Togo. Pres. Moussa Touré (Senegal).

Union monétaire ouest-africaine—UMOA (West African Monetary Union): established by Treaty of November 1973, entered into force 1974; in 1990 the UMOA Banking Commission was established, which is responsible for supervising the activities of banks and financial institutions in the region, with the authority to prohibit the operation of a banking institution. UMOA constitutes an integral part of UEMOA.

Banque centrale des états de l'Afrique de l'ouest—BCEAO: ave Abdoulaye Fadiga, BP 3108, Dakar, Senegal; tel. 839-05-00; fax 823-93-35; e-mail akangni@bceao.int; internet www.bceao.int; f. 1962; central bank of issue for the mems of UEMOA; cap. and res 844,377m. francs CFA (Dec. 1999). Mems: Benin, Burkina Faso, Côte d'Ivoire, Guinea-Bissau, Mali, Niger, Senegal and Togo. Gov. Charles Konan Banny (Côte d'Ivoire); Sec.-Gen. Michel K. Klousseh (Togo). Publs *Annual Report, Notes d'Information et Statistiques* (monthly), *Annuaire des banques, Bilan des banques et établissements financiers* (annually).

Banque ouest-africaine de développement—BOAD: 68 ave de la Libération, BP 1172, Lomé, Togo; tel. 221-42-44; fax 221-52-67; e-mail boadsiege@boad.org; internet www.boad.org; f. 1973 to promote the balanced development of mem. states and the economic integration of West Africa; auth. cap. 35,000m. francs CFA, subscribed cap. 33,680m. francs CFA (Dec. 2000). A Guarantee Fund for Private Investment in West Africa, established jtly by BOAD and the European Investment Bank, was inaugurated in Dec. 1994. The Fund aims to guarantee medium- and long-term credits to private sector businesses in the region. Mems: Benin, Burkina Faso, Côte d'Ivoire, Guinea-Bissau, Mali, Niger, Senegal, Togo. Pres. Dr Yayi Boni (Benin); Vice-Pres. Alpha Touré. Publs *Rapport Annuel, BOAD en Bref* (quarterly).

Bourse Régionale des Valeurs Mobilières—BRVM: 18 ave Joseph Anoma, BP 3802, Abidjan 01, Côte d'Ivoire; tel. 32-66-85; fax 32-66-84; e-mail brvm@brvm.org; internet www.brvm.org; f. 1998; Pres. Coulibaly Tiemkoko Yade; Man. Jean-Paul Gillet.

CENTRAL AFRICA

Communauté économique et monétaire de l'Afrique centrale—CEMAC: BP 969, Bangui, Central African Republic; tel. and fax 61-21-35; e-mail sgudeac@intnet.cf; internet www.socatel.intnet.cf/accueil1.html; f. 1998; formally inaugurated as the successor to the Union douanière et économique de l'Afrique centrale (UDEAC, f. 1966) at a meeting of heads of state held in Malabo, Equatorial Guinea, in June 1999; aims to promote the process of sub-regional integration within the framework of an economic union and a monetary union; CEMAC was also to comprise a parliament and sub-regional tribunal. UDEAC established a common external tariff for imports from other countries and administered a common code for investment policy and a Solidarity Fund to counteract regional disparities of wealth and economic development. Mems: Cameroon, Central African Republic, Chad, Republic of the Congo, Equatorial Guinea, Gabon. Sec.-Gen. Jean Nkuete.

At a summit meeting in December 1981, UDEAC leaders agreed in principle to form an economic community of Central African states (Communauté économique des états d'Afrique centrale—CEEAC), to include UDEAC members and Burundi, Rwanda, São Tomé and Príncipe and Zaire (now Democratic Republic of the Congo). CEEAC (q.v.) began operations in 1985.

Banque de développement des états de l'Afrique centrale—BDEAC: place du Gouvernement, BP 1177, Brazzaville, Republic of the Congo; tel. 81-18-85; fax 81-18-80; f. 1975; cap. 20,716m. francs CFA (Dec. 2000); shareholders: Cameroon, Central African Republic, Chad, Republic of the Congo, Gabon, Equatorial Guinea, ADB, BEAC, France, Germany and Kuwait; Chair. Eric Sorongope; Gen. Man. Anicet G. Dologuele.

Banque des états de l'Afrique centrale—BEAC: ave Mgr François Xavier Vogt, BP 1917, Yaoundé, Cameroon; tel. 23-40-30; fax 23-33-29; f. 1973 as the central bank of issue of Cameroon, the Central African Republic, Chad, Republic of the Congo, Equatorial Guinea and Gabon; a monetary market, incorporating all national financial institutions of the BEAC countries, came into effect on 1 July 1994; cap. 45,000m. francs CFA (Dec. 1998). Gov. Jean-Félix Mamalepot. Publs *Rapport annuel, Etudes et statistiques* (monthly).

CENTRAL ISSUING BANKS

Banque centrale des Comores: place de France, BP 405, Moroni, Comoros; tel. (73) 1002; fax (73) 0349; e-mail bcc@snpt.km; f. 1981; cap. 1,100m. Comoros francs (Dec. 1997); Gov. Saïd Ahmed Saïd Ali.

Banque centrale des états de l'Afrique de l'ouest: see above.

Banque des états de l'Afrique centrale: see above.

Institut d'émission d'outre-mer—IEOM: 5 rue Roland Barthes, 75598 Paris Cédex 12, France; tel. 1-53-44-41-41; fax 1-43-47-51-34; internet www.iedom-ieom.com; f. 1966; issuing authority for the French Overseas Territories; Pres. Jean-Paul Redouin; Dir-Gen. Jean-Michel Severino; Dir Christian Teysseyre.

FRENCH ECONOMIC AID

France's connection with the African Franc Zone countries involves not only monetary arrangements, but also includes comprehensive French assistance in the forms of budget support, foreign aid, technical assistance and subsidies on commodity exports.

Official French financial aid and technical assistance to developing countries is administered by the following agencies:

Agence française de développement—AFD: 5 rue Roland Barthes, 75598 Paris Cédex 12, France; tel. 1-53-44-31-31; fax 1-44-87-99-39; e-mail com@afd.fr; internet www.afd.fr/; f. 1941; fmrly the Caisse française de développement—CFD; French development bank which lends money to member states and former member states of the Franc Zone and several other states, and executes the financial operations of the FAC (see below). Following the devaluation of the franc CFA in January 1994, the French Government cancelled some 25,000m. French francs in debt arrears owed by member states to the CFD. The CFD established a Special Fund for Development and the Exceptional Facility for Short-term Financing to help alleviate the immediate difficulties resulting from the devaluation. A total of FFr 4,600m. of financial assistance was awarded to Franc Zone countries in 1994. In early 1994 the CFD made available funds totalling 2,420m. francs CFA to assist the establishment of CEMAC (see above). Serves as the secretariat for the Fonds français pour l'environnement mondial (f. 1994). Since 2000 the AFD has been implementing France's support of the World Bank's HIPC initiative. Dir-Gen. JEAN-MICHEL SEVERINO.

Fonds de Solidarité Prioritaire (FSP): 20 rue Monsieur, 75007 Paris, France; tel. 1-53-69-00-00; fax 1-53-69-43-82; f. 2000, taking over from the Fonds d'aide et de coopération (f. 1959) the administration of subsidies and loans from the French Government to the former French African states. FSP is administered by the Ministry of Co-operation, which allocates budgetary funds to it.

INTER-AMERICAN DEVELOPMENT BANK—IDB

Address: 1300 New York Ave, NW, Washington, DC 20577, USA.

Telephone: (202) 623-1000; **fax:** (202) 623-3096; **internet:** www.iadb.org.

The Bank was founded in 1959 to promote the individual and collective development of Latin American and Caribbean countries through the financing of economic and social development projects and the provision of technical assistance. Membership was increased in 1976 and 1977 to include countries outside the region.

MEMBERS

Argentina	Ecuador	Norway
Austria	El Salvador	Panama
Bahamas	Finland	Paraguay
Barbados	France	Peru
Belgium	Germany	Portugal
Belize	Guatemala	Slovenia
Bolivia	Guyana	Spain
Brazil	Haiti	Suriname
Canada	Honduras	Sweden
Chile	Israel	Switzerland
Colombia	Italy	Trinidad and Tobago
Costa Rica	Jamaica	United Kingdom
Croatia	Japan	USA
Denmark	Mexico	Uruguay
Dominican Republic	Netherlands	Venezuela
	Nicaragua	

Organization

(April 2002)

BOARD OF GOVERNORS

All the powers of the Bank are vested in a Board of Governors, consisting of one Governor and one alternate appointed by each member country (usually ministers of finance or presidents of central banks). The Board meets annually, with special meetings when necessary. The 43rd annual meeting of the Board of Governors took place in Fortaleza, Brazil, in March 2002.

BOARD OF EXECUTIVE DIRECTORS

The Board of Executive Directors is responsible for the operations of the Bank. It establishes the Bank's policies, approves loan and technical co-operation proposals that are submitted by the President of the Bank, and authorizes the Bank's borrowings on capital markets.

There are 12 executive directors and 12 alternates. Each Director is elected by a group of two or more countries, except the Directors representing Canada and the USA. The USA holds 30% of votes on the Board, in respect of its contribution to the Bank's capital. The Board has four standing committees, relating to: Policy and evaluation; Organization, human resources and board matters; Budget, financial policies and audit; and Programming. A steering committee was established in 1997.

ADMINISTRATION

The Bank comprises three Regional Operations Departments, as well as the following principal departments: Finance; Legal; Research; Integration and Regional Programmes; Private Sector; External Relations; Sustainable Development; Information Technology and General Services; Strategic Planning and Budget; and Human Resources. There are also Offices of the Auditor-General, the Multilateral Investment Fund, and the External Relations Advisor. An Office of Evaluation and Oversight, reporting directly to the Board of Executive Directors, was established in 2000 as part of a reorganization of the Bank's evaluation system. The Bank has country offices in each of its borrowing member states, and special offices in Paris, France and in Tokyo, Japan. At the end of 2001 there were 1,730 Bank staff (excluding the Board of Executive Directors and the Evaluation Office). The administrative budget for 2002 amounted to US $347m.

President: ENRIQUE V. IGLESIAS (Uruguay).

Executive Vice-President: K. BURKE DILLON (USA).

Activities

Loans are made to governments, and to public and private entities, for specific economic and social development projects and for sectoral reforms. These loans are repayable in the currencies lent and their terms range from 12 to 40 years. Total lending authorized by the Bank by the end of 2001 amounted to US $110,565m. During 2001 the Bank approved loans totalling $7,854m., compared with $5,266m. in 2000. Disbursements on authorized loans amounted to $6,459m. in 2001, compared with $7,069m. in the previous year.

The subscribed ordinary capital stock, including inter-regional capital, which was merged into it in 1987, totalled US $100,959.4m. at the end of 2001, of which $4,340.7m. was paid-in and $96,618.7m. was callable. The callable capital constitutes, in effect, a guarantee of the securities which the Bank issues in the capital markets in order to increase its resources available for lending. Replenishments are usually made every four years. In July 1995 the eighth general increase of the Bank's authorized capital was ratified by member countries: the Bank's resources were to be increased by $41,000m. to $102,000m.

In 2001 the Bank borrowed the equivalent of US $7,097m. on the international capital markets, bringing total borrowings outstanding to more than $42,186m. at the end of the year. During 2001 net earnings amounted to $1,009m. in ordinary capital resources and $129m. from the Fund for Special Operations (see below), and at the end of that year the Bank's total reserves were $8,922m.

The Fund for Special Operations enables the Bank to make concessional loans for economic and social projects where circumstances call for special treatment, such as lower interest rates and longer repayment terms than those applied to loans from the ordinary resources. The Board of Governors approved US $200m. in new contributions to the Fund in 1990, and in 1995 authorized $1,000m. in extra resources for the Fund. During 2001 the Fund made 24 loans totalling $443m., compared with loans amounting to $297m. in the previous year.

In January 1993 a Multilateral Investment Fund was established, as an autonomous fund administered by the Bank, to promote private sector development in the region. The 21 Bank members who signed the initial draft agreement in 1992 to establish the Fund pledged to contribute US $1,200m. The Fund's activities are undertaken through three separate facilities concerned with technical co-operation, human resources development and small enterprise development. In 2000 a specialist working group, established to consider MIF operations, recommended that it target its resources on the following core areas of activity: small business development; microenterprise; market functioning; and financial and capital markets. During 2001 the Fund approved $94m. for 66 projects.

In 1998 the Bank agreed to participate in a joint initiative by the International Monetary Fund and the World Bank to assist heavily indebted poor countries (HIPCs) to maintain a sustainable level of debt (see p. 174). Four member countries were eligible for assistance under the initiative (Bolivia, Guyana, Honduras and Nicaragua). Also in 1998, following projections of reduced resources for the Fund for Special Operations, borrowing member countries agreed to convert about US $2,400m. in local currencies held by the Bank, in order to maintain a convertible concessional Fund for poorer countries, and to help to reduce the debt-servicing payments under the HIPC initiative. In mid-2000 a committee of the Board of Governors endorsed a financial framework for the Bank's participation in an Enhanced HIPC Initiative, which aimed to broaden the eligibility criteria and accelerate the process of debt reduction. The Bank's total contribution to the initiative was estimated to be $1,100m. By December 2001 the Bank had approved interim debt relief for all four eligible member countries under the enhanced HIPC initiative, and had assisted the preparation of national Poverty Reduction Strategy Papers, a condition of reaching the 'completion point' of the process.

The Bank supports a range of consultative groups, in order to strengthen donor co-operation with countries in the Latin America and Caribbean region. In December1998 the Bank established an emergency Consultative Group for the Reconstruction and Transformation of Central America to co-ordinate assistance to countries that had suffered extensive damage as a result of Hurricane Mitch. The Bank hosted the first meeting of the group in the same month, which was attended by government officials, representatives of donor agencies and non-governmental organizations and academics. A total of US $6,200m. was pledged in the form of emergency aid, longer-term financing and debt relief. A second meeting of the group was held in May 1999, in Stockholm, Sweden, at which the assistance package was increased to some $9,000m., of which the Bank and World Bank committed $5,300m. In March 2001 the group convened, in Madrid, Spain, to promote integration and foreign investment in Central America. The meeting, organized by the Bank, was also used to generate $1,300m. in commitments from international donors to assist emergency relief and reconstruction efforts in El Salvador following an earthquake earlier in the year. In October the Bank organized a consultative group meeting in support of a Social Welfare and Alternative Preventive Development Programme for Ecuador, to which donor countries committed $266m. Other consultative groups co-ordinated by the Bank include ones to support the peace process in Colombia, and in Guatemala. In November the Bank hosted the first meeting of a Network for the Prevention and Mitigation of Natural Disasters in Latin America and the Caribbean, which was part of a regional policy dialogue, sponsored by the Bank to promote broad debate on strategic issues.

An increasing number of donor countries have placed funds under the Bank's administration for assistance to Latin America, outside the framework of the Ordinary Resources and the Bank's Special Operations. These trust funds, totalling some 58 in 2000, include the Social Progress Trust Fund (set up by the USA in 1961); the Venezuelan Trust Fund (set up in 1975); the Japan Special Fund (1988); and other funds administered on behalf of Austria, Belgium, Canada, Denmark, Finland, France, Israel, Italy, Japan, the Netherlands, Norway, Portugal, Spain, Sweden, Switzerland, the United Kingdom and the EU. A Program for the Development of Technical Co-operation was established in 1991, which is financed by European countries and the EU. Total cumulative lending from all these trust funds was $1,719.3m. for loans approved by the end of 2001, of which $1,646.6m. had been disbursed. During 2001 cofinancing by bilateral and multilateral sources amounted to $628.8m., which helped to finance 22 national and two regional projects.

The Bank provides technical co-operation to help member countries to identify and prepare new projects, to improve loan execution, to strengthen the institutional capacity of public and private agencies, to address extreme conditions of poverty and to promote small- and micro-enterprise development. The Bank has established a special co-operation programme to facilitate the transfer of experience and technology among regional programmes. In 2001 the Bank approved 376 technical co-operation operations, totalling US $71m., mainly financed by income from the Fund for Special Operations and donor trust funds. The Bank supports the efforts of the countries of the region to achieve economic integration and has provided extensive technical support for the formulation of integration strategies in the Andean, Central American and Southern Cone regions. The Bank is also supporting the initiative to establish a Free Trade Area of the Americas (FTAA) by 2005 and has provided technical assistance, developed programming strategies and produced a number of studies on relevant integration and trade issues. During the period 1998–2000 the Bank contributed an estimated $15,000m. to projects in support of the goals of the summit meetings of the Americas, for example, strengthening democratic systems, alleviating poverty, and promoting economic integration. In 2001 the Bank took a lead role in a Central American regional initiative, the Puebla-Panama Plan, which aimed to consolidate integration and support for social and economic development.

Distribution of loans (US $ million)

Sector	2001	%	1961–2001	%
Productive Sectors				
Agriculture and fisheries	683.2	8.7	12,278.1	11.1
Industry, mining and tourism	1,060.2	13.5	11,367.7	10.3
Science and technology	6.8	0.1	1,616.7	1.5
Physical Infrastructure				
Energy	303.7	3.9	16,022.2	14.5
Transportation and communications	391.7	5.0	12,870.1	11.6
Social Sectors				
Sanitation	123.0	1.6	8,803.5	8.0
Urban development	168.8	2.1	6,622.3	6.0
Education	711.5	9.1	4,911.7	4.4
Social investment	1,784.8	22.7	8,910.7	8.1
Health	110.3	1.4	2,107.7	1.9
Environment	79.5	1.0	1,541.8	1.4
Microenterprise	0.0	0.0	381.2	0.3
Other				
Public-sector reform and modernization	2,419.1	30.8	19,309.0	17.4
Export financing	11.0	0.1	1,536.7	1.4
Other	0.0	0.0	2,285.4	2.1
Total	7,853.5	100.0	110,564.8	100.0

Source: *Annual Report, 2001.*

INSTITUTIONS

Instituto para la Integración de América Latina y el Caribe (Institute for the Integration of Latin America and the Caribbean): Esmeralda 130, 17°, 1035 Buenos Aires, Argentina; tel. (11) 4320-1850; fax (11) 4320-1865; e-mail int/inl@iadb.org; internet www.iadb.org/intal; f. 1965 under the auspices of the Inter-American Development Bank; forms part of the Bank's Integration and Regional Programmes Department. The Institute undertakes research on all aspects of regional integration and co-operation and issues related to international trade, hemispheric integration and relations with other regions and countries of the world. Activities come under four main headings: regional and national technical co-operation projects on integration; policy fora; integration fora; and journals and information. Maintains an extensive Documentation Center and various statistical databases. Dir JUAN JOSÉ TACCONE. Publs *Integración y Comercio/Integration and Trade* (3 a year), *Intal Newsletter, Informe Mercosur/Mercosur Report* (2 a year).

Inter-American Institute for Social Development—INDES: 1350 New York Ave, NW, Washington, DC, 20057, USA; e-mail indes@iadb.org; internet www.iadb.org/indes; commenced operations in 1995; aims to support the training of senior officials from public sector institutions and organizations involved with social policies and social services. INDES organizes specialized sub-regional courses and seminars and national training programmes. It produces teaching materials and also serves as a forum for the exchange of ideas on social reform. During 2001 four courses were conducted, and other national training programmes were organized in six countries. Dir NOHRA REY DE MARULANDA.

Inter-American Investment Corporation—IIC: 1300 New York Ave, NW, Washington, DC 20057, USA; tel. (202) 623-3900; fax (202) 623-2360; e-mail iicmail@iadb.org; internet www.iadb.org/iic; f. 1986 as a legally autonomous affiliate of the Inter-American Development Bank, to promote the economic development of the region; commenced operations in 1989. The IIC's initial capital stock was US $200m., of which 55% was contributed by developing member nations, 25.3% by the USA, and the remainder by non-regional members. In total, the IIC has 42 shareholders (26 Latin American and Caribbean countries, 13 European countries, Israel, Japan and the USA). Emphasis is placed on investment in small and medium-sized enterprises without access to other suitable sources of equity or long-term loans. In 2001 the IIC approved equity investments and loans totalling $128m. for 19 transactions. In that year the Board of Governors of the IADB agreed to increase the IIC's capital by $500m. Gen. Man. JACQUES ROGOZINSKI. Publ. *Annual Report* (in English, French, Portuguese and Spanish).

Publications

Annual Report (in English, Spanish, Portuguese and French).

Annual Report on Oversight and Evaluation.

Annual Report on the Environment and Natural Resources (in English and Spanish).

Economic and Social Progress in Latin America (annually, in English and Spanish).

Equidad (2 a year).

IDB América (monthly, English and Spanish).

IDB Projects (10 a year, in English).

IFM (Infrastructure and Financial Markets) Review (quarterly).

Latin American Economic Markets (quarterly).

Proceedings of the Annual Meeting of the Boards of Governors of the IDB and IIC (in English, Spanish, Portuguese and French).

Social Development Newsletter (2 a year).

Brochure series, occasional papers, working papers, reports.

Yearly and cumulative loans and guarantees, 1961–2001(US $ million; after cancellations and exchange adjustments)

	Total Amount		Ordinary Capital*		Fund for Special Operations		Funds in Administration	
Country	2001	1961–2001	2001	1961–2001	2001	1961–2001	2001	1961–2001
Argentina	1,655.9	16,757.2	1,655.9	16,063.3	—	644.9	—	49.0
Bahamas	46.2	334.6	46.2	332.6	—	—	—	2.0
Barbados	8.8	377.5	8.8	315.7	—	42.8	—	19.0
Belize	7.0	92.2	7.0	92.2	—	—	—	—
Bolivia	113.2	2,832.8	—	970.5	113.2	1,791.1	—	71.2
Brazil	2,055.5	23,651.5	2,055.5	21,963.8	—	1,558.5	—	129.2
Chile	60.4	4,602.3	60.4	4,357.2	—	203.3	—	41.8
Colombia	800.0	8,471.0	800.0	7,651.5	—	759.3		60.2
Costa Rica	22.4	2,088.6	22.4	1,598.8	—	351.8	—	138.0
Dominican Republic	275.0	2,234.7	275.0	1,450.5	—	699.0	—	85.2
Ecuador	65.1	3,615.0	65.1	2,596.6	—	931.1	—	87.3
El Salvador	277.0	2,792.6	277.0	1,902.7	—	745.8	—	144.1
Guatemala	32.2	2,212.0	32.2	1,514.4	—	627.5	—	70.1
Guyana	53.3	747.6	—	102.3	53.3	638.4	—	6.9
Haiti	—	752.8	—	—	—	746.5	—	6.3
Honduras	96.4	2,175.5	—	484.3	96.4	1,625.8	—	65.4
Jamaica	112.0	1,618.6	112.0	1,255.8	—	163.8	—	199.0
Mexico	1,102.0	14,401.5	1,102.0	13,791.2	—	559.0	—	51.3
Nicaragua	180.0	1,841.4	—	243.0	180.0	1,533.5	—	64.9
Panama	35.7	1,866.0	35.7	1,543.4	—	280.0	—	42.6
Paraguay	22.2	1,699.7	22.2	1,116.2	—	571.7	—	11.8
Peru	343.3	5,408.0	343.3	4,768.9	—	418.1	—	221.0
Suriname	14.7	72.6	14.7	70.3	—	2.3	—	—
Trinidad and Tobago	—	951.1	—	895.3	—	30.6	—	25.2
Uruguay	303.9	2,576.8	303.9	2,430.9	—	104.1	—	41.8
Venezuela	97.5	3,730.3	97.5	3,556.0	—	101.4	—	72.9
Regional	74.0	2,660.6	74.0	2,450.3	—	197.2	—	13.1
Total	7,853.5	110,564.8	7,410.8	93,518.0	442.7	15,327.5	—	1,719.3

* Includes private sector loans, net of participations.

INTERGOVERNMENTAL AUTHORITY ON DEVELOPMENT—IGAD

Address: BP 2653, Djibouti.

Telephone: 354050; **fax:** 356994; **e-mail:** igad@igadregion.org; **internet:** www.igadregion.org.

The Intergovernmental Authority on Development (IGAD) was established in 1996 to supersede the Intergovernmental Authority on Drought and Development (IGADD), founded in 1986 to co-ordinate measures to combat the effects of drought and desertification and attain regional food security.

MEMBERS

Djibouti	Kenya	Sudan
Eritrea	Somalia	Uganda
Ethiopia		

Organization

(April 2002)

ASSEMBLY

The Assembly, consisting of heads of state and of government of member states, is the supreme policy-making organ of the Authority. It holds a summit meeting at least once a year. The ninth Assembly meeting of heads of state and of government was held in Khartoum, Sudan in January 2002.The chairmanship of the Assembly rotates among the member countries on an annual basis.

Chairman (2002/03): Lt-Gen. OMAR HASSAN AHMAD AL-BASHIR (Sudan).

COUNCIL OF MINISTERS

The Council of Ministers is composed of the minister of foreign affairs and one other minister from each member state. It meets at least twice a year and approves the work programme and the annual budget of the Secretariat.

COMMITTEE OF AMBASSADORS

The Committee of Ambassadors comprises the ambassadors or plenipotentiaries of member states to Djibouti. It convenes as regularly as required to advise and assist the Executive Secretary concerning the interpretation of policies and guide-lines and the realization of the annual work programme.

SECRETARIAT

The Secretariat, the executive body of IGAD, is headed by the Executive Secretary, who is appointed by the Assembly for a term of four years, renewable once. In addition to the Office of the Executive Secretary, the Secretariat comprises the following three divisions: Agriculture and Environment; Economic Co-operation; and Political and Humanitarian Affairs.

Executive Secretary: Dr ATTALLA HAMAD BASHIR (Sudan).

Activities

IGADD was established in 1986 by Djibouti, Ethiopia, Kenya, Somalia, Sudan and Uganda, to combat the effects of aridity and desertification arising from the severe drought and famine that has periodically affected the Horn of Africa. Eritrea became a member of IGADD in September 1993, following its proclamation as an independent state. In April 1995, at an extraordinary summit meeting held in Addis Ababa, Ethiopia, heads of state and of government resolved to reorganize and expand the Authority. In March 1996 IGAD was endorsed to supersede IGADD, at a second extraordinary summit meeting of heads of state and of government, held in Nairobi, Kenya. The meeting led to the adoption of an agreement for a new organizational structure and the approval of an extended mandate to co-ordinate and harmonize policy in the areas of economic co-operation and political and humanitarian affairs, in addition to its existing responsibilities for food security and environmental protection.

IGAD aims to achieve regional co-operation and economic integration. To facilitate this IGAD assists the governments of member states to maximize resources and co-ordinates efforts to initiate and implement regional development programmes and projects. In this context, IGAD promotes the harmonization of policies relating to agriculture and natural resources, communications, customs, trade and transport; the implementation of programmes in the fields of social sciences, research, science and technology; and effective participation in the global economy. Meetings between IGAD foreign affairs ministers and the IGAD Joint Partners' Forum, comprising the grouping's donors, are convened periodically to discuss issues such as food security and humanitarian affairs.

FOOD SECURITY AND ENVIRONMENTAL PROTECTION

IGAD seeks to achieve regional food security, the sustainable development of natural resources and environmental protection, and to encourage and assist member states in their efforts to combat the consequences of drought and other natural and man-made disasters. The region suffers from recurrent droughts, which severely impede crop and livestock production. Natural and man-made disasters increase the strain on resources, resulting in annual food deficits. About 80% of the IGAD sub-region is classified as arid or semi-arid, and some 40% of the region is unproductive, owing to severe environmental degradation. Activities to improve food security and preserve natural resources have included: the introduction of remote-sensing services; the development of a Marketing Information System and of a Regional Integrated Information System (RIIS); the establishment of training and credit schemes for fishermen; research into the sustainable production of drought-resistant, high-yielding crop varieties; transboundary livestock disease control and vaccine production; the control of environmental pollution; the promotion of alternative sources of energy in the home; the management of integrated water resources; the promotion of community-based land husbandry; training programmes in grain marketing; and the implementation of the International Convention to Combat Desertification.

ECONOMIC CO-OPERATION

The Economic Co-operation division concentrates on the development of a co-ordinated infrastructure for the region, in particular in the areas of transport and communications, to promote foreign, cross-border and domestic trade and investment opportunities. IGAD seeks to harmonize national transport and trade policy and thereby facilitate the free movement of people, goods and services. The improvements to infrastructure also aim to facilitate more timely interventions to conflicts, disasters and emergencies in the sub-region. Projects to be undertaken by the end of 2001 included: the construction of missing segments of the Trans-African Highway and the Pan African Telecommunications Network; the removal of barriers to trade and communications; improvements to ports and inland container terminals; and the modernization of railway and telecommunications services. In November 2000 the IGAD Assembly determined to establish an integrated rail network connecting all member countries. In addition, the heads of state and government considered the possibility of drafting legislation to facilitate the expansion of intra-IGAD trade. The development of economic co-operation has been impeded by persisting conflicts in the sub-region (see below).

POLITICAL AND HUMANITARIAN AFFAIRS

The field of political and humanitarian affairs focuses on conflict prevention, management and resolution through dialogue. The division's primary aim is to restore peace and stability to member countries affected by conflict, in order that resources may be diverted for development purposes. Efforts have been pursued to strengthen capacity for conflict prevention and to relieve humanitarian crises. In September 1995 negotiations between the Sudanese Government and opposition leaders were initiated, under the auspices of IGAD, with the aim of resolving the conflict in southern Sudan; these were subsequently reconvened periodically. In March 2001 IGAD's mediation committee on southern Sudan, chaired by President Daniel arap Moi of Kenya, publicized a seven-point plan for a peaceful settlement of the conflict. In early June, at a regional summit on the situation in Sudan convened by IGAD, it was agreed that a permanent negotiating forum comprising representatives of the parties to the conflict would be established at the Authority's secretariat. It was reported in the following month that a peace initiative sponsored by Egypt and Libya had also been accepted by the Sudanese Government and main opposition groupings; it was hoped that this and the IGAD initiative would be complementary. In May–August 2000 a conference aimed at securing peace in Somalia was convened in Arta, Djibouti, under the auspices of IGAD. The conference appointed a transitional Somali legislature, which then elected an interim national president. The eighth summit of IGAD heads of state and government, held in Khartoum, Sudan, in November, welcomed the conclusion in September of an agreement of reconciliation between the new Somali interim administration and a prominent opposition alliance, and determined that those member countries that neighboured Somalia (Djibouti, Ethiopia and Kenya) should co-operate in assisting the process of reconstruction and reconciliation in that country. The summit appointed a special envoy to implement IGAD's directives concerning the Somali situation. Following the violent escalation of a border dispute between Eritrea and Ethiopia in mid-1998 IGAD supported efforts by the Organization of African Unity (q.v.) to mediate a cease-fire between the two sides. This was achieved in mid-2000. The ninth IGAD summit meeting, held in Khartoum in January 2002, adopted a protocol to IGAD's founding agreement establishing a conflict early warning and response mechanism (CEWARN). CEWARN was to collect and analyse information for the preparation of periodic early warning reports concerning the potential outbreak of violent conflicts in the region. The summit meeting determined that a new conference for promoting reconciliation in Somalia (where insecurity continued to prevail) should be convened shortly, under IGAD's auspices. The leaders also issued a statement condemning international terrorism and urged Somalia in particular to make a firm commitment to eradicating terrorism. A meeting of IGAD ministers of foreign affairs in February established a technical committee to prepare for the conference, which was scheduled to be held in late April.

Publications

Annual Report.

IGAD News (2 a year).

Proceedings of the Summit of Heads of State and Government.

Reports of the Council of Ministers' Meetings.

INTERNATIONAL CHAMBER OF COMMERCE—ICC

Address: 38 Cours Albert 1er, 75008 Paris, France.

Telephone: 1-49-53-28-28; **fax:** 1-49-53-29-42; **e-mail:** icc@iccwbo.org; **internet:** www.iccwbo.org.

The ICC was founded in 1919 to promote free trade and private enterprise, provide practical services and represent business interests at governmental and intergovernmental levels.

MEMBERS

ICC membership comprises corporations, national professional and sectoral associations, business and employer federations, chambers of commerce, and individuals involved in international business from more than 130 countries. National Committees or Groups have been formed in some 70 countries and territories to co-ordinate ICC objectives and functions at the national level.

Organization

(April 2002)

COUNCIL

The Council is the governing body of the organization. It meets twice a year and is composed of members nominated by the National Committees. Ten direct members, from countries where no National Committee exists, may also be invited to participate. The Council elects the President and Vice-President for terms of two years.

President: RICHARD D. MCCORMICK (USA).

EXECUTIVE BOARD

The Executive Board consists of 15–30 members appointed by the Council on the recommendation of the President and nine *ex-officio* members. Members serve for a three-year term, one-third of the members retiring at the end of each year. It ensures close direction of ICC activities and meets at least three times each year.

INTERNATIONAL SECRETARIAT

The ICC secretariat is based at International Headquarters in Paris, with additional offices maintained in Geneva and New York principally for liaison with the United Nations and its agencies. The Secretary-General is appointed by the Council on the recommendation of the Executive Board.

Secretary-General: MARIA LIVANOS CATTAUI (Switzerland).

NATIONAL COMMITTEES AND GROUPS

Each affiliate is composed of leading business organizations and individual companies. It has its own secretariat, monitors issues of concern to its national constituents, and draws public and government attention to ICC policies.

CONGRESS

The ICC's supreme assembly, to which all member companies and organizations are invited to send senior representatives. Congresses are held regularly, in a different place on each occasion, with up to 2,000 participants. The 33rd Congress was held in Budapest, Hungary, in May 2000, on the theme of 'The New Europe in the World Economy'.

CONFERENCES

ICC Conferences was created in 1996 to disseminate ICC expertise in the fields of international arbitration, trade, banking and commercial practice, by means of a world-wide programme of conferences and seminars.

Activities

The various Commissions of the ICC (listed below) are composed of at least 500 practising business executives and experts from all sectors of economic life, nominated by National Committees. ICC recommendations must be adopted by a Commission following consultation with National Committees, and then approved by the Council or Executive Board, before they can be regarded as official ICC policies. Meetings of Commissions are generally held twice a year. Working Parties are frequently constituted by Commissions to undertake specific projects and report back to their parent body. Officers of Commissions, and specialized Working Parties, often meet in the intervals between Commission sessions. The Commissions produce a wide array of specific codes and guide-lines of direct use to the world business community; formulate statements and initiatives for presentation to governments and international bodies; and comment constructively and in detail on proposed actions by intergovernmental organizations and governments that are likely to affect business. In January 1997 the ICC opened its first regional office, in the Hong Kong Special Administrative Region.

ICC works closely with other international organizations. ICC members, the heads of UN economic organizations and the OECD convene for annual discussions on the world economy. The Commission on International Trade and Investment Policy campaigns against protectionism in world trade and in support of the World Trade Organization (WTO, q.v.). The ICC also works closely with the European Union, commenting on EU directives and making recommendations on, for example, tax harmonization and laws relating to competition.

ICC plays a part in combating international crime connected with commerce through its Commercial Crime Services, based in London, United Kingdom, and Kuala Lumpur, Malaysia. These comprise: the Commercial Crime Bureau; the International Maritime Bureau, which combats maritime fraud, including insurance fraud and the theft of cargoes; and the Counterfeiting Intelligence Bureau, established in 1985 to investigate counterfeiting in trade-marked goods, copyrights and industrial designs. The ICC provides a framework for international commercial disputes, mainly through the ICC International Court of Arbitration, which was established in 1923. The Court received some 566 requests for arbitration in 2001. Other ICC services for dispute resolution include its Rules of Arbitration, its Alternative Dispute Resolution, and the International Centre for Expertise, which administers ICC Rules of Expertise and Rules for Documentary Credit and Dispute Resolution Expertise (DOCDEX).

The ICC has developed rules and guide-lines relating to electronic transactions, including guide-lines for ethical advertising on the internet and for data protection. In September 1999 it presented model clauses for company contracts involving the electronic transfer of personal information. The Geneva Business Dialogue was held in Switzerland in September. The primary subjects discussed were the importance of globalization in business and the need to avoid protectionist reactions to recent economic upheaval. The ICC has also devised a system of standard trade definitions most commonly used in international sales contracts. A fully revised and updated version of these, Incoterms 2000, entered into effect on 1 January 2000.

Policy and Technical Commissions:

Commission on Air Cargo
Commission on Air Transport
Commission on Arbitration
Commission on Banking Technique and Practice
Commission on Business in Society
Commission on Competition
Commission on Customs and Trade Regulations
Commission on Energy
Commission on Environment
Commission on Extortion and Bribery
Commission on Financial Services and Insurance
Commission on Intellectual and Industrial Property
Commission on International Commercial Practice
Commission on Maritime Transport
Commission on Marketing, Advertising and Distribution
Commission on Surface Transport
Commission on Taxation
Commission on Telecommunications and Information Technologies

Commission on Trade and Investment Policy

Special Groups:

Corporate Economist Advisory Group
Electronic Commerce Project
Standing Committee on Extortion and Bribery

Bodies for the Settlement of Disputes:

International Centre for Technical Expertise
International Court of Arbitration
International Maritime Arbitration Organization

Other Bodies:

ICC Centre for Maritime Co-operation
ICC Commercial Crime Bureau
ICC Corporate Security Services
ICC Counterfeiting Intelligence Bureau
ICC Cybercrime Unit
ICC Institute of International Business Law and Practice
ICC International Maritime Bureau
ICC-WTO Economic Consultative Committee
Institute of World Business Law
World Chambers Federation

Finance

The International Chamber of Commerce is a private organization financed partly by contributions from National Committees and other members, according to the economic importance of the country which each represents, and partly by revenue from fees for various services and from sales of publications.

Publications

Annual Report.

Business World (electronic magazine).

Documentary Credits Insight (quarterly).

Handbook.

ICC Contact (newsletter).

ICC International Court of Arbitration Bulletin.

IGO Report.

Numerous publications on general and technical business and trade-related subjects.

INTERNATIONAL CONFEDERATION OF FREE TRADE UNIONS—ICFTU

Address: 5 blvd Roi Albert II, 1210 Brussels, Belgium.

Telephone: (2) 224-02-11; **fax:** (2) 201-58-15; **e-mail:** internet po@icftu.org; **internet:** www.icftu.org.

ICFTU was founded in 1949 by trade union federations which had withdrawn from the World Federation of Trade Unions (see p. 512). It aims to promote the interests of working people and to secure recognition of workers' organizations as free bargaining agents; to reduce the gap between rich and poor; and to defend fundamental human and trade union rights. It campaigns for the adoption by the World Trade Organization of a social clause, with legally-binding minimum labour standards, and regularly provides economic analysis and proposals at international meetings. In March 2001 ICTFU launched a two-year campaign to promote the eradication of child labour. In March 2002 it presented a report on the social dimensions of globalization, at the first meeting of the ILO World Commission on Globalization. See also the World Confederation of Labour (p. 509).

MEMBERS

226 organizations in 148 countries with 157m. members (April 2002).

Organization

(April 2002)

WORLD CONGRESS

The Congress, the highest authority of ICFTU, normally meets every four years. The 17th Congress was held in Durban, South Africa, in April 2000.

Delegations from national federations vary in size according to membership. The Congress examines past activities, maps out future plans, elects the Executive Board and the General Secretary, considers the functioning of the regional machinery, examines financial reports and social, economic and political situations. It works through plenary sessions and through technical committees which report to the plenary sessions.

EXECUTIVE BOARD

The Board meets not less than once a year, for about three days, usually at Brussels, or at the Congress venue; it comprises 53 members elected by Congress and nominated by areas of the world. The General Secretary is an *ex-officio* member. After each Congress the Board elects a President and at least seven Vice-Presidents.

The Board considers administrative questions; hears reports from field representatives, missions, regional organizations and affiliates, and makes resultant decisions; and discusses finances, applications for affiliation, and problems affecting world labour. It elects a steering committee of 19 to deal with urgent matters between Board meetings.

President: FACKSON SHAMENDA (Zambia).

PERMANENT COMMITTEES

Steering Committee. Administers the General Fund, comprising affiliation fees, and the International Solidarity Fund, constituting additional voluntary contributions.

Economic and Social Committee.

Human and Trade Union Rights Committee.

***ICFTU/ITS Working Party on Trade Union Education.**

***ICFTU/ITS Occupational Health, Safety, and the Environment Working Party.**

***ICFTU/ITS Working Party on Multinational Companies.**

Peace, Security and Disarmament Committee.

Youth Committee.

Women's Committee.

*A joint body of the ICFTU and International Trade Secretariats.

SECRETARIAT

Departments at headquarters include: Economic and Social Policy; Trade Union Rights; Projects, Co-ordination and Education (comprising units for Projects and Trade Union Education); Equality (including Youth); Finance and Administration; Press and Publications. There are also the Co-ordination Unit for Central and Eastern Europe, the Electronic Data Processing Unit, Personnel, Co-ordination and Regional Liaison Desks for the Americas, Africa and Asia.

General Secretary: GUY RYDER (United Kingdom).

BRANCH OFFICES

ICFTU Geneva Office: 46 ave Blanc, 1202 Geneva, Switzerland; tel. (22) 7384202; fax (22) 7381082; e-mail icftu-ge@geneva.icftu.org; Dir DAN CUNNIAH.

ICFTU Moscow Office: Leninsky Prospekt 42, 117119 Moscow, Russia; tel. (95) 9387356; fax (95) 9387304; e-mail icftumos@cq.ru.

ICFTU United Nations Office: 211 East 43rd St, Suite 710, New York, NY 10017, USA; tel. (212) 370-0180; fax (212) 370-0188; e-mail icftuny@igc.org; Perm. Rep. GEMMA ADABA.

There are also Permanent Representatives accredited to FAO (Rome) to the UN, UNIDO and IAEA (Vienna) and to UNEP and UN-Habitat (Nairobi).

REGIONAL ORGANIZATIONS

ICFTU African Regional Organization—AFRO: POB 67273, Kenya-re Towers, 4th Floor, Upper Hill, Nairobi, Kenya; tel. (2) 244336; fax (2) 215072; e-mail info@ictfuafro.org; internet www.icftuafro.org; f. 1957. Mems: 5m. workers in 36 African countries. Gen. Sec. ANDREW KAILEMBO (Tanzania).

ICFTU Asian and Pacific Regional Organization—APRO: 73 Bras Basah Rd, 4th Floor, Singapore 189556; tel. (65) 62226294; fax (65) 62217380; e-mail gs@icftu-apro.org; internet www.icftu-apro.org; f. 1951. Mems: 33m. in 38 orgs in 29 countries. Gen. Sec. NORIYUKI SUZUKI.

Inter-American Regional Organization of Workers—ORIT: Edif. José Vargas, Avda Andrés Eloy Blanco No 2, 15°, Los Caobos, Caracas, Venezuela; tel. (2) 578-3538; fax (2) 578-1702; e-mail secgenorit@cantv.net; internet www.chioslorit.org; f. 1951. Mems: national unions in 28 countries and territories. Gen. Sec. LUIS A. ANDERSON.

There are Field Representatives in various parts of Africa. In addition, a number of Project Planners for development co-operation travel in different countries.

Finance

Affiliated federations pay a standard fee of €165.1 (2002), or its equivalent in other currencies, per 1,000 members per annum, which covers the establishment and routine activities of the ICFTU headquarters in Brussels, and partly subsidizes the regional organizations.

An International Solidarity Fund was set up in 1956 to assist unions in developing countries, and workers and trade unionists victimized by repressive political measures. It provides legal assistance and supports educational activities. In cases of major natural disasters affecting workers token relief aid is granted.

Publications

Survey of Trade Union Rights (annually).

Trade Union World (official journal, monthly).

These periodicals are issued in English, French and Spanish. In addition the Congress report is issued in English. Numerous other publications on labour, social protection and trade union training have been published in various languages.

Associated International Trade Secretariats

Education International—EI: 5 blvd Roi Albert II (8ème étage), 1210 Brussels, Belgium; tel. (2) 224-06-11; fax (2) 224-06-06; e-mail headoffice@ei-ie.org; internet www.ei-ie.org; f. 1993 by merger of the World Confederation of Organizations of the Teaching Profession (f. 1952) and the International Federation of Free Teachers' Unions (f. 1951). Mems: 309 national orgs of teachers' trade unions representing 25m. members in 157 countries and territories. Holds Congress (every three years): July 2001 in Kathmandu, Nepal. Pres. MARY HATWOOD FUTRELL (USA); Sec.-Gen. FRED VAN LEEUWEN (Netherlands). Publs *EI Monitor* (monthly), *Education International* (quarterly) (both in English, French and Spanish).

International Federation of Building and Woodworkers—IFBWW: 54 route des Acacias, 1227 Carouge, Switzerland; tel. (22) 8273777; fax (22) 8273770; e-mail info@ifbww.org; internet www.ifbww.org; f. 1934. Mems: 289 national unions with a membership of more than 11.0m. workers in 127 countries. Organization: Congress, Executive Committee. Pres. ROEL DE VRIES (Netherlands); Sec.-Gen. ANITA NORMARK (Sweden). Publ. *IFBWW News* (2 a month).

International Federation of Chemical, Energy, Mine and General Workers' Unions—ICEM: 109 ave Emile de Béco, 1050 Brussels, Belgium; tel. (2) 626-20-20; fax (2) 648-43-16; e-mail info@icem.org; internet www.icem.org; f. 1995 by merger of the International Federation of Chemical, Energy and General Workers' Unions (f. 1907) and the Miners' International Federation (f. 1890). Mems: 403 trade unions covering approximately 20m. workers in 115 countries. Main sectors cover energy industries; chemicals; pharmaceuticals and biotechnology; mining and extraction; pulp and paper; rubber; ceramics; glass; building materials; and environmental services. Pres. JOHN MAITLAND; Gen. Sec. FRED HIGGS. Publs *ICEM Info* (quarterly), *ICEM Focus on Health, Safety and Environment* (2 a year), *ICEM Update* (Irregular).

International Federation of Journalists—IFJ: International Press Centre, 155 rue de la Loi, 1040 Brussels, Belgium; tel. (2) 235-22-19; fax (2) 235-22-00; e-mail ifj@icj.org; internet www.ifj.org; f. 1952 to link national unions of professional journalists dedicated to the freedom of the press, to defend the rights of journalists, and to raise professional standards; it conducts surveys, assists in trade union training programmes, organizes seminars and provides information; it arranges fact-finding missions in countries where press freedom is under pressure, and issues protests against the persecution and detention of journalists and the censorship of the mass media; Holds Congress (every three years): June 2001 in Seoul, Republic of Korea. Mems: 143 unions in 104 countries, comprising 450,000 individuals. Pres. CHRIS WARREN (Australia); Gen. Sec. AIDAN WHITE (UK). Publ. *IFJ Direct Line* (every two months).

International Metalworkers' Federation—IMF: CP 1516, Route des Acacias 54 bis, 1227 Geneva, Switzerland; tel. (22) 3085050; fax (22) 3085055; e-mail info@imfmetal.org; internet www.imfmetal.org; f. 1893. Mems: national orgs covering 24.8m. workers in 207 unions in 101 countries. Holds Congress (every four years); has six regional offices; seven industrial departments; World Company Councils for unions in multinational corporations. Pres. K. ZWICKEL (Germany); Gen. Sec. MARCELLO MALENTACCHI. Publs *IMF NewsBriefs* (weekly), *Metal World* (quarterly).

International Textile, Garment and Leather Workers' Federation—ITGLWF: rue Joseph Stevens 8 (Boîte 4), 1000 Brussels, Belgium; tel. (2) 512-26-06; fax (2) 511-09-04; e-mail office@itglwf.org; internet www.itglwf.org; f. 1970. Mems: 220 unions covering 10m. workers in 110 countries. Holds Congress (every four years): June 2000 in Norrköping, Sweden. Pres. PETER BOOTH (UK); Gen. Sec. NEIL KEARNEY (Ireland). Publ. *ITGLWF Newsletter* (quarterly).

International Transport Workers' Federation—ITF: 49-60 Borough Rd, London, SE1 1DR, United Kingdom; tel. (20) 7403-2733; fax (20) 7357-7871; e-mail mail@itf.org.uk; internet www.itf.org.uk; f. 1896. Mems: national trade unions covering 5m. workers in 579 unions in 132 countries. Holds Congress (every four years); has eight Industrial Sections. Pres. UMRAOMAL PURDIT (India); Gen. Sec. DAVID COCKROFT (UK). Publ. *Transport International* (quarterly).

International Union of Food, Agricultural, Hotel, Restaurant, Catering, Tobacco and Allied Workers' Associations—IUF: 8 rampe du Pont-Rouge, 1213 Petit-Lancy, Switzerland; tel. (22) 7932233; fax (22) 7932238; e-mail iuf@iuf.org; internet www.iuf.org; f. 1920. Mems: 331 affiliated organizations covering about 2.6m workers in 112 countries. Holds Congress (every five years). Pres. FRANK HURT (USA); Gen. Sec. RON OSWALD. Publs bi-monthly bulletins.

Public Services International—PSI: 45 ave Voltaire, BP9, 01211 Ferney-Voltaire Cédex, France; tel. 4-50-40-64-64; fax 4-50-40-73-20; e-mail psi@world-psi.org; internet www.world-psi.org; f. 1907; Mems: 601 unions and professional associations covering 20m. workers in 146 countries (at 31 Dec. 2001). Holds Congress (every five years). Pres. WILLIAM LUCY (USA); Gen. Sec. HANS ENGELBERTS (Netherlands). Publ. *Focus* (quarterly).

Union Network International—UNI: 8-10 ave Reverdil, 1260 Nyon, Switzerland; tel. (22) 3652100; fax (22) 3652121; e-mail contact@union-network.org; internet www.union-network.org; f. 2000 by merger of Communications International (CI), the International Federation of Commercial, Clerical, Professional and Technical Employees (FIET), the International Graphical Federation (IGF), and Media and Entertainment International (MEI). Mems: 900 unions in more than 140 countries, representing 15.5m. people. Activities cover the following 12 sectors: commerce; electricity; finance; graphical; hair and beauty; professional and information technology staff; media, entertainment and the arts; postal; property services; social insurance and private health care; telecommunications; and tourism. First World Congress convened in Berlin, Germany, in September 2001. Pres. M.-L. REMAHL (Finland); Gen. Sec. PHILIP JENNINGS (United Kingdom). Publs *UNIinfo* (quarterly), *UNInet News* (monthly).

INTERNATIONAL OLYMPIC COMMITTEE

Address: Château de Vidy, 1007 Lausanne, Switzerland.

Telephone: (21) 6216111; **fax:** (21) 6216216; **internet:** www.olympic.org.

The International Olympic Committee was founded in 1894 to ensure the regular celebration of the Olympic Games.

Organization

(April 2002)

INTERNATIONAL OLYMPIC COMMITTEE

The International Olympic Committee (IOC) is a non-governmental international organization comprising 128 members, who are representatives of the IOC in their countries and not their countries' delegates to the IOC. In addition there are 25 Honorary members and five Honor members. The members meet in session at least once a year. In accordance with reforms adopted in December 1999, the Committee was to comprise a maximum of 115 members (130 until 31 December 2003), including 15 active Olympic athletes, 15 National Olympic Committee presidents, 15 International Sports Federation presidents, and 70 other individuals. A nominations committee has been established under the reform programme to select qualified candidates to stand for election to the IOC.

The IOC is the final authority on all questions concerning the Olympic Games and the Olympic movement. There are 199 recognized National Olympic Committees, which are the sole authorities responsible for the representation of their respective countries at the Olympic Games. The IOC may give recognition to International Federations which undertake to adhere to the Olympic Charter, and which govern sports that comply with the IOC's criteria.

An International Council for Arbitration for Sport (ICAS) has been established. ICAS administers the Court of Arbitration for Sport which hears cases brought by competitors.

EXECUTIVE BOARD

The session of the IOC delegates to the Executive Board the authority to manage the IOC's affairs. The President of the Board is elected for an eight-year term, and is eligible for re-election once for an additional term of four years. The Vice-Presidents are elected for four-year terms, and may be re-elected after a minimum interval of four years. Members of the Board are elected to hold office for four years. The Executive Board generally meets four to five times per year.

President: JACQUES ROGGE (Belgium).

Vice-Presidents: RICHARD KEVAN GOSPER (Australia); THOMAS BACH (Germany); JAMES L. EASTON (USA); VITALY SMIRNOV (Russia).

Members of the Board:
SERGEI BUBKA (Ukraine)
FRANCO CARRARO (Italy)
OTTAVIO CINQUANTA (Italy)
ZHENLIANG HE (People's Republic of China)
TONI KHOURY (Lebanon)
GUNILLA LINDBERG (Sweden)
LAMBIS W. NIKOLAOU (Greece)
DENIS OSWALD (Switzerland).
TOMAS AMOS GANDA SITHOLE (Zimbabwe).
MARIO VÁZQUEZ RAÑA (Mexico).

IOC COMMISSIONS

Olympic Solidarity Commission: f. 1961; assists National Olympic Committees (NOCs); responsible for managing and administering the share of television rights allocated to NOCs.

Athletes' Commission: f. 1981; comprising active and retired athletes, represents their interests; may issue recommendations to the Executive Board.

Olympic Collectors' Commission: f. 1993; aims to increase awareness of Olympic philately, numismatics, and other memorabilia.

Co-ordination Commissions for the Olympic Games: f. after the election of a host city to oversee and assist the organizing committee in the planning and management of the games.

Commission for Culture and Olympic Education: f. 2000 by merger of the Culture Commission (f. 1968) and the IOC Commission for the International Olympic Academy and Olympic Education (f. 1961).

Ethics Commission: f. 1999 to develop and monitor rules and principles to guide the selection of hosts for the Olympic Games, and the organization and execution of the Games.

Women and Sport Working Group: f. 1995 to advise the Executive Board on policies to promote women in sport.

Medical Commission: f. 1961; concerned with the protection of the health of athletes, respect for medical and sport ethics, and equality for all competing athletes.

Sport and Environment Commission: f. 1995 to promote environmental protection and sustainable development.

Sport for All Commission: f.1983 to encourage and support the principles of Sport for All.

ADMINISTRATION

The administration of the IOC is under the authority of the Director-General and the Secretary-General, who are appointed by the Executive Board, on the proposal of the President.

Director-General: FRANÇOIS CARRARD.

Secretary-General: FRANÇOISE ZWEIFEL.

Activities

The fundamental principles of the Olympic movement are:

> Olympism is a philosophy of life, exalting and combining, in a balanced whole, the qualities of body, will and mind. Blending sport with culture, education and respect for the environment, Olympism seeks to create a way of life based on the joy found in effort, the educational value of good example and respect for universal fundamental ethical principles.
>
> Under the supreme authority of the IOC, the Olympic movement encompasses organizations, athletes and other persons who agree to be guided by the Olympic Charter. The criterion for belonging to the Olympic movement is recognition by the IOC.
>
> The goal of the Olympic movement is to contribute to building a peaceful and better world by educating youth through sport practised without discrimination of any kind and in the Olympic spirit, which requires mutual understanding with a spirit of friendship, solidarity and fair-play.
>
> The activity of the Olympic movement is permanent and universal. It reaches its peak with the bringing together of the athletes of the world at the great sport festival, the Olympic Games.
>
> The Olympic Charter is the codification of the fundamental principles, rules and bye-laws adopted by the IOC. It governs the organization and operation of the Olympic movement and stipulates the conditions for the celebration of the Olympic Games.

In March 1998, at a meeting organized with other international sports governing bodies, it was agreed to form a working group to defend the principle of self-regulation in international sports organizations, against possible interference by the EU. At a meeting in August methods of containing the increase in drugs abuse in sport were discussed. In January 1999, following publication of the results of an investigation into allegations of corruption and bribery, six members of the Committee were recommended for expulsion while investigations into the conduct of other officials were to be pursued. In March an extraordinary session of the IOC was convened, at which the six Committee members were expelled for violating rules relating to Salt Lake City's bid to host the Olympic Winter Games in 2002 (four other members had already resigned, while Executive Board member Un Yong

Kim had received disciplinary action). The President of the IOC retained his position after receiving a vote of confidence. The session approved far-reaching reforms, including the introduction of an interim procedure to select the host city for the Winter Games in 2006, by means of which an election college was to choose two finalists from the six cities submitting bids. Visits by IOC members to any of the bid cities were prohibited. In addition, the meeting approved the establishment of an independent Ethics Commission to oversee cities' bids to host the Olympic Games (see above) and an IOC 2000 Commission to review the bidding process after 2006 and the internal structure of the organization. A declaration on drugs and sport was also adopted by the meeting. In November 1999, an independent World Anti-Doping Agency (WADA, see below) was established by the IOC, and an Anti-Doping Code entered into effect on 1 January 2000. In December 1999 the IOC adopted 50 reforms proposed by the IOC 2000 Commission during the Extraordinary 110th Session. The changes aimed to create a more open, responsive and accountable organization, and included the elimination of member visits to bid cities, the application of terms of office, limiting the expansion of the Summer Games, and the election of 15 active athletes to the IOC membership. In 2000, prior to the Sydney 'Summer' Olympic Games, held in September of that year, WADA conducted about 2,200 out-of-competition drugs tests, involving competitors from more than 80 nations and supplementing significantly the IOC's ongoing out-of-competition drugs testing programme. The Agency established a 15-member team of independent observers to oversee doping control operations at the Sydney Games. A new president of the IOC's Executive Board was elected at the 112th Session, held in Moscow, Russia, in July 2001.

ASSOCIATED AGENCY

World Anti-Doping Agency (WADA): f. 1999 to promote and co-ordinate efforts to achieve drug-free sport; has five committees: Ethics and Education; Finance and Administration; Health, Medical and Research; Legal; Standards and Harmonization; Chair. RICHARD W. POUND; Sec.-Gen. HARRI SYVÄSALMI.

THE GAMES OF THE OLYMPIAD

The Olympic Summer Games take place during the first year of the Olympiad (period of four years) which they are to celebrate. They are the exclusive property of the IOC, which entrusts their organization to a host city seven years in advance.

1896	Athens	1960	Rome
1900	Paris	1964	Tokyo
1904	St Louis	1968	Mexico City
1908	London	1972	Munich
1912	Stockholm	1976	Montreal
1920	Antwerp	1980	Moscow
1924	Paris	1984	Los Angeles
1928	Amsterdam	1988	Seoul
1932	Los Angeles	1992	Barcelona
1936	Berlin	1996	Atlanta
1948	London	2000	Sydney
1952	Helsinki	2004	Athens
1956	Melbourne	2008	Beijing

The programme of the Games must include at least 15 of the total number of Olympic sports (sports governed by recognized International Federations and admitted to the Olympic programme by decision of the IOC at least seven years before the Games). The Olympic summer sports are: archery, athletics, badminton, baseball, basketball, boxing, canoeing, cycling, equestrian sports, fencing, football, gymnastics, handball, field hockey, judo, modern pentathlon, rowing, sailing, shooting, softball, swimming (including water polo and diving), table tennis, tae kwondo, tennis, triathlon, volleyball, weight-lifting, wrestling.

OLYMPIC WINTER GAMES

The Olympic Winter Games comprise competitions in sports practised on snow and ice. From 1994 onwards, they were to be held in the second calendar year following that in which the Games of the Olympiad take place.

1924	Chamonix	1972	Sapporo
1928	St Moritz	1976	Innsbruck
1932	Lake Placid	1980	Lake Placid
1936	Garmisch-Partenkirchen	1984	Sarajevo
1948	St Moritz	1988	Calgary
1952	Oslo	1992	Albertville
1956	Cortina d'Ampezzo	1994	Lillehammer
1960	Squaw Valley	1998	Nagano
1964	Innsbruck	2002	Salt Lake City
1968	Grenoble	2006	Turin

The Winter Games may include skiing, skating, ice hockey, bobsleigh, luge, curling and biathlon.

Finance

The operational budget for the International Olympic Committee for 1998 was 37,240m. Swiss francs.

Publication

Olympic Review (6 a year)

INTERNATIONAL ORGANIZATION FOR MIGRATION—IOM

Address: 17 route des Morillons, CP 71, 1211 Geneva 19, Switzerland.

Telephone: (22) 7179111; **fax:** (22) 7986150; **e-mail:** uinfo @iom.int; **internet:** www.iom.int.

The Intergovernmental Committee for Migration (ICM) was founded in 1951 as a non-political and humanitarian organization with a predominantly operational mandate, including the handling of orderly and planned migration to meet specific needs of emigration and immigration countries; and the processing and movement of refugees, displaced persons and other individuals in need of international migration services to countries offering them resettlement opportunities. In 1989 ICM's name was changed to the International Organization for Migration (IOM). IOM was admitted as an observer to the UN General Assembly in October 1992.

MEMBERS

Albania	Finland	Paraguay
Algeria	France	Peru
Angola	Georgia	Philippines
Argentina	Germany	Poland
Armenia	Greece	Portugal
Australia	Guatemala	Romania
Austria	Guinea	Senegal
Bangladesh	Guinea-Bissau	Slovakia
Belgium	Haiti	Slovenia
Belize	Honduras	South Africa
Benin	Hungary	Sri Lanka
Bolivia	Israel	Sudan
Bulgaria	Iran	Sweden
Burkina Faso	Italy	Switzerland
Canada	Japan	Tajikistan
Chile	Jordan	Tanzania
Colombia	Kenya	Thailand
Congo, Democratic Republic	Korea, Republic	Tunisia
Congo, Republic	Kyrgyzstan	Uganda
Costa Rica	Latvia	Ukraine
Côte d'Ivoire	Liberia	USA
Croatia	Lithuania	Uruguay
Cyprus	Luxembourg	United Kingdom
Czech Republic	Madagascar	Venezuela
Denmark	Mali	Yemen
Dominican Republic	Morocco	Yugoslavia, Federal Republic
Ecuador	Netherlands	Zambia
Egypt	Nicaragua	
El Salvador	Norway	
	Pakistan	
	Panama	

Observers: Afghanistan, Belarus, Bhutan, Bosnia and Herzegovina, Brazil, Cambodia, Cape Verde, People's Republic of China, Cuba, Estonia, Ethiopia, Ghana, Holy See, India, Indonesia, Ireland, Jamaica, Kazakhstan, former Yugoslav republic of Macedonia, Malta, Mexico, Moldova, Mozambique, Namibia, New Zealand, Papua New Guinea, Russia, Rwanda, San Marino, São Tomé and Príncipe, Somalia, Sovereign Military Order of Malta, Spain, Turkey, Turkmenistan, Viet Nam, Zimbabwe. In addition, some 50 international governmental and non-governmental organizations hold observer status with IOM.

Organization

(April 2002)

IOM is governed by a Council which is composed of representatives of all member governments, and has the responsibility for making final decisions on policy, programmes and financing. An Executive Committee of nine member governments elected by the Council prepares the work of the Council and makes recommendations on the basis of reports from the Sub-Committee on Budget and Finance and the Sub-Committee on the Co-ordination of Transport. IOM supported a network of more than 100 country offices in 2001; 19 field offices were designated as Missions with Regional Functions to support country and specific-purpose missions through the provision of resources and expertise.

Director-General: BRUNSON MCKINLEY (USA).

Deputy Director-General: NDIORO NDIAYE (Senegal).

Activities

IOM aims to provide assistance to member governments in meeting the operational challenges of migration, to advance understanding of migration issues, to encourage social and economic development through migration and to work towards effective respect of the human dignity and well-being of migrants. It provides a full range of migration assistance to, and sometimes *de facto* protection of, migrants, refugees, displaced persons and other individuals in need of international migration services. This includes recruitment, selection, processing, medical examinations, and language and cultural orientation courses, placement, activities to facilitate reception and integration and other advisory services. IOM co-ordinates its refugee activities with the UN High Commissioner for Refugees (UNHCR, q.v.) and with governmental and non-governmental partners. In May 1997 IOM and UNHCR signed a memorandum of understanding which aimed to facilitate co-operation between the two organizations. Since it commenced operations in February 1952 IOM has provided assistance to an estimated 11m. migrants.

IOM operates within the framework of the main service areas outlined below. It also administers special programmes. In June 2001 IOM established Migration Policy and Research Programme to strengthen the capacity of governments to manage migration effectively, and to contribute to a better understanding of migration issues. IOM was designated one of the implementing organizations of the settlement agreement concluded between survivors of the Nazi holocaust and Swiss banks. IOM established the Holocaust Victim Assets Programme (HVAP) to process claims made by certain target groups. A German Forced Labour Compensation Programme (GFLCP) was established to process applications for claims of forced labour and personal injury and for property loss. The deadline for filing claims under both programmes was 31 December 2001.

MOVEMENTS

IOM's constitution mandates the organization to provide for the organized transfer of migrants, refugee displaced persons, and others to countries offering to receive them. Accordingly, IOM provides assistance to persons fleeing conflict situations, to refugees being resettled in third countries or repatriated, to stranded individuals, , to internally and externally displaced persons, to other persons compelled to leave their homelands, to individuals seeking to reunite with other members of their families and to migrants involved in regular migration, including qualified migrants travelling under the Facilitated Passage Programme. IOM provides these individuals with secure, reliable, cost-effective resettlement services, including counselling, document processing, medical examination, language training, and cultural orientation and integration assistance. IOM offer discounted transport services and assistance during departure, transit and arrival.

IOM movements are undertaken by the Movement Management Department, which is also responsible for statistical recording of IOM activities and for the development of effective procedures and operational guide-lines. In a humanitarian emergency situation, the department assumes the focal point of IOM operations until field missions are prepared to co-ordinate activities. From April–June 1999 IOM co-operated with UNHCR and the OSCE to facilitate the evacuation of refugees from Kosovo and Metohija, a southern Serbian province of Yugoslavia, following an escalation of violence against the local Albanian population by Serbian forces and the initiation of a NATO military offensive. The joint Humanitarian Evacuation Programme included land transportation to move substantial numbers of refugees away from over-crowded camps in the border region of the former Yugoslav republic of Macedonia (FYRM), and the provision of charter flights to evacuate those refugees most at need to third countries. IOM was also involved in implementing a programme to register the refugees in Albania, the FYRM and Montenegro, and to reissue identification documents where necessary.

ASSISTED RETURNS SERVICE

IOM assists migrants to return home, on a voluntary basis. These people may include unsuccessful asylum seekers, stranded students, labour migrants, and qualified nationals. IOM provides return services directly to the migrant, as well as in co-operation with other organizations to assist wider groups of people. As with its movements service, IOM provides assistance at each stage of the process, i.e. pre-departure, transportation, and post-arrival. It aims to act in a mediating role between the countries and governments of origin, transit and destination and often extends assistance through a period of rehabilitation, to longer-term reconstruction and development efforts.

Since its establishment IOM has been involved in the voluntary repatriation of refugees, displaced persons, and other vulnerable groups. Between 1996 and 1998 more than 160,000 Bosnians were assisted to return voluntarily under IOM auspices. In June 1999, following the end of the conflict in Kosovo and Metohija (see above) IOM co-ordinated the return movement of refugees and worked with the UN mission and UNHCR to assist returnees to move to their final destination in Kosovo. From July 1999–December 2000 IOM assisted an estimated 170,000 Kosovars to return to the province. In the period October 1999–December 2000 IOM assisted 115,000 East Timorese, who had fled violence between Indonesian forces and separatist groups in September 1999, to return to the territory from camps in West Timor, and participated in rehabilitation and reconstruction activities.

A joint IOM/UNHCR programme to facilitate the return of Afghan refugees from Iran commenced in April 2000. In late 2001 the IOM was actively involved in assisting Afghans who had left their homes during renewed fighting between Taliban and opposition forces and the US bombing raids against Taliban and other military targets in Afghanistan. IOM was the co-ordinating agency for the largest camp, located in Maslakh, which had an estimated population of 120,000. A registration process was conducted in February 2002. By mid-April IOM had assisted 16,883 people to return home from Maslakh. Thousands more internally displaced people and refugees located in camps and in neighbouring countries were increasingly returning to their home areas. By the end of 2002 IOM expected to have provided transport assistance, in co-operation with UNHCR, to 400,000 Afghan refugees from Iran. In early 2001 IOM was assisting with the repatriation of Sierra Leonean refugees from Guinea, following an escalation of violence in the south of that country which had rendered refugee camps vulnerable to attack and largely inaccessible to humanitarian aid agencies.

IOM aims to contribute towards alleviating economic and social problems through recruitment and selection of high-level workers and professionals to fill positions in priority sectors of the economy in developing countries for which qualified persons are not available locally, taking into account national development priorities as well as the needs and concerns of receiving communities. IOM screens possible returnees, identifies employment opportunities and provides reintegration assistance. Selection Migration programmes help qualified professionals migrate to countries in need of specific expertise when the country cannot find the required skills from within or through the return of nationals. Integrated Experts programmes provide temporary expatriate expertise to states for up to six years: these experts transfer their skills to their working partners and contribute directly to productive output. Programmes of Intraregional Co-operation in the field of qualified human resources encourage collective self-reliance among developing countries by fostering the exchange of governmental experts and the transfer of professionals and technicians within a given region. IOM maintains recruitment offices throughout the world. In November 1996 IOM established a Return of Qualified Nationals (RQN) programme to facilitate the employment of refugees returning to Bosnia and Herzegovina. By December 1999, when the programme was terminated, more than 750 professionals had been placed in jobs in that country. In 2001 IOM initiated a Programme for the Return of Judiciary and Prosecutors to Minority Areas in Bosnia and Herzegovina. An RQN has been established for East Timor, and a programme to encourage the Return and Reintegration of Qualified Afghan Nationals is under way. In addition, IOM operates a Return of Qualified African Nationals scheme. IOM and the EU jointly fund a scheme to support Rwandan students abroad and encourage their return to Rwanda.

In recent years IOM has increasingly assisted in the return home and reintegration of demobilized soldiers, police officials, and their dependents. In 1997 IOM provided assistance to demobilized soldiers and their families in Angola; by the end of that year IOM had helped to resettle 40,621 soldiers and 107,197 dependents. The assistance programme continued in 1998, when IOM launched a major appeal for funding of the initiative. However, at the end of March 1999 IOM ended its work in Angola, owing to a lack of resources and a deterioration of the security situation in that country. IOM was also involved in the resettlement of demobilized forces in Guatemala in 1998. In mid-1999 IOM established an Information Counselling and Referral Service (ICRS) to undertake the registration of former combatants in Kosovo and assist their rehabilitation. From July–November 1999 the ICRS registered 25,723 demobilized soldiers from the Kosovo Liberation Army; during that period IOM helped 4,122 of the former combatants to start their own businesses or to find other permanent employment.

COUNTER TRAFFICKING

IOM aims to counter the growing problem of smuggling and trafficking in migrants, which has resulted in several million people being exploited by criminal agents and employers. IOM aims to provide shelter and assistance for victims of trafficking; to provide legal and medical assistance to migrants uncovered in transit or in the receiving country; and to offer voluntary return and reintegration assistance. IOM organizes mass information campaigns in countries of origin, in order to highlight the risks of smuggling and trafficking, and aims to raise general awareness of the problem. It also provides training to increase the capacity of governments and other organizations to counter irregular migration. Since 1996 IOM has worked in Cambodia and Thailand to help victims of trafficking to return home. A transit centre has been established on the border between the two countries, where assessments are carried out, advice given, and the process of tracing families is undertaken. During 2001 IOM operated a pilot project for the return of trafficked migrants to Bosnia and Herzogovina.

TECHNICAL CO-OPERATION ON MIGRATION

Through its technical co-operation programmes IOM offers advisory services on migration to governments, intergovernmental agencies and non-governmental organizations. They aim to assist in the formation and implementation of effective and coherent migration policy, legislation and administration. IOM technical co-operation also focuses on capacity building projects such as training courses for government migration officials, and analysis of and suggestions for solving emerging migration problems. Throughout these activities IOM aims to maintain an emphasis on the rights and well-being of migrants, and in particular to ensure that the specific needs of migrant women are incorporated into programmes and policies.

MASS INFORMATION

IOM furthers the understanding of migration through mass information campaigns, in particular to provide migrants with enough knowledge to make informed decisions. In recent years information campaigns have addressed migrant rights, trafficking in women and children, migration and health, promoting the image of migrants, and amnesty programmes. Information campaigns may also inform refugees and displaced persons on the nature and extent of humanitarian aid during an emergency. Information programmes may be implemented to address a specific need, or as part of a wider strategy for migration management.

Through its research IOM has developed mechanisms to gather information on potential migrants' attitudes and motivations, as well as on situations which could lead to irregular migration flows. Trends in international migration point to information as an essential resource for individuals making life-changing decisions about migrating; for governments setting migration policies; for international, regional or non-governmental organizations designing migration programmes; and for researchers, the media and individuals analyzing and reporting on migration.

MIGRATION HEALTH

IOM's migration health services aim to ensure that migrants are fit to travel, do not pose a danger to those traveling with them, and that they receive medical attention and care when necessary. IOM also undertakes research and other technical support and policy development activities in the field of health care. Medical screening of prospective migrants is routinely conducted, along with immunizations and specific counselling, e.g. for HIV/AIDS. IOM administers programmes for disabled refugees and undertakes medical evacuation of people affected by conflict. Under its programmes for health assistance and advice, IOM conducts health education programmes, training for health professionals in post-conflict regions, and assessments of availability and access to health care for migrant populations.

IOM provides assistance for post-emergency returning populations, through the rehabilitation of health infrastructures, provision of medical supplies, mental health programmes, and training of personnel. In September 1999 IOM established a one-year Psychosocial and Trauma Response in Kosovo project, to enhance the local capacity to respond to problems arising from the conflict and mass displacement. Following the end of the project, during which 37 people graduated as counsellors, IOM developed a new programme to establish community psychosocial centres, to train a further 40 counsellors and to enhance access to psychosocial support for ethnic minorities.

IOM collaborates with government health authorities and relevant intergovernmental and non-governmental organizations. In September 1999 IOM and UNAIDS signed a co-operation framework to promote awareness on HIV/AIDS issues relating to displaced populations, and to ensure the needs of migrants are incorporated into national and regional AIDS strategies. In October IOM and WHO signed an agreement to strengthen collaborative efforts to improve the health care of migrants. IOM maintains a database of its tuberculosis diagnostic and treatment programmes, which facilitates the management of the disease. An information system on immigration medical screening data was being developed to help to analyse disease trends among migrants.

INTERNATIONAL CENTRE FOR MIGRATION AND HEALTH

Address: 11 route du Nant-d'Avril, 1214 Geneva, Vernier, Switzerland; **tel.:** (22) 7831080; **fax:** (22) 7831087; **e-mail:** icmh@worldcom.ch; **internet:** www.icmh.ch.

Established in March 1995, by IOM and the University of Geneva, with the support of WHO, to respond to the growing needs for information, documentation, research, training and policy development in migration health; designated a WHO collaborating centre, in August 1996, for health-related issues among people displaced by disasters.

Co-ordinator: Dr MANUEL CARBALLO.

Finance

The approved IOM budget for 2000 amounted to US $208.4m. for operations and 34.1m. Swiss francs for administration.

Publications

International Migration (quarterly).

IOM Latin American Migration Journal (3 a year, in English and Spanish).

IOM News (quarterly, in English, French and Spanish).

IOM News—North American Supplement.

Migration and Health (quarterly).

Report by the Director-General (in English, French and Spanish).

Trafficking in Migrants (quarterly).

World Migration Report (annually).

Research reports, *IOM Info Sheets,* surveys and studies.

INTERNATIONAL RED CROSS AND RED CRESCENT MOVEMENT

The International Red Cross and Red Crescent Movement is a world-wide independent humanitarian organization, comprising three components: the International Committee of the Red Cross (ICRC), founded in 1863; the International Federation of Red Cross and Red Crescent Societies (the Federation), founded in 1919; and National Red Cross and Red Crescent Societies in 176 countries.

Organization

INTERNATIONAL CONFERENCE

The supreme deliberative body of the Movement, the Conference comprises delegations from the ICRC, the Federation and the National Societies, and of representatives of States Parties to the Geneva Conventions (see below). The Conference's function is to determine the general policy of the Movement and to ensure unity in the work of the various bodies. It usually meets every four to five years, and is hosted by the National Society of the country in which it is held. The 27th International Conference was held in Geneva in October/November 1999.

STANDING COMMISSION

The Commission meets at least twice a year in ordinary session. It promotes harmony in the work of the Movement, and examines matters which concern the Movement as a whole. It is formed of two representatives of the ICRC, two of the Federation, and five members of National Societies elected by the Conference.

COUNCIL OF DELEGATES

The Council comprises delegations from the National Societies, from the ICRC and from the Federation. The Council is the body where the representatives of all the components of the Movement meet to discuss matters that concern the Movement as a whole.

In November 1997 the Council adopted an Agreement on the organization of the activities of the Movement's components. The Agreement aimed to promote increased co-operation and partnership between the Movement's bodies, clearly defining the distribution of tasks between agencies. In particular, the Agreement aimed to ensure continuity between international operations carried out in a crisis situation and those developed in its aftermath.

Fundamental Principles of the Movement

Humanity. The International Red Cross and Red Crescent Movement, born of a desire to bring assistance without discrimination to the wounded on the battlefield, endeavours, in its international and national capacity, to prevent and alleviate human suffering wherever it may be found. Its purpose is to protect life and health and to ensure respect for the human being. It promotes mutual understanding, friendship, co-operation and lasting peace amongst all peoples.

Impartiality. It makes no discrimination as to nationality, race, religious beliefs, class or political opinions. It endeavours to relieve the suffering of individuals, being guided solely by their needs, and to give priority to the most urgent cases of distress.

Neutrality. In order to continue to enjoy the confidence of all, the Movement may not take sides in hostilities or engage in controversies of a political, racial, religious or ideological nature.

Independence. The Movement is independent. The National Societies, while auxiliaries in the humanitarian services of their governments and subject to national laws, must retain their autonomy so that they may always be able to act in accordance with the principles of the Movement.

Voluntary Service. It is a voluntary relief movement not prompted by desire for gain.

Unity. There can be only one Red Cross or Red Crescent Society in any one country. It must be open to all. It must carry on its humanitarian work throughout the territory.

Universality. The International Red Cross and Red Crescent Movement, in which all National Societies have equal status and share equal responsibilities and duties in helping each other, is world-wide.

In 1997 all constituent parts of the Movement (National Societies, the ICRC and the International Federation of Red Cross and Red Crescent Societies) adopted the Seville Agreement on co-operation in the undertaking of international relief activities. The Agreement excludes activities that are entrusted to individual components by the statutes of the Movement or the Geneva Conventions.

International Committee of the Red Cross—ICRC

Address: 19 avenue de la Paix, 1202 Geneva, Switzerland.

Telephone: (22) 7346001; **fax:** (22) 7332057; **e-mail:** press.gva@icrc.org; **internet:** www.icrc.org.

Founded in 1863, the ICRC is at the origin of the Red Cross and Red Crescent Movement, and co-ordinates all international humanitarian activities conducted by the Movement in situations of conflict. New statutes of the ICRC, incorporating a revised institutional structure, were adopted in June 1998 and came into effect in July.

Organization

(April 2002)

INTERNATIONAL COMMITTEE

The ICRC is an independent institution of a private character composed exclusively of Swiss nationals. Members are co-opted, and their total number may not exceed 25. The international character of the ICRC is based on its mission and not on its composition.

President: JAKOB KELLENBERGER.

Vice-Presidents: Prof. JACQUES FORSTER, ANNE PETITPIERRE.

ASSEMBLY

Under the new decision-making structures, approved in 1998, the Assembly was defined as the supreme governing body of the ICRC. It formulates policy, defines the Committee's general objectives and strategies, oversees its activities, and approves its budget and accounts. The Assembly is composed of the members of the ICRC, and is collegial in character. The President and Vice-Presidents of the ICRC hold the same offices in the Assembly.

ASSEMBLY COUNCIL

The Council (formally the Executive Board) is a subsidiary body of the Assembly, to which the latter delegates certain of its responsibilities. It prepares the Assembly's activities and takes decisions on matters within its competence. The Council is composed of five members elected by the Assembly and is chaired by the President of the ICRC.

Members: JAKOB KELLENBERGER, Prof. JACQUES FORSTER, JAKOB NÜESCH, JEAN ABT, JEAN DE COURTEN.

DIRECTORATE

Comprising four members appointed by the Assembly, the Directorate is the executive body of the ICRC, overseeing the efficient running of the organization and responsible for the application of the general objectives and institutional strategies decided by the Assembly. The Director of Operations is responsible for running the following divisions at headquarters: the Central Tracing Agency and Protection Division; Health and Relief Division; Logistics Division; International Organizations Division; and the External Resources Division.

Director-General: ANGELO GNAEDINGER (from 1 July 2002).

Members: JEAN-DANIEL TAUXE (Director of Operations), FRANÇOIS BUGNION (Director for International Law and Communication), JACQUES STROUN (Director of Human Resources and Finance).

Activities

The International Committee of the Red Cross was founded in 1863 in Geneva, by Henry Dunant and four of his friends. The original purpose of the Committee was to promote the foundation, in every country, of a voluntary relief society to assist wounded soldiers on the battlefield (the origin of the National Societies of the Red Cross or Red Crescent), as well as the adoption of a treaty protecting wounded soldiers and all those who come to their rescue. The mission of the ICRC was progressively extended through the Geneva Conventions (see below). The present activities of the ICRC consist in giving legal protection and material assistance to military and civilian victims of wars (international wars, internal strife and disturbances) and in promoting and monitoring the application of international humanitarian law. The ICRC takes into account the legal standards and the specific cultural, ethical and religious features of the environment in which it operates. It aims to influence the conduct of all actual and potential perpetrators of violence by seeking direct dialogue with combatants. In 1990 the ICRC was granted observer status at the United Nations General Assembly. The ICRC overall programme of activities covers the following areas:

The protection of vulnerable individuals and groups under international humanitarian law, including activities related to ensuring respect for detainees (monitoring prison conditions), respect for civilians, reuniting relatives separated in conflict situations and restoring family links, and tracing missing persons.

The implementation of assistance activities, aimed at restoring a sufficient standard of living to victims of armed conflict, including the provision of medical aid and emergency food supplies, initiatives to improve water supply, basic infrastructure and access to health care, and physical rehabilitation assistance (for example to assist civilians injured by land-mines).

Preventive action, including the development and implementation of international humanitarian law and dissemination of humanitarian principles, with a view to protecting non-combatants from violence.

Co-operation with National Societies.

In August 1993 an international conference organized by the ICRC adopted a Declaration for the Protection of War Victims (civilians affected by armed conflict in which they are not directly involved), to confirm adherence to the fourth Geneva Convention. In January 1996 an ICRC Advisory Service became operational; this was intended to assist national authorities in their implementation of humanitarian law and to provide a basis for consultation, analysis and harmonization of legislative texts. A Documentation Centre has also been established for exchanging information on national measures and activities aimed at promoting humanitarian law in countries. The Centre is open to all states and National Societies, as well as to interested institutions and the general public.

The ICRC has fully supported efforts to establish a permanent International Criminal Court, with the authority to try serious violations of international humanitarian law. The Statute on the establishment of the Court, adopted in July 1998 by representatives of 120 countries, meeting in Rome, Italy, under UN auspices, attained its 60th ratification in April 2002, enabling its entry into effect in July.

In 1996 the ICRC launched the 'Avenir' project to define the organization's future role, in recognition of significant changes in the world situation and the consequent need for changes in humanitarian action. Four main priorities were identified: improving the status of international humanitarian action and knowledge of and respect for humanitarian law; carrying out humanitarian action in closer proximity to victims, with long-term plans and identified priorities; strengthening dialogue with all parties (including launching joint appeals with other organizations if necessary, and the establishment of a combined communication and information dissemination unit); and increasing the ICRC's efficiency. In April 1998 the Assembly endorsed a plan of action, based on these priorities. In November 1999 the 27th International Conference of the Red Cross and Red Crescent adopted a further plan of action for the movement, covering the four-year period 2000–03. The plan incorporated the following three main objectives: to strengthen respect for international humanitarian law, including the conformity of weapons with legal guide-lines, in order to protect victims of armed conflict; to improve national and international preparedness to respond effectively to disaster situations, as well as to improve mechanisms of co-operation and protection of humanitarian personnel working in the field; and strategic partnerships to improve the lives of vulnerable people through health initiatives, measures to reduce discrimination and violence, and strengthening National Societies' capacities and their co-operation with other humanitarian organizations.

The ICRC consistently reviews the 1980 UN Convention on prohibitions or restrictions on the use of certain conventional weapons which may be deemed to be excessively injurious or to have indiscriminate effects (ratified by 89 states at April 2002) and its protocols. In April 1993 the ICRC organized a symposium in Montreux, Switzerland, to consider the use of anti-personnel mines, and experts meetings were convened to consider the issue in the context of incorporating the use of anti-personnel mines into the review of the 1980 conventional weapons Convention. In October 1995 a session of the Review Conference on the Convention adopted a Protocol prohibiting the use and transfer of laser weapons (which can cause permanent blindness or irreparable damage to the eyesight), as recommended by the ICRC in February 1994. In May 1996 the Conference approved an amended protocol on prohibitions or restrictions on the use of land-mines. The ICRC subsequently resolved to continue its efforts to achieve a world-wide ban on the use of land-mines, and other anti-personnel devices. In October the ICRC supported an International Strategy Conference, organized by the Canadian Government in Ottawa, which was the first formal meeting of states committed to a comprehensive ban on land-mines. In September 1997 the ICRC participated in an international conference, held in Oslo, Norway, at which a Convention was adopted, prohibiting 'the use, stockpiling, production and transfer of anti-personnel mines' and ensuring their destruction. The treaty was opened for signature in December and became legally-binding on 1 March 1999 for the 66 states that had ratified it. By October 2001 the treaty had been ratified by 122 states. In April 1998 the Swiss Government established a Geneva International Centre for Humanitarian Demining, in co-operation with the United Nations and the ICRC, to co-ordinate the destruction of land-mines world-wide.

In 1995 the ICRC adopted a 'Plan of Action concerning Children in Armed Conflicts', to promote the principle of non-recruitment and non-participation in armed conflict of children under the age of 18 years. A co-ordinating group was established, with representatives of the individual National Societies and the International Federation of Red Cross and Red Crescent Societies. The UN Commission of Human Rights invited the ICRC to participate in drafting the Optional Protocol to the Convention on the Rights of the Child. The Optional Protocol, which was adopted by the UN General Assembly in May 2000 and entered into force in February 2002, raises from 15 to 18 the minimum age for recruitment in armed conflict. The ICRC also co-operated with the UN to draw up the 'Guiding Principles on Internal Displacement', finalized in early 1998.

The ICRC's presence in the field is organized under the following three categories: responsive action, aimed at addressing the immediate effects of crises; remedial action, with an emphasis on rehabilitation; and environment-building activities, aimed at creating political, institutional, humanitarian and economic situations that are suitable for generating respect for human rights. ICRC operational delegations focus on responsive action and remedial action, while environment-building is undertaken by ICRC regional delegations. The regional delegations undertake humanitarian diplomacy efforts (e.g. networking, promoting international humanitarian law and distributing information), logistical support to operational delegations, and their own operations; they also have an early warning function, alerting the ICRC to developing conflict situations. The ICRC targets its activities at the following groups: 'victims', comprising civilians affected by violent crises, people deprived of their freedom, and the wounded and sick; and institutions and individuals with influence, i.e. national and local authorities, security forces, representatives of civil society, and Red Cross or Red Crescent National Societies. Children, women and girls, internally displaced people and missing persons are of particular concern to the ICRC.

During 2000 the ICRC distributed around 200,000 metric tons of relief supplies, including food, blankets and tents, in 48 countries; Yugoslavia received about 72,000 tons. In that year ICRC representatives visited some 216,000 prisoners held in more than 65 countries. Contacts were mediated between around 439,000 family members separated by conflict, and more than 2,000 persons reported as missing were traced. Assistance including medicines and equipment was provided for 168 hospitals in 39 countries world-wide, permanent surgical teams were maintained in medical centres in Afghanistan, East Timor, Kenya, Sierra Leone and Sudan, and short-term surgical presences were funded in eight African countries. During the year the ICRC participated in orthopaedic projects in 14 countries, including the manufacturing and fitting of artificial limbs. In early 2002 the ICRC was actively concerned with around 60 conflicts and was undertaking major operations in Afghanistan, the Caucasus, Colombia, the Democratic Republic of the Congo, Israel and the Palestinian territories, Rwanda, Somalia, Sudan and Yugoslavia. For that year operations in Africa were allocated some 39.7% of the total field budget; Europe and North America 19.2%; Asia and the Pacific 17.4%; the Middle East and North Africa 9.3%; and Latin America and the Caribbean 6.3%. (Some 8.1% of field expenditure was held as an operational reserve.)

THE GENEVA CONVENTIONS

In 1864, one year after its foundation, the ICRC submitted to the states called to a Diplomatic Conference in Geneva a draft international treaty for 'the Amelioration of the Condition of the Wounded in Armies in the Field'. This treaty was adopted and signed by twelve states, which thereby bound themselves to respect as neutral wounded soldiers and those assisting them. This was the first Geneva Convention.

With the development of technology and weapons, the introduction of new means of waging war, and the manifestation of certain phenomena (the great number of prisoners of war during World War I; the enormous number of displaced persons and refugees during World War II; the internationalization of internal conflicts in recent years) the necessity was felt of having other international treaties to protect new categories of war victims. The ICRC, for more than 134 years, has been the leader of a movement to improve and complement international humanitarian law.

There are now four Geneva Conventions, adopted on 12 August 1949: I—to protect wounded and sick in armed forces on land, as well as medical personnel; II—to protect the same categories of people at sea, as well as the shipwrecked; III—concerning the treatment of prisoners of war; IV—for the protection of civilians in time of war; and there are two Additional Protocols of 8 June 1977, for the protection of victims in international armed conflicts (Protocol I) and in non-international armed conflicts (Protocol II).

By March 2002 189 states were parties to the Geneva Conventions; 159 were parties to Protocol I and 152 to Protocol II.

In April 2000 a joint working group on the emblems of the National Red Cross and Red Crescent Societies recommended the formulation of a Third Additional Protocol to the Geneva Conventions, designating a new official emblem so that National Societies could be recognized in countries that did not wish to be represented by either current symbol or did not wish to choose between the two.

Finance

The ICRC's work is financed by a voluntary annual grant from governments parties to the Geneva Conventions, voluntary contributions from National Red Cross and Red Crescent Societies and by gifts and legacies from private donors. The ICRC's budget for 2002 totalled 915.6m. Swiss francs, of which 149.8m. Swiss francs were allocated to headquarters (62% for field support services and 22% for the promotion of international humanitarian law) and 765.8m. Swiss francs were allocated to field operations.

Publications

Annual Report (editions in English, French and Spanish).

The Geneva Conventions: texts and commentaries.

ICRC News (weekly, French, English, Spanish and German editions).

International Review of the Red Cross (quarterly in French and English; annually in Russian, Arabic and Spanish).

The Protocols Additional.

Yearbook of International Humanitarian Law (annually).

Various publications on subjects of Red Cross interest (medical studies, international humanitarian law, etc.), some in electronic form.

International Federation of Red Cross and Red Crescent Societies

Address: 17 chemin des Crêts, Petit-Saconnex, CP 372, 1211 Geneva 19, Switzerland.

Telephone: (22) 7304222; **fax:** (22) 7330395; **e-mail:** secretariat@ifrc.org; **internet:** www.ifrc.org.

The Federation was founded in 1919 (as the League of Red Cross Societies). It works on the basis of the Principles of the Red Cross and Red Crescent Movement to inspire, facilitate and promote all forms of humanitarian activities by the National Societies, with a view to the prevention and alleviation of human suffering, and thereby contribute to the maintenance and promotion of peace in the world. The Federation acts as the official representative of its member societies in the field. The Federation maintains close relations with many inter-governmental organizations, the United Nations and its Specialized Agencies, and with non-governmental organizations. It has permanent observer status with the United Nations.

MEMBERS

National Red Cross and Red Crescent Societies in 176 countries in April 2002, with a total of 97m. members and volunteers.

Organization

(April 2002)

GENERAL ASSEMBLY

The General Assembly is the highest authority of the Federation and meets every two years in commission sessions (for development, disaster relief, health and community services, and youth) and plenary sessions. It is composed of representatives from all National Societies that are members of the Federation.

President: JUAN MANUEL SUÁREZ DEL TORO RIVERO (Spain).

GOVERNING BOARD

The Board (formerly the Executive Council) meets every six months and is composed of the President of the Federation, nine Vice-Presidents, representatives of 16 National Societies elected by the Assembly, and the Chairman of the Finance Commission. Its functions include the implementation of decisions of the General Assembly; it also has powers to act between meetings of the Assembly.

COMMISSIONS

Development Commission.
Disaster Relief Commission.
Finance Commission.
Health and Community Services Commission.
Youth Commision.

The Commissions meet, in principle, twice a year, just before the Governing Board. Members are elected by the Assembly under a system that ensures each Society a seat on one Commission.

SECRETARIAT

The Secretariat assumes the statutory responsibilities of the Federation in the field of relief to victims of natural disasters, refugees and civilian populations who may be displaced or exposed to abnormal hardship. In addition, the Secretariat promotes and co-ordinates assistance to National Societies in developing their basic structure and their services to the community. From 2000 the Secretariat underwent a process of restructuring. In 2002 there were some 230 staff at the Secretariat, employed in the following divisions (created in 2000): programme and co-ordination, disaster management and co-ordination, knowledge-sharing, monitoring and evaluation, advocacy and communication, and corporate services.

Secretary-General: DIDIER J. CHERPITEL (France).

Activities

In October 1999 the Assembly adopted Strategy 2010, outlining the Federation's objectives and strategies for the next ten years, in order to address new demands placed on it, for example by the proliferation of other humanitarian groups, restricted finance, and pressure from donors for efficiency, transparency and results. The Strategy involved a significant restructuring of the organization.

DISASTER RESPONSE

The Federation supports the establishment of emergency response units, which aim to act effectively and independently to meet the needs of victims of natural or man-made disasters. The units cover basic health care provision, referral hospitals, water sanitation, logistics, telecommunications and information units. The Federation advises National Societies in relief health. In the event of a disaster the following areas are covered: communicable disease alleviation and vaccination; psychological support and stress management; health education; the provision of medicines; and the organization of mobile clinics and nursing care. The Societies also distribute food and clothing to those in need and assist in the provision of shelter and adequate sanitation facilities and in the management of refugee camps.

DEVELOPMENT

The Federation undertakes capacity-building activities with the National Societies to train and develop staff and volunteers and to improve management structures and processes, in particular in the area of disaster-preparedness. Blood donor programmes are often undertaken by National Societies, sometimes in conjunction with WHO. The Federation supports the promotion of these programmes and the implementation of quality standards. Other activities in the health sector aim to strengthen existing health services and promote community-based health care and first aid; the prevention of HIV/AIDS and substance abuse; and health education and family planning initiatives. The Federation also promotes the establishment and development of education and service programmes for children and for other more vulnerable members of society, including the elderly and disabled. Education projects support the promotion of humanitarian values.

Finance

The permanent Secretariat of the Federation is financed by the contributions of member Societies on a pro-rata basis. Each relief action is financed by separate, voluntary contributions, and development programme projects are also financed on a voluntary basis.

Publications

Annual Report.

Handbook of the International Red Cross and Red Crescent Movement (with the ICRC).

Red Cross, Red Crescent (quarterly, English, French and Spanish).

Weekly News.

World Disasters Report (annually).

Newsletters on several topics; various guides and manuals for Red Cross and Red Crescent activities.

Convention on the Prohibition of the Use, Stockpiling, Production and Transfer of Anti-personnel Mines and on their Destruction

(entered into force 1 March 1999)

The State Parties,

Determined to put an end to the suffering and casualties caused by anti-personnel mines, that kill or maim hundreds of people every week, mostly innocent and defenceless civilians and especially children, obstruct economic development and reconstruction, inhibit the repatriation of refugees and internally displaced persons, and have other severe consequences for years after emplacement,

Believing it necessary to do their utmost to contribute in an efficient and co-ordinated manner to face the challenge of removing anti-personnel mines placed throughout the world, and to assure their destruction,

Wishing to do their utmost in providing assistance for the care and rehabilitation, including the social and economic reintegration of mine victims,

Recognizing that a total ban of anti-personnel mines would also be an important confidence-building measure,

Welcoming the adoption of the Protocol on Prohibitions or Restrictions on the Use of Mines, Booby-Traps and Other Devices, as amended on 3 May 1996, annexed to the Convention on Prohibitions or Restrictions on the Use of Certain Conventional Weapons Which May Be Deemed to Be Excessively Injurious or to Have Indiscriminate Effects, and calling for the early ratification of this Protocol by all States which have not yet done so,

Welcoming also United Nations General Assembly Resolution 51/45 S of 10 December 1996 urging all States to pursue vigorously an effective, legally-binding international agreement to ban the use, stockpiling, production and transfer of anti-personnel land-mines,

Welcoming furthermore the measures taken over the past years, both unilaterally and multilaterally, aiming at prohibiting, restricting or suspending the use, stockpiling, production and transfer of anti-personnel mines,

Stressing the role of public conscience in furthering the principles of humanity as evidenced by the call for a total ban of anti-personnel mines and recognizing the efforts to that end undertaken by the International Red Cross and Red Crescent Movement, the International Campaign to Ban Landmines and numerous other non-governmental organizations around the world,

Recalling the Ottawa Declaration of 5 October 1996 and the Brussels Declaration of 27 June 1997 urging the international community to negotiate an international and legally binding agreement prohibiting the use, stockpiling, production and transfer of anti-personnel mines,

Emphasizing the desirability of attracting the adherence of all States to this Convention, and determined to work strenuously towards the promotion of its universalization in all relevant fora including, *inter alia,* the United Nations, the Conference on Disarmament, regional organizations, and groupings, and review conferences of the Convention on Prohibitions or Restrictions on the Use of Certain Conventional Weapons Which May Be Deemed to Be Excessively Injurious or to Have Indiscriminate Effects,

Basing themselves on the principle of international humanitarian law that the right of the parties to an armed conflict to choose methods or means of warfare is not unlimited, on the principle that prohibits the employment in armed conflicts of weapons, projectiles and materials and methods of warfare of a nature to cause superfluous injury or unnecessary suffering and on the principle that a distinction must be made between civilians and combatants,

Have agreed as follows:

Article 1

General obligations

1. Each State Party undertakes never under any circumstances:
   (a) To use anti-personnel mines;
   (b) To develop, produce, otherwise acquire, stockpile, retain or transfer to anyone, directly or indirectly, anti-personnel mines;
   (c) To assist, encourage or induce, in any way, anyone to engage in any activity prohibited to a State Party under this Convention.
2. Each State Party undertakes to destroy or ensure the destruction of all anti-personnel mines in accordance with the provisions of this Convention.

Article 2

Definitions

1. "Anti-personnel mine" means a mine designed to be exploded by the presence, proximity or contact of a person and that will incapacitate, injure or kill one or more persons. Mines designed to be detonated by the presence, proximity or contact of a vehicle as opposed to a person, that are equipped with anti-handling devices, are not considered anti-personnel mines as a result of being so equipped.
2. "Mine" means a munition designed to be placed under, on or near the ground or other surface area and to be exploded by the presence, proximity or contact of a person or a vehicle.
3. "Anti-handling device" means a device intended to protect a mine and which is part of, linked to, attached to or placed under the mine and which activates when an attempt is made to tamper with or otherwise intentionally disturb the mine.
4. "Transfer" involves, in addition to the physical movement of anti-personnel mines into or from national territory, the transfer of title to and control over the mines, but does not involve the transfer of territory containing emplaced anti-personnel mines.
5. "Mined area" means an area which is dangerous due to the presence or suspected presence of mines.

Article 3

Exceptions

1. Notwithstanding the general obligations under Article 1, the retention or transfer of a number of anti-personnel mines for the development of and training in mine detection, mine clearance, or mine destruction techniques is permitted. The amount of such mines shall not exceed the minimum number absolutely necessary for the above-mentioned purposes.
2. The transfer of anti-personnel mines for the purpose of destruction is permitted.

Article 4

Destruction of stockpiled anti-personnel mines

Except as provided for in Article 3, each State Party undertakes to destroy or ensure the destruction of all stockpiled anti-personnel mines it owns or possesses, or that are under its jurisdiction or control, as soon as possible but not later than four years after the entry into force of this Convention for that State Party.

Article 5

Destruction of anti-personnel mines in mined areas

1. Each State Party undertakes to destroy or ensure the destruction of all anti-personnel mines in mined areas under its jurisdiction or control, as soon as possible but not later than ten years after the entry into force of this Convention for that State Party.
2. Each State Party shall make every effort to identify all areas under its jurisdiction or control in which anti-personnel mines are known or suspected to be emplaced and shall ensure as soon as possible that all anti-personnel mines in mined areas under its jurisdiction or control are perimeter-marked, monitored and protected by fencing or other means, to ensure the effective exclusion of civilians, until all anti-personnel mines contained therein have been destroyed. The marking shall at least be to the standards set out in the Protocol on Prohibitions or Restrictions on the Use of Mines, Booby-Traps and Other Devices, as amended on 3 May 1996, annexed to the Convention on Prohibitions or Restrictions on the Use of Certain Conventional Weapons Which May Be Deemed to Be Excessively Injurious or to Have Indiscriminate Effects.
3. If a State Party believes that it will be unable to destroy or ensure the destruction of all anti-personnel mines referred to in paragraph 1 within that time period, it may submit a request to a Meeting of the States Parties or a Review Conference for an extension of the deadline for completing the destruction of such anti-personnel mines, for a period of up to ten years.
4. Each request shall contain:
   (a) The duration of the proposed extension;
   (b) A detailed explanation of the reasons for the proposed extension, including:
      (i) The preparation and status of work conducted under national demining programmes;
      (ii) The financial and technical means available to the State Party for the destruction of all the anti-personnel mines; and
      (iii) Circumstances which impede the ability of the State Party to destroy all the anti-personnel mines in mined areas;
   (c) The humanitarian, social, economic, and environmental implications of the extension; and
   (d) Any other information relevant to the request for the proposed extension.
5. The Meeting of the States Parties or the Review Conference shall, taking into consideration the factors contained in paragraph 4, assess the request and decide by a majority of votes of States

Parties present and voting whether to grant the request for an extension period.

6. Such an extension may be renewed upon the submission of a new request in accordance with paragraphs 3, 4 and 5 of this Article. In requesting a further extension period a State Party shall submit relevant additional information on what has been undertaken in the previous extension period pursuant to this Article.

Article 6

International co-operation and assistance

1. In fulfilling its obligations under this Convention each State Party has the right to seek and receive assistance, where feasible, from other States Parties to the extent possible.

2. Each State Party undertakes to facilitate and shall have the right to participate in the fullest possible exchange of equipment, material and scientific and technological information concerning the implementation of this Convention. The States Parties shall not impose undue restrictions on the provision of mine clearance equipment and related technological information for humanitarian purposes.

3. Each State Party in a position to do so shall provide assistance for the care and rehabilitation, and social and economic reintegration, of mine victims and for mine awareness programmes. Such assistance may be provided, *inter alia,* through the United Nations system, international, regional or national organizations or institutions, the International Committee of the Red Cross, national Red Cross and Red Crescent societies and their International Federation, non-governmental organizations, or on a bilateral basis.

4. Each State Party in a position to do so shall provide assistance for mine clearance and related activities. Such assistance may be provided, *inter alia,* through the United Nations system, international or regional organizations or institutions, non-governmental organizations or institutions, or on a bilateral basis, or by contributing to the United Nations Voluntary Trust Fund for Assistance in Mine Clearance, or other regional funds that deal with demining.

5. Each State Party in a position to do so shall provide assistance for the destruction of stockpiled anti-personnel mines.

6. Each State Party undertakes to provide information to the database on mine clearance established within the United Nations system, especially information concerning various means and technologies of mine clearance, and lists of experts, expert agencies or national points of contact on mine clearance.

7. States Parties may request the United Nations, regional organizations, other States Parties or other competent intergovernmental or non-governmental fora to assist its authorities in the elaboration of a national demining programme to determine, *inter alia*:

(a) The extent and scope of the anti-personnel mine problem;

(b) The financial, technological and human resources that are required for the implementation of the programme;

(c) The estimated number of years necessary to destroy all anti-personnel mines in mined areas under the jurisdiction or control of the concerned State Party;

(d) Mine awareness activities to reduce the incidence of mine-related injuries or deaths;

(e) Assistance to mine victims;

(f) The relationship between the Government of the concerned State Party and the relevant governmental, inter-governmental or non-governmental entities that will work in the implementation of the programme.

8. Each State Party giving and receiving assistance under the provisions of this Article shall co-operate with a view to ensuring the full and prompt implementation of agreed assistance programmes.

Article 7

Transparency measures

1. Each State Party shall report to the Secretary-General of the United Nations as soon as practicable, and in any event not later than 180 days after the entry into force of this Convention for that State Party on:

(a) The national implementation measures referred to in Article 9;

(b) The total of all stockpiled anti-personnel mines owned or possessed by it, or under its jurisdiction or control, to include a breakdown of the type, quantity and, if possible, lot numbers of each type of anti-personnel mine stockpiled;

(c) To the extent possible, the location of all mined areas that contain, or are suspected to contain, anti-personnel mines under its jurisdiction or control, to include as much detail as possible regarding the type and quantity of each type of anti-personnel mine in each mined area and when they were emplaced;

(d) The types, quantities and, if possible, lot numbers of all anti-personnel mines retained or transferred for the development of and training in mine detection, mine clearance or mine destruction techniques, or transferred for the purpose of destruction, as well as the institutions authorized by a State Party to retain or transfer anti-personnel mines, in accordance with Article 3;

(e) The status of programmes for the conversion or de-commissioning of anti-personnel mine production facilities;

(f) The status of programmes for the destruction of anti-personnel mines in accordance with Articles 4 and 5, including details of the methods which will be used in destruction, the location of all destruction sites and the applicable safety and environmental standards to be observed;

(g) The types and quantities of all anti-personnel mines destroyed after the entry into force of this Convention for that State Party, to include a breakdown of the quantity of each type of anti-personnel mine destroyed, in accordance with Articles 4 and 5, respectively, along with, if possible, the lot numbers of each type of anti-personnel mine in the case of destruction in accordance with Article 4;

(h) The technical characteristics of each type of anti-personnel mine produced, to the extent known, and those currently owned or possessed by a State Party, giving, where reasonably possible, such categories of information as may facilitate identification and clearance of anti-personnel mines; at a minimum, this information shall include the dimensions, fusing, explosive content, metallic content, colour photographs and other information which may facilitate mine clearance; and

(i) The measures taken to provide an immediate and effective warning to the population in relation to all areas identified under paragraph 2 of Article 5.

2. The information provided in accordance with this Article shall be updated by the States Parties annually, covering the last calendar year, and reported to the Secretary-General of the United Nations not later than 30 April of each year.

3. The Secretary-General of the United Nations shall transmit all such reports received to the States Parties.

Article 8

Facilitation and clarification of compliance

1. The States Parties agree to consult and co-operate with each other regarding the implementation of the provisions of this Convention, and to work together in a spirit of co-operation to facilitate compliance by States Parties with their obligations under this Convention.

2. If one or more States Parties wish to clarify and seek to resolve questions relating to compliance with the provisions of this Convention by another State Party, it may submit, through the Secretary-General of the United Nations, a Request for Clarification of that matter to that State Party. Such a request shall be accompanied by all appropriate information. Each State Party shall refrain from unfounded Requests for Clarification, care being taken to avoid abuse. A State Party that receives a Request for Clarification shall provide, through the Secretary-General of the United Nations, within 28 days to the requesting State Party all information which would assist in clarifying this matter.

3. If the requesting State Party does not receive a response through the Secretary-General of the United Nations within that time period, or deems the response to the Request for Clarification to be unsatisfactory, it may submit the matter through the Secretary-General of the United Nations to the next Meeting of the States Parties. The Secretary-General of the United Nations shall transmit the submission, accompanied by all appropriate information pertaining to the Request for Clarification, to all States Parties. All such information shall be presented to the requested State Party which shall have the right to respond.

4. Pending the convening of any meeting of the States Parties, any of the States Parties concerned may request the Secretary-General of the United Nations to exercise his or her good offices to facilitate the clarification requested.

5. The requesting State Party may propose through the Secretary-General of the United Nations the convening of a Special Meeting of the States Parties to consider the matter. The Secretary-General of the United Nations shall thereupon communicate this proposal and all information submitted by the States Parties concerned, to

all States Parties with a request that they indicate whether they favour a Special Meeting of the States Parties, for the purpose of considering the matter. In the event that within 14 days from the date of such communication, at least one-third of the States Parties favours such a Special Meeting, the Secretary-General of the United Nations shall convene this Special Meeting of the States Parties within a further 14 days. A quorum for this Meeting shall consist of a majority of States Parties.

6. The Meeting of the States Parties or the Special Meeting of the States Parties, as the case may be, shall first determine whether to consider the matter further, taking into account all information submitted by the States Parties concerned. The Meeting of the States Parties or the Special Meeting of the States Parties shall make every effort to reach a decision by consensus. If despite all efforts to that end no agreement has been reached, it shall take this decision by a majority of States Parties present and voting.

7. All States Parties shall co-operate fully with the Meeting of the States Parties or the Special Meeting of the States Parties in the fulfilment of its review of the matter, including any fact-finding missions that are authorized in accordance with paragraph 8.

8. If further clarification is required, the Meeting of the States Parties or the Special Meeting of the States Parties shall authorize a fact-finding mission and decide on its mandate by a majority of States Parties present and voting. At any time the requested State Party may invite a fact-finding mission to its territory. Such a mission shall take place without a decision by a Meeting of the States Parties or a Special Meeting of the States Parties to authorize such a mission. The mission, consisting of up to 9 experts, designated and approved in accordance with paragraphs 9 and 10, may collect additional information on the spot or in other places directly related to the alleged compliance issue under the jurisdiction or control of the requested State Party.

9. The Secretary-General of the United Nations shall prepare and update a list of the names, nationalities and other relevant data of qualified experts provided by States Parties and communicate it to all States Parties. Any expert included on this list shall be regarded as designated for all fact-finding missions unless a State Party declares its non-acceptance in writing. In the event of non-acceptance, the expert shall not participate in fact-finding missions on the territory or any other place under the jurisdiction or control of the objecting State Party, if the non-acceptance was declared prior to the appointment of the expert to such missions.

10. Upon receiving a request from the Meeting of the States Parties or a Special Meeting of the States Parties, the Secretary-General of the United Nations shall, after consultations with the requested State Party, appoint the members of the mission, including its leader. Nationals of States Parties requesting the fact-finding mission or directly affected by it shall not be appointed to the mission. The members of the fact-finding mission shall enjoy privileges and immunities under Article VI of the Convention on the Privileges and Immunities of the United Nations, adopted on 13 February 1946.

11. Upon at least 72 hours notice, the members of the fact-finding mission shall arrive in the territory of the requested State Party at the earliest opportunity. The requested State Party shall take the necessary administrative measures to receive, transport and accommodate the mission, and shall be responsible for ensuring the security of the mission to the maximum extent possible while they are on territory under its control.

12. Without prejudice to the sovereignty of the requested State Party, the fact-finding mission may bring into the territory of the requested State Party the necessary equipment which shall be used exclusively for gathering information on the alleged compliance issue. Prior to its arrival, the mission will advise the requested State Party of the equipment that it intends to utilize in the course of its fact-finding mission.

13. The requested State Party shall make all efforts to ensure that the fact-finding mission is given the opportunity to speak with all relevant persons who may be able to provide information related to the alleged compliance issue.

14. The requested State Party shall grant access for the fact-finding mission to all areas and installations under its control where facts relevant to the compliance issue could be expected to be collected. This shall be subject to any arrangements that the requested State Party considers necessary for:

(a) The protection of sensitive equipment, information and areas;

(b) The protection of any constitutional obligations the requested State Party may have with regard to proprietary rights, searches and seizures, or other constitutional rights; or

(c) The physical protection and safety of the members of the fact-finding mission.

In the event that the requested State Party makes such arrangements, it shall make every reasonable effort to demonstrate through alternative means its compliance with this Convention.

15. The fact-finding mission may remain in the territory of the State Party concerned for no more than 14 days, and at any particular site no more than 7 days, unless otherwise agreed.

16. All information provided in confidence and not related to the subject matter of the fact-finding mission shall be treated on a confidential basis.

17. The fact-finding mission shall report, through the Secretary-General of the United Nations, to the Meetings of the States Parties or the Special Meeting of the States Parties the results of its findings.

18. The Meeting of the States Parties or the Special Meeting of the States Parties shall consider all relevant information, including the report submitted by the fact-finding mission, and may request the requested State Party to take measures to address the compliance issue within a specified period of time. The requested State Party shall report on all measures taken in response to this request.

19. The Meeting of the States Parties or the Special Meeting of the States Parties may suggest to the States Parties concerned ways and means to further clarify or resolve the matter under consideration, including the initiation of appropriate procedures in conformity with international law. In circumstances where the issue at hand is determined to be due to circumstances beyond the control of the requested State Party, the Meeting of the States Parties or the Special Meeting of the States Parties may recommend appropriate measures, including the use of co-operative measures referred to in Article 6.

20. The Meeting of the States Parties or the Special Meeting of the States Parties shall make every effort to reach its decisions referred to in paragraphs 18 and 19 by consensus, otherwise by a two-thirds majority of States Parties present and voting.

Article 9

National implementation measures

Each State Party shall take all appropriate legal, administrative and other measures, including the imposition of penal sanctions, to prevent and suppress any activity prohibited to a State Party under this Convention undertaken by persons or on territory under its jurisdiction or control.

Article 10

Settlement of disputes

1. The States Parties shall consult and co-operate with each other to settle any dispute that may arise with regard to the application or the interpretation of this Convention. Each State Party may bring any such dispute before the Meeting of the States Parties.

2. The Meeting of the States Parties may contribute to the settlement of the dispute by whatever means it deems appropriate, including offering its good offices, calling upon the States Parties to a dispute to start the settlement procedure of their choice and recommending a time-limit for any agreed procedure.

3. This Article is without prejudice to the provisions of this Convention on facilitation and clarification of compliance.

Article 11

Meetings of the States Parties

1. The States Parties shall meet regularly in order to consider any matter with regard to the application or implementation of this Convention, including:

(a) The operation and status of this Convention;

(b) Matters arising from the reports submitted under the provisions of this Convention;

(c) International co-operation and assistance in accordance with Article 6;

(d) The development of technologies to clear anti-personnel mines;

(e) Submissions of States Parties under Article 8; and

(f) Decisions relating to submissions of States Parties as provided for in Article 5.

2. The First Meeting of the States Parties shall be convened by the Secretary-General of the United Nations within one year after the entry into force of this Convention. The subsequent meetings shall

be convened by the Secretary-General of the United Nations annually until the first Review Conference.

3. Under the conditions set out in Article 8, the Secretary-General of the United Nations shall convene a Special Meeting of the States Parties.

4. States not parties to this Convention, as well as the United Nations, other relevant international organizations or institutions, regional organizations, the International Committee of the Red Cross and relevant non-governmental organizations may be invited to attend these meetings as observers in accordance with the agreed Rules of Procedure.

Article 12

Review Conferences

1. A Review Conference shall be convened by the Secretary-General of the United Nations five years after the entry into force of this Convention. Further Review Conferences shall be convened by the Secretary-General of the United Nations if so requested by one or more States Parties, provided that the interval between Review Conferences shall in no case be less than five years. All States Parties to this Convention shall be invited to each Review Conference.

2. The purpose of the Review Conference shall be:

(a) To review the operation and status of this Convention;

(b) To consider the need for and the interval between further Meetings of the States Parties referred to in paragraph 2 of Article 11;

(c) To take decisions on submissions of States Parties as provided for in Article 5; and

(d) To adopt, if necessary, in its final report conclusions related to the implementation of this Convention.

3. States not parties to this Convention, as well as the United Nations, other relevant international organizations or institutions, regional organizations, the International Committee of the Red Cross and relevant non-governmental organizations may be invited to attend each Review Conference as observers in accordance with the agreed Rules of Procedure.

Article 13

Amendments

1. At any time after the entry into force of this Convention any State Party may propose amendments to this Convention. Any proposal for an amendment shall be communicated to the Depositary, who shall circulate it to all States Parties and shall seek their views on whether an Amendment Conference should be convened to consider the proposal. If a majority of the States Parties notify the Depositary no later than 30 days after its circulation that they support further consideration of the proposal, the Depositary shall convene an Amendment Conference to which all States Parties shall be invited.

2. States not parties to this Convention, as well as the United Nations, other relevant international organizations or institutions, regional organizations, the International Committee of the Red Cross and relevant non-governmental organizations may be invited to attend each Amendment Conference as observers in accordance with the agreed Rules of Procedure.

3. The Amendment Conference shall be held immediately following a Meeting of the States Parties or a Review Conference unless a majority of the States Parties request that it be held earlier.

4. Any amendment to this Convention shall be adopted by a majority of two-thirds of the States Parties present and voting at the Amendment Conference. The Depositary shall communicate any amendment so adopted to the States Parties.

5. An amendment to this Convention shall enter into force for all States Parties to this Convention which have accepted it, upon the deposit with the Depositary of instruments of acceptance by a majority of States Parties. Thereafter it shall enter into force for any remaining State Party on the date of deposit of its instrument of acceptance.

Article 14

Costs

1. The costs of the Meetings of the States Parties, the Special Meetings of the States Parties, the Review Conferences and the Amendment Conferences shall be borne by the States Parties and States not parties to this Convention participating therein, in accordance with the United Nations scale of assessment adjusted appropriately.

2. The costs incurred by the Secretary-General of the United Nations under Articles 7 and 8 and the costs of any fact-finding mission shall be borne by the States Parties in accordance with the United Nations scale of assessment adjusted appropriately.

Article 15

Signature

This Convention, done at Oslo, Norway, on 18 September 1997, shall be open for signature at Ottawa, Canada, by all States from 3 December 1997 until 4 December 1997, and at the United Nations Headquarters in New York from 5 December 1997 until its entry into force.

Article 16

(Ratification, acceptance, approval or accession)

Article 17

(Entry into force)

Article 18

(Provisional application)

Article 19

Reservations

The Articles of this Convention shall not be subject to reservations.

Article 20

Duration and withdrawal

1. This Convention shall be of unlimited duration.

2. Each State Party shall, in exercising its national sovereignty, have the right to withdraw from this Convention. It shall give notice of such withdrawal to all other States Parties, to the Depositary and to the United Nations Security Council. Such instrument of withdrawal shall include a full explanation of the reasons motivating this withdrawal.

3. Such withdrawal shall only take effect six months after the receipt of the instrument of withdrawal by the Depositary. If, however, on the expiry of that six-month period, the withdrawing State Party is engaged in an armed conflict, the withdrawal shall not take effect before the end of the armed conflict.

4. The withdrawal of a State Party from this Convention shall not in any way affect the duty of States to continue fulfilling the obligations assumed under any relevant rules of international law.

INTERNATIONAL SEABED AUTHORITY

Address: 14–20 Port Royal St, Kingston, Jamaica.

Telephone: 922-9105; **fax:** 922-0195; **e-mail:** postmaster@isa.org.jm; **internet:** www.isa.org.jm.

The Authority is an autonomous international organization established in accordance with the 1982 United Nations Convention on the Law of the Sea and 1994 Agreement Relating to the Implementation of Part XI of the Convention. The Authority was founded in November 1994 and became fully operational in June 1996.

Organization

(April 2002)

ASSEMBLY

The Assembly is the supreme organ of the Authority, consisting of representatives of all member states. It formulates policies, approves the budget and elects Council members. The first session of the Assembly was initiated in November 1994 and was continued at a meeting in February/March 1995. The session was concluded in August 1995, having failed to reach agreement on the composition of the Council (see below) and to elect a Secretary-General of the Authority. In March 1996 the Assembly concluded the first part of its second session, having constituted the 36-member Council and elected, by consensus, the first Secretary-General of the Authority. The seventh session of the Assembly was held in July 2001.

COUNCIL

The Council, elected by the Assembly, acts as the executive organ of the Authority. It consists of 36 members, comprising the four states that are the largest importers or consumers of seabed minerals, the four largest investors in seabed minerals, the four major exporters of seabed minerals, six developing countries representing special interests, and 18 members covering all the geographical regions.

LEGAL AND TECHNICAL COMMISSION

The Legal and Technical Commission, comprising 24 experts, assists the Council by making recommendations concerning seabed activities, assessing the environmental implications of activities in the area and proposing measures to protect the marine environment.

FINANCE COMMITTEE

The Committee, comprising 15 experts, was established to make recommendations to the Assembly and the Council on all financial and budgetary issues.

SECRETARIAT

The Secretariat provides administrative services to all the bodies of the Authority and implements the relevant work programmes. It comprises the Office of the Secretary-General, Offices of Resources and Environmental Monitoring, Legal Affairs, and Administration and Management. Under the terms of the 1994 Agreement Relating to the Implementation of Part XI of the Convention, the Secretariat is performing the functions of the Enterprise, the organ through which the Authority carries out deep sea-bed mining operations (directly or through joint ventures). It is envisaged that the Enterprise will eventually operate independently of the Secretariat.

Secretary-General: SATYA N. NANDAN (Fiji).

Activities

The Authority, functioning as an autonomous international organization in relationship with the UN, implements the Convention on the Law of the Sea (which was adopted in April 1982 and entered into force in November 1994). All states party to the Convention (138 at February 2002) are members. The Convention covers the uses of ocean space: navigation and overflight, resource exploration and exploitation, conservation and pollution, and fishing and shipping; as well as governing conduct on the oceans; defining maritime zones; establishing rules for delineating sea boundaries; assigning legal rights, duties and responsibilities to states; and providing machinery for the settlement of disputes. Its main provisions are as follows:

Coastal states are allowed sovereignty over their territorial waters of up to 12 nautical miles in breadth; foreign vessels are to be allowed 'innocent passage' through these waters.

Ships and aircraft of all states are allowed 'transit passage' through straits used for international navigation.

Archipelagic states (composed of islands) have sovereignty over a sea area enclosed by straight lines drawn between the outermost points of the islands.

Coastal states and inhabited islands are entitled to proclaim a 200-mile exclusive economic zone with respect to natural resources and jurisdiction over certain activities (such as protection and preservation of the environment), and rights over the adjacent continental shelf, up to 350 miles from the shore under specified circumstances.

All states have freedom of navigation, overflight, scientific research and fishing on the high seas, but must co-operate in measures to conserve living resources.

A 'parallel system' is to be established for exploiting the international seabed, where all activities are to be supervised by the International Seabed Authority.

States are bound to control pollution and co-operate in forming preventive rules, and incur penalties for failing to combat pollution.

Marine scientific research in the zones under national jurisdiction is subject to the prior consent of the coastal state, but consent may be denied only under specific circumstances.

States must submit disputes on the application and interpretation of the Convention to a compulsory procedure entailing decisions binding on all parties. An International Tribunal for the Law of the Sea is to be established.

In July 1994 the UN General Assembly adopted the Agreement Relating to the Implementation of Part XI of the Convention. The original Part XI, concerning the exploitation of the international ocean bed, and particularly the minerals to be found there (chiefly manganese, cobalt, copper and nickel), envisaged as the 'common heritage of mankind', had not been supported by the USA and other industrialized nations on the grounds that countries possessing adequate technology for deep-sea mining would be insufficiently represented in the Authority; that the operations of private mining consortia would be unacceptably limited by the stipulations that their technology should be shared with the Authority's 'Enterprise' and that production should be limited in order to protect land-based mineral producers. Under the 1994 Agreement there was to be no mandatory transfer of technology, the Enterprise was to operate according to commercial principles and there were to be no production limits, although a compensation fund was to assist land-based producers adversely affected by seabed mining. Several industrial nations then ratified the Convention and Agreement (which entered into force in July 1996), although the USA had not yet ratified either by early 2002. An agreement on the implementation of the provisions of the Convention relating to the conservation and management of straddling and highly migratory fish stocks was opened for signature in December 1995 and entered into force in December 2001.

In July 2000 the Authority adopted the Regulations for Prospecting and Exploration for Polymetallic Nodules in the Area. In 2001, pursuant to the Regulations, exploration contracts were signed with six out of seven registered pioneer investors who had submitted plans of work for deep seabed exploration. During 1998–2001 the Authority organized four workshops on (i) development of guide-lines for the assessment of the possible environmental impacts arising from exploration for polymetallic nodules; (ii) proposed technologies for deep seabed mining of polymetallic nodules; (iii) the available knowledge on mineral resources other than polymetallic nodules in the deep seabed; and (iv) a standardized system of data interpretation. A fifth workshop was scheduled to be held in July 2002 on international co-operation and collaboration in marine scientific research on the deep oceans. The Authority is developing a database on polymetallic nodules (POLYDAT), and has also made significant progress towards the establishment of a central data repository for all marine minerals in the seabed.

Finance

The Authority's budget is the responsibility of the Finance Committee. The budget for the Authority for the biennium 2001–02 was US $10.5m. The administrative expenses of the Authority are met by assessed contributions of its members.

Publications

Handbook (annually)
The Law of the Sea: Compendium of Basic Documents.
Selected decisions of sessions of the Authority, consultations, documents, rules of procedure, etc.

Associated Institutions

The following were also established under the terms of the Convention:

Commission on the Limits of the Continental Shelf: Division for Ocean Affairs and the Law of the Sea, Room DC2-0450, United Nations, New York, NY 10017, USA; tel. (212) 963-3966; fax (212) 963-5847; e-mail doalos@un.org; internet www.un.org/Depts/los/clcs_new/clcs_home.htm; 21 members, serving a five-year term (the first election of members took place in March 1997 and the second was scheduled to be held in late April 2002); responsible for making recommendations regarding the establishment of the outer limits of the continental shelf of a coastal state, where the limit extends beyond 200 nautical miles (370 km).

International Tribunal for the Law of the Sea: Am internationalen Seegerichtshof 1, Hamburg, Germany; tel. (40) 356070; fax (40) 35607275; e-mail itlos@itlos.org; internet www.itlos.org; inaugurated in Oct. 1996; 21 judges; responsible for interpreting the Convention and ruling on disputes brought by states party to the Convention on matters within its jurisdiction. Registrar: PHILIPPE GAUTIER (Belgium).

INTER-PARLIAMENTARY UNION—IPU

Address: CP 438, 1211 Geneva 19, Switzerland.

Telephone: (22) 9194150; **fax:** (22) 9194160; **e-mail:** postbox@mail.ipu.org; **internet:** www.ipu.org.

Founded in 1889, the IPU aims to promote peace, co-operation and representative democracy by providing a forum for multilateral political debate between representatives of national parliaments.

MEMBERS

National parliaments of 142 sovereign states; five international parliamentary associations (Associate Members).

Organization

(April 2002)

INTER-PARLIAMENTARY CONFERENCE

The Conference is the main statutory body of the IPU, comprising eight to 10 representatives from each member parliament. It meets twice a year to discuss current issues in world affairs and to make political recommendations. Other specialized conferences may also be held. The Conference is assisted by the following four plenary Study Committees: on Political Questions, International Security and Disarmament; Parliamentary, Juridical and Human Rights Questions; Economic and Social Questions; and Education, Science, Culture and the Environment.

INTER-PARLIAMENTARY COUNCIL

The Council comprises two representatives of each member parliament, usually from different political groups. It is responsible for approving membership and the annual programme and budget of the IPU, and for electing the Secretary-General. The Council may consider substantive issues and adopt resolutions and policy statements, in particular on the basis of recommendations from its subsidiary bodies.

President: NAJMA HEPTULLA (India).

MEETING OF WOMEN PARLIAMENTARIANS

The Meeting is a mechanism for co-ordination between women parliamentarians. Since 1975 the Meeting has been convened twice a year, on the occasion of IPU statutory meetings, to discuss subjects of common interest, to formulate strategies to develop the IPU's women's programme, to strengthen their influence within the organization and to ensure that women are elected to key positions. The Meeting is assisted by a Co-ordinating Committee.

SUBSIDIARY BODIES

In addition to the thematic Study Committees of the IPU Conference, various other committees and groups undertake and co-ordinate IPU activities in specific areas. All these bodies are subsidiary to the IPU Council:

Committee on the Human Rights of Parliamentarians
Committee for Sustainable Development
Committee on Middle East Questions
Group of Facilitators for Cyprus
Ad hoc Committee to Promote Respect for International and Humanitarian Law
CSCM Process and CSCM Co-ordinating Committee (concerned with security and co-operation in the Mediterranean)
Co-ordinating Committee of the Meeting of Women MPs
Gender Partnership Group
Management Board of the Staff Pension Fund

EXECUTIVE COMMITTEE

The Committee, comprising 12 members and presided over by the President of the Council, oversees the administration of the IPU and advises the Council on membership, policy and programme, and any other matters referred to it.

SECRETARIAT

Secretary-General: ANDERS B. JOHNSSON (Sweden).

Activities

PROMOTION OF REPRESENTATIVE DEMOCRACY

This is one of the IPU's core areas of activity, and covers a wide range of concerns, such as democracy, gender issues, human rights and ethnic diversity, parliamentary action to combat corruption, and links between democracy and economic growth. In September 1997 the Council adopted a Universal Declaration on Democracy. The IPU subsequently published a study entitled *Democracy: Its Principles and Achievements.*

The IPU administers a Programme for the Study and Promotion of Representative Institutions, which aims to improve knowledge of the functioning of national parliaments by gathering and disseminating information on their constitutional powers and responsibilities, structure, and membership, and on the electoral systems used. The IPU also organizes international seminars and gatherings for parliamentarians, officials, academics and other experts to study the functioning of parliamentary institutions. A Technical Co-operation Programme aims to mobilize international support in order to improve the capabilities, infrastructure and technical facilities of national parliaments and enhance their effectiveness. Under the Programme, the IPU may provide expert advice on the structure of legislative bodies, staff training, and parliamentary working procedures, and provide technical equipment and other resources. In 1999 technical assistance projects were implemented in Burundi, Ethiopia, Fiji, Gabon, The Gambia, Kyrgyzstan, Laos, Malawi, Viet Nam and Yemen.

IPU teams of observers have overseen elections in Namibia, in 1989, in Cambodia, 1993, and in El Salvador, in 1994. Their duties included observing the process of voter registration, the election campaign and voting, and verifying the results. In 1993 the Council resolved that the IPU be present at all national elections organized, supervised or verified by the United Nations. The IPU has reported on the rights and responsibilities of election observers and issued guide-lines on the holding of free and fair elections. These include a *Declaration on Criteria for Free and Fair Elections,* together with a study on the subject, and Codes of Conduct for Elections.

The IPU maintains a special database (PARLINE) on parliaments of the world, giving access to information on the structure and functioning of all existing parliaments, and on national elections. It conducts regular world studies on matters regarding the structure and functioning of parliaments. It also maintains a separate database (PARLIT) comprising literature from around the world on constitutional, electoral and parliamentary matters.

In August/September 2000 the IPU organized the first international conference of speakers of national parliaments.

INTERNATIONAL PEACE AND SECURITY

The IPU aims to promote conflict resolution and international security through political discussion. Certain areas of conflict are monitored by the Union on an ongoing basis (for example, Cyprus and the Middle East), while others are considered as they arise. In the 1990s the IPU was particularly concerned with the situation in the former Yugoslavia, and condemned incidents of violations of humanitarian law and supported efforts to improve the lives of those affected by the conflict. In March 2002 the 107th Inter-Parliamentary Conference urged both sides in the escalating conflict in the Middle East to observe a cease-fire, to resume political negotiations, and to ensure the safety of all Israeli and Palestinian people. An extensive programme of activities is undertaken by the IPU with regard to the Mediterranean region. In June 1992 the first Conference on Security and Co-operation in the Mediterranean (CSCM) took place; the objectives outlined at the Conference have been integrated as a structured process of the IPU. A second CSCM was held in Valletta, Malta, in November 1995, and a third was convened at Marseilles, France, in March/April 2000. Intermediary thematic meetings are held between plenary conferences, while consultations among parties to the CSCM process take place every six months.

The IPU has worked constantly to promote international and regional efforts towards disarmament, as part of the process of enhancing peace and security. Issues that have been discussed by the Conference include nuclear non-proliferation, a ban on testing of nuclear weapons, and a global register of arms transfers.

SUSTAINABLE DEVELOPMENT

The Committee for Sustainable Development guides the IPU's work in this area, with a broad approach of linking economic growth with social, democratic, human welfare and environmental considerations. Issues of world economic and social development on which the IPU has approved recommendations include employment in a globalizing world, the globalization of economy and liberalization of trade, Third World debt and its impact on the integration of those countries affected into the process of globalization, international mass migration and other demographic problems, and the right to food. The IPU co-operates with programmes and agencies of the UN, in particular in the preparation of major socio-economic conferences, including the World Summit for Social Development, which was held in Copenhagen, Denmark, in March 1995, the Fourth World Conference on Women, held in Beijing, People's Republic of China, in September 1995, and the World Food Summit, held in Rome, Italy, in November 1996. In September 1996 a tripartite meeting of parliamentary, governmental and inter-governmental representatives, convened at the UN headquarters in New York, considered legislative measures to pursue the objectives of the World Summit for Social Development; a follow-up meeting was held in March 1999. In November/December 1998 the IPU, in co-operation with FAO, organized an Inter-Parliamentary Conference concerned with 'Attaining the World Food Summit's Objectives through a Sustainable Development Strategy'.

Activities to protect the environment are undertaken within the framework of sustainable development. In 1984 the first Inter-Parliamentary Conference on the Environment, convened in Nairobi, Kenya, advocated the inclusion of environmental considerations into the development process. The IPU was actively involved in the preparation of the UN Conference on Environment and Development (UNCED), which was held in Rio de Janeiro, Brazil, in June 1992. Subsequently the IPU's environment programme has focused on implementing the recommendations of UNCED, and identifying measures to be taken at parliamentary level to facilitate that process. The IPU also monitors the actual measures taken by national parliaments to pursue the objective of sustainable development, as well as emerging environmental problems. In 1997 the IPU published the *World Directory of Parliamentary Bodies for Environment.*

HUMAN RIGHTS AND HUMANITARIAN LAW

The IPU frequently considers human rights issues and makes relevant recommendations at its statutory Conferences and during specialized meetings, and aims to incorporate human rights concerns, including employment, the rights of minorities, and gender issues, in all areas of activity. A five-member Committee on the Human Rights of Parliamentarians is responsible for the consideration of complaints relating to alleged violations of the human rights of members of parliament, for example state harassment, arbitrary arrest and detention, unfair trail and violation of parliamentary immunity, based on a procedure adopted by the IPU in 1976. The Committee conducts hearings and site missions to investigate a complaint and communicates with the authorities of the country concerned. If no settlement is reached at that stage, the Committee may then publish a report for the Inter-Parliamentary Council and submit recommendations on specific measures to be adopted. By the end of 1998 1,097 cases had been declared admissible, in 87 countries, of which the majority had reached a satisfactory settlement, often through the support of IPU member parliaments.

The IPU works closely with the International Committee of the Red Cross to uphold respect for international humanitarian law. It supports the implementation of the Geneva Conventions and their Additional Protocols, and the adoption of appropriate national legislation. In 1995 the Council adopted a special resolution to establish a reporting mechanism at the parliamentary level to ensure respect for international humanitarian law. Consequently IPU initiated a world survey on legislative action regarding the application of international humanitarian law, as well as efforts to ban anti-personnel land-mines. In April and September 1998 the Council adopted special resolutions on parliamentary action to secure the entry into force and implementation of the Convention on the Prohibition of the Use, Stockpiling, Production and Transfer of Anti-personnel Mines and on their Destruction, which was signed by representatives of some 120 countries meeting in Ottawa, Canada, in December 1997. Further resolutions to that effect were adopted by the Inter-Parliamentary Conference in October 1999 and in April 2001.

In 1998 the IPU published a *World Directory of Parliamentary Human Rights Bodies.*

WOMEN IN POLITICS

The IPU aims to promote the participation of women in the political and parliamentary decision-making processes, and, more generally, in all aspects of society. It organizes debates and events on these issues and compiles a statistical database on women in politics, compiled by regular world surveys. The IPU also actively addresses wider issues of concern to women, such as literacy and education, women in armed conflicts, women's contribution to development, and women in the electoral process. The eradication of violence against women was the subject of a special resolution adopted by the Conference in 1991. The Meeting of Women MPs has monitored efforts by national authorities to implement the recommendations outlined in the resolution. In 1996 the IPU promoted the Framework for Model Legislation on Domestic Violence, formulated by the UN Special Rapporteur on the issue, which aimed to assist national parliaments in preparing legislation to safeguard women. At the Fourth World Conference on Women, held in Beijing, in September 1995, the IPU organized several events to bring together parliamentarians and other leading experts, diplomats and officials to promote the rights of women and of children. In February 1997 the IPU organized a Specialized Inter-Parliamentary Conference, in New Delhi, India, entitled 'Towards partnership between men and women in politics'. Following the Conference the IPU decided to establish a Gender Partnership Group, comprising two men and two women, within the Executive Committee, to ensure that IPU activities and decisions serve the interests and needs of all members of the population. The Group was authorized to report to the IPU Council.

The IPU aims to promote the importance of women's role in economic and social development and their participation in politics as a democratic necessity, and recognizes the crucial role of the media in presenting the image of women. Within the context of the 1997 New Delhi Conference, the IPU organized a second Round Table on the Image of Women Politicians in the Media (the first having been convened in November 1989). The debate urged fair and equal representation of women politicians by the media and for governments to revise their communications policies to advance the image of female parliamentarians.

EDUCATION, SCIENCE AND CULTURE

Activities in these sectors are often subject to consideration by statutory Conferences. Resolutions of the Conference have focused on the implementation of educational and cultural policies designed to foster greater respect for demographic values, adopted in April 1993; on bioethics and its implications world-wide for human rights protection, adopted in April 1995; and on the importance of education and culture as prerequisites for securing sustainable development (with particular emphasis on the education of women and the application of new information technologies), necessitating their high priority status in national budgets, adopted in April 2001. Specialized meetings organized by the IPU have included the Asia and Pacific Inter-Parliamentary Conference on 'Science and technology for regional sustainable development', held in Tokyo, Japan, in June 1994, and the Inter-Parliamentary Conference on 'Education, science, culture and communication on the threshold of the 21st century', organized jointly with UNESCO, and held in Paris, France, in June 1996.

Finance

The IPU is financed by its members from public funds. The 2002 annual budget totalled 9m. Swiss francs. In addition external financial support, primarily from UNDP, is received for some special activities.

Publications

Activities of the Inter-Parliamentary Union (annually).

IPU Information Brochure (annually).

World Directory of Parliaments (annually).

The World of Parliaments (quarterly).

Other handbooks, reports and surveys, documents, conference proceedings.

ISLAMIC DEVELOPMENT BANK

Address: POB 5925, Jeddah 21432, Saudi Arabia.

Telephone: (2) 6361400; **fax:** (2) 6366871; **e-mail:** archives@isdb.org.sa; **internet:** www.isdb.org.

The Bank is an international financial institution that was established following a conference of Ministers of Finance of member countries of the Organization of the Islamic Conference (OIC, q.v.), held in Jeddah in December 1973. Its aim is to encourage the economic development and social progress of member countries and of Muslim communities in non-member countries, in accordance with the principles of the Islamic *Shari'a* (sacred law). The Bank formally opened in October 1975.

MEMBERS

There are 53 members.

Organization

(April 2002)

BOARD OF GOVERNORS

Each member country is represented by a governor, usually its Minister of Finance, and an alternate. The Board of Governors is the supreme authority of the Bank, and meets annually.

BOARD OF EXECUTIVE DIRECTORS

The Board consists of 14 members, seven of whom are appointed by the seven largest subscribers to the capital stock of the Bank; the remaining seven are elected by Governors representing the other subscribers. Members of the Board of Executive Directors are elected for three-year terms. The Board is responsible for the direction of the general operations of the Bank.

ADMINISTRATION

In addition to the President of the Bank, there are three Vice-Presidents, responsible for Operations, Trade and Policy, and Finance and Administration.

President of the Bank and Chairman of the Board of Executive Directors: Dr AHMED MOHAMED ALI.

Vice-President Operations: Dr AMADOU BOUBACAR CISSE.

Vice-President Trade and Policy: Dr SYED JAAFAR AZNAN.

Vice-President Finance and Administration: MUZAFAR AL HAJ MUZAFAR.

REGIONAL OFFICES

Kazakhstan: c/o Director, External Aid Co-ordination Dept, 93–95 Ablay-Khan Ave, 480091 Almaty; tel. (3272) 62-18-68; fax (3272) 69-61-52; Dir ZEINAL ABIDIN.

Malaysia: Level 11, Front Wing, Bank Industri, Jalan Sultan Ismail, POB 13671, 50818 Kuala Lumpur; tel. (3) 2946627; fax (3) 2946626; Dir SALEH AMRAN BIN JAMAN (acting).

Morocco: 177 Ave John Kennedy, Souissi 10105, POB 5003, Rabat; tel. (7) 757191; fax (7) 775726; Dir HANI SALIM SUNBUL.

FINANCIAL STRUCTURE

The authorized capital of the Bank is 6,000m. Islamic Dinars (divided into 600,000 shares, having a value of 10,000 Islamic Dinars each). The Islamic Dinar (ID) is the Bank's unit of account and is equivalent to the value of one Special Drawing Right of the IMF (SDR 1 = US $1.24539 at 5 March 2002).

Subscribed capital amounts to ID 4,000m.

SUBSCRIPTIONS (million Islamic Dinars, as at 5 April 2000)

Afghanistan	5.00	Maldives	2.50
Albania	2.50	Mali	4.92
Algeria	124.26	Mauritania	4.92
Azerbaijan	4.92	Morocco	24.81
Bahrain	7.00	Mozambique	2.50
Bangladesh	49.29	Niger	12.41
Benin	4.92	Oman	13.78
Brunei	12.41	Pakistan	124.26
Burkina Faso	12.41	Palestine	9.85
Cameroon	12.41	Qatar	49.23
Chad	4.92	Saudi Arabia	997.17
Comoros	2.50	Senegal	12.42
Djibouti	2.50	Sierra Leone	2.50
Egypt	346.00	Somalia	2.50
Gabon	14.77	Sudan	19.69
The Gambia	2.50	Suriname	2.50
Guinea	12.41	Syria	5.00
Guinea-Bissau	2.50	Tajikistan	2.50
Indonesia	124.26	Togo	2.50
Iran	349.97	Tunisia	9.85
Iraq	13.05	Turkey	315.47
Jordan	19.89	Turkmenistan	2.50
Kazakhstan	2.50	Uganda	12.41
Kuwait	496.64	United Arab Emirates	283.03
Kyrgyzstan	2.50	Yemen	24.81
Lebanon	4.92		
Libya	400.00	**Total**	4,060.54
Malaysia	79.56		

Activities

The Bank adheres to the Islamic principle forbidding usury, and does not grant loans or credits for interest. Instead, its methods of project financing are: provision of interest-free loans (with a service fee), mainly for infrastructural projects which are expected to have a marked impact on long-term socio-economic development; provision of technical assistance (e.g. for feasibility studies); equity participation in industrial and agricultural projects; leasing operations, involving the leasing of equipment such as ships, and instalment sale financing; and profit-sharing operations. Funds not immediately needed for projects are used for foreign trade financing. Under the Import Trade Financing Operations (ITFO) scheme, funds are used for importing commodities for development purposes (i.e. raw materials and intermediate industrial goods, rather than consumer goods), with priority given to the import of goods from other member countries (see table). The Longer-term Trade Financing Scheme (LTTFS) was introduced in 1987/88 to provide financing for the export of non-traditional and capital goods. During AH 1419 the LTTFS was renamed the Export Financing Scheme (EFS). A special programme under the EFS became operational in AH 1419, on the basis of a memorandum of understanding signed between the Bank and the Arab Bank for Economic Development in Africa (BADEA), to finance Arab exports to non-Arab League members of the OAU.

The Bank's Special Assistance programme was initiated in AH 1400 to support the economic and social development of Muslim communities in non-member countries, in particular in the education and health sectors. It also aimed to provide emergency aid in times of natural disasters, and to assist Muslim refugees throughout the world. Operations undertaken by the Bank are financed by the Waqf Fund (formerly the Special Assistance Account). Other assistance activities include scholarship programmes, technical co-operation projects and the sacrificial meat utilization project.

By 5 April 2000 the Bank had approved a total of ID 4,947.98m. for project financing and technical assistance, a total of ID 11,125.24m. for foreign trade financing, and ID 402.59m. for special assistance operations, excluding amounts for cancelled operations. During the Islamic year 1420 (17 April 1999 to 5 April 2000) the Bank approved a total of ID 1,522.80m., for 230 operations.

The Bank approved 39 loans in the year ending 5 April 2000, amounting to ID 179.70m. (compared with 38 loans, totalling ID 159.79m., in the previous year). These loans supported projects concerned with the construction and modernization of schools and health centres, infrastructural improvements, and

Operations approved, Islamic year 1420 (17 April 1999–5 April 2000)

Type of operation	Number of operations	Total amount (million Islamic Dinars)
Ordinary operations . . .	112	725.49
Project financing . . .	77	718.31
Technical assistance . .	35	7.19
Trade financing operations* .	64	805.85
Waqf Fund operations . .	54	21.46
Total†	230	1,522.80

* Including ITFO, the EFS, the Islamic Bank's Portfolio and the UIF.
† Excluding cancelled operations.

Project financing and technical assistance by sector, Islamic year 1420 (17 April 1999–5 April 2000)

Sector	Number of operations	Amount (million Islamic Dinars)	%
Agriculture and agro-industry	18	87.51	12.1
Industry and mining . .	4	71.40	9.8
Transport and communications . . .	17	99.25	13.7
Public utilities	18	222.18	30.6
Social sectors	39	183.74	25.3
Financial services/Other* .	16	61.41	8.5
Total†	112	725.49	100.0

* Mainly approved amounts for Islamic banks.
† Excluding cancelled operations.

agricultural developments. During the year ending 5 April 2000 the Bank's disbursements totalled ID 871m., bringing the total cumulative disbursements since the Bank began operations to ID 11,010m.

During AH 1420 the Bank approved 35 technical assistance operations for 19 countries (as well as six regional projects) in the form of grants and loans, amounting to ID 7.19m.

Import trade financing approved during the Islamic year 1420 amounted to ID 651.34m. for 39 operations in 12 member countries. By the end of that year cumulative import trade financing amounted to ID 9,480.37m., of which 37.4% was for imports of crude petroleum, 26.4% for intermediate industrial goods, 7.5% for vegetable oil and 6.4% for refined petroleum products. Export financing approved under the EFS amounted to ID 61.32m. for 15 operations in nine countries in AH 1420. In the same year the Bank's Portfolio for Investment and Development, established in AH 1407 (1986–87), approved eight operations amounting to US $106.6m. (or approximately ID 79.1m.). Since its introduction, the Portfolio has approved net financing operations amounting to $1,490.1m. (or ID 1,106.0m.).

The Bank's Unit Investment Fund (UIF) became operational in 1990, with the aim of mobilizing additional resources and providing a profitable channel for investments conforming to *Shari'a*. The initial issue of the UIF was US $100m., which has subsequently been increased to $325m. The Fund finances mainly private-sector industrial projects in middle-income countries. The UIF also finances short-term trade financing operations: two were approved in AH 1420, amounting to $19.0m. In October 1998 the Bank announced the establishment of a new fund to invest in infrastructure projects in member states. The Bank committed $250m. to the fund, which was to comprise $1,000m. equity capital and a $500m. Islamic financing facility. In September 1999 the Bank's Board of Executive Directors approved the establishment of an Islamic Corporation for the Development of the Private Sector, which aimed to identify opportunities in the private sector, provide financial products and services compatible with Islamic law, and expand access to Islamic capital markets for private companies in member countries. The Bank was to retain 50% of the authorized capital of $1,000m., with the remainder owned by member countries (30%) and public financial institutions (20%). In November 2001 the Bank signed an agreement with Malaysia, Bahrain, Indonesia and Sudan for the establishment of an Islamic financial market.

During AH 1420 the Bank approved 54 Waqf Fund operations, amounting to ID 21.5m. Of the total financing, 28 operations provided assistance for Muslim communities in 18 non-member countries.

By the end of AH 1420 the Bank's scholarships programme for Muslim communities in non-member countries had benefited some 5,343 students, at a cost of ID 27m., since it began in 1983. The Merit Scholarship Programme, initiated in AH 1412 (1991–92), aims to develop scientific, technological and research capacities in member countries through advanced studies and/or research. During the second five-year phase of the initiative, which commenced in January 1997, 20 scholars each year were expected to be placed in academic centres of excellence in Australia, Europe and the USA under the programme. In December 1997 the Board of Executive Directors approved a new scholarship programme designed specifically to assist scholars from 18 least-developed member countries to study for a masters degree in science and technology. A total of 190 scholarships were expected to have been awarded by AH 1423. The Bank's Programme for Technical Co-operation aims to mobilize technical capabilities among member countries and to promote the exchange of expertise, experience and skills through expert missions, training, seminars and workshops. During AH 1420 74 projects were implemented under the programme. The Bank also undertakes the distribution of meat sacrificed by Muslim pilgrims: in AH 1420 meat from approximately 416,699 animals was distributed to the needy in 26 countries.

SUBSIDIARY ORGANS

Islamic Corporation for the Insurance of Investment and Export Credit—ICIEC: POB 15722, Jeddah 21454, Saudi Arabia; tel. (2) 6445666; fax (2) 6379504; e-mail idb.iciec@isdb.org.sa; internet www.iciec.org; f. 1994; aims to promote trade and the flow of investments among member countries of the OIC through the provision of export credit and investment insurance services; auth. cap. ID 100m., subscribed cap. ID 95.0m. (March 2001). Man. Dr ABDEL RAHMAN A. TAHA. Mems: 29 OIC member states.

Islamic Research and Training Institute: POB 9201, Jeddah 21413, Saudi Arabia; tel. (2) 6361400; fax (2) 6378927; e-mail maljarhi@isdb.org.sa; internet www.irti.org; f. 1982 to undertake research enabling economic, financial and banking activities to conform to Islamic law, and to provide training for staff involved in development activities in the Bank's member countries. The Institute also organizes seminars and workshops, and holds training courses aimed at furthering the expertise of government and financial officials in Islamic developing countries. Dir Dr MABID ALI AL-JARHI. Publs *Annual Report*, *Journal of Islamic Economic Studies*, various research studies, monographs, reports.

Publication

Annual Report.

LATIN AMERICAN INTEGRATION ASSOCIATION—LAIA

(ASOCIACIÓN LATINOAMERICANA DE INTEGRACIÓN—ALADI)

Address: Cebollatí 1461, Casilla 577, 11000 Montevideo, Uruguay.

Telephone: (2) 4101121; **fax:** (2) 4190649; **e-mail:** sgaladi@aladi.org; **internet:** www.aladi.org.

The Latin American Integration Association was established in August 1980 to replace the Latin American Free Trade Association, founded in February 1960.

MEMBERS

Argentina	Colombia	Paraguay
Bolivia	Cuba	Peru
Brazil	Ecuador	Uruguay
Chile	Mexico	Venezuela

Observers: People's Republic of China, Costa Rica, Dominican Republic, El Salvador, Guatemala, Honduras, Italy, Nicaragua, Panama, Portugal, Romania, Russia, Spain and Switzerland; also the UN Economic Commission for Latin America and the Caribbean (ECLAC), the UN Development Programme (UNDP), the European Union, the Inter-American Development Bank, the Organization of American States, the Andean Development Corporation, the Inter-American Institute for Co-operation on Agriculture, the Latin American Economic System, and the Pan American Health Organization.

Organization

(April 2002)

COUNCIL OF MINISTERS

The Council of Ministers of Foreign Affairs is responsible for the adoption of the Association's policies. It meets when convened by the Committee of Representatives.

EVALUATION AND CONVERGENCE CONFERENCE

The Conference, comprising plenipotentiaries of the member governments, assesses the Association's progress and encourages negotiations between members. It meets when convened by the Committee of Representatives.

COMMITTEE OF REPRESENTATIVES

The Committee, the permanent political body of the Association, comprises a permanent and a deputy representative from each member country. Permanent observers have been accredited by 15 countries and eight international organizations (see above). The Committee is the main forum for the negotiation of ALADI's initiatives and is responsible for the correct implementation of the Treaty and its supplementary regulations. There are the following auxiliary bodies:

Advisory Commission on Customs Valuation.

Advisory Commission on Financial and Monetary Affairs.

Advisory Council for Export Financing.

Advisory Council for Customs Matters.

Budget Commission.

Commission for Technical Support and Co-operation.

Council for Financial and Monetary Affairs: comprises the Presidents of member states' central banks, who examine all aspects of financial, monetary and exchange co-operation.

Council on Transport for Trade Facilitation.

Entrepreneurial Advisory Council.

Labour Advisory Council.

Meeting of Directors of National Customs Administrations.

Nomenclature Advisory Commission.

Sectoral Councils.

Tourism Council.

GENERAL SECRETARIAT

The General Secretariat is the technical body of the Association; it submits proposals for action, carries out research and evaluates activities. The Secretary-General is elected for a three-year term, which is renewable. There are two Assistant Secretaries-General.

Secretary-General (2002–05): JUAN FRANCISCO ROJAS PENSO (Venezuela).

Activities

The Latin American Free Trade Association (LAFTA) was an intergovernmental organization, created by the Treaty of Montevideo in February 1960 with the object of increasing trade between the Contracting Parties and of promoting regional integration, thus contributing to the economic and social development of the member countries. The Treaty provided for the gradual establishment of a free-trade area, which would form the basis for a Latin American Common Market. Reduction of tariff and other trade barriers was to be carried out gradually until 1980.

By 1980, however, only 14% of annual trade among members could be attributed to LAFTA agreements, and it was the richest states which were receiving most benefit. In June it was decided that LAFTA should be replaced by a less ambitious and more flexible organization, the Latin American Integration Association (Asociación Latinoamericana de Integración—ALADI), established by the 1980 Montevideo Treaty, which came into force in March 1981, and was fully ratified in March 1982. Instead of across-the-board tariff cuts, the Treaty envisaged an area of economic preferences, comprising a regional tariff preference for goods originating in member states (in effect from 1 July 1984) and regional and partial scope agreements (on economic complementation, trade promotion, trade in agricultural goods, scientific and technical co-operation, the environment, tourism, and other matters), taking into account the different stages of development of the members, and with no definite timetable for the establishment of a full common market.

The members of ALADI are divided into three categories: most developed (Argentina, Brazil and Mexico); intermediate (Chile, Colombia, Peru, Uruguay and Venezuela); and least developed (Bolivia, Cuba—which joined the Association in August 1999, Ecuador and Paraguay), enjoying a special preferential system. In 2000 the value of exports within ALADI amounted to US $42,860m., compared with $34,776m. in 1999. The countries of the Southern Common Market (Mercosur) accounted for more than one-half of this total. The value of exports within ALADI was estimated at $43,210m. in 2001, an increase of only 0.8% compared with the previous year. By 2004 75% of all intra-ALADI trade was expected to be free of trade restrictions.

Certain LAFTA institutions were retained and adapted by ALADI, e.g. the Reciprocal Payments and Credits Agreement (1965, modified in 1982) and the Multilateral Credit Agreement to Alleviate Temporary Shortages of Liquidity, known as the Santo Domingo Agreement (1969, extended in 1981 to include mechanisms for counteracting global balance-of-payments difficulties and for assisting in times of natural disaster).

By August 1998 98 agreements had entered into force. Seven were 'regional agreements' (in which all member countries participate). These agreements included a regional tariff preference agreement, whereby members allow imports from other member states to enter with tariffs 20% lower than those imposed on imports from other countries, and a Market Opening Lists agreement in favour of the three least developed member states, which provides for the total elimination of duties and other restrictions on imports of certain products. The remaining 91 agreements were 'partial scope agreements' (in which two or more member states participate), including: renegotiation agreements (pertaining to tariff cuts under LAFTA); trade agreements covering particular industrial sectors; the agreements establishing Mercosur (q.v.) and the Group of Three (G3); and agreements covering agriculture, gas supply, tourism, environmental protection, books, transport, sanitation and trade facilitation. A new system of tariff nomenclature, based on the 'harmonized system', was adopted from 1 January 1990 as a basis for common trade negotiations and statistics. General regimes on safeguards and rules of origin entered into force in 1987.

The Secretariat convenes meetings of entrepreneurs in various private industrial sectors, to encourage regional trade and co-operation. In early 2001 ALADI conducted a survey on small and medium-sized enterprises in order to advise the Secretary-General in formulating a programme to assist those businesses and enhance their competitiveness.

A feature of ALADI is its 'outward' projection, allowing for multilateral links or agreements with Latin American non-member countries or integration organizations, and with other developing countries or economic groups outside the continent. In February 1994 the Council of Ministers of Foreign Affairs urged that ALADI should become the co-ordinating body for the various bilateral, multilateral and regional accords (the Andean Community, Mercosur and G3 etc.), with the aim of eventually forming a region-wide common market. The General Secretariat initiated studies in preparation for a programme to undertake this co-ordinating work. At the same meeting in February there was a serious disagreement regarding the proposed adoption of a protocol to the Montevideo Treaty to enable Mexico to participate in the North American Free Trade Agreement (NAFTA), while remaining a member of ALADI. Brazil, in particular, opposed such a solution. However, in June the first Interpretative Protocol to the Montevideo Treaty was signed by the Ministers of Foreign Affairs: the Protocol allows member states to establish preferential trade agreements with developed nations, with a temporary waiver of the most-favoured nation clause (article 44 of the Treaty), subject to the negotiation of unilateral compensation.

Mercosur (which comprises Argentina, Brazil, Paraguay and Uruguay, with Chile and Bolivia as associate members) aims to conclude free-trade agreements with the other members of ALADI. In March 2001 ALADI signed a co-operation agreement with the Andean Community to facilitate the exchange of information and consolidate regional and sub-regional integration.

Publications

Empresarios en la Integración (monthly, in Spanish).

Noticias ALADI (monthly, in Spanish).

Estadísticas y Comercio (quarterly, in Spanish).

Reports, studies, brochures, texts of agreements.

LEAGUE OF ARAB STATES

Address: POB 11642, Arab League Bldg, Tahrir Square, Cairo, Egypt.

Telephone: (2) 5750511; **fax:** (2) 5775626; **internet:** www.leagueofarabstates.org.

The League of Arab States (more generally known as the Arab League) is a voluntary association of sovereign Arab states, designed to strengthen the close ties linking them and to co-ordinate their policies and activities and direct them towards the common good of all the Arab countries. It was founded in March 1945.

MEMBERS

Algeria	Lebanon	Somalia
Bahrain	Libya	Sudan
Comoros	Mauritania	Syria
Djibouti	Morocco	Tunisia
Egypt	Oman	United Arab Emirates
Iraq	Palestine*	Yemen
Jordan	Qatar	
Kuwait	Saudi Arabia	

* Palestine is considered an independent state, and therefore a full member of the League.

Organization

(April 2002)

COUNCIL

The supreme organ of the Arab League, the Council consists of representatives of the member states (normally ministers of foreign affairs), each of which has one vote, and a representative for Palestine. Unanimous decisions of the Council shall be binding upon all member states of the League; majority decisions shall be binding only on those states which have accepted them.

The Council may, if necessary, hold an extraordinary session at the request of two member states. Invitations to all sessions are extended by the Secretary-General. The ordinary sessions are presided over by representatives of the member states in turn.

The Council is supported by technical and specialized committees which advise on financial and administrative affairs, information affairs and legal affairs. In addition, specialized ministerial councils have been established to formulate common policies for the regulation and the advancement of co-operation in the following areas: information; home affairs; legal affairs; health; housing; social affairs; transport; the youth and sports sectors; environmental affairs; and telecommunications.

GENERAL SECRETARIAT

The administrative and financial offices of the League. The Secretariat carries out the decisions of the Council, and provides financial and administrative services for the personnel of the League. General departments comprise: the Bureau of the Secretary-General, Arab Affairs, Economic Affairs, International Affairs, Palestine Affairs, Legal Affairs, Military Affairs, Social and Cultural Affairs, Information Affairs and Administrative and Financial Affairs. In addition, there are Units for Internal Auditing and Institutional Development, a Documentation and Information Centre, Arab League Centres in Tunis and, for Legal and Judicial Research, in Beirut, and a Special Bureau for the Boycott of Israel, based in Damascus, Syria (see below).

The Secretary-General is appointed by the League Council by a two-thirds' majority of the member states, for a five-year, renewable term. He appoints the Assistant Secretaries-General and principal officials, with the approval of the Council. He has the rank of ambassador, and the Assistant Secretaries-General have the rank of ministers plenipotentiary.

Secretary-General: AMR MUHAMMAD MOUSSA (Egypt).

DEFENCE AND ECONOMIC CO-OPERATION

Groups established under the Treaty of Joint Defence and Economic Co-operation, concluded in 1950 to complement the Charter of the League.

Arab Unified Military Command: f. 1964 to co-ordinate military policies for the liberation of Palestine.

Economic and Social Council: compares and co-ordinates the economic policies of the member states; supervises the activities of the Arab League's specialized agencies. The Council is composed of ministers of economic affairs or their deputies; decisions are taken by majority vote. The first meeting was held in 1953.

Joint Defence Council: supervises implementation of those aspects of the treaty concerned with common defence. Composed of foreign and defence ministers; decisions by a two-thirds' majority vote of members are binding on all.

Permanent Military Commission: established 1950; composed of representatives of army general staffs; main purpose: to draw up plans of joint defence for submission to the Joint Defence Council.

ARAB DETERRENT FORCE

Created in June 1976 by the Arab League Council to supervise successive attempts to cease hostilities in Lebanon, and afterwards to maintain the peace. The mandate of the Force has been successively renewed. The Arab League Summit Conference in October 1976 agreed that costs were to be paid in the following percentage contributions: Saudi Arabia and Kuwait 20% each, the United Arab Emirates 15%, Qatar 10% and other Arab states 35%.

OTHER INSTITUTIONS OF THE LEAGUE

Other bodies established by resolutions adopted by the Council of the League:

Administrative Tribunal of the Arab League: f. 1964; began operations 1966.

Arab Fund for Technical Assistance to African Countries: f. 1975 to provide technical assistance for development projects by providing African and Arab experts, grants for scholarships and training, and finance for technical studies.

Higher Auditing Board: comprises representatives of seven member states, elected every three years; undertakes financial and administrative auditing duties.

Investment Arbitration Board: examines disputes between member states relating to capital investments.

Special Bureau for Boycotting Israel: POB 437, Damascus, Syria; f. 1951 to prevent trade between Arab countries and Israel, and to enforce a boycott by Arab countries of companies outside the region that conduct trade with Israel.

SPECIALIZED AGENCIES

All member states of the Arab League are also members of the Specialized Agencies, which constitute an integral part of the Arab League. (See also entries on the Arab Fund for Economic and Social Development, the Arab Monetary Fund, the Council of Arab Economic Unity and the Organization of Arab Petroleum Exporting Countries.)

Arab Academy for Science, Technology and Maritime Transport—AASTMT: POB 1029, Alexandria, Egypt; tel. (3) 5602388; fax (3) 5622525; internet www.aast.edu/web/main.jsp; f. 1975 as Arab Maritime Transport Academy; provides specialized training in marine transport, engineering, technology and management. Dir-Gen. Dr GAMAL ED-DIN MOUKHTAR. Publs *Maritime Research Bulletin* (monthly), *Journal of the Arab Academy for Science, Technology and Maritime Transport* (2 a year).

Arab Administrative Development Organization—ARADO: POB 2692 Al-Horreia, Heliopolis, Cairo, Egypt; tel. (2) 4175401; fax (2) 4175407; e-mail arado@arado.org; internet www.arado.org; f. 1961 (as Arab Organization of Administrative Sciences), although became operational in 1969; administration development, training, consultancy, research and studies, information, documentation; promotes Arab and international co-operation in administrative sciences; includes Arab Network of Administrative Information; 20 Arab state members; Library of 26,000 volumes, 400 periodicals. Dir-Gen. Dr MOHAMED IBRAHIM AL-TWEGRI. Publs *Arab Journal of Administration* (biannual), *Management Newsletter* (quarterly), research series, training manuals.

Arab Atomic Energy Agency—AAEA: 4 rue Mouaouiya ibn Abi Soufiane, al-Menzah 8, POB 402, 1004 Tunis, Tunisia; tel. (71) 709464; fax (71) 711330; e-mail aaea@aaea.org.tn; f. 1988 to co-ordinate research into the peaceful uses of atomic energy. Dir-Gen. Prof. Dr MAHMOUD NASREDDINE (Lebanon). Publs *The Atom and Development* (quarterly), other publs in the field of nuclear sciences and their applications in industry, biology, medicine, agriculture, food irradiation and seawater desalination.

Arab Bank for Economic Development in Africa (Banque arabe pour le développement économique en Afrique—BADEA): Sayed Abd ar-Rahman el-Mahdi St, POB 2640, Khartoum, Sudan; tel. (11) 773646; fax (11) 770600; e-mail badea@badea.org; internet www.badea.org; f. 1973 by Arab League; provides loans and grants to African countries to finance development projects; paid-up cap. US $1,500m. (Dec. 1999). In 1999 the Bank approved loans and grants totalling $119.5m. By the end of 2000 total loans and grants approved since funding activities began in 1975 amounted to $2,298.1m. Subscribing countries: all countries of Arab League, except the Comoros, Djibouti, Somalia and Yemen; recipient countries: all countries of Organization of African Unity (q.v.), except those belonging to the Arab League. Chair. AHMAD ABDALLAH AL-AKEIL (Saudi Arabia); Dir-Gen. MEDHAT SAMI LOTFY (Egypt). Publs *Annual Report, Co-operation for Development* (quarterly), Studies on Afro-Arab co-operation, periodic brochures.

Arab Centre for the Study of Arid Zones and Dry Lands—ACSAD: POB 2440, Damascus, Syria; tel. (11) 5323087; fax (11) 5323063; e-mail ruacsad@net.sy; f. 1971 to conduct regional research and development programmes related to water and soil resources, plant and animal production, agro-meteorology, and socio-economic studies of arid zones. The Centre holds conferences and training courses and encourages the exchange of information by Arab scientists. Dir-Gen. Dr HASSAN SEOUD.

Arab Industrial Development and Mining Organization: rue France, Zanagat Al Khatawat, POB 8019, Rabat, Morocco; tel. (7) 772600; fax (7) 772188; e-mail aidmo@arifonet.org.ma; internet www.arifonet.org.ma; f. 1990 by merger of Arab Industrial Development Organization, Arab Organization for Mineral Resources and Arab Organization for Standardization and Metrology. Comprises a 13-member Executive Council, a High Consultative Committee of Standardization, a High Committee of Mineral Resources and a Co-ordination Committee for Arab Industrial Research Centres; a Ministerial Council, of ministers of member states responsible for industry, meets every two years. Dir-Gen. TALA'AT BEN DAFER. Publs *Arab Industrial Development* (monthly and quarterly newsletters).

Arab Labour Organization: POB 814, Cairo, Egypt; f. 1965 for co-operation between member states in labour problems; unification of labour legislation and general conditions of work wherever possible; research; technical assistance; social insurance; training, etc.; the organization has a tripartite structure: governments, employers and workers. Dir-Gen. IBRAHIM GUDIR. Publs *ALO Bulletin* (monthly), *Arab Labour Review* (quarterly), *Legislative Bulletin* (annually), series of research reports and studies concerned with economic and social development issues in the Arab world.

Arab League Educational, Cultural and Scientific Organization—ALECSO: POB 1120, Tunis, Tunisia; tel. (71) 784-466; fax (71) 784-965; e-mail alecso@email.ati.tn; internet www.slis.uwm.edu/ALECSO/; f. 1970 to promote and co-ordinate educational, cultural and scientific activities in the Arab region. Regional units: Arab Centre for Arabization, Translation, Authorship, and Publication—Damascus, Syria; Institute of Arab Manuscript—Cairo, Egypt; Institute of Arab Research and Studies—Cairo, Egypt; Khartoum Institute for Arabic Language—Khartoum, Sudan; and the Arabization Co-ordination Bureau—Rabat, Morocco. Sec.-Gen. WAGDI MAHMOUD. Publs *Arab Journal of Culture, Arab Journal of Science, Arab Bulletin of Publications, Statistical Yearbook, Journal of the Institute of Arab Manuscripts, Arab Magazine for Information Science.*

Arab Organization for Agricultural Development: St no. 7, Al-Amarat, POB 474, Khartoum, Sudan; tel. (11) 472176; fax (11) 471402; e-mail aoad@sudanmail.net; internet www.aoad.org; f. 1970; began operations in 1972 to contribute to co-operation in agricultural activities, and in the development of natural and human resources for agriculture; compiles data, conducts studies, training and food security programmes; includes Arab Institute of Forestry and Range, Arab Centre for Information and Early Warning, and Arab Centre for Agricultural Documentation. Dir-Gen. Dr YAHIA BAKOUR. Publs *Agricultural Statistics Yearbook, Annual Report on Agricultural Development, the State of Arab Food Security* (annually), *Agriculture and Development in the Arab World* (quarterly), *Accession Bulletin* (every 2 months), *AOAD Newsletter* (monthly), *Arab Agricultural Research Journal, Arab Journal for Irrigation Water Management* (2 a year).

Arab Satellite Communications Organization—ARABSAT: King Fahd Express Rd (Ollaya St), POB 1038, Riyadh, 11431 Saudi Arabia; tel. (1) 4820000; fax (1) 4887999; e-mail albidnah@arabsat.com; internet www.arabsat.com; f. 1976; regional satellite telecommunications organization providing television, telephone and data exchange services to members and private users; operates three satellites, which cover all Arab and Mediterranean countries, controlled by a Primary Control Station in Dirab, Saudi Arabia, and a Secondary Control Facility, based in Dkhila, Tunisia. Dir-Gen. SAAD IBN ABD AL-AZIZ AL-BIDNAH (Saudi Arabia).

Arab States Broadcasting Union—ASBU: POB 250, 1080 Tunis Cedex; 6 rue des Entrepreneurs, zone industrielle Charguia 2, Ariana Aéroport, Tunisia; tel. (71) 703854; fax (71) 704203; f. 1969 to promote Arab fraternity, co-ordinate and study broadcasting subjects, to exchange expertise and technical co-operation in broadcasting; conducts training and audience research. Mems: 23 Arab radio and TV stations and eight foreign associates. Sec.-Gen. RAOUF BASTI. Publ. *ASBU Review* (quarterly).

Inter-Arab Investment Guarantee Corporation: POB 23568, Safat 13096, Kuwait; tel. 4844500; fax 4815741; internet www.iaigc.org; f. 1975; insures Arab investors for non-commercial risks, and export credits for commercial and non-commercial risks; undertakes research and other activities to promote inter-Arab trade and investment; cap. p.u. US $81m. (Dec. 1999). Mems: 22 Arab governments. Dir-Gen. MAMOUN IBRAHIM HASSAN. Publs *News Bulletin* (monthly), *Arab Investment Climate Report* (annually).

External Relations

ARAB LEAGUE OFFICES AND INFORMATION CENTRES ABROAD

Established by the Arab League to co-ordinate work at all levels among Arab embassies abroad.

Austria: Grimmelshausengasse 12, 1030 Vienna.

Belgium: 89 ave de l'Uruguay, 1000 Brussels.

China, People's Republic: 14 Liang Male, 1-14-2 Tayuan Diplomatic Building, Beijing 100600.

Ethiopia: POB 5768, Addis Ababa.

France: 36 rue Fortuny, 75017 Paris.

Germany: Rheinallee 23, 53173 Bonn.

India: B-8/19 Vasant Vihar, New Delhi.

Italy: Piazzale delle Belle Arti 6, 00196 Rome.

Russia: 28 Koniouch Kovskaya, 132242 Moscow.

Spain: Paseo de la Castellana 180, 60°, 28046 Madrid.

Switzerland: 9 rue du Valais, 1202 Geneva.

Tunisia: 93 ave Louis Braille, el-Khadra, 1003 Tunis.

United Kingdom: 52 Green St, London, W1Y 3RH.

USA: 1100 17th St, NW, Suite 602, Washington, DC 20036; 17 Third Ave, 35th Floor, New York, NY 10017 (UN Office).

Record of Events

1945 Pact of the Arab League signed, March.

1946 Cultural Treaty signed.

1950 Joint Defence and Economic Co-operation Treaty.

1952 Agreements on extradition, writs and letters of request, nationality of Arabs outside their country of origin.

1953 Formation of Economic and Social Council.
Convention on the privileges and immunities of the League.

1954 Nationality Agreement.

1956 Agreement on the adoption of a Common Tariff Nomenclature.

1962 Arab Economic Unity Agreement.

1964 First Summit Conference of Arab kings and presidents, Cairo, January.
First meeting of Council of Arab Economic Unity, June.
Arab Common Market Agreement endorsed by the Council, August.
Second Summit Conference welcomed establishment of Palestine Liberation Organization (PLO), September.

1969 Fifth Summit Conference, Rabat. Call for mobilization of all Arab nations against Israel.

1977 Tripoli Declaration, December. Decision of Algeria, Iraq, Libya and Yemen PDR to boycott League meetings in Egypt in response to President Sadat's visit to Israel.

1979 Council meeting resolved to withdraw Arab ambassadors from Egypt; to recommend severance of political and diplomatic relations with Egypt; to suspend Egypt's membership of the League on the date of the signing of its formal peace treaty with Israel (26 March); to transfer the headquarters of the League to Tunis; to condemn US policy regarding its role in concluding the Camp David agreements (in September 1978) and the peace treaty; to halt all bank loans, deposits, guarantees or facilities, as well as all financial or technical contributions and aid to Egypt; to prohibit trade exchanges with the Egyptian state and with private establishments dealing with Israel.

1981 In November the 12th Summit Conference, held in Fez, Morocco, was suspended owing to disagreement over a Saudi Arabian proposal known as the Fahd Plan, which included not only the Arab demands on behalf of the Palestinians, as approved by the UN General Assembly, but also an implied *de facto* recognition of Israel.

1982 The 12th Summit Conference was reconvened in September. It adopted a peace plan, which demanded Israel's withdrawal from territories occupied in 1967, and removal of Israeli settlements in these areas; freedom of worship for all religions in the sacred places; the right of the Palestinian people to self-determination, under the leadership of the PLO; temporary supervision for the west bank and the gaza strip; the creation of an independent Palestinian state, with Jerusalem as its capital; and a guarantee of peace for all the states of the region by the UN Security Council.

1983 The summit meeting due to be held in November was postponed owing to members' differences of opinion concerning Syria's opposition to Yasser Arafat's chairmanship of the PLO, and Syrian support of Iran in the war against Iraq.

1984 In March an emergency meeting established an Arab League committee to encourage international efforts to bring about a negotiated settlement of the Iran–Iraq war. In May ministers of foreign affairs adopted a resolution urging Iran to stop attacking non-belligerent ships and installations in the Gulf region: similar attacks by Iraq were not mentioned.

1985 In August an emergency Summit Conference was boycotted by Algeria, Lebanon, Libya, Syria and Yemen PDR, while of the other 16 members only nine were represented by their heads of state. Two commissions were set up to mediate in disagreements between Arab states (between Jordan and Syria, Iraq and Syria, Iraq and Libya, and Libya and the PLO).

1986 In July King Hassan of Morocco announced that he was resigning as chairman of the next League Summit Conference, after criticism by several Arab leaders of his meeting with the Israeli Prime Minister earlier that month. A ministerial meeting, held in October, condemned any attempt at direct negotiation with Israel.

1987 An extraordinary Summit Conference was held in November, mainly to discuss the war between Iran and Iraq. Contrary to expectations, the participants unanimously agreed on a statement expressing support for Iraq in its defence of its legitimate rights, and criticizing Iran for its procrastination in accepting the UN Security Council Resolution 598 of July, which had recommended a cease-fire and negotiations on a settlement of the conflict. The meeting also stated that the resumption of diplomatic relations with Egypt was a matter to be decided by individual states.

1988 In June a Summit Conference agreed to provide finance for the PLO to continue the Palestinian uprising in Israeli-occupied territories. It reiterated a demand for the convening of an international conference, attended by the PLO, to seek to bring about a peaceful settlement in the Middle East (thereby implicitly rejecting recent proposals by the US Government for a conference that would exclude the PLO).

1989 In January an Arab League group, comprising six ministers of foreign affairs, began discussions with the two rival Lebanese governments on the possibility of a political settlement in Lebanon. At a Summit Conference, held in May, Egypt was readmitted to the League. The Conference expressed support for the chairman of the PLO, Yasser Arafat, in his recent peace proposals made before the UN General Assembly, and reiterated the League's support for proposals that an international conference should be convened to discuss the rights of Palestinians: in so doing, it accepted UN Security Council Resolutions 242 and 338 on a peaceful settlement in the Middle East and thus gave tacit recognition to the State of Israel. The meeting also supported Arafat in rejecting Israeli proposals for elections in the Israeli-occupied territories of the West Bank and the Gaza Strip. A new mediation committee was established, with a six-month mandate to negotiate a cease-fire in Lebanon, and to reconvene the Lebanese legislature with the aim of holding a presidential election and restoring constitutional government in Lebanon. In September the principal factions in Lebanon agreed to observe a cease-fire, and the surviving members of the Lebanese legislature (originally elected in 1972) met at Ta'if, in Saudi Arabia, in October, and approved the League's proposed 'charter of national reconciliation'.

1990 In May a Summit Conference, held in Baghdad, Iraq (which was boycotted by Syria and Lebanon), criticized recent efforts by Western governments to prevent the development of advanced weapons technology in Iraq. In August an emergency Summit Conference was held to discuss the invasion and annexation of Kuwait by Iraq. Twelve members (Bahrain, Djibouti, Egypt, Kuwait, Lebanon, Morocco, Oman, Qatar, Saudi Arabia, Somalia, Syria and the United Arab Emirates) approved a resolution condemning Iraq's action, and demanding the withdrawal of Iraqi forces from Kuwait and the reinstatement of the Government. The 12 states expressed support for the Saudi Arabian Government's invitation to the USA to send forces to defend Saudi Arabia; they also agreed to impose economic sanctions on Iraq, and to provide troops for an Arab defensive force in Saudi Arabia. The remaining member states, however, condemned the presence of foreign troops in Saudi Arabia, and their ministers of foreign affairs refused to attend a meeting, held at the end of August, to discuss possible solutions to the crisis. The dissenting countries also rejected the decision, taken earlier in the year, to return the League's headquarters from Tunis to Cairo. None the less, the official transfer of the League's headquarters to Cairo took place on 31 October. In November King Hassan of Morocco urged the convening of an Arab Summit Conference, in an attempt to find an 'Arab solution' to Iraq's annexation of Kuwait. However, the divisions in the Arab world over the issue meant that conditions for such a meeting could not be agreed.

1991 The first meeting of the Arab League since August 1990 took place in March, attended by representatives of all 21 member nations, including Iraq. Discussion of the recently-ended war against Iraq was avoided, in an attempt to re-establish the unity of the League. In September, despite deep divisions between member states, it was agreed that a committee should be formed to co-ordinate Arab positions in preparation for the US-sponsored peace talks between Arab countries and Israel. (In the event, an *ad hoc* meeting, attended by Egypt, Jordan, Syria, the PLO, Saudi Arabia—representing the Gulf Co-operation Council (GCC), and Morocco—representing the Union of the Arab Maghreb, was held in October, prior to the start of the talks.) In December the League expressed solidarity with Libya, which was under international pressure to extradite two government agents who were suspected of involvement in the explosion which destroyed a US passenger aircraft over Lockerbie, United Kingdom, in December 1988.

1992 The League attempted to mediate between the warring factions in Somalia. In March the League appointed a committee to seek to resolve the disputes between Libya and the USA, the United Kingdom and France over the Lockerbie bomb and the explosion which destroyed a French passenger aircraft over Niger in September 1989. The League condemned the UN's decision, at the end of March, to impose sanctions against Libya, and appealed for a negotiated solution. In September the League's Council issued a condemnation of Iran's alleged occupation of three islands in the Persian (Arabian) Gulf that were claimed by the United Arab Emirates, and decided to refer the issue to the UN.

1993 In April the Council approved the creation of a committee to consider the political and security aspects of water supply in Arab countries. In the same month the League pledged its commitment to the Middle East peace talks, but warned that Israel's continued refusal to repatriate the Palestinians based in Lebanon remained a major obstacle to the process. The League sent an official observer to the independence referendum in Eritrea, held in April. In September the Council admitted the Comoros as the 22nd member of the League. Following the signing of the Israeli-PLO peace accord in September the Council convened in emergency session, at which it approved the agreement, despite opposition from some members, notably Syria. In November it was announced that the League's boycott of commercial activity with Israel was to be maintained.

1994 The League condemned a decision of the GCC, announced in late September, to end the secondary and tertiary trade embargo against Israel, by which member states refuse to trade with international companies which have investments in Israel. A statement issued by the League insisted that the embargo could be removed only on the decision of the Council. Earlier in September the Council endorsed a recommendation that the UN conduct a census of Palestinian refugees, in the absence of any such action taken by the League.

1995 In March Arab ministers of foreign affairs approved a resolution urging Israel to renew the Nuclear Non-Proliferation Treaty (NPT). The resolution stipulated that failure by Israel to do so would cause Arab states to seek to protect legitimate Arab interests by alternative means. In May an extraordinary session of the Council condemned a decision by Israel to confiscate Arab-owned land in East Jerusalem for resettlement. Arab heads of state and government were scheduled to convene in emergency session later in that month to formulate a collective response to the action. However, the meeting was postponed, following an announcement by the Israeli Government that it was suspending its expropriation plans. In September the Council discussed plans for a regional court of justice and for an Arab Code of Honour to prevent the use of force in disputes between Arab states. The Council expressed its support for the Algerian Government in its efforts to combat Muslim separatist violence. In October the League was reported to be in financial difficulties, owing to the non-payment of contributions by seven member states. In November the Arab League dispatched 44 observers to oversee elections in Algeria as part of an international monitoring team.

1996 In March, following protests by Syria and Iraq that extensive construction work in southern Turkey was restricting water supply in the region, the Council determined that the waters of the Euphrates and Tigris rivers be shared equitably between the three countries. In April an emergency meeting of the Council issued a further endorsement of Syria's position in the dispute with Turkey. The main objective of the meeting, which was convened at the request of Palestine, was to attract international attention to the problem of radiation from an Israeli nuclear reactor. The Council requested an immediate technical inspection of the site by the UN, and further demanded that Israel be obliged to sign the NPT to ensure the eradication of its nuclear weaponry. In June a Summit Conference was convened, the first since 1990, in order to formulate a united Arab response to the election, in May, of a new government in Israel and to the prospects for peace in the Middle East. At the Conference, which was attended by heads of state of 13 countries and senior representatives of seven others (Iraq was excluded from the meeting in order to ensure the attendance of the Gulf member states), Israel was urged to honour its undertaking to withdraw from the Occupied Territories, including Jerusalem, and to respect the establishment of an independent Palestinian state, in order to ensure the success of the peace process. A final communiqué of the meeting warned that Israeli co-operation was essential to prevent Arab states' reconsidering their participation in the peace process and the re-emergence of regional tensions. Meanwhile, there were concerns over increasing inter-Arab hostility, in particular between Syria and Jordan, owing to the latter's relations with Israel and allegations of Syrian involvement in recent terrorist attacks against Jordanian targets. In early September the League condemned US missile attacks against Iraq as an infringement of that country's sovereignty. In addition, it expressed concern at the impact on Iraqi territorial integrity of Turkish intervention in the north of Iraq. Later in September the League met in emergency session, following an escalation of civil unrest in Jerusalem and the Occupied Territories. The League urged the UN Security Council to prevent further alleged Israeli aggression against the Palestinians. In November the League criticized Israel's settlement policy, and at the beginning of December convened in emergency session to consider measures to end any expansion of the Jewish population in the West Bank and Gaza.

1997 In March the Council met in emergency session, in response to the Israeli Government's decision to proceed with construction of a new settlement at Har Homa (Jabal Abu-Ghunaim) in East Jerusalem. The Council pledged its commitment to seeking a reversal of the decision and urged the international community to support this aim. At the end of March ministers of foreign affairs of Arab League states agreed to end all efforts to secure normal diplomatic relations with Israel (although binding agreements already in force with Egypt, Jordan and Palestine were exempt) and to close diplomatic offices and missions while construction work continued in East Jerusalem. In addition, ministers recommended reactivating the economic boycott against Israel until comprehensive peace was achieved in the region and suspending Arab participation in the multilateral talks that were initiated in 1991 to further the peace process. Earlier in the year, in February, the Economic and Social Council adopted the Executive Programme of the (1981) Agreement to Facilitate and Develop Trade Among Arab Countries, with a view to creating a Greater Arab Free Trade Area (GAFTA), which aimed to facilitate and develop inter-Arab trade through the reduction and eventual elimination of customs duties over a 10-year period (at a rate of 10% per year), with effect from 1 January 1998. The Council agreed to supervise the implementation of the free trade agenda and formally to review its progress twice a year. In June a 60-member delegation from the Arab League participated in an international mission to monitor legislative elections in Algeria. In the same month the League condemned Turkey's military incursion into northern Iraq and demanded a withdrawal of Turkish troops from Iraqi territory. In September ministers of foreign affairs of member states advocated a gradual removal of international sanctions against Libya, and agreed that member countries should permit international flights to leave Libya for specific humanitarian and religious purposes and when used for the purposes of transporting foreign nationals. Ministers also voted to pursue the decision, adopted in March, not to strengthen relations with Israel. Several countries urged a formal boycott of the forthcoming Middle East and North Africa economic conference, in protest at the lack of progress in the peace process (for which the League blamed Israel, which was due to participate in the conference). However, the meeting upheld a request by the Qatari Government, the host of the conference, that each member should decide individually whether to attend. In the event, only seven Arab League countries participated in the conference, which was held in Doha in mid-November, while the Secretary-General of the League decided not to attend as the organization's official representative. In November the League criticized the decision of the US Government to impose economic sanctions against Sudan. The League also expressed concern at the tensions arising from Iraq's decision not to co-operate fully with UN weapons inspectors, and held several meetings with representatives of the Iraqi administration in an effort to secure a peaceful conclusion to the impasse.

1998 In early 1998 the Secretary-General of the League condemned the use or threat of force against Iraq and continued to undertake diplomatic efforts to secure Iraq's compliance with UN Security Council resolutions. The League endorsed the agreement concluded between the UN Secretary-General and the Iraqi authorities in late February, and reaffirmed its commitment to facilitating the eventual removal of the international embargo against Iraq. A meeting of the Council in March, attended by ministers of foreign affairs of 16 member states, rejected Israel's proposal to withdraw from southern Lebanon, which was conditional on the deployment by the Lebanese Government of extra troops to secure Israeli territory from attack, and, additionally, urged international support to secure Israel's withdrawal from the Golan Heights. In April Arab League ministers of the interior and of justice adopted the Arab Convention for the Suppression of Terrorism, which incorporated security and judicial measures, such as extradition arrangements and the exchange of evidence. The agreement was to enter into effect 30 days after being ratified by at least seven member countries. (This was achieved in May 2000.) In August the League denounced terrorist bomb attacks against the US embassies in Kenya and Tanzania. Nevertheless, it condemned US retaliatory military action, a few days later, against suspected terrorist targets in Afghanistan and Sudan, and endorsed a request by the Sudanese Government that the Security Council investigate the incident. In the same month the USA and United Kingdom accepted a proposal of the Libyan Government, supported by the Arab League, that the suspects in the Lockerbie case be tried in The Hague, Netherlands, under Scottish law. In September the Council discussed the conditions for the suspension of sanctions against Libya. Other items concluded by the Council were condemnation of Turkey's military co-operation with Israel, support for efforts to maintain unity in the Comoros, rejection of further Israeli construction in the Golan Heights, and a request that the UN dispatch a fact-finding mission to examine conditions in the Israeli-occupied territories and alleged violations of Palestinian property rights. In November, following an escalation of tensions between the Iraqi authorities and UN weapons inspectors, the Secretary-General reiterated the League's opposition to the use of force against Iraq, but urged Iraq to maintain a flexible approach in its relations with the UN. The League condemned the subsequent bombing of strategic targets in Iraq, conducted by US and British military aircraft from mid-December, and offered immediate medical assistance to victims of the attacks. An emergency summit meeting of the League was scheduled to be held at the end of December, further to a request by the Yemeni Government to formulate a unified Arab response to the bombings; however, it was postponed, reportedly at the request of Gulf Arab states. The League has subsequently repeatedly reiterated its condemnation of the aerial attacks.

1999 The postponed emergency meeting of ministers of foreign affairs was held in late January, attended by representatives of 18 member states. The meeting expressed concern at the military response to the stand-off between Iraq and the UN, and agreed to establish a seven-member *ad hoc* committee to consider the removal of punitive measures against Iraq within the framework of UN resolutions. However the Iraqi delegation withdrew from the meeting in protest at the final statement, which included a request that Iraq recognize Kuwait's territorial integrity. In March the League's Council determined that member states would suspend sanctions imposed against Libya, once arrangements for the trial of the suspects in the Lockerbie case had been finalized. (The suspects were transferred to a detention centre in the Netherlands in early April, whereupon the UN Security Council suspended its sanctions against Libya.) The meeting also expressed support for a UN resolution convening an international conference to facilitate the implementation of agreements applying to Israel and the Occupied Territories, condemned Israel's refusal to withdraw from the Occupied Territories without a majority vote in favour from its legislature, as well as its refusal to resume the peace negotiations with Lebanon and Syria that had ended in 1996, and advocated the publication of evidence of Israeli violence against Palestinians. The Council considered other issues, including the need to prevent further Israeli expansion in Jerusalem and the problem of Palestinian refugees, and reiterated demands for international support to secure Israel's withdrawal from the Golan Heights. In May the League expressed its concern at the political situation in the Comoros, following the removal of the government and establishment of a new military regime in that country at the end of April. In June the League condemned an Israeli aerial attack on Beirut and southern Lebanon. In September Iraq chaired a meeting of the Ministerial Council for the first time since 1990. The meeting considered a range of issues, including the Middle East peace process, US military aid to Israel, and a dispute with the Walt Disney corporation regarding a forthcoming exhibition which appeared to depict Jerusalem as the capital of Israel. Later in September an extraordinary meeting of League senior media and information officials was convened to discuss the latter issue. Negotiations with representatives of Disney were pursued and the implied threat of an Arab boycott of the corporation was averted following assurances that the exhibition would be apolitical. In October the Secretary-General of the League condemned the Mauritanian authorities for concluding an agreement with Israel to establish diplomatic relations. In November the League, in conjunction with the Arab Monetary Fund and the Palestinian Monetary Authority, convened a symposium on the planned issuance of a Palestinian currency. The League demanded that Israel compensate Palestinians for alleged losses incurred by their enforced use of the Israeli currency. The League reported in December that it was owed some US $135m. in arrears by its members, announcing that only six of the 22 states were up-to-date with their contributions. In late December, prior to a short-lived resumption of Israeli-Syrian peace negotiations, the League reaffirmed its full support for Syria's position.

2000 In February the League strongly condemned an Israeli aerial attack on southern Lebanon; the League's Council changed the venue of its next meeting, in March, from its Cairo headquarters to Beirut as a gesture of solidarity with Lebanon. During March the Secretary-General of the League expressed regret over Iraq's failure to join the *ad hoc* committee established in early 1999 (see above) and also over Iraq's refusal to co-operate with the recently established UN Monitoring, Verification and Inspection Commission (UNMOVIC). The League welcomed the withdrawal of Israeli forces from southern Lebanon in May, although in mid-June it questioned the UN's official verification of the operation, citing reported continuing territorial violations by Israeli troops. In late June the League concluded a co-operation accord with UNHCR; the two bodies agreed to exchange documents and data. Meeting in early September League foreign ministers approved a draft amendment to the League's charter, providing for an annual summit conference of heads of state to take place every March. In addition, resolutions were passed urging international bodies to avoid participating in conferences in Jerusalem, reiterating a threatened boycott of a US chain of restaurants which was accused of operating a franchise in an Israeli settlement in the West Bank, and opposing an Israeli initiative for a Jewish emblem to be included as a symbol of the International Red Cross and Red Crescent Movement. At an emergency summit convened in late October in response to mounting insecurity in Jerusalem and the Occupied Territories, 15 Arab heads of state, senior officials from six countries and Yasser Arafat, the Palestinian National Authority leader, strongly rebuked Israel, which was accused of inciting the ongoing violent disturbances by stalling the progress of the peace process. The summit determined to 'freeze' co-operation with Israel, requested the formation of an international committee to conduct an impartial assessment of the situation, urged the UN Security Council to establish a mechanism to bring alleged Israeli 'war' criminals to trial, and requested the UN to approve the creation of an international force to protect Palestinians residing in the Occupied Territories. The summit also endorsed the establishment of an 'Al-Aqsa Fund', with a value of US $800m., which was to finance initiatives aimed at promoting the Arab and Islamic identity of Jerusalem, and a smaller 'Jerusalem Intifada Fund' to support the families of Palestinians killed in the unrest. A follow-up committee was subsequently established to implement the resolutions adopted by the emergency summit. Iraq and Somalia both participated in the gathering, each sending high-level representation to a summit meeting of the League for the first time since 1990.

2001 In early January a meeting of League foreign ministers reviewed a proposed framework agreement, presented by outgoing President Clinton of the USA, which aimed to resolve the continuing extreme tension between the Israeli and Palestinian authorities. The meeting agreed that the issues dominating the stalled Middle East peace process should not be redefined, strongly objecting to a proposal that, in exchange for Palestinian assumption of control over Muslim holy sites in Jerusalem, Palestinians exiled at the time of the foundation of the Israeli state in 1948 should forgo their claimed right to return to their former homes. At the end of January, following the completion of the trial in The Hague, Netherlands, of the two Libyans accused of complicity in the Lockerbie case (one of whom was found guilty and one of whom was acquitted), the Arab League Secretary-General urged the UN Security Council fully to terminate the sanctions against Libya that had been suspended in 1999. Meeting in mid-March the League's Council pledged that member states would not consider themselves bound by the (inactive) UN sanctions. The Council also reiterated the League's opposition to the economic sanctions maintained by the USA against Sudan, welcomed the political *rapprochement* achieved in the Comoros in February, and accused Iran of threatening regional security by conducting military manoeuvres on the three disputed islands in the Persian (Arabian) Gulf that were also claimed by the United Arab Emirates. In late March the League's first annual summit meeting of heads of state was convened, in Amman, Jordan. The summit issued the Amman Declaration, which emphasized the promotion of Arab unity, and demanded the reversal of Israel's 1967 occupation of Arab territories and the removal of the UN sanctions against Iraq. The Declaration also urged all member states to accelerate implementation of the GAFTA initiative. (It was reported prior to the summit that 15 of the League's 22 member states were making sufficient progress in realizing the requisite trade liberalization measures.) Heads of state attending the summit meeting requested that the League consider means of reactivating the now relaxed Arab economic boycott of Israel, and agreed that the Jordanian King should mediate contacts between Iraq and Kuwait. At the summit Amr Moussa, hitherto Egypt's minister of foreign affairs, was appointed as the League's new Secretary-General. In May a meeting of League ministers of foreign affairs determined that all political contacts with Israel should be suspended in protest at aerial attacks by Israel on Palestinian targets in the West Bank. In July representatives of 13 member countries met in Damascus, Syria, under the auspices of the Special Bureau for Boycotting Israel. The meeting declared unanimous support for reactivated trade measures against Israeli companies and foreign businesses dealing with Israel. In August an emergency meeting of ministers of foreign affairs of Arab League states was convened at the request of the Palestinian authorities to address the recent escalation of hostilities and Israel's seizure of institutions in East Jerusalem. The meeting, which was attended by the League's Secretary-General and the leader of the Palestinian National Authority, Yasser Arafat, aimed to formulate a unified Arab response to the situation. The meeting followed an emergency gathering of information ministers of member countries, at which it was agreed to provide political and media support to the Palestinian position. An emergency meeting of the League's Council convened in mid-September in response to recent major terrorist attacks on the USA allegedly perpetrated by militant Islamist fundamentalists, condemned the atrocities, while urging respect for the rights of Arab and Muslim US citizens. The Secretary-General subsequently emphasized the need for co-ordinated global anti-terrorist action to have clearly defined goals and to be based on sufficient consultations and secure evidence. He also deplored anti-Islamic prejudice, stated that US-led military action against any Arab state would not be supported and that Israeli participation in an international anti-terrorism alliance would be unacceptable, and urged a review of the UN sanction regime against Iraq and an accelerated settlement to the Palestinian-Israeli crisis. A meeting of League foreign ministers in Doha, in early October, condemned international terrorism but did not express support for retaliatory military action by the USA and its allies. In December a further emergency meeting of League foreign affairs ministers was held to discuss the deepening Middle East crisis.

2002 In January the League appointed a commissioner responsible for promoting dialogue between civilizations. The commissioner was mandated to encourage understanding in Western countries of Arab and Muslim civilization and viewpoints, with the aim of redressing perceived negative stereotypes (especially in view of the Islamist fundamentalist connection to the September 2001 terrorist atrocities). In early March a meeting of League foreign ministers agreed to support an initiative proposed by Crown Prince Abdullah of Saudi Arabia aimed at brokering a peaceful settlement to the by now critical Palestinian-Israeli crisis. The Saudi-backed plan—entailing the restoration of 'normal' Arab relations with Israel and acceptance of its right to exist in peace and security, in exchange for a full Israeli withdrawal from the Occupied Territories, the establishment of an independent Palestinian state with East Jerusalem as its capital, and the return of refugees—was unanimously endorsed, as the first ever pan-Arab Palestinian-Israeli peace initiative, by the summit meeting of heads of state held in Beirut in late March. The plan urged compliance with Security Council Resolution 194 concerning the return of Palestinian refugees to Israel, or appropriate compensation for their property; however, precise details of eligibility criteria for the proposed return, a contentious issue owing to the potentially huge numbers of refugees and descendants of refugees involved, were not elaborated. Conditions imposed by Israel on Yasser Arafat's freedom of movement deterred him from attending the summit. The Egyptian and Jordanian leaders failed to attend. The Arab leaders also agreed that external threats to the security of any Arab country (with particular reference to Iraq) would be regarded as an attack on the security of all Arab states, demanded respect for Iraq's sovereignty, and reiterated demands for the withdrawal of international sanctions against Iraq. A *rapprochement* between Iraq and Kuwait occurred at the summit meeting when the Iraqi envoy representing Saddam Hussain declared Iraq's respect for Kuwait's sovereignty and security. At the end of March the League's Secretary-General condemned the Israeli military's siege of Yasser Arafat's headquarters in Ramallah (initiated in retaliation against a succession of Palestinian bomb attacks on Israeli civilians), and, in early April, he denounced mounting Israeli military activity in the West Bank.

Publications

Arab Perspectives—Sh'oun Arabiyya (monthly).

Journal of Arab Affairs (monthly).

Bulletins of treaties and agreements concluded among the member states, essays, regular publications circulated by regional offices.

The Pact of the League of Arab States

(22 March 1945)

Article 1. The League of Arab States is composed of the independent Arab States which have signed this Pact.

Any independent Arab state has the right to become a member of the League. If it desires to do so, it shall submit a request which will be deposited with the Permanent Secretariat-General and submitted to the Council at the first meeting held after submission of the request.

Article 2. The League has as its purpose the strengthening of the relations between the member states; the co-ordination of their policies in order to achieve co-operation between them and to safeguard their independence and sovereignty; and a general concern with the affairs and interests of the Arab countries. It has also as its purpose the close co-operation of the member states, with due regard to the organization and circumstances of each state, on the following matters:

(*a*) Economic and financial affairs, including commercial relations, customs, currency, and questions of agriculture and industry.

(*b*) Communications: this includes railways, roads, aviation, navigation, telegraphs and posts.

(*c*) Cultural affairs.

(*d*) Nationality, passports, visas, execution of judgments, and extradition of criminals.

(*e*) Social affairs.

(*f*) Health problems.

Article 3. The League shall possess a Council composed of the representatives of the member states of the League; each state shall have a single vote, irrespective of the number of its representatives.

It shall be the task of the Council to achieve the realization of the objectives of the League and to supervise the execution of agreements which the member states have concluded on the questions enumerated in the preceding article, or on any other questions.

It likewise shall be the Council's task to decide upon the means by which the League is to co-operate with the international bodies to be created in the future in order to guarantee security and peace and regulate economic and social relations.

Article 4. For each of the questions listed in Article 2 there shall be set up a special committee in which the member states of the League shall be represented. These committees shall be charged with the task of laying down the principles and extent of co-operation. Such principles shall be formulated as draft agreements, to be presented to the Council for examination preparatory to their submission to the aforesaid states.

Representatives of the other Arab countries may take part in the work of the aforesaid committees. The Council shall determine the conditions under which these representatives may be permitted to participate and the rules governing such representation.

Article 5. Any resort to force in order to resolve disputes arising between two or more member states of the League is prohibited. If there should rise among them a difference which does not concern a state's independence, sovereignty, or territorial integrity, and if the parties to the dispute have recourse to the Council for the settlement of this difference, the decision of the Council shall then be enforceable and obligatory.

In such a case, the states between whom the difference has arisen shall not participate in the deliberations and decisions of the Council.

The Council shall mediate in all differences which threaten to lead to war between two member states, or a member state and a third state, with a view to bringing about their reconciliation.

Decisions of arbitration and mediation shall be taken by majority vote.

Article 6. In case of aggression or threat of aggression by one state against a member state, the state which has been attacked or threatened with aggression may demand the immediate convocation of the Council.

The Council shall by unanimous decision determine the measures necessary to repulse the aggression. If the aggressor is a member state, its vote shall not be counted in determining unanimity.

If, as a result of the attack, the government of the state attacked finds itself unable to communicate with the Council, that state's representative in the Council shall have the right to request the convocation of the Council for the purpose indicated in the foregoing paragraph. In the event that this representative is unable to communicate with the Council, any member state of the League shall have the right to request the convocation of the Council.

Article 7. Unanimous decisions of the Council shall be binding upon all member states of the League; majority decisions shall be binding only upon those states which have accepted them.

In either case the decisions of the Council shall be enforced in each member state according to its respective basic laws.

Article 8. Each member state shall respect the systems of government established in the other member states and regard them as exclusive concerns of those states. Each shall pledge to abstain from any action calculated to change established systems of government.

Article 9. States of the League which desire to establish closer co-operation and stronger bonds than are provided by this Pact may conclude agreements to that end.

Treaties and agreements already concluded or to be concluded in the future between a member state and another state shall not be binding or restrictive upon other members.

Article 10. The permanent seat of the League of Arab States is established in Cairo. The Council may, however, assemble at any other place it may designate.

Article 11. The Council of the League shall convene in ordinary session twice a year, in March and in September. It shall convene in extraordinary session upon the request of two member states of the League whenever the need arises.

Article 12. The League shall have a permanent Secretariat-General which shall consist of a Secretary-General, Assistant Secretaries, and an appropriate number of officials.

The Council of the League shall appoint the Secretary-General by a majority of two-thirds of the states of the League. The Secretary-General, with the approval of the Council, shall appoint the Assistant Secretaries and the principal officials of the League.

The Council of the League shall establish an administrative regulation for the functions of the Secretariat-General and matters relating to the Staff.

The Secretary-General shall have the rank of Ambassador and the Assistant Secretaries that of Ministers Plenipotentiary.

Article 13. The Secretary-General shall prepare the draft of the budget of the League and shall submit it to the Council for approval before the beginning of each fiscal year.

The Council shall fix the share of the expenses to be borne by each state of the League. This share may be reconsidered if necessary.

Article 14. (confers diplomatic immunity on officials).

Article 15. The first meeting of the Council shall be convened at the invitation of the head of the Egyptian Government. Thereafter it shall be convened at the invitation of the Secretary-General.

The representatives of the member states of the League shall alternately assume the presidency of the Council at each of its ordinary sessions.

Article 16. Except in cases specifically indicated in this Pact, a majority vote of the Council shall be sufficient to make enforceable decisions on the following matters:

(*a*) Matters relating to personnel.

(*b*) Adoption of the budget of the League.

(*c*) Establishment of the administrative regulations for the Council, the Committees, and the Secretariat-General.

(*d*) Decisions to adjourn the sessions.

Article 17. Each member state of the League shall deposit with the Secretariat-General one copy of every treaty or agreement concluded or to be concluded in the future between itself and another member state of the League or a third state.

Article 18. (deals with withdrawal).

Article 19. (deals with amendment).

Article 20. (deals with ratification).

ANNEX REGARDING PALESTINE

Since the termination of the last great war, the rule of the Ottoman Empire over the Arab countries, among them Palestine, which has become detached from that Empire, has come to an end. She has come to be autonomous, not subordinate to any other state.

The Treaty of Lausanne proclaimed that her future was to be settled by the parties concerned.

However, even though she was as yet unable to control her own affairs, the Covenant of the League (of Nations) in 1919 made provision for a regime based upon recognition of her independence.

Her international existence and independence in the legal sense cannot, therefore, be questioned, any more than could the independence of the Arab countries.

Although the outward manifestations of this independence have remained obscured for reasons beyond her control, this should not be allowed to interfere with her participation in the work of the Council of the League.

The states signatory to the Pact of the Arab League are therefore of the opinion that, considering the special circumstances of Palestine and until that country can effectively exercise its independence, the Council of the League should take charge of the selection of an Arab representative from Palestine to take part in its work.

ANNEX REGARDING CO-OPERATION WITH COUNTRIES WHICH ARE NOT MEMBERS OF THE COUNCIL OF THE LEAGUE

Whereas the member states of the League will have to deal in the Council as well as in the committees with matters which will benefit and affect the Arab world at large;

And whereas the Council has to take into account the aspirations of the Arab countries which are not members of the Council and has to work toward their realization;

Now therefore, it particularly behoves the states signatory to the Pact of the Arab League to enjoin the Council of the League, when considering the admission of those countries to participation in the committees referred to in the Pact, that it should do its utmost to co-operate with them, and furthermore, that it should spare no effort to learn their needs and understand their aspirations and hopes; and that it should work thenceforth for their best interests and the safeguarding of the future with all the political means at its disposal.

NORDIC COUNCIL

Address: Store Strandstraede 18, 1255 Copenhagen K, Denmark.

Telephone: 33-96-04-00; **fax:** 33-11-18-70; **e-mail** nordisk-rad@nordisk-rad.dk; **internet:** www.norden.org.

The Nordic Council was founded in 1952 for co-operation between the Nordic parliaments and governments. The four original members were Denmark, Iceland, Norway and Sweden; Finland joined in 1955, and the Faroe Islands and Åland Islands were granted representation in 1970 within the Danish and Finnish delegations respectively. Greenland had separate representation within the Danish delegation from 1984. Co-operation was first regulated by a Statute, and subsequently by the Helsinki Treaty of 1962. The Nordic region has a population of about 24m.

MEMBERS

Denmark (with the autonomous territories of the Faroe Islands and Greenland)
Finland (with the autonomous territory of the Åland Islands)
Iceland
Norway
Sweden

Organization

(April 2002)

COUNCIL

The Nordic Council is not a supranational parliament, but a forum for co-operation between the parliaments and governments of the Nordic countries. The Nordic Council of Ministers (see below) co-ordinates the activities of the governments of the Nordic countries when decisions are to be implemented.

The Council comprises 87 members, elected annually by and from the parliaments of the respective countries (Denmark 16 members; Faroes 2; Greenland 2; Finland 18; Åland 2; Iceland 7; Norway 20; Sweden 20). The various parties are proportionately represented in accordance with their representation in the national parliaments. Sessions of the Council consider proposals submitted by Council members, by the Council of Ministers or national governments. The sessions also follow up the outcome of past decisions and the work of the various Nordic institutions. The Plenary Assembly, which convenes once a year, is the highest body of the Nordic Council. Government representatives participate in the Assembly, but do not have the right to vote.

The Council has initiated and overseen extensive efforts to strengthen Nordic co-operation at the political, economic and social level. In 1995 the following were adopted as the priority focus areas ('pillars') of Nordic co-operation: intra-Nordic co-operation, with the emphasis on cultural, education and research co-operation; co-operation with the EU and the European Economic Area, focusing on promoting Nordic values and interests in a broader European context; and co-operation with the Adjacent Areas, i.e. the Baltic States, north-west Russia and the Arctic Area/Barents Sea, where Nordic governments are committed to furthering democracy, security and sustainable development. In September 2000 a Nordic Advisory Panel, appointed in 1999, recommended that the three-pillar basis of Nordic co-operation should be replaced by a theme-based, 'circular' structure. Meeting in Copenhagen, Denmark, in November 2000, the Council endorsed new guide-lines for policy and administrative reforms, in order to develop a better correspondence between the work of the Council and national parliaments. The reform process was also intended to facilitate co-operation with the Nordic Council of Ministers and the implementation of recommendations. Co-operation with non-member states remained a priority focus of the Council's activities.

STANDING COMMITTEES

Council members are assigned to the following Standing Committees: the Culture and Education Committee, Citizens and Consumer Rights Committee, Environment and Natural Resource Committee, Welfare Committee, and the Business and Industry Committee.

PRESIDIUM

The day-to-day work of the Nordic Council is directed by a Presidium, consisting of 13 members of national legislatures. The Presidium is the Council's highest decision-making body between sessions. The Presidium secretariat is headed by a Council Director. Each delegation to the Nordic Council has a secretariat at its national legislature.

Publications

Note: the titles listed below are joint publications of the Nordic Council and Nordic Council of Ministers.

Norden this Week (electronic newsletter in the languages of the region and English).

Norden the Top of Europe (monthly newsletter in English, German and French).

Politik i Norden (magazine in the languages of the region).

Yearbook of Nordic Statistics (in English, Finnish and Swedish).

Books and pamphlets on Nordic co-operation; summaries of Council sessions.

NORDIC COUNCIL OF MINISTERS

Address: Store Strandstraede 18, 1255 Copenhagen K, Denmark.

Telephone: 33-96-02-00; **fax:** 33-96-02-02; **internet:** www.norden.org.

The Governments of Denmark, Finland, Iceland, Norway and Sweden co-operate through the Nordic Council of Ministers. This co-operation is regulated by the Treaty of Co-operation between Denmark, Finland, Iceland, Norway and Sweden of 1962 (amended in 1971, 1974, 1983, 1985, 1993 and 1995) and the Treaty between Denmark, Finland, Iceland, Norway and Sweden concerning cultural co-operation of 1971 (amended in 1983 and 1985). Although the Prime Ministers do not meet formally within the Nordic Council of Ministers, they have decided to take a leading role in overall Nordic co-operation. The Ministers of Defence and Foreign Affairs do not meet within the Council of Ministers. These ministers, however, meet on an informal basis.

MEMBERS

Denmark Finland Iceland Norway Sweden

Greenland, the Faroe Islands and the Åland Islands also participate as autonomous regions.

Organization

(April 2002)

COUNCIL OF MINISTERS

The Nordic Council of Ministers holds formal and informal meetings and is attended by ministers with responsibility for the subject under discussion. Each member state also appoints a minister in its own cabinet as Minister for Nordic Co-operation.

Decisions of the Council of Ministers must be unanimous, except for procedural questions, which may be decided by a simple majority of those voting. Abstention constitutes no obstacle to a decision. Decisions are binding on the individual countries, provided that no parliamentary approval is necessary under the constitution of any of the countries. If such approval is necessary, the Council of Ministers must be so informed before its decision.

Meetings are concerned with: agreements and treaties, guidelines for national legislation, recommendations from the Nordic Council, financing joint studies, setting up Nordic institutions.

The Council of Ministers reports each year to the Nordic Council on progress in all co-operation between member states, as well as on future plans.

SECRETARIAT

The Office of the Secretary-General is responsible for co-ordination and legal matters (including co-ordination of work related to the European integration process and to the development of eastern Europe).

The work of the Secretariat is divided into the following departments:

Cultural and educational co-operation, research, advanced education, computer technology;

Budget and administration;

Environmental protection, finance and monetary policy, fisheries, industry and energy, regional policy, agriculture and forestry;

Information;

Labour market issues, social policy and health care, occupational environment, consumer affairs, equal opportunities.

Secretary-General: SØREN CHRISTENSEN (Denmark).

COMMITTEES

Nordic Co-operation Committee: for final preparation of material for the meetings of Ministers of Nordic Co-operation

Senior Executives' Committees: prepare the meetings of the Council of Ministers and conduct research at its request. There are a number of sub-committees. The Committees cover the subjects listed under the Secretariat (above).

Activities

A long-term cross-sectoral Strategy for a Sustainable Nordic Region and the Adjacent Areas covering the period 2001–20 was adopted in 2001. The strategy established targets for regional sustainable development, focusing on climate change, biodiversity, genetics, cultural environment, the oceans, chemicals and food safety. The new Nordic strategy for sustainable development was a priority area of activity for the Nordic Council of Ministers in 2002, alongside children and young people, and food safety.

ECONOMIC AND FINANCIAL CO-OPERATION

Nordic economic and financial co-operation aims to promote regional economic, ecological and socially sustainable growth, without inflation, with high employment, and supporting the Nordic social welfare model. It also aims to continue preparing the way for economic integration within the Nordic area and with Europe, and to promote issues of common Nordic concern internationally. Co-operation is undertaken in the following areas: freer markets for goods and services; measures on training and employment; elimination of trade barriers; liberalization of capital movements; research and development; export promotion; taxes and other levies; and regional policy. The Environment and Economics Group commissions environmental and economic analyses of areas of joint Nordic interest, e.g. ecological taxes and duties, cost-effective solutions to international environmental problems, and financing; and disseminates internationally analyses of and other information on Nordic environmental/economic issues.

Nordic Development Fund: f. 1989; supports activities by national administrations for overseas development with resources amounting to €330m.

Nordic Environmental Finance Corporation (NEFCO): f. 1990 to finance environmental projects in Central and Eastern Europe; cap. €80m.; administers the Nordic Environmental Development Fund (NEDF, authorized in 1999 to finance environmental projects in the Barents Sea and Baltic Sea areas during 1999–2003).

Nordic Industrial Fund: f. 1973 to provide grants, subsidies and loans for industrial research and development projects of interest to more than one member country.

Nordic Investment Bank (NIB): f. under an agreement of December 1975 to provide finance and guarantees for the implementation of investment projects and exports; total assets €15,024m. (Dec. 2001). The main sectors of the Bank's activities are energy, metal and wood-processing industries (including petroleum extraction) and manufacturing. In 1982 a separate scheme for financing investments in developing countries was established. In 1997 an Environmental Loan Facility was established to facilitate environmental investments in the Nordic Adjacent Areas.

Nordic Project Fund (NoPEF): f. 1982 to strengthen the international competitiveness of Nordic exporting companies, and to promote industrial co-operation in international projects (e.g. in environmental protection). Grants loans to Nordic companies for feasibility expenses relating to projects.

NORDTEST: f. 1973 as an inter-Nordic agency for technical testing and standardization of methods and of laboratory accreditation.

RELATIONS WITH THE EU AND EASTERN EUROPE

In 1991 the theme 'Norden in Europe' was identified as an area of high priority for the coming years by the Council. Nordic co-operation was to be used to co-ordinate member countries' participation in the western European integration process, based on EC and EC/EFTA co-operation. Since 1995, when Finland and Sweden acceded to the European Union (joining Denmark, already a member of that organization), Europe and the EU have been an integrated part of the work of Nordic co-operation. Under the Finnish presidency of the EU in the second half of 1999 the 'Northern Dimension', a strategy covering the Nordic region and Adjacent Areas, was adopted by the EU.

Since 1991 the Nordic Council of Ministers has developed its co-operation relating to the Baltic countries and north-west Russia, in order to contribute to peace, security and stability in Europe. Co-operation measures aim to promote democracy, the establishment of market economies, respect for civil rights and the responsible use of resources in these areas. The Nordic Council of Ministers has co-operated with the Arctic Council since that body's establishment in 1996. The Nordic 'Working Programme of the Adjacent Areas' comprises the following major components: Nordic Information Offices in Tallinn, Riga, Vilnius and St Petersburg, which co-ordinate Nordic projects and activities, promote regional contact at all levels and provide information about the Nordic countries in general and Nordic co-operation specifically; the Nordic Grants Scheme for the Baltic States and Northwest Russia, which supports networks linking universities and research institutions, and also awards grants to facilitate network-building in the NGO sector; a grants scheme for public servants and an exchange programme for parliamentarians; and the Nordic Council of Ministers Project Activities. Project activities for 1998–2002 were divided into the following theme areas: democracy and welfare policy; culture mediation (i.e. disseminating knowledge of Nordic culture and Nordic shared values); promotion of the development of the market economy; sustainable utilization of resources; and co-operation with the Arctic. In 2000 the Council of Ministers implemented a review of the strategic goals for co-operation with the Adjacent Areas in view of the administrative, democratic and economic reforms implemented by the Baltic States and their planned accession to the EU; progress achieved towards strengthening regional and EU co-operation with Russia; and an increase in Nordic and international bilateral co-operation measures in the Adjacent Areas. A new strategy for activities in the Adjacent Areas and an Arctic Programme of Co-operation was approved by the Council of Ministers in 2001. It was agreed that co-operation should focus primarily on the following themes: the Nordic welfare model (including healthcare and gender equality); sustainable utilization of resources (including environmental and energy issues); children and youth issues; culture mediation; and consumer policy and food safety. It was envisaged that cross-border co-operation along the boundaries with Russia and Belarus would assume a growing significance. The programme for co-operation with the Arctic was to take into account subsequent developments since the formation of the Arctic Council. In March 2000 the Nordic Investment Bank and the Nordic Environmental Finance Corporation signed a framework agreement with the EU and other partners on providing funding to assist the planned accession to the EU of the Baltic states and other central and east European countries. The Council of Ministers adopted a Framework Action Plan for Children and Young Adults in the Adjacent Areas in 1998.

Budgetary expenditure on co-operation with the Adjacent Areas totalled 70m. Danish kroner in 2001.

COMMUNICATIONS AND TRANSPORT

The main areas of co-operation have been concerned with international transport, the environment, infrastructure, road research, transport for the disabled and road safety.

EMPLOYMENT

In 1954 an agreement entered into force on a free labour market between Denmark, Finland, Norway and Sweden. Iceland became a party to the agreement in 1982 and the Faroe Islands in 1992. In 1982 an agreement on worker training and job-oriented rehabilitation came into effect. There is a joint centre for labour market training at Övertorneå in Sweden. A convention on the working environment was signed in 1989. The Nordic Institute for Advanced Training in Occupational Health is based in Helsinki, Finland.

GENDER EQUALITY

A Nordic co-operation programme on equality between women and men began in 1974. The main areas of co-operation have been the integration of equality aspects into all activities covered by the organization (i.e. 'mainstreaming'), working conditions, education, social welfare and family policy, housing and social planning, and women's participation in politics. In June 2000 the Council of Ministers determined that each ministerial group should take responsibility for gender equality in its own sphere of activities. In 2001–05 the main areas of concern were: incorporating the equality dimension into national budgetary policy; men and equality; and the prevention of violence against women.

ENVIRONMENT

A Nordic Environmental Action Plan constituted the overall guide-lines for Nordic co-operation in this field over the period 2001–04. The long-term cross-sectoral Strategy for a Sustainable Nordic Region and the Adjacent Areas covering the period 2001–20, adopted in 2001, had a strong focus on climate change, biodiversity, and the oceans. Under the Strategy environmental considerations were applied across a wide spectrum of issues, such as globalization, communications technology, natural resources, consumption patterns, renewable resources, air and sea pollutants and poverty reduction. During 2002 priority areas in the environment sector included work on a proposal to establish a testing ground for the mechanisms of the Kyoto Protocol to the UN Framework Convention on Climate Change; Nordic co-operation on chemicals; and Nordic co-operation on products and waste. The preparation of a Nordic Millennium Ecosystem Assessment was to commence in that year. The Nordic countries promote a high level of ambition as the basis for the environmental work conducted in the EU and at an international level.

ENERGY AND INDUSTRY

Co-operation in the energy sector focuses on energy-saving, energy and the environment, climate policy, the energy market, and the introduction of new and renewable sources of energy. A Nordic Co-operation Programme on Business Policy for 2002–05 represented the first joint Nordic initiative concerning the trade and industry sector.

CONSUMER AFFAIRS

The main areas of co-operation are in safety legislation, consumer education and information and consumers' economic and legal interests. In 2002 the Nordic Council of Ministers was promoting changes in consumption habits and production that would benefit sustainable development.

AGRICULTURE, FORESTRY, FISHERIES AND FOOD

Efforts to develop co-operation in both the fisheries and agriculture and forestry sectors have been undertaken with the aim of integrating environmental aspects into the relevant policies and strategies. In 2002 work was under way to promote sustainable development in agricultural production within the framework of the Strategy for a Sustainable Nordic Region and the Adjacent Areas for 2001–20. Priorities included ensuring food security through ecologically and economically sustainable production methods and an emphasis on quality, with reference to related areas such as food safety, biological diversity and genetic resources. A conference of Nordic ministers with responsibility for food was to be convened during 2002 to discuss the development of a regional action plan for food safety. Nordic co-operation on forestry issues includes joint participation in international processes concerned with forestry management. Co-operation on fisheries aims to promote the sustainable development of the fishing industry as an important economic asset and to ensure a balanced approach to the exploitaton of regional marine resources.

LAW

The five countries have similar legal systems and tend towards uniformity in legislation and interpretation of law. Much of the preparatory committee work within the national administrations on new legislation involves consultation with the neighbour countries.

Citizens of one Nordic country working in another are in many respects given the status of nationals. In all the Nordic countries they already have the right to vote in local elections in the country of residence. The changing of citizenship from one Nordic country to another has been simplified, and legislation on marriage and on children's rights amended to achieve the greatest possible parity.

There are special extradition facilities between the countries and further stages towards co-operation between the police and the courts have been adopted. In October 1996 justice ministers of the Nordic countries agreed to strengthen police co-operation in order to counter an increase in violent crime perpetrated by gangs. Emphasis is also placed on strengthening co-operation to combat the sexual abuse of children.

There is a permanent Council for Criminology and a Nordic Institute for Maritime Law in Oslo.

In 2002 the following were priority areas of co-operation: addressing criminal activity motivated by Nazi or racist ideologies; family law; and debt collection issues.

REGIONAL POLICY

The Council of Ministers has aimed to develop cross-border co-operation between the Nordic countries and co-operation with the EU and the Baltic countries, and to give greater priority to exchanging knowledge and information.

SOCIAL WELFARE AND HEALTH

Existing conventions and other co-operation directives ensure that Nordic citizens have the same rights, benefits and obligations in each Nordic country, with regard to sickness, parenthood, occupational injury, unemployment, disablement and old-age pension. Uniform provisions exist concerning basic pension and supplementary pension benefits when moving from one Nordic country to another. In 1993 Nordic representatives signed an agreement providing for a common Nordic labour market for health professionals. Numerous joint initiatives have been undertaken in the social welfare and health sectors within the framework of the co-operating institutions. A programme on Nordic co-operation on illicit drugs for 2001–05 aimed to include the Adjacent Areas in the Council of Ministers' activities in this field.

Institutions:

Nordic Committee on Disability
Nordic Committee on Social Security Statistics
Nordic Council for Alcohol and Drug Research, Helsinki, Finland
Nordic Council on Medicines, Uppsala, Sweden
Nordic Education Programme for Social Service Development, Gothenburg, Sweden
Nordic Medico-statistical Committee, Copenhagen, Denmark
Nordic School of Public Health, Gothenburg, Sweden
Nordic Staff Training Centre for Deaf-blind Services, Dronninglund, Denmark
Scandinavian Institute of Dental Materials, Haslum, Norway.

EDUCATIONAL AND SCIENTIFIC CO-OPERATION

Education: Nordic co-operation in the educational field includes the objective content and means of education, the structure of the educational system and pedagogical development work. Strategic, long-term investment in human resources, particularly education and research, form part of the basis of the Nordic welfare model. Nordic co-operation on information and communication technology aims to promote universal access to information, with a view to strengthening democracy, Nordic culture, electronic commerce and business networking.

The Nordic Council of Ministers finances the following co-operating bodies, permanent institutions and joint programmes:

Nordic-Baltic Scholarship Scheme
Nordic Folk Academy
Nordic Institute in Finland
Nordic Language and Literature Courses
NORDPLUS (Nordic Programme for Mobility of University Students and Teachers)
Nordic programmes for mobility of pupils, students, and teachers at primary and secondary school level (NORDPLUS-Junior and others)
Nordic School Data Network (ODIN)
Nordic Summer University
Programme of Action for Nordic Language Co-operation
Steering Committee for Nordic Co-operation on General and Adult Education
Steering Committee for Nordic Co-operation in Higher Education
Steering Committee for Nordic Educational Co-operation (primary and secondary school)

Research: Nordic co-operation in research comprises information on research activities and research findings, joint research projects, joint research institutions, the methods and means in research policy, the organizational structure of research and co-ordination of the national research programmes.

Much of the research co-operation activities at the more permanent joint research institutions consists of establishing science contacts in the Nordic areas by means of grants, visiting lecturers, courses and symposia.

The research institutions and research bodies listed below receive continuous financial support via the Nordic cultural budget. In many cases, these joint Nordic institutions ensure a high international standard that would otherwise have been difficult to maintain at a purely national level.

Nordic Academy for Advanced Study
Nordic Committee for Bioethics
Nordic Council for Scientific Information and Research Libraries
Nordic Institute of Asian Studies
Nordic Institute of Maritime Law
Nordic Institute for Theoretical Physics
Nordic Programme for Arctic Research
Nordic Sámi Institute
Nordic Science Policy Council
Nordic Vulcanological Institute
Research Programme on the Nordic Countries and Europe

Cultural activities: Cultural co-operation is based on the Nordic Agreement on Cultural Affairs Co-operation, adopted in 1971, and aims to promote the linguistic and cultural heritage of the Nordic nations. Co-operation includes artistic and other cultural exchange between the Nordic countries; activities relating to libraries, museums, radio, television, film and digitalized culture; promotion of activities within organizations with general cultural aims, including youth and sports organizations; the improvement of conditions for the creative and performing arts; and encouragement for artists and cultural workers. Exhibitions and performances of Nordic culture are organized abroad. Efforts were under way in 2002 to establish a Nordic Multimedia Fund. In 2000 Nordic ministers responsible for Sámi affairs and the leaders of Sámi parliaments (the Sámi being the indigenous population of the northern areas of Norway, Sweden, Finland and north-western Russia) established a permanent co-operation, with the aim of strengthening Sámi languages, culture, business and community life. The Sámi co-operation was to be informally linked to the Nordic Council of Ministers. In October 2001 the ministers for Sámi affairs agreed to appoint a committee of experts to present (by 2003) the draft text of a Nordic Sámi Convention.

Joint projects include:

Fund for Mobility of Young Nordic Artists—SLEIPNIR
Nordic Amateur Theatre Council
Nordic Art Centre
Nordic Co-operation in Athletics
Nordic Council Literature Prize
Nordic Council Music Prize
Nordic Documentation Centre for Mass Communication Research
Nordic Film and Television Fund
Nordic House in the Faroe Islands
Nordic House in Reykjavík
Nordic Institute in Åland
Nordic Institute of Contemporary Art
Nordic Institute in Greenland
Nordic Literature and Libraries Committee
Nordic Music Committee
Nordic Theatre and Dance Committee
Nordic Visual Art Committee
Steering Committee on Culture and Mass Media
Steering Committee on Nordic Cultural Projects Abroad
Valhalla (a network for children's and youth culture)

NORDIC CULTURAL FUND

The Nordic Cultural Fund was established through a separate agreement between the governments of the Nordic countries in 1966, and began operating in 1967, with the aim of supporting the needs of cultural life in the Nordic countries. A Board of 11 members administers and distributes the resources of the Fund and supervises its activities. Five of the members are appointed by the Nordic Council and five by the Nordic Council of Ministers (of culture and education), for a period of two years. The autonomous territories (the Åland islands, the Faroe Islands and Greenland) are represented by one member on the Board, appointed alternately by the Nordic Council and the Nordic Council of Ministers. The Fund is located within and administered by the Secretariat of the Nordic Council of Ministers. It considers applications for assistance for research, education and general cultural activities; grants may also be awarded for the dissemination of information concerning Nordic culture within and outside the region.

Finance

Joint expenses are divided according to an agreed scale in proportion to the relative national product of the member countries. The 2002 budget of the Nordic Council of Ministers amounted to 774m. Danish kroner. Various forms of co-operation are also financed directly from the national budgets.

NORTH AMERICAN FREE TRADE AGREEMENT—NAFTA

Canadian section: Royal Bank Centre, 90 Sparks St, Suite 705, Ottawa, ON, K1P 5B4; **tel.:** (613) 992-9388: **fax:** (613) 992-9392.

Mexican section: Blvd Adolfo López Mateos 3025, 2°, Col Héroes de Padierna, 10700 Mexico, DF; **tel.:** (5) 629-9630; **fax:** (5) 629-9637.

US section: 14th St and Constitution Ave, NW, Room 2061, Washington, DC 20230; **tel.:** (202) 482-5438; **fax:** (202) 482-0148.

E-mail: info@nafta-sec-alena.org; **internet:** www.nafta-sec-alena.org.

The North American Free Trade Agreement (NAFTA) grew out of the free-trade agreement between the USA and Canada that was signed in January 1988 and came into effect on 1 January 1989. Negotiations on the terms of NAFTA, which includes Mexico in the free-trade area, were concluded in October 1992 and the Agreement was signed in December. The accord was ratified in November 1993 and entered into force on 1 January 1994. The NAFTA Secretariat is composed of national sections in each member country.

MEMBERS

Canada Mexico USA

MAIN PROVISIONS OF THE AGREEMENT

Under NAFTA almost all restrictions on trade and investment between Canada, Mexico and the USA were to be gradually removed over a 15-year period. Most tariffs were eliminated immediately on agricultural trade between the USA and Mexico, with tariffs on 6% of agricultural products (including corn, sugar, and some fruits and vegetables) to be abolished over the 15 years. Tariffs on automobiles and textiles were to be phased out over 10 years in all three countries. Mexico was to open its financial sector to US and Canadian investment, with all restrictions to be removed by 2007. Barriers to investment were removed in most sectors, with exemptions for petroleum in Mexico, culture in Canada and airlines and radio communications in the USA. Mexico was to liberalize government procurement, removing preferential treatment for domestic companies over a 10-year period. In transport, heavy goods vehicles were to have complete freedom of movement between the three countries by 2000. An interim measure, whereby transport companies could apply for special licences to travel further within the borders of each country than the existing limit of 20 miles (32 km), was postponed in December 1995, shortly before it was scheduled to come into effect. The postponement was due to concerns, on the part of the US Government, relating to the implementation of adequate safety standards by Mexican truck-drivers. The 2000 deadline for the free circulation of heavy goods vehicles was not met, owing to the persistence of these concerns. In February 2001, however, a five-member NAFTA panel of experts appointed to adjudicate on the dispute ruled that the USA was violating the Agreement. The panel demanded that the US authorities consider entry applications from Mexican-based truck companies on an individual basis. In April 1998 the fifth meeting of the three-member ministerial Free Trade Commission (see below), held in Paris, France, agreed to remove tariffs on some 600 goods, including certain chemicals, pharmaceuticals, steel and wire products, textiles, toys, and watches, from 1 August. As a result of the agreement, a number of tariffs were eliminated as much as 10 years earlier than had been originally planned.

In the case of a sudden influx of goods from one country to another that adversely affects a domestic industry, the Agreement makes provision for the imposition of short-term 'snap-back' tariffs.

Disputes are to be settled in the first instance by intergovernmental consultation. If a dispute is not resolved within 30 to 40 days, a government may call a meeting of the Free Trade Commission. In October 1994 the Commission established an Advisory Committee on Private Commercial Disputes to recommend procedures for the resolution of such disputes. If the Commission is unable to settle the issue a panel of experts in the relevant field is appointed to adjudicate. In June 1996 Canada and Mexico announced their decision to refer the newly-enacted US 'Helms-Burton' legislation on trade with Cuba to the Commission. They claimed that the legislation, which provides for punitive measures against foreign companies that engage in trade with Cuba, imposed undue restrictions on Canadian and Mexican companies and was, therefore, in contravention of NAFTA. However, at the beginning of 1997 certain controversial provisions of the Helms-Burton legislation were suspended for a period of six months by the US administration. In April these were again suspended, as part of a compromise agreement with the European Union. The relevant provisions continued to be suspended at six-monthly intervals, and remained suspended in early 2002. An Advisory Committee on Private Commercial Disputes Regarding Agricultural Goods was formed in 1998.

In December 1994 NAFTA members issued a formal invitation to Chile to seek membership of the Agreement. Formal discussions on Chile's entry began in June 1995, but were stalled in December when the US Congress failed to approve 'fast-track' negotiating authority for the US Government, which was to have allowed the latter to negotiate a trade agreement with Chile, without risk of incurring a line-by-line veto from the US Congress. In February 1996 Chile began high-level negotiations with Canada on a wide-ranging bilateral free-trade agreement. Chile, which already had extensive bilateral trade agreements with Mexico, was regarded as advancing its position with regard to NAFTA membership by means of the proposed accord with Canada. The bilateral agreement, which provided for the extensive elimination of customs duties by 2002, was signed in November 1996 and ratified by Chile in July 1997. However, in November 1997 the US Government was obliged to request the removal of the 'fast-track' proposal from the legislative agenda, owing to insufficient support within Congress.

In April 1998 heads of state of 34 countries, meeting in Santiago, Chile, agreed formally to initiate the negotiating process to establish a Free Trade Area of the Americas (FTAA). The US Government had originally proposed creating the FTAA through the gradual extension of NAFTA trading privileges on a bilateral basis. However, the framework agreed upon by ministers of trade of the 34 countries, meeting in March, provided for countries to negotiate and accept FTAA provisions on an individual basis and as part of a sub-regional economic bloc. It was envisaged that the FTAA would exist alongside the sub-regional associations, including NAFTA. In April 2001, meeting in Quebec City, Canada, leaders of the participating countries agreed to conclude the negotiations on the FTAA by January 2005 to enable it to enter into force by the end of that year.

ADDITIONAL AGREEMENTS

During 1993, as a result of domestic pressure, the new US Government negotiated two 'side agreements' with its NAFTA partners, which were to provide safeguards for workers' rights and the environment. A Commission for Labour Co-operation was established under the North American Agreement on Labour Co-operation (NAALC) to monitor implementation of labour accords and to foster co-operation in that area. The North American Commission for Environmental Co-operation (NACEC) was initiated to combat pollution, to ensure that economic development was not environmentally damaging and to monitor compliance with national and NAFTA environmental regulations. Panels of experts, with representatives from each country, were established to adjudicate in cases of alleged infringement of workers' rights or environmental damage. The panels were given the power to impose fines and trade sanctions, but only with regard to the USA and Mexico; Canada, which was opposed to such measures, was to enforce compliance with NAFTA by means of its own legal system. In 1995 the North American Fund for Environmental Co-operation (NAFEC) was established. NAFEC, which is financed by the NACEC, supports community environmental projects.

In February 1996 the NACEC consented for the first time to investigate a complaint brought by environmentalists regarding non-compliance with domestic legislation on the environment. Mexican environmentalists claimed that a company that was planning to build a pier for tourist ships (a project that was to involve damage to a coral reef) had not been required to supply adequate environmental impact studies. The NACEC was limited to presenting its findings in such a case, as it could only make a ruling in the case of complaints brought by one NAFTA government against another. The NACEC allocates the bulk of its resources to research undertaken to support compliance with legislation and agreements on the environment. However, in October 1997 the council of NAFTA ministers of the environment, meeting in Montréal, Canada, approved a new structure for the NACEC's activities. The NACEC's main objective was to be the provision of advice concerning the environmental impact of trade issues. It was also agreed that the Commission was further to promote trade in environmentally-sound products and to encourage private-sector investment in environmental trade issues.

With regard to the NAALC, National Administration Offices have been established in each of the three NAFTA countries in order to monitor labour issues and to address complaints about non-compliance with domestic labour legislation. However, punitive measures in the form of trade sanctions or fines (up to US $20m.) may only be imposed in the specific instances of contravention of national legislation regarding child labour, a minimum wage or health and safety standards. A Commission for Labour Co-operation has been established (see below) and incorporates a council of ministers of labour of the three countries.

In August 1993 the USA and Mexico agreed to establish a Border Environmental Co-operation Commission (BECC) to assist with the co-ordination of projects for the improvement of infrastructure and to monitor the environmental impact of the Agreement on the US–Mexican border area, where industrial activity was expected to intensify. The Commission is located in Ciudad Juárez, Mexico. By early 2002 the BECC had certified 57 projects, at a cost of US $1,158.34m. In October 1993 the USA and Mexico concluded an agreement to establish a North American Development Bank (NADB or NADBank), which was mandated to finance environmental and infrastructure projects along the US–Mexican border.

Commission for Labour Co-operation: 1211 Connecticut Ave, NW Suite 200, Washington, DC 20036, USA; tel. (202) 464-1100; fax (202) 464-9487; e-mail info@naalc.org; internet www.naalc.org; f. 1994; Exec. Dir Dr ALFONSO ONATE LABORDE (Mexico). Publ. *Annual Report.*

North American Commission for Environmental Co-operation (NACEC): 393 rue St Jacques West, Bureau 200, Montréal, QC H2Y IN9, Canada; tel. (514) 350-4300; fax (514) 350-4314; e-mail info@ccemtl.org; internet www.cec.org; f. 1994; Exec. Dir JANINE FERRETI; Dir GREG BLOCK. Publ. *Annual Report.*

North American Development Bank (NADB or NADBank): 203 St Mary's, Suite 300, San Antonio, TX 78205, USA; tel. (210) 231-8000; fax (210) 231-6232; internet www.nadbank.org. At March 2002 the NADB had authorized capital of US $3,000m., subscribed equally by Mexico and the USA, of which $450m. was paid-up; Man. Dir RAUL RODRIGUEZ (Mexico). Publ. *Annual Report, NADBank News.*

NORTH ATLANTIC TREATY ORGANIZATION—NATO

Address: blvd Léopold III, 1110 Brussels, Belgium.

Telephone: (2) 707-41-11; **fax:** (2) 707-45-79; **e-mail:** natodoc@hq.nato.int; **internet:** www.nato.int.

The Atlantic Alliance was established on the basis of the 1949 North Atlantic Treaty as a defensive political and military alliance of a group of European states (then numbering 10) and the USA and Canada. The Alliance aims to provide common security for its members through co-operation and consultation in political, military and economic fields, as well as scientific, environmental, and other non-military aspects. The objectives of the Alliance are implemented by NATO. Following the collapse of the communist governments in central and eastern Europe, from 1989 onwards, and the dissolution of the Warsaw Pact (which had hitherto been regarded as the Alliance's principal adversary) in 1991, NATO has undertaken a fundamental transformation of its structures and policies to meet the new security challenges in Europe.

MEMBERS*

Belgium	Hungary	Poland
Canada	Iceland	Portugal
Czech Republic	Italy	Spain
Denmark	Luxembourg	Turkey
France	Netherlands	United Kingdom
Germany	Norway	USA
Greece		

* Greece and Turkey acceded to the Treaty in 1952, and the Federal Republic of Germany in 1955. France withdrew from the integrated military structure of NATO in 1966, although remaining a member of the Atlantic Alliance; in 1996 France resumed participation in some, but not all, of the military organs of NATO. Spain acceded to the Treaty in 1982, but remained outside the Alliance's integrated military structure until 1999. The Czech Republic, Hungary and Poland were formally admitted as members of NATO in March 1999.

Organization

(April 2002)

NORTH ATLANTIC COUNCIL

The Council, the highest authority of the Alliance, is composed of representatives of the 16 member states. It meets at the level of Permanent Representatives, ministers of foreign affairs, or heads of state and government, and, at all levels, has effective political and decision-making authority. Ministerial meetings are held at least twice a year. Occasional meetings of defence ministers are also held. At the level of Permanent Representatives the Council meets at least once a week.

The Secretary-General of NATO is Chairman of the Council, and each year a minister of foreign affairs of a member state is nominated honorary President, following the English alphabetical order of countries.

Decisions are taken by common consent and not by majority vote. The Council is a forum for wide consultation between member governments on major issues, including political, military, economic and other subjects, and is supported by the Senior or regular Political Committee, the Military Committee and other subordinate bodies.

PERMANENT REPRESENTATIVES

Belgium: Thierry de Gruben
Canada: David Wright
Czech Republic: Karel Kovanda
Denmark: Niels Egelund
France: Benoît d'Aboville
Germany: Gebhardt von Moltke
Greece: Vassilis Kaskarelis
Hungary: János Herman
Iceland: Gunnar Pálsson
Italy: Amedeo de Franchis
Luxembourg: Jean-Jacques Kasel
Netherlands: Michiel Patijn
Norway: Jakken Biørn Lian
Poland: Jerzy Nowak
Portugal: Fernando Andresen-Guimarães
Spain: Juan Prat y Coll
Turkey: Onur Öymen
United Kingdom: Dr Emyr Jones Parry
USA: R. Nicholas Burns

Note: NATO partner countries are represented by heads of diplomatic missions or liaison officers located at NATO headquarters.

DEFENCE PLANNING COMMITTEE

Most defence matters are dealt with in the Defence Planning Committee, composed of representatives of all member countries except France. The Committee provides guidance to NATO's military authorities and, within the field of its responsibilities, has the same functions and authority as the Council. Like the Council, it meets regularly at ambassadorial level and assembles twice a year in ministerial sessions, when member countries are represented by their ministers of defence.

NUCLEAR PLANNING GROUP

Defence ministers of countries participating in the Defence Planning Committee meet regularly in the Nuclear Planning Group (NPG) to discuss specific policy issues relating to nuclear forces, such as safety, deployment issues, nuclear arms control and proliferation. The NPG is supported by a Staff Group, composed of representatives of all members participating in the NPG, which meets at least once a week.

OTHER COMMITTEES

There are also committees for political affairs, economics, military medical services, armaments, defence review, science, the environment, infrastructure, logistics, communications, civil emergency planning, information and cultural relations, and civil and military budgets. In addition, other committees consider specialized subjects such as NATO pipelines, air traffic management, etc. Since 1992 most of these committees consult on a regular basis with representatives from central and eastern European countries.

INTERNATIONAL SECRETARIAT

The Secretary-General is Chairman of the North Atlantic Council, the Defence Planning Committee and the Nuclear Planning Group. He is the head of the International Secretariat, with staff drawn from the member countries. He proposes items for NATO consultation and is generally responsible for promoting consultation and co-operation in accordance with the provisions of the North Atlantic Treaty. He is empowered to offer his help informally in cases of disputes between member countries, to facilitate procedures for settlement.

Secretary-General: Lord Robertson of Port Ellen (United Kingdom).

Deputy Secretary-General: Alessandro Minuto Rizzo (Italy).

There is an Assistant Secretary-General for each of the operational divisions listed below.

PRINCIPAL DIVISIONS

Division of Political Affairs: maintains political liaison with national delegations and international organizations. Prepares reports on political subjects for the Secretary-General and the Council, and provides the administrative structure for the management of the Alliance's political responsibilities, including disarmament and arms control. Asst Sec.-Gen. Günther Altenburg (Germany).

Division of Defence Planning and Operations: studies all matters concerning the defence of the Alliance, and co-ordinates the defence review and other force planning procedures of the Alliance. Asst Sec.-Gen. Dr Edgar Buckley (United Kingdom).

Division of Defence Support: promotes the most efficient use of the Allies' resources in the production of military equipment and its standardization. Asst Sec.-Gen. ROBERT BELL (USA).

Division of Security Investment, Logistics and Civil Emergency Planning: supervises the technical and financial aspects of the security investment programme. Provides guidance, co-ordination and support to the activities of NATO committees or bodies active in the field of consumer logistics and civil emergency planning. Asst Sec.-Gen. JUAN MARTINEZ-ESPARZA (Spain).

Division of Scientific and Environmental Affairs: advises the Secretary-General on scientific matters of interest to NATO. Responsible for promoting and administering scientific exchange programmes between member countries, research fellowships, advanced study institutes and special programmes of support for the scientific and technological development of less-advanced member countries. Asst Sec.-Gen. JEAN FOURNET (France).

Military Organization

MILITARY COMMITTEE

Composed of the allied Chiefs-of-Staff, or their representatives, of all member countries: the highest military body in NATO under the authority of the Council. Meets at least twice a year at Chiefs-of-Staff level and remains in permanent session with Permanent Military Representatives. It is responsible for making recommendations to the Council and Defence Planning Committee and Nuclear Planning Group on military matters and for supplying guidance on military questions to Supreme Allied Commanders and subordinate military authorities. The Committee is supported by an International Military Staff.

In December 1995 France agreed to rejoin the Military Committee, which it formally left in 1966.

Chairman: Adm. GUIDO VENTURONI (Italy).

COMMANDS

Allied Command Europe (ACE): Casteau, Belgium—Supreme Headquarters Allied Powers Europe—SHAPE. Supreme Allied Commander Europe—SACEUR: Gen. JOSEPH W. RALSTON (USA).

Allied Command Atlantic (ACLANT): Norfolk, Virginia, USA. Supreme Allied Commander Atlantic—SACLANT: Gen. WILLIAM F. KERNAN (USA).

Activities

The common security policy of the members of the North Atlantic Alliance is to safeguard peace through the maintenance of political solidarity and adequate defence at the lowest level of military forces needed to deter all possible forms of aggression. Each year, member countries take part in a Defence Review, designed to assess their contribution to the common defence in relation to their respective capabilities and constraints. Allied defence policy is reviewed periodically by ministers of defence.

Since the 1980s the Alliance has been actively involved in co-ordinating policies with regard to arms control and disarmament issues designed to bring about negotiated reductions in conventional forces, intermediate and short-range nuclear forces and strategic nuclear forces. A Verification Co-ordinating Committee was established in 1990. In April 1999 the summit meeting determined to improve co-ordination on issues relating to weapons of mass destruction through the establishment of a separate centre at NATO headquarters.

Political consultations within the Alliance take place on a permanent basis, under the auspices of the North Atlantic Council (NAC), on all matters affecting the common security interests of the member countries, as well as events outside the North Atlantic Treaty area.

Co-operation in scientific and technological fields as well as co-operation on environmental challenges takes place in the NATO Science Committee and in its Committee on the Challenges of Modern Society. Both these bodies operate an expanding international programme of science fellowships, advance study institutes and research grants. NATO has also pursued co-operation in relation to civil emergency planning. These activities represent NATO's 'Third Dimension'.

At a summit meeting of the Conference on Security and Co-operation in Europe (CSCE, now renamed as the Organization for Security and Co-operation in Europe, OSCE, see p. 445) in November 1990, the member countries of NATO and the Warsaw Pact signed an agreement limiting Conventional Armed Forces in Europe (CFE), whereby conventional arms would be reduced to within a common upper limit in each zone. The two groups also issued a Joint Declaration, stating that they were no longer adversaries and that none of their weapons would ever be used 'except in self-defence'. Following the dissolution of the USSR the eight former Soviet republics with territory in the area of application of the CFE Treaty committed themselves to honouring its obligations in June 1992. In March 1992, under the auspices of the CSCE, the ministers of foreign affairs of the NATO and of the former Warsaw Pact countries (with Russia, Belarus, Ukraine and Georgia taking the place of the USSR) signed the 'Open Skies' treaty. Under this treaty, aerial reconnaissance missions by one country over another were to be permitted, subject to regulation. At the summit meeting of the OSCE in December 1996 the signatories of the CFE Treaty agreed to begin negotiations on a revised treaty governing conventional weapons in Europe. In July 1997 the CFE signatories concluded an agreement on Certain Basic Elements for Treaty Adaptation, which provided for substantial reductions in the maximum levels of conventional military equipment at national and territorial level, replacing the previous bloc-to-bloc structure of the Treaty.

An extensive review of NATO's structures was initiated in June 1990, in response to the fundamental changes taking place in central and eastern Europe. In November 1991 NATO heads of government, convened in Rome, recommended a radical restructuring of the organization in order to meet the demands of the new security environment, which was to involve further reductions in military forces in Europe, active involvement in international peace-keeping operations, increased co-operation with other international institutions and close co-operation with its former adversaries, the USSR and the countries of eastern Europe. The basis for NATO's new force structure was incorporated into a new Strategic Concept, which was adopted in the Rome Declaration issuing from the summit meeting. The concept provided for the maintenance of a collective defence capability, with a reduced dependence on nuclear weapons. Substantial reductions in the size and levels of readiness of NATO forces were undertaken, in order to reflect the Alliance's strictly defensive nature, and forces were reorganized within a streamlined integrated command structure. Forces were categorized into immediate and rapid reaction forces (including the ACE Rapid Reaction Corps—ARRC, which was inaugurated in October 1992), main defence forces and augmentation forces, which may be used to reinforce any NATO region or maritime areas for deterrence, crisis management or defence. In December the NAC, meeting at ministerial level, endorsed a new military structure, which envisaged a reduction in the number of NATO command headquarters from 65 to 20, and instructed the military authorities of the Alliance to formulate a plan for the transitional process. During 1998 work was undertaken on the formulation of a new Strategic Concept, reflecting the changing security environment and defining NATO's future role and objectives, which recognized a broader sphere of influence of NATO in the 21st century and confirmed NATO to be the principal generator of security in the Euro-Atlantic area. It emphasized NATO's role in crisis management and a renewed commitment to partnership and dialogue. The document was approved at a special summit meeting, convened in Washington, USA, in April 1999, to commemorate the 50th anniversary of the Alliance. A separate initiative was approved to assist member states to adapt their defence capabilities to meet changing security requirements, for example improving the means of troop deployment and equipping and protecting forces. A High-Level Steering Group was established to oversee implementation of the Defence Capabilities Initiative. The Washington meeting, which had been envisaged as a celebration of NATO's achievements since its foundation, was, however, dominated by consideration of the situation in the southern Serbian province of Kosovo and Metohija and the conduct of its military offensive against the Federal Republic of Yugoslavia, initiated in late March (see below).

In January 1994 NATO heads of state and government welcomed the entry into force of the Maastricht Treaty, establishing the European Union (EU, superseding the EC). The Treaty included an agreement on the development of a common foreign and security policy, which was intended to be a mechanism to strengthen the European pillar of the Alliance. NATO subsequently co-operated with the Western European Union (WEU) in support of the development of a European Security and Defence Identity. In June 1996 NATO ministers of foreign affairs reached agreement on the implementation of the 'Combined Joint Task Force (CJTF) concept', which had been adopted in January 1994. Measures were to be taken to establish the 'nuclei' of these task forces at certain NATO headquarters, which would provide the basis for missions that could be activated at short notice for specific purposes such as crisis management and peace-keeping. It was also agreed to make CJTFs available for operations undertaken by WEU. In conjunction with this, WEU was to be permitted to make use of Alliance hardware and capabilities (in practice, mostly belonging to the USA) subject to the endorsement of the NAC. The summit meeting, held in April 1999, confirmed NATO's willingness to establish a direct NATO-EU relationship. In February 2000 the first joint NATO-WEU crisis management exercise was conducted. However, in accordance with decisions taken by the EU in late 1999 and 2000 to implement a common security and defence policy, it was agreed that routine NATO-WEU consultation mechanisms were to be suspended. The first formal meeting of the Military Committees of the EU and NATO took place in June 2001 to exchange information relating to the development of EU-NATO security co-operation. In order to support an integrated security structure in Europe, NATO also co-operates with the OSCE and has provided assistance for the development of the latter's conflict prevention and crisis management activities.

In January 2001 NATO established an *ad hoc* working committee in response to concerns expressed by several member governments regarding the health implications of the use of depleted uranium munitions during the Alliance's military intervention in the Balkans. The committee was to co-ordinate the compilation of information regarding the use of depleted uranium and to co-operate with the Yugoslav authorities in the rehabilitation of the local environment. An extraordinary meeting of chiefs of military medical services, including surgeons-general and medical experts, was also convened to consider the issue.

On 12 September 2001 the NAC agreed to invoke, for the first time, Article 5 of the North Atlantic Treaty, providing for collective self-defence, in response to the terrorist attacks against targets in the USA of the previous day. The measure was formally implemented in early October after the US authorities presented evidence substantiating claims that the attacks had been directed from abroad. The NAC endorsed eight specific US requests for logistical and military support in its efforts to counter terrorism, including enhanced sharing of intelligence and full access to airfields and ports in member states. It also agreed to dispatch five surveillance aircraft to help to patrol US airspace and directed the standing naval force to the Eastern Mediterranean. In December NATO ministers of defence initiated a review of military capabilities and defences with a view to strengthening its ability to counter international terrorism.

PARTNERSHIPS

In May 1997 a Euro-Atlantic Partnership Council (EAPC) was inaugurated as a successor to the North Atlantic Co-operation Council (NACC), that had been established in December 1991 to provide a forum for consultation on political and security matters with the countries of central and eastern Europe, including the former Soviet republics. An EAPC Council was to meet monthly at ambassadorial level and twice a year at ministerial level. It was to be supported in its work by a steering committee and a political committee. The EAPC was to pursue the NACC Work Plan for Dialogue, Partnership and Co-operation and incorporate it into a new Work Plan, which was to include an expanded political dimension of consultation and co-operation among participating states. The Partnership for Peace (PfP) programme, which was established in January 1994 within the framework of the NACC, was to remain an integral element of the new co-operative mechanism. The PfP incorporated practical military and defence-related co-operation activities that had originally been part of the NACC Work Plan. Participation in the PfP requires an initial signature of a framework agreement, establishing the common principles and objectives of the partnership, the submission of a presentation document, indicating the political and military aspects of the partnership and the nature of future co-operation activities, and thirdly, the development of individual partnership programmes establishing country-specific objectives. In June 1994 Russia, which had previously opposed the strategy as being the basis for future enlargement of NATO, signed the PfP framework document, which included a declaration envisaging an 'enhanced dialogue' between the two sides. Despite its continuing opposition to any enlargement of NATO, in May 1995 Russia agreed to sign a PfP Individual Partnership Programme, as well as a framework document for NATO-Russian dialogue and co-operation beyond the PfP. During 1994 a Partnership Co-ordination Cell (PCC), incorporating representatives of all partnership countries, became operational in Mons, Belgium. The PCC, under the authority of the NAC, aims to co-ordinate joint military activities and planning in order to implement PfP programmes. The first joint military exercises with countries of the former Warsaw Pact were conducted in September. NATO began formulating a PfP Status of Forces Agreement (SOFA) to define the legal status of Allies' and partners' forces when they are present on each other's territory; the PfP SOFA was opened for signature in June 1995. The new EAPC was to provide a framework for the development of an enhanced PfP programme, which NATO envisaged would become an essential element of the overall European security structure. Accordingly, the military activities of the PfP were to be expanded to include all Alliance missions and incorporate all NATO committees into the PfP process, thus providing for greater co-operation in crisis management, civil emergency planning and training activities. In addition, all PfP member countries were to participate in the CJTF concept through a structure of Partners Staff Elements, working at all levels of the Alliance military structure. Defence ministers of NATO and the 27 partner countries were to meet regularly to provide the political guidance for the enhanced Planning and Review Process of the PfP. In December 1997 NATO ministers of foreign affairs approved the establishment of a Euro-Atlantic Disaster Response Co-ordination Centre (EDRCC), and a non-permanent Euro-Atlantic Disaster Response Unit. The EDRCC was inaugurated in June 1998 and immediately commenced operations to provide relief to ethnic Albanian refugees fleeing the conflict in the Serbian province of Kosovo. In November the NAC approved the establishment of a network of PfP training centres, the first of which was inaugurated in Ankara, Turkey. The centres were a key element of a Training and Education Programme, which was endorsed at the summit meeting in April 1999. During 2000 *ad hoc* working groups were convened to consider EAPC involvement in global humanitarian action against mines, the challenge of small arms and light weapons, and prospects for regional co-operation in South-Eastern Europe and in the Caucasus. The EAPC Action Plan for 2002–04 aimed to promote new approaches to co-operation in the combating of international terrorism.

The enlargement of NATO, through the admission of new members from the former USSR and eastern and central European countries, was considered to be a progressive means of contributing to the enhanced stability and security of the Euro-Atlantic area. In December 1996 NATO ministers of foreign affairs announced that invitations to join the Alliance would be issued to some former eastern bloc countries during 1997. The NATO Secretary-General and member governments subsequently began intensive diplomatic efforts to secure Russia's tolerance of these developments. It was agreed that no nuclear weapons or large numbers of troops would be deployed on the territory of any new member country in the former Eastern bloc. In May 1997 NATO and Russia signed the Founding Act on Mutual Relations, Co-operation and Security, which provided for enhanced Russian participation in all NATO decision-making activities, equal status in peace-keeping operations and representation at the Alliance headquarters at ambassadorial level, as part of a recognized shared political commitment to maintaining stability and security throughout the Euro-Atlantic region. A NATO-Russian Permanent Joint Council (PJC) was established under the Founding Act, and met for the first time in July; the Council provided each side the opportunity for consultation and participation in the other's security decisions, but without a right of veto. In March 1999 Russia condemned NATO's military action against the Federal Republic of Yugoslavia and announced the suspension of all relations within the framework of the Founding Act, as well as negotiations on the establishment of a NATO mission in Moscow. The PJC convened once more in May 2000, and subsequent meetings were held in June and December. In February 2001 the NATO Secretary-General agreed with the then acting Russian President a joint statement of commitment to pursuing dialogue and co-operation. A NATO information office was opened in Moscow in that month. The PJC condemned major terrorist attacks perpetrated against the USA in September and pledged to strengthen Russia-NATO co-operation with a view to combating international terrorism. In December an agreement was concluded by NATO ministers of foreign affairs and their Russian counterpart to establish an eventual successor body to the PJC, with a greater decision-making role.

In May 1997 NATO ministers of foreign affairs, meeting in Sintra, Portugal, concluded an agreement with Ukraine providing for enhanced co-operation between the two sides; the so-called Charter on a Distinctive Relationship was signed at the NATO summit meeting held in Madrid, Spain, in July. In May 1998 NATO agreed to appoint a permanent liaison officer in Ukraine to enhance co-operation between the two sides and assist Ukraine to formulate a programme of joint military exercises. The first NATO-Ukraine meeting at the level of heads of state took place in April 1999. A NATO-Ukraine Commission met for the first time in March 2000.

The Madrid summit meeting in July 1997 endorsed the establishment of a Mediterranean Co-operation Group to enhance NATO relations with Egypt, Israel, Jordan, Mauritania, Morocco and Tunisia. The Group was to provide a forum for regular political dialogue between the two groupings and to promote co-operation in training, scientific research and information exchange. In April 1999 NATO heads of state endorsed measures to strengthen the so-called Mediterranean Dialogue. Algeria joined the Mediterranean Dialogue in February 2000.

In July 1997 heads of state and government formally invited the Czech Republic, Hungary and Poland to begin accession negotiations, with the aim of extending membership to those countries in April 1999. During 1997 concern was expressed on the part of some member governments with regard to the cost of expanding the Alliance; however, in November the initial cost of incorporating the Czech Republic, Hungary and Poland into NATO was officially estimated at US $1,300m. over a 10-year period, which was widely deemed to be an acceptable figure. Accession Protocols for the admission of those countries were signed in December and required ratification by all member states. The three countries formally became members of NATO in March 1999. In April the NATO summit meeting, held in Washington, DC, USA, initiated a new Membership Action Plan to extend practical support to aspirant member countries and to formalize a process of reviewing applications. Albania, Bulgaria, Estonia, Latvia, Lithuania, Romania, Slovakia, Slovenia and the former Yugoslav republic of Macedonia were participating in the Membership Action Plan in 2001.

PEACE-KEEPING ACTIVITIES

During the 1990s NATO increasingly developed its role as a mechanism for peace-keeping and crisis management. In June 1992 NATO ministers of foreign affairs, meeting in Oslo, Norway, announced the Alliance's readiness to support peace-keeping operations under the aegis of the CSCE on a case-by-case basis: NATO would make both military resources and expertise available to such operations. In July NATO, in co-operation with WEU, undertook a maritime operation in the Adriatic Sea to monitor compliance with the UN Security Council's resolutions imposing sanctions against the Yugoslav republics of Serbia and Montenegro. In October NATO was requested to provide, staff and finance the military headquarters of the United Nations peace-keeping force in Bosnia and Herzegovina, the UN Protection Force in Yugoslavia (UNPROFOR). In December NATO ministers of foreign affairs expressed the Alliance's readiness to support peace-keeping operations under the authority of the UN Security Council. From April 1993 NATO fighter and reconnaissance aircraft began patrolling airspace over Bosnia and Herzegovina in order to enforce the UN prohibition of military aerial activity over the country. In addition, from July NATO aircraft provided protective cover for UNPROFOR troops operating in the 'safe areas' established by the UN Security Council. In February 1994 NATO conducted the first of several aerial strikes against artillery positions that were violating heavy-weapons exclusion zones imposed around 'safe areas' and threatening the civilian populations. Throughout the conflict the Alliance also provided transport, communications and logistics to support UN humanitarian assistance in the region.

The peace accord for the former Yugoslavia, which was initialled in Dayton, USA, in November 1995, and signed in Paris in December, provided for the establishment of a NATO-led Implementation Force (IFOR) to ensure compliance with the treaty, in accordance with a strictly defined timetable and under the authority of a UN Security Council mandate. In early December a joint meeting of allied foreign and defence ministers endorsed the military structure for the peace mission, entitled Operation Joint Endeavour, which was to involve approximately 60,000 troops from 31 NATO and non-NATO countries. The mission was to be under the overall authority of the Supreme Allied Commander Europe (ACE), with the Commander of the ACE Rapid Reaction Corps providing command on the ground. IFOR, which constituted NATO's largest military operation ever, formally assumed responsIbility for peace-keeping in Bosnia and Herzegovina from the UN on 20 December.

By mid-1996 the military aspects of the Dayton peace agreement had largely been implemented under IFOR supervision, including the withdrawal of former warring parties to behind agreed lines of separation and the release of prisoners of war. Substantial progress was achieved in the demobilization of soldiers and militia and in the cantonment of heavy weaponry. However, in August and September the Bosnian Serbs obstructed IFOR weapons inspections and the force was obliged to threaten the Serbs with strong military retaliation to secure access to the arms sites. During 1996 IFOR personnel undertook many activities relating to the civilian reconstruction of Bosnia and Herzegovina, including the repair of roads, railways and bridges; reconstruction of schools and hospitals; delivery of emergency food and water supplies; and emergency medical transportation. IFOR also co-operated with, and provided logistical support for, the Office of the High Representative of the International Community in Bosnia and Herzegovina, which was charged with overseeing implementation of the civilian aspects of the Bosnian peace accord. IFOR assisted the OSCE in preparing for and overseeing the all-Bosnia legislative elections that were held in September, and provided security for displaced Bosnians who crossed the inter-entity boundary in order to vote in their towns of origin. In December NATO ministers of foreign affairs approved a follow-on operation, with an 18-month mandate, to be known as the Stabilization Force (SFOR). SFOR was to be about one-half the size of IFOR, but was to retain 'the same unity of command and robust rules of engagement' as the previous force. SFOR became operational on 20 December. Its principal objective was to maintain a safe environment at a military level to ensure that the civil aspects of the Dayton peace accord could be fully implemented, including the completion of the de-mining process, the repatriation of refugees and preparations for municipal elections. In July 1997 NATO heads of government expressed their support for a more determined implementation of SFOR's mandate permitting the arrest of people sought by the International Criminal Tribunal for the Former Yugoslavia (ICTY, see p. 15) if they were discovered within the normal course of duties. A few days later troops serving under SFOR seized two former Serb officials who had been indicted on charges of genocide. SFOR has subsequently undertaken this objective as part of its operational activities. From mid-1997 SFOR assisted efforts to maintain the security and territorial integrity of the Republika Srpska in the face of violent opposition from nationalist supporters of the former President, Radovan Karadžić, based in Pale. In August NATO authorized SFOR to use force to prevent the use of the local media to incite violence, following attacks on multinational forces by Serb nationalists during attempts to regain control of police buildings. In November SFOR provided the general security framework, as well as logistical and communications assistance, in support of the OSCE's supervision of legislative elections that were conducted in the Republika Srpska. In December NATO ministers of defence confirmed that SFOR would be maintained at its current strength of some 31,000 troops, subject to the periodic six-monthly reviews. In February

1998 NATO resolved to establish within SFOR a specialized unit to respond to civil unrest and uphold public security. At the same time the NAC initiated a series of security co-operation activities to promote the development of democratic practices and defence mechanisms in Bosnia and Herzegovina. In October 1999 the NAC formally agreed to implement a reduction in SFOR's strength to some 20,000 troops, as well as a revision of its command structure, in response to the improved security situation in Bosnia and Herzegovina. In 2001 some 35 countries contributed troops to SFOR. Its main activities continued to be in support of the peace process, assisting the collection and disposal of illegal weapons, distributing humanitarian aid, and rebuilding the country's infrastructure.

In March 1998 an emergency session of the NAC was convened at the request of the Albanian Government, which was concerned at the deteriorating security of its border region with the Serbian province of Kosovo and Metohija, following intensified action by the Kosovo Liberation Army (KLA) and retaliatory attacks by Serbian security forces. In mid-June NATO defence ministers authorized the formulation of plans for airstrikes against Serbian targets. A few days later some 80 aircraft dispatched from 15 NATO bases flew close to Albania's border with Kosovo, in an attempt to demonstrate the Alliance's determination to prevent further reprisals against the ethnic Albanian population. In September NATO defence ministers urged a diplomatic solution to the conflict, but insisted that, with an estimated 50,000 refugees living without shelter in the mountainous region bordering Albania, their main objective was to avert a humanitarian disaster. In late September the UN Security Council issued a resolution (1199) demanding an immediate cease-fire in Kosovo, the withdrawal of the majority of Serbian military and police forces, co-operation by all sides with humanitarian agencies, and the initiation of political negotiations on some form of autonomy for the province. Plans for NATO airstrikes were finalized in early October. However, the Russian Government remained strongly opposed to the use of force and there was concern among some member states whether there was sufficient legal basis for NATO action without further UN authorization. Nevertheless, in mid-October, following Security Council condemnation of the humanitarian situation in Kosovo, the NAC agreed on limited airstrikes against Serbian targets, with a 96-hour delay on the 'activation order'. At the same time the US envoy to the region, Richard Holbrooke, concluded an agreement with President Milošević to implement the conditions of UN Resolution 1199. A 2,000-member international observer force, under the auspices of the OSCE, was to be established to monitor compliance with the agreement, supported by a NATO Co-ordination Unit, based in the former Yugoslav republic of Macedonia (FYRM), to assist with aerial surveillance. In mid-November NATO ambassadors approved the establishment of a 1,200–1,800 strong multinational force, under French command, to assist in any necessary evacuation of OSCE monitors. A NATO Kosovo Verification Command Centre was established in Kumanovo, north-east FYRM, in late November; however, President Milošević warned that the dispatch of foreign troops into Kosovo would be treated as an act of aggression.

In January 1999 NATO ambassadors convened in an emergency session following the discovery of the bodies of 45 ethnic Albanians in the Kosovan village of Racak. The meeting demanded that Serbia co-operate with an inquiry into the incident by the Prosecutor of the ICTY, guarantee the security and safety of all international personnel, withdraw security forces (which had continued to undertake offensives within Kosovo), and uphold the cease-fire. Intensive diplomatic efforts, co-ordinated by the six-country 'Contact Group' on the former Yugoslavia, succeeded in bringing both sides in the dispute to talks on the future of Kosovo. During the first stage of negotiations, held in Rambouillet, France, a provisional framework for a political settlement was formulated, based on a form of autonomy for Kosovo (to be reviewed after a three-year period), and incorporating a mandate for a NATO force of some 28,000 troops to monitor its implementation. The talks were suspended in late February with neither side having agreed to the accord. On the resumption of negotiations in mid-March representatives of the KLA confirmed that they would sign the peace settlement. President Milošević, however, continued to oppose the establishment of a NATO force in Kosovo and, despite further diplomatic efforts by Holbrooke, declined to endorse the agreement in accordance with a deadline imposed by the Contact Group. Amid reports of renewed Serbian violence against Albanian civilians in Kosovo, the NAC subsequently reconfirmed its support for NATO military intervention.

On 24 March 1999 an aerial offensive against the Federal Republic of Yugoslavia was initiated by NATO, with the declared aim of reducing that country's capacity to commit attacks on the Albanian population. The first phase of the allied operation was directed against defence facilities, followed, a few days later, by the second phase which permitted direct attacks on artillery positions, command centres and other military targets in a declared exclusion zone south of the 44th parallel. The escalation of the conflict prompted thousands of Albanians to flee Kosovo, while others were reportedly forced from their homes by Serbian security personnel, creating massive refugee populations in neighbouring countries. In early April NATO ambassadors agreed to dispatch some 8,000 troops, as an ACE Mobile Force Land operation (entitled 'Operation Allied Harbour'), to provide humanitarian assistance to the estimated 300,000 refugees in Albania at that time and to provide transportation to relieve overcrowded camps, in particular in border areas. Refugees in the FYRM were to be assisted by the existing NATO contingent (numbering some 12,000 troops by early April), which was permitted by the authorities in that country to construct new camps for some 100,000 displaced Kosovans. An additional 1,000 troops were transferred from the FYRM to Albania in mid-May in order to construct a camp to provide for a further 65,000 refugees. In mid-April NATO ministers of foreign affairs, meeting in special session, expressed extreme concern at the refugee situation throughout the region. The ministers also clarified the conditions necessary to halt the offensive, which included Serbia's agreement to an international military presence in Kosovo, provision for the safe return of all refugees and an undertaking to work on the basis of the Rambouillet accord. Russia continued to pursue diplomatic efforts to secure a peaceful settlement to the conflict, however, Milošević's reported agreement to allow an unarmed international force in Kosovo, conditional on the immediate end to the NATO campaign, was dismissed by NATO governments. From early April there was increasing evidence of civilian casualties resulting from NATO's aerial bombing of transport, power and media infrastructure and suspected military targets. In mid-April NATO initiated an inquiry following the bombing of a convoy of lorries which resulted in the deaths of some 69 refugees. In the following month NATO was obliged to apologise to the authorities of the People's Republic of China after the accidental bombing of its embassy in Belgrade. At the same time there was widespread concern among governments at increasing evidence of systematic killings and ethnic violence being committed by Serbian forces within Kosovo, and at the estimated 100,000 Albanian men unaccounted for among the massive displaced population. NATO's 50th anniversary summit meeting, held in Washington, USA, in late April, was dominated by consideration of the conflict and of the future stability of the region. A joint statement declared the determination of all Alliance members to increase economic and military pressure on President Milošević to withdraw forces from Kosovo. In particular, the meeting agreed to prevent shipments of petroleum reaching Serbia through Montenegro, to complement the embargo imposed by the EU and a new focus of the bombing campaign which aimed to destroy the fuel supply within Serbia. However, there was concern on the part of several NATO governments on the legal and political aspects of implementing the embargo. The meeting failed to adopt a unified position on the use of ground forces, which many expert commentators insisted, throughout the campaign, were necessary to secure NATO's objectives. In May ministers of foreign affairs of the Group of Seven industrialized nations and Russia (the G-8) agreed on general principles for a political solution, which was to form the basis of UN Security Council resolution. Later in that month NATO estimated that a future Kosovo Peace Implementation Force (KFOR), installed to guarantee a settlement, would require at least 48,000 troops. Following further intensive diplomatic efforts to secure a cease-fire in Kosovo, on 9 June a Military Technical Agreement was signed between NATO and the Federal Republic of Yugoslavia, incorporating a timetable for the withdrawal of all Serbian security personnel. On the following day the UN Security Council adopted Resolution 1244, which authorized an international security presence in Kosovo, under NATO, and an international civilian presence, the UN Interim Administration Mission in Kosovo (UNMIK). The NAC subsequently suspended the airstrike campaign, which, by that time, had involved some 38,000 sorties. KFOR was organized into six brigades, under the leadership of France, Germany, Italy, USA and the United Kingdom (with responsibility for two brigades). An initial force of 20,000 troops entered Kosovo on 12 June. A few days later an agreement was concluded with Russia, whose troops had also entered Kosovo and taken control of Pristina airport, which provided for the joint responsibility of the airstrip with a NATO contingent and for the participation of some 3,600 Russian troops in KFOR, reporting to the country command in each sector. On 20 June the withdrawal of Yugoslav troops from Kosovo was completed, providing for the formal ending of NATO's air campaign. The KLA undertook to demilitarize and transform the force, as required under Resolution 1244, which was reported to have been achieved in September. KFOR's immediate responsibility was to provide a secure environment to facilitate the safe return of refugees, and, pending the full deployment of UNMIK, to assist the reconstruction of infrastructure and civil and political institutions. In addition, NATO troops were to assist personnel of the international tribunal to investigate sites of alleged violations of human rights and mass graves. From August an escalation of ethnic violence and deterioration of law and order in some parts of the province was an outstanding concern. In January 2000 NATO agreed that the Eurocorps defence force (see under WEU) would assume command of KFOR headquarters in April. At that time KFOR's main concerns were to protect the minority populations, maintain security and reintegrate members of the KLA into civilian life. KFOR was also to continue to work closely with UNMIK in the provision of humanitarian aid, the rehabilitation of infrastructure and the development of civil administration. In February an emergency meeting of the NAC was convened to review the situation in the divided town of Titova Mitrovica, northern Kosovo, where violent clashes had occurred between the ethnic populations and five people had died during attempts by KFOR to impose order. The NAC expressed its determination to reinforce KFOR's troop levels. In September KFOR undertook to protect ethnic Serbians who were eligible to vote in a general election in the Federal Republic of Yugoslavia, and in the following month KFOR worked with OSCE and UN personnel to maintain a secure environment and provide logistical assistance for the holding of municipal elections in Kosovo. During the year KFOR attempted to prevent the movement and stockpiling of illegal armaments in the region. In November there was a marked deterioration in the security situation in Kosovo, and KFOR attempted to halt several outbreaks of cross-border violence. In February 2001 NATO conducted negotiations with the Yugoslav Government regarding new security arrangements to prevent further attacks on the local population in southern Serbia and to counter illegal arms-trafficking. A Weapons Destruction Programme was successfully conducted by KFOR between April 2000–December 2001; a second programme was initiated in March 2002, while an Ammunition Destruction Programme commenced in January.

In March 2001 Albanian separatists in the FYRM escalated their campaign in the north of that country. KFOR troops attempted to prevent Kosovo Albanians from supporting the rebels, fighting as the National Liberation Army (NLA), in order to avert further violence and instability. NATO dispatched military and political missions to meet with the Macedonian authorities, and agreed that Serbian troops were to be permitted to enter the ground safety zone in the Presevo valley (bordering on Kosovo and the FYRM) to strengthen security and prevent it becoming a safe haven for the rebel fighters. The Secretary-General also requested an additional 1,400 troops from member countries to reinforce border security. In mid-March the NLA seized strategic positions around Tetovo, in north-west FYRM. After several days of conflict Macedonian troops initiated an offensive against the rebel strongholds, prompting thousands of Albanians to flee into Kosovo. Nevertheless, hostilities intensified again from late April, resulting in further population displacements. In June NATO troops supervised the withdrawal of some 300 armed Albanian rebels who had been besieged in a town neighbouring Skopje, the Macedonian capital. A cease-fire agreement, mediated by NATO, was concluded by the Macedonian authorities and Albanian militants in early July, as a prelude to negotiations on a political settlement. Meanwhile, NATO, at the request of the Macedonian Government, was drafting contingency plans to deploy troops in the FYRM with a mandate to supervise the voluntary disarmament of the Albanian militants and to collect and destroy their weapons, on condition that both sides showed commitment to maintaining the cease-fire and pursuing peace talks. In mid-July, however, ethnic Albanian insurgents in the Tetovo area were reportedly violating the cease-fire accord. An agreement regarding disarmament and conditions for ethnic minorities, as well as for the immediate withdrawal of troops, was concluded in August. Some 3,800 NATO troops were deployed at the end of that month, under so-called Operation Essential Harvest. At the end of the operation's 30-day mandate almost 4,300 guns had been surrendered, together with 400,000 mines, grenades and ammunition rounds. The NLA formally disbanded, in accordance with the peace agreement. The NAC approved a successor mission, comprising 700 troops with a three-month mandate, to protect the civilian observers of the accord (to be deployed by the EU and OSCE). The mission's mandate was subsequently extended until 26 June 2002.

Nato Agencies

1. Civilian production and logistics organizations responsible to the NAC:

Central Europe Pipeline Management Agency—CEPMA: BP 552, 78005 Versailles, France; tel. 1-39-24-49-00; fax 1-39-55-65-39; f. 1957; responsible for the 24-hour operation of the Central Europe Pipeline System and its storage and distribution facilities.

NATO Air Command Control System Management Agency—NACMA: 8 rue de Genève, 1140 Brussels, Belgium; tel. (2) 707-41-11; fax (2) 707-87-77; internet www.nacma.nato.int; conducts planning, system engineering, implementation and configuration management for NATO's ACCS programme.

NATO Airborne Early Warning and Control Programme Management Organisation—NAPMO: Akerstraat 7, 6445 CL Brunssum, Netherlands; fax (45) 5254373; f. 1978; responsible for the management and implementation of the NATO Airborne Early Warning and Control Programme.

NATO Consultation, Command and Control Agency—NC3A: 1110 Brussels, Belgium; tel. (2) 707-43-58; fax (2) 708-87-70; internet www.nc3a.nato.int; works within the framework of the NATO C3 Organization (f. 1996 by restructuring of the NATO Communications and Information Systems Organization and the Tri-Service Group on Communications and Electronics, incorporating the former Allied Data Systems Interoperability Agency, the Allied Naval Communications Agency and the Allied Tactical Communications Agency); provides scientific advice and assistance to NATO military and political authorities; helps to develop, procure and implement cost-effective system capabilities to support political consultations and military command and control functions. Also maintains offices in The Hague.

NATO CIS Operating and Support Agency—NACOSA: Maintains NATO's communications and information system (CIS); supervised by the NC3 Board.

NATO CIS School: 04010 Borgo Riave, Latina, Italy; tel. (0773) 6771; fax (0773) 662467; f. 1959; provides advanced training to civilian and military personnel in the operation and maintenance of NATO's communications and information system. Conducts orientation courses for partner countries.

NATO EF 2000 and Tornado Development, Production and Logistics Management Agency—NETMA: Insel Kammerstrasse 12–14, Postfach 1302, 82008 Unterhaching, Germany; tel. (89) 666800; fax (89) 6668055; replaced the NATO Multirole Combat Aircraft (MRCA) Development and Production Management Agency (f. 1969) and the NATO European Fighter (EF) Aircraft Development, Production and Logistics Management Agency (f. 1987); responsible for the joint development and production of the European Fighter Aircraft and the MRCA (Tornado).

NATO HAWK Management Office: 26 rue Galliéni, 92500 Rueil-Malmaison, France; tel. 1-47-08-75-00; fax 1-47-52-10-99; f. 1959 to supervise the multinational production and upgrading programmes of the HAWK surface-to-air missile system in Europe; Gen. Man. A. BOCCHI.

NATO Helicopter Design and Development Production and Logistics Management Agency—NAHEMA: Le Quatuor, Bâtiment A, 42 route de Galice, 13082 Aix-en-Provence Cédex 2, France; tel. 4-42-95-92-00; fax 4-42-64-30-50.

NATO Maintenance and Supply Agency—NAMSA: 8302 Capellen, Luxembourg; tel. 30-631; fax 30-87-21; internet www.namsa.nato.int; f. 1958; supplies spare parts and logistic support for a number of jointly-used weapon systems, missiles and electronic systems; all member nations except Iceland participate.

2. Responsible to the Military Committee:

NATO Defense College—NADEFCOL: Via Giorgio Pelosi 1, 00143 Rome-Cecchiguola, Italy; tel. (06) 505259; f. 1951 to train officials for posts in NATO organizations or in national ministries.

NATO Frequency Management Sub-Committee—FMSC: 1100 Brussels, Belgium; tel. (2) 707-55-28; replaced the Allied Radio Frequency Agency (f. 1951); the FMSC is the frequency authority of the Alliance and establishes and co-ordinates all policy concerned with the military use of the radio frequency spectrum.

NATO Standardization Agency—NSA: 1110 Brussels, Belgium; tel. (2) 707-55-76; fax (2) 707-57-18; e-mail nsa@hq.nato.int; lead agent for the development, co-ordination and assessment of operational standardization, in order to enhance interoperability; initiates, co-ordinates, supports and administers standardization activities conducted under the authority of the NATO Committee for Standardization.

Research and Technology Organization—RTO: BP 25, 7 rue Ancelle, 92201 Neuilly-sur-Seine Cédex, France; tel. 1-55-61-22-00; fax 1-55-61-22-99; e-mail mailbox@rta.nato.int; internet www.rta.nato.int; f. 1998 by merger of the Advisory Group for Aerospace Research and Development and the Defence Research Group; brings together scientists and engineers from member countries for exchange of information and research co-operation (formally established 1998); provides scientific and technical advice for the Military Committee, for other NATO bodies and for member nations; comprises a Research and Technology Board and a Research and Technology Agency, responsible for implementing RTO's work programme.

3. Responsible to Supreme Allied Commander Atlantic (SACLANT):

NATO SACLANT Undersea Research Centre—SACLANTCEN: Viale San Bartolomeo 400, 19138 La Spezia, Italy; tel. (0187) 5271; fax (0187) 527420; e-mail library@saclantc.nato.int; internet www.saclantc.nato.int; f. 1959 to conduct research in support of NATO operational requirements in antisubmarine warfare and mine counter-measures.

4. Responsible to Supreme Allied Commander Europe (SACEUR):

NATO (SHAPE) School: Am Rainenbichl 54, 82487 Oberammergau, Germany; tel. (88) 224477; fax (88) 221035; e-mail postmaster@natoschool-shape.de; internet www.natoschool-shape.de; f. 1975; acts as a centre for training military and civilian personnel of NATO countries, and, since 1991, for officials from partner countries, in support of NATO policies, operations and objectives.

Finance

As NATO is an international, not a supra-national, organization, its member countries themselves decide the amount to be devoted to their defence effort and the form which the latter will assume. Thus, the aim of NATO's defence planning is to develop realistic military plans for the defence of the alliance at reasonable cost. Under the annual defence planning process, political, military and economic factors are considered in relation to strategy, force requirements and available resources. The procedure for the co-ordination of military plans and defence expenditures rests on the detailed and comparative analysis of the capabilities of member countries. All installations for the use of international forces are financed under a common-funded infrastructure programme. In accordance with the terms of the Partnership for Peace strategy, partner countries undertake to make available the necessary personnel, assets, facilities and capabilities to participate in the programme. The countries also share the financial cost of military exercises in which they participate. The administrative (or 'civil') budget, which includes the NATO Science Programme, amounted to US $133m. in 2000. The total military budget approved for 2001 amounted to $716m. (including the operating costs of NATO command structures in the former Yugoslavia, but excluding the costs of assignment of military personnel, met by the contributing countries).

Publications

NATO publications (in English and French, with some editions in other languages) include:

NATO Basic Fact Sheets.

NATO Final Communiqués.

NATO Handbook.

NATO in the 21st Century.

NATO Review (quarterly in 11 languages; annually in Icelandic).

NATO Update (weekly, electronic version only).

Economic and scientific publications.

North Atlantic Treaty

(4 April 1949, as amended by Protocols signed on the accession of Greece, Turkey, Germany and Spain.)

The Parties to this Treaty reaffirm their faith in the purposes and principles of the Charter of the United Nations and their desire to live in peace with all peoples and all governments.

They are determined to safeguard the freedom, common heritage and civilization of their peoples, founded on the principles of democracy, individual liberty and the rule of law.

They seek to promote stability and well-being in the North Atlantic area. They are resolved to unite their efforts for collective defence and for the preservation of peace and security.

They therefore agree to this North Atlantic Treaty:

Article 1

The Parties undertake, as set forth in the Charter of the United Nations, to settle any international dispute in which they may be involved by peaceful means in such a manner that international peace and security and justice are not endangered, and to refrain in their international relations from the threat or use of force in any manner inconsistent with the purposes of the United Nations.

Article 2

The Parties will contribute toward the further development of peaceful and friendly international relations by strengthening their free institutions, by bringing about a better understanding of the principles upon which these institutions are founded, and by promoting conditions of stability and well-being. They will seek to eliminate conflict in their international economic policies and will encourage economic collaboration between any or all of them.

Article 3

In order more effecitvely to achieve the objectives of this Treaty, the Parties, separately and jointly, by means of continuous and effective self-help and mutual aid, will maintain and develop their individual and collective capacity to resist armed attack.

Article 4

The Parties will consult together whenever, in the opinion of any of them, the territorial integrity, political independence or security of any of the Parties is threatened.

Article 5

The Parties agree that an armed attack against one or more of them in Europe or North America shall be considered an attack against them all and consequently they agree that, if such an armed attack occurs, each of them, in exercise of the right of individual or collective self-defence recognised by Article 51 of the Charter of the United Nations, will assist the Party or Parties so attacked by taking forthwith, individually and in concert with the other Parties, such action as it deems necessary, including the use of armed force, to restore and maintain the security of the North Atlantic area.

Any such armed attack and all measures taken as a result thereof shall immediately be reported to the (UN) Security Council. Such measures shall be terminated when the Security Council has taken the measures necessary to restore and maintain international peace and security.

Article 6

For the purpose of Article 5, an armed attack on one or more of the Parties is deemed to include an armed attack:

—on the territory of any of the Parties in Europe or North America, on the Algerian Departments of France*, on the territory of Turkey or on the Islands under the jurisdiction of any of the Parties in the North Atlantic area north of the Tropic of Cancer;

—on the forces, vessels, or aircraft of any of the Parties, when in or over these territories or any other area in Europe in which occupation forces of any of the Parties were stationed on the date when the Treaty entered into force or the Mediterranean Sea or the North Atlantic area north of the Tropic of Cancer.

Article 7

This treaty does not affect, and shall not be interpreted as affecting in any way the rights and obligations under the Charter of the Parties which are members of the United Nations, or the primary responsibility of the Security Council for the maintenance of international peace and security.

Article 8

Each Party declares that none of the international engagements now in force beween it and any other of the Parties or any third State is in conflict with the provisions of this Treaty, and undertakes not to enter into any international engagement in conflict with this Treaty.

Article 9

The Parties hereby establish a Council, on which each of them shall be represented, to consider matters concerning the implementation of this Treaty. The Council shall be so organised as to be able to meet promptly at any time. The Council shall set up such subsidiary bodies as may be necessary; in particular it shall establish immediately a defence committee which shall recommend measures for the implementation of Articles 3 and 5.

Article 10

The Parties may, by unanimous agreement, invite any other European State in a position to further the principles of this Treaty and to contribute to the security of the North Atlantic area to accede to this Treaty. Any State so invited may become a Party to the Treaty by depositing its instrument of accession with the Government of the United States of America. The Government of the United States of America will inform each of the Parties of the deposit of each such instrument of accession.

Article 11

This Treaty shall be ratified and its provisions carried out by the Parties in accordance with their respective constitutional processes. The instruments of ratification shall be deposited as soon as possible with the Government of the United States of America, which will notify all the other signatories of each deposit. The Treaty shall enter into force between the States which have ratified it as soon as the ratifications of the majority of the signatories, including the ratifications of Belgium, Canada, France, Luxembourg, the Netherlands, the United Kingdom and the United States, have been deposited and shall come into effect with respect to other States on the date of the deposit of their ratifications.

Article 12

After the Treaty has been in force for ten years, or at any time thereafter, the Parties shall, if any of them so requests, consult together for the purpose of reviewing the Treaty, having regard for the factors then affecting peace and security in the North Atlantic area, including the development of universal as well as regional arrangements under the Charter of the United Nations for the maintenance of international peace and security.

Article 13

After the Treaty has been in force for twenty years, any Party may cease to be a Party one year after its notice of denunciation has been given to the Government of the United States of America, which will inform the Governments of the other Parties of the deposit of each notice of denunciation.

Article 14

This Treaty, of which the English and French texts are equally authentic, shall be deposited in the archives of the Government of the United States of America. Duly certified copies will be transmitted by that Government to the Governments of other signatories.

* In January 1963, the North Atlantic Council noted that insofar as the former Algerian Departments of France were concerned, the relevant clauses of this Treaty had become inapplicable as from July 1962.

ORGANISATION FOR ECONOMIC CO-OPERATION AND DEVELOPMENT—OECD

Address: 2 rue André-Pascal, 75775 Paris Cédex 16, France.

Telephone: 1-45-24-82-00; **fax:** 1-45-24-85-00; **e-mail:** webmaster@oecd.org; **internet:** www.oecd.org.

OECD was founded in 1961, replacing the Organisation for European Economic Co-operation (OEEC), which had been established in 1948 in connection with the Marshall Plan. It constitutes a forum for governments to discuss, develop and attempt to co-ordinate their economic and social policies. The Organisation aims to promote policies designed to achieve the highest level of sustainable economic growth, employment and increase in the standard of living, while maintaining financial stability and democratic government, and to contribute to economic expansion in member and non-member states and to the expansion of world trade.

MEMBERS

Australia	Hungary	Norway
Austria	Iceland	Poland
Belgium	Ireland	Portugal
Canada	Italy	Slovakia
Czech Republic	Japan	Spain
Denmark	Republic of Korea	Sweden
Finland	Luxembourg	Switzerland
France	Mexico	Turkey
Germany	Netherlands	United Kingdom
Greece	New Zealand	USA

The European Commission also takes part in OECD's work.

Organization

(April 2002)

COUNCIL

The governing body of OECD is the Council, at which each member country is represented. The Council meets from time to time (usually once a year) at the level of government ministers, with the chairmanship rotated among member states. It also meets regularly at official level, when it comprises the Secretary-General and the Permanent Representatives of member states to OECD. It is responsible for all questions of general policy and may establish subsidiary bodies as required, to achieve the aims of the Organisation. Decisions and recommendations of the Council are adopted by mutual agreement of all its members.

Heads of Permanent Delegations (with ambassadorial rank):

Australia: IAN K. FORSYTH
Austria: KARL SCHRAMEK
Belgium: RÉGINE DE CLERCQ
Canada: SUZANNE HURTUBISE
Czech Republic: JAROMÍR PRIVRATSKY
Denmark: PETER BRÜCKNER
Finland: JORMA JULIN
France: JOËLLE BOURGEOIS
Germany: HANS-STEFAN KRUSE
Greece: GEORGE E. KRIMPAS
Hungary: BÉLA KÁDÁR
Iceland: SIGRIDUR ASDIS SNAEVARR
Ireland: PRÁDACI MACKERNAN
Italy: FRANCESCO OLIVIERI
Japan: MUTSUYOSHI NISHIMURA
Republic of Korea: KYUNG-TAE LEE
Luxembourg: JEAN-MARC HOSCHEIT
Mexico: JAVIER ARRIGUNAGA
Netherlands: FRANZ ENGERING
New Zealand: BRIAN WILSON (interim)
Norway: IRVIN HØYLAND (interim)
Poland: JAN BIELAWSKI
Portugal: ANA MARTINHO
Slovakia: DUSAN BELLA
Spain: ELENA PISONERO RUIZ
Sweden: ANDERS FERM
Switzerland: WILHELM B. JAGGI
Turkey: ULUÇ OZÜLKER
United Kingdom: CHRISTOPHER CRABBIE
USA: JEANNE L. PHILLIPS

Participant with Special Status:

European Commission: JOHN MADDISON (United Kingdom).

EXECUTIVE COMMITTEE

The Executive Committee prepares the work of the Council. It is also called upon to carry out specific tasks where necessary. In addition to its regular meetings, the Committee meets occasionally in special sessions attended by senior government officials.

SECRETARIAT

The Council, the committees and other bodies in OECD are assisted by an independent international secretariat headed by the Secretary-General. An Executive Director is responsible for the management of administrative support services. Some 1,850 staff were employed in the secretariat in January 2000.

Secretary-General: DONALD J. JOHNSTON (Canada).

Deputy Secretaries-General: THORVALD MOE (Norway), HERWIG SCHLÖGL (Germany), SEIICHI KONDO (Japan), SALLY SHELTON-COLBY (USA).

Executive Director: JEAN-JACQUES NOREAU (Canada).

AUTONOMOUS AND SEMI-AUTONOMOUS BODIES

Centre for Educational Research and Innovation—CERI: f. 1968; includes all member countries. Dir THOMAS J. ALEXANDER (see also under Education, Employment, Labour and Social Affairs, below).

Club du Sahel et de l'Afrique de l'Ouest: f. 1976; an informal forum of donor countries and member states of the Permanent Inter-State Committee on Drought Control in the Sahel; mandate extended to cover West Africa in April 2001 (see p. 534). Dir JACQUELINE DAMON.

Development Centre: f. 1962; includes most member countries and Argentina, Brazil and Chile. Pres. JORGE BRAGA DE MACEDO (Portugal) (see also under Development Co-operation, below).

European Conference of Ministers of Transport (see p. 593).

International Energy Agency (see p. 442).

Nuclear Energy Agency (see p. 443).

Activities

The greater part of the work of OECD, which covers all aspects of economic and social policy, is prepared and carried out in about 200 specialized bodies (committees, working parties, etc.); all members are normally represented on these bodies, except on those of a restricted nature.

ECONOMIC POLICY

Through its work on economic policy, OECD aims to promote stable macroeconomic environments in member and non-member countries and the equitable distribution of income. The main organ for the consideration and direction of economic policy is the Economic Policy Committee, which comprises governments' chief economic advisers and central bankers, and meets two or three times a year. It has several working parties and groups, the most important of which are Working Party No. 1 on Macro-Economic and Structural Policy Analysis, Working Party No. 3 on Policies for the Promotion of Better International Payments Equilibrium, and the Working Group on Short-Term Economic Prospects. In 2001 the Committee's priority work areas included the interaction between labour and product markets, tax reform, issues related to the ageing of OECD populations, and the development of human capital.

The Economic and Development Review Committee, comprising all member countries, is responsible for the annual examination of the economic situation and macro economic and structural policies of each member country. A report is issued every 12 to 18 months on each country, after an examination carried out by the Committee. The reports include specific policy recommendations. This process of peer review has been extended to other branches of the Organisation's work (agriculture, environment, manpower and social affairs, scientific policy and development aid efforts).

STATISTICS

Statistical data and related methodological information are collected from member governments and, where possible, consolidated, or converted into an internationally comparable form. The Statistics Directorate maintains data required for macroeconomic forecasting, i.e. national accounts, the labour force, foreign trade, prices, output, and monetary, financial, industrial and other short-term statistics. Work is also undertaken to develop new statistics and new statistical standards and systems in areas of emerging policy interest (such as sustainable development). In addition, the Directorate passes on to non-member countries member states' experience in compiling statistics. In 2000 a project to reform OECD's statistical system was launched, and in 2001 a new strategy began to be defined. The overall aim was to improve the efficiency and quality of the statistics produced and to counter some of the problems inherent in the decentralized system. (Other specialist directorates also collect statistics and maintain databases.) A co-ordinated framework for collecting, processing, storing, retrieving, analysing and disseminating data was to be developed, with precise guide-lines issued to all directorates and integrated programmes across the Organisation. The Directorate aims to expand contacts with other international and national statistical authorities.

DEVELOPMENT CO-OPERATION

The Development Assistance Committee (DAC) is the principal body through which the Organisation deals with issues relating to co-operation with developing countries and is one of the key forums in which the major bilateral donors work together to increase their effectiveness in support of sustainable development. The DAC holds an annual high-level meeting of ministers or heads of aid agencies. Work is supported by the Development Co-operation Directorate, which monitors aid programmes and resource flows, compiles statistics and seeks to establish codes of practice in aid. There is also a working party on aid evaluation, a working party on gender equality, a network on good governance and capacity development, a network on conflict, peace and development co-operation, and a working party on the financial aspects of development assistance.

Guided by the Development Partnerships Strategy formulated in 1996, the DAC's mission is to foster co-ordinated, integrated, effective and adequately financed international efforts in support of sustainable economic and social development. Recognizing that developing countries themselves are ultimately responsible for their own development, the DAC concentrates on how international co-operation can contribute to the population's ability to overcome poverty and participate fully in society. Principal activities include: adopting authoritative policy guide-lines; conducting periodic critical reviews of members' programmes of development co-operation; providing a forum for dialogue, exchange of experience and the building of international consensus on policy and management issues; and publishing statistics and reports on aid and other resource flows to developing countries and countries in transition. A working set of indicators of development progress has been established by the DAC, in collaboration with experts from UN agencies including the World Bank and from developing countries.

The Development Partnerships Strategy was followed up by a report entitled *Shaping the 21st Century—The Contribution Of Development Co-operation*, which outlined a series of poverty reduction and development objectives. In 2000 the Partnership for Poverty Reduction was launched, with the aim of establishing a partnership approach for bilateral co-operation with developing countries. In late 2000 the DAC established a Task Force on Donor Practices, which aimed to strengthen partner countries' ownership of development programmes by improving and co-ordinating donor practices. In April 2001 OECD adopted a Recommendation on Untying Official Development Assistance to the Least Developed Countries, whereby recipient countries may use aid to purchase goods and services from any state, not just the donor country.

The OECD Development Centre was established in 1962 to provide a focal point within the Organisation for analysis and policy dialogue on economic and social aspects of development in Africa, Asia, Latin America, the Caribbean and the Middle East. The Centre informs member countries of emerging issues and offers developing countries objective, in-depth analyses, with a view to promoting constructive policy reform. It serves as an intermediary between OECD and the developing countries by promoting the exchange of ideas and information. Research and dialogue activities are orientated towards topics with a high priority on the agenda of policy-makers. In 2001 the Centre was considering means of achieving a more equitable distribution of the benefits of globalization, and, in particular, how to strengthen the platform of developing countries in WTO negotiations. Other important issues included questions of migration and development and the impact of new technologies on developing countries.

The Club du Sahel et de l'Afrique de l'Ouest (Sahel and West Africa Club, known as the Club du Sahel until April 2001, when its mandate was extended) has provided an informal framework for dialogue and co-operation between its member countries, donor governments and concerned organizations since 1976. Its programme of studies, analysis and joint work programmes has evolved since its establishment to reflect the most pressing needs and concerns of these sub-regions. In 2001 the principal issues under consideration included local development and decentralization, market integration, food security and best practice in development assistance.

In a report to the Secretary-General in late 1997 an advisory group on the environment, comprising non-governmental experts, recommended that OECD should evolve into the principal intergovernmental organization providing the analytical and comparative framework of policy necessary for industrialized countries to make the transition to sustainable development. Through the DAC working party on development co-operation and the environment, projects are being implemented in areas relating to technology, the effects of climate change, the environmental impact of subsidies, and the creation of indicators of sustainability, in order comprehensively to address the economic, social and environmental dimensions of sustainable development.

PUBLIC MANAGEMENT

The Public Management Committee, and its secretariat, the Public Management Service (PUMA) are concerned with issues of governance, including: the formulation of policies and their implementation; the allocation of resources; building and strengthening effective government structures; human resource management; and questions of accountability, ethics and corruption, consultation and transparency. PUMA serves as a forum for senior officials responsible for the central management systems of government, providing information, analysis and recommendations on public management and governing capacity. In view of recent changes in the environment for government management, PUMA has addressed the greater role afforded to sub-national governments by decentralization and the use of new information and communication technologies. A joint initiative of OECD and the EU, operating within PUMA, supports good governance in countries of Central and Eastern Europe. The so-called Support for Improvement in Governance and Management (SIGMA) programme advises countries on improving their administrative efficiency and promotes the adherence of public-sector staff to democratic values and ethics and respect for the rule of law. SIGMA also helps to strengthen capacities at the level of central government to address the challenges of EU integration, and greater global interdependence.

CO-OPERATION WITH NON-MEMBER ECONOMIES

The Centre for Co-operation with Non-Members (CCNM) was established in January 1998, by merger of the Centre for Co-operation with Economies in Transition (founded in 1990) and the Liaison and Co-ordination Unit. It serves as the focal point for the development of policy dialogue with non-member economies, managing multi-country, thematic, regional and country programmes. In 2001 country programmes were being undertaken for Brazil, the People's Republic of China and Russia. There was also a General Programme for Asia, a General Programme for the Transition Economies of Europe and Central Asia (covering a broad range of economic and social policy issues, as well as structural adjustment), a Baltic Regional Programme, a General Programme for South Eastern Europe, and a South America General Programme. OECD also undertakes a limited number of exploratory initiatives in the Middle East and Africa. The Centre manages OECD's various Global Forums, which discuss a wide range of specific issues. An Emerging Market Economy Forum brings together non-member economies engaged in market-oriented policy reform of interest to members. Recent topics discussed have included tax evasion, the regulation of securities markets and foreign direct investment policy.

Non-member economies are invited, on a selective basis by the CCNM, to participate in or observe the work of certain OECD committees and working parties. The Centre also provides a limited range of training activities in support of policy implementation and institution building. Five multilateral tax centres provide workshops and seminars for senior officials in tax administration and policy. OECD, through the CCNM, co-sponsors the Centre for Private Sector Development in İstanbul, Turkey, with the Turkish and German Governments. This assists various countries to develop the necessary framework and policies for a market economy and integration into the world economy. The CCNM also sponsors the Joint Vienna Institute (see IMF, p. 174), which offers a variety of administrative, economic and financial management courses to participants from transition economies. The CCNM co-ordinates and maintains OECD's relations (formal and informal) with other international organizations, such as the World Bank and regional development banks.

INTERNATIONAL TRADE

OECD's Trade Committee supports the continued liberalization and efficient operation of the multilateral trading system, with the aim of contributing to the expansion of world trade on a non-discriminatory basis. Its activities include examination of issues concerning trade relations among member countries as well as relations with non-member countries, and consideration and discussion of trade measures taken by a member country which adversely affect another's interests. Through its working parties, it analyses trade issues relating to, for example, the environment and agriculture. The Committee holds regular consultations with civil society organizations.

Through its export credit agreement, OECD maintains an export credit system, stipulating generous financial terms and conditions, and serves as a forum for the discussion and co-ordination of export credit policies. The Working Party on Export Credits and Credit Guarantees works to achieve a level playing field in this area.

The Committee considers the challenges that are presented to the existing international trading system by financial or economic instability, the process of globalization of production and markets and the ensuing deeper integration of national economies. OECD provided support to the multilateral trade negotiations conducted under the General Agreement on Tariffs and Trade (GATT), assisting member countries to analyse the effects of the trade accords and promoting its global benefits. Following the entry into force of the World Trade Organization (WTO) agreements in 1995, OECD continued to study and assess aspects of the international trade agenda. In November 1999 OECD published a report on the impact of further trade liberalization on developing countries, in preparation for the next round of multilateral trade negotiations (which were initiated by WTO in November 2001).

FINANCIAL, FISCAL AND ENTERPRISE AFFAIRS

Promoting the efficient functioning of markets and enterprises and strengthening the multilateral framework for trade and investment is the responsibility of a number of OECD committees under the Directorate for Financial, Fiscal and Enterprise Affairs. The Directorate works to encourage policy convergence, provides policy guide-lines, gives examples of best practice and maintains benchmarks to measure progress.

The Committee on Capital Movements and Invisible Transactions monitors the implementation of the Codes of Liberalization of Invisible Transactions and of Current Invisible Operations as legally binding norms for all member countries. The Committee on International Investment and Multinational Enterprises monitors the observance of the OECD Guide-lines for Multinational Enterprises, a corporate Code of Conduct recommended by OECD member governments, business and labour units (the guide-lines were adopted by all OECD governments, as well as Argentina, Brazil and Chile, in 2000). A Declaration on International Investment and Multinational Enterprises, while non-binding, contains commitments on the conduct and treatment of foreign-owned enterprises established in member countries. Negotiations on a Multilateral Agreement on Investment (MAI), initiated by OECD ministers in 1995 to provide a legal framework for international investment, broke down in October 1998, although 'informal consultation' on the issue subsequently continued.

The Committee on Competition Law and Policy promotes the harmonization of national competition policies, co-operation in competition law enforcement, common merger reporting rules and pro-competitive regulatory reform, the development of competition laws and institutions, and efforts to change policies that restrain competition. The Committee on Financial Markets exercises surveillance over recent developments, reform measures and structural and regulatory conditions in financial markets. It aims to promote international trade in financial services, to encourage the integration of non-member countries into the global financial system, and to improve financial statistics. The Insurance Committee monitors structural changes and reform measures in insurance markets. Its programme of work for 2001–02 focused on the liberalization of insurance markets, financial insolvency, co-operation on insurance and reinsurance policy, the monitoring and analysis of regulatory and structural developments, and private pensions and health insurance. A working party on private pensions meets twice a year.

The Committee on Fiscal Affairs has recently focused on the tax implications of the globalization of national economies. Its activities include promoting the removal of tax barriers and monitoring the implementation and impact of major tax reforms, as well as developing a neutral tax framework for electronic commerce. Since 1998 OECD has promoted co-ordinated action for the elimination of so-called 'harmful' tax practices, designed to reduce the incidence of international money-laundering, and the level of potential tax revenue lost by OECD members. In mid-2000 it launched an initiative to abolish 'harmful tax systems', identifying a number of offshore jurisdictions as 'tax havens' lacking financial transparency, and inviting these to co-operate with the Organisation by amending national financial legislation. Several of the countries and territories named agreed to follow a timetable for reform, with the aim of eliminating such practices by the end of 2005. Others, however, were reluctant to participate. (The USA also strongly opposed the initiative.) In mid-2001 OECD threatened to impose sanctions on non-complying jurisdictions. The Organisation has also highlighted examples of preferential tax regimes in member countries. OECD provides the secretariat for the Financial Action Task Force on Money Laundering (FATF, q.v.).

The Corporate Affairs Division of the Directorate for Financial, Fiscal and Enterprise Affairs considers issues related to the development of the corporate sector in member and non-member countries, such as company law and reform; privatization and the reform of state-owned enterprises; and questions of insolvency and financial disclosure. In May 1997 the OECD Council endorsed plans to introduce a global ban on the corporate bribery of public officials; the OECD Convention on Bribery of Foreign Public Officials in International Business Transactions entered into force in February 1999. By February 2002 the Convention had been ratified by 34 countries. Conformity is monitored by a working group on bribery. In May 1999 ministers endorsed a set of OECD Principles for Corporate Governance, covering ownership and control of corporate entities, the rights of shareholders, the role of stakeholders, transparency, disclosure and the responsibilities of boards. In 2000 these became one of the 12 core standards of global financial stability and are used as a benchmark by other international financial institutions. OECD also collaborates with the World Bank and other organizations to promote good governance world-wide, for example through regional round tables and the Global Corporate Governance Forum.

FOOD, AGRICULTURE AND FISHERIES

The Committee for Agriculture reviews major developments in agricultural policies, deals with the adaptation of agriculture to changing economic conditions, elaborates forecasts of production and market prospects for the major commodities, manages a programme to develop product standards in agriculture, identifies best practices for limiting the impact of agricultural production on the environment, promotes the use of sustainable practices in the sector, considers questions of agricultural development in emerging and transition economies, and evaluates progress towards the integration of the agro-food sector into the multilateral trading system. OECD agriculture ministers have agreed on the long-term objective of seeking a substantial reduction in agricultural support. The Fisheries Committee carries out similar tasks in its sector, and, in particular, analyses the consequences of policy measures with a view to promoting responsible and sustainable fisheries. OECD is currently seeking to develop indicators measuring economic and social sustainability in the fisheries sector.

TERRITORIAL DEVELOPMENT

The Territorial Development Service assists central governments with the design and implementation of more effective, area-based strategies, encourages the emergence of locally driven initiatives for economic development, and promotes better integration of local and national approaches. Territorial policies have recently emphasized the need to mobilize local resources to enhance regional competitiveness and to create employment. The Service comprises two intergovernmental bodies—the Local Economic and Employment Development Committee and the Territorial Development Policy Committee—which share an overall work programme emphasizing the need for innovative policy initiatives and exchange of knowledge in a wide range of policies, such as entrepreneurship and technology diffusion and issues of social exclusion and urban deprivation. The two Committees select and analyse territorial data in order to produce reviews of economic performance and prospects. In 2000 the areas of focus of the Territorial Development Policy Committee included metropolitan governance.

ENVIRONMENT

The OECD Environment Directorate works in support of the Environment Policy Committee (EPOC) on environmental issues. EPOC assesses performance; encourages co-operation on environmental policy; promotes the integration of environmental and economic policies; works to develop principles, guide-lines and strategies for effective environmental management; provides a forum for member states to address common problems and share data and experience; and promotes the sharing of information with non-member states. Working parties consider a range of issues, in some cases collaborating with other Directorates (for example, the Working Parties on Trade and Environment and on Agriculture and Environment). An Experts Group on Climate Change, based in the Environment Directorate, undertakes studies related to international agreements on climate change.

In April 1998 environment ministers of member countries agreed upon a set of 'Shared Goals for Action', with four principal aims: to promote strong national policies and effective regulatory structures for the protection of the natural environment and human health; to promote an integrated policy approach, encouraging coherence among economic, environmental and social policies; to strengthen international co-operation in meeting global and regional environmental commitments; and to support participation, transparency, the provision of information and accountability in environmental policy-making at all levels. In May 2001 ministers adopted an Environmental Strategy for the 21st Century, containing recommendations for future work. The Strategy, which was to be implemented by 2010, focused on fostering sustainable development, and strengthening co-operation with non-member countries and partnerships with the private sector and civil society. Fundamental objectives included the efficient use of renewable and non-renewable resources; the avoidance of irreversible damage; the maintenance of ecosystems; and separating environmental pressures from economic growth. The Strategy identified several issues requiring urgent action, such as the generation of municipal waste, increased car and air travel, greenhouse gas emissions, groundwater pollution, and the exploitation of marine fisheries. It aimed to ensure the implementation of agreed policies and the formulation of new ones. The Environment Directorate also provides the secretariat for the Task Force for the Implementation of the Environmental Action Programme in Central and Eastern Europe, which encourages countries in Eastern Europe and the CIS to take environmental issues into consideration in the process of economic restructuring. A further part of the environment programme considers environmental data, indicators and measurement of performance. The first cycle of 32 Environmental Performance Reviews of member and selected non-member countries was completed in 2000. The second cycle commenced in 2001. The Directorate aims to improve understanding of past and future trends through the collection and dissemination of environmental data.

SCIENCE, TECHNOLOGY AND INDUSTRY

The principal objective of the Directorate for Science, Technology and Industry is to assist member countries in formulating and implementing policies that optimize the contribution of science, technology, industrial development and structural change to economic growth, employment and social development. The Committee for Scientific and Technological Policy reviews national and international policy issues relating to science and technology. It provides indicators and analysis on emerging trends in these fields, identifies and promotes best practices, and offers a forum for dialogue. Important themes include: the management and reform of science systems; the development of policies to promote the innovative capacity of members' economies; and policy responses to the globalization of science and technology.

A working party on biotechnology was established in 1993 and its mandate was renewed in 1998. Among the priority topics in its most recent work programme were scientific and technological infrastructure, and the relation of biotechnology to sustainable industrial development. In 1992 a megascience forum was established to bring together senior science policy-makers for consultations regarding large scientific projects and programmes. It was succeeded, in 1999, by the Global Science Forum. The Forum's research programme for 2002 was to include elementary particle physics, neuroinformatics, radio astronomy and the radio spectrum. In 2000 multilateral negotiations on establishing a Global Biodiversity Information Facility (GBIF) were concluded. The GBIF was to connect global biodiversity databases in order to make available a wide range of on-line data.

The Committee for Information, Computer and Communications Policy monitors developments in telecommunications and information technology and their impact on competitiveness and productivity, with a new emphasis on technological and regulatory convergence. It also promotes the development of new rules (e.g. guide-lines on information security) and analyses trade and liberalization issues. The Committee maintains a database of communications indicators and telecommunications tariffs. In December 1999 the OECD Council adopted a set of Guide-lines for Consumer Protection in the Context of Electronic Commerce. OECD's Global Conference on Telecommunications Policy for the Digital Environment, held in January 2002, stressed the importance of competition in the sector and the need for regulatory reform.

The Committee on Industry and the Business Environment focuses on industrial production; business performance; innovation and competitiveness in industrial and services sectors; and policies for private-sector development in member and selected non-member economies. In recent years the Committee has addressed issues connected with globalization, regulatory reform, small and medium-sized enterprises (SMEs), and the role of industry in sustainable development. Business and industry policy fora explore a variety of issues with the private sector and develop recommendations. Issues addressed recently include environmental strategies for industry and new technologies. A working party on SMEs conducts an ongoing review of the contribution of SMEs to growth and employment and carries out a comparative assessment of best practice policies. Databases enabling internationally comparable monitoring of structural change in areas of science and technology, investment, production, employment and trade have been prepared by a working party on statistics.

The Transport Division of the Directorate for Science, Technology and Industry considers aviation, maritime, shipbuilding, road and intermodal transport issues. A road transport research programme covers all aspects of road transport, including its integration into overall transport systems and multimodal transport strategies. Two databases on road transport research and road safety are maintained. The Maritime Transport and Steel Committees aim to promote multilateral solutions to sectoral friction and instability based on the definition and monitoring of rules. The Working Party on Shipbuilding seeks to establish normal competitive conditions in that sector, especially through dialogue with non-OECD countries. In June 1994 negotiations between leading shipbulding nations, conducted under OECD auspices, concluded a multilateral agreement to end state subsidies to the industry. However, continued failure by the US Congress to ratify the agreement disrupted its entry into force. The Tourism Committee promotes sustained growth in the tourism sector and encourages the integration of tourism issues into other policy areas.

EDUCATION, EMPLOYMENT, LABOUR AND SOCIAL AFFAIRS

The Employment, Labour and Social Affairs Committee is concerned with the development of the labour market and selective employment policies to ensure the utilization of human capital at the highest possible level and to improve the quality and flexibility of working life, as well as the effectiveness of social policies; it plays a central role in addressing OECD's concern to reduce high and persistent unemployment through the creation of high-quality jobs. The Committee's work covers such issues as the role of women in the economy, industrial relations, international migration, measurements of unemployment, and the development of an extensive social database. The Committee also carries out single-country and thematic reviews of labour-market policies and social assistance systems. It has assigned a high priority to work on the policy implications of an ageing population and on indicators of human capital investment.

The Health Policy Unit of the Employment, Labour and Social Affairs Committee's provides analysis to policymakers on health care and health expenditure issues, and analyses the organization and performance of health systems. A new OECD Health Project was launched in 2001. The Non-Member Economies and International Migration Division works on social policy issues in emerging economies and economies in transition, especially relating to education and labour market reforms and to the economic and social aspects of migration. The Education Committee analyses policies for education and training at all levels, carries out education and training policy reviews and produces education data and indicators. An adult literacy survey conducted by the Committee was concluded in June 2000. During 2001 'lifelong learning' was a priority focus area. Together, the Employment, Labour and Social Affairs and Education Committees seek to provide for the greater integration of labour market and educational policies and the prevention of social exclusion.

OECD's Centre for Educational Research and Innovation (CERI) promotes the development of research activities in education, together with experiments of an advanced nature designed to test innovations in educational systems and to stimulate research and development. A programme for the production of policy-oriented and comparable indicators of student achievement on a regular basis was established in 1998, in order to provide a profile of the knowledge, skills and competencies of students towards the end of compulsory schooling. A Programme on Educational Building provides analysis and advice on the management of educational facilities and infrastructure, while the Programme on Institutional Management in Higher Education focuses on the relation between higher education policy and the management of institutions in the sector. The Forum on Trade in Educational Services considers the implications for the educational sector of globalization. Under its work programme for 2002 CERI was to develop and analyse educational indicators and statistics, and to address innovation and the use of new technologies in schools and social exclusion in education.

RELATIONS WITH OTHER INTERNATIONAL ORGANIZATIONS

Under a Protocol signed at the same time as the OECD Convention, the European Commission generally takes part in the work of OECD. EFTA may also send representatives to OECD meetings. Formal relations exist with a number of other international organizations, including the ILO, FAO, IMF, IBRD, UNCTAD, UNIDO, WHO, IAEA, APEC and the Council of Europe. A few non-governmental organizations have been granted consultative status, notably the Business and Industry Advisory Committee to OECD (BIAC) and the Trade Union Advisory Committee to OECD (TUAC).

Finance

In 2000 OECD's total budget amounted to 1,200m. French francs.

Publications

Activities of OECD (Secretary-General's Annual Report).
Agricultural Outlook (annually).
Energy Balances (quarterly).
Energy Prices and Taxes (quarterly).
Financial Market Trends (3 a year).
Financial Statistics (Part 1 (domestic markets): monthly; Part 2 (international markets): monthly; Part 3 (OECD member countries): 25 a year).
Foreign Trade Statistics (monthly).
Higher Education Management and Policy (3 a year).
Indicators of Industry and Services Activity (quarterly).
International Trade by Commodities Statistics (5 a year).
Joint BIS-IMF-OECD-World Bank Statistics on External Debt (quarterly).
Main Developments in Trade (annually).
Main Economic Indicators (monthly).
Monthly Statistics of International Trade.
National Accounts Quarterly.
OECD Economic Outlook (2 a year).
OECD Economic Studies (2 a year).
OECD Economic Surveys (every 12 to 18 months for each country).
OECD Employment Outlook (annually).
OECD Journal of Competition Law and Policy (quarterly).
The OECD Observer (every 2 months).
Oil and Gas Statistics (quarterly).
PEB Exchange (newsletter of the Programme on Educational Building, 3 a year).
Quarterly Labour Force Statistics.
Short-term Economic Indicators: Transition Economies (quarterly).
Numerous specialized reports, working papers, books and statistics on economic and social subjects (about 130 titles a year, both in English and French) are also published.

International Energy Agency—IEA

Address: 9 rue de la Fédération, 75739 Paris Cédex 15, France.

Telephone: 1-40-57-65-00; **fax:** 1-40-57-65-59; **e-mail:** info@iea.org; **internet:** www.iea.org.

The Agency was established by the OECD Council in 1974 to develop co-operation on energy questions among participating countries.

MEMBERS

Australia	Greece	Norway*
Austria	Hungary	Portugal
Belgium	Ireland	Spain
Canada	Italy	Sweden
Czech Republic	Japan	Switzerland
Denmark	Republic of Korea	Turkey
Finland	Luxembourg	United Kingdom
France	Netherlands	USA
Germany	New Zealand	

The European Commission is also represented.

*Norway participates in the IEA under a special arrangement.

Organization

(April 2002)

GOVERNING BOARD

Composed of ministers or senior officials of the member governments. Meetings are held every two years at ministerial level and five times a year at senior official level. Decisions may be taken by a weighted majority on a number of specified subjects, particularly concerning emergency measures and the emergency reserve commitment; a simple weighted majority is required for procedural decisions and decisions implementing specific obligations in the agreement. Unanimity is required only if new obligations, not already specified in the agreement, are to be undertaken.

SECRETARIAT

The Secretariat comprises the following divisions: Standing Group on Long-Term Co-operation; Standing Group on the Oil Market; Standing Group on Emergency Questions; Committee on Energy Research and Technology (with working parties); Committee on Non-Member Countries; Coal Industry Advisory Board; and Industry Advisory Board.

Executive Director: ROBERT PRIDDLE (United Kingdom).

Activities

The Agreement on an International Energy Programme was signed in November 1974 and formally entered into force in January 1976. The Programme commits the participating countries of the International Energy Agency to share petroleum in emergencies, to strengthen their long-term co-operation in order to reduce dependence on petroleum imports, to increase the availability of information on the petroleum market, to co-operate in the development and co-ordination of energy policies, and to develop relations with the petroleum-producing and other petroleum-consuming countries. The IEA issues energy statistics and publications and provides information and analysis on the energy sector. It sponsors conferences, symposia and workshops to enhance international co-operation among member and non-member states.

An emergency petroleum-sharing plan has been established, and the IEA ensures that the necessary technical information and facilities are in place so that it can be readily used in the event of a reduction in petroleum supplies. The IEA undertakes emergency response reviews and workshops, and publishes an Emergency Management Manual to facilitate a co-ordinated response to a severe disruption in petroleum supplies. A separate division monitors and reports on short-term developments in the petroleum market. It also considers other related issues, including international crude petroleum pricing, petroleum trade and stock developments and investments by major petroleum-producing countries.

The IEA Long-Term Co-operation Programme is designed to strengthen the security of energy supplies and promote stability in world energy markets. It provides for co-operative efforts to conserve energy, to accelerate the development of alternative energy sources by means of both specific and general measures, to strengthen research and development of new energy technologies and to remove legislative and administrative obstacles to increased energy supplies. Regular reviews of member countries' efforts in the fields of energy conservation and accelerated development of alternative energy sources assess the effectiveness of national programmes in relation to the objectives of the Agency.

The IEA also reviews the energy situation in non-member countries, in particular the petroleum-producing countries of the Middle East and central and eastern European countries. In the latter states the IEA has provided technical assistance for the development of national energy legislation, regulatory reform and energy efficiency projects. The IEA has entered into co-operation agreements with Russia, the People's Republic of China and India.

The IEA aims to contribute to the energy security of member countries through energy technology and research and development projects, in particular those concerned with energy efficiency, conservation and protection of the environment. The IEA promotes international collaboration in this field and the participation of energy industries to facilitate the application of new technologies, through effective transfer of knowledge, technology innovation and training. Member states adopt Implementing Agreements, which provide mechanisms for collaboration and information exchange in specific areas, for example, electric vehicle technologies, electric demand-side management and photovoltaic power systems. Non-member states are encouraged to participate in these Agreements.

In recent years the IEA has increased its focus on issues related to the environment and sustainable development. In 2000 and 2001 it supported analysis of actions to mitigate climate change, studies of the implications of the Kyoto Protocol to the UN Framework Convention on Climate Change, and analysis of policies designed to reduce greenhouse gas emissions, including emissions trading. (In June/July 2000 it organized an emissions-trading simulation involving 17 countries.) The Agency also analyses the regulation and reform of energy markets, especially for electricity and gas. The IEA Regulatory Forum held in February 2002 considered the implications for security of supply and public service of competition in energy markets.

Publications

Coal Information (annually).

Electricity Information (annually).

Natural Gas Information (annually).

Oil Information (annually).

Oil Market Report (monthly).

World Energy Outlook (annually).

Reports, studies, statistics, country reviews.

OECD Nuclear Energy Agency—NEA

Address: Le Seine Saint-Germain, 12 blvd des Îles, 92130 Issy-les-Moulineaux, France.

Telephone: 1-45-24-10-10; **fax:** 1-45-24-11-10; **e-mail:** nea@nea.fr; **internet:** www.nea.fr.

The NEA was established in 1958 to further the peaceful uses of nuclear energy. Originally a European agency, it has since admitted OECD members outside Europe.

MEMBERS

All members of OECD (except New Zealand, Poland and Slovakia).

An application for membership by Slovakia is under review.

Organization

(April 2002)

STEERING COMMITTEE FOR NUCLEAR ENERGY

Meets twice a year. Comprises senior representatives of member governments, presided over by a chairman.

SECRETARIAT

Director-General: LUIS ENRIQUE ECHÁVARRI (Spain).

Deputy Director-General: CAROL KESSLER (USA).

MAIN COMMITTEES

Committee on Nuclear Regulatory Activities
Committee on Radiation Protection and Public Health
Committee on the Safety of Nuclear Installations
Committee for Technical and Economic Studies on Nuclear Energy Development and the Fuel Cycle
Nuclear Law Committee
Nuclear Science Committee
Radioactive Waste Management Committee.

NEA DATA BANK

The Data Bank was established in 1978, as a successor to the Computer Programme Library and the Neutron Data Compilation Centre. The Data Bank develops and supplies data and computer programmes for nuclear technology applications to users in laboratories, industry, universities and other areas of interest. Under the supervision of the Nuclear Science Committee, the Data Bank collates integral experimental data, and functions as part of a network of data centres to provide direct data services. It was responsible for co-ordinating the development of the Joint Evaluation Fission and Fusion (JEFF) data reference library, and works with the Radioactive Waste Management Division of the NEA on the Thermonuclear Database project (see below).

Activities

The mission of the Agency is to assist its member countries in maintaining and further developing—through international co-operation—the scientific, technological and legal bases required for the safe, environmentally-friendly and economical use of nuclear energy for peaceful purposes. The Agency maintains a continual survey with the co-operation of other organizations, notably the International Atomic Energy Agency (IAEA, see p. 148), of world uranium resources, production and demand, and of economic and technical aspects of the nuclear fuel cycle.

A major part of the Agency's work is devoted to the safety and regulation of nuclear power, including co-operative studies and projects related to the prevention of nuclear accidents and the long-term safety of radioactive waste disposal systems. It is also concerned with the harmonization of nuclear legislation and the dissemination of information on nuclear law issues. A Nuclear Development Committee provides members with statistics and analysis on nuclear resources, economics, technology and prospects. The NEA also co-operates with non-member countries of central and eastern Europe and the CIS in areas such as nuclear safety, radiation protection and nuclear law.

JOINT PROJECTS

Nuclear Safety

OECD Halden Reactor Project: Halden, Norway; experimental boiling heavy water reactor, which became an OECD project in 1958. From 1964, under successive agreements with participating countries, the reactor has been used for long-term testing of water reactor fuels and for research into automatic computer-based control of nuclear power stations. The main focus is on nuclear fuel safety and man-machine interface. Some 100 nuclear energy research institutions and authorities in 20 countries support the project.

OECD International Common Cause Data Exchange—ICDE Project: initiated in 1994 and formally operated by the NEA since April 1998; encourages multilateral co-operation in the collection and analysis of data on common cause failure (CCF) events occurring at nuclear power plants, with the aim of enabling greater understanding and prevention of such events; nine participating countries.

OECD-IPSN CABRI Water Loop Project: revised programme initiated in 2000; conducted at the Institute for Protection and Nuclear Safety (IPSN), based in France; investigates the capacity of high burn-up fuel to withstand sharp power peaks that may occur in power reactors owing to rapid reactivity insertion in the reactor core (i.e. reactivity-initiated accidents); 11 participating countries.

OECD MASCA Project: initiated in 2000 as a follow-up to the NEA-sponsored RASPLAV Project, which studied the behaviour of molten core material in a reactor pressure vessel during a severe accident; MASCA is undertaking additional tests in order to resolve remaining uncertainties related to the heat load that the reactor vessel can support during an accident involving core melt; scheduled for completion in 2003; 17 participating countries.

OECD Melt Coolability and Concrete Interaction—MCCI Project: initiated 2002; conducted at the Argonne National Laboratory, USA; aims to provide experimental data on severe accident molten core coolability and interaction with containment concrete, contributing to improved accident management; eight participating countries.

OECD SETH Project: covering the period 2001–05; conducted at the Paul Scherrer Institute PANDA facility, based in Switzerland, and the Siemens Primär Kreislauf, Germany; researches important thermal-hydraulic phenomena in support of accident management; 14 participating countries.

Bubbler Condenser Project: initiated 2002; conducted at the Electrogorsk Research and Engineering Centre, Russia; performs thermal-hydraulic and structural experiments to resolve outstanding issues surrounding the bubbler condenser function for VVER-213 reactors; six participating countries.

Sandia Lower Head Failure Project: initiated in 1999; conducted at the Sandia National Laboratory, USA; researches the rupture behaviour of the reactor pressure vessel lower head and, consequently, provides information for the development of severe accident management strategies; 8 participating countries.

Radioactive Waste Management

Co-operative Programme for the Exchange of Scientific and Technical Information Concerning Nuclear Installation Decommissioning Projects Programme: initiated in 1985; promotes exchange of technical information and experience for ensuring that safe, economic and optimum environmental options for decommissioning are used; 12 participating countries.

Sorption Project: phase II commenced in 2000; comprises benchmark exercises co-ordinated by the NEA; aims to evaluate various approaches used to model sorption phenomena in the context of performance assessments of geologic disposal concepts for the disposal of radioactive waste in deep geological formations; 10 participating countries and 16 participating organizations.

Thermonuclear Database—TDB Project: phase II commenced in 1998; aims to develop a quality-assured, comprehensive thermodynamic database of selected chemical elements for use in the safety assessment of radioactive waste repositories; data are selected by review teams; 13 participating countries and 17 participating organizations.

Radiation Protection

Information System on Occupational Exposure—ISOE: initiated in 1992 and co-sponsored by the IAEA; maintains largest database world-wide on occupational exposure to ionizing radiation at nuclear power plants; participants: 452 reactors in 28 countries; the system also contains information from 39 nuclear reactors which are either defunct or actively decommissioning.

Finance

The Agency's annual budget amounts to €11m.

Publications

Annual Report.

NEA News (2 a year).

Nuclear Energy Data (annually).

Nuclear Law Bulletin (2 a year).

Publications on a range of issues relating to nuclear energy, reports and proceedings.

ORGANIZATION FOR SECURITY AND CO-OPERATION IN EUROPE—OSCE

Address: 1010 Vienna, Kärntner Ring 5–7, Austria.

Telephone: (1) 514-36-0; **fax:** (1) 514-36-105; **e-mail:** info@osce.org; **internet:** www.osce.org.

The OSCE was established in 1972 as the Conference on Security and Co-operation in Europe (CSCE), providing a multilateral forum for dialogue and negotiation. It produced the Helsinki Final Act of 1975 on East–West relations (see below). The areas of competence of the CSCE were expanded by the Charter of Paris for a New Europe (1990), which transformed the CSCE from an *ad hoc* forum to an organization with permanent institutions, and the Helsinki Document 1992 (see 'Activities'). In December 1994 the summit conference adopted the new name of OSCE, in order to reflect the Organization's changing political role and strengthened secretariat. The OSCE has 55 participating states and comprises all the recognized countries of Europe, and Canada, the USA and all the former republics of the USSR.

PARTICIPATING STATES

Albania	Greece	Portugal
Andorra	Hungary	Romania
Armenia	Iceland	Russia
Austria	Ireland	San Marino
Azerbaijan	Italy	Slovakia
Belarus	Kazakhstan	Slovenia
Belgium	Kyrgyzstan	Spain
Bosnia and Herzegovina	Latvia	Sweden
Bulgaria	Liechtenstein	Switzerland
Canada	Lithuania	Tajikistan
Croatia	Luxembourg	Turkey
Cyprus	Macedonia, former Yugoslav republic	Turkmenistan
Czech Republic	Malta	Ukraine
Denmark	Moldova	United Kingdom
Estonia	Monaco	USA
Finland	Netherlands	Uzbekistan
France	Norway	Vatican City (Holy See)
Georgia	Poland	Yugoslavia*
Germany		

* The Federal Republic of Yugoslavia, suspended from the CSCE in July 1992, was admitted to the OSCE in November 2000.

Organization

(April 2002)

SUMMIT CONFERENCES

Heads of state or government of OSCE participating states normally meet every two years to set priorities and political orientation of the Organization. The most recent conference was held in İstanbul, Turkey, in November 1999.

MINISTERIAL COUNCIL

The Ministerial Council (formerly the Council of Foreign Ministers) comprises ministers of foreign affairs of member states. It is the central decision-making and governing body of the OSCE and meets at least once a year.

SENIOR COUNCIL

The Senior Council (formerly the Council of Senior Officials—CSO) is responsible for the supervision, management and co-ordination of OSCE activities. Member states are represented by senior political officers, who convene at least twice a year in Prague, Czech Republic, and once a year as the Economic Forum.

PERMANENT COUNCIL

The Council, which is based in Vienna, is responsible for day-to-day operational tasks. Members of the Council, comprising the permanent representatives of member states to the OSCE, convene weekly. The Council is the regular body for political consultation and decision-making, and may be convened for emergency purposes.

FORUM FOR SECURITY CO-OPERATION—FSC

The FSC, comprising representatives of delegations of member states, meets weekly in Vienna to negotiate and consult on measures aimed at strengthening security and stability throughout Europe. Its main objectives are negotiations on arms control, disarmament, and confidence- and security-building; regular consultations and intensive co-operation on matters related to security; and the further reduction of the risks of conflict. The FSC is also responsible for the implementation of confidence- and security-building measures (CSBMs); the preparation of seminars on military doctrine; the holding of annual implementation assessment meetings; and the provision of a forum for the discussion and clarification of information exchanged under agreed CSBMs.

CHAIRMAN-IN-OFFICE—CIO

The CIO is vested with overall responsibility for executive action. The position is held by a minister of foreign affairs of a member state for a one-year term. The CIO may be assisted by a troika, consisting of the preceding, current and succeeding chairpeople; *ad hoc* steering groups; or personal representatives, who are appointed by the CIO with a clear and precise mandate to assist the CIO in dealing with a crisis or conflict.

Chairman-in-Office: ANTONIO MARTINS DA CRUZ (Portugal).

SECRETARIAT

In 2000 the Secretariat was restructured on the basis of two departments: the Conflict Prevention Centre (including an Operations Centre), which focuses on the support of the CIO in the implementation of OSCE policies, in particular the monitoring of field activities and co-operation with other international bodies; and the Department for Support Services and Budget, responsible for technical and administrative support activities. The OSCE maintains an office in Prague, Czech Republic, which assists with documentation and information activities, and a liaison office in Central Asia, based in Tashkent, Uzbekistan.

The position of Secretary-General was established in December 1992 and the first appointment to the position was made in June 1993. The Secretary-General is the representative of the CIO and is responsible for the management of OSCE structures and operations.

Secretary-General: JÁN KUBIŠ (Slovakia).

HIGH COMMISSIONER ON NATIONAL MINORITIES

Address: POB 20062, 2500 EB The Hague, Netherlands.

Telephone: (70) 3125500; **fax:** (70) 3635910; **e-mail:** hcnm@hcnm.org; **internet:** www.osce.org/hcnm.

The establishment of the office of High Commissioner on National Minorities was proposed in the 1992 Helsinki Document, and endorsed by the Council of Foreign Ministers in Stockholm in December 1992. The role of the High Commissioner is to identify ethnic tensions that might endanger peace, stability or relations between OSCE participating states, and to promote their early resolution. The High Commissioner may issue an 'early warning' for the attention of the Senior Council of an area of tension likely to degenerate into conflict. The High Commissioner is appointed by the Ministerial Council, on the recommendation of the Senior Council, for a three-year term.

High Commissioner: ROLF EKÉUS (Sweden).

OFFICE FOR DEMOCRATIC INSTITUTIONS AND HUMAN RIGHTS—ODIHR

Address: Aleje Ujazdowskie 19, 00-517 Warsaw, Poland.

Telephone: (22) 520-06-00; **fax:** (22) 520-06-05; **e-mail:** office@odihr.osce.waw.pl; **internet:** www.osce.org.odihr.

The ODIHR, which was originally called the Office for Free Elections with a mandate to promote multiparty democracy, was assigned major new tasks under the Helsinki Document 1992, including responsibility for promoting human rights, democracy and the rule of law. The Office provides a framework for the exchange of information on and the promotion of democracy-building, respect for human rights and elections within OSCE states. In addition, it co-ordinates the monitoring of elections and provides expertise and training on constitutional and legal matters.

Director: GÉRARD STOUDMANN (Switzerland).

OFFICE OF THE REPRESENTATIVE ON FREEDOM OF THE MEDIA

Address: 1010 Vienna, Kärntner Ring 5–7, Austria.

Telephone: (1) 512-21-450; **fax:** (1) 512-21-459; **e-mail:** pmfom@osce.org; **internet:** www.osce.org/fom.

The office was founded in 1998 to strengthen the implementation of OSCE commitments regarding free, independent and pluralistic media.

Representative: FREIMUT DUVE (Germany).

PARLIAMENTARY ASSEMBLY

Address: Rädhusstraede 1, 1466 Copenhagen K, Denmark.

Telephone: 33-37-80-40; **fax:** 33-37-80-30; **e-mail:** osce@oscepa.dk; **internet:** www.osce.org/pa.

The OSCE Parliamentary Assembly, which is composed of 317 parliamentarians from 55 participating countries, was inaugurated in July 1992, and meets annually. The Assembly comprises a Standing Committee, a Bureau and three General Committees and is supported by a Secretariat in Copenhagen, Denmark.

President: ADRIAN SEVERIN (Romania).

Secretary-General: R. SPENCER OLIVER.

OSCE Related Bodies

COURT OF CONCILIATION AND ARBITRATION

Address: 266 route de Lausanne, 1292 Chambésy, Geneva, Switzerland.

Telephone: (22) 7580025; **fax:** (22) 7582510; **e-mail:** cca.osce@bluewin.ch.

The establishment of the Court of Conciliation and Arbitration was agreed in 1992 and effected in 1994. OSCE states that have ratified the OSCE Convention on Conciliation and Arbitration may submit a dispute to the Court for settlement by the Arbitral Tribunal or the Conciliation Commission.

President: ROBERT BADINTER.

JOINT CONSULTATIVE GROUP—JCG

The states that are party to the Treaty on Conventional Armed Forces in Europe (CFE), which was concluded within the CSCE framework in 1990, established the Joint Consultative Group (JCG). The JCG, which meets in Vienna, addresses questions relating to compliance with the Treaty; enhancement of the effectiveness of the Treaty; technical aspects of the Treaty's implementation; and disputes arising out of its implementation. There are currently 30 states participating in the JCG.

OPEN SKIES CONSULTATIVE COMMISSION

The Commission represents all states parties to the 1992 Treaty on Open Skies, and promotes its implementation. Its regular meetings are serviced by the OSCE secretariat.

Activities

In July 1990 heads of government of the NATO member countries proposed to increase the role of the CSCE 'to provide a forum for wider political dialogue in a more united Europe'. In November heads of government of the participating states signed the Charter of Paris for a New Europe, which undertook to strengthen pluralist democracy and observance of human rights, and to settle disputes between participating states by peaceful means. At the summit meeting the Treaty on Conventional Armed Forces in Europe (CFE), which had been negotiated within the framework of the CSCE, was signed by the member states of NATO (q.v.) and of the Warsaw Pact. The Treaty limits non-nuclear air and ground armaments in the signatory countries. It was decided at the same meeting to establish a permanent secretariat, which opened in February 1991, in Prague, Czechoslovakia. (The secretariat was moved to Vienna, Austria, in 1993.) It was also decided to create a Conflict Prevention Centre, which was established in Vienna, Austria, in March 1991, and an Office for Free Elections (later renamed the Office for Democratic Institutions and Human Rights), which was established in Warsaw, Poland, in July. In April parliamentarians from the CSCE countries agreed on the creation of a pan-European parliamentary assembly. Its first session was held in Budapest, Hungary, in July 1992.

The Council of Foreign Ministers met for the first time in Berlin, Germany, in June 1991. The meeting adopted a mechanism for consultation and co-operation in the case of emergency situations, to be implemented by the Council of Senior Officials (CSO, which was subsequently renamed the Senior Council). A separate mechanism regarding the prevention of the outbreak of conflict was also adopted, whereby a country can demand an explanation of 'unusual military activity' in a neighbouring country. These mechanisms were utilized in July in relation to the armed conflict in Yugoslavia between the Republic of Croatia and the Yugoslav Government. The CSCE appealed to all parties involved in the conflict to uphold a cease-fire. In mid-August a meeting of the CSO resolved to reinforce the CSCE's mission in Yugoslavia considerably and requested all the parties involved in the conflict to begin negotiations as a matter of urgency. In September the CSO agreed to impose an embargo on the export of armaments to Yugoslavia. In October the CSO resolved to establish an observer mission to monitor the observance of human rights in Yugoslavia.

In 1993 the First Implementation Meeting on Human Dimension Issues (the CSCE term used with regard to issues concerning human rights and welfare) took place. The Meeting, for which the ODIHR serves as a secretariat, provides a now annual forum for the exchange of news regarding OSCE commitments in the fields of human rights and democracy.

In January 1992 the Council of Foreign Ministers agreed that the Conference's rule of decision-making by consensus was to be altered to allow the CSO to take appropriate action against a participating state 'in cases of clear and gross violation of CSCE commitments'. This development was precipitated by the conflict in Yugoslavia, where the Yugoslav Government was held responsible by the majority of CSCE states for the continuation of hostilities. It was also agreed at the meeting that the CSCE should undertake fact-finding and conciliation missions to areas of tension, with the first such mission to be sent to Nagornyi Karabakh, the largely Armenian-populated enclave in Azerbaijan.

In March 1992 CSCE participating states reached agreement on a number of confidence-building measures, including commitments to exchange technical data on new weapons systems; to report activation of military units; and to prohibit military activity involving very large numbers of troops or tanks. Later in that month at a meeting of the Council of Foreign Ministers, which opened the Helsinki Follow-up Conference, the members of NATO and the former members of the Warsaw Pact (with Russia, Belarus, Ukraine and Georgia taking the place of the USSR) signed the Open Skies Treaty. Under the treaty, aerial reconnaissance missions by one country over another were permitted, subject to regulation. An Open Skies Consultative Commission was subsequently established (see above).

The Federal Republic of Yugoslavia (Serbia and Montenegro) was suspended from the CSCE immediately prior to the summit meeting of heads of state and government that took place in Helsinki, Finland, in July 1992. The meeting adopted the Helsinki Document 1992, in which participating states defined the terms of future CSCE peace-keeping activities. Conforming broadly to UN practice, peace-keeping operations would be undertaken only with the full consent of the parties involved in any conflict and only if an effective cease-fire were in place. The CSCE may request the use of the military resources of NATO, WEU, the EU, the CIS or other international bodies. (NATO and WEU had recently changed their constitutions to permit the use of their forces for CSCE purposes.) The Helsinki Document declared the CSCE a 'regional arrangement' in the sense of Chapter VIII of the UN's Charter, which states that such a regional grouping should attempt to resolve a conflict in the region before referring it to the Security Council. In December 1993 a Permanent Committee (now renamed the Permanent Council) was established in Vienna, providing for greater political consultation and dialogue through its weekly meetings. In December 1994 the summit conference redesignated the CSCE as the Organization for Security and Co-operation in Europe—OSCE, and endorsed the role of the Organization as the primary instrument for early warning, conflict prevention and crisis management in the region. The conference adopted a 'Code of Conduct on Politico-Military Aspects of Security', which set out principles to guide the role of the armed forces in democratic societies. The summit conference that was held in Lisbon, Portugal, in December 1996 agreed to adapt the CFE Treaty, in order to further arms reduction negotiations on a national and territorial basis. The conference also adopted the 'Lisbon Declaration on a Common and Comprehensive Security Model for Europe for the 21st Century' (see below), committing all parties to pursuing measures to ensure regional security. A Security Model Committee was established and began to meet regularly during 1997 to consider aspects of the Declaration, including the identification of risks and challenges to future European security; enhancing means of joint co-operative action within the OSCE framework in the event of non-compliance with OSCE commitments by participating states; considering other new arrangements within the OSCE framework that could reinforce security and stability in Europe; and defining a basis of co-operation between the OSCE and other relevant organizations to co-ordinate security enforcement. In November 1997 the Office of the Representative on Freedom of the Media was established in Vienna, to support the OSCE's activities in this field.

In November 1999 OSCE heads of state and of government, convened in İstanbul, Turkey, signed a new Charter for European Security, which aimed to formalize existing norms regarding the observance of human rights and to strengthen co-operation with other organizations and institutions concerned with international security. The Charter focused on measures to improve the operational capabilities of the OSCE in early warning, conflict prevention, crisis management and post-conflict rehabilitation. Accordingly, Rapid Expert Assistance and Co-operation (REACT) teams were to be established to enable the organization to respond rapidly to requests from participating states for assistance in crisis situations. The REACT programme became operational in April 2001. At the İstanbul meeting a revised CFE Treaty was also signed, providing for a stricter system of limitations and increased transparency, which was to be open to other OSCE states not currently signatories. The US and EU governments determined to delay ratification of the Agreement of the Adaptation of the Treaty until Russian troop levels in the Caucasus had been reduced.

In April 2000 the OSCE High Commissioner on National Minorities issued a report reviewing the problems confronting Roma and Sinti populations in OSCE member states. A programme of assistance for the Roma communities of south-eastern Europe was initiated in April 2001. In February 2001 the ODIHR established an Anti-Trafficking Project Fund to help to finance its efforts to combat trafficking in human beings. In November 2000 an OSCE Document on Small Arms and Light Weapons was adopted, aimed at curtailing the spread of armaments in member states. A workshop on implementation of the Document was held in February 2002. In July 2001 the OSCE Parliamentary Assembly adopted a resolution concerned with strengthening transparency and accountability within the Organization. The Secretary-General condemned major terrorist attacks perpetrated in September against targets in the USA, allegedly by militant Islamist fundamentalists. In early October OSCE member states unanimously adopted a statement in support of the developing US-led global coalition against international terrorism. Meanwhile, the Organization determined to establish a working group on terrorism to draft an action plan on counter-terrorism measures. In December the Ministerial Council, meeting in Romania, approved the 'Bucharest Action Plan' outlining the Organization's contribution to countering terrorism. A Personal Representative for Terrorism was appointed by the CIO in January 2002 to co-ordinate the implementation of the initiatives. Later in December 2001 OSCE sponsored, with the UN Office for Drug Control and Crime Prevention, an International Conference on Security and Stability in Central Asia, held in Bishek, Kyrgyzstan. The meeting, which was attended by representatives of more than 60 countries and organizations, was concerned with strengthening efforts to counter terrorism and providing effective support to the Central Asian states.

OSCE MISSIONS AND FIELD ACTIVITIES

In early 2002 there were long-term OSCE missions in Bosnia and Herzegovina, Croatia, Georgia, the former Yugoslav republic of Macedonia, Moldova, Tajikistan, the Federal Republic of Yugoslavia, and Kosovo. (OSCE Missions to Latvia and Estonia were terminated at the end of 2001.) The OSCE was also undertaking field activities in Albania, Armenia, Azerbaijan, Belarus, Chechnya, Kazakhstan, Kyrgyzstan, Turkmenistan, and Uzbekistan. The OSCE has institutionalized structures to assist in the implementation of certain bilateral agreements. At April 2002 there were OSCE representatives to the Russian-Latvian Joint Commission on Military Pensioners and to the Estonian Government Commission on Military Pensioners.

In August 1995 the CIO appointed a Personal Representative concerned with the conflict between Armenia and Azerbaijan in the Nagornyi Karabakh region. The OSCE provided a framework for discussions between the two countries through its 11-nation Minsk Group, which from early 1997 was co-chaired by France, Russia and the USA. In October 1997 Armenia and Azerbaijan reached agreement on OSCE proposals for a political settlement; however, the concessions granted by the Armenian President, Levon Ter-Petrossian, which included the withdrawal of troops from certain strategic areas of Nagornyi Karabakh precipitated his resignation in February 1998. The proposals were rejected by his successor, Robert Kocharian. Nevertheless, meetings of the Minsk Group continued in 1998 and both countries expressed their willingness to recommence negotiations. The then CIO, Bronisław Geremek, met with the leaders of both countries in November and persuaded them to exchange prisoners of war. In July 1999 the OSCE Permanent Council approved the establishment of an Office in Yerevan (Armenia), which began operations in February 2000. The Office works independently of the Minsk Group, to promote OSCE principles within the country in order to support political and economic stability. It aims to contribute to the development of democratic institutions and to the strengthening of civil society. An Office in Baku (Azerbaijan) opened in July 2000. In November 2001 the Office in Yerevan presented a report on trafficking in human beings in Armenia, which had been compiled as a joint effort by the OSCE, IOM and UNICEF. In March 2002 the CIO visited the region to discuss prospects for peace, and the OSCE's role in the process.

In January 1995 Russia agreed to an OSCE proposal to send a fact-finding mission to assist in the conflict between the Russian authorities and an independence movement in Chechnya. The mission criticized the Russian army for using excessive force against Chechen rebels and civilians; reported that violations of human rights had been perpetrated by both sides in the conflict; and urged Russia to enforce a cease-fire to allow the delivery of humanitarian supplies by international aid agencies to the population of the city. An OSCE Assistance Group to Chechnya mediated between the two sides, and, in July, brokered a cease-fire agreement between the Russian military authorities in Chechnya and the Chechen rebels. A further peace accord was signed, under the auspices of the OSCE, in May 1996, but the truce was broken in July. A more conclusive cease-fire agreement was signed by the two parties to the conflict in August. In January 1997 the OSCE assisted in the preparation and monitoring of general elections conducted in Chechnya. The Assistance Group remained in the territory to help with post-conflict rehabilitation, including the promotion of democratic institutions and respect for human rights. In December 1998, however, the Assistance Group relocated from its headquarters in Groznyi (also known as Dzokhar from March of that year) to Moscow, owing to the deteriorating security situation. It continued to co-ordinate the delivery of humanitarian aid and implementation of other assistance projects. In September 1999, in response to resurgent separatist activity, Russian launched a military offensive against Chechnya. In early November an OSCE mission arrived in the neighbouring republic of Ingushetia to assess the condition and needs of the estimated 200,000 refugees who had fled the hostilities; however, the officials were prevented by the Russian authorites from travelling into Chechnya. The issue dominated the OSCE summit meeting, held in İstanbul, Turkey, later in that month. The meeting insisted upon a political solution to the conflict and called for an immediate cease-fire. An agreement was reached with the Russian President to allow the CIO to visit the region, and to an OSCE role in initiating political dialogue. In February 2000 the CIO welcomed the Russian Government's appointment of a Presidential Representative for Human Rights in Chechnya. In June 2001 the Assistance Group to Chechnya resumed operations inside the territory from a new office in Znamenskoye. An OSCE/ODIHR delegation visited Chechnya during that month to evaluate the prevailing humanitarian and human rights situation.

In December 1999 the Permanent Council, at the request of the Government of Georgia expanded the mandate of the existing OSCE Mission to Georgia to include monitoring that country's border with Chechnya. The first permanent observation post opened in February 2000 and the monitoring team was fully deployed by July. In December 2001 the Permanent Council approved an expansion in the border monitoring mission to cover the border between Georgia and Ingushetia. The OSCE Mission to Georgia was established in 1992 to work towards a political settlement between disputing factions within the country. Since 1994 the Mission has contributed to efforts to define the political status of South Ossetia and has supported UN peace-keeping and human rights activities in Abkhazia.

In late 1996 the OSCE declared the constitutional referendum held in Belarus in November to be illegal and urged that country's Government to ensure political freedoms and respect for human rights. In September 1997 the Permanent Council determined to establish an OSCE Advisory and Monitoring Group to assist with the process of democratization; the Group commenced operations in February 1998. It has subsequently been active in strengthening civil society, organizing training seminars and workshops in electoral practices, monitoring the human rights situation, including the registration of political parties and the development of an independent media, and in mediating between the President and opposition parties. In October the OSCE Parliamentary Assembly formed an *ad hoc* Committee on Belarus, to act as a working group to support and intensify the organization's work in the country. The OSCE/ODIHR declared legislative elections held in Belarus in October 2000 not to have been conducted freely and fairly, and pronounced that presidential elections held in September 2001 had not met the standards required by the Organization.

An OSCE Mission to Moldova was established in February 1993, in order to assist the conflicting parties to pursue negotiations on a political settlement, as well as to observe the military situation in the region and to provide advice on issues of human and minority rights, democratization and the repatriation of refugees. In December 1999 the Permanent Council, with the approval of the Russian Government, authorized an expansion of the Mission's mandate to ensure the full removal and destruction of Russian ammunition and armaments and to co-ordinate financial and technical assistance for the withdrawal of foreign troops and the destruction of weapons. In June 2001 the Mission established a tripartite working group, with representatives of the Russian Ministry of Defence and the local authorities in Transdniestrian to assist and support the process of disposal of munitions.

In 1999 an OSCE Project Co-ordinator in Ukraine was established, following the successful conclusion of the OSCE Mission to Ukraine (which had been established in November 1994). The Project Co-ordinator is responsible for pursuing co-operation between Ukraine and the OSCE and providing technical assistance in areas including legal reform, freedom of the media, trafficking in human rights, and the work of the human rights Ombudsman. In April 2002 an ODIHR Election Observation Mission monitored parliamentary elections held in Ukraine.

In March 1997 the OSCE dispatched a fact-finding mission to Albania to help restore political and civil stability, which had been undermined by the collapse of national pyramid saving schemes at the start of the year. At the end of that month the Permanent Council agreed to establish an OSCE Presence in Albania. OSCE efforts focused on reaching a political consensus on new legislation for the conduct of forthcoming elections to establish a government of national reconciliation. Voting took place in June/July, with 500 OSCE observers providing technical electoral assistance and helping to monitor the voting. In December the Permanent Council confirmed that the Presence should provide the framework for co-ordinating other international efforts in the country. In March 1998 the OSCE Presence was mandated to monitor the country's borders with the Kosovan region of southern Serbia and to prevent any spillover effects from the escalating crisis. This role was reduced following the political settlement for Kosovo and Metohija concluded in mid-1999. In June 1998 the OSCE observed local elections in Albania. It became the Co-Chair, with the EU, of the Friends of Albania group, which then brought together countries and international bodies concerned with the situation in Albania for the first time in September. (The sixth annual meeting of the group was held in April 2002.) In October 1998 the Permanent Council determined to enhance the Presence's role in border-monitoring activities. With other organizations, the OSCE was involved in the preparation of the country's draft constitution, finalized in October, and an ODIHR Election Observation Mission was established to observe the referendum on the constitution held in November. The OSCE Presence in Albania has subsequently provided advice and support to the Albanian Government regarding democratization, the rule of law, the media, human rights, election preparation and monitoring, and the development of civil society. It supports an Economics and Environment Office. The Presence also monitors the Government's weapons collection programme.

The OSCE Mission to Bosnia and Herzegovina was established in December 1995 to achieve the objectives of the peace accords for the former Yugoslavia, in particular to oversee the process of democratization. The OSCE's efforts to organize and oversee the Bosnian national elections, which were held on 14 September 1996, was the largest-ever electoral operation undertaken by the organization, with some 1,200 electoral observers deployed. The OSCE subsequently monitored Bosnian municipal elections, twice rescheduled by the organization and eventually held in September 1997, and the elections to the National Assembly of the Serb Republic and to the Bosnian Serb presidency in November. In 1998 the mission was charged with organizing the second post-war general elections in Bosnia and Herzegovina (comprising elections to the legislature of Bosnia and Herzegovina, the Federation and the Serb Republic, and to the presidencies of Bosnia and Herzegovina and the Serb Republic). The mission assisted with the registration of voters and, in September, was responsible for the supervision of the elections at polling stations within and outside the country. The final results of the election to the Bosnian Serb presidency were delayed, owing to the unexpected victory of an extreme nationalist which, it was feared, could jeopardize the peace process. The OSCE immediately emphasized the necessity of maintaining the process. It also insisted on the need to transfer responsibility for the electoral process to the national authorities for future elections. In March 1999 the OSCE initiated an educational campaign relating to new election laws. However a permanent electoral legal framework had not been approved by the time of legislative elections held in November 2000; the OSCE was therefore active in both preparing and monitoring these. The Mission's responsibility for elections in the country ended in November 2001 when a new permanent Election Commission was inaugurated. However, it was to continue to provide support for the Commission's secretariat. Other key areas of Mission activity continued to be the promotion of democratic values, monitoring and promoting respect for human rights, and implementation of arms control and security-building measures. An Agreement on Regional Arms Control was signed in 1995, providing for confidence- and security-building measures and a reduction in excess armaments. The Mission has established consultative commissions to promote dialogue among military personnel from different entities within the country. An audit of the entities' defence budgets was conducted in 2001.

The OSCE Mission to Croatia was established in April 1996 to provide assistance and expertise in the field of human and minority rights, and to assist in the implementation of legislation and the development of democratic institutions. The Mission's mandate was extended in June 1997 in order to enhance its capacity to protect human rights, in particular the rights of minorities, to monitor the return and treatment of refugees and displaced persons, and to make specific recommendations to the Croatian authorities. In March 1998, following the integration of the disputed region into Croatia, the OSCE criticized the conditions imposed by the Croatian Government for the return of Serb refugees, stating that the right to return to one's own country was inalienable and must not depend on the fulfilment of conditions. The Mission conducts extensive field monitoring to facilitate the return of refugees and displaced persons. In October 1998 the Mission assumed the responsibilities of the United Nations Police Support Group (UNPSG). The OSCE Police Monitoring Group, comprising a maximum of 120 unarmed OSCE civilian police monitors, was deployed in the region, representing the Organization's first police-monitoring role. The Group was terminated in October 2000, although the OSCE was to continue to advise on and monitor police activities in Croatia. The OSCE was also to be responsible for monitoring the border regions, with particular concern for customs activities. The OSCE/ODIHR monitored legislative and presidential elections held in Croatia in January 2000. Local government elections were held in May 2001.

In mid-1998 the OSCE was involved in the mediation effort to resolve the conflict between the Serbian authorities and ethnic Albanian separatists in the formerly autonomous province of Kosovo and Metohija. In October, following months of diplomatic effort and the threat of NATO air strikes, Yugoslav President Slobodan Milošević agreed to comply with UN Security Council Resolution 1199, which required an immediate cease-fire, Serbian troop withdrawals, the commencement of meaningful peace negotiations, and unrestricted access for humanitarian aid. Under a peace plan proposed by the US special envoy, Richard Holbrooke, President Milošević agreed to the formation of a 2,000-member OSCE Kosovo Verification Mission (KVM) to monitor compliance, in addition to surveillance flights by unarmed NATO aircraft. The KVM was to patrol the region to ensure the withdrawal of Serbian military and police units, and to oversee the safe return of refugees and the non-harassment of ethnic Albanian inhabitants. It was also to monitor border control activities and accompany police units in Kosovo, when necessary, to assist them to perform their normal policing roles. The mission's mandate was formally established on 25 October 1998 for a period of one year. Upon achievement of a political settlement defining the area's self-government, and its subsequent implementation, the KVM was to be responsible for supervising elections in Kosovo, assisting in the establishment of democratic institutions and developing a Kosovo police force. The long-term mission was accepted in return for the eventual removal of Yugoslavia's suspension from the OSCE. However, sporadic fighting continued in the province, and the monitoring force began unofficially to assume a peace-keeping role. In January 1999 the KVM successfully negotiated for the release of eight Yugoslav soldiers held hostage by the separatist forces. Later in that month following the KVM's denunciation of the killing of some 45 ethnic Albanians by Serbian security forces in the village of Racak, President Milošević ordered the head of the mission, William Walker, to leave the region. This was later revoked. Meanwhile, OSCE monitors were forced to withdraw from Racak under fire from Serbian troops. An emergency meeting of the OSCE in Vienna agreed to maintain the mission. However, on 19 March, following the failure of negotiations to resolve the crisis, the CIO decided to evacuate the 1,380 unarmed monitors, owing to the deteriorating security situation in Kosovo. NATO commenced an aerial offensive against Yugoslavia in late March. In early April the CIO condemned the mass expulsion of ethnic Albanians from Kosovo and other violations of human rights committed by Serbian forces. Later in the same month the CIO, at a meeting of a ministerial troika attended by the Secretary-General, announced that the OSCE was willing to assist in the implementation of a political settlement in Kosovo. The OSCE was also concerned with measures to prevent the crisis affecting the other Balkan states. Within the framework of a political settlement for Kosovo, which was formally concluded in June, the OSCE (whose Mission in Kosovo, mandated to comprise 1,400 personnel, was established on 1 July) was responsible for democracy- and institution-building under the auspices of the UN Interim Administration Mission for Kosovo (UNMIK). OSCE monitors were deployed to assess the human rights situation throughout the region, and in August a new OSCE-administered police training school was inaugurated. (By the end of 2001 5,700 police officers had trained under the OSCE police education programme.) In December 1999 the OSCE published a report on the situation in Kosovo, which confirmed that Serbian forces had conducted systematic abuses of human rights but also raised suspicion against the KLA for organizing retribution attacks against Serbian civilians later in the year. In February 2000 the OSCE Mission established an Institute for Civil Administration to train public officials in principles of democratic governance. A Kosovo Law Centre was established in June to provide technical assistance to the legal community, with a view to promoting democratic principles and human rights. In the following month the Department for Democratic Governance and Civil Society was established by UNMIK, and was to be administered by the OSCE Mission. In August an Ombudsperson, nominated by the OSCE, was appointed to a new Office of the Ombudsperson, which became operational in November: the role of the Ombudsperson was to investigate and mediate claims of human rights violations arising within Kosovo. The OSCE was responsible for registering about 1m. voters prior to municipal elections that were held in Kosovo in October. During 2001 the Mission assisted the registration process for voting in a general election, and supervised the polling which took place in November. In early 2002 the Mission initiated training sessions for members of the new Kosovo Assembly. At that time the Mission was restructured, consolidating the number of field offices from 21 to nine.

In November 2000 the Federal Republic of Yugoslavia (FRY) was admitted into the OSCE. An OSCE Mission to the FRY, to assist in the areas of democracy and protection of human rights and in the restructing and training of law enforcement agencies and the judiciary, was approved by the Permanent Council in January 2001 and inaugurated in March. In March 2002 members of the Mission were facilitating the census process in southern Serbia.

The OSCE Spillover Monitor Mission to Skopje was established in 1992 to help to prevent the conflict in the former Yugoslavia from destabilizing the former Yugoslav republic of Macedonia (FYRM). Its principal mandate is to monitor the border region, as well as monitoring human rights and promoting the development of democratic institutions, including an independent media. The Mission is also concerned with mediating between inter-ethnic groups in the country, and has provided support for implementation of a framework political agreement signed in August 2001 through the deployment of international confidence-building monitors and police advisers. In December OSCE monitors accompanied multi-ethnic police officers to areas of early conflict, as part of the August agreement. In March 2002 OSCE signed its first memorandum of understanding with the European Commission, in respect to policing operations in FYRM.

In March 2000 the OSCE adopted a Regional Strategy for South-Eastern Europe, aimed at enhancing co-operation amongst its presences in the region. The OSCE was actively involved in co-ordinating the Stability Pact for South-Eastern Europe, which was initiated, in June 1999, as a collaborative plan of action by the EU, Group of Seven industrialized nations and Russia (the G-8), regional governments and other organizations concerned with the stability of the region. (This can be accessed at www.stabilitypact.org.) A meeting of participants in the Pact was convened to coincide with the OSCE summit meeting, held in November. In October 2001 the OSCE organized a Stability Pact regional conference, held in Bucharest, Romania. A memorandum of understanding between the OSCE Mission to the FRY and the Stability Pact was signed in December.

The OSCE Mission to Tajikistan was established in December 1993, and began operations in February 1994. The Mission worked with the UN Mission of Observers to Tajikistan (UNMOT) to promote a peace process in that country, and was a guarantor of the peace agreement concluded in June 1997. The Mission remained actively concerned with promoting respect for human rights, assisting the development of the local media, locating missing persons, and the fair distribution of humanitarian aid. Following multi-party parliamentary elections, held in February 2000, the Mission's focus was to be on post-conflict rehabilitation. In April 2002 the Mission initiated a one-year project to promote access to environmental information and network-building among young people concerned with ecology.

In December 2000 the Permanent Council renamed the OSCE Liaison Office in Central Asia the OSCE Centre in Tashkent. The Centre aims to promote OSCE principles within Uzbekistan; it also functions as an information exchange between OSCE bodies and participating Central Asian states and as a means of liaising with OSCE presences in the region. In July 1998 the Permanent Council determined to open OSCE Centres in Bishkent (Kyrgyzstan), Almaty (Kazakhstan), and Ashgabad (Turkmenistan), all of which opened in January 1999. In general the Centres were to encourage each country's integration into the OSCE, and implementation of its principles, and to focus on the economic, environmental, human and political aspects of security. In January 2000, for the first time, the OSCE refused to dispatch official observers to monitor presidential elections in a member state, owing to concerns about the legitimacy of elections held in Kazakhstan. Subsequently the Centre in Almaty, with the ODIHR and the OSCE Parliamentary Assembly, initiated a round table on elections project to improve electoral legislation, thus strengthening the political system. The project concluded in January 2002, when participants presented a list of recommendations to the national parliament.

Japan, the Republic of Korea and Thailand have the status of 'partners for co-operation' with the OSCE, while Algeria, Egypt, Israel, Jordan, Morocco and Tunisia are 'Mediterranean partners for co-operation'. Regular consultations are held with these countries in order to discuss security issues of common concern.

Finance

All activities of the institutions, negotiations, *ad hoc* meetings and missions are financed by contributions from member states. The budget for 2001 amounted to €198m., of which some 84% was allocated to OSCE missions and field activities.

Publications

Annual Report of the Secretary-General.

Decision Manual (annually).

OSCE Handbook (annually).

OSCE Newsletter (monthly).

Summary of the Final Act of the Helsinki Conference on Security and Co-operation in Europe

(1 August 1975)

Note: The substantive articles relating to defence and security in Europe are contained in the first part of the Final Act. Other chapters incorporate provisions relating to Co-operation in the field of economics, science and technology, and the environment, Questions relating to security and co-operation in the Mediterranean, and Co-operation in humanitarian and other fields (including human contacts, information, culture and education).

Motivated by the political will, in the interest of peoples, to improve and intensify their relations and to contribute in Europe to peace, security, justice and co-operation as well as to rapprochement among themselves and with the other States of the world,

Determined, in consequence, to give full effect to the results of the Conference and to assure, among their States and throughout Europe, the benefits deriving from those results and thus to broaden, deepen and make continuing and lasting the process of détente,

The High Representatives of the participating States have solemnly adopted the following:

QUESTIONS RELATING TO SECURITY IN EUROPE

The States participating in the Conference on Security and Co-operation in Europe,

Reaffirming their objective of promoting better relations among themselves and ensuring conditions in which their people can live in true and lasting peace free from any threat to or attempt against their security;

Convinced of the need to exert efforts to make détente both a continuing and an increasingly viable and comprehensive process, universal in scope, and that the implementation of the results of the Conference on Security and Co-operation in Europe will be a major contribution to this process;

Considering that solidarity among peoples, as well as the common purpose of the participating States in achieving the aims as set forth by the Conference on Security and Co-operation in Europe, should lead to the development of better and closer relations among them in all fields and thus to overcoming the confrontation stemming from the character of their past relations, and to better mutual understanding;

Mindful of their common history and recognizing that the existence of elements common to their traditions and values can assist them in developing their relations, and desiring to search, fully taking into account the individuality and diversity of their positions and views, for possibilities of joining their efforts with a view to overcoming distrust and increasing confidence, solving the problems that separate them and co-operating in the interest of mankind;

Recognizing the indivisibility of security in Europe as well as their common interest in the development of co-operation throughout Europe and among selves and expressing their intention to pursue efforts accordingly;

Recognizing the close link between peace and security in Europe and in the world as a whole and conscious of the need for each of them to make its contribution to the strengthening of world peace and security and to the promotion of fundamental rights, economic and social progress and well-being for all peoples;

Have adopted the following:

1.(a) Declaration on Principles Guiding Relations between Participating States

The participating States,

Reaffirming their commitment to peace, security and justice and the continuing development of friendly relations and co-operation; . . .

Declare their determination to respect and put into practice, each of them in its relations with all other participating States, irrespective of their political, economic or social systems as well as of their size, geographical location or level of economic development, the following principles, which all are of primary significance, guiding their mutual relations:

I. Sovereign equality, respect for the rights inherent in sovereignty.

The participating States will respect each other's sovereign equality and individuality as well as all the rights inherent in and encompassed by its sovereignty, including in particular the right of every State to juridical equality, to territorial integrity and to freedom and political independence. They will also respect each other's right freely to choose and develop its political, social, economic and cultural systems as well as its right to determine its laws and regulations.

Within the framework of international law, all the participating States have equal rights and duties. They will respect each other's right to define and conduct as it wishes its relations with other States in accordance with international law and in the spirit of the present Declaration. They consider that their frontiers can be changed, in accordance with international law, by peaceful means and by agreement. They also have the right to belong or not to belong to international organizations, to be or not to be a party to bilateral or multilateral treaties including the right to be or not to be a party to treaties of alliance; they also have the right to neutrality.

II. Refraining from the threat or use of force.

The participating States will refrain in their mutual relations, as well as in their international relations in general, from the threat or use of force against the territorial integrity or political independence of any State, or in any other manner inconsistent with the purposes of the United Nations and with the present Declaration. No consideration may be invoked to serve to warrant resort to the threat or use of force in contravention of this principle.

Accordingly, the participating States will refrain from any acts constituting a threat of force or direct or indirect use of force against another participating State.

Likewise they will refrain from any manifestation of force for the purpose of inducing another participating State to renounce the full exercise of its sovereign right. Likewise they will also refrain in their mutual relations from any act of reprisal by force.

No such threat or use of force will be employed as a means of settling disputes, or questions likely to give rise to disputes, between them.

III. Inviolability of frontiers.

The participating States regard as inviolable all one another's frontiers as well as the frontiers of all States in Europe and therefore they will refrain now and in the future from assaulting these frontiers.

Accordingly, they will also refrain from any demand for, or act of, seizure and usurpation of part or all of the territory of any participating State.

IV. Territorial integrity of States.

The participating States will respect the territorial integrity of each of the participating States.

Accordingly, they will refrain from any action inconsistent with the purposes and principles of the Charter of the United Nations against the territorial integrity, political independence or the unity of any participating State, and in particular from any such action constituting a threat or use of force.

The participating States will likewise refrain from making each other's territory the object of military occupation or other direct or indirect measures of force in contravention of international law, or the object of acquisition by means of such measures or the threat of them. No such occupation or acquisition will be recognized as legal.

V. Peaceful settlement of disputes.

The participating States will settle disputes among them by peaceful means in such a manner as not to endanger international peace and security, and justice.

They will endeavour in good faith and a spirit of co-operation to reach a rapid and equitable solution on the basis of international law.

For this purpose they will use such means as negotiation, enquiry, mediation, conciliation, arbitration, judicial settlement or other peaceful means of their own choice including any settlement procedure agreed to in advance of disputes to which they are parties.

In the event of failure to reach a solution by any of the above peaceful means, the parties to a dispute will continue to seek a mutually agreed way to settle the dispute peacefully.

Participating States, parties to a dispute among them, as well as other participating States, will refrain from any action which might aggravate the situation to such a degree as to endanger the maintenance of international peace and security and thereby make a peaceful settlement of the dispute more difficult.

VI. Non-intervention in internal affairs.

The participating States will refrain from any intervention, direct or indirect, individual or collective, in the internal or external affairs falling within the domestic jurisdiction of another participating State, regardless of their mutual relations.

They will accordingly refrain from any form of armed intervention or threat of such intervention against another participating State.

They will likewise in all circumstances refrain from any other act of military, or of political, economic or other coercion designed to subordinate to their own interest the exercise by another participating State of the rights inherent in its sovereignty and thus to secure advantages of any kind.

Accordingly, they will, *inter alia*, refrain from direct or indirect assistance to terrorist activities, or to subversive or other activities directed towards the violent overthrow of the regime of another participating State.

VII. Respect for human rights and fundamental freedoms, including the freedom of thought, conscience, religion or belief.

The participating States will respect human rights and fundamental freedoms, including the freedom of thought, conscience, religion or belief, for all without distinction as to race, sex, language or religion.

They will promote and encourage the effective exercise of civil, political, economic, social, cultural and other rights and freedoms all of which derive from the inherent dignity of the human person and are essential for his free and full development.

Within this framework the participating States will recognize and respect the freedom of the individual to profess and practice, alone or in community with others, religion or belief acting in accordance with the dictates of his own conscience.

The participating States on whose territory national minorities exist will respect the right of persons belonging to such minorities to equality before the law, will afford them the full opportunity for the actual enjoyment of human rights and fundamental freedoms and will, in this manner, protect their legitimate interests in this sphere.

The participating States recognize the universal significance of human rights and fundamental freedoms, respect for which is an essential factor for the peace, justice and well-being necessary to ensure the development of friendly relations and co-operation among themselves as among all States.

They will constantly respect these rights and freedoms in their mutual relations and will endeavour jointly and separately, including in co-operation with the United Nations, to promote universal and effective respect for them.

They confirm the right of the individual to know and act upon his rights and duties in this field.

In the field of human rights and fundamental freedoms, the participating State will act in conformity with the purposes and principles of the Charter of the United Nations and with the Universal Declaration of Human Rights. They will also fulfil their obligations as set forth in the international declarations and agreements in this field, including *inter alia* the International Covenants on Human Rights, by which they may be bound.

VIII. Equal rights and self-determination of peoples.

The participating States will respect the equal rights of peoples and their right to self-determination, acting at all times in conformity with the purposes and principles of the Charter of the United Nations and with the relevant norms of international law, including those relating to territorial integrity of states.

By virtue of the principle of equal rights and self-determination of peoples, all peoples always have the right, in full freedom, to determine, when and as they wish, their internal and external political status, without external interference, and to pursue as they wish their political, economic, social and cultural development.

The participating States reaffirm the universal significance of respect for and effective exercise of equal rights and self-determination of peoples for the development of friendly relations among themselves as among all States; they also recall the importance of the elimination of any form of violation of this principle.

IX. Co-operation among States.

The participating States will develop their co-operation with one another and with all States in all fields in accordance with the purposes and principles of the Charter of the United Nations. In developing their co-operation the participating States will place special emphasis on the fields as set forth within the framework of the Conference on Security and Co-operation in Europe, with each of them making its contribution in conditions of full equality.

They will endeavour, in developing their co-operation as equals, to promote mutual understanding and confidence, friendly and good-neighbourly relations among themselves, international peace, security and justice. They will equally endeavour, in developing their co-operation, to improve the well-being of peoples and contribute to the fulfilment of their aspirations through, *inter alia*, the benefits resulting from increased mutual knowledge and from progress and achievement in the economic, scientific, technological, social, cultural and humanitarian fields. They will take steps to promote conditions favourable to making these benefits available to all; they will take into account the interest of all in the narrowing of differences in the levels of economic development, and in particular the interest of developing countries throughout the world.

They confirm that governments, institutions, organizations and persons have a relevant and positive role to play in contributing toward the achievement of these aims of their co-operation.

They will strive, in increasing their co-operation as set forth above, to develop closer relations among themselves on an improved and more enduring basis for the benefit of peoples.

X. Fulfilment in good faith of obligations under international law.

The participating States will fulfil in good faith their obligations under international law, both those obligations arising from the generally recognized principles and rules of international law and those obligations arising from treaties or other agreements, in conformity with international law, to which they are parties.

In exercising their sovereign rights, including the right to determine their laws and regulations, they will conform, with their legal obligations under international law; they will furthermore pay due regard to and implement the provisions in the Final Act of the Conference on Security and Co-operation in Europe.

The participating States confirm that in the event of a conflict between the obligations of the members of the United Nations under the Charter of the United Nations and their obligations under any treaty or other international agreement, their obligations under the Charter will prevail, in accordance with Article 103 of the Charter of the United Nations.

All the principles set forth above are of primary significance and, accordingly, they will be equally and unreservedly applied, each of them being interpreted taking into account the others.

The participating States express their determination fully to respect and apply these principles, as set forth in the present Declaration, in all aspects, to their mutual relations and co-operation in order to ensure to each participating State the benefits resulting from the respect and application of these principles by all.

The participating States, paying due regard to the principles above and, in particular, to the first sentence of the tenth principle, 'Fulfilment in good faith of obligations under international law', note that the present Declaration does not affect their rights and obligations, nor the corresponding treaties and other agreements and arrangements.

The participating States express the conviction that respect for these principles will encourage the development of normal and friendly relations and the progress of co-operation among them in all fields. They also express the conviction that respect for these principles will encourage the development of political contacts among them which in time would contribute to better mutual understanding of their positions and views.

The participating States declare their intention to conduct their relations with all other States in the spirit of the principles contained in the present Declaration.

1.(b) Matters related to giving effect to certain of the above Principles

(i) The participating States,

Reaffirming that they will respect and give effect to refraining from the threat or use of force and convinced of the necessity to make it an effective norm of international life,

Declare that they are resolved to respect and carry out, in their relations with one another, *inter alia*, the following provisions which are in conformity with the Declaration on Principles Guiding Relations between Participating States:

–To give effect and expression, by all the ways and forms which they consider appropriate, to the duty to refrain from the threat or use of force in their relations with one another.

–To refrain from any use of armed forces inconsistent with the purposes and principles of the Charter of the United Nations and the provisions of the Declaration on Principles Guiding Relations between Participating States, against another participating State, in particular from invasion of or attack on its territory.

–To refrain from any manifestation of force for the purpose of inducing another participating State to renounce the full exercise of its sovereign rights.

–To refrain from any act of economic coercion designed to subordinate to their own interest the exercise by another participating State of the rights inherent in its sovereignty and thus to secure advantages of any kind.

–To take effective measures which by their scope and by their nature constitute steps towards the ultimate achievement of general and complete disarmament under strict and effective international control.

–To promote, by all means which each of them considers appropriate, a climate of confidence and respect among peoples consonant with their duty to refrain from propaganda for wars of aggression or for any threat or use of force inconsistent with the purposes of the United Nations and with the Declaration on Principles Guiding Relations between Participating States, against another participating State.

–To make every effort to settle exclusively by peaceful means any dispute between them, the continuance of which is likely to endanger the maintenance of international peace and security in Europe, and to seek, first of all, a solution through the peaceful means set forth in Article 33 of the United Nations Charter.

To refrain from any action which could hinder the peaceful settlement of disputes between the participating States.

(ii) The participating States,

Reaffirming their determination to settle their disputes as set forth in the Principle of Peaceful Settlement of Disputes;

Convinced that the peaceful settlement of disputes is a complement to refraining from the threat or use of force, both being essential though not exclusive factors for the maintenance and consolidation of peace and security;

Desiring to reinforce and to improve the methods at their disposal for the peaceful settlement of disputes;

1. Are resolved to pursue the examination and elaboration of a generally acceptable method for the peaceful settlement of disputes aimed at complementing existing methods, and to continue to this end to work upon the 'Draft Convention on a European System for the Peaceful Settlement of Disputes' submitted by Switzerland during the second stage of the Conference on Security and Co-operation in Europe, as well as other proposals relating to it and directed towards the elaboration of such a method.
2. Decide that, on the invitation of Switzerland, a meeting of experts of all the participating States will be convoked in order to fulfil the mandate described in paragraph 1 above within the framework and under the procedures of the follow-up to the Conference laid down in the chapter 'Follow-up to the Conference'.
3. This meeting of experts will take place after the meeting of the representatives appointed by the Ministers of Foreign Affairs of the participating States, scheduled according to the chapter 'Follow-up to the Conference' for 1977; the results of the work of this meeting of experts will be submitted to Governments.

2. Document on confidence-building measures and certain aspects of security and disarmament

The participating States,

Desirous of eliminating the causes of tension that may exist among them and thus of contributing to the strengthening of peace and security in the world;

Determined to strengthen confidence among them and thus to contribute to increasing stability and security in Europe;

Determined further to refrain in their mutual relations, as well as in their international relations in general, from the threat or use of force against the territorial integrity or political independence of any State, or in any other manner inconsistent with the purposes of the United Nations and with the Declaration on Principles Guiding Relations between Participating States as adopted in this Final Act;

Recognizing the need to contribute to reducing the dangers of armed conflict and of misunderstanding or miscalculation of military activities which could give rise to apprehension, particularly in a situation where the participating States lack clear and timely information about the nature of such activities;

Taking into account considerations relevant to efforts aimed at lessening tension and promoting disarmament;

Recognizing that the exchange of observers by invitation at military manoeuvres will help to promote contacts and mutual understanding;

Having studied the question of prior notification of major military movements in the context of confidence-building;

Recognizing that there are other ways in which individual States can contribute further to their common objectives;

Convinced of the political importance of prior notification of major military manoeuvres for the promotion of mutual understanding and the strengthening of confidence, stability and security;

Accepting the responsibility of each of them to promote these objectives and to implement this measure, in accordance with the accepted criteria and modalities, as essentials for the realization of these objectives;

Recognizing that this measure deriving from political decision rests upon a voluntary basis;

Have adopted the following:

I. Prior notification of major military manoeuvres.

They will notify their major military manoeuvres to all other participating States through usual diplomatic channels in accordance with the following provisions:

Notification will be given of major military manoeuvres exceeding a total of 25,000 troops, independently or combined with any possible air or naval components (in this context the word 'troops' includes amphibious and airborne troops). In the case of independent manoeuvres of amphibious or airborne troops, or of combined manoeuvres involving them, these troops will be included in this total. Furthermore, in the case of combined manoeuvres which do not reach the above total but which involve land forces together with significant numbers of either amphibious or airborne troops, or both, notification can also be given.

Notification will be given of major military manoeuvres which take place on the territory, in Europe, of any participating State as well as, if applicable, in the adjoining sea area and air space.

In the case of a participating State whose territory extends beyond Europe, prior notification need be given only of manoeuvres which take place in an area within 250 km from its frontier facing or shared with any other European participating State, the participating State need not, however, give notification in cases in which that area is also contiguous to the participating State's frontier facing or shared with a non-European non-participating State.

Notification will be given 21 days or more in advance of the start of the manoeuvre or in the case of a manoeuvre arranged at shorter notice at the earliest possible opportunity prior to its starting date.

Notification will contain information of the designation, if any, the general purpose of and the States involved in the manoeuvre, the type or types and numerical strength of the forces engaged, the area and estimated time-frame of its conduct. The participating States will also, if possible, provide additional relevant information, particularly that related to the components of the forces engaged and the period of involvement of these form.

Prior notification of other military manoeuvres.

The participating States recognize that they can contribute further to strengthening confidence and increasing security and stability, and to this end may also notify smaller-scale military manoeuvres to other participating States, with special regard for those near the area of such manoeuvres.

To the same end, the participating States also recognize that they may notify other military manoeuvres conducted by them.

Exchange of observers.

The participating States will invite other participating States, voluntarily and on a bilateral basis, in a spirit of reciprocity and goodwill towards all participating States, to send observers to attend military manoeuvres.

The inviting State will determine in each case the number of observers, the procedures and conditions of their participation, and give other information which it may consider useful. It will provide appropriate facilities and hospitality.

The invitation will be given as far ahead as is conveniently possible through usual diplomatic channels.

Prior notification of major military movements.

In accordance with the Final Recommendations of the Helsinki Consultations the participating States studied the question of prior-notification of major military movements as a measure to strengthen confidence.

Accordingly, the participating States recognize that they may, at their own discretion and with a view to contributing to confidence-building, notify their major military movements.

In the same spirit, further consideration will be given by the States participating in the Conference on Security and Co-operation in Europe to the question of prior notification of major military movements, bearing in mind, in particular, the experience gained by the implementation of the measures which are set forth in this document.

Other confidence-building measures.

The participating States recognize that there are other means by which their common objectives can be promoted.

In particular, they will, with due regard to reciprocity and with a view to better mutual understanding, promote exchanges by invitation among their military delegations.

In order to make a fuller contribution to their common objective of confidence-building, the participating States, when conducting their military activities in the area covered by the provisions for the prior notification of major military manoeuvres, will duly take into account and respect this objective.

They also recognize that the experience gained by the implementation of the provisions set forth above, together with further efforts, could lead to developing and enlarging measures aimed at strengthening confidence.

II. Questions relating to disarmament.

The participating States recognize the interest of all of them in efforts aimed at lessening military confrontation and promoting disarmament which are designed to complement political détente in Europe and to strengthen their security. They are convinced of the necessity to take effective measures in these fields which by their scope and by their nature constitute steps towards the ultimate achievement of general and complete disarmament under strict and effective international control, and which should result in strengthening peace and security throughout the world.

III. General considerations.

Having considered the views expressed on various subjects related to the strengthening of security in Europe through joint efforts aimed at promoting détente and disarmament, the participating States, when engaged in such efforts, will, in this context, proceed, in particular, from the following essential considerations:

–The complementary nature of the political and military aspects of security;

–The interrelation between the security of each participating State and security in Europe as a whole and the relationship which exists, in the broader context of world security, between security in Europe and security in the Mediterranean area;

–Respect for the security interests of all States participating in the Conference on Security and Co-operation in Europe inherent in their sovereign equality;

–The importance that participants in negotiating fora see to it that information about relevant developments, progress and results is provided on an appropriate basis to other States participating in the Conference on Security and Co-operation in Europe and, in return, the justified interest of any of those States in having their views considered.

Lisbon Declaration on a Common and Comprehensive Security Model for Europe for the Twenty-first Century

(December 1996)

1. We, the Heads of State or Government of the States participating in the OSCE and meeting in Lisbon, believe that history has offered us an unprecedented opportunity. Freedom, democracy and co-operation among our nations and peoples are now the foundation for our common security. We are determined to learn from the tragedies of the past and to translate our vision of a co-operative future into reality by creating a common security space free of dividing lines in which all States are equal partners.

2. We face serious challenges, but we face them together. They concern the security and sovereignty of States as well as the stability of our societies. Human rights are not fully respected in all OSCE States. Ethnic tension, aggressive nationalism, violations of the rights of persons belonging to national minorities, as well as serious difficulties of economic transition, can threaten stability and may also spread to other States. Terrorism, organized

crime, drug and arms trafficking, uncontrolled migration and environmental damage are of increasing concern to the entire OSCE community.

3. Drawing strength from our diversity, we shall meet these challenges together, through the OSCE and in partnership with other international organizations. Our approach is one of co-operative security based on democracy, respect for human rights, fundamental freedoms and the rule of law, market economy and social justice. It excludes any quest for domination. It implies mutual confidence and the peaceful settlement of disputes.

4. The OSCE plays a central role in achieving our goal of a common security space. Its fundamental elements—the comprehensiveness and indivisibility of security and the allegiance to shared values, commitments and norms of behaviour—inspire our vision of empowering governments and individuals to build a better and more secure future.

5. We recognize that, within the OSCE, States are accountable to their citizens and responsible to each other for their implementation of OSCE commitments.

6. We jointly commit ourselves:
–to act in solidarity to promote full implementation of the principles and commitments of the OSCE enshrined in the Helsinki Final Act, the Charter of Paris and other CSCE/OSCE documents;
–to consult promptly—in conformity with our OSCE responsibilities and making full use of the OSCE's procedures and instruments—with a participating State whose security is threatened and to consider jointly actions that may have to be undertaken in defence of our common values;
–not to support participating States that threaten or use force in violation of international law against the territorial integrity or political independence of any participating State;
–to attach importance to security concerns of all participating States irrespective of whether they belong to military structures or arrangements.

7. We reaffirm the inherent right of each and every participating State to be free to choose or change its security arrangements, including treaties of alliance, as they evolve. Each participating State will respect the rights of all others in this regard. They will not strengthen their security at the expense of the security of other States. Within the OSCE, no State, organization or grouping can have any superior responsibility for maintaining peace and stability in the OSCE region, or regard any part of the OSCE region as its sphere of influence.

8. We shall ensure that the presence of foreign troops on the territory of a participating State is in conformity with international law, the freely expressed consent of the host State, or a relevant decision of the United Nations Security Council.

9. We are committed to transparency in our actions and in our relations with one another. All our States participating in security arrangements will take into consideration that such arrangements should be of a public nature, predictable and open, and should correspond to the needs of individual and collective security. These arrangements must not infringe upon the sovereign rights of other States and will take into account their legitimate security concerns.

We may use the OSCE as a repository for declarations and agreements in regard to our security arrangements.

10. Based on these foundations, our task now is to enhance our co-operation for the future. To this end:
–We encourage bilateral or regional initiatives aimed at developing relations of good neighbourliness and co-operation. In this context, the OSCE could explore a menu of confidence- and security-building measures in support of regional security processes. We shall continue to follow the implementation of the Pact on Stability in Europe. Regional round tables can be a useful means of preventive diplomacy.
–As an important contribution to security we reaffirm our determination to fully respect and implement all our commitments relating to the rights of persons belonging to national minorities. We reaffirm our will to co-operate fully with the High Commissioner on National Minorities. We are ready to respond to a request by any participating State seeking solutions to minority issues on its territory.
–We value our co-operation with regions adjacent to the OSCE region, giving particular attention to the Mediterranean area.
–We commit ourselves to the continuation of the arms control process as a central security issue in the OSCE region.

The further strengthening of stability through conventional arms control will be decisive for future European security. We reaffirm the importance of the CFE Treaty and welcome the decision of the CFE States Parties to adapt it to a changing security environment in Europe so as to contribute to common and indivisible security.

We welcome the decisions on the 'Framework for Arms Control' and on the 'Development of the Agenda of the Forum for Security Co-operation' adopted by the Forum for Security Co-operation. We are determined to make further efforts in this Forum in order to jointly address common security concerns of participating States and to pursue the OSCE's comprehensive and co-operative concept of indivisible security.

In this context, we reaffirm that we shall maintain only such military capabilities as are commensurate with individual or collective legitimate security needs, taking into account rights and obligations under international law. We shall determine our military capabilities on the basis of national democratic procedures, in a transparent manner, bearing in mind the legitimate security concerns of other States as well as the need to contribute to international security and stability.
–We reaffirm that European security requires the widest co-operation and co-ordination among participating States and European and transatlantic organizations. The OSCE is the inclusive and comprehensive organization for consultation, decision-making and co-operation in its region and a regional arrangement under Chapter VIII of the United Nations Charter. As such it is particularly well suited as a forum to enhance co-operation and complementarity among such organizations and institutions. The OSCE will act in partnership with them, in order to respond effectively to threats and challenges in its area.

In exceptional circumstances the participating States may jointly decide to refer a matter to the United Nations Security Council on behalf of the OSCE whenever, in their judgement, action by the Security Council may be required under the relevant provision of Chapter VII of the Charter of the United Nations.
–The OSCE will strengthen co-operation with other security organizations which are transparent and predictable in their actions, whose members individually and collectively adhere to OSCE principles and commitments, and whose membership is based on open and voluntary commitments.

11. Our work on the Security Model is well under way and will actively continue. We instruct our representatives to work energetically on the Security Model and invite the Chairman-in-Office to report to the next Ministerial Council in Copenhagen. The agenda for their work will include the following:
–continuing review of the observance of OSCE principles and implementation of commitments to ensure progress toward the goals of the OSCE and towards the work outlined in this agenda;
–enhancing instruments of joint co-operative action within the OSCE framework in the event of non-compliance with the OSCE commitments by a participating State;
–defining in a Platform for Co-operative Security modalities for co-operation between the OSCE and other security organizations as set out above;
–based on the experience of OSCE instruments for preventive diplomacy and conflict prevention, refining the existing tools and developing additional ones in order to encourage participating States to make greater use of the OSCE in advancing their security;
–enhancing co-operation among participating States to develop further the concepts and principles included in this Declaration and to improve our ability to meet specific risks and challenges to security;
–recommending any new commitments, structures or arrangements within the OSCE framework which would reinforce security and stability in Europe.

Drawing on this work, remaining committed to the Helsinki Final Act and recalling the Charter of Paris, we will consider developing a Charter on European Security which can serve the needs of our peoples in the new century.

12. Our goal is to transform our search for greater security into a mutual effort to achieve the aspirations and improve the lives of all our citizens. This quest, grounded in pragmatic achievements as well as ideals, will draw on the flexible and dynamic nature of the OSCE and its central role in ensuring security and stability.

ORGANIZATION OF AFRICAN UNITY—OAU

Address: Roosevelt St, Old Airport Area, POB 3243, Addis Ababa, Ethiopia.

Telephone: (1) 517700; **fax:** (1) 517844; **internet** www.oau-oua.org.

The Organization was founded in 1963 to promote unity and solidarity among African states. In May 2001 the Constitutive Act of the African Union entered into force. The African Union was to become fully operational, replacing the OAU, in July 2002; during the intervening transitional period the OAU Charter was to remain in effect.

FORMATION

There were various attempts at establishing an inter-African organization before the OAU Charter was drawn up. In November 1958 Ghana and Guinea (later joined by Mali) drafted a Charter which was to form the basis of a Union of African States. In January 1961 a conference was held at Casablanca, attended by the heads of state of Ghana, Guinea, Mali, Morocco, and representatives of Libya and of the provisional government of the Algerian Republic (GPRA). Tunisia, Nigeria, Liberia and Togo declined the invitation to attend. An African Charter was adopted and it was decided to set up an African Military Command and an African Common Market.

Between October 1960 and March 1961 three conferences were held by French-speaking African countries, at Abidjan, Brazzaville and Yaoundé, Cameroon. None of the 12 countries that attended these meetings had been present at the Casablanca Conference. These conferences led eventually to the signing in September 1961, at Tananarive, of a charter establishing the Union africaine et malgache, later the Organisation commune africaine et mauricienne (OCAM).

In May 1961 a conference was held at Monrovia, Liberia, attended by the heads of state or representatives of 19 countries: Cameroon, Central African Republic, Chad, Congo Republic (ex-French), Côte d'Ivoire, Dahomey, Ethiopia, Gabon, Liberia, Madagascar, Mauritania, Niger, Nigeria, Senegal, Sierra Leone, Somalia, Togo, Tunisia and Upper Volta. Meeting again (with the exception of Tunisia and with the addition of the ex-Belgian Congo Republic) in January 1962 at Lagos, Nigeria, they established a permanent secretariat and a standing committee of finance ministers, and accepted a draft charter for an Organization of Inter-African and Malagasy States.

It was the Conference of Addis Ababa, convened in 1963, which finally brought together African states despite the regional, political and linguistic differences that divided them. The foreign ministers of 32 African states attended the Preparatory Meeting held in mid-May: Algeria, Burundi, Cameroon, Central African Republic, Chad, Congo (Brazzaville) (now Republic of the Congo), Congo (Léopoldville) (now Democratic Republic of the Congo), Côte d'Ivoire, Dahomey (now Benin), Ethiopia, Gabon, Ghana, Guinea, Liberia, Libya, Madagascar, Mali, Mauritania, Morocco, Niger, Nigeria, Rwanda, Senegal, Sierra Leone, Somalia, Sudan, Tanganyika (now Tanzania), Togo, Tunisia, Uganda, the United Arab Republic (Egypt) and Upper Volta (now Burkina Faso).

The topics discussed by the meeting were: (i) creation of the Organization of African States; (ii) co-operation among African states in the following fields: economic and social; education, culture and science; collective defence; (iii) decolonization; (iv) apartheid and racial discrimination; (v) effects of economic grouping on the economic development of Africa; (vi) disarmament; (vii) creation of a Permanent Conciliation Commission; and (viii) Africa and the United Nations.

The Heads of State Conference which opened on 23 May 1963 drew up the Charter of the Organization of African Unity, which was then signed by the heads of 30 states on 25 May. The Charter was essentially functional and reflected a compromise between the concept of a loose association of states favoured by the Monrovia Group and the federal idea supported by the Casablanca Group, and in particular by Ghana.

In May 1994 the Abuja Treaty Establishing the African Economic Community (signed in June 1991) entered into force. The formation of the Community was expected to be a gradual process, to be completed by 2028.

In May 2001 the Constitutive Act of the African Union entered into force. It was envisaged that the Union would be inaugurated, and would thus replace the OAU, one year after the endorsement of the Act, which occurred in July. The Union was to strengthen and advance the process of African political and economic integration initiated by the OAU. The terms of the Constitutive Act provided for the institution of a supreme body, an executive council of foreign ministers, a court of justice and a central bank. Meanwhile, it was also envisaged that the process of implementing the Abuja Treaty would be accelerated. A protocol to the Abuja Treaty establishing a Pan-African Parliament was opened for signature in March 2001.

MEMBERS*

Algeria
Angola
Benin
Botswana
Burkina Faso
Burundi
Cameroon
Cape Verde
Central African Republic
Chad
The Comoros
Congo, Democratic Republic†
Congo, Republic
Côte d'Ivoire
Djibouti
Egypt
Equatorial Guinea
Eritrea
Ethiopia
Gabon
The Gambia
Ghana
Guinea
Guinea-Bissau
Kenya
Lesotho
Liberia
Libya
Madagascar
Malawi
Mali
Mauritania
Mauritius
Mozambique
Namibia
Niger
Nigeria
Rwanda
São Tomé and Príncipe
Senegal
Seychelles
Sierra Leone
Somalia
South Africa
Sudan
Swaziland
Tanzania
Togo
Tunisia
Uganda
Zambia
Zimbabwe

* The Sahrawi Arab Democratic Republic (SADR–Western Sahara) was admitted to the OAU in February 1982, following recognition by 26 of the then 50 members, but its membership was disputed by Morocco and other states which claimed that a two-thirds majority was needed to admit a state whose existence was in question. Morocco withdrew from the OAU with effect from November 1985.

† Known as Zaire between 1971 and 1997.

Organization

(April 2002)

ASSEMBLY OF HEADS OF STATE

The Assembly of Heads of State and Government meets annually to co-ordinate policies of African states. Resolutions are passed by a two-thirds majority, procedural matters by a simple majority. A chairman is elected at each meeting from among the members, to hold office for one year.

Chairman (2001/02): LEVY MWANAWASA (Zambia).

COUNCIL OF MINISTERS

Consists of ministers of foreign affairs and others and meets twice a year, with provision for extraordinary sessions. Each session elects its own Chairman. Prepares meetings of, and is responsible to, the Assembly of Heads of State.

GENERAL SECRETARIAT

The permanent headquarters of the organization. It carries out functions assigned to it in the Charter of the OAU and by other agreements and treaties made between member states. Departments: Political; Finance; Education, Science, Culture and Social Affairs; Economic Development and Co-operation; Administration and Conferences. The Secretary-General is elected for a four-year term by the Assembly of Heads of State.

Secretary-General: AMARA ESSY (Côte d'Ivoire).

ARBITRATION COMMISSION

Commission of Mediation, Conciliation and Arbitration: Addis Ababa; f. 1964; consists of 21 members elected by the Assembly of Heads of State for a five-year term; no state may have more than one member; has a Bureau consisting of a President and two Vice-Presidents, who shall not be eligible for re-election. Its task is to hear and settle disputes between member states by peaceful means.

SPECIALIZED COMMISSIONS

There are specialized commissions for economic, social, transport and communications affairs; education, science, culture and health; defence; human rights; and labour.

Finance

Member states contribute in accordance with their United Nations assessment. No member state is assessed for an amount exceeding 20% of the yearly regular budget of the Organization. The budget for 2001–02 was US $31m. At February 2001 member states owed some $39m. in outstanding contributions. By that time the following countries had had their voting rights in the Organization suspended owing to outstanding arrears: Burundi, Central African Republic, Chad, Comoros, Democratic Republic of the Congo, Equatorial Guinea, Guinea-Bissau, Liberia, Niger, São Tomé and Príncipe, Seychelles, and Sierra Leone.

Principal Events, 1991–2002

1991

June The Assembly of Heads of State signed the Abuja Treaty Establishing an African Economic Community (AEC). The Treaty was to enter into force after ratification by two-thirds of OAU member states. The Community was to be established by 2028, following a gradual six-phase process involving the co-ordination, harmonization and progressive integration of the activities of all existing and future sub-regional economic unions. The main policy-making organ of the AEC was to be an Economic and Social Council. The meeting also established a committee of heads of state to assist national reconciliation in Ethiopia; and gave a mandate to the OAU Secretary-General to undertake a mission to assist in restoring political stability in Somalia.

1992

Feb.–March The OAU was involved, together with the UN and the Organization of the Islamic Conference (OIC, q.v.), in mediation between the warring factions in Mogadishu, Somalia. The OAU subsequently continued to assist in efforts to achieve a peace settlement in Somalia.

May An OAU mission was dispatched to South Africa to monitor the continued violence in that country.

June–July Proposals were advanced at the Assembly of Heads of State, held in Dakar, Senegal, for a mechanism to be established within the OAU for 'conflict management, prevention and resolution'. These proposals were accepted in principle; operational details were to be elaborated at a later stage.

Oct. The *Ad Hoc* Committee on Southern Africa met in Gaborone, Botswana, to discuss a report compiled by a team of OAU experts on practical steps to be taken towards the democratization of South Africa. Plans to send a mission to monitor the Mozambican peace accord were announced.

1993

May A Pan-African Conference on Reparations for the suffering caused by colonialism in Africa, organized by the OAU together with the Nigerian Government, was held in Abuja. The Conference appealed to those countries which had benefited from the colonization of Africa and the use of Africans as slaves (particularly European countries and the USA) to make reparations to Africans and their descendants, either in the form of capital transfers, or cancellation of debt.

June Eritrea was admitted as the 52nd member of the OAU. The 29th Assembly of Heads of State authorized the establishment of a mechanism for conflict prevention and resolution. The mechanism's primary objective was to be anticipation and prevention of conflict. In cases where conflicts had already occurred, the OAU was to undertake peace-making and peace-building activities, including the deployment of civilian or military monitoring missions. However, in the case of a conflict seriously degenerating, assistance would be sought from the United Nations.

Sept. The OAU announced the immediate removal of economic sanctions against South Africa, following the approval by that country's Parliament of a bill to establish a transitional executive council prior to the democratic elections, scheduled to be conducted in April 1994.

Oct. The OAU Secretary-General condemned an attempted military coup in Burundi, in which the President and six Cabinet ministers were killed, and the subsequent civil unrest.

Nov. A summit conference of African ministers of foreign affairs, conducted in Addis Ababa, resolved to establish a 200-member OAU protection and observation mission to Burundi, and appealed for international financial and material support to assist the mission.

Dec. A meeting of 11 African Heads of State approved the establishment of a Peace Fund to finance the mechanism for conflict prevention, management and resolution, and called for contributions from the international community.

1994

Feb. The Council of Ministers reaffirmed its support for the results of elections in Burundi, which were conducted in 1993, and endorsed the establishment of an OAU mission to promote dialogue and national reconciliation in that country. The Council condemned anti-government forces for the escalation of violence in Angola.

April The OAU mission to South Africa participated as observers of the electoral process. An OAU delegation visited Nigeria and Cameroon to investigate the border dispute between the two countries.

May South Africa was admitted as the 53rd member of the OAU. The Abuja Treaty Establishing the AEC entered into force on 12 May, having been ratified by the requisite number of OAU member states. The OAU was to operate henceforth on the basis of both the OAU Charter and the Abuja Treaty.

June Consultations with each of the conflicting parties in Rwanda were conducted by the OAU. The Assembly of Heads of State, meeting in Tunis, approved a code of conduct for inter-African relations, in order to strengthen political consultation and co-operation for the promotion of security and stability in the region. Nine countries were nominated to serve on the central committee (organ) of the mechanism for conflict prevention, management and resolution. The military component of the OAU mission in Burundi was now deployed in that country, and its mandate was extended until mid-September. (The mission was subsequently granted three-monthly extensions of its mandate.)

Nov. The Secretary-General, noting the Organization's serious financial situation, warned that most activities of the regular budget for 1994/95 would have to be suspended. Certain sanctions were to be imposed on any country that had not paid its contribution in full by 1 June 1995.

1995

March An extraordinary session of the Council of Ministers, held in Cairo, Egypt, adopted an Agenda for Action, which aimed to stimulate African economic and social development. The document emphasized the importance of peace, democratic government and stability in achieving development targets. It also assessed Africa's role in the world economy and the need for structural reforms of countries' economies, in particular in view of agreements reached under the GATT Uruguay Round of trade negotiations. The OAU, together with representatives of the UN and the Commonwealth Secretariat, dispatched a special mission to Sierra Leone, in order to assess means of facilitating the peace process in that country.

April A meeting of the conflict mechanism's central organ, held in Tunis, Tunisia, reviewed OAU peace initiatives. The meeting urged OAU member states to offer humanitarian aid to consolidate the peace process in Angola and for further OAU assistance for the rehabilitation and reconstruction of Somalia. A seminar, organized jointly by the OAU and the International Committee of the Red Cross, assembled military and civil experts in Yaoundé, Cameroon, to discuss the issue of land-mines.

May An 81-member OAU observer group was deployed to monitor a general election in Ethiopia. The group confirmed that the electoral process had been 'free and fair'.

June At the 31st Assembly of Heads of State, held in Addis Ababa, Ethiopia, the Secretary-General observed that the OAU's peace-keeping role had been severely affected by the failure of member states to pay their contributions. Sanctions were to be imposed on those countries which had failed to pay 25% of their arrears by the end of June. (Liberia and Somalia were exempted from this deadline.) The meeting endorsed a proposal to establish a conflict management centre, provisionally in Cairo, Egypt, to strengthen the OAU's role in conflict prevention. The situation in warring African countries was discussed, as well as the problem of large-scale refugee and displaced populations in the region. In addition, member states urged the international community to end the application of sanctions against Libya.

Sept. An extraordinary meeting of the conflict mechanism's central organ condemned the attempted assassination of Egypt's President Mubarak prior to the Heads of State meeting in June. The committee censured Sudan for protecting the alleged perpetrators of the attack and for supporting other terrorist elements in the country.

Oct. OAU observers monitored the conduct of elections in Zanzibar and attempted to mediate between the parties when the vote failed to secure a decisive result.

Nov. A 50-member OAU observer group was deployed to monitor elections in Algeria, as part of an international team.

1996

Feb. The Council of Ministers reiterated the OAU's readiness to promote and support dialogue and reconciliation in Burundi. However, the meeting did not support military intervention in that country, despite a UN report proposing international co-operation with the OAU to establish a stand-by force for Burundi.

March The UN Secretary-General launched a System-wide Special Initiative on Africa, which was based on the development objectives outlined in the OAU Agenda for Action (see above). Funds were to be allocated under the Initiative to strengthen the OAU's capacity for conflict prevention, management and resolution.

May-June The OAU assisted the International Peace Academy to conduct a meeting of international organizations, in Cape Town, South Africa, to promote the OAU's conflict mechanism, under the theme of 'Civil Society and Conflict Management in Africa'.

July The 32nd Assembly of Heads of State agreed to support a plan, formulated earlier that month by the Governments of Tanzania, Uganda and Ethiopia, to send troops to Burundi in a peace-keeping capacity. The Assembly requested logistical and financial support from the international community for the initiative. At the end of July, following a military coup in Burundi, the OAU endorsed a decision of seven east and central African states to impose economic sanctions against the new regime.

Oct. The OAU Secretary-General cautiously endorsed a US proposal to establish an African military force for the protection of civilian populations in areas of conflict. A regional committee of the OAU declared its support for the continuation of the economic embargo against Burundi.

Nov. An OAU delegation, meeting with the heads of state of eight African countries in Nairobi, Kenya, supported the establishment of an international humanitarian force, to be sent to Zaire (although this was never deployed).

1997

Jan. The UN and the OAU appointed a joint special representative for the Great Lakes Region.

Feb. The 65th session of the Council of Ministers, meeting in Libya, expressed its support of that country in the face of sanctions imposed upon it by the international community. The OAU welcomed the newly-elected Secretary-General of the UN, the Ghanaian, Kofi Annan. The situation in Zaire was discussed and an extraordinary summit of the OAU's conflict management mechanism was scheduled for March. Further donations to the OAU Peace Fund were requested.

March A special summit of the OAU organ on conflict prevention, management and resolution, which was attended by delegations from both the Zairean Government and the rebel AFDL forces, called for an immediate cease-fire and concluded a provisional agreement for negotiations between the two sides based on a five-point plan that had been formulated by the joint OAU/UN Special Representative and approved by the UN Security Council in February.

June The Assembly of Heads of State, meeting in Harare, Zimbabwe, condemned the military coup in Sierra Leone, which took place in May, and endorsed the intervention of ECOMOG troops in order to restore a democratic government in that country. The first meeting between ministers of the OAU and the European Union was held in New York, USA. The inaugural meeting of the AEC took place.

July The UNDP donated US $3m. to the OAU conflict management mechanism. An OAU observer group was deployed to monitor elections in Liberia.

Aug. The OAU appointed a special envoy to the Comoros, following a declaration of independence by separatists on the islands of Nzwani and Mwali.

Oct. Chiefs of Defence Staff, meeting in Harare, Zimbabwe, proposed a series of measures to strengthen the capacity of African countries to lead peace-keeping missions in the region, which included the establishment of operations, training and early-warning units.

Nov. A group of OAU military observers was reported to have been dispatched to the Comoros.

Dec. The OAU organized an international conference, held in Addis Ababa, Ethiopia, which aimed to resolve the dispute between the Comoran Government and the secessionists and to initiate a process of political dialogue. In a separate meeting OAU ministers of justice adopted a protocol approving the creation of a permanent African court of human rights (based on the African Charter of Human and People's Rights, entered into force 1986).

1998

Feb. The OAU concluded an agreement with La Francophonie (q.v.) to co-operate in economic and cultural areas.

March The OAU declared its support for ECOWAS efforts in restoring President Ahmed Tejan Kabbah to power in Sierra Leone. A nine-member OAU ministerial mission visited the Comoros in an attempt to further a peaceful solution to the dispute; however, it was prevented from conducting discussions with the separatist leaders in Nzwani.

June Fighting between Eritrea and Ethiopia dominated discussions at the 34th Assembly of Heads of State, held in Burkina Faso. It was agreed to send a delegation to attempt to resolve the dispute. The Assembly also considered economic issues affecting the region, and resolved to disregardcertain economic and humanitarian sanctions imposed against Libya, owing to that country's refusal to release two people suspected of the bombing of a US aircraft over the United Kingdom in 1988. The OAU leaders reiterated their support for the proposal of the Libyan authorities that the suspects be tried in a neutral venue. The OAU agreed to establish a seven-member International Panel of Eminent Personalities to examine all aspects of the genocide that occurred in Rwanda in 1994; a special trust fund was to be established to finance its activities. (The Panel was inaugurated in January 1999.)

July An OAU delegation conducted discussions with the Eritrean and Ethiopian authorities in an attempt to conclude a peace settlement. The OAU Secretary-General also expressed support for efforts to negotiate a settlement between the conflicting parties in Guinea-Bissau.

Aug. The OAU expressed its concern at the escalating violence in the Democratic Republic of the Congo (DRC), in particular the involvement of armed forces from other countries in the region, and resolved to send a mission to negotiate a cease-fire. An OAU ministerial committee (comprising representatives of Burkina Faso, Djibouti and Zimbabwe) pursued efforts to negotiate an accord between Eritrea and Ethiopia. The proposed OAU framework agreement was based on a US-Rwandan peace plan, presented to both sides in June, and included implementation of an immediate cease-fire, the initiation of peace discussions and recognition of the positions prior to the start of hostilities in May. At the end of August delegates of the SADC held talks at OAU headquarters, and urged an immediate cease-fire by all sides in the Congolese conflict.

Sept. The OAU Secretary-General supported a request of the Sudanese Government for an international commission of inquiry to be established to examine the US airstrike on a pharmaceutical plant in Khartoum, in retaliation for terrorist bombing incidents in August.

Nov. A meeting of the OAU mediation committee on the Eritrean/Ethiopian dispute was held in Ouagadougou.

Dec. A special meeting of the conflict resolution mechanism, at the level of heads of state, was held to pursue a peace settlement in the DRC. The ongoing Eritrean-Ethiopian dispute and the unstable security situation in Angola were also considered. A Special OAU Ministerial Meeting on Refugees, Returnees and Internally Displaced Persons was convened, in Khartoum; the meeting urged member states to implement efforts to mitigate problems associated with the mass movement of populations, and to promote humanitarian assistance efforts.

1999

Feb. A high-level OAU delegation, including the Chairman and Secretary-General, replaced the previous ministerial committee on a visit to Eritrea, following that country's refusal to negotiate with a representative of Djibouti. In early February an OAU delegation conducted talks with representatives of the Nzwani separatist factions and the Government of the Comoros; however, the negotiations failed to conclude an agreement on a political settlement to the conflict or on the establishment of an OAU peace-keeping mission.

March An OAU mission visited the authorities in Ethiopia and Eritrea to pursue efforts towards settling the conflict. The Chairman of the OAU cancelled a special summit meeting on African conflict scheduled to take place at the end of March, owing to controversy over the extension of invitations to rebel leaders from those countries affected by civil conflict. A meeting of the Council of Ministers appointed the President of Zambia, Frederick Chiluba, to co-ordinate efforts to resolve the conflict in the DRC. The meeting also imposed sanctions against eight countries that had failed to pay their annual contributions to the Organization for two years. The sanctions denied nationals from those countries the right to vote or to work at the OAU offices, which resulted in a substantial reduction in personnel at OAU headquarters.

April The first OAU conference on human rights, at ministerial level, was convened in Mauritius. An inter-island conference was held, under OAU auspices, in Antananarivo, Madagascar, to conclude arrangements for a new political union in the Comoros. At the end of the month, however, the Government of the Comoros was removed by army officers following renewed unrest. The OAU condemned the coup, but urged the Nzwani representatives to sign the agreed framework.

May The OAU announced the withdrawal of the military component of its observer mission in the Comoros. A new round of talks with the heads of government of Eritrea and Ethiopia was initiated to provide for a cessation of hostilities.

July The summit meeting, held in Algiers, was concerned with the economic development of Africa and prospects for greater integration, as well as ongoing conflicts in the region. The meeting requested the Secretary-General to send a fact-finding mission to Somalia to assess its post-conflict needs. The OAU also appointed a senior Algerian army general to chair a Joint Military Commission in the DRC, which was to be established according to the terms of a peace accord signed earlier in July. Heads of state declared that the Organization would not recognize any authority in a member state which assumed power illegally. An African convention for the prevention and combating of terrorism was signed, which included provisions for the exchange of information to help counter terrorism and for signatory states to refrain from granting asylum to terrorists. The meeting also declared that 2000 was to be the Year of Peace, Security and Solidarity in Africa.

Sept. An extraordinary summit meeting was convened in Sirte, Libya, at the request of the Libyan leader Col al-Qaddafi. The meeting determined to establish an African Union, based on the principles and objectives of the OAU and AEC, but furthering African co-operation, development and integration. A new charter was to be adopted by 2001. In addition, heads of state declared their commitment to accelerating the establishment of regional institutions, including a pan-African parliament, court of justice and central bank, as well as the implementation of economic and monetary union, as provided for by the Abuja Treaty Establishing the AEC. The Ethiopian Government rejected the final technical arrangements for implementation of the OAU framework agreement, which had been approved by Eritrea in August, on the grounds that they did not ensure the return of disputed territories to their status prior to the start of the conflict.

Oct. A conference on Industrial Partnerships and Investment in Africa was held in Dakar, Senegal, jointly organized by OAU with UNIDO, the ECA, the African Development Bank, and the Alliance for Africa's Industrialization.

Dec. The OAU Chairman, President Bouteflika of Algeria, urged the removal of UN sanctions against Libya. The OAU condemned the military's seizure of power in Côte d'Ivoire.

2000

Feb. The OAU imposed economic sanctions against the Nzwani separatists in the Comoros, including the immobilization of their overseas assets, and urged the co-operation of OAU members in implementing these. The OAU dispatched a special envoy to mediate between Eritrea and Ethiopia; the Ethiopian adminstration reiterated its dissatisfaction with the technical arrangements (deemed no longer negotiable by the OAU) for the framework peace agreement, which in other respects it was prepared to approve.

March An OAU conference unanimously approved a peace plan for Somalia that had been drafted in late 1999 by the Djibouti President (and then IGAD Chairman), Ismael Omar Gelleh. Further punitive measures were imposed against the Nzwani separatists in the Comoros, including the suspension of telephone communications, and restrictions on oil deliveries and on sea and air traffic.

April The OAU participated in an EU–Africa summit, held in Cairo, Egypt.

May In early May an initiative by the OAU's special envoy to mediate indirect communications ('proximity talks') between Eritrea and Ethiopia failed, and was followed by a serious escalation of their conflict. The OAU urged an immediate cessation of hostilities and commitment from both sides to pursuing a peaceful resolution. Indirect negotiations, mediated by the OAU and envoys of the EU and USA, resumed in late May.

June The OAU, EU and USA continued to mediate proximity talks between Eritrea and Ethiopia, culminating, in mid-June, in the conclusion of a cease-fire agreement, which was formalized at Algiers. The Algiers accord stipulated the immediate cessation of hostilities and withdrawal by both sides to the positions that had been held prior to the commencement of the conflict. Meanwhile, a UN peace-keepingforce was to be deployed to supervise the disputed border area. Subsequently negotiations were to be convened on the implementation of the OAU framework agreement. Following the conclusion of the accord an OAU Liaison Mission in Ethiopia and Eritrea—OLMEE—was established. During the month a committee comprising 10 OAU heads of state was appointed to address the ongoing political insecurity in Côte d'Ivoire.

July At the annual summit meeting, held at Lomé, Togo, 27 OAU heads of state signed the draft Constitutive Act of the African Union, concerning the establishment of the proposed African Union, agreed in September 1999. The Constitutive Act was to enter into force following ratification by two-thirds of member states' legislatures. It was envisaged that the Union would be inaugurated, and would thus replace the OAU, one year after the endorsement of the Act. The summit meeting also adopted a resolution in support of the ongoing Somali peace and reconciliation conference convened in Arta, Djibouti, under the auspices of IGAD. At the end of July the OAU announced that it was to send observers to the Horn of Africa to monitor the implementation of the Algiers cease-fire accord.

Sept. A special envoy appointed by the Secretary-General to address the conflict in Sierra Leone visited several West African leaders for consultations regarding the situation in that country.

Oct. The OAU declined to dispatch a team of observers to monitor presidential elections held in Côte d'Ivoire, following failure by that country's government to accept the mediation attempts of the OAU 'Committee of 10'. The Secretary-General subsequently declared that the elections had not been conducted freely and fairly and urged that the electoral process be repeated. An OAU observer team monitoring concurrent legislative and presidential elections staged in Zanzibar at the end of the month identified numerous electoral irregularities and refused to endorse the official results. (Legislative and presidential elections held at that time in mainland Tanzania were declared free and fair.)

Nov. An OAU special representative was appointed to a military co-ordination commission jointly established by the OAU and UN under the terms of Algiers accord, to facilitate the conflict settlement process in Eritrea and Ethiopia. During the month the Secretary-General expressed concern over mounting insecurity in southern Guinea.

Dec. At the beginning of the month the OAU adopted the Bamako Declaration, concerning arresting the circulation of small arms on the continent. The Organization refused to dispatch observers to monitor legislative elections that were held in Côte d'Ivoire in early December. Following continued mediation efforts by the OAU a formal peace agreement was concluded by Eritrea and Ethiopia in Algiers in mid-December.

2001

Feb. The OAU endorsed a framework agreement for reconciliation initialled in mid-February, at Fomboni on the island of Mwali, by representatives of the Comoros Government, civil society and former dissident factions. The Council of Ministers urged all Somali faction leaders who had not participated in the Arta peace conference convened in mid-2000 to support ongoing efforts towards reconciliation in that country.

March The OAU's fifth extraordinary summit, convened at the start of the month in Sirte, Libya, discussed progress towards the establishment of the African Union. The Union was officially declared, in anticipation of promptly securing the ratification of the Constitutive Act by the requisite two-thirds majority. In addition the Protocol to the Abuja Treaty Establishing the AEC relating to the Pan-African Parliament was adopted and signed by 10 member states. The protocol was to enter into effect following ratification by a majority of states. An African Summit on HIV/AIDS, Tuberculosis and other related Infectious Diseases was convened, under OAU auspices, towards the end of March.

April–May The 36th ratification of the Constitutive Act of the African Union, representing a two-thirds majority of OAU member states, was deposited on 26 April. On 26 May the Constitutive Act of the African Union entered into force. The OAU Charter was to remain in effect until the transfer of all assets and liabilities to the Union had been completed,rendering it fully operative (this was subsequently scheduled for July 2002, see below). During May the OAU suspended the punitive economic sanctions that had been imposed in February 2000 on the former Nzwani separatists in Comoros.

July Meeting in Lomé, Togo, the Assembly of Heads of State endorsed the Constitutive Act of the African Union, agreeing that the Union would become operational following a transitional period of one year, during which its main policy organs and other institutions were to be established (through protocols to the Constitutive Act and Abuja Treaty Establishing the AEC), or incorporated from the OAU (such as the mechanism for conflict prevention, management and resolution). A review of all OAU treaties was to be implemented, and those deemed relevant would be retained by the African Union. Hitherto 40 OAU member states had ratified the Constitutive Act. At the meeting in Lomé, Amara Essy, a former Côte d'Ivoire minister of foreign affairs, was elected as the new OAU Secretary-General, to replace Salim Ahmed Salim with effect from September. In addition, the Assembly authorized the establishment of an African Energy Commission—AFREC, which was to increase co-operation in energy matters between Africa and other regions, and adopted the New African Initiative. (The Initiative, subsequently renamed the New Partnership for Africa's Development—NEPAD, represented a long-term strategy for socio-economic recovery in Africa and aimed to promote the strengthening of democracy and economic management in the region. The heads of state of Algeria, Egypt, Nigeria, Senegal and South Africa have played leading roles in its preparation and management.) Heads of state urged the Government of the United Kingdom to co-operate with the Zimbabwean authorities, with a view to resolving the ongoing dispute over land ownership in Zimbabwe.

Oct. NEPAD was officially launched.

2002

Jan. The OAU requested the UN to deploy a new peace-keeping force in the Central African Republic (CAR), in view of a failed coup attempt there in May 2001 and subsequent instability. The international community was urged to provide aid to help alleviate the ongoing economic crisis in the CAR.

Feb. In mid-February the OAU declared its support for the Zimbabwean Government's reluctance to admit Western observer teams to monitor the presidential election scheduled to be held there in March. Later in February the OAU mediated talks between President Didier Ratsiraka of Madagascar and the official opposition leader Marc Ravalomanana, who had established a rival Madagascan government on 22 February, having also claimed victory at the presidential election held in that country in December 2001. During February an OAU delegation undertook a tour of the Mano River Union countries (Guinea, Liberia and Sierra Leone) in order to assess the security situation there.

March The OAU held talks with each of the disputing sides in the Madagascan political crisis and in mid-March urged the formation of an interim government of national unity, pending the staging of a new presidential election. An OAU observer team found the Zimbabwean presidential election, held in controversial circumstances in early March, to have been conducted freely and fairly.

Specialized Agencies

African Accounting Council: POB 11223, Kinshasa, Democratic Republic of the Congo; tel. (12) 33567; f. 1979; provides assistance to institutions in member countries on standardization of accounting; promotes education, further training and research in accountancy and related areas of study. Publ. *Information and Liaison Bulletin* (every two months).

Pan-African Institution of Education for Development—PIED: 29 ave de la Justice, BP 1764, Kinshasa I, Democratic Republic of the Congo; tel. (12) 34527; e-mail baseeduc@hotmail.com; f. 1973, became specialized agency of OAU in 1986, present name adopted 2001; undertakes educational research and training, focuses on co-operation and problem-solving, acts as an observatory for education. Publs *Bulletin d'Information* (quarterly), *Revue africaine des sciences de l'éducation* (2 a year), *Répertoire africain des institutions de recherche* (annually).

African Civil Aviation Commission—AFCAC: 15 blvd de la République, BP 2356, Dakar, Senegal; tel. 839-93-73; fax 823-26-61; e-mail cafac@sentoo.sn; internet www.afcac-cafac.sn; f. 1969 to encourage co-operation in all civil aviation activities; promotes co-ordination and better utilization and development of African air transport systems and the standardization of aircraft, flight equipment and training programmes for pilots and mechanics; organizes working groups and seminars, and compiles statistics. Pres. MAMDOUH HESHMAT (Egypt); Sec. CHARLES M. DIOP.

Pan-African News Agency—PANAPRESS: BP 4650, Dakar, Senegal; tel. 824-14-10; fax 824-13-90; internet www.panapress.com; regional headquarters in Khartoum, Sudan; Lusaka, Zambia; Kinshasa, Democratic Republic of the Congo; Lagos, Nigeria; Tripoli, Libya; began operations in May 1983, restructured in late 1990s; receives information from national news agencies and circulates news in English and French. Dir-Gen. BABACAR FALL. Publ. *PANA Review*.

Pan-African Postal Union—PAPU: POB 6026, Arusha, Tanzania; tel. (27) 2508603; fax (27) 2503913; e-mail papu@habari.co.tz; f. 1980 to extend members' co-operation in the improvement of postal services. Sec.-Gen. JILANI BEN HADDADA. Publ. *PAPU Bulletin*.

Pan-African Railways Union: BP 687, Kinshasa, Democratic Republic of the Congo; tel. (12) 23861; f. 1972 to standardize, expand, co-ordinate and improve members' railway services; the ultimate aim is to link all systems; main organs: Gen. Assembly, Exec. Bd, Gen. Secr., five tech. cttees. Mems in 30 African countries.

Pan-African Telecommunications Union: POB 7248, Kinshasa, Democratic Republic of the Congo; f. 1977; co-ordinates devt of telecommunications networks and services in Africa.

Supreme Council for Sports in Africa: BP 1363, Yaoundé, Cameroon; tel. and fax 23-95-80; Sec.-Gen. Dr AWOTURE ELEYAE (Nigeria). Publs *SCSA News* (6 a year), *African Sports Movement Directory* (annually).

Note: Prior to the formal establishment of the African Union, scheduled for July 2002, the OAU Secretary-General was mandated by the Assembly of Heads of State to undertake a review of the specialized agencies, in order to assess their continued relevance, and to formulate proposals where necessary on their incorporation into the African Union.

ASSOCIATED PARTNERSHIP

New Partnership for Africa's Development—NEPAD: POB 1234, Midrand, Halfway House, 1685 South Africa (secretariat); internet www.nepad.org; f. 2001 as a long-term strategy to promote socio-economic development in Africa; steering cttee, comprising Algeria, Egypt, Nigeria, Senegal and South Africa, meets once a month; Steering Cttee Chair. Prof. WISEMAN NKUHLU (South Africa).

Summary of OAU Charter

(25 May 1963)

Article I

Establishment of the Organization of African Unity. The Organization to include continental African states, Madagascar, andother islands surrounding Africa.

Article II

Aims of the OAU:

1. To promote unity and solidarity among African states.
2. To intensify and co-ordinate efforts to improve living standards in Africa.
3. To defend sovereignty, territorial integrity and independence of African states.
4. To eradicate all forms of colonialism from Africa.
5. To promote international co-operation in keeping with the Charter of the United Nations.

Article III

Member states adhere to the principles of sovereignty, non-interference in internal affairs of member states, respect for territorial integrity, peaceful settlement of disputes, condemnation of political subversion, dedication to the emancipation of dependent African territories, and international non-alignment.

Article IV

Each independent sovereign African state shall be entitled to become a member of the Organization.

Article V

All member states shall have equal rights and duties.

Article VI

All member states shall observe scrupulously the principles laid down in Article III.

Article VII

Establishment of the Assembly of Heads of State and Government, the Council of Ministers, the General Secretariat, and the Commission of Mediation, Conciliation and Arbitration.

Articles VIII–XI

The Assembly of Heads of State and Government co-ordinates policies and reviews the structure of the Organization.

Articles XII–XV

The Council of Ministers shall prepare conferences of the Assembly, and co-ordinate inter-African co-operation. All resolutions shall be by simple majority.

Articles XVI–XVIII

The General Secretariat. The Secretary-General and his staff shall not seek or receive instructions from any government or other authority external to the Organization. They are international officials responsible only to the Organization.

Article XIX
Commission of Mediation, Conciliation and Arbitration. A separate protocol concerning the composition and nature of this Commission shall be regarded as an integral part of the Charter.

Articles XX–XXII
Specialized Commissions shall be established, composed of Ministers or other officials designated by Member Governments. Their regulations shall be laid down by the Council of Ministers.

Article XXIII
The Budget shall be prepared by the Secretary-General and approved by the Council of Ministers. Contributions shall be in accordance with the scale of assessment of the United Nations. No Member shall pay more than 20% of the total yearly amount.

Article XXIV
Texts of the Charter in African languages, English and French shall be equally authentic. Instruments of ratification shall be deposited with the Government of Ethiopia.

Articles XXV
The Charter shall come into force on receipt by the Government of Ethiopia of the instruments of ratification of two-thirds of the signatory states.

Article XXVI
The Charter shall be registered with the Secretariat of the United Nations.

Article XXVII
Questions of interpretation shall be settled by a two-thirds majority vote in the Assembly of Heads of State and Government.

Article XXVIII
Admission of new independent African states to the Organization shall be decided by a simple majority of the Member States.

Articles XXIX–XXXIII
The working languages of the Organization shall be African languages, English, French, Arabic and Portuguese. The Secretary-General may accept gifts and bequests to the Organization, subject to the approval of the Council of Ministers. The Council of Ministers shall establish privileges and immunities to be accorded to the personnel of the Secretariat in the territories of Member States. A State wishing to withdraw from the Organization must give a year's written notice to the Secretariat. The Charter may only be amended after consideration by all Member States and by a two-thirds majority vote of the Assembly of Heads of State and Government. Such amendments will come into force one year after submission.

ORGANIZATION OF AMERICAN STATES—OAS

(ORGANIZACIÓN DE LOS ESTADOS AMERICANOS—OEA)

Address: 17th St and Constitution Ave, NW, Washington, DC 20006, USA.

Telephone: (202) 458-3000; **fax:** (202) 458-3967; **e-mail:** pi@oas.org; **internet:** www.oas.org.

The ninth International Conference of American States (held in Bogotá, Colombia, in 1948) established the Organization of American States by adopting the Charter (succeeding the International Union of American Republics, founded in 1890). The Charter was subsequently amended by the Protocol of Buenos Aires (creating the annual General Assembly), signed in 1967, enacted in 1970, and by the Protocol of Cartagena de Indias, which was signed in 1985 and enacted in 1988. The purpose of the Organization is to strengthen the peace and security of the continent; to promote and consolidate representative democracy, with due respect for the principle of non-intervention; to prevent possible causes of difficulties and to ensure the peaceful settlement of disputes that may arise among the member states; to provide for common action in the event of aggression; to seek the solution of political, juridical and economic problems that may arise among them; to promote, by co-operative action, their economic, social and cultural development; to achieve an effective limitation of conventional weapons; and to devote the largest amount of resources to the economic and social development of the member states.

MEMBERS

Antigua and Barbuda	Guyana
Argentina	Haiti
Bahamas	Honduras
Barbados	Jamaica
Belize	Mexico
Bolivia	Nicaragua
Brazil	Panama
Canada	Paraguay
Chile	Peru
Colombia	Saint Christopher and Nevis
Costa Rica	Saint Lucia
Cuba*	Saint Vincent and the Grenadines
Dominica	Suriname
Dominican Republic	Trinidad and Tobago
Ecuador	USA
El Salvador	Uruguay
Grenada	Venezuela
Guatemala	

* The Cuban Government was suspended from OAS activities in 1962.

Permanent Observers: Algeria, Angola, Armenia, Austria, Azerbaijan, Belgium, Bosnia and Herzegovina, Bulgaria, Croatia, Cyprus, Czech Republic, Denmark, Egypt, Equatorial Guinea, Finland, France, Germany, Ghana, Greece, the Holy See, Hungary, India, Ireland, Israel, Italy, Japan, Kazakhstan, the Republic of Korea, Latvia, Lebanon, Morocco, the Netherlands, Norway, Pakistan, Philippines, Poland, Portugal, Romania, Russia, Saudi Arabia, Spain, Sri Lanka, Sweden, Switzerland, Thailand, Tunisia, Turkey, Ukraine, the United Kingdom, Yemen and the European Union.

Organization

(April 2002)

GENERAL ASSEMBLY

The Assembly meets annually and may also hold special sessions when convoked by the Permanent Council. As the supreme organ of the OAS, it decides general action and policy.

MEETINGS OF CONSULTATION OF MINISTERS OF FOREIGN AFFAIRS

Meetings are convened, at the request of any member state, to consider problems of an urgent nature and of common interest to member states, or to serve as an organ of consultation in cases of armed attack or other threats to international peace and security. The Permanent Council determines whether a meeting should be convened and acts as a provisional organ of consultation until ministers are able to assemble.

PERMANENT COUNCIL

The Council meets regularly throughout the year at OAS headquarters. It is composed of one representative of each member state with the rank of ambassador; each government may accredit alternate representatives and advisers and when necessary appoint an interim representative. The office of Chairman is held in turn by each of the representatives, following alphabetical order according to the names of the countries in Spanish. The Vice-Chairman is determined in the same way, following reverse alphabetical order. Their terms of office are three months.

The Council acts as an organ of consultation and oversees the maintenance of friendly relations between members. It supervises the work of the OAS and promotes co-operation with a variety of other international bodies including the United Nations. The official languages are English, French, Portuguese and Spanish.

INTER-AMERICAN COUNCIL FOR INTEGRAL DEVELOPMENT—CIDI

The Council was established in 1996, replacing the Inter-American Economic and Social Council and the Inter-American Council for Education, Science and Culture. Its aim is to promote co-operation among the countries of the region, in order to accelerate economic and social development. CIDI's work focuses on eight areas: social development and education; cultural development; the generation of productive employment; economic diversification, integration and trade liberalization; strengthening democratic institutions; the exchange of scientific and technological information; the development of tourism; and sustainable environmental development. An Executive Secretary for Integral Development provides CIDI with technical and secretarial services.

Executive Secretary: RONALD SCHEMAN (USA).

Inter-American Agency for Co-operation and Development: f. November 1999 as a subsidiary body of CIDI to accelerate the development of Latin America and the Caribbean through technical co-operation and training programmes. In particular, the Agency aimed to formulate strategies for mobilizing external funds for OAS co-operation initiatives; establish criteria for the promotion and exchange of co-operation activities; prepare co-operation accords and evaluate project requests and results; and review mechanisms for promoting scholarships and professional exchange programmes. The Executive Secretary for Integral Development serves as the Agency's Director-General.

GENERAL SECRETARIAT

The Secretariat, the central and permanent organ of the Organization, performs the duties entrusted to it by the General Assembly, Meetings of Consultation of Ministers of Foreign Affairs and the Councils.

Secretary-General: CÉSAR GAVIRIA TRUJILLO (Colombia).

Assistant Secretary-General: LUIGI R. EINAUDI (USA).

INTER-AMERICAN COMMITTEES AND COMMISSIONS

Inter-American Juridical Committee: Rua Senador Vergueiro 81, Rio de Janeiro, RJ 22230-000, Brazil; tel. (21) 558-

3204; fax (21) 558-4600; e-mail cjioea@trip.com.br; composed of 11 jurists, nationals of different member states, elected for a period of four years, with the possibility of re-election. The Committee's purposes are: to serve as an advisory body to the Organization on juridical matters; to promote the progressive development and codification of international law; and to study juridical problems relating to the integration of the developing countries in the hemisphere, and, in so far as may appear desirable, the possibility of attaining uniformity in legislation. Chair. JOÃO GRANDINO RODAS.

Inter-American Commission on Human Rights: 1889 F St, NW, Washington, DC 20006, USA; tel. (202) 458-6002; fax (202) 458-3992; e-mail cidhoea@oas.org; internet www.cidh.oas.org; f. 1960. The Commission comprises seven members. It promotes the observance and protection of human rights in the member states of the OAS; it examines and reports on the human rights situation in member countries, and provides consultative services. During 2000 the Commission received 681 written complaints, and opened 110 new cases related to 25 member states. Exec. Sec. SANTIAGO CANTON.

Inter-American Court of Human Rights: Apdo Postal 6906-1000, San José, Costa Rica; tel. 234-0581; fax 234-0584; e-mail corteidh@racsa.co.cr; internet www.corteidh.or.cr; f. 1978, as an autonomous judicial institution whose purpose is to apply and interpret the American Convention on Human Rights (which entered into force in 1978: at November 1998 the Convention had been ratified by 25 OAS member states, of which 18 had accepted the competence of the Court). The Court comprises seven jurists from OAS member states. Pres. ANTÔNIO CANÇADO TRINDADE; Sec. MANUEL E. VENTURA-ROBLES.

Inter-American Drug Abuse Control Commission—CICAD: 1889 F St, NW, Washington, DC 20006–4499, USA; tel. (202) 458-3178; fax (202) 458-3658; e-mail cicad@oas.org; internet www.cicad.oas.org; f. 1986 by the OAS to promote and facilitate multilateral co-operation in the control and prevention of the trafficking, production and use of illegal drugs, and related crimes. Mems 34 countries. Exec. Sec. DAVID R. BEALL. Publs *Statistical Survey* (annually), *Directory of Governmental Institutions Charges with the Fight Against the Illicit Production, Trafficking, Use and Abuse of Narcotic Drugs and Psychotropic Substances* (annually), *Evaluation of Progress in Drug Control* (annually).

Inter-American Telecommunication Commission—CITEL: 1889 F St, NW, Washington, DC 20006, USA; tel. (202) 458-3004; fax (202) 458-6854; e-mail citel@oas.org; internet www.citel.oas.org; f. 1993 to promote the development of telecommunications in the region. Mems 35 countries. Exec. Sec. CLOVIS BAPTISTA NETO.

Inter-American Committee on Ports—CIP: 1889 F St, NW, Washington, DC 20006, USA; tel. (202) 458-3871; fax (202) 458-3517; e-mail cgallegos@oas.org; f. 1998 to further OAS activities in the sector (previously undertaken by Inter-American port conferences); aims to develop and co-ordinate member state policies in port administration and management. The first meeting of the Committee took place in October 1999; three technical advisory groups were established to advise on port operations, port security, and navigation safety and environmental protection. An Executive Board meets annually. Sec. CARLOS GALLEGOS.

Activities

In December 1994 the first Summit of the Americas was convened in Miami, USA. The meeting endorsed the concept of a Free Trade Area of the Americas (FTAA), and also approved a Plan of Action to strengthen democracy, eradicate poverty and promote sustainable development throughout the region. The OAS subsequently embarked on an extensive process of reform and modernization to strengthen its capacity to undertake a lead role in implementing the Plan. The Organization realigned its priorities in order to respond to the mandates emerging from the Summit and developed a new institutional framework for technical assistance and co-operation, although many activities continued to be undertaken by the specialized or associated organizations of the OAS (see below). In 1998, following the second Summit of the Americas, held in April, in Santiago, Chile, the OAS established an Office of Summit Follow-Up, in order to strengthen its servicing of the meetings, and to co-ordinate tasks assigned to the Organization. The third Summit, convened in Quebec City, Canada, in April 2001, reaffirmed the central role of the OAS in implementing decisions of the summit meetings and instructed the Organization to pursue the process of reform in order to enhance its operational capabilities, in particular in the areas of human rights, combating trade in illegal drugs, and enforcement of democratic values. The Summit declaration stated that commitment to democracy was a requirement for a country's participation in the summit process. The meeting also determined that the OAS was to be the technical secretariat for the process, assuming many of the responsibilities previously taken by the host country.

TRADE AND ECONOMIC INTEGRATION

A trade unit was established in 1995 in order to strengthen the Organization's involvement in trade issues and the process of economic integration, which became a priority area following the first Summit of the Americas. The unit was to provide technical assistance in support of the establishment of the FTAA, and to co-ordinate activities between regional and sub-regional integration organizations. In 2002 the unit was providing technical support to the nine FTAA negotiating groups: market access; investment; services; government procurement; dispute settlement; agriculture; intellectual property rights; subsidies, anti-dumping and countervailing duties; and competition policy. In April 2001 the third Summit of the Americas requested the OAS to initiate an analysis of corporate social responsibility. At the Summit it was agreed that negotiations to establish the FTAA should be concluded by January 2005, to allow the trade pact to enter into force no later than December of that year.

The unit operates in consultation with a Special Committee on Trade, which was established in 1993, comprising high-level officials representing each member state. The Committee studies trade issues, provides technical analyses of the economic situation in member countries and the region, and prepares reports for ministerial meetings of the FTAA. The OAS also administers an Inter-American Foreign Trade Information System which facilitates the exchange of information.

DEMOCRACY AND CIVIL SOCIETY

Two principal organs of the OAS, the Inter-American Commission on Human Rights and the Inter-American Court of Human Rights, work to secure respect for human rights in all member countries. The OAS aims to encourage more member governments to accept jurisdiction of the Court. The OAS also collaborates with member states in the strengthening of representative institutions within government and as part of a democratic civil society. The third Summit of the Americas, convened in April 2001, mandated the OAS to formulate an Inter-American Democratic Charter. The Charter was adopted in September at a special session of the Assembly. Central to the Charter's five chapters was democracy and its relationship to human rights, integral development and combating poverty.

Through its Unit for the Promotion of Democracy, established in 1990, the OAS provides electoral technical assistance to member states and undertakes missions to observe the conduct of elections. By the end of 2001 the OAS had conducted more than 60 electoral missions in 18 countries. The OAS also supports societies in post-conflict situations and recently-installed governments to promote democratic practices.

In June 1991 the OAS General Assembly approved a resolution on representative democracy, which authorized the Secretary-General to summon a session of the Permanent Council in cases where a democratically-elected government had been overthrown or democratic procedures abandoned in member states. The Council could then convene an *ad hoc* meeting of ministers of foreign affairs to consider the situation. The procedure was invoked following political developments in Haiti, in September 1991, and Peru, in April 1992. Ministers determined to impose trade and diplomatic sanctions against

Haiti and sent missions to both countries. The resolution was incorporated into the Protocol of Washington, amending the OAS charter, which was adopted in December 1992 and entered into force in September 1997. A high-level OAS mission was dispatched to Peru in June 2000 to assist with the process of 'strengthening its institutional democratic system', following allegations that the Peruvian authorities had manipulated the re-election of that country's President in May. The mission subsequently co-ordinated negotiations between the Peruvian Government and opposition organizations. In August the OAS Secretary-General undertook the first of several high-level missions to negotiate with the authorities in Haiti in order to resolve the political crisis resulting from a disputed general election in May. (An OAS electoral monitoring team was withdrawn from Haiti in July prior to the second round of voting owing to concern at procedural irregularities.) In January 2001, following a meeting with the Haitian Prime Minister, the Assistant Secretary-General recommended that the OAS renew its efforts to establish a dialogue between the government, opposition parties and representatives of civil society in that country. In May the OAS and CARICOM undertook a joint mission to Haiti in order to assess prospects for a democratic resolution to the political uncertainties, and in June the OAS General Assembly issued a resolution urging all parties in Haiti to respect democratic order. At the end of that month the OAS Secretary-General led a visit of the joint mission to Haiti, during which further progress was achieved on the establishment of a new electoral council. Following political and social unrest in Haiti in December 2001, the OAS and CARICOM pledged to conduct an independent investigation into the violence, and in March 2002 an agreement to establish a special OAS mission to Haiti was signed in the capital, Port-au-Prince.

An OAS Mine-Clearing Assistance Programme in Central America was established in 1992, as part of efforts to facilitate the social and economic rehabilitation of the region. By 2002 the programme had provided training for more than 1,100 demining experts and assisted six countries in the clearance of some 75,000 anti-personnel devices, as well as in the destruction of more than 500,000 landmines from military stock-piles. Technical support was provided by the Inter-American Defense Board (see below). In 2001 Ecuador, Peru and Colombia approved OAS programmes to support national efforts to eliminate the problem of landmines. OAS activities were to include minefield surveying, civilian awareness, mine removal, the destruction of stock-piles, and victim assistance.

The OAS formulated an Inter-American Programme of Co-operation to Combat Corruption in order to address the problem at national level and, in 1996, adopted a Convention against Corruption. The first conference of the parties to the Convention was held in Buenos Aires, Argentina, in May 2001. In June the General Assembly approved the proposed establishment of a verification mechanism, including a policy-making annual conference and an intergovernmental committee of experts. At June the Convention had been signed by 29 member states, of which 22 had ratified the treaty. A working group on transparency aims to promote accountability throughout the public sector and supports national institutions responsible for combating corruption. In 1997 the OAS organized a meeting of experts to consider measures for the prevention of crime. The meeting adopted a work programme which included commitments to undertake police training in criminology and crime investigation, to exchange legal and practical knowledge, and to measure crime and violence in member countries.

REGIONAL SECURITY

In 1991 the General Assembly established a working group to consider issues relating to the promotion of co-operation in regional security. A Special Commission on Hemispheric Security was subsequently established, while two regional conferences have been held on security and confidence-building measures. Voluntary practices agreed by member states include the holding of border meetings to co-ordinate activities, co-operation in natural disaster management, and the exchange of information on military exercises and expenditure. From 1995 meetings of ministers of defence have been convened regularly, which provide a forum for discussion of security matters. The OAS aims to address the specific security concerns of small-island states, in particular those in the Caribbean, by adopting a multidimensional approach to counter their vulnerability, for example through efforts to strengthen democracy, to combat organized crime, to mitigate the effects of natural disasters and other environmental hazards, and to address the problem of HIV/AIDS.

In June 2000 the OAS General Assembly, convened in Windsor, Canada, established a Fund for Peace in support of the peaceful settlement of territorial disputes. In 2001 the Fund was supporting efforts to resolve disputes between Belize and Guatemala and between Honduras and Nicaragua. In June an agreement was concluded to enable an OAS Civilian Verification Mission to visit Honduras and Nicaragua in order to monitor compliance with previously agreed confidence-building measures. The Mission was to be financed by the Fund for Peace.

The OAS is actively involved in efforts to combat the abuse and trafficking of illegal drugs, and in 1996 members approved a Hemispheric Anti-drug Strategy, reiterating their commitment to addressing the problem. In 1998 the Inter-American Drug Abuse Control Commission established a Multilateral Evaluation Mechanism (MEM) to measure aspects of the drug problem and to co-ordinate an evaluation process under which national plans of action to combat drugs trafficking were to be formulated. The first hemispheric drugs report was published by MEM in January 2001 and in February 34 national reports produced under MEM were issued together with a series of recommendations for action. A meeting to review and strengthen MEM was convened in April. In January 2002 MEM published a progress report on the implementation of the recommendations, in which it stated that the countries of the Americas had made a 'significant effort' to adopt the recommendations, although in some instances they had encountered difficulties owing to a lack of technical or financial resources. It was reported that advances had been made in developing national anti-drugs plans, measuring land under illicit cultivation, and adopting procedures against money-laundering. Since 1996 an OAS group of experts has undertaken efforts to assist countries in reducing the demand for illegal substances. Activities include the implementation of prevention programmes for street children; the development of communication strategies; and education and community projects relating to the prevention of drug dependence.

The first Specialized Inter-American Conference on Terrorism was held in Lima, Peru, in April 1996. A Declaration and Plan of Action were adopted, according to which member states agreed to co-operate and implement measures to combat terrorism and organized crime. A second conference was held in Mar del Plata, Argentina, in 1998, which culminated in the adoption of the Commitment of Mar del Plata. Member states recommended the establishment of an Inter-American Committee against Terrorism (CICTE) to implement decisions relating to judicial, police and intelligence co-operation. The Committee held its first session in Miami, USA, in October 1999; a second meeting was convened in January 2002. Two special sessions of the CICTE were held in October and November 2001, following the terrorist attacks on targets in the USA in September.

SOCIAL DEVELOPMENT AND EDUCATION

In June 1996 the OAS established a specialized unit for social development and education to assist governments and social institutions of member states to formulate public policies and implement initiatives relating to employment and labour issues, education development, social integration and poverty elimination. It was also to provide technical and operational support for the implementation of inter-American programmes in those sectors, and to promote the exchange of information among experts and professionals working in those fields. In June 1997 the OAS approved an Inter-American Programme to Combat Poverty. The unit serves as the technical secretariat for annual meetings on social development that were to be convened within the framework of the Programme. The unit also administers the Social Networks of Latin America and the Caribbean project, and its co-ordinating committee, which promotes sub-regional co-operation to combat poverty and discrimination. In 1999 the unit was to implement a project funded by the Inter-American Development Bank to place interns and trainees within the Social Network institutions and to promote exchanges between the institutions.

The first meeting of ministers of education of the Americas was held in Brasília, Brazil, in July 1998, based on the mandate of the second Summit of the Americas. The meeting approved an Inter-American Education Programme, formulated by the unit for social development and education, which incorporated the following six priority initiatives: education for priority social sectors; strengthening educational management and institutional development; education for work and youth development; education for citizenship and sustainability in multicultural societies; training in the use of new technologies in teaching the official languages of the OAS; and training of teachers and education administrators. Other programmes in the education sector are undertaken with international agencies and non-governmental organizations.

The OAS supports member states to formulate and implement programmes to promote productive employment and vocational training, to develop small businesses and other employment generation initiatives, and to regulate labour migration. In 1998 the OAS initiated the Labour Market Information System project, which aimed to provide reliable and up-to-date indicators of the labour situation in member countries, to determine the impact of economic policy on the labour situation, and to promote the exchange of information among relevant national and regional institutions. Labour issues were addressed by the second Summit of the Americas, and, following an Inter-American Conference of Labour Ministers, held in Viña del Mar, Chile, in October 1998, two working groups were established to consider the globalization of the economy and its social and labour dimension and the modernization of the state and labour administration.

SUSTAINABLE DEVELOPMENT AND THE ENVIRONMENT

In 1996 a summit meeting on social development adopted a plan of action, based on the objectives of the UN Conference on the Environment and Development, which was held in Rio de Janeiro, Brazil, in June 1992. The OAS was to participate in an inter-agency group to monitor implementation of the action plan. The OAS has subsequently established new financing mechanisms and networks of experts relating to aspects of sustainable development. Technical co-operation activities include multinational basin management; a strategic plan for the Amazon; natural disaster management; and the sustainable development of border areas in Central America and South America. In December 1999 the Inter-American Council for Integral Development approved a policy framework and recommendations for action of a new Inter-American Strategy for Public Participation in Decision-making for Sustainable Development.

The following initiatives have also been undertaken: a Caribbean Disaster Mitigation Project, to help those countries to counter and manage the effects of natural disasters; a Post-Georges Disaster Mitigation initiative specifically to assist countries affected by Hurricane Georges; a Natural Hazards Project to provide a general programme of support to assess member states' vulnerability, to provide technical assistance and training to mitigate the effects of a disaster, and to assist in the planning and formulation of development and preparedness policies; the Renewable Energy in the Americas initiative to promote co-operation and strengthen renewable energy and energy efficiency; an Inter-American Water Resources Network, which aims to promote collaboration, training and the exchange of information within the sector; and a Water Level Observation Network for Central America to provide support for coastal resources management, navigation and disaster mitigation in the countries affected by Hurricane Mitch.

SCIENCE AND TECHNOLOGY

The OAS supports and develops activities to contribute to the advancement of science and technology throughout the Americas, and to promote its contribution to social and sustainable development. In particular, it promotes collaboration, dissemination of information and improved communication between experts and institutions working in the sector. Specialized bodies and projects have been established to promote activities in different fields, for example metrology; co-operation between institutions of accreditation, certification and inspection; the development of instruments of measurements and analysis of science and technology; chemistry; the development of technical standardization and related activities; and collaboration between experts and institutions involved in biotechnology and food technology. The OAS also maintains an information system to facilitate access to databases on science and technology throughout the region.

TOURISM AND CULTURE

A specialized unit for tourism was established in 1996 in order to strengthen and co-ordinate activities for the sustainable development of the tourism industry in the Americas. The unit supports regional and sub-regional conferences and workshops, as well as the Inter-American Travel Congress, which was convened for the first time in 1993 to serve as a forum to formulate region-wide tourism policies. The unit also undertakes research and analysis of the industry.

In 1998 the OAS approved an Inter-American Programme of Culture to support efforts being undertaken by member states and to promote co-operation in areas such as cultural diversity; protection of cultural heritage; training and dissemination of information; and the promotion of cultural tourism. The OAS also assists with the preparation of national and multilateral cultural projects, and co-operates with the private sector to protect and promote cultural assets and events in the region.

COMMUNICATIONS

In June 1993 the OAS General Assembly approved the establishment of an Inter-American Telecommunication Commission. The body has technical autonomy, within the statute and mandate agreed by the Assembly. It aims to facilitate and promote the development of communications in all member countries, in collaboration with the private sector and other organizations, and serves as the principal advisory body of the OAS on matters related to telecommunications.

Finance

The OAS budget for 2002, approved by the General Assembly in mid-2001, amounted to US $84.4m.

Publications

(in English and Spanish)

Américas (6 a year).

Annual Report.

Catalog of Publications (annually).

Ciencia Interamericana (quarterly).

La Educación (quarterly).

Statistical Bulletin (quarterly).

Numerous cultural, legal and scientific reports and studies.

Specialized Organizations and Associated Agencies

Inter-American Children's Institute—IIN: Avda 8 de Octubre 2904, 11600 Montevideo, Uruguay; tel. (2) 4872150; fax (2) 4873242; e-mail iin@redfacil.com.uy; internet www.iin.org.uy; f. 1927; promotes the regional implementation of the Convention on the Rights of the Child, assists in the development of child-oriented public policies; promotes co-operation between states; and aims to develop awareness of problems affecting children and young people in the region. The Institute organizes workshops, seminars, courses, training programmes and conferences on issues relating to children, including, for example, the rights of children, children with disabilities, and the child welfare system. It also provides advisory services, statistical data and other relevant information to authorities and experts throughout the region. Dir-Gen. ALEJANDRO BONASSO. Publs *Boletín* (quarterly), *IINfancia* (2 a year).

Inter-American Commission of Women—CIM: 1889 F St, NW, Suite 880 Washington, DC 20006, USA; tel. (202) 458-6084; fax (202) 458-6094; f. 1928 for the extension of civil, political, economic, social and cultural rights for women. In 1991 a Seed Fund was established to provide financing for grass-roots projects consistent with the Commission's objectives. Pres. INDRANIE CHANDARPAL (Guyana); Exec. Sec. CARMEN LOMELLIN.

Inter-American Committee Against Terrorism: 17th St and Constitution Ave, NW, Washington, DC 20006, USA; tel. (202) 458-3000; fax (202) 458-3967; f. 1999 to enhance the exchange of information via national authorities (including the establishment of an Inter-American database on terrorism issues), formulate proposals to assist member states in drafting counter-terrorism legislation in all states, compile bilateral, sub-regional, regional and multilateral treaties and agreements signed by member states and promote universal adherence to international counter-terrorism conventions, strengthen border co-operation and travel documentation security measures, and develop activities for training and crisis management.

Inter-American Defense Board: 2600 16th St, NW, Washington, DC 20441, USA; tel. (202) 939-7490; internet www.jid.org; works in liaison with member governments to plan and train for the common security interests of the western hemisphere; operates the Inter-American Defense College. Chair. Maj.-Gen. CARL H. FREEMAN (USA).

Inter-American Indigenous Institute: Av. de las Fuentes 106, Col. Jardines del Pedregal, 01900 México, DF, Mexico; tel. (5) 595-8410; fax (5) 652-0089; f. 1940; conducts research on the situation of the indigenous peoples of America; assists the exchange of information; promotes indigenist policies in member states aimed at the elimination of poverty and development within Indian communities, and to secure their position as ethnic groups within a democratic society. Dir Dr JOSÉ MANUEL DEL VAL (Mexico); Exec. Co-ordinator EVANGELINA MENDIZABAL. Publs *América Indígena* (quarterly), *Anuario Indigenista*.

Inter-American Institute for Co-operation on Agriculture—IICA: Apdo Postal 55-2200 San Isidro de Coronado, San José, Costa Rica; tel. 216-0222; fax 216-0233; e-mail iicahq@iica.ac.cr; internet www.iica.int; f. 1942 (as the Inter-American Institute of Agricultural Sciences: new name 1980); supports the efforts of member states to improve agricultural development and rural well-being; encourages co-operation between regional organizations, and provides a forum for the exchange of experience. Dir-Gen. CHELSTON W. D. BRATHWAITE (Barbados). Publ. *Annual Report, Comuniica* (quarterly).

Pan American Development Foundation—PADF: 2600 16th St, NW, Washington, DC 20009-4202, USA; tel. (202) 458-3969; fax (202) 458-6316; e-mail padf-dc@padf.org; internet www.padf.org; f. 1962 to improve economic and social conditions in Latin America and the Caribbean through providing low-interest credit for small-scale entrepreneurs, vocational training, improved health care, agricultural development and reafforestation, and strengthening local non-governmental organizations; provides emergency disaster relief and reconstruction assistance. Mems: foundations and institutes in 35 countries. Pres. ALEXANDER WATSON; Exec. Dir JOHN SANBRAILO. Publ. *PADF Newsletter* (2 a year).

Pan American Health Organization: 525 23rd St, NW, Washington, DC 20037, USA; tel. (202) 974-3000; fax (202) 974-3663; e-mail webmaster@paho.org; internet www.paho.org; f. 1902; co-ordinates regional efforts to improve health; maintains close relations with national health organizations and serves as the Regional Office for the Americas of the World Health Organization. Dir Sir GEORGE ALLEYNE (Barbados).

Pan-American Institute of Geography and History: Ex-Arzobispado 29, 11860 México, DF, Mexico; tel. (5) 277-5888; fax (5) 271-6172; e-mail ipgh@laneta.apc.org; internet www.ipgh.org.mx; f. 1928; co-ordinates and promotes the study of cartography, geophysics, geography and history; it provides technical assistance, conducts training at research centres, distributes publications, and organizes technical meetings. Chair. Dr JORGE SALVADOR LARA (Ecuador); Sec.-Gen. CHESTER ZELAYA GOODMAN (Costa Rica). Publs *Boletín Aéreo* (quarterly), *Revista Cartográfica* (2 a year), *Revista Geográfica* (2 a year), *Revista Historia de América* (2 a year), *Revista de Arqueología Americana* (2 a year), *Revista Geofísica* (2 a year), *Folklore Americano* (2 a year), *Boletín de Antropología Americana* (2 a year).

Summary of the Charter of the Organization of American States

(adopted 30 April 1948, as amended by the 'Protocol of Buenos Aires', signed on 27 February 1967, at the Third Special Inter-American Conference, the 'Protocol of Cartagena de Indias', approved on 5 December 1985, at the Fourteenth Special Session of the General Assembly, the 'Protocol of Washington', approved on 14 December 1992, at the Sixteenth Special Session of the General Assembly, and by the 'Protocol of Managua', adopted on 10 June 1993, at the Nineteenth Special Session of the General Assembly.)

Note: The principal aims and activities of the Organization are contained in Part One of the Charter, and are detailed below. Part Two of the Charter is concerned with the Organs of the Organization, and Part Three General and other Miscellaneous and Transitory Provisions.

In the name of their peoples, the States represented at the Ninth International Conference of American States,

Convinced that the historic mission of America is to offer to man a land of liberty and a favorable environment for the development of his personality and the realization of his just aspirations;

Conscious that that mission has already inspired numerous agreements, whose essential value lies in the desire of the American peoples to live together in peace and, through their mutual understanding and respect for the sovereignty of each one, to provide for the betterment of all, in independence, in equality and under law;

Convinced that representative democracy is an indispensable condition for the stability, peace and development of the region;

Confident that the true significance of American solidarity and good neighborliness can only mean the consolidation on this continent, within the framework of democratic institutions, of a system of individual liberty and social justice based on respect for the essential rights of man;

Persuaded that their welfare and their contribution to the progress and the civilization of the world will increasingly require intensive continental co-operation;

Resolved to persevere in the noble undertaking that humanity has conferred upon the United Nations, whose principles and purposes they solemnly reaffirm;

Convinced that juridical organization is a necessary condition for security and peace founded on moral order and on justice; and

In accordance with Resolution IX of the Inter-American Conference on Problems of War and Peace, held in Mexico City,

have agreed upon the following

PART ONE

I. Nature and Purposes

Article 1

The American States establish by this Charter the international organization that they have developed to achieve an order of peace and justice, to promote their solidarity, to strengthen their collaboration, and to defend their sovereignty, their territorial integrity, and their independence. Within the United Nations, the Organization of American States is a regional agency.

The Organization of American States has no powers other than those expressly conferred upon it by this Charter, none of whose provisions authorizes it to intervene in matters that are within the internal jurisdiction of the Member States.

Article 2

The Organization of American States, in order to put into practice the principles on which it is founded and to fulfill its regional obligations under the Charter of the United Nations, proclaims the following essential purposes:

(a) To strengthen the peace and security of the continent;

(b) To promote and consolidate representative democracy, with due respect for the principle of non-intervention;

(c) To prevent possible causes of difficulties and to ensure the pacific settlement of disputes that may arise among the Member States;

(d) To provide for common action on the part of those States in the event of aggression;

(e) To seek the solution of political, juridical, and economic problems that may arise among them;

(f) To promote, by co-operative action, their economic, social, and cultural development;

(g) To eradicate extreme poverty, which constitutes an obstacle to the full democratic development of the peoples of the hemisphere; and

(h) To achieve an effective limitation of conventional weapons that will make it possible to devote the largest amount of resources to the economic and social development of the Member States.

II. Principles

Article 3

The American States reaffirm the following principles:

(a) International law is the standard of conduct of States in their reciprocal relations;

(b) International order consists essentially of respect for the personality, sovereignty, and independence of States, and the faithful fulfillment of obligations derived from treaties and other sources of international law;

(c) Good faith shall govern the relations between States;

(d) The solidarity of the American States and the high aims which are sought through it require the political organization of those States on the basis of the effective exercise of representative democracy;

(e) Every State has the right to choose, without external interference, its political, economic, and social system and to organize itself in the way best suited to it, and has the duty to abstain from intervening in the affairs of another State. Subject to the foregoing, the American States shall co-operate fully among themselves, independently of the nature of their political, economic, and social systems;

(f) The elimination of extreme poverty is an essential part of the promotion and consolidation of representative democracy and is the common and shared responsibility of the American States;

(g) The American States condemn war of aggression: victory does not give rights;

(h) An act of aggression against one American State is an act of aggression against all the other American States;

(i) Controversies of an international character arising between two or more American States shall be settled by peaceful procedures;

(j) Social justice and social security are bases of lasting peace;

(k) Economic co-operation is essential to the common welfare and prosperity of the peoples of the continent;

(l) The American States proclaim the fundamental rights of the individual without distinction as to race, nationality, creed, or sex;

(m) The spiritual unity of the continent is based on respect for the cultural values of the American countries and requires their close co-operation for the high purposes of civilization;

(n) The education of peoples should be directed toward justice, freedom, and peace.

III. Members

Article 4

All American States that ratify the present Charter are Members of the Organization.

Article 5

Any new political entity that arises from the union of several Member States and that, as such, ratifies the present Charter, shall become a Member of the Organization. The entry of the new political entity into the Organization shall result in the loss of membership of each one of the States which constitute it.

Article 6

Any other independent American State that desires to become a Member of the Organization should so indicate by means of a note addressed to the Secretary General, in which it declares that it is willing to sign and ratify the Charter of the Organization and to accept all the obligations inherent in membership, especially those relating to collective security expressly set forth in Articles 28 and 29 of the Charter.

Article 7

The General Assembly, upon the recommendation of the Permanent Council of the Organization, shall determine whether it is appropriate that the Secretary General be authorized to permit the applicant State to sign the Charter and to accept the deposit of the corresponding instrument of ratification. Both the recommendation of the Permanent Council and the decision of the General Assembly shall require the affirmative vote of two thirds of the Member States.

Article 8

Membership in the Organization shall be confined to independent States of the Hemisphere that were Members of the United Nations as of 10 December 1985, and the non-autonomous territories mentioned in [the OAS] document of 5 November 1985, when they become independent.

Article 9

A Member of the Organization whose democratically constituted government has been overthrown by force may be suspended from the exercise of the right to participate in the sessions of the General Assembly, the Meeting of Consultation, the Councils of the Organization and the Specialized Conferences as well as in the commissions, working groups and any other bodies established.

(a) The power to suspend shall be exercised only when such diplomatic initiatives undertaken by the Organization for the purpose of promoting the restoration of representative democracy in the affected Member State have been unsuccessful;

(b) The decision to suspend shall be adopted at a special session of the General Assembly by an affirmative vote of two-thirds of the Member States;

(c) The suspension shall take effect immediately following its approval by the General Assembly;

(d) The suspension notwithstanding, the Organization shall endeavour to undertake additional diplomatic initiatives to contribute to the re-establishment of representative democracy in the affected Member State;

(e) The Member which has been subject to suspension shall continue to fulfill its obligations to the Organization;

(f) The General Assembly may lift the suspension by a decision adopted with the approval of two-thirds of the Member States;

(g) The powers referred to in this article shall be exercised in accordance with this Charter.

IV. Fundamental Rights and Duties of States

Article 10

States are juridically equal, enjoy equal rights and equal capacity to exercise these rights, and have equal duties. The rights of each State depend not upon its power to ensure the exercise thereof, but upon the mere fact of its existence as a person under international law.

Article 11

Every American State has the duty to respect the rights enjoyed by every other State in accordance with international law.

Article 12

The fundamental rights of States may not be impaired in any manner whatsoever.

Article 13

The political existence of the State is independent of recognition by other States. Even before being recognized, the State has the right to defend its integrity and independence, to provide for its preservation and prosperity, and consequently to organize itself as it sees fit, to legislate concerning its interests, to administer its services, and to determine the jurisdiction and competence of its courts. The exercise of these rights is limited only by the exercise of the rights of other States in accordance with international law.

Article 14
Recognition implies that the State granting it accepts the personality of the new State, with all the rights and duties that international law prescribes for the two States.

Article 15
The right of each State to protect itself and to live its own life does not authorize it to commit unjust acts against another State.

Article 16
The jurisdiction of States within the limits of their national territory is exercised equally over all the inhabitants, whether nationals or aliens.

Article 17
Each State has the right to develop its cultural, political, and economic life freely and naturally. In this free development, the State shall respect the rights of the individual and the principles of universal morality.

Article 18
Respect for and the faithful observance of treaties constitute standards for the development of peaceful relations among States. International treaties and agreements should be public.

Article 19
No State or group of States has the right to intervene, directly or indirectly, for any reason whatever, in the internal or external affairs of any other State. The foregoing principle prohibits not only armed force but also any other form of interference or attempted threat against the personality of the State or against its political, economic, and cultural elements.

Article 20
No State may use or encourage the use of coercive measures of an economic or political character in order to force the sovereign will of another State and obtain from it advantages of any kind.

Article 21
The territory of a State is inviolable; it may not be the object, even temporarily, of military occupation or of other measures of force taken by another State, directly or indirectly, on any grounds whatever. No territorial acquisitions or special advantages obtained either by force or by other means of coercion shall be recognized.

Article 22
The American States bind themselves in their international relations not to have recourse to the use of force, except in the case of self-defense in accordance with existing treaties or in fulfillment thereof.

Article 23
Measures adopted for the maintenance of peace and security in accordance with existing treaties do not constitute a violation of the principles set forth in Articles 19 and 21.

V. Pacific Settlement of Disputes

Article 24
International disputes between Member States shall be submitted to the peaceful procedures set forth in this Charter.

This provision shall not be interpreted as an impairment of the rights and obligations of the Member States under Articles 34 and 35 of the Charter of the United Nations.

Article 25
The following are peaceful procedures: direct negotiation, good offices, mediation, investigation and conciliation, judicial settlement, arbitration, and those which the parties to the dispute may especially agree upon at any time.

Article 26
In the event that a dispute arises between two or more American States which, in the opinion of one of them, cannot be settled through the usual diplomatic channels, the parties shall agree on some other peaceful procedure that will enable them to reach a solution.

Article 27
A special treaty will establish adequate means for the settlement of disputes and will determine pertinent procedures for each peaceful means such that no dispute between American States may remain without definitive settlement within a reasonable period of time.

VI. Collective Security

Article 28
Every act of aggression by a State against the territorial integrity or the inviolability of the territory or against the sovereignty or political independence of an American State shall be considered an act of aggression against the other American States.

Article 29
If the inviolability or the integrity of the territory or the sovereignty or political independence of any American State should be affected by an armed attack or by an act of aggression that is not an armed attack, or by an extracontinental conflict, or by a conflict between two or more American States, or by any other fact or situation that might endanger the peace of America, the American States, in furtherance of the principles of continental solidarity or collective self-defense, shall apply the measures and procedures established in the special treaties on the subject.

VII. Integral Development

Article 30
The Member States, inspired by the principles of inter-American solidarity and co-operation, pledge themselves to a united effort to ensure international social justice in their relations and integral development for their peoples, as conditions essential to peace and security. Integral development encompasses the economic, social, educational, cultural, scientific, and technological fields through which the goals that each country sets for accomplishing it should be achieved.

Article 31
Inter-American co-operation for integral development is the common and joint responsibility of the Member States, within the framework of the democratic principles and the institutions of the inter-American system. It should include the economic, social, educational, cultural, scientific, and technological fields, support the achievement of national objectives of the Member States, and respect the priorities established by each country in its development plans, without political ties or conditions.

Article 32
Inter-American co-operation for integral development should be continuous and preferably channelled through multilateral organizations, without prejudice to bilateral co-operation between Member States.

The Member States shall contribute to inter-American co-operation for integral development in accordance with their resources and capabilities and in conformity with their laws.

Article 33
Development is a primary responsibility of each country and should constitute an integral and continuous process for the establishment of a more just economic and social order that will make possible and contribute to the fulfillment of the individual.

Article 34
The Member States agree that equality of opportunity, the elimination of extreme poverty, equitable distribution of wealth and income and the full participation of their peoples in decisions relating to their own development are, among others, basic objectives of integral development. To achieve them, they likewise agree to devote their utmost efforts to accomplishing the following basic goals:

(a) Substantial and self-sustained increase of per capita national product;
(b) Equitable distribution of national income;
(c) Adequate and equitable systems of taxation;
(d) Modernization of rural life and reforms leading to equitable and efficient land-tenure systems, increased agricultural productivity, expanded use of land, diversification of production and improved processing and marketing systems for agricultural products; and the strengthening and expansion of the means to attain these ends;
(e) Accelerated and diversified industrialization, especially of capital and intermediate goods;
(f) Stability of domestic price levels, compatible with sustained economic development and the attainment of social justice;
(g) Fair wages, employment opportunities, and acceptable working conditions for all;
(h) Rapid eradication of illiteracy and expansion of educational opportunities for all;

(i) Protection of man's potential through the extension and application of modern medical science;
(j) Proper nutrition, especially through the acceleration of national efforts to increase the production and availability of food;
(k) Adequate housing for all sectors of the population;
(l) Urban conditions that offer the opportunity for a healthful, productive, and full life;
(m) Promotion of private initiative and investment in harmony with action in the public sector; and
(n) Expansion and diversification of exports.

Article 35
The Member States should refrain from practising policies and adopting actions or measures that have serious adverse effects on the development of other Member States.

Article 36
Transnational enterprises and foreign private investment shall be subject to the legislation of the host countries and to the jurisdiction of their competent courts and to the international treaties and agreements to which said countries are parties, and should conform to the development policies of the recipient countries.

Article 37
The Member States agree to join together in seeking a solution to urgent or critical problems that may arise whenever the economic development or stability of any Member State is seriously affected by conditions that cannot be remedied through the efforts of that State.

Article 38
The Member States shall extend among themselves the benefits of science and technology by encouraging the exchange and utilization of scientific and technical knowledge in accordance with existing treaties and national laws.

Article 39
The Member States, recognizing the close interdependence between foreign trade and economic and social development, should make individual and united efforts to bring about the following:

(a) Favorable conditions of access to world markets for the products of the developing countries of the region, particularly through the reduction or elimination, by importing countries, of tariff and non-tariff barriers that affect the exports of the Member States of the Organization, except when such barriers are applied in order to diversify the economic structure, to speed up the development of the less-developed Member States, and intensify their process of economic integration, or when they are related to national security or to the needs of economic balance;
(b) Continuity in their economic and social development by means of:

(i) Improved conditions for trade in basic commodities through international agreements, where appropriate; orderly marketing procedures that avoid the disruption of markets, and other measures designed to promote the expansion of markets and to obtain dependable incomes for producers, adequate and dependable supplies for consumers, and stable prices that are both remunerative to producers and fair to consumers;

(ii) Improved international financial co-operation and the adoption of other means for lessening the adverse impact of sharp fluctuations in export earnings experienced by the countries exporting basic commodities;

(iii) Diversification of exports and expansion of export opportunities for manufactured and semi-manufactured products from the developing countries; and

(iv) Conditions conducive to increasing the real export earnings of the Member States, particularly the developing countries of the region, and to increasing their participation in international trade.

Article 40
The Member States reaffirm the principle that when the more developed countries grant concessions in international trade agreements that lower or eliminate tariffs or other barriers to foreign trade so that they benefit the less-developed countries, they should not expect reciprocal concessions from those countries that are incompatible with their economic development, financial, and trade needs.

Article 41
The Member States, in order to accelerate their economic development, regional integration, and the expansion and improvement of the conditions of their commerce, shall promote improvement and co-ordination of transportation and communication in the developing countries and among the Member States.

Article 42
The Member States recognize that integration of the developing countries of the Hemisphere is one of the objectives of the inter-American system and, therefore, shall orient their efforts and take the necessary measures to accelerate the integration process, with a view to establishing a Latin American common market in the shortest possible time.

Article 43
In order to strengthen and accelerate integration in all its aspects, the Member States agree to give adequate priority to the preparation and carrying out of multinational projects and to their financing, as well as to encourage economic and financial institutions of the inter-American system to continue giving their broadest support to regional integration institutions and programs.

Article 44
The Member States agree that technical and financial co-operation that seeks to promote regional economic integration should be based on the principle of harmonious, balanced, and efficient development, with particular attention to the relatively less-developed countries, so that it may be a decisive factor that will enable them to promote, with their own efforts, the improved development of their infrastructure programs, new lines of production, and export diversification.

Article 45
The Member States, convinced that man can only achieve the full realization of his aspirations within a just social order, along with economic development and true peace, agree to dedicate every effort to the application of the following principles and mechanisms:

(a) All human beings, without distinction as to race, sex, nationality, creed, or social condition, have a right to material well-being and to their spiritual development, under circumstances of liberty, dignity, equality of opportunity, and economic security;
(b) Work is a right and a social duty, it gives dignity to the one who performs it, and it should be performed under conditions, including a system of fair wages, that ensure life, health, and a decent standard of living for the worker and his family, both during his working years and in his old age, or when any circumstance deprives him of the possibility of working;
(c) Employers and workers, both rural and urban, have the right to associate themselves freely for the defense and promotion of their interests, including the right to collective bargaining and the workers' right to strike, and recognition of the juridical personality of associations and the protection of their freedom and independence, all in accordance with applicable laws;
(d) Fair and efficient systems and procedures for consultation and collaboration among the sectors of production, with due regard for safeguarding the interests of the entire society;
(e) The operation of systems of public administration, banking and credit, enterprise, and distribution and sales, in such a way, in harmony with the private sector, as to meet the requirements and interests of the community;
(f) The incorporation and increasing participation of the marginal sectors of the population, in both rural and urban areas, in the economic, social, civic, cultural, and political life of the nation, in order to achieve the full integration of the national community, acceleration of the process of social mobility, and the consolidation of the democratic system. The encouragement of all efforts of popular promotion and co-operation that have as their purpose the development and progress of the community;
(g) Recognition of the importance of the contribution of organizations such as labor unions, co-operatives, and cultural, professional, business, neighborhood, and community associations to the life of the society and to the development process;
(h) Development of an efficient social security policy; and

(i) Adequate provision for all persons to have due legal aid in order to secure their rights.

Article 46

The Member States recognize that, in order to facilitate the process of Latin American regional integration, it is necessary to harmonize the social legislation of the developing countries, especially in the labor and social security fields, so that the rights of the workers shall be equally protected, and they agree to make the greatest efforts possible to achieve this goal.

Article 47

The Member States will give primary importance within their development plans to the encouragement of education, science, technology, and culture, oriented toward the overall improvement of the individual, and as a foundation for democracy, social justice, and progress.

Article 48

The Member States will co-operate with one another to meet their educational needs, to promote scientific research, and to encourage technological progress for their integral development. They will consider themselves individually and jointly bound to preserve and enrich the cultural heritage of the American peoples.

Article 49

The Member States will exert the greatest efforts, in accordance with their constitutional processes, to ensure the effective exercise of the right to education, on the following bases:

(a) Elementary education, compulsory for children of school age, shall also be offered to all others who can benefit from it. When provided by the State it shall be without charge;

(b) Middle-level education shall be extended progressively to as much of the population as possible, with a view to social improvement. It shall be diversified in such a way that it meets the development needs of each country without prejudice to providing a general education; and

(c) Higher education shall be available to all, provided that, in order to maintain its high level, the corresponding regulatory or academic standards are met.

Article 50

The Member States will give special attention to the eradication of illiteracy, will strengthen adult and vocational education systems, and will ensure that the benefits of culture will be available to the entire population. They will promote the use of all information media to fulfill these aims.

Article 51

The Member States will develop science and technology through educational, research, and technological development activities and information and dissemination programs. They will stimulate activities in the field of technology for the purpose of adapting it to the needs of their integral development. They will organize their co-operation in these fields efficiently and will substantially increase exchange of knowledge, in accordance with national objectives and laws and with treaties in force.

Article 52

The Member States, with due respect for the individuality of each of them, agree to promote cultural exchange as an effective means of consolidating inter-American understanding; and they recognize that regional integration programs should be strengthened by close ties in the fields of education, science, and culture.

ORGANIZATION OF ARAB PETROLEUM EXPORTING COUNTRIES—OAPEC

Address: POB 20501, Safat 13066, Kuwait.

Telephone: 4844500; **fax:** 4815747; **e-mail:** oapec@qualitynet.net; **internet:** www.oapecorg.

OAPEC was established in 1968 to safeguard the interests of members and to determine ways and means for their co-operation in various forms of economic activity in the petroleum industry. OAPEC member states accounted for 29.3% of total world petroleum production in 2000, and for 11.9% of total global natural gas output in 1999.

MEMBERS

Algeria	Kuwait	Saudi Arabia
Bahrain	Libya	Syria
Egypt	Qatar	United Arab Emirates
Iraq		

Organization

(April 2002)

MINISTERIAL COUNCIL

The Council consists normally of the ministers of petroleum of the member states, and forms the supreme authority of the Organization, responsible for drawing up its general policy, directing its activities and laying down its governing rules. It meets twice yearly, and may hold extraordinary sessions. Chairmanship is on an annual rotation basis.

EXECUTIVE BUREAU

Assists the Council to direct the management of the Organization, approves staff regulations, reviews the budget, and refers it to the Council, considers matters relating to the Organization's agreements and activities and draws up the agenda for the Council. The Bureau comprises one senior official from each member state. Chairmanship is by rotation on an annual basis, following the same order as the Ministerial Council chairmanship. The Bureau convenes at least three times a year.

GENERAL SECRETARIAT

Secretary-General: ABDULAZIZ A. AL-TURKI (Saudi Arabia).

Besides the Office of the Secretary-General, there are four departments: Finance and Administrative Affairs, Information and Library, Technical Affairs, and Economics. The last two form the Arab Centre for Energy Studies (which was established in 1983). At the end of 2000 there were 22 professional staff members and 29 general personnel at the General Secretariat.

JUDICIAL TRIBUNAL

The Tribunal comprises seven judges from Arab countries. Its task is to settle differences in interpretation and application of the OAPEC Agreement, arising between members and also between OAPEC and its affiliates; disputes among member countries on petroleum activities falling within OAPEC's jurisdiction and not under the sovereignty of member countries; and disputes that the Ministerial Council decides to submit to the Tribunal.

President: FARIS ABDUL AL-WAGAYAN.

Registrar: Dr RIAD RASHAD AL-DAOUDI.

Activities

OAPEC co-ordinates different aspects of the Arab petroleum industry through the joint undertakings described below. It co-operates with the League of Arab States and other Arab organizations, and attempts to link petroleum research institutes in the Arab states. It organizes or participates in conferences and seminars, many of which are held jointly with non-Arab organizations in order to enhance Arab and international co-operation. OAPEC collaborates with the AFESD, the Arab Monetary Fund and the League of Arab States in compiling the annual *Joint Arab Economic Report*, which is issued by the Arab Monetary Fund.

OAPEC provides training in technical matters and in documentation and information. The General Secretariat also conducts technical and feasibility studies and carries out market reviews. It provides information through a library, 'databank' and the publications listed below.

The invasion of Kuwait by Iraq in August 1990, and the subsequent international embargo on petroleum exports from Iraq and Kuwait, severely disrupted OAPEC's activities. In December the OAPEC Council decided to establish temporary headquarters in Cairo while Kuwait was under occupation. The Council resolved to reschedule overdue payments by Iraq and Syria over a 15-year period, and to postpone the Fifth Arab Energy Conference from mid-1992 to mid-1994. The Conference was held in Cairo, Egypt, in May 1994. In June OAPEC returned to its permanent headquarters in Kuwait. The Sixth Arab Energy Conference was held in Damascus, Syria, in May 1998, with the theme of 'Energy and Arab Co-operation'. The seventh conference, focusing on the same theme, was to be convened in May 2002, in Cairo, Egypt. It was to be attended by OAPEC ministers of petroleum and energy, senior officials from other Arab states, and representatives of invited institutions and organizations concerned with energy issues.

Finance

The General Secretariat's budget for 2001 amounted to 1,465,000 Kuwaiti dinars (KD). A budget of 117,200 KD was approved for the Judicial Tribunal.

Publications

Annual Statistical Report.

Energy Resources Monitor (quarterly, Arabic).

OAPEC Monthly Bulletin (Arabic and English editions).

Oil and Arab Co-operation (quarterly, Arabic).

Secretary-General's Annual Report (Arabic and English editions).

Papers, studies, conference proceedings.

OAPEC-Sponsored Ventures

Arab Maritime Petroleum Transport Company—AMPTC: POB 22525, Safat 13086, Kuwait; tel. 4844500; fax 4842996; f. 1973 to undertake transport of crude petroleum, gas, refined products and petro-chemicals, and thus to increase Arab participation in the tanker transport industry; auth. cap. US $200m.; Gen. Man. SULAYMAN AL-BASSAM.

Arab Petroleum Investments Corporation—APICORP: POB 9599, Dammam 31423, Saudi Arabia; tel. (3) 847-0444; fax (3) 847-0022; e-mail apicorp@apicorp-arabia.com; internet www.apicorp-arabia.com; f. 1975 to finance investments in petroleum and petrochemicals projects and related industries in the Arab world and in developing countries, with priority being given to Arab joint ventures. Projects financed include gas liquefaction plants, petrochemicals, tankers, oil refineries, pipelines, exploration, detergents, fertilizers and process control instrumentation; auth. cap. US $1,200m.; subs. cap. $460m. Shareholders: Kuwait, Saudi Arabia and United Arab Emirates (17% each), Libya (15%), Iraq and Qatar (10% each), Algeria (5%), Bahrain, Egypt and Syria (3% each). Chair. ABDULLAH A. AZ-ZAID (Saudi Arabia); Gen. Man. and CEO RASHEED AL-MARAJ.

Arab Detergent Chemicals Company—ARADET: POB 27864, el-Monsour, Baghdad, Iraq; tel. (1) 541-9893; f. 1981; produces and markets linear alkyl benzene; an additional project to construct a sodium tripolyphosphate plant has been suspended temporarily owing to the trade embargo against Iraq; APICORP and the Iraqi Government each hold 32% of shares in the co; auth. cap. 72m. Iraqi dinars; subs. cap. 60m. Iraqi dinars.

Arab Petroleum Services Company—APSCO: POB 12925, Tripoli, Libya; tel. (21) 45861; fax (21) 3331930; f. 1977 to provide petroleum services through the establishment of companies specializing in various activities, and to train specialized personnel; auth. cap. 100m. Libyan dinars; subs. cap. 15m. Libyan dinars. Chair. AYAD HUSSEIN AD-DALI; Gen. Man. ISMAIL AL-KORAITLI.

Arab Drilling and Workover Company: POB 680, Suani Rd, km 3.5, Tripoli, Libya; tel. (21) 800064; fax (21) 805945; f. 1980; 40%-owned by APSCO; auth. cap. 12m. Libyan dinars; Gen. Man. MUHAMMAD AHMAD ATTIGA.

Arab Geophysical Exploration Services Company—AGESCO: POB 84224, Airport Rd, Tripoli, Libya; tel. (21) 4804863; fax (21) 4803199; f. 1985; 40%-owned by APSCO; auth. cap. 12m. Libyan dinars; subs. cap. 4m. Libyan dinars; Gen. Man. AYAD HUSSEIN AD-DALI.

Arab Well Logging Company—AWLCO: POB 6225, Baghdad, Iraq; tel. (1) 541-8259; f. 1983; wholly-owned subsidiary of APSCO; provides well-logging services and data interpretation; auth. cap. 7m. Iraqi dinars.

Arab Petroleum Training Institute—APTI: POB 6037, Al-Tajeyat, Baghdad, Iraq; tel. (1) 523-4100; fax (1) 521-0526; f. 1978 to provide instruction in many technical and managerial aspects of the oil industry. From Dec. 1994 the Institute was placed under the trusteeship of the Iraqi Government; the arrangement was scheduled to come to an end in Dec. 1998. Dir HAZIM A. AS-SULTAN.

Arab Shipbuilding and Repair Yard Company—ASRY: POB 50110, Hidd, Bahrain; tel. 671111; fax 670236; e-mail asryco@batelco.com.bh; internet www.asry.net; f. 1974 to undertake repairs and servicing of vessels; operates a 500,000 dwt dry dock in Bahrain; two floating docks operational since 1992; has recently diversified it activities, e.g. into upgrading oil rigs; cap. (auth. and subs.) US $340m.; Chair. EID ABDULLA YOUSIF (Bahrain); Chief Exec. MOHAMED M. AL-KHATEEB.

ORGANIZATION OF THE BLACK SEA ECONOMIC CO-OPERATION—BSEC

Address: Istinye Cad. Müşir Fuad Paşa Yalısı, Eski Tersane 80860 İstinye-İstanbul, Turkey.

Telephone: (212) 229-63-30; **fax:** (212) 229-63-36; **e-mail:** bsec@turk.net; **internet:** www.bsec.gov.tr.

The Black Sea Economic Co-operation (BSEC) was established in 1992 to strengthen regional co-operation, particularly in the field of economic development. In June 1998, at a summit meeting held in Yalta, Ukraine, participating countries signed the BSEC Charter, thereby officially elevating the BSEC to regional organization status. The Charter entered into force on 1 May 1999, at which time the BSEC formally became the Organization of the Black Sea Economic Co-operation, retaining the same acronym.

MEMBERS

Albania	Georgia	Russia
Armenia	Greece	Turkey
Azerbaijan	Moldova	Ukraine
Bulgaria	Romania	

Note: Observer status has been granted to Egypt, France, Germany, Israel, Italy, Poland, Slovakia and Tunisia. The BSEC Business Council, International Black Sea Club, and the Energy Charter Conference also have observer status. Iran, the former Yugoslav republic of Macedonia, the Federal Republic of Yugoslavia and Uzbekistan have applied for full membership.

Organization

(April 2002)

PRESIDENTIAL SUMMIT

The Presidential Summit, comprising heads of state or government of member states, represents the highest authority of the body.

COUNCIL

The Council of Ministers of Foreign Affairs is BSEC's principal decision-making organ. Ministers meet twice a year to review progress and to define new objectives. Chairmanship of the Council rotates among members; the Chairman-in-Office co-ordinates the activities undertaken by BSEC. The Council is supported by a Committee of Senior Officials.

PARLIAMENTARY ASSEMBLY

Address: 1 Hareket Kösku, Dolmabahçe Sarayi, Besiktas, 80680 İstanbul, Turkey.

Telephone: (212) 227-6070; **fax:** (212) 227-6080; **e-mail:** vdeiv@pabsec.org; **internet:** www.pabsec.org.

The Parliamentary Assembly, consisting of the representatives of the national parliaments of member states, was created in February 1993 to provide a legal basis for the implementation of decisions within the BSEC framework. It comprises three committees concerning economic, commercial, technological and environmental affairs; legal and political affairs; and cultural, educational and social affairs.

PERMANENT INTERNATIONAL SECRETARIAT

The Secretariat commenced operations in March 1994. Its tasks are, primarily, of an administrative and technical nature, and include the maintenance of archives, and the preparation and distribution of documentation. Much of the organization's activities are undertaken by 15 working groups, each headed by an Executive Manager, and by various *ad hoc* groups and meetings of experts.

Secretary-General: VALERI CHECHELASHVILI (Georgia).

Activities

In June 1992, at a summit meeting held in İstanbul, heads of state and of government signed the summit declaration on BSEC, and adopted the Bosphorus statement, which established a regional structure for economic co-operation. The grouping attained regional organization status in May 1999 (see above). The organization's main areas of co-operation include transport; communications; trade and economic development; banking and finance; energy; tourism; agriculture and agro-industry; health care and pharmaceuticals; environmental protection; science and technology; the exchange of statistical data and economic information; collaboration between customs authorities; and combating organized crime, drugs-trafficking, trade in illegal weapons and radioactive materials, and terrorism. In order to promote regional co-operation, the organization also aims to strengthen the business environment by providing support for small and medium-sized enterprises; facilitating closer contacts between businesses in member countries; progressively eliminating obstacles to the expansion of trade; creating appropriate conditions for investment and industrial co-operation, in particular through the avoidance of double taxation and the promotion and protection of investments; encouraging the dissemination of information concerning international tenders organized by member states; and promoting economic co-operation in free-trade zones.

BSEC aims to foster relations with other international and regional organizations, and has been granted observer status at the UN General Assembly. In 1999 BSEC agreed upon a Platform of Co-operation for future structured relations with the European Union. The main areas in which BSEC determined to develop co-operation with the EU were transport, energy and telecommunications infrastructure; trade and the promotion of foreign direct investment; sustainable development and environmental protection, including nuclear safety; science and technology; and combating terrorism and organized crime. BSEC supports the Stability Pact for South-Eastern Europe, initiated in June 1999 as a collaborative plan of action by the EU, Group of Seven industrialized nations and Russia (the G-8), regional governments and other organizations concerned with the stability of the region.

A BSEC Business Council was established in İstanbul in December 1992 by the business communities of member states. It has observer status at the BSEC, and aims to identify private and public investment projects, maintain business contacts and develop programmes in various sectors. A Black Sea Trade and Development Bank was inaugurated in June 1999, in Thessaloniki, Greece, as the organization's main funding institution, to finance and implement joint regional projects. It began operations on 1 July 1999. The European Bank for Reconstruction and Development (EBRD, see p. 313) was entrusted as the depository for all capital payments made prior to its establishment. A BSEC Co-ordination Centre, located in Ankara, Turkey, aims to promote the exchange of statistical and economic information. In September 1998 a Black Sea International Studies Centre was inaugurated in Athens, Greece, in order to undertake research concerning the BSEC, in the fields of economics, industry and technology. The transport ministers of BSEC member states adopted a Transport Action Plan in March 2001, which envisaged reducing the disparities in regional transport systems and integrating the BSEC regional transport infrastructure with wider international networks and projects.

BSEC has supported implementation of the Bucharest Convention on the Protection of the Black Sea Against Pollution, adopted by Bulgaria, Georgia, Romania, Russia, Turkey and Ukraine in April 1992. In October 1996 those countries adopted the Strategic Action Plan for the Rehabilitation and Protection of the Black Sea (BSSAP), to be implemented by the Commission of the Bucharest Convention.

ORGANIZATION OF THE ISLAMIC CONFERENCE—OIC

Address: Kilo 6, Mecca Rd, POB 178, Jeddah 21411, Saudi Arabia.

Telephone: (2) 680-0800; **fax:** (2) 687-3568; **e-mail:** info@oic-oci.org; **internet:** www.oic-oci.org.

The Organization was formally established in May 1971, when its Secretariat became operational, following a summit meeting of Muslim heads of state at Rabat, Morocco, in September 1969, and the Islamic Foreign Ministers' Conference in Jeddah in March 1970, and in Karachi, Pakistan, in December 1970.

MEMBERS

Afghanistan*	Indonesia	Palestine
Albania	Iran	Qatar
Algeria	Iraq	Saudi Arabia
Azerbaijan	Jordan	Senegal
Bahrain	Kazakhstan	Sierra Leone
Bangladesh	Kuwait	Somalia
Benin	Kyrgyzstan	Sudan
Brunei	Lebanon	Suriname
Burkina Faso	Libya	Syria
Cameroon	Malaysia	Tajikistan
Chad	Maldives	Togo
The Comoros	Mali	Tunisia
Côte d'Ivoire	Mauritania	Turkey
Djibouti	Morocco	Turkmenistan
Egypt	Mozambique	Uganda
Gabon	Niger	United Arab Emirates
The Gambia	Nigeria†	Uzbekistan
Guinea	Oman	Yemen
Guinea-Bissau	Pakistan	
Guyana		

* Afghanistan's membership of the OIC was suspended in 1996.

† Nigeria renounced its membership in May 1991; however, the OIC has not formally recognized this decision.

Note: Observer status has been granted to Bosnia and Herzegovina, the Central African Republic, Côte d'Ivoire, Thailand, the Muslim community of the 'Turkish Republic of Northern Cyprus', the Moro National Liberation Front (MNLF) of the southern Philippines, the United Nations, the Non-Aligned Movement, the League of Arab States, the Organization of African Unity, the Economic Co-operation Organization, the Union of the Arab Maghreb and the Co-operation Council for the Arab States of the Gulf.

Organization

(April 2002)

SUMMIT CONFERENCES

The supreme body of the Organization is the Conference of Heads of State, which met in 1969 at Rabat, Morocco, in 1974 at Lahore, Pakistan, and in January 1981 at Mecca, Saudi Arabia, when it was decided that summit conferences would be held every three years in future. Ninth Conference: Doha, Qatar, November 2000.

CONFERENCE OF MINISTERS OF FOREIGN AFFAIRS

Conferences take place annually, to consider the means for implementing the general policy of the Organization, although they may also be convened for extraordinary sessions.

SECRETARIAT

The executive organ of the Organization, headed by a Secretary-General (who is elected by the Conference of Ministers of Foreign Affairs for a four-year term, renewable only once) and four Assistant Secretaries-General (similarly appointed).

Secretary-General: Dr ABDELOUAHED BELKEZIZ (Morocco).

At the summit conference in January 1981 it was decided that an International Islamic Court of Justice should be established to adjudicate in disputes between Muslim countries. Experts met in January 1983 to draw up a constitution for the court; however, by 2001 it was not yet in operation.

STANDING COMMITTEES

Al-Quds Committee: f. 1975 to implement the resolutions of the Islamic Conference on the status of Jerusalem (Al-Quds); it meets at the level of foreign ministers; maintains the Al-Quds Fund; Chair. King MUHAMMAD VI of Morocco.

Standing Committee for Economic and Commercial Co-operation (COMCEC): f. 1981; Chair. AHMET NECDET SEZER (Pres. of Turkey).

Standing Committee for Information and Cultural Affairs (COMIAC): f. 1981. Chair. ABDOULAYE WADE (Pres. of Senegal).

Standing Committee for Scientific and Technological Co-operation (COMSTECH): f. 1981; Chair. Gen. PERVEZ MUSHARRAF (Pres. of Pakistan).

Other committees comprise the Islamic Peace Committee, the Permanent Finance Committee, the Committee of Islamic Solidarity with the Peoples of the Sahel, the Six-Member Committee on the Situation of Muslims in the Philippines, the Six-Member Committee on Palestine, and the *ad hoc* Committee on Afghanistan. In addition, there is an Islamic Commission for Economic, Cultural and Social Affairs and OIC contact groups on Bosnia and Herzegovina, and Kosovo, Jammu and Kashmir, and Sierra Leone.

Activities

The Organization's aims, as proclaimed in the Charter that was adopted in 1972, are:

(i) To promote Islamic solidarity among member states;

(ii) To consolidate co-operation among member states in the economic, social, cultural, scientific and other vital fields, and to arrange consultations among member states belonging to international organizations;

(iii) To endeavour to eliminate racial segregation and discrimination and to eradicate colonialism in all its forms;

(iv) To take necessary measures to support international peace and security founded on justice;

(v) To co-ordinate all efforts for the safeguard of the Holy Places and support of the struggle of the people of Palestine, and help them to regain their rights and liberate their land;

(vi) To strengthen the struggle of all Muslim people with a view to safeguarding their dignity, independence and national rights; and

(vii) To create a suitable atmosphere for the promotion of co-operation and understanding among member states and other countries.

The first summit conference of Islamic leaders (representing 24 states) took place in 1969 following the burning of the Al Aqsa Mosque in Jerusalem. At this conference it was decided that Islamic governments should 'consult together with a view to promoting close co-operation and mutual assistance in the economic, scientific, cultural and spiritual fields, inspired by the immortal teachings of Islam'. Thereafter the foreign ministers of the countries concerned met annually, and adopted the Charter of the Organization of the Islamic Conference in 1972.

At the second Islamic summit conference (Lahore, Pakistan, 1974), the Islamic Solidarity Fund was established, together with a committee of representatives which later evolved into the Islamic Commission for Economic, Cultural and Social Affairs. Subsequently, numerous other subsidiary bodies have been set up (see below).

ECONOMIC CO-OPERATION

A general agreement for economic, technical and commercial co-operation came into force in 1981, providing for the establishment of joint investment projects and trade co-ordination. This was followed by an agreement on promotion, protection and guarantee of investments among member states. A plan of action to strengthen economic co-operation was adopted at the third Islamic summit conference in 1981, aiming to promote collective self-reliance and the development of joint ventures in all sectors. In 1994 the 1981 plan of action was revised; the reformulated plan placed greater emphasis on private-sector participation in its implementation. Although several meetings of experts were subsequently held to discuss some of the 10 priority focus areas of the plan, little progress was achieved in implementing it during the 1990s.

A meeting of ministers of industry was held in February 1982, and agreed to promote industrial co-operation, including joint ventures in agricultural machinery, engineering and other basic industries. The fifth summit conference, held in 1987, approved proposals for joint development of modern technology, and for improving scientific and technical skills in the less developed Islamic countries. The first international Islamic trade fair was held in Jeddah, Saudi Arabia, in March 2001.

In 1991 22 OIC member states signed a framework agreement concerning the introduction of a system of trade preferences among member states. It was envisaged that, if implemented, this would represent the first step towards the eventual establishment of an Islamic common market. In May 2001 the OIC Secretary-General urged increased progress in the ratification of the framework agreement. An OIC group of experts was considering the implications of the proposed creation of such a common market.

CULTURAL CO-OPERATION

The Organization supports education in Muslim communities throughout the world, and was instrumental in the establishment of Islamic universities in Niger and Uganda (see below). It organizes seminars on various aspects of Islam, and encourages dialogue with the other monotheistic religions. Support is given to publications on Islam both in Muslim and Western countries. The OIC organizes meetings at ministerial level to consider aspects of information policy and new technologies.

HUMANITARIAN ASSISTANCE

Assistance is given to Muslim communities affected by wars and natural disasters, in co-operation with UN organizations, particularly UNHCR. The countries of the Sahel region (Burkina Faso, Cape Verde, Chad, The Gambia, Guinea, Guinea-Bissau, Mali, Mauritania, Niger and Senegal) receive particular attention as victims of drought. In April 1993 member states pledged US $80m. in emergency assistance for Muslims affected by the war in Bosnia and Herzegovina (see below for details of subsequent assistance). In April 1999 the OIC resolved to send humanitarian aid to assist the displaced ethnic Albanian population of Kosovo and Metohija, in southern Serbia. Several member states have provided humanitarian assistance to the Muslim population affected by the conflict in Chechnya. During 2001 the OIC was providing emergency assistance to Afghanistan.

POLITICAL CO-OPERATION

Since its inception the OIC has called for vacation of Arab territories by Israel, recognition of the rights of Palestinians and of the Palestine Liberation Organization (PLO) as their sole legitimate representative, and the restoration of Jerusalem to Arab rule. The 1981 summit conference called for a *jihad* (holy war—though not necessarily in a military sense) 'for the liberation of Jerusalem and the occupied territories'; this was to include an Islamic economic boycott of Israel. In 1982 Islamic ministers of foreign affairs decided to establish Islamic offices for boycotting Israel and for military co-operation with the PLO. The 1984 summit conference agreed to reinstate Egypt (suspended following the peace treaty signed with Israel in 1979) as a member of the OIC, although the resolution was opposed by seven states.

In August 1990 a majority of ministers of foreign affairs condemned Iraq's recent invasion of Kuwait, and demanded the withdrawal of Iraqi forces. In August 1991 the Conference of Ministers of Foreign Affairs obstructed Iraq's attempt to propose a resolution demanding the repeal of economic sanctions against the country. The sixth summit conference, held in Senegal in December 1991, reflected the divisions in the Arab world that resulted from Iraq's invasion of Kuwait and the ensuing war. Twelve heads of state did not attend, reportedly to register protest at the presence of Jordan and the PLO at the conference, both of which had given support to Iraq. Disagreement also arose between the PLO and the majority of other OIC members when a proposal was adopted to cease the OIC's support for the PLO's *jihad* in the Arab territories occupied by Israel, in an attempt to further the Middle East peace negotiations.

In August 1992 the UN General Assembly approved a non-binding resolution, introduced by the OIC, that requested the UN Security Council to take increased action, including the use of force, in order to defend the non-Serbian population of Bosnia and Herzegovina (some 43% of Bosnians being Muslims) from Serbian aggression, and to restore its 'territorial integrity'. The OIC Conference of Ministers of Foreign Affairs, which was held in December, demanded anew that the UN Security Council take all necessary measures against Serbia and Montenegro, including military intervention, in order to protect the Bosnian Muslims. In February 1993 the OIC appealed to the Security Council to remove the embargo on armaments to Bosnia and Herzegovina with regard to the Bosnian Muslims, to allow them to defend themselves from the Bosnian Serbs, who were better equipped.

A report by an OIC fact-finding mission, which in February 1993 visited Azad Kashmir while investigating allegations of repression of the largely Muslim population of the Indian state of Jammu and Kashmir by the Indian armed forces, was presented to the 1993 Conference. The meeting urged member states to take the necessary measures to persuade India to cease the 'massive human rights violations' in Jammu and Kashmir and to allow the Indian Kashmiris to 'exercise their inalienable right to self-determination'. In September 1994 ministers of foreign affairs, meeting in Islamabad, Pakistan, urged the Indian Government to grant permission for an OIC fact-finding mission, and for other human rights groups, to visit Jammu and Kashmir (which it had continually refused to do) and to refrain from human rights violations of the Kashmiri people. The ministers agreed to establish a contact group on Jammu and Kashmir, which was to provide a mechanism for promoting international awareness of the situation in that region and for seeking a peaceful solution to the dispute. In December OIC heads of state approved a resolution condemning reported human rights abuses by Indian security forces in Kashmir.

In July 1994 the OIC Secretary-General visited Afghanistan and proposed the establishment of a preparatory mechanism to promote national reconciliation in that country. In mid-1995 Saudi Arabia, acting as a representative of the OIC, pursued a peace initiative for Afghanistan and issued an invitation for leaders of the different factions to hold negotiations in Jeddah.

A special ministerial meeting on Bosnia and Herzegovina was held in July 1993, at which seven OIC countries committed themselves to making available up to 17,000 troops to serve in the UN Protection Force in the former Yugoslavia (UNPROFOR). The meeting also decided to dispatch immediately a ministerial mission to persuade influential governments to support the OIC's demands for the removal of the arms embargo on Bosnian Muslims and the convening of a restructured international conference to bring about a political solution to the conflict. In of September 1994 ministers of foreign affairs of nine countries constituting the OIC contact group on Bosnia and Herzegovina, meeting in New York, resolved to prepare an assessment document on the issue, and to establish an alliance with its Western counterpart (comprising France, Germany, Russia, the United Kingdom and the USA). The two groups met in Geneva, Switzerland, in January 1995. In December 1994 OIC heads of state, convened in Morocco, proclaimed that the UN arms embargo on Bosnia and Herzegovina could not be applied to the Muslim authorities of that Republic. The Conference also resolved to review economic relations between OIC member states and any country that supported Serbian activities. An aid fund was established, to which member states were requested to contribute between US $500,000 and $5m., in order to provide further humanitarian and economic assistance to Bosnian Muslims. In relation to wider concerns the conference adopted a Code of Conduct for Combating International Terrorism, in an attempt to control Muslim extremist groups. The code commits states to ensuring that militant groups do not use their territory for planning or executing terrorist activity against other states, in addition to states refraining from direct support or participation in acts of terrorism. In a further resolution the OIC supported the decision by Iraq to recognize Kuwait, but advocated that Iraq comply with all UN Security Council decisions.

In July 1995 the OIC contact group on Bosnia and Herzegovina (at that time comprising Egypt, Iran, Malaysia, Morocco, Pakistan, Saudi Arabia, Senegal and Turkey), meeting in Geneva, declared the UN arms embargo against Bosnia and Herzegovina to be 'invalid'. Several Governments subsequently announced their willingness officially to supply weapons and other military assistance to the Bosnian Muslim forces. In September a meeting of all OIC ministers of defence and foreign affairs endorsed the establishment of an 'assistance mobilization group' which was to supply military, economic, legal and other assistance to Bosnia and Herzegovina. In a joint declaration the ministers also demanded the return of all territory seized by Bosnian Serb forces, the continued NATO bombing of Serb military targets, and that the city of Sarajevo be preserved under a Muslim-led Bosnian Government. In November the OIC Secretary-General endorsed the peace accord for the former Yugoslavia, which was concluded, in Dayton, USA, by leaders of all the conflicting factions, and reaffirmed the commitment of Islamic states to participate in efforts to implement the accord. In the following month the OIC Conference of Ministers of Foreign Affairs, convened in Conakry, Guinea, requested the full support of the international community to reconstruct Bosnia and Herzegovina through humanitarian aid as well as economic and technical co-operation. Ministers declared that Palestine and the establishment of fully-autonomous Palestinian control of Jerusalem were issues of central importance for the Muslim world. The Conference urged the removal of all aspects of occupation and the cessation of the construction of Israeli settlements in the occupied territories. In addition, the final statement of the meeting condemned Armenian aggression against Azerbaijan, registered concern at the persisting civil conflict in Afghanistan, demanded the elimination of all weapons of mass destruction and pledged support for Libya (affected by the US trade embargo). Ministers determined that an intergovernmental group of experts should be established in 1996 to address the situation of minority Muslim communities residing in non-OIC states.

In December 1996 OIC ministers of foreign affairs, meeting in Jakarta, Indonesia, urged the international community to apply pressure on Israel in order to ensure its implementation of the terms of the Middle East peace process. The ministers reaffirmed the importance of ensuring that the provisions of the Dayton Peace Agreement for the former Yugoslavia were fully implemented, called for a peaceful settlement of the Kashmir issue, demanded that Iraq fulfil its obligations for the establishment of security, peace and stability in the region and proposed that an international conference on peace and national reconciliation in Somalia be convened. The ministers elected a new Secretary-General, Azeddine Laraki, who confirmed that the organization would continue to develop its role as an international mediator. In March 1997, at an extraordinary summit held in Pakistan, OIC heads of state and of government reiterated the organization's objective of increasing international pressure on Israel to ensure the full implementation of the terms of the Middle East peace process. An 'Islamabad Declaration' was also adopted, which pledged to increase co-operation between members of the OIC. In June the OIC condemned the decision by the US House of Representatives to recognize Jerusalem as the Israeli capital. The Secretary-General of the OIC issued a statement rejecting the US decision as counter to the role of the USA as sponsor of the Middle East peace plan. In December OIC heads of state attended the eighth summit conference, held in Iran. The Tehran Declaration, issued at the end of the conference, demanded the 'liberation' of the Israeli-occupied territories and the creation of an autonomous Palestinian state. The conference also appealed for a cessation of the conflicts in Afghanistan, and between Armenia and Azerbaijan. It was requested that the UN sanctions against Libya be removed and that the US legislation threatening sanctions against foreign companies investing in certain countries (including Iran and Libya), introduced in July 1996, be dismissed as invalid. In addition, the Declaration encouraged the increased participation of women in OIC activities.

In early 1998 the OIC appealed for an end to the threat of US-led military action against Iraq arising from a dispute regarding access granted to international weapons inspectors. The crisis was averted by an agreement concluded between the Iraqi authorities and the UN Secretary-General in February. In March OIC ministers of foreign affairs, meeting in Doha, Qatar, requested an end to the international sanctions against Iraq. Additionally, the ministers urged all states to end the process of restoring normal trading and diplomatic relations with Israel pending that country's withdrawal from the occupied territories and acceptance of an independent Palestinian state. In April the OIC, jointly with the UN, sponsored new peace negotiations between the main disputing factions in Afghanistan, which were conducted in Islamabad, Pakistan. In early May, however, the talks collapsed and were postponed indefinitely. In September the Secretaries-General of the OIC and UN agreed to establish a joint mission to counter the deteriorating security situation along the Afghan–Iranian border, following the large-scale deployment of Taliban troops in the region and consequent military manoeuvres by the Iranian authorities. They also reiterated the need to proceed with negotiations to conclude a peaceful settlement in Afghanistan. In December the OIC appealed for a diplomatic solution to the tensions arising from Iraq's withdrawal of co-operation with UN weapons inspectors, and criticized subsequent military air-strikes, led by the USA, as having been conducted without renewed UN authority. An OIC Convention on Combating International Terrorism was adopted in 1998. An OIC committee of experts responsible for formulating a plan of action for safeguarding the rights of Muslim communities and minorities met for the first time in 1998.

In early April 1999 ministers of foreign affairs of the countries comprising OIC's contact group met to consider the crisis in Kosovo. The meeting condemned Serbian atrocities being committed against the local Albanian population and urged the provision of international assistance for the thousands of people displaced by the conflict. The group resolved to establish a committee to co-ordinate relief aid provided by member states. The ministers also expressed their willingness to help to formulate a peaceful settlement and to participate in any subsequent implementation force. In June an OIC Parliamentary Union was inaugurated; its founding conference was convened in Tehran, Iran.

In early March 2000 the OIC mediated contacts between the parties to the conflict in Afghanistan, with a view to reviving peace negotiations. Talks, held under OIC auspices, ensued in May. In November OIC heads of state attended the ninth summit conference, held in Doha, Qatar. In view of the significant deterioration in relations between Israel and the Palestinian National Authority during late 2000, the summit issued a Declaration pledging solidarity with the Palestinian cause and accusing the Israeli authorities of implementing large-scale systematic violations of human rights against Palestinians. The summit also issued the Doha Declaration, which reaffirmed commitment to the OIC Charter and undertook to modernize the organization's organs and mechanisms. Both the elected Government of Afghanistan and the Taliban sent delegations to the Doha conference. The summit determined that Afghanistan's official participation in the OIC, suspended in 1996, should not yet be reinstated. In early 2001 a high-level delegation from the OIC visited Afghanistan in an attempt to prevent further destruction of ancient statues by Taliban supporters.

In May 2001 the OIC convened an emergency meeting, following an escalation of Israeli-Palestinian violence. The meeting resolved to halt all diplomatic and political contacts with the Israeli government, while restrictions remained in force against Palestinian-controlled territories. In June the OIC condemned attacks and ongoing discrimination against the Muslim Community in Myanmar. In the same month the OIC Secretary-General undertook a tour of six African countries — Burkina Faso, The Gambia, Guinea, Mali, Niger, and Senegal, — to promote co-operation and to consider further OIC support for those states. In August the Secretary-General condemned Israel's seizure of several Palestinian institutions in East Jerusalem and aerial attacks against Palestinian settlements. The OIC initiated high-level diplomatic efforts to convene a meeting of the UN Security Council in order to discuss the situation. The OIC Secretary-General strongly condemned major terrorist attacks perpetrated in September against targets on the territory of the USA. Soon afterwards the US authorities rejected a proposal by the Taliban regime that an OIC observer mission be deployed to monitor the activities of the Saudi Arabian-born exiledmilitant Islamist fundamentalist leader Osama bin Laden, who wasaccused by the US Government of having co-ordinated the attacks from alleged terrorist bases in the Taliban-administered area of Afghanistan. An extraordinary meeting of OIC ministers of foreign affairs, convened in early October, in Doha, Qatar, to consider the implications of the terrorist atrocities, condemned the attacks and declared its support for combating all manifestations of terrorism within the framework of a proposed collective initiative co-ordinated under the auspices of the UN. The meeting, which did not pronounce directly on the recently-initiated US-led military retaliation against targets in Afghanistan, urged that no Arab or Muslim state should be targeted under the pretext of eliminating terrorism. It determined to establish a fund to assist Afghan civilians. In February 2002 the Secretary-General expressed concern at statements of the US administration describing Iran and Iraq (as well as the Democratic People's Republic of Korea) as belonging to an 'axis of evil' involved in international terrorism and the development of weapons of mass destruction. In early April OIC foreign ministers convened an extraordinary session on terrorism, in Kuala Lumpur, Malaysia. The meeting issued the 'Kuala Lumpur Declaration', which reiterated member states' collective resolve to combat terrorism, recalling the organization's 1994 code of conduct and 1998 convention to this effect; condemned attempts to associate terrorist activities with Islamists or any other particular creed, civilization or nationality, and rejected attempts to associate Islamic states or the Palestinian struggle with terrorism; rejected the implementation of international action against any Muslim state on the pretext of combating terrorism; urged the organization of a global conference on international terrorism; and urged an examination of the root causes of international terrorism. In addition, the meeting strongly condemned Israel's ongoing military intervention in areas controlled by the Palestinian National Authority. The meeting adopted a plan of action on addressing the issues raised in the declaration. Its implementation was to be co-ordinated by a 13-member committee on international terrorism. Member states were encouraged to sign and ratify the Convention on Combating International Terrorism in order to accelerate its implementation.

Finance

The OIC's activities are financed by mandatory contributions from member states. The budget for 2000/01 totalled US $11.4m.

SUBSIDIARY ORGANS

Islamic Centre for the Development of Trade: Complexe Commercial des Habous, ave des FAR, BP 13545, Casablanca, Morocco; tel. (2) 314974; fax (2) 310110; e-mail icdt@icdt.org; internet www.icdt.org; f. 1983 to encourage regular commercial contacts, harmonize policies and promote investments among OIC mems. Dir-Gen. RACHDI ALLAL. Publs *Tijaris: International and Inter-Islamic Trade Magazine* (bi-monthly), *Inter-Islamic Trade Report* (annually).

Islamic Institute of Technology—IIT: GPO Box 3003, Board-Bazar, Gazipur 1704, Dhaka, Bangladesh; tel. (2) 980-0960; fax (2)980-0970; e-mail dg@iit.dhaka.edu; internet www.iitoic-dhaka.edu; f. 1981 to develop human resources in OIC mem. states, with special reference to engineering, technology, tech. and vocational education and research; 224 staff and 1,000 students; library of 23,000 vols. Dir-Gen. Prof. Dr M. ANWAR HOSSAIN. Publs *News Bulletin* (annually), annual calendar and announcement for admission, reports, human resources development series.

Islamic Jurisprudence (Fiqh) Academy: POB 13917, Jeddah, Saudi Arabia; tel. (2) 667-1664; fax (2) 667-0873; internet www.fiqhacademy.org.sa; f. 1982. Sec.-Gen. Sheikh MOHAMED HABIB IBN AL-KHODHA.

Islamic Solidarity Fund: c/o OIC Secretariat, POB 178, Jeddah 21411, Saudi Arabia; tel. (2) 680-0800; fax (2) 687-3568; f. 1974 to meet the needs of Islamic communities by providing emergency aid and the finance to build mosques, Islamic centres, hospitals, schools and universities. Chair. Sheikh NASIR ABDULLAH BIN HAMDAN; Exec. Dir ABDULLAH HERSI.

Islamic University of Niger: BP 11507, Niamey, Niger; tel. 723903; fax 733796; f. 1984; provides courses of study in *Shari'a* (Islamic law) and Arabic language and literature; also offers courses in pedagogy and teacher training; receives grants from Islamic Solidarity Fund and contributions from OIC member states. Rector Prof. ABDELALI OUDHRIRI.

Islamic University in Uganda: POB 2555, Mbale, Uganda; tel. (45) 33502; fax (45) 34452; e-mail iuiu@info.com.co.ug; Kampala Liaison Office: POB 7689, Kampala; tel. (41) 236874; fax (41) 254576; f. 1988 to meet the educational needs of Muslim populations in English-speaking African countries; mainly financed by OIC. Principal Officer Prof. MAHDI ADAMU.

Research Centre for Islamic History, Art and Culture—IRCICA: POB 24, Beşiktaş 80692, İstanbul, Turkey; tel. (212) 2591742; fax (212) 2584365; e-mail ircica@superonline.com; internet www.ircica.org; f. 1980; library of 50,000 vols. Dir-Gen. Prof. Dr EKMELEDDİN İHSANOĞLU. Publs *Newsletter* (3 a year), monographical studies.

Statistical, Economic and Social Research and Training Centre for the Islamic Countries: Attar Sok 4, GOP 06700, Ankara, Turkey; tel. (312) 4686172; fax (312) 4673458; e-mail centre@sesrtcic.org; internet www.sesrtcic.org; f. 1978. Dir-Gen. ERDINÇ ERDÜN. Publs *Journal of Economic Co-operation among Islamic Countries* (quarterly), *Inforep* (quarterly), *Statistical Yearbook* (annual).

SPECIALIZED INSTITUTIONS

International Islamic News Agency—IINA: King Khalid Palace, Madinah Rd, POB 5054, Jeddah, Saudi Arabia; tel. (2) 665-8561; fax (2) 665-9358; e-mail iina@ogertel.com; internet www.islamicnews.org; f. 1972. Dir-Gen. ABDULWAHAB KASHIF.

Islamic Educational, Scientific and Cultural Organization—ISESCO: BP 755, Rabat 10104, Morocco; tel. (7) 772433; fax (7) 772058; e-mail cid@isesco.org.ma; internet www.isesco.org.ma; f. 1982. Dir-Gen. Dr ABDULAZIZ BIN OTHMAN AL-TWAIJRI. Publs *ISESCO Newsletter* (quarterly), *Islam Today* (2 a year), *ISESCO Triennial*.

Islamic States Broadcasting Organization—ISBO: POB 6351, Jeddah 21442, Saudi Arabia; tel. (2) 672-1121; fax (2) 672-2600; f. 1975. Sec.-Gen. HUSSEIN AL-ASKARY.

The Islamic Development Bank (see p. 383) is also a Specialized Institution of the OIC.

AFFILIATED INSTITUTIONS

International Association of Islamic Banks—IAIB: King Abdulaziz St, Queen's Bldg, 23rd Floor, Al-Balad Dist, POB 9707, Jeddah 21423, Saudi Arabia; tel. (2) 651-6900; fax (2) 651-6552; f. 1977 to link financial institutions operating on Islamic banking principles; activities include training and research; mems: 192 banks and other financial institutions in 34 countries. Sec.-Gen. SAMIR A. SHAIKH.

Islamic Chamber of Commerce and Industry: POB 3831, Clifton, Karachi 75600, Pakistan; tel. (21) 5874756; fax (21) 5870765; e-mail icci@icci-oic.org; internet www.icci.org.pk/islamic/main.html; f. 1979 to promote trade and industry among member states; comprises nat. chambers or feds of chambers of commerce and industry. Sec.-Gen. AQEEL AHMAD AL-JASSEM.

Islamic Committee for the International Crescent: POB 17434, Benghazi, Libya; tel. (61) 95823; f. 1979 to attempt to alleviate the suffering caused by natural disasters and war. Sec.-Gen. Dr AHMAD ABDALLAH CHERIF.

Islamic Solidarity Sports Federation: POB 5844, Riyadh 11442, Saudi Arabia; tel. and fax (1) 482-2145; f. 1981. Sec.-Gen. Dr MOHAMMAD SALEH GAZDAR.

Organization of Islamic Capitals and Cities—OICC: POB 13621, Jeddah 21414, Saudi Arabia; tel. (2) 665-5896; fax (2) 665-7516; e-mail oiccorg@icc.net.sa; f. 1980 to promote and develop co-operation among OICC mems, to preserve their character and heritage, to implement planning guide-lines for the growth of Islamic cities and to upgrade standards of public services and utilities in those cities. Sec.-Gen. OMAR ABDULLAH KADI.

Organization of the Islamic Shipowners' Association: POB 14900, Jeddah 21434, Saudi Arabia; tel. (2) 663-7882; fax (2) 660-4920; e-mail oisa@sbm.net.sa; f. 1981 to promote co-operation among maritime cos in Islamic countries. In 1998 mems approved the establishment of a new commercial venture, the Bakkah Shipping Company, to enhance sea transport in the region. Sec.-Gen. Dr ABDULLATIF A. SULTAN.

World Federation of Arab-Islamic Schools: POB 3446, Jeddah, Saudi Arabia; tel. (2) 670-0019; fax (2) 671-0823; f. 1976; supports Arab-Islamic schools world-wide and encourages co-operation between the institutions; promotes the dissemination of the Arabic language and Islamic culture; supports the training of personnel.

ORGANIZATION OF THE PETROLEUM EXPORTING COUNTRIES—OPEC

Address: Obere Donaustrasse 93, 1020 Vienna, Austria.

Telephone: (1) 211-12-279; **fax:** (1) 214-98-27; **e-mail:** info@opec.org; **internet:** www.opec.org.

OPEC was established in 1960 to link countries whose main source of export earnings is petroleum; it aims to unify and co-ordinate members' petroleum policies and to safeguard their interests generally. The OPEC Fund for International Development is described on p. 486.

OPEC's share of world petroleum production was 41.5% in 2000 (compared with 44.7% in 1980 and 54.7% in 1974). OPEC members were estimated to possess 79.3% of the world's known reserves of crude petroleum in 2000; about two-thirds of these were in the Middle East. In 2000 OPEC members possessed about 44.4% of known reserves of natural gas.

MEMBERS

Algeria	Kuwait	Saudi Arabia
Indonesia	Libya	United Arab Emirates
Iran	Nigeria	Venezuela
Iraq	Qatar	

Organization

(April 2002)

CONFERENCE

The Conference is the supreme authority of the Organization, responsible for the formulation of its general policy. It consists of representatives of member countries, who examine reports and recommendations submitted by the Board of Governors. It approves the appointment of Governors from each country and elects the Chairman of the Board of Governors. It works on the unanimity principle, and meets at least twice a year.

BOARD OF GOVERNORS

The Board directs the management of the Organization; it implements resolutions of the Conference and draws up an annual budget. It consists of one governor for each member country, and meets at least twice a year.

MINISTERIAL MONITORING COMMITTEE

The Committee (f. 1982) is responsible for monitoring price evolution and ensuring the stability of the world petroleum market. As such, it is charged with the preparation of long-term strategies, including the allocation of quotas to be presented to the Conference. The Committee consists of all national representatives, and is normally convened four times a year. A Ministerial Monitoring Sub-committee, reporting to the Committee on production and supply figures, was established in 1993.

ECONOMIC COMMISSION

A specialized body operating within the framework of the Secretariat, with a view to assisting the Organization in promoting stability in international prices for petroleum at equitable levels; consists of a Board, national representatives and a commission staff; meets at least twice a year.

SECRETARIAT

Secretary-General: Dr ALÍ RODRÍGUEZ ARAQUE (Venezuela).

Research Division: comprises three departments:

Data Services Department: Maintains and expands information services to support the research activities of the Secretariat and those of member countries; collects, collates and analyses statistical information and provides essential data for forecasts and estimates necessary for OPEC medium- and long-term strategies.

Energy Studies Department: Energy Section monitors, forecasts and analyses developments in the energy and petrochemical industries and their implications for OPEC, and prepares forecasts of demands for OPEC petroleum and gas. Petroleum Section assists the Board of the Economic Commission in determining the relative values of OPEC crude petroleum and gases and in developing alternative methodologies for this purpose.

Petroleum Market Analysis Department: Monitors and analyses short-term oil market indicators and world economic developments, factors affecting the supply and demand balance, policy developments affecting prices and petroleum demand, crude oil and product market performance, stocks, spot price movements and refinery utilization.

Division Director: Dr ADNAN SHIHAB-ELDIN (Kuwait).

Administration and Human Resources Department: Responsible for all organization methods, provision of administrative services for all meetings, personnel matters, budgets, accounting and internal control; reviews general administrative policies and industrial relations practised throughout the oil industry; **Head:** S. J. SENUSSI.

Public Relations and Information Department: Concerned with communicating OPEC objectives, decisions and actions; produces and distributes a number of publications, films, slides and tapes; and disseminates news of general interest regarding the Organization and member countries on energy and other related issues. Operates a daily on-line news service, the OPEC News Agency (OPECNA). An OPEC Library contains an extensive collection of energy-related publications; **Head:** FAROUK U. MUHAMMED (Nigeria).

Legal Office: Provides legal advice, supervises the Secretariat's legal commitments, evaluates legal issues of concern to the Organization and member countries, and recommends appropriate action; **Legal Officer:** DOLORES DOBARRO DE TORRES (Venezuela).

Office of the Secretary-General: Provides the Secretary-General with executive assistance in maintaining contacts with governments, organizations and delegations, in matters of protocol and in the preparation for and co-ordination of meetings; **Officer-in-Charge:** KARIN CHACIN.

In September 2000 the Conference agreed that regular meetings of heads of state or government should be convened every five years.

Record of Events

1960 The first OPEC Conference was held in Baghdad in September, attended by representatives from Iran, Iraq, Kuwait, Saudi Arabia and Venezuela.

1961 Second Conference, Caracas, January. Qatar was admitted to membership; a Board of Governors was formed and statutes agreed.

1962 Fourth Conference, Geneva, April and June. Protests were addressed to petroleum companies against price cuts introduced in August 1960. Indonesia and Libya were admitted to membership.

1965 In July the Conference reached agreement on a two-year joint production programme, implemented from 1965 to 1967, to limit annual growth in output to secure adequate prices.

1967 Abu Dhabi was admitted to membership.

1969 Algeria was admitted to membership.

1970 Twenty-first Conference, Caracas, December. Tax on income of petroleum companies was raised to 55%.

1971 A five-year agreement was concluded in February between the six producing countries in the Gulf and 23 international petroleum companies (Teheran Agreement). Nigeria was admitted to membership.

1972 In January petroleum companies agreed to adjust petroleum revenues of the largest producers after changes in currency exchange rates (Geneva Agreement).

1973 OPEC and petroleum companies concluded an agreement whereby posted prices of crude petroleum were raised by 11.9% and a mechanism was installed to make monthly adjustments to prices in future (Second Geneva Agreement).
Negotiations with petroleum companies on revision of the Teheran Agreement collapsed in October, and the Gulf states unilaterally declared 70% increases in posted prices, from US $3.01 to $5.11 per barrel. In December the Conference resolved to increase the posted price by nearly 130%, to $11.65 per barrel, from 1 January 1974. Ecuador was admitted to full membership and Gabon became an associate member.

1974 As a result of Saudi opposition to the December price increase, prices were held at current level for first quarter (and subsequently for the remainder of 1974). Abu Dhabi's membership was transferred to the United Arab Emirates (UAE). A meeting in June increased royalties charged to petroleum companies from 12.5% to 14.5% in all member states except Saudi Arabia. A meeting in September increased governmental take by about 3.5% through further increases in royalties on equity crude to 16.67% and in taxes to 65.65%, except in Saudi Arabia.

1975 OPEC's first summit meeting of heads of state or government was held in Algiers in March. Gabon was admitted to full membership. A ministerial meeting in September agreed to raise prices by 10% for the period until June 1976.

1976 The OPEC Fund for International Development was created in May. In December 11 member states endorsed a rise in basic prices of 10% as of 1 January 1977, and a further 5% rise as of 1 July 1977. However, Saudi Arabia and the UAE decided to raise their prices by 5% only.

1977 Following an earlier waiver by nine members of the 5% second stage of the price increase, Saudi Arabia and the UAE announced in July that they would both raise their prices by 5%. As a result, a single level of prices throughout the organization was restored. Because of continued disagreements between the 'moderates', led by Saudi Arabia and Iran, and the 'radicals', led by Algeria, Libya and Iraq, the Conference, held in December, was unable to settle on an increase in prices.

1978 The June Conference agreed that price levels should remain stable until the end of the year. In December it was decided to raise prices in four instalments, in order to compensate for the effects of the depreciation of the US dollar. These would bring a rise of 14.5% over nine months, but an average increase of 10% for 1979.

1979 At an extraordinary meeting in March members decided to raise prices by 9%. In June the Conference agreed minimum and maximum prices that seemed likely to add between 15% and 20% to import bills of consumer countries. The December Conference agreed in principle to convert the OPEC Fund into a development agency with its own legal personality.

1980 In June the Conference decided to set the price for a marker crude at US $32 per barrel, and that the value differentials which could be added above this ceiling (on account of quality and geographical location) should not exceed $5 per barrel. The planned OPEC summit meeting in Baghdad in November was postponed indefinitely because of the Iran–Iraq war, but the scheduled ministerial meeting went ahead in Bali in December, with both Iranians and Iraqis present. A ceiling price of $41 per barrel was fixed for premium crudes.

1981 In May attempts to achieve price reunification were made, but Saudi Arabia refused to increase its US $32 per barrel price unless the higher prices charged by other countries were lowered. Most of the other OPEC countries agreed to cut production by 10% so as to reduce the surplus. An emergency meeting in Geneva in August again failed to unify prices, although Saudi Arabia agreed to reduce production by 1m. barrels per day (b/d). In October OPEC countries agreed to increase the Saudi marker price to $34 per barrel, with a ceiling price of $38 per barrel.

1982 In March an emergency meeting of petroleum ministers was held in Vienna and agreed (for the first time in OPEC's history) to defend the Organization's price structure by imposing an overall production ceiling of 18m. b/d. In December the Conference agreed to limit OPEC production to 18.5m. b/d in 1983 but postponed the allocation of national quotas pending consultations among the respective governments.

1983 In January an emergency meeting of petroleum ministers, fearing a collapse in world petroleum prices, decided to reduce the production ceiling to 17.5m. b/d, but failed to agree on individual production quotas or on adjustments to the differentials in prices charged for the high-quality crude petroleum produced by Algeria, Libya and Nigeria compared with that produced by the Gulf States. In February Nigeria cut its prices to US $30 per barrel, following a collapse in its production. To avoid a 'price war' OPEC set the official price of marker crude at $29 per barrel, and agreed to maintain existing price differentials at the level agreed on in March 1982, with the temporary exception that the differentials for Nigerian crudes should be $1 more than the price of the marker crude. It also agreed to maintain the production ceiling of 17.5m. b/d and allocated quotas for each member country except Saudi Arabia, which was to act as a 'swing producer' to supply the balancing quantities to meet market requirements.

1984 In October the production ceiling was lowered to 16m. b/d. In December price differentials for light (more expensive) and heavy (cheaper) crudes were slightly altered in an attempt to counteract price-cutting by non-OPEC producers, particularly Norway and the United Kingdom.

1985 In January members (except Algeria, Iran and Libya) effectively abandoned the marker price system. During the year production in excess of quotas by OPEC members, unofficial discounts and barter deals by members, and price cuts by non-members (such as Mexico, which had hitherto kept its prices in line with those of OPEC) contributed to a weakening of the market.

1986 During the first half of the year petroleum prices dropped to below US $10 per barrel. In April ministers agreed to set OPEC production at 16.7m. b/d for the third quarter of 1986 and at 17.3m. b/d for the fourth quarter. Algeria, Iran and Libya dissented. Discussions were also held with non-member countries (Angola, Egypt, Malaysia, Mexico and Oman), which agreed to co-operate in limiting production, although the United Kingdom declined. In August all members, with the exception of Iraq (which demanded to be allowed the same quota as Iran and, when this was denied it, refused to be a party to the agreement), agreed upon a return to production quotas, with the aim of cutting production to 14.8m. b/d (about 16.8m. b/d including Iraq's production) for the ensuing two months. This measure resulted in an increase in prices to about $15 per barrel, and was extended until the end of the year. In December members (with the exception of Iraq) agreed to return to a fixed pricing system at a level of $18 per barrel as the OPEC reference price, with effect from 1 February 1987. OPEC's total production for the first half 1987 was not to exceed 15.8m. b/d.

1987 In June, with prices having stabilized, the Conference decided that production during the third and fourth quarters of the year should be limited to 16.6m. b/d (including Iraq's production). However, total production continued to exceed the agreed levels. In December ministers decided to extend the existing agreement for the first half of 1988, although Iraq, once more, refused to participate.

1988 By March prices had fallen below US $15 per barrel. In April non-OPEC producers offered to reduce the volume of their petroleum exports by 5% if OPEC members would do the same. Saudi Arabia, however, refused to accept further reductions in production, insisting that existing quotas should first be more strictly enforced. In June the previous production limit (15.06m. b/d, excluding Iraq's production) was again renewed for six months, in the hope that increasing demand would be sufficient to raise prices. By October, however, petroleum prices were below $12 per barrel. In November a new agreement was reached, limiting total production (including that of Iraq) to 18.5m. b/d, with effect from 1 January 1989. Iran and Iraq finally agreed to accept identical quotas.

1989 In June (when prices had returned to about US $18 per barrel) ministers agreed to increase the production limit to 19.5m. b/d for the second half of 1989. However, Kuwait and the UAE indicated that they would not feel bound to observe this limit. In September the production limit was again increased, to 20.5m. b/d, and in November the limit for the first half of 1990 was increased to 22m. b/d.

1990 In May members resolved to adhere more strictly to the agreed production quotas, in response to a sharp decline in prices. By late June, however, it was reported that total production had decreased by only 400,000 b/d, and prices remained at about US $14 per barrel. In July Iraq threatened to take military action against Kuwait unless it reduced its petroleum production. In the same month OPEC members agreed to limit output to 22.5m. b/d. In August Iraq invaded Kuwait, and petroleum exports by the two countries were halted by an international embargo. Petroleum prices immediately increased to exceed $25 per barrel. Later in the month an informal consultative meeting of OPEC ministers placed the July agreement in abeyance, and permitted a temporary increase in production of petroleum, of between 3m. and 3.5m. b/d (mostly by Saudi Arabia, the UAE and Venezuela). In September and October prices fluctuated in response to political developments in the Gulf region, reaching a point in excess of $40 per barrel in early October, but falling to about $25 per barrel by the end of the month. In December a meeting of OPEC members voted to maintain the high levels of production and to reinstate the quotas that had been agreed in July, once the Gulf crisis was over. During the period August 1990–February 1991 Saudi Arabia increased its petroleum output from 5.4m. to 8.5m. b/d. Seven of the other OPEC states also produced in excess of their agreed quotas.

1991 In March, in an attempt to reach the target of a minimum reference price of US $21 per barrel, ministers agreed to reduce production from 23m. b/d to 22.3m. b/d, although Saudi Arabia refused to return to its pre-August 1990 quota. In June ministers decided to maintain the ceiling of 22.3m. b/d into the third quarter of the year, since Iraq and Kuwait were still unable to export their petroleum. In September it was agreed that OPEC members' production for the last quarter of 1991 should be raised to 23.65m. b/d, and in November the OPEC Conference decided to maintain the increased production ceiling during the first quarter of 1992. From early November, however, the price of petroleum declined sharply, owing to lower than anticipated demand.

1992 The Ministerial Monitoring Committee, meeting in February, decided to impose a production ceiling of 22.98m. b/d with immediate effect. In May ministers agreed to maintain the production restriction during the third quarter of 1992. Kuwait, which was resuming production in the wake of the extensive damage inflicted on its oil-wells by Iraq during the Gulf War, was granted a special dispensation to produce without a fixed quota. During the first half of 1992 member states' petroleum output consistently exceeded agreed levels, with Saudi Arabia and Iran (despite its stance on reducing production) the principal over-producers. In June, at the UN Conference on Environment and Development, OPEC's Secretary-General expressed its member countries' strong objections to the tax on fossil fuels (designed to reduce pollution) proposed by the EC. In September agreement was reached on a production ceiling of 24.2m. b/d for the final quarter of 1992, in an attempt to raise the price of crude petroleum to the OPEC target of US $21 per barrel. At the Conference, held in late November, Ecuador formally resigned from OPEC, the first country ever to do so, citing as reasons the high membership fee and OPEC's refusal to increase Ecuador's quota. The meeting agreed to restrict production to 24.58m. b/d for the first quarter of 1993 (24.46m. b/d, excluding Ecuador).

1993 In February a quota was set for Kuwait for the first time since the onset of the Gulf crisis. Kuwait agreed to produce 1.6m. b/d (400,000 less than current output) from 1 March, on the understanding that this would be substantially increased in the third quarter of the year. The quota for overall production from 1 March was set at 23.58m. b/d. A Ministerial Monitoring Sub-committee was established to supervise compliance with quotas. In June OPEC ministers decided to 'roll over' the overall quota of 23.58m. b/d into the third quarter of the year. However, Kuwait rejected its new allocation of 1.76m. b/d, demanding a quota of at least 2m. In July discussions between Iraq and the UN on the possible supervised sale of Iraqi petroleum depressed petroleum prices to below US $16 per barrel. The Monitoring Sub-committee urged member states to adhere to their production quotas (which were exceeded by a total of 1m. b/d in July). At the end of September an extraordinary meeting of the Conference agreed on a raised production ceiling of 24.52m. b/d, to be effective for six months from 1 October. Kuwait accepted a quota of 2m. b/d, which brought the country back into the production ceiling mechanism. Iran agreed on an allocation of 3.6m. b/d, while Saudi Arabia consented to freeze production at current levels, in order to support petroleum prices which remained persistently low. In November the Conference rejected any further reduction in production. Prices subsequently fell below $14.

1994 In March ministers opted to maintain the output quotas agreed in September 1993 until the end of the year, and urged non-OPEC producers to freeze their production levels. (Iraq failed to endorse the agreement, recognizing only the production agreement adopted in July 1990.) At the meeting Saudi Arabia resisted a proposal from Iran and Nigeria, both severely affected by declines in petroleum revenue, to reduce its production by 1m. b/d in order to boost prices. In June the Conference endorsed the decision to maintain the existing production ceiling, and attempted to reassure commodity markets by implying that the production agreement would remain in effect until the end of 1994. Ministers acknowledged that there had been a gradual increase in petroleum prices in the second quarter of the year, with an average basket price of US $15.6 per barrel for that period. In November OPEC ministers endorsed a proposal by Saudi Arabia to maintain the existing production quota, of 24.52m. b/d, until the end of 1995.

1995 In January it was reported that Gabon was reconsidering its membership of OPEC, owing to difficulties in meeting its budget contribution. During the first half of the year Gabon consistently exceeded its quota of 287,000 b/d, by 48,000 b/d, and the country failed to send a delegate to the ministerial Conference in June. At the Conference ministers expressed concern at OPEC's falling share of the world petroleum market. The Conference criticized the high level of North Sea production, by Norway and the United Kingdom, and urged collective production restraint in order to stimulate prices. In November the Conference agreed to extend the existing production quota, of 24.52m. b/d, for a further six months, in order to stabilize prices. During the year, however, output remained in excess of the production quotas, some 25.58m. b/d.

1996 The possibility of a UN-Iraqi agreement permitting limited petroleum sales dominated OPEC concerns in the first half of the year and contributed to price fluctuations in the world markets. By early 1996 output by OPEC countries was estimated to be substantially in excess of quota levels; however, the price per barrel remained relatively buoyant (the average basket price reaching US $21 in March), owing largely to unseasonal cold weather in the northern hemisphere. In May a memorandum of understanding was signed between Iraq and the UN to allow the export of petroleum, up to a value of $2,000m. over a six-month period, in order to fund humanitarian relief efforts within that country. In June the Conference agreed to increase the overall output ceiling by 800,000 b/d, i.e. the anticipated level of exports from Iraq in the first six months of the agreement. Gabon's withdrawal from the Organization was confirmed at the meeting. As a result of these developments, the new production ceiling was set at 25.03m. b/d. Independent market observers expressed concern that, without any formal agreement to reduce overall production and given the actual widespread violation of the quota system, the renewed export of Iraqi petroleum would substantially depress petroleum prices. However, the markets remained stable as implementation of the UN-Iraqi agreement was delayed. In September the monitoring group acknowledged that members were exceeding their production quotas, but declined to impose any punitive measures (owing to the steady increase in petroleum prices). In November the Conference agreed to maintain the existing production quota for a further six months. Also in that month, Iraq accepted certain disputed technical terms of the UN agreement, enabling the export of petroleum to commence in December.

1997 During the first half of the year petroleum prices declined, reaching a low of US $16.7 per barrel in early April, owing to the Iraqi exports, depressed world demand and persistent overproduction. In June the Conference agreed to extend the existing production ceiling, of 25.03m. b/d, for a further six-month period. Member states resolved to adhere to their individual quotas in order to reduce the cumulative excess production of an estimated 2m. b/d; however, Venezuela, which (some sources claimed) was producing almost 800,000 b/d over its quota of 2.4m. b/d, declined to co-operate. An escalation in political tensions in the Gulf region in October, in particular Iraq's reluctance to co-operate with UN inspectors, prompted an increase in the price of crude petroleum to some $21.2 per barrel. Price fluctuations ensued, although there was a general downward trend. In November the OPEC Conference, meeting in Jakarta, approved a proposal by Saudi Arabia, to increase the overall production ceiling by some 10%, with effect from 1 January 1998, in order to meet the perceived stable world demand and to reflect more accurately current output levels. At the same time the Iranian Government announced its intention to increase its production capacity and maintain its share of the quota by permitting foreign companies to conduct petroleum exploration in Iran.

1998 A decline in petroleum prices at the start of the year caused widespread concern, and speculation that this had resulted from the decision to increase production to 27.5m. b/d, coinciding with the prospect of a decline in demand from Asian economies that had been undermined by extreme financial difficulties and of a new Iraqi agreement with the UN with provision for increased petroleum exports. A meeting of the Monitoring Sub-committee, in late January, urged members to implement production restraint and resolved to send a monitoring team to member states to encourage compliance with the agreed quotas. (Venezuela remained OPEC's principal over-producer.) In February the UN Security Council approved a new agreement permitting Iraq to export petroleum valued at up to US $5,256m. every 180 days, although the Iraqi Government insisted that its production and export capacity was limited to $4,000m. In March Saudi Arabia, Venezuela and Mexico announced a joint agreement to reduce domestic production by 300,000 b/d, 200,000 b/d and 100,000 b/d respectively, with effect from 1 April, and agreed to co-operate in persuading other petroleum producing countries to commit to similar reductions. At the end of March an emergency ministerial meeting ratified the reduction proposals (the so-called 'Riyadh Pact'), which amounted to 1.245m. b/d pledged by OPEC members and 270,000 b/d by non-member states. Nevertheless, prices remained low, with over-production, together with lack of market confidence in member states' willingness to comply with the restricted quotas, an outstanding concern. In June Saudi Arabia, Venezuela and Mexico reached agreement on further reductions in output of some 450,000 b/d. Later in that month the Conference, having reviewed the market situation, agreed to implement a new reduction in total output of some 1.36m b/d, with effect from 1 July, reducing the total production target for OPEC members to 24.387m. b/d. Iran, which had been criticized for not adhering to the reductions agreed in March, confirmed that it would reduce output by 305,000 b/d. In early August petroleum prices fell below $12 per barrel. In September Iraq's petroleum production reached an estimated 2.4m. b/d, contributing to concerns of over-supply in the world market. In early November OPEC members attending a conference of the parties to the UN Framework Convention on Climate Change, held in Buenos Aires, Argentina, warned that they would claim compensation for any lost revenue resulting from initiatives to limit the emission of 'greenhouse gases' and reduce the consumption of petroleum. Later in November OPEC ministers, meeting in Vienna, resolved to maintain the existing production levels, but improve compliance. Subsequently, despite an escalation of tensions between the UN and Iraqi authorities, prices remained consistently around the level of $11 per barrel. Air strikes initiated in late 1998 by the USA and United Kingdom against strategic targets in Iraq in December were not considered to have interrupted petroleum supplies and therefore had little impact on prices.

1999 In March ministers from Algeria, Iran, Mexico, Saudi Arabia and Venezuela, meeting in The Hague, the Netherlands, agreed further to reduce petroleum production, owing to the continued weakness of the global market. Subsequently, petroleum prices rose by nearly 40%, after reaching the lowest price of US $9.9 per barrel in mid-February. Later in March OPEC confirmed a new reduction in output of 2.104m. b/d from 1 April, including commitments from non-OPEC members Mexico, Norway, Oman and Russia to decrease production by a total of 388,000 b/d. The agreement envisaged a total production target for OPEC member countries of 22.976m. b/d. Actual output in April was estimated at 26.38m. b/d (compared with 27.72m. in March), which contributed to prices reaching $17 per barrel. Prices continued to fluctuate, however, owing to concern at Iraq's potential production capacity. By June total production by OPEC member states (excluding Iraq) had declined to a reported 23.25m. b/d. The evidence of almost 90% compliance with the new production quotas contributed to market confidence that stockpiles of petroleum would be reduced, and resulted in sustained price increases. At the end of July a meeting of the Ministerial Monitoring Sub-committee confirmed that adherence to the production quotas in the period April to June had been strong, but reiterated the need to maintain the total production level at least until March 2000 given that the year's average basket price was under $14 per barrel and markets remained volatile. In September 1999 OPEC ministers confirmed that the existing quotas would be maintained for a further six-month period. At the end of September the reference price for petroleum rose above $24, its highest level since January 1997. Prices remained buoyant during the rest of the year; however, there was increasing speculation at whether the situation was sustainable. At the end of November Iraq temporarily suspended its petroleum exports, totalling some 2.2m. b/d, pending agreement on a new phase of the 'oil-for-food' arrangement and concern at the lack of progress on the removal of international sanctions.

2000 In March petroleum prices attained their highest level since the 1990 Gulf crisis; the reference price briefly exceeded US $34, representing more than a threefold increase over early 1999 price levels. At the end of that month OPEC ministers, meeting in Vienna, agreed to raise output by 1.45m. b/d, in order to ease supply shortages and thereby contain the surge in prices, with a view to restoring these to a more moderate level. A further increase in production, of 500,000 b/d, was approved by member states in June, to take effect from July (contingent on the reference price continuing to exceed $28 for 20 consecutive days). Prices remained high, reaching $34.6 in early September and leading to intense international pressure on OPEC to resolve the situation. OPEC ministers immediately announced that an increase in production of 800,000 b/d would take effect from 1 October and indicated that, were the reference price still to exceed $28 at the end of that month, an additional increase in output would be implemented. It was noted that a target band of $22–$28 per barrel was envisaged as an acceptable price level. The production agreement was supported by five non-OPEC member countries: Angola, Mexico, Norway, Oman and Russia. In late September both the Group of Seven industrialized nations (G-7) and the IMF issued warnings about the potential economic and social consequences of sustained high petroleum prices. Meanwhile the US administration agreed to release part of its strategic petroleum reserve. Towards the end of the month OPEC heads of state or government, convened at their first summit since 1975, issued the so-called 'Caracas Declaration' in which they resolved to promote market stability by developing 'remunerative, stable and competitive' pricing policies in conjunction with implementing a production policy that would secure OPEC member states an equitable share of world supply; by strengthening co-operation between the organization and other oil-exporting nations; and by developing communication between petroleum producers and consumers. The declaration also affirmed the organization's commitment to environmentally sound practice and to promoting sustainable global economic growth, social development and the eradication of poverty; supported research in technical and scientific fields; expressed concern that government taxation policies significantly inflate the end cost of petroleum; and agreed to convene future heads of state summits at regular five-yearly intervals on an institutionalized basis. By the end of September petroleum prices had declined to just above $30 per barrel; this was attributed in part to an announcement by the Saudi Arabian Government that it would consider unilaterally raising output if prices were to remain at a high level. However, the decline in prices was short-lived, as the politicalcrisis in the Middle East prompted a further series of increases: by 12 October the London Brent crude price exceeded $35 per barrel for the first time since 1990. From 31 October an additional increase in production, of 500,000 b/d was implemented, as planned for in early September. Meeting in mid-November the Conference appointed Dr Alí Rodríguez Araque, hitherto the Venezuelan minister of energy and mines, as the new OPEC Secretary-General, with effect from January 2001. Addressing the Conference, Rodríguez identified the following contributory factors to the high level of petroleum prices other than the relationship between production and price levels: a decline in recent years in the refining capacity of the USA (the world's largest market), the high national taxes on consumption (particularly within the European Union), and price distortions deriving from speculation on futures markets. Attending the sixth conference of parties to the UN Framework Convention on Climate Change later in November OPEC reiterated its concern over the lost revenue that limits on 'greenhouse gas' emissions and reduced petroleum consumption would represent for member states, estimating this at $63,000m. per year.

2001 In mid-January, with a view to stabilizing petroleum prices that by now had fallen back to around US $25 per barrel, the Conference agreed to implement a reduction in production of 1.5m. b/d, to take effect on 1 February. A further reduction, of 1m. b/d, effective from 1 April, was approved by the Conference in mid-March, limiting overall production to 24.2m. b/d. In early June an extraordinary meeting of the Conference determined to maintain the production level, given that prices had stabilized within the agreed price range of $22–$28 per barrel, in spite of market reports forecasting reduced demand. A further extraordinary meeting was convened in early July, following Iraq's decision temporarily to suspend its petroleum exports under the UN programme, which again resolved to make no adjustment to the output ceiling. Later in that month, however, OPEC responded to a gradual decline in petroleum prices, which reached $22.78 in mid-July, by announcing a ministerial agreement to reduce production by 1m. b/d, with effect from 1 September. Meeting in late September the Conference addressed the repercussions of recent major terrorist attacks on targets in the USA, which had caused significant market uncertainty. OPEC's spot basket reference price had fallen back to around $20 per barrel. The Conference declared its commitment to stabilizing the market and determined to leave production levels unchanged (at 23.2m. b/d) in order to ensure sufficient supplies. It agreed to establish an expert working group, comprising representatives of OPEC and non-OPEC producer countries, to evaluate future market developments. At a further meeting in December the Conference decided, in view of the prevailing global economic uncertainty and a decline in the average basket price level to $17–$18 in November and December, to prevent a further deterioration in petroleum prices by reducing output by a further 1.5m. b/d for six months from 1 January 2002, contingent upon the non-OPEC producers concurrently implementing a reduction in production amounting to 500,000 b/d. The Conference resolved to continue to develop contacts with the non-OPEC producer states. By the end of December 2001 the non-OPEC producers had committed themselves to a reduction in output totalling 462,500 b/d, which was considered by OPEC an adequate basis for lowering its own production ceiling to 21,700 b/d from the start of 2002, as planned. The new production quotas were: Algeria 693,000 b/d; Indonesia 1,125,000 b/d; Iran 3,186,000 b/d; Kuwait 1,741,000 b/d; Libya 1,162,000 b/d; Nigeria 1,787,000 b/d; Qatar 562,000 b/d; Saudi Arabia 7,053,000 b/d; UAE 1,894,000 b/d; Venezuela 2,497,000 b/d.

2002 Meeting in March the OPEC Conference welcomed a gradual improvement in the reference price (the spot basket price had averaged nearly $19 in February), attributing this to a high level of compliance by member countries with their agreed production quotas and to ongoing support from non-OPEC producers. The latter were urged to maintain their voluntarily-imposed reductions in output. Six non-OPEC producers—Angola, Egypt, Mexico, Oman, Russia and Syria—attended the meeting as observers. Concern was expressed over the potentially destabilizing effects of the ongoing Middle East crisis. Prices rose significantly in early April following the imposition by Iraq of a one-month suspension of its oil exports in protest at the ongoing Israeli military intervention in areas controlled by the Palestinian National Authority. The ensuing reduction in global supply was compounded by constraints on Venezuelan production caused by a strike in the oil sector. It was reported at this time that the Iranian Government was urging the implementation of a general embargo by the Arab states on oil exports to Western countries perceived to be supporting Israeli actions.

Finance

The budget for 2002 amounted to €16.7m., of which €3.5m. was to be financed by transfer from the Reserve Fund and the balance was to be contributed by member states.

Publications

Annual Report.

Annual Statistical Bulletin.

Monthly Oil Market Report.

OPEC Bulletin (monthly).

OPEC Review (quarterly).

Reports, information papers, press releases.

OPEC FUND FOR INTERNATIONAL DEVELOPMENT

Address: POB 995, 1011 Vienna, Austria.

Telephone: (1) 515-64-0; **fax:** (1) 513-92-38; **e-mail:** info@opecfund.org; **internet:** www.opecfund.org.

The Fund was established by OPEC member countries in 1976.

MEMBERS

Member countries of OPEC (q.v.).

Organization

(April 2002)

ADMINISTRATION

The Fund is administered by a Ministerial Council and a Governing Board. Each member country is represented on the Council by its minister of finance. The Board consists of one representative and one alternate for each member country.

Chairman, Ministerial Council: Dr PRIJADI PRAPTOSUHARDJO (Indonesia).

Chairman, Governing Board: Dr SALEH AL-OMAIR (Saudi Arabia).

Director-General of the Fund: Dr YESUFU SEYYID ABDULAI (Nigeria).

FINANCIAL STRUCTURE

The resources of the Fund, whose unit of account is the US dollar, consist of contributions by OPEC member countries, and income received from operations or otherwise accruing to the Fund.

The initial endowment of the Fund amounted to US $800m. Its resources have been replenished three times, and have been further increased by the profits accruing to seven OPEC member countries through the sales of gold held by the International Monetary Fund. The pledged contributions to the OPEC Fund amounted to $3,435m. at the end of 2001, and paid-in contributions totalled some $2,990m.

Activities

The OPEC Fund for International Development is a multilateral agency for financial co-operation and assistance. Its objective is to reinforce financial co-operation between OPEC member countries and other developing countries through the provision of financial support to the latter on appropriate terms, to assist them in their economic and social development. The Fund was conceived as a collective financial facility which would consolidate the assistance extended by its member countries; its resources are additional to those already made available through other bilateral and multilateral aid agencies of OPEC members. It is empowered to:

(*i*) Provide concessional loans for balance-of-payments support;

(*ii*) Provide concessional loans for the implementation of development projects and programmes;

(*iii*) Make contributions and/or provide loans to eligible international agencies; and

(*iv*) Finance technical assistance and research through grants.

The eligible beneficiaries of the Fund's assistance are the governments of developing countries other than OPEC member countries, and international development agencies whose beneficiaries are developing countries. The Fund gives priority to the countries with the lowest income.

The Fund may undertake technical, economic and financial appraisal of a project submitted to it, or entrust such an appraisal to an appropriate international development agency, the executing national agency of a member country, or any other qualified agency. Most projects financed by the Fund have been co-financed by other development finance agencies. In each such case, one of the co-financing agencies may be appointed to administer the Fund's loan in association with its own. This practice has enabled the Fund to extend its lending activities to 105 countries over a short period of time and in a simple way, with the aim of avoiding duplication and complications. As its experience grew, the Fund increasingly resorted to parallel, rather than joint financing, taking up separate project components to be financed according to its rules and policies. In addition, it started to finance some projects completely on its own. These trends necessitated the issuance in 1982 of guide-lines for the procurement of goods and services under the Fund's loans, allowing for a margin of preference for goods and services of local origin or originating in other developing countries: the general principle of competitive bidding is, however, followed by the Fund. The loans are not tied to procurement from Fund member countries or from any other countries. The margin of preference for goods and services obtainable in developing countries is allowed on the request of the borrower and within defined limits. Fund assistance in the form of programme loans has a broader coverage than project lending. Programme loans are used to stimulate an economic sector or sub-sector, and assist recipient countries in obtaining inputs, equipment and spare parts. Besides extending loans for project and programme financing and balance of payments support, the Fund also undertakes other operations, including grants in support of technical assistance and other activities (mainly research), and financial contributions to other international institutions. In 1998 the Fund began to extend

OPEC FUND COMMITMENTS AND DISBURSEMENTS IN 2000 (US $ million)

	Commitments	Disbursements
Public-sector lending operations:	257.30	151.50
Project financing	193.40	150.02
Programme financing	—	1.48
HIPC initiative financing*	63.90	—
Private-sector lending operations	23.23	—
Grant Programme:	3.86	3.90
Technical assistance	2.75	2.24
Research and other activities	0.36	0.31
Emergency aid	0.75	1.35
Total	284.39	155.40

* Heavily Indebted Poor Countries initiative, jointly implemented by the International Monetary Fund and World Bank.

Project loans approved in 2000 (US $ million)

	Loans approved
Sector:	
Transportation	72.80
Agriculture and agro-industry	50.52
Education	21.00
Health	6.20
Water supply and sewerage	29.50
Multisectoral	13.38
Total	193.40
Region*:	
Africa	90.50
Asia	76.90
Europe	5.00
Latin America and the Caribbean	21.00

* A total of 31 loans was approved for projects in 29 countries, benefiting 13 countries in Africa, 10 in Asia, five in Latin America and the Caribbean, and one in Europe.

lines of credit to support private-sector activities in beneficiary countries.

By the end of December 2000 the Fund had approved 867 loans since operations began in 1976, totalling US $4,548.3m., of which $3,424.5m. (or 75.3%) was for project financing, $724.2m. (15.9%) was for balance-of-payments support, $305.3m. (6.7%) was for programme financing and $94.2m. (2.1%) was allocated as financing for the Heavily Indebted Poor Countries (HIPC) initiative (see World Bank, p. 174). Private sector operations totalled $53.2m. at that time. The Fund's 14th lending programme, covering the period 2000–01, commenced on 1 January 2000; a 15th lending programme, approved for a three-year period, became effective on 1 January 2002.

Direct loans are supplemented by grants to support technical assistance, food aid and research. By the end of December 2000 531 grants, amounting to US $246.5m., had been extended, including $83.6m. to the Common Fund for Commodities (established by the UN Conference on Trade and Development—UNCTAD), $42.6m. in support of emergency relief operations and a special contribution of $20m. to the International Fund for Agricultural Development (IFAD). In addition, the OPEC Fund had committed $971.8m. to other international institutions by the end of 2000, comprising OPEC members' contributions to the resources of IFAD, and irrevocable transfers in the name of its members to the IMF Trust Fund. By the end of 2000 67.4% of total commitments had been disbursed.

During the year ending 31 December 2000 the Fund's total commitments amounted to US $284.4m. (compared with $320.5m. in 1999). These commitments included 31 public sector project loans, amounting to $193.4m., and eight loans, totalling $63.9m., to finance debt-relief under the HIPC initiative. The largest proportion ofproject loans (37.6%) was to support improvements in the transportation sector in 12 countries and included road construction andupgrading in Guinea, Madagascar, Tanzania and Zambia, improvements in rural transport infrastructure in Belize, Laos, Mali and Mozambique, and the modernization of railways in Uzbekistan. Agriculture and agro-industry loans, amounting to 26.1%, supported irrigation schemes in Burkina Faso, the Democratic People's Republic of Korea, Madagascar and Sudan, a flood protection project in Honduras, and livestock farming in Bosnia and Herzegovina and Mauritania. Some 15.3% of project loans was allocated to water supply and sewerage projects in Cape Verde, Dominican Republic, Ghana, Nepal and Turkmenistan. The education sector received 10.9% of loans, supporting projects in Egypt, Jamaica, and the Philippines; the health sector received 3.2%; while other loans, including multisectoral loans, amounted to 6.9% of the total. Private sector operations approved during 2000, including loans and equity participation, amounted to $23.2m.

During 2000 the Fund approved US $3.86m. for 24 grants, of which $2.75m. was for technical assistance activities, $356,000 for research, and $750,000m. to support emergency humanitarian operations in Ethiopia, Madagascar and Mozambique.

Publications

Annual Report (in Arabic, English, French and Spanish).

OPEC Fund Newsletter (3 a year).

Occasional papers and documents.

PACIFIC COMMUNITY

Address: BP D5, 98848 Nouméa Cédex, New Caledonia.
Telephone: 26-20-00; **fax:** 26-38-18; **e-mail:** spc@spc.int; **internet:** www.spc.org.nc/.

In February 1947 the Governments of Australia, France, the Netherlands, New Zealand, the United Kingdom, and the USA signed the Canberra Agreement establishing the South Pacific Commission, which came into effect in July 1948. (The Netherlands withdrew from the Commission in 1962, when it ceased to administer the former colony of Dutch New Guinea, now Irian Jaya, also known as West Papua, part of Indonesia.) In October 1997 the 37th South Pacific Conference, convened in Canberra, Australia, agreed to rename the organization the Pacific Community, with effect from 6 February 1998. The Secretariat of the Pacific Community (SPC) services the Community, and provides research, technical advice, training and assistance in economic, social and cultural development to 22 countries and territories of the Pacific region. It serves a population of about 6.8m., scattered over some 30m. sq km, more than 98% of which is sea.

MEMBERS

American Samoa	Niue
Australia	Northern Mariana Islands
Cook Islands	Palau
Fiji	Papua New Guinea
France	Pitcairn Islands
French Polynesia	Samoa
Guam	Solomon Islands
Kiribati	Tokelau
Marshall Islands	Tonga
Federated States of Micronesia	Tuvalu
	United Kingdom
Nauru	USA
New Caledonia	Vanuatu
New Zealand	Wallis and Futuna Islands

Organization

(April 2002)

CONFERENCE OF THE PACIFIC COMMUNITY

The Conference is the governing body of the Community (replacing the former South Pacific Conference) and is composed of representatives of all member countries and territories. The main responsibilities of the Conference, which meets annually, are to appoint the Director-General, to determine major national or regional policy issues in the areas of competence of the organization and to note changes to the Financial and Staff Regulations approved by the Committee of Representatives of Governments and Administrations (CRGA).

COMMITTEE OF REPRESENTATIVES OF GOVERNMENTS AND ADMINISTRATIONS (CRGA)

This Committee comprises representatives of all member states and territories, having equal voting rights. It meets annually to consider the work programme evaluation conducted by the Secretariat and to discuss any changes proposed by the Secretariat in the context of regional priorities; to consider and approve any policy issues for the organization presented by the Secretariat or by member countries and territories; to consider applicants and make recommendations for the post of Director-General; to approve the administrative and work programme budgets; to approve amendments to the Financial and Staff Regulations; and to conduct annual performance evaluations of the Director-General.

SECRETARIAT

The Secretariat of the Pacific Community—SPC is headed by a Director-General and two Deputy Directors-General, based in Suva and Nouméa. Three administrative Divisions cover Land Resources, Marine Resources and Social Resources. The Secretariat also provides information services, including library facilities, publications, translation and computer services. The organization has about 250 staff members.

Director-General: LOURDES PANGELINAN (Guam).

Senior Deputy Director-General: Dr JIMMIE RODGERS (Solomon Islands).

Deputy Director-General: YVES CORBEL (France).

Regional Office: Private Mail Bag, Suva, Fiji; tel. 370733; fax 370021; e-mail spcsuva@spc.org.fj.

Activities

The SPC provides, on request of its member countries, technical assistance, advisory services, information and clearing-house services aimed at developing the technical, professional, scientific, research, planning and management capabilities of the regional population. The SPC also conducts regional conferences and technical meetings, as well as training courses, workshops and seminars at the regional or country level. It provides small grants-in-aid and awards to meet specific requests and needs of members. In November 1996 the Conference agreed to establish a specific Small Islands States fund to provide technical services, training and other relevant activities. The organization's three programme divisions are: land resources, marine resources and social resources. The Pacific Community oversees the maritime programme and telecommunications policy activities of the Pacific Islands Forum Secretariat (q.v.).

In 1998 the SPC adopted a Corporate Plan for 1999–2003, the main objectives of which included developing national capabilities in 'value-adding' technology; enhancing the integration of cross-sectoral issues (such as economics, gender, culture and community education) into national planning and policy-making processes; and developing a co-ordinated human resources programme as a focal point for providing information, advice and support to the regional population. The 1999 Conference, held in Tahiti in December, adopted the 'Déclaration de Tahiti Nui', a mandate that detailed the operational policies and mechanisms of the Pacific Community, taking into account operational changes not covered by the founding Canberra Agreement. The Déclaration was regarded as a 'living document' that would be periodically revised to record subsequent modifications of operational policy. The SPC has signed memoranda of understanding with WHO, the Forum Fisheries Agency, the South Pacific Regional Environment Programme (SPREP), and several other partners. The organization participates in meetings of the Council of Regional Organizations in the Pacific (CROP, see under Pacific Islands Forum Secretariat). Representatives of the SPC, SPREP and the South Pacific Applied Geoscience Commission hold periodic 'troika' meetings to develop regional technical co-operation and harmonization of work programmes.

LAND RESOURCES

The land resources division comprises two major programmes: agriculture (incorporating advice and specific activities in crop improvement and plant protection; animal health and production services; and agricultural resource economics and information); and forestry (providing training, technical assistance and information in forestry management and agroforestry). Objectives of the agriculture programme, based in Suva, Fiji, include the promotion of land and agricultural management practices that are both economically and environmentally sustainable; strengthening national capabilities to reduce losses owing to crop pests (insects, pathogens and weeds) and animal diseases already present, and to prevent the introduction of new pests and diseases; and facilitating trade through improved quarantine procedures. Forestry activities include the implementation, jointly with other partners, of the Pacific Islands Forests and Trees Support Project, which is concerned with natural forest management and conservation, agroforestry and development and the use of tree and plant resources; and of the Pacific-German Regional Forestry Project. A Pacific Regional Agricultural Programme (PRAP), funded by the European Union, was introduced by eight member states in 1990. The SPC assumed responsibility for administering PRAP in 1998.

MARINE RESOURCES

The SPC aims to support and co-ordinate the sustainable development and management of inshore fisheries resources in the region, to undertake scientific research in order to provide member governments with relevant information for the sustainable development and management of tuna and billfish resources in and adjacent to the South Pacific region, and to provide data and analytical services to national fisheries departments. The main components of the Community's fisheries activities are the Coastal Fisheries Programme (CFP), the Oceanic Fisheries Programme (OFP), and the Regional Maritime Programme (RMP). The CFP is divided into the following sections: community fisheries (research and assessment of and development support for people occupied in subsistence and artisanal fisheries); fisheries training; sustainable fisheries development; reef fisheries assessment and management; fisheries information; and post-harvest development (offering advice and training in order to improve handling practices, storage, seafood product development, quality control and marketing). The OFP consists of the following three sections: statistics and monitoring; tuna ecology and biology; and stock assessment and modelling. The statistics and monitoring section maintains a database of industrial tuna fisheries in the region. The OFP contributed research and statistical information for the formulation of the Convention for the Conservation and Management of Highly Migratory Fish Stocks in the Western and Central Pacific, which aimed to establish a regime for the sustainable management of tuna reserves, and was opened for signature in Honolulu in September 2000. (The convention had been ratified by four states at February 2002.) The SPC and European Commission were jointly to launch the Pacific Regional Oceanic and Coastal Fisheries Project (PROCFISH) in 2002. The oceanic component of the project aimed to assist the OFP with advancing knowledge of tuna fisheries ecosystems, while the coastal element was to produce the first comparative regional baseline assessment of reef fisheries. The RMP advises member governments in the fields of policy, law and training. In early 2002 the RMP launched the model Pacific Islands Maritime Legislation and Regulations as a framework for the development of national maritime legislation. The SPC adminsters the Pacific Island Aquaculture Network, a forum for promoting regional aquaculture development.

The SPC hosts the Pacific Office of the World Fish Centre (the International Centre for Living Aquatic Resources Management—ICLARM); the SPC and the World Fish Centre have jointly implemented a number of projects.

SOCIAL RESOURCES

The Social Resources Division comprises the Community Health Programme and the Socio-economic Programme (including sub-programmes and sections on statistics; population and demography; rural energy development; youth issues; culture; women's and gender equality; community education training; and media training).

The Community Health Programme aims to implement health promotion programmes; to assist regional authorities to strengthen health information systems and to promote the use of new technology for health information development and disease control (for example, through the Public Health Surveillance and Disease Control Programme); to promote efficient health services management; and to help all Pacific Islanders to attain a level of health and quality of life that will enable them to contribute to the development of their communities. The Community Health Services also work in the areas of non-communicable diseases and nutrition (with particular focus on the high levels of diabetes and heart disease in parts of the region); environmental health, through the improvement of water and sanitation facilities; and reducing the incidence of HIV/AIDS and other sexually-transmitted diseases (STDs), tuberculosis, and vector-borne diseases such as malaria and dengue fever. The SPC operates a project (mainly funded by Australia and New Zealand), to prevent AIDS and STDs among young people through peer education and awareness. It is also responsible for implementing the Pacific Regional Vector-Borne Diseases Project, established in 1996, which focuses particularly on Fiji, Vanuatu and the Solomon Islands.

The Statistics Programme assists governments and administrations in the region to provide effective and efficient national statistical services through the provision of training activities, a statistical information service and other advisory services. A Regional Conference of Statisticians facilitates the integration and co-ordination of statistical services throughout the region.

The Population and Demography Programme provides technical support in population, demographic and development issues to member governments, other SPC programmes, and organizations active in the region. The Programme aims to assist governments effectively to analyse data and utilize it into the formulation of national development policies and programmes. The Programme organizes national workshops in population and development planning, provides short-term professional attachments, undertakes demographic research and analysis, and disseminates information.

The Rural Energy Development Programme provides technical assistance and advice to member states on the utilization of sustainable energy resources, and incorporates a regional rural renewable energy project, sponsored by Australia and France.

The Pacific Youth Resource Bureau (PWRB) co-ordinates the implementation of the Pacific Youth Strategy 2005, which aims to develop opportunities for young people to play an active role in society. The PYRB provides non-formal education and support for youth, community workers and young adults in community development subjects and provides grants to help young people find employment. It also advises and assists the Pacific Youth Council in promoting a regional youth identity. The Pacific Women's Resource Bureau (PWRB) aims to promote the social, economic and cultural advancement of women in the region by assisting governments and regional organizations to include women in the development planning process. The PWRB also provides technical and advisory services, advocacy and management support training to groups concerned with women in development and gender and development, and supports the production and exchange of information regarding women.

The Cultural Programme aims to preserve and promote the cultural heritage of the Pacific Islands. The Programme assists with the training of librarians, archivists and researchers and promotes instruction in local languages, history and art at schools in member states and territories. The SPC acts as the secretariat of the Council of Pacific Arts, which organizes the Festival of Pacific Arts on a four-yearly basis.

The SPC regional office in Suva, Fiji, administers a Community Education Training Centre (CETC), which conducts a seven-month training course for up to 36 women community workers annually, with the objective of training women in methods of community development so that they can help others to achieve better living conditions for island families and communities. The Regional Media Centre provides training, technical assistance and production materials in all areas of the media for member countries and territories, community work programmes, donor projects and regional non-governmental organizations. The Centre comprises a radio broadcast unit, a graphic design and publication unit and a TV and video unit.

In 2000 the SPC's Information Technology and Communication Unit launched ComET, a satellite communications project aimed at linking more closely the organization's headquarters in New Caledonia and regional office in Fiji. The Information and Communications Programme is developing the use of modern communication technology as an invaluable resource for problem-solving, regional networking, and uniting the Community's scattered, often physically isolated, island member states. In conjunction with the Secretariat of the Pacific Islands Forum the SPC convened the first regional meeting of Information and Communication Technology workers, researchers and policy-makers in August 2001. The meeting addressed strategies for the advancement of new information technologies in member countries.

Finance

The organization's core budget, funded by assessed contributions from member states, finances executive and administrative expenditures, the Information and Communications Programme, and several professional and support positions that contribute to the work of the three programme divisions (i.e. Land Resources, Marine Resources and Social Resources). The non-core budget, funded mainly by aid donors and in part by Community member states, mostly on a contractual basis, finances the SPC's technical services. Administrative expenditure for 2000 amounted to US $2.5m.

Publications

Annual Report.

Fisheries Newsletter (quarterly).

Pacific Aids Alert Bulletin (quarterly).

Pacific Island Nutrition (quarterly).

Regional Tuna Bulletin (quarterly).

Report of the Conference of the Pacific Community.

Women's Newsletter (quarterly).

Technical publications, statistical bulletins, advisory leaflets and reports.

PACIFIC ISLANDS FORUM

MEMBERS

Australia	Niue
Cook Islands	Palau
Fiji	Papua New Guinea
Kiribati	Samoa
Marshall Islands	Solomon Islands
Federated States of Micronesia	Tonga
Nauru	Tuvalu
New Zealand	Vanuatu

Note: New Caledonia was admitted as an observer at the Forum in 1999.

The Pacific Islands Forum (which changed its name from South Pacific Forum in October 2000) was founded as the gathering of Heads of Government of the independent and self-governing states of the South Pacific. Its first meeting was held on 5 August 1971, in Wellington, New Zealand. It provides an opportunity for informal discussions to be held on a wide range of common issues and problems and meets annually or when issues require urgent attention. The Forum has no written constitution or international agreement governing its activities nor any formal rules relating to its purpose, membership or conduct of meeting. Decisions are always reached by consensus, it never having been found necessary or desirable to vote formally on issues. In October 1994 the Forum was granted observer status by the General Assembly of the United Nations.

Since 1989 each Forum has been followed by 'dialogues' with representatives of other countries with a long-term interest in and commitment to the region. In October 1995 the Forum Governments suspended France's 'dialogue' status, following that country's resumption of the testing of nuclear weapons in French Polynesia. France was reinstated as a 'dialogue partner' in September 1996. In 2002 'dialogue partners' comprised Canada, the People's Republic of China, France, Indonesia, Japan, the Republic of Korea, Malaysia, Philippines, the United Kingdom, the USA, and the European Union.

The South Pacific Nuclear-Free Zone Treaty (Treaty of Rarotonga), prohibiting the acquisition, stationing or testing of nuclear weapons in the region, came into effect in December 1986, following ratification by eight states. The USSR signed the protocols to the treaty (whereby states possessing nuclear weapons agree not to use or threaten to use nuclear explosive devices against any non-nuclear party to the Treaty) in December 1987 and ratified them in April 1988; the People's Republic of China did likewise in December 1987 and October 1988 respectively. The other three major nuclear powers, however, intimated that they did not intend to adhere to the Treaty. In July 1993 the Forum petitioned the USA, the United Kingdom and France, asking them to reconsider their past refusal to sign the Treaty in the light of the end of the 'Cold War'. In July 1995, following the decision of the French Government to resume testing of nuclear weapons in French Polynesia, members of the Forum resolved to increase diplomatic pressure on the three Governments to sign the Treaty. In October the United Kingdom, the USA and France announced their intention to accede to the Treaty, by mid-1996. While the decision was approved by the Forum, it urged the Governments to sign with immediate effect, thus accelerating the termination of France's testing programme. Following France's decision, announced in January 1996, to end the programme four months earlier than scheduled, representatives of the Governments of the three countries signed the Treaty in March.

In 1990 five of the Forum's smallest island member states formed an economic sub-group to address their specific concerns, in particular economic disadvantages resulting from a poor resource base, absence of a skilled work-force and lack of involvement in world markets. In September 1997 the 28th Forum, convened in Rarotonga, the Cook Islands, endorsed the inclusion of the Marshall Islands as the sixth member of the Smaller Island States sub-group. Representatives of the grouping, which also includes Kiribati, the Cook Islands, Nauru, Niue and Tuvalu, meet regularly. In February 1998 senior Forum officials, for the first time, met with representatives of the Caribbean Community and the Indian Ocean Commission, as well as other major international organizations, to discuss means to enhance consideration and promotion of the interests of small island states. Small island member states have been particularly concerned about the phenomenon of global warming and its potentially damaging effects on the region (see below).

The 23rd Forum, held in Honiara, Solomon Islands, in July 1992, welcomed France's suspension of its nuclear-testing programme until the end of the year, but urged the French Government to make the moratorium permanent. Forum members discussed the decisions made at the UN Conference on Environment and Development held in June, and approved the Cook Islands' proposal to host a 'global conference for small islands'. The Niue Fisheries Surveillance and Law Enforcement Co-operation Treaty was signed by members, with the exception of Fiji, Kiribati and Tokelau, which were awaiting endorsement from their legislatures. The treaty provided for co-operation in the surveillance of fisheries resources and in defeating drugs-trafficking and other organized crime. Forum leaders also adopted a separate declaration on future priorities in law enforcement co-operation.

At the 24th Forum, held in Yaren, Nauru, in August 1993 it was agreed that effective links needed to be established with the broader Asia-Pacific region, with participation in Asia-Pacific Economic Co-operation (APEC), where the Forum has observer status, to be utilized to the full. The Forum urged an increase in intra-regional trade and asked for improved opportunities for Pacific island countries exporting to Australia and New Zealand. New Caledonia's right to self-determination was supported. Environmental protection measures and the rapid growth in population in the region, which was posing a threat to economic and social development, were also discussed by the Forum delegates.

The 25th Forum was convened in Brisbane, Australia, in August 1994 under the theme of 'Managing Our Resources'. In response to the loss of natural resources as well as of income-earning potential resulting from unlawful logging of timber by foreign companies, Forum members agreed to impose stricter controls on the exploitation of forestry resources and to begin negotiations to standardize monitoring of the region's resources. The Forum also agreed to strengthen its promotion of sustainable exploitation of fishing stocks, reviewed preparations of a convention to control the movement and management of radioactive waste within the South Pacific and discussed the rationalization of national airlines, on a regional or sub-regional basis, to reduce operational losses.

The 26th Forum, held in Madang, Papua New Guinea, in September 1995, was dominated by extreme hostility on the part of Forum Governments to the resumption of testing of nuclear weapons by France in the South Pacific region. The decision to recommence testing, announced by the French Government in June, had been instantly criticized by Forum Governments. The 26th Forum reiterated their demand that France stop any further testing, and also condemned the People's Republic of China for conducting nuclear tests in the region. The meeting endorsed a draft Code of Conduct on the management and monitoring of indigenous forest resources in selected South Pacific countries, which had been initiated at the 25th Forum; however, while the six countries concerned committed themselves to implementing the Code through national legislation, its signing was deferred, owing to an initial unwillingness on the part of Papua New Guinea and Solomon Islands. The Forum did adopt a treaty to ban the import into the region of all radioactive and other hazardous wastes, and to control the transboundary movement and management of these wastes (the so-called Waigani Convention). The Forum agreed to reactivate the ministerial committee on New Caledonia, comprising Fiji, Nauru and Solomon Islands, which was to monitor political developments in that territory prior to its referendum on independence, scheduled to be held in 1998. In addition, the Forum resolved to implement and pursue means of promoting economic co-operation and long-term development in the region. In December 1995 Forum finance ministers, meeting in Port Moresby, Papua New Guinea, discussed the issues involved in the concept of 'Securing Development Beyond 2000' and initiated an assessment project to further trade liberalization efforts in the region.

The 27th Forum, held in Majuro, the Marshall Islands, in September 1996, supported the efforts of the French Government to improve relations with countries in the South Pacific and agreed to readmit France to the post-Forum dialogue. The Forum meeting recognized the importance of responding to the liberalization of the global trading system by reviewing the region's economic tariff policies, and of assisting members in attracting investment for the development of the private sector. The Forum advocated that a meeting of economy ministers of member countries be held each year. The Forum was also concerned with environmental issues: in particular, it urged the ratification and implementation of the Waigani Convention by all member states, the promotion of regional efforts to conserve marine resources and to protect the coastal environment, and the formulation of an international, legally-binding agreement to reduce emissions by industrialized countries of so-called 'greenhouse gases'. Such gases contribute to the warming of the earth's atmosphere (the 'greenhouse effect') and to related increases in global sea-levels, and have therefore been regarded as a threat to low-lying islands in the region. The Forum requested the ministerial committee on New Caledonia (established by the 1990 Forum to monitor, in co-operation with the French authorities, political developments in the territory) to pursue contacts with all parties there and to continue to monitor preparations for the 1998 referendum.

In July 1997 the inaugural meeting of Forum economy ministers was convened in Cairns, Australia. It formulated an Action Plan to encourage the flow of foreign investment into the region by committing members to economic reforms, good governance and the implementation of multilateral trade and tariff policies. The meeting also commissioned a formal study of the establishment of a free-trade agreement between Forum island states. The 28th Forum, held in Rarotonga, the Cook Islands, in September, considered the economic challenges confronting the region. However, it was marked by a failure to conclude a common policy position on mandatory targets for reductions in 'greenhouse gas' emissions, owing to an ongoing dispute between Australia and other Forum Governments.

The 29th Forum, held in Pohnpei, Federated States of Micronesia, in August 1998, considered the need to pursue economic reforms and to stimulate the private sector and foreign investment in order to ensure economic growth. Leaders reiterated their support for efforts to implement the economic Action Plan and to develop a framework for a free-trade agreement, and endorsed specific recommendations of the second Forum Economic Ministers Meeting, which was held in Fiji, in July, including the promotion of competitive telecommunications markets, the development of information infrastructures and support for a new economic vulnerability index at the UN to help determine least developed country status. The Forum was also concerned with environmental issues, notably the shipment of radioactive wastes, the impact of a multinational venture to launch satellites from the Pacific, the need for ongoing radiological monitoring of the Mururoa and Fangataufa atolls, and the development of a South Pacific Whale Sanctuary. The Forum adopted a Statement on Climate Change, which urged all countries to ratify and implement the gas emission reductions agreed upon by UN member states in December 1997 (the so-called Kyoto Protocol of the UN Framework Convention on Climate Change), and emphasized the Forum's commitment to further measures for verifying and enforcing emission limitation.

In October 1999 the 30th Forum, held in Koror, Palau, endorsed in principle the establishment of a regional free-trade area (FTA), which had been approved at a special ministerial meeting held in June. The FTA was to be implemented from 2002 over a period of eight years for developing member countries and 10 years for smaller island states and least developed countries. The Forum requested officials from member countries to negotiate the details of a draft agreement on the FTA (the so-called Pacific Island Countries Trade Agreement), including possible extensions of the arrangements to Australia and New Zealand. The heads of government adopted a Forum Vision for the Pacific Information Economy, which recognized the importance of information technology infrastructure for the region's economic and social development and the possibilities for enhanced co-operation in investment, job creation, education, training and cultural exchange. Forum Governments also expressed concern at the shipment of radioactive waste through the Pacific and determined to pursue negotiations with France, Japan and the United Kingdom regarding liability and compensation arrangements; confirmed their continued support for the multinational force and UN operations in East Timor; and urged more countries to adopt and implement the Kyoto Protocol to limit the emission of 'greenhouse gases'. In addition, the Forum agreed to rename the grouping (hitherto known as the South Pacific Forum) the Pacific Islands Forum, to reflect the expansion of its membership since its establishment; the new designation took effect at the 31st Forum, which was convened in Tarawa, Kiribati, at the end of October 2000.

At the 31st Forum the heads of government discussed the escalation in regional insecurity that had occurred since the previous Forum. Concern was expressed over the unrest that prevailed during mid-2000 in Fiji and Solomon Islands, and also over ongoing political violence in the Indonesian province of Irian Jaya (West Papua). The Forum adopted the Biketawa Declaration, which outlined a mechanism for responding to any future such crises in the region while urging members to undertake efforts to address the fundamental causes of instability. The detrimental economic impact of the disturbances in Fiji and Solomon Islands was noted. The Forum endorsed a proposal to establish a Regional Financial Information Sharing Facility and national financial intelligence units, and welcomed the conclusion in June by the European Union and ACP states (which include several Forum members) of the Cotonou Agreement (q.v.). The Forum also reiterated support for the prompt implementation of the Kyoto Protocol.

In August 2001, convened at the 32nd Forum, in Nauru, nine regional leaders adopted the Pacific Island Countries Trade Agreement (PICTA), providing for the establishment of the FTA (as envisaged at the 30th Forum). A related Pacific Agreement on Closer Economic Relations (PACER), envisaging the phased establishment of a regional single market including the signatories to PICTA and Australia and New Zealand, was also adopted. The Forum expressed concern at the refusal of the USA (responsible for about one-quarter of world-wide 'greenhouse gas' emissions) to ratify the Kyoto Protocol. In response to an ongoing initiative by the Organisation of Economic Co-operation and Development (OECD) to eliminate the operation of 'harmful tax systems', the Forum reaffirmed the sovereign right of nations to establish individual tax regimes and urged the development of a new co-operative framework to address issues relating to financial transparency. (The OECD had identified the Cook Islands, the Marshall Islands, Nauru and Niue as so-called 'tax havens' lacking financial transparency and had demanded that they impose stricter legislation to address the incidence of international money-laundering on their territories.) Forum leaders also reiterated protests against the shipment of radioactive materials through the region.

Pacific Islands Forum Secretariat

Address: Private Mail Bag, Suva, Fiji.

Telephone: 312600; **fax:** 305573; **e-mail:** info@forumsec.org.fj; **internet:** www.forumsec.org.fj.

The South Pacific Bureau for Economic Co-operation (SPEC) was established by an agreement signed on 17 April 1973, at the third meeting of the South Pacific Forum (now Pacific Islands Forum) in Apia, Western Samoa (now Samoa). SPEC was renamed the South Pacific Forum Secretariat in 1988; this, in turn, was redesignated as the Pacific Islands Forum Secretariat in October 2000.

Organization

(April 2002)

FORUM OFFICIALS COMMITTEE

The Forum Officials Committee is the Secretariat's executive board. It comprises representatives and senior officials from all member countries. It meets twice a year, immediately before the meetings of the Pacific Islands Forum and at the end of the year, to discuss in detail the Secretariat's work programme and annual budget.

SECRETARIAT

The Secretariat undertakes the day-to-day activities of the Forum. It is headed by a Secretary-General, with a staff of some 70 people drawn from the member countries. The Secretariat comprises the following four Divisions: Corporate Services; Development and Economic Policy; Trade and Investment; and Political, International and Legal Affairs.

Secretary-General: NOEL LEVI (Papua New Guinea).

Deputy Secretary-General: IOSEFA MAIAVA (Samoa).

Activities

The Secretariat's aim is to enhance the economic and social well-being of the people of the South Pacific, in support of the efforts of national governments.

The Secretariat's trade and investment services extend advice and technical assistance to member countries in policy, development, export marketing, and information dissemination. Trade policy activities are mainly concerned with improving private sector policies, for example investment promotion, assisting integration into the world economy (including the provision of information and technical assistance to member states on WTO-related matters and supporting Pacific Island ACP states with preparations for negotiations on trade partnership with the EU under the Cotonou Agreement), and the development of businesses. The Secretariat aims to assist both island governments and private sector companies to enhance their capacity in the development and exploitation of export markets, product identification and product development. A trade exhibition was held in French Polynesia in 1997, and support was granted to provide for visits to overseas trade fairs and the development of promotional materials. A regional trade and investment database is being developed. The Trade and Investment Division of the Secretariat co-ordinates the activities of the regional trade offices located in Australia, New Zealand and Japan (see below). A representative trade office in Beijing, People's Republic of China, opened in January 2002.

In 2002 the Trade and Investment Division was preparing for the implementation of two major regional trade accords signed by Forum heads of state in August 2001: the Pacific Island Countries Trade Agreement (PICTA), providing for the establishment of a Pacific Island free-trade area (FTA); and the related Pacific Agreement on Closer Economic Relations (PACER), incorporating trade and economic co-operation measures and envisaging an eventual single regional market comprising the PICTA FTA and Australia and New Zealand. It was envisaged that negotiations on free-trade agreements between Pacific Island states and Australia and New Zealand, with a view to establishing the larger regional single market envisaged by PACER, would commence within eight years of PICTA's entry into force. SPARTECA (see below) would remain operative pending the establishment of the larger single market, into which it would be subsumed. Under the provisions of PACER, Australia and New Zealand were to provide technical and financial assistance to PICTA signatory states in pursuing the objectives of PACER.

In 1981 the South Pacific Regional Trade and Economic Co-operation Agreement (SPARTECA), came into force. SPARTECA aimed to redress the trade deficit of the Pacific Island countries with Australia and New Zealand. It is a non-reciprocal trade agreement under which Australia and New Zealand offer duty-free and unrestricted access or concessional access for specified products originating from the developing island member countries of the Forum. In 1985 Australia agreed to further liberalization of trade by abolishing (from the beginning of 1987) duties and quotas on all Pacific products except steel, cars, sugar, footwear and garments. In August 1994 New Zealand expanded its import criteria under the agreement by reducing the rule of origin requirement for garment products from 50% to 45% of local content. In response to requests from Fiji, Australia agreed to widen its interpretation of the agreement by accepting as being of local content manufactured products that consist of goods and components of 50% Australian content. A new Fiji/Australia Trade and Economic Relations Agreement (AFTERA) was concluded in March 1999 to complement SPARTECA and compensate for certain trade benefits that were in the process of being withdrawn.

In April 2001 the Secretariat convened a meeting of seven member island states—Cook Islands, the Marshall Islands, Nauru, Niue, Samoa, Tonga and Vanuatu—as well as representatives from Australia and New Zealand, to address the regional implications of the OECD's Harmful Tax Competition Initiative. Under the initiative, designed to reduce the level of potential tax revenue lost by OECD member states to offshore 'tax havens', 35 jurisdictions, including these seven Pacific Island states, were required to amend national financial legislation by the end of July. States that did not comply would be designated as 'non-co-operative' and might be targeted by 'defensive measures'. The meeting requested the OECD to engage in conciliatory negotiations with the listed Pacific Island states. At the August 2001 Forum (by which time Cook Islands, the Marshall Islands, Nauru and Niue had been identified as non-co-operative) leaders reiterated this stance, proclaiming the sovereign right of nations to establish individual tax regimes, and supporting the development of a new co-operative framework to address financial transparency concerns. In December the Secretariat hosted a workshop for officials from nine member states concerned with combating financial crime. The workshop was attended and sponsored by several partner organizations and bodies, including the IMF.

The Political, International and Legal Affairs Division of the Secretariat organizes and services the meetings of the Forum, disseminates its views, administers the Forum's observer office at the United Nations, and aims to strengthen relations with other regional and international organizations, in particular APEC and ASEAN. The Division's other main concern is to promote regional co-operation in law enforcement and legal affairs, and it provides technical support for the drafting of legal documents and for law enforcement capacity-building. In 1997 the Secretariat undertook an assessment to survey the need for specialist training in dealing with money laundering in member countries. In recent years the Forum Secretariat has been concerned with assessing the legislative reforms and other commitments needed to ensure implementation of the 1992 Honiara Declaration on Law Enforcement Co-operation. The Division assists member countries to ratify and implement the 1988 UN Convention against Illicit Trafficking in Narcotic Drugs and Psychotropic Substances. In December 1998 the Secretariat initiated a five-year programme to strengthen regional law enforcement capabilities, in particular to counter cross-border crimes such as money-laundering and drugs-trafficking. All member states, apart from Australia and New Zealand, were to participate in the initiative. In December

2001 the first ever Forum Election Observer Group was dispatched to monitor legislative elections held in Solomon Islands. A conference of Forum immigration ministers convened in that month expressed concern at rising levels of human-trafficking and illegal immigration in the region, and recommended that member states become parties to the 2000 UN Convention Against Transnational Organized Crime.

The Secretariat helps to co-ordinate environmental policy. With support from the Australian Government, it administers a network of stations to monitor sea-levels and climate change throughout the Pacific region. In recent years the Secretariat has played an active role in supporting regional participation at meetings of the Conference of the Parties to the UN Framework Convention on Climate Change.

The Development and Economic Policy Division of the Secretariat aims to co-ordinate and promote co-operation in development activities and programmes throughout the region. The Division administers a Short Term Advisory Service, which provides consultancy services to help member countries meet economic development priorities, and a Fellowship Scheme to provide practical training in a range of technical and income-generating activities. A Small Island Development Fund aims to assist the economic development of this sub-group of member countries (i.e. the Cook Islands, Kiribati, the Marshall Islands, Nauru, Niue and Tuvalu) through project financing. A separate fellowship has also been established to provide training to the Kanak population of New Caledonia, to assist in their social, economic and political development. The Division aims to assist regional organizations to identify development priorities and to provide advice to national governments on economic analysis, planning and structural reforms. The Secretariat chairs the Council of Regional Organizations in the Pacific (CROP), an *ad hoc* committee comprising the heads of eight regional organizations, which aims to discuss and co-ordinate the policies and work programmes of the various agencies in order to avoid duplication of or omissions in their services to member countries.

The Secretariat services the Pacific Group Council of ACP states receiving assistance from the EU (q.v.), and in early 1993 a joint unit was established within the Secretariat headquarters to assist Pacific ACP countries and regional organizations in submitting projects to the EU for funding.

The Forum established the Pacific Forum Line and the Association of South Pacific Airlines (see below), as part of its efforts to promote co-operation in regional transport. On 1 January 1997 the work of the Forum Maritime Programme, which included assistance for regional maritime training and for the development of regional maritime administrations and legislation, was transferred to the regional office of the South Pacific Commission (renamed the Pacific Community from February 1998) at Suva. At the same time responsibility for the Secretariat's civil aviation activities was transferred to individual countries, to be managed at a bilateral level. Telecommunications policy activities were also transferred to the then South Pacific Commission at the start of 1997. In May 1998 ministers responsible for aviation in member states approved a new regional civil aviation policy, which envisaged liberalization of air services, common safety and security standards and provisions for shared revenue.

Finance

The Governments of Australia and New Zealand each contribute some 37% of the annual budget and the remaining amount is shared by the other member Governments. Extra-budgetary funding is contributed mainly by Australia, New Zealand, Japan, the EU and France. Forum officials approved a budget of $F 15.4m. for the Secretariat's 2002 work programme.

Publications

Annual Report.

Forum News (quarterly).

Forum Trends.

Forum Secretariat Directory of Aid Agencies.

South Pacific Trade Directory.

SPARTECA (guide for Pacific island exporters).

Reports of meetings; profiles of Forum member countries.

Associated and Affiliated Organizations

Association of South Pacific Airlines—ASPA: POB 9817, Nadi Airport, Nadi, Fiji; tel. 723526; fax 720196; f. 1979 at a meeting of airlines in the South Pacific, convened to promote co-operation among the member airlines for the development of regular, safe and economical commercial aviation within, to and from the South Pacific. Mems: 16 regional airlines, two associates. Chair. SEMISI TAUMOEPEAU; Sec.-Gen. GEORGE E. FAKTAUFON.

Forum Fisheries Agency—FFA: POB 629, Honiara, Solomon Islands; tel. (677) 21124; fax (677) 23995; e-mail info@ffa.int; f. 1979 to promote co-operation in fisheries among coastal states in the region; collects and disseminates information and advice on the living marine resources of the region, including the management, exploitation and development of these resources; provides assistance in the areas of law (treaty negotiations, drafting legislation, and co-ordinating surveillance and enforcement), fisheries development, research, economics, computers, and information management. A Vessel Monitoring System, to provide automated data collection and analysis of fishing vessel activities throughout the region, was inaugurated by the FFA in 1998. On behalf of its 16 member countries, the FFA administers a multilateral fisheries treaty, under which vessels from the USA operate in the region, in exchange for an annual payment. Dir VICTORIO UHERBELAU. Publs *FFA News Digest* (every two months), *FFA Reports*.

Pacific Forum Line: POB 796, Auckland, New Zealand; tel. (9) 356-2333; fax (9) 356-2330; e-mail info@pflnz.co.nz; internet www.pflnz.co.nz; f. 1977 as a joint venture by South Pacific countries, to provide shipping services to meet the special requirements of the region; operates three container vessels; conducts shipping agency services in Australia, Fiji, New Zealand and Samoa, and stevedoring in Samoa. Chair. T. TUFUI; CEO W. J. MACLENNAN.

Pacific Islands Centre—PIC: Sotobori Sky Bldg, 5th Floor, 2-11 Ichigayahonmura-cho, Shinjuku-ku,, Tokyo 162-0845, Japan; tel. (3) 3268-8419; fax (3) 3268-6311; f. 1996 to promote and to facilitate trade, investment and tourism among Forum members and Japan. Dir HIDEO FUJITA.

South Pacific Trade Commission (Australia Office): Level 30, Piccadilly Tower, 133 Castlereagh St, Sydney, NSW 2000, Australia; tel. (2) 9283-5933; fax (2) 9283-5948; e-mail info@sptc.gov.au; internet www.sptc.gov.au; f. 1979; assists Pacific Island Governments and business communities to identify market opportunities in Australia and promotes investment in the Pacific Island countries. Senior Trade Commr AIVU TAUVASA (Papua New Guinea).

South Pacific Trade Commission (New Zealand Office): Flight Centre, 48 Emily Pl., Auckland, New Zealand; tel. (9) 3020465; fax (9) 3776642; e-mail parmeshc@sptc.org.nz; internet www.sptc.org.nz. Senior Trade Commr PARMESH CHAND.

SOUTH ASIAN ASSOCIATION FOR REGIONAL CO-OPERATION—SAARC

Address: POB 4222, Kathmandu, Nepal.

Telephone: (1) 221785; **fax:** (1) 227033; **e-mail:** saarc@saarc-sec.org; **internet:** www.saarc-sec.org.

The South Asian Association for Regional Co-operation (SAARC) was formally established in 1985 in order to strengthen and accelerate regional co-operation, particularly in economic development.

MEMBERS

Bangladesh	Nepal
Bhutan	Pakistan
India	Sri Lanka
Maldives	

Organization

(April 2002)

SUMMIT MEETING

Heads of state and of government of member states represent the body's highest authority, and a summit meeting is normally held annually. The 11th SAARC summit meeting was convened in Kathmandu, Nepal, in January 2002. (It had been postponed from November 1999 owing to a deterioration in relations at that time between India and Pakistan.)

COUNCIL OF MINISTERS

The Council of Ministers comprises the ministers of foreign affairs of member countries, who meet twice a year. The Council may also meet in extraordinary session at the request of member states. The responsibilities of the Council include formulation of policies, assessing progress and confirming new areas of co-operation.

STANDING COMMITTEE

The Committee consists of the secretaries of foreign affairs of member states. It has overall responsibility for the monitoring and co-ordination of programmes and financing, and determines priorities, mobilizes resources and identifies areas of co-operation. It usually meets twice a year, and submits its reports to the Council of Ministers. The Committee is supported by an *ad hoc* Programming Committee made up of senior officials, who meet to examine the budget of the Secretariat, confirm the Calendar of Activities and resolve matters assigned to it by the Standing Committee.

TECHNICAL COMMITTEES

SAARC's Integrated Programme of Action is implemented by seven Technical Committees (reduced from 11 since 2000) covering: Agriculture and rural development; Energy; Environment, meteorology and forestry; Human resource development; Science and technology; Social development; and Transport and communications. Each committee is headed by a representative of a member state and meets annually.

SECRETARIAT

The Secretariat was established in 1987 to co-ordinate and oversee SAARC activities. It comprises the Secretary-General and a Director from each member country. The Secretary-General is appointed by the Council of Ministers, after being nominated by a member state. The ninth summit meeting of heads of state and of government, held in Malé, Maldives, in 1997, extended the Secretary-General's term of office from two to three years. The Director is nominated by member states and appointed by the Secretary-General for a term of three years, although this may be increased in special circumstances.

Secretary-General: Q. A. M. A. RAHIM (Bangladesh).

Activities

The first summit meeting of SAARC heads of state and government, held in Dhaka, Bangladesh, in December 1985, resulted in the signing of the Charter of the South Asian Association for Regional Co-operation (SAARC). In August 1993 ministers of foreign affairs of seven countries, meeting in New Delhi, India, adopted a Declaration on South Asian Regional Co-operation and launched an Integrated Programme of Action (IPA), which identified the main areas for regional co-operation. The ninth summit meeting, held in May 1997, authorized the establishment of a Group of Eminent Persons to review the functioning of the IPA. On the basis of the group's recommendations a reconstituted IPA, to be administered by a more efficient arrangement of Technical Committees, was initiated in June 2000.

SAARC is committed to improving quality of life in the region by accelerating economic growth, social progress and cultural development; promoting self-reliance; encouraging mutual assistance; increasing co-operation with other developing countries; and co-operating with other regional and international organizations. The SAARC Charter stipulates that decisions should be made unanimously, and that 'bilateral and contentious issues' should not be discussed. Regular meetings, at all levels, are held to further co-operation in areas covered by the Technical Committees (see above). A priority objective is the eradication of poverty in the region, and in 1993 SAARC endorsed an Agenda of Action to help achieve this. A framework for exchanging information on poverty eradication has also, since, been established. In 1998 the 10th summit meeting resolved to formulate a SAARC Social Charter, which was to incorporate agreed objectives in areas such as poverty eradication, promotion of health and nutrition, and the protection of children. Representatives of civil society, academia, non-governmental organizations and government were to be involved in the process of drafting the Charter, under the auspices of an inter-governmental expert group, which met for the first time in April 2001. The 11th SAARC summit meeting, held in Kathmandu, Nepal, in January 2002, adopted a convention on regional arrangements for the promotion of child welfare in South Asia. The 11th summit also determined to reinvigorate regional poverty reduction activities in the context of the UN General Assembly's Millennium Goal of halving extreme poverty by 2015, and of other internationally-agreed commitments. The summit also urged the development of a regional strategy for preventing and combating HIV/AIDS and other communicable diseases; the SAARC Tuberculosis Centre (see below) was to play a co-ordinating role in this area.

A Committee on Economic Co-operation (CEC), comprising senior trade officials of member states, was established in July 1991 to monitor progress concerning trade and economic co-operation issues. In the same year the summit meeting approved the creation of an inter-governmental group to establish a framework for the promotion of specific trade liberalization measures. A SAARC Chamber of Commerce (SCCI) became operational in 1992, with headquarters in Karachi, Pakistan. (The SCCI headquarters were subsequently transferred to Islamabad, Pakistan.) In April 1993 ministers signed a SAARC Preferential Trading Arrangement (SAPTA), which came into effect in December 1995. The 10th summit meeting proposed a series of measures to accelerate progress in the next round of SAPTA trade negotiations, including a reduction in the domestic content requirements of SAPTA's rules of origin, greater tariff concessions on products being actively traded and the removal of certain discriminatory and non-tariff barriers. By the third, and most recent, round of trade negotiations under SAPTA, held in November 1998, 3,456 products had been identified as eligible for preferential trade tariffs. In December 1995 the Council resolved that the ultimate objective for member states should be the establishment of a South Asian Free Trade Area (SAFTA), superseding SAPTA. An *ad hoc* inter-governmental expert group was constituted to formulate a framework treaty to realize SAFTA.

The 11th summit urged that the draft treaty on a regulatory framework for SAFTA be finalized by the end of 2002.

In January 1996 the first SAARC Trade Fair was held, in New Delhi, India, to promote intra-SAARC commerce. At the same time SAARC ministers of commerce convened for their first meeting to discuss regional economic co-operation. A group on customs co-operation was established in 1996 to harmonize trading rules and regulations within the grouping, to simplify trade procedures and to upgrade facilities. In 1999 a regional action plan to harmonize national standards, quality control and measurements came into effect. A second SAARC trade fair was held at Colombo, Sri Lanka, in 1998, and the third was held in Islamabad, Pakistan, in early September 2001. In August 2001 SAARC commerce ministers met, in New Delhi, to discuss a co-ordinated approach to the World Trade Organization negotiations that were held in November.

An Agricultural Information Centre was founded in 1988, in Dhaka, Bangladesh, to serve as a central institution for the dissemination of knowledge and information in the agricultural sector. It maintains a network of centres in each member state, which provide for the efficient exchange of technical information and for strengthening agricultural research. An agreement establishing a Food Security Reserve to meet emergency food requirements was signed in November 1987, and entered into force in August 1988. The Board of the Reserve meets annually to assess the food security of the region. At March 2001 the Reserve contained some 241,580 metric tons of grain. Other regional institutions include the SAARC Tuberculosis Centre in Thimi, Nepal, which opened in July 1992 with the aim of preventing and reducing the prevalence of the disease in the region through the co-ordination of tuberculosis control programmes, research and training; a SAARC Documentation Centre, established in New Delhi in May 1994; and a SAARC Meteorological Research Centre which opened in Dhaka in January 1995. A Human Resources Development Centre was established in Islamabad, Pakistan in 1999. Regional funds include a SAARC-Japan Special Fund established in September 1993. One-half of the fund's resources, which were provided by the Japanese Government, was to be used to finance projects identified by Japan, including workshops and cultural events, and one-half was to be used to finance projects identified by SAARC member states. The eighth SAARC summit meeting, held in New Delhi in May 1996, established a South Asian Development Fund, comprising a Fund for Regional Projects, a Regional Fund and a fund for social development and infrastructure building.

A SAARC Youth Volunteers Programme (SYVOP) enables young people to work in other member countries in the agriculture and forestry sectors. The Programme is part of a series of initiatives designed to promote intra-regional exchanges and contact. A Youth Awards Scheme to reward outstanding achievements by young people was inaugurated in 1996. The theme selected for recognition in 2001 was 'Creative Photography: South Asian Diversity'. Founded in 1987, the SAARC Audio-visual Exchange Programme (SAVE) broadcasts radio and television programmes on social and cultural affairs to all member countries, twice a month, in order to disseminate information about SAARC and its members. From 2001 SAVE was to organize an annual SAARC Telefilm festival. The SAARC Consortium of Open and Distance Learning was established in 2000. A Visa Exemption Scheme, exempting 21 specified categories of person from visa requirements, with the aim of promoting closer regional contact, became operational in March 1992. A SAARC citizens forum promotes interaction among the people of South Asia. In addition, SAARC operates a fellowships, scholarships and chairs scheme and a scheme for the promotion of organized tourism.

At the third SAARC summit, held in Kathmandu in November 1987, member states signed a regional convention on measures to counteract terrorism. The convention, which entered into force in August 1988, commits signatory countries to the extradition or prosecution of alleged terrorists and to the implementation of preventative measures to combat terrorism. Monitoring desks for terrorist and drugs offences have been established to process information relating to those activities. The first SAARC conference on co-operation in police affairs, attended by the heads of the police forces of member states, was held in Colombo in July 1996. The conference discussed the issues of terrorism, organized crime, the extradition of criminals, drugs-trafficking and drug abuse. A convention on narcotic drugs and psychotropic substances was signed during the fifth SAARC summit meeting, held in Malé in 1990. The convention entered into force in September 1993, following its ratification by member states. It is implemented by a co-ordination group of drug law enforcement agencies. At the 11th SAARC summit member states adopted a convention on the prevention of trafficking of women and children for prostitution.

SAARC co-operates with other regional and international organizations. In February 1993 SAARC signed a memorandum of understanding with UNCTAD, whereby both parties agreed to exchange information on trade control measures regionally and in 50 developed and developing countries, respectively, in order to increase transparency and thereby facilitate trade. In February 1994 SAARC signed a framework co-operation agreement with ESCAP to enhance co-operation on development issues through a framework of joint studies, workshops and information exchange. A memorandum of understanding with the European Commission was signed in July 1996. SAARC has also signed co-operation agreements with UNICEF (in 1993), the Asia Pacific Telecommunity (1994), UNDP (1995), UNDCP (1995), the International Telecommunication Union (1997), the Canadian International Development Agency (1997), WHO (2000), and UNIFEM (2001). An informal dialogue at ministerial level has been conducted with ASEAN and the European Union since 1998. SAARC and WIPO hold regular consultations concerning regional co-operation on intellectual property rights, and regular consultations are convened with the WTO.

Finance

The national budgets of member countries provide the resources to finance SAARC activities. The Secretariat's annual budget is shared among member states according to a specified formula.

Publications

SAARC News (7/8 a year).

SPECTRUM (irregular).

Regional Apex Bodies

Association of Persons of the Legal Communities of the SAARC Countries—SAARCLAW: Pioneer House, Shahayog Marg, Anamnagar, Kathmandu, Nepal; tel. (1) 221340; fax (1) 226770; e-mail saarclaw@wlink.com.np; internet www.saarclaw.org; f. 1991; recognized as a SAARC regional apex body in July 1994; aims to enhance exchanges and co-operation amongst the legal communities of the sub-region and to promote the development of law. Pres. LAXMAN ARYAL (Nepal); Sec.-Gen. BHARAT RAJ UPRETI (Nepal).

SAARC Chamber of Commerce and Industry (SCCI): House 5, St 59, F-8/4, Islamabad, Pakistan; tel. (51) 2281395; fax (51) 2281390; e-mail saarc@isb.comsats.net.pk; internet www.saarcnet.org; f. 1992; promotes economic and trade co-operation throughout the sub-region and greater interaction between the business communities of member countries; organizes SAARC Economic Co-operation Conferences and Trade Fairs. Pres. PADMA JYOTI (Nepal); Sec.-Gen. ABUL HASAN.

South Asian Federation of Accountants (SAFA): f. 1984; recognized as a SAARC regional apex body in Jan. 2002; aims to develop regional co-ordination for the accountancy profession.

Other recognized regional bodies include the South Asian Association for Regional Co-operation of Architects, the Association of Management Development Institutions, the SAARC Federation of University Women, the SAARC Association of Town Planners, the SAARC Cardiac Society, the Association of SAARC Speakers and Parliamentarians, the Federation of State Insurance Organizations of SAARC Countries, the Federation of State Insurance Organizations of SAARC Countries, the SAARC Diploma Engineers Forum, the Radiological Society of SAARC Countries, the SAARC Teachers' Federation, the SAARC Surgical Care Society and the Foundation of SAARC Writers and Literature.

SOUTHERN AFRICAN DEVELOPMENT COMMUNITY—SADC

Address: SADC House, Government Enclave, Private Bag 0095, Gaborone, Botswana.

Telephone: 351863; **fax:** 372848; **e-mail:** registry@sadc.int; **internet:** www.sadc.int.

The first Southern African Development Co-ordination Conference (SADCC) was held at Arusha, Tanzania, in July 1979, to harmonize development plans and to reduce the region's economic dependence on South Africa. On 17 August 1992 the 10 member countries of the SADCC signed a treaty establishing the Southern African Development Community (SADC), which replaced the SADCC. The treaty places binding obligations on member countries, with the aim of promoting economic integration towards a fully developed common market. A tribunal was to be established to arbitrate in the case of disputes between member states arising from the treaty. By September 1993 all of the member states had ratified the treaty; it came into effect on 5 October. A protocol on the establishment of the long-envisaged SADC tribunal was adopted in 2000. The Protocol on Politics, Defence and Security Co-operation, regulating the structure, operations and functions of the Organ on Politics, Defence and Security, established in June 1996 (see under Regional Security), was adopted and opened for signature in August 2001. A troika system, comprising the current, incoming and outgoing SADC chairmanship, operates at the level of the Summit, Council of Ministers and Standing Committee of Officials, and co-ordinates the Organ on Politics, Defence and Security. Other member states may be co-opted into the troika as required. A system of SADC national committees, comprising representatives of government, civil society and the private sector, oversees the implementation of regional programmes at country level and helps to formulate new regional strategies. In 2002 SADC institutions were undergoing a process of intensive restructuring.

MEMBERS

Angola	Malawi	South Africa
Botswana	Mauritius	Swaziland
Congo, Democratic Republic	Mozambique	Tanzania
	Namibia	Zambia
Lesotho	Seychelles	Zimbabwe

Organization

(April 2002)

SUMMIT MEETING

The meeting is held at least once a year and is attended by heads of state and government or their representatives. It is the supreme policy-making organ of the SADC and is responsible for the appointment of the Executive Secretary. A report on the restructuring of the SADC, adopted by an extraordinary summit held in Windhoek, Namibia, in March 2001, recommended that biannual summit meetings should be convened.

COUNCIL OF MINISTERS

Representatives of SADC member countries at ministerial level meet at least once a year.

STANDING COMMITTEE OF OFFICIALS

The Committee, comprising senior officials, usually from the ministry responsible for economic planning or finance, acts as the technical advisory body to the Council. It meets at least once a year. Members of the Committee also act as a national contact point for matters relating to SADC.

SECRETARIAT

Executive Secretary: Dr PAKEREESAMY ('PREGA') RAMSAMY (Mauritius).

The extraordinary summit held in March 2001 determined that the mandate and resources of the Secretariat should be strengthened. A Department of Strategic Planning, Gender and Development and Policy Harmonization was established, comprising permanently-staffed Directorates covering the four priority areas of integration, as follows: trade, industry, finance and investment (established in 2001); infrastructure and services (to become operational in 2002); food, agriculture and natural resources (established 2001); and social and human development and special programmes (to become operational in 2002). The Community's 19 sectors were to be divided among the new Directorates. An Integrated Committee of Ministers (ICM) was to oversee the four priority areas of integration, monitor the Directorates, facilitate the co-ordination and harmonization of cross-sectoral activities, and provide policy guidance to the Secretariat. The ICM would be responsible to the Council of Ministers. The former Sectoral Co-ordinating Units and Sectoral Commissions were to be phased out.

Activities

In July 1979 the first Southern African Development Co-ordination Conference was attended by delegations from Angola, Botswana, Mozambique, Tanzania and Zambia, with representatives from donor governments and international agencies. In April 1980 a regional economic summit conference was held in Lusaka, Zambia, and the Lusaka Declaration, a statement of strategy entitled 'Southern Africa: Towards Economic Liberation', was approved. The members aimed to reduce their dependence on South Africa for rail and air links and port facilities, imports of raw materials and manufactured goods, and the supply of electric power. In 1985, however, an SADCC report noted that since 1980 the region had become still more dependent on South Africa for its trade outlets, and the 1986 summit meeting, although it recommended the adoption of economic sanctions against South Africa, failed to establish a timetable for doing so.

In January 1992 a meeting of the SADCC Council of Ministers approved proposals to transform the organization (by then expanded to include Lesotho, Malawi, Namibia and Swaziland) into a fully integrated economic community, and in August the treaty establishing the SADC (see above) was signed. An SADC Programme of Action—SPA was to combine the strategies and objectives of the organization's sectoral programmes. (By 2001 some 407 projects were being conducted under the SPA.) South Africa became a member of the SADC in August 1994, thus strengthening the objective of regional co-operation and economic integration. Mauritius became a member in August 1995. In September 1997 SADC heads of state agreed to admit the Democratic Republic of the Congo and Seychelles as members of the Community.

A possible merger between the SADC and the Preferential Trade Area for Eastern and Southern African States (PTA), which consisted of all the members of the SADC apart from Botswana and had similar aims of enhancing economic co-operation, was rejected by the SADC's Executive Secretary in January 1993. He denied that the two organizations were duplicating each other's work, as had been suggested. However, concerns of regional rivalry with the PTA's successor, the Common Market for Eastern and Southern Africa (COMESA, q.v.), persisted. In August 1996 an SADC–COMESA ministerial meeting advocated the continued separate functioning of the two organizations. A programme of co-operation between the secretariats of the SADC and COMESA, aimed at reducing all duplication of roles between the two organizations, was ongoing in 2002. A co-ordinating SADC/COMESA task force was established in 2001.

In September 1994 the first meeting of ministers of foreign affairs of the SADC and the European Union (EU) was held in Berlin, Germany. The two sides agreed to establish working groups to promote closer trade, political, regional and economic co-operation. In particular, a declaration issued from the meeting specified joint objectives, including a reduction of exports of weapons to southern Africa and of the arms trade within the region, promotion of investment in the region's manufacturing sector and support for democracy at all levels. A consultative meeting between representatives of the SADC and EU was held in February 1995, in Lilongwe, Malawi, at which both groupings resolved to strengthen security in the southern African region. The meeting proposed initiating mechanisms to prevent conflicts and to maintain peace, and agreed to organize a conference to address the problems of drugs-trafficking and cross-border crime in the region. A second SADC–EU ministerial meeting, held in Namibia in October 1996, endorsed a Regional Indicative Programme to enhance co-operation between the two organizations over the next five years. The third ministerial meeting took place in Vienna, Austria, in November 1998. In September 1999 the SADC signed a co-operation agreement with the US Government, which incorporated measures to promote US investment in the region, and commitments to support HIV/AIDS assessment and prevention programmes and to assist member states to develop environmental protection capabilities. The fourth SADC–EU ministerial meeting, convened in Gaborone, Botswana, in November 2000, adopted a joint declaration on the control of small arms and light weapons in the SADC region. The meeting also emphasized that the termination of illicit trading in diamonds would be a major contributory factor in resolving the ongoing conflicts in Angola and the Democratic Republic of the Congo—DRC (see below). The fifth SADC-EU forum was scheduled to be held in Copenhagen, Denmark, in November 2002.

In April 1997 the SADC announced the establishment of a Parliamentary Forum to promote democracy, human rights and good governance throughout the region. Membership was to be open to national parliaments of all SADC countries, and was to offer fair representation for women. Representatives were to serve for a period of five years. The Parliamentary Forum, with its headquarters in Windhoek, Namibia, was to receive funds from member parliaments, governments and charitable and international organizations. In September SADC heads of state endorsed the establishment of the Forum as an autonomous institution.

The SADC has adopted a strategic framework and programme of action for tackling HIV/AIDS, which are endemic in the region. In December 1999 a multisectoral sub-committee on HIV/AIDS was established.

In 2001 the recommendations of a report on the restructuring of the SADC's institutions, adopted by an extraordinary summit meeting convened in March, were being implemented, in order to facilitate the effective application of the objectives of the organization's treaty and of the SPA. The Community's sectoral system was being reorganized under four new directorates: trade, industry, finance and investment; infrastructure and services; food, agriculture and natural resources; and social and human development and special programmes. These were to be administered from the secretariat in Gaborone to ensure greater efficiency (the previous system of directorates had been decentralized). The report outlined a common agenda for the organization, which covered the promotion of poverty reduction measures and of sustainable and equitable socio-economic development, promotion of democratic political values and systems, and the consolidation of peace and security. A Regional Indicative Strategic Development Plan was to be formulated during 2002.

In August 2001 the SADC established a task force, comprising representatives of five member countries, to address the ongoing political crisis in Zimbabwe. The Community sent two separate observer teams to monitor the controversial presidential election held in Zimbabwe in March 2002; the SADC Council of Ministers team found the election to have been conducted freely and fairly, while the Parliamentary Forum group was reluctant to endorse the poll. Having evaluated both reports, the Community approved the election.

REGIONAL SECURITY

In November 1994 SADC ministers of defence, meeting in Arusha, Tanzania, approved the establishment of a regional rapid-deployment peace-keeping force, which could be used to contain regional conflicts or civil unrest in member states. In April 1997 a training programme was held, which aimed to inform troops from nine SADC countries of UN peace-keeping doctrines, procedures and strategies. The exercise took place in Zimbabwe at a cost of US $900,000, provided by the British Government and the Zimbabwe National Army. A peace-keeping exercise involving 4,000 troops was held in South Africa, in April 1999. An SADC Mine Action Committee has been established to monitor and co-ordinate the process of removing anti-personnel land devices from countries in the region.

In June 1996 SADC heads of state and government, meeting in Gaborone, Botswana, inaugurated a new Organ on Politics, Defence and Security, which was expected to enhance co-ordination of national policies and activities in these areas. The objectives of the body were, *inter alia*, to safeguard the people and development of the region against instability arising from civil disorder, inter-state conflict and external aggression; to undertake conflict prevention, management and resolution activities, by mediating in inter-state and intra-state disputes and conflicts, pre-empting conflicts through an early-warning system and using diplomacy and peace-keeping to achieve sustainable peace; to promote the development of a common foreign policy, in areas of mutual interest, and the evolution of common political institutions; to develop close co-operation between the police and security services of the region; and to encourage the observance of universal human rights, as provided for in the charters of the UN and OAU. In October the Organ convened, at summit level, to consider measures to promote the peace process in Angola; however, there were disagreements within SADC regarding its future status, either as an integrated part of the Community (favoured by South Africa) or as a more autonomous body (supported by Zimbabwe).

In August 1998 the Zimbabwean Government convened a meeting of the heads of state of seven SADC member states to discuss the escalation of civil conflict in the DRC and the threat to regional security, with Rwanda and Uganda reportedly having sent troops to assist anti-government forces. Later in that month ministers of defence and defence officials of several SADC countries declared their support for an initiative of the Zimbabwean Government to send military assistance to the forces loyal to President Kabila in the DRC. South Africa, which did not attend the meeting, rejected any military intervention under SADC auspices and insisted that the organization would pursue a diplomatic initiative. Zimbabwe, Angola and Namibia proceeded to send troops and logistical support to counter rebel Congolese forces. The Presidents of those countries failed to attend an emergency meeting of heads of state, convened by President Mandela of South Africa, which called for an immediate cease-fire and presented a 10-point-peace plan. A further emergency meeting, held in early September and attended by all SADC leaders, agreed to pursue negotiations for a peaceful settlement of the conflict. Some unity within the grouping was restored by Mandela's endorsement of the objective of supporting Kabila as the legitimate leader in the DRC. Furthermore, at the annual SADC summit meeting, held in Mauritius, it was agreed that discussion of the report on the security Organ, scheduled to have been presented to the conference, would be deferred to a specially convened summit meeting (although no date was agreed). Talks attended by Angola, the DRC, Namibia, Rwanda, Uganda, Zambia and Zimbabwe, conducted in mid-September, in Victoria Falls, agreed in principle on a cease-fire in the DRC but failed to conclude a detailed peace accord. Fighting continued to escalate, and in October Zimbabwe, Angola and Namibia resolved to send reinforcements to counter the advancing rebel forces. Meanwhile, in September representatives of the SADC attempted to mediate between government and opposition parties in Lesotho amidst a deteriorating security situation in that country. At the end of the month, following an attempt by the Lesotho military to seize power, South Africa, together with Botswana, sent troops into Lesotho to restore civil order. The operation was declared to have been conducted under SADC auspices, however it prompted widespread criticism owing to the troops' involvement in heavy fighting with opposition forces. A committee was established by SADC to secure a cease-fire in Lesotho. Also at the end of September SADC chiefs of staff agreed that the Community would assist the Angolan Government to eliminate the UNITA movement, owing to its adverse impact on the region's security. In October an SADC ministerial team, comprising representatives of South Africa, Botswana, Mozambique and Zimbabwe, negotiated an accord between the opposing sides in Lesotho providing for the conduct of democratic elections. The withdrawal of foreign troops from Lesotho was initiated at the end of April 1999, and was reported to have been completed by mid-May.

During the first half of 1999 Zambia's President Chiluba pursued efforts, under SADC auspices, to negotiate a political solution to the conflict in the DRC. Troops from the region, in particular from Angola and Zimbabwe, remained actively involved in the struggle to uphold Kabila's administration. SADC ministers of defence and of foreign affairs convened in Lusaka, in June, in order to secure a cease-fire agreement. An accord was finally signed in July between Kabila, leaders of the rebel forces and foreign allies of both sides. All foreign troops were to be withdrawn within nine months according to a schedule to be drawn up by the UN, OAU and a Joint Military Commission. However, the disengagement and redeployment of troops from front-line positions did not commence until February 2001. In August 2001 SADC heads of state resolved to support the continuing imposition of sanctions by the UN Security Council against the UNITA rebels in Angola; it was agreed to promote the international certification system for illicit trade in rough diamonds (believed to finance UNITA's activities), to install mobile radar systems that would detect illegal cross-border flights in the region, and to establish a body to compile information and to devise a strategy for terminating the supply of petroleum products to UNITA.

In August 2000 proposals were announced (strongly supported by South Africa, see above) to develop the Organ for Politics, Defence and Security as a substructure of the SADC, with subdivisions for defence and international diplomacy, to be chaired by a member country's head of state, working within a troika system; these were approved at the extraordinary summit held in March 2001. A Protocol on Politics, Defence and Security Co-operation, regulating the structure, operations and functions of the Organ, was adopted and opened for signature in August. The protocol was to be implemented by an Inter-state Politics and Diplomacy Committee.

In July 2001 SADC ministers of defence approved a draft regional defence pact, providing for a mechanism to prevent conflict involving member countries and for member countries to unite against outside aggression. In January 2002 an extraordinary summit of SADC heads of state, held in Blantyre, Malawi, adopted a Declaration against Terrorism. An SADC peace-keeping exercise was conducted in February 2002, in Tanzania, jointly with Tanzanian and Ugandan forces.

INFRASTRUCTURE AND SERVICES

The directorate of infrastructure and services was scheduled to become operational during 2002.

At the SADC's inception transport was seen as the most important area to be developed, on the grounds that, as the Lusaka Declaration noted, without the establishment of an adequate regional transport and communications system, other areas of co-operation become impractical. Priority was to be given to the improvement of road and railway services into Mozambique, so that the landlocked countries of the region could transport their goods through Mozambican ports instead of South African ones. The Southern African Transport and Communications Commission (SATCC) was established, in Maputo, Mozambique, in order to undertake SADC's activities in this sector. The successful distribution of emergency supplies in 1992/93, following a severe drought in the region, was reliant on improvements made to the region's infrastructure. The facilities of 12 ports in southern Africa, including South Africa, were used to import some 11.5m. metric tons of drought-related commodities, and the SADC co-ordinated six transport corridors to ensure unobstructed movement of food and other supplies. During 1995 the SATCC undertook a study of regional transport and communications to provide a comprehensive framework and strategy for future courses of action. A task force was also established to identify measures to simplify procedures at border crossings throughout southern Africa. In 1996 the SATCC Road Network Management and Financing Task Force was established.

The SADC's development projects in the transport and communications sector (which accounted for some 80% of total project financing in 1996/97) have aimed to address missing links and over-stretched sections of the regional network, as well as to improve efficiency, operational co-ordination and human resource development, such as management training projects. Other sectoral objectives have been to ensure the compatibility of technical systems within the region and to promote the harmonization of regulations relating to intra-regional traffic and trade. In 1997 Namibia announced plans, supported by the SADC, to establish a rail link with Angola in order to form a trade route similar to that created in Mozambique, on the western side of southern Africa. In March 1998 the final stage of the trans-Kalahari highway, linking ports on the east and west coasts of southern Africa, was officially opened. In July 1999 a 317-km rail link between Bulawayo, Zimbabwe, and the border town of Beitbridge, administered by the SADC as its first build-operate-transfer project, was opened.

The SADC promotes greater co-operation in the civil aviation sector, in order to improve efficiency and to reverse a steady decline in the region's airline industries. Within the telecommunications sector efforts have been made to increase the capacity of direct exchange lines and international subscriber dialling (ISD) services. In January 1997 the Southern African Telecommunications Regional Authority (SATRA), a regulatory authority, was established. An SADC Expedited Mail Service operates in the postal services sector. The SATCC's Technical Unit oversees the region's meteorological services and issues a regular *Drought-Watch for Southern Africa* bulletin, a monthly *Drought Overview* bulletin and forewarnings of impending natural disasters.

The tourism sector operates within the context of national and regional socio-economic development objectives. It comprises four components: tourism product development; tourism marketing and research; tourism services; and human resources development and training. The SADC has promoted tourism for the region at trade fairs in Europe, and has initiated a project to provide a range of promotional material and a regional tourism directory. By September 1993 a project to design a standard grading classification system for tourist accommodation in the region was completed, with the assistance of the World Tourism Organization, and the Council approved its implementation. A new five-year development strategy for tourism in the region was initiated in 1995, the key element of which was the establishment of a new tourism body, to be administered jointly by SADC officials and private-sector operators. The Regional Tourism Organization for Southern Africa (RETOSA) was to assist member states to formulate tourism promotion policies and strategies. A legal charter for the establishment of RETOSA was signed by ministers of tourism in September 1997. During 1999 a feasibility study on the development of the Upper Zambezi basin as a site for eco-tourism was initiated.

Areas of activity in the energy sector include: joint petroleum exploration, training programmes for the petroleum sector and studies for strategic fuel storage facilities; promotion of the use of coal; development of hydroelectric power and the co-ordination of SADC generation and transmission capacities; new and renewable sources of energy, including pilot projects in solar energy; assessment of the environmental and socio-economic impact of wood-fuel scarcity and relevant education programmes; and energy conservation. In July 1995 SADC energy ministers approved the establishment of a Southern African Power Pool, whereby all member states were to be linked into a single electricity grid. (Several grids are already integrated and others are being rehabilitated.) At the same time, ministers endorsed a Protocol to promote greater co-operation in energy development within the SADC. On receiving final approval and signature by member states, the Protocol was to replace the energy sector with an Energy Commission, responsible for 'demand-side' management, pricing, ensuring private-sector involvement and competition, training and research, collecting information, etc. The sector administers a joint SADC Petroleum Exploration Programme. In September 1997 heads of state endorsed an Energy Action Plan to proceed with the implementation of co-operative policies and strategies in four key areas of energy: trade, information exchange, training and organizational capacity-building, and investment and financing. A technical unit of the Energy Commission was to be responsible for implementation of the Action Plan.

FOOD, AGRICULTURE AND NATURAL RESOURCES

The food, agriculture and natural resources directorate, established in 2001, combines the following sectors: agricultural research and training; inland fisheries; forestry; wildlife; marine fisheries and resources; food security; livestock production and animal disease control; environment and land management; and water. According to SADC figures, agriculture contributes one-third of the region's GNP, accounts for about one-quarter of total earnings of foreign exchange and employs some 80% of the labour force. The principal objectives in this field are regional food security, agricultural development and natural resource development.

The Southern African Centre for Co-operation in Agricultural Research (SACCAR), was established in Gaborone, Botswana, in 1985. It aims to strengthen national agricultural research systems, in order to improve management, increase productivity, promote the development and transfer of technology to assist local farmers, and improve training. Examples of activity include: a sorghum and millet improvement programme; a land and water management research programme; a root crop research network; agroforestry research, implemented in Malawi, Tanzania, Zambia and Zimbabwe; and a grain legume improvement programme, comprising separate research units for groundnuts, beans and cowpeas. The SADC's Plant Genetic Resources Centre was established in 1988, near Lusaka, Zambia, to collect, conserve and utilize indigenous and exotic plant genetic resources and to develop appropriate management practices.

The sector for livestock production and animal disease control has aimed to improve breeding methods in the region through the Management of Farm Animal Genetic Research Programme. It also seeks to control diseases such as contagious bovine pleuropneumonia, foot and mouth disease and heartwater through diagnosis, monitoring and vaccination programmes. An *Animal Health Mortality Bulletin* is published, as is a monthly *Animal Disease Situation Bulletin*, which alerts member states to outbreaks of disease in the region.

The SADC aims to promote inland and marine fisheries as an important, sustainable source of animal protein. Marine fisheries are also considered to be a potential source of income of foreign exchange. In May 1993 the first formal meeting of SADC ministers of marine fisheries convened in Namibia, and it was agreed to hold annual meetings. In April 1997 it was agreed that Namibia would co-ordinate the establishment of inspectorates to monitor and control marine fisheries in the region for a period of five years. The development of fresh water fisheries is focused on aquaculture projects, and their integration into rural community activities. The environment and land management sector is concerned with sustainability as an essential quality of development. It aims to protect and improve the health, environment and livelihoods of people living in the southern African region; to preserve the natural heritage and biodiversity of the region; and to support regional economic development on a sustainable basis. The sector also focuses on capacity-building, training, regional co-operation and the exchange of information in all areas related to the environment and land management. It administers an SADC Environmental Exchange Network, which was established in 1995, and the Community's Land Degradation and Desertification Control Programme. The sector also undertakes projects for the conservation and sustainable development of forestry and wildlife.

Under the food security programme, the Harare-based Regional Early Warning Unit aims to anticipate and prevent food shortages through the provision of information relating to the food security situation in member states. As a result of the drought crisis experience, SADC member states have agreed to inform the food security sector of their food and non-food requirements on a regular basis, in order to assess the needs of the region as a whole. A regional food reserve project was also to be developed. In April 2002 the SADC predicted a regional cereals deficit of 3.2m. metric tons for 2001/02, owing to both severe drought and flooding; the SADC Regional Disaster Response Task Force recommended a number of strategies for managing the situation.

Following the severe drought in the region in 1991/92, the need for water resource development became a priority. The water sector was established as a separate administrative unit in August 1996, although the terms of reference of the sector were only formally approved by the Council, meeting in Windhoek, Namibia, in February 1997. The sector aims to promote the equitable distribution and effective management of water resources, in order to address the concern that many SADC member countries may be affected by future droughts and water scarcity. In April a workshop was held in Swaziland concerning the implementation of a new SADC Protocol on Shared Watercourse Systems. The involvement of the private sector in the region's water policies was under consideration at the Round Table Conference on Integrated Water Resources Development in October 1998.

TRADE, INDUSTRY, FINANCE AND INVESTMENT

The trade, industry, finance and investment directorate was established in 2001.

Under the treaty establishing the SADC, efforts were to be undertaken to achieve regional economic integration. The trade and industry sector aims to facilitate this by the creation of an enabling investment and trade environment in SADC countries, the establishment of a single regional market, by progressively removing barriers to the movement of goods, services and people, and the promotion of cross-border investment. The sector supports programmes for industrial research and development and standardization and quality assurance. A sector of finance and investment has been established to mobilize industrial investment resources and to co-ordinate economic policies and the development of the financial sector. During 1995 work continued on the preparation of two protocols on trade co-operation and finance and investment, which were to provide the legal framework for integration. In August 1996 SADC member states (except Angola) signed a protocol providing for the establishment of a regional free-trade area, through the gradual elimination of tariff barriers over an eight-year period, at a summit meeting held in Lesotho. In September 1999 representatives of the private sector in SADC member states, meeting in Mauritius, agreed to establish an Association of SADC Chambers of Commerce. The trade protocol entered into force in January 2000. In accordance with a revised schedule, announced in May 2000, the SADC free-trade area was launched in September of that year, comprising the 11 member states that had ratified the protocol by that time (all but Angola, the DRC and Seychelles). It was envisaged, under the new timescale, that all intra-SADC trade tariffs would be removed by 2012, with about 85% to be withdrawn by 2008. Annual meetings are convened to review the work of expert teams in the areas of standards, quality, assurance, accreditation and metrology.

In January 1992 a five-year strategy for the promotion of mining in the region was approved, with the principal objective of stimulating local and foreign investment in the sector to maximize benefits from the region's mineral resources. In December 1994 the SADC held a mining forum, jointly with the EU, in Lusaka, Zambia, with the aim of demonstrating to potential investors and promoters the possibilities of mining exploration in the region. A second mining investment forum was held in Lusaka in December 1998. Other objectives of the mining sector are the improvement of industry training, increasing the contribution of small-scale mining, reducing the illicit trade in gemstones and gold, increasing co-operation in mineral exploration and processing, and minimizing the adverse impact of mining operations on the environment. At the summit meeting, held in September 1997, SADC heads of state signed a Protocol providing for the harmonization of policies and programmes relating to the development and exploitation of mineral resources in the region.

In July 1998 a Banking Association was officially constituted by representatives of SADC member states. The Association was to establish international banking standards and regional payments systems, organize training and harmonize banking legislation in the region. In April 1999 governors of SADC central banks determined to strengthen and harmonize banking procedures and technology in order to facilitate the financial integration of the region. Efforts to harmonize stock exchanges in the region were also initiated in 1999.

It was planned that a meeting of SADC ministers of justice, scheduled to be held in April 2002, would adopt a memorandum on finance and investment as the basis of a future protocol on finance and investment.

SOCIAL AND HUMAN DEVELOPMENT AND SPECIAL PROGRAMMES

The social and human development and special programmes directorate was expected to become operational in 2002.

The SADC helps to supply the region's requirements in skilled manpower by providing training in the following categories: high-level managerial personnel; agricultural managers; high- and medium-level technicians; artisans; and instructors. The Technical Committee on Accreditation and Certification aims to harmonize and strengthen the education and training systems in the SADC through initiatives such as the standardization of curricula and examinations. The human resources development sector aims to determine active labour market information systems and institutions in the region, improve education policy analysis and formulation, and address issues of teaching and learning materials in the region. It administers an Intra-regional Skills Development Programme. The sector has initiated a programme of distance education to enable greater access to education, and operates the SADC's scholarship and training awards programme. In September 1997 heads of state, meeting in Blantyre, Malawi, endorsed the establishment of a Gender Department within the Secretariat to promote the advancement and education of women. At the same time representatives of all member countries (except Angola) signed a Protocol on Education and Training, which was to provide a legal framework for co-operation in this sector.

The employment and labour sector was founded in 1996. It seeks to promote employment and harmonize legislation concerning labour and social protection. Its activities include: the implementation of International Labour Standards, the improvement of health and safety standards in the workplace, combating child labour and the establishment of a statistical database for employment and labour issues.

A culture and information sector was established in 1990. Following the ratification of the treaty establishing the Community, the sector was expected to emphasize regional socio-cultural development as part of the process of greater integration. The SADC Press Trust was established, in Harare, Zimbabwe, to disseminate information about the SADC and to articulate the concerns and priorities of the region. Public education initiatives have commenced to encourage the involvement of people in the process of regional integration and development, as well as to promote democratic and human rights' values. In 1998 a new project —'Information 21'— was to be implemented under the sector, in collaboration with the SADC secretariat and the Southern African Research and Documentation Centre (q.v.), which aimed to promote community-building and greater participation in decision-making at all levels of government. In 1994 the SADC Festival on Arts and Culture project was initiated. In connection with this, South Africa was to organize an SADC dance festival in 2002. A draft SADC protocol on piracy and protection of copyright and neighbouring rights has been prepared.

Finance

The SADC's administrative budget for 2002–03, approved by the Council in February 2002, amounted to US $12.8m., to be financed mainly by contributions from member states. At June 2001 members reportedly owed some $10.2m. in unpaid arrears.

Publications

SACCAR Newsletter (quarterly).

SADC Annual Report.

SADC Energy Bulletin.

SADC Today (six a year)

SATCC Bulletin (quarterly).

SKILLS.

SPLASH.

SOUTHERN COMMON MARKET—MERCOSUR/MERCOSUL

(MERCADO COMÚN DEL SUR/MERCADO COMUM DO SUL)

Address: Edif. Mercosur, Dr Luis Piera 1992, 1°, 11200 Montevideo, Uruguay.

Telephone: (2) 4129024; **fax:** (2) 4180557; **e-mail:** sam@mercosur.org.uy; **internet:** www.mercosur.org.uy.

Mercosur (known as Mercosul in Portuguese) was established in March 1991 by the heads of state of Argentina, Brazil, Paraguay and Uruguay with the signature of the Treaty of Asunción. The primary objective of the Treaty is to achieve the economic integration of member states by means of a free flow of goods and services between member states, the establishment of a common external tariff, the adoption of common commercial policy, and the co-ordination of macroeconomic and sectoral policies. The Ouro Preto Protocol, which was signed in December 1994, conferred on Mercosur the status of an international legal entity with the authority to sign agreements with third countries, group of countries and international organizations.

MEMBERS

Argentina	Brazil	Paraguay	Uruguay

Chile and Bolivia are associate members.

Organization

(April 2002)

COMMON MARKET COUNCIL

The Common Market Council (Consejo del Mercado Común) is the highest organ of Mercosur and is responsible for leading the integration process and for taking decisions in order to achieve the objectives of the Asunción Treaty.

COMMON MARKET GROUP

The Common Market Group (Grupo Mercado Común) is the executive body of Mercosur and is responsible for implementing concrete measures to further the integration process.

TRADE COMMISSION

The Trade Commission (Comisión de Comercio del Mercosur) has competence for the area of joint commercial policy and, in particular, is responsible for monitoring the operation of the common external tariff (see below). The Brasília Protocol may be referred to for the resolution of trade disputes between member states.

JOINT PARLIAMENTARY COMMISSION

The Joint Parliamentary Commission (Comisión Parlamentaria Conjunta) is made up of parliamentarians from the member states and is charged with accelerating internal national procedures to implement Mercosur decisions, including the harmonization of country legislation.

CONSULTATIVE ECONOMIC AND SOCIAL FORUM

The Consultative Economic and Social Forum (Foro Consultivo Económico-Social) comprises representatives from the business community and trade unions in the member countries and has a consultative role in relation to Mercosur.

ADMINISTRATIVE SECRETARIAT

Director: SANTIAGO GONZÁLEZ CRAVINO (Argentina).

Activities

Mercosur's free-trade zone entered into effect on 1 January 1995, with tariffs removed from 85% of intra-regional trade. A regime of gradual removal of duties on a list of special products was agreed, with Argentina and Brazil given four years to complete this process while Paraguay and Uruguay were allowed five years. Regimes governing intra-zonal trade in the automobile and sugar sectors remained to be negotiated. Mercosur's customs union also came into force at the start of 1995, comprising a common external tariff of 0–20%. A list of exceptions from the common external tariff was also agreed; these products were to lose their special status and be subject to the general tarification concerning foreign goods by 2006. The value of intra-Mercosur trade was estimated to have tripled during the period 1991–95 and was reported to have amounted to US $20,400m. in 1998. However, in 1999 intra-Mercosur trade was reported to have declined to $15,200m.

In December 1995 Mercosur presidents affirmed the consolidation of free trade as Mercosur's 'permanent and most urgent goal'. To this end they agreed to prepare norms of application for Mercosur's customs code, accelerate paper procedures and increase the connections between national computerized systems. It was also agreed to increase co-operation in the areas of agriculture, industry, mining, energy, communications, transport and tourism, and finance. At this meeting Argentina and Brazil reached an accord aimed at overcoming their dispute regarding the trade in automobiles between the two countries. They agreed that cars should have a minimum of 60% domestic components and that Argentina should be allowed to complete its balance of exports of cars to Brazil, which had earlier imposed a unilateral quota on the import of Argentine cars. In June 1995 Mercosur ministers responsible for the environment agreed to harmonize environmental legislation and to form a permanent sub-group of Mercosur

In May 1996 Mercosur parliamentarians met with the aim of harmonizing legislation on patents in member countries. In December Mercosur heads of state, meeting in Fortaleza, Brazil, approved agreements on harmonizing competition practices (by 2001), integrating educational opportunities for post-graduates and human resources training, standardizing trading safeguards applied against third-country products (by 2001) and providing for intra-regional cultural exchanges. An Accord on Sub-regional Air Services was signed at the meeting (including by the heads of state of Bolivia and Chile) to liberalize civil transport throughout the region. In addition, the heads of state endorsed texts on consumer rights that were to be incorporated into a Mercosur Consumers' Defence Code, and agreed to consider the establishment of a bank to finance the integration and development of the region.

In June 1996 the Joint Parliamentary Commission agreed that Mercosur should endorse a 'Democratic Guarantee Clause', whereby a country would be prevented from participation in Mercosur unless democratic, accountable institutions were in place. The clause was adopted by Mercosur heads of state at the summit meeting held in San Luis de Mendoza, Argentina, later in the month. The presidents approved the entry into Mercosur of Bolivia and Chile as associate members. An Economic Complementation Accord with Bolivia, which includes Bolivia in Mercosur's free-trade zone, but not in the customs union, was signed in December 1995 and was to come into force on 1 January 1997. In December 1996 the Accord was extended until 30 April 1997, when a free-trade zone between Bolivia and Mercosur was to become operational. Measures of the free-trade agreement, which was signed in October 1996, were to be implemented over a transitional period commencing on 28 February 1997 (revised from 1 January). Chile's Economic Complementation Accord with Mercosur entered into effect on 1 October 1996, with duties on most products to be removed over a 10-year period (Chile's most sensitive products were given 18 years for complete tariff elimination). Chile was also to remain outside the customs union, but was to be involved in other integration projects, in particular infrastructure projects designed to give Mercosur countries access to both the Atlantic and Pacific Oceans (Chile's Pacific coast was regarded as Mercosur's potential link to the economies of the Far East).

In June 1997 the first meeting of tax administrators and customs officials of Mercosur member countries was held, with the aim of enhancing information exchange and promoting joint customs inspections. During 1997 Mercosur's efforts towards regional economic integration were threatened by Brazil's adverse external trade balance and its Government's measures to counter the deficit, which included the imposition of import duties on certain products. In November the Brazilian Government announced that it was to increase its import tariff by 3%, in a further effort to improve its external balance. The measure was endorsed by Argentina as a means of maintaining regional fiscal stability. The new external tariff, which was to remain in effect until 31 December 2000, was formally adopted by Mercosur heads of state at a meeting held in Montevideo, Uruguay, in December 1997. At the summit meeting a separate Protocol was signed providing for the liberalization of trade in services and government purchases over a 10-year period. In order to strengthen economic integration throughout the region, Mercosur leaders agreed that Chile, while still not a full member of the organization, be integrated into the Mercosur political structure, with equal voting rights. In December 1998 Mercosur heads of state agreed on the establishment of an arbitration mechanism for disputes between members, and on measures to standardize human, animal and plant health and safety regulations throughout the grouping. In March 1998 the ministers of the interior of Mercosur countries, together with representatives of the Governments of Chile and Bolivia, agreed to implement a joint security arrangement for the border region linking Argentina, Paraguay and Brazil. In particular, the initiative aimed to counter drugs trafficking, money laundering and other illegal activities in the area.

Tensions within Mercosur were compounded in January 1999 owing to economic instability in Brazil and its Government's decision effectively to devalue the national currency, the real. In March the grouping's efforts at integration were further undermined by political instability in Paraguay. As a consequence of the devaluation of its currency, Brazil's important automotive industry became increasingly competitive, to the detriment of that of Argentina. In April Argentina imposed tariffs on imports of Brazilian steel and, in July, the Argentine authorities approved a decree permitting restrictions on all imports from neighbouring countries, in order to protect local industries, prompting Brazil to suspend negotiations to resolve the trading differences between the two countries. Argentina withdrew the decree a few days later, but reiterated its demand for some form of temporary safeguards on certain products as compensation for their perceived loss of competitiveness resulting from the devalued real. An extraordinary meeting of the Common Market Council was convened, at Brazil's request, in August, in order to discuss the dispute, as well as measures to mitigate the effects of economic recession throughout the sub-region. However, little progress was made and the bilateral trade dispute continued to undermine Mercosur. Argentina imposed new restrictions on textiles and footwear, while, in September, Brazil withdrew all automatic import licences for Argentine products, which were consequently to be subject to the same quality control, sanitary measures and accounting checks applied to imports from non-Mercosur countries. The volume of intra-Mercosur trade shrank during 1999 as a consequence of the continuing dispute. In January 2000, however, the Argentine and Brazilian Governments agreed to refrain from adopting potentially divisive unilateral measures and resolved to accelerate negotiations on the resolution of ongoing differences. In March Mercosur determined to promote and monitor private accords to cover the various areas of contention, and also established a timetable for executing a convergence of regional macroeconomic policies. In June Argentina and Brazil signed a bilateral automobile agreement; however, a new sectoral trade regime failed to be approved by the summit meeting held later in that month. The Motor Vehicle Agreement, incorporating new tariffs and a nationalization index, was endorsed by all Mercosur leaders at a meeting convened in Florianopolis, Brazil, in December. The significant outcome of that meeting was the approval of criteria, formulated by Mercosur finance ministers and central bank governors, determining monetary and fiscal targets to achieve economic convergence. Annual inflation rates were to be no higher than 5% in 2002–05, and reduced to 4% in 2006 and 3% from 2007 (with an exception for Paraguay). Public debt was to be reduced to 40% of GDP by 2010, and fiscal deficits were to be reduced to no more than 3% of GDP by 2002. The targets aimed to promote economic stability throughout the region, as well as to reduce competitive disparities affecting the unity of the grouping. The Florianopolis summit meeting also recommended the formulation of social indicators to facilitate achieving targets in the reduction of poverty and the elimination of child labour. However, political debate surrounding the meeting was dominated by the Chilean Government's announcement that it had initiated bilateral free-trade discussions with the USA, which was considered, in particular by the Brazilian authorities, to undermine Mercosur's unified position at multilateral free-trade negotiations. Procedures to incorporate Chile as a full member of Mercosur were suspended.

In early 2001 Argentina imposed several emergency measures to strengthen its domestic economy, in contradiction of Mercosur's external tariffs. In March Brazil was reported to have accepted the measures, which included an elimination of tariffs on capital goods and an increase in import duties on consumer goods, as an exceptional temporary trade regime; this position was reversed by mid-2001 following Argentina's decision to exempt certain countries from import tariffs. In February 2002, at a third extraordinary meeting of the Common Market Council, held in Buenos Aires, Argentina, Mercosur heads of state expressed their support for Argentina's application to receive international financial assistance, in the wake of that country's economic crisis. Although there were fears that the crisis might curb trade and stall economic growth across the region, Argentina's adoption of a floating currency made the prospect of currency harmonization between Mercosur member countries appear more viable. During the meeting it was also agreed that a permanent panel to consider trade disputes would be established in Asunción, Paraguay, comprising one legal representative from each of Mercosur's four member countries, plus one 'consensus' member.

EXTERNAL RELATIONS

In December 1995 Mercosur and the EU signed a framework agreement for commercial and economic co-operation, which provided for co-operation in the economic, trade, industrial, scientific, institutional and cultural fields and the promotion of wider political dialogue on issues of mutual interest. In June 1997 Mercosur heads of state, convened in Asunción, reaffirmed the group's intention to pursue trade negotiations with the EU, Mexico and the Andean Community, as well as to negotiate as a single economic bloc in discussions with regard to the establishment of a Free Trade Area of the Americas (FTAA). Chile and Bolivia were to be incorporated into these negotiations. During 1997 negotiations to establish a free-trade accord with the Andean Community were hindered by differences regarding schedules for tariff elimination and Mercosur's insistence on a local content of 60% to qualify for rules of origin preferences. However, in April 1998 the two groupings signed an accord that committed them to the establishment of a free-trade area by January 2000. Negotiations in early 1999 failed to conclude an agreement on preferential tariffs between the two blocs, and the existing arrangements were extended on a bilateral basis. In March the Andean Community agreed to initiate free-trade negotiations with Brazil; a preferential tariff agreement was concluded in July. In August 2000 a similar agreement between the Community and Argentina entered into force. In September leaders of Mercosur and the Andean Community, meeting at a summit of Latin American heads of state, determined to relaunch negotiations, with a view to establishing a free-trade area by 1 January 2002. The establishment of a mechanism to support political dialogue and co-ordination between the two groupings, which aimed to enhance the integration process, was approved at the first joint meeting of ministers of foreign affairs in July 2001. In February 2002 Mercosur heads of state, convened at an extraordinary meeting of the Common Market Council in Buenos Aires, reiterated their intention to conclude negotiations with the Andean Community on the establishment of the free-trade area before June.

In March 1998 ministers of trade of 34 countries agreed a detailed framework for negotiations to establish the FTAA by 2005. Mercosur secured support for its request that a separate negotiating group be established to consider issues relating to agriculture, as one of nine key sectors to be discussed. The FTAA negotiating process was formally initiated by heads of state of the 34 countries meeting in Santiago, Chile, in April 1998. In June Mercosur and Canada signed a Trade and Investment Co-operation Arrangement, which aimed to remove obstacles to trade and to increase economic co-operation between the two signatories. In July the European Commission proposed obtaining a mandate to commence negotiations with Mercosur and Chile towards a free-trade agreement, which, it was envisaged, would provide for the elimination of tariffs over a period of 10 years. However, Mercosur requested that the EU abolish agricultural subsidies as part of any accord. Negotiations between Mercosur, Chile and the EU were initiated in April 2000. Specific discussion of tariff reductions and market access commenced at the fifth round of negotiations, held in July 2001, at which the EU proposed a gradual elimination of tariffs on industrial imports over a 10-year period and an extension of access quotas for agricultural products. The summit meeting held in December 2000 was attended by the President of South Africa, and it was agreed that Mercosur would initiate free-trade negotiations with that country. In June 2001 Mercosur leaders agreed to pursue efforts to conclude a bilateral trade agreement with the USA, an objective previously opposed by the Brazilian authorities, while reaffirming their commitment to the FTAA process. Negotiations to conclude a bilateral trade accord with the USA were ongoing in 2002.

Finance

In December 1996 the Mercosur summit meeting approved an annual budget of US $1.2m. for the Mercosur secretariat, to be contributed by the four full member countries. The annual budget for the secretariat was set at $980,887 in 1999.

Publication

Boletín Oficial del Mercosur (quarterly).

WESTERN EUROPEAN UNION—WEU

Address: 15 rue de l'Association, 1000 Brussels, Belgium

Telephone: (2) 500-44-50; **fax:** (2) 500-44-70; **e-mail:** ueo .secretarygeneral@skynet.be; **internet:** www.weu.int.

Based on the Brussels Treaty of 1948, the Western European Union (WEU) was set up in 1955 as an intergovernmental organization for European co-operation in the field of security and defence. In the 1990s WEU was developed as the defence component of the European Union (EU), and as the means of strengthening the European pillar of the Atlantic Alliance under NATO. However, in June 1999 the European Council resolved to formulate a common European security and defence policy, incorporating the main crisis management responsibilities of WEU. Consequently, WEU relinquished these functions to the EU by July 2001.

MEMBERS*

Belgium	Luxembourg
France	Netherlands
Germany	Portugal
Greece	Spain
Italy	United Kingdom

* WEU has invited the other members of the EU to join the organization and has invited other European members of NATO to become Associate Members to enable them to participate fully in WEU activities. In November 1992 Denmark and Ireland took up observer status and on 1 January 1995 Austria, Finland and Sweden became Observers following their accession to the EU. Associate member status was granted to Iceland, Norway and Turkey in November 1992. Associate Partner status was granted to Bulgaria, the Czech Republic, Estonia, Hungary, Latvia, Lithuania, Poland, Romania and Slovakia in May 1994 and to Slovenia in June 1996. The Czech Republic, Hungary and Poland became Associate Partners in March 1999.

Organization

(April 2002)

COUNCIL

The Council is the WEU's main body, responsible for addressing all security and defence matters within WEU's remit. It is organized so as to be able to function on a permanent basis and may be convened at any time at the request of a member state. The Permanent Council, chaired by the WEU Secretary-General, is the central body responsible for day-to-day management of the organization and for assigning tasks to and co-ordinating the activities of the various working groups. It is composed of permanent representatives, supported by military delegates, and meets as often as required. The presidency of the Council is rotated between member states on a six-monthly basis.

SECRETARIAT-GENERAL

Secretary-General: Dr JAVIER SOLANA MADARIAGA (Spain).

ASSEMBLY

Address: 43 ave du Président Wilson, 75775 Paris Cédex 16, France; tel. 1-53-67-22-00; fax 1-53-67-22-01; e-mail assembly@weu.int; internet www.weu.int/assembly/welcome .html.

The Assembly of Western European Union is composed of the representatives of the Brussels Treaty powers to the Parliamentary Assembly of the Council of Europe. It meets at least twice a year, usually in Paris. The Assembly may proceed on any matter regarding the application of the Brussels Treaty and on any matter submitted to the Assembly for an opinion by the Council. Resolutions may be adopted in cases where this form is considered appropriate. When so directed by the Assembly, the President transmits such resolutions to international organizations, governments and national parliaments. An annual report is presented to the Assembly by the Council. In March 2000 an extraordinary meeting of the Assembly determined to initiate a process of transforming the body into the European Security and Defence Assembly (ESDA).

President: KLAUS BUEHLER (Germany).

PERMANENT COMMITTEES OF THE ASSEMBLY

There are permanent committees on: Political Defence Questions; Technological and Aerospace Questions; Budgetary Affairs and Administration; Rules of Procedure and Privileges; and Parliamentary and Public Relations.

Activities

The Brussels Treaty was signed in 1948 by Belgium, France, Luxembourg, the Netherlands and the United Kingdom. It foresaw the potential for international co-operation in Western Europe and provided for collective defence and collaboration in economic, social and cultural activities. Within this framework, NATO and the Council of Europe (see chapters) were formed in 1949.

On the collapse in 1954 of plans for a European Defence Community, a nine-power conference was convened in London to try to reach a new agreement. This conference's decisions were embodied in a series of formal agreements drawn up by a ministerial conference held in Paris in October. The agreements entailed: arrangements for the Brussels Treaty to be strengthened and modified to include the Federal Republic of Germany and Italy, the ending of the occupation regime in the Federal Republic of Germany, and the invitation to the latter to join NATO. These agreements were ratified on 6 May 1955, on which date the seven-power Western European Union came into being. WEU was reactivated in October 1984 by restructuring its organization and by holding more frequent ministerial meetings, in order to harmonize members' views on defence questions, arms control and disarmament, developments in East-West relations, Europe's contribution to the Atlantic alliance, and European armaments co-operation.

In April 1990 ministers of foreign affairs and defence discussed the implications of recent political changes in central and eastern Europe, and mandated WEU to develop contacts with democratically elected governments there. In June 1992 an extraordinary meeting of WEU's Ministerial Council with the ministers of defence and foreign affairs of Hungary, Czechoslovakia, Poland, Romania, Bulgaria, Estonia, Latvia and Lithuania agreed on measures to enhance co-operation. The ministers were to meet annually, while a forum of consultation was to be established between the WEU Council and the ambassadors of the countries concerned, which was to meet at least twice a year. The focus of consultations was to be the security structure and political stability of Europe; the future development of the CSCE (now the OSCE); and arms control and disarmament, in particular the implementation of the Treaty on Conventional Armed Forces in Europe (the CFE Treaty) and the 'Open Skies' Treaty (see NATO for both). In May 1994 the Council of Ministers, meeting in Luxembourg, issued the Kirchberg Declaration, according the nine countries concerned (including the Czech Republic and Slovakia, which were the legal successors to Czechoslovakia) the status of Associate Partners of WEU, thereby suspending the forum of consultation.

The EC Treaty on European Union, which was agreed at Maastricht, in the Netherlands, in December 1991, and entered into force on 1 November 1993, referred to WEU as an 'integral part of the development of European Union' and requested WEU 'to elaborate and implement decisions and actions of the Union which have defence implications'. The Treaty also committed EU member countries to the 'eventual framing of a common defence policy which might in time lead to a common defence'. A separate declaration, adopted by WEU member states in Maastricht, defined WEU's role as being the defence component of the European Union but also as the instrument for strengthening the European pillar of the Atlantic Alliance, thus maintaining a role for NATO in Europe's defence and retaining WEU's identity as distinct from that of the EU. In January 1993 WEU's Council and Secretariat-General moved to Brussels (from Paris and London, respectively), in order to promote closer co-operation with both the EU and NATO, which have their headquarters there.

In June 1992 WEU ministers of defence and foreign affairs convened in Petersberg, Germany, to consider the implementation of the Maastricht decisions. In the resulting 'Petersberg Declaration' member states declared that they were prepared to make available military units from the whole spectrum of their conventional armed forces for military tasks conducted under the authority of WEU. In addition to contributing to the common defence in accordance with Article V of the modified Brussels Treaty, three categories of missions were identified for the possible employment of military units under the aegis of WEU: humanitarian and rescue tasks; peace-keeping tasks; and crisis management, including peace-making. (Missions of this kind are often described as 'Petersberg tasks'.) The Petersberg Declaration stated that the WEU was prepared to support peace-keeping activities of the CSCE and UN Security Council on a case-by-case basis. A WEU planning cell was established in Brussels in October, which was to be responsible for preparing contingency plans for the employment of forces under WEU auspices for humanitarian operations, peace-keeping and crisis-management activities. It was expected that the same military units identified by member states for deployment under NATO would be used for military operations under WEU: this arrangement was referred to as 'double-hatting'. In May 1995 WEU ministers, convened in Lisbon, Portugal, agreed to strengthen WEU's operational capabilities through new structures and mechanisms, including the establishment of a politico-military group to advise on crises and crisis management, a Situation Centre able to monitor WEU operations and support decisions taken by the Council, and an Intelligence Section within the planning cell. WEU rules of engagement, with a view to implementing the missions identified in the Petersberg Declaration, were to be formulated.

In January 1994 NATO heads of state gave their full support to the development of a European Security and Defence Identity (ESDI) and to the strengthening of WEU. They declared their readiness to make collective assets of the Alliance available for WEU operations, and endorsed the concept of Combined Joint Task Forces (CJTFs), which was to provide separable, but not separate, military capabilities that could be employed by either organization. In May 1996 NATO and WEU signed a security agreement, which provided for the protection and shared use of classified information. In June NATO ministers, meeting in Berlin, Germany, agreed on a framework of measures to enable the implementation of the CJTF concept and the development of an ESDI within the Alliance. WEU was to be permitted to request the use of a CJTF headquarters for an operation under its command and to use Alliance planning capabilities and military infrastructure. In May 1998 the Council of both organizations approved a set of consultation arrangements as a guide to co-operation in a crisis situation. A framework document on principles and guide-lines for detailed practicalities of cases where NATO assets and/or capabilities were loaned to WEU was subsequently prepared.

In November 1994 a WEU ministerial meeting in Noordwijk, the Netherlands, adopted a set of preliminary conclusions on the formulation of a common European defence policy. The role and place of WEU in further European institutional arrangements were addressed by the EU's Intergovernmental Conference, which commenced in March 1996. The process was concluded in June 1997 with agreement having been reached on the Treaty of Amsterdam (see EU chapter). The Treaty, which was signed in October and entered into force on 1 May 1999, confirmed WEU as providing the EU with access to operational capability for undertaking the Petersberg tasks, which were incorporated into the revised Treaty. It advocated enhanced EU-WEU co-operation and referred to the possible integration of the WEU into the EU, should the European Council so decide (the United Kingdom being the main opponent). Following the entry into force of the Treaty of Amsterdam WEU and the EU approved a set of arrangements for enhanced co-operation. In June the EU determined to strengthen its common security and defence policy, and initiated a process of assuming direct responsibility for the Petersberg tasks. Javier Solana was appointed as the EU's first High Representative for foreign and security policy, and subsequently named as the new WEU Secretary-General, providing for the highest level of co-operation between the two organizations. In November WEU ministers adopted a series of recommendations, based on the results of an audit of assets, to enable European countries to respond rapidly to conduct crisis management operations, to enhance collective capabilities in strategic intelligence and planning, and to strengthen military air, sea and transport equipment and capabilities for use in humanitarian and peace-keeping operations. By July 2001 the transfer of WEU's crisis management functions to the EU had been finalized, leaving commitments relating to collective defence as WEU's key focus area. The EU assumed responsibility for two former subsidiary bodies of the WEU (a Satellite Centre and the Paris-based Institute for Strategic Studies) in January 2002.

In the early 1990s WEU's operational capabilities were substantially developed. From mid-July 1992 warships and aircraft of WEU members undertook a monitoring operation in the Adriatic Sea, in co-ordination with NATO, to ensure compliance with the UN Security Council's resolutions imposing a trade and armaments embargo on Serbia and Montenegro. In mid-November the UN Security Council gave the NATO/WEU operation the power to search vessels suspected of attempting to flout the embargo. In June 1993 the Councils of WEU and NATO agreed to establish a unified command for the operation, which was to implement a Security Council resolution to strengthen the embargo against Serbia and Montenegro. Under the agreement, the Councils were to exert joint political control, and military instructions were to be co-ordinated within a joint *ad hoc* headquarters. In April WEU ministers offered civil assistance to Bulgaria, Hungary and Romania in enforcing the UN embargo on the Danube, and a monitoring mission began operations in June. In June 1996 the NATO/WEU naval monitoring mission in the Adriatic Sea was suspended, following the decision of the UN Security Council to remove the embargo on the delivery of armaments to the former Yugoslavia. WEU provided assistance for the administration of Mostar, Bosnia and Herzegovina, for which the EU assumed responsibility in July 1994.

In May 1997 WEU dispatched a Multinational Advisory Police Element (MAPE) to Albania to provide training and advice on restructuring the police force in that country. By the end of 1999 a new State Police Law, formulated with MAPE's support, had been ratified by the Albanian legislature, while some 3,000 police officers had been trained at centres in Tirana and Dürres and through field programmes. In February the WEU Council approved plans for an enhanced MAPE, with greater geographical coverage and operational mobility, with an initial mandate until April 2000. MAPE was being conducted by WEU at the request of the EU, enabling a large part of the costs to be met from the EU budget. In response to the escalation of conflict in the Serbian province of Kosovo and Metohija in 1999, MAPE assisted the Albanian authorities to establish an Emergency Crisis Group to help to administer and to assist the massive refugee population which entered Albania in March and April. MAPE terminated its operational activities in Albania on 31 May 2001.

In April 1999 WEU and Croatia signed an agreement to establish a WEU De-mining Assistance Mission (WEUDAM) in that country, upon a request by the Council of the EU. WEUDAM, which commenced activities in May, provided advice, technical expertise and training to the Croatian Mine Action Centre. WEUDAM was terminated on 31 November 2001.

In May 1992 France and Germany announced their intention to establish a joint defence force, the 'Eurocorps', which was to be based in Strasbourg, France, and which was intended to provide a basis for a European army under the aegis of WEU. This development caused concern among some NATO member countries, particularly the USA and United Kingdom, which feared that it represented a fresh attempt (notably on the part of France, which is outside NATO's military structure) to undermine the Alliance's role in Europe. In November, however, France and Germany stated that troops from the joint force could serve under NATO military command. This principle was recognized in an agreement signed in January 1993, which established links between the proposed joint force and NATO's military structure. In June Belgium opted to participate in the Eurocorps. In December Spain agreed to provide troops for the force. Luxembourg agreed to participate in May 1994. Eurocorps formally became operational on 30 November 1995. In June 1999 EU ministers decided that Eurocorps was to be transformed into a rapid reaction force, under EU authority. In May 1995 France, Italy, Spain and Portugal announced the establishment of two new forces, which were to be at the disposal of WEU as well as NATO and the UN: EUROFOR, consisting of up to 14,000 ground troops, to be based in Florence, Italy; and EUROMARFOR, a maritime force serving the Mediterranean. A number of other multinational forces are also designated as forces answerable to WEU (FAWEU) or that were to be available to WEU: the Multinational Division (Central),comprising Belgium, Germany, the Netherlands and the United Kingdom; the Headquarters of the First German-Netherlands Corps; the United Kingdom-Netherlands Amphibious Force; the Spanish-Italian Amphibious Force; and the European Air Group (EAG), comprising Belgium, France, Germany, Italy, Netherlands, Spain and the United Kingdom.

Publications

Account of the Session (WEU Assembly, 2 a year).

Annual Report of the Council.

Assembly of Western European Union: Texts adopted and Brief Account of the Session (2 a year).

Assembly documents and reports.

Treaty of Economic, Social and Cultural Collaboration and Collective Self-Defence (Brussels Treaty)

(17 March 1948, as amended by Protocol I, signed 23 October 1954, modifying and completing the Treaty)

Article I

Convinced of the close community of their interests and of the necessity of uniting in order to promote the economic recovery of Europe, the High Contracting Parties will so organize and co-ordinate their economic activities as to produce the best possible results, by the elimination of conflict in their economic policies, the co-ordination of production and the development of commercial exchanges.

The co-operation provided for in the preceding paragraph, which will be effected through the Council referred to in Article VIII as well as through other bodies, shall not involve any duplication of, or prejudice to, the work of other economic organizations in which the High Contracting Parties are or may be represented but shall on the contrary assist the work of those organizations.

Article II

The High Contracting Parties will make every effort in common, both by direct consultation and in specialized agencies, to promote the attainment of a higher standard of living by their peoples and to develop on corresponding lines the social and other related services of their countries.

The High Contracting Parties will consult with the object of achieving the earliest possible application of recommendations of immediate practical interest, relating to social matters, adopted with their approval in the specialized agencies.

They will endeavour to conclude as soon as possible conventions with each other in the sphere of social security.

Article III

The High Contracting Parties will make every effort in common to lead their peoples towards a better understanding of the principles which form the basis of their common civilization and to promote cultural exchanges by conventions between themselves or by other means.

Article IV

In the execution of the Treaty the High Contracting Parties and any organs established by them under the Treaty shall work in close co-operation with the North Atlantic Treaty Organization.

Recognising the undesirability of duplicating the military staffs of NATO, the Council and its Agency will rely on the appropriate military authorities of NATO for information and advice on military matters.

Article V

If any of the High Contracting Parties should be the object of an armed attack in Europe, the other High Contracting Parties will, in accordance with the provisions of Article 51 of the Charter of the United Nations, afford the Party so attacked all the military and other aid and assistance in their power.

Article VI

All measures taken as a result of the preceding Article shall be immediately reported to the Security Council. They shall be terminated as soon as the Security Council has taken the measures necessary to maintain or restore international peace and security.

The present Treaty does not prejudice in any way the obligations of the High Contracting Parties under the provisions of the Charter of the United Nations. It shall not be interpreted as affecting in any way the authority and responsibility of the Security Council under the Charter to take at any time such action as it deems necessary in order to maintain or restore international peace and security.

Article VII

The High Contracting Parties declare, each so far as he is concerned, that none of the international engagements now in force between him and any of the High Contracting Parties or any third State is in conflict with the provisions of the present Treaty.

None of the High Contracting Parties will conclude any alliance or participate in any coalition directed against any other of the High Contracting Parties.

Article VIII

1. For the purpose of strengthening peace and security and of promoting unity and of encouraging the progressive integration of Europe and closer co-operation between them and with other European organizations, the High Contracting Parties to the Brussels Treaty shall create a Council to consider matters concerning the execution of this Treaty and its Protocols and their Annexes.

2. This council shall be known as the "Council of Western European Union"; it shall be so organized as to be able to exercise its functions continuously; it shall set up such subsidiary bodies as may be considered necessary; in particular it shall establish immediately an Agency for the Control of Armaments, whose functions are defined in Protocol No. IV.

At the request of any of the High Contracting Parties the Council shall be immediately convened in order to permit them to consult with regard to any situation which may constitute a threat to peace, in whatever area this threat should arise, or a danger to economic stability.

The Council shall decide by unanimous vote questions for which no other voting procedure has been or may be agreed. In the cases provided for in Protocols II, III and IV it will follow the various voting procedures, unanimity, two-thirds majority, simple majority, laid down therein. It will decide by simple majority questions submitted to it by the Agency for the Control of Armaments.

Article IX

The Council of Western Union shall make an annual report on its activities and, in particular, concerning the control of armaments to an Assembly composed of representatives of the Brussels Treaty Powers to the Consultative Assembly of the Council of Europe.

Article X

In pursuance of their determination to settle disputes only by peaceful means, the High Contracting Parties will apply to disputes between themselves the following provisions:

The High Contracting Parties will, while the present Treaty remains in force, settle all disputes falling within the scope of Article 36, paragraph 2, of the Statute of the International Court of Justice by referring them to the Court, subject only, in the case of each of them, to any reservation already made by that Party when accepting this clause for compulsory jurisdiction, to the extent that that Party may maintain the reservation.

In addition, the High Contracting Parties will submit to conciliation all disputes outside the scope of Article 36, paragraph 2, of the Statute of the International Court of Justice.

In the case of a mixed dispute involving both questions for which conciliation is appropriate and other questions for which judicial settlement is appropriate, any Party to the dispute shall have the right to insist that the judicial settlement of the legal questions shall precede conciliation.

The proceeding provisions of this Article in no way affect the application of relevant provisions or agreements prescribing some other method of pacific settlement.

Article XI

The High Contracting Parties may, by agreement, invite any other State to accede to the present Treaty on conditions to be agreed between them and the State so invited.

Any State so invited may become a Party to the Treaty by depositing an instrument of accession with the Belgian Government.

The Belgian Government will inform each of the High Contracting Parties of the deposit of each instrument of accession.

Article XII

The present Treaty shall be ratified and the instruments of ratification shall be deposited as soon as possible with the Belgian Government.

It shall enter into force on the date of the deposit of the last instrument of ratification and shall thereafter remain in force for fifty years.

After the expiry of the period of fifty years, each of the High Contracting Parties shall have the right to cease to be a party thereto provided that he shall have previously given one year's notice of denunciation to the Belgian Government.

The Belgian Government shall inform the Governments of the other High Contracting Parties of the deposit of each instrument of ratification and of each notice of denunciation.

Summary of Protocols

Protocol I

This Protocol is incorporated in the text of the revised Treaty as printed above.

Protocol II

This Protocol sets upper limits on the size of the land and air forces which the members of WEU maintain on the continent of Europe in peace-time and place under the command of the Supreme Allied Commander, Europe. For Belgium, France, (the Federal Republic of) Germany, Italy and the Netherlands these limits are the same as in the Annex to the EDC Treaty; for Luxembourg the limit is one regimental combat team, while for the United Kingdom it is four divisions and the Second Tactical Air Force. The level of naval forces are determined annually by NATO. These limits are not to be increased except by unanimous agreement, and the level of internal defence and police forces are also to be established by internal agreement. Finally, the United Kingdom agreed not to withdraw or diminish her forces in Europe against the wishes of the majority of her partners, except in the event of an acute overseas emergency.

Protocol III

Under the third Protocol, (the Federal Republic of) Germany undertook not to manufacture atomic, chemical or biological weapons, or certain other weapons on a list (including guided missiles, warships and strategic bombers) which can be amended by the Council of WEU by a two-thirds majority. The Federal Republic agreed to supervision to ensure that these undertakings were respected and the other members agreed that their stocks of various weapons would be subject to control.

Protocol IV

This Protocol provided for the setting up of the Agency for the Control of Armaments, which has the task of ensuring that the commitments contained in the third Protocol are observed. A Resolution was also passed setting up the Standing Armaments Committee. (See *Organization* above.)

WORLD CONFEDERATION OF LABOUR—WCL

Address: 33 rue de Trèves, 1040 Brussels, Belgium.

Telephone: (2) 285-47-00; **fax:** (2) 230-87-22; **e-mail:** info@cmt-wcl.org; **internet:** www.cmt-wcl.org.

Founded in 1920 as the International Federation of Christian Trade Unions (IFCTU); reconstituted under present title in 1968. (See also the International Confederation of Free Trade Unions and the World Federation of Trade Unions.)

MEMBERS

Affiliated national federations and trade union internationals; about 26m. members in 116 countries.

Organization

(April 2002)

CONGRESS

The supreme and legislative authority, which convenes every four years (October 2001: Bucharest, Romania). Congress consists of delegates from national confederations and trade internationals. Delegates have votes according to the size of their organization. Congress receives official reports, elects the Executive Board, considers the future programme and any proposals.

CONFEDERAL BOARD

The Board meets annually, and consists of 47 members (including 23 representatives of national confederations and eight representatives of trade internationals) elected by Congress from among its members for four-year terms. It issues executive directions and instructions to the Secretariat.

SECRETARIAT-GENERAL

Secretary-General: WILLY THYS (Belgium).

Deputy Secretaries-General: EDUARDO ESTÉVEZ (Argentina), JAAP WIENEN (Netherlands).

REGIONAL AND OTHER OFFICES

Africa: Democratic Organization of African Workers' Trade Unions (ODSTA), BP 4401, Route International d'Atakpamé, Lomé, Togo; tel. 250710; fax 256113; e-mail odsta@café.tg. Pres. F. KIKONGI.

Asia: Brotherhood of Asian Trade Unionists (BATU), 1943 Taft Avenue, 1004 Malate, Manila, Philippines; tel. (2) 500709; fax (2) 5218335; e-mail batuasean@batunorm.org.ph. Pres. J. TAN.

Latin America: Latin-American Confederation of Workers (CLAT), Apdo 6681, Caracas 1010, Venezuela; tel. (32) 720794; fax (32) 720463; e-mail clat@telcel.net.ve; internet www.clat.org. Sec.-Gen. EDUARDO GARCÍA.

North America: c/o National Alliance of Postal and Federal Employees, 1628 11th St, NW, Washington, DC 20001, USA; tel. (202) 939-6325; fax (202) 939-6389; e-mail ptennas@patriot.net. Pres. JAMES MCGEE.

Eastern Europe Liaison Office: Bucharest, Splaiul Independentei, nr 202, cam. 324, Sector 6, Romania; tel. and fax (1) 3101586; e-mail cmtest@alfa.rtel.ro.

Geneva Liaison Office: CP 122, 1 rue de Varembé, 1211 Geneva 20, Switzerland; tel. (22) 7482080; fax (22) 7482088; e-mail Beatrice.fauchere@suisse.cmt-wcl.org.

INTERNATIONAL INSTITUTES OF TRADE UNION STUDIES

Africa: Fondation panafricaine pour le développement économique, social et culturel (Fopadesc), Lomé, Togo.

Asia: BATU Social Institute, Manila, Philippines.

Latin America:

Instituto Andino de Estudios Sociales, Lima, Peru.

Instituto Centro-Americano de Estudios Sociales (ICAES), San José, Costa Rica.

Instituto del Cono Sur (INCASUR), Buenos Aires, Argentina.

Instituto de Formación del Caribe, Willemstad, Curaçao, Netherlands Antilles.

Universidad de Trabajadores de América Latina (UTAL).

Finance

Income is derived from affiliation dues, contributions, donations and capital interest.

Publications

Tele-flash (every 2 weeks).

Labor magazine (quarterly).

Reports of Congresses; Study Documents.

International Trade Union Federations

Federation of Professional Sportsmen: Chaussée de Haecht 579, 1031 Brussels, Belgium; tel. (2) 246-35-41; fax (2) 246-35-42. Sec. MARCEL VAN MOL.

International Federation of Textile and Clothing Workers—IFTC: 27 Koning Albertlaan, 9000 Ghent, Belgium; tel. (9) 222-57-01; fax (9) 220-45-59; e-mail info@cnv.net; f. 1901. Mems: unions covering 800,000 workers in 39 countries. Organization: Congress (every three years), Board, Exec. Committee, Pres. JACQUES JOURET (Belgium); Gen. Sec. BART BRUGGEMAN (Netherlands).

International Federation of Trade Unions of Employees in Public Service—INFEDOP: 33 rue de Trèves, 1040 Brussels, Belgium; tel. (2) 230-38-65; fax (2) 231-14-72; e-mail info@infedop_eurofedop.com; f. 1922. Mems: national federations of workers in public service, covering 4m. workers. Organization: World Congress (at least every five years), World Confederal Board (meets every year), 10 Trade Groups, Secretariat. Pres. GUY RASNEUR (Belgium); Sec.-Gen. BERT VAN CAELENBERG (Belgium). Publ. *Servus* (monthly).

European Federation of Employees in Public Services—EUROFEDOP: 33 rue de Trèves, 1040 Brussels, Belgium; tel. (2) 230-38-65; fax (2) 231-14-72; e-mail info@infedop_eurofedop.com; Chair. GUY RASNEUR (Belgium); Sec.-Gen. BERT VAN CAELENBERG (Belgium).

International Federation of Trade Unions of Transport Workers—FIOST: 33 rue de Trèves, 1040 Brussels, Belgium; tel. (2) 285-47-35; fax (2) 230-87-22; e-mail freddy.pools@cmt-wcl.org; f. 1921. Mems: national federations in 28 countries covering 600,000 workers. Organization: Congress (every four years), Committee (meets twice a year), Executive Board. Pres. MICHEL BOVY (Belgium); Exec. Sec. FREDDY POOLS (Belgium). Publ. *Labor* (6 a year).

World Confederation of Teachers—WCL: 33 rue de Trèves, 1040 Brussels, Belgium; tel. (2) 285-47-29; fax (2) 230-87-22; e-mail wct@cmt-wcl.org; internet www.wctcsme.org; f. 1963. Mems: national federations of unions concerned with teaching. Organization: Congress (every four years), Council (at least once a year), Steering Committee. Pres. LOUIS VAN BENEDEN; Sec.-Gen. GASTON DE LA HAYE.

World Federation of Agriculture, Food, Hotel and Allied Workers—WFAFW: 33 rue de Trèves, 1040 Brussels, Belgium; tel. (2) 230-60-90; fax (2) 230-87-22; e-mail fmtaa@cmt-wcl.org; f. 1982 (merger of former World Federation of Agricultural Workers and World Federation of Workers in the Food, Drink, Tobacco and Hotel Industries). Mems: national federations covering 2,800,000 workers in 38 countries. Organization: Congress (every five years), World Board, Daily Management Board. Pres. ADRIAN COJOCARUN (Romania); Exec. Sec. JOSÉ GÓMEZ CERDA (Dominican Republic).

World Federation of Building and Woodworkers Unions—WFBW: 33 rue de Trèves, 1040 Brussels, Belgium; tel. (2)

285-02-11; fax (2) 230-74-43; e-mail piet.nelissen@cmt-wcl.org; f. 1936. Mems: national federations covering 2,438,000 workers in several countries. Organization: Congress, Bureau, Permanent Secretariat. Pres. JACKY JACKERS; Sec.-Gen. DICK VAN DE KAMP (Netherlands). Publ. *Bulletin.*

World Federation of Clerical Workers—WFCW: 33 rue de Trèves, 1040 Brussels, Belgium; tel. (2) 285-47-00; fax (2) 230-87-22; e-mail piet.nelissen@cmt-wcl.org; f. 1921. Mems: national federations of unions and professional associations covering 700,000 workers in 57 countries. Organization: Congress (every four years), Council, Executive Board, Secretariat. Pres. ROEL ROTSHUIZEN (Netherlands); Sec. PIET NELISSEN. Publ. *Labor.*

World Federation of Industry Workers—WFIW: 33 rue de Trèves, 1040 Brussels, Belgium; e-mail piet.nelissen@cmt-wcl.org; f. 1985. Mems: regional and national federations covering about 600,000 workers in 45 countries. Organization: Congress (every five years), World Board (every year), Executive Committee, six World Trade Councils. Pres. CARLOS GAÍTAN; Gen. Sec. ALFONS VAN GENECHTEN. Publ. *Labor.*

WORLD COUNCIL OF CHURCHES—WCC

Address: 150 route de Ferney, POB 2100, 1211 Geneva 2, Switzerland.

Telephone: (22) 7916111; **fax:** (22) 7910361; **e-mail:** info@wcc-coe.org; **internet:** www.wcc-coe.org.

The Council was founded in 1948 to promote co-operation between Christian Churches and to prepare for a clearer manifestation of the unity of the Church.

MEMBERS

There are 342 member Churches in more than 120 countries. Chief denominations: Anglican, Baptist, Congregational, Lutheran, Methodist, Moravian, Old Catholic, Orthodox, Presbyterian, Reformed and Society of Friends. The Roman Catholic Church is not a member but sends official observers to meetings.

Organization

(April 2002)

ASSEMBLY

The governing body of the World Council, consisting of delegates of the member Churches, it meets every seven or eight years to frame policy and consider some main themes. It elects the Presidents of the Council, who serve as members of the Central Committee. The eighth Assembly was held at Harare, Zimbabwe, in December 1998. The ninth Assembly was scheduled to be convened in 2006.

Presidium: Dr Agnes Aboum (Kenya), Rev Kathryn K. Bannister (USA), Bishop Jabez L. Bryce (Fiji), His Eminence Chrysostomos of Ephesus (Greece), Dr Moon-Kyu Kang (Republic of Korea), Bishop Federico J. Pagura (Argentina), Bishop Eberhardt Renz (Germany), His Holiness Ignatius Zakka I (Syria).

CENTRAL COMMITTEE

Appointed by the Assembly to carry out its policies and decisions, the Committee consists of 158 members chosen from Assembly delegates. It meets every 12 to 18 months.

The Central Committee comprises the Programme Committee and the Finance Committee. Within the Programme Committee there are advisory groups on issues relating to communication, women, justice, peace and creation, youth, ecumenical relations, and inter-religious relations. There are also five commissions and boards.

Moderator: His Holiness Aram I, Catholicos of Cilicia (Armenian Apostolic Church, Lebanon).

Vice-Moderators: Justice Sophia O. A. Adinyira (Ghana), Dr Marion S. Best (Canada).

EXECUTIVE COMMITTEE

Consists of the Presidents, the Officers and 20 members chosen by the Central Committee from its membership to prepare its agenda, expedite its decisions and supervise the work of the Council between meetings of the Central Committee. Meets every six months.

GENERAL SECRETARIAT

The General Secretariat implements the policies laid down by the WCC, and co-ordinates the work of the programme units described below. The General Secretariat is also responsible for the Ecumenical Centre Library and an Ecumenical Institute, at Bossey, which provides training in ecumenical leadership.

General Secretary: Rev. Dr Konrad Raiser (Germany).

Activities

Following the Assembly in Harare in December 1998 the work of the WCC was restructured. Activities were grouped into four 'clusters':

RELATIONSHIPS

The cluster group on relationships carries out the Council's work in promoting unity and community. There are teams on Church and Ecumenical Relations; Relations and Ecumenical Sharing; Inter-religious Relations and Dialogue; and International Relations. Two programmes—Action by Churches Together (ACT) and the Ecumenical Church Loan Fund (ECLOF)—are included in this grouping.

ISSUES AND THEMES

This grouping, dealing with issues and themes encompassed by the aims of the Council, comprises four teams: Faith and Order; Mission and Evangelism; Justice, Peace, Creation; and Education and Ecumenical Formation.

COMMUNICATION

The Communication cluster unites those parts of the Council involved in the provision of public information, documentation, and the production of publications.

FINANCE, SERVICES AND ADMINISTRATION

This grouping comprises the following teams: Finance, Human Resources, Income Monitoring and Development, Computer Information Services, and Building Services.

In February 2001 the WCC launched its Decade to Overcome Violence (2001-10) during which various events were to be held on the themes of reconciliation, peace and justice.

Finance

The main contributors to the WCC's budget are the churches and their agencies, with funds for certain projects contributed by other organizations. The 1999 budget amounted to 53.9m. Swiss francs.

Publications

Catalogue of periodicals, books and audio-visuals.

Current Dialogue (2 a year).

Echoes (2 a year).

Ecumenical News International (weekly).

Ecumenical Review (quarterly).

International Review of Mission (quarterly).

Ministerial Formation (quarterly).

Overcoming Violence (quarterly).

WCC News (quarterly).

WCC Yearbook.

WORLD FEDERATION OF TRADE UNIONS—WFTU

Address: Branická 112, 14701 Prague 4, Czech Republic.

Telephone: (2) 44462140; **fax:** (2) 44461378; **e-mail:** wftu@login.cz; **internet:** www.wftu.cz.

The Federation was founded in 1945, on a world-wide basis. A number of members withdrew from the Federation in 1949 to establish the International Confederation of Free Trade Unions (see p. 390). (See also the World Confederation of Labour, p. 509.)

MEMBERS

Affiliated or associated national federations (including the six Trade Unions Internationals) in 126 countries representing some 135m. individuals.

Organization

(April 2002)

WORLD TRADE UNION CONGRESS

The Congress meets every five years. It reviews WFTU's work, endorses reports from the executives, and elects the General Council. The size of the delegations is based on the total membership of national federations. The Congress is also open to participation by non-affiliated organizations. The 14th Congress was held in New Delhi, India, in March 2000.

GENERAL COUNCIL

The General Council meets three times between Congresses, and comprises members and deputies elected by Congress from nominees of national federations. Every affiliated or associated organization and Trade Unions International has one member and one deputy member.

The Council receives reports from the Presidential Council, approves the plan and budget and elects officers.

PRESIDENTIAL COUNCIL

The Presidential Council meets twice a year and conducts most of the executive work of WFTU. It comprises a President, elected each year from among its members, the General Secretary and 18 Vice-Presidents.

SECRETARIAT

The Secretariat consists of the General Secretary, and six Deputy General Secretaries. It is appointed by the General Council and is responsible for general co-ordination, regional activities, national trade union liaison, press and information, administration and finance.

WFTU has regional offices in New Delhi, India (for the Asia-Pacific region), Havana, Cuba (covering the Americas), Dakar, Senegal (for Africa), Damascus, Syria (for the Middle East) and in Moscow, Russia (covering the CIS countries).

General Secretary: ALEKSANDR ZHARIKOV (Russia).

Finance

Income is derived from affiliation dues, which are based on the number of members in each trade union federation.

Publication

Flashes from the Trade Unions (fortnightly, in English, French and Spanish; monthly in Arabic and Russian).

Trade Unions Internationals

The following autonomous Trade Unions Internationals (TUIs) are associated with WFTU:

Trade Unions International of Agriculture, Food, Commerce, Textile and Allied Workers: f. 1997 by merger of the TUI of Agricultural, Forestry and Plantation Workers (f. 1949), the TUI of Food, Tobacco, Hotel and Allied Industries Workers (f. 1949), the TUI of Workers in Commerce (f. 1959) and the TUI of Textile, Clothing, Leather and Fur Workers (f. 1949). Pres. FREDDY HUCK (France); Gen. Sec. DMITRII DOZORIN (Russia).

Trade Unions International of Public and Allied Employees: 4 Windsor Pl., New Delhi 110 001, India; tel. (11) 3311829; fax (11) 3311849;e-mail aisgef@ca12.vsnl.net.in; internet www.tradeunionindia.org; f. 1949. Mems: 34m. in 152 unions in 54 countries. Branch Commissions: State, Municipal, Postal and Telecommunications, Health, Banks and Insurance. Gen. Sec. SUKOMAL SEN (India). Publ. *Information Bulletin* (in three languages).

Trade Unions International of Transport Workers: Tengerszem U. 21/B, 1142 Budapest, Hungary; tel. and fax (1) 2851593; f. 1949. Holds International Trade Conference (every 4 years) and General Council (annually). Mems: 95 unions from 37 countries. Pres. NASR ZARIF MOUHREZ (Syria); Gen. Sec. JÓZSEF TÓTH (Hungary). Publ. *TUI Reporter* (every 2 months, in English and Spanish).

Trade Unions International of Workers of the Building, Wood and Building Materials Industries (Union Internationale des Syndicats des Travailleurs du Bâtiment, du Bois et des Matériaux de Construction—UITBB): Box 281, 00101 Helsinki, Finland; tel. (9) 6931130; fax (9) 6931020; e-mail rguitbb@kaapeli.fi; internet ww.uitbb.org; f. 1949. Mems: unions in 50 countries, grouping 2m. workers. Sec.-Gen. JOSÉ DINIS. Publ. *Bulletin*.

Trade Unions International of Workers in the Energy, Metal, Chemical, Oil and Related Industries: c/o 3a Calle del Maestro Antonio Caso 45, Col. Tabacatera, 06470 Mexico City, Mexico; tel. and fax (55) 55357046; e-mail uis@uis-tui.org; internet www.uis-tui.org; f. 1998 by merger of the TUI of Chemical, Oil and Allied Workers (f. 1950), the TUI of Energy Workers (f. 1949) and the TUI of Workers in the Metal Industry (f. 1949). Gen. Sec. ROSENDO FLORES FLORES (Mexico).

World Federation of Teachers' Unions: 4 Windsor Pl., New Delhi 110 001, India; tel. (11) 3311829; fax (11) 3311849; f. 1946. Mems: 132 national unions of teachers and educational and scientific workers in 85 countries, representing over 25m. individuals. Pres. LESTURUGE ARIYAWANSA (Sri Lanka); Gen. Sec. MRINMOY BHATTACHARYYA (India). Publ. *FISE-Infos* (quarterly, in English, French and Spanish).

WORLD TRADE ORGANIZATION—WTO

Address: Centre William Rappard, rue de Lausanne 154, 1211 Geneva, Switzerland.

Telephone: (22) 7395111; **fax:** (22) 7314206; **e-mail:** enquiries@wto.org; **internet:** www.wto.org.

The WTO is the legal and institutional foundation of the multilateral trading system. It was established on 1 January 1995, as the successor to the General Agreement on Tariffs and Trade (GATT). At January 2002 WTO comprised 144 members.

MEMBERS*

Albania
Angola
Antigua and Barbuda
Argentina
Australia
Austria
Bahrain
Bangladesh
Barbados
Belgium
Belize
Benin
Bolivia
Botswana
Brazil
Brunei
Bulgaria
Burkina Faso
Burundi
Cameroon
Canada
Central African Republic
Chad
Chile
China, People's Republic
China, Republic†
Colombia
Congo, Democratic Republic
Congo, Republic
Costa Rica
Côte d'Ivoire
Croatia
Cuba
Cyprus
Czech Republic
Denmark
Djibouti
Dominica
Dominican Republic
Ecuador
Egypt
El Salvador
Estonia
Fiji
Finland
France
Gabon
The Gambia
Georgia
Germany
Ghana
Greece
Grenada
Guatemala
Guinea
Guinea-Bissau
Guyana
Haiti
Honduras
Hong Kong
Hungary
Iceland
India
Indonesia
Ireland
Israel
Italy
Jamaica
Japan
Jordan
Kenya
Korea, Republic
Kuwait
Kyrgyzstan
Latvia
Lesotho
Liechtenstein
Lithuania
Luxembourg
Macau
Madagascar
Malawi
Malaysia
Maldives
Mali
Malta
Mauritania
Mauritius
Mexico
Moldova
Mongolia
Morocco
Mozambique
Myanmar
Namibia
Netherlands
New Zealand
Nicaragua
Niger
Nigeria
Norway
Oman
Pakistan
Panama
Papua New Guinea
Paraguay
Peru
Philippines
Poland
Portugal
Qatar
Romania
Rwanda
Saint Christopher and Nevis
Saint Lucia
Saint Vincent and the Grenadines
Senegal
Sierra Leone
Singapore
Slovakia
Slovenia
Solomon Islands
South Africa
Spain
Sri Lanka
Suriname
Swaziland
Sweden
Switzerland
Tanzania
Thailand
Togo
Trinidad and Tobago
Tunisia
Turkey
Uganda
United Arab Emirates
United Kingdom
USA
Uruguay
Vanuatu
Venezuela
Zambia
Zimbabwe

* The European Community also has membership status.

† Admitted as the Separate Customs Territory of Taiwan, Penghu, Kinmen and Matsu (referred to as Chinese Taipei).

Note: In early 2002 a further 27 governments had requested to join the WTO, and their applications were under consideration by accession working parties. Accession requests had also been received from Syria and Libya in late 2001, for which working parties had not yet been established.

Organization

(April 2002)

MINISTERIAL CONFERENCE

The Ministerial Conference is the highest authority of the WTO. It is composed of representatives of all WTO members at ministerial level, and may take decisions on all matters under any of the multilateral trade agreements. The Conference is required to meet at least every two years. The fourth Conference was held in Doha, Qatar, in November 2001; the fifth Conference was scheduled to be convened in Mexico in 2003.

GENERAL COUNCIL

The General Council, which is also composed of representatives of all WTO members, is required to report to the Ministerial Conference and conducts much of the day-to-day work of the WTO. The Council convenes as the Dispute Settlement Body, to oversee the trade dispute settlement procedures, and as the Trade Policy Review Body, to conduct regular reviews of the trade policies of WTO members. The Council delegates responsibility to three other major Councils: for trade-related aspects of intellectual property rights, for trade in goods and for trade in services.

TRADE NEGOTIATIONS COMMITTEE

The Committee was established in November 2001 by the Declaration of the fourth Ministerial Conference, held in Doha, Qatar, to supervise the agreed agenda of trade negotiations. It was to operate under the authority of the General Council and was mandated to establish negotiating mechanisms and subsidiary bodies for each subject under consideration. A structure of negotiating groups and a declaration of principles and practices for the negotiations were formulated by the Committee in February 2002.

SECRETARIAT

The WTO Secretariat comprises some 550 staff. Its responsibilities include the servicing of WTO delegate bodies, with respect to negotiations and the implementation of agreements, undertaking accession negotiations for new members and providing technical support and expertise to developing countries. In July 1999 member states reached a compromise agreement on the appointment of a new Director-General, having postponed the decision several times after failing to achieve the required consensus. Two candidates were appointed to serve consecutive three-year terms-in-office. In December 2001 the Director-General announced that the Secretariat was to be reorganized, in order to provide greater support to developing countries.

In June 2001 a WTO Training Institute was established, at the Secretariat, to extend the provision of training activities previously undertaken. Courses were to be held on trade policy, WTO dispute settlement rules and procedures, and other specialized topics; other programmes included training-of-trainers programmes and distance-learning services.

Director-General: Michael Moore (New Zealand); (from Sept. 2002) Supachai Panitchpakdi (Thailand).

Deputy Directors-General: Andrew Stoler (USA), Ablasse Ouédraogo (Burkina Faso), Paul-Henri Ravier (France), Miguel Rodríguez Mendoza (Venezuela).

Activities

The Final Act of the Uruguay Round of GATT multilateral trade negotiations, which were concluded in December 1993, provided for extensive trade liberalization measures and for the establishment of a permanent structure to oversee international trading procedures. The Final Act was signed in April 1994, in Marrakesh, Morocco. At the same time a separate accord, the Marrakesh Declaration, was signed by the majority of GATT contracting states, endorsing the establishment of the WTO. The essential functions of the WTO are: to administer and facilitate the implementation of the results of the Uruguay Round; to provide a forum for multilateral trade negotiations; to administer the trade dispute settlement procedures; to review national trade policies; and to co-operate with other international institutions, in particular the IMF and World Bank, in order to achieve greater coherence in global economic policy-making.

The WTO Agreement contains some 29 individual legal texts and more than 25 additional Ministerial declarations, decisions and understandings, which cover obligations and commitments for member states. All these instruments are based on a few fundamental principles, which form the basis of the WTO Agreement. An integral part of the Agreement is 'GATT 1994', an amended and updated version of the original GATT Agreement of 1947, which was formally concluded at the end of 1995. Under the 'most-favoured nation' (MFN) clause, members are bound to grant to each other's products treatment no less favourable than that accorded to the products of any third parties. A number of exceptions apply, principally for customs unions and free-trade areas and for measures in favour of and among developing countries. The principle of 'national treatment' requires goods, having entered a market, to be treated no less favourably than the equivalent domestically-produced goods. Secure and predictable market access, to encourage trade, investment and job creation, may be determined by 'binding' tariffs, or customs duties. This process means that a tariff level for a particular product becomes a commitment by a member state, and cannot be increased without compensation negotiations with its main trading partners. Other WTO agreements also contribute to predictable trading conditions by demanding commitments from member countries and greater transparency of domestic laws and national trade policies. By permitting tariffs, whilst adhering to the guide-lines of being non-discriminatory, the WTO aims to promote open, fair and undistorted competition.

The WTO aims to encourage development and economic reform among the increasing number of developing countries and countries with economies in transition participating in the international trading system. These countries, particularly the least-developed states, have been granted transition periods and greater flexibility to implement certain WTO provisions. Industrial member countries are encouraged to assist developing nations by their trading conditions and by not expecting reciprocity in trade concession negotiations. In addition, the WTO operates a limited number of technical assistance programmes, mostly relating to training and the provision of information technology.

Finally, the WTO Agreement recognizes the need to protect the environment and to promote sustainable development. A new Committee on Trade and Environment was established to identify the relationship between trade policies, environmental measures and sustainable development and to recommend any appropriate modifications of the multilateral trading provisions. There was much contention over the compatibility of environmental and free-trade concerns in 1998, which was highlighted by a dispute settlement relating to shrimp-fishing in Asia.

At the 1996 Conference representatives of some 28 countries signed a draft Information Technology Agreement (ITA), which aimed to eliminate tariffs on the significant global trade in IT products by 2000. By late February 1997 some 39 countries, representing the required 90% share of the world's IT trade, had consented to implement the ITA. It was signed in March, and was to cover the following main product categories: computers; telecommunications products; semiconductors or manufacturing equipment; software; and scientific instruments. Tariff reductions in these sectors were to be undertaken in four stages, commencing in July, and subsequently on 1 January each year, providing for the elimination of all tariffs by the start of 2000. (By February 2001 there were 56 participants in the ITA.) In February 1999 the WTO announced plans to investigate methods of removing non-tariff barriers to trade in IT products, such as those resulting from non-standardization of technical regulations. A one-year work programme on non-tariff measures was approved by the Committee of Participants on the Expansion of Trade in IT Products in November 2000.

At the end of the Uruguay Round a 'built-in' programme of work for the WTO was developed. In addition, the Ministerial Conferences in December 1996 and May 1998 addressed a range of issues. The final declaration issued from the Ministerial Conference in December 1996 incorporated a text on the contentious issue of core labour standards, although it was emphasized that the relationship between trade and labour standards was not part of the WTO agenda. The text recognized the International Labour Organization's competence in establishing and dealing with core labour standards and endorsed future WTO/ILO co-operation. The declaration also included a plan of action on measures in favour of the world's least-developed countries, to assist these countries in enhancing their trading opportunities. The second Conference, convened in May 1998, decided against imposing customs duties on international electronic transactions, and agreed to establish a comprehensive work programme to address the issues of electronic commerce. The Conference also supported the creation of a framework of international rules to protect intellectual property rights and provide security and privacy in transactions. Developing countries were assured that their needs in this area would be taken into account. Members agreed to begin preparations for the launch of comprehensive talks on global trade liberalization. In addition, following repeated mass public demonstrations against free trade, it was agreed to try to increase the transparency of the WTO and improve public understanding of the benefits of open global markets.

Formal negotiations on the agenda of a new multilateral trade 'round', which was scheduled to be launched at the third Ministerial Conference, to be held in Seattle, USA, in late November/December 1999, commenced in September. While it was confirmed that further liberalization of agriculture and services was to be considered, no consensus was reached (in particular between the Cairns Group of countries and the USA, and the EU, supported by Japan) on the terms of reference or procedures for these negotiations prior to the start of the Conference. In addition, developing countries criticized renewed efforts, mainly by the USA, to link trade and labour standards and to incorporate environmental considerations into the discussions. Efforts by the EU to broaden the talks to include investment and competition policy were also resisted by the USA. The conduct of the Ministerial Conference was severely disrupted by public demonstrations by a diverse range of interest groups concerned with the impact of WTO accords on the environment, workers' rights and developing countries. The differences between member states with regard to a formal agenda failed to be resolved during extensive negotiations, and the Conference was suspended. At a meeting of the General Council, convened later in December, member countries reached an informal understanding that any agreements concluding on 31 December would be extended. Meanwhile, the Director-General attempted to maintain a momentum for proceeding with a new round of trade negotiations, although it was considered unlikely to be initiated before 2001. In February 2000 the General Council agreed to resume talks with regard to agriculture and services, and to consider difficulties in implementing the Uruguay Accord, which was a main concern of developing member states. The Council also urged industrialized nations to pursue an earlier initiative to grant duty-free access to the exports of least developed countries. In May the Council resolved to initiate a series of Special Sessions to consider implementation of existing trade agreements, and approved more flexible provisions for implementation of TRIPS (see below), as part of ongoing efforts to address the needs of developing member states and strengthen their confidence in the multilateral trading system.

During 2001 negotiations were undertaken to reach agreement on further trade liberalization. A draft accord was approved by the General Council in October. The fourth Ministerial Conference, held in Doha, Qatar, in November, adopted a final declaration providing a mandate for a three-year agenda for negotiations on a range of subjects, commencing 1 January 2002. Most of the negotiations were to be concluded, on 1 January 2005, as a single undertaking, i.e. requiring universal agreement on all matters under consideration. A new Trade Negotiations Committee was established to supervise the process, referred to as the Doha Development Round. Several aspects of existing agreements were to be negotiated, while new issues included WTO rules, such as subsidies, regional trade agreements and anti-dumping measures, and market access. The Declaration incorporated a commitment to negotiate issues relating to trade and the environment, including fisheries subsidies, environmental labeling requirements, and the relationship between trade obligations of multilateral environment agreements and WTO rules. The Conference approved a separate decision on implementation-related issues and concerns, to address the concerns of developing countries in meeting their WTO commitments. Several implementation issues were agreed at the meeting, while others were incorporated into the Development Agenda. Specific reference was made in the Declaration to providing greater technical co-operation and capacity-building assistance to WTO developing country members. A Doha Development Agenda Global Trust Fund was established in late 2001, with a core budget of CHF 15m., to help finance technical support for trade liberalization in less developed member states.

AGRICULTURE

The Final Act of the Uruguay Round extended previous GATT arrangements for trade in agricultural products through new rules and commitments to ensure more predictable and fair competition in the sector. All quantitive measures limiting market access for agricultural products were to be replaced by tariffs (i.e. a process of 'tariffication'), enabling more equal protection and access opportunities. All tariffs on agricultural items were to be reduced by 36% by developed countries, over a period of six years, and by 24% by developing countries (excluding least-developed member states) over 10 years. A special treatment clause applied to 'sensitive' products (mainly rice) in four countries, for which limited import restrictions could be maintained. Efforts to reduce domestic support measures for agricultural products were to be based on calculations of total aggregate measurements of support (Total AMS) by each member state. A 20% reduction in Total AMS was required by developed countries over six years, and 13% over 10 years by developing countries. No reduction was required of least-developed countries. Developed member countries were required to reduce the value and quantity of direct export subsidies by 36% and 21% respectively (on 1986–90 levels) over six years. For developing countries these reductions were to be two-thirds those of developed nations, over 10 years. A specific concern of least-developed and net-food importing developing countries, which had previously relied on subsidized food products, was to be addressed through other food aid mechanisms and assistance for agricultural development. The situation was to be monitored by WTO's Committee on Agriculture. Negotiations on the further liberalization of agricultural markets were part of the WTO 'built-in' programme for 2000 or earlier, but remained a major area of contention. In March 2000 negotiations on market access in the agricultural sector commenced, under an interim chairman owing to a disagreement among participating states. By November 2001 121 countries had submitted proposals for the next stage of negotiations. The Doha Declaration, approved in that month, established a timetable for further negotiations on agriculture, which were to be concluded as part of the single undertaking on 1 January 2005. A compromise agreement was reached with the EU to commit to a reduction in export subsidies, with a view to phasing them out (without a firm deadline for their elimination). Member states agreed to aim for further reductions in market access restrictions and domestic support mechanisms, and to incorporate non-trade concerns, including environmental protection, food security and rural development, into the negotiations.

The Agreement on the Application of Sanitary and Phytosanitary Measures aims to regulate world-wide standards of food safety and animal and plant health in order to encourage the mutual recognition of standards and conformity, so as to facilitate trade in these products. The Agreement includes provisions on control inspection and approval procedures. In September 1997, in the first case to be brought under the Agreement, a dispute panel of the WTO ruled that the EU's ban on imports of hormone-treated beef and beef products from the USA and Canada was in breach of international trading rules. In January 1998 the Appellate Body upheld the panel's ruling, but expressed its support for restrictions to ensure food standards if there was adequate scientific evidence of risks to human health. The EU maintained the ban, against resistance from the USA, while it carried out scientific risk assessments.

TEXTILES AND CLOTHING

From 1974 the Multi-fibre Arrangement (MFA) provided the basis of international trade concerning textiles and clothing, enabling the major importers to establish quotas and protect their domestic industries, through bilateral agreements, against more competitive low-cost goods from developing countries. MFA restrictions that were in place on 31 December 1994 were carried over into the new agreement and were to be phased out through integration into GATT 1994, under which they would be subject to the same rules applying to other industrial products. This was to be achieved in four stages: products accounting for 16% of the total volume of textiles and clothing imports (at 1990 levels) were to be integrated from 1 January 1995; a further 17% on 1 January 1998; and not less than a further 18% on 1 January 2002, with all remaining products to be integrated by 1 January 2005.

TRADE IN SERVICES

The General Agreement on Trade in Services (GATS), which was negotiated during the GATT Uruguay Round, is the first set of multilaterally-agreed and legally-enforceable rules and disciplines ever negotiated to cover international trade in services. The GATS comprises a framework of general rules and disciplines, annexes addressing special conditions relating to individual sectors and national schedules of market access commitments. A Council for Trade in Services oversees the operation of the agreement.

The GATS framework consists of 29 articles, including the following set of basic obligations: total coverage of all internationally-traded services; national treatment, i.e. according services and service suppliers of other members no less favourable treatment than that accorded to domestic services and suppliers; MFN treatment (see above), with any specific exemptions to be recorded prior to the implementation of the GATS, with a limit of 10 years duration; transparency, requiring publication of all relevant national laws and legislations; bilateral agreements on recognition of standards and qualifications to be open to other members who wish to negotiate accession; no restrictions on international payments and transfers; progressive liberalization to be pursued; and market access and national treatment commitments to be bound and recorded in national schedules. These schedules, which include exemptions to the MFN principles, contain the negotiated and guaranteed conditions under which trade in services is conducted and are an integral part of the GATS.

Annexes to the GATS cover the movement of natural persons, permitting governments to negotiate specific commitments regarding the temporary stay of people for the purpose of providing a service; the right of governments to take measures in order to ensure the integrity and stability of the financial system; the role of telecommunications as a distinct sector of economic activity and as a means of supplying other economic activities; and air transport services, excluding certain activities relating to traffic rights.

At the end of the Uruguay Round governments agreed to continue negotiations in the following areas: basic telecommunications, maritime transport, movement of natural persons and financial services. The Protocol to the GATS relating to movement of natural persons was concluded in July 1995. In May 1996 the USA withdrew from negotiations to conclude an agreement on maritime transport services. At the end of June the participating countries agreed to suspend the discussions and to recommence negotiations in 2000.

In July 1995 some 29 members signed an interim agreement to grant greater access to the banking, insurance, investment and securities sectors from August 1996. Negotiations to strengthen the agreement and to extend it to new signatories (including the USA, which had declined to sign the agreement, claiming lack of reciprocity by some Asian countries) commenced in April 1997. A final agreement was successfully concluded in mid-December: 102 countries endorsed the elimination of restrictions on access to the financial services sectors from 1 March 1999, and agreed to subject those services to legally-binding rules and disciplines. In late January 1999 some 35 signatory states had yet to ratify the financial services agreement, and its entry into force was postponed. Negotiations on trade in basic telecommunications began in May 1994 and were scheduled to conclude in April 1996. Before the final deadline, however, the negotiations were suspended, owing to US concerns, which included greater access to satellite telecommunications markets in Asia and greater control over foreign companies operating from the domestic markets. An agreement was finally concluded by the new deadline of 15 February 1997. Accordingly the largest telecommunications markets, i.e. the USA, the EU and Japan, were to eliminate all remaining restrictions on domestic and foreign competition in the industry by 1 January 1998 (although delays were granted to Spain, until December 1998, Ireland, until 2000, and Greece and Portugal, until 2003). The majority of the 69 signatories to the accord also agreed on common rules to ensure that fair competition could be enforced by the WTO disputes settlement mechanism, and pledged their commitment to establishing a regulatory system for the telecommunications sector and guaranteeing transparency in government licensing. The agreement entered into force on 5 February 1998, having been rescheduled, owing to the delay on the part of some signatory countries (then totalling 72 states) in ratifying the accord and incorporating the principles of industry regulation into national legislation. The negotiations to liberalize trade in services were formally reopened in 2000, while new guide-lines and procedures for the negotiations were approved in March 2001. The negotiations were incorporated into the Doha Agenda and were to be concluded as part of a single undertaking by 1 January 2005.

INTELLECTUAL PROPERTY RIGHTS

The WTO Agreement on Trade-Related Aspects of Intellectual Property Rights (TRIPS) recognizes that widely varying standards in the protection and enforcement of intellectual property rights and the lack of multilateral disciplines dealing with international trade in counterfeit goods have been a growing source of tension in international economic relations. The TRIPS agreement aims to ensure that nationals of member states receive equally favourable treatment with regard to the protection of intellectual property and that adequate standards of intellectual property protection exist in all WTO member countries. These standards are largely based on the obligations of the Paris and Berne Conventions of WIPO (see p. 193), however, the agreement aims to expand and enhance these where necessary, for example: computer programmes, to be protected as literary works for copyright purposes; definition of trade marks eligible for protection; stricter rules of geographical indications of consumer products; a 10-year protection period for industrial designs; a 20-year patent protection available for all inventions; tighter protection of layout design of integrated circuits; and protection for trade secrets and 'know-how' with a commercial value.

Under the agreement member governments are obliged to provide procedures and remedies to ensure the effective enforcement of intellectual property rights. Civil and administrative procedures outlined in the TRIPS include provisions on evidence, injunctions, judicial authority to order the disposal of infringing goods, and criminal procedures and penalties, in particular for trade-mark counterfeiting and copyright piracy. A one-year period was envisaged for developed countries to bring their legislation and practices into conformity with the agreement. Developing countries were to do so in five years (or 10 years if an area of technology did not already have patent protection) and least-developed countries in 11 years. A Council for Trade-Related Property Rights monitors the compliance of governments with the agreement and its operation. During 2000 the implementation of TRIPS was one the key areas of contention among WTO members. In November WTO initiated a review of TRIPS, although this was expected to consider alteration of the regime rather than of its implementation. At that time some 70 developing countries were failing to apply TRIPS rules. In November 2001 the WTO Ministerial Conference sought to resolve the ongoing dispute regarding the implementation of TRIPS in respect of pharmaceutical patents in developing countries. A separate declaration aimed to clarify a flexible interpretation of TRIPS in order for governments to meet urgent public health priorities. The deadline for some of the poorest countries to apply provisions on pharmaceutical patents was extended to 1 January 2016. The TRIPS Council was mandated to undertake further consideration of problems of compulsory licensing. The Doha Declaration also committed the Council to concluding, by the next Ministerial Conference, scheduled to be held in 2003, negotiations on a multilateral registration system for geographical indications for wines and spirits.

LEGAL FRAMEWORK

In addition to the binding agreements mentioned above, WTO aims to provide a comprehensive legal framework for the international trading system. Under GATT 1994 'anti-dumping' measures were permitted against imports of a product with an export price below its normal value, if these imports were are likely to cause damage to a domestic industry. The WTO agreement provides for greater clarity and more-detailed rules determining the application of these measures and determines settlement procedures in disputes relating to anti-dumping actions taken by WTO members. In general, anti-dumping measures were to be limited to five years. WTO's Agreement on Subsidies and Countervailing Measures is intended to expand on existing GATT agreements. It classifies subsidies into three categories: prohibited, which may be determined by the Dispute Settlement Body and must be immediately withdrawn; actionable, which must be withdrawn or altered if the subsidy is found to cause adverse effects on the interests of other members; and non-actionable, for example subsidies involving assistance to industrial research, assistance to disadvantaged regions or adaptation of facilities to meet new environmental requirements. The Agreement also contains provisions on the use of duties to offset the effect of a subsidy (so-called countervailing measures) and establishes procedures for the initiation and conduct of investigations into this action. Countervailing measures must generally be terminated within five years of their imposition. Least-developed countries, and developing countries with gross national product per capita of less than US $1,000, are exempt from disciplines on prohibited export subsidies; however, these were to be eliminated by 2003 in all other developing countries and by 2002 in countries with economies in transition.

WTO members may take safeguard actions to protect a specific domestic industry from a damaging increase of imported products. However, the WTO agreement aims to clarify criteria for imposing safeguards, their duration (normally to be no longer than four years, which may be extended to eight years) and consultations on trade compensation for the exporting countries. At 1 December 1995 50 member states had notified the Committee on Safeguards of the WTO Secretariat of their existing domestic safeguard legislations, as required under the agreement. Any measures to protect domestic industries through voluntary export restraints or other market-sharing devices were to be phased out by the end of 1998, or a year later for one specific safeguard measure, subject to mutual agreement of the members directly concerned. Safeguard measures are not applicable to products from developing countries as long as their share of imports of the product concerned does not exceed 3%.

Further legal arrangements act to ensure the following: that technical regulations and standards (including testing and certification procedures) do not create unnecessary obstacles to trade; that import licensing procedures are transparent and predictable; that the valuation of goods for customs purposes are fair and uniform; that GATT principles and obligations apply to import preshipment inspection activities; the fair and transparent administration of rules of origin; and that no investment measures which may restrict or distort trade may be applied. A Working Group on Notification Obligations and Procedures aims to ensure that members fulfil their notification requirements, which facilitate the transparency and surveillance of the trading rules.

PLURILATERAL AGREEMENTS

The majority of GATT agreements became multilateral obligations when the WTO became operational in 1995; however, four agreements, which have a selective group of signatories, remained in effect. These so-called plurilateral agreements, the Agreement on Trade in Civil Aircraft, the Agreement on Government Procurement, the International Dairy Agreement and the International Bovine Meat Agreement, aim to increase international co-operation and fair and open trade and competition in these areas. Each of the agreements establish their own management bodies, which are required to report to the General Council.

TRADE POLICY REVIEW MECHANISM

The mechanism, which was established provisionally in 1989, was given a permanent role in the WTO. Through regular monitoring and surveillance of national trade policies the mechanism aims to increase the transparency and understanding of trade policies and practices and to enable assessment of the effects of policies on the world trading system. In addition, it records efforts made by governments to bring domestic trade legislation into conformity with WTO provisions and to implement WTO commitments. Reviews are conducted in the Trade Policy Review Body on the basis of a policy statement of the government under review and an independent report prepared by the WTO Secretariat. Under the mechanism the world's four largest traders, the European Union, the USA, Japan and Canada, were to be reviewed every two years. Special groups were established to examine new regional free-trade arrangements and the trade policies of acceding countries. In February 1996 a single Committee on Regional Trade Agreements was established, superseding these separate working parties. The Committee aimed to ensure that these groupings contributed to the process of global trade liberalization and to study the implications of these arrangements on the multilateral system. At the Ministerial Conference held in December 1996 it was agreed to establish a new working group to conduct a study of transparency in government procurement practices.

SETTLEMENT OF DISPUTES

A separate annex to the WTO agreement determines a unified set of rules and procedures to govern the settlement of all WTO disputes, substantially reinforcing the GATT procedures. WTO members are committed not to undertake unilateral action against perceived violations of the trade rules, but to seek recourse in the dispute settlement mechanism and abide by its findings.

The first stage of the process requires bilateral consultations between the members concerned in an attempt to conclude a mutually-acceptable solution to the issue. These may be undertaken through the good offices and mediation efforts of the Director-General. Only after a consultation period of 60 days may the complainant ask the General Council, convened as the Dispute Settlement Body (DSB), to establish an independent panel to examine the case, which then does so within the terms of reference of the agreement cited. Each party to the dispute submits its arguments and then presents its case before the panel. Third parties which notify their interest in the dispute may also present views at the first substantive meeting of the panel. At this stage an expert review group may be appointed to provide specific scientific or technical advice. The panel submits sections and then a full interim report of its findings to the parties, who may then request a further review involving additional meetings. A final report should be submitted to the parties by the panel within six months of its establishment, or within three months in cases of urgency, including those related to perishable goods. Final reports are normally adopted by the DSB within 60 days of issuance. In the case of a measure being found to be inconsistent with the relevant WTO agreement, the panel recommends ways in which the member may bring the measure into conformity with the agreement. However, under the WTO mechanism either party has the right to appeal against the decision and must notify the DSB of its intentions before adoption of the final report. Appeal proceedings, which are limited to issues of law and the legal interpretation covered by the panel report, are undertaken by three members of the Appellate Body within a maximum period of 90 days. The report of the Appellate Body must be unconditionally accepted by the parties to the dispute (unless there is a consensus within the DSB against its adoption). If the recommendations of the panel or appeal report are not implemented immediately, or within a 'reasonable period' as determined by the DSB, the parties are obliged to negotiate mutually-acceptable compensation pending full implementation. Failure to agree compensation may result in the DSB authorizing the complainant to suspend concessions or obligations against the other party. In any case the DSB monitors the implementation of adopted recommendations or rulings, while any outstanding cases remain on its agenda until the issue is resolved. By April 2002 254 trade complaints had been notified to the WTO since 1995, on some 180 different issues.

In late 1997 the DSB initiated a review of the WTO's understanding on dispute settlement, as required by the Marrakesh Agreement. The Doha Declaration, which was adopted in November 2001, mandated further negotiations to be conducted on the review and on additional proposals to amend the dispute procedure as a separate undertaking from the rest of the work programme. Negotiations were to be concluded by May 2003.

CO-OPERATION WITH OTHER ORGANIZATIONS

WTO is mandated to pursue co-operation with the IMF and the World Bank, as well as with other multilateral organizations, in order to achieve greater coherence in global economic policy-making. In November 1994 the preparatory committee of the WTO resolved not to incorporate the new organization into the UN structure as a specialized agency. Instead, co-operation arrangements with the IMF and World Bank were to be developed. In addition, efforts were pursued to enhance co-operation with UNCTAD in research, trade and technical issues. The Directors-General of the two organizations agreed to meet at least twice a year in order to develop the working relationship. In particular, co-operation was to be undertaken in WTO's special programme of activities for Africa, which aimed to help African countries expand and diversify their trade and benefit from the global trading system. Since 1997 WTO has co-operated with the IMF, ITC, UNCTAD, UNDP and World Bank in an Integrated Framework for trade-related technical assistance to least developed countries. In 2000 WTO led efforts to enhance activities under this grouping.

International Trade Centre UNCTAD/WTO: Palais des Nations, 1211 Geneva 10, Switzerland; tel. (22) 7300111; fax (22) 7334439; e-mail itcreg@intracen.org; internet www.intracen.org; f. 1964 by GATT; jointly operated with the UN (through UNCTAD) since 1968; ITC works with developing countries in product and market development, the development of trade support services, trade information, human resource development, international purchasing and supply management, and needs assessment and programme design for trade promotion. Publs *International Trade Forum* (quarterly), market studies, handbooks, etc.

Executive Director: J. DENIS BÉLISLE.

Finance

The WTO's 2002 budget amounted to 143m. Swiss francs (CHF), financed mainly by contributions from members in proportion to their share of total trading conducted by WTO members. Of the total budget, CHF 140.3m. was for the Secretariat and CHF 2.8m. for the Appellate Body.

Publications

Annual Report (2 volumes).

International Trade Statistics (annually).

World Trade Review (3 a year).

WTO Focus (monthly).

PART FOUR

Other International Organizations

OTHER INTERNATIONAL ORGANIZATIONS

Agriculture, Food, Forestry and Fisheries

(For organizations concerned with agricultural commodities, see Commodities, p. 527)

African Timber Organization—ATO: BP 1077, Libreville, Gabon; tel. 732928; fax 734030; e-mail oab-gabon@internetgabon.com; f. 1976 to enable members to study and co-ordinate ways of ensuring the optimum utilization and conservation of their forests. Mems: 13 African countries. Sec.-Gen. PAUL NGATSE-OBALA. Publs *ATO Information Bulletin* (quarterly), *International Magazine of African Timber* (2 a year).

Asian Vegetable Research and Development Center—AVRDC: POB 42, Shanhua, Tainan 741, Taiwan; tel. (6) 5837801; fax (6) 5830009; e-mail avrdcbox@netra.avrdc.org.tw; internet www.avrdc.org.tw; f. 1971; aims to enhance the nutritional well-being and raise the incomes of the poor in rural and urban areas of developing countries, through improved varieties and methods of vegetable production, marketing and distribution; runs an experimental farm, laboratories, gene-bank, greenhouses, quarantine house, insectarium, library and weather station; provides training for research and production specialists in tropical vegetables; exchanges and disseminates vegetable germplasm through regional centres in the developing world; serves as a clearing-house for vegetable research information; and undertakes scientific publishing. Mems: Australia, France, Germany, Japan, Republic of Korea, Philippines, Taiwan, Thailand, USA. Dir-Gen. Dr SAMSON C. S. TSOU. Publs *Annual Report, Technical Bulletin, Proceedings, Centerpoint* (4 a year).

CAB International (CABI): Wallingford, Oxon, OX10 8DE, United Kingdom; tel. (1491) 832111; fax (1491) 833508; e-mail cabi@cabi.org; internet www.cabi.org; f. 1929 as the Imperial Agricultural Bureaux (later Commonwealth Agricultural Bureaux), current name adopted in 1985; aims to improve human welfare world-wide through the generation, dissemination and application of scientific knowledge in support of sustainable development; places particular emphasis on forestry, human health and the management of natural resources, with priority given to the needs of developing countries; compiles and publishes extensive information (in a variety of print and electronic forms) on aspects of agriculture, forestry, veterinary medicine, the environment and natural resources, Third World rural development and others; maintains regional centres in Kenya, Malaysia, Pakistan, Switzerland and Trinidad and Tobago. Mems: 40 countries. Dir-Gen. Dr DENIS BLIGHT.

CABI Bioscience: Bakeham Lane, Egham, Surrey, TW20 9TY, United Kingdom; tel. (1491) 829080; fax (1491) 829100; e-mail bioscience@cabi.org; internet www.cabi.org/bioscience; f. 1998 by integration of the following four CABI scientific institutions: International Institute of Biological Control; International Institute of Entomology; International Institute of Parasitology; International Mycological Institute; undertakes research, consultancy, training, capacity-building and institutional development measures in sustainable pest management, biosystematics and molecular biology, ecological applications and environmental and industrial microbiology; maintains centres in Kenya, Malaysia, Pakistan, Switzerland, Trinidad and the United Kingdom.

Collaborative International Pesticides Analytical Council Ltd—CIPAC: c/o Dr M. D. Mueller, Swiss Federal Res. Station, 8820 Waedenswil, Switzerland; tel. (1) 7836412; fax (1) 7836439; e-mail markus.mueller@faw.admin.ca; internet www.cipac.org; f. 1957 to organize international collaborative work on methods of analysis for pesticides used in crop protection. Mems: in 46 countries. Chair. Dr W. DOBRAT (Germany); Sec. Dr M. D. MUELLER (Switzerland).

Dairy Society International—DSI: 7185 Ruritan Drive, Chambersburg, PA 17201, USA; tel. (717) 375-4392; f. 1946 to foster the extension of dairy and dairy industrial enterprise through the interchange and dissemination of scientific, technological, economic, dietary and other relevant information. Mems: in 50 countries. Pres. JAMES E. CLICK (USA); Man. Dir G. W. WEIGOLD (USA). Publs *DSI Report to Members, DSI Bulletin, Market Frontier News, Dairy Situation Review.*

Desert Locust Control Organization for Eastern Africa: POB 30023, Nairobi, Kenya; tel. (2) 501704; fax (2) 505137; e-mail delco@insightkenya.com; f. 1962 to promote effective control of desert locust in the region and to conduct research into the locust's environment and behaviour; also assists member states in the monitoring and extermination of other migratory pests. Mems: Djibouti, Eritrea, Ethiopia, Kenya, Somalia, Sudan, Tanzania, Uganda. Dir PETER O. ODHO; Co-ordinator J. M. GATIMU. Publs *Desert Locust Situation Reports* (monthly), *Annual Report*, technical reports.

European and Mediterranean Plant Protection Organization—EPPO: 1 rue Le Nôtre, 75016 Paris, France; tel. 1-45-20-77-94; fax 1-42-24-89-43; e-mail hq@eppo.fr; internet www.eppo.org; f. 1951, present name adopted in 1955; aims to promote international co-operation between government plant protection services to prevent the introduction and spread of pests and diseases of plants and plant products. Mems: governments of 43 countries and territories. Chair. OLIVER FELIX; Dir-Gen. Dr I. M. SMITH. Publs *EPPO Bulletin, Data Sheets on Quarantine Organisms, Guidelines for the Efficacy Evaluation of Pesticides, Crop Growth Stage Keys, Summary of the Phytosanitary Regulations of EPPO Member Countries, Reporting Service.*

European Association for Animal Production—EAAP (Fédération européenne de zootechnie): Via A. Torlonia 15A, 00161 Rome, Italy; tel. (06) 44238013; fax (06) 44241466; e-mail zoorec@mnet.it; internet www.eaap.org; f. 1949 to help improve the conditions of animal production and meet consumer demand; holds annual meetings. Mems: asscns in 37 countries. Pres. Prince P. ZU SOLMS-LICH (Germany). Publ. *Livestock Production Science* (16 a year).

European Association for Research on Plant Breeding—EUCARPIA: c/o POB 315, 6700 AH Wageningen, Netherlands; tel. (317) 482838; e-mail marjo.dejeu@pv.dpw.wag-ur.nl; internet www.eucarpia.org; f. 1956 to promote scientific and technical co-operation in the plant breeding field. Mems: 1,000 individuals, 64 corporate mems. Pres. Dr G. R. MACKAY (UK); Sec. Dr Ir M. J. DE JEU (Netherlands). Publ. *Bulletin.*

European Confederation of Agriculture: 23 rue de la Science, 1040 Brussels, Belgium; tel. (2) 230-43-80; fax (2) 230-46-77; e-mail cea@pophost.eunet.be; f. 1889 as International Confederation, re-formed in 1948 as European Confederation; represents the interests of European agriculture in the international field; provides social security for independent farmers and foresters in the member countries. Mems: 300 mems. in 30 countries. Pres. HANS JONSSON (Sweden); Gen. Sec. CHRISTOPHE HÉMARD (France). Publs *CEA Dialog, Annual Report.*

European Grassland Federation: c/o Dr W. H. Prins, Hollandseweg 382, 6705 BE Wageningen, Netherlands; tel. and fax (317) 416386; e-mail egf-secr@pckassa.com; internet www.europeangrassland.org; f. 1963 to facilitate and maintain liaison between European grassland organizations and to promote the interchange of scientific and practical knowledge and experience; holds General Meeting every two years and symposia at other times. Mems: 29 full and eight corresponding mem. countries in Europe. Pres. Dr CHRISTIAN HUYGHE; Sec. Dr W. H. PRINS. Publ. *Proceedings (Grassland Science in Europe).*

European Livestock and Meat Trading Union: 81A rue de la Loi, 1040 Brussels, Belgium; tel. (2) 230-46-03; fax (2) 230-94-00; e-mail uecbv@pophost.eunet.be; internet uecbv.eunet.be; f. 1952 to study problems of the European livestock and meat trade and inform members of all relevant legislation; acts as an international arbitration commission; conducts research on agricultural markets, quality of livestock, and veterinary regulations. Mems: national organizations in 26 countries, and the European Association of Livestock Markets. Pres. L. SPANGHERO; Sec.-Gen. J.-L. MERIAUX.

Inter-American Association of Agricultural Librarians, Documentalists and Information Specialists (Asociación Interamericana de Bibliotecarios, Documentalistas y Especialistas en Información Agrícolas—AIBDA): c/o IICA-CIDIA, Apdo 55-2200 Coronado, Costa Rica; tel. 216-0290; fax 216-0291; e-mail cmolesti@iica.ac.cr; internet www.iica.ac.cr; f. 1953 to promote professional improvement through technical publications and meetings, and to promote improvement of library services in agricultural sciences. Mems: c. 400 in 29 countries and territories. Pres. MAGDA SAUDÍ; Exec. Sec. CARLOS J. MOLESTINA. Publs *Boletín Informativo* (3 a year), *Boletín Especial* (irregular), *Revista AIBDA* (2 a year), *AIBDA Actualidades* (4 or 5 a year).

Inter-American Tropical Tuna Commission—IATTC: Scripps Institution of Oceanography, 8604 La Jolla Shores Drive, La Jolla, CA 92037-1508, USA; tel. (858) 546-7100; fax (858) 546-7133; e-mail rallen@iattc.org; internet www.iattc.org; f. 1950; runs two programmes, the Tuna-Billfish Programme and the Tuna-Dolphin Programme. The Tuna-Billfish Programme investigates the biology of the tunas and related species of the eastern Pacific Ocean and recommends appropriate conservation measures to maintain stocks. The Tuna-Dolphin Programme monitors dolphin levels and promotes fishing techniques and equipment likely to minimize dolphin fatalities. The Commission also investigates the effect of various fishing methods on other species of fish and aquatic animals and provides a secretariat for the International Dolphin Conservation Program. Mems: Costa Rica, Ecuador, El Salvador, France, Guatemala, Japan, Mexico, Nicaragua, Panama, USA, Vanuatu, Venezuela. Dir ROBIN L. ALLEN. Publs *Bulletin* (irregular), *Annual Report, Stock Assessment Report* (annual), *Special Report* (irregular).

International Association for Cereal Science and Technology—ICC: Wiener Strasse 22A, POB 77, 2320 Schwechat, Austria; tel. (1) 707-72-02; fax (1) 707-72-04; e-mail gen.sec@icc.or.at; internet www.icc.or.at; f. 1955 (as the International Association for Cereal Chemistry; name changed 1986); aims to promote international co-operation in the field of cereal science and technology through the dissemination of information and the development of standard methods of testing and analysing products. Mems: 50 mem. states. Sec.-Gen. Dr HELMUT GLATTES (Austria).

International Association for Vegetation Science—IAVS: Alterra, Green World Research, POB 47, 6700 AA Wageningen, Netherlands; tel. (317) 477914; fax (317) 424988; e-mail j.h.j.schaminee@alterra.wag-ur.nl; internet www.iavs.org; f. 1938. Mems: 1,500 in 70 countries. Chair. Prof. Dr E. O. BOX; Gen Sec. Dr J. H. J. SCHAMINÉE. Publs *Phytocoenologia, Journal of Vegetation Science, Applied Vegetation Science.*

International Association of Agricultural Economists—IAAE: 1211 West 22nd St, Suite 216, Oak Brook, IL 60523-2197, USA; tel. (630) 571-9393; fax (630) 571-9580; e-mail iaae@farmfoundation.org; internet www.iaae-agecon.org; f. 1929 to foster development of agricultural economic sciences; aims to further the application of research into agricultural processes; works to improve economic and social conditions for agricultural and rural life. Mems: in 96 countries. Pres. JOACHIM VON BRAUN; Sec. and Treas. WALTER J. ARMBRUSTER (USA). Publs *Agricultural Economics* (8 a year), *IAAE Newsletter* (2 a year).

International Association of Agricultural Information Specialists: c/o Margot Bellamy, 14 Queen St, Dorchester-on-Thames, Wallingford, Oxon OX10 7HR, United Kingdom; tel. (1865) 340054; e-mail margot.bellamy@fritillary.demon.co.uk; f. 1955 to promote agricultural library science and documentation and the professional interests of agricultural librarians and documentalists; affiliated to the International Federation of Library Asscns and Institutions. Mems: 600 in 84 countries. Pres. Dr JAN VAN DER BURG (Netherlands); Sec.-Treas. MARGOT BELLAMY (UK). Publs *Quarterly Bulletin, World Directory of Agricultural Information Resource Centres.*

International Association of Horticultural Producers—IAHP: Postbus 200, 2700 AG Zoetermeen, Netherlands; tel. (79) 3470707; fax (79) 3470404; e-mail pt@tuinbouw.nl; internet www.aiph.org.uk; f. 1948; represents the common interests of commercial horticultural producers in the international field; authorizes international horticultural exhibitions. Mems: national asscns in 25 countries. Pres. B. WERNER; Gen. Sec. Dr J. B. M. ROTTEVEEL. Publ. *Yearbook of International Horticultural Statistics.*

International Bee Research Association—IBRA: 18 North Rd, Cardiff, CF10 3DT, United Kingdom; tel. (29) 2037-2409; fax (29) 2066-5522; e-mail info@ibra.org.uk; internet www.ibra.org.uk; f. 1949 to further bee research and provide an information service for bee scientists and bee-keepers world-wide. Mems: 1,200 in 130 countries. Dir RICHARD JONES; Asst Dir Dr PAMELA MUNN. Publs *Bee World* (quarterly), *Apicultural Abstracts* (quarterly), *Journal of Apicultural Research* (quarterly).

International Centre for Integrated Mountain Development—ICIMOD: POB 3226, Kathmandu, Nepal; tel. (1) 525313; fax (1) 524509; e-mail dits@icimod.org.np; internet www.icimod.org.sg; f. 1983 to promote the well-being of mountain communities through effective socioeconomic development policies and programmes; advocates the sound management of fragile mountain habitats, especially in the Hindu Kush-Himalayan region. Dir-Gen. EGBERT PELINCK.

International Centre for Tropical Agriculture (Centro Internacional de Agricultura Tropical—CIAT): Apdo Aéreo 6713, Cali, Colombia; tel. (2) 445-0000; fax (2) 445-0073; e-mail ciat@cgnet.com; internet www.ciat.cgiar.org; f. 1967 to contribute to the alleviation of hunger and poverty in tropical developing countries by using new techniques in agriculture research and training; focuses on production problems in field beans, cassava, rice and tropical pastures in the tropics. Dir-Gen. Dr JOACHIM VOSS. Publs *Annual Report, Growing Affinities* (2 a year), *Pasturas Tropicales* (3 a year), catalogue of publications.

International Commission for the Conservation of Atlantic Tunas—ICCAT: Calle Corazón de Maria 8, 28020 Madrid, Spain; tel. (91) 4165600; fax (91) 4152612; internet www.iccat.es; f. 1969 under the provisions of the International Convention for the Conservation of Atlantic Tunas (1966) to maintain the populations of tuna and tuna-like species in the Atlantic Ocean and adjacent seas at levels that permit the maximum sustainable catch; collects statistics; conducts studies. Mems: 24 contracting parties. Chair. J. BARANANO; Exec. Sec. Dr A. RIBEIRO LIMA (Portugal). Publs *ICCAT Newsletter, Statistical Bulletin* (annually), *Data Record* (annually).

International Commission of Sugar Technology: c/o Dr H. van Malland, 97199 Ochsenfurt, Marktbreiter Str. 74, Germany; tel. (9331) 91450; fax (9331) 91462; f. 1949 to discuss investigations and promote scientific and technical research work. Pres. of Scientific Cttee Dr JAN MAARTEN DE BRUIJN (Netherlands); Sec.-Gen. Dr HENK VAN MALLAND.

International Committee for Animal Recording—ICAR: Villa del Ragno, Via Nomentana 134, 00161 Rome, Italy; tel. (06) 86329141; fax (06) 86329263; e-mail icar@eap.org; internet www.icar.org; f. 1951 to extend and improve the work of recording and to standardize methods. Mems: in 40 countries. Pres. Dr JOSEPH CRETTENAND (Switzerland).

International Crops Research Institute for the Semi-Arid Tropics—ICRISAT: Patancheru, Andhra Pradesh, India; tel. (40) 596161; fax (40) 241239; e-mail icrisat@cgiar.org; internet www.icrisat.org; f. 1972 to promote the genetic improvement of crops and for research on the management of resources in the world's semi-arid tropics, with the aim of reducing poverty and protecting the environment; research covers all physical and socio-economic aspects of improving farming systems on unirrigated land. Dir Dr WILLIAM D. DAR (Philippines). Publs *ICRISAT Report* (annually), *SAT News* (2 a year), *International Chickpea and Pigeonpea Newsletter, International Arachis Newsletter, International Sorghum and Millet Newsletter* (annually), information and research bulletins.

International Dairy Federation—IDF: 41 Sq. Vergote, 1030 Brussels, Belgium; tel. (2) 733-98-88; fax (2) 733-04-13; e-mail info@fil-idf.org; internet www.fil-idf.org; f. 1903 to link all dairy asscns, in order to encourage the solution of scientific, technical and economic problems affecting the dairy industry. Mems: national cttees in 40 countries. Dir. Gen. E. HOPKIN (UK). Publs *Bulletin of IDF, IDF Standards.*

International Federation of Agricultural Producers—IFAP: 60 rue St Lazare, 75009 Paris, France; tel. 1-45-26-05-53; fax 1-48-74-72-12; e-mail ifap@ifap.org; internet www.ifap.org; f. 1946 to represent, in the international field, the interests of agricultural producers; encourages the exchange of information and ideas; works to develop understanding of world problems and their effects upon agricultural producers; encourages sustainable patterns of agricultural development; holds conference every two years. Mems: national farmers' organizations and agricultural co-operatives of 60 countries. Pres. GERARD DOORNBOS (Netherlands); Sec.-Gen. DAVID KING. Publs *The World Farmer* (bimonthly), *Proceedings of General Conferences.*

International Federation of Beekeepers' Associations—APIMONDIA: Corso Vittorio Emanuele 101, 00186 Rome, Italy; tel. and fax (06) 6852286; e-mail apimondia@mclink.it; internet www.beekeeping.org/apimondia; f. 1949; collects and brings up to date documentation on international beekeeping; carries out studies into the particular problems of beekeeping; organizes international congresses, seminars, symposia and meetings; co-operates with other international organizations interested in beekeeping, in particular, with the FAO. Mems: 56 asscns from 52 countries. Pres. RAYMOND BORNECK; Sec.-Gen. RICCARDO JANNONI-SEBASTIANINI. Publs *Apiacta* (quarterly, in English, French, German and Spanish), *Dictionary of Beekeeping Terms,* AGROVOC (thesaurus of agricultural terms), studies.

International Hop Growers' Convention: c/o Inštitut za hmeljarstvo in pivovarstvo, POB 51, 3310 Žalec, Slovenia; tel. (63) 715214; fax (63) 717163; e-mail martin.pavlovic@uni-lj.si; internet www.hmelj-giz.si/ihgc/; f. 1950 to act as a centre for the collection of data on hop production, and to conduct scientific, technical and economic studies. Mems: national asscns in 19 countries. Pres. MARTIN JOLLY; Gen. Sec. Dr MARTIN PAVLOVIČ. Publ. *Hopfen-Rundschau* (fortnightly).

International Institute for Beet Research—IIRB: 195 ave de Tervueren, 1150 Brussels, Belgium; tel. (2) 737-70-90; fax (2) 737-70-99; e-mail mail@iirb.org; internet www.iirb.org; f. 1932 to promote research and the exchange of information; organizes meetings and study groups. Mems: 600 in 33 countries. Pres. of the Admin. Council J-J. MISONNE; Sec.-Gen. R. BECKERS.

International Institute of Tropical Agriculture—IITA: Oyo Rd, PMB 5320, Ibadan, Nigeria; tel. (2) 241-2626; fax (2) 241-2221; e-mail ciat@cgiar.org; internet www.iita.org; f. 1967; principal financing arranged by the Consultative Group on International Agricultural Research (CGIAR, q.v.), co-sponsored by the FAO, the IBRD and the UNDP; research programmes comprise crop management, improvement of crops and plant protection and health; conducts a training programme for researchers in tropical agriculture; maintains a library of 75,000 vols and data base; administers six agro-ecological research stations. Dir-Gen. Dr LUKAS BRADER. Publs *Annual Report, IITA Research* (quarterly), technical bulletins, research reports.

International Livestock Research Institute—ILRI: POB 30709, Nairobi, Kenya; tel. (2) 632311; fax (2) 631499; e-mail ilri-kenya@cgiar.org; internet www.cgiar.org/ilri; f. 1995 to supersede the International Laboratory for Research on Animal Diseases and the International Livestock Centre for Africa; conducts laboratory and field research on animal health and other livestock issues; carries out training programmes for scientists and technicians; maintains a specialized science library. Dir Dr HANK FITZHUGH. Publs *Annual Report, Livestock Research for Development* (newsletter, 2 a year).

International Maize and Wheat Improvement Centre—CIMMYT: Apdo Postal 6-641, 06600 México, DF, Mexico; tel. (5) 804-2004; fax (5) 804-7588; e-mail cimmyt@cgiar.org; internet www.cimmyt.mx; conducts world-wide research programme for sustainable increase in production of maize, wheat and triticale in developing countries. Dir-Gen. Prof. TIMOTHY REEVES.

International Organization for Biological Control of Noxious Animals and Plants: IOBC Permanent Secretariat, AGROPOLIS, Ave Agropolis, 34394 Montpellier Cédex 5, France; e-mail iobc@agropolis.fr; f. 1955 to promote and co-ordinate research on the more effective biological control of harmful organisms; re-organized in 1971 as a central council with world-wide affiliations and six largely autonomous regional sections. Pres. Dr J. WAAGE (UK); Sec.-Gen. Dr E. WAJNBERG (France). Publs *BioControl, Newsletter.*

International Organization of Citrus Virologists: c/o C. N. Roistacher, Dept of Plant Pathology, Univ. of California, Riverside, CA 92521-0122, USA; tel. (909) 684-0934; fax (909) 684-4324; e-mail chester.r@worldnet.att.net; f. 1957 to promote research on citrus virus diseases at international level by standardizing diagnostic techniques and exchanging information. Mems: 250. Chair. R. F. LEE; Sec. CHESTER N. ROISTACHER.

International Red Locust Control Organization for Central and Southern Africa: POB 240252, Ndola, Zambia; tel. (2) 615684; fax (2) 614285; e-mail locust@zamnet.zm; f. 1971 to control locusts in eastern, central and southern Africa; also assists in the control of African army-worm and quelea-quelea. Mems: seven countries. Dir Dr A. D. GADABU. Publs *Annual Report, Quarterly Report, Monthly Report,* scientific reports.

International Rice Research Institute—IRRI: DAPO Box 7777, Metro Manila, Philippines; tel. (2) 8450563; fax (2) 8911292; e-mail irri@cgiar.org; internet www.cgiar.org/irri; f. 1960; conducts research on rice, with the aim of developing technologies of environmental, social and economic benefit; works to enhance national rice research systems and offers training; operates Riceworld, a museum and learning centre about rice; maintains a library of technical rice literature; organizes international conferences and workshops. Dir-Gen. Dr RONALD CANTRELL. Publs *Rice Literature Update, Hotline, Facts about IRRI, News about Rice and People, International Rice Research Notes.*

International Seed Testing Association—ISTA: Zürichstrasse 50, Postfach 308, 8303 Bassersdorf, Switzerland; tel. (1) 8386000; fax (1) 8386001; e-mail ista.office@ista.ch; internet www.seedtest.org; f. 1924 to promote uniformity and accurate methods of seed testing and evaluation in order to facilitate efficiency in production, processing, distribution and utilization of seeds; organizes meetings, workshops, symposia, training courses and triennial congresses. Mems: 72 countries. Sec.-Gen. Dr M. MUSCHICK; Pres. Prof. Dr N. LEIST (Germany). Publs *Seed Science and Technology* (3 a year), *ISTA News Bulletin* (3 a year).

International Sericultural Commission: 25 quai JeanJacques Rousseau, 69350 La Mulatière, France; tel. 4-78-50-41-98; fax 4-78-86-09-57; f. 1948 to encourage the development of silk production. Mems: governments of Brazil, Egypt, France, India, Indonesia, Iran, Japan, Lebanon, Madagascar, Romania, Thailand, Tunisia, Turkey. Sec.-Gen. Dr GÉRARD CHAVANCY (France). Publ. *Sericologia* (quarterly).

International Service for National Agricultural Research—ISNAR: Laan van Nieuw Oost Indie 133, 2593 BM The Hague, Netherlands; tel. (70) 349-61-00; fax (70) 381-96-77; e-mail isnar@cgiar.org; internet www.cgiar.org/isnar; f. 1980 by the Consultative Group on International Agricultural Research (CGIAR, q.v.) to strengthen national agricultural research systems in developing countries; promotes appropriate research policies, the creation of sustainable research institutions and improved research management; provides advisory, training and research services and information. Chair. MOÏSE MENSAH; Dir-Gen. STEIN BIE.

International Society for Horticultural Science—ISHS: Decroylaan 42, POB 500, 3001 Leuven, Belgium; tel. (16) 22-94-27; fax (16) 22-94-50; e-mail info@ishs.org; internet www.ishs.org; f. 1959 to promote co-operation in horticultural science research. Mems: 54 mem. countries, 265 organizations, 3,050 individuals. Pres. Prof. Dr C. D. BRICKELL (UK); Exec. Dir Ir Jozef VAN ASSCHE (Belgium). Publs *Chronica Horticulturae* (quarterly), *Acta Horticulturae, Scientia Horticulturae* (monthly), *Horticultural Research International.*

International Union of Forest Research Organizations—IUFRO: 1131 Vienna, Seckendorff-Gudent-Weg 8, Austria; tel. (1) 877-01-51; fax (1) 877-93-55; e-mail iufro@forvie.ac.at; f. 1892. Mems: 700 organizations in 115 countries, involving more than 15,000 scientists. Pres. Prof. RISTO SEPPÄLÄ (Finland); Sec. HEINRICH SCHMUTZENHOFER (Austria). Publs *Annual Report, IUFRO News* (quarterly), *IUFRO World Series, IUFRO Occasional Paper Series.*

International Union for the Protection of New Plant Varieties (Union internationale pour la protection des obtentions végétales—UPOV): c/o 34 chemin des Colombettes, 1211

Geneva 20, Switzerland; tel. (22) 3389153; fax (22) 7330336; e-mail upov.mail@wipo.org; internet www.upov.int/; f. 1961 by the International Convention for the Protection of New Varieties of Plants (entered into force 1968, revised in 1972, 1978 and 1991); aims to encourage the development of new plant varieties and provide an effective system of protection. Admin. support provided by WIPO (q.v.). Mems: 50 signatory states. Sec.-Gen. Dr KAMIL IDRIS.

International Union of Soil Sciences: c/o Institute of Soil Science, University of Agricultural Sciences, Gregor-Mendel-Strasse 33, 1180 Vienna, Austria; tel. (1) 478-9107; fax (1) 478-9110; e-mail iusss@edv1.boku.ac.at; internet www.17wcss.ku.ac.th; f. 1924. Mems: 50,000 (including through 78 national societies) from 143 countries. Pres. Dr SOMPONG THEERAWONG; Sec.-Gen. Prof. Dr W. E. H. BLUM (Austria). Publ. *Bulletin* (2 a year).

International Whaling Commission—IWC: The Red House, 135 Station Rd, Impington, Cambridge, CB4 9NP, United Kingdom; tel. (1223) 233971; fax (1223) 232876; e-mail secretariat@iwcoffice.com; internet www.iwcoffice.org; f. 1946 under the International Convention for the Regulation of Whaling, for the conservation of world whale stocks; reviews the regulations covering whaling operations; encourages research; collects, analyses and disseminates statistical and other information on whaling. A ban on commercial whaling was passed by the Commission in July 1982, to take effect three years subsequently (in some cases, a phased reduction of commercial operations was not completed until 1988). A revised whale-management procedure was adopted in 1992, to be implemented after the development of a complete whale management scheme. Iceland left the IWC in June 1992 and Norway resumed commercial whaling in 1993. Mems: governments of 40 countries. Chair. Prof. BO FERNHOLM (Sweden); Sec. Dr NICOLA GRANDY. Publ. *Annual Report.*

North Pacific Anadromous Fish Commission: 889 W. Pender St, Suite 502, Vancouver, BC V6C 3B2, Canada; tel. (604) 775-5550; fax (604) 775-5577; e-mail secretariat@npafc.org; f. 1993. Mems: Canada, Japan, Russia, USA. Exec. Dir VLADIMIR FEDORENKO. Publs *Annual Report, Newsletter* (2 a year), *Statistical Yearbook, Scientific Bulletin.*

Northwest Atlantic Fisheries Organization—NAFO: POB 638, Dartmouth, NS B2Y 3Y9, Canada; tel. (902) 468-5590; fax (902) 468-5538; e-mail nafo@fox.nstn.ca; internet www.cafo.ca; f. 1979 (formerly International Commission for the Northwest Atlantic Fisheries); aims at optimum use, management and conservation of resources; promotes research and compiles statistics. Pres. E. OLTUSKI (Cuba); Exec. Sec. Dr L. I. CHEPEL. Publs *Annual Report, Statistical Bulletin, Journal of Northwest Atlantic Fishery Science, Scientific Council Reports, Scientific Council Studies, Sampling Yearbook, Proceedings.*

World Association for Animal Production: Villa del Ragno, Via Nomentana 134, 00162 Rome, Italy; tel. (06) 86329141; fax (06) 86329263; e-mail waap@waap.it; internet www.waap.it; f. 1965; holds world conference on animal production every five years; encourages, sponsors and participates in regional meetings, seminars and symposia. Mems: 17 mem. organizations. Pres. AKKE J. VAN DER ZIJPP (Netherlands); Sec.-Gen. JEAN GEORGES BOYAZOGLU (Greece). Publ. *WAAP Newsletter.*

World Association of Veterinary Food-Hygienists: Federal Institute for Health Protection of Consumers and Veterinary Medicine (BgVV), Diedersdorfer Weg 1, 12277 Berlin, Germany; tel. (30) 8412-2101; fax (30) 8412-2951; e-mail p.teufel@bgvv.de; f. 1955 to promote hygienic food control and discuss research. Mems: national asscns in 40 countries. Pres. Prof. PAUL TEUFEL; Sec. Treas. Dr L. ELLERBROEK.

World Association of Veterinary Microbiologists, Immunologists and Specialists in Infectious Diseases: Ecole Nationale Vétérinaire d'Alfort, 7 ave du Général de Gaulle, 94704 Maisons-Alfort Cédex, France; tel. 1-43-96-70-21; fax 1-43-96-70-22; f. 1967 to facilitate international contacts in the fields of microbiology, immunology and animal infectious diseases. Pres. Prof. C. PILET (France). Publs *Comparative Immunology, Microbiology and Infectious Diseases.*

World Fish Center (International Centre for Living Aquatic Resources Management—ICLARM): POB 500 GPO, 10670 Penang, Malaysia; tel. (4) 6261606; fax (4) 6265530; e-mail iclarm@cgiar.org; internet www.iclarm.org; f. 1973; became a mem. of the Consultative Group on International Agricultural Research (CGIAR, q.v.) in 1992; aims to contribute to food security and poverty eradication in developing countries through the sustainable development and use of living aquatic resources; carries out research and promotes partnerships. Dir-Gen. MERYL J. WILLIAMS.

World Ploughing Organization—WPO: Søkildevej 17, 5270 Odense N, Denmark; tel. 65-97-80-06; fax 65-93-24-40; e-mail ht@flbf.dk; internet www.worldploughing.org; f. 1952 to promote the World Ploughing Contest in a different country each year, to improve techniques and promote better understanding of soil cultivation practices through research and practical demonstrations; arranges tillage clinics world-wide. Mems: affiliates in 30 countries. Gen. Sec. CARL ALLESO. Publ. *WPO Handbook* (annually).

World's Poultry Science Association—WPSA: c/o Dr P. C. M. Simons, Centre for Applied Poultry Research, 'Het Spelderholt', POB 31, 7360 AA Beekbergen, Netherlands; tel. (55) 506-6534; fax (55) 506-4858; e-mail p.c.m.simons@pp.agro.nl; internet www.wpsa.com; f. 1912 to exchange knowledge in the industry, to encourage research and teaching, to publish information relating to production and marketing problems, to promote World Poultry Congresses and co-operate with governments. Mems: individuals in 95 countries, branches in 55 countries. Pres. Dr PETER HUNTON (Canada); Sec. Dr P. C. M. SIMONS (Netherlands). Publ. *The World Poultry Science Journal* (quarterly).

World Veterinary Association: Rosenlunds Allé 8, 2720 Vanløse, Denmark; tel. 38-71-01-56; fax 38-71-03-22; e-mail wva@ddd.dk; internet www.worldvet.org; f. 1959 as a continuation of the International Veterinary Congresses; organizes quadrennial congress. Mems: organizations in 76 countries, 19 organizations of veterinary specialists as associate members. Pres. Dr JIM EDWARDS (New Zealand); Exec. Sec. Dr LARS HOLSAAE. Publs *WVA Bulletin, World Veterinary Directory.*

Arts and Culture

Europa Nostra—Pan-European Federation for Heritage: Lange Voorhout 35, 2514 EC The Hague, Netherlands; tel. (70) 3024050; fax (70) 3617865; e-mail office@europanostra.org; internet www.europanostra.org; f. 1963; groups organizations and individuals concerned with the protection and enhancement of the European architectural and natural heritage and of the European environment; has consultative status with the Council of Europe. Mems: 216 mem. organizations, more than 150 associate mems, more than 40 supporting bodies, more than 1,000 individual mems. Pres. HRH The Prince Consort of Denmark; Exec. Pres. DANIEL CARDON DE LICHTBUER (Belgium); Sec.-Gen. SNESKA QUAEDVLIEG-MIHAILOVIĆ.

European Association of Conservatoires, Music Academies and Music High Schools: c/o Music House International Centre for Music and Music Education, POB 005, 3500 AV Utrecht, Netherlands; tel. (30) 236-12-42; fax (30) 236-12-90; e-mail aecinfo@aecinfo.org; internet www.aecinfo.org; f. 1953 to establish and foster contacts and exchanges between members. Mems: 133 mems, 14 associate mems. Pres. IAN HORSBRUGH; Gen. Sec. JOHANNES JOHANSSON.

European Centre for Culture (Centre européen de la culture): Maison de l'Europe, 120B rue de Lausanne, 1202 Geneva, Switzerland; tel. (22) 7322803; fax (22) 7384012; e-mail cecge@vtx.ch; internet www.europeans.ch; f. 1950 to contribute to the union of Europe by encouraging cultural pursuits, providing a meeting place, and conducting research in various fields of European Studies; holds conferences and training on European subjects, documentation and archives. Pres. JEAN-FRED BOURQUIN (Switzerland). Publ. *Newsletter* (3 a year).

European Society of Culture: Guidecca 54P (Calle Michelangelo, Villa Hériot), 30133 Venice, Italy; tel. (041) 5230210; fax (041) 5231033; e-mail soceurcultur@flashnet.it; f. 1950 to unite artists, poets, scientists, philosophers and others through mutual interests and friendship in order to safeguard and improve the conditions required for creative activity; maintains a library of 10,000 volumes. Mems: national and local centres, and 2,000 individuals, in 60 countries. Pres. Prof. VINCENZO CAPPELLETTI (Italy); Gen. Sec. Dott. MICHELLE CAMPAGNOLO-BOUVIER.

Inter-American Music Council (Consejo Interamericano de Música—CIDEM): 2511 P St NW, Washington, DC 20007, USA; f. 1956 to promote the exchange of works, performances and information in all fields of music, to study problems relative to music education, to encourage activity in the field of musicology, to promote folklore research and music creation, and to establish distribution centres for music material of the composers of the Americas. Mems: national music societies of 33 American countries. Sec.-Gen. EFRAÍN PAESKY.

International Association of Art: Maison de l'UNESCO, 1 rue Miollis, 75732 Paris Cédex 15, France; tel. 1-45-68-26-55; fax 1-45-67-22-87; f. 1954. Mems: 104 national committees. Pres. UNA WALKER; Sec.-Gen. J. C. DE SALINS. Publ. *IAA Newsletter* (quarterly).

International Association of Art Critics—AICA: 15 rue Martel, 75010 Paris, France; tel. 1-47-70-17-42; fax 1-47-70-17-81; e-mail paris.office@aica-int.org; internet www.aica-int.org; f. 1949 to increase co-operation in plastic arts, promote international cultural exchanges and protect the interests of mems. Mems: 4,062 in 77 countries. Pres. KIM LEVIN (USA); Sec.-Gen. RAMON TIO BELLIDO (France). Publs *Annuaire, Newsletter* (quarterly).

International Association of Bibliophiles: Bibliothèque nationale de France, 58 rue Richelieu, 75084 Paris Cédex 02, France; fax 1-47-03-77-57; f. 1963 to create contacts between bibliophiles and encourage book-collecting in different countries; organizes and encourages congresses, meetings, exhibitions and the award of scholarships. Mems: 450. Pres. CONDE DE ORGAZ (Spain); Sec.-Gen. JEAN-MARC CHATELAIN (France). Publs *Le Bulletin du Bibliophile* (2 a year), yearbooks.

International Association of Literary Critics: 38 rue du Faubourg St-Jacques, 75014 Paris, France; tel. 1-53-10-12-13; fax 1-53-10-12-12; internet www.aicl.org; f. 1969; national centres in 34 countries; organizes congresses. Pres. ROBERT ANDRÉ. Publ. *Revue* (2 a year).

International Association of Museums of Arms and Military History—IAMAM: c/o Dr C. Gaier, Musée d'Armes de Liège, Halles du Nord, 4 rue de la Boucherie, 4000 Liège, Belgium; tel. (4) 221-94-16; fax (4) 221-94-01; e-mail claude.gaier@museedarmes.be; f. 1957; links museums and other scientific institutions with public collections of arms and armour and military equipment, uniforms, etc.; holds triennial conferences and occasional specialist symposia. Mems: 252 institutions in 60 countries. Pres. CLAUDE GAIER (Belgium); Sec.-Gen. JAN PIET PUYPE (Netherlands). Publ. *The Mohonk Courier.*

International Board on Books for Young People—IBBY: Nonnenweg 12, Postfach, 4003 Basel, Switzerland; tel. (61) 2722917; fax (61) 2722757; e-mail ibby@eye.ch; internet www.ibby.org; f. 1953 to support and link bodies in all countries connected with children's book work; encourages the distribution of good children's books; promotes scientific investigation into problems of juvenile books; presents the Hans Christian Andersen Award every two years to a living author and a living illustrator whose work is an outstanding contribution to juvenile literature; presents the IBBY-Asahi Reading Promotion Award annually to an organization that has made a significant contribution towards the encouragement of reading; sponsors International Children's Book Day (2 April). Mems: national sections and individuals in more than 60 countries. Pres. TAYO SHIMA (Japan); Sec. LEENA MAISSEN. Publs *Bookbird* (quarterly, in English), *Congress Papers, IBBY Honour List* (every 2 years), special bibliographies.

International Centre for the Study of the Preservation and Restoration of Cultural Property—ICCROM: Via di San Michele 13, 00153 Rome, Italy; tel. (06) 585-531; fax (06) 5855-3349; e-mail iccrom@iccrom.org; internet www.iccrom.org; f. 1959; assembles documents on the preservation and restoration of cultural property; stimulates research and proffers advice; organizes missions of experts; undertakes training of specialists. Mems: 101 countries. Dir-Gen. Dr NICHOLAS STANLEY-PRICE (UK). Publ. *Newsletter* (annually, in English and French).

International Centre of Films for Children and Young People (Centre international du film pour l'enfance et la jeunesse—CIFEJ): 3774 rue Saint-Denis, Bureau 200, Montréal, QC H2W 2M1, Canada; tel. (514) 284-9388; fax (514) 284-0168; e-mail info@cifej.com; internet www.cifej.com; f. 1955; serves as a clearing house for information about: entertainment films (cinema and television) for children and young people, the influence of films on the young, and the regulations in force for the protection and education of young people; promotes production and distribution of suitable films and their appreciation; awards the CIFEJ prize at selected film festivals. Mems: 163 mems in 53 countries. Exec. Dir JO-ANNE BLOUIN. Publ. *CIFEJ Info* (monthly).

International Committee for the Diffusion of Arts and Literature through the Cinema (Comité international pour la diffusion des arts et des lettres par le cinéma—CIDALC): 24 blvd Poissonnière, 75009 Paris, France; tel. 1-42-46-13-60; f. 1930 to promote the creation and release of educational, cultural and documentary films and other films of educational value, in order to contribute to closer understanding between peoples; awards medals and prizes for films of exceptional merit. Mems: national committees in 19 countries. Pres. JEAN-PIERRE FOUCAULT (France); Sec.-Gen. MARIO VERDONE (Italy). Publs *Annuaire CIDALC, Cinéma éducatif et culturel.*

International Comparative Literature Association: c/o Paola Mildonian, Letterature Comparate, Dipartim. di Studi Anglo-Americani e Ibero-Americani, Università Ca' Foscari-Venezia, Ca' Garzoni, S. Marco 3417, 30124 Venice, Italy; tel. (041) 257-8427; fax (041) 257-8476; e-mail pamildo@unive.it; internet www.byu.edu/ icla/; f. 1954 to work for the development of the comparative study of literature in modern languages. Mems: societies and individuals in 78 countries. Pres. KOJI KAWAMOTO. Publs *ICLA Bulletin* (2 a year), *Literary Research* (2 a year).

International Confederation of Societies of Authors and Composers—World Congress of Authors and Composers (CISAC): 20–26 blvd du Parc, 92200 Neuilly-sur-Seine, France; tel. 1-55-62-08-50; fax 1-55-62-08-60; e-mail cisac@cisac.org; internet www.cisac.org; f. 1926 to protect the rights of authors and composers; organizes biennial congress. Mems: 204 mem. societies from 105 countries. Sec.-Gen. ERIC BAPTISTE.

International Council of Graphic Design Associations—ICOGRADA: POB 5, Forest 2, 1190 Brussels, Belgium; tel. (2) 344-58-43; fax (2) 344-71-38; e-mail secretariat@icograda.org; internet www.icograda.org; f. 1963; aims to raise standards of graphic design; promotes the exchange of information; organizes exhibitions and congresses; maintains library, slide collection and archive. Mems: 68 asscns in 43 countries. Pres. ROBERT L. PETERS (Canada); Sec.-Gen. TIFFANY TURKINGTON (South Africa). Publs *Newsletter* (quarterly), *Regulations and Guidelines governing International Design Competitions, Model Code of Professional Conduct,* other professional documents.

International Council of Museums—ICOM: Maison de l'UNESCO, 1 rue Miollis, 75732 Paris Cédex 15, France; tel. 1-47-34-05-00; fax 1-43-06-78-62; e-mail secretariat@icom.org; internet www.icom.org; f. 1946 to further international co-operation among museums and to advance museum interests; maintains with UNESCO the organization's documentation centre. Mems: 17,000 individuals and institutions in 139 countries. Pres. JACQUES PEROT (France); Sec.-Gen. MANUS BRINKMAN (Netherlands). Publ. *ICOM News—Nouvelles de l'ICOM—Noticias del ICOM* (quarterly).

International Council on Monuments and Sites—ICOMOS: 49–51 rue de la Fédération, 75015 Paris, France; tel. 1-45-67-67-70; fax 1-45-66-06-22; e-mail secretariat@icomos.org; internet www.international.icomos.org; f. 1965 to promote the study and preservation of monuments and sites and to arouse and cultivate the interest of public authorities and people of every country in their cultural heritage; disseminates the results of research into the technical, social and administrative problems connected with the conservation of the architectural heritage; holds triennial General Assembly and Symposium. Mems: c. 7,000, 21 international committees, 105 national committees. Pres. Dr MICHAEL PETZET (Germany); Sec.-Gen. JEAN-LOUIS LUXEN (Belgium). Publs *ICOMOS Newsletter* (quarterly), *Scientific Journal* (quarterly).

International Federation for Theatre Research: c/o Flat 7, 118 Avenue Rd, London, W3 8QG, United Kingdom; e-mail d.whitton@lancaster.ac.uk; internet www.firt-iftr.org; f. 1955 by 21 countries at the International Conference on Theatre History, London. Pres. Prof. JOSETTE FÉRAL; Joint Secs-Gen. Prof. DAVID WHITTON, Prof. CHRISTIANE PAGE. Publs *Theatre Research International* (in association with Oxford University Press; 3 a year), *Bulletin* (2 a year).

International Federation of Film Archives (Fédération internationale des archives du film—FIAF): c/o Christian Dimitriu, rue Defacqz 1, 1000 Brussels, Belgium; tel. (2) 538-30-65; fax (2) 534-47-74; e-mail info@fiafnet.org; internet www.fiafnet.org; f. 1938 to encourage the creation of audio-visual archives for the collection and conservation of the moving image heritage of every country; facilitates co-operation and exchanges between film archives; promotes public interest in the art of the cinema; aids and conducts research; compiles new documentation; holds annual congress. Mems: in 60 countries. Pres. IVAN TRUJILLO BOLIO (Mexico); Sec.-Gen. Dr STEVEN RICCI (USA). Publs *Journal of Film Preservation* (2 a year), *FIAF International Film Archive Database* (2 a year).

International Federation of Film Producers' Associations: 9 rue de l'Echelle, 75002 Paris, France; tel. 1-44-77-97-50; fax 1-42-56-16-52; e-mail infos@fiapf.org; internet fiapf.org; f. 1933 to represent film production internationally, to defend its general interests and promote its development; studies all cultural, legal, economic, technical and social problems related to film production. Mems: national asscns in 23 countries. Pres. AURELIO DE LAURENTIIS (Italy); Dir-Gen. ANDRÉ CHAUBEAU (France).

International Institute for Children's Literature and Reading Research (Internationales Institut für Jugendliteratur und Leseforschung): 1040 Vienna, Mayerhofgasse 6, Austria; tel. (1) 50503-59; fax (1) 50503-5917; e-mail kidlit@netway.at; internet www.kidlit.nwy.at; f. 1965 as an international documentation, research and advisory centre of juvenile literature and reading; maintains specialized library; arranges conferences and exhibitions; compiles recommendation lists. Mems: individual and group members in 28 countries. Pres. Dr HILDE HAWLICEK; Dir KARIN HALLER. Publ. *1000 & 1 Buch* (quarterly and 1 special issue).

International Institute for Conservation of Historic and Artistic Works: 6 Buckingham St, London, WC2N 6BA, United Kingdom; tel. (20) 7839-5975; fax (20) 7976-1564; e-mail iicon@compuserve.com; internet www.iiconservation.org; f. 1950. Mems: 3,350 individual, 450 institutional mems. Pres. ANDREW ODDY; Exec. Sec. PERRY SMITH. Publs *Studies in Conservation* (quarterly), *Reviews in Conservation* (annually).

International Liaison Centre for Cinema and Television Schools (Centre international de liaison des écoles de cinéma et de television—CILECT): 8 rue Thérésienne, 1000 Brussels, Belgium; tel. (2) 511-98-39; fax (2) 511-98-39; e-mail hverh.cilect@skynet.be; internet www.cilect.org; f. 1955 to link higher teaching and research institutes and improve education of makers of films and television programmes; organizes conferences and student film festivals; runs a training programme for developing countries. Mems: 107 institutions in 52 countries. Pres. CATERINA D'AMICO (Italy); Exec. Sec. HENRY VERHASSELT (Belgium). Publ. *Newsletter*.

International Music Council—IMC: Maison de l'UNESCO, 1 rue Miollis, 75732 Paris Cédex 15, France; tel. 1-45-68-25-50; fax 1-43-06-87-98; e-mail imc_cim@compuserve.com; internet www.unesco.org/imc; f. 1949 to foster the exchange of musicians, music (written and recorded), and information between countries and cultures. Mems: 30 international non-governmental organizations, national committees in 65 countries. Pres. FRANS DE RUITER (Netherlands); Sec.-Gen. GUY HUOT.

Members of IMC include:

European Festivals Association: 5 ch. du Sigmal, BP 26, 1296 Coppet, Switzerland; tel. (22) 7768673; fax (22) 7384012; e-mail geneva@eurofestival.net; internet www.eurofestival.net; f. 1952 to maintain high artistic standards and the representative character of art festivals; holds annual General Assembly. Mems: 88 regular music festivals in 29 European countries, Israel, Japan, Lebanan and Mexico. Pres. FRANS DE RUITER. Publ. *Festivals* (annually).

International Association of Music Libraries, Archives and Documentation Centres—IAML: c/o Cataloguing Dept, Carleton Univ. Library, 1125 Colonel By Drive, Ottawa, ON K1S 5B6, Canada; tel. (613) 520-2600; fax (613) 520-3583; e-mail alison hall@carleton.ca; internet www.cilea.it/music/iame/iamchome.htm; f. 1951. Mems: 2,003 institutions and individuals in 58 countries. Pres. JOHN H. ROBERTS (USA); Sec.-Gen. ALISON HALL (Canada). Publ. *Fontes artis musicae* (quarterly).

International Council for Traditional Music—ICTM: Dept of Ethnomusicology, UCLA, 2539 Schoenberg, Box 957178, Los Angeles, California, CA 90095-7178, USA; tel. (310) 794-1858; fax (310) 206-4738; e-mail ictm@arts.ucla.edu; internet www.ethnomusic.ucla.edu/ictm: f. 1947 (as International Folk Music Council) to further the study, practice, documentation, preservation and dissemination of traditional music of all countries; holds conference every two years. Mems: 1,650. Pres. Dr KRISTER MALM (Sweden); Sec.-Gen. Prof. ANTHONY SEEGER. Publs *Yearbook for Traditional Music, ICTM Bulletin* (2 a year), *Directory of Traditional Music* (every 2 years).

International Federation of Musicians: 21 bis rue Victor Massé, 75009 Paris, France; tel. 1-45-26-31-23; fax 1-45-26-31-57; e-mail fimparis2@compuserve.com; internet www.fim-musicians.com/; f. 1948 to promote and protect the interests of musicians in affiliated unions; promotes international exchange of musicians. Mems: 50 unions totalling 200,000 individuals in 43 countries. Pres. JOHN MORTON (UK); Gen. Sec. JEAN VINCENT (France).

International Music Centre (Internationales Musikzentrum—IMZ—Vienna): 1230 Vienna, Speisinger Str. 121–127, Austria; tel. (1) 889 03-15; fax (1) 889 03-1577; e-mail office@imz.at; internet www.imz.at; f. 1961 for the study and dissemination of music through technical media (film, television, radio, gramophone); organizes congresses, seminars and screenings on music in audio-visual media; holds courses and competitions designed to strengthen the relationship between performing artists and audio-visual media. Mems: 110 ordinary mems and 30 associate mems in 33 countries, including 50 broadcasting organizations. Pres. HENK VAN DER MEULEN (Netherlands); Sec.-Gen. FRANZ A. PATAY (Austria). Publ. *IMZ-Magazine* (5 a year, in English).

International Society for Contemporary Music—ISCM: c/o Gaudeamus, Swammerdamstraat 38, 1091 RV Amsterdam, Netherlands; tel. (20) 6947349; fax (20) 6947258; e-mail info@iscm.nl; f. 1922 to promote the development of contemporary music; organizes annual World Music Day. Mems: organizations in 48 countries. Pres. ARNE MELLNAS; Sec.-Gen. HENK HEUVELMANS.

Jeunesses Musicales International—JMI: Palais des Beaux-Arts, 10 rue Royale, 1000 Brussels, Belgium; tel. (2) 513-97-74; fax (2) 514-47-55; e-mail mail@jmi.net; internet www.jmi.net; f. 1945 to enable young people to develop, through music, and to stimulate contacts between member countries. Mems: organizations in 40 countries. Sec.-Gen. DAG FRANZÉN.

World Federation of International Music Competitions—WFIMC: 104 rue de Carouge, 1205 Geneva, Switzerland; tel. (22) 3213620; fax (22) 7811418; e-mail fmcim@iprolink.ch; internet www.wfimc.org; f. 1957 to co-ordinate the arrangements for affiliated competitions and to exchange experience; holds General Assembly annually. Mems: 107. Pres. MARIANNE GRANVIG; Sec.-Gen. RENATE RONNEVELD.

International PEN (A World Association of Writers): 9–10 Charterhouse Bldgs, Goswell Rd, London, EC1M 7AT, United Kingdom; tel. (20) 7253-4308; fax (20) 7253-5711; e-mail intpen@dircon.co.uk; internet www.oneworld.org/internatpen; f. 1921 to promote co-operation between writers. Mems: c. 13,500, 132 centres worldwide. International Pres. HOMERO ARIDJIS; International Sec. TERRY CARLBOM. Publ. *PEN International* (2 a year, in English, French and Spanish, with the assistance of UNESCO).

International Theatre Institute—ITI: Maison de l'UNESCO, 1 rue Miollis, 75732 Paris Cédex 15, France; tel. 1-45-68-26-50; fax 1-45-66-50-40; e-mail iti@unesco.org; internet iti-worldwide.org; f. 1948 to facilitate cultural exchanges and international understanding in the domain of the theatre; holds conferences. Mems: 87 member nations, each with an ITI national centre. Pres. KIM JEONG-OK (Republic of Korea); Sec.-Gen. ANDRÉ-LOUIS PERINETTI.

Organization of World Heritage Cities: 56 Saint-Pierre St, Suite 401, Quebec City, QC, G1K 4AI, Canada; tel. (418) 692-0000; fax (418) 692-5558; e-mail secretariat@ovpm.org; internet www.ovpm.org; f. 1993; aims to assist cities inscribed on the UNESCO World Heritage List to implement the Convention concerning the Protection of the World Cultural and Natural Heritage (1972); promotes co-operation between city authorities, in particular in the management and sustainable development of historic sites; holds a General Assembly, comprising the mayors of member cities, at least every two years. Mems: 164 cities world-wide. Sec.-Gen. D. S. MYRVOLL (acting).

Pan-African Writers' Association—PAWA: PAWA House, Roman Ridge, Accra, Ghana; tel. (21) 773062; fax (21) 773042; e-mail pawa@ghana.com; f. 1989 to link African creative writers, defend the rights of authors and promote awareness of literature. Sec.-Gen. ATUKWEI OKAI (Ghana); Dep. Sec.-Gen. MAHAMADU TRAORÉ DIOP (Senegal).

Royal Asiatic Society of Great Britain and Ireland: 60 Queen's Gardens, London, W2 3AF, United Kingdom; tel. (20) 7724-4742; e-mail info@royalasiaticsociety.org; internet www.royalasiaticsociety.org; f. 1823 for the study of history and cultures of the East. Mems: c. 700, branch societies in Asia. Pres. Prof. A. J. STOCKWELL; Sec. A. P. THOMAS. Publ. *Journal* (3 a year).

Society of African Culture: 25 bis rue des Ecoles, 75005 Paris, France; tel. 1-43-54-15-88; fax 1-43-25-96-67; f. 1956 to create unity and friendship among scholars in Africa, for the encouragement of their own cultures. Mems: national asscns and individuals in 44 countries and territories. Pres. AIMÉ CÉSAIRE; Sec.-Gen. CHRISTIANE YANDÉ DIOP. Publ. *La Revue Présence Africaine* (2 a year).

United World Federation of United Cities: 60 rue de la Boétie, 75008 Paris, France; tel. 1-53-96-05-80; fax 1-53-96-05-81; e-mail cites.unies@wanadoo.fr; f. 1957, as the United Towns Organization, by Le Monde Bilingue (f. 1951); aims to set up permanent links between towns throughout the world, leading to social, cultural, economic and other exchanges favouring world peace, understanding and development; involved in sustainable development and environmental activities at municipal level; mem. of the Habitat II follow-up group. Mems: 4,000 local and regional authorities throughout the world. World Pres. DABY DIAGNE; Dir-Gen. MICHEL BESCOND. Publs *Cités Unies* (quarterly, in French, English and Spanish), *Newsletter* (3 a year in English, French, Italian and Spanish).

World Crafts Council International: Anthrakitou 5 and Tsechouli Street, Kastro Ioanninon, 452 21 Ioannina, Greece; tel. (30) 651072315; fax (30) 651036695; e-mail wis@epcon.gr; internet www.wccwis.gr; f. 1964; aims to strengthen the status of crafts as a vital part of cultural life, to link crafts people around the world, and to foster wider recognition of their work. Mems: national organizations in more than 87 countries. Pres. ELENA AVEROFF. Publs *Annual Report, Newsletter* (2 a year).

Commodities

African Groundnut Council: Trade Fair Complex, Badagry Expressway Km 15, POB 3025, Lagos, Nigeria; tel. (1) 880982; fax (1) 887811; f. 1964 to advise producing countries on marketing policies. Mems: six African countries. Chair. MUSTAFA BELLO; Exec. Sec. Elhadj MOUR MAMADOU SAMB (Senegal). Publ. *Groundnut Review*.

African Oil Palm Development Association—AFOPDA: 15 BP 341, Abidjan 15, Côte d'Ivoire; tel. 25-15-18; f. 1985; seeks to increase production of, and investment in, palm oil. Mems: Benin, Cameroon, Democratic Republic of the Congo, Côte d'Ivoire, Ghana, Guinea, Nigeria, Togo. Exec. Sec. BAUDELAIRE SOUROU.

African Petroleum Producers' Association—APPA: POB 1097, Brazzaville, Republic of the Congo; tel. 83-64-38; fax 83-67-99; f. 1987 by African petroleum-producing countries to reinforce co-operation among regional producers and to stabilize prices; council of ministers responsible for the hydrocarbons sector meets twice a year. Mems: Algeria, Angola, Benin, Cameroon, Democratic Republic of the Congo, Republic of the Congo, Côte d'Ivoire, Egypt, Equatorial Guinea, Gabon, Nigeria. Publ. *APPA Bulletin* (2 a year).

Asian and Pacific Coconut Community—APCC: POB 1343, 3rd Floor, Lina Bldg, Jalan H. R. Rasuna Said Kav. B7, Kuningan, Jakarta 10002, Indonesia; tel. (21) 5221712; fax (21) 5221714; e-mail apcc@indo.net.id; internet www.apcc.org.sg; f. 1969 to promote and co-ordinate all activities of the coconut industry, to achieve higher production and better processing, marketing and research. Mems: Fiji, India, Indonesia, Kiribati, Malaysia, Federated States of Micronesia, Papua New Guinea, Philippines, Samoa, Solomon Islands, Sri Lanka, Thailand, Vanuatu, Viet Nam; assoc. mem.: Palau. Exec. Dir Dr P. RETHINAM. Publs *Cocomunity* (2 a month), *CORD* (2 a year), *Statistical Yearbook, Cocoinfo International* (2 a year).

Association of Coffee Producing Countries—ACPC: Suite B, 5th Floor, 7/10 Old Park Lane, London, W1Y 3LJ, United Kingdom; tel. (20) 7493-4790; fax (20) 7355-1690; e-mail info@acpc.org; internet www.acpc.org; f. 1993; aims to co-ordinate coffee production policies and to co-ordinate the efforts of producer countries to secure a stable situation in the world coffee market; reported to have suspended activities in Jan. 2002. Mems: 29 African, Asian and Latin American countries. Pres. JORGE CARDENAS GUTIERREZ (Colombia); Sec.-Gen. ROBÉRIO OLIVEIRA SILVA.

Association of Natural Rubber Producing Countries—ANRPC: Bangunan Getah Asli, 148 Jalan Ampang, 7th Floor, 50450 Kuala Lumpur, Malaysia; tel. (3) 2611900; fax (3) 2613014; f. 1970 to co-ordinate the production and marketing of natural rubber, to promote technical co-operation amongst members and to bring about fair and stable prices for natural rubber; holds seminars, meetings and training courses on technical and statistical subjects. A joint regional marketing system has been agreed in principle. Mems: India, Indonesia, Malaysia, Papua New Guinea, Singapore, Sri Lanka, Thailand. Sec.-Gen. GNOH CHONG HOCK. Publs *ANRPC Statistical Bulletin* (quarterly), *ANRPC Newsletter*.

Cocoa Producers' Alliance: POB 1718, Western House, 8–10 Broad St, Lagos, Nigeria; tel. (1) 2635506; fax (1) 2635684; f. 1962 to exchange technical and scientific information, to discuss problems of mutual concern to producers, to ensure adequate supplies at remunerative prices and to promote consumption. Mems: Brazil, Cameroon, Côte d'Ivoire, Dominican Republic, Ecuador, Gabon, Ghana, Malaysia, Nigeria, São Tomé and Príncipe, Togo, Trinidad and Tobago. Sec.-Gen. DJEUMO SILAS KAMGA.

Common Fund for Commodities: Postbus 74656, 1070 BR, Amsterdam, Netherlands; tel. (20) 575-4949; fax (20) 676-0231; e-mail managing.director@common-fund.org; internet www.common-fund.org; f. 1989 as the result of an UNCTAD negotiation conference; finances commodity development measures including research, marketing, productivity improvements and vertical diversification, with the aim of increasing the long-term competitiveness of particular commodities; paid-in capital US $165m. Mems: 104 countries and the EC, OAU and COMESA. Man. Dir (also Chief Exec. and Chair.) ROLF BOEHNKE.

European Aluminium Association—EAA: 12 ave de Broqueville, 1150 Brussels, Belgium; tel. (2) 775-63-63; fax (2) 779-05-31; e-mail eaa@eaa.be; internet www.eaa,net; f. 1981 to encourage studies, research and technical co-operation, to make representations to international bodies and to assist national asscns in dealing with national authorities. Mems: individual producers of primary aluminium, 17 national groups for wrought producers, the Organization of European Aluminium Smelters, representing producers of recycled aluminium, and the European Aluminium Foil Association, representing foil rollers and converters. Chair. R. BELDA; Sec.-Gen. P. DE SCHRYNMAKERS. Publs *Annual Report, EAA Quarterly Report*.

European Association for the Trade in Jute and Related Products: Adriaan Goekooplaan 5, POB 29822, 2502 LV, The Hague, Netherlands; tel. (70) 330-4659; fax (70) 351-2777; e-mail eurojute@verbondgroothandel.nl; f. 1970 to maintain contacts between national asscns, permit the exchange of information and represent the interests of the trade; carries out scientific research. Mems: enterprises in eight European countries. Sec.-Gen. H. J. J. KRUIPER.

European Committee of Sugar Manufacturers: 182 ave de Tervueren, 1150 Brussels, Belgium; tel. (2) 762-07-60; fax (2) 771-00-26; e-mail cefs@cefs.org; internet www.ib.be.cefs; f. 1954 to collect statistics and information, conduct research and promote co-operation between national organizations. Mems: national asscns in 15 European countries. Pres. RENATO PICCO; Dir-Gen. J. L. BARJOL.

Group of Latin American and Caribbean Sugar Exporting Countries—GEPLACEA: Paseo de la Reforma 1030, Lomas de Chapultepec, México DF 11000, Mexico; tel. (55) 520-9711; fax (55) 520-5089; e-mail geplacea@mail.internet.com.mx; internet www.geplacea.ipn.mx; f. 1974 to serve as a forum for consultation on the production and sale of sugar; to contribute to the adoption of agreed positions at international meetings on sugar; to provide training and the transfer of technology; to exchange scientific and technical knowledge on agriculture and the sugar industry; to co-ordinate the various branches of sugar processing; and to co-ordinate policies of action, in order to achieve fair and remunerative prices. Mems: 23 Latin American and Caribbean countries (accounting for about 45% of world sugar exports and 66% of world cane sugar production). Exec. Sec. LUIS PONCE DE LEÓN.

Inter-African Coffee Organization—IACO (Organisation internationale du café—OIAC): BP V210, Abidjan, Côte d'Ivoire; tel. 20-21-61-31; fax 20-21-62-12; e-mail oiac-iaco@aviso.ci; internet www.oiac.org; f. 1960 to adopt a common policy on the marketing and consumption of coffee; aims to collaborate on research, in particular through the African Coffee Research Network (ACRN); seeks improvement in the quality of coffee exports. Mems: 25 coffee-producing countries in Africa. Chair. ERIC-VICTOR KAHÉ KPLOHOUROU (Côte d'Ivoire); Sec.-Gen. JOSEFA LEONEL CORREIA SACKO (Angola).

International Cadmium Association: 12110 Sunset Hills Rd, Suite 110, Reston, VA 22090, USA; tel. (703) 709-1400; fax (703) 709-1402; f. 1976; covers all aspects of the production and use of cadmium and its compounds; includes almost all producers and users of cadmium. Chair. DAVID SINCLAIR (USA).

International Cocoa Organization—ICCO: 22 Berners St, London, W1P 3DB, United Kingdom; tel. (20) 7637-3211; fax (20) 7631-0114; e-mail exec.dir@icco.org; internet www.icco.org; f. 1973 under the first International Cocoa Agreement, 1972. The ICCO supervises the implementation of the agreements, and provides member governments with conference facilities and up-to-date information on the world cocoa economy and the operation of the agreements. The sixth International Cocoa Agreement was signed in March 2001; it will enter into force in October 2003. Mems: 19 exporting countries and 23 importing countries; and the European Union. Exec. Dir EDOUARD KOUAMÉ (Côte d'Ivoire); Council Chair. 2001–02 ADRIAN FRIJLINK (Netherlands). Publs *Quarterly Bulletin of Cocoa Statistics, Annual Report, World Cocoa Directory, Cocoa Newsletter*, studies on the world cocoa economy.

International Coffee Organization—ICO: 22 Berners St, London, W1P 4DD, United Kingdom; tel. (20) 7580-8591; fax (20) 7580-6129; e-mail info@ico.org; internet www.ico.org; f. 1963 under the International Coffee Agreement, 1962, which was renegotiated in 1968, 1976, 1983,1994 (extended in 1999) and 2001; aims to improve international co-operation and provide a forum for intergovernmental consultations on coffee matters; to facilitate international trade in coffee by the collection, analysis and dissemination of statistics; to act as a centre for the collection, exchange and publication of coffee information; to promote studies in the field of coffee; and to encourage an increase in coffee consumption. Mems: 45 exporting and 18 importing countries. Chair. of Council LAKSHMI VENKATACHALAM (India); Exec. Dir NÉSTOR OSORIO (Colombia).

International Confederation of European Beet Growers (Confédération internationale des betteraviers européens—CIBE): 29 rue du Général Foy, 75008 Paris, France; tel. 1-44-69-41-80; fax 1-42-93-28-93; f. 1925 to act as a centre for the co-ordination and dissemination of information about beet sugar production and the industry; to represent the interests of sugar beet growers at an international level. Mems: asscns in Austria, Belgium, Czech Republic, Denmark, Finland, France, Germany, Greece, Hungary, Ireland, Italy, Netherlands, Poland, Portugal, Romania, Slovakia, Spain, Sweden, Switzerland, United Kingdom. Pres. J. KIRSCH (Germany); Sec.-Gen. H. CHAVANES (France).

International Cotton Advisory Committee—ICAC: 1629 K St, NW, Suite 702, Washington, DC 20006, USA; tel. (202) 463-6660; fax (202) 463-6950; e-mail secretariat@icac.org; internet www.icac.org; f. 1939 to observe developments in world cotton; to collect and disseminate statistics; to suggest measures for the furtherance of international collaboration in maintaining and developing a sound world cotton economy; and to provide a forum for international discussions on cotton prices. Mems: 40 countries. Exec. Dir Dr TERRY TOWNSEND (USA). Publs *Cotton: This Month, Cotton: Review of the World Situation, Cotton: World Statistics, The ICAC Recorder.*

International Grains Council—IGC: 1 Canada Sq., Canary Wharf, London, E14 5AE, United Kingdom; tel. (20) 7513-1122; fax (20) 7513-0630; e-mail igc@igc.org.uk; internet www.igc.org.uk; f. 1949 as International Wheat Council, present name adopted in 1995; responsible for the administration of the Grains Trade Convention of the International Grains Agreement, 1995; aims to further international co-operation in all aspects of trade in grains and to promote the freest possible flow of this trade, in particular, to support developing countries; seeks to contribute to the stability of the international grain market; acts as a forum for consultations between members; provides comprehensive information on the international grain market. Mems: 28 countries and the EU. Exec. Dir. G. DENIS. Publs *World Grain Statistics* (annually), *Wheat and Coarse Grain Shipments* (annually), *Report for the Fiscal Year* (annually), *Grain Market Report* (monthly), *Grain Market Indicators* (weekly).

International Jute Study Group—IJSG: 145 Monipuriparu, Old Airport Rd, Dhaka 1215, Bangladesh; tel. (2) 9125581; fax (2) 9125248; e-mail ijoinf@bdmail.net; f. 2002 as successor to International Jute Organization (f. 1984 in accordance with an agreement made by 48 producing and consuming countries in 1982, under the auspices of UNCTAD); aims to improve the jute economy and the quality of jute and jute products through research and development projects and market promotion.

International Lead and Zinc Study Group—ILZSG: 2 King St, London, SW1Y 6QP, United Kingdom; tel. (20) 7484-3300; fax (20) 7930-4635; e-mail root@ilzsg.org; internet www.ilzsg.org; f. 1959 for intergovernmental consultation on world trade in lead and zinc; conducts studies and provides information on trends in supply and demand. Mems: 28 countries. Chair. A. IGNATOW (Canada); Sec.-Gen. DON SMALE. Publ. *Lead and Zinc Statistics* (monthly).

International Molybdenum Association—IMOA: 2 Baron's Gate, 33 Rothschild Rd, London, W4 5HT, United Kingdom; tel. (20) 8742-2274; fax (20) 8742-7345; e-mail itia.imoa@compuserve.com; internet www.imoa.org.uk/; f. 1989; collates statistics; promotes the use of molybdenum; monitors health and environmental issues in the molybdenum industry. Mems: 49. Pres. J. GRAELL; Sec.-Gen. MICHAEL MABY.

International Olive Oil Council: Príncipe de Vergara 154, 28002 Madrid, Spain; tel. (91) 59033638; fax (91) 5631263; e-mail iooc@internationaloliveoil.org; internet www.internationaloliveoil.org; f. 1959 to administer the International Agreement on Olive Oil and Table Olives, which aims to promote international co-operation in connection with problems of the world economy for olive products; works to prevent unfair competition, to encourage the production and consumption of, and international trade in, olive products, and to reduce the disadvantages caused by fluctuations of supplies on the market. Mems: of the 1986 Agreement (Fourth Agreement, amended and extended in 1993): eight mainly producing countries, one mainly importing country, and the European Commission. Dir FAUSTO LUCHETTI. Publs *Information Sheet of the IOOC* (fortnightly, in French and Spanish), *OLIVAE* (5 a year, in English, French, Italian and Spanish).

International Pepper Community—IPC: 4th Floor, Lina Bldg, Jalan H. R. Rasuna Said, Kav. B7, Kuningan, Jakarta 12920, Indonesia; tel. (21) 5224902; fax (21) 5224905; e-mail ipc@indo.net.id; internet www.ipcnet.org; f. 1972 for promoting, co-ordinating and harmonizing all activities relating to the pepper economy. Mems: six exporting countries, 30 importing countries. Exec. Dir Dr K. P. G. MENON. Publs *Pepper Statistical Yearbook, International Pepper News Bulletin* (quarterly), *Directory of Pepper Exporters, Directory of Pepper Importers, Weekly Prices Bulletin, Pepper Market Review.*

International Platinum Association: Kroegerstr. 5, 60313 Frankfurt-am-Main, Germany; tel. (69) 287941; fax (69) 283601; links principal producers and fabricators of platinum. Man. Dir MARCUS NURDIN.

International Rubber Study Group: Heron House, 109–115 Wembley Hill Rd, Wembley, HA9 8DA, United Kingdom; tel.

(20) 8903-7727; fax (20) 8903-2848; e-mail irsg@compuserve .com; internet www.rubberstudy.org; f. 1944 to provide a forum for the discussion of problems affecting synthetic and natural rubber and to provide statistical and other general information on rubber. Mems: 18 governments. Sec.-Gen. Dr A. F. S. BUDIMAN (Indonesia). Publs *Rubber Statistical Bulletin* (monthly), *International Rubber Digest* (monthly), *Proceedings of International Rubber Forums* (annually), *World Rubber Statistics Handbook, Key Rubber Indicators, Rubber Statistics Yearbook* (annually), *Rubber Economics Yearbook* (annually), *Outlook for Elastomers* (annually).

International Silk Association: 34 rue de la Charité, 69002 Lyon, France; tel. 4-78-42-10-79; fax 4-78-37-56-72; e-mail isa -silk.ais-sole@wanadoo.fr; f. 1949 to promote closer collaboration between all branches of the silk industry and trade, develop the consumption of silk, and foster scientific research; collects and disseminates information and statistics relating to the trade and industry; organizes biennial Congresses. Mems: employers' and technical organizations in 40 countries. Pres. MICHELE CANEPA (Italy); Gen. Sec. R. CURRIE. Publs *ISA Newsletter* (monthly), congress reports, standards, trade rules, etc.

International Spice Group: c/o International Trade Centre (UNCTAD/WTO), 54–56 rue de Montbrillant, 1202 Geneva, Switzerland; tel. (22) 730-01-01; fax (22) 730-02-54; e-mail itcreg@intracen.org; f. 1983 to provide a forum for producers and consumers of spices; works to increase the consumption of spices. Mems: 33 producer countries, 15 importing countries. Chair. HERNAL HAMILTON (Jamaica).

International Sugar Organization: 1 Canada Sq., Canary Wharf, London, E14 5AA, United Kingdom; tel. (20) 7513-1144; fax (20) 7513-1146; e-mail exdir@isosugar.org; internet www.isosugar.org; administers the International Sugar Agreement (1992), with the objectives of stimulating co-operation, facilitating trade and encouraging demand; aims to improve conditions in the sugar market through debate, analysis and studies; serves as a forum for discussion; holds annual seminars and workshops; sponsors projects from developing countries. Mems: 58 countries producing some 75% of total world sugar. Exec. Dir Dr P. BARON. Publs *Sugar Year Book, Monthly Statistical Bulletin, Market Report and Press Summary, Ouarterly Market Review*, seminar proceedings.

International Tea Committee Ltd: Sir John Lyon House, 5 High Timber St, London, EC4V 3NH, United Kingdom; tel. (20) 7248-4672; fax (20) 7329-6955; e-mail info@intteacomm.co.uk; internet www.intteacomm.co.uk; f. 1933 to administer the International Tea Agreement; now serves as a statistical and information centre; in 1979 membership was extended to include consuming countries. Producer mems: national tea boards or asscns in eight countries; consumer mems: United Kingdom Tea Assn, Tea Assn of the USA Inc., Comité européen du thé and the Tea Council of Canada; assoc. mems: Netherlands and UK ministries of agriculture, Cameroon Development Corpn. Chair. M. J. BUNSTON. Publs *Annual Bulletin of Statistics, Monthly Statistical Summary.*

International Tea Promotion Association: POB 20064, Tea Board of Kenya, Nairobi, Kenya; tel. (2) 220241; fax (2) 331650; f. 1979. Mems: eight countries. Chair. GEORGE M. KIMANI. Publ. *International Tea Journal* (2 a year).

International Tobacco Growers' Association—ITGA: Apdo 5, 6001-081 Castelo Branco, Portugal; tel. (72) 325901; fax (72) 325906; e-mail itga@mail.telepac.pt; internet www.tobaccoleaf .org; f. 1984 to provide a forum for the exchange of views and information of interest to tobacco producers. Mems: 22 countries producing over 80% of the world's internationally traded tobacco. Pres. MARCELO QUEVEDO (Argentina); Exec. Dir ANTONIO ABRUNHOSA (Portugal). Publs *Tobacco Courier* (quarterly), *Tobacco Briefing.*

International Tropical Timber Organization—ITTO: International Organizations Center, 5th Floor, Pacifico-Yokohama, 1-1-1, Minato-Mirai, Nishi-ku, Yokohama 220, Japan; tel. (45) 223-1110; fax (45) 223-1111; e-mail itto@itto.or.jp; internet www.itto.or.jp; f. 1985 under the International Tropical Timber Agreement (1983); a new treaty, ITTA 1994, came into force in 1997; provides a forum for consultation and co-operation between countries that produce and consume tropical timber; facilitates progress towards 'Objective 2000' (all trade in tropical timber to be derived from sustainably managed resources) financed by a special Bali Partnership Fund; conducts research and development, reafforestation and forest management projects. Mems: 31 producing and 25 consuming countries and the EU. Exec. Dir Dr MANOEL SOBRAL FILHO. Publs *Annual Review and Assessment of the World Timber Situation, Tropical Timber Market Information Service* (every 2 weeks), *Tropical Forest Update* (quarterly).

International Tungsten Industry Association—ITIA: 2 Baron's Gate, 33 Rothschild Rd, London, W4 5HT, United Kingdom; tel. (20) 8742-2274; fax (20) 8742-7345; e-mail itiaimoa @compuserve.com; internet www.itia.org.uk/; f. 1988 (fmrly Primary Tungsten Asscn, f. 1975); promotes use of tungsten; collates statistics; prepares market reports; monitors health and environmental issues in the tungsten industry. Mems: 51. Pres. D. LANDSPERGER; Sec.-Gen. MICHAEL MABY.

International Vine and Wine Office: 18 rue d'Aguesseau, 75008 Paris, France; tel. 1-44-94-80-80; fax 1-42-66-90-63; e-mail oiv@oiv.int; internet www.oiv.int; f. 1924 to study all the scientific, technical, economic and human problems concerning the vine and its products; to spread knowledge and facilitate contacts between researchers. Mems: 45 countries. Dir-Gen. GEORGES DUTRUC-ROSSET. Publs *Bulletin de l'OIV* (every 2 months), *Lettre de l'OIV* (monthly), *Lexique de la Vigne et du Vin, Recueil des méthodes internationales d'analyse des vins, Code international des Pratiques oenologiques, Codex oenologique international,* numerous scientific publications.

International Zinc Association: 168 ave de Tervueren, 1150 Brussels, Belgium; tel. (2) 776-00-70; fax (2) 776-00-89; e-mail email@iza.com; internet www.iza.com; f. 1990 to represent the world zinc industry; provide a forum for senior executives to address global issues requiring industry-wide action; consider new applications for zinc and zinc products; foster understanding of zinc's role in the environment; build a sustainable development policy. Mems: 28 zinc-producing countries. Exec. Dir EDOUARD GERVAIS. Publ. *Zinc Protects* (4 a year).

Lead Development Association International: 42 Weymouth St, London, W1G 6NP, United Kingdom; tel. (20) 7499-8422; fax (20) 7493-1555; e-mail eng@ldaint.org; internet www.ldaint .org; f. 1956; provides authoritative information on the use of lead and its compounds. Financed by lead producers and users in the United Kingdom, Europe and elsewhere. Dir Dr D. N. WILSON (UK).

Regional Association of Oil and Natural Gas Companies in Latin America and the Caribbean (Asociación Regional de Empresas de Petróleo y Gas Natural en Latinoamérica y el Caribe—ARPEL): Javier de Viana 2345, Casilla de correo 1006, 11200 Montevideo, Uruguay; tel. (2) 4106993; fax (2) 4109207; e-mail arpel@arpel.org.uy; internet www.arpel.org; f. 1965 as the Mutual Assistance of the Latin American Oil Companies; aims to initiate and implement activities for the development of the oil and natural gas industry in Latin America and the Caribbean; promotes the expansion of business opportunities and the improvement of the competitive advantages of its members; promotes guide-lines in support of competition in the sector; and supports the efficient and sustainable exploitation of hydrocarbon resources and the supply of products and services. Works in co-operation with international organizations, governments, regulatory agencies, technical institutions, universities and non-governmental organizations. Mems: state enterprises in Argentina, Bolivia, Brazil, Canada, Chile, Colombia, Costa Rica, Cuba, Ecuador, Jamaica, Mexico, Nicaragua, Paraguay, Peru, Suriname, Trinidad and Tobago, Uruguay, Venezuela. Exec. Sec. JOSÉ FÉLIX GARCÍA GARCÍA. Publ. *Boletín Técnico.*

Sugar Association of the Caribbean (Inc.): c/o Caroni (1975) Ltd, Brechin Castle, Conva, Trinidad and Tobago; tel. 636-2449; fax 636-2847; f. 1942. Mems: national sugar cos of Barbados, Belize, Guyana, Jamaica and Trinidad and Tobago, and Sugar Asscn of St Kitts–Nevis–Anguilla. Chair. KARL JAMES. Sec. AZIZ MOHAMMED. Publs *SAC Handbook, SAC Annual Report, Proceedings of Meetings of WI Sugar Technologists.*

Union of Banana-Exporting Countries—UPEB: Apdo 4273, Bank of America, piso 7, Panamá 5, Panama; tel. 263-6266; fax 264-8355; e-mail iicapan@pan.gbm.net; f. 1974 as an intergovernmental agency to assist in the cultivation and marketing of bananas and to secure prices; collects statistics. Mems: Colombia, Costa Rica, Guatemala, Honduras, Nicaragua, Panama, Venezuela. Exec. Dir J. ENRIQUE BETANCOURT. Publs *Informe UPEB, Fax UPEB, Anuario de Estadísticas*, bibliographies.

West Africa Rice Development Association—WARDA: 01 BP 2551 Bouaké 01, Côte d'Ivoire; tel. 31-63-45-14; fax 31-63-47-14; e-mail warda@cgiar.org; internet www.cgiar.org/warda; f. 1971 as a mem. of the network of agricultural research centres supported by the Consultative Group on International Agricultural Research (CGIAR, q.v.); aims to contribute to food security and poverty eradication in poor rural and urban populations, particularly in West and Central Africa, through research, partnerships, capacity strengthening and policy support on rice-based systems; promotes sustainable agricultural development based on environmentally-sound management of natural resources; maintains research stations in Côte d'Ivoire, Nigeria and Senegal; provides training and consulting services. WARDA. Mems: 17 west African countries. Dir-Gen. Dr KANAYO F. NWANZE (Nigeria). Publs *Annual Report, Current Contents at WARDA* (monthly), *Programme Report, Advances in Rice Research*, proceedings, leaflets, brochures.

West Indian Sea Island Cotton Association (Inc.): c/o Barbados Agricultural Development Corporation, Fairy Valley, Christ Church, Barbados. Mems: organizations in Antigua-Barbuda, Barbados, Jamaica, Montserrat and St Christopher and Nevis. Pres. E. LE ROACH; Sec. MICHAEL I. EDGHILL.

World Association of Beet and Cane Growers—WABCG: c/o IFAP, 60 rue St Lazare, 75009 Paris, France; tel. 1-45-26-05-53; fax 1-48-74-72-12; e-mail wabcg@ifap.org; internet www.ifap.org/wabcg; f 1983 (formal adoption of Constitution, 1984); groups national organizations of independent sugar beet and cane growers; aims to boost the economic, technical and social development of the beet- and cane-growing sector; works to strengthen professional representation in international and national fora; serves as a forum for discussion and exchange of information. Mems: 21 beet-growing organizations, 14 cane-growing organizations, from 30 countries. Sec. MIKE GARROD. Publs *World Sugar Farmer News* (quarterly), *World Sugar Farmer Fax Sheet, WABCG InfoFlash*, study reports.

World Federation of Diamond Bourses: 62 Pelikaanstraat, 2018 Antwerp, Belgium; tel. (3) 234-07-78; fax (3) 226-40-73; e-mail wfdb@iway.be; internet www.worldfed.com; f. 1947 to protect the interests of affiliated organizations and their individual members and to settle or arbitrate in disputes. Mems: 24 bourses in 15 countries. Pres. A. FISCHLER (Belgium); Sec.-Gen. G. GOLDSCHMIDT (Belgium).

World Gold Council: 45 Pall Mall, London, SW1Y 5JG, United Kingdom; tel. (20) 7930-5171; fax (20) 7839-6561; internet www.gold.org; f. 1987 as world-wide international asscn of gold producers, to promote the demand for gold. Chair. R. M. GODSELL; Chief Exec. HARUKO FUKUDA (Japan).

World Sugar Research Organisation—WSRO: Science and Technology Centre, University of Reading, Earley Gate, Whiteknights Rd, Reading, RG6 6BZ, United Kingdom; tel. (118) 935-7000; fax (118) 935-7301; e-mail info@wsro.org; internet www.wsro.org; an alliance of sugar producers, processors, marketers and users; monitors and communicates research on role of sugar and other carbohydrates in nutrition and health; organizes conferences and symposia; operates a database of information; serves as a forum for exchange of views. Mems: 73 orgs in 30 countries. Publs *WSRO Research Bulletin* (on-line, monthly), *WSRO Newsletter*, papers and conference proceedings.

Development and Economic Co-operation

African Capacity Building Foundation—ACBF: Southampton Life Centre, 7th Floor, Jason Moyo Ave/Second St, POB 1562, Harare, Zimbabwe; tel. (4) 790398; fax (4) 702915; e-mail root@acbf-pact.org; internet www.acbf-pact.org; f. 1991 by the World Bank, UNDP, the African Development Bank, African and non-African governments; assists African countries to strengthen and build local capacity in economic policy analysis and development management. In January 2000 the Partnership for Capacity Building in Africa (PACT) was integrated into the ACBF. Exec. Sec. Dr SOUMANA SAKO.

African Training and Research Centre in Administration for Development (Centre africain de formation et de recherche administratives pour le développement—CAFRAD): ave Mohamed V, BP 310, Tangier, 90001 Morocco; tel. (1) 307269; fax (9) 325785; e-mail cafrad@cafrad.org; internet www.cafrad.org; f. 1964 by agreement between Morocco and UNESCO; undertakes research into administrative problems in Africa and documents results; provides a consultation service for governments and organizations; holds workshops to train senior civil servants; prepares the Biennial Pan-African Conference of Ministers of the Civil Service. Mems: 37 African countries. Chair. M'HAMED EL KHALIFA; Dir-Gen. Prof. TIJJANI MUHAMMAD BANDE. Publs *African Administrative Studies* (2 a year), *Research Studies, CAFRAD News* (2 a year, in English, French and Arabic).

Afro-Asian Rural Development Organization—AARDO: No. 2, State Guest Houses Complex, Chanakyapuri, New Delhi 110 021, India; tel. (11) 6877783; fax (11) 6115937; e-mail aardohq@nde.vsnl.net.in; internet www.aardo.org; f. 1962 to act as a catalyst for the co-operative restructuring of rural life in Africa and Asia and to explore opportunities for the co-ordination of efforts to promote rural welfare and to eradicate hunger, thirst, disease, illiteracy and poverty; carries out collaborative research on development issues; organizes training; encourages the exchange of information; holds international conferences and seminars; awards 100 individual training fellowships at nine institutes in Egypt, India, Japan, the Republic of Korea and Taiwan. Mems: 12 African countries, 14 Asian countries, one African associate. Sec.-Gen. Dr BAHAR MUNIP. Publs *Afro-Asian Journal of Rural Development, Annual Report, Journal of Rural Reconstruction* (2 a year), *AARDO Newsletter* (2 a year).

Agence Intergouvernementale de la Francophonie: 13 quai André Citroën, 75015 Paris, France; tel. 1-44-37-33-00; fax 1-45-79-14-98; internet agence.francophonie.org; f. 1970 as l'Agence de coopération culturelle et technique; promotes co-operation among French-speaking countries in the areas of education, culture, science and technology; implements decisions of the Sommet francophone (q.v.); technical and financial assistance has been given to projects in every member country, mainly to aid rural people. Mems: 50 countries and territories. Gen. Dir ROGER DEHAYBE (Belgium). Publ. *Journal de l'Agence de la Francophonie* (6 a year).

Arab Authority for Agricultural Investment and Development—AAAID: POB 2102, Khartoum, Sudan; tel. (11) 780777; fax (11) 772600; e-mail aaidsd@sudanmail.net; f. 1976 to accelerate agricultural development in the Arab world and to ensure food security; acts principally by equity participation in agricultural projects in Iraq, Sudan and Tunisia; signed a co-operation agreement with IFAD in Nov. 2000. Mems: 16 countries. Pres. ABDULKARIM AL-AMRI. Publ. *Annual Report* (English and Arabic).

Arab Co-operation Council: POB 2640, Khartoum, Sudan; tel. (11) 73646; f. 1989 to promote economic co-operation between member states, including free movement of workers, joint projects in transport, communications and agriculture, and eventual integration of trade and monetary policies. Mems: Egypt, Iraq, Jordan, Yemen.

Arab Gulf Programme for the United Nations Development Organizations—AGFUND: POB 18371, Riyadh 11415, Saudi Arabia; tel. (1) 4418888; fax (1) 4412962; e-mail info@agfund.org; internet www.agfund.org; f. 1981 to provide grants for projects in mother and child care carried out by United Nations organizations, Arab non-governmental organizations and other international bodies, and to co-ordinate assistance by the nations of the Gulf; financing comes mainly from member states, all of which are members of OPEC. Mems: Bahrain, Iraq, Kuwait, Oman, Qatar, Saudi Arabia, UAE. Pres. HRH Prince TALAL IBN ABD AL-AZIZ AL-SAUD.

Arctic Council: c/o Ministry of Foreign Affairs, Unit for Northern Dimension, POB 176, 00161 Helsinki, Finland; tel. (9) 1341-6187; fax (9) 1341-6120; e-mail johanna.lammi@formin.fi; internet www.arctic-council.org; f. 1996 to promote co-ordination of activities in the Arctic region, in particular in the areas of education, development and environmental protection. Mems: govts of eight circumpolar countries.

Association of Caribbean States—ACS: 5–7 Sweet Briar Rd, St Clair, POB 660, Port of Spain, Trinidad and Tobago; tel.

622-9575; fax 622-1653; e-mail mail@acs-aec.org; internet www.acs-aec.org; f. 1994 by the Governments of the 13 CARICOM countries (q.v.) and Colombia, Costa Rica, Cuba, Dominican Republic, El Salvador, Guatemala, Haiti, Honduras, Mexico, Nicaragua, Suriname and Venezuela. Aims to promote economic integration, sustainable development and co-operation in the region; to co-ordinate participation in multilateral forums; to undertake concerted action to protect the environment, particularly the Caribbean Sea; and to co-operate in the areas of science and technology, health, trade, transport, tourism, education and culture. Policy is determined by a Ministerial Council and implemented by a Secretariat based in Port of Spain. In December 2001 a third Summit of Heads of State and Government was convened in Venezuela; a Plan of Action focusing on issues of sustainable tourism, trade, transport and natural disasters was agreed. Mems: 25 signatory states, three associate members, 14 observer countries. Sec.-Gen. Prof. Dr NORMAN GIRVAN (Jamaica).

Association of Development Financing Institutions in Asia and the Pacific—ADFIAP: Skyland Plaza, 2nd Floor, Sen. Gil J. Puyat Ave, Majati City, Metro Manila, 1200 Philippines; tel. (2) 816-1672; fax (2) 817-6498; e-mail inquire@adfiap.org; internet www.adfiap.org; f. 1976 to promote the interests and economic development of the respective countries of its member institutions, through development financing. Mems: 81 institutions in 35 countries. Chair. ASWIN KONGSIRI (Thailand); Sec.-Gen. ORLANDO P. PEÑA (Philippines). Publs *Asian Banking Digest, Journal of Development Finance* (2 a year), *ADFIAP Newsletter,* surveys.

Benelux Economic Union: 39 rue de la Régence, 1000 Brussels, Belgium; tel. (2) 519-38-11; fax (2) 513-42-06; e-mail r.vanimpe@benelux.be; internet www.benelux.be; f. 1960 to bring about the economic union of Belgium, Luxembourg and the Netherlands; aims to introduce common policies in the field of cross-border co-operation and harmonize standards and intellectual property legislation; structure comprises: Committee of Ministers; Council; Court of Justice; Consultative Inter-Parliamentary Council; the Economic and Social Advisory Council; and the General Secretariat. Sec.-Gen. Dr B. M. J. HENNEKAM (Netherlands). Publs *Benelux Newsletter, Bulletin Benelux.*

Caribbean Council for Europe: Westminster Palace Gardens, Suite 18, 1–7 Artillery Row, London, SW1P 1RR, United Kingdom; tel. (20) 7799-1521; e-mail caribbean@compuserve.com; f. 1992 by the Caribbean Association of Industry and Commerce and other regional organizations, to represent the interests of the Caribbean private sector in the European Union; organizes regular Europe/Caribbean Conference. Chair. YESU PERSAUD; Exec. Dir DAVID JESSOP.

Caritas Internationalis (International Confederation of Catholic Organizations for charitable and social action): Palazzo San Calisto, 00120 Città del Vaticano; tel. (06) 6988-7197; fax (06) 6988-7237; e-mail caritas.internationalis@caritas.va; internet www.caritas.org; f. 1950 to study problems arising from poverty, their causes and possible solutions; national mem. organizations undertake assistance and development activities. The Confederation co-ordinates emergency relief and development projects, and represents mems at international level. Mems: 156 national orgs. Pres. Mgr AFFONSO GREGORY, Bishop of Imperatriz (Brazil); Sec.-Gen. DUNCAN MACLAREN. Publs *Caritas Matters* (quarterly), *Emergency Calling* (2 a year).

Central European Free Trade Association—CEFTA: internet www.ijs.si/cefta; f. 1992, entered into force 1993; free-trade agreement covering a number of sectors. Mems: Bulgaria, Czech Republic, Hungary, Poland, Romania, Slovakia, Slovenia.

Colombo Plan: Bank of Ceylon Merchant Tower, 28 St Michael's Rd, Colombo 03, Sri Lanka; tel. (1) 564448; fax (1) 564531; e-mail cplan@slt.lk; internet www.colombo-plan.org; f. 1950 by seven Commonwealth countries, to encourage economic and social development in Asia and the Pacific. The Plan comprises the Programme for Public Administration, to provide training for officials in the context of a market-orientated economy; the Programme for Private Sector Development, which organizes training programmes to stimulate the economic benefits of development of the private sector; a Drug Advisory Programme, to encourage regional co-operation in efforts to control drug-related problems, in particular through human resources development; a programme to establish a South-South Technical Co-operation Data Bank, to collate, analyse and publish information in order to facilitate south-south co-operation; and a Staff College for Technician Education (see below). All programmes are voluntarily funded; developing countries are encouraged to become donors and to participate in economic and technical co-operation activities among developing mems. Mems: 24 countries. Sec.-Gen. U. SARAT CHANDRAN (India). Publs *Annual Report, Colombo Plan Focus* (quarterly), Consultative Committee proceedings (every 2 years).

Colombo Plan Staff College for Technician Education: POB 7500, Domestic Airport Post Office, NAIA, Pasay City 1300, Metro Manila, Philippines; tel. (2) 6310991; fax (2) 6310996; e-mail cpsc@skyinet.net; internet www.cpsc.org.ph; f. 1973 with the support of member Governments of the Colombo Plan; aims to enhance the development of technician education systems in developing mem. countries. Dir Dr BERNARDO F. ADIVISO. Publ. *CPSC Quarterly.*

Communauté économique des états de l'Afrique centrale—CEEAC (Economic Community of Central African States): BP 2112, Libreville, Gabon; tel. 73-35-48; f. 1983, operational 1 January 1985; aims to promote co-operation between member states by abolishing trade restrictions, establishing a common external customs tariff, linking commercial banks, and setting up a development fund, over a period of 12 years; works to combat drug abuse and to promote regional security. Mems: 10 African countries. Sec.-Gen. LOUIS-SYLVAIN GOMA (Republic of the Congo).

Community of the Sahel-Saharan States (Communauté des états du Sahel et du Sahara—CEN-SAD): Tripoli, Libya; f. 1997; fmrly known as COMESSA; aims to strengthen co-operation between signatory states; established a joint commission with the OAU, in 1998, to support mediation in the conflicts between Eritrea and Ethiopia. Mems: Burkina Faso, Central African Republic, Chad, Djibouti, Egypt, Eritrea, The Gambia, Libya, Mali, Morocco, Niger, Nigeria, Senegal, Sudan, Tunisia. Sec.-Gen. ALMADANI AL-AZHARI (Libya).

Conseil de l'Entente (Entente Council): 01 BP 3734, Abidjan 01, Côte d'Ivoire; tel. 33-28-35; fax 33-11-49; f. 1959 to promote economic development in the region. The Council's Mutual Aid and Loan Guarantee Fund (Fonds d'entraide et de garantie des emprunts) finances development projects, including agricultural projects, support for small and medium-sized enterprises, vocational training centres, research into new sources of energy and building of hotels to encourage tourism. A Convention of Assistance and Co-operation was signed in February 1996. Holds annual summit (2000: Kara, Togo). Mems: Benin, Burkina Faso, Côte d'Ivoire, Niger, Togo. Sec.-Gen. PAUL KOUAMÉ. Publ. *Rapport d'activité* (annually).

Communauté économique du bétail et de la viande (CEBV) du Conseil de l'Entente (Livestock and Meat Economic Community of the Entente Council): 01 BP 638 Ouagadougou, Burkina Faso; tel. 30-62-67; fax 30-62-68; e-mail cebv@cenatrin.bf; internet www.cenatrin.bf/cebv; f. 1970 to promote the production, processing and marketing of livestock and meat; negotiates between members and with third countries on technical and financial co-operation and co-ordinated legislation; attempts to co-ordinate measures to combat drought and cattle diseases. Mems: states belonging to the Conseil de l'Entente. Exec. Sec. Dr ELIE LADIKPO.

Council of American Development Foundations—SOLIDARIOS: Calle 6 No. 10 Paraiso, Apdo Postal 620, Santo Domingo, Dominican Republic; tel. (809) 549-5111; fax (809) 544-0550; e-mail solidarios@codetel.net.do; f. 1972; exchanges information and experience, arranges technical assistance, raises funds to organize training programmes and scholarships; administers development fund to finance programmes carried out by members through a loan guarantee programme; provides consultancy services. Mem. foundations provide technical and financial assistance to low-income groups for rural, housing and microenterprise development projects. Mems: 18 institutional mems in 14 Latin American and Caribbean countries. Pres. MERCEDES P. DE CANALDA; Sec.-Gen. ISABEL C. ARANGO. Publs *Solidarios* (quarterly), *Annual Report.*

Developing Eight—D-8: Musir Fuad Pasa Yalisi, Eski Tersane, Emirgan, Cad. 90, 80860 İstanbul, Turkey; tel. (212) 2275513;

fax (212) 2775519; internet www.developing-8.net; inaugurated at a meeting of heads of state in June 1997; aims to foster economic co-operation between member states and to strengthen the role of developing countries in the global economy; project areas include trade and industry, agriculture, human resources, telecommunications, rural development, finance (including banking and privatization), energy, environment, and health. Third Summit meeting, convened in Cairo, Egypt, in Feb. 2001, discussed reducing trade barriers amongst member states and considered the impact of external debt on member economies. Mems: Bangladesh, Egypt, Indonesia, Iran, Malaysia, Nigeria, Pakistan, Turkey. Exec. Dir AYHAN KAMEL.

Earth Council: POB 319-6100, San José, Costa Rica; tel. 205-1600; fax 249-3500; e-mail eci@terra.ecouncil.ac.cr; internet www.ecouncil.ac.cr; f. 1992, following the UN Conference on Environment and Development; aims to promote and support sustainable development; supported the establishment of National Councils for Sustainable Development (NCSDs) and administers a programme to promote co-operation and dialogue and to facilitate capacity-building and training, with NCSDs; works, with other partner organizations, to generate support for an Earth Charter. The Earth Council Institute, comprising 18 members, functions as an advisory board to the Council. Chair. MAURICE STRONG (Canada); Pres. And CEO of Earth Council Institute FRANS VAN HAREN (Netherlands).

East African Community—EAC: Arusha International Conference Centre, POB 1096, Arusha, Tanzania; tel. (57) 4253; fax (57) 4255; e-mail eac@eachq.org; internet www.eachq.org; f. Jan. 2001, following the adoption of a treaty on political and economic integration (signed in November 1999) by the heads of state of Kenya, Tanzania and Uganda, replacing the Permanent Tripartite Commission for East African Co-operation (f. 1993) and reviving the former East African Community (f. 1967; dissolved 1977); initial areas for co-operation were to be trade and industry, security, immigration, transport and communications, and promotion of investment; further objectives were the elimination of trade barriers and ensuring the free movement of people and capital within the grouping. Sec.-Gen. FRANCIS KIRIMI MUTHAURA.

Economic Community of the Great Lakes Countries (Communauté économique des pays des Grands Lacs—CEPGL): POB 58, Gisenyi, Rwanda; tel. 61309; fax 61319; f. 1976; main organs: annual Conference of Heads of State, Council of Ministers of Foreign Affairs, Permanent Executive Secretariat, Consultative Commission, Security Commission, three Specialized Technical Commissions. There are four specialized agencies: a development bank, the Banque de Développement des Etats des Grands Lacs (BDEGL) at Goma, Democratic Republic of the Congo; an energy centre at Bujumbura, Burundi; the Institute of Agronomic and Zootechnical Research, Gitega, Burundi; and a regional electricity company (SINELAC) at Bukavu, Democratic Republic of the Congo. Mems: Burundi, the Democratic Republic of the Congo, Rwanda. Publs *Grands Lacs* (quarterly review), *Journal* (annually).

Food Aid Committee: c/o International Grains Council, 1 Canada Sq., Canary Wharf, London, E14 5AE, United Kingdom; tel. (20) 7513-1122; fax (20) 7513-0630; e-mail igc-fac@igc.org.uk; internet www.igc.org.uk; f. 1967; responsible for administration of the Food Aid Convention—FAC (1999), a constituent element of the International Grains Agreement (1995); aims to make appropriate levels of food aid available on a consistent basis to maximize the impact and effectiveness of such assistance; provides a framework for co-operation, co-ordination and information-sharing among members on matters related to food aid. The 23 donor members pledge to supply a minimum of 5m. metric tons of food annually to developing countries and territories, mostly as gifts: in practice aid has usually exceeded 8m. tons annually. Secretariat support is provided by the International Grains Council (q.v.). Exec. Dir G. DENIS. Publ. *Report on shipments* (annually).

Gambia River Basin Development Organization (Organisation de mise en valeur du fleuve Gambie—OMVG): BP 2353, 13 passage Leblanc, Dakar, Senegal; tel. 822-31-59; fax 822-59-26; e-mail omvg@telecomplus.sn; f. 1978 by Senegal and The Gambia; Guinea joined in 1981 and Guinea-Bissau in 1983. A masterplan for the integrated development of the Kayanga/Geba and Koliba/Corubal river basins has been developed, encompassing a projected natural resources management project; work on a hydraulic development plan for the Gambia river commenced in late 1996 and was completed in mid-1998; a pre-feasibility study on connecting the national electric grids of the four member states has been completed, and a feasibility study for the construction of the proposed Sambangalou hydroelectric dam, providing for energy transmission to all member states, was scheduled to commence by late 2002; maintains documentation centre. Exec. Sec. MAMADOU NASSIROU DIALLO.

Group of Three—G3: Grupo de los Tres, Edif. MRE, Avda Udaneta, Esq. Carmelitas, Caracas 1010, Venezuela; e-mail dgseccc@impsat.com.ve; f. 1990 by Colombia, Mexico and Venezuela to remove restrictions on trade between the three countries. The trade agreement covers market access, rules of origin, intellectual property, trade in services, and government purchases, and entered into force in early 1994. Tariffs on trade between member states were to be removed on a phased basis. Co-operation was also envisaged in employment creation, the energy sector and the fight against cholera.

Indian Ocean Commission—IOC: Q4, Ave Sir Guy Forget, BP 7, Quatre Bornes, Mauritius; tel. 425-9564; fax 425-2709; e-mail coi7@intnet.mu; internet www.coi.intnet.mu; f. 1982 to promote regional co-operation, particularly in economic development; projects include tuna-fishing development, protection and management of environmental resources and strengthening of meteorological services; tariff reduction is also envisaged; organizes an annual regional trade fair. Mems: Comoros, France (representing the French Overseas Department of Réunion), Madagascar, Mauritius, Seychelles. Sec.-Gen. CAABI E. MOHAMED. Publ. *La Gazette de la Commission de l'Océan Indien*.

Indian Ocean Rim Association for Regional Co-operation—IOR-ARC: Sorèze House, 14 Angus Rd, Vacoas, Mauritius; tel. 698-3979; fax 697-5390; e-mail iorarchq@intnet.mu; the first intergovernmental meeting of countries in the region to promote an Indian Ocean Rim initiative was convened in March 1995; charter to establish the Asscn was signed at a ministerial meeting in March 1997; aims to promote regional economic co-operation in fields of trade, investment, the environment, tourism, and science and technology. Third meeting of Council of Ministers held in Muscat, Oman, April 2001. Mems: Australia, Bangladesh, India, Indonesia, Iran, Kenya, Madagascar, Malaysia, Mauritius, Mozambique, Oman, Seychelles, Singapore, South Africa, Sri Lanka, Tanzania, Thailand, United Arab Emirates and Yemen. Dialogue countries: People's Republic of China, Egypt, Japan, United Kingdom. Chair. Y OUSSOUF BIN ABDULLAH AL-ALAWI (Oman); Dir DEVDASLALL DUSORUTH (Mauritius).

Inter-American Planning Society (Sociedad Interamericana de Planificación—SIAP): c/o Revista Interamericana de Planificación, Casilla 01-05-1978, Cuenca, Ecuador; tel. (7) 823-860; fax (7) 823-949; e-mail siap1@siap.org.ec; f. 1956 to promote development of comprehensive planning. Mems: institutions and individuals in 46 countries. Pres. Arq. HERMES MARROQUÍN (Guatemala); Exec. Sec. LUIS E. CAMACHO (Colombia). Publs *Correo Informativo* (quarterly), *Inter-American Journal of Planning* (quarterly).

International Bank for Economic Co-operation—IBEC: 107815 GSP Moscow B-78, 11 Masha Poryvaeva St, Russia; tel. (95) 975-38-61; fax (95) 975-22-02; f. 1963 by members of the Council for Mutual Economic Assistance (dissolved in 1991), as a central institution for credit and settlements; following the decision in 1989–91 of most member states to adopt a market economy, the IBEC abandoned its system of multilateral settlements in transferable roubles, and (from 1 January 1991) began to conduct all transactions in convertible currencies. The Bank provides credit and settlement facilities for member states, and also acts as an international commercial bank, offering services to commercial banks and enterprises. Mems: Bulgaria, Cuba, Czech Republic, Hungary, Mongolia, Poland, Romania, Russia, Slovakia, Viet Nam. Chair. VITALI S. KHOKHLOV; Man. Dirs V. SYTNIKOV, S. CONSTANTINESCU.

International Co-operation for Development and Solidarity (Co-opération internationale pour le développement et la solidarité—CIDSE): 16 rue Stévin, 1000 Brussels, Belgium; tel. (2) 230-77-22; fax (2) 230-70-82; e-mail postmaster@cidse.org; internet www.cidse.org; f. 1967 to link Catholic development organizations and assist in the co-ordination of projects; co-ordinates advocacy and lobbying; provides information. Mems: 14 Catholic agencies in 13 countries and territories. Pres. JEAN-MARIE FARDEAU; Sec.-Gen. JEF FELIX.

International Investment Bank: 107078 Moscow, 7 Masha Poryvaeva St, Russia; tel. (95) 975-40-08; fax (95) 975-20-70; f. 1970 by members of the CMEA (q.v.) to grant credits for joint investment projects and the development of enterprises; following the decision in 1989–91 of most member states to adopt a market economy, the Bank conducted its transactions (from 1 January 1991) in convertible currencies, rather than in transferable roubles. The Bank focuses on production and scientific and technical progress. Mems: Bulgaria, Cuba, Czech Republic, Hungary, Mongolia, Poland, Romania, Russia, Slovakia, Viet Nam.

Inuit Circumpolar Conference: 170 Laurier Ave West, Suite 504, Ottawa, ON K1P 5V5, Canada; tel. (613) 563-2642; fax (613) 565-3089; internet www.inuit.org; f. 1977 to protect the indigenous culture, environment and rights of the Inuit people (Eskimoes), and to encourage co-operation among the Inuit; conferences held every four years. Mems: Inuit communities in Canada, Greenland, Alaska and Russia. Pres. AQQALUK LYNGE. Publ. *Silarjualiriniq.*

Lake Chad Basin Commission—LCBC: BP 727, N'Djamena, Chad; tel. 52-41-45; fax 52-41-37; e-mail lcbc@intnet.td; f. 1964 to encourage co-operation in developing the Lake Chad region and to promote the settlement of regional disputes. Work programmes emphasize the regulation of the utilization of water and other natural resources in the basin; the co-ordination of natural resources development projects and research; holds annual summit of heads of state. Mems: Cameroon, Central African Republic, Chad, Niger, Nigeria. Exec. Sec. BOBBOÏ JAURO ABUBAKAR. Publ. *Bibliographie générale de la cblt* (2 a year).

Latin American Association of Development Financing Institutions (Asociación Latinoamericana de Instituciones Financieras para el Desarrollo—ALIDE): Apdo Postal 3988, Paseo de la República 3211, Lima 100, Peru; tel. (1) 442-2400; fax (1) 442-8105; e-mail sg@alide.org.pe; internet www.alide.org.pe; f. 1968 to promote co-operation among regional development financing bodies; programmes: technical assistance; training; studies and research; technical meetings; information; projects and investment promotion. Mems: 62 active, 8 assoc. and 8 collaborating (banks and financing institutions and development organizations in 22 Latin American countries, Slovenia and Spain). Sec.-Gen. ROMMEL ACEVEDO. Publs *ALIDE Bulletin* (6 a year), *ALIDENOTICIAS Newsletter* (monthly), *Annual Report, Latin American Directory of Development Financing Institutions.*

Latin American Economic System (Sistema Económico Latinoamericano—SELA): Apdo 17035, Caracas 1010-A; Torre Europa, 4°, Urb. Campo Alegre, Av. Francisco de Miranda, Caracas 1061, Venezuela; tel. (212) 955-7111; fax (212) 951-5292; e-mail difusion@sela.org; internet sela2.sela.org; f. 1975 in accordance with the Panama Convention; aims to foster co-operation and integration among the countries of Latin America and the Caribbean, and to provide a permanent system of consultation and co-ordination in economic and social matters; conducts studies and other analysis and research; extends technical assistance to sub-regional and regional co-ordination bodies; provides library, information service and data bases on regional co-operation. The Latin American Council, the principal decision-making body of the System, meets annually at ministerial level and high-level regional consultation and co-ordination meetings are held; there is also a Permanent Secretariat. Mems: 28 countries. Perm. Sec. (1999-2003) OTTO BOYE SOTO (Chile). Publs *Capítulos del SELA* (3 a year), *Bulletin on Latin America and Caribbean Integration* (monthly), *SELA Antenna in the United States* (quarterly).

Liptako-Gourma Integrated Development Authority: POB 619, ave M. Thevenond, Ouagadougou, Burkina Faso; tel. (3) 30-61-48; f. 1972; scope of activities includes water infrastructure, telecommunications and construction of roads and railways; in 1986 undertook study on development of water resources in the basin of the Niger river (for hydroelectricity and irrigation). Mems: Burkina Faso, Mali, Niger. Dir-Gen. GISANGA DEMBÉLÉ (Mali).

Mano River Union: Private Mail Bag 133, Delco House, Lightfoot Boston St, Freetown, Sierra Leone; tel. (22) 226883; f. 1973 to establish a customs and economic union between member states to accelerate development via integration. A common external tariff was instituted in October 1977. Intra-union free trade was officially introduced in May 1981, as the first stage in progress towards a customs union. The Union was inactive for three years until mid-1994, owing to disagreements regarding funding. In January 1995 a Mano River Centre for Peace and Development was established, which was to be temporarily based in London. The Centre aims to provide a permanent mechanism for conflict prevention and resolution, and monitoring of human rights violations, and to promote sustainable peace and development. Decisions are taken at meetings of a joint ministerial council formed by the ministers of member states. Mems: Guinea, Liberia, Sierra Leone. Dir Dr KABINEH KOROMAH (Sierra Leone).

Mekong River Commission—MRC: 364 M. V. Preah Monivong, Sangkat Phsar Doerm Thkouv, Khan Chamkar Mon, POB 1112, Phnom Penh, Cambodia; tel. (23) 720979; fax (23) 720972; e-mail mrcs@mrcmekong.org; internet www.mrcmekong.org; f. 1995 as successor to the Committee for Co-ordination of Investigations of the Lower Mekong Basin (f. 1957); aims to promote and co-ordinate the sustainable development and use of the resources of the Mekong River Basin for navigational and non-navigational purposes, in order to assist the social and economic development of member states and preserve the ecological balance of the basin. Provides scientific information and policy advice; supports the implementation of strategic programmes and activities; organizes an annual donor consultative group meeting; maintains regular dialogue with Myanmar and the People's Republic of China. Mems: Cambodia, Laos, Thailand, Viet Nam. Chief Exec. JOERN KRISTENSEN.

Niger Basin Authority (Autorité du bassin du Niger): BP 729, Niamey, Niger; tel. 723102; fax 735310; f. 1964 (as River Niger Commission; name changed 1980) to harmonize national programmes concerned with the River Niger Basin and to execute an integrated development plan; compiles statistics; regulates navigation; runs projects on hydrological forecasting, environmental control; infrastructure and agro-pastoral development. Mems: Benin, Burkina Faso, Cameroon, Chad, Côte d'Ivoire, Guinea, Mali, Niger, Nigeria. Exec. Sec. OTHMAN MUSTAPHA (Nigeria). Publ. *Bulletin.*

Organisation of Eastern Caribbean States—OECS: POB 179, Morne Fortune, Castries, Saint Lucia; tel. 452-2537; fax 453-1628; e-mail oesec@oecs.org; internet www.oecs.org; f. 1981 by the seven states that formerly belonged to the West Indies Associated States (f. 1966). Aims to promote the harmonized development of trade and industry in member states; single market created on 1 January 1988. Principal institutions are: the Authority of Heads of Government (the supreme policy-making body), the Foreign Affairs Committee, the Defence and Security Committee, and the Economic Affairs Committee. There is also an Export Development and Agricultural Diversification Unit—EDADU (based in Dominica). Mems: Antigua and Barbuda, Dominica, Grenada, Montserrat, Saint Christopher and Nevis, Saint Lucia, Saint Vincent and the Grenadines; assoc. mems: Anguilla, British Virgin Islands. Dir-Gen. SWINBURNE LESTRADE.

Organization of the Black Sea Economic Co-operation—BSEC: İstinye Cad. Müşir Fuad Paşa Yalısı, Eski Tersane 80860 İstinye-İstanbul, Turkey; tel. (212) 2296330; fax (212) 2296336; e-mail bsec@turk.net; internet www.bsec.gov.tr; f.1992 as the Black Sea Economic Co-operation (name changed on entry into force of BSEC Charter on 1 May 1999); aims to strengthen regional co-operation, particularly in the field of economic development. The following institutions have been established within the framework of BSEC: a Parliamentary Assembly (established in 1993), a Business Council (1992), a Black Sea Trade and Development Bank (inaugurated in 1998), a BSEC Co-ordination Centre, and a Black Sea International Studies Centre (opened in 1998). Mems: Albania, Armenia, Azerbaijan, Bulgaria, Georgia, Greece, Moldova, Romania, Russia, Turkey, Ukraine. Sec.-Gen. VALERI CHECHELASHVILI (Georgia).

Organization for the Development of the Senegal River (Organisation pour la mise en valeur du fleuve Sénégal—OMVS): 46 rue Carnot, BP 3152, Dakar, Senegal; tel. 823-45-30; fax 823-

47-62; e-mail omvs.sphc@telecomplus.sn; internet www.omvs-hc.org; f. 1972 to promote the use of the Senegal river for hydroelectricity, irrigation and navigation. The Djama dam in Senegal provides a barrage to prevent salt water from moving upstream, and the Manantali dam in Mali is intended to provide a reservoir for irrigation of about 375,000 ha of land and for production of hydroelectricity and provision of year-round navigation for ocean-going vessels. In 1997 two companies were formed to manage the dams: Société de gestion de l'énergie de Manantali (SOGEM) and Société de gestion et d'exploitation du barrage de Djama (SOGED). Work began in 1997 on a hydro-electric power station on the Senegal River. Mems: Mali, Mauritania, Senegal; Guinea has observer status. Chair. MAAOUYA OULD SID'AHMED TAYA.

Organization for the Management and Development of the Kagera River Basin (Organisation pour l'aménagement et le développement du bassin de la rivière Kagera): BP 297, Kigali, Rwanda; tel. (7) 84665; fax (7) 82172; f. 1978; envisages joint development and management of resources, including the construction of an 80-MW hydroelectric dam at Rusumo Falls, on the Rwanda-Tanzania border, a 2,000-km railway network between the four member countries, road construction (914 km), and a telecommunications network between member states. Mems: Burundi, Rwanda, Tanzania, Uganda. Exec. Sec. JEAN-BOSCO BALINDA.

Pacific Basin Economic Council—PBEC: 900 Fort St, Suite 1080, Honolulu, HI 96813, USA; tel. (808) 521-9044; fax (808) 521-8530; e-mail info@pbec.org; internet www.pbec.org; f. 1967; an asscn of business representatives aiming to promote business opportunities in the region, in order to enhance overall economic development; advises governments and serves as a liaison between business leaders and government officials; encourages business relationships and co-operation among members; holds business symposia. Mems: 20 economies (Australia, Canada, Chile, People's Republic of China, Colombia, Ecuador, Hong Kong, Indonesia, Japan, Republic of Korea, Malaysia, Mexico, New Zealand, Peru, Philippines, Russia, Singapore, Taiwan, Thailand, USA). Chair. KOSAKU INABA; Vice-Pres. STEPHEN OLSON.

Pacific Economic Co-operation Council—PECC: 4 Nassim Rd, Singapore 258372; tel. 67379823; fax 67379824; e-mail peccsec@pecc.net; internet www.pecc.net; f. 1980; an independent, policy-orientated organization of senior research, government and business representatives from 25 economies in the Asia-Pacific region; aims to foster economic development in the region by providing a forum for discussion and co-operation in a wide range of economic areas; holds a General Meeting every 2 years. Mems: Australia, Brunei, Canada, Chile, the People's Republic of China, Colombia, Ecuador, Hong Kong, Indonesia, Japan, the Republic of Korea, Malaysia, Mexico, Mongolia (assoc. mem.), New Zealand, Peru, Philippines, Russia, Singapore, Taiwan, Thailand, USA, Viet Nam and the Pacific Island Forum; French Pacific Territories (assoc. mem.). Dir-Gen. DAVID PARSONS. Publs *PECC Highlights* (electronic newsletter, 2 a month), *Issues PECC* (quarterly), *Pacific Economic Outlook* (annually), *Pacific Food Outlook* (annually).

Pan-African Institute for Development—PAID: BP 4056, Douala, Cameroon; tel. 42-10-61; fax 42-43-35; e-mail ipd.sg@camnet.cm; internet www.paid-wa.org; f. 1964; gives training to people from African countries involved with development at grassroots, intermediate and senior levels (48 countries in 1998); emphasis is given to: development management and financing; agriculture and rural development; issues of gender and development; promotion of small and medium-sized enterprises; training policies and systems; environment, health and community development; research, support and consultancy services; and specialized training. There are four regional institutes: Central Africa (Douala), Sahel (Ouagadougou, Burkina Faso), West Africa (Buéa, Cameroon), Eastern and Southern Africa (Kabwe, Zambia) and a European office in Geneva; training was given to participants from 48 countries in 1998. Publs *Newsletter* (2 a year), *Annual Progress Report, PAID Report* (quarterly).

Permanent Inter-State Committee on Drought Control in the Sahel—CILSS: POB 7049, Ouagadougou, Burkina Faso; tel. 306758; fax 306757; e-mail cilss@fasonet.bf; internet www.cilss.org; f. 1973; works in co-operation with UN Sudano-Sahelian Office (UNSO, q.v.); aims to combat the effects of chronic drought in the Sahel region, by improving irrigation and food production, halting deforestation and creating food reserves; maintains Institut du Sahel at Bamako (Mali) and centre at Niamey (Niger). Mems: nine African countries. Pres. YAHYA A. J. J. JAMMEH (The Gambia); Exec. Sec. MOUSSA BENGA. Publ. *Reflets Sahéliens* (quarterly).

Population Council: 1 Dag Hammarskjöld Plaza, New York, NY 10017, USA; tel. (212) 339-0500; fax (212) 755-6052; e-mail pubinfo@popcouncil.org; internet www.popcouncil.org; f. 1952; aims to improve reproductive health and achieve a balance between people and resources; analyses demographic trends; conducts biomedical research to develop new contraceptives; works with private and public agencies to improve the quality and scope of family planning and reproductive health services; helps governments to design and implement population policies; communicates results of research. Five regional offices, in India, Mexico, Egypt, Kenya and Senegal, and 15 country offices. Additional office in Washington, DC, USA, carries out worldwide operational research and activities for reproductive health and the prevention of HIV and AIDS. Chair. ELIZABETH J. MCCORMACK; Pres. LINDA MARTIN. Publs *Studies in Family Planning* (quarterly), *Population and Development Review* (quarterly), *Population Briefs* (quarterly).

Society for International Development: Via Panisperna 207, 00184 Rome, Italy; tel. (06) 4872172; fax (06) 4872170; e-mail info@sidint.org; internet www.sidint.org; f. 1957; a global network of individuals and institutions wishing to promote participative, pluralistic and sustainable development; builds partnerships with civil society groups and other sectors; fosters local initiatives and new forms of social experimentation. Mems: over 3,000 in 115 countries, 60 local chapters. Pres. ENRIQUE IGLESIAS; Sec.-Gen. ROBERTO SAVIO. Publs *Development* (quarterly), *Bridges* (bimonthly newsletter).

South Centre: Chemin du Champ-d'Anier 17–19, BP 228, 1211 Geneva 19, Switzerland; tel. (22) 7918050; fax (22) 7988531; e-mail south@southcentre.org; internet www.southcentre.org; f. 1990 as a follow-up mechanism of the South Commission (f. 1987); in 1995 established as an intergovernmental body to promote South–South solidarity and co-operation by generating ideas and action-oriented proposals on major policy issues. Chair. GAMANI COREA (Sri Lanka). Publ. *South Letter* (quarterly).

Union of the Arab Maghreb (Union du Maghreb arabe—UMA): 26–27 rue Okba, Agdal, Rabat, Morocco; tel. (7) 772668; fax (7) 772693; e-mail uma@mtds.com; internet www.maghrebarabe.org; f. 1989; aims to encourage joint ventures and to create a single market; structure comprises a council of heads of state (meeting annually), a council of ministers of foreign affairs, a consultative council of 30 delegates from each country, a UMA judicial court, and four specialized ministerial commissions. Chairmanship rotates annually between heads of state. A Maghreb Investment and Foreign Trade Bank, funding joint agricultural and industrial projects, has been established and a customs union created. In April 1994 the Supreme Council agreed to undertake measures to establish a free trade zone, and to set up a Maghrebian Agency for Youth Tourism and a Maghrebian Union of Sport. Sec.-Gen. MOHAMED AMAMOU (Tunisia). Mems: Algeria, Libya, Mauritania, Morocco, Tunisia.

Vienna Institute for Development and Co-operation (Wiener Institut für Entwicklungsfragen und Zusammenarbeit): Weyrgasse 5, 1030 Vienna, Austria; tel. (1) 713-35-94; fax (1) 713-35-94-73; e-mail vidc@magnet.at; internet www.oneworld.at; f. 1987 (fmrly Vienna Institute for Development, f. 1964); disseminates information on the problems and achievements of developing countries; encourages increased aid-giving and international co-operation; conducts research. Pres. FRANZ VRANITZKY; Dir ERICH ANDLIK. Publs *Report Series, Echo.*

Economics and Finance

African Centre for Monetary Studies: 15 blvd Franklin Roosevelt, BP 4128, Dakar, Senegal; tel. 821-93-80; fax 822-73-43; e-mail caem@syfed.refer.sn; began operations 1978; aims to promote better understanding of banking and monetary matters; studies monetary problems of African countries and the effect on them of international monetary developments; seeks to enable African countries to co-ordinate strategies in international monetary affairs. Established as an organ of the Association of African Central Banks (AACB) following a decision by the OAU Heads of State and Government. Mems: all mems of AACB (q.v.). Chair. Dr PAUL A. OGWUMA (Nigeria); Dir MAMADOU SIDIBE.

African Insurance Organization: BP 5860, Douala, Cameroon; tel. 42-47-58; fax 43-20-08; e-mail aio@sprynet.com; internet www.africaninsurance.org; f. 1972 to promote the expansion of the insurance and reinsurance industry in Africa, and to increase regional co-operation; holds annual conference, periodic seminars and workshops, and arranges meetings for reinsurers, brokers, consultant and regulators in Africa; has established African insurance 'pools' for aviation, petroleum and fire risks, and created asscns of African insurance educators, supervisory authorities and insurance brokers and consultants. Sec.-Gen. YOSEPH ASEFFA.

Asian Clearing Union—ACU: c/o Central Bank of the Islamic Republic of Iran, POB 11365/8531, Tehran, Iran; tel. (21) 2842076; fax (21) 2847677; e-mail acusecret@mail.iranet.net; f. 1974 to provide clearing arrangements, whereby members settle payments for intra-regional transactions among the participating central banks, on a multilateral basis, in order to economize on the use of foreign exchange and promote the use of domestic currencies in trade transactions among developing countries; part of ESCAP's Asian trade expansion programme; the Central Bank of Iran is the Union's agent; in September 1995 the ACU unit of account was changed from SDR to US dollars, with effect from 1 January 1996. Mems: central banks of Bangladesh, Bhutan, India, Iran, Myanmar, Nepal, Pakistan, Sri Lanka. Sec.-Gen. MOHAMMAD FIROUZDOR. Publs *Annual Report, Newsletter* (monthly).

Asian Reinsurance Corporation: 17th Floor, Tower B, Chamnan Phenjati Business Center, 65 Rama 9 Rd, Huaykwang, Bangkok 10320, Thailand; tel. (2) 245-2169; fax (2) 248-1377; e-mail asianre@asianrecorp.com; internet www.asianrecorp.com; f. 1979 by ESCAP with UNCTAD, to operate as a professional reinsurer, giving priority in retrocessions to national insurance and reinsurance markets of member countries, and as a development organization providing technical assistance to countries in the Asia-Pacific region; cap. (auth.) US $15m., (p.u.) $8m. Mems: Afghanistan, Bangladesh, Bhutan, People's Republic of China, India, Iran, Republic of Korea, Philippines, Sri Lanka, Thailand. Gen. Man. A. S. MALABANAN.

Association of African Central Banks: 15 blvd Franklin Roosevelt, BP 4128, Dakar, Senegal; tel. 821-93-80; fax 822-73-43; f. 1968 to promote contacts in the monetary and financial sphere, in order to increase co-operation and trade among member states; aims to strengthen monetary and financial stability on the African continent. Mems: 36 African central banks representing 47 states. Chair. Dr PAUL A. OGWUMA (Nigeria).

Association of African Tax Administrators: POB 13255, Yaoundé, Cameroon; tel. 22-41-57; fax 23-18-55; f. 1980 to promote co-operation in the field of taxation policy, legislation and administration among African countries. Mems: 20 states. Exec. Sec. OWONA PASCAL-BAYLON.

Association of Asian Confederation of Credit Unions—AACCU: POB 24-171, Bangkok 10240, Thailand; tel. (2) 374-3170; fax (2) 374-5321; e-mail accuran@ksc.th.com; internet www.aaccu.net; links and promotes credit unions in Asia, provides research facilities and training programmes. Mems: in 10 Asian countries. Gen. Man. RANJITH HETTIARACHICHI. Publs *ACCU News* (every 2 months), *Annual Report and Directory*.

Association of European Institutes of Economic Research (Association d'instituts européens de conjoncture économique—AIECE): 3 place Montesquieu, 1348 Louvain-la-Neuve, Belgium; tel. (10) 47-34-26; fax (10) 47-39-45; e-mail olbrechts@ires.ucl.ac.be; internet www.aiece.org; f. 1957; provides a means of contact between member institutes; organizes two meetings annually, at which discussions are held on the economic situation and on a special theoretical subject. Mems: 40 institutes in 20 European countries. Admin. Sec. PAUL OLBRECHTS.

Central Asian Bank for Co-operation and Development: 115A Abay, Almaty, Kazakhstan; tel. (2) 422737; fax (2) 428627; f. 1994; to support trade and development in the sub-region. Mems: Kazakhstan, Kyrgyzstan, Uzbekistan.

Centre for Latin American Monetary Studies (Centro de Estudios Monetarios Latinoamericanos—CEMLA): Durango 54, Col. Roma, Del. Cuauhtémoc, 06700 México, DF, Mexico; tel. (55) 5533-0300; fax (55) 5525-4432; e-mail estudios@cemla.org; internet www.cemla.org; f. 1952; organizes technical training programmes on monetary policy, development finance, etc.; runs applied research programmes on monetary and central banking policies and procedures; holds regional meetings of banking officials. Mems: 31 associated members (Central Banks of Latin America and the Caribbean), 28 co-operating members (supervisory institutions of the region and non-Latin American Central Banks). Dir KENNETH GILMORE COATES SPRY. Publs *Bulletin* (every 2 months), *Monetaria* (quarterly), *Money Affairs* (2 a year).

Comité Européen des Assurances—CEA: 3 bis rue de la Chaussée d'Antin, 75009 Paris, France; tel. 1-44-83-11-83; fax 1-47-70-03-75; internet www.cea.assur.org; f. 1953 to represent the interests of European insurers, to encourage co-operation between members, to allow the exchange of information and to conduct studies. Mems: national insurance asscns of 29 countries. Pres. GIJSBERT J. SWALEF (Netherlands); Sec.-Gen. and Chief Exec. DANIEL G. SCHANTÉ (France). Publs *CEA INFO—Euro Brief* (every 2 months), *European Insurance in Figures* (annually), *The European Life Insurance Market* (annually).

East African Development Bank: 4 Nile Ave, POB 7128, Kampala, Uganda; tel. (41) 230021; fax (41) 259763; e-mail admin@eadb.com; internet www.eadb.com; f. 1967 by the former East African Community to promote development within Kenya, Tanzania and Uganda, which each hold 25.78% of the equity capital; the remaining equity is held by the African Development Bank and other institutional investors; cap. SDR 37.5m. (31 Dec. 2000). Dir-Gen. F. R. Tibeita.

Eastern Caribbean Central Bank—ECCB: POB 89, Basseterre, St Christopher and Nevis; tel. 465-2537; fax 466-8954; e-mail eccberu@caribsurf.com; internet www.eccb-centralbank.org; f. 1983 by OECS governments; maintains regional currency (Eastern Caribbean dollar) and advises on the economic development of member states. Mems: Anguilla, Antigua and Barbuda, Dominica, Grenada, Montserrat, Saint Christopher and Nevis, Saint Lucia, Saint Vincent and the Grenadines. Gov. DWIGHT VENNER.

Econometric Society: Dept of Economics, Northwestern University, Evanston, IL 60208, USA; tel. (847) 491-3615; internet www.econometricsociety.org; f. 1930 to promote studies aiming at a unification of the theoretical-quantitative and the empirical-quantitative approaches to economic problems. Mems: c. 7,000. Exec. Dir and Sec. JULIE P. GORDON. Publ. *Econometrica* (6 a year).

European Federation of Finance House Associations—Eurofinas: 267 ave de Tervueren, 1150 Brussels, Belgium; tel. (2) 778-05-60; fax (2) 778-05-79; internet www.eurofinas.org; f. 1959 to study the development of instalment credit financing in Europe, to collate and publish instalment credit statistics, and to promote research into instalment credit practice. Mems: finance houses and professional asscns in 14 European countries. Chair. GREGORIO D'OTTAVIANO (Italy); Sec.-Gen. MARC BAERT . Publs *Eurofinas Newsletter* (monthly), *Annual Report, Study Reports*.

European Federation of Financial Analysts Societies—EFFAS: Palais de la Bourse, Place de la Bourse, 75002 Paris, France; tel. 1-03-58-33-48; fax 1-03-58-33-35; e-mail claudia.stinnes@effas.com; internet www.effas.com; f. 1962 to co-ordinate the activities of European asscns of financial analysts; aims to raise the standard of financial analysis and improve the quality of information given to investors; encourages unification of national rules and draws up rules of profession; holds biennial congress. Mems: 12,000 in 18 European countries. Pres. FRITZ H. RAU.

European Financial Management and Marketing Association—EFMA: 16 rue d'Aguesseau, 75008 Paris, France; tel. 1-47-42-52-72; fax 1-47-42-56-76; e-mail info@efma.com; internet www.efma.com; f. 1971 to link financial institutions by organizing seminars, conferences and training sessions and an annual Congress and World Convention, and by providing information services. Mems: 145 European financial institutions. Pres. ALFREDO SÁENZ ABAD; Sec.-Gen. MICHEL BARNICH. Publ. *Newsletter*.

European Private Equity and Venture Capital Association—EVCA: Minervastraat 4, 1930 Zaventem, Belgium; tel. (2) 715-00-20; fax (2) 725-07-04; e-mail evca@evca.com; internet www.evca.com; f. 1983 to link private equity and venture capital companies within Europe; provides information services; supports networking; organizes lobbies and campaigns; works to promote the asset class in Europe and worldwide; holds annual symposium, seminars and training courses. Mems: over 900. Chair. MAX BURGER; Sec.-Gen. JAVIER ECHARRI. Publ. *Survey of Pan-European Private Equity and Venture Capital* (2 a year).

Fédération Internationale des Bourses de Valeurs—FIBV (International Federation of Stock Exchanges): 22 boulevard de Courcelles, 75017 Paris, France; tel. 1-44-01-05-45; fax 1-47-54-94-22; internet www.fibv.com; f. 1961; assumes a leadership role in advocating the benefits of self-regulation in the regulatory process; offers a platform for closer collaboration between member exchanges; promotes enhanced ethical and professional behaviour in the securities industry. Mems: 51, and 42 corresponding exchanges. Pres. MANUEL ROBLEDA; Sec-Gen. GERRIT H. DE MAREZ OYENS.

Financial Action Task Force on Money Laundering—FATF: 2 rue André-Pascal, 75775 Paris Cédex 16, France; tel. 1-45-24-82-00; fax 1-45-24-85-00; e-mail contact@fatf.gafi.org; internet www1.oecd.org/fatf; f. 1989, on the recommendation of the Group of Seven industrialized nations (G-7), to develop and promote policies to combat money laundering and the financing of terrorism; formulated a set of Recommendations for member countries to implement; established regional task forces in the Caribbean, Asia-Pacific, Europe, Africa and South America. Mems: 29 countries, the European Commission, and the Co-operation Council for the Arab States of the Gulf. Exec. Sec. PATRICK MOULETTE. Publ. *Annual Report*.

Fonds Africain de Garantie et de Co-opération Economique—FAGACE (African Guarantee and Economic Co-operation Fund): BP 2045, Cotonou, Benin; tel. 300376; fax 300284; e-mail fagace@intnet.bj; commenced operations in 1981; guarantees loans for development projects, provides loans and grants for specific operations and supports national and regional enterprises. Mems: nine African countries. Dir-Gen. SOULEYMANE GADO.

International Accounting Standards Board—IASB: 30 Cannon St, London, EC4M, United Kingdom; tel. (20) 7353-0565; fax (20) 7353-0562; e-mail iasb@iasb.org.uk; internet www.iasb.org.uk; f. 1973 as International Accounting Standards Committee, reorganized and present name adopted 2001; aims to develop, in the public interest, a single set of high-quality, uniform, clear and enforceable global accounting standards requiring the submission of high-quality, transparent and comparable information in financial statements and other financial reporting, in order to assist participants in world-wide capital markets and other end-users to make informed decisions on economic matters; aims also to promote the use and rigorous application of these global accounting standards, and to bring about the convergence of these with national accounting standards. Chair. and CEO Sir DAVID TWEEDIE. Publs *IASB Insight* (quarterly), *Bound Volume of International Accounting Standards* (annually), *Interpretations of International Accounting Standards*.

International Association for Research in Income and Wealth: Dept of Economics, New York University, 269 Mercer St, Room 700, New York, NY 10003, USA; tel. (212) 924-4386; fax (212) 366-5067; e-mail iariw@nyu.edu; internet www.econ.nyu.edu/iariw; f. 1947 to further research in the general field of national income and wealth and related topics by the organization of biennial conferences and other means. Mems: approx. 375. Chair. MICHAEL WARD; Exec. Sec. JANE FORMAN (USA). Publ. *Review of Income and Wealth* (quarterly).

International Bureau of Fiscal Documentation—IBFD: H. J. Wenckebachweg 201, POB 20237, 1096 AS Amsterdam, Netherlands; tel. (20) 5540100; fax (20) 6228658; e-mail info@ibfd.nl; internet www.ibfd.nl; f. 1938 to supply information on fiscal law and its application; maintains library on international taxation. Pres. J. F. AVERY JONES; Man. Dir H. M. A. L. HAMAEKERS. Publs *Bulletin for International Fiscal Documentation, Asia Pacific Tax Bulletin, Derivatives and Financial Instruments, European Taxation, International VAT Monitor, Supplementary Service to European Taxation* (all monthly), *Tax News Service* (fortnightly); studies, data bases, regional tax guides.

International Centre for Local Credit: Koninginnegracht 2, 2514 AA The Hague, Netherlands; tel. (70) 3750850; fax (70) 3454743; e-mail centre@bng.nl; f. 1958 to promote local authority credit by gathering, exchanging and distributing information and advice on member institutions and on local authority credit and related subjects; studies important subjects in the field of local authority credit. Mems: 22 financial institutions in 14 countries. Pres. F. NARMON (Belgium); Sec.-Gen. P. P. VAN BESOUW (Netherlands). Publs *Bulletin, Newsletter* (quarterly).

International Economic Association: 23 rue Campagne Première, 75014 Paris, France; tel. 1-43-27-91-44; fax 1-42-79-92-16; e-mail iea@iea-world.org; internet www.iea-world.com; f. 1949 to promote international collaboration for the advancement of economic knowledge and develop personal contacts between economists, and to encourage the provision of means for the dissemination of economic knowledge. Mems: asscns in 59 countries. Pres. Prof. ROBERT SOLOW; Sec.-Gen. Prof. JEAN-PAUL FITOUSSI (France).

International Federation of Accountants: 535 5th Ave, 26th Floor, New York, NY 10017, USA; tel. (212) 286-9344; fax (212) 286-9570; e-mail mariahermann@ifac.org; internet www.ifac.org; f. 1977 to develop a co-ordinated world-wide accounting profession with harmonized standards. Mems: 156 accountancy bodies in 114 countries. Pres. TSUGUOKI FUJINUMA; Chief Exec. PETER JOHNSTON. Publ. *International Standards on Auditing*.

International Fiscal Association—IFA: World Trade Center, POB 30215, 3001 DE Rotterdam, Netherlands; tel. (10) 4052990; fax (10) 4055031; e-mail n.gensecr@ifa.nl; internet www.ifa.nl; f. 1938 to study international and comparative public finance and fiscal law, especially taxation; holds annual congresses. Mems in 90 countries and national branches in 45 countries. Pres. S. O. LODIN (Sweden); Sec.-Gen. J. FRANS SPIERDIJK (Netherlands). Publs *Cahiers de Droit Fiscal International, Yearbook of the International Fiscal Association, IFA Congress Seminar Series*.

International Institute of Public Finance: University of the Saar, PO Box 151150, 66041 Saarbrücken, Germany; fax (681) 302-4369; e-mail sec@iipf.net; internet www.iipf.net; f. 1937; a private scientific organization aiming to establish contacts between people of every nationality, whose main or supplementary activity consists in the study of public finance; holds one meeting a year devoted to a certain scientific subject. Pres. HIROFUMI SHIBATA (Japan).

International Organization of Securities Commissions—IOSCO: CP 171, Tour de la Bourse, 800 Square Victoria, Suite 4210, Montréal, QC H4Z 1C8, Canada; tel. (514) 875-8278; fax (514) 875-2669; e-mail mail@oicv.iosco.org; internet www.iosco.org; f. 1983 to facilitate co-operation between securities and futures regulatory bodies at the international level. Mems: 163 agencies. Sec.-Gen. PETER CLARK. Publ. *IOSCO News* (3 a year).

International Securities Market Association—ISMA: Rigistr. 60, PO Box, 8033 Zürich, Switzerland; tel. (1) 3634222; fax (1) 3637772; e-mail info@isma.org; internet www.isma.org; f. 1969 for discussion of questions relating to the international securities market, to issue rules governing their functions, and to maintain a close liaison between the primary and secondary markets in international securities. Mems: 568 banks and major financial institutions in 48 countries. Chair. RIJNHARD W. F. VAN TETS (Netherlands); Chief Exec. and Sec.-Gen. JOHN L. LANGTON (Switzerland). Publs *International Bond Manual*, daily Eurobond listing, electronic price information, weekly Eurobond guide, ISMA formulae for yield, members' register, ISMA quarterly comment, reports, etc.

International Union for Housing Finance: Suite 400, 111 East Wacker Drive, Chicago, IL 60601-4389, USA; tel. (312) 946-8200; fax (312) 946-8202; e-mail iuhf@wwa.com; internet www.housingfinance.org; f. 1914 to foster world-wide interest in savings and home-ownership and co-operation among members; encourages comparative study of methods and practice in housing finance; promotes development of appropriate legislation on housing finance. Mems: 350 in 71 countries, 8 regional affiliates. Sec.-Gen. DONALD R. HOLTON. Publs *Housing Finance International* (quarterly), *Directory, International Housing Finance Factbook* (every 2 years), *IUHFI Newsletter* (3 a year).

Latin American Banking Federation (Federación Latinoamericana de Bancos—FELABAN): Apdo Aéreo 091959, Santafé de Bogotá, DE8, Colombia; tel. (1) 621-8617; fax (1) 621-8021; internet www.latinbanking.com; f. 1965 to co-ordinate efforts towards wide and accelerated economic development in Latin American countries. Mems: 19 Latin American national banking asscns. Pres. of Board MILTON AYON WONG; Sec.-Gen. Dra MARICIELO GLEN DE TOBÓN (Colombia).

West African Monetary Agency—WAMA: 11-13 ECOWAS St, PMB 218, Freetown, Sierra Leone; tel. 224485; fax 223943; e-mail wama@sierratel.sl; f. 1975 as West African Clearing House; administers transactions between its 10 member central banks in order to promote sub-regional trade and monetary co-operation; aims to establish a common central bank and single currency through monetary integration; administers ECOWAS travellers' cheques scheme. Mems: Banque Centrale des Etats de l'Afrique de l'Ouest (serving Benin, Burkina Faso, Côte d'Ivoire, Guinea-Bissau, Mali, Niger, Senegal, Togo) and the central banks of Cape Verde, The Gambia, Ghana, Guinea, Liberia, Mauritania, Nigeria and Sierra Leone. Dir-Gen. ANTOINE M. F. NDIAYE (Senegal). Publs *News Bulletin* (2 a year), progress and consultancy reports.

World Council of Credit Unions—WOCCU: POB 2982, 5710 Mineral Point Rd, Madison, WI 53705, USA; tel. (608) 231-7130; fax (608) 238-8020; e-mail mail@woccu.org; internet www.woccu.org; f. 1970 to link credit unions and similar co-operative financial institutions and assist them in expanding and improving their services; provides technical and financial assistance to credit union asscns in developing countries. Mems: 35,000 credit unions in 86 countries. CEO CHRISTOPHER BAKER. Publs *WOCCU Annual Report, Perspectives* (quarterly).

World Savings Banks Institute: 11 rue Marie Thérèse, 1000 Brussels, Belgium; tel. (2) 211-11-11; fax (2) 211-11-99; internet www.savings-banks.com/wsbi; f. 1924 as International Savings Banks Institute, present name and structure adopted in 1994; promotes co-operation among members and the development of savings banks world-wide. Mems: 107 banks and asscns in 88 countries. Pres. MANUEL PIZARRO (Spain). Publs *Annual Report, International Savings Banks Directory, Perspectives* (8–10 a year).

Education

African Association for Literacy and Adult Education—AALAE: POB 50768, Finance House, 6th Floor, Loita St, Nairobi, Kenya; tel. (2) 222391; fax (2) 340849; f. 1984, combining the former African Adult Education Association and the AFROLIT Society (both f. 1968); aims to promote adult education and literacy in Africa, to study the problems involved, and to allow the exchange of information; programmes are developed and implemented by 'networks' of educators; holds Conference every three years. Mems: 28 national education asscns and 300 institutions in 33 countries. Publs *The Spider Newsletter* (quarterly, in French and English), *Journal* (2 a year).

Agence Universitaire de la Francophonie (AUPELF–UREF): BP 400, succ. Côte-des-Neiges, Montréal, QC H3S 2S7, Canada; tel. (514) 343-6630; fax (514) 343-2107; e-mail rectorat@aupelf.refer.org; internet www.aupelf-uref.org; f. 1961; aims to develop a francophone university community, through building partnerships with students, teachers, institutions and governments. Mems: 391 institutions. Pres. ARTHUR BODSON (Canada); Dir-Gen. and Rector MICHEL GUILLOU (France). Publs *Universités* (quarterly), *UREF Actualités* (every 2 months), directories (Francophone universities, Professors from francophone universities, Departments of French studies world-wide).

Asian Confederation of Teachers: c/o FIT, 55 Abhinav Apt, Mahturas Rd Extn, Kandivli, Mumbai 400 067, India; tel. (22) 8085437; fax (22) 6240578; e-mail vsir@hotmail.com; f. 1990. Mems in 10 countries and territories. Pres. MUHAMMAD MUSTAPHA; Sec.-Gen. VINAYAK SIRDESAI.

Asian and South Pacific Bureau of Adult Education—ASPBAE: c/o H. Bhargava, 1st Floor,Shroff Chambers, 259-261 Perin Nariman St, Fort, Mumbai 400 001, India; tel. (22) 2665942; fax (22) 2679154; e-mail aspbae@vsnl.com; internet www.aspbae.org; f. 1964 to assist non-formal education and adult literacy; organizes training courses and seminars; provides material and advice relating to adult education. Mems in 36 countries and territories. Sec.-Gen. MARIA-LOURDES ALMAZAN-KHAN. Publs *ASPBAE News* (3 a year), *ASPBAE Courier* (2 a year).

Association for Childhood Education International: 17904 Georgia Ave, Suite 215, Olney, MD 20832, USA; tel. (301) 570-2111; fax (301) 570-2212; e-mail aceihq@aol.com; internet www.udel.edu/bateman/acei; f. 1892 to work for the education of children (from infancy through early adolescence) by promoting desirable conditions in schools, raising the standard of teaching, co-operating with all groups concerned with children, informing the public of the needs of children. Mems: 12,000. Pres. NANCY L. QUISENBERRY; Exec. Dir GERALD C. ODLAND. Publs *Childhood Education* (6 a year), *Professional Focus Newsletters, Journal of Research in Childhood Education* (2 a year), books on current educational subjects.

Association Montessori Internationale: Koninginneweg 161, 1075 CN Amsterdam, Netherlands; tel. (20) 6798932; e-mail ami@xs4all.nl; internet www.montessori-ami.org; f. 1929 to propagate the ideals and educational methods of Dr Maria Montessori on child development, without racial, religious or political prejudice; organizes training courses for teachers in 15 countries. Pres. RENILDE MONTESSORI; Sec. MARY P. HAYES. Publ. *Communications* (quarterly).

Association of African Universities—AAU: POB 5744, Accra North, Ghana; tel. (21) 774495; fax (21) 774821; e-mail info@aau.org; internet www.aau.org; f. 1967 to promote exchanges, contact and co-operation among African university institutions and to collect and disseminate information on research and higher education in Africa. Mems: 132 university institutions. Sec.-Gen. Prof. FRANÇOIS RAJAOSON (Mozambique). Publs *AAU Newsletter* (3 a year), *Directory of African Universities* (every 2 years).

Association of Arab Universities: POB 401, Jubeyha, Amman, Jordan; tel. (6) 5345131; fax (6) 5332994; e-mail secgen@aaru.edu.jo; internet www.aaru.edu.jo; f. 1964. Mems: 137 universities. Sec.-Gen. Dr MARWAN RASIM KAMAL. Publ. *AARU Bulletin* (annually and quarterly, in Arabic).

Association of Caribbean University and Research Institutional Libraries—ACURIL: Apdo postal 23317, San Juan 00931, Puerto Rico; tel. 764-0000; fax 763-5685; e-mail vtorres @upracd.upr.clu.edu; internet acuril.rrp.upr.edu; f. 1968 to foster contact and collaboration between mem. universities and institutes; holds conferences, meetings and seminars; circulates information through newsletters and bulletins; facilitates co-operation and the pooling of resources in research; encourages exchange of staff and students. Mems: 250. Exec.-Sec. ONEIDA R. ORTIZ. Publ. *Newsletter* (2 a year).

Association of South-East Asian Institutions of Higher Learning—ASAIHL: Secretariat, Ratasastra Bldg 2, Chulalongkorn University, Henri Dunant Rd, Bangkok 10330, Thailand; tel. (2) 251-6966; fax (2) 253-7909; e-mail oninnat@chula.ac.th; internet www.seameo.org/asaihl; f. 1956 to promote the economic, cultural and social welfare of the people of South-East Asia by means of educational co-operation and research programmes; and to cultivate a sense of regional identity and interdependence; collects and disseminates information, organizes discussions. Mems: 160 university institutions in 14 countries. Pres. Prof. Tan Sri Dr SYED JALALUDIN SYED SALIM; Sec.-Gen. Dr NINNAT OLANVORAVUTH. Publs *Newsletter, Handbook* (every 3 years).

Caribbean Examinations Council: The Garrison, St Michael 20, Barbados; tel. 436-6261; fax 429-5421; internet www.cxc.org; f. 1972; develops syllabuses and conducts examinations. Mems: govts of 16 English-speaking countries and territories.

Catholic International Education Office: 60 rue des Eburons, 1000 Brussels, Belgium; tel. (2) 230-72-52; fax (2) 230-97-45; e-mail oiec@pophost.eunet.be; internet www.ciateq.mx/~maria/oiec; f. 1952 for the study of the problems of Catholic education throughout the world; co-ordinates the activities of members; represents Catholic education at international bodies. Mems: 98 countries, 16 assoc. mems, 13 collaborating mems, 5 corresponding mems. Pres. Mgr CESARE NOSIGLIA; Sec.-Gen. ANDRÉS DELGADO HERNÁNDEZ. Publs *OIEC Bulletin* (every

3 months, in English, French and Spanish), *OIEC Tracts on Education.*

Catholic International Federation for Physical and Sports Education: 22 rue Oberkampf, 75011 Paris, France; tel. 1-43-38-50-57; f. 1911 to group Catholic asscns for physical education and sport of different countries and to develop the principles and precepts of Christian morality by fostering meetings, study and international co-operation. Mems: 14 affiliated national federations representing about 3.5m. members. Pres. DICK WIJTE (Netherlands); Sec.-Gen. CLÉMENT SCHERTZINGER (France).

Comparative Education Society in Europe: Institut für Augemeine Pädagogik, Humboldt-Universität zu Berlin, Unter den Linden 6, 10099 Berlin, Germany; tel. (30) 20934094; fax (30) 20931006; e-mail juergen.schriewer@educat.hu-berlin.de; f. 1961 to promote teaching and research in comparative and international education; organizes conferences and promotes literature. Mems: in 49 countries. Pres. Prof. J. SCHRIEWER (Belgium); Sec. and Treas. Prof. M. A. PEREYRA (Spain). Publ. *Newsletter* (quarterly).

Council of Legal Education—CLE: POB 323, Tunapuna, Trinidad and Tobago; tel. 662-5860; fax 662-0927; f. 1971; responsible for the training of members of the legal profession. Mems: govts of 12 countries and territories.

European Association for the Education of Adults: 8 rue J. Stevensstraat, B-1000 Brussels, Belgium; tel. (2) 513-5205; fax (2) 513-5734; e-mail eaea@eaea.org; internet www.eaea.org; f. 1953; aims to create a 'learning society' by encouraging demand for learning, particularly from women and excluded sectors of society; seeks to improve response of providers of learning opportunities and authorities and agencies. Mems: 110 in 30 countries. Pres. JORMA TURUNEN. Publs *EAEA Monograph Series*, newsletter.

European Cultural Foundation: Jan van Goyenkade 5, 1075 HN Amsterdam, Netherlands; tel. (20) 6760222; fax (20) 6752231; e-mail eurocult@eurocult.org; internet www.eurocult.org; f. 1954 as a non-governmental organization, supported by private sources, to promote activities of mutual interest to European countries on aspects of culture; maintains national committees in 23 countries and a transnational network of institutes and centres: European Institute of Education and Social Policy, Paris; Institute for European Environmental Policy, London, Madrid and Berlin; Association for Innovative Co-operation in Europe (AICE), Brussels; EURYDICE Central Unit (the Education Information Network of the European Community), Brussels; European Institute for the Media, Düsseldorf; European Foundation Centre, Brussels; Fund for Central and East European Book Projects, Amsterdam; Institute for Human Sciences, Vienna; East West Parliamentary Practice Project, Amsterdam; and Centre Européen de la Culture, Geneva. A grants programme, for European co-operation projects is also conducted. Pres. HRH Princess MARGRIET of the Netherlands; Sec.-Gen. Dr R. STEPHAN. Publs *Annual Report, Newsletter* (3 a year).

European Federation for Catholic Adult Education: Bildungshaus Mariatrost, Kirchbergstrasse 18, A-8044 Graz, Austria; tel. (316) 39-11-31-35; fax (316) 39-11-31-30; f. 1963 to strengthen international contact between mems and to assist with international research and practical projects in adult education; holds conference every two years. Pres. Prof. Mag. KARL KALCSICS (Austria).

European Foundation for Management Development—EFMD: 88 rue Gachard, 1050 Brussels, Belgium; tel. (2) 629-08-10; fax (2) 629-08-11; e-mail info@efmd.be; internet www.efmd.be; f. 1971 through merger of European Association of Management Training Centres and International University Contact for Management Education; aims to help improve the quality of management development, disseminate information within the economic, social and cultural context of Europe and promote international co-operation. Mems: over 390 institutions in 41 countries world-wide (26 in Europe). Dir-Gen. ERIC CORNUEL. Publs *Forum* (3 a year), *Guide to European Business Schools and Management Centres* (annually).

European Union of Arabic and Islamic Scholars: c/o Dipartimento di studi e ricerche su Africa e Paesi arabi, Istituto universitario orientale, Piazza S. Domenico Maggiore 12, 80134 Naples, Italy; tel. (081) 5517840; fax (081) 5515386; f. 1964 to organize congresses of Arabic and Islamic Studies; holds congresses every two years. Mems: 300 in 28 countries. Pres. Prof. URBAIN VERMEULEN (Belgium); Sec. Prof. CARMELA BAFFIONI (Italy).

European University Association—EUA: 10 rue du Conseil Général, 1211 Geneva 4, Switzerland; tel. (22) 3292644; fax (22) 3292821; e-mail info@eua.unige.ch; internet www.unige.ch/eua/; f. 2001 by merger of the Association of European Universities and the Confederation of EU Rectors' Conferences; serves as a platform for representation of the higher education sector and a forum for the exchange of information and good practice; supports networking; carries out peer reviews; supports development of strategies on use of IT in education; promotes academic research; holds conferences, training and leadership development seminars and workshops, and a General Assembly. Mems: 543 universities and associate members in 44 countries. Sec.-Gen. Dr ANDRIS BARBLAN. Publs *EUA-Info, EUA-Action, EUAdoc, EUAguide.*

Graduate Institute of International Studies (Institut universitaire de hautes études internationales): POB 36, 132 rue de Lausanne, Geneva, Switzerland; tel. (22) 9085700; fax (22) 9085710; e-mail info@hei.unige.ch; internet heiwww.unige.ch; f. 1927 to establish a centre for advanced studies in international relations of the present day; maintains a library of 147,000 vols. Dir Prof. PETER TSCHOPP; Dep. Dir Dr DANIEL WARNER.

Inter-American Centre for Research and Documentation on Vocational Training (Centro Interamericano de Investigación y Documentación sobre Formación Profesional—CINTERFOR): Avda Uruguay 1238, Casilla de correo 1761, Montevideo, Uruguay; tel. (2) 9020557; fax (2) 9021305; e-mail dirmvd@cinterfor.org.uy; internet www.cinterfor.org.uy; f. 1964 by the International Labour Organization (q.v.) for mutual help among the Latin American and Caribbean countries in planning vocational training; services are provided in documentation, research, exchange of experience; holds seminars and courses. Dir PEDRO DANIEL WEINBERG. Publs *Bulletin* (quarterly), *Documentation* (2 a year), *Herramientas para la transformación, Trazos de la formación*, studies, monographs and technical office papers.

Inter-American Confederation for Catholic Education (Confederación Interamericana de Educación Católica—CIEC): Calle 78 No 12–16 (ofna 101), Apdo Aéreo 90036, Santafé de Bogotá 8 DE, Colombia; tel. (1) 255-3676; fax (1) 255-0513; e-mail ciec@latino.net.co; internet www.ciec.to; f. 1945 to defend and extend the principles and rules of Catholic education, freedom of education, and human rights; organizes congress every three years. Pres. ADRIANO PACIFICO TOMASI; Sec. Gen. MARIA CONSTANZA ARANGO. Publ. *Educación Hoy.*

International Association for Educational and Vocational Guidance—IAEVG: c/o Linda Taylor, Essex Careers and Business Partnership, Westergaard House, The Matchyns, London Rd, Rivenhall, Essex, CM8 3HA, United Kingdom; tel. (1376) 391303; fax (1376) 391498; e-mail linda.taylor@careersbp.co.uk; internet www.iaevg.org; ; f. 1951 to contribute to the development of vocational guidance and promote contact between persons associated with it. Mems: 40,000 from 60 countries. Pres. Dr BERNHARD JENSCHKE (Germany); Sec.-Gen. LINDA TAYLOR (UK). Publs *Bulletin* (2 a year), *Newsletter* (3 a year).

International Association for the Development of Documentation, Libraries and Archives in Africa: Villa 2547 Dieuppeul II, BP 375, Dakar, Senegal; tel. 824-09-54; f. 1957 to organize and develop documentation and archives in all African countries. Mems: national asscns, institutions and individuals in 48 countries. Sec.-Gen. ZACHEUS SUNDAY ALI (Nigeria).

International Association of Educators for World Peace: POB 3282, Mastin Lake Station, Huntsville, AL 35810, USA; tel. (256) 534-5501; fax (256) 536-1018; e-mail mercieca@hiwaay.net; internet www.earthportals.com/portal_messenger/mercieca.html; f. 1969 to develop education designed to contribute to the promotion of peaceful relations at personal, community and international levels; aims to communicate and clarify controversial views in order to achieve maximum understanding; helps put into practice the Universal Declaration of Human Rights. Mems: 35,000 in 102 countries. Pres. Dr CHARLES MERCIECA (USA); Exec. Vice-Pres. RAJWANT SINGH SIDHU (UK); Sec.-Gen. Dr SURYA NATH PRASAD (India). Publs *Peace Progress* (annually), *IAEWP Newsletter* (6 a year), *Peace Education* (2 a year), *UN News* (monthly).

International Association of Papyrologists: Fondation Egyptologique Reine Elisabeth, Parc du Cinquantenaire 10, 1000 Brussels, Belgium; tel. (2) 741-73-64; e-mail amartin@ulb.ac.be; internet www.ulb.ac.be/assoc/aip; f. 1947; links all those interested in Graeco-Roman Egypt, especially Greek texts; mem. of the International Federation of the Societies of Classical Studies. Mems: about 400. Pres. Prof. DOROTHY THOMPSON (UK); Sec. Prof. ALAIN MARTIN (Belgium).

International Association of Physical Education in Higher Education: Institut Supérieur d'Education Physique, Bâtiment B21, Université de Liège au Sart Tilman, 4000 Liège, Belgium; tel. (4) 366-38-90; fax (4) 366-29-01; e-mail mpieron@ulg.ac.be; f. 1962; organizes congresses, exchanges, and research in physical education. Mems: institutions in 51 countries. Sec.-Gen. Dr MAURICE PIERON.

International Association of Universities—IAU/International Universities Bureau—IUB: 1 rue Miollis, 75732 Paris Cédex 15, France; tel. 1-45-68-25-45; fax 1-47-34-76-05; e-mail iau@unesco.org; internet www.unesco.org/iau; f. 1950 to allow co-operation at the international level among universities and other institutions of higher education; provides clearing-house services and operates the joint IAU/UNESCO Information Centre on Higher Education; conducts meetings and research on issues concerning higher education. Mems: about 700 universities and institutions of higher education in some 150 countries, 31 international and national university organizations. Pres. HANS VAN GINKEL; Sec.-Gen. EVA EGRON-POLAK. Publs *Higher Education Policy* (quarterly), *IAU Newsletter* (every 2 months), *International Handbook of Universities* (every 2 years), *Issues in Higher Education* (monographs), *World Academic Database* (CD-ROM, annually), *World List of Universities* (every 2 years).

International Association of University Professors and Lecturers—IAUPL: c/o F. Mauro, 18 rue du Docteur Roux, 75015 Paris, France; f. 1945 for the development of academic fraternity amongst university teachers and research workers; the protection of independence and freedom of teaching and research; the furtherance of the interests of all university teachers; and the consideration of academic problems. Mems: federations in 17 countries. Sec.-Gen. F. MAURO.

International Baccalaureate Organization—IBO: Route des Morillons 15, Grand-Saconnex 1218, Geneva, Switzerland; tel. (22) 7917740; fax (22) 7910277; e-mail ibhq@ibo.org; internet www.ibo.org; f. 1967 to plan curricula and an international university entrance examination, the International Baccalaureate, recognized by major universities world-wide; offers the Primary Years Programme for children aged between 3 and 12, the Middle Years Programme for students in the 11–16 age range, and the Diploma Programme for 17–18 year olds; Mems: over 1,180 participating schools in 101 countries. Pres. of Council GREG CRAFTER (Australia); Dir-Gen. GEORGE WALKER.

International Council for Adult Education—ICAE: 720 Bathurst St, Suite 500, Toronto, Canada ON M5S 2R4; tel. (416) 588-1211; fax (416) 588-5725; e-mail icae@icae.ca; internet www.web.net/icae; f. 1973 as a partnership of adult learners, teachers and organizations; promotes the education of adults, to support the development of individuals and communities; maintains resource centre with extensive material on literacy, adult education and development education; General Assembly meets every four years. Mems: seven regional organizations and 95 national asscns in 80 countries. Pres. PAUL BÉLANGER. Publs *Convergence*, *ICAE News*.

International Council for Open and Distance Education—ICDE: Gjerdrums Vei 12, 0484 Oslo, Norway; tel. 22-02-81-70; fax 22-02-81-61; e-mail icde@icde.no; internet www.icde.org; f. 1938 (name changed 1982); furthers distance (correspondence) education by promoting research, encouraging regional links, providing information and organizing conferences. Mems: institutions, corporations and individuals in 120 countries. Pres. MOLLY CORBETT BROAD (USA); Sec.-Gen. REIDAR ROLL (Norway). Publ. *Open Praxis* (2 a year).

International Federation for Parent Education: 1 ave Léon Journault, 92311 Sèvres Cédex, France; tel. 1-45-07-21-64; fax 1-46-26-69-27; f. 1964 to gather in congresses and colloquia experts from different scientific fields and those responsible for family education in their own countries and to encourage the establishment of family education where it does not exist. Mems: 120. Pres. MONEEF GUITOUNI (Canada). Publ. *Lettre de la FIEP* (2 a year).

International Federation of Catholic Universities (Fédération internationale d'universités catholiques—FIUC): 21 rue d'Assas, 75270 Paris Cédex 06, France; tel. 1-44-39-52-26; fax 1-44-39-52-28; e-mail sgfiuc@bureau.fiuc.org; internet www.fiuc.org/; f. 1948; aims to ensure a strong bond of mutual assistance among all Catholic universities in the search for truth; to help to solve problems of growth and development, and to co-operate with other international organizations. Mems: 191 in 41 countries. Pres. Rev. JAN PETERS (Netherlands); Sec.-Gen. GUY-RÉAL THIVIERGE (Canada). Publ. *Quarterly Newsletter*.

International Federation of Library Associations and Institutions—IFLA: POB 95312, 2509 CH The Hague, Netherlands; tel. (70) 3140884; fax (70) 3834827; e-mail ifla@ifla.org; internet www.ifla.org; f. 1927 to promote international co-operation in librarianship and bibliography. Mems: 153 asscns, 1,112 institutions and 429 individual members in 154 countries. Pres. CHRISTINE DESCHAMPS; Sec.-Gen. ROSS SHIMMON. Publs *IFLA Annual Report*, *IFLA Directory*, *IFLA Journal*, *International Cataloguing and Bibliographic Control* (quarterly), *IFLA Professional Reports*.

International Federation of Organizations for School Correspondence and Exchange: Via Torino 256, 10015 Ivrea, Italy; tel. (0125) 234433; fax (0125) 234761; e-mail fioces@ipfs.org; internet ipfs.org/fioces.htm; f. 1929; aims to contribute to the knowledge of foreign languages and civilizations and to bring together young people of all nations by furthering international scholastic correspondence. Mems: 78 national bureaux of scholastic correspondence and exchange in 21 countries. Pres. ALBERT V. RUTTER (Malta); Gen. Sec. LIVIO TONSO (Italy).

International Federation of Physical Education (Fédération internationale d'éducation physique—FIEP): c/o Prof. Robert Decker, 7–9 rue du X Octobre, 7243 Bereldange, Luxembourg; tel. and fax 33-94-81; e-mail robert.decker@in.educ.lu; f. 1923; studies physical education on scientific, pedagogic and aesthetic bases, with the aim of stimulating health, harmonious development or preservation, healthy recreation, and the best adaptation of the individual to the general needs of social life; organizes international congresses and courses; awards research prize. Mems: from 112 countries. Vice-Pres. (Europe) Prof. ROBERT DECKER. Publ. *FIEP Bulletin* (trilingual edition in French, English and Spanish, 3 a year).

International Federation of Teachers of Modern Languages: Seestrasse 247, 8038 Zürich, Switzerland; tel. (1) 4855251; fax (1) 4825054; f. 1931; holds meetings on every aspect of foreign-language teaching; has consultative status with UNESCO. Mems: 33 national and regional language asscns and six international unilingual asscns (teachers of English, French, German, Italian and Spanish). Pres. MICHAEL CANDELIER; Sec.-Gen. DENIS CUNNINGHAM. Publ. *FIPLV World News* (quarterly, in English, French and Spanish).

International Federation of University Women—IFUW: 8 rue de l'Ancien Port, 1201 Geneva, Switzerland; tel. (22) 7312380; fax (22) 7380440; e-mail ifuw@ifuw.org; internet www.ifuw.org; f. 1919 to promote understanding and friendship among university women of the world; to encourage international co-operation; to further the development of education; to represent university women in international organizations; to encourage the full application of members' skills to the problems which arise at all levels of public life. Affiliates: 72 national asscns with over 180,000 mems. Pres. Prof. REIKO AOKI (Japan). Publs *IFUW News* (6 a year), triennial report.

International Federation of Workers' Education Associations: c/o AOF Postboks 8703, Youngstorget, 0028 Oslo 1, Norway; tel. 23-06-12-88; fax 23-06-12-70; e-mail jmehlum@online.no; internet www.ifwea.org; f. 1947 to promote co-operation between non-governmental bodies concerned with workers' education; organizes clearing-house services; promotes exchange of information; holds international seminars, conferences and summer schools. Pres. DAN GALLIN (Switzerland); Gen. Sec. JAN MEHLUM (Norway).

International Institute for Adult Education Methods: POB 19395/6194, 5th Floor, Golfam St, 19156 Tehran, Iran; tel. (21) 2220313; f. 1968 by UNESCO and the Government of Iran, to collect, analyse and distribute information on activities concerning methods of literacy training and adult education; sponsors seminars; maintains documentation service and library on literacy and adult education. Dir Dr MOHAMMAD REZA HAMIDIZADE. Publs *Selection of Adult Education Issues* (monthly), *Adult Education and Development* (quarterly), *New Library Holdings* (quarterly).

International Institute of Philosophy—IIP (Institut international de philosophie): 8 rue Jean-Calvin, 75005 Paris, France; tel. 1-43-36-39-11; e-mail inst.intern.philo@wanadoo.fr; f. 1937 to clarify fundamental issues of contemporary philosophy and to promote mutual understanding among thinkers of different backgrounds and traditions. Mems: 102 in 36 countries. Pres. JAAKKO HINTIKKA (Finland); Sec.-Gen. P. AUBENQUE (France). Publs *Bibliography of Philosophy* (quarterly), *Proceedings* of annual meetings, *Chroniques, Philosophy and World Community* (series), *Philosophical Problems Today, Controverses philosophiques.*

International Institute of Public Administration: 2 ave de l'Observatoire, 75272 Paris Cédex 06; tel. 1-44-41-85-00; fax 1-44-41-86-19; e-mail iiap.bib@wanadoo.fr; f. 1966; trains high-ranking civil servants; runs administrative, economic, financial and diplomatic programmes; maintains a library of 80,000 vols and a documentation centre. Dir M. MAUS. Publ. *Revue française d'administration publique* (quarterly).

International Reading Association: 800 Barksdale Rd, POB 8139, Newark, DE 19714-8139, USA; tel. (302) 731-1600; fax (302) 731-1057; internet www.reading.org; f. 1956 to improve the quality of reading instruction at all levels, to promote the habit of lifelong reading, and to develop every reader's proficiency. Mems: 90,000 in 99 countries. Pres. CAROL M. SANTA. Publs *The Reading Teacher* (8 a year), *Journal of Adolescent and Adult Literacy* (8 a year), *Reading Research Quarterly, Lectura y Vida* (quarterly in Spanish), *Reading Today* (6 a year).

International Schools Association—ISA: CIC CASE 20, 1211 Geneva 20, Switzerland; tel. (22) 7336717; e-mail isa@amatec.ch; internet www.intschoolsasscn.com; f. 1951 to co-ordinate work in international schools and promote their development; supports the maintenance of high standards and equal opportunities in international schools; carries out curriculum research; convenes annual conferences on problems of curriculum and educational reform; organizes occasional teachers' training workshops and specialist seminars. Mems: 85 schools throughout the world. Pres. M M MANZITTI. Publs *Education Bulletin* (2 a year), *ISA Magazine* (annually), *Conference Report* (annually), curriculum studies (occasional).

International Society for Business Education: POB 20457, Carson City, NV 89721, USA; tel. (775) 882-1445; fax (775) 882-1449; e-mail lkantin@prodigy.net; internet www.siec-isbe.org; f. 1901; encourages international exchange of information; organizes international courses and congresses on business education. Mems: 2,200 national organizations and individuals in 23 countries. Pres. MICHAELA FEVERSTEIN (Germany); Gen. Sec. G. LEE KANTIN (USA). Publ. *International Review for Business Education.*

International Society for Education through Art—INSEA: c/o Peter Hermans, Citogroep, POB 1109, 6801 BC Arnhem, Netherlands; fax (26) 3521202; e-mail insea@citogroep.nl; internet www.insea.org; f. 1951 to unite art teachers throughout the world, to exchange information and to co-ordinate research into art education; organizes international congresses and exhibitions of children's art. Pres. DIEDERIK SCHÖNAU (Netherlands). Publ. *INSEA News* (3 a year).

International Society for Music Education—ISME: POB 909, Nedlands, WA 6909, Australia; tel. (8) 9389-5862; fax (8) 9386-2658; e-mail isme@iinet.net.au; internet www.isme.org; f. 1953 to organize international conferences, seminars and publications on matters pertaining to music education; acts as advisory body to UNESCO in matters of music education. Mems: national committees and individuals in 60 countries. Pres. JOHN DRUMMOND (New Zealand); Sec.-Gen. JUDY THÖNELL (Australia). Publs *ISME Newsletter, Journal.*

International Society for the Study of Medieval Philosophy: Collège Mercier, place du Cardinal Mercier 14, 1348 Louvain-la-Neuve, Belgium; tel. (10) 47-48-07; fax (10) 47-82-85; e-mail siepm@isp.vcp.ac.be; internet www.isp.ucl.ac.be/isp/siepm/siepm.html; f. 1958 to promote the study of medieval thought and the collaboration between individuals and institutions in this field; organizes international congresses. Mems: 576. Pres. Prof. DAVID LUSCOMBE (UK); Sec. Prof. JACQUELINE HAMESSE (Belgium). Publ. *Bulletin de Philosophie Médiévale* (annually).

International Youth Library (Internationale Jugendbibliothek): 81247 Munich, Schloss Blutenburg, Germany; tel. (89) 8912110; fax (89) 8117553; e-mail bib@ijb.de; internet www.ijb.de; f. 1949, since 1953 an associated project of UNESCO; promotes the international exchange of children's literature; provides study opportunities for specialists in childrens' books; maintains a library of 510,000 volumes in about 130 languages. Dir Dr BARBARA SCHARIOTH. Publs *The White Ravens, IJB Report*, catalogues.

League of European Research Libraries (Ligue des bibliothèques européennes de recherche—LIBER): c/o Prof. Elmar Mittler, Göttingen Univ. Library, 37070 Göttingen, Germany; tel. (551) 395212; fax (551) 395222; e-mail mittler@mail.sub.uni-goettingen.de; internet www.kb.dk/liber; f. 1971 to encourage collaboration between the general research libraries of Europe, and national and university libraries in particular; gives assistance in finding practical ways of improving the quality of the services provided. Mems: 310 libraries and individuals in 33 countries. Pres. Prof. ELMAR MITTLER; Sec. Dr TOBY BAINTON (UK). Publ. *LIBER Quarterly.*

Organization of Ibero-American States for Education, Science and Culture (Organización de Estados Iberoamericanos para la Educación, la Ciencia y la Cultura): Centro de Recursos Documentales e Informáticos, Calle Bravo Murillo, No 38, 28015 Madrid, Spain; tel. (91) 594-44-42; fax (91) 594-32-86; e-mail oeimad@oei.es; internet www.oei.es; f. 1949 (as the Ibero-American Bureau of Education); promotes peace and solidarity between member countries, through education, science, technology and culture; provides information, encourages exchanges and organizes training courses; the General Assembly (at ministerial level) meets every four years. Mems: govts of 20 countries. Sec.-Gen. FRANCISCO JOSÉ PIÑÓN. Publ. *Revista Iberoamericana de Educacion* (quarterly).

Organization of the Catholic Universities of Latin America (Organización de Universidades Católicas de América Latina—ODUCAL): c/o Dr J. A. Tobías, Universidad del Salvador, Viamonte 1856, CP 1056, Buenos Aires, Argentina; tel. (11) 4813-1408; fax (11) 4812-4625; e-mail udes-rect@salvador.edu.ar; f. 1953 to assist the social, economic and cultural development of Latin America through the promotion of Catholic higher education in the continent. Mems: 43 Catholic universities in 15 Latin American countries. Pres. Dr JUAN ALEJANDRO TOBÍAS (Argentina). Publs *Anuario, Sapientia, Universitas.*

Southeast Asian Ministers of Education Organization—SEAMEO: Darakarn Bldg, 920 Sukhumvit Rd, Bangkok 10110, Thailand; tel. (2) 391-0144; fax (2) 381-2587; e-mail secretariat@seameo.org; internet www.seameo.org; f. 1965 to promote co-operation among the Southeast Asian nations through projects in education, science and culture; SEAMEO has 14 regional centres including: BIOTROP for tropical biology, in Bogor, Indonesia; INNOTECH for educational innovation and technology; an Open-Learning Centre in Indonesia; RECSAM for education in science and mathematics, in Penang, Malaysia; RELC for languages, in Singapore; RIHED for higher education development in Bangkok, Thailand; SEARCA for graduate study and research in agriculture, in Los Baños, Philippines; SPAFA for archaeology and fine arts in Bangkok, Thailand; TROPMED for tropical medicine and public health with regional centres in Indonesia, Malaysia, Philippines and Thailand and a central office in Bangkok; VOCTECH for vocational and technical education; and the SEAMO Training Centre in Ho Chi Minh City, Viet Nam. Mems: Brunei, Cambodia, Indonesia, Laos, Malaysia, Philippines, Singapore, Thailand, Viet Nam; assoc. mems: Australia, Canada, France, Germany, Netherlands, New Zealand. Pres. TEO CHEE HEAN (Singapore); Dir Dr SUPARAK RACHAINTRA. Publs *Annual Report, SEAMEO Horizon.*

Union of Latin American Universities (Unión de Universidades de América Latina—UDUAL): Edificio UDUAL, Apdo postal 70-232, Ciudad Universitaria, Del. Coyoacán, 04510 México, DF, Mexico; tel. (55) 5622-0991; fax (55) 5616-1414; f. 1949 to organize the interchange of professors, students, research fellows and graduates and generally encourage good relations between the Latin American universities; arranges conferences; conducts statistical research; maintains centre for university documentation. Mems: 165 universities. Pres. Dr SALOMÓN LERNER FEBRES (Peru); Sec.-Gen. Dr JUAN JOSÉ SÁNCHEZ SOSA (Mexico). Publs *Universidades* (2 a year), *Gaceta UDUAL* (quarterly), *Censo* (every 2 years).

Universal Esperanto Association: Nieuwe Binnenweg 176, 3015 BJ Rotterdam, Netherlands; tel. (10) 4361044; fax (10) 4361751; e-mail uea@inter.nl.net; internet www.uea.org; f. 1908 to assist the spread of the international language, Esperanto, and to facilitate the practical use of the language. Mems: 62 affiliated national asscns and 19,750 individuals in 120 countries. Pres. RENATO CORSETTI (Italy); Gen. Sec. IVO OSIBOV (Croatia). Publs *Esperanto* (monthly), *Kontakto* (every 2 months), *Jarlibro* (yearbook), *Esperanto Documents*.

World Association for Educational Research: Université de Sherbrooke, Sherbrooke, QC J1K 2R1, Canada; e-mail ylenoir@courrier.usherb.ca; f. 1953, present title adopted 1977; aims to encourage research in educational sciences by organizing congresses, issuing publications and supporting the exchange of information. Mems: societies and individual members in 50 countries. Pres. Prof. Dr Y. LENOIR.

World Education Fellowship: 22A Kew Gardens, Kew, Richmond, TW9 3HD, United Kingdom; tel. (20) 8940-0131; f. 1921 to promote education for international understanding, and the exchange and practice of ideas, together with research into progressive educational theories and methods. Mems: sections and groups in 20 countries. Chair. CHRISTINE WYKES; Sec. ROSEMARY CROMMELIN. Publ. *The New Era in Education* (3 a year).

World Union of Catholic Teachers (Union mondiale des enseignants catholiques—UMEC): Piazza San Calisto 16, 00120 Città del Vaticano; tel. (06) 69887286; f. 1951; encourages the grouping of Catholic teachers for the greater effectiveness of Catholic schools, distributes documentation on Catholic doctrine with regard to education, and facilitates personal contacts through congresses, and seminars, etc., nationally and internationally. Mems: 32 organizations in 29 countries. Pres. ARNOLD BACKX; Sec.-Gen. MICHAEL EMM. Publ. *Nouvelles de l'UMEC*.

World University Service—WUS: 383 Los Jardines, Nuñoa, Santiago de Chile, Chile; tel. (2) 272375; fax (2) 2724002; internet antenna.nl/wus-i; f. 1920; links students, faculty and administrators in post-secondary institutions concerned with economic and social development, and seeks to protect their academic freedom and autonomy; seeks to extend technical, personal and financial resources of post-secondary institutions to under-developed areas and communities; provides scholarships at university level for refugees, displaced people, and returnees, and supports informal education projects for women; governed by an assembly of national committees. Pres. CALEB FUNDANGA (Zambia); Sec.-Gen. XIMENA ERAZO. Publs *WUS News*, *WUS and Human Rights* (quarterly).

Environmental Conservation

BirdLife International: Wellbrook Ct, Girton Rd, Cambridge, CB3 0NA, United Kingdom; tel. (1223) 277318; fax (1223) 277200; e-mail birdlife@birdlife.org.uk; internet www.birdlife.net; f. 1922 as the International Council for Bird Preservation; a global partnership of organizations that determines status of bird species throughout the world and compiles data on all endangered species; identifies conservation problems and priorities; initiates and co-ordinates conservation projects and international conventions. Mems: partners in 60 countries, representatives in 31 countries. Chair. GERARD A. BERTRAND; Dir Dr MICHAEL RANDS (UK). Publs *Bird Red Data Book*, *World Birdwatch* (quarterly), *Bird Conservation Series*, study reports.

Friends of the Earth International: Prins Hendrikkade 48, POB 19199, 1000 GD Amsterdam, Netherlands; tel. (20) 6221369; fax (20) 6392181; e-mail foei@foei.org; internet www.foei.org; f. 1971 to promote the conservation, restoration and rational use of the environment and natural resources through public education and campaigning. Mems: 56 national groups. Publs *Link* (quarterly), *BIFI* (monthly).

Greenpeace International: Keizersgracht 176, 1016 DW Amsterdam, Netherlands; tel. (20) 5236222; fax (20) 5236200; e-mail greenpeaceinternational@green2.greenpeace.org; internet www.greenpeace.org; f. 1971 to campaign for the protection of the environment; aims to bear witness to environmental destruction, and to demonstrate solutions for positive change. Mems: offices in 34 countries. Chair. CORNELIA DURRANT; Exec. Dir GERD LEIPOLD.

Independent World Commission on the Oceans—IWCO: c/o Palácio de Belém, 1300 Lisbon, Portugal; tel. (1) 3637141; fax (1) 3636603; e-mail secretariat@world-oceans.org; internet www.world-oceans.org; f. 1995 to study ways of protecting maritime resources and coastal areas. Chair. MÁRIO SOARÈS.

International Commission for the Protection of the Rhine: 56002 Koblenz, Hohenzollernstrasse 18, POB 200253, Germany; tel. (261) 12495; fax (261) 36572; e-mail sekretariat@iksr.de; internet www.iksr.org; f. 1950; prepares and commissions research on the nature of the pollution of the Rhine; proposes protection, ecological rehabilitation and flood prevention measures. Mems: 23 delegates from France, Germany, Luxembourg, Netherlands, Switzerland and the EU. Pres. Prof. M. KRAFFT; Sec. J. H. OTERDOOM. Publ. *Annual Report*.

International Council on Metals and the Environment—ICME: 294 Albert St, Suite 506, Ottawa, ON K1P 6E6, Canada; tel. (613) 235-4263; fax (613) 235-2865; e-mail info@icme.com; internet www.icme.com; f. 1991 by metal-producing and mining companies to promote responsible environmental practices and policies in the mining, use, recycling and disposal of metals. Mems: companies from six continents. Chair. DOUGLAS YEARLEY (USA); Sec.-Gen. GARY NASH (Canada). Publ. *ICME Newsletter* (quarterly).

South Pacific Regional Environment Programme—SPREP: POB 240, Apia, Samoa; tel. 21929; fax 20231; e-mail sprep@sprep.org.ws; internet www.sprep.org.ws; f. 1978 by the South Pacific Commission (where it was based), the South Pacific (now Pacific Islands) Forum, ESCAP and UNEP; formally established as an independent institution in June 1993 when members signed the *Agreement Establishing SPREP*; aims to promote regional co-operation in environmental matters, to assist members to protect and improve their shared environment, and to help members work towards sustainable development. Mems: 22 Pacific islands, Australia, France, New Zealand, USA. Dir TAMARI'I P. TUTANGATA (Cook Islands). Publs *SPREP Newsletter* (quarterly), *CASOLink* (quarterly), *La lettre de l'environnement* (quarterly), *South Pacific Sea Level and Climate Change Newsletter* (quarterly).

Wetlands International Africa, Europe, Middle East (AEME): POB 471, 6700 AL Wageningen, Netherlands; tel. (317) 478854; fax (317) 478850; e-mail post@wetlands.agro.nl; internet www.wetlands.org; f. 1995 by merger of several regional wetlands organizations; aims to sustain and restore wetlands, their resources and biodiversity through research, information exchange and conservation activities; promotes implementation of the 1971 Ramsar Convention on Wetlands. Publs *Wetlands* (2 a year), other studies, technical publications, manuals, proceedings of meetings.

World Conservation Union—IUCN: rue Mauverney 28, 1196 Gland, Switzerland; tel. (22) 9990001; fax (22) 9990002; e-mail mail@iucn.org; internet www.iucn.org; f. 1948, as the International Union for Conservation of Nature and Natural Resources; supports partnerships and practical field activities to promote the conservation of natural resources, to secure the conservation of nature, and especially of biological diversity, as an essential foundation for the future; to ensure wise use of the earth's natural resources in an equitable and sustainable way; and to guide the development of human communities towards ways of life in enduring harmony with other components of the biosphere, developing programmes to protect and sustain the most important and threatened species and eco-systems and assisting governments to devise and carry out national conservation strategies; maintains a conservation library and documentation centre and units for monitoring traffic in wildlife. Mems: 79 governments, 112 govt agencies, 68 international non-governmental organizations and 692 national non-governmental organizations, from a total of 141 countries; 37 non-voting affiliate mems. Pres. YOLANDA KAKABADSE (Ecuador); Dir-Gen. SIMON STUART. Publs *World Conservation Strategy*, *Caring for the Earth*, *Red List of Threatened Plants*, *Red List of Threatened Species*, *United Nations List of National Parks and Protected Areas*, *World Conservation* (quarterly).

World Society for the Protection of Animals—WSPA: 89 Albert Embankment, London, SE1 7TP, United Kingdom; tel. (20) 7793-0540; fax (20) 7793-0208; e-mail wspa@wspa.org.uk; internet www.wspa.org. uk; f. 1981, incorporating the World Federation for the Protection of Animals (f. 1950) and the International Society for the Protection of Animals (f. 1959); promotes animal welfare and conservation by humane education, practical field projects, international lobbying and legislative work. Chief Exec. ANDREW DICKSON.

World Wide Fund for Nature—WWF: ave de Mont-Blanc, 1196 Gland, Switzerland; tel. (22) 3649111; fax (22) 3643239; e-mail userid@wwfnet.org; internet www.panda.org; f. 1961 (as World Wildlife Fund); aims to conserve nature and ecological processes by preserving genetic, species and ecosystem diversity; works to ensure the sustainable use of resources, and to reduce pollution and wasteful consumption of resources and energy. Mems: 27 national organizations, five associates. Pres. Prof. RUUD LUBBERS (Netherlands); Dir-Gen. Dr CLAUDE MARTIN. Publs *Annual Report, WWF News* (quarterly).

Government and Politics

African Association for Public Administration and Management: POB 48677, Nairobi, Kenya; tel. (2) 52-19-44; fax (2) 52-18-45; e-mail aapam@africaonline.co.ke; f. 1971 to provide senior officials with a forum for the exchange of ideas and experience, to promote the study of professional techniques and to encourage research into African administrative problems. Mems: 500 individual, 50 corporate. Pres. Dr JONATHAN CHILESHE (Zambia); Sec.-Gen. HUDSON M. BIGOGO (Kenya). Publs *Newsletter* (quarterly), *Annual Seminar Report, African Journal of Public Administration and Management,* studies.

Afro-Asian Peoples' Solidarity Organization—AAPSO: 89 Abdel Aziz Al-Saoud St, POB 11559-61 Manial El-Roda, Cairo, Egypt; tel. (2) 3636081; fax (2) 3637361; e-mail aapso@idsc.gov.eg; f. 1958; acts among and for the peoples of Africa and Asia in their struggle for genuine independence, sovereignty, socio-economic development, peace and disarmament. Mems: national committees and affiliated organizations in 66 countries and territories, assoc. mems in 15 European countries. Pres. Dr MOURAD GHALEB; Sec.-Gen. NOURI ABD AR-RAZZAK HUSSEIN (Iraq). Publs *Solidarity Bulletin* (monthly), *Development and Socio-Economic Progress* (quarterly), *Human Rights Newsletter* (6 a year).

Agency for the Prohibition of Nuclear Weapons in Latin America and the Caribbean (Organismo para la Proscripción de las Armas Nucleares en la América Latina y el Caribe—OPANAL): Schiller 326, 5°, Col Chapultepec Morales, 11570, México, DF, Mexico; tel. (55) 5255-2914; fax (55) 5255-3748; internet www.opanal.org; f. 1969 to ensure compliance with the Treaty for the Prohibition of Nuclear Weapons in Latin America (Treaty of Tlatelolco), 1967; to ensure the absence of all nuclear weapons in the application zone of the Treaty; to contribute to the movement against proliferation of nuclear weapons; to promote general and complete disarmament; to prohibit all testing, use, manufacture, acquisition, storage, installation and any form of possession, by any means, of nuclear weapons. The organs of the Agency comprise the General Conference, meeting every two years, the Council, meeting every two months, and the secretariat. A General Conference is held every two years. Mems: 30 states that have fully ratified the Treaty. The Treaty has two additional Protocols: the first signed and ratified by France, the Netherlands, the United Kingdom and the USA; the second signed and ratified by China, the USA, France, the United Kingdom and Russia. Sec.-Gen. ENRIQUE ROMÁN-MOREY (Peru).

Alliance of Small Island States—AOSIS: c/o 800 Second Ave, Suite 400D, New York, NY 10017, USA; tel. (212) 599-6196; fax (212) 599-0797; e-mail samoa@un.int; internet www.sidsne.org/aosis; f. 1990 as an *ad hoc* intergovernmental grouping to focus on the special problems of small islands and low-lying coastal developing states. Mems: 43 island nations. Chair. TUILOMA NERONI SLADE (Samoa). Publ. *Small Islands, Big Issues.*

ANZUS: c/o Dept of Foreign Affairs and Trade, Locked Bag 40, Queen Victoria Terrace, Canberra, ACT 2600, Australia; tel. (2) 6261-9111; fax (2) 6273-3577; internet www.dfat.gov.au; the ANZUS Security Treaty was signed in 1951 by Australia, New Zealand and the USA, and ratified in 1952 to co-ordinate partners' efforts for collective defence for the preservation of peace and security in the Pacific area, through the exchange of technical information and strategic intelligence, and a programme of exercises, exchanges and visits. In 1984 New Zealand refused to allow visits by US naval vessels that were either nuclear-propelled or potentially nuclear-armed, and this led to the cancellation of joint ANZUS military exercises: in 1986 the USA formally announced the suspension of its security commitment to New Zealand under ANZUS. Instead of the annual ANZUS Council meetings, bilateral talks were subsequently held every year between Australia and the USA. ANZUS continued to govern security relations between Australia and the USA, and between Australia and New Zealand; security relations between New Zealand and the USA were the only aspect of the treaty to be suspended. Senior-level contacts between New Zealand and the USA resumed in 1994.

Association of Secretaries General of Parliaments: c/o Committee Office, House of Commons, London, SW1, United Kingdom; tel. (20) 7219-3754; e-mail phillipsris@parliament.uk; internet www.ipu.org/english/asgp.htm; f. 1938; studies the law, practice and working methods of different Parliaments; proposes measures for improving those methods and for securing co-operation between the services of different Parliaments; operates as a consultative body to the Inter-Parliamentary Union (q.v.), and assists the Union on subjects within the scope of the Association. Mems: c. 200 representing about 90 countries. Pres. ADELINA SA CARVALHO (Portugal); Sec. R. I. S. PHILLIPS (UK). Publ. *Constitutional and Parliamentary Information* (2 a year).

Atlantic Treaty Association: 10 rue Crevaux, 75116 Paris, France; tel. 1-45-53-28-80; fax 1-47-55-49-63; e-mail ata sg@noos.fr; internet www.atasec.org; f. 1954 to inform public opinion on the North Atlantic Alliance and to promote the solidarity of the peoples of the North Atlantic; holds annual assemblies, seminars, study conferences for teachers and young politicians. Mems: national asscns in the 19 member countries of NATO (q.v.); 19 assoc. mems from central and eastern Europe, two observer mems. Chair. ALAN LEE WILLIAMS (UK); Sec.-Gen. ANTÓNIO BORGES DE CARVALHO (Portugal).

Baltic Council: f. 1993 by the Baltic Assembly, comprising 60 parliamentarians from Estonia, Latvia and Lithuania; the Council of Ministers of the three Baltic countries co-ordinates policy in the areas of foreign policy, justice, the environment, education and science.

Celtic League: 11 Cleiy Rhennee, Kirk Michael, Isle of Man, IM6 1HT, United Kingdom; tel. (1624) 877918; e-mail b.moffatt@advsys.co.im; internet www.manxman.co.im/cleague/index.html; f. 1961 to foster co-operation between the six Celtic nations (Ireland, Scotland, Man, Wales, Cornwall and Brittany), especially those actively working for political autonomy by non-violent means; campaigns politically on issues affecting the Celtic countries; monitors military activity in the Celtic countries; co-operates with national cultural organizations to promote the languages and culture of the Celts. Mems: approx. 1,400 individuals in the Celtic communities and elsewhere. Chair. CATHAL Ó LUAIN; Gen. Sec. J. B. MOFFAT. Publ. *Carn* (quarterly).

Central European Initiative—CEI: CEI Executive Secretariat, Via Genova 9, 34121 Trieste, Italy; tel. (040) 7786777; fax (040) 360640; e-mail cei-es@cei-es.org; internet www.ceinet.org; f. 1989 as 'Pentagonal' group of central European countries (Austria, Czechoslovakia, Italy, Hungary, Yugoslavia); became 'Hexagonal' with the admission of Poland in July 1991; present name adopted in March 1992, when Croatia and Slovenia replaced Yugoslavia as mems (Bosnia and Herzegovina and the former Yugoslav republic of Macedonia subsequently became mems); the Czech Republic and Slovakia became separate mems in January 1993; Albania, Belarus, Bulgaria, Romania and Ukraine joined the CEI in June 1996 and Moldova in November; aims to encourage regional and bilateral political and economic co-operation, working within the OSCE (q.v.). Dir-Gen. Dr HARALD KREID.

Christian Democrat and Peoples' Parties International: 16 rue de la Victoire, Boîte 1, 1060 Brussels, Belgium; tel. (2) 537-13-22; fax (2) 537-93-48; internet www.idc-cdi.org; f. 1961 to serve as a platform for the co-operation of political parties of Christian Social inspiration. Mems: parties in 64 countries (of which 47 in Europe). Pres. JAVIER RUPÉREZ. Publs *DC-Info* (quarterly), *Human Rights* (5 a year), *Documents* (quarterly).

Comunidade dos Países de Língua Portuguesa (Community of Portuguese-Speaking Countries): rua S. Caetano 32, 1200 Lisbon, Portugal; tel. (1) 392-8560; fax (1) 392-8588; internet www.cplp.org; f. 1996; aims to produce close political, economic, diplomatic and cultural links between Portuguese-speaking countries and to strengthen the influence of the Lusophone commonwealth within the international community. Mems: Angola, Brazil, Cape Verde, Guinea-Bissau, Mozambique, Portugal, São Tomé e Príncipe; East Timor has observer status. Exec. Sec. Dr DULCE MARIA PEREIRA.

Eastern Regional Organization for Public Administration—EROPA: One Burgundy Plaza, Suite 12M, 307 Katipunan Ave, Loyola Heights, Quezon City 1105, Metro Manila, Philippines; tel. (2) 433-8175; fax (2) 434-9223; e-mail eropa@eropa.org.ph; internet www.eropa.org.ph; f. 1960 to promote regional co-operation in improving knowledge, systems and practices of governmental administration, to help accelerate economic and social development; organizes regional conferences, seminars, special studies, surveys and training programmes. There are three regional centres: Training Centre (New Delhi), Local Government Centre (Tokyo), Development Management Centre (Seoul). Mems: 12 countries, 102 organizations/groups, 418 individuals. Chair. CORAZON ALMA G. DE LEON (Philippines); Sec.-Gen. PATRICIA A. STO TOMAS (Philippines). Publs *EROPA Bulletin* (quarterly), *Asian Review of Public Administration* (2 a year).

European Movement: 25 Square de Meeus, 1040 Brussels, Belgium; tel. (2) 508-30-88; fax (2) 512-66-73; e-mail secretariat@europeanmovement.skynet.be; internet www.europeanmovement.org; f. 1947 by a liaison committee of representatives from European organizations, to study the political, economic and technical problems of a European Union and suggest how they could be solved and to inform and lead public opinion in the promotion of integration. Conferences have led to the creation of the Council of Europe, College of Europe, etc. Mems: national councils and committees in 27 European countries, and several international social and economic organizations. Pres. JOSÉ MARIA GIL-ROBLES (Spain); Sec.-Gen. PIER VIRGILIO DASTOLI (Italy).

European Union of Women—EUW: 2 Pittakou St, 10558 Athens, Greece; tel. (1) 3314847; fax (1454) 3314817; e-mail fpetralia@parliament.gr; f. 1955 to increase the influence of women in the political and civic life of their country and of Europe. Mems: national organizations in 21 countries. Chair. FANNY PALLI; Sec.-Gen. VASSO KOLLIA.

La Francophonie: 28 rue de Bourgogne, 75007 Paris, France; tel. 1-44-11-12-50; fax 1-44-11-12-76; e-mail oif@.francophonie.org; internet www.francophonie.org; political grouping of French-speaking countries; conference of heads of state convened every two years to promote co-operation throughout the French-speaking world (2002: Beirut, Lebanon). Mems: govts of 51 countries. Sec.-Gen. BOUTROS BOUTROS-GHALI (Egypt).

Gulf of Guinea Commission (Commission du Golfe de Guinée—CGG): f. 2001 to promote co-operation among mem. countries and the peaceful and sustainable development of natural resources in the sub-region. Mems: Angola, Cameroon, the Repub. of the Congo, Equatorial Guinea, Gabon, Nigeria, Sao Tomé e Principe.

Hansard Society: St Philips Bldg North, LSE, Sheffield St, London, WC2A 2EX, United Kingdom; tel. (20) 7955-7459; fax (20) 7955-7492; e-mail hansard@hansard.lse.ac.uk; internet www.hansardsociety.org.uk; f. 1944 as Hansard Society for Parliamentary Government; aims to promote political education and research and the informed discussion of all aspects of modern parliamentary government. Dir SHELAGH DIPLOCK. Publ. *Parliamentary Affairs—A Journal of Comparative Politics* (quarterly).

International Alliance of Women: 9/10 Queen St, Melbourne, Vic 3000, Australia; tel. (3) 9629-3653; fax (3) 9629-2904; e-mail toddsec@surfnetcity.com.au; f. 1904 to obtain equality for women in all fields and to encourage women to assume responsibilities and join in international activities. Mems: 78 national affiliates in 67 countries. Pres. PATRICIA GILES. Publ. *International Women's News* (quarterly).

International Association for Community Development—IACD: 179 rue du Débarcadère, 6001 Marcinelle, Belgium; tel. (71) 44-72-78; fax (71) 47-11-04; internet www.iacdglobal.org; organizes annual international colloquium for community-based organizations. Sec.-Gen. PIERRE ROZEN. Publ. *IACD Newsletter* (2 a year).

International Commission for the History of Representative and Parliamentary Institutions—ICHRPI: c/o John Rogister, Dept of History, 43–46 North Bailey, Durham DH1 3EX, United Kingdom; fax (191) 374-4754; internet www.univie.ac.at/ichrpi; f. 1936; promotes research into the origin and development of representative and parliamentary institutions worldwide; encourages wide and comparative study of such institutions, both current and historical; facilitates the exchange of information. Mems: 300 individuals in 31 countries. Pres. JOHN ROGISTER (UK); Sec. JOHN H. GREVER (USA). Publs *Parliaments, Estates and Representation* (annually), studies.

International Democrat Union: 32 Smith Sq., London, SW1P 3HH, United Kingdom; tel. (20) 7984-8052; fax (20) 7976-0486; e-mail rnormington@idu.org; internet www.idu.org; f. 1983 as a group of centre and centre-right political parties; facilitates the exchange of information and views; promotes networking; organizes campaigning seminars for politicians and party workers; holds Party Leaders' meetings every three or four years, also executive meetings and a Young Leaders' Forum. Mems: political parties in 37 countries, 46 assoc. mems in regions. Exec. Sec. RICHARD NORMINGTON.

International Federation of Resistance Movements: c/o R. Maria, 5 rue Rollin, 75005 Paris, France; tel. 1-43-26-84-29; f. 1951; supports the medical and social welfare of former victims of fascism; works for peace, disarmament and human rights, and against fascism and neo-fascism. Mems: 82 national organizations in 29 countries. Pres. ALIX LHOTE (France); Sec.-Gen. OSKAR WIESFLECKER (Austria). Publs *Feuille d'information* (in French and German), *Cahier d'informations médicales, sociales et juridiques* (in French and German).

International Institute for Peace: Möllwaldplatz 5, 1040 Vienna, Austria; tel. (1) 504-43-76; fax (1) 505-32-36; e-mail iip@aon.at; f. 1957; non-governmental organization with consultative status at ECOSOC (see UN) and UNESCO; studies interdependence as a strategy for peace, conflict prevention and the transformation of central and eastern Europe. Mems: individuals and corporate bodies invited by the executive board. Pres. ERWIN LANC (Austria); Dir Prof. LEV VORONKOV (Russia). Publs *Peace and the Sciences* (quarterly, in English), occasional papers (2 or 3 a year, in English and German).

International Institute for Strategic Studies—IISS: Arundel House, 13–15 Arundel St, London, WC2R 3DX, United Kingdom; tel. (20) 7379-7676; fax (20) 7836-3108; e-mail iiss@iiss.org; internet www.iiss.org; f. 1958; concerned with the study of the role of force in international relations, including problems of international strategy, the ethnic, political and social sources of conflict, disarmament and arms control, peace-keeping and intervention, defence economics, etc.; independent of any government. Mems: c. 3,000. Dir Dr JOHN M. W. CHIPMAN. Publs *Survival* (quarterly), *The Military Balance* (annually), *Strategic Survey* (annually), *Adelphi Papers* (10 a year), *Strategic Comments* (10 a year).

International Lesbian and Gay Association—ILGA: 81 rue Marché-au-charbon, 1000 Brussels 1, Belgium; tel. and fax (2) 502-24-71; e-mail ilga@ilga.org; internet www.ilga.org; f. 1978; works to abolish legal, social and economic discrimination against homosexual and bisexual women and men, and transexuals, throughout the world; co-ordinates political action at an international level; co-operates with other supportive movements; 2001 world conference: Oakland, CA, USA. Mems: 350 national and regional asscns in 75 countries. Secs-Gen. ANNA LEAH SARABIA, KURSAD KAHRAMANOGLU. Publs *ILGA Bulletin* (quarterly), *GBLT Human Rights Annual Report.*

International Peace Bureau—IPB: 41 rue de Zürich, 1201 Geneva, Switzerland; tel. (22) 7316429; fax (22) 7389419; e-mail mailbox@ipb.org; internet www.ipb.org; f. 1892; promotes international co-operation for general and complete disarmament and the non-violent solution of international conflicts; co-ordinates and represents peace movements at the UN; conducts projects on the abolition of nuclear weapons and the role of non-governmental organizations in conflict prevention and resolution. Mems: 220 peace organizations in 53 countries. Pres. CORA WEISS; Sec.-Gen. COLIN ARCHER. Publs *IPB News* (quarterly), *IPB Geneva News*.

International Political Science Association—IPSA: c/o Prof. John Coakley, Dept of Politics, Univ. College Dublin, Belfield, Dublin 4, Ireland; tel. (1) 706-8182; fax (1) 706-1171; e-mail ipsa@ucd.ie; internet www.ucd.ie/~ipsa/index.html; f. 1949; aims to promote the development of political science. Mems: 41 national asscns, 100 institutions, 1,350 individual mems. Pres. Prof. THEODORE J. LOWI (USA); Sec.-Gen. JOHN COAKLEY. Publs *Participation* (3 a year), *International Political Science Abstracts* (6 a year), *International Political Science Review* (quarterly).

International Union of Local Authorities—IULA: POB 90646, 2509 LP, The Hague, Netherlands; tel. (70) 3066066; fax (70) 3500496; e-mail iula@iula.org; internet www.iula.org; f. 1913 to promote local government, improve local administration and encourage popular participation in public affairs. Activities include organization of a biennial international congress; operation of specific 'task forces' (Association Capacity-Building, Women in Local Government, Information Technology); development of intermunicipal relations to provide a link between local authorities of countries; maintenance of a permanent office for the collection and distribution of information on municipal affairs. Mems: in over 110 countries, seven regional sections. Pres. ALAN LLOYD; Sec.-Gen. JEREMY SMITH. Publs various, on a range of local government issues.

International Union of Young Christian Democrats—IUYCD: 16 rue de la Victoire, 1060 Brussels, Belgium; tel. (2) 537-77-51; fax (2) 534-50-28; f. 1962. Mems: national organizations in 59 countries and territories. Sec.-Gen. MARCOS VILLASMIL (Venezuela). Publs *IUYCD Newsletter* (fortnightly), *Debate* (quarterly).

Jewish Agency for Israel—JAFI: POB 92, 48 King George St, Jerusalem, Israel; tel. (2) 6202297; fax (2) 6202412; e-mail elibir@jazo.org.il; internet www.jafi.org.il; f. 1929; reconstituted 1971 as an instrument through which world Jewry can work to develop a national home. Constituents are: World Zionist Organization, United Israel Appeal, Inc. (USA), and Keren Hayesod. Chair. Exec. SALLAI MERIDOR; Chair. Bd. ALEX GRASS.

Latin American Parliament (Parlamento Latinoamericano): Avda Auro Soares de Moura Andrade 564, São Paulo, Brazil; tel. (11) 38246325; fax (11) 38246324; internet www.parlatino.org; f. 1965; permanent democratic institution, representative of all existing political trends within the national legislative bodies of Latin America; aims to promote the movement towards economic, political and cultural integration of the Latin American republics, and to uphold human rights, peace and security. Publs *Acuerdos, Resoluciones de las Asambleas Ordinarias* (annually), *Revista del Parlamento Latinoamericano* (annually); statements and agreements.

Liberal International: 1 Whitehall Place, London, SW1A 2HD, United Kingdom; tel. (20) 7839-5905; fax (20) 7925-2685; e-mail li@worldlib.org; internet www.worldlib.org/li/; f. 1947; world union of 83 liberal parties in 58 countries; co-ordinates foreign policy work of member parties, and promotes freedom, tolerance, democracy, international understanding, protection of human rights and market-based economics; has consultative status at ECOSOC of United Nations and the Council of Europe. Pres. ANNEMIE NEYTS-UYTTEBROECK; Sec.-Gen. JAN WEIJERS. Publ. *London Aerogramme* (monthly).

Nato Parliamentary Assembly: 3 place du Petit Sablon, 1000 Brussels, Belgium; tel. (2) 513-28-65; fax (2) 514-18-47; e-mail secretariat@naa.be; internet www.nato-pa.int; f. 1955 as the NATO Parliamentarians' Conference; name changed 1966 to North Atlantic Assembly; renamed as above 1999; the inter-parliamentary assembly of the North Atlantic Alliance; holds two plenary sessions a year and meetings of committees (Political, Defence and Security, Economics and Security, Civil Dimension of Security, Science and Technology), where parliamentarians from North America, western Europe and eastern Europe (associate delegates) examine the problems confronting the Alliance and European security issues in general. Pres. RAFAEL ESTRELLA; Sec.-Gen. SIMON LUNN (United Kingdom).

Non-aligned Movement: c/o Permanent Representative of South Africa to the UN, 333 East 38th St, 9th Floor, New York, NY 10016, USA (no permanent secretariat); tel. (212) 213-5583; fax (212) 692-2498; e-mail soafun@worldnet.att.net; internet www.nam.gov.za; f. 1961 by a meeting of 25 Heads of State, with the aim of linking countries that had refused to adhere to the main East-West military and political blocs; co-ordination bureau established in 1973; works for the establishment of a new international economic order, and especially for better terms for countries producing raw materials; maintains special funds for agricultural development, improvement of food production and the financing of buffer stocks; 'South Commission' (q.v.) promotes co-operation between developing countries; seeks changes in the United Nations to give developing countries greater decision-making power; holds summit conference every three years; 13th conference scheduled to be held in Dakar, Bangladesh, in April 2002. Mems: 113 countries.

Open Door International (for the Economic Emancipation of the Woman Worker): 16 rue Américaine, 1060 Brussels, Belgium; tel. (2) 537-67-61; f. 1929 to obtain equal rights and opportunities for women in the whole field of work. Mems: in 10 countries. Hon. Sec. ADÈLE HAUWEL (Belgium).

Organization for the Prohibition of Chemical Weapons—OPCW: Johan de Wittlaan 32, 2517JR The Hague, Netherlands; tel. (70) 4163300; fax (70) 3063535; e-mail mediabr@opcw.org; internet www.opcw.org; f. 1997 to oversee implementation of the Chemical Weapons Convention, which aims to ban the development, production, stockpiling and use of chemical weapons. The Convention was negotiated under the auspices of the UN Conference on Disarmament and entered into force in April 1997, at which time the OPCW was inaugurated. Governed by an Executive Council, comprising representatives of 41 States Parties, elected on a regional basis; undertakes mandatory inspections of member states party to the Convention (145 at Dec. 2001). Provisional 2002 budget: €61.9m. Dir-Gen. JOSÉ MAURICIO BUSTANI (Brazil).

Organization of Solidarity of the Peoples of Africa, Asia and Latin America (Organización de Solidaridad de los Pueblos de Africa, Asia y América Latina—OSPAAAL): Apdo 4224 y 6130, Calle C No 670 esq. 29, Vedado, Havana 10400, Cuba; tel. (7) 830-5136; fax (7) 833-3985; f. 1966 at the first Conference of Solidarity of the Peoples of Africa, Asia and Latin America, to unite, co-ordinate and encourage national liberation movements in the three continents, to oppose foreign intervention in the affairs of sovereign states, colonial and neo-colonial practices, and to fight against racialism and all forms of racial discrimination; favours the establishment of a new international economic order. Mems: organizations in 10 countries. Sec.-Gen. JUAN CARRETERO IBAÑEZ. Publ. *Tricontinental* (quarterly).

Organization of the Cooperatives of America (Organización de las Cooperativas de América): Apdo Aéreo 241263, Carrera 11, No. 86-32 Of. 101, Santafé de Bogotá, DC, Colombia; tel. (1) 610-3296; fax (1) 610-1912; f. 1963 for improving socio-economic, cultural and moral conditions through the use of the co-operative system; works in every country of the continent; regional offices sponsor plans of activities based on the most pressing needs and special conditions of individual countries. Mems: organizations in 23 countries and territories. Pres. Dr ARMANDO TOVAR PARADA; Exec. Sec. Dr CARLOS JULIO PINEDA. Publs *OCA News* (monthly), *América Cooperativa* (3 a year).

Parliamentary Association for Euro-Arab Co-operation: 21 rue de la Tourelle, 1040 Brussels, Belgium; tel. (2) 231-13-00; fax (2) 231-06-46; e-mail paeac@medea.be; internet www.medea.be; f. 1974 as an asscn of 650 parliamentarians of all parties from the national parliaments of the Council of Europe countries and from the European Parliament, to promote friendship and co-operation between Europe and the Arab world; Executive Committee holds annual joint meetings with Arab Inter-Parliamentary Union; represented in Council of Europe, Western European Union and European Parliament; works for the progress of the Euro-Arab Dialogue and a settlement in the Middle East that takes into account the national rights of the Palestinian people. Joint Chair. ROSELYNE BACHELOT (France), HENNING GJELLEROD (Denmark); Sec.-Gen. JEAN-MICHEL

DUMONT (Belgium). Publs *Information Bulletin* (quarterly), *Euro-Arab and Mediterranean Political Fact Sheets* (2 a year).

Party of European Socialists—PES: 60 rue Wiertz, 1047 Brussels, Belgium; tel. (2) 284-29-76; fax (2) 230-17-66; e-mail pes@pes.org; internet www.pes.org; f. 1992 to replace the Confederation of the Socialist Parties of the EC (f. 1974); affiliated to Socialist International (q.v.). Mems: 20 member parties, 15 associate parties and 6 observer parties. Chair. ROBIN COOK (UK); Sec.-Gen. ANTONY BEUMER. Publs various, including statutes, manifestos and Congress documents.

Rio Group: f. 1987 at a meeting in Acapulco, Mexico, of eight Latin American government leaders, who agreed to establish a 'permanent mechanism for joint political action'; additional countries subsequently joined the Group (see below); holds annual summit meetings at presidential level. At the ninth presidential summit (Quito, Ecuador, September 1995) a 'Declaration of Quito' was adopted, which set out joint political objectives, including the strengthening of democracy; combating corruption, drugs-production and -trafficking and 'money laundering'; and the creation of a Latin American and Caribbean free trade area by 2005 (supporting the efforts of the various regional groupings). Opposes US legislation (the 'Helms-Burton' Act), which provides for sanctions against foreign companies that trade with Cuba; also concerned with promoting sustainable development in the region, the elimination of poverty, and economic and financial stability. The Rio Group holds annual ministerial conferences with the European Union (10th meeting held in Chile in March 2001; 11th meeting scheduled to be held in Greece in 2003). Mems: Argentina, Bolivia, Brazil, Chile, Colombia, Ecuador, Mexico, Panama, Paraguay, Peru, Uruguay, Venezuela.

Shanghai Co-operation Organization—SCO: f. 2001, replacing the Shanghai Five (f. 1996 to address border disputes); comprises People's Republic of China, Kazakhstan, Kyrgyzstan, Russia, Tajikistan and Uzbekistan; aims to achieve security through mutual co-operation: promotes economic co-operation and measures to eliminate terrorism and drugs-trafficking; agreement on combating terrorism signed June 2001; an SCO anti-terrorism centre was to be established in Bishkek, Kyrgyzstan, in 2001; holds annual summit meeting.

Socialist International: Maritime House, Clapham, London, SW4 0JW, United Kingdom; tel. (20) 7627-4449; fax (20) 7720-4448; e-mail secretariat@socialistinternational.org; internet www.socialistinternational.org; f. 1864; re-established in 1951; the world's oldest and largest asscn of political parties, grouping democratic socialist, labour and social democratic parties from every continent; provides a forum for political action, policy discussion and the exchange of ideas; works with many international organizations and trades unions (particularly members of ICFTU, q.v.); holds Congress every three years. The Council meets twice a year, and regular conferences and meetings of party leaders are also held; committees and councils on a variety of subjects and in different regions meet frequently. Mems: 89 full member, 25 consultative and 15 observer parties in 110 countries. There are three fraternal organizations and nine associated organizations, including: the Party of European Socialists (PES, q.v.), the Group of the PES at the European Parliament and the International Federation of the Socialist and Democratic Press (q.v.). Pres. ANTONIO GUTERRES (Portugal); Gen. Sec. LUIS AYALA (Chile); Publ. *Socialist Affairs* (quarterly).

International Falcon Movement—Socialist Educational International: 3 rue Quinaux, 1030 Brussels, Belgium; tel. (2) 215-79-27; fax (2) 245-00-83; e-mail contact@ifm.sei.org; internet www.ifm.sei.org; f. 1924 to help children and adolescents develop international understanding and a sense of social responsibility and to prepare them for democratic life; co-operates with several institutions concerned with children, youth and education. Mems: about 1m., 62 co-operating organizations in all countries. Pres. ÖSTEN LÖUGREN (Sweden); Sec.-Gen. UWE OSTENDORFF (Germany). Publs *IFM-SEI Bulletin* (quarterly), *IFM-SEI Documents, Flash Infos* (6 a year), *Asian Regional Bulletin, Latin American Regional Bulletin.*

International Union of Socialist Youth—IUSY: 1070 Vienna, Neustiftgasse 3/13, Austria; tel. (1) 523-12-67; fax (1) 523-12-679; e-mail iusy@iusy.org; internet www.iusy.org; f. 1907 as Socialist Youth International (present name adopted 1946), to educate young people in the principles of free and democratic socialism and further the co-operation of democratic socialist youth organizations; conducts international meetings, symposia, etc. Mems: 134 youth and student organizations in 100 countries. Pres. ALVARO ELIZALDE SOTO; Gen. Sec. LISA PELLING. Publs *IUSY Newsletter, FWG News, IUSY—You see us in Action.*

Socialist International Women: Maritime House, Old Town, Clapham, London, SW4 0JW, United Kingdom; tel. (20) 7627-4449; fax (20) 7720-4448; e-mail socintwomen@gn.apc.org; internet socintwomen.org; f. 1907 to promote the understanding among women of the aims of democratic socialism; to facilitate the exchange of experience and views; to promote programmes opposing discrimination in society; and to work for human rights in general and for development and peace. Mems: 131 organizations. Pres. DOLORS RENAU; Gen. Sec. MARLÈNE HAAS. Publ. *Women and Politics* (quarterly).

Stockholm International Peace Research Institute—SIPRI: Signalistgatan 9, 169 70 Solna, Sweden; tel. (8) 655-97-00; fax (8) 655-97-33; e-mail sipri@sipri.se; internet www.sipri.se; f. 1966; carries out studies on international security and arms control issues, including on conflict and crisis management, peace-keeping and regional security, and chemical and biological warfare. Mems: about 50 staff mems, half of whom are researchers. Dir Dr ADAM DANIEL ROTFELD (Poland); Chair. ROLF EKÉUS (Sweden). Publs *SIPRI Yearbook: Armaments, Disarmament and International Security*, monographs and research reports.

Transparency International: Otto-Suhr-Allee 97-99, 10585 Berlin, Germany; tel. (30) 3438200; fax (30) 34703912; e-mail ti@transparency.de; internet www.transparency.de; f. 1993; aims to promote governmental adoption of anti-corruption practices and accountability at all levels of the public sector; works to ensure that international business transactions are conducted with integrity and without resort to corrupt practices; formulates an annual Corruption Perception Index and a Bribe Payers Index; holds International Anti-Corruption Conference every two years. Chair. Dr PETER EIGEN.

Trilateral Commission: 1156 15th St, NW, Washington, DC 20005, USA; tel. (202) 467-5410; fax (202) 467-5415; e-mail admin@trilateral.org; internet www.trilateral.org; (also offices in Paris and Tokyo); f. 1973 by private citizens of western Europe, Japan and North America, to encourage closer co-operation among these regions on matters of common concern; by analysis of major issues the Commission seeks to improve public understanding of problems, to develop and support proposals for handling them jointly, and to nurture the habit of working together in the 'trilateral' area. The Commission issues 'task force' reports on such subjects as monetary affairs, political co-operation, trade issues, the energy crisis and reform of international institutions. Mems: about 335 individuals eminent in academic life, industry, finance, labour, etc.; those currently engaged as senior government officials are excluded. Chair. THOMAS S. FOLEY, YOTARO KOBYASHI, PETER SUTHERLAND; Dirs MICHAEL J. O'NEIL, TADASHI YAMAMTO, PAUL REVAY. Publs *Task Force Reports, Triangle Papers.*

Unrepresented Nations' and Peoples' Organization—UNPO: Javastraat, 40A, 2585 AP, Netherlands; tel. (70) 360-3318; fax (70) 360-3346; e-mail unpo@unpo.nl; internet www.unpo.org; f. 1991 to provide an international forum for indigenous and other unrepresented peoples and minorities; provides training in human rights, law, diplomacy and public relations to UNPO members; provides conflict resolution services. Mems: 52 organisations representing occupied nations, indigenous peoples and minorities. Gen. Sec. ETKIN ALPTEKIN. Publs *UNPO News, UNPO Yearbook.*

War Resisters' International: 5 Caledonian Rd, London, N1 9DX, United Kingdom; tel. (20) 7278-4040; fax (20) 7278-0444; e-mail warresisters@gn.apc.org; internet www.gn.apc.org/warresisters; f. 1921; encourages refusal to participate in or support wars or military service, collaborates with movements that work for peace and non-violent social change. Mems: approx. 150,000. Chair. JOANNE SHEEHAN; Sec. ROBERTA BACIC. Publ. *Peace News* (quarterly).

Women's International Democratic Federation (Fédération Démocratique Internationale des Femmes—FDIF): c/o 'Femmes solidaires', 25 rue du Charolais, 75012 Paris, France; tel. 1-40-

01-90-90; fax 1-40-01-90-81; e-mail fdif@fdif.eu.org; f. 1945 to unite women regardless of nationality, race, religion or political opinion; to enable them to work together to win and defend their rights as citizens, mothers and workers; to protect children; and to ensure peace and progress, democracy and national independence. Structure: Congress, Secretariat and Executive Committee. Mems: 629 organizations in 104 countries. Pres. SYLVIE JAN (France); Vice-Pres. MAYADA ABBASSI (Palestine). Publs *Women of the Whole World* (6 a year), *Newsletter*.

World Council of Indigenous Peoples: 100 Argyle Ave, 2nd Floor, Ottawa, K2P 1B6, Canada; tel. (613) 230-9030; fax (613) 230-9340; f. 1975 to promote the rights of indigenous peoples and to support their cultural, social and economic development; comprises representatives of indigenous organizations from five regions: North, South and Central America, Pacific-Asia and Scandinavia; holds General Assembly every three years. Pres. CONRADO JORGE VALIENTE. Publ. *WCIP Newsletter* (4–6 a year).

World Disarmament Campaign: 45–47 Blythe St, London, E2 6LN, United Kingdom; tel. (20) 7729-2523; f. 1980 to encourage governments to take positive and decisive action to end the arms race, acting on the four main commitments called for in the Final Document of the UN's First Special Session on Disarmament; aims to mobilize people of every country in a demand for multilateral disarmament, to encourage consideration of alternatives to the nuclear deterrent for ensuring world security, and to campaign for a strengthened role for the UN in these matters. Chair. Dr FRANK BARNABY, Dr TONY HART. Publ. *World Disarm!* (6 a year).

World Federalist Movement: 777 UN Plaza, New York, NY 10017, USA; tel. (212) 599-1320; fax (212) 599-1332; e-mail wfm@igc.apc.org; internet www.worldfederalist.org; f. 1947 to achieve a just world order through a strengthened United Nations; to acquire for the UN the authority to make and enforce laws for the peaceful settlement of disputes, and to raise revenue under limited taxing powers; to establish better international co-operation in the areas of environment, development and disarmament; and to promote federalism throughout the world. Mems: c. 25,000 in 41 countries. Pres. Sir PETER USTINOV; Exec. Dir WILLIAM R. PACE. Publ. *World Federalist News* (quarterly).

World Federation of United Nations Associations—WFUNA: c/o Palais des Nations, 1211 Geneva 10, Switzerland; tel. (22) 7330730; fax (22) 7334838; internet www.wfuna.org; f. 1946 to encourage popular interest and participation in United Nations programmes, discussion of the role and future of the UN, and education for international understanding. Plenary Assembly meets every two years; WFUNA has founded International Youth and Student Movement for the United Nations (q.v.). Mems: national asscns in 80 countries. Pres. HASHIM ABDUL HALIM (India); Sec.-Gen. DONALD BLINKEN. Publ. *WFUNA News*.

World Peace Council: 94 rue Jean-Pierre Timbaud, 75011 Paris, France; tel. 1-40-12-09-12; fax 1-40-11-57-87; e-mail 100144.1501@compuserve.com; internet www.wpc-in.org; f. 1950 at the Second World Peace Congress, Warsaw. Principles: the prevention of nuclear war; the peaceful co-existence of the various socio-economic systems in the world; settlement of differences between nations by negotiation and agreement; complete disarmament; elimination of colonialism and racial discrimination; and respect for the right of peoples to sovereignty and independence. Mems: representatives of national organizations, groups and individuals from 140 countries, and of 30 international organizations; Executive Committee of 40 mems elected by world assembly held every three years. Pres. ALBERTINA SISULU; Exec. Sec. LYSIANE ALEZARD. Publ. *Peace Courier* (monthly).

Youth of EPP—YEPP: EPP Group, European Parliament, Bureau 2F, 158 rue Wiertz, 1047, Brussels, Belgium; tel. (2) 284-36-73; fax (2) 284-49-40; e-mail yepp@eeuroparl.eu.int; internet www.yepp.org; f. 1997 to unite national youth organizations of member parties of European Young Christian Democrats and Democrat Youth Community of Europe; aims to develop contacts between youth movements and advance general political debate. Mems: 388 national organizations in 29 European countries. Exec. Officer FILIP VANCRAENENDONCK. Publ. *YEPP News* (monthly).

Industrial and Professional Relations

See also the chapters on ICFTU, WCL and WFTU.

Arab Federation of Petroleum, Mining and Chemicals Workers: POB 5339, Tripoli, Libya; tel. (21) 444-7597; fax (21) 444-9139; f. 1961 to establish industrial relations policies and procedures for the guidance of affiliated unions; promotes establishment of trade unions in the relevant industries in countries where they do not exist. Publs *Arab Petroleum* (monthly), specialized publications and statistics.

European Association for Personnel Management—EAPM: c/o CIPD, IPD House, Camp Rd, Wimbledon, London, SW19 4UX; tel. (20) 8263-3273; fax (20) 8262-3806; e-mail f.wilson@ipd.co.uk; internet www.eapm.org; f. 1962 to disseminate knowledge and information concerning the personnel function of management, to establish and maintain professional standards, to define the specific nature of personnel management within industry, commerce and the public services, and to assist in the development of national asscns. Mems: 22 national asscns. Pres. CHRISTOPH SCHAUB (Switzerland); Sec.-Gen. GEOFF ARMSTRONG (UK).

European Civil Service Federation—ECFS: 200 rue de la Loi, L 102 6/14, 1049 Brussels, Belgium; e-mail secretariat.politique@ffpe.org; internet www.ffpe.org; f. 1962 to foster the idea of a European civil service of staff of international organizations operating in western Europe or pursuing regional objectives; upholds the interests of civil service members. Mems: local cttees in 12 European countries and individuals in 66 countries. Sec.-Gen. L. RIJNOUDT. Publ. *Eurechos*.

European Construction Industry Federation: 66 ave Louise, 1050 Brussels, Belgium; tel. (2) 514-55-35; fax (2) 511-02-76; e-mail info@fiec.org; internet www.fiec.org; f. 1905 as International European Construction Federation, present name adopted 1999. Mems: 31 national employers' organizations in 24 countries. Pres. FRANCO NOBILI (Italy); Dir-Gen. ULRICH PAETZOUD. Publs *Annual Report, Construction Activity in Europe*.

European Federation of Conference Towns: POB 182, 1040 Brussels, Belgium; tel. (2) 732-69-54; fax (2) 732-58-62; e-mail efct@efct.com; internet www.efct.com; lays down standards for conference towns; provides advice and assistance to its members and other organizations holding conferences in Europe; undertakes publicity and propaganda for promotional purposes; helps conference towns to set up national centres. Exec. Dir ALINE LEGRAND.

European Federation of Lobbying and Public Affairs (Fédération européenne du lobbying et public afairs—FELPA): rue du Trône 61, 1050 Brussels, Belgium; tel. (2) 511-74-30; fax (2) 511-12-84; aims to enhance the development and reputation of the industry; encourages professionals active in the industry to sign a code of conduct outlining the ethics and responsibilities of people involved in lobbying or public relations work with the institutions of the EU. Pres. Y. DE LESPINAY.

European Industrial Research Management Association—EIRMA: 34 rue de Bassano, 75008 Paris, France; tel. 1-53-23-83-10; fax 1-47-20-05-30; e-mail info@eirma.asso.fr; internet www.eirma.asso.fr; f. 1966 under auspices of the OECD (q.v.); a permanent body in which European science-based firms meet to consider approaches to industrial innovation, support research and development, and take joint action to improve performance in their various fields. Mems: 160 in 21 countries. Pres. LARS-GÖRAN ROSENGREN; Gen. Sec. ANDREW DEARING. Publs *Annual Report, Conference Reports, Working Group Reports, Workshop Reports*.

European Trade Union Confederation—ETUC (Confédération européenne des syndicats): 5 blvd du Roi Albert II, 1210 Brussels, Belgium; tel. (2) 224-04-11; fax (2) 224-04-54; e-mail etuc@etuc.org; internet www.etuc.org; f. 1973; comprises 74 national trade union confederations and 15 European industrial federations in 33 European countries, representing 60m. workers; holds congress every four years. Gen. Sec. EMILIO GABAGLIO.

Federation of International Civil Servants' Associations—FICSA: Palais des Nations, 1211 Geneva 10, Switzerland; tel. (22) 917-3150; fax (22) 917-0660; e-mail ficsa@ficsa.org; internet www.ficsa.org; f. 1952 to co-ordinate policies and activities of member asscns and unions, to represent staff interests before inter-agency and legislative organs of the UN and to promote the development of an international civil service. Mems: 26 asscns and unions consisting of staff of UN organizations, 2 associate mems from non-UN organizations, 25 consultative asscns and 17 inter-organizational federations with observer status. Pres. BERNHARD P. GRANDJEAN; Gen. Sec. ANDRÉ J. HEITZ. Publs *Annual Report, FICSA Newsletter, FICSA Update, FICSA circulars.*

Graphical International Federation: Valeriusplein 30, 1075 BJ Amsterdam, Netherlands; tel. (20) 671-32-79; fax (20) 675-13-31; f. 1925. Mems: national federations in 15 countries, covering 100,000 workers. Pres. L. VAN HAUDT (Belgium); Sec.-Gen. R. E. VAN KESTEREN (Netherlands).

International Association of Conference Interpreters: 10 ave de Sécheron, 1202 Geneva, Switzerland; tel. (22) 9081540; fax (22) 7324151; e-mail aiic@compuserve.com; internet www.aiic.net; f. 1953 to represent professional conference interpreters, ensure the highest possible standards and protect the legitimate interests of mems; establishes criteria designed to improve the standards of training; recognizes schools meeting the required standards; has consultative status with the UN and several of its agencies. Mems: 2,300 in 53 countries. Pres. MALICK SY (Switzerland); Exec. Sec. JOSYANE CRISTINA. Publs *Code of Professional Conduct, Yearbook* (listing interpreters), etc.

International Association of Conference Translators: 15 route des Morillons, 1218 Le Grand-Saconnex, Geneva, Switzerland; tel. (22) 7910666; fax (22) 7885644; e-mail secretariat@aitc.ch; internet www.aitc.ch; f. 1962; represents revisers, translators, précis writers and editors working for international conferences and organizations; aims to protect the interests of those in the profession and help maintain high standards; establishes links with international organizations and conference organizers. Mems: 419 in 33 countries. Pres. GENEVIÈVE SÉRIOT (Switzerland); Exec. Sec. MICHEL BOUSSOMMIER (France). Publs *Directory, Bulletin.*

International Association of Crafts and Small and Medium-Sized Enterprises—IACME: c/o Centre patronal, CP 1215, 1001 Lausanne, Switzerland; tel. (21) 796-33-54; fax (21) 796-33-11; e-mail info@centrepatronal.ch; f. 1947 to defend undertakings and the freedom of enterprise within private economy, to develop training, to encourage the creation of national organizations of independent enterprises and promote international collaboration, to represent the common interests of members and to institute exchange of ideas and information. Mems: organizations in 26 countries. Chair. MARIO SECCA; Gen. Sec. JACQUES DESGRAZ.

International Association of Medical Laboratory Technologists—IAMLT: Adolf Fredriks Kyrkogata 11, 111 37 Stockholm, Sweden; tel. (8) 10-30-31; fax (8) 10-90-61; e-mail margareta.haag@iamlt.org; internet www.iamlt.org; f. 1954 to allow discussion of matters of common professional interest; aims to promote globally the highest standards in the delivery of care, of professional training, and ethical and professional practices; develops and promotes active professional partnerships in health care at the international level; promotes and encourages participation of members in international activities; holds international congress every second year. Mems: 180,000 in 40 countries. Pres. MARTHA HJÁLMARSDÓTTIR; Exec. Dir MARGARETA HAAG. Publs *MedTecInternational* (2 a year), *Newsletter* (6 a year).

International Association of Mutual Insurance Companies (Association internationale des sociétés d'assurance mutuelle—AISAM): 114 rue La Boëtie, 75008 Paris, France; tel. 1-42-25-84-86; fax 1-42-56-04-49; e-mail aisam@wanadoo.fr; internet www.aisam.org; f. 1963 for the establishment of good relations between members and the protection of the general interests of private insurance based on the principle of mutuality. Mems: over 200 in 25 countries. Pres. BENT KNIE-ANDERSEN (Denmark); Sec.-Gen. GÉRARD OUTTERS. Publs *Mutuality* (2 a year), *AISAM Directory, Newsletter.*

International Federation of Actors (Fédération internationale des acteurs—FIA): Guild House, Upper St Martin's Lane, London, WC2H 9EG, United Kingdom; tel. (20) 7379-0900; fax (20) 7379-8260; e-mail office@fia-actors.com; internet www.fia-actors.com; f. 1952. Mems: 100 performers' unions in 70 countries. Pres. TOMAS BOLME (Sweden); Gen. Sec. DOMINICK LUQUER.

International Federation of Air Line Pilots' Associations—IFALPA: Interpilot House, Gogmore Lane, Chertsey, Surrey, KT16 9AP, United Kingdom; tel. (1932) 571711; fax (1932) 570920; e-mail admin@ifalpa.org; internet www.ifalpa.org; f. 1948 to represent pilots at the ICAO and other industry fora and organizations, especially in technical and safety matters; establishes standards for air safety world-wide; seeks to ensure fair conditions of employment for pilots.. Mems: 95 asscns, over 100,000 pilots. Pres. Capt. TED MURPHY. Publs *Interpilot* (2 a year), safety bulletins and news-sheets.

International Federation of Business and Professional Women: Studio 16, Cloisters Business Centre, 8 Battersea Park Rd, London, SW8 4BG, United Kingdom; tel. (20) 7738-8323; fax (20) 7622-8528; e-mail bpwihq@cscom; internet www.bpwintl.com; f. 1930 to promote interests of business and professional women and secure combined action by such women. Mems: national federations, associate clubs and individual associates, totalling more than 200,000 mems in over 100 countries. Pres. SYLVIA G. PERRY; Exec. Dir JANIC BANCROFT. Publ. *BPW News International* (monthly).

International Federation of Insolvency Professionals—INSOL: 2/3 Philpot Lane, London, EC3M 8AQ, United Kingdom; tel. (20) 7929-6679; fax (20) 7929-6678; internet www.insol.org; f. 1982; comprises national asscns of accountants and lawyers specializing in corporate turnaround and insolvency; holds annual conference. Mems: 29 asscns, with more than 7,700 individual members. Publ. *International Insolvency Review* (2 a year).

International Industrial Relations Association—IIRA: c/o International Labour Office, 1211 Geneva 22, Switzerland; tel. (22) 7996841; fax (22) 7998541; e-mail mennie@ilo.org; internet www.iira2001.org; f. 1966 to encourage development of national asscns of specialists, facilitate the spread of information, organize conferences, and promote internationally planned research, through study groups and regional meetings; a World Congress is held every three years. Mems: 39 asscns, 47 institutions and 1,100 individuals. Pres. Prof. MANFRED WEISS; Sec. Prof. TAYO FASHOYIN. Publs *IIRA Bulletin* (3 a year), *IIRA Membership Directory, IIRA Congress proceedings.*

International Organisation of Employers—IOE: 26 chemin de Joinville, BP 68, 1216 Cointrin/Geneva, Switzerland; tel. (22) 7981616; fax (22) 7988862; internet www.ioe-emp.org; f. 1920, reorganized 1948; aims to establish and maintain contacts between mems and to represent their interests at the international level; works to promote free enterprise; and to assist the development of employers' organizations. General Council meets annually; there is an Executive Committee and a General Secretariat. Mems: 122 federations in 119 countries. Chair. JEAN-JACQUES OECHSLIN (France); Sec.-Gen. COSTAS KAPARTIS (Cyprus). Publ. *The Free Employer.*

International Organization of Experts—ORDINEX: 19 blvd Sébastopol, 75001 Paris, France; tel. 1-40-28-06-06; fax 1-40-28-03-13; e-mail contact@ordinex.org; internet www.ordinex.org; f. 1961 to establish co-operation between experts on an international level. Mems: 600. Pres. ALI EL KAÏBI (Tunisia); Sec.-Gen. PIERRE ROYER (France). Publ. *General Yearbook.*

International Public Relations Association—IPRA: Cardinal House, 7 Wolsey Rd, Kingston-upon-Thames, KT8 9EL, United Kingdom; tel. (20) 8481-7634; fax (20) 8481-7648; e-mail iprasec@compuserve.com; internet www.ipranet.org; f. 1955 to provide for an exchange of ideas, technical knowledge and professional experience among those engaged in international public relations, and to foster the highest standards of professional competence. Mems: 750 in 73 countries. Sec.-Gen. FRANS VOORHOEVE. Publs *Newsletter* (6 a year), *Frontline 21* (quarterly), *Members' Manual* (annually).

International Society of City and Regional Planners—ISoCaRP: Willem Witsenplein 6, 2596 BK, The Hague, Netherlands; tel. (70) 3462654; fax (70) 3617909; e-mail secretariat@isocarp.org; internet www.isocarp.org; f. 1965 to promote better planning practice through the exchange of knowledge. Holds annual international congress (2001: Netherlands; 2002: Greece). Mems: 450 in 64 countries. Pres. Prof. IR MAX VAN

DEN BERG (Netherlands); Sec.-Gen. Prof. Dr MILICA BAJÍC BRKOVIC (Federal Republic of Yugoslavia). Publs *News Bulletin* (quarterly), *Bulletin* (2 a year); seminar and congress reports.

International Union of Architects (Union internationale des architectes—UIA): 51 rue Raynouard, 75016 Paris, France; tel. 1-45-24-36-88; fax 1-45-24-02-78; e-mail uia@uia-architectes.org; internet www.uia-architectes.org; f. 1948; holds triennial congress. Mems: 106 countries. Pres. VASSILIS SGOUTAS (Greece); Sec.-Gen JEAN-CLAUDE RIGUET (France). Publ. *Lettre d'informations* (monthly).

Latin American Federation of Agricultural and Food Industry Workers (Federación Latinoamericana de Trabajadores Campesinos y de la Alimentación): Avda Baralt esq. Conde a Padre Cierra, Edificio Bapgel, 4°, Oficina 42, Apdo 1422, Caracas 1010A, Venezuela; tel. (2) 863-2447; fax (2) 720463; e-mail lassofeltaca@cantv.net; f. 1961 to represent the interests of agricultural workers and workers in the food and hotel industries in Latin America. Mems: national unions in 28 countries and territories. Sec.-Gen. JOSÉ LASSO. Publ. *Boletín Luchemos* (quarterly).

Nordic Industry Workers' Federation (Nordiska Industriarbetarefederationen—NIF): Olof Palmes gata 11, 5th Floor, Box 1114, 111 81 Stockholm, Sweden; tel. (8) 7868500; fax (8) 105968; e-mail henning.carlsson.nif@industrifacket.se; f. 1901; promotes collaboration between affiliates representing workers in the chemicals, energy, garment, manufacturing, mining, paper and textile sectors in Denmark, Finland, Iceland, Norway and Sweden; supports sister unions economically and in other ways in labour market conflicts. Mems: 400,000 in 17 unions. Pres. LEIF OHLSSON; Sec. HENNING CARLSSON.

Organisation of African Trade Union Unity—OATUU: POB M386, Accra, Ghana; tel. (21) 508851; fax (21) 2772621; internet www.ecouncil.ac.cr/ngoexch/oatuu2.htm; f. 1973 as a single continental trade union org., independent of international trade union organizations; has affiliates from all African trade unions. Congress, the supreme policy-making body, is composed of four delegates from all affiliated trade union centres and meets at least every four years; the General Council, composed of one representative from each affiliated trade union, meets annually to implement Congress decisions and to approve the annual budget. Mems: trade union movements in 53 independent African countries. Sec.-Gen. HASSAN SUNMONU (Nigeria). Publ. *Voice of African Workers.*

Pan-African Employers' Confederation: c/o Mauritius Employers' Federation, Cerné House, 13 la chaussée, Port Louis, Mauritius; tel. 212-1599; fax 212-6725; e-mail mef@intnet.mu; f. 1986 to link African employers' organizations and represent them at the UN, the ILO and the OAU. Sec.-Gen. AZAD JEETUN (Mauritius).

World Federation of Scientific Workers: 1–7 Great George St, London, SW1P 3AA, United Kingdom; tel. (20) 7222-7722; e-mail 100764.1427@compuserve.com; internet perso.wanadoo.fr/fmts.wfsw; f. 1946 to improve the position of science and scientists, to assist in promoting international scientific co-operation and to promote the use of science for beneficial ends; studies and publicizes problems of general, nuclear, biological and chemical disarmament; surveys the position and activities of scientists. Mems: organizations in 37 countries, totalling over 500,000 mems. Sec.-Gen. S. DAVISON (UK). Publ. *Scientific World* (quarterly, in English, Esperanto, German and Russian).

World Movement of Christian Workers—WMCW: 124 blvd du Jubilé, 1080 Brussels, Belgium; tel. (2) 421-58-40; fax (2) 421-58-49; e-mail mmtc@skynet.be; internet www.mmtc-wmcw-wbca.be; f. 1961 to unite national movements that advance the spiritual and collective well-being of workers; holds General Assembly every four years. Mems: 47 affiliated movements in 39 countries. Sec.-Gen. NORBERT KLEIN. Publ. *Infor-WMCW.*

World Union of Professions (Union mondiale des professions libérales): 38 rue Boissière, 75116 Paris, France; tel. 1-44-05-90-15; fax 1-44-05-90-17; e-mail info@umpl.com; internet www.umpl.com; f. 1987 to represent and link members of the liberal professions. Mems: 27 national inter-professional organizations, two regional groups and 12 international federations. Pres. LUIS EDUARDO GAUTERIO GALLO; Sec.-Gen. HENRY SALMON.

Law

African Bar Association: 29/31 Obafemi Awolowo Way, Ikeja, Lagos, Nigeria (temporary address); tel. (1) 4936907; fax (1) 7752202; f. 1972; aims to uphold the rule of law, maintain the independence of the judiciary, and improve legal services. Pres. PETER ALA ADJETY (Ghana); Sec.-Gen. FEMI FELANA (Nigeria).

African Society of International and Comparative Law—ASICL: Private Bag 520, Kairaba ave KSMD, Banjul, The Gambia; tel. 375476; fax 375469; e-mail asicl@compuserve.com; internet www.asicl.org; f. 1986; promotes public education on law and civil liberties; aims to provide a legal aid and advice system in each African country, and to facilitate the exchange of information on civil liberties in Africa. Pres. MOHAMED BEDJAOUI; Sec. EMILE YAKPO (Ghana). Publs *Newsletter* (every 2 months), *African Journal of International and Comparative Law* (quarterly).

Asian-African Legal Consultative Organization—AALCO: E-66, Vasant Marc, Vasant Vihar, New Delhi 110057, India; tel. (11) 6152251; fax (11) 6152041; e-mail aalco@ysnl.com; internet www.aalco.org; f. 1956 to consider legal problems referred to it by member countries and to serve as a forum for Afro-Asian co-operation in international law and economic relations; provides background material for conferences, prepares standard/model contract forms suited to the needs of the region; promotes arbitration as a means of settling international commercial disputes; trains officers of member states; has permanent UN observer status. Mems: 45 countries. Pres. Dr P. S. RAO (India); Sec.-Gen. Dr WAFIK ZAHER KAMIL (Egypt).

Centre for International Environmental Law—CIEL: 1367 Connecticut Ave, NW, Suite 300, Washington, DC 20036, USA; tel. (202) 785-8700; fax (202) 785-8701; e-mail info@ciel.org; internet www.ciel.org; f. 1989; aims to solve environmental problems and promote sustainable societies through use of law; works to strengthen international and comparative environmental law and policy and to incorporate fundamental ecological principles into international law; provides a range of environmental legal services; educates and trains environmental lawyers. Exec. Dir DANIEL MAGRAW; Pres. DURWOOD ZAELKE.

Council of the Bars and Law Societies of the European Union—CCBE: 45 rue de Trèves, 1040 Brussels, Belgium; tel. (2) 234-65-10; fax (2) 234-65-11; e-mail ccbe@ccbe.org; internet www.ccbe.org; f. 1960; the officially recognized representative organization for the legal profession in the European Union and European Economic Area; liaises between the bars and law societies of member states and represents them before the European institutions; also maintains contact with other international organizations of lawyers. The CCBE's principal objective is to study all questions affecting the legal profession in member states and to harmonize professional practice. Mems: 18 delegations (representing some 500,000 European lawyers), and observers from Bulgaria, Croatia, Cyprus, Czech Republic, Estonia, Hungary, Poland, Romania, Slovakia, Slovenia, Switzerland and Turkey. Pres. JOHN FISH; Sec.-Gen. JONATHON GOLDSMITH.

Hague Conference on Private International Law: Scheveningseweg 6, 2517 KT, The Hague, Netherlands; tel (70) 3633303; fax (70) 3604867; e-mail secretariat@hcch.net; internet www.hcch.net; f. 1893 to work for the unification of the rules of private international law; Permanent Bureau f. 1955. Mems: 38 European and 19 other countries. Sec.-Gen. J. H. A. VAN LOON. Publs *Proceedings of Diplomatic Sessions* (every 4 years), *Collection of Conventions.*

Institute of International Law (Institut de droit international): IUHEI, 132 rue de Lausanne, CP 36, 1211 Geneva 21, Switzerland; tel. (22) 9085720; fax (22) 9085710; e-mail gerardi@hei.unige.ch; f. 1873 to promote the development of international law through the formulation of general principles, in accordance with civilized ethical standards; provides assistance for the gradual and progressive codification of international law. Mems: limited to 132 members and associates world-wide. Sec.-Gen. CHRISTIAN DOMINICÉ (Switzerland). Publ. *Annuaire de l'Institut de Droit international.*

Inter-African Union of Lawyers: 12 rue du Prince Moulay Abdullah, Casablanca, Morocco; tel. (2) 271017; fax (2) 204686;

f. 1980; holds congress every three years. Pres. ABDELAZIZ BENZAKOUR (Morocco); Sec.-Gen. FRANÇOIS XAVIER AGONDJO-OKAWE (Gabon). Publ. *L'avocat africain* (2 a year).

Inter-American Bar Association—IABA: 1211 Connecticut Ave, NW, Suite 202, Washington, DC 20036, USA; tel. (202) 466-5944; fax (202) 466-9546; e-mail iaba@iaba.org; internet www.iaba.org; f. 1940 to promote the rule of law and to establish and maintain relations between asscns and organizations of lawyers in the Americas. Mems: 90 asscns and 3,500 individuals in 27 countries. Pres. ANTONO DE SOLA; Sec.-Gen. LOUIS G. FERRAND (USA). Publs *Newsletter* (quarterly), *Conference Proceedings*.

Intergovernmental Committee of the Universal Copyright Convention: Division of Creativity, Cultural Industries and Copyright, UNESCO, 7 place de Fontenoy, 75700 Paris, France; tel. 1-45-68-47-05; fax 1-45-68-55-89; e-mail r.sye@unesco.org; established to study the application and operation of the Universal Copyright Convention and to make preparations for periodic revisions of this Convention; studies other problems concerning the international protection of copyright, in co-operation with various international organizations. Mems: 18 states. Publ. *Copyright Bulletin* (quarterly).

International Association for the Protection of Industrial Property—AIPPI: Tödistrasse 16, 8027 Zürich 27, Switzerland; tel. (1) 2805880; fax (1) 2805885; e-mail mail@aippi.org; internet www.aippi.org; f. 1897 to encourage the development of legislation on the international protection of industrial property and the development and extension of international conventions, and to make comparative studies of existing legislation with a view to its improvement and unification; holds triennial congress. Mems: 8,200 (national and regional groups and individual mems) in 108 countries. Exec. Pres. J. MICHAEL DOWLING (Australia); Sec.-Gen. VINCENZO M. PEDRAZZINI (Switzerland). Publs *Yearbook*, reports.

International Association of Democratic Lawyers: 21 rue Brialmont, 1210 Brussels, Belgium; tel. and fax (2) 223-33-10; e-mail iadl@ist.cerist.dz; internet www.iadllaw.org; f. 1946 to facilitate contacts and exchange between lawyers, encourage study of legal science and international law and support the democratic principles favourable to the maintenance of peace and co-operation between nations; promotes the preservation of the environment; conducts research on labour law, private international law, agrarian law, etc.; has consultative status with UN. Mems: in 96 countries. Pres. AMAR BENTOUMI (Algeria); Sec.-Gen. JITENDRA SHARMA (India). Publ. *International Review of Contemporary Law*, (2 a year, in French, English and Spanish).

International Association of Juvenile and Family Court Magistrates: 175 Andersonstown Rd, Belfast, BT11 9EA, Northern Ireland; f. 1928 to consider questions concerning child welfare legislation and to encourage research in the field of juvenile courts and delinquency; organizes study groups, meetings and an international congress. Mems: 23 national asscns. Pres. LUCIEN BEAULIEU (Canada).

International Association of Law Libraries—IALL: POB 5709, Washington, DC 20016-1309, USA; e-mail morriso6@is.dal.ca; internet www.iall.org; f. 1959 to encourage and facilitate the work of librarians and others concerned with the bibliographic processing and administration of legal materials. Mems: 600 from more than 50 countries (personal and institutional). Pres. HOLGER KNUDSEN (Germany); Sec. ANN MORRISON (Canada). Publ. *International Journal of Legal Information* (3 a year).

International Association of Legal Sciences (Association internationale des sciences juridiques): c/o CISS, 1 rue Miollis, 75015 Paris, France; tel. 1-45-68-25-59; fax 1-43-06-87-98; f. 1950 to promote the mutual knowledge and understanding of nations and the increase of learning by encouraging throughout the world the study of foreign legal systems and the use of the comparative method in legal science. Governed by a president and an executive committee of 11 members known as the International Committee of Comparative Law; sponsored by UNESCO. Mems: national committees in 47 countries. Pres. Prof. WLADIMIR TOUMANOV (Russia); Sec.-Gen. M. LEKER (Israel).

International Association of Penal Law: 41 rue Bonado, 640000 Pau, France; tel. 5-59-98-08-24; fax 5-59-27-24-56; e-mail aidp-pau@infonie.fr; f. 1924 to promote collaboration between those from different countries working in penal law, studying criminology, or promoting the theoretical and practical development of international penal law. Mems: 1,800. Pres. Prof. M. C. BASSIOUNI; Sec.-Gen. Dr H. EPP. Publs *Revue Internationale de Droit Pénal* (2 a year), *Nouvelles Etudes Penales*.

International Bar Association—IBA: 271 Regent St, London, W1R 7PA, United Kingdom; tel. (20) 7629-1206; fax (20) 7409-0456; internet www.ibanet.org; f. 1947; a non-political federation of national bar asscns and law societies; aims to discuss problems of professional organization and status; to advance the science of jurisprudence; to promote uniformity and definition in appropriate fields of law; to promote administration of justice under law among peoples of the world; to promote in their legal aspects the principles and aims of the United Nations. Mems: 154 member organizations in 164 countries, 17,500 individual members in 173 countries. Pres. KLAUS BÖHLHOFF (Germany); Exec. Dir PAUL HODDINOTT (UK). Publs *International Business Lawyer* (11 a year), *International Bar News* (3 a year), *International Legal Practitioner* (quarterly), *Journal of Energy and Natural Resources Law* (quarterly).

International Commission of Jurists—ICJ: POB 216, 81A ave de Châtelaine, 1219 Châtelaine/Geneva, Switzerland; tel. (22) 9793800; fax (22) 9793801; e-mail info@icj.org; internet www.icj.org; f. 1952 to promote the understanding and observance of the rule of law and the protection of human rights throughout the world; maintains Centre for the Independence of Judges and Lawyers (f. 1978); contributes to the elaboration of international human rights instruments and their adoption and implementation by governments. Mems: 81 sections and affiliates. Pres. Justice CLAIRE L'HEUREUX-DUBÉ (Canada); Sec.-Gen. LOUISE DOSWALD-BECK. Publs *CIJL Yearbook, The Review, ICJ Newsletter*, special reports.

International Commission on Civil Status: 3 place Arnold, 67000 Strasbourg, France; e-mail ciec-sg@ciec1.org; internet www.ciec1.org; f. 1950 for the establishment and presentation of legislative documentation relating to the rights of individuals; carries out research on means of simplifying the judicial and technical administration with respect to civil status. Mems: governments of Austria, Belgium, Croatia, France, Germany, Greece, Hungary, Italy, Luxembourg, Netherlands, Poland, Portugal, Spain, Switzerland, Turkey, United Kingdom. Pres. H. G. KOUMANTOS (Greece); Sec.-Gen. P. LAGARDE (France). Publs *Guide Pratique international de l'état civil* (available on-line), various studies on civil status.

International Copyright Society: 81667 Munich, Rosenheimer Strasse 11, Germany; tel. (89) 4800300; fax (89) 48003969; f. 1954 to enquire scientifically into the natural rights of the author and to put the knowledge obtained to practical application world-wide, in particular in the field of legislation. Mems: 393 individuals and corresponding organizations in 52 countries. Pres. Prof. Dr REINHOLD KREILE; Gen. Sec. Dr MARTIN VOGEL. Publs *Schriftenreihe* (61 vols), *Yearbook*.

International Council for Commercial Arbitration—ICCA: c/o Ulf Franke, POB 16050, 103 21 Stockholm, Sweden; tel. (8) 55510000; fax (8) 56631650; e-mail info@arbitration-icca.org; internet www.arbitration-icca.org; promotes international arbitration and other forms of dispute resolution; convenes Congresses and Conferences for discussion and the presentation of papers. Mems: 33 mems, 12 advisory mems. Pres. FALI S. NARIMAN (India), Sec.-Gen. ULF FRANKE (Sweden). Publs *Yearbook on Commercial Arbitration, International Handbook on Commercial Arbitration, ICCA Congress Series*.

International Council of Environmental Law: 53113 Bonn, Adenauerallee 214, Germany; tel. (228) 2692240; fax (228) 2692250; e-mail 100651.317@compuserve.com; f. 1969 to exchange information and expertise on legal, administrative and policy aspects of environmental questions. Exec. Governors Dr WOLFGANG BURHENNE, Dr ABDULBAR AL-GAIN. Publs *Directory, References, Environmental Policy and Law, International Environmental Law—Multilateral Treaties*, etc.

International Criminal Police Organization—INTERPOL: 200 quai Charles de Gaulle, 69006 Lyon, France; tel. 4-72-44-70-00; fax 4-72-44-71-63; e-mail cp@interpol.int; internet www.interpol.int; f. 1923, reconstituted 1946; aims to promote and ensure mutual assistance between police forces in different countries; co-ordinates activities of police authorities of member states in international affairs; works to establish and develop institutions with the aim of preventing transnational crimes; centralizes records and information on international criminals; operates a telecommunications network of 179 stations; holds General Assembly annually. Mems: official bodies of 179 countries. Sec.-Gen. RONALD K. NOBLE (USA). Publs *International Criminal Police Review, International Crime Statistics, Stolen Works of Art* (CD Rom), *Interpol Guide to Vehicle Registration Documents* (annually).

International Customs Tariffs Bureau: 38 rue de l'Association, 1000 Brussels, Belgium; tel. (2) 501-87-74; fax (2) 218-30-25; e-mail bitd@euronet.be; internet www.bitd.org; f. 1890; serves as the executive instrument of the International Union for the Publication of Customs Tariffs; translates and publishes all customs tariffs in five languages—English, French, German, Italian, Spanish. Mems: 71. Pres. JAN DE BOCK (Belgium); Dir DAVID DAVIES (UK). Publs *International Customs Journal, Annual Report.*

International Development Law Institute—IDLI: Via di San Sebastianello 16, 00187 Rome, Italy; tel. (06) 6979261; fax (06) 6781946; e-mail idli@idli.org; internet www.idli.org; f. 1983; designs and conducts courses and seminars for lawyers, legal advisors and judges from developing countries, central and eastern Europe and the former USSR; also provides in-country training workshops; training programme addresses legal skills, international commercial law, economic law reform, governance and the role of the judiciary. Dir-Gen. WILLIAM T. LORIS.

International Federation for European Law—FIDE: 113 ave Louise, 1050 Brussels, Belgium; tel. (2) 534-71-63; fax (2) 534-28-58; e-mail pia.conseil@euronet.be; f. 1961 to advance studies on European law among members of the European Community by co-ordinating activities of member societies; organizes conferences every two years. Mems: 12 national asscns. Pres. G. O. ZACHARIAS SUNDSTRÖM; Sec.-Gen. Prof. P.-C. MÜLLER-GRAFF.

International Federation of Senior Police Officers: FISP, Ministère de l'Intérieur, 127 rue Faubourg Saint Honoré, 75008 Paris, France; tel. 1-49-27-40-67; fax 1-49-24-01-13; f. 1950 to unite policemen of different nationalities, adopting the general principle that prevention should prevail over repression, and that the citizen should be convinced of the protective role of the police; established International Centre of Crime and Accident Prevention, 1976 and International Association against Counterfeiting, 1994. Mems: 34 national organizations. Sec.-Gen. JEAN-PIERRE HAVRIN (France). Publ. *International Police Information* (quarterly, in French, German and English).

International Institute for the Unification of Private Law—UNIDROIT: Via Panisperna 28, 00184 Rome, Italy; tel. (06) 696211; fax (06) 69941394; e-mail unidroit.rome@unidroit.org; internet www.unidroit.org; f. 1926 to undertake studies of comparative law, to prepare for the establishment of uniform legislation, to prepare drafts of international agreements on private law and to organize conferences and publish works on such subjects; holds international congresses on private law and meetings of organizations concerned with the unification of law; maintains a library of 215,000 vols. Mems: govts of 58 countries. Pres. LUIGI FERRARI BRAVO (Italy); Sec.-Gen. Prof. Dr HERBERT KRONKE (Germany). Publs *Uniform Law Review* (quarterly), *Digest of Legal Activities of International Organizations,* etc.

International Institute of Space Law—IISL: 3–5 rue Mario Nikis, 75015 Paris, France; tel. 1-45-67-42-60; fax 1-42-73-21-20; e-mail rtmasson@cyberway.com.sg; internet www.iafastro.com; f. 1959 at the XI Congress of the International Astronautical Federation; organizes annual Space Law colloquium; studies juridical and sociological aspects of astronautics; makes awards. Pres. MARCIA NOGUERIA BARBOSA (Brazil). Publs *Proceedings of Annual Colloquium on Space Law, Survey of Teaching of Space Law in the World.*

International Juridical Institute—IJI: Permanent Office for the Supply of International Legal Information, Spui 186, 2511 BW, The Hague, Netherlands; tel. (70) 3460974; fax (70) 3625235; e-mail iji@worldonline.nl; f.1918 to supply information on any non-secret matter of international interest, respecting international, municipal and foreign law and the application thereof. Pres. A. V. M. STRUYCKEN; Dir A. L. G. A. STILLE.

International Law Association—ILA: Charles Clore House, 17 Russell Sq., London, WC1B 5DR, United Kingdom; tel. (20) 7323-2978; fax (20) 7323-3580; e-mail secretariat@ila-hq.org; internet www.ila-hq.org; f. 1873 for the study and advancement of international law, both public and private and the promotion of international understanding and goodwill. Mems: 4,000 in 51 regional branches; 25 international cttees. Pres. Prof. HUNGDAH CHIU (Taiwan); Chair. Exec. Council Lord SLYNN OF HADLEY (UK); Sec.-Gen. DAVID J. C. WYLD (UK).

International Maritime Committee (Comité maritime international): Markgravestraat 9, 2000 Antwerp, Belgium; tel. (3) 227-35-26; fax (3) 227-35-28; e-mail admin@cmi-imc.org; f. 1897 to contribute to the unification of maritime law and to encourage the creation of national asscns; work includes drafting of conventions on collisions at sea, salvage and assistance at sea, limitation of shipowners' liability, maritime mortgages, etc. Mems: national asscns in 50 countries. Pres. PATRICK GRIGGS (UK). Publs *CMI Newsletter, Year Book.*

International Nuclear Law Association—INLA: 29 sq. de Meeûs, 1000 Brussels, Belgium; tel. (2) 547-58-41; fax (2) 503-04-40; e-mail aidn.inla@skynet.be; internet www.aidn-inla.be; f. 1972 to promote international studies of legal problems related to the peaceful use of nuclear energy; holds conference every two years. Mems: 500 in 30 countries. Sec.-Gen. V. VERBRAEKEN. Publs *Congress reports, Une Histoire de 25 ans.*

International Penal and Penitentiary Foundation: c/o Dr K. Hobe, Bundesministerium der Justiz, 10104 Berlin, Germany; tel. (30) 20259226; fax (30) 20259525; f. 1951 to encourage studies in the field of prevention of crime and treatment of delinquents. Mems in 23 countries (membership limited to three people from each country) and corresponding mems. Pres. JORGE DE FIGUEIREDO DIAS (Portugal); Sec.-Gen. KONRAD HOBE (Germany).

International Police Association—IPA: 1 Fox Rd, West Bridgford, Nottingham, NG2 6AJ, United Kingdom; tel. (115) 945-5985; fax (115) 982-2578; e-mail isg@ipa-iac.org; internet www.ipa-iac.org; f. 1950 to permit the exchange of professional information, create ties of friendship between all sections of the police service and organize group travel and studies. Mems: 291,000 in more than 58 countries. International Sec.-Gen. A. F. CARTER.

International Society for Labour Law and Social Security—ISLLSS: CP 500, 1211 Geneva 22, Switzerland; tel. (22) 7996343; fax (22) 7998542; e-mail bromstein@ilo.org; internet www.ilo.org/isllss; f. 1958 to encourage collaboration between labour law and social security specialists; holds World Congress every three years, as well as irregular regional congresses (Europe, Africa, Asia and Americas). Mems: 66 national asscns of labour law officers. Pres. Prof. ROGER BLANPAIN (Belgium); Sec.-Gen. ARTURO BROMSTEIN.

International Union of Latin Notaries (Unión Internacional del Notariado Latino): Via Locatelli 5, 20124 Milan, Italy; internet www.uinl.org; f. 1948 to study and standardize notarial legislation and promote the progress, stability and advancement of the Latin notarial system. Mems: organizations and individuals in 70 countries. Sec. EMANUELE FERRARI. Publ. *Revista Internacional del Notariado* (quarterly), *Notarius International.*

Law Association for Asia and the Pacific—LAWASIA: GPO Box 3275, NT House, 11th Floor, 22 Mitchell St, Darwin, Northern Territory 0800, Australia; tel. (8) 8946-9500; fax (8) 8946-9505; e-mail lawasia@lawasia.asn.au; internet www.lawasia.asn.au; f. 1966; provides an international, professional network for lawyers to update, reform and develop law within the region; comprises five Sections and 21 Standing Committees in Business Law and General Practice areas, which organize speciality conferences; also holds a biennial conference (2001: Christchurch, New Zealand). Mems: national orgs in 23 countries; 2,500 mems in 55 countries. Publs *Directory* (annually), *LAWASIA Update* (quarterly), *Directory* (annually), *Journal* (annually).

Permanent Court of Arbitration: Peace Palace, Carnegieplein 2, 2517 KJ, The Hague, Netherlands; tel. (70) 3024165; fax (70) 3024167; e-mail bureau@pca-cpa.org; internet www.pca-cpa.org; f. by the Convention for the Pacific Settlement of International Disputes (1899, 1907); provides for the resolution of disputes involving combinations of states, private parties and intergovernmental organizations, under its own rules of procedure, by means of arbitration, conciliation and fact-finding. Operates a secretariat, the International Bureau, which provides registry services and legal support to ad hoc tribunals and commissions; draws up lists of adjudicators with specific expertise; and maintains documentation on mass claims settlement processes. Mems: governments of 95 countries. Sec.-Gen. TJACO VAN DEN HOUT (Netherlands). Publs *Kluwer Law International Database* (ed), *Journal of International Arbitration* (ed), *World Trade and Arbitration Materials* (ed), *Peace Palace Papers* (ed), *International Law Seminars* (2 a year).

Society of Comparative Legislation: 28 rue Saint-Guillaume, 75007 Paris, France; tel. 1-44-39-86-23; fax 1-44-39-86-28; e-mail slc@sky.fr; internet www.legiscompare.com; f. 1869 to study and compare laws of different countries, and to investigate practical means of improving the various branches of legislation. Mems: 600 in 48 countries. Pres. GUY CANIVET (France); Sec.-Gen. MARIE-ANNE GALLOT LE LORIER (France). Publ. *Revue Internationale de Droit Comparé* (quarterly).

Union Internationale des Avocats (International Association of Lawyers): 25 rue du Jour, 75001 Paris, France; tel. 1-44-88-55-66; fax 1-44-88-55-77; e-mail uiacentre@wanadoo.fr; internet www.uianet.org; f. 1927 to promote the independence and freedom of lawyers, and defend their ethical and material interests on an international level; aims to contribute to the development of international order based on law. Mems: 250 asscns and 3,000 lawyers in over 120 countries. Pres. MIGUEL ESTRADA SAMANO (Mexico); Exec. Dir MARIE-PAUL RICHARD.

Union of Arab Jurists: POB 6026, Al-Mansour, Baghdad, Iraq; tel. (1) 5372371; fax (1) 53723693; f. 1975 to facilitate contacts between Arab lawyers, to safeguard the Arab legislative and judicial heritage, to encourage the study of Islamic jurisprudence; and to defend human rights. Mems: national jurists asscns in 15 countries. Sec.-Gen. SHIBIB LAZIM AL-MALIKI. Publ. *Al-Hukuki al-Arabi* (Arab Jurist).

Union of International Associations—UIA: 40 rue Washington, 1050 Brussels, Belgium; tel. (2) 640-41-09; fax (2) 643-61-99; e-mail uia@uia.be; internet www.uia.org; f. 1907, present title adopted 1910; aims to facilitate the evolution of the activities of the world-wide network of non-profit organizations, especially non-governmental and voluntary asscns; collects and disseminates information on such organizations; promotes research on the legal, administrative and other problems common to these asscns. Mems: 200 in 54 countries. Sec.-Gen. JACQUES RAEYMAECKERS (Belgium). Publs *Transnational Associations* (6 a year), *International Congress Calendar* (quarterly), *Yearbook of International Organizations, International Organization Participation* (annually), *Global Action Network* (annually), *Encyclopedia of World Problems and Human Potential, Documents for the Study of International Non-Governmental Relations, International Congress Science* series, *International Association Statutes* series, *Who's Who in International Organizations*.

World Jurist Association—WJA: 1000 Connecticut Ave, NW, Suite 202, Washington, DC 20036, USA; tel. (202) 466-5428; fax (202) 452-8540; e-mail wja@worldjurist.org; internet www.worldjurist.org; f. 1963; promotes the continued development of international law and the legal maintenance of world order; holds biennial world conferences, World Law Day and demonstration trials; organizes research programmes. Mems: lawyers, jurists and legal scholars in 155 countries. Pres. HANS THÜMMEL (Germany); Exec. Vice-Pres. MARGARETHA M. HENNEBERRY (USA). Publs *The World Jurist* (6 a year), Research Reports, *Law and Judicial Systems of Nations*, 3rd revised edn (directory), *World Legal Directory, Law/Technology* (quarterly), *World Law Review* Vols I–V (World Conference Proceedings), *The Chief Justices and Judges of the Supreme Courts of Nations* (directory), work papers, newsletters and journals.

World Association of Judges—WAJ: 1000 Connecticut Ave, NW, Suite 202, Washington, DC 20036, USA; tel. (202) 466-5428; fax (202) 452-8540; e-mail wja@worldjurist.org; f. 1966 to advance the administration of judicial justice through co-operation and communication among ranking jurists of all countries. Pres. Prince BOLA AJIBOLA (Nigeria).

World Association of Law Professors—WALP: 1000 Connecticut Ave, NW, Suite 202, Washington, DC 20036, USA; tel. (202) 466-5428; fax (202) 452-8540; e-mail wja@worldjurist.org; internet www.worldjurist.org; f. 1975 to improve scholarship and education in matters related to international law. Pres. SERAFIN V. C. GUINGONA (Philippines).

World Association of Lawyers—WAL: 1000 Connecticut Ave, NW, Suite 202, Washington, DC 20036, USA; tel. (202) 466-5428; fax (202) 452-8540; e-mail wja@worldjurist.org; internet www.worldjurist.org; f. 1975 to develop international law and improve lawyers' effectiveness in this field. Pres. JACK STREETER (USA).

Medicine and Health

Council for International Organizations of Medical Sciences—CIOMS: c/o WHO, ave Appia, 1211 Geneva 27, Switzerland; tel. (22) 7913467; fax (22) 7913111; e-mail cioms@who.ch; internet www.cioms.ch; f. 1949 to serve the scientific interests of the international biomedical community; aims to facilitate and promote activities in biomedical sciences; runs long-term programmes on bioethics, health policy, ethics and values, drug development and use, and the international nomenclature of diseases; maintains collaborative relations with the UN; holds a general assembly every three years. Mems: 67 organizations. Pres. Prof. JOHN H. BRYANT; Sec.-Gen. Prof. J. E. IDÄNPÄÄN-HEIKKILÄ. Publs *Reports on Drug Development and Use, Proceedings of CIOMS Conferences, International Nomenclature of Diseases*.

MEMBERS OF CIOMS

Members of CIOMS include the following:

FDI World Dental Federation: 7 Carlisle St, London, W1V 5RG, United Kingdom; tel. (20) 7935-7852; fax (20) 7486-0183; internet www.fdi.org.uk; f. 1900. Mems: 129 national dental asscns and 29 affiliates. Pres. Dr KATSUO TSURUMAKI (Japan); Exec. Dir Dr P. Å. ZILLÉN (Sweden). Publs *International Dental Journal* (every 2 months) and *FDI World* (every 2 months).

International Association for the Study of the Liver: c/o Prof. June W. Halliday, Queensland Institute of Medical Research, The Bancroft Centre, PO Royal Brisbane Hospital, Brisbane, Australia 4029; tel. (7) 3362-0373; fax (7) 3362-0191; e-mail jhallid@tpgi.com.au; internet www.powerup.com.au/~iasl; Pres. Dr JOHN L. GOLLAN; Sec. Prof. JUNE W. HALLIDAY.

International College of Surgeons—ICS: 1516 N. Lake Shore Drive, Chicago, IL 60610, USA; tel. (312) 642-3555; fax (312) 787-1624; e-mail info@icsglobal.org; internet www.icsglobal.org; f. 1935, as a world-wide federation of surgeons and surgical specialists for the advancement of the art and science of surgery; aims to create a common bond among the surgeons of all nations and promote the highest standards of surgery, without regard to nationality, creed, or colour; sends teams of surgeons to developing countries to teach local surgeons; provides research and scholarship grants, organizes surgical congresses around the world; manages the International Museum of Surgical Science in Chicago. Mems: c. 10,000 in 112 countries. Pres. Prof. CHUN-JEAN LEE (Taiwan); Exec. Dir MAX DOWNHAM (USA). Publ. *International Surgery* (quarterly).

International Diabetes Federation—IDF: 1 rue Defacqz, 1000 Brussels, Belgium; tel. (2) 538-55-11; fax (2) 538-51-14; e-mail luc.hendrickx@idf.org; internet www.idf.org; f. 1949 to help in the collection and dissemination of information on diabetes and to improve the welfare of people suffering from diabetes. Mems: 175 asscns in 138 countries. Pres. Sir GEORGE ALBERTI; Exec. Dir LUC HENDRICKX. Publs *Diabetes Voice, Bulletin of the IDF* (quarterly).

International Federation of Clinical Neurophysiology: c/o Prof. G. Caruso, Clinica Neurologica, Univ. di Napoli 'Federico II', Via S. Panini 5, 80131 Naples, Italy; tel. (081) 746-3793; fax (081) 546-9861; internet www.elsevier.nl/homepage/sah/ifcn; f. 1949 to attain the highest level of knowledge in the field of electro-encephalography and clinical neurophysiology in all the countries of the world. Mems: 48 organizations. Pres. Prof. MARC NUWER; Sec. Prof. HIROSHI SHIBASAKI. Publs *The EEG Journal* (monthly), *Evoked Potentials* (every 2 months), *EMG and Motor Control* (every 2 months).

International Federation of Oto-Rhino-Laryngological Societies—IFOS: Oosterveldlaan 24, 2610 Wilrijk, Belgium; tel. and fax (3) 443-36-11; e-mail ifos@uia.ua.ac.be; internet www.ifosworld.org; f. 1965 to initiate and support programmes to protect hearing and prevent hearing impairment; holds Congresses every four years. Pres. G. J. MCCAFFERTY (Australia); Sec.-Gen. P. W. ALBERTI. Publ. *IFOS Newsletter* (quarterly).

International Federation of Surgical Colleges: c/o Prof. S. W. A. Gunn, La Panetiere, 1279 Bogis-Bossey, Switzerland; tel. (22) 7762161; fax (22) 7766417; e-mail muldoon@mail.med.upenn.edu; f. 1958 to encourage high standards in surgical training; accepts volunteers to serve as surgical teachers in developing countries and co-operates with the WHO (q.v.) in these countries; provides journals and text books for needy medical schools; conducts international symposia; offers travel grants. Mems: colleges or asscns in 77 countries, 420 individual associates. Pres. Prof. JONATHAN MEAKINS (Canada); Hon. Sec. Prof. S. W. A. GUNN. Publ. *World Journal of Surgery*.

International League of Associations for Rheumatology—ILAR: c/o Dr J. Sergent, Chief Medical Officer, Vanderbilt Univ., 3810 Nashville, TN 37232-5545, USA; tel. (615) 343-9324; fax (615) 343-6478; internet www.ilar.org; f. 1927 to promote international co-operation for the study and control of rheumatic diseases; to encourage the foundation of national leagues against rheumatism; to organize regular international congresses and to act as a connecting link between national leagues and international organizations. Mems: 13,000. Pres. Dr ROBERTO ARINOVICHE (Chile); Sec.-Gen. Dr JOHN SERGENT (USA). Publs *Annals of the Rheumatic Diseases* (in the UK), *Revue du Rhumatisme* (in France), *Reumatismo* (in Italy), *Arthritis and Rheumatism* (in the USA), etc.

International Leprosy Association (ILA): c/o ALM, 1 ALM Way, Greenville, SC 29601, USA; tel. (864) 271-7040; fax (864) 271-7062; e-mail amlep@leprosy.org; f. 1931 to promote international co-operation in work on leprosy; holds congress every five years (2002: Brazil). Pres. Dr YO YUASA (Japan); Sec. Dr PIETER FEENSTRA (Netherlands). Publ. *International Journal of Leprosy and Other Mycobacterial Diseases* (quarterly).

International Pediatric Association—IPA: c/o Univ. of Rochester School of Medicine and Dentistry, Dept. of Pediatrics (Rm 4-8104), 601 Elmwood, Rochester NY 14642-8777, USA; tel. (716) 275-0225; fax (716) 273-1038; internet www.ipa-france.net; f. 1912; holds triennial congresses and regional and national workshops. Mems: 135 national paediatric societies in 131 countries, 9 regional affiliate societies, 9 paediatric specialty societies. Pres. Prof. GAVIN C. ARNEIL (UK); Exec. Dir Dr ROBERT J. HAGGERTY. Publ. *International Child Health* (quarterly).

International Rhinologic Society: c/o Prof. Clement, ENT-Dept, AZ-VUB, Laarbeeklaan 101, 1090 Brussels, Belgium; tel. (2) 477-60-02; fax (2) 477-64-23; e-mail knoctp@az.vub.ac.be; f. 1965; holds congress every four years. Pres. I. Y. PARK (Republic of Korea); Sec. Prof. P. A. R. CLEMENT (Belgium). Publ. *Rhinology*.

International Society of Audiology: University Hospital Rotterdam, Audiological Centre, Molewaterplein 40, 3015 GD Rotterdam, Netherlands; tel. (10) 463-4586; fax (10) 463-3102; e-mail verschuure@kno.fgg.eur.nl; internet www.eur.nl/fgg/kno/isa; f. 1952 to facilitate the knowledge, protection and rehabilitation of human hearing and to represent the interests of audiology professionals and of the hearing-impaired; organizes biannual Congress and workshops and seminars. Mems: 300 individuals. Pres. Prof. A. QUARANTA; Gen. Sec. Dr J. VERSCHUURE. Publ. *International Journal of Audiology* (every 2 months).

International Society of Dermatopathology: c/o International Society of Veterinary Dermatopathology, Dept of Dermatology, Univerisity of Graz, Auenbruggerplatz 8, A-8036, Graz, Austria; tel. (316) 385-2423; fax (316) 2466; e-mail lorenzo.cerroni@kfunigraz.ac.at; internet www.vetcutis.freeserve.co.uk/vetcutis.freeserve.co.uk; f. 1958; groups professionals interested in the microscopic interpretation of skin diseases; aims to advance veterinary and comparative dermatopathology; encourages the development of technologies for the diagnosis of skin diseases in animals; promotes professional training. Pres. Dr LORENZO CERRONI; Sec. Dr NOREEN WALSH.

International Society of Internal Medicine: Dept. of Medicine, Regionalspital, 4900 Langenthal, Switzerland; tel. (62) 9163102; fax (62) 9164155; e-mail r.streuli@sro.ch; internet www.acponline.org/isim; f. 1948 to encourage research and education in internal medicine. Mems: 51 national societies, 3,000 individuals in 54 countries. Congresses: Kyoto, Japan (2002); Granada, Spain (2004). Pres. Prof. JOSEF E. JOHNSON (USA); Sec. Prof. ROLF A. STREULI (Switzerland).

International Society of Physical and Rehabilitation Medicine—ISPRM: c/o Dr J. Jimenez, 600 University Ave, Rm 215, Toronto, M5G 1XJ, Canada; internet www.isprm.org; f. 1999 by merger of International Federation of Physical Medicine and Rehabilitation (f. 1952) and International Rehabilitation Medicine Association (f. 1968). Mems: in 68 countries.

International Union against Cancer (Union internationale contre le cancer—UICC): 3 rue du Conseil Général, 1205 Geneva, Switzerland; tel. (22) 8091811; fax (22) 8091810; e-mail info@uicc.org; internet www.uicc.org; f. 1933 to promote the campaign against cancer on an international level; organizes International Cancer Congress every four years; administers the American Cancer Society UICC International Fellowships for Beginning Investigators (ACSBI), the Astrazeneca and Novartis UICC Transnational Cancer Research Fellowships (TCRF), the UICC International Cancer Technology Transfer Fellowships (ICRETT), the Yamagiwa-Yoshida Memorial UICC International Cancer Study Grants (YY), the Trish Greene UICC International Oncology Nursing Fellowships (IONF), the UICC Asia-Pacific Cancer Society Training Grants (APCASOT), and the Latin America UICC COPES Training and Education Fellowship (LACTEF); conducts worldwide programmes of campaign organization; public and professional education; and patient support, detection and diagnosis; and programmes on epidemiology and prevention; tobacco and cancer; the treatment of cancer; and tumour biology. Mems: voluntary national organizations, cancer research and treatment organizations, institutes and governmental agencies in more than 80 countries. Pres. Dr E. ROBINSON (Israel); Sec.-Gen. Dr S. KVINNSLAND (Norway); Exec. Dir I. MORTARAL (Switzerland). Publs *UICC International Directory of Cancer Institutes and Organizations* (electronic version), *International Journal of Cancer* (36 a year), *UICC News* (quarterly), *International Calendar of Meetings on Cancer* (2 a year).

Latin American Association of National Academies of Medicine: Carrera 7, No 69-05, Santafé de Bogotá, Colombia; tel. and fax (1) 345-8890; internet anm.fepafem.org/alanam.htm; f. 1967. Mems: 11 national Academies. Pres. Dr ROLANDO CALDERÓN VELASCO (Peru); Sec. Dr ZOILO CUELLAR-MONTOYA (Colombia).

Medical Women's International Association—MWIA: 44141 Dortmund, Wilhelm-Brand-Str.3, Germany; e-mail mwia@aol.com; internet members.aol.com/mwia/index.htm; f. 1919 to facilitate contacts between women in medicine and to encourage co-operation in matters connected with international health problems. Mems: national asscns in 43 countries, and individuals. Pres. Dr SHELLEY ROSS (Canada); Sec.-Gen. Dr WALTRAUD DIEKHAUS (Germany). Publ. *MWIA UPDATE* (3 a year).

Organisation panafricaine de lutte contre le SIDA—OPALS: 15/21 rue de L'Ecole de Médecine, 75006 Paris, France; tel. 1-43-26-72-28; fax 1-43-29-70-93; e-mail opals@croix-rouge.fr; f. 1988; disseminates information relating to the treatment and prevention of AIDS; provides training of medical personnel; promotes co-operation between African medical centres and specialized centres in the USA and Europe. Publ. *OPALS Liaison*.

World Allergy Organization—IAACI: 611 East Wells St, Milwaukee, WI 53202, USA; tel. (414) 276-1791; fax (414) 276-3349; f. 1945, as International Association of Allergology and Clinical Immunology, to further work in the educational, research and practical medical aspects of allergic and immunological diseases; 2003 Congress: Vancouver, Canada. Mems: 54 national societies and four regional orgs. Pres. ALLEN P. KAPLAN (USA); Sec.-Gen. Prof. G. WALTER CANONICA (Italy). Publ. *Allergy and Clinical Immunology International* (6 a year).

World Federation for Medical Education: University of Edinburgh Centre for Medical Education, 11 Hill Square, Edinburgh, EH8 9DR, United Kingdom; tel. (131) 650-6209; fax (131) 650-6537; internet www.sund.ku.dk/wfme; f. 1972; aims to promote and integrate medical education world-wide; links regional and international asscns; has official relations with WHO, UNICEF, UNESCO, UNDP and the World Bank. Pres. Prof. H. J. WALTON.

World Federation of Associations of Paediatric Surgeons: c/o Prof. J. Boix-Ochoa, Clinica Infantil 'Vall d'Hebron', Departamento de Cirugía Pediátrica, Valle de Hebron 119-129, Barcelona 08035, Spain; f. 1974. Mems: 80 asscns. Pres. Prof. T. MIYANO; Sec. Prof. J. BOIX-OCHOA.

World Federation of Neurology—WFN: 12 Chandos St, London, W1G 9DR, United Kingdom; tel. (20) 7323-4011; fax (20) 7323-4012; e-mail wfnlondon@aol.com; internet www.wfneurology.org; f. 1955 as International Neurological Congress, present title adopted 1957. Aims to assemble members of various congresses associated with neurology and promote co-operation among neurological researchers. Organizes Congress every four years. Mems: 23,000 in 89 countries. Pres. J. KIMURA (Japan); Sec.-Treas. Dr R. GODWIN-AUSTEN (UK); Admin. K. M. NEWTON (UK). Publs *Journal of the Neurological Sciences, World Neurology* (quarterly).

World Heart Federation: 34 rue de l'Athénée, CP 117, 1211 Geneva 12, Switzerland; tel. (22) 3476755; fax (22) 3471028; e-mail admin@worldheart.org; internet www.worldheart.org; f. 1978 as International Society and Federation of Cardiology, through merger of the International Society of Cardiology and the International Cardiology Federation, name changed as above 1998; aims to promote the study, prevention and relief of cardiovascular diseases through scientific and public education programmes and the exchange of materials; organizes world congresses every four years. Mems: national cardiac societies and heart foundations in 84 countries. Pres. Dr MARIO MARANHAO (Brazil); Sec. Dr J. G. PAPP (Hungary). Publs *CVD Prevention, Heartbeat* (quarterly).

World Medical Association—WMA: 13 chemin du Levant, 01210 Ferney-Voltaire, France; tel. 4-50-40-75-75; fax 4-50-40-59-37; e-mail info@wma.net; internet www.wma.net; f. 1947 to achieve the highest international standards in all aspects of medical education and practice, to promote closer ties among doctors and national medical asscns by personal contact and all other means, to study problems confronting the medical profession, and to present its views to appropriate bodies; holds an annual General Assembly. Mems: 73 national medical asscns. Pres. Dr E. TSUBOI ; Sec.-Gen. Dr DELON HUMAN (South Africa). Publ. *The World Medical Journal* (6 a year).

World Organization of Gastroenterology: II Medizinische Klinik und Poliklinik der Technischen Universität München, Ismaninger Str. 22, 81675 Munich, Germany; tel. (89) 41402250; fax (89) 41404871; internet www.omge.org; f. 1958 to promote clinical and academic gastroenterological practice throughout the world, and to ensure high ethical standards. Mems: in 80 countries. Pres. MEINHARD CLASSEN.

World Psychiatric Association—WPA: Mt Sinai School of Medicine, 5th Ave and 100th St, New York, NY 10029-6574, USA; tel. (718) 334-5094; fax (718) 334-5096; e-mail wpa@dti_net; internet www.wpanet.org; f. 1961 for the exchange of information on problems of mental illness and to strengthen relations between psychiatrists in all countries; organizes World Psychiatric Congresses and regional and inter-regional scientific meetings. Mems: 150,000 psychiatrists in 100 countries. Pres. Prof. JUAN J. LÓPEZ-IBOR (Spain); Sec.-Gen. Prof. JUAN ENRIQUE MEZZICH (USA).

ASSOCIATE MEMBERS OF CIOMS

Associate members of CIOMS include the following:

Asia Pacific Academy of Ophthalmology: c/o Prof. Arthur S. M. Lim, Eye Clinic Singapura, 6A Napier Rd, 02-38 Gleneagles Annexe Block, Gleneagles Hospital, Singapore 258500; tel. 64666666; fax 67333360; f. 1956; holds Congress every two years. Pres. I. C ONSTABLE (Australia); Sec.-Gen. Prof. ARTHUR S. M. LIM (Singapore).

International Association of Medicine and Biology of the Environment: c/o 115 rue de la Pompe, 75116 Paris, France; tel. 1-45-53-45-04; fax 1-45-53-41-75; e-mail celine.abbou@free.fr; f. 1971 with assistance from the UN Environment Programme; aims to contribute to the solution of problems caused by human influence on the environment; structure includes 13 technical commissions. Mems: individuals and organizations in 73 countries. Hon. Pres. Prof. R. DUBOS; Pres. Dr C. ABBOU.

International Committee of Military Medicine—ICMM (Comité international de médecine militaire—CIMM): Hôpital Militaire Reine Astrid, rue Bruyn, 1120 Brussels, Belgium; tel. (2) 264-43-48; fax (2) 264-43-67; e-mail cimm.icmm@smd.be; internet www.cimm-icmm.org; f. 1921 as Permanent Committee of the International Congresses of Military Medicine and Pharmacy; name changed 1990. Aims to increase co-operation and promote activities in the field of military medicine; considers issues relating to mass medicine, dentistry, military pharmacy, veterinary sciences and the administration and organization of medical care missions, among others. Mems: official delegates from 94 countries. Chair. Brig.-Gen. T. SAHI (Finland); Sec.-Gen. Col Dr J. SANABRIA (Belgium). Publ. *Revue Internationale des Services de Santé des Forces Armées* (quarterly).

International Council for Laboratory Animal Science—ICLAS: Canadian Council on Animal Care, 315-350 Albert Street, Ottawa, ON, K1R 1B1, Canada; tel. (613) 238-4031 ext. 28; fax (613) 238-2837; e-mail gdemers@ccac.ca; internet www.iclas.org; f. 1956; promotes the ethical care and use of laboratory animals in research, with the aim of advancing human and animal health; establishes standards and provides support resources; encourages international collaboration to develop knowledge. Pres. Prof. STEVEN PAKES (USA); Sec.-Gen. Dr GILLES DEMERS (Canada).

International Federation of Clinical Chemistry and Laboratory Medicine—IFCC: 30 rue Lionnois, 54000 Nancy, France; tel. 3-83-35-26-16; fax 3-83-32-13-22; e-mail thirion@ifccts.unancy.fr; internet www.ifcc.org; f. 1952. Mems: 78 national societies (about 33,000 individuals) and 33 corporate mems. Pres. Prof. M. MÜLLER (Austria); Sec. Dr R. BAIS (Australia). Publs *Journal* (electronic version), *Annual Report.*

International Medical Society of Paraplegia—IMSOP: National Spinal Injuries Centre, Stoke Mandeville Hospital, Aylesbury, Bucks, HP21 8AL, United Kingdom; tel. (1296) 315866; fax (1296) 315870; e-mail imsop@bucks.net; internet www.imsop.org.uk; studies all problems relating to traumatic and non-traumatic lesions of the spinal cord, including causes, prevention, research and rehabilitation; promotes the exchange of information; assists in efforts to guide and co-ordinate research. Pres. Prof. T. IKATA; Hon. Sec. Prof. J. J. WYNDALE. Publ. *Spinal Cord.*

International Society of Blood Transfusion—ISBT: c/o Eurocongres Conference Management, Jan van Goyenkade 11, 1075 HP Amsterdam, Netherlands; tel. (20) 6794311; fax (20) 6737306; e-mail isbt@eurocongres.org; internet www.isbt-web.org; f. 1937. Mems: c. 1,000 in 100 countries. Pres. Dr PAUL F. W. STRENGERS (Netherlands); Sec.-Gen. P. V. HOLLAND. Publ. *Transfusion Today* (quarterly).

Rehabilitation International: 25 East 21st St, New York, NY 10010, USA; tel. (212) 420-1500; fax (212) 505-0871; internet www.rehab-international.org; f. 1922 to improve the lives of disabled people through the exchange of information and research on equipment and methods of assistance; organizes international conferences and co-operates with UN agencies and other international organizations. Mems: organizations in 92 countries. Pres. Dr ARTHUR O'REILLY; Sec.-Gen. SUSAN PARKER. Publs *International Rehabilitation Review, Rehabilitación* (2 a year).

Transplantation Society: c/o Dr Felix Rapaport, PR Transplant Program, University Hospital, Health Science Centre, State Univ. of New York at Stony Brook, Stony Brook, NY 11794-8192, USA; tel. (516) 444-2209; fax (516) 444-3831; e-mail rapaport@surg.som.sunysb.edu; internet www.transplantation-soc.org; Sec. EDUARDO A. SANTIAGO-DELPÍN.

World Federation of Associations of Poison Centres and Clinical Toxicology Centres: c/o Prof. Louis Roche, CIRC, 150 cours Albert-Thomas, F-69372 Lyon, Cédex 2, France; f. 1975 as World Federation of Associations of Clinical Toxicology Centres and Poison Control Centres. Mems: 37. Pres. Dr. HANS PERSSON. Publ. *Bulletin of the World Federation* (quarterly).

OTHER ORGANIZATIONS

Aerospace Medical Association: 320 S. Henry St, Alexandria, VA 22314, USA; tel. (703) 739-2240; fax (703) 739-9652; e-mail rrayman@asma.org; internet www.asma.org; f. 1929 as Aero Medical Association; aims to advance the science and art of aviation and space medicine; establishes and maintains co-operation between medical and allied sciences concerned with aerospace medicine; works to promote, protect, and maintain safety in aviation and astronautics. Mems: individual, constituent and corporate in 75 countries. Pres. ROGER F. LANDRY (USA); Exec. Dir RUSSELL B. RAYMAN (USA). Publ. *Aviation Space and Environmental Medicine* (monthly).

Asian-Pacific Dental Federation: 242 Tanjong Katong Rd, Singapore 437030; tel. 63453125; fax 63442116; e-mail bibi@pacific.net.sg; f. 1955 to establish closer relationships among dental asscns in Asian and Pacific countries and to encourage research on dental health in the region; holds Congress every year. Mems: 23 national asscns. Sec.-Gen. Dr OLIVER HENNEDIGE. Publ. *Asian Dentist* (every 2 months).

Association for Paediatric Education in Europe: c/o Dr Claude Billeaud, Dept. Néonatal Médicine, Maternité-CHU Pellegrin, 33076 Bordeaux Cédex, France; fax 5-56-79-61-56; e-mail claude.billeaud@neonata.u-bordeaux2.fr; internet www.atinternet.com/apee; f. 1970 to promote research and practice in educational methodology in paediatrics. Mems: 127 in 20 European countries. Pres. Dr JUAN BRINES (Spain); Sec.-Gen. Dr CLAUDE BILLEAUD (France).

Association of National European and Mediterranean Societies of Gastroenterology—ASNEMGE: c/o Mrs A. C. M. van Dijk-Meijer, Wolkendek 5, 3454 TG De Meern, Netherlands; tel. (30) 6667400; fax (30) 6622808; e-mail info@asnemge.org; internet www.asnemge.org; f. 1947 to facilitate the exchange of ideas between gastroenterologists and to disseminate knowledge; organizes International Congress of Gastroenterology every four years. Mems: in 37 countries, national societies and sections of national medical societies. Pres. Prof. COLM D'MORAÍN (Ireland); Sec. Prof. JØRGEN RASK-MADSEN (Denmark).

Balkan Medical Union: POB 149, 1 rue G. Clémenceau, 70148 Bucharest, Romania; tel. (1) 3137857; fax (1) 3121570; f. 1932; studies medical problems, particularly ailments specific to the Balkan region; promotes a regional programme of public health; facilitates the exchange of information between doctors in the region; organizes research programmes and congresses. Mems: doctors and specialists from Albania, Bulgaria, Cyprus, Greece, Moldova, Romania, Turkey and the former Yugoslav republics. Pres. Prof. H. CIOBANU (Moldova). Publs *Archives de l'union médicale Balkanique* (quarterly), *Bulletin de l'union médicale Balkanique* (6 a year), *Annuaire*.

European Association for Cancer Research—EACR: c/o P. Saunders, Cancer Research Laboratories, University of Nottingham, University Park, Nottingham, NG7 2RD, United Kingdom; tel. and fax (115) 9515114; e-mail paul.saunders@nottingham.ac.uk; internet www.oncoweb.com/EACR; f. 1968 to facilitate contact between cancer research workers and to organize scientific meetings in Europe. Mems: over 3,000 in more than 40 European and other countries. Pres. E. OLAH; Sec. Dr HELGA ÖGMUNDSDÓTTIR (Iceland).

European Association for the Study of Diabetes—EASD: 40223 Düsseldorf, Merowingerstr. 29, Germany; tel. (211) 316738; fax (211) 3190987; e-mail easd@uni-duesseldorf.de; internet www.easd.org; f. 1965 to support research in the field of diabetes, to promote the rapid diffusion of acquired knowledge and its application; holds annual scientific meetings within Europe. Mems: 6,000 in 101 European and other countries. Pres. Prof. J. NERUP (Denmark); Exec. Dir Dr VIKTOR JOERGENS. Publ. *Diabetologia* (13 a year).

European Association of Radiology: c/o Prof. Dr P. Vock, Institut für Diagnostische Radiologie der Universität Bern, Inselspital, 3010 Bern, Switzerland; tel. (31) 632-24-35; fax (31) 632-48-74; e-mail peter.vock@insel. ch; internet www.ear-online.org; f. 1962 to develop and co-ordinate the efforts of radiologists in Europe by promoting radiology in both biology and medicine, studying its problems, developing professional training and establishing contact between radiologists and professional, scientific and industrial organizations. Mems: national asscns in 38 countries. Sec.-Gen. Prof. Dr PETER VOCK. Publs *EAR Newsletter*, *European Radiology* (monthly).

European Association of Social Medicine: Corso Bramante 83, 10126 Turin, Italy; f. 1953 to provide co-operation between national asscns of preventive medicine and public health. Mems: asscns in 14 countries. Pres. Dr JEAN-PAUL FOURNIER (France); Sec.-Gen. Prof. Dr ENRICO BELLI (Italy).

European Brain and Behaviour Society—EBBS: c/o Dr M. Ammassari-Teule, Istituto di Psicobiologia e Psicofarmacologia, CNR, IRCCS S. Lucia Foundation, Via Ardeatina 306, 00179 Rome, Italy; tel. (06) 51501511; fax (06) 5034038; e-mail ebbs@hsantalucia.it; internet www.ebbs-science.org; f. 1969; holds one conference a year and organizes workshops. Pres. WOLFROM SCHULTZ; Sec.-Gen. Dr AMMASSARI-TEULE. Publ. *Newsletter*.

European Federation of Internal Medicine—EFIM: c/o Dr Davidson, Royal Sussex County Hospital, Eastern Rd, Brighton, BN2 5BE, United Kingdom; tel. (1273) 696955; fax (1273) 684554; e-mail chris.davidson@brighton-healthcare.nhs.uk; internet www.efim.org; f. 1969 as European Asscn of Internal Medicine (present name adopted 1996); aims to bring together European specialists, and establish communication between them, to promote internal medicine; organizes congresses and meetings; provides information. Mems: 27 European societies of internal medicine. Pres. Prof. JAIME MERION; Sec. Dr CHRISTOPHER DAVIDSON. Publ. *European Journal of Internal Medicine* (2 a month).

European Health Management Association—EHMA: Vergemount Hall, Clonskeagh, Dublin 6, Ireland; tel. (1) 2839299; fax (1) 2838653; e-mail pcberman@ehma.org; internet www.ehma.org; f. 1966; aims to improve health care in Europe by raising standards of managerial performance in the health sector; fosters co-operation between health service organizations and institutions in the field of health-care management education and training. Mems: 225 in 30 countries. Pres. Prof. JOAN HIGGINS; Dir PHILIP C. BERMAN. Publs *Newsletter, Eurobriefing* (quarterly).

European League against Rheumatism—EULAR: Witikonerstr. 15, 8032 Zürich, Switzerland; tel. (1) 3839690; fax (1) 3839810; e-mail secretariat@eular.org; internet www.eular.org; f. 1947 to co-ordinate research and treatment of rheumatic complaints; holds an annual Congress. Mems: in 41 countries. Exec. Sec. F. WYSS. Publ. *Annals of the Rheumatic Diseases*.

European Organization for Caries Research—ORCA: c/o Lutz Stösser, Dept of Preventive Dentistry, Dental School of Erfurt, Univ. of Jena, Nordhauser Str. 78, 99089 Erfurt, Germany; tel. (361) 7411205; e-mail stoesser@zmkh.ef.uni-jena.de; internet www.orca-caries-research.org; f. 1953 to promote and undertake research on dental health, encourage international contacts, and make the public aware of the importance of care of the teeth. Mems: research workers in 23 countries. Pres. Prof. BIRGIT ANGMAR-MANSSON (Sweden); Sec.-Gen. Prof. L. STÖSSER (Germany). Publ. *Caries Research*.

European Orthodontic Society—EOS: Flat 20, 49 Hallam St, London, W1W 6JN, United Kingdom; tel. (20) 7935-2795; fax (20) 7323-0410; e-mail eoslondon@compuserve.com; internet www.umds.ac.uk/physiology/eos; f. 1907 (name changed in 1935), to advance the science of orthodontics and its relations with the collateral arts and sciences. Mems: 2,700 in 80 countries. Sec. Prof. J. MOSS. Publ. *European Journal of Orthodontics* (6 a year).

European Union of Medical Specialists—UEMS: 20 ave de la Couronne, Brussels 1050, Belgium; tel. (2) 649-51-64; fax (2) 640-37-30; e-mail uems@skynet.be; internet www.uems.be; f. 1958 to harmonize and improve the quality of medical specialist practices in the EU and safeguard the interests of medical specialists; seeks formulation of common training policy. Mems: two representatives each from Austria, Belgium, Denmark, Finland, France, Germany, Greece, Iceland, Ireland, Italy, Luxembourg, Netherlands, Norway, Portugal, Spain, Sweden, Switzerland, United Kingdom. Pres. Dr C. TWOMEY (Ireland); Sec.-Gen. Dr C. LEIBBRANDT (Netherlands).

Eurotransplant International Foundation: POB 2304, 2301 CH Leiden, Netherlands; tel. (71) 5795795; fax (71) 5790057; internet www.eurotransplant.nl; f. 1967; co-ordinates the exchange of organs for transplants in Austria, Belgium, Germany, Luxembourg, Netherlands and Slovenia; keeps register of c. 15,000 patients with all necessary information for matching with suitable donors in the shortest possible time; organizes transport of the organ and transplantation; collaborates with similar organizations in western and eastern Europe. Dirs Dr B. COHEN, Dr G. G. PERSIJN.

Federation of French-Language Obstetricians and Gynaecologists (Fedération des gynécologues et obstetriciens de langue française—FGOLF): Clinique Baudelocque, 123 blvd de Port-Royal, 75674 Paris Cédex 14, France; tel. 1-42-34-11-43; fax 1-42-34-12-31; f. 1920 for the scientific study of phenomena having reference to obstetrics, gynaecology and reproduction in general. Mems: 1,500 in 50 countries. Pres. Prof. H. RUF (France); Gen. Sec. Prof. J. R. ZORN (France). Publ. *Journal de Gynécologie Obstétrique et Biologie de la Reproduction* (8 a year).

Federation of the European Dental Industry: 50858 Cologne, Kirchweg 2, Germany; tel. (221) 9486280; fax (221) 483428; f. 1957 to promote the interests of the dental industry. Mems: national asscns in 10 European countries.. Pres. and Chair. Dr J. EBERLEIN (Germany); Sec. HARALD RUSSEGGER (Germany).

General Association of Municipal Health and Technical Experts: 83 ave Foch, BP 3916, 75761 Paris Cédex 16, France; tel. 1-53-70-13-53; fax 1-53-70-13-40; e-mail aghtm@aghtm.org; internet www.aghtm.org; f. 1905 to study all questions related to urban and rural health. Mems: in 35 countries. Dir-Gen. ALAIN LASALMONIE (France). Publ. *TSM-Techniques, Sciences, Méthodes* (monthly).

Inter-American Association of Sanitary and Environmental Engineering: Rua Nicolau Gagliardi 354, 05429-010 São Paulo, SP, 05429-010 Brazil; tel. (11) 3812-4080; fax (11) 3814-2441; e-mail aidis@unisys.com.br; internet www.aidis.org.br; f. 1948 to assist in the development of water supply and sanitation. Mems: 32 countries. Exec. Dir LUIZ AUGUSTO DE LIMA PONTES. Publs *Revista Ingeniería Sanitaria* (quarterly), *Desafío* (quarterly).

International Academy of Aviation and Space Medicine—IAASM: 21 Antares Dr., Suite 112, Ottawa, ON K2E 7T8, Canada; tel. (613) 228-9345; fax (613) 228-0242; e-mail g.takahashi@sympatico.ca; internet www.iaasm.org; f. 1955 to facilitate international co-operation in research and teaching in the fields of aviation and space medicine. Mems: in 41 countries. Sec.-Gen. Dr GEORGE TAKAHASHI.

International Academy of Cytology: 79104 Freiburg, Burgunderstr. 1, Germany; tel. (761) 292-3801; fax (761) 292-3802; internet www.cytology-iac.org; f. 1957 to facilitate the international exchange of information on specialized problems of clinical cytology, to stimulate research and to standardize terminology. Mems: 2,400. Pres. HARUBUMI KATO; Sec. VOLKER SCHNEIDER. Publs *Acta Cytologica, Analytical and Quantitative Cytology and Histology* (both every 2 months).

International Agency for the Prevention of Blindness—IAPB: L. V. Prasad Eye Institute, L. V. Prasad Marg, Banjara Hills, Hyderabad 500 034, India; tel. (40) 3545389; fax (40) 3548271; e-mail IAPB_SECT/eye@lvp.lvpeye.stph.net; internet www.iapb.org; f. 1975; promotes advocacy and information sharing on the prevention of blindness; aims to encourage the formation of national prevention of blindness committees and programmes; has an official relationship with WHO. Pres. Dr HANNAH FAAL; Sec.-Gen. Dr GULLAPALLI N. RAO. Publ. *IAPB News*.

International Anatomical Congress: c/o Prof. Dr Wolfgang Kühnel, Institut für Anatomie, Medizinische Universität zu Lübeck, Ratzeburger Allee 160, 23538 Lübeck, Germany; tel. (451) 500-4030; fax (451) 500-4034; e-mail buchuel@anet.mu-luebeck.de; internet www.anet.mu-luebeck.de/anetpes.html; f. 1903; runs international congresses for anatomists to discuss research, teaching methods and terminology in the fields of gross and microscopical anatomy, histology, cytology, etc. Pres. J. ESPERENCA-PINE (Portugal); Sec.-Gen. Prof. Dr WOLFGANG KÜHNEL (Germany). Publ. *Annals of Anatomy*.

International Association for Child and Adolescent Psychiatry and Allied Professions—IACAPAP: c/o Prof. Helmut Remschmidt, Dept of Child and Adolescent Psychiatry, Philipps-University Marburg, Hans-Sachs-Str.6, D-35033 Marburg, Germany; tel. (6421) 2866260; fax (6421) 2868975; e-mail remschm@post.med.uni-marburg.de; internet www.iacapap.org; f. 1937 to promote scientific research in the field of child psychiatry by collaboration with allied professions. Mems: national asscns and individuals in 42 countries. Pres. Prof. HELMUT REMSCHMIDT; Sec.-Gen. IAN M. GOODYER. Publs *The Child in the Family* (Yearbook of the IACAPP), *Newsletter*.

International Association for Dental Research—IADR: 1619 Duke St, Alexandria, VA 22314, USA; tel. (703) 548-0066; fax (703) 548-1883; e-mail research@iadr.com; internet www.iadr.com; f. 1920 to encourage research in dentistry and related fields; holds annual meetings, triennial conferences and divisional meetings. Pres. Dr SALLY MARSHALL; Exec. Dir Dr ELI SCHWARZ.

International Association of Agricultural Medicine and Rural Health—IAAMRH: Biuro Poselskie AWS, Stronnictwo Konservatywno-Ludowe, 62-800 Kalisz. ul. Targowa 24, Poland; tel. and fax (62) 767-2604; e-mail kris@krus.gov.pl; internet www.iaamrh.org; f. 1961 to study the problems of medicine in agriculture in all countries and to prevent the diseases caused by the conditions of work in agriculture. Mems: 405. Pres. ASHOK PATIL (India); Gen. Sec. ANDRZEJ WOJTYLA (Poland).

International Association of Applied Psychology—IAAP: c/o Prof. J. M. Prieto, Colegio Oficial de Psicólogos, Cuesta de San Vicente 4, 5-28008 Madrid, Spain; fax (91) 3510091; e-mail iaap@cop.es; internet www.iaapsy.org; f. 1920, present title adopted in 1955; aims to establish contacts between those carrying out scientific work on applied psychology, to promote research and to encourage the adoption of measures contributing to this work. Mems: 2,200 in 94 countries. Pres. Prof. C. D. SPIELBERGER (USA); Sec.-Gen. Prof. J. M. PRIETO (Spain). Publ. *Applied Psychology: An International Review* (quarterly).

International Association of Asthmology—INTERASMA: c/o Prof. Hugo Neffen, Irigoyen Freyre 2670, 3000 Santa Fé, Argentina; tel. (42) 453-7638; fax (42) 456-9773; e-mail interasm@neffen.satlink.net; internet www.asmanet.com/interasma; f. 1954 to advance medical knowledge of bronchial asthma and allied disorders. Mems: 1,100 in 54 countries. Pres. Prof. GAETANO MELILLO (Italy); Sec./Treas. Prof. H. NEFFEN. Publs *Journal of Investigative Allergology and Clinical Immunology* (every 2 months), *Allergy and Clinical Immunology International* (every 2 months).

International Association of Gerontology—IAG: Centre for Ageing Studies, Flinders Univ. of S. Australia, Lafter Dr., Science Park, Bedford Park, S. Australia; tel. (618) 8201-7552; fax (618) 8201-7551; e-mail iag@flinders.edu.au; internet www.cas.flinders.edu.au/iag; f. 1950 to promote research and training in all fields of gerontology and to protect the interests of gerontologic societies and institutions; holds World Congress every four years. Mems: 60 national societies in 51 countries. Pres. Prof. GARY ANDREWS; Sec.-Gen. Prof. MARY LUSZCZ. Publ. *International Newsletter* (2 a year).

International Association of Group Psychotherapy: c/o Dr E. Hopper, 11 Heath Mansions, The Mount, London, NW3 6SN, United Kingdom; internet www.psych.mcgill.ca/labs/iagp; f. 1954; holds congresses every three years. Mems: in 35 countries. Pres. Dr E. HOPPER; Sec. Dr C. SANDAHL (Sweden). Publs *Newsletter, Yearbook of Group Psychotherapies*.

International Association of Hydatidology: Florida 460, 3°, 1005 Buenos Aires, Argentina; tel. (11) 4322-2030; fax (11) 4325-8231; f. 1941. Mems: 1,200 in 41 countries. Pres. Dr RAÚL MARTÍN MENDY; Sec.-Gen. Dr JORGE ALFREDO IRIARTE (Argentina). Publs *Archivos Internacionales de la Hidatidosis* (every 2 years), *Boletín de Hidatidosis* (quarterly).

International Association of Logopedics and Phoniatrics—IALP: 43 Louis de Savoie, 1110 Morges, Switzerland; fax (21) 3209300; e-mail h.k.schutte@med.rug.nl; internet www1.ldc.lu.se/logopedi/IALP; f. 1924 to promote standards of training and research in human communication disorders, to establish information centres and communicate with kindred organizations. Mems: 125,000 in 60 societies from 54 countries. Pres. Prof. HARM SCHUTTE (Netherlands). Publ. *Folia Phoniatrica et Logopedica* (6 a year).

International Association of Oral and Maxillofacial Surgeons—IAOMS: 9700 W. Bryn Mawr, Suite 210, Rosemont, ILL 60018-5701, USA; tel. (847) 678-9370; fax (847) 678-9380; e-mail lsavler@iaoms.org; internet www.iaoms.org; f. 1963 to advance the science and art of oral and maxillofacial surgery; organizes biennial international conference. Mems: over 3,000. Pres. JOHN HELFRICK (USA); Exec. Dir VICTOR MONCARZ (Canada). Publs *International Journal of Oral and Maxillofacial Surgery* (every 2 months), *Newsletter* (every 6 months).

International Brain Research Organization—IBRO: 51 blvd de Montmorency, 75016 Paris, France; tel. 1-46-47-92-92; fax 1-45-20-60-06; e-mail ibro@wanadoo.fr; internet www.ibro.org; f. 1958 to further all aspects of brain research. Mems: 45 corporate, 16 academic and 51,000 individual. Pres. Prof. T. N. WIESEL (USA); Sec.-Gen. Prof. A. J. AGUAYO (Canada). Publs *IBRO News, Neuroscience* (bi-monthly).

International Bronchoesophagological Society: Mayo Clinic, 13400 E. Shea Blvd, Scottsdale, AZ 85259, USA; f. 1951 to promote the progress of bronchoesophagology and to provide a forum for discussion among bronchoesophagologists with various medical and surgical specialities; holds Congress every two years. Mems: 500 in 37 countries. Exec. Sec. Dr DAVID SANDERSON.

International Bureau for Epilepsy—IBE: POB 21, 2100 AA Heemstede, Netherlands; tel. (23) 5237411; fax (23) 5470119; e-mail ibe@xs4all.nl; internet www.ibe-epilepsy.org; f. 1961; collects and disseminates information about social and medical care for people with epilepsy; organizes international and regional meetings; advises and answers questions on social aspects of epilepsy. Mems: 59 national epilepsy organizations. Sec.-Gen. ESPER CAVALHEIRO. Publ. *International Epilepsy News* (quarterly).

International Catholic Committee of Nurses: 43 Square Vergote, 1040 Brussels, Belgium; tel. (2) 732-10-50; fax (2) 734-84-60; f. 1933 to group professional Catholic nursing asscns; to represent Christian thought in the general professional field at international level; to co-operate in the general development of the profession and to promote social welfare. Mems: 49 full, 20 corresponding mems. Pres. R. LAI; Gen. Sec. AN VERLINDE. Publ. *Nouvelles/News/Nachrichten* (3 a year).

International Cell Research Organization—ICRO: c/o UNESCO, SC/BES/LSC, 1 rue Miollis, 75015 Paris, France; e-mail icro@unesco.org; internet www.unesco.org/icro; f. 1962 to create, encourage and promote co-operation between scientists of different disciplines throughout the world for the advancement of fundamental knowledge of the cell, normal and abnormal; organizes international laboratory courses on modern topics of cell and molecular biology and biotechnology for young research scientists. Mems: 400. Pres. Prof. J. E. ALLENDE (Chile); Exec. Sec. Prof. G. N. COHEN (France).

International Centre for Diarrhoeal Disease Research, Bangladesh (ICDDR, B): GPO Box 128, Dhaka 1000, Bangladesh; tel. (2) 8811751; fax (2) 8823116; e-mail info@icddrb.org; internet www.icddrb.org; f. 1960; undertakes research, training and information dissemination on diarrhoeal diseases, child health and child survival, reproductive health, women's health, nutrition, emerging infectious diseases, environmental health, vaccine evaluation and case management, with particular reference to developing countries; supported by 55 governments and international organizations. Dir Prof. DAVID SACK. Publs *Annual Report, Journal of Health, Population and Nutrition* (quarterly), *Glimpse* (quarterly), *Shasthya Sanglap* (3 a year), *DISC Bulletin* (weekly), scientific reports, working papers, monographs.

International Chiropractors' Association: 1110 North Glebe Rd, Suite 1000, Arlington, VA 22201, USA; tel. (703) 528-5000; internet www.chiropractice.org; f. 1926 to promote advancement of the art and science of chiropractors. Mems: 7,000 individuals, and affiliated asscns. Pres. FRED BARGE; Exec. Vice-Pres. RON HENRIKSON. Publs *International Review of Chiropractic* (every 2 months), *ICA Today* (every 2 months).

International Commission on Occupational Health—ICOH: Dept of Community, Occupational and Family Medicine, MD3, National University of Singapore, 16 Medical Drive, Singapore 117597; tel. 68744915; fax 67791489; e-mail icohsg@singnet.com.sg; internet www.icoh.org.sg; f. 1906, present name adopted 1985; aims to study and prevent pathological conditions arising from industrial work; arranges congresses on occupational medicine and the protection of workers' health; provides information for public authorities and learned societies. Mems: 1,944 in 89 countries. Pres. Prof. BENGT KNAVE(Sweden); Sec.-Gen. Prof. CHIA KEE SENG (Singapore). Publ. *Newsletter* (electronic version).

International Commission on Radiological Protection—ICRP: 17116 Stockholm, Sweden; tel. (8) 729-72-75; fax (8) 729-72-98; e-mail jack.valentin@ssi.se; internet www.icrp.org; f. 1928 to provide technical guidance and promote international co-operation in the field of radiation protection; committees on Radiation Effects, Doses from Radiation Exposure, Protection in Medicine, and the Application of Recommendations. Mems: c. 70. Chair. Prof. R. H. CLARKE (UK); Scientific Sec. Dr J. VALENTIN (Sweden). Publ. *Annals of the ICRP.*

International Council for Physical Activity and Fitness Research—ICPAFR: Faculty of Physical Education and Physiotherapy, Catholic Univ. of Leuven, 3001 Heverlee (Leuven), Belgium; tel. (16) 32-90-83; fax (16) 32-91-97; e-mail albrecht.claessens@flok.kuleuven.ac.be; internet http://sites.huji.ac.il/cosell/icpafr; f. 1964 to construct international standardized physical fitness tests, to encourage research based upon the standardized tests and to enhance participation in physical activity. Mems: some 35 countries. Pres. Prof. ALBRECHT L. CLAESSENS (Belgium); Sec. Treas. Prof. ANDREW HILLS (Australia). Publs *International Guide to Fitness and Health*, proceedings of seminars and symposia, other fitness and health publs.

International Council of Nurses—ICN: 3 place Jean-Marteau, 1201 Geneva, Switzerland; tel. (22) 8090100; fax (22) 8090101; e-mail icn@icn.ch; internet www.icn.ch; f. 1899 to allow national asscns of nurses to work together to develop the contribution of nursing to the promotion of health; holds quadrennial Congresses. Mems: 124 national nurses' asscns. Pres. CHRISTINE HANCOCK (UK); Exec. Dir JUDITH OULTON. Publ. *The International Nursing Review* (4 a year, in English).

International Cystic Fibrosis (Mucoviscidosis) Association: POB 2290, 5600 MD Eindhoven, Netherlands; tel. (492) 520241; fax (492) 599060; e-mail steenkamer.gina@kpmg.nl; internet www.icfma.org; f. 1964 to disseminate information on cystic fibrosis and to stimulate the work of scientific and medical researchers attempting to discover a cure; conducts annual medical symposia. Mems: 54 national organizations, 14 associate mems. Pres. HERMAN WEGGEN (Netherlands); Sec. GINA STEENKAMER (Netherlands). Publ. *Annual Review.*

International Epidemiological Association—IEA: Suite 840, 111 Market Place, Baltimore, MD 21202-6709, USA; tel. (410) 223-1600; fax (410) 223-1620; e-mail harmenia@jhsph.edu; internet www.dundee.ac.uk/iea; f. 1954. Mems: 2,237. Pres. and Chair. Dr RODOLFO SARACCI; Sec. Prof. HAROUTUNE ARMENIAN. Publ. *International Journal of Epidemiology* (6 a year).

International Federation for Medical and Biological Engineering—IFMBE: c/o Prof. Jos A. E. Spaan, Faculty of Medicine, Meibergdreef 15, 1105 AZ Amsterdam, Netherlands; tel. (20) 566-5200; fax (20) 691-7233; e-mail ifmbe@amc.uva.nl; internet www.vub.vub.oc.be/~ifmbe/ifmbe-html; f. 1959. Mems: organizations in 40 countries. Sec.-Gen. Prof. JOS A. E. SPAAN (Netherlands).

International Federation for Medical Psychotherapy: c/o Prof. E. Heim, Tannackstr. 3, 3653 Oberhofen, Switzerland; tel. and fax (33) 2431141; e-mail senf-blum@t-online.de; internet www.psychotherapy.de/html/general-information.html; f. 1946 to further research and teaching of psychotherapy; organizes international congresses. Mems: c. 6,000 psychotherapists from around 40 countries, 36 societies. Pres. Dr EDGAR HEIM (Switzerland); Sec.-Gen. Prof. Dr WOLFGANG SENE (Germany).

International Federation of Fertility Societies—IFFS: c/o CSI, 337 rue de la Combe Caude, 34090 Montpellier, France; tel. 4-67-63-53-40; fax 4-67-41-94-27; e-mail algcsi@mnet.fr; internet www.mnet.fr/iffs; f. 1951 to study problems of fertility and sterility. Sec.-Gen. Prof. BERNARD HEDON. Publ. *Newsletter* (2 a year).

International Federation of Gynecology and Obstetrics—FIGO: 70 Wimpole St, London, W1X 8AG, United Kingdom; tel. (20) 7224-3270; fax (20) 7935-0736; e-mail figo@figo.org; internet www.figo.org; f. 1954; aims to improve standards in gynaecology and obstetrics, promote better health care for women, facilitate the exchange of information, and perfect methods of teaching. Mems: national societies in 102 countries. Pres. Dr SHIRISH S. SHETH (India); Sec.-Gen. Prof. G. BENAGIANO (Italy). Publ. *International Journal of Obstetrics and Gynecology.*

International Federation of Ophthalmological Societies: c/o Dr Bruce E. Spivey, One Beekman Pl., New York, NY 10022, USA; tel. (212) 326-8804; fax (212) 326-8773; e-mail icoph@icoph.org; internet www.icoph.org; f. 1927; works to support and develop ophthalmology, especially in developing countries; carries out education and assessment projects; promotes clinical standards; holds International Congress every four years. Pres. Prof. G. O. H. NAUMANN (Germany); Sec. Dr BRUCE E. SPIVEY.

International Hospital Federation: 46 Grosvenor Gdns, London, SW1 0EB, United Kingdom; tel. (20) 7881-9222; fax (20) 7881-9223; e-mail ihf@hospitalmanagement.net; internet www.hospitalmanagement.net; f. 1947 for information exchange and education in hospital and health service matters; represents institutional health care in discussions with WHO; conducts conferences and courses on management and policy issues. Mems in five categories: national hospital and health service organizations; professional asscns, regional organizations and individual hospitals; individual mems; professional and industrial mems; honorary mems. Dir-Gen. Prof. PER-GUNNAR SVENSSON. Publs *World Hospitals and Health Services* (quarterly), *Hospitals International* (quarterly), *Hospital Management International (Yearbook1)*, *New World Health (Yearbook 2)*.

International League against Epilepsy—ILAE: c/o Prof. Peter Wolf, Klinik Mara I, Epilepsie-Zentrum Bethel, Maraweg 21, 33617 Bielefeld, Germany; tel. (521) 144-4897; fax (521) 144-4637; e-maililae-secretariat@mara.de; internet www.ilae-epilepsy.org; f. 1909 to link national professional asscns and to encourage research, including classification and the development of anti-epileptic drugs; collaborates with the International Bureau for Epilepsy (q.v.) and with WHO. Mems: 72 asscns. Pres. JEROME ENGEL, Jr (USA); Sec.-Gen. P. WOLF.

International Narcotics Control Board—INCB: 1400 Vienna, POB 500, Austria; tel. (1) 260-60-42-77; fax (1) 260-60-58-67; e-mail secretariat@incb.org; internet www.incb.org; f. 1961 by the Single Convention on Narcotic Drugs, to supervise implementation of drug control treaties by governments. Mems: 13 individuals. Pres. HAMID GHODSE (Iran); Sec. HERBERT SCHAEPE (Germany). Publ. *Annual Report* (with three technical supplements).

International Opticians' Association: Godmersham Park Mansion, Godmersham, Canterbury, Kent, CT4 7DT, United Kingdom; tel. (1227) 733901; fax (1227) 733900; e-mail general@abdo. org.uk; internet www.abdo.org.uk; f. 1951 to promote the science of opthalmology, and to maintain and advance standards and effect co-operation in optical dispensing. Gen. Sec. Sir ANTHONY GARRETT; Vice-Pres. C. J. PACKFORD. Publs *ABDO Frame Rule*, *Dispensing Optics* (monthly).

International Organization for Medical Physics—IOMP: c/o Prof. Gary D. Fullerton, UTHSCSA, Dept of Radiology, MSC 7800, 7703 Floyd Curl Drive, San Antonio, TX 78229-3900, USA; tel. (210) 567-5551; fax (210) 567-5549; e-mail iomp@uthscsa.edu; internet www.iomp.org; f. 1963 to organize international co-operation in medical physics, to promote communication between the various branches of medical physics and allied subjects, to contribute to the advancement of medical physics in all its aspects and to advise on the formation of national organizations. Mems: national organizations of medical physics in over 70 countries. Pres. Prof. OSKAR CHORNICKI (Poland); Sec.-Gen. Prof. GARY FULLERTON. Publ. *Medical Physics World*.

International Pharmaceutical Federation: POB 84200, 2508 AE The Hague, Netherlands; tel. (70) 3021970; fax (70) 3021999; e-mail int.pharm.fed@fip.nl; internet www.fip.nl; f. 1912; aims to represent and serve pharmacy and pharmaceutical sciences world-wide; holds Assembly of Pharmacists every two years and International Congress every year. Mems: 86 national pharmaceutical organizations in 62 countries, 55 associate, supportive and collective mems, 4,000 individuals. Dir A. H. M (TON) HOEK (Netherlands). Publ. *International Pharmacy Journal* (every 2 months).

International Psycho-Analytical Association—IPA: Broomhills, Woodside Lane, London, N12 8UD, United Kingdom; tel. (20) 8446-8324; fax (20) 8445-4729; e-mail ipa@ipa.org.uk; internet www.ipa@ipa.org.uk; f. 1908; holds meetings to define and promulgate the theory and teaching of psychoanalysis; acts as a forum for scientific discussions; controls and regulates training; contributes to the interdisciplinary area common to the behavioural sciences. Mems: 10,000. Pres. Dr OTTO KERNBERG; Sec. Dr ROBERT TYSON. Publs *Bulletin*, *Newsletter*.

International Society for Cardiovascular Surgery: 13 Elm St, Manchester, MA 01944-1314, USA; tel. (978) 526-8330; fax (978) 526-4018; e-mail iscvs@prri.com; f. 1950 to stimulate research on the diagnosis and therapy of cardiovascular diseases and to exchange ideas on an international basis. Sec.-Gen. Dr LAZAR J. GREENFIELD (USA). Publ. *Cardiovascular Surgery*.

International Society for Oneiric Mental Imagery Techniques: c/o Odile Dorkel, 56 rue Sedaine, 75011 Paris, France; tel. 1-47-00-16-63; links a group of research workers, technicians and psychotherapists using oneirism techniques under waking conditions, with the belief that a healing action cannot be dissociated from the restoration of creativity. Mems: in 17 countries. Pres. ODILE DORKEL (France); Sec.-Gen. JEAN-FRANÇOIS CESARO (France).

International Society of Developmental Biologists: c/o Dr Paul T. van der Saag, Hubrecht Laboratorium/Netherlands Institute for Developmental Biology, Uppsalalaan 8, 3584 CT, Utrecht, Netherlands; tel. (30) 2510-211; e-mail directie@niob.knaw.nl; internet www.elsevier.com/inca/homepage/sah/isdb; f. 1911 as International Institute of Embryology. Aims to promote the study of developmental biology and to encourage international co-operation among investigators in the field. Mems: 850 in 33 countries. Pres. Prof. WALTER GEHRING (Switzerland); Sec.-Treas. Prof. SIEGFRIED DE LAAT (Netherlands). Publ. *Mechanisms of Development*.

International Society of Lymphology: Room 4406, University of Arizona, 1501 North Campbell Ave, POB 245063, Tucson, AZ 85724-5063, USA; tel. (520) 626-6118; fax (520) 626-0822; e-mail lymph@u.arizona.edu; internet www.u.arizona.edu/witte/isl.htm; f. 1966 to further progress in lymphology through personal contacts and the exchange of ideas. Mems: 400 in 43 countries. Pres. A. PISSAS (France); Sec.-Gen. M. H. WITTE (USA). Publ. *Lymphology* (quarterly).

International Society of Neuropathology: c/o Prof. Hannu Kalimo, Dept of Pathology, Turku University Hospital, 20520 Turku, Finland; tel. (2) 2611685; fax (2) 3337456; e-mail hkalimo@mailhost.utu.fi. Pres. Prof. SAMUEL LUDWIN (Canada); Sec.-Gen. Prof. HANNU KALIMO.

International Society of Orthopaedic Surgery and Traumatology: 40 rue Washington, 1050 Brussels, Belgium; tel. (2) 648-68-23; fax (2) 649-86-01; internet www.sicot.org; f. 1929; convenes world congresses every three years. Mems: 102 countries, 3,000 individuals. Pres. RAINER KOTZ (Austria); Sec.-Gen. ANTHONY J. HALL (UK). Publ. *International Orthopaedics* (every 2 months).

International Society for the Psychopathology of Expression and Art Therapy—SIPE: c/o Dr G. Roux, 27 rue du mal Joffre, 64000 Pau, France; tel. and fax 5-59-27-69-74; e-mail sipearther@aol.com; internet monsite.ifrance.com/art-therapy/art-therapy/000018124. htm; f. 1959 to bring together specialists interested in the problems of expression and artistic activities in connection with psychiatric, sociological and psychological research. Mems: 625. Pres. Dr G. ROUX (France); Sec.-Gen. J. L. SUDRES (France). Publ. *Newsletter* (quarterly).

International Society of Radiology—ISR: 7910 Woodmont Ave, Suite 800, Bethesda, Maryland 20814-3095, USA; tel. (301) 657-2652; fax (301) 907-8768; e-mail isr@isradiology.org; internet www.isradiology.org; f. 1953 to promote radiology worldwide. International Commissions on Radiation Units and Measurements (ICRUM), on Radiation Protection (ICRP), and on Radiological Education (ICRE); organizes biannual International Congress of Radiology; collaborates with WHO. Mems: more than 50 national radiological societies. Pres. C.-G. SANDERT-SKÖJOLD-NORDENSTAM; Sec.-Gen. FRANCISCO ARREDONDO. PUBL *Newsletter*.

International Society of Surgery—ISS: Netzibodenstr. 34, POB 1527, 4133 Pratteln, Switzerland; tel. (61) 8159666; fax (61) 8114775; e-mail surgery@iss-sic.ch; internet www.iss-sic.ch; f. 1902 to promote understanding between surgical disciplines; groups surgeons to address issues of interest to all surgical specialists; supports general surgery as a training base for abdominal surgery, surgery with integuments and endocrine surgery; organizes congresses: 40th World Congress of Surgery, Bangkok, Thailand (August 2003). Mems: 4,000. Admin. Dir. VICTOR BERTSCHI; Sec.-Gen. Prof. FELIX HARDER. Publ. *World Journal of Surgery* (monthly).

International Union against Tuberculosis and Lung Disease—IUATLD: 68 blvd St Michel, 75006 Paris, France; tel. 1-44-32-03-60; fax 1-43-29-90-87; e-mail iuatldparis@compuserve.com; internet www.iuatld.org; f. 1920 to co-ordinate the efforts of anti-tuberculosis and respiratory disease asscns, to mobilize public interest, to assist control programmes and research around the world, to collaborate with governments and WHO and to promote conferences. Mems: asscns in 165 countries, 3,000 individual mems. Pres. Prof. S. SUPCHAROEN; Exec. Dir Dr NILS BILLO. Publs *The International Journal of Tuberculosis and Lung Disease* (in English, with summaries in French and Spanish; incl. conference proceedings), *Newsletter*.

International Union for Health Promotion and Education—IUHPE: Immeuble le Berry, 2 rue Auguste Comte, 92170 Vanves, France; tel. 1-46-45-00-59; fax 1-46-45-00-45; e-mail iuhpecj@worldnet.fr; internet www.iuhpe.org; f. 1951; provides an international network for the exchange of practical information on developments in health promotion and education; promotes research; encourages professional training for health workers, teachers, social workers and others; holds a World Conference on Health Promotion and Health Education every three years; organizes regional conferences and seminars. Mems: in more than 90 countries. Pres. Prof. MAURICE MITTELMARK (Norway). Publ. *Promotion and Education* (quarterly, in English, French and Spanish).

International Union of Therapeutics: c/o Prof. A. Pradalier, Hôpital Louis Mourier, 178 rue des Renouillers, 92701 Colombes, France; tel. 1-47-60-67-05; e-mail secretariat.medecine4@emr.ap-hop-paris.fr; f. 1934; international congress held every other year. Mems: 500 from 22 countries. Pres. Prof. A. PRADALIER.

Middle East Neurosurgical Society: c/o Dr Fuad S. Haddad, Neurosurgical Department, American University Medical Centre, POB 113-6044, Beirut, Lebanon; tel. (1) 347348; fax (1) 342517; e-mail gfhaddad@aub.edu.lb; f. 1958 to promote clinical advances and scientific research among its members and to spread knowledge of neurosurgery and related fields among all members of the medical profession in the Middle East. Mems: 684 in nine countries. Pres. Dr FUAD S. HADDAD; Hon. Sec. Dr GEDEON MOHASSEB.

Multiple Sclerosis International Federation—MSIF: 3rd Floor, Skyline House, 200 Union St, London, SE1 0LX, United Kingdom; tel. (20) 7620-1911; fax (20) 7620-1922; e-mail info@msif.org; internet www.msif.org; f. 1965; co-ordinates the work of national multiple sclerosis organizations throughout the world; encourages scientific research into multiple sclerosis and related neurological diseases; helps to develop new and existing multiple sclerosis organizations; collects and disseminates information. Pres. PETER SCHWEITZER; Chief Exec. CHRISTINE PURDY. Publs *Making Connections* (annually), *MS Research in Progress* (every 2 years), *MS Management* (2 a year), *MS: The Guide to Treatment and Management* (annually).

Organization for Co-ordination in the Struggle against Endemic Diseases in Central Africa (Organisation de coordination pour la lutte contre les endémies en Afrique Centrale—OCEAC): BP 288, Yaoundé, Cameroon; tel. 23-22-32; fax 23-00-61; e-mail oceac@mnet.cm; internet www.refer.org/camer_ct/site_oceac; f. 1965 to standardize methods of controlling endemic diseases, to co-ordinate national action, and to negotiate programmes of assistance and training on a regional scale. Mems: Cameroon, Central African Republic, Chad, Republic of the Congo, Equatorial Guinea, Gabon. Pres. L. ESSO (Cameroon); Sec.-Gen. Dr AUGUSTE BILONGO MANENE. Publ. *Bulletin de Liaison et de Documentation* (quarterly).

Pan-American Association of Ophthalmology—PAAO: 1301 South Bowen Rd, Suite 365, Arlington, TX 76013, USA; tel. (817) 265-2831; fax (817) 275-3961; e-mail info@paao.org; internet www.paao.org; f. 1939 to promote friendship within the profession and the dissemination of scientific information; holds biennial Congress (2003: Puerto Rico). Mems: national ophthalmological societies and other bodies in 39 countries. Pres. Dr RUBENS BELFORT, Jr (USA); Exec. Dir Dr CRISTIAN LUCO (Chile). Publs *The Pan American* (2 a year), *El Noticiero* (quarterly).

Pan-Pacific Surgical Association: 2000 L. St, NW, Suite 200, Washington, DC 20036, USA; tel. (202) 416-1866; fax (202) 416-1867; e-mail ppsa@slackinc.com; internet www.ppsa.org; f. 1929 to bring together surgeons to exchange scientific knowledge relating to surgery and medicine, and to promote the improvement and standardization of hospitals and their services and facilities; congresses are held every two years. Mems: 2,716 regular, associate and senior mems from 44 countries. Chair. ALLAN KUNIMOTO.

Society of French-speaking Neuro-Surgeons (Société de neuro-chirurgie de langue française): c/o Prof. Jacques Lagarrigue, Service de Neurochirurgie, CHU de Toulouse Rangueil, 1 ave Jean-Poulhès, F-31054 Toulouse Cédex, France; tel. 5-61-32-26-32; fax 5-31-32-22-40; f. 1949; holds annual convention and congress. Mems: 700. Pres. M. CHOUX (France); Sec. Prof. JACQUES LAGARRIGUE (France). Publ. *Neurochirurgie* (6 a year).

World Association for Disaster and Emergency Medicine—WADEM: c/o Marvin L. Birnbaum, E5/615 CSC, 600 Highland Avenue, Madison, WI 53791-9744, USA; tel. (608) 263-2069; fax (608) 265-3037; e-mail mlb@medicine.wisc.edu; internet www.pdm.medicine.wisc.edu; f. 1976 to improve the world-wide delivery of emergency and humanitarian care in mass casualty and disaster situations, through training, symposia, and publications.Mems: 600 in 62 countries. Hon. Sec. Prof. W. DICK (Germany). Publ. *Prehospital and Disaster Medicine.*

World Association of Societies of (Anatomic and Clinical) Pathology—WASP: c/o Japan Clinical Pathology Foundation for International Exchange, Sakura-Sugamo Bldg 7F, Sugamo 2-11-1, Toshima-ku, Tokyo 170, Japan; tel. (3) 3918-8161; fax (3) 3949-6168; internet www.dokkyomed.ac.jp/dep-k/cli-path/wasp.html; f. 1947 to link national societies and co-ordinate their scientific and technical means of action; promotes the development of anatomic and clinical pathology, especially by convening conferences, congresses and meetings, and through the interchange of publications and personnel. Mems: 54 national asscns. Pres. PETER B. HERDSON; Sec. WALTER TIMPERLEY. Publ. *Newsletter* (quarterly).

World Confederation for Physical Therapy—WCPT: 46–48 Grosvenor Gdns, London, SW1W 0EB, United Kingdom; tel. (20) 7881-9234; fax (20) 7881-9239; e-mail wcpt@dial.pipex.com; f. 1951; represents physical therapy internationally; encourages high standards of physical therapy education and practice; promotes exchange of information among members, and the development of a scientific professional base through research; aims to contribute to the development of informed public opinion regarding physical therapy; holds seminars and workshops and quadrennial General Assembly. Mems: national organizations in 54 countries. Pres. Prof. D. P. G. TEAGER; Sec.-Gen. B. J. MYERS. Publ. *Newsletter* (2 a year).

World Council of Optometry—WCO: 8360 Old York West, 4th Floor, Elkins Park, PA 19027, USA; e-mail wco@pco.edu; internet www.worldoptometry.org; f. 1927 to co-ordinate efforts to provide a good standard of ophthalmic optical (optometric) care throughout the world; enables exchange of ideas between different countries; focuses on optometric education; gives advice on standards of qualification; considers optometry legislation throughout the world. Mems: 70 optometric organizations in 47 countries and four regional groups. Exec. Dir Dr ANTONY DI STEFANO. Publ. *Interoptics* (quarterly).

World Federation for Mental Health—WFMH: 1021 Prince St, Alexandria, VA 22314, USA; tel. (703) 838-7543; fax (703) 519-7648; e-mail wfmh@erols.com; internet www.wfmh.org; f. 1948 to promote the highest standards of mental health; works with agencies of the United Nations in promoting mental health; assists other voluntary asscns in improving mental health services. Mems: 250 national and international asscns in 115 countries. Pres. and Chief Exec. PIRKKO LAHTI. Publs *Newsletter* (quarterly), *Annual Report*.

World Federation of Hydrotherapy and Climatotherapy: Cattedra di Terapia Med. E Medic. Termal, Università degli Studi, via Cicognara 7, 20129 Milan, Italy; tel. (02) 733880; fax (02) 70100398; internet www.naturmed.unimi.it/femtec.html; f. 1947 as International Federation of Thermalism and Climatism; present name adopted 1999. Mems: in 36 countries. Pres. M. NIKOLAI A. STOROJENKO; Gen. Sec. Prof. UMBERTO SOLIMENE.

World Federation of Neurosurgical Societies—WFNS: c/o Prof. Edward R. Laws, Dept. of Neurological Surgery, Univ. of

Virginia, Box 212, Health Science Center, Charlottesville, VA 22908, USA; tel. (804) 924-2650; fax (804) 924-5894; internet www.wfns.org; f. 1957 to assist in the development of neurosurgery and to help the formation of asscns; facilitates the exchange of information and encourages research. Mems: 57 societies in 56 countries. Pres. Prof. ARMANDO BASSO; Sec. Prof. EDWARD R. LAWS, Jr.

World Federation of Occupational Therapists—WFOT: c/o Carolyn Webster, Disabilities Services Comm., PO Box 441, West Perth, 6872 Western Australia, Australia; tel. (8) 9426-9200; fax (8) 9490-5223; e-mail wfot@multiline.com.au; internet wfot.org.au; f. 1952 to further the rehabilitation of the physically and mentally disabled by promoting the development of occupational therapy in all countries; facilitates the exchange of information and publications; promotes research in occupational therapy; holds international congresses every four years. Mems: national professional asscns in 50 countries, with total membership of c. 100,000. Pres. CAROLYN WEBSTER (Australia); Hon. Sec. CLEPHANE HUME (UK). Publ. *Bulletin* (2 a year).

World Federation of Public Health Associations: c/o Allen Jones, APHA, 800 I St, NW, Washington, DC 20001-3710, USA; tel. (202) 777-2487; fax (202) 777-2534; e-mail allen.jones@apha.org; internet www.apha.org; f. 1967; brings together researchers, teachers, health service providers and workers in a multidisciplinary environment of professional exchange, studies and action; endeavours to influence policies and to set priorities to prevent disease and promote health; holds a triennial Congress: United Kingdom (2004). Mems: 64 national public health asscns. Sec.-Gen. ALLEN JONES (USA). Publs *WFPHA News* (in English), and occasional technical papers.

World Federation of Societies of Anaesthesiologists—WFSA: Imperial House, 8th Floor, 15–19 Kingsway, London, WC2B 6TH, United Kingdom; tel. (20) 7836-5652; fax (20) 7836-5616; e-mail wfsa@compuserve.com; internet www.nda.ox.ac.uk/wfsa; f. 1955; aims to make available the highest standards of anaesthesia to all peoples of the world. Mems: 106 national societies. Pres. Dr K. BROWN (Australia); Sec. Dr A. E. E. MEURSING. Publs *World Anaesthesia Newsletter* (2 a year), *Annual Report.*

Posts and Telecommunications

African Telecommunications Union: Posta Sacco Plaza, 11th Floor, Uhuru Highway, POB 35282 Nairobi, Kenya; tel. (2) 216678; fax (2) 219478; e-mail sg@atu-uat.org; internet www.atu-uat.org; f. 1999 as successor to Pan-African Telecommunications Union (f. 1977); promotes the rapid development of information communications in Africa, with the aim of making Africa an equal participant in the global information society; works towards universal service and access and full inter-country connectivity; promotes development and adoption of appropriate policies and regulatory frameworks; promotes financing of development; encourages co-operation between members and the exchange of information; advocates the harmonization of telecommunications policies. Mems: in 46 countries. Sec.-Gen. M. JAN MUTAI.

Arab Permanent Postal Commission: c/o Arab League Bldg, Tahrir Sq., Cairo, Egypt; tel. (2) 5750511; fax (2) 5775626; f. 1952; aims to establish stricter postal relations between the Arab countries than those laid down by the Universal Postal Union, and to pursue the development and modernization of postal services in member countries. Publs *APU Bulletin* (monthly), *APU Review* (quarterly), *APU News* (annually).

Arab Telecommunications Union: POB 2397, Baghdad, Iraq; tel. (1) 555-0642; f. 1953 to co-ordinate and develop telecommunications between member countries; to exhange technical aid and encourage research; promotes establishment of new cable telecommunications networks in the region. Sec.-Gen. ABDUL JAFFAR HASSAN KHALAF IBRAHIM AL-ANI. Publs *Arab Telecommunications Union Journal* (2 a year), *Economic and Technical Studies.*

Asia-Pacific Telecommunity: No. 12/49, Soi 5, Chaengwattana Rd, Thungsonghong, Bangkok 10210, Thailand; tel. (2) 573-0044; fax (2) 573-7479; e-mail aptmail@aptsec.org; internet www.aptsec.org;. 1979 to cover all matters relating to telecommunications in the region. Mems: Afghanistan, Australia, Bangladesh, Brunei, the People's Republic of China, India, Indonesia, Iran, Japan, the Republic of Korea, Laos, Malaysia, Maldives, Myanmar, Nauru, Nepal, Pakistan, the Philippines, Singapore, Sri Lanka, Thailand, Viet Nam; assoc. mems: Cook Islands, Hong Kong; two affiliated mems each in Indonesia, Japan and Thailand, three in the Republic of Korea, four in Hong Kong, one in Maldives and six in the Philippines. Exec. Sec. JONG-SOON LEE.

Asian-Pacific Postal Union: Post Office Bldg, 1000 Manila, Philippines; tel. (2) 470760; fax (2) 407448; f. 1962 to extend, facilitate and improve the postal relations between the member countries and to promote co-operation in the field of postal services. Mems: 23 countries. Dir JORGE SARMIENTO. Publs *Annual Report, Exchange Program of Postal Officials, APPU Newsletter.*

European Conference of Postal and Telecommunications Administrations: Ministry of Transport and Communications, Odos Xenofontos 13, 10191 Athens, Greece; tel. (1) 9236494; fax (1) 9237133; internet www.cept.org; f. 1959 to strengthen relations between member administrations and to harmonize and improve their technical services; set up Eurodata Foundation, for research and publishing. Mems: 26 countries. Sec. Z. PROTOPSALTI. Publ. *Bulletin.*

European Telecommunications Satellite Organization—EUTELSAT: 70 rue Balard, 75015, Paris Cédex 15, France; tel. 1-53-98-47-47; fax 1-53-98-37-00; internet www.eutelsat.com/; f. 1977 to operate satellites for fixed and mobile communications in Europe; EUTELSAT's in-orbit resource comprises 18 satellites; commercialises capacity in three satellites operated by other companies. Mems: public and private telecommunications operations in 47 countries. Dir-Gen. GIULIANO BERRETTA.

INMARSAT—International Mobile Satellite Organization: 99 City Rd, London, EC1Y 1AX, United Kingdom; tel. (20) 7728-1000; fax (20) 7728-1044; internet www.inmarsat.org; f. 1979, as International Maritime Satellite Organization, to provide (from February 1982) global communications for shipping via satellites on a commercial basis; satellites in geo-stationary orbit over the Atlantic, Indian and Pacific Oceans provide telephone, telex, facsimile, telegram, low to high speed data services and distress and safety communications for ships of all nations and structures such as oil rigs; in 1985 the operating agreement was amended to include aeronautical communications, and in 1988 amendments were approved which allow provision of global land-mobile communications. In April 1999 INMARSAT was transferred to the private sector and became a limited company; an intergovernmental secretariat was to be maintained to monitor INMARSAT's public service obligations. Mems: 86 countries. Chair. RICHARD VOS; Dir of Secretariat JERZY VONAU (Poland).

International Telecommunications Satellite Organization—INTELSAT: 3400 International Drive, NW, Washington, DC 20008-3098, USA; tel. (202) 944-6800; fax (202) 944-7860; internet www.intelsat.com; f. 1964 to establish a global commercial satellite communications system. Assembly of Parties attended by representatives of member governments, meets every two years to consider policy and long-term aims and matters of interest to members as sovereign states. Meeting of Signatories to the Operating Agreement held annually. Twenty-four INTELSAT satellites in geosynchronous orbit provide a global communications service; INTELSAT provides most of the world's overseas traffic. In 1998 INTELSAT agreed to establish a private enterprise, incorporated in the Netherlands, to administer six satellite services. Mems: 143 governments. Dir-Gen. and Chief Exec. CONNY KULLMAN (Sweden).

Internet Corporation for Assigned Names and Numbers—ICANN: 4676 Admiralty Way, Suite 330, Marina del Rey, CA 90292-6601, USA; tel. (310) 823-9358; fax (310) 823-8649; e-mail icann@icann.org; internet www.icann.org; f. 1998; non-profit, private-sector body; aims to co-ordinate the technical management and policy development of the internet; comprises three Supporting Organizations to assist, review and develop recommendations on internet policy and structure relating to addresses, domain names, and protocol. Pres. and CEO STUART LYNN.

Pacific Telecommunications Council—PTC: 2454 S. Beretania St, 302 Honolulu, HI 96826, USA; tel. (808) 941-3789;

fax (808) 944-4874; e-mail info@ptc.org; internet www.ptc.org; f. 1980 to promote the development, understanding and beneficial use of telecommunications and information systems/services throughout the Pacific region; provides forum for users and providers of communications services; sponsors annual conference and seminars. Mems: 650 (corporate, government, academic and individual). Pres. JANE HURD; Exec. Dir HOYT ZIA. Publ. *Pacific Telecommunications Review* (quarterly).

Postal Union of the Americas, Spain and Portugal (Unión Postal de las Américas, España y Portugal): Cebollatí 1468/70, 1°, Casilla de Correos 20.042, Montevideo, Uruguay; tel. (2) 4100070; fax (2) 4105046; e-mail secretariat@upaep.com.uy; internet www.upaep.com.uy; f. 1911 to extend, facilitate and study the postal relationships of member countries. Mems: 27 countries. Sec.-Gen. MARIO FELMER KLENNER (Chile).

Press, Radio and Television

Asia-Pacific Broadcasting Union—ABU: POB 1164, 59700 Kuala Lumpur, Malaysia; tel. (3) 22823592; fax (3) 22825292; e-mail sg@abu.org.my; internet www.abu.org.my; f. 1964 to foster and co-ordinate the development of broadcasting in the Asia-Pacific area, to develop means of establishing closer collaboration and co-operation among broadcasting orgs, and to serve the professional needs of broadcasters in Asia and the Pacific; holds annual General Assembly. Mems: 102 in 50 countries and territories. Pres. KATSUJI EBISAWA (Japan); Sec.-Gen. HUGH LEONARD. Publs *ABU News* (every 2 months), *ABU Technical Review* (every 2 months).

Association for the Promotion of the International Circulation of the Press—DISTRIPRESS: 8002 Zürich, Beethovenstrasse 20, Switzerland; tel. (1) 2024121; fax (1) 2021025; e-mail info@distripress.ch; internet www.distripress.ch; f. 1955 to assist in the promotion of the freedom of the press throughout the world, supporting and aiding UNESCO in promoting the free flow of ideas. Organizes meetings of publishers and distributors of newspapers, periodicals and paperback books, to promote the exchange of information and experience among members. Mems: 458. Pres. ALFRED HEINTZE (Germany); Man. HEINZ E. GRAF (Switzerland). Publs *Distripress Gazette, Who's Who.*

Association of European Journalists—AEJ: Balistraat 46, Den Haag, 2585 Netherlands; tel. (70) 3635875; fax (70) 3107217; e-mail hhetzel@atglobal.net; internet www.aej.org; f. 1963 to participate actively in the development of a European consciousness; to promote deeper knowledge of European problems and secure appreciation by the general public of the work of European institutions; and to facilitate members' access to sources of European information. Mems: 2,100 individuals and national asscns in 23 countries. Pres. HELMUT HETZEL (Netherlands); Sec.-Gen. NIKOS ROUSSIS (Greece). Publ. *Newsletter.*

Association of Private European Cable Operators: 1 blvd Anspach, boîte 25, 1000 Brussels, Belgium; tel. (2) 223-25-91; fax (2) 223-06-96; f. 1995 aims to promote the interests of independent cable operators and to ensure exchange of information on cable and telecommunications; carries out research on relevant technical and legal questions. Mems: 27 organizations in 19 countries. Pres. M. DE SUTTER.

Broadcasting Organization of Non-aligned Countries—BONAC: c/o Cyprus Broadcasting Corpn, POB 4824, 1397 Nicosia, Cyprus; tel. (2) 422231; fax (2) 314050; e-mail rik@cybc.com.cy; f. 1977 to ensure an equitable, objective and comprehensive flow of information through broadcasting; Secretariat moves to the broadcasting organization of host country. Mems: in 102 countries.

European Alliance of Press Agencies: c/o Agence Belga, rue F. Pelletier 8B, 1030 Brussels, Belgium; tel. (2) 743-13-11; fax (2) 735-18-74; e-mail dir@belganews.be; internet www.press alliance.com; f. 1957 to assist co-operation among members and to study and protect their common interests; annual assembly. Mems: in 30 countries. Sec.-Gen. RUDI DE CEUSTER.

European Broadcasting Union—EBU: CP 45, Ancienne-Route 17A, 1218 Grand-Saconnex, Geneva, Switzerland; tel. (22) 7172033; fax (22) 7474033; e-mail ebu@ebu.ch; internet www.ebu.ch; f. 1950 in succession to the International Broadcasting Union; a professional asscn of broadcasting organizations, supporting the interests of members and assisting the development of broadcasting in all its forms; activities include the Eurovision news and programme exchanges and the Euroradio music exchanges. Mems: 70 active (European) in 51 countries, and 46 associate in 29 countries. Pres. ARNE WESSBERG (Finland); Sec.-Gen. JEAN STOCK (France). Publs *EBU Technical Review* (annually), *Diffusion* (quarterly).

IFRA: Washingtonplatz 1, 64287 Darmstadt, Germany; tel. (6151) 7336; fax (6151) 733800; e-mail info@ifra.com; internet www.ifra.com; f. 1961 as Inca-Fiej Research Asscn to develop methods and techniques for the newspaper industry; to evaluate standard specifications for raw materials for use in newspaper production; and to investigate economy and quality improvements for newspaper printing and publishing. Mems: more than 1,300 newspapers, 400 suppliers. Pres. MURDOCH MACLENNAN; Man. Dir REINER MITTELBACH. Publ. *Newspaper Techniques* (monthly, in English, French and German).

Inter-American Press Association—IAPA (Sociedad Interamericana de Prensa): Jules Dubois Bldg, 1801 SW 3rd Ave, Miami, FL 33129, USA; tel. (305) 634-2465; fax (305) 635-2272; e-mail info@sipiapa.org; internet www.sipiapa.org; f. 1942 to guard the freedom of the press in the Americas; to promote and maintain the dignity, rights and responsibilities of the profession of journalism; to foster a wider knowledge and greater interchange among the peoples of the Americas. Mems: 1,400. Exec. Dir JULIO E. MUÑOZ. Publ. *IAPA News.*

International Association of Broadcasting (Asociación Internacional de Radiodifusión—AIR): Cnel Brandzen 1961, Office 402, 11200 Montevideo, Uruguay; tel. (2) 4088129; fax (2) 4088121; e-mail airiab@distrinet.com.uy; internet www .airiab.com; f. 1946 to preserve free and private broadcasting; to promote co-operation between the corporations and public authorities; to defend freedom of expression. Mems: national asscns of broadcasters. Pres. Dr LUIS H. TARSITANO; Dir-Gen. Dr HÉCTOR OSCAR AMENGUAL. Publ. *La Gaceta de AIR* (every 2 months).

International Association of Sound and Audiovisual Archives: c/o Albrecht Häfner, Südwestrundfunk, Documentation and Archives Dept, 76522 Baden-Baden, Germany; tel. (7221) 9293487; fax (7221) 9294199; e-mail albrecht.haefner @swr.de; internet www.llgc.org.uk/iasa; f. 1969; supports the professional exchange of sound and audiovisual documents, and fosters international co-operation between audiovisual archies in all field, in particular in the areas of acquisition, documentation, access, exploitation copyright, and preservation; holds annual conference. Mems: 380 individuals and institutions in 48 countries. Sec.-Gen. ALBRECHT HÄFNER. Publs *IASA Journal* (2 a year), *IASA Information Bulletin* (quarterly).

International Catholic Union of the Press (Union catholique internationale de la presse—UCIP): 37–39 rue de Vermont, Case Postale 197, 1211 Geneva 20, Switzerland; tel. (22) 7340017; fax (22) 7340053; e-mail helo@ucip.ch; internet www.ucip.ch; f. 1927 to link all Catholics who influence public opinion through the press, to inspire a high standard of professional conscience and to represent the interest of the Catholic press at international organizations. Mems: Federation of Catholic Press Agencies, Federation of Catholic Journalists, Federation of Catholic Dailies, Federation of Catholic Periodicals, Federation of Teachers in the Science and Technics of Information, Federation of Church Press Associations, Federation of Book Publishers, eight regional asscns. Pres. RERESA EE-CHOOI; Sec.-Gen. JOSEPH CHITTILAPPILLY (India). Publ. *UCIP-Information.*

International Council for Film, Television and Audiovisual Communication (Conseil international du cinema de la television et de la communication audiovisuelle): 1 rue Miollis, 75732 Paris Cédex 15, France; tel. 1-45-68-48-55; fax 1-45-67-28-40; e-mail cict@unesco.org; internet www.occam.org/french/ cict.html; f. 1958 to arrange meetings and co-operation generally. Mems: 36 international film and television organizations. Pres. JEAN ROUCH; Sec.-Gen. Dr ROBERT E. KALMAN. Publ. *Letter of Information* (monthly).

International Council of French-speaking Radio and Television Organizations (Conseil international des radios-télévisions d'expression française): 52 blvd Auguste-Reyers, 1044 Brussels, Belgium; tel. (2) 732-45-85; fax (2) 732-62-40; f. 1978 to establish links between French-speaking radio and television organizations. Mems: 46 organizations. Sec.-Gen. ABDELKADER MARZOUKI (Tunisia).

International Federation of Press Cutting Agencies: Streulistr. 19, POB 8030 Zürich, Switzerland; tel. (1) 3888200; fax (1) 3888201; e-mail fibep@swissline.ch; f. 1953 to improve the standing of the profession, prevent infringements, illegal practices and unfair competition; and to develop business and friendly relations among press cuttings agencies throughout the world. Annual meeting, 2002: Berlin. Mems: 71 agencies. Pres. CARLOS BEGAS (Israel); Gen. Sec. THOMAS HENNE (Switzerland).

International Federation of the Cinematographic Press—FIPRESCI: Schleissheimerstr. 83, 80797 Munich, Germany; tel. (89) 182303; fax (89) 184766; e-mail keder@fipresci.org; internet www.fipresci.org; f. 1930 to develop the cinematographic press and promote cinema as an art; organizes international meetings and juries in film festivals. Mems: national organizations or corresponding members in 68 countries. Pres. DEREK MALCOLM (UK); Sec.-Gen. KLAUS EDER (Germany).

International Federation of the Periodical Press—FIPP: Queen's House, 55/56 Lincoln's Inn Fields, London, WC2A 3LJ, United Kingdom; tel. (20) 7404-4169; fax (20) 7404-4170; e-mail info@fipp.com; internet www.fipp.com; f. 1925; works through national asscns to promote optimum conditions for the development of periodical publishing; fosters formal and informal alliances between magazine publishers. Mems: 35 national asscns representing 2,500 publishing cos and 75 international publishing cos and assoc. mems. Pres. and CEO PER R. MORTENSEN; Chair. AXEL GANZ (Germany). Publ. *Magazine World* (6 a year).

International Federation of the Socialist and Democratic Press: CP 737, 1-2021 Milan, Italy; tel. (02) 8050105; f. 1953 to promote co-operation between editors and publishers of socialist newspapers; affiliated to the Socialist International (q.v.). Mems: about 100. Sec. UMBERTO GIOVINE.

International Institute of Communications: 3rd Floor, Westcott House, 35 Portland Place, London, W1B 1AE, United Kingdom; tel. (20) 7323-9672; fax (20) 7323-9625; e-mail enquiries@iicom.org; internet www.iicom.org; f. 1969 (as the International Broadcast Institute) to link all working in the field of communications, including policy makers, broadcasters, industrialists and engineers; holds local, regional and international meetings; undertakes research. Mems: over 1,000 corporate, institutional and individual. Pres. BERNARD COURTOIS (Canada); Chair. BÄASHIR SHARIFF (Malaysia). Publs *Intermedia* (quarterly), *Communications Technology Decisions* (2 a year).

International Maritime Radio Association: South Bank House, Black Prince Rd, London, SE1 7SJ, United Kingdom; tel. (20) 7587-1245; fax (20) 7587-1436; e-mail secgen@cirm.org; internet www.cirm.org; f. 1928 to study and develop means of improving marine radio communications and radio aids to marine navigation. Mems: over 70 organizations and companies are involved in marine electronics in the areas of radio communications and navigation. Mems: companies in the major maritime nations. Pres. G. SEUTIN (Belgium); Sec.-Gen. and Chair. of Technical Cttee Capt. C. K. D. COBLEY.

International Press Institute—IPI: Spiegelgasse 2/29, 1010 Vienna, Austria; tel. (1) 5129011; fax (1) 5129014; e-mail ipi@freemedia.at; internet www.freemedia.at; f. 1951 as a non-governmental organization of editors, publishers and news broadcasters supporting the principles of a free and responsible press; aims to defend press freedom; conducts training programmes and research; maintains a library; holds regional meetings and an annual World Congress. Mems: about 2,000 from 110 countries. Pres. HUGO BUETLER (Switzerland); Dir JOHANN FRITZ (Austria). Publs *IPI Global Journalist* (quarterly), *World Press Freedom Review* (annually).

International Press Telecommunications Council—IPTC: Royal Albert House, Sheet St, Windsor, Berks, SL4 1BE, United Kingdom; tel. (1753) 705051; fax (1753) 831541; e-mail m_director_iptc@dial.pipex.com; internet www.iptc.org/iptc; f. 1965 to safeguard and promote the interests of the Press on all matters relating to telecommunications; keeps its members informed of current and future telecommunications developments; to act as the news information formal standards body. The Council meets three times a year and maintains four committees and 10 working parties. Mems: 44 press asscns, newspapers, news agencies and industry vendors. Chair. PETER MÜLLER; Man. Dir DAVID ALLEN. Publs *IPTC Spectrum* (annually), *IPTC Mirror* (monthly).

Latin-American Catholic Press Union: Apdo Postal 17-21-178, Quito, Ecuador; tel. (2) 548046; fax (2) 501658; f. 1959 to co-ordinate, promote and improve the Catholic press in Latin America. Mems: national asscns and local groups in most Latin American countries. Pres. ISMAR DE OLIVEIRA SOARES (Brazil); Sec. CARLOS EDUARDO CORTÉS (Colombia).

Organization of Asia-Pacific News Agencies—OANA: c/o Xinhua News Agency, 57 Xuanwumen Xidajie, Beijing 100803, People's Republic of China; tel. (10) 3074762; fax (10) 3072707; internet www.oananews.com; f. 1961 to promote co-operation in professional matters and mutual exchange of news, features, etc. among the news agencies of Asia and the Pacific via the Asia-Pacific News Network (ANN). Mems: Anadolu Ajansi (Turkey), Antara (Indonesia), APP (Pakistan), Bakhtar (Afghanistan), BERNAMA (Malaysia), BSS (Bangladesh), ENA (Bangladesh), Hindustan Samachar (India), IRNA (Iran), ITAR-TASS (Russia), Kaz-TAG (Kazakhstan), KABAR (Kyrgyzstan), KCNA (Korea, Democratic People's Republic), KPL (Laos), Kyodo (Japan), Lankapuvath (Sri Lanka), Montsame (Mongolia), PNA (Philippines), PPI (Pakistan), PTI (India), RSS (Nepal), Samachar Bharati (India), TNA (Thailand), UNB (Bangladesh), UNI (India), Viet Nam News Agency, Xinhua (People's Republic of China), Yonhap (Republic of Korea). Pres. GUO CHAOREN; Sec.-Gen. MIKHAIL GUSMANN.

Press Foundation of Asia: POB 1843, S & L Bldg, 3rd Floor, 1500 Roxas Blvd, Manila, Philippines; tel. (2) 5233223; fax (2) 5224365; e-mail pfa@pressasia.org; internet www.pressasia.org; f. 1967; an independent, non-profit making organization governed by its newspaper members; acts as a professional forum for about 200 newspapers in Asia; aims to reduce cost of newspapers to potential readers, to improve editorial and management techniques through research and training programmes and to encourage the growth of the Asian press; operates *Depthnews* feature service. Mems: 200 newspapers. Exec. Chair. MAZLAN NORDIN (Malaysia); Chief Exec. MOCHTAR LUBIS (Indonesia). Publs *Pressasia* (quarterly), *Asian Women* (quarterly).

Reporters sans Frontières: 5 rue Geoffroy Marie, 75009 Paris, France; tel. 1-44-83-84-84; fax 1-45-23-11-51; e-mail rsf@rsf.org; internet www.rsf.org; f. 1985 to defend press freedoms throughout the world; generates awareness of violations of press freedoms and supports journalists under threat or imprisoned as a result of their work. Mems in 77 countries. Dir ROBERT MÉNARD. Publs *Annual Report, La Lettre de Reporters sans Frontières* (monthly).

Union of National Radio and Television Organizations of Africa—URTNA: 101 rue Carnot, BP 3237, Dakar, Senegal; tel. 821-16-25; fax 822-51-13; e-mail urtnadkr@telecomplus.sn; f. 1962; co-ordinates radio and television services, including monitoring and frequency allocation, the exchange of information and coverage of national and international events among African countries; maintains programme exchange centre (Nairobi, Kenya), technical centre (Bamako, Mali), a centre for rural radio studies (Ouagadougou, Burkina Faso) and a centre for the exchange of television news (Algiers, Algeria). Mems: 48 organizations and six associate members. Sec.-Gen. ABDELHAMID BOUKSANI. Publ. *URTNA Review* (2 a year, in English and French).

World Association for Christian Communication—WACC: 357 Kennington Lane, London, SE11 5QY, United Kingdom; tel. (20) 7582-9139; fax (20) 7735-0340; e-mail wacc@wacc.org.uk; internet www.wacc.org.uk; f. 1975 to promote human dignity, justice and peace through freedom of expression and the democratization of communication; offers professional guidance on communication policies; interprets developments in and the consequences of global communication methods; works towards the empowerment of women; assists the training of Christian communicators. Mems: more than 800 corporate and personal mems in 115 countries, organized in eight regional assocs. Pres. ALBERT VAN DEN HEUVEL; Gen.-Sec. R. L. NAYLOR. Publs *Action* newsletter (10 a year), *Media Development* (quarterly), *Communication Resource, Media and Gender Monitor* (both occasional).

World Association of Newspapers—WAN: 25 rue d'Astorg, 75008 Paris, France; tel. 1-47-42-85-00; fax 1-47-42-49-48; e-mail tbalding@wan.asso.fr; internet www.wan-press.org; f. 1948 to defend the freedom of the press, to safeguard the ethical and economic interests of newspapers and to study all questions of interest to newspapers at international level. Mems: 66 national newspaper asscns, individual newspaper executives in 93 countries, 17 news agencies and seven regional and world-wide press groups. Pres. BENGT BRAUN (Sweden); Dir-Gen. TIMOTHY BALDING. Publ. *Newsletter*.

Religion

Agudath Israel World Organisation: Hacherut Sq., POB 326, Jerusalem 91002, Israel; tel. (2) 5384357; fax (2) 5383634; f. 1912 to help solve the problems facing Jewish people all over the world in the spirit of the Jewish tradition; holds World Congress (every five years) and an annual Central Council. Mems: over 500,000 in 25 countries. Chair. J. M. ABRAMOWITZ (Jerusalem); Secs Rabbi MOSHE GEWIRTZ, Rabbi CHAIM WEINSTOCK. Publs *Hamodia* (Jerusalem daily newspaper, in Hebrew; weekly in English), *Jewish Tribune* (London, weekly), *Jewish Observer* (New York, monthly), *Dos Yiddishe Vort* (New York, monthly), *Coalition* (New York), *Perspectives* (Toronto, monthly), *La Voz Judia* (Buenos Aires, monthly), *Jüdische Stimme* (Zürich, monthly).

All Africa Conference of Churches—AACC: POB 14205, Waiyaki Way, Nairobi, Kenya; tel. (2) 441483; fax (2) 443241; e-mail aacc-secretariat@maf.org; f. 1958; an organ of co-operation and continuing fellowship among Protestant, Orthodox and independent churches and Christian Councils in Africa. 1997 Assembly: Addis Ababa, Ethiopia. Mems: 147 churches and affiliated Christian councils in 39 African countries. Pres. The Very Rev. Prof. KWESI DICKSON (Ghana); Gen. Sec. Canon CLEMENT JANDA (Uganda). Publs *ACIS/APS Bulletin, ACLCA News, Tam Tam*.

Alliance Israélite Universelle—AIU: 45 rue La Bruyère, 75425 Paris Cédex 09, France; tel. 1-53-32-88-55; fax 1-48-74-51-33; e-mail info@aiu.org; internet www.aiu.org; f. 1860 to work for the emancipation and moral progress of the Jews; maintains 40 schools in eight countries; library of 120,000 vols. Mems: 8,000 in 16 countries. Pres. ADY STEG; Dir JEAN-JACQUES WAHL (France). Publs *Les Cahiers de l'Alliance Israélite Universelle* (3 a year, in French), *Les Cahiers du Judaïsme, The Alliance Review* (in English).

Bahá'í International Community: Bahá'í World Centre, POB 155, 31 001 Haifa, Israel; tel. (4) 8358394; fax (4) 8313312; e-mail opi@bwc.org; internet www.bahai.org; f. 1844 in Persia to promote the unity of mankind and world peace through the teachings of the Bahá'í religion, including the equality of men and women and the elimination of all forms of prejudice; maintains schools for children and adults world-wide, operates educational and cultural radio stations in the USA, Asia and Latin America; has 32 publishing trusts throughout the world. Governing body: Universal House of Justice (nine mems elected by 182 National Spiritual Assemblies). Mems: in 129,949 centres (in 190 countries and 45 dependent territories or overseas departments). Sec.-Gen. ALBERT LINCOLN (USA). Publs *Bahá'í World* (annually), *One Country* (quarterly, in 6 languages).

Baptist World Alliance: 6733 Curran St, McLean, VA 22101-6005, USA; tel. (703) 790-8980; fax (703) 893-5160; e-mail bwa@bwanet.org; internet www.bwanet.org; f. 1905; aims to unite Baptists, lead in evangelism, respond to people in need and defend human rights. Mems: 191 Baptist unions and conventions comprising 42m. people in 200 countries and territories. Pres. Dr NILSON DO AMARAL FANINI (Brazil); Gen. Sec. Dr DENTON LOTZ. Publ. *The Baptist World* (quarterly).

Caribbean Conference of Churches: POB 876, Port of Spain, Trinidad and Tobago; tel. 628-202; fax 628-2031; e-mail caconftt@trinidad.net; internet www.cariblife.com/pub/ccc; f. 1973; holds Assembly every five years; conducts study and research programmes; supports education and community projects. Mems: 34 churches. Gen. Sec. GERARD GRANADO. Publ *Christian Action Newsletter* (quarterly).

Christian Conference of Asia—CCA: 96, 2nd District, Pak Tin Village, Mei Tin Rd, Shatin, NT, Hong Kong; tel. 26911068; fax 26924378; e-mail cca@cca.org.hkt; internet www.cca.org.hk; f. 1957 (present name adopted 1973) to promote co-operation and joint study in matters of common concern among the Churches of the region and to encourage interaction with other regional Conferences and the World Council of Churches. Mems: more than 100 churches and councils of churches from 18 Asian countries. Gen. Sec. Dr AHN JAE WOONG. Publ. *CCA News* (quarterly).

Christian Peace Conference: Prokopova 4, 130 00 Prague 3, Czech Republic; tel. (2) 22781800; fax (2) 22781801; e-mail christianpeace@volny.cz; internet www.volny.cz/christianpeace; f. 1958 as an international movement of theologians, clergy and lay-people, aiming to bring Christendom to recognize its share of guilt in both world wars and to dedicate itself to the service of friendship, reconciliation and peaceful co-operation of nations, to concentrate on united action for peace and justice, and to co-ordinate peace groups in individual churches and facilitate their effective participation in the peaceful development of society. It works through five continental asscns, regional groups and member churches in many countries. Moderator Dr SERGIO ARCE MARTÍNEZ; Co-ordinator Rev. BRIAN G. COOPER. Publs *CPC INFORMATION* (8 a year in English and German), occasional *Study Volume*.

Conference of European Churches—CEC: POB 2100, 150 route de Ferney, 1211 Geneva 2, Switzerland; tel. (22) 7916111; fax (22) 7916227; e-mail cec@cec-kek.org; internet www.cec-kek.org; f. 1959 as a regional ecumenical organization for Europe and a meeting-place for European churches, including members and non-members of the World Council of Churches; holds assemblies every few years. Mems: 128 Protestant, Anglican, Orthodox and Old Catholic churches in all European countries. Gen. Sec. Rev. Dr KEITH CLEMENTS. Publs *Monitor* (quarterly), CEC communiqués, reports.

Conference of International Catholic Organizations: 37–39 rue de Vermont, 1202 Geneva, Switzerland; tel. (22) 7338392; f. 1927 to encourage collaboration and agreement between the different Catholic international organizations in their common interests, and to contribute to international understanding; organizes international assemblies and meetings to study specific problems. Permanent commissions deal with human rights, the new international economic order, social problems, the family health, education, etc. Mems: 36 Catholic international organizations. Administrator PAUL MORAND (Switzerland).

Consultative Council of Jewish Organizations—CCJO: 420 Lexington Ave, New York, NY 10170, USA; tel. (212) 808-5437; f. 1946 to co-operate and consult with the UN and other international bodies directly concerned with human rights and to defend the cultural, political and religious rights of Jews throughout the world. Sec.-Gen. WARREN GREEN (USA).

European Baptist Federation—EBF: Postfach 610340, 22423 Hamburg, Germany; tel. (40) 5509723; fax (40) 5509725; e-mail office@ebf.org; internet www.ebf.org; f. 1949 to promote fellowship and co-operation among Baptists in Europe; to further the aims and objects of the Baptist World Alliance; to stimulate and co-ordinate evangelism in Europe; to provide for consultation and planning of missionary work in Europe and elsewhere in the world. Mems: 49 Baptist Unions in European countries and the Middle East. Pres. DAVID COFFEY; Sec.-Treas. Rev. KARL-HEINZ WALTER (Germany).

European Evangelical Alliance: Wilhelmshoeher Allee 258, 34131 Kassel, Germany; tel. (561) 3149711; fax (561) 9387520; e-mail 100341.550@compuserve.com; internet www.hfe.org; f. 1953 to promote understanding and co-operation among evangelical Christians in Europe and to stimulate evangelism. Mems: 25 national alliances from 24 countries, 6 pan-European asscns. Pres. DEREK COPLEY (UK); Sec. GORDON SHOWELL-ROGERS.

Friends World Committee for Consultation: 4 Byng Pl., London, WC1E 7LE, United Kingdom; tel. (20) 7388-0497; fax (20) 7383-4644; e-mail world@fwcc.quaker.org; internet www.quaker.org/fwcc/; f. 1937 to encourage and strengthen the spiritual life within the Religious Society of Friends (Quakers); to help Friends to a better understanding of their vocation in the world; and to promote consultation among Friends of all countries; representation at the United Nations as a non-governmental organization. Mems: appointed representatives and individuals from 70 countries. Gen. Sec. ELIZABETH DUKE.

Publs *Friends World News* (2 a year), *Calendar of Yearly Meetings* (annually), *Quakers around the World* (handbook).

Initiatives of Change: POB 3, 1211 Geneva 20, Switzerland; tel. (22) 7330920; fax (22) 7330267; e-mail media@caux.ch; internet www.caux.ch; other international centres at Panchgani, India, Petropolis, Brazil, London and Tirley Garth, UK, and Gweru, Zimbabwe; f. 1921; aims to develop a new social order for better human relations and the elimination of political, industrial and racial antagonism. Legally incorporated bodies in 20 countries. Pres. of Swiss foundation CORNELIO SOMMARUGA. Publs *Changer* (French, 6 a year), *For a Change* (English, 6 a year), *Caux Information* (German, monthly).

International Association for Religious Freedom—IARF: 2 Market St, Oxford OX1 3EF, United Kingdom; tel. (1865) 202-744; fax (1865) 202-746; e-mail hq@iarf.net; internet iarf-religiousfreedom.net; f. 1900 as a world community of religions, subscribing to the principle of openness and upholding the United Nation's Universal Declaration on freedom of religion or belief; conducts intercultural encounters, inter-religious dialogues and a series of religious freedom programmes; holds regional conferences and triennial congress. Mems: 90 groups in 27 countries. Pres. EIMERT VAN HERWIJNEN (Netherlands); Gen. Sec. ANDREW C. CLARK (UK). Publ. *IARF World* (2 a year).

International Association of Buddhist Studies—IABS: c/o Prof. Oskar von Hinüber, Orientalisches Seminar, Indologie, Humboldtstr. 5, Freiburg 79085, Germany; tel. (761) 203-3158; fax (761) 203-3152; e-mail iabs.treasurer@orient.unil.ch; f. 1976; supports studies of Buddhist religion, philosophy and literature; holds international conference every three or four years. Gen. Sec. OSKAR VON HINÜBER. Publ. *Journal* (2 a year).

International Council of Christians and Jews—ICCJ: Martin Buber House, Werléstrasse 2, 64646 Heppenheim, Germany; tel. (6252) 93120; fax (6252) 68331; e-mail iccj_buberhouse@t-online.de; internet www.iccj.org; f. 1947 to promote mutual respect and co-operation; holds annual international colloquium, seminars, meetings for young people and for women; maintains a forum for Jewish–Christian–Muslim relations. Mems: 36 national councils in 32 countries. Pres. Rabbi Prof. DAVID ROSEN; Sec.-Gen. Rev. FRIEDHELM PIEPER. Publs *ICCJ History*, *ICCJ Brochure*, conference documents.

International Council of Jewish Women: 24–32 Stephenson Way, London, NW1 2JW, United Kingdom; tel. (20) 7388-8311; fax (20) 7387-2110; e-mail hq@icjw.demon.co.uk; internet www.icjw.org.uk; f. 1912 to promote friendly relations and understanding among Jewish women throughout the world; campaigns for human and women's rights, exchanges information on community welfare activities, promotes volunteer leadership, sponsors field work in social welfare, co-sponsors the International Jewish Women's Human Rights Watch and fosters Jewish education. Mems: affiliates totalling over 1.5m. members in 46 countries. Pres. JUNE JACOBS. Publs *Newsletter, Links around the World* (2 a year, English and Spanish), *International Jewish Women's Human Rights Watch* (2 a year).

International Fellowship of Reconciliation—IFOR: Spoorstraat 38, 1815 BK Alkmaar, Netherlands; tel. (72) 512-30-14; fax (72) 515-11-02; e-mail office@ifor.org; internet www.ifor.org; f. 1919; international, spiritually-based movement committed to active non-violence as a way of life and as a means of building a culture of peace and non-violence; maintains branches, affiliates and groups in more than 50 countries. Int. Pres. VIRGINIA BARON (USA). Publs *Reconciliation International* (quarterly), *Patterns in Reconciliation, Cross the Lines* (3 a year, in English, French and Spanish), occasional paper series.

International Humanist and Ethical Union—IHEU: 47 Theobald's Rd, London, WC1X 8SP, United Kingdom; tel. (20) 7831-4817; fax (20) 7404-8641; internet www.iheu.org; f. 1952 to bring into asscn all those interested in promoting ethical and scientific humanism and human rights. Mems: national organizations and individuals in 37 countries. Exec. Dir BABU R. R. GOGINENI. Publ. *International Humanist News* (quarterly).

International Organization for the Study of the Old Testament: c/o Prof. Gordon, St Catherine's College, Cambridge CB2 1RL, United Kingdom; tel. (1223) 338300; fax (1223) 338340; f. 1950. Holds triennial congresses. Pres. Prof. A. VAN DER KOOIJ (Netherlands); Sec. Prof. R. P. GORDON (UK). Publ. *Vetus Testamentum* (quarterly).

Latin American Council of Churches (Consejo Latinoamericano de Iglesias—CLAI): Casilla 17-08-8522, Calle Inglaterra 943 y Mariana de Jesús, Quito, Ecuador; tel. and fax (2) 553996; e-mail israel@clai.ecuanex.net.ec; internet www.clai.org.ec; f. 1982. Mems: 147 churches in 19 countries. Gen. Sec. Rev. ISRAEL BATISTA.

Latin American Episcopal Council: Apartado Aéreo 51086, Santafé de Bogotá, Colombia; tel. (1) 612-1379; fax (1) 612-1929; e-mail celam@celam.org; internet www.celam.org; f. 1955 to study the problems of the Roman Catholic Church in Latin America and to co-ordinate Church activities. Mems: the Episcopal Conferences of Central and South America and the Caribbean. Pres. Mgr JORGE E. JIMÉNEZ CARVAJAL (Colombia). Publ. *CELAM* (6 a year).

Lutheran World Federation: 150 route de Ferney, POB 2100, 1211 Geneva 2, Switzerland; tel. (22) 7916111; fax (22) 7988616; e-mail info@lutheranworld.org; internet www.lutheranworld.org; f. 1947; groups 128 Lutheran Churches in 70 countries; provides inter-church aid and relief work in various areas of the globe; gives service to refugees, including resettlement; carries out theological research, conferences and exchanges; grants scholarship aid in various fields of church life; conducts inter-confessional dialogue with Roman Catholic, Seventh-day Adventist, Anglican and Orthodox churches. Pres. Rt Rev. Dr CHRISTIAN KRAUSE (Germany); Gen. Sec. Rev. Dr ISHMAEL NOKO (Zimbabwe). Publs *Lutheran World Information* (English and German, every 2 weeks), *LWF Today* and *LWF Documentation* (both irregular).

Middle East Council of Churches: Makhoul St, Deep Bldg, POB 5376, Beirut, Lebanon; tel. and fax (1) 344894; internet www.mecchurches.org; f. 1974. Mems: 28 churches. Pres Pope SHENOUDAH III, Patriarch PETROS VII PAPAPETRO, Rev. Dr SELIM SAHYOUNI, Archbishop KYRILLOS BUSTROS; Gen. Sec. Rev. Dr RIAD JARJOUR. Publs *MECC News Report* (monthly), *Al Montada News Bulletin* (quarterly, in Arabic), *Courrier oecuménique du Moyen-Orient* (quarterly), *MECC Perspectives* (3 a year).

Muslim World League—MWL (Rabitat al-Alam al-Islami): POB 537–538, Makkah, Saudi Arabia; tel. (2) 5422733; fax (2) 5436619; e-mail mwlhq@aol.com; internet www.arab.net/mwl; f. 1962; aims to advance Islamic unity and solidarity, and to promote world peace and respect for human rights; provides financial assistance for education, medical care and relief work; has 30 offices throughout the world. Sec.-Gen. Dr ABDULLAH BIN ABDULMOSHIN AL-TURKI. Publs *Majalla al-Rabita* (monthly, Arabic), *Akhbar al-Alam al Islami* (weekly, Arabic), *Journal* (monthly, English).

Opus Dei (Prelature of the Holy Cross and Opus Dei): Viale Bruno Buozzi 73, 00197 Rome, Italy; tel. (06) 808961; e-mail newyork@opusdei.org; internet www.opusdei.org; f. 1928 by Blessed Josemaría Escrivá de Balaguer to spread, at every level of society, an increased awareness of the universal call to sanctity and apostolate in the exercise of one's work. Mems: 82,443 Catholic laypeople and 1,763 priests. Prelate Most Rev. JAVIER ECHEVARRÍA. Publ. *Romana, Bulletin of the Prelature* (every six months).

Pacific Conference of Churches: POB 208, 4 Thurston St, Suva, Fiji; tel. 3311277; fax 3303205; e-mail pacific@is.com.fj; f. 1961; organizes assembly every five years, as well as regular workshops, meetings and training seminars throughout the region. Mems: 36 churches and councils. Moderator Pastor REUBEN MAGEKON; Gen. Sec. Rev. VALAMOTU PALU.

Pax Romana International Catholic Movement for Intellectual and Cultural Affairs—ICMICA; and International Movement of Catholic Students—IMCS: 15 rue du Grand-Bureau, POB 315, 1211 Geneva 24, Switzerland; tel. (22) 8230707; fax (22) 8230708; e-mail miicmica@paxromana.int.ch; internet www.pax-romana.org; f. 1921 (IMCS), 1947 (ICMICA), to encourage in members an awareness of their responsibilities as people and Christians in the student and intellectual milieux; to promote contacts between students and graduates throughout the world and co-ordinate the contribution of Catholic intellectual circles to international life. Mems: 80 student and 60 intellectual organizations in 80 countries. ICMICA—Pres. MARY J. MWINGIRA (Tanzania); Gen. Sec. ANSELMO LEE SEONG-HOON (Republic of Korea); IMCS—Gen. Secs WALTER PRYSTHON

(Brazil), ROLAND RANAIVOARISON (Madagascar). Publ. *Convergence* (3 a year).

Salvation Army: International HQ, 101 Queen Victoria St, London, EC4P 4EP, United Kingdom; tel. (20) 7332-0022; fax (20) 7236-4981; e-mail websa@salvationarmy.org; internet www.salvationarmy.org.uk; f. 1865 to spread the Christian gospel and relieve poverty; emphasis is placed on the need for personal discipleship, and to make its evangelism effective it adopts a quasi-military form of organization. Social, medical and educational work is also performed in the 107 countries where the Army operates. Pres. Gen. JOHN GOWANS; Chief of Staff Commissioner JOHN LARSSON. Publs 132 periodicals in 31 languages.

Soroptimist International: 87 Glisson Rd, Cambridge, CB1 2HG, United Kingdom; tel. (1223) 311833; fax (1223) 467951; e-mail sorophq@dial.pipex.com; internet www.sorop.org/; f. 1921 to strive for the advancement of the status of women, high ethical standards, human rights for all, equality and development of peace through international goodwill, understanding and friendship. Convention held every 4 years; 2003: Sydney, Australia. Mems: 95,000 in 3,000 clubs in 122 countries and territories. International Pres. IRHELI TORSSONEN (Finland); Exec. Officer JANET BILTON. Publ. *International Soroptimist* (quarterly).

Theosophical Society: Adyar, Chennai 600 020, India; tel. (44) 4915552; fax (44) 4902706; e-mail theossoc@satyam.net.in; internet www.ts-adyar.org; f. 1875; aims at universal brotherhood, without distinction of race, creed, sex, caste or colour; study of comparative religion, philosophy and science; investigation of unexplained laws of nature and powers latent in man. Mems: 35,000 in 70 countries. Pres. RADHA S. BURNIER; Int. Sec. DOLORES GAGO. Publs *The Theosophist* (monthly), *Adyar News Letter* (quarterly), *Brahmavidya* (annually).

United Bible Societies: 7th Floor, Reading Bridge House, Reading, RG1 8PJ, United Kingdom; tel. (118) 950-0200; fax (118) 950-0857; e-mail jphillips@ubs-wsc.org; internet www.biblesociety.org; f. 1946; co-ordinates the translation, production and distribution of the Bible by Bible Societies world-wide; works with national Bible Societies to develop religious programmes. Mems: 138 Bible Societies in more than 200 countries. Pres. Dr SAMUEL ESCOBAR (Peru/USA); Gen. Sec. NEIL CROSBIE (UK). Publs *Bulletin (1 or 2 a year), The Bible Translator* (quarterly), *Publishing World* (3 a year), *Prayer Booklet* (annually), *Special Report* (3 or 4 a year), *World Report* (monthly).

Watch Tower Bible and Tract Society: (British section) The Ridgeway, London, NW7 1RN, United Kingdom; tel. (20) 8906-2211; fax (20) 8371-0051; e-mail pr@wtbts.org.uk; internet www.watchtower.org; f. 1881; 110 branches; serves as legal agency for Jehovah's Witnesses. Pres. RON DRAGE; Sec. and Treas. TOM CRUSE. Publs *The Watchtower* (2 a month, in 144 languages), *Awake!* (2 a month, in 87 languages).

World Alliance of Reformed Churches (Presbyterian and Congregational): Box 2100, 150 route de Ferney, 1211 Geneva 2, Switzerland; tel. (22) 7916240; fax (22) 7916505; e-mail sn@warc.ch; internet www.warc.ch; f. 1970 by merger of WARC (Presbyterian) (f. 1875) with International Congregational Council (f. 1891) to promote fellowship among Reformed, Presbyterian and Congregational churches. Mems: 214 churches in 106 countries. Pres. Prof. CHOAN-SENG SONG; Gen. Sec. Rev. Dr SETRI NYOMI (Ghana). Publs *Reformed World* (quarterly), *Up-Date.*

World Christian Life Community: Borgo S. Spirito 8, Casella Postale 6139, 00195 Rome, Italy; tel. (06) 6868079; e-mail mcvx.wclc@agora.stm.it; f. 1953 as World Federation of the Sodalities of our Lady (first group f. 1563) as a lay movement based on the teachings of Ignatius Loyola, to integrate Christian faith and daily living. Mems: groups in 55 countries representing about 100,000 individuals. Pres. JOSÉ MARÍA RIERA; Exec. Sec. GILLES MICHAUD. Publ. *Progressio* (in English, French and Spanish).

World Conference on Religion and Peace: 777 United Nations Plaza, New York, NY 10017, USA; tel. (212) 687-2163; fax (212) 983-0566; internet www.wcrp.org; f. 1970 to co-ordinate education and action of various world religions for world peace and justice. Mems: religious organizations and individuals in 100 countries. Sec.-Gen. Dr WILLIAM VENDLEY. Publ. *Religion for Peace.*

World Congress of Faiths: 2 Market St, Oxford, OX1 3EF, United Kingdom; tel. (1865) 202751; fax (1865) 202746; e-mail worldconfaiths@aol.com; internet www.worldfaiths.org; f. 1936 to promote a spirit of fellowship among mankind through an understanding of one another's religions, to bring together people of all nationalities, backgrounds and creeds in mutual respect and tolerance, to encourage the study and understanding of issues arising out of multi-faith societies, and to promote welfare and peace. Mems: about 400. Pres Prof. KEITH WARD, Rev. MARCUS BRAYBROOKE; Chair. RICHARD BOEKE. Publ. *World Faiths Encounter* (3 a year).

World Evangelical Alliance: 141 Middle Rd 05-05, GSM Bldg, Singapore 188976, Singapore; tel. 3397900; fax 3383756; e-mail 100012.345@compuserve.com; internet www.worldevangelical.org; f. 1951 as World Evangelical Fellowship, on reorganization of World Evangelical Alliance (f. 1846), reverted to original name Jan. 2002; an int. grouping of national and regional bodies of evangelical Christians; encourages the organization of national fellowships and assists national mems in planning their activities. Mems: national evangelical asscns in 110 countries. International Dir AUGUSTIN B. VENCER, Jr. Publs *Evangelical World* (monthly), *Evangelical Review of Theology* (quarterly).

World Fellowship of Buddhists: 616 Benjasiri Pk, Soi Medhinivet off Soi Sukhumvit 24, Bangkok 10110, Thailand; tel. (2) 661-1284; fax (2) 661-0555; e-mail wfb-hq@asianet.co.th; internet www.wfb-hq.org; f. 1950 to promote strict observance and practice of the teachings of the Buddha; holds General Conference every 2 years; 140 regional centres in 37 countries. Pres. PHAN WANNAMETHEE; Hon. Sec.-Gen. Dr NANTASARN SEESALAB. Publs *WFB Journal* (6 a year), *WFB Review* (quarterly), *WFB Newsletter* (monthly), documents, booklets.

World Hindu Federation: c/o Dr Jogendra Jha, Pashupati Kshetra, Kathmandu, Nepal; tel. (1) 470182; fax (1) 470131; e-mail hem@karki.com.np; f. 1981 to promote and preserve Hindu philosophy and culture; to protect the rights of Hindus, particularly the right to worship. Executive Board meets annually. Mems: in 45 countries and territories. Sec.-Gen. Dr JOGENDRA JHA (Nepal). Publ. *Vishwa Hindu* (monthly).

World Jewish Congress: 501 Madison Ave, New York, NY 10022, USA; tel. (212) 755-5770; fax (212) 755-5883; internet www.wcj.org.il; f. 1936 as a voluntary asscn of representative Jewish communities and organizations throughout the world; aims to foster the unity of the Jewish people and ensure the continuity and development of their heritage. Mems: Jewish communities in 84 countries. Pres. EDGAR M. BRONFMAN; Sec.-Gen. ISRAEL SINGER. Publs *Gesher* (Hebrew quarterly, Israel), *Boletín Informativo OJI* (fortnightly, Buenos Aires).

World Methodist Council: International Headquarters, POB 518, Lake Junaluska, NC 28745, USA; tel. (704) 456-9432; fax (704) 456-9433; e-mail georgefreeman@mindspring.com; internet www.worldmethodistcouncil.org; f. 1881 to deepen the fellowship of the Methodist peoples, encourage evangelism, foster Methodist participation in the ecumenical movement and promote the unity of Methodist witness and service. Mems: 77 churches in 132 countries, comprising 36m. individuals. Gen. Sec. GEORGE H. FREEMAN (USA). Publ. *World Parish* (6 a year).

World Sephardi Federation: 13 rue Marignac, 1206 Geneva, Switzerland; tel. (22) 3473313; fax (22) 3472839; f. 1951 to strengthen the unity of Jewry and Judaism among Sephardi and Oriental Jews, to defend and foster religious and cultural activities of all Sephardi and Oriental Jewish communities and preserve their spiritual heritage, to provide moral and material assistance where necessary and to co-operate with other similar organizations. Mems: 50 communities and organizations in 33 countries. Pres. NESSIM D. GAON; Sec.-Gen. SHIMON DERY.

World Student Christian Federation—WSCF: 5 route des Morillons, Grand-Saconnex, 1218 Geneva, Switzerland; tel. (22) 7988953; fax (22) 7982370; e-mail wscf@worldcom.ch; internet www.wscf.net; f. 1895 to proclaim Jesus Christ as Lord and Saviour in the academic community, and to present students with the claims of the Christian faith over their whole life; holds General Assembly every four years. Mems: 67 national Student Christian Movements, and 34 national correspondents. Chair. Rev. EJIKE OKORD (Nigeria); Secs-Gen. BEATE FAGERLI (Norway), LAWRENCE BREW (Ghana).

World Union for Progressive Judaism: 633 Third Ave, New York, NY 10017, USA; tel. (212) 249-0100; fax (212) 650-4099; internet wupj.org; f. 1926; promotes and co-ordinates efforts of Reform, Liberal, Progressive and Reconstructionist congregations throughout the world; supports new congregations; assigns and employs rabbis; sponsors seminaries and schools; organizes international conferences; maintains a youth section. Mems: organizations and individuals in 30 countries. Pres. AUSTIN BEUTEL; Exec. Dir Rabbi RICHARD G. HIRSCH (Israel). Publs *News Updates, International Conference Reports, European Judaism* (bi-annual).

World Union of Catholic Women's Organisations: 18 rue Notre-Dame-des-Champs, 75006 Paris, France; tel. 1-45-44-27-65; fax 1-42-84-04-80; e-mail wucwoparis@wanadoo.fr; internet home.pi.net/ wucwo; f. 1910 to promote and co-ordinate the contribution of Catholic women in international life, in social, civic, cultural and religious matters. Mems: 20m. Pres. MARÍA EUGENIA DÍAZ DE PFENNICH (Mexico); Sec.-Gen. GILLIAN BADCOCK (UK). Publ. *Newsletter* (quarterly, in four languages).

Science

International Council for Science—ICSU: 51 blvd de Montmorency, 75016 Paris, France; tel. 1-45-25-03-29; fax 1-42-88-94-31; e-mail secretariat@icsu.org; internet www.icsu.org; f. 1919 as International Research Council; present name adopted 1931; new statutes adopted 1996; to co-ordinate international co-operation in theoretical and applied sciences and to promote national scientific research through the intermediary of affiliated national organizations; General Assembly of representatives of national and scientific members meets every three years to formulate policy. The following committees have been established: Cttee on Science for Food Security, Scientific Cttee on Antarctic Research, Scientific Cttee on Oceanic Research, Cttee on Space Research, Scientific Cttee on Water Research, Scientific Cttee on Solar-Terrestrial Physics, Cttee on Science and Technology in Developing Countries, Cttee on Data for Science and Technology, Programme on Capacity Building in Science, Scientific Cttee on Problems of the Environment, Steering Cttee on Genetics and Biotechnology and Scientific Cttee on International Geosphere-Biosphere Programme. The following services and Inter-Union Committees and Commissions have been established: Federation of Astronomical and Geophysical Data Analysis Services, Inter-Union Commission on Frequency Allocations for Radio Astronomy and Space Science, Inter-Union Commission on Radio Meteorology, Inter-Union Commission on Spectroscopy, Inter-Union Commission on Lithosphere. National mems: academies or research councils in 98 countries; Scientific mems and assocs: 26 international unions (see below) and 28 scientific associates. Pres. W. ARBER; Sec.-Gen. H. A. MOONEY. Publs *ICSU Yearbook, Science International* (quarterly), *Annual Report*.

UNIONS FEDERATED TO THE ICSU

International Astronomical Union—IAU: 98 bis blvd d'Arago, 75014 Paris, France; tel. 1-43-25-83-58; fax 1-43-25-26-16; e-mail iau@iap.fr; internet www.iau.org; f. 1919 to facilitate co-operation between the astronomers of various countries and to further the study of astronomy in all its branches. Mems: organizations in 65 countries, and 9,000 individual mems. Pres. FRANCO PACINI (Italy); Gen. Sec. HANS RICKMAN (Sweden). Publs *IAU Information Bulletin* (2 a year), *Symposia Series* (6 a year), *Highlights* (every 3 years).

International Geographical Union—IGU: Dept of Geography, University of Bonn, 53115 Bonn, Meckenheimer Allee 166, Germany; tel. (228) 739287; fax (228) 739272; e-mail secretariat@igu.bn.eunet.be; internet www.helsinki.fi/science/igu; f. 1922 to encourage the study of problems relating to geography, to promote and co-ordinate research requiring international co-operation, and to organize international congresses and commissions. Mems: 83 countries, 11 associates. Pres. Prof. BRUNO MESSERLI (Switzerland); Sec.-Gen. Prof. ECKART EHLERS (Germany). Publ. *IGU Bulletin* (2 a year).

International Mathematical Union—IMU: c/o Institute for Advanced Study (IAS), Einstein Drive, Princeton, NJ 08540, USA; e-mail imu@ias.edu; internet elib.zib.de/imu; f. 1952 to support and assist the International Congress of Mathematicians and other international scientific meetings or conferences and to encourage and support other international mathematical activities considered likely to contribute to the development of mathematical science—pure, applied or educational. Mems: 63 countries. Pres. Prof. JACOB PALIS; Sec.-Gen. Prof. PHILLIP GRIFFITHS.

International Union for Physical and Engineering Sciences in Medicine—IUPESM: c/o Prof. G. Fullerton, UTHSCSA, Dept of Radiology, MSC 7800, 7703 Floyd Curl Drive, San Antonio, TX 78229-3900, USA; tel. (210) 567-5551; fax (210) 567-5549; e-mail fullerton@uthscsa.edu; internet www.iupesm.org; f. 1980 by its two constituent orgs (International Federation for Medical and Biological Engineering, see p.556, and International Organization for Medical Physics, see p.557); promotes international co-operation in health care science and technology and represents the professional interests of members; organizes seminars, workshops, scientific conferences; holds World Congress every three years (2003: Sydney, Australia). Sec.-Gen. Prof. GARY FULLERTON (USA). Publs *IUPESM Newsletter* (2 a year), Congress proceedings.

International Union for Pure and Applied Biophysics—IUPAB: School of Biochemistry and Molecular Biology, University of Leeds, Leeds, LS2 9JT, United Kingdom; tel. (113) 2333023; fax (113) 2333167; e-mail a.c.t.north@leeds.ac.uk; internet www.iupab.org; f. 1961 to organize international co-operation in biophysics and promote communication between biophysics and allied subjects, to encourage national co-operation between biophysical societies, and to contribute to the advancement of biophysical knowledge. Mems: 50 adhering bodies. Pres. I. PECHT (Israel); Sec.-Gen. Prof. A. C. T. NORTH (UK). Publ. *Quarterly Reviews of Biophysics*.

International Union of Biochemistry and Molecular Biology—IUBMB: Institute for Biophysical Chemistry and Biochemistry, Technical University Berlin, Franklinstr. 29, 10587 Berlin, Germany; tel. (30) 31424205; fax (30) 31424783; e-mail kleinkauf@chem.tu-berlin.de; internet www.iubmb.unibe.ch; f. 1955 to sponsor the International Congresses of Biochemistry, to co-ordinate research and discussion, to organize co-operation between the societies of biochemistry and molecular biology, to promote high standards of biochemistry and molecular biology throughout the world and to contribute to the advancement of biochemistry and molecular biology in all its international aspects. Mems: 65 bodies. Pres. W. WHELAN (USA); Gen. Sec. Prof. Dr H. KLEINKAUF (Germany).

International Union of Biological Sciences—IUBS: 51 blvd de Montmorency, 75016 Paris, France; tel. 1-45-25-00-09; fax 1-45-25-20-29; e-mail iubs@paris7.jussieu.fr; internet www.iubs.org; f. 1919; serves as an international forum for the promotion of biology; runs scientific programmes on subjects including biosystematics, bionomenclature, reproductive biology and aquaculture; carries out international collaborative research programmes; convenes General Assembly every 3 years. Mems: 44 national bodies, 80 scientific bodies. Exec. Dir Dr T. YOUNES. Publs *Biology International* (4 a year), *IUBS Monographs, IUBS Methodology, Manual Series*.

International Union of Crystallography: c/o M. H. Dacombe, 2 Abbey Sq., Chester, CH1 2HU, United Kingdom; tel. (1244) 345431; fax (1244) 344843; internet www.iucr.org; f. 1947 to facilitate the international standardization of methods, units, nomenclature and symbols used in crystallography; and to form a focus for the relations of crystallography to other sciences. Mems: in 40 countries. Pres. Prof. H. SCHENK (Netherlands); Gen. Sec. S. LARSEN (Denmark); Exec. Sec. M. H. DACOMBE. Publs *Acta Crystallographica, Journal of Applied Crystallography, Journal of Synchrotron Radiation, International Tables for Crystallography, World Directory of Crystallographers, IUCr/OUP Crystallographic Symposia, IUCr/OUP Monographs on Crystallography, IUCr/OUP Texts on Crystallography*.

International Union of Food Science and Technology: 522 Maple Ave, Oakville, Ontario, L6J 2J4, Canada; tel. (905) 815-1926; fax (905) 815-1574; e-mail iufost@inforamp-net; internet home.inforamp.net/-iufost; f. 1970; sponsors international symposia and congresses. Mems: 60 national groups. Pres. Prof. WALTER SPIESS (Germany); Sec.-Gen. JUDITH MEECH (Canada). Publ. *IUFOST Newsline* (3 a year).

International Union of Geodesy and Geophysics—IUGG: Cires Campus Box 216, University of Colorado, Boulder, CO 80309, USA; tel. (303) 497-51-47; fax (303) 497-36-45; e-mail jjoselyn@cires. colorado.edu; internet www.iugg.org; f. 1919; federation of seven asscns representing Geodesy, Seismology and Physics of the Earth's Interior, Physical Sciences of the Ocean, Volcanology and Chemistry of the Earth's Interior, Hydrological Sciences, Meteorology and Atmospheric Physics, Geomagnetism and Aeronomy, which meet in committees and at the General Assemblies of the Union. The Union organizes scientific meetings and sponsors various permanent services to collect, analyse and publish geophysical data. Mems: in 66 countries. Pres. Prof. MASARU KONO (Japan); Sec.-Gen. Dr JOANN JOSELYN (USA). Publs *IUGG Yearbook, Journal of Geodesy* (quarterly), *IASPEI Newsletter* (iregular), *Bulletin Volcanologique* (2 a year), *Hydrological Sciences Journal* (quarterly), *Bulletin de l'Association Internationale d'Hydrologie Scientifique* (quarterly), *IAMAP News Bulletin* (irregular).

International Union of Geological Sciences—IUGS: c/o Norges Geologiske Underskelse, N-7491 Trondheim, Norway; tel. 73-90-40-40; fax 73-50-22-30; e-mail iugs.secretariat.ngu.no; internet www.iugs.org/; f. 1961 to encourage the study of geoscientific problems, facilitate international and inter-disciplinary co-operation in geology and related sciences, and support the quadrennial International Geological Congress; organizes international meetings and co-sponsors joint programmes, including the International Geological Correlation Programme (with UNESCO). Mems: in 114 countries. Pres. Prof. ED DE MULDER (Netherlands); Sec.-Gen. Prof. A. BORIANI (Italy).

International Union of Immunological Societies—IUIS: Executive Manager, IUIS Central Office, c/o Vienna Academy of Postgraduate Medical Education and Research, Alser Strasse 4, 1090 Vienna, Austria; tel. (1) 405-13-83-13; fax (1) 405-13-83-23; e-mail iuis-central-office@medacad.org; internet www .iuisonline.org f. 1969; holds triennial international congress. Mems: national societies in 50 countries and territories. Pres. PHILIPPA MARRACK; Sec.-Gen. Dr MOHAMED R. DAHA; Exec. Man. SYLVIA TRITTINGER.

International Union of Microbiological Societies—IUMS: c/o Prof. John S. Mackenzie, Dept of Microbiology, University of Queensland, Brisbane QLD 4072, Australia; tel. (7) 3365-4648; fax (7) 3365-6265; e-mail jmac@biosci.uq.edu.au; internet www.iums.org; f. 1930. Mems: 106 national microbiological societies. Pres. P. HELENA MÄKELÄ (Finland); Sec.-Gen. Prof. JOHN S. MACKENZIE. Publs *International Journal of Systematic Bacteriology* (quarterly), *International Journal of Food Microbiology* (every 2 months), *Advances in Microbial Ecology* (annually), Archives of Virology.

International Union of Nutritional Sciences—IUNS: c/o Dr Galal, UCLA School of Public Health, 10833 Le Conte Ave, POB 951772, Los Angeles, CA 90095-1772, USA; tel. (310) 2069639; fax (310) 7941805; e-mail ogalal@ucla.edu; internet www.iuns.org; f. 1946 to promote international co-operation in the scientific study of nutrition and its applications, to encourage research and exchange of scientific information by holding international congresses and issuing publications. Mems: 69 organizations. Pres. Dr MARK WHALQVIST; Sec.-Gen. Dr OSMAN GALAL. Publs *Annual Report, IUNS Directory, Newsletter.*

International Union of Pharmacology: c/o Prof. Paul M. Vanhoutte, IRIS, 6 pl. des Pléiades, 92415 Courbevoie Cédex, France; tel. 1-55-72-61-23; fax 1-55-72-72-76; internet www .iuphar.org; f. 1963 to promote co-ordination of research, discussion and publication in the field of pharmacology, including clinical pharmacology, drug metabolism and toxicology; co-operates with WHO in all matters concerning drugs and drug research; holds international congresses. Mems: 54 national and three regional societies. Pres. W. W. FLEMING (USA); Sec.-Gen. Prof. PAUL M. VANHOUTTE (France). Publ. *PI (Pharmacology International).*

International Union of Physiological Sciences—IUPS: IUPS Secretariat, LGN, Bâtiment CERVI, Hôpital de la Pitié-Salpêtrière, 83 blvd de l'Hôpital, 75013 Paris, France; tel. 1-42-17-75-37; fax 1-42-17-75-75; e-mail svorsoni@infobiogen.fr; internet iups.mcw.edu; f. 1955. Mems: 50 national, six assoc., four regional, two affiliated and 14 special mems. Pres. Prof. EWALD WEIBEL (Switzerland); Sec. Prof. DENIS NOBLE.

International Union of Psychological Science: c/o Prof. P. L.-J. Ritchie, Ecole de psychologie, Université d'Ottawa, 145 Jean-Jacques-Lussier, CP 450, Succ. A, Ottawa, ON KIN 6N5, Canada; tel. (613) 562-5289; fax (613) 562-5169; e-mail pritchie @uottawa.ca; internet www.aix1.uottawa.ca~pritchie; f. 1951 to contribute to the development of intellectual exchange and scientific relations between psychologists of different countries. Mems: 68 national and 12 affiliate orgs. Pres. Prof. M. DENIS (France); Sec.-Gen. Prof. P. L.-J. RITCHIE (Canada). Publs *International Journal of Psychology* (quarterly), *The IUPsyS Directory* (irregular), *Psychology CD Rom Resource File* (annually).

International Union of Pure and Applied Chemistry—IUPAC: Bldg 19, 104 T. W. Alexander Dr., Research Triangle Park, POB 13757, NC 27709-3757, USA; tel. (919) 485-8700; fax (919) 485-8706; e-mail secretariat@iupac.org; internet www.iupac.org; f. 1919 to organize permanent co-operation between chemical asscns in the member countries, to study topics of international importance requiring standardization or codification, to co-operate with other international organizations in the field of chemistry and to contribute to the advancement of all aspects of chemistry. Holds a biennial General Assembly. Mems: in 43 countries. Pres. Prof. P. S. STEYN (South Africa); Sec.-Gen. Dr E. D. BECKER (USA). Publs *Chemistry International* (2 a month), *Pure and Applied Chemistry* (monthly).

International Union of Pure and Applied Physics—IUPAP: c/o ESRF, BP 220, 38043 Grenoble Cedex, France; tel. 4-76-88-20-30; fax 4-76-88-24-18; e-mail petroff@esrf.fr; internet www.iupap.org; f. 1922 to promote and encourage international co-operation in physics and facilitate the world-wide development of science. Mems: in 46 countries. Pres. Y. PETROFF; Sec.-Gen. Dr RENÉ TURLAY (France).

International Union of Radio Science: c/o INTEC, Ghent University, Sint-Pietersnieuwstraat 41, 9000 Ghent, Belgium; tel. (9) 264-33-20; fax (9) 264-42-88; e-mail ursi@intec.rug.ac.be; internet www.intec.rug.ac.be/ursi; f. 1919 to stimulate and co-ordinate, on an international basis, studies, research, applications, scientific exchange and communication in the field of radio science; aims to encourage the adoption of common methods of measurement and the standardization of measuring instruments used in scientific work; represents radio science at national and international levels. There are 48 national committees. Pres. Prof. H. MATSUMOTO (Japan); Sec.-Gen. Prof. P. LAGASSE (Belgium). Publs *The Radio Science Bulletin* (quarterly), *Proceedings of General Assemblies* (every 3 years), *Handbook on Radiopropagation related to Satellite Communications in Tropical and Subtropical Countries, Review of Radio Science* (every 3 years).

International Union of the History and Philosophy of Science: Division of the History of Science (DHS): Centre d'Histoire des Sciences et des Techniques, 5 quai Banning, 4000 Liège, Belgium; tel. (4) 366-94-79; fax (4) 366-94-47; e-mail chst@ulg .ac.be; Division of the History of Logic, Methodology and Philosophy of Science (DLMPS): 161 rue Ada, 34392 Montpellier, France; f. 1956 to promote research into the history and philosophy of science. DHS has 44 national committees and DLMPS has 35 committees. DHS Council: Pres. Prof. B. V. SUBBARAYAPPA (India); Sec. Prof. R. HALLEUX (Belgium). DLMPS Council: Pres. Prof. M. RABIN (Israel); Sec.-Gen. Prof. D. WESTERSTAHL (Sweden).

International Union of Theoretical and Applied Mechanics: c/o Prof. Dick H. van Campen, Dept of Mechanical Engineering, Eindhoven University of Technology, POB 513, 5600 Eindhoven, Netherlands; tel. (40) 2472768; fax (40) 2461418; e-mail sg@ iutam.net; internet www.iutam.net; f. 1947 to form links between those engaged in scientific work (theoretical or experimental) in mechanics or related sciences; organizes international congresses of theoretical and applied mechanics, through a standing Congress Committee, and other international meetings; engages in other activities designed to promote the development of mechanics as a science. Mems: from 49 countries. Pres. Prof. H. K. MOFFATT (UK); Sec.-Gen. Prof. D. H. van CAMPEN (Netherlands). Publs *Annual Report, Newsletter.*

International Union of Toxicology: c/o Dept of Environmental and Occupational Health, Graduate School of Public Health, University of Pittsburgh, Pittsburgh, PA 15261, USA; tel. (412) 383-9473; fax (412) 624-3040; e-mail mhk@pitt.edu; internet www.iutox.org; f. 1980 to foster international co-operation among toxicologists and promote world-wide acquisition, dissemination and utilization of knowledge in the field; sponsor International Congresses, and other education programmes. Mems: 43 national societies. Sec.-Gen. MERYL H. KAROL. Publs *IUTOX Newsletter*, Congress proceedings.

OTHER ORGANIZATIONS

Association for the Taxonomic Study of the Flora of Tropical Africa: National Botanic Garden of Belgium, Domein van Bouchout, 1860 Meise, Belgium; tel. (2) 260-09-28; fax (2) 260-08-45; e-mail rammeloo@br.fgov.be; f. 1950 to facilitate co-operation and liaison between botanists engaged in the study of the flora of tropical Africa south of the Sahara including Madagascar; maintains a library. Mems: c. 800 botanists in 63 countries. Sec.-Gen. Prof. J. RAMMELOO. Publs *AETFAT Bulletin* (annually), *Proceedings*.

Association of European Atomic Forums—FORATOM: 15–17 rue Belliard, 1040 Brussels, Belgium; tel. (2) 502-45-95; fax (2) 502-39-02; e-mail foratom@foratom.org; internet www.foratom.org; f. 1960; promotes the peaceful use of nuclear energy; provides information on nuclear energy issues to the EU, the media and the public; represents the nuclear industry within the EU institutions; holds periodical conferences. Mems: atomic forums in 12 countries. Pres. FRANCIS TÉTREAU; Sec.-Gen. Dr PETER HAUG. Publ. *Almanac* (annually).

Association of Geoscientists for International Development—AGID: Institute of Geoscience, University of São Paulo, Rua do Lago 562, São Paulo, 05508-900 Brazil; tel. (11) 818-4206; fax (11) 210-4958; e-mail kmellito@usp.br; internet agid.igc.usp.br; f. 1974 to encourage communication and the exchange of knowledge between those interested in the application of the geosciences to international development; contributes to the funding of geoscience development projects; provides postgraduate scholarships. Mems: 2,000 individual and institutional mems in over 120 countries. Pres. Dr S. D. LIMAYE (India); Sec. Dr A. J. REEDMAN (UK). Publs *Geoscience and Developments* (2 or 3 a year), reports on geoscience and development issues.

Council for the International Congresses of Entomology: c/o FAO, POB 3700 MCPO, 1277 Makati, Philippines; tel. (2) 8134229; fax (2) 8127725; e-mail joliver@gasou.edu; f. 1910 to act as a link between quadrennial congresses and to arrange the venue for each congress; the committee is also the entomology section of the International Union of Biological Sciences (q.v.). Chair. Dr M. J. WHITTAM (Australia); Sec. Dr J. OLIVER (USA).

European Association of Geoscientists and Engineers—EAGE: c/o EAGE Holdings, 3990 DB Houten, Netherlands; tel. (30) 6354055; fax (30) 6343524; e-mail eage@eage.nl; internet www.eage.nl; f. 1997 by merger of European Asscn of Exploration Geophysicists and Engineers (f. 1951) and the European Asscn of Petroleum Geoscientists and Engineers (f. 1988); these two organizations have become, respectively, the Geophysical and the Petroleum Divisions of the EAGE; aims to promote the applications of geoscience and related subjects and to foster co-operation between those working or studying in the fields; organizes conferences, workshops, education programmes and exhibitions; seeks global co-operation with organizations with similar objectives. Mems: approx. 5,400 in 95 countries. Exec. Dir A. VAN GERWEN. Publs *Geophysical Prospecting* (6 a year), *First Break* (monthly), *Petroleum Geoscience* (quarterly).

European Molecular Biology Organization—EMBO: Meyerhofstr. 1, Postfach 1022.40, 69012 Heidelberg, Germany; tel. (6221) 383031; fax (6221) 384879; e-mail embo@embo.org; internet www.embo.org; f. 1962 to promote collaboration in the field of molecular biology and to establish fellowships for training and research; has established a European Molecular Biology Laboratory where a majority of the disciplines comprising the subject are represented. Mems: 965. Exec. Dir Prof. FRANK GANNON. Publ. *EMBO Journal* (24 a year).

European Organization for Nuclear Research—CERN: European Laboratory for Particle Physics, 1211 Geneva 23, Switzerland; tel. (22) 7676111; fax (22) 7676555; internet www.cern.ch; f. 1954 to provide for collaboration among European states in nuclear research of a pure scientific and fundamental character, for peaceful purposes only; Council comprises two representatives of each member state. Major experimental facilities: Proton Synchrotron (of 25–28 GeV), Super Proton Synchrotron (of 450 GeV), and a Large Electron-Positron Collider (LEP) of 27 km circumference (of 94 GeV per beam). Budget (1998) 875m. Swiss francs. Mems: 20 European countries, Observers: Israel, Japan, Russia, Turkey, USA, European Commission, UNESCO. Dir-Gen. LUCIANO MAIANI (Italy). Publs *CERN Courier* (monthly), *Annual Report, Scientific Reports*.

European-Mediterranean Seismological Centre: c/o LDG, BP 12, 91680 Bruyères-le-Châtel, France; tel. 1-69-26-78-14; fax 1-69-26-70-00; e-mail csem@mail.csem.fr; internet www.emsc-csem.org; f. 1976 for rapid determination of seismic hypocentres in the region; maintains data base. Mems: institutions in 21 countries. Pres. C. BROWITT; Sec.-Gen. F. RIVIERE. Publ. *Newsletter* (two a year).

Federation of Arab Scientific Research Councils: POB 13027, Al Karkh/Karadat Mariam, Baghdad, Iraq; tel. (1) 8881709; fax (1) 8866346; f. 1976 to encourage co-operation in scientific research, promote the establishment of new institutions and plan joint regional research projects. Mems: national science bodies in 15 countries. Sec.-Gen. Dr TAHA AL-NUEIMI. Publs *Journal of Computer Research, Journal of Environmental and Sustained Development, Journal of Biotechnology*.

Federation of Asian Scientific Academies and Societies—FASAS: c/o Indian National Science Academy, Bahadur Shah Zafar Marg, New Delhi 110 002, India; tel. (11) 3232066; fax (11) 3235648; e-mail insa@giasdlo1.vsnl.net.in; f. 1984 to stimulate regional co-operation and promote national and regional self-reliance in science and technology, by organizing meetings, training and research programmes and encouraging the exchange of scientists and of scientific information. Mems: national scientific academies and societies from Afghanistan, Australia, Bangladesh, People's Republic of China, India, Republic of Korea, Malaysia, Nepal, New Zealand, Pakistan, Philippines, Singapore, Sri Lanka, Thailand. Pres. Prof. C. S. DAYRIT (Philippines); Sec. Prof. INDIRA NATH (India).

Federation of European Biochemical Societies: c/o Institute of Cancer Biology and Danish Centre for Human Genome Research, Danish Cancer Society, Strandboulevarden 49, 2100 Copenhagen Ø, Denmark; tel. 3525-7363; fax 3525-7376; e-mail febs@cancer.dk; internet www.febs.unibe.ch; f. 1964 to promote the science of biochemistry through meetings of European biochemists, advanced courses and the provision of fellowships. Mems: 40,000 in 34 societies. Chair. Prof. G. DIRHEIMER; Sec.-Gen. Prof. JULIO E. CELIS. Publs *European Journal of Biochemistry, FEBS Letters, FEBS Bulletin*.

Foundation for International Scientific Co-ordination (Fondation 'Pour la science', Centre international de synthèse): 12 rue Colbert, 75002 Paris, France; tel. 1-42-97-50-68; fax 1-42-97-46-46; e-mail synthese@libertysurf.fr; internet synthese.pour-le-science.org; f. 1925. Dirs MICHEL BLAY, ERIC BRIAN. Publs *Revue de Synthèse, Revue d'Histoire des Sciences, Semaines de Synthèse, L'Evolution de l'Humanité*.

Intergovernmental Oceanographic Commission: UNESCO, 1 rue Miollis, 75732 Paris Cédex 15, France; tel. 1-45-68-39-83; fax 1-45-68-58-10; internet ioc.unesco.org/iocweb; f. 1960 to promote scientific investigation of the nature and resources of the oceans through the concerted action of its members. Mems: 127 govts. Chair. SU JILAN (China); Exec. Sec. Dr PATRICIO BERNAL. Publs *IOC Technical Series* (irregular), IOC *Manuals* and *Guides* (irregular), *IOC Workshop Reports* (irregular) and *IOC Training Course Reports* (irregular), annual reports.

International Academy of Astronautics—IAA: 6 rue Galilee, POB 1268-16, 75766 Paris Cédex 16, France; tel. 1-47-23-82-15; fax 1-47-23-82-16; internet www.iaanet.org; f. 1960; fosters the development of astronautics for peaceful purposes, holds scientific meetings and makes scientific studies, reports, awards and book awards; maintains 19 scientific cttees and a multilingual terminology data base (20 languages). Mems: 681, and 382 corresponding mems, in basic sciences, engineering sciences, life sciences and social sciences, from 57 countries. Sec.-Gen. Dr JEAN-MICHEL CONTANT. Publ. *Acta Astronautica* (monthly).

International Association for Biologicals—IABS: CP 456, 1211 Geneva 4, Switzerland; tel. (22) 702-93-21; fax (22) 702-93-55; e-mail iabs@iabs.org; internet www.iabs.org; f. 1955 to connect producers and controllers of immunological products (sera, vaccines, etc.), for the study and development of methods of standardization; supports international organizations in their efforts to solve problems of standardization. Mems: c. 500. Pres. J. PETRICCIANI (USA); Sec.-Gen. D. GAUDRY (France). Publs *Newsletter* (quarterly), *Biologicals* (quarterly).

International Association for Earthquake Engineering: Kenchiku Kaikan, 3rd Floor, 5-26-20, Shiba, Minato-ku, Tokyo 108, Japan; tel. (3) 453-1281; fax (3) 453-0428; internet www.iaee.or.jp; f. 1963 to promote international co-operation among scientists and engineers in the field of earthquake engineering through exchange of knowledge, ideas and results of research and practical experience. Mems: national cttees in 49 countries. Pres. SHELDON CHERRY (Canada); Sec.-Gen. Dr TSUNEO KATAYAMA.

International Association for Ecology—INTECOL: Lunigiana Museum of Natural History, 54011 Aulla, Italy; tel. (0187) 400252; fax (0187) 420727; e-mail afarina@tamnet.it; internet www.intecol.org; f. 1967 to provide opportunities for communication between ecologists world-wide; to co-operate with organizations and individuals having related aims and interests; to encourage studies in the different fields of ecology; affiliated to the International Union of Biological Sciences (q.v.). Mems: 35 national and international ecological societies, and 1,000 individuals. Pres. J. A. LEE (UK); Sec.-Gen. A. FARINA (Italy).

International Association for Mathematical Geology—IAMG: c/o T. A. Jones, POB 2189, Houston, TX 77252-2189, USA; tel. (713) 431-6546; fax (713) 431-6336; internet www.iamg.org; f. 1968 for the preparation and elaboration of mathematical models of geological processes; the introduction of mathematical methods in geological sciences and technology; assistance in the development of mathematical investigation in geological sciences; the organization of international collaboration in mathematical geology through various forums and publications; educational programmes for mathematical geology; affiliated to the International Union of Geological Sciences (q.v.). Mems: c. 600. Pres. Dr R. A. OLEA (USA); Sec.-Gen. Dr T. A. JONES (USA). Publs *Mathematical Geology* (8 a year), *Computers and Geosciences* (10 a year), *Natural Resources Research* (quarterly), *Newsletter* (2 a year).

International Association for Mathematics and Computers in Simulation: c/o Free University of Brussels, Automatic Control, CP 165, 50 ave F. D. Roosevelt, 1050 Brussels, Belgium; tel. (2) 650-20-97; fax (2) 650-35-64; internet www.first.gmd.de/imacs97/imacs; f. 1955 to further the study of mathematical tools and computer software and hardware, analogue, digital or hybrid computers for simulation of soft or hard systems. Mems: 1,100 and 27 assoc. mems. Pres. R. VICHNEVETSKY (USA); Sec. Prof. RAYMOND HANUS. Publs *Mathematics and Computers in Simulation* (6 a year), *Applied Numerical Mathematics* (6 a year), *Journal of Computational Acoustics*.

International Association for the Physical Sciences of the Ocean—IAPSO: POB 820440, Vicksburg, MS 39182-0440, USA; tel. (601) 636-1363; fax (601) 629-9640; e-mail camfield@vicksburg.com; internet www.olympus.net/IAPSO; f. 1919 to promote the study of scientific problems relating to the oceans and interactions occurring at its boundaries, chiefly in so far as such study may be carried out by the aid of mathematics, physics and chemistry; to initiate, facilitate and co-ordinate research; to provide for discussion, comparison and publication; affiliated to the International Union of Geodesy and Geophysics (q.v.). Mems: 81 member states. Pres. PAOLA RIZZOLI; Sec.-Gen. Dr FRED E. CAMFIELD (USA). Publ. *Publications Scientifiques* (irregular).

International Association for Plant Physiology—IAPP: c/o Dr D. Graham, Div. of Food Science and Technology, CSIRO, POB 52, North Ryde, NSW, Australia 2113; tel. (2) 9490-8333; fax (2) 9490-3107; e-mail douglasgraham@dfst.csiro.au; f. 1955 to promote the development of plant physiology at the international level through congresses, symposia and workshops, by maintaining communication with national societies and by encouraging interaction between plant physiologists in developing and developed countries; affiliated to the International Union of Biological Sciences (q.v.). Pres. Prof. S. MIYACHI; Sec.-Treas. Dr D. GRAHAM.

International Association for Plant Taxonomy—IAPT: c/o Prof. Tod F. Stuessy, Institut für Botanik und Botanischer Garten, Universität Wien, Rennweg 14, A-1030 Wien, Austria; e-mail iapt@s1.botanik.univie.ac.at; internet www.botanik.univie.ac.at/iapt; f. 1950 to promote the development of plant taxonomy and encourage contacts between people and institutes interested in this work; affiliated to the International Union of Biological Sciences (q.v.). Mems: institutes and individuals in 85 countries. Publs *Taxon* (quarterly), *Regnum vegetabile* (irregular).

International Association of Botanic Gardens—IABG: c/o Prof. J. E. Hernández-Bermejo, Córdoba Botanic Garden, Avda de Linneo, s/n, 14004 Córdoba, Spain; tel. (957) 200077; fax (957) 295333; e-mail jardinbotcord@cod.servicom.es; f. 1954 to promote co-operation between scientific collections of living plants, including the exchange of information and specimens; to promote the study of the taxonomy of cultivated plants; and to encourage the conservation of rare plants and their habitats; affiliated to the International Union of Biological Sciences (q.v.). Pres. Prof. KUNIO IWATSUKI (Japan); Sec. Prof. J. ESTEBAN HERNÁNDEZ-BERMEJO (Spain).

International Association of Geodesy: Dept of Geophysics, Juliane Maries Vej 30, 2100 Copenhagen Oe, Denmark; tel. (45) 3532-0582; fax (45) 3536-5357; e-mail iag@gfy.ku.dk; internet www.gfy.ku.dk/~iag/; f. 1922 to promote the study of all scientific problems of geodesy and encourage geodetic research; to promote and co-ordinate international co-operation in this field; to publish results; affiliated to the International Union of Geodesy and Geophysics (q.v.). Mems: national committees in 73 countries. Pres. F. SANSÓ (Italy); Sec.-Gen. C. C. TSCHERNING (Denmark). Publs *Journal of Geodesy, Travaux de l'AIG*.

International Association of Geomagnetism and Aeronomy—IAGA: c/o Dr JoAnn Joselyn, NOAA Space Environment Center, 325 Broadway, Boulder, CO 80303, USA; tel. (303) 497-5147; fax (303) 494-0980; e-mail jjoselyn@sec.noaa.gov; internet www.ngdc.noaa.gov/iaga; f. 1919 for the study of questions relating to geomagnetism and aeronomy and the encouragement of research; holds General and Scientific Assemblies every two years; affiliated to the International Union of Geodesy and Geophysics (IUGG, q.v.). Mems: countries that adhere to the IUGG. Pres. M. KONO (Japan); Sec.-Gen. Dr JOANN JOSELYN. Publs *IAGA Bulletin* (including annual *Geomagnetic Data), IAGA News* (annually).

International Association of Hydrological Sciences: Dept of Geography, Wilfrid Laurier Univ., Waterloo, ON N2L 3C5, Canada; tel. (519) 884-1970; fax (519) 846-0968; e-mail 44iahs@mach1.wlu.ca; internet www.wlu.ca/~wwwiahs/index.html; f. 1922 to promote co-operation in the study of hydrology and water resources. Pres. Dr J. C. RODDA (UK); Sec.-Gen. Dr GORDON J. YOUNG (Canada). Publs *Journal* (every 2 months), *Newsletter* (3 a year).

International Association of Meteorology and Atmospheric Sciences—IAMAS: Dept of Physics, Univ. of Toronto, Toronto, ON M5S 1A7, Canada; internet iamas.org; f. 1919; maintains permanent commissions on atmospheric ozone, radiation, atmospheric chemistry and global pollution, dynamic meteorology, polar meteorology, clouds and precipitation, climate, atmospheric electricity, planetary atmospheres and their evolution, and meteorology of the upper atmosphere; holds general assemblies every four years, special assemblies between general assemblies; affiliated to the International Union of Geodesy and Geophysics (q.v.). Pres. Prof. R. DUCE (USA); Sec.-Gen. Prof. R. LIST (Canada).

International Association of Sedimentologists: c/o Prof. A. Strasser, Institut de Géologie, Pérolles, 1700 Fribourg, Switzerland; tel. (26) 3008978; fax (26) 3009742; e-mail andreas.strasser@unifr.ch; internet www.blackwell-science.com/uk/society/ias; f. 1952; affiliated to the International Union of Geological Sciences (q.v.). Mems: 2,200. Pres. Prof. M. E. TUCKER (UK); Gen. Sec. Prof. A. STRASSER (Switzerland). Publ. *Sedimentology* (every 2 months).

International Association of Theoretical and Applied Limnology (Societas Internationalis Limnologiae): Dept of Biology, University of Alabama, Tuscaloosa, AL 35487-0206, USA; tel. (205) 348-1793; fax (205) 348-1403; e-mail rwetzel@biology.as.ua.edu; internet www.limnology.org; f. 1922 for the study of physical, chemical and biological phenomena of lakes and rivers; affiliated to the International Union of Biological Sciences (q.v.). Mems: c. 3,200. Pres. G. E. LIKENS (USA); Gen. Sec. and Treas. ROBERT G. WETZEL (USA).

International Association of Volcanology and Chemistry of the Earth's Interior—IAVCEI: Geophysical Institute, University of Alaska Fairbanks, POB 757320, Fairbanks, AK 99775,

USA; tel. (907) 474-7131; fax (907) 474-5618; f. 1919 to examine scientifically all aspects of volcanology; affiliated to the International Union of Geodesy and Geophysics (q.v.). Pres. R. S. J. SPARKS (UK); Sec.-Gen. S. R. MCNUTT (USA). Publs *Bulletin of Volcanology, Catalogue of the Active Volcanoes of the World, Proceedings in Volcanology.*

International Association of Wood Anatomists: USDA Forest Service, Forest Products, Laboratory, 1 Gifford Pinchot Drive, Madison WI 53705-2398, USA; tel. (608) 231-9200; fax (608) 231-9508; f. 1931 for the purpose of study, documentation and exchange of information on the structure of wood; holds annual conference. Mems: 650 in 68 countries. Exec. Sec. REGIS B. MILLER. Publ. *IAWA Journal.*

International Astronautical Federation—IAF: 3–5 rue Mario-Nikis, 75015 Paris, France; tel. 1-45-67-42-60; fax 1-42-73-21-20; e-mail iaf@wanadoo.fr; internet www.iafastro.com; f. 1950 to foster the development of astronautics for peaceful purposes at national and international levels. The IAF has created the International Academy of Astronautics (IAA) and the International Institute of Space Law (IISL). Mems: 153 national astronautical societies in 45 countries. Pres. Dr TOMIFUMI GODAI (Japan); Exec. Sec. CLAUDE GOURDET.

International Biometric Society: c/o Prof. E. Baráth, Chair. of Statistics, 2103 Gödöllö, Hungary; tel. (28) 410-694; fax (28) 430-336; internet www.tibs.org; f. 1947 for the advancement of quantitative biological science through the development of quantitative theories and the application, development and dissemination of effective mathematical and statistical techniques; the Society has 16 regional organizations and 17 national groups, is affiliated with the International Statistical Institute and WHO, and constitutes the Section of Biometry of the International Union of Biological Sciences (q.v.). Mems: over 6,000 in more than 70 countries. Pres. Prof. SUE WILSON (Australia); Sec. Prof. E. BARÁTH (Hungary). Publs *Biometrics* (quarterly), *Biometric Bulletin* (quarterly), *Journal of Agricultural, Biological and Environmental Statistics* (quarterly).

International Botanical Congress: c/o Dr Peter Hoch, Missouri Botanical Garden, PO Box 299, St Louis, MO 63166-0299, USA; tel. (314) 577-5175; fax (314) 577-9589; e-mail ibc16@mobot.org; f. 1864 to inform botanists of recent progress in the plant sciences; the Nomenclature Section of the Congress attempts to provide a uniform terminology and methodology for the naming of plants; other Divisions deal with developmental, metabolic, structural, systematic and evolutionary, ecological botany; genetics and plant breeding; 2005 Congress: Vienna, Austria; affiliated to the International Union of Biological Sciences (q.v.). Sec. Dr PETER HOCH.

International Bureau of Weights and Measures (Bureau international des poids et mesures—BIPM): Pavillon de Breteuil, 92312 Sèvres Cédex, France; tel. 1-45-07-70-70; fax 1-45-34-20-21; e-mail info@bipm.org; internet www.bipm.org; f. 1875 works to ensure the international unification of measurements and their traceability to the International System of Unification; carries out research and calibration; organizes international comparisons of national measurement standards. Mems: 51 member states and 6 associates. Pres. J. KOVALEVSKY (France); Sec. R. KAARLS (Netherlands). Publs *Le Système International d'Unités* (in French and English), *Metrologia* (6 a year), scientific articles, reports and monographs, committee reports.

International Cartographic Association: 136 bis rue de Grenelle, 75700 Paris 07 SP, France; tel. 1-43-98-82-95; fax 1-43-98-84-00; internet www.icaci.org; f. 1959 for the advancement, instigation and co-ordination of cartographic research involving co-operation between different nations. Particularly concerned with furtherance of training in cartography, study of source material, compilation, graphic design, drawing, scribing and reproduction techniques of maps; organizes international conferences, symposia, meetings, exhibitions. Mems: 80 countries. Pres. MICHAEL WOOD. Publ. *ICA Newsletter* (2 a year).

International Centre of Insect Physiology and Ecology: POB 30772, Nairobi, Kenya; tel. (2) 861680; fax (2) 803360; e-mail icipe@africaonline.co.ke; internet www.icipe.org; f. 1970; specializes in research and development of environmentally sustainable and affordable methods of managing tropical arthropod plant pests and disease vectors, and in the conservation and utilisation of biodiversity of insects of commercial and ecological importance; organizes training programmes. Dir-Gen. Dr HANS RUDOLPH HERREN. Publs *Insect Science and its Application* (quarterly), *Annual Report*, training manuals, technical bulletins, newsletter.

International Commission for Optics—ICO: Institut d'Optique/CNRS, POB 147, 91403 Orsay Cédex, France; tel. 1-69-35-87-41; fax 1-69-35-87-00; e-mail Pierre.chavel@iota.u-psud.fr; internet www.ico-optics.org; f. 1948 to contribute to the progress of theoretical and instrumental optics, to assist in research and to promote international agreement on specifications; holds Gen. Assembly every three years. Mems: committees in 42 territories, and four international societies. Pres. Prof. A. H. GUEUTHER (USA); Sec.-Gen. Dr P. CHAVEL (France). Publ. *ICO Newsletter.*

International Commission for Plant-Bee Relationships: c/o Prof. I. Williams, Entomology-Nematology Dept, Rothamsted Experimental Station, Harpenden, Herts, AL5 2JQ, United Kingdom; e-mail ingrid.williams@bbsrc.ac.uk; f. 1950 to promote research and its application in the field of bee botany, and collect and spread information; to organize meetings, etc., and collaborate with scientific organizations; affiliated to the International Union of Biological Sciences (q.v.). Mems: 175 in 34 countries. Pres. Prof. INGRID WILLIAMS; Sec. Dr J. N. TASEI.

International Commission for the Scientific Exploration of the Mediterranean Sea (Commission internationale pour l'exploration scientifique de la mer Méditerranée—CIESM): 16 blvd de Suisse, 98000 Monaco; tel. 93-30-38-79; fax 92-16-11-95; e-mail fbriand@ciesm.org; internet www.ciesm.org; f. 1919 for scientific exploration of the Mediterranean Sea; organizes multilateral research investigations; includes 6 scientific committees. Mems: 22 member countries, 2,500 scientists. Pres. SAS Prince ALBERT of MONACO; Sec.-Gen. Prof. F. DOUMENGE; Dir-Gen. Prof. F. BRIAND. Publs Congress reports, science and workshop series.

International Commission on Physics Education: c/o Prof. J. Barojas, POB 55534, 09340 México DF, Mexico; tel. (5) 686-35-19; internet www.physics.umd.edu/ripe/icpe; f. 1960 to encourage and develop international collaboration in the improvement and extension of the methods and scope of physics education at all levels; collaborates with UNESCO and organizes international conferences. Mems: appointed triennially by the International Union of Pure and Applied Physics. Sec. Prof. J. BAROJAS.

International Commission on Radiation Units and Measurements—ICRU: 7910 Woodmont Ave, Suite 800, Bethesda, MD 20814, USA; tel. (301) 657-2652; fax (301) 907-8768; e-mail icru@icru.org; internet www.icru.org; f. 1925 to develop internationally acceptable recommendations regarding: (1) quantities and units of radiation and radioactivity, (2) procedures suitable for the measurement and application of these quantities in clinical radiology and radiobiology, (3) physical data needed in the application of these procedures. Makes recommendations on quantities and units for radiation protection (see below, International Radiation Protection Association). Mems: from about 18 countries. Chair. A. ALLISY; Sec. R. S. CASWELL. Publs *Reports.*

International Commission on Zoological Nomenclature: c/o The Natural History Museum, Cromwell Rd, London, SW7 5BD, United Kingdom; tel. (20) 7942-5653; e-mail iczn@nhm.ac.uk; internet www.iczn.org; f. 1895; has judicial powers to determine all matters relating to the interpretation of the International Code of Zoological Nomenclature and also plenary powers to suspend the operation of the Code where the strict application of the Code would lead to confusion and instability of nomenclature; also responsible for maintaining and developing the Official Lists and Official Indexes of Names in Zoology; affiliated to the International Union of Biological Sciences (q.v.). Pres. Dr N. L. EVENHUIS (USA); Exec. Sec. Dr A. WAKEHAM-DAWSON (UK). Publs *Bulletin of Zoological Nomenclature* (quarterly), *International Code of Zoological Nomenclature, Official Lists and Indexes of Names and Works in Zoology, Towards Stability in the Names of Animals.*

International Council for Scientific and Technical Information: 51 blvd de Montmorency, 75016 Paris, France; tel. 1-45-25-65-92; fax 1-42-15-12-62; e-mail icsti@dial.oleane.com; internet www.icsti.org; f. 1984 as the successor to the International Council of Scientific Unions Abstracting Board (f. 1952); aims to increase accessibility to scientific and technical information; fosters communication and interaction among all participants in the information transfer chain. Mems: 50 organizations. Pres. DAVID RUSSON (UK); Gen. Sec. MARIE WALLIN (Sweden).

International Council for the Exploration of the Sea—ICES: Palægade 2–4, 1261 Copenhagen K, Denmark; tel. 33-15-42-25; fax 33-93-42-15; e-mail ices.info@ices.dk; internet www.ices.dk; f. 1902 to encourage and facilitate research on the utilization and conservation of living resources and the environment in the North Atlantic Ocean and its adjacent seas; publishes and disseminate results of research; advises member countries and regulatory commissions. Mems: 19 mem. countries and five countries or bodies with observer status. Gen. Sec. D. DE G. GRIFFITH. Publs *ICES Journal of Marine Science, ICES Marine Science Symposia, ICES Fisheries Statistics, ICES Cooperative Research Reports, ICES Oceanographic Data Lists and Inventories, ICES Techniques in Marine Environmental Sciences, ICES Identification Leaflets for Plankton, ICES Identification Leaflets for Diseases and Parasites of Fish and Shellfish, ICES/CIEM Information.*

International Council of Psychologists: Dept of Psychology, Southwest Texas State University, San Marcos, TX 78666, USA; tel. (512) 245-7605; fax (512) 245-3153; internet www.geocities.com/icpsych; f. 1941 to advance psychology and the application of its scientific findings throughout the world; holds annual conventions. Mems: 1,200 qualified psychologists. Sec.-Gen. Dr JOHN M. DAVIS. Publs *International Psychologist* (quarterly), *World Psychology* (quarterly).

International Council of the Aeronautical Sciences—ICAS: 66 route de Verneuil, BP 3002, 78133 Les Mureaux Cédex, France; tel. 1-39-06-34-23; fax 1-39-06-36-15; e-mail secr.exec@icas.org; internet www.icas.org; f. 1957 to encourage free interchange of information on all phases of mechanical flight; holds biennial Congresses. Mems: national asscns in 27 countries. Pres. JEAN-PIERRE MAREC (France); Exec. Sec. CLEMENT DOUSSET (France).

International Earth Rotation Service: Central Bureau, Paris Observatory, 61 ave de l'Observatoire, 75014 Paris, France; tel. 1-40-51-22-26; fax 1-40-51-22-91; e-mail iers@obspm.fr; internet hpiers.obspm.fr; f. 1988 (fmrly International Polar Motion Service and Bureau International de l'Heure); maintained by the International Astronomical Union and the International Union of Geodesy and Geophysics; defines and maintains the international terrestrial and celestial reference systems; determines earth orientation parameters (terrestrial and celestial co-ordinates of the pole and universal time) connecting these systems; monitors global geophysical fluids; organizes collection, analysis and dissemination of data. Pres. Directing Bd Prof. C. REIGBER.

International Federation for Cell Biology: c/o Dr Ivan Cameron, Dept of Cellular and Structural Biology, Univ. of Texas Health Science Center, 7703 Floyd Curl Drive, San Antonio, Texas 78229, USA; internet lonestar.texas.net/icameron/ifcb.htm; f. 1972 to foster international co-operation, and organize conferences. Pres. Dr JUDIE WALTON; Sec.-Gen. Dr IVAN CAMERON. Publs *Cell Biology International* (monthly), reports.

International Federation of Operational Research Societies—IFORS: c/o Loretta Peregrina, Richard Ivey School of Business, University of Western Ontario, London, ON N6A 3K7, Canada; tel. (519) 661-4220; fax (519) 661-3485; e-mail ifors@ivey.uwo.ca; internet www.ifors.org; f. 1959 for development of operational research as a unified science and its advancement in all nations of the world. Mems: c. 30,000 individuals, 44 national societies, four kindred societies. Pres. Prof. PAOLO TOTH (Italy); Sec. LORETTA PEREGRINA. Publs *International Abstracts in Operational Research, IFORS Bulletin, International Transactions in Operational Research.*

International Federation of Science Editors: School for Scientific Communication, Abruzzo Science Park, Via Antica Arischia 1, 67100 L'Aquila, Italy; tel. (0862) 3475308; fax (0862) 3475213; e-mail miriam.balaban@aquila.infn.it; f. 1978; links editors in different branches of science with the aim of improving scientific writing, editing, ethics and communication internationally. Pres. MIRIAM BALABAN (Italy).

International Federation of Societies for Electron Microscopy—IFSEM: Dept of Materials, Univ. of Oxford, Parks Rd, Oxford, OX1 3PH, United Kingdom; tel (1865) 273654; fax (1865) 283329; e-mail david.cockayne@materials.ox.ac.uk; internet www.materials.ox.ac.uk/ifsem; f. 1955 to contribute to the advancement of all aspects of electron microscopy; promotes and co-ordinates research; sponsors meetings and conferences; holds International Congress every four years. Mems: representative organizations of 40 countries. Pres. Prof. A. HOWIE (UK); Gen.-Sec. D. J. H. COCKAYNE (Australia).

International Food Information Service—IFIS: UK Office (IFIS Publishing), Lane End House, Shinfield Rd, Shinfield, Reading, RG2 9BB, United Kingdom; tel. (118) 988-3895; fax (118) 988-5065; e-mail ifis@ifis.org; internet www.ifis.org; f. 1968; board of governors comprises two members each from CAB-International (UK), Bundesministerium für Landwirtschaft, Ernährung und Forsten (represented by Deutsche Landwirtschafts-Gesellschaft e.V.) (Germany), the Institute of Food Technologists (USA), and the Centrum voor Landbouwpublikaties en Landbouwdocumentaties (Netherlands); collects and disseminates information on all disciplines relevant to food science, food technology and human nutrition. Man. Dir Prof. J. D. SELMAN. Publ. *Food Science and Technology Abstracts* (monthly, also available via the internet and on CD-ROM).

International Foundation of the High-Altitude Research Stations Jungfraujoch and Gornergrat: Sidlerstrasse 5, 3012 Berne, Switzerland; tel. (31) 6314052; fax (31) 6314405; e-mail louise.wilson@phim.unibe.ch; internet www.ifjungo.ch; f. 1931; international research centre which enables scientists from many scientific fields to carry out experiments at high altitudes. Six countries contribute to support the station: Austria, Belgium, Germany, Italy, Switzerland, United Kingdom. Pres. Prof. E. FLÜCKIGER.

International Glaciological Society: Lensfield Rd, Cambridge, CB2 1ER, United Kingdom; tel. (1223) 355974; fax (1223) 336543; e-mail int_glaciol_soc@compuserve.com; internet www.spri.cam.ac.uk/igs/home.htm; f. 1936 to stimulate interest in and encourage research into the scientific and technical problems of snow and ice in all countries. Mems: 850 in 30 countries. Pres. Dr R. A. BINDSCHADLER; Sec.-Gen. C. S. L. OMMANNEY. Publs *Journal of Glaciology* (quarterly), *Ice* (News Bulletin—3 a year), *Annals of Glaciology.*

International Hydrographic Organization—IHO: 4 quai Antoine 1er, BP 445, Monte Carlo, 98011 Monaco; tel. 93-10-81-00; fax 93-10-81-40; e-mail info@ihb.mc; internet www.iho.shom.fr; f. 1921 to link the hydrographic offices of member governments and co-ordinate their work, with a view to rendering navigation easier and safer; seeks to obtain, as far as possible, uniformity in charts and hydrographic documents; fosters the development of electronic chart navigation; encourages adoption of the best methods of conducting hydrographic surveys; encourages surveying in those parts of the world where accurate charts are lacking; provides IHO Data Centre for Digital Bathymetry; and organizes quinquennial conference. Mems: 70 states. Directing Committee: Pres. Rear-Adm. GIUSEPPE ANGRISANO (Italy); Dir Rear-Adm. N. GUY (South Africa). Publs *International Hydrographic Bulletin* (monthly), *IHO Yearbook.*

International Institute of Refrigeration: 177 blvd Malesherbes, 75017 Paris, France; tel. 1-42-27-32-35; fax 1-47-63-17-98; e-mail iifiir@ibm.net; internet www.iifiir.org; f. 1908 to further the development of the science of refrigeration and its applications on a world-wide scale; to investigate, discuss and recommend any aspects leading to improvements in the field of refrigeration; maintains FRIDOC data-base (available on CD-ROM). Mems: 61 national, 1,500 associates. Dir FRANÇOIS BILLIARD (France). Publs *Bulletin* (every 2 months), *International Journal of Refrigeration* (8 a year), books, proceedings, recommendations.

International Mineralogical Association: Institute of Mineralogy, University of Marburg, 3550 Marburg, Germany; tel. 28-5617; fax 285831; internet www.dst.unipi.it/ima; f. 1958 to further international co-operation in the science of mineralogy; affiliated to the International Union of Geological Sciences (q.v.). Mems: national societies in 31 countries. Sec. Prof. S. S. HAFNER.

International Organization of Legal Metrology: 11 rue Turgot, 75009 Paris, France; tel. 1-48-78-12-82; fax 1-42-82-17-27; internet www.oiml.org; f. 1955 to serve as documentation and information centre on the verification, checking, construction and use of measuring instruments, to determine characteristics and standards to which measuring instruments must conform for their use to be recommended internationally, and to determine the general principles of legal metrology. Mems: governments of 50 countries. Dir B. ATHANÉ (France). Publ. *Bulletin* (quarterly).

International Palaeontological Association: c/o Prof. D. L. Bruton, Paleontologisk Museum, Box 1172 Blindern, 0318 Oslo, Norway; tel. 2285-1668; fax 2285-1810; e-mail d.l.bruton @nhm.uio.no; internet ipa.geo.ukans.edu; f. 1933; affiliated to the International Union of Geological Sciences and the International Union of Biological Sciences (q.v.). Pres. Dr J. TALENT (Australia); Sec.-Gen. D. L. BRUTON (Norway). Publs *Lethaia* (quarterly), *Directory of Paleontologists of the World, Directory of Fossil Collectors of the World.*

International Peat Society: Vapaudenkatu 12, 40100 Jyväskylä, Finland; tel. (14) 3385440; fax (14) 3385410; e-mail ips@peat society.fi; internet www.peatsociety.fi; f. 1968 to encourage co-operation in the study and use of mires, peatlands, peat and related material, through international meetings, research groups and the exchange of information. Mems: 18 Nat. Cttees, research institutes and other organizations, and individuals from 35 countries. Pres. GERRY HOOD (Canada); Sec.-Gen. RAIMO SOPO (Finland). Publs *Peatlands International* (2 a year), *International Peat Journal* (annually).

International Phonetic Association—IPA: Dept of Linguistics, University of Victoria, POB 3045, Victoria, V8W 3P4, Canada; e-mail esling@uvic.ca; internet www.arts.gla.ac.uk/ipa/ipa.html; f. 1886 to promote the scientific study of phonetics and its applications. Mems: 1,000. Pres. K. KOHLER (Germany). Publ. *Journal* (2 a year).

International Phycological Society: c/o Harbor Branch Oceanographic Institution, 5600 Old Dixie Highway, Fort Pierce, FL 34946, USA; fax (561) 468-0757; e-mail hanisak@hboi.edu; internet seaweed.ucg.ie/phycologia/ips.html; f. 1961 to promote the study of algae, the distribution of information, and international co-operation in this field. Mems: about 1,000. Pres. C. J. BIRD; Sec. M. D. HANISAK. Publ. *Phycologia* (every 2 months).

International Primatological Society: c/o Dr D. Fragaszy, Dept of Psychology, Univ. of Georgia, Athens, GA 30602, USA; tel. (706) 542-3036; fax (706) 542-3275; e-mail doree@arches .uga.edu; internet www.primate.wisc.edu/pin/ips.html; f. 1964 to promote primatological science in all fields. Mems: about 1,500. Pres. Dr D. FRAGASZY; Sec.-Gen. Dr J. A. R. A. M. VAN HOOFF. Publs *Bulletin, International Journal of Primatology, Codes of Practice.*

International Radiation Protection Association—IRPA: POB 662, 5600 AR Eindhoven, Netherlands; tel. (40) 247-33-55; fax (40) 243-50-20; e-mail irpa.exof@sbd.tue.nl; internet www .irpa.net; f. 1966 to link individuals and societies throughout the world concerned with protection against ionizing radiations and allied effects, and to represent doctors, health physicists, radiological protection officers and others engaged in radiological protection, radiation safety, nuclear safety, legal, medical and veterinary aspects and in radiation research and other allied activities. Mems: 16,000 in 42 societies. Pres. Prof. K. DUFTSCMID (Austria); Sec.-Gen. C. J. HUYSKENS (Netherlands). Publ. *IRPA Bulletin.*

International Society for General Semantics: POB 728, Concord, CA 94522, USA; tel. (925) 798-0311; e-mail isgs@general semantics.org; internet www.generalsemantics.org; f. 1943 to advance knowledge of and inquiry into non-Aristotelian systems and general semantics. Mems: 2,000 individuals in 40 countries. Pres. CHARLES RUSSELL, Jr (USA); Exec. Dir PAUL D. JOHNSTON (USA).

International Society for Human and Animal Mycology—ISHAM: Mycology Unit, Women's and Children's Hospital, N. Adelaide 5006, Australia; tel. (8) 8204-7365; fax (8) 8204-7589; e-mail dellis@mad.adelaide.edu.au; internet www.leeds.ac.uk/ isham; f. 1954 to pursue the study of fungi pathogenic for man and animals; holds congresses (2003 Congress: San Antonio, USA). Mems: 1,100 in 70 countries. Pres. Prof. M. R. MCGINNIS; Gen. Sec. Dr D. H. ELLIS. Publ. *Medical Mycology* (6 a year).

International Society for Rock Mechanics: c/o Laboratório Nacional de Engenharia Civil, 101 Av. do Brasil, 1799 Lisboa Codex, Portugal; tel. (21) 8482131; fax (21) 8497660; e-mail isrm@lnec.pt; internet www.lnec.pt/isrm; f. 1962 to encourage and co-ordinate international co-operation in the science of rock mechanics; assists individuals and local organizations in forming national bodies; maintains liaison with organizations representing related sciences, including geology, geophysics, soil mechanics, mining engineering, petroleum engineering and civil engineering; organizes international meetings; encourages the publication of research. Mems: c. 6,000. Pres. Prof. MARC PANET; Sec.-Gen. JOSÉ DELGADO RODRIGUES. Publ. *News Journal* (3 a year).

International Society for Stereology: c/o Dr Jens R. Nyengaard, Stereological Research Laboratory, Bartholin Bldg, Aarhus Univ., 8000 Århus C, Denmark; tel. 89-49-36-54; fax 89-49-36-50; e-mail stereo@svfcd.aau.dk; internet www.health.aau.dk/stereology/ iss; f. 1962; an interdisciplinary society gathering scientists from metallurgy, geology, mineralogy and biology to exchange ideas on three-dimensional interpretation of two-dimensional samples (sections, projections) of their material by means of stereological principles; tenth Congress: Melbourne, Australia, 1999. Mems: 300. Pres. BENTE PAKKENBERG; Treas. JENS R. NYENGAARD.

International Society for Tropical Ecology: c/o Botany Dept, Banaras Hindu University, Varanasi, 221 005 India; tel. (542) 368399; fax (542) 368174; e-mail tropecol@banaras.ernet.in; f. 1956 to promote and develop the science of ecology in the tropics in the service of humanity; to publish a journal to aid ecologists in the tropics in communication of their findings; and to hold symposia from time to time to summarize the state of knowledge in particular or general fields of tropical ecology. Mems: 500. Sec. Prof. J. S. SINGH (India); Editor Prof. K. P. SINGH. Publ. *Tropical Ecology* (2 a year).

International Society of Biometeorology—ISB: Dept of Physical Geography, Div. of Environmental and Life Sciences, Macquarie Univ., Sydney, NSW 2109, Australia; tel. (2) 9850-8399; fax (2) 9850-8420; e-mail paul.beggs@mq.edu.au; internet www.biometeorology.org; f. 1956 to unite all biometeorologists working in the fields of agricultural, botanical, cosmic, entomological, forest, human, medical, veterinarian, zoological and other branches of biometeorology. Mems: 250 individuals, nationals of 46 countries. Pres. Dr PETER HÖPPE (Germany); Sec. Dr PAUL J. BEGGS (Australia). Publs *Biometeorology* (Proceedings of the Congress of ISB), *International Journal of Biometeorology* (quarterly), *Biometeorology Bulletin.*

International Society of Criminology (Société internationale de criminologie): 4 rue Ferrus, 75014 Paris, France; tel. 1-45-88-00-23; fax 1-45-88-96-40; e-mail crim.sic@wanadoo.fr; f. 1934 to promote the development of the sciences in their application to the criminal phenomenon. Mems: in 63 countries. Sec.-Gen. GEORGES PICCA. Publ. *Annales internationales de Criminologie*.

International Union for Quaternary Research—INQUA: Dept of Soil and Water Sciences, Agricultural University of Norway, POB 3028, 1432, Aas, Norway; e-mail sylvi.haldorsen@ ijvf.nlh.no; internet inqua.nlh.no; f. 1928 to co-ordinate research on the Quaternary geological era throughout the world; holds congress every four years (2003: Reno, USA). Mems: in 38 countries and states. Sec.-Gen. Prof. SYLVI HALDORSEN (Norway). Publs *Quarternary International, Quarternary Perspectives.*

International Union of Photobiology: c/o Dr Tom Dubbelman, POB 9503, 2300 RA Leiden, Netherlands; tel. (71) 5276053; fax (71) 5276125; e-mail t.m.a.r.dubbelman@mcb.medfac.leiden univ.nl; internet www.pol.us.net/iupb; f. 1928 (frmly International Photobiology Asscn); stimulation of scientific research concerning the physics, chemistry and climatology of non-ionizing radiations (ultra-violet, visible and infra-red) in relation to their biological efffects and their applications in biology and medicine; 18 national committees represented; affiliated to the International Union of Biological Sciences (q.v.). International Congresses held every four years. Pres. Prof. PILL SOON SONG; Sec.-Gen. Dr TOM DUBBELMAN.

International Water Association—IWA: Alliance House, 12 Caxton St, London SW1H OQS, United Kingdom; tel. (20) 7654-5500; fax (20) 7654-5555; e-mail water@iwahq.org.uk; internet www.iwahq.org.uk; f. 1999 by merger of the International Water Services Association and the International Association on Water Quality; aims to encourage international communication, co-operative effort, and exchange of information on water quality management, through conferences, electronic media and publication of research reports. Mems: c. 9,000 in 130 countries. Pres. Prof. N. TAMBO (Japan); Exec. Dir ANTHONY MILBURN (UK). Publs *Water Research* (monthly), *Water Science and Technology* (24 a year), *Water 21* (6 a year), *Yearbook, Scientific and Technical Reports.*

Pacific Science Association: 1525 Bernice St, POB 17801, Honolulu, HI 96817; tel. (808) 848-4139; fax (808) 847-8252; e-mail psa@bishop.bishop.hawaii.org; internet www.pacificscience.org/psa.shtml; f. 1920 to promote co-operation in the study of scientific problems relating to the Pacific region, more particularly those affecting the prosperity and well-being of Pacific peoples; sponsors Pacific Science Congresses and Inter-Congresses. Mems: institutional representatives from 35 areas, scientific societies, individual scientists. Ninth Inter-Congress: Taipei, Taiwan, Nov. 1998; 19th Congress: Sydney, Australia, 1997. Pres. Dr AKITA ARIMA (Japan); Exec. Sec. Dr LUCIUS G. ELDREDGE. Publ. *Information Bulletin* (2 a year).

Pan-African Union of Science and Technology: POB 2339, Brazzaville, Republic of the Congo; tel. 832265; fax 832185; f. 1987 to promote the use of science and technology in furthering the development of Africa; organizes triennial congress. Pres. Prof. EDWARD AYENSU; Sec.-Gen. Prof. LÉVY MAKANY.

Pugwash Conferences on Science and World Affairs: 63A Great Russell St, London, WC1B 3BJ, United Kingdom; tel. (20) 7405-6661; fax (20) 7831-5651; e-mail pugwash@qmw.ac.uk; internet www.pugwash.org; f. 1957 to organize international conferences of scientists to discuss problems arising from the development of science, particularly the dangers to mankind from weapons of mass destruction. Mems: national Pugwash groups in 38 countries. Pres. Sir MICHAEL ATIYAH; Sec.-Gen. Prof. GEORGE RATHJENS. Publs *Pugwash Newsletter* (quarterly), occasional papers, monographs.

Scientific, Technical and Research Commission—STRC: Nigerian Ports Authority Bldg, PMB 2359, Marina, Lagos, Nigeria; tel. (1) 2633430; fax (1) 2636093; e-mail oaustrc@rcl.nig.com; f. 1965 to succeed the Commission for Technical Co-operation in Africa (f. 1954). Supervises the Inter-African Bureau for Animal Resources (Nairobi, Kenya), the Inter-African Bureau for Soils (Lagos, Nigeria) and the Inter-African Phytosanitary Commission (Yaoundé, Cameroon) and several joint research projects. The Commission provides training in agricultural man., and conducts pest control programmes. Exec. Sec. Dr ROBERT N. MSHANA.

Unitas Malacologica (Malacological Union): c/o Dr P. B. Mordan, The Natural History Museum, Science Depts, Zoology: Mollusca, Cromwell Rd, London, SW7 5BD, United Kingdom; tel. (20) 7938-9359; fax (20) 7938-8754; e-mail p.mordan@nhm.ac.uk; f. 1962 to further the study of molluscs; affiliated to the International Union of Biological Sciences (q.v.); holds triennial congress. Mems: 400 in over 30 countries. Pres. Dr F. WELLS (Australia); Sec. Dr PETER B. MORDAN (UK). Publ. *UM Newsletter* (2 a year).

World Organisation of Systems and Cybernetics—WOSC: c/o Prof. R. Vallée, 2 rue de Vouillé, 75015 Paris, France; tel. and fax 1-45-33-62-46; internet www.cybsoc.org/wosc; f. 1969 to act as clearing-house for all societies concerned with cybernetics and systems, to aim for the recognition of cybernetics as fundamental science, to organize and sponsor international exhibitions of automation and computer equipment, congresses and symposia, and to promote and co-ordinate research in systems and cybernetics; sponsors an honorary fellowship and awards a Norbert Wiener memorial gold medal. Mems: national and international societies in 30 countries. Pres. Prof. S. BEER (UK); Dir-Gen. Prof. R. VALLÉE (France). Publs *Kybernetes, the International Journal of Cybernetics and Systems.*

Social Sciences

International Council for Philosophy and Humanistic Studies—ICPHS: Maison de l'UNESCO, 1 rue Miollis, 75732 Paris Cédex 15, France; tel. 1-45-68-26-85; fax 1-40-65-94-80; internet www.unesco.org/cipsh; f. 1949 under the auspices of UNESCO to encourage respect for cultural autonomy by the comparative study of civilization and to contribute towards international understanding through a better knowledge of humanity; works to develop international co-operation in philosophy, humanistic and kindred studies; encourages the setting up of international organizations; promotes the dissemination of information in these fields; sponsors works of learning, etc. Mems: organizations (see below) representing 145 countries. Pres. JEAN D'ORMESSON (France); Sec.-Gen. TILO SCHABERT (Germany). Publs *Bulletin of Information* (biennially), *Diogenes* (quarterly).

UNIONS FEDERATED TO THE ICPHS

International Association for the History of Religions—IAHR: c/o Prof. Armin W. Geertz, Institut for Religionsvidenskab, Aarhus Universitet, Taasingegade 3, 8000 Aarhus C, Denmark; tel. 89-42-23-06; fax 86-13-04-90; e-mail geertz@teologi.au.dk; internet www.iahr.dk; f. 1950 to promote international collaboration of scholars, to organize congresses and to stimulate research. Mems: 33 countries. Pres. PETER ANTES; Gen. Sec. Prof. ARMIN W. GEERTZ.

International Committee for the History of Art: 13 rue de Seine, 75006 Paris, France; e-mail philippe.senechal@inha.fr; internet www.esteticas.unam.mx/ciha; f. 1930 by the 12th International Congress on the History of Art, for collaboration in the scientific study of the history of art; holds international congress every four years, and at least two colloquia between congresses. Mems: National Committees in 34 countries. Pres. Prof. STEPHEN BANN (United Kingdom); Sec. PHILIPPE SENECHAL (France). Publ. *Bibliographie d'histoire de l'Art* (quarterly).

International Committee of Historical Sciences: Bâtiment Laplace, École Normale Supérieure de Cachan, 94235 Cachan Cédex, France; e-mail cish@ihtp-cnrs.ens-cachan.fr; internet www.cish.org; f. 1926 to work for the advancement of historical sciences by means of international co-ordination; holds international congress every five years. Mems: 53 national committees, 22 affiliated international organizations and 18 internal commissions. Pres. IVAN T. BEREND (USA); Sec.-Gen. FRANÇOIS BÉDARIDA (France). Publ. *Bulletin d'Information du CISH.*

International Congress of African Studies: c/o International African Institute, School of Oriental and African Studies, Thornhaugh St, London, WC1H OXG, United Kingdom; tel. (20) 7898-4420; fax (20) 7898-4419; e-mail iai@soas.ac.uk; f. 1962.

International Federation for Modern Languages and Literatures: c/o D. A. Wells, Dept of German, Birkbeck College, Malet St, London, WC1E 7HX, United Kingdom; tel. (20) 7631-6103; fax (20) 7383-3729; e-mail d.wells@bbk.ac.uk; internet vicu.utoronto.ca/staff/kushner/fillm.htm; f. 1928 to establish permanent contact between historians of literature, to develop or perfect facilities for their work and to promote the study of modern languages and literature; holds Congress every three years. Mems: 19 asscns, with individual mems in 98 countries. Sec.-Gen. D. A. WELLS (UK).

International Federation of Philosophical Societies: c/o I. Kuçuradi, Ahmet Rasim Sok. 8/4, Çankaya, 06550 Ankara, Turkey; tel. (312) 4407408; fax (312) 4410297; e-mail ioanna@fisp.org.tr; internet www.fisp.org.tr; f. 1948 under the auspices of UNESCO, to encourage international co-operation in the field of philosophy; holds World Congress of Philosophy every five years. Mems: 120 societies from 50 countries; 27 international societies. Pres. IOANNA KUÇURADI (Turkey); Sec.-Gen. PETER KEMP (Denmark). Publs *Newsletter, International Bibliography of Philosophy, Chroniques de Philosophie, Contemporary Philosophy, Philosophical Problems Today, Philosophy and Cultural Development, Ideas Underlying World Problems.*

International Federation of Societies of Classical Studies: c/o Prof. F. Paschoud, 6 chemin aux Folies, 1293 Bellevue, Switzerland; tel. (22) 7742656; fax (22) 7742734; e-mail zosime@isuisse.com; f. 1948 under the auspices of UNESCO. Mems: 79 societies in 44 countries. Pres. C. J. CLASSEN; Sec. Prof. F. PASCHOUD (Switzerland). Publs *L'Année Philologique, Thesaurus linguae Latinae.*

International Musicological Society—IMS: CP 1561, 4001 Basel, Switzerland; fax (1) 9231027; e-mail imsba@swissonline.ch; internet www.ims-online.ch; f. 1927; holds international congresses every five years. Pres. LÁSZLÓ SOMFAI; Sec.-Gen. Dr DOROTHEA BAUMANN (Switzerland). Publ. *Acta Musicologica* (2 a year).

International Union for Oriental and Asian Studies: Közraktar u. 12A 11/2, 1093 Budapest, Hungary; f. 1951 by the 22nd International Congress of Orientalists under the auspices of UNESCO, to promote contacts between orientalists throughout the world, and to organize congresses, research and publications. Mems: in 24 countries. Sec.-Gen. Prof. GEORG HAZAI. Publs *Philologiae Turcicae Fundamenta, Materialien zum Sumerischen Lexikon, Sanskrit Dictionary, Corpus Inscriptionum Iranicarum, Linguistic Atlas of Iran, Matériels des parlers iraniens, Turcology Annual, Bibliographie égyptologique.*

International Union of Academies—IUA (Union académique internationale—UAI): Palais des Académies, 1 rue Ducale, 1000 Brussels, Belgium; tel. (2) 550-22-00; fax (2) 550-22-05; e-mail info@uai-iua.org; internet www.uai-iua.org; f. 1919 to promote international co-operation through collective research in philology, archaeology, art history, history and social sciences. Mems: academic institutions in 49 countries. Pres. S. SHAKED (Israel); Secs L. HOUZIAUX, J.-L. DE PAEPE.

International Union of Anthropological and Ethnological Sciences—IUAES: c/o Dr P. J. M. Nas, Faculty of Social Sciences, Univ. of Leiden, Wassenaarseweg 52, POB 9555, 2300 RB Leiden, Netherlands; tel. (71) 5273992; fax (71) 5273619; e-mail nas@rulfsw.leidenuniv.nl; internet lucy.ukc.ac.uk/IUAES; f. 1948 under the auspices of UNESCO, to enhance exchange and communication between scientists and institutions in the fields of anthropology and ethnology; aims to promote harmony between nature and culture; organizes 22 international research commissions. Mems: institutions and individuals in 100 countries. Pres. Prof. ERIC SUNDERLAND (UK); Sec.-Gen. Dr P. J. M. NAS (Netherlands). Publ. *IUAES Newsletter* (3 a year).

International Union of Prehistoric and Protohistoric Sciences: c/o Prof. J. Bourgeois, Dept of Archaeology and Ancient History of Europe, University of Ghent, Blandijnberg 2, 9000 Ghent, Belgium; tel. (9) 264-41-06; fax (9) 264-41-73; e-mail jean.bourgeois@rug.ac.be; internet www.geocities.com/athens/ithaca/7152; f. 1931 to promote congresses and scientific work in the fields of pre- and proto-history. Mems: 120 countries. Pres. Prof. P. BONENFANT (Belgium); Sec.-Gen. Prof. J. BOURGEOIS (Belgium).

Permanent International Committee of Linguists: Instituut voor Nederlandse Lexicologie, Matthias de Vrieshof 2, 2311 BZ Leiden, Netherlands; tel. (71) 5141648; fax (71) 5272115; e-mail secretariaat@inl.nl; f. 1928; aims to further linguistic research, to co-ordinate activities undertaken for the advancement of linguistics, and to make the results of linguistic research known internationally; holds Congress every five years. Mems: 48 countries and two international linguistic organizations. Pres. S. A. WURM (Australia); Sec.-Gen. P. G. J. VAN STERKENBURG (Netherlands). Publ. *Linguistic Bibliography* (annually).

OTHER ORGANIZATIONS

African Social and Environmental Studies Programme: Box 4477, Nairobi, Kenya; tel. (2) 747960; fax (2) 740817; f. 1968; develops and disseminates educational material on social and environmental studies in eastern and southern Africa. Mems: 18 African countries. Chair. Prof. WILLIAM SENTEZA-KAJUBI; Exec. Dir Prof. PETER MUYANDA MUTEBI. Publs *African Social and Environmental Studies Forum* (2 a year), teaching guides.

Arab Towns Organization—ATO: POB 68160, Kaifan 71962, Kuwait; tel. 4849705; fax 4849322; e-mail ato@ato.net; internet www.ato.net; f. 1967; aims to promote co-operation and the exchange of expertise with regard to urban administration; works to improve the standard of municipal services and utilities in Arab towns and to preserve the character and heritage of Arab towns. Administers an Institute for Urban Development (AUDI), based in Riyadh, Saudi Arabia, which provides training and research for municipal officers; the Arab Towns Development Fund, to help member towns implement projects; and the ATO Award, to encourage the preservation of Arab architecture. Mems: 413 towns. Dir-Gen. MOHAMMED ABDUL HAMID AL-SAQR; Sec.-Gen. ABD AL-AZIZ Y. AL-ADASANI. PUBL. *Al-Madinah Al-Arabiyah* (every 2 months).

Association for the Study of the World Refugee Problem—AWR: Piazzale di Porta Pia 121, 00198 Rome, Italy; tel. (06) 44250159; f. 1951 to promote and co-ordinate scholarly research on refugee problems. Mems: 475 in 19 countries. Pres. FRANCO FOSCHI (Italy); Sec.-Gen. ALDO CLEMENTE (Italy). Publs *AWR Bulletin* (quarterly, in English, French, Italian and German), treatises on refugee problems (17 vols).

Council for the Development of Social Science Research in Africa—CODESRIA: BP 3304, Dakar, Senegal; tel. 825-98-22; fax 824-12-89; e-mail codesria@telecomplus.sn; internet www.sas.upenn.edu / african_studies / codesria / codes_menu.html; f. 1973; promotes research, organizes conferences, working groups and information services. Mems: research institutes and university faculties in African countries. Exec. Sec. ACHILLE MBEMBE. Publs *Africa Development* (quarterly), *CODESRIA Bulletin* (quarterly), *Index of African Social Science Periodical Articles* (annually), directories of research.

Council for Research in Values and Philosophy—CRVP: c/o Prof. G. F. McLean, School of Philosophy, Catholic University of America, Washington, DC 20064, USA; tel. and fax (202) 319-6089; e-mail cua-rvp@cua.edu; internet www.crvp.org. Mems: 33 teams from 24 countries. Pres. Prof. KENNETH L. SCHMITZ (Canada); Sec.-Gen. Prof. GEORGE F. MCLEAN (USA). Publ. *Cultural Heritage and Contemporary Change* series.

Eastern Regional Organisation for Planning and Housing: POB 10867, 50726 Kuala Lumpur, Malaysia; tel. (3) 718-7068; fax (3) 718-3931; f. 1958 to promote and co-ordinate the study and practice of housing and regional town and country planning; maintains offices in Japan, India and Indonesia. Mems: 57 organizations and 213 individuals in 28 countries. Sec.-Gen. JOHN KOH SENG SIEW. Publs *EAROPH News and Notes* (monthly), *Town and Country Planning* (bibliography).

English-Speaking Union of the Commonwealth: Dartmouth House, 37 Charles St, Berkeley Sq., London, W1J 5ED, United Kingdom; tel. (20) 7529-1550; fax (20) 7495-6108; e-mail esu@esu.org; internet www.esu.org; f. 1918 to promote international understanding between Britain, the Commonwealth, the United States and Europe, in conjunction with the ESU of the USA. Mems: 70,000 (incl. USA). Chair. Lord ALAN WATSON; Dir-Gen. VALERIE MITCHELL. Publ. *Concord.*

European Association for Population Studies—EAPS: POB 11676, 2502 AR The Hague, Netherlands; tel. (70) 3565200; fax (70) 3647187; e-mail eaps@nidi.nl; internet www.nidi.nl/eaps; f. 1983 to foster research and provide information on European population problems; organizes conferences, seminars and workshops. Mems: demographers from 40 countries. Exec. Sec. GYS BEETS. Publ. *European Journal of Population/Revue Européenne de Démographie* (quarterly).

European Society for Rural Sociology: c/o C. Ray, Centre for Rural Economy, Univ. of Newcastle upon Tyne, NE1 7RU, United Kingdom; tel. (191) 222-6460; fax (191) 222-6720; e-mail christopher.ray@newcastle.ac.uk; internet cc.joensuu.fi/ alma/ esrs; f. 1957 to further research in, and co-ordination of, rural sociology and provide a centre for documentation of information. Mems: 300 individuals, institutions and asscns in 29 European countries and nine countries outside Europe. Pres. Dr HILARY TOVEY (Ireland); Sec. CHRISTOPHER RAY (United Kingdom). Publ. *Sociologia Ruralis* (quarterly).

Experiment in International Living: POB 595, Main St, Putney, VT 05346, USA; tel. (802) 387-4210; fax (802) 387-5783; e-mail federation@experiment.org; internet www.experiment.org; f. 1932 as an international federation of non-profit educational and cultural exchange institutions; works to create mutual understanding and respect among people of different nations, as a means of furthering peace. Mems: organizations in 20 countries. Dir ROBIN BITTERS.

International African Institute—IAI: School of Oriental and African Studies, Thornhaugh St, Russell Sq., London, WC1H 0XG, United Kingdom; tel. (20) 7898-4420; fax (20) 7898-4419; e-mail iai@soas.ac.uk; internet www.oneworld.org/iai; f. 1926 to promote the study of African peoples, their languages, cultures and social life in their traditional and modern settings; organizes an international seminar programme bringing together scholars from Africa and elsewhere; links scholars in order to facilitate research projects, especially in the social sciences. Mems: 1,500 in 97 countries. Chair. Prof. V. Y. MUDIMBE; Dir Prof. PAUL SPENCER. Publs *Africa* (quarterly), *Africa Bibliography* (annually).

International Association for Media and Communication Research: c/o Ole Prehn, Aalborg University, Kroghstr. 3, 9220 Aalborg East, Denmark; tel. 9635-9038; fax 9815-6869; e-mail prehn@hum.auc.dk; internet www.humfak.auc.dk/iamcr; f. 1957 (frmly International Asscn for Mass Communication Research) to stimulate interest in mass communication research and the dissemination of information about research and research needs, to improve communication practice, policy and research and training for journalism, and to provide a forum for researchers and others involved in mass communication to meet and exchange information. Mems: over 2,300 in c. 70 countries. Pres. FRANK MORGAN; Sec.-Gen. OLE PREHN. Publ. *Newsletter*.

International Association of Applied Linguistics (Association internationale de linguistique appliquée—AILA): c/o Prof. Andrew D. Cohen, Dept of ESL, 331E Nolte Center, University of Minnesota, 315 Pillsbury Drive SE, Minneapolis, MN 55455, USA; tel. (612) 624-3806; fax (612) 624-4579; e-mail adcohen@tc.umn.edu; internet www.aila.ac; f. 1964; organizes seminars on applied linguistics, and a World Congress every three years. Mems: asscns in 38 countries. Pres. Prof. CHRISTOPHER CANDLIN (Hong Kong); Sec.-Gen. Prof. ANDREW D. COHEN (USA). Publs *AILA Review* (annually), *AILA News* (2 a year).

International Association of Metropolitan City Libraries—INTAMEL: c/o Jan Boman, Swedish National Council for Cultural Affairs, POB 7843, S-103 98 Stockholm, Sweden; tel. (8) 679-31-31; fax (8) 679-31-10; e-mail jan.boman@kur.se; f. 1967; serves as a platform for libraries in cities of over 400,000 inhabitants or serving a wide and diverse geographical area; promotes the exchange of ideas and information on a range of topics including library networks, automation, press relations and research. Mems: 98 libraries in 28 countries. Sec. and Treas. JAN BOMAN. Publs *INTAMEL Metro* (2 a year), conference reports.

International Committee for Social Sciences Information and Documentation: c/o Dr A. F. Marks, Herengracht 410 (Swidoc), 1017BX Amsterdam, Netherlands; tel. (20) 6225061; fax (20) 6238374; internet www.unesco.org/most/icssd.htm; f. 1950 to collect and disseminate information on documentation services in social sciences, to help improve documentation, to advise societies on problems of documentation and to draw up rules likely to improve the presentation of documents. Mems: from international asscns specializing in social sciences or in documentation, and from other specialized fields. Sec.-Gen. ARNAUD F. MARKS (Netherlands). Publs *International Bibliography of the Social Sciences* (annually), *Newsletter* (2 a year).

International Council on Archives—ICA: 60 rue des Francs-Bourgeois, 75003 Paris, France; tel. 1-40-27-63-06; fax 1-42-72-20-65; e-mail ica@ica.cia.org; internet www.ica.org; f. 1948 to develop relationships between archivists in different countries; aims to protect and enhance archives, to ensure preservation of archival heritage; facilitates training of archivists and conservators; promotes implementation of a professional code of conduct; encourages ease of access to archives; has 12 regional branches. Mems: 1,680 in 180 countries. Pres. ELISA DE SANTOS (Spain); Sec.-Gen. JOAN VAN ALBADA. Publ. *Comma* (4 a year).

International Ergonomics Association—IEA: BP 2025, 3500 HA Utrecht, Netherlands; tel. (30) 35-44-55; fax (30) 35-76-39; internet www.iea.cc; f. 1957 to bring together organizations and persons interested in the scientific study of human work and its environment; to establish international contacts among those specializing in this field, to co-operate with employers' asscns and trade unions in order to encourage the practical application of ergonomic sciences in industries, and to promote scientific research in this field. Mems: 17 federated societies. Pres. ILKKA KUORINKA (Finland); Sec.-Gen. Prof. D. P. ROOKMAAKER. Publ. *Ergonomics* (monthly).

International Federation for Housing and Planning—IFHP: Wassenaarseweg 43, 2596 CG The Hague, Netherlands; tel. (70) 3244557; fax (70) 3282085; e-mail ifhp.nl@inter.nl.net; internet www.ifhp.org; f. 1913 to study and promote the improvement of housing and the theory and practice of town planning; holds world congress and international conference every 2 years. Mems: 200 organizations and 300 individuals in 65 countries. Pres. IRENE WIESE-VON OFEN (Germany); Sec.-Gen. E. E. VAN HYLCKAMA VLIEG (Netherlands). Publ. *Newsletter* (quarterly).

International Federation of Institutes for Socio-religious Research: 1 pl. Montesquieu, bte 13, 1348 Louvain-la-neuve, Belgium; e-mail gendebien@anso.ucl.ac.be; f. 1958; federates centres engaged in scientific research in order to analyse and discover the social and religious phenomena at work in contemporary society. Mems: institutes in 26 countries. Pres. Canon Fr. HOUTART (Belgium); Sec. F. GENDEBIEN. Publ. *Social Compass (International Review of Sociology of Religion)* (quarterly, in English and French).

International Federation of Social Science Organizations—IFSSO: Institute of Law, nardoni 18, 110 000 Prague 1, Czech Republic; tel. (2) 24913858; fax (2) 24913858; f. 1979 to assist research and teaching in the social sciences, and to facilitate co-operation and enlist mutual assistance in the planning and evaluation of programmes of major importance to members. Mems: 31 national councils or academies in 29 countries. Pres. Prof. CARMENCITA T. AGUILAR; Sec.-Gen. Prof. J. BLAHOZ. Publs *IFSSO Newsletter* (2 a year), *International Directory of Social Science Organizations*.

International Federation of Vexillological Associations: Box 580, Winchester, MA 01890, USA; tel. (781) 729-9410; fax (781) 721-4817; e-mail vexor@mediaone.net; internet www.crwflags.com/fotw/flags/vex-fiav.html; f. 1967 to promote through its member organizations the scientific study of the history and symbolism of flags; sanctions international standards for scientific flag study; holds International Congresses every two years. Mems: 42 institutions and asscns in 27 countries. Pres. Prof. MICHEL LUPANT (Belgium); Liaison Officer WHITNEY SMITH. Publs *Recueil* (every 2 years), *The Flag Bulletin* (every 2 months), *Info FIAV* (every 4 months).

International Institute for Ligurian Studies: Via Romana 39, 18012 Bordighera, Italy; tel. (0184) 263601; fax (0184) 266421; e-mail istituto@üsl.it; internet www.üsl.it; f. 1947 to conduct research on ancient monuments and regional traditions in the north-west arc of the Mediterranean (France and Italy); maintains library of 80,000 vols. Mems: in France, Italy, Spain, Switzerland. Dir Prof. CARLO VARALDO (Italy).

International Institute of Administrative Sciences—IIAS: 1 rue Defacqz, 1000 Brussels, Belgium; tel. (2) 538-91-65; fax (2) 537-97-02; e-mail iias@iiasiisa.be; internet www.iiasiisa.be; f. 1930 for the comparative examination of administrative experience; carries out research and programmes designed to improve administrative law and practices; maintains library of 15,000 vols; has consultative status with UN, UNESCO and ILO; organizes international congresses. Mems: 46 mem. states, 55 national sections, nine international governmental organizations, 51 corporate mems, 13 individual members. Pres. IGNACIO PICHARDO PAGAZA (Mexico); Dir-Gen. GIANCARLO VILELLA (Italy). Publs *International Review of Administrative Sciences* (quarterly), *Newsletter* (3 a year).

International Institute of Sociology—IIS: c/o Dr K. Cook, Dept of Sociology, Stanford University, Stanford CA 94305, USA; f. 1893 to enable sociologists to meet and to study sociological questions. Mems: c. 300 in 47 countries. Pres. PAOLO AMMASSARI (Italy); Sec.-Gen. Dr KAREN COOK. Publ. *The Annals of the IIS*.

International Numismatic Commission: Coins and Medals Dept, British Museum, London, WC1B 3DG, United Kingdom; tel. (20) 7323-8227; fax (20) 7323-8171; internet www.amnumsoc.org/inc; f. 1936; facilitates co-operation between scholars studying coins and medals. Mems: numismatic organizations in 35 countries. Pres. A. BURNETT; Sec. M. AMANDRY.

International Peace Academy—IPA: 777 United Nations Plaza, New York, NY 10017, USA; tel. (212) 687-4300; fax (212) 983-8246; e-mail ipa@ipacademy.org; internet www.ipacademy.org; f. 1970 to promote the prevention and settlement of armed conflicts between and within states through policy research and development; educates government officials in the procedures needed for conflict resolution, peace-keeping, mediation and negotiation, through international training seminars and publications; off-the-record meetings are also conducted to gain complete understanding of a specific conflict. Chair. RITA E. HAUSER; Pres. OLARA A. OTUNNU. Publs *Annual Report, Newsletter* (2 a year).

International Peace Research Association—IPRA: c/o Copenhagen Peace Research Institute, University of Copenhagen, Fredericiagade 18, 1310 Copenhagen, Denmark; tel. 3345-5052; fax 3345-5060; e-mail bmoeller@copn.dk; internet www.copn.dk/ipra/ipra.html; f. 1964 to encourage interdisciplinary research on the conditions of peace and the causes of war. Mems: 150 corporate, five regional branches, 1,000 individuals, in 93 countries. Pres. URSULA OSWALD (Mexico); Sec.-Gen. BJOERN MOELLER (Denmark). Publ. *IPRA Newsletter* (quarterly).

International Social Science Council—ISSC: Maison de l'UNESCO, 1 rue Miollis, 75732 Paris Cédex 15, France; tel.

1-45-68-25-58; fax 1-45-66-76-03; e-mail issclak@unesco.org; internet www.unesco.org/ngo/issc; f. 1952; aims to promote the advancement of the social sciences throughout the world and their application to the major problems of the world; encourages co-operation at an international level between specialists in the social sciences. ISSC has a Senior Board; and programmes on International Human Dimensions of Global Environmental Change (IHDP), co-sponsored by the International Council of Scientific Unions (q.v.), and Comparative Research on Poverty (CROP). Mems: 14 asscns (listed below), 17 national organizations, 16 associate member organizations. Pres. KURT PAWLIK (Germany); Sec.-Gen. LESZEK A. KOSINSKI (Canada).

Associations Federated to the ISSC

(details of these organizations will be found under their appropriate category elsewhere in the International Organizations section)

International Association of Legal Sciences (p. 549).
International Economic Association (p. 536).
International Federation of Social Science Organizations (p. 574).
International Geographical Union (p. 565).
International Institute of Administrative Sciences (p. 574).
International Law Association (p. 550).
International Peace Research Association (p. 574).
International Political Science Association (p. 544).
International Sociological Association (p. 575).
International Union for the Scientific Study of Population (p. 575).
International Union of Anthropological and Ethnological Sciences (p. 573).
International Union of Psychological Science (p. 566).
World Association for Public Opinion Research (p. 575).
World Federation for Mental Health (p. 558).

International Society of Social Defence and Humane Criminal Policy—ISSD: c/o Centro nazionale di prevenzione e difesa sociale, Piazza Castello 3, 20121 Milan, Italy; tel. (02) 86460714; fax (02) 72008431; e-mail cnpds.ispac@iol.it; f. 1945 to combat crime, to protect society and to prevent citizens from being tempted to commit criminal actions. Mems: in 43 countries. Pres. SIMONE ROZÈS (France); Sec.-Gen. EDMONDO BRUTI LIBERATI (Italy). Publ. *Cahiers de défense sociale* (annually).

International Sociological Association: c/o Faculty of Political Sciences and Sociology, Universidad Complutense, 28223 Madrid, Spain; tel. (91) 3527650; fax (91) 3524945; e-mail isa@sis.ucm.es; internet www.ucm.es/info/isa; f. 1949 to promote sociological knowledge, facilitate contacts between sociologists, encourage the dissemination and exchange of information and facilities and stimulate research; has 53 research committees on various aspects of sociology; holds World Congresses every four years (15th Congress: Brisbane, Australia, 2002). Pres. A. MARTINELLI (Italy); Exec. Sec. IZABELA BARLINSKA. Publs *Current Sociology* (3 a year), *International Sociology* (quarterly), *Sage Studies in International Sociology* (based on World Congress).

International Statistical Institute—ISI: POB 950, Prinses Beatrixlaan 428, 2270 AZ Voorburg, Netherlands; tel. (70) 3375737; fax (70) 3860025; e-mail isi@cbs.nl; internet www.cbs.nl/isi; f. 1885; devoted to the development and improvement of statistical methods and their application throughout the world; administers a statistical education centre in Calcutta, in co-operation with the Indian Statistical Institute; executes international research programmes. Mems: 2,000 ordinary mems, 10 hon. mems, 110 *ex-officio* mems, 75 corporate mems, 45 affiliated organizations, 32 national statistical societies. Pres. DENNIS TREWIN; Dir Permanent Office M. P. R. VAN DEN BROECKE. Publs *Bulletin of the International Statistical Institute* (proceedings of biennial sessions), *International Statistical Review* (3 a year), *Short Book Reviews* (3 a year), *Statistical Theory and Method Abstracts* (quarterly), *ISI Newsletter* (3 a year), *Membership Directory* (every 2 years).

International Studies Association—ISA: Social Science 324, Univ. of Arizona, Tucson, AZ 85721, USA; tel. (520) 621-7715; fax (520) 621-5780; e-mail isa@u.arizona.edu; internet www.isanet.org; f. 1959; links those whose professional concerns extend beyond their own national boundaries (government officials, representatives of business and industry, and scholars). Mems: 3,500 in 60 countries. Pres. MICHAEL BRECHER; Exec. Dir THOMAS J. VOLGY. Publs *International Studies Quarterly, International Studies Perspectives, International Studies Review, ISA Newsletter.*

International Union for the Scientific Study of Population—IUSSP: 34 rue des Augustins, 4000 Liège, Belgium; tel. (4) 222-40-80; fax (4) 222-38-47; e-mail iussp@iussp.org; internet www.iussp.org; f. 1928 to advance the progress of quantitative and qualitative demography as a science. Mems: 1,917 in 121 countries. Pres. JOSÉ ALBERTO M. DE CARVALHO. Publs *IUSSP Bulletin* and books on population.

Mensa International: 15 The Ivories, 6–8 Northampton St, London, N1 2HY, United Kingdom; tel. (20) 7226-6891; fax (20) 7226-7059; internet www.mensa.org/mensa-international; f. 1946 to identify and foster intelligence for the benefit of humanity. Mems: individuals who score in a recognized intelligence test higher than 98% of people in general may become mems; there are 100,000 mems world-wide. Exec. Dir E. J. VINCENT (UK). Publ. *Mensa International Journal* (monthly).

Third World Forum: 39 Dokki St, POB 43, Orman Giza, Cairo, Egypt; tel. (2) 7488092; fax (2) 7480668; e-mail 20sabry2 @gega.net; internet www.egypt2020.org; f. 1973 to link social scientists and others from the developing countries, to discuss alternative development policies and encourage research; currently undertaking Egypt 2020 research project; maintains regional offices in Egypt, Mexico, Senegal and Sri Lanka. Mems: individuals in more than 50 countries. Chair. ISMAIL-SABRI ABDALLA.

World Association for Public Opinion Research: c/o University of Nebraska-Lincoln, UNL Gallup Research Center, 200 N 11th St, Lincoln, NE 68588-0241, USA; tel. (402) 458-2030; fax (402) 458-2038; e-mail wapor@unl.edu; internet www.wapor .org; f. 1947 to establish and promote contacts between persons in the field of survey research on opinions, attitudes and behaviour of people in the various countries of the world; works to further the use of objective, scientific survey research in national and international affairs. Mems: 450 from 72 countries. Man. Dir RENAE REIS. Publs *WAPOR Newsletter* (quarterly), *International Journal of Public Opinion* (quarterly).

World Society for Ekistics: c/o Athens Centre of Ekistics, 24 Strat. Syndesmou St, 106 73 Athens, Greece; tel. (1) 3623216; fax (1) 3629337; e-mail ekistics@otenet.gr; internet www.ekistics .org; f. 1965; aims to promote knowledge and ideas concerning human settlements through research, publications and conferences. Mems: 159 individuals. Pres. Prof. UDO E. SIMONIS; Sec.-Gen. P. PSOMOPOULOS. Publs *The Ekistics Journal, Ekistic Index of Periodicals.*

Social Welfare and Human Rights

African Commission on Human and People's Rights: Kairaba Ave, POB 673, Banjul, The Gambia; tel. 392962; fax 390764; f. 1987; mandated to monitor compliance with the African Charter on Human and People's Rights (ratified in 1986); investigates claims of human rights abuses perpetrated by govts that have ratified the Charter (claims may be brought by other African govts, the victims themselves, or by a third party); meets twice a year for 10 days in March and Oct.; Mems: 11. Sec. GERMAIN BARICAKO (Burundi).

Aid to Displaced Persons and its European Villages: 35 rue du Marché, 4500 Huy, Belgium; tel. (85) 21-34-81; fax (85) 23-01-47; e-mail aidepersdepl.huy@proximedia.be; internet www.proximedia.com/aideperso.html; f. 1957 to carry on and develop work begun by the Belgian asscn Aid to Displaced Persons; aims to provide material and moral aid for refugees; European Villages established at Aachen, Bregenz, Augsburg, Berchem-Ste-Agathe, Spiesen, Euskirchen, Wuppertal as centres for refugees. Pres. LUC DENYS (Belgium).

Amnesty International: 1 Easton St, London, WC1X ODW, United Kingdom; tel. (20) 7413-5500; fax (20) 7956-1157; e-mail amnestyis@amnesty.org; internet www.amnesty.org/; f. 1961; an independent world-wide movement that campaigns impartially for the release of all prisoners of conscience, for fair and prompt trials for all political prisoners, for the abolition of torture and the death penalty and for an end to extrajudicial executions and 'disappearances'; also opposes abuses by opposition groups (hostage-taking, torture and arbitrary killings); financed by donations. Mems: 1m. represented by 7,500 local, youth, student and other specialist groups, in more than 100 countries and territories; nationally organized sections in 56 countries. Sec.-Gen. IRENE KHAN (Bangladesh). Publs *International Newsletter* (monthly), *Annual Report*, other country reports.

Anti-Slavery International: Thomas Clarkson House, The Stableyard, Broomgrove Rd, London, SW9 9TL, United Kingdom; tel. (20) 7501-8920; fax (20) 7738-4110; e-mail antislavery@antislavery.org; internet www.antislavery.org; f. 1839 to eradicate slavery and forced labour in all their forms, to generate awareness of such abuses, to promote the well-being of indigenous peoples, and to protect human rights in accordance with the Universal Declaration of Human Rights, 1948. Mems: 1,800 members in 30 countries. Chair. REGGIE NORTON; Dir MIKE DOTTRIDGE. Publs *Annual Report, Anti-Slavery Reporter* (quarterly), special reports on research.

Associated Country Women of the World—ACWW: Clutha House, 10 Storey's Gate, London, SW1P 3AY, United Kingdom; tel. (20) 7834-8635; internet www.acww.org.uk; f. 1933; aims to aid the economic and social development of countrywomen and home-makers of all nations, to promote international goodwill and understanding, and to work to alleviate poverty, and promote good health and education. Gen. Sec. ANNA FROST. Publ. *The Countrywoman* (quarterly).

Association Internationale de la Mutualité—AIM (International Association of Mutual Health Funds): 50 rue d'Arlon, 1000 Brussels, Belgium; tel. (2) 234-57-00; fax (2) 234-57-08; e-mail aim.secretariat@aim-mutual.org; internet www.aim-mutual.org; f. 1950 as a grouping of autonomous health insurance and social protection bodies; aims to promote and reinforce access to health care by developing the sound management of mutualities; serves as a forum for exchange of information and debate. Mems: 43 national federations in 27 countries. Pres. UELI MÜLLER (Switzerland); Dir WILLY PALM (Belgium). Publs *AIMS* (newsletter), reports on health issues.

Aviation sans frontières—ASF: Brussels National Airport, Brucargo 706, POB 7339, 1931 Brucargo, Belgium; tel. (2) 753-24-70; fax (2) 753-24-71; e-mail office@asfbelgium.org; internet www.asfbelgium.org; f. 1983 to make available the resources of the aviation industry to humanitarian organizations, for carrying supplies and equipment at minimum cost, both on long-distance flights and locally. Pres. PHILIPPE DEHENNIN; Gen. Man. XAVIER FLAMENT.

Co-ordinating Committee for International Voluntary Service—CCIVS: Maison de l'UNESCO, 1 rue Miollis, 75732 Paris Cédex 15, France; tel. 1-45-68-49-36; fax 1-42-73-05-21; e-mail ccivs@unesco.org; internet www.unesco.org/ccivs; f. 1948 to co-ordinate youth voluntary service organizations world-wide. Organizes seminars and conferences; publishes relevant literature; undertakes planning and execution of projects in collaboration with UNESCO, the UN, the EU etc; generates funds for member organizations' projects. Affiliated mems: 140 orgs in more than 90 countries. Pres. G. ORSINI; Dir S. COSTANZO-SOW. Publs *News from CCIVS* (3 a year), *The Volunteer's Handbook*, other guides, handbooks and directories.

EIRENE—International Christian Service for Peace: 56503 Neuwied, Postfach 1322, Germany; tel. (2631) 83790; fax (2631) 31160; e-mail eirene-int@eirene.org; internet www.eirene.org; f. 1957; carries out professional training, apprenticeship programmes, agricultural work and work to support co-operatives in Africa and Latin America; runs volunteer programmes in co-operation with peace groups in Europe and the USA. Gen. Sec. ECKEHARD FRICKE.

European Federation of the Elderly—EURAG: Wielandgasse 9, 1 Stock, 8010 Graz, Austria; tel. (316) 81-46-08; fax (316) 81-47-67; e-mail eurag.europe@aon.at; internet www.eurag-europe.org; f. 1962 as the European Federation for the Welfare of the Elderly (present name adopted 1996); serves as a forum for the exchange of experience and practical co-operation among member organizations; represents the interests of members before international organizations; promotes understanding and co-operation in matters of social welfare; draws attention to the problems of old age. Mems: organizations in 33 countries. Pres. EDMÉE MANGERS-ANEN (Luxembourg); Sec.-Gen. GREGOR HAMMERL (Austria). Publs (in English, French, German and Italian) *EURAG Newsletter* (quarterly), *EURAG Information* (monthly).

Federation of Asia-Pacific Women's Associations—FAWA: Centro Escolar University, 9 Mendiola St, San Miguel, Manila, Philippines; tel. (2) 741-04-46; e-mail zmaustria@ceu.edu.ph; f. 1959 to provide closer relations, and bring about joint efforts among Asians, particularly women, through mutual appreciation of cultural, moral and socio-economic values. Mems: 415,000. Pres. SUSY CHIA-ISAI (Singapore); Sec. WOO CHOON MEI (Singapore). Publ. *FAWA News Bulletin* (quarterly).

Inclusion Europe: Galeries de la Toison d'Or, 29 ch. d'Ixelles, Ste 393/32, 1050 Brussels, Belgium; tel. (2) 502-28-15; fax (2) 502-80-10; e-mail secretariat@inclusion-europe.org; internet www.inclusion-europe.org; f. 1988 to advance the human rights and defend the interests of people with learning or intellectual disabilities, and their families, in Europe. Mems: 20 societies in 15 EU member states. Publs *INCLUDE* (bi-monthly newsflash), *Information Letter* (monthly), *Human Rights Observer* (available on-line), *Enlargement Update* (every 2 weeks, in English and French), other papers and publs.

Interamerican Conference on Social Security (Conferencia Interamericano de Seguridad Social—CISS): Calle San Ramon s/n esq. Avda San Jerónimo, Unidad Independencia, Col. San Jerónimo Lídice, Deleg. Magdalena Contreras, CP 10100 México DF, Mexico; tel. (55) 5595-0177; fax (55) 5683-8524; e-mail ciss@data.net.mx; internet www.ciss.org.mx; f. 1942 to contribute to the development of social security in the countries of the Americas and to co-operate with social security institutions. CISS bodies are: the General Assembly, the Permanent Interamerican Committee on Social Security, the Secretariat General, six American Commissions of Social Security and the Interamerican Center for Social Security Studies. Mems: 77 social security institutions in 38 countries. Pres. Dr SANTIAGO LEVY ALGAZI (Mexico); Sec.-Gen. Dr JOSÉ LUIS STEIN VELASCO (Mexico) (acting). Publs *Social Security Journal/Seguridad Social* (every 2 months), monographs, study series.

International Abolitionist Federation: Gasvaerksvej 24, 1656 Copenhagen V, Denmark; tel. 33-23-40-52; fax 33-23-40-51; e-mail iaf@iaf-online.org; f. 1875; aims to abolish traffic in persons, the exploitation of the prostitution of others, state regulation of prostitution, degradation, humiliation and marginalizing of women and children, all forms of discrimination based on gender, and all contemporary forms of slavery and slavery-like practices; holds international congress every three years and organizes regional conferences to raise awareness of the cultural, religious and traditional practices that affect adversely the lives of women and children. Affiliated organizations in 17 countries, corresponding mems in 40 countries. Pres. DORIS OTZEN (Denmark); Exec. Sec. BENOIT OMONT (France). Publ. *IAF Information* (1-2 a year).

International Association against Noise: Hirschenplatz 7, 6004 Lucerne, Switzerland; tel. (41) 4103013; fax (41) 4109093; f. 1959 to promote noise-control at an international level; encourages co-operation and the exchange of experience; prepares supranational measures; issues information; carries out research; organizes conferences; and assists national anti-noise asscns. Mems: four, and one associate mem. Pres. KAREL NOVOTNÝ (Czech Republic); Sec. Dr WILLY AECHERLI (Switzerland).

International Association for Education to a Life without Drugs (Internationaler Verband für Erziehung zu suchtmittelfreiem Leben—IVES): c/o Uljas Syväniemi, Haiharankatu 15 G 64, 33710 Tampere, Finland; e-mail uljas.syvaniemi@koti.tpo.ti; f. 1954 (as the International Association for Temperance Education) to promote international co-operation in education on the dangers of alcohol and drugs; collects and distributes information on drugs; maintains regular contact with national and international organizations active in these fields; holds conferences. Mems: 77,000 in 10 countries. Pres. ULJAS SYVÄNIEMI; Sec. DAG MAGNE JOHANNESSEN.

International Association for Suicide Prevention: c/o Ms M. Campos, IASP Central Administrative Office, 1725 West Harrison St, Suite 955, Chicago, IL 60612, USA; tel. (312) 942-

7208; fax (312) 942-2177; internet www.iasp1960.org; f. 1960; serves as a common platform for interchange of acquired experience, literature and information about suicide; disseminates information; arranges special training; encourages and carries out research; organizes the Biennial International Congress for Suicide Prevention. Mems: 340 individuals and societies, in 55 countries of all continents. Pres. Dr DIEGO DE LEO. Publ. *Crisis* (quarterly).

International Association of Children's International Summer Villages—CISV International Ltd: Mea House, Ellison Pl., Newcastle upon Tyne, NE1 8XS, United Kingdom; tel. (191) 232-4998; fax (191) 261-4710; e-mail international@cisv.org; internet www.cisv.org; f. 1950 to promote peace, education and cross-cultural friendship; conducts International Camps for children and young people mainly between the ages of 11 and 19. Mems: c. 49,000. International Pres. CATHY KNOOP ; Sec.-Gen. GABRIELLE MANDELL. Publs *CISV News, Annual Review, Local Work Magazine, Interspectives* (all annually).

International Association of Schools of Social Work: c/o Dept of Social Work Studies, University of Southampton, Highfield, Southampton SO17 1BJ, United Kingdom; tel. (2380) 595000; fax (2380) 593939; e-mail ld@socsci.soton.ac.uk; internet www.iassw.soton.ac.uk; f. 1928 to provide international leadership and encourage high standards in social work education. Mems: 1,600 schools of social work in 70 countries, and 25 national asscns of schools. Pres. LENA DOMINELLI (UK); Sec. BERTHA MARY RODRIGUEZ VILLA. Publs *Newsletters* (in English, French and Spanish), *Directory of Schools of Social Work, Journal of International Social Work*, reports and case studies.

International Association of Workers for Troubled Children and Youth: 22 rue Halévy, 59000 Lille, France; tel. 3-20-93-70-16; fax 3-20-09-18-39; e-mail aieji@nordnet.fr; f. 1951 to promote the profession of specialized social workers for troubled children and youth; provides a centre of information about child welfare; encourages co-operation between members; 1997 Congress: Brescia, Italy. Mems: national and regional public or private asscns from 22 countries and individual members in many other countries. Pres. GUSTAVO VELASTEGUI (France); Sec.-Gen. LARS STEINOV (Denmark).

International Catholic Migration Commission: CP 96, 37–39 rue de Vermont, POB 96, 1211 Geneva 20, Switzerland; tel. (22) 9191020; fax (22) 9191048; e-mail secretariat@icmc.dpn.ch; f. 1951; offers migration aid programmes; grants interest-free travel loans; assists refugees on a world-wide basis, helping with social and technical problems. Mems: in 85 countries. Pres. Prof. STEFANO ZAMAGNI (Italy); Sec.-Gen. WILLIAM CANNY (USA). Publ. *Annual Report.*

International Christian Federation for the Prevention of Alcoholism and Drug Addiction: 20A Ancienne Route, Apt. No 42, 1218 Grand-Saconnex, Geneva, Switzerland; tel. (22) 7888158; fax (22) 7888136; e-mail jonathan@iprolink.ch; f. 1960, reconstituted 1980 to promote world-wide education and remedial work through the churches and to co-ordinate Christian concern about alcohol and drug abuse, in co-operation with the World Council of Churches and WHO. Chair. KARIN ISRAELSSON (Sweden); Gen. Sec. JONATHAN N. GNANADASON.

International Civil Defence Organization—ICDO (Organisation internationale de protection civile—OIPC): POB 172, 10–12 chemin de Surville, 1213 Petit-Lancy 2, Geneva, Switzerland; tel. (22) 8796969; fax (22) 8796979; e-mail icdo@icdo.org; internet www.icdo.org; f. 1931, present statutes in force 1972; aims to contribute to the development of structures ensuring the protection of populations and the safeguarding of property and the environment in the face of natural and man-made disasters; promotes co-operation between civil defence organizations in member countries. Sec.-Gen. ZNAÏDI SADOK (Tunisia). Publ. *International Civil Defence Journal* (quarterly, in English, French, Spanish, Russian and Arabic).

International Commission for the Prevention of Alcoholism and Drug Dependency: 12501 Old Columbia Pike, Silver Spring, MD 20904-6600 USA; tel. (301) 680-6719; fax (301) 680-6707; e-mail 74617.1663@compuserve.com; internet www.adventist.org/icpa; f. 1952 to encourage scientific research on intoxication by alcohol, its physiological, mental and moral effects on the individual, and its effect on the community; tenth World Congress: Cape Town, South Africa, 2000. Mems: individuals in 120 countries. Exec. Dir Dr PETER N. LANDLESS. Publ. *ICPA Quarterly.*

International Council of Voluntary Agencies—ICVA: 48 Chemin du Grand-Montfleury, 1290 Versoix, Switzerland; tel. (22) 9509600; fax (22) 9509609; e-mail secretariat@icva.ch; internet www.icva.ch; f. 1962 to provide a forum for voluntary humanitarian and development agencies. Mems: 78 non-governmental organizations. Chair. ANDERS LADEKARL; Co-ordinator ED SCHENKENBERG VAN MIEROP; Publ. *Talk Back* (newsletter; available on website).

International Council of Women—ICW (Conseil international des femmes—CIF): 13 rue Caumartin, 75009 Paris, France; tel. 1-47-42-19-40; fax 1-42-66-26-23; e-mail icw-cif@wanadoo.fr; internet www.icw-cif.org; f. 1888 to bring together in international affiliation Nat. Councils of Women from all continents, for consultation and joint action; promotes equal rights for men and women and the integration of women in development and decision-making; has five standing committees. Mems: 59 national councils. Pres. PNINA HERZOG; Sec.-Gen. MARIE-CHRISTINE LAFARGUE. Publ. *Newsletter.*

International Council on Alcohol and Addictions—ICAA: CP 189, 1001 Lausanne, Switzerland; tel. (21) 3209865; fax (21) 3209817; e-mail secretariat@icaa.ch; internet www.icaa.de; f. 1907; provides an international forum for all those concerned with the prevention of harm resulting from the use of alcohol and other drugs; offers advice and guidance in development of policies and programmes; organizes training courses, congresses, symposia and seminars in different countries. Mems: affiliated organizations in 74 countries, as well as individual members. Pres. Dr IBRAHIM AL-AWAJI (Saudi Arabia); Exec. Dir Dr JÖRG SPIELDENNER (Germany). Publs *ICAA News, Alcoholism* (2 a year).

International Council on Jewish Social and Welfare Services—INTERCO: World Jewish Relief, The Forum, 74–80 Camden St, London, NW1 OEG, United Kingdom; tel. (20) 7691-1771; fax (20) 7691-1780; e-mail wjr1@wjr.org.uk; f. 1961; functions include the exchange of views and information among member agencies concerning the problems of Jewish social and welfare services; represents views to governments and international organizations. Mems: organizations in France, Switzerland, United Kingdom and the USA. Exec. Sec. CHERYL MARINER.

International Council on Social Welfare—ICSW: 380 St Antoine St West, Suite 3200, Montreal H2Y 3X7, Canada; tel. (514) 287-3280; fax (514) 287-9702; e-mail icsw@icsw.org; internet www.icsw.org; f. 1928 to provide an international forum for the discussion of social work and related issues and to promote interest in social welfare; holds international conference every two years; provides documentation and information services. Mems: 45 national committees, 12 international organizations, 33 other organizations. Pres. JULIAN DISNEY (Australia); Exec. Dir STEPHEN KING (UK). Publ. *Social Development Review* (quarterly).

International Dachau Committee: 2 rue Chauchat, 75009 Paris, France; tel. 1-45-23-39-99; fax 1-48-00-06-73; f. 1958 to perpetuate the memory of the political prisoners of Dachau; to manifest the friendship and solidarity of former prisoners whatever their beliefs or nationality; to maintain the ideals of their resistance, liberty, tolerance and respect for persons and nations; and to maintain the former concentration camp at Dachau as a museum and international memorial. Mems: national asscns in 20 countries. Pres. Gen. ANDRÉ DELPECH; Sec.-Gen. JEAN SAMUEL. Publ. *Bulletin Officiel du Comité International de Dachau* (2 a year).

International Federation of the Blue Cross: CP 6813, 3001 Bern, Switzerland; tel. (31) 3005860; fax (31) 3005869; e-mail ifbc.bern@bluewin.ch; internet www.eurocare.org/bluecross; f. 1877 to aid the victims of intemperance and drug addicts, and to take part in the general movement against alcoholism. Pres. Pastor RAYMOND BASSIN (Switzerland); Gen. Sec. HANS RÜTTIMAN.

International Federation of Educative Communities—FICE: Piazza S.S. Annunziale 12, 50122 Florence, Italy; tel. (055) 2469162; fax (055) 2347041; e-mail fice@lycosmail.com; f. 1948 under the auspices of UNESCO to co-ordinate the work of national asscns, and to promote the international exchange of knowledge and experience in the field of childcare. Mems: national asscns from 21 European countries, India, Israel, Canada, Morocco, the USA and South Africa. Pres. ROBERT SOISSON (Luxembourg); Gen. Sec. GIANLUCA BARBANOTTI (Italy). Publ. *Bulletin* (2 a year).

International Federation of Human Rights Leagues—FIDH: 17 passage de la Main d'Or, 75011 Paris, France; tel. 1-43-55-25-28; fax 1-43-55-18-80; e-mail fidh@csi.com; internet www.fidh.imaginet.fr; f. 1922; promotes the implementation of the Universal Declaration of Human Rights and other instruments of human rights protection; aims to raise awareness and alert public opinion to issues of human rights violations; undertakes investigation and observation missions; carries out training; uses its consultative and observer status to lobby international authorities. Mems: 105 national leagues in over 86 countries. Pres. PATRICK BAUDOUIN. Publs *Lettre* (2 a month), mission reports.

International Federation of Persons with Physical Disability—FIMITIC: 53173 Bonn, Beethovenallee 56–58, Germany; tel. (228) 95640; fax (228) 9564132; e-mail fimitic@t-online.de; internet www.fimitic.org; f. 1953 to bring together representatives of the disabled and handicapped into an international non-political organization under the guidance of the disabled themselves; to promote greater opportunities for the disabled; to create rehabilitation centres; to act as a co-ordinating body for all similar national organizations. Mems: national groups from 27 European countries, corresponding mems from eight countries. Pres. MARCEL ROYEZ (France); Gen. Sec. MARIJA ŠTIGLIC (Germany). Publs *Bulletin, Nouvelles.*

International Federation of Social Workers—IFSW: POB 6875, Schwarztorstrasse 20, 3000 Bern, Switzerland; tel. (31) 3826015; fax (31) 3811222; e-mail secr.gen@ifsw.org; internet www.ifsw.org; f. 1928 as International Permanent Secretariat of Social Workers; present name adopted 1956; aims to promote social work as a profession through international co-operation on standards, training, ethics and working conditions; organizes international conferences; represents the profession at the UN and other international bodies; supports national asscns of social workers. Mems: national asscns in 77 countries. Pres. IMELDA DODDS (Australia); Sec.-Gen. TOM JOHANNESEN (Switzerland). Publs *Newsletter, IFSW update* (both available on-line), policy statements and manifestos.

International League against Racism and Antisemitism: CP 1754, 1211 Geneva 1, Switzerland; tel. (22) 7310633; fax (22) 7370634; e-mail licra@mnet.ch; internet www.licra.ch; f. 1927. Mems in 17 countries. Pres. PIERRE AIDENBAUM (France).

International League for Human Rights: 823 UN Plaza Suite 717, New York, NY 10017, USA; tel. (212) 661-0480; fax (212) 661-0416; e-mail info@ilhr.org; internet www.ilhr.org; f. 1942 to implement political, civil, social, economic and cultural rights contained in the Universal Declaration of Human Rights adopted by the United Nations and to support and protect defenders of human rights world-wide. Mems: individuals, national affiliates and correspondents throughout the world. Exec. Dir CATHERINE A. FITZPATRICK. Publs various human rights reports.

International Planned Parenthood Federation—IPPF: Regent's College, Inner Circle, Regent's Park, London, NW1 4NS, United Kingdom; tel. (20) 7487-7900; fax (20) 7487-7950; e-mail info@ippf.org; internet www.ippf.org; f. 1952; aims to promote and support sexual and reproductive health and family planning services throughout the world, with a particular focus on the needs of young people; works to bring relevant issues to the attention of the media, parliamentarians, academics, governmental and non-governmental organizations, and the general public; mobilizes financial resources to fund programmes and information materials; offers technical assistance and training; collaborates with other international organizations. The International Medical Panel of the IPPF formulates guide-lines and statements on current medical and scientific advice and best practices. Mems: independent family planning asscns in over 150 countries. Pres. ANGELA GÓMEZ; Dir-Gen. INGAR BRUEGGEMANN.

International Prisoners Aid Association: c/o Dr Ali, Department of Sociology, University of Louisville, Louisville, KY 40292, USA; tel. (502) 588-6836; fax (502) 852-7042; f. 1950; works to improve prisoners' aid services, with the aim of promoting the rehabilitation of the individual and increasing the protection of society. Mems: national federations in 29 countries. Pres. Dr WOLFGANG DOLEISCH (Austria); Exec. Dir Dr BADR-EL-DIN ALI. Publ. *Newsletter* (3 a year).

International Scout and Guide Fellowship—ISGF: 9 rue du Champ de Mars, bte 14, 1050 Brussels, Belgium; tel. (2) 511-46-95; fax (2) 511-84-36; e-mail isgf-aisg@euronet.be; internet www.isgf.org; f. 1953 to help adult scouts and guides to keep alive the spirit of the Scout and Guide Promise and Laws in their own lives and to bring that spirit into the communities in which they live and work; promotes liaison and co-operation between national organizations for adult scouts and guides; encourages the founding of an organization in any country where no such organization exists. Mems: 90,000 in 46 mem. states. Chair. of Cttee NIELS ROSENBOM; Sec.-Gen. NAÏC PIRARD. Publ. *World Gazette Mondiale* (quarterly).

International Social Security Association—ISSA: CP 1, 1211 Geneva 22, Switzerland; tel. (22) 7996617; fax (22) 7998509; internet www.issa.int; f. 1927 to promote the development of social security throughout the world, mainly through the improvement of techniques and administration, in order to advance social and economic conditions on the basis of social equality. Mems: 270 institutions in 150 countries. Pres. JOHAN VERSTRAETEN (Belgium); Sec.-Gen. DALMER D. HOSKINS (USA). Publs *International Social Security Review* (quarterly, in English, French, German, Spanish), *Trends in Social Security* (quarterly, in English, French, German, Spanish), *Social Security Documentation* (African, Asian-Pacific and European series), *Social Security Worldwide* (CD Rom and internet), *Compendia of Conference Reports* (in English, French, German, Spanish), various news bulletins.

International Social Service—ISS (Service social international—SSI): 32 quai du Seujet, 1201 Geneva, Switzerland; tel. (22) 9067700; fax (22) 9067701; e-mail iss.gs@span.ch; internet www.iss-ssi.org; f. 1921 to aid families and individuals whose problems require services beyond the boundaries of the country in which they live, and where the solution of these problems depends upon co-ordinated action on the part of social workers in two or more countries; studies from an international standpoint the conditions and consequences of emigration in their effect on individual, family, and social life; operates on a non-sectarian and non-political basis. Mems: branches in 14 countries, six affiliated offices, and correspondents in some 100 other countries. Pres. Prof. Dr RAINER FRANK (Germany); Sec.-Gen. DAMIEN NGABONZIZA. Publs *ISS Reports, Newsletter* (available on-line).

International Union of Family Organisations: 28 place Saint-Georges, 75009 Paris, France; tel. 1-48-78-07-59; fax 1-42-82-95-24; f. 1947 to bring together all organizations throughout the world working for family welfare; maintains commissions and working groups on issues including standards of living, housing, marriage guidance, rural families, etc.; there are six regional organizations: the Pan-African Family Organisation (Rabat, Morocco), the North America organization (Montreal, Canada), the Arab Family Organisation (Tunis, Tunisia), the Asian Union of Family Organisations (New Delhi, India), the European regional organization (Berne, Switzerland) and the Latin American Secretariat (Curitiba, Brazil). Mems: national asscns, groups and governmental departments in over 55 countries. Pres. MARIA TERESA DA COSTA MACEDO (Portugal).

International Union of Tenants: Box 7514, 10392 Stockholm, Sweden; tel. (8) 791-02-00; fax (8) 20-43-44; e-mail magnus.hammar@hyresgasterna.se; internet www.iut.nu; f. 1955 to collaborate in safeguarding the interests of tenants; participates in activities of UN-Habitat; has working groups for EC matters, eastern Europe, developing countries and for future development; holds annual council meeting and triennial congress. Mems: national tenant organizations in 24 European countries, Australia, Benin, Canada, India, Kenya, New Zealand, Tanzania and Uganda. Chair. ELISABET LÖNNGREN; Sec.-Gen. MAGNUS HAMMAR. Publ. *The Global Tenant* (quarterly).

Inter-University European Institute on Social Welfare—IEISW: 179 rue du Débarcadère, 6001 Marcinelle, Belgium; tel. (71) 44-72-67; f. 1970 to promote, carry out and publicize scientific research on social welfare and community work. Pres. JOSEPH GILLAIN; Gen. Dir SERGE MAYENCE. Publ. *COMM.*

Lions Clubs International: 300 West 22nd St, Oak Brook, IL 60523-8842, USA; tel. (630) 571-5466; fax (630) 571-8890; e-mail lions@lionsclubs.org; internet www.lionsclubs.org; f. 1917 to foster understanding among people of the world; to promote principles of good government and citizenship and an interest in civic, cultural, social and moral welfare and to encourage service-minded people to serve their community without financial reward. Mems: 1.4m. in over 44,500 clubs in 185 countries and geographic areas. Exec. Admin. WIN HAMILTON. Publ. *The Lion* (10 a year, in 20 languages).

Médecins sans frontières—MSF: 39 rue de la Tourelle, 1040 Brussels, Belgium; tel. (2) 280-18-81; fax (2) 280-01-73; internet www.msf.org; f. 1971; independent medical humanitarian org composed of physicians and other members of the medical profession; aims to provide medical assistance to victims of war and natural disasters; operates longer-term programmes of nutrition, immunization, sanitation, public health, and rehabilitation of hospitals and dispensaries; awarded the Nobel peace prize in Oct. 1999. Mems: national sections in 18 countries in Europe, Asia and North America. Pres. Dr NORTEN ROSTRUP; Sec.-Gen. RAFAEL VILASANJUAN. Publ. *Activity Report* (annually).

Pan Pacific and South East Asia Women's Association—PPSEAWA: POB 119, Nuku'alofa, Tonga; tel. 24003; fax 41404; e-mail nanasi@kalianet.to; internet www.ppseawa.org; f. 1928 to foster better understanding and friendship among women in the region, and to promote co-operation for the study and improvement of social conditions; holds international conference every three years. Mems: 19 national member organizations. Pres. HRH Princess NANASIPAU'U TUKU'AHO. Publ. *PPSEAWA Bulletin.*

Rotary International: 1560 Sherman Ave, Evanston, IL 60201, USA; tel. (847) 866-3000; fax (847) 328-8554; e-mail wenerm@rotaryintl.org; internet www.rotary.org; f. 1905 to carry out activities for the service of humanity, to promote high ethical standards in business and professions and to further international understanding, goodwill and peace. Mems: over 1,195,000 in 30,462 Rotary Clubs in 162 countries. Pres. RICHARD D. KING; Gen. Sec. EDWIN H. FUTA (USA). Publs *The Rotarian* (monthly, English), *Rotary World* (5 a year, in 9 languages), *News Basket* (weekly).

Service Civil International—SCI: St-Jacobsmarkt 82, 2000 Antwerp, Belgium; tel. (3) 266-57-27; fax (3) 232-03-44; e-mail sciint@sciint.org; internet www.sciint.org; f. 1920 to promote peace and understanding through voluntary service projects. Mems: 14,000 in 36 countries. Pres. M. RAJUDEEN. Publ. *Action* (quarterly).

Society of Saint Vincent de Paul: 5 rue du Pré-aux-Clercs, 75007 Paris, France; tel. 1-44-55-36-55; fax 1-42-61-72-56; e-mail stvincent.cgi@wanadoo.fr; internet www.cef.fr/vincenpaul; f. 1833 to conduct charitable activities such as childcare, youth work, work with immigrants, adult literacy programmes, residential care for the sick, handicapped and elderly, social counselling and work with prisoners and the unemployed, through personal contact. Mems: over 800,000 in 132 countries. Pres. JOSÉ RAMÓN DÍAZ TORREMOCHA; Sec.-Gen. YVES VERRÉ. Publ. *Vincenpaul* (quarterly, in French, English and Spanish).

SOLIDAR: 22 rue de Commerce, 1000 Brussels, Belgium; tel. (2) 500-10-20; fax (2) 500-10-30; e-mail solidar@skynet.be; internet www.solidar.org; f. 1951 (frmly International Workers' Aid); an asscn of independent development and social welfare agencies based in Europe, linked to the labour and democratic socialist movements; aims to contribute to the creation of radical models of economic and social development, and to advance practical solutions that enable people to have increased control over their future. Mems: agencies in 90 countries. Sec.-Gen. GIAMPIERO ALHADEFF.

World Blind Union: c/o CBC ONCE, 18 La Coruña, 28020 Madrid, Spain; tel. (91) 5713675; fax (91) 5715777; e-mail umc@once.es; internet www.once.es/wbu; f. 1984 (amalgamating the World Council for the Welfare of the Blind and the International Federation of the Blind) to work for the prevention of blindness and the welfare of blind and visually-impaired people; encourages development of braille, talking book programmes and other media for the blind; organizes rehabilitation, training and employment; works on the prevention and cure of blindness in co-operation with the International Agency for the Prevention of Blindness; co-ordinates aid to the blind in developing countries; maintains the Louis Braille birth-place as an international museum. Mems: in 146 countries. Pres. EUCLID HERIE (Canada); Sec.-Gen. PEDRO ZURITA (Spain). Publ. *World Blind* (2 a year, in English, English Braille and on cassette, in Spanish and Spanish Braille and on cassette, and in French).

World Federation of the Deaf—WFD: POB 65, 00401 Helsinki, Finland; e-mail carol-lee.aquiline@wfdnews.org; internet www.wfdnews.org; f. 1951 to serve the interests of deaf people and their national organizations and represent these in international fora; works towards the goal of full participation by deaf people in society; encourages deaf people to set up and run their own organizations; priority is given to the promotion of the recognition and use of national sign languages, the education of deaf people and deaf people in the developing world. Mems: 120 member countries. Pres. LIISA KAUPPINEN; Gen. Sec. CAROL-LEE AQUILINE. Publ. *WFD News* (3 a year).

World ORT: ORT House, 126 Albert St, London, NW1 7NE, United Kingdom; tel. (20) 7446-8500; fax (20) 7446-8650; internet www.ort.org; f. 1880 for the development of industrial, agricultural and artisanal skills among Jews; now, a highly developed educational and training organization active in over 60 countries throughout the world; conducts vocational training programmes for adolescents and adults, including instructors' and teachers' education and apprenticeship training in more than 40 countries, including technical assistance programmes in co-operation with interested governments. Mems: committees in over 40 countries. Dir-Gen. ROBERT SINGER. Publs *Annual Report, Frontline News, World ORT Times*

World Veterans Federation: 17 rue Nicolo, 75116 Paris, France; tel. 1-40-72-61-00; fax 1-40-72-80-58; e-mail fmawvf@cybercable.fr; f. 1950 to maintain international peace and security by the application of the San Francisco Charter and work to help implement the Universal Declaration of Human Rights and related international conventions; aims to defend the spiritual and material interests of war veterans and war victims; promotes practical international co-operation in disarmament, legislation concerning war veterans and war victims, and development of international humanitarian law, etc; in 1986 established International Socio-Medical Information Centre (United Kingdom) for psycho-medical problems resulting from stress. Regional committees for Africa, Asia and the Pacific, and Europe and Standing Committee on Women. Mems: national organizations in 84 countries, representing about 27m. war veterans and war victims. Pres. ABDUL HAMID IBRAHIM; Sec.-Gen. MAREK HAGMAJER (Poland). Publs special studies (disarmament, human rights, rehabilitation).

Zonta International: 557 W. Randolph St, Chicago, IL 60661-2206, USA; tel. (312) 930-5848; fax (312) 930-0951; e-mail zontaint@zonta.org; internet www.zonta.org; f. 1919; links executives in business and the professions, with the aim of advancing the status of women world-wide; carries out local and international projects; supports women's education and leadership; makes fellowship awards in various areas. Mems: 34,000 in 70 countries. Pres. MARGIT WEBJORN; Exec. Dir JANET HALSTEAD. Publ. *The Zontian* (quarterly).

Sport and Recreations

Arab Sports Confederation: POB 62997, Riyadh 11442, Saudi Arabia; tel. (1) 482-9427; fax (1) 482-3196; f. 1976 to encourage regional co-operation in sport. Mems: 20 national Olympic Committees, 36 Arab sports federations. Sec.-Gen. OTHMAN M. AS-SAAD. Publ. *Annual Report.*

Fédération Aéronautique Internationale—FAI (World Air Sports Federation): 24 ave Mon Repos, 1005 Lausanne, Switzerland; e-mail sec@fai.org; internet www.fai.org; f. 1905 to promote all aeronautical sports; organizes world championships; develops rules through Air Sports Commissions; endorses world aeronautical and astronautical records. Mems: in 96 countries and territories. Pres. WOLFGANG WEINREICH; Sec.-Gen. MAX BISHOP. Publ. *Air Sports International.*

General Association of International Sports Federations—GAISF (Association générale de fédérations internationales de sports): 4 blvd du Jardin Exotique, Monte Carlo, Monaco; tel. 97-97-65-10; fax 93-25-28-73; e-mail info@agfisonline.com; internet www.agfisonline.com; f. 1967 to act as a forum for the exchange of ideas and discussion of common problems in sport; collects and circulates information; and provides secretarial, translation, documentation and consultancy services for members. Mems: 95 international sports organizations. Pres. Dr UN YONG KIM (Republic of Korea); Sec.-Gen. DON PORTER (USA). Publs *Calendar of International Sports Competitions* (2 a year), *Sportvision Magazine* (quarterly, in English and French), *GAISF Calendar, Sport and Education* and *Sport and Media*.

International Amateur Athletic Federation—IAAF: 17 rue Princesse Florestine, BP 359, 98007 Monte Carlo Cédex, Monaco; tel. 93-10-88-88; fax 93-15-95-15; e-mail headquarters @iaaf.org; f. 1912 to ensure co-operation and fairness and to combat discrimination in athletics; compiles athletic competition rules and organizes championships at all levels; frames regulations for the establishment of World, Olympic and other athletic records; settles disputes between members; conducts a programme of development consisting of coaching, judging courses, etc.; and affiliates national governing bodies. Mems: national asscns in 210 countries and territories. Gen. Sec. ISTVÁN GYULAI (Hungary). Publs *IAAF Handbook* (every 2 years), *IAAF Review* (quarterly), *IAAF Directory* (annually), *New Studies in Athletics* (quarterly).

International Amateur Boxing Association—AIBA: POB 76343, Atlanta, GA 30358, USA; tel. (770) 455-8350; fax (770) 454-6467; e-mail lbaker27@mindspring.com; internet www.aiba .net; f. 1946 as the world body controlling amateur boxing for the Olympic Games, continental, regional and inter-nation championships and tournaments in every part of the world. Mems: 191 national asscns. Pres. Prof. A. CHOWDHRY (Pakistan); Sec.-Gen. LORING K. BAKER (USA). Publ. *World Amateur Boxing Magazine* (quarterly).

International Amateur Radio Union: POB 310905, Newington, CT 06131-0905, USA; tel. (860) 594-0200; fax (860) 594-0259; internet www.iaru.org; f. 1925 to link national amateur radio societies and represent the interests of two-way amateur radio communication. Mems: 150 national amateur radio societies. Pres. LARRY E. PRICE; Sec. DAVID SUMNER.

International Archery Federation (Fédération internationale de tir à l'arc—FITA): 135 ave de Cour, 1007 Lausanne, Switzerland; tel. (21) 6143050; fax (21) 6143055; e-mail info@archery .org; internet www.archery.org; f. 1931 to promote international archery; organizes world championships and Olympic tournaments; holds Biennial Congress (2001: Beijing, People's Republic of China). Mems: national amateur asscns in 130 countries. Pres. JAMES L. EASTON (USA); Sec.-Gen. GIUSEPPE CINNIRELLA (Italy). Publs *Information FITA* (monthly), *The Arrow* (bulletin, quarterly), *The Target* (annually).

International Automobile Federation (Fédération internationale de l'automobile—FIA): 2 chemin de Blandonnet, CP 296, 1215 Geneva, Switzerland; tel. (22) 5444400; fax (22) 5444450; internet www.fia.com; f. 1904; manages world motor sport and organizes international championships. Mems: 157 national automobile clubs and asscns in 119 countries. Pres. MAX MOSLEY; Sec.-Gen. (Sport) PIERRE DE CONINCK; Sec.-Gen. (Tourism) PETER DOGGWILER.

International Badminton Federation—IBF: Manor Park Place, Rutherford Way, Cheltenham, Gloucestershire, GL51 9TU, United Kingdom; tel. (1242) 234904; fax (1242) 221030; e-mail info@intbadfed.org; internet www.intbadfed.org; f. 1934 to oversee the sport of badminton world-wide. Mems: affiliated national organizations in 147 countries and territories. Pres. LU SHENGRONG; Chief Exec. NEIL CAMERON (UK). Publs *World Badminton* (available on internet), *Statute Book* (annually).

International Basketball Federation (Fédération internationale de basketball): POB 700607, 81306 Munich, Germany; tel. (89) 7481580; fax (89) 74815833; e-mail secretariat@office .fiba.com; internet www.fiba.com; f. 1932 as International Amateur Basketball Federation (present name adopted 1989); aims to promote, supervise and direct international basketball; organizes quadrennial congress. Mems: affiliated national federations in 211 countries. Sec.-Gen. BORISLAV STANKOVIC. Publs *FIBA Assist* (monthly), *FIBA Media Guide*.

International Canoe Federation: Dozsa György ut. 1-3, 1143 Budapest, Hungary; tel. (1) 363-4832; fax (1) 221-4130; e-mail icf-hq-budapest@mail.datanet.hu; internet www.datanet.hu/icf-hq; f. 1924; administers canoeing at the Olympic Games; promotes canoe/kayak activity in general. Mems: 108 national federations. Pres. ULRICH FELDHOFF; Sec.-Gen. OTTO BONN.

International Council for Health, Physical Education, Recreation, Sport and Dance—ICHPERSD: 1900 Association Drive, Reston, VA 20191, USA; tel. (800) 213-7193; internet www.ichpersd.org; f. 1958 to encourage the development of programmes in health, physical education, recreation, sport and dance throughout the world, by linking teaching professionals in these fields.

International Cricket Council: Lord's Cricket Ground, London, NW8 8QN, United Kingdom; tel. (20) 7266-1818; fax (20) 7266-1777; internet www.cricket.org; f. 1909 as the governing body for international cricket; holds an annual conference. Mems: Australia, England, India, New Zealand, Pakistan, South Africa, Sri Lanka, West Indies, Zimbabwe, and 23 associate and 13 affiliate mems. Chief Exec. D. L. RICHARDS.

International Cycling Union: 37 route de Chavannes, 1007 Lausanne, Switzerland; tel. (21) 6220580; fax (21) 6220588; e-mail admin@uci.ch; internet www.uci.ch; f. 1900 to develop, regulate and control all forms of cycling as a sport. Mems: 158 federations. Pres. HEIN VERBRUGGEN (Netherlands). Publs *International Calendar* (annually), *Velo World* (6 a year).

International Equestrian Federation: CP 157, ave Mon-Repos 24, 1000 Lausanne 5, Switzerland; tel. (21) 3104747; fax (21) 3104760; e-mail info@horsesport.org; internet www.horse sport.org; f. 1921; international governing body of equestrian sport recognized by the International Olympic Committee; establishes rules and regulations for conduct of international equestrian events, including on the health and welfare of horses. Mems: 127 member countries. Sec.-Gen. Dr BO HELANDER.

International Federation of Associated Wrestling Styles: 17 ave Juste-Olivier, 1006 Lausanne, Switzerland; tel. (21) 3128426; fax (21) 3236073; e-mail filalausanne@bluewin.ch; internet www.fila_wrestling.org; f. 1912 to encourage the development of amateur wrestling and promote the sport in countries where it is not yet practiced and to further friendly relations between all members. Mems: 142 federations. Pres. MILAN ERCEGAN; Sec.-Gen. MICHEL DUSSON. Publs *News Bulletin, Wrestling Revue*.

International Federation of Association Football (Fédération internationale de football association—FIFA): Hitzigweg 11, POB 85, 8030 Zürich, Switzerland; tel. (1) 3849595; fax (1) 3849696; internet www.fifa.com; f. 1904 to promote the game of association football and foster friendly relations among players and national asscns; to control football and uphold the laws of the game as laid down by the International Football Association Board; to prevent discrimination of any kind between players; and to provide arbitration in disputes between national asscns; organizes World Cup competition every four years. Mems: 204 national asscns, six regional confederations. Pres. JOSEPH S. BLATTER (Switzerland); Gen. Sec. MICHEL ZEN-RUFFINEN. Publs *FIFA News* (monthly), *FIFA Magazine* (every 2 months) (both in English, French, Spanish and German).

International Federation of Park and Recreation Administration—IFPRA: Globe House, Crispin Close, Caversham, Reading, Berks, RG4 7JS, United Kingdom; tel. and fax (118) 946-1680; e-mail ifpraworld@yahoo.co.uk; internet www.ifpra.org; f. 1957 to provide a world centre for members of government departments, local authorities, and all organizations concerned with recreational services to discuss relevant matters. Mems: 550 in over 50 countries. Gen. Sec. ALAN SMITH (UK). Publ. *IFPRA Bulletin*.

International Fencing Federation (Fédération internationale d'escrime—FIE): ave Mon-Repos 24, CP 128, 1000 Lausanne 5, Switzerland; tel. (21) 3203115; fax (21) 3203116; e-mail contact@fie.ch; internet www.fie.ch; f. 1913; promotes development and co-operation between amateur fencers; determines rules for international events; organizes World Championships. Mems: 109 national federations. Pres. RENÉ ROCH.

International Gymnastic Federation: rue des Oeuches 10, CP 359, 2740 Moutier 1, Switzerland; tel. (32) 4946410; fax (32) 4946419; e-mail gymnastics@fig.worldsport.org; f. 1881 to promote the exchange of official documents and publications on gymnastics. Mems: in 122 countries and territories. Pres. BRUNO GRANDI; Gen. Sec. NORBERT BUECHE (Switzerland). Publs *FIG Bulletin* (quarterly), *World of Gymnastics Magazine* (quarterly).

International Hockey Federation: 1 ave des Arts, Boîte 5, 1210 Brussels, Belgium; tel. (2) 219-45-37; fax (2) 219-27-61; e-mail fih@fihockey.org; internet www.fihockey.org; f. 1924 to fix the rules of outdoor and indoor hockey for all affiliated national asscns; to control the game of hockey and indoor hockey and to control the organization of international tournaments, such as the Olympic Games and the World Cup. Mems: 120 national asscns. Pres. JUAN ANGEL CALZADO; Sec.-Gen. ELS VAN BREDA-VRIESMAN. Publ. *World Hockey* (quarterly).

International Judo Federation: 12 rue Maamoun, 1082 Tunis, Tunisia; tel. (1) 781-057; fax (1) 801-517; e-mail dhouib @gnet.tn; internet www.ijf.org; f. 1951 to promote cordial and friendly relations between members; to protect the interests of judo throughout the world; to organize World Championships and the judo events of the Olympic Games; to develop and spread the techniques and spirit of judo throughout the world; and to establish international judo regulations. Pres. YONG SUNG PARK (Republic of Korea); Gen. Sec. Dr HEDI DHOUIB (Tunisia).

International Paralympic Committee: Adenauerallee 212–214, 53113 Bonn, Germany; tel. (228) 2097200; fax (228) 2097209; e-mail info@paralympic.org; internet www.paralympic .org; f. 1989; responsible for organizing the paralympic games for sportspeople with disabilities, which are held alongside the Olympic Games. Mems: 160 national paralympic committees and 5 disability-specific international sports federations. Pres. PHILIP CRAVEN (UK); Chief Operating Officer THOMAS REINECKE (Germany). Publ. *The Paralympian* (quarterly).

International Philatelic Federation: Jupiterstrasse 49, 9032 Zürich, Switzerland; tel. (1) 4223839; fax (1) 4223843; e-mail heiri@f-i-p.ch; internet www.f-i-p.ch/; f. 1926 to promote philately internationally. Pres. KNUD MOHR; Sec.-Gen. MARIE-LOUISE HEIRI.

International Rowing Federation (Fédération internationale des sociétés d'aviron—FISA): 135 ave de Cour, CP 18, 1000 Lausanne 3, Switzerland; tel. (21) 6178373; fax (21) 6178375; e-mail info@fisa.org; internet www.worldrowing.com; f. 1892 to establish contacts between rowers in all countries and to draw up racing rules; serves as the world controlling body of the sport of rowing. Mems: national federations in 112 countries. Pres. DENIS OSWALD; Sec.-Gen. and Exec. Dir MATTHEW SMITH. Publs *FISA Guide* (annually), *FISA World Rowing Magazine* (quarterly), *FISA Bulletins*(annually).

International Sailing Federation—ISAF: Ariadne House, Town Quay, Southampton, Hants, SO14 2AQ, United Kingdom; tel. (2380) 635111; fax (2380) 635789; e-mail sail@isaf.co.uk; internet www.sailing.org; f. 1907; serves as the controlling authority of sailing in all its forms throughout the world; establishes and amends international yacht racing rules; organizes the Olympic Sailing Regatta and other championships. Mems: 117 national yachting federations. Pres. PAUL HENDERSON; Sec.-Gen. ARVE SUNDHEIM. Publ *Making Waves*.

International Shooting Sport Federation—ISSF: 80336 Munich, Bavariaring 21, Germany; tel. (89) 5443550; fax (89) 54435544; e-mail munich@issf-shooting.org; internet www.issf -shooting.org; f. 1907 to promote and guide the development of amateur shooting sports; organizes World Championships and controls the organization of continental and regional championships; supervises the shooting events of the Olympic and Continental Games under the auspices of the International Olympic Committee. Mems: 151 federations in 146 countries. Pres. OLEGARIO VÁZQUEZ-RAÑA (Mexico); Sec.-Gen. HORST G. SCHREIBER (Germany). Publs *ISSF News, International Shooting Sport* (6 a year).

International Skating Union—ISU: chemin de Primerose 2, 1007 Lausanne, Switzerland; tel. (21) 6126666; fax (21) 6126677; e-mail info@isu.ch; internet www.isu.org; f. 1892; holds regular conferences. Mems: 72 national federations in 56 countries. Pres. OTTAVIO CINQUANTA; Gen.-Sec. FREDI SCHMID. Publs Judges' manuals, referees' handbooks, general and special regulations.

International Ski Federation (Fédération internationale de ski—FIS): 3653 Oberhofen am Thunersee, Switzerland; tel. (33) 2446161; fax (33) 2446171; internet www.fis-ski.com; f. 1924 to further the sport of skiing; to prevent discrimination in skiing matters on racial, religious or political grounds; to organize World Ski Championships and regional championships and, as supreme international skiing authority, to establish the international competition calendar and rules for all ski competitions approved by the FIS, and to arbitrate in any disputes. Mems: 100 national ski asscns. Pres. GIAN-FRANCO KASPER (Switzerland); Sec.-Gen. SARAH LEWIS (UK). Publ. *FIS Bulletin* (quarterly).

International Swimming Federation (Fédération internationale de natation—FINA): POB 4, ave de l'Avant, 1005 Lausanne, Switzerland; tel. (21) 3126602; fax (21) 3126610; internet www.fina.org; f. 1908 to promote amateur swimming and swimming sports internationally; administers rules for swimming sports, competitions and for establishing records; organizes world championships and FINA events; runs a development programme to increase the popularity and quality of aquatic sports. Mems: 180 federations. Pres. MUSTAPHA LARFAOUI (Algeria); Exec. Dir CORNEL MARCULESCU. Publs *Handbook* (every 4 years), *FINA News* (monthly), *World of Swimming* (quarterly).

International Table Tennis Federation: ave Mon-Repos 30, 1005 Lausanne, Switzerland; tel. (21) 3407090; fax (21) 3407099; e-mail ittf@ittf.com; internet www.ittf.com; f. 1926. Pres. ADHAM SHARARA. Publs *Table Tennis Illustrated, Table Tennis Legends*.

International Tennis Federation: Bank Lane, Roehampton, London, SW15 5XZ, United Kingdom; tel. (20) 8878-6464; fax (20) 8878-7799; e-mail communications@itftennis.com; internet www.itftennis.com; f. 1913 to govern the game of tennis throughout the world, promote its teaching and preserve its independence of outside authority; produces the Rules of Tennis; promotes the Davis Cup Competition for men, the Fed. Cup for women, the Olympic Games Tennis Event, wheelchair tennis, 16 cups for veterans, the ITF Sunshine Cup and the ITF Continental Connelly Cup for players of 18 years old and under, the World Youth Cup for players of 16 years old and under, and the World Junior Tennis Tournament for players of 14 years old and under; organizes tournaments. Mems: 141 full and 57 associate. Pres. FRANCESCO RICCI BITTI. Publs *World of Tennis* (annually), *Davis Cup Yearbook, ITF World* (quarterly), *ITF This Week* (weekly).

International Volleyball Federation (Fédération internationale de volleyball—FIVB): ave de la Gare 12, 1001 Lausanne, Switzerland; tel. (21) 3453535; fax (21) 3453545; e-mail info@mail.fivb.ch; internet www.fivb.org; f. 1947 to encourage, organize and supervise the playing of volleyball, beach volleyball, and park volley; organizes biennial congress. Mems: 218 national federations. Pres. Dr RUBÉN ACOSTA HERNÁNDEZ; Gen. Man. JEAN-PIERRE SEPPEY. Publs *VolleyWorld* (every 2 months), *X-Press* (monthly).

International Weightlifting Federation—IWF: PF 614, 1374 Budapest, Hungary; tel. (1) 3530530; fax (1) 3530199; e-mail iwf@iwf.net; internet www.iwf.net; f. 1905 to control international weightlifting; draws up technical rules; trains referees; supervises World Championships, Olympic Games, regional games and international contests of all kinds; registers world records. Mems: 167 national organizations. Pres. Dr THOMÁS AJAN (Hungary); Gen. Sec. YANNIS SGOUROS (Greece). Publs *IWF Constitution and Rules* (every 4 years), *World Weightlifting* (quarterly).

International World Games Association: Ekeby House, Luiksestraat 23, 2587 The Hague, Netherlands; tel. (70) 3512774; fax (70) 3509911; e-mail iwga@hetnet.nl; internet www.worldgames-iwga.org; f. 1980; organizes World Games every four years (2001: Akita, Japan), comprising 26 sports that are not included in the Olympic Games. Sec.-Gen. J. A. P. KOREN.

Union of European Football Associations—UEFA: route de Genève 46, 1260 Nyon 2, Switzerland; tel. (22) 9944444; fax (22) 9944488; internet www.uefa.com; f. 1954; works on behalf of Europe's national football asscns to promote football; aims to foster unity and solidarity between national asscns. Mems: 51 national asscns. Pres. LENNART JOHANSSON; CEO GERHARD AIGNER. Publ *Magazine* (available on-line).

World Boxing Organization: c/o 100 West Randolph St, 9th Floor, Chicago, IL 60601, USA; tel. (312) 814-3145; fax (312)

814-2719; internet www.wbo-int.com; f. 1962; regulates professional boxing.

World Bridge Federation: 56 route de Vandoeuvres, 1253 Geneva, Switzerland; tel. (22) 7501541; fax (22) 7501620; internet www.bridge.gr; f. 1958 to promote the game of contract bridge throughout the world; federates national bridge asscns in all countries; conducts world championships competitions; establishes standard bridge laws. Mems: 89 countries. Pres. ERNESTO D'ORSI (Brazil). Publ. *World Bridge News* (quarterly).

World Chess Federation (Fédération internationale des echecs—FIDE): POB 166, 1000 Lausanne 4, Switzerland; tel. (21) 3103900; e-mail fide@fide.ch; internet www.fide.com; f. 1924; controls chess competitions of world importance and awards international chess titles. Mems: national orgs in more than 160 countries. Pres. KIRSAN ILYUMZHINOV. Publs *FIDE Forum* (every 2 months), *FIDE Handbook* (annually), *International Rating List* (2 a year).

World Squash Federation Ltd: 6 Havelock Rd, Hastings, East Sussex, TN34 1BP, United Kingdom; tel. (1424) 429245; fax (1424) 429250; e-mail squash@wsf.cablenet.co.uk; internet www.worldsquash.org; f. 1966 to maintain quality and reputation of squash and increase its popularity; monitors rules and makes recommendations for change; trains, accredits and assesses international and world referees; sets standards for all technical aspects of squash; co-ordinates coaching training and awards; runs World Championships. Mems: 115 national organizations. Exec. Dir EDWARD J. WALLBUTTON.

World Underwater Federation: Viale Tiziano 74, 00196 Rome, Italy; tel. (06) 36858480; fax (02) 22110595; e-mail amasmond@tin.it; internet www.cmas2000.org; f. 1959 to develop underwater activities; to form bodies to instruct in the techniques of underwater diving; to perfect existing equipment, encourage inventions and experiment with newly marketed products; and to organize international competitions. Mems: organizations in 90 countries. Pres. ACHILLE FERRERO (Italy); Sec. PIERRE DERNIER (Belgium). Publs *International Year Book of CMAS, Scientific Diving: A Code of Practice,* manuals.

Technology

International Union of Technical Associations and Organizations (Union internationale des associations et organismes techniques—UATI): UNESCO House, 1 rue Miollis, 75015 Paris Cédex 15, France; tel. 1-45-68-27-70; fax 1-43-06-29-27; e-mail uati@unesco.org; internet www.unesco.org/uati; f. 1951 (fmrly Union of International Technical Associations) under the auspices of UNESCO; aims to promote and co-ordinate activities of member organizations and represent their interests; facilitates relations with international organizations, notably UN agencies; receives proposals and makes recommendations on the establishment of new international technical asscns. Mems: 25 organizations. Chair. PHILIPPE AUSSOURD (France). Publ. *Convergence* (3 a year).

MEMBER ORGANIZATIONS

Members of UATI include the following:

International Association of Hydraulic Engineering and Research—IAHR: Paseo Bajo Virgen del Puerto 3, 28005 Madrid, Spain; tel. (91) 3357908; fax (91) 3357935; e-mail iahr@iahr.org; internet www.iahr.org; f. 1935; promotes advancement and exchange of knowledge on hydraulic engineering; holds biennial congresses and symposia. Mems: 1,850 individual, 300 corporate. Sec.-Gen. C. MATCOS (Spain). Publs *IAHR Bulletin, Journal of Hydraulic Research, Proceedings of Biennial Conferences.*

International Association of Lighthouse Authorities: 20 ter rue Schnapper, 78100 St Germain en Laye, France; tel. 1-34-51-70-01; fax 1-34-51-82-05; e-mail aismiala@easynet.fr; internet www.iala-aism.org; f. 1957; holds technical conference every four years; working groups study special problems and formulate technical recommendations, guide-lines and manuals. Mems in 80 countries. Sec.-Gen. TORSTEN KRUUSE. Publ. *Bulletin* (quarterly).

International Bridge, Tunnel and Turnpike Association: 1146 19th St, NW, Suite 800, Washington, DC 20036-3725, USA; tel. (202) 659-4620; fax (202) 659-0500; e-mail ibtta@ibtta.org; internet www.ibtta.org; f. 1932 to serve as a forum for sharing knowledge, with the aim of promoting toll-financed transportation services. Mems: 240 mems in 22 countries. Exec. Dir. PATRICK D. JONES. Publ. *Tollways* (monthly).

International Commission of Agricultural Engineering—CIGR: Institut für Landtechnik, Universität Bonn, Nussallee 5, 53 115 Bonn, Germany; tel. (228) 732389; fax (228) 739644; e-mail cigr@uni-bonn.de; internet www.cigr.org; f. 1930; aims to stimulate development of science and technology in agricultural engineering; encourages education, training and mobility of professionals; facilitates exchange of research; represents profession at international level. Mems: asscns from more than 60 countries. Pres. Prof. E. H. BARTALI (Morocco); Sec.-Gen. P. SCHULZE LAMMERS (Germany). Publs *Bulletin de la CIGR, Newsletter* (quarterly), technical reports.

International Commission on Glass: Stazione Sperimentale del Vetro, Via Briati 10, 30141 Murano, Venice, Italy; tel. (041) 739422; fax (041) 739420; e-mail spevetro@ve-nettuno.it; internet www.nettuno.it/fiera/spevetro; f. 1933 to co-ordinate research in glass and allied products, exchange information and organize conferences. Mems: 30 organizations. Pres. D. PYE; Sec.-Gen. F. NICOLETTI.

International Commission on Irrigation and Drainage: 48 Nyaya Marg, Chanakyapuri, New Delhi 110 021, India; tel. (11) 6115679; fax (11) 6115962; e-mail icid@icid.org; internet www.icid.org; f. 1950; holds triennial congresses. Mems: 70 national committees. Pres. BART SCHULTZ (Netherlands); Sec.-Gen. C. D. THATTE (India). Publs *Journal* (quarterly), *World Irrigation, Multilingual Technical Dictionary, World Flood Control,* technical books.

International Federation for the Promotion of Mechanism and Machine Science: PO Box 4200, Univ. of Oulu, 90014 Oulu, Finland; tel. (8) 553-2050; fax (8) 553-2026; e-mail tatu@me.oulu.fi; internet www.caip.rutgers.edu/iftomm; f. 1969 to study robots, man-machine systems, etc. Pres. K. WALDRON; Sec.-Gen. T. LEINONEN. Publ. *Mechanism and Machine Theory.*

International Federation of Automatic Control—IFAC: 2361 Laxenburg, Schlossplatz 12, Austria; tel. (2236) 71447; fax (2236) 72859; e-mail secr@ifac.co.at; internet www.ifac-control.org; f. 1957 to serve those concerned with the theory and application of automatic control and systems engineering. Mems: 48 national asscns. Pres. Prof. YONG ZAI LU (China); Sec. G. HENCSEY. Publs *Automatica and Control Engineering Practice* (bi-monthly), *Newsletter* and affiliated journals.

International Gas Union: c/o N.V. Nederlandse Gasunie, POB 19, 9700 MA Groningen, Netherlands; tel. (50) 5212999; fax (50) 5255951; e-mail secr.igu@gasnie.nl; internet www.igu.org; f. 1931 to study all aspects and problems of the gas industry, with a view to promoting international co-operation and the general improvement of the industry. Mems: national organizations in 59 countries. Pres. C. DÉTOURNÉ (France); Sec.-Gen. J. F. MEEDER (Netherlands).

International Institute of Welding: 90 rue des Vanesses, ZI Paris Nord II, 93420 Villepinte, France; tel. 1-49-90-36-08; fax 1-49-90-36-80; e-mail iiw@wanadoo.fr; internet www.iiw-iis.org; f. 1948. Mems: 52 societies in 40 countries. Pres. Y. FUJITA (Japan); Chief Exec. M. BRAMAT (France). Publ. *Welding in the World* (7 a year).

International Measurement Confederation—IMEKO: POB 457, 1371 Budapest 5, Hungary; tel. and fax (1) 353-1562; e-mail imeko.ime@mtesz.hu; internet www.imeko.org; f. 1958 as a federation of member organizations concerned with the advancement of measurement technology; aims to promote exchange of scientific and technical information in field of measurement and instrumentation and to enhance co-operation between scientists and engineers; holds World Congress every 3 years (2003: Dubrovnik; 2006: Rio de Janeiro). Mems: 36 orgs. Pres. Prof. M. PETERS (Germany); Sec.-Gen. Dr TAMÁS KEMÉNY (Hungary). Publs *Acta IMEKO* (proccedings of World Congresses), *IMEKO TC Events Series, Measurement* (quarterly), *IMEKO Bulletin* (2 a year).

International Navigation Association: Graaf de Ferraris, 11e étage, bte 3, 156 blvd Roi Albert II, 1000 Brussels, Belgium; tel. (2) 553-71-60; fax (2) 553-71-55; e-mail navigation-aipcn-pianc@tornado.be; internet www.tornado.be/~navigation-aipcn

-pianc/; f. 1885; fmrly Permanent International Assoc. of Navigation Congresses (PIANC); fosters progress in the construction, maintenance and operation of inland and maritime waterways, of inland and maritime ports and of coastal areas; holds Congresses every four years. Mems: 40 governments, 2,780 others. Pres. Ir R. DE PAEPE; Sec.-Gen. C. VAN BEGIN. Publs *Bulletin* (quarterly), *Illustrated Technical Dictionary* (in 6 languages), technical reports, Congress papers.

International Union for Electricity Applications: Espace Elec. CNIT, BP 10, 2 place de la Défense, 92053 Paris, France; tel. 1-41-26-56-48; fax 1-41-26-56-49; e-mail uie@uie.org; internet www.uie.org; f. 1953, present title adopted 1994; aims to study all questions relative to electricity applications, except commercial questions; links national groups and organizes international congresses on electricity applications. Mems: national committees, corporate associated and individual members in 18 countries. Pres. RONNIE BELMANS (Belgium); Gen. Sec. Prof. MICHEL MACHIELS. Publs UIE and Electra Collection of reports, UIE proceedings.

International Union of Air Pollution Prevention and Environmental Protection Associations: 44 Grand Parade, Brighton, BN2 2QA, United Kingdom; tel. (1273) 878772; fax (1273) 606626; e-mail iuappa@nsca.org.uk; internet www.iuappa.fsnet.co.uk; f. 1963; organizes triennial World Clean Air Congress and regional conferences for developing countries (several a year). Pres. Dr W. H. PARK (Korea); Dir-Gen. R. MILLS. Publs *IUAPPA Newsletter* (quarterly), *Clean Air around the World.*

International Union of Testing and Research Laboratories for Materials and Structures: Ecole Normale Supérieure, 61 ave du Président Wilson, 94235 Cachan Cédex, France; tel. 1-47-40-23-97; fax 1-47-40-01-13; e-mail sg@rilem.ens-cachan.fr; internet www.iabse.ethz.ch/lc/rilem.html; f. 1947 for the exchange of information and the promotion of co-operation on experimental research concerning structures and materials; studies research methods with a view to improvement and standardization. Mems: laboratories and individuals in 73 countries. Pres. Dr JACQUES BRESSON (France); Sec.-Gen. M. BRUSIN (France). Publ. *Materials and Structures—Testing and Research* (10 a year).

Union of the Electricity Industry—EURELECTRIC: Blvd de l'Impératrice 66, Box 2, 1000 Brussels, Belgium; tel. (2) 515-1000; fax (2) 510-1010; e-mail eurelectric@eurelectric.org; internet www.eurelectric.org; f. 1999 by merger of International Union of Producers and Distributors of Electrical Energy (UNIPEDE, f. 1925) and European Grouping of the Electricity Industry (EEIG, f. 1989); aims to study all questions relating to the production, transmission and distribution of electrical energy, and to promote the image of and defend the interests of the electricity supply industry. Pres. Dr ROLF BIERHOFF; Sec.-Gen. PAUL BULTEEL. Publ. *Watt's New* (newsletter).

World Energy Council: 5th Floor, Regency House, 1–4 Warwick St, London, W1B 5LT, United Kingdom; tel. (20) 7734-5996; fax (20) 7734-5926; e-mail info@worldenergy.org; internet www.worldenergy.org; f. 1924 to link all branches of energy and resources technology and maintain liaison between world experts; holds congresses every three years. Mems: 99 committees. Pres. M. GÓMEZ DE PABLOS (Spain); Sec.-Gen. GERALD DOUCET (Canada). Publs *Annual Report*, energy supply and demand projections, resources surveys, technical assessments, reports.

World Foundrymen Organization—WFO: Bordesley Hall, The Holloway, Avechurch, Birmingham B48 7QA, United Kingdom; tel. (1527) 596100; fax (1527) 596102; e-mail wfo@icme.org.uk; internet www.thewfo.com; Pres. C. W ARREN; Gen. Sec. Eng. A. TURNER.

World Road Association (PIARC): La Grande Arche, Paroi Nord, Niveau 8, 92055 La Défense Cédex, France; tel. 1-47-96-81-21; fax 1-49-00-02-02; e-mail piarc@wanadoo.fr; internet www.piarc.org; f. 1909 as the Permanent International Association of Road Congresses; aims to promote the construction, improvement, maintenance, use and economic development of roads; organizes technical committees and study sessions. Mems: governments, public bodies, organizations and private individuals in 100 countries. Pres. O. MICHAUD (Switzerland); Sec.-Gen. J. F. COSTE (France). Publs *Bulletin, Technical Dictionary, Lexicon,* technical reports.

OTHER ORGANIZATIONS

African Organization of Cartography and Remote Sensing: 5 Route de Bedjarah, BP 102, Hussein Dey, Algiers, Algeria; tel. (2) 77-79-34; fax (2) 77-79-34; e-mail oact@wissal.dz; f. 1988 by amalgamation of African Association of Cartography and African Council for Remote Sensing; aims to encourage the development of cartography and of remote sensing by satellites; organizes conferences and other meetings, promotes establishment of training institutions; maintains four regional training centres (in Burkina Faso, Kenya, Nigeria and Tunisia). Mems: national cartographic institutions of 24 African countries. Sec.-Gen. UNIS MUFTAH.

African Regional Centre for Technology: Imm. Fahd, 17th Floor, blvd Djilly Mbaye, BP 2435, Dakar, Senegal; tel. 823-77-12; fax 823-77-13; e-mail arct@sonatel.senet.net; f. 1977 to encourage the development of indigenous technology and to improve the terms of access to imported technology; assists the establishment of national centres. Mems: govts of 31 countries. Exec. Dir Dr OUSMANE KANE. Publs *African Technodevelopment, Alert Africa.*

AIIM International: 1100 Wayne Ave, Suite 1100, Silver Spring, USA; internet www.aiim.org; f. 1999 by merger of the Association for Information and Image Management (f. 1943) and the International Information Management Congress (f. 1962); serves as the international body of the document technologies industry. Chief Exec. JOHN H. MANCINI.

Bureau International de la Recupération et du Recyclage (Bureau of International Recycling): 24 ave Franklin Roosevelt, 1050 Brussels, Belgium; tel. (2) 627-57-70; fax (2) 627-57-73; e-mail bir@bir.org; internet www.bir.org; f. 1948 as the world federation of the reclamation and recycling industries; promotes international trade in scrap iron and steel, non-ferrous metals, paper, textiles, plastics and glass. Mems: asscns and individuals in 53 countries. Dir-Gen. FRANCIS VEYS.

ECMA—Standardizing Information and Communication Systems: 114 rue de Rhône, 1204 Geneva, Switzerland; tel. (22) 8496000; fax (22) 8496001; e-mail helpdesk@ecma.ch; internet www.ecma.ch; f. 1961 to develop standards and technical reports, in co-operation with the appropriate national, European and international organizations, in order to facilitate and standardize the use of information processing and telecommunications systems; promulgates various standards applicable to the functional design and use of these systems. Mems: 28 ordinary and 18 associate mems. Sec.-Gen. JAN VAN DEN BELD. Publs *ECMA Standards, ECMA Memento.*

EUREKA: 107 rue Neerveld, bte 5, 1200 Brussels, Belgium; tel. (2) 777-09-50; fax (2) 770-74-95; e-mail eureka.secretariat@es.eureka.be; internet www.eureka.be; f. 1985; aims to promote industrial collaboration between member countries on non-military research and development activities; enables joint development of technology; supports innovation and systematic use of standardization in new technology sectors. Mems: 32 in 31 countries. Sec.-Gen. Dr HEIKKI KOTILAINEN. Publs *Annual Report, Eureka Bulletin.*

European Convention for Constructional Steelwork—ECCS: 32-36 ave des Ombrages, bte 20, 1200 Brussels, Belgium; tel. (2) 762-04-29; fax (2) 762-09-35; e-mail eccs@steelconstruct.com; internet www.steelconstruct.com; f. 1955 for the consideration of problems involved in metallic construction. Mems: in 25 countries. Sec.-Gen. G. GENDEBEN. Publs Information sheets and documents, symposia reports, model codes.

European Federation of Chemical Engineering: c/o Institution of Chemical Engineers, Davis Bldg, 165–189 Railway Terrace, Rugby, Warwickshire, CV21 3HQ, United Kingdom; tel. (1788) 578214; fax (1788) 560833; internet www.icheme.org; f. 1953 to encourage co-operation between non-profit-making scientific and technical societies, for the advancement of chemical engineering and its application in the processing industries. Mems: 65 societies in 25 European countries, 15 corresponding societies in other countries. Chief Exec. Dr T. J. EVANS.

European Federation of Corrosion: 1 Carlton House Terrace, London, SW1Y 5DB, United Kingdom; tel. (20) 7839-4071; fax (20) 7839-1702; internet www.materials.org; f. 1955 to encourage co-operation in research on corrosion and methods of combating this. Mems: societies in 20 countries. Hon. Secs

J. P. BERGE (France), G. KREYSA (Germany), B. A. RICKINSON (UK); Scientific Sec. P. MCINTYRE (UK).

European Federation of National Engineering Associations (Fédération européenne d'associations nationales d'ingénieurs—FEANI): 21 rue du Beau Site, 1000 Brussels, Belgium; tel (2) 639-03-90; fax (2) 639-03-99; e-mail barbel.hakimi@feani.org; internet www.feani.org; f. 1951 to affirm the professional identity of the engineers of Europe and to strive for the unity of the engineering profession in Europe. Mems: 27 mem. countries. Pres. K. ALEXOPOULOS (Greece); Sec.-Gen. PHILIPPE WAUFERS (Belgium). Publs *FEANI News*, *INDEX*.

European Metal Union: Einsteinbaan 1, POB 2600, 3430 GA Nieuwegein, Netherlands; tel. (30) 605-33-44; fax (30) 605-31-15; e-mail info@metaalunie.nl; f. 1954 as International Union of Metal; liaises between national craft organizations and small and medium-sized enterprises in the metal industry; represents members' interests at a European level; provides for the exchange of information and ideas. Mems: national federations from Austria, Belgium, Germany, Luxembourg, Netherlands and Switzerland. Pres. WILLEMIEN VAN GARDINGEN (Netherlands); Sec. HARM-JAN KEIJER (Netherlands).

European Organisation for the Exploitation of Meteorological Satellites—EUMETSAT: 64295 Darmstadt, Am Kavalleriesand 31, Germany; tel. (6151) 807377; fax (6151) 807304; e-mail ops@eumetsat.de; internet www.eumetsat.de; f. 1986; maintains and exploits European systems of meteorological satellites, including the Meteosat programme for gathering weather data. Mems: 18 European countries and four co-operating states. Chair. Dr HENRI MALCORPS (Belgium); Dir Dr TILLMANN MOHR. Publs *Annual Report*, *IMAGE Newsletter*, brochures, conference and workshop proceedings.

European Organization for Civil Aviation Equipment—EUROCAE: 17 rue Hamelin, 75783 Paris Cédex 16, France; tel. 1-45-05-71-88; fax 1-45-05-72-30; e-mail eurocae@eurocae.com; internet www.eurocae.org; f. 1963; studies and advises on problems related to the equipment used in aeronautics; assists international bodies in the establishment of international standards. Mems: 92 manufacturers, organizations and research bodies. Pres. ALAN GARCIA; Sec.-Gen. FRANCIS GRIMAL. Publs Reports, documents and specifications on civil aviation equipment.

Eurospace: 15-17 ave de Ségur, 75005 Paris, France; tel. 1-44-42-00-70; fax 1-44-42-00-79; e-mail letterbox@eurospace.org; internet www.eurospace.org; f. 1961 as an asscn of European aerospace industrial companies responsible for promotion of European Space activity; carries out studies on the legal, economic, technical and financial aspects of space activity; acts as an industrial adviser to the European Space Agency, in particular with regard to future space programmes and industrial policy matters. Mems: 60 in 13 European countries. Pres. IVAN ÖFVERHOLM (Sweden); Sec.-Gen. ALAIN GAUBERT.

International Association for Bridge and Structural Engineering—IABSE: ETH—Hönggerberg, 8093 Zürich, Switzerland; tel. (1) 6332647; fax (1) 6331241; e-mail secretariat@iabse.ethz.ch; internet www.iabse.ethz.ch; f. 1929 to exchange knowledge and advance the practice of structural engineering world-wide. Mems: 4,400 government departments, local authorities, universities, institutes, firms and individuals in over 100 countries. Pres. MANABU ITO (Japan); Exec. Dir A. GOLAY. Publs *Structural Engineering International* (quarterly), *Congress Report*, *IABSE Report*, *Structural Engineering Documents*.

International Association for Cybernetics (Association internationale de cybernétique): Palais des Expositions, ave Sergent Vrithoff 2, 5000 Namur, Belgium; tel. (81) 71-71-71; fax (81) 71-71-00; e-mail cyb@info.fundp.ac.be; internet pespmc1.vub.ac.be/iac.html; f. 1957 to ensure liaison between research workers engaged in various sectors of cybernetics; promotes the development of the science and its applications; disseminates information. Mems: firms and individuals in 42 countries. Chair. J. RAMAEKERS; Gen. Sec. CARINE AIGRET. Publ. *Cybernetica* (quarterly).

International Association of Technological University Libraries—IATUL: c/o Dr Judith Palmer, Radcliffe Science Library, Oxford University, Parks Rd, Oxford OX1 3QP, United Kingdom; tel. (1865) 272820; fax (1865) 272832; e-mail judith.palmer@bodley.ox.ac.uk; internet www.iatul.org; f. 1955 to promote co-operation between member libraries and stimulate research on library problems. Mems: 202 university libraries in 41 countries. Pres. Dr MICHAEL BREAKS (UK); Sec. Dr JUDITH PALMER (UK). Publs *IATUL Proceedings*, *IATUL Newsletter* (electronic version only).

International Cargo Handling Co-ordination Association—ICHCA: Suite 2, 85 Western Rd, Romford, Essex RM1 3LS, United Kingdom; tel. (1708) 734787; fax (1708) 734877; e-mail info@ichca.org.uk; internet www.ichca.org.uk; f. 1952 to foster economy and efficiency in the movement of goods from origin to destination. Mems: 2,000 in 90 countries. Pres. KEN HOGGAT; Chief Exec. GERRY ASKHAM. Publs *Cargo Tomorrow: Cargo Handling News* (bimonthly), *World of Cargo Handling* (annually), *Who's Who in Cargo Handling* (annually), technical publs and reviews.

International Colour Association: c/o Frank Rochow, LMT Lichtmesstechnik GmbH Berlin, Helmholtzstr. 9, 10587 Berlin, Germany; tel. (30) 3934028; fax (30) 3918001; f. 1967 to encourage research in colour in all its aspects, disseminate the knowledge gained from this research and promote its application to the solution of problems in the fields of science, art and industry; holds international congresses and symposia. Mems: organizations in 28 countries. Pres. PAULA ALESSI (USA); Sec. and Treas. FRANK ROCHOW (Germany).

International Commission on Illumination—CIE: Kegelgasse 27, 1030 Vienna, Austria; tel. (1) 714-31-87-0; fax (1) 713-08-38-18; e-mail ciecb@ping.at; internet www.cie.co.at; f. 1900 as International Commission on Photometry, present name adopted 1913; aims to provide an international forum for all matters relating to the science and art of light and lighting; serves as a forum for the exchange of information; develops and publishes international standards and provides guidance in their application. Mems: 40 national committees and 12 individuals. Gen. Sec. C. HERMANN. Publs standards, technical reports.

International Commission on Large Dams: 151 blvd Haussmann, 75008 Paris, France; tel. 1-40-42-68-24; fax 1-40-42-60-71; e-mail secretaire.general@icold-cigb.org; internet www.icold-cigb.org./; f. 1928; holds triennial congresses (2000 congress: Beijing, People's Republic of China). Mems: in 80 countries. Pres. C. V. J. VARMA (India); Sec.-Gen. JACQUES LECORNU. Publs *Technical Bulletin* (3 or 4 a year), *World Register of Dams*, *World Register of Mine and Industrial Wastes*, *Technical Dictionary on Dams*, studies.

International Committee on Aeronautical Fatigue—ICAF: c/o Prof. O. Buxbaum, Fraunhofer-Institut für Betriebsfestigkeit LBF, 64289 Darmstadt, Bartningstrasse 47, Germany; tel. (6151) 7051; fax (6151) 705214; internet www.icaf2001.com; f. 1951 for collaboration between aeronautical bodies and laboratories on questions of fatigue of aeronautical structures; organizes periodical conferences. Mems: national centres in 13 countries. Sec. Prof. O. BUXBAUM (Germany).

International Council on Large High-Voltage Electric Systems (Conseil international des grands réseaux électriques—CIGRE): 21 rue d'Artois, 75008 Paris, France; tel. 1-53-89-12-90; fax 1-53-89-12-99; e-mail secretary-general@cigre.org; internet www.cigre.org; f. 1921 to facilitate and promote the exchange of technical knowledge and information in the general field of electrical generation and transmission at high voltages; holds general sessions (every 2 years) and symposia. Mems: 5,000 in 80 countries. Pres. D. CROFT (Australia); Sec.-Gen. J. KOWAL (France). Publ. *Electra* (every 2 months).

International Council for Research and Innovation in Building and Construction: Postbox 1837, 3000 BV Rotterdam, Netherlands; tel. (10) 4110240; fax (10) 4334372; e-mail secretariat@cibworld.nl; internet www.cibworld.nl; f. 1953 to encourage and facilitate co-operation in building research, studies and documentation in all aspects. Mems: governmental and industrial organizations and qualified individuals in 70 countries. Pres. Dr S. A. BARAKAT (Canada); Sec.-Gen. W. J. P. BAKENS. Publs *Information Bulletin* (bi-monthly), conference proceedings and technical, best practice and other reports.

International Electrotechnical Commission—IEC: 3 rue de Varembé, POB 131, 1211 Geneva 20, Switzerland; tel. (22) 9190211; fax (22) 9190300; e-mail info@iec.ch; internet www.iec.ch; f. 1906 as the authority for world standards for electrical and electronic engineering: its standards are used as the basis for regional and national standards, and are used in the preparation of specifications for international trade. Mems: national committees representing all branches of electrical and electronic activities in some 60 countries. Gen.-Sec. A. AMIT. Publs *International Standards and Reports, IEC Bulletin, Annual Report, Catalogue of Publications.*

International Special Committee on Radio Interference: British Electrotechnical Committee, British Standards Institution, 389 Chiswick High Rd, London, W4 4AL, United Kingdom; tel. (20) 8996-9000; fax (20) 8996-7400; e-mail chris_beckley@electricity.org.uk; f. 1934; special committee of the IEC, promoting international agreement on the protection of radio reception from interference by equipment other than authorized transmitters; recommends limits of such interference and specifies equipment and methods of measurement. Mems: national committees of IEC and seven other international organizations. Sec. CHRISTOPHER BECKLEY.

International Federation for Information and Documentation: POB 90402, 2509 LK The Hague, Netherlands; tel. (70) 3140671; fax (70) 3140667; e-mail fid@fid.nl; internet www.fid.nl; f. 1895; aims to promote, and improve, through international co-operation, research in and development of information science, information management and documentation; maintains regional commissions for Latin America, North America and the Caribbean, Asia and Oceania, Western, Eastern and Southern Africa, North Africa and the Near East, and for Europe. Mems: 62 national, five international, 330 institutional and individual mems. Pres. MARTHA STONE; Exec. Dir J. STEPHEN PARKER. Publs *FID Review* (every 2 months), *FID Directory* (every 2 years).

International Federation for Information Processing—IFIP: Hofstrasse 3, 2361 Laxenburg, Austria; tel. (2236) 73616; fax (2236) 736169; e-mail ifip@ifip.or.at; internet www.ifip.or.at; f. 1960 to promote information science and technology; encourages research, development and application of information processing in science and human activities; furthers the dissemination and exchange of information on information processing. Mems: 45 organizations, 3 corresponding mems, 1 assoc. mem. and 11 affiliate mems. Pres. P. BOLLERSLEV (Denmark); Exec. Dir PLAMEN NEDKOV.

International Federation of Airworthiness—IFA: 14 Railway Approach, East Grinstead, West Sussex RH19 1BP, United Kingdom; tel. (1342) 301788; fax (1342) 317808; e-mail sec@ifairworthy.org; internet www.ifairworthy.org; f. 1964 to provide a forum for the exchange of international experience in maintenance, design and operations; holds annual conference; awards international aviation scholarship annually. Mems: 120, comprising 50 airlines, 17 airworthiness authorities, 23 aerospace manufacturing companies, 17 service and repair organizations, three consultancies, six professional societies, two aviation insurance companies, one aircraft leasing company, and the Flight Safety Foundation (USA). Pres. JOHN K LAUBER (USA); Exec. Dir J. W. SAULL (UK). Publ. *IFA News* (quarterly).

International Federation of Automotive Engineering Societies—FISITA: 1 Birdcage Walk, London SW1H 9JJ, United Kingdom; tel. (20) 7973-1275; fax (20) 7973-1285; e-mail info@fisita.com; internet www.fisita.com; f. 1947 to promote the technical and sustainable development of all forms of automotive transportation; maintains electronic job centre for automotive engineers (www.fisitajobs.com); holds congresses every two years. Mems: national orgs in 33 countries. Chief Exec. IAN DICKIE. Publ. *Global Automotive Network.*

International Federation of Consulting Engineers (Fédération internationale des ingénieurs-conseils): 13C ave du Temple, POB 86, 1000 Lausanne 12, Switzerland; tel. (21) 6544411; fax (21) 6535432; e-mail fidic@fidic.org; internet www.fidic.org; f. 1913 to encourage international co-operation and the establishment of standards for consulting engineers. Mems: national asscns in 66 countries, comprising some 500,000 design professionals. Pres. EIGIL STEEN PEDERSEN. Publs *FIDIC Report, Annual Survey, Annual Review.*

International Federation of Hospital Engineering: 2 Abingdon House, Cumberland Business Centre, Northumberland Rd, Portsmouth, PO5 1DS, United Kingdom; tel. (2392) 823186; fax (2392) 815927l; e-mail iheem@btconnect.com; f. 1970 to promote internationally standards of hospital engineering and to provide for the exchange of knowledge and experience in the areas of hospital and healthcare facility design, construction, engineering, commissioning, maintenance and estate management. Mems: 50, in more than 30 countries. Pres. BRUCE NOSEDA (Australia); Gen. Sec. BERNARD SHAPIRO (South Africa). Publ. *Hospital Engineering* (quarterly).

International Institute of Seismology and Earthquake Engineering—IISEE: Building Research Institute, 1 Tatehara, Tsukuba City, Ibaraki Pref., Japan; tel. (298) 79-0677; fax (298) 64-6777; e-mail iisee@kenken.go.jp; internet iisee.kenken.go.jp; f. 1962 to work on seismology and earthquake engineering for the purpose of reducing earthquake damage in the world; trains seismologists and earthquake engineers from the earthquake-prone countries; undertakes surveys, research, guidance and analysis of information on earthquakes and related matters. Mems: 75 countries. Dir T. FUKUTA. Publs *Year Book, Bulletin* (annually), *Individual Studies* (annually).

International Institution for Production Engineering Research: 9 rue Mayran, 75009 Paris, France; tel. 1-45-26-21-80; fax 1-45-26-92-15; e-mail cirp@cirp.net; internet www.cirp.net; f. 1951 to promote by scientific research the study of the mechanical processing of all solid materials; carries out checks on efficiency and quality of work. Mems: 510 in 40 countries. Pres. R. WERTHEIM (Israel); Sec.-Gen. M. VÉRON (France). Publ. *Annals* (2 a year).

International Iron and Steel Institute—IISI: 120 rue Col Bourg, 1140 Brussels, Belgium; tel. (2) 702-89-00; fax (2) 702-88-99; e-mail steel@iisi.be; internet www.worldsteel.org; f. 1967 to promote the welfare and interests of the world's steel industries; undertakes research into all aspects of steel industries; serves as a forum for exchange of knowledge and discussion of problems relating to steel industries; collects, disseminates and maintains statistics and information; serves as a liaison body between international and national steel organizations. Mems: in over 50 countries. Sec.-Gen. IAN CHRISTMAS. Publs *Worldsteel Newsletter,* policy statements and reports.

International Organization for Standardization: POB 56, 1 rue de Varembé, 1211 Geneva 20, Switzerland; tel. (22) 7490111; fax (22) 7333430; e-mail central@iso.org; internet www.iso.org; f. 1947 to reach international agreement on industrial and commercial standards. Mems: national standards bodies of c. 140 countries. Pres. MARIO GILBERTO CORTOPASSI (Brazil); Sec.-Gen. LAWRENCE D. EICHER. Publs *ISO International Standards, ISO Memento* (annually), *ISO Management Systems* (6 a year), *ISO Bulletin* (monthly).

International Research Group on Wood Preservation: Box 5607, 114 86 Stockholm, Sweden; tel. (8) 10-14-53; fax (8) 10-80-81; internet www.irg-wp.com; f. 1965 as Wood Preservation Group by OECD; independent since 1969; consists of five sections; holds plenary annual meeting. Mems: 315 in 51 countries. Pres. Prof. JOHN N. R. RUDDICK (Canada); Sec.-Gen. JÖRAN JERMER (Sweden). Publs *Annual Report,* technical documents and books.

International Rubber Research and Development Board—IRRDB: POB 10150, 50908 Kuala Lumpur, Malaysia; fax (3) 21620414; e-mail draziz@pop.jaring.my; internet www.irrdb.org; f. 1937. Mems: 15 research institutes. Sec. Datuk Dr A. AZIZ.

International Society for Photogrammetry and Remote Sensing—ISPRS: c/o Ian Dowman, Dept of Geomatic Engineering, University College London, Gower St, London, WC1E 6BT, United Kingdom; fax (20) 7679-7226; e-mail idowman@ge.ucl.ac.uk; internet www.isprs.org/; f. 1910; holds congress every four years, and technical symposia. Mems: 103 countries. Pres. JOHN C. TRINDER (Australia); Sec.-Gen. IAN DOWMAN (UK). Publs *Photogrammetry and Remote Sensing* (6 a year), *ISPRS Highlights* (quarterly), *International Archives of Photogrammetry and Remote Sensing* (every 2 years).

International Society for Soil Mechanics and Geotechnical Engineering: City University, Northampton Sq., London, EC1V 0HB, United Kingdom; tel. (20) 7040-8154; fax (20) 7040-8832; e-mail secretariat@issmge.org; internet www.issmge.org; f. 1936 to promote international co-operation among scientists and engineers in the field of geotechnics and its engineering applications; maintains 30 technical committees; holds quadrennial international conference, regional conferences and specialist conferences. Mems: 17,000 individuals, 71 national societies, 23 corporate members. Pres. Prof. KENJI ISHIHARA; Sec.-Gen. Prof. R. NEIL TAYLOR. Publs *ISSMGE News* (quarterly), *Lexicon of Soil Mechanics Terms* (in eight languages).

International Solar Energy Society: Wiesentalstrasse 50, 79115 Freiburg, Germany; tel. (761) 459060; fax (761) 4590699; e-mail hq@ises.org; internet www.ises.org; f. 1954; aims to bring recent developments in renewable energy, both in research and applications, to the attention of decision-makers and the general public, in order to increase the understanding and use of this non-polluting resource; holds international conferences. Mems: c. 30,000 in some 100 countries. Pres. Prof. ANNE GRETE HESTNES (Norway); Exec. Dir. RIAN VAN STADEN (South Africa). Publs *Solar Energy Journal* (monthly), *Refocus Magazine* (6 a year), *Conference Proceedings* (annually).

International Solid Waste Association—ISWA: Overgaden Oven Vandet 48E, 1415 Copenhagen K, Denmark; tel. 32-96-15-88; fax 32-96-15-84; e-mail iswa@iswa.dk; internet www.iswa.org; f. 1970 to promote the exchange of information and experience in solid waste management, in order to protect human health and the environment; promotes research and development activities; provides advice; organizes conferences. Pres. CHRISTOPH SCHARFF (Austria); Man. Dir SUZANNE ARUP VELTZÉ (Denmark). Publs *Waste Management World, Waste Management and Research* (6 a year).

International Union for Vacuum Science, Technique and Applications—IUVSTA: 7 Mohawk Cres., Nepean, ON K2H 7G7, Canada; tel. (613) 829-5790; fax (613) 829-3061; e-mail westwood@istar.ca; internet www.vacuum.org/iuvsta.html; f. 1958; collaborates with the International Standards Organization in defining and adopting technical standards; holds triennial International Vacuum Congress, European Vacuum Conference, triennial International Conference on Thin Films, and International Conference on Solid Surfaces; administers the Welch Foundation scholarship for postgraduate research in vacuum science and technology. Mems: organizations in 30 countries. Pres. Prof. D. P. WOODRUFF (UK); Sec.-Gen. Dr W. D. WESTWOOD (Canada). Publ. *News Bulletin* (quarterly).

International Water Resources Association—IWRA: University of New Mexico, 1915 Roma NE, Albuquerque, NM 87131-1436, USA; tel. (505) 277-9400; fax (505) 277-9405; e-mail iwra@unm.edu; internet www.iwra.siu.edu; f. 1972 to promote collaboration in and support for international water resources programmes; holds conferences; conducts training in water resources management. Pres. GLENN E. STOUT (USA); Sec.-Gen. VICTOR DE KOSINSKY (Belgium). Publ. *Water International* (quarterly).

Latin-American Energy Organization (Organización Latinoamericana de Energía–OLADE): Avda Mariscal Antonio José de Sucre, No N58–63 y Fernándes Salvador, Edif. OLADE, Sector San Carlos, POB 17-11-6413 CCI, Quito, Ecuador; tel. (2) 598-122; fax (2) 531-691; e-mail oladel@olade.org.ec; internet www.olade.org.ec; f. 1973 to act as an instrument of co-operation in using and conserving the energy resources of the region. Mems: 26 Latin-American and Caribbean countries. Exec. Sec. Dr JULIO HERRERA. Publ. *Energy Magazine.*

Latin-American Iron and Steel Institute: Benjamín 2944, 5°, Las Condes, Santiago, Chile; tel. (2) 233-0545; fax (2) 233-0768; e-mail ilafa@entelchile.net; internet www.ilafa.org; f. 1959 to help achieve the harmonious development of iron and steel production, manufacture and marketing in Latin America; conducts economic surveys on the steel sector; organizes technical conventions and meetings; disseminates industrial processes suited to regional conditions; prepares and maintains statistics on production, end uses, prices, etc., of raw materials and steel products within this area. Mems: 18 hon. mems; 63 mems; 68 assoc. mems. Chair. JULIO CÉSAR VILLARREAL; Sec.-Gen. ENRIQUE ALVAREZ. Publs *Acero Latinoamericano* (every 2 months), *Statistical Year Book, Directory of Latin American Iron and Steel Companies* (every 2 years).

Regional Centre for Mapping of Resources for Development: POB 18118, Nairobi, Kenya; tel. (2) 803320; fax (2) 802767; e-mail rcmrd@meteo.go.ke; internet www.rcmrd.org; f. 1975; present name adopted 1997; provides services for the professional techniques of map-making and the application of satellite and remote sensing data in resource analysis and development planning; undertakes research and provides advisory services to African governments. Mems: 14 signatory and 10 non-signatory governments. Dir-Gen. Prof. SIMON NDYETABULA.

Regional Centre for Training in Aerospace Surveys—RECTAS: PMB 5545, Ile-Ife, Nigeria; tel. (36) 230050; fax (36) 230481; e-mail rectas@oauife.edu.ng; f. 1972; provides training, research and advisory services; administered by the ECA. Mems: eight governments. Dir J. A. OGUNLAMI.

Regional Council of Co-ordination of Central and East European Engineering Organizations: c/o MTESZ, 1055 Budapest, Kossuth Lajos tér 6–8, Hungary; tel. (361) 353-4795; fax (361) 353-0317; e-mail mtesz@mtesz.hu; f. 1992. Hon. Pres. JÁNOS TÓTH.

World Association of Industrial and Technological Research Organizations—WAITRO: c/o Danish Technological Institute, POB 141, 2630 Taastrup, Denmark; tel.72-20-20-85; fax 72-20-20-80; e-mail waitro@dti.dk; internet www.waitro.org; f. 1970 by the UN Industrial Development Organization to encourage co-operation in industrial and technological research; provides financial assistance for training and joint activities; arranges international seminars; facilitates the exchange of information. Mems: 200 research institutes in 80 countries. Pres. ÖMER KAYMAKCALAN (Turkey); Contact MOSES MENGU. Publs *WAITRO News* (quarterly), *WAITRO Outline.*

World Association of Nuclear Operators—WANO-CC: Kings Bldgs, 16 Smith Sq., London, SW1P 3JG, United Kingdom; tel. (20) 7828-2111; fax (20) 7828-6691; internet www.wano.org.uk; f. 1989 by operators of nuclear power plants; aims to improve the safety and operability of nuclear power plants through the exchange of operating experience; operates four regional centres (in France, Japan, Russia and the USA) and a co-ordinating centre in the UK. Mems: in 34 countries. Dir (Co-ordinating Centre) V. J. MADDEN.

World Bureau of Metal Statistics: 27A High St, Ware, Herts, SG12 9BA, United Kingdom; tel. (1920) 461274; fax (1920) 464258; e-mail wbms@dircon.co.uk; internet www.wbms.dircon.co.uk; f. 1949; produces statistics of production, consumption, stocks, prices and international trade in copper, lead, zinc, tin, nickel, aluminium and several other minor metals. Gen. Man. J. L. T. DAVIES. Publs *World Metal Statistics* (monthly), *World Tin Statistics* (monthly), *World Nickel Statistics* (monthly), *World Metal Statistics Yearbook, World Metal Statistics Quarterly Summary, World Stainless Steel Statistics* (annually), *World Wrought Copper Statistics* (annually).

World Federation of Engineering Organizations—WFEO: Maison de l'UNESCO, 1 rue Miollis, 75015 Paris, France; tel. 1-45-68-31-92; fax 1-45-68-31-14; e-mail pdeboigne@fmoi.org; internet www.unesco.org/ngo/fmoi/; f. 1968 to advance engineering as a profession; fosters co-operation between engineering organizations throughout the world; undertakes special projects in co-operation with other international bodies. Mems: 80 national mems, nine international mems. Pres. JOSÉ MEDEM SANJUAN (Spain); Exec. Dir PIERRE EDOUARD DE BOIGNE (France). Publ. *WFEO Newsletter* (2 a year).

World Petroleum Congresses: 4th floor, Suite 1, 1 Duchess St, London, W1N 3DE, United Kingdom; tel. (20) 7637-4958; e-mail pierce@world-petroleum.org; internet www.world-petroleum.org; f. 1933 to serve as a forum for petroleum science, technology, economics and management; undertakes related information and liaison activities; 2002 Congress: Rio de Janeiro, Brazil. Mems: Permanent Council includes 59 mem. countries. Pres. Ir D. VAN DER MEER (Netherlands); Dir-Gen. Dr PIERCE W. F. RIEMER (UK).

Tourism

Alliance Internationale de Tourisme: 2 Chemin de Blandonnet, CP 111, 1215 Geneva 15, Switzerland; tel. (22) 5444501; fax (22) 5444550; e-mail webmaster@aitfia.ch; internet www.aitgva.ch; f. 1898, present title adopted 1919; represents motoring organizations and touring clubs around the world; aims to study all questions relating to international touring and to suggest reforms. Mems: 140 asscns with 100m. members in 102 countries. Pres. B. DARBELNET (USA); Dir Gen. P. DOGGWILER (Switzerland). Publ. *AIT News.*

Asia Travel Marketing Association—ATMA: c/o Japan National Tourist Organization, 2-10-1 Yurakucho, Chiyoda-ku, Tokyo, Japan; tel. (3) 3216-1902; fax (3) 3216-1846; e-mail atma@jnto.go.jp; internet www.asiatravel.org; f. 1966 as East Asia Travel Association, present name adopted 1999; aims to promote tourism in the East Asian region, encourage and facilitate the flow of tourists to that region from other parts of the world, and to develop regional tourist industries by close collaboration among members. Mems: six national tourist organizations and one travel asscn. Pres. ICHIRO TANAKA; Sec.-Gen. JOÃO MANUEL COSTA ANTUNES.

Caribbean Tourism Organization: Sir Frank Walcott Bldg, 2nd Floor, Culloden Farm Complex, St Michael, Barbados; tel. 427-5242; fax 429-3065; e-mail ctobar@caribsurf.com; internet www.onecaribbean.org; f. 1989, by merger of the Caribbean Tourism Association (f. 1951) and the Caribbean Tourism Research and Development Centre (f. 1974); aims to encourage tourism in the Caribbean region; organizes annual Caribbean Tourism Conference, Sustainable Tourism Development Conference and Tourism Investment Conference; conducts training and other workshops on request; maintains offices in New York, Canada and London. Mems: 33 Caribbean governments, 400 allied mems. Sec.-Gen. JEAN HOLDER. Publs *Caribbean Tourism Statistical News* (quarterly), *Caribbean Tourism Statistical Report* (annually).

European Travel Commission: 61 rue du Marché aux Herbes, 1000 Brussels, Belgium; tel. (2) 504-03-03; fax (2) 514-18-43; e-mail etc@planetinternet.be; internet www.etc-europe-travel.org; f. 1948 to promote tourism in and to Europe, to foster co-operation and the exchange of information, and to organize research. Mems: national tourist organizations in 31 European countries. Exec. Dir WALTER LEU (Switzerland).

International Association of Scientific Experts in Tourism: Varnbüelstrasse 19, 9000 St Gallen, Switzerland; tel. (71) 2242530; fax (71) 2242536; e-mail aiest@unisg.ch; internet www.aiest.org; f. 1949 to encourage scientific activity in tourism, to support tourist institutions of a scientific nature and to organize conventions. Mems: 400 from 40 countries. Pres. Prof. Dr PETER KELLER (Switzerland); Gen. Sec. Prof. Dr THOMAS BIEGER (Switzerland). Publ. *The Tourism Review* (quarterly).

International Congress and Convention Association—ICCA: Entrada 121, 1096 EB Amsterdam, Netherlands; tel. (20) 398-19-19; fax (20) 699-07-81; e-mail icca@icca.nl; internet www.icca.nl; f. 1963 to establish world-wide co-operation between all involved in organizing congresses, conventions and exhibitions. Mems: over 500 from 71 countries. Pres. TUUIA LINDBERG; Exec. Dir. TOM HULTON. Publ. *International Meetings News* (6 a year).

International Hotel and Restaurant Association: 251 rue du Faubourg St Martin, 75010 Paris, France; tel. 1-44-89-94-00; fax 1-40-36-73-30; e-mail members@ih-ra.com; internet www.ihra.com; f. 1946 to act as the authority on matters affecting the international hotel industry, to promote its interests and to contribute to its growth, profitability and quality; membership extended to restaurants in 1996. Mems: 120 national hospitality asscns, 100 national and international hotel and restaurant chains, also independent hotels and restaurant and allied members. Dir and CEO ALAIN-PHILIPPE FEUTRÉ. Publs *Hotels* (monthly), *Yearbook and Directory* (annually).

Latin-American Confederation of Tourist Organizations (Confederación de Organizaciones Turísticas de la América Latino—COTAL): Viamonte 640, 8°, 1053 Buenos Aires, Argentina; tel. (11) 4322-4003; fax (11) 4393-5696; e-mail cotal@cscom.com.ar; internet www.cotal.org.ar; f. 1957 to link Latin American national asscns of travel agents and their members with other tourist bodies around the world. Mems: in 21 countries. Pres. ENZO U. FURNARI. Publ. *Revista COTAL* (every 2 months).

Pacific Asia Travel Association—PATA: Unit B1, 28th floor, Siam Tower, 989 Rama 1 Rd, Pratumwan, Bangkok 10330, Thailand; tel. (2) 658-2000; fax (2) 658-2010; e-mail patabkk@pata.th.com; internet www.pata.org; f. 1951; aims to enhance the growth, value and quality of Pacific Asia travel and tourism for the benefit of PATA members; holds annual conference; divisional offices in Monaco, Sydney, USA. Mems: more than 1,800 governments, carriers, tour operators, travel agents and hotels. Publs *PATA Compass* (every 2 months), *Statistical Report* (quarterly), research reports, directories, newsletters.

South Pacific Tourism Organization: POB 13119, Suva, Fiji; tel. 3304177; fax 3301995; e-mail info@spto.org; internet www.tcsp.com; frmly the Tourism Council of the South Pacific; aims to foster regional co-operation in the development, marketing and promotion of tourism in the island nations of the South Pacific; receives EU funding and undertakes sustainable activities. Mems: 13 countries in the South Pacific. Chief Exec. LISIATE AKOLO.

Universal Federation of Travel Agents' Associations—UFTAA: 1 ave des Castelans, Stade Louis II-Entrée H, 98000 Monaco; tel. 92-05-28-29; fax 92-05-29-87; e-mail uftaamc@tekworld.mc; internet www.uftaa.com; f. 1966 to unite travel agents' asscns; represents the interests of travel agents at the international level; helps in international legal differences; issues literature on travel. Mems: national asscns of travel agencies in 112 countries. Sec.-Gen. BIRGER BÄCKMAN. Publs *UFTAA Newsletter*, *UFTAA Courier*, *Directory*.

World Association of Travel Agencies—WATA: 14 rue Ferrier, 1202 Geneva, Switzerland; tel. (22) 7314760; fax (22) 7328161; e-mail wata@wata.net; internet www.wata.net; f. 1949 to foster the development of tourism, to help the rational organization of tourism in all countries, to collect and disseminate information and to participate in commercial and financial operations to foster the development of tourism. Individual travel agencies may use the services of the world-wide network of 200 mems. Pres. ADEL ZAKI (Egypt); Sec.-Gen. MARCO AGUSTONI (Switzerland). Publ. *WATA Gazette* (quarterly).

World Tourism Organization: Calle Capitán Haya 42, 28020 Madrid, Spain; tel. (91) 5678100; fax (91) 5713733; e-mail comm@world-tourism.org; internet www.world-tourism.org; f. 1975 to promote travel and tourism; co-operates with member governments; secures financing for and carries out tourism development projects; provides training in tourism-related issues; works for sustainable and environmentally-friendly tourism development; encourages the liberalization of trade in tourism services; considers health and safety issues related to tourism; collects, analyses and disseminates data and operates a Documentation Centre. Mems: governments of 138 countries and territories, also associate members, observers and over 300 affiliated mems. Sec.-Gen. FRANCESCO FRANGIALLI. Publs *Yearbook of Tourism Statistics*, *Compendium of Tourism Statistics*, *Travel and Tourism Barometer*, *WTO News*, *Tourism Market Trends*, *Directory of Multilateral and Bilateral Sources of Financing for Tourism Development*, guidelines and studies.

World Travel and Tourism Council—WTTC: 1–2 Queen Victoria Tce, Sovereign Ct, London, E1W 3HA, United Kingdom; tel. (870) 7279882; fax (870) 7289882; e-mail enquiries@wttc.org; internet www.wttc.org; f. 1989; promotes the development of the travel/tourism industry; analyses impact of tourism on employment levels and local economies and promotes greater expenditure on tourism infrastructure; administers a 'Green Globe' certification programme to enhance environmental management throughout the industry. Mems: 57 global mems, five hon. mems. Pres. JEAN-CLAUDE BAUMGARTEN; Chair. Sir IAN PROSSER. Publs *WTTC Backgrounder*, *Travel and Tourism Review*, *Viewpoint* (quarterly), regional and country reports.

Trade and Industry

African Regional Organization for Standardization: POB 57363, Nairobi, Kenya; tel. (2) 224561; fax (2) 218792; e-mail arso@nbnet.co.ke; internet www.nbnet.co.ke/test/arso; f. 1977 to promote standardization, quality control, certification and metrology in the African region, to formulate regional standards, and to co-ordinate participation in international standardization activities. Mems: 24 states. Sec.-Gen. Dr ADEBAYO O. OYEJOLA. Publs *ARSO Bulletin* (2 a year), *ARSO Catalogue of Regional Standards* (annually), *ARSO Annual Report*.

Arab Iron and Steel Union—AISU: BP 4, Chéraga, Algiers, Algeria; tel. (21) 371580; fax (21) 371975; e-mail relex@solbarab.com; internet www.solbarab.com; f. 1972 to develop commercial and technical aspects of Arab steel production by helping member asscns commercialize their production in Arab markets, guaranteeing them high quality materials and intermediary products, informing them of recent developments in the industry and organizing training sessions; also arranges two annual symposia. Mems: 80 companies in 15 Arab countries. Gen. Sec. MUHAMMAD LAID LACHGAR. Publs *Arab Steel Review* (monthly), *Information Bulletin*, *News Steel World* (2 a month), *Directory* (annually).

Asian Productivity Organization: 2/F Hirakawa-cho Dai-ichi Seimei Bldg, 1-2-10, Hirakawa-cho, Chiyoda-ku, Tokyo 102–0093, Japan; tel. (3) 3408-7221; fax (3) 3408-7220; e-mail apo@gol.com; internet www.apo-tokyo.com; f. 1961 to strengthen the productivity movement in the Asian and Pacific regions and to disseminate technical knowledge on productivity. Mems: 18 countries. Sec.-Gen. TAKASHI TAJIMA. Publs *APO News* (monthly), *Annual Report*, *APO Productivity Journal* (2 a year), *Directory of National Productivity Organizations in APO member countries* (irregular), other related studies.

Association of African Trade Promotion Organizations—AATPO: Pavillion International, BP 23, Tangier, Morocco; tel. (9) 324465; fax (9) 943779; e-mail aoapc@mtds.com; f. 1975 under the auspices of the OAU and the ECA to foster regular contact between African states in trade matters and to assist in the harmonization of their commercial policies, in order to promote intra-African trade; conducts research and training; organizes meetings and trade information missions. Mems: 26 states. Sec.-Gen. Prof. ADEYINKA W. ORIMALADE. Publs *FLASH: African Trade* (monthly), *Directory of African Consultants and Experts in Trade Promotion*, *Directory of Trade Information Contacts in Africa*, *Directory of Trade Information Sources in Africa*, *Directory of State Trading Organizations*, *Directory of Importers and Exporters of Food Products in Africa*, *Basic Information on Africa*, studies.

Association of European Chambers of Commerce and Industry (EUROCHAMBRES): 5 rue d'Archimède, 1000 Brussels, Belgium; tel. (2) 282-08-50; fax (2) 230-00-38; e-mail eurochambres@eurochambres.be; internet www.eurochambres.be; f. 1958 to promote the exchange of experience and information among its members and to bring their joint opinions to the attention of the institutions of the European Union; conducts studies and seminars; co-ordinates EU projects. Mems: 15 full and 18 affiliated mems. Pres. JÖRG MITTELSTEN SCHEID (Germany); Sec.-Gen. ARNALDO ABRUZZINI (Italy).

Cairns Group: c/o Department of Foreign Affairs and Trade, GPO Box 12, Canberra, ACT 2601, Australia; tel. (2) 6263-2222; fax (2) 6261-3111; internet www.dfat.gov.au/trade/negotiations/cairns_group/index.html; f. 1986 by major agricultural exporting countries; aims to bring about reforms in international agricultural trade, including reductions in export subsidies, in barriers to access and in internal support measures; represents members' interests in WTO negotiations. Mems: Argentina, Australia, Bolivia, Brazil, Canada, Chile, Colombia, Costa Rica, Fiji, Guatemala, Indonesia, Malaysia, New Zealand, Paraguay, Philippines, South Africa, Thailand, Uruguay. Chair. MARK VAILE (Australia).

Caribbean Association of Industry and Commerce—CAIC: POB 442, Trinidad Hilton and Conference Centre, Rooms 1238-1241, Lady Young Rd, St Ann's, Trinidad and Tobago; tel. (868) 623-4830; fax (868) 623-6116; e-mail sifill@wow.net; internet www.caic.wow.net; f. 1955; aims to encourage economic development through the private sector; undertakes research and training and gives assistance to small enterprises; encourages export promotion. Mems: chambers of commerce and enterprises in 20 countries and territories. Exec. Dir SEAN IFILL. Publ. *Caribbean Investor* (quarterly).

Committee for European Construction Equipment—CECE: c/o Diamont Bldg, blvd Reyers 80, 1030 Brussels, Belgium; tel. (2) 706-82-25; fax (2) 706-82-29; e-mail cece@skynet.be; f. 1959 to further contact between manufacturers, to improve market conditions and productivity and to conduct research into techniques. Mems: representatives from 10 European countries. Sec.-Gen. PIERRE JULIENS.

Committee of Associations of European Foundries—CAEF: Sohnstrasse 70, D-40237 Düsseldorf, Germany; tel. (211) 687-1215; fax (211) 687-1205; e-mail info@caef-eurofoundry.org; internet www.caef-eurofoundry.org; f. 1953 to safeguard the common interests of European foundry industries and to collect and exchange information. Mems: asscns in 17 countries. Sec.-Gen. Dr KLAUS URBAT. Publ. *The European Foundry Industry* (annually).

Confederation of Asia-Pacific Chambers of Commerce and Industry—CACCI: 9th Floor, 3 Sungshou Rd, Taipei 110, Taiwan; tel. (2) 27255663; fax (2) 27255665; e-mail cacci@iplus.net.tw; internet www.cacci.org.tw; f. 1966; holds biennial conferences to examine regional co-operation; liaises with governments to promote laws conducive to regional co-operation; serves as a centre for compiling and disseminating trade and business information; encourages contacts between businesses; conducts training and research. Mems: national chambers of commerce and industry in 22 countries in the region, also affiliate and special mems. Dir-Gen. Dr WEBSTER KIANG. Publs *CACCI Profile* (monthly), *CACCI Journal of Commerce and Industry* (2 a year).

Confederation of International Soft Drinks Associations—CISDA: 79 blvd St Michel, 1040 Brussels, Belgium; tel. (2) 743-40-50; fax (2) 732-51-02; e-mail mail@unesda-cisda.org; internet www.unesda-cisda.org; f. 1951 to promote co-operation among the national asscns of soft drinks manufacturers on all industrial and commercial matters, to stimulate the sales and consumption of soft drinks, to deal with matters of interest to all member asscns and to represent the common interests of member asscns; holds a congress every year. Gen. Sec. ALAIN BEAUMONT.

Consumers International: 24 Highbury Cres., London, N5 1RX, United Kingdom; tel. (20) 7226-6663; fax (20) 7354-0607; internet www.consumersinternational.org; f. 1960 as International Organization of Consumers' Unions—IOCU; links consumer groups world-wide through information networks and international seminars; supports new consumer groups and represents consumers' interests at the international level; maintains five regional offices. Mems: 215 asscns in 93 countries. Dir-Gen. JULIAN EDWARDS. Publs *Consumer Currents* (10 a year), *World Consumer* (quarterly), *Consumidores y Desarollo* (10 a year), *Consommation-Developpement* (quarterly).

Energy Charter Secretariat: blvd de la Woluwe 56, 1200 Brussels, Belgium; tel. (2) 775-98-00; fax (2) 775-98-01; e-mail info@encharter.org; internet www.encharter.org; f. 1995 under the provisions of the Energy Charter Treaty (1994); aims to promote trade and investment in the energy industries. Mems: 51 signatory states. Sec.-Gen. RIA KEMPER (Germany). Publs *Promoting Energy Efficiency*, *Trade in Energy*, reports.

European Association of Advertising Agencies—EAAA: 152 blvd Brand Whitlock, 1200 Brussels, Belgium; tel. (2) 740-07-10; fax (2) 740-07-17; e-mail stig.carlson@eaaa.be; internet www.eaaa.be; f. 1960 to maintain and raise the standards of service to advertisers of all European advertising agencies; to strive towards uniformity in fields where this would be of benefit; and to serve the interests of all agency members in Europe. Mems: 18 national advertising agency asscns and 23 multinational agency groups. Pres. ALBERT WINNINGHOFF (Netherlands); Sec.-Gen. STIG CARLSON (Sweden). Publ. *Next Steps* (monthly).

European Association of Manufacturers of Radiators—EURORAD: Konradstr. 9, 8023 Zürich, Switzerland; tel. (1) 2719090; fax (1) 2719292; f. 1966 to represent the national asscns of manufacturers of radiators made of steel and cast iron, intended to be attached to central heating plants and which convey heat by natural convection and radiation without the need for casing. Mems: in 15 countries. Pres. Dr H. GASSER (Belgium); Gen. Sec. K. EGLI (Switzerland).

European Association of National Productivity Centres—EANPC: 60 rue de la Concorde, 1050 Brussels, Belgium; tel. (2) 511-71-00; fax (2) 511-02-97; e-mail eanpc@skynet.be; internet www.eanpc.org; f. 1966 to enable members to pool knowledge about their policies and activities. Mems: 19 European centres. Pres. PETER REHNSTRÖM; Sec.-Gen. A. C. HUBERT. Publs *EPI* (quarterly), *Annual Report*.

European Brewery Convention: POB 510, 2380 BB Zoeterwoude, Netherlands; tel. (71) 545-60-47; fax (71) 541-00-13; e-mail secretariat@ebc-nl.com; internet www.ebc-nl.com; f. 1947, present name adopted 1948; aims to promote scientific co-ordination in malting and brewing. Mems: national asscns in 22 European countries. Pres. E. PAJUNEN (Finland); Sec.-Gen. M. VAN WIJNGAARDEN (Netherlands). Publs *Analytica*, *Thesaurus*, *Dic-*

tionary of Brewing, monographs, conference proceedings, manuals of good practice.

European Chemical Industry Council: ave E. van Nieuwenhuyse 4, 1160 Brussels, Belgium; tel. (2) 676-72-11; fax (2) 676-73-00; e-mail mail@cefic.be; internet www.cefic.org; f. 1972; represents and defends the interests of the chemical industry in legal and trade policy, internal market, environmental and technical matters; liaises with intergovernmental organizations; provides secretariat for some 100 product sector groups. Mems: 16 national federations. Dir.-Gen. Dr HUGO LEVER; Sec.-Gen. JEAN-MARIE DEVOS.

European Committee for Standardization (Comité européen de normalisation—CEN): 36 rue de Stassart, 1050 Brussels, Belgium; tel. (2) 550-08-11; fax (2) 550-08-19; e-mail infodesk@cenorm.be; internet www.cenorm.be; f. 1961 to promote European standardization; works to eliminate obstacles caused by technical requirements, in order to facilitate the exchange of goods and services. Mems: 20 national standards bodies, 7 associated and 13 affiliated bodies in central and eastern Europe and 4 corresponding organizations. Sec.-Gen. GEORG HONGLER. Publs *Catalogue of European Standards*, *Work Programme* (both 2 a year), *CEN Networking* (newsletter, every 2 months), *Bulletin* (monthly), *Directories and related standards* (in English, French and German), *New Approach* (CD ROM).

European Committee of Associations of Manufacturers of Agricultural Machinery: 19 rue Jacques Bingen, 75017 Paris, France; tel. 1-42-12-85-90; fax 1-40-54-95-60; e-mail cema@syma.org; f. 1959 to study economic and technical problems in field of agricultural machinery manufacture, to protect members' interests and to disseminate information. Mems: 13 mem. countries. Pres. A. TASSINARI (Italy); Sec.-Gen. J. DEHOLLAIN (France).

European Committee of Textile Machinery Manufacturers—CEMATEX: POB 190, 2700-AD Zoetermeer, Netherlands; tel. (79) 531-100; fax (79) 531-365; f. 1952; promotes general interests of the industry. Mems: organizations in eight European countries. Pres. Dr F. PAETZOLD (Germany); Gen. Sec. R. BICKER CAARTEN.

European Confederation of Iron and Steel Industries—EUROFER: 211 rue du Noyer, 1000 Brussels, Belgium; tel. (2) 738-79-20; fax (2) 736-30-01; e-mail mail@eurofer.be; internet www.eurofer.org; f. 1976 as a confederation of national federations and companies in the European steel industry; aims to foster co-operation between the member federations and companies and to represent their common interests to the EU and other international organizations. Mems: in 13 European countries, assoc. mems from central and eastern European countries. Dir-Gen. D. VON HÜLSEN.

European Confederation of Woodworking Industries: Hof-Ter-Vleestdreef 5, Bo^te 4, 1070 Brussels, Belgium; tel. (2) 556-25-85; fax (2) 556-25-95; e-mail info@cei-bois.org; internet www.cei-bois.org; f. 1952 to liaise between national organizations, undertake research and defend the interests of the industry. Mems: national federations in 19 European countries. Pres. BO BORGSTRÖM (Finland); Sec.-Gen. Dr G. VAN STEERTEGEM. Publ. *Brochure*.

European Council of Paint, Printing Ink and Artists' Colours Industry: ave E. van Nieuwenhuyse 4, 1160 Brussels, Belgium; tel. (2) 676-7480; fax (2) 676-7490; e-mail secretariat@cepe.org; internet www.cepe.org; f. 1951 to study questions relating to the paint and printing ink industries, to take or recommend measures for the development of these industries or to support their interests, and to exchange information. Mems: national asscns in 17 European countries and 13 company members. Pres. N. PETERSEN ; Gen. Sec. J. SCHODER. Publs *Annual Review*, guidance documents.

European Federation of Associations of Insulation Enterprises: Kurfürstenstr. 129, 10785 Berlin, Germany; tel. (30) 212-86163; fax (30) 212-86160; e-mail bfa.wksb@bauindustrie.de; f. 1970; groups organizations in Europe representing insulation firms; aims to facilitate contacts between member asscns; studies problems of interest to the profession; works to safeguard the interests of the profession and represent it in international fora. Mems: professional organizations in 16 European countries. Sec.-Gen. M. SCHMOLDT.

European Federation of Marketing Research Organisations—EFAMRO: Studio 38, Wimbledon Business Centre, Riverside Road, London, SW17 0BA, United Kingdom; tel. (20) 8879-0709; fax (20) 8947-2637; internet www.efamro.org; f. 1965 (frmly known as FEMRA) to facilitate contacts between researchers; maintains specialist divisions on European chemical marketing research, European technological forecasting, paper and related industries, industrial materials, automotives, textiles, methodology, and information technology. Mems: 500. Pres. DAVID A. CLARK (Belgium).

European Federation of Management Consultants' Associations: 3–5 ave des Arts, 1210 Brussels, Belgium; tel. (2) 250-06-50; fax (2) 250-06-51; e-mail feaco@feaco.org; internet www.feaco.org; f. 1960 to bring management consultants together and promote a high standard of professional competence, by encouraging discussions of, and research into, problems of common professional interest. Mems: 24 asscns. Pres. and Chair. GIL GIDRON; Exec. Man. ELSE GROEN. Publs *Newsletter* (3 a year), *Annual Survey of the European Management Consultancy Market*.

European Federation of Material Handling Industries: Diamant Bldg, 80 blvd A. Reyers, 1030 Brussels, Belgium; tel. (2) 706-82-30; fax (2) 706-82-50; e-mail guy.vandoorslaer@orgalirne.org; internet www.fem-eur.com; f. 1953 to facilitate contact between members of the profession, conduct research, standardize methods of calculation and construction and promote standardized safety regulations. Mems: organizations in 14 European countries. Pres. TONY GRESHAM JONES; Sec.-Gen. GUY VAN DOORSLAER.

European Federation of the Plywood Industry—FEIC: Allée Hof-ter-Vleest, bte 4, 1070 Brussels, Belgium; tel. (2) 556-25-84; fax (2) 556-25-95; e-mail danny.croon@europlywood.org; internet www.europlywood.org; f. 1957 to organize joint research between members of the industry at the international level. Mems: asscns in 15 European countries. Pres. F. ALLIN; Sec.-Gen. D. CROON.

European Federation of Tile and Brick Manufacturers: Obstgartenstrasse 28, 8035 Zürich, Switzerland; tel. (1) 3619650; fax (1) 3610205; e-mail office@tbe-euro.ch; internet www.tbe-euro.com; f. 1952 to co-ordinate research between members of the industry, improve technical knowledge and encourage professional training. Mems: asscns in 23 European and east European countries. Chair. VITTORIO VITOLO; Dir Dr W. P. WELLER.

European Furniture Manufacturers Federation (Union européenne de l'ameublement—UEA): 35 chaussé de Haecht, 1210 Brussels; tel. (2) 218-18-89; fax (2) 219-27-01; e-mail secretariat@uea.be; internet www.ueanet.com; f. 1950 to determine and support the general interests of the European furniture industry and facilitate contacts between members of the industry. Mems: organizations in 19 European countries. Pres. J. ENGELS; Sec.-Gen. B. DE TURCK. Publs *UEA Newsletter* (bi-monthly), *Focus on Issues*, *Strategy Survey*.

European General Galvanizers Association—EGGA: Croudace House, Godstone Rd, Caterham, Surrey, CR3 6RE, United Kingdom; tel. (1883) 331277; fax (1883) 331287; e-mail mail@egga.com; internet www.egga.com; f. 1955 to promote co-operation between members of the industry, especially in improving processes and finding new uses for galvanized products. Mems: asscns in 19 European countries. Pres. E. HOFFMANN (Germany). Publ. *Worldgalv Newsletter*.

European Glass Container Manufacturers' Committee: Northumberland Rd, Sheffield, S10 2UA, United Kingdom; tel. (114) 268-6201; fax (114) 268-1073; e-mail l.roe@britglass.co.uk; internet www.britglass.co.uk; f. 1951 to facilitate contacts between members of the industry and inform them of relevant legislation. Mems: representatives from 15 European countries. Sec. Dr W. G. A. COOK.

European Organization for Quality—EOQ: 3 rue de Luxembourg, 1000 Brussels, Belgium; tel. (2) 501-07-35; fax (31) 501-07-36; e-mail bjouslin@compuserve.com; internet www.eoq.org; f. 1956 to encourage the use and application of quality management, with the aim of improving quality, lowering costs and increasing productivity; organizes the exchange of information and documentation. Mems: organizations in 31 European countries. Sec.-Gen. BERTRAND JOUSLIN DE NORAY. Publs *European Quality* (6 a year), *Annual Report.*

European Packaging Federation: c/o Institut Français de l'Emballage et du Conditionnement IFEC, 33 rue Louis Blanc, 93582 St-Ouen Cédex, France; tel. 1-40-11-22-12; fax 1-40-11-01-06; e-mail info@ifecpromotion.tm.fr; internet www.ifecpromotion.tm.fr/epf.htm; f. 1953 to encourage the exchange of information between national packaging institutes and to promote technical and economic progress. Mems: organizations in 12 European countries. Pres. J. P. POTHET (France); Sec.-Gen. A. FREIDINGER-LEGAY (France).

European Panel Federation: Hof-ter-Vleestdreef 5, 1070 Brussels, Belgium; tel. (2) 556-25-89; fax (2) 556-25-94; e-mail info@europanels.org; internet www.europanels.org; f. 1958 as European Federation of Associations of Particle Board Manufacturers; present name adopted 1999; works to develop and encourage international co-operation in the particle board and MDF industry. Pres. F. DE COCK; Sec.-Gen. G. VAN STEERTEGEM (Belgium). Publ. *Annual Report.*

European Patent Office—EPO: 80331 Munich, Erhardtstrasse 27, Germany; tel. (89) 2399-0; fax (89) 23994560; internet www.european-patent-office.org; f. 1977 to grant European patents according to the Munich convention of 1973; conducts searches and examination of patent applications. Mems: 19 European countries. Pres. INGO KOBER (Germany); Chair. Admin. Council SEAN FITZPATRICK. Publs *Annual Report, Official Journal* (monthly), *European Patent Bulletin, European Patent Applications, Granted Patents.*

European Society for Opinion and Marketing Research—ESOMAR: Vondelstraat 172, 1054 GV Amsterdam, Netherlands; tel. (20) 664-21-41; fax (20) 664-29-22; e-mail email@esomar.nl; internet www.esomar.nl; f. 1948 to further professional interests and encourage high technical standards. Mems: over 4,000 in 100 countries. Pres. JOHN KELLY (UK); Dir-Gen. JUERGEN SCHWOERER. Publs *Research World* (monthly), *ESOMAR Directory* (annually).

European Union of Coachbuilders: 46 Woluwedal, bte 14, 1200 Brussels, Belgium; tel. (2) 778-62-00; fax (2) 778-62-22; e-mail mail@federauto.be; f. 1948 to promote research on questions affecting the industry, exchange information, and establish a common policy for the industry. Mems: national federations in eight European countries. Pres. J. BLYWEERT (Belgium); Sec.-Gen. HILDE VANDER STICHELE (Belgium).

European Union of the Natural Gas Industry—EUROGAS: 4 ave Palmerston, 1000 Brussels, Belgium; tel. (2) 237-11-11; fax (2) 230-62-91; e-mail eurogas@eurogas.org; internet www.eurogas.org/. Mems: organizations in 17 European countries. Pres. P. GADONNEIX (France); Gen. Sec. PETER CLAUS (Belgium).

Federación de Cámaras de Comercio del Istmo Centroamericano (Federation of Central American Chambers of Commerce): 10a Calle 3-80, Zona 1, 01001 Guatemala City, Guatemala; internet www.fecamco.com; f. 1961; plans and co-ordinates industrial and commercial exchanges and exhibitions. Pres. EMILIO BRUCE JIMÉNEZ (Costa Rica); Sec. JORGE E. BRIZ ABULARACH (Guatemala).

General Union of Chambers of Commerce, Industry and Agriculture for Arab Countries—GUCCIAAC: POB 11-2837, Beirut, Lebanon; tel. (1) 814269; fax (1) 862841; e-mail gucciaac@destination.com.lb; internet www.gucciaac.org.lb; f. 1951 to enhance Arab economic development, integration and security through the co-ordination of industrial, agricultural and trade policies and legislation. Mems: chambers of commerce, industry and agriculture in 22 Arab countries. Sec. Gen. Dr ELIAS GHANTOUS. Publs *Arab Economic Report, Al-Omran Al-Arabi* (every 2 months), economic papers, proceedings.

Global Crop Protection Federation—GCPF: ave Louise 143, 1050 Brussels, Belgium; tel. (2) 542-04-10; fax (2) 542-04-19; e-mail gcpf@pophost.eunet.be/; internet www.gcpf.org; f. 1960 as European Group of National Asscns of Pesticide Manufacturers, international body since 1967, present name adopted in 1996; aims to harmonize national and international regulations concerning crop protection products; supports the development of the industry; promotes observation of the FAO Code of Conduct on the Distribution and Use of Pesticides; holds an annual General Assembly. Mems: 6 regional asscns covering Africa/Middle East, Asia-Pacific, Europe, Latin America, North America and Japan. Pres. WILLIAM J. MURRAY; Dir-Gen. K. P. VLAHODIMOS.

Gulf Organization for Industrial Consulting—GOIC: POB 5114, Doha, Qatar; tel. 4858888; fax 4831465; e-mail goic@goic.org.qa; internet www.goic.org.qa; f. 1976 by the Gulf Arab states to encourage industrial co-operation among Gulf Arab states, to pool industrial expertise and to encourage joint development of projects; undertakes feasibility studies, market diagnosis, assistance in policy-making, legal consultancies, project promotion, promotion of small and medium industrial investment profiles and technical training; maintains industrial data bank. Mems: mem. states of Gulf Co-operation Council (q.v.). Sec.-Gen. MOHAMED BIN ALI BIN ABDULLAH AL-MUSALLAM. Publs *GOIC Monthly Bulletin* (in Arabic), *Al Ta'awon al Sina'e* (quarterly, in Arabic and English).

Instituto Centroamericano de Administración de Empresas—INCAE (Central American Institute for Business Administration): Apdo 960, 4050 Alajuela, Costa Rica; tel. 443-0506; fax 433-9101; e-mail artauiar@mail.incae.ac.cr; internet www.incae.ac.cr; f. 1964; provides a postgraduate programme in business administration; runs executive training programmes; carries out management research and consulting; maintains a second campus in Nicaragua; libraries of 85,000 vols. Rector Dr ROBERTO ARTAVIA. Publs *Alumni Journal* (in Spanish), *Bulletin* (quarterly), books and case studies.

Inter-American Commercial Arbitration Commission: OAS Administration Bldg, Rm 211, 19th and Constitution Ave, NW, Washington, DC 20006, USA; tel. (202) 458-3249; fax (202) 458-3293; f. 1934 to establish an inter-American system of arbitration for the settlement of commercial disputes by means of tribunals. Mems: national committees, commercial firms and individuals in 22 countries. Dir-Gen. Dr ADRIANA POLANIA POLANIA.

International Advertising Association Inc: 521 Fifth Ave, Suite 1807, New York, NY 10175, USA; tel. (212) 557-1133; fax (212) 983-0455; e-mail iaa@iaaglobal.org; internet www.iaaglobal.org; f. 1938 as a global partnership of advertisers, agencies, the media and other marketing communications professionals; aims to protect freedom of commercial speech and consumer choice; holds World Congress every 2 years (2004: China). Mems: more than 3,600 in 99 countries. Pres. DAVID HANGER (UK); Dir-Gen. WALLY O'BRIEN (USA). Publs *IAA Membership Directory and Annual Report, IAA World News.*

International Association of Buying and Marketing Groups: Vorgebirgsstr. 43, 53119 Bonn, Germany; tel. (228) 9858420; fax (228) 9858410; e-mail g.olesch@zgv-online.de; f. 1951 to research, document and compile statistics; holds annual conference. Mems: 300 buying groups in 13 countries. Sec.-Gen. Dr GÜNTER OLESCH.

International Association of Department Stores: 4 rue de Rome, 75008 Paris, France; tel. 1-42-94-02-02; fax 1-42-94-02-04; e-mail iads@iads.org; internet www.iads.org; f. 1928 to conduct research and exchange information and statistics on management, organization and technical problems; maintains a documentation centre. Mems: large-scale retail enterprises in 14 countries. Pres. L. MANDAC (Germany); Gen. Sec. M. DE GROOT VAN EMBDEN (Netherlands). Publ. *Retail News Letter* (monthly).

International Association of Electrical Contractors: 5 rue Hamelin, 75116 Paris, France; tel. 1-44-05-84-20; fax 1-44-05-84-05; e-mail aie@wanadoo.fr. Mems: national asscns in 18 countries and territories Pres. AAGE KJAERGAARD; Gen. Sec. DENIS HANNOTIN. Publ. *AIE Brochure* (every 2 years).

International Association of Scholarly Publishers: c/o Fred C. Bohm, Michigan State University Press, 1405 South Harrison Rd, East Lansing, MI 48823-5202, USA; tel. (517) 355-9543; fax (517) 432-2611; e-mail bohm@pilot.msu.edu; f. 1972 for the exchange of information and experience on scholarly and academic publishing by universities and others; assists in the transfer of publishing skills to developing countries. Mems: over 140 in 38 countries. Pres. MICHAEL HUTER (Austria); Sec.-Gen. FRED C. BOHM (USA). Publs *IASP Newsletter* (every 2 months), *International Directory of Scholarly Publishers.*

International Association of the Soap, Detergent and Maintenance Products Industry (Association internationale de la savonnerie, de la détergence et des produits d'entretien—AISE): 49 sq. Marie-Louise, 1000 Brussels, Belgium; tel. (2) 230-83-71; fax (2) 230-82-88; e-mail aise.main@aise-net.org; internet www.aise-net.org; f. 1967 to promote the manufacture and use of a wide range of cleaning products, polishes, bleaches, disinfectants and insecticides, to develop the exchange of statistical information and to study technical, scientific, economic and social problems of interest to its members. Mems: 31 national asscns in 25 countries. Dir. M. GLABBERTON. Publs *Annual Review*, technical documents and reports.

International Booksellers Federation—IBF: rue du Grand Hospice 34a, 1000 Belgium; tel. (2) 223-49-40; fax (2) 223-49-41; e-mail eurobooks@skynet.be; internet www.ibf-world.org; f. 1956 to promote the book trade and the exchange of information, and to protect the interests of booksellers when dealing with other international organizations; special committees deal with questions of postage, resale price maintenance, book market research, advertising, customs and tariffs, the problems of young booksellers, etc. Mems: 200 in 22 countries. Pres. YVONNE STEINBERGER; Sec.-Gen. CHRISTIANE VUIDAR. Publs *IBF-bulletin* (2 a year), *Booksellers International.*

International Bureau for the Standardization of Man-Made Fibres (BISFA): 4 ave van Nieuwenhuyse, 1160 Brussels, Belgium; tel. (2) 676-74-55; fax (2) 676-74-54; e-mail van@cirfs.org; internet www.bisfa.org; f. 1928 to examine and establish rules for the standardization, classification and naming of various categories of man-made fibres. Mems: 49. Sec.-Gen. J. SPIJKERS.

International Butchers' Confederation: bte 10, 4 rue Jacques de Lalaing, 1040 Brussels, Belgium; tel. (2) 230-38-76; fax (2) 230-34-51; e-mail info@cibc.be; f. 1907; aims to defend the interests of small and medium-sized enterprises in the meat trading and catering industry. Pres. BRUNO KAMM; Sec.-Gen. INGOLF JAKOBI.

International Confederation for Printing and Allied Industries—INTERGRAF: 18 sq. Marie-Louise, bte 25, 1040 Brussels, Belgium; tel. (2) 230-86-46; fax (2) 231-14-64; internet www.intergraf.org; f. 1983 (frmly EUROGRAF, f. 1975) to defend the common interests of the printing and allied interests in mem. countries. Mems: federations in 20 countries. Pres. MARTIN HANDGRAAF; Sec.-Gen. GEOFFREY WILSON.

International Confederation of Art Dealers: 33 rue Ernest-Allard, 1000 Brussels, Belgium; tel. (2) 511-67-77; internet www.cinoa.org; f. 1936 to co-ordinate the work of asscns of dealers in works of art and paintings and to contribute to artistic and economic expansion. Mems: asscns in 24 countries. Pres. WALTER FEILCHENFELDT; Sec.-Gen. DORIS AMMANN.

International Co-operative Alliance—ICA: 15 route des Morillons, 1218 Grand-Saconnex, Geneva, Switzerland; tel. (22) 929-88-88; fax (22) 798-41-22; e-mail ica@coop.org; internet www.coop.org; f. 1895 for the pursuit of co-operative aims. A General Assembly and four Regional Assemblies meet every two years, on an alternating basis; a 20-member ICA Board controls the affairs of the organization between meetings of the General Assembly. Specialized bodies have been established to promote co-operative activities in the following fields: agriculture, banking, fisheries, consumer affairs, energy, tourism, communications, co-operative research, health, human resources, wholesale distribution, housing, insurance, women's participation and industrial, artisanal and service producers' co-operatives. Mems: 242 affiliated national orgs, with a total membership of more than 760m. individuals in 100 countries, and four int. orgs. Pres. ROBERTO RODRIGUES (Brazil); Dir-Gen. BRUCE THORDARSON (Canada). Publs *Review of International Co-operation* (quarterly), *ICA News* (every 2 months), *Co-op Dialogue* (2 a year).

International Council of Societies of Industrial Design—ICSID: Erottajankatu 11A, 00130 Helsinki, Finland; tel. (9) 6962290; fax (9) 69622910; e-mail icsidsec@icsid.org; internet www.icsid.org; f. 1957 to encourage the development of high standards in the practice of industrial design; works to improve and expand the contribution of industrial design throughout the world. Mems: 150 in 53 countries. Pres. AUGUSTO MORELLO (Italy); Sec.-Gen. KAARINA POHTO. Publs *ICSID News, World Directory of Design Schools.*

International Council of Tanners: Leather Trade House, Kings Park Rd, Moulton Park, Northampton, NN3 6JD, United Kingdom; tel. (1604) 679917; fax (1604) 679998; e-mail sec@tannerscouncilict.org; internet www.tannerscouncilict.org; f. 1926 to study all questions relating to the leather industry and maintain contact with national asscns. Mems: national tanners' organizations in 33 countries. Pres. TONY MOSSOP (South Africa); Sec. PAUL PEARSON (UK).

International Emissions Trading Association: 20 Eglinton Ave West, Suite 1305, POB 2017, Toronto, Canada, ON M4R 1K8; tel. (416) 487-8591; fax (416) 481-2625; e-mail marcu@ieta.org; internet www.ieta.org; f. 1999; aims to establish a functional international framework for trading greenhouse gas emissions, in accordance with the objectives of the UN Framework Convention on Climate Change; serves as a specialized information centre on emissions trading and the greenhouse gas market. Mems: 45 international companies from all sectors of the industry. Exec. Dir ANDREI MARCU.

International Exhibitions Bureau: 56 ave Victor Hugo, Paris 16e, France; tel. 1-45-00-38-63; fax 1-45-00-96-15; e-mail bie@bie-paris.org; internet www.bie-paris.org; f. 1931, revised by Protocol 1972, for the authorization and registration of international exhibitions falling under the 1928 Convention. Mems: 88 states. Pres. GILLES NOGHES; Sec.-Gen. VICENTE GONZALES LOSCERTALES.

International Federation of Associations of Textile Chemists and Colourists—IFATCC: Postfach 403, 4153 Reinach 1, Switzerland; e-mail markus.krayer@cibasc.com; f. 1930 for liaison on professional matters between members and the furtherance of scientific and technical collaboration in the development of the textile finishing industry and the colouring of materials. Mems: in 22 countries. Pres. LIONEL DUCROCQ (France); Sec. MARKUS KRAYER (Switzerland).

International Federation of Grocers' Associations—IFGA: Vakcentrum, Woerden, Netherands; tel. (348) 419771; fax (348) 421801; f. 1927; initiates special studies and works to further the interests of members, with special regard to conditions resulting from European integration and developments in consuming and distribution. Mems: 500,000.

International Federation of Insurance Intermediaries (Bureau international des producteurs d'assurances et de réassurances—BIPAR): 40 ave Albert-Elisabeth, 1200 Brussels, Belgium; tel. (2) 735-60-48; fax (2) 732-14-18; e-mail bipar@skynet.be; internet www.bipar.org; f. 1937 to represent, promote and defend the interests of national asscns of professional insurance agents and brokers at the international level; works to co-ordinate members' activities. Mems: 43 asscns from 27 countries, representing approx. 250,000 brokers and agents. Pres. GÉRARD LEBEGUE; Dir HARALD KRAUSS. Publ. *BIPAR Intern* (quarterly).

International Federation of Pharmaceutical Manufacturers Associations—IFPMA: 30 rue de St Jean, POB 758, 1211 Geneva 13, Switzerland; tel. (22) 3383200; fax (22) 3383299; e-mail admin@ifpma.org; internet www.ifpma.org; f. 1968 for the exchange of information and international co-operation in all questions of interest to the pharmaceutical industry, particularly in the field of health legislation, science and research; develops ethical principles and practices; co-operates with national and international organizations. Mems: the national pharmaceutical asscn of 60 countries and one regional asscn (representing Latin America). Pres. Prof. ROLF KREBS (Germany); Dir-Gen. Dr HARVEY E. BALE, Jr (USA). Publs *IPFMA Code of Pharmaceutical Marketing Practices,* action papers, occasional publications.

International Federation of the Phonographic Industry—IFPI: 54 Regent St, London, W1R 5PJ, United Kingdom; tel. (20) 7878-7900; fax (20) 7878-7950; e-mail info@ifpi.org; internet www.ifpi.org; f. 1933; represents the interests of record producers by campaigning for the introduction, improvement and enforcement of copyright and related rights legislation; co-ordinates the recording industry's anti-piracy activities. Mems: 1,476 in 73 countries. Chair. and Chief Exec. JASON BERMAN.

International Fertilizer Industry Association: 28 rue Marbeuf, 75008 Paris, France; tel. 1-53-93-05-00; fax 1-53-93-05-45; e-mail ifa@fertilizer.org; internet www.fertilizer.org; Pres. C. E. CHILDERS; Sec.-Gen. L. M. MAENE.

International Fragrance Association—IFRA: 48 sq. Marie Louise, 1000 Brussels, Belgium; tel. (2) 2389904; fax (2) 2300265; e-mail secretariat@ifraorg.org; internet www.ifraorg .org; f. 1973 to collect and study scientific data on fragrance materials and to make recommendations on their safe use. Mems: national asscns in 14 countries. Pres. J. BOYDEN; Exec. Dir M. WAGNER. Publs *Code of Practice, Information Letters.*

International Fur Trade Federation: POB 495, Weybridge, KT13 8WD, United Kingdom; internet www.iftf.com; f. 1949 to promote and organize joint action by fur trade organizations in order to develop and protect the trade in fur skins and the processing of skins. Mems: 33 organizations in 27 countries. Exec. Dir J. BAILEY.

International Meat Secretariat (Office international de la viande): 17 pl. des Vins de France, 75012 Paris, France; tel. 1-44-68-84-54; fax 1-44-68-84-53; e-mail ims@wanadoo.fr; internet www.meat-ims.org. Pres. PHILIP M. SENG; Sec.-Gen. LAURENCE WRIXON.

International Organization of Motor Manufacturers (Organisation internationale des constructeurs d'automobiles—OICA): 4 rue de Berri, 75008 Paris; tel. 1-43-59-00-13; fax 1-45-63-84-41; e-mail oica@oica.net; internet www.oica.net; f. 1919 to co-ordinate and further the interests of the automobile industry, to promote the study of economic and other matters affecting automobile construction, and to control automobile manufacturers' participation in international exhibitions in Europe. Mems: manufacturers' asscns of 16 European countries, China, Japan, the Republic of Korea and the USA; 40 assoc. mems. Gen. Sec. Y. van der SRAATEN. Publ. *Yearbook of the World's Motor Industry.*

International Organization of the Flavour Industry—IOFI: 49 sq. Marie Louise, 1000 Brussels, Belgium; tel. (2) 2389902; fax (2) 2300265; e-mail secretariat@iofiorg.org; f. 1969 to support and promote the flavour industry; active in the fields of safety evaluation and regulation of flavouring substances. Mems: national asscns in 21 countries. Pres. M. DAVIS; Exec. Dir M. WAGNER. Publs *Documentation Bulletin, Information Letters, Code of Practice.*

International Publishers' Association: 3 ave de Miremont, 1206 Geneva, Switzerland; tel. (22) 3463018; fax (22) 3475717; e-mail secretariat@ipa-uie.org; internet www.ipa-uie.org; f. 1896 to defend the freedom of publishers, promote their interests and foster international co-operation; promotes the international trade in books and music; carries out work on international copyright and translation rights. Mems: 74 professional book publishers' organizations in 65 countries and music publishers' asscns in 20 countries. Pres. ALAIN GRÜND; Sec.-Gen. J. ALEXIS KOUTCHOUMOW.

International Rayon and Synthetic Fibres Committee (Comité international de la rayonne et des fibres synthétique—CIRFS): 4 ave E. van Nieuwenhuyse, 1160 Brussels, Belgium; tel. (2) 676-74-55; fax (2) 676-74-54; e-mail info@cirfs.org; internet www.cirfs.org; f. 1950 to improve the quality and promote the use of man-made fibres and products made from fibres. Mems: individual producers in 24 countries. Pres. GIANCARLO BERTI; Dir-Gen. C. PURVIS (UK). Publs *Statistical Booklet* (annually), market reports, technical test methods.

International Shopfitting Organisation: Gladbachstr. 80, 8044 Zürich, Switzerland; tel. (1) 2678100; fax (1) 2678150; e-mail petra.isenberg@vssm.ch; internet www.shopfitting.org; f. 1959 to promote the interchange of ideas between individuals and firms concerned with shopfitting. Mems: companies in 13 countries. Pres. J. BREITENMOSER; Sec. PETRA ISENBERG.

International Textile Manufacturers Federation—ITMF: Am Schanzengraben 29, Postfach, 8039 Zürich, Switzerland; tel. (1) 2017080; fax (1) 2017134; e-mail secretariat@itmf.org; internet www.itmf.org; f. 1904, present title adopted 1978; aims to protect and promote the interests of its members, disseminate information, and encourage co-operation. Mems: national textile trade asscns in c. 50 countries. Pres. HERBERT SCHMID (Brazil); Dir-Gen. Dr HERWIG STROLZ (Austria). Publs *State of Trade Report* (quarterly), *Country Statements, Annual Conference Report, Directory*, various statistics, sectoral reports and guidelines.

International Union of Marine Insurance—IUMI: Gotthardstr. 3, POB 6304, Zug, Switzerland; tel. (41) 7293966; fax (41) 7293967; e-mail mail@iumi.com; internet www.iumi.com; f. 1873 to collect and distribute information on marine insurance on a world-wide basis. Mems: 54 asscns. Pres. GEORG MEHL (Germany); Gen. Sec. STEFAN PELLER.

International Wool Textile Organisation—IWTO (Fédération lanière internationale—FLI): 19–21 rue du Luxembourg, Boite 13, 1000 Brussels, Belgium; tel. (2) 513-06-20; fax (2) 514-06-65; e-mail info@iwto.org; internet www.iwto.org; f. 1929 to link wool textile organizations in member-countries and represent their interests; holds annual International Wool Conference (2002: Barcelona; 2003: Buenos Aires). Mems: in 23 countries. Pres. DIETER J. VOLLSTEDT (Germany); Sec.-Gen. W. H. LAKIN (UK). Publs *Wool Statistics* (annually), *Global Wool Supplies and Wool Textile Manufacturing Activity* (annually), *Blue Book, Red Book.*

International Wrought Copper Council: 6 Bathurst St, Sussex Sq., London, W2 2SD, United Kingdom; tel. (20) 7724-7465; fax (20) 7724-0308; e-mail iwcc@coppercouncil.org; internet www.coppercouncil.org; f. 1953 to link and represent copper fabricating industries and represent the views of copper consumers to raw material producers; organizes specialist activities on technical work and the development of copper. Mems: 17 national groups in Europe, Australia, Japan and Malaysia, 13 corporate mems. Chair. A. BAGRI; Sec.-Gen. SIMON PAYTON. Publs *Annual Report*, surveys.

Liaison Group of the European Mechanical, Electrical, Electronic and Metalworking Industries—Orgalime: Diamant Bldg, 80 blvd Reyers, 1030 Brussels, Belgium; tel. (2) 511-34-84; fax (2) 512-99-70; e-mail secretariat@orgalime.be; internet www.orgalime.org; f. 1954 to provide a permanent liaison between the mechanical, electrical and electronic engineering, and metalworking industries of member countries. Mems: 25 trade asscns in 16 European countries. Pres. ENRICO MASSIMO CARLE (Italy); Sec.-Gen. PATRICK KNOX-PEEBLES.

Union des Foires Internationales—UFI (Union of International Fairs): 35 bis, rue Jouffroy d'Abbans, 75017 Paris, France; tel. 1-42-67-99-12; fax 1-42-27-19-29; e-mail info@ufinet.org; internet www.ufinet.org; f. 1925; represents the show and fairground industry worldwide; works to increase co-operation between international trade fairs/exhibitions, safeguard their interests and extend their operations; imposes quality criteria and defines standards. Mems: 191 organizers and managers with 621 approved events, 33 assoc. mems in 72 countries. Pres. SANDY ANGUS (UK); Man. Dir VINCENT GÉRARD (Belgium).

Union of Industrial and Employers' Confederations of Europe—UNICE: 40 rue Joseph II, 1000 Brussels, Belgium; tel. (2) 237-65-11; fax (2) 231-14-45; e-mail main@unice.be; internet www.unice.org; f. 1958; aims to ensure that European Union policy-making takes account of the views of European business; committees and working groups develop joint positions in fields of interest to business and submit these to the Community institutions concerned. The Council of Presidents (of member federations) lays down general policy; the Executive Committee (of Directors-General of member federations) is the managing body; and the Committee of Permanent Delegates, consisting of federation representatives in Brussels, ensures permanent liaison with mems. Mems: 20 industrial and employers' federations from the EU member states, and 14 federations from non-EU countries. Pres. GEORGES JACOBS. Publ. *UNICE@News* (monthly, by e-mail).

World Customs Organization—WCO: 30 rue du Marché, 1210 Brussels, Belgium; tel. (2) 209-92-11; fax (2) 209-92-92; e-mail info@wcoomd.org; internet www.wcoomd.org; f. 1952 as Customs Co-operation Council; aims to enhance the effectiveness and efficiency of customs administrations in the areas of compliance with trade regulations, the protection of society and revenue collection. Mems: governments of 159 countries. Chair. Dr PRAVIN GORDHAN (South Africa); Sec.-Gen. MICHEL DANET (France). Publ. *WCO News* (quarterly).

World Federation of Advertisers: 120 ave Louise, 1050 Brussels; tel. (2) 502-57-40; fax (2) 502-56-66; e-mail info@wfanet .org; internet www.wfanet.org; f. 1953; promotes and studies advertising and its related problems; holds World Congress (2001: Tokyo, Japan). Mems: asscns in 46 countries and 29 international companies. Pres. ANTHONY GORTZIS; Dir-Gen. BERNHARD ADRIAENSENS. Publ. *E-Monitor* (monthly).

World Packaging Organisation: 481 Carlisle Dr., Herndon, VA 20170-4823, USA; tel. (703) 318-5512; fax (703) 814-4961; e-mail wpo@pkgmatters.com; internet www.packinfo-world.org; f. 1967 to provide a forum for the exchange of knowledge of packaging technology and, in general, to create conditions for the conservation, preservation and distribution of world food production; holds annual congress and competition. Mems: Asian, North American, Latin American, European and South African packaging federations. Pres. SERGIO HABERFELD (Brazil); Gen. Sec. WILLIAM C. PFLAUM (USA).

World Trade Centers Association: 60 East 42nd St, Suite 1901, New York, NY 10165, USA; tel. (212) 432-2626; fax (212) 488-0064; internet www.wtca.org; f. 1968 to promote trade through the establishment of world trade centres, including education facilities, information services and exhibition facilities; operates an electronic trading and communication system (WTC On-Line). Mems: trade centres, chambers of commerce and other organizations in 95 countries. Pres. GUY F. TOZZOLI; Chair. BRYAN MONTGOMERY. Publ. *WTCA News* (monthly).

Transport

African Airlines Association: POB 20116, Nairobi, Kenya; tel. (2) 604925; fax (2) 601173; e-mail afraa@africaonline.co.ke; internet www.afraa.org; f. 1968 to give African air companies expert advice in technical, financial, juridical and market matters; to improve air transport in Africa through inter-carrier co-operation; and to develop manpower resources. Mems: 34 national carriers. Publs *Newsletter*, reports.

Airports Council International—ACI: POB 16, 1215 Geneva 15-Airport, Switzerland; tel. (22) 7178585; fax (22) 7178888; e-mail aci@airports.org; internet www.airports.org; f. 1991, following merger of Airport Operators Council International and International Civil Airports Association; aims to represent and develop co-operation among airports of the world. Mems: 554 mems operating more than 1,400 airports in 170 countries and territories. Chair. A. GHANEM AL-HAJRI; Dir-Gen. JONATHAN HOWE; Sec.-Gen. ALEXANDER STRAHL. Publs *World Report* (8–10 a year), *Airport World Magazine*, *Policy Handbook*, reports.

Arab Air Carriers' Organization—AACO: PO Box 13-5468, Beirut, Lebanon; tel. (1) 861297; fax (1) 863168; e-mail info@aaco.org; internet www.aaco.org; f. 1965 to promote co-operation in the activities of Arab airline companies. Mems: 20 Arab air carriers. Pres. AKBAR AL-BAKER (Qatar); Sec.-Gen. ABDUL WAHAB TEFFAHA. Publs *bulletins, reports and research documents.*

Association of Asia Pacific Airlines: 9th Floor, Kompleks Antarabangsa, Jalan Sultan Ismail, 50250 Kuala Lumpur, Malaysia; tel. (3) 2145-5600; fax (3) 2145-2500; e-mail aapahdg@aapa.org.my; internet www.aapairlines.org; f. 1966 as Orient Airlines Asscn; present name adopted in April 1997; represents the interests of Asia Pacific airlines; encourages the exchange of information and increased co-operation between airlines; seeks to develop safe, efficient, profitable and environmentally friendly air transport. Mems: 17 scheduled international airlines. Dir.-Gen. RICHARD T. STIRLAND. Publs *Annual Report*, *Annual Statistical Report*, *Monthly International Statistics*, *Orient Aviation* (10 a year).

Association of European Airlines: 350 ave Louise, bte 4, 1050 Brussels, Belgium; tel. (2) 639-89-89; fax (2) 639-89-90; e-mail aea.secretariat@aca.be; internet www.aea.be; f. 1954 to carry out research on political, commercial, economic and technical aspects of air transport; maintains statistical data bank. Mems: 29 airlines. Chair. LEO M. VAN WIJK (Netherlands); Sec.-Gen. KARL-HEINZ NEUMEISTER (Germany).

Baltic and International Maritime Council—BIMCO: Bagsvaerdvej 161, 2880 Bagsvaerd, Denmark; tel. 44-36-68-00; fax 44-36-68-68; e-mail mailbox@bimco.dk; internet www.bimco.dk; f. 1905 to unite shipowners and other persons and organizations connected with the shipping industry. Mems: in 122 countries, representing over 65% of world merchant tonnage. Pres. MICHAEL EVERARD (UK); Sec.-Gen. TRULS W. L'ORANGE. Publs *BIMCO Review* (annually), *BIMCO Bulletin* (6 a year), *Vessel* (CD-ROM), manuals.

Central Commission for the Navigation of the Rhine: Palais du Rhin, Place de la République, 67000 Strasbourg, France; tel. 3-88-52-20-10; fax 3-88-32-10-72; e-mail ccmr@ccr-zkr.org; internet www.ccr-zkr.org; f. 1815 to ensure free movement of traffic and standard river facilities for ships of all nations; draws up navigational rules; standardizes customs regulations; arbitrates in disputes involving river traffic; approves plans for river maintenance work; there is an administrative centre for social security for boatmen. Mems: Belgium, France, Germany, Netherlands, Switzerland. Sec.-Gen. JEAN-MARIE WOEHRLING (France). Publs Guides, rules and directives (in French and German).

Danube Commission: Benczúr utca 25, 1068 Budapest, Hungary; tel. (1) 352-1835; fax (1) 352-1839; e-mail secretariat@danubecom-intern.org; internet www.dunacom.matav.hu; f. 1948; supervises implementation of the Belgrade Convention on the Regime of Navigation on the Danube; approves projects for river maintenance; supervises a uniform system of traffic regulations on the whole navigable portion of the Danube and on river inspection. Mems: Austria, Bulgaria, Croatia, Germany, Hungary, Moldova, Romania, Russia, Slovakia, Ukraine, Yugoslavia. Pres. Dr H. STRASSER; Dir-Gen. Capt. D. NEDIALKOV. Publs *Basic Regulations for Navigation on the Danube*, *Hydrological Yearbook*, *Statistical Yearbook*, proceedings of sessions.

European Civil Aviation Conference—ECAC: 3 bis Villa Emile-Bergerat, 92522 Neuilly-sur-Seine Cédex, France; tel. 1-46-41-85-44; fax 1-46-24-18-18; e-mail ecac@compuserve.com; internet www.ecac-ceac.org; f. 1955; aims to promote the continued development of a safe, efficient and sustainable European air transport system. Mems: 38 European states. Pres. ALFREDO ROMA; Exec. Sec. RAYMOND BENJAMIN.

European Conference of Ministers of Transport—ECMT: 2 rue André Pascal, 75775 Paris Cédex 16, France; tel. 1-45-24-82-00; fax 1-45-24-97-42; e-mail ecmt.contact@oecd.org; internet www.oecd.org/cem; f. 1953 to achieve the maximum use and most rational development of European transport; aims to create a safe, sustainable, efficient, integrated transport system; provides a forum for analysis and discussion; holds round tables, seminars and symposia;. shares Secretariat staff with OECD (q.v.). Mems: 41 member countries, 6 associate mems, 2 observer countries. Sec.-Gen. JACK SHORT. Publs *Activities of the Conference* (annually), *ECMT News* (2 a year), *Catalogue of Publications*, various statistical publications and surveys.

European Organisation for the Safety of Air Navigation—EUROCONTROL: 96 rue de la Fusée, 1130 Brussels, Belgium; tel. (2) 729-90-11; fax (2) 729-90-44; internet www.eurocontrol.int; f. 1960; aims to develop a coherent and co-ordinated air traffic control system in Europe. A revised Convention was signed in June 1997, incorporating the following institutional structure: a General Assembly (known as the Commission in the transitional period), a Council (known as the Provisional Council) and an Agency under the supervision of the Director General; there are directorates, covering human resources and finance matters and a general secretariat. A special organizational structure covers the management of the European Air Traffic Management Programme. EUROCONTROL also operates the Experimental Centre (at Brétigny-sur-Orge, France), the Institute of Air Navigation Services (in Luxembourg), the Central Route Charges Office, the Central Flow Management Unit (both in Brussels) and the Upper Area Control Centre (in Maastricht, Netherlands). Mems: 28 European countries. Dir-Gen. VICTOR M. AGUADO (Spain).

European Railway Wagon Pool—EUROP: SNCB/NMBS, B-Cargo 407, Section 2014, 60 rue du Trôme, 1050 Brussels, Belgium; tel. (2) 525-88-55; fax (2) 525-86-91; f. 1953 for the common use of wagons put into the pool by member railways. Mems: national railway administrations of Austria, Belgium, Denmark, France, Germany, Italy, Luxembourg, Netherlands, Switzerland. Managing railway: Belgian Railways. Pres. A. MARTENS.

Forum Train Europe—FTE: Direction générale des chemins de fer fédéraux suisses, Hochschulstrasse 6, 3030 Berne, Switzerland; internet www.fte-rail.com; f. 1923 as the European Passenger Train Time-Table Conference to arrange international passenger connections by rail and water; since 1997 concerned also with rail freight. Mems: rail and steamship companies and administrations. Administered by the Directorate of the Swiss Federal Railways. Pres. P. A. URECH.

Institute of Air Transport: 103 rue la Boétie, 75008 Paris, France; tel. 1-43-59-38-68; fax 1-43-59-47-37; e-mail contac@ita-paris.com; internet www.ita-paris.com; f. 1945 as an international centre of research on economic, technical and policy aspects of air transport, and on the economy and sociology of transport and tourism; acts as economic and technical consultant in research requested by members on specific subjects; maintains a data bank, a library and a consultation and advice service; organizes training courses on air transport economics. Mems: organizations involved in air transport, production and equipment, universities, banks, insurance companies, private individuals and government agencies in 79 countries. Dir-Gen. JACQUES PAVAUX. Publs (in French and English), *ITA Press* (2 a month), *ITA Studies and Reports* (quarterly), *Aviation Industry Barometer* (quarterly).

Intergovernmental Organization for International Carriage by Rail: Gryphenhübeliweg 30, 3006 Berne, Switzerland; tel. (31) 3591010; fax (31) 3591011; e-mail otif@otif.ch; internet www.otif.ch; f. 1893 as Central Office for International Carriage by Rail, present name adopted 1985; aims to establish and develop a uniform system of law governing the international carriage of passengers, luggage and goods by rail in member states. Mems: 40 states. Dir-Gen. HANS RUDOLF ISLIKER. Publ. *Bulletin des Transports Internationaux ferroviaires* (quarterly, in French and German).

International Air Transport Association—IATA: 33 route de l'Aéroport, CP 416, 1215 Geneva 15, Switzerland; tel. (22) 7992525; fax (22) 7983553; e-mail information@iata.org; internet www.iata.org; f. 1945 to represent and serve the airline industry. Aims to promote safe, reliable and secure air services; to assist the industry to attain adequate levels of profitability while developing cost-effective operational standards; to promote the importance of the industry in global social and economic development; and to identify common concerns and represent the industry in addressing these at regional and international level; maintains regional offices in Amman, Brussels, Dakar, London, Nairobi, Santiago, Singapore and Washington, DC. Mems: 258 airline cos. Dir-Gen. PIERRE JEANNIOT; Corporate Sec. LORNE CLARK. Publ. *Airlines International* (every 2 months).

International Association for the Rhine Vessels Register—IVR: Vasteland 12E, 3011 BL Rotterdam (POB 23210, 3001 KE Rotterdam), Netherlands; tel. (10) 4116070; fax (10) 4129091; e-mail info@ivr.ne; internet www.ivr.ne; f. 1947 for the classification of Rhine ships, the organization and publication of a Rhine ships register, the unification of general average rules, and the harmonization of European inland navigation law. Mems: shipowners and asscns, insurers and asscns, shipbuilding engineers, average adjusters and others interested in Rhine traffic. Gen. Sec. T. K. HACKSTEINER.

International Association of Ports and Harbors—IAPH: Kono Bldg, 1-23-9 Nishi-Shimbashi, Minato-ku, Tokyo 105, Japan; tel. (3) 3591-4261; fax (3) 3580-0364; e-mail iaph@msn.com; internet www.iaph.or.jp; f. 1955 to increase the efficiency of ports and harbours through the dissemination of information on port organization, management, administration, operation, development and promotion; encourages the growth of water-borne commerce; holds conference every two years. Mems: 350 in 85 states. Pres. DOMINIC J. TADDEO (Canada); Sec.-Gen. SATOSHI INOUE (Japan). Publs *Ports and Harbors* (10 a year), *Membership Directory* (annually).

International Association of Public Transport: 17 ave Herrmann-Debroux, 1160 Brussels, Belgium; tel. (2) 673-61-00; fax (2) 660-10-72; e-mail administration@uitp.com; internet www.uitp.com; f. 1885 to study all problems connected with the urban and regional public passenger transport industry. Mems: 2,000 in 80 countries. Pres. JEAN-PAUL BAILLY (France); Sec.-Gen. HANS RAT. Publs *Public Transport International* (every 2 months), *EUExpress, Mobility News* (monthly, electronic), statistics reports.

International Chamber of Shipping: Carthusian Court, 12 Carthusian St, London, EC1M 6EZ, United Kingdom; tel. (20) 7417-8844; fax (20) 7417-8877; e-mail ics@marisec.org; internet www.marisec.org; f. 1921 to co-ordinate the views of the international shipping industry on matters of common interest, in the policy-making, technical and legal fields of shipping operations. Mems: national asscns representing free-enterprise shipowners and operators in 39 countries. Sec.-Gen. J. C. S. HORROCKS.

International Container Bureau: 167 rue de Courcelles, 75017 Paris, France; tel. 1-47-66-03-90; fax 1-47-66-08-91; f. 1933 to group representatives of all means of transport and activities concerning containers, to promote combined door-to-door transport by the successive use of several means of transport, to examine and bring into effect administrative, technical and customs advances, and to centralize data on behalf of mems. Mems: 800. Sec.-Gen. JEAN REY. Publ. *Container Bulletin*.

International Federation of Freight Forwarders' Associations: Baumackerstr. 24, POB 8050 Zürich, Switzerland; tel. (1) 3116511; fax (1) 3119044; e-mail info@fiata.com; internet www.fiata.com; f. 1926 to protect and represent its members at international level. Mems: 95 organizations and more than 2,500 associate members in 150 countries. Pres. ALDO DA ROS; Dir MARCO A. SANGALETTI. Publ. *FIATA Review* (every 2 months).

International Rail Transport Committee (Comité international des transports ferroviaires—CIT): 10A Bahnhofplatz, 3000 Berne 65, Switzerland; tel. (512) 202806; fax (512) 203457; e-mail cit@sbb.ch; internet www.cit.ch; f. 1902 for the development of international law relating to railway transport, on the basis of the Convention concerning International Carriage by Rail (COTIF) and its Appendices (CIV, CIM), and for the adoption of standard rules on other questions relating to international transport law. Mems: 300 transport undertakings in 37 countries. Pres. M. WEIBEL (Switzerland); Sec. M. LEIMGRUBER (Switzerland).

International Railway Congress Association: Section 10, 85 rue de France, 1060 Brussels, Belgium; tel. (2) 520-78-31; fax (2) 525-40-84; e-mail secretariat@aiccf.org; internet www.aiccf.org; f. 1885 to facilitate the progress and development of railways. Mems: governments, railway administrations, national and international organizations. Pres. E. SCHOUPPE; Sec.-Gen. A. MARTENS. Publ. *Rail International* (monthly).

International Road Federation—IRF: Washington office: 1010 Massachusetts Ave, NW, Suite 410, Washington, DC 20037, USA; tel. (202) 371-5544; fax (202) 371-5565; e-mail info@irfnet.org; internet www.irfnet.org; Geneva Office: 2 chemin de Blandonnet 1214, Vernier, Geneva, Switzerland; tel. (22) 3060260; fax (22) 3060270; f. 1948 to encourage the development and improvement of highways and highway transportation; organizes IRF world and regional meetings. Mems: 70 national road asscns and 500 individual firms and industrial asscns. Dir-Gen. (Washington) GERALD P. SHEA; Dir-Gen. (Geneva) M. W. WESTERHUIS. Publs *World Road Statistics* (annually), *World Highways* (8 a year).

International Road Safety Association (La prevention routière internationale—PRI): Estrada da Luz , 90-1°, 1600-160 Lisbon, Portugal; tel. (21) 7222230; fax (21) 7222232; e-mail info@lapri .org; internet www.lapri.org; f. 1959 for exchange of ideas and material on road safety; organizes international action and congresses; assists non-member countries. Mems: 74 national organizations. Pres. JOSÉ MIGUEL TRIGOSO (Portugal); Sec.-Gen. MARTINE PETERS. Publ. *Newsletter* (6 a year).

International Road Transport Union—IRU: Centre International, 3 rue de Varembé, BP 44, 1211 Geneva, Switzerland; tel. (22) 9182700; fax (22) 9182741; e-mail iru@iru.org; internet www.iru.org; f. 1948 to study all problems of road transport, to promote unification and simplification of regulations relating to road transport, and to develop the use of road transport for passengers and goods; represents and promotes the industry at an international level. Mems: 150 national asscns in 68 countries. Dir MARTIN MARMY. Publs *IRU Handbook of International Road Transport*, studies, congress and conference reports, regulations and statistics.

International Shipping Federation: Carthusian Court, 12 Carthusian St, London, EC1M 6EZ, United Kingdom; tel. (20) 7417-8844; fax (20) 7417-8877; e-mail isf@marisec.org; internet www.marisec.org; f. 1909 to consider all personnel questions affecting the interests of shipowners; responsible for Shipowners' Group at conferences of the International Labour Organisation. Mems: national shipowners' organizations in 34 countries. Pres. R. WESTFAL-LARSON (Norway); Sec.-Gen. J. C. S. HORROCKS. Publs *Guide to International Shipping Registers*, conference papers, guidelines and training records.

International Union for Inland Navigation: 7 quai du Général Koenig, 67085 Strasbourg Cédex, France; tel. 3-88-36-28-44; fax 3-88-37-04-82; f. 1952 to promote the interests of inland waterways carriers. Mems: national waterways organizations of

Austria, Belgium, France, Germany, Italy, Luxembourg, Netherlands, Switzerland. Pres. P. GRULOIS (Belgium); Sec. M. RUSCHER. Publs annual and occasional reports.

International Union of Railways (Union internationale des chemins de fer —UIC): 16 rue Jean-Rey, 75015 Paris, France; tel. 1-44-49-20-20; fax 1-44-49-20-29; e-mail communication@uic.asso.fr; internet www.uic.asso.fr; f. 1922 for the harmonization of railway operations and the development of international rail transport; aims to ensure international interoperability of the rail system; compiles information on economic, management and technical aspects of railways; co-ordinates research and collaborates with industry and the EU; organizes international conferences. Mems: 150 railways in 87 countries. Pres. ETIENNE SCHOUPPE; Chief Exec. PHILIPPE ROUMEGUÈRE. Publs *Rail International,* jointly with the International Railway Congress Association (IRCA) (monthly, in English, French and German), *International Railway Statistics* (annually), *Activities Reports, UIC Panorama* (newsletter).

Northern Shipowners' Defence Club (Nordisk Skibsrederforening): Kristinelundv. 22, POB 3033 El., 0207 Oslo, Norway; tel. 22-13-56-00; fax 22-43-00-35; e-mail post@nordisks-skibsrederforening.no; internet www.nordisk.org; f. 1889 to assist members in disputes over charter parties, contracts and sale and purchase, taking the necessary legal steps on behalf of members and bearing the cost of such claims. Mems: mainly Finnish, Swedish and Norwegian and some non-Scandinavian shipowners, representing about 1,800 ships and drilling rigs with gross tonnage of about 50m.. Man. Dir GEORG SCHEEL; Chair. MORTEN WERRING. Publ. *A Law Report of Scandinavian Maritime Cases* (annually).

Organisation for the Collaboration of Railways: Hozà 63–67, 00681 Warsaw, Poland; tel. (22) 6573600; fax (22) 6573654; e-mail osjd@osjd.org.pl; f. 1956; aims to improve standards and co-operation in railway traffic between countries of Europe and Asia; promotes co-operation on issues relating to traffic policy and economic and environmental aspects of railway traffic; ensures enforcement of a number of rail agreements; aims to elaborate and standardize general principles for international transport law. Conference of Ministers of mem. countries meets annually; Conference of Gen. Dirs of Railways meets at least once a year. Mems: ministries of transport of 27 countries world-wide. Chair. TADEUSZ SZOZDA. Publ. *OSShD Journal* (every 2 months, in Chinese, German and Russian).

Pan American Railway Congress Association (Asociación del Congreso Panamericano de Ferrocarriles): Av. 9 de Julio 1925, 13°, 1332 Buenos Aires, Argentina; tel. (11) 4381-4625; fax (11) 4814-1823; e-mail acpf@nat.com.ar; f. 1907, present title adopted 1941; aims to promote the development and progress of railways in the American continent; holds Congresses every three years. Mems: government representatives, railway enterprises and individuals in 21 countries. Pres. JUAN CARLOS DE MARCHI (Argentina); Gen. Sec. LUIS V. DONZELLI (Argentina). Publ. *Boletín ACPF* (5 a year).

Union of European Railway Industries—UNIFE: 221 ave Louise, 1050 Brussels, Belgium; tel. (2) 626-12-60; fax (2) 626-12-61; e-mail mail@unife.org; internet www.unife.org; f. 1975 to represent companies concerned in the manufacture of railway equipment in Europe to European and international organizations. Mems: 140 companies in 14 countries. Chair. ROLF ECKRODT; Dir Gen. DREWIN NIEUWENHUIS.

World Airlines Clubs Association—WACA: c/o IATA, 800 Pl. Victoria, POB 113, Montréal, Québec, Canada H3A 2R4; tel. (514) 874-0202; fax (514) 874-1753; internet www.waca.org; f. 1966; holds a General Assembly annually, regional meetings, international events and sports tournaments. Mems: clubs in 38 countries. Man. AUBREY WINTERBOTHAM. Publs *WACA World, WACA Contact, WACA World News,* annual report.

Youth and Students

AIESEC International: Teilingerstraat 126–128, 3032 Rotterdam, Netherlands; tel. (10) 443-43-83; fax (10) 265-13-86; e-mail info@ai.aiesec.org; internet www.aiesec.org; f. 1948 as International Association of Students in Economics and Management; works to develop leadership skills and socio-economic and international understanding among young people, through exchange programmes and related educational activities. Mems: 50,000 students in more than 650 higher education institutions in 88 countries and territories. Pres. SAHIL KAUL; Vice-Pres. ANDREW SCHURGOTT. Publ. *Annual Report.*

Asia Students Association: 353 Shangai St, 14/F, Kowloon, Hong Kong; tel. 23880515; fax 27825535; e-mail asasec@netvigator.com; f. 1969; aims to promote students' solidarity in struggling for democracy, self-determination, peace, justice and liberation; conducts campaigns, training of activists, and workshops on human rights and other issues of importance. There are Student Commissions for Peace, Education and Human Rights. Mems: 40 national or regional student unions in 25 countries and territories. Secretariat: LINA CABAERO (Philippines), STEVEN GAN (Malaysia), CHOW WING-HANG (Hong Kong). Publs *Movement News* (monthly), *ASA News* (quarterly).

Council on International Educational Exchange—CIEE: 205 East 42nd St, New York, NY 10017, USA; tel. (212) 661-1414; fax (212) 972-3231; e-mail strooboff@ciee.org; internet www.ciee.org; f. 1947; issues International Student Identity Card entitling holders to discounts and basic insurance; arranges overseas work and study programmes for students; co-ordinates summer work programme in the USA for foreign students; administers programmes for teachers and other professionals and sponsors conferences on educational exchange; operates a voluntary service programme. Mems: 307 colleges, universities and international educational organizations. Pres. and CEO STEVAN TROOBOFF. Publs include *Work, Study, Travel Abroad: The Whole World Handbook, Update, Volunteer!, High-School Student's Guide to Study, Travel and Adventure Abroad.*

European Law Students' Association—ELSA: 1 rue Defacqz, 1050 Brussels, Belgium; tel. (2) 534-56-79; fax (2) 534-65-86; internet www.elsa-online.org; f. 1981 to foster mutual understanding and promote social responsibility of law students and young laywers. Publs *ELSA Law Review, Legal Studies in Europe.*

European Students' Forum (Association des états généraux des étudiants de l'Europe): 15 rue Nestor de Tiere, 1040 Brussels, Belgium; tel. (2) 245-23-00; fax (2) 245-62-60; e-mail info@aegee.org; internet www.aegee.org; promotes cross-border communication and integration between students; holds specialized conferences. Mems: 17,000 students in 271 university cities in 40 countries.

European Youth Forum: 120 rue Joseph II, 1000 Brussels, Belgium; tel. (2) 286-94-12; fax (2) 233-37-09; e-mail youthforum@youthforum.org; internet www.europeanyouthforum.com; f. 1996; promotes development of a coherent and integrated youth policy; promotes the rights of young people, as well as understanding and respect for human rights; consults with international organizations and governments on issues relevant to young people.

International Association for the Exchange of Students for Technical Experience—IAESTE: e-mail webmaster@iaeste.org; internet www.iaeste.org; f. 1948. Mems: 63 national committees. Publs *Activity Report, Annual Report.*

International Association of Dental Students—IADS: c/o FDI World Dental Federation, 7 Carlisle St, London, W1V 5RG, United Kingdom; tel. (20) 7935-7852; fax (20) 7486-0183; internet www.iads.ndirect.co.uk; f. 1951 to represent dental students and their opinions internationally, to promote dental student exchanges and international congresses. Mems: 60,000 students in 45 countries, 15,000 corresponding mems. Pres. VALENTINA STERJOVA (UK). Publ. *IADS Newsletter* (3 a year).

International Federation of Medical Students' Associations—IFMSA: Institute of Social Medicine, Academisch Medisch Centrum, Meibergdreef 15, 1105 Amsterdam, Netherlands; tel. (20) 5665366; fax (20) 6972316; e-mail f.w.hilhorst@amc.uva.nl; internet www.ifmsa.org; f. 1951 to promote international co-operation in professional treatment and the achievement of humanitarian ideals; provides forum for medical students; maintains standing committees on professional exchange, electives exchange, medical education, public health, refugees and AIDS; organizes annual General Assembly. Mems: 57 asscns. Sec.-Gen. MIA HILHORST. Publ. *IFMSA Newsletter* (quarterly).

International Pharmaceutical Students' Federation—IPSF: POB 84200, 2508 AE The Hague, Netherlands; tel. (70) 3021992; fax (70) 3021999; e-mail ipsf@fip.nl; internet www.pharmweb.net/ipsf.html; f. 1949 to study and promote the interests of pharmaceutical students and to encourage international co-operation. Mems: 31 full mems from national organizations and 23 mems in assoc. from national or local organizations. Pres. GONÇALO SOUSA PINTO; Sec.-Gen. HELENA WESTERMARK. Publ. *IPSF News Bulletin* (3 a year).

International Union of Students: POB 58, 17th November St, 110 01 Prague 01, Czech Republic; tel. (2) 312812; fax (2) 316100; internet www.stud.uni-hannover/delgruppen/ius; f. 1946 to defend the rights and interests of students and strive for peace, disarmament, the eradication of illiteracy and of all forms of discrimination; operates research centre, sports and cultural centre and student travel bureau; activities include conferences, meetings, solidarity campaigns, relief projects; awards 30–40 scholarships annually. Mems: 140 organizations from 115 countries. Pres. JOSEF SKALA; Vice-Pres. MARTA HUBIČKOVÁ; Gen. Sec. GIORGOS MICHAELIDES (Cyprus). Publs *World Student News* (quarterly), *IUS Newsletter, Student Life* (quarterly), *DE—Democratization of Education* (quarterly).

International Young Christian Workers: 4 ave G. Rodenbach, 1030 Brussels, Belgium; tel. (2) 242-18-11; fax (2) 242-48-00; e-mail jociycw@skynet.be; internet www.skynet.be/sky34197; f. 1925, on the inspiration of the Priest-Cardinal Joseph Cardijn; aims to educate young workers to take on present and future responsibilities in their commitment to the working class, and to confront all the situations which prevent them from fulfilling themselves. Pres. DESROSIERS JOSÉ (Canada); Sec.-Gen. LANGWIESNER GERTRAUD (Austria). Publs *International INFO* (3 a year), *IYCW Bulletin* (quarterly).

International Youth and Student Movement for the United Nations—ISMUN: c/o Palais des Nations, 16 ave Jean-Trembly, 1211 Geneva 10, Switzerland; tel. (22) 7985850; fax (22) 7334838; internet www.ismun.org; f. 1948 by the World Federation of United Nations Associations, independent since 1949; an international non-governmental organization of students and young people dedicated especially to supporting the principles embodied in the United Nations Charter and Universal Declaration of Human Rights; encourages constructive action in building economic, social and cultural equality and in working for national independence, social justice and human rights on a world-wide scale; maintains regional offices in Austria, France, Ghana, Panama and the USA. Mems: asscns in 53 countries. Sec.-Gen. JAN LÖNN. Publ. *ISMUN Newsletter* (monthly).

International Youth Hostel Federation: 1st floor, Fountain House, Parkway, Welwyn Garden City, Herts., AL8 6QW, United Kingdom; tel. (1707) 324170; fax (1707) 323980; e-mail iyhf@iyhf.org; internet www.iyhf.org; f. 1932; facilitates international travel by members of the various youth hostel asscns; advises and helps in the formation of youth hostel asscns in countries where no such organizations exist; records over 34m. overnight stays annually in around 4,300 youth hostels. Mems: 58 national asscns with over 3.2m. national members and 1m. international guest members; 12 associated national organizations. Pres. Dr HARISH SAXENA (India); Sec.-Gen. ULRICH BUNJES (Germany). Publs *Annual Report, Guidebook on World Hostels* (annually), *Manual, News Bulletin.*

Junior Chamber International (JCI), Inc.: 400 University Drive (POB 140-577), Coral Gables, FL 33114-0577, USA; tel. (305) 446-7608; fax (305) 442-0041; e-mail jciwhq@ix.netcom.com; internet www.juniorchamber.org; f. 1944 to encourage and advance international understanding and goodwill; aims to solve civic problems by arousing civic consciousness; Junior Chamber organizations throughout the world provide opportunities for leadership training and for the discussion of social, economic and cultural questions. Mems: 400,000 in 90 countries. Pres. SALVADOR BATLLE (Spain); Sec.-Gen. BENNY ELLERBE. Publ. *JCI News* (quarterly, in English and more than six other languages).

Latin American and Caribbean Confederation of Young Men's Christian Associations (Confederación Latinoamericana y del Caribe de Asociaciones Cristianas de Jóvenes): Culpina 272, 1406 Buenos Aires, Argentina; tel. (11) 4373-4156; fax (11) 4374-4408; e-mail clacj@wamani.apc.org; f. 1914; aims to encourage the moral, spiritual, intellectual, social and physical development of young men; to strengthen the work of national Asscns and to sponsor the establishment of new Asscns. Mems: affiliated YMCAs in 25 countries (comprising 350,000 individuals). Pres. GERARDO VITUREIRA (Uruguay); Gen. Sec. MARCO ANTONIO HOCHSCHEIT (Brazil). Publs *Diecisiete/21* (bulletin), *Carta Abierta, Brief*, technical articles and other studies.

Pan-African Youth Movement (Mouvement pan-africain de la jeunesse): 19 rue Debbih Chérif, BP 72, Didouch Mourad, 16000 Algiers, Algeria; tel. and fax (2) 71-64-71; f. 1962; aims to encourage the participation of African youth in socio-economic and political development and democratization; organizes conferences and seminars, youth exchanges and youth festivals. Mems: youth groups in 52 African countries and liberation movements. Publ. *MPJ News* (quarterly).

World Alliance of Young Men's Christian Associations: 12 clos. Belmont, 1208 Geneva, Switzerland; tel. (22) 8495100; fax (22) 8495110; e-mail office@ymca.int; internet www.ymca.int; f. 1855 to unite the National Alliances of Young Men's Christian Associations throughout the world. Mems: national alliances and related asscns in 128 countries. Pres. MARTIN VÖGLER (Switzerland); Sec.-Gen. NICK NIGHTINGALE (UK). Publ. *YMCA World* (quarterly).

World Assembly of Youth: International Youth Centre, Jalan Tenteram, Bandar Tun Razak, 56000 Kuala Lumpur, Malaysia; tel. (3) 9732722; fax (3) 9736011; internet www.jaring.my/way; f. 1949 as co-ordinating body for youth councils and organizations; organizes conferences, training courses and practical development projects. Pres. Datuk ALI RUSTAM; Sec.-Gen. HEIKKI PAKARINEN. Publs *WAY Information* (every 2 months), *Youth Roundup* (monthly), *WAY Forum* (quarterly).

World Association of Girl Guides and Girl Scouts—WAGGGS: World Bureau, Olave Centre, 12C Lyndhurst Rd, London, NW3 5PQ, United Kingdom; tel. (20) 7794-1181; fax (20) 7431-3764; e-mail wagggs@wagggsworld.org; internet www.wagggsworld.org; f. 1928 to enable girls and young women to develop their full potential as responsible citizens, toand support friendship and mutual understanding among girls and young women world-wide; World Conference meets every three years. Mems: about 10m. individuals in 140 organizations. Chair. World Board GINNY RADFORD ; Dir World Bureau LESLEY BULMAN. Publs *Triennial Report, Annual Report, Trefoil Round the World* (every 3 years), *Our World News* (quarterly).

World Council of Service Clubs: POB 148, Wallaroo, South Australia 5556, Australia; e-mail kelly@kadina.mtx.net.au; internet www.woco.org; f. 1946 to provide a means for the exchange of information and news, with the aim of furthering international understanding and co-operation; aims to create in young people a sense of civic responsibility; works to facilitate the extension of service clubs. Mems: over 3,000 clubs in 83 countries. Sec.-Gen. SHANE KELLY.

World Federation of Democratic Youth—WFDY: POB 147, 1389 Budapest, Hungary; tel. (1) 3502202; fax (1) 3501204; e-mail wfdy@mail.matav.hu; internet www.wfdy.org; f. 1945 to strive for peace, disarmament and joint action by democratic and progressive youth movements and for the creation of a new and more just international economic order; promotes national independence, democracy, social progress and youth rights; supports the liberation struggles in Asia, Africa and Latin America. Mems: 152 members in 102 countries. Pres. IRAKLIS TSAVDARIDIS (Greece). Publ. *WFDY News* (every 3 months, in English, French and Spanish).

World Organization of the Scout Movement: Case Postale 241, 1211 Geneva 4, Switzerland; tel. (22) 7051010; fax (22) 7051020; e-mail worldbureau@world.scout.org; internet www.scout.org; f. 1922 to promote unity and understanding of scouting throughout the world; to develop good citizenship among young people by forming their characters for service, co-operation and leadership; and to provide aid and advice to members and potential member asscns. The World Scout Bureau (Geneva) has regional offices in Chile, Egypt, Kenya and the Philippines (the European Region has its offices in Brussels and Geneva). Mems: over 25m. in 215 countries and territories. Sec.-Gen. Dr JACQUES MOREILLON (Switzerland). Publs *World Scouting News* (every 2 months), *Triennial Report.*

World Union of Jewish Students—WUJS: Rechov Alkalai 9, POB 4498, 91045 Jerusalem, Israel; tel. (2) 5610133; fax (2) 5610741; e-mail office@wujs.org.il; internet www.wujs.org.il; f. 1924 (by Albert Einstein); organization for national student bodies concerned with educational and political matters, where possible in co-operation with non-Jewish student organizations, UNESCO, etc.; divided into six regions; organizes Congress every two years. Mems: 52 national unions representing over 1,500,000 students. Chair. PELEG RESHEF. Publs *The Student Activist Yearbook, Heritage and History, Forum, WUJS Report.*

World Young Women's Christian Association—World YWCA: 16 Ancienne Route, 1218 Grand-Saconnex, Geneva, Switzerland; tel. (22) 9296040; fax (22) 9296044; e-mail worldoffice@worldywca.org; internet www.worldywca.org; f. 1894 for the linking together of national YWCAs (now in 98 countries) for their mutual help and development and the initiation of work in countries where the Association does not yet exist; works for international understanding, for improved social and economic conditions and for basic human rights for all people. Pres. JANE WOLFE; Gen. Sec. MUSIMBI KANYORO. Publs *Annual Report, Common Concern.*

Youth for Development and Co-operation—YDC: Rijswijkstrasse 141, 1062 HN Amsterdam, Netherlands; tel. (20) 6142510; fax (20) 6175545; e-mail ydc@geo2.geonet.de; aims to strengthen youth structures promoting co-operation between young people in the industrialized and developing worlds, in order to achieve development that is environmentally sustainable and socially just; holds seminars, conferences and campaigns on issues related to youth and development. Mems: 51 organizations. Sec.-Gen. B. AUER. Publ. *FLASH Newsletter* (irregular).

PART FIVE

Who's Who in International Organizations

ABDULAI, Yesufu Seyyid Momoh; Nigerian economist; b. 19 June 1940, Auchi; m. Zene Makonnen Abdulai 1982; three s. one d.; ed. Mount Allison Univ. and McGill Univ., Canada; Tech. Asst to Exec. Dir for Africa Group 1, World Bank Group, Washington, DC, USA 1971–73, Adviser to Exec. Dir 1973–78, Alt. Exec. Dir for Africa Group 1 1978–80, Exec. Dir 1980–82, Vice-Chair. Jt Audit Cttee Exec. Bd 1980–82; Chair. Jt Secr. African Exec. Dirs of the World Bank Group and the IMF 1975–77; Man. Dir and CEO Fed. Mortgage Bank of Nigeria Jan. 1982–83; Dir-Gen. OPEC Fund for Int. Devt 1983–.
Address: OPEC Fund for International Development, POB 995, 1011 Vienna, Austria.
Telephone: (1) 515-64-0; **fax:** (1) 513-92-38; **internet:** www.opecfund.org.

ALEGRETT, Sebastián, B.ECONS.; Venezuelan diplomatist; b. 1942, Caracas; ed. Andrés Bello Catholic Univ., Caracas, Univ. of Paris, France; private consultant; Pres. Export Financing Fund of Venezuela (FINEXPO); mem. of Bd of Dirs, Central Bank of Venezuela, CVG Siderúrgica del Orinoco, CA (SIDOR) Iron and Steel Plant, CVG Internacional, Extebandes; Integration Dir Inst. of Foreign Trade of Venezuela 1971–74, Pres. 1979–83; Prof. Andrés Bello Catholic Univ. and Central Univ. of Venezuela 1973–79; Perm. Sec. Latin American Economic System 1983–87; Amb. to Brazil 1990–94, to Colombia 1996–97; Perm. Rep. to Org. of American States 1994–96; Rep. of Venezuela to the Acuerdo de Cartagena (the Cartagena Agreement, or the Andean Community of Nations) and Corporación Andina de Fomento (CAF); Sec.-Gen. Andean Community of Nations Aug. 1997–.
Address: Andean Community of Nations, Avda Paseo de la República 3895, San Isidro, Lima 27, Peru.
Telephone: (1) 4111400; **fax:** (1) 2213329; **e-mail:** contacto@comunidadandina.org; **internet:** www.comunidadandina.org.

AMOAKO, Kingsley Y., M.SC., PH.D.; Ghanaian economist; b. 1947; ed. Univ. of Ghana, Univ. of California, Berkeley, USA; with IBRD (World Bank) from the 1970s, Dir, Dept of Education and Social Policy 1993–95; UN Under-Sec.-Gen. and Exec. Sec., Economic Commission for Africa (ECA) July 1995–.
Address: ECA, Africa Hall, POB 3001, Addis Ababa, Ethiopia.
Telephone: (1) 517200; **fax:** (1) 514416; **e-mail:** ecainfo@uneca.org; **internet:** www.uneca.org.

ANNAN, Kofi A., B.A.(ECONS)., M.SC.; Ghanaian international civil servant; b. 8 April 1938, Kumasi; m. Nane Cronstedt; one s. two d.; ed. Univ. of Science and Tech., Kumasi, Macalester Coll., St. Paul, Minn., USA, Institut des Hautes Etudes Internationales, Geneva, Switzerland, Massachusetts Inst. of Tech. (MIT), USA; Alfred P. Sloan Fellow, MIT 1971–72; held post in UN Economic Commission for Africa (ECA), Addis Ababa, Ethiopia, UN, New York, USA, WHO, Geneva, Switzerland 1962–71, Admin. Man. Officer, UN, Geneva 1972–74; Chief Civilian Personnel Officer, UN Emergency Force, Cairo, Egypt 1974; Man. Dir Ghana Tourist Devt Co 1974–76; Dep. Chief of Staff Services, Office of Personnel Services, Office of UNHCR, Geneva 1976–80, Dep. Dir Div. of Admin., and Head Personnel Service 1980–83; Dir of Admin. Man. Service, then Dir of Budget, Office of Financial Services, UN, New York 1984–87, Asst Sec.-Gen., Office of Human Resources Man. 1987–90; Controller, Office of Programme Planning, Budget and Finance 1990–92; Asst Sec.-Gen. Dept of Peace-Keeping Operations 1992–93; Under-Sec.-Gen. 1993–96; UN Special Envoy (a.i.) to former Yugoslavia 1995–96; Sec.-Gen. of UN Jan. 1997–. Awarded Nobel Peace Prize, jointly with UN, Dec. 2001.
Address: United Nations, New York, NY 10017, USA.
Telephone: (212) 963-1234; **fax:** (212) 963-4879; **internet:** www.un.org/News/ossg/sg/.

ARAM I (KESHISHIAN), Catholicos of Cilicia, His Holiness, PH.D.; Lebanese ecclesiastic; b. 1947; ed. Seminary of the Armenian Apostolic Church, Antelias, Near East School of Theology, Beirut, American Univ. of Beirut, Fordham Univ., New York, USA, World Council of Churches (WCC) Graduate School of Ecumenical Studies, Bossey, Switzerland, Univ. of Oxford, United Kingdom; ordained priest 1968; named to WCC Faith and Order Comm. 1975; *locum tenens* of diocese of Lebanon 1978; primate 1979; ordained bishop 1980; elected to Central Cttee of WCC 1983, youngest person and first Orthodox to be elected Moderator of Central Cttee of WCC 1991, re-elected 1998; Catholicos of the See of Cilicia of the Armenian Apostolic Church 1995–; mem. Oriental–Eastern Orthodox and Oriental Orthodox–Roman Catholic bilateral dialogues; Hon. mem. Pro-Oriente Catholic Ecumenical Foundation, Vienna, Austria. *Publications:* 12 incl. Conciliar Fellowship: A Common Goal 1990, The Challenge to be a Church in a Changing World 1997.
Address: WCC, 150 route de Ferney, POB 2100, 1211 Geneva 2, Switzerland.
Telephone: (22) 7916111; **fax:** (22) 7910361; **internet:** www.wcc-coe.org.

ATTIYA, Abdul Rahman ibn Hamad al-; Qatari politician and international official; fmr Min. of Energy, Industry, Water and Electricity; Sec.-Gen. Co-operation Council for the Arab States of the Gulf (GCC) 2002–.
Address: Co-operation Council for the Arab States of the Gulf, POB 7153, Riyadh 11462, Saudi Arabia.
Telephone: (1) 482-7777; **fax:** (1) 482-9089; **internet:** www.gcc-sg.org.

BAGE, Lennart; Swedish diplomatist; Assistant Under-Sec. Ministry of Foreign Affairs; Amb. to Zimbabwe; Head Dept for Int. Co-operation, Ministry of Foreign Affairs, Dep. Dir-Gen. Ministry of Foreign Affairs–2001; Pres. and CEO Int. Fund for Agricultural Development (IFAD) April 2001–.
Address: IFAD, Via del Serafico 107, 00142 Rome, Italy.
Telephone: (06) 54591; **fax:** (06) 5043463; **e-mail:** ifad@ifad.org; **internet:** www.ifad.org.

BAKER, James Addison, III, LL.B.; US government official and lawyer; b. 28 April 1930, Texas; m. Susan Garrett 1973; eight c.; ed. Princeton Univ. and Univ. of Texas Law School; served with US Marine Corps 1952–54; with law firm Andrews, Kurth, Campbell and Jones, Houston, Texas 1957–75; Under-Sec. of Commerce under Pres. Ford 1975; Nat. Chair. Ford's presidential campaign 1976; Campaign Dir for George Bush in primary campaign 1980, later joined Reagan campaign; White House Chief of Staff and on Nat. Security Council 1981–85; Trustee, Woodrow Wilson Int. Center for Scholars, Smithsonian Inst. 1977–; Sec. of the Treasury 1985–88, Sec. of State 1989–92; White House Chief of Staff and Sr Counsellor 1992–93; Gov. Rice Univ. 1993; Sr Partner Baker and Botts 1993–; Personal Envoy of the UN Sec.-Gen., UN Mission for the Referendum in Western Sahara (MINURSO) 1997–. *Publication:* The Politics of Diplomacy 1995.
Address: c/o Dept of Peace-keeping Operations, Room S-3727-B, United Nations, New York, NY 10017, USA.
Telephone: (212) 963-9222; **fax:** (212) 963-8079.

BARADEI, Mohamed M. el-, PH.D.; Egyptian diplomatist; b. 1942; m.; one s. one d.; ed. Univ. of Cairo, Egypt, New York Univ., USA; with diplomatic service incl. Perm. Rep. to UN (New York and Geneva, Switzerland); Rep. of Dir-Gen. of the Int. Atomic Energy Agency (IAEA) to UN, New York 1984–87, Legal Adviser to IAEA, Dir of IAEA's Legal Div., Asst Dir-Gen. for External Rels 1993–97, Dir-Gen. IAEA Dec. 1997–; mem. Int. Law Asscn, American Soc. of Int. Law, Nuclear Law Asscn.
Address: IAEA, POB 100, Wagramerstr. 5, 1400 Vienna,Austria.
Telephone: (1) 26000; **fax:** (1) 26007; **e-mail:** official.mail@iaea.org; **internet:** www.iaea.org/worldatom.

BASHIR, Attalla Hamad, B.SC., M.A., PH.D; Sudanese diplomatist and international official; b. 23 Aug. 1946, Dongola, Sudan; m.; one s. one d.; ed. Khartoum Univ. –1970, Syracuse Univ., New York, USA –1979, Academy of Commerce, Bucharest, Romania –1986; joined diplomatic service 1971; served Kuwait, Bahrain, Czechoslovakia, Hungary, Malta, Italy, Romania, Ethiopia; Amb. to German Democratic Republic 1989–90; Amb. to Rep. of Korea 1990–93; Amb. to Saudi Arabia and Perm. Rep. to Islamic Development Bank and Organization of the Islamic Conference 1995–97; Amb. to Netherlands and Resident Rep. to ICJ 1997–2000; Dir-Gen. Bilateral and Regional Relations, Ministry of External Relations –2000; Exec. Sec. Intergovernmental Authority on Devt (IGAD) June 2000–.
Address: IGAD, BP 2653, Djibouti.
Telephone: 354050; **fax:** 356994; **e-mail:** igad@igadregion.org; **internet:** www.igadregion.org.

BELLAMY, Carol, J.D.; US agency administrator; b. 1942, Plainfield, NJ; ed. Gettysburg Coll. and New York Univ.; Asst Commr, Dept of Mental Health and Mental Health Retardation Service, New York; with Peace Corps, Guatemala; Assoc. Cravath, Swaine and Moore, New York; mem. New York State Senate; Man. Dir Morgan Stanley and Co, New York; Dir Peace Corps, Washington, DC 1993–95; Exec. Dir UNICEF 1995–.
Address: UNICEF, 3 United Nations Plaza, New York, NY 10017, USA.
Telephone: (212) 326-7000; **fax:** (212) 888-7465; **e-mail:** netmaster@unicef.org; **internet:** www.unicef.org.

BELKEZIZ, Abdelouahed, DR.JUR; Moroccan international organization official; b. 5 July 1939, Marrakesh, Morocco; ed. Univ. of Rennes, France; Dean Moroccan Univ. (Rabat) 1966, Hassan II Univ. (Casablanca) 1985, Ibn Tofail Univ. (Kenitra) 1992, Univ. Muhammad V (Rabat) 1997-2000; Pres. Exec. Cttee Islamic World Univs Fed. 1997–2000; Amb. to Iraq 1977–79; Min. of Information 1979–81, Min. of Information, Min. of Youth and Sports 1981–83, Min. of Foreign Affairs 1983–85; Sec.-Gen. Org. of the Islamic Conf. (OIC) Jan. 2001–.
Address: General Secretariat, Organization of the Islamic Conference, Kilo 6, Mecca Road, P.O. Box 178, Jeddah 21411, Saudi Arabia.
Telephone: (2) 680-0800; **fax:** 687-3568; **e-mail:** info@oic-oci.org; **internet:** www.oic-oci.org.

BRAHIMI, Lakhdar; Algerian United Nations official and politician; b. 1 Jan. 1934; m.; 3 c.; Amb. to Egypt and Sudan 1963–1970Amb. to United Kingdom 1971–79; diplomatic advisor 1982–84; Under-Sec. Gen. League of Arab States 1984–91; Min. of Foreign Affairs 1991–93; Special Rep. of the UN Sec.-Gen. for Haiti 1994–96; Under Sec.-Gen. for Special Assignments in Support of Preventive and Peacemaking Efforts of the Sec.-Gen. (appointed Jan. 1997); Special Envoy of the UN Sec.-Gen. in Afghanistan, UN Special Mission to Afghanistan (UNSMA) July 1997–Oct. 1999, Special Envoy of UN Sec.-Gen. in Angola (appointed July 1998); Chair. UN panel for evaluation of peace-keeping operations March–Aug. 2000; Special Rep. of the UN Sec.-Gen. for Afghanistan Oct. 2001–.
Address: Dept of Peace-keeping Operations, Room S-3727B, UN, New York, NY 10017, USA.
Telephone: (212) 963-9222; **fax:** (212) 963-8079.

BRUNDTLAND, Gro Harlem, M.D., M.P.H.; Norwegian politician and physician; b. 20 April 1939, Oslo; m. Arne Olav Brundtland 1960; three s. (one deceased) one d.; ed. Oslo Univ. and Harvard Univ., USA; Consultant, Ministry of Health and Social Affairs 1965–67; Medical Officer, Oslo City Health Dept 1968–69; Dep. Dir School Health Services, Oslo 1969; Min. of Environment 1974–79; Dep. Leader Labour Party 1975–81, Leader Labour Parl. Group 1981–92; Prime Min. of Norway Feb.–Oct. 1981, 1986–89, 1990–96; mem. Parl. Standing Cttee on Foreign Affairs, former mem. Parl. Standing Cttee on Finance; mem. of Storting (Parl.) 1977–97; Dir-Gen. World Health Org. (WHO) July 1998–; Chair. UN World Comm. on Environment and Devt; former Vice-Chair. Sr Secondary Schools' Socialist Asscn, Students' Asscn of Labour Party; Third World Prize for Work on Environmental Issues 1989, Indira Gandhi Prize 1990, Onassis Foundation Award 1992. *Publications:* articles on preventive medicine, school health and growth studies.
Address: WHO, Ave Appia, 1211 Geneva 27, Switzerland.
Telephone: (22) 7912111; **fax:** (22) 7913111; **e-mail:** info@who.ch; **internet:** www.who.int.

BUERGENTHAL, Thomas, B.A., LL.D; American judge; b. 11 May 1934, Lubochna, fmr Czechoslovakia (became US citizen 1957); m.; three s.; mem. (Judge, then Pres.) Inter-American Court on Human Rights 1979–91; mem. (Judge, then Pres.) Admin. Tribunal Inter-American Devt Bank 1989–94; mem. UN Human Rights Comm. 1995–99; mem. Claims Resolution Tribunal for Dormant Accounts, Switzerland 1998–99, Vice-Chair. 1999; mem. (Judge) Int. Court of Justice March 2000–.
Address: Peace Palace, Carnegieplein 2, 2517 KJ The Hague, Netherlands.
Telephone: (70) 302-23-23; **fax:** (70) 364-99-28; **e-mail:** information@icj-cij.org; **internet:** www.icj-cij.org.

CAPELING-ALAKIJA, Sharon, B.ED.; Canadian international official; b. 6 May 1944, Moose Jaw, Saskatchewan; m. 1985 (died); three s.; ed. Univ. of Saskatchewan; Teacher, Saskatchewan 1966–67; Volunteer Dept Head and Teacher in Tanzania and Barbados, Canadian Univ. Service Overseas (CUSO) 1967–72, Co-ordinator Local Cttee, London, Ontario 1972–74, Co-ordinator Orientation Dept, Ottawa 1974–77, Dir Public Affairs and Programme Funding 1977–82, Dir Human Resources Div. 1978–79, Dir West Africa Region, Lomé, Togo 1982–89; Dir UN Devt Fund for Women, New York, USA 1989–94; Dir Office of Evaluation and Strategic Planning, UNDP, New York 1994–97; Exec. Co-ordinator UN Volunteers (UNV) 1998–; affiliated to Bd of Dirs of North/South Inst., Ottawa, and Daimler/Benz Foundation Kolleg, Ladenburg, Germany; Patron of Global Co-operation Council, Nord-Süd-Forum e.V. Feb. 1998; Hon. Ph.D. (Univ. of Saskatchewan) May 1998.
Address: UNV, Martin-Luther-King-Str. 8, POB 260111, 53153 Bonn, Germany.
Telephone: (228) 8152000; **fax:** (228) 815001; **e-mail:** information@unvolunteers.org; **internet:** www.unvolunteers.org.

CARRARD, François Denis Etienne, LL.D.; Swiss lawyer; b. 19 Jan. 1938, Lausanne; ed. Lausanne, John Muir High School, Pasadena, California, USA, Univ. of Lausanne; with audit co., Lausanne 1962; with attorney's practice, Stockholm, Sweden 1963–64; Attorney, Lausanne 1965–, admitted to bar of Vaud (Swiss bar) 1967, Sr partner Etude Carrard, Paschoud, Heim et Associés; Dir and Chair. of Bds of several cos; Dir-Gen. Int. Olympic Cttee Sept. 1989–; fmrly mem. Swiss Federal Comm. of Foreign Indemnities, Vice-Pres. Bd of Vintage Brands of Vaud; Pres. Automobile-Club de Suisse; Chair. Montreux Jazz Festival Foundation, Gabriella Giorgi-Cavaglieri Foundation; mem. Ordre des Avocats Vaudois, Fédération Suisse des Avocats, Int. Bar Asscn, Asscn Suisse de l'Arbitrage, Union Internationale des Avocats; Commdr, Order of Mérito Civil (Spain) 1992, Officer, Order of Saint-Charles (Monaco) 1993.
Address: Int. Olympic Cttee, Château de Vidy, 1007 Lausanne, Switzerland.
Telephone: (21) 6216111; **fax:** (21) 6216216; **internet:** www.olympic.org.

CARRINGTON, Edwin Wilberforce, M.SC.; Tobagonian economist; b. 23 June 1938; m.; two s. one d.; ed. Univ. of the West Indies, McGill Univ., Canada; Administrative Cadet, Central Planning Unit, Prime Min.'s Office 1964; Chief of Econ. and Statistics, CARICOM 1973–76, Dir Trade and Integration Div. 1973–76, Dep. Sec.-Gen. ACP 1976–85, Sec.-Gen. 1985; High Commissioner to Guyana 1991; Sec.-Gen. CARICOM 1992; Sec.-Gen. Caribbean Forum ACP states. *Publications:* Industrialization by Invitation: the case of Trinidad and Tobago 1968, The Solution of Economic Problems through Regional Groupings (jointly), Tourism as a Vehicle for Economic Development 1975.
Address: CARICOM, Bank of Guyana Bldg, POB 10827, Georgetown, Guyana.
Telephone: (2) 69281; **fax:** (2) 67816; **e-mail:** carisec3@caricom.org; **internet:** www.caricom.org.

CATTAUI, Maria Livanos; Swiss foundation executive; b. 25 June 1941, New York, USA; m.; two s.; ed. Harvard Univ., USA; fmrly staff writer and researcher, Encyclopædia Britannica, Time Life Books, editorial supervisor and planner; freelance writer 1963–68; at World Economic Forum, Geneva, Switzerland from 1977, mem. Exec. Bd, Exec. Dir, Man. Dir 1980–96; Sec.-Gen. Int. Chamber of Commerce (ICC) 1996–.
Address: ICC, 38 Cours Albert 1er, 75008 Paris, France.
Telephone: 1-49-53-28-28; **fax:** 1-49-53-29-42; **e-mail:** icc@iccwbo.org; **internet:** www.iccwbo.org.

CHAMBAS, Mohamed Ibn; LL.B., PH.D.; Ghanaian lawyer and political scientist; b. 7 Dec. 1950; m.; ed. Univ. of Ghana, Legon, Cornell Univ., New York, Western Reserve Univ., Cleveland, U.S.A.; teacher Oberlin Coll., Ohio; practised law with Forbes, Forbes and Teamor L.P., Ohio; Deputy Foreign Sec. of Ghana 1987; M.P. for Bimbilla 1993–96, 2000–; First Deputy Speaker Ghanaian Parl. 1993–94; Deputy Foreign Min. 1994–, Chair. Foreign Affairs Cttee. 1993–94; Deputy Min. of Educ. 1997–2000; Exec. Sec. ECOWAS Jan. 2002–; fmr. Del. to UN Gen. Ass., OAU, Non-aligned Movt., Commonwealth; mem. Nat. Democratic Congress.

Address: Economic Community of West African States, ECOWAS Secretariat and Conference Centre, 60 Yakubu Gowon Crescent, Asokoro, Abuja, Nigeria.
Telephone: (9) 3147647; **fax:** (9) 3147646; **e-mail:** info@ecowasmail.net; **internet:** www.ecowas.int.

CHECHELASHVILI, Valeri; PH.D.; Georgian diplomatist and international organization official; b. 17 March 1961, Tbilisi; m. Marine Neparidze; two s. one d.; ed. Kyiv State Univ., Ukraine; mem. staff Foreign Econ. Relations Dept., Ministry of Light Industry 1987–88; Deputy Head of Foreign Econ. Relations section, Jt. Stock Co. Gruzkurort 1988–89; First Sec. Dept. of Int. Econ. Relations, Ministry of Foreign Affairs 1989–90, Deputy Dir. 1990–91, First Deputy Dir. 1991–92, Dir. 1992–94, Deputy Min. of Foreign Affairs 1998–2000; Amb. to Ukraine 1994–98; Sec.-Gen. of the Org. of the Black Sea Econ. Co-operation (BSEC) 2000–; Second Degree Order for Service, Ukraine 1998. *Publications: several articles in learned journals on econ. co-operation.*
Address: BSEC, İstinye Cad. Müşir Fuad Paşa Yalısı, Eski Tersane 80860 İstinye-İstanbul, Turkey.
Telephone: (212) 229-63-30; **fax:** (212) 229-63-36; **e-mail:** bsec@turk.net; **internet:** www.bsec.gov.tr.

CHERPITEL, Didier J.; French Red Cross official; b. 24 December 1944, Paris; m. Nicole Estrangin 1973; two d.; banking career with J.P. Morgan, Head of Private Banking Europe June 1996–97; Man. Dir of Security Cap. Markets Group Ltd 1998–99; Sec.-Gen. Int. Fed. of Red Cross and Red Crescent Socs Jan. 2000–.
Address: International Federation of Red Cross and Red Crescent Societies, 17 chemin des Crêts, Petit-Saconnex, CP 372, 1211 Geneva 19, Switzerland.
Telephone: (22) 7304222; **fax:** (22) 7330395; **e-mail:** secretariat@ifrc.org; **internet:** www.ifrc.org.

CHINO, Tadao, B.A., B.L.; Japanese banker; b. 1934; m.; two d.; ed. Stanford Univ., USA, Tokyo Univ.; at Economic Comm. for Asia and the Far East (based in Thailand, now ESCAP) for several years from 1964; at Ministry of Finance from 1960, Dep. Dir-Gen. of Banking Bureau 1987–89, Dir-Gen. of Int. Finance Bureau 1989–91, Vice Min. of Finance for Int. Affairs 1991–93, Special Adviser to the Min. of Finance 1993–94; Dep. Gov., Agriculture, Forestry and Fisheries Finance Corpn 1994; Pres. Asian Devt Bank (ADB) Jan. 1999–; head of several economic delegations to Asian countries.
Address: ADB, 6 ADB Ave, Manadaluyong City 0401, Metro Manila, Philippines.
Telephone: (2) 6324444; **fax:** (2) 6362444; **e-mail:** information@adb.org; **internet:** www.adb.org.

CHRISTENSEN, Søren, LL.B.; Danish civil servant; b. 31 Oct. 1940, Copenhagen; m. Inge Rudbeck 1964; ed. Univ. of Copenhagen; Sec., Secr. of Lord Mayor, Municipality of Copenhagen 1968–71, Dep. Office Man. 1971–73; Head of Secr. Municipality of Randers 1973–78, CEO 1978–86; Perm. Under-Sec. Ministry of Finance 1986–94; Head of Danish Supreme Admin. Authority, Copenhagen 1994–97; Sec.-Gen. Nordic Council of Mins 1997–.
Address: Nordic Council of Ministers, Store Strandstraede 18, 1255 Copenhagen K, Denmark.
Telephone: 33.96.02.00. **fax:** 33.96.02.02; **internet:** www.norden.org.

CONNOR, Joseph E., A.B., M.S.; US international official and accountant; b. 23 Aug. 1931, New York; m. Cornelia B. Camarata 1958 (died 1983); two s. one d.; m. Sally Howard Johnson 1992; ed. Univ. of Pittsburgh and Columbia Univ.; joined Price Waterhouse and Co, New York 1956, Partner 1967–, Man. Partner, Western region, Los Angeles 1976–78, Chair. Policy Bd 1978–88, Chair. World Firm 1988–92; Pres. ICC 1990–92; Under-Sec.-Gen. UN, New York 1994–; Distinguished Prof. of Business, Georgetown Univ. 1992–94; Consultant Foreign Direct Investment Programme, US Dept of Commerce; mem. Pres.'s Man. Advisory Council, Pres.'s Private Sector Survey on Cost Control.
Address: United Nations, New York, NY 10017, USA.
Telephone: (212) 963-1234; **fax:** (212) 963-4879.

CÓRDOVEZ, Diego; Ecuadorean diplomatist and lawyer; b. 3 Nov. 1935, Quito; m. Maria Teresa Somavia 1960; one s.; ed. Univ. of Chile; admitted to bar 1962; foreign service of Ecuador until 1963; joined UN as Econ. Affairs Officer 1963; political officer on special missions to Dominican Repub. 1965, Pakistan 1971; Dir UN Econ. and Social Council Secr. 1973–78, Asst Sec.-Gen. for Econ. and Social Matters, UN 1978–81; Special Rep. of UN Sec.-Gen. on Libya-Malta dispute 1980–82; Sec.-Gen.'s rep. on UN Comm. of Inquiry on hostage crisis in Tehran 1980; sr officer responsible for efforts to resolve Iran/Iraq war 1980–88; Under-Sec.-Gen. for Special Political Affairs 1981–88; Special Envoy to Grenada 1983; UN Mediator, Afghanistan 1982–88, Rep. for implementation of Geneva Accords 1988–89; Min. for Foreign Affairs 1988–92; Pres. World Trade Center (Ecuador) 1993–; Special Counsel Le Boeuf, Lamb, Greene and Macrae 1993–; Special Adviser to UN Sec.-Gen., UN Peace-keeping Force in Cyprus (UNFICYP) 1997–99; Special Adviser to UN Sec.-Gen. on Latin American Affairs April 1999–; mem. American Soc. of Int. Law; Order of Merit (Ecuador), Légion d'honneur, Grand Cross (Argentina, Brazil, Chile, Colombia, Peru, Portugal, Spain, Venezuela). *Publications:* UNCTAD and Development Diplomacy 1971, Out of Afghanistan: The Inside Story of the Soviet Withdrawal (jointly) 1995.
Address: c/o Dept of Peace-keeping Operations, Room S-3727B, UN, New York, NY 10017, USA.
Telephone: (212) 963-9222; **fax:** (212) 963-8079.

CORELL, Hans, LL.B.; Swedish diplomatist and lawyer; b. 7 July 1939, Västermo; m. Inger Peijfors 1964; one s. one d.; ed. Univ. of Uppsala; court clerk, Eksjö District Court and Göta Court of Appeal 1962–67; Asst Judge, Västervik District Court 1968–72; Legal Adviser, Ministry of Justice 1972, 1974–79; Additional mem. and Assoc. Judge of Appeal, Svea Court of Appeal 1973; Asst Under-Sec. Div. for Constitutional and Admin. Law, Ministry of Justice 1979–81; Judge of Appeal 1980; Under-Sec. for Legal Affairs, Ministry of Justice 1981–84; Amb. and Under-Sec. for Legal and Consular Affairs, Ministry of Foreign Affairs 1984–94; mem. Perm. Court of Arbitration, The Hague, Netherlands 1990–; Under-Sec.-Gen. for Legal Affairs, Legal Counsel of the UN 1994–; Hon. LL.D. (Stockholm) 1997. *Publications:* Sekretesslagen (co-author) 1992, Proposal for an Int. War Crimes Tribunal for the Former Yugoslavia (CSCE Report) (co-author) 1993; various legal publs.
Address: Room S-3427, United Nations, New York, NY 10017, USA.
Telephone: (212) 963-5338.

COSTA, Antonio Maria, PH.D.; Italian economist; b. 16 June 1941, Mondovi; s. of Francesco Costa and Maria Costa; m. Patricia Agnes Wallace 1971; two s. one d.; ed. Univ. of California, Berkeley, U.S.A., Acad. of Sciences of the U.S.S.R. and Univ. of Turin; Visiting Prof. of Econs., Moscow Univ. and Acad. of Sciences of the U.S.S.R. 1965–67; Instructor of Econs., Univ. of Calif., Berkeley 1968–70; Prof. of Econs., New York Univ. 1976–83; Sr. Econ. Adviser to the UN 1970–83; Special Counsellor in Econs. to Sec.-Gen. of OECD 1983–87; Dir-Gen. Econ. and Financial Affairs, EC 1987–90; Sec-.Gen. EBRD –2002; Dir.-Gen. UN Office at Vienna (UNOV) June 2002–, Dir-Gen. UN Office for Drug Control and Crime Prevention (ODCCP) June 2002–. *Publications:* articles on econs. and politics.
Address: UN Office for Drug Control and Crime Prevention, Vienna International Centre, P.O. Box 500, 1400 Vienna, Austria.
Telephone: (1) 26060-4266; **fax:** (1) 26060-5866; **e-mail:** odccp@odccp.org; **internet:** www.odccp.org.

COSTA PEREIRA, Renato Claudio; Brazilian civil aviation official; b. 30 Nov. 1936; m.; ed. Brazilian Air Force Academy; Personnel Commdr, Belo Horizonte Air Force Base 1961–67; Officer, Brazilian Air Force Gen. Personnel Command 1967–70, Instructor Officer, Brazilian Air Force Improvement Officer School 1970–74; Pilot Instructor, Brazilian Air Force Academy 1974–77; Man. and Co-ordinator of Research and Devt project 1978–84; Dir Flight Protection Inst. 1984–85; Logistics Adviser to Min. of Aeronautics 1985–87; Chief, Brazilian Air Comm., London, United Kingdom 1987–89; Sec. of Planning and Contracting, Secretariat of Economy and Finance, Ministry of Aeronautics 1989–90; Dir Operations Sub-dept, Civil Aviation Dept 1990–92, Dir Planning Sub-dept 1990–94; Pres. Latin American Comm. of Civil Aviation 1990–97, responsible for establishing the basis for the enlargement of the Comm. to a Pan-American body in 1997; Pres. Brazilian govt agency for int. air navigation affairs, CERNAI, 1990–97; Sec.-Gen. Int. Civil Aviation Org. (ICAO) 1997–.

Address: ICAO, 999 Univ. St, Montréal, QC H3A 5H7, Canada. **Telephone:** (514) 954-8219; **fax:** (514) 954-6077; **e-mail:** icaohq@icao.int; **internet:** www.icao.int.

COX, Pat; Irish politician and fmr television journalist; m.; 6 c.; ed. Trinity Coll. Dublin; economics lecturer Inst. of Public Admin. Dublin and Limerick Univ., current affairs reporter on Irish television 1982–86; founding Gen. Sec. Progressive Democrats 1985; mem. European Parl. (MEP) 1989; mem. Dail Eireann Nov. 1992; re-elected MEP 1994 (independent), nominated as Dep. Leader European Liberal Democrats, Pres. Liberal Democrat Group (now Group of the European Liberal, Democrat and Reform Party) 1998, Pres. European Parl. Jan. 2002–.
Address: Centre Européen, Plateau du Kirchberg, BP 1601, 2929 Luxembourg.
Telephone: 4300-1; **fax:** 4300-29494; **internet:** www.europarl.eu.int.

COX, Winston A., M.SC. (Econs); Barbadian banker and international official; m.; five c.; ed. Univ. of the West Indies, Inst. of Social Studies, Netherlands; joined Central Bank of Barbados 1974, Adviser to Governor 1982–87; Director of Finance, Ministry of Finance 1987–91; served on Exec. Bd IBRD (World Bank) 1994–97; Governor Central Bank of Barbados 1997; Dep. Sec.-Gen. (Development Co-operation) of the Commonwealth Sept. 2000–.
Address: Commonwealth Secretariat, Marlborough House, Pall Mall, London, SW1Y 5HX, United Kingdom.
Telephone: (20) 7839-3411; **fax:** (20) 7930-0827; **e-mail:** w.cox@commonwealth.int; **internet:** www.thecommonwealth.int.

CROCKETT, Andrew Duncan, M.A.; British banker; b. 23 March 1943; m. Marjorie Hlavacek 1966; two s. one d.; ed. Queens' Coll. Cambridge and Yale Univ., USA; Bank of England 1966–72, Exec. Dir 1989–93; IMF 1972–89; Gen. Man. Bank for Int. Settlements (BIS) Jan. 1994–. *Publications:* Money: Theory, Policy, Institutions 1973, International Money: Issues and Analysis 1977; contributions to professional journals.
Address: Bank for International Settlements, Centralbahnplatz 2, 4052 Basel, Switzerland.
Telephone: (61) 2808080; **fax:** (61) 2809100; **e-mail:** -mailmaster@bis.org; **internet:** www.bis.org.

DE LA PENA NAVARRETE, Alejandro; b. 1951, Chihuahua; m.; two s.; Dep. Perm. Rep. to GATT 1987–92; Min. of Trade and Ind. Promotion Rep. to EC 1992–93; Perm. Rep. to WTO 1995–2001; Dep. Exec. Dir Asia-Pacific Econ. Co-operation (APEC) May–Dec. 2001, Exec. Dir Jan. 2002–.
Address: APEC Secretariat, 438 Alexandra Rd, 14th Floor, Alexandra Point, Singapore 119958.
Telephone: 62761880; **fax:** 62761775; **e-mail:** info@mail.apecsec.org.sg; **internet:** www.apecsec.org.sg.

DEL PONTE, Carla; Swiss criminal prosecutor; b. 9 February 1947, Lugano; investigating magistrate from 1981, then public prosecutor at Lugano District Attorney's Office; Fed. Attorney-Gen. April 1994–; Chief Prosecutor, UN Int. Criminal Tribunals for Rwanda and fmr Yugoslavia, Arusha, Tanzania and The Hague, Netherlands, Sept. 1999–.
Address: United Nations International Criminal Tribunal for former Yugoslavia, Public Information Unit, POB 13888, 2501 The Hague, Netherlands.
Telephone: (70) 512-5233; **fax:** (70) 512-5355; **internet:** www.un.org/icty.

DESAI, Nitin Dayalji, B.A., M.SC.; Indian international official, economist and civil servant; b. 5 July 1941, Bombay; m. Aditi Gupta 1979; two s.; ed. Univ. of Bombay and London School of Econs, United Kingdom; lecturer in Econs, Univ. of Liverpool, United Kingdom 1965–67, Univ. of Southampton, United Kingdom 1967–70; consultant, Tata (India) Econ. Consultancy Services 1970–73; consultant/adviser, Planning Comm. Govt of India 1973–85; Sr adviser, Brundtland Comm. 1985–87; Special Sec. Planning Comm. India 1987–88; Sec./Chief Econ. Adviser, Ministry of Finance 1988–90; Dep. Under-Sec.-Gen. UN Conference on Environment and Devt, Geneva, Switzerland 1990–92; Under-Sec.-Gen. Dept. for Policy Co-ordination and Sustainable Devt, UN 1993–97, Under-Sec.-Gen. for Economic and Social Affairs 1997–.
Address: Room DC2-2320, United Nations, New York, NY 10017, USA.

DE SOTO, Alvaro; Peruvian diplomatist; b. 16 March 1943, Argentina; m. Irene Philippi 1981 (divorced); two s. one d.; ed. Int. School, Geneva, Catholic Univ., Lima, San Marcos Univ., Lima, Diplomatic Acad., Lima and Inst. of Int. Studies, Geneva; Acting Dir Maritime Sovereignty Div. Ministry of Foreign Affairs 1975–78; Dep. Perm. Rep. at UN Geneva Office 1978–82; Special Asst to UN Sec.-Gen. 1982–86, Exec. Asst 1987–91; Asst Sec.-Gen. UN Office for Research and Collection of Information 1991; Sr Political Adviser to UN Sec.-Gen. 1992–94, Special Adviser on Cyprus 2000–.
Address: Room S-3527 A, United Nations, New York, NY 10017, USA.
Telephone: (212) 963-5034.

DHANAPALA, Jayantha C. P., B.A., M.A.; Sri Lankan diplomatist; b. 30 Dec. 1938, Colombo; m. Maureen Elhart 1938; one s. one d.; ed. Univ. of Peradeniya, Univ. of London, United Kingdom, American Univ., Washington, DC, USA; private sector corporate exec. 1962–65; diplomatic appointments in the People's Repub. of China, United Kingdom and USA 1965–77; Dir Non-aligned Movt Div., Ministry of Foreign Affairs 1978–80, Additional Foreign Sec. 1992–95; Dep. High Commr to India 1981–83; Amb. and Perm. Rep. to UN, Geneva, Switzerland 1984–87, Dir UN Inst. for Disarmament Research 1987–92; Amb. to USA (also accredited to Mexico) Jan. 1995–April 1997; UN Under-Sec.-Gen. for Disarmament Affairs Feb. 1998–; Rep. of UN to Conference on Disarmament; Pres. Review and Extension Conference of Treaty on the Non-proliferation of Nuclear Weapons 1995; served as mem. of Canberra Comm., Australia; Diplomat-in-Residence, Centre for Non-proliferation Studies, Monterey Inst. of Int. Studies, California, USA; 'Jit' Trainor Award for Distinction in the Conduct of Diplomacy. *Publications include:* China and the Third World 1984, Nuclear War, Nuclear Proliferation and their Consequences (jointly) 1985.
Address: UN, United Nations Plaza, New York, NY 10017, USA.
Telephone: (212) 963-1232; **fax:** (212) 963-4879.

DIABRÉ, Zéphirin, PH.D.; Burkina Faso politician; ed. École Supérieure de Commerce de Bordeaux, France; Head, Business Dept, Univ. of Ouagadougou; Min. of Industry, Trade and Mines 1992–94, of Economy, Finance and Planning 1994–96; Pres. ECOSOC 1996–97, Economic Adviser to Pres.; Assoc. Administrator, UN Devt Programme (UNDP) Jan. 1999–; Visiting Scholar Harvard Inst. for Int. Devt, USA 1997; Fellow, Weatherhead Centre for Int. Studies 1997.
Address: UNDP, One United Nations Plaza, New York, NY 10017, USA.
Telephone: (212) 906-5295; **fax:** (212) 906-5364; **e-mail:** hq@undp.org; **internet:** www.undp.org.

DIOUF, Jacques; Senegalese international civil servant and agronomist; b. 1 Aug. 1938, Saint-Louis; m. Aissatou Seye 1963; one s. four d.; ed. Lycée Faidherbe, Saint-Louis, Ecole Nationale d'Agriculture, Paris/Grignon, France, Ecole Nationale d'Application d'Agronomie Tropicale, Paris/Nogent, and Sorbonne, Paris; Exec. Sec. African Groundnut Council, Lagos, Nigeria 1965–71; Exec. Sec. West African Rice Devt Asscn, Monrovia, Liberia 1971–77; Sec. of State for Science and Tech., Govt of Senegal, Dakar 1978–83; mem. Nat. Assembly, Chair. Foreign Relations Comm. and elected Sec., Dakar 1983–84; Sec.-Gen. Banque centrale des états de l'Afrique de l'ouest, Dakar 1985–90; Perm. Rep. of Senegal to UN 1991; Dir-Gen. Food and Agriculture Org. (FAO) Jan. 1994–; led Senegalese delegations to UN Conferences on Science and Tech., Vienna, Austria 1979 (Chair. of 1st Comm.), Industrial Devt, New Delhi, India 1980, New and Renewable Energy Sources, Nairobi, Kenya (Vice-Chair.) 1981, Peaceful Use of Space, Vienna 1982; African Rep., Consultative Group on Int. Agricultural Research, Washington, DC, USA; mem. Bd of Dirs ISNAGUE, The Hague, Netherlands, IITA, Lagos, Nigeria, IIRSDA, Abidjan, Côte d'Ivoire, I.C.R.A.F., Nairobi, Kenya, Int. Foundation for Science, Stockholm, Sweden, African Capacity Building Foundation, Harare, Zimbabwe, World Inst. for Devt Econs, Research, Helsinki, Council of African Advisers of IBRD (World Bank), Washington, DC, USA; Chair. SINAES, Dakar; mem. Consultative Cttee on Medical Research, WHO, Geneva, Switzerland; Officier Légion d'honneur, des Palmes Académiques (France); Grand Commdr, Order of the Star of Africa (Liberia). *Publications:* La détérioration du pouvoir d'achat de l'Arachide 1972, Les fondements du dialogue scientifique entre les civilisa-

tions Euro-occidentale et Négro-Africaine 1979, The Challenge of Agricultural Development in Africa 1989.
Address: FAO, Viale delle Terme di Caracalla, 00100 Rome, Italy.
Telephone: (06) 57051; **fax:** (06) 5705-3152; **e-mail:** fao.hq@fao.org; **internet:** www.fao.org.

DUISENBERG, Willem (Wim) Frederik, D.ECONS.; Netherlands economist; b. 9 July 1935, Heerenveen; m. Gretta Nieuwenhuizen 1987; two s. one d.; ed. State Univ. of Groningen; Scientific Asst, State Univ., Groningen 1961–65; with IMF 1966–69; Special Adviser De Nederlandsche Bank NV 1969–70; Prof. of Macro-econs, Univ. of Amsterdam 1970–73; Min. of Finance 1973–77; Pres. De Nederlandsche Bank 1982; Chair. EC Bank Govs; Pres. European Cen. Bank May 1998–; Chevalier Légion d'honneur. *Publications:* Economic Consequences of Disarmament 1965, The IMF and the International Monetary System 1966, The British Balance of Payments 1969, Some Remarks on Imported Inflation 1970.
Address: European Central Bank, Kaiserstrasse 29, 60066 Frankfurt-am-Main, Germany.
Telephone: (69) 13440; **fax:** (69) 13446000; **internet:** www.ecb .int.

ECHAVARRI, Luis Enrique, B.SC., M.SC.; Spanish nuclear scientist; b. 1950; m.; two c.; ed. Univ. of Madrid; Project and Nuclear Plants Man., Westinghouse Electric, Madrid; Man. Lemóniz, Sayago and Almaraz nuclear power plants; Tech. Dir, Consejo de Seguridad Nuclear (Spanish nuclear regulatory comm.), Commr, Man. Dir; Dir-Gen. Org. of Econ. Co-operation and Devt (OECD) Nuclear Energy Agency July 1997–; rep. of Spain at int. fora on nuclear energy, incl. OECD Nuclear Energy Agency, Int. Atomic Energy Agency and EU.
Address: OECD Nuclear Energy Agency, le Seine Saint-Germain, 12 blvd des Iles, 92130 Issy-les-Moulineux, France.
Telephone: 1-45-24-10-10; **fax:** 1-45-24-11-10; **e-mail:** nea@nea.fr; **internet:** www.nea.fr.

ESSY, Amara; Côte d'Ivoirian diplomatist; b. 20 Dec. 1944, Bouake; m. Lucie Essy 1971; three s. three d.; Head, Div. of Econ. Relations 1970; First Counsellor, Côte d'Ivoirian Embassy, Brazil 1971–73, Mission to the UN 1973–75; Perm. Rep. to UN Office, Geneva 1975–81, to UNIDO, Vienna 1975–81; Amb. to Switzerland 1978–81; Perm. Rep. to UN, New York 1981–91; Pres. UN Security Council 1990–91; Min. of Foreign Affairs 1990; Pres. 49th Session UN Gen. Ass.; Sec.-Gen. OAU Sept. 2001–; participated in numerous UN confs. including Law of the Sea (Caracas, Geneva, New York), Int. Women's Year (Mexico City), Econ. Co-operation among Developing Countries, UNCTAD (Nairobi, Manila) and of the codification of int. law.
Address: Organization of African Unity, Roosevelt St, Old Airport Area, P.O. Box 3243, Addis Ababa, Ethiopia.
Telephone: (1) 517700; **fax:** (1) 517844; **internet:** www.oau-oua.org.

FALL, Ibrahima; Senegalese politician and educator; b. 1942, Tivaouane, Thies; m. Déguène Fall; four c.; ed. Univ. of Dakar, Inst. of Political Science, Paris, France, Faculty of Law, Univ. of Paris; Prof. of Int. Law and Int. Relations, Dean of Faculty of Law, Univ. of Dakar 1975–81; Min. of Higher Education 1983–84, of Foreign Affairs 1984–89; Adviser, Supreme Court of Senegal; Asst Gen.-Sec. UN Dept of Political Affairs, Special Envoy of UN Sec.-Gen. to Côte d'Ivoire Jan. 2000–; Consultant, UNESCO; mem. African Council for Higher Education. *Publications:* articles in professional journals.
Address: United Nations, New York, NY 10017, USA.
Telephone: (212) 963-1234; **fax:** (212) 963-4879.

FLEISCHHAUER, Carl-August, DR.JUR.; German lawyer; b. 9 Dec. 1930, Düsseldorf; m. Liliane Sarolea 1957; two d.; ed. Univ. of Heidelberg, Univs of Grenoble and Paris, France and Univ. of Chicago, USA; Research Fellow, Max-Planck Inst. for Comparative Foreign Public Law and Int. Law, Heidelberg 1960–62; with Foreign Service of Fed. Repub. of Germany 1962–83, Legal Adviser to Fed. Foreign Office 1975, Legal Adviser and Dir-Gen. Legal Dept 1976; Under-Sec.-Gen. for Legal Affairs, Legal Counsel of the UN 1983–94; mem. (Judge) Int. Court of Justice 1994–; mem. numerous orgs; Bundesverdienstkreuz and foreign decorations. *Publications:* various legal publications.
Address: c/o International Court of Justice, Peace Palace, Carnegieplein 2, 2517 KJ The Hague, Netherlands.
Telephone: (70) 302-23-23; **fax:** (70) 364-99-28; **e-mail:** information@icj-cij.org; **internet:** www.icj-cij.org.

FRÉCHETTE, Louise, B.A.; Canadian international official and politician; b. 16 July 1946, Montréal, QC; ed. Collège Basile Moreau, Univ. de Montréal; with Dept of External Affairs, Govt of Canada early 1970s–, envoy to Argentina 1985; Asst Dep. Min. for Latin America and the Caribbean, Ministry of Foreign Affairs, for Int. Econ. and Trade Policy 1990–92; Perm. Rep. to UN 1992–94; Assoc. Dep. Min., Dept of Finance 1994–95, Dept of Defence 1995–98; Dep. Sec.-Gen. UN March 1998–.
Address: United Nations, New York, NY 10017, USA.
Telephone: (212) 963-1234; **fax:** (212) 963-4879.

GAVAHI, Abdolrahim, B.A., M.B.A., PH.D.; Iranian diplomatist and international official; ed. Abadan Inst. of Technology, Iran, and Iran Center for Management Studies; with Ministry of Oil, Govt of Iran, 1979; Amb. to Sweden (accredited concurrently to Denmark, Finland, Iceland and Norway) 1980–82; Amb. to Japan 1982–84; with Ministry of Foreign Affairs 1987–89, Ministry of Int. and Economic Affairs 1989–; Amb. to Norway 1994; Sec.-Gen. Iran Chamber of Commerce, Industries and Mines 1998; with Ministry of Foreign Affairs 2000; Sec.-Gen. of the Economic Co-operation Organization (ECO) June 2000–.
Address: ECO, 1 Golbou Alley, Kamranieh St, POB 14155-6176, Tehran, Iran.
Telephone: (21) 2831733; **fax** (21) 2831732; **e-mail:** registry@ecosecretariat.org; **internet:** www.ecosecretariat.org.

GAVIRIA TRUJILLO, César, B.ECONS.; Colombian economist; m. Milena Gaviria; two c.; ed. Roosevelt High School, California, USA and Univ. de Los Andes; mem. town council of Pereira, later Mayor; elected to House of Reps 1974, Vice-Min. of Economic Devt 1978, Speaker 1983; journalist 'La Tarde' (Pereira) and 'El Tiempo' (Santafé de Bogotá) in early 1980s; managed presidential campaigns of Virgilio Barco Vargas 1986 and Dr Luis Carlos Galán Sarmiento (assassinated) 1989; Min. of Finance and Public Credit 1986–87, of Govt (Interior) 1987–89; Pres. of Colombia 1990–94; Sec.-Gen. Organization of American States (OAS) 1994–; Hon. LL.B., Univ. Libre de Colombia.
Address: OAS, 17th St and Constitution Ave, NW, Washington, DC 20006, USA.
Telephone: (202) 458-3000; **fax:** (202) 458-3967; **e-mail:** pi@oas.org; **internet:** www.oas.org.

GOULONGANA, Jean-Robert; Gabonese politician and diplomatist; b. 30 April 1953, Lambarene, Gabon; m.; three c.; ed. Dakar Univ., Aix-Marseille III Univ.; Min. of Waters, Forests and the Environment 1990–91; Amb. to Italy 1992; Amb. to Belgium 1996; Head of Gabonese Mission to European Union; Sec.-Gen. African, Caribbean and Pacific (ACP) states 2000–; Officier dans l'Ordre du Mérite Maritime Gabonais.
Address: ACP Secretariat, ACP House, 451 ave Georges Henri, Brussels, Belgium.
Telephone: (2) 743-06-00; **fax** (2) 735-55-73; **e-mail:** info@acpsec.org; **internet:** www.acpsec.org.

GOWEILI, Ahmed; Egyptian politician; frmly Min. of Trade and Supply in Egyptian Govt; Gen. Sec. Council of Arab Economic Unity June 2000–.
Address: Council of Arab Economic Unity, 1191 Corniche en-Nil, 12th Floor, POB 1, Mohammed Fareed, Cairo, Egypt.
Telephone: (2) 5755321; **fax:** (2) 5754090.

GUÉHENNO, Jean-Marie; French diplomatist; b. 30 Oct. 1949, Boulogne-sur-Seine; m. Michèle Fahy Moss; one d.; ed. Ecole normale supérieure de la rue d'Ulm, Institut d'etudes politiques de Paris; joined Ministry of Foreign Affairs 1979; Perm. Rep. to the Western European Union 1993–95; mem. UN consultative council on disarmament questions; Under-Sec.-Gen. for Peace-keeping Operations, UN Secr., New York, June 2000–.
Address: United Nations, Department of Peace-keeping Operations, Room S-3727B, New York, NY 10017, USA.
Telephone: (212) 963-8079; **fax:** (212) 963-9222.

GUILLAUME, Gilbert, L.EN D.; French judge; b. 4 Dec. 1930, Bois-Colombes; m. Marie-Anne Hidden 1961; one s. two d.; ed.

Univ. of Paris, Paris Inst. of Political Studies and Ecole Nationale d'Administration; mem. Council of State 1957; Legal Adviser, State Secr. for Civil Aviation 1968–79; French Rep. Legal Cttee of Int. Civil Aviation Org. (ICAO) 1968–69, Chair. of Cttee 1971–75; Chair. Conciliation Comm. OECD 1973–78; Dir of Legal Affairs, OECD 1979; mem. European Space Agency Appeals Bd 1975–78; French Rep., Central Comm. for Navigation of the Rhine 1979–87, Chair. 1981–82; Dir of Legal Affairs, Ministry of Foreign Affairs 1979–87; Conseiller d'Etat 1981–96; Prof., Paris Inst. of Political Studies 1983–95; Counsel/agent for France in int. arbitration proceedings, numerous cases before European Courts etc.; mem. Perm. Court of Arbitration 1980–; delegate to numerous int. legal and diplomatic conferences; Prof. Inst. of Political Studies, Univ. of Paris and other lecturing appointments; mem. various legal asscns, institutes etc.; mem. (Judge) Int. Court of Justice 1987–, Pres. Feb. 2000–; Officier, Légion d'honneur, Chevalier, Ordre nat. du Mérite, du Mérite agricole, du Mérite maritime, Commdr des arts et des lettres. *Publications:* numerous books and articles on administrative and int. law.
Address: c/o International Court of Justice, Peace Palace, Carnegieplein 2, 2517 KJ The Hague, Netherlands.
Telephone: (70) 302-23-23; **fax:** (70) 364-99-28; **e-mail:** information@icj-cij.org; **internet:**www.icj-cij.org.

HAMAD, Abdlatif Yousuf al-, B.A.; Kuwaiti international official, banker and politician; b. 1936; m.; four c.; ed. Claremont Coll., California and Harvard Univ., USA; mem. delegation to UN 1962; Dir-Gen. Kuwait Fund for Arab Economic Devt 1963–81; Dir Kuwait Investment Co 1963–71, Man. Dir 1965–74; Chair. Kuwait Prefabricated Bldg Co 1965–78, United Bank of Kuwait Ltd, London, United Kingdom 1966–84; Exec. Dir Arab Fund for Econ. and Social Devt 1972–81, Dir-Gen. and Chair. Bd of Dirs 1985–; Chair. Compagnie Arabe et Internationale d'Investissements, Luxembourg 1973–81; mem. Bd of Trustees, Corporate Property Investors, New York 1975–; mem. Governing Body, Inst. of Devt Studies, Sussex, United Kingdom 1975–87; mem. Ind. Comm. on Int. Devt Issues (Brandt Comm.) 1976–79; mem. Bd Int. Inst. for Environment and Devt, London 1976–80; Min. of Finance and Planning 1981–83; Gov. for Kuwait, IBRD (World Bank) and IMF 1981–83; mem. UN Cttee for Devt Planning 1982–91, Chair. 1987; mem. IFC Banking Advisory Bd Group 1987–, Advisory Group on Financial Flows for Africa (UN) 1987–88, South Comm. 1987–89, Group of Ten (African Devt Bank) 1987–, World Bank's Pvt. Sector Devt Review Group 1988–, UN Panel for Public Hearings on Activities of Transnat. Corpns in S. Africa and Namibia 1989–92, Bd of Trustees, Stockholm Environment Inst. 1989–92, Comm. on Global Governance 1992–.
Address: Arab Fund for Economic and Social Development, POB 21923, Safat 13080, Kuwait.
Telephone: 4844500; **fax:** 4815760; **e-mail:** hq@arabfund.org; **internet:** www.arabfund.org.

HAN SEUNG-SOO, PH.D.; South Korean politician, economist and United Nations official; b. Chunchon, Kangwon Prov.; m.; two c.; ed. Yonsei Univ., Seoul Nat. Univ. and Univ. of York, U.K.; taught econs. at Univ. of York, England 1965–68, Univ. of Cambridge 1968–70; Prof. of Econs., Seoul Nat. Univ. 1970–88; Pres. Korea Int. Econ. Asscn. 1983–84; First Chair. Korea Trade Comm. 1987–88; elected mem. Nat. Ass., Repub. of Korea 1988; Min. of Trade and Industry 1988–90; Amb. to U.S.A. 1993–94; Chair. Council of Repub. of Korea Group of the Interparl. Union (IPU); Chief of Staff to Pres. of Repub. of Korea 1994–95; Deputy Prime Min. and Min. of Finance and Economy 1996–97; Min. of Foreign Affairs and Trade 2001–02; Pres. 56th Session of UN Gen. Assembly Sept. 2001–; Pres. Korea-Britain Soc., Korea-UK Forum for the Future; mem. Royal Econ. Soc., Korean Econ. Asscn., Int. Inst. of Public Finance, Seoul Forum for Int. Affairs, Korean Council on Foreign Relations, Korean Soc. for Future Studies. *Publications:* Taxes in Britain and the EEC: The Problem of Harmonization 1968 (jtly.), Britain and the Common Market (jtly.) 1971, The Growth and Function of the European Budget 1971, The Health of Nations 1985; numerous articles in learned journals and press commentaries in both Korean and English.
Address: General Assembly, United Nations, New York, NY 10017, USA.
Telephone: (212) 963-1234; **fax:** (212) 963-4879; **internet:** www.un.org/ga.

HANSEN, Peter, B.SC.; Danish international official; b. 2 June 1941, Aahlborg; m.; one s. two d.; ed. Aarhus Univ.; Assoc. Prof. Aarhus Univ. 1966–68, Chair. Dept of Political Science 1968–70, Sr Research Fellow 1970–74; Prof. Int. Rels, Odense Univ.; Adviser, Ministry of Foreign Affairs; Chair. UN Consultative Cttee on Substantive Questions of the Administrative Cttee on Co-ordination and of the Appointment and Promotion Bd, mem. UN Programme Budgeting Bd, Asst Sec.-Gen., Programme Planning and Co-ordination 1978–85, Asst Sec.-Gen. and Exec. Dir UN Centre on Transnat. Corpns 1985–92, Rep. of UN Sec.-Gen. to Food Aid and Policies Cttee, World Food Programme, Team Leader UN Operation in Somalia 1992, Exec. Dir Comm. on Global Governance, Geneva, Switzerland 1992–94, Special Rep. of Sec.-Gen., *Ad Hoc* Liaison Cttee in support of Middle East peace process 1993–; Under-Sec.-Gen. for Humanitarian Affairs and UN Emergency Relief Co-ordinator, New York, USA March 1994–Jan. 1996; Commr-Gen. UNRWA Jan. 1996–; mem. delegation to UN Gen. Assembly. *Publications:* World Politics 1969, International Organization 1975.
Address: Bayader Wadi Seer, POB 140157, Amman 11814; Gamal Abdul Nasser St, Gaza City, Jordan.
Telephone: (6) 5826171 (Amman), (7) 6777333 (Gaza City); **fax:** (6) 5826177 (Amman), (7) 6777555 (Gaza City); **e-mail:** unrwapio@unrwa.org; **internet:** www.un.org/unrwa.

HERCZEGH, Géza Gábor, PH.D.; Hungarian judge; b. 17 Oct. 1928, Nagykapos; m. Melinda Petnehazy 1961; one s. one d.; ed. French Grammar School, Gödöllö, Univ. of Szeged; Research Fellow in public int. law Inst. of Political Science, Budapest 1951–67; Prof. of Law, Head Int. Law Dept, Univ. of Pécs 1967–90; Judge, Vice-Pres. Constitutional Court 1990–93; mem. (Judge) Int. Court of Justice, The Hague, Netherlands 1994–; mem. Hungarian Academy of Sciences 1985; Dr h.c. (Marburg) 1990. *Publications:* The Colonial Question and International Law 1962, General Principles of Law and the International Legal Order 1969, Development of International Humanitarian Law 1984, Foreign Policy of Hungary 896–1919 1987.
Address: c/o International Court of Justice, Peace Palace, Carnegieplein 2, 2517 KJ The Hague, Netherlands.
Telephone: (70) 302-23-23; **fax:** (70) 364-99-28; **e-mail:** information@icj-cij.org; **internet:** www.icj-cij.org.

HEYZER, Noeleen, PH.D.; Singaporean international official; m.; two d.; ed. Univ. of Singapore and Univ. of Cambridge, United Kingdom; Fellow and Research Officer, Inst. of Devt Studies, Univ. of Sussex, United Kingdom 1979–81; with Social Devt Div., ESCAP, Bangkok, Thailand; Dir, Gender and Devt Programme, Asian and Pacific Devt Centre, Kuala Lumpur, Malaysia 1984–94; Substantive Co-ordinator for the Asia-Pacific NGO Working Group for the UN Fourth World Conference on Women, Beijing, China; Exec. Dir UN Devt Fund for Women (UNIFEM) Oct. 1994–; served on Bds of several humanitarian orgs, incl. Devt Alternatives with Women for a New Era (DAWN), the Global South, ISIS, OXFAM, Panos and Soc. for Int. Devt. *Publications include:* Gender, Economic Growth and Poverty, The Trade in Domestic Workers, Working Women in South-east Asia.
Address: UNIFEM, 15th Floor, 304 East 45th St, New York, NY 10017, USA.
Telephone: (212) 906-6400; **fax:** (212) 906-6705; **e-mail:** unifem@undp.org; **internet:** www.unifem.undp.org.

HIGGINS, Dame Rosalyn, D.B.E., J.S.D., Q.C., F.B.A.; British judge and professor of international law; b. 2 June 1937; m. Rt Hon. Terence L. Higgins 1961; one s. one d.; ed. Burlington Grammar School, London, Girton Coll. Cambridge and Yale Law School, USA; UK Intern, Office of Legal Affairs, UN 1958; Commonwealth Fund Fellow 1959; Visiting Fellow, Brookings Inst., Washington, DC 1960; Jr Fellow in Int. Studies, LSE 1961–63; staff specialist in int. law, Royal Inst. of Int. Affairs 1963–74; Visiting Fellow, LSE 1974–78; Prof. of Int. Law, Univ. of Kent at Canterbury 1978–81; Prof. of Int. Law, LSE 1981–95; mem. (Judge) Int. Court of Justice 1995–; mem. UN Cttee on Human Rights 1985–; Visiting Prof. Stanford Univ. 1975, Yale Univ. 1977; Vice-Pres. American Soc. of Int. Law 1972–74; Dr h.c. (Paris XI); Hon. D.C.L. (Dundee) 1994, (Durham, LSE) 1995, (Cambridge, Sussex, Kent, City Univ., Greenwich, Essex)

1996, (Birmingham, Leicester, Glasgow) 1997; Ordre des Palmes Académiques, Yale Law School Medal of Merit 1997, Manley Hudson Medal (ASIC) 1998. *Publications:* incl. The Development of International Law through the Political Organs of the United Nations 1963, Conflict of Interests 1965, The Administration of the United Kingdom Foreign Policy through the United Nations 1966, Law in Movement–essays in memory of John McMahon (editor, with James Fawcett) 1974, UN Peacekeeping: documents and commentary: (Vol. I) Middle East 1969, (Vol. II) Asia 1971, (Vol. III) Africa 1980, (Vol. IV) Europe 1981, Problems and Process—International Law and How We Use It 1994; articles in law journals and journals of int. relations.
Address: c/o International Court of Justice, Peace Palace, Carnegieplein 2, 2517 KJ The Hague, Netherlands.
Telephone: (70) 302-23-23; **fax:** (70) 364-99-28; **e-mail:** information@icj-cij.org; **internet:** www.cij-icj.org.

IDRIS, Kamil E., B.A., PH.D.; Sudanese diplomatist and lawyer; ed. Univs of Cairo, Egypt, Khartoum, Ohio, USA and Geneva, Switzerland and Inst. of Public Admin., Khartoum; part-time journalist El-Ayam and El-Sahafa newspapers in Sudan 1971–79; lecturer Univ. of Cairo 1976–77, Ohio Univ. 1978, Univ. of Khartoum 1986; Asst Dir Arab Dept, Ministry of Foreign Affairs, Khartoum 1977–78, Asst Dir Research Dept Jan.–June 1978, Dep. Dir Legal Dept July–Dec. 1978; mem. Perm. Mission of Sudan to UN Office, Geneva 1979–82; Vice-Consul of Sudan, Switzerland 1979–82; Sr Program Officer, Devt Co-operation and External Relations Bureau for Africa, World Intellectual Property Org. (WIPO) 1982–85, Dir Devt Co-operation and External Relations Bureau for Arab and Cen. and Eastern European Countries 1985–94, Dep. Dir-Gen. WIPO 1994–97, Dir-Gen. Nov. 1997–; mem. UN Int. Law Comm. (ILC) 1991–96 (Vice-Chair. 45th session 1993); served on numerous cttees of int. orgs including WHO, ILO, ITU, UNHCR, OAU, Group of 77 etc. and Sudanese delegations to numerous int. and regional conferences; Prof. of Public Int. Law, Univ. of Khartoum; mem. African Jurists Asscn; Scholars and Researchers State Gold Medal (Sudan) 1983, Scholars and Researchers Gold Medal, Egyptian Academy of Scientific Research and Tech. 1985. *Publications include:* State Responsibility in International Law 1977, North-South Insurance Relations: The Unequal Exchange 1984, The Law of Non-navigational Uses of International Water Courses; the ILC's draft articles: An Overview 1995, The Theory of Source and Target in Child Psychology 1996 and articles on law, economics, jurisprudence and aesthetics in newspapers and periodicals.
Address: WIPO, 34 chemin des Colombettes, 1211 Geneva 20, Switzerland.
Telephone: (22) 3389111; **fax:** (22) 7335428; **e-mail:** public inf@wipo.int; **internet:** www.wipo.int.

IGLESIAS, Enrique V.; Uruguayan international official; b. 26 July 1931, Asturias, Spain; ed. Univ. de la República, Montevideo; held several positions including Prof. Agregado, Faculty of Political Economy, Prof. of Econ. Policy and Dir Inst. of Econs, Univ. de la República, Montevideo 1952–67; Man. Dir Unión de Bancos del Uruguay 1954; Tech. Dir Nat. Planning Office of Uruguay 1962–66; Pres. (Gov.), Banco Central del Uruguay 1966–68; Chair. Council, Latin American Inst. for Economic and Social Planning (ILPES), UN 1967–72, Interim Dir-Gen. 1977–78; Head, Advisory Mission on Planning, Govt of Venezuela 1970; Adviser UN Conference on Human Environment 1971–72; Exec. Sec. Econ. Comm. for Latin America and the Caribbean (ECLAC) 1972–85; Min. of External Affairs 1985–88; Pres. Inter-American Devt Bank April 1988–; Acting Dir-Gen. ILPES 1973–78; Pres., Third World Forum 1973–76; mem. Steering Cttee, Soc. for Int. Devt 1973–92, Pres. 1989, Selection Cttee, Third World Prize 1979–82; Sec.-Gen. UN Conference on New and Renewable Sources of Energy Feb.–Aug. 1981; Chair. UN Inter-Agency Group on Devt of Renewable Sources of Energy; mem. North-South Round Table on Energy; Chair. Energy Advisory Panel, Brundtland Comm. 1984–86; Hon. LL.D. (Liverpool) 1987; Prince of Asturias Award 1982.
Address: Inter-American Development Bank, 1300 New York Ave, NW, Washington, DC 20577, USA.
Telephone: (202) 623-1000; **fax:** (202) 623-3096; **internet:** www.iadb.org.

JOHNSSON, , Anders B., LL.B.; Swedish international official; b. 1948, Lund; m.; 3 c.; with UNHCR –1991; Asst Sec.-Gen. Inter-Parliamentary Union (IPU) 1991–94, Dep. Sec.-Gen. and Legal Adviser 1994–98, Sec.-Gen. July 1998–.

JOHNSTON, Rt. Hon. Donald J., P.C., Q.C., B.A., LL.B.; Canadian politician, lawyer and international civil servant; b. 1936, Cumberland, Ont.; m. Heather Bell Maclaren; four d.; ed. McGill Univ. and Univ. of Grenoble, France; joined Stikeman, Elliott (int. law firm) 1961; subsequent f. own law firm, Johnston, Heenan and Blaikie; teacher of law, McGill Univ. 1963–76; mem. Parl. 1978–88; Pres. Treasury Bd 1980–82; Min. for Econ. Devt and Min. of State for Science and Tech. 1982–83; Min. of State for Econ. Devt and Tech. 1983–84; Min. of Justice and Attorney-Gen. June–Sept. 1984; elected Pres. Liberal Party of Canada 1990, re-elected 1992; Counsel, Heenan, Blaikie (law firm), Montréal 1988–96; Sec.-Gen. Org. for Econ. Co-operation and Devt (OECD) June 1996–. *Publications:* Up the Hill (political memoirs) 1986; one book on taxation; numerous professional papers.
Address: OECD, 2 rue André-Pascal, 75775 Paris Cédex 16, France.
Telephone: 1-45-24-82-10; **fax:** 1-45-24-85-00; **e-mail:** webmaster@oecd.org; **internet:** www.oecd.org.

JORDA, Claude Jean Charles; French judge; b. 16 Feb. 1938, Bône, Algeria; m. (divorced); two s.; ed. Institut d'Etudes Politiques, Toulouse, Barreau de Toulouse and Ecole Nationale de la Magistrature; with central admin. Ministry of Justice 1966–70; with Ecole Nationale de la Magistrature 1970–82 (Sec.-Gen. 1970–74, Dep. Dir 1978–82); Dir of Legal Services, Ministry of Justice 1982–85; Chief Prosecutor Bordeaux Appeals Court 1985–92; Chief Prosecutor Paris Appeals Court 1992–94; mem. (Judge) UN International Criminal Tribunal for the fmr Yugoslavia (ICTY) Jan. 1994–, Pres. Jan. 2000–; mem. Société FranÇaise de Droit International; has participated in several judicial co-operation missions; awarded Légion d'honneur, l'ordre nationale du Mérite, Chevalier des Palmes académiques.
Address: United Nations International Tribunal for former Yugoslavia, Public Information Unit, POB 13888, 2501 The Hague, Netherlands.
Telephone: (70) 512-5233; **fax:** (70) 512-5355; **internet:** www.un.org/icty.

KABBAJ, Omar; Moroccan business executive, public servant and international official; m.; four s.; held various positions in national research, banking and trade and industry sectors –1974; Man. Dir Sucrerie Nationale de Canne de Sebou 1974–79; with Moroccan Ministry of Finance –1979; mem. Exec. Bd IBRD (World Bank) 1979–80; mem. Exec. Bd, IMF 1980–93; economic affairs specialist, Prime Min.'s Office 1993–95; Exec. Pres., Chair. Bd of Dirs, African Devt Bank (ADB) Sept. 1995–; Knight of the Order of the Throne of Morocco.
Address: African Development Bank, 01 BP 1387, Abidjan 01, Côte d'Ivoire.
Telephone: 20-20-44-44; **fax:** 20-20-40-06; **e-mail:** comuadb@afdb.org; **internet:** www.afdb.org.

KALOMOH, Tuliameni; Namibian diplomatist; b. 18 Feb. 1948, Onamutai; m.; three c.: ed. Indian Acad. of Int. Law and Diplomacy, New Delhi, India; Special Asst to Regional Election Dir, Oshakati; Chief Rep. to W. Africa, S.W. Africa People's Org. (SWAPO) 1976–81, Chief Rep. to France 1981–86, SWAPO Amb. to India 1986-90; Amb. to USA (concurrently High Commr to Canada) 1991–96; Under-Sec. for Political and Econ. Affairs 1990–91, Acting Min. for Foreign Affairs 2000–01, Deputy Min. for Foreign Affairs 2001–02; UN Special Rep. for Liberia 1997–; UN Asst. Sec.-Gen. for Political Affairs 2002–.
Address: Department of Political Affairs, United Nations, New York, NY 10017, USA.**Telephone:** (212) 963-1234; **fax:** (212) 963-4879; **internet:** www.un.org.

KELLENBERGER, Jakob, PH.D.; Swiss politician and diplomatist; b. 1944; ed. Univs of Zürich, Tours and Granada; joined Swiss diplomatic service 1974; Head Graduate Inst. of Devt Studies, Geneva 1980–92; various diplomatic posts; fmrly Head of the Integration Office of the Fed. Dept of Foreign Affairs; Sec. of State for Foreign Affairs 1992–99; Pres. of the Int. Cttee of the Red Cross (ICRC) Jan. 2000–.
Address: ICRC, 19 ave de la Paix, 1202 Geneva, Switzerland.

Telephone: (22) 7346001; **fax:** (22) 7332057; **e-mail:** press.gva@icrc.org; **internet:** www.icrc.org.

KHASAWNEH, Awn Shawkat al-, M.A., LL.M.; Jordanian judge; b. 22 Feb. 1950, Amman; ed. Islamic Educational Coll. of Amman, Queens' Coll. Cambridge, United Kingdom; entered diplomatic service 1975; with Perm. Mission of Jordan to the UN 1976–80, later as First Sec.; with Ministry of Foreign Affairs 1980–90, Head of Legal Dept 1985–90; Legal Adviser to Crown Prince 1990–1995, Adviser to the King 1995, Chief of the Royal Hashemite Court 1996–98; mem. (Judge) Int. Court of Justice Feb. 2000–; mem. Arab Int. Law Comm. 1982–89; mem. (Chair. 1993) Subcomm. on Prevention of Discrimination and Protection of Minorities, Comm. on Human Rights 1984–93, Special Rapporteur of Comm. on Human Rights on the human rights dimensions of forcible population transfer; mem. Int. Law Comm. 1986–; mem. Jordanian Royal Comm. on Legislative and Admin. Reform 1994–96; has participated and lectured in academic seminars; awarded Istiqlal Order 1st Class (1993), Kawkab Order 1st Class (1996), Nahda Order 1st Class (1996), Légion d'Honneur, Grand Officier (France, 1997).
Address: International Court of Justice, Peace Palace, Carnegieplein 2, 2517 KJ The Hague, Netherlands.
Telephone: (70) 302-23-23; **fax:** (70) 364-99-28; **e-mail:** information@icj-cij.org; **internet:** www.icj.cij.org.

KIM, Hak-Su, M.A., PH.D.; South Korean economist, banker, govt official and co. dir; b. Wonju, Rep. of Korea; ed. Yonsei Univ., Edinburgh Univ, South Carolina Univ.; economist at Bank of Korea (central bank) 1960; with the Ministry of Commerce and Industry 1969; with London Rep. Office of Bank of Korea 1971–73; Exec. Dir Daewoo Corpn 1977; Pres. ACWOO Int. Corpn; Chief Planning Officer and Chief Tech. Adviser for UN Dept for Tech. Co-operation and Devt during 1980s; Senior Research Fellow Korea Inst. for Int. Economic Policy 1989–93; Pres. Hanil Banking Inst.; Sec.-Gen. Colombo Plan 1995–99; Amb. for Int. Economic Affairs 1999; Exec. Sec. UN Economic and Social Comm. for Asia and the Pacific (ESCAP) June 2000–.
Address: ESCAP, United Nations Bldg, Rajdamnern Ave, Bangkok 10200, Thailand.
Telephone: (2) 288-1234; **fax:** (2) 288-1000 **e-mail:** unisbkk .unescap@un.org; **internet:** www.unescap.org.

KING, Angela; Jamaican United Nations official; fmrly Chief of UN Observer Mission in South Africa; Dir Div. of Advancement of Women; Asst-Sec.-Gen., Special Adviser on Gender Issues and the Advancement of Women Jan. 1997–.
Address: UN, Dept of Economic and Social Affairs, United Nations, New York, NY 10017, USA.

KÖHLER, Horst, DR. RER. POL.; German banker; b. 22 Feb. 1943, Skierbieszow, Poland; m. Eva Köhler; two c.; ed. Univ. of Tübingen; Research Asst Inst. for Applied Economic Research, Tübingen 1969–76; Sec. of State, Ministry of Finance, Bonn until 1993; Pres. Deutsche Sparkassen-und-Giroverband, Bonn 1993–98; mem. Advisory Bd, Treuhandanstalt; Dep. German Gov., IBRD and European Bank for Reconstruction and Devt (EBRD), Pres. EBRD 1998–2000; Pres. European Asscn of Savings Banks 1993–98; Man. Dir International Monetary Fund (IMF) May 2000–.
Address: IMF, 700 19th St, NW, Washington, DC 20431, USA.
Telephone: (202) 623-7300; **fax:** (202) 623-6220; **e-mail:** publicaffairs@imf.org; **internet:** www.imf.org.

KOOIJMANS, Pieter Hendrik, DR.JUR.; Netherlands politician and lawyer; b. 6 July 1933, Heemstede; m. A. Kooijmans-Verhage; four c.; ed. Free Univ. Amsterdam; mem. Faculty of Law, Free Univ. of Amsterdam 1960–65, Prof. of European Law and Public Int. Law 1965–73; State Sec. for Foreign Affairs 1973–77; Prof. of Public Int. Law, Univ. of Leiden 1978–92, 1995–97; Min. for Foreign Affairs 1993–94; mem. (Judge) Int. Court of Justice 1997–; Chair. or mem. numerous orgs. including Chair. Bd. Carnegie Foundation, Netherlands Disaster Relief Agency; Head Netherlands del. to UN Comm. on Human Rights 1982–85, 1992, Chair. Comm. 1984–85, Special Rapporteur on questions relevant to torture 1985–92; mem. various UN and CSCE missions to fmr Yugoslavia 1991–92. *Publications:* various textbooks and articles on int. law and human rights.
Address: International Court of Justice, Peace Palace, Carnegieplein 2, 2517 KJ The Hague, The Netherlands.
Telephone: (70) 392-44-11; **fax:** (70) 364-99-28; **e-mail:** information@icj-cij.org; **internet:** www.icj-cij.org.

KOROMA, Abdul G.; Sierra Leonean diplomatist and lawyer; b. 29 Sept. 1943; ed. King's Coll., Univ. of London, Kiev State Univ.; barrister and Hon. Bencher (Lincoln's Inn) and legal practitioner, High Court of Sierra Leone; joined Sierra Leone govt. service 1964, Int. Div., Ministry of External Affairs 1969; del., UN Gen. Assembly; mem. Int. Law Comm. (Chair. 43rd Session); mem. of dels to 3rd UN Conf. on the Law of the Sea, UN Conf. on Succession of States in Respect of Treaties, UN Comm. on Int. Trade Law, Special Cttee. on the Review of the UN Charter and on the Strengthening of the Role of the Org., Cttee. on the Peaceful Uses of Outer Space; Vice-Chair. UN Charter Cttee. 1978; Chair. UN Special Cttee. of 24; Dep. Perm. Rep. of Sierra Leone to the UN 1978–81, Perm. Rep. 1981–85; fmr Amb. to EEC and Perm. Del. to UNESCO; Amb. to Ethiopia and OAU 1988; Perm. Rep. to UN –1993; mem. (Judge) Int. Court of Justice 1994–; High Commr in Zambia and Tanzania; Chair., UN 6th Cttee. (Legal); Vice-Pres. African Soc. of Int. and Comparative Law, African Soc. of Int. Law; del. to numerous int. confs.; lecturer at numerous univs.; mem. Int. Planning Council of Int. Ocean Inst.; mem. American Soc. of Int. Law; Hon. LL.D. (Kiev State Univ.); Insignia of Commdr of Rokel 1991. *Publications:* articles on int. law.
Address: International Court of Justice, Peace Palace, Carnegieplein, 2517 KJ The Hague, Netherlands.
Telephone: (70) 302-23-23; **fax:** (70) 302-24-09; **e-mail:** information@icj-cij.org; **internet:** www.icj-cij.org.

KOTAITE, Assad, LL.D.; Lebanese international aviation official and lawyer; b. 6 Nov. 1924, Hasbaya; s. of Adib Kotaite and Kamle Abousamra; m. Monique Ayoub 1983; ed. French Univ., Beirut, Univ. of Paris and Acad. of Int. Law, The Hague; Head of Legal and Int. Affairs, Directorate of Civil Aviation, Lebanon 1953–56; Rep. of Lebanon, Council of Int. Civil Aviation Org. (ICAO) 1956–70; Sec.-Gen. ICAO 1970–76, Pres. Council 1976–; Pres. Int. Court of Aviation and Space Arbitration, Paris 1995–.
Address: c/o International Civil Aviation Organisation, 999 University Street, Suite 12.20, Montréal, QC H3C 5H7, Canada.
Telephone: (514) 954-8011; **fax:** (514) 954-6077; **e-mail:** icaohq@icao.int; **internet:** www.icao.int.

KRUEGER, Anne; M.S., PH.D.; American economist; ed. Oberlin Coll. and Univ. of Wisconsin; Vice-Pres. for Econ. and Research IBRD 1982–86; taught Univ. of Minnesota and Duke Univ.; Herald L. and Caroline L. Ritch Prof. Humanities and Sciences, Dept of Econ. Stanford Univ.; Dir Center for Research on Econ. Devt and Policy Reform, Stanford Univ; Dist. Fellow American Economic Asscn, mem. Nat. Acad. Sciences, Research Asst, Nat. Bureau of Econ. Research; First Dep. Man. Dir IMF Sept. 2001–.
Address: IMF, 700 19th St, NW, Washington, DC 20431, USA.
Telephone: (202) 623-7300; **fax:** (202) 623-6220; **e-mail:** publicaffairs@imf.org; **internet:** www.imf.org.

KUBIŠ, Ján, Slovak diplomatist; b. 12 November 1952, Bratislava, fmr Czechoslovakia; ed. Moscow State Inst. for Int. Affairs; entered diplomatic service 1976; Perm. Rep. of Slovakia at the UN's Geneva Office 1993–94; Dir of the Conflict Prevention Centre at the Organization for Security and Co-operation in Europe (OSCE) 1994–98; Special Rep. of the UN Sec.-Gen. for Tajikstan, Head UN Observer Mission in Tajikstan 1998–99; Sec.-Gen. of OSCE June 1999; awarded OSCE Medal 1998.
Address: OSCE, 1010 Vienna, Kärntner Ring 5–7, Austria.
Telephone: (1) 514-36-0; **fax:** (1) 514-36-105; **e-mail:** info@osce.org; **internet:** www.osce.org.

LEAVEY, Thomas Edward, M.A., PH.D.; American international postal official; b. 10 Nov. 1934, Kansas City.; m. Anne Roland 1968; ed. Josephinum Coll., Columbus, Ohio, Inst. Catholique, Paris and Princeton Univ.; Prof. Farleigh Dickinson Univ., Teaneck, NJ and George Washington Univ., Washington, DC 1968–70; various man. and exec. positions in US Postal Services (USPS), Los Angeles, Chicago and Washington DC 1970–87; Asst Postmaster-Gen. Int. Postal Affairs, USPS HQ 1987–94; Chair. Exec. Council, Universal Postal Union (UPU) 1989–94; Dir-Gen. Int. Bureau of UPU 1995–; John Wanamaker Award 1991, Heinrich von Stephan Medal.
Address: Universal Postal Union, Weltpoststr. 4, 3000 Berne 15, Switzerland.

Telephone: (31) 3503111; **fax:** (31) 3503110; **e-mail:** info@upu.int; **internet:** www.upu.int.

LEES, Martin; British engineer and international official; b. 1941; m.; four c.; ed. Univ. of Cambridge, Coll. of Europe, Belgium; Rector UN Univ. for Peace Jan. 2001–.
Address: POB 138, Ciudad Colón, Costa Rica.
Telephone: 249-1072; **fax:** 249-1929; **e-mail:** info@upeace.org; **internet:** www.upeace.org.

LEMIERRE, Jean; French economist and financial official; m.; two c.; ed. Institut d'Etudes Politiques de Paris; Ecole Nationale d'Administration; with Ministry of Economy and Finance 1995, headed French Treasury Oct. 1995–May 2000; mem. European Monetary Cttee 1995–98; Chair. European Economic and Financial Cttee; Chair. Paris Club; Pres. European Bank for Reconstruction and Devt (EBRD) June 2000–.
Address: EBRD, One Exchange Square, 175 Bishopsgate, London, EC2A 2EH, United Kingdom.
Telephone: (20) 7338-6000; **fax:** (20) 7338-6100; **internet:** www.ebrd.com.

LEVI, Noel; B.A., C.B.E.; Papua New Guinean diplomatist; b. 6 Feb. 1947, Nonopai, New Ireland Province; m.; four c.; ed. Univ. of Papua New Guinea, Port Moresby 1970–73; Asst Sec. (Defence Policy), Chief Min.'s Dept, Govt of Papua New Guinea 1973–74; Sec. Defence Dept. 1974–77; mem. of Papua New Guinea Parl. 1977–87; Min. of Foreign Affairs 1980–82; Amb. to the People's Repub. of China 1987–90; High Commr to the United Kingdom 1991–95; Perm. Sec. Prime Min.'s Council and Nat. Exec. Council; Sec.-Gen. Pacific Islands Forum Secr. Jan. 1998–.
Address: Pacific Islands Forum Secretariat, Private Mail Bag, Suva, Fiji.
Telephone: 3312600; **fax:** 3305573; **e-mail:** info@forumsec.org.fj; **internet:** www.forumsec.org.fj.

LUBBERS, Rudolphus (Ruud) Franciscus Marie; Netherlands politician and international official; b. 7 May 1939, Rotterdam; m. Maria E. J. Hoogeweegen 1962; two s. one d.; ed. Canisius College, Nijmegen, Netherlands School of Economics; Sec. to Man. Bd Lubbers Construction Workshops and Machinery Fabricators Hollandia 1963-65, Co-Dir 1965; Chair. Catholic Asscn of Metalwork Employers; mem. Bd Netherlands Christian Employers' Fed.; Min. of Econ. Affairs 1973-77; mem. Second Chamber of States-Gen. (Parl.) May 1977-94; Parl. Leader Christian Democratic Appeal 1978; Prime Min. of the Netherlands 1982-94; Vice-Chair. Independent World Commission on the Oceans; Int. Pres. World Wide Fund for Nature 1999–; Chair. Globus and Prof. of Globalization, Tilburg Univ.; Visiting Prof. Harvard Univ.; UN High Commr for Refugees Jan. 2001–.
Address: Office of the United Nations High Commissioner for Refugees, CP 2500, 1211 Geneva 2 dépôt, Switzerland.
Telephone: (22) 7398111; **fax:** (22) 7397312; **e-mail:** unhcr@unhcr.ch; **internet:** www.unhcr.ch.

McKINLEY, Brunson; American diplomatist; b. 1943; m.; one s. one d.; ed. Univ. of Chicago, Univ. of Harvard; joined Dept of State after military service; diplomatic appointments in China, Germany, Italy, Viet Nam and the United Kingdom; Amb. to Haiti, responsible for US refugee and migration budget and migration policy 1991–95, incl. establishment of temporary protection regime for Cuban and Haitian immigrants and provision of emergency assistance to the Central African refugee crisis 1994; Humanitarian Co-ordinator for Bosnia and Herzegovina 1995–98, incl. significant responsibility for the formulation of Annex 7 (relating to refugees) of Gen. Framework Agreement for Peace in Bosnia and Herzegovina, establishment of the Bosnian Comm. for Real Property Claims of Displaced Persons and Refugees and initiation of Int. Org. for Migration (IOM) Out-of-Country Voting Programme; Dir-Gen. IOM Oct. 1998–.
Address: IOM, 17 route des Morillons, CP 71, 1211 Geneva 19, Switzerland.
Telephone: (22) 7179111; **fax:** (22) 7986150; **e-mail:** info@iom.int; **internet:** www.iom.int.

McKINNON, Donald Charles (Don); New Zealand politician; b. 1939, London, United Kingdom; m. 2nd Clare de Lore 1995; one s; one s. three d. from 1st marriage; ed. Nelson Coll., New Zealand, Woodrow Wilson High School, Washington D.C., USA, Lincoln Univ., New Zealand; fmrly estate agent and farm management consultant; Nat. Party MP 1978–2000; held posts of Jr. and Sr Govt Whip, Spokesperson for Health; Sr Opposition Whip 1984–87, Dep. Prime Min. 1990–96, Leader of the House 1993–96, Min. of Foreign Affairs and Trade, of Pacific Island Affairs 1991–99, for Disarmament and Arms Control 1996–99, of Trade 1998–99; Dep. Chair. Commonwealth Ministerial Action Group on the Harare Declaration (CMAG) 1995–2000, Sec.-Gen. of Commonwealth April 2000–.
Address: Commonwealth Secretariat, Marlborough House, Pall Mall, London SW1Y 5HX, United Kingdom.
Telephone: (20) 7839-3411; **fax:** (20) 7930-0827; **e-mail:** info@commonwealth.int; **internet:** www.thecommonwealth.org.

MAGARIÑOS, Carlos Alfredo, M.B.A.; Argentine international civil servant; b. 16 August 1962, Buenos Aires, Argentina; m. María José Santambrogio 1989; ed. Nat. Univ. of Buenos Aires; analyst, Office of Strategic Planning and Foreign Trade, Banco Ciudad de Buenos Aires 1984–86; Assoc. Prof. of Argentine and Latin American Economic Problems, Univ. of Salvador 1990; Nat. Dir for Foreign Trade 1991–92; joined Ministry of Economy 1992, Under-Sec. of State for Industry 1992–93, Sec. of State for Mining and Industry 1993–96; Econ. and Trade Rep. of Argentina, Washington, D.C., USA 1996–97; rank of Amb. 1996; Dir-Gen. UN Industrial Devt Org. (UNIDO) 1997–. *Publications:* El Rol del Estado en la Política Industrial de los 90; articles on econ. and industrial issues.
Address: United Nations Industrial Development Organization, Vienna International Centre, POB 300, A-1400 Vienna, Austria.
Telephone: (1) 26026; **fax:** (1) 2692669; **e-mail:** unido@unido.org; **internet:** www.unido.org.

MALLOCH BROWN, Mark, B.A., M.A.; British international official; ed. Magdalene Coll., Univ. of Cambridge, Univ. of Michigan, USA; at UNHCR 1979–83 (which received the Nobel Peace Prize 1981), responsible for field operations for Cambodian refugees, Thailand 1979–81, Dep. Chief of Emergency Unit, Geneva, Switzerland 1981–83; founder, Economist Devt Report, editor 1983–86; Partner responsible for int. practice, incl. provision of political advice to presidential candidates and advice on privatization in eastern Europe, Sawyer Miller Group (communications management firm); mem. Soros Advisory Cttee on Bosnia and Herze-govina 1993–94; Dir of External Affairs, IBRD 1994–96, Vice-Pres. for External Affairs Jan. 1996–99, for UN Affairs Feb. 1996–99; Administrator UN Devt Programme (UNDP) 1 July 1999–; Vice-Chair. Bd of Refugees Int., Washington, DC, USA.
Address: UNDP, One United Nations Plaza, New York, NY 10017, USA.
Telephone: (212) 906-5295; **fax:** (212) 906-5364; **e-mail:** hq@undp.org; **internet:** www.undp.org.

MANNAI, Jassim Abdullah al-, PH.D.; Dir-Gen. and Chair. of Bd of Exec. Dirs, Arab Monetary Fund.
Address: Arab Monetary Fund, POB 2818, Abu Dhabi, United Arab Emirates.
Telephone: (2) 215000; **fax:** (2) 326454; **e-mail:** centralmail@amfad.org.ae; **internet:** www.amf.org.ae.

MATSUURA, Koichiro, Japanese diplomatist; b. 1937, Tokyo, Japan; ed. Univ. of Tokyo, Haverford Coll., Pennsylvania, USA; with Ministry of Foreign Affairs, Govt of Japan 1988–94; Amb. to France 1994–1998; Chair. UNESCO Heritage Cttee 1998–99, UNESCO Dir-Gen. 1999–.
Address: Office of the Director-General, UNESCO, 7 place de Fontenoy, 75352 Paris, France.
Telephone: 1-45-68-10-00; **fax:** 1-45-67-16-90; **e-mail:** scg@unesco.org; **internet:** www.unesco.org.

MOORE, Michael Kenneth (Mike); New Zealand politician; b. 28 Jan. 1949, Whakatane, North Island, New Zealand; m. Yvonne Dereaney; fmrly social worker, printer, trade union researcher; mem. New Zealand Labour Party; mem. New Zealand Parl. 1972–1999, Min. of Overseas Trade and Marketing 1984–90, also Min. of Tourism and Publicity, and of Recreation and Sport 1984–87, Min. of Foreign Affairs 1990, Prime Min. Sept.–Oct. 1990, Leader of the Opposition 1990–93, Opposition Spokesperson on Foreign Affairs and Overseas Trade 1993–99; Dir.-Gen. World Trade Organization (WTO) Sept. 1999–. *Publications:* A Pacific Parliament, Hard Labour, Fighting for New

Zealand, Children of the Poor, The Added Value Economy, A Brief History of the Future.
Address: WTO, Centre William Rappard, rue de Lausanne 154, 1211 Geneva, Switzerland.
Telephone: (22) 7395111; **fax:** (22) 7314206; **e-mail:** enquiries@wto.org; **internet:** www.wto.org.

MORRIS, James T., B.S., M.B.A.; American international organization official and business executive; b. 18 April 1943, Terre Haute, Ind.; m. Jacqueline Harrell Morris; three c.; ed. Indiana Univ., Butler Univ.; Chief of Staff to Mayor of Indianapolis 1967–73; Dir of Community Devt, Lilly Endowment 1973, Vice-Pres., Pres. 1984–89; Chair. and CEO. IWC Resources Corpn, Indiana Water Co. 1989–; Exec. Dir World Food Programme (WFP) April 2002–; Chair. Bd of Trustees Indiana Univ.; Treas. U.S. Olympic Cttee; mem. Bd of Govs. American Red Cross.
Address: WFP, Via Cesare Giulio Viola 68, Parco dei Medici, 00148 Rome, Italy.
Telephone: (06) 6513-1; **fax:** (06) 6590-632; **e-mail:** wfpinfo@wfp.org; **internet:** www.wfp.org.

MOUSSA, Amr Muhammad, B.A.; Egyptian diplomatist and politician; b. 3 October 1936, Cairo, Egypt; ed. Univ. of Cairo; joined Ministry of Foreign Affairs 1958 as civil servant; Amb. to India 1987–90; Perm. Rep. to the UN 1990–91; Min. of Foreign Affairs 1990–2001; Sec.-Gen. League of Arab States May 2001–.
Address: League of Arab States, POB 11642, Arab League Bldg, Tahrir Sq., Cairo, Egypt.
Telephone: (2) 5750511; **fax:** (2) 5775626; **internet:** www.leagueofarabstates.org.

MUGASHA, Florence; Ugandan civil servant and international official; joined Ugandan Public Service in 1970s; govt rep. to numerous regional and int. confs and summits; Head of Public Service and Sec. to Cabinet Nov. 1996–2002(first woman to head public services in Africa); Deputy Sec.-Gen. (Political) of the Commonwealth May 2002–; mem. Bd of Dirs Commonwealth Asscn for Public Admin. and Man.
Address: Commonwealth Secretariat, Marlborough House, Pall Mall, London, SW1Y 5HX, United Kingdom.
Telephone: (20) 7839-3411; **fax:** (20) 7930-0827; **email:** info@commonwealth.int; **internet:** www.commonwealth.org.

MWENCHA, J. E. O. (Erastus), B.A., M.A.; Kenyan economist and international official; m.; three c.; ed. Univ. of Nairobi, York Univ., Canada; entered civil service 1974, becoming Prin. Industrial Devt Officer; Dir, various parastatal orgs; mem. of research cttee, Nat. Council of Science and Tech.; Dir, Kenya Medical Research Inst.; Dir, Kenya Industrial Research and Devt Inst.; Sec., Industrial Sciences Advisory Council; appointed Sr Industrial Expert, ECA 1983; Dir of Industry, Energy and Environment, Preferential Trade Area (PTA) for Eastern and Southern Africa 1987–97; acting Sec.-Gen. COMESA Jan. 1997–June 1998, Sec.-Gen. June 1998–; awarded Order of the Moran of the Burning Spear (1998).
Address: COMESA Centre, Ben Bella Rd, POB 30051, 10101 Lusaka, Zambia.
Telephone: (1) 229726; **fax:** (1) 225107; **e-mail:** comesa@comesa.int; **internet:** www.comesa.int.

NANDAN, Satya Nand, C.B.E.; Fijian diplomatist; b. 10 July 1936, Suva; m. Sreekumari Nandan 1966 (died 1971); m. Zarine Merchant 1976; one s.; ed. John McGlashan Coll., Dunedin, New Zealand, D.A.V. Coll., Suva and Univs of Wellington and London; called to Bar, Lincoln's Inn, London 1965; barrister and solicitor, Supreme Court of Fiji 1966–; pvt. law practice, Suva 1965–70; Counsellor then Amb. Perm. Mission of Fiji to UN 1970–76; Leader, Fiji del. to Third UN Conf. on Law of the Sea 1973–82; Amb. to EEC (also accred. to Belgium, France, Italy, Luxembourg, Netherlands) 1976–80; Perm. Sec. for Foreign Affairs, Fiji 1981–83; UN Under-Sec.-Gen. for Ocean Affairs and the Law of the Sea and Special Rep. of UN Sec.-Gen. for Law of the Sea 1983–92; mem. Perm. Mission of Fiji at UN 1993–95; Chair. UN Conf. on Straddling Fish Stocks and Highly Migratory Fish Stocks 1993–95; Rep. of Fiji to Int. Seabed Authority 1994–95, elected first Sec.-Gen. of the Authority March 1996; Int. Law Adviser to Govt of Fiji 1994–95; del. to numerous int. confs etc.; Visiting lecturer, Columbia Univ., New York and Univ. of Virginia, Charlottesville; Sr Visiting Fellow, US Inst. of Peace 1992; many other professional appts; Hon.LL.D. (Newfoundland) 1995. *Publications include:* Commentary on 1982 UN Convention on Law of the Sea (7 vols.) (ed.); numerous articles on UN and aspects of Law of the Sea.
Address: International Seabed Authority, 14-20 Port Royal St, Kingston, Jamaica.
Telephone: 922-9105; **fax:** 922-0195; **e-mail:** postmaster@isa.org.jm; **internet:** www.isa.org.jm.

NOYER, Christian; French banker and civil servant; b. 6 Oct. 1950, Soisy; m. Martine Broyet; three s. one d.; ed. Univs of Rennes and Paris, Inst. of Political Science, Ecole Nat. d'Admin.; joined Treasury 1976, Chief of Banking Office, then of Export Credit Office 1982–85, Dep. Dir in charge of Int. Multilateral Issues 1988–90, then of Debt Man., Monetary and Banking Affairs 1990–92, Dir of Dept responsible for public holdings and financing 1991–93, Dir of Treasury 1993–95; financial attaché French del. to EC, Brussels 1980–82; tech. adviser, then sr adviser to Min. for Econ. Affairs, Finance and Privatization, Edouard Balladur 1986–88, Chief of Staff to E. Alphandéry 1993, to Jean Arthuis 1995–97; Dir Ministry for Econ. Affairs, Finance and Industry 1997–98; Vice-Pres. European Cen. Bank June 1998–; Alt. Gov. IMF and World Bank 1993–95; alt. mem. European Monetary Cttee 1988–90, mem. 1993–95, 1998–; alt. mem. G-7 and G-10 1993–95; mem. working party no. 3, OECD 1993–95; Chair. Paris Club of Creditor Cos 1993–97; Kt. Légion d'honneur, Ordre nat. du Mérite, Commdr, Nat. Order of Lion, Senegal. *Publications:* Banks: The Rules of the Game 1990, various articles.
Address: European Central Bank, Kaiserstrasse 29, 60066 Frankfurt-am-Main, Germany.
Telephone: (69) 13-44-0; **fax:** (69) 13-44-6000; **internet:** www.ecb.int.

OBAID, Thoraya Ahmed, B.A., M.A., PH.D; Saudi Arabian international official; b. 2 March 1945, Baghdad, Iraq; m.; two d.; ed. Mills Coll., Oakland, USA, Wayne State Univ., Detroit, USA; mem. League of Arab States working group for formulating the Arab Strategy for Social Devt 1984–85; mem. editorial bd *Journal of Arab Women* 1984–90; mem. Int. Women's Advisory Panel, Int. Planned Parenthood Federation 1993; Chair. UN Inter-agency Task Force on Gender, Amman 1996; mem. UN Inter-agency Gender Mission to Afghanistan Nov. 1997; mem. UN Strategic Framework Mission to Afghanistan 1997; Assoc. Social Affairs Officer (Women and Development), ESCWA Social Devt and Population Div. (SDPD) 1975–81, Women and Devt Programme Manager ESCWA SDPD 1981–92, Chief ECSWA SDPD 1992–93, Dep. Exec. Sec. ESCWA 1993–98; Dir UNFPA Div. for Arab States and Europe 1998–2000, Exec. Dir UNFPA Jan. 2001–.
Address: United Nations Population Fund, 220 East 42nd Street, 19th Floor, New York, NY 10017, USA.
Telephone: (212) 297-5020; **fax:** (212) 297-4911; **internet:** www.unfpa.org.

OBASI, Godwin Olu Patrick, PH.D.; Nigerian meteorologist and statistician; b. 24 Dec. 1933, Ogori; m.; one s. five d.; ed. McGill Univ., Montréal, Canada and Massachusetts Inst. of Tech., USA; joined Nigerian Meteorological Dept as Asst Meteorological Officer 1956, later apptd Sr Meteorologist in charge of Research and Training and of Nat. Meteorological Centre for Forecasting Services; Visiting Research Scientist, Fla. State Univ., and Nat. Center for Atmospheric Research, Boulder, Colo., USA 1973; Sr. Lecturer in Meteorology for WMO/UNDP, Univ. of Nairobi, Kenya 1967–74, Prof., Chair. Dept. of Meteorology, and Dean Faculty of Science 1974–76; Adviser in Meteorological Research and Training, Fed. Govt of Nigeria, Head Nigerian Inst. for Meteorological Research and Training 1976–78; Dir Educ. and Training Dept, World Meteorological Org. (WMO) Secr., Geneva 1978–84, Sec.-Gen. WMO 1984–; mem. British Inst. of Statisticians, Int. Acad. of Sciences of Nature and Society (Armenia br.) 1998; Fellow African Acad. of Sciences 1993, Third World Acad. of Sciences 1996 (Vice-Pres. 1999–), meteorological socs of Dominican Repub., Ecuador, Colombia, Nigeria, Africa, America, Hon. Fellow meteorological socs of Cuba, Burkina Faso, India; Hon. mem. Acad. of Agricultural and Forestry Sciences, Romania, Kenya meteorological soc.; Hon. Dr Physics (Bucharest) 1991; Hon. LL.D. (Univ. of Philippines) 1992; Hon. D.Sc. (Fed. Univ. of Tech., Nigeria) 1992, (Alpine Geophysical Research Inst., Russian Fed.) 1993, (Univ. of Nairobi) 1998;

Gold Plaque Merit Award for Science and Art, Czechoslovakian Acad. of Sciences 1986, Gold Medal for Meteorology and Hydrology, Paraguay 1988, Cross Medal of Air Force, Venezuela 1989, Ogori Merit Award, Kogi State, Nigeria 1991, Washington Climate Award, U.S.A. 1990, Gold Medal Award, African Meteorological Soc. 1993, Recognition of Merit, Nat. Univ. of Asunción, Paraguay 1993, Medal of Merit for Devt of Hydrology and Meteorology, Slovak Hydrometeorological Inst. 1994, Balkan Physical Union Golden Medal Award, Greece 1997, Medal of Honour and Certificate of Merit, Front for Ebira Solidarity, Okene, Nigeria 1995, Award for Promotion of Hydrometeorology, Viet Nam 1998; Officer, Order of Fed. Repub. of Nigeria; Commdr, Nat. Order of Côte d'Ivoire, Benin, Burkina Faso; Commdr, Nat. Order of Lion, Senegal, Medal of Freedom of Ho Chi Minh City, Viet Nam, Order of Grand Duke of Gediminas and Medal Order of Gediminas, Lithuania, Presidential Award Medal of Friendship, Viet Nam and other distinctions. *Publications:* many scientific and tech. papers on meteorology and hydrometeorology.
Address: World Meteorological Organization, CP 2300, 7 bis, ave de la Paix, 1211 Geneva 2, Switzerland.
Telephone: (22) 7308111; **fax:** (22) 7308181; **e-mail:** ipa@wmo.ch; **internet:** www.wmo.ch.

OCAMPO, José Antonio, PH.D.; Colombian United Nations official; b. 20 Dec. 1952; m.; three c.; ed. Univ. of Notre Dame, Yale Univ., USA; Researcher, Centre for Devt Studies, Univ. de los Andes 1976–80, Dir 1980–82; at Foundation for Higher Education and Devt (FEDESARROLLO) 1983–93, Dep. Dir 1983–84, Exec. Dir 1984–88, Senior Researcher and mem. of Bd of Dirs; Min. of Agriculture 1993–94, of Planning 1994–96, of Finance and Public Credit 1996–97; Exec. Sec. UN Econ. Comm. for Latin America and the Caribbean (ECLAC) Jan. 1998–; Nat. Dir, Employment Mission 1985–86; Adviser to Colombian Foreign Trade Bd 1990–91; Adviser, Colombian Nat. Council of Entrepreneurial Asscn; mem. Tech. Comm. on Coffee Affairs, Public Expenditure Comm., Advisory Comm. for Fiscal Reform., Mission on Intergovernmental Finance; consultant to IBRD, IDB and UN; appointed mem. Colombian Academy of Econ. Science 1987; awarded Nat. Science Prize 1988; Visiting Fellow Univ. of Oxford, United Kingdom and Yale Univ.; Visiting Researcher, UNCTAD; Dir of several academic journals. *Publications:* various, covering economics, politics, trade and commerce.
Address: ECLAC, Edif. Naciones Unidas, Avda Dag Hammarskjöld, Casilla 179D, Santiago, Chile.
Telephone: (2) 2102000; **fax:** (2) 2080252; **e-mail:** dpisantiago@eclac.cl; **internet:** www.eclac.org.

ODA, Shigeru, LL.M., J.S.D., LL.D.; Japanese lawyer; b. 22 Oct. 1924; m. Noriko Sugimura 1950; one s. one d.; ed. Univ. of Tokyo, Yale Univ.; Research Fellow, Univ. of Tokyo 1947–49; Lecturer Univ. of Tôhoku 1950–53, Assoc. Prof. 1953–59, Prof. 1959–76, Prof. Emer. 1985–; Tech. Adviser, Atomic Energy Comm. 1961–64; Special Asst to Min. for Foreign Affairs 1973–76; mem. Science Council of Ministry of Educ. 1969–76, of Council for Ocean Devt in Prime Min.'s Office 1971–76, Advisory Cttee for Co-operation with UN Univ. 1971–76; mem. (Judge), Int. Court of Justice 1976–85, 1985–94, 1994–, Vice-Pres. 1991–94; del. to UN Confs on Law of the Sea 1958, 1960, 1973–75; Rep. at 6th Gen. Conf. of Inter-Governmental Oceanographic Comm. 1969; consultative positions with bodies concerned with marine questions; Counsel for Fed. Repub. of Germany before Int. Court of Justice 1968; Editor-in-Chief, Japanese Annual of International Law 1973–77; Assoc. Inst. de Droit Int. 1969 (mem. 1979); mem. Curatorium, Hague Acad. of Int. Law 1989–, Bd. of Dirs., Int. Devt Law Inst., Rome 1994–, Int. Council of Arbitration for Sport 1994–; Hon. mem. American Soc. of Int. Law 1975; mem. Japan Acad. 1994; Hon. D.Jur. (Bhopal Univ.) 1980, (New York Law School) 1981. *Publications:* in Japanese: International Law of the Sea 1956–85 (8 vols), International Law and Maritime Resources 1971–75, Judicial Decisions relating to International Law before Japanese Courts 1978; in English: International Control of Sea Resources 1962, The International Law of Ocean Development (4 vols) 1972–79, The Law of the Sea in Our Times (2 vols) 1977, The Practice of Japan in International Law 1961–70 1982, The International Court of Justice 1987; various articles.
Address: International Court of Justice, Peace Palace, Carnegieplein 2, 2517 KJ The Hague, Netherlands.
Telephone: (70) 302-23-23; **fax:** (70) 364-99-28; **e-mail:** information@icj-cij.org; **internet:** www.icj-cij.org.

O'NEIL, William Andrew, O.C., B.SC., F.R.S.A.; Canadian international public servant and engineer; b. 6 June 1927, Ottawa; m. Dorothy Muir 1950; one s. two d.; ed. Univ. of Toronto; engineer, Fed. Dept of Transport, Ottawa 1949–53, Resident Engineer, Special Projects Br. 1954; Div. Engineer, St Lawrence Seaway Authority 1955–59, Regional Dir 1960–63, Dir of Construction 1964–70; Dep. Admin., Marine Services, Canadian Marine Transportation Admin. 1975–79; Commr, Canadian Coast Guard and Dep. Admin., Marine Admin. 1979–89; Pres. St Lawrence Seaway Authority 1980–89; Chair. Council Int. Maritime Org (IMO) 1980–89, Sec.-Gen. 1990–; mem. Bd of Govs., World Maritime Univ. 1983–89, subsequently mem. Exec. Council of Bd of Govs. and Bd of Trustees of Capital Fund; Chair. Governing Bd, Int. Maritime Law Inst., Malta 1991–; Canadian del. to Perm. Int. Asscn of Navigation Congresses 1984–90; Chair. Canadian Cttee, Lloyd's Register of Shipping 1987–88; mem. Int. Maritime Bureau 1991–; Chancellor World Maritime Univ. 1991–; Dir Canarctic Shipping Co; Pres. Seaway Int. Bridge Corpn; mem. Bd of the Thousand Islands Bridge Authority 1980–90; mem. Asscn of Professional Engineers of Ont., American Soc. of Civil Engineers; Foreign mem. Royal Acad. of Eng. (UK); Fellow, Chartered Inst. of Transport (UK); Hon. Commodore, Canadian Coast Guard; Hon. mem. Canadian Maritime Law Asscn, Honourable Co of Master Mariners, UK, Int. Maritime Pilots Asscn, Int. Fed. of Shipmasters' Asscns, NUMAST (Nat. Union of Marine Aviation and Shipping Transport Officers) (UK), Soc. of Naval Architects and Marine Engineers (USA), Soc. of Naval Architects and Marine Engineers, Singapore, Int. Asscn of Lighthouse Authorities, Co of Master Mariners, India 1998; Hon. Fellow, The Nautical Inst., UK, Royal Inst. of Naval Architects 1998; Hon. Dip. Canadian Coast Guard Coll.; Hon. LL.D. (Malta), (Memorial Univ. of Newfoundland) 1996; Hon. D.Sc. (Nottingham Trent) 1994; Eng. Medal, Asscn of Professional Engineers of Ont., Distinguished Public Service Award, US Govt, Admirals' Medal 1994, Seatrade Personality of the Year Award 1995, NUMAST Award (UK) 1995, Professional Engineers Ont. Gold Medal, mem. Eng. Alumni Hall of Distinction, Univ. of Toronto 1996, Silver Bell Award, Seamen's Church Inst., New York 1997; Commdr, Ordre Nat. des Cèdres (Lebanon) 1995, Grand Cross, Orden Vasco Nuñez de Balboa (Panama) 1998, Cdre Award, Conn. Maritime Asscn. 1998, Dioscun Prize, Lega Nowali Italiana (Italy) 1998.
Address: International Maritime Organization, 4 Albert Embankment, London, SE1 7SR, United Kingdom.
Telephone: (20) 7735-7611; **fax:** (20) 7587-3210; **e-mail:** info@imo.org; **internet:** www.imo.org.

ORDZHONIKIDZE, Sergey Aleksandrovich; Russian politician and diplomatist; b. 14 March 1946, Moscow; m.; one d.; ed. Moscow State Inst. of Int. Relations; mem. staff Ministry of Foreign Affairs until 1991, later Head Dept. of Int. Orgs. 1996–99, Deputy Min. of Foreign Affairs 1999–2002; Deputy Perm. Rep. to UN, New York 1991–96; Dir-Gen. UN Office at Geneva (UNOG) March 2002–.
Address: United Nations Office at Geneva, Palais de Nations, 1211 Geneva 10, Switzerland.
Telephone: (22) 9171234; **fax:** (22) 9179012; **internet:** www.unog.ch.

OSHIMA, Kenzo; Japanese diplomatist; b. 1943; ed. Tokyo Univ.; served in diplomatic posts in Australia, France, India, USA and at Perm. Mission to the UN; Dir-Gen. Economic Co-operation Bureau, Ministry of Foreign Affairs; Sec.-Gen. Secr. for Int. Peace Co-operation HQ, Office of the Prime Min. –2000; UN Under-Sec.-Gen. for Humanitarian Affairs and Emergency Relief Co-ordinator Jan. 2001–.
Address: : Office for the Co-ordination of Humanitarian Affairs, United Nations Plaza, New York, NY 10017, USA.
Telephone: (212) 963-1234; **fax:** (212) 963-1312; **e-mail:** ochany@un.org.

O'SULLIVAN, David; Irish European Union (EU) official; b. 1 March 1953; m. Agnes O'Hare 1984; one s. one d.; ed. Trinity Coll., Dublin, Coll. of Europe, Bruges, Belgium; with Dept. of

Foreign Affairs 1977–79; with Comm. of EC, later EU (European Comm.) 1979–; Dep. chef de cabinet 1995–96; with Directorate-Gen. Employment, Industrial Relations and Social Affairs 1996–99, Dir European Social Fund policy 1996–97, Dir Resources 1997–99; Dir-Gen. DGXXII 1999; chef de cabinet of Pres. of the European Comm. 1999–2000; European Comm. Sec.-Gen. 2000–

Address: European Commission Secretariat, 200 rue de la Loi, 1049 Brussels, Belgium.

Telephone: (2) 299-11-11; **fax** (2) 295-01-38; **internet:** www.europa.eu.int/comm/index.htm.

OTUNNU, Olara; diplomatist; b. Sept. 1950, Mucwini, northern Uganda (became Côte d'Ivoire citizen in late 1980s); guardian of six c.; ed. Makerere Univ. (Uganda), Univ. of Oxford (United Kingdom), Harvard Law School (USA); practised law in USA; Asst Prof. of Law at Albany Law School, USA; participated in resistance activities against the regime of Idi Amin; Perm. Rep. to the UN 1980–85, Pres. Security Council 1981, Vice-Pres. Gen. Assembly 1982–83; Min. of Foreign Affairs 1985–86; Pres. Int. Peace Academy 1990–97; appointed Special Rep. of UN Sec.-Gen. for Children and Armed Conflict Aug. 1997; UN Under-Secretary-General for Children and Armed Conflict Sept. 1998–.

Address: United Nations, United Nations Plaza, New York, NY 10017, USA.

Telephone: (212) 963-1234; **fax:** (212) 963-4879.

PANGELINAN, Lourdes; Guam international official; held various positions in the judicial, legislative and executive branches of the Guam Govt, incl. Chief of Staff in the Office of the Governor; Dep. Dir.-Gen. Pacific Community 1996–99, Dir.-Gen. Jan. 2000–.

Address: Pacific Community, BP D5, 98848 Nouméa Cédex, New Caledonia.

Telephone: 26-20-00; **fax** 26-38-18; **e-mail:** lourdesp@spc.int; **internet:** www.spc.org.nc/.

PANITCHPAKDI, Supachai; B.A., M.A., PH.D.; Thai banker and politician; b. 1946, Bangkok, Thailand; ed. Erasmus Univ., Rotterdam, the Netherlands; held various positions at Bank of Thailand (central bank) until 1986; Dep. Min. of Finance, Thai Govt 1986–88; Pres. Thai Military Bank 1988–92; Dep. Prime Min. 1992–95; Dep. Prime Min. and Min. of Commerce 1997–; appointed Dir-Gen. designate of World Trade Organization (WTO) 1999 (to commence term of office in Sept. 2002); awarded Knight Grand Cordon (Special Class) of the Most Exalted Order of the White Elephant.

Address: c/o WTO, Centre William Rappard, rue de Lausanne 154, 1211 Geneva, Switzerland.

Telephone: (22) 7395111; **fax:** (22) 7314206; **e-mail:** enquiries@wto.org; **internet:** www.wto.org.

PARRA-ARANGUREN, Gonzalo; Venezuelan judge and university professor; b. 5 Dec. 1928, Caracas; ed. Cen. Univ. of Venezuela, Inter-American Law Inst., Univ. of New York, Ludwig-Maximilians Univ., Munich; Prof., Cen. Univ. of Venezuela, Caracas 1956–, Andrés Bello Catholic Univ., Caracas 1957–96; Judge, Second Court of First Instance (commercial matters), Fed. Dist. and State of Miranda, Caracas 1958–71; First Assoc. Judge, Chamber of Cassation (civil, commercial and labour matters) of Supreme Court of Justice 1988–92, elected Alt. Judge 1992; mem. nat. group for Venezuela, Perm. Court of Arbitration, The Hague 1985–; mem. (Judge) Int. Court of Justice 1991–; has acted as arbitrator in Venezuela and abroad on pvt. commercial matters; mem. Legal Advisory Cttee. of Ministry of Foreign Affairs 1984–, of Nat. Congress 1990–; mem. Acad. of Political and Social Sciences of Caracas 1966– (Pres. 1993–95), Inst. of Int. Law 1979–; rep. Venezuela at several sessions of The Hague Conf. on Pvt. Int. Law. *Publications:* several books and numerous articles in Venezuelan and foreign journals on law of nationality, pvt. int. law and int. civil procedural law.

Address: International Court of Justice, Peace Palace, Carnegieplein 2, 2517 KJ The Hague, Netherlands.

Telephone: (70) 392-44-41; **fax:** (70) 364-99-28; **e-mail:** information@icj-cij.org; **internet:** www.icj-cij.org.

PILLAY, Navanethem, B.A., LL.B; South African judge; b. 1941, Durban, South Africa; ed. Natal Univ.; founded own law practice 1967, practised law 1967–95; Acting Judge Supreme Court of South Africa 1995; mem. (Judge) UN International Criminal Tribunal for Rwanda (ICTR) May 1995–, Pres. July 1999–.

Address: United Nations International Criminal Tribunal for Rwanda, Arusha International Conference Centre, POB 6016, Arusha, Tanzania.

Telephone: (57) 4207; **fax:** (57) 4000; **e-mail:** public@un.org; **internet:** www.ictr.org.

PRENDERGAST, Sir (Walter) Kieran, K.C.V.O., C.M.G.; British diplomatist; b. 2 July 1942, Campbeltown, Scotland; m. Joan Reynolds 1967; two s. two d.; ed. Salesian Coll., Chertsey and St Edmund Hall, Oxford; Asst Pvt. Sec. to successive Secs of State, Foreign and Commonwealth Office 1976–78; has served at Istanbul, Ankara, Nicosia, The Hague, UK Mission to UN, New York and Tel Aviv; seconded to Staff of last Gov. of Rhodesia (Lord Soames) during transition to independence in Zimbabwe; High Commr in Zimbabwe 1989–92, in Kenya 1992–95; Amb. to Turkey 1995–97; UN Under-Sec.-Gen. for Political Affairs 1997–.

Address: United Nations, New York, NY 10017, USA.

Telephone: (212) 963-5055; **fax:** (212) 963-5065.

PRIDDLE, Robert; British international official; b. 9 Sept. 1938; m. Janice Elizabeth Gorham 1962; two c.; ed. King's Coll. School, Wimbledon, Univ. of Cambridge; Min. of Aviation 1960; at Dept of Trade and Industry 1973 and 1985–89; Dep. Sec., Dept of Energy from 1974, Dir-Gen., Energy Resources 1989–92; Pres. Conference of European Posts and Telecommunications Admins 1987–89; Chair. of Gov. Bd, International Energy Agency (IEA) 1991–92, now Exec. Dir; mem. Financial Reporting Council 1992–94. *Publication:* Victoriana (2nd Edn) 1963.

Address: IEA, 9 rue de la Fédération, 75739 Paris Cédex 15, France.

Telephone: 1-40-57-65-00; **fax:** 1-40-57-65-59; **e-mail:** info@iea.org; **internet:** www.iea.org.

PRODI, Romano; Italian industrialist and politician; b. 9 Aug. 1939, Scandiano, Italy; m. Flavia Prodi Franzoni; two s.; ed. Univ. Cattolica del Sacro Cuore, Milan; Visiting Prof., Harvard Univ., USA; Researcher, London School of Economics, United Kingdom; Prof. of Econ. and Industrial Policy, Univ. degli Studi, Bologna; Min. for Industry 1978–79; Chair. Istituto per la Ricostruzione Industriale (IRI—state industrial and banking holding) 1982–89 and 1993–94; endorsed Leader, L'Ulivo (The Olive Tree) political alliance July 1995, Prime Min. May 1996–Oct. 1998; Pres. European Comm. Sept. 1999–; mem. Bd of Trustees of Massachusetts Inst. of Tech., USA. *Publications:* numerous scientific publs on European industrial policy, public enterprise, energy and economic systems.

Address: European Commission, 200 rue de la Loi, 1049 Brussels, Belgium.

Telephone: (2) 299-11-11; **fax:** (2) 295-01-38; **internet:** www.europa.eu.int/comm/index.htm.

RAHIM, Q. A. M. A.; Bangladeshi diplomatist; High Commr to Pakistan 1993–98, to Australia (concurrent accreditation to New Zealand and Fiji) 1998–99; Prin. Foreign Service Training Acad. 1999–2000; Sec. to the Govt 1999–2000; retd from govt service 2000; Officer on Special Duty (Sec.), Ministry of Foreign Affairs 2000–01; Dir Secr. SAARC 1990–92, Sec.-Gen. Jan. 2002–; fmr Del. Bangladesh Missions to Tokyo, London, Doha, Washington, D.C., UN, and Islamabad.

Address: SAARC, POB 4222, Kathmandu, Nepal.

Telephone: 221785; **fax:** 227033; **e-mail:** saarc@saarc.sec.org; **internet:** www.saarc-sec.org.

RALSTON, Gen. Joseph W., B.A., M.A.; US air force officer; b. 4 Nov., Hopkinsville, Kentucky; m. Diane Dougherty; two s. two d.; ed. Miami Univ. (Ohio), Univ. of Central Michigan, Army Command and Gen. Staff Coll., Fort Leavenworth, Kansas, Nat. War Coll., Fort Lesley J. McNair, Washington DC, Harvard Univ.; joined US air force 1965, various air force positions -1987; Asst Dep. Chief of Staff for Operations, then Dep. Chief of Staff for Requirements at HQ Tactical Air Command, Langley 1987–90; Dir Tactical Programms at Office of the Asst Sec. of the Air Force for Acquisition 1990–91, Dir of Operational Requirements, Office of the Dep. Chief of Staff for Plans and Operations, HQ US Air Force 1991–92; Commdr, Alaskan Command, Alaskan North American Aerospace Defense Command

Region, 11th Air Force and Jt Task Force Alaska 1992–94; Dep. Chief of Staff for Plans and Operations, HQ US Air Force 1994–95, Commdr, HQ Air Combat Command 1995–96; Vice-Chair. Jt Chiefs of Staff 1996–Apr. 2000; Commdr-in-Chief US European Command; NATO Supreme Allied Commdr Europe (SACEUR) May 2000–; awarded Defense Distinguished Service Medal, Distinguished Service Medal, Legion of Merit, Distinguished Flying Cross, Meritorious Service Medal, Air Medal, Air Force Medal.
Address: blvd Léopold III, 1110 Brussels, Belgium.
Telephone: (2) 707-41-11; **fax:** (2) 707-45-79; **e-mail:** nato doc@hq.nato.int; **internet:** www.nato.int.

RAMSAMY, Pakereesamy (Prega); Mauritian economist; b. 1950, Mauritius; with Preferential Trade Area for Eastern and Southern Africa, then Common Market for Eastern and Southern Africa for 14 years; Chief Economist, Southern African Devt Community (SADC) 1997–98, Dep. Exec. Sec. Sept. 1998–99, Exec. Sec. Jan. 2000– (acting –April 2001).
Address: SADC Bldg, Private Bag 0095, Gaborone, Botswana.
Telephone: 351863; **fax:** 372848; **e-mail:** registry@sadc.int; **internet:** www.sadc.int.

RANJEVA, Raymond, B.L.L., LL.D.; Malagasy lawyer; b. 31 Aug. 1942, Antananarivo; m. Yvette Madeleine R. Rabetafika 1967; five c.; ed. Univ. of Madagascar, Madagascar Nat. School of Admin., Univ. of Paris, France; Trainee, Judicial Div., Conseil d'Etat, Paris; Civil Administrator, Univ. of Madagascar 1966, Asst Lecturer 1966–72, Lecturer 1972, Dir Dept of Legal and Political Science 1973–82, Prof. 1981–91, Dean of Faculty of Law, Econ., Management and Social Sciences 1982–86, reappointed 1986–88; Prof., Madagascar Military Academy, Madagascar School of Admin.; Dir Public Law and Political Science Study Centre; First Rector, Univ. of Antananarivo 1988–90; Assoc. or Visiting Lecturer at several overseas univs; Man. Dir, Jureco (economic, financial and legal databank for advisory and research bodies) 1986–90, Editor 'Lettre mensuelle de Jureco' 1986–88; Conciliator, IBRD (World Bank) Int. Centre for Settlement of Investment Disputes 1970–; Attorney to Mali, Border Dispute (Burkina Faso/Mali); Consultant on the transfer to the State of the activities of Eau-Electricité de Madagascar and Electricité de France 1973; mem. (Judge) Int. Court of Justice Feb. 1991–; mem. Malagasy delegations at numerous int. conferences etc.; founder mem. Malagasy Human Rights Cttee 1971; mem. and Vice-Pres. Malagasy Academy 1974, Pres. Ethics and Political Science section 1975–91; mem. Nat. Constitutional Cttee 1975; mem. Court of Arbitration for Sport 1995–; legal adviser to Catholic Bishop's Conference, Madagascar; mem. Governing Body of African Soc. of Int. and Comparative Law, French Soc. of Int. Law, Québec Soc. (Canada); Sec.-Gen. Malagasy Legal Studies Soc.; Commdr, Ordre Nat. Malgache of Madagascar; Chevalier, Ordre de Mérite of Madagascar; Officier, Ordre Nat. of Mali. *Publications:* numerous works.
Address: International Court of Justice, Peace Palace, Carnegieplein 2, 2517 KJ The Hague, Netherlands.
Telephone: (70) 302-23-23; **fax:** (70) 364-99-28; **e-mail:** information@icj-cij.org; **internet:** www.icj-cij.org.

REZEK, Francisco, LL.B.; Brazilian judge and politician; b. 18 Jan. 1944, Cristina, Minas Gerais; ed. Fed. Univ. of Minas Gerais, Sorbonne, Oxford Univ., Harvard Univ., The Hague Acad. of Int. Law; Attorney of the Repub., Supreme Court 1972–79; Prof. of Int. and Constitutional Law, Univ. of Brasilia 1971–, Chair. Law Dept. 1974–76, Dean Faculty of Social Studies 1978–79; Prof. of Int. Law, Rio Branco Inst. 1976–; Justice of Supreme Court 1983–90, 1992–97; Foreign Min. 1990–92; mem. Perm. Court of Arbitration 1987–; mem. (Judge) Int. Court of Justice, The Hague Feb. 1997–. *Publications:* Droit des traités: particularités des actes constitutifs d'organisations internationales 1968, La conduite des relations internationales dans le droit constitutionnel latino-américain 1970, Direito dos Tratados 1984, Public International Law 1989.
Address: International Court of Justice, Peace Palace, Carnegieplein 2, 2517 KJ The Hague, Netherlands.
Telephone: (70) 302-23-23; **fax:** (70) 364-99-28; **e-mail:** information@icj-cij.org; **internet:** icj-cij.org.

RICUPERO, Rubens; Brazilian diplomatist, politician and international civil servant; b. 1 March 1937, São Paulo; m. Marisa Parolari; four c.; Prof. of Theory of Int. Relations, Univ. of Brasilia 1979–95; Prof. of History of Brazilian Diplomatic Relations, Rio Branco Inst. 1980–95; with Ministry of Foreign Relations 1981–85; Perm. Rep. to the UN in Geneva 1987–91; Amb. to USA 1991–93; Min. of the Environment and Amazonian Affairs 1993–94, of Finance March–Sept. 1994; Amb. to Italy 1995; Sec.-Gen. of UNCTAD Sept. 1995–.
Address: Office of the Secretary-General, UNCTAD, Palais des Nations, 1211 Geneva 10, Switzerland.
Telephone: (22) 9071234; **fax:** (22) 9070057; **e-mail:** ers@unctad.org; **internet:** www.unctad.org.

RIZA, Iqbal, M.A.; Pakistani international civil servant; b. 20 May 1934, India; m. 1959; two s.; ed. Pakistan and USA; Pakistan Foreign Service 1958–77; served Spain, Germany, Sudan, UK, USA; Dir Foreign Service Acad., Lahore 1968–71; Dep. Chief of Mission, Washington, D.C. 1972–76; Chargé d'Affaires, Paris 1977; joined UN 1978; assigned to negotiations in Iran-Iraq war 1981–87; Dir UN Gen. Ass. 1988; Chief, UN Electoral Mission, Nicaragua 1988–90; Special Rep. of UN Sec.-Gen. in El Salvador 1991–93; Asst Sec.-Gen. for Peace-keeping Operations 1993–97, Under-Sec.-Gen., Chief of Staff in Exec. Office of Sec.-Gen. 1997–.
Address: Exec. Office of the UN Sec.-Gen., United Nations, New York, NY 10017, USA.

ROBERTSON OF PORT ELLEN, Baron (Life Peer); George Islay Macneill, M.A.; British politician; b. 12 April 1946, Port Ellen, Isle of Islay, Scotland; m. Sandra Wallace 1970; two s. one d.; ed. Dunoon Grammar School, Argyll, Univ. of Dundee; Asst, Tayside Study 1968–69; Scottish Resident Officer, General, Municipal and Boilermakers' Union 1968–70, Scottish organizer 1979–78; MP for Hamilton 1979–99, Parl. Pvt. Sec. to Sec. of State for Social Services 1979; Opposition Spokesman on Scottish Affairs 1979–80, on Defence 1980–81; on Foreign and Commonwealth Affairs 1981–93, Prin. Spokesman on European Affairs 1984–93, Shadow Sec. of State for Scotland 1993–97, Sec. of State for Defence May 1997–99; Sec.-Gen. of NATO October 1999–; Chair. Scottish Council of the Labour Party 1977–78; Sec, Manifesto Group of Parl. Labour Party 1979-84; Chair. British-German Parl. Group 1992–93 (Hon. Pres. 1973–); Vice-Chair. British Council 1985–94; Vice-Pres. Raleigh Int. 1982–; many other appointments; awarded Commander's Cross, Order of Merit (Germany).
Address: NATO International Secretariat, blvd Léopold III, 1110 Brussels, Belgium.
Telephone: (2) 707-41-11; **fax:** (2) 707-45-79; **e-mail:** nato doc@hq.nato.int; **internet:** www.nato.int.

ROBINSON, Mary, LL.M.; Irish international civil servant and fmr head of state; b. 21 May 1944, Ballina, Co. Mayo; m. Nicholas Robinson 1970; two s. one d.; ed. Mount Anville, Trinity Coll. Dublin, King's Inns, Dublin and Harvard Univ., USA; Barrister 1967, Sr Counsel 1980; called to English Bar (Middle Temple) 1973; Reid Prof. of Constitutional and Criminal Law, Trinity Coll. Dublin 1969–75, lecturer in European Community Law 1975–90; Founder and Dir, Irish Centre for European Law 1988–90; Senator 1969–89; Pres. of Ireland 1990–97; UN High Commr for Human Rights 1997–; mem. Dublin City Council 1979–83; mem. New Ireland Forum 1983–84; mem. Irish Parl. Jt Cttee. on EC Secondary Legislation 1973–89; mem. Vedel Cttee on Enlargement of European Parl., EC 1971–72, Saint-Geours Cttee on Energy Efficiency, EC 1978–79, Advisory Bd of Common Market Law Review 1976–90, Irish Parl. Jt Cttee on Marital Breakdown 1983–85, Editorial Bd of Irish Current Law Statutes Annoted 1984–90, Advisory Cttee of Interights, London 1984–90, Int. Comm. of Jurists, Geneva 1987–90, Cttee. of Man., European Air Law Asscn 1989–90, Scientific Council of European Review of Public Law 1989–90, Euro Avocats, Brussels 1989–90; Gen. Rapporteur, Human Rights at the Dawn of the 21st Century, Council of Europe, Strasbourg 1993; Pres. Cherish (Irish Asscn of Single Parents) 1973–90; mem. Royal Irish Acad.; Hon. Bencher King's Inns, Dublin, Middle Temple, London; Hon. Prof. of Law, Manchester Univ.; Hon. Fellow Trinity Coll. Dublin, Inst. of Engineers of Ireland, Royal Coll. of Physicians in Ireland, Hertford Coll. Oxford, Royal Coll. of Psychiatrists, London, Royal Coll. of Surgeons, Ireland, Royal Coll. of Obstetricians and Gynaecologists, London; Hon. mem. N.Y. Bar Asscn, Bar of Tanzania; LL.D. h.c. (Nat. Univ. of

Ireland, Cambridge, Brown, Liverpool, Dublin, Montpellier, St Andrews, Melbourne, Columbia, Nat. Univ. of Wales, Poznań, Toronto, Fordham, Queens Univ. Belfast); Dr. h.c. of Public Services (Northeastern Univ.); Hon. Doctorat en Sciences Humaines (Rennes) 1996, Hon. LL.D. (Coventry) 1996; Berkeley Medal, Univ. of Calif., Medal of Honour, Univ. of Coimbra, Medal of Honour, Ordem dos Advogados, Portugal, Gold Medal of Honour, Univ. of Salamanca, Andrés Bello Medal, Univ. of Chile, New Zealand Suffrage Centennial Medal, Freedom Prize, Max Schmidheiny Foundation (Switzerland), UNIFEM Award, Noel Foundation, Los Angeles, Marisa Bellisario Prize, Italy 1991, European Media Prize, The Netherlands 1991, Special Humanitarian Award, CARE, Washington, D.C. 1993, Int. Human Rights Award, Int. League of Human Rights, New York 1993, Liberal Int. Prize for Freedom 1993, Stephen P. Duggan Award (USA) 1994; Freedom of the City of Cork; Hon. A.O.

Address: Office of the UN High Commissioner for Human Rights, Palais des Nations, United Nations, 1211 Geneva 10, Switzerland.

Telephone: (22) 9179290; **fax:** (22) 9179022; **e-mail:** scrt.hchr@unog.ch; **internet:** www.unhchr.ch.

RODOTÁ, Antonio, B.SC.; Italian administrator and engineer; b. 24 Dec. 1935, Cosenza; ed. Univ. of Rome; Asst Lecturer in radio engineering, Univ. of Rome 1959–61; electronic design, SISPRE SpA from 1959; delegate to NATO (Paris, France) 1965–66; Head, Electronic Design Group, Selenia Spazio SpA 1966–71, with Radar and Systems Div. 1971–76, Head of Div. from 1976, Jt Man. Dir 1983–90; Dir-Gen. Compagnia Nazionale Satelliti (CNS) SpA 1980–83; Jt Man. Dir, Alenia Spazio SpA (now Alenia Aerospazio) 1990–95, Man. Dir 1995; Head of Space Div., Finmeccanica 1996 (with responsibility for co-ordination of the relevant activities of subsidiaries Laben and Space Software Italia–SSI); Chair. and Man. Dir, Quadrics Supercomputer World Ltd (jt venture between Alenia Spazio SpA and Meiko Ltd); mem. of Bds of Dirs, Alelco, Arianespace, Marconi/Alenia Comm., SSI, Space System Loral; Dir-Gen. European Space Agency (ESA) July 1997–; fmrly mem. Man. Cttee, Italian Aerospace Asscn; fmrly mem. High-performance Computer Group, Ministry of Research; fmrly Vice-Chair., Defence and Space Group, Italian Nat. Asscn of Electrical Industries.

Address: ESA, 8–10 rue Mario Nikis, 75738 Paris Cédex 15, France.

Telephone: 1-53-69-76-54; **fax:** 1-53-69-75-60; **e-mail:** mail com@esa.int; **internet:** www.esa.int.

RODRÍGUEZ ARAQUE, Alí; Venezuelan politician and lawyer; d. Univ. Cen. de Venezuela, Univ. de los Andes; practised law; mem. Parl. 1983; mem. Nat. Council of Energy; Chair. Chamber of Deputies Comm. of Energy and Mines 1994–97; Vice-Chair. Bicameral Comm. of Energy and Mines; Senator 1999–; fmr Min. of Energy and Mines; Pres. of OPEC Conf. 2000; Sec.-Gen. of OPEC Jan. 2001–.

Address: OPEC, Obere Donaustrasse 93, 1020 Vienna, Austria.

Telephone: (1) 211-12-279; **fax:** (1) 214-98-27; **e-mail:** prid@opec.org.

ROGGE, Jacques; Belgian surgeon and international official; b. 2 May 1942, Ghent; m. Anne Bovijn; two c.; orthopaedic surgeon and lecturer in sports medicine; fmr competitor in international yachting competitions, participating in the Finn class event at the following Olympic Summer Games: Mexico City (1968), Munich (1972) and Montréal (1976); mem. Belgian national rugby team; Pres. Nat. Olympic Cttee 1989–1992; Pres. European Olympic Cttees 1989; mem. Int. Olympic Cttee 1991–, mem. Exec. Bd 1998–2001; Pres. July 2001–.

Address: International Olympic Committee, Château de Vidy, 1007 Lausanne, Switzerland.

Telephone: (21) 6216111; **fax:** (22) 6216216; **internet:** www.olympic.org.

ROSSIER, William; Swiss diplomatist; b. 1942; ed. Univ. of Lausanne; joined diplomatic service 1970; served with Mission to the European Community 1976–80; with Fed. Office for External Economic Affairs 1981–88, Head of Div. in Charge of Relations with Western Europe; Plenipotentiary Amb. in Geneva 1988, Perm. Rep. to WTO, EFTA, ECE and UNCTAD; Chair. WTO Gen. Council; Sec.-Gen. European Free Trade Asscn (EFTA) Sept. 2000–.

Address: EFTA, 9–11 rue de Varembé, 1211 Geneva 20, Switzerland.

Telephone: (22) 7491111; **fax:** (22) 7339291; **e-mail:** efta -mailbox@efta.int; **internet:** www.efta.int.

ROJAS PENSO, Juan Francisco; Venezuelan economist; b. 18 Sept. 1952; ed. Andrés Bello Catholic Univ., Caracas and CENDES; Prof. Univ. Central de Venezuela and Univ. Simón Bolivar; Official, Council of the Acuerdo de Cartagena (the Cartagena Agreement, now the Andean Community of Nations) 1977–79 and 1982–85, Alt. Plenipotentiary Rep. and Dir Corporación Andina de Fomento (CAF) 1985–87; Councillor (Economic Affairs) to Colombia 1980–81; Dir-Gen. of Economic Integration, Venezuelan Inst. of Foreign Trade 1985–87; Dir, Commercial Policy Dept, Latin American Integration Asscn (LAIA) 1989–93, Dep. Sec.-Gen. 1993–99, Sec.–Gen. March 1999–; independent consultant to various orgs incl. the Andean Community of Nations, LAIA, Organization of American States (OAS) and the Friedrich Ebert Foundation.

Address: LAIA, Cebollatí 1461, Casilla 577, Montevideo, Uruguay.

Telephone: (2) 4101121; **fax:** (2) 4190649; **e-mail:** sgaladi@ aladi.org; **internet:** www.aladi.org.

RYDER, Guy; British international trade union official; b. 3 Jan. 1956, Liverpool; ed. Univ. of Cambridge; Asst Int. Dept, Trade Union Congress (TUC) 1981–85; Sec. Industry Trade Section, Int. Fed. of Commercial, Clerical, Professional and Tech. Employees (FIET), Geneva 1985–88; Sec. Workers' Group, Int. Labour Office (ILO) 1993–96, 1996–98, Sec. Worker's Group, Int. Labour Conf. 1994–98, Dir. of Bureau for Workers' Activities, ILO 1998–99, Chief of Cabinet 1999–2001, Special Adviser to the Dir.-Gen. –2001; Asst Dir, then Dir Int. Confed. of Free Trade Unions (ICFTU), Geneva 1988–98, Gen.-Sec. Feb. 2002–.

Address: ICFTU, 5 blvd Roi Albert II, 1210 Brussels, Belgium.

Telephone: (2) 224-02-11; **fax:** (2) 201-58-15; **e-mail:** internet po@icftu.org; **internet:** www.icftu.org.

SCHMÖGNEROVA, Brigita, PH.D.; Slovakian politician and international official; b. 17 Nov. 1947, Bratislava; m.; one s.; ed. School of Economics, Bratislava; teacher Univ. of Athens, Greece and Georgetown Univ., Washington, U.S.A.; researcher Inst. of Econs., Slovak Acad. of Sciences; lecturer Univ. of Econs., Bratislava; Econ. Adviser to Pres. of Slovak Repub. 1993; Deputy Prime Min. 1994; M.P. 1995–98; Min. of Finance 1998–2002; Exec. Sec. UN Econ. Comm. for Europe (ECE) 2002–; adviser to IMF, IBRD and EBRD; mem. OECD 2000; World Finance Min. of the Year Award, Euromoney Inst. Investor 2000.

Address: Economic Commission for Europe, Palais des Nations, 1211 Geneva 10, Switzerland.

Telephone: (22) 9174444; **fax:** (22) 9170505; **email:** info .ece@unece.org; **internet:** www.unece.org.

SCHWIMMER, Walter; Austrian politician; b. 16 June 1942, Vienna; m.; two s.; ed. Universität Wien; with Law Dept, Austrian Private Employees Trade Union; Dep. Dir-Gen. Vienna Health Insurance Fund; mem. Austrian Parl. 1971–99; Vice-Chair. Austrian People's Party Parl. Group 1986–94; mem. Council of Europe Parl. Assembly 1991–99, Vice-Pres. 1996 and 1999); Sec.-Gen. Council of Europe 1999–.

Address: Council of Europe, 67075 Strasbourg Cédex, France.

Telephone: 3-88-41-20-00; **fax:** 3-88-41-27-81; **e-mail:** point_i@coe.int; **internet:** www.coe.int.

SEVAN, Benon V., M.A.; Cypriot international civil servant; b. 18 Dec. 1937; m.; one d.; ed. Melkonian Educational Inst., and Columbia Coll. and School of Int. and Public Affairs, Colombia Univ., New York, USA; joined UN in 1965; Dept of Public Information 1965–66; secr. of the Special Cttee on Decolonization 1966–68; served UN in West Irian (Irian Jaya), Indonesia 1968–72; secr. of the UN Economic and Social Council 1973–88; Dir and Senior Political Adviser to the Rep. of the Sec.-Gen. on the Settlement of the Situation relating to Afghanistan April 1988–89; Personal Rep. of the Sec.-Gen. in Afghanistan and Pakistan May 1989–92; Rep. of the Sec.-Gen. on the Implementation of the Geneva Accords on Afghanistan Jan. 1990–92; Dir Office for the Co-ordination of the UN Humanitarian and Economic Assistance Programmes in Afghanistan Jan. 1991–92; Asst Sec.-Gen., Dept of Political Affairs Aug. 1992–March 1994; Asst

Sec.-Gen. for Conference and Support Services July 1994–Oct. 1997; Asst Sec.-Gen., Office of Security Co-ordination July 1994–; Exec. Dir, Office of the Iraq Programme Oct. 1997–.
Address: Office of the Iraq Programme, United Nations, New York, NY 10017, USA.

SEVERINO, Rodolfo Certeza, Jr., M.A.; Philippine diplomatist; m. Rowena V. Romero; ed. Ateneo de Manila Univ., Johns Hopkins Univ. School of Advanced Int. Studies, Washington, D.C.; Assoc. Ed. Manor Press Inc. 1956–59, Philippine Int. 1957–59, Marketing Horizons 1961–64; with Operation Brotherhood, Laos 1959–61; special asst to Senator Raul S. Manglapus, Philippine Senate 1961–64; information asst, UN Information Centre, Manila 1964–65; Third, then Second and First Sec. Embassy, Washington, D.C. 1967–74; special asst to Under-Sec. of Foreign Affairs 1974–76, Under-Sec. 1992–97; Chargé d'Affaires Embassy, Beijing 1976–78; Consul-Gen., Houston, Texas 1979–86; Asst Sec. for Asian and Pacific Affairs 1986–88; Amb. to Malaysia 1988–92; Sec.-Gen. Asscn of S.E. Asian Nations (ASEAN) 1997–.
Address: Association of South East Asian Nations, 70A Jalan Sisingamangaraja, POB 2072, Jakarta 12110, Indonesia.
Telephone: (21) 726-2991; **fax:** (21) 739-8234; **e-mail:** public@asean.or.id; **internet:** www.aseansec.org.

SHI JIUYONG, M.A.; Chinese lawyer; b. 9 Oct. 1926, Zhejiang; m. Zhang Guoying 1956; one s.; ed. St John's Univ. Shanghai and Columbia Univ., New York, USA; Asst Research Fellow, Inst. of Int. Relations, Beijing 1956–58; Sr lecturer, Assoc. Prof. of Int. Law, Foreign Affairs Coll., Beijing 1958–64; Research Fellow in Int. Law, Inst. of Int. Law, Beijing 1964–73, Inst. of Int. Studies, Beijing 1973–80; Prof. of Int. Law, Foreign Affairs Coll., Beijing 1984–93, Foreign Econ. Law Training Centre of Ministry of Justice; Legal Adviser, Ministry of Foreign Affairs 1980–93, Chinese Centre of Legal Consultancy, Office of Chinese Sr Rep. Sino-British Jt Liaison Group (on question of Hong Kong) 1985–93; Adviser to Chinese Soc. of Int. Law, Inst. of Hong Kong Law of Chinese Law Soc.; mem. American Soc. of Int. Law, mem. Standing Cttee, Beijing Cttee. of CPCC 1988–93, mem. 8th Nat. Cttee. 1993; mem. Int. Law Comm. (ILC) 1987–93, Chair. 1990; mem. (Judge) Int. Court of Justice 1994–, Vice-Pres. Feb. 2000–; legal adviser to Chinese dels. at numerous int. confs, etc. *Publications:* numerous publs on int. law.
Address: International Court of Justice, Peace Palace, Carnegieplein 2, 2517 KJ The Hague, Netherlands.
Telephone: (70) 302-23-23; **fax:** (70) 364-99-28; **e-mail:** information@icj-cij.org; **internet:** www.icj-cij.org.

SOLANA MADARIAGA, Javier; Spanish politician; b. 14 July 1942, Madrid; m. Concepción Jiménez; two c.; ed. Colegio del Pilar, Universidad Complutense de Madrid; won Fulbright scholarship to study physical sciences in USA until 1968; Asst to Prof. Nicolas Cabrera, Univ. of Valencia 1968–71, then at Universidad Autónoma de Madrid (where contract was cancelled for political reasons); mem. Exec., Federación Socialista Madrileña and Federación de Trabajadores de la Enseñanza, Unión General de Trabajadores; Prof. of Physical Sciences, Universidad Complutense de Madrid; mem. Congress of Deputies for Madrid; mem. Fed. Exec. Comm., Partido Socialista Obrero Español, former Press Sec. and Sec. for Research and Programmes; Min. of Culture and Govt Spokesman 1982–88; Min. of Educ. and Science 1988–92, of Foreign Affairs 1992–95; Sec.-Gen. NATO Dec. 1995–Oct. 1999; Sec.-Gen. Council of the European Union, 'High Representative' for Common Foreign and Security Policy Oct. 1999–; Sec.-Gen. Western European Union (WEU) Nov. 1999–.
Address: General Secretariat, Council of the European Union, Justus Lipsius Bldg, 175 rue de la Loi, 1048 Brussels, Belgium.
Telephone: (2) 285-61-11; **fax:** (2) 285-73-97; **e-mail:** public .relations@consilium.eu.int; **internet:** www.ue.eu.int.

SOMAVÍA, Juan O.; Chilean diplomatist; m.; two c.; ed. Catholic Univ. of Chile, Univ. of Paris; various posts in Ministry of Foreign Relations; Founder and Exec. Dir Latin American Inst. for Transnat. Studies, Mexico, Co-ordinator Third World Forum, mem. Bd of Dirs and Vice-Pres. for Latin America of Inter-Press Service 1976–87; Sec.-Gen. South American Peace Comm. 1987; Press. Int. Comm. of Chilean opposition No Campaign for Referendum 1988–89; Perm. Rep. to UN, New York 1990–98; Dir Gen. Int. Labour Organization (ILO) 1999–; fmr consultant to GATT and UNDP; mem. Bd of Dirs, Int. Foundation for Devt Alternatives; mem. MacBride Comm. on communication problems; Leonidas Proaño Prize, Latin American Human Rights Asscn for contrib. to peace and regional security.
Address: International Labour Organization, 4 route des Morillons, 1211 Geneva 22, Switzerland.
Telephone: (22) 7996111; **fax:** (22) 7988685.

SUTHERLAND, Dame Veronica Evelyn, D.M.G., M.A.; British diplomatist; b. 25 April 1939; m. Alex J. Sutherland 1981; ed. Royal School, Bath, Univs of London and Southampton; joined diplomatic service 1965, Second Sec., then First Sec., Copenhagen 1967–70, New Delhi 1975–78; with Foreign and Commonwealth Office 1970–75, 1978–80, Counsellor 1981, 1984–87, Asst Under-Sec. of State (Personnel) 1990–95; Perm Del. to UNESCO 1981–84; Amb. to Côte d'Ivoire 1987–90, to Ireland 1995–99; Dep. Sec.-Gen. (Economic and Social) of the Commonwealth Feb. 1999–; Hon. LL.D. (Trinity Coll., Dublin) 1998.
Address: Commonwealth Secretariat, Marlborough House, Pall Mall, London, SW1Y 5HX, United Kingdom.
Telephone: (20) 7839-3411; 27678; **fax:** (20) 7930-0827; **e-mail:** info@commonwealth.int; **internet:** www.thecom monwealth.org.

TALLAWY, Mervat M.; Egyptian diplomatist and politician; b. 1 Dec. 1937; m.; one d.; ed. American Univ. Cairo, Inst. for Diplomatic Studies, Cairo and Grad. Inst. of Int. Studies, Geneva; joined Ministry of Foreign Affairs 1963; served Geneva, New York and Caribbean countries, Vienna and Tokyo; Dep. Dir UN Inst. for the Advancement of Women 1982–85; Min. Plenipotentiary, Dep. Dir Dept. of Int. Organizations, Ministry of Foreign Affairs 1985–88; Amb. to Austria and Resident Rep. to IAEA, UNIDO and UN Centre for Social and Humanitarian Affairs 1988–91; Dir of Int. Economics Dept, Ministry of Foreign Affairs 1991; Asst Min. for Int. Political and Economic Affairs 1992–93; Amb. to Japan 1993–97; Asst UN Sec. for UNDP, Arab countries 1997; Min. of Insurance and Social Affairs 1997–99; Exec. Dir UN Economic and Social Comm. for Western Asia (ESCWA) 2000–.
Address: ESCWA, Riad es-Solh Sq., POB 11-8575, Beirut, Lebanon.
Telephone: (1) 981301; **fax:** (1) 981510; **e-mail:** unescwa@escwa.org.lb; **internet:** www.escwa.org.lb.

THYS, Willy; Belgian trade unionist; b. 18 July 1943; m.; three c.; ed. FOPES/UCL; elected shop steward of ACV–CSC trade union, Société Nationale des Chemins de Fer Belges 1963, joined Exec. Cttee, railway workers' fed. of ACV–CSC 1970, Sec.-Gen. Syndicat Chrétien des Communications et de la Culture 1976–87, Nat. Sec. ACV–CSC 1987–96; Sec.-Gen. WCL Dec. 1996–.
Address: WCL, 33 rue de Trèves, 1040 Brussels, Belgium.
Telephone: (2) 285-47-00; **fax:** (2) 230-87-22; **e-mail:**willy.-thys@cmt-wcl.org; **internet:** www.cmt-wcl.org.

TIBAIJUKA, Anna Kajumulo; Tanzanian agricultural economist; m. (died); four c.; ed. Swedish Univ. of Agricultural Sciences, Uppsala; Assoc. Prof. Dar-es-Salaam Univ. 1993–98; founding Chair. Tanzanian Nat. Women's Council; UNCTAD Special Co-ordinator for Least Developed Countries, Landlocked and Small Island Developing Countries 1998–2000; Exec. Dir of UN Human Settlements Programme (UN-Habitat) 2000–; appointed Exec. Sec. for Third UN Conference on Least Developed Countries held May 2001 in Brussels, Belgium.
Address: POB 30030, Nairobi, Kenya.
Telephone: (2) 621234; **fax:** (2) 624266; **e-mail:** infohabitat@ unhabitat.org; **internet:** www.unhabitat.org.

TÖPFER, Klaus, PH.D.; German politician; b. 29 July 1938, Waldenburg, Silesia; m.; three c.; ed. Univs of Mainz, Frankfurt-am-Main and Munster; family expelled from Silesia, settled in Höxter/Weser 1945; Head, Political Economy Dept, Inst. of Devt Planning, Munster 1970–71; Head, Planning and Information Section, Saarland State Chancellery, Saarbrucken; lecturer, Coll. of Admin., Speyer 1971–78; Prof. Ordinarius, Hanover Univ., Dir. Inst. of Environmental Research and Regional Planning 1978–79; Hon. Prof. Mainz Univ. 1985–; joined Christian Democratic Union (CDU) 1972, CDU Dist Chair., Saarbrucken,

mem. CDU State Exec., Saar 1977–79; State Sec., Rhineland Palatinate, Ministry of Social Affairs, Health and Environment, Mainz 1978–85; Dep. Chair. CDU Fed. Cttee of Experts on the Environment 1983; Min. of Environment and Health, Rhineland Palatinate 1985–87; CDU Dist Chair., Rhein-Hunsrück 1987–; Fed. Min. for the Environment, Nature Conservation and Nuclear Safety 1987–94, of Regional Planning, Housing and Urban Devt Nov. 1994–Jan. 1998; UN Under-Sec.-Gen. and Exec. Dir of UN Environment Programme Feb. 1998–; Dir-Gen. of UN Office in Nairobi Feb. 1998–; Acting Exec. Dir UN Centre for Human Settlements (Habitat) July 1998–2000.
Address: UN Office in Nairobi, POB 30552, Nairobi, Kenya.
Telephone: (2) 621234; **fax:** (2) 624349; **e-mail:** cpiinfo@unep.org; **internet:** www.unep.org.

TURKI, Abdulaziz Al-Abdullah al-, B.A.; Saudi Arabian oil official; b. 12 Aug. 1936, Jeddah; m.; two d.; ed. Univ. of Cairo; US Embassy, Jeddah 1953–54; ARAMCO 1954–66; Dir Office of Min. of Petroleum and Mineral Resources 1966–68; Dir of Gen. Affairs, Directorate of Mineral Resources 1968–70; Asst Sec.-Gen. Organization of Arab Petroleum Exporting Countries (OAPEC) 1970–75; Sec.-Gen. Supreme Advisory Council for Petroleum and Mineral Affairs, Saudi Arabia 1975–90; Saudi Gov. for OPEC 1975–90; Dep. Min., Ministry of Petroleum and Mineral Resources 1975–; Chair. Arab Maritime Petroleum Transport Co, Kuwait 1981–87, Pemref 1982–89; mem. Bd of Dirs Petromin 1975–89, ARAMCO 1980–89; Sec.-Gen. OAPEC 1990–.
Address: Organization of Arab Petroleum Exporting Countries, POB 20501, Safat 13066, Kuwait.
Telephone: 4844500; **fax:** 4815747; **e-mail:** oapec@qualitynet.net; **internet:** www.oapecorg.org.

UTSUMI, Yoshio, B.L., M.A.; Japanese lawyer, politician and telecommunications official; b. 14 Aug. 1942; m. Masako Utsumi; one s. one d.; ed. Univ. of Tokyo, Univ. of Chicago, USA; joined Ministry of Posts and Telecommunications (MPT); Prof. of Public Admin., MPT Postal Coll. 1972; responsible for country's largest investment fund, MPT Postal Life Insurance Bureau 1986–88; Head Gen. Affairs Div. of MPT Broadcasting Bureau; with MPT Communication Policy Bureau; Dir-Gen. of Int. Affairs, MPT, Dir-Gen., Asst Vice-Min., Dep. Min.; First Sec. (responsible for ITU affairs) to UN, Geneva, Switzerland; Sec.-Gen. Int. Telecommunication Union (ITU) 1999–; Chair. ITU plenipotentiary conference 1994.
Address: ITU, Place des Nations, 1211 Geneva 2, Switzerland.
Telephone: (22) 7305111; **fax:** (22) 7337256; **e-mail:** itumail@itu.int; **internet:** www.itu.int.

VENTURONI, Adm. Guido; Italian naval officer; b. 10 April 1934, Teramo; m. Giuliana Marinozzi; two s. one d.; ed. Naval Academy 1952–56; Navigator; Communications Officer; maritime patrol pilot and tactical instructor; Head of Naval Helicopter Studies and Projects Office; Exec. Asst to Chief of Navy Staff, to Chief of Defence at Naval Personnel Directorate; Head of Plans and Operation Dept at Navy Gen. Staff, at Defence Gen. Staff 1982–86; Commdr, First Naval Div. 1986–87; Head, Financial Planning Bureau, Naval Gen. Staff 1987–89; Dep. Chief of Staff of Navy 1989–90; Vice-Adm. 1990–91; Commdr-in-Chief of Fleet and NATO Commdr of Central Mediterranean 1991–92; Chief of Staff of Navy 1992–93, Chief of Defence Gen. Staff from 1994; Over Commdr, Int. Security Mission to Albania from 1997; Chair. Military Cttee, NATO May 1999–; Knight of the Grand Cross of the Order of Merit of the Italian Republic; Medal for Merit (Mauritius); Silver Medal for sea-duty service; Gold Medal for air service; Officer of the Legion of Merit (France); Grand Cross of the Orden de Mayo al Mérito Naval (Argentina); 1st class Cross of the Order of Mérito Naval (Spain); 2nd class Decoration of the Order of Mérito Naval (Venezuela).
Address: NATO, blvd Léopold III, 1110 Brussels, Belgium.
Telephone: (2) 707-41-11; **fax:** (2) 707-45-79; **e-mail:** natodoc@hq.nato.int; **internet:** www.nato.int.

VERESHCHETIN, Vladlen Stepanovich; Russian professor of law; b. 8 Jan. 1932, Briansk; m.; one d.; mem. staff, Presidium of USSR Acad. of Sciences 1958–67; First Vice-Chair. and Legal Counsel, Intercosmos, USSR Acad. of Sciences 1967–81; Prof. of Int. Law, Univ. of Friendship of Peoples 1979–82; mem. USSR dels to the UN Cttee on the Peaceful Uses of Outer Space and its Legal Sub-cttee 1979–90; Dep. Dir and Head, Dept of Int. Law, Inst. of State and Law, Russian Acad. of Sciences 1981–95, Chair. Scientific Council on Int. and Comparative Law 1981–95; mem. Perm. Court of Arbitration, The Hague 1984–95; Vice-Pres. Russian (fmrly Soviet) UN Asscn 1984–; Vice-Pres. Russian (fmrly Soviet) Asscn of Int. Law 1985–97; Distinguished Visiting Prof., Univ. of Akron, USA 1991; mem. UN Int. Law Comm. 1992–95, Chair. 1994; mem. (Judge) Int. Court of Justice 1995–. *Publications:* numerous books and 150 articles on int. law, law of the sea, space law, state responsibility, int. criminal law and constitutional law.
Address: International Court of Justice, Peace Palace, Carnegieplein 2, 2517 KJ The Hague, Netherlands.
Telephone: (70) 302-23-23; **fax:** (70) 364-99-28; **e-mail:** information@icj-cij.org; **internet:** www.icj-cij.org.

VIEIRA DE MELLO, Sergio, PH.D.; Brazilian United Nations official; b. 15 March 1948; m.; two s.; ed. Brazil, Univ. of Paris (Panthéon-Sorbonne), France; fmrly UN Regional Humanitarian Co-ordinator for Great Lakes region, Head of Civil Affairs of the UN Protection Force (UNPROFOR), Dir of Repatriation for the UN Transitional Authority in Cambodia (UNTAC), Special Envoy for the UNHCR for Cambodia; involvement with humanitarian and peace-keeping missions in Bangladesh, Cyprus, Lebanon, Mozambique, Peru and Sudan; UN Asst High Commr for Refugees 1996–97; Under Sec.-Gen. and Emergency Relief Co-ordinator, UN Office for the Co-ordination of Humanitarian Affairs (UNOCHA) Jan. 1998–; Special Rep. of the UN Sec.-Gen. for East Timor and Head of the UN Transitional Admin. in East Timor (UNTAET) Nov. 1999–.
Address: Dept of Peace-keeping Operations, Room S-3727B, United Nations, New York, NY 10017, USA.
Telephone: (212) 963-9222; **fax:** (212) 963-8079.

WELLINK, Arnout H.E.M., PH.D.; Dutch international banking executive; b. 1943; m. M.V. Volmer; five c.; ed. Leyden Univ., Univ. of Rotterdam; teaching asst, staff mem. Leyden Univ. 1965–70; staff mem. Ministry of Finance 1970–75, Head of Directorate Gen. Financial and Econ. Policy 1975–77, Treas.-Gen. 1977–81; Exec. Dir. The Netherlands Bank 1982–, Pres. 1997–; Chair. of Bd and Pres. Bank of Int. Settlements (BIS) March 2002–; mem. Council, European Cen. Bank; mem. Bd of Trustees Museum Meermanno-Westreenianum; Knight of the Order of the Netherlands.
Address: Bank for International Settlements, Centralbahnplatz 2, 4002 Basel, Switzerland.
Telephone: (61) 2808080; **fax:** (61) 2809100; **e-mail:** emailmaster@bis.org; **internet:** www.bis.org

WOICKE, Peter L.; German banker; with J. P. Morgan for over 30 years, in particular in Latin America and the Middle East, headed banking div. of affiliate in Beirut, Lebanon, man. of J. P. Morgan's global gas and petroleum gp, fmrly mem. J. P. Morgan exec. management gp, Chair. J. P. Morgan Securities Asia, Singapore; Exec. Vice-Pres. Int. Finance Corpn (IFC) 1999–.
Address: IFC, 2121 Pennsylvania Ave, NW, Washington, DC 20433, USA.
Telephone: (202) 477-1234; **fax:** (202) 974-4384; **e-mail:** information@ifc.org; **internet:** www.ifc.org.

WOLFENSOHN, James D. (Jim), B.A., LL.B., M.B.A.; American international official, business executive and arts administrator; b. 1 Dec. 1933, Sydney, Australia; m. Elaine Botwinick 1961; one s. two d.; ed. Univ. of Sydney, Harvard Business School; Pres. J. Henry Schroder Banking Corpn. 1970–76; Chair. Salomon Bros Int. 1977–81; owner, Pres. James D. Wolfensohn Inc. 1981–, fmr Chair., also CEO; Bd Carnegie Hall; Chair. Kennedy Center for the Performing Arts 1990–95; Chair. Emer. 1995–; Pres. Int. Bank for Reconstruction and Devt (IBRD) June 1995–, Int. Devt Asscn, Int. Finance Corpn, Multilateral Guarantee Agency; Trustee, Rockefeller Univ. 1985–94, Howard Hughes Medical Inst. 1987–96; Montblanc de la Culture Award 1992.
Address: IBRD, 1818 H Street, NW, Washington, DC 20433, U.S.A.
Telephone: (202) 477-1234; **fax:** (202) 477-6391; **e-mail:** pic@worldbank.org; **internet:** www.worldbank.org.

YAROV, Yurii Fedorovich; Russian politician; b. 2 April 1942, Mariinsk, Kemerovo Region; m.; one s. one d.; ed. Leningrad Tech. Inst., Leningrad Eng. Econ. Inst.; worked in factories in Latvia 1964–68, Leningrad Region 1968–76; Dir factory Burevestnik 1978–85; First Sec. Gatchina City CPSU Cttee 1985–87; Dep. Chair. Exec. Cttee Leningrad Regional Soviet of Deputies 1987–89, Chair. 1989–90; Chair. Leningrad Regional Soviet of People's Deputies 1990–91; People's Dep. of Russian Fed. 1990–92; Dep. Chair. Supreme Soviet of Russia 1991–92; Dep. Prime Min. 1992–96; Dep. Head of Pres. Yeltsin's Admin. 1996–, First Dep. 1997–98; Plenipotentiary Rep. of Pres. of the Russian Fed. in Council of Fed. 1998; Exec. Sec. Commonwealth of Independent States (CIS) 1999–.
Address: CIS, 220000 Minsk, Kirana 17, Belarus.
Telephone: (172) 22-35-17; **fax:** (172) 27-33-39; **e-mail:** postmaster@www.cis.minsk.by; **internet:** www.cis.minsk.by.

YONGJIAN JIN; Chinese diplomatist; b. 15 Sept. 1934, Jiangsu Prov.; m. Youping Wang 1955; two s.; ed. Beijing Univ.; joined diplomatic service 1954, officer, People's Inst. of Foreign Affairs 1954–63, Attaché, Embassy of PRC to Kenya 1964–67, officer, African Dept, Ministry of Foreign Affairs 1967–71, Third then Second Sec. Embassy of PRC to Nigeria 1971–76; Rep. of PRC to UN Security Council Cttee 1977, UN Special Cttee on Decolonization, and UN Council for Namibia 1977–84; Alt. Rep. of PRC to UN Security Council; Second, First Sec. then Counsellor, Perm. Mission of PRC to UN; Dep. Dir-Gen. then Dir-Gen. African Dept, Ministry of Foreign Affairs 1984–88, Dir-Gen. Dept of Int. Orgs and Confs 1988–90; Dep. Perm. Rep. and Amb. of PRC to UN, Dep. Rep. of PRC to Security Council 1990–92; Amb. and Perm. Rep. of PRC to UN Office, Geneva and other int. orgs 1992–96; UN Under-Sec.-Gen. for Devt Support and Man. Services 1996–97, Under-Sec.-Gen. for Gen. Assembly Affairs and Conf. Services June 1997–.
Address: Room S-2963A, United Nations, New York, NY 10017, USA.
Telephone: (212) 963-8362; **fax:** (212) 963-8196.

ZHARIKOV, Alexander Nikolayevich; Russian trade union official and engineer; b. 2 Jan. 1945, Arsenjevo; m. Olga Borisovna Suhova 1975; one s.; ed. Leningrad Shipbldg Inst.; mil. service 1962–66; Sec. of Youth and Student Org. of Leningrad 1971–74; Chair. Student Council of USSR 1974–78; Vice-Pres. Int. Union of Students 1978–84; official, Int. Dept, Cen. Cttee of CPSU 1984–88; Dir Int. Dept USSR All-Union Council 1988–90; Sec.-Gen. World Fed. of Trade Unions (WFTU) 1990–; Order of Honour (Russia) 1974. *Publications:* book on world student movt 1979; numerous articles on social issues, labour and trade union relations in newspapers and magazines.
Address: Branická 112, 14701 Prague 4, Czech Republic.
Telephone: (2) 44462140; **fax:** (2) 44461378; **e-mail:** wftu@login.cz; **internet:** www.wftu.cz.

INDEX OF INTERNATIONAL ORGANIZATIONS

(Main reference only)

B

C

D

F

G

H

I

J

K

L

M

N

Y

Z

For Product Safety Concerns and Information please contact our EU representative GPSR@taylorandfrancis.com Taylor & Francis Verlag GmbH, Kaufingerstraße 24, 80331 München, Germany

* 9 7 8 1 8 5 7 4 3 1 1 0 0 *

T - #0066 - 270225 - C0 - 280/208/35 [37] - CB - 9781857431100 - Gloss Lamination